THE
CAMBRIDGE
GUIDE TO

LITERATURE IN
ENGLISH

THE CAMBRIDGE

GUIDE TO

LITERATURE IN ENGLISH

Ian Ousby

Foreword by Doris Lessing

CAMBRIDGE
UNIVERSITY PRESS

Published by the Press Syndicate of the University of Cambridge
The Pitt Building, Trumpington Street, Cambridge CB2 1RP
40 West 20th Street, New York, NY 10011-4211, USA
10 Stamford Road, Oakleigh, Melbourne 3166, Australia

This edition first published 1993
Reprinted with corrections 1995

Printed in Great Britain by The Bath Press, Avon

A catalogue record for this book is available from the British Library

Library of Congress cataloging-in-publication data
Cambridge guide to literature in English / edited by Ian Ousby. – [rev ed]
1072p.   24.7cm
1. English literature – Dictionaries
2. Commonwealth literature (English) – Bio-bibliography
3. Commonwealth literature (English) – Dictionaries
4. Authors, Commonwealth – Biography – Dictionaries
5. Authors, American – Biography – Dictionaries
6. Authors, English – Biography – Dictionaries
7. American literature – Bio-bibliography
8. English literature – Bio-bibliography
9. American literature – Dictionaries
1. Ousby, Ian, 1947–
PR85.C29   1993
820.9'0003 – dc20

ISBN 0 521 440866 hardback

Contributors

Michael Abbott
Robert Ackerman
James Aikens
Stephen M. Archer
Christopher Baldick
Cameron Bardrick
Gillian Beer
Alan Bell
Misha Berson
Alison Blair-Underwood
Jeremy Black
M. H. Black
Paul Bongiorno
John L. Bradley
Andrew Brown
Frances Bzowski
Jo-Anne Carty
Paul Chipchase
Jean Chothia
David Christie
Henry Claridge
Alan Clark
Larry D. Clark
Michael Collie
Graham Coster
David Daniell
Geoffrey Day
Seamus Deane
Nicholas Drake
Dorothy Driver
Rod Edmond
Colin Edwards
John Elsom
Geraint Evans
Mark Fisher
Michael Freeman
Helen Fulton
Colin Gardner
Robin Gilmour
Jon Glover
Andrew Gurr

Paul Hartle
Laura Henigman
Ann Hill
Errol G. Hill
Anna Hodson
Meridel Holland
Richard Hollick
Coral Ann Howells
Robin Howells
Jane Hughes
C. L. Innes
Russell Jackson
Elizabeth Jay
David Johnston-Jones
Douglas Killam
Philip Kolin
Grevel Lindop
Tony Lopez
Eric Lott
James Lynn
James Malpas
Robyn Marsack
Desmond Maxwell
David McKitterick
Paul McNeil
Tice L. Miller
Isobel Murray
Michael Grosvenor Myer
Valerie Grosvenor Myer
Alastair Niven
Christopher Norris
Nancy Nystul
Ian Ousby
W. R. Owens
Geoffrey Parrinder
Graham Parry
Neil Powell
David Profumo
Richard Proudfoot
Gay Raines
Arthur Ravenscroft
Bronwen Rees

Jane Remus
Peggy Reynolds
Lucy Rinehart
Gareth Roberts
Jane Roberts
Allan Rodway
Anne Rooney
Clare Rossini
George Rowell
Frank Salmon
Jack Salzman
Andrew Sanders
Christopher Scarles
Raman Selden
Robert Sheppard
Mark Sherman
C. H. Sisson
Iain Crichton Smith
Brian Stableford
David Staines
Sarah Stanton
Simon Stevens
Margarita Stocker
Ann Stonehouse
Bernard Stonehouse
Sally Stonehouse
Barbara Strang
Jordan Sullivan
John Thieme
Peter Thomson
Nicholas Tredell
Nicholas Tucker
Ann Turner
Norman Vance
Lindeth Vasey
Judy Weiss
Don B. Wilmeth
Barry B. Witham
Barry Wood
Robert Wyke
Alan Young

Foreword

It is an awesome thing to be asked to contribute a foreword to a reference book that will be as widely used as the *Cambridge Guide*, particularly when literature has meant so much to me and in so many different ways. Literature has dimensions that we take for granted and hardly notice. In order to consider the most interesting, I want briefly to set aside the question of excellence. A dangerous thing to do now, when excellence is under attack. Recently a long article in a respectable newspaper complained that 'romantic novels' are dismissed and – here is the point – claimed that this is illogical since the Brontës wrote romantic novels and *Anna Karenina* is a romantic novel. Before reading this article I had not ever thought there might be people really unable to tell the difference between *Anna Karenina* and novels written to a romantic or sentimental formula. Of course the political correctors deny that excellence exists, but politics has always had to pursue lines of logic that go off and away from life and common sense. But I shall hold on to my faith that enough people can tell the difference between a good novel and a bad one, and take the risk of saying that literary excellence is the chief pleasure in reading, but another is how one may use a novel or tale for information. Literature maps the world for us, fleshing out what we get from newspaper articles and television reports, giving us a parallel landscape infinitely rich and various where we may stroll any time we like, tourists in imaginary worlds that mirror real ones. What did we know about the feel, taste, texture, the airs and aromas of South America before the recent explosion of wonderful South American novels, most translated into English? Or about Africa until the novels written by Africans in English, which issued from one end of the continent to the other? Nigeria, Ghana, Kenya, Somalia, Zimbabwe, South Africa – we are invited in, for writers are like hosts: come and share this with me. In the last decade or two we have felt at home in Canada. The USA has always been part of our literary domain, because of a language which – though developing so fast – remains a cousin of our own.

It is interesting to imagine what our vision of the world would be like had there been no novelists, no storytellers. Like the dark side of the moon, or the sea floors where fishes still unknown to science live, or reports from unexplored countries where maps said 'Here be monsters'. Literature makes us all kin, because every tale is a report from people whose differences are only variations on the theme of our humanity. Without the explorations of writers we would not know them. When I went to Brazil and was enclosed suddenly in a storm of irridescent butterflies the size of kingfishers, and children began to clap and dance; when in London I met a black girl who only by the accident of a brother's death got an education; when I met in Canada a woman frozen in grief because her love-child was given away for adoption; when in an Irish provincial town an elderly woman with a drinker's face sat by herself in the corner of a hotel lounge sipping a prim sherry while her eyes confessed a world of private lunacies – then I could say, 'Oh there you are, I already know you, you are part of my inner world, because I've read your story.'

While I read a novel, enjoying all the skills that go with literary excellence – the design, the complexities, the ironies, the insights – I am saying, 'But wait a minute, here's a region of the world (or of society or of psychology) I haven't been in before.'

If we can say, 'No human behaviour is alien to me', then it is because we know it all from literature.

Doris Lessing 1993

Editor's Note

What to find in *The Cambridge Guide to Literature in English* and where to find It

Like the previous edition published in 1988, this revised edition aims to provide a handy reference guide to the literature in English produced by all the various English-speaking cultures throughout the world. Its scope thus extends beyond the United Kingdom and Ireland, and beyond the traditional 'English Literature syllabus', to represent the USA, Canada, the Caribbean, Africa, India, Australia and New Zealand as well. There is no cut-off date for writers and works noticed either in passing or in detail. Within these pages you will find many writers who are still living and publishing, as well perhaps a few of the younger generation whose major work, we may soon be concluding, had not yet been done when this edition was compiled. The processes of publication make it impossible for any book to claim to be truly up-to-the-minute, but every effort has been to make coverage as contemporary as possible. Revision and expansion of the previous edition, though extending to virtually all aspects of its coverage, has made particularly marked changes in this area.

Writers in foreign languages are, of course, considered in the context of the genres or movements which they originated or assisted. But they are not given separate consideration except in the case of Anglo-Saxon (Old English) literature, here treated as part of the 'English tradition', and major examples of British medieval literature written in Latin, Anglo-Norman and the Gaelic languages, which influenced or flourished beside literature in English.

The entries fall into the following categories:

Writers. The term here embraces not just poets, novelists and playwrights but also those who, while not strictly producing 'literature', were closely allied to literary culture and often influenced it: theologians (Alcuin, John Henry Newman); authors of religious or devotional works (John Foxe, Jonathan Edwards); philosophers (David Hume, G. E. Moore); economists (David Ricardo, John Maynard Keynes); scientists (Charles Darwin, William James); naturalists (John James Audubon) and social theorists, journalists, scholars, critics, travel writers, essayists, historians, art historians too numerous to mention even selectively. You will also find entries for major publishers, book illustrators, artists closely associated with the literary life, book collectors and even the occasional forger.

Individual plays, poems, novels, treatises and other works. Entries range from the deliberately generous treatment accorded established giants and the more selective approach adopted with writers whose works have become modern classics (Graham Greene, Chinua Achebe, Robertson Davies) down to an instance like Stella Gibbons's *Cold Comfort Farm*, where the very title has overshadowed the writer's own name.

Literary groups or schools, such as the Lake Poets, the Bloomsbury Group and the Black Mountain School.

Wider literary movements, such as neoclassicism, Romanticism, modernism and post-modernism.

Critical schools or movements, such as the New Criticism, structuralism, post-structuralism and deconstruction.

Literary genres, such as comedy and tragedy, fable, farce, melodrama and miracle play.

Poetic forms and sub-genres of drama and fiction, such as acrostic, the elegy, the revenge tragedy, the Gothic novel and the *Bildungsroman*.

Critical concepts, such as dissociation of sensibility, hamartia, metaphor and symbol.

Rhetorical terms, such as anaphora, bathos, chiasmus, euphuism, litotes, synedoche and zeugma.

Theatres from the Globe onwards and **theatre companies** from the King's Men to the Federal Theatre Project and the Sistren Theatre Collective.

Literary magazines from *The Quarterly Review* and *Punch* to *The New Masses* and *Staffrider*.

Some of the wider or less obvious topics which receive entries include:		
alienation	Cruelty, Theatre of	Lollards, The
Arthurian literature	deconstruction	Marxist criticism
Baconian heresy	detective fiction	metre
Bible in English	dub poetry	New Criticism
bluestocking	dumb show	pantomime
Booker Prize	English dictionaries	psychoanalytic criticism
boys' companies	English language	Pulitzer Prizes
children's literature	estates satire	rhyme
Cockney School, The	expressionism	science fiction
conceit	feminist criticism	Shakespeare apocrypha
conduct books	genre fiction	Shakespeare: performance
confessional poetry	imitation	and criticism
copyright	irony	Utilitarianism
courtesy book	Left Book Club	well-made play
courtly love	libraries	wit

Entries

Entries are listed in alphabetical word-by-word order.

Entries on people come before those on works when names and titles are the same.

Headings for writers, movements, literary terms, and so forth, appear in **bold face**. Headings for titles of books and magazines in ***bold face italics***. The appearance of SMALL CAPITALS or *SMALL ITALIC CAPITALS* in the course of an entry indicates that the topic receives an entry of its own elsewhere in the *Guide*.

In the case of writers who published under an abbreviated version of their full name, the heading supplies the unused part in brackets; thus T. S. Eliot appears as Eliot, T(homas) S(tearns). Writers like George

Eliot and Mark Twain, who are remembered by the pseudonyms under which they commonly wrote, are listed under their pseudonyms with their real names given afterwards in square brackets. People who published under their real names as well, or used more than one pseudonym, or adopted an obviously fanciful pseudonym ('Q' or 'Phiz'), appear under their real names. Names beginning 'Mc' have been put with those beginning 'Mac'; St has been ordered as Saint; Dr as Doctor. Medieval writers who take their last name from a place are listed under their first name: Geoffrey of Monmouth rather than Monmouth, Geoffrey of.

Works commonly known by the name of the protagonist which appears in their title are listed under that name: *Huckleberry Finn, The Adventures of* not *Adventures of Huckleberry Finn, The.* Works like *Comus* and *Gulliver's Travels,* which have been retitled by posterity, appear under the names by which they are popularly known. Archaic spelling has in general been modernized but phrases and titles still universally known and recognized in their original form – *The Compleat Angler, The Faerie Queene* – have not been tampered with.

Acknowledgements

Updating this guide has expanded the list both of contributors and of those who helped with advice and encouragement in addition to or instead of contributions. They are: Martin Banham, Andrew Brown, Elinor Cole, Geoffrey Day, Andrew Gurr, Paul Hartle, Mark Hendy, Ann Hill, Ann Mason, Don B. Wilmeth and Robert Wyke. Sarah Stanton and Ann Stonehouse, my editors at Cambridge University Press for the first edition, proved invaluable. Their successors, Adrian du Plessis, Anna Hodson and Caroline Bundy, have been equally long-suffering, as have the copyeditor, Stephen Adamson, and the proofreaders, Sue Philpott and Michael Coultas. Those readers of the first edition who took the trouble to contact me with encouragement or chastisement also deserve my thanks. I can only hope this edition will find so helpful an audience.

À Beckett, Gilbert (Abbott) 1811–56 Humorist. Born in London of an old Wiltshire family claiming descent from the father of St Thomas à Becket, he attended Westminster School and was called to the Bar at Gray's Inn. He combined a distinguished legal career with comic writing, particularly for *PUNCH*, of which he was a founding member. *The Comic History of England* (1847) and *The Comic History of Rome* (1852), published by but not in *Punch*, were his most successful works; both were illustrated by JOHN LEECH. À Beckett also wrote over 50 plays.

À Wood, Anthony See WOOD, ANTHONY À.

Aaron's Rod A novel by D. H. LAWRENCE, first published in 1922.

Aaron Sisson, an amateur flautist, works as check-weighman and secretary to the Miners' Union in a Midlands colliery. He abandons this position, also his wife and his children, in order to join the orchestra of a London opera house. His life thereafter is spent searching for emotional freedom and a fuller sense of 'being'. His quest takes him to Italy and to the Marchesa del Torre, whose lover he becomes, but he is unable to liberate himself from the emotional bondage of conventional relationships. He meets Rawdon Lilly, again in Florence, who tries to persuade Sisson to be his follower. A portrait of NORMAN DOUGLAS, as James Argyle, and his friends is included; this portion of the novel was censored by Lawrence's English and American publishers. At the end of the novel his flute ('Aaron's rod') is symbolically destroyed as a result of an anarchist bomb explosion in Florence.

The biblical Aaron, brother of Moses, was the founder of the priesthood and the first high priest. His rod, the rod of Levi, was made to blossom by God as a sign of his spiritual authority over the children of Israel. He was not permitted to enter Canaan, however, because he doubted God's ability to bring the water of Meribah out of a rock.

Abbey Theatre A Dublin theatre, named after the street in which it stood and opened in 1904 as headquarters of the Irish National Theatre Society, originally founded as the Irish Literary Theatre by W. B. YEATS, GEORGE MOORE and EDWARD MARTYN in 1899. Productions of work by the Abbey's directors, Yeats, LADY GREGORY and J. M. SYNGE, quickly made the Abbey a focus of the new Irish drama. A second phase, dominated by the work of SEAN O'CASEY, began with *THE SHADOW OF A GUNMAN* in 1923 and ended with the decision of the directors to reject *THE SILVER TASSIE* in 1928. Between then and the destruction by fire of the Abbey in 1951, the work of lesser dramatists, like LENNOX ROBINSON and GEORGE SHIELS, sustained the theatre. It was not until 1966 that a second Abbey was opened.

Abbot, The See SCOTT, SIR WALTER.

Abercrombie, Lascelles 1881–1938 Poet and critic. The son of a stockbroker from Ashton upon Mersey, Cheshire, he was educated at Malvern College and the University of Manchester. After some years as a journalist he became a lecturer in poetry at the University of Liverpool (1919), professor of English literature at Leeds University (1922) and Goldsmith's Reader in English at Oxford (1935).

As poet and critic Abercrombie belongs to the Georgian period, before the revolution brought about by POUND and ELIOT. A collected volume, *The Poems of Lascelles Abercrombie* (1930), was supplemented by the posthumous *Lyrics and Unfinished Poems* (1940). Among his critical works were a study of THOMAS HARDY (1912), *The Idea of Great Poetry* (1925) and *Principles of Literary Criticism* (1932).

Abinger Harvest A collection of essays, reviews, poems and miscellaneous pieces by E. M. FORSTER, published in 1936.

The book takes its title from the village of Abinger Hammer in Surrey with which Forster's family had been connected 'for nearly 60 years' and in which he himself lived at the time. About 80 items are reprinted, all of which had appeared in various periodicals between 1903 and 1935. They are arranged not in their order of composition but according to subjects, in five sections:

(1) *The Present*, 'a commentary on passing events', which includes 'Notes on the English Character' (1920), 'Our Diversions' (1917–34) and 'Liberty in England', an address delivered at the Congrès International des Ecrivains at Paris in June 1935;

(2) *Books*, which includes essays and reviews on Ibsen, T. S. ELIOT, Proust, CONRAD, T. E. LAWRENCE and JANE AUSTEN;

(3) *The Past*, including a delightful note on 'The Consolations of History' (1920), and early essays on Gemistus Pletho, Girolamo Cardan (a 16th-century Italian scientist), Voltaire and GIBBON;

(4) *The East*, a salute to the Orient and Asia, with essays on Marco Polo (1931) and 'The Mind of the Indian Native State' (1922);

(5) *The Abinger Pageant*, a romantic pastoral celebration of local history, and a nostalgic evocation of 'another England, green and eternal'.

Abrahams, Peter 1919– South African novelist. Born in Vrededorp township, he worked as a ship's stoker in 1939–41 and as a journalist in London in 1941–57 before settling in Jamaica. His fiction usually features isolated individuals hungering for fellowship. Early work, such as the stories in *Dark Testament* (1942) and the novels *Song of the City* (1945) and *The Path of Thunder* (1948), is often marred by sentimentality. Black deprivation under apartheid is vividly detailed in another novel, *Mine Boy* (1946), as well as in his account of a visit to South Africa in 1952, *Return to Goli* (1953), and an autobiography, *Tell Freedom* (1954). An acute understanding of Third World politics informs: *Wild Conquest* (1950), a historical novel about 19th-century white–black confrontation; *A Wreath for Udomo* (1956), about post-independence Africa; *A Night of Their Own* (1965), about resistance to apartheid; *This Island Now* (1966), about neo-colonialism; and *The View from Coyaba* (1985), about the world-wide black struggle.

Absalom, Absalom! A novel by WILLIAM FAULKNER, published in 1936. From their room at Harvard, Quentin Compson (see THE SOUND AND THE FURY) and Shreve McCannon reconstruct the story of Thomas Sutpen's failed attempt to found a dynasty in Jefferson, Mississippi. Sutpen manages to build a mansion but is finally defeated by the complex, violent pattern of miscegenation embodied in his sons, Henry and Charles. Dividing its attention between Sutpen and Quentin's attempt to understand him, the novel is about the ambition and self-destructive capacity of the old South.

Absalom and Achitophel A poem by JOHN DRYDEN, written in HEROIC COUPLETS and published in 1681. It adapts characters and story from the Old Testament (2 Kings) to create an allegory satirizing contemporary politics. Dryden's main target is the efforts of Lord Shaftesbury and his party to exclude the future James II, a Catholic, from the succession in favour of Charles II's bastard son, the Duke of Monmouth. The poem is famous for its verse portraits of Monmouth (Absalom), Shaftesbury (Achitophel), the DUKE OF BUCKINGHAM (Zimri) and Charles II (David). Other figures include: Edward Seymour, Speaker of the House of Commons (Amiel, Chief of the Sanhedrin); Titus Oates, fabricator of the Popish Plot (Corah); and Bethel, Sheriff of London (Shimei). A second part (1682) was written chiefly by NAHUM TATE and revised by Dryden, who contributed 200 lines of savage satire against two of his rivals, THOMAS SHADWELL (Og) and ELKANAH SETTLE (Doeg).

Abse, Dannie (Daniel) 1923– Poet. Born into a Welsh-Jewish family in Cardiff, he was educated locally and at the University of Wales before training as a doctor at King's College, London, and Westminster Hospital. With Howard Sergeant he was joint editor of *Mavericks* (1957), an anthology designed to show the MOVEMENT as limited and unrepresentative of the time and to stress the importance of 'image and Dionysian excitement' rather than irony and understatement. Abse's own work, begun in *After Every Green Thing* (1949), continued with *Funland and Other Poems* (1973) and *Collected Poems 1948–76* (1977), *White Coat, Purple Coat: Collected Poems 1948–88* (1989) and *Remembrance of Crimes Past: Poems 1986–89* (1990). Without loss of discipline, his work attempts to include a wider range of experience – including that of a doctor and a Jewish cultural outsider – in a poetry that remains rooted in the English tradition of intimate address to the reader. *A Poet in the Family* (1974) and *There was a Young Man from Cardiff* (1991) are autobiographical.

Absentee, The A novel by MARIA EDGEWORTH, published in the second series of *Tales of Fashionable Life* in 1812. It is set on a large landholding in Ireland, whose absentee landlord, Lord Clonbrony, is finally persuaded to return to his responsibilities by his son.

Absurd, Theatre of the Literally meaning 'out of harmony', absurd was Albert Camus's designation for the dilemma of modern man, a stranger in an inhuman universe. Recognizing such strangers in stage characters in the 1950s, critic Martin Esslin's influential *Theatre of the Absurd* (1961) applied the term to contemporary playwrights who presented man's metaphysical absurdity in an aberrant dramatic style mirroring the situation. His main examples were Adamov, Ionesco, Genet and BECKETT, whose WAITING FOR GODOT brought international acclaim to the Theatre of the Absurd. ALBEE and PINTER received less attention. Journalists soon seized upon the term, confusing it with the everyday meaning of absurd as outrageously comic and applying it to almost every non-realistic modern dramatist.

A shared recognition of the incongruity of human life is not enough to create a distinct or distinguishable group of writers, which is to say that the Theatre of the Absurd remains, however it is employed, a critical invention. Certain of the techniques used by absurdist writers have nevertheless established themselves in the contemporary theatre, and it is in this formal sense, rather than in any philosophical one, that the idea of a 'Theatre of the Absurd' has maintained a critical currency-value. The carrying of logic *ad absurdum*, the dissolution of language, the bizarre relationship of stage properties to dramatic situation, the diminution of sense by repetition or unexplained intensification, the rejection of narrative continuity and the refusal to allow characters or even scenery to be self-defining have become acceptable stage conventions. Beckett's question, 'What has one thing to do with another?', is quite as much a formal matter as a philosophical one. The techniques are of the disruptive kind associated with FARCE, but there is no presiding context of harmony to give reassurance to an audience. Instead there are stage images of extraordinary concreteness, dissociated from the milieu that normally defines them.

Abt Vogler A DRAMATIC MONOLOGUE by ROBERT BROWNING, published in *Dramatis Personae* (1864). The speaker is the Abbé Georg Josef Vogler (1749–1814), advocate of a new system of harmony based on mathematics and precursor of the musical theories of Liszt and Wagner.

Academy, The A periodical founded by Charles Edward Cutts Birch Appleton in 1869. Covering a wide range of topics in art, literature and the sciences, it included MARK PATTISON, MATTHEW ARNOLD and THOMAS HENRY HUXLEY among its contributors and LORD ALFRED DOUGLAS among its editors.

accentual metre See METRE.

Achebe, Chinua 1930– Nigerian novelist, short-story writer, essayist, editor and writer of CHILDREN'S LITERATURE. Born at Ogidi, Eastern Nigeria, he attended secondary school at Government College, Umuahia, and graduated from University College, Ibadan, in 1953. He worked in Nigerian broadcasting from 1954 and was Director of External Broadcasting until 1967. During the Nigerian Civil War (1967–70) he was in Biafran government service. After the war he taught in United States and Nigerian universities.

Achebe's indignation at European representations of Africans in fiction prompted him to write his first novel, now a classic, *THINGS FALL APART* (1958). *ARROW OF GOD* (1964, revised 1974) deals more extensively with similar themes, but *No Longer at Ease* (1960) and *A Man of the People* (1966) treat modern Nigerian urban and political problems satirically. He has also published *The Sacrificial Egg and Other Stories* (1962) and *Girls at War and Other Stories* (1972), and children's books: *Chike and the River* (1966), *How the Leopard Got His Claws* (1972), *The Flute* and *The Drum* (1977). Achebe's war experience is astringently expressed in *Beware, Soul Brother* (1971; as *Christmas in Biafra and Other Poems* in the USA, 1972).

Some of his many lectures and essays appeared in *Morning Yet on Creation Day: Essays* (1975) and *Hopes and Impediments: Selected Essays, 1965–87* (1988). He became founding editor of the African Writers Series for Heinemann Educational Books in 1962 and of *OKIKE: AN AFRICAN JOURNAL OF NEW WRITING* in 1971. He has co-edited: *The Insider: Stories of War and Peace from Nigeria* (1971); *Don't Let Him Die* (1978), a commemorative volume for his friend CHRISTOPHER OKIGBO; *African Short Stories* (1985); and

Chinua Achebe

Contemporary African Short Stories. During the 1983 Nigerian elections he was elected Deputy National President of the People's Redemption Party and wrote a political statement, *The Trouble with Nigeria.* *ANTHILLS OF THE SAVANNAH* (1987) is a novel about the failures of contemporary African politicians and intellectuals.

Ackerley, J(oseph) R(andolph) 1896–1967 Literary editor. He was born in London and educated at Rossall School and (after serving in World War I) at Cambridge, where he studied law. During the 1920s he wrote a play, *Prisoners of War* (1925), and visited India as private secretary and tutor in a maharaja's household. His experiences were recorded in *Hindoo Holiday* (1932). As literary editor of *THE LISTENER* from 1932 until 1959 he published contributions from many distinguished writers, including E. M. FORSTER and CHRISTOPHER ISHERWOOD. *My Dog Tulip* (1956) and the novel *We Think the World of You* (1960) are about his relationship with a pet Alsatian. *My Father and Myself,* published posthumously in 1968, gives a fascinating account of his father, who managed to live a secret life behind the trappings of respectability.

Ackroyd, Peter 1949– Novelist and biographer. While his lives of EZRA POUND (1980), T. S. ELIOT (1984) and DICKENS (1990) have found separate acclaim, a principle of literary and biographical criticism also informs much of his fiction. *The Great Fire of London* (1982) attempts to apply a Dickensian narrative idiom to a story of a modern attempt to film *LITTLE DORRIT* in the City of London (the capital is often a resonant location in Ackroyd's fiction). *The Last Days of Oscar Wilde* (1983) is an eloquent pastiche of WILDE's final diary. *Hawksmoor* (1985) explores the life of the architect in convincingly 18th-century prose, and *Chatterton* (1987) the life of THOMAS CHATTERTON. Subsequent novels are *First Light* (1989), which uses rural England as the setting to speculate on landscape and antiquity, and *English Music* (1992). His prolific output has also included poetry and television criticism.

Acorn, Milton 1923–86. Canadian poet. Born in Charlottetown, Prince Edward Island, he was disabled in World War II and subsequently worked as a carpenter, living in Montreal, Toronto and Charlottetown. He was briefly married to GWENDOLYN MACEWEN. In the 1960s he was a staunch Canadian nationalist and an advocate of counter-culture values, reacting (like IRVING LAYTON and LEONARD COHEN) against the elitist views which he believed had dominated Canadian literature. His verse is informed by socialist politics and a strong sense of the need for literature to be committed to populist causes. It also vividly chronicles the boarding-house world in which he spent much of his life. Volumes include *I've Tasted My Blood* (1969), *More Poems for People* (1972), *This Island Means Minago* (1975), *Jackpine Sonnets* (1977), *Dig Up My Heart* (1983) and a number of posthumous publications, including *Whiskey Jack* (1986), *The Uncollected Acorn* (1987) and *Hundred Proof Earth* (1988).

acrostic A poem in which letters in successive lines make a word or pattern. In a true acrostic, like the 'Argument' at the beginning of BEN JONSON's *VOLPONE*, the word is formed by the first letter of each line. Variants are the mesostich, which uses the middle letters to form a word, and the telestich, using the final letters. See also PALINDROME.

Acton, Sir Harold (Mario Mitchell) 1904– Poet, novelist and self-styled 'aesthete'. Acton was born at 'La Pietra', the 14th-century villa in the hills above Florence which is still his home. He was educated at Eton and Christ Church, Oxford. During his second term at Oxford he published a volume of poetry, *Aquarium* (1923); another volume, *This Chaos*, appeared in 1930.

From 1932 to 1939 Acton travelled extensively, visiting Europe, the United States and China – a country with which he felt a special affinity. He translated several works of Chinese poetry and wrote on Oriental art and culture. A novel, *Peonies and Ponies* (1941), was also set in China 'to illustrate the effect of Peking on a typical group of foreigners and the effect of these foreigners on a few Chinese'.

During World War II he served in the Royal Air Force, and afterwards began work on the first part of his autobiography, *Memoirs of an Aesthete* (1948), covering the years 1904–39. The label 'aesthete' had been applied to him since leaving school, but he was careful to associate it with its 'original' meaning. He considered himself a 'citizen of the world' with a duty to 'remind... fellow creatures of what they are fast forgetting, that true culture is universal'. A second volume of autobiography, *More Memoirs of an Aesthete*, appeared in 1970.

Acton's historical studies included *The Last Medici* (1932) and *The Bourbons of Naples* (1957). He also published volumes of short stories (*The Soul's Gymnasium and Other Stories* and *Tit for Tat and Other Tales*) and a 'memoir' of NANCY MITFORD. He was awarded the CBE in 1965.

Acton, Sir John (Emerich Edward Dalberg), 1st Baron Acton 1834–1902 Historian. The son of Sir Ferdinand Acton and his German wife, Acton was born in Naples and brought up a Roman Catholic. He received an international education, at Paris, the new Roman Catholic College in Oscott, Edinburgh, and Munich, where he studied under the liberal theologian and historian von Döllinger. Elected Whig MP for Carlow in 1859, he was created Baron Acton on Gladstone's recommendation in 1869. From the 1860s he acquired a reputation as a writer and teacher of liberal Catholic ideas, many of which brought him into conflict with the ecclesiastical authorities, notably his rejection of Papal infallibility in *Letters from Rome on the Council* (1870). In 1886 he was instrumental in founding the *English Historical Review*, to which he contributed the article 'German Schools of History'. He was appointed Regius Professor of Modern History at Cambridge in 1895, and became first editor of the *Cambridge Modern History* (1899–1900). Acton's influential series of lectures on modern history and the French Revolution were published posthumously in 1906 and 1910.

Acts and Monuments A work of Protestant history and propaganda by JOHN FOXE, formally entitled *Acts and Monuments of These Latter and Perilous Days, Touching Matters of the Church* in its first English edition (1563), but soon popularly known as 'Foxe's Book of Martyrs'. It had largely been written while Foxe was in exile during Queen Mary's reign, a period which supplied part of its subject and fuelled its fervent tone. Two Latin versions had appeared on the Continent: *Commentarii rerum in ecclesia gestarum* (Strasburg, 1554), taking the history as far as WYCLIF and John Hus, and *Rerum in ecclesia gestarum* (Basle, two parts, 1559 and 1563), an expanded version continuing the story almost to the end of Mary's reign.

Expanded again in 1570 and many times reprinted, *Acts and Monuments* proved enormously popular, especially in Puritan households. Its account of Roman Catholic persecution and Protestant martyrdom, illustrated with graphic woodcuts, helped to shape anti-Catholic – particularly anti-Spanish – sentiment in the 16th century and afterwards.

Adam Bede GEORGE ELIOT's first full-length novel, published in 1859. The idea for the story came from the account her aunt Elizabeth Evans, a Methodist preacher, gave of the night she had spent in the condemned cell at Nottingham jail with a girl awaiting execution for the murder of her child.

Adam Bede, a carpenter in the Midland village of Hayslope, is in love with Hetty Sorrel, niece of the farmer Martin Poyser. The squire, Arthur Donnithorne, is attracted to Hetty and she is vain enough to dream of becoming the squire's wife. Adam watches Arthur's flirtation with growing anxiety and tries unsuccessfully to intervene. Arthur abandons Hetty after seducing her. Adam earns the reward of his loyalty to Hetty when, heartbroken at Arthur's desertion, she agrees to marry him. But she finds herself pregnant and flies from home in a desperate search for her lover. Adam is supported in his grief by Dinah Morris, a young Methodist preacher, with whom his brother Seth is hopelessly in love. Unable to find Arthur Donnithorne, the unfortunate Hetty is arrested, charged with the murder of her child and convicted. Dinah becomes her comforter and the close of the novel describes how Hetty, with Dinah's help, faces her final ordeal. But she is reprieved and her sentence commuted to transportation. Adam later marries Dinah.

The novel was exceptionally well received by contemporary reviewers, who praised its evocation of English rural life and its character studies, particularly Martin's wife, Mrs Poyser.

Adams, Andy 1859–1935 American novelist. Born in Indiana, he spent much of his life in the Texas cattle country and the mining centres of Colorado. He is best known for his authentic, unsentimental depictions of cowboy life in the days of the open range and of the westward expansion of the railroad. His most notable book is *The Log of a Cowboy* (1903). His other works include *The Outlet* (1905), *Cattle Brands* (1906), *Reed Anthony, Cowman* (1907), *Wells Brothers* (1911) and *The Ranch on the Beaver* (1927).

Adams, Arthur Henry 1872–1936 Novelist and poet. Born at Laurence, New Zealand, he worked as a journalist in Australia and New Zealand and visited China in 1900 during the Boxer rebellion. He published several volumes of fiction with an Australasian background including *Tussock Land* (1904), *The New Chum and Other Stories* (1909), *Galahad Jones* (1910),

The Australians (1920) and *A Man's Life* (1929). His verse included a war poem, *My Friend, Remember* (1914). He wrote *Three Plays for the Australian Stage* (1914) with a view to helping the establishment of Australian commercial theatre. He also produced light fiction under the pseudonyms of Henry James James and James James.

Adams, Francis William Lauderdale 1862–93 Australian poet. Born in Malta and educated at Shrewsbury School, he went to Australia in 1884. His poetry, represented by three volumes, *Henry and Other Tales* (1884), *Poetical Works* (1887) and *Songs of the Army of the Night* (1888), was admired by WILLIAM MICHAEL ROSSETTI for its 'intensity and fierceness of tone'. Adams also wrote several novels, among them *John Webb's End: Australian Bush Life* (1891), and two volumes of essays on contemporary Australian society and culture, *Australian Essays* (1886) and *The Australians* (1893). A play, *Tiberius*, was published posthumously with an introduction by Rossetti.

Adams, Henry (Brooks) 1838–1918 American historian and man of letters. He was born in Boston, the grandson of John Quincy Adams, the sixth President of the United States, and the great-grandson of John Adams, the second President. He wrote numerous histories and political essays, but his two most important works are MONT-SAINT-MICHEL AND CHARTRES (privately printed 1904, published 1913), a study of 13th-century culture, and THE EDUCATION OF HENRY ADAMS (privately printed 1907, published 1918), an autobiographical exploration of his heritage and a critical examination of the age in which he lived.

His first publication, an essay on Captain John Smith, appeared in 1867. From 1870 to 1877 he taught history at Harvard, where he had himself been educated, and edited THE NORTH AMERICAN REVIEW. During this period he produced *Chapters of Erie and Other Essays* (with his brother Charles Francis Adams; 1871) and edited *Essays on Anglo-Saxon Law* (1876) and *Documents Relating to New England Federalism 1800–15* (1877). Discouraged by his experiences as a teacher, he left Harvard and went to Washington to observe the political scene at first hand. In 1879 he wrote *The Life of Albert Gallatin* and *The Writings of Albert Gallatin*, both of which examine the career of the émigré Swiss who became a controversial politician, Jefferson's Secretary of the Treasury, and the author of a pioneering study of the North American Indian. In the following year he anonymously published *Democracy*, a novel about political life in Washington. In 1884 he published the novel *Esther* under the pseudonym of Frances Snow Compton. The heroine was modelled on his wife, Marian, whose subsequent suicide in 1885 apparently brought to a head the discontent that he had been feeling for some time with life in America. He began to travel, first in the

Orient with the artist John La Farge and then in the Sierras with the geologist Clarence King.

He returned to Washington to complete his largest-scale historical study, the nine-volume *History of the United States of America during the Administrations of Thomas Jefferson and James Madison* (1889–91). Further travels in the Pacific and in Europe led to *Memoirs of Marau Taaroa, Last Queen of Tahiti* (1893) and *Mont-Saint-Michel and Chartres* (1904). In 1910 he published *A Letter to American Teachers of History*, which was later reprinted in *The Degradation of the Democratic Dogma* (1919) by his brother Brooks Adams. In *The Education of Henry Adams* he self-consciously presents himself as being representative of the American mind at a particular historical moment; he has taken his place as such in the literary and critical tradition.

Adams, Richard (George) 1920– Novelist and writer of CHILDREN'S LITERATURE. Born in Berkshire, the son of a doctor, Adams served in World War II before graduating from Oxford to become a successful civil servant. *WATERSHIP DOWN* (1972) – his first and most famous book, about the wanderings of a group of rabbits – was rejected by many publishers before appearing to acclaim from both children and adults. *Shardik* (1974) is an ambitious novel about a humanized bear; it horrific accounts of man's cruelty to beasts reflect a major preoccupation in Adams's work. Since then he has written some long, humorous ballads for children but otherwise moved towards adult fiction, with *The Plague Dogs* (1977) and *The Girl in a Swing* (1980), his first exclusively adult book. *Day Gone By* (1990) is his autobiography.

Adamson, Robert (Henry) 1944– Australian poet. He was born in Sydney. Experience in reform school and prison provided material for an experimental novel, *Zimmer's Essays* (with Bruce Hanford; 1974), and his first collection of poems, *Canticles on the Skin* (1970). *Where I Came From* (1979) and *The Law at Heart's Desire* (1983) resemble his earliest verse in content and manner but intervening work, eclectic and experimental, has been seen as the platform on which the Australian 'new poetry' of the 1970s stands. *The Rumour* (1971), *Swamp Riddles* (1974), *Theatre I–XIX* (1976) and *Cross the Border* (1977) constantly explore themes of metamorphosis and poetry as deception. *Selected Poems 1970–1989* (1990) contains what Adamson wishes to preserve. As editor of *Poetry Magazine* he transformed it into the modernist *New Poetry*.

Adcock, Fleur 1934– New Zealand/English poet. Born in Papakura on New Zealand's North Island, she studied at Victoria University in Wellington. After briefly working as an assistant lecturer in classics at the University of Otago, she held various library posts

in New Zealand and Britain, where she has lived since 1963. Her poetry is notable for its unsentimental treatment of personal and family relationships, its psychological insights and its interest in classical themes. In her work an ostensibly low-key, ironic manner often takes on a chilling quality as she comments on subjects such as love and the death of relationships. Her volumes of verse include *The Eye of the Hurricane* (1964), *Tigers* (1967), *High Tide in the Garden* (1971), *The Scenic Route* (1974), *The Inner Harbour* (1979), *Selected Poems* (1983), *The Incident Book* (1986), *Hotspur* (1986), *Meeting the Comet* (1988) and *Time Zones* (1991). She has translated a medieval Latin poem, *The Virgin and the Nightingale* (1983), and the work of the Romanian poet Grete Tartler, in *The Orient Express* (1989), as well as editing *The Oxford Book of New Zealand Verse* (1982) and *The Faber Book of Twentieth Century Women's Poetry* (1987).

Adding Machine, The A play by ELMER RICE, first presented by the Theatre Guild in 1923 at the Garrick Theatre, New York. It was among the earliest experiments with EXPRESSIONISM in the American theatre. The central character, Mr Zero, is a slave to routine. When he learns that he has been replaced by an adding machine in the department store where he works, he murders his boss with a bill file. Condemned to death and executed, he goes to a pastoral heaven, but is unable to adjust until he is set to work on a giant adding machine. Finally the authorities there decide to send him back to earth, where he will operate an even better and more efficient machine.

The point of the play lies not in its plot but in Rice's portrayal of Zero's over-mechanized, joyless existence through carefully chosen, symbolic detail. Even though Zero is not an entirely sympathetic character, the play is a clear indictment of the systematic application of commercial values to crush the individual soul.

Addison, Joseph 1672–1719 Essayist, poet and playwright. Son of the Dean of Lichfield, he was educated at Charterhouse (where one of his schoolfellows was RICHARD STEELE) and at Magdalen College, Oxford, where he became a fellow. Addison was a notable classical scholar, and his Latin verse was commended by DRYDEN. From 1699 to 1703 he travelled on the Continent, with a mind to entering the diplomatic service. *The Campaign* (1704) is a poem in HEROIC COUPLETS celebrating the English victory at Blenheim.

His Whig supporters in London secured Addison an appointment as Commissioner of Excise in 1705; he entered Parliament in 1708 and remained an MP until his death. In 1709 he went to Ireland as chief secretary to Lord Wharton, the Lord Lieutenant, though he lost office with the collapse of the Whig government in 1710, when he returned to London. He became a member of the KIT-CAT CLUB, where his close acquaintances included SWIFT and Steele. The latter was then editor of THE TATLER, to which Addison contributed papers between 1709 and 1711, when the two friends founded THE SPECTATOR, which ran until 1712, and was revived in 1714. Addison also contributed to Steele's THE GUARDIAN during 1713. One of the leading editorial journalists of his age, he wrote urbane and familiar prose, a model of the 'middle style' so admired in that period.

CATO (1713), his BLANK-VERSE tragedy, was staged to great success at DRURY LANE but his later prose-comedy, The Drummer (1715), was a failure. When the Whigs returned to power in 1715, Addison was appointed Chief Secretary for Ireland, becoming a Lord Commissioner of Trade in 1716, the year in which he married the Countess of Warwick. He started a political newspaper The Freeholder (1715–16), his last journalistic venture being The Old Whig, which reveals a growing estrangement from his old friend Steele. He is buried in Westminster Abbey.

Ade, George 1866–1944 American humorist, short-story writer and playwright. Born in Kentland, Indiana, Ade began his career by writing for the Chicago Record. Interested in stories of everyday characters, he achieved success with his extensive use of colloquialism in Fables in Slang (1899). This form of fable became his trademark and the substance of several more books, including Forty Modern Fables (1901), People You Know (1903), and Hand-Made Fables (1920). Ade was also a popular writer of both musical and dramatic comedies, of which the best known are probably The Sultan of Sulu (1903) and The College Widow (1904).

Adelphi, The A journal founded by JOHN MIDDLETON MURRY in 1923, appearing monthly at first and then from 1927 as a quarterly (under the title The New Adelphi until 1930). Its purpose was chiefly to air the literary and philosophical views of Murry himself and of his friend D. H. LAWRENCE. Murry handed over the editorship in 1930 to Max Plowman and Richard Rees. Before it ceased publication in 1955 it had counted W. H. AUDEN, T. S. ELIOT, GEORGE ORWELL and W. B. YEATS among its contributors.

Admirable Crichton, The A comedy by J. M. BARRIE, first performed at the Duke of York's Theatre, London, in 1902. A model butler in the household of Lord Loam, Crichton becomes, by a social reversal based on his adaptability and ingenuity, lord of the island when the family is shipwrecked. After supervising the rescue in the last act, he reverts to his subservient role.

Adonais: An Elegy on the Death of John Keats SHELLEY's lament for his fellow poet, published in 1821. Written in SPENSERIAN STANZAS, the ELEGY moves from an account of the mourning at KEATS's bier to a triumphant affirmation of his immortality.

Advancement of Learning, The A treatise by FRANCIS BACON, properly titled The Two Books of Francis Bacon: Of the Proficiency and Advancement of Learning, Divine and Humane, published in 1605. It constitutes the preliminary section of Bacon's great scheme for intellectual and scientific reform, the Instauratio magna ('Great Instauration'), continued in NOVUM ORGANUM (1620). The Advancement of Learning itself was extended in the Latin version, De augmentis scientiarum (1623).

It begins by disposing of objections to the idea of learning and championing its advantages. Bacon goes on to attack the various methods of education currently in practice, based on the Aristotelian structures of knowledge, and to suggest they would be improved if the student worked from experiment and observation rather than theory. The principal subdivisions of knowledge (history, poetry and philosophy) are then considered.

AE [A. E.] See RUSSELL, GEORGE WILLIAM.

Aelfric fl. c. 955–c. 1010 Aelfric Grammaticus, 'the grammarian', studied with the Benedictine order at Winchester under St Aethelwold, whose example he followed in promoting the monastic reforms of the 10th century. His authority was recognized in his own lifetime. His best-known works were written while he was a teacher at Cerne Abbey: a Latin Grammar and Glossary, and the Colloquy, a primer with a parallel Old English/Latin text. Consisting of dialogues between a teacher and pupils who adopt the characters of working people, the Colloquy gives a vivid picture of everyday life. Other writings included: two sets of homilies in English, largely based on the works of BEDE, Augustine, Jerome and Gregory; a translation of Bede's De temporibus; a collection of SAINTS' LIVES; and translations from the Old and New Testaments (see THE BIBLE IN ENGLISH). As abbot of Eynsham, he wrote a life of St Aethelwold and several minor treatises. The lucidity of his style and the variety of religious topics on which he wrote ensured Aelfric's lasting popularity: copied throughout the Middle Ages, his writings became the first Old English works to be printed.

Aelred [Ailred] **of Rievaulx** 1110–67 Abbot of Rievaulx. Born of a long line of married Benedictine priests in Northumbria, he spent his boyhood at Hexham, went to school in Durham, and entered the household of David I of Scotland, whose steward he became. On his way back from a visit to York in 1134, Aelred visited the new Cistercian foundation at Rievaulx and decided to stay on as a novice monk. He became the confidential adviser of Abbot William and, in 1142, novice master. He wrote *Speculum caritatis* at this time, a book inspired by two friends, the prior and another monk; its introductory letter was written by Bernard of Clairvaux. In 1143 he was appointed abbot of St Laurence, a daughter house of Rievaulx, returning to Rievaulx as its abbot in 1147. In 1152–3 he wrote *Genealogia regum anglorum*, containing a eulogy of King David. In 1155 he wrote on the saints of Hexham, to celebrate their translation. Between 1158 and 1163 he composed sermons on Isaiah and *De spirituali amicitia*, in which he wrote of monastic friendships. He also wrote *De institutione inclusarum* for his sister. In 1163 he wrote a life of Edward the Confessor at the request of Laurence, Abbot of Westminster. *De anima* was apparently unfinished at his death. Aelred's biography was written by Walter Daniel, who entered Rievaulx in 1150.

Aesthetic Movement A movement of mind, or shift in sensibility, arising in the 1880s. Its credo of 'Art for Art's sake' and its aspirations in verse and prose, and on canvas, ran counter to powerful high-Victorian optimism, UTILITARIANISM and the belief that art should be moral. Touched with melancholy and pessimism, and stirred by exotic art forms, novel precepts and remote cultures, it was shaped by the work of WALTER PATER as well as by contemporary activities in France. Anti-bourgeois, escapist, dandiacal, flamboyant, placing form before content and ever seeking aesthetic originality, the movement progressively stressed pure sensation and deified the intensity of the moment. Talents as varied as OSCAR WILDE, LIONEL JOHNSON and ERNEST DOWSON were attracted to various phases of the movement; also associated with it were the young YEATS, MAX BEERBOHM, ARTHUR SYMONS, AUBREY BEARDSLEY and RICHARD LE GALLIENNE. *THE YELLOW BOOK* and *The Savoy*, both short-lived publications, were important outlets of the movement, and the RHYMERS' CLUB a nucleus for its adherents.

Agard, John 1949– Guyanese poet, performer and writer of CHILDREN'S LITERATURE. Born and educated in Georgetown, where he worked as a journalist, he published a collection of poetry, *Shoot Me with Flowers* (1973), exhibited paintings and toured the Caribbean with a performance group before coming to Britain in 1977. He has toured as a lecturer for the Commonwealth Institute, performing Caribbean poetry in schools and other venues. He also writes in a more reflective voice, combining scribal and oral influences, in sequences of short poems on common themes. *Man to Pan* (1982) traces the origins of the steel band pan. *Limbo Dancer in Dark Glasses* (1983) follows WILSON HARRIS and EDWARD BRATHWAITE in connecting the limbo dance with the Atlantic slave-ship crossings. *Lovelines for a Goat-Born Lady* (1990), dedicated to GRACE NICHOLS, celebrates Caribbean sensuality and the language in which it expresses itself. His children's books include *Quetzy de Saviour* (1976), *Letters from Lettie* (1979) and *I Din Do Nuttin* (1983).

Agate, James (Evershed) 1877–1947 Drama critic. Born in Manchester, he began his career as reviewer for *The Manchester Guardian*. It was as drama critic of *The Sunday Times* from 1923 until his death that Agate established himself as the most feared and most courted of theatrical judges. His exemplary determination to write well did not prevent an occasional waywardness in deciding what to say nor a preparedness to resist radical change in the London theatre. He became too conscious of his own personality, as is disarmingly confessed in the very title of his nine-volume selection from his diary, *Ego* (1938–47). Among his volumes of selected criticism are *Brief Chronicles* (1943), *Red-Letter Nights* (1944) and *Immoment Toys* (1945).

Age of Innocence, The A novel by EDITH WHARTON, published in 1920 and awarded a PULITZER PRIZE the following year. Mainly set in New York during the 1870s, it tells the story of Newland Archer, a lawyer, and his involvement with two women: May Welland, who becomes his wife, and her cousin, Ellen Olenska, the wife of a Polish count. Ellen, having left her husband, appears in New York, where her unconventional behaviour displeases society. Newland, on behalf of the Welland family, is called upon to dissuade her from divorcing the count. Attracted by her foreign exoticism, Newland falls in love with her, but the constraints of society and his impending marriage to May keep them apart. His interest in Ellen, however, continues after his marriage and prompts May to disclose to her cousin that she is pregnant, whereupon Ellen quickly leaves New York to live in Paris. Visiting the city 30 years later, the widowed Newland decides to preserve his idealized memories rather than call on her.

Age of Reason, The A tract by THOMAS PAINE, written during his imprisonment in Paris and published in 1794–6. Showing his inclination towards DEISM, it makes a stark critique of accepted religious belief and practices. The first part argues that a rational knowledge of God does not accord with traditional conceptions of the Deity; the second illuminates various inconsistencies in the Bible in order to invalidate both literal and figurative readings of the text. The book estranged Paine from many of his more orthodox American friends.

Agee, James 1909–55 American journalist, social critic, poet and novelist. Born in Knoxville, Tennessee, he was educated at Harvard and then moved to New York City, where he worked as a staff writer and eventually as a film critic for *Fortune* and *Time* (1932–48), as well as for THE NATION (1943–8). He also wrote several filmscripts, including *The African Queen* (with John Huston, 1951), *The Bride Comes to Yellow Sky* (based on STEPHEN CRANE's short story, 1953) and *The Night of the Hunter* (1955). He is perhaps best known for *Let Us Now Praise Famous Men* (1941), the product of an eight-week collaboration with the photographer Walker Evans, which sympathetically depicts the plight of three rural Alabama families during the Depression. Agee's poems and short stories were collected and edited by Robert Fitzgerald in 1968. His two novels, *The Morning Watch* (1951) and *A Death in the Family*, which was published posthumously in 1957 and won the PULITZER PRIZE the following year, are partly autobiographical, the first dealing with religious piety and the second with the effects on a family of a father's early death.

Agnes Grey A novel by ANNE BRONTË, published in 1847. It is based on her experiences as a governess. Agnes Grey, a rector's daughter employed by the Murray family, is badly treated and her loneliness is relieved only by the kindness of the curate, Weston, whom she eventually marries.

Ahlberg, Alan 1938– Writer of CHILDREN'S LITERATURE. With his illustrator-wife Janet, he has produced many picture books, popular with small children and highly successful with critics. Their first great success, *Each Peach Pear Plum* (1978), is an accumulative verse using characters from nursery rhymes and fairy tales. The *Happy Families* series, warmly affectionate but never cloying, stretches from *Mr Biff the Boxer* (1980) to *Mr Creep the Crook* (1988). Other titles extend the concept of what a book can do. In *Peepo!* (1981) each page contains a small opening through which it is possible to spy on the events happening overleaf. Most successfully of all, *The Jolly Postman* (1987) is made up of amusing and incongruous letters, each in their individual envelope, addressed to and from famous fairy-tale characters. They are delivered by the jolly postman himself, whose progress is described in RHYME.

Aidoo, Ama Ata 1942– Ghanaian playwright, novelist, short-story writer and poet. Born in the Central Region of Ghana, and originally known as Christina Ama Aidoo, she is a graduate of the University of Ghana, where she was later made a fellow of the Institute of African Studies. She has held other academic posts in West and East Africa and in the USA. She was briefly Minister of Education in the government of Jerry Rawlings, but fell out with him and settled in Zimbabwe. Aidoo has proved a versatile writer. Her first play and still her best-known work, *The Dilemma*

of a Ghost (1965), is a serious comedy about the pitfalls faced by a black American girl who marries into a Ghanaian family. Marriage, slavery and Western influences are also the subjects of *Anowa* (1969), a play based on a traditional legend. Aidoo's other works include short stories, *No Sweetness Here* (1970); novels, *Our Sister Killjoy* (1977) and *Changes* (1991); poems, *Someone Talking to Sometime* (1985); and CHILDREN'S LITERATURE. She is one of the leading writers to be concerned about the position of women in modern Africa, but has also castigated all forms of corruption, chauvinism and inequality.

Aiken, Conrad (Potter) 1889–1973 American poet, short-story writer and novelist. Born in Savannah, Georgia, Aiken was educated at Harvard, where his contemporaries included T. S. ELIOT and WALTER LIPPMANN. Both his fiction and his poetry reflect his interest in psychology, and his reading of Freud, WILLIAM JAMES and French SYMBOLISM, as well as of EDGAR ALLAN POE, his most obvious American antecedent.

His first collection of verse, *Earth Triumphant, and Other Tales in Verse*, was published in 1914, and was followed by *Turns and Movies* and *The Jig of Forslin: A Symphony* (both 1916). His 16 subsequent volumes include *Selected Poems* (1929), for which he won the PULITZER PRIZE; *And in the Human Heart* (1940), a SONNET sequence; *Collected Poems* (1929); and *Thee* (1967), a book-length poem. He also published several collections of short stories, including *Bring! Bring!* (1925), *Costumes by Eros* (1928) and *Among the Lost People* (1934); five novels, which appeared together in *The Collected Novels* (1964); and numerous critical essays, collected in *Scepticisms: Notes on Contemporary Poetry* (1919), and *A Reviewer's ABC* (1958). *Ushant*, an autobiographical piece, appeared in 1952.

Aiken, Joan (Delano) 1924– Novelist and writer of CHILDREN'S LITERATURE. Born in Sussex, the daughter of CONRAD AIKEN, she was educated at home by her mother until finally going to school at the age of 12. Her first collection of short stories for children, *All You've Ever Wanted*, was published in 1953. In a series of vividly imaginative children's novels, beginning with *The Wolves of Willoughby Chase* (1962) and including *Black Hearts in Battersea* (1964) and *The Cuckoo Tree* (1981), she invented not just convincing characters but whole new periods of history where 19th-century England is ruled by a line of Stuart–Tudor monarchs and train journeys are regularly threatened by hordes of marauding wolves. In the foreground, meanwhile, strong melodramas are enacted mixed with unpredictable, quirky humour. Other novels for children include *Midnight is a Place* (1974), an impressive evocation of Victorian industrial brutality, and the supernatural tale of *The Shadow Guests* (1980). More ghostly stories have included *A Goose on Your Grave* (1987) and *A Foot on the Grave* (1989). Her writing for younger children includes *A Necklace of Raindrops* (1968). She has also written many novels for adults.

Aikin, John 1747–1822 Essayist and physician. An MD of the University of Leiden, Aikin early engaged in polemical pamphleteering which offended his patients. A stroke led him to abandon medicine for letters and he produced a number of ephemeral volumes. He wrote several reports on prisons for John Howard and became his literary executor. He is perhaps best known as the brother of ANNA LAETITIA BARBAULD, with whom he collaborated on *Miscellaneous Pieces* (1773) and the six-volume *Evenings at Home* (1792–6).

Ailred See AELRED.

Ainger, Alfred 1837–1904 Essayist, editor and critic. Born in London, the son of a Unitarian family, and educated at University College School and privately. As a boy Ainger was much influenced by DICKENS, with whose sons he was educated and for whom he acted in the Tavistock House amateur theatricals. Having abandoned his family's Unitarianism, he studied at King's College, London, under F. D. MAURICE. In 1856 he matriculated at Trinity Hall, Cambridge, and was ordained on graduation in 1860. He became a canon of Bristol in 1887 and Master of the Temple in 1894. Ainger was an early contributor to *Macmillan's Magazine*. As an editor and critic he was particularly drawn to the work of CHARLES LAMB, contributing a *Life* to the English Men of Letters series (1882) and editing the *Essays* (1883), the *Poems and Plays* (1884) and the *Letters* (1888, 1904). He also wrote a life of CRABBE for the English Men of Letters series (1903). Ainger's collected *Lectures and Essays* were published in two volumes in 1905.

Ainsworth, William Harrison 1805–82 Novelist. The son of a solicitor, he was born in Manchester and educated at the grammar school there. His first novel, *Rookwood* (1834), which gave a romanticized account of the highwayman Dick Turpin, was a great commercial and popular success. He became editor of *BENTLEY'S MISCELLANY* in 1840 and, at different periods, also edited *Ainsworth's Magazine* and *The New Monthly Magazine*. But he continued to exploit the vein of historical romance he had first tapped with *Rookwood* and wrote 39 novels in all. They include: *Jack Sheppard* (1839), which features another notorious criminal and so helped to fuel the controversy about the NEWGATE NOVEL; *The Tower of London* (1840), about the short reign of Lady Jane Grey; *Old St Paul's* (1841), which uses the Plague and Great Fire of London; *Windsor Castle* (1843), set in the reign of Henry VIII; and *The Lancashire Witches* (1849), set in Pendle Forest. GEORGE CRUIKSHANK and Phiz (HABLOT BROWNE) were notable illustrators of his work. Ainsworth's reputation, which made him the friend of DICKENS and other notable contemporaries, began to sink even in his own lifetime and has not risen since.

Akenside, Mark 1721–70 Poet. The son of a butcher, he himself turned to medicine and conducted a successful practice as a physician in London. Most of his poetry is minor, but *The Pleasures of Imagination* (1744) – revised as *The Pleasures of the Imagination* in 1757 – is remembered for anticipating the concerns of later Romantic poets.

Alabaster, William 1567–1640 Divine, scholar, mystical exegete and poet. Alabaster was educated at Westminster School and Trinity College, Cambridge, which he entered as a scholar in 1584. In 1596 he accompanied the Earl of Essex on his Cadiz expedition as chaplain. The rest of his life saw extraordinary religious vacillations, conversions, reconversions and recantations, beginning with his conversion to Roman Catholicism in 1597 and ending with his appointment as Anglican chaplain to JAMES I in 1618. In between he was deprived of Anglican orders, was imprisoned for some time in the Tower of London and visited Rome, where one of his works was denounced by the Inquisition and put on the Index. This latter incident caused a typical recantation, this time of his Roman Catholicism.

Alabaster's Senecan Latin tragedy *Roxana* was performed at Trinity, Cambridge, *c.* 1592 and printed in 1632. JOHNSON praised it as the only Latin work by an Englishman worthy of note before MILTON's elegies. *Elisaeis*, his unfinished Latin epic glorifying Elizabeth I, was praised by SPENSER in *COLIN CLOUT'S COME HOME AGAIN*, although Spenser's comment that Alabaster was then 'known yet to few' is still true. Alabaster was interested in mystical theology and particularly in eschatology and the Apocalypse. His *Apparatus in revelationem Jesu Christi* (Antwerp, 1607) was the work put on the Index; *Ecce sponsus venit* (1633) is concerned with the end of the world, and *De bestia Apocalypsis* was printed at Delft in 1621. His devotional poems were not printed in his lifetime. They are METAPHYSICAL in their tone and their use of paradox and typology; many resemble the religious poems of JOHN DONNE.

Alastor: or, The Spirit of Solitude A poem by SHELLEY, published in 1816. It reflects his interest in the figure of the contemplative idealist, condemning his attitude as self-centred while at the same time lamenting the condition of the real world.

Albee, Edward (Franklin) 1928– American playwright. Born in Washington, DC, he was adopted by the owner of a chain of vaudeville theatres. He rose to prominence with four one-act plays, *THE ZOO STORY* (1959), *The Death of Bessie Smith* (1960), *The Sandbox* (1960) and *The American Dream* (1961), angrily disenchanted with American middle-class values and influenced by the THEATRE OF THE ABSURD. His reputation was confirmed by *WHO'S AFRAID OF VIRGINIA WOOLF?* (1962), an account of marital conflict and reconciliation, and *Tiny Alice* (1964), an enigmatic story of a murder in which fantasy begins to reassert itself over the claims of REALISM. Later work, aiming at formal elegance rather than emotional intensity, has not always been so highly acclaimed. It includes experimental chamber plays such as *Box* (1968), *Quotations from Mao-Tse Tung* (1968), *Listening* (1975) and *Counting the Ways* (1976), and more substantial work, notably *A Delicate Balance* (1966), about a family's vain search for happiness and purpose, *Seascape* (1975) and *The Lady from Dubuque* (1980). Albee has also dramatized CARSON MCCULLERS's *The Ballad of the Sad Café* (1963), JAMES PURDY's *Malcolm* (1966) and NABOKOV's *LOLITA* (1981).

Alchemist, The A comedy by BEN JONSON, first produced in 1610 and published in 1612. During an outbreak of the plague in London, Lovewit leaves the city and the care of his house to his servant, Face. Face is a confidence trickster and with his henchman, Subtle, uses Lovewit's house as a centre for his frauds. Subtle poses as an alchemist with possession of the philosopher's stone and therefore the ability to confer knowledge of secret processes for increasing wealth, restoring youth, and generally realizing the dreams of the gullible. Taking part in their operations is Subtle's woman, Doll Common. Their victims represent the foolish and greedy from different walks of life: Sir Epicure Mammon, a knight, is a greedy voluptuary; Abel Drugger a tobacconist; Dapper a lawyer's clerk; Ananias and Tribulation Wholesome are two hypocritical Puritans; young Kastril is newly rich and quarrelsome, looking for a suitable match for Dame Pliant, his sister. The villains come close to exposure when Surly, a gambler, sees through their imposture; and they are finally confounded when Lovewit returns to his house without notice. Subtle and Doll take to their heels and Face is left to explain to his master. Lovewit finds the booty from the frauds in his house and decides to keep it. Face cleverly puts Dame Pliant, who is comely as well as rich, in Lovewit's way. Lovewit marries her and Face is at peace with his master.

Alcott, (Amos) Bronson 1799–1888 American educationalist. Born in Connecticut, and perhaps best known as the father of LOUISA MAY ALCOTT, he was a pioneer of new educational methods in America. Although he himself had little formal schooling, he became a teacher in 1823, and in 1834 founded his own Temple School. At a time when American education consisted mostly of strict discipline, codified moral instruction, and memorization of texts, Alcott was devoted above all to instilling the joy of learning in his students. Adhering to TRANSCENDENTALIST principles that upheld the unlimited potential of every human being, he encouraged his students to look into themselves to realize their individual intellects. After 11 years at the Temple School he became school superintendent of Concord, Massachusetts, in 1859. There his work initiated the Concord School of Philosophy (1879–88), which was run by his disciple William T. Harris. His books are no longer widely read, but his ideas have had a lasting influence on American education. His major works include *Observations on the Principles and Methods of Infant Instruction* (1830), *Record of a School* (with ELIZABETH PEABODY; 1835), *The Doctrine and Discipline of Human Culture* (1836) and *Tablets* (1868). *Sonnets and Canzonets* (1882) was written in memory of his wife, Abigail May.

Alcott, Louisa May 1832–88 American novelist and writer of CHILDREN'S LITERATURE. Daughter of BRONSON ALCOTT, she was born in Germantown, Pennsylvania, and grew up in Boston and Concord, Massachusetts. She completed her first book, *Flower Fables*, when she was 16, though it was not published until 1855. During the Civil War she worked as an army nurse in a Union hospital (1861–3), an experience she documented in *Hospital Sketches* (1863).

Louisa May Alcott

From 1867 she edited a children's magazine, *Merry's Museum*.

Although she produced nearly 300 titles in a variety of genres, Alcott generally is remembered as a writer of domestic novels, of which the best known is *LITTLE WOMEN: or, Meg, Jo, Beth, and Amy*. (The novel originally was published in two parts: the first part, *Little Women*, appeared in 1868; the second part, *Good Wives*, came out the following year. In 1871, the two appeared as a single volume entitled *Little Women and Good Wives*.) She drew upon her own life and family experiences in writing this and her other wholesome domestic tales: *Little Men: Life at Plumfield with Jo's Boys* (1871), *Jo's Boys and How They Turned Out* (1886), *Eight Cousins: or, The Aunt-Hill* (1875), *Rose in Bloom* (1876) and others. Under various pseudonyms, she also wrote melodramatic adventure stories. *Work: A Study of Experience* (1873) is a feminist and autobiographical novel. When, as she noted in her journal, she became 'tired of providing moral pap for the young', she wrote *A Modern Mephistopheles* (1877), in which an innocent young woman resists seduction by the diabolic genius with whom her poet-husband has made a Faustian pact. This novel was republished posthumously with another, *A Whisper in the Dark* (1889), which has a similar theme. She died on 6 March 1888, the day of her father's funeral.

Alcuin [Albinus] *c.* 735–804 Theologian and educationalist. His Anglo-Saxon name was Ealhwine. He studied at the episcopal school in York, was later involved in running it and became its head in 778. After meeting Charlemagne at Parma in 781, he went to Aachen as head of the palace school and did not return to England except for a diplomatic visit to renegotiate peace between Charlemagne and Offa, King of Mercia, in 790–2. He retired to be abbot of Tours in 796 and built up the reputation of the school there, remaining its head until his death.

From Aachen he supervised reforms to the educational system in France which quickly spread throughout Europe; his *quadrivium* and *trivium* shaped the pattern of education throughout the Middle Ages. Under his scheme, study centred on religious texts and Latin and profane subjects which could be of use in religious studies, but not secular topics in their own right. The matter taught consisted of remnants of classical culture preserved by Boethius, St Augustine, Isidore, Capella and Cassiodorus, and the grammar of Priscian and Donatus. He was active in denouncing the Adoptian heresy and in securing its condemnation at the Council of Frankfurt. By revising the liturgy, introducing the sung Creed, re-editing the Vulgate Bible and arranging votive masses for days of the week, he played an influential part in the development of Catholicism.

Alcuin's own writing includes handbooks to aid the teaching of Latin, religion, arithmetic and computation, and dialogues on rhetoric and dialectic. He also wrote several SAINTS' LIVES, some mediocre verses in Latin, biblical commentaries and studies in theology and philosophy. Over 300 of his letters survive, a valuable historical source.

Aldhelm, St d. 709 or 710 Writer of Latin prose and verse. Little is known of Aldhelm's life. He acquired a very good education, apparently spending some time at the school of Canterbury, and became abbot of Malmesbury in 675. An enthusiastic and sympathetic churchman, he is said to have stood on bridges and sung vernacular popular songs to attract a crowd, then switched to religious subjects once he had their attention. He instigated and supervised the building of several churches and monasteries. In 705 he was instrumental in drawing in the Welsh to the orthodox Catholic faith. After this he accepted an extensive bishopric covering Somerset and parts of Devon and Dorset – half of Wessex – with his see at Sherborne. A brilliant and famous scholar, he was partly responsible for the resurgence of learning in England. He wrote treatises, letters and verse in Latin, and probably some verses in English which no longer survive. His treatises include *De laude virginitate*, about virginity; a version of it in verse; a work about writing verse which includes a collection of riddles in Latin; and an examination of the Pentateuch. Aldhelm's language is repetitious, bombastic and difficult, showing frequent evidence of his Celtic knowledge and training, but it set the style for the Anglo-Latin poets who came after him.

Aldington, Richard 1892–1962 Poet, novelist and biographer. A member of the group which pioneered IMAGISM, he published *Images 1910–1915* (1915) and *Collected Poems* (1928). He was married to the imagist poet HILDA DOOLITTLE (H. D.) from 1913 to 1937.

During World War I Aldington suffered the effects of gas and shell-shock. His powerful anti-war novel, *Death of a Hero* (1929), presents a savage indictment of the social and intellectual climate of the pre-war era, which so disgusts the 'hero' that he invites his own death by exposing himself to enemy fire. Other novels include *The Colonel's Daughter* (1931), satirizing English village life, and *All Men are Enemies* (1933). Aldington also translated Julien Benda's *La Trahison des clercs* as *The Great Betrayal* (1928) and wrote controversial biographies of D. H. LAWRENCE (*Portrait of a Genius, But...*, 1950) and T. E. LAWRENCE (1955). *Life for Life's Sake* (1941) is an autobiography. His correspondence with LAWRENCE DURRELL, *Literary Lifelines*, was published in 1981.

Aldiss, Brian W(ilson) 1925– Writer of SCIENCE FICTION. Novels like *Non-Stop* (1958) and *Greybeard*

(1964) develop stock themes of science fiction in a thoughtful and stylish manner, but in other work Aldiss has pushed the conventions of the genre to new limits. *Hothouse* (1962) is a fantasia of the far future; *The Primal Urge* (1961) and *The Dark Light-Years* (1964) are boisterous satires; *Report on Probability A* (1968) is an exercise in the anti-novel; and *Barefoot in the Head* (1969) is an extravaganza influenced by JOYCE, set in the aftermath of a psycho-chemical war. His most sustained exercise in invention is the trilogy *Helliconia Spring* (1982), *Helliconia Summer* (1983) and *Helliconia Winter* (1985), and his versatility is amply displayed in several short-story collections. His non-fantastic fiction includes *The Hand-Reared Boy* (1970), *Life in the West* (1980) and *Forgotten Life* (1989). He has also written a history of science fiction, *Billion-Year Spree* (1973; revised with David Wingrove as *Trillion-Year Spree*, 1986).

Aldrich, Thomas Bailey 1836–1907 American novelist and journalist. Born in Portsmouth, New Hampshire, he edited the *Illustrated News* during the Civil War, becoming editor of *Every Saturday* in 1866 and THE ATLANTIC MONTHLY in 1881. His first book, a collection of poems entitled *The Bells*, was published in 1855. His best-known work is *The Story of a Bad Boy* (1870), a novel based on his childhood. Other notable works are *Marjorie Daw and Other People* (1873), a collection of short stories, and *The Stillwater Tragedy* (1880), a detective novel.

Alexander, Meena 1951– Indian poet and novelist. Though born in India, she spent part of her childhood in Sudan and has followed an academic career in the USA. Her verse includes *Stone Roots* (1980), *House of a Thousand Doors* (1988) and *The Storm: A Poem in Five Parts* (1989). *Nampally Road* (1991), a novel, describes an educated woman returning to India after years in Britain. *Fault Lines* (1993) is an autobiography examining 'a life left scattered by multiple migrations and uprootings'. Her other work includes a study of women Romantic writers.

Alexander, Sir William, Earl of Stirling *c.* 1567–1640 Poet and playwright. Courtier to JAMES I and Charles I, he became Secretary of State in 1626 and was created Earl of Stirling in 1633, but died in poverty. His best-known work is *Aurora* (1604), a book of songs and SONNETS. Other works include *The Monarchick Tragedies* (1603–7), four plays on the theme of destructive ambition, and a long poem, *Doomsday* (1614); these have been described by Maurice Lindsay as 'unactable plays' and 'an unreadable poem'.

Alexander of Hales *c.* 1170 or 1180–1245 Philosopher and theologian. Born at Hales in Gloucestershire, he probably trained for the church and held various offices; he became archdeacon of Canterbury in 1235. He studied and taught in Paris, becoming a Master of Arts before 1210 and Master of Theology in 1229. In 1236 he joined the Franciscan order and founded the Schola Fratrum Minorum in Paris. He held the first Franciscan chair in the university, and was largely responsible for establishing the Franciscan order as a teaching body. Basically an Augustinian, he absorbed some Aristotelian doctrines and brought knowledge of this to bear on his theological studies. The contemporary attempt to combine Christian philosophy with classical metaphysics and the Arabic commentaries caused an enduring controversy and debate largely centred on Paris. Although Alexander's name was traditionally attached to the *Summa Theologica*, ROGER BACON denies his authorship; it is a composite work of which Alexander wrote some sections. His works include a commentary on the *Sententiae*, part of an *Expositio Regulae*, and sermons. His work influenced St Bonaventure among others, and earned him the title *doctor irrefragibilis*.

alexandrine See METRE.

Alfred, King *c.* 848–99 King of Wessex (871–99), largely responsible for the restoration of learning in England after the decay in scholarship which the Norse raids had accelerated.

Alfred's own written works were translations, though he often added new material to his sources. Their order is uncertain, but those that survive are: (1) his translation of Gregory the Great's *Cura pastoralis*, a manual of instruction for the clergy, to which Alfred added a preface describing the contemporary decline in learning and outlining his intention to make education more readily available; (2) a translation of the *Historia adversus pagonos* of Paulus Orosius, a textbook of universal history, to which Alfred added accounts of the experiences of contemporary travellers; (3) a version of Boethius' *De consolatione philosophiae*, originally written entirely in prose but with verse renderings of Boethius' metrical passages added later; (4) a translation of Augustine's *Soliloquia*, which was probably Alfred's final work. The last two include much additional material, and his authorship of the last has been questioned, though it now seems likely that he did write it. Alfred probably had a hand in translating a shortened version of BEDE's *Historia ecclesiastica gentis anglorum*, at one time attributed wholly to him but written largely in a dialect not his own. He may have been instrumental in planning the ANGLO-SAXON CHRONICLE, begun during his reign, but there is nothing to suggest he was involved in writing it.

A great deal of information about the king is given in *De rebus gestis Aelfredi Magni* by ASSER, a Welsh monk who became his friend and teacher. Written in Latin, it chronicles Alfred's life from his birth to 887. The account of national events is largely the same as in the *Anglo-Saxon Chronicle*, but Asser added a great deal about Alfred's character and actions. This is at times naive, subjective and fulsome in its praise of the king, but nevertheless remains an invaluable source.

Alger, Horatio 1832–99 American novelist and writer of CHILDREN'S LITERATURE. Born into a strict Puritan family in Massachusetts, he graduated from Harvard Divinity School but spent several Bohemian years in Paris before becoming a Unitarian minister in 1864. He left the ministry in 1866, following alleged liaisons with choirboys, and moved to New York where he became chaplain of the Newsboys' Lodging House, a position to which he devoted most of his remaining years.

His adult novels were largely unsuccessful, in striking contrast to more than 100 novels he wrote for boys, most of them based on a rags-to-riches theme and the moral that a boy can rise from poverty to wealth if he has a good character. The most popular were *Ragged Dick* (1867), *Luck and Pluck* (1869) and *Tattered Tom* (1871), all of which first appeared in serial form. In the same vein as his fiction he wrote several biographies of famous self-made men, under such titles as *From Canal Boy to President* (about Abraham Lincoln; 1881) and *From Farm Boy to Senator* (about James Garfield; 1882).

Algerine Captive, The A novel by ROYALL TYLER, published in 1797. It provides a satiric commentary on contemporary American life. In the first part, Underhill, the narrator, tells of his inappropriately classical education in New England, his own attempts to teach school, and his study and practice of medicine, exposing along the way various instances of American pretension and quackery. He then travels south, serves as a doctor on a slave ship, and sharply condemns American slavery. Abandoned by the ship in Africa, he is himself taken into slavery by the Algerians. The second part of the novel, interspersed with observations about Muslim life, comments obliquely on American culture, as Underhill recounts his first-hand experience of slavery, his resistance of attempts to convert him to Islam, and his various plans to escape. He finally gains his freedom and returns to America.

Algren, Nelson 1909–81 American novelist. He was born in Detroit, but his work is associated with Chicago, the city where he lived and worked. He graduated from the University of Illinois School of Journalism in 1931 and spent much of the Depression as a migratory worker in the South-west, an experience which contributed to his earliest fiction. In 1935 he returned to Chicago and published his first novel, *Somebody in Boots*. He became co-editor of *The New Anvil Magazine* in 1939, and his second novel, *Never Come Morning*, appeared in 1942. He is best known for his novel about drug addiction, *The Man with the Golden Arm* (1949), which won the National Book Award. Other books are *The Neon Wilderness* (1947), *Chicago: City on the Make* (1951), *A Walk on the Wild Side* (1956), *Who Lost an American?* (1963), *Notes from a Sea Diary: Hemingway All the Way* (1965) and *The Last Carousel* (1973). His last novel, *The Devil's Stocking*, was published posthumously in 1983.

Ali, Ahmed 1912– Indian/Pakistani novelist. Born in India, he was educated at Aligarh and Lucknow. He became involved in Urdu cultural affairs while still a student, and has translated much Urdu poetry into English as well as writing short stories in Urdu. After Partition he moved to Pakistan and must now be considered a Pakistani writer. His most important novel, however, is *Twilight in Delhi* (1940), written while he was still an Indian. A magnificent historical novel about Muslim life in Delhi, it remains one of the centrepieces of Indian writing in English. *Ocean of Night* (1964), less well received, is set in Lucknow and depicts the decline of an aristocratic way of life. *Rats and Diplomats* (1985) is a novella, while *The Prison House* (1985) translates a selection of his Urdu stories. A lyrical writer with strong undercurrents of melancholy, Ali has presented the characteristics of Muslim life in India with consummate skill.

Alice B. Toklas, The Autobiography of A fictionalized account by GERTRUDE STEIN, published in 1933, of her life with Alice B. Toklas, the ostensible author-narrator of the book. Stein adopts the persona and even the manner of her secretary and long-time companion, but the story she tells is essentially about her own life, as seen from Toklas's point of view.

Stein and Toklas were, as the narrator claims, 'in the heart of an art movement', and *The Autobiography* catalogues the many famous artists and intellectuals with whom they came into contact. The narrator notes how many wives of geniuses she has had to sit with while Stein – also a genius – has been with their husbands; among them the wives of Picasso, Matisse, Braque, Gris, ERNEST HEMINGWAY, SHERWOOD ANDERSON and FORD MADOX FORD. The book also tells of the visit Stein and Toklas made to Alfred North Whitehead's home in England, where they met LYTTON STRACHEY and BERTRAND RUSSELL, and of their wartime involvement with the American Fund for the French Wounded, when they visited French hospitals and were decorated by the French government. It also provides an account of their busy life from 1919 to 1932 – the years of 'constantly seeing people' such as EZRA POUND, Tristan Tzara, T. S. ELIOT, DJUNA BARNES, Jacques Lipschitz, Jean Cocteau, Marcel Duchamp and EDITH SITWELL.

Alice's Adventures in Wonderland A fantasy by Lewis Carroll, originally published as *Alice's Adventures Under Ground* (1865).

Beginning famously as a story told to children on a boating picnic in 1862, it is half dream, half nightmare and always highly diverting. Plunging down a rabbit hole the seven-year-old Alice grows first too large and then too small. When turning for help or enlightenment from the strange characters around her she usually becomes caught up in logic-chopping, PARODY or pun, whether this be with the Cheshire Cat, the Mad Hatter, the March Hare or the King and Queen of Hearts. Finally she loses her temper, bringing down this dream world and so waking up. Illustrated by Sir John Tenniel, this unique book was an immediate best-seller – much to the surprise of its shy, reclusive author. Its effect on CHILDREN'S LITERATURE, in particular the way it favoured good-humoured iconoclasm at the expense of the conventional didacticism of the time, can hardly be exaggerated. Favourite moments include the parodies 'You are Old, Father William' and 'Twinkle Twinkle Little Bat', the Lobster Quadrille, the Hatter's Tea Party and Alice's own understandable comment, 'Curiouser and curiouser'. See also *THROUGH THE LOOKING-GLASS AND WHAT ALICE FOUND THERE*.

alienation The use of the word 'alienation' (or 'alienation effect') to describe a particular theatrical intention (or technique) derives from the critical writing of the German playwright, Bertolt Brecht. His alienation effects were dramatic or theatrical devices, deployed in order to bring home to audiences the strangeness of social and economic conditions they took for granted. The basic aim is to draw attention to social structures, ideas, principles, motives or conflicts that would normally be ignored, and to draw attention in such a way as to prove them alterable.

Some confusion has inevitably arisen through translation. Brecht coined the word *Verfremdung* to carry his meaning. A kindred word, *Entfremdung*, was already in familiar use. Brecht would certainly have known its application by Marx to the condition of the proletariat in a capitalist economy. Many of Brecht's plays concern themselves with alienation in this sense, and that has confounded the problem. For Brecht, *Entfremdung* was a condition and *Verfremdung* a method of making that condition clear to audiences. He argued that the alienation of the proletariat was not perceived because it was taken for granted, just as an industrialist might honestly believe that a woman's place is in the home despite the fact that he employed women in his factory. Already believing that the alienation of the proletariat was strange, he wished to have people recognize it as strange. That is to say that he wished to alienate alienation – to make strange the condition of proletarian estrangement.

Brecht's use of alienation effects influenced all the major political writers of the post-war English theatre from John Arden and John McGrath to David Edgar and Howard Brenton.

All Fools A comedy by George Chapman, published in 1605 but possibly first performed as early as 1599, and known to have been in the repertoire of the Children of the Revels at the Blackfriars Theatre in 1604. Chapman's source was the *Heautontimorumenos* of Terence, though he imported characters from the same author's *Adelphi*. Gostanzo, a dictatorial father, is gulled into collaborating in the love-affairs of his son and daughter.

All for Love: *or, The World Well Lost* A tragedy in blank verse by John Dryden, first performed in December 1677 and published in 1678. Dryden's chief source is Shakespeare's *Antony and Cleopatra*, from which he borrows freely; but the two plays are very different. Under the influence of French neoclassical theory, Dryden has regularized Shakespeare, confining the action of the play to the period following the battle of Actium. In *All for Love*, Cleopatra struggles for possession of Antony with his general Ventidius, his friend Dolabella and his wife Octavia. The latter nearly succeeds; Caesar (Octavian) is prepared to come to terms with Antony but requires him to separate from Cleopatra and return to his wife, Octavian's sister. The plan founders when Antony grows jealous of Dolabella, thinking the younger man may supplant him in Cleopatra's affections. His suspicions are skilfully fed by Octavia but, with the desertion of the Egyptian fleet and the report that Cleopatra is dead, the play returns to historical fact and the tragedy runs its course.

All the Year Round A weekly magazine edited by Charles Dickens from 1859, when it took over from *Household Words*, until his death in 1870. Like its predecessor, it offered a blend of serialized fiction (including some of Dickens's own later novels) and journalism.

All's Well That Ends Well A comedy by William Shakespeare, probably written or revised in 1602–4. Claims for an earlier date are based on the proposal that this is the *Love's Labour's Won* referred to by Francis Meres in *Palladis Tamia* (1598). It was not published until the First Folio of 1623. The source is a story from Boccaccio's *Decameron*, probably read in the English version in William Painter's *The Palace of Pleasure*.

Helena, ward of the Countess of Rousillon, vainly loves the young count Bertram. She succeeds in marrying him only when she follows him to the French court and cures the sick with a remedy inherited from her father. Invited to choose a husband from among the courtiers, she selects Bertram. He grudgingly complies but escapes immediately afterwards with the help of the cowardly braggart Parolles. He promises to accept her fully as his wife only if she can get a treasured ring from his finger and bear him a child. She succeeds by taking the place in his bed of Diana, a widow's daughter whom he has been courting; she persuades him to exchange rings with her. Unaware of the trick and believing Helena dead, Bertram plans to remarry, but his possession of Helena's ring arouses suspicions of foul play. Matters are resolved when the pregnant Helena appears, with his ring. Confronted by the evidence of his wife's persistence, Bertram accepts her with good grace.

All's Well That Ends Well has never been a favourite among Shakespeare's plays. Often grouped with *MEASURE FOR MEASURE* and *TROILUS AND CRESSIDA*, it shares with these other PROBLEM PLAYS an implied challenge to ideas of romantic love as a basis for marriage. Some of the plotting is perfunctory and the verse uneven, while neither Helena nor Bertram wins ready sympathy from an audience, particularly an audience that has lost confidence in the 'change-of-heart' convention. It is more fairly viewed as a satirical comedy than as a romantic comedy that has lost its way.

Allan Quatermain A novel by SIR HENRY RIDER HAGGARD, published in 1887. A sequel to *KING SOLOMON'S MINES*, it is more sombre in tone and more scholarly in its delineation of a 'primitive' people.

Curtis and Good return to Africa because of a deep disillusion with 'civilized' living which anticipates the primitivism of D. H. LAWRENCE; Quatermain joins the expedition because his life has become meaningless since the death of his only son. After various preliminary adventures, they reach the lost land of Zu-Vendis by a journey along an underground river. The land of Zu-Vendis is ruled by two queens, one dark, the other fair. Both fall in love with Curtis, who chooses the fair queen, Nyleptha. Her dark sister, Sorais, declares civil war but Curtis and Nyleptha are victorious, and Sorais kills herself. Curtis assumes the kingship, but the price to be paid is the death of both Quatermain and the heroic 'primitive', Umslopogaas. When Umslopogaas smashes his battle-axe, 'Inkosi-Kaas' ('Chieftainess'), to fragments on the sacred stone of the palace he fulfils an ancient prophecy, and a new dynasty rules in Zu-Vendis.

In its disillusionment with Western civilization, its glorification of the 'primitive' in the figure of Umslopogaas and its theme of rebirth through sacrifice, the novel presents a fantasy of an uncorrupted new kingdom, free from the gathering storm of modern degenerate trends.

allegory Description or narrative – in verse, prose or drama – presenting literal characters and events which contain sustained reference to a simultaneous structure of other ideas or events. The intention may be didactic, political or humorous, and the subject of the secondary level(s) may be philosophical, historical, theological or moral. Allegory does not consist in the simple substitution of one object or action for another, but relies upon a correspondence between the literal and metaphorical levels to help elucidate the meaning. In figural allegory the form and structure of what is described correspond to the features and structure of what is intended; thus the goddess Fortune is blind to indicate the arbitrary nature of luck. In narrative allegory the sequence of events on the literal level corresponds to a psychological, spiritual, moral or historic progression.

Allegory has its origins in myths, fictional narratives which attempt to explain and contain universal facts of human nature and the material world. All religions therefore have a large allegorical content. In the Middle Ages a fourfold scheme of allegory was seen to operate in the Bible and was emulated in some literary texts. The levels of meaning are (1) the literal, (2) the allegorical, (3) the tropological or moral and (4) the anagogical. These correspond to (1) the historical account, (2) the life of Christ and the Church Militant, (3) the individual soul and moral virtue, (4) the divine schema and the Church Triumphant. The fourfold reading was formulated by John Cassian (AD 360–435), although a similar scheme was proposed by Sallastius (4th century AD). It is a development from exegesis, the explication of biblical passages to develop theological and spiritual significances contained within the literal account of the events of biblical history. Another common method of reading the Bible allegorically is typology, in which the stories of the Old Testament are seen both as historical fact and simultaneously as foreshadowing events of the New Testament.

Although sometimes difficult to penetrate, allegory is generally intended to elucidate rather than obscure, its original purpose being to make universal or divine mysteries accessible to human understanding. The qualities and characteristics of a similar object or event are used to hint at the nature of the unknown. In literary texts allegory appears in a wide variety of forms. The simplest and most explicit is found in EXEMPLA and FABLES, where the relationship between the literal narrative (usually fictional) and a spiritual or moral lesson is deliberately indicated or explained by the author. In other cases (e.g. *PIERS PLOWMAN*), the relation of literal to other levels is complex and shifting as the author searches for appropriate ways of exploring difficult concepts. At other times the intellectual conceit offers a new insight into an idea or event while its actual interpretation is not challenging. Despite the original explanatory intentions of allegory, some 16th-century poets wrote deliberately unfathomable allegories, and sometimes a poet's individual mythological system may render his work almost unintelligible to the reader not supplied with the necessary personal information (e.g. WILLIAM BLAKE). Although it is predominantly associated with the Middle Ages, many later writers have used it in both conventional and original ways (e.g. THE FAERIE QUEENE, PILGRIM'S PROGRESS, THE SCARLET LETTER, MOBY-DICK, ANIMAL FARM).

Allen, (Charles) Grant (Blairfindie) 1848–99 Novelist and popularizer of science. Born in Kingston, Ontario, the son of a clergyman of Irish descent, Allen was educated in America, France and England, at King Edward's School, Birmingham, and Merton College, Oxford. He was for many years a teacher, part of the time in Jamaica. He returned to England in the 1870s, and started publishing scientific and evolutionary works, as a follower of HERBERT SPENCER. Among them were *Physiological Aesthetics* (1877), *The Colour Sense* (1879), which won him high praise from the scientific community, *The Evolutionist at Large* (1881) and *The Evolution of the Idea of God* (1897). Allen is usually remembered now for *The Woman Who Did* (1895), one of nearly 30 novels. Its heroine chooses to live unmarried with her lover and bear his child, but suffers the miseries of the outcast when he dies. It enjoyed a brief *succès de scandale*, though not the approval of feminists.

Allen, James Lane 1849–1925 American novelist and short-story writer. Allen was born in Kentucky and taught there until he moved to New York in 1893. His first attempts at writing, mostly for HARPER'S NEW MONTHLY MAGAZINE, were the short stories, descriptive articles, and critical essays collected in the volume *Flute and Violin* (1891).

In an 1886 article, 'Realism and Romance', which appeared in the New York *Evening Post*, Allen attacked claims for the primacy of REALISM as practised by WILLIAM DEAN HOWELLS and others, defending the older romance tradition associated with NATHANIEL HAWTHORNE and carried on to some extent by the non-urban, regional writers of his own time. He himself is best known for his romances set in the South, especially *A KENTUCKY CARDINAL* (1894) and its sequel, *Aftermath* (1895). His other works include *Summer in Arcady* (1896), *The Choir Invisible* (1897), *The Mettle of the Pasture* (1903), *The Bride of the Mistletoe* (1909) and *The Kentucky Warbler* (1918). His last collection of short stories, *The Landmark*, was published in the year of his death.

Allen, Paula Gunn 1939– American poet. She was born in Cubero, New Mexico, of Laguna Pueblo, Sioux and Chicano parentage. Her collections of poetry are *The Blind Lion* (1974), *Coyote's Daylight Trip* (1978), *Starchild* (1981), *A Cannon between My Knees* (1981), *Shadow Country* (1982), *Skins and Bones* (1988) and

Grandmothers of the Light: A Medicine Woman's Sourcebook (1991). Much of her verse attempts a modern transformation of the mythic heritage of her people. She explores the nature of the Native American past, the alienation of the *mestizo* and the trauma of biculturation, the influence of contemporary white consumer culture on the Native American and, in particular, the dual role of Native American women as victims and reformers of their culture. A novel, *The Woman Who Owned the Shadows: The Autobiography of Ephanie Atencio* (1983), tells the story of one woman's psychological journey towards spiritual rebirth and her attempt to adapt to a biculturated world. Allen has also edited an anthology of Native American women's writing, *Spider Woman's Granddaughters* (1989), and written a scholarly study, *The Sacred Hoop: Recovering the Feminine in American Indian Traditions* (1987).

Allen, Walter (Ernest) 1911– Critic and novelist. Born in Birmingham and educated at King Edward's Grammar School, Aston, and Birmingham University, he worked as a teacher and university lecturer in England, and spent some time in the USA as a visiting lecturer and professor of English at American universities. He published his first novel, *Innocence is Drowned*, in 1938. This and the two which followed, *Blind Man's Ditch* (1939) and *Living Space* (1940), are pictures of working-class life in England on the eve of World War II. His later fiction includes *The Black Country* (1946), *Rogue Elephant* (1946), *Dead Man over All* (1950; as *The Square Peg* in USA) and *All in a Lifetime* (1959; as *Threescore and Ten* in USA).

Allen's critical work was well known through his contributions to THE TIMES LITERARY SUPPLEMENT, *The New Statesman*, and *New Writing* before he published his study of ARNOLD BENNETT in 1948. In the same year came *Writers on Writing* (as *The Writer on His Art* in USA). This was followed by *Reading a Novel* (1949), a study of JOYCE CARY (1953), *The English Novel: A Short Critical History* (1954), *The Novel Today* (1955), *Six Great Novelists* (biographical studies of DEFOE, FIELDING, SCOTT, DICKENS, STEVENSON and CONRAD, 1955), a study of GEORGE ELIOT (1964), and *Tradition and Dream* (1964; as *The Modern Novel in Britain and the United States* in USA).

Alleyn, Edward 1566–1626 Actor, known to have been with Worcester's Men in 1583 and with the Admiral's Men at the ROSE by, at the latest, 1592. It was above all as the creator, for the latter company, of MARLOWE's towering heroes that Alleyn was celebrated. Friendship with the Rose's manager, PHILIP HENSLOWE, was strengthened by marriage to Henslowe's step-daughter and by a business partnership that eventually made Alleyn a rich man. He retired from the stage in 1597, probably to concentrate on some of Henslowe's business enterprises. Together they ran the Bear Garden, possibly from as early as 1594, and built the Fortune as a new home for the Admiral's Men. Alleyn returned to the stage when the Fortune opened in 1600, but his highly rhetorical style may by then have seemed old-fashioned, particularly by comparison with his rival, RICHARD BURBAGE. He had probably retired finally from acting by 1604, when he and Henslowe received a joint patent as Masters of the Royal Game of Bears, Bulls and Mastiff Dogs. In 1605 Alleyn was involved in negotiations to purchase the Manor of Dulwich, where, in 1613, he began the building of the College of God's Gift. The papers he deposited there, including Henslowe's *Diary*, provide unique evidence of business practices in the contemporary theatre. Alleyn's social status, confirmed by his second marriage to JOHN DONNE's daughter, demonstrates the upward social mobility of actors during the reigns of Elizabeth I and James I.

Allingham, Margery (Louise) 1904–66 Writer of DETECTIVE FICTION. Born in London, she was educated at the Perse School for Girls in Cambridge and married the artist and editor Philip Youngman Carter in 1927. She made her reputation during the so-called Golden Age of detective fiction with *The Crime at Black Dudley* (1929), *Mystery Mile* (1930), *Look to the Lady* (1931), *Police at the Funeral* (1931), *Sweet Danger* (1933), *Death of a Ghost* (1934), *Flowers for the Judge* (1936), *Dancers in Mourning* (1937), *The Case of the Late Pig* (1937) and *The Fashion in Shrouds* (1938). Her hero, Albert Campion, is a light-hearted aristocrat modelled on DOROTHY L. SAYERS's Lord Peter Wimsey, but from the start Margery Allingham showed an unusually strong grasp of characterization and a Dickensian eye for the idiosyncrasies of London life. Her post-war novels, particularly *The Tiger in the Smoke* (1952), greatly modify Campion and shed many of her earlier mannerisms. Her last novel, *Cargo of Eagles* (1968), was completed by her husband.

Allingham, William 1824–89 Poet. Born in County Donegal, Ireland, he worked in the customs service until 1870, when he retired to become sub-editor of *FRASER'S MAGAZINE*; he was editor in 1874–9. By then he had published *Poems* (1850), *Day and Night Songs* (1854), several other volumes of poetry and the rhymed novel of Irish life, *Laurence Bloomfield: or Rich and Poor* (1864). His six volumes of *Collected Poems* (1888–93) are culled from these various earlier works. Allingham's poetry, some of it illustrated by DANTE GABRIEL ROSSETTI (a close friend), Arthur Hughes and Millais, is graceful and charged with lyric simplicity; it can also become national in spirit and touched by local colour. Through LEIGH HUNT, Allingham came to know CARLYLE, TENNYSON and other literary lions so that, not surprisingly, his *Diary* (first published in 1907) is a mine of information about Victorian aesthetic life. In 1874 he married the watercolourist and illustrator Helen Paterson.

alliteration The repetition of a sound in two or more words. In its commonest form, initial consonants are repeated: 'Peter Piper picked a peck of pickled peppers'. The repetition of initial vowels tends to make less impact and is therefore less frequent; it is no less alliterative. In the example 'An Austrian army awfully arrayed', it is to be noted that though 'army' begins with the same letter as the other words it does not alliterate with any of them, while 'Austrian/awfully' and 'An/arrayed' alliterate only with each other. Such repetition of initial sounds is sometimes styled initial-rhyme or head-rhyme (see RHYME). The repetition of internal sounds (like the second 'p' in 'Piper' and 'pepper') is sometimes styled hidden alliteration. Often, though not always, this latter kind of alliteration is also an example of consonance or assonance.

Consonance (apart from its unspecialized sense of agreement or harmony) consists in the repetition of similar consonants along with different vowels ('pipe/pep' or 'rife/reef'), assonance being the reverse ('grope/throne'). Since both by definition avoid rhyme, consonance and assonance are the main forms of that near rhyme (or para-rhyme or half-rhyme) which features so prominently in modernist poetry and old-fashioned nursery rhymes alike.

Initial, internal, and final repetitions are often inextricably intertwined (as in 'life's fitful fever') or the effect of one is almost identical with that of another (as with the internal alliteration of the 'Peter Piper' example). It seems sensible, where it is critically convenient, to speak of alliteration for all cases, including those that are also examples of consonance, assonance, or para-rhyme – using those terms for cases where the intertwining, if it exists, is not inextricable or the effects are significantly different. Such does, in fact, seem to be normal critical usage.

alliterative verse Originally Old English, alliterative verse continued to be composed until the end of the 15th century in England and into the early 16th century in Scotland. Between the Old English works and those of the late 13th century no examples of alliterative verse survive, but it is usually thought that it continued to be composed orally before enjoying a revival in the later Middle Ages.

Initially the unrhymed alliterative line had four major stresses, two in each half-line. Any number of minor stresses could be included. Usually the two major stresses of the first half-line and the first of the second half-line alliterate, but this was subject to variation for effect. Consonants alliterate with the same consonant, but all vowels (and some words beginning with 'h') were deemed to alliterate with each other. Towards the end of the period in which alliterative verse was being written, variations in the line form and the use of rhyme began to appear. A special poetic vocabulary, marked by a wide range of synonyms for common nouns, with different initial letters, developed to allow the poet greater flexibility; many of these words are not found outside alliterative poetry.

The best-known examples in Middle English are *SIR GAWAIN AND THE GREEN KNIGHT* and *PIERS PLOWMAN*; all Old English verse is alliterative.

Alther, Lisa 1944– Novelist. She was born in Kingsport, Tennessee, and educated at Wellesley College, Massachusetts. *Kinflicks* (1976) and *Original Sins* (1981), set in the Deep South but using the point of view of a protagonist who has left for the North, as well as *Other Women* (1985) and *Bedrock* (1990), have been praised as a substantial and witty addition to feminist literature.

Alton Locke: *Tailor and Poet* A novel by CHARLES KINGSLEY, published in 1850. It reflects the social and political turbulence of the 1840s, expressing Kingsley's CHRISTIAN SOCIALISM and making a significant contribution to the CONDITION OF ENGLAND NOVEL.

Alton Locke, the son of a small shopkeeper, is apprenticed to a tailor and experiences the squalid conditions of sweated labour. A talent for poetry develops with his consciousness of the need for social reform and he takes readily to Chartism. His poetry brings him into contact with Eleanor Staunton, her cousin Lillian, and Saunders Mackaye, a Scottish bookseller loosely modelled on THOMAS CARLYLE. At the urging of Lillian and her well-to-do father, Alton allows his revolutionary verse to be made innocuous before publication; this earns him the contempt of his Chartist comrades. Their taunts lead him to undertake a mission that provokes a riot, and he is sentenced to three years in prison. Lillian, with whom he has fallen in love, marries someone else during his imprisonment, and it is Eleanor who stands by him when he falls ill with typhus. She nurses him back to health and explains to him her own views on reform and the role of Christianity. Disillusioned by demagogy and violence, Alton becomes a Christian Socialist, and at the close of the story dies on his way to the USA.

Aluko, T(imothy) M(ofolorunso) 1918– Nigerian novelist. A Yoruba, he was born in Ilesha, Nigeria, and educated at Government College, Ibadan, and Higher College, Yaba, Lagos, before undertaking training in civil engineering and town planning at the University of London. He has held senior positions in Nigeria, including that of Director of Public Works in Western Nigeria. He has written many satirical novels, among them *One Man, One Wife* (1959), the first full-length novel in English to be published by a Nigerian publisher, *One Man, One Matchet* (1964), *Kinsman and Foreman* (1966), *Chief the Honourable Minister*

(1970), *His Worshipful Majesty* (1973) and *Wrong Ones in the Park* (1982). Aluko's is a contemporary world, one in which the clash between old and new values gives rise to comedy. Perhaps because his tone is hardly ever judgemental, Aluko has not been regarded as one of the most important African novelists, but he has enjoyed consistent popularity.

Alvarez, A(lfred) 1929– Critic, anthologist and poet. Born in London, he was educated at Oundle and Corpus Christi College, Oxford. He was poetry editor of *The Observer* in 1956–66 and drama critic of *The New Statesman* in 1958–60. His most famous book is *The New Poetry* (1962), an anthology whose combative introduction rejects the gentility of the MOVEMENT and most current English verse, preferring the work of ROBERT LOWELL, JOHN BERRYMAN and SYLVIA PLATH. Plath's suicide is a major element in *The Savage God: A Study of Suicide* (1971), which, with *Beyond All This Fiddle: Essays 1955–1967* (1968), defines his taste for poetry and art which expresses extreme states of psychic disorder. His own poetry reveals an acute understanding of FROST, T. S. ELIOT and DONNE, of whom he has written a study, *The School of Donne* (1961). In *Fantasy Poets 15* (1952), *Apparition* (1971) and *Autumn to Autumn, and Selected Poems 1953–76* (1978) dark IRONY and mordant WIT are used to treat the ebb and flow of human relationships, often simple enough in themselves but made monumental by the economies of his language. He has also published several novels, *Hers* (1974), *Hunt* (1978) and *The Day of Atonement* (1991), and a work of non-fiction, *Off-Shore: A North Sea Journey* (1987).

Amadi, Elechi 1934– Nigerian novelist and playwright. Of the Ekwerri people, he was born in Aluu near Port Harcourt in Eastern Nigeria and educated at Government College, Umuahia, and the University of Ibadan. He spent his early career as a land surveyor and then as a teacher in the Military Academy in Zaria. Although he left the army in 1965 to teach at the Anglican Grammar School in Igrito, Port Harcourt, he later rejoined it, on the Federal side, during the Civil War – though only after having been twice detained in Biafra. He wrote about his experiences of this period in *Sunset in Biafra* (1973), an unusual account of the war because few people from Eastern Nigeria shared Amadi's political perspective. He has written a trilogy of novels, *The Concubine* (1966), *The Great Ponds* (1969) and *The Slave* (1978), which draws on the traditional spiritual and mythic life of his area. *Estrangement* (1986), his fourth novel, portrays the desolation and confusion in society and personal relationships which followed the Nigerian Civil War. His plays, which include *Isiburu* (1973), *The Road to Ibadan* (1977) and *Dancer of Johannesburg* (1978), are slight in scale and not well known. Amadi is regarded as one of the leading African novelists, but perhaps because there is a deliberate lack of historical specificity in much of his work he has tended to languish in the shade of CHINUA ACHEBE.

Amazing Marriage, The A novel by GEORGE MEREDITH, published in 1895.

Carinthia Jane Kirby is the daughter of a sea captain and a runaway countess. She is the charge of her uncle, the miserly Lord Levellier. Lord Fleetwood, immensely rich and spoiled, meets Carinthia at a ball and is so charmed that he proposes to her during a quadrille and is accepted. Fleetwood, realizing his own irresponsibility, hopes Carinthia will realize it too. But she doesn't, and Lord Levellier is determined to hold Fleetwood to the engagement so he can be rid of her. Fleetwood goes through with the marriage – and treats her abominably, eventually abandoning her and their child. Carinthia makes her way to Whitechapel to the house of Gower Woodseer, whom she met in Europe. Woodseer's father is a minister among the poor and Carinthia is given shelter there. Gower, also a friend of Fleetwood, tries to effect a reconciliation, but when he succeeds with Fleetwood it is already too late: Carinthia has determined to go as an army nurse to Spain with her brother Chillon. Fleetwood ends his days as a Roman Catholic monk.

Ambassadors, The A novel by HENRY JAMES, serialized in THE NORTH AMERICAN REVIEW and published, with revisions, in volume form in 1903. James considered it his most 'perfect' work of art.

Lambert Strether is sent to Paris by Mrs Newsome, a wealthy widow, to persuade her son Chad to return to Massachusetts and his responsibilities as head of the family business. Strether's success as an ambassador will ensure his marriage to Mrs Newsome when he returns. On the way he meets Maria Gostrey, an expatriate American whose witty and sympathetic observations introduce him to the pleasure of European life. In Paris he finds Chad an assured and sophisticated young man who is not eager to return to America. Madame de Vionnet has clearly been the refining influence on Chad's life.

Strether's letters to Mrs Newsome reveal his declining enthusiasm for his embassy, and she sends her daughter Sarah, with Sarah's husband and sister-in-law, to appeal to Chad. They receive little help from Strether and their lack of success further estranges him from Mrs Newsome. In the ensuing action Strether makes two discoveries: that Chad's liaison with Madame de Vionnet is an intimate one, and that his own sympathies rest with Chad. However, he remains content to observe life rather than participate in it and ultimately returns to Massachusetts.

Ambler, Eric 1909– Novelist. Born and educated in London, he became an apprentice engineer and advertising copywriter before devoting himself to writing after the success of his first novel, *The Dark Frontier* (1936). His many popular thrillers are all sustained by a successful formula, usually involving an ordinary Englishman who becomes caught up in a web of international espionage and intrigue. With their fast-moving plots and carefully controlled suspense, the novels were early models for subsequent writers in the genre. His many titles include *Epitaph for a Spy* (1938), *The Mask of Dimitrios* (1939; called *A Coffin for Dimitrios* in USA), *Journey into Fear* (1940), *Judgment on Deltchev* (1951), *The Night-Comers* (1956), *Passage of Arms* (1959) and *Dirty Story* (1967). He has also written many screenplays, beginning with *The Way Ahead* (with Peter Ustinov; 1944).

Amelia The last novel by HENRY FIELDING, published in 1751.

William Booth, an attractive but impetuous young army officer, has married the virtuous and beautiful Amelia against her mother's wishes. The couple run away and fall foul of the predatory world of London, which is the focus of the book's intense social scrutiny. Unjustly imprisoned in Newgate, William is seduced by Miss Matthews, an unscrupulous adventuress; his weakness is contrasted to the resolute behaviour of Amelia in rejecting the attentions of several men. She forgives William, but their situation grows still more miserable as his folly then leads him to gambling in an attempt to release them from poverty, and he is imprisoned for debt. Their desperate suffering is alleviated by the happy discovery that her mother's will was a forgery and that Amelia, not her sister, is the rightful heiress to her property. William is released, and the couple retire to the country.

Unlike Fielding's other fiction, *Amelia* is a domestic novel set in one place. It is less sprightly than his previous works, and its depiction of social evil and legal injustice is generally gloomy, although certain minor characters (Dr Harrison the honest clergyman, the brave Colonel Bath) do enliven the representation of human behaviour.

American, The A novel by HENRY JAMES, published in THE ATLANTIC MONTHLY between June 1876 and May 1877, and as a volume in 1877.

Christopher Newman, a bachelor who has become wealthy through shrewd business dealings in America, travels to Paris to find a wife. Though an accomplished businessman, he is naive about European ways. Mrs Tristram, an expatriate American, serves as a sort of guide and confidante to him, much as Maria Gostrey serves Lambert Strether in THE AMBASSADORS.

Newman becomes engaged to Claire de Cintré, a widow and the daughter of an aristocratic French family, the Bellegardes. But the Bellegardes decide they cannot sacrifice the family pride, even to Newman's wealth, and they terminate the engagement. Meanwhile Newman has introduced Valentin Bellegarde, Claire's brother and his own friend and ally, to Noémie Nioche, a young woman who copies great paintings for a living. Because of his involvement with Noémie, Valentin fights and dies in a duel. Just before dying, however, he provides Newman with the means of compelling the Bellegarde family to allow him to marry Claire: he sends Newman to Mrs Bread, the Dowager Marquise's maid, who reveals that the Marquise had caused her husband's death by withholding his medicine. In the end, however, Newman decides not to use this information to force the marriage, and the novel closes with Claire's becoming a Carmelite nun.

American Crisis, The A series of 16 pamphlets by THOMAS PAINE, published between 1776 and 1783. Written during the War of Independence, 'the times that try men's souls', they discuss human nature and the individual's proper relationship to the state, tyranny, the spirit of liberty and the future of colonialism. The pamphlets made an important contribution to the American Revolutionary cause and influenced the young nation's political and philosophical ideology.

American Mercury, The An American magazine of literary criticism and social commentary founded in 1924 by H. L. MENCKEN and GEORGE JEAN NATHAN. When Nathan left the journal in 1925 Mencken assumed sole editorship, a position he retained until his own departure in 1933. The journal, which ceased publication in 1975, featured fiction, essays, and social and political commentary by such authors as VACHEL LINDSAY, THEODORE DREISER, W. E. B. DU BOIS, BEN HECHT, JAMES T. FARRELL, EDGAR LEE MASTERS, WILLIAM FAULKNER, WILLIAM SAROYAN, LIONEL TRILLING, MARK VAN DOREN, THOMAS WOLFE, PEARL S. BUCK, CONRAD AIKEN, EUGENE O'NEILL, DOROTHY PARKER and SHERWOOD ANDERSON.

American Notes CHARLES DICKENS's account of his first visit to America in 1842, published later the same year. It is based on notebooks and letters home, and so mainly takes the form of a casual travel journal, but also includes serious consideration of the treatment of the blind at the Perkins Institute in Boston, the prison system in Philadelphia and slavery in the southern states. Although Dickens had originally travelled to America in hope and had planned to correct the hostile accounts given by earlier visitors from England, his own book becomes savagely critical as it proceeds. Its views are supplemented by the satirical American episodes in his next novel, MARTIN CHUZZLEWIT.

American Senator, The A novel by ANTHONY TROLLOPE, serialized in *Temple Bar* from May 1876 to July 1877.

Senator Gotobed comes to England at the invitation of John Morton, whom he has met in Washington, in order to study English institutions. He stays in the town of Dillborough and visits Bragton Hall. His comments are outspoken and diverting, but some contemporary reviewers thought the novel spoiled by the addition of two love-affairs.

American Tragedy, An A novel by THEODORE DREISER, published in 1925. It is based on the Chester Gillette–Grace Brown murder case of 1906.

Clyde Griffiths, anxious to escape his family's dreary life, goes to work as a bellboy in a luxury hotel. He enjoys the lively society of his more sophisticated co-workers until he is involved in a car accident and found to be legally culpable. Fleeing the scene, he meets his uncle Samuel Griffiths, a successful manufacturer in New York State, who gives him a job in his Eastern factory. Clyde falls in love with Sondra Finchley, a rich girl from a nearby town, who represents the elegance and culture to which he has always aspired. Meanwhile, however, he has seduced a young factory worker, Roberta, who becomes pregnant and demands that he marry her. Seeing marriage to Sondra within his grasp, Clyde decides to dispose of the unfortunate Roberta. He takes her to a lake resort, deserted at that time of year, where he plans to murder her. He lacks the resolution to carry out his plan, but when the boat accidentally overturns he swims away and leaves Roberta to drown. He is accused of her murder, and the rest of the novel traces, in relentless detail, the investigation of the case, and Clyde's indictment, trial, conviction and execution.

Amis, Sir **Kingsley** 1922– Novelist and poet. Born in Clapham, he was educated at the City of London School and St John's College, Oxford. He became a lecturer in English at Swansea, then at Cambridge, and during the 1940s and 1950s was associated with writers of the ANGRY YOUNG MEN generation and poets of the MOVEMENT. His own poetry was represented in ROBERT CONQUEST's influential anthology, *New Lines* (1956). Volumes include *Bright November* (1947), *A Frame of Mind* (1953), *A Case of Samples* (1956) and *Collected Poems 1944–1979* (1979).

It was with his first novel, *LUCKY JIM* (1954), that Amis achieved wider popular recognition. *That Uncertain Feeling* (1955), *I Like it Here* (1958), set in Portugal, and *Take a Girl Like You* (1960) displayed his talent for comic and mildly satiric writing, continued with increasing vehemence in *One Fat Englishman* (1963), *Ending Up* (1974) and *Jake's Thing* (1978). *Colonel Sun* (1968), published under the pseudonym of Robert Markham, is a James Bond thriller in imitation of IAN FLEMING, whose work he had praised in *The*

Kingsley Amis

James Bond Dossier (1965). *The Riverside Villas Murder* (1973) is a pastiche of DETECTIVE FICTION, set in the author's childhood in the 1930s. More sober novels were *The Anti-Death League* (1966), an atheistic protest cast in the form of a spy story; *The Green Man* (1969), about the supernatural; and *The Alteration* (1976), set in a parallel contemporary world in which there has been no Reformation and the Papacy still wields supreme power. Later novels, such as *Stanley and the Women* (1984), *The Old Devils* (BOOKER PRIZE, 1986), *The Folks That Live on the Hill* (1990) and *The Russian Girl* (1992), have shown comic exuberance increasingly supplanted by gloomy FARCE.

Amis's non-fiction covers a variety of topics, including SCIENCE FICTION (*New Maps of Hell*, 1960, and *The Golden Age of Science Fiction*, 1981) and wine. A critical study of KIPLING (1975) was followed by a biography (1986). *The New Oxford Book of Light Verse* (1978) is one of several poetry anthologies he has edited. His vitriolic *Memoirs* (1991) attracted much admiring disapproval. He was knighted in 1990.

Amis, Martin 1949– Novelist. The son of KINGSLEY AMIS, he went to Exeter College, Oxford, and turned to full-time writing following a period of editorial work with THE TIMES LITERARY SUPPLEMENT and *The New Statesman*. His first three novels, *The Rachel Papers* (1973), *Dead Babies* (1975) and *Success* (1978), are ferociously witty, scabrously scatological and balefully satirical of modern-day metropolitan torpor and cultural trendiness. Amis's fourth, *Other People* (1981), is a fragmented, nightmarish psychological thriller, while *Money* (1984) is a longer work set in high-life America, which revives his penchant for gross, excessive comedy. *London Fields* (1989) revives his disgusted affection for urban low life, navigating a byzantine London underworld somewhat in the manner of a Gothic COLIN MACINNES. *Time's Arrow* (1991) is a much-acclaimed shorter novel about the Nazi death camps; its reverse plot shows a continuing sensitivity to the enlarged perspectives which result from forsaking conventionally linear narrative. *Einstein's Monsters* (1986) is a collection of short stories on the theme of nuclear destruction. Amis also writes astringent literary journalism. His non-fictional pieces on contemporary America have been collected in *The Moronic Inferno* (1986).

Amis and Amiloun A Middle English VERSE RO-MANCE of the late 13th century, adapted from *Amis et Amile*, a 12th-century French romance. Amis and Amiloun are foster-brothers of noble birth, separated after the death of Amiloun's parents. Amis is subjected to trial by combat after succumbing to advances from the daughter of his overlord and foster-father, but is unable to defend himself because of his guilt. Despite a divine warning that he will be stricken with leprosy and reduced to beggary, Amiloun impersonates him in the combat and kills his accuser. Years later, the leprous Amiloun eventually finds his foster-brother who obeys the bidding of an archangel to cure him with the blood of his own children, but as Amiloun is cured Amis's children are restored.

Ammons, A(rchie) R(andolph) 1926– American poet. Born near Whiteville, North Carolina, he was educated at Wake Forest College, North Carolina, and the University of California at Berkeley. For 12 years he worked as an executive of a New Jersey company making biological glass. He has taught at Cornell University since 1964. His first book of poetry, *Ommateum with Doxology* (the title refers to the compound eye of an insect), appeared in 1955 but it was his second, *Expressions of Sea Level* (1964), which established him as a major poet. Since then his output has been prolific. Precise description of the natural world characterizes the work in *Corson's Inlet* (1965), *Northfield Poems* (1966), *Uplands* (1970), *Diversifications* (1975), *The Snow Poems* (1977), *Highgate Road* (1977) and *A Coast of Trees* (1981). He has published two long poems as books, *Tape for the Turn of the Year* (1965) and *Sphere: The Form of a Motion* (1974). An early volume of selected poetry (1968) has been superseded by *Collected Poems: 1951–1971* (1972), *The Selected Poems 1951–1977* (1977) and *Selected Longer Poems* (1980). Subsequent volumes include *Worldly Hopes* (1982), *Lake Effect Country* (1983) and *Sumerian Vistas* (1987). Ammons has won both the Bollingen Award and the National Book Award for poetry.

Amoretti SPENSER'S contribution to the English SONNET vogue of the late 16th century was published together with *EPITHALAMION* in 1595. It consists of 89 sonnets (83 repeating 35) followed by four short lyrics.

Amoretti ('little loves') is a record of a courtship which reflects Spenser's wooing of Elizabeth Boyle: Spenser's three Elizabeths, his mother, queen and love, are mentioned in 74. Earlier sonnets follow PETRARCHAN conventions: love's warfare (11), with its ambush (12), siege (14) and archers (16), and the cruel tyrannical mistress (10). The sequence covers a period of just over two years, beginning in a New Year (4) and punctuated by another New Year (62) and two Easters (22 and 68). It is remarkable among English Renaissance sonnet cycles for this chronological narrative, its comparatively unconventional and characterized mistress and its innovative rhyme scheme of linked quatrains (abab bcbc cdcd ee). The courtship and the time scheme may well be intended to culminate in the marriage-day celebrated in *Epithalamion*.

Amory, Thomas *c.* 1691–1788 Irish novelist. Educated at Trinity College, Dublin, and acquainted with JONATHAN SWIFT, he studied medicine but could afford a life of leisure in Dublin and London. *The Memoirs of Several Ladies of Great Britain* (1755) describes the adventures of Mrs Marinda Benlow, a BLUE-STOCKING, before wandering off into a curious tour of the Hebrides, where Amory places a Green Island of exotic flora on which stands a ladies' academy. *The Life and Opinions of John Buncle, Esquire* (1756 and 1766), is practically a sequel but purports to be an autobiography, describing the travels and matrimonial adventures of the amorous but virtuous narrator.

Amours de Voyage A verse novel in five CANTOS by ARTHUR HUGH CLOUGH, first published in 1858. It is narrated chiefly by Claude, a doubting intellectual, in letters written from Rome, Florence, Bagni di Lucca and other towns visited by the middle-class English in the last century. Such story as there is concerns the tenuous relationship between Claude and Mary Trevellyn, a tepid affair that comes to nothing at the end of the book. *Amours de Voyage* is primarily a series of reflections on contemporary problems. Claude is a condescending, self-mocking, critical young man who loftily contemplates art, ancient and modern Rome, patriotism, love, politics, Christian belief and other topics which absorbed the attention of Clough himself during his short life.

amphibrach See METRE.

amphimacer See METRE.

anacreontic A poem celebrating wine, love and song, after the example of the Greek lyric writer Anacreon of Teos (6th century BC) and his subsequent classical imitators. COWLEY first used the English term in his *Anacreontiques* (1656), though JONSON and HERRICK had already been notable practitioners of the form. THOMAS MOORE published a famous verse translation, the *Odes of Anacreon* (1800), for which BYRON dubbed him 'Anacreon Moore'.

anagnorisis The term used by Aristotle in the *Poetics* for the moment in TRAGEDY when a character moves from ignorance to knowledge, particularly knowledge of his or her tragic error (HAMARTIA). More loosely, it refers to the DÉNOUEMENT of a drama.

Anand, Mulk Raj 1905– Indian novelist. Born in Peshawar, he divided his time from 1930 to 1945 between literary London and Gandhi's India, until undertaking his long editorship of the Bombay arts magazine *Marg*. Sophisticated and cosmopolitan, impatient of transcendentalism, sceptical of religion, Anand looks Indian life fully in the face. His realistic novels, angry at injustice, satirical yet warm, reveal generosity of heart and great sympathy with the unfortunate: a hereditary latrine-cleaner in *Untouchable* (1935), an itinerant labourer in *Coolie* (1936) and a simple villager in the trilogy headed by *The Village* (1939). *Across the Black Waters* (1940) is involved in Europe's mud in Flanders. In *The Sword and the Sickle* (1942) profit and loss have replaced traditional moral imperatives. *The Big Heart* (1945) shows traditional coppersmiths under pressure from factory owners. Anand's sympathies embrace even the privileged in *Private Life of an Indian Prince* (1953). His art engages fully with the physical and emotional destitution of a peasant woman in *The Woman and the Cow* (1960; reissued as *Gauri*, 1976). A projected series of autobiographical novels, *The Seven Ages of Man*, has so far included *Seven Summers* (1951), *Morning Face* (1968), *Confessions of a Lover* (1976), *The Bubble* (1984) and the first section of a fifth, *Little Plays of Mahatma Gandhi* (1990), a rare excursion into dramatic dialogue. Anand has also published over half-a-dozen volumes of short stories. *Conversations in Bloomsbury* (1981) contains his recollections of T. S. ELIOT, D. H. LAWRENCE and VIRGINIA WOOLF.

anapaest See METRE.

anaphora The rhetorical device of repeating the first word or words of successive sentences or clauses. Famous examples are John of Gaunt's eulogy on England in SHAKESPEARE'S *RICHARD II* ('This royal throne of kings, this scept'red isle,/ This earth of majesty...') and the opening paragraphs of DICKENS'S *BLEAK HOUSE* ('Fog everywhere. Fog up the river...').

Anastasius See HOPE, THOMAS.

Anatomy of Abuses, The See STUBBES, PHILIP.

Anatomy of Melancholy, The A colourfully written paramedical treatise by ROBERT BURTON, pub-

lished in 1621. This curious work is elaborately subdivided but comprises three main parts: the first deals with the causes and symptoms of melancholy, the second with its cures and the third with specific melancholies attaching to love and religion. Physical and mental health are only the starting point of Burton's study, which digresses continually to encompass topics such as politics and religion, its pages abounding in quotations from wide-ranging sources including the Bible, the classics and learned works by contemporaries. The style is both comic and serious in flavour, lively as well as informed.

Ancients and Moderns, The A literary and cultural debate of the AUGUSTAN AGE. See SIR WILLIAM TEMPLE, RICHARD BENTLEY and *THE BATTLE OF THE BOOKS*.

Ancrene Riwle [*Ancrene Wisse*] A devotional manual in Middle English prose (*c.* 1200), also extant in French and Latin versions. It was written for a small group of anchoresses – women who, after a period of instruction, took vows of chastity and obedience and were confined to an eremitical cell to spend the rest of their lives in devotion. The anchoress was considered dead: she received the last rites before entering her cell and the burial service was used at her inclusion. The cell was sometimes sealed.

The work deals with the 'inner' and 'outer' rules of the anchorite life, i.e. both the psychological and physical aspects of devotion and conduct. Its approach reflects the change which took place in the 12th century, subordinating the rules of formal prayer to the private meditations of the individual. Despite its austere subject matter, the work is enlivened with many graphic details of everyday life and with brief ALLEGORIES and EXEMPLA. Its highly accomplished style has sophistication and charm.

Anderson, Jessica 1925– Australian novelist and short-story writer. Born in Brisbane, she has lived most of her adult life in Sydney, apart from a period in London. Before turning to writing novels she had worked at a variety of occupations, including that of drama scriptwriter for the Australian Broadcasting Commission, for whom she adapted several classic novels. *An Ordinary Lunacy* (1963), *The Last Man's Head* (1970) and *The Commandant* (1975) were followed by *Tirra Lirra by the River* (1978) and *The Impersonators* (1980; called *The Only Daughter* in the USA), the two novels for which she is best known, and *Taking Shelter* (1990). *Tirra Lirra* is an elderly woman's account of a life in Queensland, Sydney and London which appears to have been a series of escapes from one constricting environment to another; gradually, she comes to terms with herself in her present situation, bedridden in Queensland after a serious illness. *The Impersonators*, about an Australian woman who has lived abroad rediscovering her native Sydney, also offers a vivid portrait of a divided Australian family. Like *Tirra Lirra*, it embodies a strong, albeit delicately realized, feminist vision in its portrayal of the constrictions to which women are subject. *Stories from the Warm Zone and Sydney Stories* (1987) draws on her childhood and frequently explores breakdown in marriage. Her stories are less economic and controlled than her novels, which have a flair for the poetic and a laconic IRONY, reflecting her admiration for HENRY GREEN, EVELYN WAUGH and MURIEL SPARK. CHRISTINA STEAD is the most significant Australian influence on her work.

Anderson, Maxwell 1888–1959 American playwright. Born in Pennsylvania, he spent much of his childhood travelling through Pennsylvania, Ohio, Iowa and North Dakota, following the 'call' of his father, a Baptist preacher. He attended the University of North Dakota, and then taught school in North Dakota and California. Newspaper work in San Francisco led to the offer of an editorship on THE NEW REPUBLIC. He moved to New York City, where he soon began writing for the theatre.

His first play, *White Desert* (1923), about struggling North Dakota miners, was a failure, but a second, *What Price Glory?* (1924), written in collaboration with Lawrence Stallings, won acclaim for its realistic portrayal of soldiers during wartime. The 1930s were successful years for Anderson: he wrote and saw produced *Elizabeth the Queen* (1930), a blank-verse tragedy; *Night over Taos* (1932); *Both Your Houses* (1932); *Mary of Scotland* (1933); *Valley Forge* (1934); *Winterset* (1935), a verse tragedy based on the Sacco and Vanzetti case; *Wingless Victory* (1937); *High Tor* (1937), a comedy about a struggle over land rights; *The Masque of Kings* (1937); *The Star Wagon* (1937); *Knickerbocker Holiday* (1938), a musical comedy written in collaboration with his close friend Kurt Weill; *Key Largo* (1939), another tragedy; and *Journey to Jerusalem* (1940), a retelling of the story of Christ's childhood.

During World War II he produced two anti-Nazi plays, *The Miracle of the Danube* (1941) and *Candle in the Wind* (1941), and two more plays about the lives of soldiers, *The Eve of St Mark* (1942) and *Storm Operation* (1944). 1946 saw the appearance of *Truckline Café* and *Joan of Lorraine*; in 1948 he completed his Elizabethan trilogy with *Anne of the Thousand Days*. *Lost in the Stars* (1950), another collaboration with Weill, was an adaptation of ALAN PATON's novel, *Cry the Beloved Country*. Among his last plays were *Barefoot in Athens* (1951), about Socrates, and *The Bad Seed* (1954).

Anderson, Robert W(oodruff) 1917– American playwright. He was born in New York and educated at Harvard. He first drew attention with *Come Marching Home* (1945) but is best known for *Tea and Sympathy* (1953), a sensitive study of a young man's growth from innocence into experience, and the autobiographical *I Never Sang for My Father* (1968). He wrote screenplays for the film versions of the last two plays (1956 and 1970 respectively). Other work includes *Silent Night, Lonely Night* (1959), *The Days Between* (1965) and two evenings of one-act plays, *You Know I Can't Hear You When the Water's Running* (1967) and *Solitaire/Double Solitaire* (1970).

Anderson, Sherwood 1876–1941 American novelist and short-story writer. Anderson was born in Camden, Ohio, and completed his education at the age of 14. He drifted from job to job, served in the Spanish-American War (1898–9), married, and managed a paint factory in Elyria, Ohio. Then, apparently, he left family and job and went to pursue a literary career in Chicago, where he met CARL SANDBURG, BEN HECHT, FLOYD DELL and others.

Anderson's first book, *Windy McPherson's Son*, was published in 1916. Other early works include *Marching Men* (1917), a novel about coal miners in Pennsylvania, and *Mid-American Chants* (1918), a volume of unrhymed verse. He received his greatest recognition following the publication of WINESBURG, OHIO (1919), a collection of interrelated stories of small-town life, and the novel POOR WHITE (1920), which explores the effects of technological change on American culture. His later work includes collections of short stories – *The Triumph of the Egg* (1921), *Horses and Men* (1923) and *Death in the Woods* (1933) – and the novels *Many Marriages* (1923), *Dark Laughter* (1925), *Tar: A Midwest Childhood* (1926) and *Beyond Desire* (1932). His autobiography, *A Story Teller's Story*, was published in 1924. A volume of *Letters* was issued in 1953, and a critical edition of his Memoirs in 1973. The influence of his flat, minimalist prose style, evocative of a bleaker vision of life than had previously been characteristic of American writing, can be seen in such writers as ERNEST HEMINGWAY and WILLIAM FAULKNER.

Andrea del Sarto A DRAMATIC MONOLOGUE by ROBERT BROWNING, published in *Men and Women* (1855). Andrea del Sarto (1486–1531) was a contemporary of Michelangelo and Raphael; Browning's subtitle, *The Faultless Painter*, echoes the description he earned during his lifetime. In *The Lives of the Painters* Vasari wrote that Andrea del Sarto was less devoted to his art than to his wife Lucrezia. Browning's poem makes him aware of his deficiencies, talking to Lucrezia with sad resignation about his enslavement to her.

Andreas Old English poem preserved in the VERCELLI BOOK. It relates the deeds of Sts Andrew and Matthew, its ultimate source being the Greek *Acts of*

Andrew and Matthias. Matthew, persecuted, blinded, imprisoned and condemned by the cannibal Mermedonians, prays for help and God instructs Andrew to go to him. At first he protests that he cannot travel fast enough, but Christ steers his ship and with divine aid he reaches Matthew, restores his sight and releases him and other prisoners. Andrew is betrayed to the angry cannibals by a demon and tortured, but he has divine protection and cannot be killed. He is miraculously healed, flowers spring from the trace of his blood and the city is destroyed by a flood which only recedes when Andrew, at the bidding of some of the citizens, requires it. The dead are resurrected and the whole race converted. The poet takes every opportunity to expand the narrative with description and dialogue and pays great attention to the creation of atmosphere, setting and sentiment. The style shows the influence of CYNEWULF, to whom the poem has sometimes been attributed.

Andrew of Wyntoun *c.* 1355–1422 Scots chronicler. Little is known of his life but he was a canon regular at St Andrews and prior of St Serfs Inch, Lochleven, in 1395–1413. His single surviving work, the *Orygynale Cronykil*, was written in the late 14th century and is probably the earliest surviving example of Scots verse. It relates in octosyllabic couplets the history of Scotland from the Creation to the reign of Robert I. It is in nine books, the first five dealing with events from the Creation and mythical genealogies of the Britons, and the last four tracing the history of Scotland from the time of Malcolm III. There is some inaccuracy in the relation of historical fact, but the *Cronykil* is nevertheless interesting as a record of early events in the history of Scotland. (See also CHRONICLE.)

Andrewes, Lancelot 1555–1626 Churchman and translator of the Bible. Educated at the Merchant Taylors' School, he went to Pembroke Hall, Cambridge, where he became a fellow in 1576. In 1589 he became both master of his college and vicar of St Giles, Cripplegate. The living was attached to a prebend of St Paul's Cathedral and it was there that his preaching brought him to the attention of Queen Elizabeth. She offered him two bishoprics, which Andrewes declined, though he did become Dean of Westminster in 1601.

A distinguished scholar and master of 15 languages, Andrewes was foremost among the translators selected to work on the Authorized Version of the Bible in 1604 (see THE BIBLE IN ENGLISH). King James made him Bishop of Chichester (1605), then of Ely (1609) and of Winchester (1619).

Andrewes recoiled from the extremism of the Puritans, and was one of the shaping influences in Anglican theology. His sermons are classics of Anglican homiletic, though their appeal has been limited by Andrewes's classical scholarship and his taste for exhaustive textual analysis. *Ninety-Six Sermons* was published in 1629, *A Pattern of Catechistical Doctrine* in 1630, and *Preces Privatae* (*Private Devotions*) in 1648. T. S. ELIOT's essay (1928) is an important modern reappraisal of Andrewes's work.

Angel in the House, The A loosely constructed sequence of poems in praise of married love by COVENTRY PATMORE, published at intervals between 1854 and 1863. Its first two parts, *The Betrothal* (1854) and *The Espousals* (1856), follow the courtship and marriage of Felix Vaughan and Honoria, a dean's daughter. This deliberately everyday narrative is interspersed with preludes and epigrams setting forth Patmore's philosophy of love and proclaiming the beneficent power of women to make 'brutes men, and men divine'. *Faithful for Ever* (1860) and *The Victories of Love* (1863) continue the story but in a markedly different manner, being written in octosyllabic couplets and taking the form of letters by Felix, Honoria, her unsuccessful former suitor Frederick Graham, and his wife Jane. Although many readers found the two later books weaker than their predecessors, *The Angel in the House* was among the most popular and highly praised poems of its day.

Angelou, Maya 1928– Black American actress, director, playwright, autobiographer and poet. Born Marguerita Johnson in St Louis, Missouri, she attended schools in Arkansas and California. Her work for several media tackles the problems of racism and survival. Plays include *Cabaret for Freedom* (with Godfrey Cambridge; 1960), an adaptation of Sophocles' *Ajax* (1974), *And Still I Rise* (1976), and *King* (1990). *All Day Long* (1974) is a film. *Blacks, Blues, Black* (1968), *Assignment America* (1975), *The Legacy* (1976) and *The Inheritors* (1976) are television documentaries. She is best known for her lyrical and painful autobiographies: *I Know Why the Caged Bird Sings* (1969), *Gather Together in My Name* (1974), *Singin' and Swingin' and Gettin' Merry Like Christmas* (1976), *The Heart of a Woman* (1981) and *All God's Children Need Travelling Shoes* (1986). She has also published poetry in *Just Give Me a Cool Drink of Water 'Fore I Dine* (1971) and *Oh Pray My Wings are Gonna Fit Me Well* (1975).

Anglo-Norman The variety of French spoken in England from the time of the Norman Conquest until the end of the Middle Ages. The Norman officials appointed by the conquerors to positions of power naturally spoke Norman. During the ensuing centuries, this insular version of French became increasingly corrupt as it absorbed features of English and developed separately from European French. At first Norman (and then Anglo-Norman) was the sole language of the aristocracy and, with Latin, the language of official business and of all but the most popular of literature. The growth of English as a literary language during the 13th and particularly the 14th centuries was accompanied by a decline in Anglo-Norman. English was finally re-established as the language of the court, and courtly literature was again written in English. The earliest major writer to favour English as a literary language was GEOFFREY CHAUCER.

The Anglo-Norman language developed from pure Norman as it was infiltrated by English forms and words. There is no point of stasis at which the language can be identified as Anglo-Norman in a 'final' form; corruption continued until the language died out. Anglo-Norman is characterized by a proliferation of variant spellings, and a mixture of English and French constructions. Many types of work were written in it, the *Lais* of MARIE DE FRANCE being perhaps the most famous. See also ENGLISH LANGUAGE.

Anglo-Saxon Chronicle The main literary source for Anglo-Saxon history, beginning in the reign of KING ALFRED (871–99) and continuing, in the Peterborough version, until 1134. It is written in Old English prose. The earliest compiler(s) had access to various sources including some universal histories and a set of Frankish annals from the late 9th century. Manuscripts of the first section were in circulation in the early 890s, and some were continued in various religious houses throughout the country. There are seven versions and a fragment extant, some containing common material and others preserving matter of local interest. The quantity and quality of the material recorded vary: the early 9th and mid-10th centuries are least well represented, while the reign of Aethelred and the years from Edward Confessor's reign onwards are treated most fully. Copies of the chronicle were apparently available to ASSER, William of Malmesbury, Henry of Huntingdon and Florence of Worcester. (See also CHRONICLE.)

Angry Young Men A group of writers of the late 1950s, characterized by what Kenneth Allsop defined in *The Angry Decade* (1958) as 'irreverence, stridency, impatience with tradition, vigour, vulgarity, sulky resentment against the cultivated'. These feelings were founded in the sense of betrayal and futility which succeeded the exalted aspirations generated by post-war reforms. COLIN WILSON's study of alienation, *The Outsider* (1956), was judged by many an important manifesto for the movement. The classic dramatic embodiment is in JOHN OSBORNE's *LOOK BACK IN ANGER* (1956), whose anti-hero Jimmy Porter has come to represent the definitive 'angry young man'. The seminal novels are JOHN WAIN's *Hurry on Down* (1953), KINGSLEY AMIS's *LUCKY JIM* (1954), JOHN

BRAINE's *Room at the Top* (1957) and ALAN SILLITOE's *Saturday Night and Sunday Morning* (1958).

The prototypical action occurs in a provincial, lower-middle- or working-class setting, around a solitary, rootless male protagonist whose persistent conflicts with and contempt for authority are rendered with a sardonic humour frequently verging on luxuriant scorn. Posterity's critical judgements, however, have tended to see the anger of such works as no more than dissent, less the product of a coherent or constructive social critique than the virtuoso indulgence of sensibility.

Animal Farm A novel by GEORGE ORWELL, published in 1945.

The novel is a satirical ALLEGORY or FABLE directed primarily against Stalin's Russia. The animals on Mr Jones's farm revolt against their human masters and violently expel them. Led by the pigs, they decide to run the farm themselves on egalitarian principles. However, in time the pigs themselves become corrupted by power and, under their leader, Napoleon (Stalin), a new tyranny is established. Revolutionary idealism is undermined and the slogans which had embodied the new revolutionary order are cynically rewritten ('All animals are equal, but some animals are more equal than others'). Snowball (Trotsky), an idealist, is driven out, and Boxer, the noble carthorse whose courage and strength had helped to make the revolution possible, is sent to the knacker's yard. The final betrayal occurs when the pigs engineer a *rapprochement* with Mr Jones.

The book was originally rejected for publication by T. S. ELIOT in 1944, though many hailed it as a classic during the Cold War era. It represented Orwell's rejection of all revolutionary change, and has remained very popular, especially with younger readers.

Anna of the Five Towns A novel by ARNOLD BENNETT, published in 1902.

The cultural and economic realities of Bursley, a Potteries town, weigh heavily on the heroine as do the harsh codes of her father, Ephraim Tellwright, and of evangelical Methodism. The prospect of her inheriting £50,000 makes her the more attractive in the eyes of the successful businessman Henry Mynors. Anna is impressed by Mynors, so that she excludes thoughts of her other suitor, Willie Price, an industrial tenant of her father. But her eventual engagement to Mynors is primarily a means of escape for herself and her sister Agnes; Mynors's religious fervour wins her respect rather than her love.

Anna's awakening to her true feelings for the helpless Willie Price is cut across by the constraints of class and money. Ephraim sends her to demand payment from Willie and his devious father, Titus; to some extent, she shares her father's distaste for the debtors' predicament. Her love for Price is real, though ineffectual; yet she acts to save him from public disgrace by destroying the forged bill of credit which the Prices have sent to her father. Ephraim disinherits her for this.

While Anna's marriage to Mynors goes ahead, Willie Price learns that his father has embezzled £50 from the chapel building fund before committing suicide. When Willie disappears, the Bursley community believes he has emigrated to Australia. But he has followed his father's example of self-destruction, throwing himself into a disused pitshaft.

Annals of the Parish, The A novel by JOHN GALT, published in 1821. The Rev. Micah Balwhidder records life in his Lowland parish of Dalmailing, often in an unintentionally humorous way, over a period of 50 years (1760–1810).

Anne of Geierstein See SCOTT, SIR WALTER.

Anne of Green Gables A novel by L. M. MONTGOMERY, published in 1908.

Matthew and Marilla Cuthbert, an elderly Canadian bachelor and his sister farming on Prince Edward Island, decide to take in an orphan boy to help with the daily chores. By mistake they are sent Anne Shirley instead, an 11-year-old redhead who quickly charms the shy Matthew by her vivacious prattle. His sister is not so easily won over but eventually Anne's vulnerable but deeply affectionate character wins her heart too, with the rest of the novel detailing the mini-adventures of an adolescent girl and her peer group, from attempts at amateur dramatics to first courtship. Anne's long-winded, romantic soliloquies are regularly brought down to earth by Marilla's dry interjections, only to soar to new imaginative heights the next moment. Subsequent novels follow Anne's career from teaching college to marriage and domesticity, but without recapturing the charm of the original book.

Annual Register, The An annual review of the year's events, in its early years also containing literary essays and poetry, founded by ROBERT DODSLEY and EDMUND BURKE in 1758 and still in publication. From a literary point of view *The Annual Register*'s importance derives from the fact that for the first eight years of publication it was edited by Burke, though anonymously, and he continued as a reviewer probably till at least 1773.

Anson, George, Baron 1697–1762 Sailor and travel-writer. Born at Colwich in Staffordshire, Anson served in the Navy and finally became First Lord of the Admiralty. His journal of an eventful and hazardous expedition made in 1740–4 was edited as *Voyage round the World* (1748) by his chaplain, Richard Walter. It includes accounts of the storms at Cape Horn which wrecked four of the seven ships in the squadron, and of the capture in the Pacific of a Spanish galleon with a million and a half dollars.

Anstey, Christopher 1724–1805 Poet. Born at Brinkley in Cambridgeshire and educated at Eton and King's College, Cambridge, Anstey made his reputation with *The New Bath Guide* (1766). It describes the comic adventures of the Blunderhead family at the fashionable spa town in a series of verse letters.

Anstey, F. [Guthrie, Thomas Anstey] 1856–1934 Humorist. Educated at King's College School and Trinity Hall, Cambridge, Anstey was called to the Bar but diverted from the law by the success of *Vice Versa: or A Lesson to Fathers* (1882), the story of a father and son who exchange ages and personalities. He contributed regularly to *PUNCH* and joined the staff of the magazine in 1887. His large output included *The Brass Bottle* (1900), a comedy about an inefficient jinnee.

Anthills of the Savannah, The A novel by CHINUA ACHEBE, published and shortlisted for the BOOKER PRIZE in 1987. Set in the imaginary West African country of Kangan (to all intents and purposes Nigeria), it centres on the tragic story of three boyhood friends: Sam, who becomes the military leader; Ikem Osodi, a poet and editor of the *National Gazette*; and Chris Oriko, Minister of Government in Sam's administration. Through their ruminations, and the dramatic encounters which make up the novel, Achebe continues the examination of politics initiated in *A Man of the People* (1966). Here he is concerned with the consequences of military rule in a country where constitutional processes have come to an impasse: political chaos has been replaced by dictatorship and cynical self-interest by megalomania. Future hope lies in the faint but predictable certainty that power corrupts and corrupt power destroys itself.

Anthony, Michael 1932– Trinidadian novelist. He was born in Mayaro and had his secondary education until the age of 15 at the Junior Technical School in San Fernando. These two places feature centrally in his fiction. Four novels are concerned with childhood or adolescence. Probably the best known is *The Year in San Fernando* (1965), one of the acknowledged classics of Caribbean literature and a brilliant study of the maturing process whereby a young country boy acquires insight into adult and urban middle-class life. His other novels of growing up are *The Games were Coming* (1963), *Green Days by the River* (1967) and *All That Glitters* (1981). After living in Brazil for some time Anthony wrote *Streets of Conflict* (1976), which is set in Rio de Janeiro in the late 1960s. He is also the author of many short stories; some appeared early in his career in such publications as *The Trinidad*

Guardian and *BIM*. These are collected in *Cricket in the Road and Other Stories* (1973). His gentle but shrewdly observant talent is perhaps more recognized outside the Caribbean than within it. He has also published *The Bright Road to Eldorado* (1982).

Anti-Jacobin, The A weekly journal published from 20 November 1797 to 7 July 1798 with the aim of opposing the radical politics and philosophy encouraged by the French Revolution. It was founded by GEORGE CANNING and edited by WILLIAM GIFFORD, who, together with JOHN HOOKHAM FRERE and George Ellis, were responsible for its lively blend of news and satirical verse. Notable items included Canning's anti-French *The New Morality* and Canning and Frere's *The Loves of the Triangles*, a witty PARODY of ERASMUS DARWIN.

Antiquary, The A novel by SIR WALTER SCOTT, published in 1816.

Major Neville, calling himself William Lovel, follows Isabella Wardour to Scotland. She has rejected him in deference to her father, Sir Arthur, who believes Neville to be illegitimate. On the way to Scotland, Neville falls in with the Wardours' neighbour, Jonathan Oldbuck, the antiquary of the title, and with him meets the king's bedesman, Edie Ochiltree. Sir Arthur has fallen under the influence of Dousterswivel, a plausible German scoundrel. Lovel saves Sir Arthur and Isabella from drowning, quarrels with Oldbuck's nephew, Hector M'Intyre, and with Ochiltree's help exposes Dousterswivel. Lovel proves to be the heir of Glenallan and all ends happily.

The success of *The Antiquary*, the author's own chief favourite among all his novels, owes much to the character of the talkative and eccentric Oldbuck.

antithesis A rhetorical device which uses opposites balanced and contrasted to create sharpness of effect. Antithetical expression is a particularly marked feature of style in neoclassical poetry, and is an important element in the structure of the 'closed couplet' (see HEROIC COUPLET): 'Tis the first Virtue, Vices to abhor/ And the first Wisdom, to be Fool no more' (POPE, *Imitations of Horace*). See also CHIASMUS.

Antonio and Mellida and **Antonio's Revenge** A play in two distinct but related parts by JOHN MARSTON, written for the Boys of St Paul's, first performed in 1599 or 1600 and published in 1602.

Antonio and Mellida is essentially a love-story, though with dark aspects. Antonio, son of Andrugio, Duke of Genoa, loves Mellida, daughter of Piero, Duke of Venice. Genoa and Venice are at war, and Piero puts a price on the heads of Andrugio and Antonio. Disguised as an Amazon, Antonio goes to Venice and persuades Mellida to run away with him. They are captured, and Andrugio offers himself to the enemy in order to save his son's life. To general surprise, Piero relents and consents to the marriage of Antonio and Mellida. This happy ending is overthrown in *Antonio's Revenge*, which is formally a REVENGE TRAGEDY. Piero kills Andrugio and wins the hand of his widow. He also thwarts Antonio's happiness by contriving to dishonour his own daughter, Mellida, who dies of grief. Antonio is visited by the ghost of his murdered father, whom he avenges by killing Piero. The relationship of *Antonio's Revenge* to KYD's earlier *THE SPANISH TRAGEDY* and to SHAKESPEARE's *HAMLET* has been often noted.

Antony and Cleopatra A tragedy by WILLIAM SHAKESPEARE, first performed *c.* 1607 and published in the First Folio of 1623. The sole source is SIR THOMAS NORTH's translation of Plutarch, on which it relies for much of the language as well as for the story.

Infatuated with Cleopatra, Antony neglects his duties as a Roman triumvir and lingers in Alexandria. Only when news of Pompey's rebellion is added to news of the death of Antony's own wife, Fulvia, does he decide, despite Cleopatra's pleas, to leave for Rome with his loyal general, Enobarbus. The uneasy triumvirate of the scheming Octavius Caesar, the foolish Lepidus and the hedonistic Antony is patched up, and Antony agrees to marry Octavius' sister, Octavia. Even Pompey accepts peace terms. Abandoned in Alexandria, Cleopatra beats the messenger who brings news of Antony's marriage.

In Athens with Octavia, Antony hears that Octavius has ridiculed him and sent an army against Pompey. Octavia returns to Rome on a peace mission, and Antony goes back to Egypt and Cleopatra. There he promises the eastern provinces of the Roman Empire to her and her children. Given such a pretext for open hostility, Octavius embarks his army. Against advice from Enobarbus, Antony combines with the Egyptian fleet to engage Octavius at sea. The battle at Actium is turned into a fiasco when Cleopatra's ships turn tail and Antony follows her back to Egypt.

In despair, Enobarbus deserts his leader and dies soon afterwards. More at home in a land battle, Antony recovers his firmness of purpose but, after an initial victory, is again drawn into defeat by the Egyptian army's defection. The fearful Cleopatra hides in her monument and sends Antony a message that she is dead. Defeated and despairing, he falls on his sword, and is carried to the monument, where he dies in Cleopatra's arms. Octavius visits Cleopatra and leaves confident that she will return as his prisoner to Rome. But Cleopatra achieves a new dignity at last, robbing Octavius of his triumph (over Antony as well as herself) by arranging for her own death. She has deadly asps smuggled into the monument, dresses herself in her finest robes, and holds the asps to her body. The outwitted Octavius concedes that she be buried with Antony.

Shakespeare's imagination was excited by the contrast between Egyptian opulence and Roman regulation, and he portrays Antony as a man torn between love and duty. The triumph of love is complete only when Cleopatra finds the resolution to kill herself. Richer in language and imagery than the Roman tragedies, *JULIUS CAESAR* and *CORIOLANUS*, with which it is inevitably associated, *Antony and Cleopatra* is more appropriately viewed as one of the group of great tragedies Shakespeare wrote *c.* 1603-7 than as part of a scattered group of Roman plays.

Apologia pro Vita Sua The spiritual autobiography of JOHN HENRY NEWMAN, serialized in 1864 and published in book form in 1865. The full title of the serial version, *Apologia pro Vita Sua: Being a Reply to a Pamphlet Entitled: 'What, Then, Does Dr Newman Mean?'*, reflected its origin in Newman's public quarrel with the militantly Protestant CHARLES KINGSLEY. In a review of J. A. FROUDE's *History of England* (vols. 7 and 8), contributed to *Macmillan's Magazine* in January 1864, Kingsley had written: 'Truth for its own sake has never been a virtue of the Roman clergy. Father Newman informs us that it need not and on the whole ought not to be.' The next month Newman published *Mr Kingsley and Dr Newman*, the record of his unsatisfactory correspondence with Kingsley and his publishers over the offending passage. Kingsley issued his pamphlet and so provoked Newman to write the *Apologia*. The volume edition (1865) detached the book from the original controversy by omitting the first two parts and the appendix, where he had not spared his opponent, and by using a new subtitle: *Being a History of his Religious Opinions*.

Yet the underlying purpose remained the same. Newman had found in Kingsley's jibe a clear statement of the distrust with which the English public had long regarded his career as an Anglican clergyman, his conversion to Roman Catholicism and his subsequent career as a Catholic priest. The response it demanded went beyond theology and polemic, and involved personal justification. Newman's account of himself is designed to assert the sincerity and consistency of his spiritual development. In addition to its value as a record of personal faith, the *Apologia* is also a primary historical source for the OXFORD MOVEMENT.

Apology for Poetry, An A critical treatise by SIR PHILIP SIDNEY, published in 1595 in two separate editions, one bearing the title *The Defence of Poesy*. Few of the ideas it presents are original, being Renaissance critical commonplaces. However, the work is a masterpiece of elegant persuasion, and its easy and engaging style conceals a careful rhetorical structure. Sidney claims that imaginative literature is a better teacher than philosophy or history. He defends it against the charges of time-wasting, lying and allurement to vice, and deals also with Plato's famous decision to ban poets from the state in his *Republic*. In Sidney's view, literature has the power to reproduce an ideal golden world, not just the brazen one we know, and so to offer 'a speaking picture – with this end, to teach and delight'. A digression looks at the state of English literature and finds it sadly wanting, but makes honourable exceptions of CHAUCER's *TROILUS AND CRISEYDE*, SURREY's poems, *THE MIRROR FOR MAGISTRATES*, SPENSER's *SHEPHEARDES CALENDER* and the play *GORBODUC*.

Apostles, The Officially 'The Cambridge Conversazione Society', formed at Cambridge in 1820 to promote formal discussion between friends. Early members included TENNYSON and ARTHUR HENRY HALLAM. The turn of the century was a period of particular brilliance for the society, largely through the influence of G. E. MOORE. Among the BLOOMSBURY GROUP, members included Roger Fry, DESMOND MACCARTHY, E. M. FORSTER, LEONARD WOOLF, Saxon Sydney-Turner, LYTTON STRACHEY and JOHN MAYNARD KEYNES.

Apperley, C(harles) J(ames) 1779-1843 Writer on sport and rural life, under the pseudonym Nimrod. Educated at Rugby, Apperley turned from his life as a Shropshire squire to journalism when the income from his land declined. He contributed to *THE QUARTERLY REVIEW* and *The Sporting Magazine*, and became a staff editor on *The Sporting Review*. His first book, *Memoirs of the Life of John Mytton* (1837), was about a Shropshire neighbour. *The Life of a Sportsman* (1842) contains a vivid picture of country life. His books were illustrated by Henry Alkne. His friend and rival R. S. SURTEES lampooned Apperley in *JORROCKS'S JAUNTS AND JOLLITIES* and *HANDLEY CROSS*.

Arbuthnot, John 1667-1735 Physician and creator of 'John Bull', the archetypal Englishman. Born in Kincardineshire, he studied medicine at Oxford and then took his MD at St Andrews University, after which he pursued a distinguished medical career. He was elected a Fellow of the Royal Society in 1704, and was appointed physician to Queen Anne in the following year. A humane man with diverse talents, he was not only progressive in the field of science, but known as a wit and writer of considerable ability. He became a convivial member of the SCRIBLERUS CLUB and a valued friend of SWIFT and POPE, whose *Epistle from Mr Pope to Dr Arbuthnot* (1735) is a magnificent final testimony to their intimacy. Arbuthnot himself was a leading contributor to the *Memoirs of Martinus Scriblerus* (published in Pope's *Works* in 1741) and to the collaborative comedy *THREE HOURS AFTER MARRIAGE* (1717). But he is best known for *THE HISTORY OF JOHN BULL* (1712), a popular collection of five satirical pamphlets designed to end

Marlborough's European campaign, and advocating a return to peace and common sense. His 'A Sermon Preached to the People at Mercat Cross, Edinburgh' (1706) supported the union of Scotland with England. His scientific works include *An Essay concerning the Nature of Ailments* (1731), which stressed the value of proper diet in the treatment of patients, *An Essay concerning the Effects of Air on Human Bodies* (1733), and *An Essay on the Usefulness of Mathematical Learning* (1701). He published a single poem, 'Know Thyself', in 1734.

Arcadia, The A prose romance, interspersed with poems, by SIR PHILIP SIDNEY. Enormously popular in its age, it appealed to the Renaissance love of PASTORAL but was also read as a COURTESY BOOK, a moral treatise, a discussion of love and philosophy, and even a rhetorical handbook. Sidney wrote the bulk of it in 1580 while staying at Wilton House with his sister, the Countess of Pembroke, to whom it is dedicated; he subsequently began but never finished a careful revision. As a result, the work exists in three different forms.

The first, unrevised version, the *Old Arcadia*, was never printed in the 16th century, though copies circulated in manuscript. It was devised as a tragicomedy in five acts, with ECLOGUES scattered in the text and groups of eclogues as dividing entr'actes. The story has a serious double plot and a comic underplot. Duke Basilius is warned by an oracle of enigmatic disasters and retires to Arcadia with his wife Gynecia and his two daughters, Philoclea and Pamela. Two princes, Pyrocles and Musidorus, first cousins and devoted friends, arrive and fall in love respectively with Philoclea and Pamela. Pyrocles disguises himself as an Amazon, Cleophila, to be near Philoclea. Basilius falls in love with his disguise: Gynecia and Philoclea, seeing through the disguise, fall in love with Pyrocles. Musidorus decides to elope with Pamela and his attempt to rape her is interrupted by rebels. Pyrocles attempts to solve his amatory entanglements by arranging to meet both Basilius and Gynecia in a cave. There, as the oracle predicted, the Duke commits adultery with his own wife. Pyrocles seduces Philoclea, Basilius apparently dies from a love philtre, and Pamela and Musidorus are carried off by rebels. At the end of the work all the major characters are arraigned before Euarchus. Gynecia confesses to killing her husband and is to be buried alive. Pyrocles and Musidorus are condemned to death; Philoclea is to go to a nunnery. Euarchus, the upholder of strict justice, will not alter his verdict even when he realizes that he has condemned his son Pyrocles and his nephew Musidorus. Tragedy is averted and turns to comedy when Basilius revives and asserts the strange workings of providence. A general pardon is extended.

Like *ASTROPHIL AND STELLA*, the *Old Arcadia* examines the various workings of love on the human char-

acter. It can be an ennobling and educative passion, but it can also bring shame, overthrow reason and undermine the life of heroic action. The trial scene at the end raises acute problems of justice and equity.

The second version, known as the *New Arcadia*, was published posthumously in 1590, perhaps under the supervision of Sidney's friend FULKE GREVILLE. It presented the revised text of the first three books, all that the author had lived to complete. Sidney's changes, often done painstakingly sentence by sentence, make the unfinished *New Arcadia* longer by 50,000 words than the finished *Old Arcadia* and introduce major differences. There is no attempted rape of Pamela or successful seduction of Philoclea. The opening of the work is different and new subsidiary stories are interlaced, including that of the blind Paphlagonian king which SHAKESPEARE borrowed for the Gloucester subplot in *KING LEAR*. The revised *Arcadia* is a more serious work than the first; moral earnestness is constantly deepened, especially in the depiction of Pamela.

In 1593 *The Countess of Pembroke's Arcadia* was published, perhaps under the supervision of the Countess herself. It brought together the first three revised books of the *New Arcadia* and the last two books of the unrevised *Old Arcadia*, thus making a third hybrid version of the text.

Sidney's sources were recognized as early as the 1590s. From Sannazaro's *Arcadia* he took his title and the pastoral setting; from *Amadis of Gaule* he took chivalric romance and Pyrocles' disguise as an Amazon. Heliodorus' *Aethiopica* influenced the work in many ways, especially in its revised version.

Archer, William 1856-1924 Scottish journalist and dramatic critic. His alliance with GEORGE BERNARD SHAW in championing Ibsen helped to raise the literary standards of British drama at the end of the 19th century. The first of his translations from Ibsen, *Quicksands: or, The Pillars of Society*, was performed in London in 1880, and a collected edition in 11 volumes was published in 1906-8. Archer was a fierce defender of the best of contemporary drama against what he considered a dangerous and indiscriminate preference for the old. *The Old Drama and the New* (1923) vigorously argues that the English drama since THOMAS WILLIAM ROBERTSON has a greater claim for stage performance than all but a tiny minority of earlier plays.

archetypal criticism See FRYE, NORTHROP.

Arden, John 1930- Playwright and novelist. Born in Barnsley and educated at Sedbergh School, Cambridge University and Edinburgh College of Art, where he trained as an architect. His first play, *All Fall Down* (1955), was performed by Edinburgh students. It was followed by a radio play, *The Life of Man*

(1956), and his first professionally staged work, *The Waters of Babylon* (1957), which brought him into membership of the Writers' Group at the ROYAL COURT THEATRE. *Live Like Pigs* (1958) and the powerful *SERJEANT MUSGRAVE'S DANCE* (1959) established him as the most allusive and original new playwright of the socially conscious renaissance of English drama. *The Happy Haven* (1960), the first of several collaborations with his wife Margaretta D'Arcy, makes adventurous use of halfmasks in order to allow young actors to impersonate old people. *The Workhouse Donkey* (1963) used the context of local government to explore a recurrent concern: the conflict between rigid values and anarchic subversion. As in *Armstrong's Last Goodnight* (1964) and a play about King John and the barons, *Left-Handed Liberty* (1965), Arden allows his preference for 'curvilinear' Celtic disorder to emerge without his having totally to discredit 'rectilinear' Roman order. In *The Hero Rises Up* (1968) and, unmistakably, in the overtly political plays about Ireland, like *The Ballygombeen Bequest* (1972), the six-part *The Non-Stop Connolly Show* (1975) and *Vandaleur's Folly* (1978), the Roman rigidity of the rulers of British society receives short shrift. Arden has consciously progressed from a liberal socialism to the politics of revolution, particularly with regard to the British 'occupation' of Northern Ireland. The essays in *To Present the Pretence* (1978) record some of that progress. Arden's ventures into fiction, notably *Silence among the Weapons* (1982) and *Books of Bale* (1988), show the same combination of topical commitment with sense of history that informs his plays.

Arden of Feversham, The Tragedy of Mr

An anonymous play, published in 1592 and probably performed the same year; at one time it was attributed to Shakespeare (see SHAKESPEARE APOCRYPHA). It is an early example of domestic tragedy and, in so far as it is based on an actual murder which took place at Faversham in Kent, is a forerunner of the popular criminal drama of the 18th and 19th centuries. The play shows the initially frustrated but eventually successful attempts of Mistress Arden to rid herself of an unloved husband. The murder is discovered and she is executed for the crime, together with her lover and fellow conspirator. GEORGE LILLO, whose own work made both domestic tragedy and criminal dramas fashionable, adapted the play for the 18th-century stage.

Ardizzone, Edward

1900–79 Writer and illustrator of CHILDREN'S LITERATURE. Born in China of an Italian father and Scots mother, Ardizzone settled in England at the age of five, first in Ipswich and later in London. After an unsuccessful period of office work he became an artist, specializing in scenes of low life around London pubs and street corners. His first children's book, *Little Tim and the Brave Sea Captain* (1936), was devised for the amusement of his own small son and daughter. Its success established him as a leading author–illustrator with a good eye for adventure and a brilliant, elusive drawing style concentrating on the essentials of line and form, leaving readers to provide the rest from their own imaginations. More books about Little Tim followed after a period as official war artist, when Ardizzone travelled (often under hazardous conditions) in France, Italy, Libya and Germany. He went on to illustrate over 100 books by other writers, but remained best loved for his children's work.

Areopagitica: A Speech of Mr John Milton for the Liberty of Unlicensed Printing to the Parliament of England

JOHN MILTON's celebrated plea for a free press and free discussion (1644) takes its title from the Greek *Areopagus*, the hill of Ares in Athens where the highest judicial tribunal of the city used to meet. Having abolished the Star Chamber in 1641, the Parliamentarians effectively reimposed censorship in 1643, and Milton opens his objection by demonstrating that the government was using the methods of those they most decried, namely the Papal regimes. He argues that freedom to pursue learning is essential

The frontispiece to the third edition of *Arden of Feversham*, 1633. The murderers attack Arden as he plays backgammon with Mosbie, his wife's lover.

to the Christian 'ethos', that to read freely is necessary to the development of virtue, and that licensing will in any case prove ineffectual. He appeals rousingly to the 'Lords and Commons of England' not to act repressively upon 'a nation not slow and dull, but of a quick, ingenious and piercing spirit'.

Areopagus Letters exchanged between EDMUND SPENSER and GABRIEL HARVEY in 1579–80 refer allusively to an 'Areopagus', an association of aristocratic courtiers and poets which took its name from the hill in Athens where the earliest aristocratic council met. Spenser himself seems to have been on the fringes of the group, but the best-known members were EDWARD DYER, FULKE GREVILLE and Sir PHILIP SIDNEY. The group's exact nature and constitution is not clear, though it was certainly concerned with prosody and classical metres, perhaps in imitation of the French 16th-century academies. Its members may also have discussed political and religious matters as well as exclusively literary ones.

Argument against Abolishing Christianity, An
A satirical pamphlet by JONATHAN SWIFT, written in 1708 and published in 1711. Pretending to be a mild objection to an imaginary campaign to remove Christianity altogether, this ironical performance points out that such a move might be 'attended with some Inconveniences'. Concerned at the extremes of religious thinking then current, Swift attacks both the 'low' churchmen (freethinkers and Deists: see DEISM) and the high Tories (NONJURORS and Jacobites) who in their different ways threaten the strength of the established Anglican church.

Arlen, Michael [Kouyoumdjian, Dikran] 1895 –1956 Novelist and short-story writer. Born in Bulgaria of Armenian parents, he was educated at Malvern College and Edinburgh but chose to live in the South of France from the time of his marriage in 1928. He achieved a brief popularity with his acerbic but stylish portrait of London life in collections of short stories such as *The Romantic Lady* (1921) and *These Charming People* (1923), and particularly in his best-selling novel *The Green Hat* (1924). His last novel, *The Flying Dutchman*, was published in 1939. Arlen settled in New York after World War II.

Armah, Ayi Kwei 1939– Ghanaian novelist. Born in Takoradi, he was educated in Ghana, at Harvard University and in New York. He worked as scriptwriter, schoolmaster, translator, journalist and lecturer in Ghana, Algeria, France and the USA before settling for some years in Tanzania. His vivid, eloquent novels lament centuries of African suffering and cultural obliteration. In THE BEAUTYFUL ONES ARE NOT YET BORN (1969), from a slogan on a Ghanaian bus, and *Fragments* (1970) recurrent imagery of ex-crement, decay, disease, and society's condemnation of individual integrity as insanity, suggest Armah's total disillusion with independent Africa. *Why are We So Blest?* (1972) explores the failure of would-be revolutionaries and westernized intellectuals in Nigeria. In *Two Thousand Seasons* (1973), however, he rewrites as simple epic the history of both Islamic and Christian assaults upon Africa and, by representing traditional *griots* as inspired seers, advocates the true African way as selfless, mutual caring. *The Healers* (1975), about the crumbling 19th-century Ashanti empire, implies the need for a truly African cultural integrity. Armah has also written numerous essays on African literature, culture and politics.

Armin, Robert *c.* 1580-1612 One of the actors in SHAKESPEARE's company, the Lord Chamberlain's Men, Armin became the principal comedian after WILL KEMP's departure. He contributed a considerable portion to a play that gave him a fine part, *The History of the Two Maids of More-Clacke* (published 1609). He was also the author of the satirical prose tract *Fool upon Fool: or, Six Sortes of Sots* (1605), which he later enlarged as *A Nest of Ninnies* (1608), and a verse translation of an Italian tale, *The Italian Taylor and his Boy* (1609).

Armitage, Simon 1963– Poet. Born in Huddersfield, brought up in West Yorkshire and educated at Portsmouth Polytechnic and the University of Manchester, he works as a probation officer in Oldham. As well as several pamphlets, he has published longer collections in *Zoom* (1989) and *Kid* (1992). No casual observer of life, he writes in direct and forceful language from experience and engagement with his subjects. A pamphet of 1991 introduced the character of Robinson, a shifting figure who appears sometimes in the 'action' of his poems and sometimes in dialogue with the author. *Xanadu* (1992), a group of poems written for a BBC2 series, *Words on Film*, is about the Ashfield Valley Estate in Rochdale.

Armstrong, John *c.* 1709-79 Poet and physician. The son of a minister from Roxburghshire, Armstrong studied medicine at Edinburgh and practised in London. He wrote *The Oeconomy of Love* (1736), a blank-verse sex manual for the newly married, and *The Art of Preserving Health* (1744), a didactic work pleasantly done in the manner of his friend JAMES THOMSON, who included a portrait of Armstrong in THE CASTLE OF INDOLENCE.

Arnold, Sir Edwin 1823-1904 Poet and translator. Born at Gravesend in Kent and educated at King's College, London, and University College, Oxford, Arnold won the Newdigate Prize in 1852 with his poem 'Belshazzar's Feast'. In 1856 he became

Principal of Deccan College, Poona, and in 1861 joined the staff of *The Daily Telegraph*. Arnold studied Eastern languages and published his first translation, from Sanskrit, in 1861: *Hitopadésa* (*The Book of Good Counsels*). His BLANK-VERSE epic on the life and teachings of the Buddha, *The Light of Asia* (1879), was enormously popular. He did not repeat his success with *The Light of the World* (1891).

Arnold, Matthew 1822–88 Poet, critic and educational administrator. The son of THOMAS ARNOLD of Rugby, he was born at Laleham in Middlesex and educated at Winchester, Rugby and Balliol College, Oxford, where in 1843 he won the Newdigate Prize for poetry with 'Cromwell'. He became a fellow of Oriel College in 1845 but left the university shortly afterwards to be private secretary to Lord Lansdowne. He travelled abroad in the late 1840s, and met the Swiss girl Marguerite who haunts much of his earlier lyric poetry. By 1851 he was an inspector of schools, a post which brought him the financial security to marry Frances Lucy Wightman.

Arnold's poetic career began in 1849 with the publication of *The Strayed Reveller, and Other Poems* by 'A', but by *New Poems* (1867) it was over. Between these dates, however, he published *Empedocles on Etna, and Other Poems* (1852), *Poems* (1853), *Poems Second Series* (1855) and *Merope* (1858). The variety of poetic expression in these volumes is apparent: lyrics (the 'Marguerite' poems, THE FORSAKEN MERMAN, DOVER BEACH, 'Philomela'); poetic drama (*EMPEDOCLES ON ETNA* and *Merope*); narrative poems (*TRISTRAM AND ISEULT* and *SOHRAB AND RUSTUM*); elegies (*THYRSIS*, THE SCHOLAR-GIPSY and 'Memorial Verses'). Often deriving from classical subjects, Arnold's poetry is frequently informed by alienation, stoicism, despair and spiritual emptiness.

In 1858 Arnold became professor of poetry at Oxford, perhaps appreciating the mild irony that, save for the 1867 volume, he wrote prose for the rest of his life. Like other Victorian polymaths sensitive to the stresses of the age, he sought to deal with these problems in literary, political, religious and educational writings. Holding an inspectorate in education until his retirement in 1886 and possessed of European rather than insular vision, Arnold contemplated the British and Continental pedagogical scenes through a series of reports on differing educational problems, marked by clear writing, advocacy of the humane disciplines and emphasis on the Bible as a moral and a literary strength. He was also a trenchant critic of elementary and secondary education, of teacher training, and an advocate of state instruction at home and abroad. Above all, his educational writings put the case for a national instruction rising above local and political interests.

In 1865 Arnold produced the first series of his *ESSAYS IN CRITICISM* (the second appearing posthumously in 1888). Here, particularly in 'The Function of Criticism at the Present Time' in the first volume, he develops his view of criticism as a disinterested and flexible mode of thought whose application extends far beyond literature. Such a view leads naturally to the broad consideration of the dilemmas of English society in his great prose work, *CULTURE AND ANARCHY* (1869), where culture is recommended as 'the great help out of our present difficulties' and defined as 'the pursuit of total perfection by means of getting to know, on all the matters which most concern us, the best which has been thought and said in the world'. By the 1870s Arnold had joined the long list of Victorian thinkers who turned their attention to the theological controversies of the age, with *Saint Paul and Protestantism* (1870), *Literature and Dogma* (1873), *God and the Bible* (1875) and *Last Essays on Church and Religion* (1877).

Of the major Victorian poets Arnold is perhaps the least generous, but what he lacks in abundance he compensates for in subtlety and variety. His melancholy, delicately moving stanzas are an exquisite register of the feelings of those intellectuals 'wandering between two worlds,/ One dead, the other powerless to be born'. The despairing gentleness of Arnold's poetry renders it unique in the Victorian canon. And as a prose writer tackling insuperable problems – in language often sardonic and invariably articulate – Arnold is forthright, courageous and impervious to hostility. In their advocacy of culture, his appeals are as applicable in our own day as a century ago.

Arnold, Thomas 1795–1842 Educator, historian and father of MATTHEW ARNOLD. Born in the Isle of Wight and educated at Winchester College and Corpus Christi College, Oxford, Arnold became a fellow of Oriel College in 1815. In 1828 he was appointed headmaster of Rugby School, and set about raising its standards and reputation with characteristic energy. Arnold's regime stressed the importance of classical education and, particularly, religious training; its purpose was to develop the boys' sense of duty and their character. Its success made Rugby the first choice of middle-class parents seeking a public school for their sons; in a larger sense, Rugby became the model for the English public-school system in the 19th century. Arnold returned to Oxford as Regius Professor of Modern History in 1841. His edition of Thucydides was published in 1830–5 and his *History of Rome* (1838–42) left unfinished. Admiringly described by his former pupil THOMAS HUGHES in TOM BROWN'S SCHOOLDAYS and made the subject of a respectful biography by ARTHUR PENRHYN STANLEY, Arnold was caricatured for a later generation by LYTTON STRACHEY in *Eminent Victorians* (1918).

Arrow of God A novel by CHINUA ACHEBE, published in 1964 and revised in 1974. It develops the theme of his first novel, *THINGS FALL APART*: the impact of British colonialism on traditional Igbo life. Set in Eastern Nigeria during the entrenchment of colonial rule, it tells the tragic story of Ezeulu, Chief Priest of the god Ulu. His attempt to reconcile the demands of his god and his own quest for personal power brings calamity on himself, his family and his clan, and inadvertently fosters the hegemony of Christianity.

Arthur Mervyn A GOTHIC NOVEL by CHARLES BROCKDEN BROWN, published in two volumes in1799 and 1800.

Dr Stevens, the narrator, cares for the 18-year-old Arthur Mervyn, a farmboy who has come to Philadelphia and fallen ill during the plague year of 1793. Soon, however, a friend voices the suspicion that Mervyn is not the country innocent he seems, but has been involved in criminal dealings with an embezzler named Thomas Welbeck. Mervyn then tells Stevens his story.

He worked for Welbeck on first arriving in Philadelphia, but soon began to suspect him of criminal activities. His suspicions were confirmed one night when Welbeck shot a man in his study. At this point Welbeck confessed that, despite his ideals, he had been guilty of seduction, the theft of $20,000, forgery, and now murder. He then tried to escape by boat but was apparently drowned. Mervyn returned to the country, taking with him a manuscript of Welbeck's; he found a new home on the farm of a Mr Hadwin, and fell in love with his daughter Eliza. Later he discovered the stolen $20,000 in the manuscript. Back in Philadelphia on an errand, he found Welbeck still alive, but burned the money. By now ill with yellow fever, he wandered into the streets and was found by Dr Stevens.

Mervyn's account dispels suspicion and he returns to the Hadwin farm to find that only Eliza has escaped the epidemic, inheriting the farm. Back in Philadelphia he has a final confrontation with the now dying and repentant Welbeck. Meanwhile, fresh suspicions about Mervyn's character and activities have arisen, and this time his explanations prove somewhat less satisfactory. Indeed, the second part of the book in general casts some doubt on the validity of the version of his life he had given originally. The novel ends when Mervyn, having re-evaluated his love for Eliza (she turns out not to have inherited the farm after all), falls in love with Mrs Fielding, a widow of means whom he finally marries.

Arthurian literature Our fairly unified picture of Arthurian legend derives from SIR THOMAS MALORY's 15th-century *LE MORTE DARTHUR*. Before Malory this unity does not exist; there is only a great mass of fable, legend and pseudo-history. Arthur's first 'biography' is in Latin, in the *Historia regum Britanniae* (c. 1135) by GEOFFREY OF MONMOUTH. Before Geoffrey, Arthur makes only scattered appearances in chronicle, folktale and art.

1 The Pseudo-Historical Arthur

The earliest portrait of Arthur is of a British commander of Roman descent repelling the Saxon invaders at the siege of Mons Badonicus, probably c. 500. *De excidio et conquestu Britanniae* (c. 540) by Gildas depicts such an unnamed leader, probably Ambrosius Aurelianus whom he elsewhere praises and who is made Arthur's uncle in later chronicles. The early 9th-century *Historia Brittonum* by Nennius, perhaps using Welsh tradition, has the first direct mention of Arthur, depicted as a Christian *dux bellorum* winning 12 battles against the Saxons; the last of these is at Mons Badonis. Nennius also tells the story of the British king Vortigern and a marvellous boy, Ambrosius, the original of Merlin. The mid-10th-century *Annales Cambriae* refers to two battles: Badon in 516, with Arthur victorious, and Camlann in 537, where Arthur and Medraut fell. The Welsh triads, which preserve early, pre-Norman traditions about Arthur, depict him, accompanied by his principal warriors Cei and Bedwyr, as a defender of his country; and it is to this tradition that William of Malmesbury's *Gesta regum anglorum* also refers, in 1125.

The 12th century sees the flowering of the 'historical' Arthur through the work of Geoffrey of Monmouth, who presents him as king and leader of a group of mounted knights, a very Norman image. Geoffrey used Gildas, BEDE, Nennius and insular tradition to create a picture of a great medieval monarch, conqueror of many peoples including the French and the Romans, a descendant of Constantine and a king who made his court a hub of civilization. He retained the story of the Saxon wars, identifying Badon with Bath. Arthur is the son of Uter Pendragon and Ygraine, with a capital at Caerleon; he possesses the sword Caliburn (Excalibur), the shield Pridwen and the lance Ron; he is married to Guanhumara and his principal warriors are the Normanized Kai and Bedivere, while Gualguanus (Gawain) and Mordred are his sister Morgan's sons by King Lot. Merlin Ambrosius appears as a prophet aiding Uter, but never meets Arthur. After a battle with Mordred, who has attempted to usurp his kingdom and marry his queen, Arthur is wounded and translated to Avalon; he is succeeded by Constantine of Cornwall.

The Jersey writer Wace in his *Roman de Brut* (1155) translated Geoffrey's *History* into French, greatly enlarging it. Drawing on other sources, he added more marvels to the story, especially the round table, and under the influence of the new and fashionable romance genre made Arthur's court a centre of *courtoisie*. His Arthur is still in Avalon, his return awaited by the Bretons: references to this belief appear from

1113 onwards. In 1191 fraudulent 'discoveries' of Arthur and Guinevere's tombs at Glastonbury sought both to identify it with Avalon and to quash the idea of Arthur's survival. LAYAMON, a priest in the Severn valley, is the first to put the legend of Arthur into English in his late 12th-century *Brut*, a free and expanded adaptation of Wace.

The pseudo-historical Arthur of chronicle is now swamped by the popularity of the Arthur of romance, and surfaces only briefly in the Saxon wars of *Arthour and Merlin* (English, 13th–14th century) before re-emerging in splendour in the epic alliterative *MORTE ARTHURE* (beginning of the 15th century). Here Arthur's conquests increase to include Italy, but his aggressive wars and reckless pride are depicted as causing Gawain's death and his own downfall.

2 The Arthur of Romance

Twelfth-century romance presents Arthur as the head of a brilliant chivalric court from which individual knights leave on adventures. Much of the material for these romances derives ultimately from Celtic tradition. Welsh poetry before Geoffrey of Monmouth mostly depicts Arthur as the leader of a group of monster-killing heroes. The earliest fleeting reference is in the 7th-century *Gododdin*. Nennius, besides recounting Arthur's battles, alludes to his dog Cabal and the tomb of his son Anir/Amr. Cai and Bedwyr, early associated with Arthur, reappear in the pre-Norman *Spoils of Annwyn*, where Arthur leads an expedition to the Otherworld, and in the Welsh triads, where Gwalchmei (Gawain) and Drystan, lover of Essylt, also occur; here would seem to be the first loose association of the Tristan story with the Arthurian legend.

Culhwch and Olwen (*c.* 1100), a story contained in the Red Book of Hergest and the White Book of Rhydderch, depicts Arthur as a ruler of Britain able to summon armies from France, who helps Culhwch to overcome supernatural obstacles to win his bride. Beside Cai, Bedwyr and Gwalchmei, Gwenhwyfar makes her appearance here. The figure of Merlin derives in part from the Welsh prophet Myrddin, originally unconnected to the Arthurian legend and the subject of various prophetic poems, contained in the Black Book of Carmarthen and the Red Book of Hergest, which refer back to 9th-century sources. A story of the abduction of Guinevere, recurrent in the romances, first appears in written form in the *Vita Gildae* (*c.* 1130), by Caradoc of Lancarvan, though, surprisingly, preceded in sculptural form on an archivolt of Modena Cathedral. Welsh Arthurian literature written after Geoffrey of Monmouth, like *Rhonabwy's Dream* (early 13th century), is influenced by him.

The earliest writer of Arthurian romance, and one of the greatest, was the Northern French Chrétien de Troyes, writing in the last quarter of the 12th century. Before him, though the poetry of Southern France has many allusions to the 'Matter of Britain' from 1137

onwards, the troubadours left no romance except the 13th-century *Jaufré*. There is only *Lanval* among the *lais* of MARIE DE FRANCE (*c.* 1155–89) – interestingly depicting Arthur's queen as unfaithful, which indicates the vogue of the legend among the Anglo-Normans. Chrétien's five verse romances – *Erec et Enide*, *Yvain*, *Lancelot*, *Le Conte du Graal* and *Cligés* – introduce many of the permanent features of the legend: Lancelot and his love for Guinevere; Gawain as a model of prowess and courtesy, often, however, surpassed by the eponymous heroes; Kay as a churlish boaster; Perceval and the quest for the mysterious *graal*; and a king subordinated to his knights, inactive and increasingly ignoble. The degradation of Arthur, and of some of his best warriors, has begun. Guinevere has already appeared in an ambiguous light through her forcible annexation by Mordred in Geoffrey's *History*, which Layamon interprets as willing treachery to Arthur; the *Lai du cor* (1150–75) shows her failing a chastity test.

Chrétien's influence is huge, not least perhaps on a group of Welsh stories, *c.* 1200, about Owain, Peredur and Geraint, part of the so-called *MABINOGION*, which may, however, derive from his sources, not him. There are many continuations of his unfinished Grail story and several romances inspired by the theme, notably Wolfram von Eschenbach's *Parzival* (1200–12), *Perlesvaus* (1225–50), the *Didot Perceval* (*c.* 1202), and Robert de Boron's *Joseph d'Arimathie* (*c.* 1200). This last interprets the *graal* as the vessel used at the Last Supper and also to catch Christ's last drops of blood at the Crucifixion, and which is brought to England by Bron, the Rich Fisher, Joseph's brother-in-law. Boron's *Merlin* introduced yet more elements to the legend, such as Arthur's fostering by Antor (Ector) and the sword in the stone which designates his kingship.

A version of it forms part of the so-called Vulgate Cycle, a huge 13th-century collection of prose romances by various authors, in five parts: *Estoire del Saint Graal*, *Merlin*, *Lancelot*, *Queste del Saint Graal* and *Mort Artu*. These portray Arthur and his court as embodying a worldly chivalry doomed to be surpassed by the spiritual chivalry of the Grail knights, and flawed from the start: Arthur unwittingly and incestuously begets Mordred on his sister Morgause. The quest for the Grail by most of Arthur's hitherto praiseworthy knights, above all Gawain, is barren; Lancelot is displaced as the greatest knight by his son Galaad, and his adulterous love for Guinevere leads to the collapse of the Round Table. Only Galaad, Perceval and Bors achieve the Grail, and only Bors returns to the secular life of Camaalot.

The Vulgate and its successors, such as the *Roman du Graal*, are attempts to combine some of the branches of the Arthurian legend, but there are also vast numbers of miscellaneous romances. In French these range from *Le Bel Inconnu* (1185–90) to Froissart's *Meliador* (1388); there are four in Latin, from the 12th to the 14th century, and many in other languages such as Spanish, Portuguese, Dutch, Norwegian and Icelandic. Though Italy provides us with evidence of early diffusion of the legend in the form of the baptismal names of Artusius and Walwanus, from 1100 on, and in the Modena archivolt (1099–1120), there is no accompanying literary record until the 13th-century prose romances. Arthur's popularity is then plain in literature and art (witness the Pisanello frescoes in Mantua) and leads to his later celebration by Boiardo. German versions of the legend appear from the end of the 12th century, at first influenced by Chrétien, and include, in addition to the *Parzival*, Hartmann von Aue's *Erek* and *Iwein* (c. 1190, c. 1202); Ulrik von Zatzikhoven's *Lanzelet* (from 1194); *Wigalois* and *Diu Krône* (13th century). English romances, in verse and prose, featuring Arthur and his knights range from the second half of the 13th century (*Arthur and Merlin*) to the 16th century. Most notable of these are Thomas Chestre's *Sir Launfal* (c. 1350), *Ywain and Gawain* (c. 1350), the stanzaic *Morte Arthur* (c. 1400), *Sir Gawain and the Green Knight* (late 14th century), and *The Awntyrs of Arthure* (late 14th century) with its reproach of the 'covetous' Arthur and its hint of an adulterous Guinevere. Many of the English romances use French originals but compress and adjust their material to give a clear and action-packed storyline.

Sir Thomas Malory's *Le Morte Darthur*, completed in 1469 or 1470, distils these sources, drawing on both French texts (the Vulgate Cycle, the *Roman du Graal* and the prose *Tristan*) and English ones (the alliterative *Morte Arthure* and the stanzaic *Morte Arthur*). It is the culmination of the tradition, the last and greatest attempt to consolidate all the Arthurian material into a unified cycle. In Caxton's printed text of 1485 it achieves a wider circulation than any of its predecessors, and later reworkings of the legend – such as Tennyson's *Idylls of the King* and T. H. White's *The Once and Future King* – take it as their model.

As I Lay Dying A novel by William Faulkner, published in 1930. It treats the events surrounding the illness, death and burial of Addie Bundren, wife of Anse and mother of Cash, Darl, Jewel, Dewey Dell, and Vardaman. Experimental in both subject and narrative structure, it is divided into 59 short interior monologues (see stream of consciousness) from members of the family and various other characters, including the Reverend Whitfield, Dr Peabody, and the Bundrens' neighbours, Vernon and Cora Tull.

As the novel opens, Addie lies in her bed watching Cash construct her coffin outside the window. Dewey Dell stands beside her, musing about a sexual encounter with Lafe. Jewel, Addie's illegitimate son by the Reverend Whitfield, and Darl, the most devoted son, who is considered 'queer' by the townspeople, are hauling a load of lumber to a Northern town.

While they are away, Addie dies. Anse is stubbornly insistent that her wish to be buried in her home town of Jefferson, Mississippi, should be respected, despite the setbacks which the family encounters on its 10-day journey with the coffin. In one accident Cash is crippled for life. Addie is finally buried in the family plot. Darl, who tried to cremate the body during the journey, is taken away to an asylum. Anse confiscates the money which Lafe had given to Dewey Dell to get an abortion and buys himself the set of false teeth he has always wanted. As the family prepares to leave for home, he appears with a strange woman and introduces her as the new 'Mrs Bundren'.

As You Like It A comedy by William Shakespeare, first performed c. 1599 and published in the First Folio of 1623. The source is Thomas Lodge's *Rosalynde*.

Oliver de Boys has deprived his younger brother, Orlando, of his birthright, and plans to have him killed by tempting him into a match with the champion wrestler of the ducal court. At the court Orlando meets Rosalind, daughter of the deposed duke, and her cousin and friend Celia, daughter of the usurping duke. Orlando wins his bout and Rosalind falls in love with him; but their love is hopeless in Duke Frederick's unjust court. Orlando flies to the Forest of Arden. Rosalind is banished by the duke. She decides to disguise herself as a boy (Ganymede) and Celia leaves with her, in the role of Ganymede's sister, Aliena. Together with the court fool, Touchstone, they, like Orlando, reach the Forest of Arden.

The forest is also the refuge of the banished duke, whose court in exile includes the solitary and wryly speculative Jaques. Orlando is welcomed by the duke and the unexpected comfort gives him leisure to write love poems for his lost Rosalind and post them on trees. Rosalind and Celia find them, and Rosalind uses her male disguise as a pretext for gently testing Orlando's love. She is disturbed to find her new persona loved by the pastoral Phebe. The forest idyll is threatened when Duke Frederick sends Oliver to track down his brother; but Oliver undergoes a change of heart, is saved from death by Orlando and falls in love with Celia. In a joyful scene, Rosalind oversees the matching of Celia and Oliver, Phebe and her equally pastoral lover Silvius, Touchstone and his wench Audrey, and Orlando and herself. Duke Frederick, suddenly repentant, restores his banished brother to the dukedom and himself takes refuge from the world, accompanied by Jaques.

Despite the subtlety of its construction *As You Like It* acknowledges the more primitive pull of fertility rituals and folk festivities. The release from the pressures and constraints of the court brings to all its leading characters a new understanding of their true priorities. However improbable its incidents may seem on a purely narrative level, the harmony of their outcome is profoundly satisfying. *As You Like It* is the most charitable of Shakespeare's mature comedies.

Ascension, The See CHRIST.

Ascham, Roger 1515–68 Scholar and teacher. Ascham was educated at St John's College, Cambridge, and was associated with both the college and the university for many years. He graduated as a BA in 1534 (MA 1537). He taught Greek there, even as an undergraduate, to the younger students, and became instrumental in establishing the importance of Greek at St John's, becoming Greek reader at the college in 1538. He became a fellow of the college and later public orator to the university, resigning both posts only on his marriage in 1554. As well as being an authority on Greek, Ascham was thoroughly versed in Latin literature, an accomplished musician and a fine calligrapher.

In 1548 he became tutor to Princess Elizabeth, a position to which he was reappointed on her accession. With her he read Cicero, Livy and the Greek New Testament. He was also Latin secretary to Queen Mary, with the extraordinary dispensation that he was permitted to continue in the reformed religion.

Ascham wrote two important works in English. *Toxophilus* (1545), a dialogue on archery, stresses the importance of physical exercise in education and pleads for the use of English. *The Schoolmaster*, printed in 1570 after Ascham's death, was apparently provoked by tales of boys running away from Eton for fear of flogging. It argues against excessive discipline in education, warns against idleness and Italian travel, and recommends a method of teaching Latin grammar. Although Ascham's English prose style was praised by GABRIEL HARVEY for its elegance and polish, the modern reader is likely to find it pleasingly plain and clear. Among his writings in Latin are translations of commentaries on the epistles to Titus and Philemon (1542), a treatise against the Mass (1577) and volumes of letters.

Ash, John 1948– Poet. Born in Manchester, he was educated at Birmingham University, and lived in Cyprus before returning to Manchester and then moving to New York. *Casino* (1978) was an attempt to assimilate, and exorcize, the ghosts of French SYMBOLISM. *The Bed* (1981) displays an uncertainty of style as Ash works through various modes of European MODERNISM and approximates the work of the few British poets he feels to have acknowledged this tradition, including ROY FISHER and LEE HARWOOD. The poems in *The Goodbyes* (1982) stress their own artifice, fashioning social detail into an often humorous mode that Ash has called 'urban pastoral'. *The Branching Stairs* (1984) resembles the work of his mentor, JOHN ASHBERY. A commitment to

innovation, which avoids the autobiographical and anecdotal, is manifest in *Disbelief* (1987) and *The Burnt Pages* (1991), where he achieves a clear voice of his own, eclectically knowledgeable and intellectually challenging.

Ashbery, John (Lawrence) 1927– American poet. Born in Rochester, New York, he attended Deerfield Academy in Massachusetts and then Harvard, Columbia and New York universities. He worked as a copywriter for Oxford University Press and then the McGraw-Hill Book Company from 1951 to 1955, when a Fulbright Scholarship enabled him to study in France. He became an art critic for the European edition of *The New York Herald Tribune* and for *Art International*, and was for three years an editor of *Art and Literature*. He returned to the USA in 1965. He is presently a professor of creative writing at Brooklyn College, art critic for *Newsweek* and a frequent contributor to THE NEW YORKER.

The best-known member of the NEW YORK SCHOOL, he presents an essentially sceptical view of the world in verse that is generally self-referential and self-enclosed but still capable of humour and dazzling playfulness. His first volume, *Turandot and Other Poems* (1953), published shortly after his graduation from Columbia, has been followed by *Some Trees* (1956), *The Poems* (1960), *The Tennis Court Oath* (1962; Harriet Monroe Memorial Prize), *Rivers and Mountains* (1966), *Sunrise in Suburbia* (1966), *Three Madrigals* (1966), *Fragment* (1969), *The Double Dream of Spring* (1970), *The New Spirit* (1970), *Three Poems* (1972; Shelley Memorial Award), *The Vermont Notebook* (with Joe Brainard; 1975), *Self-Portrait in a Convex Mirror* (1975; PULITZER PRIZE), *The Serious Doll* (1975), *Houseboat Days* (1977), *As We Know* (1979), *Shadow Train* (1981), *A Wave* (1984), *Selected Poems* (1985), *The Ice Storm* (1987), *April Galleons* (1987) and *Hotel Lautreamont* (1992). He has also published: a novel, *Nest of Ninnies* (with James Schuyler; 1969); drama, collected as *Three Plays* (1978); *Repeated Sightings: Art Chronicles, 1957–1987* (1989); and translations from the French, including Jean-Jacques Mayoux's *Melville* (1960), about the film director, and Jacques Dupin's study of Giacometti (1963). In addition to the poetry awards noted above Ashbery has received many academic and literary honours, including the National Book Award and the Bollingen Prize. He was elected to the American Academy of Arts and Sciences in 1983.

Ashford, Daisy 1881–1972 Juvenile novelist. Born in Surrey, the daughter of a War Office employee, she spent her childhood in Lewes, Sussex. She dictated her first story at the age of four and thereafter constantly wrote or told stories for her own pleasure. At the age of 13 she went off to boarding-school, putting aside writing for the rest of her life. But in

1919, shortly before she married, she came across *The Young Visiters*, a long-forgotten, imperfectly spelled manuscript written when she was nine. It was published the same year with an introduction by J. M. BARRIE. Within its pages Ethel Monticue, an attractive 17-year-old, is courted by both Bernard Clark, her favourite, and Mr Salteena, crushingly described as 'not quite a gentleman'. In search of self-improvement Mr Salteena visits London to stay with the Earl of Clincham as a paying pupil, leaving the field clear for Bernard to propose to Ethel during a romantic riverside picnic. The young author's lively eye for detail and occasional understandable confusions combine to make this book a classic of unconscious humour, never out of print since its first appearance. Other manuscripts written when she was a child and since published are *Love and Marriage* (1965) and *The Hangman's Daughter* (1982).

Ashley, Bernard 1935– Writer of CHILDREN'S LITERATURE. Born and educated in London, he became headmaster of an inner-city primary school. His knowledge of grim urban realities has always made itself evident in his tough, unsentimental writing, starting with *The Trouble with Donovan Croft* (1974). His next books focused on juvenile thieves (*Terry on the Fence*, 1977), bullying (*All My Men*, 1978) and parental neglect (*A Kind of Wild Justice*, 1978). While his young heroes and heroines face serious problems, they still manage to emerge from their adventures stronger and wiser. The world they live in is dangerous but is more manageable when individuals decide to take responsibility for their own actions. *Running Scared* (1986) shows young characters faced with the necessity of making difficult and often dangerous moral decisions. Works for younger readers, such as *Linda's Lie* (1982), adopt a more light-hearted approach.

Ashmole, Elias 1617–92 Antiquary and virtuoso. He was born at Lichfield, Staffordshire, and educated at the grammar school there. While in the service of the king's excise at Oxford in 1645 he entered himself as a student of natural philosophy, mathematics, astronomy and astrology at Brasenose College. He knew the astrologer WILLIAM LILLY. It was with this background of judicial astrology that Ashmole became, in 1646, one of the earliest English Freemasons. Scientific interests (including alchemy) brought him into the company of Rosicrucians and led him to publish his *Theatrum chemicum britannicum* in 1652. Alchemy and astrology later gave way to Hebrew, engraving and heraldry: Ashmole was appointed Windsor Herald in 1660, by which time he was already amassing material for *The Institution, Laws and Ceremonies of the Order of the Garter* (1672). In 1650 Ashmole met the naturalist John Tradescant, whose collections he later inherited. In 1677 he decided to give the collection and his own additions to it to the University of Oxford, provided a suitable building was made available. The twelve carts bearing Ashmole's collections arrived at the museum in March 1683 and the Ashmolean was opened, with Dr Robert Plot as curator, in May of that year.

Ashton-Warner, Sylvia 1908–84 New Zealand novelist. Born in Stratford on North Island, she was educated at small country schools and subsequently, after training at the Teachers' College, Auckland, worked in such schools herself. For 17 years she taught Maori infant classes in the same school as her husband, Keith Henderson. After retiring she was a visiting professor of education at Aspen Community School Teaching Center in Colorado. Her first novel, *Spinster* (1958), did not appear until she was nearly 50, but immediately made an impact in New Zealand as a ROMAN À CLEF and internationally for its STREAM-OF-CONSCIOUSNESS presentation of the teacher-protagonist's turbulent inner life and its relationship to her professional life. Her next novels, *Incense to Idols* (1960) and *Bell Call* (1965), employ Romantic narrative modes which complement the challenge offered to conventional society and its notions of communication and education. *Teacher* (1963) and *Myself* (1967), supposedly the author's diary from the early 1940s, employ a documentary mode but give the impression of being at least partly fictive. Both focus on the narrator's intensely emotional response to the various aspects of her life. *Greenstone* (1966) is a romance that draws heavily on Maori myth and also, in the title theme which refers to an Old English rune, on Germanic cultures. Through a technique which moves between fantasy and realism, it makes a plea for racial and cultural harmony. Ashton-Warner's other works include *Three* (1970) and *I Passed This Way* (1979).

Asimov, Isaac 1920–92 American writer of SCIENCE FICTION. Born in Russia, he was taken to the USA in infancy. A child prodigy, he graduated from Columbia University in 1939. His academic career was interrupted by the war, but he obtained his doctorate in 1948 and became an associate professor of biochemistry at Boston. He has become one of the leading exponents of the popularization of science, prolifically producing essays and books in which explanation of scientific matters is enlivened by his remarkable relish for the excitement of enlightenment. Some of his pulp science fiction stories are among the most popular ever produced, especially those collected in the three-volume Foundation series (1942–50; in book form 1951–3) and the classic collection *I, Robot* (1950), which made famous the 'three laws of robotics'. This programmed ethical system has been further elaborated in the science fiction detective stories *The Caves of Steel* (1954) and *The Naked*

Sun (1956) and in the more philosophically inclined robot stories in *The Bicentennial Man and Other Stories* (1976). His other science fiction novels include *The Currents of Space* (1952), *The End of Eternity* (1955), *The Gods Themselves* (1972) and *Nemesis* (1989). In the years before his death he attempted to bind his two most famous series together into a single pattern of future history, as *Foundation's Edge* (1982), *The Robots of Dawn* (1983), *Robots and Empire* (1985), *Foundation and Earth* (1986) and *Prelude to Foundation* (1988).

Aspern Papers, The A story by HENRY JAMES, published in *THE ATLANTIC MONTHLY* from March to May 1888, and as the title piece of a volume of stories in the same year. The narrator, an American editor, travels to Venice to recover the letters written by Jeffrey Aspern, a Romantic poet of the early 19th century, to his mistress, 'Juliana'. He rents rooms from Juliana, now the aged Miss Bordereau, who lives with her niece, Tina, an unattractive spinster. After Miss Bordereau dies Tina says that she could give the letters only to 'a relative' of the family. The editor balks at the veiled proposal and when they next meet Tina reveals that she has burned them.

Assembly of Ladies, The A poem of unknown authorship once attributed to CHAUCER and probably written in the third quarter of the 15th century in the London area. It is a DREAM-VISION presented as the work of a woman. A lady tells a knight about her dream of an assembly held by Lady Loyalty in the palace of Pleasaunt Regard at which women air their grievances. Nothing is resolved, and another meeting is planned for finding suitable remedies. (See also CHAUCERIAN APOCRYPHA.)

Asser d. 908 or 910 Reputed author of a Latin biography of KING ALFRED, *De rebus gestis Aelfredi Magni*. A monk of St David's and a renowned scholar, he was invited to join the king's household in 885 and took up the offer (after a year of sickness) in 887, dividing his time between home and the royal household. Asser became Alfred's teacher, friend and adviser. He was appointed abbot of monasteries in Congresbury and Banwell, and later Bishop of Devon and Cornwall. At his death he held the bishopric of Sherborne in Dorset.

Although Asser's authorship of *De rebus gestis Aelfredi Magni* has been contested, the work is generally accepted as his. It comprises a chronicle of events in England between 849 and 887, and an account of Alfred's life to 887. The historical material comes largely from the *ANGLO-SAXON CHRONICLE* but the account of Alfred presents the observations of a man who knew him well. The work is thus an important historical source, as well as being the earliest biography of a secular figure written in England.

The only known manuscript was destroyed in the Cotton library fire of 1731 (see COTTON, SIR ROBERT). Of the two editions based on it, that of 1574 is full of arbitrary alterations while that of 1722, though more reliable, preserves many errors from the earlier edition. The work survives in various corrupt versions with extra passages interpolated by other writers. It was, for example, incorporated virtually in its entirety into the chronicles of Florence of Worcester and extensively copied by Simeon of Durham and in the *Annals* of St Neots.

assonance See ALLITERATION.

Astley, Thea 1925– Australian novelist and short-story writer. Born in Brisbane, she was brought up as a Roman Catholic, an important factor in her fiction. She studied arts at the University of Queensland and taught English in Queensland (1944–8) and in New South Wales (1948–67). She was subsequently fellow in Australian literature at Macquarie University from 1968 to 1980, when she moved to Kurando, near Cairns, Queensland. She has won the prestigious Miles Franklin Award for fiction three times. Her novels frequently focus on outsiders and misfits, and attack the philistinism and hypocrisy of middle-class, small-town Australia. *The Well-Dressed Explorer* (1962) and *The Acolyte* (1972) are studies in individual selfishness. *A Kindness Cup* (1974) exposes the criminal past of leading citizens in a small Queensland town. *An Item from the Late News* (1982) attacks several sacred cows of Australian society, including the 'mateship' ethos. Her other novels include *Girl with a Monkey* (1958), *A Descant for Gossips* (1960), *The Slow Natives* (1965), *A Boat Load of Home Folk* (1968), *Beach-masters* (1985), *Reaching Tin River* (1989), *Slow Nature* (1990) and *Vanishing Points* (1992). *Hunting the Wild Pineapple* (1979) and *It's Raining for Mango* (1987) are collections of related short stories. She has also published a volume of essays on BRUCE DAWE, BARBARA BAYNTON and PATRICK WHITE (1979).

Astrophil and Stella A SONNET sequence by SIR PHILIP SIDNEY, the first in English, probably composed in 1582 but not printed until 1591. A preface by THOMAS NASHE introduced it as 'the tragicomedy of love... performed by starlight... The argument cruel chastity, the prologue hope, the epilogue despair'. The sequence of 108 sonnets and 11 songs has as its heroine Stella ('star'). Punning use of the word 'rich' in sonnets 24, 35 and 37 invites the reader to identify her with Penelope Devereux, who became Lady Rich on her marriage in 1581. She is courted by Astrophil ('star-lover'), self-consciously preoccupied not only with Stella but also with poetry. He makes a concise list of 16th-century poetic conventions and styles in sonnet 6. He debates the claims of will and wit, reason and passion (4 and 52). He professes originality: the first sonnet has lines of 14 syllables, the second denies that he fell in love at first sight, and he proclaims independence of PETRARCHAN predecessors (15). The sequence presents an unsuccessful courtship in a series of scenes and emotional attitudes. It is also, implicitly, a critical account of conventional attitudes to love and love poetry in the late 16th century.

Atalanta in Calydon A verse drama by ALGERNON CHARLES SWINBURNE, published in 1865. His intention was 'to do something original in English which might in some degree reproduce for English readers the likeness of a Greek tragedy with something of the true poetic life and charm'. The subject is the myth of Meleager and the hunt for the Calydonian boar, a monster sent by the goddess Artemis to punish King Oeneus for neglecting to honour her. His queen, Althaea, is the mother of Meleager; at his birth the Fates promised him strength and good fortune but warned that his life would last no longer than the stick burning in the hearth fire. When they had left Althaea snatched the stick from the fire, put out the flames, and hid it. When a great hunt was organized to kill the boar, one of the participants was the virgin huntress Atalanta, daughter of Iasius of Arcadia and a favourite of Artemis; Meleager fell in love with her. The boar was killed but a quarrel arose over the distribution of the spoils. When the besotted Meleager gave everything to Atalanta his uncles, Toxeus and Phlexippus (Althaea's brothers), objected. Meleager killed them, and in revenge Althaea burned the stick that measured her son's life and so destroyed him.

Several lyrics from *Atalanta in Calydon* achieved a fame beyond their original context: the chief huntsman's address to Artemis and Apollo ('Maiden, and mistress of the months and stars'); the choric hymn to the goddess that follows ('When the hounds of spring are on winter's traces'); and the chorus's comment when Althaea goes to prepare her son for the hunt ('Before the beginning of years/ There came to the making of man').

Atheist's Tragedy, The: *or, The Honest Man's Fortune* A REVENGE TRAGEDY ascribed to CYRIL TOURNEUR on the title page of the edition published in 1611. Scholars have found it difficult to accept that the author of the sombrely splendid *REVENGER'S TRAGEDY* also wrote this uneven and often lifeless play.

The atheist of the title is D'Amville, whose determination to provide for his family leads him to kill his brother and to arrange for his own sickly son to marry the wealthy Castabella in place of his nephew, Charlemont, to whom Castabella is betrothed. D'Amville's plans are thwarted by his son's impotence, and there follows an extraordinary graveyard scene in which D'Amville's attempt on the honour of his daughter-in-law is prevented by Charlemont.

Charlemont is condemned to death for killing D'Amville's servant. D'Amville himself offers to serve as executioner and 'As he raises up the axe strikes out his own brains'. This (presumably authorial) stage direction is followed by a moralizing speech from the unusually ineffective hero, Charlemont, which concludes that 'patience is the honest man's revenge'.

Athelston A short VERSE ROMANCE of the mid-14th century based on an Old English story. Four men meet and swear brotherhood, and when one of them, Athelston, becomes King of England he makes the others Archbishop of Canterbury, Earl of Dover and Earl of Stane. Stane marries Athelston's sister and Dover, out of jealousy, tells Athelston that the couple are plotting against him. The King imprisons them and when his queen intercedes for them he assaults her, killing her unborn child. Canterbury now intercedes; Athelston orders him to resign his office and is excommunicated. The threat of a popular rising makes Athelston give way. A trial by ordeal proves Stane innocent, but in the same test Dover is proved guilty and is executed. Stane's son is made Athelston's heir; the poem makes a romantic connection with history by identifying him with St Edmund.

Athenaeum, The A weekly literary review founded by James Silk Buckingham in 1828. Its distinguished character was moulded by CHARLES WENTWORTH DILKE, the editor from 1830 to 1846. ROBERT BROWNING, THOMAS CARLYLE, CHARLES LAMB and WALTER PATER were among its contributors in the 19th century. Probably its finest hour came with the brief editorship of JOHN MIDDLETON MURRY (1919–21), when *The Athenaeum* published work by BERTRAND RUSSELL, T. S. ELIOT, ALDOUS HUXLEY and KATHERINE MANSFIELD. In 1921 it merged with *Nation*, appearing as the *Nation and Athenaeum* until it was finally absorbed by *The New Statesman* in 1931.

Atlantic Monthly, The A magazine devoted to literature and current affairs, founded in Boston in 1857 by OLIVER WENDELL HOLMES and JAMES RUSSELL LOWELL. Its editors have included WILLIAM DEAN HOWELLS and THOMAS BAILEY ALDRICH. It regularly features the work of America's most prominent writers, and since 1938 has included articles and essays on international as well as national affairs.

Atterbury, Francis 1662–1732 Churchman and theologian. Born at Middleton Keynes, Buckinghamshire, he was educated at Westminster School and Christ Church, Oxford. After ordination his progress in the church was rapid, and he became Bishop of Rochester and Dean of Westminster in 1713. In 1720 he was imprisoned for alleged complicity in a plot to restore the Stuarts; he was deprived of his offices and banished in 1723, to die in exile. He was a notable contributor to the Phalaris controversy (see SIR WILLIAM TEMPLE) and a preacher of renown. His chief published works were concerned with church dogma, and include *Sermons* (1740) and *Miscellaneous Works* (1789–98).

Atwood, Margaret (Eleanor) 1939– Canadian novelist, poet, short-story writer and critic. Born in Ottawa, she studied at the University of Toronto under NORTHROP FRYE and JAY MACPHERSON and at Harvard, and subsequently taught at several Canadian universities. She first attracted attention as a poet with volumes such as *The Circle Game* (1966), *The Animals in That Country* (1968) and *The Journals of Susanna Moodie* (1970), belonging to the mythopoeic tradition of Jay Macpherson. Her best-known novel, *SURFACING* (1972), traverses similar terrain in relating its narrator-protagonist's quest for personal truth to a journey into the national past and ultimately prehistory – also a concern in a later novel, *Life before Man* (1979). *Lady Oracle* (1976) is a social comedy in which the heroine once again 'escapes' from contemporary consumer society. *The Handmaid's Tale* (1986), set in the near future, is a SCIENCE-FICTION ALLEGORY which comments on the rise of right-wing fundamentalism and new forms of patriarchy in North America in the 1980s. Like much of Atwood's fiction, it demonstrates her capacity for focusing on newly emerging social trends before they have been generally appreciated. *Cat's Eye* (1989) is based on flashback, as the narrator, like earlier Atwood protagonists, reviews and reassesses her past. Now, however, the method is altogether more complex, since conventional notions of time are destroyed by references to contemporary physics.

Atwood's other works include: novels, *The Edible Woman* (1969) and *Bodily Harm* (1981); volumes of verse, *Procedures for Underground* (1970), *Power Politics* (1971), *Two-Headed Poems* (1978), *True Stories* (1981), *Interlunar* (1984) and *Selected Poems: 1966–1984* (1990); and the short-story collections *Dancing Girls* (1977) and *Bluebeard's Egg* (1983). *Survival: A Thematic Guide to Canadian Literature* (1972) is a work of archetypal criticism which shows the influence of Northrop Frye's *The Bush Garden*. Atwood edited *The New Oxford Book of Canadian Verse in English* (1982). *Second Words* (1982) is a collection of her shorter critical pieces.

Aubrey, John 1626–97 Biographer and antiquary. He was born at Easton Pierse, Wiltshire, and received his early education mainly at home, with brief periods at the 'latin schoole' at Yatton Keynell (1633) and under THOMAS HOBBES's old teacher, Robert Latimer, at Leigh Delamere (1634). In 1638 he went to William Sutton's school at Blandford. He entered Trinity College, Oxford, in May 1642 and, though he stayed for only four months, formed a lifelong attachment to the place. He died in Oxford in 1697 and is buried in the church of St Mary Magdalen.

He was admitted as a student of the Middle Temple in 1646. In the late 1640s Aubrey found himself developing a special association with the intellectual *avant-garde* of his day. Although fundamentally royalist, he managed to move easily, in London and Oxford, between groups of various political shadings. He was on terms with such men as Hobbes, Samuel

Margaret Atwood

Hartlib, William Petty and John Wilkins. It is no surprise that he was elected a Fellow of the Royal Society in 1663 and presented many papers before it in the years to come.

Aubrey was strongly drawn both by the Society's empirical approach (with its basis in the work of FRANCIS BACON) and by his own profound sense of history. He never felt any contradiction between these two major aspects of his highly original imagination. Aubrey's scientific impulse to record led him to prepare works of natural history and comparative religion. He made topographical and archaeological collections in the tradition of CAMDEN: his discovery and survey of Avebury (the most reliable before those of this century) give him some claim to be among the first field archaeologists in Britain. But he is best known for the so-called *Brief Lives*. What began in 1667 as compilations of notes for ANTHONY À WOOD's *Historia et antiquitates universitatis oxoniensis* (1674) and *Athenae oxonienses* (1691–2) survived to occupy a far more interesting place in the history of biography. Although he took account of certain figures of the previous age (SHAKESPEARE and SIR WALTER RALEIGH, for example), Aubrey's principal aim was to set down accurate records of the foremost men of his own day. The *Lives* are a serious exercise in biographical truth-telling (perhaps the first in English), packed with detail, mostly observed at first hand and conveyed in an inimitable style. Aubrey's sense of the force of individual personality to which the *Lives* are a monument also informs another of his pioneering works, *An Idea of Education of Young Gentlemen* (manuscript completed 1684), which anticipates much that was thought novel in the educational writings of JOHN LOCKE.

It is to be regretted that Aubrey published only one book in his lifetime: *Miscellanies* (1696). His *Lives, Idea of Education* and other work remained in manuscript for a variety of later editors, not all of them equal to the task, to prepare for publication; some remain unedited to this day. The standard, though somewhat bowdlerized, edition of the *Brief Lives* is that by Andrew Clark (2 vols., Oxford, 1898). *A Perambulation of the County of Surrey*, edited and enlarged by Richard Rawlinson, appeared in 1719 (reprinted 1975). The work on Wiltshire has appeared as *The Natural History of Wiltshire* (1847; reprinted 1969) and *Wiltshire: The Topographical Collections* (1862). *Aubrey on Education* appeared, poorly edited, in 1972. JOHN FOWLES has supervised an edition of *Monumenta Britannica. Miscellanies, Remaines of Gentilisme and Judaisme* and *Observations* are printed as *Three Prose Works*, edited by John Buchanan-Brown (1972). Aubrey is the subject of a biography, *John Aubrey and his Friends* (1948; revised 1963), by ANTHONY POWELL, who has also edited the best selection from the *Lives* and other works (1949).

Audelay, John Early 15th-century poet. Nothing is known of his life beyond the information in the unique manuscript of his poems. He apparently lived at Haughmond Abbey near Shrewsbury. He was blind, deaf and, at least towards the end of his poetic career, ill. The collection bears a colophon dated 1426, and he was at some time first priest to Lord Strange (who held the title 1397–1449).

Audelay's poems comprise 55 religious pieces on various themes, though it is possible that the last two are the work of a different writer. The majority of the poems are penitential; while one tells of the joys of the true religious life, most are inspired by a fear of damnation. Their treatment of religious matters is completely orthodox and generally symptomatic of a popular interpretation. The poems fall into three broad categories, the didactic, the narrative and descriptive, and a group of 25 poems labelled as carols for Christmas. The poems show little originality of thought and borrow extensively from each other and from other writers. They exhibit a fondness for metrical experimentation and use a wide variety of verse forms. Audelay's skill in metre was not, however, matched by his use of rhyme, which was often careless and uninspired.

Auden, W(ystan) H(ugh) 1907–73 Poet, playwright and critic. He was born in York, the youngest son of a doctor and a devoutly Anglo-Catholic mother. His father moved the family to Birmingham a year later to take up a post as schools medical officer for the district. Auden was educated at St Edmund's preparatory school in Surrey (1915–20), where CHRISTOPHER ISHERWOOD was a fellow pupil, at Gresham's School, Holt, Norfolk (1920–5), and at Christ Church, Oxford (1925–8), where he changed from science to English and gained a third class honours degree in 1928. Contemporaries at Oxford included REX WARNER, JOHN BETJEMAN, STEPHEN SPENDER, C. DAY-LEWIS and LOUIS MACNEICE. Auden began to make a name for himself as a poet while still a student: he twice edited *Oxford Poetry* and his first book of poems was printed by Spender in 1928. After Oxford he spent some time in Berlin, where Isherwood was living. On his return to England in 1929 he worked as a tutor and then as a schoolmaster until he obtained work with the GPO film unit who produced *Night Mail*, a documentary film with Auden's text.

His early collections of verse, *Poems* (1930), *The Orators* (1932), *The Dance of Death* (1933) and *Look Stranger!* (1936), established him as the leading figure of his generation. In collaboration with Isherwood he wrote three plays, *The Dog beneath the Skin* (1935), *The Ascent of F6* (1936) and *On the Frontier* (1939). His brief service as an ambulance driver for the Republicans in the Spanish Civil War resulted in *Spain* (1937). Other travels produced *Letters from*

Iceland (with Louis MacNeice, 1937) and *Journey to a War* (with Isherwood, 1939), about China. He emigrated to the United States with Isherwood in 1939 and became an American citizen in 1946.

Auden's early work is socially committed left-wing writing with a purpose and direction that is uncommon in its uniformity and power. *The Orators* shows that, apart from his early interest in Old English vocabulary and metrical forms, he was working through and applying the model of T. S. ELIOT's *THE WASTE LAND* to his own preoccupation with science and psychology. There is a deliberate materialism derived from his reading of Marx and Freud, but also a complicating wealth of latent thematic material that has to do with the concealment (necessary in that time) of a homosexual writing about his own and his friends' emotional lives.

Auden married Erika Mann in 1935 to provide her with a British passport and thus help her escape from Nazi Germany. His lifelong companion, however, was Chester Kallman, whom he met in America. Once settled in New York, he left behind the conflict between his relatively privileged background and his early political sympathies, though his interest in Freud continued. He became increasingly attracted to his mother's faith, and his Anglicanism left its mark on his poetry. While he could successfully adopt American verse forms, he remained unmistakably a British poet. *New Year Letter* (1941; as *The Double Man* in USA) was the first of his American books, followed by *For the Time Being: A Christmas Oratorio* (1944), *The Age of Anxiety: A Baroque Eclogue* (1947), *Nones* (1951), *The Shield of Achilles* (1955), *The Old Man's Road* (1956) and *Homage to Clio* (1960).

He was professor of poetry at Oxford in 1956-60, becoming a Student (i.e. fellow) of Christ Church in 1962 and returning to live in his old college in 1972. Part of his later life was spent in Kirchstetten, Austria, and his life with Chester Kallman there is celebrated in *About the House* (1967). Final volumes were *City Walls and Other Poems* (1969), *Academic Graffiti* (1971) and *Epistle to a Godson* (1972). He also extensively revised his early work from his later viewpoint as a Christian, presenting his personal canon in *Collected Shorter Poems* (1966), *Collected Longer Poems* (1968) and *Collected Poems* (1976). A useful collection is thus *The English Auden* (1977), which reissued his early poetry and some prose in the versions in which it was first read.

Auden edited *The Oxford Book of Light Verse* (1938) and many other collections and anthologies. His critical writing includes *The Enchafèd Flood* (1951), *The Dyer's Hand* (1963) and *Secondary Worlds* (1968). He also collaborated with Chester Kallman on the libretto for Stravinsky's *The Rake's Progress* (1951).

Audubon, John James 1785-1851 American naturalist and artist. Born in Haiti, he was educated in the USA and later in France, where he studied with Jacques-Louis David. Audubon spent much of his life travelling throughout the USA and Canada to find materials for his wildlife drawings, which became celebrated for their accurate detail and delicate use of watercolour. Many were included in his most famous book, *The Birds of America*, which was published in England between 1827 and 1838. Sections of his journals also have been published, including *Delineations of American Scenery and Character* (1926), *Journal of John James Audubon, Made during His Trip to New Orleans in 1820-21* (1929) and *Audubon's America* (1940).

Augie March, The Adventures of A novel by SAUL BELLOW, published in 1953.

Augie March is one of three sons born to a feeble-minded Jewish woman on Chicago's West Side. He attends but does not finish college, becomes involved briefly in union organizing, travels to Mexico, returns to the USA and joins the navy, marries and, after leaving the service, goes to Europe to write his 'memoir'. In it he records his encounters with the people who have shaped (or tried to shape) his life. The first, and perhaps most important, is his Grandma Lausch, a Machiavellian *grande dame* who lives with the Marches. There are also William Einhorn, the brilliant and wealthy cripple for whom the teenaged Augie works; the wealthy Renlings from Evanston, who want to adopt him; Mini Villar, the tough waitress who becomes pregnant by another man and whom he helps to obtain an abortion; Thea Fenchel, the rich married woman who takes him with her to Mexico, where she plans to divorce her husband; the millionaire Robey, who hires Augie to help him write a masterwork defining the nature of man; Stella Chesney, the showgirl he marries; and the lunatic scientist Bateshaw, with whom he shares a lifeboat after their ship has been torpedoed.

Augustan Age, The A term applied loosely to the literature and art of the Restoration and early 18th century, though some scholars object sharply to its vagueness. It denotes a period of literary excellence, and refers back to the heyday of classical writing during the reign of the Roman emperor Augustus (27 BC-AD 14) and the stylistic achievements of the Latin poets of the golden age, Virgil, Horace and Ovid, whose writings were much admired and imitated by the authors of this later period of NEOCLASSICISM.

Although the term is imprecise, it is none the less convenient for bracketing together the writings and styles of many authors from DRYDEN and SAMUEL BUTLER to SAMUEL JOHNSON, and is most frequently applied to the work of POPE and JONATHAN SWIFT. Common literary concerns, especially among the poets, included: the development of an elegant, well-turned style; the pursuit of fluency, precision of expression and a dislike of cant or slang; the observation of decorum; and the cultivation of good taste and the refinement of manner.

The period is characterized by a general desire for common sense and compromise in the face of the wilder extremes of contemporary fashion and thought, and this moderation is sometimes referred to as the *via media* or golden mean, its artistic manifestation being a delight in proportion, poise and WIT. Pope's poem 'The First Epistle of the Second Book of Horace Imitated' (1737) is dedicated 'To Augustus' as a specific reference to the monarch George II, whose other name was Augustus, but this was an ironic inversion of the otherwise complimentary implications of the Latin original since the Hanoverian king ignored rather than patronized the arts, and scarcely even spoke English. GOLDSMITH's essay on the 'Augustan Age in England' is a *locus classicus* for contemporary discussion.

Auld Lang Syne See AYTON, SIR ROBERT and BURNS, ROBERT.

Aureng-Zebe A heroic tragedy by JOHN DRYDEN, first produced in 1675 and published the following year. It was the last and best of Dryden's plays in HEROIC COUPLETS.

Set in Mogul India, it concerns the love of Aureng-Zebe for Indamora, a captive queen. Their love becomes entangled with a struggle for power in the court of Aureng-Zebe's father, the Mogul emperor, Shah Jehan. Both the emperor and Morat, his son by his second wife Nourmahal, pursue Indamora. Despite this, Aureng-Zebe remains loyal to his father, and after the struggle for the throne has led to the deaths of both Morat and Nourmahal, Shah Jehan rewards Aureng-Zebe by abandoning his pursuit of Indamora.

Aurora Leigh A novel in verse by ELIZABETH BARRETT BROWNING, published in 1856 (postdated 1857).

Conceived at least 10 years before publication, this is her most sustained piece of work, confronting many contemporary issues (the role of women, the plight of the poor and the efficacy of Utopian socialism) and embodying her 'highest convictions upon Life and Art'. The heroine, though a poet, is not an autobiographical portrait. The story traces her development as an artist in opposition to the active philanthropy of her cousin Romney. The resolution lies in the recognition by both cousins that each has placed too great an emphasis on limited aspects of man's character: Romney in considering and supplying only the physical needs of the under-privileged, Aurora in relinquishing love and companionship to pursue her ambitious ideal of the poet's vocation.

Austen, Jane 1775–1817 Novelist. She was born at Steventon in Hampshire where her father, who was also her tutor, was rector. On his retirement in 1801 the family moved to Bath, a city that frequently appears in her fiction, but returned to Hampshire after his death in 1805. With her mother and sister, she lived first in Southampton and then in Chawton, near Alton, remaining there until she died. Her life was conspicuous for its lack of event – allowing biographers to make it a study in quiet contemplation or quiet frustration – and for the strength of her family ties, most importantly with her sister Cassandra. She died in Winchester at the age of 41 and is buried in the cathedral.

She began her literary career at the age of 15 with *Love and Friendship*, a BURLESQUE of SAMUEL RICHARDSON; other pieces belonging to the 1790s caricature the excessive 'sensibility' fashionable in the 18th-century SENTIMENTAL NOVEL. Her eye for the ridiculous in contemporary taste also inspired *NORTHANGER ABBEY* (published posthumously in 1818 but probably her earliest extended work of fiction), which satirizes her heroine's penchant for GOTHIC FICTION, and *SENSE AND SENSIBILITY* (begun in 1797 but not published until 1811).

Begun in 1796 or 1797 and published after revision in 1813, *PRIDE AND PREJUDICE* has the same high spirits as its predecessors but, more clearly than they, marks out the territory, the subject and the mode of her mature work. It looks forward to her later novels: *MANSFIELD PARK* (begun 1811, published 1814), *EMMA* (begun 1814, published 1816) and *PERSUASION* (begun 1815, published posthumously in 1818). In these works she chose deliberately to portray small groups of people in a limited, perhaps confining, environment, and to mould the apparently trivial incidents of their lives into a poised comedy of manners. Her characters are middle-class and provincial; their most urgent preoccupation is with courtship and their largest ambition is marriage. The task she set herself required careful shaping of her material, delicate economy and precise deployment of IRONY to point the underlying moral commentary. She developed not by obvious enlargement of her powers but by the deepening subtlety and seriousness with which she worked inside the formal boundaries she had established.

Although her novels did not prove especially popular in her own day, *Emma* was reviewed favourably by SIR WALTER SCOTT and was dedicated to another admirer of her work, the Prince Regent. *Lady Susan*, an EPISTOLARY NOVEL, and *The Watsons* were not published until they appeared in the second edition of J. E. Austen Leigh's *Memoir of Jane Austen* (1871). The fragment of *SANDITON*, on which she was working in the last months of her life, was first published in 1925.

Austin, Alfred 1835–1913 Poet. Though educated at Stonyhurst and Oscott College, he abandoned his Roman Catholicism; he later qualified as a barrister. An inheritance gave him sufficient income to turn instead to being a man of letters. An Imperialist and supporter of DISRAELI, he was joint editor of *The National Review* from 1883 and sole editor from 1887 to 1895. He published 20 volumes of poetry between 1871 and 1908, and, to general mockery, was appointed POET LAUREATE in 1896. He was especially parodied for his ode on the Jameson Raid. His autobiography appeared in 1911.

Authorized Version, The See BIBLE IN ENGLISH, THE.

Autobiography of a Super-Tramp, The See DAVIES, W. H.

Autocrat of the Breakfast Table, The A collection of essays, poems, and occasional pieces by OLIVER WENDELL HOLMES, first published in THE ATLANTIC MONTHLY in 1857–8 and in volume form in 1858, though it expands two youthful papers written while he was studying medicine at Harvard. It takes the form of table talk in a Boston boarding house; besides the autocrat himself, those present at the breakfast table include the landlady, her daughter, a poor relation, a schoolmistress, a divinity student and an old gentleman. The autocrat is generally seen as a vehicle for Holmes's own wit and social commentary.

Ave atque Vale An ELEGY by ALGERNON CHARLES SWINBURNE to Baudelaire, based on a false report of the French poet's death. It was published in THE FORTNIGHTLY REVIEW for January 1868 and reprinted in the second series of *Poems and Ballads* (1878).

Avison, Margaret (Kirkland) 1918– Canadian poet. Born in Galt, Ontario, and educated at the University of Toronto, she has held a variety of posts as secretary, librarian, lecturer, researcher and social worker. Her literary output has been small, consisting of contributions to magazines and the volumes *Winter Sun* (1960), *The Dumbfounding* (1966), *Sunblue* (1978) and *No Time* (1990). Nevertheless, she is recognized as one of Canada's finest poets, concentrating with delicate precision upon the nature of imaginative perception in the bleak landscapes of the 20th century. From *The Dumbfounding* onwards, her poetry is informed by her conversion to Christianity in the 1960s.

Avowynge of King Arthur, Sir Gawan, Sir Kaye, and Sir Bawdewyn of Bretan, The An anonymous poem in TAIL-RHYME stanzas, probably written around 1425 in the North of England. Arthur and his three knights are hunting near Carlisle when they hear of a great boar. The four make various vows: Arthur to kill it single-handed before morning, Gawain to watch at the Tarn Wadling and Kay to ride the forest all night, while Bawdewyn, who becomes the central figure, extravagantly vows never to be jealous of his wife, never to deny his food to any man and not to fear death. The poem tells of their adventures, and culminates in three anecdotes by Bawdewyn explaining why he made and honoured such vows. The work has no known single source. (See also ARTHURIAN LITERATURE.)

Awake and Sing! A play by CLIFFORD ODETS, first performed by the Group Theatre in New York in 1935. It was one of the major pieces in the repertoire of that short-lived but important company.

The play describes a crisis in the lives of a Jewish family living in the Bronx during the Depression. Bessie Berger determines to sustain her impoverished family by the force of her own belief in a tolerable present and a better future. Her communist father sees hope only in changing society and makes his grandson Ralph his ally. It is only after his grandfather has committed suicide that Ralph finds the energy to fight for the cause.

Awakening, The A novel by KATE CHOPIN, published in 1899. It is a study of the inner life and rebellion of Edna Pontellier, the wife of a successful Creole speculator in Louisiana, and the mother of two small boys.

While spending the summer at Grand Isle, she flirts with Robert Lebrun, the son of the resort owner, who awakens her to a new sense of spiritual and physical self-awareness. She begins to question the importance of the traditional roles of wife and mother that she has always fulfilled and that she sees embodied in her friend Adele Ratignolle. On her return to New Orleans, she begins to assert her new sense of identity. She develops her artistic nature by painting and attains some financial independence by selling her work. She moves out of the family house, and has sexual relations with another man. Lebrun returns and their intimacy is renewed, but the consummation of their love is prevented when Edna is called to help Adele through the birth of her child. Profoundly distressed by the birth scene, she returns home to find Lebrun gone. She realizes that a succession of lovers will not lead to fulfilment, and that, though she feels neither loyalty nor guilt towards her husband, she cannot escape from her responsibilities to her sons. In a final desperate assertion of her independence, she returns to Grand Isle, and the novel closes as she swims far out to sea to her death.

Awdry, Rev. **W(ilbert) V(ere)** 1911– Writer of CHILDREN'S LITERATURE. Born in Hampshire and educated at Oxford, he was first a schoolmaster and then an Anglican clergyman. His first book, *The Three Railway Engines* (1945), arose from stories which he told his infant son. Every page was accompanied by an illustration showing the different engines, with faces but otherwise trains in every other detail. Its success spawned a series, including *Gordon, the Big Engine* (1953) and *Edward, the Blue Engine* (1954), in which the Fat Controller repeatedly tries to supervise the characters. Succeeding illustrators have maintained the idyllic tradition laid down by C. Reginald Dalby, who worked on the series from 1948 to 1956. *Starlight Express* (1984), a stage musical by Andrew Lloyd Webber and Richard Stilgoe loosely based on Awdry's train characters, has since proved extremely successful.

Awkward Age, The A novel by HENRY JAMES, published serially in *Harper's Weekly* from October 1898 to January 1899 (as a volume, revised, 1899). It is written almost entirely in the form of dialogue. Its heroine, Nanda Brookenham, is a 'knowing' young woman brought up in the permissive and worldly atmosphere of her mother's salon. Aggie, a 'pure' young lady who has been raised strictly, in the Continental manner, by her aunt the Duchess, serves as her foil. The action of the novel revolves around the relations between Nanda and Aggie and two men, Mr Vanderbank and Mr Mitchett.

Nanda loves Mr Vanderbank, but he does not return her feeling. Mr Longdon, an elderly gentleman who once cared for Nanda's grandmother, encourages Vanderbank to marry Nanda, even offering to provide her with a dowry. But Nanda, out of the worldly wisdom that has perhaps made her less marriageable than Aggie, realizes Vanderbank does not love her and, in a typically Jamesian renunciation scene, graciously gives him up. Meanwhile, Mr Mitchett, who had hoped to marry Nanda himself, has been sought by the Duchess as a match for Aggie. Accepting that he cannot have Nanda, Mitchett marries Aggie. Nanda leaves the marriage market and retires to Longdon's country house.

Awntyrs of Arthure at the Terne Wathelyne, The An alliterative poem of the late 14th century written in Northern England or Scotland. Some have identified it with the *Awntyre of Gawayn* mentioned in ANDREW OF WYNTOUN's *Cronykil* (*c.* 1420) as the work of HUCHOWN OF THE AWLE RYALE.

The Terne Wathelyne is Wadling Tarn near Hesket in Cumbria. There are two *awntyrs* (adventures), but Arthur features only in the second and Gawain is the central figure in each. Arthur and his court are at Carlisle and are hunting when a storm separates Dame Gaynoure (Guinevere) and Gawain from the remainder of the hunting party. They are confronted by a fearsome figure which emerges from the waters of the tarn, the tormented spirit of Gaynoure's mother.

Before vanishing, she warns Gaynoure that she is paying the price for her life of pride and lechery and prophesies the end of the Round Table, Arthur's last battle and Gawain's death. The second adventure tells of the combat between Galleron of Galway and Gawain. Arthur had taken Galleron's lands and given them to Gawain, but peace is restored when Arthur returns Galleron's lands and makes Gawain lord of Wales in recompense. The work has been the subject of controversy, the disparate nature of the two adventures causing some critics to see it as two works brought together. However, the two illuminate each other and share a moral criticism of Arthur's court. See also ARTHURIAN LITERATURE.

Awoonor, Kofi 1935– Ghanaian poet and novelist, formerly known as George Awoonor Williams. Born in Wheta, he was educated in Ghana, London and New York. Under different Ghanaian regimes he has been both political detainee and ambassador. He writes in both English and Ewe. The lucid, lyrical English verse in *Rediscovery* (1964), *Night of My Blood* (1971), *Ride Me Memory* (1973) and *The House by the Sea* (1978) celebrates African communality as 'the feast of oneness' and tries to bridge modern and precolonial African culture by writing, in Williams's own words, 'traditional oral poetry of the Ewes, with emphasis on lyricism, the chant, repetition of lines, symbolism, and imagery transfused into English through the secondary influence of POUND and DYLAN THOMAS'. Joint editor of *Messages: Poems from Ghana* (1970), he has also written *Guardians of the Sacred Word* (1974), about traditional Ewe poetry, and *The Breast of the Earth: A Survey of the History, Culture, and Literature of Africa* (1975). *This Earth, My Brother...* (1972), his novel about Ghana before and after independence, has been admired for its experimental form and its complex portrayal of cultural alienation and corruption.

Ayala's Angel A novel by ANTHONY TROLLOPE, published in three volumes in 1881.

The romantic Ayala and her more practical sister Lucy are the pretty but penniless orphan daughters of Egbert Dormer, an improvident artist. Ayala is taken into the home of her wealthy City uncle, Sir Thomas Tringle, and Lucy goes to stay in the pennypinching household of another uncle, Reginald Dosett. Ayala's attitude to her rich relations is disrespectful, and when her vulgar but good-natured cousin Tom falls in love with her, and she rejects his persistent proposals of marriage, the two sisters change places. The novel concerns the romantic idealism which leads Ayala to reject her available suitors for an 'Angel of Light' of her imagination, and the comic reversal which comes when she discovers this angel in the ugly, fiery-complexioned but devoted soldier Jonathan Stubbs. Her sister, although living in luxury, remains true to the young sculptor she loves, and is enabled to marry him through the generosity of her uncle Sir Thomas. His own children fare less happily and are the subject of the novel's secondary action.

A playful and self-mocking novel, *Ayala's Angel* shows Trollope lightly experimenting with many of the characteristic themes and situations of his earlier novels.

Ayckbourn, Alan 1939– Playwright. He began his career as an actor, became a producer of radio drama and then, in 1970, artistic director of the Stephen Joseph Theatre in Scarborough. Since *Relatively Speaking* (1967), his increasingly sour FARCES about middle-class anxiety and neurosis have transferred to London and enjoyed extraordinary critical acclaim. Outstanding among them are *How the Other Half Loves* (1969), *Absurd Person Singular* (1972), the trilogy grouped under the title *The Norman Conquests* (1973), *Bedroom Farce* (1975), *Joking Apart* (1978), *A Chorus of Disapproval* (1985), *A Small Family Business* (1987), *Henceforward...* (1988) and *Man of the Moment* (1990).

Ayenbite of Inwyt A religious tract in prose, written by Dan Michel of Northgate, Kent, and completed in 1340. It is a translation and adaptation of *Le Somme des vices et des vertues*, written by Frère Lorens for Philip II of France in 1279. The title means the 'again-biting' (remorse) of the 'inner wit' (conscience). The tract aims to teach the basis of good Christian living and the nature of sin. It is divided into discourses on each of the Ten Commandments, the twelve articles of the Creed and the seven deadly sins, and on learning to die, the knowledge of good and evil, and the virtues. Each discourse is further subdivided. ALLEGORY is sometimes used but, unlike many similar works, *Ayenbite* prefers to explain the vices and virtues by analysis of their structure and character rather than by anecdote and EXEMPLUM.

Ayer, Sir A(lfred) J(ules) 1910–89 Philosopher. He was educated at Eton and Christ Church, Oxford, with further study in Vienna; his professorial career was spent mainly at London (1946–59) and Oxford (1959–78). His first book, *Language, Truth and Logic* (1936, revised 1946), forcefully argued but notably elegant and lucid, provided a link between the logical positivism of the Vienna Circle and nascent English linguistic analysis. *The Problem of Knowledge* (1956) deals with questions of scepticism in philosophy. His autobiographies (1977, 1984) cover his varied social life as well as his intellectual career. A prominent atheist, he was knighted in 1951.

Aylwin See WATTS-DUNTON, THEODORE.

Ayrshire Legatees, The A novel by JOHN GALT, published in 1820. It takes the form of letters from Dr Zachariah Pringle and his family in London to their friends in Scotland, describing their impressions of the capital and the events of 1820, when George IV succeeded George III.

Ayton [Aytoun], Sir **Robert** 1570–1638 Scottish poet. Educated at St Andrews University, Ayton served as secretary to Anne of Denmark, JAMES I's queen, and then to Henrietta Maria, and was a friend of BEN JONSON and THOMAS HOBBES. Fluent in several languages, he was probably the first Scot to write in the English of the south as opposed to the Scottish of his contemporaries; his verses are popular with anthologists; best known is the song 'Should Old Acquaintance be Forgot', credited to him by James Watson in 1711. 'Auld Lang Syne', the melody to which BURNS's more famous version is sung, is an old Scots air and would have been known to Ayton.

Aytoun, William Edmonstoune 1818–65 Scottish poet and critic. He taught at Edinburgh University as professor of rhetoric and belles lettres and contributed to BLACKWOOD'S EDINBURGH MAGAZINE. Aytoun coined the term 'spasmodic' (see SPASMODIC SCHOOL OF POETRY) in unflattering description of the febrile Romantic verse of SYDNEY DOBELL, PHILIP JAMES BAILEY and ALEXANDER SMITH, whom he satirized in *FIRMILIAN: or, The Student of Badajoz: A Spasmodic Tragedy* (1854). With Theodore Martin, he was author of the *Bon Gaultier Ballads* (1855), which contain parodies of TENNYSON and ELIZABETH BARRETT BROWNING. Aytoun's *Lays of the Scottish Cavaliers* (1849) and *The Ballads of Scotland* (1858) were extremely popular in the 19th century.

Bab Ballads, The A series of humorous verses by W. S. GILBERT, originally contributed to *Fun* and other periodicals between 1862 and 1871, many with illustrations by the author signed 'Bab' (the version of 'Baby' by which he had been known as a child). A first collected edition was published in 1868, *More Bab Ballads* in 1872, and a comprehensive edition in 1882. The ironic tone and many of the themes of the ballads helped to form the characteristic style and content of Gilbert's lyrics for the SAVOY OPERAS. For *The Bab Ballads with Which are Included the Songs of a Savoyard* (1898) he redrew many of the original illustrations, which he claimed had 'erred gravely in the direction of unnecessary extravagance'.

Babbitt A novel by SINCLAIR LEWIS, published in 1922. It depicts the complacency and materialism of George F. Babbitt, a real-estate agent and representative middle-class family man from the city of Zenith in the American Midwest. After his only real friend, the artist-turned-businessman Paul Riesling, shoots his wife and is sent to prison, Babbitt rebels against commonplace values: he begins a love affair with the widow Tanis Judique, refuses to join the Good Citizens' League, and becomes influenced by the socialist lawyer Seneca Doane. But he soon finds the price of nonconformity too great and once again resigns himself to the superficial values of his business culture. His reconciliation with society is completed by his acceptance back into the Booster Club. At the end of the novel, his son (ironically named Theodore Roosevelt Babbitt) himself rebels against the wishes of his family and the town by leaving college and marrying hastily. Babbitt supports him in this rebellion, hoping that, unlike himself, his son will be able to do as he wants and lead a more independent and fulfilled life.

Babbitt, Irving 1865–1933 American scholar and critic. Born in Ohio, Babbitt graduated from Harvard in 1889 and then taught at Williams College (1893–4) and Harvard (1894–1933). With Paul Elmer More he was a leading figure among the New Humanists. His criticism emphasized the ethical component of art, rejecting more romantic ideals which, in his view, tended too much to establish art or science as objects of veneration. His ideas influenced T. S. ELIOT, who was his student at Harvard. His major works are *Literature and the American College* (1908), *The New Laokoön* (1910), *Masters of Modern French Criticism* (1912), *Rousseau and Romanticism* (1919), *Democracy and Leadership* (1924), *On Being Creative* (1932) and *The Spanish Character and Other Essays: with a Bibliography of His Publications and an Index to His Collected Works* (1940).

Back to Methuselah: *A Metabiological Pentateuch* A five-part play by GEORGE BERNARD SHAW, published in 1921 and first produced at the Garrick Theatre, New York, in 1922. It was given its first English production by Barry Jackson at the Birmingham Repertory Theatre in 1923. The five parts, each separately titled, stretch from the Garden of Eden to the year 21,920, allowing Shaw ample space to dramatize the essential opposition, in the development of human society, between stagnation and creative evolution. He defined the modern world's dilemma in a 1944 postscript to *Back to Methuselah*: 'Civilization means stabilization; and creative evolution means change. As the two must operate together we must carefully define their spheres, and coordinate them instead of quarrelling and persecuting as we do at present.' Shaw's aim was to demonstrate the capacity of humankind to will its own betterment.

Bacon, Sir **Francis** 1st Viscount St Albans 1561–1626 Philosopher and essayist. The youngest son of Nicholas Bacon, Lord Keeper of the Seal to Elizabeth I, he was born at York House in the Strand, London, and educated at Trinity College, Cambridge. He entered Gray's Inn in 1576 and, failing to secure any official position in public service, turned to practising the law. He was an ambitious man, and though he enjoyed the patronage of the Earl of Essex, and became an MP in 1584, his career saw no dramatic advances until the death of Elizabeth, partly because he had opposed her tax programme in Parliament. Appointed to prepare the case against his own patron following the Essex revolt, in 1601 he dispassionately brought his formidable legal skills to bear upon his friend and secured a conviction. In 1606 he married Alice Barnham. Under JAMES I Bacon's talents were rewarded. He became Solicitor-General in 1607, Attorney-General in 1613, Lord Keeper of the Seal in 1617, and, finally, Lord Chancellor in 1618. In the same year he was created Baron Verulam, and in 1621 Viscount St Albans. But Bacon was not popular among many of his peers. His most jealous rival was SIR EDWARD COKE, formerly Chief Justice of the King's Bench, who in 1621 successfully instigated a charge of corruption against him. Bacon admitted accepting bribes, but denied he had ever perverted the course of justice. He was dismissed from office, debarred from Parliament, fined, and sent briefly to the Tower, thence retiring into private life, disgraced.

Bacon devoted much of his subsequent life to writing. His first writing had been political: the *Temporis Pastus Masculus* (1584) outlined a policy of tolerance and moderation, but a *Letter of Advice to Queen Elizabeth* later advocated tough anti-Catholic measures. His *ESSAYS*, published in 1597 in a book of 10, were reprinted in a 1625 edition which contained 58. After *THE ADVANCEMENT OF LEARNING* (1605) he turned to Latin for *DE SAPIENTIA VETERUM* (1609), later translated as *The Wisdom of the Ancients* (1619). Latin was also chosen for his celebrated *NOVUM ORGANUM* (1620). He returned to English in *The History of the Reign of King Henry the Seventh* (1622) and *Apophthegms New and Old* (1624). *Sylva Sylvarum: or, A Natural History* and an unfinished Utopian fiction, *THE NEW ATLANTIS*, were both published in 1627, the year after he died on his estate at Gorhambury, from a chill contracted while studying the properties of snow.

Sir Francis Bacon as portrayed on the frontispiece to the first volume of *The Works of Francis Bacon*, edited by James Spedding and others, 1857–9

His works are suffused with the curiosity of a scientific mind and are written in an accomplished, ever beautiful, style that is concise and frequently epigrammatic. Bacon's greatest achievement is the programme of intellectual and scientific reform proposed under the title of *Instauratio Magna* ('Great Instauration'), begun in *The Advancement of Learning* and continued in *Novum Organum* and *Sylva Sylvarum*, as well as informing *The New Atlantis*. These works reject the older, Aristotelian structures of knowledge and seek to discover a new system of philosophic instruction based upon a clearer, empirical perception of nature. Ironically, it was Bacon's reputation for polymathic intelligence that gave rise to the so-called BACONIAN HERESY.

Bacon, Roger *c.* 1220–*c.* 1292 Philosopher and scientist. Born at either Ilchester in Somerset or Bisley in Gloucestershire, Bacon studied the *quadrivium* at Oxford before going to Paris where he lectured on Aristotle and pseudo-Aristotelian works. After 1247, under the influence of ROBERT GROSSETESTE, Adam de Marisco and Thomas the Welshman, he was in Oxford engaged in experimental work, studying mathematics, optics, alchemy and astronomy as well as languages. In 1257 he became a Franciscan friar and suffered a long period of illness; his literary and university careers virtually ended. In 1266 he sought the patronage of Pope Clement IV for a projected encyclopaedia of all known science and for reforming the teaching of science. Over the next two years he sent the *Opus Majus, Opus Minus* and *Opus Tertium* to the Pope, but the death of Clement IV in 1268 frustrated Bacon's desire to see the sciences fully recognized as part of the university curriculum. Other projected encyclopaedias proved abortive. He was condemned to prison at some time between 1277 and 1279 on account of his unorthodox teaching, probably his attacks on theologians and scholars and his interest in alchemy and astrology. Exaggerated accounts of his experiments made him a figure in popular literature (like *FRIAR BACON AND FRIAR BUNGAY*), and he acquired the title *doctor admirabilis* after his death. His influence was principally as a promoter of science and the teaching of science.

Baconian Heresy The theory that FRANCIS BACON wrote the works of SHAKESPEARE was first publicly advanced by the suitably named Delia Bacon, an American living in England, in her *Philosophy of the Plays of Shakespeare Unfolded* (1857). NATHANIEL HAWTHORNE contributed a cautious preface to the book, more in his capacity as American consul at Liverpool than as literary critic. Miss Bacon died insane after haunting Shakespeare's grave in the belief its opening would settle the question of authorship, but her theory flourished and enjoyed a considerable vogue among amateur scholars, particularly in the closing years of the 19th and the early years of the 20th century. In the hands of supporters like Sir Edwin Durning-Lawrence (*Bacon is Shakespeare*, 1910; *The Shakespeare Myth*, 1912) it rests on a variety of arguments. As a rustic from Stratford, Shakespeare is seen as too boorishly illiterate to make a poet; Francis Bacon, on the other hand, was a man of admittedly wide learning who would have had political reasons for concealing any involvement in the contemporary theatre. The connection between the two is made by pointing out linguistic similarities between Bacon and Shakespeare's work, and by discovering cryptogrammatic references to Bacon's name in the text of the plays. The first stage of this argument, the attack on Shakespeare the man, has also been used to serve rival theories attributing authorship to the Earls of Derby and Oxford, a committee including either or both of these peers, and – in Calvin Hoffman's *The Man Who Was Shakespeare* (1955) – CHRISTOPHER MARLOWE.

Bage, Robert 1728–1801 Novelist. Son of a papermaker at Darley, near Derby, Bage was educated at a common school. Married at 23, he set up a paper-mill at Elford, near Tamworth, with his wife's money and continued in this business throughout his life. For a period of 14 years from 1765 he was also engaged in the manufacture of iron, an exercise which was not profitable. He produced six novels: *Mount Henneth* (1781), *Barham Downs* (1784), *The Fair Syrian* (1787), *James Wallace* (1788), *Man As He Is* (1792) and *Hermsprong: or, Man As He is Not* (1796). Of these works only the last has been edited this century. Like all Bage's novels, it is radical if simplistic in its political and social messages. Hermsprong claims to be an American Indian, and has fixed views on the importance of physical fitness, the corruption endemic among the rich, and the necessity of female education and equality. At the end he proves to be acceptable in polite society. Characterization is not a strong point, but Bage successfully combined polemic and humour, the latter very much in the vein of STERNE. This and his command of dialogue were praised by SIR WALTER SCOTT. In his private life he was, according to Scott, an impeccable exemplar of his beliefs.

Bagehot, Walter 1826–77 Political thinker, economist and literary critic. Born at Langport in Somerset, Bagehot went to school in Bristol, attended University College, London, and was called to the Bar in 1852 but chose instead to enter his father's bank. In 1855 he became joint editor of *The National Review* with R. H. HUTTON, a friend from University College, and in 1860–77 he edited *The Economist*. His most famous work, *The English Constitution* (1867), is a classic appraisal of the workings of government. *Physics or Politics* (1872) attempts to relate contemporary theories of natural selection and inheritance to the workings of the state; *Lombard Street* (1873) and *Economic Studies* (edited by Hutton, 1880) examine the money market and commerce. Bagehot's literary criticism, represented by *Estimates of Some Englishmen and Scotchmen* (1858) and *Literary Studies* (edited by Hutton, 1879), adopts the same stance of the worldly, moderate man which marks his approach to economic and political affairs.

Bagnold, Enid 1889–1981 Playwright and novelist. At the outbreak of World War I she turned from art studies to nursing. Her *Diary without Dates* (1917), based on her nursing experience, offended some of the hospital authorities by its frankness. Her first literary success was with a novel, *Serena Blandish* (1925); it was dramatized by S. N. BEHRMAN (1929). She herself dramatized a more famous novel, *National Velvet* (1935), about a girl who wins the Grand National; it also became a popular film. *Lottie Dundas* was both a novel (1941) and a play (1943). *The Chalk Garden* (1955), a social comedy, was the last of her plays to achieve theatrical success.

Bail, Murray 1941– Australian short-story writer and novelist. Born in Adelaide, he lived abroad in Bombay from 1968 to 1970 and in London from 1970 to 1974. Widely regarded as one of the most cosmopolitan of contemporary Australian writers, he had been publishing fiction in magazines for several years when his short-story collection *Contemporary Portraits* (republished as *The Drover's Wife and Other Stories* in 1986) appeared in 1975. Bail's *avant-garde* fiction frequently takes issue with the realist tradition in the Australian short story, as can be seen in one of his best-known stories, 'The Drover's Wife', which, while it is ostensibly a response to Russell Drysdale's painting of this name, may also be seen as an ironic rebuttal of the narrative manner and values of the classic HENRY LAWSON story with the same title. Much of his work offers a playful, Borgesian treatment of definitions, encyclopaedism and literary tradition. His novel *Homesickness* (1980) takes a group of 13 assorted Australians on a package tour of the world's museums. While this situation affords opportunities for satire, the novel is mainly concerned with the way experience is perceived, specifically the perspectives engendered by tourism, and gradually the motley travellers begin to react to the often absurdist stimuli with which they are confronted in an increasingly uniform way. His most recent novel, *Holden's Performance* (1987), is a comic epic about the passage of an innocent through Australian society. Non-fictional works are *Longhand* (1989), a writer's diary of his years in London, and a study of the artist Ian Fairweather (1981).

Bailey, Paul 1937– Novelist. He was a professional actor before he turned to writing austere and painstaking novels. The first, *At the Jerusalem* (1967), poignantly depicts old age, a subject he returned to in *Old Soldiers* (1980). *Trespasses* (1971), *A Distant Likeness* (1973) and *Peter Smart's Confessions* (1977) share a preoccupation with madness and neurotic despair. Other novels include *Gabriel's Lament* (1986), a grave study of bereavement which nevertheless manipulates a Dickensian multiplicity of eccentric characters with quixotic humour, and *Sugar Cane* (1993). *An English Madam* (1982) is an affectionate biography of the brothel-keeper Cynthia Payne, and *An Immaculate Mistake* (1990) a wistful memoir of his early life, the title wryly summing up his unplanned arrival to elderly parents.

Bailey, Philip James 1816–1902 Poet. 'Festus' Bailey was born in Nottingham, educated at Glasgow University and called to the Bar in 1840. In 1839 he published *Festus*, a blank-verse epic based on the Faust legend. Progressively enlarged editions appeared throughout his lifetime, and by the last (1889) *Festus* had swollen to 52 scenes and 40,000 lines, incorporating much of the verse earlier published in *The Angel World* (1850), *The Mystic* (1855) and *The Universal Hymn* (1867). Originally praised by the reviewers, *Festus* was effectively ridiculed by WILLIAM AYTOUN, who identified Bailey as father of the SPASMODIC SCHOOL OF POETRY.

Baillie, Joanna 1762–1851 Poet and playwright. She was born at Hamilton in Lanarkshire. The first volume of her *Plays on the Passions* (1798) included *De Montfort*, which was produced by Kemble in 1800 and in which Mrs Siddons enjoyed considerable success. A second volume of plays appeared in 1802 and a third in 1812. Her drama *The Family Legend* was produced in 1810 and her *Miscellaneous Plays* was published in 1836. Her most notable collections of verse appeared as *Fugitive Verses* (1790) and *Metrical Legends* (1821). She was a close friend of SIR WALTER SCOTT.

Bain, Alexander 1818–1903 Philosopher. Born in Aberdeen and educated at Marischal College, he was appointed Professor of Logic in the University of Aberdeen in 1860. A friend of JOHN STUART MILL and biographer of JAMES MILL (1882), he developed the ideas of UTILITARIANISM in his own writings, which include *The Senses and the Intellect* (1855), *The Emotions and the Will* (1859), *Mental and Moral Science* (1868) and *Logic* (1870).

Bainbridge, Beryl 1934– Novelist. She grew up in Liverpool in a conflict-ridden but united family whose oddity she has evoked memorably in non-fictional essays and a claustrophobic novel, *A Quiet Life* (1976). Works such as *The Dressmaker* (1973), *The Bottle Factory Outing* (1974), *Injury Time* (1977), *Mum and Mrs Armitage* (1985), *Filthy Lucre* (1986) and *An Awfully Big Adventure* (1989), are terse black comedies in which innocent, inadequate characters confront situations of incipient menace and grotesque violence. Several novels tackle historical subjects: Hitler's possible stay in Liverpool in *Young Adolf* (1978); a notorious Victorian murder case in *Watson's Apology* (1984); and Captain Scott's Antarctic expedition in *The Birthday Boys* (1991).

Baker, Father Augustine 1571–1641 Catholic mystic and author of more than 40 treatises, or 'Directions for the Prayer of Contemplation'. His work was published posthumously as the *Sancta Sophia* (1657), a kind of Catholic parallel to TRAHERNE's *Centuries of Meditations*.

James Baldwin

Baldwin, James (Arthur) 1924–87 Black American novelist, playwright and essayist. The son of a preacher, he was born in Harlem, New York, and left home at 17, eventually making his way to Paris. His first novel, *Go Tell It on the Mountain* (1953), recounts a young boy's coming to terms with the religious beliefs of his father, a storefront preacher incapable of controlling his desires. His father's lusts and inability to communicate with his children have kept the Lord away from the boy, for before kneeling to the Lord he must kneel to his father, something he cannot bring himself to do. After a long series of conflicts, he is finally able to reject his father and turn to the Lord at one stroke, and he feels something die in him as well as come alive. He has achieved faith through struggle.

The promise of this first book was borne out in further novels, plays, short stories and essays, which showed him as a powerful and articulate enemy of racial discrimination. After *Giovanni's Room* (1956), which is set in Paris, he returned to black America as a setting for his fiction. *Another Country* (1962) is set in New York and focuses mainly on Harlem society. The death – perhaps suicide – of the main character, Rufus Scott, is representative of the treatment individuals receive in an environment which is essentially hostile and which erects barriers to their desire for love. Other works of fiction by Baldwin include *Going to Meet the Man* (1965), *Tell Me How Long the Train's Been Gone* (1968), *If Beale Street Could Talk*

(1974) and *Just above My Head* (1979). His essays were published in *Notes of a Native Son* (1955), *Nobody Knows My Name: More Notes of a Native Son* (1961; as *No Name in the Streets* in Britain, 1972), *The Fire Next Time* (1963), *The Devil Finds Work* (1976), *The Evidence of Things Not Seen: An Essay* (1985) and *The Price of the Ticket: Collected Nonfiction, 1948–1985* (1986). He also wrote four plays: *Blues for Mr Charlie* (produced and published 1964), *The Amen Corner* (produced 1965, published 1968), *One Day, When I was Lost* (produced 1972, published 1973) and *A Deed from the King of Spain* (produced 1974). *Jimmy's Blues* (1986) is a volume of poetry.

Baldwin, Joseph G(lover) 1815–64 American jurist. Born in Virginia, he educated himself in both literature and law, and in 1836 decided to seek work in the comparatively uncivilized region of Mississippi. In 1853 he published *The Flush Times of Alabama and Mississippi*, a collection of sketches and anecdotes about frontier law, which combines serious and moralistic portraits of great men Baldwin admired with comic tales of infamous rascals. The latter pieces remain better-known, and include 'Ovid Bolus, Esq.', about a chronic liar, and 'Simon Suggs, Jr, Esq.: A Legal Biography', about a lawyer who cleverly cheats his way to success. Encouraged by the volume's favourable reception, he published *Party Leaders* (1855), a more sober work containing studies of THOMAS JEFFERSON, Alexander Hamilton and Andrew Jackson.

Bale, John 1495–1563 Playwright. The son of poor parents from Suffolk, he trained for the church but became a vigorous supporter of the English Reformation. His Protestant polemics earned him the patronage of Thomas Cromwell, for whose troupe of itinerant players Bale wrote several anti-Catholic plays between 1537 and Cromwell's fall in 1540. Five of these works survive. *The Three Laws* and the trilogy comprising *God's Promises, John the Baptist* and *The Temptation of Our Lord* are MORALITY PLAYS in an already well-established style. It is the fifth, *King John*, which earns Bale an important place in the history of English drama, for although such abstract characters as Dissimulation, Private Wealth and Sedition look back to the morality tradition, the portraits of the King, Stephen Langton and Cardinal Pandulphus look forward to the English history plays of MARLOWE and SHAKESPEARE. Unlike Shakespeare's, Bale's King John is an idealized Christian hero battling with the Pope and the whole 'heap of adders of Antichrist's generation'. Bale's historical researches brought him in contact with the antiquary LELAND, whom he mentions in *King John*.

Balfour, Arthur James, 1st Earl of Balfour 1848–1930 Statesman and philosopher. Born at Whittingehame in East Lothian, he was educated at Eton and Trinity College, Cambridge. He was leader of the Conservative Party (1902–11), Prime Minister (1902–5) and Foreign Secretary (1916–19). His works included *A Defence of Philosophic Doubt* (1879), expressing his belief that the ultimate convictions of mankind rest on religious faith and are not susceptible to the probing of logic and science. In 1893 he became President of the Society for Psychical Research. He developed his religious position in *The Foundation of Belief* (1895) and in two series of Gifford Lectures, *Theism and Humanism* (1915) and *Theism and Thought* (1923). His other works included *Decadence* (1908), *Criticism and Beauty* (1910) and *Essays Speculative and Political* (1920). His incomplete *Chapters of Autobiography* (edited by Mrs Dugdale) was published posthumously in 1930.

ballad Two main types are to be distinguished, the least unsatisfactory names for them, perhaps, being 'traditional' and 'street'. There is no proof that the first type is earlier than the second, though internal evidence points that way. Both have been transmitted mainly through printed BROADSIDES (the earliest known example dating from 1513), both have influenced major poets and been imitated by them, but as a popular creative form the traditional ballad seems unlikely to have been composed after the 16th century, while street ballads are still being composed today. The difference may be briefly summed up as follows: the former, deriving from a pre-literate rural community, tended to be tragic, romantic and heroic, telling its story in arbitrary narrative fragments, whereas the latter, developing with the growth of towns and the printing press, tended to be comic, realistic and unheroic, its narrative more leisurely and circumstantial. But frequent and contemporaneous reprinting by publishers unconcerned with authenticity ensures blurring and overlapping – as indeed occurs with the distinction between ballad and folk-song.

All ballads, of whatever type, must not only tell a story in verse but also lend themselves to being sung (if not actually accompanied by a tune). These two defining conditions imply a third: the narrative and style must be simple enough to be followed at a hearing. So most ballads – but by no means all – are written in simple ballad metre: that is to say, in QUATRAINS of alternating lines of iambic tetrameter and iambic trimeter (see METRE). Musical evidence, the fact that most such quatrains rhyme only the second and fourth lines (especially in earlier periods), and the prevalence of 'fourteeners' in the early Elizabethan period, suggest that the normal ballad form, to begin with, was that of long 14-syllable couplets, whose lines were later split into the 8- and 6-syllable lines of the familiar quatrain form. The split led to an increasing tendency to rhyme the first and third lines as well as the second and fourth. Though ballad metre is basically iambic, much syllabic irregularity is common – presumably owing to the demands of music, the early origins of the ballad and the popular audience it mainly catered for.

ballad metre See BALLAD.

Ballad of Reading Gaol, The A poem by OSCAR WILDE, published in 1898, about the hanging of a murderer, Charles Thomas Wooldridge, while Wilde was himself a convict. Its harsh eloquence is in contrast to the aestheticism of Wilde's earlier poems, but shows the same technical control. It concludes with a plea for Christ's forgiveness and a protest against prison conditions.

ballad opera A dramatic form pioneered by GAY, whose *BEGGAR'S OPERA* (1728) was the most popular play of the 18th century. A combination of FARCE, PANTOMIME, street literature, delightful lyrics and musical comedy, the ballad opera enjoyed an intense vogue, and was designed to counteract the modishness of imported Italian opera by offering an entertainment that was British, topical, anti-heroic and satirical of contemporary politics.

ballade An Old French verse form, consisting of three eight-line STANZAS, rhyming ababbcbC, and a four-line envoy, rhyming bcbC (the capital letter indicating that the line is used as a refrain). They are not common in English, and even the best – probably those by CHAUCER and SWINBURNE – fall far short of the power and mastery of the greatest French exemplar, François Villon.

Ballantyne, R(obert) M(ichael) 1825–94 Scottish writer of CHILDREN'S LITERATURE. Born and educated in Edinburgh, the son of a newspaper editor, he travelled to Canada at the age of 16 in the service of the Hudson's Bay Company, trading with local Indians in remote areas. Returning to Britain, he produced his first adventure story for boys, *The Young Fur-Traders* (1856), based on these memories. This best-seller was followed two years later by his most famous title, *THE CORAL ISLAND* (1858). Afterwards, he often returned to writing from first-hand knowledge, whether this involved three weeks on Bell Rock (*The Lighthouse*, 1865) or a short spell as a London fireman (*Fighting the Flames*, 1867).

With over 80 books to his credit, written in less than 40 years, Ballantyne was one of the most popular adventure-story writers of all time. Today his books seem over-concerned with details of local flora and fauna, as well as obtrusively pious. *The Gorilla Hunters* (1861), sequel to *The Coral Island*, is disturbing in its callous enthusiasm for every sort of wild-animal slaughter. But in his day Ballantyne provided entertainment popular with both child and adult, the fruits of his own hard work, adventurous life and strong conviction of his importance as a mentor to the young.

Ballard, J(ames) G(raham) 1930– Novelist and short-story writer. Born in Shanghai, he spent part of his childhood in a Japanese internment camp during World War II. Early novels such as *The Drowned World* (1962), *The Drought* (1965) and *The Crystal World* (1966), and the short stories in *The Four-Dimensional Nightmare* (1963) and *The Terminal Beach* (1964), are stylish and highly sophisticated exercises in *avant-garde* SCIENCE FICTION, preoccupied with the psychological adaptations which natural catastrophes demand of their central characters. *The Atrocity Exhibition* (1970), a collection of 'fragmented novels', and *Crash* (1973) pursued this vein of experimentalism to its surreal extreme. The relative conventionality of *The Unlimited Dream Company* (1979) paved the way for the semi-autobiographical realism of Ballard's two finest and most widely known novels: *Empire of the Sun* (1984), drawing on his boyhood experience of World War II, and a sequel, *The Kindness of Women* (1991), which follows the life of the protagonist, Jim, in post-war Britain.

Bancroft, George 1800–91 American historian. Born in Massachusetts, Bancroft graduated from Harvard at the age of 17, and the following year went to Germany, to study history in Berlin under Hegel and in Göttingen under Heeren and Eichhorn. Though trained for the ministry, he held a variety of government positions: Secretary of the Navy (1845–6), Minister to England (1846–9) and Minister to Germany (1867–74). A Jacksonian Democrat, he supported the Manifest Destiny policy in the 1840s.

His life work, the 10-volume *History of the United States* (1834–75), tells the story of the progressive tendency towards liberty exemplified by American history, culminating in the American Revolution. Bancroft's progressivist notions of history, imbibed in Germany, his extensive use of manuscript sources, and his interest in the human characters underlying historical events place him in a class with his major American contemporaries, WILLIAM HICKLING PRESCOTT, JOHN LATHROP MOTLEY, and FRANCIS PARKMAN JR, whose historiographical ideas and practices were similar. *The History*, highly nationalistic and characterized by a resounding rhetoric, was a popular work in its own day.

Banim, John 1798–1842 Irish playwright and novelist. He collaborated with his elder brother MICHAEL BANIM on *Tales by the O'Hara Family* (1825–7). His tragedy *Damon and Pythias* was produced at COVENT GARDEN in 1821, and his satirical essays, *Revelations of the Dead Alive*, appeared in 1824.

Banim, Michael 1796–1874 Irish novelist. He collaborated with his younger brother JOHN BANIM in *Tales by the O'Hara Family* (1825–7). *The Croppy* (1828) is a novel set in the Irish rebellion of 1798. His other fiction includes *Father Connell* (1842) and *The Town of the Cascades* (1864).

Banks, Iain (Menzies) 1954– Novelist. Born in Fife, he worked as a testing technician in Scotland and a solicitor's clerk in England before attracting equal measures of fame and notoriety with his first novel, *The Wasp Factory* (1984). A gruesome Gothic fantasy about a maladjusted adolescent who visits unspeakable horrors on his young relatives and the surrounding wildlife, it is distinguished by its tactile descriptive prose. Subsequent novels range from colourful and visceral horror thrillers like *Walking on Glass* (1985) to cybernetic science fantasy, in *Consider Phlebas* (1987). None has repeated the success of his début.

Bannatyne, George 1545–?1608 Anthologist. Bannatyne was born in Newtyle, Angus, and became a prosperous merchant in Edinburgh. While isolated by the plague in 1568 he compiled a manuscript anthology of Scottish poetry of the 15th and 16th centuries. The 'Bannatyne Manuscript' of some 800 pages is now in the Advocates' Library, Edinburgh. It contains works by major poets such as DUNBAR, HENRYSON and SIR DAVID LINDSAY, works by minor poets (like Alexander Scot) who would otherwise be unknown, and much anonymous verse. This collection influenced the revival of interest in Scottish poetry in the 18th century. In Edinburgh in 1823 the Bannatyne Club was founded, under the presidency of SIR WALTER SCOTT, to encourage the study of Scottish history and literature.

Bannerman, Helen (Brodie Cowan) 1862–1946 Writer and illustrator of CHILDREN'S LITERATURE. Born in Edinburgh and educated at the University of St Andrews, she lived in India from 1889 as the wife of an army doctor.

Her first book, *The Story of Little Black Sambo* (1890), published in a small format with her own brightly coloured illustrations, was an immediate success. Little Black Sambo himself, with his new red coat, blue trousers, purple shoes and green umbrella, cut a dashing figure in the then still rather staid world of children's books. The four tigers who so nearly devour him are both menacing and finally ridiculous as they reduce themselves to butter by chasing each other round a tree. The stories which followed include *Little Black Mingo* (1902), *Little Black Quibba* (1902) and *Little Black Quasha* (1908). Arguments over their relish for violent incident were overshadowed by the charge of racism in the 1960s. Little Black Sambo was particularly criticized for his name and his guileless enjoyment of bright new clothes.

Banville, John 1945– Irish novelist. Born in Wexford, and for some years literary editor of *The Irish Times*, he has published *Long Lankin* (1970), a collection of short stories, and novels notable for their quizzical, burnished prose and their fabulous inhabitation of historical worlds. *Birchwood* (1974), a self-consciously quirky variation on the Irish country-house narrative, has been followed by a loose tetralogy of novels essaying the fictional biography of a pre-eminent scientific figure: *Doctor Copernicus* (1976), *Kepler* (1981), *The Newton Letter* (1982) and *Mefisto* (1987). *The Book of Evidence* (1989), a psychological thriller about a middle-aged art thief's gratuitous murder of a young chambermaid, has been acclaimed as his most substantial work.

Baraka, (Imamu) Amiri [Jones, LeRoi] 1934– Black American playwright, poet, novelist and essayist. Born LeRoi Jones in Newark, New Jersey, he studied at Rutgers and Howard universities. He changed his name on converting to Islam in 1965. Activities have included founding the Totem Press (1958), which prints the work of contemporary poets; directing the Black Arts Repertory Theatre in Harlem; and teaching contemporary poetry and creative writing at Columbia, the New School for Social Research, and the State University of New York at Buffalo. He has been a prominent voice in the black movement since the mid-1950s and is one of America's most prolific black writers.

He established his reputation with plays – *A Good Girl is Hard to Find* (1958), *Dante* (1961; adapted as a novel, *The System of Dante's Hell*, 1965), DUTCHMAN (1964), *The Slave* (1964) and *Slave Ship: A Historical Pageant* (1967) – dealing with with black–white relations and using drama as a weapon against racism. *The Baptism* (1964) and *The Toilet* (1964) explore his preoccupation with personal identity. After 1974 his political ideology underwent a change: his separatist fervour gave way to a commitment to the overthrow, by blacks and whites alike, of an oppressive capitalist system. Plays like *S-1* (1976), *The Motion of History* (1977) and *What was the Relationship of the Lone Ranger to the Means of Production?* (1979) exemplify this stage of his career. His volumes of verse include *Preface to a Twenty Volume Suicide Note* (1961), *The Dead Lecturer* (1964), *A Poem for Black Hearts* (1967), *It's Nation Time* (1970), *Spirit Reach* (1972), *Afrikan Revolution* (1973), *Hard Facts* (1976) and *Reggae or Not!* (1982). *Selected Poems* (1979) reprints most of his best work. He has written on music in *Blues People: Negro Music in White America* (1963) and *Black Music* (1968). Other essays appear in *Raise Race Rays Raze: Essays Since 1965* (1971) and *Daggers and Javelins: Essays 1974–1979* (1984). *The Autobiography of LeRoi*

Jones (1984) explores many of his social and political concerns in relation to his life. The most ambitious of his later works is *Money: A Jazz Opera* (1982), in collaboration with George Gruntz.

Barbauld, Anna Laetitia 1743–1825 Editor, poet and anthologist. Born Anna Aikin at Kibworth, Leicestershire, she was educated by her father and learned, unusually for a girl in her times, French, Italian, Latin and Greek. She collaborated with her brother, JOHN AIKIN, on two collections of essays, mainly on literary topics, *Miscellaneous Pieces* (1773) and the six-volume *Evenings at Home* (1792–6); published a collection of poems (1773) and produced the didactic, highly successful *Hymns in Prose for Children* (1781). After her husband's death she undertook a 50-volume anthology, *The British Novelists* (1810), introduced by a lengthy and intelligently argued essay 'On the Origin and Progress of Novel-writing' attempting to define the genre. The works of the selected authors were prefixed by a biographical and critical notice, in several cases the first critical discussion of the writer in question. Possibly her most important contribution to literature was her six-volume edition of SAMUEL RICHARDSON's correspondence (1804), never superseded. Her own slightly less voluminous correspondence with, among others, HESTER CHAPONE, MARIA EDGEWORTH, PRIESTLEY, CRABB ROBINSON, SIR WALTER SCOTT and WORDSWORTH, throws interesting light on contemporary literary and moral concerns.

Barbellion, W. N. P. [Bruce Frederick Cummings] 1889–1919 Diarist. Born at Barnstaple, Devon, Cummings was a self-educated biologist who eventually became an official of the British Museum (Natural History), London. Disseminated sclerosis impaired his scientific work and he turned an increasingly self-critical eye on himself. *The Journal of a Disappointed Man*, covering the years 1903–17, was published a few months before his death in 1919 as extracts from the diaries of Wilhelm Nero Pilate Barbellion. It reveals a brave, intelligent personality whose ambitions and aspirations are bedevilled by lack of opportunity and poor health. It is vivid, humorous and objective: 'a self-portrait in the nude' was the author's phrase for it. *A Last Diary* (1920) gives additional information.

Barbour, John *c.* 1320–95 Scottish poet. Probably born in Aberdeen, he spent most of his life there and was appointed archdeacon of Aberdeen in or before 1357. In 1364, 1365 and 1368 he studied in Oxford and Paris; in 1372 he was appointed Clerk of Audit and Auditor of the Exchequer to Robert II. His surviving poem, *THE BRUCE*, gives a patriotic account of the life of Robert the Bruce (Robert I) and his liberation of Scotland from English domination. Two other works, *The Brut* and *The Stewartis Original*, are lost, a record

of them surviving only in ANDREW OF WYNTOUN's *Orygynale Cronykil*. The first related mythical history of Britain from its foundation by Brutus and the second traced the pedigree of the Stewarts from Banquo. *The Alexander Buik*, a Scottish version of the life of Alexander the Great, was once attributed to Barbour (see KING ALISAUNDER).

Barchester Towers A novel by ANTHONY TROLLOPE, the second of his BARSETSHIRE NOVELS, published in 1857.

A sequel to *THE WARDEN*, it opens with the death of the Bishop of Barchester and the fall of the Conservative ministry which would appoint his son Archdeacon Grantly to succeed him. The incoming Whigs appoint the timeserving Dr Proudie, who comes to Barchester with his Low Church wife and evangelical chaplain Obadiah Slope, an unctuous hypocrite. Mrs Proudie and Mr Slope set about reforming the easygoing diocese, and battle is joined between them and the traditionalists led by Dr Grantly. Mrs Proudie wants to appoint the hard-pressed Mr Quiverful to the vacant wardenship of Hiram's Hospital, but the ambitious Slope, discovering that the newly widowed Eleanor Bold has £1200 a year, manoeuvres to reappoint her father Mr Harding to his old post. When the absentee cleric Dr Vesey Stanhope returns to Barchester, however, Slope becomes infatuated with his *femme fatale* daughter, the crippled Signora Neroni. In the ensuing complications Slope and Mrs Proudie fall out, Quiverful is appointed to the wardenship, and Slope fails in his schemes and is dismissed by the Bishop. Pursued by Slope and Bertie Stanhope, a charming wastrel, Eleanor chooses instead Francis Arabin, a shy cleric brought from Oxford to Barchester to be Dr Grantly's High Church champion. They marry and Arabin becomes Dean of Barchester. A classic comic novel, dealing with the clash between old and new ways, *Barchester Towers* made Trollope's reputation with the Victorian reading public.

Barclay, Alexander ?1475–1552 Poet and translator. Barclay was a monk and priest at the college of Ottery St Mary, Devon, and later a Benedictine at Ely. He survived the Reformation and in 1546 was presented with a vicarage at Great Baddow in Kent, and with another vicarage in Somerset in the same year. He was a prolific translator: Pierre Gringore's allegorical DREAM-VISION *The Castle of Labour* (?1505), Sallust's *Jugurthine War* and Mancinus' *The Mirror of Good Manners* (?1523). His two most important works are his translation of Sebastian Brant's *Das Narrenschiff* as *The Ship of Fools* (1509) and his *Egloges*, which are partly a translation of the work of Aeneas Piccolomini (later Pope Pius II) on the miseries of courtiers and partly an imitation of the pastorals of Mantuan. *The Ship of Fools*, illustrated with woodcuts, is ESTATES SATIRE and contains some personal attacks on local Devon clergy and JOHN SKELTON. The *Egloges* are important as early English attempts at the PASTORAL form later to be used by SPENSER in *THE SHEPHEARDES CALENDER*.

Barclay, John 1582–1621 Miscellaneous writer in Latin. The son of a Scottish jurist, he was born in France at Pont-à-Mousson and was connected with the court of James I. His *Euphormionis Satyricon* (1603–7) is an episodic collection of satire, adventures and discourses modelled on Petronius. *Icon Animorum* (1614), translated by THOMAS MAY as *The Mirror of Minds* (1631), is a book of essays on national and temperamental types. *Argenis* (1621) is an allegorical romance with a contemporary setting. It was printed over 40 times in the original Latin, but none of the many English translations secured a lasting place; the last, by CLARA REEVE, was a revision of Kingsmill Long's translation of 1625 and was published as *The Phoenix* (1772).

Barclay, Robert 1648–90 Quaker apologist. He was born at Gordonstown in Elginshire and educated at the Scottish Catholic College in Paris. In 1667 he followed his father in joining the Quaker movement and, because of his wide learning, became its leading theologian. His first published work was his *Catechism and Confession of Faith* (1673). In 1676 he published a Latin apologia supporting the Quaker theses he had circulated and defended at Aberdeen; the English version was called *Apology for the True Christian Religion, as the Same is Set Forth and Preached by the People Called in Scorn 'Quakers'* (1678). It is the main exposition of Quaker principles and also contains a strong attack on Calvinism. Barclay was held in favour by James II, and assisted WILLIAM PENN in the founding of Pennsylvania; he was himself appointed governor of East New Jersey in 1683.

Barfoot, Joan 1946– Canadian novelist. Born and brought up in rural Ontario, she subsequently worked as a journalist in London, Ontario. *Abra* (1978; reissued in Britain as *Gaining Ground*, 1980), *Dancing in the Dark* (1982), *Duet for Three* (1985) and *Family News* (1990) are women-centred fictions which present female protagonists isolated by choice, insanity or old age from defining social contexts. In her explorations of women's search for an identity apart from society, Barfoot offers an interesting variant of a pattern which has loomed large in Canadian women's fiction since 1970. *Abra* has clear affinities with such works as MARGARET ATWOOD's *SURFACING* and MARIAN ENGEL's *Bear*.

Barham, Rev. R(ichard) H(arris) 1788–1845 Poet and novelist. Born in Canterbury, he inherited the 'moderate estate, somewhat encumbered' of Tappington Everard at the age of seven. After attending St Paul's School and Brasenose College, Oxford, he became a clergyman in Kent and later, in 1821, a minor canon of St Paul's. While recovering from a carriage accident he wrote and published an unsuccessful novel, *Baldwin: or A Miser's Heir* (1820). He contributed to *BLACKWOOD'S MAGAZINE* and edited *The London Chronicle* – work he described in his diary as 'rubbish' – but achieved fame only with *THE INGOLDSBY LEGENDS*, appearing in *BENTLEY'S MISCELLANY* and *The New Monthly Magazine* from 1837 onwards and in various collections from 1840. Barham was a friend of THACKERAY, DICKENS, SAMUEL ROGERS and SYDNEY SMITH. His son published his life and letters in 1870.

Baring, Maurice 1874–1945 Novelist and playwright. Born in London, he was educated at Eton and Trinity College, Cambridge. From 1898 to 1904 he served in the Foreign Office, mainly in Moscow, and then became foreign correspondent for *The Morning Post* and *The Times* (1904–12). While in Moscow he discovered the works of Chekhov and helped to introduce these and other works of Russian literature to the West. *Landmarks in Russian Literature* (1910) was followed by *An Outline of Russian Literature* (1914) and *The Oxford Book of Russian Verse* (1924).

Baring was closely associated with two better remembered contemporaries, HILAIRE BELLOC and G. K. CHESTERTON, whose social and religious preoccupations he shared. His own creative output included the novels *Passing By* (1921), *C* (1924) and *Cat's Cradle* (1925), and a novella, *The Lonely Lady of Dulwich* (1934), often cited as his best work. His plays – like the novels, reflecting the liberal humanism of his social milieu – include *The Black Prince* (1902) and *Diminutive Dramas* (1911). Two historical tales, *Robert Peckham* (1930) and *In My End is My Beginning* (1931), show the influence of Roman Catholicism, to which he became a convert. Baring's autobiography, *The Puppet Show of Memory*, was published in 1922.

Baring-Gould, Sabine 1834–1924 Novelist, amateur antiquary and writer of hymns. He was born in Exeter and educated at Clare College, Cambridge. Ordained in 1864, he was rector of Lewtrenchard in Devon for the last 40 years of his life. His first novel, *Through Fire and Flame* (1868), described his marriage to a mill girl in 1867, and this was followed by over 30 others, of which *Mehalan* (1880) is often considered most noteworthy. Among his non-fictional works were several volumes of *The Lives of the Saints* (1872–7), a biography of R. S. HAWKER, *The Vicar of Morwenstow* (1876), and numerous works of travel, folklore and local legend (see FOLK REVIVAL). His many hymns included 'Onward Christian Soldiers'.

Barker, George (Granville) 1913–91 Poet. Born in Loughton, Essex, he was educated at Regent Street Polytechnic. Although he held university posts in Japan and the USA, he lived mainly by his writing. His initial volumes were *Thirty Preliminary Poems* (1933), *Poems* (1935) and *Calamiterror* (1937). This early work is marked by a superficial, misunderstood surrealism, garbled rhetoric and a facile fluency with evocative, musical words. He was sometimes associated with the NEW APOCALYPSE movement and compared to DYLAN THOMAS, mistakes which dogged him throughout his career. *Lament and Triumph* (1940) and *Eros in Dogma* (1944) are better books, and *News of the World* (1950) showed a new limpidity of language. His first masterpiece, however, was the notorious *True Confession of George Barker* (1950), omitted from *Collected Poems 1930–1955* (1957). Later volumes frequently show his mastery of the ELEGY as well as autobiographical forms: *The View from a Blind I* (1962), *Dreams of a Summer Night* (1966), *The Golden Chains* (1968), *In Memory of David Archer* (1973), *Dialogues, Etc.* (1976), *Villa Stellar* (1978) and another masterpiece, *Anno Domini* (1983). *Collected Poems* (1987) brought most of his work back into print. He also published *Essays* (1970) and novels, including *The Dead Seagull* (1950). *Street Ballads* appeared posthumously in 1992. ELIZABETH SMART's novel, *By Grand Central Station I Sat Down and Wept* (1945), was inspired by her long liaison with Barker.

Barker, Harley Granville See GRANVILLE-BARKER, HARLEY.

Barker, Howard 1946– Playwright. Born in Dulwich, he was educated at Battersea Grammar School and read history at the University of Sussex. His first plays, produced at the ROYAL COURT THEATRE and the Open Space, looked at British society from the stance of the underworld as well as the underdog – twin gangsters in *Alpha Alpha* (1972), pimps in *Claw* (1975) and a criminal who invades the house of the judge who condemned him in *Stripwell* (1975). Barker is adept at choosing telling dramatic situations in which many different incidents can take place, but he reverses what might be regarded as the moral expectations. The prison governor in *The Hang of the Gaol* (1978) becomes an arsonist, while an entrepreneur who capitalizes on graveyard mementoes in *The Love of a Good Man* is the hero of a black comedy set in 1920, after the carnage of World War I. In *No End of Blame* (1981) he debates the issue of the different censorships, East and West. Work for other media includes *Scenes from an Execution* (radio, 1984; staged, 1988).

Barker, James Nelson 1784–1858 American playwright. Born in Philadelphia, Barker followed his father's example by becoming mayor of that city in 1819 after a distinguished military career. He later served as Comptroller of the United States Treasury. Only five of his 10 plays have survived. *Tears and Smiles* (1807), a comedy of manners, was first produced in Philadelphia. His operatic play, *The Indian Princess: or, La Belle Sauvage*, was produced in 1808; the first extant play to deal with American-Indian life, it was mounted in London in 1820 as *Pocahontas: or, The Indian Princess*. Barker's biggest success, *Marmion: or, The Battle of Flodden Field* (1812), was based on SIR WALTER SCOTT's poem. Although he originally advertised the play under the pen name of Thomas Morton, Barker acknowledged his authorship after its implicit criticism of the British stance towards the United States during the war of 1812 was enthusiastically received by the public. His second romantic comedy, adapted from a French novel about medieval Spain, was published as *How to Try a Lover* in 1817, and produced as *The Court of Love* in 1836. *Superstition: or, The Fanatic Father* (1824), a tragedy in verse, is about a Puritan refugee who leads attacks against the Indians, and deals with religious intolerance and witch-hunting.

Barlaam and Josaphat A SAINT'S LIFE written in Middle English in the 14th century. When it is prophesied that Josaphat, son of a heathen king, will become a Christian his father keeps him in seclusion. He eventually releases him, however, and Josaphat is converted by a holy man, Barlaam. Josaphat converts his dying father, gives up his kingdom and ends his life as a hermit.

The origin of the story is Greek but this English version is translated from the *Legenda Aurea*, later translated again by CAXTON as *The Golden Legend*. The text appears in the Vernon *Golden Legend* of *c.* 1385, which translates selected stories, and in one manuscript of each of THE SOUTH ENGLISH LEGENDARY and *The Northern Verse Homily*.

Barlow, Joel 1754–1812 American poet. He is best remembered as one of the CONNECTICUT WITS, though he eventually became politically estranged from the group. Born in Redding, Connecticut, he attended Dartmouth College and in 1774 transferred to Yale, where he met others of the Wits, with whose orthodox Calvinism and aristocratic politics he sympathized. After the Revolutionary War, in which he served as chaplain for the Third Massachusetts Brigade, he founded *The American Mercury* with Elisha Backock, studied law, and was admitted to the Bar in 1786. Throughout this period he maintained contact with the Wits and contributed to their most notable production, *The Anarchiad*, a satire in MOCK-HEROIC verse which attacked democratic liberalism in favour of federalist conservatism and was published between 1786 and 1787 in *The New Haven Gazette* and *The Connecticut Magazine*. In 1787 Barlow published *The Vision of Columbus*, an epic poem in which he envisages America's glorious future.

In 1788 he went to France, where he lived periodically for 17 years, an experience which changed his political perspective. Contact with prominent European liberals – HORNE TOOKE, MARY WOLLSTONECRAFT, WILLIAM GODWIN – and a re-evaluation of the writings of THOMAS JEFFERSON and of his friend THOMAS PAINE transformed him into a champion of democracy, a change evident in three pamphlets in the 1790s: *Advice to the Privileged Orders*; *The Conspiracy of Kings*; and *A Letter to the National Convention of France*, for which he was awarded French citizenship. In 1796 he published his renowned *Hasty Pudding*, a mock EPIC in three CANTOS which celebrates a native American dish as well as 'simplicity of diet'. He returned to the USA in 1805 and in 1807 published *THE COLUMBIAD*, a revision of *The Vision of Columbus*. Accepting an appointment as US minister to France in 1811, he went back to Europe and died in Poland on his way to negotiate a treaty with Napoleon.

Barnaby Rudge A novel by CHARLES DICKENS, first published serially in *MASTER HUMPHREY'S CLOCK*, February–November 1841.

Set at the time of the 'No Popery' riots of 1780 provoked by Lord George Gordon, the narrative of *Barnaby Rudge* derives from the unsolved murder of Reuben Haredale, a crime committed 20 years before the start of the novel. Reuben's brother Geoffrey is a fundamentally upright Roman Catholic gentleman hostile towards the hypocritical, unprincipled Mr (later Sir John) Chester whose honourable son, Edward, loves Geoffrey's niece, Emma. Although markedly at odds, the two older men conspire to frustrate this match. Approximately halfway through the novel the Gordon riots erupt and Geoffrey Haredale's house, The Warren, is razed to the ground by an anti-Catholic mob. Emma and her confidante, the beguiling Dolly Varden, daughter of the hale and hearty locksmith Gabriel Varden, are kidnapped. Ultimately both are rescued by Edward Chester and Joe Willet, Dolly's one-armed soldier–suitor. When the riots are quelled it is revealed that Mr Rudge, Reuben Haredale's former steward and a shadowy figure throughout the novel, had murdered his master. He is hanged and his son Barnaby, a poor half-crazed youth who has been unwittingly drawn into the anti-Papist camp, only narrowly escapes the gallows. Sir John Chester dies in a duel with Haredale.

A rich cast of characters includes the snivelling Miss Miggs (servant to the Vardens), Simon Tappertit ('captain of the "Prentice Knights"'), John Willet (Joe's father and a stupid, obstinate old publican), Mrs Varden (the locksmith's tiresome wife), Gashford (the treacherous secretary to Lord George Gordon), Dennis

(the despicable and cowardly hangman), Hugh (the intelligent but undisciplined, irresponsible apprentice) and John Grueby (loyal servant to Lord George).

Barnes, Barnabe ?1569–1609 Poet and playwright. The son of Richard Barnes, Bishop of Durham, he had an eventful life, travelling with Essex to Normandy in 1591 and being arraigned before the Star Chamber for poisoning in 1598. His poetic works are a SONNET sequence *Parthenophil and Parthenope* (?1594), which exists in a unique copy, and *A Divine Century of Spiritual Sonnets* (1595). He wrote one prose work, *Four Books of Offices* (1606). One play, *The Battle of Hexham*, is lost but *The Devil's Charter* survives. An anti-Catholic portrayal of the magician and poisoner Pope Alexander VI, it was performed only once, before King James at Whitehall in 1607.

Barnes, Djuna 1892–1982 American novelist, playwright and poet. Born in Cornwall-on-Hudson, New York, Barnes began her career in New York City as a journalist and graphic artist, but spent much of her later life among the post-war Paris expatriates. In her early years in New York she was associated with the experimental Provincetown Players, who produced three of her one-act plays in 1919 and 1920. Her first publication was a collection of poems, *The Book of Repulsive Women* (1915). Her stories and short plays were collected in *A Book* (1923); the stories were revised and reissued subsequently as *A Night among the Horses* (1929) and later still as *Spillway* (1972). In 1929 she published her first novel, *Ryder*, a satiric chronicle of family history; and *Ladies' Almanack*, a celebration of lesbian life and love in the form of a quasi-medieval calendar or miscellany. Her best-known work is the novel *Nightwood* (1936), which concerns the relationships of a group of expatriates in Paris and Berlin. *The Antiphon* (1958) is a REVENGE TRAGEDY in blank verse, which again takes up issues of family history.

Barnes, Julian 1946– Novelist. He began his career as one of the group of urbane, precociously witty young writers on IAN HAMILTON's *NEW REVIEW*, for which he wrote the infamous 'Edward Pygge' gossip column. His first two novels, *Metroland* (1981) and *Before She Met Me* (1982), combine flamboyant wit and scatological comedy with a psychological sensitivity that recalls Flaubert, Barnes's acknowledged master. Flaubert is obliquely the subject of his third novel, *Flaubert's Parrot* (1984), which mixes biographical investigation, historical speculation and whimsical fantasy in a highly original manner. *Staring at the Sun* (1986) is comparably heterogeneous, ranging through history and different literary modes, as does the more elegantly accomplished *A History of the World in 10 ½ Chapters* (1989). *Talking It Over* (1991) returns to a realistic idiom and *The*

Porcupine (1992) is a novella about a politicial trial in a former Soviet satellite country.

Barnes, Juliana See THE BOOK OF ST ALBANS.

Barnes, Peter 1931– Playwright. He was educated at Stroud Grammar School. His plays combine trenchant satire with a delight in shock effects. His first play, *Sclerosis* (1965), an attack on British colonialism, was seen in Edinburgh and London, but Barnes achieved much greater success with his second play, *The Ruling Class* (1968), which contained many distinguishing features of his style: fierce parody of the English upper classes, rapid changes of mood and atmosphere from the farcical to the macabre, an unusual delight in rhetoric and several *coups de théâtre*. In subsequent plays, he has chosen major moral and historical themes as subjects for black comedy: the Spanish Succession in *The Bewitched* (1974), the Holocaust in *Laughter!* (1978) and the Black Death in *Red Noses* (1985). *Barnes' People* (1981, 1983, 1986) is a continuing series of radio monologues which show his affinity for the medium. Despising NATURALISM, he consciously looks back to the Jacobeans and to the German dramatist Frank Wedekind. He has adapted plays by BEN JONSON (whom he admires more than SHAKESPEARE) and Wedekind's *Lulu* plays (1971).

Barnes, William 1801–86 Dialect poet and philologist. Born into a family of farmers near Sturminster Newton in the Blackmoor Vale, Dorset, Barnes became a schoolteacher, was ordained in 1838 and graduated as a 'ten-year man' from St John's College, Cambridge, in 1850. From 1862 until his death he served as rector of Winterbourne Came, near Dorchester. His writings on philology – most notably *Tiw: or A View of the Roots and Stems of English as a Teutonic Tongue* (1861) – reject the importation of foreign words and advocate a return to the purity of Anglo-Saxon English. To Barnes, the speech of his native county was the truest survival of Anglo-Saxon, and so he turned to it in his three collections of *Poems in the Dorset Dialect* (1844, 1859, 1862). His command of folk idiom and lyric form gave his poetry more than a philological value, and helped attract a distinguished, if small, circle of admirers. His neighbour THOMAS HARDY contributed an obituary to THE ATHENAEUM, a poem about his funeral ('The Last Signal') and a selection of his poetry (1908).

Barnfield, Richard 1574–1627 Poet. Barnfield graduated from Brasenose College, Oxford, in 1592. He was the author of *The Affectionate Shepherd* (1594), a series of homoerotic ECLOGUES telling of the love of Daphnis for Ganymede; *Cynthia*, published together with 20 sonnets in 1595; and a satire, *The Encomion of Lady Pecunia* (1598), in mock-praise of money. Two of Barnfield's poems appeared in THE

PASSIONATE PILGRIM (1599). He was a friend of THOMAS WATSON and later of MICHAEL DRAYTON, and is mentioned as a pastoral poet by FRANCIS MERES in *Palladis Tamia*.

Barrack-Room Ballads and Other Verses A collection of poems by RUDYARD KIPLING, first published in 1892. It contains some of Kipling's most popular verse, as do later collections which also deal with the life of the British soldier overseas: *The Seven Seas* (1896), *The Five Nations* (1903) and *The Years Between* (1919). Influenced by ROBERT BROWNING, Kipling uses the DRAMATIC MONOLOGUE; Irish and Scottish accents are heard as well as comic Cockney dialect. The popular traditions of the BALLAD and street-song help give the speakers representative rather than individualized voices. The rhythms of the hymn tune or, in 'Mandalay', the music-hall song can be felt. Looking beneath the patriotic surface of poems like 'The Widow at Windsor', recent criticism has begun to acknowledge the satirical force and originality of Kipling's depiction of the harsh life of the ill-paid common soldier. *The Complete Barrack-Room Ballads of Rudyard Kipling*, collected by Charles Carrington, was published in 1973.

Barren Ground A novel by ELLEN GLASGOW, published in 1925.

It tells the story of Dorinda Oakley, a lower-middle-class country woman who goes to work in Nathan Pedlar's store, hoping the money she earns will restore her father's farm – the barren ground. She falls in love with Jason Greylock, but he is committed to another woman. Dorinda travels from her native rural Virginia to New York, where, after a street accident, she supports herself by caring for her doctor's children. Another doctor proposes to her, but she refuses him. In her spare time she studies new techniques in agriculture. When her father dies, she returns to Virginia and singlehandedly establishes a prosperous dairy farm. After her mother's death, she marries Nathan Pedlar, the man for whom she once worked and a widower with children. After his death, Dorinda, out of kindness, shelters the degenerate Jason Greylock. But she no longer loves him, and in fact plans never to marry again, being thankful 'to have finished with all that'. The title takes on further significance when one considers that Dorinda, although she nurtures other people's children and restores fertility to her family's farm, has no offspring of her own.

Barrett, Elizabeth See BROWNING, ELIZABETH BARRETT.

Barrie, Sir J(ames) M(atthew) 1860–1937 Scottish playwright and novelist. The ninth of the 10 children of a Scottish handloom weaver, he described the early encouragement he received from his mother in his admiring biography of her, *Margaret Ogilvy* (1896). He called his native Kirriemuir 'Thrums' in a series of homely stories and novels which identified him as a member of the KAILYARD SCHOOL: *Auld Licht Idylls* (1888), *A Window in Thrums* (1889) and *The Little Minister* (1891). Subsequent work included *Sentimental Tommy* (1896) and *Tommy and Grizel* (1900). Barrie, meanwhile, had married the actress Mary Ansell in 1894; his painful divorce in 1907, like his close relationship with his mother, is sometimes cited in explanation of his tendency to shrink from the realities of adult life in his writing. Theatrical recognition came with a dramatization of *The Little Minister* in 1897, and a profitable association with the American impresario Charles Frohman determined him to devote his talent to the stage. Two of his best plays, QUALITY STREET and THE ADMIRABLE CRICHTON, were produced in London in 1902, followed two years later by the overwhelming triumph of PETER PAN. A story, *Peter Pan in Kensington*, appeared in 1906. It is unfortunate that Barrie has become so identified with Peter Pan. He was always too ready to resort to cloying fantasy, as he did again in *Dear Brutus* (1917) and *Mary Rose* (1920), but however sentimental his solutions may have been, the problems he investigated were real enough. There is a shrewd feeling for the theatre in WHAT EVERY WOMAN KNOWS (1908), the single completed act of *Shall We Join the Ladies?* (1921) and the excellent one-act comedy *The Twelve-Pound Look* (1910). Barrie was knighted in 1913.

Barrow, Isaac 1630–77 Divine. The son of a linen merchant, he entered Trinity College, Cambridge, in 1647, during the Civil War; despite his Royalist sympathies he became a fellow of the college in 1649, and was ordained in 1659. A notable scholar, he became professor of Greek at Cambridge in 1660 and professor of geometry at Gresham College, London, in the same year, and was appointed the first Lucasian Professor of Mathematics at Cambridge in 1663. He resigned the last post in 1669 to his pupil, SIR ISAAC NEWTON, preferring to concentrate on theological studies. Charles II made him a royal chaplain, a DD by royal mandate (1670) and Master of Trinity (1673). His sermons were famous for their reasonable views in an age of pious recrimination. As well as two works on geometry, *Exposition of the Creed, Decalogue and Sacraments* (1669) was published during his lifetime; theological works edited after his death include *A Treatise on the Pope's Supremacy* (1680). Barrow's prose style was praised by COLERIDGE in his *Anima Poetae*.

Barry, Philip 1896–1949 American playwright. Born in Rochester, New York, he attended both Harvard and Yale. *You and I* (1923) was his first professional production. A number of his other plays – such as *Holiday* (1929), *Tomorrow and Tomorrow* (1931), and *The Animal Kingdom* (1932) – are comedies that puncture the snobbish pretensions of wealthy society. His other works include *Here Come the Clowns* (1938), *The Philadelphia Story* (1939), *Liberty Jones* (1941) and *The Foolish Notion* (1945). *Second Threshold*, another comedy, unfinished at his death, was completed in 1951 by ROBERT SHERWOOD.

Barry Lyndon A novel by W. M. THACKERAY, serialized as *The Luck of Barry Lyndon* in FRASER'S MAGAZINE in 1844, subsequently revised and reprinted as *The Memoirs of Barry Lyndon* (2 vols., 1852).

Set in the 18th century, the novel is the autobiography of an Irish adventurer whose boastful accounts of his exploits serve only to reveal the extent of his villainy. Redmond Barry of Brady's Town fights a duel and escapes to Dublin, where he changes his name to Barry Redmond, lives a fast life and falls into debt. He enlists as a soldier and fights on both sides in the Seven Years War, eventually meeting up with his lost uncle, Cornelius Barry, who as the Chevalier de Balibari joins him in cardsharping. After various adventures abroad, he lays siege to, and by subterfuge succeeds in marrying, a wealthy widow, the Countess of Lyndon. He changes his name again to Barry Lyndon and embarks on a career of extravagance, illtreating his wife, bullying his stepson, and wasting their fortune. With the death of his son Bryan in a riding accident, Barry's luck starts to run out. The family regains control of the estate, and Barry is forced to live abroad on a pension. With the death of Lady Lyndon he becomes penniless, and ends his life in the Fleet prison, tended by his faithful old mother.

The novel is a notable contribution to rogue literature, after the manner of JONATHAN WILD by Thackeray's admired master, FIELDING, and is interesting as a sustained exercise in the use of the unreliable narrator.

Barsetshire Novels, The A sequence of novels by ANTHONY TROLLOPE, set in the fictional West Country county of Barsetshire, or Barset, and particularly the cathedral city of Barchester, whose clergy are the main characters. It consists of THE WARDEN (1855), BARCHESTER TOWERS (1857), DOCTOR THORNE (1858), FRAMLEY PARSONAGE (1860–1), THE SMALL HOUSE AT ALLINGTON (1862–4) and THE LAST CHRONICLE OF BARSET (1866–7).

Barstow, Stan(ley) 1928– Novelist. Born into a Yorkshire mining family and educated in Ossett, he has written many novels about Yorkshire life, but remains best known for his first, *A Kind of Loving* (1960), a later example of the provincial working-class realist fiction developed by JOHN BRAINE and ALAN SILLITOE in the late 1950s. Barstow's novel follows the fortunes of office-worker Vic Brown, who is forced to marry his pregnant girlfriend, and also the changes brought to a conservative Northern town by television, pop music, immigration and new money.

Barth, John (Simmons) 1930– American novelist and short-story writer. He was born in Cambridge, Maryland, and educated at the Johns Hopkins University, where he now teaches. After publishing short stories in various periodicals, he attracted considerable critical attention with a novel, *The Floating Opera* (1956). This book, about a nihilist who, contemplating suicide, decides not to kill himself after all, is informed by the sense of the absurd which has coloured all his work. Other fiction, fluent in pastiche and helping to establish POST-MODERNISM by its narrative contingency, includes *The End of the Road* (1958), *The Sot-Weed Factor* (1960), *Giles Goat-Boy: or, The Revised New Syllabus* (1966), *Lost in the Fun-house* (1968), *Chimera* (1972; National Book Award), *Letters* (1979), *Sabbatical* (1982), *The Tidewater Tales* (1987) and *The Last Voyage of Somebody the Sailor* (1991). *The Friday Book*, a collection of non-fiction pieces, was published in 1984.

Barthelme, Donald 1931–89 American short-story writer and novelist. He was born in Philadelphia and brought up in Texas. His first book, *Come Back, Dr Caligari*, a collection of stories, appeared in 1964. *Snow White* (1967), a novel set in Greenwich Village, is a contemporary reworking of the popular fairy-tale. The fragmented narrative is made up of word games and random allusions to both literature and popular culture, taking the disintegration of language as a central metaphor for the breakdown of personal relationships. His later collections of stories – *Unspeakable Practices, Unnatural Acts* (1968), *City Life* (1970), *Guilty Pleasures* (1974) and *Amateurs* (1976) – continue his satiric commentary on contemporary American life and language. His second novel, *The Dead Father* (1975), is a humorous story about paternity and the fragmentation of the self. His other publications include *Great Days* (1979), *Sixty Stories* (1981), *Over Night to Many Distant Cities* (1983), *Paradise* (1986) and the posthumously published *The King* (1991), a short comic novel about the reappearance of King Arthur during World War II.

Barthes, Roland See POST-STRUCTURALISM, SEMIOTICS and STRUCTURALISM.

Bartholomew Fair A comedy by BEN JONSON, performed in 1614 but not published until 1631. The fair of the title was held annually at Smithfield on St Bartholomew's Day, 24 August. Jonson takes it as the setting for one of his most adventurous and original plays. The play contains a number of stories, but spreads them so loosely that it seems scarcely dependent upon plot at all. Jonson gives us a gallery of vivid characters. Adam Overdo, a justice, comes to the fair to spy out its iniquities and is engulfed by them. The country squire, Bartholomew Cokes, brings his lively betrothed, Grace Wellborn, but, simpleton that he is, is easily outwitted by her rival suitors, Winwife and Quarlus, and robbed of everything including his future wife. His servant Waspe has a biting tongue, but in the topsy-turvy world of the fair the biter is bitten, and Waspe ends up in the stocks, as does the hypocritical Puritan Zeal-of-the-Land Busy, his mind more fixed on food than on fastidious faith. Like all the other characters, but more greedily, Busy is drawn to the stall of the foul-mouthed pig-woman, Ursula, whose roast pork and small beer attract the crowds. Almost as if beguiled by the earthy liveliness of the fair, Jonson in this play is more intent on observing than correcting the behaviour of his contemporaries.

Bartleby the Scrivener See PIAZZA TALES, THE.

Barton, Bernard 1784–1849 Poet. Born in Carlisle and educated at a Quaker school in Ipswich, Barton worked for most of his life as a bank clerk in Woodbridge, Suffolk. Although collections such as *Metrical Effusions* (1812), *Poems* (1820) and *Devotional Verses* (1826) secured him a steady following as a writer of homely and unaffected religious verse, he is now hardly read and is chiefly remembered for his friendship and correspondence with SOUTHEY and CHARLES LAMB. Lamb was intrigued by his staunch Quakerism and his advice, 'Keep to your bank, and the bank will keep you,' was undoubtedly sound. EDWARD FITZGERALD wrote Barton's biography (1849) and, at the elder poet's earnest wish, made an unhappy marriage with Barton's daughter.

Bartram, John (1699–1777) and **Bartram, William** (1729–1823) American naturalists and travellers. A Philadelphia Quaker, John Bartram went on various expeditions in his official capacity as botanist for the American colonies, keeping records in his journals and publishing *Observations on the Inhabitants, Climate, Soil... Made by John Bartram in His Travels from Pensilvania to Lake Ontario* (1751). On his later trips he was accompanied by his son William, who made ornithological and anthropological as well as botanical contributions, and painted some of the flora and fauna he observed. William is most remembered, though, for his descriptions of the American landscape and imaginative, romantic reflections on the wilderness and natural man in his *Travels through North and South Carolina, Georgia, East and West Florida, the Cherokee Country, the Extensive Territories of the Muscogulges, or Creek Confederacy, and the Country of the Chactaws* (1791).

Bates, H(erbert) E(rnest) 1905–74 Novelist and short-story writer. He was born in Rushden,

Northamptonshire, and used the rural Midlands as a setting for much of his work. Outstanding among his 19 collections of stories are *The Woman Who Had Imagination and Other Stories* (1934), *My Uncle Silas: Stories* (1939), *Colonel Julian and Other Stories* (1951), *The Daffodil Sky* (1955) and *The Enchantress and Other Stories* (1961). His wartime experiences in the RAF prompted two more collections, *The Greatest People in the World* (1942) and *How Sleep the Brave* (1943), and his best-known novel, *Fair Stood the Wind for France* (1944), all originally published under the pseudonym of 'Flying Officer X'. *The Jacaranda Tree* (1949) is the most successful of three novels about the Far East. *The Darling Buds of May* (1958), *A Breath of French Air* (1959), *Hark, Hark, the Lark* (originally called *When the Green Woods Laugh*; 1960), *Oh! To Be in England* (1963) and *A Little of What You Fancy* (1970) are a popular series of novels about the Larkin family which celebrate the same hedonistic values as the earlier Uncle Silas stories.

Bateson, F(rederick) (Noel) W(ilse) 1901–78 Critic. Born in Styal, Cheshire, and educated at Charterhouse and at Trinity College, Oxford, Bateson undertook during the 1930s the huge task of editing *The Cambridge Bibliography of English Literature* (1940). He spent the war as an agricultural administrator, also writing articles on agricultural policy. In 1946 he took up a fellowship at Corpus Christi College, Oxford, which he held until his death in 1978. In 1951 he founded the periodical *ESSAYS IN CRITICISM*, which assumed the leading position in academic criticism soon vacated by the demise of *SCRUTINY* (in which Bateson had debated the principles of literary criticism with F. R. LEAVIS). As the title of his book *The Scholar-Critic* (1972) suggests, Bateson aimed to inform literary-critical judgements with higher standards of historical and linguistic scholarship. His other major works, *English Poetry and the English Language* (1934), *English Poetry: A Critical Introduction* (1950) and *Essays in Critical Dissent* (1972), all stress the importance of the context, historical and linguistic, in which literary works were written.

bathos An unwitting drop from elevation into triteness or triviality, or pathos so overdone that it tumbles into the ludicrous. Many enjoyable excruciating examples are to be found in *The Stuffed Owl* (1930), an anthology of bad verse, edited by D. B. Wyndham Lewis and C. Lee.

Battle Hymn of the Republic, The An American patriotic song, written by JULIA WARD HOWE in 1861, after visiting a Union army camp near Washington. The melody was provided by *John Brown's Body*, a song popular with the soldiers. The hymn was given its title by James T. Fields, who published it in *THE ATLANTIC MONTHLY* in 1862.

Battle of Brunanburh, The An Old English poem of 73 lines giving an account of a battle between an army of Norsemen and Scots and another of West Saxons and Mercians, which took place in 937. The location of Brunanburh is unknown, but it was apparently near the sea. The poem employs conventional motifs and rhetoric without singling out specific individuals or feats; nevertheless it is a vivid account, perhaps by an eyewitness. TENNYSON wrote a version of *The Battle of Brunanburh* in modern verse.

Battle of Life, The A Christmas story by CHARLES DICKENS, published in 1846 and collected in *CHRISTMAS BOOKS* (1852).

The story follows the fortunes of Dr Anthony Jeddler, who regards the world as 'a gigantic practical joke', and his two daughters, Grace and Marion. Into the girls' lives come Alfred Heathfield, an honest young medical student, and Michael Warden, a wastrel who later reforms. The narrative depicts the two interrelated love-affairs, the absences and returns of the suitors, the hazards of developing love, the nobility of sacrifice and, in Dr Jeddler's case, a modification of his reading of life. Lesser figures – the lawyer Snitchey, the sour servant Benjamin Britain (known as 'Little Britain') and the worthy servant Clemency Newcombe – round off a brisk, expressive tale.

Battle of Maldon, The A fragment of a poem in Old English, probably composed at the end of the 10th century; the manuscript was lost in a fire in 1731, but a transcript had been made. The beginning and end of the poem are lost; the surviving section occupies 325 lines. The battle, which took place in 991, is also described in the *ANGLO-SAXON CHRONICLE*.

The poem tells how the Vikings landed near Maldon in Essex and demanded tribute; this was contemptuously rejected by the Saxon leader Byrhtnoth. The ensuing battle was delayed by the tide, but the over-confident Byrhtnoth allowed the Danes to cross the causeway before joining battle. He was killed and the Saxons fled, led by Godric. Aelfwin drew them together again to rejoin the fight but the Saxon leaders continued to fall. The fragment breaks off at this point.

Despite its late date, the work is heroic and archaic in character. Its presentation of values and the type of the warrior recalls *BEOWULF* and the Germanic epics, though here the traditional values are seen to be in decline. In contrast to *THE BATTLE OF BRUNANBURH*, the poem relates the actions of individuals and presents a short series of speeches of explanation, encouragement and boasting.

Battle of the Books, The A prose SATIRE by JONATHAN SWIFT, written in 1697 and published in 1704. It remains the classic, humorous treatment of the debate between Ancients and Moderns, then treated as a serious cultural issue. Swift's patron, SIR WILLIAM TEMPLE, had published in 1690 his *Essay upon the Ancient and Modern Learning* in which the majority of contemporary writers and philosophers were unfavourably and condescendingly compared with their ancient classical counterparts. Temple was utterly opposed to the New Learning and all it represented, the attitude initiated by FRANCIS BACON's challenging of the Aristotelian system and subsequently developed by Descartes, and the work of the Royal Society. In extolling the virtues of the ancient authors, he unfortunately singled out the epistles of Phalaris, which were later proved to be spurious; RICHARD BENTLEY and William Wotton, leading scholars of the 'modern' camp, launched an attack upon him, and Swift replied in kind on his patron's behalf.

The satire takes the form of a MOCK-HEROIC drama set in the Royal Library, where the books championing the ancient and modern causes are preparing to fight over which party should rightfully occupy the higher peak of Parnassus. A dispute meanwhile arises between a resident spider and a bee entangled in his web, and the matter is summarized by the intervention of Aesop who identifies the spider with the Moderns (who spin out empty pedantry) while the bee, going directly to Nature, like the Ancients, succeeds in producing honey and wax, which are 'sweetness and light'. The verdict goads the Moderns into attack, and battle commences. Under the protection of Pallas, Homer leads the Ancients against the Moderns (patronized by the Goddess 'Criticism') under the leadership of MILTON. Individual duels are nicely matched, as when Virgil takes on his translator DRYDEN (whose helmet is nine times too large for him) and Aristotle shoots Descartes while aiming at Bacon. The book ends in mid-battle, supposedly because of a defective manuscript.

Though similarly sceptical about ideas of progress, Swift's spirited defence of Temple's position was largely dictated by personal loyalty, and the *Battle* is closely modelled on the latter's *Essay*. The Preface opens with Swift's memorable contention that 'Satire is a sort of glass, wherein beholders do generally discover everybody's face but their own.'

Battle-Pieces and Aspects of the War A book of
poems by HERMAN MELVILLE, published in 1866. The 72 poems commemorate the tragedy of the American Civil War and its impact on the nation. The sense of Northern victory and celebration is muted; many poems dwell upon the tragic loss of young men cut down in battle. Among the more notable pieces are 'The Portent', on the hanging of John Brown; 'Misgivings', on slavery; and 'Shiloh: A Requiem'. The volume also contains a prose appendix appealing to Northern readers for a humane rather than vengeful attitude toward the South during Reconstruction.

Baughan, Blanche 1870–1958 New Zealand poet.
Born in Putney, London, she was educated at Brighton High School and Royal Holloway College, University of London. Her finest poetry belongs to the decade after she emigrated to New Zealand in 1900 and appeared in *Reuben and Other Poems* (1903) and *Shingle-Short and Other Verses* (1908). The latter contains DRAMATIC MONOLOGUES written in a colloquial style and penetrating studies of society's pariahs and misfits. Its success in rendering aspects of the New Zealand experience represents a remarkable achievement for a comparatively recent immigrant. After an illness in 1910 she felt that her gift for poetry had deserted her. In subsequent years she mainly devoted herself to social work and became an important figure in the movement for prison reform. She also wrote many works on New Zealand rural life and topography, of which *Brown Bread from a Colonial Oven* (1912) is the best known.

Baum, L(yman) Frank 1856–1919 American
writer of CHILDREN'S LITERATURE. Born in New York, the son of a wealthy businessman, Baum worked as a journalist and playwright before setting off across America doing a variety of jobs including selling crockery and general shop-keeping. His first children's book, *Mother Goose in Prose* (1897), was based on stories told to his own children. Its last chapter introduced Dorothy, the farm-girl who then reappeared in *The Wonderful Wizard of Oz* (1900). This was immediately successful, leading to 14 more titles in the same vein. In 1902 Baum wrote the lyrics for a musical based on his famous book, and later three different film versions followed, the last starring Judy Garland in 1939. After Baum's death 26 more adventures of Oz appeared, written by various authors including Baum's own son. The series had sold over seven million copies when it finished in 1951. Never particularly well written, Baum's stories succeeded through their racy good humour and their straightforward moral framework in which virtue and loyalty are always finally rewarded.

Bawden, Nina 1925– Novelist and writer of CHIL-
DREN'S LITERATURE. Born in London, she completed her education at Oxford. Her novels for adults provide a consistently incisive analysis of life among the upper middle classes, concentrating on the way that emotional disturbances can threaten or destroy an otherwise comfortable existence. *The Birds in the Trees* (1969) describes how a tormented adolescent puts intolerable pressure on himself and his family, while *Anna Apparent* (1972) explores the way illegitimacy and subsequent adoption can present lifelong problems – a point also taken up in *Familiar Passions* (1979). *Circles of Deceit* (1987) was shortlisted for the BOOKER PRIZE. The principal characteristic of her novels for children is a good-humoured understanding of

the child's point of view. Adventure stories such as *The Witch's Daughter* (1966) that start with obvious heroes and villains soon introduce greater complexity. Her most successful novel, *Carrie's War* (1973), drew on autobiographical memories of wartime evacuation to Wales. Mr Evans, a penny-pinching and initially antipathetic grocer with whom the book's young characters are billeted, comes to appear in time a rather sad person, finally inspiring sympathy. *Keeping Henry* (1988) also features three wartime childen living in the country.

Baxter, James K(eir) 1926–72 New Zealand poet, playwright and critic. Born in Dunedin, he was educated in Quaker schools in New Zealand and England and at Otago University, Dunedin, and Victoria University, Wellington, where he obtained his BA in 1952. He worked as a labourer, journalist and teacher and edited the Wellington magazine *Numbers* from 1954 to 1960. Much of his career represented a crusade against what he saw as his country's lack of spirituality. Early bohemianism and Christian concern found a focus when he was converted to Roman Catholicism in 1958. He subsequently founded a religious commune on the Wanganui River and was active in various social-welfare schemes, including projects to house the homeless in Wellington and Auckland.

One of New Zealand's finest poets, Baxter achieved early recognition with the appearance of his volume of verse, *Beyond the Palisade* (1944), when he was just 18. This was the first of more than 30 books of poetry published before his death at the age of 46. His early verse is notable for its lyrical rendition of the New Zealand rural world and the effect of this landscape on its inhabitants. It was followed by a period in which Baxter concentrated on narrative, BALLADS and other poems about local figures like the mill girl, the hotel licensee and the hermit. The poetry he wrote before his conversion is collected in *In Fires of No Return* (1958). After 1958 he went through what by his own standards was a comparatively unproductive period, but his career was reinvigorated when he took up a Burns Fellowship at the University of Otago in 1966. *Pig Island Letters* (1966) and *Jerusalem Sonnets* (1970) are outstanding works from his later period. In the latter volume he evolved a fluid version of the SONNET to express his highly personal sense of religious conviction. *Howrah Bridge* (1961) and *Autumn Testament* (1972) are among his other notable volumes of verse. Baxter began to write plays in the late 1950s, but it was during his time at the University of Otago, when seven of his plays were performed in Dunedin, that his talent as a dramatist first received recognition. These plays included *The Band Rotunda* (1967), *The Sore-Footed Man* (1967), *The Devil and Mr Mulcahy* (1967) and *The Temptations of Oedipus* (1970). His criticism includes *Recent Trends in New Zealand Poetry* (1951) and *Aspects of Poetry in New Zealand* (1967).

Baxter, Richard 1615–91 Presbyterian divine. A military chaplain during the Civil War, Baxter disliked the growth of sectarianism in the Commonwealth and contributed to the change of feeling that led to the Restoration. He accepted the position of royal chaplain, but refused a bishopric and suffered persecution under James II for his uncompromising conscience. He was sentenced to imprisonment in 1685 and vilified by Judge Jeffreys for libelling the established church. A prolific writer of devotional literature, Baxter is best known for *The Saint's Everlasting Rest* (1651), *A Call to the Unconverted* (1658) and his moving, intimate tribute to his beloved wife who died in 1681, *A Breviate of the Life of Margaret Baxter* (1681). His own account of his turbulent life, *Reliquiae Baxterianae*, was published in 1696.

Bay Psalm Book, The: or, *The Whole Book of Psalms Faithfully Translated into English Meter* The authoritative hymnal of the Massachusetts Bay Colony and the first book published in America (Cambridge, Massachusetts, 1640). The translation, by RICHARD MATHER, JOHN ELIOT and Thomas Weld, replaced the Sternhold and Hopkins version, which the Bay Puritans rejected because it sacrificed the literal rendering of the Hebrew text to poetic effect. *The Bay Psalm Book*'s motto, 'God's Altar needs not our Polishings', makes clear the Puritan translators' insistence on a direct confrontation with the Word of God, unmediated by added ornaments. Following a second printing in 1647, it was revised by Henry Dunster (the president of Harvard) and Richard Lyon, and reprinted in 1651 with the title *The Psalms, Hymns and Scriptural Songs of the Old and New Testament*, an edition which was reissued several times over a period of almost a century. See also PSALTERS.

Bayly, (Nathaniel) Thomas Haynes 1797–1839 Poet, playwright and novelist. Born at Bath and educated at Winchester and St Mary Hall, Oxford, he was celebrated in his time as the author of sentimental songs and BALLADS, most notably 'I'd be a Butterfly', 'She Wore a Wreath of Roses', and 'Oh No, We Never Mention Her'. Among his 36 plays *Perfection: or, the Lady of Munster*, a FARCE, enjoyed considerable commercial success. His novels include *The Aylmers* (1827). A collected edition of his *Songs, Ballads and Other Poems* was published in 1844.

Baynton, Barbara 1857–1929 Australian short-story writer. Born in Scone, New South Wales, the daughter of a staunch Presbyterian mother, she was brought up in the Hunter River area. She married a selector who, after they had had three children, left her. She moved to Sydney and married again, this time to a retired surgeon, Thomas Baynton, in 1890. In the decade that followed, she first began to write fiction and her stories appeared in the *Bulletin*, along with the work of such important shapers of the Australian myth of the bush as HENRY LAWSON and A. B. PATERSON. In the first years of the 20th century she visited London where her volume of short stories, *Bush Studies*, the work on which her reputation rests, was published in 1902. After the death of her husband in 1904, she moved between London and Australia and in 1921 entered into a third, short-lived marriage to Lord Headley. Baynton's picture of the bush, while not without humour, presents it as a harsh, inimical environment. It represents a contrast to the robust nationalism of Paterson and even to the equivocal treatment of the bush which characterizes many of Lawson's short stories. In classic stories such as 'Squeaker's Mate' and 'The Chosen Vessel' she vividly dramatizes the plight of bush women, frequently regarding them as victims of both malevolent nature and male brutality. Baynton also published a novel, *Human Toll* (1907). Despite the slender nature of her output, she occupies an important place in Australian literature as an early critic of the romantic view of the bush.

Be Domes Daege (*'Of Doomsday'*) An Old English poem of 300 lines based on the Latin *De Die Judicii* attributed formerly to both ALCUIN and BEDE; the translation is eloquent and capable. It urges men to contemplate the torments of Hell and the bliss of Heaven awaiting them at Doomsday, and to shun luxury in favour of the hardships which promise salvation.

Beaman, S(ydney) G(eorge) Hulme 1886–1932 Writer and illustrator of CHILDREN'S LITERATURE. Born and educated in London, he trained as an artist and worked as a toymaker before he turned to writing picture books. His deftly humorous *Tales of Toytown* (1928) describes a small town where a stuffy mayor and a very slow policeman try to govern a cast of adult eccentrics. The chief troublemaker is Larry the Lamb, portrayed as a cunning would-be innocent child, expert in getting his own way while causing maximum havoc. Toytown became famous through adaptations on BBC radio's *Children's Hour* from 1929 to 1963, with Beaman himself writing over 30 episodes before his early death. Several books were made from these scripts, using Beaman's own drawings.

Beardsley, Aubrey (Vincent) 1872–98 Illustrator and writer. In a career that began virtually in childhood but was cut short by his early death from tuberculosis, Beardsley created a visual style for the 1890s with his sensuous black-and-white drawings. He illustrated WILDE's *SALOME* and became art editor

of *THE YELLOW BOOK* in 1894, but lost the job when Wilde's public disgrace began the following year. He also illustrated POPE's *THE RAPE OF THE LOCK* (1896) and JONSON's *VOLPONE* (1898). A censored version of Beardsley's erotic novel *The Story of Venus and Tannhauser* originally appeared in *The Yellow Book* as *Under the Hill*; it was privately printed without expurgation in 1907.

Beats, The A group of writers centred in San Francisco and New York in the latter half of the 1950s. The term 'beat' was first used by JOHN CLELLON HOLMES in his 1952 novel, *Go*, the first literary description of the people of the Beat movement and their milieu. The name 'beat' has been variously interpreted as meaning 'beaten down' and 'beatific'; members of the group shared an antagonism towards middle-class values, commercialism and conformity, as well as an enthusiasm for the visionary states produced by religious meditation, sexual experience, jazz or drugs. The poet ALLEN GINSBERG and the novelist JACK KEROUAC were perhaps the most prominent spokesmen for the movement, which also included WILLIAM S. BURROUGHS, GREGORY CORSO, GARY SNYDER, and LAWRENCE FERLINGHETTI, whose City Lights Bookstore, founded in San Francisco in 1953, was a gathering-place for Beat writers.

Beattie, James 1735–1803 Philosopher and poet. Born a farmer's son in Kincardineshire, he rose steadily in the academic world to become Professor of Moral Philosophy at Marischal College, Aberdeen, in 1760. His *Essay on the Nature and Immutability of Truth* (1770) was a celebrated attack on the philosophy of DAVID HUME. In 1771 Beattie published the first book of *The Minstrel*, a poem in SPENSERIAN STANZAS on the development of an imaginary poet in past times. The second book appeared in 1774 and Beattie became an honoured poet in his lifetime, praised by SAMUEL JOHNSON. Like the rest of his verse, *The Minstrel* is largely forgotten, though it shows what one critic has called 'a thin-coloured talent for nature-painting'.

Beauchamp's Career A novel by GEORGE MEREDITH, published serially in *THE FORTNIGHTLY REVIEW* (August 1874–December 1875) and in volume form in 1876. Nevil Beauchamp's career is traced from an early commission in the navy through his attempt to stand for Parliament after the Crimean War. Nevil is also torn between two loves, for a married Frenchwoman, Renée de Croisnel, and for Cecilia Halkett. He resists the temptation to join Renée in her flight from her husband, but loses Cecilia to a cousin. After recovering from a severe illness, during which he manages to reconcile his aristocratic uncle to his Radical friend Dr Shrapnel, Nevil marries Shrapnel's ward but is drowned while attempting to rescue a child from the sea. The novel offers a powerful picture of the workings of contemporary political life.

Beaumont, Francis 1584–1616 Playwright. Beaumont was born into the rural gentry of Elizabethan England, left Oxford without a degree in 1598 and entered the Inner Temple to study law in 1600. He probably studied very little, and there is no evidence that he ever practised law. His fashionable interest in sub-erotic Ovidian verse was expressed in *Salmacis and Hermaphroditus* (published in 1602). His first play, a prose comedy called *The Woman Hater* (1605) written for the boys of St Paul's, may reflect the onslaught of a need for money on a writer who would have preferred to be a poet. It is a servile imitation of the work of BEN JONSON, in whose company Beaumont was often seen. THE KNIGHT OF THE BURNING PESTLE (1607), the other piece of which Beaumont is now believed to have been sole author, is altogether finer. It is a witty outcome of avid theatre-going in which the dramatic taste of unsophisticated audiences is mocked without much malice.

Beaumont's collaboration with JOHN FLETCHER marks a separate and substantial stage in his dramatic career. They seem to have replaced SHAKESPEARE in about 1609 as chief dramatists of the KING'S MEN, for whom they probably wrote *PHILASTER* (*c.* 1609), *THE MAID'S TRAGEDY* (*c.* 1610) and *A KING AND NO KING* (1611). The collaborators were sufficiently sensitive to the shifts in public taste to become leaders of it. Their plays exploited the scenic scope of the indoor theatre at the BLACKFRIARS THEATRE, sacrificing Shakespearean profundity to the less durable appeal of the decorated stage, ambiguity to intrigue, and the complexity of metaphor to the easy flow of language. Their influence carried over into post-Restoration drama. It is dangerously easy to detect in their plays the transition from Elizabethan popular drama to the elitist drama of Jacobean and Caroline England. By any but the highest standards, the collaborative work of Beaumont and Fletcher is impressive.

The popularity of the Beaumont and Fletcher plays tempted contemporary publicists and publishers to ascribe to the partnership more work than belonged to it. Beaumont probably abandoned the theatre soon after his marriage to an heiress in 1613, while Fletcher continued to write, either singly or with other collaborators, for over 10 years. Of the 50 or more 'Beaumont and Fletcher plays', only seven or eight can be confidently attributed, in any significant part, to Beaumont. These include *Cupid's Revenge* (*c.* 1611), *The Coxcomb* (1612), *The Scornful Lady* (*c.* 1613) and *The Captain* (1613), in addition to the three finer works already mentioned. Despite this, a folio containing 34 plays and a masque was published under the joint names of Beaumont and Fletcher in 1647, and *Fifty Comedies and Tragedies*, again ascribed to Beaumont and Fletcher and containing 18 additional pieces, was published in 1679. Through such a casual approach to authorship, Beaumont's reputation was increased and, in particular, that of MASSINGER diminished.

Beautyful Ones are Not Yet Born, The A novel by AYI KWEI ARMAH, published in 1969. The title is taken from a slogan on a Ghanaian bus. A bitter indictment of Nkrumah's post-colonial betrayal of Ghana's independence, the story is set in Accra, where the physical filth of the environment adumbrates the moral corruption of an indolent ruling class. The desire for Western goods tempts government and municipal officials to embezzle funds and engage in bribery and fraud on a massive scale. The anonymous hero, the Man, is a modern urbanized African whose integrity is scorned by his family and his wife's relations. The friends who shared his hopes for independent Ghana have opted out of society altogether (Teacher), gone mad (Manaan) or retreated into dysfunctional spirituality (Rama Krishna). Some hope for the future is suggested, though ambiguously, by the final scenes dealing with the anti-Nkrumah coup.

Beaux' Stratagem, The A comedy by GEORGE FARQUHAR, first performed at DRURY LANE in 1707, two months before its author's death. Durable and good-humoured, the play is often revived in the modern theatre.

Two improvident friends, Archer and Aimwell, arrive at an inn in Lichfield in quest of a change of fortune. They decide that Aimwell shall pose as his titled brother and Archer as 'Lord' Aimwell's servant. The pretence does not fend off speculation as to who they are, and they are taken for Jesuits and, by the landlord, for highwaymen. Dorinda, daughter of the local Lady Bountiful, falls in love with Aimwell when she sees him in church, and the wife of her oafish brother Sullen is attracted to Archer. When Lady Bountiful's house is attacked by highwaymen, Archer and Aimwell rescue the ladies. Struck by love and remorse, Aimwell confesses the deception to Dorinda, whose love survives the revelation. However, it requires the arrival of a DEUS EX MACHINA in the person of Mrs Sullen's brother, Sir Charles Freeman, to resolve the difficulties. Not only does he bring news that Aimwell's brother is dead and Aimwell's title therefore real, but he also persuades the drunken Sullen to consent to the dissolution of his marriage, thus leaving the way clear for Archer to ask for Mrs Sullen's hand.

Beaver, Bruce 1928– Australian poet. Born and educated in Sydney, he worked at various occupations before going to New Zealand in 1958. After his return to Australia four years later, he published three volumes of verse before achieving major recognition with *Letters to Live Poets* (1969). He has worked as a freelance journalist. Beaver's rough-hewn early verse is essentially personal and documents a struggle to reconcile the conflicting pressures of modern urban life in a morally responsible vision. *Letters to Live Poets* extended his range to a broader consideration of the conflicts involved in artistic perception itself. The formally innovative *Lauds and Plaints* (1974) shows the influence of modern American poets, particularly WILLIAM CARLOS WILLIAMS. His other books include *Under the Bridge* (1961), *Seawall and Shoreline* (1964), *Odes and Days* (1975), *Death's Directive* (1978), the autobiographical *As It Was* (1979), *Charmed Lives* (1988), *New and Selected Poems: 1960–1990* (1991) and the novels *The Hot Spring* (1965) and *You Can't Come Back* (1966). He has been an important influence on the younger generation of Australian poets.

Samuel Beckett photographed in Paris two days before his death

Beckett, Samuel (Barclay) 1906–89 Irish-born playwright and novelist. One of the most individual voices of the post-war European theatre, he left Dublin for Paris after graduating from Trinity College in 1927. As a young man, he was an associate and assistant of JAMES JOYCE, with whom he shares a relentless urge to test and extend the scope of words. He usually wrote in French and translated his own work into English. His first published works were a volume of verse, *Whoroscope* (1930), and a critical study of Proust (1931). *More Pricks than Kicks* (1934) was a volume of short stories. Beckett's first novel, *Murphy* (1938), made little impact on its first publication. It is almost entirely on his work after 1950 that his fame rests. It earned him the Nobel Prize for Literature in 1969.

Beckett's major novels, the French 'trilogy' *Molloy* (1951; translated 1955), *Malone meurt* (1951; *Malone Dies*, 1956) and *L'Innommable* (1953; *The Unnameable*, 1958) and the English *Watt* (1953), exist in and through their narrators: social misfits, old and ill, embarked on a quest for the explanation of 'I'. Although distinct from the plays, they are not cut off from them. *The Unnameable*, for example, searches for an escape from writing in the spoken word, and the difficult *Comment c'est* (*How It Is*, 1961) is insistently aural. The short prose fictions that followed *How It Is* replace the puzzled subjectivity of the novels with a bleak objectivity.

Beckett is probably more widely known for his plays, above all for *WAITING FOR GODOT* (first produced in French in 1953 and in English in 1955), than for his novels. They introduced to the post-war theatre a philosophical dimension that bemused and intrigued audiences. Martin Esslin saw Beckett as a leading exponent of the THEATRE OF THE ABSURD, arguing that his depiction of characters struggling doggedly with beginnings and, especially, with endings, represented a perception of meaninglessness and incoherence. The three full-length plays, *Waiting for Godot*, *ENDGAME* (first produced in French in 1957 and in English in 1958) and *HAPPY DAYS* (1961), if not exactly a trilogy, are all concerned with human suffering, survival – and immobility. The shorter, but still substantial, *Krapp's Last Tape* (1958) and *Play* (1963) seek to identify moments in the characters' past when something actually happened, as does the uncharacteristically rich radio play *All That Fall* (1957). All of Beckett's stage plays replace conventional decor with stark images. In the fragmentary *Breath* (1970) the image is all we have. The mysterious *Come and Go* (1966), which Beckett calls a 'dramaticule', shows three women behaving according to a regular pattern but not allowing the audience to hear the whispers that might (or might not) motivate their behaviour. In *Not I* (1972) and *Footfalls* (1976), it is the detailed direction of stage lighting that dictates what the audience sees (a mouth and feet respectively) as the spoken words reverberate.

Beckford, William 1759–1844 Connoisseur and man of letters. Beckford was born at Fonthill, Wiltshire, the son of an immensely wealthy alderman from whom he inherited a vast fortune. A compulsive builder and collector, he reconstructed his Wiltshire mansion as an elaborate Gothic fantasy, Fonthill Abbey, substantially completed in 1809 but abandoned after the fall of its immense tower in 1825. His travel book *Dreams, Waking Thoughts and Incidents* (1783) was reissued in amended form as the first volume of *Italy, with Sketches of Spain and Portugal* (1834). Beckford's fantastic story *VATHEK* was written in French and published in an English translation by Samuel Henley in 1786. Two pseudo-nymous BURLESQUES, *Modern Novel Writing: or, the Elegant Enthusiast* (1796) and *Azemia* (1797), were followed by another travel book, *Recollections of an Excursion to the Monasteries of Alcobaça and Batalha* (1835).

Beddoes, Thomas Lovell 1803–49 Poet. A nephew of the novelist MARIA EDGEWORTH, he was born at Clifton near Bristol and educated at Charterhouse and Pembroke College, Oxford. He studied medicine in several European cities and prac-tised in Zurich but was denied a university post be-cause of his revolutionary ideas. An anomalous, solitary figure of unique, even bizarre, qualities, Beddoes seemed incapable of carrying through his literary plans and designs. He published *The Impro-visatore* (1821) and *The Bride's Tragedy* (1822) but is best known for *DEATH'S JEST-BOOK*, a REVENGE TRAGEDY in the Jacobean manner which he began in 1825, re-peatedly revised and left unpublished when he com-mitted suicide. It appeared in 1850.

Bede [Baeda] *c.* 673–735 Historian, known as 'The Venerable Bede'. Probably born at Monkton, Durham, he went to the monastery in Wearmouth at the age of seven and in 682 to the monastery in Jarrow, where he became a deacon at the age of 19 and a priest at 30. He remained in Jarrow for the rest of his life, leaving the area only for occasional short visits. His Latin *Historia Ecclesiastica Gentis Anglorum*, finished in 731, was a pioneering work which earned him the title of 'The Father of English History'. It traces the development of Christianity in Britain from the barbarous, dis-parate Christian and heathen groups left after the withdrawal of the Roman Empire to the conversion of the British, the unification and consolidation of their Christian faith under the influence of such fig-ures as Sts Patrick, David, Augustine, Ninian, Aidan and Columba. With Christianity came the enriching civilization and culture of Rome, and the decay of Celtic tribalism. During the period covered by Bede church administration changed from the strictly spir-itual and hierarchical monastic structure of the Celtic saints to the cohesive and stable administrative diocesan form of the Roman church, which fused spir-itual and temporal power in one body. Bede was a thorough and scholarly historian, collating evidence and verifying his facts wherever possible. He treats his material sympathetically, to produce a lively account full of insights into daily life in the 7th century. Although his predominant concerns were theologi-cal, Bede's other writings reflect wide-ranging inter-ests. They include: *De Orthographia*, perhaps his earliest work, about spelling; *De Natura Rerum*, about natural science; a hagiographic account of the early Northumbrian abbots; biblical commentaries and translations; homilies; and hymns.

Bede, Cuthbert [Bradley, Edward] 1827–89 Humorist. Born at Kidderminster and educated at University College, Durham, he was ordained in 1850 and served from 1871 as rector of Stretton in Rutland. *The Adventures of Mr Verdant Green, an Oxford Freshman* (1853–6), a comic account of undergradu-ate life, was very popular in its day.

Beecher, Henry Ward 1813–87 American preacher and brother of HARRIET BEECHER STOWE. After serving as minister to several Indiana churches, in 1847 he was called to the Plymouth Church in Brooklyn, New York, where he remained for the rest of his life. There he preached a theology of love rather than fear, exploiting the emotional Protestant revival tradition while addressing social issues such as edu-cation, temperance and slavery. His fame grew as he spoke on lecture tours as well as from the pulpit, and wrote weekly columns for *The Independent*, a widely read sectarian newspaper. In the 1850s he emerged as a major moral spokesman on secular issues of na-tional concern, especially slavery; and though a mod-erate, he became associated in the popular mind with the radical Abolitionists.

His sermons were published periodically in *The Plymouth Pulpit* throughout the 1860s, and in 1870 he began editing a new journal, *Christian Union*. He was a prominent proponent of votes for women, and became active in the American Women's Suffrage Association. His novel, *Norwood: or, Village Life in New England* (1867), whose characters have long con-versations about religious values, sold well. In the 1870s he incorporated many of CHARLES DARWIN's ideas to support his old teachings of evangelical liber-alism, the benefits of virtuous self-improvement and the moral value of material success.

Beer, Patricia 1924– Poet. Born in Exmouth, she was educated at Exmouth Grammar School, Exeter University and St Hugh's College, Oxford. She has worked as a lecturer in English in Italy and at Goldsmiths' College, London. An autobiography, *Mrs Beer's House* (1969), describes her childhood. Her verse, in *Loss of the Magyar* (1959), *The Survivors* (1963), *Just Like the Resurrection* (1967), *The Estuary* (1971), *Driving West* (1975), *Selected Poems* (1979), *The Lie of the Land* (1983), *Collected Poems* (1988) and *Moon's Ottery* (1988), is marked by a development away from traditional forms. Precise and economical, her poems observe everyday matters and West Country scenes. She has also published *Reader, I Married Him* (1974), an influential study of JANE AUSTEN, CHARLOTTE BRONTË, ELIZABETH GASKELL and GEORGE ELIOT.

Beerbohm, Sir (Henry) Max(imilian) 1872–1956 Humorist, essayist and cartoonist. Half-brother of the actor-manager Herbert Beerbohm Tree, he was born in London and educated at Charterhouse and Merton College, Oxford. A friend of OSCAR WILDE and AUBREY BEARDSLEY, and a precociously poised figure in the decadent literary world of the 1890s, he began by publishing caricatures in THE STRAND MAGAZINE and essays in THE YELLOW BOOK, the latter facetiously gathered as The Works of Max Beerbohm (1896). After publishing The Happy Hypocrite (1897) he succeeded SHAW as dramatic critic of THE SATURDAY REVIEW in 1898. Three works best epitomize his acute but sunny and gentle wit: his Oxford novel, ZULEIKA DOBSON (1911); A Christmas Garland (1912), containing PARODIES of JAMES, CONRAD, WELLS and BENNETT, among others; and Seven Men (1919), which includes 'Enoch Soames' and a spoof of portentous historical drama in 'Savonarola Brown'. The Poets' Corner (1904), a collection of cartoons, wryly comments on major writers. After his marriage in 1910 Beerbohm lived mainly in Italy, returning home during the two world wars and establishing a reputation as a broadcaster. A selection of his talks appeared as Mainly on the Air (1946). He was knighted in 1939.

Beeton, Mrs **Isabella Mary** 1836–65 Author of Household Management. It was first published in The Englishwoman's Domestic Magazine in 1859–61 and as a separate volume in 1861. Usually remembered for its sections on cookery, which have been reprinted many times, the book in its original form gives a full picture of the duties of the Victorian middle-class housewife.

Beggar's Opera, The A BALLAD OPERA by JOHN GAY, with songs arranged by John Christopher Pepusch, who also composed an overture. It was first staged by John Rich at Lincoln's Inn Fields in 1728 to such success that, according to the contemporary tag, it made 'Rich gay and Gay rich'. SWIFT had suggested the idea of a 'Newgate pastoral' to Gay and The Beggar's Opera was apparently his response, an original and astonishing work which combines a riposte to the fashionable excesses of Italian opera with satire of corrupt government. Sir Robert Walpole and his colleagues were sufficiently concerned to refuse a performing licence for its sequel, POLLY, in 1729.

Peachum, a receiver of stolen goods, whose creation owed much to the historical character of Jonathan Wild, is mortified when his daughter Polly marries the highwayman Macheath, with whom Peachum has a profitable business arrangement. True to the style of Jonathan Wild, he informs against Macheath. Sentenced to death and imprisoned in Newgate, Macheath is rescued by the warder's pretty daughter, Lucy Lockit. The rivalry between Polly Peachum and Lucy maintains the piece's characteristic balance of romance and cynicism. Recaptured in a brothel, Macheath is saved a second time from the gallows by the improbable intervention of a compulsory

happy ending, demanded on behalf of the audience by one of the players.

The Beggar's Opera has been frequently revived, and its musical score set by Benjamin Britten and, for a disappointing film version, by Arthur Bliss. It provided the formal inspiration for Bertolt Brecht's The Threepenny Opera (1928), a satire on corrupt capitalism, with original music by Kurt Weill.

Behan, Brendan 1923–64 Irish playwright. Behan was born in Dublin, a child of the tenements. He credited his education to his prison terms, though he owed much to his family, well-read, and of strong Republican sympathies. At 14 he joined the IRA, and spent two years in an English Borstal, convicted in 1939 of carrying explosives. Released and deported, in 1942 he got 14 years for shooting at a policeman during an IRA ceremony.

Amnestied in 1947, Behan continued the writing begun in prison, mainly short stories in an inventive stylization of Dublin vernacular. His plays brought him celebrity. In 1954 the Pike Theatre presented The Quare Fellow, a grimly comic drama of the hours preceding a prison hanging. Much more than propaganda against judicial execution, it captures, with remarkable economy of form and neutrality of tone, the condition of the outcast and the emotions excited by barbaric revenge. Joan Littlewood's 1956 Theatre Workshop production in London made Behan famous. Success was unmanageable. Behan's irresolute discipline collapsed into prolonged drinking bouts. THE HOSTAGE (1958), his next play, derived from his one-act Gaelic play An Giall, was acclaimed in London, Paris and New York. Much influenced by Joan Littlewood's improvisational theatre, it travesties with song and dance – and Behan's easy connivance – the tragic simplicity of its original. His last serious work, Borstal Boy (1958), is an imaginatively controlled account of his Borstal years, itself the testimony to a sophisticated creative power and great generosity of feeling.

A clamorous Dublin presence, belligerent or convivial, Behan illuminated the theatrical drabness of the 1950s. He subdued his vivid personality to an objective form, and his work, however brief, is continuous with a tradition, that of O'CASEY's urban drama.

Behn, Aphra 1640–89 Playwright, novelist and translator. Probably the first Englishwoman to see herself as a professional writer, she led an adventurous life, although our knowledge of its details is unreliable. A childhood in the West Indies apparently suggested the setting for her best prose romance, OROONOKO. The date of her marriage to a merchant of Dutch extraction is uncertain, as is the exact nature of her spying mission in Antwerp in 1666. Imprisoned for debt in the late 1660s, she turned to writing plays soon after her release.

Her early work was in what Restoration England took to be the style of BEAUMONT and FLETCHER. Even the more distinguished comedies, like *The Town Fop* (1676), *The Rover* (1677), *Sir Patient Fancy* (1678), *The Second Part of the Rover* (1681) and *The Lucky Chance* (1686), are variously derivative from the work of earlier writers. The political piece *The City Heiress* (1682) borrows from MIDDLETON's *A Mad World, My Masters*. The farce *The Emperor of the Moon* (1687), based on a scenario from Italian COMMEDIA DELL' ARTE, helped make popular the harlequinade, forerunner of the English style of PANTOMIME. Behn's plays were successful in their time and several of them merit revival, not least because her advocacy of mature relationships between the sexes is a reminder of the social seriousness that underlies the licentiousness of Restoration drama. Her translations from French and Latin were money-making ventures and have no special claims. Of her fiction, only *The Fair Jilt* (1688), a lively account of a *femme fatale*, and *Oroonoko* rival the plays.

Behrman, S(amuel) N(athaniel) 1893–1973 American playwright. Born in Worcester, Massachusetts, and educated at Harvard and Columbia, he began his theatrical career as an actor. When ill health forced him to give up the stage he took to writing – mostly sophisticated social comedies dealing with success, wealth, love and marriage. His first play, *Bedside Manners*, written with J. Kenyon Nicholson, was produced in New York in 1923; in the following year the two of them collaborated on *A Night's Work*. Behrman's third play, *The Man Who Forgot*, written with Owen Davis, appeared in 1926. Others of his plays include *Serena Blandish: or, The Difficulty of Getting Married* (adapted from ENID BAGNOLD's novel, 1929), *Meteor* (1929), *Love Story* (1933), *End of Summer* (1936), *Wine of Choice* (1938), *No Time for Comedy* (1939), *Jacobowsky and the Colonel* (New York Drama Critics Circle Award, 1944), *Jane* (adapted from a SOMERSET MAUGHAM short story, 1952), *Fanny* (with Joshua Logan, 1954) and his last play, *But for Whom Charlie* (1964). Behrman also wrote more than 25 screenplays between 1930 and 1962. He published several collections of essays which had first appeared in THE NEW YORKER, as well as volumes of short stories. *People in a Diary: A Memoir* appeared in 1972.

Bekederemo, J. P. Clark See CLARK BEKEDEREMO, J. P.

Belasco, David 1853–1931 American playwright, theatrical impresario, director and actor. Born and educated in San Francisco, he became a powerful figure in its theatrical life before moving in 1882 to New York, where he enjoyed an equally successful Broadway career. He was famous for devising sensational stage effects at the Belasco Theatre, which he owned and managed from 1907 until his death. He also wrote or co-wrote more than 50 plays, notably: *Chums* (1879; retitled *Hearts of Oak*, 1880) with JAMES A. HERNE; *The Wife* (1880), *Lord Chumley* (1888) and other works with Henry C. De Mille; *The Girl I Left Behind Me* (1893) with Franklin Fyles; and *Madame Butterfly* (1900), *The Darling of the Gods* (1902) and *Adrea* (1904) with John L. Long. *The Girl of the Golden West* (1905) and *Madame Butterfly* were turned into operas by Puccini. *The Return of Peter Grimm* (1911) was based on an idea by Cecil B. De Mille.

Bell, (Arthur) Clive (Howard) 1881–1964 Critic of art and literature. He was born at East Shefford, Bedfordshire, and educated at Marlborough College and Cambridge, where he was influenced by the philosopher G. E. MOORE's advocacy of 'the pleasures of human intercourse and the enjoyment of beautiful objects'. A central figure in the BLOOMSBURY GROUP, he married VIRGINIA WOOLF's sister Vanessa Stephen in 1907. With Roger Fry, Bell was one of the first critics to recognize the achievements of the Post-Impressionists. His first book, *Art* (1914), introduced his concept of 'Significant Form', which separated and elevated the element of form above content in works of art. His other works of criticism include *Since Cézanne* (1922), *Civilization* (1928), *Proust* (1929) and *Account of French Painting* (1931). *Old Friends: Personal Recollections* (1956) includes reminiscences of his friends among the Bloomsbury Group, though it also rejects the label as an invention by journalists.

Bell, Currer, Ellis and **Acton** Pseudonyms of CHARLOTTE, EMILY and ANNE BRONTË.

Bell, Gertrude (Margaret Lowthian) 1868–1926 Travel-writer. The daughter of a rich ironmaster, Gertrude Bell was born in Washington, County Durham, and educated in London and at Lady Margaret Hall, Oxford. Having learned Persian and Arabic on early travels, she undertook archaeological work in the Middle East and became an influential liaison officer between British and Arab interests during World War I. Among the books describing her travels are *Safar Nameh: Persian Pictures* (1894), *The Desert and the Sown* (1907) and *Amurath to Amurath* (1911). She died in Baghdad. Her vivid personality is well conveyed in her posthumously published letters (1927).

Bell, Martin 1918–78 Poet. Born in Southampton, he was educated at Taunton School and University College, Southampton. A member of the Communist Party 1935–9, he worked as a teacher and lecturer, and became Gregory Fellow in Poetry at Leeds University in 1967. He was a leading member of the GROUP, and it was under his influence that it developed into the Poets' Workshop. Though his work was frequently anthologized *Collected Poems 1938-67* (1967) was his only major book. Deliberately populist, he wrote many poems about his peers, including a satire on the Group's meetings called 'Mr Hobsbaum's Monday Evening Meeting'. His most famous poem is the corruscating attack, 'Headmaster: Modern Style'.

Bellamy, Edward 1850-98 American novelist. Born in Massachusetts, Bellamy was working as a journalist when in 1888 he wrote *LOOKING BACKWARD: 2000-1887*, an immensely popular Utopian romance. For the rest of his life he developed and disseminated the political principles set forth in this book. Above all, these involved a government programme of strict state capitalism, resulting in non-revolutionary socialist reform. Bellamy clubs and a Nationalist party were established to advocate his ideas; in support he founded the journal *The New Nation* (1891), and later wrote *Equality* (1897), a more theoretical sequel to *Looking Backward*. His earlier, less political writings include *The Duke of Stockbridge* (1879), about Shay's Rebellion, and *Dr Heidenhoff's Process* (1880) and *Miss Ludington's Sister* (1884), novels dealing with psychic phenomena in the tradition of NATHANIEL HAWTHORNE. *The Blind Man's World and Other Stories* (1898) was published just before his death from tuberculosis.

Belloc, (Joseph) Hilaire (Pierre René) 1870-1953 Poet, novelist, biographer, historian and travel-writer. Born of half-French parentage in St Cloud, France, he was educated at Cardinal Newman's Oratory School near Birmingham and Balliol College, Oxford. He became a British citizen in 1902. His close friendship with CHESTERTON, whom he met in 1900, was based on common beliefs and interests; their anti-Imperial, pro-Boer contributions to *The Speaker* made SHAW nickname them the 'Chesterbelloc'. After serving as a Liberal MP for Salford in 1906-10 Belloc recorded his disillusionment with party politics in *The Party System* (with Cecil Chesterton, 1911) and *The Servile State* (1912).

His other writings cover many genres. His literary career began with *Verses and Sonnets* and *The Bad Child's Book of Beasts* (both 1896). His other verse includes *Cautionary Tales* (1907) and *Sonnets and Verses* (1923). His many biographies, often lively and partisan, include *Danton* (1899), *Robespierre* (1901), *Marie Antoinette* (1909) and *Cromwell* (1927) and he wrote several histories, notably *The French Revolution* (1911) and a *History of England* (1915). Books of travel include *Paris* (1900), *The Path to Rome* (1902), *The Pyrenees* (1909), *The Cruise of the Nona* (containing many personal reflections; 1925) and *Return to the Baltic* (1938). Among his essays, memorable collections are *Hills and the Sea* (1906), *First*

Saul Bellow

and Last (1911), *Short Talks with the Dead* (1926) and *The Silence of the Sea* (1940). His novels, many of which were illustrated by Chesterton, included *Mr Clutterbuck's Election* (1908), *The Girondin* (1911), *The Green Overcoat* (1912) and *Belinda* (1928).

Bellow, Saul 1915- American novelist. The son of immigrant Russian parents, he was born in Quebec. His family moved to Chicago in 1924, and he was educated at the University of Chicago, Northwestern University, and the University of Wisconsin. He has followed an academic career since 1938. Two early novels, *Dangling Man* (1944) and *The Victim* (1947), were followed by the exuberant PICARESQUE of *THE ADVENTURES OF AUGIE MARCH* (1953), which won him his first National Book Award, and by *Seize the Day* (1956). *Henderson the Rain King* (1959), about a middle-aged American's travails in Africa, further illustrates Bellow's penchant for expansive, occasionally sentimental comedy, while a later novel, *The Dean's December* (1982), partly set in Eastern Europe, shows him confronting with a graver, bleaker tone the austere question of living a good life. *HERZOG* (1964) and *Humboldt's Gift* (1975), his most widely admired novels, best exemplify his reputation for interpreting the struggles of city dwellers to define their roles and responsibilities in the modern world. His other fiction includes the novels *Mr Sammler's Planet* (1970), which won the National Book Award, and *More Die of Heartbreak* (1987), and several collections of shorter work: *Mosby's Memoirs and Other Stories* (1968), *Him* with *His Foot in His Mouth and Other Short Stories* (1984) and *Something to Remember Me By* (1993). He is also the author of several plays, including *The Wrecker* (1954), *The Last Analysis* (1965) and *A Wen* (1965), and a travel book about modern Israel, *To Jerusalem and Back: A Personal Account* (1976). His academic publications include *Recent American Fiction: A Lecture* (1963), *The Future of the Moor* (1970) and *Technology and the Frontiers of Knowledge* (1975), and he is the editor of *Great Jewish Short Stories* (1963). He was awarded the Nobel Prize for Literature in 1976.

Bells, The A MELODRAMA adapted by LEOPOLD LEWIS from a French play, *Le Juif polonais*, by Erckmann and Chatrian. It was first staged at the Lyceum Theatre, London, in 1871. Its success established Sir Henry Irving as a leading actor, and the role of Mathias remained in his repertoire until his death in 1905.

The bells are the sleigh-bells of the Polish Jew, whom Mathias, now a respected burgomaster of the small German town where he was once a poor servant, murdered many winters ago. They ring in his mind, tormenting him with the memory of his crime, eventually driving him to a remorseful death.

Belton Estate, The A novel by ANTHONY TROLLOPE, serialized in *THE FORTNIGHTLY REVIEW* from May 1865 to January 1866 and published in volume form in 1866.

Clara Amedroz is the daughter of the squire of Belton Castle, Bernard Amedroz, whose spendthrift son and heir has committed suicide. Her cousin Will Belton, a hearty Norfolk farmer, becomes heir to the entailed estate, and on a visit to her father falls in love with Clara and proposes marriage. Clara, however, is in love with Captain Aylmer, an MP and nephew of her wealthy adopted aunt Mrs Winterfield, and she refuses Will. When Mrs Winterfield dies, it transpires that she has left her money to Captain Aylmer, and has committed him by a deathbed promise to propose marriage to Clara. This he does and is accepted, but Clara comes to question his conventional attitudes and lukewarm courtship; when she goes to stay at Aylmer Park after her father's death, and encounters insolent condescension from Aylmer's mother, she breaks off the engagement. Will Belton has meanwhile proved his devotion and generosity by his determination to surrender the Belton estate to her, and Clara finds that she truly loves him. The novel ends with their marriage.

Although not rated highly by Trollope himself, *The Belton Estate* is of some interest for its characteristically sympathetic exploration of the plight of the single, dependent woman.

Ben-Hur: *A Tale of the Christ* A historical novel by LEW WALLACE, published in 1880. Judah Ben-Hur and

Messala the Roman are apparently devoted friends, but Messala, in search of advancement, accuses Ben-Hur of an attempt on the life of the Roman governor. Ben-Hur is sent to the galleys for life, and his mother and sister are also imprisoned. In the slave train to the coast he is given water by a stranger outside a carpenter's workshop. Years later he returns to Judaea a free man and a Roman officer; soon after, he challenges Messala in the chariot races in Caesarea. His mother and sister, meanwhile, have contracted leprosy. Ben-Hur wins the chariot race; Messala, who has staked everything on the victory, is crippled and ruined. Ben-Hur rescues his mother and sister, and they return to Jerusalem on the day of the Crucifixion. The condemned man is the same one who once aided Ben-Hur as a slave; he dies on the cross, but his passing cures the lepers. Ben-Hur and his family embrace Christianity.

Benchley, Robert (Charles) 1889–1945 American humorist, drama critic and actor. After graduating from Harvard in 1912 he began his career as a journalist, working on several New York newspapers and magazines. He was theatre critic for *Life* (1920–9) and then for *THE NEW YORKER* (1929–40). During these years he also wrote and published humorous sketches, based on the daily lives of ordinary people and marked by an ironic appreciation of life in an era of rapid and often confusing change. They were collected in *Of All Things* (1921), *Love Conquers All* (1922), *Pluck and Luck* (1925), *The Early Worm* (1927), *20,000 Leagues Under The Sea: or, David Copperfield* (1928), *The Treasurer's Report* (1930), *My Ten Years in a Quandary* (1936), *After 1903 – What?* (1938), *Inside Benchley* (1942) and *Benchley beside Himself* (1943). In addition to his writing, Benchley made frequent appearances in films and on the radio.

Benét, Stephen Vincent 1898–1943 American poet, short-story writer and novelist. He was born in Bethlehem, Pennsylvania. *John Brown's Body* (1928) is a PULITZER PRIZE-winning collection of verse about the Civil War. *Western Star* (1943), unfinished at his death but also awarded a Pulitzer Prize, deals with American roots in 17th-century European migrations. A collection of short stories, *Thirteen O'Clock* (1937), includes the popular 'The Devil and Daniel Webster', which has been made into an opera and a film. Other volumes of his stories are *Tales before Midnight* (1939) and *The Last Cycle* (1946). He also wrote five novels, and a number of radio scripts which appeared in a posthumous collection, *We Stand United, and Other Radio Scripts* (1945).

Benét, William Rose 1886–1950 American poet, founder of the *SATURDAY REVIEW* (1924) and elder brother of STEPHEN VINCENT BENÉT. He published several books of poetry, including *Merchants from*

Cathay (1913), *Moons of Grandeur* (1920), *Days of Deliverance* (1944) and *The Stairway of Surprise* (1947). An experimental verse novel, *Rip Tide*, appeared in 1932. He won a PULITZER PRIZE for his verse autobiography, *The Dust Which is God* (1941).

Benito Cereno See PIAZZA TALES, THE.

Benlowes, Edward 1602–76 Religious poet. The heir of a rich Roman Catholic family, he changed his faith at the age of 25. Staunch support of the Royalist cause in the Civil War reduced him to poverty. His long religious poem, *Theophilia: or, Love's Sacrifice* (1652), is a rambling theological romance containing many curious expressions and the occasional fine line.

Bennett, Alan 1934– Playwright and actor. Born and educated in Yorkshire, Bennett was a student at Oxford when he contributed to the successful revue *Beyond the Fringe* (1960). Despite his own self-effacing qualities, he has remained in the public eye ever since. *Forty Years On* (1968) and *Getting On* (1971) are intelligent political comedies, *Habeas Corpus* (1973) a FARCE. Their half-ironic, half-senti-mental preoccupation with British institutions has an obvious counterpart in the interest in post-war traitors expressed by *The Old Country* (1977), *An Englishman Abroad* (TV, 1983; stage, 1988) and *A Question of Attribution* (stage, 1988 ; TV, 1991). The confrontation between Sir Anthony Blunt and the Queen in the last led the way to an ambitious treatment of monarchy, *The Madnesss of George III* (1992), in which easy sentiment predominates. More promising, despite the failure of *Enjoy* (1980), are works derived from his northern, working-class roots, triumphantly examined in *Talking Heads* (TV, 1988; stage, 1992), which, like so much of his best work to date, establishes a two-way communication between TV and the stage.

Bennett, (Enoch) Arnold 1867–1931 Novelist, short-story writer, playwright and journalist. He was born at Hanley in the Staffordshire Potteries, where his father Enoch had trained himself as a solicitor. Bennett's decision, made when he was 21, to leave his father's firm was crucial for his future, but he still worked as a solicitor's clerk on moving to London. Although literary success came slowly, he was able to change careers in 1893, becoming assistant editor of

Arnold Bennett, photograph by E. O. Hoppé

Woman magazine. A short story, 'A Letter Home', was accepted by THE YELLOW BOOK and a first, highly autobiographical novel, *A Man from the North* (1898), was accepted by John Lane.

Bennett's literary mentors were mostly French, notably Maupassant, Zola and Flaubert. A three-volume *Journal* (1932–3), inspired by the example of the Goncourt brothers, was begun in 1896. His first major achievement, ANNA OF THE FIVE TOWNS (1902), was set in the Potteries of his boyhood, the scene for much of his best work. It was joined by novels of a different sort: *The Grand Babylon Hotel* (1902), a comedy thriller about the problems of a millionaire, and *The Gates of Wrath* (1903). Two collections of short stories followed: *Tales of the Five Towns* (1905) and *The Grim Smile of the Five Towns* (1907). His greatest achievement came with THE OLD WIVES' TALE (1908) and CLAYHANGER (1910). The fortunes of the Clayhanger family are followed further in *Hilda Lessways* (1911), *These Twain* (1916) and *The Roll Call* (1918).

Following the death of his dominating father, Bennett had moved to Paris in 1903. His marriage to Marguerite Soulie in 1907 lasted until their separation in 1921. Bennett had a daughter by the companion of his later years, Dorothy Cheston.

Bennett's interest in the theatre began as a critic, but he was to see many of his own plays produced and took an active part in the management of the Lyric Theatre, Hammersmith, in the 1920s. His greatest success came with *Milestones* (1912), written in collaboration with Edward Knoblock. With his lesser novels, *The Card* (1911), *Mr Prohack* (1922) and *Imperial Palace* (1930), he returned to the subject of the rich and the worldly; the more highly regarded political novel *Lord Raingo* (1926) reflects his knowledge of powerful men like Lord Beaverbrook, who became a close friend. In 1918 Bennett served as Director of Propaganda in the Ministry of Information. It was owing to Beaverbrook that he undertook the influential 'Books and Persons' series for *The Evening Standard* from 1926 until his death. His reputation as a novelist was enhanced by RICEYMAN STEPS (1923), in which he again considered the lives of ordinary and undistinguished people, the subject for which he is chiefly remembered.

Bennett, Louise 1919– Jamaican poet, performer and folklorist. Born in Kingston, she lived in Britain in 1945–55, studying drama at RADA and working for the BBC West Indian section. In Jamaica she has been a radio broadcaster, newspaper columnist and drama teacher at Excelsior College and the Extra-Mural Department of the University of the West Indies. She has frequently lectured on Jamaican culture in Britain and North America. The awards she has received include the MBE and the Order of Jamaica.

She occupies a unique place in Caribbean cultural history for pioneering an interest in 'dialect' and the culture it articulates. Her richly comic Creole verse frequently adopts the persona of 'Miss Lou', a garrulous Jamaican *diseuse*, and draws on a broad range of popular forms, including folk-songs, riddles, proverbs, legends and ring-games. Classics such as 'Back to Africa' and 'Colonization in Reverse', about post-war Caribbean emigration to Britain, treat issues of cultural identity with warmth and IRONY. Her most substantial volumes are *Jamaica Labrish* (1966) and *Collected Poems* (1982). *Anancy and Miss Lou* (1979) brings together many of her popular versions of traditional stories about Anancy, the spider-trickster hero. Her work is also available on a number of record albums, including *Jamaican Folk Songs* (1954) and *Yes M'Dear* (1982).

Benson, A(rthur) C(hristopher) 1862–1925 Man of letters. The elder brother of E. F. BENSON, he was born at Wellington College, Berkshire, and educated at Eton and King's College, Cambridge. He was Master of Magdalene College, Cambridge, from 1915 until his death. His prolific writings include *The Schoolmaster* (1902), on education, and studies of ROSSETTI, FITZGERALD and PATER for the English Men of Letters series in 1904–6. He is best remembered as a poet and hymn-writer, and particularly for his words to Elgar's first 'Pomp and Circumstance' march, 'Land of Hope and Glory' (1902), originally forming part of the Coronation Ode for Edward VII.

Benson, E(dward) F(rederic) 1867–1940 Novelist and younger brother of A. C. BENSON. He was born at Wellington College, Berkshire, and educated at Marlborough and King's College, Cambridge. He wrote some 93 books, the most popular being his comic novels about Dodo (*Dodo, Dodo the Second* and *Dodo Wonder*, 1914–21) and Lucia, starting with *Queen Lucia* (1920) and *Lucia in London* (1927). Between 1911 and 1940 he also published five volumes of personal and family reminiscences.

Bentham, Jeremy 1748–1832 Philosopher. Born in London and educated at Westminster and Queen's College, Oxford, he studied law at Lincoln's Inn but never practised as a barrister. In 1776 his legal studies bore fruit in the anonymously published *A Fragment on Government: Being an Examination of What is Delivered in William Blackstone's Commentaries* in which he outlined his theory of government and a programme of future reform. The arguments were substantially expanded in the *Introduction to the Principles of Morals and Legislation* (1789), much of the editorial work being done by the Swiss scholar Étienne Dumont. After a period of travel in Russia and eastern Europe (1785–8) Bentham published a plan for prison reform, *The Panopticon: or, Inspection House* (1791). But lack of official interest in his scheme gradually dislodged Bentham's early faith in enlightened monarchic reform and stimulated him to develop the 'philosophical radicalism' known as UTILITARIANISM. This system was based on the dual ideas that all reform should be dictated by the greatest happiness of the greatest number as a measure of right and wrong, and that human motivation was founded on self-interest. The coincidence of interest and duty became an ideal of social and moral reform. Bentham's *Poor Laws and Pauper Management* (in *Annals of Agriculture*, 1797) was to provide the guiding principles for the New Poor Law of 1834 (which was so bitterly attacked by DICKENS in *OLIVER TWIST*). Among Bentham's other influential tracts are *Chrestomathia* (1816), which discussed education, *A Catechism of Parliamentary Reform* (1817), *A Radical Reform Bill, with Explanations* (1819) and *A Constitutional Code for the Use of All Nations* (1830). His *Rationale of Evidence* (1825) was edited by JOHN STUART MILL, the son of Bentham's closest Utilitarian colleague, JAMES MILL. Bentham founded *THE WESTMINSTER REVIEW* in 1824 with the latter's assistance as the organ of the Philosophical Radicals and was a guiding force behind the establishment of the University of London. His skeleton is preserved in University College, London.

Bentley, E(dmund) C(lerihew) 1875–1956 Journalist, writer of light verse and DETECTIVE FICTION. Born in London, he was educated at St Paul's School and Merton College, Oxford, becoming President of the Oxford Union in 1898. He was called to the Bar in 1902 but spent most of his working life as a journalist, first with *The Daily News* (1902–12) and then as leader writer for *The Daily Telegraph* (1912–34), returning to the paper to serve as its chief literary critic 1940–7. Bentley earned a minor place in literary history by inventing the comic verse form known as the CLERIHEW, after the middle name he used as pseudonym for his first collection, *Biography for Beginners* (1905). *Trent's Last Case* (1903), dedicated to his friend G. K. CHESTERTON and recommended for publication by JOHN BUCHAN, was intended as an exposure of detective stories but was quickly hailed as a classic of the genre. Bentley revived his artist–detective, with much less success, in *Trent's Own Case* (with H. Warner Allen, 1936) and a collection of short stories, *Trent Intervenes* (1938). *Elephant's Work: An Enigma* (1950) is a thriller. More enduring than these works is 'Greedy Night' (1939), a wickedly accurate PARODY of DOROTHY L. SAYERS.

Bentley, Phyllis 1894–1977 Novelist. The daughter of a textile manufacturer, she was born in Halifax and brought up in Huddersfield in the West Riding of Yorkshire. She completed her education at Cheltenham Ladies' College, where she passed a University of London external examination which granted her a BA. She began her largely autobio-

graphical first novel, *Environment* (1915), while teaching in north London. She subsequently worked as a librarian and a writer for *John O'London's Weekly*. *The World's Bane* (1918), a volume of four allegorical stories influenced by OLIVE SCHREINER, was followed by more novels, including *Cat-in-the-Manger* (1918), *The Spinner of the Years* (1928) and *The Partnership* (1928). Her love for the West Riding was encouraged by her friendship with WINIFRED HOLTBY and her career was helped by VERA BRITTAIN. 1932 saw the publication of her best-known novel, *Inheritance*, which chronicles the lives of Yorkshire families involved in the textile industry and draws on her mother's family recollections. Phyllis Bentley also wrote several studies of the BRONTËS.

Bentley, Richard 1662–1742 Scholar and antiquarian. Born at Oulton in Yorkshire, he entered St John's College, Cambridge, at the age of 14, and became tutor to the son of Edward Stillingfleet, Dean of St Paul's and Bishop of Worcester.

Bentley's scholarly reputation dates from 1691, when his *Epistola ad Millium* – a learned appendix on the Greek dramatists – was contributed to John Mill's edition of John Malalas, a Byzantine chronicler. In 1692 he became the first Boyle lecturer, taking as his subject 'A Confutation of Atheism', which established him as a skilful defender of orthodox Christianity. He became keeper of the Royal Library in 1694. During the years 1697–9 he was embroiled in the dispute provoked by SIR WILLIAM TEMPLE's *Essay upon the Ancient and Modern Learning*, his own contribution being to show that the epistles of Phalaris which Sir William had praised as examples of classical excellence were spurious. (See *THE BATTLE OF THE BOOKS*.)

Bentley was appointed Master of Trinity College, Cambridge, in 1700, a post he despotically enjoyed for some 40 years despite repeated controversy. As an editor Bentley was renowned for his diligent work on Horace and Manilius, but his arbitrary edition of MILTON's *PARADISE LOST* (1732) discredited him. He was caricatured by POPE in *THE DUNCIAD* as a 'mighty scholiast, whose unwearied pains/ Made Horace dull, and humbled Milton's strains'.

Bentley's Miscellany A monthly magazine issued by the publisher Richard Bentley from 1837 to 1869. It had originally been proposed that it should be called 'The Wits' Miscellany'. CHARLES DICKENS, its first editor, was succeeded in January 1839 by another novelist, WILLIAM HARRISON AINSWORTH. Contributors included FRANCIS MAHONY (Father Prout) and R. H. BARHAM, many of whose *INGOLDSBY LEGENDS* first appeared in its pages.

Beowulf The most famous and the longest surviving poem in Old English, written *c.* 1000 in the West Saxon dialect. The story probably developed orally, achieving its present form during the 8th century in Mercia or Northumberland. The poem makes no reference to Britain, but is set in southern Scandinavia during the migrations of the 5th and 6th centuries. It is an EPIC recording the great deeds of Beowulf in his youth and maturity.

Beowulf tells how the monster Grendel terrorizes the Scyldings of Hrothgar's Danish kingdom until the young Geatish warrior Beowulf eventually defeats him. When Grendel's mother comes to wreak revenge on Hrothgar's men Beowulf is summoned again and in her underwater lair kills both her and the wounded Grendel. After receiving his rewards Beowulf returns to his native Geatland and relates his story. His king, Hygelac, gives him lands which he rules for 50 years. A dragon, which had guarded its hoard in peace for 300 years, is stirred by the theft of a goblet to attack the Geats. Beowulf, now Lord of the Geats, battles with the dragon and, with the help of Wiglaf, kills it. Beowulf is fatally wounded in the fight, but Wiglaf recovers the dragon's hoard before his lord's death. The poem ends with Beowulf's funeral pyre and barrow, and a prophesy of disaster for the Geats.

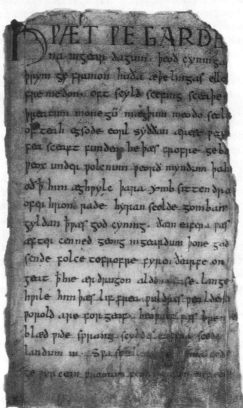

The opening lines of *Beowulf*. Line four introduces Scyld Scefing who arrived mysteriously over the sea to found the Scylding dynasty in Denmark.

The central story is linked by the names of characters in peripheral episodes to a network of other European legends and epics. Some of the names are historical (as Hygelac, d. 521) and the action is firmly attached at many points to the history of Germanic Europe. The poet sets it in the wider context of the founding of the Scylding dynasty and the Danish race and the imminent destruction of the Geats. As the genealogies of men and monsters root the poem in human and supernatural history, the sustained spatial and temporal precision creates a sense of immediacy and physical reality.

The poem's central preoccupations are with the prowess and glory of the hero Beowulf, his well-deserved fame, and with the feasting and fighting which characterize masculine feudal society, yet the many peripheral episodes introduce conflicts inside the feudal code and with outside forces. The poem incorporates the larger considerations of life and death, war and peace, society and the individual, good and evil. These, and Beowulf's supernatural acts (such as fighting under water for days), have encouraged Christian, mythic and allegorical interpretations. The progress of the action is slow, with elaboration of other episodes, inset stories and the rhetorical development of laments and speeches reducing the pace. The second half – after Beowulf's return to the Geats – is often considered inferior, but it is generally accepted that originally *Beowulf* was the work of a single poet.

Beppo: *A Venetian Story* A poem by BYRON in OTTAVA RIMA, published in 1818. It satirizes both English and Italian life, telling of the return during a carnival of a long-lost soldier, Beppo (Giuseppe). Disguised as a Turkish merchant, he finds that his wife has consoled herself with a *cavaliere servente*. The scene is set for a violent confrontation, but the dilemma is resolved over a cup of coffee. MOCK-HEROIC in manner and pervaded by gentle irony, the poem marks an important change from Byron's early work and introduces the style (and verse form) he developed and refined in DON JUAN and THE VISION OF JUDGEMENT.

Berenson, Bernard 1865–1959 American art historian. Born Bernhard Valvrojenski in Lithuania, he moved to Boston with his parents at the age of 10. With the help of CHARLES ELIOT NORTON he transferred from Boston University to Harvard. After graduating in 1888 he visited Paris, London and Oxford before settling in Italy, where he quickly established a reputation as a connoisseur, particularly of Italian Renaissance painting. His expertise in attributing and authenticating paintings brought wealthy buyers and dealers as clients. His scholarly works include *Venetian Painters of the Renaissance* (1894), *Florentine Painters of the Renaissance* (1896), *Central Italian Painters of the Renaissance* (1897), *The Study and Criticism of Italian Art* (1902) and *Drawings of the Florentine Painters* (1903). *Sketch for a Self-Portrait* (1949) is autobiographical. Berenson entertained EDITH WHARTON, HENRY ADAMS and KENNETH CLARK at his Florentine villa, I Tatti, which he bequeathed with its library and collections to Harvard.

Berger, John 1926– Novelist and art critic. Born in London, he studied at the Central and the Chelsea Schools of Art before becoming a painter and teacher of drawing. His preoccupation with the nature and possibilities of individual freedom, social, political or sexual, is expressed in several novels. *A Painter of Our Time* (1958) charts the crises and breakthrough in an artist's career, while *Corker's Freedom* (1964) depicts the hero's attempts to break free of a stultifying suburban existence. *G* (1972), a winner of the BOOKER PRIZE and his most substantial work, mixes narrative, reflection, political treatise and historical reconstruction in pursuing the fortunes of an ambiguous central figure who is variously Garibaldi, the pioneering aviator Geo Chavez and Don Giovanni. Berger's life in a farming community in the French Jura has prompted *Into Their Labours*, a spare, often elegiac trilogy combining fiction, poetry and reportage. The constituent volumes are *Pig Earth* (1979), *Once in Europa* (1989) and *Lilac and Flag* (1991). His interest in photography has led to collaborations with Jean Mohr in *A Fortunate Man* (1967) and *Another Way of Telling* (1982). His art criticism, influenced by Marxism and sometimes combative, includes *Permanent Red* (1960), *Ways of Seeing* (1972), *The White Bird* (1985) and *Keeping a Rendezvous* (1991).

Berkeley, George 1685–1753 Philosopher. The son of an English family settled in Ireland, George Berkeley was born at Dysert Castle, near Kilkenny, and attended the same school as CONGREVE and SWIFT. Like them he went on to Trinity College, Dublin, where he was ordained and where he became a junior fellow in 1707. His first published works dealt with mathematics, a subject in which he maintained an interest throughout his life; *The Analyst* (1734), written late in his career, asserted that the assumptions of mathematicians were harder to understand than Christian dogma.

But Berkeley's fame was earned as a philosopher. His first book, *An Essay towards a New Theory of Vision* (1709), advanced a psychological theory of perception based on two propositions: the objects and ideas of sight have nothing in common with the objects and ideas of touch; the connection between them comes only from experience and there is no abstract element common to both. Like LOCKE, Berkeley

hated abstractions, and he wrote in English prose that has commanded admiration ever since for its lucidity.

The first part of *The Treatise Concerning the Principles of Human Knowledge* followed in 1710. The second part, concerning morals, existed in a first draft but this was lost while Berkeley was travelling in Italy and he never found the inclination to 'do so disagreeable a thing as writing twice on the same subject'. In essence, the treatise insists that mind is the creative force: rather than being representations of reality, ideas are reality. This theory of immaterialism is based on the principle *esse est percipi* (to be is to be perceived) which holds that there is no external reality independent of man's mental perception of things. As a distinguished member of the church (he was later Dean of Derry in 1724, and then Bishop of Cloyne) Berkeley was concerned to oppose any philosophical theories that might nurture atheism or scepticism, and he therefore ranged himself against HOBBES and Locke, especially the latter's concept of the dualism of spirit and matter. His argument for belief in the existence of God is an idealistic one, resting upon the notion that Nature is a regular series of material objects that exist continuously in God's own perception, which lends them uniformity. *Three Dialogues between Hylas and Philonus* (1713) further defended the theory. BOSWELL records that, in reply to Berkeley's 'ingenious sophistry to prove the non-existence of matter', DR JOHNSON forcefully kicked a large stone and pronounced, 'I refute it thus.'

In 1713 Berkeley was in England and soon became the friend of ADDISON, POPE, SWIFT and STEELE, and contributed to the latter's *GUARDIAN*. On appointment as Dean of Derry in 1724 Berkeley launched a scheme to found a missionary college in Bermuda, described in his *Proposal for the Better Supplying of Churches in our Foreign Plantations* (1725); he sailed for America in 1728 with the promise of an essential grant from Robert Walpole. Three years went by, which Berkeley spent in Newport, Rhode Island, but the grant never materialized. He formed a Literary and Philosophical Society and wrote the popular *Alciphron: or, the Minute Philosopher* (1832), Platonic dialogues on his philosophical principles in the defence of religion. His model for a college was put to excellent use in founding King's College in New York City; it later became Columbia University. After returning to England Berkeley published his *Theory of Vision: or, Visual Language Vindicated and Explained* (1733).

In 1734 Berkeley was given the bishopric of Cloyne, a remote diocese in the county of Cork in Ireland, where he remained until 1752, his mind occupied with questions of social reform and religious speculation. *The Querist* (1735) shows the reformer asking penetrating questions about the matter of Ireland. *Siris: A Chain of Philosophical Reflexions* (1744) examines both physical and metaphysical questions chiefly concerning the virtues of tar-water. Berkeley retired to Oxford, where he died. His notes, *The Commonplace Book*, were first published in 1871.

Berkoff, Steve(n) 1937– Playwright, actor and director. Born in London, he first became known with the formation of the London Theatre Group in 1968. Its tightly choreographed productions of well-known texts, adapted by Berkoff and often with Berkoff himself in the leading role, have featured in the programme of major alternative theatres from the Roundhouse to the Mickery in Amsterdam. They include works by Kafka (*The Penal Colony*, 1968; *Metamorphosis*, 1969; and *The Trial*, 1970), SHAKESPEARE, Aeschylus and EDGAR ALLAN POE, whose *Fall of the House of Usher* (1974) transferred to the ROYAL NATIONAL THEATRE. As a guest director he has staged *CORIOLANUS* (1989) at New York's Public Theatre and WILDE'S *SALOME* (1989) at the Gate Theatre in Dublin, a production which did much to rescue the play from nearly a century of neglect. His own plays, which often use mannered PARODY of other styles, include: *East* (1975), about his East End boyhood, written in a BLANK VERSE which simultaneously echoes Shakespeare and the football terraces; *Greek* (1979); *Decadence* (1981), in which he writhed in the coils of upper-class vowel sounds; *Kvetch* (1987); and *Acapulco* (1992).

Berners, 2nd Baron See BOURCHIER, JOHN.

Berners, Juliana See *THE BOOK OF ST ALBANS*.

Berrigan, Ted (Edmund Joseph Michael, Jr) 1934–83 American poet. Born in Providence, Rhode Island, and educated at the University of Tulsa, he moved in 1960 to New York, where he came under the influence of JOHN ASHBERY and other poets of the NEW YORK SCHOOL. He first attracted attention with *The Sonnets* (1964) and *Bean Spasms* (with Ron Padgett; 1967), which use a technique resembling collage in the way it cuts and rearranges lines of verse. *Many Happy Returns* (1967) contains one of his best-known experimental poems, 'Tambourine Life'. *So Going around Cities* (1980) gathers old and new work.

Berry, James 1924– Poet. Born in Jamaica, he was among the first immigrants to arrive in Britain after World War II. He has lived in England since 1948 and has become a cultural leader in the black community. His collections of poetry include *Fractured Circles* (1979), *Lucy's Letters and Loving* (1982; an enlarged version of *Lucy's Letter*, 1975), *Chain of Days* (1985), *When I Dance* (1988) and *Future-Telling Lady* (1991). He is also a prolific editor of poetry, his anthologies including *News for Babylon* (1984), a selection of West Indian–British poetry. His poem 'Fantasy of an African Boy' won the National Poetry Competition in

Britain in 1981. Berry is often humorous, particularly in his ability to capture Caribbean speech, but there is also a plangent aspect to some of his poems. He is regarded as the doyen, and possibly as the best, of the black poets who made a significant mark on British culture in the 1980s. *A Thief in the Village* (1987) is a collection of short stories.

Berryman, John 1914–72 American poet. Born in McAlester, Oklahoma, he was educated at Columbia University and at Clare College, Cambridge. He taught at Princeton, Harvard, the University of Cincinnati and, from 1955 until his death, at the University of Minnesota. His poems appeared in small magazines and reviews during the 1930s, and then in 1940 his work was published in *Five American Poets*. His first collected volume was *Poems* (1942), followed in 1948 by *The Dispossessed*. Widespread recognition came with *Homage to Mistress Bradstreet* (1956), and in 1965 he was awarded the PULITZER PRIZE for *77 Dream Songs* (1964). The poems in the latter volume became the first section of a sequence, THE DREAM SONGS, continued in *His Toy, His Dream, His Rest* (1968) and published in its entirety in 1969. *Delusions* (1972), published after his suicide, shows him looking toward the end of his life, also the subject of his novel, *Recovery* (1973). *The Freedom of the Poet*, a collection of his essays on poets and poetry, appeared in 1976. He also wrote a notable biography of STEPHEN CRANE (1950; revised and reissued, 1962).

Bertrams, The A novel by ANTHONY TROLLOPE, published in 1859.

After a brilliant undergraduate career, George Bertram takes time off to visit the Holy Land. There he meets and falls in love with Caroline Waddington, the granddaughter of his wealthy City uncle, also called George Bertram. They plan to marry but she insists that he establish himself financially first, encouraging him in a legal career despite his own inclination to the church. Their engagement drags on for three years until it is broken by mutual consent, and soon after Caroline marries Sir Henry Harcourt, the Solicitor-General and an ambitious politician. Harcourt is disappointed when he fails to gain access to Caroline's grandfather's fortune to support his extravagant way of life, and he becomes jealous of George Bertram, eventually committing suicide after Caroline leaves him and he loses his political position. In due course Caroline and George are reconciled and marry. Secondary plots deal with George's father Sir Lionel, a plausible but irresponsible diplomat, and his attempts to marry a wealthy spinster, and with the love-affair between George's friend Arthur Wilkinson and Adela Gauntlet.

Although Trollope considered the plot of *The Bertrams* 'more than ordinarily bad', the novel is redeemed by his unconventional handling of the hero and heroine as disenchantment overtakes their initial high hopes.

Besant, Sir **Walter** 1836–1901 Novelist and historian. He was born at Portsmouth and educated at Christ's College, Cambridge. His early novels, of which *Ready Money Mortiboy* (1872) and *The Golden Butterfly* (1876) were the most popular, were collaborations with James Rice. His own later historical fiction was less widely read than two realistic works, *All Sorts and Conditions of Men* (1882) and *Children of Gibeon* (1886), which exposed conditions in the East End of London. Sincere and tireless in his philanthropic interests, he helped found the 'People's Palace' in the Mile End Road and was knighted in 1895. A founder in 1884 of the Society of Authors, he campaigned to secure better legal protection for literary works, exposed the fraudulent practices of disreputable publishers and wrote and argued constantly for an agreed system of international copyright. Besant's Royal Institution lecture of 1884 on the status of the novel provoked HENRY JAMES's famous reply, 'The Art of Fiction'. An authority on Rabelais and Montaigne and on the exploration of Palestine, Besant planned and inaugurated a great 10-volume topographical survey of London, which appeared under other editors after his death (1902–12).

Best, George d. ?1584 Navigator. He accompanied Martin Frobisher in his three attempts to find the Northwest Passage in 1576, 1577 and 1578. His account, *A True Discourse of the Late Voyages of Discovery* (1578), was dedicated to Sir Christopher Hatton and was later included in the collection of RICHARD HAKLUYT.

Bestall, Alfred (Edmeades) 1892–1986 Writer and illustrator of CHILDREN'S LITERATURE. Born in India and educated at Birmingham Central School of Art, he contributed cartoons to *PUNCH* and other leading periodicals. In 1935 he took over the *Rupert Bear* comic strip from MARY TOURTEL, who had been producing it since 1920. The popularity of the series stayed high, and by the time he retired in 1965 over 34 million *Rupert Bear* annuals had been sold.

Bestiary, The A poem of the late 12th or early 13th century, the only surviving English example of a form widespread throughout medieval Europe, represented by many Latin and French works. Probably dating back to the 4th century but influenced more directly by the 7th-century *Etymologiae* of Isidore of Seville and the 11th-century *Physiologus* of Thetbaldus, bestiaries studied the natural world as a means of understanding God. The animals and animal behaviour they described are sometimes real and sometimes fictitious. It was believed, for example, that the elephant had no knees and slept leaning

against a tree; to kill or capture it, the hunter had only to fell the tree and the animal would fall over. Its fate was an allegory of fallen mankind's dependence on the supportive power of Christ. Fictitious beasts included the unicorn, phoenix and cockatrice, but also the bizarre manticora with scorpion's tail, lion's body, man's head, gleaming red eyes, triple row of teeth and taste for human flesh. Such accounts are not always pure invention. Many of the non-existent animals bear some resemblance to real ones and may be based on distorted reports, like the fantastic characteristics attributed to real animals. The belief that an animal's nature could be derived etymologically from its name was a frequent source of misunderstanding: barnacle geese were supposed to hatch from barnacles, and the crocodile was saffron- (crocus-) coloured.

Bethell, Ursula 1874–1945 New Zealand poet. Born in England, she spent most of her life in a family of farmers in the South Island. In the 1930s she established a 'house of Christian learning', a community of women of the Church of England, in Christchurch. In some degree it reflected her own search for a community of like-minded spirits; in that regard, it was not a success. Known as the poet of the Cashmere Hills, near Christchurch, she produced domestic, unassertive, openly meditative verse. Her first book of New Zealand poetry, published in London in 1929 under the pseudonym 'Evelyn Hayes', was *From a Garden in the Antipodes*. The recipient of these poems was an English friend, and the shape this epistolary format gave the poems in the volume, as well as the acknowledgement of foreignness and distance, created a delicate balance of inward- and outward-looking meditation. This book and two later volumes, published by the Caxton Press in Christchurch, contain her best work. Her *Collected Poems* appeared posthumously in New Zealand in 1950, also from Caxton.

Betjeman, Sir **John** 1906–84 Poet, critic of architecture, journalist and broadcaster. He was born in Highgate and educated at Marlborough and Magdalen College, Oxford, where he came into contact with the group of young poets led by W. H. AUDEN without being influenced by their political and artistic stance. He became a schoolmaster and, during World War II, United Kingdom press attaché in Dublin before earning his living as a writer, journalist and broadcaster.

Betjeman's first volume of verse, *Mount Zion* (1931), was followed by *Continual Dew* (1937), *Old Lights for New Chancels* (1940), *New Bats in Old Belfries* (1945), *A Few Late Chrysanthemums* (1954), *Poems in the Porch* (1954), the autobiographical *Summoned by Bells* (1960), *High and Low* (1966), *A Nip in the Air* (1974) and *Church Poems* (1981), among others. His immensely popular *Collected Poems*

(1958; revised 1962), edited by the Earl of Birkenhead, was reprinted many times and sold close to a million copies. He succeeded CECIL DAY-LEWIS as POET LAUREATE in 1972.

Particularly after his success as a broadcasting personality, Betjeman's very popularity often stood in the way of serious recognition, though this came from fellow poets like Auden and LARKIN. Technically conservative and deceptively simple in its reliance on regular rhythms and well-worn rhymes, his poetry creates a wry comedy of middle-class life and aspirations that is shot through with sadness. His sense of the smallness and superficiality of contemporary life, his melancholy Christianity and, above all, the abiding sustenance he took from English landscape and English architecture found a voice, too, in his large output of prose from *Ghastly Good Taste* (1933) onwards. His architectural writings were notable for their unfashionable advocacy of Victorian buildings, often in danger of obliteration, and their discerning eye for churches, perhaps best displayed in the introduction to *Collins Guide to English Parish Churches* (1958). *The Best of Betjeman* (edited by John Guest; 1989), an edition of *Summoned by Bells* illustrated by Sir Hugh Casson (1989) and *Betjeman's Oxford* (1990) are evidence of continuing interest in his writings.

Betrothed, The See SCOTT, SIR WALTER.

Between the Acts VIRGINIA WOOLF's last novel, published posthumously in 1941.

Pointz Hall, an English country house owned by the ageing Bartholomew Oliver and his widowed sister, Lucy Swithin, is also home to their nephew, Giles Oliver, a stockbroker, and his wife, Isa, whose poetic inner thoughts are rendered in STREAM OF CONSCIOUS-NESS and correspond to the metaphorical impulse which underlies the main action. This centres on the performance of a village pageant during a June afternoon in 1939 in the grounds of Pointz Hall. It is directed by Miss La Trobe, a lesbian artist whose creative aspirations are continually thwarted by reality. The pageant itself occupies the bulk of the novel, a fragmentary re-enactment of English history by means of songs and tableaux. Naively comic aspects are offset by an underlying nostalgia as a communal image of rural England is interwoven with the spectators' varying interpretations.

The author's intention seems to be to celebrate the lasting values in English country life ('We act different parts; but are the same') and to indict the contemporary age for its shallow pretensions. The imminent threat of annihilation in World War II is a recurrent background theme.

When the pageant reaches its climax in the present day (June 1939) the audience is confronted by mirrors and asked how 'orts, scraps and fragments like our-

selves' can build the great wall of civilization. A gramophone runs down ambiguously ('*Unity – Dispersity*. It gurgled *Un... dis...* And ceased') but the novel closes on a note of qualified optimism: 'Before they slept, they must fight; after they had fought, they would embrace. From that embrace another life might be born.'

Bevis of Hampton [*Beves of Hamtoun*] A VERSE ROMANCE in TAIL-RHYME stanzas and octosyllabic couplets, probably written in Southampton *c.* 1300. The story exists in several European languages; the source of the Middle English romance is an Anglo-Norman version.

Bevis's father is murdered by his mother's lover and he is taken by pirates and sold as a slave to the Saracen King of Armenia. He gains favour at court and the King's daughter Josian falls in love with him and renounces her faith. Her father objects and contrives to have Bevis imprisoned; Josian is forcibly married but manages to preserve her virginity. After seven years Bevis escapes from prison, rescues her and subdues a giant, Ascopart, who becomes their ally. Bevis goes to England to aid the faithful steward against his father's murderer, now the new Earl of Southampton, but has to return when Josian is condemned to burn for murdering a knight who forced her to marry him. Bevis succeeds in defeating his stepfather and mother, marries Josian and becomes Earl of Southampton, but he is forced to flee again when his horse kills King Edgar's son. In his absence Josian gives birth to twins and is abducted by Ascopart. After many years the family is reunited. Despite being needlessly long and packed with spurious incident, the romance is enlivened by touches of humour and the characters of its hero and heroine are sympathetically drawn.

Bewick, Thomas 1753–1828 Engraver. The son of a small farmer, Bewick was born and educated at Ovingham, Northumberland, and was apprenticed to Thomas Beilby (1744–1817), a Newcastle engraver whose partner he later became. He is credited with having revived wood engraving, a neglected art when he began his career. His first cuts for GAY's *Fables* were completed before the end of his apprenticeship and gained a prize from the Society of Arts. They were published in 1779, and followed by the *Select Fables* of 1784. Although his early work is based on previous illustrators, he invariably improved on their technique, and swiftly developed into an artist of remarkable facility as an interpreter of animal life, and a humorist in the tradition of HOGARTH. His most original and characteristic work is to be found in the lovingly executed wild-life illustrations and vignettes of country life in *A General History of Quadrupeds* (1790), and *A History of British Birds* (2 vols., 1797, 1804). He also cut blocks for poems by GOLDSMITH and PARNELL (1795), THOMSON's *THE SEASONS* (1805) and Aesop's fables (1818). His admirers included WORDSWORTH, CARLYLE, RUSKIN and the ornithologist AUDUBON, who visited him in his workshop in 1827. Apart from a brief period in London in his youth, Bewick spent his life in Newcastle. His *Memoir* (1862) contains absorbing descriptions of his Northumberland childhood and the development of the techniques of his craft.

Bhattacharya, Bhabani 1906–88 Indian novelist. Born in Bhagalpur, he studied in Patna and London before travelling widely as journalist and lecturer. The Bengal famine of 1942–3 shocked him into writing his first, uncompromisingly realistic novel, *So Many Hungers* (1947), about 3 million deaths making 'thirty new millionaires'. His fiction confronts many Indian social problems, always with compassion for the victims of injustice: the young wife in an arranged marriage in *Music for Mohini* (1952), villagers resisting greedy businessmen in *A Goddess Named Gold* (1960). This compassion blends with social satire in *He Who Rides a Tiger* (1954), about caste and wealth, and, less convincingly, within a broadly political dimension, in *Shadow from Ladakh* (1967). In *A Dream in Hawaii* (1978) a holy man paradoxically retains his integrity within American-style commercialized religion. *Steel Hawk* (1968) is a volume of short stories. Bhattacharya also published non-fiction and translated RABINDRANATH TAGORE.

Bible in English, The The task of translating the Bible into English has been in hand in almost every decade since the 1520s. Then, it was a dangerous thing to do. Now, many modern English versions compete for a publishing market.

Before the Reformation, for over 1000 years, the Bible existed primarily in Latin, descended from Jerome's 4th-century versions, known as the Vulgate. Parts were paraphrased or translated, sometimes with some brilliance, into Anglo-Saxon (by AELFRIC, for example) and Middle English; in the late 14th century JOHN WYCLIF and his LOLLARD followers translated the entire Vulgate into English for the first time. The Lollard Bibles (*c.* 1376–96) were in two versions, hand-written and prohibitive in cost, yet with a pastoral aim not far from the spirit of the Protestant Reformation, and, in particular, the work of WILLIAM TYNDALE. His urgent need to enable 'the boy that driveth the plough' to know Scripture impelled him to give his life to the work, in two senses. His translations of the New Testament, between 1525 and 1534, were from the original Greek (of which a good text had just been established by ERASMUS), and his translations of the Old Testament books of the Pentateuch (1530 and 1534), Jonah (1531) and Judges to 2 Chronicles were from the Hebrew. This work set a norm.

It is remarkable that the very first printed translations into English remain in many ways the best, even though the language was then considered hardly worthy enough and scholarship has since provided better original texts. Tyndale was a good scholar of Greek and Hebrew at a time when to be so was rare. His sense of how those languages might go into English produced phrases often so clear and arresting that all but the most bizarre of later attempts, even down to our own day, stand in some relation to his work. This is often imperceptibly familiar, because later translations took it over. Yet there have been enough later changes to make his translations still have extraordinary freshness. His serpent says to Eve not 'Ye shall not surely die' as in the Authorized Version (Genesis 3.4) but 'Tush ye shall not die'; of Joseph in Egypt Tyndale says not, as in the Authorized Version, 'and the Lord was with Joseph and he was a prosperous man' (Genesis 39.2) but 'the Lord was with Joseph and he was a luckie felawe'. The sixth chapter of Matthew, part of the Sermon on the Mount, does not end with the Authorized Version's remote and Latinate 'Sufficient unto the day is the evil thereof', but with 'For each day hath enough of his owne trouble.'

Only one copy of Tyndale's first complete New Testament of 1526 survives, so ruthless were the authorities; readers in England were persecuted, and there was a public burning of books at St Paul's Cross in London. Tyndale worked in permanent exile, often in hiding and even on the run. His enemies caught him in May 1535 and blocked attempts to release him: he was strangled and burned at the stake at Vilvorde, near Brussels, in October 1536. His dying words were, 'Lord, open the King of England's eyes.'

His fellow worker MILES COVERDALE, whose Englishing of the Psalms is cherished to this day in the BOOK OF COMMON PRAYER, used Tyndale's work, some then unpublished, to produce a complete Bible – the first to be printed in English – at Cologne in 1535. A year later Henry VIII gave royal licence for an English Bible. Known as Matthew's Bible, it was said to have been edited by John Rogers, but these names were devices to conceal the work of Tyndale – the elaborate initials 'W. T.' at the end of Malachi, and thus between the Testaments, perhaps covertly indicate this. A revised version by Richard Taverner followed in 1539. Later in the same year the first Great Bible, the only 'official' Bible in English, was ordered to be set up in churches. It was prepared by Coverdale as another revision of Matthew's Bible (and thus again of Tyndale) and carried a prologue by the Archbishop of Canterbury, THOMAS CRANMER.

Two decades later the most international of all English Bibles appeared, a remarkable result of humanist and Reformation scholarship. English Protestants escaping from Mary had arrived in Geneva, which was then a powerhouse of textual research and translation into European vernaculars, of secular classics as well as Scripture. The English exiles, including Coverdale, worked on a new translation into English which they were able to present to Queen Elizabeth soon after her accession, in 1560. This, the Geneva Bible, had indexes, copious explanatory notes on every page, maps and elucidatory pictures, in a tradition going back to Tyndale – illumination, as a preface frankly said, 'of all the hard places'. It was a Bible for readers at all levels, and for nearly a century it was the Bible of the English people, influencing SHAKESPEARE, MILTON and many others. It set a new standard in Greek and Hebrew scholarship. In 1576 the New Testament was revised, with only slight changes to the text but complete reworking of the notes, now full and often surprisingly engaging, by Laurence Tomson of Magdalen College, Oxford. In 1599 the Book of Revelation was given vast new notes by the European theologian 'Junius'. In the hundred years of its life, the Geneva Bible came in many forms, large and small, black-letter and Roman, but – especially when it had Tomson's New Testament – it was encyclopaedic. A whole world of learning, often including concordances, the Book of Common Prayer, Sternhold and Hopkins's metrical psalms (see PSALTERS) and changing but usually impressive preliminary matter, it made a *locus* of Reformation and Renaissance scholarship. Even the two Roman Catholic, Vulgate-based retorts to Geneva – a New Testament from Rheims in 1582 and an Old Testament from Douai in 1609 – make use of it, for all their huffing against Protestants. Yet the Geneva Bible has been quite forgotten. Worse, it was replaced for political reasons, being dismissed as bitterly Calvinistic, which it is not. Worst of all, it has been shrivelled to a vulgar nickname and called the Breeches Bible because in Genesis 2.7 it says (as did the Lollard Bibles, incidentally) that Adam and Eve 'made themselves breeches'.

The Bishops' Bible, an attempt led by Archbishop MATTHEW PARKER to rival Geneva with a more Latinate, Vulgate-based translation, with few notes, appeared in 1568 but did not establish itself. JAMES I, however, decided that he found the Geneva Bible objectionable, and at the Hampton Court Conference of 1604 he initiated a new translation. A panel of 54 scholars was appointed, divided into six groups. LANCELOT ANDREWES was head of one of the groups at Westminster. The Authorized Version (so called, although it was never authorized) or King James Bible appeared in 1611, incidentally to broadside attacks on its accuracy. It carried an obsequious dedication to James which contrasts unhealthily with the urgent religious concern of the dedication of the Geneva Bible to Elizabeth. This translation was in fact largely a revision heavily dependent on the scholarship of the Geneva Bible and the phrasing of Tyndale but taking from the Bishops' Bible and Rheims New Testament a more lofty, Latinate orotundity. The translators' declared aim, 'to make a good one better', was often doubtfully achieved. The Authorized Version certainly contains many famous beauties, such as 'And the glory of the Lord shall be revealed, and all flesh shall see it together: for the mouth of the Lord hath spoken it' (Isaiah 40.5), or Jesus's 'Father, forgive them, for they know not what they do' (Luke 23.34) or 'In my Father's house are many mansions' (John 14.2). But that phrase from Isaiah comes from the Geneva Bible, and the two New Testament phrases come from Tyndale. The much-loved Christmas stories in Matthew 2 and Luke 3 are virtually unchanged from Tyndale and Geneva. Where the Authorized Version differs, whether or not from the Bishops' Bible, it can in fact be very unlovely: 'Nevertheless the dimness shall not be such as was in her vexation' (Isaiah 9.1); 'The treacherous dealers have dealt treacherously; yea, the treacherous dealers have dealt very treacherously' (Isaiah 24.16); 'We do you to wit' (2 Corinthians 8.1); 'I long after you all in the bowels of Jesus Christ' (Philippians 1.8). Though King James had set his translators specifically to avoid marginal notes, the Authorized Version was later printed eight times with Geneva's notes.

The Authorized Version gradually ousted the Geneva Bible. Its overwhelming impact on English literature since its first appearance, though commonly asserted, is in fact quite hard to substantiate. Certainly a reader who does not know an earlier Bible in English will miss much of the meaning of religious writing like the poems of GEORGE HERBERT or the poetry and much of the prose of HENRY VAUGHAN, or of a satire like DRYDEN's *ABSALOM AND ACHITOPHEL*. In spite of what is sometimes said, BUNYAN's English comes from common speech rather than the Authorized Version. SWIFT, however, in *A Proposal for Correcting the English Tongue* (1712), wrote that 'the translators of the Bible were masters of an English stile much fitter for the work, than we see in any of our present writings' and praised 'the simplicity of the whole'; COLERIDGE believed that 'without this holdfast, our vitiated imaginations would refine away language to mere abstractions'. By the time of its first official revision in the Revised Version of 1881–5, the Authorized Version had become a hallowed classic of English literature, and the revisers could state, wrongly, that it had been revered from its first appearance.

Between the Authorized Version of 1611 and the Revised Version of 1881–5 there were some 150 published translations of all or part of the Bible, some admirable and some odd. Some, like Dr Challoner's revisions of Douai and Rheims, were influential in their time. Between the 1880s and 1939 at least seven 'one-man' translations of the whole Bible into English were printed. Two dozen 'one-man' New Testaments have appeared in the last hundred years, not to mention a host of parts of the Bible. In the last 25 years, for example, over 150 translations of sections of the Bible into English have been published. Modern printing techniques can conceal the sheer size of the undertaking, to say nothing of the necessity of professional expertise in textual scholarship and so many different kinds of Hebrew and Greek. In this century, the modern translations by Moffatt, by Weymouth, by Ferrar Fenton, by Goodspeed, by Knox and by Barclay have been influential and are still well regarded. Just after World War II, the English editions of the (American) Revised Standard Version were widely used; the translations of Paul's letters by J. B. Phillips alerted a generation to the fact that Paul did not write in an archaic code, but made vivid modern sense (as did his original Greek). As the Bible in local vernaculars spreads now across the world – the Bible, or part of it, is to date in over 1700 languages – so more is learned about how the special revelations of the Old and New Testaments might best come across to late 20th-century English-reading people. There are now many different versions of the Bible in English in print, including several attempts to modernize the Authorized Version. Those with greatest impact have been: The New English Bible (1970), which is lucid but sometimes disliked; The Living Bible (1971), a paraphrase; Today's English Version (1976), popularly known by its American title, the Good News Bible, which combines accuracy with a relaxed readability that is a long way from the Authorized Version; The Jerusalem Bible (1966), an often ponderous antidote to raciness; and the rather patchwork New International Version (1979). New Testament scholars often use the excellent Translator's New Testament (1973), which hits the theological nail on the head every time; it is designed to help those who translate the New Testament into remoter languages.

More Bibles in English are now sold than ever before. The number of English readers has risen from six million under Elizabeth I to 600 million now. Whether the proportion of Bible students has changed is arguable. It is debatable whether it matters that now so many people do not know that 'the scales fell from his eyes', for example, comes from Acts 9.18 (Tyndale, via the Authorized Version). It is an emotive question whether men and women who lack Greek should have the clear access to the doctrines of the Epistle to the Romans that they can find in very modern translations, rather than a reverential knowledge of the Authorized Version. Certainly the Bible in English has had an effect on our literature that is beyond fathoming. Many hundreds of fine phrases have passed into the language, to form a body of allusions of lapidary beauty unmatched by anything from any other source. In the study of English literature, not to know them is to be deprived of a rich store, as a student is deprived who does not know Virgil. But the greatest impact of the Bible in English has always been from the message and its accessibility. Shakespeare used Bible cadences, of course – from the Geneva and Bishops' Bibles. Deep in him, however, were the roots of the Bible doctrines. This is something of far greater significance than a sentimental regret for the passing of the Authorized Version – with which Shakespeare, in any case, had no connection.

Bible in Spain, The GEORGE BORROW's colourful narrative of his travels through Portugal and Spain, published in 1843. Ostensibly an account of his five years' service (1835–40) as an agent of the British and Foreign Bible Society, committed to distributing a Protestant New Testament in a Catholic country where it was not wanted, the book describes adventures in remote regions, encounters with gypsies and bandits and frequent confrontations with authority. The inherent absurdity, indeed illegality, of the enterprise added spice to stories often told with great vivacity and directness, the reader having no means of distinguishing between fact and fiction. Based partly on his Spanish notebooks, and partly on the set of remarkable reports he had sent his employers from Spain, it was accepted as authentic both by JOHN MURRAY, a publisher ill-disposed to fiction, and by an Evangelical reading public that most enjoyed sensational adventures when they could be thought to have happened in reality. The book was a best-seller on both sides of the Atlantic and was never out of print during the 19th century.

Bickerstaff, Isaac A character invented by SWIFT, and supposedly the author of *Predictions for the Ensuing Year* (1708), a collection of spoof prophecies at the expense of John Partridge, a cobbler turned astrologer, currently fashionable for his almanac. In Swift's version, Partridge's death is foretold for 29 March and, despite the hapless quack's protestations to the contrary, Bickerstaff successfully 'proved' that his prediction had been fulfilled. STEELE adopted the nickname of Bickerstaff when he started *THE TATLER* in 1709.

Bickerstaffe, Isaac 1733–c. 1808 Playwright. He was largely responsible for the emergence and fashionable acceptance of English comic opera. His early successes, *Thomas and Sally* (1760) and the excellent *Love in a Village* (1762), had accompanying music by Thomas Arne. *The Maid of the Mill* (1765) and *The Royal Garland* (1768) were provided with music, in part and in whole respectively, by Samuel Arnold. Bickerstaffe's other music dramas were written chiefly in collaboration with CHARLES DIBDIN. The best of these is *Lionel and Clarissa* (1768). Two serenatas, written by Bickerstaffe and Dibdin for performance at Ranelagh House, *The Ephesian Matron* (1769) and *The Recruiting Serjeant* (1770), promised new developments in the collaboration, but Bickerstaffe's career was brought to a sudden end in 1772, when he was threatened with arrest as a homosexual. He fled to the Continent, where he lived in obscurity for a further 40 years.

Bidart, Frank 1939– American poet. Born in Bakersfield, California, he was educated at the University of California at Riverside and at Harvard, where he studied writing with ROBERT LOWELL. Notable for its attempt to dramatize ordinary speech, his work often uses the DRAMATIC MONOLOGUE in the tradition of ROBERT BROWNING and ROBERT FROST. His volumes are *Golden State* (1973), *The Book of the Body* (1977), *The Sacrifice* (1983) and *In the Western Night: Collected Poems, 1965–1990* (1990). Now at Wellesley College, he has also taught at Brandeis and Berkeley.

Bierce, Ambrose (Gwinnett) 1842–c. 1914 American journalist and short-story writer. Born in Horse Cave Creek, Ohio, he fought in the Civil War, and reached the rank of major, but saw his part as a soldier as little more than that of a paid assassin. This bitterness (his nickname was 'Bitter Bierce') later informed his Civil War stories – stories of defeat and disillusionment. When the war ended Bierce went to California and eventually became a journalist, contributing to the celebrated *OVERLAND MONTHLY*, which BRET HARTE had helped to establish. Later he published his own newsletter, and with Harte, MARK TWAIN and JOAQUIN MILLER constituted a Western literary circle. With the departure of Twain and Harte for the East, his position as chief arbiter of the Western literary establishment (and later, chief short-story writer) was unchallenged.

He went to England in 1872, where he lived and wrote until 1876. Although he was a busy contributor to periodicals, his success did not match that of his San Francisco period, and he returned there to write for William Randolph Hearst's *Examiner*. In 1891 he published *Tales of Soldiers and Civilians* (entitled *IN THE MIDST OF LIFE* in England and in the 1898 US edition), and *Can Such Things Be?* in 1893. He moved to Washington in 1897 as the capital correspondent for the Hearst papers. He contributed to *Cosmopolitan* and in 1906 published *The Cynic's Word Book*, a volume of ironic definitions. He also published verse and essays. Estranged from all family connections and discontented with life in America, Bierce disappeared in Mexico during its Civil War. It is not known exactly when or how he died.

Big Money, The See *USA*.

Bigg, John Stanyon 1828–65 Journalist and poet of the SPASMODIC SCHOOL OF POETRY. Born at Ulverston in the Lake District, he became editor of its local paper in 1848. In the same year he published his first work,

The Sea King, a metrical romance in six CANTOS. He later worked as a journalist in Ulster but returned to his home town in 1860. His other writings include *Night and Soul* (1854), the novel *Alfred Staunton* (1860) and a final volume of poetry, *Shifting Scenes and Other Poems* (1862).

Biglow Papers, The Two series of popular satirical verses by JAMES RUSSELL LOWELL, written in Yankee dialect. The first series (1848) opposes the Mexican War, and the second (1867) attacks the policy of the Confederate states in the Civil War.

Bildungsroman A 'novel of development', tracing the protagonist's growth, usually from birth or early childhood, into adulthood and maturity. The prototype is Goethe's *Wilhelm Meister's Apprenticeship* (1795–6), translated into English by THOMAS CARLYLE in 1824. Even an incomplete list of major examples suggests how important a part the form has played in English fiction since then: DICKENS's *DAVID COPPERFIELD* and *GREAT EXPECTATIONS*, SAMUEL BUTLER's *THE WAY OF ALL FLESH*, D. H. LAWRENCE's *SONS AND LOVERS*, JOYCE's *PORTRAIT OF THE ARTIST AS A YOUNG MAN* and E. M. FORSTER's *THE LONGEST JOURNEY*.

Billings, Josh [Shaw, Henry Wheeler] 1818–85 American comic writer. Born in Lanesboro, Massachusetts, he began his career as a humorist with contributions to local newspapers, like PETROLEUM V. NASBY, MARK TWAIN and ARTEMUS WARD, who helped him publish his first collection, *Josh Billings: Hiz Sayings* (1865). Thereafter he became a favourite exponent of agrarian folk wisdom and reached an immense public with his comments on government, fashionable pretension and political corruption. His publications include *Josh Billings on Ice, and Other Things* (1868), *Everybody's Friend* (1874), *Josh Billings' Trump Kards* (1877) and *Josh Billings' Spice Box* (1881). From 1869 to 1880 he published a PARODY annual called *Farmer's Allminax*. In the tradition of the vernacular humorists of his day, he lectured widely in his Josh Billings persona and commanded a large popular audience.

Billy Budd, Sailor A short novel by HERMAN MELVILLE, begun in 1886 and left in a semi-final draft at his death in 1891. It was first published in 1924.

The story is set aboard HMS *Bellipotent* in 1797, a tense period following mutinies in the navy during the war between England and France. Billy Budd, the 'Handsome Sailor' of sailors' folklore, is impressed from a merchantman, the *Rights-of-Man*. He quickly adjusts to life aboard a man-of-war and is a favourite of the crew, but he becomes the target of the envious and brutal master-at-arms, John Claggart. Claggart concocts a plot of a supposed mutiny and accuses Billy of being involved in it before the ship's commander, Captain Vere. The innocent Billy, unable to answer the charge because of a chronic stammer, strikes Claggart on the forehead and kills him. Vere, though recognizing the falsity of Claggart's story and sympathizing with the agonized Billy, fears reaction among the crew if Billy is not punished for assaulting a superior. He calls a drumhead court and in effect instructs it to find Billy guilty of a capital crime. The court, though troubled by the ambiguities of the case and by Vere's precipitate action, condemns Billy, who is hanged from the yardarm after crying out, 'God bless Captain Vere!' Some time later Vere is killed during an engagement with the French; his last murmured words are Billy's name.

Bingham, Joseph 1668–1723 Church historian. Born at Wakefield in Yorkshire, he attended Wakefield Grammar School, and completed his education at University College, Oxford, where he became a fellow in 1689. In literature he is remembered for his exhaustive *Origines Ecclesiasticae: or, The Antiquities of the Christian Church*, a 20-year labour (10 vols., 1708–22).

Binyon, (Robert) Laurence 1869–1943 Poet, playwright and art historian. He was born in Lancaster and educated at Trinity College, Oxford. He worked at the British Museum in 1893–1933, first in the Department of Printed Books and later as Keeper of the Department of Oriental Prints and Books. His poetry includes *Lyric Poems* (1894), *Winnowing Fan: Poems of the Great War* (1914), *The Anvil* 1916), *The Cause* (1917), *The New World* (1918) and *The Burning of the Leaves and Other Poems* (1944), as well as two collections of ODES, *The Sirens* (1924) and *The Idols* (1928). His subjects are often classical and his themes frequently mutability and decay, as in his famous ELEGY for the dead of World War I, 'For the Fallen': 'They shall not grow old, as we that are left grow old.' In addition to works of art history, he also wrote several verse dramas, including *Arthur* (1923) with music by Elgar, *Brief Candles* (1938) and the unfinished *Madness of Merlin* (1947). His translation of Dante's *Divine Comedy* appeared in 1933–43.

Biographia Literaria A philosophical and autobiographical work by SAMUEL TAYLOR COLERIDGE, published in 1817. Originally conceived in 1814 as a brief critical preface to *Sibylline Leaves*, it rapidly grew into a two-volume *causerie* on his 'literary life and opinions'. Unsystematic, inexhaustibly communicative, and untied to a single literary register, it is entirely lacking in the aesthetic and recapitulatory 'finish' of conventional autobiography. Whether his subject matter is his youthful admiration for the SONNETS of WILLIAM BOWLES, his early friendship with and domestic proximity to WORDSWORTH, or the 'associa-

tionist' tradition in philosophy from Aristotle to HARTLEY and the challenge to it issuing from Kant and his German Romantic successors, Coleridge invariably begins, and not infrequently ends, in *medias res*. Important theoretical matters are forced to queue behind passages of advice to would-be writers and the detailed enumeration of the practical difficulties of publishing and editing journals. As in the lectures and *Table Talk*, his method is excitingly oblique and inspirational, the moment of insight sudden and often wonderfully incandescent.

The underlying philosophical concern of the *Biographia* is the process, as opposed to the fact, of human creativity. The predominantly empirical English tradition of literary and philosophical thought bequeathed by the 18th to the early 19th century had tended, for Coleridge, to view culture and creativity as simple givens rather than as the products of a specifically constituted intelligence. His famous definition of the creative intelligence, or the 'Imagination', issues from an exploration (which takes him through pioneering readings of Kant, Fichte, Schelling and the brothers Schlegel) of the structure of the relations between subjectivity and objectivity, self and world, speculative reason and rational understanding (chapters IX, XII, XIII). As the universal human faculty through which these antinomies are reconciled, or rendered merely apparent, the Imagination is by no means the monopoly of a particular group or a specific practice, though Coleridge is in no doubt that it finds its greatest adepts among poets, and its highest form of expression in poetry and aesthetic culture. Like Friedrich Schiller before him, in the celebrated *Letters on the Aesthetic Education of Man* (1794), though in a more fragmentary form, he envisages the substitution – spearheaded by the greatest among the poetic *avant-garde* of the time – of a dynamic and progressive aesthetic culture for the grievously divided political cultures of the revolutionary and post-revolutionary era.

Having come to the central point of his theoretical meditations, Coleridge abruptly drops it, and Volume II of the book consists largely of a critique of his erstwhile collaborator Wordsworth, interspersed with essays on SHAKESPEARE, and the 'origin and elements of metre' and the differences between poetry and prose. Here he turns from the theory to the psychology of the creative process, and the question of the inner preconditions and workings of authentic imagination.

Before SHELLEY's unpublished *Philosophical View of Reform* of 1820, Coleridge's theory of the imagination and the commitments it enjoined was English ROMANTICISM's most carefully articulated response to the multiple contradictions of early industrial society. Its influence upon later 19th- and 20th-century cultural theory has been, to say the least, pervasive, and its model of the creative process is the one with which students of poetry and literature are still most readily familiar.

Bird, Robert (Montgomery) 1806–54 American novelist and playwright. Born in Delaware, he attended the University of Pennsylvania, where he received an MD in 1827. He taught for a short period at Pennsylvania Medical College (1841–3) but left to take up a career as a writer. He began with romantic plays about Philadelphia life, including *The City Looking Glass* (1828, first published 1933), and historical dramas: *Pelopidas, The Gladiator* and *Oralloosa* (1830, 1831 and 1832, respectively; all published in 1919), and *The Broker of Bogota* (1834, first published 1917). His first novel, *Calavar: or, the Knight of the Conquest*, was published anonymously in 1834 and its favourable reception prompted him to write a sequel, *The Infidel: or, The Fall of Mexico* (1835). He then turned to stories of Pennsylvania society: *The Hawks of Hawk-Hollow* (1835), about a well-to-do family's fatal lack of patriotism; and *Sheppard Lee* (1836), a satire on contemporary society, informed by Bird's Whig politics.

Nick of the Woods: or, The Jibbenainosay (1837) is generally considered to be his best novel. Set at the end of the American Revolution, it concerns the abduction of a white woman by Indians who, unlike those of JAMES FENIMORE COOPER, are not in the least noble. Its leading character is a Quaker known as Bloody Nathan or Nick of the Woods, who kills Indians mercilessly to avenge the murder of his family. Bird published two other books: *Peter Pilgrim: or, A Rambler's Recollections* (travel sketches, 1838); and *The Adventures of Robin Day* (a novel, 1839).

Birmingham, George A. [Hannay, James Owen] 1865–1950 Irish novelist and playwright. Born in Belfast, he attended Trinity College, Dublin, and was ordained as a Church of Ireland clergyman in 1889. From 1892 to 1913 he was rector of Westport, County Mayo. He settled in England in 1924. His early novels – such as *Hyacinth* (1906) and *The Bad Times* (1908) – are serious, compassionate explorations of the tangle of recent Irish history and contemporary politics from a moderate nationalist standpoint. With the success of the more light-hearted *Spanish Gold* (1908) he won a large popular audience, but he unintentionally offended Roman Catholic and extreme nationalist sensibilities with the social criticism of *The Seething Pot* (1905), *Red Hand of Ulster* (1912) and a stage comedy, *General John Regan* (1913). In all he wrote more than 80 books and countless articles and pamphlets on many subjects. His autobiography, *Pleasant Places*, appeared in 1934.

Birney, (Alfred) Earle 1904– Canadian poet. Born in Calgary, he lived as a boy on farms in Northern Alberta and in British Columbia. After working at a range of jobs, including those of bank clerk and farm labourer, he attended the University of British Columbia and went on to do postgraduate work at the University of Toronto and the University of California, Berkeley. He became a prominent Trotskyist in the 1930s and, while teaching at University of Utah, was embroiled in controversy because of his political affiliations. During a year at the University of London as a Royal Society of Canada Fellow he travelled to Norway to interview Trotsky. During World War II he served as a personnel selection officer with the Canadian army and afterwards supervised broadcasts to Europe for the Canadian Broadcasting Corporation. From 1946 to 1965 he was professor of English at the University of British Columbia, where he introduced Canada's first creative writing department.

Birney did not begin writing verse until the late 1930s, but he has come to be regarded as one of Canada's most important poets. His verse deals with an encyclopaedic range of Canadian subjects, but he has also travelled extensively and written poems about virtually every area of the globe. His early writing is characterized by a belief that art can change the course of experience, and frequently supposes knowledge of myth and early English cultural traditions. More recently these attitudes have been replaced by an absurdist view of the human experience, and from *Ice Cod Bell and Stone* (1962) onwards he has written in a more colloquial North American voice. Birney has used a wide variety of styles, showing considerable technical virtuosity in all of them. His best work includes a verse drama, *Trial of a City* (1952; reissued as *The Damnation of Vancouver*), in which the 'trial' debates whether Vancouver, representing modern urban civilization, ought to be destroyed, and a comic 'military picaresque', *Turvey* (1977). His other volumes of poetry include *David and Other Poems* (1942), *Near False Mouth* (1964) and *Collected Poems* (1975).

Birrell, Augustine 1850–1933 Politician and essayist. The son of a Baptist minister in Liverpool, Birrell became a barrister in 1875 and entered Parliament as MP for West Fife in 1889. He became President of the Board of Education (1905) and Chief Secretary for Ireland (1907), a post he resigned after the Parliamentary storm following the Easter Rising of 1916. Birrell's collections of literary essays, *Obiter Dicta* (1884, 1887 and 1924), were popular; his other writings include a biography of CHARLOTTE BRONTË (1887) and studies of WILLIAM HAZLITT (1902) and ANDREW MARVELL (1905) for the English Men of Letters series.

Birth of Merlin, The See ROWLEY, WILLIAM and SHAKESPEARE APOCRYPHA.

Birthday Party, The A play by HAROLD PINTER, originally staged at the Arts Theatre, Cambridge, in 1957. It was his first work to attract attention (and abuse).

In a seaside boarding-house belonging to a deck-chair attendant and his eccentric wife, Meg, the only boarder is Stanley, who claims to have been a concert pianist and who suffers from the persecution mania of a neurotic refugee. When two new boarders, a Jew called Goldberg and an Irishman called McCann, come to lodge at the house, Stanley is terrified. At a birthday party, given in his honour, he is driven to hysteria during a game of blind man's buff. The next day Goldberg and McCann remove him to an unknown destination.

Bishop, Elizabeth 1911–79 American poet. Following the early death of her father and her mother's mental illness, she was raised by grandparents in Nova Scotia and in her birthplace of Worcester, Massachusetts. *Questions of Travel* (1965) contains a number of poems about her experiences in Brazil, where she spent 16 years. *Poems: North and South a Cold Spring* (1955) won her the PULITZER PRIZE. Another product of her time in Brazil is a translation from the Portuguese of *The Diary of 'Helena Morley'* (1957), the diary of a young Brazilian girl at the end of the 19th century, whom Bishop met when she was an old woman. The *Complete Poems* (1969) won the National Book Award; *Geography III* appeared in 1976. The *Collected Prose* was published in 1984 and includes autobiographical sketches, travel accounts, a memoir of MARIANNE MOORE, and several short stories.

Bishop Blougram's Apology A DRAMATIC MONOLOGUE by ROBERT BROWNING, published in *Men and Women* (1855). The worldly, comfort-loving but highly intelligent Bishop treats his listener, the journalist Gigadibs, to a virtuoso performance that leaves him and the reader still uncertain of the extent or nature of his religious faith. In the process, the poem offers a minute and skilful examination of the various grounds for faith and doubt in the 19th century. Contemporaries widely assumed, and Browning did not deny, that the model for Blougram was Nicholas Wiseman, who in 1850 had become Archbishop of Westminster and Primate of the Roman Catholic Church in England.

Bishop Orders His Tomb at Saint Praxed's Church, The A DRAMATIC MONOLOGUE by ROBERT BROWNING, included in *Dramatic Romances and Lyrics* (1845). Even as he is dying, the Renaissance bishop still clings desperately to the world of the senses. In a well-known passage in *MODERN PAINTERS* JOHN RUSKIN wrote: 'I know of no other piece of modern English, prose or poetry, in which there is so much told, as in these lines, of the Renaissance spirit – its worldliness, inconsistency, pride, hypocrisy, ignorance of itself, love of art, of luxury and of good Latin. It is nearly all that I have said of the central Renaissance in thirty pages, of THE STONES OF VENICE, put into as many lines.'

Bishops' Bible, The See BIBLE IN ENGLISH, THE.

bissett, bill 1939– Canadian poet. Born in Halifax, Nova Scotia, he attended Dalhousie University and the University of British Columbia. He is best known as a poet of the Canadian West Coast, where he first came to the fore as a writer of the 1960s counter-culture. Since *We Sleep Inside Each Other All* (1966) he has published more than 50 volumes, including *Awake in the Red Desert* (1968), *Drifting into War* (1971), *Pomes for Yoshi* (1972), *Plutonium Missing* (1976), *Sailor* (1978), *Northern Birds in Colour* (1981), *What We Have* (1988) and *Hard 2 Beleev* (1990), all characterized by an attempt to expand the physical properties of poetry. His experiments include sound poems, attempts at scribal renditions of native Canadian chanting, unorthodox orthography and visual formations which mimic the sentiments they are expressing. He is particularly known as a performer whose repetitive incantations can divest words of their usual associations. His poetry celebrates spontaneity and nature, and attacks the constrictions of conventional society and class oppression.

Bissoondath, Neil 1955– Trinidadian/Canadian novelist and short-story writer. A nephew of V. S. NAIPAUL, he left Trinidad in 1973 to study French at York University, Toronto. He has published two volumes of short stories, *Digging Up the Mountains* (1985) and *On the Eve of Uncertain Tomorrows* (1990), and a novel, *A Casual Brutality* (1988). His fiction revolves around three pivotal points: India, the fictional Caribbean island of Casaquemada and Canada. They are as much psychic possibilities for his characters as physical locations, though Bissoondath is a master of realized social detail. His central themes are the inevitability of pursuing and the impossibility of fulfilling a quest for origins, the drift towards apocalypse in contemporary Caribbean life and the dislocation of immigrants in Canadian society. *On the Eve of Uncertain Tomorrows* also contains stories reflecting on the Holocaust and the Spanish Civil War.

Black, William 1841–98 Scottish novelist. He was born in Glasgow and educated at Glasgow School of Art. His first novel, *James Merle: An Autobiography* (1864), was followed by *Love or Marriage* (1867). He is best remembered for his novels with a Scottish setting, most notably *A Daughter of Heth* (1871), *A Princess of Thule* (1874) and *Macleod of Dare* (1878). The miscellaneous *The Strange Adventures of a Phaeton* (1872) combines elements of fiction, romance, guidebook and natural description. He contributed a study of GOLDSMITH to the English Men of Letters series in 1878. See also CELTIC REVIVAL.

Black Arrow, The A novel by ROBERT LOUIS STEVENSON, serialized in *Young Folks* between June and October 1883 and issued in book form in 1888. It is set in late 15th-century England, during the final stages of the Wars of the Roses. Stevenson himself ridiculed it as a potboiler, an example of what he called pseudo-historic 'tushery'.

Brutally reduced, the diffuse plot has three main strands. The first concerns the conflict between Yorkists and Lancastrians, and the second a group of outlaws, the Brotherhood of the Black Arrow, led by 'John Amend-All' (Ellis Duckworth). The third strand concerns the hero, Richard Shelton, and heroine, Joanna Sedley, and their relations with her treacherous uncle and guardian, Sir Daniel Brackley. Dick rescues Joanna from Sir Daniel, at first believing that she is a boy called 'John Matcham'. The activities of Duckworth and his band eventually lead Dick to suspect that his father was murdered by Sir Daniel. The three stories are eventually resolved after the Battle of Shoreby, where the Yorkists are victorious and Dick is knighted by Richard of Gloucester. He spares his uncle's life but Sir Daniel is killed by Duckworth and the last Black Arrow. The book ends with the marriage of Dick and Joanna and his retreat into private life, as he abandons the 'heroism' which the whole novel has shown to be self-seeking and treacherous.

Black Beauty A novel by ANNA SEWELL, published in 1877.

One of the best animal stories ever written, *Black Beauty* charts the decline and fall of a well-bred horse brought low by neglectful grooms and overwork in the cab trade. He also suffers sadly throughout from the hated 'bearing rein', a harness designed to keep a horse's head up however hard the effect upon its breathing. Although the story's gentle Quaker author died a few months after her book was published, with the horses at her own funeral still forced to suffer from the same hated bearing rein, this practice ended soon after partly as a result of her book. Black Beauty himself is finally saved from the knacker's yard to enjoy an honourable retirement. Less fortunate is his high-spirited friend in harness Ginger, whose ignoble death in the streets of London makes for one of the most powerful passages in all CHILDREN'S LITERATURE.

Black Dwarf, The See SCOTT, SIR WALTER.

Black Elk 1863–1950 Sioux warrior and priest. He was born into the Oglala division of the Teton Dakota. His youth coincided with the last years of territorial freedom for the Plains Indians. Black Elk had been instructed as a child in the ancient tribal religions, and his mission to defend the embattled Indian cultures involved both active resistance to US encroachments – he fought at Little Big Horn and Wounded Knee – and the perpetuation of the spiritual vision and commitment of his forefathers. His oral autobiography, *Black Elk Speaks* (recorded and edited by John Neihardt, 1932), is a moving account of his life and mission. He also delivered an account of the religious rites of the Oglala Sioux, *The Sacred Pipe* (recorded and edited by John Epes Brown, 1953).

Black Mask, The A magazine of DETECTIVE FICTION, founded by H. L. MENCKEN and GEORGE JEAN NATHAN in 1920. It began by publishing stories in the traditional English mould, but with the introduction of Carroll John Daly's Race Williams, the first of the hard-bitten detectives, it began to reflect the realities of post-war America. DASHIELL HAMMETT's Continental Op stories, which began to appear in 1923, and Sam Spade, the hero of *The Maltese Falcon*, mirrored the cynical, detached and disillusioned times of Prohibition. RAYMOND CHANDLER also published extensively in *The Black Mask*, and by the time Philip Marlowe made his appearance in 1939 the magazine had fathered a unique American hero – the private eye. Other contributors included Erle Stanley Gardner, George Harmon Coxe, Frederick Nebel, Lester Dent and Horace McCoy.

Black Mountain school A group of American poets attracted to the experimental Black Mountain College near Asheville, North Carolina, in the early 1950s to study with CHARLES OLSON, a faculty member from 1948 and rector in 1951–6. His theory of 'projective verse' advocated 'open forms' and 'composition by field' which abandoned conventional METRE. The group included ROBERT CREELEY, ROBERT DUNCAN and DENISE LEVERTOV. Its work appeared in the *Black Mountain Review*, published from 1954 to 1957.

Blackburn, Paul 1926–71 American poet. Born in St Albans, Vermont, the son of the poet Frances Frost, he was educated at the University of Wisconsin and then attended the University of Toulouse from 1954 to 1955 on a Fulbright fellowship. His early work appeared in *The Dissolving Fabric* (1955), *Brooklyn–Manhattan Transit* (1960) and *The Nets* (1961). His middle-period poems were collected in *The Cities* (1967) and *In. On. Or about the Premises* (1968). A substantial number of late poems appeared in *Halfway down the Coast* and *The Journals* (both 1975). *The Collected Poems of Paul Blackburn* appeared in 1985. Before his early death Blackburn had also established a reputation as a translator of the Provençal troubadours and the works of Julio Cortázar and Antonio Jiménez-Landi.

Blackfriars Theatre The first Blackfriars theatre opened in 1576 to house performances by the Children of the Chapel Royal. The converted room was probably the old refectory of the dissolved Blackfriars monastery inside London's city walls. There are no surviving plans or drawings on which to base reconstructions of this indoor theatre, the first of its kind known to have been open to a paying public. It closed in 1584. Twelve years later James Burbage, who had built the outdoor THEATRE in 1576, leased several rooms in the Blackfriars with the intention of converting them to an indoor theatre for an adult company. The work was halted after a protest by the Blackfriars residents, and it was not completed until 1600, when his son RICHARD BURBAGE (famous as the creator of many of Shakespeare's greatest roles) returned the lease to the Children of the Chapel Royal. For several years, the boy actors at the Blackfriars rivalled and sometimes out-stripped the adult companies in popularity, but their tenure of the theatre (probably in the converted Parliament Chamber) ended in disarray in 1608. It was then that Richard Burbage led the KING'S MEN into occupation of the Blackfriars, which they continued to run in tandem with the outdoor GLOBE until the closure of the theatres in 1642, after which it fell into disrepair.

Blackmore, Sir Richard c. 1655-1729 Poet. A well-meaning but long-winded writer, as well as physician to Queen Anne, he published a *Satyr against Wit* (1700), which was admired by his friend, Samuel Wesley. Blackmore's uncontrolled EPIC verses, pious and patriotic, include *The Creation* (1712) and *Redemption* (1722), which attempt to promote adherence to religion on the basis of natural reason.

Blackmore, R(ichard) D(oddridge) 1825-1900 Novelist. He was born at Longworth in Oxfordshire and spent most of his childhood on Exmoor in the West Country; after attending Blundell's School in Tiverton he went to Exeter College, Oxford. Called to the Bar in 1852, Blackmore preferred instead to divide his time between writing and market gardening. His earliest published works were poems and translations but he gained his first real success, and lasting fame, as a novelist with *LORNA DOONE* (1869), a historical novel set on Exmoor. His other books, all overshadowed by the popularity of *Lorna Doone*, include *Clara Vaughan* (1864), *Alice Lorraine* (1875), *Cripps the Carrier* (1877), *Christowell: A Dartmoor Tale* (1881) and *Springhaven: A Tale of the Great War* (1887), set in southern England during the Napoleonic era.

Blackstone, Sir William 1723-80 Jurist. Born in London, and educated at Charterhouse and Pembroke College, Oxford, he became a fellow of All Souls College and the first Vinerian Professor of English Law at Oxford in 1758-66. Appointed a judge in 1770, he had the misfortune to have the loudly sociable GOLDSMITH as a neighbour in the Middle Temple. He is buried at Wallingford.

Blackstone's four-volume *Commentaries on the Laws of England* (1765-9), derived from his annual lectures at Oxford, was admired for its lucid, eloquent exposition, and regarded for many years as a definitive historical account. In it, he advances from the law of nature (being either the revealed or the inferred will of God) to municipal law, which he defines as a rule of civil conduct prescribed by the supreme power in the state, commanding what is right and what is wrong. Yet Blackstone was by no means a scientific jurist. His attempt to find a basis in history and reason for all the most characteristic English institutions was attacked by JEREMY BENTHAM in *A Fragment on Government* (1776).

Blackwood's (Edinburgh) Magazine A monthly periodical started in July 1817 by the Edinburgh publisher William Blackwood in response to the success of Constable's *EDINBURGH REVIEW* and MURRAY'S *QUARTERLY REVIEW*. JOHN GIBSON LOCKHART, JOHN WILSON ('Christopher North') and JAMES HOGG shaped its character, giving it a reputation for bitter attacks on those of whom it disapproved: Whig intellectuals in the *Chaldee MS* and the so-called COCKNEY SCHOOL of writers in a series of venomous articles. Wilson, Lockhart and Hogg were joined by WILLIAM MAGINN in writing *Noctes Ambrosianae*, a series of lively imaginary conversations whose appearance between 1822 and 1835 greatly contributed to the magazine's success. In later years GEORGE ELIOT'S *SCENES OF CLERICAL LIFE* first appeared in its pages. Known familiarly as the 'Maga', *Blackwood's* dropped the 'Edinburgh' from its title in 1906 and survived, though without its former influence, until 1980.

Blair, Robert 1699-1746 Poet. Born the son of a clergyman in Edinburgh, Blair became a clergyman himself. While minister at Athelstaneford in East Lothian he wrote *The Grave* (1743), a blank-verse poem which owed much to EDWARD YOUNG'S *NIGHT THOUGHTS* and identified him with the GRAVEYARD POETS. Its morbid meditation was popular with middle-class Dissenters for many years, and one edition (1808) was illustrated by WILLIAM BLAKE.

Blaise, Clark 1940- Canadian novelist and short-story writer. Born in Fargo, North Dakota, to Canadian parents, he grew up in the southern United States with summers spent in Winnipeg, Manitoba. He studied at Denison University, Ohio, and the University of Iowa, and taught English for one year at the University of Wisconsin before going to Canada. He took out Canadian citizenship in 1966 and has taught at Concordia University, Montreal,

York University, Toronto, and Columbia University. Blaise is married to the Indian novelist Bharati Mukherjee.

His short-story collections, *A North American Education* (1973) and *Tribal Justice* (1974), and his novels, *Lunar Attractions* (1979) and *Lusts* (1983), focus on the often victimized outsider, the isolated individual struggling to find a place in an increasingly bizarre contemporary society. *Resident Alien* (1986) combines autobiographical essays and autobiographical fiction in a further exploration of geographical and personal identity. With Bharati Mukherjee, he wrote *Days and Nights in Calcutta* (1977), a fascinating account of a stay in India where their different approaches and attitudes provide intriguing and complementary analyses.

Blake, Nicholas See DAY-LEWIS, C.

Blake, William 1757–1827 Poet and painter. Blake's father, James, was a successful London hosier and a Dissenter attracted by the doctrines of Emmanuel Swedenborg; nevertheless his son William was baptized at St James's Church in Piccadilly. Blake never went to school but was educated at home, chiefly by his mother. He read widely in SHAKESPEARE, MILTON, BEN JONSON and the Bible, and somehow picked up a knowledge of French, Italian, Latin, Greek and Hebrew. This learning, randomly acquired and independently held, underlay his later writing.

At the age of 14 Blake was apprenticed to James Basire, an engraver specializing in antiquarian and topographical work. Basire sent his pupil to make drawings of Westminster Abbey and other old churches, thus exposing him to the influence of Gothic art. At this time also Blake's fascination with the nude began, through a study of Henry Fuseli's *Reflections on the Painting and Sculpture of the Greeks*. He stayed with Basire until he was 21, but aimed higher than being a journeyman engraver; he was accepted at the recently founded Royal Academy at Somerset House, though he would soon become restless with its traditional approach.

In 1782 he married Catherine Boucher, and the Blakes had their first home in Leicester Fields,

William Blake

London. Among their neighbours were Jane Hogarth, widow of the artist, the pioneer surgeon and anatomist John Hunter, and SIR JOSHUA REYNOLDS, the painter whose *Discourses on Art* epitomized the NEO-CLASSICISM Blake rejected.

In 1783 two of Blake's friends, the artist John Flaxman and a BLUESTOCKING named Mrs Mathew, decided to print a collection of his poems. *Poetical Sketches* contained such poems as 'To the Muses' and 'My Silks and Fine Array'. In 1789 he published *Songs of Innocence*, the gentlest of all his volumes of lyrics, and *The Book of Thel*, which illustrates his early mysticism and use of emblems. *Tiriel*, written in 1788–9, is the first of his elaborately symbolic writings. Blake added *Songs of Experience* to an edition of *Songs of Innocence* in 1794; the full title of the volume was SONGS OF INNOCENCE AND OF EXPERIENCE *Shewing the Two Contrary States of the Human Soul*. The poems set the world of pastoral innocence and childhood against the world of adult corruption and repression; they contrast the meek virtue of 'The Lamb' with the darker forces of energy in 'The Tyger'.

Blake's dislike of human authority and his radical sympathies found natural expression in friendships with WILLIAM GODWIN and THOMAS PAINE, and increasingly in his writing. He published two sets of prose aphorisms under the title *There is No Natural Religion*, and a third called *All Religions are One* (all *c.* 1788), as well as *The French Revolution: A Poem in Seven Books* (*c.* 1791), only one book of which survived. 1790 was the year in which he engraved THE MARRIAGE OF HEAVEN AND HELL, his principal prose work.

The Blakes moved south of the Thames to Lambeth in 1793, the period when he began to work on his 'prophetic books'. In his new home Blake executed some of his most famous engravings, including those for *The Book of Job* and for EDWARD YOUNG'S *NIGHT THOUGHTS*, though his early admiration for the GRAVE-YARD POETS waned and he came to regard their work as insipid. He wrote *The Visions of the Daughters of Albion* (1793), introducing the figures of his personal mythology: Urizen, the grim symbol of restrictive morality, and Orc, the arch-rebel. Urizen appears with all his depressing characteristics in *America: A Prophecy* (1793).

The ideas of *The Marriage of Heaven and Hell* and the personified symbols encountered in *The Visions of the Daughters of Albion* are developed in *Europe* and *The Book of Urizen* (1794), *The Book of Ahania*, *The Book of Los* and *The Song of Los* (1795), in which Blake pursued his exposure of the errors of the moral code. Urizen has been expelled from the abode of the immortals and has taken possession of man; his agent, or archangel, is Enitharmon. Los is apparently the champion of light and the lord of time, but is held in bondage. Orc is the symbol of anarchy, opposed to Urizen. The whole sequence is an inversion of MILTON's *PARADISE LOST*, which Blake denounced for trying to justify the evil committed by God. His criticism of Christianity is strongest in *Europe* and *The Song of Los*. *Vala* was probably begun in 1795; its rewritten version, *The Four Zoas: The Torments of Love and Jealousy in the Death and Judgement of Albion the Ancient Man*, appeared in 1797. The four Zoas of the title – Urizen (reason), Urthonah (spirit), Luvah (passion) and Tharmas (body) – are traced in a great cloud of symbols. Urizen and Orc oppose each other: the oppressive moral code is condemned; Orc and liberty triumph, and the figure of Jesus as Redeemer is introduced.

In 1800 Blake was taken up by the wealthy WILLIAM HAYLEY, a bad poet but a patron of good ones, and the Blakes went to live in Hayley's house at Felpham in Sussex. They stayed three years but the association was not a success, and Blake's time at Felpham was soured by his arrest on trumped-up charges of sedition; they returned again to London in 1803. Blake remained there for the rest of his life. At Felpham he had worked on *Milton: A Poem in Two Books, To Justify the Ways of God to Men*; it was finished and engraved between 1803 and 1808. The most famous part of this poem, when Milton returns to earth and in the person of the living poet corrects the spiritual error glorified in *Paradise Lost*, appears at the conclusion of the preface in the lines beginning 'And did those feet in ancient time'. *Jerusalem: The Emanation of the Giant Albion*, written between 1804 and 1820, is a complex account of Albion (Man), continually torn between the forces of imagination and the forces of natural religion. *The Ghost of Abel* (1822) came the year after BYRON's *CAIN* and challenges the younger poet's views in a minute poetic drama of 70 lines. The shadow of Cain is seen as Satan's work, not Jehovah's, and the atonement is made on Calvary.

Other notable poems by Blake are difficult to place in the chronology of his career. *Auguries of Innocence* probably dates from 1802, for example, and *The Everlasting Gospel* perhaps from 1810. Some works were unknown until his papers were examined after his death, while many were not issued in the conventional way. Defying the usual methods of publication,

Blake became a one-man industry, designing, engraving and producing his own works like the medieval craftsmen who so intrigued him. Now famous, his engraved books then did not reach more than a small circle of readers. To fellow writers he remained an eccentric and a curiosity, known more through rumour and report than directly through his writings.

The years after Blake's return to London were trying, if only because he never shook off the poverty which had accompanied him through life. The publisher Robert Hartley Cromek cheated him over the commission of 'The Canterbury Pilgrims'; an exhibition of his work in 1809 was a commercial fiasco, though the *Descriptive Catalogue* is a prized addition to his output. But in spite of these discouragements, he remained tenaciously independent. At his death he left no debts, though he was buried in an unmarked grave at the public cemetery of Bunhill Fields.

One of the most difficult artists to assess, Blake was a mixture of extremes in both thought and work, by turns profound and naive. Though the mythology he evolved was highly complex, its allusive sources only now being unravelled by scholars, it was never meant to be private and impenetrable, and the image of Blake as a totally isolated figure is no longer acceptable. His vision of the contradictory forces beneath the appearance of human civilization mirrors the intense political turmoil of Europe (and the New World) during his lifetime. His interest in legend and antiquity was revived with the Romantics' rediscovery of the past, especially the Gothic and the medieval. His insistence on the need to remake those legends in the poet's own terms, and the need to find a new language for expressing them, has pointed the way to the poetry of later generations. But it was left to later generations to recognize his importance.

Bland, Peter 1934– Anglo-New Zealand poet and playwright. Born in Britain, he went to New Zealand in the 1950s and lived in Wellington, where he was associated with the group of writers around LOUIS JOHNSON. His main volumes from this period, *Domestic Interiors* and *My Side of the Story* (both 1964), deal largely with contemporary urban themes. In 1961 he helped to found Downstage, New Zealand's first local professional theatre, acting for it and contributing plays such as *Father's Day* (1966) until the end of the decade. After working in Britain as a stage and TV actor, he returned to New Zealand in the 1980s. Later poetry, less explicitly social and more inventive than his earlier work, includes *Mr Maui* (1976) and *The Crusoe Factor* (1985). He has also written radio plays.

blank verse Verse in unrhymed iambic pentameters (see METRE and RHYME). A flexible form able to accommodate a variety of English speech rhythms, it is used in most Elizabethan drama (including the plays of SHAKESPEARE) and many long narrative poems (MILTON's *PARADISE LOST*, WORDSWORTH's *THE PRELUDE* and TENNYSON's *IDYLLS OF THE KING*).

Blast: The Review of the Great English Vortex Intended as a periodical of art and literature, it lasted for only two issues, in July 1914 and July 1915. Its advocacy of VORTICISM signalled an important stage in the development of MODERNISM in Britain. The first issue attacked Victorianism and the BLOOMSBURY GROUP, promoting in their place mechanical, geometric and non-representational elements derived from such art movements as EXPRESSIONISM, cubism and futurism. It carried a manifesto signed by EZRA POUND and RICHARD ALDINGTON, both adherents of imagism, as well as WYNDHAM LEWIS, Henri Gaudier-Brzeska, Edward Wadsworth and several other artists. Lewis and Pound were largely responsible for the dynamically and radically authoritarian tone of the issue, and for its futurist typography and layout. It contained poems by Pound, Lewis's 'vorticist drama' *The Enemy of the Stars*, and contributions from FORD MADOX FORD and REBECCA WEST. There were also illustrations of vorticist art, including sculpture by Gaudier-Brzeska and Jacob Epstein and works by Wadsworth, Lewis and William Roberts. The second issue, published as a 'War Number', was mostly written by Lewis, though it contained some poems by T. S. ELIOT.

Bleak House A novel by CHARLES DICKENS, published in monthly parts from March 1852 to September 1853 and in volume form in 1853.

Although the fortunes of three pedestrian characters – Esther Summerson (who narrates much of the story), Ada Clare and Richard Carstone – are central to the plot, it is Dickens's merciless indictment of the Court of Chancery and its bungling, morally corrupt handling of the endless case of Jarndyce *v.* Jarndyce that gives the novel its scope and meaning. Starting with Esther's account of her lonely, unhappy childhood, her role as protégée of the worthy John Jarndyce (the guardian of Richard and Ada), the tale develops the relations between the three young people, all inhabitants of the Jarndyce household. Ada and Richard marry but he, always vacillating in his choice of career, becomes enmeshed in the Jarndyce lawsuit and dies worn out by its frustrations. The story is enlarged by the introduction of the pompous Sir Leicester Dedlock and his proud wife. Her guilty past – an affair with the now dead Captain Hawdon that produced Esther – is slowly unravelled by the coldly calculating lawyer Tulkinghorn. Before Tulkinghorn can expose Lady Dedlock, he is murdered by Mademoiselle Hortense, waiting woman to her ladyship, who is brought to book by Inspector Bucket. Although Sir Leicester in fact behaves with compassion and understanding when he learns his wife's secret, she flees from home and is found dead by Bucket and Esther, not far from where the Captain lies. In due course Esther, released from an understanding with John Jarndyce, marries the surgeon Allan Woodcourt.

Numerous other characters contribute to the complex portrait of society which emerges from the novel. They include the selfish leech on others, Harold Skimpole (based on LEIGH HUNT), and the boisterous Boythorn (based on WALTER SAVAGE LANDOR); Krook, the rag-and-bottle shopkeeper who dies a hideous death by 'Spontaneous Combustion'; Gridley and the crazed Miss Flite, both ruined by Chancery; Mrs Jellyby, neglectful of domestic responsibilities in favour of 'Telescopic Philanthropy'; the greasy Mr Chadband, a parson 'of no particular denomination'; the grasping Smallweed family; Conversation Kenge and Mr Vholes, lawyers both; and the two sons of Sir Leicester Dedlock's stately old housekeeper, Mrs Rouncewell. Of particular importance to the moral design of the novel is Jo, the crossing-sweeper whose brutish life and death are the instrument for one of Dickens's most savage judgements on an indifferent society.

Bleasdale, Alan 1946– Playwright. His comedies, musicals and dramas are often set in his home town, Liverpool. *The Party's Over* (1975), *Down the Dock Road* (1976), *It's a Madhouse* (1976) and *No More Sitting on the Old School Bench* (1977) were produced in the north of England but failed to make an impact in London. Despite the popularity of *Having a Ball* (1981), about four men waiting for treatment in a vasectomy clinic, his greatest success came with two television drama series: *Boys from the Blackstuff* (1983), about the unemployed on Merseyside, and *GBH* (1991), about the rise and fall of the leader of a far-left faction in the Liverpool Labour Party. Both show his gift for comedy veering towards FARCE and for lively rather than subtle characterization. His fellow-feeling for people down on their luck informs *Are You Lonesome Tonight?* (1985), his musical about the last days of Elvis Presley.

Blessed Damozel, The A poem by DANTE GABRIEL ROSSETTI, first published in 1850 in the shortlived literary magazine *THE GERM*. The Damozel leans out 'from the gold bar of Heaven' yearning for her earthly lover, whose reflections are expressed parenthetically throughout. This highly symbolic work is the embodiment of PRE-RAPHAELITE verse, and it is complemented by a Rossetti painting of the same name.

Blessington, Marguerite, Countess of 1789–1849 Woman of letters. One of the most colourful Regency figures, she was born at Knockbrit near Clonmel, Co. Tipperary. Her father, a dissolute small landowner, forced her to marry the equally dissolute

Captain Maurice St Leger Farmer when she was only 14. She left him after three months, and shortly after his death in 1817 married Charles John Gardiner, the 1st Earl of Blessington; their town mansion in St James's Square, London, became a centre of social attraction. Her first work, *The Magic Lantern: or, Sketches of Scenes in the Metropolis*, was published anonymously in 1822. In August of the same year she and Blessington embarked on a tour of the Continent, accompanied by the young Count d'Orsay, with whom she was intimately associated until the end of her life. At Genoa in 1823 the Blessingtons struck up a brief though extremely cordial friendship with BYRON, the details of which were recorded by the Countess in her *Journal of Conversations with Lord Byron* (1832), the work for which she is now chiefly remembered. Towards the end of 1828, the Blessington menage shifted its centre of operations to Paris, where the Earl died of apoplexy in 1829. Returning with d'Orsay to London in 1831, she eventually established court at Gore House, Kensington, where for 13 years she was hostess to literary, political and artistic London. Restricted by her husband's death to a jointure that left her merely well-off she began to write in order to maintain her position. Her prolific output over the next 15 years included countless pieces for periodicals, annuals and magazines; the editorship of *The Book of Beauty* and *The Keepsake*; highly successful travel books such as *The Idler in Italy* (1839) and *The Idler in France* (1841); and numerous novels in three volumes. Although considerable, her earnings failed to keep pace with her needs, and when the inevitable crash came in April 1849 she fled with d'Orsay to Paris, where she died in June of that year.

Blickling Homilies, The A series of 19 Old English HOMILIES (or sermons) found in a manuscript of 971. Their date of composition is not known; since it is not unusual to find archaisms in Old English prose, the fact that their language belongs to the 9th century is far from decisive. The homilies deal largely with stories from the Bible and religious festivals, but one takes as its theme the imminent end of the world, another the futility of worldly pleasures and the importance of the life of the soul, and a third treats the life and incarnation of Christ.

Blind Harry c. 1440–c. 1492 The author of *WALLACE* (c. 1477), an epic poem in 12 books describing the life of the Scottish hero William Wallace and his struggle against the English. Little is known of Blind Harry's life but the vividness of some descriptive passages in the poem suggests that he had not been blind from birth. His work shows familiarity with the geography of Central Scotland and with contemporary scholarship, and a strong anti-English sentiment.

Blithedale Romance, The A novel by NATHANIEL HAWTHORNE, published in 1852.

The narrator, Miles Coverdale, goes to the Utopian community of Blithedale (based on BROOK FARM), where he meets the famous Zenobia, an exotic feminist (based on MARGARET FULLER), Hollingsworth, a blacksmith turned philanthropist, and Priscilla, a mysterious and fragile seamstress. Zenobia passionately loves the egotistic Hollingsworth, who wishes to turn Blithedale into an institution for criminal reform. Priscilla has escaped to Blithedale from the control of the evil Westervelt, who forced her to pose as the mysterious 'Veiled Lady', through whom he demonstrated his mesmeric powers to Boston audiences. Westervelt also has a mysterious past connection with Zenobia. Sensing competition for Hollingsworth from Priscilla, Zenobia delivers her back to Westervelt. Hollingsworth, however, intervenes to save Priscilla, and pledges himself to her. Meanwhile, it is revealed to all that Priscilla is Zenobia's half-sister, and that apparently she has been chosen to receive the inheritance that Zenobia thought was hers. Hollingsworth has chosen her over Zenobia because he needs the inheritance money to realize his reform scheme. The spurned and impoverished Zenobia drowns herself. Hollingsworth and Priscilla marry, but the egotistical reformer, overcome by guilt for Zenobia's suicide, is a broken man. Coverdale lapses back into a lonely bachelor's life, offering as explanation for his obsession with his three friends that all along he has been in love with Priscilla.

Blitzstein, Marc 1905–64 American composer, librettist and lyricist. He is best remembered for his contributions to the theatre of social protest in the 1930s. His first major work was the oratorio *The Condemned* (1932), based on the martyrdom of Sacco and Vanzetti. This was followed by *I've Got the Tune* (1937), a radio play. His best-known work is the musical play *THE CRADLE WILL ROCK* (1937), which fused elements of opera and popular music to portray the tyranny of a wealthy businessman over all aspects of life in a small city. *No for an Answer* (1941) was soon censored and shut down by the authorities because of its political content. After World War II, during which he served in the US Air Force, he completed a ballet, *The Guests* (produced by The New York City Ballet in 1949), and an adaptation of the text of Brecht's *The Threepenny Opera*, produced off Broadway in 1954 with Lotte Lenya as Jenny. His musical *Regina*, based on LILLIAN HELLMAN's play *THE LITTLE FOXES*, was first produced in 1949 and later became part of the repertory at The New York City Opera. Hellman's plot and characterizations allowed Blitzstein to continue his criticism of capitalism in America by focusing on the way greed can lead members of a family to destroy one another.

Blixen, Karen See DINESEN, ISAK.

Bloody Tenet of Persecution, The A tract by ROGER WILLIAMS, written and published in London in 1644. Provoked by JOHN COTTON's defence of persecution to preserve orthodoxy, Williams presents a two-part dialogue between Truth and Peace. The first part constitutes both a point-by-point rebuttal of Cotton's argument, and a defence of freedom of conscience as an inalienable right. On the grounds that civil power derives from the people and not from God, the second part denounces the ministerial intervention in secular affairs sanctioned by the Puritan theocracy of Massachusetts Bay. Thus, *The Bloody Tenet* subverts the idea of a national church, the basis of New England's theocratic practices. Cotton replied in *The Bloody Tenet Washed and Made White in the Blood of the Lamb* (1647).

Bloomfield, Robert 1766–1832 Poet. Born in the village of Honington, Suffolk, Bloomfield was the son of a tailor, and was taught to read and write by his mother, who ran the village school. After a period as a farm labourer, he ran away to join his older brothers in London, where he became a cobbler, and improved himself by attending meetings of Dissenters, and by reading 'the long and beautiful speeches of BURKE, Fox, or North'. He is now chiefly remembered as the author of *The Farmer's Boy* (1800), in imitation of THOMSON's *THE SEASONS*, which had come to the attention of Capel Lofft, who arranged for its publication in a fine quarto edition with wood engravings by THOMAS BEWICK. No fewer than 26,000 copies were sold in three years, and translations appeared in French, Italian, and even Latin. Despite the prevailing demand for authentic rustic poetry, Bloomfield was unable to repeat the success of his life of the orphan ploughboy, Giles, and did not develop significantly as a writer during the two decades after its appearance. Later works include *Rural Tales* (1802), *Good Tidings or News from the Farm* (1804) and *The Banks of the Wye* (1811). His last years were dogged by illness and partial blindness, and he died in extreme poverty.

Bloomsbury Group, The The name given to a group of friends – writers, artists and intellectuals – who began meeting in about 1905 at the Bloomsbury house of the Stephen sisters, Vanessa Bell and VIRGINIA WOOLF. Accurate dating of the group's existence is difficult, the broadest estimate being 1905–41. In 1899 Thoby Stephen, CLIVE BELL, LYTTON STRACHEY, Saxon Sydney-Turner and LEONARD WOOLF had all entered Trinity College, Cambridge. By 1905 Thoby had initiated his 'Thursday evenings' when he brought his Cambridge friends to meet his sisters at Gordon Square. After Vanessa's marriage to Clive Bell, Virginia moved to Fitzroy Square and then to Brunswick Square, where she lived with her younger brother Adrian and where MAYNARD KEYNES had a

pied à terre which Duncan Grant also used as a studio. Leonard Woolf rented rooms on the top floor. E. M. FORSTER was a frequent visitor. This was 'Old Bloomsbury'. Thoby's friends, Strachey, Sydney-Turner and WOOLF, serious-minded and heavily influenced by G. E. MOORE's *Principia Ethica*, formed one element, enlivened by the more worldly and sophisticated Clive Bell and DESMOND MACCARTHY.

By 1910 Clive Bell had met Roger Fry, through whom the group's interest broadened to encompass a greater involvement in the visual arts – the first Post-Impressionist exhibition also took place in that year. During World War I a second generation began to make its appearance, in particular, DAVID GARNETT, and after the war the circle grew larger and became geographically more dispersed. The Bells, Woolfs and Lytton Strachey all took country houses which members of the group visited, and they also met at the Garsington home of LADY OTTOLINE MORRELL. Lytton Strachey's death in 1932 and Virginia Woolf's suicide in 1941 can both be seen as ends of an era.

Although its members denied being a group in any formal sense, they were united in an abiding belief in the importance of the arts. Their philosophy can perhaps best be summarized in Moore's statement that 'one's prime objects in life were love, the creation and enjoyment of aesthetic experience and the pursuit of knowledge'. They were sceptical and tolerant, reacting against the artistic and social restraints of Victorian society. Through writing (biography, novels, art criticism, economics, political theory), painting (in the works of Vanessa Bell and Duncan Grant), publishing (the Hogarth Press started in 1917 and in 1923 published ELIOT's *THE WASTE LAND*) and support of new developments in the arts, they exercised a considerable influence on the *avant-garde* of the early 20th century. Some accused the group of intellectual elitism. Its reputation faltered in the 1940s and 1950s, but from the 1960s critical interest in their achievements began to revive.

bluestocking This term for a woman of pronounced literary or intellectual interests gained currency in the 1750s, when ELIZABETH MONTAGU held assemblies at her home to which 'literary and ingenious' figures were invited. Conversation on intellectual matters prevailed, instead of cards or entertainments. Among the members of Mrs Montagu's circle were HANNAH MORE, FANNY BURNEY, HESTER CHAPONE and HORACE WALPOLE. The group was nicknamed 'The Blue Stocking Society' probably because of the costume of one of its male members. The term has also come to mean a female pedant.

Blume, Judy 1938– American writer of CHILDREN'S LITERATURE. She was born in New Jersey and educated at New York University. Her first successful book, *Are You There, God? It's Me, Margaret* (1970), is about an

A female salon: by the 1750s such groups of women were derisively known as BLUESTOCKINGS. Frontispiece to vol. 1 of *The Female Spectator*, edited by Eliza Haywood from 1744–6

11-year-old girl who longs to reach puberty so that she can wear a bra. Such comparative outspokenness on personal problems or worries became a feature of later novels, and *Forever* (1975) provoked controversy by describing an adolescent girl's first sexual experience in explicit detail. *Letters to Judy: What Kids Wish They Could Tell You* (1986) is a selection from her correspondence with children.

Blunden, Edmund (Charles) 1896–1974 Poet and critic. Born in London, he moved to Kent, which later became the inspiration for much of his poetry. After serving in the Royal Sussex Regiment, he became assistant editor of THE ATHENAEUM until 1922. He left England to teach in Tokyo, and became professor of English literature in Hong Kong in 1953, and professor of poetry at Oxford in 1966.

His early verse appeared in GEORGIAN POETRY. Volumes include *The Waggoner and Other Poems* (1920), *The Shepherd and Other Poems of Peace and War* (1922), *English Poems* (1929), *Collected Poems* (1930), *After the Bombing and Other Short Poems* (1950) and *A Hong Kong House Poem* (1962). His autobiographical account of World War I, *Undertones of War*, appeared in 1928, and *Votive Tablets*, a collection of essays on English poetry, in 1931. He published biographies of LEIGH HUNT (1930) and SHELLEY (1943), a study of THOMAS HARDY (1941), pioneering editions of the poetry of JOHN CLARE (1920), WILFRED OWEN (1931) and IVOR GURNEY (1954), autobiographical writings (1931), and *Cricket Country* (1944) and *English Villages* (1947) for the Britain in Pictures series.

Blunt, Wilfrid Scawen 1840–1922 Poet, diplomat and Arabist. Born into a landed Roman Catholic family in Sussex, he joined the diplomatic service at 18 and married Annabella King-Noel, BYRON's granddaughter, in 1869. His first verse collection, *Sonnets and Songs by Proteus* (1875), contained addresses to women, poems on the Sussex countryside, and adaptations from the Arabic. He wrote and worked in support of Egyptian, Indian and Irish independence, publishing *The Future of Islam* (1882), *Ideas about India* (1885) and *The Secret History of the English Occupation of Egypt* (1907). During a spell in an Irish prison he wrote the SONNET sequence *In Vinculis* (1899). *My Diaries*, published in two volumes in 1919–20, referred to his friendships with Lord Lytton (EDWARD ROBERT LYTTON), Curzon, WILLIAM MORRIS, LADY GREGORY, ALICE MEYNELL and OSCAR WILDE. His *Poetical Works* appeared in 1914, and in the same year a birthday celebration, at which roasted peacocks in full plumage were served, was attended by EZRA POUND, W. B. YEATS, RICHARD ALDINGTON, T. STURGE MOORE and F. S. Flint.

Bly, Robert 1926– American poet. He was born in Madison, Minnesota, and educated at Harvard and the University of Iowa. His verse is filled with images of rural Minnesota, which often become figures for the poet's unconscious; his exploration of interior 'landscapes' can give his work a mystical or surreal quality. He has published many volumes since *Silence in the Snowy Fields* (1962), together with a distinguished body of work translating poetry from Swedish, German (Rilke), Spanish (Neruda and Machado) and Russian.

Blythe, Ronald (George) 1922– Miscellaneous writer. Born in Acton, Suffolk, he has written a novel (*A Treasonable Growth*, 1960), short stories (collected in 1985) and essays on literature, but is principally known for *Akenfield: Portrait of an English Village* (1969). Blythe used its technique of transcribed interviews with linking commentary again in *The View in Winter: Reflections on Old Age* (1979). *The Age of Illusion* (1963) is a social history of England between the two world wars.

Blyton, Enid (Mary) 1897–1968 Writer of CHIL-DREN'S LITERATURE. Born in London, she was educated at a girls' school in Beckenham, anticipating the heroines of her later stories by becoming both head girl and captain of games. She then trained as an infant teacher, but soon became known as a writer of stories, poems, journalism and full-length books as well as an energetic organizer of competitions and charitable appeals. Her 'Famous Five' adventures, appearing from 1942, feature a gang of well-born, privately educated children who solve various mysteries during their largely unsupervised vacations. Little Noddy and Big Ears, introduced after the war, are humanized toys enjoying mild adventures in a bland, domestic setting. Critics have questioned the effect of Blyton's limited literary style on young children and pointed to her racist and snobbish attitudes, but without destroying her popularity, which continues even today.

bob and wheel A wheel is a group of short lines at the end of a longer stanza of longer lines. If its first line is even shorter than the others, it is known as a bob and the whole group is then styled a 'bob and wheel'. The medieval romance SIR GAWAIN AND THE GREEN KNIGHT provides the best-known example.

Bodkin, (Amy) Maud 1875–1967 Critic. She was born in Chelmsford, Essex, and educated at the University College of Wales, Aberystwyth. Of the later life of this amateur psychologist little is known: she held no public position or academic post. Her book *Archetypal Patterns in Poetry* (1934) was the first and most important English work on literature to emerge from the psychological school of C. G. Jung. Applying Jung's concept of the collective unconscious to the reading of COLERIDGE'S THE RIME OF THE ANCIENT MARINER, she discerned underlying patterns and cycles of death and rebirth also to be found in ancient literatures and religions. Surveying the endurance of these and other 'archetypes' in poetry and drama from Sophocles to T. S. ELIOT, she argued that poetry, as the objectification of 'universal forces of our nature', allows special access to the collective unconscious of the race. A sequel, *Studies of Type-Images in Poetry, Religion, and Philosophy* (1951), developed these Jungian theories in the direction of a synthesis between poetry and religion.

Bodley, Sir **Thomas** 1545–1613 Scholar and diplomat. Born at Exeter, Bodley was brought up on the Continent, chiefly at Geneva, where his parents had taken their family to avoid the persecutions of Mary. In Geneva Bodley was taught divinity by Calvin and Beza. He entered Magdalen College, Oxford, and became a fellow in 1565. A fine Hebrew scholar, he was also instrumental in encouraging the study of Greek at Oxford. In the 1570s he travelled abroad and subse-

quently became a diplomat. He was Elizabeth I's permanent resident at The Hague in 1589–96, though he found his later years there tiresome and pressed to be recalled. Bodley withdrew from active political service after 1596 and channelled his energies into the establishment at Oxford of the great library which was opened in 1603 and given his name in 1604. SIR HENRY SAVILE assisted him in the project. Bodley later extended the library building and endowed it with other property, as well as making the university chief beneficiary of his will. (See also LIBRARIES.)

Boece Translation by GEOFFREY CHAUCER of the *Consolatione Philosophiae* of the 6th-century Roman philosopher Boethius, undertaken *c.* 1380. While not following the original closely Chaucer's prose version testifies to his deep sympathy for and engagement with Boethius' work. Its discussion of the 'true good' and the apparent paradox of man's free will and God's foreknowledge influenced his own writing, most notably *TROILUS AND CRISEYDE* and *The Knight's Tale* (see *CANTERBURY TALES*).

Boece [Boethius], **Hector** ?1465–1536 Scottish historian. Boece's family came from Dundee. He was educated at the University of Paris and later helped Bishop Elphinstone in his plans to set up a university at Aberdeen. His major work was the compilation of a history of Scotland, *Historia Scotorum* (1527), which shows a humanist concern with narrative and rhetoric rather than historical accuracy. LELAND commented that Boece wrote as many lies as there are waves or stars. HOLINSHED found the story of Macbeth in the *Historia* and it was thus transmitted to SHAKESPEARE.

Bogan, Louise 1897–1970 American poet. Born in Maine, Bogan was educated at Boston University and spent most of her life in New York. She was the regular poetry reviewer for *THE NEW YORKER* from 1931 to 1968, and in 1951 published the highly regarded *Achievement in American Poetry 1900–1950*. Her own poetry was strongly influenced by her study of 16th- and 17th-century English verse, and is characterized by its dramatic structure and highly refined metrical forms. She published six volumes of poems: *Body of This Death* (1923), *Dark Summer* (1929), *The Sleeping Fury* (1937), *Poems and New Poems* (1941), *Collected Poems 1923–1953* (1954) and *The Blue Estuaries: Poems 1923–1968* (1968). A prose collection, *A Poet's Alphabet*, appeared in 1970.

Boker, George Henry 1823–90 American playwright and poet. Born into a wealthy Pennsylvania family, he was educated at the College of New Jersey (later Princeton University) and went on to study law but aspired to the life of a poet. He published his first collection of verse, *The Lesson of Life*, in 1848. Only six of his 11 plays were produced professionally. The first, *Calaynos*, was staged without authorization in London in 1849. He wrote two comedies in verse, *The Betrothal* (1850), set in Renaissance Italy, and *The Widow's Marriage* (1852, unproduced), and one in prose about contemporary London, *The World a Mask* (1851). His two most successful plays were the historical verse tragedies *Leonor de Guzman* (1853), about the rivalry between the mistress of Alfonso XII and his wife Maria, and *Francesca da Rimini* (1855), based on Dante's story of the lovers Paolo and Francesca. The latter play was unsuccessful at first, but its revival in 1882 won great critical acclaim. Boker's last two plays, *Nydia* (1885) and *Glaucus* (1886), were both based on EDWARD BULWER LYTTON's novel *The Last Days of Pompeii* (1834); both were unproduced. His patriotism during the Civil War was rewarded by his appointment as United States Ambassador to Turkey (1871–5) and to Russia (1875–8).

Boland, Eavan (Aisling) 1944– Irish poet. Born in Dublin, the daughter of a diplomat, she was schooled in London, New York and Killiney, County Dublin, before reading English at Trinity College, Dublin. She has worked as a freelance lecturer, and reviews regularly for *The Irish Times* and *PN Review*. After her 'truly frightful' pamphlet, *23 Poems* (1962), her first full-length book was *New Territory* (1967). Her range of themes is wide: Irish myth and legend, suburbia, the intimacies of love and motherhood. The distinctive development from volume to volume – *The War Horse* (1975), *In Her Own Image* (1980), and *Night Feed* (1982) – is a deepening internal response to external phenomena. *The Journey and Other Poems* (1987), her first book to be published in Britain, has been followed by *Selected Poems* (1989) and *Outside History* (1990). Recognized as one of her country's leading writers, she returned to national concerns in *A Kind of Scar: Woman Poet in a National Tradition* (1989).

Boldrewood, Rolf [Browne, Thomas Alexander] 1826–1915 Australian novelist. Browne was born in London but his family emigrated in 1830 and he was educated in Sydney. From 1843 to 1871 he speculated as a squatter on property in Victoria and the Riverina, New South Wales. Drought ended this career and he became a police magistrate and goldfields commissioner. He was 40 before he began to write. Browne's best-known novel, *Robbery under Arms*, was published as a serial in the *Sydney Mail* (1881) and in volume form in 1888. This racy tale about an infamous bush-ranger, Captain Starlight, with authentic scenes and dialogue, soon established itself as a classic adventure story. Of some 17 other novels the most popular were *The Miner's Right* (1890), *A Colonial Reformer* (1890) and *The Squatter's Dream* (1890), first published in 1878 as *Ups and Downs of Australian Life*.

Bolingbroke, 1st Viscount [St John, Henry] 1678–1751 Statesman and historian. Born at Battersea, he was educated at Eton and (probably) Christ Church, Oxford, and then made the fashionable tour of Europe. He entered Parliament in 1701, supporting ROBERT HARLEY and the Tories with his powerful oratory. He became Secretary of State in 1710 and was created 1st Viscount Bolingbroke in 1712. An opponent of the Hanoverian succession, who wanted the crown to remain with the Stuarts, Bolingbroke was impeached when George I came to the throne in 1714. He fled to France, where he became Secretary of State to Prince James Stuart (the Old Pretender), though the Prince dismissed him in 1716 and Bolingbroke wisely severed his connection with the Stuarts. His friends managed to secure his pardon, and he returned to England in 1725; his property was restored but he was banned from holding office.

Most of his writing dates from his return to England but during his political ascendancy he was the friend and patron of writers. In 1711 he founded the Brothers Club, which included SWIFT, ARBUTHNOT and MATTHEW PRIOR, as well as adherents of the Tory Party, among its members. In exile Bolingbroke wrote *A Letter to Sir William Wyndham* (1717; published in 1753), about the Jacobite question. While not entirely honest in its handling of fact, it is persuasively written and of interest for Bolingbroke's comments on his former colleagues – particularly Harley – and for the description of the Old Pretender's court. *Reflections in Exile* was written the year before, in 1716. After he returned to England Bolingbroke was soon in active opposition to the Whigs, then securely in power under Robert Walpole. His attacks on the administration for Nicholas Amherst's periodical, *The Craftsman*, were collected in *A Dissertation upon Parties* (1735) and *Remarks upon the History of England* (1743).

Disillusioned with party politics, Bolingbroke retired to live in his French wife's home at Chanteloup, Touraine, in 1735. *Letters on the Study and Use of History* (published in 1752) argued that, since history teaches philosophy by example, England should follow the example of her European neighbours and produce written histories. The book was widely read, and not only in England, for Bolingbroke's friend and protégé Voltaire acknowledged its influence. *A Letter on the True Use of Retirement and Study* and *A Letter on the Spirit of Patriotism* were both written in 1736. The latter (published in 1749) looks hopefully to a future Tory Party inspired by patriotism, an influential argument developed in *The Idea of a Patriot King* (written in 1738, published in 1749). *Some Reflections on the Present State of the Nation* (1749) examines the question of the public debt. The collection of Bolingbroke's writings edited by DAVID MALLET in 1754 included *Philosophical Works*, the occasional writings believed to have influenced POPE in his *ESSAY ON MAN*.

Bolt, Robert (Oxton) 1924– Playwright. He studied history at Manchester University before becoming a schoolteacher. The success of *Flowering Cherry* (1957), a domestic play, encouraged him to become a professional writer. *The Tiger and the Horse* (1960) reflected his concern for nuclear disarmament. Bolt's best work for the stage includes large-scale historical plays distinguished by their immediately effective stagecraft: *A Man for All Seasons* (1960), about THOMAS MORE, *Vivat! Vivat! Regina* (1970), about Elizabeth I and Mary, Queen of Scots, and *State of Revolution* (1977), about Lenin, Trotsky and the Russian Revolution. The dilemmas of conscience make a recurrent theme. Bolt's screenplays, which have involved him in highly successful collaboration with the director Sir David Lean, include *Lawrence of Arabia* (1962), *Dr Zhivago* (1965), *Ryan's Daughter* (1970) and *The Mission* (1986).

Bond, Edward 1934– Playwright. He left school at the age of 14. His farm-working parents had been drawn to London in search of work, and Bond's plays are powerfully aware of both rural and urban deprivation. Several caused controversy. Bond received his first encouragement as a member of the Writers' Group at the ROYAL COURT THEATRE, where *The Pope's Wedding* (1962) was given a Sunday night performance. *Saved* (1965) is a bleak presentation of the effects of cultural deprivation. Banned by the Lord Chamberlain because of the scene in which a group of bored youths stone a baby, it brought Bond's name into theatrical prominence. *Early Morning* (1968), a surreal historical fantasy, was the last play to be banned in its entirety by the Lord Chamberlain, whose legal control of theatrical performance was discontinued in the year of its first production. *Narrow Road to the Deep North* (1968), radically revised as *The Bundle* (1978), impartially compares fascism and imperialism as modes of government. As in *Early Morning*, Bond is here attacking the legacy of Victorian prejudice and pride. *Lear* (1971) is a startlingly cruel reappraisal of SHAKESPEARE's *KING LEAR* and *Bingo* (1973) takes Shakespeare himself as its central character, speculating on his complicity in the agricultural enclosures that disinherited the rural population. A concern with the relationship between artist and society is also central to *The Fool* (1975), a disturbing dramatization of scenes in the life of JOHN CLARE. Other plays in which Bond uses historical settings to expose modern injustices include *The Woman* (1978) and *Restoration* (1981). Bond has also written the libretti for two operas by Hans Werner Henze, *We Come to the River* (1976) and *The English Cat* (1983), as well as adapting work by Chekhov and Wedekind for the English stage.

Bond, (Thomas) Michael 1926– Writer of CHILDREN'S LITERATURE. Born and educated in Berkshire, he was a television cameraman before becoming an author. His success began with *A Bear Called Paddington* (1958), which created a favourite character later to appear in numerous sequels popular both in Britain and abroad. Other successful characters Bond has invented include an orphan mouse, first appearing in *Here Comes Thursday* (1966), and a guinea-pig named Olga da Polga.

Bonifacius A pamphlet by COTTON MATHER, subtitled *An Essay Upon the Good*, published anonymously in Boston in 1710 and discussing the meaning of true Christian conduct. Invoking the traditional Puritan idea that every person has a social as well as a spiritual calling, Mather suggests ways in which people of diverse callings – ministers, lawyers, doctors, magistrates, merchants – may translate Christian principles into their daily lives and activities. He stresses that true Christians fulfil their callings for the good of the whole community, and should direct their energies in responsible and cooperative rather than competitive ways. He pays particular attention to the nurture of pious principles in the family and to the value of organized church prayers.

Although Mather retains his Puritan orthodoxy in *Bonifacius*, his concern with worldly activity is an attempt to apply traditional Puritan teachings to the immediate concerns of his changing society, with its increasingly complex and diversified secular activities. The book went through many printings both during and after Mather's lifetime, and provided something of a programmatic statement of the social vision of the American Protestant sensibility.

Bontemps, Arna (Wendell) 1902–73 Black American novelist. Born in Louisiana and raised in California, he received an MA from the University of Chicago in 1943, and spent much of his professional life working at Fisk University, first as a librarian, then as public relations director. His writing is dedicated to portraying the life of black people in America. *Black Thunder* (1936) and *Drums at Dusk* (1939) are novels about slave revolts in Virginia and in Haiti. *God Sends Sunday* (1931) was dramatized by COUNTEE CULLEN as *St Louis Woman* (1946). The CHILDREN'S LITERATURE he wrote with JACK CONROY includes *Sam Patch* (1951). His non-fiction includes *They Seek a City* (with Conroy; 1945), *The Story of the Negro* (1948) and *100 Years of Negro Freedom* (1961).

Book Named the Governor, The See ELYOT, SIR THOMAS.

Book of Common Prayer, The The name for the service-book used by the Church of England from 1549 until the mid-1970s, when it was largely replaced by Alternative Services, and in particular one called Series 3.

Christian service-books can be traced from the earliest times. The first chapters of Luke's gospel contain four great hymns, later called the Magnificat (1.46–55), the Benedictus (1.66–79), the Gloria (2.14) and the Nunc Dimittis (2.29–32), and there are many evidences of Christian worship in the New Testament: fragments of hymns throughout Revelation, corporate prayer in Acts 4.23–30. Examination of the service-books of the Fathers, for example in 6th-century Rome, reveals eight daily services, mostly of Scripture reading. Complication, accretion and local variation followed over the centuries. Scripture was often replaced by legends – 'some be untrue, some uncertain, some vain and superstitious', as THOMAS CRANMER wrote. Additional services, for the Virgin Mary, or for the dead, or of other kinds, multiplied so much in number and length as to demand at least four different service-books; all were in Latin.

At the English Reformation, there was great need for simplification and for standardization over the country – for an agreed order in one book in English. The large number of daily Latin 'uses' was clarified into Matins and Evensong (Morning and Evening Prayer after 1552), Holy Communion and Baptism (two, not seven, sacraments) and five other services, all in English. The first Book of Common Prayer of 1549, under the young Edward VI, was the work, as always, of committees, based on the best 'use', that of Sarum (Salisbury), and influenced by several service-books from the Continent. The special gifts, however, of the Archbishop of Canterbury, Thomas Cranmer, especially in the making in English of the brief, beautiful daily prayers known as 'collects', link his name for ever with the Prayer Book. Though many sentences translate earlier Latin forms, it is wrong to think of the Book of Common Prayer as the Latin-in-English: it is a Reformed book, with much that is simple, fresh and 'new' only in the sense that it restored earlier forms. This first Edwardian Book of Common Prayer, and all Prayer Books that follow, put daily Bible reading in the House of God first in importance, as the Fathers had done: all the Psalms to be read through once a month, the whole New Testament three times a year, and most of the Old Testament once a year. The Bible was to be read from the Great Bible of 1540, which was MILES COVERDALE's printing and continuation of the work of WILLIAM TYNDALE (see THE BIBLE IN ENGLISH). The Psalms, though based on Coverdale, made use of earlier Middle English PSALTERS and carried forward a more ancient tradition.

Innumerable phrases have come into the language from the Book of Common Prayer, many of them now taken to be proverbial: 'through fire and water', 'the iron entered into his soul', 'like a giant refreshed', 'all sorts and conditions', 'peace in our time'. Cranmer's genius can be felt in the beauty of one collect for Evensong: 'Lighten our darkness, we beseech thee, O Lord, and by thy great mercy defend us from all perils

and dangers of this night, for the love of thy only son, our saviour Jesus Christ. Amen.' Such timeless simplicity is found everywhere: 'we have done those things which we ought not to have done', or 'pour into our hearts such love toward thee' or 'that peace which the world cannot give', or 'serve thee with a quiet mind'.

In 1550 John Merbecke's music for the Prayer Book was printed. Composed on the sound principle of 'one syllable, one note', it was used whenever the services were sung for over 400 years. The First, 1549, Prayer Book was revised in 1552 and, though hardly used, this Second Prayer Book influenced later revisions. After the savagery of Queen Mary's five years, during which Cranmer, among hundreds of others, was martyred, the Third Prayer Book of 1559 was instituted on the accession of Elizabeth. Under her, there was some revision, and additional services and other matter were bound in: the 39 Articles (setting out Anglican belief), some hymns, and sometimes metrical psalms. The compulsory Sunday attendance of almost everyone at church meant that the ideas and phrases of Cranmer's English liturgy bit deep into the nation's consciousness. The same Hampton Court Conference of 1604 which initiated the Authorized Version under King James produced also the Fourth Prayer Book, with some fresh variations. In 1637 the Scottish Prayer Book was printed in Edinburgh, to local hostility; it later influenced Scottish, English and American liturgies. From 1645 to 1660 the use of the Book of Common Prayer was forbidden by law. Its place was taken by the Directory for Public Worship, which gave only general directions to the minister.

At the Restoration the old Book of Common Prayer was instantly in demand, and quickly revised and lavishly reissued. The Fifth Prayer Book was completed in 1661, but as it became attached to the Act of Uniformity of 1662, it has been known ever since as '1662'. This Prayer Book – and Parliament – went a little way towards incorporating the professions of opponents, but then threw tolerance away and hardened the divisions in the nation, making non-adherence to the Prayer Book a most serious handicap for several following centuries. JOHN BUNYAN and thousands of others suffered harshly, and it was a long time before being a Dissenter, a Roman Catholic, a Jew, or what became known as an agnostic, and thus unable to subscribe to the Prayer Book through conscience, did not bring penalties.

The 1662 Prayer Book introduced several hundred alterations, changing obsolete phrases, transferring the source for all the Bible except the Psalms to the Authorized Version, and giving new directions to the minister. The tendency of the revision can be seen in the change from 'Bishops, pastors and ministers' to 'Bishops, priests and deacons'. State services, particularly those for remembering 'King Charles the Martyr' and the Restoration, joined the revised older service commemorating the Gunpowder Treason of 1605. New collects were introduced. Some revision, usually towards elaboration of ritual, was the work of Bishop John Cosin. It was '1662' which represented Anglicanism for three centuries, and transmitted Cranmer's prose and the Prayer Book Psalms across the world; it was the basis of the service-books for what were to become nearly 20 independent Anglican churches around the globe.

'1662' was richly and frequently issued. In the 100 years from 1660, some 350 fresh editions were published, about 25 of them with full-page engravings, sometimes very lavish. These illustrate Bible events throughout the Church Calendar – the angels appearing to the shepherds, Christ riding into Jerusalem, and so on – followed by pictures of saints. About half the illustrated editions have also, against the appropriate services, an engraving of Guy Fawkes under the eye of God and pictures of the martyrdom of Charles I and the Restoration of Charles II.

Proposals for the further revision of the Book of Common Prayer continued. An attempt under William and Mary in 1689 did not succeed. Movements for Prayer Book reform were strong in the 18th century. A new Scottish liturgy was accepted in 1764, an American Prayer Book in 1789, an Irish Prayer Book in 1877, and the Scottish Prayer Book in 1912. Reform of the Book of Common Prayer was discussed urgently in the 19th century. In 1859 the Gunpowder Treason and Stuart services were dropped. Later proposals were in the direction of more universally Protestant evangelicalism, and more powerfully in the opposite direction, by those who wished that the Reformation had never happened. The wholesale revision proposed in the 1920s was twice rejected by the House of Commons in 1928. The arguments continued, notwithstanding, and some of the 1928 proposals resurfaced in the 1960s, when moves towards alternative services produced three sets. One from the Bishops was called the First Series, and another from the Liturgical Commission was called the Second Series. International religious commissions, dominated by the United States, made proposals which the Church of England largely incorporated in what it called Series 3. This has become standard in many Anglican churches, which now use '1662' for perhaps one early Holy Communion a month. Cranmer and the Reformers (and Merbecke) have been replaced. So, often, have Morning and Evening Prayer. The emphasis is frequently on one weekly 'Parish' or 'Family Eucharist'. The supposed 'popularizing' of the words and order of the services has been in line with the Englishing of the Roman Catholic Mass, but the Church of England must be held responsible for the ugliness of Series 3. Words for people to use together repeatedly in enacting worship have to be specially crafted. The sense of mystery, essential in worship, has in Series 3 been replaced by baffling blocks of language, like the unpunctuated 'You are God we praise you' in the Te Deum. Cranmer's 'The Lord be with you: and with thy spirit' has become in Series 3 'The Lord be with you: and also with you', which is tautological, vacuous, and the result, apparently, of an international commission's insistence that 'spirit' would be misunderstood in English (it remains in European revisions).

Book of Martyrs, Foxe's See ACTS AND MONUMENTS.

Book of St Albans, The Four verse treatises, which had existed separately since *c.* 1400, published together at St Albans in 1486. They deal with hawking, hunting, coat-armour and blazoning of arms; WYNKYN DE WORDE's 1496 edition added a treatise on fishing. The collection proved enduringly popular, appearing only slightly altered under various titles in the 16th and 17th centuries. Juliana Berners (or Barnes), whose name appears at the end of the miscellanea following the hunting treatise in the 1486 edition, was once claimed as author of the whole collection, but it is unlikely she contributed more than the 'company terms' and other terminology. The details usually offered about her life are fabrications by early editors.

Book of Snobs, The Satirical sketches by W. M. THACKERAY, published in PUNCH as *The Snobs of England by One of Themselves* from 28 February 1846 to 27 February 1847, with his own illustrations, and revised for book publication in 1848.

The portraits range from 'The Snob Royal', 'Military Snobs' and 'Clerical Snobs' to 'Country Snobs' and 'Club Snobs'. Although crude and repetitive in places, these sketches have a keen satirical edge, and prefigure both the social concerns of VANITY FAIR and Thackeray's mature narrative stance of involved spectator, implicated in the vices he satirizes.

Book of the Duchess, The A poem by GEOFFREY CHAUCER on the death of Blanche, Duchess of Lancaster, the first wife of John of Gaunt, in 1368. It was composed within a few years of the duchess's death and is one of the poet's earliest works.

The poem is a DREAM-VISION with a long prologue. Unable to sleep because of some sickness or depression, the narrator reads a truncated version of Ovid's story of Ceyx and Alcyone. He tells the story, which ends before the metamorphosis, and prays to Morpheus. He falls asleep and narrates a dream in which he first watches and then wanders away from the hunt of the Emperor Octavian and comes upon a knight in black, lamenting. The latter (probably intended to represent John of Gaunt) describes his love for the lady White and his life with her, and tells the dreamer, at first in a metaphor but finally explicitly, of her death. At this point the dream ends and the narrator awakes and determines to write the poem.

Booker Prize An annual award open to new novels by British and Commonwealth writers, inaugurated in 1969. It is administered by the Book Trust (formerly the National Book League) and sponsored by the multinational conglomerate Booker McConnell. The most widely known literary prize in Britain, its rise to fame since its early years of scarce publicity has been aided by occasional controversies between the judges, or their bizarre decisions as well as by the live television coverage given to the award ceremony since 1981. Publishers now regard the Booker as the most reliable way of securing a novelist's name and the most effective boost to sales, not just for the winner but also for the other five shortlisted authors and titles. Winners have been: P. H. Newby, *Something to Answer For* (1969); BERNICE RUBENS, *The Elected Member* (1970); V. S. NAIPAUL, *In a Free State* (1971); JOHN BERGER, *G* (1972); J. G. FARRELL, *The Siege of Krishnapur* (1973); NADINE GORDIMER, THE CONSERVATIONIST with STANLEY MIDDLETON, *Holiday* (1974); RUTH PRAWER JHABVALA, *Heat and Dust* (1975); DAVID STOREY, *Saville* (1976); PAUL SCOTT, *Staying On* (1977); IRIS MURDOCH, *The Sea, The Sea* (1978); PENELOPE FITZGERALD, *Offshore* (1979); WILLIAM GOLDING, *Rites of Passage* (1980); SALMAN RUSHDIE, *MIDNIGHT'S CHILDREN* (1981); THOMAS KENEALLY, *Schindler's Ark* (1982); J. M. COETZEE, *The Life and Times of Michael K* (1983); ANITA BROOKNER, *Hôtel du Lac* (1984); KERI HULME, *The Bone People* (1985); KINGSLEY AMIS, *The Old Devils* (1986); PENELOPE LIVELY, *Moon Tiger* (1987); PETER CAREY, *Oscar and Lucinda* (1988); KAZUO ISHIGURO, *The Remains of the Day* (1989); A. S. BYATT, *Possession* (1990); BEN OKRI, *The Famished Road* (1991); Barry Unsworth, *Sacred Hunger* with MICHAEL ONDAATJE, *The English Patient* (1992); Roddy Doyle, *Paddy Clarke Ha Ha Ha* (1993); and James Kelman, *How Late It Was, How Late* (1994).

Boorde, Andrew ?1490–1549 Writer on medicine and travel. A Carthusian, he was released from his vows in 1529 and was practising medicine in Glasgow in 1536, though much of his time was spent in Continental travel. His medical works are *A Dietary of Health* (1542), which ran through many editions, and *The Breviary of Health* (1547). His travels led to the first Continental guidebook in English, *The First Book of the Introduction of Knowledge* (?1548), in prose with verse portraits of national types. His other works include a book on astronomy. Boorde is sometimes identified with the 'A. B.' who wrote THE MERRY TALES OF THE MAD MEN OF GOTHAM, a collection of popular jests first printed in 1630.

Booth, Charles 1840–1916 Social critic and reformer. Born in Liverpool to a prosperous Unitarian family, he made his fortune in the shipping business. His interest in public issues developed into active concern about poverty after he opened a London branch of his business in the 1880s. The result was a monumental survey in the tradition of HENRY MAYHEW, taking 17 years and growing to 17 volumes, published in its final form as *Life and Labour of the People in London* (1902–3). BEATRICE WEBB, his wife's cousin, was one of his researchers for the early volumes. Enough of a Manchester liberal to dislike state intervention in business and trade, Booth nevertheless welcomed measures to regulate incomes (he coined the term 'poverty line') and his advocacy of old-age pensions eased the way for their introduction in 1908.

Borough, The A poem by GEORGE CRABBE, published in 1810. It takes the form of 24 letters from 'a residing burgess in a large sea-port', describing various aspects of life in a town which is clearly based on Crabbe's native Aldeburgh. Much of the poem is rather shapeless and meandering, but it comes to life towards the end with seven letters dealing exclusively with the life history of a single person – either one of the 'Inhabitants of the Alms-House' or one of 'The Poor of the Borough'. Particularly powerful are *Clelia*, about the moral and social decline of an irredeemably trivial flirt, *Ellen Orford* and *Peter Grimes* (Letter XXII). Grimes is a fisherman driven by the desire to inflict pain and hurt. The apprentices he buys from the London workhouses perish under his brutal treatment. Eventually forced to live and work in solitude, he is visited by the ghosts of his father and the tormented boys. He goes insane with guilt and remorse, and dies in mental agony. The story was made into an opera by Benjamin Britten (1945).

Borrow, George (Henry) 1803–81 Autobiographer, translator, linguist and traveller. Born in East Dereham, Norfolk, son of a recruiting officer in the militia, Borrow experienced little childhood stability because of the frequent movements of the regiment around Britain. He had only three or four years of formal schooling, after which he was articled to a firm of solicitors in Norwich, though apparently without any intention of practising law. By 1824, when his father died and the articling period ended, he had a working knowledge of at least 12 languages, including Latin, Greek, French, Welsh, Irish, Italian, German, Danish and Dutch; he later added Portuguese, Russian, Arabic and Spanish. Borrow habitually called himself a philologist or 'Lavengro', throughout his life dabbling in comparative linguistics and verse translation. At least by the time of the family's return to Norwich in 1816, he had begun to associate with gypsies, soon having a good knowledge of their ways.

The years 1824–32 were divided between Norwich and London, where he made a number of attempts to establish himself as a writer. He compiled a six-volume edition of *THE NEWGATE CALENDAR* (1826); published a translation of *Faustus: His Life, Death, and Descent into Hell* (1825), banned by some libraries because of antisocial interpolations; engaged in hackwork for London booksellers, producing the *Life and Adventures of the Famous Colonel Blood* (1825) and probably other such pamphlets; and put out, by subscription, his *Romantic Ballads, Translated from the Danish* (1826). Not a great deal is known about his personal life: he continued to read widely, he may have travelled, he was certainly from time to time ill, for he was throughout his life the victim of a severe nervous disorder which he and his mother called 'the horrors'.

His linguistic proficiency resulted in an introduction to the British and Foreign Bible Society in 1832. Financially supported by an extensive network of local Bible groups, this interdenominational, but predominantly Evangelical organization was committed to the world-wide distribution of the Bible, and particularly the New Testament, usually in specially prepared editions in the appropriate language. Borrow worked for the Society for seven years, first in St Petersburg (1833–5), where he issued a translation of the New Testament into Manchu and produced two volumes of his own verse translations, *Targum* and *The Talisman* (both 1835), and then in Portugal and Spain (1835–40), where he supervised the printing and distribution of the New Testament in Spanish and Basque. For these activities he was arrested on several occasions, and at least once spent some time in gaol. By travelling extensively through dangerous, little-known areas of Portugal and western Spain, Borrow also had those adventures that were soon to give imaginative substance to the two books which made him famous: *The Zincali* (1841) and *THE BIBLE IN SPAIN* (1843).

Borrow married Mrs Mary Clarke in 1840 and for the rest of his life resided on her estate at Oulton, Norfolk, albeit with long periods in Yarmouth (1853–60) and London (1860–?70). During this period, he wrote the three works on which his literary reputation chiefly depends: *LAVENGRO* (1851), *THE ROMANY RYE* (1857) and *WILD WALES* (1857). Though he declined to provide the literal autobiography he at one time promised, these works, especially the first two, for many years enjoyed the status of established classics, simultaneously delighting and puzzling the reader with a racy, convincing, but impenetrable amalgam of fact and fiction. He spent his later years in further forays into translation (a second edition of his *Gypsy Luke*) and philology *(Romano Lavo-Lil)*, at the same time consolidating his reputation as a traveller by means of walking tours through Norfolk, Wales, Ireland and Scotland.

Bosman, Herman Charles 1905–51 South African short-story writer, essayist and novelist. He was born at Kuils River, Cape Province. With Afrikaner background but English-medium education, he worked as a schoolmaster in a remote Afrikaner district near Groot Marico, Transvaal. After four and a half years in jail for fatally shooting his stepbrother in a quarrel, he spent nine years in Europe, then practised journalism in South Africa. His literary reputation rose steadily after his death. It rests especially upon *Mafeking Road* (1947), *Unto Dust* (1963), *Jurie Steyn's Post Office* (1971) and *A Bekkersdal Marathon* (1971) – collections of spirited stories about rural Afrikaner life, original, versatile treatments that include sardonic detachment, shrewd observation, social satire, irony and folk comedy. With humour and pathos *Cold Stone Jug* (1949) recounts his prison experience; *A Cask of Jerepigo* (1957) gathers essays and sketches together; *Jacaranda in the Night* (1947) and *Willemsdorp* (1977) are novels. *Collected Works* (2 vols.) appeared in 1981.

Boston, Lucy (Maria) 1892–1990 Writer of CHILDREN'S LITERATURE. Born in Southport, and educated at a Quaker school and Oxford, she trained as a nurse before turning to poetry and painting. In 1939 she took up residence at the 12th-century manor house at Hemingford Grey, near Cambridge, which later featured in her children's books. The first of these, *The Children of Green Knowe* (1954), was published when she was over 60. Its successors include *The River at Green Knowe* (1959), *A Stranger at Green Knowe* (1961), *An Enemy at Green Knowe* (1964) and *The Stones of Green Knowe* (1976), which brings the series to an end by describing how the house was originally built. *The Sea Egg* (1967), more strikingly original, tells the story of a greenish stone that hatches a small triton under the gaze of two children holidaying in Cornwall.

Bostonians, The A novel by Henry James, serialized in *THE CENTURY MAGAZINE* in 1885–6 and published in volume form in 1886. It is a satirical study of the movement for female emancipation in New England. In searching for a tale which would be characteristic of social conditions in the USA, James concluded that the most striking aspect of American life at the time was 'the situation of women, the decline of the sentiment of sex, and the agitation in their behalf'.

The novel recounts the story of a young lawyer from the South, Basil Ransom, who comes to Boston on business. He becomes acquainted with his two cousins, the feminist Olive Chancellor and her sister, the widow Mrs Luna, who soon falls in love with him. Olive takes Basil to a suffragette meeting, where he meets the altruistic philanthropist, Miss Birdseye, a character modelled on ELIZABETH PEABODY. Both Olive and Basil are immediately interested by a beautiful young woman speaker, Verena Tarrant. Verena is easily persuaded to share Olive's luxurious home, and

Olive sets out to make her a leader of the feminist cause, pleading with her to forswear the thought of marriage. Basil, however, increasingly irritated by the attentions of Mrs Luna, falls in love with Verena and attempts to counter Olive's sway over her. As a result, hostility develops between Olive and Basil. Verena is preparing to deliver a course of lectures, but when Miss Birdseye dies she loses confidence in her purpose. She is about to begin her first lecture when Basil's appearance in the hall unnerves her. Forced to choose between Olive and Basil, she accepts Basil's proposal, to Olive's bitter disappointment.

Boswell, Sir **Alexander** 1775–1822 Poet. Born at Auchinleck, the eldest son of JAMES BOSWELL, he inherited his father's interest in literature. Like many of his contemporaries, he was a collector of songs. He also wrote occasional verse and political squibs. One of them, 'The New Whig Song', offended James Stuart of Dunearn, who killed him in a duel. Boswell took a particular interest in his fellow Ayrshireman ROBERT BURNS, and campaigned for the monument to Burns on the banks of the River Doon.

Boswell, James 1740–95 Journal writer and biographer of SAMUEL JOHNSON. Born in Edinburgh, the son of Alexander Boswell (later Lord Auchinleck), judge of the Court of Session, he was educated at Edinburgh High School and studied law, with little enthusiasm, at the Universities of Edinburgh and Glasgow. His father intended a legal career for him, but Boswell had set his mind on other things and left for London in 1760. By turns libertine and puritanical, his colourful life there involved him in a protracted battle of wills with his formidable father, without whose help he was unable to purchase the commission in the Footguards he so desired. He was also ambitious for literary and political reputation, and began to mix in the appropriate social circles.

Already a friend of Thomas Sheridan and GARRICK, Boswell made the most important literary acquaintance of his life on 16 May 1763, when he met Samuel Johnson. Although Boswell started recording closely the activities and conversation of Johnson almost at once, the impression that he had little literary or even social life independent of his friend is wrong. It was largely with the latter's encouragement, though, that he recorded his elaborate view of contemporary London life, published in 1950 as *Boswell's London Journal 1762–3*.

Boswell toured the Continent in 1763–6, completing his legal studies in Utrecht, meeting Rousseau and WILKES, and visiting Corsica in October 1765. There he gained an introduction to the redoubtable General Paoli, whose independent spirit greatly impressed him, and as a direct result of which he championed the Corsican cause in an *Account of Corsica* (published 1768) and *Essays in Favour of the Brave*

Corsicans (1769). Returning to England in 1766 on the death of his mother, Boswell was admitted to the Scottish Bar where, to his father's relief, he began to practise as an advocate in Edinburgh. In 1767 he published *Dorando*, an allegorical romance, set in Spain, concerning the Douglas inheritance case, and in 1769, after numerous well-documented philanderings, he married his cousin, Margaret Montgomerie.

He remained closely in touch with Johnson, however, paying frequent visits to London, and continuing to move in literary circles. Boswell made the acquaintance of GOLDSMITH and BURKE, and in 1773 became a member of the celebrated literary coterie 'the Club'. He wrote essays under the name 'Hypochondriack' from 1777 to 1783, and continued to pursue a legal career in Scotland, where he succeeded to his father's estate in 1782.

Samuel Johnson died in December 1784, and in the following year Boswell published THE JOURNAL OF A TOUR TO THE HEBRIDES, a record of their travels through Scotland in 1773. He was called to the English Bar in 1786, and unsuccessfully entertained hopes of a political career in London. During this time, though, with the encouragement of the scholar EDMOND MALONE, he completed the magnificent work for which he is best remembered, THE LIFE OF SAMUEL JOHNSON LL.D., published in 1791. Boswell spent his remaining years in London where he died on 19 May 1795, after a short illness. He was renowned as good company, with his lively mind and formidable memory, a man exuberant and melancholy by turns. His several journals and private papers, many discovered at Malahide Castle, have been collected and edited by Frederick A. Pottle; they confirm Boswell as a talented writer and a man worth remembering in his own right.

Bottomley, Gordon 1874–1948 Playwright and poet. Born and educated in Keighley, Yorkshire, Bottomley was prevented by ill health from pursuing a career in banking. In enforced leisure, he wrote poetry and plays, and became a contributor to GEORGIAN POETRY. Bottomley's interest in Celtic folklore is already evident in his first published collection of poetry, *The Mickle Drede and Other Verses* (1896). His plays are always historically and geographically distanced. The first three to be performed are certainly among his best. *The Crier by Night* (published in 1902; first performed 1916) resolves the cruel conflict between the sadistic wife of a farmer and an Irish servant-girl with the aid of a water-spirit. *King Lear's Wife* (published in 1920; first performed 1915), also much concerned with brutality, invents an adulterous affair for King Lear while his wife is dying. *Gruach* (published 1921; first performed 1923) describes the courtship of Macbeth and Lady Macbeth. Bottomley's later dramatic work was written for and confined to amateur performance. It showed the influence of

W. B. YEATS, in particular his *Plays for Dancers*. Some of the best of it is collected in *Lyric Plays* (1932).

Boucicault, Dion(ysius) (Lardner) 1820–90 Irish playwright, actor and theatre manager. His first success came early when *LONDON ASSURANCE* (1841) was staged at the Theatre Royal, COVENT GARDEN. Another five-act comedy, *Old Heads and Young Hearts* (1844), offers further evidence of his proficiency. A series of hastily written but clever versions of French plays, including *The Corsican Brothers* (1852) and *The Vampire* (1852), had established him as a leading dramatist in England before his emigration to the United States in 1853. There he began a separate and equally successful career, particularly with the MELO-DRAMAS *The Poor of New York* (1857), *Jessie Brown: or, The Relief of Lucknow* (1858) and *THE OCTOROON* (1859). Three outstanding Irish melodramas, the *COLLEEN BAWN* (1860), *Arrah-na-Pogue* (1864) and *THE SHAUGHRAUN* (1874), confirmed his position at the head of the dramatic profession. It was a position that did not survive him. Boucicault wrote too much – nearly 200 plays have been ascribed to him – and too opportunistically, but he had the facility to disguise imitation as innovation and was, at his best, a superb theatrical storyteller.

Bourchier, John, 2nd Baron Berners ?1469–1533 Translator and statesman. When young he was involved in a premature attempt to make Henry Tudor king, and in 1497 he helped in the suppression of the Cornish rebellion against the then Henry VII in support of the pretender Perkin Warbeck. He served the next Tudor monarch, Henry VIII, in various military and diplomatic capacities, including the post of deputy at Calais, and was present at the Field of the Cloth of Gold. In 1516 he became Chancellor of the Exchequer; Holbein painted him in the robes of that office.

As a translator he favoured the works of medieval chivalry and romance, COURTESY BOOKS and CHRONI-CLES. His vigorous translation of Froissart's *Chronicles*, faithful in spirit to its original, appeared in two parts in 1523 and 1525. The later chronicles of EDWARD HALL and RAPHAEL HOLINSHED are indebted to it. The chivalric romance *HUON OF BORDEAUX*, which introduced the fairy prince Oberon to English readers, was not printed until after Berners's death, probably by WYNKYN DE WORDE in 1534. From the French Berners translated *The History of the Most Noble and Valiant Knight Arthur of Little Brittain* (i.e. of Brittany). *The Castle of Love*, of which the first edition was *c.* 1540, was a translation of a courtesy book by Diego de San Pedro. Berners's most popular work was *The Golden Book of Marcus Aurelius*, a translation from the French version of Antonio de Guevara's original Spanish. This appeared in 1535 and went through many editions in the 16th century.

Bourne, George See STURT, GEORGE.

Bourne, Randolph 1886–1918 American essayist and social critic. He was born in Bloomfield, New Jersey, and educated at Columbia. His first articles, on the revolutionary character of youth, were published in *THE ATLANTIC MONTHLY* and collected in *Youth and Life* (1913). As his reputation as an essayist rose, he found audiences through *THE NEW REPUBLIC*, *THE DIAL*, and the *Seven Arts*. He was an eclectic reader, and his writings reflected broad interests, notably education (*The Gary Schools*, 1916, and *Education and Living*, 1917), the development of socially responsible fiction, and the depreciation of an ethnically diverse American culture ('Trans-National America', 1916). He was also a fervent pacifist, and after Woodrow Wilson's abandonment of neutrality in 1917 he became an eloquent and increasingly isolated advocate of American non-intervention in World War I (for example in *Untimely Papers*, 1919). His prowess as a conversationalist impressed a generation of writers and critics, including Van Wyck Brooks, Lewis Mumford, and JOHN DOS PASSOS. Among these figures Bourne developed an almost mythic stature. Disfigured – his spine had been deformed at birth by an incompetent doctor – but brilliant, he seemed to represent to them the spirit of 1910 which could not outlive the war.

Bowdler, Thomas 1754–1825 Editor. Bowdler's edition of SHAKESPEARE, *The Family Shakespeare* (1818), made drastic cuts in the text of the plays by omitting 'whatever is unfit to be read aloud by a gentleman to a company of ladies' and so gave rise to the term 'to bowdlerize'. He also prepared an edition of GIBBON's *DECLINE AND FALL OF THE ROMAN EMPIRE* on the same principles.

Bowen, Elizabeth (Dorothea Cole) 1899–1973 Novelist and short-story writer. She was born in Dublin at Bowen's Court, an 18th-century manor where she spent much of her early childhood and which she eventually inherited in 1930. She was educated at Downe House School in Kent, and lived in Ireland, London, France and Italy until her marriage in 1923. For the next 10 years she was based in London, the setting for many of her novels and short stories. Early volumes of stories, which already displayed a subtle use of language, were *Encounters* (1923), *Ann Lee's* (1926), *Joining Charles* (1929) and *The Cat Jumps* (1934). Later collections included *Look at All Those Roses* (1941) and *The Demon Lover* (1945). Her *Collected Stories*, introduced by ANGUS WILSON, appeared in 1980.

Early novels included *The Hotel* (1927), *The Last September* (1929), *Friends and Relations* (1931) and *The House in Paris* (1935). Best known, however, are *THE DEATH OF THE HEART* (1938) and *The Heat of the Day* (1949), the latter being a tragic love-story set in war-time London. Later novels were *A World of Love* (1955) and *Eva Trout* (1969). Her writing follows HENRY JAMES in its attention to style and its subtle delineation of character (especially female character) and setting. Her impressionistic descriptions of the landscape, both urban and rural, and its seasonal changes add a highly effective dimension to her work. She also wrote *Seven Winters* (1942), a partial autobiography, and *Bowen's Court* (1942), a history of the family seat.

Bowering, George 1935– Canadian poet, novelist and critic. Born and brought up in the Okanagan Valley of British Columbia, he was a Royal Canadian Air Force aerial photographer before attending the University of British Columbia. His early volumes of poetry, strongly influenced by the BLACK MOUNTAIN SCHOOL, include *Points on the Grid* (1964), *Baseball* (1967), *Rocky Mountain Foot* (1968) and *The Gangs of Kosmos* (1969). He has been involved in the publication of a number of influential little magazines and was founding editor of *Tish*, an iconoclastic poetry journal of the 1960s. He has worked in various Canadian universities and now teaches at Simon Fraser University, Vancouver. Around 1970 Bowering turned to longer, book-length poems; these include *George Vancouver* (1970) and *Autobiology* (1972), collected in *The Catch* (1976) and *West Window* (1982). The navigator and explorer GEORGE VANCOUVER fascinates him and his most acclaimed novel, *Burning Water* (1980), is a deconstructionist account of Vancouver's search for the Northwest Passage. His fiction, which includes *A Short Sad Book* (1977), *A Place to Die* (1983) and *Harry's Fragments* (1990), adopts a playful stance towards narrative conventions, showing the influence of GERTRUDE STEIN. *In the Flesh* (1974) and *Another Mount* (1979) are among his other volumes of verse. His critical books include *A Way with Words* (1982) and *Imaginary Hand* (1988).

Bowles, Paul 1910– American novelist and short-story writer. Born in New York, he attended the University of Virginia before going to Paris, where his first poetry was published in the magazine *transitions*. After some years as a composer and music critic, he published his first novel, *The Sheltering Sky* (1949). Subsequent works, notably *The Delicate Prey* (1950; as *A Little Stone* in Britain), *Let It Come Down* (1952) and *The Spider's House* (1955), continue to explore the theme of spiritually weary Westerners attempting to escape the ennui of their lives only to find themselves displaced in an Orient they find unsatisfying and even frightening.

Resident in Tangier since 1952, Bowles has tape-recorded, transcribed and translated original accounts of indigenous life, including *A Life Full of Holes* by Driss ben Hamad Charhadi (1964), *For Bread Alone* by Mohammad Chourkil (1973) and several by

Mohammad Mrabet: *M'Hashish* (1969), *The Boy Who Set the Fire* (1974), *Harmless Poisons, Blameless Sins* (1976) and *The Beach Café and the Voice* (1980). His other work includes: short stories in *Pages from Cold Point and Other Stories* (1968), *Collected Stories* (1979), *Midnight Mass* (1985), *Call at Corazón* (1988) and *A Thousand Days for Mokhtar* (1989); travel sketches in *Their Heads are Green and Their Hands are Blue* (1963); and poetry in *Scenes* (1968). *Without Stopping* (1972) is an autobiography and *Two Years beside the Strait* (1990) a journal of the years 1987-9.

Bowles, William Lisle 1762-1850 Poet. Educated at Winchester School and at Trinity College, Oxford, in 1804 Bowles was appointed vicar of Bremhill in Wiltshire and prebendary of Salisbury Cathedral; he later became a canon and was made chaplain to the Prince Regent in 1818. *Fourteen Sonnets, Elegiac and Descriptive, Written during a Tour* (1789) revived the SONNET, a neglected form, and influenced both COLERIDGE and SOUTHEY. His edition of ALEXANDER POPE (1806) brought him into conflict with THOMAS CAMPBELL, to whom he replied in *The Invariable Principles of Poetry* (1819). BYRON joined Campbell, but Bowles effectively defended his views.

Bowra, Sir **(Cecil) Maurice** 1898-1971 Scholar and critic. The son of a customs official, he was born in China and educated at Cheltenham and at New College, Oxford. A fellow of Wadham College, Oxford, from 1922 and its warden from 1938 until 1970, he was a celebrated host, raconteur and wit. His many works on classical literature include *Tradition and Design in the Iliad* (1930), *Ancient Greek Literature* (1933), *The Greek Experience* (1957) and *Landmarks in Greek Literature* (1966); his more modern interests appear in *The Heritage of Symbolism* (1943) and *The Romantic Imagination* (1949). Bowra also published translations of Greek and Russian poetry, and edited *The Oxford Book of Greek Verse in Translation* (1938).

Boyd, John 1912– Irish playwright. Born in Belfast, and educated at Queen's University, Belfast, and Trinity College, Dublin, he became director of the Lyric Theatre, Belfast. His major theme is the North's divided heritage, mainly in an urban setting and expressed in the local idiom paradoxically common to the antagonistic faiths. *The Assassin* (1969) explores the psychology of a clerical demagogue; *The Flats* (1971) places domestic tragedy in the collective violence of the Belfast streets. These naturalistic plays, with *The Farm* (1972) and *The Street* (1977), are acutely discerning of the brutalities behind factional slogans and their travesty of political action.

Boyd, Martin (A'Beckett) 1893-1969 Australian novelist. Born in Lucerne and brought up in Melbourne, Boyd divided his time between Australia and

Europe. He was studying architecture when World War I broke out; he enlisted in the British army and later transferred to the RFC. In a period of post-war indecision he tried life as a journalist and spent some time in a Franciscan community before becoming a novelist. *The Montforts* (1928), one of the early novels published under the pseudonym of Martin Mills, is a dense but elegant and ironic family chronicle of Anglo-Australian life. Its preoccupations recur in much of his best work, which includes *Lucinda Brayford* (1946), *Such Pleasure* (1949), *The Cardboard Crown* (1952), *A Difficult Young Man* (1955), *Outbreak of Love* (1957) and *When Blackbirds Sing* (1962). Of his other novels the most notable is *Such Pleasure* (1949). He published two volumes of autobiography, *A Single Flame* (1939) and *Day of My Delight* (1965).

Boyd, William 1952– Novelist. Born in Accra, he grew up in Ghana and Nigeria and was educated at Gordonstoun, an experience he drew on for his television play *Good and Bad at Games* (1985). Until 1982 he was a lecturer in English literature at St Hilda's College, Oxford. A fluent and good-humoured writer, he has several times used Africa as the setting for his work. *A Good Man in Africa* (1981), his first novel, chronicles the misadventures of the dishevelled and lecherous Morgan Leafy, who reappears in a collection of short stories, *On the Yankee Station* (1981). *An Ice-Cream War* (1982) is a detailed, often whimsically comic novel about an obscure African interstice of World War I. *Brazzaville Beach* (1990) is a sober tale of a female animal behaviourist in West Africa, whose fictional observations of chimpanzees in the wild owe much to the examples of research scientists like Jane Goodall. *Stars and Bars* (1984) is a more predictable Englishman-abroad comedy set in the USA. Boyd's most substantial book, *The New Confessions* (1987), is a long, ambitious and energetic fictive history of the 20th century, constituted as the memoirs of a pioneering film director concerned to create filmic adaptations of the works of Rousseau, whose *Confessions* provides the novel with a literary paradigm.

Boyer, Abel 1667–1729 Historian. A Huguenot, he was educated in the Netherlands and came to England in 1689. In 1703–13 he published an annual calendar of events. He made his mark as a historian with *The History of King William III* (1702) and *The History of the Life and Reign of Queen Anne* (1722). His translation of the *Mémoires de la vie du Comte de Gramont* (1714) was revised and annotated by SIR WALTER SCOTT (1811).

Boyle, Kay 1903–93 American novelist and short-story writer. Born in St Paul, Minnesota, she lived in Europe for 30 years before and after World War II. From 1946 to 1954 she was a foreign correspondent for THE NEW YORKER. Among the 24 volumes of fiction she published between 1929 and 1975 were several collections of short stories: *Short Stories* (1929), *Wedding Day and Other Stories* (1930), *The First Lover and Other Stories* (1936), *The White Horse of Vienna and Other Stories* (1936) and *Thirty Stories* (1946). In 1935 and 1941 she was the recipient of the O. Henry Award. Among her novels are *Year before Last* (1932), *My Next Bride* (1934), *Monday Night* (1938), *The Crazy Hunter: Three Short Novels* (1940), *Avalanche* (1944) and *A Frenchman Must Die* (1946). She often took as her subject a young and unworldly American who travels to Europe, and made extraordinary instances of brutality or absurdity a particular characteristic of her work. She also published: verse, most recently in *This is Not a Letter* (1985); non-fiction, including a selection of essays, *Words That Must Somehow be Said* (1985); and CHILDREN'S LITERATURE.

Boyle, Robert 1627–91 Chemist and philosopher. The 14th child of the Earl of Cork, he was educated at Eton and by private tutors. Around 1655 he moved to Oxford to join the group of proto-scientists centred on John Wilkins, Warden of Wadham, which included Christopher Wren, Seth Ward, William Petty and later Robert Hooke. His early interests were in alchemy. However, following the lead given by Descartes and Gassendi, he became convinced that the structure of matter was corpuscular, and its operations open to rational investigation. His work would be instrumental in turning chemistry from an occult science to a recognizably modern discipline in which theory and practical experiment supported and advanced each other. His method of experiment, observation and hypothesis owed much to BACON's proposals for a regulated scientific programme. Assisted by Hooke, his most rewarding research was into the behaviour of air and gases. Boyle's law, which stemmed from his work on atmospheric pressure and the vacuum in the 1650s, established the relationship between the pressure and the volume of a gas at a constant temperature. As a founder-member of the Royal Society in 1660, he was associated with all the leaders of the early scientific movement in England.

Boyle was a prolific writer, his most enduring works being *The Sceptical Chymist* (1661), a dialogue in which he attacked the theories of matter based on elements and qualities that derived from Aristotle and Paracelsus, and approached the question of how change occurred in the material world. The book contains a somewhat florid recommendation of the experimental method. *The Origin of Forms and Qualities* (1666) offered a defence of the corpuscular theory of matter, falling back on to Greek atomic theory for support. Boyle's concern with the bases of scientific classification expressed in this book had some influence over LOCKE's ESSAY CONCERNING HUMAN UNDERSTANDING. Later in his life his religious concerns began to merge with his scientific interests, and he was anxious to refute the suspicion that atomism led to atheism. He was a declared opponent of HOBBES. His desire to demonstrate the intellectual compatibility between scientific enquiry and revealed Christianity led him to endow the Boyle Lectures, which became a vehicle for those who strove to maintain a consensus between science and religion in the early 18th century. His *Occasional Reflections on Several Subjects* (1665) provided material for Book Three of *GULLIVER'S TRAVELS*, and was also satirized by SWIFT in *Meditations on a Broomstick*. His sentimental religious romance, *The Martyrdom of Theodora and Didymus* (1687), was later adapted to provide a libretto for Handel's opera *Theodora*.

boys' companies Surviving records show that the choristers of the Chapel Royal, London, were performing occasional plays by 1516 and those of St Paul's by about 1525, but the significant decision to present plays in public was taken in 1576, when Richard Farrant, Master of the Children of the Chapel at Windsor, purchased a lease on rooms in the Blackfriars with the aim of converting them for indoor performance. The BLACKFRIARS THEATRE was closed in about 1585, perhaps overshadowed by the greater success of the St Paul's Boys in the plays of JOHN LYLY. Increasingly involved in controversy during the 1580s, the boys' companies fell seriously out of favour over their part in the MARPRELATE debate (1588–9) and for nearly 10 years (*c.* 1590–8) they ceased to act in public. But the popularity of boy actors reached a new peak during the first decade of the 17th century. MARSTON, DEKKER, MIDDLETON, CHAPMAN, WEBSTER, JONSON, BEAUMONT and FLETCHER were among the playwrights who wrote for them. By 1613, fashionable interest had so diminished that the once-great Children of the Chapel Royal were absorbed by an adult company.

Boz The early pseudonym of DICKENS, derived from his infant mispronunciation of 'Moses' as 'Boses'. His longest-standing illustrator, HABLOT K. BROWNE, adopted the pseudonym of Phiz.

Bracebridge Hall: or, The Humorists: A Medley A book of 49 tales and sketches by WASHINGTON IRVING, published in 1822 under the pseudonym, Geoffrey Crayon, Gent., that he had used for its predecessor, *THE SKETCH BOOK*. Though the collection uses English, French and Spanish settings, the best-remembered tales, 'Dolph Heylinger' and 'The Storm-Ship', are set in America.

Brackenbury, Alison 1953– Poet. Born in Gainsborough, Lincolnshire, she was educated at St Hugh's College, Oxford. She worked as a librarian until the birth of her daughter in 1983. After publishing two pamphlets, *Journey to a Cornish Wedding* (1977) and

Two Poems (1979), she has produced a series of major collections which have established her as one of the leading poets of her generation: *Dreams of Power and Other Poems* (1981), in which the title-poem is a DRAMATIC MONOLOGUE by one of history's victims, Arabella Stuart, granddaughter of Bess of Hardwick; *Breaking Ground and Other Poems* (1984), in which the title-poem evokes episodes from the life of JOHN CLARE; and *Christmas Roses and Other Poems* (1988), dealing confidently with urban and rural themes, individually or united in a delicate twist. Her poems about her daughter are poignant but refreshingly free of sentimentality. *Selected Poems* appeared in 1991.

Brackenridge, Hugh Henry 1748–1816 American novelist and poet. Brackenridge was born in Scotland; his family emigrated to Pennsylvania when he was five. He educated himself in the classics while growing up on the frontier, and in 1768 entered Princeton University where he collaborated with PHILIP FRENEAU on *Father Bembo's Pilgrimage to Mecca* (1770), a prose SATIRE on American manners, and on a patriotic poem, *The Rising Glory of America* (1772). During the Revolutionary War he wrote several patriotic works, including *A Poem on Divine Revelation* (1774) and two plays, *The Battle of Bunkers-Hill* (1776) and *The Death of General Montgomery* (1777). In 1779 he went to Philadelphia and founded the *United States Magazine*, which published patriotic speeches and state constitutions, as well as his own series of fictional essays on Revolutionary themes, 'The Cave of Vanhest'.

He soon moved to Pittsburgh to practise law. There he became involved in politics, but was a true partisan of neither political party. Having founded *The Pittsburgh Gazette* (1786), the first Western newspaper, he frequently contributed satires on both Eastern and Western manners, both Federalist and Republican politics. He acted as mediator during the Whiskey Rebellion provoked by Alexander Hamilton's excise tax on liquor, and his account of the rebellion was published as *Incidents of the Insurrection in the Western Parts of Pennsylvania, in the Year 1794* (1795). He served on the Pennsylvania Supreme Court from 1799 to 1814, continuing to publish instalments of *MODERN CHIVALRY* (1792–1815), the satirical novel on which his literary reputation chiefly rests.

Bradbrook, M(uriel) C(lara) 1909–93 Critic. Born in Wallasey, near Liverpool, where her father was a coastguard officer, she attended schools in Wallasey and Glasgow before going to study at Cambridge University. She began a long association with Girton College as an undergraduate, becoming a fellow in 1932 and eventually Mistress from 1968 to 1976. She was also professor of English from 1965 to

1976. Her many works include studies of Ibsen (1946), T. S. ELIOT (1950), SIR THOMAS MALORY (1957), MALCOLM LOWRY (1974) and JOHN WEBSTER (1980), as well as a history of Girton College. However, she is best known as an authority on SHAKESPEARE and the Elizabethan theatre. *Themes and Conventions of Elizabethan Tragedy* (1934), *The Growth and Structure of Elizabethan Comedy* (1955) and *The Rise of the Common Player* (1962) have been gathered with *Shakespeare the Craftsman* (1969) and two other works on Shakespeare as the six-volume *History of Elizabethan Drama* (1979).

Bradbury, Malcolm (Stanley) 1932– Novelist and critic. He was born in Leicester. His first novel, *Eating People is Wrong* (1959), and *Stepping Westward* (1965), set in the USA, are PICARESQUE novels of academic life in the manner of KINGSLEY AMIS's *LUCKY JIM*. *The History Man* (1975), with its bitter portrait of a manically trendy sociology lecturer, was hailed as the definitive fictional response to the culture of the 1960s. *Rates of Exchange* (1982) continues the preoccupation with the academic life but displays greater technical self-consciousness. The tendency has grown in subsequent work: *Why Come to Slaka?* (1986), a pastiche guidebook to the fictional Eastern European setting of *Rates of Exchange*; *Cuts* (1987), a novella developing the metaphoric consonances between monetarism and STRUCTURALISM; *Mensonge* (1987), a monograph on a fictional structuralist philosopher; an anthology of personal *Unsent Letters* (1988); and *Dr Criminale* (1992), a novel.

Since 1970 Bradbury has been professor of American Studies at the University of East Anglia, where with ANGUS WILSON he has presided over Britain's only notable university course in creative writing. Students have included IAN MCEWAN, KAZUO ISHIGURO, Adam Mars-Jones, Clive Sinclair and MAGGIE GEE. His academic publications include: monographs on EVELYN WAUGH (1962) and SAUL BELLOW (1982); a collection of essays on contemporary fiction, *Possibilities* (1973); and *The Modern American Novel* (1983). *No, Not Bloomsbury* (1987) is a collection of literary journalism.

Bradbury, Ray (Douglas) 1920– American novelist and short-story writer. Born in Waukegan, Illinois, he became a full-time writer in 1943 and contributed numerous short stories to periodicals before publishing a collection, *Dark Carnival* (1947). His reputation as a leading writer of SCIENCE FICTION was established with the publication of *The Martian Chronicles* (1950; called *The Silver Locusts* in Britain), which describes the first attempts of Earth people to conquer and colonize Mars during the years 1999–2026, the constant thwarting of their efforts by the gentle, telepathic Martians, the eventual colonization, and finally the effect on the Martian settlers of a massive nuclear war

on Earth. As much a work of social criticism as of science fiction, *The Martian Chronicles* reflects some of the prevailing anxieties of America in the early 1950s: the fear of nuclear war, the longing for a simpler life, and reactions against racism and censorship. Another of Bradbury's best-known works, the novel *Fahrenheit 451* (1953), is set in a future when the written word is forbidden: resisting a totalitarian state which burns all the books, a group of rebels memorize entire works of literature and philosophy. Among his other works are the novel *Something Wicked This Way Comes* (1962), and numerous collections of short stories: *The Illustrated Man* (1951), *The Golden Apples of the Sun* (1953), *The October Sky* (1955), *A Medicine for Melancholy* (1959; called *The Day It Rained Forever* in Britain), *The Machineries of Joy* (1964), *I Sing The Body Electric!* (1969), *The Last Circus and the Electrocution* (1980) and *A Memory of Murder* (1984). His poetry is collected in *The Complete Poems of Ray Bradbury* (1982). *Death is a Lonely Business* (1985) is a Californian murder mystery.

Braddon, Mary Elizabeth 1835–1915 Novelist. She was born in London (two years earlier than she later liked to admit), the daughter of an unsuccessful solicitor who eventually deserted his family. In youth she took to the stage, but without abandoning her interest in writing: she began her first novel, not published until several years afterwards, when she was 19. In 1860 she met John Maxwell, a publisher of journals, and lived with him for 14 years before the death of his wife allowed them to marry. *LADY AUDLEY'S SECRET* (1862), her first published novel, was started in an attempt to rescue one of Maxwell's journals; the journal failed but the novel became the most popular example of Victorian SENSATION FICTION. Its success overshadowed the rest of a long and hard-working career in which she produced some 80 novels. Some were in the same vein as *Lady Audley's Secret*: *Aurora Floyd* (1863), *John Marchmont's Legacy* (1863), *Henry Dunbar: The Story of an Outcast* (1864), *Sir Jasper's Tenant* (1865), *Birds of Prey* (1867) and *Charlotte's Inheritance* (1868). Others demonstrate a greater range and seriousness than public or reviewers fully recognized: *The Doctor's Wife* (1864) adapts Flaubert's *Madame Bovary*; *The Lady's Mile* (1866) and *The Lovels of Arden* (1871) are novels of society; *Vixen* (1871) is a SATIRE; *Ishmael* (1884) is a historical romance; and *Dead Love Has Chains* (1907) is a tragedy. She also contributed to many journals and edited *Belgravia* and *Temple Bar*.

Bradford, William 1590–1657 Governor and historian of Plymouth Colony. Born in Yorkshire, he sailed to America on board the *Mayflower* in 1620. At Plymouth, on the death of John Carver, Bradford was elected governor, an office which he held from 1621 to 1656 except for five years when he voluntarily stepped down to serve as assistant governor. In 1627, together with seven fellow emigrants and four London merchants, he assumed the colony's debt of £1800 from the original investors. His *History of Plymouth Plantation* describes the origins of the Separatist movement in England, the settlement in Leyden, the plans to emigrate to New England, the voyage of the *Mayflower*, and the sacred and secular affairs of the colony in the years 1620–46. Written between 1630 and 1651, it remained unpublished until 1856, though his nephew, NATHANIEL MORTON, consulted it when writing *New England's Memorial* (1669). Bradford's incomplete *Letter Book* (1624–30) and his letters to John Winthrop show a leader working out the colony's internal problems as well as negotiating with England, the neighbouring Massachusetts Bay Colony and the Indians.

Bradley, A(ndrew) C(ecil) 1851–1935 Critic. Bradley was born in Cheltenham, the son of a clergyman, and the younger brother of the philosopher F. H. BRADLEY. He was educated at Cheltenham College and at Balliol College, Oxford, where he became a fellow in 1874, lecturing in philosophy and English. In 1882 he became the first professor of literature and history at Liverpool, and he was later professor of English language and literature at Glasgow from 1890, and professor of poetry at Oxford from 1901 until 1906, when he retired from academic life.

Bradley is best known for his *Oxford Lectures on Poetry* (1909) and especially for *Shakespearean Tragedy* (1904), a series of lectures in which he approached the major tragedies of SHAKESPEARE through an extended study of the characters, who were presented as personalities independent of their place in the plays. The value of this approach has often been questioned since the 1930s, but Bradley's book is still read.

Bradley, F(rancis) H(erbert) 1846–1924 Philosopher. Born at Clapham in London and educated at Marlborough and University College, Oxford, he was elected a fellow of Merton College in 1870. His essay, *The Presuppositions of Critical History*, which contributed to the debate about the HIGHER CRITICISM (the study of the Gospels as historical records), appeared in 1874. Bradley's most important philosophical works were *Ethical Studies* (1876), *The Principles of Logic* (1883), *Appearance and Reality* (1893) and *Essays on Truth and Reality* (1914), the last two being a discussion of the state of contemporary metaphysical speculation. Bradley's thought was the subject of T. S. ELIOT's Harvard PhD thesis, eventually published as *Knowledge and Experience in the Philosophy of F. H. Bradley* (1964).

Bradshaigh, Lady *c.* 1706–85 Letter-writer. Born Dorothy Bellingham, she married Sir Roger Brad-

shaigh of Haigh, near Wigan, in 1731. On the publication of the first two volumes of *CLARISSA* in December 1747 she wrote to RICHARDSON, under the pseudonym 'Mrs Belfour', to suggest that Lovelace be reformed by Clarissa's excellence and that the conclusion of the work be their happy marriage. This started an extensive correspondence centring mainly on *Clarissa* and *THE HISTORY OF SIR CHARLES GRANDISON*, during the course of which Richardson attempted to explain his intentions in the two works. It is believed that the development of *Sir Charles Grandison* was much influenced by her constant adjurations that Richardson write a book about a good man. Although she considered intelligence to be a defect in a woman, Lady Bradshaigh nevertheless managed to evoke from Richardson some remarkable pieces of self-analysis. Recognizing the commercial and literary value of the correspondence, he persuaded her to edit it for publication. The letters were eventually incorporated into ANNA LAETITIA BARBAULD's edition of Richardson's letters (6 vols., 1804).

Bradstreet, Anne 1612–72 America's first published poet. She was born and grew up in aristocratic surroundings in England as the daughter of Thomas Dudley, who had been steward to the Earl of Lincoln. She married Simon Bradstreet at 16, and two years later sailed for America with her husband and father on the *Arbella*. Living in Ipswich, Massachusetts, and then in Andover, she became the mother of eight children. Both her father and her husband eventually became governors of Massachusetts.

Bradstreet's collection of poems, *The Tenth Muse Lately Sprung Up in America*, was published without her knowledge by her brother-in-law in London in 1650. A second edition, with corrections and additional poems, entitled *Several Poems Compiled with a Great Variety of Wit*, appeared in Boston six years after her death. The poems generally follow Elizabethan models, and show the influence of SPENSER, SIDNEY, Du Bartas and RALEIGH. There are, for example, quaternions such as 'The Four Elements', 'The Four Humours', 'The Four Ages of Man' and 'The Four Seasons'; a series of emblematic stanzas on the themes of time and mutability; and elegies on Sidney, Du Bartas and Queen Elizabeth. Many of the later poems are more personal in subject and less conventional in form, often meditating on domestic topics from a religious point of view. This group includes poems to her husband and ELEGIES on her dead children.

Bragg, Melvyn 1939– Novelist and broadcaster. Born and educated in Wigton, Cumbria, he went to Wadham College, Oxford, before setting out on a highly successful broadcasting career whose principal achievement has been the creation of a distinguished television arts programme, *The South Bank*

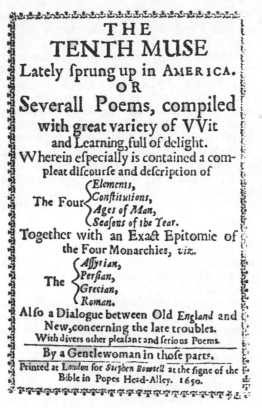

THE
TENTH MUSE
Lately fprung up in AMERICA.
OR
Severall Poems, compiled
with great variety of VVit
and Learning, full of delight.
Wherein efpecially is contained a com-
pleat difcourfe and defcription of
The Four {
Elements,
Conftitutions,
Ages of Man,
Seafons of the Year.

Together with an Exact Epitomie of
the Four Monarchies, viz.
The {
Affyrian,
Perfian,
Grecian,
Roman.

Alfo a Dialogue between Old England and
New, concerning the late troubles.
With divers other pleafant and ferious Poems.

By a Gentlewoman in thofe parts.

Printed at London for Stephen Bowtell at the figne of the
Bible in Popes Head-Alley. 1650.

The title-page of Anne Bradstreet's
The Tenth Muse, 1650

Show. As a novelist, he is unashamedly provincial, returning to his native Cumbria for the settings of works which range from *The Hired Man* (1969), sober and emotionally exact, to the breathless *A Time to Dance* (1990). *The Silken Net* (1974) is a sensitive study of a woman's inter-war life and *The Maid of Buttermere* (1987) an ingenious treatment of an episode from Lake District history. Bragg also wrote the screenplay for the film version of the musical *Jesus Christ Superstar* and an aptly titled biography of the actor Richard Burton, *Rich* (1988).

Braine, John 1922–86 Novelist. He was born and educated in Bradford. Before World War II he worked in a shop, a laboratory and a factory; afterwards he became a librarian in Northumberland and Yorkshire. He is still best known for his first novel, *Room at the Top* (1957), which brought him immediate recognition and was successfully filmed in 1959. One of the classic ANGRY YOUNG MEN novels, it features an unscrupulous and opportunistic hero, Joe Lampton, who chooses to marry wealth and success rather than his true love, and offers a sharp picture of Northern life in the 1950s, obsessed with wealth and social status. A sequel, *Life at the Top*, appeared in

1962. None of Braine's subsequent work attracted comparable attention; later novels include *The Vodi* (1959), set in a tuberculosis sanatorium, *The Crying Game* (1964), *First and Last Love* (1981) and *The Two of Us* (1984).

Braithwaite, William Stanley (Beaumont)
1879–1962 Black American poet, novelist, short-story writer and editor. Born in Boston, the son of West Indian parents, he began his literary career with *The Canadian* (1901), a novel which received little attention. His first collection of poetry, *Lyrics of Life and Love*, appeared in 1904; his second, *The House of Falling Leaves*, followed in 1908. He also produced a volume of short stories, *Frost on the Green Tree* (1928), a second novel, *Going over Tindel* (1924), and an autobiography, *The House under Arcturus* (1941). *Selected Poems* appeared in 1948.

In the first few decades of the century, Braithwaite was influential as an editor and literary critic. For 16 years he published the annual *Anthology of Magazine Verse and Year Book of American Poetry* (1913–29), which served as a major outlet for black writers and poets. He also became a mentor to the younger generation of black writers. In an article entitled 'Some Contemporary Poets of the Negro Race', published in *The Crisis* in 1919, he wrote about the dawning of a 'new movement' in black letters, a flourishing of creative activity which was later termed the HARLEM RENAISSANCE. He subsequently joined the faculty of the first black graduate school at Atlanta University, where he taught until his retirement.

Brathwaite, Edward (Kamau) [L. Edward] 1930– Caribbean poet and historian. Born in Bridgetown, Barbados, he was educated at Harrison College, Barbados, Pembroke College, Cambridge, and the University of Sussex. Between 1955 and 1962 he worked in Ghana, an experience which, he says, helped him complete his 'triangular trade' of origins. He then returned to the Caribbean to teach at the Jamaica campus of the University of the West Indies, where he is professor of social and cultural history.

Unlike DEREK WALCOTT, he tries to establish a Caribbean aesthetic by retrieving and re-orchestrating surviving and submerged echoes of African culture. His shorter poems appear in *Other Exiles* (1975), *Days and Nights* (1975), *Black and Blues* (1976) and *Third World Poems* (1983), but his excellence as an accomplished and visionary poet was established by three long poems: *Rights of Passage* (1967), *Masks* (1968) and *Islands* (1969), reprinted together as *The Arrivants: A New World Trilogy* (1973). Each of the three parts consists of 'movements' containing varying numbers of shorter poems rhythmically, verbally and thematically interrelated. Brathwaite interweaves popular Caribbean genres like worksongs and calypso with modern 'literary' verse forms. Through the voices of representative personae, *Rights of Passage* meditates upon the slavery-induced rootlessness of West Indians and the dispossession generally of black people. In *Masks* he finds in West African music, dance and ritual the origins of African cultural fragments, still extant in the Caribbean, which enabled African vitality to transcend the horrors of slavery. In *Islands* Caribbean history is reconsidered, not as pain and despair, but as coral growth; present-day dancing, drumming and masquerade become the means of 'now waking/ making/ making/ with their/ rhythms some-/ thing torn/ and new'. *Mother Poem* (1977), first in a new trilogy, is similar in technique and structure, though the concept of Barbados as 'mother' is somewhat strained. *Sun Poem* (1982), more persuasive and cohesive, evokes a Barbadian childhood. The more wide-ranging *X-Self* (1987), which brings together African, European, Amerindian and Maroon landscapes, completes the second trilogy. Historical writings include *The Development of Creole Society in Jamaica, 1770–1820* (1970), from which *The Folk Culture of the Slaves of Jamaica* (1970) is extracted.

In addition to being a professional historian and, with Walcott, one of the Caribbean's two most important poets, he is also a prolific literary critic. He has particularly concerned himself with the oral aspects of Caribbean discourse, notably in *History of the Voice: The Development of Nation Language in Anglophone Caribbean Poetry* (1984).

Brautigan, Richard 1935–84 American novelist and poet. Born in Tacoma, Washington, he came to prominence in the mid-1960s as a leading exponent of a new social order. His poetry, of which the best-known collection is *The Pill versus the Springhill Mine Disaster* (1968), paid homage to an unconstrained sexuality and to the enrichment derived from personal encounters. His novel *Trout Fishing in America* (1967), which sold over two million copies, describes the narrator's nostalgic search for a morning of good fishing in a crystal-clear stream. His quest takes him through a variety of American landscapes – San Francisco city parks, Oregon forests, Idaho campgrounds, a Filipino laundry, and a wrecking yard that sells used trout streams by the foot. The fact that his idiosyncratic quest is never realized becomes a metaphor for the unpromising and unappealing cultural environment that surrounds his journey. *In Watermelon Sugar* (1968) portrays a mode of life in a commune that shuns all standard American values, the residents defining themselves largely in opposition to the social structure of the outside world.

Many of his novels display a childlike conception of a world in which one can rearrange, ridicule, or ignore elements that are threatening or irrelevant. His other works of fiction include *A Confederate General from Big Sur* (1964), *Revenge of the Lawn: Stories,*

1962–1970 (1971), *The Abortion: An Historical Romance 1966* (1971), *The Hawkline Monster: A Gothic Western* (1974), *Willard and His Bowling Trophies: A Perverse Mystery* (1974), *Sombrero Fallout: A Japanese Novel* (1976), *Dreaming of Babylon: A Private Eye Novel, 1942* (1977), *The Tokyo-Montana Express* (1980) and *So The Wind Won't Blow It All Away* (1982). Among his other collections of poetry are *The Galilee Hitch-Hiker* (1958), *The Return of the Rivers* (1958), *Lay the Marble Tea* (1959), *The Octopus Frontier* (1960), *All Watched Over by Machines of Loving Grace* (1967), *Please Plant This Book* (a combination of poems and seed packets, 1968), *Rommel Drives Deep into Egypt* (1970), *Loading Mercury with a Pitchfork* (1976) and *June 30th, June 30th* (1978). He died from a self-inflicted gunshot wound.

Brave New World A novel by ALDOUS HUXLEY, first published in 1932. The title is taken from Miranda's words in THE TEMPEST: 'O brave new world/ That has such people in't!'

In the year 632 After Ford (i.e. the 26th century) the world has attained a kind of Utopia, in which the means of production are in state ownership and the principle 'from each according to his ability, to each according to his need' is rigorously applied. Biological engineering fits different categories of workers – Alphas, Betas, Gammas, etc. – to their stations in life, and universal happiness is preserved by psychotropic drugs. As a stranger into this world comes the Savage, raised in a reservation of American Indian primitives. He takes up the arguments introduced by the disaffected intellectuals Bernard Marx and Helmholtz Watson, debating the merits of freedom and passion with World Controller Mustapha Mond. In the end, though, the Savage yields to the temptations of the carefree world, and kills himself in disgust.

Brave New World is frequently cited as a horrific work, though it is really a black comedy. It provides a scathing criticism of the values implicit in the myth of social salvation through technological expertise. Modern developments in biological engineering and psycho-chemistry have preserved, and perhaps increased, its relevance as an exercise in alarmism.

Brazil, Angela 1868–1947 Writer of CHILDREN'S LITERATURE. Born in Lancashire, the daughter of a cotton manufacturer, Angela Brazil was educated at Manchester High School and then at art college. After her father's early death she became a companion to her mother, with whom she travelled extensively in Europe. She began writing at the age of 36, scoring her first success two years later with *The Fortunes of Philippa* (1906), a story about a 10-year-old girl attending boarding-school for the first time. In the more than 50 school novels which followed Angela Brazil created an idealized world, which emphasized hearty games-playing and the strong emotions that often spring up between pupils of the same sex. Her books also contained snippets of general knowledge, and while a few headmistresses banned them for their use of schoolgirl slang, most accepted them as a wholesome influence. Her last story, *The School on the Loch* (1946), appeared a year before her death.

Breeches Bible, The See BIBLE IN ENGLISH, THE.

Brennan, Christopher John 1870–1932 Australian poet. Born in Sydney of Irish parents, Brennan was educated at Sydney University and in Berlin after winning a travelling scholarship. From 1921 to 1925 he was associate professor in German and comparative literature at Sydney University. His work was greatly influenced by the German Romantics and the French symbolist, Mallarmé, with whom he corresponded. Brennan's erudite and crafted verse still possesses considerable lyricism, as his best-known sequence, 'The Wanderer', shows. He published little in his lifetime. His first publication was *XVIII Poems, Being the First Collection of Verse and Prose* (1897), of which only eight copies were issued by the author, and his most important collection was *Poems 1913* (1914).

Brent-Dyer, Elinor M. [Dyer, Gladys Eleanor May] 1894–1969 Writer of CHILDREN'S LITERATURE. Born in Durham and educated at the City of Leeds Training College, she started teaching in 1912, finally retiring as a headmistress in 1948. In 1922 she began writing girls' school stories with breezy titles, such as *The Feud in the Fifth Remove* (1931) and *Monica Turns up Trumps* (1936), which give a fair idea of their uncomplicated content. In 1925 she wrote the first of 58 stories about Chalet School, an international girls' school romantically situated in the Austrian Alps and forcefully led by a young British headmistress. Dramatic mountain scenery made a good backdrop for action-packed plots. Little read now, her fiction is a testament to the type of undemanding reading once thought suitable for adolescent girls. However, her emphasis on internationalism as an ideal acted as a useful corrective to the strong belief in national superiority found in other popular writing for British children of the time.

Brenton, Howard 1942– Playwright. A leading spokesman for the political drama that flourished during and after the revolutionary year of 1968, he began writing while he was a student at Cambridge, but came to prominence with *Christie in Love* (1969) and *Revenge* (1969). *Magnificence* (1973) is an exploration of urban terrorism. The structures of political power are also the subject of *The Churchill Play* (1974) and *The Weapons of Happiness* (1976), one of the first plays staged in the ROYAL NATIONAL THEATRE's new premises. The sweep of *Epsom Downs* (1977) is broader, though the focus on class divisions remains. Brenton writes under the influence of Brecht, a fact which is implicitly acknowledged by his translation for the National Theatre of the German playwright's *Galileo* (1980). For *The Romans in Britain* (1980) Brenton provided an elaborate analogy between the Roman invasion and the British 'occupation' of Northern Ireland. The sexual explicitness of one scene gave rise to a private prosecution (eventually dropped) of its director, Michael Bogdanov. *The Genius* (1983) is a provocative, though flawed, confrontation of the political expediency that threatens the tentative balance of nuclear deterrence. *Pravda* (1985), about the corruptions of newspaper ownership and written in collaboration with DAVID HARE, scored a striking success, which eluded *Moscow Gold* (with Tariq Ali; 1990), an ambitious study of political change in the Soviet Union.

Breton, Nicholas ?1555–1626 Poet and miscellaneous writer. Breton's mother was married first to a wealthy tradesman and then to the poet GEORGE GASCOIGNE, who influenced Breton's early work. He possibly went to Oxford and then settled in London. His early poetry of the 1570s is laboured with poetic diction and excessive alliteration but improves by the 1590s so that FRANCIS MERES in *Palladis Tamia* (1598) can rank him (undeservedly) with SHAKESPEARE, SPENSER and DRAYTON as a lyricist. Some of his best poems appeared in *ENGLAND'S HELICON* (1600). Breton's earliest work is *A Small Handful of Fragrant Flowers* (1575), his last, *Strange News out of Divers Countries* (1622). Between them he produced over 60 works of pastoral and religious poetry, pamphlets, satires, dialogues and letters. His prose works have a moral and pious tone, and the poverty of poets is a constant theme in his poetry.

Breton lay The precise form of the original Breton lay is not known; it was apparently a narrative accompanied by music. The name has become attached to those poems which claim to be adapted from these earlier lyric lays or are Breton in origin. They are exemplified by the collection of MARIE DE FRANCE's *Lais*, written in the late 12th century – simple, relatively short narrative poems, usually treating of love and often involving some elements of magic. Most of the extant English lays were written during the 14th century, and are in couplets or TAIL-RHYME stanzas. They are *SIR LAUNFAL* and *LAI LE FREINE* (both translated from Marie's *Lais*), *SIR ORFEO*, *EMARE*, *SIR DEGARE*, *SIR GOWTHER* and *THE EARL OF TOULOUS*. CHAUCER's *Franklin's Tale* (see *THE CANTERBURY TALES*), while claiming to be a Breton lay, has an Italian source and an uncharacteristically complex narrative structure.

Brewer's Dictionary of Phrase and Fable A reference book or 'Treasury of Literary bric-à-brac' compiled by the educational writer Ebenezer Cobham Brewer (1810–97), published in 1870 and revised by Brewer in 1881 and 1895. It forms a unique compendium of folklore, slang, etymology, mythology and 'words with a tale to tell', as Brewer put it. Since a major revision in 1952, the much-expanded modern editions (notably Ifor H. Evans's Centenary Edition of 1970) have added new curiosities from Australia and America, while some of Brewer's original entries have been omitted.

As a glossary of names from fiction and myth, the *Dictionary* drew heavily on William A. Wheeler's *Noted Names of Fiction* (1866), and has since been superseded by more thorough guides; but its miscellany of adages, superstitions and catchphrases is unrivalled – and delightfully odd. Few other reference books can provide us with a list of German archbishops supposedly devoured by mice (under 'Hatto'), or remind us of the unlucky days of the week for cutting our fingernails (under 'Nail-paring').

Bridal of Triermain, The A poem by SIR WALTER SCOTT, published in 1813, one of his immensely successful verse romances which take their subjects from legend and history. Framed by the bland courtship of Lucy by Arthur (the poor man and the lady), the central narrative describes Sir Roland de Vaux of Triermain's quest for Gyneth, daughter of King Arthur and the enchantress Guendolen, who lies sleeping in the Valley of St John as the result of a spell by Merlin.

Bride of Abydos, The: *A 'Turkish Tale'* A poem by BYRON, published in 1813. It describes the tragic love affair of Selim and his supposed half-sister Zuleika, daughter of the Pasha Giaffir. Giaffir intends her to marry his fellow tyrant, the elderly Bey of Carasman. When Selim appears in pirate costume to reveal he is not Zuleika's brother but her cousin, and to plead that she join him on the high seas, he is killed by Giaffir and his men. Zuleika dies of a broken heart and the Pasha is left with his impotent grief. The poem contributed to the late 18th-century and Romantic cult of Orientalism, while also encouraging the fascination with piracy that runs through the work of Byron and his fellow Romantics.

Bride of Lammermoor, The A novel by SIR WALTER SCOTT, published in 1818 in the third series of *Tales of My Landlord*. It tells the story of the Master of Ravenswood's unhappy and eventually tragic love for Lucy Ashton, daughter of a family with whom he has an inherited feud. Lady Ashton, Lucy's mother, opposes the romance and tricks her daughter into marriage with the Laird of Bucklaw by convincing her that Ravenswood has abandoned her. He returns after the wedding to demand vengeance; Lucy becomes insane and stabs her husband. He goes into exile.

Donizetti used the story as the basis for his opera, *Lucia di Lammermoor* (1835).

Brideshead Revisited: *The Sacred and Profane Memories of Captain Charles Ryder* A novel by EVELYN WAUGH, published in 1945. Described in the preface to the revised edition of 1959 as 'an attempt to trace the workings of the divine purpose in a pagan world', it marked a departure from his earlier satirical works.

Billeted at Brideshead during the war, Ryder recalls his past experiences there as a guest of the Marchmains, a great Roman Catholic family. His acquaintance with them begins at Oxford, where he is dazzled by the good looks and whimsicality of Sebastian Flyte, the younger son of the Marquis of Marchmain. Lord Marchmain has deserted the family to live in Venice with his mistress. Sebastian holds himself aloof from his mother – a fervent Catholic – and sisters Julia and Cordelia, and sinks into alcoholism as the story progresses. He flees to North Africa and, after Lady Marchmain's death, becomes a menial in an African monastery.

Ryder has meanwhile continued to visit Brideshead, where his feelings are centred upon Julia. She, however, marries a non-Catholic, a vulgar politician who fails to qualify as a Catholic convert. With the death of his wife, Lord Marchmain returns to Brideshead and, on his deathbed, is restored to the faith. Julia, who might have married Ryder after her divorce, witnesses her father's reconciliation and she too returns to Catholicism. Ryder's doubts about his own faith are resolved by her renunciation of him, and his agnosticism withers.

Bridge, The A long poem by HART CRANE, published in 1930. Begun in 1923, it seeks to present an affirmative, epic vision of America; New York's Brooklyn Bridge is its central image. In his prefatory 'Proem' Crane describes the bridge as both 'harp and altar' which will 'lend a myth to God', and he returns to this affirmative vision in 'Atlantis', the final part of the sequence. In the intervening seven sections, however, he explores the negative as well as the positive aspects of the American experience, which are symbolized by literary and historical figures, geographical features and place names, and technological inventions. In the section entitled 'Powhatan's Daughter', for example, the Indian princess Pocahontas comes to represent the beauty of the American landscape; in a subsection entitled 'The River' the Mississippi River is transformed into a natural force fusing history with eternal time; and in 'The Tunnel' the New York subway becomes a hellish underworld haunted by the ghost of EDGAR ALLAN POE.

Bridges, Robert (Seymour) 1844–1930 Poet and critic. Born in Walmer, Kent, he was educated at Eton and Corpus Christi College, Oxford, where he met GERARD MANLEY HOPKINS. He practised medicine until 1881. His first volume of *Poems* appeared in 1873, followed by a SONNET sequence, *The Growth of Love* (1876), and further collections of short poems and several long poems including *Prometheus the Firegiver* (1883), *Eros and Psyche* (1885) and *Demeter* (1905). During the next decade he wrote eight plays, and his influential criticism included studies of MILTON's prosody (1893) and KEATS (1895). He was interested in the musical setting of poetry, and between 1895 and 1908 wrote four poems set by Parry. He edited the Yattendon Hymnal and wrote *A Practical Discourse on Hymn Singing* (1901).

A one-volume edition of his *Collected Poems* (1912) was very successful, and made his work available to a wider audience. In 1913 he was appointed POET LAUREATE, and appropriately produced *The Spirit of Man* (1916), an anthology of prose and verse intended to console and encourage the nation. It included six poems by Gerard Manley Hopkins, whose original and unorthodox work Bridges finally published in 1918. After the war, while living at Boar's Hill, near Oxford, where his neighbours included ROBERT GRAVES, JOHN MASEFIELD and ROBERT NICHOLS, he published *October and Other Poems* (1920). His experiments in prosody led to the 'loose alexandrines' of *The Testament of Beauty* (1929), a poem in four books on spiritual and artistic wisdom. It was very popular, going through 14 impressions in the first year of publication.

Bridges's poetry is distinguished by its subtle metrics, expert craftsmanship and rationally intelligent subject matter. Much-anthologized poems are 'London Snow', 'Awake My Heart' and 'The Storm is Over'.

Bridges, Roy(al) 1885–1952 Australian novelist. Born and educated in Tasmania, Bridges worked as a journalist in Melbourne and Sydney. His first novel, *The Barb of an Arrow* (1909), dealt with the convict days of Tasmania. Many of the more than 30 novels he went on to publish returned to the period of the early settlement. They include *By His Excellency's Command* (1909), *Mr Barrington* (1911), *Rat's Castle* (1924) and *The League of the Lord* (1950).

Bridie, James [Mavor, Osborne Henry] 1888–1951 Scottish playwright. Mavor combined an active career as a doctor with an equally active career in the theatre, during which he wrote over 50 plays, many of them first performed in Glasgow despite the fact that he was already well established in London's West End. This regionalism has contributed to the neglect of a writer whose humour has more often a Shavian sharpness than is allowed by critics who compare him to his compatriot J. M. BARRIE.

Bridie's first major success was *The Anatomist* (1930), a witty scrutiny of medical ethics in the light of Dr Knox and the bodysnatchers Burke and Hare. *A Sleeping Clergyman* (1933) also directs its iconoclasm against the medical profession. In *Tobias and the Angel* (1930) and *Jonah and the Whale* (1932) Bridie's target is the humourless fundamentalism that makes of the Bible a book for threatening sinners, and he calls on the Devil to do some of his work for him in *Mr Bolfry* (1943). There are many other effective plays, including *Colonel Wotherspoon* (1934), *Susannah and the Elders* (1937), *Daphne Laureola* (1949) and *Mr Gillie* (1950). Bridie's genial humour is an easily penetrated disguise for his IRONY.

Briggs, Raymond (Redvers) 1934– Writer and illustrator of CHILDREN'S LITERATURE. Born in London the son of a milkman, Briggs studied at art college before becoming a successful illustrator, particularly of nursery rhymes. He was first noticed as a writer in *Jim and the Beanstalk* (1970), which introduces one of his many proletarian heroes in the shape of a genial cockney giant. There followed *Father Christmas* (1973), detailing in comic strip a day in the life of an equally working-class Santa Claus who, despite grumbling, has a good heart and is devoted to his pets. He reappeared in *Father Christmas Goes on Holiday* (1975) but was eclipsed by *Fungus the Bogeyman* (1977), which brought Briggs fame amongst adults as well as children by breaking several taboos. *The Snowman* (1979) was another popular creation; but later books, notably *When the Wind Blows* (1982), a bitter SATIRE on government advice about how to survive a nuclear war, and *The Tin Pot Foreign General and the Old Iron Woman* (1984), an attack on the politics behind the Falklands War, make no pretence of being written for children.

Brighouse, Harold 1882–1958 Playwright. Born near and educated in Manchester, he was working in the cotton trade when Manchester's Gaiety Theatre opened in 1908, providing him with the impetus to write. Of the 70 or so plays he produced between 1909 and 1952, the majority are one-act comedies. The best known of his full-length works is *HOBSON'S CHOICE* (1915). Its durable popularity has eclipsed the almost equally accomplished *Lonesome-Like* (1911), *The Odd Man Out* (1912) and *Sack* (1916).

Brighton Rock A novel by GRAHAM GREENE, published in 1938.

The story is set in the criminal underworld of Brighton. Pinkie ('The Boy'), a 17-year-old gang leader hell-bent on establishing himself, plans to murder Fred Hale, a journalist who indirectly caused the death of the gang's former leader. During the attack Hale dies of heart failure, and Pinkie later realizes that he has left a clue in a café which could establish his guilt. He visits the café and, to allay suspicion, dates the innocent young waitress Rose. Later he reluctantly agrees to marry her, thus preventing her from appearing as a future witness against him.

A brief acquaintance of Hale's, the middle-aged Ida Arnold, determines to establish the truth about his death. She attempts (unsuccessfully) to persuade Rose to abandon Pinkie, but he panics and arranges a fake suicide pact with the girl as a means of eliminating her. In the event Rose's conscience will not permit her to go through with the suicide, and Ida Arnold arrives with a policeman to arrest the youth. Pinkie attempts a desperate escape bid by throwing a bottle of vitriol. This is smashed before he does so and the acid blinds Pinkie instead. He falls to his death over the edge of a cliff.

Though Greene called the novel an 'entertainment' (in the US edition), it is profoundly influenced by his Catholicism. Pinkie himself is a nominal Catholic, still deeply superstitious, and Rose almost a saintly figure, while Ida Arnold is a fun-loving hedonist who believes in a secular notion of decency. The tensions between them create an ambiguous moral drama foreshadowing his later novels.

Brink, André 1935– South African novelist. An Afrikaans writer, born in Vrede, he has also written in English, especially after his seventh novel, *Kennis van die aand* (1973), became the first Afrikaans book to be banned in South Africa. He translated it as *Looking on Darkness* (1974) and has since published his novels in both languages: *'n Oomblik in die wind* as *Rumours of Rain* (both 1978), *'n Droë wit seisoen* as *A DRY WHITE SEASON* (both 1979), *Houd-den-bek* as *A Chain of Voices* (both 1982) and *Die muur van die pes* as *The Wall of the Plague* (both 1984). Despite his considerable skill in anatomizing Afrikaner history and morality, his fiction is sometimes ungainly and occasionally even gauche. He has also produced six volumes of Afrikaans short stories, 12 Afrikaans plays, CHILDREN'S LITERATURE, travel books, academic criticism and some 50 translations of English, French and Spanish books into Afrikaans. A selection of his essays on Afrikaans and English writing in South Africa, and on politics and culture, appeared as *Mapmakers: Writing in a State of Siege* (1983).

Brinkelow, Henry d. 1546 Satirist. Brinkelow left his religious order and joined the Protestant reformers. His satires include complaints against land enclosures and clerical abuses. Under the pseudonym Roderigo Mors he wrote *The Lamentation of a Christian* (1542) and *The Complaint of Roderick Mors* (?1542), both first published abroad.

Britannia A work of history and topography by the antiquary WILLIAM CAMDEN; its scope is indicated by the subtitle, translated as 'A Chorographical Description of the Most Flourishing Kingdoms of England, Scotland, and Ireland, and the Islands Adjoining, out of the Depth of Antiquity'. It was first published in Latin in 1586 and went through six Latin editions in Camden's lifetime. PHILEMON HOLLAND's English translation, made under Camden's supervision, appeared in 1610.

Encouraged by SIR PHILIP SIDNEY, Camden began to gather the materials which were later included in *Britannia* as early as 1571. Holidays from his schoolmastering left him free to make the expeditions on which he observed antiquities at first hand. Initially he had no plans for publication, but he began systematically to compile *Britannia* in 1577 after meeting the geographer Abraham Ortelius. The result was the first practical and historical guide to the British Isles, arranged county by county. Camden treated not only topography and monuments (most famously Stonehenge), but also such subjects as coins and language. He made liberal use of genealogies, maps and illustrative plates. Subsequent copious additions by Camden himself and by succeeding scholars caused later editions to bear less and less resemblance to the first edition of 1586; but the fact that *Britannia* survived so long as the model for antiquarian studies is a tribute to its practicality and usefulness.

Brittain, Vera (Mary) 1893–1970 Author of autobiography, poetry and fiction. She was born at Newcastle under Lyme, Staffordshire, the daughter of a wealthy manufacturer, and was educated at Kingswood and Somerville College, Oxford. She married Professor George Catlin in 1925.

During World War I she served as a VAD (Voluntary Aid Detachment) nurse, an experience which interrupted her studies at Oxford and which she recounted in her autobiographical *Testament of Youth* (1933). The book deals with her girlhood, during which she was strongly influenced by OLIVE SCHREINER, and her early struggles to get an education. It was immediately acclaimed and has become an important feminist text. Although she wrote numerous volumes of poetry and fiction, Brittain is more widely known for two later works: *Testament of Friendship* (1940), a memorial to WINIFRED HOLTBY, with whom she developed a close friendship at Oxford; and *Testament of Experience* (1957), a sequel to her early autobiography, covering the years 1925–50.

broadside A song or poem printed on one side of a large single sheet of paper, offered for sale on the streets by ballad sellers and hawkers from the Renaissance onwards. Generally doggerel verse or BALLADS to popular airs, broadsides in particular enjoyed a great circulation during the second part of the 17th century when the production of street literature was at a peak.

Brodber, Erna 1942– Jamaican novelist. Born in Woodside in the parish of St Mary, Jamaica, she studied sociology at the Jamaica campus of the University of the West Indies and psychiatric anthropology in Washington. She has been a social caseworker in Kingston and published a number of articles and monographs on social conditions. Since the mid-1970s she has been a member of a Rastafarian sect, the Twelve Tribes of Israel. Her first novel, *Jane and Louisa Will Soon Come Home* (1980), written in a distinctively original poetic prose, shows how the folk traditions of Jamaica have been undervalued and how negative stereotyping has stultified the emotional and intellectual development of black women. *Myal* (1988), also about the need to repossess buried identities, takes the Afro-Caribbean religious cult of Myalism (formerly criminalized by the colonial authorities) as the central metaphor for black Jamaican spiritual survival.

Brodsky, Joseph (Iosif Alexandrovich) 1940– Russian-born American poet. Born in Leningrad (St Petersburg) of Jewish parents – his father was a naval officer – he started writing poetry in the late 1950s. Convicted in 1962 of dissident activities, he was first sentenced to imprisonment with hard labour and then sent into internal exile. After being forced to leave the USSR in 1972 he migrated via Vienna and London to the USA, where he has been honoured by many universities and currently teaches Russian language and literature at Mount Holyoke College in Massachusetts. He received the Nobel Prize for Literature in 1987 and was US POET LAUREATE in 1991–2. His work, which frequently treats the themes of exile and loss, is distinguished by its IRONY and WIT. Collections of his verse in English include *A Halt in the Wilderness* (1970), *Brodsky: Selected Poems* (1974), *A Part of Speech* (1977) and *To Urania* (1984). He has also written: a play, *Marbles* (1989); the prose writings collected in *Less Than One: Selected Essays* (1986); and a book-length essay, *Watermark* (1992).

Broken Heart, The A tragedy by JOHN FORD. The play was first produced about 1629 and published in 1633.

The setting of the play is Laconia, where Penthea is married to a brutal and jealous nobleman, Bassanes. Penthea was in love with Orgilus; they intended to marry but Penthea's brother Ithocles had forced her to marry Bassanes. She cannot bring herself to return Orgilus' love, feeling herself prostituted in her marriage. Ithocles, meanwhile, has been successful in war; he returns from the conquest of Messene and is greatly favoured by the King, who gives him the Princess Calantha as a bride. Orgilus, whose life has been wrecked, watches Penthea die of self-starvation and is determined to have revenge on Ithocles. At a feast, Calantha hears of the death of Penthea and, soon after, news is brought of the death of her father, the King. A third blow is news of the murder of Ithocles and the apprehension of Orgilus. She continues at the feast, her feelings under control, and waits until the feast is over before ordering the execution of Orgilus. Then she dies of a broken heart.

Brome, Richard *c.* 1590–1652 Playwright. One of the many efficient professional dramatists who continued to provide the Caroline stage with plays until the closing of the theatres in 1642, Brome is known only by his writing. According to *Biographia Dramatica* (1764) 'his extraction was mean, he having originally been no better than a menial servant to the celebrated BEN JONSON', and a Jonsonian influence is certainly detectable in much of his work, though the geniality is Brome's own. The best of his surviving plays are *The Northern Lass* (1629), *The City Wit* (*c.* 1630), *The Late Lancashire Witches* (with THOMAS HEYWOOD; 1634), *The Antipodes* (1638) and *A Jovial Crew* (1641). That Brome's talent was recognized in his own time is clear from the earliest extant playwright's contract, drawn up in his name on 20 July 1635.

Bromfield, Louis 1896–1956 American novelist and short-story writer. Born in Mansfield, Ohio, he began studying journalism at Columbia University in 1916 but left to serve in World War I. Between 1922 and 1925 he worked as foreign editor of *Musical America*. He subsequently wrote columns for THE NEW YORKER and The Bookman (of which he was also a music and drama critic). His first novel, *The Green Bay Tree*, was published in 1924, and was followed by numerous others, including *Possession* (1925), *Early Autumn* (1926), for which he was awarded the PULITZER PRIZE, *The Farm* (1933), *The Rains Came* (1937), *Night in Bombay* (1940), *Wild is the River* (1941), *Mrs Parkinson* (1943) and *Pleasant Valley* (1945). He also published collections of short stories, including *Awake and Rehearse* (1929), *It Takes All Kinds* (1939) and *The World We Live In* (1944), and such plays as *The House of Women* (1927) and *De Luxe* (1935). Bromfield's fiction often reflects a profound distrust of industrialism and materialism, which he saw as dehumanizing factors in 20th-century American life.

Brontë, Charlotte 1816–55; **Brontë, Emily (Jane)** 1818–48; **Brontë, Anne** 1820–49 Novelists and poets. They were daughters of the Reverend Patrick Brontë, a Church of England clergyman born in Northern Ireland, and of Maria Branwell, a Cornishwoman. The couple's other children were Maria (1813–25), Elizabeth (1815–25) and Patrick Branwell (1817–48). Maria and Elizabeth were born in Hartshead, near Dewsbury in Yorkshire, where Mr

Brontë was curate; the rest were born at Mr Brontë's next curacy in Thornton, near Bradford. In 1820, the year before his wife's death, Mr Brontë took up the living of Haworth, a bleak weaving village a few miles north-west of Thornton. The Haworth parsonage and its surrounding moorland became, as it always remained, the centre of his children's lives.

All the girls save Anne attended the Clergy Daughters' School run by the Reverend William Carus Wilson at Cowan Bridge, near Kirkby Lonsdale. Its harsh regime contributed to the early deaths of Maria and Elizabeth, which left Charlotte the oldest child in the motherless family. In 1831–2 she was sent to Miss Wooler's school at Roe Head, near Dewsbury, where she met her lifelong friends Mary Taylor and Ellen Nussey. During Charlotte's subsequent time as governess there (1835–8), Emily also went along as a pupil but was quickly replaced by Anne.

The girls' real education, however, was at the Haworth parsonage, where they had the run of their father's books and were thus nurtured on the Bible, Homer, Virgil, SHAKESPEARE, MILTON, BYRON, SIR WALTER SCOTT and many others. They enthusiastically read articles on current affairs, lengthy reviews and intellectual disputes in BLACKWOOD'S EDINBURGH MAGAZINE, FRASER'S MAGAZINE and THE EDINBURGH REVIEW. They also ranged freely in Aesop and in the colourfully bizarre world of *The Arabian Nights' Entertainments*; and they pored over lavishly illustrated keepsakes and annuals like *The Gem*, *The Amulet* and *Friendship's Offering*, among whose contributors were such artists as the epic painter John Martin, master of the boundless romantic canvas. Over this household presided the forbidding figure of their aunt, Elizabeth Branwell, who had been invited to live with them soon after the death of her sister, and the family servant, Tabitha Aykroyd, who arrived in 1825 and remained until her death 30 years later. Elizabeth Branwell's relentless Calvinistic world – with its threats of eternal punishment, of fiery furnaces and of a vengeful God – had a powerful influence on the young children, while Tabitha's knowledge of folk-tales and superstitions provided another sort of nourishment for their imaginations.

In June 1826 Mr Brontë came back from a visit to Leeds with a box of 12 wooden soldiers he had promised Branwell, and around them his children wove tales and legends associated with remote Africa (where they situated their imaginary Glass Town). Later came other narratives about the kingdom of Angria, whose stories Charlotte and Branwell recorded in minute notebooks two inches by one in size. Yet another 'saga' – the Gondal saga – was created by Emily and Anne. Replete with melodrama and violence, the wondrous and the fantastic, this juvenilia still showed a strong moral strain suggestive of parsonage life and of their aunt's stern Methodism. Much, too, from these youthful writings

informs the later fiction and poetry of the Brontë sisters.

The strength of the children's attachment to each other and to the Haworth parsonage is shown by the desultory and usually unhappy nature of their forays into the world beyond. Branwell went to London to study painting at the Royal Academy in 1835 but stayed only a few days; thereafter he failed as a portrait painter in Bradford and as a clerk on the local railway. His sisters, meanwhile, worked as governesses. Anne's longest stint (1840–5) was with the Robinson family at Thorp Green Hall, near York, where she was lonely and unhappy in the situation; she left when Branwell, for whom she had secured a tutorial post in the same household, became involved with its mistress. He was dismissed a month later. But the most important sojourn away from home for any of the family was Charlotte's time in Brussels at the *pensionnat* run by M. Constantin Heger and his wife. Helped by money from her aunt, Charlotte went there with Emily in February 1842 and remained until Elizabeth Branwell's illness demanded her return nine months later. A slightly longer stay to improve her French and German and to develop her teaching of English followed in 1843, though she was back home by January 1844. For much of her stay she was anxious, melancholy and hostile to the atmosphere around her. Her position at the *pensionnat* was not improved by her growing attachment for M. Heger, who broke off the correspondence she attempted after her return to England.

Charlotte had shown her literary ambition while still at Roe Head by sending her poems to SOUTHEY, who responded with sage advice. In 1845 her discovery of poems written by Emily further encouraged her to propose a joint volume by all three sisters. In the face of Emily's reluctance, *Poems by Currer, Ellis and Acton Bell* appeared in 1846 but passed unnoticed by the reading public. It was Charlotte who again urged publication of the novels which each of them had by then finished. Her own work, THE PROFESSOR, which drew heavily on her experiences in Brussels, was rejected and did not appear until its posthumous publication in 1857. But the encouragement she received from GEORGE SMITH of Smith, Elder and Co. emboldened her to complete and submit *JANE EYRE*. It appeared in October 1847, two months before Emily Brontë's WUTHERING HEIGHTS and Anne Brontë's lesser known AGNES GREY, which (unsurprisingly) concerned a governess unhappy in a family she disliked. Anne's second novel, THE TENANT OF WILDFELL HALL, appeared in July 1848.

These works, particularly *Jane Eyre*, attracted the public interest that the volume of poems had so signally failed to provoke. It was made the more piquant by the sisters' continued use of their apparently male pseudonyms, Currer, Ellis and Acton Bell, though in July 1848 Charlotte and Anne visited GEORGE SMITH to reveal their identity and to help quell rumours that a single author lay behind the pseudonyms. By this time, however, the family was involved in private sorrow. Branwell's alcoholism, which so clearly cast its shadow over *The Tenant of Wildfell Hall*, contributed to his early death in September 1848. He was followed by Emily, who died of tuberculosis in December, stubbornly resisting the encroachments of the illness until virtually her last hours, and by Anne, who died calmly and resignedly at Scarborough in July 1849.

Charlotte survived to cope with a father now sorely tried and going blind. She published *SHIRLEY* in October 1849 and, in 1853, *VILLETTE*, a novel which, like *THE PROFESSOR*, drew upon her life in Brussels. Despite her nervous self-consciousness she began to move in literary society, meeting THACKERAY (to whom she had dedicated *Jane Eyre*) and G. H. LEWES, and becoming friendly with HARRIET MARTINEAU and, particularly, ELIZABETH GASKELL, her future biographer. In June 1854 she overcame her father's entrenched opposition and married his curate, the Reverend Arthur Bell Nicholls, at Haworth church; the couple lived together with Mr Brontë at the parsonage. She died the following March, apparently from the complications of a chill caught during early pregnancy. Her father survived until 1861 and her husband until 1906.

Brook Farm A co-operative reform community, founded in 1841 by GEORGE RIPLEY and other followers of TRANSCENDENTALISM on a farm in West Roxbury, Massachusetts, about eight miles from Boston, and set up as a joint-stock company. The Brook Farmers' aim was to simplify and purify economic relations by retreating from an increasingly commercial society and working the farm together to achieve a near-subsistence existence which would leave time for intellectual and spiritual self-improvement. Those who lived on the farm or visited it included MARGARET FULLER, RALPH WALDO EMERSON, WILLIAM ELLERY CHANNING, THEODORE PARKER, ORESTES BROWNSON and NATHANIEL HAWTHORNE, who based *THE BLITHEDALE ROMANCE* on his Brook Farm experience. The Brook Farmers produced two periodicals, *The Phalanx* (1843–5) and *The Harbinger* (1845–9). The community disbanded in 1847.

Brooke, Charlotte 1740–93 Irish translator and poet. The youngest daughter of HENRY BROOKE, and the only one of his 22 children to survive him, she was educated at home by her father. From him she caught an enthusiasm for Irish antiquities, further stimulated by the controversies surrounding JAMES MACPHERSON's alleged *Poems of Ossian* (1765), the Irish antecedents of which were demonstrated by her godfather Sylvester O'Halloran. Her anonymous translation of a poem attributed to the famous Irish bard O'Carolan was included in Joseph Walker's *Historical*

Memoirs of *the Irish Bards* (1786). With her friend THOMAS PERCY's *Reliques of Ancient English Poetry* (1765) as model she published *Reliques of Ancient Irish Poetry* (1789). This contains not merely some of the earliest verse translations of traditional Irish poems about the Red Branch Knights and the Fenians but also an original composition, *Maön, an Irish Tale*, coloured by this material. While she has been censured for slack paraphrase and conventionally elegant English metres, her polished translations were often reprinted and did much to stimulate an emerging Irish literature in English. Her other, less noted, works include an unacted tragedy, *Belisarius*, and dialogues for children, *A School for Christians* (1791), as well as an edition of her father's works (1792).

Brooke, Henry 1703–83 Irish poet, playwright and novelist. Brooke came from County Cavan in Ireland and was educated at Trinity College, Dublin. He spent 10 years in London, and began to write when he returned to Dublin. *Design and Beauty: An Epistle* (1734) was followed by a more ambitious poem in six parts, *Universal Beauty* (1734–6), on the perfection of design in the universe. His translation of Tasso's *Gerusalemme Liberata*, Books I and II, followed in 1738 and a tragedy, *Gustavus Vasa*, appeared in 1739. The play was banned, however, because Sir Robert Walpole fancied a likeness to himself in the villain of the piece. It was produced in Dublin as *The Patriot* in 1744. Brooke's SENTIMENTAL NOVEL, *THE FOOL OF QUALITY* (1766–72), attracted considerable attention but a second novel, *Juliet Grenville* (1774), was soon forgotten.

Brooke, Rupert (Chawner) 1887–1915 Poet. Born in Rugby, he was educated at Rugby School (where his father was a master) and at King's College, Cambridge. He then travelled in Germany and published *Poems* (1911) before taking up a fellowship at King's in 1912. While there he wrote *Lithuania*, a one-act play published posthumously in 1935, and began work on *John Webster and the Elizabethan Drama* (1916). Following a nervous breakdown, he travelled in the United States, Canada and the Pacific during 1913, and joined the RNVR after the outbreak of World War I. His five 'war sonnets', published in *New Numbers* in 1915, included his famous 'The Soldier' ('If I should die, think only this of me'), which drew from his Cambridge contemporary CHARLES HAMILTON SORLEY the comment that 'he has clothed his attitude in fine words; but he has taken the sentimental attitude'. He died of blood-poisoning *en route* to the Dardanelles and was buried at Scyros.

Brooke's good looks and early death ensured his transformation into a symbol of romantic patriotism, a process encouraged by the posthumous appearance of *1914 and Other Poems* (1915), *Letters from America* (1916), with a preface by HENRY JAMES, and *Collected*

Poems (1918), edited with a memoir by his friend SIR EDWARD MARSH, with whom Brooke had been associated in the anthologies of *GEORGIAN POETRY*. His verse is characteristically Georgian, colloquial and nostalgic; well-known anthology poems include 'The Old Vicarage, Grantchester' (1912), 'Clouds' (1913) and 'The Dead' (1914). A *Complete Poems* edited by Geoffrey Keynes appeared in 1946.

Brooke-Rose, Christine 1926– Novelist and critic. Born in Geneva, she was educated at Somerville College, Oxford, and University College, London. In 1956–68 she worked as a freelance journalist in London and since 1975 she has been professor of American literature at the University of Paris VIII, Vincennes. She is a European intellectual, influenced by the French *avant-garde* of the 1950s. Although she rejects the label of 'experimental novelist', the SATIRE of her early work, beginning with *The Languages of Love* (1957), has given way to a concern with the nature of words and the meanings invested in them. *Such* (1966), *Between* (1968), and *Thru* (1975) have been followed by *Amalgamemnon* (1984), *Xorander* (1986) and *Verbivore* (1990). She has also translated Alain Robbe-Grillet's *In the Labyrinth* (1968) and Juan Goytisolo's *Children of Chaos* (1958). Her works of criticism include *A Grammar of Metaphor* (1958), *A ZBC of Ezra Pound* (1971) and *A Rhetoric of the Unreal: Studies in Narrative and Structure, Especially the Fantastic* (1981).

Brookner, Anita 1928– Novelist. A lecturer at London's Courtauld Institute of Art, and before that the first woman to be Slade Professor at Cambridge, she turned to fiction only in 1980, but has written prolifically since then. Her plangent tales of single, solitary women and their failure to secure lasting close relationships, or even reliable friends, have been compared to the novels of BARBARA PYM and ELIZABETH TAYLOR. The first four, *A Start in Life* (1981), *Providence* (1982), *Look at Me* (1983) and *Hôtel du Lac* (1984), which won the BOOKER PRIZE, are all unashamedly literary in their allusions, and counterpoint wry, delicate comedy with a remorselessly pessimistic insistence on the disadvantages of opting for timid moral rectitude over worldly self-advancement. *Family and Friends* (1985) differs in attempting a concentrated family saga, based on her own East European ancestry. Subsequent novels include *A Misalliance* (1986), *A Friend from England* (1987), *A Closed Eye* (1991) and *Fraud* (1992).

Brooks, Cleanth 1906–94 American critic. A Kentuckian by birth, he was educated at Vanderbilt and Tulane universities before going to Oxford as a Rhodes Scholar in 1929. He taught for 15 years at the Louisiana State University, Baton Rouge, where he edited (with ROBERT PENN WARREN) the influential *Southern Review*. From 1947 he taught at Yale University, as Gray Professor of Rhetoric from 1960 to 1975.

A leader of the NEW CRITICISM, Brooks elaborated the critical principles of T. S. ELIOT in *Modern Poetry and the Tradition* (1939), examining the poetry of YEATS and Eliot as a revival of Metaphysical 'wit'. His other important book, *The Well-Wrought Urn* (1947), comprises a series of close readings of poems from DONNE to Yeats, concentrating on their ironies and ambiguities in the manner of WILLIAM EMPSON. With Robert Penn Warren, Brooks wrote *Understanding Poetry: An Anthology for College Students* (1938; revised editions 1950, 1960 and 1976) and *Understanding Fiction* (1943; revised editions 1959 and 1979), two college textbooks which helped to entrench the New Criticism as an academic orthodoxy. His long (and too modestly titled) *Literary Criticism: A Short History* (with W. K. Wimsatt; 1957) still commands wide respect. Brooks's other works include *The Hidden God* (1963), *A Shaping Joy* (1971), *The Language of the American South* (1985) and *Historical Evidence and the Reading of Seventeenth-Century Poetry* (1991).

Brooks, Gwendolyn 1917– Black American poet. Born in Topeka, Kansas, she moved to Chicago as a child and was educated at Wilson Junior College. She has taught at Northeastern Illinois State College, the University of Wisconsin and City College, New York. In 1986 she was consultant in poetry to the Library of Congress. Her first volume, *A Street in Bronzeville* (1945), was followed by *Annie Allen* (1949; PULITZER PRIZE). *Bronxville Girls and Boys* (1956) and *The Bean Eaters* (1960) were written for children. She succeeded CARL SANDBURG as POET LAUREATE of Illinois, and in 1968 published the celebratory *For Illinois 1968: A Sesquicentennial Poem*. Subsequent volumes, showing her command of direct, colloquial language inside complex formal structures, are *Riot* (1970), *Family Pictures* (1970), *Aloneness* (1971), *Aurora* (1972), *Beckonings* (1975), *To Disembark* (1981) and *Blacks* (1991). An updated edition of her *Selected Poems* appeared in 1982. She has also published *Maud Martha* (1953), an early work of fiction, and *Report from Part One: An Autobiography* (1972).

Brophy, Brigid (Antonia) 1929– Novelist and critic. She was born in London and educated at St Paul's Girls' School and St Hugh's College, Oxford, where she was a Jubilee Scholar. She married Sir Michael Levey in 1954. A lively writer with the disciplined mind of a classical scholar, she uses the term 'baroque' for her technique of presenting contrasted forces and unexpected views. Her novels include *Hackenfeller's Ape* (1954), *Flesh* (1963), *The Snowball* (1964), *In Transit* (1970) and *Palace without Chairs* (1978). Her criticism includes studies of Mozart (1964),

AUBREY BEARDSLEY (1969) and RONALD FIRBANK (1973), and *Baroque 'n' Roll* (1987). She has been vice-president of the Anti-Vivisection Society of Great Britain and was active in the successful Public Lending Right campaign.

Brougham, Henry Peter, Baron Brougham and Vaux 1778–1868 Lawyer, politician and journalist. Born in Edinburgh and educated at Edinburgh High School and Edinburgh University, he became an advocate in 1800. With FRANCIS JEFFREY, SYDNEY SMITH and FRANCIS HORNER he founded THE EDINBURGH REVIEW in 1802, contributing three of the 29 articles in the first issue. He published *The Colonial Policy of European Nations* in 1803 and in the same year became a member of Lincoln's Inn. In 1805 he settled in London but continued to contribute regularly to *The Edinburgh Review*, including the notorious review of BYRON's *Hours of Idleness* which prompted the poet to respond with *English Bards and Scotch Reviewers*. Brougham also became active in the movement to abolish slavery. He was called to the English Bar in 1808 and elected MP for Camelford in 1810. In 1810 he successfully defended LEIGH HUNT in a libel action following the publication of an article on military flogging in THE EXAMINER, but in 1812 a second court defence of Hunt failed when the essayist was indicted for a libel on the Prince Regent. Brougham became MP for Winchelsea in 1815 and a prominent member of the Whig opposition. In 1820 he defended Queen Caroline before the House of Lords in the matter of the Queen's degradation and divorce, and in the following year he unsuccessfully argued her right to coronation before the Privy Council. Brougham was appointed Lord Chancellor by Lord Grey and was created Baron Brougham and Vaux. A leading advocate of the founding of the University of London and of Parliamentary Reform (his speech on the second reading of the Reform Bill in October 1831 was much praised and was often regarded as a classic of English Parliamentary oratory), he gradually withdrew from politics in the 1850s but was elected Chancellor of the University of Edinburgh in 1859. His published works include: *Practical Observations on the Education of the People* (1825), *Historical Sketches of Statesmen* (1839), *Political Philosophy and Other Essays* (1832), *Albert Lunel: or, the Chateau of Languedoc* (a novel, 1844), *Lives of Men of Letters and Science* (1845, second series 1846) and *Contributions to the Edinburgh Review* (1856). His memoirs, *Life and Times of Henry, Lord Brougham*, appeared posthumously in 1871.

Brougham, John 1810–80 American playwright. Born and educated in Dublin, he wrote or adapted at least 125 plays. His greatest popularity, both as an actor and as a dramatist, was in the years preceding the Civil War, and he is best known for his two-act musical BURLESQUE, *Po-ca-hon-tas! or, Ye Gentle Savage* (1855). Also notable are *A Row at the Lyceum: or, Green Room Secrets* (1851), an innovative one-act skit in which a rehearsal is interrupted by an objection from a plant in the audience; and the *Game of Love* (1855), a five-act social satire about marriage between upper and lower classes. His other burlesques include *Metamora: or, The Last of the Pollywoags* (1847), *Columbus* (1857) and *Much Ado about the Merchant of Venice* (1869). He also adapted several contemporary British and American novels for the stage: *DOMBEY AND SON* (1848), *JANE EYRE* (1849), *VANITY FAIR* (1849) and *Dred* (1856). His other successes include *Temptation* (1849), *The Irish Immigrant* (1857) and *The Mustard Ball: or, Love at the Academy* (1858).

Broughton, Rhoda 1840–1920 Novelist. The daughter of a parson, she was born in Wales and wrote copiously from an early age. Two novels, *Not Wisely But Too Well* and *Cometh Up As a Flower* (both published in 1867), were considered audacious in their time and offended Victorian propriety. She said of her own writing that she began as Zola and finished as CHARLOTTE YONGE, itself a revealing comment on 19th-century shifts in sensibility. TROLLOPE in his *Autobiography* praises the mildly rebellious authoress for her ability 'to make her personages stand upright on the ground. And', he continues, 'she has the gift of making them speak as men and women do speak.'

Brown, Charles Brockden 1771–1810 Novelist, often considered America's first professional author. Born in Philadelphia into a family of prosperous Quakers, he studied law, and during his brief practice in Philadelphia met Elihu Smith, one of the CONNECTICUT WITS, with whom in 1790 he formed the Society for the Attainment of Useful Knowledge. Contemptuous of the legal profession, he moved to New York in 1796 and began writing. His first publication, *Alcuin: A Dialogue* (1798), was a treatise on the rights of women which shows the influence of WILLIAM GODWIN. Further stimulated by Godwin's philosophy of rational individualism, and by the novels of MRS RADCLIFFE, Brown wrote feverishly for the next two years and produced four novels, all of which translate the English GOTHIC NOVEL into an American idiom: *WIELAND* (1798), *ARTHUR MERVYN* (1799–1800), *Ormond* (1799) and *Edgar Huntly* (1799).

Although widely read in America and England, these novels were not commercial successes. Brown invested in an import business, which collapsed in 1806, and simultaneously engaged himself in more lucrative literary ventures. From 1799 he served as editor of *The Monthly Magazine and American Review*, and at the turn of the century produced two more traditional romances which sold well but lacked the artistic innovation of his previous fiction: *Clara*

Howard (1801; in England as *Philip Stanley*) and *Jane Talbot* (1801). *Memoirs of Carwin*, a sequel to *Wieland*, appeared serially (1803–5) in his newly founded and highly successful *The Literary Magazine and American Register* (1803–7), but remained unfinished at his death in 1810.

Brown, E(dward) K(illoran) 1905–51 Canadian critic. Born in Toronto, he was educated at the Universities of Toronto and Paris. He subsequently worked in the English departments of the Universities of Toronto and Manitoba, before moving to the United States, where he was chairman of the English department at Cornell and later worked at the University of Chicago. Brown was a wide-ranging critic, but is best remembered for his work on Canadian literature at a time before the discipline had become fashionable. From 1932 to 1942 he was editor of the *University of Toronto Quarterly*. His *On Canadian Poetry* (1943), in addition to helping to construct a canon of what was valuable in Canadian poetry and offering important revaluations of earlier poets' work, did much to establish parameters for Canadian criticism. He particularly stressed the problems that faced the writer in a materialistic society.

Brown, George Mackay 1921– Scottish poet and novelist. He was born in Stromness, on the Orkney mainland, where he still lives. He was educated at Stromness Academy and Newbattle Abbey, an adult education college near Edinburgh, where EDWIN MUIR encouraged his early work. After graduating from Edinburgh University in 1960, he did postgraduate research on GERARD MANLEY HOPKINS. Growing out of his life in the Orkney Islands, his poems are influenced by the *Orkneyinga Saga* (13th-century Icelandic tales of the Earls of Orkney and of Magnus, the Orkney saint), the work of Hopkins and Muir, and the symbolic structures of his own Roman Catholic faith. Early volumes, such as *The Storm* (1954), *Loaves and Fishes* (1959) and *The Year of the Whale* (1965), have been followed by *Fishermen with Ploughs* (1971), *Winterfold* (1976), *Voyages* (1983), *Andrina* (1983) and several limited editions: *Stone: Poems* (1987), *Seven Poems* (1989), *Songs for St Magnus* (1988) and *Two Poems for Kenna* (1988). His novels include *Greenvoe* (1972), an evocation of an imaginary Orkney village; *Magnus* (1973), a lyrical account of the saint's martyrdom; and *Time in a Red Coat* (1984), a richly textured fable about war. Short stories include *A Calendar of Love* (1967), *The Golden Bird: Two Orkney Stories* (1987) and *The Masked Fisherman and Other Stories* (1989).

Brown, Dr John 1810–82 Scottish essayist. Born in Lanarkshire, he attended Edinburgh High School and Edinburgh University and practised medicine in the city. His three-volume collection of essays, *Horae*

Subsecivae ('Hours of Leisure', 1858–62), was particularly admired by contemporaries for two items, *Marjorie Fleming* and a story of a dog, *Rab and His Friends*.

Brown, Rita Mae 1944– American novelist and poet. Born in Hanover, Pennsylvania, she attended universities in Florida and New York as well as the New York School of Visual Arts. Her first novel, *Rubyfruit Jungle* (1973), put her at the forefront of the feminist and gay rights movements. Its comic treatment of the homosexual life influenced, for example, the work of ARMISTEAD MAUPIN. Other novels include: *In Her Day* (1976); *Six of One* (1978); *Southern Discomfort* (1982); *Sudden Death* (1983), an uncompromising ROMAN À CLEF about the world of professional tennis, drawing on her relationship with Martina Navratilova; *High Hearts* (1986); *Bingo* (1988); and *Wish You were Here* (1990). Her poetry has appeared in collections such as *The Hand That Cradles the Rock* (1971) and *Songs to a Handsome Woman* (1973). *A Plain Brown Rapper* (1976) is a collection of essays.

Brown, Sterling A(llen) 1901–89 Black American poet and critic. Born in Washington DC, he was educated at Williams College, Massachusetts, and Harvard. He taught at Lincoln University in Jefferson City, Missouri, and at Fisk University in Nashville, and from 1929 was professor of English at Howard University in Washington. His first volume, *Southern Road* (1932), with its direct style and use of folk material, shows the influence of CARL SANDBURG. A leading characteristic of Brown's poetry is the appropriation of folk idioms, such as work-songs and BALLADS, which he transforms into contemporary statements of social protest. Most of his work appeared in magazines, with few published volumes, though it was anthologized in JAMES WELDON JOHNSON's *The Book of American Negro Poetry* (1922). *The Last Ride of Wild Bill, and Eleven Narrative Poems* appeared in 1975 and *The Collected Poems*, edited by Michael S. Harper, in 1980. An active and prolific critic of black literature in the 1930s, he also wrote *The Negro in American Fiction* (1937) and *Negro Poetry and Drama* (1939) and co-edited the influential anthology of HARLEM RENAISSANCE writers, *The Negro Caravan* (1941). The recipient of several academic and literary awards, he became POET LAUREATE of Washington DC in 1984.

Brown, Thomas 1663–1704 Translator and satirist. Born in Shropshire, Brown went to Christ Church, Oxford. Dr John Fell, the Dean, threatened to expel him for some misdemeanour and Brown adapted one of Martial's EPIGRAMS to make a famous jingle ('I do not love you, Dr Fell'). He was one of the team who wrote an English version of Paul Scarron's *Le Roman Comique* and, also with others, translated works by Petronius and Lucian. Brown's sketches of London life were published as *Amusements Serious and Comical* (1700). His collected works were published in four volumes (1707–11).

Brown, William Hill 1765–93 American novelist, poet and essayist. He was born in Boston, the great-great-grandson of INCREASE MATHER. His first book, *THE POWER OF SYMPATHY* (1789), is generally considered to be the first American novel. Before his early death, probably of malaria, at the age of 28 he contributed prose and poetry to the *Massachusetts Magazine* and the *New England Palladium*, occasionally using the pseudonym Pollio. As The Yankee he wrote literary and political essays for Boston's *Columbian Sentinel*. Several works were published posthumously: a tragedy, *West Point Preserved: or, the Treason of Arnold* (1797); various poems and prose pieces published in the *Boston Magazine* and the *Emerald* (1805–7); and a second novel, *Ira and Isabella: or, The Natural Children* (1807), whose plot is similar to that of *The Power of Sympathy* except that it has a happy ending.

Brown, William Wells *c.* 1816–84 Black American writer. Born into slavery in Kentucky and raised in St Louis, he helped runaway slaves in Ohio after gaining his own freedom. His autobiographical *Narrative of William W. Brown, a Fugitive Slave* was published in 1847 by the Massachusetts Antislavery Society, and he soon became widely known, both in the USA and abroad, as a leading black advocate of Abolition.

Soon after the publication of his *Narrative* Brown turned to other forms of writing. A collection of poems, *The Anti-Slavery Harp*, appeared in 1848, and *Three Years in Europe: or, Places I Have Seen and People I Have Met* in 1852. *Clotel: or, The President's Daughter* was published in London in 1853. Long thought to have been the first novel published by a black American, this story of the mulatta daughter of THOMAS JEFFERSON's black slave was issued in the USA in 1864, without reference to the President, as *Clotel: A Tale of the Southern States*. Brown's other works are a play, *The Escape: or, A Leap for Freedom* (1858), and the essay *The Black Man: His Antecedents, His Genius, and His Achievements* (1863), later expanded as *The Rising Son* (1873).

Browne, Hablot K(night) 1815–80 Illustrator. Under the pseudonym of Phiz he took over the illustrations for *PICKWICK PAPERS* after the suicide of the artist Robert Seymour in 1836, and went on to provide the plates for many other novels by DICKENS: *NICHOLAS NICKLEBY, MARTIN CHUZZLEWIT, DOMBEY AND SON, DAVID COPPERFIELD, BLEAK HOUSE, LITTLE DORRIT* and *A TALE OF TWO CITIES*. He also illustrated works by WILLIAM HARRISON AINSWORTH, CHARLES LEVER and R. S. SURTEES.

Browne, Sir Thomas 1605–82 Scientific and religious writer. Born in London and educated at Winchester and Oxford, he studied medicine at Montpellier, Padua and Leyden, qualified as a doctor and practised first in Oxford, then in Norwich, where he settled in 1637. A fervent Royalist and anti-Puritan, Browne remained in Norwich through the Civil War, and eventually became a celebrated local figure, knighted by Charles II during the royal visit of 1671.

Browne was the author of several prose tracts distinguished by a widely enquiring intelligence and liveliness of expression, the first of which, *RELIGIO MEDICI* (an examination of his religious beliefs), was published in 1642 (though written several years earlier). This was followed by *PSEUDODOXIA EPIDEMICA* (or *Vulgar Errors*) in 1646. *HYDRIOTAPHIA* (or *Urn Burial*), a reflection on burial ceremonies, and *The Garden of Cyrus*, a treatise on the application of the quincunx, both appeared in 1658. The latter was the last of the author's works to be published during his lifetime; posthumous publications included *Certain Miscellany Tracts* (1684) and *Christian Morals* (1716; later edited by JOHNSON in 1756). He also conducted an extensive and interesting correspondence with such distinguished contemporaries as AUBREY, EVELYN and ASHMOLE.

Browne, William 1591–*c.* 1643 Poet. Born in Tavistock, Devon, and educated at Exeter College, Oxford, and at the Middle Temple, Browne was a scholarly admirer of SPENSER, SIDNEY and DRAYTON, and was himself the author of PASTORAL verse which influenced MILTON and KEATS. His principal work is *Britannia's Pastoral*, a long poem in three books (the first published in 1613, the next in 1616, but the third not until 1852) combining stock motifs of the rural tradition with occasional descriptive freshness. He collaborated with GEORGE WITHER and others on *The Shepherd's Pipe* (1614), a collection of pastorals, and was also the author of several epitaphs, including the famous one on the Countess of Pembroke beginning 'Underneath this sable hearse', formerly attributed to his friend BEN JONSON.

Browning, Elizabeth Barrett 1806–61 Poet. The eldest of the 12 children of Edward Moulton-Barrett and his wife Mary, she was born at Coxhoe Hall, near Durham. While she was still quite young her father purchased the estate of Hope End, near Malvern, and it was there that most of her childhood and youth were passed. A precocious and ardent student, Elizabeth Barrett studied with a governess and shared her brothers' lessons in Latin and Greek. At the age of 15 she suffered a serious illness, but recovered sufficiently to take full part in family life. She began to write verse at an early age, celebrating family feast days as the 'Poet Laureate' of Hope End. Her first volume, *The Battle of Marathon*, was privately printed in

1820, and her second was published in 1826; both are undeniably juvenile, but in the latter Elizabeth Barrett's distinctive style begins to emerge. She later repudiated her translation of Aeschylus' *Prometheus Bound* (1833) as 'cold as Caucasus, and as flat as the nearest plain', and expiated her sin by making a new version (published in *Poems*, 1850).

In 1832 business difficulties forced Edward Moulton-Barrett to leave Hope End and, after a period at Sidmouth, he finally moved his family to London in 1835. There, Elizabeth Barrett enjoyed a moderately full literary life, corresponding with MARY RUSSELL MITFORD, R. H. HORNE and her cousin and literary confidant, John Kenyon. *The Seraphim and Other Poems* was favourably received when it appeared in 1838. In the same year she suffered a lung haemorrhage which required a long convalescence at Torquay. Against the wishes of their father, her brother Edward spent much time with her. She suffered a relapse when her brother Samuel died on the family estates in Jamaica in 1840, made more severe by Edward's death in a sailing accident shortly afterwards. She returned in 1841 to the family home at 50 Wimpole Street in London as an invalid, tied to the household of a father reluctant to grant any of his children independence. Nevertheless, she embarked on a productive period, contributing a notable series of essays on English literature and the Greek Christian poets to *THE ATHENAEUM* (1842) and collaborating with Horne on the *New Spirit of the Age* (1843).

Poems (1844), which included 'A Drama of Exile' and 'Lady Geraldine's Courtship', received considerable acclaim. One of her admirers was ROBERT BROWNING, whose verse she had complimented in 'Lady Geraldine'. A correspondence soon developed, growing rapidly into love after Browning's first visit in May 1843. In order to avoid her father's expected prohibition, the poets were married secretly in September 1846 and left for Italy a week later. After staying in Pisa they moved to Florence and settled at Casa Guidi, where their son Robert Wiedemann Barrett Browning was born in 1849. In 1850 Elizabeth Barrett Browning published a further volume of *Poems*, among them the SONNETS FROM THE PORTUGUESE, written during her courtship. This was followed by *Casa Guidi Windows* (1851). On the death of WORDSWORTH in 1850 *The Athenaeum* had proposed Elizabeth Barrett Browning as an appropriate successor to the post of POET LAUREATE (on the grounds that the appointment of a woman poet would be a fitting compliment to the Queen, and would assist two poets for the price of one), but it was not until the publication of *AURORA LEIGH* (1856) that her recognition as the foremost woman poet in English was secure. However, her political *Poems before Congress* (1860) was received with dismay as hysterical and unwomanly. Saddened by the deaths of her sister Henrietta and the Italian leader, Cavour,

she fell ill and died at Casa Guidi. She was buried in Florence's Protestant Cemetery. Robert Browning prepared her *Last Poems* (1861) for publication.

Browning, Oscar 1837–1923 Historian and teacher. He was educated at Eton under WILLIAM JOHNSON CORY and became an assistant master there from 1860 to 1875. He then became a history lecturer at King's College, Cambridge, gaining notoriety for his snobbery and argumentativeness. Among his works were a biography of GEORGE ELIOT (1890), a childhood acquaintance, and various historical studies. He is frequently mentioned in memoirs by his former students; see, for example, A. C. BENSON's *Memories and Friends* (1924) and E. F. BENSON's *As We Were* (1930).

Browning, Robert 1812–89 Poet. Born at Camberwell in South London, the son of a scholarly man whose estrangement from his own father led to his taking a post as clerk in the Bank of England. Largely educated at home, Browning read widely among the books of his father's extensive library. At 16 he began to study at the newly established London University, but returned home after a brief period.

He wrote verse from an early age, taking as his literary hero SHELLEY, who influenced much of his work and prompted him to adopt vegetarian and atheist principles for a time. In 1833 he published anonymously *Pauline: A Fragment of a Confession*. It was briefly noticed in a few journals, but more important was the reaction of JOHN STUART MILL, who noted in the young poet 'a more intense and morbid self-consciousness than I ever knew in any sane human being'. Such censure may have encouraged Browning to turn to the dramatic creation of character and the use of the DRAMATIC MONOLOGUE, which characterizes his best work. His next poem, *PARACELSUS* (1835), dealt with the life of the Swiss alchemist, a subject suggested by the poet's friend Amédée de Ripert-Monclar.

In 1837 Browning wrote a play, *Strafford*, for the actor William Macready. In spite of the efforts of Macready and JOHN FORSTER, who assisted in revising the work for the stage, it was not a popular success. After a visit to Italy (1838), he published *SORDELLO* (1840), which concentrated on 'the incidents in the development of a soul' as evinced in the life of the poet who was Dante's contemporary. From 1841 to 1846 Browning's work was published by Moxon as pamphlets in a series bearing the general title of *Bells and Pomegranates*. These included *PIPPA PASSES* (1841), *Dramatic Lyrics* (1842), *Dramatic Romances and Lyrics* (1845), *Luria and A Soul's Tragedy* (1846) and the plays *King Victor and King Charles* (1842), *The Return of the Druses* (1843), *A Blot on the 'Scutcheon* (1843) and *Colombe's Birthday* (1844). Many of Browning's best-known poems date from this early period; 'Porphyria's Lover' and 'Johannes Agricola'

Robert Browning

had already appeared in the *Monthly Repository* (1836) and were reprinted in *Dramatic Lyrics* along with MY LAST DUCHESS, SOLILOQUY OF THE SPANISH CLOISTER and THE PIED PIPER OF HAMELIN. *Dramatic Romances and Lyrics* included HOW THEY BROUGHT THE GOOD NEWS FROM GHENT TO AIX, 'Home Thoughts from Abroad', THE BISHOP ORDERS HIS TOMB IN ST PRAXED'S CHURCH and 'The Flight of the Duchess'.

Browning paid another visit to Italy in 1844, returning to take part in the chorus of admiration greeting the publication of Elizabeth Barrett's *Poems* that year (see ELIZABETH BARRETT BROWNING). His enthusiastic first letter to her led to a correspondence, friendship and eventually marriage, which took place in September 1846. Leaving England for Italy, the Brownings settled in Florence where their son was born in 1849, but a few days after the death of Browning's mother.

1850 saw the publication of *Christmas-Eve and Easter-Day* which received little attention but was well reviewed by Joseph Milsand in the *Revue des deux mondes*. *Men and Women* (1855) received grudging reviews, though it was read enthusiastically by a small group of adherents, not least DANTE GABRIEL ROSSETTI. It included FRA LIPPO LIPPI, A TOCCATA OF GALUPPI'S, 'CHILDE ROLAND TO THE DARK TOWER CAME', BISHOP BLOUGRAM'S APOLOGY, ANDREA DEL SARTO, 'Love among the Ruins', 'Saul', 'Cleon' and the eloquent dedication 'One Word More: To E.B.B.'. RUSKIN, though a friend of the Brownings, made the familiar complaint of obscurity that dogged Browning throughout his career.

After Elizabeth Barrett Browning died in 1861, Browning resolved to leave Italy and settled in England with his son. A year previously he had discovered on a Florentine stall an 'old yellow book' of documents relating to a 17th-century murder trial and he now began to contemplate his 'Roman murder-story'. Meanwhile *Dramatis Personae* (1864) included 'James Lee's Wife', *ABT VOGLER*, 'Prospice' and 'Rabbi Ben Ezra', 'A Death in the Desert', 'Mr Sludge, 'The Medium' and *CALIBAN UPON SETEBOS*. The 'murder-story', *THE RING AND THE BOOK*, was published in monthly instalments from November 1868 to February 1869. The poem received complimentary reviews and Browning, 'king of the mystics', was at last popular with the reading public.

His vitality continued undiminished as he produced a remarkable series of later works, too frequently undervalued: *Balaustion's Adventure* (1871), *Prince Hohenstiel-Schwangau* (1871), *Fifine at the Fair* (1872), *Red Cotton Night-Cap Country* (1873), *Aristophanes' Apology* (1875), *THE INN ALBUM* (1875), *Pacchiarotto and How He Worked in Distemper* (1876), *La Saisiaz* and *The Two Poets of Croisic* (1878), *Dramatic Idyls* (1879 and 1880), *Jocoseria* (1883), *Ferishtah's Fancies* (1884), *Parleyings with Certain People of Importance in Their Day* (1887) and *Asolando: Fancies and Facts* (1889).

Browning's prolific output during these years nevertheless left him time to produce a translation of Aeschylus' *Agamemnon* (1877), to watch anxiously over the career of his painter son, and to lead a demanding social life. The foundation of the Browning Society (1881) is an indication of the status he had achieved as sage and celebrity in old age. He died while visiting his son in Venice and, his wish to be buried in Florence proving impossible to fulfil, his body was returned to England and buried in Westminster Abbey.

Brownjohn, Alan 1931– Poet. Born in Catford, South London, and educated there and at Merton College, Oxford (1950–3), he taught at London schools before becoming a lecturer at Battersea College of Education. He has served as a councillor and stood as a Labour candidate for Richmond, Surrey, in the 1964 Parliamentary election. His volumes since *The Railings* (1961) include *Collected Poems 1952–83* (1983) and *Collected Poems* (1988). Associated with the GROUP, he has been influenced principally by HARDY and LARKIN. His verse is scrupulous and controlled in its use of a rather flat language to record and to satirize contemporary British life.

Brownson, Orestes (Augustus) 1803–76 American novelist and social critic. Born in Stockbridge, Vermont, into an old Connecticut family, he received no formal education. In 1824 he left the Presbyterian church and became a Universalist. By 1832 he had joined the Unitarian church, and finally, in 1844, he became a Roman Catholic. Although he was associated with TRANSCENDENTALISM and the BROOK FARM experiment, and shared the Transcendentalists' be-

lief that moral reform had to be the basis of political change, his own activities were often more radical than those emanating from that movement. He helped organize the Workingmen's Party in the early 1830s; he agitated for the reform of the penal code and inheritance laws; and in 1836 he founded a church for the working classes in Boston called the Society for Christian Union and Progress.

Brownson provided forums for these ideas in several of the magazines he edited: *Boston Quarterly Review*, *Democratic Review* and *Brownson's Quarterly Review*. Many of his works put forth his religious and social beliefs and describe his changes of faith. In *New Views of Christianity, Society and the Church* (1836), he attacked organized Christianity; *Charles Elwood: or, The Infidel Converted* (1840) is a semi-autobiographical novel about a man's conversion to Unitarianism; *The Meditational Life of Jesus* (1842) outlines his Roman Catholic tendencies; *The Spirit Rapper: An Autobiography* (1854) is less an autobiography than a novel about the Satanic influences evident in contemporary spiritualism; *The Convert: or, Leaves from My Experiences* (1857) is an account of his religious growth.

Bruce, The Poem by JOHN BARBOUR in octosyllabic couplets. It is an epic account of the struggle of Robert the Bruce (Robert I) and Sir James Douglas against the English domination of Scotland. The poem is intensely patriotic, yet avoids elevating the figure of Robert to such mythic status as to undermine his credibility. The descriptions of battles are spirited and vigorous, and the account of Bannockburn is usually judged the poem's finest passage. The tone combines chivalric elements from VERSE ROMANCE with touches of humour and a strong historical interest. Apart from some minor errors the poem gives a relatively accurate account of events. It is also notable for Barbour's strong sense of the high value of personal freedom.

Bruce, James 1730–94 Explorer. Educated at Harrow, Bruce travelled extensively in northern Africa and spent two years in Abyssinia, where he succeeded in tracing the source of the Blue Nile. In 1790 he published an account of his journeys, *Travels to Discover the Source of the Nile*, which was considered fanciful until verified by SIR RICHARD BURTON and J. H. SPEKE.

Bruce, Mary Grant 1878–1958 Australian writer of CHILDREN'S LITERATURE. Born in Victoria the daughter of an Irish surveyor, she began writing as a child and later settled into journalism in Melbourne. As editor of a children's page in *The Leader*, she also contributed her own short stories and serials, the most successful of which eventually appeared in book form as *A Little Bush Maid* (1910). This described Billabong, a fictional station in Victoria inhabited by two motherless children, Jim and Norah Linton, with their father, various friends, visiting relatives and servants. Independent, hard-working and adventurous, the Lintons soon became firm favourites with readers, the last of their 15 stories appearing in 1942. Against a physically tough setting, the author creates an idealized rural existence highly acceptable to generations of readers many of whom lived in more urban surroundings. *The Stone Age of Burkamukk* (1922) is a book of Aboriginal legends, and *The Happy Traveller* (1929) the story of a resourceful boy escaping from his orphanage.

Brut An alliterative verse chronicle by LAYAMON, written in the late 12th century. The poem is adapted from the French of Wace's *Le Roman de Brut* (1155), itself an adaptation of GEOFFREY OF MONMOUTH's *Historia Regum Britanniae* (*c.* 1135). It narrates the history of England from its foundation by the legendary Brutus, great-grandson of Aeneas, who left Italy to seek a new land, destroyed the giants then living in England and built London. King Lear and Cymbeline both appear, but the narrative is memorable for being the first to tell the story of King Arthur in English (see ARTHURIAN LITERATURE). *Brut* lacks much of Wace's courtliness, resembling more closely the vigorous epic character of Old English poetry.

Brutus, Dennis 1924– South African poet. Born in Zimbabwe, but educated in South Africa, he became a schoolmaster and vigorous opponent of apartheid. He was banned in 1961, arrested in 1963, shot in the back while trying to escape, and imprisoned on Robben Island. He went into exile in 1966 and successfully campaigned abroad for South Africa's exclusion from the Olympic Games. Since 1970 he has taught at universities in the USA.

His first book of poems, *Sirens, Knuckles, Boots* (1962), was published in Nigeria. It vigorously records the strident noises and police violence which accompany black South African life under apartheid, estranging blacks from a lover-like possession of their land. The central idea of the poet as troubadour, the land as his mistress, integrates his vatic, sometimes bitter utterance on public themes with the great tenderness of his personal love poetry. *Letters to Martha and Other Poems from a South African Prison* (1968) contains some of the most honest and disturbing poetry in English about prison life: spare, largely nonfigurative, relying on subtle, conversational rhythms and delicate verbal nuances. *Poems from Algiers* (1970), *China Poems* (1970) and *Thoughts Abroad* (1970) are poems of exile in which foreign views contain hints of South African landmarks. *A Simple Lust* (1973) collects all the former verse and adds previously unpublished poems. *Stubborn Hope* (1979) and *Strains* (1981) reiterate the exile's concern with his

country but also dramatize a personal conflict between sensual indulgence and spiritual discipline.

Bryant, William Cullen 1794–1878 American poet and editor. Born in Cummington, Massachusetts, he began writing poetry at the age of 13. His first work, *The Embargo* (1808), satirizes THOMAS JEFFERSON's government. He attended Williams College, then studied law and followed a legal career until he was 31. He was still a young lawyer when the first version of *Thanatopsis*, which he had written when he was 16, appeared in *THE NORTH AMERICAN REVIEW* in 1817. He published a collection, *Poems*, in 1821, and from 1824 to 1825 contributed regularly to the *United States Literary Gazette*. It was during this period that his reputation as a leading American poet was established.

A vigorous opponent of slavery and an advocate of the new Republican Party, he became an editor of the *New York Review* and *Athenaeum Magazine* in 1825, and chief editor of the *New York Evening Post* in 1829, a position he held for nearly 50 years. His career as a poet continued with the publication of a second collection, *Poems*, in 1832. Late in life he produced blank verse translations of the *Iliad* (1870) and the *Odyssey* (1871–2). Though he was strongly influenced by European ROMANTICISM, and by WORDSWORTH in particular, his verse reveals a concern with distinctively American political and philosophical issues.

Bryce, James, 1st Viscount 1838–1922 Historian. Educated at the University of Glasgow, Trinity College, Oxford, and the University of Heidelberg, he became a barrister in 1867 and was appointed Regius Professor of Civil Law at Oxford (1870–93). Bryce entered politics in 1880 and was Chief Secretary for Ireland (1905–6) and ambassador to Washington (1907–13). As a historian, Bryce is remembered for *The Holy Roman Empire* (1864) and *The American Commonwealth* (1888, revised 1920). Other works include *Studies in History and Jurisprudence* (1901) and *Impressions of South Africa* (1897), a sharply observed picture of the country on the eve of the Boer War.

Bryden, Bill (Campbell Rough) 1942– Playwright and director. Born in Greenock, he began his career as a documentary writer for Scottish television before being appointed assistant director at the Belgrade Theatre, Coventry (1965–7) and at the ROYAL COURT THEATRE (1967–9) and an associate director at the Royal Lyceum Theatre in Edinburgh (1971–4). Notable among many Lyceum productions were those of Bryden's own two plays, *Willie Rough* (1972), about the Greenock shop steward who led a shipyard strike during World War I, and *Benny Lynch* (1974). Both plays are distinguished by naturalistic detail, clear handling of complex historical material and socialist fervour which never becomes blindly polemical. In 1975 he joined the ROYAL NATIONAL THEATRE, where his play *Old Movies* (1977) was staged. He became Head of TV Drama for BBC Scotland in 1984.

Buchan, John 1875–1940 Scottish novelist, biographer, historian, essayist, journalist, editor, poet and publisher. Son of a Lowland manse, he received a classical education in Glasgow and Oxford and worked with Milner in South Africa, later becoming a practising London lawyer and virtually editing *The Spectator*. He revitalized Nelson's the publishers, particularly through pocket editions of great literature. In World War I he served in Intelligence, and was then MP for the Scottish Universities. As Lord Tweedsmuir he became Governor-General of Canada.

Buchan is famous for his five Richard Hannay thrillers, particularly the first, *The Thirty-Nine Steps* (1915), his 27th book. His 100 books include nearly 30 novels and seven collections of short stories; many are still widely praised and read, both historical fiction, like *Salute to Adventurers* (1915), *Midwinter* (1923), *Witch Wood* (1927) and *The Blanket of the Dark* (1931), and contemporary tales, like the charming *Huntingtower* (1922) or *Castle Gay* (1930), and the profounder Sir Edward Leithen novels, especially Buchan's last, *Sick Heart River* (1941). His fiction has clarity, atmosphere, good characterization, a grasp of large affairs and an acute sense of landscape. His 24-volume *Nelson's History of the War* (1915–19), partly written from the Front, has a global view free from jingoism. Biographies of Montrose (1913, 1928), Oliver Cromwell (1934), Augustus (1937) and others are admired; that of SIR WALTER SCOTT (1932) is definitive. He was a prolific contributor to journals. His fine autobiography, *Memory Hold-the-Door* (1940), may be amplified by the biography by Janet Adam Smith and memoirs by his daughter and sons.

Buchanan, George 1506–82 Historian and scholar. Buchanan is the most important of the 16th-century Scottish humanists. He was educated at St Andrews and Paris, where he became an MA in 1528. His career was characteristically humanist: that of teacher, tutor to boys of noble families (including the future JAMES I), translator, poet and grammarian. He corresponded with the leading scholars of the day, including Languet, ASCHAM and Tycho Brahe. He returned from the Continent to Scotland in 1536 as tutor to the natural son of James V, and with the King's encouragement wrote *Franciscanus et Fratres* attacking the morals of the clergy. Consequently, he had to flee the persecution of Cardinal Beaton to London, Paris and Bordeaux. There in the early 1540s he composed four tragedies: *Baptistes* and *Jephthes* on biblical subjects, and two Latin versions of Euripides, *Alcestis* and *Medea*. While confined in a Portuguese monastery for writing against the

Franciscans he produced a Latin paraphrase of the Psalms.

Buchanan returned to Scotland in 1562 and took part in public life. He celebrated the marriage of Mary and Darnley in an epithalamion, but after Darnley's death participated in the commissions against Mary and authenticated her handwriting in the incriminating 'Casket Letters'. He wrote *De Maria Scotorum Regina... Conjuratione*, which appeared simultaneously in Scottish as *Ane Detection of the Duinges of Marie Queene of Scottes* in 1571. His later years saw the publication of *De Jure Regni*, a defence of limited monarchy, and his major work, *Rerum Scotiarum Historia*, printed at Edinburgh in the year of his death, 1582.

Buchanan, Robert (Williams) 1841–1901 Poet, novelist and playwright. The son of an Ayrshire freethinker, Buchanan was born in Staffordshire and after high-school and university education in Edinburgh sought fame in London. Several strands are detectable in his varied output of verse. *London Poems* (1866) shows the attraction to mean streets and squalid city lives that became a literary obsession in the 1890s. *Idyls and Legends of Inverburn* (1865), *Ballad Stories of the Affections* (1866) and *North Coast and Other Poems* (1867) often deal with the Scottish peasantry and the exacting northern life. Several mystical works, *The Book of Orm* (1870), *Balder the Beautiful* (1877) and *The City of Dream* (1888), betray an affinity with the SPASMODIC SCHOOL OF POETRY in their penchant for verse on an epic scale. More down-to-earth were *Saint Abe and His Seven Wives* (1872) and *White Rose and the Red* (1873), which deal with life in the New World. Buchanan also wrote plays, with varying success, such as *Lady Clare* (1883), *Sophia* (an adaptation of TOM JONES; 1886) and *The Charlatan* (1894). There were, in addition, a good many novels, among them *The Shadow of the Sword* (1876), *God and the Man* (1881), *Foxglove Manor* (1885) and *Effie Hetherington* (1886). The literary histories usually remember Buchanan for 'The Fleshly School of Poetry', a scurrilous attack on the PRE-RAPHAELITES which was developed from an article for *The Contemporary Review* into a pseudonymous pamphlet (1872). DANTE GABRIEL ROSSETTI, the chief target, was stung into replying with 'The Stealthy School of Criticism'. SWINBURNE supported Rossetti in *Under the Microscope* (1872).

Buck, Pearl S(ydenstricker) 1892–1973 American novelist. Born in Hillsboro, West Virginia, she was taken to China as a child by her parents, who were missionaries, and spent much of her life there, teaching at various universities. Many of her works of fiction are set in China, including *The Good Earth* (1931), probably her best-known novel, for which she was awarded the PULITZER PRIZE in 1932. An epic story about a peasant's relationship with the soil, it is the first in a trilogy called *The House of Earth*, of which the others are *Sons* (1932) and *A House Divided* (1935). Her first novel about Chinese life was *East Wind, West Wind* (1930). Subsequent novels about China include *The Mother* (1934), *This Proud Heart* (1938), *Dragon Seed* (1941) and *Kinfolk* (1949).

A prolific writer, Buck produced over 100 titles: novels, collections of stories, plays, screenplays, one book of verse, CHILDREN'S LITERATURE, biographies, two autobiographies, a cookbook, and works of non-fiction about the mentally retarded, her philanthropic activities, Russia and missionaries. She also translated and edited works by various Chinese writers. The biographies of her parents, *The Exile* (1936) and *Fighting Angel: Portrait of a Soul* (1936), are considered classics. In 1938 she became the first American woman to win the Nobel Prize for Literature.

Buckeridge, Anthony 1912– Writer of CHILDREN'S LITERATURE. Born in London and educated at London University, he became a schoolmaster teaching principally in boys' preparatory schools. The stories about Jennings he used to tell his pupils during or after lessons became radio plays broadcast on the BBC's *Children's Hour* from 1948. The first of many Jennings books appeared in 1950. The amiable adventures of the 10-year-old Jennings and Darbyshire, his fellow pupil at Linbury Court School, usually centre on the chaos created by Jennings's well-intentioned efforts to help. Of the two masters in charge, Mr Carter always manages to restore order just at the moment when his irritable colleague Mr Wilkins has reached the end of his tether. The stories are further enlivened by Jennings's spirited use of schoolboy slang, with the author substituting his own inventions ('Crystallized cheesestraws!') for the type of contemporary argot that would soon seem dated.

Buckingham, 2nd Duke of [Villiers, George] 1628–87 Playwright. Son of James I's ennobled favourite, he was born in the year of his father's assassination and brought up in the royal household of Charles I. Constantly involved in intrigue, both before and after the Restoration, Buckingham also found time for literary pursuits. Perhaps in collaboration with SAMUEL BUTLER and others, he wrote THE REHEARSAL (1671), a BURLESQUE of the excesses of heroic tragedy which long outlived the dramatic taste it satirized, providing a model a century later for SHERIDAN'S THE CRITIC (1779). DRYDEN, mocked in the person of Bayes, took his revenge by portraying Buckingham as Zimri in ABSALOM AND ACHITOPHEL. The only other of Buckingham's dramatic works to merit attention is his adaptation of JOHN FLETCHER'S *The Chances* (1667).

Buckle, Henry Thomas 1821–62 Historian. Born at Lee in Kent, he was for most of his life a Londoner. A solitary man, largely without formal education, he used the small fortune inherited from his father to devote himself to studying history from a scientific standpoint influenced by JOHN STUART MILL. The first volume of his ambitious *History of Civilization* appeared in 1857 and the second in 1861, but he died in Damascus with the work unfinished. Buckle's *History* enjoyed a brief popularity before its approach came to appear dated even to those who shared its author's scientific precepts.

Buckler, Ernest (Redmond) 1908–84 Canadian novelist. A farmer in Nova Scotia, he was educated at Dalhousie University and the University of Toronto. His best-known work, *The Mountain and the Valley* (1952), is a classic novel of life in maritime Canada, describing the protagonist's desire for an artistic existence outside his rural world. Other works include *The Cruelest Month* (1963), *Ox Bells and Fireflies: A Memoir* (1968) and *Whirligig: Selected Prose and Verse* (1977). Some of his engaging short stories were collected in *The Rebellion of Young David and Other Stories* (1975).

Buckley, Vincent 1925–88 Australian poet and critic. Born of Irish parents in Romsey, Victoria, Buckley was educated by Jesuits in Melbourne and later at the Universities of Melbourne and Cambridge. During World War II he served with the Royal Australian Air Force. He subsequently worked in the public service and then took up an appointment at the University of Melbourne, where he spent all his academic life. Early work, such as *The World's Flesh* (1954), *Masters in Israel* (1961) and *Arcady and Other Poems* (1966), is concerned with the state of contemporary culture, particularly in religion and politics. After *Golden Builders and Other Poems* (1975) he dealt more directly with the process of perception and the way art constructs and enacts meanings. Volumes include *Late Winter Child* (1979), *The Pattern* (1979) and the posthumous *Last Poems* (1991). As a critic, he wrote *Essays in Poetry* (1957), an influential commentary on the state of Australian poetry, and, as poetry editor of the *Bulletin* in 1961–3, he published poets who questioned the prevailing orthodoxies. His edition of *The Faber Book of Modern Australian Verse* appeared posthumously in 1991. He also wrote an autobiography, *Cutting Green Hay* (1983), and *Meaning Ireland: Insights into the Contemporary Irish Condition* (1985).

Buckstone, John Baldwin 1802–79 Playwright, actor and theatre manager. He was born and brought up in London's East End. After three seasons in the provinces, he made his London debut at the Surrey Theatre in 1823–4, establishing himself in the 'low comedian' line which he sustained for over 50 years. Of the 100 or so dramatic pieces Buckstone wrote between 1825 and 1850, most were short FARCES, operettas or burlettas but one of the earliest, *Luke the Labourer* (1826), helped set the fashion for domestic MELODRAMA. *The Wreck Ashore* (1830) is an adventure story larded with low-life comic characters. Here, as in the lively comedy of *The Irish Lion* (1838) and *Single Life* (1839) and in the tear-jerking of *The Green Bushes* (1845), Buckstone upholds manly fortitude and decency, assuring his heroes and heroines the satisfaction of victory or of superior self-sacrifice in defeat. As manager of the HAYMARKET THEATRE in 1853–76 he made it the home of comedy, staging the work of TOM TAYLOR, WESTLAND MARSTON, and, after 1870, W. S. GILBERT.

Buke of the Howlat, The An alliterative poem in Middle Scots, written around 1450 by SIR RICHARD HOLLAND. The poem is a moral ALLEGORY indicating the dangers of pride and ambition. The owl complains of its dull plumage to the peacock and a parliament of birds is called. They decide nothing can be done, but Dame Nature descends and allows each bird to donate a feather to the owl. The owl becomes too proud of its new appearance and Nature revokes the favour, leaving it in its former state. The poem contains a passage praising the Douglas family to whom Holland was allied.

Bukowski, Charles 1920– American poet, novelist and screenwriter. Born in Germany, he was brought to the USA by his parents in 1922, and raised in Los Angeles. His screenplay for the film *Barfly* (1987) introduced a wider audience to a writer descended from the BEATS, whose life has been that of an angry, irreverent outsider and whose work has largely been published in limited editions and magazines designed for an underground rather than a commercial readership. Collections have included *Drowning in Flame: Selected Poems 1955–1973* (1974), *Love is a Dog from Hell: Poems 1974–1977* (1977), *War All the Time: Poems 1981–1984* (1984), *Roominghouse Madrigals: Early Selected Poems 1946–1966* (1988) and *Septuagenarian Stew: Stories and Poems* (1990). His novels include *Post Office* (1971), *Factotum* (1975), *Women* (1978) and *Ham on Rye* (1982).

Bullins, Ed 1935– Black American playwright. He was born in Philadelphia and educated there and in California. He joined the New Lafayette Theatre in Harlem as resident playwright in 1967, becoming its associate director, and edited its periodical, *Black Theatre*. He moved to San Francisco in 1982. Originally inspired to turn to the theatre by the example of AMIRI BARAKA, he showed his sensitivity to life in the ghetto in his first piece, *Clara's Ole Man* (1965), and has since become one of the most prolific

and internationally known American playwrights. Among his best-known works are *Goin' a Buffalo* (1966), *In the Wine Time* (1968), *The Duplex* (1970), *In New England Winter* (1971), *The Fabulous Miss Marie* (1971) and *The Taking of Miss Janie* (1975). They combine formal discipline with an improvisatory energy which embraces black ritual, jazz and blues. Bullins has also published a collection of stories, *The Hungered One: Early Writings* (1971), and a novel, *The Reluctant Rapist* (1973).

Bulwer Lytton, Edward (George Earle Lytton), 1st Baron Lytton 1803–73 Novelist, playwright and poet. Few English writers are known by such a variety of names. He began as plain Edward Bulwer, though he often called himself Edward Lytton Bulwer (Lytton being his mother's maiden name and one of his several Christian names). He was knighted in 1837, and on his mother's death in 1843 expanded his surname to Bulwer Lytton: hence Sir Edward (Lytton) Bulwer Lytton. Raised to the peerage in 1866, he was known thereafter as Lord Lytton. His son, EDWARD ROBERT BULWER LYTTON, with whom he is sometimes confused, was created the 1st Earl of Lytton in 1880.

One of the most accomplished authors of his day, he is marked above all by the versatility of his talents. His two dozen novels, written over an active career of 45 years, tackle almost every genre popular with his contemporaries. They include: historical romances, notably THE LAST DAYS OF POMPEII (1834), *Rienzi* (1835), THE LAST OF THE BARONS (1843) and *Harold* (1848); tales of magic, spiritualism and SCIENCE FICTION like *Zanoni* (1842), *A Strange Story* (1862) and THE COMING RACE (1871); SILVER-FORK NOVELS of high society like *Pelham* (1828); light novels of middle-class domestic life like *The Caxtons* (1849), *My Novel* (1853) and *What Will He Do with It?* (1858); NEWGATE NOVELS like *Paul Clifford* (1830) and *Eugene Aram* (1832); and philosophical novels about gifted young men seeking the meaning of life, like *Godolphin* (1833), *Ernest Maltravers* (1837) and *Alice* (1838). In almost every instance he was immensely successful. 'Everything he wrote,' remarked EDMUND GOSSE, 'sold as though it were bread displayed to a hungry crowd.'

He also published 10 plays, of which *The Lady of Lyons* (1838), *Richelieu* (1839) and *Money* (1840) were regularly performed throughout the 19th century, 11 volumes of poetry, two collections of essays, numerous short stories, a history of Athens, translations of Horace and Schiller, and a pioneering sociological study, *England and the English* (1833). From 1831 to 1833 he edited *The New Monthly Magazine*. He entered Parliament in 1831 as a Liberal, resigned 10 years later, returned in 1852 as a Tory, and in 1858 became Secretary for the Colonies. He was a lifelong friend of DICKENS, and is often remembered for persuading him to change the ending of GREAT EXPECTATIONS. That he is not much remembered in his own right would have surprised his contemporaries, for during the mid-19th century he was widely regarded as England's leading man of letters.

Bulwer Lytton, Edward Robert, 1st Earl of Lytton 1831–91 Diplomat and poet. The son of EDWARD BULWER LYTTON, he pursued a successful career in the diplomatic service, eventually becoming Viceroy of India (1876–80). In his youth he served in Italy where he met ROBERT BROWNING and ELIZABETH BARRETT BROWNING, whose work influenced his poetry. His volumes include *Wanderer* (1857), *Lucile* (1860), *Glenaveril* (1885) and *King Poppy* (1892). His early work was published under the pseudonym of Owen Meredith.

Bunting, Basil 1900–85 Poet. Born in Northumberland and educated at Quaker schools and at the London School of Economics, he went to prison as a conscientious objector during World War I. He worked in London as a music critic and in Paris as an editor on *The Transatlantic Review* before seeking out EZRA POUND in Rapallo, Italy, where he lived for some time. He published his first poems in the 1930s, and during World War II went to Persia to serve first with the British forces and later with the diplomatic service as an interpreter. After being expelled from Persia, he worked as a journalist in Newcastle until his retirement.

His reputation was well established abroad before he became widely known in Britain for his long autobiographical poem *Briggflatts* (1966), celebrating and seeking to define a distinct Northumbrian community with its own language and history. *Collected Poems* appeared in 1968 and Richard Caddel's edition of his *Uncollected Poems*, which includes some fine translations, in 1991. Influenced both by Pound and LOUIS ZUKOFSKY, Bunting also took many of his poetic concerns from the tradition of WORDSWORTH.

Bunting, Edward 1773–1843 Irish musicologist and collector of folk music. Born in Armagh, he was commissioned at the age of 18 to take down the music at the Belfast Harp Festival. This experience determined him to collect the rich treasures of the Irish folk-music tradition. His three volumes, *A General Collection of the Ancient Irish Music* (1796), *A General Collection of the Ancient Music of Ireland* (1809) and *The Ancient Music of Ireland, Arranged for the Piano Forte* (1840), form the basis for the attempt to preserve Irish traditional music. Bunting's work, continued by GEORGE PETRIE, is an integral part of the CELTIC REVIVAL which is a marked feature of 19th- and 20th-century Irish literature. Bunting settled in Dublin in 1819, where he was organist at St George's Church.

Bunyan, John 1628–88 Nonconformist preacher and writer. Bunyan was born at Elstow, near Bedford, the eldest of three children of Thomas Bunyan, a brasier or tinker, and his second wife Margaret Bentley. He was sent to a local school where he learned to read and write before taking up his father's trade. BALLADS and CHAPBOOK versions of chivalric romances were his favourite reading. In 1644 Bunyan was enrolled into the Parliamentary army to serve in the Civil War; he spent the next two-and-a-half years as a soldier in the garrison town of Newport Pagnell. Little is known of Bunyan's military career: his only reference to it is to record a providential escape from death when a fellow soldier who had taken his place at a siege was killed. It is likely, however, that he was influenced by radical sectarian preachers who were active in the army.

In 1647, following his discharge from the army, Bunyan returned to Elstow to resume his trade as a tinker. During the next few years he underwent a severe psychological crisis, the progress of which he later recorded in his spiritual autobiography, *Grace Abounding to the Chief of Sinners* (1666). His first wife, whom he married in 1648, possessed a couple of popular religious books, Arthur Dent's *The Plain Man's Path-Way to Heaven* and Lewis Bayley's *The Practice of Piety*, and reading these Bunyan became convinced that he was a sinful creature destined for hell. He tried repeatedly to reform his life, giving up dancing and bell-ringing which were his favourite pastimes, and devoted himself to an intensive study of the Bible. Searching for spiritual enlightenment and fellowship, he came into contact with members of some of the religious sects which had emerged in the 1650s, such as Ranters and Quakers, and read their books, though later coming to reject their doctrines. He was much influenced by reading Luther's *Commentary on Galatians*, finding there his own spiritual condition 'so largely and profoundly handled, as if his book had been written out of my heart'. About 1653 he joined an Independent (or Congregational) church in Bedford, but it took several more years of struggle, alternately swinging from moods of blackest despondency to moments of ecstatic vision, before he felt assured that his sins were forgiven and that he was an elect child of God.

The Bedford congregation of which he became a member had been formed in 1650. It developed a comparatively tolerant attitude towards matters which were deemed to be inessential, not insisting, for example, on adult baptism as a requirement for fellowship. Two or three years after joining, Bunyan began to preach in public. His early sermons evidently drew upon his own experience of spiritual conflict. The right of unlearned and unordained men to preach was a fiercely controversial matter in the 17th century, and Bunyan, like other 'mechanick preachers', repeatedly came into conflict with the regular clergy.

He also engaged in doctrinal disputes with other sectarian preachers, and his earliest published works, *Some Gospel-Truths Opened* (1656) and *A Vindication of Some Gospel-Truths* (1657), were written against the Quakers. These provoked replies from Edward Burrough, a young Quaker polemicist, and from GEORGE FOX. Bunyan's first non-controversial work, *A Few Sighs from Hell: or, The Groans of a Damned Soul* (1658), took as its text the parable of Dives and Lazarus, and in it he vigorously castigated the rich for their pride and covetousness, and for their oppression of the poor. This was followed by his most important theological statement, *The Doctrine of the Law and Grace Unfolded* (1659), a lengthy exposition of the Calvinist doctrine of the two covenants of works and grace. He married his second wife, Elizabeth, in 1659, following the death the previous year of his first wife who had borne four children.

With the restoration of Charles II in 1660 the comparative freedom which religious sects had enjoyed under Cromwell came to an end. Bunyan was one of the first Nonconformist preachers to suffer. He was arrested at a meeting at Lower Samsell in Bedfordshire in November 1660 and brought before the local magistrate, who remanded him in custody to appear at the quarter sessions in Bedford in January 1661. The charge was that he did not attend the established church and that he preached without licence to unlawful assemblies, or 'conventicles'. Bunyan's own account of his arrest and trial is to be found in the penultimate section of *Grace Abounding*, and in *A Relation of My Imprisonment*, taking the form of a series of verbatim reports of his trial and subsequent interviews with officials of the court, written for his friends in the Bedford congregation and not published until the middle of the 18th century. Bunyan stubbornly refused to give an undertaking to cease preaching, and spent most of the next 12 years in Bedford jail in consequence. He occupied himself making shoe laces to help support his family, preaching to his fellow prisoners, and writing. His first prison book, *Profitable Meditations* (1661), presented theological doctrine in verse form in an attempt to reach a wider audience, since, as Bunyan remarked, 'Man's heart is apt in metre to delight.' This was followed by *I Will Pray with the Spirit* (c. 1662), a defence of extempore prayer, and *Christian Behaviour* (1663), a conduct manual. In 1665 he published two more volumes of poetry, as well as *The Holy City*, a millenarian vision of the approaching establishment of the true church on earth, when the saints would no longer suffer persecution. His last and most important prison work was *Grace Abounding*. It is likely that he also began writing his masterpiece of religious ALLEGORY, *THE PILGRIM'S PROGRESS*, during these years.

He was released in 1672 as a result of a royal pardon following Charles II's first Declaration of Indulgence. As pastor of the Bedford congregation, he obtained a licence to preach and for the remainder of his life was an active Nonconformist organizer, travelling throughout Cambridgeshire, Hertfordshire and Bedfordshire, and earning for himself the nickname 'Bishop Bunyan'. His reputation brought him invitations to preach in London, where, however, he became embroiled in doctrinal disputes with the Strict Baptists. He also engaged in controversy with the latitudinarian Anglican divine, Edward Fowler, publishing *A Defence of the Doctrine of Justification by Faith* (1672) in response to Fowler's *Design of Christianity* (1670).

The threat of further imprisonment was always present, though the warrant issued for his arrest in 1675 seems not to have been executed. He was jailed again for six months in 1677, and it was during this second imprisonment that he put the finishing touches to *The Pilgrim's Progress* (1678). Such was its success that its publisher, Nathaniel Ponder, became known in the trade as 'Bunyan Ponder'. In the 10 years before Bunyan's death more than 11 authorized editions had appeared, the book had been published in New England, and it had been translated into French, Dutch and Welsh. Following the success of his allegory of the Christian life, Bunyan turned his attention to the ungodly, publishing in 1680 a realistic tale of *THE LIFE AND DEATH OF MR BADMAN*. Though lacking the imaginative fervour of the earlier work, it presents an unsparing condemnation of the vices of Restoration society. *THE HOLY WAR*, published two years later, is in many ways Bunyan's most ambitious work. In 1684, following the appearance of spurious 'continuations' to *The Pilgrim's Progress*, Bunyan published his own Second Part.

As well as these works for which he is remembered, Bunyan continued to publish theological treatises, sermons, verse and controversial works. His bibliography runs to nearly 60 titles, 14 of which were published posthumously. In addition to writing and preaching, Bunyan devoted much energy to the pastoral care of his group of congregations. *The Church Book of Bunyan Meeting* contains entries in his handwriting admonishing wayward professors and recording congregational visits. The latter years of Charles II's reign saw renewed persecution of Nonconformists, and Bunyan's fears for his own security are indicated by the deed of gift which he had drawn up in December 1685, making over all his worldly possessions to his wife. In 1687 the situation was reversed again, when James II offered toleration to both Protestant and Catholic Dissenters. In an attempt to ensure the return of a Parliament which would accept this, he instituted a reorganization of the corporations. Bunyan himself, it is said, was approached by James's agent, Lord Aylesbury, and offered 'a place of public trust', but he evidently refused, no doubt believing that James's real ambition was to enhance the political power of Catholicism in England. He did not live to see the overthrow of James II and the achievement of toleration for Protestant Dissenters under William III. His death in August 1688 was brought about by a fever contracted while riding from Reading to London in heavy rain. He was buried in the famous Dissenting burial ground at Bunhill Fields, Finsbury.

Burbage, Richard c. 1569–1619 The leading member of the company to which SHAKESPEARE belonged. Burbage's father was the builder of the first English playhouse, the THEATRE, and his son seems to have inherited business sense as well as acting talent. As a founder member of the Lord Chamberlain's Men, later the KING'S MEN, and a shareholder in both the GLOBE and the BLACKFRIARS THEATRE, he guided the company to unparalleled fame and remarkable financial equilibrium. Considered by contemporaries a more lifelike actor than his chief rival, EDWARD ALLEYN, Burbage is known to have played the title roles in HAMLET, OTHELLO, KING LEAR and RICHARD III, Ferdinand in WEBSTER'S THE DUCHESS OF MALFI, and Malevole in MARSTON'S THE MALCONTENT. It is reasonable to suppose that he created many other major Shakespearean roles. He was also a painter of reputation and it is probably a self-portrait which can now be seen in the Dulwich picture gallery.

Burgess, Anthony [Wilson John] 1917–93 Novelist and critic. Born in Manchester, he was educated at the Xaverian College and Manchester University, graduating in philology and literature. After service in World War II he worked as an instructor for the Central Advisory Council for Forces Education and as a grammar-school teacher. From 1954 to 1960 he was an educational officer in the Colonial Service, stationed in Borneo and Malaya. During these years he completed his first three novels, *Time for a Tiger* (1956), *The Enemy in the Blanket* (1958) and *Beds in the East* (1959), published together as *The Malayan Trilogy* (1972; reissued as *The Long Day Wanes*, 1982).

His bleak dystopian novel *A Clockwork Orange* (1962) marked a new development in the Joycean tradition. Its popularity reached the level of a cult after the film version by Stanley Kubrick in 1972. Burgess's prolific output during the 1960s and 1970s also included *The Wanting Seed* (1962), *Nothing Like the Sun* (about SHAKESPEARE; 1964), *Napoleon Symphony* (1974) and *ABBA ABBA* (1977). The verbal inventiveness and pointed social SATIRE which characterize his fiction are displayed in a comic sequence about the poet Enderby, whose carnal and cultural career spans England, Rome, Tangiers and New York: *Inside Mr Enderby* (published under the pseudonym Joseph Kell in 1963), *Enderby Outside* (1968) and *The Clockwork Testament* (1974). *Enderby's Dark Lady* (1984) resurrected its hero after he had been dispatched by the author. Notably ambitious are *Earthly Powers* (1980), about 20th-century life, and *The Kingdom of the*

Wicked (1985), about early Christianity. *The Devil's Mode* (1989) is a collection of short stories.

His many other works include: studies of JOYCE in *Here Comes Everybody* (1965) and *Joysprick* (1973); *The Novel Today* (1963) and *The Novel Now* (1967); biographies of HEMINGWAY (1978) and D. H. LAWRENCE (1985); *Urgent Copy* (1968) and *Homage to Qwertyuiop* (1987), culled from his relentless output of reviews and essays; screenplays; and translations of foreign drama. Two volumes of autobiography, *Little Wilson and Big God* (1987) and *You've Had Your Time* (1990), are teeming, bawdy and often hilarious recapitulations of his National Service and teaching career abroad.

Burgoyne, John 1722–92 Soldier and playwright. In command of the British forces at Saratoga in 1777 General Burgoyne lost both an army and a well-earned reputation as a soldier. He had had one play, *The Maid of the Oaks* (1774), staged before the American debacle. Soon after his return to England, he provided what is virtually a libretto for the music of William Jackson of Exeter, *The Lord of the Manor* (1780). It is a slight piece, with a redeeming trio of soldiers among its characters. A second and more serious musical piece, *Richard Coeur de Lion* (1786), is undistinguished. Burgoyne's dramatic reputation rests on his witty comedy, THE HEIRESS (1786), whose trivial plot does not obstruct pertinent social comment. SHAW made Burgoyne a character in his play *The Devil's Disciple*.

Burke, Edmund 1729–97 Political philosopher. Born in Dublin, the second son of a Roman Catholic mother and an Irish Protestant lawyer, Burke was educated as a Protestant, attending Trinity College, Dublin, and then studying law at the Middle Temple in 1750. He was never called to the Bar. His first published works were *A Vindication of Natural Society* (1756), an ironical treatise examining the divisions in society, and *A Philosophical Enquiry into the Origin of Our Ideas of the Sublime and the Beautiful* (1757). He married Jane Nugent in 1756, and was a founding editor of THE ANNUAL REGISTER in 1758. He associated freely in the literary circles of London, befriended JOHNSON and REYNOLDS, and was an early member of 'the Club'.

Burke was a Whig, and became secretary to the Marquis of Rockingham, then Prime Minister, in 1765, entering Parliament as MP for Wendover in the same year. In the Commons he was an outspoken opponent of Lord North's Tory administration, especially over its attempts to repress the American colonies. His published views on the American question, supporting the colonists' cause, include: *Observations on 'The Present State of the Nation'* (1769), *On American Taxation* (1774) and *On Conciliation with the Colonies* (1775). He was strongly opposed to the control exercised over the House by the friends of George III, and forcibly expressed concern in his *Thoughts on the Cause of the Present Discontents* (1770).

At the invitation of the people of Bristol he became their MP in 1774, during which time he made himself famous as an orator, especially for his speech on economic reform in February 1780. But he espoused the cause of free trade with Ireland, became unpopular in his constituency, and lost his seat in the Commons in that year, a defence of his views appearing in *Two Letters... to Gentlemen in the City of Bristol* (1778) and the *Speech at the Guildhall* (1780). He also championed the cause of the Irish Catholics, another controversial alignment, of which his letters *To a Peer of Ireland on the Penal Laws* (1782) and *To Sir Hercules Langrishe* (1792) are evidence.

Re-entering the Commons in 1781 as member for Malton, Burke rose to become Paymaster of the Forces (his highest public office) in 1782. Thereafter, two of his chief interests were to be the emancipation of British India and the abolition of the slave trade. In the former matter he became an expert authority, supporting Fox's Bill for reforming the administration, and delivering a celebrated speech in 1785 'On the Nabob of Arcot's Private Debts'. He was a formidable critic of Warren Hastings, the first Governor-General of India, who was impeached for corruption in 1788; Burke led the prosecution, but Hastings was acquitted after a trial lasting 145 days. Always an eloquent defender of the oppressed, Burke then supported William Wilberforce from 1788 to 1789 in his campaign against the slave trade.

In opposition to the principles behind the French Revolution of 1789, Burke published his most famous treatise, REFLECTIONS ON THE REVOLUTION IN FRANCE (1790), a forceful attack on the drastic action of the revolutionaries. He argued against the charge that his attitudes towards the French and the American Revolutions were inconsistent, publishing in 1791 *A Letter... to a Member of the National Assembly* and an *Appeal from the New to the Old Whigs*, further discussion of French revolutionary politics appearing in his *Thoughts on French Affairs* (1791), *Remarks on the Policy of the Allies* (1793) and *Letters on a Regicide Peace* (1795–7).

Dogged throughout his career by financial difficulties, Burke was even criticized when, on retiring from Parliament in 1794, he was awarded a pension. He defended himself against the Duke of Bedford and the Earl of Lauderdale with characteristic vigour in *A Letter to a Noble Lord*, in 1796. His published speeches and writings were collected in eight volumes between 1792 and 1827. Burke is remembered for the spirited manner in which he consistently defended the cause of civil justice, for his intellectual integrity and for the magnificent power of his rhetoric; he was a master of persuasive prose.

Burke, Kenneth 1897–1986 American critic, short-story writer, novelist and poet. Born in Pittsburgh, Pennsylvania, Burke was educated at Columbia University. He wrote essays, short fiction and poetry before becoming the music critic of the *Dial* magazine and, later, THE NATION. He is best known as a theorist of literary forms, whose studies also encompass history, rhetoric and philosophy. His most famous books, *A Grammar of Motives* (1945) and *A Rhetoric of Motives* (1950), are enquiries into the ways in which all human activity is ordered in language.

Apart from his early fiction and poetry, Burke's first works were *Counter-Statement* (1931), *Permanence and Change* (1935), *Attitudes toward History* (1937) and *The Philosophy of Literary Form* (1941). His fiction and poetry are collected in *The Complete White Oxen* (1968) and *Collected Poems, 1915–1967* (1968). *Towards a Better Life* (1932) is his only novel. His other books include *The Rhetoric of Religion* (1961), *Perspective by Incongruity* (1964), *Terms for Order* (1964) and *Language as Symbolic Action* (1966).

burlesque A kind of mockery found in all the arts, and in life too. In literature, a mocking, but not a bitter or contemptuous, imitation of some literary species or specific work or author. In its widest sense, then, it covers MOCK-HEROIC, travesty, and PARODY. But as the demands of critical precision often require a distinction within this usage, between high-burlesque (otherwise mock-heroic) and low-burlesque (otherwise travesty or burlesque), there seems good reason for following DRYDEN and Boileau, in restricting burlesque to cases where a high theme or subject is travestied by a low style (as in the 'Pyramus and Thisbe' episode in *A MIDSUMMER NIGHT'S DREAM*). Mock-heroic does the reverse, treating a low theme in a high style (as in POPE's *RAPE OF THE LOCK*). Parody, then, is distinguished as the mockery of specific works or authors.

Burnet, Gilbert 1643–1715 Historian and divine. Of an Aberdeenshire family, Burnet was born in Edinburgh, but returned to Aberdeen for his education at Marischal College. He became professor of divinity at Glasgow University in 1669, and came to England in 1675 as chaplain to the Rolls Chapel, a position he held until 1684. Burnet was on familiar terms with Charles II and James, Duke of York, and was a well-known preacher. However, he offended Charles by remonstrating with him about his conduct and was dismissed in 1684. He went abroad in the following year, where he enjoyed the confidence of William of Orange and Mary, and sailed for England in 1688. He was rewarded with the bishopric of Salisbury (1689).

Burnet's chief works are *The History of the Reformation of the Church of England*, published in three parts (1679, 1681 and 1714) and *The History of My Own Times* (published posthumously, 1724-34). His *Reformation* was begun during the years of the 'Popish Plot', when English Catholics endured a reign of terror. *The History of My Own Times* is the work of a good storyteller; his style is conversational, anecdotal, and often prejudiced, but it makes valuable reading. Burnet's contributions to English literature began in history and biography with *The Memoires of the Lives and Actions of James and William Dukes of Hamilton and Castleherald* (1677), constructed from documents and, in the French manner, held together by Burnet's narrative links. The results of his conversations with the dying ROCHESTER appeared in 1680 and his biography of SIR MATTHEW HALE in 1682. His admired translation of MORE's *UTOPIA* was published in 1684. Burnet was a notable moderate and his *Exposition of the Thirty-Nine Articles* (1699) became a standard work in English divinity studies.

Burnet, Thomas ?1635-1715 Theologian. Born at Croft in Yorkshire, he was an undergraduate first at Clare Hall, Cambridge, where TILLOTSON taught him, and then of Christ's College, of which he became a fellow in 1657. He was appointed Master of the Charterhouse in 1685. *Telluris Theoria Sacra*, which he published in Latin in 1681-9 and translated as *The Sacred Theory of the Earth* in 1684-90, argued that the world was smooth and egg-shaped at the Creation but given its present form when waters burst out of its interior during the biblical Flood. Though Burnet intended to reconcile religion and science, his book confirmed the reputation for freethinking which dogged him throughout his career. It remained influential for well over a century, if only because of the sombrely magnificent prose in which Burnet conjured up his vision of mountains and rivers as 'Ruins of a Broken World'. He also wrote three series of *Remarks* (1697, 1697, 1699) in answer to LOCKE's *ESSAY CONCERNING HUMAN UNDERSTANDING*.

Burnett, Frances (Eliza) Hodgson 1849-1924 American novelist and writer of CHILDREN'S LITERATURE. She was born in Manchester and moved to Tennessee in 1865. Although she became popular with her first book, a sentimental novel entitled *That Lass o'Lowrie's* (1877), she is remembered for her children's books: *Little Lord Fauntleroy* (1886), *The Little Princess* (1905) and *The Secret Garden* (1911). In *Little Lord Fauntleroy* the title character is Cedric Erroll, curly-haired and velvet-suited, affectionate and loved by all, who comes to England from New York to win the heart of his estranged grandfather, the Earl of Dorincourt. In *The Secret Garden* the orphaned Mary and her cousin Colin achieve happiness reviving an abandoned garden. Other works include *Editha's Burglar* (1888), *The White People* (1917), a novel about

the supernatural, and *The One I Knew Best of All* (1893), an autobiography. Burnett was also instrumental in establishing the legal precedent which gave American authors control over the English publication of their work.

Burney, Fanny [Frances] 1752-1840 Novelist and woman of letters. Daughter of the musician Dr Charles Burney, she was born in King's Lynn and seems to have largely educated herself. Her father was part of SAMUEL JOHNSON's circle and she assumed a place in it by right. Her first novel, *EVELINA: or, The History of a Young Lady's Entrance into the World* (1778), made her famous and her second, *CECILIA: or, Memoirs of an Heiress* (1782), confirmed her reputation. In 1786 she became Second Keeper of the Robes to Queen Charlotte. Her *Diary* vividly records how uncongenial she found the position; it was only with some difficulty that she obtained permission to retire in 1791.

She married a French refugee officer, General Alexandre Gabriel Jean-Baptiste d'Arblay, in 1793, and in 1796 published her third novel, *CAMILLA: or, A Picture of Youth*. D'Arblay, who had been adjutant general to Lafayette, returned to France with his English wife in 1802 and Fanny Burney lived there for 10 years, returning to England in 1812, where she published her last and least successful novel, *The Wanderer*, in 1814. She spent her time in Bath and, after her husband's death, in London, devoting much of her later career to editing *The Memoirs of Dr Burney* (1832). Of her eight plays only one, *Edwy and Elgiva*, was produced during her lifetime.

Fanny Burney's diaries are not the least of her literary achievements. The *Early Diary 1768-78* (1889) gives firsthand accounts of Johnson and GARRICK, and the *Diary and Letters 1778-1840* (1842-6) includes the years at court. As a novelist, she inherited the form from RICHARDSON and FIELDING and handled it in a way that would prove useful to JANE AUSTEN. Her strength lay in comedy and the comedy of domestic life, developed around innocent heroines like Evelina as they enter a sophisticated social world. 'To read Miss Burney,' wrote WALTER ALLEN, 'is rather like having a mouse's view of the world of cats: the cats are very terrifying, but the mouse's sense of the ridiculous could not be keener.'

Burningham, John (Macintosh) 1926- Writer and illustrator of CHILDREN'S LITERATURE. He was born in Surrey and educated in Suffolk and at London's Central School of Art. His first book, *Borka: The Adventures of a Goose with No Feathers* (1963), announced a distinctive visual style in which bright colours and naive, almost clumsy shapes combine to create a strong sense of the primitive, in welcome contrast to the more refined art often thought suitable for younger readers. Burningham's imagination also comes very close to children's various dreams of wish-fulfilment. In *Mr Gumpy's Outing* (1970), the gentle, rather muddled title character just about manages to satisfy a series of near-impossible requests from a variety of animals. *Come Away from the Water, Shirley* (1977) contrasts the dull world of Shirley's parents with the imaginative excesses going on in their daughter's mind. The element of fantasy expresses itself differently in *Avocado Baby* (1982), where an infant thrives on mashed avocado to the extent of becoming able to perform tasks of Herculean strength. *Oi! Get Off Our Train* (1990) shows strong feelings for threatened species of wild animals.

Burns, Robert 1759–96 Scottish poet. Born the son of a small farmer, William Burnes (the poet was the first to adopt the more familiar spelling), he was brought up in agricultural poverty and strict Calvinism at the village of Alloway in Ayrshire. Educated by his father, Burns started work as a farm labourer but became a flax-dresser at the age of 22. On his father's death in 1784, he went into farming with his brother Gilbert at Mossgiel for four years, a period which saw the composition of some of his first verse, such as 'The Twa Dogs' and the striking cantata *THE JOLLY BEGGARS*. It was a time, too, of apparent promiscuity, and Burns formed an attachment to Jean Armour, who became pregnant.

It was not until 1786 that Burns's poetry began to appear in print; this early, 'Kilmarnock' edition of *Poems Chiefly in the Scottish Dialect* contained many of the varied and entertaining pieces of his Mossgiel period, such as 'The Cotter's Saturday Night' and 'Halloween'. The volume brought him fame, and he went to Edinburgh, where the success of his poems led to a new edition being published by William Creech in 1787. Burns was lionized as an untutored rustic genius (HENRY MACKENZIE hailed him as 'a heaven-taught ploughman'), but he disliked hypocrisy and never trusted in that brief fame. During this time he immortalized himself as a songwriter by contributing some hundreds of songs, new and reworked, to James Johnson's *The Scots Musical Museum* (1787–1803), including 'Auld Lang Syne' and 'A Red, Red Rose'.

Having earned sufficient money to buy a small farm at Ellisland, Burns settled there in 1788 with his erstwhile consort Jean, now his wife (in the intervening years a number of liaisons had given rise to some passionate verse, addressed to Alison Begbie and Mary Campbell). They led a hard life, had four children, and Burns became an excise man to supplement their meagre income. He developed a pronounced sympathy with the French revolutionary movement, which caused him to be regarded with some suspicion. Poverty forced him to abandon the farm in 1791 and move to Dumfries, where he wrote little of importance except for *TAM O'SHANTER*, 'Captain Matthew

Henderson' and the 100 or so lyrics he contributed to George Thomson's *A Select Collection of Original Scottish Airs* (1793–1811). He died at the age of 37, his health undermined by rheumatic fever.

Although his origins were genuinely rustic, and he has become a cult figure as a ploughman poet, Burns was proud of his background and had taught himself to read widely among the English and French poets. In the tradition of ALLAN RAMSAY and ROBERT FERGUSSON, whom he admired, he was also skilful in the Scots vernacular, many of his most celebrated lyrics working from the strong native material of Scottish folklore and daily life. His poems about animals are famous, and often anthropomorphic ('To a Mouse'); he also penned some vigorous satires on religion ('The Ordination' and *HOLY WILLIE'S PRAYER*) and at least one narrative masterpiece, the late *Tam O'Shanter*. His rural poems dating from the late 1780s are consistently the best, with a blend of humour and sadness that have made him accepted as the Scottish national poet.

Burroughs, Edgar Rice 1875–1950 American novelist. Burroughs was educated at a military academy and served briefly in the US cavalry, but failed to find a successful career until he began to write for pulp magazines in 1912, when he published the first of many SCIENCE-FICTION fantasies (reprinted in 1917 as *A Princess of Mars*) and the first of many novels about Tarzan, an English aristocrat raised by apes in the African jungle. He wrote extravagant and exotic adventure stories, which might be considered the ultimate daydreams. The Tarzan novels remain his most enduring success, having some significance as a modern hero-myth despite the injury done to the character by many poor films. Burroughs's work deteriorated after 1925, thereafter consisting mainly of lack-lustre sequels, but his early books have an appealing escapist verve which overrides their essential silliness.

Burroughs, William S(eward) 1914– American novelist. Born in St Louis and educated at Harvard, he has spent much of his life in Paris and Tangier. Before leaving the USA he was friendly with JACK KEROUAC, ALLEN GINSBERG, and the circle of writers later known as the BEATS.

He wrote of his experience of heroin addiction in *Junkie* (under the pseudonym of William Lee; 1953) and *Naked Lunch* (1959). The latter became notorious for its frank treatment of the life of the addict, and was banned on grounds of obscenity. Its bitter rendering not only of the horrors of addiction, but of the far-reaching cultural illusions for which addiction is a metaphor, has made it his most famous book. His subsequent work includes *The Exterminator* (with Brion Gysin; 1960), *The Soft Machine* (1961), *The Ticket That Exploded* (1962), *The Yage Letters* (a collection of letters with Allen Ginsberg; 1963), *Dead Fingers Talk* (1963), *Nova Express* (1964), *The Job* (1970; an interview), *The Wild Boys* (1971), *Exterminator!* (1973), *Port of Saints* (1973), *The Last Words of Dutch Schultz* (1975), *The Third Mind* (1978), *Ah Pook Is Here and Other Texts* (1979), *Blade Runner: A Movie* (1979), *With William Burroughs: A Report from the Bunker* (1981; interviews), *Cities of the Red Night* (1981), *Letters to Allen Ginsberg 1953–1957* (1982), *The Place of Dead Roads* (1983), *Queer* (1984) and *The Western Lands* (1987).

Burton, Sir **Richard (Francis)** 1821–90 Orientalist, traveller, diplomat and eccentric. He was born at Torquay and baptized at Elstree. His childhood was spent wandering France and Italy, where he became a collector of patois. Largely self-educated, he was wayward, original and brilliant. In 1840, he went up to Trinity College, Oxford, but was rusticated for his unconventional behaviour (which included challenging a fellow student who criticized his moustache to a duel). While at Oxford, Burton had started to study Arabic, without a tutor. A remarkable linguist, he is variously estimated to have mastered 35 languages, or 25 with their various dialects. In October 1842 he joined the Bombay Native Infantry as a subaltern, having worked in London at Hindustani. In India he mastered Gujarati and Marathi, as well as Persian. Appointed assistant in the Sind survey, he frequently mixed in disguise with the people, passing as a native. He contributed to government reports and on his return published four books on India. In 1853 he made the pilgrimage to Mecca, disguised as an Indian Pathan and relying on his intimate acquaintance with Eastern customs and etiquette. Although he was not the first Englishman to achieve this feat, Burton became famous as a result. The following year he explored the Somali desert, encountering considerable dangers. The Foreign Office commissioned him to search for the sources of the Nile and in February 1858, along with SPEKE, he discovered Lake Tanganyika. Three years later he explored West Africa. In 1861 he entered the Foreign Office as consul, service which produced numerous further books. His most famous literary works, however, were his translations of *The Kama Sutra* (1883), *The Arabian Nights* (1885–8) and *The Perfumed Garden* (from the French; 1886). For the last 14 years of his life he worked on a translation of *The Perfumed Garden* from the Arabic but his widow, who had suffered from his drunkenness and frequent absences, chose to burn it after his death. As a memorial, she built an Arab tent in stone and marble at Mortlake Crematorium, and set up the 'Burton Memorial Lecture Fund', inaugurated in 1921.

Burton, Robert 1577–1640 Author of THE ANATOMY OF MELANCHOLY (1621). Born at Lindley in Leicestershire, he was educated at Nuneaton and Sutton Coldfield, then at Brasenose College, Oxford. He was elected a student (i.e. a fellow) of Christ Church in 1599 and remained there for the rest of his life, despite becoming vicar of St Thomas's, Oxford, and later rector of Seagrave in his home county. *The Anatomy of Melancholy*, much admired by subsequent writers for its curious and colourful mixture of psychological speculation and allusive learning, was his only book. Little more is known of Burton beyond the occasional facts he let drop in the splendidly digressive course of his *Anatomy* and these brief (and perhaps unreliable) remarks by Bishop Kennett in his *Register and Chronicle* (1728): 'The Author is said to have labour'd long in the Writing of this Book to suppress his own Melancholy, and yet did but improve it... In an interval of Vapours he would be extremely pleasant, and raise Laughter in any Company. Yet I have heard that nothing at last could make him laugh, but going down to the Bridge-foot in *Oxford*, and hearing the Barge-men scold and storm and swear at one another, at which he would set his Hands to his Sides, and laugh most profusely: Yet in his College and Chamber so mute and mopish that he was suspected to be *Felo de se.*'

Bussy D'Ambois A tragedy by GEORGE CHAPMAN, written for performance by a BOYS' COMPANY in 1604 and published in 1607. Its hero (played in the first production by the actor and playwright NATHAN FIELD) has earned comparison with the hero of MARLOWE'S *TAMBURLAINE*. He is based on the historical figure of Louis de Clermont Bussy-d'Amboise, favourite of the Duc d'Alençon, brother of the French king Henri III.

Bussy D'Ambois is introduced to the court as the protégé of Monsieur (Alençon) and proves himself courageous but insolent. In a quarrel he is forced to defend himself against three courtiers, and kills them; he also quarrels with the Duc de Guise. Monsieur is in love with the Countess of Montsurry (Monsorcau) but she favours Bussy D'Ambois. Giving way to jealousy, Monsieur tells Montsurry that his wife has dishonoured him, and the Count tortures his wife into sending a letter of summons to her lover. Bussy d'Ambois is overpowered and murdered on his arrival.

Butler, Joseph 1692–1752 Divine. Born at Wantage in Berkshire, the son of Presbyterian parents, he attended the Dissenting Academy at Tewkesbury. He abandoned Presbyterianism and entered Oriel College, Oxford, in 1714; he was ordained at Salisbury in 1718 and appointed Clerk of the Closet to Queen Caroline in 1736. He became Bishop of Bristol in 1738 and of Durham in 1750.

Butler published *Fifteen Sermons* in 1726. These were delivered while he was preacher at the Rolls Chapel, London (1718–26) and gained him a reputation as an exponent of natural theology and ethics. Butler's most famous work, *The Analogy of Religion, Natural and Revealed, to the Constitution and Course of Nature* (1736), is a defence of Christianity against the 'natural' religion of DEISM.

Butler, Samuel 1612–80 Satirist. Born the son of a farmer at Strensham in Worcestershire, he was educated at King's School, Worcester, and served in the household of Elizabeth, Countess of Kent, where he met JOHN SELDEN. Butler seems subsequently to have served as secretary to various gentlemen, becoming steward to the Earl of Carbery by 1661. His fame rests on the long burlesque poem *HUDIBRAS*, the first part of which appeared in 1663, the second in 1664 and the third in 1678. Charles II liked it and granted him a pension; Butler also became secretary to the DUKE OF BUCKINGHAM in 1670, accompanied him to France, and may have assisted in the composition of his topical satirical play, *THE REHEARSAL*. He is reputed, however, to have died penniless, and is buried in Westminster Abbey.

Butler's other works include numerous prose 'characters', epigrammatic 'thoughts' and various verses, the most accomplished of which is his poem *The Elephant in the Moon*, a satire on Sir Paul Neale (of the Royal Society) that concerns a mouse which gets into a telescope. It was printed, along with much of the writing unpublished during his life, in Robert Thyer's collected edition of 1759, *The Genuine Remains in Verse and Prose of Mr Samuel Butler*.

Butler, Samuel 1835–1902 Novelist, satirical poet, painter, art critic, amateur scientist and philosopher. A clergyman's son, he was born at Langar Rectory, Nottinghamshire, and educated at Shrewsbury where his grandfather, later a bishop, had been headmaster. After attending St John's College, Cambridge, he rejected his father's wish that he take holy orders, alleging doubts as to the efficacy of baptism, and emigrated to New Zealand, where he became a successful sheep-farmer. This period also saw his first publication, *A First Year in Canterbury Settlement* (1863), and the composition of an anonymous pamphlet, *The Evidence for the Resurrection of Jesus Christ as Given by the Four Evangelists Critically Examined* (1865), which was to become the core of *Fair Haven* (1873), a mock defence of miracles, so veiled in its SATIRE that some orthodox readers missed the joke entirely.

Returning home in 1865, Butler could now afford to embark on the painting career his family had so strongly disapproved of. At Heatherley's Art School Butler won for himself the nickname of 'the incarnate bachelor'. Although he struggled to find other emotionally satisfying friendships he remained sharply critical of family ties. For seven years he continued to paint, exhibiting at the Royal Academy, and

later turned art critic in *Alps and Sanctuaries* (1881) and *Ex Voto* (1888), written during prolonged visits to Italy.

Unsuccessful investments necessitated a journey to Canada in 1874–5, where Butler found the material for the satirical poem 'A Psalm of Montreal' (1878) and started *Life and Habit* (1877), the first of a series of works – which included *Evolution Old and New* (1879), *Unconscious Memory* (1880), *Luck or Cunning* (1886) – to pursue his critical debate with DARWIN's theory of evolution. Butler's contention, later applauded by G. B. SHAW in his preface to *BACK TO METHUSELAH* (1921), was that where variation occurred in the reproductive chain this was not a matter of random chance but a product of the 'Life Force' working through heredity and memory, conscious and unconscious, towards the breeding of the highest form of 'Continuous Personality'.

Butler's eclectic interests and unfocused talent, best displayed in the *Notebooks* (1912), next surfaced in the field of music. In collaboration with his closest friend H. Festing Jones, he composed Handelian pieces and a comic oratorio, *Narcissus* (1888). Two further areas of study produced *The Authoress of the 'Odyssey'* (1897), in which Butler argued that internal evidence proclaimed a female author, and *Shakespeare's Sonnets Reconsidered* (1899), in which he represented the recipient of the sonnets as a plebeian lover.

Butler's habits of obsessively revisiting his past life and reworking his literary material emerge most clearly in *EREWHON REVISITED* (1901), a sequel to *EREWHON* (1872), and his most influential work, the posthumously published, semi-autobiographical novel, *THE WAY OF ALL FLESH* (1903).

Buzo, Alex(ander) (John) 1944– Australian playwright. Of Albanian extraction, he was born in Sydney. His style and wit initially aligned him with DAVID WILLIAMSON but his work has moved through phases of surrealism and romanticism. *The Revolt* (1966) was followed by *Norm and Ahmed* (1968), the object of one of several obscenity test cases which opened the way to greater freedom in the use of Australian vernacular. Subsequent plays are *The Front Room Boys* (1968), *Rooted* (1969), *The Roy Murphy Show* (1971), *Macquarie* (1972), *Tom* (1972), *Batman's Beach-head* (1973), *Coralie Landsdown Says No* (1974), *Martello Towers* (1976), *Makassar Reef* (1978), *Big River* (1980), *The Marginal Farm* (1983), *Stingray* (1987) and *Shellcove Road* (1989). He has also written a novel, *The Search for Harry Allway* (1985), among other work.

Byars, Betsy (Cromer) 1928– American writer of CHILDREN'S LITERATURE. Born in Charlotte, North Carolina, and educated at Queen's College, she began writing as her own family was growing up. Following the success of *The Summer of the Swans* (1970) she established herself as a prolific novelist with a strong line in racy humour and realistic dialogue. Each novel is seen from a child's point of view and takes up some of children's typically urgent concerns, such as fear of bullying, feelings of rejection or worries about parents' marriages. In her most famous novel, *The Summer of the Eighteenth Emergency* (1973), a bright pupil named Benjie deals with the repercussions of making one joke too many at the expense of a slow, thuggish classmate.

Byatt, A(ntonia) S(usan) 1936– Novelist and critic. Like her sister, MARGARET DRABBLE, she was educated in York and at Newnham College, Cambridge. She lectured at the Central School of Art and Design and then became lecturer in English and American literature at University College, London. Her fiction is densely peopled, intricately detailed, unafraid of literary allusion and frequently concerned with the nature of art and our perception of it. *Possession* (1990), which won the BOOKER PRIZE, uses a biographical investigation of an imaginary 19th-century poet to explore the process of literary interpretation. Its predecessors are *Shadow of a Sun* (1964) and *The Game* (1967), and two parts of a projected sequence tracing English life from the mid-1950s to the present day, *The Virgin in the Garden* (1978) and *Still-Life* (1985). *Sugar* (1987), a collection of short stories on the theme of repetition, shows the weight of family history, tradition and literature recurring over several generations. *Angels and Insects* (1992) consists of two novellas on Victorian themes. Byatt has also published a monograph on IRIS MURDOCH (1965), a critical study of WORDSWORTH and COLERIDGE (1970) and *Passions of the Mind* (1991), a collection of essays.

Byng, The Honourable **John,** 5th Viscount Torrington 1742–1813 Travel-writer. The son of the 3rd Viscount, he was orphaned in early childhood and brought up by his uncle, the Admiral Byng who was executed for neglect of duty in 1757. He inherited his title from his older brother only a few weeks before his own death, having lived the unremarkable life of a younger son, first as an officer in the Foot Guards and then (from 1780) as a place-holder with the Inland Revenue at Somerset House. 'His early days were spent in Camps,/ His latter days were pass'd at Stamps', was his own glum summary of his career. What is remarkable about Byng is the written record he left of his 15 tours through England and Wales between 1781 and 1794, unpublished until C. Bruyn Andrews's four-volume edition in 1934. Byng's journals show him to have been a natural writer with an unaffected style that finds room for both sharp local observation and pithy utterance of his own firmly held views about taste, architecture and society, which frequently anticipate WILLIAM COBBETT in both

their nature and the explosive bluntness with which they are expressed.

Byrd, William 1674–1744 American diarist and travel-writer. He lived for long periods in England as well as in Virginia, where he served in various public offices, including, from 1709 to his death, on the Royal Council of Virginia.

Byrd's writings, though not published during his lifetime, provide a vivid picture of his milieu, as well as a satiric commentary on some of his experiences. His journal was discovered in the 20th century, and two portions were published as *The Secret Diary of William Byrd of Westover 1709–1712* (1941) and *Another Secret Diary 1739–1741* (1942). He also wrote important narratives of American travel and exploration. The most famous of these, *The History of the Dividing Line*, is his reworking of a journal he kept while serving on a surveying commission in 1728 to determine the boundary between Virginia and North Carolina. It includes a history of Virginia, satiric digs at North Carolinians, observations on the countryside and Indians, and humorous anecdotes from the surveying expedition. *The Secret History of the Dividing Line*, probably an earlier version, is shorter, and its humour more racy. *A Progress to the Mines in the Year 1732* and *A Journey to the Land of Eden in the Year 1733* are also travel accounts, probably reworked from his journals of the late 1730s.

Byrom, John 1692–1763 Poet. A native of Cheshire, he received his early education at Chester and later went to Merchant Taylors' School. At Cambridge he became a fellow of Trinity College, though he lived chiefly in Manchester. He is remembered best for the hymn 'Christians Awake', and for the EPIGRAM on King and Pretender showing his Jacobite sympathies: 'But who Pretender is, or who is King,/ God bless us all – that's quite another thing.' Byrom studied medicine in Montpellier but never practised. He taught shorthand in Manchester and wrote a quantity of religious verse that is now forgotten, and a pastoral in ANAPAESTS (1714). *The Private Journal and Literary Remains of John Byrom* (first published 1854–7) is an important source of information on WILLIAM LAW, whom he admired.

Byron, George Gordon, 6th Lord 1788–1824 Poet. He was born in London, the son of Catherine Gordon, a Scottish heiress descended from James I of Scotland, and Captain 'Mad Jack' Byron, a profligate who squandered his wife's money as well as his own. Soon after his son's birth Captain Byron fled from his creditors to France, and Catherine took her son to her home in Aberdeenshire, where they lived in straitened circumstances. Byron's father died when he was three, and the boy was educated at home and later at Aberdeen Grammar School. Scottish scenery and Scottish Calvinism both left their mark on his character.

In 1798 Byron's great-uncle William, the 5th Baron Byron, died, leaving the 10-year-old boy the barony and the family home at Newstead Abbey in Nottinghamshire but very little fortune. He went to Harrow in 1801 and his first poems were written while a pupil there. In 1805 Byron proceeded to Trinity College, Cambridge, where he cultivated a reputation for high-spirited and profligate behaviour that belied the real achievements of his undergraduate years. In January 1807 he published a small volume of verse, *Fugitive Pieces*. A friend advised him that some of the contents were too sensual and Byron destroyed most of the printing; only four copies have survived. The revised volume was published the same year; 'miraculously chaste' was how he described his *Poems on Various Occasions* (1807), which contained 12 new pieces. With remarkable speed Byron published *Hours of Idleness* the same March, a collection of lyrics more distinguished than any of his previous work.

In January 1808 a notice of *Hours of Idleness* appeared in THE EDINBURGH REVIEW, savaging his work and scorning his pretensions. On the title-page Byron had mentioned his minority and the reviewer, HENRY BROUGHAM, was at pains to point out that this was no excuse for bad verse. Byron responded by revising and extending *British Bards*, a satirical poem he had written, as *English Bards and Scotch Reviewers* (1809). It attacked SOUTHEY, COLERIDGE, WORDSWORTH and SCOTT, though he was later generous in admitting the hastiness of his judgements.

Soon after the publication of *English Bards* Byron came of age and took his seat in the House of Lords; then he left on a tour of the Mediterranean in June 1809 with his friend from Cambridge, John Cam Hobhouse, whose expenses he paid. His letters from Spain, Portugal and the eastern Mediterranean are remarkably vivid. *Hints from Horace* was published in 1811, and after visiting the tyrant of Ioannina, Ali Pasha, he began work on another poem; at the same time he encouraged Hobhouse, who was writing his *Journey through Albania*.

After returning to England Byron completed the first two CANTOS of the poem begun in Albania. *CHILDE HAROLD'S PILGRIMAGE* (1812) made him not just a celebrity but the most sought-after figure in English society. Between then and the uproar of 1816 he published *The Curse of Minerva* (1812), *The Giaour* and THE BRIDE OF ABYDOS (1813), THE CORSAIR, *Lara* and *Jacqueline* (1814), *Hebrew Melodies* (1815), and *The Siege of Corinth and Parisina* (1816).

In 1815 Byron married Annabella (Anne Isabella) Milbanke. The unimaginative Annabella was scarcely an ideal wife for the poet, nor he an ideal husband, and their marriage lasted little more than a year. After the birth of their daughter in December 1815

she left him and obtained a separation. The English public was seized with 'one of its periodical fits of morality', as MACAULAY put it, and, without knowledge of the facts, supported Lady Byron. He left England on 25 April 1816 and never returned.

After sailing up the Rhine to Switzerland Byron joined MARY SHELLEY and PERCY SHELLEY. The third canto of *Childe Harold* and *The Prisoner of Chillon* were written in 1816. In January 1817 Mary Shelley's stepsister, Claire Clairmont, bore Byron a daughter who was named Allegra. The liaison continued throughout the year, and Byron agreed to be responsible for supporting Claire and Allegra, but he did not pretend any real attachment. When the Shelley household returned to England in 1817, Byron continued to Venice.

To this period belong *The Lament of Tasso* (1817), *MANFRED* (1817), the fourth canto of *Childe Harold* (1818), *Beppo* (1818), *Mazeppa* (1819) and the first cantos of DON JUAN. His connection with Teresa, Countess Guiccioli, whose home was in Ravenna, began in Venice in April 1819 and proved a lasting one. Byron moved to Ravenna in December of the same year. He remained, meanwhile, in close touch with England despite his exile. Letters to and from friends – his publisher JOHN MURRAY, Hobhouse, Scott, THOMAS MOORE and others – were important to him and he was an avid reader of the English literary reviews. Of the friends who visited him in Venice, Moore wrote a vivid account of Byron's domestic life at this time. Teresa inspired *The Prophecy of Dante* (1821), chiefly by interesting him in the cause of Italian nationalism. His tragedies, *MARINO FALIERO* and THE TWO FOSCARI (both 1821), take Venice as their subject. The latter was published with two more dramatic poems or CLOSET DRAMAS, *SARDANAPALUS* and *CAIN*. His reputation had by now spread beyond England and Byron was famous throughout Europe. After reading *Manfred*, Goethe started a correspondence with the younger poet; *Sardanapalus* is dedicated to Goethe and Byron was honoured in the second part of *Faust*, where he appears as Euphorion, the child of Faust and Helen.

Teresa Guiccioli obtained a separation from her husband and moved to the house of her brother Pietro, Count Gamba. She and Byron, now 15 miles from Ravenna, became more closely involved with the Carbonari, a militant nationalist movement of which Count Gamba was a leader. Byron was a ready adherent and supported it with his money and influence. However, the Carbonari foundered and the Gamba property was confiscated; they fled to Pisa and set up house in the Palazzo Lanfranchi in autumn 1821. Byron found Shelley living in the same city and also made the acquaintance of EDWARD TRELAWNY, who later wrote a memoir of both poets.

In 1822 a literary quarrel with Southey, begun by a hostile article the older poet contributed to

Byron in Albanian
costume: a detail
from the portrait
by T. Phillips, 1813

BLACKWOOD'S MAGAZINE in August 1819, reached a head. Byron had replied in *Some Observations* (1820), accusing him of slander and apostasy. The next year Southey published *A VISION OF JUDGEMENT*, and prefaced it with an ill-considered, almost hysterical attack on *Don Juan* and its author as the founder of 'the Satanic school'. Byron's answer was to satirize, with devastating ease, Southey's encomium on the passing of George III in *THE VISION OF JUDGEMENT*, published in LEIGH HUNT's magazine *THE LIBERAL* in 1822. Charges were brought against the publisher for 'calumniating the late King and wounding the feelings of his present Majesty'. The same year brought Byron news of the death of his daughter Allegra, and saw the departure of the Shelleys and Trelawny for Spezia in May. Byron and the Gambas went to Leghorn, and two months later Shelley was drowned in the Bay of Spezia. After moving on to Genoa, Byron resumed work on *Don Juan*, a new part of which was completed in March 1823. The domestic tragedy *Werner*, the

verse tale *The Island* and the satirical poem *The Age of Bronze* were also published in 1823. *The Deformed Transformed*, Byron's unfinished drama, followed in 1824.

The end of the Carbonari and of Italian aspirations to independence from their Austrian overlords in 1821 saw Byron embracing another cause – one perhaps closer to his heart and dating back to his travels in the eastern Mediterranean (1810–11). His interest was apparent in *Childe Harold* and *Don Juan*, and the new cause took on reality in 1821. Greek liberation from centuries of Turkish oppression found a sympathetic response in England and a committee was formed to organize aid. The committee asked Byron, probably the most famous Englishman in Europe, to help; without hesitation he turned all his energies to aiding the Greeks. He armed a brig, the *Hercules*, and set sail from Leghorn with Trelawny and Gamba on 24 July 1823. He reached Cephalonia 10 days later. The factional quarrels which had plagued the Greek rebels dissolved, and some even hinted that he could become king of a free Greece. Byron worked ceaselessly and in January 1824 joined Alexander Mavrocordato (to whom Shelley dedicated his *Hellas*) at Missolonghi on the north shore of the Gulf of Patras. The Greek leader had brought a fleet of ships, and Byron's plan was to attack the Turkish stronghold at Lepanto. But in April he caught a severe chill after being soaked to the skin in an open boat. Rheumatic fever set in and Byron died on 19 April 1824. The Greeks wished to bury him in Athens, but only his heart stayed in Greece. His body was returned to England but was refused burial in Westminster Abbey. He was buried in the family vault in the church of Hucknall Torkard, near Newstead Abbey in Nottinghamshire.

TENNYSON, a boy of 14 when he heard the news of Byron's death, said 'the whole world darkened to me'; on a rock near his home in Somersby he inscribed the words 'Byron is dead'. He spoke for his generation, and indeed for several generations who would labour admiringly or uneasily in the shadow of the legend Byron had left. It was Byron's achievement, as much by his life as his poetry, to organize the new feelings of ROMANTICISM into a stance, a style that the wider public could easily recognize and secretly admire even while publicly condemning it. He bequeathed to posterity the image of the Byronic hero, a Childe Harold or Cain or Manfred, an outcast from his own kind and a wanderer in foreign lands, gloomily absorbed in the memory of his past sins and the injustices done him by society. Like all satisfying legends, it was no less powerful for bearing only a partial resemblance to the man and the poet who inspired it. In personal life, Byron was practical and resilient, fully engaged in the social and political affairs of the world about him. In poetry, he found his characteristic voice not in *Childe Harold* but in mature works like *The Vision of Judgement* and *Don Juan*, where he presents himself as the poised and urbane satirist – heir to the Augustan tradition of DRYDEN and POPE.

Byron, Henry James 1834–84 Playwright. He made a notable contribution to the development of the peculiarly British style of PANTOMIME (Buttons and Widow Twankey are his inventions). Byron's contemporary reputation rested on his prodigiously punning BURLESQUES, written for the Strand and Adelphi Theatres in London between 1857 and 1865. Among the most popular of these were *The Maid and the Magpie* (1858), *Blue Beard from a New Point of Hue* (1860) and *Ali Baba: or, The Thirty-Nine Thieves* (1863). *The Lancashire Lass* (1867) is an unabashed MELODRAMA of the kind he delighted to burlesque and *Our Boys* (1875), an accomplished comedy, broke all records with its four-year run at the Vaudeville Theatre.

Byron, Robert 1905–41 Travel-writer and journalist. Born at Wembley, he was educated at Eton and Merton College, Oxford. He travelled extensively in Greece, India, Tibet, Afghanistan, Persia, Russia, China and Egypt, and his books, largely the result of these travels, are enthusiastic appreciations of the ancient world. They include *The Byzantine Achievement* (1929), *An Essay on India* (1931) and *The Road to Oxiana* (1937). The last, widely considered his best work, pursues the origins of Islamic architecture and culture from Venice to India. He was killed during World War II when his ship was torpedoed.

Cabell, James Branch 1879–1958 American novelist. Born in Richmond, Virginia, Cabell is best known for the creation of a mythical French province Poictesme, whose 'history' from 1234 to 1750 he chronicled in a series of allegorical novels which comment obliquely on American life. He went into great detail about the life, customs and liberal morality of the people of Poictesme, and one novel in the series, *JURGEN* (1919), was suppressed as being immoral. The case stirred public curiosity, and Cabell enjoyed a large popular following in the 1920s. He published his first novel, *The Eagle's Shadow*, in 1904. *The Soul of Melicent*, the first in the Poictesme series, appeared in 1913; the last, *Straws and Prayer-Books*, in 1924. He also wrote poetry and non-fiction throughout his career.

Cable, George Washington 1844–1925 American novelist and short-story writer. Born in New Orleans, Cable served in the Mississippi Cavalry during the Civil War, and then worked as a surveyor, as a reporter and columnist for the New Orleans Picayune (using the pseudonym 'Drop Shot'), and as an accountant and clerk. Though he contributed stories of Louisiana life to *Scribner's Monthly* and *Appleton's Journal* from 1873, he did not take up writing as a career until 1879. He established himself as one of the leading local-colour writers of the 'New South' with 18 volumes of fiction. The best of these are generally thought to be the collection of short stories entitled *OLD CREOLE DAYS* (1879) and the novels *THE GRANDISSIMES* (1880) and *MADAME DELPHINE* (1881). He also wrote a history, *The Creoles of Louisiana* (1884), and *The Silent South* (1885), a treatise advocating reforms for improving the lives of blacks. Because of the offence these books caused to some of his Southern neighbours Cable moved to Northampton, Massachusetts, in 1885. Several novels – *Dr Sevier* (1884), *Bonaventure* (1888), *John March, Southerner* (1894) and *Bylow Hill* (1902) – treat the collision between Northern and Southern manners and morals. From 1885 he made annual reading tours of the USA.

Cadenus and Vanessa A poem by JONATHAN SWIFT, written in 1713. Vanessa was Esther Vanhomrigh and Cadenus (an anagram of *decanus* or dean) was Dean Swift. Vanessa fell in love with Swift but he did not return her passion, though he treated her with respect and honoured her with his esteem. The poem gives an equivocal account of their relationship in mock-classical form. Esther Vanhomrigh preserved the poem and it was published in 1726.

Caedmon *fl.* 670–80 All that is known of Caedmon is what BEDE relates in Book 4 of his *Historia Ecclesiastica*: that he was a herdsman ignorant of poetry and unable to sing until one night he was inspired in a dream. On waking he retained his new talent and was advised by Abbess Hild to become a monk. He joined the abbey at Whitby during her rule (657–80), and wrote more hymns. The nine-line hymn in praise of God the Creator quoted by Bede is his only definite work, FRANCIS JUNIUS's attribution of other poems being no longer accepted. Bede seems to imply that Caedmon was the first to write hymns in Old English, but this has been challenged.

caesura In Greek or Latin prosody, the division of a metrical foot between two words, usually toward the middle of the line. In English, it denotes the natural pause or breathing space occurring almost anywhere in the line, though most often near the middle, as in these lines from SHAKESPEARE's Sonnet 73:

This thou perceiv'st, ‖ which makes thy love
  more strong,
To love that well ‖ which thou must leave ere
  long.

Cahan, Abraham 1860–1951 American novelist and short-story writer. Having emigrated to the USA from Russia, in 1897 Cahan founded the *Jewish Daily Forward*, a pioneering Jewish newspaper in New York. He had just published his first novel, *Yekl: A Tale of the New York Ghetto* (1896), which had won the enthusiastic support of WILLIAM DEAN HOWELLS. Its realistic treatment of the experience of Jewish immigrants became the hallmark of Cahan's work. *The Imported Bridegroom and Other Stories of the New York Ghetto* (1898) further established him as a leader in Jewish American fiction, a position exemplified by his best-known work, *The Rise of David Levinsky* (1917), which portrays a rich but dissatisfied garment manufacturer looking back at his rise from poverty in Russia and in the New York ghetto.

Cain A CLOSET DRAMA by BYRON, published in 1821 to a storm of abuse. It was widely considered blasphemous, partly because of Byron's readiness to deploy Cuvier's arguments on the creation of the earth and partly because he so obviously preferred Cain to Abel. *Cain* follows its hero's rebellion against the post-lapsarian life of toil, his turning to Lucifer to find out more than God will reveal, his journey through the Universe under the guidance of Lucifer, his killing of Abel and the remorse and exile that is the murder's consequence.

Cain, James M(allahan) 1892–1977 American novelist, journalist and screenwriter. Born in Annapolis, Maryland, he worked as a coalminer, teacher and reporter before serving in France as a private in World War I. In 1924 he began to write editorials for the New York *World* under the supervision of WALTER LIPPMANN. After briefly serving as managing editor of *THE NEW YORKER*, he moved to Hollywood in 1931, where he remained for 17 years writing filmscripts as well as articles, syndicated columns and novels, which combine NATURALISM in the tradition of NORRIS and DREISER with features of the hard-boiled school of DETECTIVE FICTION. *The Postman Always Rings Twice* (1934) was adapted for the stage in 1936 and became a movie in 1946. It is the story of Frank Chambers and Cora Papadakis, lovers who murder Cora's wealthy husband for money, making his death look like an accident. Cora then dies in a car crash, and ironically Frank is convicted of murder for her truly accidental death. In *Double Indemnity* (serialized in *Liberty* in 1936, and made into a movie in 1943), an unmarried man and a married woman again plan and execute the husband's 'accidental' death, in this case for the insurance money. Cain's other novels include *Serenade* (1937), *Career in C Major* (1938), *The Embezzler* (1940), *Mildred Pierce* (1941), *Love's Lovely Counterfeit* (1942), *The Butterfly* (1947) and *The Root of His Evil* (1951). *Past All Dishonor* (1946) and *Mignon* (1962) are historical novels set in the period following the Civil War.

Caine, (Sir Thomas Henry) Hall 1853–1931 Novelist. He was born at Runcorn in Cheshire, the son of a Manx blacksmith. He became a trusted friend of DANTE GABRIEL ROSSETTI in the last years of the older man's life, and was with him at his death in 1882. *Recollections of Rossetti* was published the same year. Caine's melodramatic novels, popular in their day but soon forgotten, include *The Shadow of a Crime* (1885), *The Deemster* (1887), *The Bondman* (1890), *The Scapegoat* (1891), *The Manxman* (1894), *The Prodigal Son* (1904) and *The Woman Thou Gavest Me* (1913). *My Story* (1908) gives an account of his early literary career.

Caird, Edward 1835–1908 Scottish philosopher. Born at Greenock, he was educated at Greenock Academy, the Universities of Glasgow and St Andrews, and Balliol College, Oxford, where his tutor was BENJAMIN JOWETT. He became fellow and tutor of Merton College and, in 1866, professor of moral philosophy at Glasgow. He succeeded Jowett as Master of Balliol in 1893. He published *The Philosophy of Kant* (1878), *The Critical Philosophy of Kant* (1899), a monograph on Hegel (1883) and *The Religious and Social Philosophy of Comte* (1885). *The Evolution of Religion* (1893) is based on his Gifford lectures.

Caird, John 1820–98 Scottish theologian. The elder brother of EDWARD CAIRD, he became a minister of the Church of Scotland in 1845, professor of divinity at Glasgow University in 1862 and Principal in 1873. *An Introduction to the Philosophy of Religion* (1880) seeks to demonstrate the rationality of religion.

Caldecott, Randolph 1846–86 Children's illustrator. The son of an accountant, he first worked in a bank before resigning to become an artist. His success in illustrating WASHINGTON IRVING's *Old Christmas* (1876) prompted Edmund Evans, the eminent printer and engraver who had previously engaged WALTER CRANE, to invite him to illustrate a series of picture-books. Caldecott's illustrations for WILLIAM COWPER's *John Gilpin* (1876) and *The House That Jack Built* (1878), combining lively action with infectious good humour, soon made his reputation. Other famous commissions to follow included OLIVER GOLDSMITH's *Elegy on a Mad Dog* (1879), *Sing a Song of Sixpence* (1880), *The Fox Jumps over the Parson's Gate* (1883) and SAMUEL FOOTE's *The Great Panjandrum* (1885). Following this last work Caldecott travelled to America for health reasons, only to die soon afterwards of rheumatic fever. Many of his works are still in print, popular not just because of his nostalgic evocation of former rural life but also because of his ingenious ways of commenting on and generally expanding a text, with one line of verse sometimes made to stretch out over a number of pages. It was entirely fitting that the Caldecott Medal, awarded annually to the artist of the most distinguished American picture-book, should take its name from so brilliant and lively an illustrator.

Caldwell, Erskine 1903–87 American novelist and short-story writer. Born in Georgia, he is best known for his portrayal of the experiences of poor whites and blacks in the rural deep South. *Tobacco Road* (1932), the novel which first brought him to prominence, is about a family of white sharecroppers driven to desperate and degenerate acts by the oppression of a changing economic system. It was successfully dramatized by Jack Kirkland in 1933 and ran for over 3000 consecutive Broadway performances. In the same year Caldwell published his second novel, *God's Little Acre*, which consolidated his reputation. *Journeyman* (1935), *Trouble in July* (1940), *A House in the Uplands* (1946), and *Jenny by Nature* (1961) are among his many other novels with Southern settings. He also wrote numerous short stories; collections include *American Earth* (1930), *Jackpot* (1940) and *The Courting of Susie Brown* (1952). Among his works of non-fiction is the documentary study of Southern sharecroppers, *You Have Seen Their Faces* (1937). *All Out On the Road to Smolensk* (1942) is Caldwell's personal account of his work as a war correspondent in Russia. *Call It Experience* (1951) is his literary autobiography. The essays collected in *Around About America* (1964) and *Afternoons in Mid-America* (1976) tell of his travels throughout the USA.

Caleb Williams, The Adventures of: *or, Things as They Are* A novel by WILLIAM GODWIN, first published in 1794. As the alternative title indicates, Godwin intended the book as a radical critique of an unjust social system, but he went beyond his merely polemical purpose by his effective use of the conventions associated with the GOTHIC NOVEL.

The story is told by Caleb Williams, the self-educated son of humble parents who has risen to become secretary to the polished and accomplished local squire, Falkland. Out of admiration for his master, and concern for the man's recurrent fits of melancholy, he begins to enquire into Falkland's past. He learns of the violent behaviour of a neighbouring squire, Tyrrel, who humiliated Falkland publicly and was later found murdered. Hawkins and his son, tenants whom Tyrrel had ruined, were tried and hanged for the crime. But Caleb discovers that Falkland is the murderer. Falkland becomes aware of Caleb's knowledge, falsely accuses him of theft and uses his influence to have him imprisoned. Caleb escapes and goes into hiding. Hunted from place to place, he at last confronts Falkland and accuses him of his crimes. Though he has no proof the strength of Caleb's manner makes Falkland confess. He collapses and dies, leaving Caleb to feel not triumphant but guilty at what he has done to his master.

Calendar of Modern Letters, The A monthly literary journal published from 1925 to 1927. The *Calendar* was edited by EDGELL RICKWORD, Douglas Garman and Bertram Higgins, and published poems, fiction and essays by E. M. FORSTER, ROBERT GRAVES, D. H. LAWRENCE, WYNDHAM LEWIS and EDWIN MUIR. It questioned the reputations of several established writers – J. M. BARRIE, JOHN GALSWORTHY and RUDYARD KIPLING, among others – in its celebrated 'Scrutinies' (some of them published after the *Calendar*'s closure in *Scrutinies by Various Writers*, 2 vols., 1928 and 1931) and inspired the founders of *SCRUTINY*, including F. R. LEAVIS, who edited *Towards Standards of Criticism: Selections from the Calendar of Modern Letters* (1933).

Caliban upon Setebos: *or, Natural Theology in the Island* A DRAMATIC MONOLOGUE by ROBERT BROWNING, published in *Dramatis Personae* (1864). Browning borrowed the character of Caliban from SHAKESPEARE'S *THE TEMPEST*. His 'natural theology' – primitive speculation about the character of his god, Setebos – allows the poet to glance obliquely at several strands of religious thought: stern Calvinism, the HIGHER CRITICISM and the contemporary debate about evolution.

Calisher, Hortense 1911– American novelist and short-story writer. She was born in New York and graduated from Barnard College in 1932. Her work is wide-ranging in subject and includes notable studies of family relationships and racial conflict. She began her career with short stories; her early collections include *In the Absence of Angels: Stories* (1952), *Tale for the Mirror: A Novella and Other Stories* (1963) and *Extreme Magic: A Novella and Other Stories* (1964). Her first novel, *False Entry* (1962) was followed by *Textures of Life* (1963), *Journal from Ellipsia* (1965), *The Railway Police and The Last Trolley Ride* (1966), *The New Yorkers* (1969) and *Queenie* (1971). Subsequent work includes *Herself* (1972), *Standard Dreaming* (1972), *Eagle Eye* (1973), *The Collected Stories of Hortense Calisher* (1975), *On Keeping Women* (1977), *Mysteries of Motion* (1983), *Saratoga Hot* (1985), *The Bobby-Soxer* (1986) and *Age* (1987). *Kissing Cousins* (1988) is a memoir.

Calisto and Melibea: *A New Comedy in English in Manner of an Interlude* A comedy (or INTERLUDE) printed by John Rastell, who may also have been its author, in 1530. It is adapted from *Celestina* by Fernando de Rojas, a Spanish novel written entirely in dialogue and obviously suitable for dramatization, which was translated again by JAMES MABBE in 1631.

Calisto is a high-born young man who loves Melibea from the moment of first meeting her. She is deterred by the violence of his passion, and Calisto enlists the aid of Celestina, a bawd, to bring Melibea to his arms. Melibea is soon as violently in love as Calisto, and Celestina is rewarded, only to be murdered by Calisto's servants, who steal the reward and are executed for their crime. Meanwhile Calisto and Melibea continue with their guilty love until Calisto, keeping a tryst in a tower, falls off a ladder and is killed. The broken-hearted Melibea leaps to her death. The play version is softened by the introduction of a moralizing ending, in which Melibea is persuaded by her father Danio to step no further into vice. He brings her to a timely repentance by telling her the details of a vision, in which the horrors of her avoidable damnation have been revealed to him.

Call of the Wild, The A novel by JACK LONDON, published in 1903. Buck, the 'hero', is a dog who is kidnapped from his comfortable existence on a California estate, and sold into service as a sledge dog in the Klondike. He proves himself among the other dogs, but is brutally mistreated by a series of cruel masters before being rescued by John Thornton, a gold prospector who treats him with kindness. Fiercely loyal to Thornton, Buck performs several heroic exploits for him, most notably saving him from drowning and winning a wager by drawing a 1000-lb sledge. Later, he fends off an Indian attack during which Thornton is nevertheless killed.

Masterless, but now at home in the Alaskan wilds, Buck abandons human civilization to become the leader of a wolf pack.

Callaghan, Morley (Edward) 1903–90 Canadian novelist and short-story writer. Born in Toronto and educated at St Michael's College, University of Toronto, he studied law, but began to write seriously in 1923. As a reporter on the Toronto *Star* he met ERNEST HEMINGWAY, who influenced his early work and encouraged him to publish his first novel, *Strange Fugitive* (1928). Other titles include *They Shall Inherit the Earth* (1935), *More Joy in Heaven* (1937), *The Loved and the Lost* (1951), *The Many-Coloured Coat* (1960), *Close to the Sun Again* (1975) and *A Wild Old Man on the Road* (1988). His distinctively spare prose is displayed to greatest advantage in the collections of short stories, *A Native Argosy* (1929), *No Man's Meat* (1931), *Now That April's Here* (1936) and *Morley Callaghan's Stories* (1959).

Calverley, Charles Stuart 1831–84 Poet and parodist. Born at Martley, Worcestershire, he went to school at Marlborough and Harrow. Calverley's practical jokes resulted in his being sent down from Balliol College, Oxford, and he finished his education at Christ's College, Cambridge, where he later became a fellow. He was called to the Bar in 1865 but a severe accident, sustained while skating, disabled him for the rest of his life. He made a reputation as a translator from Greek and Latin, publishing, among other volumes, *Theocritus Translated into English Verse* (1869). But he was best known for the parodies of poets such as TENNYSON, ROBERT BROWNING and JEAN INGELOW which appeared in *Fly Leaves* (1872).

Cambises, King of Persia The long title page of the 1569 edition of this play by THOMAS PRESTON describes it as a 'lamentable tragedy mixed full of mirth'. It also contains a table showing how eight actors can play all the 38 parts. For the main plot, Preston has drawn on the racy account of Cambises' reign in Book Three of Herodotus' *Histories*. The Cambises of Herodotus is as erratic as he is vengeful, drawn Tamburlaine-like to conquest, sinking into madness and dying exactly as had been predicted by a deceitful oracle. But Preston has added to the characters of his Persian chronicle play abstract figures – Murder, Cruelty, Commons Cry – familiar from MORALITY PLAYS, a vice called Ambidexter and the vice's companions in fooling, Huf, Ruf and Snuff. *Cambises* was sufficiently familiar to Elizabethan audiences to draw from Falstaff the warning that 'I must speak in passion, and I will do it in king Cambyses' vein.' The reference is less to the story than to the already stilted and archaic verse form in which Preston wrote it: rhyming couplets composed of seven iambic feet per line, familiarly known as 'fourteeners' (see METRE).

Cambridge Platonists A group of 17th-century Anglican divines at the University of Cambridge, notably HENRY MORE, RALPH CUDWORTH, JOHN NORRIS and John Smith, who evolved a philosophical approach marking a path between High Anglicanism and Puritanism. The chief contemporary influence was the philosophy of Descartes, though they could not accept his materialistic view of the inanimate world. The Cambridge Platonists advocated tolerance and insisted on the need for comprehension, seeing reason as the arbiter of both natural and revealed religion. Morality itself is based on reason, and reason and religion are essentially in harmony.

Camden, William 1551–1623 Historian and antiquary, justly praised by SPENSER as 'the nurse of antiquity/ And lantern unto late succeeding age'. Camden attended both Christ's Hospital and St Paul's School and, at Oxford, both Magdalen College and Christ Church. He was second master at Westminster School in 1575 and headmaster in 1593.

Camden travelled the country noting its antiquities, and acquired a knowledge of both Welsh and Anglo-Saxon so that he might read ancient accounts of Britain. The two major results of his erudite and persistent researches were his Latin works, *BRITANNIA* and *Annales*. *Britannia*, a description of England, Scotland and Ireland, first appeared in 1586 and was translated into English under Camden's supervision in 1610. The *Annales* describe and eulogize the reign of Elizabeth I. The first part was printed in 1615, the second at Leyden in 1625 and at London in 1627; the two parts were translated into English in 1625 and 1629 respectively, and the whole work appeared in English in 1635. Camden's minor works include editions of chronicles and other histories, an account of the trial of the conspirators in the Gunpowder Plot, a list of epitaphs in Westminster Abbey, a poem on the marriage of the Thames and the Isis, and his *Remains* (1605), which he described as the 'rubble' of a greater work. In 1621 he endowed a chair of history at Oxford. He is buried in Westminster Abbey.

Camilla: or, A Picture of Youth FANNY BURNEY's third novel, published in 1796. The tale involves a large cast of diverse characters, but concentrates upon the fortunes of Camilla Tyrold, daughter of the respectable but modestly placed rector of Etherington in Hampshire, her sisters Eugenia and Lavinia, her brother Lionel, cousins Indiana and Clermont Lynmere, and her eligible suitor Edgar Mandlebert. With an eye upon the potential market for her novel, Burney calculatedly introduced tender sentiment, dramatic incident and Gothic colour into this work. Nevertheless, as the preface makes clear, the primary interest and skill of the story lie in its delicate and perceptive rendering of 'the human heart in its feelings and changes'.

Campaspe A prose comedy by JOHN LYLY, first performed under the title *Alexander and Campaspe* by a BOYS' COMPANY in *c.* 1584. It was probably Lyly's first play, an elegant dramatization of the story told in Pliny's *Natural History*.

Attracted by his Theban prisoner Campaspe, Alexander the Great commissions Apelles to paint her portrait. Apelles and Campaspe fall in love and Apelles spoils the completed portrait so that Campaspe will have to go on sitting for him. Having tricked Apelles into revealing what he has done, Alexander releases Campaspe to him and returns to war on the famous grounds that 'It were a shame Alexander should desire to command the world, if he cannot command himself.'

Campbell, Alistair 1925– New Zealand poet and novelist. Born in Rarotonga in the Cook Islands, he moved to New Zealand in 1933 and was educated in Dunedin and at the Victoria University of Wellington. He worked as an editor for the Schools Publication Branch of the Department of Education in Wellington from 1955 to 1972 and as a senior editor for the New Zealand Council for Educational Research from 1972. His first marriage was to FLEUR ADCOCK. Originally seen as a member of the 'Wellington group' of poets and associated with LOUIS JOHNSON in the 1950s, he went on to carve out a more distinctive reputation for himself, without being a prolific writer. One of New Zealand's finest writers of lyric verse, he has been deeply influenced by Maori oral culture, as can be seen in his sequence *Sanctuary of Spirits* (1963), which deals with the history of the Maori chief Te Raupahara. A latter-day Romantic, Campbell has demonstrated a strong empathy for nature since the publication of his first volume of poetry, *Mine Eyes Dazzle* (1950). Later volumes include *Wild Honey* (1964), *Kapiti* (1972), *Dreams, Yellow Lions* (1975) and *Collected Poems* (1982). *The Dark Lord of Savaika* (1980) and *Soul Traps* (1985) return to the legends of his native Rarotonga for inspiration. *Island to Island* (1984) is an autobiography of his early years. *The Frigate Bird* (1989) is the first novel in a projected trilogy. He has also written plays, television documentaries and CHILDREN'S LITERATURE.

Campbell, David 1915–79 Australian poet. Of pioneer stock, he was born and raised on an isolated sheep-farm near Adelong, New South Wales. He was educated at the King's School, Sydney, and Cambridge University, where his interest in poetry first developed. He was a distinguished athlete who played rugby for England. During World War II he was a pilot in the Royal Australian Air Force and was awarded the DFC and bar. In later life he farmed property near Canberra. Campbell's poetry draws heavily on his formative years. His early verse is mainly nature poetry conveying a strong sense of equipoise

and serenity. It attempts to bring together the Elizabethan tradition and the Australian ballad tradition of A. B. PATERSON. The treatment of the bush is notable for its incorporation of Aboriginal elements. Campbell's distinctive poetic manner changed in the 1960s, becoming more involved with contemporary social issues. Volumes include *Speak with the Sun* (1949), *The Miracle of Mullion Hill* (1956), *The Branch of Dodonna* (1970), *Selected Poems* (1973) and *Devil's Rock* (1974). He also translated several volumes of Russian poetry with ROSEMARY DOBSON.

Campbell, (Ignatius) Roy (Dunnachie) 1902–57 South African poet. Born in Durban, he studied privately in Oxford, travelled in France and married in 1921. During two penurious years he wrote *The Flaming Terrapin* (1924), a 1400-line rhymed poem about a mythic terrapin which draws Noah's Ark into a revitalized world, symbolizing the released energy of created nature, writ large in images of volcanic flames, lightning and electric current. Back in Durban in 1924–7, he briefly collaborated with WILLIAM PLOMER on a radical magazine, *Voorslag* ('Whiplash'), and wrote pungent verse about South African provincialism, collected as *The Wayzgoose* (1928). Literary London never forgave him *The Georgiad* (1931), which flays Georgian literature as emasculated, its practitioners as treacherous. *Adamastor* (1931) had revealed Campbell's muse under greater control, capable of savouring calmer experience and defter satire, of expressing a pained sense of exile from sub-tropical climes, yet recognizing 'spirits of power and beauty and delight' in southern Europe. This affinity leads to more contemplative poetry and tauter versification in *Flowering Reeds* (1933) and *Mithraic Emblems* (1936). Although he cuts an uneasy figure as a Franco-apologist in *Flowering Rifle* (1939), he served the anti-Fascist cause in 1939–45. *Talking Bronco* (1946) includes war themes and, in 'Luis de Camões', some of his best poetry. He handsomely repays his debts to Spanish and French literature in translations of *Poems of St John of the Cross* (1951) and Baudelaire's *Les Fleurs du mal* (1952). The swaggering autobiography, *Light on a Dark Horse* (1951), has contributed to Campbell's undervaluation as a poet.

Campbell, Thomas 1777–1814 Poet. Born in Glasgow and educated at Glasgow University, he wrote a number of poems written before he was 30, some of which have remained popular. His first success was *The Pleasures of Hope* (1799), which has ensured his inclusion in dictionaries of quotations ('Tis distance lends enchantment to the view'). He was skilful and might have achieved more had his inclination to poetry been stronger. He is remembered best for such poems as 'The Battle of Hohenlinden', 'Lord Ullin's Daughter', and 'Ye Mariners of England'.

Campbell, Wilfred 1858–1918 Canadian poet. The son of an Anglican clergyman, Campbell was born in Berlin, Canada West (now Kitchener, Ontario). He attended the University of Toronto and the Episcopal Theological School in Cambridge, Massachusetts, and was ordained in 1886. After five years working in various parishes in the United States and Canada, he left the ministry and became a civil servant in Ontario for the remainder of his life. Campbell was influenced by the HIGHER CRITICISM of the Bible and his poetry reflects the religious doubt of the late Victorian period. His style is often rough and uneven, but he justified such a mode on the grounds that it made for a more spontaneous expression of human emotions than was possible in formally correct poetry. LONGFELLOW and the English Romantic poets were significant influences on his work, and during his time in New England he became familiar with TRANSCENDENTALISM. His volumes of poetry include *Snowflakes and Sunbeams* (1888), *Lake Lyrics and Other Poems* (1889) and *The Dread Voice* (1893), painting a very unromantic picture of a nonpantheistic Canadian Nature which represents a marked shift from the view taken in his earlier verse. In his later years Campbell became a staunch advocate of imperialist values, a stance which can be seen particularly in his last volume of verse, *Sagas of Vaster Britain: Poems of the Race, the Empire and the Divinity of Man* (1914). He also wrote in many other genres, including verse drama, the novel and the travel book. Campbell wrote the Eastern Canada volume of *The Scotsman in Canada* (1911) and edited *The Oxford Book of Canadian Verse* (1913).

Campion, Thomas 1567–1620 Poet and musician. Campion was educated at Cambridge in 1581–4 but left apparently without taking a degree. In 1586 he was admitted to Gray's Inn to study law, participated in its revels of 1588 and contributed some songs to the *Gesta Grayorum* revels of 1594. He studied medicine in France and was practising as a doctor in London in 1606. He became innocently implicated in the scandal surrounding the murder of Sir Thomas Overbury, but was cleared of suspicion in 1615.

His lute songs, which make him a worthy rival to John Dowland, were published as *A Book of Airs* (1601), in collaboration with Philip Rossiter, *Two Books of Airs* (?1613) and *The Third and Fourth Books of Airs* (?1617). These books contain great variety: BALLADS, courtly airs, English versions of Horace, Virgil and Catullus, and spiritual and moral songs. Among the justly famous airs are 'Follow Your Saint', 'Break Now My Heart and Die' and 'There is a Garden in Her Face'.

Poemata (1595) was a collection of Latin poems, mainly ELEGIES and EPIGRAMS. *Observations in the Art of English Poesy* (1602) was answered by SAMUEL DANIEL. In it Campion argued against rhyme and was fighting the cause, already lost, for the application of classical quantitative metres and forms to English verse. Campion also wrote MASQUES: *The Lord Hay's Masque*, performed at court in 1607; *The Lords' Masque* for the wedding of Princess Elizabeth (1613); and *The Somerset Masque* for the marriage of the Earl of Somerset to the Countess of Essex (1613).

Can You Forgive Her? A novel by ANTHONY TROLLOPE, the first of his PALLISER NOVELS, serialized in monthly parts from January 1864 to August 1865.

The novel deals with three related love-triangles, in each of which a woman hesitates between a 'wild' and a 'worthy' lover. In the main plot, Alice Vavasor breaks off her engagement to an honourable country gentleman, John Grey, and is pursued by her reckless cousin George, to whom she was once engaged, and who now seeks her fortune to pay off his debts and enter Parliament. She is attracted to the political life and offers to lend him money, agreeing to marry him after the lapse of a year, but he is disinherited by his grandfather, wins and then loses an expensively contested seat, and escapes to America a ruined man. Grey, who survives George Vavasor's attempts to shoot him, proposes again to Alice and is accepted. The second plot concerns Alice's cousin and friend, Lady Glencora, who has made a prudent marriage with Plantagenet Palliser, a rising Liberal politician, despite her continuing attraction to the charming wastrel Burgo Fitzgerald. She is about to elope with him at Lady Monk's ball when her husband, warned of the danger, arrives to take her home. Realizing that his devotion to politics has made married life dull for her, Palliser refuses the coveted post of Chancellor of the Exchequer to take Lady Glencora on an extended European holiday. The novel ends with the birth of their son, Lord Silverbridge, thus ensuring a succession to the Omnium title, and with Mr Grey's election to the Palliser pocket borough of Silverbridge, thereby satisfying Alice's political interests. A third, comic plot reverses the pattern of the other two, when Alice's aunt, a wealthy widow, chooses a dashing suitor in preference to a solid one.

The novel, which reworks material from Trollope's blank-verse comedy *The Noble Jilt*, shows his subtle understanding of the discontents engendered by conventional Victorian courtship and marriage.

Canning, George 1770–1827 Tory politician and writer. He was educated at Eton and Christ Church, Oxford. Entering Parliament in 1793, he served as Foreign Secretary from 1822 until 1827 and as Prime Minister for a brief and troubled spell in 1827. He founded *THE ANTI-JACOBIN*, where some of his wittiest verse appeared, and contributed regularly to *THE QUARTERLY REVIEW*. His *Collected Poems* appeared in 1823.

Canon's Yeoman's Tale, The See CANTERBURY TALES, THE.

Canterbury Tales, The GEOFFREY CHAUCER's most famous work is an unfinished collection of tales told in the course of a pilgrimage to Becket's shrine at Canterbury. A General Prologue briefly describes the 30 pilgrims and introduces the framework: each pilgrim is to tell two tales on the way to Canterbury and two more on the way back, the teller of the best tale winning a free supper. There follow 24 tales, including two told by Chaucer himself. They are of various types – including VERSE ROMANCE, FABLIAU, EXEMPLUM, FABLE, HOMILY, SAINT'S LIFE – and from widely differing sources, though usually written in verse with rhyming couplets the favourite form. The use of a single framework to link a series of stories in this way was not uncommon in medieval literature and there is no reason to suppose Chaucer had a specific model for it. His work is remarkable, however, for its integration of framework and tales; the characters established in the General Prologue are developed through linking passages and through the tales they tell, making the collection a sustained piece of social drama.

The structure of *The Canterbury Tales* probably began to emerge *c.* 1387, but the individual stories cannot be dated. The final order Chaucer intended for them has not been definitely established; they are usually given in the order in which they appear in the Ellesmere manuscript. Similarly, some tales were apparently intended for narrators other than the ones who tell them in the text we have.

The General Prologue gives an account of the pilgrims as they meet at the Tabard in Southwark and begin their journey under the guidance of the Host, Harry Bailly. They come from all sections of society. Some are described in vivid and realistic detail, combining elements from the traditional representation of social types with individual characterization.

The Knight's Tale is a romance based on Boccaccio's *Teseida*. Not originally intended for the collection, it was adapted to suit the character of the Knight. It tells how sworn brothers, Palamon and Arcite, become rivals for the love of Emelye, the niece of Theseus, whom they first see from their prison window. Out of prison, they are discovered fighting by Theseus, who arranges a tournament to decide their quarrel. Arcite prays to Mars for victory, while Palamon prays to Venus for Emelye. Both requests are granted, as Arcite falls from his horse and dies after his victory and Palamon is later married to Emelye.

The Miller's Tale is a bawdy fabliau told by a drunken and quarrelsome character. Like *The Reeve's Tale* which follows, it has several analogues but no known individual source. It describes the cuckolding of an Oxford carpenter by a clerk, Nicholas. Nicholas tricks him into believing that Noah's flood is about to recur, and the carpenter sleeps in a tub suspended under the rafters, leaving Alisoun, his wife, free to sleep with Nicholas. The amorous Absolon also tries to win her love, and Alisoun and Nicholas humiliate him. When Absolon stands under the window craving a kiss, Alisoun thrusts out her backside. But when he returns and Nicholas does the same, Absolon brands him with a red-hot iron. The noise of his screaming wakes the carpenter, who cuts the cord suspending him and plunges from the attic.

The Reeve's Tale answers the Miller's abuse of carpenters, for the Reeve is himself a carpenter. It tells how a miller is tricked by two clerks whom he has cheated of some of their flour. One sleeps with the miller's daughter and the other rearranges the furniture so that the miller's wife gets into his bed instead of her husband's. The first clerk goes to the miller's bed thinking his companion is in it and boasts of his conquest. The furious miller finds his wife with the other clerk and she accidentally beats him. The clerks further beat him and escape with their retrieved flour, baked into a cake.

The Cook's Tale is a fragment of 57 lines, opening with an account of an apprentice who loses his position because of his riotous living and moves in with a prostitute and her husband.

The Man of Law's Tale begins the second fragment of *The Canterbury Tales*. After a prologue in which he complains that Chaucer has spoiled all the good stories and announces that he will speak in prose, the Man of Law tells the tale of the unfortunate Constance. She is married to a sultan, converted to Christianity, whose evil mother destroys all the Christians in the court and sets the widowed Constance adrift in a boat. She lands in Northumberland, where she miraculously cures a blind man and converts her heathen host. A knight in love with Constance, but spurned by her, murders her host's wife and puts the blame on Constance. A mysterious voice condemns him when he swears falsely to her guilt. He is killed, and Constance marries the king and bears a child while the king is away. The king's evil mother interferes with his messages, so that Constance and her child are set adrift again. The king returns and kills his mother. Constance and her son finally come to Rome, where they live with a senator and his wife. They are eventually reunited with Constance's husband and father when these two come to Rome in later years. The story is also told by JOHN GOWER in *CONFESSIO AMANTIS* and is the basis of *EMARE*, but Chaucer's immediate source was the Anglo-Norman CHRONICLE by Nicholas Trivet.

The Wife of Bath's Tale, the first tale of the third fragment, is preceded by a prologue in which the Wife's character – domineering, licentious and pleasure-seeking – is fully developed as she gives an account of her eventful life with five husbands. Her tale continues the theme of women's mastery over men.

As a punishment for rape the hero has to discover, within a year, what women most desire. Eventually he promises to grant a wish to an old hag in return for the right answer. When he has given the answer in court, 'maistrie' or sovereignty, she demands that he marry her. As they lie in bed together she asks him if he would prefer her ugly and faithful or beautiful and faithless; he allows her the choice and is rewarded by having her beautiful and faithful all the time. The story is a version of THE WEDDING OF SIR GAWEN AND DAME RAGNELL.

The Friar's Tale, an animated and original version of a fabliau from an unknown source, is an attack on the Summoner. A corrupt summoner enters into fellowship with a fiend disguised as a bailiff and agrees to work with him even after learning his true identity. They see a carter cursing his horses but the fiend refuses to take them because the curse is not sincere. The summoner tries to cheat an old woman and when she sincerely wishes him damned the fiend carries him off to hell.

The Summoner's Tale answers the Friar with another fabliau from an unknown source about a corrupt mendicant friar. The friar asks a dissatisfied benefactor for more donations and angers him. After preaching against anger he promises to divide whatever he is given among all 12 members of his chapter, and the man tricks him into accepting a fart. A squire, Jankin, wins a new coat by explaining how it may be divided – by seating 12 friars around a cartwheel, each with his nose at the end of a spoke, and letting off the fart from the centre.

The Clerk's Tale begins the fourth fragment and gives a version of the folk-tale of Patient Griselda, derived from Petrarch's Latin translation of Boccaccio's version of it in the Decameron. Griselda's husband subjects her to various cruelties, including the feigned murder of her children and his intended divorce and remarriage, in order to test her love and patience. Griselda bears his cruelty to the end, when her children are finally restored to her and her husband again accepts her as his wife. The character of Griselda is stylized to the point of implausibility, a fault recognized in the six stanzas called Lenvoy de Chaucer which follow the tale and plead that wives show more independent spirit in the face of stupid, cruel or stubborn husbands.

The Merchant's Tale also has its source in folk-tale, though it is richly elaborated and expanded. The ancient January marries the young May but is cuckolded by Damyan. He is struck blind and becomes jealous but does not discover Damyan's affair with May until they are in the garden one day and May asks him to help her up into a pear tree to pick pears. Damyan waits in the tree and they make love, at which point January's sight is miraculously restored by Pluto. Proserpina gives May the ability to convince January that she was only struggling with Damyan and had been told that to do so would restore January's sight.

The Squire's Tale begins the fifth fragment. It is an unfinished verse romance of no known source, though there are similarities with the story of Cleomades. The King of Arabia and India sends to King Cambyuskan a magic horse, sword, mirror and ring. The brass horse can carry a man anywhere he wishes to go at incredible speed, the sword can cut through all armour and heal wounds, the mirror reveals future misfortunes and the ring gives its wearer the power to understand the speech of birds. The King's daughter wears the ring and hears a falcon complaining of her betrayal by a fickle and dissimulating lover. She takes the bird to court and nurses its self-inflicted wounds. The tale breaks off at this point.

The Franklin's Tale is introduced as a BRETON LAY but its source is in Boccaccio's Filocolo. It tells the story of Dorigen, wooed by a clerk, Aurelius, in her husband's absence. She refuses the clerk but promises him her love if he can remove all the rocks from the coast of Brittany, so making her husband's return safe. Secure in her belief that the preposterous condition cannot be met, she is horrified when, by enlisting a magician's help, Aurelius makes the rocks disappear. On Arveragus' return he tells his distraught wife she must keep her promise; Aurelius, touched by her love and fidelity to her husband, releases her from her obligation. The tale ends with an appeal to the audience to say which character is most 'fre'.

The Physician's Tale is the first in the sixth fragment. It gives a version of the story of Virginia adapted from Le Roman de la rose. The corrupt judge Apius falls in love with the chaste Virginia and invents a charge of abduction to force her father to give the girl to the judge's servant Claudius. However, her father kills Virginia to protect her honour and sends the head to Apius. The corruption uncovered, Apius is imprisoned and kills himself and Claudius is exiled.

The Pardoner's Tale is preceded by a prologue in which he explains how he preaches against all types of sin but himself indulges in various vices and begs from the poor. His tale takes the form of an exemplum inserted in a rhetorically flamboyant sermon. It tells how three drunken men set out to find and destroy Death after one of their friends has died of the plague. An old man directs them to an oak tree, where they find a hoard of gold and kill each other through trickery and treachery born of their greed. The Pardoner ends his sermon by displaying his false relics and appealing to the other pilgrims to buy them.

The Shipman's Tale, which begins the seventh fragment, is a fabliau. A merchant's wife borrows 100 francs from a monk, who in turn borrows it from her husband. In the merchant's absence his wife and the monk sleep together. On his return the monk tells him he gave the money to his wife; she tells her husband that she thought it a gift and spent it on clothes.

The Prioress's Tale follows a polite request by the Host to her to tell the next story. It begins with an invocation to the Virgin and tells how, when a Christian child is killed by Jews, the Virgin grants the body the power of song, so that it can be discovered and the murderers exposed.

Sir Thopas is the first of Chaucer's tales. A pastiche of verse romance at its most trite, it tells how Sir Thopas rides in search of an elf-queen and is challenged by a giant. He retreats, promising to return. After a conventional arming scene he leaves court again, but the tale is interrupted by the Host in exasperation.

The Tale of Melibee, Chaucer's second tale, is a prose homily, closely translated from the *Livre de Melibé et de Dame Prudence* ascribed to Renaud de Louens, which is itself based on Albertanius of Brescia's *Liber consolationis et consilii*. It is long and, to the modern reader, unremittingly dull, but receives an enthusiastic response from the Host. When the house of Melibeus is attacked and his daughter injured, his wife Prudence persuades him to abandon thoughts of revenge and be reconciled with his enemies. Her advice is delivered largely in proverbs.

The Monk's Tale follows a prologue in which the Host asks him to tell a story in keeping with his character, perhaps about hunting. Instead the Monk relates a series of tragedies and is interrupted by the Knight because he cannot bear such dismal stories. The sources of the biblical, classical and contemporary figures are Boccaccio's *De casibus virorum et feminarum illustrium*, *De mulieribus claris*, *Le Roman de la rose*, the Bible, Boethius and Dante.

The Nun's Priest's Tale is a vivid fable related to the French *Roman de Renart*. After a premonitory dream which Chauntecleer the cock repeats to his favourite hen, Pertelote, he is approached by a fox who appeals to his vanity to make him close his eyes and crow. The fox seizes him and carries him off, but Chauntecleer tricks him into speaking and so escapes from his mouth. The fable is set against a background of world history and philosophy (notably about the meaning of dreams), and is enlivened with humour.

The Second Nun's Tale is the first of two in the eighth fragment. It is a saint's life, relating the story of St Cecilia from the *Legenda Aurea* (later translated by WILLIAM CAXTON as *THE GOLDEN LEGEND*) and following its source closely. The prologue has an invocation to the Virgin based in part on lines from Dante's *Paradiso*. The tale tells how the virgin Cecilia converted her husband and his brother to Christianity and then some of their persecutors, and was eventually martyred for refusing to honour the pagan gods. After this tale the Canon and his Yeoman join the party, though the Canon soon leaves again.

The Canon's Yeoman's Tale tells of his own experiences helping his master in alchemy. The tale gives details of alchemical processes and relates how the canon cheated a priest, tricking him into believing he could transmute mercury into silver and selling him the method for £40.

The Manciple's Tale is the only one in the ninth fragment. It tells the story of the tell-tale bird found in *THE SEVEN SAGES OF ROME* but adapted by Chaucer from Ovid's *Metamorphoses*. Phebus has a white crow which sings sweetly and talks. Phebus' wife sleeps with a churl in her husband's absence and is betrayed by the crow. Phebus kills his wife. Overcome by anger and remorse, he plucks and curses the bird so that all its descendants are black with a coarse voice.

The Parson's Tale, comprising the tenth fragment, is the final tale. It is a prose sermon of great length on the Seven Deadly Sins, treating them in a manner common in manuals of penance. The sources are the *De poenitentia* of Raymond de Pennaforte and Guilielmus Peraldus' *Summa de vitiis*. The Parson's Tale is followed by *Chaucer's Retraccions*, a much-debated passage in which the poet renounces all his secular works except *THE LEGEND OF GOOD WOMEN* and asks that they may be excused on account of the many moral works he has written. The sincerity and reliability of the *Retracciouns* must be considered in view of contemporary convention and in their relation to Chaucer's projected character in *The Canterbury Tales*, as well as their position immediately after the overtly moral and didactic *Parson's Tale*.

canto A sub-division of a long poem, used by Dante in Italian and in English by, among others, SPENSER in *THE FAERIE QUEENE* and BYRON in *CHILDE HAROLD'S PILGRIMAGE* and *DON JUAN*.

Cantos, The The major work of EZRA POUND, widely regarded as one of the most influential poetic achievements of the 20th century, published in *A Draft of XVI Cantos… for the Beginning of a Poem of Some Length* (1925), *A Draft of Cantos XVII to XXVII* (1928), *A Draft of XXX Cantos* (1933), *Eleven New Cantos, XXXI–XLI* (1934), *The Fifth Decad of Cantos* (1937), *Cantos LII–LXXI* (1940), *The Pisan Cantos* (1948), *Section: Rock-Drill: 85–95 de los Cantares* (1956) and *Thrones: 96–109 de los Cantares* (1959). A collection, *The Cantos of Ezra Pound*, appeared in 1970. A total of 117 thematically and stylistically varied poems, they deal with people and events in ancient, Renaissance and modern history, employ diverse languages, and comment on various political and moral problems. The effect is often that of a series of evocative fragments. At other times, such as in the *Pisan Cantos*, the focus is on one subject: in this case, Pound's incarceration in an Italian prisoner-of-war camp during World War II.

Cantwell, Robert 1908–78 American novelist. Born in Little Falls (now Vader), Washington, Cantwell attended the University of Washington. He then served in the coastguard for two years before going to work in a lumber mill. In 1931 he became literary editor of *New Outlook*, and in 1935 literary editor of *Time*. He also worked on the staffs of *Fortune*, *Newsweek*, and *Sports Illustrated*. He is best known as a proletarian writer. His first novel, *Laugh and Lie Down* (1931), describes life in a lumber mill. His second, *The Land of Plenty* (1934), about factory life, is widely considered one of the finest novels to come out of the left-wing movement in the USA. In addition to a few uncollected short stories, he also wrote biography and criticism.

Canute, The Song of

Canute, The Song of [*Canute Song*] Four lines of Middle English verse said to have been composed by King Cnut as he rowed past Ely and heard the monks sing. It was recorded by a monk of Ely *c.* 1167 although the actual date of its composition is not known.

Capell, Edward

Capell, Edward 1713–81 Shakespearean scholar. He was born at Troston, near Bury St Edmunds in Suffolk, and educated at Bury Grammar School and St Catharine's College, Cambridge. With the passing of Walpole's Licensing Act in 1737 he became Deputy Inspector of Plays, but it was with the age of SHAKESPEARE that his real theatrical interests lay. *Prolusions: or Select Pieces of Ancient Poetry* (1760) reprinted the anonymous EDWARD III and considered the case for Shakespeare's authorship (see also SHAKESPEARE APOCRYPHA). Twenty years' work was brought to a triumphant conclusion with Capell's 10-volume edition of Shakespeare's plays in 1767–8. The preface is important for attempting a contextual study of Shakespeare and challenging 'some good writer' to undertake a biography, a challenge accepted by EDMOND MALONE.

Capell could hardly have expected to survive unscathed in the vicious world of 18th-century Shakespeareans. He prepared an acting edition of ANTONY AND CLEOPATRA with GARRICK in 1758, but their friendship turned sour. STEEVENS and Malone, it was later alleged, used his notes with unwarrantable freedom. Ironically, Capell had produced *Reflections on Originality in Authors* in 1766. He never published his edition of Shakespeare's poems, and a lack of subscribers delayed full publication of his three-volume commentary on the plays until 1783, after his death. He bequeathed the finer parts of his library to Trinity College, Cambridge, and would no doubt have been pleased that a modern society of Cambridge bibliophiles should bear his name.

See also SHAKESPEARE: PERFORMANCE AND CRITICISM.

Capgrave, John

Capgrave, John 1393–1464 Historian and religious writer. Born in King's Lynn, Norfolk, he entered the Augustinian order at an early age and was ordained a priest in 1417 or 1418. He became Provincial of the Augustinian friars in England some time before 1456. His works are largely in Latin and comprise theological, historical, hagiographical writings and biblical commentaries. In English he wrote a verse life of St Catharine, a prose life of St Gilbert of Sempringham and a guide for pilgrims to Rome, but his most important contribution to English literature is his prose *Chronicle of England*. It is written in a plain, clear style and is a valuable historical authority on the reign of Henry IV.

Capote, Truman

Capote, Truman 1924–84 American novelist and short-story writer. Born in New Orleans, Capote moved to New York in 1942. He got a job at THE NEW YORKER and also submitted stories to the magazine, but none was accepted. He did publish elsewhere, however, and his short story 'Miriam' won the O. Henry Award in 1946. This distinction led to a book contract, and in 1948 *Other Voices, Other Rooms*, his first novel, was published. This study of youthful innocence in a decadent world was followed by *A Tree of Night and Other Stories* (1949) and *The Glass Harp* (1951), both set in the South. In 1956 he published *The Muses are Heard*, an account of an officially sponsored tour of Russia by an American company performing *Porgy and Bess*. He turned away from Southern settings with his next novel, *Breakfast at Tiffany's* (1958), a comedy of life in New York City. His next collection of short stories *A Christmas Memory*, was published in 1966. His major publication of that year, however, was *In Cold Blood*, an investigation of the apparently motiveless murder of a Kansas family by two youths. Capote also worked as a journalist and published collections of his pieces in *Local Color* (1950), *Selected Writings* (1963), *The Dogs Bark* (1973) and *Music for Chameleons* (1981). *Answered Prayers*, a final, incomplete novel on which he had made desultory progress for many years, appeared to general disappointment in 1986.

Captain Singleton, The Life, Adventures and Piracies of the Famous

Captain Singleton, The Life, Adventures and Piracies of the Famous A novel by DANIEL DEFOE, published in 1720, it is a narrative of romantic adventure, told in the first person.

Singleton is kidnapped as a child and sent to sea. Off Madagascar he and some of the other sailors mutiny, but their venture fails and they are put ashore. From there he reaches Africa, which he manages to cross, obtaining a fortune in gold on the way. He squanders it recklessly in England and turns to piracy. He sails the high seas as far as China and once more puts together a large fortune. At the end of the novel he is back in England, his adventures over, and married to his shipmate's sister.

Defoe's hero is a man without 'sense of virtue or religion' because of his upbringing. Virtue is represented by his shipmate and friend William Walters, who is nevertheless a character of considerable charm. In the end William is Singleton's saviour, both morally and physically. The adventures, many culled from Defoe's wide reading, are compellingly recounted and include escapes, rescues and bizarre encounters in the heart of Africa.

Cardinal, The A tragedy by JAMES SHIRLEY, first performed in 1641. Often considered Shirley's best tragedy, it has an unremarkable plot and a title part strong enough to fill the play with a brooding evil.

The Cardinal, ambitious for his family, enlists the support of the King of Navarre in arranging the marriage of Columbo (the Cardinal's nephew) to Rosaura. During Columbo's absence, Rosaura persuades the King to permit her to marry Alvarez, whom she loves, but Columbo kills Alvarez on the wedding night. Rosaura takes her revenge by having the disaffected Hernando kill Columbo in a duel and the Cardinal becomes the new avenger. His attempt to rape and kill Rosaura is prevented by Hernando, but he succeeds in poisoning her by a trick. Hernando kills the Cardinal before taking his own life.

Caretaker, The A play by HAROLD PINTER, first performed at the Arts Theatre, London, in 1960. It is set in a shabby room which belongs to either or both of two brothers, Aston and Mick. A derelict, who may be called Davies, makes desperate but futile attempts to establish a role for himself and a hold on the room.

Carew, Thomas ?1595–?1639 CAVALIER POET. Son of a Master in Chancery, Carew (pronounced 'Carey') was educated at Oxford, and entered the Inner Temple in 1612 to study law. About a year later he was attached as secretary to Sir Dudley Carleton, the ambassador to Venice and, later, to the Netherlands, but he returned to London in 1616. He was subsequently employed by the British ambassador to France, LORD HERBERT OF CHERBURY, and was accepted at court, where his reputation as a lyric poet and stylish personality won him the friendship of Charles I. His MASQUE, *Coelum Britannicum*, was performed before the king in 1634. Best remembered as a love poet (for 'The Rapture', in particular) on a par with the other court poets SUCKLING and LOVELACE, Carew was a disciple of DONNE and JONSON, with whom he was a fellow-member of FALKLAND's circle at Great Tew.

Carey, Henry *c.* 1681–1743 Poet. A music teacher for whom poetry was a pastime, Carey is remembered for his song 'Sally in Our Alley'. He wrote *Poems on Several Occasions* (1713) and a BURLESQUE tragedy, *Chrononhotonthologos* ('the Most Tragical Tragedy that ever was tragediz'd'), produced in 1734. He invented the nickname 'Namby-Pamby' for AMBROSE PHILIPS, and may have been the author of 'God Save the King'.

Peter Carey

Carey, Peter 1943– Australian novelist and short-story writer. Born in Bacchus Marsh, near Melbourne, he was educated at Geelong Grammar School and studied science at Monash University. He subsequently worked in advertising in Sydney, and lived in the mountainous rainforest country of Queensland and in London. He won immediate recognition as an important new voice with the appearance of his first collection of short stories, *The Fat Man in History* (1974).

It was subsequently combined with a second collection, *War Crimes* (1979), as *Exotic Pleasures* (1980). The novels which followed confirmed his gift for endowing fantasy with a concrete particularity rare in POST-MODERNIST writing. *Bliss* (1981) is a sardonic black comedy. *Illywhacker* (1985), the story of a 139-year-old confidence trickster looking back over his life, is a comic novel of epic scope, a fable that attempts to extend reality to the limit. *Oscar and Lucinda* (1988), which won the BOOKER PRIZE, begins in the world of 19th-century REALISM (pinpointed by references to GEORGE ELIOT and EDMUND GOSSE's *Father and Son*) but crosses the seas to Australia and a fantastic adventure into the bush. *The Tax Inspector* (1991) is set during the audit of Catchprice Motors in the Sydney of the 1990s.

Carleton, William 1794–1869 Irish novelist. Born of a poor family in Tyrone, he was an acute observer of peasant life. He contributed a number of sketches of the Irish scene to the *Christian Examiner* which were collected and published in 1832 as *Traits and Stories of the Irish Peasantry*. There followed a second series in 1833 and *Tales of Ireland* in 1834. He also wrote a number of novels, of which *Fardorougha the Miser* (1839) is best known. His other novels include *The Misfortunes of Barry Branagan* (1841), *Valentine McClutchy* (1845) and *The Evil Eye* (1860).

Carlyle, Jane Welsh 1801–66 Letter-writer and wife of THOMAS CARLYLE. Born at Haddington, East Lothian, she showed herself a precocious scholar in childhood. She inherited her father's estate in Dumfriesshire in 1819 and married Carlyle in 1826. Her shrewdness and astringent wit made her an excellent letter-writer, and her circle of correspondents included many eminent Victorians. *The Letters and Memorials of Jane Welsh Carlyle*, edited by her husband, appeared in 1883.

Carlyle, Thomas 1795–1881 Historian, philosopher, essayist and critic. The son of a stonemason in the little village of Ecclefechan, near Dumfries, he was educated at the village school, Annan Grammar School and Edinburgh University, which he entered at the age of 15. After completing an arts course he began to study for the ministry but abandoned this course and taught, first at Annan and later at Kircaldy, where he became friends with EDWARD IRVING. Returning to the university he studied law for a while, but began to concentrate upon literary work. He wrote contributions for Brewster's *Edinburgh Encyclopaedia* and undertook a thorough study of German literature. His first considerable essay, on Goethe's *Faust*, was published in *The New Edinburgh Review* (April 1822). From 1822 to 1824 Carlyle held a post as a private tutor; during this time he worked at his *Life of Schiller*, published by *The London Magazine* in 1823–4 (and in volume form in 1825), and a translation of Goethe's *Wilhelm Meister's Apprenticeship*, published in Edinburgh in 1824. This was followed by *German Romance* (1827) which included his translation of *Wilhelm Meister's Travels*. In 1826 he married Jane Welsh, whom he had met through Irving in 1821 (see JANE WELSH CARLYLE). For two years they lived in Edinburgh, during which time Carlyle wrote for THE EDINBURGH REVIEW, producing, among others, two well-known essays on Jean Paul and on German literature (published June and October 1827).

In 1828 the Carlyles, oppressed by financial difficulties, returned to Jane's farm at Craigenputtock where Carlyle began to write SARTOR RESARTUS, published in FRASER'S MAGAZINE (November 1833–August 1834), while continuing to contribute to *The Edinburgh Review* and other literary journals; *Signs of the Times* (1829) and *Characteristics* (1831) were published during this period. While staying in London in 1831 Carlyle became acquainted with JOHN STUART MILL, who later introduced him to EMERSON. Correspondence with Mill interested Carlyle in the French Revolution and, after 1834 when the Carlyles moved to Cheyne Row in Chelsea, he began work in earnest on his history of THE FRENCH REVOLUTION. The manuscript of the first volume was accidentally destroyed while on loan to Mill in 1835, but Carlyle rewrote it and the work was published in 1837.

From 1837 to 1840 Carlyle undertook several series of lectures of which the most significant and successful was that ON HEROES, HERO-WORSHIP AND THE HEROIC IN HISTORY, published in 1841. *Chartism* (1839) dealt with contemporary agitation and outlined Carlyle's views on the political and social problems of the day. In *PAST AND PRESENT* (1843) he drew on the recently published chronicle of JOCELIN OF BRAKELOND to argue that the proper regulation of society depended upon the leadership of a strong man of genius. In *Latter-Day Pamphlets* (1850) these views were repeated in more vehement form. With the publication of *Oliver Cromwell's Letters and Speeches* (1845) Carlyle's literary reputation was firmly established. The biography *The Life of John Sterling*, the friend of TENNYSON and Mill, followed in 1851. Fourteen years and an immense amount of labour were spent on Carlyle's most ambitious work, *The History of Frederick the Great* (1858–65).

In 1865 Carlyle was invited by the students of Edinburgh University to become their Lord Rector and he delivered his inaugural speech on 2 April 1866. He published one more book, *The Early Kings of Norway* (1875), but it is not a notable one. For the most part his writing was confined to letters to *The Times*; one of these, on behalf of Germany in her war against France, impressed Bismarck so much that the Order of Merit of Prussia was conferred on the author. Carlyle refused DISRAELI's offer to secure him an honour in England. During his last few years Carlyle completely ceased writing, having lost the use of his right hand; he died on 4 February 1881. His friends wanted a burial at Westminster Abbey but his wishes were honoured and his grave is in Ecclefechan.

In his lifetime, and indeed until the end of the 19th century, Carlyle enjoyed a reputation in striking contrast to his present largely neglected status. To contemporaries he was the leading thinker of his day, a challenging, commanding, if at times exasperating figure to reckon with. There are few Victorians whose work does not reflect his ideas – if only in the process of rejecting them – or echo the colourful, quirky turns of phrase in which he wrote. The social writings of RUSKIN and the mature novels of DICKENS are perhaps the strongest examples of his influence. The secret of Carlyle's appeal lay in his affirmation of moral certainties in an age of profound change.

Victorian England saw the social upheavals of industrialism, the political turbulence of the demand for wider democracy and the challenge to established religion from the natural sciences. Carlyle responded, not with a philosophical system or with a political programme, but with a list of values to which people could adhere: work, duty and self-abnegation. Above all, in an age of mass movements and mass democracy, he refused to see society in these terms but insisted on the importance of the individual, the private life of service by the ordinary man and the public life of heroism by the leader. From his early lectures on heroism until his last great work, the biography of Frederick the Great, he searched for a satisfactory model of the hero to put before the eyes of contemporaries. The search at first inspired them but, by removing Carlyle from the liberal and democratic tendencies of his age, finally isolated him and paved the way for later neglect.

Carman, (William) Bliss 1861–1929 Canadian poet. Born at Fredericton, he was a cousin of SIR CHARLES G. D. ROBERTS. He studied at the University of New Brunswick and as an external student at London University, left Canada for Harvard, and worked for a time as a journalist in New York. His career as a prolific and popular writer of verse celebrating the outdoor life began with *Low Tide on Grand Pré* (1893), three works in collaboration with RICHARD HOVEY – *Songs from Vagabondia* (1894), *More Songs from Vagabondia* (1896) and *Last Songs from Vagabondia* (1901) – and a series of BALLADS and myths, *The Pipes of Pan* (1898–1905). Other works include *Behind the Arras* (1895), *A Book of the Sea* (1897), *April Airs* (1916), *Later Poems* (1921), *Far Horizons* (1925) and *Sanctuary* (1929). He also translated the lyrics of Sappho (1904), collaborated on the masques *Daughter of the Dawn* (1913) and *Earth's Deities and Other Masques* (1914), and wrote several books of essays.

carpe diem Literally, a Latin imperative meaning 'seize the day', an exhortation to make the best use of time before it is too late. The motif derives from Horace, but was frequently imitated by the erotic and devotional poetry of the Renaissance and 17th century; classic expressions of it include MARVELL's 'To his Coy Mistress' and HERRICK's 'Gather Ye Rose-Buds While Ye May', both of which cite the urgency of passing time to dissuade a lady from chastity.

Carpenter, Edward 1844–1929 Poet, author and socialist reformer. Born at Brighton, he was educated at Trinity Hall, Cambridge, where he became a fellow and was curate to F. D. MAURICE. In 1874 he abandoned the church to pursue his own brand of primitive communism, much influenced by the writings of WHITMAN and THOREAU. Among English writers, he was indebted to RUSKIN and WILLIAM MORRIS. He eventually settled at Millthorpe, near Chesterfield, where he earned his living as a lecturer, farmer and controversial author in support of numerous progressive causes (sexual reform, women's rights, vegetarianism) aimed at subverting middle-class convention. He attracted a considerable number of admirers, notably E. M. FORSTER, for his overt homosexuality; and he was an early influence on D. H. LAWRENCE.

Carpenter's best-known prose works were *England's Ideal* (1887), *Civilization: Its Cause and Cure* (1889) and *Love's Coming of Age* (1896). Collections of his poetry included *Narcissus* (1873), *Towards Democracy* (1883–1902) – a long poem, published in four parts, which reflected his Whitmanic sense of 'cosmic consciousness' and 'spiritual democracy' – and *Sketches from Life in Town and Country* (1908). His autobiography, *My Days and Dreams*, was published in 1916.

Carr, Emily 1871–1945 Canadian writer and painter. The daughter of a stern Victorian father, she was born and brought up in Victoria, British Columbia, and gives a vivid, though partly fictionalized, account of her early years in *The Book of Small* (1942) and the first part of her posthumously published 'autobiography', *Growing Pains* (1946). After studying art in San Francisco, London and Paris, she went on to become Canada's best-known woman painter, taking her early subjects mainly from the culture of the Western Canadian Indians and developing a style characterized by vivid use of colour and sweeping brush-strokes. Recognition did not come easily and she supported herself by a variety of means, including running a boarding house in Victoria, an experience described in *The House of All Sorts* (1944). It was in her later years, when she was bedridden after a series of strokes and heart attacks, that she turned to writing. Her first book, *Klee Wyck* (1941), is a volume of short stories about the Indians of British Columbia. 'Klee Wyck', or 'Laughing One', was the name given to Carr by her Indian friends. She occupies a particular place in Canadian literature as a fond chronicler of late 19th-century and early 20th-century life, as well as for the close affinity she demonstrates for Indian peoples.

Carr, J(ames) (Joseph) L(loyd) 1912–94 Novelist. Born and educated in the North Riding of Yorkshire, he served on a West African flying boat station during the war and then worked as a schoolteacher in England and in South Dakota, finally settling in Northamptonshire. He did not begin writing fiction until the age of 50. *A Month in the Country* (1980), his best-known novel, is an intricately symbolic love story involving a World War I veteran who comes to a Yorkshire village to restore the ancient mural in the church. Carr's fiction is notable for its discreet articulation of Englishness, found in institutions like the small town and the Established Church and in sports like cricket (*A Season in Sinji*, 1967) or football (in *How Steeple Sinderby Wanderers Won the FA Cup*, 1975). Other novels include *The Battle of Pollocks Crossing* (1985), *What Hetty Did* (1988) and *Harpole and Foxberrow, Publishers* (1992). *Carr's Dictionary of Extraordinary Cricketers* (1977), one of the series of tiny literary pamphlets he published himself, has won a deserved reputation.

Carroll, Lewis [Dodgson, Charles Lutwidge] 1832–98. Humorist and writer of CHILDREN'S LITERATURE. The child of a scholarly country parson, he was born at Daresbury in Cheshire and attended a Yorkshire grammar school and Rugby. At home during his holidays he took a leading part in family amusements, producing a home-made magazine largely consisting of his own comic verse. At Christ Church, Oxford, he studied mathematics, obtaining a university post but lecturing and teaching with difficulty because of his habitual shyness and bad stammer. For the same reasons he preached only occasionally after his ordination in 1861. He produced mathematical textbooks and some occasional comic writing. Both he and his friends were surprised by the immediate success of his masterpiece, *Alice's Adventures under Ground* (now usually known as ALICE'S ADVENTURES IN WONDERLAND; 1865), a book which revolutionized children's literature by putting all previous literary pieties aside and opening the door to entertainment for its own sake. At this stage in his life he also took great interest in photography and in the company of young children, particularly girls. Later successes were equally original, notably THROUGH THE LOOKING-GLASS AND WHAT ALICE FOUND THERE (1871) and a long nonsense poem, THE HUNTING OF THE SNARK (1876). After these Dodgson's genius faded, although his fame continued to grow. Today, while his life has become a quarry for psychological speculation, his best works remain as fresh and ultimately elusive as they have always been.

Carroll, Paul Vincent 1900–68 Irish playwright. Born in Dundalk, he emigrated when he was 21 and taught in Glasgow until 1937, when his plays gave him financial independence. He was a co-founder of the Glasgow Citizens' Theatre. His early plays – *Things That are Caesar's* (1932), *Shadow and Substance* (1937) and *The White Seed* (1939) – satirize the clerical authoritarianism of his Irish childhood. Apart from two lightly satiric comedies, *The Devil Came from Dublin* and *The Wayward Saint* (1955), his later work is heavily didactic. The acrid scenes from provincial life in his first three plays put him worthily in the line of COLUM and THOMAS CORNELIUS MURRAY.

Angela Carter

Carter, Angela 1940–92 Novelist and essayist. Born in Sussex, she read English at the University of Bristol. She taught and was writer-in-residence at universities in America and Australia; she wrote extensively about her two years' residence in Japan in essays for *New Society* later included in her collection of journalism, *Nothing Sacred* (1982). Her fiction, often cited as MAGIC REALISM, mounts a witty, resourceful attack on received notions of 'reality' in the novel. It uses extravagant Gothic fantasy, a baroque multiplicity of characters who change role, status and even sex, and pastiches of genres from SCIENCE FICTION to 18th-century PICARESQUE. Outstanding novels include *Heroes and Villains* (1969), *Nights at the Circus* (1984) and her last, *Wise Children* (1991). *Bloody Chamber* (1979), a collection of stories retelling classic fairy-tales in full modern awareness of their symbolism of the unconscious, exemplifies her predilection for myth-making, the unforced feminist imperative that underlies her fiction, and her measured, sensual prose style. Her essay *The Sadeian Woman* (1979) considers the Marquis de Sade's ideas of repression in the light of what Carter describes as 'the culturally determined nature of women and the relations between men and women that result from it'. *Expletives Deleted* (1992) is a posthumous collection of non-fiction.

Carter, Elizabeth 1717–1806 Translator, linguist and poet. Educated by her father, the perpetual curate of Deal chapel, she learned Latin, Greek, Hebrew,

French, German, Italian and Spanish, and subsequently taught herself Portuguese and Arabic. At the age of 17 she started to contribute poems to *THE GENTLEMAN'S MAGAZINE*, which was edited by her father's friend Edward Cave. A small collection of her verse was published in 1738 as *Poems upon Particular Occasions*; it was followed in 1762 by *Poems on Several Occasions*. Cave introduced her to JOHNSON, and she wrote articles for *THE RAMBLER*, Nos. 44 and 100. Johnson thought very highly of her and their friendship lasted nearly 50 years. Similar longstanding friendships with Catherine Talbot and ELIZABETH MONTAGU resulted in *A Series of Letters between Mrs Elizabeth Carter and Miss Catherine Talbot from the Year 1741 to 1770* (4 vols., 1809), and of *Letters from Mrs Elizabeth Carter to Mrs Montagu, between the Years 1755 and 1800* (3 vols., 1817), collections valuable for their detailed comments upon contemporary literature and social conventions. In 1739 she published anonymously her translation of Jean Pierre de Crousaz's discussion of POPE's *ESSAY ON MAN*, which led to Warburton's defensive response, *A Vindication of Mr Pope's Essay on Man, from the Misrepresentations of Mr de Crousaz*. In the same year she produced, also anonymously, *Sir Isaac Newton's Philosophy Explained for the Use of Ladies*, a translation of Algarotti's *Newtonianismo per le dame*.

Her most important work is a translation of the works of Epictetus (1758). It is a reflection upon 18th-century attitudes that the reviewers seemed more concerned to express surprise that a woman knew any Greek than to comment on the excellence of the work. Johnson considered her knowledge of the language superior to that of anybody he had met.

Carter, Martin 1927– Guyanese poet. He was born in Georgetown, and educated there at Queen's College. After a career in the civil service he turned to radical political activity and was detained in 1953. After independence he became for a while Minister of Information and Culture in Prime Minister Burnham's government. It was during his period as a detainee that he wrote *Poems of Resistance* (1954), which first made him a poet of more than local reputation, though this he had in abundance on the basis of *Hills of Fire Glow Red* (1951), *The Kind Eagle* (1952) and *Returning* (1953). Later collections include *Poems of Shape and Motion* (1955), *Conversations* (1961), *Jail Me Quickly* (1963), *Poems of Succession* (1977) and *Poems of Affinity* (1980). There are many influences upon Carter's writing from both American and European sources, but he is indisputably a Caribbean poet, and it has been accurately said that he combines a tradition of public poetry with an uncomfortable private anguish.

Cartwright, Jim 1958– Playwright. His first play, *Road* (1986), is a study of the unemployed in Lancashire, as witnessed by its narrator Scully, in short but telling scenes with a lyrical commentary which reminded some observers of DYLAN THOMAS. *Bed* (1989) presents the thoughts and dreams of seven elderly people. *To* (1990) is a less ambitious collection of sketches about working-class life but *The Rise and Fall of Little Voice* (1992), staged at the ROYAL NATIONAL THEATRE, offers two splendid comic roles for actresses as the little voice of the title and the mother who exploits her skill in impersonating the stars.

Cartwright, William 1611–43 Poet, playwright and preacher, Cartwright was much admired by 17th-century Royalists. Educated at Westminster School and Oxford, where he lived from 1628 until his death, he was claimed as a poetic 'son' by BEN JONSON. His comedy, *The Ordinary* (c. 1634), is Jonsonian in style. Two tragicomedies, *The Siege* (c. 1636) and *The Lady-Errant* (c. 1636), are not without ingenuity. *The Royal Slave* (1636) was acted before Charles I and Henrietta Maria in the hall of Christ Church, Oxford. The occasion was a splendid one, with Henry Lawes providing music for the play and Inigo Jones designing it.

Cartwright took holy orders in 1638 and wrote no more plays. He became a noted preacher whose fiery loyalty to the King survives in a Passion Sermon preached at Oxford. The 1651 edition of his works contains 51 commendatory verses by writers of the day.

Carver, Raymond 1939–88 American short-story writer and poet. He was born in Clatskanie, Oregon. His poetry, usually focused on a particular object or aspect of daily life, appeared in five collections: *Near Klamath* (1968), *Winter Insomnia* (1970), *At Night the Salmon Move* (1976), *Where Water Comes Together with Other Water* (1985) and *Ultramarine* (1986). A prime example of DIRTY REALISM, his fiction navigates the apparently contingent lives of its small-town protagonists in quizzical, unadorned prose. His short stories are collected in *Will You Please be Quiet, Please?* (1976), *What We Talk About When We Talk About Love* (1981), *Cathedral* (1983) and *Fires: Essays, Stories, Poems* (1983). Carver's uncollected writings appeared posthumously as *No Heroics, Please* (1992).

Cary, Henry Francis 1772–1844 Poet and translator. Born in Gibraltar, he was educated at Christ Church, Oxford, and ordained in 1796. He served as assistant librarian at the British Museum in 1826–37. Although he published a slight volume of verse at the age of 16 (*Sonnets and Odes*, 1788), Cary is best known for his BLANK-VERSE translation of Dante's *Divina Commedia* (*Inferno*, 1805–6; *Purgatorio* and *Paradiso*, 1814).

Cary, (Arthur) Joyce (Lunel) 1888–1957 Novelist. Born in Londonderry, educated at Clifton and Trinity College, Oxford, he studied art in Edinburgh and Paris (1904–9). He served with a British Red Cross unit in Montenegro during the Balkan war of 1912–13 and later joined the Nigerian political service as a district magistrate and administrative officer. Resigning from the colonial service in 1920, he settled in Oxford with the intention of serving an apprenticeship as a novelist.

His first four novels – *Aissa Saved* (1932), *An American Visitor* (1933), *The African Witch* (1936) and *Mister Johnson* (1939) – were set in West Africa and dealt with the confrontation between tribal culture and British administration. Then followed *Castle Corner* (1938), the only completed novel of a planned trilogy on the decline of the British Empire, and two novels about childhood, *Charley is My Darling* (1940) and *House of Children* (1941). But his best-known works are the trilogies which explore the worlds of art – *Herself Surprised* (1941), *To be a Pilgrim* (1942) and *THE HORSE'S MOUTH* (1944) – and politics – *Prisoner of Grace* (1952), *Except the Lord* (1953), *Not Honour More* (1955). In both trilogies the story is told through first-person narratives by each of the three main characters. Cary's disciplined presentation of the subjective viewpoint is much admired.

Cary also published two volumes of poetry, *Marching Soldier* (1945) and *The Drunken Sailor* (1947), and several political works including *Power in Men* (1939), *The Case for African Freedom* (1941) and *Britain and West Africa* (1946). His last works, published posthumously, were a book on aesthetics, *Art and Reality* (1958), and an incomplete novel, *The Captive and the Free* (1959).

Cary, Patrick ?1623–57 Poet. Son of Henry, Viscount Falkland and younger brother to the famous LUCIUS FALKLAND, Patrick Cary was born in Dublin. His early years were tempestuous, largely owing to his mother's conversion to Roman Catholicism and subsequent estrangement from her husband. When the latter died in 1633, Patrick went to live at Great Tew with Lucius, a staunch Anglican. In 1636, he and his younger brother were abducted by their mother and sent to St Edmund's Priory in Paris. Patrick travelled to Rome, where he remained until 1650; while in residence, he met MILTON, CRASHAW and JOHN EVELYN. He entered monastic life briefly, but returned to the world, and England, married and took employment in government service in Ireland, where he died from causes unknown. His poems, written in 1650 and 1651, were unpublished in his lifetime and first printed in 1771. His secular work, the *Trivial Ballads*, embraces satire, PASTORAL and love-lyric, and exhibits skilful metrical variety and gentlemanly wit. His devotional meditations are deeply felt, if of uneven quality, echoing both DONNE's vigour and JONSON's el-

egance; the manuscript is embellished with interesting emblematic illustrations in Cary's hand.

Caste A comedy by THOMAS WILLIAM ROBERTSON, first performed at the Prince of Wales's Theatre, London, in 1867. It is the outstanding example of Robertson's innovative realism in the presentation of domestic detail, the 'cup-and-saucer drama'.

Esther Eccles and her lively sister, Polly, are impoverished by their idle, drunken father. Polly may flirt with George's snooty friend, Captain Hawtrey, but she loves her gas-fitter, Sam Gerridge. Esther, on the other hand, is persuaded almost against her will to marry the genteel George d'Alroy. Transported from Lambeth to Mayfair, she is ill at ease, and her plight is worsened when George is reported missing, believed dead in battle. But George returns, and the problems are resolved.

Castle Dangerous See SCOTT, SIR WALTER.

Castle of Indolence, The A poem in SPENSERIAN STANZAS by JAMES THOMSON, published in 1748, though he had begun it 15 years before. The first CANTO tells of the wizard, Indolence, and the castle into which he lures world-weary pilgrims. There they surrender to idleness in an atmosphere of delicious ease, until they degenerate and are thrown into the dungeons. The second tells of the Knight of Arts and Industry and his destruction of the castle. Thomson introduces himself ('A bard here dwelt, more fat than bard beseems') and several of his friends into the action of the first canto.

Castle of Otranto, The: *A Gothic Story* A novel by HORACE WALPOLE, published in 1764. In the first edition it was offered as a translation from an imaginary Italian original, but Walpole acknowledged his authorship in the second edition. These circumstances suggest that *The Castle of Otranto* was playfully conceived, at least in part, but it proved influential in establishing the fashion for the GOTHIC NOVEL.

The story is set in the 13th century. Manfred, Prince of Otranto, is the grandson of a usurper and has no lawful claim to the realm; his grandfather had poisoned the rightful prince, Alfonso. A prophecy foretold that the usurpers would remain in power as long as they had male issue to continue their line and while the castle remained large enough to hold the lawful ruler. Manfred has arranged the marriage of his only son, Conrad, to the beautiful Isabella, daughter of the Marquis of Vicenzo, but on the night before the wedding Conrad is mysteriously killed. Manfred knows that a gigantic figure haunts the castle and, now suddenly bereft of an heir, he determines to marry Isabella himself and beget another. But Isabella, terrified of Manfred, escapes from the castle with the help of a young peasant, Theodore, who is under suspicion of being connected with Conrad's death. Manfred's daughter, Matilda, loves the handsome peasant, and when he is arrested she releases him. Manfred is convinced that Isabella and Theodore are in love; he learns that Theodore is keeping a tryst by Alfonso's tomb. He goes there, stabs the lady – and discovers that he has murdered his daughter Matilda. The ghost of Alfonso, now grown too enormous to be contained by the castle, overthrows it and rises from the ruins. Manfred confesses the usurpation by his family, and the ghost proclaims Theodore the lawful prince. The tale ends with Theodore and Isabella's marriage.

Castle of Perseverance, The A MORALITY PLAY, dating from *c.* 1405–25. The surviving manuscript, some 3500 lines of rhyming stanzas, includes a crude drawing of the appropriate stage setting, from which we learn that the play was performed in the round, with the castle in the centre and various scaffolds on the circumference, housing respectively Flesh, World, Belial, Covetousness and God. Beneath the castle there is a bench-bed for the protagonist, Humanum Genus. The play describes the competition between forces of Good and Evil for the soul of humankind. Saved from the scaffold of the World by the Good Angel, Humanum Genus takes refuge in the castle, which offers the protection of Perseverance, a kind of Christian patience in the face of temptation. The castle is assaulted by Satan and his cohorts, who are driven away by the Virtues hurling emblematic roses, but Humanum Genus is drawn towards worldly riches by Covetousness. Death proves the transitoriness of worldly wealth. Defended at the throne of God by Mercy and Justice, Humanum Genus is admitted to Heaven and the play ends with a Te Deum.

Castle Rackrent A novel by MARIA EDGEWORTH, published in 1801. Thady Quirk, steward to the Rackrents, tells the story of the family's path to ruin, beginning three generations before with the hard-drinking Sir Patrick. Like *THE ABSENTEE*, it criticizes 18th-century Irish landlords, vividly depicting the results of profligacy and corruption.

Castle Richmond A novel by ANTHONY TROLLOPE, published in 1860. Set in 1846–7, it is of interest for its portrayal of the Irish Famine and for the character of Lady Desmond and her hopeless love for a younger man, Owen Fitzgerald, who wishes to marry her daughter Clara.

Cat on a Hot Tin Roof A play by TENNESSEE WILLIAMS, first performed in New York in 1955 and awarded a PULITZER PRIZE. It was revised for a revival in 1974.

The action centres on the wealthy and chaotic Pollitt family in Mississippi, and on the question of the inheritance of Big Daddy Pollitt's 28,000-acre estate. Big Daddy has stipulated that to inherit a share of the estate each of his sons must have children. Brick, the younger son, and his wife Maggie, the 'cat' of the title, are childless, in sharp contrast to Gooper Pollitt and his wife Mae, who already have five children and are expecting another. The discovery that Big Daddy is terminally ill forces the family to confront the tensions and hostilities which have developed as a result of his rigid control of their lives. Obsessed with guilt over his homosexuality, Brick has turned to alcohol. This in turn worsens his relationship with the passionate Maggie, which has already been damaged by the vindictiveness of Gooper and Mae. At the end of the play there is a suggestion that Maggie will be able to seduce Brick and conceive a child.

catachresis The misapplication of a word, sometimes ineptly, as in mixed metaphors (see METAPHOR), but often with striking rhetorical effect (as in MILTON's 'Blind mouths!' in *LYCIDAS*). It is sometimes called 'Clevelandism', from JOHN CLEVELAND's love of implausible and far-fetched metaphors.

catalexis (truncation) The omission of the last syllable or syllables from a line in a passage of generally regular verse (see METRE). Such a line is said to be catalectic when it is one syllable short, brachycatalectic when it is two short. The regular lines of the passage are acatalectic. A line with one or two syllables in excess of the regular number would be hypercatalectic.

Catch-22 An anti-war novel by JOSEPH HELLER, published in 1961. Its non-chronological plotting technique, intended to emphasize the displacements that war produces, makes for a disjointed, fragmented narrative. The story is set in a US army air force base hospital on the fictional island of Pinosa during World War II. Captain John Yossarian is determined to survive the war and will use any means at his disposal to do so. He hopes to get a medical discharge by pretending to be insane, but the 'Catch-22' rule – which says that anyone rational enough to want to be grounded cannot be insane and is therefore capable of returning to flight duty – keeps him in the war. Finally, after all his friends are killed or go missing, he decides to desert to Sweden.

Catcher in the Rye, The A novel by J. D. SALINGER, published in 1951.

The 16-year-old Holden Caulfield narrates his own story of rebellion against the banality and 'phoniness' of middle-class values. Expelled from his private school in Pennsylvania, the caustic but quixotic teenager goes to New York City. He has an unsuccessful encounter with a prostitute and ends up in a skirmish with her pimp. The next day he meets an old girlfriend, Sally Hayes, and takes her skating. His spirits lifted, he suggests that the two of them escape to the New England countryside. Sally rejects this impractical offer and Holden, completely discouraged, gets drunk and then sneaks home to see his sister Phoebe, telling her that he plans to 'go West'. Later that night he has an unsettling reunion with his former schoolteacher, Mr Antolini, who makes homosexual advances to him. The next morning he goes to Phoebe's school to say goodbye, but he is overwhelmed by his love for her and decides to stay. He then has a nervous breakdown, and tells his story as he is recovering.

catharsis From the Greek, a purging or cleansing. In Aristotle's theory of TRAGEDY, it refers specifically to the release of emotion caused in the audience by the fate of the tragic hero.

Cather, Willa (Siebert) 1873–1947 American novelist. Born in rural Virginia, she moved with her family to Red Cloud, Nebraska, in 1883. In an attempt to escape the conservatism of the small

Willa Cather

town, she moved to Lincoln in 1890 and the following year entered the University of Nebraska. After graduating, she moved to Pittsburgh to pursue a career in journalism. She spent 10 years there, first as a newspaper woman and then as a high-school teacher of English and Latin. *April Twilights*, her only volume of poetry, appeared in 1903. Two years later she published *The Troll Garden*, a collection of short stories which showed the influence of HENRY JAMES. She later reissued four of these stories and added four more in a collection entitled *Youth and the Bright Medusa* (1920).

When she was 32, Cather moved to New York City and joined the staff of *McClure's Magazine*. Over the next seven years she published stories in *THE CENTURY MAGAZINE* and *HARPER'S MONTHLY MAGAZINE*, as well as in *McClure's*. In 1912 her first novel, *Alexander's Bridge*, was published. She resigned from McClure's and travelled to the Southwest. Her second novel, *O PIONEERS!*, appeared in 1913. She returned to the Southwest in the summer of 1915, and her novel of that year, *The Song of the Lark*, is partly set in the ancient cliff-dwellings of Walnut Canyon, Arizona. In her next novel, *MY ANTONIA* (1918), she returns to the Nebraska of her childhood.

Her first popular success was *One of Ours* (1922), which won the PULITZER PRIZE. It tells the story of a boy from the Western plains who joins the army and is killed in France in World War I. Her next novel, *A Lost Lady* (1923), deals with stages of the moral decline of a woman from a small Nebraska town. *The Professor's House* (1925) is set in a small Midwestern college and in New Mexico in the post-war years. *My Mortal Enemy* (1926) is set in New York and on the West Coast in the early 1900s. The New Mexico landscapes in *DEATH COMES FOR THE ARCHBISHOP* (1927) reflect Cather's continuing love for the Southwest. Composed after several visits to Quebec, and set in French Canada at the end of the 17th century, *Shadows on the Rock* (1931) won her the first Prix Femina Americaine in 1933. The three tales that make up *Obscure Destinies* (1932) take place in the Midwest. *Lucy Gayheart* (1935) tells the story of the daughter of a German-born watchmaker who leaves a small Nebraska town to study music in Chicago. *Not Under Forty* (1936; later retitled *Literary Encounters*) is a volume of critical essays. Her last novel, *Sapphira and the Slave* (1940), is the only one set in the Virginia of her grandmothers.

Catherine: *A Story, by Ikey Solomons, Esq., Junior* A short novel by W. M. THACKERAY, first published in *FRASER'S MAGAZINE* (May 1839–February 1840). It is a deliberately sordid tale of criminal life, based on the career of Catherine Hayes, executed in 1726 for the murder of her husband. Thackeray wrote it in reaction against the sentimental view of criminals offered by the NEWGATE NOVEL.

Catiline His Conspiracy A tragedy by BEN JONSON, first produced in 1611 and published the same year. The play, rarely revived, follows the events of Roman history in the days of the republic, specifically the conspiracy of 63 BC. Catiline (Lucius Sergius Catilina) was a patrician who had been praetor and governor of Africa but whose dissolute life ruined him financially. He was defeated when he stood for the consulship in 64 BC, the votes going to Cicero and Antonius. Catiline renewed his candidature in the following year but was again rejected. Jonson's play begins at this point.

The impoverished and desperate Catiline, with the secret encouragement of Caesar and Crassus, is preparing to overthrow the government. But Cicero is warned by Fulvia of the intention to assassinate him as the first part of the conspiracy; he summons the Senate and accuses Catiline, who immediately leaves the city for Faesulae, where his supporters have raised an army. Proof is delivered to Cicero by the ambassadors of the Allobroges (a Gallic tribe), who had been approached by Catiline for aid. The evidence is submitted to the Senate; Catiline and the other conspirators are sentenced to death. However, Catiline is defeated and killed in battle by the government general Petreius.

Catnach, James 1792–1841 Printer and publisher. He was born at Alnwick, Northumberland, the son of John Catnach (1769–1813), a printer there, and, later, at Newcastle upon Tyne. In 1813 James set up business in Seven Dials, London, and prospered with innumerable cheap publications, including ABCs and children's tracts. Some of his output was in the old BALLAD-publishing tradition, and he helped to preserve the texts of nursery rhymes and carols. He was notorious, however, for his output of topical and sensational material – on crimes, scandals, villainies, prize-fights and political events – which with its crude woodcut illustrations was very widely distributed by itinerant hawkers. Some of his work derives from his own historical collections, and he stands late in a long line of succession in the trade, but his emphasis on the sensational did much to kill off the long-established ballad market. He retired from his lucrative business in 1838.

Cato A tragedy in BLANK VERSE by JOSEPH ADDISON, first produced and published in 1713. It enjoyed considerable success in the climate of the time; Queen Anne was dying and the succession was a question that divided the country into two opposing parties. The play has not been revived and is now better known for quotations such as "Tis not in mortals to command success,/ But we'll do more, Sempronius; we'll deserve it.' It is based on the last weeks of the life of Cato (Marcus Porcius Cato, the republican), besieged in Utica by Caesar in 46 BC. Cato has been betrayed by Sempronius, a senator, and the Numidian general Syphax. Faithful to him is Juba, Prince of Numidia. Addison introduces romantic interest in the character of Marcia, Cato's daughter, who is loved by Juba, and in the rivalry of Cato's two sons for the hand of Lucia.

Catriona See KIDNAPPED.

Caudwell, Christopher [Sprigg, Christopher St John] 1901-37. Critic, journalist, poet and detective novelist. Sprigg was born in Putney, the son of a journalist. After leaving school at the age of 15, he worked as a reporter on *The Yorkshire Observer*, and then in London as a writer on aeronautics, launching his own journal, *Aircraft Engineering*. Under his real name he wrote DETECTIVE FICTION and textbooks on aircraft. In 1934 he discovered the writings of Marx, Engels and Lenin, and joined the Communist Party the following year. He drove an ambulance to Spain and joined the International Brigade in 1936, but was killed manning a machine gun in the battle of the Jamara river in 1937. His literary reputation rests on his posthumous book *Illusion and Reality* (1937), which attempted to develop a Marxist theory of poetry as a product of the human struggle with nature. *Studies in a Dying Culture* (1938) includes analyses of Freud, SHAW and D. H. LAWRENCE; it was followed by the philosophical essays in *Further Studies in a Dying Culture* (edited by EDGELL RICKWORD, 1949). His other works include *The Crisis in Physics* (1939). *Poems* (1939), edited by his friend Paul Beard, has been superseded by *Collected Poems* (1986). Lacking literary sophistication and sometimes falling into stilted earnestness, Caudwell's plain language and simple forms have an unsentimental realism and urgency. The only directly political poem, 'Heil Baldwin', is often merely propaganda.

Causley, Charles 1917- Poet. Born and educated in Launceston, Cornwall, he worked briefly as a builder and played piano in a dance-band before spending six years in the Royal Navy, during which he began to write poetry. He then returned to Launceston and spent the rest of his working life as a teacher. *Hands to Dance* (1951), his first collection, was followed by *Farewell, Aggie Weston* (1951), *Survivor's Leave* (1953), *Union Street* (1957), *Johnny Alleluia* (1961), *Underneath the Water* (1968), *Figgie Hobbin* (1970), *Collected Poems* (1975), *Early in the Morning* (1988) and *Collected Poems* (1992). Well known as a poet of the sea, he uses simple diction, firm rhythms and traditional forms (especially the BALLAD) with great facility. These techniques, together with his recurrent interest in the survival of innocence, have helped to make his poetry for children immensely popular.

Cavalier poets A term loosely describing a group of lyric poets who flourished during the reign of Charles I (1625-49). These courtiers wrote about love and loyalty to the monarch, usually in complimentary poems or lighthearted lyrics. LOVELACE, SUCKLING and CAREW were the most prominent, while HERRICK and WALLER, though not of their social coterie, often resemble them in literary style and attitude. All owe a debt to DONNE and JONSON.

Cave, Edward See GENTLEMAN'S MAGAZINE, THE.

Cavendish, George 1500-?61 The biographer of Wolsey, Cavendish was a gentleman usher in the Cardinal's household, which he joined in 1527. He accompanied Wolsey on an embassy to France and was with him when he died at Leicester. *The Life of Cardinal Wolsey* was not printed until 1641 but manuscript copies circulated in the 16th century, making it known to writers like JOHN STOW, who drew on it for his *Annales*. Cavendish's biography is in the medieval tradition of historical writing describing the fall of a great man. Wolsey's sometime glory and magnificence are contrasted with his later disgrace. The work portrays the fickleness of fortune and the transience of honour.

Caxton, William c. 1415/24-c. 1491/2 Printer and translator. Caxton was born in the Weald of Kent and apprenticed to Robert Large, a London cloth merchant, in or before 1438. Large died in 1441 and Caxton seems to have gone to Bruges where he followed a prosperous career. He probably learned to print in Cologne in 1471-2, but he acquired his experience and bought type in Bruges before returning to England to set up his own press near Westminster Abbey in 1476-7, the first printing press in England. When he died it passed to WYNKYN DE WORDE.

Caxton's early printing ventures included an involvement in the production of *Bartholomaeus anglicus* and perhaps *De vera nobilitate* in Cologne, and, in Bruges, the first part of his own translation *Recuyell of the Histories of Troy* (1471-6) from the *Recueil des histoires de Troyes* by Raoul Lefevre (1464) and a 15th-century version of Guido delle Colonne's *Historia troiana*. In England he printed a few works in Latin, but these were religious works, a book of grammar and one of rhetoric, and not the Greek or Latin classics, which appeared only in translation (Ovid, Virgil and Cato). In English he printed works by CHAUCER, GOWER and LYDGATE (but not LANGLAND), books on history and geography, SAINTS' LIVES and didactic works, including the FABLES of Aesop (1483/4), prose romances (most notably *The Knight of the Tower*, 1483) and several miscellaneous treatises. He did not print the original work of any living English writer. He was a prolific translator and all the prose romances he printed, except MALORY's *MORTE DARTHUR*, were his own work. Best known are his translations of part of the French Renard cycle as *REYNARD THE FOX* (1481), of the *Legenda Aurea* as *THE GOLDEN LEGEND* (1483), his *Recuyell* and *Esop*, and his *The Game and Play of the Chess* (1474/5). He included some critical comment in the prologues and epilogues he attached to some of the works he printed, and though his criticism is unoriginal and uninspired, his prose style is vigorous and fluent.

Cecil, Lord (Edward Christian) David (Gascoyne) 1902–86 Critic and biographer. The son of the Marquess of Salisbury, Cecil was educated at Eton and Christ Church, Oxford. He taught at Wadham College and New College, Oxford, where he occupied the Goldsmiths' Chair of English Literature from 1948 to 1969. He wrote studies of WILLIAM COWPER (1929), Lord Melbourne (1939, 1954), THOMAS HARDY (1943), Thomas Gray and SIR WILLIAM TEMPLE's wife Dorothy Osborne (*Two Quiet Lives*, 1948), JANE AUSTEN (1978) and CHARLES LAMB (1983), but is best remembered for *Early Victorian Novelists* (1934). His approach to literature was that of an amateur enthusiast emulating the refined impressionism of WALTER PATER, a gentlemanly style which earned him the scorn of the Cambridge School led by F. R. LEAVIS. Several of his Oxford lectures were collected in *The Fine Art of Reading* (1957).

Cecilia:* or, *Memoirs of an Heiress FANNY BURNEY's second novel, published in 1782. The story concerns the fortunes of Cecilia Beverley, who is victimized by her three unscrupulous guardians, Harrel, Briggs and the Hon. Compton Delvile. Driven by ill usage to insanity and the point of death, Cecilia eventually finds a modicum of happiness with her lover Mortimer Delvile. In spite of its scenes of frantic excitement, hysteria and farce, Burney intended the work to be realistic: 'I meant... to blend upon paper, as I have frequently seen blended in life, noble and rare qualities with striking and incurable defects.' The result was highly successful, receiving praise from DR JOHNSON, EDMUND BURKE, HESTER CHAPONE, MRS DELANY and EDWARD GIBBON.

Celebrated Jumping Frog of Calaveras County, The A collection of stories by MARK TWAIN, his first book, published in 1867. The title sketch, which first appeared in the New York *Saturday Press* in 1865, was based on an old California folk-tale. Dan'l Webster, the champion jumping frog, is owned by Jim Smiley. A stranger claims that any frog could beat him, and sends Smiley off to catch another one to have a contest. Dan'l is defeated, but only because, as Smiley discovers after the race, the stranger had managed to fill his gullet with quail shot to weigh him down.

Celtic revival, the The reawakening of interest in the literature and culture of the Celtic people in the 19th and 20th centuries. It had its origins in ROMANTICISM and the 18th-century antiquarianism which preceded it. A number of works in English exploiting what was perceived as the Gothic element in early Celtic literature appeared in the mid 18th century. THOMAS GRAY's Pindaric ODE 'The Bard' (1757) and 'The Triumphs of Owen' (1768) are typical. The latter drew on the first substantial selection of Welsh poetry to be published: *Some Specimens of the Poetry of the Ancient Welsh Bards. Translated into English...* (1764), by Ieuan Brydydd Hir (Evan Evans, 1731–88). The growing interest was fuelled by the literary forgeries of the Welsh antiquarian and poet Iolo Morganwg (Edward Williams, 1747–1826) and particular of the Scotsman JAMES MACPHERSON, whose 'Ossian' poems were the subject of enormous enthusiasm and then fierce controversy. Reliable translations began to appear in the 19th century: Lady Charlotte Guest's *THE MABINOGION* was published between 1838 and 1849, Hersart de la Villemarqué's *Barzaz Breiz* and *Les Bardes bretons du sixième siècle* in 1839 and 1850 and EUGENE O'CURRY's *Lectures on the Manuscript Materials of Ancient Irish History* in 1861.

Translations provided the basis for MATTHEW ARNOLD's important 'Lectures on Celtic Literature' at Oxford in 1865–6. His linking together of all the Celtic literatures – Irish, Welsh, Scottish, Cornish, Breton and Manx – was one of the founding steps of modern Celtic scholarship, though many of his other ideas were anticipated by Ernest Renan (1823–92) in *La Poésie des races celtiques* (1854). However eccentric some of Arnold's assumptions and conclusions may have been, his lectures led directly to the founding of the Chair of Celtic at Jesus College, Oxford, in 1877, which in turn helped in the establishment of further chairs in the University of Wales and elsewhere. The popular view of Celtic literature and people as mysteriously romantic also owes much to Arnold's description of their gift for style, 'natural magic' and 'Celtic melancholy'.

Throughout the 19th century English authors made use of Celtic material, real or imaginary, in works as various as THOMAS LOVE PEACOCK's *THE MISFORTUNES OF ELPHIN* (1829), TENNYSON's *IDYLLS OF THE KING* (1842–85) and GERARD MANLEY HOPKINS's 'St Winifred's Well' (written 1879–85). At the same time Irish, Scottish and Welsh writers were exploiting the same material in their English writing. YEATS's collection of stories and folklore, *The Celtic Twilight* (1893), provided a descriptive term for Irish literary activity in the 1890s and early 1900s, although it was made to seem anachronistic by the new generation of writers such as JOYCE and SEAN O'CASEY. In Scotland this kind of writing, with its implicit belief in ancient heroes and spirits, was produced by WILLIAM BLACK and WILLIAM SHARP. In the 20th century English writers have continued to make use of Celtic material, and there have been literary revivals – often linked with strongly nationalist feeling – in many of the Celtic countries, both in Celtic languages and in English. See also FOLK REVIVAL.

Cenci, The A five-act tragedy by PERCY BYSSHE SHELLEY, published in 1819. The single most impressive stage play to have been written by any of the Romantic poets, its subject made performance unlikely in the theatre of the time, though it was considered by COVENT GARDEN. It was first produced privately by the Shelley Society in 1886 and has been occasionally revived since then. It provided the French visionary Antonin Artaud (1896–1948) with the basis for a scenario which can be seen as the central text in his THEATRE OF CRUELTY.

The play is based on the savage history of a 16th-century Roman family. Count Francesco Cenci, a vicious husband and father with a sadistic taste for punishment, combines hatred for his daughter Beatrice with incestuous lust. The family conspires to have him killed. Suspected and tortured, they are brought to trial, and, despite the compassion aroused by their pitiful story and by Beatrice's self-conduct, they are executed. The executions took place on 11 September 1599. Shelley makes Beatrice, whose portrait by Guido Reni he had seen in the Colonna palace in Rome, the central figure of his tragedy.

Centlivre, Susannah 1669–1723 Playwright. Susannah Freeman was probably born at Holbeach, Lincolnshire. She was first married at the age of 16 and twice widowed before her marriage to Joseph Centlivre, Queen Anne's cook at Windsor, in 1706. She became an actress but achieved no great distinction, and began writing for the stage under her second married name, Susannah Carroll. Eighteen of her plays were produced, to considerable success, during her lifetime. They include *The Gamester* (1705), adapted from *Le Joueur* by Jean-François Regnard; *The Wonder: A Woman Keeps a Secret* (1714); and *A Bold Stroke for a Wife* (1718). The last two provided successful parts for DAVID GARRICK and Anne Oldfield.

Century Magazine, The An American journal, first published in November 1870 as *Scribner's Monthly, an Illustrated Magazine for the People*, founded by Roswell Smith, Charles Scribner, and Dr Josiah Gilbert Holland, who served as its editor until his death in 1881. Under Holland's control *Scribner's Monthly* featured essays on politics, religion, and current affairs; serial fiction; and numerous high-quality illustrations. Contributors included GEORGE MAC-DONALD, MARGARET OLIPHANT and Jules Verne. It also published most of the *Nights with Uncle Remus* by JOEL CHANDLER HARRIS.

In 1881 the name was changed to *The Century Illustrated Monthly Magazine*, under the editorship of Richard Watson Gilder. Under Gilder *The Century* displayed an increased concern with public events, but continued to serialize novels, among them WILLIAM DEAN HOWELLS's *A MODERN INSTANCE*, *THE RISE OF SILAS LAPHAM* and *The Minister's Charge*; HENRY JAMES's *THE BOSTONIANS*; JACK LONDON's *THE SEA WOLF* and GEORGE WASHINGTON CABLE's *Dr Sevier*. In 1925 the title became *The Century Monthly Magazine*, and from May through August 1929 *The Century Magazine*. In the autumn of 1929 it became a quarterly publication called *The Century Quarterly*; it was merged with *Forum* in 1930.

Chamberlayne, William 1619–89 Poet. He was a physician in Shaftesbury, Dorset. *Pharonnida* (1659) is a heroic romance in couplets – the poetic fashion of his day – which runs to 14,000 lines. His play *Love's Victory* was published in 1658.

Chambers, Sir E(dmund) K(erchever) 1866–1956 Literary scholar. Born in Berkshire, the son of a clergyman, Chambers was educated at Marlborough and at Corpus Christi College, Oxford, where he began his work on SHAKESPEARE with an edition of *RICHARD II* (1891). His working life from 1892 to 1926 was spent as a civil servant in the Education Department (later reconstituted as the Board of Education), and although his researches into the history of English drama were conducted in his spare time, they were outstanding contributions to scholarship. He was the first president (1906–39) of the Malone Society founded by W. W. GREG for the reprinting of early English plays, and to this field of learning he brought a civil servant's deliberative care in sifting the evidence of authorship and chronology, as shown in his major works *The Medieval Stage* (2 vols., 1903), *The Elizabethan Stage* (4 vols., 1923) and *William Shakespeare: A Study of the Facts and Problems* (2 vols., 1930). He wrote a survey of Arthurian legend, *Arthur of Britain* (1927), and biographies of S. T. COLERIDGE and MATTHEW ARNOLD, produced editions of Shakespeare, DONNE and MILTON, and also edited *The Oxford Book of Sixteenth-Century Verse* (1932).

Chance A novel by JOSEPH CONRAD, published in 1913. Marlow is the chief of several narrators who tell the story of Flora de Barral, a victim of emotional isolation.

An uncaring governess undermines her self-confidence, and her father's financial ruin and imprisonment leave her feeling insipid and unlovable. She is rescued from depression by Captain Roderick Anthony, but their marriage is blighted by doubts about her own worth and remains unconsummated. Anthony, moreover, is told by her friends, Mr and Mrs

Fyne, that Flora's motives are self-interested and pru-
dential. After her father's release from prison all
three live on board Anthony's ship, the *Ferndale*. But
de Barral, unbalanced by imprisonment, regards his
daughter's marriage as a betrayal. He tries to poison
Anthony and takes his own life when discovered by
Powell, the second mate. Though she is unaware of
these facts, her father's death helps Flora communicate with Anthony. When Anthony dies in an accident
at sea several years later, there is some prospect of a
romance between Powell and Flora. However, it is the
forces which control and over-determine conduct
which mostly engage Conrad in a novel whose title is
strongly ironic.

Chances, The A comedy by JOHN FLETCHER, apparently *c.* 1617 but not published until 1647, when it appeared with a prologue and epilogue by another
hand. Based on a novel by Cervantes, it contains some
of his best writing. The 'chances' are the coincidences
and complications that beset Constantia and the
Duke of Ferrara when they decide to elope. Others
concerned are Vecchio, a wizard, Dame Gillian, the
hostess, and two Spanish gallants, Don John and Don
Frederick.

Chandler, Raymond (Thornton) 1888–1959
American writer of DETECTIVE FICTION. Born in
Chicago and brought up in England, he worked as a
journalist and businessman before starting to write
fiction at the age of 45. His stories, published regularly in *THE BLACK MASK* magazine until 1939, are col-
lected in *Trouble is My Business* (1950), *Killer in the
Rain* (1964) and *The Smell of Fear* (1965). *The Big Sleep*
(1939) introduced his most famous character, the dis-
illusioned but chivalric detective Philip Marlowe,
who reappeared in *Farewell, My Lovely* (1940), *The
High Window* (1942), *The Lady in the Lake* (1943), *The
Little Sister* (1949), *The Long Goodbye* (1953) and
Playback (1958). Chandler discusses his work in *The
Simple Art of Murder* (1950) and the posthumous
Raymond Chandler Speaking (1962).

Changeling, The A tragedy by THOMAS MIDDLETON
and WILLIAM ROWLEY, first performed in 1622 and
published in 1653. The uncertainly related sub-plot,
possibly Rowley's contribution to the play, is often
omitted in performance.

Beatrice Joanna, daughter of the Governor of
Alicant, loves Alsemero. In order to avoid her
arranged marriage to Alonzo de Piracquo she enlists
the dangerous support of her father's physically repulsive servant, De Flores. It is the first in a train of
events that draws her, with a terrible logic, into the
clutches of De Flores, by whom she is both revolted
and fascinated. With Alonzo dead, killed by De Flores,
Beatrice Joanna can marry Alsemero, but the marriage is followed by a grotesque scene of feigned vir-

Raymond Chandler

ginity, which requires the complicity of her maid
Diaphanta. As a dangerous witness to the truth,
Diaphanta is also killed by De Flores; but Alsemero
has been growing suspicious and it is he who un-
masks the pair. Bound together to the end, Beatrice
Joanna and De Flores kill themselves.

The sub-plot concerns the efforts of Antonio to
seduce Isabella, the wife of an old and jealous doctor
who runs a lunatic asylum. In pursuit of his prey,
Antonio (he is the 'changeling' of the sub-plot as
Beatrice Joanna, in a subtler sense, is of the main
plot) pretends to be an idiot. But Isabella frustrates
the attempts to corrupt her, retaining the control of
her life that is utterly surrendered by Beatrice
Joanna.

Channing, William Ellery 1780–1842 American
minister and social reformer. Born in Newport, Rhode
Island, he studied at Harvard Divinity School, and was
ordained as a Congregational minister in 1803. His
'Baltimore Sermon' (*A Sermon Delivered at the
Ordination of the Rev Jared Sparks*, 1819) and *The
Moral Argument against Calvinism* (1820) state
plainly his opposition to the dogma and coercion of
strict Calvinist theology, and his rejection of the tenet
that man is essentially depraved. These revisionist
ideas were common among many of Channing's
circle, which included such important New England
writers as RALPH WALDO EMERSON, HENRY DAVID

THOREAU, MARGARET FULLER and BRONSON ALCOTT. He put forth his ideas on pacifism, prison reform, child labour, education and slavery – which he opposed fiercely – in many pamphlets and sermons. In his time his views were widely discussed, and his influence was considerable.

chapbooks Popular literature, especially profuse during the 18th century, sold by wandering dealers ('chapmen') and comprising BALLADS, folk-tales, assorted tracts, fairy-tales, contemporary legends and short biographical pieces. Generally illustrated with woodcuts, they numbered 16 or 24 pages depending on format, and were priced at a few pennies.

Chapman, George c. 1560–1634 Poet, translator and playwright. His considerable learning, combined with a belief that the true meaning of poetry need reveal itself only to the few, made his work notoriously difficult and often obscure. Very little is known of his life, but his creative output is clearly divisible.

Of his poetry, as distinct from his translations, the two poetical hymns combined in *The Shadow of Night* (1594) are the earliest to have survived. The three-level ALLEGORY, philosophical, political and poetic, of the second is particularly complex. *Ovids Banquet of Sence* (1595) obliquely advocates true Platonism as a counter to Ovidian eroticism. The correction and completion of MARLOWE's *HERO AND LEANDER* (1598) was undertaken in order to confirm and strengthen the poem's moral seriousness. *Euthymiae Raptus* (1609), better known by its alternative title *The Teares of Peace*, is a carefully constructed defence of learning in which the poetic form of the medieval DREAM-VISION is the vehicle for Platonic, Stoic and Christian speculation. *An Epicede or Funerall Song on the Death of Henry Prince of Wales* (1612) laments the loss of a valuable patron.

Of Chapman's translations, the most famous, not least because of a much-quoted sonnet by JOHN KEATS, are Homeric. *Seven Books of the Iliad* (1598) and *Achilles' Shield* (1598) announced the beginning of what Chapman called 'The Worke that I was borne to doe'. The complete *Iliads* (1611) and *Homer's Odyssey* (1614–15) are translations not only from one language to another, but also from one age and culture to another. Chapman interprets the ethical and philosophical views which he believed to be inherent in the Homeric original. Such monumental labour inevitably eclipses the shorter translations from Petrarch (1612), Musaeus (1616), Hesiod (1618) and Juvenal (1629).

The date of Chapman's first involvement with the theatre is uncertain. He was certainly associated with PHILIP HENSLOWE and the Admiral's Men in 1595–6, when *The Blind Beggar of Alexandria* was produced, and he was considered among the best poets for both tragedy and comedy in FRANCIS MERES's *Palladis Tamia* (1598). Some early plays have obviously been lost. *An Humorous Day's Mirth* (1597) strongly supports claims that Chapman's friendship with BEN JONSON was mutually influential. Other surviving comedies, probably written for the BOYS' COMPANIES with which Chapman was associated in the first decade of the 17th century, are *The Gentleman Usher* (c. 1602), *ALL FOOLS* (1599 or 1604), *Monsieur D'Olive* (1604), *Sir Giles Goosecap, Knight* (c. 1604), *THE WIDOW'S TEARS* (c. 1605) and *May Day* (1609). For his part-authorship, with Jonson and JOHN MARSTON, of *EASTWARD HO* (1605), a splendid city comedy, Chapman was imprisoned in the Tower of London. In his tragedies he writes repeatedly of deeply flawed Titanic heroes, philosophically removed from the recent French history in which they figured. It is these overreachers who give their names to *BUSSY D'AMBOIS* (1604), *THE CONSPIRACY AND TRAGEDY OF CHARLES, DUKE OF BYRON, MARSHAL OF FRANCE* (1608), *THE REVENGE OF BUSSY D'AMBOIS* (c. 1610) and *Chabot, Admiral of France* (c. 1613). To earn Jonson's commendation, Chapman probably wrote more masques than the single surviving *Memorable Masque of the Middle Temple and Lyncolnes Inn* (1613).

Chapone, Hester 1727–1801 Moralist and BLUE-STOCKING. Daughter of Thomas Mulso, a country gentleman, she was taught Latin, French and Italian, and wrote her first fiction at nine. She met ELIZABETH CARTER, the linguist, and became a friend of SAMUEL RICHARDSON. In Susannah Highmore's sketch of Richardson reading *THE HISTORY OF SIR CHARLES GRANDISON* aloud to female friends, she is in the centre. She married John Chapone, an attorney and friend of Richardson, but he died soon afterwards.

Author of tales in verse and essays, she is remembered chiefly for her *Letters on the Improvement of the Mind* (1773), a seminal work in the moral education of generations of girls (see CONDUCT BOOKS). Lydia Languish, in SHERIDAN's *THE RIVALS*, pushes SMOLLETT's and FIELDING's novels out of sight, and pretends to be reading Mrs Chapone. Among Mrs Chapone's exhortations are the necessity for humility, sincerity and uprightness of heart; pride and vanity are to be subdued by reason and grace. The affections must be 'regulated' and the temper 'governed'. She also published *A Letter to a New Married Lady* (1777). Her correspondence and a memoir were published posthumously (1807, 1808).

Charles, Duke of Byron, Marshal of France, The Conspiracy and Tragedy of A double play by GEORGE CHAPMAN, first performed by a BOYS' COMPANY in 1608, when its references to recent history (the Marshal of France had been executed in 1602) gave grave offence to the French ambassador, who succeeded in getting the play banned. Chapman protested to the Office of the Revels of 'Illiterate

Authority' that 'sets up his Bristles against Poverty', adding the interesting claim that 'I see not mine own plays; nor carry the Actors' Tongues in my mouth.'

In the first play, the restlessly ambitious Herculean hero is discovered in his conspiracy against the French king, Henri IV, asks forgiveness and is pardoned. In the second play he again conspires, is again discovered and dwindles into cringing despair before being executed.

Charley's Aunt An immensely successful FARCE, the only play by which its author, BRANDON THOMAS, is remembered. It ran for four years after its opening in London in 1892. Lord Fancourt Babberly, an amiable Oxford aristocrat, is prevailed upon to aid the amorous designs of two friends by impersonating his rich aunt. The troubles begin when the real aunt arrives in Oxford.

Charlotte Temple: *A Tale of Truth* A novel by SUSANNA ROWSON, published in England in 1791 and in America in 1794. Modelled on SAMUEL RICHARDSON's *CLARISSA*, it sold poorly in England but was a great success in the USA. Intended as a warning against the dangers of seduction, the book is full of authorial admonitions.

Charlotte, a 15-year-old pupil at Mme Du Pont's school for young ladies, is wooed by Montraville, an army officer. They elope to New York, where Montraville, despite qualms of conscience, soon deserts Charlotte for an heiress, Julia Franklin. Charlotte is now stranded, and pregnant. She looks in vain for help, and is even rebuffed by her former schoolteacher, Mlle La Rue, the woman of moral laxity who had introduced her to Montraville in the first place. Charlotte dies in poverty after giving birth to Montraville's illegitimate child, Lucy. Montraville is conscience-stricken, but returns to Julia. Mlle La Rue dies in ignominy. Charlotte's father adopts Lucy.

Chaste Maid in Cheapside, A A comedy by THOMAS MIDDLETON, first performed in 1611 and published in 1630. One of the richest CITIZEN COMEDIES, it parades mercantile double-dealing as if it were the norm, exposing its characters' obsessive concern with sex, procreation and genteel inheritance. As so often in the work of Middleton, there is not so much a plot as a variety of plots, unified (if at all) by the shared involvement and eventual discomforting of Sir Walter Whorehound.

Whorehound hopes to marry Moll Yellowhammer, daughter of an avaricious goldsmith. He encourages a strategic marriage between his own discarded mistress (the 'chaste' maid of the title) and Moll's birdbrained brother Tim. But Moll loves Touchwood Junior, and a major strand in the play details their eventually successful struggles to be united. Another follows the adventures of the childless Sir Oliver and

Lady Kix, whose fortune Whorehound will inherit. Once again, however, the dissolute Whorehound is worsted when, after some hilarious trickery, Lady Kix is impregnated by Touchwood Senior while the impotent Sir Oliver takes medicine and exercise. Having lost his inheritance and his hopes of marriage, Whorehound turns for help to the Allwits – Mistress Allwit's affair with him has been happily condoned by Allwit because Whorehound has 'maintained my house this ten years' – and is roundly rejected. Now that Whorehound is impecunious, the Allwits plan to set up a bawdy-house in the Strand. Whorehound is arrested for debt. The play's realistic vision is nicely conveyed by the fact that the complacent Allwit comes nearer than any other character to being its 'hero'.

Chatterton, Thomas 1752–70 Poet. He was born in Bristol, the son of a schoolmaster, and published his first poem when he was 11. He was educated at a charity school, Colston's Hospital, and apprenticed to an attorney when he was 14. His family was associated with the church of St Mary Redcliffe, and Chatterton, who could fabricate pedigrees and coats of arms from supposed originals, became interested in the archives of the parish. He made 15th-century Bristol the setting for the supposed poems of 'Thomas Rowley, a Secular Priest of St John's'. His principal source was the documents relating to a 15th-century merchant and mayor of Bristol, William Canynges, who became the imaginary patron of the imaginary Rowley.

In April 1770 he went to London. A practised writer – he had been contributing to London journals since the year before – he might have succeeded in earning a living, but the poems which he offered to DODSLEY and the document he offered to HORACE WALPOLE were refused, and only one of the Rowley poems, 'Elinoure and Juga', was published in Chatterton's lifetime (in *The Town and Country Magazine* in 1769). In a fit of depression Chatterton took arsenic and died in a room in Holborn, London, on 24 August 1770. He was not yet 18.

A single poem, 'Bristowe Tragedie: or The Dethe of Syr Charles Bawdin', was published in 1772; the remainder of the Rowley poems were collected and edited by the CHAUCER scholar THOMAS TYRWHITT in 1777. Tyrwhitt and many others were persuaded that the poems were genuine, but GRAY, PERCY and THOMAS WARTON THE YOUNGER doubted their authenticity. Tyrwhitt himself was induced to reconsider, and the 1778 edition of *Poems, Supposed to Have Been Written at Bristol, by Thomas Rowley, and Others, in the Fifteenth Century* contained 'An Appendix Tending to Prove that They Were Written by Chatterton'.

With their archaic vocabulary and Spenserian style, the poems none the less reveal a genuine talent. Chatterton became an object of admiration to the Romantics, who recognized his youthful genius and were impressed by the histrionic circumstances of his death. WORDSWORTH remembered him as 'the marvellous boy... that perished in his pride' and KEATS dedicated *ENDYMION* to his memory.

Chatwin, Bruce 1940–89 Travel writer and novelist. He worked for Sotheby's auction house and *The Sunday Times* before developing into a maverick and splendidly uncategorizable talent, notable for having challenged the conventions of travel writing, autobiography, history and fiction with a succession of *sui generis* works which frequently combine all four genres. The alternation of minute esoterica with vast imaginative leaps in his first book, *In Patagonia* (1977), characterized his customary voice. His introduction to a reprint of ROBERT BYRON's *The Road to Oxiana* in 1981 paid homage to an equivalently iconoclastic and magpie-like sensibility. *The Viceroy of Ouidah* (1980) is a predominantly historical monograph about the African slave kingdom of Dahomey. *On the Black Hill* (1982) is ungainsayably a novel, in PASTORAL mode, about twin brothers running a Welsh hill farm. Chatwin finally incorporated the prolonged and hitherto indeterminate thesis on nomadism which had impelled his own travels from Afghanistan to Africa into *The Songlines* (1987). It develops a partly fictionalized investigation of the psychic mapping traditions of the Australian Aborigines into arcane but passionately felt speculation about nothing less than the origins of human civilization. *Utz* (1988) is a brief, lapidary novel about a collector of Dresden china. Shorter pieces were posthumously gathered in *What am I Doing Here* (1989).

The Knight's Tale from Chaucer's *Canterbury Tales*: an illustration from Richard Pynson's 1526 edition

Chaucer, Geoffrey Before 1346–1400 The son of a wealthy London vintner, he was perhaps educated at St Paul's Cathedral School and later studied at the Inner Temple. He became a page to Elizabeth, Countess of Ulster, and Prince Lionel, but it is not known how long he remained in this service. It was at least until he was involved in military campaigns in France in 1359–60; he was ransomed in March 1360 and returned to England but was again in France later that year. Nothing is known of his life between 1360 and 1367 except that he entered the king's service; he received a pension from Edward III in 1367. He married Philippa, probably in 1366, and apparently had two sons, Lewis (to whom he dedicated *A TREATISE ON THE ASTROLABE*) and Thomas.

Between *c.* 1368 and 1378 he conducted diplomatic missions to Europe, including Italy, which he first visited *c.*1373; Italian culture was to become a strong influence on his poetry. During this period he was also connected with John of Gaunt, either receiving his patronage or being in his service, or both. In 1374 he received a house in Aldgate where he lived until 1385 or 1386. Also in 1374 he undertook a series of professional and official appointments including a post as a customs official. His appointments increased in importance and he became prosperous, but in 1385 he left the Custom House and retired to Kent where he was a justice of the peace and, in 1386, knight of the shire and MP. Whether his retirement was voluntary is unrecorded, but he was not re-elected to Parliament after his only session in 1386. Only after Richard II reached the age of majority and took over from Gloucester in 1389 did Chaucer receive any new preferments. In that year he was appointed Clerk of the King's Works and supervised construction, maintenance and renovation work, travelling constantly for two years. He left the post in 1391 and became deputy forester of the royal forest of North Petherton, Somerset. This was his last regular office; his appointment was renewed in 1398 but it is not known for how long he maintained it. Late in 1399 he moved to Westminster, dying there the following year; his tomb in Westminster Abbey became the nucleus of Poets' Corner.

Generally considered to be the greatest English poet of the Middle Ages, Chaucer was recognized during his lifetime and remained extremely influential throughout the 15th century. The canon of his writings has now been established, with only a few short pieces and the translation *THE ROMAUNT OF THE ROSE* remaining uncertain, but from the 15th to the 19th centuries much spurious material was attributed to him (see CHAUCERIAN APOCRYPHA). The chronology of his poetry is less certain, and of the longer pieces only *THE BOOK OF THE DUCHESS* can be attached to a definite event, the death of Blanche, Duchess of Lancaster in 1368. The other works can be put into an approximate order by their relation to each other, the dates of known sources and the influence of French and Italian literary traditions. *The Book of the Duchess*, some of the short poems and *The ABC* were written before 1372 and show the influence of French poets. Italian influence begins to appear in the works ascribed to the period 1372–80: *THE HOUSE OF FAME*, *Anelida and Arcite*, early versions of *The Second Nun's Tale* and *The Monk's Tale*, and some of the lyrics form this group. Between 1380 and 1386 *THE PARLEMENT OF FOULES*, *BOECE*, *TROILUS AND CRISEYDE*, an early version of *The Knight's Tale*, *THE LEGEND OF GOOD WOMEN* and some short poems were written, in all of which the Italian influence appears fully assimilated. *The General Prologue* and the early stories of *THE CANTERBURY TALES* were written between 1387 and 1392, and *A Treatise on the Astrolabe* in 1391–2. The later *Canterbury Tales* and final short poems date from 1393–1400. The doubtful translation of *Le Roman de la rose* cannot be placed with certainty; it may belong with *The Book of the Duchess* in the period of French influence, but the Prologue to *The Legend of Good Women* links it with *Troilus and Criseyde* (c. 1385).

Although frequently imitated, Chaucer's blend of humour, realism, philosophical depth, poetic virtuosity, and masterful control of dialogue and character was never matched. The pervasive humour (sometimes vulgar) is directed at various targets, and the poet appears as the butt of his own jokes throughout the canon; in *The Canterbury Tales* it is Chaucer who cannot tell a tale competently and in the DREAM-VISIONS he appears as naive, ignorant and foolish. His translations are highly workmanlike and his use of philosophical ideas, though sometimes derived from intermediate texts, consistently demonstrates his understanding of them. As a storyteller he is supreme, and it is for this that he is known best. In the framework of *The Canterbury Tales* he develops both character and dialogue, and the extended characterization in *Troilus and Criseyde* has made critics liken the poem to a novel. His favourite verse forms are the decasyllabic couplet and RHYME ROYAL, but *The Romaunt of the Rose* is in octosyllabic couplets; he also wrote in prose, though less well, in *Boece* and *A Treatise on the Astrolabe*, as well as *The Tale of Melibee* and *The Parson's Tale*.

Chaucer made a crucial contribution to English literature in using English at a time when much court poetry was still written in ANGLO-NORMAN or Latin. His confidence in the language encouraged his followers and imitators also to write in English and speeded the transition from French as the language of literature.

Chaucerian apocrypha Body of material once attributed to GEOFFREY CHAUCER, much of it included in early editions of his works. It includes over 100 pieces of verse. The 15th-century manuscript distributor John Shirley instigated many of the early erroneous attributions and remains the only authority for some poems still accepted as the work of Chaucer. Early editions such as those of Pynson (1526), Thynne (1532) and Stow (1561) contain several apocryphal works and the canon was not revised until the 19th century. The apocrypha includes works by other known poets such as JOHN LYDGATE (*THE SIEGE OF THEBES*, *THE FALL OF PRINCES* and others), ROBERT HENRYSON (*THE TESTAMENT OF CRESSEID*), THOMAS USK (*The Testament of Love*) and JOHN GOWER. There are also additions to *THE CANTERBURY TALES* – *THE PLOWMAN'S TALE*, *The Tale of Beryn* and *THE TALE OF GAMELYN* – and anonymous pieces on various themes, including *THE ASSEMBLY OF LADIES*, *THE CUCKOO AND THE NIGHTINGALE*, *THE FLOWER AND THE LEAF* and *JACK UPLAND*. The degree to which these poems are Chaucerian in style and content varies, and some resemble the presently established canon hardly at all.

Chaudhuri, Nirad C(handra) 1897– Indian writer. He was born in Kishorganj, Bengal. His literary career began late, with *The Autobiography of An Unknown Indian* (1951), described by V. S. NAIPAUL as 'the one great book to come out of the Anglo-Indian encounter'. A massive second volume, *Thy Hand, Great Anarch!* (1987), contains an affecting estimate of TAGORE's place in Bengali culture. A travel book, *A Passage to England* (1960), and two biographies, *Clive of India* (1975) and his account of F. M. Muller, *Scholar Extraordinary* (1975), unravel many strands in British–Indian relations. *The Continent of Circe* (1965) argues that Indians are displaced Europeans at odds with their Indian geography. His energy found further exercise in *Culture in the Vanity Bag* (1976) and *Hinduism: A Religion to Live By* (1979). The British Government awarded him an honorary CBE in 1992.

Cheever, John 1912–82 American short-story writer and novelist. He was born in Quincy, Massachusetts, and educated at Thayer Academy. Much of his fiction deals humorously and compassionately with the spiritually and emotionally impoverished life in materially affluent communities. His first novel, *The Wapshot Chronicle* (1957), won the 1958 National Book Award. In 1965 he received the Howells Medal for Fiction from the National Academy of Arts and Letters. His other novels include *The Wapshot Scandal* (1964), *Bullet Park* (1969), *Falconer* (1977) and *Oh, What a Paradise It Seems* (1982). His short stories, many of which appeared originally in *THE NEW YORKER* and *THE NEW REPUBLIC*, were collected in *The Way Some People Live: A Book of Short Stories* (1943), *The Enormous Radio and Other Stories*

(1953), *Stories* (1956), *The Housebreaker of Shady Hill and Other Stories* (1958), *Some People, Places, and Things That Will Not Appear in My Next Novel* (1961), *The Brigadier and the Golf Widow* (1964), *Homage to Shakespeare* (1965), *The World of Apples* (1973) and *The Day the Pig Fell into the Well* (1978). *The Stories of John Cheever* (1978) received a PULITZER PRIZE and a National Book Critics Circle Award. His posthumously published letters (edited by Benjamin Cheever; 1988) and journals (1991) revealed a tormented private life apparently at odds with the often urbane character of his fiction.

Chesney, Sir George Tomkyns 1830–95 Novelist. Born in Devon, he pursued a distinguished military career in India. His first novel, *The Battle of Dorking*, a fictional account of an enemy attack on England, was published by *BLACKWOOD'S MAGAZINE* in 1871 and frequently reprinted. Other novels were *The Dilemma* (1876), set at the time of the Indian mutiny, *The New Ordeal* (1879), *The Private Secretary* (1881) and *The Lesters* (1893).

Chesnutt, Charles W(addell) 1858–1932 Black American short-story writer and novelist. He was born in Cleveland, Ohio, to parents who recently had left Fayetteville, North Carolina, to escape the repression of free blacks in the South at the time. After the Civil War, the family returned to Fayetteville, where Chesnutt's education included instruction in German, French and Greek. After some years as a schoolteacher in the Carolinas, in 1883 he went to New York City to work as a reporter, and then moved to Cleveland, where he began his career as a writer.

His work came to the attention of a national audience when his story 'The Goophered Grapevine' was published in *THE ATLANTIC MONTHLY* in 1887. He rapidly mastered the conventions of the short narrative aimed at readers of the popular literary magazines of his day, and this urbane, fluent style is seen in his first two collections of stories, *The Conjure Woman* and *The Wife of His Youth and Other Stories of the Color Line*, both published in 1899. Despite his adoption of prevailing literary forms, Chesnutt is considered a pioneer of black fiction, with his probing exploration of racial themes and his realistic view of slavery and the Reconstruction era. In his later works he focused on the problems of racial and class identity in a changing society. He wrote three novels, *The House behind the Cedars* (1900), *The Marrow of Tradition* (1901) and *The Colonel's Dream* (1906), and regularly published essays and reviews in various journals.

Chester cycle See MIRACLE PLAYS.

Chesterfield, Philip Dormer Stanhope, 4th Earl of 1694–1773 Statesman and writer. Born in St James's Square, Westminster, he was educated at home and at Trinity College, Cambridge. After the customary Grand Tour for the sons of gentlemen he entered Parliament (1716) and became England's ambassador at The Hague from 1728 to 1732. With the fall of Walpole's government Lord Chesterfield (he succeeded to the title in 1726) entered Newcastle's cabinet as Secretary of State (1744), and became Lord Lieutenant of Ireland from 1745 to 1746. In that difficult post he acquitted himself with honour, earning the gratitude of the people for his tolerance. Although he found Newcastle a difficult colleague, he served as Secretary of State again from 1746 until 1748, when he retired.

A kindly and witty man who mixed in literary circles, Chesterfield was one of the most pleasant letter-writers in English. His most famous letters were written to his illegitimate son Philip Stanhope (1732–68) and published by his son's widow as *Letters to his Son, Philip Stanhope, Together with Several Other Pieces on Various Subjects* (1774). Affectionate, spontaneous and shrewd, they are full of advice and guidance which amount to a CONDUCT BOOK in the ways of the world. A second and similar series of letters to his godson and heir, also Philip Stanhope, first appeared as *The Art of Pleasing: in a Series of Letters to Master Stanhope* (1774).

Chesterfield has also acquired an undeserved literary notoriety as the epitome of churlish patrons for his treatment of SAMUEL JOHNSON. On his publisher's advice Johnson addressed his original *Plan* (1747) for his *DICTIONARY OF THE ENGLISH LANGUAGE* to Chesterfield, who failed to respond but belatedly commended the work on its publication in 1755. Johnson expressed his anger in a famous letter of 7 February 1755: 'Is not a patron, my lord, one who looks with unconcern on a man struggling for life in the water, and, when he has reached ground, encumbers him with help? The notice which you have been pleased to take of my labours, had it been early, had been kind; but it has been delayed... till I am known and do not want it.'

Chesterton, G(ilbert) K(eith) 1874–1936 Poet, novelist, writer of DETECTIVE FICTION, critic, journalist and essayist. Born on Camden Hill, London, he was educated at St Paul's School and the Slade. His talent as an illustrator can be seen in his contributions to the novels of his friend, HILAIRE BELLOC, but he made a more definite mark by his own prolific writings. He first published articles in *The Bookman* and *The Illustrated London News* and, like Belloc, contributed to *The Speaker*, in which he made known his anti-imperial sentiments during the Boer War. His first book was a collection of verse and sketches, *Greybeards at Play – Literature and Art for Old Gentlemen* (1900). This was followed by *The Wild Knight and Other Poems* (1900). Most of his verse, which tends to celebrate the 'Englishness' of England, can be found in

Collected Poems, published in 1933. Chesterton's first novel, *The Napoleon of Notting Hill* (1904), was a political fantasy which, like much of his work, reflected his distaste for the modern world of business and centralized power and celebrated the romance of an earlier pre-industrial world. Similar sentiments informed *The Man Who was Thursday: A Nightmare* (1908). *The Innocence of Father Brown* (1911) started an enduringly popular series of detective stories about an unassuming Catholic priest whose gift for solving complex mysteries springs largely from his insight into evil. Chesterton himself became a Roman Catholic in 1922.

Of his literary criticism, Chesterton's book about CHARLES DICKENS (1906) was particularly influential and is still by no means a period piece; other studies include books on ROBERT BROWNING (1903), GEORGE BERNARD SHAW and WILLIAM BLAKE (both 1910), and CHAUCER (1932). Works on social, political and religious subjects include *Heretics* (1905), *Orthodoxy* (1909), *St Francis of Assisi* (1923) and *St Thomas Aquinas* (1933). Collections of his essays appeared as *All Things Considered* (1908), *A Miscellany of Men* (1912), *The Uses of Diversity* (1920), and *As I was Saying* (1936). His *Autobiography* appeared in 1936.

Chestre, Thomas 14th-century poet who wrote SIR LAUNFAL and possibly also LIBEAUS DESCONUS. Nothing else is known about him.

Chettle, Henry *c.* 1560–*c.* 1607 Particularly active as a playwright – he had a hand in about 50 plays – Chettle made his first significant contribution to Elizabethan literature as a printer, when he prepared *Greene's Groatsworth of Wit* for publication in 1592. When the printing house in which he was a partner failed, Chettle turned to writing. His satirical dream-fable *Kind Harts Dreame* (1593) is best remembered for its preface, in which he expresses regret for GREENE's abuse of SHAKESPEARE. *Piers Plainnes Seaven Yeres Prentiship* (1595) is a picaresque romance better than many of its voguish kind.

By 1598 Chettle was providing plays for PHILIP HENSLOWE and the Admiral's Men. That he was living hand-to-mouth is clear from his imprisonment for debt in the Marshalsea that year. Most of his plays are lost. Of those that survive only *Hoffman: or, A Revenge for a Father* (*c.* 1603) is believed to be his alone. It is a REVENGE TRAGEDY. Two pieces written in collaboration with ANTHONY MUNDAY are generally regarded as his most interesting work, not only because they deal with the ROBIN HOOD legend. Both performed in 1598, *The Downfall of Robert, Earl of Huntingdon* and *The Death of Robert, Earl of Huntingdon* illustrate the Elizabethan theatre's avidity to capitalize on success. As well as contributing to SIR THOMAS MORE, Chettle collaborated with William Haughton and THOMAS DEKKER on PATIENT GRISSEL

(1600) and with JOHN DAY on *The Blind Beggar of Bednal-Green* (1600). His elegy on the death of Elizabeth I, *England's Mourning Garment* (1603), is charming but slight.

chiasmus A type of ANTITHESIS. Where the contrasting parts of the normal antithesis stand in the relation ab/ab, those of a chiasmus form a mirror-image, ab/ba: 'A Fop[a] their Passion[b]/ but their Prize[b] a Sot[a]' (POPE, MORAL ESSAYS).

Child, F(rancis) J(ames) 1825–96 American scholar. He was born in Boston and educated at Harvard University, where he became Boylston professor of rhetoric in 1851 and professor of English in 1876. His friends and colleagues included CHARLES ELIOT NORTON, JAMES RUSSELL LOWELL and LONGFELLOW. The editor of SPENSER and the author of philological studies of CHAUCER and GOWER, he is remembered for his collections of BALLADS, particularly the five-volume *English and Scottish Popular Ballads*, originally issued in 10 parts between 1883 and 1898. See also FOLK REVIVAL.

Child, Lydia M(aria) 1802–80 American social reformer and novelist. Born in Medford, Massachusetts, Child is best remembered as a leading Abolitionist. She achieved her greatest success with her 'Appeal in Favor of that Class of Americans Called Africans' (1833). Her persuasive letters to the governor of Virginia were later published as *Correspondence* (1860), and won many adherents to the anti-slavery cause. She also wrote several novels, including *Hobomok* (1824), a didactic story about the Indians of colonial Massachusetts, *The Rebels: or, Boston before the Revolution* (1825), about the Stamp Tax agitation, and *Philothea* (1836), a romance set in classical Greece.

Child of the Jago, A A novel by ARTHUR MORRISON, published in 1896. 'The Jago', Morrison's name for 'The Nichol' in London's Bethnal Green, is the setting for this story about the childhood of Dick ('Dicky') Perrott. A boy with good intentions, he is constantly frustrated by his environment – a 'violent jungle' in which his father is hanged for murder and Dicky himself is killed in a street fight at the age of 17. Morrison's terse, straightforward style owes something to GEORGE MOORE and looks ahead to the social realism of a later generation of writers. His refusal to impose his own moral judgements on the various criminals in the book distinguished him from most of his late-Victorian contemporaries.

Childe Harold's Pilgrimage A poem by BYRON, written in SPENSERIAN STANZAS. The first two CANTOS were published in 1812, the third in 1816, and the fourth in 1818. The poem was begun in Albania in

1809 during Byron's visit to the eastern Mediterranean with John Cam Hobhouse.

It describes the wanderings of a young man, disillusioned with his empty pleasure-seeking existence, who looks for distraction in foreign scenes, travelling through Spain, Portugal, Albania and Greece whose 'haunted, holy ground' had made an indelible impression on the poet's mind. The third canto follows the pilgrim to Belgium on the eve of Waterloo, along the Rhine and to the Alps and Jura. Finally, speaking in his own voice, Byron describes a literary and historical tour of Italy invoking the associations of Venice, Arqua, Florence and Rome.

Childe Harold's Pilgrimage was immediately popular – after the publication of the first two cantos Byron 'woke one morning and found myself famous' – and made the melancholy 'Byronic hero' one of the most recognizable figures in English and European ROMANTICISM.

Childe Roland to the Dark Tower Came A poem by ROBERT BROWNING published in *Men and Women* (1855). The title is taken from SHAKESPEARE'S *KING LEAR* (III, iv, 173). This masterful and enigmatic nightmare poem was apparently one result of a resolution made by Browning in 1852 to write a poem a day.

Childers, (Robert) Erskine 1870–1922 Novelist and political pamphleteer. Born of an Anglo-Irish family in London, and educated at Haileybury College and Trinity College, Cambridge, Childers served in the Boer War and World War I. After working as a clerk in the House of Commons (1895–1910), he settled in Dublin in 1919 and devoted himself to the cause of Irish Home Rule. He joined the Irish Republican Army after the establishment of the Irish Free State, and was arrested and executed. Although his political pamphlets on military affairs and the Irish question are forgotten, his one novel, *The Riddle of the Sands* (1903), is not. A slow-paced thriller, packed with yachting lore and polemical warnings of Germany's military ambitions, it remains notable for its portrait of the two well-contrasted heroes, the dandified civil servant Carruthers and the homespun amateur sailor Davies.

Children of the New Forest, The See MARRYAT, FREDERICK.

children's companies of actors See BOYS' COMPANIES.

children's literature Stories and poems aimed at children have an exceedingly long history: lullabies, for example, were sung in Roman times, and a few nursery games and rhymes are almost as ancient. Yet so far as written-down literature is concerned, while there were stories in print before 1700 that children

often seized on when they had the chance, such as translations of Aesop's fables, fairy-stories and popular BALLADS and romances, these were not aimed at young people in particular. Since the only genuinely child-oriented literature at this time would have been a few instructional works to help with reading and general knowledge, plus the odd Puritanical tract as an aid to morality, the only course for keen child readers was to raid adult literature. This still occurs today, especially with adult thrillers or romances that include more exciting, graphic detail than is normally found in literature for younger readers. For the boy or girl in the early 18th century the equivalent could have been BUNYAN'S *THE PILGRIM'S PROGRESS* (1678), DEFOE'S *THE ADVENTURES OF ROBINSON CRUSOE* (1719) or SWIFT'S *GULLIVER'S TRAVELS* (1726). The fact that all these classics soon appeared in simplified form suggests that such popularity among young readers had not been overlooked.

By the middle of the 18th century there were enough eager child readers, and enough parents glad to cater to this interest, for publishers to specialize in children's books whose first aim was pleasure rather than education or morality. In Britain, a London merchant named Thomas Boreham produced *Cajanus, The Swedish Giant* in 1742, while the more famous JOHN NEWBERY published *A Little Pretty Pocket Book* in 1744. Its contents – rhymes, stories, children's games plus a free gift ('A ball and a pincushion') – in many ways anticipated the similar lucky-dip contents of children's annuals this century. It is a tribute to Newbery's flair that he hit upon a winning formula quite so quickly, to be pirated almost immediately in America.

Such pleasing levity was not to last. Influenced by Rousseau, whose *Émile* (1762) decreed that all books for children save *Robinson Crusoe* were a dangerous diversion, contemporary critics saw to it that children's literature should be instructive and uplifting. Prominent among such voices was Mrs Sarah Trimmer, whose magazine *The Guardian of Education* (1802) carried the first regular reviews of children's books. It was she who condemned fairy-tales for their violence and general absurdity; her own stories, *Fabulous Histories* (1786), described talking animals who were always models of sense and decorum. In less fanciful vein, MARY SHERWOOD'S *The History of the Fairchild Family* (1818–47) contained dark moral warnings together with regular reference to biblical verses. That her book stayed in print so long is a tribute to her powers as a writer; a famous passage, where the Fairchild father takes his children to see a corpse on a gibbet as a final Awful Warning, had actually to be softened in later editions. Not for the first time, children may have thrilled to this part of the text with its horrific, Gothic overtones rather more wholeheartedly than its author intended. The stories of Captain FREDERICK MARRYAT too, such as *Masterman*

Ready (1841) or *Children of the New Forest* (1847), were popular for more reasons than their lengthy digressions on flora, fauna and British history. They also included passages of exciting action where both reader and writer could temporarily forget about self-improvement.

So the moral story for children was always threatened from within, given the way children have of drawing out entertainment from the sternest moralist. But the greatest blow to the improving children's book was to come from an unlikely source indeed: early 19th-century interest in folklore. Both nursery rhymes, selected by JAMES ORCHARD HALLIWELL for a folklore society in 1842, and collections of fairy-stories by the scholarly Grimm brothers, swiftly translated into English in 1823, soon rocketed to popularity with the young, quickly leading to new editions, each one more child-centred than the last. But another folklorist, Sir George Dasent, insisted on keeping his translation of Norse fairy-tales intact, merely suggesting – no doubt unrealistically – that all good children should ignore the two slightly racy examples at the end of the book. Later on, American children also had the chance of enjoying the legends of ROBIN HOOD (1883) and *King Arthur* (1903) skilfully reworked by HOWARD PYLE – another revivalist who provided rich fare for children, however occasionally worrying for the puritan conscience.

Those latter-day followers of Rousseau who still battled for 'sensible' stories continued to have a certain success despite the wrath of CHARLES DICKENS in his memorable essay of 1853, 'Frauds on the Fairies'. But by now history was against them: 1846, for example, saw the publication of EDWARD LEAR's *Book of Nonsense*, as anarchic as any rebellious child could wish, while THACKERAY's *THE ROSE AND THE RING* (1855) and CHARLES KINGSLEY's *THE WATER BABIES* (1863) continued to make an unanswerable case for fantasy and the imagination first, moral lessons second. All it needed was a masterpiece that not only avoided didacticism but actually made fun of it, and two years later this duly arrived with the appearance of LEWIS CARROLL's *ALICE'S ADVENTURES IN WONDERLAND* (1865).

From now on younger children could expect stories written for their particular interest and with the needs of their own limited experience of life kept well to the fore. In Britain, MRS JULIANA EWING, MRS MARY MOLESWORTH and CHARLOTTE M. YONGE produced excellent stories aimed at young girl readers in this spirit, and their success was repeated in America by SUSAN COOLIDGE in *What Katy Did* (1872), KATE DOUGLAS WIGGIN in *Rebecca of Sunnybrook Farm* (1903), Eleanor H. Porter in *Pollyanna* (1913), and by the Canadian writer L. M. MONTGOMERY in *ANNE OF GREEN GABLES* (1908). For boys, THOMAS HUGHES's classic *TOM BROWN'S SCHOOLDAYS* (1857) spawned a new generation of school-stories.

But while such books for younger children stood out on their own as the next stage after the large picture-books now available for fortunate infants from homes wealthy enough to afford such fare, older child readers and adults still tended to share each other's principal fare. R. M. BALLANTYNE's adventure stories were popular with all ages, for example, while Gladstone was an enthusiastic fan of ROBERT LOUIS STEVENSON's *TREASURE ISLAND* (1883), although on hearing this news the ungrateful author merely remarked, 'He would do better to attend to the Imperial affairs of England.' GEORGE MACDONALD's strange, mystical stories, such as *At the Back of the North Wind* (1871), also intrigued a wide audience, while ANNA SEWELL's *BLACK BEAUTY* (1877) was once set as compulsory reading material in prison by way of reform for an adult guilty of animal cruelty.

What eventually determined the reading of older children was often not the availability of special, children's literature as such but access to books that contained characters, such as young people or animals, with whom they could more easily identify, or action, such as exploring or fighting, that made few demands on adult maturity or understanding. Such a list encompassed G. A. HENTY's imperialistic adventures or FENIMORE COOPER's *The Last of the Mohicans* (1826; see *LEATHERSTOCKING TALES*), HARRIET BEECHER STOWE's *UNCLE TOM'S CABIN* (1852), LOUISA M. ALCOTT's *LITTLE WOMEN* (1868), MARK TWAIN's *THE ADVENTURES OF HUCKLEBERRY FINN* (1884) and FRANCES HODGSON BURNETT's *Little Lord Fauntleroy* (1885), also greatly admired by Gladstone. Mention must also be made of Dickens's novels, with a poll as late as 1888 still revealing him to be the most popular author with older children by a generous margin.

In time, however, adults themselves moved on to a narrower spectrum of imaginative literature, leaving genres they had once freely enjoyed – such as animal or fairy-stories – to a younger audience. In this way, masterpieces such as RUDYARD KIPLING's *THE JUNGLE BOOK* (1894), KENNETH GRAHAME's *THE WIND IN THE WILLOWS* (1908) or ANDREW LANG's collection of folk-stories would more often be found on children's than adults' bookshelves. At the same time magazines specifically directed at children sprang up in Britain and America, while a new generation of writers such as E. NESBIT took the children's story into the details of family life, imaginative games and domestic adventures that adults found less relevant to their current interests. In America FRANK L. BAUM's *The Wonderful Wizard of Oz* (1900) was another determinedly child-centred success, despite its doctrinaire morality, while Australian children could enjoy a comic masterpiece without adult pretensions, NORMAN LINDSAY's *The Magic Pudding* (1918). In poetry Robert Louis Stevenson's *A Child's Garden of Verses* (1885) set a standard unequalled until WALTER DE LA MARE's *Peacock Pie* (1913). More knockabout fare was provided by HILAIRE BELLOC's *The Bad Child's Book of Beasts* (1896), only rivalled in popularity years later by the publication of T. S. ELIOT's *Old Possum's Book of Practical Cats* (1939). At the same time sentimental verses for and about children, also very popular since the 19th century, finally touched bottom with the saccharine cadences of Rose Fyleman's *Fairies and Chimneys* (1918).

The inter-war period saw a further consolidation of children's literature as an exclusive empire, a process helped by the growing popularity of children's annuals, children's picture-books and the children's comic, now moving well away from its rougher, penny-dreadful origins towards something far gentler in taste. With books, plots became considerably softened, with the dangers of Kenneth Grahame's Wild Wood or Kipling's jungle giving way to the gentler concerns of A. A. MILNE's Ashdown Forest in *Winnie-the-Pooh* (1926) and HUGH LOFTING's amiably eccentric collection of humans and animals in *The Story of Doctor Dolittle* (1922). In ARTHUR RANSOME's adventure stories young people wrestled with sailing boats rather than with hostile enemies, while in NOEL STREATFEILD's *Ballet Shoes* (1936) the chief fear was failing an audition rather than encountering adult ostracism or family ruin. In America, though, LAURA INGALLS WILDER's *The Little House* series (1932–43) described a past that could be tough as well as warm and loving. Picture-books also lost some of the matter-of-fact treatment of danger and death found earlier in BEATRIX POTTER's stories for small children. Instead, EDWARD ARDIZZONE and William Nicholson in Britain or Munro Leaf and later DR SEUSS in America painted a world both safe and ultimately welcoming to all.

The final apotheosis of literary childhood as something to be protected from unpleasant reality came with the arrival in the late 1930s of child-centred bestsellers intent on entertainment at its most escapist. In Britain novelists such as ENID BLYTON and RICHMAL CROMPTON described children who were always free to have the most unlikely adventures, secure in the knowledge that nothing bad could ever happen to them in the end. The fact that war broke out again during her books' greatest popularity fails to register at all in the self-enclosed world inhabited by Enid Blyton's young characters, and for Richmal Crompton's mischievous creation, William, a country in arms just offers more opportunities for being a nuisance. Reaction against such dream-worlds was inevitable after World War II, coinciding with the growth of paperback sales, children's libraries and a new spirit of moral and social concern. Urged on by committed publishers and progressive librarians, writers slowly began to explore new areas of interest while also shifting the settings of their plots from the middle-class world to which their chiefly adult patrons had always previously belonged. In the realms

of fantasy a similar spirit of moral toughness is evident in the stories of C. S. LEWIS and J. R. R. TOLKIEN and later in the stories of ALAN GARNER and URSULA LEGUIN. Picture-books also began to experiment with off-beat stories and characters. Artist-illustrators like MAURICE SENDAK and RAYMOND BRIGGS explored the small child's timeless concern with death and aggression as well as lighter preoccupations.

Critical emphasis, during this development, has been divided. For some the most important task was to rid children's books of the social prejudice and exclusiveness no longer found acceptable. Others concentrated more on the positive achievements of contemporary children's literature, in particular those of British novelists like WILLIAM MAYNE, LEON GARFIELD, PHILIPPA PEARCE, JOAN AIKEN and NINA BAWDEN; American novelists like VIRGINIA HAMILTON, PAULA FOX and BETSY BYARS; and Australian novelists like PATRICIA WRIGHTSON, IVAN SOUTHALL and NAN CHAUNCY. That such writers are now often recommended to the attentions of adult as well as child readers echoes the 19th-century belief that children's literature can be shared by the generations, rather than being a defensive barrier between childhood and the necessary growth towards adult understanding.

Chillingworth, William 1602–44 Divine. A godson of LAUD, Chillingworth became a Roman Catholic in 1630 but returned to the Protestant fold and accepted preferment at Salisbury in 1638. In 1637 he published *The Religion of Protestants a Safe Way to Salvation*, which argued that disagreements among Protestants were not a spiritual hazard and caused heated controversy. A Royalist, he fought at the siege of Gloucester; he was captured at Arundel Castle, where he lay ill, and died the same year. NATHANIEL HAWTHORNE may have been remembering his reputation for Protestant polemic when he called one of his characters in *THE SCARLET LETTER* Chillingworth.

Chimes, The A Christmas story by CHARLES DICKENS, published in 1844 and collected in *CHRISTMAS BOOKS* (1852).

The Chimes is an uneasy amalgam of realism and fantasy built around the adventures of the simple, good-hearted Toby ('Trotty') Veck who, mesmerized by chiming bells and influenced by spirits, 'dwarf phantoms' and elfin creatures, witnesses the hardships of his daughter Meg, the falsely accused Will Fern and the orphaned Lilian. These good characters are maltreated or condescended to by Sir Joseph Bowley, Alderman Cute, Mr Filer and others. But the plight of the poor, as well as an appeal for deeper human feeling to be directed towards social improvement, is eloquently voiced by Will Fern. A final burst of goodwill resolves the various problems and effects a happy ending.

Ch'indaba See TRANSITION.

Chinodya, Shimmer 1957– Zimbabwean novelist. He was born in Gweru. *Harvest of Thorns* (1989) is a complex and compelling novel about the rite of passage, or 'harvest of thorns', of Benjamin Tichafa as he grows to maturity against the background of Rhodesia in the 1970s.

Chinweizu 1943– Nigerian critic and poet. Born in Eluama-Isuikwuato in Imo State, he was educated at Government College, Afikpo, the Massachusetts Institute of Technology and the State University of New York at Buffalo. He was Rockefeller Research Fellow in Environmental Economics at MIT in 1976 and taught Afro-Amerian studies at San Jose State University in 1978–9. He has published *The West and the Rest of Us* (1975), *Energy Crisis and Other Poems* (1978) and, with Onwuchekwa Jemie and Ihechukwu Madubuike, *Toward the Decolonization of African Literature* (1980). Unabashedly polemical, the last book denounces the Eurocentricity of non-African critics and the apostasy of their African sympathizers in repudiating the aesthetics of Negritude and thus the African inheritance. The discussion bridges the gap between universalists and localists by defining what is distinctively African in African literature, including examples of the central element of 'orature' and describing the multi-cultural dynamic which operates within the African context and its written literary expression.

Chomsky, Noam (Avram) 1928– American linguist and political activist. Born in Pennsylvania and educated at the University of Pennsylvania, he has taught at the Massachusetts Institute of Technology since 1955. As a linguist, he rehabilitated the study of grammar in such seminal works as *Syntactic Structures* (1957), *Aspects of the Theory of Syntax* (1965), *Cartesian Linguistics* (1966) and *Reflections on Language* (1976). Arguing that grammar is not learned but genetically innate, Chomsky's theory approximates to Cartesian theories of a 'universal grammar' in which psychological structures permit the formation of linguistic sentences. Later works include *Language and Problems of Knowledge* (1987) and *Language in a Psychological Setting* (1987).

Chomsky became a prominent political activist by his opposition to America's role in the Vietnam War. *At War with Asia* (1970) has been followed by a number of trenchant polemical works, which include: *Toward a New Cold War* (1982); *The Fateful Triangle* (1983), about the USA's relationship with Israel and the Palestinians; *Turning the Tide* (1985), about the USA's involvement in Central America; *Necessary Illusions* (1989); and *Deterring Democracy* (1991). *The Chomsky Reader* (1988) presents extracts from a wide range of his works.

Chopin, Kate 1851–1904 American novelist and short-story writer. Born Kate O'Flaherty in St Louis, Missouri, to an Irish father and French mother, she moved to New Orleans following her marriage to Oscar Chopin. After the death of her mother and husband, she began to devote herself to writing. Her first novel, *At Fault* (1890), showed the influence of Guy de Maupassant. This was followed by two collections of short stories set among Creoles and Acadians in Louisiana, *Bayou Folk* (1894) and *A Night in Acadie* (1897), which helped establish her as a leading exponent of the 'local colour' school. She also contributed regularly to popular and literary magazines. Her best-known work, THE AWAKENING, was published in 1899. Its sympathetic portrayal of a woman who rejects the constraints of marriage and motherhood provoked hostile criticism. The book was banned from the library shelves in Chopin's home town of St Louis, and following a reprint in 1906 went out of print for over 50 years.

Chrétien de Troyes See ARTHURIAN LITERATURE and COURTLY LOVE.

Christ An Old English poem in three parts, dealing with the Nativity, the Ascension and Doomsday. It is preserved in the EXETER BOOK. CYNEWULF's runic signature appears in the second section; it is not certain whether he also wrote the other two parts. The *Nativity* is freely adapted from the Church antiphon for Advent, the *Ascension* is based principally on a HOMILY of Pope Gregory the Great, and the third part, a powerful description of the Day of Judgement with Christ's address to the sinners, has various sources. The dialogue between Mary and Joseph in the first part is the earliest extant dramatic scene in English.

Christ and Satan An Old English poem in three parts, or perhaps three separate pieces, found in the Junius manuscript (see JUNIUS, FRANCIS). They deal with the Fall of the Angels, the Harrowing of Hell and the Temptation of Christ. The first and third have biblical sources, while the second draws upon the apocryphal *GOSPEL OF NICODEMUS*.

Christabel An unfinished poem by SAMUEL TAYLOR COLERIDGE, begun during the period of his collaboration with WORDSWORTH on the LYRICAL BALLADS (1798) but first published in *Christabel and Other Poems* (1816). Making evocative use of Gothic and supernatural themes, it tells how the enchantress Geraldine deceives all but the virtuous Christabel. It uses a new metre, the rhyming four-stressed line.

Christian Socialism A 19th-century religious and social movement. In response to the Chartist agitation of 1848, it set out to help the working man to help himself and to avert revolution by improving social conditions. Its practical outcome was the founding of the Working Men's College in 1854, the establishment of small self-governing workshops and a revival of the Co-operative Movement. The leader was FREDERICK DENISON MAURICE; his associates were CHARLES KINGSLEY, who wrote under the pseudonym Parson Lot, THOMAS HUGHES, author of TOM BROWN'S SCHOOLDAYS, and 'John Townsend', whose real name was John Malcolm Ludlow (1821–1911). Although Maurice was the figurehead, Ludlow was the mainspring. A barrister, educated in Paris, he was largely responsible for promoting the Industrial and Provident Societies Act of 1852. Kingsley's socialism, as evinced in his novels YEAST (1848) and ALTON LOCKE (1850), was paternalistic and ultimately impermanent, though his enthusiasm for sanitary reform was passionate. Christian Socialism did not imply radical social change, though Marx's famous phrase about religion being 'the opium of the people' (1844) is echoed by Kingsley: in Letters to the Chartists (1848) he wrote that the Bible had been used as 'an opium dose for keeping beasts of burden patient'. The Christian Socialists produced several short-lived journals: Politics for the People (1848), The Christian Socialist (1850), Tracts for Christian Socialists (1850) and The Journal of Association (1852).

Christian Year, The See KEBLE, JOHN.

Christie, Dame **Agatha (Mary Clarissa)** 1890–1976 Writer of DETECTIVE FICTION. Born in Torquay, Devon, of an American father and English mother, she enjoyed a quiet, middle-class childhood that set the keynote for her adult life and personality. Only the much-publicized episode of her temporary disappearance in 1926 offers any encouragement to those wishing to connect the author and her work. The more than 80 books she produced made her beyond doubt the most famous detective novelist of the century. Her first novel, The Mysterious Affair at Styles (1920), introduced the Belgian private detective Hercule Poirot, whose fictional career extended through many books to Curtain (1975). The Murder at the Vicarage (1930) introduced the shrewd, gentle Miss Marple, whose fictional career rivalled Poirot's in length and popularity, ending with Sleeping Murder (1976). Other detective heroes (Superintendent Battle, Tommy and Tuppence Beresford) proved less durable. Agatha Christie's classic books – The Murder of Roger Ackroyd (1926), Peril at End House (1932), Lord Edgeware Dies (1933), Murder on the Orient Express (1934), Why Didn't They Ask Evans? (1934), The ABC Murders (1936) and Ten Little Niggers (1939) – epitomize the so-called Golden Age of detective fiction in the 1920s and 1930s. Perfunctory in setting and characterization, they concentrate almost exclusively on tantalizing ingenuity of plot. Of the several short stories Agatha Christie adapted for the stage, The Mousetrap (first produced 1952) and Witness for the Prosecution (first produced 1953) were prodigiously successful. She also wrote light romantic novels as Mary Westmacott.

Christmas Books A collection of Christmas stories by CHARLES DICKENS, published together for the first time in 1852: A CHRISTMAS CAROL (1843), THE CHIMES (1844), THE CRICKET ON THE HEARTH (1845), THE BATTLE OF LIFE (1846) and THE HAUNTED MAN AND THE GHOST'S BARGAIN (1848).

Christmas Carol, A A novella by CHARLES DICKENS, published in 1843. The first and most popular of his Christmas stories, it was gathered together with its successors in CHRISTMAS BOOKS (1852).

This 'ghostly little book', as Dickens called A Christmas Carol, starts on Christmas Eve when the miserly Ebenezer Scrooge is visited by the shade of his dead partner, Jacob Marley. This uninvited guest warns Scrooge he is to be haunted by three spirits, without whose visits he cannot avoid the endless wanderings now inflicted upon Marley himself. The trio consists of The Ghost of Christmas Past, The Ghost of Christmas Present, and The Ghost of Christmas Yet to Come. Escorted by each in turn Scrooge goes back, invisibly, to the scenes of his youth and, later, to the family life of his loyal clerk, Bob Cratchit, whose household includes the sadly crippled Tiny Tim. With the third Ghost the old miser surveys the ominous shape of things to come. Chastened by his experiences, and now taught how others suffer in adversity, Scrooge resolves to lead a better life, sending a turkey to the Cratchits, visiting his honest nephew, donating to charity and raising Bob's salary. The tale ends in a glow of warmth and bonhomie.

chronicle Historical writing of the Middle Ages, in either verse or prose, varying in scope from the universal history to the local record. Written in English, Latin and ANGLO-NORMAN, the British chronicles borrowed from each other and adapted each other freely. Despite their large mythic and fictional content, they can be valuable historical sources for contemporary and near-contemporary events.

THE ANGLO-SAXON CHRONICLE is the earliest vernacular English example and records events from the 9th century to, in one version, 1134. The first important Latin chronicle was the Historia Regum Britanniae (c. 1135) by William of Malmesbury. William's sceptical reference to King Arthur was developed by GEOFFREY OF MONMOUTH into a full 'history' of the king and his court imitating the form of the ostensibly accurate historical chronicle (see ARTHURIAN LITERATURE). Arthur's place in history was consolidated by Wace's Anglo-Norman Roman de Brut (1155) and its Middle English version, LAYAMON's BRUT (c. 1190). Although the chronicles begin with a mythic past, they end in recent history and here they are more trustworthy. ANDREW OF WYNTOUN's *Orygynale Cronykil*, for example, begins with biblical history but culminates in a fairly accurate account of Scottish political history.

Many chronicles are by several hands. Thus the Latin chronicle of Florence of Worcester (d. 1148) was continued by John of Worcester until 1141, then by Henry of Huntingdon until 1152 and thereafter by the monks of Bury St Edmunds. Similarly, in the Middle English chronicle of ROBERT OF GLOUCESTER the work of at least two other compilers can be detected.

Chronicles of the Canongate The inclusive title given by SIR WALTER SCOTT to stories presented as the recollections of Mrs Bethune, Baliol of the Canongate in Edinburgh. They are written down by her friend Mr Chrystal Croftangry, whose own remarkable story serves as an introduction. The first series, consisting of three stories, was published in 1827 and the second, *The Fair Maid of Perth*, in 1828.

The Highland Widow. The story of a widow's struggle to make her son adhere to the traditions of his dead father, one of the Highland rebels in 1745. When the son enlists in an English regiment, her attempts to stop him succeed only in provoking him to kill his sergeant. He is shot for desertion and murder, and she dies alone in her grief.

The Two Drovers. Two drovers – a Highlander, Robin Oig M'Combich, and a Yorkshireman, Harry Wakefield – quarrel on their way to England. Robin finally kills his companion and surrenders himself to justice.

The Surgeon's Daughter. Richard Middlemass, adopted son of a surgeon, goes to India and falls under the influence of a procuress, Madame Montreville. He attempts to lure Janet Gray, the surgeon's daughter, out to India and into the clutches of Tippoo Sahib, but she is saved by Adam Hartley, Richard's fellow pupil who is in love with Janet. Richard is put to death for his crime.

St Valentine's Day: or, The Fair Maid of Perth. A story of Scotland in the 14th century, in the reign of Robert III. The fair maid of Perth is Catharine Glover. The worthless Duke of Rothsay, the king's son, and his evil friend, Sir John Ramorny, try to kidnap Catharine but are driven off by Henry Smith, tan armourer, who loves her; Henry strikes off Ramorny's hand during the fight. Ramorny is determined on vengeance: first on Henry, and also on Rothsay whom he blames as the author of his misfortune. He lures Rothsay to Falkland Tower, with the promise of Catharine, and has him murdered. The gentle Catharine, meanwhile, in spite of her father's urging, refuses Henry; his great strength and love of combat are not for her. Henry is finally confronted by his rival, Conachar, in an arranged battle. Conachar's courage deserts him and

Henry wins the day when Conachar runs from the field. But Henry is sickened by the carnage and, when he learns that Conachar has killed himself in shame, he resolves to hang up his broadsword for ever. Catharine accepts him in the light of this vow.

Church, Richard (Thomas) 1893–1972 Poet and novelist. Born in London, Church attended Dulwich Hamlet School. He was a civil servant for 24 years before becoming a publisher's reader; he was also the Examiner for Voice Production and Verse Speaking for London University. His novels include *The Porch* (1937) and *The Nightingale* (1952). His essentially Georgian poetry is characterized by sturdy craftsmanship and limited ambition; now neglected, he is doomed to oblivion. His many collections include *The Flood of Life* (1917), *The Lamp* (1946), *Collected Poems* (1948) and *The Burning Bush* (1967).

Churchill, Caryl 1938– Playwright. She began by writing radio plays in the early 1960s about 'bourgeois middle-class life and [its] destruction'. A hatred of injustice characterized her first works for the stage, notably *Owners* (1972). Subsequently she wrote for left-wing and feminist companies: Monstrous Regiment performed *Vinegar Tom* (1976) and Joint Stock *Light Shining in Buckinghamshire* (1976). She accepted the then standard connection between the class struggle and the role of women in an imperialist and capitalist society, a broad-brush approach which helps to explain the leaps in associative logic which occur in *Cloud Nine* (1979), about sexual role-playing, and *Top Girls* (1982), in which famous women from different epochs describe their struggles in a male world. Some left-wing admirers found the lack of didacticism in *Serious Money* (1987), her SATIRE of City financiers, a weakness. *Mad Forest* (1990), a play about Romania developed onsite in the weeks following the downfall of the Ceauçescus, is a rare example of a British play attempting to understand the havoc left by totalitarianism in Eastern Europe.

Churchill, Charles 1731–64 Satirist. The son of a curate of St John's, Westminster, he attended Westminster School and went on to St John's College, Cambridge, but blighted his academic prospects by a secret marriage at the age of 17 to Martha Scott. Though hardly better suited to the Church, he succeeded his father in 1758 as incumbent of St John's. To help support his family Churchill soon turned to writing. Two poems, 'The Bard' and 'The Conclave', failed to find publishers but he published *The Rosciad* with his own money in 1761. A verse SATIRE praising DAVID GARRICK at the expense of other contemporary actors, it was an overnight success.

It also led to his friendship with JOHN WILKES, whose rakish example Churchill (now estranged from his wife) lost no time in following. THE NORTH BRITON, Wilkes's political weekly, owed a great deal of its success to Churchill, who wrote at least half of it. The Prophecy of Famine (1763) was a satirical blast at Bute; but Wilkes made sure that his friend escaped prosecution in the uproar which followed the publication of No. 45 of The North Briton, asserting that Churchill had not written it. Throughout this turbulent period Churchill continued his social and political satires: The Apology and Night (1761) and The Ghost (1762–3), attacking WILLIAM WHITEHEAD, preceded the suppression of The North Briton, while The Conference, The Author, An Epistle to William Hogarth (1763), The Duellist, The Candidate, Gotham, Independence, The Times and The Farewell (1764) followed it. He died at Boulogne on his way to visit Wilkes. The Journey, a fragment, and some satirical verses directed at Bishop Warburton appeared in 1765.

Churchill, Sir **Winston (Leonard Spencer)** 1874–1965 Politician and historian. Born at Blenheim Palace, the eldest son of Lord Randolph Churchill, he was educated at Harrow and Sandhurst. He served with the British forces in India and the Sudan, and was captured by the Boers while acting as a war correspondent in South Africa. He entered Parliament in 1900 and thereafter held the offices of among others, Home Secretary (1910–11), First Lord of the Admiralty (1911–15), Secretary of State for War (1918–21), Chancellor of the Exchequer (1924–9) and Prime Minister (1940–5 and 1951–5). He published several historical studies including The World Crisis 1916–18 (6 vols., 1923–31), The Second World War (6 vols., 1948–54) and A History of the English-Speaking Peoples (4 vols., 1956–8). His biographies include Lord Randolph Churchill (1906) and Marlborough: His Life and Times (4 vols., 1933–8). He also wrote a novel, Savrola (1900), and several books dealing with his early career, among them My African Journey (1908) and My Early Life (1930). He was awarded the Nobel Prize for Literature in 1953.

Churchyard, Thomas ?1520–1604 Poet. He started writing poetry in the reign of Edward VI and lived long enough to celebrate James I's public entry to Westminster in 'A Paean Triumphal' (1603). In COLIN CLOUT'S COME HOME AGAIN, SPENSER portrayed him as Palaemon, who 'sung so long until quite hoarse he grew'. Trained as a soldier, Churchyard campaigned in Scotland, Ireland, the Low Countries and France. Some of his military experiences appear in his works, e.g. General Rehearsal of Wars (1579). He wrote pageant verses, epitaphs, tracts and broadsides. His best works are the 'Legend of Shore's Wife' which appeared in THE MIRROR FOR MAGISTRATES, the voluminous collection The First Part of Churchyard's Chips (1575) and The Worthiness of Wales (1587), which has some historical interest.

Cibber, Colley 1671–1757 Actor, playwright and poet. The son of an immigrant Danish sculptor, Cibber joined the company of actors at DRURY LANE in 1691 and made a major success in the role of Lord Foppington in VANBRUGH's The Relapse. There is some irony in that, since Vanbrugh's play was a riposte to Cibber's own LOVE'S LAST SHIFT (1696), but it accurately illustrates Cibber's ability to deflect hostility by his provocative and sometimes outrageous good humour. It was an ability that stood him in good stead during his controversial years as co-manager of Drury Lane (1708–32) and as POET LAUREATE (from 1730). The latter appointment earned him the dubious immortality of POPE's scorn in THE DUNCIAD.

Few people, even among his contemporaries, believed that Cibber's verse merited the laureateship, but his services to the theatre have been often underrated. Love's Last Shift, his first play, heralded the long reign of SENTIMENTAL COMEDY on the English stage. It is among the best of its now unfashionable kind, together with The Careless Husband (1704), The Lady's Last Stake (1707) and The Provoked Husband (1728), a completion of Vanbrugh's A Journey to London. Cibber's understanding of contemporary theatrical taste is further exemplified in his cleverly compiled version of SHAKESPEARE's RICHARD III (1700), which replaced the original on the English stage for 150 years, and in his much-loved version of Molière's Tartuffe as The Non Juror (1717). His discursive autobiography, An Apology for the Life of Mr Colley Cibber, Comedian (1740, revised 1750 and 1756), gives an unrivalled account of the English theatre over four decades.

citizen [city] **comedy** The term is used to describe a group of Elizabethan and Jacobean plays whose setting is London and whose characters are predominantly the day-to-day tradesmen of the city. The satire of mercantile values and financial opportunism is, for the most part, good-humoured, but no quarter is given to social overreaching or the pursuit of commercial success by fraud. Citizen comedy is characteristically moral and determined to castigate whatever or whoever discredits the good name of London. Outstanding examples include DEKKER's THE SHOEMAKER'S HOLIDAY (1599), EASTWARD HO (1605), on which CHAPMAN, JONSON and MARSTON collaborated – and which outdoes the two joint works of Dekker and WEBSTER, WESTWARD HO (1604) and NORTHWARD HO (1605) – and MIDDLETON's A CHASTE MAID IN CHEAPSIDE (1611). The combination of a romantic plot and plain characters was sufficiently familiar by 1607 to provoke the lively mockery of BEAUMONT's THE KNIGHT OF THE BURNING PESTLE, but citizen comedy was both durable and adaptable. It reflected the secure London base of many of the public stage's greatest dramatists. Jonson, too various and too original to be confined within a category, evoked the teeming life of the city in *EPICOENE* (1609), *THE ALCHEMIST* (1610) and *BARTHOLOMEW FAIR* (1614). The increasing tensions of London under the Stuarts, which contributed to the hardening tone and eventual decline of citizen comedy, are well represented by the distance between *Eastward Ho* and MASSINGER's altogether darker version of the same plot in *THE CITY MADAM* (c. 1632).

City Madam, The A CITIZEN COMEDY by PHILIP MASSINGER, first performed c. 1632 and published in 1659.

Sir John Frugal is a successful merchant; his wife and daughters have grown in affectation and vanity as his wealth has increased. Living in his household is his younger brother, Luke, a ruined prodigal Sir John has helped and whose manner is one of humble gratitude. Exasperated by his family, Sir John pretends to retire to a monastery and hands the management of the household over to his brother. Luke shows his true colours at once, appropriating his brother's fortune and displaying a remarkable rapacity in calling in debts. He ridicules Lady Frugal and her daughters, and is prepared to sell them to three 'Indians' who want three women for human sacrifice. The Indians, however, are in fact Sir John and two young men who unsuccessfully wooed his daughters, so Luke is unmasked. He is driven unrepentant from the house, and the relieved and repentant ladies promise to behave better in future.

The play gives a realistic picture of London society at various levels in the Caroline period, ranging from the integrity of Sir John, the honest merchant, and his family to the stews where the prostitutes Shavem and Secret are ready to fight with knives against fashionable ruffians who would make victims of them. The pretensions of aristocracy are given utterance by one suitor, Sir Maurice Lacy, and vigorously challenged by the other, Master Plenty, a yeoman farmer's son whose wealth and station come from hard work.

City of Dreadful Night, The A poem by JAMES THOMSON, first published in Charles Bradlaugh's secularist magazine, *The National Reformer*, in 1874. It takes its motto from Leopardi: 'In thee, O Death, our naked nature finds repose; not joyful, but safe from the old sadness.' *The City of Dreadful Night* is a work of profound desolation, a requiem to disillusionment and negation. Written in contrasting sections of episodic and ruminative verse, the poem envisages London both topographically and as a terrifying City of Dis, dark, tenebrous and forbidding. It reflects on the meaninglessness of the human condition, on the

death-in-life Thomson believed man must endure. Sinister imagery, dramatic scenes, and brooding despair (as in Thomson's arresting description of Dürer's 'Melancholia') render the poem unique in the literature of despondency as well as a landmark in late-Victorian pessimism.

Civil Disobedience, On the Duty of An essay by HENRY DAVID THOREAU, originally published as *Resistance to Civil Government* in 1849 and given its familiar title when it appeared in a posthumous collection of essays, *A Yankee in Canada, with Anti-Slavery and Reform Papers* (1866). Citing the controversial Mexican War, slavery and the treatment of Indians, and referring to the night he himself spent in gaol for refusing to pay his poll tax, Thoreau argues that an individual may refuse to participate in a government that does not uphold his or her moral standards.

Clampitt, Amy 1920– American poet. She was born in Providence, Iowa, and educated at Grinnell College in the same state. After graduation she worked in publishing with Oxford University Press and the Audubon Society before establishing herself as freelance writer. It was not until 1973 that *Multitudes,* her first, privately printed volume appeared. A number of her poems were originally printed in *THE NEW YORKER*, a forum which brought her a wider audience and growing reputation. Her intelligent, elegiac, frequently intense verse has since appeared in several commercially published volumes: *The Kingfisher* (1973), *What the Light was Like* (1985), *Archaic Figure* (1987), *Westward* (1990) and *Predecessors* (1991).

Clandestine Marriage, The A comedy by GEORGE COLMAN THE ELDER and DAVID GARRICK, first performed at DRURY LANE in 1766. While it is generally agreed that the original idea of basing a play on the first plate of HOGARTH's *Marriage à la Mode* was Colman's and that the brilliant fifth act was written by Garrick, there is no certainty about the sharing out of the rest of the play. Its best part, that of Lord Ogleby, was intended for Garrick, and may have been invented by him, though illness prevented him from playing it.

The wealthy merchant, Sterling, plans to increase his social standing by marrying his elder daughter to Sir John Melvil, nephew of the impecunious Lord Ogleby. At the last moment, Melvil expresses a preference for the younger daughter, Fanny, and Sterling complies, to the indignation of his rich sister, Mrs Heidelberg. What no one knows is that Fanny is secretly married to her father's clerk, Lovewell. A series of misfortunes culminate in Lovewell's being found in Fanny's bedroom, and it is Lord Ogleby who unexpectedly saves the situation.

Clanvowe, Sir John *c.* 1341–91 Poet and religious writer. Of Welsh ancestry, he inherited an estate on the southern Welsh border. He fought in military campaigns in France, including the battle of Lussac Bridge in 1369. He was knight bachelor to the Earl of Hereford and entered the service of Edward III on Hereford's death in 1373. He was later in the service of Richard II and held political offices in England and abroad. He died near Constantinople in 1391; it is reported that his lover, Sir William Neville, refused food and died a few days later. His two known works are quite disparate in character. THE CUCKOO AND THE NIGHTINGALE, or *The Book of Cupid*, is a secular poem on the nature of love modelled on CHAUCER'S *PARLEMENT OF FOULES* and a part of the CHAUCERIAN APOCRYPHA. His other work is a religious tract in prose condemning luxury and worldliness and exhorting his readers to obey the commandments and to love God. Although Clanvowe is counted with Neville, Sir Thomas Latimer, Sir Lewis Clifford, Sir John Montagu and Sir Richard Sturry as one of the 'Lollard knights', the tract does not express LOLLARD sympathies.

Clare, John 1793–1864 Poet. The son of an agricultural labourer in receipt of poor relief, Clare was born at Helpston, Northamptonshire, where he worked as a thresher, farm labourer and gardener. His life and work are marked by an intimate sense of place: in his *Autobiography* he describes how, as a child, he once strayed beyond the parish boundary, until he found himself 'out of his knowledge', the sun seeming to shine from a 'different quarter of the sky'. The formative years of his youth were contemporary with the passing of an Act for the enclosure of Helpston and several neighbouring villages, and by the time he began to write a new landscape had been created. His *Poems Descriptive of Rural Life* appeared in 1820, and in the following year he produced *The Village Minstrel*, a long poem in SPENSERIAN STANZAS. Both works contain moving descriptions of the conditions of the rural poor, together with poignant evocations of the old village landscape of open fields. Although Clare was producing verse that shows him as already the equal of his models, GOLDSMITH and THOMSON, he was at length dissatisfied with this mode, feeling that their poetic diction was at odds with his own sensibility. In THE SHEPHERD'S CALENDAR (1827), *The Rural Muse* (1835) and the posthumous collection *The Midsummer Cushion* he attempted to blend the physical with the linguistic textures of Helpston, employing grammar, vocabulary and syntax that are pronouncedly, though by no means naively, athwart the dominant conventions of PASTORAL.

In 1820 Clare married Martha Turner, and, though he never adjusted to the breakdown of an earlier relationship with Mary Joyce, he seems to have been a dutiful husband and a good father. In 1832 he was offered a cottage in Northborough, a village just three miles northeast of Helpston, but in a landscape so different that he felt wholly estranged there. The poems written at Northborough communicate a deep melancholy and a sense of irretrievable loss. In 1837 he became mentally ill, and was admitted to an asylum in High Beach, Epping. He escaped in 1841 and walked to Northamptonshire, having convinced himself that he would there be reunited with Mary Joyce, to whom he believed himself married. He was committed to the county asylum at Northampton, where he remained for the rest of his life, enjoying considerable freedom and continuing to write poetry. He seems to have recognized his illness as a loss of 'self-identity', in which the enclosures, the move from Helpston and the decline in the sales of his work, with the passing of the vogue for 'peasant' poetry at the end of the 1820s, all played a part. His poetry, much of which was distorted by his publisher's editorial interventions, remained virtually unread until this century, when its reception as a pre-figuration of modern, or 'alienated', aesthetic consciousness did much to stimulate the production of new editions based on the original manuscripts.

Clarel: *A Poem and Pilgrimage in the Holy Land* A 7000-line poem by HERMAN MELVILLE in octosyllabic couplets, published in two volumes in 1876. Inspired by Melville's reflections on his visit to the Holy Land 20 years earlier, the poem is an enquiry into and search for faith. Its various characters represent a range of attitudes: some express religious doubts arising from their personal experience or philosophy; others are comfortably certain of their faith. None, however, is able to assist Clarel, an American theology student visiting Jerusalem, to resolve his own uncertainties.

Clarendon, 1st Earl of [Hyde, Edward] 1609–74 Historian and statesman. The son of a Wiltshire country gentleman, Clarendon attended Magdalen Hall, Oxford, and then practised law. He entered Parliament in 1640 and sat in the Commons throughout the Short and Long Parliaments, first for Wootton Bassett and then for Saltash. He began by being opposed to the King's policies, but soon fell out of sympathy with the tenor of the opposition and with the Presbyterians. By 1641 he had become one of the King's chief advisers.

When Charles I gave the Prince of Wales a council and court of his own in the West Country during the Civil War (1645), Hyde was appointed to it. He followed the Prince into exile and, while in the Scilly Isles, began in 1646 to write his *True Historical Narrative of the Rebellion and Civil Wars in England* – the HISTORY OF THE REBELLION, as it is usually known.

At the Restoration he became Lord Chancellor, and at Charles II's coronation was created Earl of

Clarendon; he was Charles's chief minister until 1667. The mismanagement of the war with the Dutch (which Clarendon had opposed) gave political enemies a chance to bring about his downfall. Because they feared his possible return to power – his daughter, Anne, was married to James, Duke of York and later James II – Lord Arlington and others moved his impeachment. Charles did not intervene and Clarendon again went into exile, living at Montpellier and then Rouen, where he died. During these years he finished his *History*, though it was not published until 1702–4. It eventually incorporated two other works belonging to this period, *The History of the Irish Rebellion and Civil Wars in Ireland* and his autobiography, *The Life of Edward, Earl of Clarendon* (separately published in 1759). His speeches, political tracts and essays were published as *A Collection of Several Tracts* (1727), while his criticism of HOBBES, in *Leviathan: A Brief View and Survey*, appeared two years after his death. From the Restoration until his flight from England Clarendon was Chancellor of the University of Oxford, which inherited his manuscripts. The profits from publication of his work provided the funds for the building of the Clarendon Press.

***Clarissa:** or, The History of a Young Lady* A novel by SAMUEL RICHARDSON, the first two volumes published in 1747, the last five in 1748. Like *PAMELA*, it is an EPISTOLARY NOVEL, consisting of a four-way correspondence between the principal characters: Clarissa Harlowe's letters to her friend Miss Howe and Robert Lovelace's to his friend John Belford predominate.

Clarissa is a well-bred young lady attracted to the dashing Lovelace, an unscrupulous man of whom her parents strongly disapprove. In deference to their wishes, Clarissa resists his advances, but also refuses to marry the man they have selected instead, the detestable Mr Solmes. Confined to her room (for the first 500 pages of the plot) she secretly corresponds with Lovelace, and runs away with him, only to discover his real nature. He instals her under the watchful eye of Mrs Sinclair, a bawd, and woos her ardently. When his subtlety gives way to impatience he drugs and then rapes her. Denounced by her family, she rejects Lovelace totally, ignores the pleas of his family and friends to accept his proposal of marriage, and retires into solitude. She dies of shame and grief, and Lovelace is killed in a duel with her cousin. Belford, the libertine correspondent, turns over a new leaf, becomes Clarissa's executor, and edits her letters.

Though the action of the novel encompasses less than a year, the intense degree of characterization is extraordinarily sustained, buoyed up by Richardson's careful unification of the narrative elements. *Clarissa* is widely regarded as his masterpiece, and, running to over a million words, is the longest novel in the English language.

Samuel Richardson's *Clarissa*: an illustration from the 1768 edition

Clark Bekederemo, J(ohn) P(epper) [Clark, John Pepper] 1936– Nigerian poet and playwright. He was born in Kiagbodo, Niger Delta. Despite wide reading in European literatures, his imagination, idiom and even themes are nurtured by traditional Ijaw culture. *Poems* (1962), *A Reed in the Tide* (1965), and *Casualties: Poems 1966/68* (1970) contain some well-wrought, crisp, economical poems. *A Decade of Tongues* (1981) is a selection. The collection *State of the Union* appeared in 1985, *Mandela and Other Poems* in 1988. *Song of a Goat* (1961; reissued with *The Masquerade* and *The Raft* in *Three Plays*, 1964) is the finest of his verse tragedies, in which supra-human fate overwhelms human endeavour. *Ozidi* (1966), a verse play about revenge that dehumanizes, is adapted from the seven-day Ijaw epic drama he translated as *The Ozidi Saga* (1975). In image-laden prose, *The Boat*, *The Return Home* and *Full Circle* constitute *The Bikoroa Plays* (1985), about fratricide and family strife across three generations in a traditional riverine community. *America, Their America* (1964) angrily describes a year at Princeton. The critical essays in *The Example of Shakespeare* (1970) include a seminal piece, 'The Legacy of Caliban'.

Clark, Kenneth (Mackenzie), Baron 1903–83 Art historian and critic. Born in Oxford, educated at

Winchester and Trinity College, Oxford, he held various distinguished appointments in the course of a long career, being director of the National Gallery (1934–45), Surveyor of the King's Pictures (1934–44) and chairman of the Arts Council of Great Britain (1953–60). As a writer he first attracted attention with *The Gothic Revival* (1928); the many works that followed include *Florentine Painting* (1945), *Landscape into Art* (1949), *The Nude: A Study of Ideal Art* (1953), *Moments of Vision* (1954) and *Civilisation* (1969), based on a successful television series. His interest in RUSKIN, which lay behind his first book, was again expressed in the introduction he provided for an edition of *PRAETERITA* (1949) and in the selection *Ruskin Today* (1964). *Another Part of the Wood* (1974) and *The Other Half* (1977) are volumes of autobiography.

Clarke, Arthur C(harles) 1917– Writer of SCIENCE FICTION. He was born in Minehead, Somerset, and served in the RAF during the war. He graduated from King's College, London, in physics and mathematics in 1948 and since 1956 has lived in Sri Lanka. As a writer and popularizer of science he has been an ardent champion of the cause of technological progress; a strong interest in space exploration dates from the 1940s, when he first published plans for a hypothetical communications satellite. His early works, *Childhood's End* (1953) and *The City and the Stars* (1956), show the influence of OLAF STAPLEDON, but most of his novels aim at technological realism. They include *Rendezvous with Rama* (1973), *Imperial Earth* (1975), *The Fountains of Paradise* (1979) and *The Songs at Distant Earth* (1986). Clarke worked closely with Stanley Kubrick on the film *2001: A Space Odyssey* (1968), carrying the story forward in *2010: Odyssey Two* (1982) and *2061: Odyssey Three* (1988). *Cradle* (1988) and *Rama II* (1989) were written with Gentry Lee.

Clarke, Austin 1896–1974 Irish playwright, poet and novelist. Born and educated in Dublin, he worked as a journalist in England before returning in 1937 to found the Dublin Verse-Speaking Society and, later, the Lyric Theatre Company. Clarke's aim was to revive poetic drama. The first of his verse plays, *The Son of Learning* (1927), is based on a medieval Irish story, as are most of those that followed. Two exceptions are the delicate one-act Pierrot plays, *The Kiss* (1942) and *The Second Kiss* (1946). For the three-act *The Moment Next to Nothing* (1958) he returned to a Gaelic story that had already furnished him with the plot for a novel, *The Sun Dances at Easter* (1952), which was banned in Ireland. *The Plot Succeeds* (1950), particularly interesting for its experiments with RHYME, is one of a small number of plays by Clarke that might sustain revival. *The Vengeance of Fionn* (1917), first of several volumes of verse before and after *Collected Poems* (1936), is a product of his enthusiasm for Irish legend and folk-tales. An autobiography, *Twice around the Black Church* (1960), and a volume of memoirs, *A Penny in the Clouds* (1968), also show the range and intensity of his Irish studies.

Clarke, Austin 1934– Barbadian/Canadian novelist and short-story writer. He worked as a schoolteacher before leaving Barbados in 1955 for Canada, where he attended the University of Toronto and worked in journalism and broadcasting. He has taught at a number of American universities. His fiction vividly renders the speech of Barbadians and Barbadian immigrants in Canada and blends humour and anger in its criticism of colonial Barbados and contemporary Canada. *Survivors of the Crossing* (1964) is about a strike on a Barbadian plantation, while *Among Thistles and Thorns* (1965) is about a Caribbean boyhood. *The Meeting Point* (1967), *Storm of Fortune* (1973) and *The Bigger Light* (1975) form a trilogy, his major work to date, about Caribbean immigrants in Canada. Other works include *The Prime Minister* (1977), *Proud Empires* (1988) and several collections of stories: *When He was Free and Young and He Used to Wear Silks* (1971), *When Women Rule* (1985) and *Nine Men Who Laughed* (1986). His memoirs are *Growing Up Stupid under the Union Jack* (1980), about his early life in Barbados, and *Colonial Innocency* (1982).

Clarke, Charles Cowden 1787–1877 Scholar and critic. Born in Enfield, Middlesex, he became a friend of KEATS, who attended his father's school. Later he became acquainted with LEIGH HUNT, SHELLEY, HAZLITT and DICKENS. He was a London bookseller and publisher who wrote and lectured on SHAKESPEARE. With his wife MARY COWDEN CLARKE he wrote *Recollections of Writers* (1878).

Clarke, Gillian 1937– Poet. Born in Cardiff, she read English Literature at University College, Cardiff, and has lived in South Wales all her life, apart from two years with the BBC in London. Until 1984 she combined work as a part-time teacher with editing *The Anglo-Welsh Review*. Two early books of poems, *Snow on the Mountain* (1971) and *The Sundial* (1978) established a strong following in Wales but it was her third collection, *Letter from a Far Country* (1982), which brought a wider audience. *Selected Poems* (1985) and *Letting in the Rumour* (1989) have established her as a leading woman poet of her generation. Although strongly rooted in both the urban and rural experience of her native Wales, her work transcends regional concerns and approaches archetypal themes of love, death and family life from intimate, almost casual angles. She combines the traditional skills of versification with a sharply accurate, at times visionary use of imagery and language.

Clarke, Marcus 1846–81 Australian novelist. Born in London, he was educated at Highgate School, where he was a schoolfellow of GERARD MANLEY HOPKINS. He emigrated to Victoria in 1863 and, after four years on a station in the Wimmera, joined *The Melbourne Argus*. He contributed a weekly column as 'the Peripatetic Philosopher' to *The Australian* and, in 1868, became owner and editor of *The Colonial Monthly*, where his first novel, *Long Odds* (1869), was serialized. A commission from *The Australian Journal* led to his best-known work, *HIS NATURAL LIFE* (serialized, 1870–2; revised for book publication, 1874), which presented a vivid picture of the penal settlement in Tasmania. His other works included collections of short stories – *Old Tales of a Young Country* (1871) and *The Man with the Oblong Box* (1878) – and a PANTOMIME, *Twinkle, Twinkle Little Star* (1873).

Clarke, Mary (Victoria) Cowden 1809–98 Scholar and critic. Her *Concordance to Shakespeare's Plays* was published in monthly parts in 1844–5. *Recollections of Writers* (1878) was written in collaboration with CHARLES COWDEN CLARKE, whom she had married in 1828.

Clarke, Samuel 1675–1729 Divine. Clarke was born in Norwich and educated at Gonville and Caius College, Cambridge. He was appointed chaplain to the Bishop of Norwich in 1698. In 1704 and 1705 he delivered the Boyle lectures known in their published form (1716) as *A Discourse Concerning the Being and Attributes of God*, a carefully reasoned defence of rational theology against the empiricism of JOHN LOCKE.

Claverings, The A novel by ANTHONY TROLLOPE, serialized in *THE CORNHILL MAGAZINE* from February 1866 to May 1867.

Harry Clavering, a schoolmaster resolved to become an engineer, is jilted by the beautiful Julia Brabazon in favour of Lord Ongar, a wealthy debauchee. After a year abroad Ongar dies and Julia returns to London. In the meantime Harry has fallen in love with Florence Burton, the homely daughter of a partner in his engineering firm. He is drawn into contact with Julia again through his concern to protect her from the sinister Count Pateroff and his scheming sister Sophie Gordeloup, who are after her money, and the old feeling between them revives. Julia now wants to marry him and Harry is drawn into a second proposal, but conscience and domesticity win when he realizes that Florence will be a better wife for him. Julia surrenders her claim and fortune smiles on Harry when his two cousins drown in a boating accident, and he finds himself heir to the Clavering estate.

Despite its conventional ending, *The Claverings* offers what was for its time an unconventional and penetrating exploration of the mind of a man in love with two women.

Clayhanger A novel by ARNOLD BENNETT, published in 1910. The first of a trilogy, it was followed by *Hilda Lessways* (1911) and *These Twain* (1916). A fourth novel, *The Roll Call* (1918), is loosely connected with the series.

Edwin Clayhanger's life over 20 years is traced, from the day he leaves school in 1872 aged 16. The central relationship of Edwin and his father, Darius, was inspired by Bennett's own struggles with a dominating parent. Crucially for their relationship, Edwin is unaware of Darius's cruel upbringing in the workhouse during the 1840s and of the chance in life that came to him from Mr Shushions, the Sunday school teacher, now poor and decrepit himself.

Edwin's dreams of escaping the Potteries town of Bursley, the family printing business, the narrow company of his downtrodden sisters Mary and Clara, and the pious hypocrisies of Auntie Hamps, are held in contempt by Darius. Edwin's association with the cultivated Orgreaves family has introduced him to ideas and unattainable prospects: one of these, at first, is Hilda Lessways. When marriage seems possible, Edwin's request for a rise in salary brings a climactic, unsuccessful encounter with Darius. But Hilda departs mysteriously and he hears of her subsequent marriage. Years later, Edwin traces Hilda and her son to a Brighton boarding house, and learns of her ruin at the hands of the bigamous George Cannon. The novel ends with their plan to marry. The earlier account of Darius's slow and painful decline into death is more characteristic of the novel than is the note of romance.

Cleanness [*Purity*] A late 14th-century poem in ALLITERATIVE VERSE and the dialect of the West Midlands. Preserved in the same manuscript as *SIR GAWAIN AND THE GREEN KNIGHT*, *PATIENCE* and *PEARL*, it is usually grouped with them as the work of the same, unidentified author, known as the *GAWAIN*-POET. Its theme is the supreme value of spiritual purity and God's rejection of the impure. The 'cleanness' of the title is not simply chastity, but freedom from all kinds of vices which defile the soul in the eyes of God. The poet draws on biblical narratives to illustrate his theme, using the parable of the Guest without a Wedding Garment, the Flood, the destruction of Sodom and Gomorrah and finally Belshazzar's Feast. These narratives are enlivened by vivid description and given a medieval English setting. The result is powerful and dynamic, the austere subject matter enriched by gentle humour, sincere faith and tenderness. Alone among the four poems attributed to the *Gawain*-poet, *Cleanness* draws on the Apocrypha for some of its material and is clearly dependent on known secular works, citing Jean de Meun's part of the *Roman de la rose* and borrowing from an early French version of *MANDEVILLE'S TRAVELS* for the description of the Dead Sea.

Cleary, Jon (Stephen) 1917– Australian novelist. Born in Sydney, he joined the army in 1940 and served in the Middle East and New Guinea. His first published volume was a collection of short stories entitled *These Small Glories* (1945). His many novels are tales of adventure or DETECTIVE FICTION in the manner of Simenon, generally set in exotic locations and often distinguished by their subtle interest in personal dilemmas of indecision and fear of responsibility. They include *You Can't See Round Corners* (1947), *Just Let Me Be* (1950), *The Sun-downers* (1952), *Forests of the Night* (1963), *The High Commissioner* (1966), *Season of Doubt* (1968), *Remember Jack Hoxie* (1969), *The Safe House* (1975), *A Very Private War* (1980), *Spearfield's Daughter* (1982), *Phoenix Tree* (1984), *Now and Then Amen* (1988), *Murder Song* (1990) and *Pride's Harvest* (1991). He also writes for film, television and radio.

Cleland, John 1709–89 Novelist. Educated at Westminster School, he held minor government posts in Smyrna and Bombay before becoming a professional writer in London. He is best known for *Memoirs of a Woman of Pleasure* (1748–9), usually called *Fanny Hill*, for long suppressed as obscene, though it was one of the most popular novels of the 18th century. *Memoirs of a Coxcomb: or, The History of Sir William Delamere* (1751) and *The Surprises of Love* (1764) are his other novels. Cleland also wrote dramatic pieces and philological studies.

Clemo, Jack (Reginald John) 1916– Poet. A native of St Austell, he still lives in the cottage in which he was born. Unhelpfully, his poetic career has sometimes been seen merely as a triumph over deafness, blindness (since 1955), heart trouble and cerebral paralysis. His father's death and religious indoctrination by his mother have significantly shaped his verse, which is concerned with the conflict between grace and nature, and the assimilation of sexuality into Christianity. A novel, *Wilding Craft* (1948) and an autobiography, *Confession of a Rebel* (1949), were followed by two volumes of poetry, *The Clay Verse* (1951) and *The Wintry Priesthood* (1951), featuring a tortured Christian existentialism and devastated, metaphysical Cornish landscapes. Clemo's late discovery of MODERNISM is evident in *Cactus on Carmel* (1967); other volumes include *Broad Autumn* (1975), *The Bouncing Hills* (1983), *The Shadowed Bed* (1986), *Selected Poems* (1988), *Banner Poems* (1989) and *Approach to Murano* (1992). Although Clemo has been praised by DONALD DAVIE and CHARLES CAUSLEY, the unusual and individual directions in which he has proceeded account in part for the lack of a proper assessment of his work.

Cleopatra A Senecan CLOSET DRAMA by SAMUEL DANIEL, published in 1594. It deals with events following the death of Antony. Octavius tries to persuade Cleopatra to leave the monument in which she has taken refuge; he wants to parade her in triumph in Rome. But after a last celebration of great magnificence she takes her life by the application of a venomous serpent. At the same time her son by Julius Caesar, Caesarion, is murdered by Octavius and the line of Ptolemy is extinguished.

clerihew A comic verse form invented by EDMUND CLERIHEW BENTLEY, consisting of two rhyming couplets designed to sum up a subject or character: 'The art of Biography/ Is different from Geography./ Geography is about maps,/ Biography is about chaps.'

Clerk of Pennecuik, Sir **John** 1676–1755 Man of letters. Clerk was one of the circle of friends who grouped around ALLAN RAMSAY in the reviving literary life of Edinburgh in the early 18th century. A pupil of Corelli, he composed a set of five cantatas for solo voice in 1698; he also wrote a number of songs. His *Memoirs* give an illuminating picture of his times; they were published by The Roxburghe Club in 1895. Clerk was also the author of *Observations on the Present State of Scotland* (1730).

Clerk's Tale, The See CANTERBURY TALES, THE.

Cleveland, John 1613–58 Poet. The son of a Yorkshire clergyman, he was educated at Christ's College, Cambridge (where he was a contemporary of MILTON), and became a fellow of St John's in 1634, though he was later deprived of this post for his opposition to Cromwell. He went to Oxford and later joined the Royalist garrison at Newark. Robustly loyal to the cause of the Crown, he was imprisoned by the Parliamentarians in 1655–6, but released after a personal appeal to Cromwell.

As a political satirist and poet he was both formidable and popular. His verse portraits were often anti-Presbyterian and his best poems are 'The Rebel Scot' and 'The King's Disguise'. Though collections of his work continued to appear after the Restoration of the monarchy, he was ridiculed by DRYDEN for the roughness of his effects, and his conceits are often extreme and 'far-fetch't', giving rise to the term 'Clevelandism' to denote implausible comparison, or CATACHRESIS. Sometimes dubbed 'the last METAPHYSICAL POET', he is not widely read today, though some of his verse is memorably vigorous.

cliché From the French, 'a stereotype plate'. A trite expression which has lost its cutting edge.

Cliff-Dwellers, The A novel by HENRY BLAKE FULLER, published in 1893, and one of the earliest American novels to have as its setting the monstrous and impersonal city. A satire on greed and social striving set in Chicago, it depicts the lives of the 'cliff-dwellers' – those inhabiting a skyscraper called the Clifton Building. The characters include Arthur Ingles, the rich owner of the Clifton; Erasmus Brainard, an antisocial banker; Eugene H. McDowell, a crooked real estate agent; George Ogden, an ambitious clerk who works in Brainard's bank; and the various women who contribute to their fortunes and misfortunes.

Clive, Caroline 1801–73 Poet and novelist. Born Caroline Meysey-Wigley, she married Archer Clive in 1840. Under the pseudonym V she published *IX Poems* (1840), well received and followed by several other volumes. Her most popular work was a SENSATION NOVEL, *Paul Ferroll* (1855), whose wealthy and cultured hero is forced to confess to the murder of his wife many years after the event. A sequel, *Why Paul Ferroll Killed His Wife* (1860), describes the provocation that drove him to the crime.

Cloete, Stuart 1897–1976 South African novelist. Born in Paris, he was educated in England. British army service (1914–25) was followed by farming in South Africa. A prolific author of non-fictional works, novels of adventure, and collections of stories, he is at his best in a sequence of realistic, unsentimental novels covering 19th-century Afrikaner history. His first novel, *Turning Wheels*, published in 1937, just before the Voortrekker centenary, was banned for depicting sacrosanct pioneer heroes as human and fallible. Other fictional themes include elephant-hunting (*The Curve and the Tusk*, 1953) and white-slave trafficking (*The Abductors*, 1970). *A Victorian Son* (1971) and *The Gambler* (1973) are autobiographies.

Cloister and the Hearth, The: *A Tale of the Middle Ages* A historical romance by CHARLES READE, published in 1861 but expanded from a story, 'The Good Fight', which had appeared in *Once a Week* in 1859. The tale is set in the 15th century in Tergou, Holland, and concerns Gerard, a mercer's son, who loves Margaret, the daughter of a poor scholar, Peter Brandt. Both the burgomaster and Gerard's family oppose the marriage and contrive to have Gerard imprisoned. He escapes to join Margaret, but is later forced to flee the country. Gerard wanders through Europe, the incidents of his exile enlivened by atmospheric scenes in taverns, stews, castles and monasteries. In Italy, he hears a false report of Margaret's death and surrenders to debauchery before repenting and becoming a Dominican monk. Gerard returns to Holland, where he discovers Margaret. She has borne him a son who will grow up to be ERASMUS. No longer able to marry, Gerard spends the rest of his life at Gouda near his family. Reade based the novel on his studies of ERASMUS's *Life* and *Colloquies*, and the works of Froissart and Luther.

closet drama Plays written to be read rather than performed. There is scholarly dispute over the question of whether Seneca's work provides a classical precedent. English examples include MILTON's *SAMSON AGONISTES*, SHELLEY's *PROMETHEUS UNBOUND*, MATTHEW ARNOLD's *EMPEDOCLES ON ETNA* and HARDY's *THE DYNASTS*.

Cloud of Unknowing, The A mystical treatise of unknown authorship written in the second half of the 14th century, probably in the east Midlands. It is concerned with the preparation of the mind and soul for mystical experience, requiring the obliteration of the Christian's sense of self. The 'cloud' of the title is the gulf between man and God which can be crossed only by love and not by reason. The treatise aims to correct misleading notions drawn from the work of RICHARD ROLLE (d. 1349) and was itself later criticized by WALTER HILTON (d. 1395). Six other works are attributed to the author: *The Epistle of Privy Counsel*, *The Epistle of Prayer*, *Deonise Hid Divinite*, *Benjamin*, *The Epistle of Discretion in the Stirrings of the Soul* and *The Treatise of the Discerning of Spirits*. See also MYSTICAL WRITING.

Clough, Arthur Hugh 1819–61 Poet. Born in Liverpool, the son of a cotton merchant who emigrated to South Carolina, Clough spent his early years in the USA. During a family visit to England in 1828 he attended school in Chester and the following year was sent to Rugby, then under the headship of THOMAS ARNOLD whose son, MATTHEW ARNOLD, became one of his friends. In 1837 Clough went up to Balliol College, Oxford, and, after taking an undistinguished degree, he became in 1842 a fellow and tutor of Oriel College. But his orthodox faith was challenged, and in 1848 his perplexities over the interpretation of the 39 Articles compelled him to resign both his posts at Oriel. In 1849–51 he was principal of a student hostel at University College, London. Shortly thereafter he went as a tutor to Cambridge, Massachusetts, where he was friendly with such New England intellectuals as RALPH WALDO EMERSON and CHARLES ELIOT NORTON. Ever restless, Clough returned to England in 1853 to become Examiner in the Education Office, an office he held until his early death in Florence from a cerebral attack complicated by fever. Clough is commemorated in Matthew Arnold's elegiac poem, *THYRSIS*.

Clough wrote almost as much poetry as Matthew Arnold, but only two volumes appeared during his lifetime: *The Bothie of Tober-na-Vuolich* (1848), a verse-novel in hexameters, and *Ambarvalia* (1849), 29 shorter poems printed together with some verses by Thomas Burbidge. *AMOURS DE VOYAGE* first appeared in *THE ATLANTIC MONTHLY* in 1858 and the unfinished *DIPSYCHUS*, although mostly written in Venice in 1850, did not come out until 1865. Two other longer poems, both unfinished, *Mari Magno* and *Adam and*

Eve, and some lesser prose round off his writings. Long neglected, Clough's poetry has recently received recognition for its lyric quality and for its interpretation of the Victorian spiritual malaise.

Cobbe, Frances Power 1822–1904 Religious writer and philanthropist. Her first work, published anonymously, was *The Theory of Intuitive Morals* (1855–7). She travelled widely, producing, among other titles, *Italics* (1864), based on her observation of Italian life. Turning to philanthropic work, she supported female suffrage and opposed vivisection. Most of her numerous published works deal with these topics. Her autobiography appeared in 1894.

Cobbett, William 1763–1835 Political activist, journalist, farmer and MP. The son of an innkeeper in Farnham, Surrey, who taught him shorthand and arithmetic, as well as to read and write, Cobbett, otherwise self-educated, acquired at an early age a vigorous, plain style on which his whole career was based. It was 'vehement and brisk... free from affectation, loose, irregular and bold'. It was also witty, in the sense that Cobbett perceived connections of which others were unaware. Through the use of his pen he came to be acknowledged as one of the most powerful political influences of his day, writing some 20 million words in all.

He ran away from home at the age of 10 or 11 to work in the Royal Gardens at Kew (where he said he first read SWIFT's *TALE OF A TUB*) and then for a second time to London, where he worked as a clerk. Cobbett was posted to America soon after enlisting in the 54th Regiment of Foot in 1784. Though only a sergeant, he soon had effective responsibility for the garrison at Fredericton in New Brunswick because he could read, write and think more clearly than his officers. Back in England in 1792, and married to Anne (Nancy) Reid whom he had met in New Brunswick, Cobbett brought charges of corruption and peculation against his former officers, but had to flee, first to France and then to America, when counter-charges were brought against him by the military establishment.

This confrontation with authority set the pattern of his life: 'It is the system, the vermin-breeding system, that I for my part am at war with.' Always a loyalist and a patriot, and never a revolutionary, he became nevertheless what someone called 'a fiercely independent radical reformer', openly and energetically opposed to government corruption, to the vote-buying and patronage that was then normal, to the manipulation of the press by those in power, and to all types of social injustice, irrespective of the actual political system prevailing at the time. In 1792–1800, first in Wilmington and then in Philadelphia, though he earned his living by teaching English to French emigrés, he became as 'Peter Porcupine' (his pseudonym) the outstanding journalist in support of the Washington administration. But in his newspaper, *Porcupine's Gazette* (1797–9), and in pamphlets such as the outspoken *Observations on the Emigration of Dr Joseph Priestley* (1794) he so frequently tracked corruption and hypocrisy to its source in the personal abuse of power that his entertaining scurrility and outspokenness were bound to result, sooner or later, in court action. Libel actions brought against him in 1800 by Judge McKean and Benjamin Rush forced him to leave Philadelphia, ending the first phase of his career as an influential political journalist.

Whereas in Philadelphia Cobbett had attacked the American adulation of Napoleon, urging the case for the continuing interdependence of Britain and America, back in England he changed his tune and through his newspaper, *The Political Register*, regularly savaged the British government for corruption and incompetence. Although Cobbett consequently enjoyed immense popularity in the country as a whole, the fact that the government controlled both the press and the courts meant he was soon in trouble. 'Laws grind the poor, and rich men rule the law,' said Cobbett. Tried by one of the infamous special juries in an action brought against him by Spencer Perceval, a cabinet minister, Cobbett was found guilty of seditious libel, fined heavily and sent to Newgate Prison for two years, after which, Habeas Corpus having been suspended, he fled again to America. On Long Island he rented a small farm and lived almost at subsistence level, though continuing to write.

When Cobbett returned to England (with the disinterred mortal remains of TOM PAINE in his baggage) it was to re-engage fearlessly with British political life once again. His target now was to a much greater extent what he took to be the mismanagement of an economy characterized by alarming fluctuations in the price of wheat and the over-production of paper money. During the turbulent period leading to the Reform Bill of 1832, this political involvement never abated. Nevertheless, he lived more prudently. The farm at Botley he had acquired in 1805 proving impractical because distant from London, he took possession of a small-holding in Kensington, selling seeds and saplings of trees at that time unfamiliar in England – the ability, indeed the right, of a man to live off the soil by means of his own labour being one of the principal tenets of his belief.

At the same time he continued to write and publish practical primers, treatises and handbooks for the use of the literate poor. He had earlier published *A Grammar of the English Language* (1818) and *Cottage Economy* (1822). To these he now added *A French Grammar* (1824), *Cobbett's Poor Man's Friend* (1826–7), *The Woodlands* (1828), *The English Gardener* (1828), *Advice to Young Men and (Incidentally) Young Women* (1830) and *A Spelling Book* (1831), to give these only their short titles. The poor would always be poor, he thought, but by their own efforts they could improve the quality of their existence. Late in life he realized one of his principal ambitions by being elected MP for Oldham in the Reformed Parliament of 1832. By that time he had already made the travels that resulted in his best-known work, *RURAL RIDES* (1830). The social indignation of his earlier work is expressed here in more mellow terms. Indeed, for any reader who believes Cobbett's political battles to have been won, this must stand as his literary masterpiece.

Cockburn, Henry 1779–1854 Scottish judge and writer of autobiography. Born in Edinburgh, he became Solicitor-General for Scotland in 1830 and was appointed to the bench in 1834, with the judicial title of Lord Cockburn. Though he wrote a life of his friend FRANCIS JEFFREY (1852), he did not make his literary gifts widely known in his lifetime. A posthumously published volume of reminiscences, *Memorials of His Time* (1856), continued by two volumes of his *Journal* (1874) and one of *Circuit Journeys* (1888), established his reputation. He was the recorder of a rapidly vanishing Scotland whose characters, especially among Edinburgh legal dignitaries, he captured in memorable vignettes. His nostalgia for the 18th century and respect for Scottish rural peculiarities were tempered by a commonsensical view of the 19th century and a strong feeling for the metropolitan elegance of Edinburgh, where a civic society, the Cockburn Association, was founded in his memory in 1875.

Cockney School, The An abusive label for LEIGH HUNT and his friends KEATS and HAZLITT, apparently coined by *BLACKWOOD'S EDINBURGH MAGAZINE* in October 1817 in the first of a series of venomous attacks which portrayed Hunt as the debauched ringleader of a group of literary upstarts, whose humble (i.e. lower middle-class) origins ill fitted them for the poetic calling. Hazlitt was so angered that he sued the editors, who settled out of court. Keats's work, notably *Poems* (1817) and *ENDYMION* (1818), was cruelly combed for immature verses and 'Cockney' rhymes, and the poet derided as an apprentice apothecary 'of pretty abilities, which he has done everything in his power to spoil' – a sneer tastelessly repeated after his death.

Cocktail Party, The A verse drama by T. S. ELIOT, first performed at the Edinburgh Festival in 1949. It is loosely based on the *Alcestis* of Euripides. The outer shell of the play concerns a quartet of lovers temporarily adrift from the fashionable society to which they belong, but Eliot's deeper concern is with modes of spiritual reconciliation for individual Christians. A knowing psychoanalyst, Sir Henry Harcourt-Reilly, restores the unsatisfactory marriage of Lavinia and Edward Chamberlayne. This achievement requires, in

a way uneasily assimilated by the accomplished triviality of the poetic dialogue, the Christian martyrdom of Edward's lover Celia, a sacrifice which permits the predominantly secular life of the community to continue.

Cockton, Henry 1807–53 Novelist. Nothing is known of Cockton's early life except that he was born in London. He achieved temporary success with broadly comic novels in the manner of the early DICKENS – notably *The Life and Adventures of Valentine Vox the Ventriloquist* (1840) – but lost the money they earned him by an unsuccessful venture into the malting business at Bury St Edmunds, Suffolk, where he died.

Coetzee, J(ohn) M(ichael) 1940– South African novelist. Born in Cape Town, he is professor of general literature at the University of Cape Town. His deliberately disorienting, linguistically explosive writing is as much about the nature of language and the techniques of fiction as about the victims of imperialism, neo-colonialism, and apartheid. *Dusklands* (1974) consists of two closely related novellas, one about America and Vietnam, the other about an 18th-century Boer pioneer, both protagonists exercising power brutally over people considered inferior. *In the Heart of the Country* (1977; as *From the Heart of the Country* in the USA) presents the patricidal fantasies of a rebellious Afrikaner spinster, trying vainly to reorder her life imaginatively; it is an overwritten book. The Crusoe-like fear of unidentifiable footprints dominates *Waiting for the Barbarians* (1980), with neither humane imperial-frontier magistrate nor brutal security chief able to discover the external 'enemy' they mistake for their corrosive power-sickness. *Life and Times of Michael K* (1983), which won the BOOKER PRIZE, describes its despised hero's almost epic survival. *Foe* (1986) retells DEFOE's *ROBINSON CRUSOE* from the viewpoint of a woman castaway excluded from the original story. *Age of Iron* (1990) is narrated by a woman dying of cancer, linked to the malignancy at the heart of South African society. Coetzee has also published translations and literary criticism, including the essays in *White Writing* (1988).

Cogswell, Fred 1917– Canadian poet and editor. Born in East Centreville, New Brunswick, he served in the Canadian army in World War II and subsequently attended the Universities of New Brunswick and Edinburgh, from which he received his doctorate in 1952. He then returned to the University of New Brunswick to teach English and spent his entire career there. He was editor of the magazine *Fiddlehead* from 1952 to 1967 and founded Fiddlehead Books, a publishing house which provided an outlet for many young Maritime writers. He was made a member of the Order of Canada in 1981. Cogswell has published numerous volumes of poetry since his first book, *The Stunted Strong*, appeared in 1954. They include *Descent from Eden* (1959), *Lost Dimension* (1960), *Star-People* (1968), *A Long Apprenticeship: Collected Poems* (1980) and *The Best Notes Merge* (1988). His best work describes the lives of Maritime villagers in a witty, laconic style. Other poems are more personal, recording a subjective response to a variety of everyday experiences. His translations, which include *One Hundred Poems of Modern Quebec* (1970) and *Confrontations* (1976), have helped stimulate interest in Quebec poetry in anglophone Canada. With Jo-Anne Elder he has edited *Unfinished Dreams: Contemporary Poetry of Acadie* (1990).

Cohen, Leonard 1934– Canadian poet, novelist and composer-singer. The son of a prominent Jewish clothier, he was born and brought up in an affluent district of Montreal and attended McGill University, graduating in 1955. His first volume of verse, *Let Us Compare Mythologies*, appeared the following year. He embarked on graduate study at Columbia University but dropped out to write and perform music. Internationally known as an entertainer, Cohen has also published important works of poetry and fiction. His poetry includes *The Spice-Box of Earth* (1961), *Flowers for Hitler* (1964), *The Energy of Slaves* (1972), *Death of a Lady's Man* (1978) and *Book of Mercy* (1984). Like his songs, it explores contemporary mythologies but frequently uses traditional forms. Cohen's novel *The Favourite Game* (1963) was followed by *Beautiful Losers* (1968), a counter-cultural religious epic. He declined a Canadian Governor-General's Award for his *Selected Poems* (1968). In 1983 he completed an opera with the Montreal composer Louis Furey. His record albums include *Songs of Leonard Cohen* (1967), *Songs of Love and Hate* (1971), *New Skins for the Old Ceremony* (1974), *The Best of Leonard Cohen* (1975) and *Death of a Lady's Man* (1977).

Cohen, Matt 1942– Canadian novelist and short-story writer. Born in Kingston, Ontario, he grew up in Ottawa, attended the University of Toronto and spent a year teaching the sociology of religion at McMaster University, Hamilton. He has mainly lived in Toronto and on a farm in Verona, Ontario, but has also spent periods in France, Italy and the Queen Charlotte Islands, the setting for his fourth novel *Wooden Hunters* (1975). His first two novels, *Korsoniloff* (1969) and *Johnny Crackle Sings* (1971), use experimental forms to explore the dehumanizing pressures of contemporary society. His four 'Salem' novels – *The Disinherited* (1974), *The Colours of War* (1977), *The Sweet Second Summer of Kitty Malone* (1979) and *Flowers of Darkness* (1981) – are

written in a realistic mode, which he believes is the dominant tradition in Canadian fiction, and deal with family relationships in a community in rural Ontario. Dispossession and self-exploration are major themes of these and other works. *The Spanish Doctor* (1984) is an epic novel about the Jewish diaspora in medieval Europe. *Emotional Arithmetic* (1990) is the story of a woman scarred by her internment by the Nazis in World War II. Other books include short-story collections: *Columbus and the Fat Lady* (1972), *Night Flights* (1978), *Café le Dog* (1983) and *Living on Water* (1988).

Coke [Cook], Sir **Edward** 1552–1634 Legal writer. Born in Norfolk, he completed his education at Trinity College, Cambridge, and became a barrister of the Inner Temple. His future was assured when he attracted the attention of Lord Burghley, who made him Attorney-General. His rival for the office was FRANCIS BACON, whose opponent in law he remained. Coke became Chief Justice of the Court of Common Pleas in 1606, and waged a steady war against the courts of privilege; one of his triumphs was the acceptance of the principle that the King could not change the common law by proclamation. JAMES I, and all the adherents of the idea of government by *rex*, were determined to overcome the champion of *lex* and James 'promoted' him to Chief Justice of the King's Bench in 1613. Coke and the other judges were involved in a direct challenge to the King in 1616, when they decided that he could not command the common-law courts to desist from hearing cases pending, even if the royal interest was involved. When summoned before the King's council Coke was the only judge who stood his ground, and the King dismissed him.

Coke's place as a writer on English law is a proud one. His *Reports* (13 vols., 1600–15) and *Institutes* (4 vols., 1628–44) contain a superb exposition of the rules of English common law.

Cold Comfort Farm The first and most famous novel by Stella Gibbons (1902–89), *Cold Comfort Farm* appeared in 1932 and won the Femina Vie Heureuse Prize. An acute and witty PARODY of the rural fiction made popular by writers like MARY WEBB, it both mocks and exploits the hysterical intrigue, emotional turmoil and lugubriousness of the genre.

Colenso, John William 1814–83 Theologian. Born into a poor family at St Austell he entered St John's College, Cambridge, as a sizar and was elected a fellow in 1837. After some years as a mathematics teacher at Harrow and a tutor in his own college, Colenso became vicar of Forncett St Mary in Norfolk. In 1853 he was appointed bishop of the new diocese of Natal, where his attitude to race relations and his broadminded approach to tribal customs in marriage caused controversy. Colenso provoked a larger storm by his contribution to the HIGHER CRITICISM in *A Commentary on the Epistle to the Romans* (1861) and *The Pentateuch and Book of Joshua Critically Examined* (1862–79), which challenged the historical accuracy of those books and concluded that they were written during the post-Exile period. In 1863 Bishop Gray of Cape Town deposed Colenso, who in turn challenged Gray's jurisdiction. Colenso was confirmed as holder of the see by the law courts in 1866 and he continued in the affection of his diocese until he died.

Coleridge, Derwent 1800–83 Editor, biographer and poet. The son of SAMUEL TAYLOR COLERIDGE, he was educated at St John's College, Cambridge, and ordained in 1825. As master of the grammar school at Helston in Cornwall, he taught CHARLES KINGSLEY. He contributed poetry to *Knight's Quarterly Magazine* from 1822. He also published *The Scriptural Character of the English Church* (1839) and a biography of his brother HARTLEY COLERIDGE (1849), whose works he edited (1851).

Coleridge, Hartley David 1796–1849 Poet. The eldest son of SAMUEL TAYLOR COLERIDGE, who named him after the philosopher DAVID HARTLEY. Born at Clevedon, Somerset, he attended Ambleside school where his education was supervised by ROBERT SOUTHEY. He went on to Merton College, Oxford, and later became a probationer fellow of Oriel, but was dismissed for 'intemperance'. He eked out a living by contributing to *BLACKWOOD'S EDINBURGH MAGAZINE* and *The London Magazine*. He attempted to run a school at Ambleside 1823–8, but finally retired as a recluse to Grasmere. He published *Biographia Borealis* (1833), republished in 1852 as *Lives of Northern Worthies* with marginal observations by S. T. Coleridge. Other works included a slight volume of *Poems* (1833) and a biography of ANDREW MARVELL (1835). Two volumes of *Poems* were published in 1851, accompanied by a memoir by his brother DERWENT COLERIDGE.

Coleridge, Mary Elizabeth 1861–1907 Novelist and poet. She was born in London, the great-granddaughter of SAMUEL TAYLOR COLERIDGE's brother. Educated at home, partly by W. J. CORY, she began to write verse as a child, publishing her first volumes *Fancy's Following* (1896) and *Fancy's Guerdon* (1897) under the pseudonym Anodos. Her first novel, *The Seven Sleepers of Ephesus* (1893), was praised by ROBERT LOUIS STEVENSON; other titles include *The King with Two Faces* (1897), *The Fiery Dawn* (1901) and *The Lady on the Drawing Room Floor* (1906). Her *Poems Old and New* (1907) and *Gathered Leaves* (1910) were published posthumously.

Coleridge, Samuel Taylor 1772–1834 Poet, critic and philosopher. He was born at Ottery St Mary,

Devon, where his father was vicar. After his father's death in 1781 he was sent to preparatory school in London and then to Christ's Hospital, where his schoolfellows included CHARLES LAMB and LEIGH HUNT. Intended for the church, he entered Jesus College, Cambridge, in 1791, joining in the reformist fervour stimulated by the French Revolution. He abandoned his studies in December 1793, enlisting in the Light Dragoons under the name of Silas Tomkyn Comberbache. He was bought out after two wretched months but did not return to Cambridge to take his degree, despite reinstatement in autumn 1794.

In June 1794 Coleridge met ROBERT SOUTHEY in Oxford. They decided to establish a commune in New England based on the ideas of WILLIAM GODWIN. The scheme – which Coleridge called 'Pantisocracy' – came to nothing, though at Bristol Coleridge allowed Southey to talk him into pledging himself to Sara Fricker, sister of Southey's fiancée Edith. Coleridge's first poems appeared in *The Morning Chronicle* in December 1794. On leaving Cambridge for good that winter, he went to London and then Bristol, lodging with Southey and lecturing on politics, religion and education. His lectures won him the respect of local democrats, including the publisher Joseph Cottle and Thomas and Josiah Wedgwood of the pottery dynasty. After his marriage to Sara Fricker in October 1795 he settled at nearby Clevedon. His first volume, *Poems on Various Subjects*, was published by Cottle in April 1796 and his first son, HARTLEY DAVID COLERIDGE, was born in September. Coleridge preached throughout the region, produced 10 issues of a radical Christian weekly, *The Watchman*, wrote philosophical and religious 'conversation poems' and began to read German literature and philosophy. He also took opium during bouts of illness and depression.

In December 1796 the Coleridges moved to Nether Stowey on the edge of the Quantock Hills. WILLIAM WORDSWORTH and his sister DOROTHY WORDSWORTH, whom he first visited in June 1797, were living nearby. The literary partnership that began laid the foundations of English ROMANTICISM. The two poets planned a joint volume of 'experimental' poems, the *LYRICAL BALLADS*, eventually published in 1798, to which Coleridge's most important contribution was *THE RIME OF THE ANCIENT MARINER*. He also began, though never completed, three other BALLADS in the same idiom, the finest of which is *CHRISTABEL*. Visitors included Charles and Mary Lamb, the radical John Thelwall and the young HAZLITT. The year 1797–8 was a happy, creative period. His second son was born in May 1798 and an annuity from the Wedgwoods allowed him to write full-time. He produced another sequence of conversation poems, addressed to friends: 'This Lime-Tree Bower My Prison', 'Frost at Midnight', 'Fears in Solitude' and 'The Nightingale'. The enigmatic fragment *KUBLA KHAN* was written in 1797.

Other work included the verse tragedy *Osirio*, leading articles for *The Morning Post* on foreign policy, the political ode 'France' and the anti-war poem 'Fire, Famine, Slaughter: A War Eclogue'.

In September 1798 Coleridge visited Germany with the Wordsworths, proceeding alone to Göttingen to attend lectures and read deeply in Kant, Schiller, Schelling and A. W. Schlegel. These studies made him the most influential English interpreter of German Romanticism and the foremost exponent of its organicist doctrines. Back in England the next year, he translated part of Schiller's *Wallenstein* trilogy, contracted for a biography of Lessing and planned an ambitious work of Romantic metaphysics. He also wrote some 50 articles for *The Morning Post* between December 1799 and October 1800. He moved his family to London and then to Keswick in the Lake District to be near Wordsworth. By this time Coleridge's marriage had begun to fail and he fell in love with Sara Hutchinson, whose sister Mary married Wordsworth in 1802. The guilt and stress of this love profoundly affected him over the next decade, forming the background to such poems as 'The Keepsake' (1800), 'On Revisiting the Seashore' (1801), 'To Asra' (1801), 'The Picture, or, The Lovers' Resolution' (1802) and 'A Daydream' (1801–2). A more authentic voice breaks through in 'Dejection: An Ode' (1802), answered by Wordsworth in his 'Intimations of Immortality' ode. Coleridge now became more or less addicted to opium. His energies flowed away from systematic work and into the meditative, confessional *Notebooks*.

In spring 1804 he left Southey to take care of his family (which by then included another son, DERWENT COLERIDGE, and SARA COLERIDGE) and spent two years in the wartime Civil Service at Malta. Little was heard of him in England during this exile. He increased his intake of opium, visited Sicily and Italy, wrote nothing but his notebooks and vainly tried to forget Sara Hutchinson. On his return to England in August 1806 he formalized his separation from his wife. From December 1806 to June 1807 he stayed with the Wordsworths and Sara Hutchinson, then living at Coleorton, Leicestershire, and was present at Wordsworth's reading of the 'Poem to Coleridge' which became THE PRELUDE; he replied with the conversation poem 'To William Wordsworth'. In 1808 he delivered 18 lectures 'On Poetry and the Principles of Taste' at the Royal Institute, the first of many series in the next decade. The form was particularly congenial to him, and he drew large, distinguished audiences. Especially significant were the lectures on SHAKESPEARE (first published as a two-volume collection of *Shakespearean Criticism* in 1907), developing the idea of a poet's work as epiphenomena, or particular emanations, of a single creative mind and the concept, then completely new, of 'Organic' form. In autumn 1808 Coleridge joined the Wordsworths for the last time, spending 18 months at Grasmere. Here he produced *The Friend*, a 'literary, moral and political paper' running for 28 issues in 1809–10 and appearing in book form in 1812, perhaps the closest he came to fulfilling his dream of a synthesis. Politically and intellectually, its project of educating the English mind in post-Kantian idealism showed his development towards a new conservatism.

The final break with Wordsworth, and the last crisis of his relationship with Sara Hutchinson, came in 1810. Coleridge lodged in London, lecturing and writing despite periods of near suicidal despair and his ever-increasing opium addiction. The few poems of the next years include 'The Visionary Hope' (1810), 'The Suicide's Argument' (1811) and 'Time, Real and Imaginary' (1812). His pro-Government articles in *The Courier* and his attacks on the English Jacobins caused Hazlitt to denounce him as a political turncoat. His play *Remorse*, a reworking of *Osirio*, was produced at DRURY LANE in 1813. After a physical and mental breakdown in December 1813 Coleridge underwent treatment at Bristol and spent the summer of 1814 with friends near Bath. To this period belong the marginal commentaries added to *The Rime of the Ancient Mariner*, three short essays 'On the Principles of Genial Criticism Concerning the Fine Arts' and *BIOGRAPHIA LITERARIA*, a kaleidoscope of philosophy, criticism and autobiography, and one of the key texts of English Romanticism.

In the spring of 1816 Coleridge settled at the Highgate home of Dr James Gillman, remaining there for the rest of his life. A chastened but also clarified figure, he became something of a living legend to younger Romantic poets. At BYRON'S initiative, *Christabel and Other Poems* appeared in 1816, printing 'Kubla Khan' and 'The Pains of Sleep' for the first time. *Sibylline Leaves*, his collected poems, was published in 1817 (and expanded in 1828 and 1834), along with the *Biographia* and *Zapolyta*, a 'dramatic poem... in humble imitation of "The Winter's Tale" of Shakespeare'. Yet Coleridge's poetic career was largely over. The philosopher, preacher-lecturer and critic, on the other hand, flourished. He became the centre of a circle of friends and disciples that included Godwin, CRABB ROBINSON and the faithful Charles Lamb.

Coleridge's view of society, culture and religion became more concrete and programmatic. His two *Lay Sermons* (1816–17) develop ideas on morality, national education and the 'organic' structure of society. His 'Treatise on Method', written as introduction to the *Encyclopaedia Metropolitana* and included in the final three-volume edition of *The Friend* (1818), ranges through every conceivable branch of knowledge in dizzying pursuit of the 'self-organizing purpose' of nature, man and science. In 1818–19 he lectured on 'The History of Philosophy' and gave a 'General Course on Literature', described in the *Literary Remains* (1836). *Aids to Reflection* (1824), emphasizing the importance of Christianity as 'personal revelation', influenced the development of the Broad Church movement and the CHRISTIAN SOCIALISM of John Sterling, F. D. MAURICE and CHARLES KINGSLEY. In his last years Coleridge renewed his friendship with Wordsworth, with whom he went on a short tour of Germany in 1828, made memorable by a meeting with Friedrich Schlegel. 'Work without Hope', 'Constancy to an Ideal Object', 'Coeli Enarrant' and 'Love's Apparition' are among the most representative of his few late poems. His last major publication, *On the Constitution of the Church and State* (1830), proposed the removal of education and learning from both ecclesiastical and state control and the establishment of teachers, scholars, scientists, artists and priests as an independent 'estate of the Realm' called the 'clerisy' or 'National Church'. Some idea of Coleridge's conversation is given in *Table Talk* (1836), edited by his nephew Henry Coleridge.

Coleridge's reputation as a poet is secured by a small, though radiant, corpus of major works. The distinctively Continental cast of his thought was excitingly new to British contemporaries. His theory of the poetic imagination as a unifying and mediating power within divided modern cultures provided one of the central ideas of Romantic aesthetics, and his dialectical juxtapositions of reason and understanding, culture and civilization, and mechanical and organic form shaped the vocabulary of its recoil from UTILITARIANISM. Yet much of Coleridge's work is shot through with self-doubt and fears for his Christian belief, a metaphysical anxiety that seems to anticipate modern existentialism.

Coleridge, Sara 1802–52 Miscellaneous writer. Born at Keswick, the only daughter of SAMUEL TAYLOR COLERIDGE, she married her cousin, Henry Nelson Coleridge, in 1829. She translated Dobrizhoffer's *Account of the Abipones* (1822) and the history of the Chevalier Bayard (1825). Her most important work was a romantic fairy-tale in prose and verse, *Phantasmion* (1837). She also published *Pretty Lessons for Good Children* (1845) and edited her father's *Poems* (1852) with her brother DERWENT COLERIDGE.

Colet, John ?1467–1519 Humanist and scholar. He was educated at Oxford and travelled abroad for three years in France and Italy. He lectured in 1496–1504 at Oxford, first on the Epistle to the Romans and (with ERASMUS among his audience) on 1 Corinthians. His exposition abandoned the minute exegesis and allegorical interpretation of the schoolmen. As a humanist he extolled the virtues of pure classical Latin and was influenced by Platonic and neo-Platonic thought. In 1504 Colet became Dean of St Paul's, and *c.*1509 he founded St Paul's School with William Lily as its first headmaster. He and Lily prepared a Latin grammar, later revised by Erasmus. Colet was a close friend and correspondent of THOMAS MORE as well as Erasmus.

Colin Clout's Come Home Again A PASTORAL poem (1595) by SPENSER, it is evidently designed to recall the major character in *THE SHEPHEARDES CALENDER*. Colin gives a first-hand account of his adventures to his fellow shepherds, some of whose names, Hobbinol and Cuddy, also recall Spenser's earlier poem. It offers compliments to Queen Elizabeth (Cynthia) and Raleigh (the Shepherd of the Ocean), laments the death of SIR PHILIP SIDNEY (Astrophel), and alludes to notable personages of the poet's time, such as the Countess of Pembroke (Urania). It is ambivalent in its feeling about the court which it alternately compliments and criticizes, and is one of Spenser's most autobiographically allusive poems.

Colleen Bawn, The A MELODRAMA by DION BOUCICAULT, based on GERALD GRIFFIN's 'true-life' crime novel, *The Collegians* (1829). The play was first performed at Laura Keene's Theatre, New York, in 1860.

Hardress Cregan, secretly married to Eily O'Connor, the poor but honest colleen bawn (Anglo-Irish for 'fair girl'), needs to marry the heiress, Anne Chute, in order to redeem the family's fortunes. He instructs his devoted hunchbacked servant to kill Eily, but the attempt is frustrated by the comic vagabond Myles-na-Coppaleen. Although Myles loves Eily, it is enough for him to see her happily restored to her repentant husband. The creation of Myles gave new life to the figure of the stage Irishman.

Collier, Arthur 1680–1732 Churchman and philosopher. A native of Wiltshire, Collier was educated at Pembroke and Balliol colleges, Oxford, and held the living of Langford Magna until his death. His *Clavis Universalis: or, A Demonstration of the Non-Existence and Impossibility of the External World* (1713) showed that Collier had arrived independently at the same conclusions as BERKELEY's *Principles of Human Knowledge*.

Collier, Jeremy 1650–1726 Moralist and divine. Educated at Ipswich school and Gonville and Caius College, Cambridge, Collier became rector of Ampton in Suffolk (1679) and lecturer at Gray's Inn (1685). He remained loyal to James II, refusing to take the oath of loyalty to William and Mary, and was imprisoned in 1689 and 1692; in 1696 he incurred further wrath by giving absolution on the scaffold, to two men charged with attempting to assassinate King William. Collier was outlawed and fled the country; but he returned in 1697 and became a bishop in 1713, though still without taking the oath of loyalty.

A man of unwavering courage, Collier was author of *Essays upon Several Moral Subjects* (3 parts, 1698-1705), *The Great Historical, Geographical, Genealogical and Poetical Dictionary* (1701) and *The Ecclesiastical History of Great Britain* (2 vols., 1708 and 1714). He is best known for his controversial *Short View of the Immorality and Profaneness of the English Stage* (1698), an attack on the leading playwrights of the day, including DRYDEN, CONGREVE, VANBRUGH, JOHN DENNIS and THOMAS D'URFEY. Both Congreve and Vanbrugh replied to Collier.

Collier, John Payne 1789-1883 Scholar and forger. Born in London, he qualified as a barrister despite receiving little formal education. He chose instead to work as a journalist, for *The Times* and later *THE MORNING CHRONICLE*. His scholarly writings on SHAKESPEARE and Renaissance drama were supported by researches in noblemen's private libraries and vigorous work for various literary and historical publishing societies. A Second Folio Shakespeare (1632) with supposedly contemporary annotations was the basis for his later work and reputation. The annotations were exposed as forgeries only after embittered controversy. Collier was taken to be the perpetrator rather than the victim of the fraud and, as well as blighting the end of his life, the revelation rendered his previous work permanently suspect.

Collins, Anthony 1676-1729 Philosopher. Collins was born in Heston, Middlesex, and educated at Eton and King's College, Cambridge. He became Deputy-Lieutenant of Essex in 1715.

A close friend and admirer of JOHN LOCKE, Collins became a freethinker and influential advocate of DEISM in his own right. His *Essay Concerning the Use of Reason* (1707) denied the accepted separation between those things that are beyond human reason and those that are not. *A Discourse of Freethinking, Occasioned by the Rise and Growth of a Sect Call'd Freethinkers* (1713) sharply attacked ministers of all denominations and was in its turn attacked by many churchmen, including RICHARD BENTLEY and JONATHAN SWIFT. Collins's *A Philosophical Inquiry concerning Human Liberty and Necessity* (1715) is a statement of determinism.

Collins, John Churton 1848-1908 Critic. The son of a doctor, Collins was born in Gloucestershire and attended King Edward's School, Birmingham, before studying at Balliol College, Oxford. Until his appointment as professor of English at Birmingham in 1904, he made his living as a private tutor and extension lecturer in London, contributing articles to *THE CORNHILL MAGAZINE*, *THE QUARTERLY REVIEW* and, later, to *THE SATURDAY REVIEW*. A ruthless critic, he wrote damaging attacks on EDMUND GOSSE and even on his friend SWINBURNE, and offended Oxford

University with his agitation for the establishment of an English school there, in his book *The Study of English Literature* (1891) and in earlier articles for *THE PALL MALL GAZETTE*.

Collins edited works by ROBERT GREENE, TOURNEUR, LORD HERBERT OF CHERBURY and MILTON, and published *Ephemera Critica* (1901), *Studies in Shakespeare* (1904) and other critical works. Morbidly interested in murder, spiritualism and graveyards, and depressive in temperament, he drowned himself near Lowestoft.

Collins, Tom See MURPHY, JOSEPH.

Collins, (William) Wilkie 1824-89 Novelist. Born in London, son of the landscape painter William Collins, he was named after his father's friend Sir David Wilkie. Educated privately, with generous interruptions for travel abroad, he entered Lincoln's Inn in 1846 but quickly showed the real direction of his interest by publishing three books: a memoir of his father (1848); *Antonina: or, The Fall of Rome* (1850), a historical novel in the manner of BULWER LYTTON; and the charming *Rambles beyond Railways* (1851), about a walking tour of Cornwall. He first met DICKENS in 1851, joining the older novelist in amateur theatricals and becoming a regular contributor to *HOUSEHOLD WORDS*; the two men also collaborated in writing, among other pieces, *The Lazy Tour of Two Idle Apprentices* (1857) and two MELODRAMAS, *The Lighthouse* (1855) and *The Frozen Deep* (1857). By himself Collins produced a succession of short stories and several novels: *Basil: A Story of Modern Life* (1852), *Hide and Seek* (1854) and *The Dead Secret* (1857). They were the prelude to his work of the 1860s, when he emerged as the most skilful writer of SENSATION FICTION, with *THE WOMAN IN WHITE* (1860), *No Name* (1862), *Armadale* (1866) and *THE MOONSTONE* (1868). Vigorously observing his own advice to the novelist – 'Make 'em laugh, make 'em cry, make 'em wait' – these books made him one of the most popular writers of the day.

His triumph ended with the decade. Various reasons have been suggested for Collins's subsequent decline in power and the near-eclipse of his former popularity: the death of Dickens in 1870 robbed him of a powerful mentor; his recurrent ill health was aggravated by addiction to laudanum; and his unconventional private life became further entangled, with two mistresses, Caroline Graves and Martha Rudd, apparently sharing his house. Above all, his determination to tackle social issues disconcerted his audience and, at times, dispersed his narrative powers. SWINBURNE commented in a famous doggerel: 'What brought good Wilkie's genius nigh perdition?/ Some devil whispered – "Wilkie, have a mission."' Collins attacked athleticism in *Man and Wife* (1870), attitudes to fallen women in *The New Magdalen* (1873), the Jesuits in *The Black Robe* (1881) and vivisection in *Heart and Science* (1883). *The Evil Genius* (1886) dealt with adultery and divorce, *The Legacy of Cain* (1889) with heredity and environment. Not all his later works were failures – though Swinburne thought *The Fallen Leaves* (1879) 'something too absurdly repulsive for comment and endurance' – and Collins periodically returned to mystery and suspense, with varying success, in *Poor Miss Finch* (1872), *The Law and the Lady* (1875), *My Lady's Money* (1878) and *I Say No* (1884). His last novel, *Blind Love* (1890), was completed by WALTER BESANT.

Collins, William 1721–59 Poet. The son of a hatter, Collins was born in Chichester and was educated at Winchester College and then at Magdalen College, Oxford. He went to London in 1744 with almost no money, determined on a literary career.

Collins began to write poetry as a schoolboy and completed the *Persian Eclogues* (published in 1742) when he was 17. In London he published *Odes on Several Descriptive and Allegoric Subjects* (1746) but did not gain recognition immediately; he accepted an advance from a London bookseller for a translation of Aristotle's *Poetics* and retired to Chichester. Then in 1749 he inherited £2000 and promptly repaid the advance; he also abandoned the translation of Aristotle, but his plans for future work halted when his mental and physical health began to fail. He broke down completely after a journey in France (1750) and died insane at the age of 38, at his sister's house in Chichester.

Collins's temperament was unstable and, for most of his life, his circumstances uncertain: he was always 'doubtful of his dinner and trembling at a creditor', anxieties that his inheritance came too late to allay. Even before his career as a poet broke off, he had never been prolific and he left less than 1500 lines of verse. Yet they show he had the makings of an original artist, struggling to escape the conventions of his time and often succeeding. The works which have a permanent place in English poetry show him above all a master of the ODE: 'Ode to Simplicity', 'Dirge in Cymbeline', 'Ode to Evening', 'How Sleep the Brave' ('Ode, Written in the Beginning of the Year 1746') and especially the posthumous 'Ode on the Popular Superstitions of the Highlands' (1788).

Colman, George, the elder 1732–94 Playwright, journalist and theatre manager. Colman trained, rather casually, as a lawyer in the expectation that he would inherit riches from his uncle, William Pulteney, Earl of Bath. His early involvement with the theatre, a product of his friendship with the equally clubbable DAVID GARRICK, was amateur. The one-act *Polly Honeycombe* (1760) is light and charming. *The Jealous Wife* (1761), inspired by rather than based on

FIELDING's *TOM JONES*, is more ambitious. Its extraordinary success, in a style more acerbic than that of SENTIMENTAL COMEDY, may have tempted Colman towards the theatre and away from his legal practice. If the Earl of Bath was displeased, we have a ready explanation of his leaving Colman, in 1764, a much smaller inheritance than he had hoped for. Colman's disappointment silenced the carefree tone of his life and work. He was sufficiently provided to abandon the law, but he had now to rely on the patronage of the public. His translation of *The Comedies of Terence* (1765) enhanced his reputation, as did a successful collaboration with Garrick in *THE CLANDESTINE MARRIAGE* (1766), but Colman was temperamentally inclined to spend more than he had. It was the need to make money that persuaded him to put his friendship with Garrick at risk by buying a share in the management of COVENT GARDEN, chief rival to Garrick's DRURY LANE.

Colman was the active and effective manager of Covent Garden for seven years, 1767–74. His own plays during this period were mostly adaptations, though *The Man of Business* (1774) was a notable exception. Two years after leaving Covent Garden he was tempted back into management when the death of SAMUEL FOOTE left vacant the Little Theatre in the HAYMARKET. His last two considerable plays, *The Suicide* (1778) and *The Separate Maintenance* (1779), were first performed there. Increasingly subject to bouts of insanity from 1785, Colman eventually surrendered the management of the Haymarket to his son, GEORGE COLMAN THE YOUNGER, in 1790.

Colman, George, the younger 1762–1836 Playwright and theatre manager. He was the son of GEORGE COLMAN THE ELDER, from whom he inherited the Little Theatre in the HAYMARKET in 1794, having already assumed the responsibilities of management five years earlier. Gregarious, hard-drinking and improvident, he nevertheless defended and improved the status of the Little Theatre, with which he remained associated until 1817. His fourth play, *Inkle and Yarico* (1787), was a deserved success there. Described as an opera, it is a comedy with songs, humanely if uninsistently critical of the slave trade. Colman was a fluent writer of comic verse, as his collection of 'tales in verse', *My Nightgown and Slippers* (1797) shows. This talent enlivens, with some strain on plausibility, the historical romances, *The Battle of Hexham* (1789) and *The Surrender of Calais* (1791), as well as colouring the otherwise sombre adaptation of GODWIN's *CALEB WILLIAMS*, *The Iron Chest* (1796). Colman's more traditional five-act comedies, *The Heir at Law* (1797), *The Poor Gentleman* (1801) and particularly *John Bull* (1803), are not without incidental merits, but he was at his best as a popular entertainer. It is ironic that his work as Examiner of Plays in 1824–36 should have left him with the reputation of a spoiler of other people's entertainment.

Colonel Jack [*The History and Remarkable Life of the Truly Honourable Colonel Jacque, Commonly Called Colonel Jack*] A novel by DANIEL DEFOE, published in 1722. Like the earlier CAPTAIN SINGLETON, it is a romantic adventure told in the first person. The early chapters are among the finest in Defoe's fiction.

Abandoned by his parents while a small child, 'Colonel Jack' falls into bad company, becomes a pickpocket, and reaches early manhood living on his wits. To escape this way of life, he enlists as a soldier but promptly deserts when faced with the prospect of fighting in Flanders. Next he is abducted and shipped to Virginia, where he is sold as a slave to a planter. Promoted to overseer and eventually freed, he becomes a planter himself and is so successful that he is able to return to England a rich man. By the end of the tale he is prosperous and mellow.

Colton, Charles Caleb ?1780–1832 Author of the immensely popular *Lacon: or, Many Things in Few Words*(1820), a collection of aphorisms, EPIGRAMS and essays. Educated at Eton and Cambridge, Colton was a clergyman who felt little inclination for the calling.

Colum, Padraic 1881–1972 Irish poet, playwright, folklorist and writer of CHILDREN'S LITERATURE. The son of a workhouse master in Longford, he worked in Dublin as a railway clerk until helped by a wealthy American and Arthur Griffith, a nationalist politician whose biography he eventually wrote (1959). Early plays such as *Broken Soil* (1903), *The Land* (1905) and *Thomas Muskerry* (1910) are sombrely realistic pieces prompted by his association with YEATS and LADY GREGORY at the ABBEY THEATRE. *Wild Earth* (1907) is the first of many collections of poems chiefly remembered for the simple rhythmic lyricism of his early work. He left Ireland in 1914 and lived thereafter chiefly in the USA, though temporary residence in Paris brought him the friendship of JAMES JOYCE, commemorated in *Our Friend James Joyce* (1958). His commissioned study of Polynesian folklore in Hawaii resulted in three volumes of stories in the 1920s. He lectured on comparative literature and published many volumes for children retelling Irish, Welsh, classical and Scandinavian myths and legends, while also continuing to write poems and plays. *The Flying Swans* (1957) is an ambitious, neglected novel.

Columbiad, The An EPIC poem in HEROIC COUPLETS by JOEL BARLOW published in 1807, 20 years after it first appeared as *The Vision of Columbus*. The two versions, however, have little in common. In nine books, *The Vision* presents a dialogue between an angel and Christopher Columbus, both of whom ascend the Mount of Vision and survey human history. The angel argues that all historical events, particularly Columbus's discovery, lead to the future glory of America. The poem thus reaffirms America's manifest destiny; it offers an essentially conservative vision congenial to Federalists of the new republic.

By 1807 Barlow had changed his political orientation and had revised the poem accordingly into *The Columbiad*. Now a liberal democrat, he replaced the simple dialogue with a colloquy of different voices, each intended to represent a different political or social interest. He also included further classical allusions, often explained in lengthy scholarly footnotes, and developed the prefaces to each of the nine books into extensive political and philosophical arguments. Ironically, these revisions, which aimed at widening the poem's audience, in fact limited it, and made *The Columbiad* read more like a political treatise than a poem.

Colvin, Sir Sidney 1845–1927 Critic of art and literature. Born in Norwood, he attended Trinity College, Cambridge. He served as Slade Professor of Fine Art at Cambridge (1873–85), director of the Fitzwilliam Museum (1876–84) and Keeper of Prints and Drawings at the British Museum (1884–1912). In addition to his art criticism, chiefly on engravers and engraving, he published volumes on LANDOR (1881) and KEATS (1887) for the English Men of Letters series, a biography of Keats (1917), and memorials to his friend ROBERT LOUIS STEVENSON in editions of the *Vailima Letters*(1895) he had received from Stevenson and in editions of Stevenson's works (1894–7) and correspondence (1899–1911).

Combe, William 1741–1823 Satirical poet and writer of miscellaneous prose. Combe was born in Bristol and educated at Eton, and then Oxford, which he left without taking a degree. He travelled in France and Italy, where he met STERNE, and then proceeded to squander his substantial inheritance in London; after which he seems to have been successively a common soldier, a waiter, a teacher of elocution, a cook and a private in the French army. He turned to writing around 1772, and enjoyed his first success as a satirist with *The Diaboliad* (1776), dedicated to Lord Imham, 'the worst man in His Majesty's dominion', in settlement of a private score. He followed it up with *Diabo-lady* (1777), *Anti-diabolady* (1778), and numerous other works in verse and prose, including *The Devil upon Two Sticks* (1790) and the topographical *Microcosm of London* (1808). His most famous work, THE TOUR OF DR SYNTAX IN SEARCH OF THE PICTURESQUE, on which he collaborated with Thomas Rowlandson, appeared in Ackermann's *Poetical Magazine* in 1809, and was followed in 1820 by *The Second Tour of Dr Syntax in Search of*

Consolation, and in 1821 by *The Third Tour of Dr Syntax in Search of a Wife*. Combe again combined his talents with Rowlandson's in *The English Dance of Death* (1815–16), which contains some of his best verse; *The Dance of Life* (1816); and *Johnny Quae Genius* (1822), the last, and feeblest, of the Syntax series.

comedy The term is applied to a great variety of work, of which the simplest common denominator is a happy ending; a more complex feature is a greater interest in society and its values than in individuals and their destiny.

The Greeks originally used the word from which 'comedy' derives to describe a choric song of celebration or revel. The transition of the word, from describing a song and dance within a play to describing a kind of play distinct from TRAGEDY, was complete by the second half of the 5th century BC. The earliest surviving examples are the satiric comedies of Aristophanes (*c.* 448–*c.* 380 BC). The form of 'old comedy', of which the plays of Aristophanes are the unique evidence, was elaborate, but the content has an air of improvisatory freedom. There was licence for parody, personal abuse and invective, and a direct treatment of contemporary social and political issues as well as for the traditional obscenity of fertility rituals. In 'new comedy', as exemplified by the surviving work of Menander (*c.* 342–293 BC) and his Roman successors, Plautus (*c.* 254–184 BC) and Terence (*c.* 190–159 BC), plot is altogether more central, and stock characters of fiction replace the portraits of living people.

It is the much more easily imitable 'new comedy' that lies behind British and Continental comedy. The earliest substantial example in English, RALPH ROISTER DOISTER, was written in conscious imitation of Terence, who continued to serve as a model to the writers of intrigue comedy for the Elizabethan stage. By exaggerating Terentian stereotypes, BEN JONSON invented the 'humours' comedy that was immensely popular after the 1598 performance of *EVERY MAN IN HIS HUMOUR*. CITIZEN COMEDY, like *THE SHOEMAKER'S HOLIDAY*, also reflects the influence of Terence and Plautus, whose *Menaechmi* provided SHAKESPEARE with the plot of one of his earliest successes, *THE COMEDY OF ERRORS*. Shakespeare's later comedies, as well as the unclassifiable 'last plays', mark a departure from strict classical form. But English comedy followed Jonsonian rather than Shakespearean lines. The comedy of manners that dominated the English stage for four decades after the restoration of Charles II rests on the foundation of a Jonsonian contrast between the truly witty and those who pretend to wit. Too bawdy and too mordant for many of its critics, RESTORATION COMEDY gave way to 18th-century SENTIMENTAL COMEDY, in which the emphasis is shifted from the exposure of fools and villains to the rewarding of virtue and prudence.

It has been the tendency, in criticism at least, to celebrate only those writers who have challenged the dominance of sentimental comedy in the 18th and 19th centuries – GOLDSMITH, SHERIDAN, the BOUCICAULT of *LONDON ASSURANCE*, OSCAR WILDE – and to neglect or question the achievements

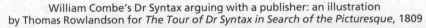

William Combe's Dr Syntax arguing with a publisher: an illustration by Thomas Rowlandson for *The Tour of Dr Syntax in Search of the Picturesque*, 1809

of such 'sentimental' writers as STEELE, CIBBER, CUMBERLAND, O'KEEFFE, T. W. ROBERTSON, PINERO and HENRY ARTHUR JONES. It was the more robust work of SHAW that carried the reputation of comedy into the 20th century, but a distinctive kind of play, formally classifiable as comedy, is hard to identify in the modern theatre. It survived longer in Ireland, where the plays of SYNGE and FITZMAURICE gave impetus to a uniquely Irish comic drama.

Comedy of Errors, The A comedy by WILLIAM SHAKESPEARE, first performed c. 1593 and published in the First Folio of 1623. The main source is the *Menaechmi* of Plautus, presumably in an English translation.

Antipholus of Syracuse arrives in Ephesus unaware that the city holds his twin brother, another Antipholus. To complicate matters further the two brothers are served by twin slaves, both named Dromio. The whole purpose of the plot is thus to create scenes of mistaken identity – handled dexterously and with a mature sense of comic timing – before the confusions are finally resolved in an ending which reunites the brothers and frees their father Egeon from sentence of death.

This early comedy was immensely successful in the Elizabethan theatre. It was still popular enough in 1604 to be called for performance at James I's court, and it probably remained in the repertoire of the KING'S MEN for many years after that.

Comical Revenge, The: or, Love in a Tub A comedy by SIR GEORGE ETHEREGE, first produced in March 1664 and published the same year. The play shows the influence of Molière's early style and is set in the last months of the Commonwealth.

The very slight comic plot concerns Sir Frederick Frolick's wooing by a rich widow, the impudence of a valet, Dufoy, who is wedged into a tub by his irritated fellow servants, and the cheating of a country knight, Sir Nicholas Cully, by Palmer and Wheadle. Cully is married off to Sir Frederick's former mistress Lucy. Sir Frederick decides to marry the rich widow. The serious plot, in rhymed couplets, is almost a satire of heroic drama: Aurelia loves Colonel Bruce, who loves Aurelia's sister Graciana, who loves Lord Beaufort. Bruce and Beaufort quarrel over Graciana and fight a duel; Beaufort wins, and Bruce tries to kill himself in despair. Beaufort takes Graciana; Bruce recovers from wounds both physical and mental, and is comforted by Aurelia.

Coming Race, The A novel by EDWARD BULWER LYTTON, published in 1871. An American mining engineer descends to the centre of the earth and encounters a subterranean people with control over a mysterious kinetic energy, called 'Vril', which gives them unbounded powers. The book is in part a satire on Darwinian evolutionary theory and on contemporary ideas about the emancipation of women. For a time the word 'Vril' became associated with any strength-giving elixir: hence Bo(vine)vril.

commedia dell'arte The name given to a style of improvised comedy which flourished in Italy from the mid 16th to the mid 18th century, and whose influence was felt throughout Europe. The performed pieces were based, not on an established text (though certain set speeches were commonly learned by heart), but on a scenario which left room for improvised action and dialogue. Commedia companies toured Italy and, later, France. Each member adopted a vivid mask, generally retaining that mask throughout his or her career. It was always possible to add a new mask to such well-established ones as Arlecchino, Pantalone, the pedantic Dottore and the bragging Capitano. Thus, Tiberio Fiorilli (1608–94) virtually invented Scaramuccia, who was adopted in France as Scaramouche, and another (unknown) Neapolitan invented Cetrulo, who was modified into Pulcinella, reaching England as Punchinel in about 1650 and becoming familiar as the fairground Punch. Such modifications of a mask are typical. The English Harlequin, though derived from the quick-witted Italian Arlecchino, was utterly unlike him. John Rich (c. 1692–1761), who popularized the harlequinade during his long tenure of COVENT GARDEN theatre, played Harlequin as a dumb acrobat, endowed with sufficient magical powers to win his Columbine. The triumph of love in the English harlequinade was an acting out of the 'real' struggles of young lovers in the framing play, and it is in the evolution of the harlequinade and the PANTOMIME that the influence of *commedia dell'arte* in England can be most clearly seen. A divergent tradition is that of Pierrot, derived from the mask of Pedrolino by way of Paris.

Commentaries on the Laws of England See BLACKSTONE, SIR WILLIAM.

Common Sense A political pamphlet by THOMAS PAINE, published anonymously in Philadelphia on 10 January 1776. The first public statement to urge America's immediate and unqualified separation from Britain, it sold over half a million copies and helped to galvanize the forces which only seven months later began to fight the American Revolution. Paine's argument divides into four parts. The first insists that in so far as governments are established only to protect the freedom and security of citizens, Britain has violated its mandate by its economic and political enslavement of the colonies. The second part rejects hereditary succession in favour of democratic election, a process which respects individual talents rather than family lineage in the designation of a ruler. The third and fourth parts celebrate both

America's economic security and its potential to safe-guard, by example, the inalienable rights of all people.

complaint A conventional poetic expression of personal complaint common in the Middle Ages and used also by the CAVALIER POETS in the 17th century. A first-person narrator describes his sorrow and its causes, often by telling his story. The theme is frequently unrequited or betrayed love, but may also be some other personal grief or a general dissatisfaction with the state of the world or the vicissitudes of Fortune. A complaint may be part of a longer work, like the knight's complaint in CHAUCER's *THE BOOK OF THE DUCHESS*, or may be self-contained, as in his *Complaint unto Pity*.

Complaint of the Black Knight, The A poem usually accepted as the work of JOHN LYDGATE, mainly written in RHYME ROYAL. The narrator walks through a park and overhears a knight in black complaining of the cruelty of his mistress. The poet prays to Venus to make the knight's beloved have mercy on him. The work shows the influence of GEOFFREY CHAUCER and the French poet Froissart.

Compleat Angler, The: or, The Contemplative Man's Recreation The classic work on fish and fishing by IZAAK WALTON was first published in 1653, and there were four further editions carefully supervised by the author during his lifetime, the last in 1676. It has become one of the most reprinted books in the history of British letters.

Three sportsmen, a fisherman (Piscator, who is Walton himself), a huntsman (Venator), and a fowler (Auceps), travel north through the countryside from Tottenham to Ware along the river Lea on the first day in May; they discuss the relative merits of their respective pastimes. Venator becomes a pupil of Piscator, and is systematically introduced to the arts of angling for various species of freshwater fish, along with a wealth of advice about watercraft, pisciculture and country lore. In the fifth edition there appeared a continuation of Walton's expanded original, a second part by his younger friend CHARLES COTTON, which largely concerns fly-fishing on the river Dove, a subject Walton himself knew little about.

The book is often wrongly assumed to be the first of its kind in the language, but is in fact partly an anthology of previous writers on fishing and the mass of related subjects. As well as numerous borrowings and adaptations from the extensive tradition of piscatorial literature, it includes about 40 songs and verses and contains some fine examples of both PASTORAL and devotional writing. It is a unique combination of manual and meditation, and the way in which the personality of the author, both widely read and practically experienced, pervades the whole shape and flavour of the book is the reason for its lasting appeal to sportsman and general reader alike.

Compton-Burnett, Dame **Ivy** 1892–1969 Novelist. She was born in Pinner, Middlesex, and educated privately before attending the Royal Holloway College in 1902. Her family background was difficult. The children (five by her father's first wife, seven by his second) were divided by conflicting emotional allegiances. There were numerous family tragedies: her brother, Noel, was killed on the Western Front during World War I, and two of her sisters committed suicide in 1917. In 1919 she began to live with the writer Margaret Jourdain, a relationship which lasted until the latter's death in 1951.

Her first novel, *Dolores* (1911), which she later rejected, was a pale imitation of GEORGE ELIOT, and it was not until *Pastors and Masters* (1925) that she emerged as a writer with a distinct and highly individual style. From the late 1920s until her death she produced a new novel almost every two years: *Brothers and Sisters* (1929), *Men and Wives* (1931), *More Women Than Men* (1933), *A House and Its Head* (1935), *Daughters and Sons* (1941), *A Family and a Fortune* (1939), *Parents and Children* (1941), and so on, a total of over 20 novels. *Mother and Son* (1955) won the James Tait Black Memorial Prize.

As their titles suggest, her novels are preoccupied with domestic scenes and family strife: she confines her characters to an Edwardian setting, and isolates them within a claustrophobic and frequently violent world. Her plots are realized almost exclusively through dialogue, dispensing with conventional authorial comment, yet at their best her novels achieve a brilliantly incisive irony, occasionally broadening into satire. Her central theme is the abuse of power (ranging from the petty to the diabolical), and some have found in her work remarkably acute and universal insights into the psychology of persecution.

Comus The popular title for a PASTORAL entertainment by MILTON, published in 1637. Its original title explains the circumstances of its first production: *A Masque Presented at Ludlow Castle 1634: On Michaelmas Night, Before the Right Honourable, John Earl of Bridgewater, Viscount Brackley Lord President of Wales...* Milton wrote it at the request of his friend Henry Lawes, who provided the music, to celebrate the earl's appointment as Lord President, and the parts of the lady and her brothers were taken by the earl's children. *Comus* is not a MASQUE in the court sense, in which singing and spectacle were more important than words. Its theme, the confrontation between virtue and evil, is both serious and recurrent in the rest of Milton's poetry.

Three travellers, a lady and her two brothers, are stranded in a forest by nightfall. The brothers go in search of a spring and, attracted by sounds of revelry, the lady finds a shepherd who offers her shelter in his cottage. He is Comus, son of Circe and Bacchus, and he has dismissed his rout at sight of the lady, his passion having been aroused by her beauty. When the brothers return they are told of what has happened by the benign Attendant Spirit, who has taken the form of a shepherd, Thyrsis. He warns them that Comus is an evil sorcerer who lies in wait for travellers and, in the guise of hospitality, gives them a potion that changes their faces into those of wild beasts. The Attendant Spirit gives the brothers the root of the Haemony plant, of use against all enchantments, and shows them the way to the palace of Comus.

Comus has placed the lady in a chair that holds her fast by magic. His rout is enjoying a feast and the sorcerer presses a glass, containing the potion, on the lady. She refuses it and struggles to rise but he tells her that only his wand can release her. The brothers burst in with drawn swords; they subdue the rout but Comus escapes, taking the wand with him. However, the Attendant Spirit invokes Sabrina, goddess of the nearby River Severn, who releases the lady with pure drops of water from her own spring. After a song of thanks to Sabrina the lady and her brothers, guided by the Spirit, complete their journey to Ludlow Castle.

conceit An intricate metaphorical figure which makes ingenious comparison between two apparently incongruous things or concepts. Originating from the Italian '*concetto*', it featured prominently in Petrarch's love poetry (see PETRARCHAN). In England it became one of the exercises of fancy admired by 16th-century poets and was developed by the METAPHYSICAL POETS, particularly DONNE, whose conceits are sometimes extended throughout an entire poem in a virtuoso display of similitude (the figure of the compasses, for example, in 'A Valediction: Forbidding Mourning'). In other instances the effect is compressed and paradoxical, requiring an imaginative and intellectual act on the part of the reader to unravel the analogies. The latter type of conceit has characterized much recent British poetry.

concrete poetry An experimental form of poetry, flourishing in the 1960s, which concentrated on isolated and particular aspects of visual, phonetic or kinetic structure, abandoning normal forms of meaning for those disclosed at or below the level of the single word. Its pioneers were Eugen Gomringer and the Brazilian Noigandres group, though the *Calligrammes* (1918) of Apollinaire were perhaps equally influential. The leading British practitioner was IAN HAMILTON FINLAY, whose work has notably moved on to other fields.

Different accounts of concrete poetry have either stressed its novel and experimental nature, making links with STRUCTURALISM and SEMIOTICS, or else have claimed a long tradition stemming from older texts whose visual aspects contributed to their meaning. Now that the moment of concrete poetry is past, it can most usefully be seen as an episode in the continuing assertion of an internationalist *avant-garde* that has sought to break with the past and establish formal structures reflecting the scale of alteration that technology has unleashed on the world.

Condell, Henry See HEMINGES, JOHN.

Condition of England novel A type of novel reflecting concern about the 'Condition of England' in the 19th century, particularly in the restless and insecure 1840s. The concern was largely stimulated by CARLYLE's message in *Chartism* (1839) and *PAST AND PRESENT* (1843) that *laissez-faire* policies, combined with neglect of the industrial poor, were driving the ranks of society further apart and could easily lead to revolution. Recurrent preoccupations of the Condition of England novel are: the use of power, mechanical and social; the sense of a breach between man and man and the importance of healing it; the need for education; and the fear of revolution. Examples include: DISRAELI's *CONINGSBY* (1844) and *SYBIL* (1845); CHARLES KINGSLEY's *YEAST* (1848) and *ALTON LOCKE* (1850); GASKELL's *MARY BARTON* (1848) and *NORTH AND SOUTH* (1855); CHARLOTTE BRONTË's *SHIRLEY* (1849); DICKENS's *HARD TIMES* (1854); and DINAH MULOCK's *JOHN HALIFAX, GENTLEMAN* (1857).

conduct books 'Improving reading' urged upon young people, particularly girls of the leisured class, and especially in the 18th century. Like the Renaissance COURTESY BOOK, they touch on manners and deportment, but in the main deal with religion, morality and self-control. In this they differ from the Victorian etiquette book, which instructed social climbers. Probably the most famous and influential conduct books were Fordyce's *Sermons to Young Women* (1767) and HESTER CHAPONE's *Letters on the Improvement of the Mind* (1773). Other examples widely read in the 18th century include HENRY HOME's *Loose Hints upon Education, Chiefly concerning the Culture of the Heart* (1781), CLARA REEVE's *Plans of Education* (1792) and HANNAH MORE's didactic novel, *Coelebs in Search of a Wife* (1809). Against this background of discussion of female education and female duties, MARY WOLLSTONECRAFT's *A Vindication of the Rights of Woman* (1792) may be seen as both traditional in its concerns and revolutionary in its stance.

Conduct of the Allies, The A political pamphlet by JONATHAN SWIFT, published anonymously in 1711 under the full title, *The Conduct of the Allies, and of* *the Late Ministry, in Beginning and Carrying on the Present War.*

Swift's most famous political pamphlet, it was also the single most polished contribution to the propaganda machine controlled by the Tory ministry of ROBERT HARLEY, EARL OF OXFORD, in its determination to end the ruinous war with France. Swift had already alleged, in essays for THE EXAMINER (November 1710–June 1711), a Whig conspiracy by the Duke of Marlborough and others to prolong the war and aggrandize themselves and other 'monied men' at the expense of Britain's true interests. In the *Conduct*, begun in August 1711, he extends the theory to implicate the Allies (the Dutch, Austrians and Portuguese) as fellow conspirators of the Whig grandees. He builds up the case for peace by artful selection and manipulation of facts, revelation of previously secret information, subtle innuendo and audacious logic. Britain is portrayed as the losing party, and the fact that she would emerge with distinct advantages is played down; even the failure to secure Spain for the Habsburgs is justified.

Swift's pamphlet greatly strengthened the Tory case, helping to smooth the way for Marlborough's dismissal at the end of 1711 and the Treaty of Utrecht in 1713. The first edition of 1000 copies, appearing on 27 November 1711 but dated 1712, disappeared in two days and a second edition in five hours. 11,000 copies had been sold by the time the sixth edition sold out in January 1712.

Confederacy, The A comedy by JOHN VANBRUGH, adapted from *Les Bourgeoises à la mode* (1692) by Florent Dancourt. It was first produced in October 1705, and published the same year.

Gripe and Moneytrap are both mean moneylenders, grown rich by charging high interest. Gripe falls in love with Mrs Moneytrap; Moneytrap falls in love with Mrs Gripe. The ladies confide in each other and resolve to exploit their husbands' weaknesses. To pay her debts, Mrs Gripe has pawned her necklace to Mrs Amlet, a seller of cosmetics, whose unprincipled son Dick poses as a colonel and pursues Corinna, Mrs Gripe's daughter.

Dick has enlisted the help of Mrs Gripe's maid, Flippanta; his friend Brass acts as his footman. Mrs Gripe and Mrs Moneytrap use the maid and the footman as go-betweens, and each succeeds in extracting money from the other's spouse. Dick Amlet, meanwhile, has stolen Mrs Gripe's necklace from his mother and sends Brass out to sell it. But the goldsmith recognizes it as the one reported lost and takes it to Gripe. His wife, Moneytrap and Mrs Moneytrap are present when the exposure takes place; the wives close ranks and challenge their husbands about the money, freely given though one wife has been forced to pawn her necklace. Dick Amlet's true character being exposed also, his prospects look bleak; but

Corinna loves him and his mother makes him a generous cash settlement.

Confessio Amantis ('The Lover's Confession') JOHN GOWER's major English poem, in rhyming octosyllabic couplets, was probably completed in 1390. He later revised it, replacing the dedicatory preface praising Richard II with praise of Henry of Lancaster.

The poem makes a notable contribution to the literature of COURTY LOVE in English. Its prologue contains a complaint at the state of the world and times, and the first book announces the poet's intention to write about love instructively and entertainingly. The narrator, Amans (or the Lover), complains that he has served love too long and wishes for death. Venus instructs him to confess to her priest, Genius. The poem progresses through confession and enquiry from the Lover, answered by the priest's instruction and exposition, each point being explained through the use of one or more tales. (They include the source for SHAKESPEARE's *PERICLES*, in which Gower appears as the Chorus.) The work deals with the seven deadly sins and the sins of the five senses, but although they provide a structural framework the material treated often bears little relation to them. The seventh book is on Aristotle's counsel to Alexander and the eighth deals with the laws of marriage and incest. Finally the Lover is won over to reason and abandons his cause, being too old to be a lover.

The poem's central interest lies in the collection of tales, taken from various classical and medieval sources. The use of a framework designed to embrace such various elements was not unusual in the Middle Ages and, indeed, several stories used by Gower also appear in another famous example, CHAUCER's *CANTERBURY TALES*.

confessional poetry Verse which reveals intimate details of the poet's life. It has played a major part in American poetry since the 1950s, in the work of such writers as W. D. SNODGRASS, ROBERT LOWELL, THEODORE ROETHKE, JOHN BERRYMAN, SYLVIA PLATH, ANNE SEXTON and ADRIENNE RICH. They focus on particularly painful moments or experiences, often related to more general historical or cultural problems.

Confessions of an English Opium Eater An autobiographical work by THOMAS DE QUINCEY, first published in two parts in THE LONDON MAGAZINE in 1821, and as a single volume (with an appendix) in 1822. In 1856 De Quincey considerably extended the *Confessions* for a collected edition of his works, but, on his later admission, succeeded more in damaging than enhancing his original slender text.

De Quincey's account of his opium addiction is interwoven with a description of his life, from early childhood to the present in which he writes. Inevitably, perhaps, the book is open to interpretation as an apology for opium-taking in view of its pragmatic advocacy of the drug as the most efficient available artificial means of inducing intellectual clarity and, above all, visionary waking dreams. What the latter confirm, according to De Quincey, is that 'there is no such a thing as *forgetting* possible to the mind'. The tumultuous symbolic actions facilitated by the opium are a retelling of the manifold, and more often than not terrifying, experiences of childhood that have moulded the mind of the adult.

The work was an overnight success and quickly established De Quincey's reputation as a writer. A slight aura of scandal hangs over it to this day, for he does not offer the story of his addiction as a cautionary tale. Not only are the 'pains of opium' too inextricably bound up with its pleasures for that, but its claims to literary significance rest on the lofty, sonorous, and 'impassioned prose' of its climactic dream descriptions. Among his more famous disciples were Branwell Brontë and FRANCIS THOMPSON, though he had a deterrent effect on the more cautious CARLYLE. The *Tales* of POE are profoundly influenced by De Quincey, and a large part of Baudelaire's *Paradis artificiels* consists of verbatim translations of the *Confessions* and *Suspiria de Profundis*.

Confidence-Man, The: *His Masquerade* A novel by HERMAN MELVILLE, published in 1857, the last to appear during his lifetime. It is a complex exploration of the dialectic between trust and sincerity on the one hand, and manipulation and violation of trust on the other – a conflict which Melville saw as pervading contemporary American society.

The action takes place on the Mississippi river steamer *Fidèle*, and involves a large number of characters, many of whom are different manifestations of a single figure, the confidence-man. He makes his initial appearance as a deaf-mute on the riverboat landing in St Louis. Holding up a chalkboard sign advertising the virtues of charity, he is derided by the crowd, but in his later appearances he proves to be more persuasive. For example, in the guise of a herb doctor he succeeds in persuading a distrusting miser to buy his worthless tonic; in other disguises he sells phoney stock to passengers, petitions for a loan to alleviate alleged hardship, and solicits contributions to Indian missions. In some of his appearances, however, he merely encourages the more disaffected and cynical passengers to keep faith and to trust in the goodness of others.

Throughout the second half of the novel the confidence-man is in the costume of a friendly 'cosmopolitan', Frank Goodman, who engages in philosophical conversations with other passengers, occasionally digressing to tell long stories related to the central themes of the book, especially to that of trust in personal relationships. The narrative ends with a discussion between him and an old man about the status of the apocryphal scriptures, thus fusing the book's thematic concern with trust with the literary issue of narrative as a bearer of meaning.

Congreve, William 1670–1729 Playwright. Born in Yorkshire into a military family, he was educated at Kilkenny School and Trinity College, Dublin, where SWIFT was a near-contemporary. He entered the Middle Temple in 1690, but never practised law, preferring a fashionable life (he was the lover of Henrietta, Duchess of Marlborough, who bore him a daughter) and the pursuit of literature, which he began by publishing a novel, *Incognita* (1692). His first play, THE OLD BACHELOR (1693), was shaped for performance with the help of DRYDEN. It made Congreve famous, a status confirmed by the success of two further comedies, THE DOUBLE DEALER (1693) and LOVE FOR LOVE (1695), and his single tragedy, THE MOURNING BRIDE (1697). The tragedy is, after the fashion of the time, inflated and self-consciously poetic, but Congreve's comedies are distinguished by the wit and elegance of their dialogue as well as by their skilful plotting and the crafty deployment of contrasting characters and themes. They are mannered explorations of social values, marital practices and the scope given to intrigue and deceit by prurience in high places. It was on Congreve and VANBRUGH that JEREMY COLLIER concentrated his fury in his *Short View of the Immorality and Profaneness of the English Stage* (1698). That Congreve was stung by Collier's attack is evident in his own *Amendments of Mr Collier's False and Imperfect Citations* (1698) and, regrettably, in the diminution of his interest in the theatre. He remained involved in the management of Lincoln's Inn Theatre until 1705, but added only one important comedy to the repertoire. This was THE WAY OF THE WORLD (1700), a masterpiece of the comedy of manners, less lucidly plotted than *Love for Love* but lively with brilliantly drawn characters and firmly moral in its corrective satire of high society. Its comparative failure on its first performance combined with Collier's continuing grumbles and Congreve's own financial security (he had been granted three lucrative sinecures through the influence of a patron) to hasten Congreve's abandonment of drama. He lived in comfort, numbered POPE, Swift and STEELE among his friends and the actress Anne Bracegirdle among his lovers, and continued to write at leisure. His 18th-century work includes a MASQUE, *The Judgement of Paris* (1701), an operatic piece, *Semele* (1710), which, with additions by Pope, provided Handel with the libretto of his secular oratorio (1744), a prose tale, *An Impossible Thing* (1720), an edition of *The Dramatic Works of John Dryden* (1717) and several poems. Congreve never fully recovered from a fall suffered when his carriage overturned in Bath in 1728. He is buried in Westminster Abbey.

Coningsby: *or, The New Generation* A novel by BENJAMIN DISRAELI, published in 1844. It addresses the problem of leadership for England under a regenerated, idealistic Conservative Party. The answer, for Disraeli, lies in the symbolic marriage of his hero, the aristocratic Harry Coningsby, with a daughter of the 'millocracy', Edith Millbank. Originally Edith's father opposes the match, but later comes round. The true hero of the book, however, is the aloof Sidonia, fiercely proud of his Jewish race and its purity, who looks down on mere Normans and Saxons as *parvenus,* and who combines wealth, wisdom and cosmopolitan culture. However, while Coningsby and his brother-in-law, Oswald Millbank, go into Parliament, Sidonia does not enter public service, although shown to be the superior of everybody in the book. He has reverted to the faith of his fathers, thus cutting him off from his place as a natural leader in England, and guards the purity of his race by not marrying.

Connecticut Wits, The A group of 18th-century American poets, often referred to as the Hartford Wits (because they were centred in Hartford, Connecticut), and drawn together at Yale by shared academic, literary and political values. They advocated a revision of Yale's curriculum to include the study of American literature, and they sought themselves to produce poetry which would simultaneously proclaim and signify America's literary independence. They also adhered to the orthodox Calvinism and conservative Federalism which had found a home in Connecticut.

The group espoused its causes in numerous publications, three of which stand out in American literary history: *The Anarchiad,* 12 papers in MOCK-HEROIC verse printed serially between 1786 and 1787 in *The New Haven Gazette* and *The Connecticut Magazine; The Echo,* a verse satire against anti-Federalists, as well as against THOMAS JEFFERSON, and printed in *The American Mercury* between 1791 and 1805; and *The Practical Greenhouse,* a Federalist satire printed in 1799 in the *Connecticut Courant.* All three represent the collaborative efforts of the group's members: JOHN TRUMBULL, TIMOTHY DWIGHT, JOEL BARLOW, Lemuel Hopkins, David Humphreys, Richard Alsop, Theodore Dwight, E. H. Smith and Dr Mason F. Cogswell.

Connecticut Yankee in King Arthur's Court, A A satirical fantasy by MARK TWAIN, published in 1889.

It tells the story of Hank Morgan, a master mechanic and chief superintendent at the Colt arms factory in Hartford, Connecticut, who is knocked unconscious during a fight with one of his workmen and awakes to find himself near Camelot in 6th-century England. The Yankee uses his knowledge of history and 19th-century technology to convince King Arthur and the knights of the Round Table that he has magical powers. Having earned the nickname 'The Boss', he then sets himself, in the author's words, to 'the task of introducing the great and beneficent civilization of the nineteenth century' into the chivalric order of Camelot.

Originally conceived by Twain as a comic experiment in anachronistic contrast, the novel gradually developed into a darker, more violent story. Hank's introduction to Camelot of 19th-century 'enlightenment', with its ideology of progress and its powerful gadgets, leads to civil war in Arthur's England, and to an apocalyptic last battle in which both sides are destroyed by advanced technology.

Connell, Evan (Shelby) Jr 1924– American novelist. Born in Kansas City, he is best known for *Mrs Bridge* (1959) and *Mr Bridge* (1969). Other novels include *The Patriot* (1960), *The Diary of a Rapist* (1966) and *The Connoisseur* (1974). His short stories are collected in *The Anatomy Lesson and Other Stories* (1957) and *At the Crossroads* (1965). His verse includes *Notes from a Bottle Found on a Beach at Carmel* (1963) and *Points From a Compass Rose* (1973). *Son of the Morning Star* (1984) is a historical study of General Custer and the battle of Little Big Horn. His essays are collected in *A Long Desire* (1979) and *The White Lantern* (1980).

Connelly, Marc(us) (Cook) 1890–1980 American playwright. Born and educated in Pennsylvania, he had his first play produced in 1913, two years before he moved to New York to work as a journalist. His first real success as a dramatist came in a series of 10 collaborations with GEORGE S. KAUFMAN, beginning with *Dulcy* (1921) and including *Merton of the Movies* (1922) and a notable piece of EXPRESSIONISM, *Beggar on Horseback* (1924), staged in the year in which the partnership broke up. Connelly continued to write plays and screenplays, but only the Broadway production of *The Green Pastures* (1930) confirmed his place in any history of American drama. Based on Roark Bradford's stories of Louisiana blacks and framed by scenes in a Sunday school, it retells Old Testament stories through the innocent voices of uneducated blacks. Flawed by sentimentality, the play retains humour and dignity.

Connolly, Cyril (Vernon) 1903–74 Critic and literary editor. Born in Coventry, he was educated as a scholar both of Eton and of Balliol College, Oxford. His reputation for intellectual precocity set him a target of promise that his actual literary output consistently failed to fulfil. His main books are a novel, *The Rock Pool* (1936), the partly autobiographical *Enemies of Promise* (1938) and the nostalgic-hedonist maxims of *The Unquiet Grave* (by 'Palinurus', 1944). *Horizon* (1939–50), a wartime literary monthly magazine which he founded and edited, was one of the most influential intellectual organs of its period. He became principal book reviewer of *The Sunday Times* and published several collections of his reviews and essays, which showed him a skilled arbiter of taste, even if he made a career of under-fulfilment.

Conquest, (George) Robert (Acworth) 1917– Poet, historian and critic. Born in Malvern and educated at Winchester and Magdalen College, Oxford, Conquest served in World War II, worked for the Diplomatic Service (1946–56), held academic posts in Britain and the United States, and was for a time literary editor of *The Spectator*. He edited and introduced the influential anthology *New Lines* (1956), which helped to establish the poets of the MOVEMENT. His own verse, in *Poems* (1955), *Between Mars and Venus* (1962) and *Arias from a Love Opera* (1969), shows him a typical Movement poet in his concern for traditional forms and ordinary language, less so in his variety of subjects, which include SCIENCE FICTION. He has written and edited many works on Marxism and the USSR.

Conquest of Canaan, The A poem by TIMOTHY DWIGHT, written between 1771 and 1773 but not published until 1785. Dwight claimed it as the first American EPIC. Its 11 books of heroic verse elaborate upon the biblical account of Joshua's conquest of Canaan and, by allusion to people and events of the 18th century, draw a parallel between the Hebrew invasion of Canaan and the English settlement of New England. The poem thus confirms the Puritan conception of America as the seat of the New Jerusalem and in turn provides theological justification for the American Revolution.

Conrad, Joseph [Korzeniowski, Jozef Teodor Konrad] 1857–1924 Novelist and short-story writer. He was born in Podolia in the Ukraine, the child of Polish parents – Apollo Korzeniowski and Evelina Bobrowski – opposed to the Tsarist domination of their country. Apollo's involvement in political conspiracy prior to the nationalist insurrection of 1863 resulted in exile to Volgoda, north-west of Moscow. Here Conrad's mother died when he was seven. Apollo returned to Poland, dying of tuberculosis four years later. It was Conrad's uncle, Tadeusz Bobrowski, who acted as his guide in major decisions at this time, but the early influence of Apollo (notably in introducing him to the works of DICKENS, FENIMORE COOPER and MARRYAT in either Polish or French translation) may have shaped his deeper aspirations. Conrad's wish to go to sea, to serve on French vessels, certainly had the advantage of sparing him service in the Russian army. He went to Marseilles in 1874 and began a 20-year career as a sailor.

Conrad later discouraged interpretation of his sea novels from the evidence of his life, but he was proud of his qualifications and experiences as a sailor. In 1878 he began service on English ships; in 1880 he passed the second mate's examination, and in 1884 that for first mate. He became a naturalized British subject in 1886, and received his master's certificate from the Board of Trade. His early sea career had not promised this steady progress, however. While in Marseilles he was employed by the shipowning firm of Delestang, a family having strong sympathies with the claimant to the Spanish throne, Don Carlos VII. While making his first voyages to the West Indies in the *Mont Blanc* in 1875, and the *Sainte-Antoine* in 1876, Conrad met the Corsican Dominic Cervoni, who became a model for central figures of romantic daring in his fiction. Conrad and Cervoni were involved in a number of gun-running voyages to Spain for the Carlists, which ended in disaster. These events were depicted impressionistically in Conrad's reminiscences, *The Mirror of the Sea* (1906) and in *The Arrow of Gold* (1919). These reckless and improvident years for the young Conrad culminated in a suicide attempt in 1878.

During his service with the British merchant navy Conrad worked on a variety of ships: first with the *Mavis*, on a journey to Constantinople, and then on more than one wool clipper bound for Sydney. Particularly eventful voyages came in 1881, during service with the *Palestine*, when Conrad had his first experience of the East, and with the *Narcissus* in 1884, when he sailed from Bombay to Dunkirk. These experiences underlay the novels *Youth* (1902) and THE NIGGER OF THE *'NARCISSUS'* (1897), respectively. His later experience as first mate on the *Vidar*, sailing through the Malay archipelago, and as master of the *Otago* in 1888, was to show a wide influence on his fiction: notably the *Otago*'s voyage from Bangkok to Singapore, which is directly discernible within *The Shadow Line* (1917).

Before his experiences of 1890 as captain of a river steamer in the Congo – later to form the basis of HEART OF DARKNESS (published with *Youth*, 1902) – he began writing his first novel, *Almayer's Folly* (1895). When this had been published, with the help of EDWARD GARNETT, he was settled in England; in 1896 he married Jessie George.

The period between *The Nigger of the 'Narcissus'* (1897) and UNDER WESTERN EYES (1911) is commonly regarded as his major phase, producing, apart from works already mentioned: LORD JIM (1900), *Typhoon* (1903), NOSTROMO (1904), THE SECRET AGENT (1907) and *The Secret Sharer* (1910). These works earned little money or praise from reviewers but brought him the recognition of leading contemporaries such as ARNOLD BENNETT, JOHN GALSWORTHY and FORD MADOX FORD, with whom he wrote *The Inheritors* (1901) and *Romance* (1903), as well as his fellow expa-

Joseph Conrad

with Arna Bontemps; including *The Fast Sooner Hound* (1942) and *Sam Patch* (1951).

Conscious Lovers, The A comedy by SIR RICHARD STEELE, first performed at DRURY LANE in 1722 and published the following year. The plot is based on the *Andria* of Terence, but Steele has softened and moralized his original. Soon translated into French, the play influenced the development of the *comédie larmoyante*. In England, its success helped to oust the comedy of manners from the stage and to pave the way for SENTIMENTAL COMEDY.

In Bevil, the hero, Steele has created an ethical absolute of surpassing dullness. What life the play has is confined to below-stairs interludes. Bevil, affianced to Lucinda, heiress to the wealthy Sealand, loves his own ward, Indiana, a destitute orphan whom he found and has brought up. Bevil's worthy friend Myrtle loves Lucinda, who is pestered by the fortune-hunting Cimberton. When Bevil, with the utmost decency, tells Lucinda of his love for Indiana, Myrtle takes offence on Lucinda's behalf and challenges Bevil to a duel. Bevil's refusal of the challenge permits him (and Steele) to ridicule the fashion for duelling, but it requires a timely revelation to resolve the play's problems. Indiana is discovered to be Sealand's lost child, a daughter from his first marriage. With the dowry shared between the half-sisters, each is free to marry the man who loves her, and Cimberton, dissatisfied with half a fortune, is happy to withdraw his suit.

Conservationist, The A novel by NADINE GORDIMER, published in 1974 and awarded the BOOKER PRIZE. Many critics consider it her most complex critique of the conservative and capitalist patriarchy which governs South Africa and of the white liberals who collaborate with it. The title is ironic since Mehring, a wealthy white businessman who has bought a small farm near Johannesburg as a weekend retreat, is concerned with preserving the land for his own use and enjoyment only. Preoccupied with the ecology of his farm and the interdependence of varieties of animal life on one another, he tries to ignore the interdependence of human beings and is indifferent to the uprooting and dislocation of whole groups of peoples within South Africa. The novel portrays his increasing self-removal from meaningful human contact – with his liberal mistress, his conscientious-objector son and especially with the black farm workers – leading to paranoia, mental breakdown and, finally, his flight from the country.

consonance See ALLITERATION.

Constable, Henry 1562–1613 Poet. Constable came from a family distinguished for military and public service. He graduated from St John's College, Cambridge, in 1580 and went to Paris, with

triates in Sussex and Kent, STEPHEN CRANE and HENRY JAMES. Wider public recognition came with the publication of *CHANCE* (1913) and *VICTORY* (1915), in which some critics find the first signs of the weakening apparent in *The Rescue* (1920) and *The Rover* (1923).

Conroy, Jack 1899– 1980 American novelist and editor. He was born at Monkey Nest coal camp near Moberly, Missouri, and spent several years as a migrant worker in steel mills, rubber factories and coal mines. When the Depression came, he drew on his experiences to write poems and articles about unemployment, which were published in periodicals such as *Northern Lights*, *Unrest* and *THE NEW MASSES*. In 1933 his novel *The Disinherited* appeared. A classic of proletarian literature, it explores working-class life in the Depression with unsentimental directness, and is widely considered to be Conroy's greatest achievement. He later founded *The Anvil* and *The New Anvil*, important left-wing magazines which published work by writers such as RICHARD WRIGHT, ERSKINE CALDWELL, FRANK YERBY, JAMES T. FARRELL, MICHAEL GOLD, LANGSTON HUGHES and MERIDEL LE SUEUR. Conroy's other books include *A World to Win* (1935), *Anyplace but Here* (with ARNA BONTEMPS; 1966) and *Writers in Revolt: The Anvil Anthology* (with Curt Johnson; 1973). He also wrote CHILDREN'S LITERATURE

Walsingham as his patron, in 1583. In the late 1580s he converted to Catholicism, and having again crossed to France in 1591 did not return to England until JAMES I's accession in 1603. He had hopes of the king's conversion to Rome, was well received at court, but was confined briefly to the Tower in 1604 after some of his letters were seized. He left England in 1610 and died at Liège. *Diana*, his collection of SON-NETS, was printed in 1592 and reissued in 1594 with additional sonnets dubiously ascribed to Constable and contributions by other poets. He also wrote sonnets to such noble ladies as the Countess of Pembroke and Penelope Rich, and 16 'Spiritual Sonnets', not printed until 1815. His work is represented in *ENGLAND'S HELICON*.

Constantine, David (John) 1944– Poet. Born in Salford, he read modern languages at Oxford, and has lectured at Durham and Oxford. Influenced by ROBERT GRAVES, he brings a classical and European sensibility to his work. *A Brightness to Cast Shadows* (1980), *Watching for Dolphins* (1983), *Madder* (1987) and *Selected Poems* (1991) are erudite and culturally wide-ranging. *Space Displaced* (1992) contains translations from Henri Michaux. An initial work on Hölderlin (1979) has been followed by a major critical study (1988). Constantine has also published *Early Greek Travellers and the Hellenic Ideal* (1984).

Contarini Fleming: *A Psychological Romance* A novel by BENJAMIN DISRAELI, published in 1832. It purports to be the autobiography of Contarini Fleming, a romantic and idealistic young man, the son of a Venetian noblewoman and an aristocratic British father active in political circles. After a failed marriage to his cousin, Alceste, and a prolonged tour of Europe and the East, he settles in Rome, devoting himself to art.

Contrast, The A play by ROYALL TYLER, produced in 1787 and published in 1790. The first comedy by a native American writer to be staged professionally, it is indebted to the 18th-century English comedy of manners, particularly SHERIDAN's *THE SCHOOL FOR SCANDAL*.

The 'contrast' of the title is that between Bill Dimple, the representative of European affectation, and Colonel Manly, the representative of American straightforwardness and honesty. Maria van Rough is to marry Dimple, the match having been arranged by her father. The intensely Anglophilic Dimple is carrying on flirtations with two other women, Letitia and Charlotte. Charlotte's brother, Colonel Manly, is in love with Maria. Dimple gambles away his fortune and decides to marry the wealthy Letitia. Maria's father discovers his baseness and gives his blessing to Manly's suit. Dimple is finally thwarted in his ambition when Letitia learns of his flirtation with

Charlotte. The subplot reproduces the contrast between national manners in the amorous rivalry of Dimple's servant, the devious and conceited Jessamy, and Manly's servant Jonathan, the prototype of the naive, goodhearted Yankee.

Cook, Eliza 1818–89 Poet. Born in London of a poor family, she was self-educated and began to write verse as a child. Her first volume, *Lays of a Wild Harp*, was published in 1835. *Melaia* (1838) and *New Echoes* (1864) followed. Her best-known poem, 'The Old Arm Chair', appeared in *The Weekly Dispatch* in 1836. She conducted *Eliza Cook's Journal* from 1849 to 1854.

Cook, Captain **James** 1728–79 Navigator. As well as writing *Sailing Directions* (1766–8), Cook left records of his three principal voyages, published as: *Journal during his First Voyage* (1893), edited by Captain W. J. L. Wharton; *A Voyage towards the South Pole and round the World in 1772–1775* (1777); and *A Voyage to the Pacific Ocean in 1776–1780* (1784), completed by Captain T. King after Cook's death in Hawaii.

Cook, Michael 1933– English-born Canadian playwright. He spent 12 years in the British Army where he wrote, directed and acted in troop entertainments. After teacher training in drama at Nottingham University he emigrated to Canada and settled in Newfoundland, where he was associated with Memorial University. He became deeply involved in local theatre and started writing radio plays. His works are passionate and unsubtle attacks on the emotions that 'celebrate the elemental and instinctive', particularly as found in indigenous cultures. *Colour the Flesh the Colour of Dust* (1972), his first stage play, is a Brechtian examination of the political turmoil in Newfoundland in 1762 as it went from a British to a French to a British colony. *Head, Guts and Soundbone Dance* (1974) is a powerful folk play which captures both the colourful Newfoundland speech and the fatalistic attitudes engendered by the island's harsh life. *The Gayden Chronicles* (1979), commissioned by Festival Lennoxville, tells the story of a British Navy rebel who was hanged in St John's in 1812. His other plays include *Jacob's Wake* (1975), *Quiller* (1975), *On the Rim of the Curve* (1977) and *This Damned Inheritance* (1983).

Cook's Tale, The See *CANTERBURY TALES, THE*.

Cooke, John (Esten) 1830–86 American novelist. He wrote historical novels of colonial Virginia in the manner of JAMES FENIMORE COOPER: *Leather Stocking and Silk* (1854), *The Virginia Comedians* (1854) and *Henry St John, Gentleman* (1859). While fighting for the Confederates in the Civil War he wrote a life of Stonewall Jackson (1863), and later a biography of

Robert E. Lee (1871). A series of novels about the Civil War appeared in the late 1860s, but he returned to the colonial history of Virginia in: *Her Majesty The Queen* (1872), about the Cavaliers; *Canolles* (1877), about Virginia during the Revolution; and *My Lady Pokahontas* (1885).

Coolbrith, Ina Donna 1842–1928 American poet. *A Perfect Day* (1881), *The Singer of the Sea* (1894) and *Songs from the Golden Gate* (1895), written in a simple lyrical style, are the first published verses from California. She also shared the editorship of the *OVERLAND MONTHLY* with BRET HARTE.

Coolidge, Susan [Woolsey, Sarah Chauncy] 1845–1905 American writer of CHILDREN'S LITERATURE. Born in Ohio, the oldest daughter of a close family, she was educated at private schools and served as a nurse in the Civil War. She became popular with several generations of young readers for the heroine she introduced in her second book, *What Katy Did* (1872) – the tall, rebellious daughter of a small-town family very much like its creator's own. Katy's adventures in succeeding books cover her schooldays, foreign travel and engagement. Susan Coolidge also published several volumes of poetry and edited the correspondence of FANNY BURNEY and JANE AUSTEN.

Cooper, Giles (Stannus) 1918–66 Playwright. Cooper was born at Carrickmines, County Dublin, and educated at Lancing College. After service in World War II, he worked first as an actor and then as a television script editor. Although best known in his lifetime as a prolific adapter for television (notably the *Maigret* series, which won him a Writer of the Year award in 1961), he produced 70 original plays for radio, television and the stage. He had some critical success in the theatre with *Everything in the Garden* (1962) and created one of the most spectacular television plays of its time, *The Other Man* (1964), an alternative history of Anglo-Nazi relations. But his best work, like *Unman, Wittering and Zigo* (1958), was in radio, a medium whose extreme flexibility suited his acerbic mixture of the absurd and the naturalistic. Pushing out radio's technical frontiers, Cooper pioneered electronic sound-effects to reinforce the cartoon-like nature of some of his stories; he moved adroitly between his characters' inner and outer lives, between dream and reality. A prestigious award for radio drama bears his name.

Cooper, James Fenimore 1789–1851 American novelist. He was born in Burlington, New Jersey, the son of Judge William Cooper, an enterprising and wealthy land agent who founded Cooperstown in upstate New York, where Cooper spent much of his childhood. He attended a school in Albany and studied for a time at Yale until he was expelled in 1805. He

spent the next five years at sea, first on a merchant ship and then as a midshipman in the US Navy. He left the sea in 1811 to marry Susan Delancy, who was descended from the early governors of New York colony. The Coopers settled in Scarsdale and then New York.

His first novel was *Precaution* (1820), a study of manners in English society in the tradition of JANE AUSTEN, written after his wife challenged him to improve on an English novel he had criticized. THE SPY (1821), set during the American Revolution, and *The Pilot* (1823), a tale of the sea, were more characteristic of the vein of romance he would develop. *The Pioneers* (1823) began the LEATHERSTOCKING TALES, the series of novels for which he is chiefly remembered; subsequent volumes were *The Last of the Mohicans* (1826), *The Prairie* (1827), *The Pathfinder* (1840) and *The Deerslayer* (1841). *Lionel Lincoln* (1825) a story of Boston during the Revolution, was the only novel in a projected series which would have dealt with each of the 13 original states.

Cooper soon established a reputation as one of America's leading authors. The long stay in Europe which he began in 1826 made him one of the first American writers to become widely popular outside his own country. He was hailed as an American counterpart of SIR WALTER SCOTT, who became his friend. The years in Europe were also intensely productive. Cooper published: *The Red Rover* (1827), a sea story; *The Wept of Wishton-Wish* (1829), a novel of early American frontier life; *The Water Witch* (1830), another sea story; *Notions of America* (1828), an essay partly inspired by his friend the Marquis de Lafayette; and a historical trilogy, *The Bravo* (1831), *The Heidenmauer* (1832) and *The Headsman* (1833).

In 1832 he returned to the USA, where his conservative political essays made him less popular. Non-fictional works of social commentary such as *The Monikins* (1835) and *The American Democrat* (1838) contain sharp criticism of American society and the abuses of democracy. The novels *Homeward Bound* (1838) and *Home as Found* (1838) also dramatize his aristocratic, social and political beliefs. The 21 books he produced during the last decade of his life include two more sea novels, *Afloat and Ashore* and *Miles Wallingford*, and a historical trilogy known as the 'Littlepage Manuscripts', about a New York family. *Satanstoe* (1845) explores problems of property rights in America from the Colonial period to the 1840s. *The Chainbearer* (1845) is set during the Revolution. *The Redskins* (1846) tells how the Littlepage family manages, with the help of Indians, to deal with the exploitations of agents and lawyers in developing American society.

Cooper, Thomas 1805–92 Poet. A Chartist imprisoned for sedition in 1842, he wrote, while serving his sentence, *The Purgatory of Suicides* (1845), an epic on political themes, and *Wise Saws and Modern*

Instances (1845). He also published an *Autobiography* in 1872.

Cooper, William [Huff, Harry Summerfield] 1910–
Novelist. Born in Crewe, he worked as a schoolmaster in Leicester before entering the civil service in 1945 and becoming Personnel Consultant to the Atomic Energy Research Authority in 1958. Cooper's most important novel is his fifth, *Scenes from Provincial Life*, which appeared in 1950. With its cynical and pragmatic hero, Joe Lunn, lower-middle-class provincial milieu and quiet realism, it was a seminal influence on writers like JOHN BRAINE and the genesis of the ANGRY YOUNG MEN novel. Three sequels have since been added, continuing Joe Lunn's story through his marriage and later years in London: *Scenes from Married Life* (1961), *Scenes from Metropolitan Life* (actually the second of the sequence, but not published until 1982) and *Scenes from Later Life* (1983). *From Early Life* (1990) is his autobiography.

Coover, Robert (Lowell) 1932– American novelist. Born in Iowa, he studied at Southern Illinois, Indiana, and Chicago universities, serving in the US Navy from 1953 to 1957, and then taught philosophy at several universities. His novels, with their particular emphasis on culture patterns and movements, are representative of POST-MODERNISM. *The Origin of the Brunists* (1966), which received the William Faulkner Award for best first novel, describes the founding of a religious cult by the survivor of a mining disaster. *The Universal Baseball Association, Inc., J. Henry Waugh, Prop.* (1968) uses baseball as a central metaphor to satirize American religious attitudes. *The Public Burning* (1977), set in the 1950s, treats the impulses that lead to dogmatic extremism, an interest that has been integral to most of Coover's fiction. *Spanking the Maid* (1981) is a dark story of the obsessive relationship between a man and his maid. Subsequent novels are *Gerald's Party* (1986) and *Pinocchio in Venice* (1991). He has also published short stories in *Pricksongs and Descants* (1969), *You Must Remember This* (1987) and *Whatever Happened to Gloomy Gus of the Chicago Bears?* (1988).

Cope, Wendy (Mary) 1945– Poet. Born in Kent and educated at St Hilda's College, Oxford, she has worked as a primary school teacher, arts editor for the ILEA magazine, *Contact,* and TV columnist for THE SPECTATOR. The witty, satirical, occasionally desperate poems in *Making Cocoa for Kingsley Amis* (1986), *Men and Their Boring Arguments* (1988), *Does She Like Word Games* (1988) and *Serious Concerns* (1992) quickly won her popularity. She uses her invented character, Jason Strugnell, an unpleasant South London poet, to dissect traditional attitudes and expose British anti-intellectualism. Cope has also written CHILDREN'S LITERATURE in *Twiddling Your*

Thumbs (1988) and *The River Girl* (1991) and edited an anthology, *Is That the New Moon* (1989).

Coppard, A(lfred) E(dgar) 1878–1957 Short-story writer and poet. He received a rudimentary education at Board schools in Folkestone and Brighton before leaving at the age of nine to become apprentice to a tailor in Whitechapel at the time of the Jack the Ripper killings. Subsequently he worked as a paraffin vendor's assistant, auctioneer, cheesemonger and soap agent. In 1907 he moved to Oxford to become a clerk at the Eagle Ironworks, where he stayed until he became a full-time writer in 1919. His friends in Oxford included Harold Laski and L. P. HARTLEY, but his nearest literary kin is perhaps W. H. DAVIES. Warm and friendly, with an immense capacity for enjoying life, Coppard added sophistication to the lyrical power which both men possessed. The first of his volumes of poetry, *Hips and Haws*, appeared in 1922, but he is chiefly remembered for the collections of short stories that began with *Adam and Eve and Pinch Me* (1921) and included *The Black Dog and Other Stories* (1923), *Fishmonger's Fiddle: Tales* (1925) and *The Field of Mustard* (1926). They contain tales as diverse as the rich and mysterious 'Dusky Ruth' and 'The Presser', about a 10-year-old boy apprenticed to a Whitechapel tailor, but above all Coppard's work conveys the flavour of the English countryside.

copyright In simple terms, copyright is ownership of and right of control over all possible ways of reproducing a work – a work in this context being an object which is the product of an original creative act by one or more people, in a form which makes it subject to one or other means of copying. In particular, but not exclusively, copyright protection is given to literary works, dramatic works, artistic works (paintings, drawings, photographs, and so on), sound recordings, films, television and sound broadcasts, and various productions of the new technology.

Beyond this basic definition matters become less easy, because of the inherent complexity of copyright (at least in its modern manifestations), and because of its tendency to mean different things at different times in different countries and even in different minds. In terms of existing laws, for instance, copyright in the UK and in France differs in important respects, despite many common characteristics; and copyright in both countries differs significantly from copyright as a system of international protection. In historical terms, copyright is an evolving legal concept determined by the peculiarities of each particular nation's history, by the growing ease of international communications and by technological developments (the invention of the gramophone, television, the photocopier and so on). And in more general conceptual terms there is unresolvable debate as to whether copyright is properly seen primarily as a negative right (the right to stop), or as a monopoly, or as property, or as uniquely personal (dealing above all with the control of the creator over his creation). Copyright is fixed and final only in so far as it happens to be frozen, for the time being, within the laws of those countries which grant it recognition, and within certain international conventions. Beyond that, there is continuing debate as to the proper nature of copyright as an abstract entity which in turn affects debate as to the correct legislative balance to be struck between the interests of different parties.

To a large extent, the history of copyright begins when you want it to begin. Those who have been interested in dignifying the concept of authors' rights with as long a genealogy as possible have gone back to classical Greek culture, to around the sixth century BC, when it is said that intellectual works began to be considered as the product of one mind rather than as the anonymous property of a whole society. Others have argued that 'true' copyright began in 1709, with the passing of the first national copyright Act in England. However that may be, copyright has been an important subject since the invention of movable type and continues to grow in importance as the world finds more and better ways in which to multiply images, to record, to transmit and to receive. We are all copiers and receivers now: both the large institutions with their photocopiers and visual terminals, and the average individual, with an accessible photocopier at work or in the nearest library, a computer in his spare-room, a videocassette recorder, a television and a radio in his living-room and a tape-recorder close at hand or even in his pocket. What is being devoured insatiably, what is being copied, often illegally – plays, novels, films, poems, operas, computer programs – is the very lifeblood of our culture. The main, almost the sole, legal safeguard of that lifeblood is the law of copyright.

Under most national copyright laws there are two major qualifications for protection. First, that the work is 'original', which does not mean so much being novel in subject matter as being the product of some skill and labour in composition other than the skill and labour involved in mere copying. In the main, emphasis here is on expression rather than content. For example, the copyright in an article expressing a new philosophical theory lies in its unique sequence of words rather than in the theory as such. It does not infringe copyright to paraphrase this theory and publish the paraphrase (although it may be plagiarism). Indeed, the paraphrase secures its own copyright protection as another sequence of words. A common, but over-simple, catchphrase in this context is 'copyright is in words and not ideas'. This is certainly true in the example that has just been given, and in the case of any single 'idea'. But if it were generally true, then to translate an English novel into French, or to turn it into a play, would not be an infringement of copyright. It is a matter of degree, and at one extreme a particularly distinctive sequence of events in a play, or whole collection of philosophical ideas, can be regarded as a substantial part of a work, and to express them, or a significant part of them, in other words, or with other characters, or in another medium, will be to infringe copyright.

The creator of a work is normally the copyright owner, and no special act (e.g. registration) is required in order to establish ownership. The main exceptions are where the creator has already assigned copyright to another party, via a contract entered into before the work was begun, or at least before it was finished, or where the act of creation was a legitimate part of the creator's role under a contract of employment (broadly speaking, what US copyright legislation refers to as a 'work made for hire').

The second qualification for protection concerns time. In the main, copyright is finite: after a given period a work goes out of copyright and falls into 'the public domain'. Different countries define the period very differently – from 20 years after first publication at one extreme to 80 years after the author's death at the other – but all would probably justify it in a similar fashion. It is right for the author to control the use of his work during his lifetime and that his immediate dependants or successors should also have some measure of control over it, or at least some financial reward from it. Yet if it still remains in circulation at some stage after his death, then the work must be assumed to have the makings of some kind of classic: it is a candidate for permanent membership of a nation's culture, and should, in some sense, belong to everybody.

Copyright protection extends to all forms of writing, regardless of quality and of character. The hurried, banal letter is safeguarded as strongly as the great novel. The practical consequences are dictated by the writer's intent. If he is not writing for the public, then copyright merely acts as a protection against unauthorized publication (an unlikely event, but we would not want a law which attempted to discriminate between our letters and the letters of D. H. LAWRENCE). If he is writing for the public, then copyright not only protects his work from the pirate but also provides him with a means by which he can control and encourage the maximum exploitation of his work. For copyright is not one right but a bundle of different rights. The copyright in a novel, for example, will include the prime right to publish in the novel's original language in volume form. But it will also include the right to publish it in translation; the right to turn it into a stage play, and a television play, and a film; the right to read it on radio; the right to take one or more of its characters and 'merchandize' them (as toys, or on T-shirts, for example); and so on.

This potential lies in every just completed novel. For the majority, alas, it remains merely potential: nobody offers publication. For the rest, the offer of publication leads to a publishing contract, one of whose major objects will be to bring about, by a transfer of rights, a state of affairs where some of the potential can be realized.

One important element in the history of publishing in the UK has been a growing concern for the lot of the author. Until 1694, printing and publishing were carried out only with the direct authority of the Crown through the Star Chamber, by a designated group of printers, publishers and booksellers – the Stationers' Company. The official emphasis, that is to say, was not on the rights of the author but on the control of what could be published and the establishment within the Company of a mutually beneficial system whereby each member respected the other's copyrights. It was the expiration of the Act granting the Company this monopoly which led to the making of the first national copyright law in 1709, and it is not to be wondered at that the main thrust of this Act is the protection of the entrepreneur rather than the creator. Compared with the present day, the contractual relationship between the bookseller/publisher and the author, then and for many generations to come, was very simple: the publisher purchased the copyright from the author for one flat fee, and there was an end of it. A typical arrangement of the early 1800s, for example, would have the publisher commissioning a novel in serial form for so many guineas a sheet (16 pages). The guineas bought the copyright as well as the author's time. No further payment would be made if the serial was eventually published in volume form, nor if that volume was reprinted. The growing concern for the author found expression towards the end of the 19th century in a collective sense with the founding of the Society of Authors and in an individualistic sense in the new profession of author's agent. This, together with the growth in international publishing and the proliferation of separate exploitable rights (film, television, video-cassette, etc.), means that the modern contract between author and publisher will tend to be complex, and will ensure that the author retains a permanent financial interest in the sales of his book and in the leasing of and proceeds from the various subsidiary rights. There are exceptions, which may be well founded, but in the main the transfer of rights will be piecemeal and reversible. Instead of an outright sale, there will be separate leasings of different rights (usually achieved by the publisher or agent on the author's behalf) or of the same rights in different exclusive markets.

Most countries now have their own copyright laws and most belong to one or other, if not both, of the two major international conventions. These act as a kind of club in which member countries agree to respect each other's copyrights, thereby making international publishing possible. None the less, piracy survives – particularly in developing countries – and with it the need for continued vigilance.

'Piracy' is usually taken to mean the theft of the copyright of a whole work. However, almost as big a threat is posed by the theft of parts of a copyright – by the photocopying or electronic scanning of a large number of pages without permission or payment, for example. Electronic scanning presents a new and particularly difficult challenge to meet, since the possessor of a work in electronic form has the power to edit it, combine it with other texts, print it out repeatedly, download it to a data base, and so forth. In this, as in other manifestations of the new technology, the problem facing publishers and others is to find controlled and legitimate ways in which these exciting possibilities can be realized. Without sensible control (and proper payment) the whole copyright system could be dangerously weakened. The effect on our cultural life would be devastating.

Coral Island, The An adventure story by R. M. BALLANTYNE, published in 1858.

Three youths, Ralph, Jack and Peterkin, are wrecked on a desert island and set about surviving in true *ROBINSON CRUSOE* fashion. They make a fire by rubbing two sticks together and climb palm trees to gather obligingly thin-skinned coconuts (a mistake in detail Ballantyne was bitterly to regret). Later adventures include rescuing natives from cannibals and escaping from a shark when fishing on a log. Finally the three heroes return to civilization, none the worse for their ordeal and as chummy still as the day on which they were marooned. Writers since have acknowledged the book's influence, most memorably WILLIAM GOLDING in his pessimistic reworking of a similar situation, *LORD OF THE FLIES*.

corantos See NEWSPAPER, THE RISE OF THE ENGLISH.

Corbett [Corbet], **Richard** 1582–1635 Poet and divine. Son of a Surrey gardener, Corbett was educated at Westminster and Christ Church, Oxford, and through the powerful patronage of the royal favourite the Duke of Buckingham he became chaplain to JAMES I, Dean of Christ Church, Bishop of Oxford and finally Bishop of Norwich. He was a celebrated figure of fun, convivial and witty, and a friend of DONNE, JONSON and CORYATE. His occasional verse is sprightly and ironical, and was published posthumously in *Certain Elegant Poems* (1647) and *Poëtica Stromata* (1648); he is best remembered for 'Farewell, Rewards and Fairies', a nostalgic and accomplished poem on the theme of England's past.

Corelli, Marie 1855–1924 Novelist. Born Mary Mackay, the daughter of CHARLES MACKAY, she was originally trained for a musical career, but at the age of 30 published her first novel, *A Romance of Two Worlds* (1886). Although disparaged by the critics, her wildly over-written romantic fiction achieved extraordinary popularity. A habit of creating exotic legends about her own life and an unfailing talent for publicity-seeking helped to keep her in the public eye. She spent her latter years in Stratford-upon-Avon, vying with SHAKESPEARE as a tourist attraction. Although Queen Victoria was convinced that Marie Corelli's fame would be lasting, her books are now forgotten. In their day, *Barabbas* (1893) and *The Sorrows of Satan* (1895) were perhaps the most famous; others include *Vendetta* (1886), *Thelma* (1887), *Ardath* (1889), *The Soul of Lilith* (1892), *The Mighty Atom* (1896), *The Master Christian* (1900) and *Temporal Power* (1902).

Coriolanus A tragedy by WILLIAM SHAKESPEARE, first performed *c.* 1608 and published in the First Folio of 1623. The main source is SIR THOMAS NORTH's translation of Plutarch's *Lives*.

Rome's plebeians are a constant, though inconsistent, force in the play. When it opens, they are on the verge of rebellion against their patrician rulers. Persuaded by the tactful Menenius Agrippa to work for the common good, they are immediately incensed by the arrogant scorn of Caius Martius. But crisis is temporarily averted by the appointment of five Tribunes of the People and by the dispatching of Caius Martius to put down a Volscian uprising. His success in capturing the Volscian city of Corioli wins him glory in Rome and the honourable name of Coriolanus. Election to the Senate seems certain, but Coriolanus is too proud to observe the traditional rites of public humility, and the Tribunes refuse to support him.

The Volscian leader Tullus Aufidius, who is Coriolanus' sworn enemy, prepares another attack on Rome. Hated by the plebeians, Coriolanus is finally persuaded by Volumnia, his mother, to face them and ask for their support, but it is a role he cannot sustain. His outburst in the Forum forces the Tribunes to demand his banishment, and Coriolanus presents himself to Tullus Aufidius in Antium, either as a sacrifice or as an ally. He becomes the leader of the Volscian army against Rome, rejects the desperate pleas of the Senators and is persuaded to spare the city only after an astonishing confrontation with his mother, Volumnia. Aufidius sees the peace treaty as a betrayal, and when Coriolanus taunts him, he and the Volscians kill him as an enemy.

The story of Coriolanus was much less familiar to the Elizabethans than that of Julius Caesar or Antony and Cleopatra. This fact alone would distinguish *Coriolanus* from those other Roman plays. It is a stark political tragedy, in which Shakespeare gives unusual attention to the claims of the people on those who undertake to rule them. It is a consideration that relates the play more obviously to KING LEAR among the great tragedies than to ANTONY AND CLEOPATRA. On the other hand, the making and breaking of the individual Coriolanus is told so barely as to invite comparison with TIMON OF ATHENS, which was probably the next play Shakespeare wrote.

Corkery, Daniel 1878–1964 Irish critic, short-story writer and man of letters. Born in Cork, he was professor of English at University College, Cork, from 1931 to 1947. His book on SYNGE (1931), and his other scholarly works – *The Hidden Ireland* (1925) and *The Fortunes of the Irish Language* (1954) – constitute the most sustained attempt to formulate a nationalist version of the Irish literary tradition. He was mentor to younger writers such as FRANK O'CONNOR and SEAN O'FAOLAIN. His own fiction can be highly sentimental, as in his novel *The Threshold of Quiet* (1917) and his volume of short stories *The Hounds of Banba* (1920); at other times it was broodingly impressive. His best stories are to be found in *A Munster Twilight* (1916), *The Stormy Hills* (1929) and, to a lesser extent, in *Earth out of Earth* (1939). He published a number of plays, of which those in *The Yellow Bittern and Other Plays* (1920) are the most notable.

Cormier, Robert 1925– American writer of CHILDREN'S LITERATURE. Born and educated in Massachusetts, he worked as a scriptwriter and journalist. After publishing three adult novels, he turned to writing children's books which created immediate controversy by their attempt to extend the boundaries of what was thought acceptable or suitable in the genre. In *The Chocolate War* (1974), his first, the portrayal of corruption and bullying at a Roman Catholic boys' school is unrelieved by a happy or morally just ending. In *I am the Cheese* (1977) another boy suffers as a pawn in a battle between organized crime, government bureaucracy and parental callousness. *After the First Death* (1979) enters into the mind of a young terrorist. *The Bumblebee Flies Anyway* (1985) is set in a hospital ward for terminally ill children. Many children find Cormier's books compelling, not simply because they offer a stark contrast to other children's books but also because they are tautly written and move at a uniformly fast pace.

Corn Law Rhymer, The See ELLIOTT, EBENEZER.

Cornford, Frances 1886–1960 Poet. The granddaughter of CHARLES DARWIN and the mother of JOHN CORNFORD, she was born and lived in Cambridge. Her *Collected Poems* (1954) includes the famous TRIOLET 'To a Fat Lady Seen from a Train'.

Cornford, (Rupert) John 1915–36 Poet and writer on politics. Born in Cambridge, he was educated at Stowe School, Trinity College, Cambridge, and the London School of Economics. He joined the Communist Party in 1933 and in August 1936 he became the first Englishman to go to Spain to fight against Franco, serving with the POUM and the International Brigade before his death at the Cordoba Front. He began writing poetry at an early age, much influenced by his mother, FRANCES CORNFORD; his work still kept its clarity and direct simplicity after he rebelled in favour of the MODERNISM of GRAVES, ELIOT and AUDEN. A few love-poems and 'Poems from Spain, 1936' are the best, though even some of the earlier poems indicate much talent unrealized because of his allegiance to Communism and his premature death. Jonathan Galassi has edited *Understand the Weapon, Understand the Wound: Selected Writings of John Cornford* (1976).

Cornhill Magazine, The A monthly periodical founded by GEORGE SMITH in 1860, with THACKERAY as its first editor. He established a distinctive brand of family literature for the journal, and contributed two novels of his own, *DENIS DUVAL* and *THE ADVENTURES OF PHILIP*. Other contributors included ELIZABETH BARRETT BROWNING, ROBERT BROWNING, SWINBURNE, ELIZABETH GASKELL, RUSKIN, GEORGE ELIOT, CHARLES READE, MATTHEW ARNOLD, TROLLOPE and, under the editorship (1871–82) of LESLIE STEPHEN, THOMAS HARDY.

Cornwall, Barry [Procter, Bryan Waller] 1787–1874 Poet. Born in Leeds and educated at Harrow, he enjoyed a successful practice as a London solicitor before changing to the profession of barrister. He was a Commissioner of Lunacy from 1832 to 1861. He began to contribute to *The Literary Gazette* in 1815 and thereafter produced several volumes of poetry, chiefly lyrics and songs, among them *Dramatic Scenes* (1819), *Marcian Colonna* (1820), *The Flood of Thessaly* (1823) and *English Songs* (1832). He also wrote a tragedy, *Mirandola* (1821). His daughter was the poet ADELAIDE ANNE PROCTER.

Corsair, The A poem by BYRON, published in 1814. It belongs with *THE BRIDE OF ABYDOS* in its use of the pirate as Romantic hero. Conrad, an Aegean pirate, is captured by his enemy, the Turkish Pasha Seyd, but chivalrously refuses Gulnare's offer to kill her master. She kills the Pasha herself and flees with Conrad, who finds that his beloved Medora has died of grief after a mistaken report of his death. He leaves home and disappears, but returns in disguise as the title character of *Lara* (1814).

Corso, Gregory (Nunzio) 1930– American poet. The son of poor immigrants, he was born and raised in Greenwich Village, New York. His youth was difficult, and by the age of 20 he had served three years in

prison for attempted robbery. His poetry, which is associated with that of the BEATS in its concern with political and social issues, often adopts the stance of a sophisticated child who looks upon a world gone mad. His first volume, *The Vestal Lady on Brattle and Other Poems* (1955), was followed by *Gasoline* (1958), *Bomb* (1958), *The Happy Birthday of Death* (1960), *Long Live Man* (1962), *Selected Poems* (1962) and *There is Yet Time to Run Back through Life and Expiate All That's been Sadly Done* (1965). One of his most important volumes is *Elegiac Feelings American* (1970), dedicated to JACK KEROUAC, which assembles completed poems, drafts of poems and casual drawings. It also marks the beginning of his interest in Egyptology and Eastern religions, apparent in *Egyptian Cross* (1971), *Ankh* (1971), *The Night Last Night was at its Nightest...* (1972), and *Earth Egg* (1974). Later volumes include *Writings from Ox* (1981) and *Mindfield: New and Selected Poems* (1989). He has also written a play, *This Hung-Up Age* (1955), and a volume of memoirs, *The American Express* (1961).

Corvo, Baron See ROLFE, FREDERICK WILLIAM.

Cory, William Johnson 1823–92 Poet. Born William Johnson in Torrington, Devon, he was educated at Eton and King's College, Cambridge. He worked as an assistant master at Eton for over 26 years. On inheriting an estate in 1872 he assumed the name of Cory and settled in Hampstead. *Ionica*, a collection of lyrics, was published anonymously in 1858. His *Letters and Journals* appeared in 1897. His best-known works are the poem 'Heraclitus', paraphrasing Callimachus, and the 'Eton Boating Song', written in 1863.

Coryate, Thomas c. 1577–1617 Traveller and writer. Son of the rector of Odcombe, Somerset, Coryate was educated at Gloucester Hall, Oxford, and became an inveterate traveller. In 1608 he journeyed through Europe, largely on foot, visiting France, Italy, Switzerland, Germany and Holland. On his return in 1611 he published a vivacious account entitled *Coryats Crudities, Hastily Gobbled up in Five Months Travels*, a mishmash of entertaining curiosities and opinionated reportage still of considerable interest as a period piece. It was prefaced with an extravagant number of commendatory verses including contributions from several of the leading poets of the day; these were reprinted separately as *The Odcombian Banquet* (1611). In the following year he embarked on an overland expedition to India, by way of Greece, Turkey, Egypt, Mesopotamia and Persia. He reached Agra, the court of the Mogul Emperor, in 1616, but died exhausted in Surat on his way home. His notes on this journey were preserved in his correspondence, and in *Thomas Coriate Traveller for the*

English Wits: Greeting from the Court of the Great Mogul (1611).

Cotton, Charles 1630–87 Poet, translator and angler. Son of a generous landowner and *literatus*, who numbered DONNE, JONSON and HERRICK among his friends, he was born at the family home, Beresford Hall in Staffordshire. Staunchly Anglican and Royalist, he lived most of his life in retirement, and his few ventures into public life brought him no eminent success. Constantly plagued by financial problems of his father's making, he obtained modest pecuniary relief from his writing, particularly his burlesque of the *Aeneid, Scarronnides*, the first Book of which appeared in 1664, to instant and lasting popular success, only ceasing to command reprints in the 19th century. A burlesque of Lucian, *The Scoffer Scoft*, followed in 1675. His translations from the French include military memoirs, Corneille's *Pompey*, and an excellently racy version of Montaigne's *Essays* (3 vols., 1685), which largely supplanted JOHN FLORIO's 1603 translation until this century. The bulk of his original poetry appeared posthumously, in *Poems on Several Occasions* (1689); it is a true miscellany, but his particular gifts are best represented in burlesques, conversational epistles and poems of retirement. These last bear eloquent witness to his love of angling, and his enduring fame has been as IZAAK WALTON's friend and protégé, and as author of the dialogue between Piscator and Viator which forms the Second Part of the renowned fifth edition of *THE COMPLEAT ANGLER* (1676).

Cotton, John 1584–1652 American Puritan minister. Born in Derbyshire, Cotton entered Trinity College, Cambridge, at the age of 13. Subsequently awarded a fellowship at Emmanuel College for his proficiency in Hebrew, he served as a lecturer, dean and catechist (1608–12), and in 1612 was appointed vicar of St Botolph's Church in Boston, Lincolnshire, a post which he resigned 20 years later when the Court of High Commission summoned him for instituting Puritan reforms in his parish. In July 1633 he emigrated to Massachusetts Bay aboard the *Griffin* and was chosen to be minister of the Boston church, where he remained until his death. He was the father-in-law of INCREASE MATHER and the grandfather of COTTON MATHER.

A distinguished preacher, he took up the issues most pressing to the Puritan consciousness in edifying and affective sermons. *A Brief Exposition on the Whole Book of Canticles* (1642) reads the history of the Christian church in the biblical *Song of Solomon*, an interpretation which theologically justifies the Puritan enterprise in Massachusetts. The sermons collected in *Christ the Fountain of Life: or, Sundry Choice Sermons on Part of the Fifth Chapter of the First Epistle of St John* (1651) describe Cotton's ideas about religious conversion, revealing the emphasis he placed throughout his ministry on the irrelevance of good works to salvation. He also wrote several widely read theological tracts. *The Keys of the Kingdom of Heaven* (1644) was written to persuade the Westminster Assembly to adopt the New England Way of church governance, and *The Way of Churches of Christ in New England* (1645) in an attempt to define Congregational theology and ecclesiology. In 1646 he published *Milk for Babes, Drawn from the Breasts of Both Testaments*, one of the authoritative catechisms which was used widely throughout the 17th century in America. The following year, he responded to ROGER WILLIAMS's criticisms of New England church policies in *THE BLOODY TENET OF PERSECUTION* with *The Bloody Tenet Washed and Made White in the Blood of the Lamb*. Having been attacked for the views expressed in *The Way of Churches of Christ in New England* by Robert Baille, whose critique was published as *A Dissuasive from the Errors of the Time* (1645), Cotton refuted Baille's charges in *The Way of the Congregational Churches Cleared* (1648). That same year he published his most thorough ecclesiastical statement, *A Survey of the Sum of Church Discipline*.

Cotton, Sir Robert Bruce 1571–1631 Author of political tracts, antiquary and collector of manuscripts. Educated at Westminster School and Jesus College, Cambridge, Cotton became a Parliamentarian during the reign of James I. He was less important for his own writings than for his library of manuscripts from the dissolved monasteries, precious material which might otherwise have been destroyed or lost. Cotton allowed BACON, RALEIGH, CAMDEN, SELDEN and USSHER access to his collection and gave manuscripts to the newly founded Bodleian Library at Oxford in 1602. The Cottonian Library was left to the nation by his grandson, Sir John Cotton, and housed first in Essex House and then in Ashburnham House, where some of it was destroyed in a disastrous fire of 1731. The remainder passed to the British Museum in 1753. Among the treasures to survive are the single manuscript of *BEOWULF*, the manuscripts of *SIR GAWAIN AND THE GREEN KNIGHT* and *PEARL*, several biblical manuscripts and the Lindisfarne Gospels. See also LIBRARIES.

Coulter, John 1888–1980 Irish-Canadian playwright. Born in Belfast, he taught art and textile design there and in Dublin, and wrote plays influenced by the ABBEY THEATRE before moving to London and then Canada. *The House in the Quiet Glen* won several awards at the 1937 Dominion Drama Festival. His best-known work is *Riel* (1950), an epic play about the leader of the 19th-century Métis rebellion in Western Canada. The same episode also yielded *The Crime of Louis Riel* (1966) and *The Trial of Louis Riel*

(1968). Other work included the libretti for two operas by Healey Willan, *Transit through Fire* (1942) and *Deirdre* (1946), and scripts for radio and television in Canada, the USA and Britain.

Count Robert of Paris See SCOTT, SIR WALTER.

Country of the Pointed Firs, The A novel by SARAH ORNE JEWETT, published in 1896. The unnamed female narrator takes a summer vacation in the imaginary town of Dunnet Landing in rural Maine, where the townspeople, at first somewhat distant, gradually include her in their daily lives. The novel reveals the dramatic depth and intensity in the life of an apparently placid community. It concentrates in particular on the characters and abilities of women and on ageing.

Country Wife, The A comedy by WILLIAM WYCHERLEY, first produced in January 1675 and published in the same year. One of the greatest examples of RESTORATION COMEDY, the play gave some offence even in its own day, and was toned down by DAVID GARRICK when he presented it as *The Country Girl* in 1766. Wycherley's original is certainly bawdy and the humour is not without savagery, but the play is constructed by a master of comedy.

Pinchwife and his wife Margery go to London for the marriage of Pinchwife's sister, Alithea, to Sparkish. Pinchwife is paying his sister's dowry, the real reason for Sparkish wanting to marry her. He is a foolish character who bores his acquaintances, among them Horner, a cynical libertine who has put it about that he suffers from impotence; jealous and suspicious husbands are content to trust their wives to Horner's company, believing him harmless. Pinchwife has married a country girl much younger than himself, and Margery is agog with excitement at being in London. Sparkish takes Alithea for granted and eventually loses her to Harcourt (the love of Harcourt and Alithea is the play's still centre). The fashionable ladies soon discover that Horner is far from impotent but keep their apparent secret to themselves. Horner finds Margery irresistible; she is driven into his arms by the jealousy of Pinchwife. In a brilliant closing scene the wives discover to their wrath that they all share the same secret, but they have to close ranks and swear to Horner's impotence in order to protect themselves from their husbands' rage. The curtain comes down to a dance of cuckolds.

court theatres The various entertainments at the Tudor and Stuart courts were often elaborate enough to demand the temporary adaptation of indoor spaces. The Great Hall at Hampton Court, the Banqueting Hall as well as the Great Chamber at Whitehall and the Great Halls at Greenwich, Richmond and Windsor were all put to use, particularly during the Christmas festivities at which professional theatre companies were privileged to perform and rewarded well for doing so. Under Charles I, more permanent structures were adapted or built. Inigo Jones converted the Cockpit-in-Court (1629–30) into an intimate theatre along lines already tested at the Cockpit in Drury Lane, and the Stuart delight in MASQUES was gratified by the costly erection of the Masquing House (1637) close to the Banqueting Hall. Under Charles II and his successors, the custom of adaptation declined and the court theatres dwindled into insignificance.

courtesy book A type of literature particularly popular in the Middle Ages, defining the rules of polite behaviour and the general demeanour and duties of a courtier. Often written in verse and in dialogue, examples are extant in most European vernaculars and in Latin. Courtesy books were intended for the young gentry and aspiring courtiers, and dealt with personal hygiene and cleanliness as well as matters of etiquette, courtly duties and codes of behaviour. In the Renaissance the form changed slightly, following the influential work of Castiglione, *Il libro del cortegiano* (1528, translated 1561; see THE COURTIER). These later works were concerned with the integration of a wide variety of intellectual and practical attributes and skills in the ideal man of the age. The last courtesy book in the traditional mould is LORD CHESTERFIELD's *Letters to His Son* (1774).

Courtier, The Baldessare Castiglione's dialogue *Il libro del cortegiano* was first printed at Venice in 1528. It describes conversations at the court of Urbino, supervised by the Duchess Elisabetta Gonzaga, aimed at defining the perfect courtier. It had numerous Italian editions and was translated into the major European languages. The English translation made in 1561 by Sir Thomas Hoby (1530–66) ran through several editions and it was enormously popular as a COURTESY BOOK. Its immediate influence is discernible in such educational treatises as ELYOT's *The Book Named the Governor* and ASCHAM's *The Schoolmaster*, and JONSON bases a scene in *EVERY MAN OUT OF HIS HUMOUR* on it.

courtly love The modern name for a literary and social concept, originating in the Middle Ages, of a particular kind of love between men and women, involving service and veneration on the part of the man, and a nominal or actual domination on the part of the woman. This reversal of the usual medieval marital relationship took place between a lady who might or might not be married and a man sometimes but not invariably her social inferior. Descriptions consequently insist on its private, discreet and secret nature, on the frustrations and obstacles intensifying it, and on the dangers of its discovery by spies and slanderers. Its aristocratic system of values envisaged love as an educative and ennobling experience, the source of prowess and refinement, and consequently beneficial to society.

Some critics have denied that such a concept ever existed and point to Gaston Paris's coining of the term *amour courtois* in 1883. More widely held is the view that some such variation of romantic love was discussed, and existed as an ideal, if not as a historical fact, from the 12th century onwards, though usually called fine (or *verai*, or *bon*) *amour*. Definitions of it have varied according to literary fashion and have proliferated in the 20th century, when increasingly specialized knowledge of the Middle Ages has also resulted in scepticism and an unwillingness to make grandiose hypotheses.

Theories on the origins of courtly love have also proliferated. Dronke has asserted that it is a timeless human experience that transcends geographical boundaries (thus removing its 'courtly' label), and can be found in the earliest poetry. But C. S. LEWIS and most critics have seen it as a phenomenon arising at the end of the 11th century in the courts of Southern France. Influences contributing to its formation are multiple, probably including the ironical love treatises of Ovid, and Hispano-Arabic literature. Southern France had many and various connections with Spain, and the Norman kingdom of Sicily also provided a bridge to the Arab world. The idea of love melancholy or *amor hereos* is a Graeco-Arabic one that passed into standard European medical knowledge through Avicenna and thence to literature. Both Troubadour and Arabic poetry express similar ideas about love, as simultaneously beneficial and distressing, in similar oxymorons: delight/torment; sickness/medicine; freedom/slavery; life/death.

Whereas the Arab poets frequently wrote of their love for slave girls, the Christians address themselves to noble ladies and use the terminology of feudalism to make the relationship resemble one between vassal and overlord. Here the growth of the concept of courtly love has perhaps been influenced by certain 12th-century social factors. The households of territorial magnates were often full of young men, landless younger sons, receiving their education and chivalric training there and as yet unable to afford marriage. There was often a shortage of women in such households; and in the absence of the overlord on crusade, his wife or sister frequently acted as suzerain. Such a situation may have nurtured love affairs between people of different social standing. The medieval practice of arranged marriages might also have encouraged the ladies to look elsewhere for love, but it is important to remember too that despite the famous dictum (allegedly by Marie de Champagne in 1174) that love and marriage were incompatible, there is much literary evidence to suggest that they were not. Jan Huizinga has widened the discussion of sociological factors contributing to the growth of courtly love by envisaging it as an aristocratic game, played by members of a class who had the leisure to indulge in it, and containing all the satisfying game elements of contest, chance, make-believe and risk.

The poetry of the Troubadours of Southern France, which flourished for about 250 years before being dealt a mortal blow by the onset of the Albigensian Crusade in 1209, is responsible for the earliest formulation of courtly ideas about love and for their subsequent wide dissemination throughout Europe. But their poetry shows right from its beginnings, in the literate and civilized court at Poitiers at the end of the 11th century, a range of amorous attitudes: Guilhem IX of Poitou, Duke of Aquitaine, writes both bawdily and seriously, of sensual and aspiring lovers. Distinctions between *Amors* (carnal, treacherous, sterile) and *Fin'Amors* (spiritual, distant, inspiring) continue to be made in the 12th century by poets like Jaufré Rudel (*fl.* 1140s), with his *amor de lonh* (love from afar), and the moralist Marcabru (*fl.* 1138–50). Bernart de Ventadorn (*fl.* 1145–80), on the other hand, accepts love's service completely and identifies *Fin'Amors* as no quasi-religious ideal but true, mutual, fulfilled love, a source of improvement for the submissive and patient lover.

The Troubadour ideal of *cortesia* as a high moral code of behaviour based on profane love spread to the Northern French lyric poets and to England, to the *lais* of MARIE DE FRANCE (*fl.* 1160–90) and the story of Tristan, both based on Celtic legends. These stories in their outlines are often uncourtly: they depict mutual passion and women often both attainable and active, even (as in Marie's *Lanval* and *Eliduc*) making the first advances; and the linchpin of aristocratic society, the queen, is removed by Tristan to temporary exile. The uncourtly material of legend has in other respects, however, been modified or used to enhance other powerful constituents of courtly love. Hopeless passion makes young men accomplish all kinds of deeds; their suffering due to separation is intensified by all kinds of obstacles – mountains, jealous husbands, jealous wives. The Tristan story, above all, contributes three details endlessly imitated in courtly literature: the body/heart *(cors/cuers)* pun expressing Iseut's dilemma of body possessed by husband and heart by lover; the words '*En vus e ma mort e ma vie*'; and the love potion, expressing the sudden and inexorable force of passion. The romances of Chrétien de Troyes (*fl.* 1170–81) likewise link Celtic material and the terminology of courtly love, but much of his work (*Erec, Yvain, Cligés*) portrays married lovers. The immoral adulterous love of Tristan and Iseut may have inspired his *Cligés*, where the dilemma of *cors/cuers* is ingeniously solved. Marriage is seen as the proper, socially celebrated expression of romantic love, even if there is a subsequent danger that satisfied desire may lead, not to prowess on the knight's part, but inertia

(*Erec*). Chrétien's *Lancelot* is the great exception to the rest of his work, and still arouses controversy, since it is the first romance to depict the adulterous love of Lancelot and Guinevere, with hauteur and scorn on the latter's part when her submissive lover does not at once undergo a humiliating ordeal for her sake.

The subject of the romance may well have been imposed on Chrétien by his patroness Marie de Champagne, depicted as denying the compatibility of love and marriage in a much more controversial work, Andreas Capellanus's *De arte honeste amandi* (1175–80). Two-thirds of this popular and much-translated treatise expounds courtly love, its rules and etiquette, to an unknown young man called Walter; the last third claims it has been expounded only so that it should be rejected, as harmful to the soul. Is it a scholastic joke, a seduction manual, a moralistic work or an early documenting of the game of love? Its structure, and some of its sentiments, undoubtedly owe something to Ovid's cynical *Ars amatoria* and *Remedia amoris*, and for this reason alone it is probably not worth attaching too much importance to Andreas; certainly we should not assume that his rules present an inflexible code. By the 1180s and 1190s some of the courtly attitudes to love were being parodied, as the romances of the Anglo-Norman poet Hue de Rotelande bear witness. The hugely influential 13th-century *Roman de la rose*, the work of Guillaume de Lorris and Jean de Meun, is no romance but ALLEGORY used for the first time to convey the courtly experience of love. It presents a garden of love which excludes old age and poverty but is open to the rich and leisured; a Lover who falls in love with a Rose (the lady) and has to find a way of wooing and seducing her; and a gamut of Opinions on the emotion, from varying characters, which range from the idealistic to the downright cynical.

In medieval English literature, expressions of the courtly ideal of love, other than in the work of CHAUCER, are less frequently found than on the Continent. An early and delightful use of the *amor de lonh* motif appears in a little story in the ANCRENE RIWLE (*c.* 1200) about a disdainful lady wooed patiently by a king from a distant land – Christ wooing the soul. Courtly terminology often appears in English lyric only to lead us to the supreme Lady, the Virgin Mary. Secular lyrics refer to some of the courtly attitudes and attributes, but often in a modified form: the lady may still be described in terms of *largesse, prouesse* and *lealte* as if she were a feudal overlord; the necessary secrecy of the love affair may be emphasized; but it is not necessarily extramarital and the lady seems attainable, not aloof. English VERSE ROMANCES, taking their cue perhaps from the 12th- and 13th-century Anglo-Norman ones, which they often adapted or translated, are not notably courtly. The great exception is the 14th-century *IPOMADON*, which translated Hue de Rotelande's *Ipomédon* and retains its extensive reflection on the problems of courtly love and its emphasis on the thoughts and emotions of its characters. The romance portrays its hero and heroine as learning and maturing through the suffering entailed in love, whose natural fulfilment comes in marriage.

But this courtly theme of education through love is comparatively rare in English romances, which are more commonly homiletic in character or, when they use French originals, are less interested in love problems than adventures. So *YWAIN AND GAWAIN* (*c.* 1350), a version of Chrétien's *Yvain*, omits the long self-questioning monologues of the original, and the late 13th-century *SIR TRISTREM* is predominantly not a love story. The Lancelot story is not taken up till around 1400, in the stanzaic *LE MORTE ARTHUR*, where although love is the chief source of Lancelot's greatness, it is also firmly established as responsible for the fall of Arthur and the Round Table. SIR THOMAS MALORY too, who used the stanzaic *Morte* in his *LE MORTE DARTHUR*, was not entirely happy with the relationship of Lancelot and Guinevere and at times seems to deny the possibility of any carnal union between them. A group of 14th-century romances – *SIR EGLAMOUR OF ARTOIS, THE EARL OF TOULOUS, SIR DEGREVANT, SIR TORRENT OF PORTYNGALE* and *GUY OF WARWICK* – all portray the hero in love with his social superior, and *GUY*, like its 13th-century Anglo-Norman original, shows him taking to his bed with all the symptoms of love-melancholy. His lady will not return his love until he has proved worthy of her, and is anxious lest her premature yielding should check his prowess, a concern reminiscent of Chrétien's Erec. But these courtly features only occur in the first quarter of the romance; the rest is entirely given up to Guy's martial adventures, eventually performed for the greater glory of God rather than for the lady. The 14th-century *WILLIAM OF PALERNE* is a fairly faithful translation of its French original and so retains the description of the symptoms of 'courtly love' evinced by its hero. The courtly elements in these works make them exceptional cases among English romances, where the heroines often take the lead in wooing and the heroes may be initially reluctant.

The work of the greatest 14th-century English writers, however, makes it clear that they were thoroughly familiar with and sympathetic to the aristocratic ideal of love. We may not think of the relationship between Gawain and Bertilak's lady, in *SIR GAWAIN AND THE GREEN KNIGHT*, as one of *fine amour*, especially as she is the one who woos, yet the 'luf-talkyng' expected of Gawain and indulged in by both of them is undoubtedly an essential ingredient of *courtoisie* and reminds us of Huizinga's theory of courtly love as an aristocratic game. In JOHN GOWER's *CONFESSIO AMANTIS* the Lover is questioned about his amorous behaviour. He 'confesses' his sentiments and experiences and demonstrates his refined manners and 'fair speech' in his long and devoted service to his lady. But the Lover has grown old in this service and by the end of the poem Love will have no more of him.

This realistic and clear-sighted attitude that accompanies a sympathetic depiction of courtly love is also shared by Gower's friend Chaucer. His first poem, THE BOOK OF THE DUCHESS, indebted in part to the French love-visions of Machaut and Froissart, celebrates the relationship between yearning knight and virtuous but aloof lady which leads to a happy marriage but is abruptly terminated by death. The knight's feelings are intensified by loss and threaten to overwhelm him. A more detached and comic view of courtly relationships is expressed in THE PARLEMENT OF FOULES. The poet dreams of a garden containing a great gathering of birds of all classes, assembled to witness the formel (i.e. female) eagle select a mate from among her three noble suitors, all of whom suitably express their devotion in terms of service, fidelity and obedience. Amid ribald comments from the lower orders of birds, the timid formel cannot bring herself to abandon the chaste life as yet, and the decision is postponed for another year. In such a company idealistic posturing has to take its place next to perhaps equally acceptable and more down-to-earth points of view: each perspective on love qualifies the other.

This sympathetic but critical viewpoint is also characteristic of Chaucer's mature works, TROILUS AND CRISEYDE and THE CANTERBURY TALES. Many of the tales in the latter offer a variety of attitudes to love, from the sensual and bawdy to the idealistic, from secular to religious. The two tales which most exemplify courtly attitudes are The Knight's Tale, where Emelye's attitude to her two noble lovers reminds us a little of the formel eagle's, and The Franklin's Tale, frequently cited as Chaucer's last word on ideal marriage. The Roman de la rose (which Chaucer translated as THE ROMAUNT OF THE ROSE) has influenced The Franklin's Tale: Jean de Meun puts into the cynical mouth of Amis a discussion of the reversal of roles endured by a woman when courtship is followed by marriage. The maistrie, or sovereignty, passes from her to her husband and as a result love dies. The Franklin's Tale envisages a union where the husband refuses to exert maistrie over his wife and tries to preserve within marriage the mutual honour and tolerance characteristic of their courtship. Their happy relationship is the source of their adherence to trouthe, the highest standard of honourable behaviour, by which they act in times of stress and which inspires similarly honourable behaviour in others. Troilus and Criseyde is Chaucer's most extended portrayal of a courtly love affair, ending in grief because one of the partners fails to adhere to trouthe. With that ending constantly in mind, Chaucer paints a complex, critical picture of his lovers and the ideals by which they talk and strive to act. Courtly behaviour in love is both high-principled and silly, noble and ineffectual. It cannot survive too much pressure from the violent world of war; seen from the cosmic viewpoint Troilus is granted when he ascends to the eighth sphere after death, it is indistinguishable from fleshly lust; seen from the Christian perspective which closes the poem, it is infinitely surpassed by Divine love. Yet courtly love at its greatest is celebrated, as the lovers consummate their union, in an unforgettable scene where the aspirations and desires of both mind and body have been fully satisfied. The patience, suffering, self-abnegation and self-control imposed by courtly ideals have led directly to this transient but intense joy: by no other road could the lovers arrive at their temporary heaven upon earth.

Covent Garden, Theatre Royal A theatre built and opened in 1732 by John Rich, who brought from his previous theatre in Lincoln's Inn Fields the patent entitling him to share with DRURY LANE the monopoly of legitimate drama in London (see PATENT THEATRES). Sustained with varying intensity, the rivalry with Drury Lane continued until 1843, when the patent monopoly was abolished by Act of Parliament. By then, the first theatre, with its capacity of nearly 2000, had been replaced by a second, with a capacity of 3000. This second theatre, designed by Richard Smirke and opened in 1809, was immediately threatened by the most famous of all popular resistance to increased admission charges, the Old Price Riots. John Philip Kemble, acting manager, had to give in to public demand and even to apologize to his victorious audience.

Even under the management of the actor Macready (1837–9), Covent Garden struggled to overcome the costliness of its ambition and soon after the 1843 act it became primarily an opera-house. After a fire had destroyed the building in 1856, a third theatre, designed by Sir Edward Barry, was erected on the site, and it is this theatre, considerably altered, that now carries the name of the Royal Opera House.

Coventry, Francis d. ?1759 Satirist. Educated at Magdalene College, Cambridge, he became vicar of Edgware, near London. His prose tale, The History of Pompey the Little (1751), gives a lap-dog's observation of life as he is passed from one owner to another with bewildering speed and treated in different ways.

Coventry cycle See MIRACLE PLAYS.

Coverdale, Miles ?1488–1569 Protestant reformer and translator of the Bible. Coverdale was ordained priest in 1514 and became an Augustinian friar in Cambridge. But he developed enthusiasm for reform and by 1528 was preaching against the Mass and devotion to images. A fellow worker with WILLIAM TYNDALE in the translation of the Bible, Coverdale was responsible for the English version of the Psalms preserved in the BOOK OF COMMON PRAYER. Using Tyndale's work, he published at Cologne in 1535 the first complete English Bible to be printed, and he was editor of the Great Bible of 1539. He became Bishop of Exeter in 1551, but lost the bishopric in Mary's reign and left England to live in Germany and Switzerland. There he joined the group of exiles who worked on the Geneva Bible, presented to Queen Elizabeth in 1560. He had returned to England in 1559 but his Puritanism prevented his ever regaining a bishopric. He was made a DD of Cambridge in 1563, the same year that he became rector of St Magnus at London Bridge; he held the post until 1566. See also BIBLE IN ENGLISH and PSALTERS.

Coward, Sir **Noël (Pierce)** 1899–1973 Playwright, actor, lyricist and composer. Educated privately and at a stage school, he had already written several plays and sketches, including some for *The Co-Optimists* (1922), when his comedy *The Young Idea* (1922) announced a distinctive voice of the 1920s. Much better than the more celebrated but contrived *The Vortex* (1924), *The Young Idea* was the first of a succession of stylish comedies, which include *Fallen Angels* (1925), HAY FEVER (1925), PRIVATE LIVES (1930), *Design for Living* (1933), *Blithe Spirit* (1941) and *Present Laughter* (1942).

It was not by his plays alone that Coward earned for himself the admiration, and often the envy, of the theatrical profession. He was also a gifted and notably relaxed actor, a showman who learned how to sell a song without singing it and a master of revue. His lyrics, particularly those that look with wry affection at English eccentricity ('The Stately Homes of England', 'Mad Dogs and Englishmen', 'Let's Not be Beastly to the Germans'), are among the best of their kind. Except in *Bitter-Sweet* (1929), he found it hard to sustain a whole piece with music of his own composition, but individual tunes linger ('Some Day I'll Find You', 'I'll See You Again').

Of Coward's patriotic plays, the ambitious *Cavalcade* (1931) has more admirers than *This Happy Breed* (1942) and *Peace in Our Time* (1947). The best of his later work includes *Look after Lulu* (1959), an adaptation of a Feydeau farce, and the three plays performed under the general title *Suite in Three Keys* (1966). Coward also published two lively autobiographies, *Present Indicative* (1937) and *Future Indefinite* (1954), several volumes of short stories (*The Collected Short Stories*, 1962) and a novel, *Pomp and Circumstance* (1960). Under the pseudonym of Hernia Whittlebot, he published *Poems* (1923) and *Chelsea Buns* (1925). *The Coward Song-Book* (1953) and *The Lyrics of Coward* (1965) are useful collections. Coward was knighted in 1970.

Cowley, Abraham 1618–67 Poet. The posthumous son of a wealthy London stationer, Cowley was educated at Westminster School and Trinity College, Cambridge, where he took his BA in 1639, was made a fellow in 1640 and became MA in 1643. Like CLEVELAND and CRASHAW, he was deprived of his fellowship by the Parliamentary party during the Civil War, but had already left Cambridge when this happened. He joined the King at Oxford, and departed for France as secretary to Queen Henrietta Maria in 1644. Ten years later he came back to England and was immediately imprisoned; upon his release he appears to have submitted to the Cromwellian regime but he may have been a Royalist spy. During this time he studied medicine at Oxford and became an MD in 1657. At the Restoration Cowley's fellowship was restored and he was granted land by Henrietta Maria. Thereafter he lived a retired life at Chertsey, devoting his time to botany and to the writing of essays.

Cowley was writing at the age of 10 and had published two romantic epics by the time he was 15; a pastoral drama appeared when he was 20 and he wrote a Latin comedy in the same year. His first collection of verse was *The Mistress: or, Several Copies of Love Verses* (1647). In 1656 a multiple collection was published in which *The Mistress* was included; it contained also *Miscellanies, Pindaric Odes* and four books of an epic on an Old Testament subject, *Davideis*. Cowley wrote an 'Ode upon the Blessed Restoration' in 1660 and *A Discourse by Way of Vision Concerning the Government of Oliver Cromwell* in 1661. In the same year he published his *Proposition for the Advancement of Experimental Philosophy*. A folio edition of his works published in 1668, the year after his death, contained *Several Discourses by way of Essays, in Verse and Prose*, the essays that kept his name alive.

The poet's reputation earned him a splendid funeral and burial in Westminster Abbey beside CHAUCER and SPENSER, but after his death his fame quickly dwindled, though he was a formative influence on SWIFT, and the first subject of SAMUEL JOHNSON's THE LIVES OF THE POETS. His imitations of the high metaphysical style of DONNE and the difficult measures of Pindar are energetic, learned and difficult to read.

Cowley, Hannah 1743–1809 Playwright and poet. Born in Tiverton, Devon, she began writing for the stage eight years after her marriage to a captain in the East India Company. Her first play, *The Runaway* (1776), is a lively comedy, dedicated to DAVID GARRICK, who may have 'improved' it. *Who's the Dupe?* (1779), her second performed play, remained popular as a two-act afterpiece until the end of the century. In an age of generally turgid SENTIMENTAL COMEDY, her plays are refreshingly sprightly. The best of them, *The Belle's Stratagem* (1780), held its own on the 19th-century stage and was revived in London in 1913. Her characters are recognizably stereotypes, but their dialogue is deft and the contrast between a witty couple and a sentimental one, repeated in *Which is the Man?* (1783) and *More Ways Than One* (1783), is effective. Hannah Cowley's career as poet involved her in a sentimental verse correspondence with Robert Merry, leader of the so-called DELLA CRUSCANS.

Cowper, William 1731–1800 Poet. Cowper (pronounced 'Cooper') was born in his father's rectory at Great Berkhampstead, Hertfordshire. As a child he attended a private school – where he suffered from bullying – and then Westminster School. His vehement dislike of public school education was later the subject of 'Tirocinium' (1785). He studied law at the Inner Temple, was called to the Bar in 1754, but made no attempt to practise. He fell in love with his cousin, Theodora Cowper, but his father forbade them to marry on the grounds of consanguinity.

Already suffering from fitful periods of depression, Cowper deteriorated into unmistakable mania when, at the age of 32, an uncle tried to help him by nominating him for a sinecure as Clerk of the Journals of the House of Lords: the prospect of a formal examination drove him to attempt suicide. He was cured, and settled in comfortable lodgings at Huntingdon, with a small income. Throughout his life, the poet was fortunate to have a wide circle of friends who cared for his welfare. In Huntingdon he met Morley Unwin, a retired Evangelical clergyman, and his wife Mary, with whom he went to live. After Unwin's death in 1767, Cowper moved to Olney in Buckinghamshire, along with Mary and her children, and here he came under the powerful influence of John Newton, a formidable Evangelical pastor with an inclination to Calvinism. The intellectual pressures of this association were not fortunate for Cowper and he declined again into melancholy, though his poetic talents were channelled into several notable contributions to Newton's *Olney Hymns* (1779), including 'God Moves in a Mysterious Way'.

Cowper again suffered mental collapse but Mary Unwin, to whom he was engaged, nursed him to recovery, and by 1776 he was again corresponding with his friends. Many of his letters are of exceptional quality, and are of importance in revealing his true personality; Cowper did not cultivate the 'art of letter-writing' like many literary correspondents of that century. His letters talk directly and personally to his friends, and show him, when not unwell, cheerfully intent upon a simple country existence. At this period he began to write verse again. His cousin, Martin Madan, had published a book supporting polygamy, and Cowper replied with *Anti-Thelyphthora: A Tale in Verse* (1781), and, at Mary

Unwin's instigation, began the series of eight satires contained in *Poems* (1782). They are weakened by his restricted experience of life but illustrate his skill with the couplet; 'Retirement' is the most accomplished. Shorter poems include 'The Shrubbery', 'Boadicea' and *Verses Supposed to be Written by Alexander Selkirk*. At the suggestion of a new friend, Lady Austen, Cowper wrote THE TASK, in six books, published in 1785 in a volume which included THE DIVERTING HISTORY OF JOHN GILPIN (1782), also the result of Lady Austen's initiative.

Cowper and Mary Unwin never married, but they remained together and moved in 1786 to nearby Weston Underwood. There he composed a number of short poems published after his death, including 'The Poplar Field', 'On the Loss of the Royal George' and the fine sonnet 'To Mrs Unwin'. In 1785 he started to translate Homer, beginning with a blank-verse version of the *Iliad*. The project was well subscribed and was published in 1791, though it is not among his best achievements. He also translated works from Latin, Italian and French.

When Mary Unwin died in 1794, he became a physical and mental invalid for the rest of his life. He was awarded a royal pension in 1794, and died at East Dereham, Norfolk, his last years yielding the depressingly powerful poem, 'The Castaway'. It is sometimes thought that Cowper did not take seriously enough his vocation as a poet, yet his quiet, direct verse addressing simple human and rural themes marked the point at which English poetry moved away from the concerns of NEOCLASSICISM towards those of ROMANTICISM.

Cozzens, James Gould 1903–78 American novelist. Born in Chicago, he attended Harvard and began his writing career early, publishing in THE ATLANTIC MONTHLY when he was 16. His novels explore the social order of American life and its potential for stability and hierarchy, by portraying professional men caught in moral and cultural dilemmas: *The Last Adam* (1933) is about the medical profession, *Men and Brethren* (1936) about the ministry and *The Just and the Unjust* (1942) about the law. *Guard of Honor* (1948), an ambitious novel set during World War II, won Cozzens the PULITZER PRIZE. In 1957 he published *By Love Possessed*, about a lawyer, his most controversial and widely read book. Cozzens has long been the object of controversy; his enquiries into the possibilities of social stability have been criticized by some as dangerously right-wing. His last publications were *Children and Others* (children's stories; 1964) and *Morning, Noon and Night* (a novel; 1968).

Crabbe, George 1755–1832 Poet. He was born at Aldeburgh, Suffolk, where his father was a collector of salt duties, and educated at schools in Bungay and Stowmarket, before being apprenticed to surgeons at

Bury St Edmunds and Woodbridge. In 1772 Crabbe met and became engaged to Sarah Elmy, and published his first verse in *Wheble's Magazine*. His first significant poem, *Inebriety*, a didactic SATIRE in the manner of POPE on the perils of drink, was published anonymously in 1775. In the same year he returned to Aldeburgh to set up practice as a surgeon, making little money but continuing to read, write and pursue botanical studies.

In 1780 he determined upon a literary career and, with £5 in his pocket, a sheaf of manuscripts and a case of surgical instruments, set off for London, where, but for the timely intervention of BURKE, to whom he appealed as a complete stranger, he would have been imprisoned for debt. With the help of Burke's recommendation and literary connections, *The Library*, another work showing the influence of Pope, was published in 1781, and Crabbe went to stay with his patron at Beaconsfield, where he began work on his next publication, *THE VILLAGE*. Burke introduced him to Charles James Fox and SIR JOSHUA REYNOLDS and encouraged him to enter the church. After a brief period as curate at Aldeburgh, Crabbe took holy orders and was from 1782 to 1785 chaplain to the Duke of Rutland at Belvoir. In 1783 he married Sarah Elmy, and in the same year met SAMUEL JOHNSON who read, praised and slightly 'corrected' *THE VILLAGE*, a work in HEROIC COUPLETS, which established his reputation following its publication in May. In 1784 he published a brief memoir of Lord Robert Manners, Rutland's brother, who had been killed in action at sea in 1782; and in 1785 a satire, *The Newspaper*.

There now followed a period of 22 years during which Crabbe published nothing of importance, although he wrote and destroyed three novels and continued to be intellectually active, particularly as a botanist and entomologist. In 1789 he took up the living of Muston, Leicestershire, which he held until 1814, but absented himself to Suffolk between 1792 and 1805. *The Parish Register* appeared in 1807, and inaugurated the second phase of Crabbe's literary career, in which he emerged as a gifted exponent of verse narrative. The main part of the collection narrates the memories of a country parson as he leafs through the register of births, marriages and deaths. It includes 'Sir Eustace Grey', a remarkable poem portraying the hallucinations of a patient in a madhouse. The extraordinary vividness of the dream sequences suggests that they may have been written under the influence of opium, which Crabbe is known to have begun taking in 1790. *THE BOROUGH* (1810) consists of 24 'letters' describing the scenery and life of a country town based on his native Aldeburgh; *Peter Grimes* is the most memorable. *Tales* followed in 1812.

His wife, who had suffered from manic depression for many years, died in 1813, following which he was himself for a while dangerously ill. In 1814 he became vicar of Trowbridge, Wiltshire, and was briefly engaged to Charlotte Ridout. He now began to travel more frequently to London, where he became acquainted with THOMAS MOORE, SAMUEL ROGERS, SOUTHEY and WORDSWORTH. His *London Journal* of 1817 was later printed in the *Life* by his son. *The World of Dreams* was written in 1817, and 1819 saw the publication of *Tales of the Hall*. In 1822 he went to Edinburgh to visit SIR WALTER SCOTT, with whom he enjoyed a close friendship. In the same year he wrote *In a Neat Cottage*, and in 1823 a collected edition of his *Works* appeared in five- and eight-volume formats. He died in Trowbridge, leaving much unpublished work, some of which was incorporated into the last volume of *The Poetical Works* (8 vols., 1834).

Although Crabbe first gained his reputation as a poet in the age of Johnson, his best work was contemporary with that of the Romantics. He was not, however, simply a survival from the AUGUSTAN AGE, despite his almost unbroken fidelity to the heroic couplet, and firm commitment to that period's values of sense, judgement, moderation and balance. His tales are an original achievement in a new art form through which he probed the psychological, social and moral textures of the post-classical epoch. He was much admired by JANE AUSTEN (who thought she could see herself as Mrs Crabbe), Scott and BYRON, who saw him as 'Nature's sternest painter yet the best'.

Cradle Will Rock, The A musical drama of social protest, with lyrics and music by MARC BLITZSTEIN, first produced in 1937. Blitzstein brought techniques of classical opera together with elements of popular music to tell the story of a strike in 'Steeltown, USA'. The characters are representative types rather than realistic individuals. Mr Mister, who owns the steel mill and everything else in town, is trying to break the strike with the aid of his 'Liberty Committee' – Reverend Salvation, Editor Daily, Yasha (a musician), Dauber (an artist), Dr Specialist, and Professor Trixie and President Prexy from the local university. Most of the play takes place in a courtroom to which the Liberty Committee has been taken, mistakenly arrested along with 'the man who made the speech' – Larry Foreman, a union organizer and the hero of the piece. Through a series of flashbacks the sympathetic Harry Druggist, a former drugstore owner who has become a bum after the death of his son in an explosion caused by Mr Mister's henchmen, explains to Moll, a poor woman who is being framed for soliciting, how each member of the Liberty Committee came to sell his soul and his profession to Mr Mister and his family. At the end of the play, Mr Mister appears and attempts unsuccessfully to buy off Larry Foreman; we are left with the impression that the union will be successful.

Craik, Dinah Maria See MULOCK, DINAH.

Crane, (Harold) Hart 1899–1932 American poet. Crane was born in Ohio but spent most of his life in New York City. His parents' unhappy marriage deeply troubled him; alcoholism and his inability to support himself in New York further undermined his stability. He committed suicide at the age of 33.

Strongly influenced by French SYMBOLISM and by T. S. ELIOT, Crane produced in his relatively brief career a body of poetry that has received considerable critical attention and acclaim. Characterized by dramatic rhetoric and exotic diction, his work often drew on images of water and the sea, which provided him with material for his symbolic and psychological speculations. He is best known for his long poem THE BRIDGE (1930), written partly in response to the negativism of Eliot's THE WASTE LAND. Each section of the poem focuses on a particular aspect of American history or culture, which Crane then unifies in the figure of the Brooklyn Bridge, which he called 'a symbol of our constructive Future'. His first book of poetry, *White Buildings*, was published in 1926, his *Collected Poems* in 1933.

Crane, Stephen 1871–1900 American novelist and short-story writer. He was born in Newark, New Jersey, the son of a Methodist minister. After leaving high school he moved to New York City and worked as a journalist for the *Tribune* and the *Herald* before starting on his first novel, eventually published as *MAGGIE: A GIRL OF THE STREETS* (1893). Though *Maggie* was not widely noticed, his second novel, *THE RED BADGE OF COURAGE* (1895), was a critical and popular success. In 1896 he published a collection of short stories, *The Little Regiment*, focusing on the Civil War. In the same year, working-class life in New York provided material for the novel *George's Mother*. The *Third Violet* (1897) is a short novel about a young artist.

Crane's career as a journalist continued during these years and he travelled to the Southwest, to Mexico, and, in 1896, to Cuba. On this last journey he was shipwrecked, spending nearly three days in an open boat at sea, an experience which formed the basis for one of his most famous stories, the title piece of *The Open Boat and Other Stories* (1898). In 1897 he and his companion Cora Taylor travelled to Greece, where he served as a war correspondent. His poor health forced them to leave and they moved to England, where he met JOSEPH CONRAD and HENRY JAMES, two of his most distinguished admirers. A novel, *Active Service* (1899), was derived from his experience of the Graeco-Turkish War. In 1899 he returned to Cuba, to cover the Spanish-American War, but was again obliged to return to England due to poor health. He died of tuberculosis at the age of 29. Some of his most highly regarded stories appeared in *The Monster* (1898). His poetry was collected in *The*

Black Rider (1895) and *War is Kind* (1900). Posthumous publications include the sketches and stories from his life as a correspondent in *Wounds in the Rain* (1900), and *Whilomville Stories* (1900), about a childhood in a small town in New York state.

Crane, Walter 1845–1915 Artist and illustrator of CHILDREN'S LITERATURE. Born in Liverpool, the son of a portrait painter, Crane first trained as a wood engraver before illustrating a children's book at the age of 18. The pioneer colour printer Edmund Evans asked him to illustrate a series of children's picture-books, which appeared between 1865 and 1873 and included classics like *The Railroad Alphabet*, *The House That Jack Built* and *Sing a Song of Sixpence*. While somewhat static in design, they appealed to children because of their strong line, bold colour and the intricate decorative borders which added an extra commentary to each picture. Most popular of all, and still in print today, was *The Baby's Opera* (1877), a collection of traditional nursery rhymes where text, music and illustration come together in one diminutive but pleasing whole. A friend of WILLIAM MORRIS, Crane also designed mosaics, friezes and wallpapers and became the first president of the Arts and Crafts Society. Best remembered for his children's work, Crane was an important figure in the movement to bring picture-books to a pitch of excellence never seen before and only rarely equalled since.

Cranford A novel by ELIZABETH GASKELL, first published serially in HOUSEHOLD WORDS in 1851–3.

Set in early 19th-century England, it presents a series of vignettes of life in a community of genteel ladies, a world into which very few gentlemen are admitted. A strict social hierarchy obtains among the well-intentioned, basically kind spinsters and widows whose weaknesses and attributes extend across the pages of this mild and gentle book. At the centre of Cranford is Miss Matilda (Miss Matty) Jenkyns whose warm heart and tender ways compel affection and regard from all about her. Her quiet life of 'elegant economy' is seen through the eyes of a sympathetic narrator. Revealed, too, are the foibles and attributes of others in Miss Matty's circle: the pompous Mrs Jamieson and her awesome butler, Mulliner; the genial, straightforward Captain Brown, killed while looking up too late from reading; Miss Deborah Jenkyns, Miss Matty's elder sister and an ardent Johnsonian; Martha, the cumbersome but loyal housemaid; and several others. The cast is replete with fundamentally decent people touched by the lesser weaknesses of the human animal. But above all, it is Miss Matty, free from any taint of hypocrisy, affectation or unkindness, who emerges as a true Christian.

Although there is a tenuous narrative in *Cranford* that takes Miss Matty from quiet satisfaction through minor crises rising to serious personal adversity and retreating to calm security through the reappearance of a long lost brother, it is the individual moment of revelation that marks Cranford as a minor triumph. The passing of Mr Holbrook (a yeoman-farmer who loved Miss Matty), the permission granted Martha to have a follower, and Miss Matty's conduct towards a farmer deprived by a bank failure: these and other scenes are deftly, quietly, and economically written.

Cranmer, Thomas 1489-1556 Divine. Cranmer was educated at Cambridge and became a fellow of Jesus College in 1510 or 1511. He found favour with Henry VIII, who sent him on embassies to the Pope in 1530 and the Emperor Charles V in 1532. In 1533 he became Archbishop of Canterbury and remained in office through the Reformation, thus becoming Canterbury's first Anglican archbishop. In cooperation with Thomas Cromwell he promoted publication of the BIBLE IN ENGLISH and wrote a prologue to the Great Bible of 1540. He composed a litany for the reformed church of 1545, was responsible for the publication of the *Homilies* in 1547 and supervised the first and second Edwardian prayer-books of 1549 and 1552 (see BOOK OF COMMON PRAYER). His other works include a controversy with Stephen Gardiner, a catechism and a treatise on the Eucharist. Under Queen Mary he was condemned for treason in 1553, degraded from ecclesiastical office and burned as a heretic.

Crashaw, Richard 1612-49 Poet. The son of William Crashaw, a Puritan preacher, he spent his short adult life in increasing reaction against the austerity of his father's religion. He entered Pembroke College, Cambridge, graduated in 1634, and was awarded a fellowship of Peterhouse in the following year. With the defeat of the Royalists in the Civil War he was deprived of his fellowship (1644) but had already left Cambridge the previous year. After two years, mostly in exile, he became a Roman Catholic, and ended his days in a minor office at the Cathedral of Loreto.

Crashaw is best remembered as a religious poet. He sometimes achieves a memorable sequence of lines but the matter of his poetry is, as D. J. ENRIGHT says, 'lovingly handled, but sometimes too lovingly fondled'. This is clearly seen in his only original secular lyric 'Wishes: To His (Supposed) Mistress'; other lyrics, like 'Love's Duel', are versions from foreign languages. But there are fine lines to be found, especially when the poet's intensity of feeling imposes its own discipline on his baroque extravagance. His first collection, *Steps to the Temple. Sacred Poems with Other Delights of the Muses*, was published in 1646; a revised and enlarged edition followed two years later. In 1652 Crashaw's friend Miles Pinkney published a

more complete collection, the posthumous volume *Carmen Deo Nostro*.

Crawford, Francis Marion 1854-1909 American novelist. Son of the sculptor Thomas Crawford and nephew, on his mother's side, of JULIA WARD HOWE, Crawford was born in Italy. He was educated in the USA and at Cambridge and Heidelberg universities. An accomplished linguist, he travelled extensively, sometimes gathering material for his novels.

His first novel, *Mr Isaacs: A Tale of Modern India* (1882), was an immediate success, and he went on to write almost 50 more romances, historical novels and tales of cosmopolitan adventure which enjoyed a large following. His aim, as he argued in *The Novel: What It Is* (1893), was not to moralize or to paint life in the realistic mode that was then becoming popular, but simply to entertain. Among his other novels are *A Tale of a Lonely Parish* (1886), *Don Orsini* (1891), *Corleone: A Tale of Sicily* (1896), *Via Crucis* (1898), *In the Palace of the King: A Love Story of Old Madrid* (1900) and *The White Sister* (1909). Many of his novels were adapted for the stage. He wrote *Francesca da Rimini* (1902), a play in four acts, for Sarah Bernhardt. His tales of the supernatural, *Wandering Ghosts*, were published posthumously in 1911.

Crawford, Isabella Valancy 1850-87 Canadian poet. She was born in Dublin, but her parents settled in Canada in about 1858. After her father's death in 1875 she was the sole support of her mother and sister and began to write for a living. In Toronto she wrote short stories and contributed poems to *The Globe* and *The Telegram*. In 1884 she published a paper-bound collection, *Old Spookses' Pass, Malcolm's Katie and Other Poems*, at her own expense. It was well reviewed in England, but only some 50 copies were sold before the author's death. Her *Collected Poems* appeared in 1905 with an introduction by John Garvin. One of Canada's finest early writers, Crawford combines in her poetry exuberance and vigour with a wide range of mythological material drawn from classical legend, biblical and folk-stories.

Creeley, Robert 1926- American poet. Born in Arlington, Massachusetts, he was educated at Harvard (though he did not graduate), Black Mountain College in North Carolina, and the University of New Mexico at Albuquerque. During World War II he served for two years with the American Field Service in Burma and India. In 1954 he joined the faculty of Black Mountain College, where he was associated with the BLACK MOUNTAIN SCHOOL of poets. After the college closed in 1956 he moved to San Francisco and quickly established his presence in the city's poetry revival, alongside writers such as GREGORY CORSO, ALLEN GINSBERG, LAWRENCE FERLINGHETTI and JACK KEROUAC. Creeley has acknowledged his debt to other American poets such as WILLIAM CARLOS WILLIAMS and CHARLES OLSON. His own work is noted for its syntactic compression. It includes *Le Fou* (1952), *If You* (1956), *For Love: Poems 1950–1960* (1962), *Words* (1965), *Poems, 1950–1965* (1966), *Divisions and Other Early Poems* (1968), *Pieces* (1968), *The Finger: Poems 1966–1969* (1970), *St Martin's* (1971), *Selected Poems* (1976), *Later: New Poems* (1979), *Mirrors* (1983), *Memories* (1984) and *Memory Gardens* (1986). *The Collected Poems of Robert Creeley, 1945–1975* (1982) brings together all his important early work. Prose works include: a novel, *The Island* (1963); a collection of short stories, *The Gold Diggers* (1954); *Was That a Real Poem and Other Essays* (1979), edited by Donald Allen; and *The Collected Prose* (1984). *Charles Olson and Creeley: The Complete Correspondence* (1980–3), a five-volume edition by George F. Butterick, is invaluable. Creeley has taught at the University of New Mexico, the University of British Columbia and, since 1978, the State University of New York at Buffalo.

Creevey, Thomas 1768–1838 Politician. Born in Liverpool, he was elected MP for Thetford in 1802, and later held the seat for Appleby. He was also treasurer for Greenwich Hospital. *The Creevey Papers: A Selection from the Correspondence and Diaries of the Late Sir Thomas Creevey* was published in 1903. This gossipy and irreverent volume is interesting for the light it sheds on the principal figures of the late Georgian period.

Creighton, Mandell 1843–1901 Historian. Born in Carlisle and educated at Merton College, Oxford, he became professor of ecclesiastical history at Cambridge (1884), Bishop of Peterborough (1891) and Bishop of London (1897). He made his reputation with *A History of the Papacy during the Period of the Reformation* (1882–94), praised for its detachment and erudition. Other works include *A History of Rome* (1875), *The Tudors and the Reformation* (1876), *Cardinal Wolsey* (1888), *Queen Elizabeth* (1896), *A History of the Papacy from the Great Schism to the Sack of Rome* (1897) and *The Life of Simon de Montfort* (published posthumously, 1905).

Cresswell, Helen 1934– Writer of CHILDREN'S LITERATURE. Born in Nottingham and educated at London University, she worked as a teacher before turning to full-time writing. Her first success, *The Piemakers* (1967), mixed fantasy with earthy realism in its description of a family of hereditary cooks faced with the task of baking a pie to feed 2000 people. Several distinctive fantasy stories followed. In *The Night-Watchmen* (1969) two indigent workmen manage to catch a magical night-train after a fierce battle with Greeneyes, their mysterious but fearsome

enemy. *Lizzy Dripping* (1973) features a plain but dreamy girl who manages to create a live witch from her imagination. Originally devised for television, it spawned a number of successful sequels. *The Bagthorpe Saga*, beginning with *Ordinary Jack* (1977), has also proved popular. Stories for much younger readers include *Two Hoots* (1989) and *Rosie and the Boredom Eater* (1990).

Crèvecoeur, J. Hector St John de 1735–1813 American essayist. Born in Normandy, and educated in France and England, in 1754 he went to Quebec to serve in Montcalm's army. He subsequently travelled around the Great Lakes and the Ohio River Valley, New York and Pennsylvania, describing his experiences in *Voyage dans la Haute Pennsylvanie et dans l'état de New York* (Paris, 1801). He became naturalized as an American colonial citizen in New York in 1764. In 1769 he married and settled on a farm in Orange County, New York.

In 1780 the American Revolution forced Crèvecoeur to leave America for Europe, where he moved in fashionable circles and published, under the name J. Hector St John, a collection of his impressions of America called LETTERS FROM AN AMERICAN FARMER (London, 1782; not published in America until 1793). Returning to the USA after the war in 1783, he found his farm burned, his wife dead, and his children dispersed. He served as French consul and eventually went back to France in 1790. Further letters and essays written during his American period were published in 1925 as *Sketches of Eighteenth Century America*.

Cricket on the Hearth, The A Christmas story by CHARLES DICKENS, published in 1845 and collected in *CHRISTMAS BOOKS* (1852).

After he introduces an elderly stranger into his house John Peerybingle, a stolid but worthy carrier, is urged into jealousy of his younger wife Dot by the interference of the odious toy-merchant Tackleton. The 'Cricket on the Hearth in Faery shape' prevents Peerybingle from wreaking vengeance. Meanwhile, Tackleton woos Dot's friend, May Fielding, but is forestalled by the stranger, really her fiancé, the young Edward Plummer. Another narrative strand concerns Edward's blind sister Bertha and their father, the simple Caleb, who works for Tackleton. The story ends with reconciliation and rejoicing, in which even Tackleton joins.

Criterion, The A literary journal founded and edited by T. S. ELIOT. It appeared quarterly from 1922 to 1939, with a short period in 1926 and 1927 as *The New Criterion*, and from 1927 to 1928 as *The Monthly Criterion*. Financial backing came first from Viscountess Rothermere and later from Eliot's employer, Faber and Faber. It was launched with the publication of *THE WASTE LAND* in its first issue. Eliot's editorial 'Commentary' in each issue expounded his right-wing, Anglo-Catholic and classicist doctrine of order, and at times expressed admiration for fascism. This did not prevent him from opening *The Criterion* to contributions from younger writers of very different persuasions: W. H. AUDEN, HART CRANE, WILLIAM EMPSON, D. H. LAWRENCE and STEPHEN SPENDER were represented, along with Eliot's mentor EZRA POUND. To many who had hailed Eliot's promise in the early 1920s, *The Criterion* proved to be a disappointment, and by 1939 Eliot himself was too dispirited to carry on with it.

Critic, The: *or, A Tragedy Rehearsed* A comedy-burlesque by RICHARD BRINSLEY SHERIDAN, first performed at DRURY LANE in 1779. The piece is modelled on the DUKE OF BUCKINGHAM'S *THE REHEARSAL* (1671), which had set the fashion for topical jokes about pompous playwrights and theatrical stupidity. *The Critic* is given added point by the exasperation Sheridan must often have felt as manager of Drury Lane. 'It was to be regarded', according to the compilers of *Biographia Dramatica* (1811 edn), 'in the light of an advertisement published by the manager of Drury Lane, signifying his wish that no more *modern tragedies* might be offered for representation at his theatre.'

The Critic is in three acts. In the first, Dangle, a man obsessed with theatrical affairs, reads the paper and discusses the issues of the day. Various figures of the day, in particular RICHARD CUMBERLAND as Sir Fretful Plagiary, are mocked. In the second and third, Puff introduces and then exhibits a rehearsal of his appalling tragedy, the hilarious *The Spanish Armada*.

Critical Quarterly, The A literary journal founded by C. B. Cox and A. E. Dyson in 1959. It publishes poems, reviews and critical articles with a strong emphasis on modern literature. Its contributing poets have included TED HUGHES, PHILIP LARKIN, R. S. THOMAS and CHARLES TOMLINSON, and it has published articles by W. H. AUDEN, WILLIAM EMPSON, RAYMOND WILLIAMS and DAVID LODGE, among many others.

Crock of Gold, The A prose fantasy by JAMES STEPHENS, published in 1912. It blends Irish faery and folk idioms with ancient legend to create a meandering tale which depends upon inconsequential asides and false trails for its elusive charm. The central characters are the Two Philosophers, who live in the centre of a pine wood called Coilla Doraca and are married to the Grey Woman of Dun Gortin and the Thin Woman of Inis Magrath. Other characters arrive and vanish at will, among them the Philosophers' children Seumas Beg and Brigid Beg, the farmer

Meehawl MacMurrachu and his daughter Caitlin, who follows Pan and marries the god Angus Og.

Crockett, S. R. See KAILYARD SCHOOL.

Croker, John Wilson 1780–1857 Essayist and critic. Born in Galway and educated at Trinity College, Dublin, he became a Tory MP, held various offices, and was Secretary of State for the Navy for 20 years. He was a founder of and regular contributor to *THE QUARTERLY REVIEW*, and the author of the notorious attack on KEATS'S *ENDYMION*. *Essays on the Early Period of the French Revolution* (1857) was a collection of *Quarterly* papers. He edited *Royal Memoirs of the French Revolution* (1823) and BOSWELL'S *LIFE OF JOHNSON* (1831). Croker is said to have been the model for Rigby in DISRAELI'S *CONINGSBY*.

Croker, T(homas) Crofton 1798–1854 Irish folklorist. Born in Cork, he received little formal education and served as an apprentice in a mercantile firm from the age of 15. He moved to London in 1818 and gained a clerkship at the Admiralty, where he worked until 1850. Croker was the first collector of folk-tales (chiefly from Munster) to make his material attractive to a wide range of readers. His *Fairy Legends and Traditions of the South of Ireland* (1825) is a classic of its kind. Although he altered the tales to suit his own taste, his work is valuable both as an act of preservation and as a stimulus to further researches and to writers as various as Wilhelm Grimm, SIR WALTER SCOTT, MARIA EDGEWORTH and W. B. YEATS, all of whom praised Croker highly. He was a contributor to *FRASER'S MAGAZINE* and a member of the Camden Society, the Percy Society, the British Archaeological Association and a Fellow of the Society of Antiquaries of London. He died at Brompton.

Croly, George 1780–1860 Poet and playwright. Born in Dublin and educated at Trinity College, he became rector of St Stephen's Walbrook in 1810. He wrote a tragedy, *Catiline* (1822), and a number of romantic and narrative poems. In *Salathiel* (1829) he employs the theme of the 'wandering Jew' to describe life in Rome under Nero, and Jerusalem at the time of its destruction by Titus. *Marton* (1846) is set during the days of the French Revolution and the Napoleonic wars.

Crompton, Richmal [Lamburn, Richmal Crompton] 1890–1969 Novelist and writer of CHILDREN'S LITERATURE. Born in Lancashire, she was educated first in Cheshire and later at London University. While teaching classics at Bromley High School for Girls she wrote short stories for magazines in her spare time. The mischievous small boy called William whom they introduced proved popular enough to justify a collection, *Just William* (1922). It was an instant success, far outselling the adult fiction which Richmal Crompton also began to produce. At first, the 'William' stories were also aimed at a grown-up audience, allowing his creator to enjoy the mayhem he brings to his family and its suburban environs without adding any admonitory note of the sort still expected in books written exclusively for the young. More 'William' books followed in quick succession after she became a full-time writer, a decision forced on her by a serious attack of polio in 1923. Although she occasionally tired of William, turning instead to her more modestly successful adult fiction, she continued the series until her death. By this time more than 8 million copies had been sold, and William's tussles with his irritable father, long-suffering mother and permanently suspicious older brother and sister had also been featured on radio, film and television.

Cronin, A(rchibald) J(oseph) 1896–1981 Novelist. Cronin was born in Cardross, Scotland, and educated at Dumbarton Academy and Glasgow University, where he studied medicine. He graduated as a physician in 1919, after working in the naval medical service during World War I. He practised medicine in South Wales, making a special study of industrial medicine, from 1921 to 1924, when he was appointed Medical Inspector of Mines. In 1928-30 he practised in London. After the success of his first novel, *Hatter's Castle* (1931), Cronin gave up medicine for writing. In the years that followed he produced a large number of popular novels which drew upon his Scottish childhood and his experiences in the Welsh coal-mining valleys. Many were subsequently made into successful films: *Hatter's Castle* in 1941, *The Stars Look Down* (1935) in 1939, *The Keys of the Kingdom* (1942) in 1944 and *The Green Years* (1944) in 1946. A play, *Jupiter Laughs*, was produced in 1940. His autobiography, *Adventures in Two Worlds*, appeared in 1952. His later works included *The Judas Tree* (1961) and *A Pocketful of Rye* (1969).

Crossing the Bar A short poem by ALFRED TENNYSON, published in 1889. Written in 20 minutes while crossing the Solent, a journey he often made to and from his home on the Isle of Wight, it contemplates the prospect of death. It was his wish that it should appear at the end of all editions of his poems.

Crossley-Holland, Kevin (John William) 1941– Poet, translator and writer of CHILDREN'S LITERATURE. Born in Norfolk and educated at St Edmund Hall, Oxford, he has worked for the BBC and in publishing, as well as being visiting professor at St Olaf's College, Minnesota, since 1988 and St Thomas's College, Minnesota, since 1991. Firmly rooted in his native East Anglia, he draws on its folklore, traditions and landscape in both his poetry and prose. His prolific

writing for children includes *Havelok the Dane* (1964), *The Green Children* (1966; subsequently the libretto for a children's opera by Nicola Lefanu), *The Stones Remain* (1989) and *Long Tom and the Dead Hand* (1992). His poetry, at once resolute and tender, earthy and lyrical, has appeared in *The Rain-Giver* (1972), *The Dream House* (1976), *Time's Oriel* (1983), *Waterslain* (1986), *The Painting-Room* (1988) and *New and Selected Poems 1965–1990* (1990). As a translator, he is recognized for his editions of THE BATTLE OF MALDON (with Bruce Mitchell; 1965), BEOWULF (1968) and the riddles in THE EXETER BOOK (1978). He has also edited anthologies, including *The Faber Book of Northern Legends* (1977), *The Riddle Book* (1982) and *The Oxford Book of Travel Verse* (1986).

Crotchet Castle A novel by PEACOCK, published in 1831. As in NIGHTMARE ABBEY and GRYLL GRANGE, the plot is minimal and subordinate to a conversation about conservatism and progress which serves as vehicle for Peacock's highly individual brand of SATIRE. The chief participant is the Rev. Dr Folliott, gourmet, classicist and Tory, who disputes with other characters, notably Mr Skionar, a transcendental philosopher resembling COLERIDGE, Mr MacQuedy, a Scottish political economist, and Mr Chainmail, in love with the Middle Ages.

Crothers, Rachel 1878–1958 American playwright. She was born in Illinois. Her plays brought box-office success throughout her long career; with their realistic characterization, dialogue and settings, their central concern was always the possibility of freedom for the modern woman in a world dominated by men. In her first major drama, *The Three of Us* (1906), she relates the story of a determined spinster's attempt to save her and her brothers' interests in a Nevada mine. In *A Little Journey* (1918), a self-centred young woman's world is changed by the experience of a train wreck. *He and She* (1920) examines the conflicts in a woman's life between her artistic career and her role as wife and mother. *Nice People* (1921) describes the rebellion and reform of three flappers. *Mary the Third* (1923) recounts another flapper's feelings about love and marriage. In one of her more enduring social comedies, *Let Us be Gay* (1929), she examines a woman's attempt to gain freedom through marital infidelity. Her last successful production, *Susan and God* (1937), is the story of another woman's search for independence through religion. Among her other notable plays are: *A Man's World* (1910), *Young Wisdom* (1914), *Old Lady 31* (1916), *39 East* (1919), *Expressing Willie* (1924), *A Lady's Virtue* (1925), *As Husbands Go* (1931) and *When Ladies Meet* (1932).

Crowe, Catherine 1800–76 Novelist, short-story writer and writer of CHILDREN'S LITERATURE. Born

Catherine Stevens, at Borough Green in Kent, she published children's books, dramas and novels, including *Susan Hopley* (1841) and *Lilly Dawson* (1847). But her most popular work was a collection of stories on ghostly and supernatural themes, *The Night Side of Nature* (1848).

Crowne, John *c.* 1640–1712 Playwright. His family emigrated to Nova Scotia in 1656, but returned in 1660 when the land granted to them by Cromwell was seized by the French. Crowne's dislike of court manners may have resulted from his service as a gentleman usher to a London lady. Nevertheless, he wrote an impressive court MASQUE, *Calisto* (1675). His comedies, much better than his tragedies, are unusually firm in their moral judgements. They include *The Country Wit* (1676), *City Politiques* (1683), the excellent *Sir Courtly Nice* (1685) and *The Married Beau* (1694).

Crucible, The A play by ARTHUR MILLER, first performed in New York in 1953. Written at the height of Senator McCarthy's campaign against Communists and their associates, it draws a clear analogy between McCarthyism and the witch-trials in Salem in 1692. Abigail, the niece of Reverend Parris and a mischief-maker, has led some of the girls of Salem in a naked frolic. To protect herself she claims to be the victim of witchcraft, and frightens the other girls into making the claim. When the witch-finders are brought to Salem, Abigail and the girls denounce any member of the community who resists them. One by one the weak and the virtuous are brought to trial, condemned, and hanged. The strongest resistance comes from John Proctor, a good-hearted man whom Abigail had seduced when she was working for his wife. His confession of adultery promises to end Abigail's reign of terror, but his wife lovingly denies it, and Proctor goes to his death knowing that society has lost its ability and its right to distinguish between good and evil.

Cruden, Alexander 1701–70 Compiler of *Cruden's Concordance* to the Bible. A strict Presbyterian, he was born in Aberdeen and educated at the university there before moving to London as a tutor and bookseller. He began compiling his Concordance in 1736, presenting the first copy to Queen Caroline in 1737; it long remained the standard word-guide to the Authorized Version (see BIBLE IN ENGLISH). Thorough and accurate, but eccentric and sometimes mad, he elevated his career of proof-reading into 'Alexander the Corrector's' campaign of moral castigation. He died disappointed.

Cruelty, Theatre of An idea of the anti-rational scope of theatrical performance was outlined by the French actor and writer, Antonin Artaud, in a *First Manifesto of the Theatre of Cruelty* (1932) and a *Second Manifesto* (1933). Believing that 'the theatre only exists on a level which is not quite human', Artaud sought for ways of uprooting the complacency of audiences by drawing attention to the precariousness of conventional moral values. His theatre is concerned with human behaviour under extreme threat of provocation, and his ideas have been influential, even when only partially comprehended, in the modern theatre. No prominent English playwrights can be properly called disciples of Artaud, though he himself enlisted in the prospective repertoire of his theatre SHELLEY's *THE CENCI*, TOURNEUR's *THE REVENGER'S TRAGEDY* and JOHN FORD's *'TIS PITY SHE'S A WHORE*.

Cruikshank, George 1792–1878 Caricaturist and illustrator. He was born in London, son of the artist Isaac Cruikshank. In addition to a long and successful career in political caricature, and the impassioned advocacy of temperance which occupied much of his later years, Cruikshank also illustrated books by many contemporaries. These include: PIERCE EGAN's *LIFE IN LONDON* (1821), though Cruikshank was so dismayed by Egan's departure from any moral design that he left completion of the plates to his brother Robert (?1790–1856); DICKENS's *SKETCHES BY BOZ* (1836–7) and *OLIVER TWIST* (1839), in which he is reputed to have used himself as the model for his depiction of Fagin; *Jack Sheppard* (1839) and other novels by WILLIAM HARRISON AINSWORTH; the first three series of R. H. BARHAM's *INGOLDSBY LEGENDS*; and HARRIET BEECHER STOWE's *UNCLE TOM'S CABIN* (1853).

Cuckoo and the Nightingale, The [*The Boke of Cupide*] A poem once attributed to GEOFFREY CHAUCER but now generally accepted as the work of SIR JOHN CLANVOWE, whose name appears at the end of the poem in one of its manuscripts. It was probably written between 1390 and 1403. The poem is a DREAM-VISION and records an overheard debate between a cuckoo who is opposed to love and a nightingale who praises it. The narrator drives away the cuckoo and the nightingale pledges loyalty to him. The poem shows the influence of *THE OWL AND THE NIGHTINGALE* and Chaucer's *PARLEMENT OF FOULES*. See also CHAUCERIAN APOCRYPHA.

Cudworth, Ralph 1617–88 Philosopher. One of the more prominent of the CAMBRIDGE PLATONISTS, Cudworth had a distinguished academic career. Elected a fellow of Emmanuel College, Cambridge, in 1639, he was appointed master of Clare Hall by the parliamentary commission in 1645; he became Regius Professor of Hebrew in the same year and master of Christ's College in 1654. He rejected the Hobbesian type of atheism and was a steadfast opponent of religious dogmatism. His chief work (left unfinished) was *The True Intellectual System of the Universe* (1678); it argues that the Christian religion is the only real source of knowledge. His *Treatise concerning Eternal and Immutable Morality* was published posthumously (1731).

Cullen, Countee 1903–46 Black American poet. A leading figure of the HARLEM RENAISSANCE, Cullen was reared by foster parents in Harlem, New York. He was educated at New York University and at Harvard. His first verse collections were *Color* (1925), *Copper Sun* (1927), and *The Ballad of the Brown Girl: An Old Ballad Retold* (1927). While in France on a Guggenheim scholarship he wrote *The Black Christ, and Other Poems* (1929), the title piece of which recounts the lynching of a black youth for a crime he did not commit. Cullen's only novel, *One Way to Heaven* (1932), is a social comedy of lower-class blacks and the bourgeoisie in New York. *The Medea and Some Poems* (1935) is a collection of SONNETS and short lyrics together with a translation of Euripides' tragedy (in prose, with the choruses in verse). He also edited the magazine *Opportunity* and an anthology of black poetry, *Caroling Dusk* (1927).

Culture and Anarchy A volume of essays by MATTHEW ARNOLD, originating in Oxford lectures and articles for *THE CORNHILL MAGAZINE*, published as a book in 1869.

Its sub-title, *An Essay in Political and Social Criticism*, points to Arnold's intentions, for he saw the England of his time as being in political, social and religious ferment, and sought to show that the remedy lay in culture – the supreme realization of the human spirit under reason. Observing in his first chapter, 'Sweetness and Light', that culture is 'a study of perfection' whose 'motto' should be 'To render an intelligent being more intelligent', Arnold avers that a second view of it ought to be 'To make reason and the will of God prevail'. Then follow chapters showing the imbalances, inequities and confusions of English life that impede the advance of culture. Arnold fears a drift towards anarchy through an excess of liberty, of freedom unrestrained by any centre of authority. No one, he believes, has an idea of the state, 'of the nation in its collective and corporate character of controlling, as government, the free swing of this or that one of its members in the name of the higher realm of all of them, his own as well as that of others'. None of the various classes – barbarians (aristocracy), philistines (middle class) and populace (lower class) – provides an adequate centre of authority. Similarly, the two great traditions of Hebraism, with its 'strictness of conscience', and Hellenism, with its 'spontaneity of consciousness', have vied with each other in English life down the centuries instead of being mutually

complementary. Concluding chapters attempt some pragmatic solutions, but Arnold returns to culture as the true saving grace – culture with its development of the individual self in the interests of the greater whole, with its aspiration to a 'fair chance' for the growth of the moral life and with its constant movement towards perfection.

Cumberland, Richard 1732–1811 Playwright, too often identified with SHERIDAN's cruel portrait of him as Sir Fretful Plagiary in *THE CRITIC*. He was educated at Westminster School and Trinity College, Cambridge, of which he became a fellow in 1752. His subsequent political career was not sufficiently successful to spare him the toil of writing for a living. His SENTIMENTAL COMEDIES, or 'bastard tragedies' as GOLDSMITH called them, often avert disaster only because of a villain's unlikely change of heart in the fifth act. Plays popular in their own time, like *The Brothers* (1769), *The West Indian* (1771) and *The Jew* (1794), can best be read as transitional pieces, carrying sentimental comedy towards MELODRAMA. Cumberland wrote nearly 50 plays as well as three novels, *Arundel* (1789), *Henry* (1795) and *John de Lancaster* (1809), a few volumes of negligible verse, two volumes of *Memoirs* (1806–7), scores of journalistic essays and two books on Spanish painters and painting.

Cummings, Bruce Frederic See BARBELLION, W. N. P.

cummings, e(dward) e(stlin) 1894–1962 American poet. He was born in Cambridge, Massachusetts, and graduated from Harvard in 1916. He drove an ambulance in France during World War I, and stayed on in Paris after the armistice. His first published work was a novel, *The Enormous Room* (1922), based on his mistaken imprisonment in a French detention centre during the war. This was followed by collections of verse, *Tulips and Chimneys* (1923) and *XLI Poems* (1925).

& and *is 5* (both 1925) presented cummings's new style, which was influenced by jazz and contemporary slang and characterized by an innovative use of punctuation and typography, as in the use of lower case letters for his own name. Features of this poetry include the use of capital letters and punctuation in the middle of single words, phrases split by parentheses, and stanzas arranged to create a visual design on the page. Formal devices were often used as visual manifestations of theme or tone; the poem's typographical dimension itself becomes a new level of meaning.

cummings's other works include *Vi Va* (1931), *No Thanks* (1935), *1/20* (1936), *Collected Poems* (1938), *50 Poems* (1940), *1 x 1* (1944), *Poems 1923–1954* (1954), *Ninety-Five Poems* (1958), *73 Poems* (1963) and

Complete Poems 1913–1962 (1972). He also published two plays, a book of drawings and paintings, a travel book, and *i, six nonlectures* (1953).

Cunningham, Alan 1784–1842 Miscellaneous writer. Born at Keir, Dumfriesshire, Cunningham was apprenticed at age 11 to his brother as a stonemason. As a boy he walked in BURNS's funeral procession and nourished his literary ambitions on the works of SCOTT. He became a friend of the self-taught bard JAMES HOGG, who, together with Scott, suspected his authorship of *Remains of Nithsdale and Galloway Songs* (1810), a volume of poems which were innocently published by Cromek as authentic old Scottish BALLADS. In 1813 he published *Songs, Chiefly in the Rural Dialect of Scotland* and in 1814 he was tempted down to London by Cromek, who introduced him to the sculptor Sir Francis Chantrey. From 1814 to 1841 he was Chantrey's trusted assistant, secretary and occasional artistic adviser, pursuing his literary interests in his spare time. From 1819 to 1821 he contributed a series of stories called 'Recollections of Mark Macrabin' to *BLACKWOOD'S EDINBURGH MAGAZINE*, and then changed to *THE LONDON MAGAZINE*, becoming associated with a circle of writers that included DE QUINCEY, LAMB, HAZLITT and THOMAS HOOD. He collected old ballads and stories, published as *Traditional Tales of the English and Scottish Peasantry* (1822) and *Songs of Scotland, Ancient and Modern* (1825). His *Lives of the Most Eminent British Painters, Sculptors and Architects* appeared in six volumes in 1829–33, and in 1834 he produced his edition of *The Works of Robert Burns*, prefaced with a biography of Burns that contained much important new material. His romances and longer dramatic poems are little read today and he is chiefly remembered by a handful of poems and ballads, which include 'A Wet Hat Sheet and a Flowering Sea' and 'Hame, Hame, Hame'.

e e cummings: a self-portrait

Cunningham, J(ames) V(incent) 1911–85 American poet. Born in Cumberland, Maryland, and educated at Stanford, he taught at the Universities of Hawaii, Chicago, Virginia, and, from 1953 until his retirement, at Brandeis. His first volume of poetry, *The Helmsman*, was published in 1942 and was followed by *The Judge is Fury* (1947) and *Doctor Drink* (1950). The poems in all three volumes are notable for their economy of presentation, and their use of precise METRES and traditional verse forms. An accomplished Renaissance scholar, Cunningham was drawn to the EPIGRAM, publishing *Trivial, Vulgar, & Exalted: Epigrams* (1957). His later collections include *The Exclusions of a Rhyme; Poems and Epigrams* (1960), *To What Strangers, What Welcome: A Sequence of Short Poems* (1964) and *Some Salt: Poems and Epigrams* (1967). *The Collected Poems and Epigrams of J. V. Cunningham* and *Selected Poems* were both published in 1971. His *Collected Essays* appeared in 1976.

Cunninghame Graham, R(obert) B(ontine) 1852–1936 Short-story writer, essayist, traveller and social reformer. Born in London, the son of a Scottish laird and a half-Spanish mother, he was educated at Harrow and in Brussels. He visited South America at the age of 17 and became an expert horseman. Later he was Liberal MP for North-West Lanarkshire, but became a socialist and disciple of WILLIAM MORRIS, receiving a six weeks' prison sentence for assaulting the police during a demonstration.

He is chiefly remembered for *Mogreb-el-Aksa* (1898), an extraordinary account of his dangerous journey to discover the forbidden city of Tarudant in Morocco. The book was much admired by GEORGE BERNARD SHAW and JOSEPH CONRAD. His other works include *Thirteen Stories* (1900), *A Vanished Arcadia* (the story of the Jesuit settlements in Paraguay, 1901), *Success* (1902) and *Scottish Stories* (1914).

cup-and-saucer drama See ROBERTSON, THOMAS WILLIAM.

Curnow, Allen 1911– New Zealand poet, playwright, critic and editor. Born in Timaru in the South Island, the son of an Anglican vicar and writer of light verse, he worked as a journalist before studying at St John's College, Auckland, an Anglican theological college, and at Auckland University. His early poetry was published in *Phoenix*, an important Auckland journal which appeared in 1932–3 and published other important young poets such as R. A. K. MASON, A. R. D. FAIRBURN and ROBIN HYDE. Curnow worked as a journalist in New Zealand and Britain until joining the Auckland University English Department in 1950. He remained there until his retirement in 1976.

Curnow's poetry of the 1930s and 1940s was concerned with New Zealand's cultural identity and attempted to create a national tradition or myth for New Zealand writers. Notable collections of this period include *Not in Narrow Seas* (1939), *Island and Time* (1941) and *At Dead Low Water* (1949). Two anthologies he edited, *A Book of New Zealand Verse* (1945) and *The Penguin Book of New Zealand Verse* (1960), defined a canon in terms of his belief that the best poetry must be local. His introduction to the 1960 anthology called on New Zealand poets 'to name those "nameless native hills"'. This poetic has been the biggest single influence on post-World War II poetry in New Zealand.

By the 1950s, however, Curnow's own work was becoming more personal, and, influenced by WALLACE STEVENS, slowly moved away from its founding preoccupation with establishing a distinctive national poetic identity. *Poems 1949–57* (1957) and *A Small Room with Large Windows* (1962) are the main volumes of this period. A decade's silence was then followed by a series of volumes, notably *An Incorrigible Music* (1979), *You Will Know When You Get There* (1982), *The Loop in Lone Kauri Road* (1986) and *Continuum* (1988), which together constitute the most sustained achievement in New Zealand poetry. They do not abandon the concerns of his earlier work but treat them less self-consciously, more dispassionately, with greater openness of form and in language more obviously influenced by MODERNISM. Curnow has also published four verse dramas and five volumes of satirical verse under the pseudonym Whim-Wham, originally issued weekly in the *Auckland Herald*.

Cursor Mundi (*The Course of the World*) An anonymous Middle English poem in rhyming couplets, probably written in the early 14th century in the North of England. Dedicated to the Virgin Mary, the work is a spiritual history of the world from the Creation to Doomsday. It deals at length with all the principal episodes of both Testaments as well as including apocryphal material. The historical section ends with an exhortation to all people to repent and live a good Christian life, and with a prayer to the Virgin. There follow various miscellaneous pieces, differing from one manuscript to another.

The work was widely known, and survives in several manuscripts. The poet maintains his sense of purpose and the structure of the work despite its length and succeeds in creating a unified poem from diverse material and sources. The work is characterized by the author's humanity and his plain language skilfully written into fluent and regular verse.

Curzon, Robert, 14th Baron Zouche 1810–73 Traveller, writer, manuscript collector. He was born in London, and educated at Charterhouse, then Christ Church, Oxford. He travelled to the Levant in 1833–4 and again in 1837–8. These journeys resulted in *Visits to Monasteries in the Levant* (1849), an entertaining account of travel in the Near East and the joys and problems of manuscript collecting in the decaying libraries of Greek monasteries. He wrote *Armenia* (1854) after going there in 1841 as private secretary to Sir Stratford Canning. The manuscripts he collected were deposited in the British Museum after his death. Curzon's life and interests are well documented by a collection of letters (deserving of publication) to his friend the Rev. Walter Sneyd; these are now in Keele University Library. Curzon spent his last years quietly at his family home, Parham in Sussex.

Cymbeline A play by WILLIAM SHAKESPEARE, first performed *c.* 1610 and published in the First Folio of 1623. There are various sources, of which HOLINSHED's *Chronicles* is primary only in the sense that it deals with the reign of the early Christian king, Cymbeline.

The emotional centre of the play is the relationship of Imogen, Cymbeline's daughter, and Posthumus Leonatus, whom the king has raised. Angered by their marriage, Cymbeline banishes Posthumus almost as the play opens. The intrigues and complications that delay their reunion make the matter of the play, which can be seen as a prolonged testing of their love. The many strands are kept separate until the extraordinary (and in some eyes clumsy) final act.

Taking refuge in Rome, the banished Posthumus finds solace in the company of the cynical Iachimo but wagers Imogen's virtue against Iachimo's boast that he will seduce her. She does, indeed, resist all Iachimo's wiles, and he is forced to cheat by hiding in a trunk to gain access to her bedroom. There he observes the mole on the breast of the sleeping Imogen, takes note of the room's furnishings and steals a bracelet. Confronted with this evidence of Imogen's infidelity, Posthumus swears vengeance and sails for England intent on killing her.

Iachimo is not the only schemer against the marriage. Cymbeline's second wife, a wicked queen of fairy-tale proportions, wants Posthumus dead so that her oafish son Cloten can marry Imogen. The desperate Imogen learns of her husband's anger from his servant Pisanso while they are travelling to Milford Haven for what she had supposed to be a love-tryst. She disguises herself as a boy (significantly named Fidele). Cloten pursues her, determined to kill Posthumus and rape Imogen; but 'Fidele', lost in Wales, has fallen among friends. Neither she nor they know that the two 'sons' of the exiled general Belarius are, in fact, Cymbeline's own lost sons, Guiderius and Arviragus, but the love between them protects Imogen from Cloten, who is killed and beheaded by one of the boys.

It can be appreciated that the final act has to work hard to achieve all the necessary reconciliations, as well as to achieve a political peace between Rome and Britain. It is not only credibility which the plot strains, but also comprehension. *Cymbeline* is a difficult play to categorize. The editors of the First Folio grouped it among the tragedies, but its outcome is comedic and even its deeper tones are dependent more on peril than on actual pain. It stands with the group of last plays, PERICLES, THE WINTER'S TALE and THE TEMPEST, written to satisfy the new fashion, encouraged by the staging facilities of the indoor theatre at the BLACKFRIARS, for spectacle and romance.

Cynewulf An Old English poet of the late 8th and early 9th centuries, Cynewulf is known through the inscription of his name in runic characters after four poems in the EXETER BOOK and the VERCELLI BOOK. One of them, *ELENE*, contains the ony information known about his life: he was old at the time of writing and, after leading what he considered a sinful life, had experienced some sort of spiritual enlightenment which granted him grace and his poetic gift. The other three poems bearing Cynewulf's signature are *The Ascension* (the second part of *CHRIST*), *JULIANA*, and *The Fates of the Apostles*. Various other poems have been attributed to him at different times, but without evidence.

Cynthia's Revels: *or, The Fountain of Self Love* A comedy by BEN JONSON, first performed by a BOYS' COMPANY in 1600 and published in 1601. The play was a contribution to the war of the theatres, and much of the satire has lost its point. Virtually plotless, it is chiefly memorable for its self-portrait of Jonson as Crites, an impartial judge of social and artistic standards, and for the lyric hymn to Diana, 'Queen and huntress, chaste and fair'.

dactyl See METRE.

Dafydd ap Gwilym *c.* 1320–80 Welsh Poet. In English his name means 'David son of William'. He was born in the parish of Llanbadarn Fawr, just outside Aberystwyth. Few details of his life are known but his family certainly belonged to the influential class of Welsh landed gentry known as *uchelwyr*, who maintained their prestige after the English conquest of Wales in 1284 by serving the crown as highly placed administrators. References in the poems indicate that Dafydd moved in a circle of poets and their noble patrons in Cardiganshire but also travelled widely throughout Wales. He had access to English, French and Latin literary traditions, often in oral rather than written form, and probably through the medium of Welsh in many cases.

He composed entirely in Welsh. His collected works, edited by Thomas Parry, consist of about 150 poems, a relatively large number testifying to his stature and popularity long after his death. Only a handful survive in contemporary manuscripts. Even if there were more early manuscripts now lost, it must be assumed that oral transmission played a crucial part in disseminating and preserving his work. Composed within a bardic tradition which had been absorbing Continental themes at least since the Norman Conquest, his poems therefore have affinities with the Middle English HARLEY LYRICS and with CHAUCER, his contemporary. His themes cover almost the entire range of medieval genres and *topoi*: COURTLY LOVE, dialogues between lovers, nature description, DREAM-VISION, humorous poems in a FABLIAU style. Most of his lyrics use a traditional Welsh bardic metre called the *cywydd*, widely practised in the 14th and 15th centuries. He often employs *dyfalu*, a series of compressed and striking images describing a particular object, and extended metaphors which develop a witty central image throughout the poem. The obligatory bardic device of *cynghanedd*, a complex and highly specific set of alliterative and rhyming patterns within each line of verse, adds richness to a poetry intended to be spoken or sung aloud. His work suggests the concerns of his *uchelwyr* audiences. The recurrent motifs of bardic patronage, the desirability of possessing women and land, and the unremitting satire of bourgeois values, all point to a context in which a traditional Welsh nobility is guarding its privileges as rulers and landowners while aligning itself with the governing English aristocracy.

The complete works of Dafydd ap Gwilym have been translated by R. M. Loomis (1982). Rachel Bromwich has produced a selection with textual notes (1982).

D'Aguiar, Fred 1960– Guyanese/British poet. Born in London of Guyanese parents, he spent his early years in Guyana, returning to England, where he received his secondary school education in 1972. After training and working as a psychiatric nurse, he read English at the University of Kent. Many of the poems in *Mama Dot* (1985) and *Airy Hall* (1989) deal with the Guyana of his youth, lyrically rekindling both its landscape and family relationships in lively images. His most vivid creation is the title-character of *Mama Dot*, an archetypal grandmother-figure. He has also written plays, *High Life* (1986) and *A Jamaican Airman Sees His Death* (1989), and edited the Black British section of *The New British Poetry* (1988).

Dahl, Roald 1916–90 Writer of CHILDREN'S LITERATURE. Born in Wales of Norwegian parentage, Dahl was educated at Repton School before serving as a fighter pilot during World War II. In 1943 a children's book *The Gremlins* was published, followed by many adult short stories. He returned to children's fiction with *James and the Giant Peach* (1961), a good-humoured fantasy about a boy travelling around the world in an enormous fruit. This was followed by *Charlie and the Chocolate Factory* (1964), which became an international best-seller as well as a successful film. It deals with one small boy's search for the ultimate prize in fierce competition with other, highly unpleasant children, many of whom come to sticky ends as a result of their greediness. The cruelty involved in such descriptions upset many adult critics, as did some of Dahl's grotesque characterizations in other books. But young readers often relish just those excesses that critics tend to deplore; they also enjoy Dahl's immense verbal facility, much in evidence in *Revolting Rhymes* (1982) and *Dirty Beasts* (1984), which take a typically unsentimental look at favourite animals. *The BFG* (1982) won him his first literary prize, although some critics objected to what they saw as sexism in *The Witches* (1983) and snobbery in *Matilda* (1988). *Boy* (1984) and *Going Solo* (1986) are vivid autobiographies of his early years.

Dahlberg, Edward 1900–77 American novelist and critic. Born in Boston, the illegitimate son of a lady barber from Kansas City, he was sent at an early age to an orphanage in Cleveland, Ohio. He ran away and later enrolled at the University of California and then at Columbia. In 1926 he settled in Europe, where he wrote his first book, *Bottom Dogs* (1929), a semi-autobiographical novel about a childhood in slums and orphanages. This was followed by *From Flushing to Calvary* (1932), about the slums of New York City, and *Those Who Perish* (1934), about the effects of Nazism upon American Jews. Dahlberg's interests were wide-ranging: his literary criticism is collected in *Do These Bones Live?* (1941); studies of 'classical sensuality' and myth comprise *The Sorrows of Priapus* (1957) and *The Carnal Myth* (1968); and essays on modern society and modern writers are collected in *The Flea of Sodom* (1950), *Truth is More Sacred* (1961) and *Alms for Oblivion* (1964). *Because I was Flesh* (1964) is his autobiography. Other books include *Cipango's Hinder Door* (1965, poems), *Epitaphs of Our Times* (1967, letters), *The Confessions of Edward Dahlberg* (1971) and *The Olive of Minerva* (1976).

Daily News, The A radical newspaper founded by CHARLES DICKENS and edited by him from January until October 1846. He was succeeded by his friend JOHN FORSTER. The newspaper was absorbed by *The Daily Chronicle* in 1930 and became *The News Chronicle*, continuing publication under this name until 1960.

Daisy Chain, The A novel by CHARLOTTE M. YONGE, published in 1856. The story concerns the large family (the 'Daisy Chain' of the title) of Dr May, tragically widowed in the early chapters. His ugly but warm-hearted daughter, Ethel, with her untidiness, her clumsiness and her marked capacity for scholarship, is the most memorable and best loved of the characters.

Daisy Miller A short novel by HENRY JAMES, published in 1879. Daisy Miller is touring Europe with her mother and brother. The expatriate American community interprets her innocence and lack of concern for social convention as immodesty and forwardness, and she is ostracized. One of its number, Frederick Winterbourne, though agreeing with that judgement, is also charmed by her innocence. In Rome Daisy takes up with Giovanelli, a young Italian of no social position. Winterbourne meets them one evening viewing the Coliseum by moonlight without a chaperone, and berates Daisy for her lack of social decorum. Shocked and hurt by his reaction, she returns at once to her hotel, where she contracts malaria and dies after a week.

Dallas, E(neas) S(weetland) 1828–79 Journalist and literary critic. Born in Jamaica, he was brought to England at the age of four and educated at Edinburgh University, where he studied philosophy under SIR WILLIAM HAMILTON. As a journalist, he worked on *The Times* during the editorship of J. T. DELANE. His critical writing, represented by *Poetics: An Essay on Poetry* (1852) and *The Gay Science* (1866),

took a scientific approach to aesthetics, viewing the aim of art as pleasure and the imagination as a function of the unconscious mind.

D'Alpuget, Blanche 1944– Australian novelist and biographer. Born in Sydney, she has lived in Malaysia and Indonesia. Her novels include: *Monkeys in the Dark* (1980) and *Turtle Beach* (1981), dramatizing the details of Australian relationships with the Far East; *Winter in Jerusalem* (1986), about a young woman's attempt to understand the place where she was born; and *White Eye* (1991). She has also written biographies of Sir Richard Kirby (1977) and Bob Hawke (1982).

Dalrymple, Sir David, Lord Hailes 1726–92 Scottish jurist, historian and man of letters. He was born at Edinburgh and educated at Eton and at Utrecht, where he studied civil law. He enjoyed the financial independence simply to have pursued his literary interests, but he became a judge notable for his humanity and an expert legal historian.

Uncomfortable with the major Scottish literary figures (DAVID HUME, ADAM SMITH and WILLIAM ROBERTSON), Dalrymple looked south for more congenial correspondents. Political and religious differences did not deter him from forming friendships with such men as JOHNSON, BURKE, HORACE WALPOLE, and Bishops Hurd, PERCY and Warburton. It was Dalrymple who fired the young JAMES BOSWELL with the desire to know Johnson. Thought by Burke 'a clever man and generally knowing', Dalrymple published many works, chiefly of legal history and anti-sceptical Christian antiquarianism. He contributed to *The World* and *THE GENTLEMAN'S MAGAZINE*. He edited BALLADS and other ancient Scottish poetry. His most significant historical work was *Annals of Scotland* (1776–9). The *Annals* were praised for their exactness and lightly revised by Johnson, who found the narrative 'clear, lively, and short'. GIBBON, too, thought well of Dalrymple's diligence and accuracy as a historian, though Dalrymple later took issue with him in *An Inquiry into the Secondary Causes Which Mr Gibbon Has Assigned for the Rapid Growth of Christianity* (1786).

Daly, (John) Augustin 1838–99 American playwright and theatre manager. Born in North Carolina and educated in New York City, he was first a drama critic, then a professional playwright. *Leah the Forsaken* (1862) was the first of about 100 plays which he wrote or, more often, adapted, in regular collaboration with his brother Joseph. The best include spectacular MELODRAMAS like *Under the Gaslight* (1867), *The Flash of Lightning* (1868), and *The Red Scarf* (1868) and comedies about American high society like *Divorce* (1871), *Pique* (1875) and *Love on Crutches* (1884). *Horizon* (1871) is a frontier drama. Daly's major contribution to the American theatre was as a company manager and director. At the Fifth Avenue Theatre from 1869 to 1873, and then, particularly, at Daly's Theatre from 1879 until his death, he established ensemble companies, the finest in America, increasing the prestige of his country's actors during tours to London and Paris.

Dame Sirith A Middle English FABLIAU written c. 1272–83. It tells how Wilekin unsuccessfully tries to seduce Margery in her husband's absence and then goes to Dame Sirith for assistance. She feeds her dog mustard and pepper and takes it to Margery, saying that it is her daughter transformed by a clerk whose advances she refused and showing her the dog's tears as proof. In horror, Margery tells her to bring Wilekin to her and submits to his desires. Much of the poem is in dialogue: it may have been intended for performance, either by several actors, or, which is perhaps more likely, by a minstrel using mime to distinguish the different characters.

Damnation of Theron Ware, The See THERON WARE, THE DAMNATION OF.

Dampier, William 1652–1715 Voyager, discoverer and privateer. He was born in the West Country, near Yeovil. His career took him to the West Indies, South America, the Pacific, Australia and the East Indies. During one of Dampier's early voyages (1703–4) a Scottish seaman named Alexander Selkirk asked to be put ashore on the Pacific island of Juan Fernández after a quarrel with his captain. (See also ROGERS, WOODES and *ROBINSON CRUSOE*.) Dampier's accounts of his travels and adventures are vivid, entertaining and of considerable historical interest: *A New Voyage round the World* (1697), *Voyages and Descriptions* (1699) and *A Voyage to New Holland* (1703–9).

Dana, Richard Henry, Jr 1815–82 American social reformer. The son of a minor poet and journalist of the same name, he was born in Cambridge, Massachusetts, and went to Harvard. Forced to withdraw by eye trouble at the end of his second year (1834), he signed on as a seaman for a voyage from Boston to California around Cape Horn. After working on the Pacific coast for a year, collecting and curing hides, he returned to Harvard Law School and qualified as a lawyer. His first work, 'Cruelty to Seamen', published in the *American Jurist* in 1839, expressed a deeply felt anger at what he had seen on his voyages. *TWO YEARS BEFORE THE MAST* (1840), the book that made him famous, described the life of the ordinary seaman as it was lived day by day. It was followed by *The Seaman's Friend* (1841; as *The Seaman's Manual* in Britain), instructing sailors in their rights as well as their duties, and a less successful account of a later voyage, *To Cuba and Back* (1859).

A champion of the underprivileged, Dana opposed slavery in word and deed. He helped fugitive slaves and in doing so antagonized the Boston mill-owners, because cheap raw materials from the South boosted their profits. His hopes of a political career were dashed by accusations of plagiarism levelled at his edition of Henry Wheaton's *Elements of International Law* (1866), and his appointment as ambassador to Great Britain was withdrawn by the Senate. He withdrew to Europe in 1878 and died a disappointed man. *Speeches in Stirring Times* (1910) and *An Autobiographical Sketch* (1953) were published posthumously.

Dance to the Music of Time, A A sequence of 12 novels by ANTHONY POWELL, consisting of *A Question of Upbringing* (1951), *A Buyer's Market* (1952), *The Acceptance World* (1955), *At Lady Molly's* (1957), *Casanova's Chinese Restaurant* (1960), *The Kindly Ones* (1962), *The Valley of Bones* (1964), *The Soldier's Art* (1966), *The Military Philosophers* (1968), *Books Do Furnish a Room* (1971), *Temporary Kings* (1973) and *Hearing Secret Harmonies* (1975).

The sequence is a ROMAN FLEUVE, or 'river novel', intended to be read as a unity. It constitutes a history of 20th-century English life as observed by Nicholas Jenkins, a member of the post-World War I generation and a fashionable set in which the life of the artist overlaps with that of polite society. He begins the narrative, in *A Question of Upbringing*, at public school and subsequently broadens its focus to include a panoramic and satirical view of the changes in the lives and fortunes of the English upper middle classes over the next 50 years. His own life takes place 'off stage', but as narrator he is constantly present as the selective recorder of the temporal flow of events, eventually formalizing them into the pattern of a dance like the painting by Poussin from which the sequence takes its title. Among the memorable characters in this epic enterprise are the power-hungry Kenneth Widmerpool, whose beginnings are inauspicious, but who eventually achieves formidable influence through a series of ruthless manoeuvres, and Sir Magnus Donners, at whose mansion World War II is fanfared with a charade of the seven deadly sins.

Dane, Clemence [Ashton, Winifred] 1888–1965 Playwright and novelist. Born at Blackheath, she was educated in England and France; after teaching in Geneva for a year, she studied art at the Slade and in Dresden. She gave up painting for acting, then devoted herself to writing. Her first and second novels, *Regiment of Women* (1917) and *Legend* (1919), were widely acclaimed, but she turned her attention to drama before returning to fiction with *Broome Stages* (1931), *The Moon is Feminine* (1938) and *He Brings Great News* (1944).

Dane's career as a playwright began with *A Bill of Divorcement* (1921), about a woman who divorces her husband on grounds of insanity in order to remarry, but comes up against the moral prejudices of the older generation. It was an outstanding success, never quite repeated by subsequent plays like the blank-verse *Will Shakespeare* (1921), *Granite* (1926) and *Wild Decembers* (1932), about the BRONTËS. She also wrote a study of HUGH WALPOLE (1929) and a stage adaptation of MAX BEERBOHM's story *The Happy Hypocrite* (1936).

Dangarembga, Tsitsi 1959– Zimbabwean playwright, novelist and film-maker. Educated in Britain, Zimbabwe and the USA, she attended the University of Cambridge before returning to her native country in 1980, shortly before independence. While a student at the University of Zimbabwe she contributed three plays to its Drama Group. After receiving a Commonwealth Writers' Award in 1989 she left for Berlin to study film. She has published a play, *She No Longer Weeps* (1987), and a novel, *Nervous Conditions* (1988).

Daniel An Old English poem preserved in the Junius manuscript (see JUNIUS, FRANCIS). It tells the story of Daniel from Exodus, which it usually follows closely. Beginning with the fall of the Israelites into sin and Nebuchadnezzar's plundering of Jerusalem, the poem goes on to give an account of Daniel's interpretation of the king's dreams, a vigorous description of the ordeal in the furnace and an incomplete account of Belshazzar's feast. In general the style is flat and uninspiring, but there are occasional redeeming passages.

Daniel, Samuel 1562/3–1619 Poet, translator, literary critic, historian and playwright. Tradition has it that Daniel was born near Taunton and that his father was a music master. His brother John was also a musician. Daniel tutored the future Earl of Pembroke, SHAKESPEARE's patron, and also Lady Anne Clifford, daughter of the Countess of Cumberland.

Twenty-eight of his sonnets appeared without his authority at the end of the 1591 edition of SIDNEY's *ASTROPHIL AND STELLA*. In 1592 Daniel first issued the work for which he is best remembered, *Delia*, a SONNET sequence showing the influence of Desportes and Tasso. Revised and expanded over the years, the number of sonnets had grown from its original 50 to 57 by the 1601 edition of his *Works*. In 1592 Daniel also published *The Complaint of Rosamond*, in the manner of poems in *THE MIRROR FOR MAGISTRATES*, adding to it in 1594 his Senecan closet tragedy *Cleopatra*. *Civil Wars*, an epic poem about the Wars of the Roses, was printed in 1595 and expanded from four to five books the same year; it was never completed, though its narrative had reached the marriage

of Edward IV by 1609. Written partly under the influence of Lucan, it in turn influenced Shakespeare's *RICHARD II* and the *HENRY IV* plays. Daniel's *Poetical Essays* (1599) included two new works: *Musophilus*, a verse colloquium on the literary life, and *Octavia*, a verse epistle in the manner of Ovid's *Heroides*.

A Defence of Rhyme (1603) made sensible answer to THOMAS CAMPION's *Observations in the Art of English Poesy*. *Certain Small Poems* (1605) contains *Philotas*, a tragedy on the story of a rebellion against Alexander the Great, which got Daniel into trouble for its apparent sympathy with Essex's rebellion. It did not permanently damage his position at court, where his MASQUES were popular. *The Vision of the Twelve Goddesses* was performed at Hampton Court and printed in 1604. *Tethys's Festival* (1610), for the creation of Prince Henry as Prince of Wales, had scenery by Inigo Jones. *Hymen's Triumph* was played at Somerset House in 1614 and printed in 1615. His masques gained Daniel the favour of Queen Anne, who danced in the Hampton Court masque. She gave him the office of licensing all entertainments played by the Children of the Queen's Revels; he probably resigned this post to his brother in 1618. Daniel's last work was the ambitious *Collection of the History of England*, a prose narrative which had reached Edward III's reign by the enlarged edition of 1618.

Daniel was admired by his contemporaries for his poetic skill and choice of language. The range of his literary productions and his choice of subjects and forms invite comparison with his contemporary MICHAEL DRAYTON. Daniel's own assessment of his work is modestly confident, 'I know I shall be read among the rest / So long as men speak English.'

Daniel Deronda GEORGE ELIOT's last novel, published in eight parts between February and September 1876. The story is principally concerned with the destinies of two characters: Daniel Deronda, the adopted child of an English aristocrat, and Gwendolen Harleth, the spoiled and selfish elder daughter of a widow. In order to avoid penury as her family approaches destitution, Gwendolen agrees to marry Henleigh Grandcourt, fully aware that he has children by his mistress and that his mistress has a prior claim to his hand. The marriage proves unhappy and Gwendolen finds herself drawn for spiritual guidance to Deronda. Deronda, who has rescued the Jewish girl, Mirah Lepidoth, from suicide, gradually discovers a dense Jewish world through Mirah and through her brother, Mordecai. He eventually learns that he too is a Jew and the novel ends with his determination to seek for his ancient racial and religious roots in Palestine.

Although the novel has seemed awkward and unbalanced to some critics, it has also been acknowledged to be George Eliot's most ambitious work, combining profound scholarship and an original power in describing character and thought. The novelist sought both a challenging shape for her narrative and a contrast between the lax, aristocratic mores of her English characters and the fervour and moral intensity of her Jewish ones. Unlike the novelist's earlier work, *Daniel Deronda* has a contemporary setting and radiates disquiet about the future of English society.

Dark, Eleanor 1901–85 Australian novelist. Her novels, which frequently explore the results of catastrophes preceding the action and which experiment with time, include *Slow Dawning* (1932), *Prelude to Christopher* (1933), *Sun across the Sky* (1937), *Waterway* (1938), *Return to Coolami* (1935) and *The Little Company* (1945). *The Timeless Land* (1941), *Storm of Time* (1948) and *No Barrier* (1953) form a trilogy covering the first 25 years of the Sydney settlement. Republished in 1988, it has been recognized as a masterpiece of carefully researched historical REALISM. *Lantana Lane* (1959), a collection of Queensland tales, was her last work.

Darley, George 1795–1846 Irish poet and critic. He was born in Dublin and educated at Trinity College. From the 1820s he contributed essays, mainly on drama, to *THE LONDON MAGAZINE* and later to *THE ATHENAEUM*. His poetry includes *The Errors of Ecstasie: A Dramatic Poem, with Other Pieces* (1822), *Sylvia: or, the May Queen: A Lyrical Drama* (1827) and *Nepenthe* (1835). His tragedy *Thomas à Becket: A Dramatic Chronicle* and his notable edition of the plays of BEAUMONT and FLETCHER appeared in 1840. Darley was also an accomplished mathematician, publishing four popular guides to the subject.

Darwin, Charles (Robert) 1809–82 Natural historian. Grandson of ERASMUS DARWIN and son of a doctor, Robert Darwin, he was born at Shrewsbury, where he later went to school. He attended Christ's College, Cambridge, in 1828–31, after a period as a medical student at Edinburgh. Though not seen by his family or himself as intellectual at this time, he impressed James Henslow, professor of botany at Cambridge, who encouraged him to study geology and subsequently recommended him as naturalist for the voyage of the survey ship *Beagle* (1831–6), the most important formative period of his intellectual life. Darwin's wide interests – in geology, zoology, botany and wild-life (especially beetles) – prepared him for an extraordinarily wide-ranging career of observation and theorizing. His sea and land voyage of five years round the world produced his *Journal of Researches into the Geology and Natural History of the Various Countries Visited by HMS Beagle* (1839), a highly readable and thoughtful account of his response to the tropics, his encounters with 'primitive' peoples, and his realization of how complex are the

relations between living forms within an environment. These forms include the human and he writes movingly about enslavement and about the conflicts between indigenous Indians and colonizing Spaniards.

Darwin declared that his reading of MALTHUS's *Essay on Population* precipitated the formulation of his theory of natural selection, though there are indications in his journals of the late 1830s that he had more or less reached the concept some months earlier. Darwin long delayed publication of his findings: because of the disturbing cultural and religious implications of his views he wished to render his theories as near as possible impregnable by adducing manifold and various evidences. He recognized from the start that 'descent with modification' removed humankind from its centrality in the natural order and undermined the time-honoured religious myths of Genesis. He wrote *THE ORIGIN OF SPECIES* (1859) rapidly, under the impetus of knowing that Alfred Russel Wallace had reached conclusions similar to his concerning the mechanism of evolutionary development.

Responses to Darwin's theories immediately recognized their implications for humankind, although he had deliberately excluded discussion of 'man's place in nature' from his argument. In particular, objection was made to the implied kinship with other species.

Much of Darwin's later work emphasizes this kinship. In *The Descent of Man and Selection in Relation to Sex* (1871) and in *The Expression of the Emotions in Man and Animals* (1872) he juxtaposes material from anthropology, primate studies, and sociology. All these new disciplines had themselves been partly formed by the ideas in *The Origin of Species*. The emphasis on 'sexual selection' opened up connections between evolutionary theory and aesthetics and cultural studies. It also stimulated 'social Darwinism', developed by HERBERT SPENCER as much as Darwin himself, which shifts the definition of 'fitness' from that of the aptness of the organism to its current environment to a quasi-moral concept of 'fitness' as physical and mental power. The result stresses a hierarchical order in society, a constant struggle for dominance by strong individuals, and a readiness to jettison the weak. Such views form part of the debate in the work of JACK LONDON and THEODORE DREISER and coloured many later literary responses to Darwin's work.

Among his own contemporaries and at the turn of the century GEORGE ELIOT, SAMUEL BUTLER, THOMAS HARDY and JOSEPH CONRAD were writers who energetically responded to – and in Butler's case, contended against – Darwin's work. GEORGE BERNARD SHAW, H. G. WELLS and VIRGINIA WOOLF demonstrate how differently Darwin could be read in literary terms. In the 20th century his ideas have become part of the apparatus of assumptions to a degree which makes it difficult to track them independently, though their power is still manifest, particularly among writers of SCIENCE FICTION such as ISAAC ASIMOV and Stanislaw Lem.

Darwin, Erasmus 1731–1802 Botanist, poet and grandfather of CHARLES DARWIN. He was born at Elston in Lincolnshire and educated at St John's College, Cambridge. He became a physician and practised for most of his life at Lichfield, where he established a botanical garden and wrote *The Botanic Garden*, a poem in HEROIC COUPLETS which embodied Linnaeus's system. Part 2, *The Loves of the Plants*, appeared first, in 1789 and Part 1, *The Economy of Vegetation*, in 1791. It was ridiculed by JOHN HOOKHAM FRERE and GEORGE CANNING in *The Loves of the Triangles*, published in THE ANTI-JACOBIN. Darwin published his theory of the laws of organic life on the evolutionary principle in *Zoonomia* (1794–6) and *Phytologia* (1799).

Daryush, Elizabeth 1887–1977 Poet. The daughter of ROBERT BRIDGES, she married in 1923 and lived in Persia until returning to England in 1927. An isolated figure, she staunchly ignored the innovations of POUND and ELIOT, clinging to traditional poetic procedures and archaic diction in *Charitessi 1911* (1912), seven books of *Verses* (1930–71), *The Last Man* (1936), *Selected Poems* (1972) and *Collected Poems* (1976). But she is important for her pioneering technical experiments with syllabic verse (see METRE), which predate those of MARIANNE MOORE, AUDEN and THOM GUNN, and her quiet stoicism has been admired by YVOR WINTERS (who called her 'one of the few distinguished poets of our century'), ROY FULLER and DONALD DAVIE.

Das, Kamala 1934– Indian poet. Born in Malabar, she can, in her own words, 'speak three languages, write in/ Two, dream in one'. Her work can be both acerbic and tempestuous, radical and traditionally minded. Collections of verse in English include *Summer in Calcutta* (1965), *The Descendants* (1968), *The Old Playhouse and Other Poems* (1973) and a volume of love poems, *Tonight, This Savage Rite* (with Pritish Nandy; 1979). Her work in Malayalam includes many short stories and an autobiography, *Ente Katha* ('My Story'; 1975).

D'Avenant, Sir William 1606–68 Playwright, poet and theatre manager. Son of the keeper of the Crown Inn in the Cornmarket at Oxford, he took pains to encourage the rumour that SHAKESPEARE was his true father. In fact, he was the poet's godson. D'Avenant was educated at grammar school in Oxford, then became page to the Duchess of Richmond and later to FULKE GREVILLE, who encouraged his interest in the theatre. His plays include *The Tragedy of Albovine* (1629), *The Cruel Brother* (1630) and *The Wits* (1636).

From 1635, following the pleasure occasioned at court by the best of his MASQUES, *The Temple of Love*, he was given charge of all such entertainments during Charles I's reign. *Madagascar, with Other Poems* was published in 1638, when he also succeeded BEN JONSON as unofficial POET LAUREATE. He fought as a Royalist in the Civil War and was knighted at the siege of Gloucester in 1643. With COWLEY, WALLER and THOMAS HOBBES he was one of the group of exiles in Paris with Henrietta Maria from 1646 until his appointment as governor of Maryland in 1649. He was captured at sea by Cromwell's forces and imprisoned in the Tower, where he continued work on his verse epic *Gondibert* (1651). His pardon in 1654 was probably the result of JOHN MILTON's intervention.

Free once more and with his love for the theatre unimpaired by vicissitude, D'Avenant organized clandestine theatrical performances. Cromwell's personal rule had only two years to run and the Puritan attitude to the theatre seems to have relaxed; at any rate D'Avenant secured authority for the presentation of an entertainment which, though given at a private house, could be attended by anyone who paid for admission. So THE SIEGE OF RHODES was performed at Rutland House in 1656, and drama began to return to life in England after being suppressed for 14 years. At the Restoration D'Avenant received one of Charles II's Letters Patent to form a company of players (see PATENT THEATRES). At his theatre in Lincoln's Inn Fields he introduced new ideas of presentation such as the proscenium, elaborate scenery, and the use of machinery. He produced adaptations of Shakespeare that infuriated many but did serve to bring Shakespeare back to the stage and to nourish the reawakened English theatre. D'Avenant will, and should, always be remembered for the part he played in that reawakening, though his own contributions to English drama have not held the stage. His patent passed in the next century to John Rich, who invested it in COVENT GARDEN.

David Copperfield A novel by CHARLES DICKENS, published in 19 monthly parts from May 1849 to November 1850 and in volume form in 1850. Its full title, *The Personal History, Experience and Observations of David Copperfield the Younger, of Blunderstone Rookery, Which He Never Meant to be Published On Any Account*, suggests the degree to which Dickens sought to frame his narrative around the personal memoirs of an observant professional writer. David traces his childhood and youth, marred by his widowed mother's remarriage to Mr Murdstone and death, and by his distressing experience working in a London factory (an incident modelled on Dickens's own boyhood suffering). Escaping from London, David takes refuge at Dover with his aunt, Betsey Trotwood, and, after a period of conventional schooling and a brief legal career, becomes a novelist. His marriage to Dora Spenlow proves unhappy but David is none the less devastated by her early death. His friendship for James Steerforth is equally disturbed by Steerforth's elopement with Emily, the niece of the Yarmouth fisherman, Mr Peggotty. The novel gradually reveals David's slow grasp of the meaning of his 'Experience', and the disciplining of his heart. He finally finds happiness with the faithful Agnes Wickfield, whom he has known since childhood and whose own future had seemed to be threatened by the wiles of her father's sometime clerk, Uriah Heep. The improvidence and verbal extravagance of Wilkins Micawber, with whom David lodges during his unhappy London days, is to some extent modelled on that of the novelist's own father, John Dickens. Dickens himself proclaimed that this novel was his own 'favourite child'.

David Simple, The Adventures of: Containing an Account of His Travels through the Cities of London and Westminster in the Search of a Real Friend. A moral romance by SARAH FIELDING, first published in 1744.

David Simple learns that his younger brother, to whom he is devoted, has used a forged will in an attempt to rob him of his inheritance. Disillusioned, David sets out on a journey to rediscover honest friendship. His encounters with Mr Orgueil and his insolent wife, Mr Spatter, who is the chief critic of Orgueil, and Mr Varnish, the chief critic of Spatter, nearly drive him to despair. Then he meets Cynthia, excluded from her father's will and ill-treated by her employer, and Camilla and Valentine, brother and sister who have become the victims of their stepmother's perfidy. David helps them, and the four become friends. David and Camilla, and Valentine and Cynthia gently fall in love and become betrothed. Camilla and Valentine are reconciled to their father, and the two couples settle down in a happy community established by David's generosity. The novel gives an excellent picture of the London scene, and its moralizing is skilfully controlled. It was very popular in France.

Davidson, Donald (Grady) 1893-1968 American poet, critic and historian. Born in Tennessee, he became a strongly committed member of the FUGITIVES, editing the group's magazine, *The Fugitive* (1922-5), and contributing to JOHN CROWE RANSOM's collection, *I'll Take My Stand: The South and the Agrarian Tradition* (1930). His poems were published in *An Outland Piper* (1924), *The Tall Men* (1927), *Lee in the Mountains, and Other Poems* (1938), *The Long Street* (1961) and *Poems, 1922-1961* (1966). His other writings include *The Attack on Leviathan: Regionalism and Nationalism in the United States* (1938), *Still Rebels, Still Yankees, and Other Essays* (1957), *Southern Writers in the Modern World* (1958)

and *The Spyglass: Views and Reviews, 1924-1930* (1963).

Davidson, John 1857-1909 Poet, playwright, novelist and essayist. Born near Glasgow the son of a minister in the Evangelical Union, Davidson briefly attended Edinburgh University and subsequently, in 1877, became a schoolmaster, a calling he reluctantly followed until 1889 when he left Scotland to pursue a literary career in London. Writing extensively from an early age, he was first published in 1885 when a farcical novel, *The North Wall*, and a verse drama, *Diabolus Amans*, appeared. A year later came a chronicle play, *Bruce*, and in 1889, *Plays*, which included a striking fantasy, *Scaramouch in Naxos*.

Settled in London, Davidson was an occasional visitor at the RHYMERS' CLUB where he had the company of YEATS, BEERBOHM, GOSSE and others of that circle; he also contributed to THE YELLOW BOOK. He wrote more novels and a great deal of poetry: *Fleet Street Eclogues* (1893), *Ballads and Songs* (1894), *A Second Series of Fleet Street Eclogues* (1896), *New Ballads* (1897) and *The Last Ballad* (1899). 'Thirty Bob a Week' is the best-known poem to show his satiric bent, colloquial language and fascination with the meaner aspects of urban life.

The last decade of his life was exceptionally fertile. As well as short stories, adaptations from the French, journalism and prose sketches, Davidson produced a series of poetic dramas, including *Godfrida* (1898), *Self's the Man* (1901), *The Knight of the Maypole* (1903), *The Theatrocrat* (1905), *The Triumph of Mammon* (1907) and *Mammon and His Message* (1908), the last two forming part of an unpublished trilogy. Of greater significance were the *Testaments* propounding his philosophy of life, fashioned from contemporary science, revolt against Christianity and perhaps his reading of Nietzsche: *The Testament of a Vivisector* (1901), *The Testament of a Man Forbid* (1901), *The Testament of an Empire-Builder* (1902), *The Testament of a Prime Minister* (1904) and *The Testament of John Davidson* (1908). Ever at odds with the world, he drowned himself off the Cornish coast.

Davie, Donald (Alfred) 1922- Poet and critic. He was born in Barnsley, Yorkshire, and educated there and at St Catharine's College, Cambridge. After military service, he lectured at Trinity College, Dublin (1950-77), and Cambridge (1958-64), and became professor of English at Essex (1964-8), where he was also Pro-Vice Chancellor (1965-8). He then emigrated to the United States to become professor at Stanford and later Vanderbilt Universities, returning to Britain on his retirement in 1988.

Davie was the major theorist of the MOVEMENT: his critical books *Purity of Diction in English Verse* (1952; revised, 1992) and *Articulate Energy* (1955) were instrumental in establishing an 'Augustinian' discipline of chastened poetic language as the measure for what poetry should be in recent times. His own poetry appeared in *Brides of Reason* (1955), *A Winter Talent* (1957), *The Forests of Lithuania* (1959), *New and Selected Poems* (1961), *To Scorch or Freeze* (1988) and successive versions of *Collected Poems* (1972, 1983 and 1990). His later poetry is more experimental and less cerebral, Davie having partially repudiated the enthusiasm and special 'romanticism' of his early 'Augustinian' protest. Travel and consideration of European and American literatures have also made him critical of what he describes as 'Little-Englandism' among his contemporaries. Other critical studies include books on SCOTT (1961), POUND (1964) and HARDY (1972), *Czeslaw Milosz and the Insufficiency of Lyric* (1986), *Under Briggflatts: A History of Poetry in Britain 1940–1980* (1989) and *Slavic Excursions* (1990). *These the Companions* (1982) is a volume of memoirs.

Davies, Idris 1905–53 Poet. Born in Rhymney, Monmouthshire, he was the son of a miner and went into the pits himself at the age of 14. After the 1926 General Strike he went to teachers' college and Nottingham University, becoming a schoolteacher in London in 1928. One of the few genuinely working-class poets to emerge from the 1930s, he produced two sequences about the valleys, *Gwalia Deserta* (1938) and *Angry Summer* (1943), as well as *Tonypandy* (1945) and *Selected Poems* (1953). His early death was caused by cancer.

Davies, John *c.* 1565–1618 Poet, usually called John Davies of Hereford (his birthplace) to distinguish him from his contemporary SIR JOHN DAVIES. He wrote a philosophical poem, *Mirum in Modum: A Glimpse of God's Glory and the Soul's Shape* (1602), the physiological and psychological *Microcosmos* (1603) and *Humours Heaven on Earth* (1605), a description of the plague of 1603. *The Scourge of Folly* (c. 1610) is a book of complimentary EPIGRAMS addressed to distinguished figures of his time, including SHAKESPEARE, JOHN DONNE, BEN JONSON and SAMUEL DANIEL.

Davies, Sir John 1569–1626 Poet. He was educated at Winchester and the Queen's College, Oxford, which he entered in 1585. He stayed there only a year and a half and did not take a degree. He studied law at the New Inn and then the Middle Temple, which he entered in 1588, and became a barrister in 1595. He was disbarred in 1598 for a fight in which he hit a friend with a cudgel. The friend was Richard Martin, to whom Davies refers as my 'better half, my dearest friend' and to whom he dedicated *Orchestra*. Davies was reinstated in 1601 after apologizing and with the insistent support of Lord Keeper Egerton. During this period he became a founder member of the Society of

Antiquaries. One of the messengers who carried the news of Elizabeth's death to James VI in 1603, he gained the new king's favour. His legal career flourished as he became successively Solicitor General of Ireland and Speaker of the Irish Parliament. He would have become Lord Chief Justice of England but died the day before he was to have assumed office.

Davies's most intense period of poetic activity was between 1593 and 1599. *Orchestra: or, A Poem of Dancing* (1596) has traditionally been read as a solemn celebration of the harmonious and hierarchical 'Elizabethan world picture', although Davies's contemporaries saw it as a frivolous poem, and the author himself invokes 'Terpsichore, my light muse'. *Nosce Teipsum* ('Know Thyself', 1599) is an expository poem on natural philosophy and the immortality of the soul, its faculties and its relation to the body and to the senses. There was a family tradition that Davies wrote it after his expulsion from the Middle Temple. *Hymns of Astraea* (1599) is a collection of ACROSTIC poems spelling out 'Elisabetha Regina'. Davies's other poetry includes the usual SONNETS produced by poets in the 1590s, and also 'Gulling Sonnets' which mock PETRARCHAN conventions. He also wrote occasional verse, verse paraphrases of the Psalms and satirical EPIGRAMS which earned for him the description of 'our English Martial'. The *Epigrams and Elegies* (?1590), which also included posthumous works by MARLOWE, were burned on the instruction of the Archbishop of Canterbury in 1599.

Davies, Robertson 1913– Canadian novelist, essayist and playwright. The son of a newspaper proprietor, he was born in Thamesville in southwestern Ontario. He attended one of Canada's leading schools, Upper Canada College in Toronto, and subsequently Queen's University, Kingston and Balliol College, Oxford. After leaving Oxford he stayed in England, acting with the Old Vic Company and teaching the history of drama. *Shakespeare's Boy Actors* was published in 1939. He returned to Canada in 1940, working first as literary editor of *Saturday Night* in Toronto and then as a writer for and, from 1946, editor of *The Peterborough Examiner*, a paper previously owned by his father. The articles he wrote under the pseudonym of Samuel Marchbanks have been collected as *The Diary of Samuel Marchbanks* (1947), *The Table Talk of Samuel Marchbanks* (1949) and *Marchbanks' Almanack* (1967). He also achieved considerable success as a stage director, playing an important part in the annual Ontario Stratford Shakespeare Festival. His plays include *Fortune, My Foe* (1949), *A Jig for the Gypsy* (1954) and *Hunting Stuart and Other Plays* (1972). From 1963 until 1981 he was master of Massey College in the University of Toronto.

Notwithstanding his success in other fields, his major reputation is as a novelist, even though he was

38 before he published *Tempest-Tost* (1951), centred on a little theatre's production of THE TEMPEST. Together with *Leaven of Malice* (1954) and *A Mixture of Frailties* (1958), it makes up *The Salterton Trilogy*, the first of three major novel trilogies. The second and finest is THE DEPTFORD TRILOGY: *Fifth Business* (1970), *The Manticore* (1972) and *World of Wonders* (1975). *The Cornish Trilogy* consists of *The Rebel Angels* (1981), *What's Bred in the Bone* (1985) and *The Lyre of Orpheus* (1988). *Murther and Walking Spirits* (1991) makes thoughtful, witty use of the supernatural. Strongly influenced by his interest in Jungian archetypes, his fiction is about myth, magic and miracles, the relationship between the world of theatre and that of everyday life. It contrasts the limited mental perspectives offered by provincial Canada with the psychic fulfilment to be discovered through encounters with the 'world of wonders'.

Davies, W(illiam) H(enry) 1871–1940 Poet and writer of autobiography. He was born at Newport, Monmouthshire, the son of a publican, and was educated at elementary school before drifting through a series of labouring jobs. In his twenties he took to the road, making his way to New York, then to the Klondike. In Canada he was injured while jumping a train and had a leg amputated. He returned to England and lived in dosshouses for sixpence a night. A prolific poet, he published at his own expense, and sent *The Soul's Destroyer* (1905) to well-known people asking them to forward the price of the book. *New Poems* (1907) and *Nature Poems and Others* (1908) followed, attracting praise from EDWARD THOMAS among others. 600 poems appeared in his *Collected Poems* of 1943, some of which were brief nature lyrics, and others which reflected the harsher side of his life on the road. His *Complete Poems* appeared in 1963, with an introduction by OSBERT SITWELL.

The *Autobiography of a Super-Tramp* (1908) appeared with a preface by SHAW and has become Davies's best-known book. He was also the author of two novels, *A Weak Woman* (1911) and *Dancing Mad* (1927), and further autobiography in *Beggars* (1909), *The True Traveller* (1912), *A Poet's Pilgrimage* (1918) and *Later Days* (1925). *Young Emma* (posthumously published, 1980) describes his courtship and marriage to his young wife in 1923.

Davin, Dan(iel) 1913–90 New Zealand novelist and short-story writer. Born in Invercargill of Irish parents, he was educated at Roman Catholic schools and at the University of Otago, before attending Balliol College, Oxford, as a Rhodes Scholar from 1936 to 1939. During World War II he served first with the Royal Warwickshire Regiment and then with the New Zealand Division in Greece, Crete (where he was wounded), North Africa and Italy. He was awarded the MBE and three times mentioned in dispatches. After the war he returned to Oxford and worked for the University Press, rising to become Director of its Academic Division in 1974. He continued to live in Oxford until his death. Davin established his reputation as one of the leading New Zealand writers of his generation in the late 1940s, with the publication of his novels, *Cliffs of Fall* (1945), *For the Rest of Our Lives* (1947) and *Roads from Home* (1949), and a volume of short stories, *The Gorse Blooms Pale* (1947). Much of his work deals with his Irish Catholic New Zealand upbringing, but he has also written fiction based on the war experiences of the New Zealand Division in *For the Rest of Our Lives* and on the experiences of New Zealanders in post-war London in *The Sullen Bell* (1956). Whatever the locale the characteristic mode of Davin's fiction is realist and his concerns are primarily social and psychological. His later work included the novels *Not Here, Not Now* (1970) and *Brides of Price* (1972) and a volume of short stories, *Breathing Spaces* (1975). He also edited several collections of short stories, contributed to the New Zealand official war history, and published a volume of memoirs, *Closing Times* (1975).

Daviot, Gordon See MACKINTOSH, ELIZABETH.

Davis, Dick 1945– Poet. Born in Portsmouth, he was educated at King's College, Cambridge, where he met ROBERT WELLS and CLIVE WILMER, sharing the volume *Shade Mariners* (1970) with them. He has travelled widely, teaching in Teheran (1970–8), California and Durham. A practitioner of the 'plain style', he reached maturity early, and it is difficult to date individual poems from *In the Distance* (1975), *Seeing the World* (1980), *The Covenant: Poems 1979–1983* (1984), and *Devices and Desires* (1988). In a tradition running through BEN JONSON, YVOR WINTERS, J. V. CUNNINGHAM and THOM GUNN, Davis's poems have clarity of diction and syntax, use traditional forms and METRE, and are morally evaluative. He has also edited a selection of TRAHERNE's writings (1980), written *Wisdom and Wilderness: The Achievement of Yvor Winters* (1983) and with his wife, Alkham Darbandi, translated *The Conference of the Birds* (1984) from a 12th-century Persian religious ALLEGORY by Farid Attar.

Davis, Jack (Leonard) 1917– Australian playwright and poet. Born in Perth, he was director of its Aboriginal centre in 1967–71 and has actively supported Aboriginal political and cultural causes. He is – with MUDROOROO (Colin Johnson) and OODGEROO (Kath Walker) – one of the few prominent Aboriginal authors who express themselves in print rather than orally. He draws much from the traditions of his own people, the Nyoongarah of the south-west of Western Australia, but writes in English. The central motif in his work is a pride in being Aboriginal and a belief that his people can restore much of their cultural dignity in a contemporary Australia that will itself be enriched by this renewed infusion. The poetry in *The Firstborn* (1970), *Jagardoo (Poems from Aboriginal Australia)* (1978), *John Pat and Other Poems* (1988) and *Black Life: Poems* (1992) expresses Aboriginal attitudes in a direct and personal manner. He is best known, however, as a playwright. *Kullark (Home)* (1979) portrays the devastating impact of European settlers on traditional Nyoongarah life, and *The Dreamers* (1982) the squalor of contemporary Aboriginal life, contrasted with nostalgia for the past. *No Sugar* (1985), *Barungin: Smell the Wind* (1989) and *Our Town* (1990) continue the re-vision of Aboriginal history.

Davis [Davys], John ?1550–1605 Davis was a navigator and explorer, one of the many who made attempts to discover the Northwest Passage. On one such trip in 1587 he established friendly relations with the Eskimos. Seeking a passage through the Straits of Magellan he discovered the Falkland Islands in 1592. Davis commanded one of the ships sent against the Armada and sailed with RALEIGH to the Azores and Cadiz. He was killed by Japanese pirates on a voyage to the Indies. *The Seaman's Secret* (1595) is a treatise on navigation and *The World's Hydrographical Description* (1595) deals with the Northwest Passage.

Davis, Rebecca (Blane) Harding 1831–1910 American novelist and short-story writer. Much of her fiction is set in her native Philadelphia, including her best-known story, 'Life in the Iron Mills' (published in THE ATLANTIC MONTHLY in 1861), which portrays the frustrated and tragic life of Hugh Wolfe, a furnace-tender in an industrial mill, and his cousin Deborah, who brings herself to ruin when she tries to help him. One of the earliest exponents of the American realist school, Davis again portrayed the bleak lives of industrial workers in her novel *Margaret Howth* (1862), and of blacks in *Waiting for the Verdict* (1868). *John Andross* (1874) is a tale about political corruption.

Davis, Richard Harding 1864–1916 American journalist, novelist, short-story writer and playwright – one of the most prolific and popular writers of his day. Born in Philadelphia, the son of REBECCA HARDING DAVIS, he became at a young age one of the leading journalists in America. In 1890 he was appointed managing editor of *Harper's Weekly*, and his travels in that capacity provided the material for *The West from a Car Window* (1892), *The Rulers of the Mediterranean* (1893), *Our English Cousins* (1894), *About Paris* (1895) and *Three Gringos in Venezuela and Central America* (1896). His subsequent experiences as a war correspondent gave rise to *Cuba in War Time* (1897), *A Year from a Reporter's Note-Book* (1898), *The Cuban and Porto Rican Campaigns* (1898), *With Both Armies in South Africa* (1900), *Notes of a War Correspondent* (1910), *With the Allies* (1914) and *With the French in France and Salonika* (1916).

Davis also published over 80 short stories, seven novels and 25 plays – successful in their day, though quickly forgotten. His novels include *Soldiers of Fortune* (1897; dramatized in collaboration with AUGUSTUS THOMAS, 1902), *The Bar Sinister* (1903) and *Vera the Medium* (1908). *Ranson's Folly* (1902) and *Miss Civilization* (1905) were among his most popular plays.

Davis, Thomas (Osborne) 1814–45 Irish poet and journalist. Posthumous son of an English army doctor and an Irish mother, Davis was born in Mallow and educated at Trinity College, Dublin. He was called to the Bar in 1837 but made his living chiefly by writing. Despite Protestant Tory antecedents and later Benthamite leanings he emerged in the early 1840s as the leading literary exponent of romantic nationalism in verse and prose. Much of his writing first appeared in *The Nation*, the patriotic newspaper he helped to found in 1842. Despite the historically well-informed reasonableness of his essays, stressing English and Scottish as well as Gaelic ingredients in Irish nationality, his verse could be bombastic and even racialist in its attempt to provide new songs and BALLADS popularizing the spirit and sentiment of the old Gaelic tradition. His political fervour as much as his poetry deeply influenced later poets such as YEATS, who commended his 'moral radiance', and PATRICK PEARSE, who saw him as one of the four evangelists of Irish separatism. His best work, such as his poetic 'Lament for Eoghan Ruadh O'Neill' and *The Patriot Parliament of 1689* (1843), explores the disasters and achievements of the Irish past as a stirring commentary on present possibilities.

Dawe, (Donald) Bruce 1930– Australian poet. Born at Geelong in Victoria, he left school at an early age and held a variety of jobs, including farmhand and copyboy. Later he became a lecturer at Toowomba in Queensland. His inventive, witty poems use the everyday structures of Australian speech with new resourcefulness and achieve a simple nobility. 'Drifters' and 'Homecoming', an elegy for the dead of the Vietnam War, are well known. Collections include *No Fixed Address* (1962), *A Need of Similar Name* (1965), *An Eye for a Tooth* (1968), *Beyond the Subdivision* (1969), *Heatwave* (1970), *Condolences of the Season* (1971), *Just a Dugong at Twilight* (1975), *Sometimes Gladness: Bruce Dawe. Collected Poems 1954–1978* (1978), *Towards Sunrise: Poems 1979–1986* (1986) and *This Side of Silence: Poems 1978–90* (1990). He has also published *Over Here, Harv and Other Stories* (1983) and *Bruce Dawe: Essays and Opinions* (1990).

Day, Clarence (Shepard) 1874–1935 American humorist. The son of a stockbroker, he was born in New York City and educated at Yale. He served in the US Navy during the Spanish-American War, then worked as a businessman in New York, and eventually became a regular writer for THE NEW YORKER. He is best known for his autobiographical writings, which include *God and My Father* (1932), *Life with Father* (1935), *Life with Mother* (1937) and *Father and I* (1940) – all characterized by their humorous examination of upper-class life in 19th-century New York. *Life with Father* was dramatized in 1939 by Howard Lindsay and Russel Crouse, and became a long-running success. Day's other publications include *This Simian World* (1920), *Thoughts without Words* (1928), *In the Green Mountain Country* (1934), *Scenes from the Mesozoic and Other Drawings* (1935) and *The Crow's Nest* (1921), which was enlarged in 1936 as *After All*.

Day, John 1574–1640 Playwright and poet. Born in Norfolk and educated at school in Ely and at Gonville and Caius College, Cambridge, Day was active in the London theatre for a decade after 1598, initially as one of PHILIP HENSLOWE's circle of writers. Of six extant plays in which he is known to have had a hand, four are probably his alone. They are: *Law Tricks* (1604) and *The Isle of Gulls* (1606), satiric comedies written for BOYS' COMPANIES; the attractive *Humour out of Breath* (c. 1608); and the pastoral dialogues of *The Parliament of Bees* (published in 1641), which exhibits Day's poetic skills at their most fanciful. With HENRY CHETTLE, Day wrote *The Blind Beggar of Bednal-Green* (1600) and with WILLIAM ROWLEY and George Wilkins the patriotic picaresque piece *The Travails of the Three English Brothers* (1607), based on the adventures of the extraordinary Shirley family. This play contains an interesting scene in which the Shakespearean clown WILL KEMP exhibits his skills, though it is not known whether Day was the author of it. THE PARNASSUS PLAYS have also been attributed to him.

Day, Thomas 1748–89 Educationalist and writer of CHILDREN'S LITERATURE. Born in London of wealthy parents and educated at Oxford, Day was an early, eccentric disciple of Rousseau. Attempting to bring up two orphan girls on the lines laid down in Emile with a view to marrying the more apt pupil, Day eventually chose a more conventional heiress when neither of his protegees wished to fall in with his scheme. In 1783 he wrote the first part of *The History of Sandford and Merton*, the second part following in 1786 and the final instalment in 1789. Totally didactic in purpose, the story followed the lives of Tommy Merton, the idle son of a rich gentleman, and Harry Sandford, the industrious son of a hardworking farmer. Tommy always does everything wrong, a

point in no danger of being lost on the good Harry, ever on hand to set a better example. This unlikely tale became a best-seller during the next century, although it was probably always more popular with parents than with children. Day subsequently wrote another moral tale, *The History of Little Jack* (1788), about a child suckled by goats and raised by a God-fearing old man before returning to civilization to make his fortune.

Day of Doom, The A didactic poem by MICHAEL WIGGLESWORTH, published in 1662. Subtitled 'A Poetical Description of the Great and Last Judgement', it describes how God rewards the virtuous sheep with eternal life and condemns the sinful goats to eternal damnation. Cast in BALLAD lines of seven feet, it was easily memorized and was soon selected to supplement the catechism in the education of the young American Puritan: within a year of the first printing all 1800 copies had been sold, which suggests that one out of 35 New Englanders owned the poem by 1663. During the next 100 years it was reprinted frequently, and found its way into virtually all Puritan homes.

Day-Lewis, C(ecil) 1904–72 Poet and writer of DETECTIVE FICTION. Born in Ballintubber, now in the Republic of Ireland, he was educated at Sherborne School and Wadham College, Oxford. At Oxford he first came into contact with W. H. AUDEN and the group of young poets around him. He worked reluctantly as a teacher in private schools until 1935, when he became a freelance writer. Of all the left-wing Auden group he was the only one to join and be active in the Communist Party, from 1935 until 1938. His first mature collections, *Transitional Poem* (1929) and *From Feathers to Iron* (1931), are lyric sequences, and in *The Magnetic Mountain* (1933) and *A Time to Dance* (1935), there is a clash between his Marxist politics and his tendency to Romanticism. *Overtures to a Death* (1938) contains his best political poems, 'Newsreel' and 'The Bombers'. Despite *An Italian Visit* (1953), with its chatty, travelogue poems, and *Collected Poems* (1954), his reputation declined after the war, as the intriguing conflicts of his Marxist poems were replaced by the dry formalism of *Pegasus* (1957), *The Gate* (1962) and *The Room* (1965). Increasing respectability brought many honours: he delivered the Clark lectures at Cambridge in 1946 (published as *The Poetic Image* the following year), served as professor of poetry at Oxford in 1951–6 and was appointed POET LAUREATE in 1968 after the death of JOHN MASEFIELD. His collection *The Whispering Roots* (1970), if unexciting, showed that public office had not dimmed his skill. *The Poems of C. Day-Lewis 1925–1972* appeared in 1977. He also made verse translations of Virgil, with *The Georgics* (1941), *The Aeneid* (1952) and *The Eclogues* (1952). Under the pseudonym of Nicholas Blake he made a distinguished contribution to detective fiction with some 20 novels, beginning with *A Question of Proof* (1935). Their hero Nigel Strangeways was originally modelled on Auden. *The Buried Day* (1960) is a volume of autobiography.

De Boissière, Ralph 1907– Trinidadian novelist of French Creole descent. Born and educated in Trinidad, he became involved in trade union activity and was a member of the influential Beacon Group, which helped to promote a sense of local cultural identity. The best of his novels, published in Australia after he migrated there in 1948, is *Crown Jewel* (1952), long neglected but successfully republished in 1981. Set in Trinidad on the eve of World War II, when the colonial presence is concealing injustices on a huge scale, it deals with political aspirations and popular culture. Later novels are *Rum and Coca-Cola* (1956), a sequel to *Crown Jewel*, and *No Saddles for Kangaroos* (1964), about the attempt to suppress the Communist Party in Australia. He has been compared to the masters of Russian fiction, whom he greatly admired, but his historical sensitivity is firmly rooted in the Caribbean.

De Forest, John W. 1826–1906 American novelist. Born in Connecticut, he went to live in Syria when ill health prevented him from attending college. He began to write after his return to the USA. His *History of the Indians of Connecticut* (1851) was marked by a strict objectivity which later became a characteristic of his fiction. *Miss Ravenel's Conversion from Secession to Loyalty* (1867), a romance set during the Civil War and Reconstruction, includes grimly realistic battle scenes which anticipate those of STEPHEN CRANE. Among De Forest's later novels are *Kate Beaumont* (1872), about South Carolina plantation society, and *Honest John Vane* (1875), a SATIRE of political corruption. His Civil War memoirs, *A Volunteer's Adventures*, appeared posthumously in 1946; *A Union Officer in the Reconstruction* followed in 1948.

De Jong, Meindert 1906– American writer of CHILDREN'S LITERATURE. Born in Holland, he emigrated with his family to America at the age of eight. But his best book, *The Wheel on the School* (1954), is set in his native country and describes how a group of Dutch schoolchildren plan to entice a stork back to nest on the roof of their school – a traditional sign of good fortune. By contrast, *The House of Sixty Fathers* (1956) memorably describes the plight of an abandoned Chinese boy during World War II, drawing on the author's experiences as a war historian in the Far East. Subsequent novels have returned to a Dutch setting: *Far out the Long Canal* (1964) deals with a village frozen up during the winter and *Journey from Peppermint Street* (1968) is a lovingly detailed account of a boy's trip through North Holland on a visit to relatives.

de la Mare, Walter 1873–1956 Poet, writer of CHILDREN'S LITERATURE and anthologist. Born at Charlton, Kent, and educated at St Paul's Choir School, he worked for an oil company, and wrote poems for children, and poems about childhood for adults. His first volume, *Songs of Childhood*, was published in 1902 under the pseudonym Walter Ramal. Eighteen further volumes, including five of collected poems, were published before the definitive *The Complete Poems of Walter de la Mare* (1969). The best-known single volumes are *Peacock Pie: A Book of Rhymes* (1913), *Memory and Other Poems* (1938), *The Burning Glass and Other Poems* (1945) and *Winged Chariot* (1951). His lyrical poems of childhood and fantasy use a great variety of verse forms, and were described by EDWARD THOMAS as 'the most original featherweight poetry of our time'. His volumes of short stories include *Broomsticks* (1925), *The Lord Fish* (1933) and *The Scarecrow* (1945). His main anthologies are *Come Hither* (1923), for children; *Behold This Dreamer* (1939); and *Love* (1943). De la Mare also published three novels, *Henry Brocken* (1904), *The Return* (1910) and *Memoirs of a Midget* (1921); critical works on RUPERT BROOKE and LEWIS CARROLL; and an edition of CHRISTINA ROSSETTI. He is buried in St Paul's Cathedral.

de la Roche, Mazo 1879–1961 Canadian novelist. Born in Toronto, she grew up on a fruit farm in Ontario. This experience gave her the background and setting for her novels, best characterized as regional idylls. Her early works, *Explorers of the Dawn* (1922), *Possession* (1923) and *Delight* (1926), attracted little attention, but *Jalna* (1927), set in an old house of that name, won *The Atlantic Monthly*'s $10,000 prize. Its sequel, *The Whiteoaks of Jalna* (1929), continued her success and another 14 novels were eventually added to the series. She also wrote CHILDREN'S LITERATURE, one-act plays, historical studies and an autobiography, *Ringing the Changes* (1957). The romantic and optimistic character of her works ensured their popularity for some time.

De Lisser, H(erbert) G(eorge) 1878–1944 Jamaican novelist. Of mixed Portuguese, Jewish and African descent, he was born in Falmouth. For many years he edited *The Daily Gleaner*, Jamaica's leading newspaper, and played a prominent part in public life, chairing the Institute of Jamaica, helping to found the Jamaica Imperial Association and, when his youthful liberalism had yielded to staunch conservatism, opposing the nationalist movement. The most popular Jamaican novelist of his day, he mainly wrote historical romances about such subjects as *obeah* (magic) and piracy. The best-known, *The White*

Witch of Rosehall (1929), was based on Annie Palmer, a 19th-century white Creole plantation owner. Only occasionally, as in his most highly regarded novel, *Jane's Career* (1914), or *Susan Proudleigh* (1915) and *Under the Sun* (1937), did he turn his attention to contemporary society. Other novels include: *Triumphant Squalitone* (1917); *Revenge* (1919), about the 1865 Morant Bay rebellion; *Psyche* (1952); and *Morgan's Daughter* (1953). From 1920 he edited *Planter's Punch*, an annual in which he published a full-length novel of his own each year. His non-fiction includes *In Jamaica and Cuba* (1910) and *Twentieth-Century Jamaica* (1913).

de Morgan, William (Frend) 1839–1917 Artist and novelist. Born in London, he attended University College, London, and studied at the Royal Academy School. A friend and colleague of WILLIAM MORRIS in the Arts and Crafts Movement, he made stained glass and, after 1870, the decorative tiles for which he is still remembered. Only in retirement did he turn to writing, achieving considerable success with *Joseph Vance* (1906) and eight more novels; the last two were completed by his wife, the artist Evelyn de Morgan. Digressive and reminiscential, they cast a Dickensian eye over the London of de Morgan's youth.

De Profundis An extended letter by OSCAR WILDE to LORD ALFRED DOUGLAS ('Bosie'), written during the author's imprisonment in Reading Gaol. It complains of Bosie's selfishness, shallowness, parasitism, greed, extravagance, tantrums, pettiness and neglect, while praising the selfless devotion of Robert Ross ('Robbie'). Ross, who became Wilde's literary executor, gave the work its present title (from the opening line of Psalm 130) and published an edited version in 1905. A fuller text appeared in 1949.

De Quincey, Thomas 1785–1859 Essayist and critic. The son of a linen merchant, he was born in Manchester and received his first education from one of the guardians appointed after his father's death in 1793. From 1796 he lived with his mother at Bath, where he attended the grammar school and quickly acquired a reputation as an outstanding classicist. Following a trivial accident he was moved to an inferior school at Winkfield, Wiltshire, where he lost interest in formal education, and then to Manchester Grammar School from which he ran away in July 1802. Two years earlier he had first read LYRICAL BALLADS and now thought of presenting himself to WORDSWORTH in the Lake District, but decided that he could in the circumstances hardly expect to make a favourable impression on his hero and embarked instead on a tour of Wales. Completely destitute, he reached London in November, suffered extreme deprivations and befriended a young prostitute named Ann. The story of this London venture is told in the first part of the CONFESSIONS OF AN ENGLISH OPIUM EATER.

In March 1803 he was reconciled with his mother and guardians, and in December he entered Worcester College, Oxford. He read voraciously, made few friends at college and frequently absented himself to London, where in 1804 he first took opium to alleviate a prolonged attack of facial neuralgia. He experimented intermittently and secretly with the drug over the next nine years. He had begun a correspondence with Wordsworth in 1803, and in the summers of 1805 and 1806 travelled to the Lakes in order to visit him, but was on each occasion overcome at the last moment by feelings of his own inadequacy which forced him to turn back. A similar diffidence seems to have caused him to absent himself from the second part of his final examinations at Oxford in the spring of 1808, when success seemed certain.

In August 1806 he came of age and inherited a modest sum which he soon spent, largely on books. He also made an anonymous loan of £300 to COLERIDGE, whom he met in Bridgwater in the summer of 1807 and through whom he finally met Wordsworth at Dove Cottage, Grasmere, the first encounter leaving very favourable impressions on both parties, and on DOROTHY WORDSWORTH. He now became totally devoted to his new friends, and when they moved to Allan Bank he took over the lease of Dove Cottage, which he held until 1834. The next few years were devoted to reading, social life and the performance of literary services for Wordsworth and Coleridge. Anticipating the exhaustion of his private means, he made a desultory attempt in 1812–15 to obtain legal qualifications. By 1813 he was a confirmed opium-addict, which estranged him from the Wordsworths, who also looked with disfavour on his affair with Margaret Simpson, a local farmer's daughter, whom he married in 1817, following the birth of a son in November 1816.

But for the need to support a family, De Quincey might never have become a writer. His work consisted almost entirely of contributions to magazines, and was collected only in the last years of his life in the 14-volume *Selections Grave and Gay from Writings Published and Unpublished* (1853–60). From 1821 to 1824 he wrote mainly for THE LONDON MAGAZINE, where *Confessions of an English Opium Eater* appeared in 1821, bringing him immediate notoriety and recognition. His 48 pieces for the periodical are remarkably varied both in quality and character, and include articles on Goethe, Herder, Richter, MALTHUS, Rosicrucians and Freemasons, English and German dictionaries, education, and one of his best critical essays, *On the Knocking at the Gate in Macbeth*. Following the demise of *The London Magazine* he turned to Edinburgh, and with the appearance of the first part of his article on Lessing in BLACKWOOD'S EDINBURGH MAGAZINE in November 1826 began the association which was to produce some of his best work in the next 23 years, including his long historical series entitled *The Caesars, The Last Days of Immanuel Kant*, an important article *Rhetoric*, and one of his humorous masterpieces, ON MURDER CONSIDERED AS ONE OF THE FINE ARTS. His GOTHIC NOVEL, *Klosterheim*, appeared as a separate volume in 1832.

Despite his productivity, De Quincey led a hand-to-mouth existence: he was briefly imprisoned for debt in 1832, forced into bankruptcy in 1833 and even harassed by creditors at the funeral of his son Julius in September of the same year. He now switched to *Tait's Edinburgh Magazine* in which he began publishing the 'Sketches... from the Autobiography of an English Opium Eater' (later entitled *Autobiographic Sketches*), and RECOLLECTIONS OF THE LAKES AND THE LAKE POETS (1834–9), which effectively set the seal on his alienation from Wordsworth, Coleridge and SOUTHEY. *The Revolt of the Tartars* (1837), the uncompleted series *Suspiria de Profundis* (1845) with its magnificent dream-visions, and the two remarkable articles on *The Glory of Motion* and *The Vision of Sudden Death*, which make up *The English Mail Coach* (1849), appeared with *Blackwood's*, which also published his book, *The Logic of Political Economy* (1844); for *Tait's* he wrote an account of his gradual estrangement from Wordsworth and a criticism of his poetry, as well as articles on GODWIN, HAZLITT, SHELLEY, KEATS and POPE.

De sapientia veterum A Latin treatise by FRANCIS BACON, published in 1609 and translated into English by SIR ARTHUR GORGES as *The Wisdom of the Ancients* in 1619. Like many Renaissance philosophers, Bacon believed that the Greek myths formed a repository of ancient wisdom concerning the phenomena of the physical world and the principles of human nature that had been coded into their narrative. Like the parables of the Bible, the fables of the myths relate an engaging story that pleases the common hearer, but communicates also a knowledge of profounder matters to a philosophic audience. The Greeks, Bacon maintained, had known many of the secrets of nature that were coming to light again in his own time; the Egyptians too had possessed much secret wisdom that they had recorded in their hieroglyphic inscriptions. In *De sapientia veterum* Bacon attempted to interpret a number of the most notable fables to reveal their esoteric content. The story of Cupid is read as an allegory of the atomistic nature of matter and of the causes of motion in the physical world. Proteus tells of the properties of matter and of the transformations that matter may undergo. Pan describes the state of nature and the unity of the natural world beneath the variety of appearances. The Orpheus myth hints at the civilizing effects of philosophy: 'persuasion and eloquence insinuate the love of virtue, equity and con-

cord in the minds of men' and inspire the achievements of high culture. These achievements are destroyed by the vicissitudes of time, though they may with difficulty be restored. Proserpina explains the perpetual fertility of the earth. Other myths provide evidence of the profound knowledge of political behaviour and of the difficulties of the moral life possessed by the poets of antiquity and preserved in their fictions. The work now serves as a useful key for deciphering the meaning of mythological figures in Renaissance art and poetry.

De Vere, Aubrey Thomas 1814–1902 Irish poet and essayist. The son of another poet, Sir Aubrey de Vere, he was born at Curragh Chase in County Limerick and educated at Trinity College, Dublin. In England he became a close friend of TENNYSON and BROWNING. His conversion to Roman Catholicism in 1851 was followed in 1854 by his appointment as professor of social and political science at the new Catholic University in Dublin, where NEWMAN was rector. De Vere's works include *The Waldenses and Other Poems* (1842), *English Misrule and Irish Misdeeds* (1848) and three volumes of *Critical Essays* (1887–9). His *Recollections* appeared in 1897.

Death and the King's Horseman A play by WOLE SOYINKA, published in 1975. It is based on events which took place in Oyo, Western Nigeria, in 1944, when the British authorities intervened in a customary burial ritual observing the death of the Alafin of Oyo to prevent his faithful servant, the Master of Horse, following his master by committing suicide. After the British Resident had the Horseman arrested, the Alafin's son fulfilled the servant's role by killing himself. Soyinka uses these events to explore both Nigerian/Yoruban religious belief and the arrogance of the British administration.

Death Comes for the Archbishop A novel by WILLA CATHER, published in 1927. It is based on the careers of two French missionaries, Jean-Baptiste Lamy and Joseph Machebeuf, who worked in the New Mexico territory in the mid 19th century.

Bishop Jean Latour arrives in the New Mexico territory shortly after it has been annexed by the USA. With his vicar, Father Joseph Vaillant, who is also his long-time friend, he establishes a new diocese. Latour is withdrawn and ascetic; Vaillant is practical, vigorous and cheerful. Together they overcome the persistence with which the native Navajo and Hopi Indians cling to their ancient superstitions, and they confront the antagonism of the corrupt Mexican priests already present in the territory. They establish mission schools in remote areas and, after some years, succeed in building a cathedral at Santa Fe.

The cathedral is the outer symbol of the achievement of these two devoted men – of their success in adapting an Old World religion to the New World. Though Latour brings two architects from France to design the cathedral, it is very much inspired by the landscape of the Southwest, a landscape Cather vividly evokes for her readers. Shortly after gold is discovered at Pike's Peak, Vaillant becomes bishop in Colorado, and the two friends part. Later, Latour is made an archbishop. Vaillant is the first to die, and the novel closes with Latour's own death, mourned by all in his diocese, Mexicans, Indians and Americans alike.

Death of a Salesman A play by ARTHUR MILLER, first performed and published in 1949. It won instant critical acclaim, running for 742 performances at the Morosco Theatre in New York and winning both the PULITZER PRIZE and the New York Drama Critics Circle Award.

It relates the tragic story of a salesman named Willy Loman, who is not the great success that he claims to be to his family and friends. After 35 years on the road trying to earn money and recognition, and measuring his own worth by the volume of his sales, Willy has begun to lose his way on trips and to run off the side of the road in his car. His devoted wife Linda and his two grown sons, Biff and Happy, who are home for a visit, worry about him. He is eventually fired because he no longer brings in the business that he used to when he was younger. He begins to hallucinate about significant events from his past: he remembers encouraging his sons to lie if it helped them to be successful and well liked; he recalls the pathetic scene of being discovered with a prostitute by his older son, who arrives unexpectedly at his hotel room seeking fatherly advice; he has imaginary conversations with his successful brother Ben. Finally, deciding that he is worth more dead than alive (the insurance money will support his family and help Biff get a new start in life), he kills himself in his car on a last trip. Critics have disagreed whether his suicide is meant to be seen as a last desperate and tragic assertion of the American dream or as an act of cowardice and selfishness.

Death of the Heart, The A novel by ELIZABETH BOWEN, published in 1938. A sensitive study of adolescence, it shows the influence of HENRY JAMES, particularly *WHAT MAISIE KNEW*, but does not suffer by the comparison.

After her father's death Portia Quayne, an innocent and emotionally vulnerable girl, has spent her childhood in dreary hotels with her mother Irene. When Irene dies Portia, then 16, is sent to London under the care of her half-brother Thomas and his wife Anna. They are a sophisticated couple, unable to cope with the terrifying honesty of Portia's emotional life and ill-equipped to show real warmth or understanding. Her only ally is an elderly female servant, Matchett,

inherited along with the furniture after old Quayne's death.

Enrolled at a private academy, Portia befriends Lilian and falls in love with Eddie, an admirer of Anna's, who in his conceited but despairing way encourages her to depend upon him. Unknown to Portia, Anna has already discovered her diary, a naive but searching account of the shallow lives around her. The girl's misplaced trust in Eddie prompts her to show him her diary, over which he and Anna gain much mirth. During a holiday on the South Coast, she is shaken when Eddie flirts with Daphne Heccomb, the daughter of the house. Portia's blind faith in him is destroyed completely when she later learns how her diary has been used. In desperation she flees to the hotel room of Major Brutt, a sympathetic but equally helpless acquaintance. She refuses to return home unless Thomas and Anna 'do the right thing'. After deliberating what this might be, they decide that the right thing to do is to dispatch Matchett to bring her back.

Death's Jest-Book: or, the Fool's Tragedy A play by THOMAS LOVELL BEDDOES, begun in 1825, continually revised and posthumously published in 1850. No less than three versions exist in manuscript. A REVENGE TRAGEDY in the Jacobean manner, its convoluted plot centres on two brothers, Wolfram and Isbrand, who enter the service of Duke Melveric in order to pursue their vengeance against him for the death of their father and the dishonour of their sister. Apart from its macabre atmosphere, the play is striking for some fine BLANK VERSE and some lyrics influenced by SHELLEY, notably the song 'Dream Pedlary' and the dirges for Sibilla and Wolfram.

debate poem Medieval poetic tradition in which opposed parties contest one or more issues. The debate form is very old, dating back to Plato and the Old Testament. Boethius' *De consolatione Philosophiae* provided the most popular philosophical debate of the Middle Ages, and the form was also very common in secular Latin poetry. In the vernacular it was used for both serious and humorous ends. Often the opposed characters are animals, birds, inanimate objects or allegorical personifications, and the subject of debate ranges from spiritual problems (see *VICES AND VIRTUES*) to personal relationships (*De Clerico et Puella*) and petty squabbling covering a variety of topics (*THE OWL AND THE NIGHTINGALE*). The form was used for political ALLEGORY and SATIRE (as in *WYNNERE AND WASTOURE*), for serious philosophical debate and for humour; *The Owl and the Nightingale* is a brilliant comic use of the genre. The debate may be inconclusive or it may be resolved by a third party. A related form is the parliament involving more than two participants (see *THE PARLIAMENT OF THE THREE AGES*, *THE PARLEMENT OF FOULES*).

Decline and Fall The first novel by EVELYN WAUGH, published in 1928.

It recounts the 'decline and fall' of Paul Pennyfeather, a theology undergraduate at Oxford when the story begins. Debagged by fellow students, Paul is caught running through the quadrangle of 'Scone College' and sent down for indecent behaviour. He becomes a schoolmaster at Llanabba Castle, a small boarding school in Wales hopelessly administered by an outrageous staff which includes Mr Prendergast, a former clergyman, and Captain Grimes, a one-legged drunkard who commits bigamy with the headmaster's daughter, Flossie Fagan. Paul is taken up by the sophisticated and wealthy Margot Beste-Chetwynde, mother of Peter, one of Paul's pupils. He is offered and accepts the position of private tutor to Peter, and is initiated into Margot's high-society life in Mayfair and at King's Thursday, a 'modernized' Tudor mansion. She and Paul become engaged, but he finds himself under arrest for having unwittingly involved himself in her activities in the white-slave trade. Tried and convicted, Paul is sentenced to seven years in prison – a natural enough environment, he feels, for anyone brought up in an English public school. There he finds Captain Grimes, a fellow prisoner, and Prendergast, now the prison chaplain. Shortly after his confinement, however, Margot engineers Paul's escape and he is transported to her villa in Corfu. At the end of the novel he returns as a very distant cousin of Paul Pennyfeather – and bearing his own name – to resume his studies at Oxford.

Decline and Fall of the Roman Empire, The History of the EDWARD GIBBON's great work of classical history was published in three instalments: vol. 1 in 1776, vols. 2 and 3 in 1783, and vols. 4, 5 and 6 in 1788. These correspond to the major divisions in his narrative, which covers more than 13 centuries: from Trajan and the age of the Antonines to the reign of Constantine; from the foundation of Constantinople to the Western Empire of Charlemagne; from the revival of the Western (Holy Roman) Empire to the long history of the Eastern (Byzantine) Empire and the capture of Constantinople by the Turks in 1453. Gibbon examines the encroachment of the Teutonic tribes who eventually held the Western Empire in fee, the rise of Islam, and the Crusades. He looks backward in history to illuminate the period of his work and forward from it to show what has been its legacy.

The Decline and Fall is a model of clarity and completeness, as accurate as the condition of historical research in Gibbon's day could make it. He is scrupulous in acknowledging his sources, and only in respect of available knowledge has he been superseded. The vast subject is finely organized, the narrative power unflagging, and the viewpoint elegantly detached – nowhere more so than in the sceptical treatment of Christianity, which provoked much contemporary criticism.

deconstruction Practice of reading which owes its development mainly to the writings of Jacques Derrida (1930–). His paper 'Structure, Sign, and Play' (1966) inaugurated a new critical movement in the United States (especially at Yale University).

Key Derridean concepts include 'presence', 'logocentrism', 'phonocentrism', 'supplement' and 'differance'. Since Plato, Western thought has used various concepts – such as 'substance', 'essence', 'end', 'cause', 'form', 'being' and so on – in order to centre discourses and to permit distinctions between truth and falsehood. Logocentrism is the desire for a centre. This principle involves the privileging of one term over another. For example, speech, in Rousseau and others, is placed hierarchically above writing. This particular 'violent hierarchy' is called 'phonocentrism' (centring on the voice). The deconstructor begins by reversing the hierarchy (writing before speech) and then by displacing the new hierarchy, thus leaving a certain indeterminacy in the particular discursive field. The term 'differance' describes the process which prevents signs from achieving a full 'presence'. 'Differance' in French combines two meanings: to 'differ' and to 'defer'. Signs acquire meanings within a system of differences, and at the same time meaning is deferred by the endless chain of signifiers which is generated as soon as we begin to interpret. The 'supplement' describes the unstable relationship which exists between terms like 'speech' and 'writing'. One term both takes the place of and supplements the other.

The Yale deconstructors include Barbara Johnson, Paul de Man, Geoffrey Hartman and J. Hillis Miller. Johnson has written excellent essays on Barthes, Derrida and Lacan. She deconstructs POE's 'The Purloined Letter' via a reading of Derrida's deconstruction of Lacan's reading of the story, showing that both readings of Poe unconsciously privilege particular concepts. De Man's work (e.g. *Blindness and Insight*, 1971 and *Allegories of Reading*, 1979) explores the way rhetoric (especially figurative language) prevents discourse from unequivocally referring to things or communicating meanings. Criticism itself is caught up in the same figurative dislocation of meaning. Critical commentary is always allegory: it stands in the place of another discourse. De Man also believes that literary texts are 'self-deconstructing', and that therefore the critic has only to collude with the text's own literary processes. Hartman takes to an extreme the post-structuralist view of criticism as an activity within literature. He combines a fondness for verbal play and a reluctance to abandon the humanistic tradition of anglophone criticism. Hillis Miller preserves some of the rigorous textualism of his New Critical phase, which was followed by a period of phenomenological criticism. However, he accepted Derrida's criticism of the former critical methods' faith in the stability and unity of text or consciousness. His recent work explores the unpredictability and heterogeneity of literary language.

Deeping, (George) Warwick 1877–1950 Novelist. Born in Southend, he was educated at the Merchant Taylors' School in London and at Trinity College, Cambridge, where he read science and medicine, finishing his medical training at the Middlesex Hospital. A prolific writer, he produced 70 novels and five volumes of short stories, which attempt to keep alive the idea and spirit of Edwardian Britain. Early novels like *Uther and Igraine* (1903), *Bertrand of Brittany* (1908) and *The Red Saint* (1909) were popular historical romances. Deeping's experiences in the Royal Army Medical Corps during World War I were the inspiration for his most famous work, *Sorrell and Son* (1925), the moving story of Captain Sorrell trying to make a life for his young son Kit in severely reduced circumstances. Later novels included *Old Pybus* (1928), *Corn in Egypt* (1941) and *The Laughing House* (1947).

Deerslayer, The See LEATHERSTOCKING TALES, THE.

Defence of Guenevere and Other Poems, The The first collection of verse by WILLIAM MORRIS, published in 1858. The title poem and the three which follow it represent the beginning of a projected cycle based on ARTHURIAN LITERATURE. It was probably TENNYSON's publication of *IDYLLS OF THE KING* in 1859, coupled with the harsh critical judgement of *The Defence of Guenevere* as 'Pre-Raphaelite minstrelsy', which dissuaded Morris from continuing his cycle. The larger part of the other poems in the collection are either taken from or based on the chronicles of Jean Froissart. A third group reflects Morris's interest in the worlds of dream and fantasy, deriving from his childhood reveries and reading of the Romantics. Two of these poems, 'The Blue Closet' and 'The Tune of Seven Towers', were written in imaginative juxtaposition with watercolours by DANTE GABRIEL ROSSETTI.

Defence of Poetry, The An essay by SHELLEY, written in Italy in 1821 and posthumously published in *Essays, Letters from Abroad, Translations and Fragments*, edited by MARY SHELLEY (1840). Shelley's most famous prose work is an amplification of arguments first advanced in earlier essays and prefaces, notably the first two chapters of *A Philosophical View of Reform* (1820), and was written as a rejoinder to his friend THOMAS LOVE PEACOCK's *The Four Ages of Poetry* which had appeared in Charles Ollier's *Literary Miscellany* (1820). Somewhat tongue-in-cheek,

Peacock had suggested that since poetry had degenerated into the pursuit of a sort of pseudo-simplicity, the brightest talents of the age would be far more usefully employed in the new sciences of economics and political and social theory, which could help to improve the world.

Shelley's use of 'poetry' is inclusive, referring to literature as a genre *per se*, imaginative writing in general, and poetry considered as a human faculty. The essay is essentially aimed against UTILITARIAN definitions of value and happiness accompanying the growth of industrial culture. Poetry is the 'expression of the Imagination', whose unifying and synthesizing operations are distinguished from Reason's neutral observation of differences and calculation with known quantities. In a rapid review of classical and European literature Shelley discusses the characteristic features of poetic thought and inspiration, the problems of literary translation, the function of erotic writing in periods of social decline and the wider connections between poetry and politics.

The case for the 'Defence' as a whole rests on the role of poetry as a force for social freedom and creative eros. The modern age, as Shelley sees it, possessed more knowledge than it could cope with. The science of economics had not led to the 'just distribution of the produce which it multiplies', while the question of meaning was subordinated to the 'accumulation of facts and calculating processes'. 'We want the creative faculty to imagine that which we know... we want the poety of life.' In burnished passages on CHAUCER, Dante and MILTON, he argues that, with their special capacity to sense connections between individual experience and social and intellectual change, poets both anticipated and provided the ideas by which subsequent ages lived. The celebrated (though often misunderstood) peroration hails them as unconscious 'ministers' of a benificent 'Power which is seated on the throne of their own soul', as 'mirrors of the gigantic shadows which futurity casts upon the present' and as 'the unacknowledged legislators of the World'.

Defoe, Daniel 1660–1731 Novelist, journalist and entrepreneur. Born in the year of the Restoration, the son of James Foe, a butcher of Stoke Newington, Daniel altered his surname to the more fashionable Defoe in 1703, the year he began depending on writing for his living. The Act of Uniformity was passed when he was two, and Defoe – a lifelong Presbyterian – was educated at Stoke Newington Academy, a school for Dissenters. He had a contemporary there by the name of Timothy Cruso. He went into trade and travelled extensively in Europe until his marriage in 1683 to Mary Tulfley, when he was a hosiery merchant in Cornhill. He took part in Monmouth's rebellion in 1685, but later became a supporter of William III, joining his army in 1688 – the first of several changes of allegiance that subsequently earned him a mercenary reputation.

Throughout his remarkably varied life, Defoe was fascinated by trade and mercantile projects. His first writing was on economics (the *Essay on Projects* of 1697) by which time he had gone bankrupt as a hosier, though in 1700 he started up a tile factory in Tilbury. His first literary success was *The True-Born Englishman* (1701), a satiric poem championing the cause of the foreign-born monarch, but (unusually among the famous writers of his period) he subsequently wrote little SATIRE. His skills in stylistic impersonation and IRONY, however, were superlative; in 1702 he published a pamphlet entitled *The Shortest Way with the Dissenters* in which Defoe (himself a Dissenter, and therefore in favour of religious toleration) mimicked the extreme attitudes of High Anglican Tories and pretended to argue for the extermination of all Dissenters. In the politically volatile atmosphere of the time the leaders of neither party were amused; the author was fined, imprisoned and pilloried, but it

Daniel Defoe: an engraving by J. Thomson

made him a popular hero. While in prison Defoe wrote a mock ODE, *Hymn to the Pillory* (1703).

His spell in prison put paid to his Tilbury project, and Defoe appears subsequently to have been wary of partisan affiliations in his politics. The politically moderate ROBERT HARLEY, EARL OF OXFORD, was astute enough to recognize the early propagandist potential of the press. In 1704 he helped Defoe to publish his first issue of THE REVIEW, a thrice-weekly newspaper which survived until 1713. Defoe contributed articles on an impressive variety of topics from the commercial to the moral, pioneering examples of the literary essay, which was emerging as one of the distinctive genres of the period. Harley began to employ him as an undercover field-agent, in particular monitoring activities in the North accompanying the Union with Scotland (1707), a clandestine occupation that suited Defoe's personality.

Defoe changed his allegiance once more in 1712, when the Tories were ousted by the Whigs, and he entered the service of Godolphin. His own political beliefs remained resolute, despite party changes. A committed anti-Jacobite, he published *Reasons against the Succession of the House of Hanover* (1712),

a satirical piece that was again mistaken by the authorities. He was imprisoned for treasonable publication, and *The Review* ceased publication. Defoe went on to edit *Mercator*, a trade journal, and in 1714 supported the notion of free trade in his *A General History of Trade*. After the death of Queen Anne and the accession of the Hanoverians, he became agent to Lord Townshend, the Whig Secretary of State, thereby escaping punishment for his libel against Lord Annesley. During this period he may have been operating in a double capacity as informer, reporter and monitor of events.

By 1720 Defoe had ceased to be politically controversial in his writings. *The Family Instructor* (1715–18) was a CONDUCT BOOK, *The History of the Wars of His Present Majesty Charles XII King of Sweden*, *Memoirs of the Church of Scotland* (1717) and *The Life and Death of Count Puktil* (1717) were all works of historical interest. His earliest venture into fiction had been *A True Relation of the Apparition of One Mrs Veal* (1706), an embroidered account of a current ghost story. No rigid barriers between fact, fiction or rumour were then considered important, but in his 60th year Defoe seems to have discovered a new well of talent for writing fictional narrative, and during the next five years he produced a flow of important books. They began with with ROBINSON CRUSOE and *The Farther Adventures of Robinson Crusoe* (1719), followed shortly by *The Serious Reflections... of Robinson Crusoe*, MEMOIRS OF A CAVALIER and CAPTAIN SINGLETON (1720), MOLL FLANDERS, *A JOURNAL OF THE PLAGUE YEAR* and COLONEL JACK (1722), and ROXANA (1724). As if these were not enough, he also produced: *The Great Law of Subordination Considered* (1724), an examination of the treatment of servants; *A Tour Thro the Whole Island of Great* Britain (3 vols., 1724–7), an outstanding guide book; *The Complete English Tradesman* (1726), which identifies the new respectability of the merchant classes; and *Augusta Triumphans* (1728), an optimistic Utopian project.

It has proved difficult to establish the full extent of his output but, with over 500 verified publications to his name, Defoe is the most prolific author in the language. His enduring reputation rests now upon his novels, the genre in which he was one of the great innovators, but he was also an outstanding journalist, producing over 250 pamphlets alone, in an age where such publications had a crucial and positive power. He brought versatile skills to the essay but he was recognizably unlike most of his important contemporaries in the AUGUSTAN AGE. Street-wise where they tended to be aesthetic, he was a master of the plain style, with almost, in fact, a utilitarian clarity, rather than the politely allusive mode cultivated by SWIFT and POPE. That he was superbly ignored by Swift – himself a propagandist of Harley – is perhaps a measure of the way he was regarded: 'the Fellow that was Pilloryed, I have forgot his name' was the extent of the Dean's recognition in 1709.

Phenomenally industrious, Defoe seemed capable of turning his hand to any endeavour. As a novelist he was interested in social man rather than individual psychology, and his fiction reveals a swashbuckling love of travel, adventure and piracy that has subsequently become the stock material of many books. As a writer on economics he championed mercantile expansion and the concept of self-sufficiency, and was later (misleadingly) hailed as a prophet of the Industrial Revolution. But in the end little is really known about him as a person, except that he was a phenomenon of literature, a prodigious one-man industry of great variety and skill.

Deighton, Len 1929– Novelist. He worked variously as a railway clerk, waiter, illustrator in New York and director of an advertising agency before achieving success with spy thrillers such as *The Ipcress File* (1962) and *Funeral in Berlin* (1964), praised for their laconic style and apparent authenticity. His subsequent output has alternated between exhaustively researched, bulky novels about World War II air combat, such as *Bomber* (1970) and *Goodbye Mickey Mouse* (1982), and more spy thrillers, notably the trilogies *Game, Set and Match* (1983–5) and *Hook, Line and Sinker* (1989–91).

Deirdre of the Sorrows A tragedy by J. M. SYNGE, posthumously produced at the ABBEY THEATRE in 1910. Had he lived, he would certainly have revised the text, written during illness and depression.

The story comes from the Saga of Cuchulain; Synge would have known the verse plays on the same subject by YEATS and AE (GEORGE WILLIAM RUSSELL) as well as SIR SAMUEL FERGUSON's poem. Deirdre, destined to be the wife of Conchubor, High King of Ulster, runs away with her lover Naisi. After seven years in Alban, they are enticed back to Conchubor's court. Naisi and his brothers are killed there, and Deirdre kills herself with Naisi's knife.

Deism A theological position which accepted the Supreme Being as the source of finite existence but denied the supernatural element in Christianity, as well as rejecting Christian revelation as the only way

to salvation. EDWARD HERBERT (Lord Herbert of Cherbury) was the first English philosopher to advance these ideas, and JOHN LOCKE's *The Reasonableness of Christianity* (1695) gave support by its contention that man and his use of reason are evidence enough for the existence of God, who must have given man the capacity. Deism played an important role in 18th-century thought and controversy, influencing Voltaire, Rousseau and Diderot in France and spreading to Germany through a translation of MATTHEW TINDAL's *Christianity as Old as the Creation* (1730). See also JOSEPH BUTLER, SAMUEL CLARKE, ANTHONY COLLINS, CONYERS MIDDLETON and JOHN TOLAND.

Dekker, Thomas *c.* 1570–1632 Playwright and pamphleteer. His vivid accounts of London life make plausible the assumption that he was a Londoner by birth and upbringing. Nothing more certain is known of him before references in PHILIP HENSLOWE's *Diary* to his plays (and to his debts) in the period 1598–1602. Dekker was prodigiously busy in these early years – Henslowe lists 16 plays in which he had a hand in 1598 – but his industry could not keep pace with his expenditure. He was briefly imprisoned in the Poultry Counter in 1599 (Henslowe arranged his release), and problems with money were probably constant, worst of all in 1613–19, when he was in the King's Bench Prison.

Of the 50 or so plays to which Dekker's name is linked, only 20 have survived, together with various MASQUES. The earliest, *OLD FORTUNATUS* (?1598), is a rambling moral tale describing the misfortunes that follow the decision of an old beggar and his sons to choose riches from among the benefits offered them by Fortune. The second, *THE SHOEMAKER'S HOLIDAY* (1599), is Dekker's masterpiece. Both in its variety and in its boisterous portraits of London's citizens it advanced the development of a distinctive comic form. The other plays of which Dekker was sole author are, in comparison, disappointing. *SATIROMASTIX* (1601) is an unattractive rejoinder to JONSON's wittier abuse of Dekker (in *THE POETASTER* as well as the earlier *EVERY MAN OUT OF HIS HUMOUR*), notable only for its contribution to the war of the theatres. The structural weaknesses of this play are shared by *The Whore of Babylon* (*c.* 1606), *If It be Not Good the Devil is in It* (*c.* 1610) and *The Wonder of a Kingdom* (published in 1636).

Of Dekker's many collaborations the most effective include: with WEBSTER, *WESTWARD HO* (1604), *THE FAMOUS HISTORY OF SIR THOMAS WYATT* (*c.* 1604) and *NORTHWARD HO* (*c.* 1605); with MIDDLETON, *THE HONEST WHORE* (1604; a second part, probably by Dekker alone, was produced in 1605) and *THE ROARING GIRL* (1610); with MASSINGER, *THE VIRGIN MARTYR* (1620); with FORD and WILLIAM ROWLEY, *THE WITCH OF EDMONTON* (*c.* 1621); and with CHETTLE and

William Haughton *PATIENT GRISSEL* (1600). He was also one of the several playwrights who had a hand in *SIR THOMAS MORE* (c. 1593–5).

The moralizing occasionally observable in his plays becomes explicit in his pamphlets, of which the best were written in 1603–10. *The Wonderful Year* (1603) describes the effects of the plague on London. *The Seven Deadly Sins of London* (1606) gives a bustling picture of city life and the seven-day triumph of the traditional sins, with new names and in modern guise. *The Bellman of London* (1608) exposes the criminal underworld, and finds nothing to choose between the town and the country for villainy. A continuation and Dekker's greatest publishing success, *Lantern and Candlelight* (1608), includes an early account of English gypsies in its description of low life. *Work for Armourers* (1609) describes the assault by the army of Poverty on the army of Money. *The Gull's Horn-Book* (1609) parodies COURTESY BOOKS, giving satiric instructions to gallants on how to behave in taverns and playhouses. *The Four Birds of Noah's Ark* (1609) is a collection of prayers, the birds being the eagle, dove, phoenix and pelican. At his best Dekker writes with exuberance, and always with affection for erring humanity.

Delafield, E. M. [Dashwood (*née* De La Pasture), Edmée Elizabeth Monica] 1890–1943 Novelist. She was born in Monmouthshire, and worked as a nurse during World War I. After the war she became a civil servant in the Ministry of National Service, then served as a magistrate. Her prolific career as a writer of mildly satiric novels about the day-to-day upheavals of provincial life began with numerous books which found a small but devoted readership. *Messalina of the Suburbs* (1923) was based upon a famous murder case. The success of *The Diary of a Provincial Lady* (1930) launched a series which provided the basis for popular films. Delafield's other works included: *Faster! Faster!* (1936) and *Nothing is Safe* (1937); three plays, *To See Ourselves* (1930), *The Glass Wall* (1933) and *The Mulberry Bush* (1935); and a study of the BRONTËS (1938).

Delane, J(ohn) T(haddeus) 1817–79 Newspaper editor. Born in London, he was educated at King's College, London, and Magdalen Hall, Oxford, and called to the Bar in 1847. The most famous Victorian editor of *The Times* (1841–77), he assembled a distinguished team of journalists around him and took an influential public role, particularly in his attacks on the mishandling of the Crimean War. According to ALEXANDER KINGLAKE, historian of the War, Delane was 'passionately imbued with the spirit of journalism'.

Delaney, Shelagh 1939– Playwright. Born in working-class Salford, she left school at 16 and began writing her first and best-known play a year later. *A Taste of Honey*, staged by Joan Littlewood's Theatre Workshop in 1958, tells the story of a white teenage girl's coming to terms with her loveless home and her pregnancy after a brief encounter with a black sailor. Its success was the result of its unadorned contemporaneity. Neither Delaney's second play, *The Lion in Love* (1960), nor her later work has achieved equal acclaim, though since adapting *A Taste of Honey* for the screen in 1961 she has produced notable screenplays for *Charlie Bubbles* (1968) and *Dance with a Stranger* (1985).

Delany, Mary 1700–88 Letter-writer. She was married first to Alexander Pendarves (d. 1725) and then to Patrick Delany, Dean of Down (d. 1768). Mary Delany was famous for intricate paper mosaics of flowers, but her lasting reputation rests upon her six-volume *Autobiography and Correspondence* (1861–2), which includes letters to and anecdotes of SWIFT, and an extensive correspondence on literary and social matters with other BLUESTOCKINGS such as ELIZABETH CARTER, ELIZABETH MONTAGU and HESTER CHAPONE.

Delany, Samuel R(ay) 1942– Black American writer of SCIENCE FICTION. He was born in New York and educated at the City College of New York. His early work – which includes novels, *Babel-17* (1966), *The Einstein Intersection* (1967) and *Nova* (1968), and the short stories collected in *Driftglass* (1971) and *Distant Stars* (1981) – displays an extraordinarily vivid romanticism. He broke new ground with the counter-cultural epic *Dhalgren* (1975), set in an imaginary decaying city. His intense interest in the language of science fiction is displayed in his critical writings, including *The Jewel-Hinged Jaw* (1977), *The American Shore* (1978) and *Starboard Wine* (1984), and his academic explorations in SEMIOTICS and POST-STRUCTURALISM have strongly influenced more recent works, especially the fantasy series which includes *Tales of Nevèrÿon* (1979), *Neveryóna* (1983), *Flight from Nevèrÿon* (1985) and *The Bridge of Lost Desire* (1987). His autobiography of the years 1957–65, *The Motion of Light in Water* (1988), provides striking documentation of the homosexual subculture of the period. A long two-volume science-fiction novel begun with *Stars in My Pocket Like Grains of Sand* (1984) is still to be completed.

DeLillo, Don 1936– American novelist. He was born in New York and educated at Fordham. Widely recognized as leading examples of American POST-MODERNISM, his novels are highly self-aware evocations of a contemporary society which defines itself through the pseudo-religious rituals of its subcultures: American football in *End Zone* (1973), for example, and rock music in *Great Jones Street* (1974). The pervasive climate of DeLillo's fictional world is fear, betraying his and his characters' conviction that social order and personal equanimity can be subverted at any time by indiscriminate catastrophe. *White Noise* (1986) is his version of a disaster novel, *Libra* (1988) deals with the assassination of President Kennedy and *Mao II* (1991) explores the relations between literature and terrorism. His other works are *Americana* (1971), *Ratner's Star* (1976), *Players* (1977), *Running Dog* (1979) and *The Names* (1983).

Dell, Floyd 1887–1969 American novelist. Born in Illinois, he settled in New York in 1913. A radical journalist, he edited *The Masses* (1914–17) and *The Liberator* (1918–24). After the success of his first novel, *Moon-Calf* (1920), about the disillusionment of the postwar generation, he turned most of his energy to fiction. *The Briary-Bush* (1921) is a sequel to *Moon-Calf*, and *Janet March* (1923) and *Runaway* (1925) are also about the confusion and turmoil of life in the Jazz Age. His other works include *An Old Man's Folly* (1926), *Upton Sinclair* (1927) and *Love in the Machine Age* (1930). Together with Thomas Mitchell, Dell dramatized his novel *An Unmarried Father* (1927) as *Little Accident* (1928). *Homecoming* (1933) is his autobiography.

Della Cruscans A short-lived school of sentimental poetry, founded by Robert Merry (1755–98). After an undistinguished career at Harrow and Christ's College, Cambridge, he toyed with the Horse Guards, gambling and travel, before arriving in Florence in 1784. There he edited two miscellanies, the *Arno* (1784) and the *Florence* (1785), containing his own effusions and those of Mrs Piozzi and other dilettanti. He managed to join the Florentine Accademia della Crusca ('of the chaff' or 'bran'), founded in 1583 to guard the purity of the Italian language. Its emblem, a sieve, emphasized its sifting function – to which Merry seems to have been engagingly blind. Having offended the English Florentines, he returned to England in 1787 and published his 'Adieu and Recall to Love' over the signature 'Della Crusca' in *The World* for 29 June of that year. Its depth of sentiment so moved the playwright HANNAH COWLEY that she responded in *The World* a fortnight later with 'The Pen', signing herself 'Anna Matilda'. Pseudonymous imitators rushed to swell the poetical correspondence, and the English Della Cruscans were launched.

A collection by 'Anna Matilda' and 'Della Crusca' was published in 1788. Bell published *The British Album*, containing examples of the school's productions, in 1789. This went quickly through four editions, the last prompted by WILLIAM GIFFORD's *The Baviad* (1791). This satire on Della Cruscan excess and nonsense was reinforced by the same author's *Maeviad* of 1795. Merry and Mrs Cowley met, apparently for the first time, in 1789. Thereafter 'Della Crusca' produced 'The Interview' and 'Anna Matilda' replied in saddened strain, but their literary affair, their influence on poetry and their school soon ended.

Deloney, Thomas ?1543–1600 Author of BALLADS, pamphlets and prose fiction. Deloney was by trade a silk-weaver: THOMAS NASHE calls him the 'balletting silk-weaver of Norwich'. Nothing is known of his early life and education, but his works suggest that he knew Latin and some French. Some of the contemporary university-educated writers of prose fiction regarded him as a mere ballad-maker and popular romancer, an opinion which continued in a subsequent low critical regard for Deloney's works as 'popular'. Nevertheless, he has good claim to have formed the English 'novel'.

His early works were ballads and BROADSIDES, including three on the Spanish Armada, and many of them were of the kind that Autolycus has in his pack in THE WINTER'S TALE. *The Lamentation of Beckles* and *The Death and Execution of Fourteen Most Wretched Traitors* (both 1586) may have been the kind of ballads which earned ROBERT GREENE's oblique and disdainful dig at 'such trivial trinkets and threadbare trash'. *Canaan's Calamity* is an attempt at a poem of greater length and sustained construction.

His prose fiction draws on popular works such as jest-books, the chronicles of EDWARD HALL and HOLINSHED, and FOXE's ACTS AND MONUMENTS, with occasional excursions into fashionable EUPHUISM and romance, to describe and glorify the English artisan. *Thomas of Reading* (licensed 1602) depicts the clothier's craft, *Jack of Newbury* (licensed 1597, first extant edition 1619) that of the weaver, and *The Gentle Craft* (licensed 1597, first extant edition 1637) shoemakers. The last contains his finest creation, Long Meg of Westminster, and also the story of Simon Eyre, a shoemaker who became Lord Mayor of London, which served as the source for DEKKER's THE SHOEMAKER'S HOLIDAY. KEMP said that Deloney 'died poorly... and was decently buried'.

Deloria, Vine, Jr 1933– American Indian writer. A Standing Rock Sioux, he was born and raised on a South Dakota reservation. He has taught political science at the University of Arizona and the University of Colorado. His writings consistently advocate a separatist political strategy for American Indians. These include the satiric *Custer Died for Your Sins: An Indian Manifesto* (1969); *We Talk, You Listen: New Tribes, New Turf* (1970); *God is Red* (1973), a critique of the Judaeo-Christian religious tradition; *Behind the Trail of Broken Treaties: An Indian Declaration of Independence* (1974), an examination of the events which led to the 1973 conflict at Wounded Knee; *Indians of the Pacific Northwest: From the Coming of the Whiteman to the Present Day* (1977); *The*

Metaphysics of Modern Existence (1979); and *American Indian Policy in the Twentieth Century* (1985).

Democracy in America (*La Démocratie en Amérique*) A classic interpretation of American civilization by Comte Alexis de Tocqueville (1805–59), published in two parts in 1835 and 1840. De Tocqueville's predictions about the course democracy would follow in the USA were based not only on what he had read about America but also on his own observations, made while on an official visit to the USA to study its penal system.

In the first part he discusses America's geography, political institutions and processes, and society. He argues that Anglo-Americans have been able to take possession of and settle such a large portion of the continent because they have the habit of democratic self-government that he considers essential to civilization, and he predicts that they will continue successfully to expand their territory. Noting that the tendency toward equality is advancing throughout the western world, he declares that – at the time he writes – equality is most advanced in the USA. In the second part he analyses the effect of democracy on intellectual movements, art, religion, taste and mores. He concludes that democracy and increasing equality will lead to greater mediocrity of individual achievement, even as it makes possible greater general comfort and greater achievements by the state.

Demos: *A Story of English Socialism* A novel by GEORGE GISSING, published in 1886. It is in fact an attack on the validity of socialism, portraying its leaders as short-sighted, self-deceived, self-serving and ultimately corrupt. Gissing shows individual members of the working class (especially women) as sensitive, high-principled and altogether noble, but his working-class agitators, such as Richard Mutimer and Daniel Dabbs, take to capitalist practices as soon as they have the chance. The story hinges on the establishment by Mutimer of an ironworks in an unspoiled valley, a model community in the tradition of ROBERT OWEN. The complex plot involves a will which is lost and found, its acknowledgement by the finder's husband becoming a test of honour. The socialist-capitalist loses his money, which reverts to the rightful, aristocratic owner, and the ironworks is closed, with loss of jobs. The peasantry have become unsettled, but the beauty of the landscape is restored, a solution to the problem of industrial relations which Gissing seems to endorse.

Denham, Sir John 1615–69 Poet. Born in Dublin and educated at Trinity College, Oxford, Denham studied law at Lincoln's Inn and was called to the Bar in 1639. He was a staunch Royalist, and his fortunes rose and fell with the king's. The Restoration saw him rewarded with a knighthood and a post as Surveyor of the Royal Works; he also served as MP for Sarum.

Denham was 26 when his blank-verse tragedy, *The Sophy*, was published. In the same year his most famous work, the long poem *Cooper's Hill*, appeared. Set in the country near his home at Egham and concentrating on landscape description, the work influenced the topographical poetry of the 18th century and, in SAMUEL JOHNSON's words, conferred on Denham 'the rank and dignity of an original author'. His use of the couplet strengthened the case for its adoption in the interest of discipline and rhythm. Denham also translated Homer and Virgil.

Denis Duval An unfinished novel by W. M. THACKERAY. The completed parts were published in *THE CORNHILL MAGAZINE* from April to June 1864. The author had died in December 1863.

The setting is Rye in the late 18th century. Denis Duval tells of his involvement with the smugglers of the area, of his love for Agnes de Saverne and the story of her victimized mother, and of the villainous de la Motte. Thackeray left sketches for the remainder of the book, which took him back to the sort of full-scale historical novel he had attempted so successfully in *HENRY ESMOND*.

Dennis, Clarence Michael James 1876–1938 Australian poet and journalist. Educated in Adelaide, Dennis followed a varied career before joining the staff of *The Melbourne Herald* in 1922. His first volume was *Backblock Ballads* (1913), followed by *The Songs of a Sentimental Bloke* (1915) and *The Moods of Ginger Mick* (1916). Their everyday language, teasing humour and use of bush themes made them immensely popular, particularly with soldiers in the trenches. Later volumes were *Digger Smith* (1918) and *Rose of Spadgers* (1924), a sequel to *Ginger Mick*.

Dennis, John 1657–1734 Critic. The son of a prosperous saddler, Dennis was born in London and attended Harrow School. At Cambridge, he was expelled from Gonville and Caius College for stabbing a fellow student, but finished his education at Trinity Hall. After university he travelled in France and Italy and became a member of DRYDEN's circle when he returned to England. A failed dramatist (he wrote eight plays, including *Appius and Virginia*, 1709, satirized by POPE), Dennis had more success as a critic, though he became cantankerous in later life and was ridiculed by Pope in *THE DUNCIAD*. His principal essays are *The Impartial Critic* (1693), an attack on THOMAS RYMER; *The Advancement and Reformation of Modern Poetry* (1701); *The Grounds of Criticism in Poetry* (1704); and *Three Letters on the Genius and Writings of Shakespeare* (1711). Dennis's *Original*

Letters, Familiar, Moral and Critical (1721) remains a valuable source of information on the literary world of his time.

Dennis, Nigel (Forbes) 1912–89 Novelist, playwright and journalist. He was born in Surrey, brought up in Rhodesia and educated partly in Austria. In 1931–49 he worked as a journalist in the USA, publishing his first novel, *Boys and Girls Come Out to Play* (1949), shortly after his return to England. The startlingly inventive *Cards of Identity* (1955) established him as a satirical novelist, but he then turned to the theatre, writing plays which deplored the debasement of standards under facile democracies and denounced left-wing totalitarianism. In *Cards of Identity* (1956), which he adapted from his novel, the target is the manipulation of mass opinion. *The Making of Moo* (1957) derides the idolatry of religion, Christianity included. In *August for the People* (1961) an aristocratic landowner who denounces the common man finds himself besieged by common men who agree with him. A witty journalist, Dennis also co-edited *ENCOUNTER* and contributed reviews and columns to *The Sunday Telegraph*.

dénouement The final resolution (literally, 'untying' or 'unravelling') of a complex plot, usually involving revelations of such things as mistaken identity, lost children, disguised motives, etc. Though the term refers most accurately to the formula of the WELL-MADE PLAY, it is also broadly applied to the closing scenes of many plays, and indeed of novels and other narratives. See also ANAGNORISIS.

Deor A short Old English poem found in the EXETER BOOK. It is written in the form of a first-person narrative by a minstrel called Deor. The narrator tells of five well-known miserable situations from history and mythology and then of his own misfortune, probably fictional: his position as official poet and its attendant benefits have been given to another. He comforts himself with the thought that God will soon improve his fortunes and offers solace throughout in a refrain which says that these other sorrows passed and so shall his own. *Deor* is similar in form and function to a longer poem, *WIDSITH*.

Deptford Trilogy, The A trilogy of novels by ROBERTSON DAVIES, consisting of *Fifth Business* (1970), *The Manticore* (1972) and *World of Wonders* (1975). Events in the fictional village of Deptford, Ontario, link the lives of the three central characters from childhood onwards: Dunstan Ramsey, narrator of the first volume and the central arbitrating consciousness of the sequence; Percy 'Boy' Staunton, whose flamboyant career ends in his mysterious death; and Paul Dempster, son of the disgraced wife

of the Baptist minister, who transforms himself into the master-magician Magnus Eisengrim. All three volumes focus on metamorphoses of identity, on characters who are 'born again', whether through the agency of myth, magic, theatre or Jungian psychology. The use of specialist knowledge – the saints' lives which preoccupy Dunstan in *Fifth Business*, the Jungian analysis undergone by Staunton's son David in *The Manticore* and the illusionism practised by Eisengrim in *World of Wonders* – is closely related to the psychic development of the characters and the author's concern with myth and moral philosophy. Also central is the contrast between provincial Presbyterian society and the alternative values of the 'world of wonders'.

Derrida, Jacques See DECONSTRUCTION.

Desai, Anita 1937– Indian novelist. She was born in Mussoorie. Her work describes surface realities sharply while using them as markers for her characters' interior lives; indeed, *The Village by the Sea* (1982), though intended for children, achieves social commitment simply through the clarity of its scenes of poverty. *Cry, the Peacock* (1963) and *Voices in the City* (1965) feature sensitive Hindu women of orthodox background seeking unorthodox means of fulfilment that lead to despair and insanity. In *Bye-Bye, Blackbird* (1971) two Indians in England gradually understand their relationship with India. The claustrophobia of family-bound women is explored in *Where Shall We Go This Summer?* (1975) and *Fire on the Mountain* (1977). Particularly distinguished is *Clear Light of Day* (1980), about an embittered woman discovering her own human shortcomings. *In Custody* (1984), her first novel centred on a male character, is a humorous and poignant study of a provincial lecturer. *Baumgartner's Bombay* (1988), focusing on a German protagonist, gives a vibrant portrait of Bombay.

Desani, G(ovindas) V(ishnoodas) 1909– Indian novelist. Born in Nairobi, Kenya, he spent World War II in Britain and now lives in the USA. He is ranked among the most important 20th-century Indian writers in English on the strength of one novel, *All About H. Hatterr* (1948), an eccentric and comic book about an Anglo-Indian in search of wisdom which combines linguistic dexterity and philosophical curiosity. Its admirers include T. S. ELIOT, ANTHONY BURGESS and SALMAN RUSHDIE. Desani has written nothing else substantial, though he has been a regular contributor from abroad to *The Illustrated Weekly of India* and is the author of a play, *Hali* (1950).

Deserted Village, The A poem by OLIVER GOLDSMITH, published in 1770. This pastoral elegy takes as its theme the vanished rural past of England,

Anita Desai

destroyed by the Enclosure Acts and by the depopulation of agrarian communities as the Industrial Revolution concentrated workers into the cities. Revisiting an idealized village, Auburn, the poet laments that money and progress should have become more important than human destinies, and that such a previously happy place has decayed. CRABBE's *THE VILLAGE* was in part a reaction to the mood of this poem.

Desperate Remedies The first published novel by THOMAS HARDY, appearing in 1871. Having failed to find a publisher for his first attempt at fiction, *The Poor Man and the Lady*, Hardy deliberately adopted the popular formulas of the SENSATION NOVEL.

Set mainly in Dorset, this complicated narrative of intrigue, violence and deception follows the welfare of Cytherea Graye, a young woman forced to become lady's maid and later companion to the imperious Miss Aldclyffe, mistress of Knapwater House, who years earlier had an illegitimate son given the name Aeneas Manston. It is Miss Aldclyffe's hope that Manston, whose post as her land agent she arranges, should marry Cytherea, although the latter is in love with Edward Springrove, a fledgling architect and son of a neighbouring farmer. But Manston is already married to a down-at-heel American woman named Eunice who pursues him to the West Country where she is presumed to have perished in a fire at the Three Tranters Inn; in fact, Manston murdered her and placed her remains in the smouldering ashes of the fire. A combination of circumstances moves Cytherea to accept Manston in marriage, at which point it is re-vealed that Springrove, who had unwisely attached himself to a local girl, has been jilted. After much investigative work Manston is brought to book as the murderer of Eunice and hangs himself in his cell. Miss Aldclyffe dies and Cytherea and Springrove are reunited.

detective fiction A sub-genre of fiction which presents a mysterious event or crime, usually but not necessarily murder, at first concealing the solution from the reader but finally revealing it through the successful investigations of the detective. W. H. AUDEN summarizes a typical plot: 'a murder occurs; many are suspected; all but one suspect, who is the murderer, are eliminated; the murderer is arrested or dies'.

Historians of the form have tried to trace its origin to the puzzle tales of the Enlightenment (Voltaire's *Zadig*) or even to the Bible (Daniel, Susanna and the elders), but there is a general agreement that its real history starts in the 19th century. EDGAR ALLAN POE brought all the basic ingredients together in his 'tales of ratiocination' of the 1840s. His detective, the brilliant and eccentric Dupin, is accompanied by an obligingly imperceptive friend who narrates the story; he confronts mystery with a coherent, though not exclusively scientific, methodology of detection; and he produces the solution with a triumphant flourish that both surprises and satisfies the reader. Without providing either a murder or an infallible detective, WILKIE COLLINS showed in *THE MOONSTONE* (1868) how the formula could be expanded to fit the requirements of the full-length novel. In his SHERLOCK HOLMES STORIES, begun in the late 1880s, SIR ARTHUR

CONAN DOYLE masterfully orchestrated the hints Poe had sketched out.

The success of Sherlock Holmes rapidly bred imitation, ranging from distinguished contributions like G. K. CHESTERTON's Father Brown stories and E. C. BENTLEY's *Trent's Last Case* (1913) to forgotten works like ARTHUR MORRISON's Martin Hewitt stories and M. P. SHIEL's tales of Prince Zaleski. It also bred new awareness of the form, a new attempt to distinguish detective fiction from all the other types of popular fiction which dabble in crime and mystery. According to Monsignor Ronald Knox (1888–1957) and his followers in the Detection Club, detective fiction should be concerned with puzzles rather than crime as such, and it should elaborate its puzzles in strict obedience to the rules of logic and fair play. From such prescriptions arose the so-called Golden Age of the detective novel in the 1920s and 1930s. Writers became known for their expert refinements of the puzzle: R. Austin Freeman (1862–1943) for his scientific expertise; Freeman Wills Crofts (1879–1957) for his juggling with timetables and alibis; John Dickson Carr (1905–77) for his variations on the locked-room mystery; and, most famous of all, AGATHA CHRISTIE for her ingenuity in making the least likely suspect turn out to be the murderer.

Setting and characterization inevitably took second place, but they, too, followed well-worn paths. Detectives tended to be gentleman amateurs rather than policemen or private enquiry agents. H. C. Bailey (1878–1961) was perhaps the first, in his Reggie Fortune stories, to make his gentleman amateur a facetious dandy, but Fortune was soon joined by a lengthening list of detectives who owed as much to SAKI and P. G. WODEHOUSE as they did to Conan Doyle: Lord Peter Wimsey (DOROTHY L. SAYERS), Albert Campion (MARGERY ALLINGHAM) and even Nigel Strangeways (Nicholas Blake, the pseudonym of CECIL DAY-LEWIS). Settings were equally genteel, with country houses and Oxbridge colleges among the favourites, and with the work of Michael Innes (J. I. M. STEWART) offering perhaps the best representative selection.

Detective stories in this classic mould were not confined to England, as the popularity of S. S. Van Dine (Willard Huntington Wright, 1880–1939), Ellery Queen (Frederic Dannay, 1905–82, and Manfred B. Lee, 1905–71) and Rex Stout (1886–1975) in America showed. Nor did they entirely disappear after the 1930s. Christie, Allingham, Blake, Innes and NGAIO MARSH all continued their careers after the war, with some adjustment to the change in public taste, and were joined by Edmund Crispin (Robert Bruce Montgomery, 1921–78) and Michael Gilbert (1912–). Contemporaries like P. D. JAMES in England and Emma Lathen (Mary J. Latsis and Martha Henissart) in America can still follow the classic formula. But it came increasingly under challenge from writers who,

whatever else they may not have shared, were agreed in finding it restrictive and in wishing to break down the barriers that separated detective fiction from other popular forms like the thriller, adventure story, chase novel and spy story, or from the concerns of serious literature.

By far the most significant challenge came from America, where DASHIELL HAMMETT, RAYMOND CHANDLER and other contributors to *THE BLACK MASK* pioneered 'hard-boiled' detective fiction. Its aims were succinctly indicated by Chandler when he praised Hammett for putting murder back in the hands of people who commit it with real weapons for real reasons, not just to provide the reader with a puzzle. With its tough, down-at-heel private eyes and its sleazy urban world of vice and hoodlums, hard-boiled detective fiction quickly rooted itself in American popular culture, not least because of its strong links with Hollywood and the *film noir*, and has attracted distinguished practitioners from Ross MacDonald (the most important of several pseudonyms used by Kenneth Millar, 1915–83) to Robert B. Parker (1932–). Though struggling, and not always succeeding, to adapt to new cultural phenomena like feminism and gay rights, its formulas still dominate the American approach as thoroughly as Conan Doyle once did the English.

In England itself the form has never properly taken root, but two other tendencies – both with international ramifications – are worth noting. The first is the 'crime novel', so called because an interest in the criminal and criminal psychology can overshadow or even replace the element of mystery. Pioneered by Anthony Berkeley Cox (1893-1971), writing as Francis Iles in the 1930s, it has since attracted distinguished adherents in the American PATRICIA HIGHSMITH, Julian Symons (1912–) and RUTH RENDELL. The second is the 'police novel', in which a determination to make good the genre's earlier neglect of the police can produce works ranging from strictly procedural novels like those of John Creasey (1908–73) or the American Ed McBain (EVAN HUNTER), to the atmospheric fiction of NICOLAS FREELING. Indeed, Freeling's work, with its policemen-heroes at odds with the bureaucracy that gives them authority, its enquiry into the social and personal origins of crime and its ability to propound a neat puzzle when the occasion requires, comes as close as any to epitomizing the eclectic variety open to the contemporary detective novelist.

deus ex machina (The god from the machine) It refers to the practice on the classical Greek stage of lowering the gods in a large crane, or 'mechane', as if they were flying down to earth. It was often the task of a god to resolve problems insoluble by human agency, and so the phrase has become more widely applied to describe any character, or even any device, used arbitrarily by a playwright in order to bring a plot to its desired end.

Devil is an Ass, The A comedy by BEN JONSON, first performed in 1616 but not published until 1631. The play exposes the activities of 'projectors' (fixers and confidence tricksters), witch-finders and those who claim to heal demoniacs, or victims of satanic possession. The plot concerns Meercraft, a projector, who proposes a scheme for reclaiming land. His victim is Fitzdottrel, who parts with his estate on the promise of being made Duke of Drowndland. Fitzdottrel, in turn, deceives the law by pretending to be bewitched. Another character in the plot is Pug, a minor devil allowed out by Satan for one day to practise his wickedness on earth. But the wickedness he encounters on earth is worse than his own; he is completely outwitted by human knaves and ends up in Newgate.

Dewey, John 1859–1952 American philosopher and educationalist, born in Burlington, Vermont. He taught at the University of Michigan and then at the University of Chicago, where he founded the Laboratory School for experimental education. He was a professor of philosophy at Columbia University from 1905 until his retirement in 1929.

Many of his works are concerned with reforms in education, politics and religion. His numerous writings greatly influenced the development of educational techniques both in the USA and abroad. His publications in this field include *Psychology* (1887), *Moral Principles in Education* (1909), *Interest and Effort in Education* (1913), *Democracy and Education* (1916), *Experience and Education* (1938), *The Public Schools and Spiritual Values* (1944). Dewey started out as a Hegelian, but his study of DARWIN led him to a philosophical pragmatism more in the tradition of WILLIAM JAMES. His philosophy, which he termed 'instrumentalism', with its emphasis on the practical problems of social construction, is elaborated in such works as *Outlines of a Critical Theory of Ethics* (1891), *Studies in Logical Theory* (1903), *Reconstruction in Philosophy* (1920), *Human Nature and Conduct* (1922), *Experience and Nature* (1925), *The Quest for Certainty* (1929), *Art as Experience* (1934) and *Freedom and Culture* (1939).

Dial, The A New England quarterly magazine started in 1840, and the chief periodical of the TRANSCENDENTALIST movement. It published the literary, philosophical and religious statements of its founders, who included MARGARET FULLER and RALPH WALDO EMERSON, as well as the poetry of JONES VERY and WILLIAM ELLERY CHANNING. Although it was published for only four years, *The Dial* had a major influence on the intellectual life of 19th-century New England. In addition to Fuller and Emerson, its editors included HENRY DAVID THOREAU.

Dialogues concerning Natural Religion A work by DAVID HUME, written in the 1750s but not published until 1779, three years after his death.

The narrator is Pamphilus, and the interlocutors are the philosopher Cleanthes, the sceptic Philo and the orthodox Christian Demea. The subject is the nature of God (the existence of God is not in question) and the dialogues examine further the questions raised in the essay on miracles in *AN ENQUIRY CONCERNING HUMAN UNDERSTANDING* and *THE NATURAL HISTORY OF RELIGION*. In particular, the issue of divine providence is debated and held in doubt. With their varying pace and rhythm, sharp exchanges and interruptions, the dialogues achieve a remarkable impression of recorded discussion.

Diana of the Crossways A novel by GEORGE MEREDITH published in 1885. The central character, Diana Warwick, is accused of adultery by her husband, a government official of limited sensibilities. An action for divorce is brought, citing the eminent Lord Dannisburgh, but fails and the couple agree to live apart. Diana forms a close relationship with a rising young politician, Percy Dacier, and their affair ends only when Dacier discovers that Diana has betrayed to the press a political secret confided in her. After the death of her husband she marries an old admirer, Thomas Redworth. The nervous, impulsive, inconsistent character of the heroine, admired by critics of the novel, is said to have been modelled on CAROLINE NORTON.

Diaper, William c. 1686–1717 Poet. The author of *Nereides: or, Sea-Eclogues* (1712), a whimsical production in verse where the speakers are mermaids and mermen. Diaper is best known for his translation of the first part of Oppian's *Halieuticks*, a Greek poem of epic proportions describing and classifying fish and methods of fishing.

Diary of a Nobody, The A comic novel of late-Victorian manners by GEORGE AND WEEDON GROSSMITH, published in 1892. 'Why should I not publish my diary... because I do not happen to be a "Somebody"?' demands city clerk Charles Pooter, the unreliable narrator. The humour derives from the socially and physically accident-prone Pooter's unconsciousness of how ridiculous he makes himself by his petty snobberies, and from his invariably unsuccessful wrangles with his rebellious son Lupin. Nevertheless, a character of respectability and even integrity emerges, so that the reader rejoices in the eventual rise in the fortunes of Pooter and his faithful, though frequently irritated, wife Carrie.

The current fashion for bicycling is exemplified by Pooter's dignified but dull friend Cummings, and that for imitations of the famous contemporary actor Irving by Lupin's friend Fosselton. Among the host of other characters who cross the Pooters' path are the hearty Mr Gowing, and his vulgar friend Padge, 'who appeared to be all moustache'.

Dibdin, Charles 1745–1814 Playwright, actor and composer. Dibdin had his first comic opera, *The Shepherd's Artifice* (1764), produced at COVENT GARDEN before he was 20. Much of his early work was done in collaboration with ISAAC BICKERSTAFFE, for whose *The Padlock* (1768) he not only wrote the music but also created the role of Mungo. He provided both text and music for *The Wedding Ring* (1773), *The Deserter* (1773), the excellent BALLAD OPERA *The Waterman* (1774) and upwards of 40 subsequent pieces. A commercial venture into equestrian drama at the Royal Circus in 1782 ended in failure and imprisonment for debt, but the series of one-man shows which Dibdin wrote and performed in 1788–93 helped to restore his uncertain fortunes. Among the many ballads for which he was famous in his time, 'Tom Bowling' has proved the most durable. His prose work included a five-volume *History of the Stage* (1795) and several forgotten novels, of which *Henry Hooka* (1806) was the last.

Dick, Philip K(endred) 1928–82 American writer of SCIENCE FICTION. Dick spent most of his life in California. His early paperback novels were written quickly to earn a living, but *The World Jones Made* (1956) and *Eye in the Sky* (1957) contain striking material. His mature work often studies the effect on human life and values of the gradual mechanization of the environment. Another theme is the unreliability of perception, and Dick's novels are most impressive when they deal with false realities created by hallucinogenic drugs or schizophrenic delusion. They include *The Man in the High Castle* (1962), *Martian Time-Slip* (1964), *Now Wait for Last Year* (1966), *Do Androids Dream of Electric Sheep?* (1969), *Flow My Tears, the Policeman Said* (1974) and *A Scanner Darkly* (1977). In his last years, having had his own problems with schizophrenia, Dick turned with deepening interest to metaphysics and hypothetical theology in *Valis* (1981) and *The Divine Invasion* (1981). His non-science fiction work, including *Confessions of a Crap Artist* (1975) and *The Transmigration of Timothy Archer* (1982), shows his concern for the plight of meek people confronted by the uncaring hostility of others.

Dickens, Charles (John Huffam) 1812–70 Novelist. Born at Portsmouth, the son of John Dickens, a well-intentioned but irresponsible clerk in the Navy Office, and his wife Elizabeth, he had an unsettled childhood in London, Chatham and London again. At Chatham from 1817 until 1821/2 the boy came under the beneficent eye of the schoolmaster William Giles, who recognized his talent and gave him particular attention. Always a voracious reader, the young Dickens fell upon the works of SMOLLETT, FIELDING and Cervantes; his restless imagination also responded to exotic tales like *The Arabian Nights*, public recitations, play-acting, colourful pageantry and magic-lantern displays. But with his father's transfer to London, he was for several years neglected while his feckless parents slid further into financial difficulties that resulted in John Dickens's imprisonment for debt in the Marshalsea. Two days after his 12th birthday Dickens was put to work in Warren's blacking factory, a humiliating experience which he nursed in memory until the end of his life. So profound a mark did his father's imprisonment and his own miserable months at Warren's leave on him that it was not until the publication of the biography by JOHN FORSTER, after Dickens's death, that his family knew of these early experiences.

When he was released from the Marshalsea John Dickens sent his son to Wellington House Academy, an institution of negligible value to the boy but an improvement on his recent mode of living, and there he remained until the spring of 1827. He then became office boy in a firm of attorneys, mastering shorthand and rising swiftly to work as reporter in that 'confusion of different courts', Doctors' Commons. In 1829 he had met and fallen in love with Maria Beadnell. Her family disapproved of her literary suitor and their association ended after four difficult years – although, like so much of Dickens's early experience, it provided material for later fiction.

Characteristically alert to self-advancement, the young Dickens was by 1832 working for his uncle's Hansard-style publication, *The Mirror of Parliament*, and also reporting for *The True Sun*. Shortly afterwards, in 1833, he was parliamentary journalist for the Liberal THE MORNING CHRONICLE, often travelling into the country to report political meetings for the paper. During the 1830s he also wrote sketches for a variety of journals, among them *The Monthly Magazine* edited by his friend George Hogarth. From these reportorial experiences and writings came his first book, SKETCHES BY BOZ (1836–7), in which he for the first time adopted the pseudonym derived from his own infant pronunciation of 'Moses' as 'Boses'. Of note, too, is that Dickens from his earliest years developed a wide knowledge of the squares, highways, courts, alleys, markets and gardens of London. His endless wanderings, literally from one end of the city to the other, not only contributed to *Sketches by Boz* but gave rise to situation after situation and description after description in his later writing.

Welcomed into George Hogarth's family, Dickens courted the eldest daughter of the household, the pretty Catherine, and the couple were married at St Luke's, Chelsea, in April 1836. The same month saw the inauspicious beginning of *The Posthumous Papers of the Pickwick Club*, better known as *THE*

Dickens' tomb in Poets' Corner, Westminster Abbey, London: an engraving from
The Illustrated London News of 25 June 1870

PICKWICK PAPERS. Its fourth number, introducing Sam Weller, elevated Dickens to a literary and financial position from which he never descended. With success assured, Dickens worked and lived with even greater intensity and purpose than before. Overlapping with the serialization of *Pickwick Papers* came first *OLIVER TWIST* (1837–9) and then *NICHOLAS NICKLEBY* (1838–9). In the autumn of 1839, as *Nicholas Nickleby* came to its conclusion, Dickens conceived the ill-fated *MASTER HUMPHREY'S CLOCK*, a weekly miscellany with its framework of an antiquarian extracting tales, sketches and stories from his 'old quaint queer-cased clock'. Sales very soon fell off and Dickens had to expand a short story originally designed for the miscellany into a full-length serial, *THE OLD CURIOSITY SHOP* (1840–1); this he quickly followed with *BARNABY RUDGE* (1841).

Dickens's business and personal life were equally busy. Ever prickly with publishers, he quarrelled with John Macrone and in 1839 friction with RICHARD BENTLEY caused him to resign the editorship of *BENTLEY'S MISCELLANY*. He moved in 1837 to Doughty Street and two years later to something more palatial on Devonshire Terrace. He enlarged his family, was elected to the Athenaeum, met his future biographer John Forster, rescued his parents several times from financial difficulties and widened his circle of friends beyond the humbler spheres of journalism.

In January 1842 Dickens arrived to an enthusiastic welcome in Boston for his first American visit. He travelled to New York, Philadelphia, Baltimore, Washington, DC, and Richmond, Virginia, as well as various smaller cities and towns; he went down the Ohio river to Cincinnati and briefly up to Canada. But his *AMERICAN NOTES* (1842) and the American episodes in his next novel, *MARTIN CHUZZLEWIT* (1843–4), caused lasting resentment among his American audience. In 1843, prompted by the sight of the Ragged Schools, he produced his first and most famous Christmas story, *A CHRISTMAS CAROL*. In the spring of the next year he went to live in Genoa – partly, he claimed, for financial reasons – and, with his usual energetic curiosity, made a round of visits to Vesuvius, Rome, Naples, Florence and Venice before returning to England in 1845. *PICTURES FROM ITALY*, published that year, was less controversial than *American Notes*. In the mid 1840s, too, Dickens produced *THE CHIMES*, *THE CRICKET ON THE HEARTH*, *THE BATTLE OF LIFE* and *THE HAUNTED MAN*, which were republished together with *A Christmas Carol* as *CHRISTMAS BOOKS* in 1852. As a journalist, he edited the newly founded *DAILY NEWS* for a mere 17 numbers in 1846 before a disagreement with the publishers, Bradbury and Evans, caused him to withdraw. In 1850 he founded his own magazine, *HOUSEHOLD WORDS*, succeeded by *ALL THE YEAR ROUND* in 1859.

More important was the publication of *DOMBEY AND SON* (1846–8), the novel which ushered in the mature period of his art and was followed in the next decade by *DAVID COPPERFIELD* (1849–50), *BLEAK HOUSE* (1852–3), *HARD TIMES* (1854), *LITTLE DORRIT* (1855–7) and *A TALE OF TWO CITIES* (1859). Where his early work had overflowed with improvisatory energy, the novels of the 1850s and beyond are more tightly controlled. No less wide-ranging in their subjects, they are unified by theme, image and symbol as much as by their complex and ramifying plots.

Outside literature, Dickens's energy continued unabated. He indulged his love for the theatre and delighted in assembling companies, mounting productions at Knebworth House and Rockingham Castle, arranging theatrical benefits for the bankrupt dramatist SHERIDAN KNOWLES and the penniless widow of DOUGLAS JERROLD, and acting in *The Frozen Deep* (a play he wrote in collaboration with his friend WILKIE COLLINS) and other pieces. He also continued his interest in social problems, concerning himself with capital punishment, the reform of prostitutes and model flats in Bethnal Green among other issues. Inevitably, he moved again – to Tavistock House – and then, in the spring of 1857, to Gad's Hill in his beloved Kent. He toured Switzerland and Italy with Wilkie Collins and the painter Augustus Egg, and visited France several times. By the late 1850s, too, he had met and been captivated by the young actress Ellen Ternan, whose shadow hovers over his later fiction. His marriage, which had deteriorated over the years, came to an end with the notorious revelation in *Household Words* (June 1858) of 'Some domestic troubles of mine, of long-standing' and a permanent separation from Catherine.

Ever aware of his inability to rest or settle, even if beset with domestic difficulties, Dickens planned a series of public readings from his work, the first of them given in 1858. Highly successful, they were repeated throughout England and on his second visit to the United States in 1867. Further readings took place on his return to England, but by then the strain had grown too great and they were curtailed. It is ironic that the 1860s should also have produced some of his best work: *GREAT EXPECTATIONS* (1860–1), *OUR MUTUAL FRIEND* (1864–5) and the tantalizingly incomplete *MYSTERY OF EDWIN DROOD*, halted in its serialization by his death in June 1870.

It is hard to accept that in the space of 58 years Dickens should have written even as much as the foregoing, though his canon also includes: pamplets such as the anti-Sabbatarian *Sunday under Three Heads* (1836); *A Child's History of England* (1851–3); short stories such as 'To be Read at Dusk' (1852), 'Hunted Down' (1859), 'A Holiday Romance' (1868), 'George Silverman's Explanation' (1868); pieces for *Household Words* and *All the Year Round*, some of them gathered in *The Uncommercial Traveller* (1860; enlarged in 1865 and 1875); several comic plays; and speeches and letters which have occupied the attention of modern editors. So prolific is his output and so frenzied his life, it seems miraculous he lived as long as he did.

Dickens, Monica (Enid) 1915–92 Novelist. The granddaughter of CHARLES DICKENS, she was brought up in London. Her five volumes of autobiography include the highly successful sequence *One Pair of Hands* (1939), *One Pair of Feet* (1942) and *My Turn to Make the Tea* (1951). The most famous of her novels is *The Happy Prisoner* (1946), one of several inspired by her wartime nursing career. She emigrated to the USA with her husband in 1959 but, after his death, returned to Britain in 1985 and broke many years' silence with *Closed at Dusk* (1990) and *Scarred* (1991), among other novels. She also wrote for children.

Dickey, James (Lafayette) 1923– American poet and novelist. Born in Atlanta, Georgia, he was educated at Clemson and Vanderbilt universities. He has taught at various colleges, including Rice University, Reed College, the University of Florida at Gainesville and the University of Wisconsin, as well as working in advertising. Much of his work is concerned with the causes and consequences of guilt arising from the cruelties of life in the Southern backwoods, and from the collective cruelties of nations. His first volume of poetry was *Into the Stone and Other Poems* (1960) but his reputation was secured by *Drowning with Others* (1962) and *Helmets* (1964), dealing with his experiences as a pilot in the US Air Force during World War II. His prolific output has since included *Two Poems of the Air* (1964), *Buckdancer's Choice* (1965), *Poems 1957–1967* (1968), *The Eye-Beaters, Blood, Victory, Madness, Buckhead and Mercy* (1970), *The Zodiac* (1976), *The Strength of Fields* (1977), *Veteran Birth: The Gadfly Poems, 1947–1949* (1978), *Falling, May Day Sermon, and Other Poems* (1981), *The Early Motion* (1981), *Puella* (1982), *The Central Motion: Poems, 1968–1979* (1983), *False Youth – Four Seasons* (1983) and *God's Images* (1984). He has also written several volumes of verse for children. *Whole Motion: Collected Poems, 1948–1992* (1992) gathers virtually all his work. *Babel to Byzantium: Poets and Poetry Now*, a collection of critical pieces, appeared in 1968 and *Self-Interviews*, edited by Barbara and James Reiss, in 1970. Dickey is, however, best known for his first novel, *Deliverance* (1970), a bestseller about a violent Georgia canoe trip; his screenplay for the film version was published in 1981. *Alniham* (1987) is his second novel. Consultant in Poetry to the Library of Congress in 1966–8, Dickey is currently a professor at the University of South Carolina.

Dickinson, Emily 1830–86 American poet. One of the three children of Edward Dickinson, a respected state legislator, US congressman and judge, she was born and lived all her life in Amherst, Massachusetts.

Emily Dickinson: this daguerreotype of 1848 is the only known photographic likeness of the poet

She attended Amherst Academy and the Mount Holyoke Female Seminary. Although her early years were filled with the normal social activities of the daughter of a prominent citizen, she began to withdraw from the world outside her home. By the age of 30 she had become an almost total recluse, never leaving her father's house and garden, dressing completely in white, receiving very few visitors, and carrying on most of her many friendships, like those with the novelist HELEN HUNT JACKSON and the Reverend Charles Wadsworth, through a regular correspondence. At the age of 32, at the end of what seems to have been the most intense and prolific period of her creative life, Dickinson sent some of her poems to Thomas Wentworth Higginson, a minister, author and critic. This marked the beginning of a long and sustained correspondence between the two that only twice (in 1870 and 1873) actually resulted in meetings. Although he encouraged her writing and assumed the role of her mentor, Higginson did not attempt to get her work published. In fact, only seven of her poems were published during her lifetime.

After her death, her sister Lavinia found over a thousand poems in her room, all bound neatly in home-made booklets. Almost all were short lyrics, typically consisting of just two four-line stanzas. Most were untitled and undated, and some survived in several versions. The first volumes of Dickinson's poetry to be published were edited by Higginson and Mabel L. Todd, an Amherst friend, in 1890 and 1891. Uncertain about public reaction to her work, Higginson and

Todd changed metres and rhymes, altered metaphors, and substituted conventional grammar for the original complex syntax. Despite their caution the critical reception was mostly unfavourable. Other volumes, also marred by insensitive and unnecessary editing, were prepared by Dickinson's niece, Martha Dickinson Bianchi, and Alfred Leete Hampson, and published in 1914, 1924, 1929, 1930, 1935 and 1937. *Bolts of Melody: New Poems of Emily Dickinson*, edited by Todd and her daughter, Millicent Todd Bingham, was published in 1945; it was more faithful than previous volumes to Dickinson's original texts, and included many poems that had been suppressed by her relatives. In 1955 Thomas H. Johnson prepared a three-volume variorum edition, *The Poems of Emily Dickinson*, containing all 1775 known poems, and this text is now accepted as the authoritative edition. Johnson and Theodora Ward edited her massive correspondence, *The Letters of Emily Dickinson*, which appeared in 1958.

The subjects of Dickinson's poetry are the traditional ones of love, nature, religion and mortality, seen through Puritan eyes, or, as she described it, 'New Englandly'. Much of the dramatic tension stems from her religious doubt: she was unable to accept the orthodox religious faith of her friends and schoolmates yet longed for the comfort and emotional stability that such faith could bring. Many lyrics mix rebellious and reverent sentiments. The eccentricities and technical irregularities which alarmed her early editors and reviewers include: frequent use of dashes; sporadic capitalization of nouns; convoluted and ungrammatical phrasing; off-rhymes; broken metres; bold, unconventional and often startling metaphors; and aphoristic wit. These have greatly influenced 20th-century poets and contributed to Dickinson's reputation as one of the most innovative 19th-century American poets.

Dickinson, Peter (Malcolm de Brissac) 1927– Writer of CHILDREN'S LITERATURE and DETECTIVE FICTION. Born in Zambia and educated at Eton and Cambridge, he was assistant editor of *PUNCH* before turning to full-time writing. His first children's novel, *The Weathermonger* (1968), describes a Britain which has returned to the Dark Ages, a disturbing theme continued in *Heartsease* (1969) and *The Devil's Children* (1970). More orthodox historical fiction includes *The Dancing Bear* (1972), about a young slave from Byzantium, and *Tulku* (1979), set in China at the time of the Boxer rebellion. Dickinson's unpredictable imagination and gift for making the unusual seem credible also inform his quirky detective novels, of which two, *Skin Deep* (1968) and *A Pride of Heroes* (1969), have won the Crime Writers' Association Golden Dagger Award.

dictionaries See ENGLISH DICTIONARIES.

Dictionary of the English Language, A A monumental work by SAMUEL JOHNSON, first published in 1755. The project had been announced in a *Plan* of 1747, dedicated at the prompting of the bookseller ROBERT DODSLEY to the EARL OF CHESTERFIELD; Johnson's own uneasiness about patronage was justified by his later quarrel with Chesterfield. The *Dictionary* represented eight years' labour, and the work was done while Johnson had several other projects on hand, driven as he was by the need to earn his living. One of these was *THE RAMBLER*, and he concluded that series of essays with a declaration that he had striven to refine the language to grammatical purity 'and to clear it from colloquial barbarisms, licentious idioms, and irregular combinations' (1752).

The *Dictionary's* full title reflected the extent of Johnson's purpose: *A Dictionary of the English Language: In Which the Words are Deduced from Their Originals, and Illustrated in Their Different Significations by Examples from the Best Writers. To Which are Prefixed a History of the Language, and an English Grammar.* His earliest authorities were SIR PHILIP SIDNEY and SPENSER, for he held firmly that the golden age of the English language began with the Elizabethans; he also honoured, as fully as the knowledge of his time permitted, provincialisms and dialect. He set himself to reject all the 'Gallick structure and phraseology' which the language had absorbed since the Restoration and which threatened to make the English 'babble a dialect of France'. In the 18th century there was only scant etymological knowledge to help Johnson but he brought to his task massive common sense, just as he brought his extraordinary wealth of reading to bear on the choice of illustrative quotations. The result was not definitive but pioneering, a dictionary which has influenced and inspired all later attempts in the field. See also ENGLISH DICTIONARIES.

Didion, Joan 1934– American essayist and novelist. Born in Sacramento, California, and educated at Berkeley, she is perhaps best known for her essays, prime examples of the New Journalism which coolly explore the spookier fringes of American society. *Slouching toward Bethlehem* (1969) and *The White Album* (1979) deal mainly with California and the wilder manifestations of 1960s culture, such as the Black Panthers and the Charles Manson murders. Three novels – *Run, River* (1964), *Play It As It Lays* (1971) and *Democracy* (1984) – are also set mainly in California, chronicling exhausted marriages and peripatetic lives on the edge of violence. *A Book of Common Prayer* (1977), which takes place in a fictional South American republic, draws on the story of the millionaire heiress for its study of guerrilla warfare. Two full-length works of non-fiction, *Salvador* (1983) and *Miami* (1988), also show her capacity for extended diagnosis of disordered societies. *Sentimental Journeys* (1993) is a later collection of essays. With her husband John Gregory Dunne, she has also written screenplays for films such as *Panic in Needle Park* (1971).

Digby, Sir Kenelm 1603–65 Writer on science and religion. A Roman Catholic, Digby was educated at Gloucester Hall (now Worcester College), Oxford, and became a successful naval commander. He interested himself in science and became a founder-member of the Royal Society in 1660. His first work, not published until 1827, was his *Private Memoirs*, written in 1628 to refute gossip about his wife, Venetia Stanley. In 1638 he published a reaffirmation of his Catholic faith, *Conference with a Lady about Choice of Religion*, after toying with Protestantism, and a criticism of SIR THOMAS BROWNE'S *RELIGIO MEDICI* (*Observations upon Religio Medici*) in 1643. A Royalist, he pleaded the cause of King Charles in Rome, and was banished in 1649, the year of the king's execution. He lived in Paris, where he became a friend of Descartes, until the Restoration, when he returned to England as Chancellor to Queen Henrietta Maria. Other works were *Of the Immortality of Man's Soul* (1644), *On the Cure of Wounds* (1658) and *A Discourse concerning the Vegetation of Plants* (1660), an address to the Royal Society on the necessity of oxygen to plant life.

Digby, Kenelm Henry ?1797–1880 Enthusiast for medieval culture. A descendant of SIR KENELM DIGBY, he was born in Ireland and educated at Trinity College, Cambridge. He converted to Roman Catholicism in 1825. Digby combined admiration for medieval religion with a love of chivalry that he had already announced during his undergraduate years by holding mock tournaments and keeping an all-night vigil in King's College Chapel. *The Broad Stone of Honour: or, Rules for the Gentlemen of England* (1822) set forth his ideals with copious quotation from classical and medieval sources – and at greater and greater length, swelling to four volumes in 1828–9 and to five in 1877. It had considerable influence on the 19th-century cult of medievalism, particularly among the PRE-RAPHAELITES. The 11-volume *Mores Catholici: or, Ages of Faith* (1831–42) dealt with the Catholic virtues. Digby later turned to verse and religious painting.

Dilke, Charles Wentworth 1789–1864 Critic and editor. Following exactly in his father's footsteps, Dilke entered the Navy Pay Office, where he remained until its abolition in 1836. His liberal sympathies and literary interests brought him into contact with LEIGH HUNT and his circle, and he is particularly remembered for his close friendship with KEATS, who enjoyed the freedom of his home at Hampstead and often used to go there to write. His continuation and completion of DODSLEY's *Old Plays* (1814–16) was, in its time, an important contribution to the rediscovery of forgotten dramatists of the Elizabethan age. Although most of his numerous contributions to periodicals such as *The London Review, THE LONDON MAGAZINE* and *Colburn's New Monthly* were on literary topics, he wrote, in 1821, a political pamphlet, in the form of a letter to Russell, calling for the repeal of the Corn Laws. From 1830 to 1846 he was editor-in-chief of *THE ATHENAEUM*, introducing the then comparatively new principle of complete editorial independence, and vastly improving the paper's circulation. In 1846 he was called in to manage the affairs of *THE DAILY NEWS*, following the departure of its founder-editor, CHARLES DICKENS. In 1849 he retired from newspaper management and was, for the remainder of his life, chiefly active as a literary historian, publishing mainly in his own *Athenaeum* and Thoms's recently founded *Notes and Queries*. He is best known for his detective work on the *Letters of Junius* (see JUNIUS), and researches into the early life and career of POPE.

Dillon, Wentworth, 4th Earl of Roscommon *c.* 1633–85 Translator. The nephew and godson of Thomas Wentworth, Earl of Strafford, Dillon was born in Ireland and educated at the University of Caen. He was interested in founding a British Academy on the lines of the Académie Française to 'refine and fix the standard of our language'. He wrote an *Essay on Translated Verse* (1684) and a blank-verse translation of Horace's *The Art of Poetry* (1680), and was among the first to recognize the greatness of MILTON's *PARADISE LOST*.

dimeter See METRE.

Dinesen, Isak [Blixen (*née* Dinesen), Karen Christentze] 1885–1962 Danish-born writer. She wrote in English, rewriting her work for Danish publication. Born to well-to-do parents living at Rungsted (on the coast between Copenhagen and Elsinore), she was educated at home, then at Lausanne. She attended the Royal Academy of Fine Arts in Copenhagen, and studied art there and later, spasmodically, in Paris and Rome. At the beginning of 1913 she went to East Africa to marry her cousin, Baron Blor von Blixen-Finecke, and farmed coffee outside Nairobi, in a district subsequently named 'Karen' after her. In 1931 she returned to Denmark, divorced and with the farm bankrupt. Her first book, *Seven Gothic Tales*, appeared in 1934, a collection of sometimes portentous neo-Gothic stories in which reality is distorted, the macabre ever-present, and desire never naturally fulfilled. *Out of Africa* followed in 1937, drawing upon her own experiences, and written in an episodic style remarkable for its clarity of phrase and intellectual breadth. *Shadows*

on the Grass (1960) continued the same theme. Other collections, *Winter's Tales* (1942), *Last Tales* (1957) and *Anecdotes of Destiny* (1958), deal with provincial as well as sophisticated situations and the insoluble difficulty of reconciling art and nature, while demonstrating erotic tension and many facets of alienation.

Dipsychus A verse drama by ARTHUR HUGH CLOUGH, written in 1850 and first published in 1865. Set in a Venetian palazzo, it takes the form of a near-plotless duologue of 13 scenes between Dipsychus (an individual of two natures) and the Spirit. The discussion ranges across problems of society, religion, the professions and the contemplative life, as the protagonist searches his inner self. The Spirit often acts as a tempter and summoner to the worldly, asserting itself as a presence conducive to SATIRE. Like Clough's other writings, *Dipsychus* articulates the role of the intellectual adrift in the world.

Dirty Realism A term coined by Bill Buford, editor of *GRANTA*, as the title for a special 1987 issue of the magazine devoted to new American fiction. It denotes a comparatively small school of downbeat, minimalist American short fiction represented by authors such as RAYMOND CARVER, RICHARD FORD and Tobias Wolff. TOM WOLFE has proposed 'K-Mart Realism' as an alternative label. Dirty Realism owes its laconic prose and elliptical narrative style to HEMINGWAY, but further pares down its range to concentrate on shabby, rootless communities and inconclusive encounters. It has been linked with POST-MODERNISM and viewed as an indirect response to the inequalities of the Reagan era. The term Dirty Realism is usually reserved for the short story, the form which best suits its brevity and selectivity.

Disch, Thomas M(ichael) 1940– American writer of SCIENCE FICTION. He was born in Des Moines and educated at Cooper Union and New York Universities. He began with sarcastic black comedies, including the apocalyptic novel *The Genocides* (1965) and the short stories in *Under Compulsion* (1968; also known as *Fun with Your New Head*). Later novels like *Camp Concentration* (1968) and *On Wings of Song* (1979) are more subtly and elegantly satirical, as are the short stories in *Getting into Death* (1973), *Fundamental Disch* (1980) and *The Man Who Had No Idea* (1982). *334* (1972) collects stories about the inhabitants of a New York apartment building in a bleakly dystopian near future. With John Sladek (initially as 'Thom Demijohn') Disch wrote a satirical comedy about racism, *Black Alice* (1968), and with Charles Naylor he wrote a historical novel about the world of Victorian letters, *Neighbouring Lives* (1981). As 'Leonie Hargrave' he wrote a pastiche GOTHIC NOVEL, *Clara Reeve* (1975). *The Businessman: A Tale of Terror*

(1984) and *The M. D.: A Horror Story* (1990) are gruesome black comedies. Collections of poetry include *The Right Way to Figure Plumbing* (1971), *Burn This* (1982) and *Here I am, There You are, Where were We?* (1984).

Disraeli, Benjamin, 1st Earl of Beaconsfield 1804–81 Novelist and politician. The eldest son of ISAAC D'ISRAELI, he was born in London and, despite his Jewish descent, was baptized at the age of 13. Aged 17, he was articled to a firm of solicitors, but by the time he was 20 he had given up the law. He gambled on the Stock Exchange, lost, attempted to found a new daily paper, *The Representative*, and lost money again. In 1826 he published his first novel, *VIVIAN GREY*, which gave the youthful hero his own wit and arrogance and (like several later works) introduced society figures under transparent disguises. The novel succeeded. Disraeli toured Italy and in 1827 published a satirical work, *The Voyage of Captain Popanilla*. He entered Lincoln's Inn to read for the Bar but, still in debt, succumbed to depression and went back to his father's house. In 1831 he published another society novel, *The Young Duke*. A tour of Spain, Greece, Albania and Egypt proved a formative experience, leaving its mark on much of his later writing, including his next novels, *CONTARINI FLEMING* (1832) and *Alroy* (1833).

In 1832 Disraeli took up politics as his main career, unsuccessfully contesting his first two seats as a Radical and then switching to the Tories. He was defeated twice more, but established a political reputation with pamphlets and letters to *The Times* arguing that the Tories were really the champions of national liberty against an oligarchy. He published a lighthearted SATIRE of contemporary politics, *The Infernal Marriage* (1834), and two more novels, *HENRIETTA TEMPLE* (1837) and *Venetia* (1837), a fictionalized account of events in the lives of SHELLEY and BYRON. In that year Queen Victoria ascended the throne and Disraeli succeeded in becoming Conservative MP for Maidstone. In 1839 he married Mrs Mary Anne Wyndham Lewis, widow of a previous Conservative member for Maidstone. During his early years in the Commons Disraeli showed his concern for the condition of the working class and associated himself with other reforming Tories in the 'Young England' group. The same attitudes underlie the trilogy of novels for which he is best known: *CONINGSBY: or, The New Generation* (1844), *SYBIL: or, the Two Nations* (1845) and *TANCRED: or, The New Crusade* (1847). They are characterized by the strength of their interest in current social problems, their informed historical discussion and their search for a true morality, a true patriotism.

Disraeli first achieved political office in Lord Derby's Conservative administration of 1852. He was twice Prime Minister, in 1868 and in 1874–80. In 1876 he took the title Earl of Beaconsfield, one he had invented for a character in his first novel. His success in politics overshadowed, but did not end, his writing career. *LOTHAIR* (1870) is a novel about religious conflict; *ENDYMION* was published in 1880, the year before his death. He also left nine chapters of an unfinished novel, *Falconet*.

d'Israeli, Isaac 1766–1848 Man of letters and father of BENJAMIN DISRAELI. He was born at Enfield, of Jewish descent, but quarrelled with the elders of his synagogue and had his children baptized, thus making his son's political career possible. He spent his teens studying philosophy with a tutor in Amsterdam and wrote a poem against commerce, which offended his father, a merchant. He went to Paris, where he frequented literary circles. He spent his life as a literary gentleman and married Maria Besevi, who gave him five children. He died at his home in Buckinghamshire.

His published works are *Curiosities of Literature* (1791), *Essay on the Literary Character* (1795), *Miscellanies, or Literary Recreations* (1796), *The Calamities of Authors* (1812–13) and *Quarrels of Authors* (1814). He also wrote historical works on JAMES I (1816) and on Charles I (1828–31). In 1833 he published *The Genius of Judaism*. Three volumes of his projected history of English literature appeared in 1841 under the title *Amenities of Literature*. He also wrote four unsuccessful novels.

dissociation of sensibility A term coined by T. S. ELIOT in his influential essay 'The Metaphysical Poets' (1921). Eliot argued that writers of the late 16th and early 17th centuries, particularly JOHN DONNE, had possessed a unity of thought and feeling, making for 'a direct sensuous apprehension of thought' and 'a mechanism of sensibility which could devour any kind of experience'. After Donne's time, with the influence of MILTON and DRYDEN, English poetry was impoverished by a dissociation of sensibility. Poets of the 18th and 19th centuries, Eliot concluded, thought but could not feel their thoughts.

dithyramb Originally a Greek choric hymn accompanied by music and describing the adventures of Dionysus, the term is now used for verse or prose of a wild, passionate or excited nature, or for any wild chant or song. Perhaps the finest example of dithyrambic verse in English is DRYDEN's 'Alexander's Feast'.

Dixon, H(enry) H(all) 1822–70 Sporting journalist. Educated at Rugby and Cambridge, he flirted with the law but turned to sporting journalism, writing as 'The Druid', and carved himself a niche in the middle ground between the aristocratic world of C. J. APPERLEY ('Nimrod') and the debased pugilistic arena of PIERCE EGAN THE ELDER. He traversed England and Scotland indefatigably on foot or pony, writing largely of bourgeois sporting personalities, professional hunt-servants and jockeys, sporting dogs, racehorses and the like; he also discoursed on cattle-dealers and farm stock. His best-known books are: *Post and Paddock* (1856), *Silk and Scarlet* (1859), *Scott and Sebright* (1862), *Field and Fern* (1865) and *Saddle and Sirloin* (1870). Some of his allusions are obscure today but his work still provides a vivid picture of mid-century, middle-class sporting and farming life.

Dixon, Richard Watson 1833–1900 Poet. He was educated at King Edward VI School, Birmingham, and Pembroke College, Oxford, where he became close friends with WILLIAM MORRIS, Burne-Jones and DANTE GABRIEL ROSSETTI. After his ordination he was assistant master at Highgate School, where he taught G. M. HOPKINS in 1861. He maintained his friendship with Hopkins, praising his poetry for 'forcibly and delicately giving the essence of things in nature' and trying to get 'The Loss of the Euridyce' printed in a Carlisle newspaper. Dixon's own first collection of verse, *Christ's Company* (1861), was praised by Rossetti and SWINBURNE. He later held various preferments in the North of England and published several more volumes, including *Historical Odes* (1864), *Mano: A Poetical History* (1883), *Odes and Eclogues* (1884) and *Lyrical Poems* (1887). *Mano* was a long narrative poem set in the 10th century, recounting the adventures of a Norman knight. Favourite anthology pieces include 'Dream', 'The Wizard's Funeral' and 'Love's Consolation'. His main prose work was a *History of the Church of England from the Abolition of Roman Jurisdiction* (1878–1902). ROBERT BRIDGES edited a selection, *The Last Poems* (1905).

Dobell, Sydney (Thompson) 1824–74 Poet. He was born at Cranbrook in Kent and privately educated in Cheltenham. *The Roman: A Dramatic Poem* (1850) supported the cause of Italian nationalism. *Balder* (1853) was left unfinished, so damaging was the ridicule inflicted by WILLIAM AYTOUN, who parodied its plot in *FIRMILIAN* (1854) and identified its author as part of the SPASMODIC SCHOOL OF POETRY. Dobell's other volumes included *Sonnets on the War* (with ALEXANDER SMITH, 1855) and *England in Time of War* (1856), about the Crimean campaign. *Thoughts on Art, Philosophy, and Religion* appeared posthumously in 1876.

Dobson, Austin (Henry) 1840–1921 Poet and biographer. Educated at Beaumaris Grammar School and in Strasburg, he served with GOSSE at the Board of Trade. His knowledge of the 18th century is apparent in his biographies of HOGARTH (1879), STEELE (1886), GOLDSMITH (1888), HORACE WALPOLE (1890), RICHARDSON (1902) and FANNY BURNEY (1903). His

verse often used French forms such as the TRIOLET and RONDEAU. His volumes include *Vignettes in Rhyme* (1873), *Proverbs in Porcelain* (1877) and *At the Sign of the Lyre* (1885). *Collected Poems* appeared in 1897, and a collection of later essays in 1921.

Dobson, Rosemary 1920– Australian poet. Born in Sydney of Australian and English parents, she is the granddaughter of AUSTIN DOBSON. After studying art at the University of Sydney, she taught art at her former school, was employed on cipher work during World War II and then entered publishing. Though it has not received a great deal of popular attention, her detached, reflective verse has few rivals in Australian literature for its craftsmanship and formal elegance. Her training in art frequently manifests itself in poems about painters, painting and design. The title-poem of one of her finest volumes, *The Ship of Ice* (1948), illustrates the timelessness of art, its power to immortalize a fleeting moment. Later poetry is increasingly concerned with her personal experiences, especially that of motherhood, and Greek themes. Her other volumes include *In a Convex Mirror* (1944), *Child with a Cockatoo* (1955), *Cock Crow* (1965), *Collected Poems* (1973), *Three Poems on Water Springs* (1973), *Greek Coins* (1977), *Over the Frontier* (1978), *The Continuance of Poetry* (1981), *Three Fates and Other Poems* (1984), *Summer Press* (1987) and *Collected Poems* (1991). She has also translated several volumes of Russian poetry with DAVID CAMPBELL and edited a feminist anthology, *Sister Poets* (1979).

Doctor Faustus, The Tragical History of A tragedy in blank verse and prose by CHRISTOPHER MARLOWE, first produced c. 1589 but not published until 1604. An edition of 1616 is more reliable, but both are faulty. The medieval legend of the bargain with the Devil first found its way into printed form at Frankfurt in 1587, when the chief character was identified with a Doctor Georg Faust, a necromancer of the late 15th and early 16th centuries in Germany. In the Frankfurt *Faustbuch* he is called Johann Faust and Marlowe uses the same name (John) in his (the first) dramatization of the story. The play was acted by the same company who produced TAMBURLAINE, The Admiral's Men, who were now called the Earl of Nottingham's Men – in recognition of their patron's new eminence. EDWARD ALLEYN played Doctor Faustus.

Faustus is weary of scientific study and turns to magic. He invokes the aid of the Devil, who sends his agent Mephistophilis in the form of an ugly beast. Faustus commands him to change his shape to that of a friar, which Mephistophilis meekly does. Faustus makes his bargain: Lucifer will give him 24 years of life, with Mephistophilis to do his bidding, but at the end of that time Faustus will be taken, body and soul, by Lucifer. The contract gives Faustus everything he asks for, except for certain questions Mephistophilis will not answer ('Now tell me, who made the world?'). Faustus's guardian angel goes on trying to redeem him, while a Bad Angel goes on persuading him he is damned. Lucifer himself comes to Faustus and shows him the pleasures of the seven deadly sins. After a confrontation with the Pope and cardinals in Rome, Faustus invokes the ghost of Helen of Troy. An Old Man pleads with Faustus to step back from the brink – there is still hope of redemption. Faustus makes his choice: he invokes the spirit of Helen again and embraces her ('Her lips suck forth my soul'). The climax of the play is Faustus's monologue anticipating the terrors that await him in his last hour of mortal life ('See, see, where Christ's blood streams in the firmament! One drop would save my soul, half a drop. Ah, my Christ!') and his descent into hell. Despite a collapse into crude farce in the middle section – charitably regarded as the additions for which SAMUEL ROWLEY was paid in 1602 – *Faustus* is a magnificent poem, a great theme expressed in language that is equal to it.

Dr Jekyll and Mr Hyde, The Strange Case of

A novel by ROBERT LOUIS STEVENSON, published in 1886. Apart from TREASURE ISLAND, it is probably his best-known work.

The mystery of Jekyll and Hyde is gradually revealed to the reader through the disparate narratives of Mr Enfield, Mr Utterson, Dr Lanyon and Poole, the butler at Jekyll's house. The respectable Dr Jekyll wants to separate the good and evil aspects of his nature. By means of a transforming drug he has secretly developed in his laboratory, he succeeds in freeing his evil propensities into the repulsive form of Mr Hyde. Initially he finds it easy to return to the personality of Jekyll, but in time this becomes more difficult and he finds himself slipping involuntarily into being Hyde. Eventually his supplies of the drug run out and he cannot manage to reduplicate the chemical formula. Hyde is now wanted for murder, and Jekyll kills himself. The body discovered in his sanctum is that of Hyde, but the confession Jekyll leaves behind establishes that the two men were versions of the same person.

The story has attracted much commentary, being read as a version of the Scottish Arminianism of JAMES HOGG's PRIVATE MEMOIRS AND CONFESSIONS OF A JUSTIFIED SINNER, a variant of the *Doppelgänger* myth, and a pre-Freudian study of ego and libido. G. K. CHESTERTON noted, however, that Hyde is not a diabolic *alter ego* but a diminished part of Jekyll's whole personality, pure evil where Jekyll is a mixture of good and evil. Jekyll's deluded belief that, because man is dual rather than whole, the good in him can hence be separated from the evil, provides a study in degeneration and ultimate human responsibility.

Dr Syntax in Search of the Picturesque, The Tour of

A verse satire by WILLIAM COMBE, published in 1809. Between 1809 and 1811 Rudolph Ackermann produced his *Poetical Magazine*, for which Thomas Rowlandson offered him a series of plates depicting the comic adventures of a village schoolmaster. Combe was asked to write the letterpress for the illustrations, and thus began a collaboration between the writer and artist which lasted for over a decade. *The Schoolmaster's Tour*, as it was first called, was an enormous popular success, and was reissued in book form in 1812. Astride a shiftless old horse called Grizzle, the clergyman-schoolmaster sets out 'to make a *tour* and *write it*', in the course of which he suffers a series of absurd misfortunes. The book is perhaps in the first instance a satire of WILLIAM GILPIN's well-known expeditions to picturesque Britain, but it also feeds off the host of 18th- and early 19th-century writers whose 'Tours', 'Travels' and 'Journeys' were vehicles of sententious moralizing, fake rapture and self-indulgent sentiment. It was followed by *The Second Tour of Dr Syntax in Search of Consolation* (1820), Mrs Syntax having expired at the end of the first tour, and *The Third Tour of Dr Syntax in Search of a Wife* (1821). The three were published together in 1826.

Doctor Thorne

A novel by ANTHONY TROLLOPE, the third of his BARSETSHIRE NOVELS, published in 1858.

The unmarried Dr Thorne, a country practitioner, lives in Greshamsbury with his niece Mary. He alone knows the secret of her birth, that she is the illegitimate child of his brother Henry by the sister of a local stonemason, Roger Scatcherd. Imprisoned for murdering his sister's seducer, Scatcherd, now Sir Roger, has risen to eminence as a successful railway contractor, although his life is vitiated by the drunkenness he has passed on to his enfeebled only son Louis. Mary has grown up as the friend of the local squire's family, the Greshams, and she and the young heir Frank are in love; but the estate is burdened with debt and Frank is required to marry money. The novel deals with the trials the young couple have to endure, as Frank's relatives first ostracize Mary, then aided by their aristocratic relations, the De Courcys, plot a marriage between him and the much older Miss Dunstable, the shrewd and kindly heiress to a patent medicine fortune. When Sir Roger dies, however, soon followed by his son Louis, Mary falls heir to his fortune, and the obstacles to her marriage with Frank dissolve, his family choosing to ignore the fact of her low birth now that money is in prospect. A subsidiary plot deals with the relations between Frank's sister and a social-climbing lawyer, and his eventual marriage to her treacherous De Courcy cousin.

Doctor Thorne was Trollope's best-selling novel in his own lifetime, and represents an extension of the Barsetshire range to take in the life of county society.

Dr Wortle's School A novel by ANTHONY TROLLOPE, serialized in *BLACKWOOD'S MAGAZINE* from May to December 1880, and published in two volumes in 1881.

Dr Jeffrey Wortle, a high-spirited and worldly clergyman, runs a successful private school to which he appoints Mr Peacocke as an assistant master, and Peacocke's beautiful American wife as matron. Although Peacocke proves an excellent master, mystery surrounds the couple's history and it is revealed early in the novel that they are not in fact married. While teaching in Missouri he had met and befriended the ill-treated and deserted wife of one Ferdinand Lefroy, a soldier of fortune, and had married her when news came of his death – an event Peacocke made every effort to verify. But Lefroy reappears, and the scandal of their seeming bigamy follows the couple to England. The novel deals with Dr Wortle's courage in standing by his conviction of the Peacockes' integrity against pressure from his bishop, the press and the malevolent gossip of an ex-parent. His stand is rewarded when Peacocke goes to America and returns with proof of a rumour that Lefroy had subsequently died. The scandal subsides when the couple are married again in London. Conventional love interest is provided by a romance between the doctor's daughter Mary and one of his former pupils, Lord Carstairs.

Dr Wortle's School deals impressively with a subject peculiarly congenial to Trollope's art, the clash between social convention and the intricacies of the individual case.

Doctorow, E(dgar) L(awrence) 1931– American novelist. Born in New York and educated at Kenyon College and Columbia University, he now teaches at New York University. *Welcome to Hard Times* (1960; as *Bad Man from Bodie* in Britain) was followed by *The Book of Daniel* (1971), the novel which first brought him wide acclaim, about the espionage trial of Julius and Ethel Rosenberg and its aftermath. His fiction is typified by its use of historical figures, most notably in *Ragtime* (1975), in which the lives of three fictional families at the beginning of the 20th century are entwined with figures such as Henry Ford, Emma Goldman, Harry Houdini, THEODORE DREISER and Sigmund Freud. Other novels are *Big as Life* (1966), *Loon Lake* (1980), *World's Fair* (1985) and *Billy Bathgate* (1989), about the New York gangland of the 1930s. *Drinks before Dinner* (1979) is a play. *Lives of the Poet, Six Stories and a Novella* (1984) addresses the position of the writer as both participant in and observer of society.

Doddridge, Philip 1702–51 Nonconformist divine. Born in London the twentieth and final offspring of an oilman, he was always delicate, and only one of his siblings reached adulthood. Educated pri-

vately, then at the school at Kingston founded by his grandfather, he finally moved to a school at St Albans. The Duchess of Bedford offered to fund a university course but he felt unable to conform. In 1723 he received his certificate of approbation and was ordained a presbyter in 1730. He was a major influence on the unification of Nonconformist groups. In an attempt to alleviate ill health he voyaged to Lisbon, but died there. He wrote *The Rise and Progress of Religion in the Soul* (1745), *Some Remarkable Passages in the Life of Colonel James Gardiner* (1747), an account of a reformed rake, and over 350 hymns, which may be compared to those of ISAAC WATTS. His collected works appeared in 10 volumes in 1802–5.

Dodgson, Charles Lutwidge See CARROLL, LEWIS.

Dodsley, Robert 1703–64 Publisher and author. Born near Mansfield, Nottinghamshire, educated at the free school where his father was headmaster, and apprenticed to a stockingmaker who ill-treated him, the young Dodsley ran away and found work as a servant, eventually becoming footman to the Hon. Mrs Lowther. He was fortunate in his employer, for she helped him publish his poem *Servitude* (1729) and called attention to her footman's gifts. Literary London became interested in Dodsley, and the friendship of POPE and SWIFT eventually brought him to the notice of John Rich.

Dodsley's play *The Toyshop: A Dramatic Satire* (written about 1732) was successfully produced by Rich at COVENT GARDEN in 1735 and Dodsley used his modest success to open a bookshop at Tully's Head in Pall Mall. Pope invested £100 and HORACE WALPOLE, LORD LYTTELTON and Joseph Spence helped him select poetry when he became a publisher. In addition to the works of Pope, Dodsley issued those of THOMAS GRAY, MARK AKENSIDE, WILLIAM COLLINS, EDWARD YOUNG and WILLIAM SHENSTONE; he also published work by SAMUEL JOHNSON and OLIVER GOLDSMITH. His great service to the poets of his time was the publication of their work in permanent volumes called *A Collection of Poems by Various Hands*, the first of which was published in 1748; six volumes appeared in 10 years. They are valuable to students of the period, as his collection of *Old Plays* (12 vols., 1744) is to students of drama. Dodsley's tragedy *Cleone* was produced in 1758. In the same year he founded, with EDMUND BURKE, *THE ANNUAL REGISTER*, which still continues to appear.

Dodsworth A novel by SINCLAIR LEWIS, published in 1929. Sam Dodsworth, a successful car manufacturer in the city of Zenith in the American Midwest, sells out to a larger company and retires. Still vigorous in his middle age, a dreamer and an idealist, he travels with his wife Fran to Europe.

Fran is spoiled, affected, and easily awed by European manners and titles. Wishing to appear a woman of the world – to become European – she flirts with other men and becomes increasingly impatient with Sam's supposed gaucheness. Eventually they separate and she plans to marry Kurt von Obersdorf, a young Austrian aristocrat. But the marriage does not take place: Kurt's mother disapproves of Fran, a soon-to-be-divorced, middle-aged American. She begs Sam's forgiveness, and though in the meantime he has met Edith Cortright, a refined and understanding American living in Italy, he takes Fran back. Soon, however, her shallowness and petulance make him realize how much he cares for Edith. He divorces Fran and returns to Edith in Europe.

Dombey and Son A novel by CHARLES DICKENS, published in 20 monthly parts from October 1846 until April 1848 (and in volume form, 1848). Its full title, *Dealings with the Firm of Dombey and Son, Retail, Wholesale and for Exportation*, is deliberately ambiguous in its reference to both a family and a family business. The stern, unbending Mr Dombey, preoccupied with his desire for a son and heir to the firm, ignores and resents his eldest child, a daughter, Florence. When a son is born at the beginning of the book, Mrs Dombey dies in childbirth and the boy, Paul, proves to be constitutionally weak. He grows to be more fond of his sister than of his father, and has the habit of disconcerting those who attempt to instruct him by his quick perceptions. Little Paul Dombey dies in the fifth number (chapter 16) and the bereavement further alienates Florence from her father, despite her desperate eagerness for his love. Dombey's second marriage, to the widowed Edith Grainger, proves loveless and childless. The passionate Edith finally runs away with the manager of Dombey's business, the predatory Carker, though she soon abandons him and he is killed in a railway accident. Dombey's ensuing mental and physical decline parallels his business difficulties. Only as a ruined man can he at last respond to Florence's enduring love.

Dombey and Son is commonly taken to herald the start of Dickens's maturity as a novelist, for its careful planning marks a break from the high-spirited improvisation which often sustains his early fiction. The central idea – that 'Dombey and Son should be a Daughter after all' – controls the book's shape, though Dickens is also deeply concerned with the theme of pride. The novel contrasts the cold unhappiness of the Dombey household with the cheerful homes of the Toodle family and of Sol Gills and his nephew Walter Gay (Florence's future husband). The story of Paul's birth, education and death was edited as 'The Story of Little Dombey' to make a favourite set-piece in Dickens's immensely successful public readings.

Domett, Alfred 1811–77 Politician and poet. He was born at Camberwell Grove, Surrey, and became a barrister of the Middle Temple after leaving St John's College, Cambridge. He emigrated to New Zealand, where he became Prime Minister. After his return to England in 1871 he published two books of poetry reflecting his experiences, *Ranolf and Amohia* (1872) and *Flotsam and Jetsam* (1877). 'A Christmas Hymn', which was once a familiar anthology piece, was one of the occasional poems published by BLACKWOOD'S MAGAZINE before Domett went to New Zealand. A friend of ROBERT BROWNING, Domett is the 'Waring' of Browning's well-known poem (1842).

Don Juan BYRON's unfinished 'epic satire' in OTTAVA RIMA, published in 16 CANTOS between 1819 and 1824. Cantos 1–2 appeared in 1819, 3–5 in 1821, 6–14 in 1823 and 15–16 in 1824.

Byron's central character is not the aggressive libertine of tradition, but a passive, if unprincipled, innocent who learns through the variety of his complex international experience. The poem opens with the 16-year-old Juan being sent away from his native Seville by his mother as a result of an intrigue with Donna Julia. On the way from Cadiz his ship is wrecked in a storm and the crew and passengers are obliged to drift in the ship's longboat; their privations lead to the consumption first of Juan's spaniel then of his tutor, Pedrillo.

Byron's description of both the storm and the subsequent cannibalism contains some of his most powerful, as well as his most wry, descriptive verse. Juan is eventually cast up on a Greek island where he meets Haïdée, the daughter of a pirate. The two fall in love, but their passion is disrupted by the return of Haïdée's pirate-father, who sends Juan away in chains to be sold as a slave. Haïdée dies of grief. Juan is sold in Constantinople to a sultana who has fallen in love with him, but their relationship is soured by her perpetual jealousy and Juan is obliged to escape to the Russian army then besieging Ismail. Distinguishing himself in the Russian service, he is sent with dispatches to St Petersburg where he inevitably attracts the attentions of the Empress Catherine. He is sent to England on a diplomatic mission; the last cantos of the unfinished poem recount his amorous adventures and contain much satirical comment on contemporary English society, politics and literature.

Don Juan is Byron's most sustained masterpiece. Its tone is varied and its loose structure allows the poet to intermix his gifts as a lyrical, satirical, comic and narrative writer. The poem offers a wide-ranging ironic comment on human passions, whims and shortcomings. It also contains the much-anthologized lyric 'The Isles of Greece' (canto 3), Byron's powerful song to a nation still occupied by the Ottomans.

Donleavy, J(ames) P(atrick) 1926– Novelist, short-story writer and playwright. Born of Irish parents in Brooklyn, New York, he served in the US Navy before going to Trinity College, Dublin, and settling in Ireland. He remains best known for a determinedly Rabelaisian novel of Dublin literary life, *The Ginger Man*, first published in Paris in 1955, then in a revised edition in New York in 1958 and in a 'complete and unexpurgated' edition in New York in 1965. Other work has included: *A Singular Man* (1961), *The Saddest Summer of Samuel S.* (1966), *The Beastly Beatitudes of Balthazar B.* (1968), *The Destinies of Darcy Dancer, Gentleman* (1977) and *That Darcy, That Dancer, That Gentleman* (1990), all novels; *Meet My Maker the Mad Molecule* (1964), short stories; and a play, *Fairy Tales of New York* (1961).

Donne, John *c.* 1572–1631 METAPHYSICAL POET and divine. He was born in Bread Street, London, his father a prosperous ironmonger and his mother the daughter of JOHN HEYWOOD, the dramatist. Donne was brought up as a Roman Catholic. He was educated at Hart Hall, Oxford, and left in 1584 without a degree, which would have required him to take the Oath of Supremacy. According to his earliest biographer, IZAAK WALTON (whose *Life* appeared in 1640), Donne then went to Cambridge and travelled abroad. He entered Lincoln's Inn in 1592, and embarked on a period of womanizing and writing verse. In 1596 he sailed on the Cadiz expedition when the Spanish fleet was defeated, and in the following year he joined an inconclusive expedition to the Azores, where he wrote 'The Calm'. The dating of his poetry is largely problematic, but to the 1590s apparently belong: most of the love poems contained in *Songs and Sonnets* (including 'The Good Morrow', 'The Canonization', 'The Bait' and songs such as 'Go and Catch a Falling Star'); the *Elegies*, characteristically sinuous, colloquial and racy poems which have none of the smoothness later identified with the ELEGY; and his five verse *Satires*, among the first formal verse satires in the language. In 1601 he published an ambitious but unfinished poem, *Metempsychosis*, a complicated explanation of the nature of good and evil as manifested in the progressive metamorphoses of the soul, from its vegetable origins in Eden to its embodiment in mankind.

On his return from the Azores expedition he became chief secretary to Sir Thomas Egerton, a former lawyer, Lord Keeper of the Great Seal. Donne now lived next to the Palace of Whitehall, and he met Ann Moore, 14-year-old daughter of Lady Egerton's brother, Sir George Moore. In 1601 Donne became MP for Brackley, one of Egerton's pocket boroughs, but he was not active in the House. At the end of this year he drastically altered the course of his life by marrying Ann (at 17 still a minor) in secret. This amounted to social suicide. The union was discovered, and in 1602 Egerton had the poet briefly imprisoned and permanently dismissed from office. At the age of 30, Donne was married and jobless.

Doubts have been raised about the happiness of this fateful marriage, but they had 12 children, of whom seven survived. Their domestic circumstances were impecunious, and the poet was dogged by intermittent illness. In 1605 he travelled to Europe with Sir Walter Chute, returning in 1606 and settling in Mitcham. Donne preferred the busy life of the metropolis to rural calm; he tried to attract the attention of potential patrons such as the Countesses of Bedford and Huntingdon, but advancement was not forthcoming. He cultivated a convivial circle of literary acquaintances centred on the Mitre Tavern, including JONSON, DRAYTON and Inigo Jones. He also made an important new friend in Sir Robert Drury, a vivacious landowning gentleman with whom Donne travelled to Amiens and Paris in 1611, returning the next year via Germany. He wrote two notable poems commemorating the death of Sir Robert's daughter Elizabeth, 'The First Anniversary' (1611) and 'The Progress of the Soul' (1612). In general, his writings record a preoccupation with religion and a movement away from Catholicism. *Biathanatos* (1607) is an erudite prose-work about Christianity and suicide. *Pseudo-Martyr* (1610), his most notable prose-work, urged English Catholics to take the Oath of Supremacy, while *Ignatius His Conclave* (1611) satirized the Jesuits. The *Holy Sonnets* reveal spiritual struggle and, at times, near-despair, as well as the hard-won triumph of the famous 'Death, be Not Proud'.

He and his wife settled in a small house in Drury Lane, and Donne assiduously presented complimentary verses to individuals in court circles, but failed to find preferment. The Church looked increasingly like the only prospect for professional success, and on 23 January 1615 he took Holy Orders. JAMES I (who had approved of *Pseudo-Martyr* and *Ignatius His Conclave*) appointed him a royal chaplain, and Donne began to acquire a reputation as a fine preacher. In 1616 he was made reader in divinity at Lincoln's Inn, a post which suited his combination of talents, and he held two livings, one in Kent and the other in Huntingdon.

Just when his fortunes appeared to be improving, Donne's wife died, on 15 August 1617, after giving birth to a stillborn child. The poet's grief at her death is powerful proof of his devotion to her; he never quite recovered, and according to Walton he was thereafter 'crucified to the world'. The religious dimension to his life certainly seems to have deepened. In 1619 Donne spent seven months travelling with Viscount Doncaster in an unsuccessful attempt to mediate between the Catholic Emperor of Germany and the troublesome Protestant subjects in Bohemia. He returned to London in 1620, his depression somewhat alleviated, and in the following year was made Dean of St Paul's, a busy administrative and spiritual occupation at which he excelled. His financial position was finally secure. In 1623 his eldest daughter, Constance, married the celebrated actor EDWARD ALLEYN (by then 58) who was the founder of Dulwich College.

Late in 1623 Donne became seriously ill during an epidemic, and began work on his *Devotions upon Emergent Occasions* (1624) consisting of meditations, expostulations and prayers. Meditation 17, which begins 'Perchance he for whom the bell tolls', has become one of the best-known passages of English prose. He also wrote some verse, including the poem 'In Sicknesse'. In 1624 he was made vicar of St Dunstan's-in-the-West, where Walton was a parishioner. On 27 March 1625 James I died, and Donne preached his first sermon before Charles I. He retired from London to Chelsea to avoid the plague, but later delivered some of his most powerful sermons on the theme of suffering. Donne became unwell again in 1630, but, emaciated and suffering from infections of the mouth, he nevertheless insisted on preaching the sermon 'Death's Duel' on the first Friday in Lent, 1631, before the king at Whitehall. It was to be his last: he died on 31 March 1631. His monument in St Paul's, which he designed himself, survived the Great Fire.

John Donne

Very little of Donne's verse appeared in print during his lifetime, and the posthumous *Collected Poems* (1633) was by no means complete. His verse is generally divided into the love poetry of his youth and the religious poetry of later years, though both clearly belong to the same process of organic development. The love poetry is original, energetic and highly rhetorical, full of passionate thought and intellectual juggling, paradox and punning designed to work forcefully against the tired conventions of the PETRARCHAN school. It is often erotic and physically urgent: Donne was the first writer to use 'sex' in its present sense. The same adroitness in argument and dramatic skill in impersonating different states of mind that make his love poetry intense and often riddling animate his religious verse. But as a devotional poet Donne is less stylistically arresting, less facetious, and less sure of his direction: the poems mirror what was evidently a fierce struggle of the spirit to conquer doubt and achieve faith. As a writer of reli-

gious prose he is best known for his *Sermons*, 160 of which were published after his death, in 1640, 1649 and 1660 successively. They are often brilliant and severe.

Doolittle, Hilda 1886–1961 American poet, who used the pseudonym H. D. Born in Bethlehem, Pennsylvania, she went to live in Europe in 1911, marrying RICHARD ALDINGTON in 1913 and becoming involved in IMAGISM through her association with EZRA POUND, to whom she had been briefly engaged. He arranged for her poems to appear in HARRIET MONROE'S *POETRY* magazine and the anthology *Des Imagistes* (1914). Her first collection, *Sea Garden* (1916), drew heavily on a passion for classical Greek literature. Indeed, all her early collections include translations from – and poems inspired by – Sappho, Meleager and Euripides among others. All reveal her gift for concise and direct visual description. Natural objects, such as a plant, a rock, a wave or a bee, are often used to stand for a human mood or emotion, a method consistent both with the principles of imagism and with the practice of the Greek poets.

She stayed in England throughout World War I, which brought many changes to her life, including the dissolution of her marriage, the birth of her daughter and the beginning of her association with Bryher (Winifred Ellerman), novelist and patron of MODERNISM, who became her lifelong companion. More collections of poetry followed: *Hymen* (1921), *Heliodora and Other Poems* (1924), and *Red Roses for Bronze* (1929). In the 1920s she also began to write prose fiction. *Palimpsest* (1926) consists of three sections narrated through STREAM OF CONSCIOUSNESS, one set in classical Rome, one in post-war London and one in the Egypt of the excavators. It is unified by themes of sexual betrayal and women's attempt to find personal fulfilment through love and art. *Hedylus* (1928), set in ancient Alexandria, deals with the relationship between a woman poet and courtesan and her son, also a poet. *Pilate's Wife, Asphodel* and *Her* are prose works with explicitly lesbian themes which she chose not to publish during her lifetime; they appeared posthumously as *Hermione* (1981).

Psychoanalysis by Freud (1933–4) and experience of London during the blitz of World War II provided two of the main sources for a long poem *Trilogy*, which comprised *The Walls Do Not Fall* (1944), *Tribute to the Angels* (1945) and *The Flowering of the Rod* (1946). Her other works include *Hippolytus Temporizes* (1927), a drama in classical form; *By Avon River* (1949), a tribute in verse and prose to SHAKESPEARE and the Elizabethans; another novel, *Bid Me to Live* (1960), treating life in London during World War I; *Helen in Egypt* (1961), a long poem about Helen of Troy; three memoirs: *Tribute to Freud* (1956), *End to Torment: A Memoir of Ezra Pound* (1979) and *The Gift* (1982); and a final set of poetic sequences, *Hermetic Definition* (1972).

Dorn, Ed(ward) 1929– American poet. Born in Villa Grove, Illinois, he was educated at the University of Illinois and Black Mountain College, where he studied with contemporaries such as ROBERT DUNCAN and CHARLES OLSON. He has taught at Idaho State University, Northeastern University, the University of Essex and, since 1977, the University of Colorado. His poetry first came to notice in Donald Allen's anthology *The New American Poetry* (1960), where it appeared with the work of other members of the BLACK MOUNTAIN SCHOOL, notably Duncan and ROBERT CREELEY. *The Newly Fallen* (1961) and *Hands Up!* (1964) were followed by *From Gloucester Out* (1964), which established him as the most important younger poet extending the possibilities of Olson's theories of 'projective verse'. Later volumes include *Geography* (1965), *The North Atlantic Turbine* (1967), *Twenty-Four Love Poems* (1969), *Songs, Set Two* (1970), *Hello La Jolla* (1978), *Selected Poems* (1978), *Views* (1980), *Abhorrence* (1990) and *By the Sound* (1991). *The Collected Poems, 1956–1974* (1975) reprints all the verse from the first 18 years of his career except *Gunslinger* (1968–1972), a dramatic narrative which first appeared as four separate books and then as *Slinger* (1975). *What I See in the Maximus Poems* (1961) is a critical study of Olson. *The Rite of Passage* (1965) is a novel.

Dos Passos, John (Roderigo) 1896–1970 American novelist. The illegitimate son of a prominent American attorney, he was born in Chicago but spent much of his early life living abroad with his mother. He returned to the USA to attend Harvard, and then served as an ambulance driver in France and Italy during World War I. He drew upon his war experiences for his first two novels, *One Man's Initiation: 1917* (1920) and *Three Soldiers* (1921), both of which portray revolt against mindless discipline. In 1922 he published a collection of essays, *Rosinante to the Road Again*, and a volume of poems, *A Pushcart at the Curb*. *Streets of Night*, a novel he had begun while still a student at Harvard, appeared in 1923. He came to

prominence with MANHATTAN TRANSFER (1925), a novel whose aim of providing a 'collective' portrait of New York embodied his left-wing views. A similar purpose underlay his most important work, *USA*, a trilogy consisting of *The 42nd Parallel* (1930), *1919* (1932) and *The Big Money* (1936), which together seek to provide a portrait of American life in the first decades of the century. *The Moon is a Gong* (1926; later renamed *The Garbage Man*), *Airways, Inc.* (1928) and *Fortune Heights* (1934) are plays stemming from his involvement with experimental theatre.

Dos Passos became disillusioned with communism and broke completely with the left at the time of the Spanish Civil War, as is made clear in *The Adventures of a Young Man* (1939). This novel began another trilogy, *District of Columbia*, completed by *Number One* (1943), about the dangers of demagogy, and *The Grand Design* (1949), about the threat of bureaucracy. Later novels include *Chosen Country* (1951) and *Midcentury* (1961). He also wrote numerous works of non-fiction: *The Head and Heart of Thomas Jefferson* (1954), a full-length biography of one of his heroes; *The Best of Times: An Informal Memoir* (1966); and several collections of essays and reportage, which reflect his increasingly conservative political stance. *The Fourteenth Chronicle* (1973) contains selections from his letters and diaries.

Double Dealer, The A comedy by WILLIAM CONGREVE, first performed in 1693. More satirical and more rigidly classical in form than his first play, *THE OLD BACHELOR* (1693), it was, according to DRYDEN, who admired it, 'much censured by the greater part of the town'. The malice of Maskwell, the double dealer, and the rhetorical force of the Touchwoods' passion are certainly more than can be easily resolved by a happy ending.

Lady Touchwood, a woman motivated by passion, desires Mellefont, who is her husband's nephew and heir. Mellefont prefers Cynthia, daughter of Sir Paul Plyant. Determined to obstruct their marriage, Lady Touchwood enlists the aid of Maskwell, a former lover expert in deceit. Playing the part of Mellefont's friend, Maskwell tricks both Sir Paul Plyant and Lord Touchwood into suspecting that Mellefont is having affairs with their wives. The ruse works and Mellefont is disinherited and banned from marrying Cynthia. But Maskwell overreaches when he claims Cynthia for himself. The jealous Lady Touchwood cannot accept being supplanted and their plotting is discovered when Lord Touchwood overhears her furious attack on Maskwell's duplicity. Mellefont and Cynthia are at last free to marry, and Maskwell and Lady Touchwood are consigned to the ignominy of oblivion.

Double Falsehood, The See SHAKESPEARE APOCRYPHA and THEOBALD, LEWIS.

Douce, Francis 1757–1834 Antiquary. A student of Gray's Inn, Douce became keeper of manuscripts at the British Museum where he catalogued the Lansdowne Manuscripts and revised the catalogue of the Harleian Manuscripts (see EDWARD HARLEY), but left after a disagreement. His *Illustrations of Shakespeare* (1807) was a collection of the principal sources and analogues of the plays. In 1823 he was left a considerable sum by the sculptor Nollekens which enabled him to indulge his passion for acquiring books, manuscripts, prints, coins and *objets d'art*. He left his collection to the Bodleian Library.

Doughty, Charles Montagu 1843–1926 Travel-writer and poet. Born at Theberton Hall, Suffolk, and educated at Gonville and Caius College, Cambridge, he began travelling as a student, visiting North Africa, Syria and Arabia in 1870. After settling in Damascus in 1875 in order to learn Arabic, he made the pilgrimage to Mecca in 1876 by joining a camel caravan. He continued with the caravan to central Arabia, finishing his journey at Jedda. The account of his journey is contained in his most famous work, *Travels in Arabia Deserta* (1888), a book written in a self-consciously archaic style and in the manner of Elizabethan travel-writers. Doughty's poetry includes *The Dawn in Britain* (6 vols., 1906–7), *Adam Cast Forth* (1908), *The Clouds* (1912) and *Mansoul: or, The Riddle of the World* (1920).

Douglas A blank-verse tragedy by JOHN HOME, first performed in Edinburgh in 1756 and in London the following year to great success. It remained popular for almost a century and leading tragedians played the parts of Young Norval (Douglas) and Lady Randolph, who exhibit the exalted sentiments that satisfied Home's quest for a 'celestial melancholy'.

The plot is based on an old Scottish ballad. After his birth, the hero is exposed to the elements and presumed dead, but brought up by a shepherd, as Young Norval. He wins the favour of Lord Randolph by saving his life and is briefly restored to his loving mother, now Lady Randolph. But Lord Randolph's heir, the villainous Glenalvon, is jealous of Young Norval. After his various attempts to calumniate him have failed, Glenalvon tries to kill him, but Young Norval kills Glenalvon, only to be killed by the deceived Lord Randolph. Lady Randolph commits suicide.

Douglas, Lord Alfred (Bruce) 1870–1945 Poet. He was born near Worcester and educated at Winchester and Magdalen College, Oxford. His intimacy with OSCAR WILDE, to whom he was introduced in 1891 by LIONEL JOHNSON, eventually provoked Douglas's father, Lord Queensberry, to intervene; Wilde's unsuccessful suit against Queensberry brought about his own downfall. In prison Wilde addressed the bitter *DE PROFUNDIS* to Douglas. Apart from his translation of *SALOME* into English (1894) and his two books, *Oscar Wilde and Myself* (1914) and *Oscar Wilde: A Summing-Up* (1940), Douglas produced several volumes of verse, notably *The City of the Soul* (1899), *Sonnets* (1909), *Sonnets – In Excelsis* (1924) and *Sonnets and Lyrics* (1935). He was editor of *THE ACADEMY* in 1907–10 and published *The Autobiography of Douglas* in 1929.

Douglas, Gavin ?1475–1522 Scottish poet. Douglas came of a noble and powerful family: his father was Earl of Angus. He graduated MA from St Andrews (1494) and probably also studied at Paris. Among ecclesiastical offices he held were the deanery of Dunkeld, the provostship of St Giles Cathedral in Edinburgh, and finally the bishopric of Dunkeld to which he was consecrated in 1515. The last was a post he sought for some time and had difficulty in obtaining. After Flodden Douglas's attention became more and more engaged by politics, as the dowager Queen Margaret, widow of James IV, married Douglas's nephew. He was ambitious but was often disappointed or hampered in his hopes for high office by clan and ecclesiastical rivalries. In 1515 he was charged with irregularities in obtaining benefices and imprisoned, despite the protestations of the Pope and Queen Margaret. In 1521 he went to London, apparently to gain Henry VIII's support for his interests, and was accused of high treason by the Scottish Lords of Council in 1522. He died in exile, probably from the plague.

As a poet he is usually grouped with the SCOTTISH CHAUCERIANS. He says that his translation of the *Aeneid* was completed 22 July 1513. His other major work, *The Palace of Honour*, was probably finished by 1501, but was not printed until later (London *c.* 1553, Edinburgh 1579). This poem was designed for a courtly audience and dedicated to James IV. It is an allegorical DREAM-VISION in which the poet sees first the pageants of Minerva, Diana and Venus. He is tried on a charge of blasphemy before the Court of Venus and only saved by the intervention of the muse Calliope. The poet's quest for Honour is finally achieved in the third part, as the poet reaches Honour's palace on a high mountain.

King Hart is only doubtfully ascribed to Douglas. It was first printed in 1786 and is a homiletic ALLEGORY at times very like *EVERYMAN*. King Hart (the soul) is imprisoned in mid-life by Lady Plesaunce and finally faces mortality. *Conscience*, probably by Douglas, is an attack on the cupidity of churchmen. BALE's *Index Britanniae Scriptorum* mentions other works by Douglas, but these are now lost.

Douglas, George [Brown, George Douglas] 1869–1902 Scottish novelist. Born in Ayrshire, he was educated at Glasgow University and Balliol College, Oxford. In London he earned his living contributing short stories and boys' stories to magazines. His realistic story of Scottish life, *THE HOUSE WITH GREEN SHUTTERS*, appeared in 1901.

Douglas, Keith (Castellain) 1920–44 Poet. Born in Tunbridge Wells and educated at Christ's Hospital and Oxford, where EDMUND BLUNDEN was his tutor, Douglas served during World War II in North Africa and was injured by a land-mine. He soon returned to active service in Normandy, where he died. His war poems face the prospect of death without recourse to heightened rhetoric or mournful sentiment. *Selected Poems* appeared in 1943 and *Alamein to Zem Zem*, an account of his experience in the desert campaign, was published posthumously in 1946. TED HUGHES's enthusiastic introduction to a selection of Douglas's verse (1964) brought him a wider audience. A revised *Collected Poems* was issued in 1966 and a *Complete Poems* in 1979.

Douglas, (George) Norman 1868–1952 Novelist and travel-writer. His father was Scottish and his mother Scottish-German. Born in Austria, he was educated at Uppingham School and Karlsruhe. From 1893–1901 he served in the British Foreign Office, working as a diplomat to St Petersburg, then settled in Italy on the island of Capri.

His career as a writer began with books on zoology, but in 1901 he published *Unprofessional Tales* (under the pseudonym Normy), which was not successful. *Siren Land* (1911), like his subsequent two works (*Fountains in the Sand*, 1912, about Tunisia, and *Old Calabria*, 1915), was essentially a travel book which reflected Douglas's wide-ranging interests as biologist, geologist, art lover, archaeologist and classicist. However, it was with *SOUTH WIND* (1917) that he achieved his first, and only popular success. The novel caused considerable debate because of its frank discussion of moral and sexual questions. *They Went* (1920) and *In the Beginning* (1927) are fantasies about early mankind, and *Looking Back* (1933) is a fragmentary autobiography.

Douglass, Frederick 1817–95 Black American writer. Born into slavery on a plantation in Maryland, he received no formal education but learned to read first by bribing young white schoolchildren to help him, then by studying a copy of the journal *The Columbian Orator*. He worked for a while in a Baltimore shipyard, and then taught school to fellow slaves before escaping in 1838 to Massachusetts, where he was employed as a lecturer by anti-slavery societies.

He became known as one of the most eloquent anti-slavery orators of his day, and in 1845 published the *Narrative of the Life of Frederick Douglass, an American Slave*, which was circulated widely and soon translated into a number of languages. Fearing

capture as a fugitive, he spent two years in England and Ireland, returning to the USA in 1847 to purchase his freedom and to establish an anti-slavery journal in Rochester, New York, *The North Star* (1847–64), later called *Frederick Douglass' Paper*. In 1858 he founded a second journal, *Douglass' Monthly*, which continued until 1863. His editorial essays in these publications comprise a substantial portion of his writing. His position as a leading spokesman against slavery was strengthened by the appearance of his enlarged autobiography, *My Bondage and My Freedom* (1855). His influence in American political life at this time was considerable. He was in personal contact with Abraham Lincoln, and during the Civil War he organized two black regiments for the Union. In 1881 he published his third autobiographical work, *The Life and Times of Frederick Douglass*, a central text of the slave narrative tradition and of American autobiography in general. He continued in public service late in life as recorder of deeds for the District of Columbia (1881–6), and as US minister to Haiti (1889–91). BOOKER T. WASHINGTON wrote his biography (1906).

Dover Beach A poem by MATTHEW ARNOLD, published in *New Poems* (1867). Despite its brevity, it is probably the best known of all his works. The poet contemplates the sea, finding in it melancholy reminders of the uncertainties of belief brought about by modern life. He turns instead to faith in human relationships: 'Ah, love, let us be true to one another!'

Dowden, Edward 1843–1913 Critic and scholar. Born in Cork and educated at Queen's College and at Trinity College, Dublin, he was appointed professor of English studies at Trinity College in 1867. The editor of 12 SHAKESPEARE plays for the original Arden edition, he also wrote *Shakespeare: A Critical Study of His Mind and Art* (1875) and *A Shakespeare Primer* (1877). His other critical works include a study of SOUTHEY (1879) for the English Men of Letters series, a substantial biography of SHELLEY (1886) and a life of BROWNING (1905) for the Temple Biographies. His *Poems* appeared in 1876.

Down Second Avenue An autobiography by ES'KIA MPHAHLELE, published in 1959, and a classic South African literary text. Writing the book (completed in Nigeria to which Mphahlele had emigrated in 1957), was partly a cathartic exercise. It tells of the intolerableness of life under white domination and of the inevitability of 'voluntary' exile. Reviewing his first 40 years, Mphahlele describes Maupaneng, where he herded goats; Marabastad, where Second Avenue is, near Pretoria; and Orlando, near Johannesburg, His story covers the complexity of township life, his education, his various contacts with whites (many of them painful) and his jobs, including teaching (from which he was dismissed for campaigning against impending apartheid legislation) and writing for *DRUM*. Mphahlele continued the story of his life in the novel *The Wanderers* (1971) and *Afrika My Music* (1984), without achieving the same resonance.

Dowson, Ernest (Christopher) 1867–1900 Poet. Born in Kent and educated at the Queen's College, Oxford, he left without taking a degree, and joined the London society of BEARDSLEY, WILDE and RICHARD LE GALLIENNE. He was a member of the RHYMERS' CLUB, and contributed poems to THE YELLOW BOOK and *The Savoy*. In 1891 he met the 12-year-old Adelaide Foltinowicz, and she became the symbol of love and innocence in his otherwise world-weary poetry. He became a Roman Catholic in 1891–2, and after the suicides of both his parents within a few months of each other in 1895, he travelled aimlessly between France, Ireland and London. YEATS described him as 'timid, silent, a little melancholy'.

His verse first achieved attention with *Poems* (1896). *Decorations* (1899) included some experiments with prose-poems, and *The Pierrot of the Minute* (1897) was a one-act verse play. His *Poetical Works* appeared in 1934, and his *Letters* (1967) were edited by H. Maas and D. Flower. The poems are written in a variety of stanza-forms, and express *ennui* (as in 'Non Sum Qualis Eram' and 'Vitae Summa Brevis') and a correspondingly idealized love (in 'Poet's Road').

Doyle, Sir **Arthur Conan** 1859–1930 Novelist and writer of DETECTIVE FICTION and SCIENCE FICTION. Born in Edinburgh, son of an unsuccessful architect and nephew of the artist RICHARD DOYLE, he attended the Jesuit Stonyhurst College but had abandoned his family's Roman Catholicism by the time he had completed his medical studies at Edinburgh University. Much of his writing reflects the scientific rationalism he adopted until his latter-day conversion to spiritualism. Doyle practised briefly in Plymouth, an experience reflected in *The Stark Munro Letters* (1894), and then at Southsea (1882–90), where the lack of patients gave him time to write. The first of his SHERLOCK HOLMES STORIES was *A Study in Scarlet*, published in *Beeton's Christmas Annual* for 1887. It was followed by another novel, *The Sign of Four* (1890), but the popularity of his detective really dated from the series of short stories he contributed to THE STRAND MAGAZINE from 1891, collected as *The Adventures of Sherlock Holmes* (1892) and *The Memoirs of Sherlock Holmes* (1894). Doyle's attempt to kill off his creation was unsuccessful and Holmes reappeared in two novels, *The Hound of the Baskervilles* (1902) and *The Valley of Fear* (1915), and several collections of short stories, *The Return of Sherlock Holmes* (1905), *His Last Bow* (1917) and *The Case-Book of Sherlock Holmes* (1927).

Doyle's resentment at being identified solely as the creator of Sherlock Holmes was excessive but understandable. Just as his life reflected the many interests of the Edwardian gentleman – particularly sport and military affairs – so his career established him as a versatile and hardworking writer. His historical fiction comprises *Micah Clarke* (1889), *The White Company* (1891), *Rodney Stone* (1896), *The Exploits of Brigadier Gerard* (1896), *Uncle Bernac* (1897), *The Adventures of Gerard* (1903) and *Sir Nigel* (1906). *The Tragedy of the 'Korosko'* (1898) is an adventure story. He also turned his hand to SCIENCE FICTION in the Professor Challenger stories, *The Lost World* (1912), *The Poison Belt* (1913) and *The Land of Mist* (1926). The last of these reflects the belief in spiritualism which occupied much of his still formidable energy in later years. As well as writing a history of spiritualism in 1926, he campaigned and lectured on its behalf in Britain and the USA with a characteristically generous disregard for the otherwise safe position his achievements had earned him in public life.

Doyle, Sir **Francis Hastings Charles** 1810–88 Poet. Born at Nunappleton in Yorkshire, and educated at Eton and Christ Church, Oxford, he became a fellow of All Souls and succeeded MATTHEW ARNOLD as professor of poetry. He was the author of popular BALLADS, notably the patriotic 'Private of the Buffs' and 'The Red Thread of Honour', and one about racing, 'The Doncaster St Leger'.

Doyle, Richard 1824–83 Cartoonist and illustrator. Born in London, 'Dicky' Doyle was son of the artist John Doyle. At the age of 19 he joined the staff of *PUNCH* and designed its famous cover, but resigned in 1850 because of the journal's anti-Catholic bias. Thereafter he became a distinguished book illustrator – his light, playful sketches accompanied RUSKIN's *King of the Golden River* (1851) and THACKERAY's *THE NEWCOMES* (1853–5), among other works – though he did not live long enough to collaborate with his nephew, SIR ARTHUR CONAN DOYLE.

Drabble, Margaret 1939– Novelist. She was born in Sheffield and, like her sister, A. S. BYATT, educated at the Mount School, York, and Newnham College, Cambridge. A prominent figure on the contemporary literary scene – in, for example, her work as chairman of the National Book League – she was awarded the CBE in 1980. She is married to MICHAEL HOLROYD.

Her novels, often preoccupied with the individual's struggle against a conventional or repressive background, have grown steadily broader in their consideration of the contemporary social climate. They include: *A Summer Birdcage* (1963); *The Garrick Year* (1964); *The Millstone* (1965); *Jerusalem the Golden* (1967), about a young woman's rebellious quest for experience in London; *The Waterfall* (1969); *The Ice Age*

St George and the dragon: an illustration by Richard Doyle for *The Scouring of the White Horse* by Thomas Hughes, 1859

(1977), a tragicomedy about the *Angst*-ridden middle age of Anthony Keating, onetime producer of TV 'social conscience' programmes; and a trilogy following the friendship of three women, *The Radiant Way* (1987), *A Natural Curiosity* (1989) and *The Gates of Ivory* (1991). She has also written studies of Wordsworth (1966) and Arnold Bennett (1974) and edited the fifth edition of *The Oxford Companion to English Literature* (1984). *A Writer's Britain* (1979) is an account of the relationship between the writer and landscape. Other works include a play, *Bird of Paradise* (1969), and a book for children, *For Queen and Country* (1978).

Dracula A novel by Bram Stoker, published in 1897.

Presented in diaries, letters and news items, this story of a bloodsucking vampire who preys on the living and can be repelled by garlic and crucifixes, is both absurd and powerful. It opens with the diary of Jonathan Harker, a London solicitor who falls victim to Count Dracula in his Transylvanian castle. The Count then travels to England, arriving at Whitby, where the story is taken up in accounts by Harker's fiancée Mina Murray, her friend Lucy Westenra and Dr John Seward. Van Helsing, a Dutch doctor and expert in vampirism, leads the attempt to frustrate the Count. Lucy falls a victim to Dracula and becomes, in her turn, a vampire, but a merciful stake through the heart brings her peace. He turns his attention to Mina, but is followed back to Transylvania and finally vanquished.

There are effective passages describing Dracula's midnight landing at Whitby and his mastery over the zoophagous lunatic in Seward's private asylum, but in general the English scenes do not compare in power with those set in Transylvania. The episode where Harker sees Dracula crawling face downwards, like a giant bat, along the stone wall of his castle is particularly memorable.

Like *Frankenstein*, *Dracula* has become modern myth – the subject of many film versions, imitations and parodies. Tourists to Romania, a country Stoker himself never visited, are now shown 'Dracula's Castle' as tourists to Verona are shown 'Juliet's balcony'.

dramatic irony See Irony.

dramatic monologue A development of the Soliloquy, but not written for the stage or forming part of a play, the dramatic monologue is a poem consisting of a speech by a single character who reveals his thoughts, character and situation. In the 19th century, when literature became increasingly preoccupied with the individual viewpoint, Robert Browning found it an ideal form and Tennyson several times used it (in, for example, *Tithonus*). In the 20th century, T. S. Eliot and others have turned to the dramatic monologue.

Drapier's Letters, The A group of seven pamphlets by Jonathan Swift, five published in March–December 1724 and two in 1735, written in the character of a Dublin draper, M. B. Drapier. The original five attack the patent acquired by William Wood for supplying Ireland with copper coinage. George I had given the patent to his ageing mistress, the Duchess of Kendal, and she in turn had sold it to Wood, a mineowner and dealer in iron, for the then enormous sum of £10,000. When the Irish Parliament protested to the King in 1723 he promised an enquiry, which opened in April 1724. By then the first of Swift's pamphlets against the 'obscure Ironmonger' had appeared. The scheme to coin 'Wood's ha'pence' was withdrawn and the satirist became a national hero. Swift's interest in the matter was part of his campaign against the arrogant and thoughtless treatment of Ireland by the English.

Drayton, Michael 1563–1631 Poet and playwright. Drayton's youth was spent in the service of Sir Henry Goodeere to whom he was indebted for his education. Goodeere's daughter Anne was partly the inspiration for the figure of 'Idea' who appears in Drayton's work.

Drayton's career covers a wide span of time: his first published work appeared in 1591 and his last in 1630. He wrote in nearly all the kinds of poetry available in his time, was sensitive and responsive to fashions in poetic taste and open to influence from a great diversity of sources. He constantly revised and reissued poems, often giving them different titles. As well as there being several separate editions of various works, there are also two collections of his poems by Drayton himself, printed in 1605 and 1619. These collections often contain yet further versions of poems, and a poem by Drayton can exist in as many as five different forms.

The Harmony of the Church (1591) is a dull metrical version, marred by excessive alliteration, of some songs and prayers from the Old Testament and the Apocrypha. Drayton responded to the fondness for PASTORAL in the 1590s with Idea: The Shepherds' Garland (1593), whose nine ECLOGUES show the strong influence of SPENSER's THE SHEPHEARDES CALENDER. It was revised and reissued in 1606. Idea's Mirror (1594) is the first version of the SONNET sequence IDEA, his contribution to the sonnet vogue of the 1590s. Endimion and Phoebe (1595) is an EPYLLION, a fashionable form used by MARLOWE in HERO AND LEANDER and SHAKESPEARE in VENUS AND ADONIS. It was revised and appeared again as The Man in the Moon (1606 and 1619). The 1590s also saw Drayton's first attempts at historical poetry with the 'legends' of Piers Gaveston (?1594) and Matilda (1594). For his historical poems Drayton thoroughly researched his chronicle sources. RAPHAEL HOLINSHED was a favourite source for him as for Shakespeare. Robert of Normandy (1596, revised 1605 and 1619) is his most medieval legend: Robert's story is told, in the presence of his ghost, by Fame and Fortune. Mortimeriados (1596), rewritten and much altered as The Barons' Wars (1603), is much indebted to Marlowe's EDWARD II. The first version is a series of scenes and tableaux, the revision is several hundred lines longer, changes its form from RHYME ROYAL to OTTAVA RIMA and displays a more serious interest in the subject of civil war. Mortimer and the queen also become more prominent figures. The 1603 text was again revised for the 1619 collection.

The First Part of Sir John Oldcastle (published 1600) is Drayton's only extant play, although there are records of others which are now lost. These, like the surviving play, seem to have been collaborations with other dramatists; many treated historical subjects. As Drayton responded to popular taste in his poetry, so Sir John Oldcastle cashed in on the success of Shakespeare's HENRY IV plays. England's Heroical Epistles (1597) earned for Drayton the title of 'our English Ovid'. Its classical model is Ovid's Heroides, and like Ovid's work it is a collection of letters exchanged by notable lovers. Instead of Ovid's mythological characters Drayton gives us figures from English history: Henry II and Fair Rosamond, Richard II and Isabel, the Earl of Surrey and Geraldine, and so forth. The couplets are full of elaborated conceits and rhetorical balance. These poems are among Drayton's most immediately readable works. The Legend of Great Cromwell (1607), drawn from FOXE's ACTS AND MONUMENTS, sees Drayton returning to legends. It shows the precarious rise to power of a 'new man' of the Tudor age, and is remarkable for its detached view of Henry VIII's reign and its refusal of easy 'Protestant' bias. It is the only one of Drayton's historical legends to be included in THE MIRROR FOR MAGISTRATES (1610 edition). The Owl (1604 and 1619) emulates the medieval FABLE. Poems Lyric and Pastoral (1606) contains imitations of Horace's Odes, the first attempted by an English Renaissance poet. Drayton's major work, POLY-OLBION, appeared in two parts in 1612 and 1622.

In 1627 a number of new poems appeared together: The Battle of Agincourt is an attempt at epic which again drew on chronicle sources, and The Miseries of Queen Margaret is indebted to Holinshed and Shakespeare's HENRY VI plays. Also in this volume is Nimphidia, which has won Drayton more popularity than any of his other works. It is a MOCK-HEROIC series of 'Nimphalls' or fairy poems. The influence of A MIDSUMMER NIGHT'S DREAM is everywhere apparent, especially in the quarrel of Oberon and his queen. The Muses' Elizium (1630) sees Drayton, like Shakespeare, returning to pastoral at the end of his career and describing the poet's paradise.

Dream of Gerontius, The A poem by JOHN HENRY NEWMAN, published in two parts in The Month (April and May 1865) and in book form in 1866. It is the DRAMATIC MONOLOGUE of a just soul on the point of death. Sir Edward Elgar's oratorio setting was composed in 1900.

Dream of John Ball, A A tale by WILLIAM MORRIS, serialized in The Commonweal from 13 November 1886 to 22 January 1887 and published in book form in 1888.

Morris describes a dream transporting him back to Kent during the 1381 Peasants' Revolt. He witnesses a battle in which the Sheriff of Kent's men are repulsed by peasants inspired by the words of John Ball, a dissenting priest. Later Morris and John Ball discuss the peasants' hopes for change and, as Morris describes the Industrial Revolution and 19th-century society, John Ball realizes he is himself dreaming of the future course of history and of still unfulfilled ideals. In its use of the dream motif for the exploration of both historical and future aspiration, *A Dream of John Ball* is the forerunner of Morris's greatest socialist work, NEWS FROM NOWHERE. However, the implicit alliance of Christian morality and socialist ethics is an unusual retrospective glance at his earlier religious beliefs.

Dream of the Rood, The An Old English poem preserved in the VERCELLI BOOK, probably dating from 750 or earlier. The narrator describes a dream in which he saw the Holy Cross alternately as a beautifully adorned symbol and as the historical, bloodstained cross. The cross speaks to him, telling him the history of the Crucifixion in terms of its own experience, and its emergence as a glorious symbol of Christ's Passion. After the dream, the poet says, he felt a longing for his own death and salvation, and determined to live a pure life. The poem is the most original, imaginative and moving of Old English religious poems.

Dream Songs, The An open-ended sequence of poems by JOHN BERRYMAN, first published in its entirety in 1969 and made up of two earlier volumes entitled *77 Dream Songs* (1964) and *His Toy, His Dream, His Rest* (1968). Through the dreams of a character called Henry, Berryman presents a meditation on American literary and cultural history. Several of the 'songs' are dedicated to Berryman's contemporaries, including JOHN CROWE RANSOM, SAUL BELLOW, ROBERT LOWELL and ADRIENNE RICH. Many of the details of Henry's character and life reflect those of Berryman himself, including the profound impact of a father's suicide and the difficulties of overcoming alcoholism.

dream-vision A medieval poem about a dream. Its substance is allegorical – though the extent to which ALLEGORY is sustained depends largely on the skill of the poet – and may be secular or religious, comic or serious. Though differing widely in form and content, medieval dream-visions share a few common features: they are told in the first person, they have a certain supernatural or surreal content and they involve some kind of instruction for the dreamer. In many the dreamer is naive or ignorant, has a companion or guide and encounters a beautiful dream landscape.

The chief influences on the form were the Latin *Somnium Scipionis* of Cicero with Macrobius' commentary on it, and the French *Roman de la rose* by Guillaume de Lorris and Jean de Meun, but the classi-

cal and biblical traditions of revelations and visions were equally important. The three greatest medieval poets all wrote dream-visions: GEOFFREY CHAUCER (who translated the *Roman de la rose* as THE ROMAUNT OF THE ROSE) in THE BOOK OF THE DUCHESS, THE PARLEMENT OF FOULES, THE HOUSE OF FAME and the Prologue to THE LEGEND OF GOOD WOMEN; WILLIAM LANGLAND in PIERS PLOWMAN; and the GAWAIN-POET in PEARL. Chaucer's dream poems were widely copied and the form continued into the 16th century, with such writers as GAVIN DOUGLAS (*The Palace of Honour*), JOHN SKELTON (*The Garland of Laurel*) and WILLIAM BAR (*The Thrissil and the Rois*). It did not then vanish but later dream-visions, like WILLIAM MORRIS's NEWS FROM NOWHERE, are usually the result of deliberate medievalizing. The preoccupation with dreams in modern literature – JAMES JOYCE's FINNEGANS WAKE, for example – often acknowledges the medieval tradition but instances are likely to be influenced by psychological theory.

Dreiser, Theodore (Herman Albert) 1871–1945 American novelist. He was born in Terre Haute, Indiana, the ninth child of German-speaking parents. The poverty of his childhood and the harsh bigotry of his father are reflected in his fiction. He briefly attended Indiana University, and then obtained a job on the *Chicago Globe* as a reporter before moving to New York City in 1894.

His first novel, SISTER CARRIE (1900), was accepted by FRANK NORRIS for Doubleday Page & Co., but Mrs Doubleday objected to its realistic style and subject matter, and interfered with its publication, with the result that it was not widely distributed. Continuing to work as a journalist, Dreiser managed to earn a fairly comfortable living as an editor for Butterick, a company specializing in women's magazines, and 10 years passed before the publication of his next novel, *JENNIE GERHARDT* (1911). Like *Sister Carrie*, it was attacked for its candid and uncompromising NATURALISM. *The Financier* (1912) and *The Titan* (1914) were the first two volumes of Dreiser's *Cowperwood* trilogy, based on the life of the business magnate, Charles T. Yerkes; it was completed by *The Stoic*, posthumously published in 1947. *The Genius* (1915) is a partly autobiographical novel examining the artistic temperament. Dreiser at last earned popular acclaim with AN AMERICAN TRAGEDY (1925), based on the Chester Gillette–Grace Brown murder case of 1906. *The Bulwark* appeared posthumously in 1946.

Apart from his novels, Dreiser wrote an account of a visit to the Soviet Union, *Dreiser Looks at Russia* (1928), and gave further expression to his growing hopes for socialism in *Tragic America* (1931) and *America is Worth Saving* (1941). He also published *Plays of the Natural and Supernatural* (1916), the tragedy *The Hand of the Potter* (1918), and books of verse, short stories, essays and autobiography.

Drennan, William 1754–1820 Irish pamphleteer and poet. The son of a prominent Presbyterian minister, he was born in Belfast and educated at Glasgow and Edinburgh universities, where he was a pupil and close friend of DUGALD STEWART and met DAVID HUME. He qualified as a doctor in 1778 and returned to practise in Ireland. Proudly conscious of his radical heritage as a Dissenter, he made his mark as a spirited, libertarian political writer with his *Letters of an Irish Helot* (1784) and was a founder and active member of the society of United Irishmen. One of his best poems, 'The Wake of William Orr' (1797), is an ELEGY for the first United Irishman to be executed. Drennan himself was tried for sedition in 1794 but acquitted. After the defeat of the United Irishmen's Rising in 1798, in which Drennan played no part, he withdrew from active politics but maintained his leading role in the cultural and intellectual life of Belfast. His verse is lyrical, witty, iconoclastic or fiercely patriotic by turns; for the last quality at least it won the admiration of THOMAS DAVIS. His most famous poem, 'Erin to Her Own Tune and Words' (1795), set to a traditional air, is the source of the phrase 'the Emerald Isle'. His *Fugitive Pieces in Verse and Prose* appeared in 1815, a translation of Sophocles' *Electra* in 1817 and *Glendalloch and Other Poems*, incorporating poems by his two sons, posthumously in 1859. A selection of his vividly informative letters was published in 1931.

Drewe, Robert (Duncan) 1943– Australian novelist, short-story writer and journalist. His experience in journalism gives his fiction a straightforward, visual style and the habitual stance of an outside observer. The stories in *The Body Surfers* (1983), his best-known work, first identified Australian culture as drawn from the beach rather than the bush. His novels include: *The Savage Crows* (1976), contrasting a contemporary journalist with a 19th-century 'protector' of Aborigines; *A Cry in the Jungle* (1979), about an insensitive Australian 'expert' let loose in Asia; *Fortune* (1986), a 'faction' based on his experience of America; and *Our Sunshine* (1991). *The Bay of Contented Men* (1989) is a further collection of stories.

Drinkwater, John 1882–1937 Playwright and poet. Born at Leytonstone, Essex, and educated at Oxford High School, he worked for the Northern Assurance Company in Nottingham and Birmingham before accepting Sir Barry Jackson's offer of the post of manager of what was to become the Birmingham Repertory Company (1909). His early verse plays, like *Cophetua* (1911) and *X = O: A Night of the Trojan War* (1917), are mostly short experimental pieces. His major achievement is a sequence of historical plays written in prose. *Abraham Lincoln* (1919) enjoyed an international reputation. His other plays include *Mary Stuart* (1921), *Oliver Cromwell* (1921), *Robert E. Lee* (1923) and the comedy *Bird in Hand* (1927). His volumes of verse include *The Death of Leander and Other Poems* (1906), *Lyrical and Other Poems* (1908), *Cromwell and Other Poems* (1913) and the wartime volume *Swords and Ploughshares* (1915). Drinkwater's critical work includes a study of WILLIAM MORRIS (1912) and biographies of SAMUEL PEPYS (1930) and SHAKESPEARE (Great Lives series, 1933).

Drum A monthly magazine, started as *African Drum* in 1951 and published in South African and (until the early 1960s) West African editions. It began by reproducing the white policy toward ethnicity and tribalism but took a different direction under the editorship of Anthony Sampson and then Sylvester Stein. Illustrated features on boxers, gangsters, beauty queens and 'nice-time girls' rubbed shoulders with courageous political exposés and fiction which marked the beginning of the modern short story in black South African writing. ES'KIA MPHAHLELE was its fiction editor. Contributors included Arthur Maimane, Nat Nakasa, LEWIS NKOSI, Can Themba, Todd Matshikiza, Peter Clarke, James Matthews, Bloke Modisane, Richard Rive, Jordan Ngubane, Dyke Sentso and Guybon Sinxo.

Drummond, William Henry 1854–1907 Canadian poet. Drummond's family emigrated from Ireland to Canada when he was 11 years old. The boy studied telegraphy and found his first job at Bord-à-Plouffe on the Rivière des Prairies. In this region, not far from the American border, Drummond was fascinated by the stories told by the travellers, backwoodsmen, and French-Canadian dwellers in the small town. He resumed his education by 1876 and graduated in medicine at Bishop's College, Montreal, in 1884. He practised as a doctor for some years and lectured in medical jurisprudence at his old college; in 1905 he became rich through a successful venture, with his brother, in a silver mine at Cobalt in Ontario.

As a poet, Drummond succeeded in capturing the patois of the French-Canadian people. His four volumes of verse were *The Habitant* (1897), *Johnny Courteau* (1901), *The Voyageur* (1905) and *The Great Fight* (1908). A collected volume, *The Poetical Works*, was published in 1912.

Drummond of Hawthornden, William 1585–1649 Poet. Born at the manor of Hawthornden near Edinburgh, he was educated at Edinburgh University and studied law in France. He lived at Hawthornden from 1610 and was to have married Mary Cunningham of Barns in 1615. She died on the eve of the wedding and much of Drummond's work reflected his grief.

Drummond was a Royalist and anti-Presbyterian and wrote many pamphlets in support of his views. His first published poem was a lament on the death of Prince Henry in 1613, *Tears on the Death of*

Moeliades. The year after the death of Mary Cunningham he published *Poems, Amorous, Funereal, Divine, Pastoral, in Sonnets, Songs, Sextains, Madrigals* (1616), and in 1617 contributed to the verses written to celebrate the visit of James I to Edinburgh ('Forth Feasting', published in *The Muses' Welcome*, 1618). Drummond corresponded with MICHAEL DRAYTON, and BEN JONSON's visit to Hawthornden in the winter of 1618/19 prompted him to keep notes of the occasion, eventually published in 1832. A collection of religious verse, *Flowers of Sion* (1623), contains the religious sonnets 'Saint John Baptist' and 'For the Magdalene', which are among his best-known works, and the prose essay on death *A Cypress Grove.* Drummond married Elizabeth Logan in 1632 and wrote the words for the entertainment staged for the Scottish coronation of Charles I in 1633. He died in 1649, the year of the King's execution. His poetry echoes his wide reading, and is in places elegant and musical.

Drury Lane, Theatre Royal It originally opened as a PATENT THEATRE in 1662, housing the KING'S MEN under THOMAS KILLIGREW's management. A second building (1674), possibly designed by Sir Christopher Wren, enlarged its capacity from 700 to 2000. It prospered, particularly from 1708–32 under the management of COLLEY CIBBER and others, and from 1747–76, under DAVID GARRICK. Garrick was succeeded by RICHARD BRINSLEY SHERIDAN, whose tenure began with a production of *THE SCHOOL FOR SCANDAL.* Increasingly involved in politics, Sheridan entrusted the management from 1788 to the actor John Philip Kemble, who supervised rebuilding in 1791–4 to a design by Henry Holland.

This third theatre burned down in 1809, leaving Sheridan in financial difficulties. An enterprising brewer, Samuel Whitbread, led the fund-raising for the building of a fourth theatre, designed by Benjamin Wyatt and opened in 1812. Its capacity was 2283. Despite many alterations, it still stands. Considered too big and too uneconomic as a home for legitimate drama after the loss of its monopoly in 1843, Drury Lane became famous as the home of spectacle and PANTOMIME during the successive managements of Augustus Harris (1879–96) and Arthur Collins (1896–1923). It is now reliant on musicals.

Dry White Season, A A novel by ANDRÉ BRINK, published in 1979. Like many of his novels, it charts the gradual distancing of an ordinary Afrikaner from the conservative attitudes of his community. Ben Du Toit is moved by the distress of a black servant to investigate her husband's disappearance and death in police custody. He continues despite threats from the police and the hostility of his wife and daughter, becoming increasingly caught up in the politics and lives of members of the black community and involved with a white journalist. Brink uses some of the appeal and narrative technique of DETECTIVE FICTION to draw the reader into sharing Du Toit's rejection of apartheid and the structures which sustain it. *A Dry White Season* was filmed in 1989.

Dryden, John 1631–1700 Poet and playwright. Born at the vicarage of Aldwinkle in Northamptonshire, Dryden came from a family of moderate Parliamentary supporters with Puritan inclinations. He was educated at Westminster when the formidable Richard Busby was the headmaster, and there he read voraciously, especially among the classical poets. While still at school he published his first verses, an ELEGY 'Upon the Death of Lord Hastings' (1649), but he was not prolific while young. He went to Trinity College, Cambridge, in 1650 and took a BA in 1654. In 1659 he wrote his impressive 'Heroic Stanzas' on the death of the Lord Protector, though he readily adapted to the Royalist climate of the Restoration, and wrote *Astraea Redux* in 1660 to welcome back the monarch. This was later interpreted as a mercenary move, but it was merely the product of common sense and moderation; from the start, Dryden's attitudes were ranged against extremism of any kind, and he became an exponent of the golden mean in art, politics and morality.

Much of Dryden's Restoration verse is professionally tailored to specific public occasions; he was a born Laureate. At the coronation he wrote 'To His Sacred Majesty, A Panegyric... ' (1661), followed by verses addressed tactfully 'To My Lord Chancellor', CLARENDON, in 1662. He began assiduously to write plays, a good way of drawing the attention of the public, since the playhouses (under the imported French tastes of the court) were busily fashionable. *The Wild Gallant*, his first, was a prose piece started in 1663 – the year he married his theatrical partner's sister, Lady Elizabeth Howard – but is otherwise unremarkable. *The Rival Ladies* (1664) used the rhymed couplet, and proved more popular. In 1665, the theatres closed owing to the plague, and the court removed to Oxford, where Dryden presented *The Indian Emperor*, which established his reputation and announced his distinctive style of heroic drama.

Well liked as a person, Dryden was rather a modest, private character, though he has been chastised (notably by JOHNSON) as a mere professional opportunist. The 'wonders' of 1666, the year of the naval war with the Dutch and the Fire of London, were commemorated in *Annus Mirabilis* (1667), a poem which proved instrumental in securing him the position of POET LAUREATE on the death of SIR WILLIAM D'AVENANT in 1668. He was the first poet officially to hold the title. Already a Fellow of the Royal Society, he also became Historiographer Royal in 1670.

From 1668 onwards Dryden enjoyed a busy period of dramatic and critical writing. His many plays include *Secret Love* (1667), a comedy popular with Charles II; *Tyrannic Love* (1669), a heroic drama about the martyrdom of St Catherine and the lust of Emperor Maximin, full of histrionic touches; and the two-part *The Conquest of Granada* (1670–1), a controversial study of religious and civil disorder. *Marriage à la Mode* (1672) is the most durable of his earlier comedies. *Amboyna* (1673), a flimsy piece of anti-Dutch propaganda, was followed in 1674 by the poet's bizarre tribute to Milton in the form of a musical adaptation of *Paradise Lost*, entitled *The State of Innocence*; perhaps an apt title for the idealistic spirit in which it was conceived for the new Theatre Royal. It was never performed. With *Aureng-Zebe* (1676) and *All for Love* (1678) – the latter his first in blank verse – Dryden returned to real drama, and wrote some of his most stirring verse, but he was beginning to be disenchanted with the cut-throat competitiveness between the theatrical companies, and the personal criticism his opponents began directing at him. He was lampooned by Rochester, and his heroic style satirized mercilessly as bombast in Buckingham's *The Rehearsal* (1671). On 18 December 1679, he was physically ambushed and badly beaten in a mysterious attack in Rose Alley, Covent Garden, an incident generally taken as proof of the seriousness with which his public position was beginning to be regarded. His unfortunate adaptation (1679) of Shakespeare's *Troilus and Cressida* earned him, excusably, additional ridicule.

By 1681 Dryden was beginning to direct his interests towards politics and that quickly maturing political adjunct, satire. He effectively discredited Shaftesbury and the supporters of Monmouth during the Exclusion Crisis with *Absalom and Achitophel* (1681), a miniature epic of ingenious exactitude supporting the legitimacy of James, Duke of York, to succeed his brother to the throne despite his Catholic sympathies. Dryden found himself once again the target for personal vituperation, but Charles II was pleased at his onslaught against the Whigs, and at his next poem *The Medal* (1682) a dutiful but baldly partisan attack on Shaftesbury's supporters, which in turn provoked a spate of counterattacks of which Thomas Shadwell's *The Medal of John Bayes* was the sharpest. The 'paper war' was now in full swing, and Dryden replied with *Mac Flecknoe*, his most entertaining poem, written around 1678, pirated in 1682 and officially published in 1684.

In *Religio Laici* (1682) he examined the squabbling history of religious factions and, in 1686, after a period of spiritual uncertainty, embraced Roman Catholicism. Since this was the year after the Catholic James II ascended the throne, Dryden was attacked as a turncoat, though in fact it was an act of courage. Apart from several 'official' odes in this period he composed in 1686 a movingly lyrical ode 'To the Pious Memory of... Mrs Anne Killigrew', a painter who drowned in the Thames, and he began to translate from the classics. *The Hind and the Panther* (1687) is a lengthy allegorical fable about Protestant and Papist beliefs in which Dryden criticizes the Anglican church. With the (Protestant) Revolution of 1688, Dryden was deprived of the Laureateship because of his religious beliefs and, ironically, replaced by Shadwell. He was now in his fifties and, having published his convictions in verse, he turned himself afresh to the theatre.

He contributed the libretto to Henry Purcell's operatic celebration of the English monarchy, *King Arthur* (1691), and wrote a tragicomedy about sin, *Don Sebastian* (produced in 1690), a comedy of errors, *Amphitryon* (1690), *Cleomenes: The Spartan Hero* (1692), and finally the unsuccessful *Love Triumphant* (1694), announcing in the prologue that it was to be his last play. Dryden's productions were by then coming into competition with the work of younger playwrights such as Congreve. In his later years Dryden turned to translations: most significant was his commercially profitable edition of Virgil (1697), but his handsome volume of translations from the satires of Persius and Juvenal (1693) is additionally valuable for its preface, the excellent *Discourse concerning the Original and Progress of Satire*. In 1693 he also published his second ode for St Cecilia's Day, 'Alexander's Feast'. His last major achievement was *Fables, Ancient and Modern* (1700), paraphrases of Ovid, Boccaccio and Chaucer, the preface to which is a fine example of his prose. Indeed, much of his prose is distinguished for its critical acuity, taking the form of essays or prefaces to plays; his *Essay of Dramatic Poesy* (1668) and *Essay of Heroic Plays* (1672) are the foremost. He also wrote a life of Plutarch (1683).

A self-critical and civilized writer, Dryden brought to the language a clarity and balance of phrase that influenced many of the 18th century who followed him in his admiration of reasonableness and common sense, as well as his stringent cultivation of the heroic couplet. Nowadays he is admired but not quite enjoyed. He summarized his aesthetic in his preface to the play *Evening's Love*: 'The employment of a poet is like that of a curious gunsmith, or watchmaker: the iron or silver is not his own; but they are the least part of that which gives the value: the prize lies wholly in the workmanship.'

Du Bois, W(illiam) E(dward) B(urghardt)

c. 1868–1963 Black American writer. He was born in Great Barrington, Massachusetts, and educated at Fisk University and at Harvard. He taught economics and history at Atlanta University from 1896 to 1910 and soon became famous for his studies of the status of black people in the USA: *John Brown* (1909), *The Negro* (1915), *The Gift of Black Folk* (1924) and *Black Reconstruction* (1935). Sketches and verses about the life of blacks make up *The Souls of Black Folk* (1903) and *Darkwater* (1920). *Color and Democracy: Colonies and Peace* (1945) argues for the rights of small nations and rejects all aspects of imperialism. He also wrote a novel, *Dark Princess* (1928), about a black man who becomes involved in a struggle to unify the 'dark peoples' of the world. With Guy Benton Johnson he co-edited the *Encyclopedia of the Negro* (1945). The autobiographical *Dusk of Dawn* (1940) was, he declared, 'the autobiography of a concept of race'. For 24 years he edited the magazine *Crisis*.

He left Atlanta University to help found the National Association for the Advancement of Colored People, but later became impatient with the association's moderation. In 1949 he became director of the Peace Information Center in New York, and in 1961, at the age of 93, joined the Communist Party. He died in Ghana where, as editor of *Encyclopedia Africana*, he had gone to live in 1961. He became a Ghanaian citizen in the year of his death.

du Fresne, Yvonne 1929– New Zealand short-story writer and novelist. Of French Huguenot origin, she grew up in a Danish community in the Manawatu region and worked as a schoolteacher. *Farvel* (1982), a collection of short stories which marked the late start of her writing career, won the PEN International award for the Best First Book of Prose. Her first novel, *The Book of Ester* (1982), and second collection of stories, *The Growing of Astrid Westergaard* (1985), both draw on her own mixed cultural background for their themes. Later work includes *Frederique* (1987), a novel, and *The Bear from the North: Tales of a New Zealand Childhood* (1989).

Du Maurier, Dame Daphne 1907–89 Novelist. Born in London, daughter of the actor Sir Gerald Du Maurier and granddaughter of GEORGE DU MAURIER, she was educated privately in Paris. For most of her adult life she lived in Cornwall, whose wild weather and scenery contribute the setting and atmosphere for her tense romances. The most famous are *Jamaica Inn* (1936), *Rebecca* (1938) and *My Cousin Rachel* (1951). Her short story 'The Birds' was given a classic film treatment by Alfred Hitchcock in 1963. Her memoirs were published in 1967 as *Vanishing Cornwall*.

Du Maurier, George (Louis Palmella Busson) 1834–96 Novelist and artist. He was born in Paris, the grandson of refugees from the French Revolution and the son of a naturalized Englishman. In 1851 he entered University College, London, studying chemistry and becoming an analytical chemist, but returned to Paris in 1856, later living in Belgium and Holland. Although the sight of his left eye was almost gone, he turned to drawing and in 1860 sent his first work to *PUNCH*, becoming a regular contributor. His most famous novel was *TRILBY* (1894); his others were *Peter Ibbetson* (1891) and *The Martian* (1897). He also wrote

humorous verse. He was the father of the actor Gerald Du Maurier and grandfather of DAPHNE DU MAURIER.

dub poetry A popular form of Caribbean oral poetry which originated in Jamaica and Britain in the 1970s. It began with Jamaican disc-jockeys rapping over the 'dub' (or instrumental B-side) version of singles, which emphasized bass and drum rhythms. This practice – known as 'toasting' – and the influence of reggae musicians such as Bob Marley provided the inspiration for a new kind of African-orientated performance poetry. Closely associated with the 'dread talk' of Rastafarianism, dub has been viewed as political poetry voicing the concerns of underprivileged black youths. In fact, while such concerns are central, its range is a good deal broader: a practitioner like Jean Binta Breeze has used dub for personal love lyrics. Leading exponents include LINTON KWESI JOHNSON, Benjamin Zephaniah and Levi Tafari in Britain and the late MICHAEL SMITH, Mutabaruka and Oku Onuora in Jamaica. Since dub is a performance art, scribal versions provide only a hint of its oral and dramatic qualities. Among the more important printed collections are Johnson's *Dread, Beat and Blood* (1975), Michael Smith's *It a Come* (1986), Breeze's *Riddym Ravings* (1988), Tafari's *Liverpool Experience* (1989) and Christian Habekost's anthology, *Dub Poetry: 19 Poets from England and Jamaica* (1986).

Dubliners A volume of short stories by JAMES JOYCE, published in 1914. Some had originally appeared in the magazine *Irish Homestead*, under the pseudonym Stephen Dedalus, in 1904 and the last, 'The Dead', was finished in 1907. The book's publication was delayed, much to Joyce's exasperation, because a printer objected to passages in the story 'Two Gallants'. Joyce told his publisher, GRANT RICHARDS, that it was not his fault if 'the odour of ashpits and old weeds and offal' hung around his attempt to 'write a chapter in the moral history of my country'. The stories were arranged to present Dublin in four of its aspects – childhood, adolescence, maturity and public life – and he claimed to have written them in a style of 'scrupulous meanness'.

Duchess of Malfi, The A tragedy by JOHN WEBSTER, published in 1623. The date of the first production is not known but is believed to have been before 1614. The plot is based on a story by Matteo Bandello.

The Duchess of Malfi is a widow. One of her brothers is a Cardinal; the other, her twin brother Ferdinand, is Duke of Calabria. Both are inordinately jealous of their noble status and warn their sister that she must not remarry. They also hope to inherit her territory. But the Duchess has fallen in love with her steward, Antonio, and secretly marries him. The suspicious brothers introduce a spy into her household in the person of Bosola, an escaped galley slave.

Linton Kwesi Johnson (left): one of Britain's most popular dub poets

Suspecting his mistress is pregnant, Bosola seeks confirmation by offering her fresh apricots which the Duchess devours greedily. Shortly afterwards she gives birth to a son. Some time later, aware of gathering suspicion, she and Antonio separate and flee. The Duchess is captured and confined to her house, where she and her children are eventually murdered.

After the murder of the Duchess, Ferdinand and the Cardinal decide they must remove Bosola, who has been shaken by his victim's courage and now regards his masters with loathing. When he realizes that they are in a hurry to be rid of him he determines on revenge. He kills the man he believes is the Cardinal, finding to his horror that it is in fact Antonio, whom he had determined to save; despair is added to remorse. The unbalanced Ferdinand now descends into total insanity. Bosola succeeds in murdering the Cardinal but is himself killed by the mad Ferdinand; his single consolation is to see the madman killed by Antonio's friends.

Duck, Stephen 1705–56 Poet. An untutored agricultural labourer, Duck taught himself by reading books on arithmetic and PARADISE LOST, using a dictionary, and began to write doggerel verse based on BALLADS as well as classical models. His patrons included Joseph Spence, professor of poetry at Oxford, and Lord Macclesfield, who brought the 'thresher poet' to the attention of Queen Caroline. She settled him at Windsor with a pension. When EUSDEN died in 1730, Duck and COLLEY CIBBER were considered for the vacant post of POET LAUREATE, which gave rise to some humorous letters between POPE and SWIFT at their expense. Duck became a clergyman after the death of the Queen in 1737, and as a preacher at Kew Chapel he drew considerable crowds, chiefly out of curiosity. Most of his verse is occasional, and much is absurd; his early *The Thresher's Labour* has some pastoral merit, but Duck is notable mainly as a peasant poet, a phenomenon intriguing to the Romantics. In 1756 he drowned himself in a trout stream outside the Black Lion Inn at Reading.

Duckworth, Marilyn 1935– New Zealand novelist. Her early novels include: *A Gap in the Spectrum* (1959), published when she was only 24, whose heroine is amnesiac and isolated in London; *A Barbarous Tongue* (1963), also concerned with questions of individual identity and language; and *Over the Fence is Out* (1969). The last, in turning from experiment towards realism, anticipates the mode of the novels which followed, after a long silence, in the second phase of her career. These include *Disorderly Conduct* (1984), set against the background of the divisive South African rugby tour in 1981, and *Married Alive* (1985). She has also published a collection of stories, *Explosions on the Sun* (1989), and a volume of poetry, *Other Lovers' Children* (1975). FLEUR ADCOCK is her sister.

Dudek, Louis 1918– Canadian poet and critic. Born in Montreal of Polish parents, he attended McGill University and Columbia University, and taught in New York at City College before returning to Montreal in 1951. He lectured at McGill until his retirement in 1982. Dudek published his first volume of poetry, *East of the City*, in 1946. His early work is realistic and shows strong egalitarian sympathies. In 1952, with RAYMOND SOUSTER and IRVING LAYTON, he founded Contact Press, the leading publisher of Canadian poetry in the 1950s. *Delta*, the literary magazine he published from 1957 to 1966, advocates the ideal of an urbane and morally responsible art which appears in his later poetry, a marked departure from his early work. By this time Dudek was also influenced by MODERNISM and particularly by EZRA POUND, with whom he conducted a lengthy correspondence. His best work is to be found in his long poems, *Europe* (1954), *En Mexico* (1958) and *Atlantis* (1967). Other volumes include *The Transparent Sea* (1956), *Laughing Stalks* (1958), *Collected Poetry* (1971), *Cross-Section* (1980), *Continuation 1* (1981) and *Infinite Worlds* (1988). His literary criticism, which adopts a 'social realist' approach, includes *Literature and the Press* (1960), *Selected Essays and Criticism* (1978) and *Technology and Culture* (1979).

Duenna, The A comic opera with text by RICHARD BRINSLEY SHERIDAN and music by Thomas Linley. It was first produced at COVENT GARDEN in November 1775, and published in the same year. The plot concerns Don Jerome and his desire for a match between his daughter Louisa and Isaac. But Louisa is in love with Antonio and enlists the help of her duenna as intermediary with him. Don Jerome finds out; he locks up Louisa and dismisses her duenna. Louisa escapes from the house disguised as the duenna, who takes her place. Isaac is deceived into marrying the duenna and into bringing about the marriage of Louisa to her Antonio.

Duffy, Carol Ann 1955– Poet and playwright. Born in Glasgow and educated in Stafford and at the University of Liverpool, she is currently editor of the

literary magazine *Ambit*. In her poetry she excels at the DRAMATIC MONOLOGUE, sometimes delivered by a morally suspect speaker. *Fleshweathercock and Other Poems* (1973), her first volume, has been followed by: *Fifth Last Song* (1982); *Standing Female Nude* (1985), one of her best-known collections, tackling a wide range of subjects which include history, persecution, death, the family, loneliness and the artist; *Thrown Voices* (1986); *Selling Manhattan* (1987), praised for the originality of its love poetry; and *The Other Country* (1990), which explores the landscape of fantasy, memory and the imagination. *Take My Husband* (1982), *Cavern of Dreams* (1984) and *Little Women and Big Boys* (1986) are plays.

Duffy, Maureen (Patricia) 1933– Novelist and poet. Born in Worthing, Sussex, she read English at King's College, London, and worked as a schoolteacher from 1956 to 1961. Her first novel, *That's How It Was* (1962), is the story of an illegitimate child's relationship with her mother, recounted with simplicity, directness and great feeling. *The Paradox Players* (1967) displays Duffy's talent for making her characters live, describing the people who inhabit a Thames houseboat during a bitter winter. The novel which attracted most attention was *The Microcosm* (1966), a study of lesbianism centred on the lives of three women and the club where they meet. Duffy's topics have ranged widely over the years. *Gorsaga* (1981), set in the future, follows the life of Gor, a young gorilla created in a laboratory and brought up as a human child. *Change* (1987), about young people in wartime Britain, was followed by *Illuminations* (1991). *Collected Poems* appeared in 1985. She has also written a major study of APHRA BEHN, *The Passionate Shepherdess* (1977), and a history of the publishing house of Methuen, *A Thousand Capricious Chances* (1989). A champion of the rights of authors, she played a leading role in the campaign for Public Lending Right.

Dugdale, Sir William 1605–86 Antiquary. Born at Shustoke, near Coleshill in Warwickshire, he became a pursuivant extraordinary in the reign of Charles I. Dugdale's *The Antiquities of Warwickshire* (1656) is regarded as the fullest and most accurate of its kind until that date, setting a new standard for local antiquarianism. His *Monasticon Anglicanum*, an account of English monastic foundations, was published in three volumes in 1655, 1661 and 1673; and the valuable record of old St Paul's before it was destroyed by fire, *The History of St Paul's Cathedral*, appeared in 1658. *The History of Imbanking and Drayning of Divers Fenns and Marshes* (1662) goes far beyond the brief suggested by the title and includes an account of Hereward the Wake. His other works were *Origines Juridicales* (1666), a history of the administration of law in England (1675–6); and *A Short View of the Late*

Troubles in England (1681), an expression of his Royalist principles. Dugdale has a high place among English antiquarians for his careful scholarship and clear, attractive style.

Duggan, Eileen 1894–1972 New Zealand poet. Born in Tua Marina on South Island into an Irish immigrant family, she was educated at Marlborough High School and Victoria University, where she received a first-class honours degree in history. She subsequently worked as a teacher and as a lecturer in history at Victoria University and wrote a regular page for *The New Zealand Tablet* for many years. One of the first New Zealand poets to establish an international reputation, she was awarded the OBE in 1943. Duggan's work is characterized by its Roman Catholicism, its interest in Maori culture and its attempt to pioneer a sense of a local identity in New Zealand verse, which was an important influence on the following generation of poets. Her work demonstrates a strong feeling for the landscape in which she grew up, as well as an optimistic religious faith. Her volumes of verse include *New Zealand Bird Songs* (1929), *Poems* (1937), *New Zealand Poems* (1940) and her best collection, *More Poems* (1951), which transcends the Georgian simplicities of her early work.

Duke's Children, The A novel by ANTHONY TROLLOPE, the sixth and last of his PALLISER NOVELS, serialized in *ALL THE YEAR ROUND* from October 1879 to July 1880 and published in volume form in 1880.

Now a widower and no longer prime minister, the Duke of Omnium (Plantagenet Palliser) is left alone to adjust to his children's generation and its freer ways. His eldest son, Lord Silverbridge, has been expelled from Oxford and has fallen in with the disreputable Major Tifto, through whom he loses heavily in gambling on horses. He causes further heartache to his father by standing for Silverbridge as a Conservative rather than as a Liberal. The Duke is tolerant of his son's waywardness, and pays his gambling debts, but advises an early marriage to steady him. He approves of Silverbridge's attraction to the poor but well-connected Lady Mabel Grex, but when he falls in love with the beautiful and wealthy American girl, Isabel Boncassen, the granddaughter of an obscure Dutch immigrant, the Duke's pride of caste is stung. His daughter, Lady Mary Palliser, also disappoints him by falling in love with Frank Tregear, a young man of promise but without wealth or social rank, who had been encouraged by Lady Glencora before her death. The Duke refuses his consent to Silverbridge's marriage to Isabel, and she will not marry without it; but gradually the girl's charm and his son's determination win him over. Recognizing in his two older children something of their mother's stubborn spirit, he surrenders gracefully, and the novel ends with the two marriages. This closing harmony is shadowed by the loneliness of Lady Mabel Grex, who loses both the man she loves, Tregear, and the man who could have given her wealth and social position, Silverbridge.

The Duke's Children is concerned more with family relationships than with politics, and shows the Duke of Omnium coming to terms with a generation in many ways less principled and public-spirited than his own. Isabel Boncassen anticipates HENRY JAMES's American girl, Isabel Archer, in *THE PORTRAIT OF A LADY* (1881).

dumb show Dumb shows flourished as a feature of tragedies in Tudor England, making a spectacular element in the actionless plays that followed in the wake of *GORBODUC* (1562). Early dumb shows were typically allegorical, employing symbolic figures rather than characters from the play itself, but the professional playwrights of Elizabethan England saw the theatrical advantage to be gained by using dumb shows to focus the audience's attention on significant deeds outside the strict time-sequence of the play. There are famous examples in KYD's *THE SPANISH TRAGEDY* (*c.* 1589), PEELE's *THE OLD WIVES' TALE* (published 1595) and the anonymous *A Warning for Fair Women* (1599). Like other writers of plays on legendary heroes, ANTHONY MUNDAY found the dumb show a valuable means for introducing episodes without spreading his plots too wide. SHAKESPEARE was less addicted to them than many of his contemporaries, although the dumb show that introduces the play-within-the-play in *HAMLET* is much the best-known example in Elizabethan drama. It is deployed in a consciously archaic way, since the vogue for introductory dumb shows had long passed. Still more unusual is its pre-enactment of the whole substance of the ensuing play rather than of a single episode. During the Jacobean period, the dumb show became increasingly associated with the MASQUE, although WEBSTER and MIDDLETON are among the dramatists who continued to exploit it to sensational effect.

Dunbar, Paul (Laurence) 1872–1906 Black American poet and novelist. The son of former slaves, he was born in Dayton, Ohio. His first collection of verse, *Oak and Ivy*, was printed privately in 1893, and was followed by *Majors and Minors* in 1895. WILLIAM DEAN HOWELLS became interested in his work and wrote the preface to a third volume, *Lyrics of Lowly Life* (1896). Dunbar soon received national recognition and embarked on a number of lecture tours.

Known in his day primarily as a writer of dialect verse, he has been severely criticized for his nostalgic and sentimental depiction of black life in the South. He himself, however, was dissatisfied with the limited basis of his reputation, and in some of his works he reveals a concern with the troubled social climate of his times. His other collections of poetry include *Lyrics of the Hearthside* (1899), *Lyrics of Love and*

Laughter (1903) and *Lyrics of Sunshine and Shadow* (1905). He wrote four novels: *The Uncalled* (1898), *The Love of Landry* (1900), *The Fanatics* (1901) and *The Sport of the Gods* (1902).

Dunbar, William ?1465–?1530 Very little is known of Dunbar's life: even the dates of his birth and death are uncertain. He graduated MA from St Andrews in 1479, probably became a Franciscan novice and travelled abroad for some period between 1479 and 1500. In 1501 he went to England, probably in connection with the arrangements for the marriage of James IV of Scotland and Margaret, daughter of Henry VII.

Dunbar is usually considered to be one of the most important SCOTTISH CHAUCERIANS. He refers to 'noble CHAUCER of makaris (i.e. poets) all' in *Lament for the Makaris* and Chaucer as 'rose of rethoris (i.e. rhetoricians) all' in *The Goldyn Targe*. His main debt to English poets, as the second apostrophe to Chaucer suggests, is to their rhetoric and diction. This is mainly seen in his court poetry. *The Thrissil and the Rois* is a nuptial song for the marriage of James IV and Margaret Tudor in 1503. It is an allegorical DREAM-VISION in Chaucer's RHYME ROYAL stanza and is at times reminiscent of *THE PARLEMENT OF FOULES*. Amid heraldic animals and flowers Nature crowns a lion, eagle and thistle preeminent among animals, birds and plants. The thistle is James and the rose Margaret. Similarly courtly is *The Goldyn Targe* with its aureate diction, 'Up sprang the goldyn candill matutyne/ With clere depurit bemes cristallyne.' In this allegorical dream the poet finds himself at the court of Venus, only temporarily defended by the golden shield of reason against the arrows of beauty. Nature, Venus and classical deities mingle with personified abstractions.

At the other extreme from the diction and style of these dream-visions is *The Flyting of Dunbar and Kennedie*, although this too was probably intended for a courtly audience. SIR WALTER SCOTT thought it the most repellent poem he knew in any language. It is a stylized *tour de force* of mutually exchanged abuse, each contestant striving to outdo the other in brilliantly inventive invective: 'Chittirlilling, ruch rilling, like schilling in the milhous/ Baird rehator, theif of nator, fals tratour, feyindis gett.' The flyting is not to be taken as indicating personal animus, for Dunbar's fellow poet Walter Kennedy is referred to fondly in *Lament for the Makaris*. *The Tretis of the Twa Mariit Wemen and the Wedo* seduces its reader into an expectation of the courtly with its opening on midsummer eve and its picture of fair ladies gathering garlands in an arbour. But the poem mixes high and low styles, for there follows a deliberately gross and cynical discussion of marriage and sex by the three speakers. The poet asks his audience at the end to choose one of the speakers as wife.

Among Dunbar's other longer poems is *Dance of the Sevin Deidly Synnes*, a dream, or rather trance, in which the poet sees the devil Mahoun goading unshriven sinners into a *danse macabre*. The seven deadly sins, headed by Pride, the most deadly, appear in turn and dance. Mahoun finally calls for a Highland fling but the Highlanders make such a noise with their Gaelic that they are smothered in smoke in the deepest pit of hell. *Lament for the Makaris* is a familiar medieval meditation on the transitoriness and mutability of life, 'The flesch is brukle (fragile).' The poem is also known by its originally liturgical refrain, '*Timor mortis conturbat me.*' Among those taken by death we find Chaucer, HENRYSON and GOWER.

Dunbar's poetry includes those kinds well established in the Middle Ages: dream-vision, the court poem and moralizing reflection (especially on 'this warld unstabille'). He also wrote religious poems, some of which are typically medieval macaronic lyrics (poems which mix the vernacular with Latin). These include 'Et Nobis Puer Natus Est' on the Nativity and a poem on the Resurrection with its splendid opening line 'Done is a battell on the dragon blak'.

Duncan, Robert (Edward) 1919–88 American poet. He was born in Oakland, California, orphaned in early childhood (he took the name Robert Duncan in 1941) and educated at the University of California at Berkeley. He edited various 'little' magazines in the late 1930s and the 1940s, notably the *Experimental Review*, *Phoenix* and *The Berkeley Miscellany*. His first volume, *Heavenly City, Earthly City* (1947), was followed by *Medieval Scenes* (1950), *Poems 1948–49* (1950), *The Song of the Border-Guard* (1951) *Fragments of a Disordered Devotion* (1952) and *Caesar's Gate: Poems 1949–50* (1955). He lived on Mallorca from 1955 to 1956, when he joined the faculty of Black Mountain College and became associated with the BLACK MOUNTAIN SCHOOL of poets. Mysticism and a preoccupation with major writers of the past – Dante in particular – emerged as the hallmark of his writing in volumes such as *Letters* (1958), *Selected Poems* (1959), *The Opening of the Field* (1960), which he said announced the beginning of his mature work, and *Roots and Branches* (1964). His prolific output in the 1960s included *Of the War: Passages 22–27* (1966), *The Years as Catches: First Poems, 1939–1946* (1966), *Bending the Bow* (1968), *Names of People* (1968), *The First Decade: Selected Poems, 1940–1950* (1968) and *Deviations: Selected Poems, 1950–1956* (1968). *Ground Work: Before the War* (1984), arguably his most important volume since *The Opening of the Field* , broke a long, self-imposed silence. With *Ground Work II* (1987), it contains improvisations on Dante and the METAPHYSICAL POETS expressing his horror at his country's involvement in Vietnam. Duncan also wrote plays and several volumes of prose, the most important of which are *Fictive Certainties: Five Essays in Essential Autobiography* (1979) and *Toward an Open Universe* (1982).

Duncan, Sara Jeanette 1861–1922 Canadian novelist. She grew up in Brantford and was educated there and in Toronto. After teaching for some years, she became a journalist, writing for *The Toronto Globe* and *The Washington Post*. In 1888 she became parliamentary correspondent for *The Montreal Star*. In 1891 she married Everard Charles Cotes, a British journalist in India, which provided the setting for some of her novels. Of more than 20 titles, the most notable are *A Social Departure: or, How Orthodocia and I Went Round the World by Ourselves* (1890), *An American Girl in London* (1891), *The Imperialist* (1904), set in the small Canadian town of 'Elgin', and *Cousin Cinderella: A Canadian Girl in London* (1908).

Dunciad, The A satirical poem by ALEXANDER POPE, first published anonymously in three books in 1728; it was expanded in 1729 and a fourth book, *The New Dunciad*, added in 1742. The complete work was re-published in 1743.

The subject of the SATIRE is dullness, but the object was Pope's desire to hit back at LEWIS THEOBALD, who had severely (and accurately) criticized his edition of SHAKESPEARE. Pope made him the original 'hero' of *The Dunciad* but moved COLLEY CIBBER into that position in the poem's final form. Cibber had alluded to the play, THREE HOURS AFTER MARRIAGE, to which Pope had contributed, in his production of THE REHEARSAL. The body of the satire is full of ridicule for those writers who had earned the poet's displeasure or disapproval, but it is also a brilliantly wrought attack on literary vices.

The four books describe the triumph of dullness. In Book I the character Bayes (Colley Cibber) is trying to decide where his talents will best be deployed. The POET LAUREATE, LAURENCE EUSDEN, has died and Bayes's decision is made for him; the goddess anoints him king in place of Eusden, who now 'sleeps among the dull of ancient days'. Book II describes the celebrations following the enthronement of Bayes as King of the Dunces; his domain is the empire of Emptiness and Dullness. The celebrations as described are a BURLESQUE of the funeral games for Anchises in the *Aeneid*, just one of the poem's many MOCK-HEROIC features. Everyone falls asleep while poetry is being read. In Book III Bayes, sleeping in the goddess's lap, sees in his dreams the past and future triumphs of the empire of Dullness extended to all arts and sciences, the theatre, and the court. Bayes's guide in his dream is ELKANAH SETTLE, who had been one of DRYDEN's literary opponents. Book IV sees the dream realized: the goddess gives her messengers instructions to discover silly pursuits that will be encouraged. Thought is discouraged and Dullness triumphs. The final vision of cultural chaos is a triumph of Pope's art, part comic and part serious.

Dunlap, William 1766–1839 One of the earliest American playwrights, and the first to make the theatre his profession. Dunlap was born in Perth Amboy, New Jersey. He studied painting in New York and then in London under Benjamin West (1784–6), but abandoned art for the theatre soon after his return to the USA. His democratic patriotism is evident in the first of his plays to be produced, *The Father: or, American Shandyism* (1789), and in the military tragedy, *André* (1798), which concerns an incident in the Revolutionary War. Dunlap wrote over 65 plays, many of them adaptations from foreign works, particularly the fashionable shocking dramas of the German August von Kotzebue. In 1805 he turned to management but was plagued by financial problems. He left the theatre in 1811, and from 1816 until his death resumed his interrupted career as a painter. His advocacy of native art is voluminously represented in *A History of the American Theatre* (1832) and *A History of the Rise and Progress of the Arts of Design in the United States* (1834).

Dunn, Douglas (Eaglesham) 1942– Poet. Born in Inchinnan, Renfrewshire, he was educated locally, becoming a librarian before reading English at Hull University (1966–9). After graduating he worked as a librarian there until 1971, when he became a freelance writer, returning to Scotland in 1984. The poems in his fine first collection, *Terry Street* (1969), influenced by PHILIP LARKIN, are detailed observations of underprivileged lives. After *The Happier Life* (1972), his third collection, *Love or Nothing* (1974), shows strong elements of fantasy. *Barbarians* (1979) articulates, like TONY HARRISON's work, the resentment of the working class towards 'a culture of contrivance'. *St Kilda's Parliament* (1981) is a surrealistic, if uneven treatment of Scottish obsessions, and *Elegies* (1985) mourns the death of his wife. *Selected Poems 1964–83* (1986) was followed by the less political *Northlight* (1988). He has also published *Secret Villages* (1985), a volume of stories, and edited *A Rumoured City: New Poets from Hull* (1982) and *The Faber Book of Twentieth-Century Scottish Poetry* (1992), a comprehensive and much-needed anthology. *The Poll Tax: The Fiscal Fake* (1990) is a political broadside.

Duns Scotus, John ?1265–1308 Schoolman. He was born in Scotland, possibly at Duns near Berwick. After completing his studies at the universities of Scotland and England between 1291 and 1293, he went to the University of Paris for further studies under Gonsalvus of Spain and James of Quarcheto. He commented on the Sentences of Peter Lombard at Cambridge between 1297 and 1300. Between 1300 and 1301 he lectured on the *Sentences* at Oxford (*Opus Oxoniense*), breaking off after Book III to go to Paris where he finally completed the commentary on Book IV (*Reportata Parisiensia*, 1303). He commented, in addition, on Aristotle and Porphyry. He returned to Oxford in 1303, after refusing to subscribe to a petition against Boniface VIII; he then returned to Paris, where he took his *magisterium*, recommended by Gonsalvus. He travelled to Cologne in 1307, dying there on 8 November 1308. In spite of his being much venerated by the Friars Minor, he was accused in 1315 of holding opinions that came dangerously close to Pelagianism, and ten '*temerariae opiniones*' were put forward for condemnation.

It is in his commentaries, particularly on the *Sentences*, that Scotus elucidates his own complex synthesis of Aristotelian, Thomistic and Augustinian ideas. He rejected an Aristotelian emphasis on knowledge and intellect, substituting an emphasis on freedom, love and the will. He is thought of as a philosopher of 'realism', positing the close correspondence of our concepts to the real, and seeking to establish a more perfect foundation for our universal concepts. He attempted to construct a valid and complete proof of the existence of God. GERARD MANLEY HOPKINS's understanding of Scotus's ideas on *haecceitas* (the individuating differences in a thing, as opposed to those features it shares in common with other individuals) contributed to the development of his own ideas about individuation.

Dunton, John 1659–1733 Bookseller. A characteristic publisher of his times, Dunton strove to print material that would satisfy the newly expanding readership of the AUGUSTAN AGE. In 1690 he started publishing *The Athenian Gazette* (later *The Athenian Mercury*), a journal initially dealing with intellectual and philosophical curiosities, but deteriorating with popularity into a sometimes preposterous triviality. The *Mercury* was the place where SWIFT first appeared in print, with an inferior encomiastic ode. Dunton was also the author of many political pamphlets, and *The Life and Errors of John Dunton* (1705).

Durang, Christopher 1949– American playwright and actor. Born in Montclair, New Jersey, he was educated at Harvard and Yale. He emerged as one of the new breed of American playwrights in the late 1970s and early 1980s with anarchic and satirical pieces whose attacks on religion, in particular, have provoked controversy and attempts at censorship. They include *A History of the American Film* (1976), the Obie-Award winning *Sister Mary Ignatius Explains It All for You* (1979), *The Actor's Nightmare* (1981), *Beyond Therapy* (1981), *Baby with the Bath Water* (1983) and *The Marriage of Bette and Boo* (1973; revised, 1985).

D'Urfey, Thomas 1653–1723 Playwright and songwriter, remembered above all as the editor of the influential collection of ballads in six volumes, *Wit and Mirth: or, Pills to Purge Melancholy* (1719–20). Born in Exeter, D'Urfey moved to London and became an intimate of both Charles II and James II. He was a versatile dramatist, always willing to adapt to changing tastes. *Madame Fickle* (1676) and *A Fond Husband* (1677) are intrigue comedies in the style of WYCHERLEY and ETHEREGE, *Squire Oldsapp* (1678) and *The Virtuous Wife* (1679) are more farcical, *Sir Barnaby Whigg* (1681) and *The Royalist* (1682) are political satires, while D'Urfey's best plays, *Love for Money* (1691) and *The Richmond Heiress* (1693), reflect the move towards a greater respect for moral standards in the drama.

Durham The latest datable poem in Old English, written between 1104 and 1109. It describes Durham's position in terms of the countryside surrounding the city, and the relics of the famous saints, bishops and scholars kept there.

Durrell, Gerald (Malcolm) 1925– Traveller and naturalist. The younger brother of LAWRENCE DURRELL, he was born in Jamshedpur, India, and brought up in France, Italy, Switzerland, Greece and Britain. From 1947 he travelled widely on expeditions to collect animals for zoos. He founded the Jersey Zoo in 1959 and the Jersey Wildlife Trust in 1964 to breed rare and threatened species. Although he has written novels, journalism and programmes for television and radio, he remains best known for light-hearted, informative books about his travels and experiences with animals. They include *The Overloaded Ark* (1951), *The Bafut Beagles* (1953), *The Drunken Forest* (1955) and *My Family and Other Animals* (1956).

Durrell, Lawrence (George) 1912–90 Novelist, poet and travel-writer. The elder brother of GERALD DURRELL, he was born in India and educated at Darjeeling and at St Edmund's School, Canterbury. In Paris he was a friend of HENRY MILLER and ANAÏS NIN. His first volume of poetry, *Quaint Fragment: Poems Written between the Ages of Sixteen and Nineteen*, was published in 1931. His first novel, *Panic Spring*, appeared under the pseudonym Charles Norden in 1935, though a second novel, *Pied Piper of Lovers*, was published the same year under his own name. The Eastern Mediterranean, where he spent a great deal of his life, formed the background to much of his best-known work, notably his books on Greece, *Prospero's Cell* (1945) and *Bitter Lemons* (1957), and the four novels forming the *Alexandria Quartet*: *Justine* (1957), *Balthazar* (1958), *Mountolive* (1958) and *Clea* (1960). Later volumes of poetry include *The Ikons* (1966) and *Vega and Other Poems* (1973); *Collected Poems* appeared in 1960. Subsequent fiction includes *Tunc* (1968), *Nunquam* (1970) and the posthumously collected *Avignon Quintet* (1992): *Monsieur* (1974), *Livia* (1978), *Constance* (1982), *Sebastian* (1983) and *Quinx* (1985), five novels organized in relation to one another in the manner of the cabbalistic figure of the quincunx. Lectures delivered while he was teaching for the British Council in Greece and Argentina were published as *A Key to Modern Poetry* (1952).

Dutch Courtesan, The A comedy by JOHN MARSTON, first published in 1605. It was first produced at least two years before that, in the reign of Elizabeth I; the title-page states that it was played 'by the children of her Majesties revels'.

The Dutch courtesan of the title is Franceschina. Her protector is Freevill, who falls in love with Beatrice, the daughter of Sir Hubert Subboys, and decides that he must end the liaison with Franceschina. Meanwhile he takes his stiff-necked friend Malheureux with him on a visit to Franceschina; he intends to amuse himself at his friend's uneasiness, but Malheureux conceives a violent passion for her. When Franceschina discovers Freevill's plans to marry she uses Malheureux's passion for her; she will respond if he will kill Freevill and bring her proof by taking from his hand a ring given him by Beatrice.

Malheureux recoils from the proposal and reveals it to Freevill, who arranges a mock fight, gives his friend the ring, and goes into hiding. But when Malheureux takes the ring to Franceschina she denounces him as a murderer to Sir Hubert and Freevill's father. Malheureux finds himself charged with Freevill's death and sentenced to the gallows. Freevill reappears in time to rescue him.

Freevill, who comments on the motives and emotions of the others and manipulates them some of the time, is one of the most unpleasant characters in Jacobean drama. Late in the action he declares himself enchanted with the prospect of marriage to Beatrice, while looking forward to the confounding of Franceschina: 'Providence all wicked art o'er tops.' If that were true he could expect to find himself brought down very hard some time in the future. But there is no such moral framework in *The Dutch Courtesan*: expedience is all in Marston's play.

Dutchman A one-act play by AMIRI BARAKA, first performed in 1964, when the author was still known as LeRoi Jones. Set in the New York subway in summer, it depicts the fatal encounter of Lula, a provocative white woman, and Clay, a somewhat naive, middle-class black man. Their initially flirtatious conversation becomes more antagonistic as Lula taunts Clay for playing the role which the dominant white society has handed him. He finally responds to her with all the force of the racial hatred that he has suppressed in order to survive. Furious at losing control of the situa-

tion, Lula fatally stabs him and orders the other subway riders to remove his body. As they are doing so, another young black man enters the subway car and Lula begins her act again. The constant references to Adam and Eve, fairy-tales and the Flying Dutchman make the play mythic rather than realistic.

Dwight, Timothy 1752–1817 American poet. One of the founding members of the CONNECTICUT WITS and the grandson of JONATHAN EDWARDS, Dwight was born in Massachusetts and matriculated at Yale at the age of 13. At 19 he was made tutor, a position he filled with such zeal that he suffered a nervous breakdown at 25. To aid his recuperation he undertook extensive walking and horseback journeys, which provided the material for his *Travels in New England and New York* (4 vols., 1821–2). During the Revolutionary War he served as an army chaplain and in 1783 became pastor of the Congregational church at Greenfield Hill, Connecticut. While serving there, he wrote his most widely read poems, which attempt to inculcate Calvinist and Federalist values: THE CONQUEST OF CANAAN (1785), *Greenfield Hill* (1794) and *The Triumph of Infidelity* (1788). In 1795 he became president of Yale, in which capacity he successfully advocated the enlargement of the curriculum and published a number of statements of his political views, among them *The True Means of Establishing Public Happiness* (1795) and *The Duty of Americans, at the Present Crisis* (1798). *Theology, Explained and Defended* (1818-19), a five-volume collection of 173 sermons, makes a complete statement of his theology.

Dyce, Alexander 1798–1869 Scholar. Born in Edinburgh, educated at the High School there and at Exeter College, Oxford, he took Anglican orders and served as a curate until 1825, after which he devoted himself to literary work in London. His editorial work, which had begun as an undergraduate, was mainly concerned with the early dramatists: FLETCHER, WEBSTER, GREENE, SHIRLEY, MIDDLETON, MARLOWE and especially SHAKESPEARE (9 vols., 1857). Other publications include an edition of the play SIR THOMAS MORE for the Shakespeare Society (1844). His extensive library, strong in classical and European verse as well as Elizabethan authors, was bequeathed to the South Kensington (Victoria and Albert) Museum.

Dyer, Sir Edward 1543–1607 Poet, courtier and diplomat. A Somerset gentleman, he was educated at Oxford, and gained access to the court as a protégé of the Earl of Leicester. A man of speculative interests, he was one of the backers of Frobisher's expeditions to the far north of America in the 1570s; later in life he became fascinated by alchemy, and developed a strong friendship with the magus John Dee. In 1575 Dyer participated in the Woodstock entertainment for Queen Elizabeth; concealed in an oak, and accompanying himself on his lute, he sang an exquisite song complaining of his neglect at court. Thereafter he prospered. He was a close friend of SIR FULKE GREVILLE and SIR PHILIP SIDNEY, who composed a song in praise of their three-in-one friendship, 'Join Mates in Mirth to Me'. Sidney also introduced Dyer into his ARCADIA as the shepherd Coridon, and Dyer wrote a moving ELEGY on the death of Sidney, 'Silence Augmenteth Grief'.

Only a handful of his poems survive, preserved in commonplace-books. NASHE wrote of Dyer that he was the first 'that repurified Poetrie from Art's pedantism, and instructed it to speak Courtly'. He liked a plain style, but his lyrics have sweetness and good measure. Their prevailing character is introspective and melancholy. Like so much Elizabethan courtier verse, his lines require a musical accompaniment to achieve their full effect. The most famous lyric ascribed to him, 'My Mind to Me a Kingdom Is' (printed in 1588), was set to music by William Byrd.

Dyer, John *c.* 1700–58 Poet. A native of Dyfed, Dyer was educated at Westminster School. He studied painting with Jonathan Richardson but was an unsuccessful artist. He was ordained in 1741, and was the incumbent of Coningsby and Kirkby in Lincolnshire when he died. Dyer is remembered for *Grongar Hill* (1727), a poem celebrating the valley of the River Towy in Dyfed. It uses the octosyllabic couplet of MILTON'S *L'ALLEGRO* and brings a remarkable freshness of observation to topographical poetry, anticipating some of the spirit of ROMANTICISM. Later, unsuccessful poems were *The Ruins of Rome* (1740) and *The Fleece* (1757), a faintly absurd treatment of the wool trade.

Dylan, Bob [Robert Allen Zimmerman] 1941– Singer, song-writer and poet. Educated at the University of Minnesota, he made his reputation with his early albums, *Bob Dylan* (1962), *Freewheelin' Bob Dylan* (1963), *The Times They are A-Changin'* (1964) and *Another Side of Bob Dylan* (1964). *Bob Dylan's Greatest Hits* was released in 1967 and *Bob Dylan's Greatest Hits, Volume 2* in 1971. *Biograph* (1987) is the most synoptic compilation of his work so far. To begin with, he was thought of as a singer of folk songs, protest songs and country blues, but his appearance at the Newport Folk Festival in 1965 announced a shift towards rock music, confirmed by the albums *Highway 61 Revisited* (1965) and *Blonde on Blonde* (1966). His later phases have included flirtations with Country and Western music, notably in *John Wesley Harding* (1968), *Nashville Skyline* (1969) and *New Morning* (1970), and – despite his Jewish upbringing – evangelical Christianity. The words to his songs have received a considerable amount of critical attention as poetry in their own right. More lyrical than GINSBERG and less self-tortured than KEROUAC, he has much in common with the BEATS. His books include: *Tarantula* (1966), a series of verbal collages intended as a quasi-autobiographical novel; *Approximately Complete Works* (1970); *Writings and Drawings* (1971); *Poem to Joanie* (1972); *XI Outlined Epitaphs and Off the Top of My Head* (1981); and *Road Drawings* (1992). *Lyrics, 1962–1985* (1985) collects his lyrics from the 20 or so years of his greatest achievement as a song-writer. Dylan has also written film music and appeared in films such as Sam Peckinpah's *Pat Garrett and Billy the Kid* (1971).

Dynasts, The THOMAS HARDY's 'Epic-Drama of the War with Napoleon', a long poem or CLOSET DRAMA, published in three parts in 1904, 1906 and 1908. Its 19 acts and 130 scenes trace Napoleon's career from 1805 until his defeat at Waterloo some 10 years later, a period that had fascinated Hardy for many years. The structure of *The Dynasts* embodies what he liked to call his philosophical 'impressions'. The actions of the huge cast of human characters, from Napoleon down to the common soldiers and ordinary people of Wessex, are subject to the Immanent Will, the controlling power of the universe and a blind, unheeding force which bears no resemblance to the Christian God. Events are commented on by 'impersonated abstractions or Intelligences, called Spirits', including the Ancient Spirit of the Years, the Spirit of the Pities the Spirit of Rumour and the Spirits Sinister and Ironic. *The Dynasts* combines a variety of verse forms with scenes and descriptions in prose.

Earl of Toulous, The A VERSE ROMANCE written around 1400 in the north-east Midlands. It is, by its own account, a BRETON LAY. The Earl promises a prisoner freedom in exchange for a meeting with his beautiful Empress, the wife of the Earl's enemy. He goes disguised as a hermit and she gives him a ring as a love-token. The Emperor later goes away and entrusts his wife to knights who try unsuccessfully to woo her. They hide a naked youth in her chamber then vociferously 'discover' and kill him; the Empress is accused of adultery. Hearing of her need of a champion the Earl disguises himself as a monk, hears her confession and, assured of her innocence, successfully defends her. The Emperor accepts the Earl's friendship and on his death the couple marry.

The story is based loosely on historical fact. In 831 the Empress Judith, second wife of Louis le Debonnaire, was accused of adultery with Bernard I, Count of Barcelona and Toulouse, but acquitted, and later Bernard offered battle with anyone who doubted his innocence.

Earle, John c. 1601–55 Essayist. A fellow of Merton College, Oxford, at the age of 18, Earle wrote *Microcosmography: or, A Piece of the World Discovered in Essays and Characters* (1628). Although the book appeared anonymously, its author's identity was no secret and Earle became famous. It is a collection of 'characters', or descriptions of behavioral types, a form much in fashion at the time. Easily recognizable from the day-to-day life he knew, Earle's characters are presented with insight and reckoned to be among the best of their kind. *Microcosmography* ran to four editions in 1628 and enlarged editions in 1629 and 1633.

Earle became tutor to Prince Charles, remaining loyal to him throughout the Civil War. He translated *EIKON BASILIKE* into Latin during his 16 years' exile as a Royalist. At the Restoration he became Dean of Westminster and later Bishop of Salisbury.

Earthly Paradise, The A poem by WILLIAM MORRIS, published in three volumes between 1868 and 1870. It consists of 24 tales in verse, with a prologue and linking narrative.

A group of Norsemen flee the plague by setting sail across the western sea in search of the Earthly Paradise where nobody grows old. After long and fruitless journeying they at last arrive, old and tired, at 'a nameless city in a distant sea' where Greek culture and civilization have been preserved. They are made welcome and spend their remaining years there. Twice a month they meet their hosts at a feast and exchange stories. One of the Norsemen tells a tale of their past and one of their hosts relates a classical legend. Lyric poems connect the months and describe the landscape of the changing year.

Obviously medieval in both its form and content, *The Earthly Paradise* deliberately creates a dreamlike atmosphere. In a famous passage the prologue offers the reader an escape from the industrial society that Morris himself so despised: 'Forget six counties overhung with smoke,/ Forget the snorting steam and piston stroke.' The appeal was popular with the Victorian public and *The Earthly Paradise* helped establish Morris as one of the leading poets of the day.

East Lynne A novel by MRS HENRY WOOD, published in 1861. Immensely popular in its day, it was also dramatized with great success. Lady Isobel Vane marries Archibald Carlyle but deserts him to go abroad with Sir Francis Levison. After he abandons her, she is disfigured in a train crash. Returning to England, she works unrecognized as governess to her own children and asks for Carlyle's forgiveness on her deathbed.

Eastman, Charles (Alexander) 1858–1939 Native American writer. Born of mixed Santee Sioux and white parentage, he received his BA from Dartmouth in 1887 and his MD from Boston University Medical School in 1890. He treated the victims of the Wounded Knee Massacre in 1890, and that same year married Elaine Goodale, with whom he collaborated on all his books (though only *Wigwam Evenings* bears both their names). Between 1890 and 1910 he held a number of positions connected with the Bureau of Indian Affairs; he also lectured in America and England, meeting many of the great literary and political figures of his day.

Through his writings Eastman attempted to bridge the gap between Indian and white culture by describing the life, customs and legends of his people for a primarily white audience. Four of his books were for children: *Indian Boyhood* (1902), *Red Hunters and the Animal People* (1904), *Old Indian Days* (1907) and *Wigwam Evenings: Sioux Folktales Retold* (1909). In *The Soul of the Indian: An Interpretation* (1911) he describes the Indian system of ethics and Indian attitudes towards nature. *The Indian To-day: The Past and Future of the First Americans* (1915) is an overview of Indian history. *From the Deep Woods to Civilization: Chapters in the Autobiography of an Indian* appeared in 1916. *Indian Heroes and Great Chieftains* (1918) is a collection of short biographies of Sioux leaders.

Eastman, Max 1883–1969 American critic, poet and essayist. Born in New York City, he came to prominence as the author of *Enjoyment of Poetry* (1913), a critical study which is still his best-known work. He co-founded and edited the left-wing magazines *The Masses* (1913–17) and *The Liberator* (1918–22), and later published *Marx, Lenin, and The Science of Revolution* (1926). With the rise of Stalin, however, he turned against the Left, publishing *Artists in Uniform: A Study of Literature and Bureaucratism* (1934), a collection of literary and political essays; *Marxism, is It Science?* (1940); and *Reflections on the Failure of Socialism* (1955). From 1941 to his death he was an editor for *Reader's Digest*. His memoirs of famous friends, including Isadora Duncan, Anatole France, Charlie Chaplin and Leon Trotsky, appeared in *Heroes I Have Known* (1942) and *Great Companions* (1959). His poems were collected as *Poems of Five Decades* (1954). *Love and Revolution* (1964) is an autobiography.

Eastward Ho A comedy by GEORGE CHAPMAN, BEN JONSON and JOHN MARSTON, first performed at BLACKFRIARS by the Children of the Revels and published in 1605. By dealing with tradesmen and their lives, it made an important – if partly parodic – contribution to the popular form of CITIZEN COMEDY. A passage about the Scots in Act III so offended JAMES I that Chapman and Jonson were briefly imprisoned.

The plot tells of Touchstone, a goldsmith, his two daughters, Mildred and Gertrude, and his two apprentices, Golding and Quicksilver. Gertrude, who wants to be fashionable and ride in her own coach, marries Sir Petronel Flash, who turns out to be a penniless adventurer. The industrious apprentice, Golding, has eyes for the unpretentious Mildred, who is happy to marry him and proud to see him become deputy alderman. Sir Petronel filches Gertrude's dowry and sends her off on a coach to an imaginary castle. As soon as she is gone he sets off for Virginia in company with the idle apprentice, Quicksilver, who has robbed his master. They are arrested when their ship is wrecked on the Isle of Dogs and brought up before Golding, the deputy alderman. A term in prison makes them repent and they are eventually released through Golding's good offices.

Eberhart, Richard 1904– American poet and playwright. Born in Austin, Minnesota, he was educated at the University of Minnesota at Minneapolis, Dartmouth College, St John's College and Harvard. In 1942–6 he served with the US Naval Reserve. His career has included teaching as well as working as assistant manager, and later vice-president, of a company in Boston. His poetry, often seen as in open combat with MODERNISM, has doggedly pursued a personal, neo-Romantic style which tends to be con-templative and lyrical. Themes range from confrontation with death to meditations inspired by nature; later work is frequently concerned with the poetic process itself. *A Bravery of Earth* (1930), his first volume, has been followed by *Poems: New and Selected* (1944), *Brotherhood of Men* (1949), *Undercliff: Poems 1946–1956* (1956), *The Oak: A Poem* (1957), *Collected Poems 1930–1960, Including 51 New Poems* (1960), *The Vastness and Indifference of the World* (1965), *Selected Poems, 1930–1965* (1965, PULITZER PRIZE), *Thirty-One Sonnets* (1967), *Shifts of Being* (1968), *Fields of Grace* (1972), *Collected Poems, 1930–1976, Including 43 New Poems* (1976), *Survivors* (1979), *Ways of Light: Poems 1972–1980* (1980), *New Hampshire: Nine Poems* (1980), *Florida Poems* (1981), *The Long Reach: New and Uncollected Poems 1948–1983* (1984) and *Throwing Yourself Away* (1984). His *Collected Verse Plays* appeared in 1962, though he has done little in the medium since then except *Chocorua* (1982). *Collected Poems* (1988), published by Oxford University Press, summarizes his poetic career. Eberhart has received many academic and literary awards, including the Harriet Monroe Poetry Award, the Bollingen Prize, and the National Book Award; he was elected to the American Academy of Arts and Sciences in 1967 and was made POET LAUREATE of New Hampshire in 1979.

Ecce Homo See SEELEY, J. R.

eclogue From the Greek word for 'selection', hence originally referring to a short poem or section of a longer poem. The term was later applied to the PASTORAL poems of Virgil and, in the Renaissance, to verse dialogues on pastoral themes, like SPENSER's *THE SHEPHEARDES CALENDER*. By the 18th century a distinction was drawn between pastoral, which described a context, and eclogue, which described a verse form. The term can also mean merely a dramatic argument in verse, not necessarily connected with pastoral.

Eden, Richard ?1521–76 Collector and translator of accounts of travel. He was educated at Queens' College, Cambridge, and for a while held a position in the Treasury. His translations include: part of Munster's *Cosmographiae* as *A Treatise of the New India* (1553); *The Decades of the New World* (1555), a collection of travels mainly from Peter Martyr of Angleria; Martin Cortes's *Arte de navegar* as *The Art of Navigation* (1561); and *The History of Travel in the West and East Indies* (1577).

Edgar, David 1948– Playwright. Born in Birmingham, he was educated at Oundle and Manchester University, where he studied drama. After a spell as a reporter in Bradford he began writing agit-prop plays for The General Will, a touring political theatre company. The best of his early work found popular forms to match his political arguments: *Tedderella* (1971) is a PANTOMIME about Edward Heath and *Dick Deterred* (1974) a MELODRAMA about President Nixon and Watergate. Edgar's work for the ROYAL SHAKESPEARE COMPANY tackled more ambitious subjects. *Destiny* (1976) concerns the rise of Nation Forward, a neo-fascist group resembling the National Front, while *Maydays* (1983) charts the growing disillusion of British socialists since World War II. His greatest success at the RSC was his adaptation of DICKENS's NICHOLAS NICKLEBY (1981), a mammoth project which spread over two evenings and recreated Victorian London in a manner which suggested that the evils of capitalism have changed little since then. Another aspect of his work is shown by *Mary Barnes* (1979), a story about a disturbed child based on a case study by R. D. LAING. While showing difficulty in sustaining the confident assumptions of his early work, *That Summer* (1987), about the effect on the left wing of the failure of the 1984 Miners' Strike, and *The Shape of the Table* (1990), about changes in Eastern Europe, maintained his reputation as the most prolific and skilled socialist playwright in contemporary Britain. In 1991 Edgar adapted STEVENSON's THE STRANGE CASE OF DR JEKYLL AND MR HYDE for the ROYAL NATIONAL THEATRE.

Edgell, Zee 1940– Belizean novelist. Born and educated in Belize City, she became the first Belizean woman to qualify as a journalist from, what was then, the Regent Street Polytechnic in London. She worked as a journalist in Jamaica and Britain and as schoolteacher and newspaper editor in Belize. After living abroad for many years, she returned to Belize in the 1980s as director of the Women's Bureau and then of the Department of Women's Affairs. *Beka Lamb* (1982) became the first Belizean novel to find an international audience. Covering a period of just a few months, it deals with the heroine's transition from unreflective child to responsible young woman. The connection made between her growing pains and the forces of social change links it with work by ERNA BRODBER, JAMAICA KINCAID and GRACE NICHOLS. *In Times Like These* (1991) also entwines personal and public crises in its account of an overseas-educated Belizean woman's return to her country as its Independence approaches.

Edgeworth, Maria 1767–1849 Novelist. Though she was born at Black Bourton in Oxfordshire and attended school in Derby (1775–80) and London (1780–2), she spent most of her life at Edgeworthstown in County Longford, where her father, the eccentric and radical Richard Lovell Edgeworth, was a wealthy landowner. He was a powerful influence on his daughter, shaping her interests and literary career. She collaborated with him on *Practical Education* (1798), adapting and modifying Rousseau's theories, and completed the second volume of her father's *Memoirs* in 1820. Her first work, *Letters to Literary Ladies* (1795), was a defence of female education. *The Parent's Assistant* (1796–1800) is a collection of stories for children, to which she later added a volume of *Little Plays*. CASTLE RACKRENT (1800), THE ABSENTEE (in the second series of *Tales of Fashionable Life*, 1812) and *Ormond* (1817) are novels of Irish life, which won the admiration of SIR WALTER SCOTT and influenced his 'Waverley' novels. *Belinda* (1801), *Leonora* (1806), *Patronage* (1814) and *Helen* (1834) deal with English society. Although they never met, JANE AUSTEN commended *Belinda* in NORTHANGER ABBEY and sent Maria Edgeworth a copy of *EMMA* in 1816.

Edinburgh Review, The A quarterly magazine founded in 1802 by FRANCIS JEFFREY, SYDNEY SMITH, HENRY BROUGHAM and FRANCIS HORNER. It was published by Constable in Edinburgh and by Longman in London, the first issue appearing on 10 October 1802 as *The Edinburgh Review and Critical Journal*. Circulation rose to 13,500 by 1818. SIR WALTER SCOTT, a notable early contributor whose Tory views brought him into conflict with the Whig editors, withdrew his support and played a part in founding the rival QUARTERLY REVIEW. Apart from Jeffrey and his co-founders, other contributors included HAZLITT, HENRY HALLAM, FRANCIS HORNER and, in later years, MACAULAY, CARLYLE and THOMAS ARNOLD. The *Edinburgh Review* was the most influential magazine of its day, setting new standards for outspoken and deliberate criticism; its demand for disciplined literary feeling made it particularly harsh on the work of WORDSWORTH, COLERIDGE and SOUTHEY, the so-called LAKE POETS. An unfavourable review of BYRON's *Hours of Idleness* by Brougham provoked the poet's *English Bards and Scotch Reviewers*. The *Edinburgh Review* ceased publication in 1929.

Edmond, Lauris 1924– New Zealand poet. Born and brought up in the Hawkes Bay region, she trained as a teacher and speech therapist, had six children, and did not start publishing until *In the Middle Air* (1975). Since then her prolific output has included *The Pear Tree* (1977) and *Wellington Letter* (1980) – two fine death sequences – as well as *Catching It* (1983), *Selected Poems* (1984; winner of the Commonwealth Poetry Prize), *Summer Near the Arctic Circle* (1988) and *New and Selected Poems* (1991). Technically conservative, carefully crafted and often familial or domestic in its themes, her poetry is written from a woman's point of view and for an implied female readership. She has also published a novel, *High Country Weather* (1984), and two volumes of autobiography.

Edmond, Murray 1949– New Zealand poet. He was born in Hamilton and studied at Auckland University, where he helped to produce *Freed*, the magazine whose appearance in 1969 announced the arrival of American MODERNISM and counter-culture on the New Zealand literary scene. After working with the Half Moon Theatre in London in the mid-1970s, he founded and ran Town and Country Players on his return to New Zealand. He is currently lecturer in drama at Auckland. Like the early work of BILL MANHIRE and IAN WEDDE, his first collection, *Entering the Eye* (1973), is influenced by the rhetoric and informality of the BLACK MOUNTAIN SCHOOL. Later poetry, which includes *End Wall* (1981), *Letters and Paragraphs* (1987) and *From the Word Go* (1992), suggests the influence of drama in its range of language and voices. It also engages with local history and geography in a way that recalls, though not stylistically, the work of KENDRICK SMITHYMAN. He has edited an anthology of New Zealand verse, *The New Poets* (1987).

Education of Henry Adams, The: *A Study of Twentieth-Century Multiplicity* The autobiography of HENRY ADAMS, privately printed in 1907, published in 1918 and awarded a PULITZER PRIZE for biography. Among other things, it describes his experience as both student and teacher at Harvard, his impressions of England during the years of the American Civil War, and the impact of CHARLES DARWIN's theories on him, but omits his marriage and his wife's suicide. Writing about himself in the third person, Adams deliberately presents his own life and experiences as representative of modernity. A crucial chapter contrasts the dynamo, the symbol of the accelerating forces of modern life, with the Virgin, the symbol of the 13th century and the subject of his earlier book, *MONT-SAINT-MICHEL AND CHARTRES*.

Edward II, King of England, The Troublesome Reign and Lamentable Death of A historical tragedy in blank verse by CHRISTOPHER MARLOWE, first produced by the Earl of Pembroke's Men *c.* 1592 and published in 1594. SHAKESPEARE's success with *HENRY VI* in 1592 had helped to make the English history play an attractive medium for dramatists. Though its detractors complain it lacks the grandeur and lofty language associated with Marlowe, it is also the best constructed of all his works.

The play begins with Edward's recall of his favourite Gaveston upon his accession to the throne (Gaveston had been banished by the King's father, Edward I), and follows the grim events that succeed. These include: the growing hatred of his queen, Isabella of France (the She-Wolf); the revolt of the barons culminating in their capture and murder of Gaveston; the rise of Hugh le Despenser in Edward's affections; the Queen's alliance with her lover Mortimer and their successful rebellion; the execution of Despenser and his father; Edward's confinement in Berkeley Castle and his degradation and murder.

Edward III, The Reign of A chronicle play published in 1596. The authorship is unknown, though the suggestion that SHAKESPEARE had a hand in it has not been completely rejected (see SHAKESPEARE APOCRYPHA). Apart from its historical content, dealing with Edward III and the Hundred Years War, the play is concerned with the King's unwelcome attentions to the Countess of Salisbury, which nearly drive her to suicide.

Edwards, Jonathan 1703–58 American Puritan minister and religious philosopher. He was born in East Windsor, Connecticut, and educated at Yale. In 1727 he was ordained minister of the church in Northampton, Massachusetts, where he served jointly with his grandfather, SOLOMON STODDARD, until Stoddard's death in 1729. His early sermons include *God Glorified in the Work of Redemption* (1731) and *A Divine and Supernatural Light* (1734), the latter notable for its emphasis on the aesthetic dimension of religious experience. His preaching helped precipitate the religious revival that swept through western Massachusetts in 1734–5, and later contributed to the 'Great Awakening' (1740), which spread through the colonies in general (see *SINNERS IN THE HANDS OF AN ANGRY GOD*). These awakenings prompted Edwards to reflect on the nature of religious experience. His *Faithful Narrative of Surprising Conversions* (1737) and *The Distinguishing Marks* (1741) describe and defend the 1735 revival and the Great Awakening, respectively. *Some Thoughts concerning the Present Revival* (1743) speculates on the millennial possibilities raised by the Awakening. *A Treatise concerning Religious Affections* (1746) is a systematic exposition of his understanding of religious psychology, while his diary and *Personal Narrative* (*c.* 1740, not intended for publication) tell the story of his own conversion.

Dismissed by his Northampton congregation in 1750 for his unorthodox views, he went to Stockbridge, where he ministered to an Indian mission. During this period he wrote *Freedom of the Will* (published 1754), *The Great Christian Doctrine of Original Sin Defended* (published 1758), *The Nature of True Virtue* (published 1765) and *The Great End for Which God Created the World* (published 1765), works of religious philosophy which expand on his conception of religious experience. Fusing an orthodox Calvinism with Lockean psychology and Newtonian physics, he explains religious conversion in 18th-century rationalist terms. In 1757 he was appointed president of the College of New Jersey (later Princeton University), but died from a smallpox inoculation soon after taking office. At the time of his death he was working on his systematic sacred history, *The History of the Work of Redemption*, based on sermons delivered in 1739. The series was published in 1774 and held an important place in American millennial thought.

Egan, Pierce, the elder 1772–1849 Comic writer and sporting journalist. Born in London, he first established a reputation as a sports reporter for the newspapers. In 1818 he began the serial publication of *Boxiana: or, Sketches of Modern Pugilism*, which continued until 1824. In 1820 he began monthly publication of the book by which he is best remembered, *LIFE IN LONDON: or, The Day and Night Scenes of Jerry Hawthorn Esq. and His Elegant Friend Corinthian Tom*. This comic portrait of Regency manners proved enormously popular. Egan's weekly newspaper, *Life in London and Sporting Guide*, later merged into *Bell's Life in London*, first appeared in 1824.

Egan, Pierce, the younger 1814–80 Novelist and son of PIERCE EGAN THE ELDER. His many historical novels include *Wat Tyler* (1841) and *Paul Jones* (1842). He was editor of *Home Circle* in 1849–51 and from 1857 contributed serial novels to *The London Journal*, among them *Love Me, Leave Me Not* (1859–60), *The Poor Girl* (1862–3) and *Eve: or, The Angel of Innocence* (1867). Egan is recognized as one of the pioneers of cheap literature.

Eger and Grime A VERSE ROMANCE of the mid-15th century written in the North of England; it survives only in 17th-century copies. Eger's lady Winglaine wants a supreme warrior as her husband. Going into a strange land, Eger is attacked by a giant knight, Graysteele, who cuts off his finger; he is cared for by Loosepaine, who gives him shirts and wine as tokens. On Eger's return his sworn brother Grime goes to avenge him and takes the tokens to Loosepaine, but she sees his hands are intact and he tells her his errand. She tells him that Gray-steele grows weaker from noon to night, which enables Grime to slay the giant and return to Eger with the proof. Eger marries Winglaine on the strength of his supposed victory, and Grime marries Loosepaine. The romance is notable for its use of direct discourse, often humorous and realistic, which gives the narrative a dramatic quality.

Egerton, George [Dunne, Mary Chevelita] 1859–1945 Short-story writer. Born in Australia, daughter of a spendthrift cashiered Irish army officer and a Welsh mother, she had some schooling in Germany before nursing briefly in London, struggling for a living in New York and eloping to Norway with a bigamist. In Norway she encountered the advanced social and sexual views of Ibsen and Strindberg. She also met Knut Hamsun, whose novel *Hunger* she translated in 1899 and to whom she dedicated her first and best collection of short stories, *Keynotes*. This was published by John Lane in 1893, with illustrations by AUBREY BEARDSLEY, on the strong recommendation of RICHARD LE GALLIENNE. The following year Lane published a further collection, *Discords*, and persuaded her to contribute to the first number of *THE YELLOW BOOK*. She published two more volumes of short stories, *Symphonies* (1896) and *Fantasies* (1898), and two novels, *The Wheel of God* (1898) and *Rosa Amorosa: The Love-Letters of a Woman* (1901) which, like her stories, drew heavily on her own varied and colourful experiences. Her first marriage to George Egerton Clairmonte broke up in 1895. After her second marriage (1901) to Golding Bright, a drama critic turned theatrical agent, she wrote for the stage, accepting trenchant advice from G. B. SHAW and attracting the interest of actresses such as Lillie Langtry but failing to win either commercial success or critical approval. In her stories an impressionist technique identifies moments of significant female – and feminist – consciousness, blending realistic structures and detail with Utopian fantasies of self-realization and freedom for the 'new woman'.

Eggleston, Edward 1837–1902 American novelist. Born into a strict Methodist family in rural Indiana, Edward and his brother GEORGE EGGLESTON were educated in back-country schools. Edward had a busy career as a Bible agent and then as a Methodist minister on circuit; he also wrote and edited juvenile magazines as an extension of his Sunday-school teaching. He was 37 when he abandoned Methodism and went to New York, where he founded a Church of Christian Endeavour in Brooklyn. He remained its pastor for five years, before retiring to devote himself entirely to writing.

His first success, and the novel for which he is best known, was *The Hoosier Schoolmaster* (1871), a realistic if somewhat pious presentation of rural life in Indiana which made excellent use of local dialect. His next novels were also set in the Midwest during the period of the country's expansion: *The End of the World* (set in Indiana, 1872), *The Mystery of Metropolisville* (set in Minnesota, 1873), *The Circuit Rider* (set in Ohio, 1874) and *Roxy* (set in Indiana, 1878). For a brief period he devoted his attention to writing history and biography, an enterprise which produced several works, among which the uncompleted *History of Life in the United States* (1888) is the most memorable. Before his death he wrote three more novels: *The Hoosier Schoolboy* (1883), a boy's view of the life described in *The Hoosier Schoolmaster*; *The Graysons: A Story of Illinois* (1888), based on Abraham Lincoln's days as a lawyer in Springfield, Illinois, when he successfully defended a man accused of murder, and *The Faith Doctor* (1891), a satirical view of the wealthy devotees of the then-new Christian Science movement.

Eggleston, George Cary 1839–1911 American novelist and editor. The younger brother of EDWARD EGGLESTON, George became a teacher in back-country Indiana at the age of 16. His experiences provided his brother with the material for two novels, *The Hoosier Schoolmaster* (1871) and *The Hoosier Schoolboy* (1883). After serving in the Confederate army during the Civil War, he practised law for a time before becoming a journalist. He served as editor of the New York *Evening Post* and worked for Joseph Pulitzer on the *New York World* for 11 years. He also wrote a number of books for boys, and several novels set in the South, including *A Man of Honour* (1873), *Dorothy South* (1902), *The Master of Warlock* (1903) and *Evelyn Byrd* (1904). With Dorothy Marbourg he co-wrote the novel *Juggernaut* (1891), which is set in Indiana. His autobiographical volume, *A Rebel's Recollections*, based on his experiences during the Civil War, appeared in 1874.

Eglinton, John [Magee, William K.] 1868–1961 Irish essayist and critic. Born in Dublin, he was for a time a schoolmate of YEATS at the High School before going on to a distinguished career at Trinity College. From 1895 to 1921 he worked as a librarian at the National Library, Dublin, appearing in this role in the 'Scylla and Charybdis' chapter of JOYCE's ULYSSES. A friend of many leading figures of the Irish revival, particularly GEORGE RUSSELL (AE), GEORGE MOORE and Stephen MacKenna, he founded and edited the literary magazine *Dana* (1904–5) in which he declined to serialize Joyce's PORTRAIT OF THE ARTIST AS A YOUNG MAN.

Yeats admired Eglinton's criticism and published a selection as *Some Essays and Passages by John Eglinton* (1905), drawing on *Two Essays on the Remnant* (1894) and *Pebbles from a Brook* (1901). Eglinton's best work appeared in *Anglo-Irish Essays* (1917), but he wrote little of importance for many years afterwards. He moved to England after the founding of the new Irish state in 1922 and it was there that he produced his most notable later works, *Irish Literary Portraits* (1935) and *Memoir of AE* (1937).

Egoist, The A novel by GEORGE MEREDITH, published in 1879.

The central character of Meredith's 'comedy in narrative' is Sir Willoughby Patterne, rich, handsome, selfish, fatuous, and conceited. He is loved by Laetitia Dale and does nothing to discourage her, but he has proposed to Constantia Durham, who has accepted him. Constantia, however, learns in time what sort of man he is and elopes with an officer of Hussars. Sir Willoughby recovers from the humiliation and turns his attention to Clara Middleton, enlisting her epi-curean father Dr Middleton on his side. She remains equivocal and he proposes to Laetitia, but is overheard and exposed by the boy Crossjay. Clara has in any case fallen in love with Vernon Whitford, a handsome scholar. Stripped of his pretensions, Sir Willoughby finally persuades Laetitia to marry him.

The character of Dr Middleton is modelled on THOMAS LOVE PEACOCK, Meredith's father-in-law, and that of Vernon on SIR LESLIE STEPHEN. ROBERT LOUIS STEVENSON thought he recognized himself in Sir Willoughby, but Meredith insisted he was all of us.

Egoist, The: *An Individualist Review* A feminist journal founded in 1913 by Dora Marsden and REBECCA WEST as *The New Freewoman*. At the prompting of POUND and ALDINGTON it changed its name in 1919 and became, under the editorship of Harriet Shaw Weaver, a vehicle for Pound's IMAGISM. HILDA DOOLITTLE, Aldington and T. S. ELIOT served as assistant editors. *The Egoist's* most notable achievement was its serialization of JOYCE's A PORTRAIT OF THE ARTIST AS A YOUNG MAN in 1914–15. After its closure in 1919, its name survived in Harriet Shaw Weaver's Egoist Press, which published ULYSSES in 1922.

Eikon Basilike 'The royal image', sub-titled *The Portraiture of His Sacred Majesty in His Solitudes and Sufferings*. It was presented as the prayers and meditations of Charles I during his imprisonment and was published on the day of his burial, 9 February 1649, running to 40 editions before the Restoration. John Gauden, Bishop of Winchester, who later claimed authorship, probably compiled it from Charles's notes and memoranda, succeeding remarkably well in presenting him as a royal martyr. It was translated into Latin by EARLE and prompted a reply from MILTON.

Ekwensi, Cyprian 1921– Nigerian novelist. Born in Minna, he was educated in Nigeria, Ghana and London. He attracted some acclaim with *People of the City* (1954), a novel about rural Nigerians corrupted by the city. A popular writer, he registers and dramatizes the attitudes of ordinary people buffeted by historical change, as in his best-known novel, *Jagua Nana* (1962), about a Lagos prostitute. Others include: *Beautiful Feathers* (1963), satirizing politicians; *Burning Grass* (1962), dealing with wandering Fulani herdsmen; *Iska* (1966), illustrating the dangers of tribalism; *Survive the Peace* (1976), chronicling Biafran defeat in 1970; and *For a Roll of Parchment* (1976), set in London. He has also written short stories and CHILDREN'S LITERATURE.

Eldershaw, M. Barnard [Eldershaw, Flora Sydney Patricia (1897–1956) and Barnard, Marjorie Faith (1897–1987)] Australian novelists. Educated in Sydney, Flora Eldershaw was senior mistress at the Presbyterian Ladies College, Croydon. Marjorie

Barnard was also educated at Sydney University and was librarian at the Commonwealth Scientific and Industrial Research Organization. Their best-known novels, *A House is Built* (1929) and *Green Memory* (1931), are set in 19th-century Australia. They also wrote *The Glass House* (1936), *Plaque with Laurel* (1937), *Tomorrow and Tomorrow* (1947; unexpurgated edition, 1982) and *But Not for Love* (1989), a posthumously published short stories. Other works include *Phillip of Australia: An Account of the Settlement at Sydney Cove 1788–92* (1938), *The Life and Times of Captain John Piper* (1939), *My Australia* (1939) and *Essays in Australian Fiction* (1938). Barnard wrote a seminal biography of MILES FRANKLIN (1967) and a collection of stories, *The Persimmon Tree* (1943), frequently anthologized.

elegy In Greek and Roman literature, any poem using the 'elegiac couplet' (a dactylic hexameter followed by a dactylic pentameter). Since the Renaissance it has come to mean a sustained poetic meditation on a solemn theme, particularly on death (e.g. MILTON's *LYCIDAS* and SHELLEY's *ADONAIS*). The 'elegiac stanza' (a quatrain of iambic pentameters, rhyming abab) takes its name from GRAY's *ELEGY WRITTEN IN A COUNTRY CHURCHYARD*.

Elegy Written in a Country Churchyard A poem by THOMAS GRAY, first published in 1751. The churchyard in question is at Stoke Poges, Buckinghamshire, where Gray himself is now buried. The poem is melancholy and reflective, as the poet muses upon the conditions of rural life, human potential, and mortality. At its close, the elegy casts forward to the prospect of the poet's own death, and considers the possibility that Art – in the shape of the poem itself – might offer a durable memorial against time. The elegy's gentle gloominess is characteristic of the style cultivated by the so-called GRAVEYARD POETS, though their work rarely achieved such refinement elsewhere.

Elene An Old English poem by CYNEWULF preserved in the VERCELLI BOOK, it tells of St Helena's discovery of the Cross in the Holy Land. The story occupies 14 sections of the poem; a 15th provides the only information known about Cynewulf and contains his runic signature. At the time of writing, he says, he was old and dying; his early life was sinful but a spiritual experience brought him enlightenment and the gift of poetry.

Eliot, George [Evans, Mary Anne (Marian)] 1819–80 Novelist, critic and poet. She was born at South Farm, Arbury, Warwickshire, where her father, Robert Evans, was a land agent. She was educated at several schools, among them Miss Wallington's Boarding School in Nuneaton, where she came under the beneficent influence of a Miss Maria Lewis, her own mother having died when she was 16. She also attended the Misses Franklins' School in Coventry, where she shed her provincial accent and studied the piano and French. During her early years she also read widely in theology, the Romantic poets and German literature. When her father retired in 1841 they went to live at Foleshill near Coventry, and there Mary Anne Evans was drawn to

George Eliot

an intellectual circle that included Charles Bray and Charles Hennell, whose influences directed her towards free-thinking in religious opinion. In 1842 she refused to attend church with her father and in 1846 she completed a translation of Strauss's *Leben Jesu*, a central document of the HIGHER CRITICISM. Then followed Continental travel with the Brays, after which she went to London and was closely associated with the amorous Chapman, now proprietor and publisher of the radical *WESTMINSTER REVIEW*, of which she was assistant editor from January 1852 until January 1854. For her services she received no salary but board and lodging at 142 Strand, where Chapman conducted a curious ménage-cum-boarding-house which was a haven for middle-class intellectuals. George Eliot's next publication of consequence was a translation of Feuerbach's *Essence of Christianity* (1854). By this time she had met GEORGE HENRY LEWES, with whom she went to live in October 1853. Their union, happy despite Lewes's irregular marital situation, lasted until his death in 1878.

George Eliot's interest in writing fiction went back to her schooldays in the early 1830s but she did not make her début until the serialization of 'The Sad Fortunes of the Reverend Amos Barton', 'Mr Gilfil's Love-Story' and 'Janet's Repentance' in BLACKWOOD'S EDINBURGH MAGAZINE in 1857. These tales were collected, and well received, as SCENES OF CLERICAL LIFE (1858). They were followed by ADAM BEDE (1859), THE MILL ON THE FLOSS (1860) and SILAS MARNER (1861). After a brief Florentine visit George Eliot deserted her native literary landscapes to publish ROMOLA in THE CORNHILL MAGAZINE in 1862–3. Next came FELIX HOLT THE RADICAL (1866) in some respects anticipating MIDDLEMARCH, published in independent parts in 1871–2, and DANIEL DERONDA, which appeared in the same way in 1874–6. Her last work was The Impressions of Theophrastus Such (1879), a series of essays linked by a narrator. George Eliot also wrote some novellas and a surprising amount of poetry, including THE SPANISH GYPSY (1868), the product of a trip to Spain in 1867, and The Legend of Jubal and Other Poems (1874). In addition, she was one of the finest letter-writers in the language.

After the death of Lewes in the spring of 1880, she married John Walter Cross, a man many years her junior; she died in December of the same year. Cross's biography was published in 1885. In a century of gifted women writers George Eliot stands pre-eminent.

Eliot, John 1604–90 American Puritan minister. Born in England and educated at Cambridge, he emigrated to Massachusetts in 1631 and became minister at the church in Roxbury the following year. He contributed, along with several other New England ministers, to the English translations in the BAY PSALM BOOK (1640). Over the next decade he learned the language of the Massachusetts Indians and began attempts to Christianize them. His missionary efforts received some support from the Massachusetts General Court, and in 1651 he established the first of a series of 'praying Indian Towns', at Natick. His pamphlet The Christian Commonwealth, written in 1649 and published in 1659, set forth his notions for the governance of these Indian communities. He also compiled a primer to teach the Indians to read, and translated the Bible into the Algonquian dialect. Known as the 'Apostle to the Indians', Eliot was a venerable figure in the Massachusetts Bay community. A youthful COTTON MATHER, who knew him in his old age, memorialized him in a biography included in the MAGNALIA CHRISTI AMERICANA.

Eliot, T(homas) S(tearns) 1888–1965 Poet, critic and playwright. He was born and brought up in St Louis, Missouri, though his Unitarian family had strong ties with Massachusetts. In 1906 he went to Harvard University, where his teachers included GEORGE SANTAYANA and IRVING BABBITT. The latter in particular influenced his ideas about the dynamic re-lationship between past and present, as well as his bias against ROMANTICISM. At Harvard he also became interested in Dante, Jules Laforgue and French SYMBOLISM. His formal studies were in philosophy, and after gaining his BA and MA he began a doctoral thesis but chose not to take the degree. The thesis was eventually published as Knowledge and Experience in the Philosophy of F. H. Bradley (1964).

Eliot left America in 1914, and after studying briefly in Germany, at the Sorbonne and at Merton College, Oxford, settled in London the following year. His troubled marriage to Vivien Haigh-Wood lasted from June 1915 until their separation in the early 1930s. She died in 1947 and Eliot was married a second time, to Valerie Fletcher, in 1957. During his early years in London he taught at Highgate School, reviewed books for THE TIMES LITERARY SUPPLEMENT, and, from 1917, worked for Lloyds Bank. After a short term as assistant editor of THE EGOIST, he became editor of a newly founded quarterly review, THE CRITERION, in 1922 and held the post until it ceased publication in 1939. He also worked as a director of its publisher, Faber and Faber, aiding many younger poets in their careers.

He himself had begun to publish poetry with the help and encouragement of EZRA POUND. THE LOVE SONG OF J. ALFRED PRUFROCK, written while he was at Harvard, appeared in 1915 in the American magazine POETRY and in 1917 was collected in his first volume, Prufrock and Other Observations, published by Harriet Shaw Weaver. It was followed by two more collections: Poems (1919), which contained 'Gerontion', printed by LEONARD WOOLF and VIRGINIA WOOLF at their Hogarth Press and published in the USA the following year, and Ara Vos Prec (1920). His next major work was THE WASTE LAND, published in the first issue of The Criterion in 1922 and dedicated to Pound in acknowledgement of his considerable editorial role in crafting the final version. After the initial controversy it provoked by its innovatory technique and its apparently pessimistic tone, the poem came to be accepted as a central text of MODERNISM. Eliot's position as a major force in 20th-century letters was confirmed by the critical essays which, throughout his career, offered a theoretical counterpart to the example of his own poetry. His first collection, The Sacred Wood (1920), reprinted the essay on HAMLET (with its concept of the OBJECTIVE CORRELATIVE) and the highly influential 'Tradition and the Individual Talent', rejecting Romantic individualism in favour of a belief in the 'impersonality' of poetry. Homage to John Dryden (1924) contained his essays on MARVELL and the METAPHYSICAL POETS, praised for their unified sensibility in contrast to the DISSOCIATION OF SENSIBILITY which afflicted later writers.

For Lancelot Andrewes: Essays on Style and Order (1928), in which Eliot described himself as 'classical in literature, royalist in politics, and Anglo-Catholic in religion', emphasized the main direction of his development during the 1920s, a direction neither anticipated nor welcomed by many of his first admirers. He had joined the Church of England in 1927, the same year that he became a British citizen. The increasingly religious tendency of his poetry can be traced in *Poems 1909–25* (1925), which includes 'The Hollow Men', and *Collected Poems 1909–35* (1936), which added 'The Journey of the Magi' (1927) and 'Ash Wednesday' (1930). Its chief fruit – and the major achievement of Eliot's later career – was FOUR QUARTETS, consisting of 'Burnt Norton' (1935), 'East Coker' (1940), 'The Dry Salvages' (1941) and 'Little Gidding' (1942), first published together in 1943. *Old Possum's Book of Practical Cats*, a collection of humorous verse for children, appeared in 1939. *Collected Poems 1909–62* was published in 1963.

Cultural problems absorbed much of Eliot's energies as critic after he joined the church. *The Use of Poetry and the Use of Criticism* (1933), based on lectures delivered at Harvard, and the incautious *After Strange Gods: A Primer of Modern Heresy* (1934) both show the fascination that authority and control in life and literature had for him during this troubled period of his life. They were followed by *The Idea of a Christian Society* (1939), but his most influential

exercise in social criticism is undoubtedly *Notes Towards a Definition of Culture* (1948). Other collections include *On Poetry and Poets* (1957) and *To Criticize the Critic* (1965).

Eliot's attempt to revive verse drama, foreshadowed in *Sweeney Agonistes: An Aristophanic Fragment* (1932) and advanced further by his pageant play *The Rock* (1934), was perhaps most successful in MURDER IN THE CATHEDRAL (1935), where Yeatsian spiritual vigour and dramatic crispness helped carry off the historicism. This was not always the case in his later plays – *The Family Reunion* (1939), THE COCKTAIL PARTY (1950), *The Confidential Clerk* (1954) and *The Elder Statesman* (1959) – in which the burden of philosophical ideas and the conventions of the contemporary stage sit uneasily together.

In 1948 Eliot received both the Nobel Prize for Literature and the Order of Merit. Such honours acknowledged his vital role in showing poetry how to become modern. 'Tradition and the Individual Talent' spoke of tradition not as inertly inherited but as achieved 'by great labour' and as bringing a perception 'not only of the pastness of the past, but of its presence'. With its dense, even riddling, allusions to earlier literature *The Waste Land* had crucially redefined the traditions of use to the modern poet, aban-

T. S. Eliot

doning Victorianism and the lingering traces of Romanticism. Eliot's praise of the Elizabethan dramatists and the metaphysical poets in his criticism confirmed a preference for intellectual toughness, energy and WIT that left its mark on most of the poets (as well as the critics) who immediately followed him. Yet the rightwards tendency of his beliefs in politics and religion, though shared by several poets of his own generation, limited his influence over younger writers from AUDEN onwards. Since his death it has further diminished, with the lyricism of YEATS and the stubborn individuality of HARDY exerting their rival claims with increasing power.

elision In verse, the slurring or omission of an unstressed syllable so that a line may conform to a metrical pattern, or the omission of part of a word for ease of pronunciation. The effect is most frequently accomplished by the omission of a final vowel preceding an initial vowel, as in 'th'Eternal', but it also occurs between syllables in a single word, as in 'ne'er' for 'never'.

Elkin, Stanley (Lawrence) 1930– American novelist and short-story writer. He was born in New York and educated at the University of Illinois. His novels tend to explore the nature of evil, frequently through a comic examination of both ordinary and extraordinary situations. His first novel, *Boswell* (1964), traces its protagonist's struggle to satisfy the needs of his ego, which culminates in a wrestling match with the Grim Reaper. His second novel, *A Bad Man* (1968), treats a salesman's compulsion to make 'the ultimate sale' regardless of its consequences. Subsequent novels include *The Dick Gibson Show* (1971), *The Franchiser* (1976), *The Living End* (1980), *The Magic Kingdom* (1985), *The Rabbi of Lud* (1987), *The MacGuffin* (1991) and *Pieces of Soap* (1993). *Searches and Seizures* (1973), published as both *Eligible Men* (1974) and *Alex and the Gypsy* (1977), and *Van Gogh's Room at Arles* (1993) are collections of novellas. Elkin has also published short stories in *Criers and Kibitzers, Kibitzers and Criers* (1966) and *The Making of Ashendon* (1972). *Stanley Elkin's Greatest Hits*, an omnibus collection, appeared in 1980.

Elliott, Ebenezer 1781–1849 The Corn Law Rhymer. Born at Rotherham in Yorkshire and largely self-educated, he ran an iron business in Sheffield for much of his working life. A Chartist, he derived his nickname from his simple, direct verses attacking the Corn Laws and describing rural poverty: *The Village Patriarch* (1829), *Corn-Law Rhymes* (1831) and *The Splendid Village* (1833–5).

Ellis, Alice Thomas [Haycraft, Anna] 1932– Novelist. Born in Liverpool and educated in Bangor, she subsequently studied at the Liverpool College of Art. *The Sin Eater* (1977) established her characteristic fictional components of neurotic religion, chintzy eccentricity and suddenly graceful insight. It has been followed by *The 27th Kingdom* (1982), often considered her most successful novel, *The Fly in the Ointment* (1989) and *The Inn at the End of the World* (1990). She has also published four volumes collecting her regular 'Home Life' columns for *The Spectator* and two cookery books. *A Welsh Childhood* (1990) is autobiographical.

Ellis, (Henry) Havelock 1859–1939 Sexual scientist. Born at Croydon and educated at private schools in Surrey, he was advised at the age of 16 to make a year's sea voyage for reasons of health. Travelling in a ship under his father's command he reached Australia and settled there for four years, working as a teacher. He returned to England in 1879 to become a medical student, but after qualifying eight years later he rarely practised professionally. During his time as a medical student he became acquainted with many prominent socialists and began writing for magazines. Ellis acted as the first editor of the Mermaid series of unexpurgated reprints of Elizabethan and Jacobean drama. He also edited the Contemporary Science series. *The New Spirit* (1890) reflected his interest in scientific and social progress and, particularly, the concern with sex which produced: *Man and Woman* (1894), *Sexual Inversion* (which included the case history of J. A. SYMONDS; 1897), *Studies in the Psychology of Sex* (1897–1910) and *The Erotic Rights of Women* (1918). These works were at once influential and notorious. Three series of essays entitled *Impressions and Comments* appeared in 1914, 1921 and 1924. *My Life* was published posthumously in 1940.

Ellison, Ralph (Waldo) 1914–94 Black American novelist, essayist and short-story writer. Born in Oklahoma City, he attended Tuskegee Institute in Alabama (1933–6), where he studied music and became an accomplished trumpet player. He then moved to New York to study sculpture, and soon began writing book reviews, essays and short stories, encouraged by RICHARD WRIGHT. In 1942 he helped to found and edit the short-lived *Negro Quarterly*.

After World War II he worked for seven years on the novel that made him famous, *INVISIBLE MAN* (1952). This semi-autobiographical account of a black man's gradual self-discovery remains Ellison's only major work of fiction to date. For over two decades he has reportedly been working on a second novel, parts of which have been published, including one entitled 'And Hickman Arrives'. His short stories have never been collected, though several are widely anthologized, among them 'Flying Home' and 'King of the Bingo Game'. He did, however, collect some of his many essays on black music, literature and American culture in *Shadow and Act* (1964) and *Going to the Territory* (1986), as well as publishing *The Writer's Experience* (with KARL SHAPIRO; 1964).

Ellison's reputation as the most important literary heir to Richard Wright – matched only by that of JAMES BALDWIN – remains strong. *Invisible Man* was attacked by the radical left in the 1950s and by black nationalists in the 1960s, but it has weathered critical controversy and remains one of the central texts of the 20th-century Afro-American experience.

Ellwood, Thomas 1639–1713 Poet and early Quaker. A friend of WILLIAM PENN, Ellwood was for some years reader to the blind MILTON, to whom he suggested the theme of *PARADISE REGAINED*. He was himself the author of *Davideis* (1712), a religious poem about King David, as well as *A Collection of Poems on Various Subjects* (1710) and *The History of the Life of Thomas Ellwood* (1714), an account of his imprisonment for his religious beliefs.

Elsie Venner: *A Romance of Destiny* A novel by OLIVER WENDELL HOLMES, published serially in *THE ATLANTIC MONTHLY* (as *The Professor's Story*, January 1860–April 1861), and as a volume in 1861. Holmes sought to 'test the doctrine of "original sin"': to question the belief that holds individuals responsible for antenatal influences upon them. The heroine of his fable was modelled on MARGARET FULLER.

Elsie Venner, whose mother was bitten by a rattlesnake three weeks before Elsie's birth, has been infected with the venom and now exhibits peculiar, snake-like qualities: she is wild and seemingly insane, with glittering eyes and the capacity to fascinate and frighten those around her. A professor of medicine becomes interested in her abnormal behaviour through Bernard Langdon, a student who has temporarily taken a job as a teacher at the school Elsie attends. Elsie falls in love with Bernard, saving his life by using her snake-like powers to enchant a rattlesnake that is about to strike and kill him. But he does not love her and Elsie falls ill, gradually losing her snake-like strangeness as she dies. Helen Darley, a schoolteacher whose sympathy is stirred by the strange, motherless girl, attends her to the end. When Old Sophy, a faithful servant, dies a few days afterwards, an earthquake buries Rattlesnake Ledge with all its poisonous snakes.

Elyot, Sir **Thomas** ?1499–1546 Lexicographer and administrator, best known for *The Book Named the Governor* (1531), remembered by his remote descendant and near-namesake T. S. ELIOT in 'East Coker', second of his *FOUR QUARTETS*. Dedicated to Henry VIII and drawn in part from Castiglione's *THE COURTIER*, Elyot's book sets out a plan for bringing up gentlemen's sons and manifests the usual humanist concern for education. Perhaps as a result of the favourable reception of this book Elyot, who had worked as clerk to the Privy Council in 1523–30 and been knighted in 1530, was made ambassador to Emperor Charles V. Elyot's Latin–English Dictionary is as important as *The Book Named the Governor;* it was published in 1538 and revised as the *Bibliotheca Eliotae* (1542), which formed the basis for the work of later English lexicographers. His translations include a work of Isocrates, as *The Doctrinal of Princes* (1534), and *The Image of Governance* (1541) from Eucolpius. Elyot's *Castle of Health* (1539) is a medical treatise written by a layman and adorned with anecdotes. He also wrote Platonic dialogues and produced translations of parts of Plutarch and a sermon on mortality by St Cyprian.

Emare A VERSE ROMANCE dating from about 1400. Emare's father is a widowed emperor with an incestuous obsession for his only child. He gives her a richly embroidered robe which endows her with an unearthly beauty, but when she rejects his advances he sets her adrift in an open boat with her robe. She lands in Galys where she eventually marries the king, against his mother's advice. While he is away at battle Emare gives birth to a son, Segramour. Her mother-in-law contrives to have Emare set adrift again. Emare and Segramour come to Rome and are taken in by a merchant; they are eventually reunited with both the king and emperor when they come to Rome on pilgrimages.

The poet says his source was a BRETON LAY, but no French version analogous to *Emare* is known. The story is substantially the same as that of the 'constant' Constance, well known in the Middle Ages, and told by GOWER in *CONFESSIO AMANTIS* and CHAUCER in *The Man of Law's Tale* (see *THE CANTERBURY TALES*).

emblem book A book made up of symbolic pictures or engravings to which mottoes and verbal explanations are attached, of a proverbial or gnomic nature. The earliest European example was *Emblematum Liber* (1531) of Andrea Alciati, but Geoffrey Whitney's *Choice of Emblemes* (1586) was the first to appear in English. The most popular was FRANCIS QUARLES's *Emblems* (1635), consisting of pictures, verses and verbal illustrations from previous authorities. Emblem books offered instruction on religious and moral subjects, and they became valuable sourcebooks for poetic imagery.

Emecheta, Buchi 1944– Nigerian novelist. Born in Lagos, she moved to Britain in 1962. Her struggle to overcome appalling social conditions gives power and authenticity to her first two novels, *In the Ditch* (1972) and *Second-Class Citizen* (1974), published together as *Adah's Story* (1983). Her championship of women's rights provides the compassion, and occasionally unrelieved anger, of her other novels, mostly set in West Africa: *The Bride Price* (1976), *The Slave Girl* (1977), *The Joys of Motherhood* (1979), *Destination Biafra* (1982), *Naira Power* (1982), *Double Yoke* (1982) and *The Rape of Shavi* (1983). She has also written CHILDREN'S LITERATURE and television plays.

Emerson, Ralph Waldo 1803–82 American essayist, philosopher and poet. He was the son of William Emerson, the minister of the First Unitarian Church of his native Boston. After completing his education at Harvard, Emerson himself became a minister in 1829. The orthodoxy of Unitarianism, however, though far moved from the original Calvinism of New England, was something he could not accept. In 1832, shortly after the death of his first wife, he resigned his ministry and sailed to Europe, his mind disturbed by personal grief and religious confusion. During the year he spent in Europe, he met SAMUEL TAYLOR COLERIDGE and WILLIAM WORDSWORTH, and commenced a lifelong friendship with THOMAS CARLYLE.

Contact with European thought stimulated his interest in religion and philosophy, and back in Boston he drifted away from preaching into the broader field of lecturing. With the growth of the lyceum movement in the Northeast and Middle West in the early 1830s, he found that he could command large audiences who came to hear him expound his natural philosophy. He drew much of his lecture material from his personal journals, which he had begun in 1820 and continued throughout his life. In 1835 he married Lydia Jackson and moved to Concord, Massachusetts, where his ancestors had first settled in the New World and where TRANSCENDENTALISM took form. He became part of the circle which included NATHANIEL HAWTHORNE, BRONSON ALCOTT, HENRY DAVID THOREAU and MARGARET FULLER.

Emerson's first book, *NATURE*, was published in 1836; *The American Scholar*, an oration in which he applied Transcendentalist views to national and cultural questions, followed in 1837. His assertion that human thought and action proceed from Nature was a radical departure from tradition; OLIVER WENDELL HOLMES referred to his philosophical position as an 'intellectual declaration of independence'. In 1838 he delivered the 'Divinity School Address' at Harvard. The statement of his belief that the individual's intuitive spiritual experience was of more importance than any formal church ensured his exclusion from that university for almost 30 years. In 1840 he became involved in the publication of the Transcendentalist quarterly magazine, *THE DIAL*, and two years later became its editor. His reputation, already considerable in the USA, became firmly established in Europe, too, with the publication of two volumes of essays in 1841 and 1844. He earned further distinction as a poet with his first collection, *Poems* (1847), and later with *May-Day and Other Pieces* (1867).

He went to England in 1847 and lectured in Oxford and London, where he renewed his friendship with Carlyle and met other English intellectuals. The lectures were published under the title REPRESENTATIVE MEN (1850). *English Traits* (1856) contains his observations on the English character. During this period, as his journals show, he became deeply interested in the issue of slavery and saw Abolition as a matter of paramount importance. Two further volumes of his lectures were published as *The Conduct of Life* (1860) and *Society and Solitude* (1870). In 1866 Harvard conferred on him the degree of Doctor of Law. His *Journals* were published in 10 volumes (1909–14).

Emma A novel by JANE AUSTEN, begun in January 1814, completed in March the following year and published in 1816. The author said she feared that nobody but herself would like the heroine, an indication that she had deliberately subdued the high-spirited comedy of manners practised in earlier novels to offer instead a study in development and education. Emma Woodhouse changes from being vain and self-satisfied, blind to her own feelings and dangerously insensitive to the feelings of others, in a slow, painful progress toward maturity.

Emma is left alone with her hypochondriacal father and feels bereft of companionship when her governess, Miss Taylor, leaves the household to marry a neighbour, Mr Weston. She makes a protégée of Harriet Smith, an illegitimate girl of no social status, and sets about arranging Harriet's life. George Knightley of Donwell Abbey is a friend of the Woodhouse family and his younger brother John is married to Emma's sister Isabella. He disputes Emma's smug assumption that Anne Taylor's marriage is largely due to her skill as a matchmaker and frowns on her attempts to manipulate Harriet into what she decides is a good marriage. One of his tenants, a young farmer named Robert Martin, proposes to Harriet but Emma sees to it that she turns him down. In spite of Knightley's warning, she tries instead to effect a match for Harriet with Mr Elton, a young clergyman. Elton, however, despises Harriet and has set his sights on Emma herself.

For her part, Emma half fancies herself in love with Mr Weston's son by his first marriage, Frank Churchill, who has now appeared on the scene. Harriet, meanwhile, has become interested in Knightley's unaffected warmth and intelligence. Emma, reassuring Harriet after the departure of Elton, is now considering Frank Churchill for her. Without giving the thought expression, she has always regarded Knightley as hers and the realization that Harriet might supplant her in Knightley's affections, together with the discovery that Frank Churchill is engaged to Jane Fairfax, forces Emma to examine her own conduct and resolve to behave better. Knightley proposes to her while Harriet, left to decide for herself, marries Robert Martin.

Empedocles on Etna A poem by MATTHEW ARNOLD, published in 1852. The philosopher Empedocles (c. 450 BC) journeys to the volcano, Etna, in Sicily with the physician Pausanias. They are joined by the poet Callicles. The philosopher's despair does not yield to the wisdom of the physician or the strength of poetry and at the end he kills himself in the crater of Etna. The songs of the poet Callicles were published separately by Arnold in 1855 in *Poems: Second Series* before he republished the whole poem in 1867.

Emperor Jones, The A play in eight scenes by EUGENE O'NEILL, produced by the Provincetown Players in 1920 and published in 1921. It is an early example of O'Neill's EXPRESSIONISM and of his progressively more experimental use of dramatic devices. Brutus Jones, a black man who has escaped from an American prison, becomes the emperor of a West Indian island. When he learns from his cockney major-domo, Henry Smithers, that his subjects have rebelled, he boasts that he can escape through the forest. He has stored money and food in various places, foreseeing that his reign would be short, and has created the legend that he can be killed only by a silver bullet. The reduction of the proud bully to a terrified savage as he is hunted down to the relentless beating of native drums is a theatrical *tour de force*.

Empson, Sir **William** 1906–84 Critic. A Yorkshireman born in Yokefleet, Empson was educated at Winchester College and at Magdalene College, Cambridge, where he studied mathematics and then, under I. A. RICHARDS, English. Here he wrote his best-known critical work, *Seven Types of Ambiguity* (1930), a detailed study of multiple shades of meaning in poetry, which encouraged the trend towards close verbal analysis in modern criticism. During the 1930s he taught English at the Universities of Tokyo and Peking, returning to Peking after working for the BBC Far Eastern Section during the war. In 1953 he returned to England as professor of English literature at the University of Sheffield, where he remained until his retirement in 1971.

His poetry, especially in *Poems* (1935), is as complex as his critical theories demanded it should be: a modern counterpart of the work of the METAPHYSICAL POETS in its use of scientific conceits and cerebral puzzles. Empson's second volume of poems, *The Gathering Storm* (1940), draws upon his experiences in the East as the world drifted towards war; he revised these works for *Collected Poems* (1955). In his critical work Empson was something of a maverick: *Some Versions of Pastoral* (1935) extends the definition of PASTORAL to embrace proletarian fiction and *ALICE IN WONDERLAND*; *The Structure of Complex Words* (1951) outlines an elaborate system for analysing the different senses of certain versatile words; and *Milton's God* (1961) uses the theological problems of *PARADISE LOST* to launch an assault upon the cruelty and 'wickedness' of Christianity. The essays in his posthumous *Using Biography* (1984) defend the use of biographical information in criticism against the dogmas of NEW CRITICISM. He was knighted in 1979.

encomium Originally a Greek choral song in praise of a hero: now, any composition in verse or prose which praises a person, idea or occasion. Encomiastic poetry enjoyed a minor vogue in the 17th and 18th centuries, DRYDEN's 'A Song for Saint Cecilia's Day' being perhaps the most famous example.

Encounter A political, cultural and literary journal founded in 1953. Editors and co-editors have included STEPHEN SPENDER, NIGEL DENNIS, Frank Kermode, ANTHONY THWAITE and Melvin Lasky. Its stance has always been Anglo-American, both in political concerns and literary interests. A controversy in the 1960s following the revelation of CIA involvement in its funding caused Spender to disassociate himself from it. The magazine is notable for having published NANCY MITFORD's 'U and non-U' treatise on acceptable and infra-dig behaviour (1955) and C. P. SNOW's defence of his 'Two Cultures' thesis (1959–60), as well as much distinguished modern poetry.

end-stopped line A line of verse in which both the sense and grammatical structure are self-contained, without the need for ENJAMBEMENT, or running-on. End-stopped couplets occur frequently in 18th-century poetry, as in these lines from the fourth of POPE's *MORAL ESSAYS*:

Who then shall grace, or who improve the soil? –
Who plants like Bathurst, or who builds like Boyle.
'Tis use alone that sanctifies expense,
And splendour borrows all her rays from sense.

Endgame A play by SAMUEL BECKETT, given its first performance in French (as *Fin de partie*) in London in 1957. Beckett's own English translation was first presented in New York in 1958.

In a room, evidently isolated from all external contact, sits Hamm, immobile and dependent on his servant Clov for everything from painkillers to conversation. Master and servant are locked in resentful symbiosis: if Hamm cannot stand, Clov cannot sit. Towards the end of the play, Clov tells Hamm that he can see a boy in the wasteland outside the room. Before his last exit he asserts to Hamm that he is leaving for ever, but we have not sufficient confidence in an ending to believe him.

Endymion BENJAMIN DISRAELI's last novel, published in 1880. Set in the political world of the 1830s, it describes the rise to positions of eminence of Endymion and Myra Pitt Ferrars, twin children of a promising politician who dies penniless. Myra succeeds because she is beautiful and captivating; her husband, the Foreign Secretary Lord Roehampton, is able to help Endymion. Contemporaries could recognize a portrait of Lord Palmerston in Lord Roehampton and a satirical portrait of THACKERAY as St Barbe.

Endymion: A Poetic Romance A poem in four books by JOHN KEATS, published in 1818. It is dedicated to the memory of THOMAS CHATTERTON.

Its basis is the Greek legend of Endymion, the young shepherd whom the moon goddess Selene puts to sleep eternally so that she may always enjoy his beauty. In Keats's poem Selene becomes Cynthia, and takes Endymion away to eternal life with her. Into this fabric are woven the stories of Venus and Adonis, Glaucus and Scylla, and Arethusa, as well as an ambitious, if not completely successful, ALLEGORY of the quest for perfection and the distraction of human beauty. The famous 'Hymn to Pan' is in Book 1; the roundelay 'O Sorrow', leading into the lovely song of the Indian maid, 'Beneath My Palm Trees, by the River Side', is in Book 4.

The poem was savagely attacked by *BLACKWOOD'S EDINBURGH MAGAZINE* and by JOHN WILSON CROKER in *THE QUARTERLY REVIEW*.

Endymion: The Man in the Moon A prose comedy by JOHN LYLY, first performed in 1588 by the Boys of St Paul's. An elaboration of the classical myth of the sleeping shepherd loved by the moon goddess, *Endymion* owed its contemporary reputation to its easily read ALLEGORY of court intrigue rather than to its slender plot. Lyly cleverly exploited the skills of his chorister-actors by incorporating several songs as well as a dance of fairies, and stage directions reveal the importance of scenic effects and spectacular costume, not least in a DUMB SHOW depicting a dream. Endymion (the Earl of Leicester) abandons Tellus, the earth (Mary Queen of Scots), for love of Cynthia, the moon (Queen Elizabeth). Tellus employs the witch Dipsas to put Endymion to sleep for 40 years, but Cynthia kisses Endymion to break the spell. There is further allegorical reference to such court notables as SIR PHILIP SIDNEY (Eumenides) and Lady Rich (Semele).

Engel, Marian 1933–85 Canadian novelist. Born in Toronto, she grew up in various towns in Ontario. After attending McMaster and McGill Universities she lived abroad for a number of years, studying French literature in Provence and teaching in the United States and Cyprus. On her return to Canada she took an active part in the Canadian writers' movement and was first chairperson of the Writers' Union of Canada. Most of her novels focus on the roles of women in contemporary consumer society. Her best-known work, *Bear* (1976), is about a woman who leaves her urban life and her job in a historical institute to do research on the northern shore of Lake Superior and discovers her identity through an erotic relationship with a large pet bear. Sometimes regarded as a parody of female quest novels, such as MARGARET ATWOOD's *SURFACING*, in which a return to animal roots provides a new sense of identity, *Bear* is at the same time a penetrating and witty exploration of this theme itself. Engel's other novels include *The Honeymoon Festival* (1970), a study of motherhood, *Monodromos* (1973; reissued as *One-Way Street*, 1974), a tragicomic account of a Canadian woman's life on a Greek island, and *The Glassy Sea* (1978), in which the protagonist joins an Anglican order of nuns. She also published two short-story collections, *Inside the Easter Egg* (1975) and *The Tattooed Woman* (1985). She was posthumously awarded the Order of Canada.

England's Helicon A collection of mainly PASTORAL poems, printed in 1600. It depicts a world of love, music and dance and is generally acknowledged to be the finest of the Elizabethan poetic miscellanies, containing verses by SIR PHILIP SIDNEY, SPENSER, MARLOWE, DRAYTON, PEELE, GREENE, BRETON, CONSTABLE and THOMAS WATSON. Some poems are taken from Elizabethan song-books and appear later with musical accompaniment. Titles of a number of the lyrics ('jig', 'roundelay' and 'madrigal') testify to their musical nature. The collection does not seem, however, to have achieved the popularity of predecessors like *THE PARADISE OF DAINTY DEVICES*. A second edition, adding nine new poems, came out in 1614.

English dictionaries Behind today's dictionaries lies a long tradition that began with the glossing of Latin. From glosses written over Latin texts there grew up separate collections, organized sometimes alphabetically and sometimes by meaning. As Englishmen became eager to learn the languages of the modern world, publishers brought out dictionaries for Italian and Spanish, and even polyglot dictionaries, but the first English dictionary did not appear until as late as 1604: Robert Cawdrey's *A Table Alphabetical, Containing and Teaching the True Writing, and Understanding of Hard Usual English Words*. As the title suggests, its immediate forerunners were teaching manuals and works on grammar and orthography. Cawdrey was indebted to the title-page of Coote's *The English Schoolmaster* (1596) for the phrase 'unskilfull persons', which must designate a part of the readership he aimed at. In their turn Bullokar's *An English Expositor* (1616), Cockeram's *The English Dictionary* (1623), Blount's *Glossographia* (1656) and Phillips's *New World of English Words*

(1658) depend on one another for basic materials, growing in bulk and pretension but still concentrating on difficult words. In the next century, recognizing the need for general treatment of the vocabulary, compilers admitted more everyday words into their dictionaries.

SAMUEL JOHNSON's *The Plan of a Dictionary of the English Language* (1747) signals a new direction. His introduction reads almost like a programme for an English Academy, and it marks the culmination of a long campaign for just such a body on the French or Italian model, a campaign that numbered many writers among its advocates – CHAPMAN, COTTON, DRAYTON, DRYDEN, EVELYN, COWLEY, WELLER and SWIFT, for example. With the publication of Johnson's *DICTIONARY OF THE ENGLISH LANGUAGE* (1755), the idea of an Academy lost ground, evidence of the immediate recognition commanded by his two folio volumes. The most notable innovation was his systematic use of quotations, taken largely from literature 1560–1660, to illustrate usage and justify definitions. (The next major step forward was taken over half a century later with Charles Richardson's inclusion of quotations from 1250 onwards in his *Encyclopaedia Metropolitana*, published in 1819.) Some contemporaries labelled Johnson 'the man who has conferred stability on the language of his country', but Johnson himself recognized that a dictionary cannot 'embalm' language or 'secure it from corruption and decay'. He acknowledged the usefulness to him of one preceding 18th-century dictionary in particular – Bailey's *Dictionarium Brittanicum: A More Complete Universal Etymological Dictionary Than Any Extant* – and he greatly increased the representation of everyday words in his own work. More importantly, he produced a dictionary in which encyclopaedic entries play little part. With him, the English dictionary has moved on from the 'difficult words' tradition.

Although Johnson's achievement was pioneering, not definitive, his dictionary cast a long shadow. Its status was not challenged until the appearance of the *OXFORD ENGLISH DICTIONARY* and, to a lesser extent, *WEBSTER'S DICTIONARY*.

English Humorists of the Eighteenth Century, The Lectures by W. M. THACKERAY, first delivered in 1851 and published in 1853. He discusses SWIFT, CONGREVE, ADDISON, STEELE, PRIOR, GAY, POPE, HOGARTH, SMOLLETT, FIELDING, STERNE and GOLDSMITH, largely in biographical and anecdotal terms which nevertheless reveal the extent of his own debt to 18th-century literature.

English language, the To every human being his mother tongue is of unique importance. Objectively, however, we can claim that English is unique among the languages of the world. It has at present the widest use of any language in history, both in num-

bers of users (among whom native speakers are probably in a minority) and in range of uses. The corollary of this is that it has an extraordinary diversity of forms. Only mankind's exceptional capacity for abstraction enables us to conceive of such a thing as the English language underlying the hugely different realizations we are liable to encounter. But the right-hand man of this capacity for abstraction is the written form of the language. This prevails worldwide, with only trivial divergences, and of course has long been the vehicle of literature. Even where writers attempt to portray dialect their portrayal has for centuries been mediated by the conventions of standard orthography.

What is true of the current range of English is almost matched by the duration and diversity of the historical record. At 1400 years this is by no means the longest in the world, but it is among those of high duration, and it incorporates changes, sometimes obvious, sometimes covert, of immense extent and profundity.

External history
The language came to England in the mouths of Germanic settlers who arrived in substantial numbers from the mid 5th century, though some had certainly come earlier. They were of various tribes, including Angles and Saxons, from a long stretch of the northern European littoral. Their dialects, which were closely related but not uniform, belonged to the wider Germanic (Gmc) family, itself a subgroup of Indo-European (IE), whose membership includes the Celtic (the antecedent language family in Britain), the Italic-Romance (including Latin and all its modern descendants), the Hellenic, the Balto-Slavonic, the Indo-Iranian, and many others. As always happens, the new societies in what is now England developed their own linguistic norms; their members converged in usage, and in doing so diverged from that of the Germanic communities they left behind. Extension of settlements throughout the country was a protracted business. Once settlements were made the village would constitute, for most people, their effective circle of communication. Under such conditions distinct dialects develop in two or three generations, and it is natural to suppose that this happened from village to village in pre-Conquest England. Customarily four large dialect areas are recognized, not because speech in these areas can have been internally uniform, but because this is as much as we can detect from the surviving written records: these are the South-eastern, South-western, Mercian (Midland) and Northumbrian. The language from the settlement to the Norman Conquest is called Old English (OE), and in late OE West Saxon had national currency as a standard for written prose.

The first settlers were only minimally literate. A tiny minority of them were masters of the runic method of inscription in angular symbols designed for carving, developed in the Gmc world probably about AD 200. Literacy in the normal sense was a by-product of the conversion to Christianity, beginning in the south with the Roman mission of Augustine in 597, and almost simultaneously with Celtic missions in the north. The alphabet developed for OE was basically Roman, omitting *j*, *q*, *v*, and usually *k* and *x*, and adding one Celtic and two runic symbols. The first written English words in it date from 597, but continuous documents in English are considerably later, though some incorporate 6th-century material which at first had been transmitted orally. Literacy remained rare, the province of two minority groups, the clergy and a handful of well-born laymen. Surviving pre-Conquest manuscripts are a small fraction of what must have existed, but even if all had survived their representation of the language would have been selective. Manuscript production was costly in materials and skilled labour and would have been authorized only for purposes which seemed convincing to ecclesiastical authorities or landowners. The surviving records are also unevenly distributed over a period of five centuries and a wide geographical area.

From the close of the 8th century, Viking raids and eventual settlement over most of northern and eastern England brought into contact two languages closely related in origin and mutually comprehensible. In 1066 came a shock as profound but wholly different in kind. The Normans (themselves originally Vikings – Northmen) were, by comparison with 11th-century Englishmen, barbarians whose strength lay in military and administrative success, the bringer of wealth. Once again the great religious houses were as much a target as the great secular estates – now not for plunder but for takeover. In most parts of the country control of the leading scriptoria soon passed into Norman hands; documents not written in Latin were for the most part written in French, and original English texts are rare from 1066 to *c.* 1200. We have least documentation for the century that seems to have witnessed the deepest and swiftest changes ever to have affected the language. Norman influence was not, like Scandinavian influence, variable by locality, but variable by class, affecting most those who had most to do with centres of wealth and power, where ANGLO-NORMAN, or Norman-French, was current. In 1204 new legislation prevented the holding of estates in both England and France. Thenceforth those who stayed were committed to England. Their families grew up English-speaking and English began to extend into public and governmental functions. During the same period English took its first small step overseas, to Ireland, with the settlement of an English landowning cadre in 1210.

In the following centuries two developments proceeded hand in hand – a vast increase in the number and types of English documents and an extension of the use of English for all public purposes. Generally, the forms of writing show marked discontinuities from those current in OE, mainly under French influence; what is more, the national currency of one standard form has been lost. Most scribes clearly wrote within a tradition they had learned, but these traditions were local, and so diverse that a recent survey has identified over 1100 of them in a single century. However, the increased public role of English created a need for standardization. From 1330 to 1430 four successive and competing standards have been identified. Type III is familiar today as CHAUCER's English, and Type IV is the ancestor of the modern standard. When printing was introduced in 1476 the existence of identical multiple copies made standardization even more important. Neither 15th-century nor 16th-century printed English is standard in the modern sense of being virtually self-consistent and uniform, but it is broadly true that, punctuation apart, CAXTON established the range of options within which the modern system would be selected. In large measure the spellings we now use are those favoured by JOHNSON in his *DICTIONARY OF THE ENGLISH LANGUAGE* (1755), but he correctly claimed that most of his preferences were determined by tradition.

English from about the Norman Conquest to the emergence of Type IV is known as Middle English (ME), and from the mid 15th century to the present as Modern English (ModE), within which present-day English (PE) is distinguished. There are long periods of overlap and transition, and change takes place at different rates from dialect to dialect; the dates are not meant to be precise.

The 16th century saw the inception of two main developments which were to continue to the present day. Externally these involved the first planting of the language outside Europe, through exploration, trade, settlement and colonization, in Africa, America and the Far East. In most of these distant places the English were preceded by and interacted with other Europeans – Portuguese, Spanish, Italian, French and Dutch. They encountered new flora, fauna, topographical and climatic features, commodities, processes, social organizations, and languages, not only the languages of Africa, Asia and America; there was greater linguistic influence from other Europeans than there had ever been in Europe, except from the French. They developed new institutions and established new kinds of official post. Everything had to be named. The linguistic effect was overwhelmingly on the repertoire of nouns.

Among the commodities were human cargo, slaves from many African tribes transported in conditions where inevitably their African linguistic heritage was blended with the language of the owners; in so doing they created new languages whose Englishness is hotly disputed.

In the late 18th century Australia and New Zealand were settled, and in the 19th century southern and eastern Africa. Meanwhile, the War of Independence in America was rapidly followed by Webster's declaration that 'our honor requires us to have a system of our own, in language as well as government' (1789). *WEBSTER'S DICTIONARY* encoded this, establishing the source of the differences in written standard English between America and Britain to this day.

English was therefore in an unprecedented position when the 19th-20th-century explosion of scholarship, scientific discovery and technical development took place. So many of the early advances were made by English speakers and published in England that researchers everywhere had to know English, and its scholarly use snowballed. When a language of worldwide currency was required for international air traffic it had to be English. In many countries where English has no native speakers it is the only practicable medium of higher education. Its world-wide role has increased, not shrunk, with the decline of the Empire.

Reverting to the 16th century, we can state that the second main development is preoccupation with the identification and fostering of a spoken standard on a par with the written one. Commentators agree in giving it a socio-geographical basis: it is the speech of courtly (not ordinary) Londoners, but it can also be heard from a thinly scattered population of gentry in every county. Though there were to be many modifications, we recognize for the first time a distinctively modern variety-structure typical of England – not of Britain, and certainly not of English world-wide.

Internal structure

A systematic account of a language needs to describe two interdependent systems – systems of transmission and of meaning. The primary means of transmission is speech; secondary, less widely distributed but not necessarily derivative, is writing. The meanings and distinctions which can or must be transmitted are organized in two ways: they may be realized by open-class items, infinitely extensible rapidly changing repertoires, the vocabulary of a language, notably nouns, verbs, adjectives and adverbs; or closed-system items, each set few in number, rarely added to or lost, its members interdependent. These constitute the grammar and may be realized by abstract contrasts, such as tense, or by wordlike items, such as prepositions, conjunctions and personal pronouns.

Only the briefest characterization of the English sound system is possible. Writing in English centres on letters, and it may be for this reason that we tend to think of strings of distinctive segments (phonemes) as the essential constituents of speech. They do indeed have an important function; changing the initial segment enables us to distinguish *bin* from *din*, *kin*, *gin*, etc., the middle one *bin* from *ban*, *bun*, *bean*,

etc., and the final one *bin* from *bid*, *big*, etc. Most varieties of English have at all times had rather more than 40 of these distinctive sounds, and though their lexical distribution has changed through time the overall shape of the system has been remarkably constant. But in many ways the suprasegmentals, which writing largely ignores, are more primary in English than the segmental sounds. These involve syllables, what shapes they can take, how stress contrasts are distributed over them, and temporal patterning (rhythm) and, pitch movement (intonation). An example of the dominance of suprasegmentals can be seen in the vowel system: stressed syllables are the domain of a system of some 20 different vowels; unstressed syllables of only two. With minor variations this has been true for 1000 years.

In what we do know of OE vocabulary over half the words (normally the commonest) are of IE origin, about one sixth Gmc, one sixth borrowed from Latin (usually the rarest), and the rest from minor or unknown sources. Vocabulary then, as at all times, responded to new demands to a large extent by word formation (WF) (chiefly compounding, as in modern *blackbird*, or derivation, as in *blacking*). In late OE clearly Scandinavian influence must have been great in the north and east, but few loanwords appear in the record till ME; those that have stayed in the language include basic words of every grammatical class, e.g. *law* (replacing OE *ae*), *egg* (replacing OE *aeg*), *ill*, *take*, *till*, *they*, *their*, *them*; hundreds have been lost. The influence of French, mainly after the Norman Conquest, was also slow to appear in the record. However, by the late 14th century Chaucer alone uses some 4000 French loans, which represent almost all semantic fields. In subsequent centuries loans flooded into English from over 100 other languages, but at all times French and classical loans have been most numerous.

Since the Norman Conquest additional methods of formation have come into prominence: zero-derivation, in which a word is established in a new grammatical class without change of form (cf. *look*, *walk*, *love*, sbs. and vs.); back-derivation, as when *peddle*, *burgle* are formed from *pedlar*, *burglar*; various sorts of sound-motivation, such as vowel gradation in *flimflam*, *shilly-shally*, or of graphic motivation, as in the acronyms *radar*, *NATO*; there are also invented and blended words (e.g. *blatant*, *brunch*). In the present century about 30 words a day, on average, have been added to the repertoire. Naturally there are losses as well as gains – of the recorded OE stock about seven items have been lost for every four preserved. Survivals may not be obvious – they can undergo radical change of shape (OE *nafo-gar*, PE *auger*) or meaning (OE *thing*, 'meeting').

It is in grammatical structure that English has undergone the most sweeping changes. Three are of central importance. First the structure of the noun phrase (NP), which in OE was more like its Latin than its PE counterpart in its range of declensions, genders, cases, and rules of concord. By early ME the present simplified system was complete in essentials. What have remained constant are rules of order (*the duke's large well-built timber-framed hunting-lodge*, for instance).

In the verb phrase (VP) Gmc had diverged sharply from IE. An older system of rich inflectional contrasts gave way to an oversimplified tense system inherited by OE. The past tense was marked either by internal change or, following a Gmc innovation, by adding a suffix; thus OE *he rad* (corresponding to PE *he rode, was riding, has ridden, had ridden*) or *he lufode* (*he loved*, etc.). In contrast with the past was the non-past tense, corresponding to everything else (he rideþ, PE *he rides, is riding, will/shall ride*). This drastically reduced system was already being re-expanded in Gmc and the process has continued ever since, using not inflection but pre-verbal particles, auxiliaries, forming at any one time a closed system. The perfective (forms in *has/ have/had* plus past participle) is pre-English, and so is a new passive (in OE with *weorþan*, 'become', later with *be*, plus past participle). Within OE clearly modal uses begin (those now involving *will, would, shall, should, can, could, may, might, must*) but the modals did not emerge as a system till early ModE nor take their full present functions till *c.* 1700. The aspect contrast (*he is riding* carved out of the former territory of *he rides*) did not come into its own till the 17th century (though scattered examples are frequent before that) and is still evolving. The semantico-syntactic categories have been refined; referential distinctions (number and person) have declined. Except in be (*was, were*, a pure number contrast) only the non-past is affected, distinguishing third person singular from the rest – singular or plural – by addition of *-s*. However, the largely syntactic contrast of subjunctive with indicative has also been almost completely lost.

Verbs are central to the functioning of negation, and here too change has been profound. OE negated by putting *ne* before the verb, a pattern that goes back to IE. This changed steadily and *c.* 1600 began to take on its present shape, which has two essential features – first the use of *not, n't* after the finite verb; second, the requirement that *not, n't* be attached only to auxiliaries, so that if no auxiliary is present the dummy *do/does/did* must be inserted (*he isn't riding* but *he doesn't ride*). The interrogative was made in OE by simple inversion of subject and verb; now this too must have an auxiliary as its domain and calls on *do/does/did* in the absence of any other (*he's riding, isn't he?* but *he rides, doesn't he?*).

The third major area of change is clause structure. In OE, as in Latin for the same reason, the subject did not always need to be expressed. The nucleus of the clause, the prime domain of rules of order, was therefore the verb and whatever nominal structure was needed to complete it. With the reduction of verb inflections expression of the subject became indispensable; it was given initial position, and if it had no semantically required realization a dummy was inserted (*It's raining; There isn't enough*). From the 15th century the nucleus of the sentence has been subject-verb, in that order (except for interrogation or special effect). Rules of order were also much affected in OE, as in modern German, by the nature of the clause and its type of onset. All these special patterns were abandoned in favour of the nuclear type.

It is no wonder that a language which has been the vehicle of much of the experience of so much of humanity should also be the vehicle of the world's richest literature, not only English literature but that of English-speaking communities in every continent and of an unparalleled number of great writers whose mother tongue was not English. Yet, as we have seen, 'English' subsumes many Englishes. Each has in its repertoire many 'false friends', words and structures that look familiar but have quite different functions in the text from those the reader expects. Constant vigilance is needed to save the inexhaustible well from turning into a snake-pit.

English Review, The A literary periodical founded in 1908 by FORD MADOX FORD with the financial backing of Arthur Marwood. Ford's editorship lasted little over a year (to 1910), but it was the most promising period for the journal, which published work by THOMAS HARDY, HENRY JAMES, H. G. WELLS and WYNDHAM LEWIS, and introduced the poems of D. H. LAWRENCE to the reading public. Ford's successor, Austin Harrison, continued to publish Lawrence's stories and essays, but Lawrence dismissed the *Review* after Ford's departure as 'piffling'. The journal was finally absorbed into *The National Review* in 1937.

enjambement From the French, 'in-striding', it refers in English poetry to the continuation of the sense and grammatical structure from one line (or couplet) to the next. Enjambement thus gives, for example, the BLANK VERSE of SHAKESPEARE's plays much of its fluidity and forward movement. The opposite practice is the END-STOPPED LINE.

Enoch Arden A poem by ALFRED TENNYSON, written in 1861 and 1862 and published in 1864. Based on a prose sketch written for the poet by his friend, the painter Thomas Woolner, it became one of his most popular works. A similar theme appears in ELIZABETH GASKELL's novel *SYLVIA'S LOVERS* (1863) and in ADELAIDE ANNE PROCTER's poem 'Homeward Bound' (1858).

Enoch Arden marries Annie Lee but, when he can no longer support his family from his work as a fisherman, is forced to set sail on a merchantman. In his absence Annie falls into financial difficulties and is helped by Philip Ray, once Enoch's rival for her love. Enoch's ship is wrecked and he is believed dead, so Annie finally marries Philip. But Enoch has survived and, after being rescued from a desert island, returns. He sees the happiness of Annie and Philip and the children, and quietly resolves to leave them be. Nobody recognizes him but he confides his secret to Miriam, the local innkeeper, when he knows he is dying. She conveys his last blessing to his wife and children, and to Philip.

Enquiry concerning Human Understanding, An

A philosophical work by DAVID HUME, originally published as *Philosophical Essays concerning Human Understanding* in 1748 and retitled in 1758. It recasts the arguments in Book I of *A TREATISE OF HUMAN NATURE* and adds an essay on miracles, once considered notorious for its scepticism, which denies that miracles can be proved with any amount or type of evidence and concludes that they cannot be part of a reasonable foundation for a system of religion.

Enquiry concerning Political Justice

A libertarian philosophical treatise by WILLIAM GODWIN, completed and published in 1793, with revised second and third editions appearing in 1796 and 1798. It is Godwin's major theoretical work and brought him immediate, though short-lived, fame upon its publication during the critical years of the French Revolution. Impressed by PAINE's *RIGHTS OF MAN* (1791), yet dissatisfied with its lack of conceptual rigour, he embarked upon a work that would philosophically 'place the principles of politics on an immovable basis and annihilate all oppositions'.

Its methodological springboard is a strongly Rousseauian attack on the 'natural' rights tradition since LOCKE, and on the idea of the origin of human society in a contract founded upon promise. Promises according to Godwin merely postponed into a vague future the exercise of virtue, performance of duty and promotion of the happiness and moral well-being of others, which he saw as the sole purpose of human existence, leaving the individual indefinitely free to pursue his own selfish interests. What he goes on to recommend, however, is in many ways the opposite of Rousseau's advocacy, in the famous *Social Contract*, of popular sovereignty and state sponsorship of economic justice and civic sensibility. *Political Justice* represents the fulfilment of the anarchic potential of classical enlightenment rationalism: itself systematic to the point of pedantry, it is essentially a repudiation of political systems as such. Although its political programme was revolutionary in that it projected the abolition of law, government, marriage and all apparatuses of inequity and coercion, there could be no question of bringing this about by insurrection, political agitation or even group solidarity. Reason's means could not differ from reason's end, which was the universal rejection of institutionalized justice itself rather than the violent or inflammatory confrontation of specific cases of its fallibility. People might, therefore, influence each other to embrace the good solely through informal reasoned persuasion: once a person became a member of a political association, he committed his reason to the care of others, and was thus self-estranged. The ultimate triumph of rationality and correct moral sentiment was inevitable, however, and with it injustices would fall away of themselves.

The book's meteoric fall from grace in the second half of the 1790s is, to some extent, explained by the conservative mobilization of British public opinion against radical and dissenting intellectuals, but it was also soon under attack from liberals and radicals as well, to whom it gave little ideological support in the new era of counter-revolutionary repression. Today the work is seen as a canonical text of anarchism. Its influence on the Romantic generation of writers was profound, and its themes echo in the writings of Tolstoy, Proudhon, Kropotkin and THOREAU.

Enright, D(ennis) J(oseph)

1920– Poet. Born in Leamington and educated at Leamington College and Downing College, Cambridge, he taught English Literature overseas before returning to Britain to take up posts at the Universities of Leeds and Warwick in the 1970s. *Memoirs of a Mendicant Professor* (1969) relates his experiences from post-war Berlin to Thailand and Singapore. An anthology, *Poets of the 1950s* (1955), helped to establish the MOVEMENT. His own work, beginning with *The Laughing Hyena* (1953), is gathered in *Collected Poems* (1981; reissued 1987). Typically set in the landscape of the East, his poems are often concerned with inequality in human circumstances and speak passionately for the poor and oppressed. His treatment of this theme avoids sentimentalism, using understatement and IRONY to carry the load of pity or indignation. He has edited a selection of MILTON (1975), JOHNSON's *RASSELAS* (1976), *The Oxford Book of Contemporary Verse 1945–80* (1980), *The Oxford Book of Death* (1987), and *The Oxford Book of Friendship* (1991), and written novels for children, including *The Joke Shop* (1976), *Wild Ghost Chase* (1978) and *Beyond Land's End* (1979).

Entail, The

A novel by JOHN GALT, published in 1823. Claud Walkinshaw, a packman, is obsessed with recovering the estates which formerly belonged to his family and can achieve this only by disinheriting his eldest son in favour of his second, an idiot. The story follows the disastrous recoil on the Walkinshaw children and grandchildren.

Eothen

See KINGLAKE, ALEXANDER WILLIAM.

epic One of the earliest literary forms, and the subject of critical discussion since Aristotle. Most critics have agreed that an epic should be a long narrative, normally in verse, dealing with one important major theme or action – however much it may be amplified or buttressed by subsidiary actions. It should also normally have a certain sublimity of style and grandeur of content. The work of Homer and Virgil provides the main precedent in classical literature, while the most obvious examples in English are *Beowulf*, Spenser's *The Faerie Queene* and Milton's *Paradise Lost*. 'A comic epic in prose' therefore carries an implication of paradox. Yet this claim, made by Fielding for *Joseph Andrews* but best exemplified by Joyce's *Ulysses*, is not quite a contradiction in terms, since it does indicate something of the scope and endeavour of these novels.

epic simile (or Homeric simile) A simile, characteristic of epic but not confined to the genre, so long and elaborate that it seems to function as a small inserted lyric, or separate ornament to the narrative. Unlike the normal brief simile, it deliberately suspends the action – giving pause for contemplation – instead of advancing or vivifying it. The extended comparison between Satan and Leviathan (the whale) in Book I of Milton's *Paradise Lost* provides a famous example.

Epicoene: or, The Silent Woman A comedy by Ben Jonson, first produced in 1609 and published in 1616.
  The plot concerns the deception of Morose, a self-centred bachelor who hates noise. Suspecting that his nephew, Sir Dauphine Eugenie, finds him ridiculous, Morose plans to remove him from his will; he also intends to marry if he can find a woman who is quiet enough. His barber, Cutbeard, tells him of such a woman and brings Epicoene, soft-spoken and of few words. Morose marries her and she immediately becomes talkative and quarrelsome. Then the house is invaded by noisy well-wishers, among them Sir Jack Daw and Sir Amorous LaFoole, who both claim to have enjoyed Epicoene's favours in the past. In the end Morose is forced to accept his nephew's offer of help in getting rid of Epicoene, and to agree to restore his nephew's inheritance. Sir Dauphine then removes Epicoene's wig and reveals that 'she' is a youth trained for the plot. Morose has to abide by his bargain, while Daw and LaFoole cover their embarrassment as best they can.

epigram 'Her whole life is an epigram, smart, smooth and neatly penn'd,/ Platted quite neat to catch applause with a sliding noose at the end.' This example by Blake both exploits and defines what the epigram has come to signify: a witty and well-turned saying with a sting in its tail. The word's Greek derivation, however, means simply an 'inscription', terse and lapidary by necessity, suitable for funerary or cel-ebratory monuments, and the collection gathered in *The Greek Anthology* (which consists of 6000 poems from 7th century BC to 10th century AD) includes many non-satirical poems. Greatest and most influential of the classical epigrammatists is the Latin poet Martial (*c.* AD 38–104), whose epigrams fully reflect the capaciousness of the genre, both in form (many are pithy distichs, others extend to 50 lines or more) and in variety of content. His scurrility has been much exaggerated, and his work embodies Camden's definition of the epigram: 'short and sweet poems, framed to praise or dispraise'. With Catullus, Martial provided the model during the vogue for the epigram in the Renaissance, with Thomas More (writing in Latin) as the acknowledged master and Sir John Harington a lively practitioner. Ben Jonson's *Epigrams* (1616) brilliantly vivify the spirit of Martial in English; Robert Herrick, in *Hesperides* (1648), was perhaps the last English poet to master the epigram's full tonal range. Later epigrammatists emphasized satirical wit at the expense of serious directness. They include Prior, Pope, Swift, Goldsmith, Cowper, Burns, Byron, Landor and Coleridge, with the last offering a famous definition: 'What is an epigram? a dwarfish whole,/ Its body brevity, and wit its soul.' Hilaire Belloc, Robert Graves and Stevie Smith have been among the distinguished exponents in this century.

Epigrams A collection of poems by Ben Jonson, published in the 1616 edition of his works. The Epigrams themselves, strongly influenced by Martial, show the poet's sharp and satirical view of contemporary manners. Better known are the sweeter-toned addresses, compliments and epitaphs; in the last category are poems on the poet's son ('On My First Son') and a child actor ('On Salomon Davy, a Child of Queen Elizabeth's Chapel').

epistolary novel A novel in which the story is told through an exchange of letters between the characters. The form was made fashionable in the 18th century by Samuel Richardson, though he used it loosely enough to allow his characters' letters to grow into private journals; Smollett's *Expedition of Humphry Clinker* shows that it was still popular towards the end of the century. Since then it has been used occasionally – in, for example, Swinburne's *Love's Cross Currents* (1877) and John Barth's *Letters* (1979) – but has not been consistently favoured by major novelists.

Epithalamion Spenser's marriage song was published together with *Amoretti* (1595) and may well be intended as the culmination of the sonnet sequence. Spenser himself had married Elizabeth Boyle in June 1594. The poem begins with the invocation of the muses before dawn, describes the awakening of the bride, the progress to church, the wedding ceremony and the onset of night, and ends with a prayer in the bridal chamber for 'fruitful progeny'. Blending classical formulas with Christian sentiment, it is a poem of jubilant festivity, full of music and light, and is considered one of Spenser's finest minor poems.

epyllion The word (from the Greek, 'little epic') was first used in the 19th century to describe classical poems that told a story whose subject was love, with mythological allusions and at least one major digression. The tradition dated from the time of Theocritus (d. 250 BC); *Peleus and Thetis* by Catullus (d. *c.* 54 BC) is a late Roman example. The term became applied to post-classical literature, especially the erotic treatment of mythological narratives in Renaissance poetry. SHAKESPEARE's *VENUS AND ADONIS* and MARLOWE's *HERO AND LEANDER* are major English examples, THOMAS LODGE's *Scillaes Metamorphosis* (1589) and FRANCIS BEAUMONT's *Salmacis and Hermaphroditus* (1602) minor ones.

Erasmus, Desiderius ?1466–1536 Humanist and scholar. He was born in Rotterdam and went to school at Deventer in 1475–83 with the Brethren of the Common Life, whose *devotio moderna* with its emphasis on personal piety and works of charity influenced his later thinking. He became an Augustinian canon and was ordained priest in 1492, but obtained dispensations throughout his life which enabled him to leave the cloister and live in the world. His experiences at the University of Paris 1495–9, where he studied for the degree of Doctor of Theology, were less than happy. He complained of addled eggs and the stench of the bedrooms. More importantly, he was irritated by the wrangling subtleties of the scholastic theologians there. His career displayed all the facets of the Renaissance humanist. He became Latin secretary to the Bishop of Cambrai in 1494, and was tutor to boys of noble families, including two English boys.

His achievements won him recognition as the greatest humanist of the northern Renaissance. He edited or translated Pliny, Seneca and Lucian as well as a long list of Church Fathers: Jerome (1516), Cyprian (1520), Hilary (1523), Ambrose (1527), Chrysostom (1530) and Origen (1536). His edition of Lorenzo Valla's *Adnotationes* on the New Testament appeared in 1505. His *Novum instrumentum*, an edition of the Greek text of the New Testament with a parallel Latin version which superseded the Vulgate in its elegance and accuracy, was printed in 1516. It also contained notes by Erasmus, some of which criticized the state of the Roman Catholic church. In his prefatory essay Erasmus wishes that every woman might read the Gospel and that the farmer at his plough might sing snatches of scripture. Erasmus made a vast collection of Greek and Latin proverbs, the *Adagia*, which grew and grew so that the Venetian Aldine edition of 1508 contained over 3000. Towards the end of his life he made a similar collection of classical anecdotes, the *Apophthegmata* (1531). The *Enchiridion militis christiani* or 'dagger of the Christian soldier' (1503) is a manual of simple piety intended, in Erasmus' words, to kindle a warm love of the scriptures in generous hearts. *Institutio principis christiani* (1516) is a work on the education of the Christian prince. *Colloquia* are dialogues on various subjects.

Erasmus' relations with England were close. On his first stay in 1499–1500 he met the future Henry VIII, and made the acquaintance of English humanists, finding congenial friends in WILLIAM GROCYN, THOMAS LINACRE, William Latimer, JOHN COLET and above all THOMAS MORE. He was in England again in 1505 and 1509–14. During this last visit he lectured at Cambridge on Greek and theology, and to this third visit belongs the composition of the *Moriae encomium* (Praise of Folly, 1511) which in its title puns on the name of his greatest English friend. Its paradoxical self-praise by Folly herself satirizes clerical abuses, corruption and ignorance, and ends with praise of Christian folly, the simple Christian and the ultimate folly of Christ's crucifixion.

Erasmus' other works are too numerous to mention. There were many 16th-century English translations of the *Colloquia* and of his devotional works, and selections from the *Adagia* were also Englished. A translation of the *Enchiridion* as *The Manual of the Christian Knight* (1533) is attributed to WILLIAM TYNDALE, and MILES COVERDALE's *A Short Recapitulation of the Enchiridion* was printed at Antwerp in 1545. UDALL's *Apophthegmes* appeared in 1542 and a complete Latin and English *Adagia* in 1621. There were also Chaloner's *Praise of Folly* (1549) and Paynell's *Complaint of Peace* (1559), a translation of *Querimonia pacis*.

Despite his constant criticism of clerical abuse and folly and theological over-niceties, Erasmus could never bring himself to join Luther and finally opposed him in a treatise on free will, *De libero arbitrio* (1524). However, there is much truth in the cliché that the Reformation was an egg laid by Erasmus and hatched by Luther.

Erdrich, (Karen) Louise 1954– American novelist. Born in Little Falls, Minnesota, partly of Chippewa ancestry, she attended Dartmouth College and the Johns Hopkins University. Though she has also published poetry in *Jacklight* (1990) and *Baptism of Desire* (1991), she secured her reputation with three novels, combining social realism with dreamlike sequences, about the Chippewa community in North Dakota: *Love Medicine* (1985), *The Beet Queen* (1988) and *Tracks* (1988), considered the most accomplished. Another novel, *Crown of Columbus* (1991), was written in collaboration with her husband, Michael Dorris.

Erewhon A satirical novel by SAMUEL BUTLER, published in 1872. Erewhon (an anagram of 'nowhere') is discovered by Higgs, the narrator, on the far side of a chain of unexplored mountains in a remote colony. His description embodies Butler's attack on the mental and moral stagnation and hypocrisy he found in England, and on his society's attitudes to crime, religion and the rearing of children. Higgs escapes in a balloon he has constructed himself, accompanied by the girl with whom he has fallen in love. In a belated sequel, *Erewhon Revisited* (1901), he returns 20 years later to discover that his ascent in the balloon has called into being a religion, Sunchildism, and that a great temple to him is about to be dedicated. He is horrified at the way people's credulity is being exploited by the Professors Hanky and Panky.

Ervine, St John (Greer) 1883–1971 Irish playwright, novelist and critic. Born in Belfast, he was a drama critic in Dublin when he began writing plays. *Mixed Marriage* (1911), the first produced at the ABBEY THEATRE, is a bold treatment of Catholic–Protestant relationships and their likely cost in human happiness. *Jane Clegg* (1913) and *John Ferguson* (1915), though obeying the fashion for the WELL-MADE PLAY, are not afraid to address serious problems seriously. Ervine became manager of the Abbey Theatre in 1915. After World War I he settled in London, working as drama critic for *The Observer* in 1919–23 and for the BBC for some years after 1932. He continued to produce social dramas but turned as well to comedies, like *The First Mrs Fraser* (1929), almost in the style of NOËL COWARD, and *Boyd's Shop* (1936), a gentle study of Irish village life. He also wrote novels and biographies.

Essay concerning Human Understanding A philosophical treatise by JOHN LOCKE, published in 1690. Further editions, with important revisions by the author, were published in 1694, 1700 and 1706. *Some Thoughts on the Conduct of the Understanding in the Search of Truth*, originally designed as a chapter of the *Essay*, was published posthumously in 1762.

Locke rejected the doctrine of inborn ideas or knowledge, maintaining that the source of knowledge is experience. His intention in the *Essay* was to enquire into the origin and extent of man's knowledge; he also examined the nature and limits of knowledge, what man can hope to know and what he cannot. In the course of his argument Locke threw new light on the working of the human mind and the association of ideas, and thereby influenced generations of poets and novelists. His philosophy is conveyed in lucid and unadorned prose.

Essay of Dramatic Poesy A critical symposium by JOHN DRYDEN, written while he was living at Charlton in Wiltshire to escape the plague in London. It was first published in 1668. Those taking part are CHARLES SACKVILLE, EARL OF DORSET (Eugenius), SIR ROBERT HOWARD (Crites), SIR CHARLES SEDLEY (Lisideius) and Dryden himself (Neander). The four friends are boating on the Thames. After discussing the fighting between the Dutch and English fleets in the Thames estuary (June 1665), they go on to discuss the English drama of earlier days and in their own time, comparing English drama with French. There is lively discussion of the use of RHYME in drama and a fine appreciation of the art of SHAKESPEARE. The *Essay* is a fine example of Dryden's succinct prose.

Essay on Criticism, An A poem in HEROIC COUPLETS by ALEXANDER POPE, written when he was 21 and first published in 1711. Didactic in purpose, it contains a description of the rules of taste and the principles by which a critic should be guided; a demonstration follows showing departures from these principles by certain critics. The classical inspiration for the poem was Horace's *Ars poetica* and it is a remarkably sophisticated performance; the skill with which Pope used the form and the concentration of witty utterance it contained made him famous. Some of the lines have the status of proverbs: 'A little learning is a dangerous thing' and 'Some praise at morning what they blame at night;/ But always think the last opinion right.'

Essay on Man A poem by ALEXANDER POPE, in four epistles. The first three were published anonymously in 1733; the fourth appeared under Pope's name in 1734. They are partly inspired by the philosophical writings of BOLINGBROKE, to whom they are addressed. The first epistle is concerned with the nature of man and his place in the universe; the second with man as an individual; the third with man in society; and the fourth with man and the pursuit of happiness. The purpose is to demonstrate the essential rightness of the world as ordered by God; man's inability to realize this is the fault of his limited perception. The result is conventional enough in its thought, but its expression is enlivened by Pope's gift for witty aphorism. Pope did not continue his original plan for a philosophical poem on a more ambitious scale.

Essays, The: or, Counsels, Civil and Moral FRANCIS BACON's essays were first published in a book of 10 in 1597, followed by a book of 38 in 1612 and a third in 1625 containing 58. They are mostly reflections and observations shaped into advice for the conduct of a successful life. Some deal with matters of great importance, such as government ('Greatness of Kingdoms'); others with topics such as architecture ('Of Building') and aspects of human behaviour including ambition and cunning. Incorporating numerous quotations from earlier writers, the essays are full of acute intelligence and wit. The turn of phrase is aphoristic: 'If the hill will not come to Mahomet, Mahomet will go to the hill'; 'Money is like muck, not good except it be spread.' The celebrated essay 'Atheism' was first published in the edition of 1612.

Essays and Reviews A collection of theological essays, published in 1860. The editor was Henry Bristow Wilson and his eminent contributors were: BENJAMIN JOWETT, professor of Greek at Oxford; MARK PATTISON, rector of Lincoln College, Oxford; Baden Powell, professor of geometry at Oxford; Frederick Temple, chaplain to the Queen and to the Earl of Denbigh, and headmaster of Rugby; Rowland Williams; and C. W. Goodwin. Influenced by the HIGHER CRITICISM, the authors argued for a liberal Christianity which took account of modern biblical research and modern science. In the ensuing controversy they were nicknamed the 'Seven against Christ' and Jowett's essay, 'The Interpretation of Scripture' was discovered to give the greatest offence; he never wrote on theological subjects again. The book was condemned by a meeting of bishops in 1861 and by the Synod of the Church of England in 1864.

Essays in Criticism Two collections of essays by MATTHEW ARNOLD, the first series published in 1865 and the second posthumously in 1888.

Of the nine essays in the first volume, mainly devoted to Continental and classical subjects, the most important is 'The Function of Criticism at the Present Time', a sustained attempt to broaden and elevate the role of criticism. According to Arnold, criticism 'obeys an instinct prompting it to know the best that is known and thought in the world, irrespective of practice, politics, and everything of the kind'. Disinterested and flexible, it can 'see the object as in itself it really is' and 'make the best ideas prevail'. Criticism can thus not only shape 'the creative epochs of literature' but play its role in other areas of knowledge and in society, whose contemporary problems Arnold eloquently notes.

The second collection likewise begins with a challenging essay, 'The Study of Poetry', notable for its theory of 'touchstones' of poetic excellence: one should 'have always in one's mind lines and expressions of the great masters... and apply them as a touchstone to other poetry'. Brief passages from Homer, Dante, Virgil, SHAKESPEARE and MILTON demonstrate the theory and assert the 'penetrative power' of poetry, whose attributes are matter and substance, manner and style, and 'high seriousness' (a quality which Arnold, surprisingly, denies to CHAUCER). Otherwise, the aim of the volume is more narrowly informative than its predecessor. It includes essays on Tolstoy, Amiel, Milton, GRAY, KEATS, WORDSWORTH and BYRON (the latter two 'first and pre-eminent in actual performance, a glorious pair, among the English poets of this century') and SHELLEY ('a beauti-

ful and ineffectual angel, beating in the void his luminous wings in vain').

Essays in Criticism A quarterly journal founded by the Oxford critic F. W. BATESON in 1951, partly in emulation of and partly in rivalry with the Cambridge-based *SCRUTINY*. The title is borrowed from MATTHEW ARNOLD. T. S. ELIOT and J. M. MURRY were among the first contributors, and since then *Essays in Criticism* has published articles by WILLIAM EMPSON, DONALD DAVIE and many other leading literary critics.

Essays of Elia, The Miscellaneous essays by CHARLES LAMB, contributed under the pseudonym of Elia to *THE LONDON MAGAZINE* between August 1820 and December 1823, beginning with 'Recollections of the South-Sea House'. They contain much observant social and literary criticism, and are also prized for the reminiscences of childhood ('Christ's Hospital Five and Thirty Years Ago', 'Blakesmoor in H--shire') and for the descriptions of characters from Lamb's wide range of acquaintances. Also included are the purely fanciful or melancholy exercises which have become famous anthology pieces: 'Dream Children', 'A Dissertation upon Roast Pig' and 'A Chapter on Ears'.

The first collection of *The Essays of Elia* was published in 1823; the remainder appeared, with other essays, as *The Last Essays of Elia* (1833).

Esson, (Thomas) Louis (Buvelot) 1879–1943 Australian playwright. Educated in Melbourne, he left university without a degree and became a journalist. More significant to his writing was his interest in the Australian outback. A political comedy, *The Time is Not Yet Ripe* (1912), was given an amateur performance, and Esson became one of the founders of a distinct Australian drama. The Pioneer Players, which he helped establish and run in Melbourne from 1922 to 1926, staged his second full-length play, *The Bride of Gospel Place* (1926). This, like the one-act *The Woman Tamer* (1910), is set in Melbourne. Esson's outback plays include the full-length *Mother and Son* (1923) and two one-act tragedies, *Dead Timber* (1911) and *The Drovers* (1920).

Essop, Ahmed 1931– South African short-story writer and novelist. Born at Dahbel, near Surat in India, he went to South Africa in 1934, studied at the University of South Africa and taught at schools in Johannesburg. He is now a full-time writer. His fiction, combining a remarkable range and variety of tones, is located almost entirely in Johannesburg, usually in the Indian areas of Fordsburg, Vrededorp and the apartheid-created Lenasia. He has published two volumes of stories: *The Hajji and Other Stories* (1978), winner of the Olive Schreiner Prize, and *Noorjehan and Other Stories* (1990). *The Visitation*

(1980) is a satirical yet partly sympathetic novel about a rich merchant, Emil Sufi, liberated by painful experiences from his material obsessions. *The Emperor* (1984) is about the tragi-comic rise and fall of the headmaster of a South African Indian school, destroyed by an authoritarianism which feeds on the bureaucratic attitudes generated by apartheid.

estates satire A medieval satirical tradition expounding the characteristics, duties and failings of the different social 'estates' or classes. Society is divided by function (often occupation) rather than social rank, typical categories being pope, priest, prince, knight, nun and wife. All the religious classes were placed at the top of the hierarchy, all classes of laymen beneath them, and all classes of women at the bottom. Characteristics were attributed to each social group, and the estates were criticized for failing to fulfil their duties to each other and society as a whole. Works dealing explicitly and solely in estates satire are mostly Latin, but many other works use material from the tradition, for example, *Piers Plowman*, the General Prologue to *The Canterbury Tales*, *Mum and the Sothsegger* and *Wynnere and Wastoure*.

Esther Waters A novel by Georgde Moore, first published in 1894. Strongly influenced by French literature and particularly by the naturalism of Zola, it gave the author his first great success and is still usually regarded as his most important work.

Esther Waters is a religious girl, a member of the Plymouth Brethren, who leaves home to escape from a drunken stepfather. She goes into service at Woodview, the home of the Barfield family whose main interest is their racing stables; the exception is Mrs Barfield, who – like Esther – belongs to the Plymouth sect. Esther, aged only 17, is easily seduced by the footman, William Latch, who then deserts her. Esther is dismissed, and only Mrs Barfield tries to be kind. She bears a son and endures a bitter and humiliating struggle to rear him. Esther is admired by a respectable man, a Salvationist, who wants to marry her; but William Latch comes back into her life and for their son's sake she marries him. William makes a good husband and father; but he is a publican in Dean Street in Soho as well as a bookmaker, and his constant attendance at races ruins his health. Further misfortune comes when he is suspected of using the pub as an unlicensed betting centre and the house is closed. William dies, leaving his family penniless; but Esther's son is soon able to fend for himself and at the close of the novel Esther returns to Woodview. Mrs Barfield, now an impoverished widow, lives alone in a corner of the old house, and there at last Esther finds peace.

Ethan Frome A novel by Edith Wharton, published in 1911. On a poor farm in western Mas-sachusetts Ethan Frome struggles to wrest a living from the soil. His slatternly wife Zeena (Zenobia) is a whining hypochondriac and spends much of Ethan's hard-earned money on quack remedies. Her cousin, Mattie Silver, is left destitute when her parents die and the farm is the only place she can go. Ethan and Mattie are attracted to each other and Zeena's jealousy is aroused. After a year Zeena drives Mattie off the farm to make way for a hired woman, and Ethan takes her to the railroad station through the snow. Realizing that he cannot bear to part from her, he causes an accident that he hopes will kill them, but the pair survive the crash and spend the remainder of their lives as invalids under the care of Zeena.

Etherege, Sir George c. 1635–91 Playwright. Little is known of Etherege's early life. He came from an Oxfordshire family of modest means and may well have spent some time in France. Certainly his knowledge of French manners and literature was sufficient to justify such an assumption. His work profoundly influenced the development of Restoration comedy.

Etherege's first play, *The Comical Revenge* (1664), was sufficiently successful to win him a place in society. He entered whole-heartedly into the rakish world of Charles II's London, had a daughter by the actress Elizabeth Barry and included the dissolute Earl of Rochester among his intimates. His second play, *She Would If She Could* (1668), is more characteristically a Restoration comedy than his first. It won him further acclaim and may have contributed to his being appointed secretary to the ambassador to Constantinople from 1668–71. The responsibility did nothing to reform him and he resumed his wild life in London on his return to England. His last and greatest play, *The Man of Mode* (1676), is a fully fledged Restoration comedy, more intolerant of dullness and affectation than of libertinism.

On the death of Charles II in 1685, Etherege was appointed ambassador to the Imperial Court at Ratisbon. He may have been knighted in the same year. The letters he wrote to friends in England, first collected in *The Letterbook of Sir George Etherege* (1928), are among the best of the period. A fuller selection of *Letters* (1974) and a volume of slight but elegant *Poems* (1963), together with the three plays, complete the literary output of one of the leaders of Restoration taste.

Ettrick Shepherd, The See Hogg, James.

Eugene Aram A novel by Edward Bulwer Lytton, published in 1832, and based on a true story. Aram is a high-minded scholar who, some 14 years earlier, had been driven by extreme poverty to become an accomplice to a murder, and is now racked by guilt. He falls in love but is denounced on his wedding day and sentenced to death. As a sensational example of

NEWGATE FICTION the book was furiously condemned in some quarters as immoral, but it confirmed Bulwer Lytton's standing, in the year of SIR WALTER SCOTT's death, as England's most popular novelist.

Euphues: or, The Anatomy of Wit A prose romance by LYLY, probably first published in 1578. With its equally popular sequel, *Euphues and His England* (1580), it gave its name to the exaggeratedly elegant style known as EUPHUISM. Lyly probably found the word 'euphues', Greek for 'well-endowed', in ASCHAM's *The Schoolmaster*.

The slight plot of *The Anatomy of Wit* is borrowed from Boccaccio, though it is also a variation on the popular Reformation story of the Prodigal Son who wastes his talents. Euphues, a young Athenian, leaves his native city (which may represent Oxford) to visit Naples (which may represent London). There he makes the acquaintance of Philautus and they pledge friendship. Unfortunately, Euphues takes the place of Philautus in the affections of Lucilla. On his return to Naples Philautus discovers this and reproaches Euphues, and there is a mutual exchange of letters. Euphues visits Lucilla only to find that he in turn has been replaced by Curio. Lucilla's father berates her, Euphues and his friend are reconciled, and the book ends with a series of letters. These events are only the skeleton of the book, which is fleshed out with discourses on wit, religion and education, all expressed with the most elaborate rhetorical artifices. Above all, Lyly treats the familiar Renaissance themes of love, friendship and the possible conflicts between them.

In the sequel, *Euphues and His England*, Euphues and Philautus visit England and the narrative chronicles Philautus's love-affairs. Lyly is fervent in praise of English virtue, and especially the virtue of the English gentlewoman. Euphues ends the story by returning to Greece and entering a monastery, while Philautus gets married. GREENE, who dabbled in most things, attempted a continuation in *Euphues, His Censure of Philautus* (1587).

euphuism A prose style fashionable in the late 16th century. It takes its name from LYLY's *EUPHUES*, where it first appears in full flower, though there are earlier hints of it in *The Dial of Princes* by SIR THOMAS NORTH and in GEORGE PETTIE's *Petite Palace of Pettie His Pleasure*. Its characteristic quality is an obvious and exaggerated artifice complete with the figures and 'flowers' of rhetoric, and a fondness for *sententiae* (moral maxims). Lyly has an especial liking for allusions to myth and history, often couched in what SIDNEY called 'strange similes', and for balanced antitheses reinforced by alliteration: 'Here may you see, gentlemen, the falsehood in fellowship, the fraud in friendship, the painted sheath with the leaden dagger, the fair words that make fools vain.'

Europeans, The A novel by HENRY JAMES, published serially in *THE ATLANTIC MONTHLY* (July–October 1878), and as a volume, in slightly revised form, later that same year.

Felix Young, an artist, and his sister Eugenia, the wife of a German nobleman who is about to renounce her for reasons of state, come from Europe to Massachusetts to visit their relatives, the Wentworths. Though concerned about the 'peculiar influence' these European cousins may exert on his family, the elder Wentworth establishes Felix and Eugenia in a nearby house. Relations between the cousins become friendly. Wentworth's daughter Gertrude falls in love with Felix, and he with her; his son Clifford becomes infatuated with Eugenia, who is looking for a wealthy husband and welcomes his attentions. Gertrude, however, already has an 'understanding' with Mr Brand, the Unitarian minister. Although she does not in fact care for Mr Brand, her sister Charlotte does. Robert and Lizzie Acton further complicate matters: Robert is drawn – but not unreservedly – to Eugenia; Lizzie hopes to win Clifford Wentworth.

At the end of the novel, Mr Wentworth consents to the marriage of Felix and Gertrude; Clifford, having overcome his infatuation for Eugenia, marries Lizzie Acton; Mr Brand discovers that he cares not for Gertrude but for Charlotte, and marries her. Robert Acton and Eugenia do not, however, make a fourth happy couple. Though attracted to her, Acton cannot overcome his scruples about her past and about the calculating way in which she uses her feminine wiles. Eugenia returns to Europe alone.

Eusden, Laurence 1688–1730 POET LAUREATE from 1718 until his death. Eusden was a writer of minor verse whose work is dwarfed by the achievements of contemporaries like POPE, who assigned him a place in the realms of Dullness in his reductive satire on contemporary culture, *THE DUNCIAD*.

Eustace Diamonds, The A novel by ANTHONY TROLLOPE, the third of his PALLISER NOVELS, serialized in *THE FORTNIGHTLY REVIEW* from July 1871 to February 1873, and published in three volumes in 1873.

The beautiful but shallow Lizzie Eustace is left a wealthy widow when her husband of a few months, Sir Florian Eustace, dies. The plot centres on the Eustace family diamonds which Lizzie claims belong to her, a claim denied by the family lawyer, Mr Camperdown. She turns for protection first to Lord Fawn, a dull but ambitious politician in need of money, and they become engaged, Fawn all the while insisting, however, that she return the diamonds. She turns next to her cousin Frank Greystock, another poor man with political ambitions, and he becomes attracted to Lizzie and her fortune while visiting her at her Scottish castle, despite his existing engagement to Lucy Morris, governess to the Fawn family. On the journey south Lizzie's hotel bedroom is robbed at Carlisle, and she claims that the diamonds have been stolen, although in fact she has secreted them under her pillow. But when her London home is robbed, and the diamonds taken in earnest, her dishonesty becomes apparent in the subsequent police investigations.

Lord Fawn breaks his engagement and she loses the disillusioned Frank, who finally marries Lucy. Rejected even by the Byronic Lord George Carruthers, to whose 'Corsair' charms she has been attracted, Lizzie ends by marrying the shady Mr Emilius, a converted Jew turned fashionable preacher. *The Eustace Diamonds* is one of Trollope's darker novels, a study in moral duplicity with a plot that owes something to WILKIE COLLINS's *THE MOONSTONE*.

Evan Harrington A novel by GEORGE MEREDITH, published in 1861.

Although the death of Melchisedec ('the Great Mel') Harrington – an exquisitely mannered tailor once mistaken for a marquis – occurs on the first page of the book, his elegant ghost hovers over the subsequent narrative. Melchisedec had four children: Caroline (now married to Major Strike), Harriet (wife of the rich brewer Andrew Cogglesby), Louisa (wife of the Portuguese Count de Saldar) and Evan, the only son. The sisters – particularly Louisa – are dedicated to furthering his fortunes by having him marry the eligible Rose Jocelyn of Beckley Court. Although he comes to love Rose, Evan wants to clear his late father's name of debt. Countless sisterly sacrifices are made to conceal their humble background while Evan, who has turned tailor, through a characteristically Meredithian twist of plot falls heir to Beckley Court. Together with misleading letters, renunciation of the estate by Evan (which earns him 'the soul of a gentleman') and other conveniences allowed by the Comic Muse, the novel concludes with the hero gaining both Rose and a diplomatic post in Naples.

Evan Harrington is too long to sustain its attenuated narrative, though the story does gain momentum in its later stages. Nevertheless, the book remains notable for its crispness of language, comedy, analysis of snobbery and the lively characterization of lesser figures like Jack Raikes, George Uploft and Mr Parsley, as well as the striking effect of Louisa, the wily Countess.

Evangeline: *A Tale of Acadie* A narrative poem by HENRY WADSWORTH LONGFELLOW, published in 1847. It is set in Acadia, a province of Canada roughly corresponding to present-day Nova Scotia. In unrhymed hexameters, the story describes the frustrated love of Evangeline Bellefontaine and Gabriel Lajeunesse, whom the French and Indian Wars have separated. Gabriel and his father, a blacksmith, make their way to Louisiana. Evangeline follows them and eventually finds Gabriel's father, but he has become separated from his son. Together they fruitlessly search for Gabriel. After many years, Evangeline, prematurely aged, becomes a Sister of Mercy in Philadelphia. During a pestilence there she recognizes a dying old man as her lover. She dies of grief and they are buried together.

Eve of St Agnes, The A narrative poem in SPENSERIAN STANZAS by KEATS, written in 1819, published in 1820. The tale's setting is a night of dancing and revelry in a medieval mansion on a freezing winter's evening in the distant past. Madeline has learned that on this night, St Agnes's Eve, a virgin may be granted a vision of her lover, and she prepares to leave the ball and retire to bed. Unknown to her, her lover Porphyro, a son of her family's deadliest enemy, has stolen unseen into the castle, where he pours out his heart to Angela, a sympathetic old 'beldame'. He persuades her to hide him in a place in Madeline's apartments from where he can observe her undressing for sleep, and to prepare an exotic supper for two. Enticed by his soft lute-playing, Madeline emerges from her dreams to find him by her bedside. Silently they slip through the sleeping halls and 'away into the storm', leaving old Angela to die 'palsy-twitched' and the Baron to his dreams of 'many a woe'.

LEIGH HUNT's judgement that it was 'the most delightful and complete specimen' of Keats's genius is shared by many of the poem's modern readers. It is an extraordinarily skilful Romantic montage of popular legend, SHAKESPEARE's *ROMEO AND JULIET*, motifs from CHAUCER and Boccaccio, and the atmospherics of Gothic romance. The narrative is fast moving, at times even dramatic; most striking of all, however, is the richness and radiant sensuousness of the imagery, particularly in the central bed-chamber sequence.

Evelina: *or, A Young Lady's Entrance into the World* An EPISTOLARY NOVEL by FANNY BURNEY, published anonymously in 1778. Her first published work, it was written, she said, for 'private recreation' and printed 'for a frolic, to see how a production of her own would figure in that author-like form'. Its germ lay in an early story, apparently entitled 'The History of Caroline Evelyn', which followed the unhappy career of Evelina's mother. Fanny Burney destroyed it along with other juvenile works.

After her mother's death, Evelina was brought up by the Rev. Arthur Villars in the rural seclusion of Berry Hill. When she reaches 17 the sensible Lady Howard declares that 'it is time that she should see something of the world. When young people are too rigidly sequestered from it, their lively and romantic imaginations paint it to them as a paradise of which they have been beguiled; but when they are shown it properly, and in due time, they see it such as it really is, equally shared by pain and pleasure, hope and disappointment.' In seven months (and three volumes) Evelina undergoes her education in self-knowledge, prudence and discretion under the tutelage of Villars, Lady Howard and the judicious Lord Orville, whom she eventually marries.

The novel rapidly became a fashionable success, sold many copies, and attracted the admiration of EDMUND BURKE, JOSHUA REYNOLDS and DR JOHNSON, who said that it gave the impression of 'long experience and deep and intimate knowledge of the world'. The work still offers sophistication and sensibility, an accomplished and witty style, and vivid portraits of the undesirable relatives, Sir John Belmont, Mme Duval and the Branghtons, who embarrass and disconcert the heroine.

Eveling, (Harry) Stanley 1925– Playwright. He teaches philosophy at the University of Edinburgh. *The Lunatic, the Secret Sportsman and the Woman Next Door* (1968) and *Dear Janet Rosenberg, Dear Mr Kooning* (1969) were made popular by their intelligent dialogue and striking imagery. Though he writes in many styles and often in a comic vein, Eveling is connected to the THEATRE OF THE ABSURD by his sense of meaninglessness and despair. *Caravaggio, Buddy* (1972), *Shivvers* (1974) and *The Dead of Night* (1975) are about suicide. *Union Jack (and Bonzo)* (1973) is a black FARCE about a Boy Scout camp and a serial killer.

Evelyn, John 1620–1706 Diarist and early Fellow of the Royal Society. The son of Richard Evelyn, a Surrey gentleman, he was educated at Balliol College, Oxford, and travelled extensively on the Continent. He was a Royalist supporter, a civilized and elegant-minded man of means, who left England after the execution of Charles I in 1649, to avoid living under the Commonwealth. During his years of exile he conducted a correspondence with Charles II, returning to England in 1652 for the rest of the Interregnum. Following the death of his son at the age of five, Evelyn translated from the Greek *The Golden Book of St John Chrysostom* (1659), a work on the education of children; the 'Epistle Dedicatory' is an early example of the evocative powers of his style, 'My tears mingle so fast with my inke that I am forced to breake off here, and be silent'.

Evelyn was elected one of the first Fellows of the Royal Society, formed shortly after the Restoration, and he interested himself in a wide variety of topics with the enthusiasm of an intelligent amateur. In 1661 he published *Fumifugium: or, The Inconvenience of the Air and Smoke of London Dissipated*, proposing certain practical remedies for metropolitan pollution, none of which was implemented by the authorities. The following year he wrote *Sculptura*, a book on engraving. The Royal Society was consulted by the Navy Office (where, coincidentally, Evelyn's friend SAMUEL PEPYS was working) over the impending shortage of timber for shipbuilding, and Evelyn was allocated the problem. The result was his influential and informed *Sylva: or, A Discourse of Forest Trees* (1664), a manual of arboriculture. After the Great Fire of 1666, he submitted some constructive proposals for the rebuilding of the capital, and he also wrote a treatise on *Navigation and Commerce* (1674), as well as essays on topics from vineyards to medals.

He is best remembered, though, for his diary. Its inevitable comparison with the diaries secretly kept at the same time by Pepys is not a helpful one, since the two documents are a totally different pair of records. Evelyn's annals are never risqué nor intimate: the record covers the whole span of his life, and started as a series of jottings and memoirs which he began to organize in 1660. The resulting volume, *Kalendarium*, reveals little about the personality of its author – a carefully remote figure – but offers a fascinating account of the principal events of his lifetime, and some penetrating character sketches of public figures. He frequently draws material from contemporary publications to illustrate events, but after 1684 the document becomes more like a diary proper.

It was not published until 1818. The papers had remained unrecognized by generations of Evelyn's family, but were rediscovered by the antiquarian William Upcott and edited by William Bray as *The Memoirs of John Evelyn*. The immediate interest in Evelyn led directly to the rediscovery of Pepys's diaries in Cambridge shortly thereafter. The definitive edition, by E. S. de Beer, was published in 1955 and runs to six volumes.

Every Man in His Humour A comedy by BEN JONSON, first performed in 1598 by the Lord Chamberlain's Men (KING'S MEN). SHAKESPEARE was a member of the company and his name appears on a surviving cast-list of the play. In a revised version published in 1616, Jonson changed the names and the setting from Italy to London. The great popularity of the play created a fashion for 'humours' comedy (see WIT). Characters whose behaviour is governed by a single dominant emotion or 'humour', grotesquely obsessive, became familiar figures on the contemporary stage, though few writers could match the relish with which Jonson exhibited and exploited the foibles of the foolish.

The merchant, Kitely, has a younger brother who brings his boisterous friends to the house. Dame Kitely is young and pretty and her husband is jealous, thinking that his brother's friends have designs on her. One of the young men, Edward Knowell, suffers from his father's excessive concern for his moral welfare; he woos Kitely's pretty sister, Bridget. An associate of the group of young men is Captain Bobadill, an old soldier who is both vain and cowardly, forever boasting of his valour. Knowell's servant, Brainworm, maliciously plays on Kitely's jealousy and Dame Kitely's credulity to bring about a confrontation between them in a house where each believes the other present for an immoral purpose. Captain Bobadill's pretensions are exposed. Misunderstandings are resolved at the end by Justice Clement, a shrewd observer of human folly, and Knowell wins Bridget's hand.

Every Man out of His Humour An almost plotless comedy by BEN JONSON, first performed at the GLOBE in 1599. Obviously intended to capitalize on the success of EVERY MAN IN HIS HUMOUR, it is a much less attractive piece, though certain foolish 'humours' are nicely hit off in Fungoso, Sogliardo and Sir Fastidious Brisk, and Jonson's adversaries in the war of the theatres, MARSTON and DEKKER, are waspishly portrayed as Clove and Olive.

Everyman This best known of all English MORALITY PLAYS dates from around the end of the 15th century. It is closely related to a Flemish play, first printed in 1495. *Everyman* survives in four versions, two of them fragmentary. It combines rhymed couplets and stanzaic forms that may seem rhythmically crude at times but rarely impede the dramatic movement.

The play details the progress of its hero from complacency through fear and despair at the prospect of his death to a Christian resignation that is the prelude to redemption. Seeking for companions on his last journey, he finds only one, Good Deeds, prepared to accompany him all the way to the grave.

Ewart, Gavin (Buchanan) 1916– Poet. He was born in London and educated at Wellington College and Christ's College, Cambridge, where he read Classics and English and was taught by F. R. LEAVIS and I. A. RICHARDS. After serving in North Africa and Italy during World War II, he worked briefly in publishing and for a longer spell in advertising, becoming a freelance writer in 1971. Ewart contributed to GEOFFREY GRIGSON's *New Verse* at the age of 17. A skilful writer of light, comic verse and PARODY, he has published a succession of volumes culminating in *Collected Poems* (1991). They include *Poems and Songs* (1939), the erotic *Pleasures of the Flesh* (1966), *The Collected Ewart 1933–80* (1980), *Other People's Clerihews* (1983) and *Cluster of Clerihews* (1986) and *Penultimate Poems* (1989). *The Learned Hippopotamus* (1988) is a book of children's poetry. He has also edited *The Penguin Book of Light Verse* (1980).

Ewing, Juliana (Horatia) 1841–85 Writer of CHILDREN'S LITERATURE. Born Juliana Gatty, the oldest daughter of MARGARET GATTY, she frequently told stories to her younger siblings before getting into print at the age of 20 in CHARLOTTE M. YONGE's magazine *The Monthly Packet*. In 1866 her mother launched her own children's journal, *Aunt Judy's Magazine*, to which Juliana contributed a serial later published as *Mrs Overtheway's Remembrances* (1869), a charming family story told with conviction and a rare feeling of accuracy for the normal ups and downs of family life. A succeeding novel, *Jan of the Windmill* (1876), told the story of a foundling later to become a celebrated artist. But perhaps Mrs Ewing is best remembered now by association, in that *The Brownies and Other Tales* (1870) influenced Sir Robert Baden-Powell and gave him the name for the junior section of the Girl Guide Movement. Following marriage and a posting with her husband overseas, Mrs Ewing died prematurely after a long period of ill health. Although little read today, she was an important figure in the history of children's literature, helping begin the long process of rejecting didacticism in favour of unsentimental realism.

Examiner, The A weekly journal begun in August 1710, as an instrument of Tory propaganda, by ROBERT HARLEY with the help of BOLINGBROKE, FRANCIS ATTERBURY, MATTHEW PRIOR and other willing Tory pens. SWIFT edited it anonymously from 2 November 1710 to 14 June 1711, contributing 33 issues which provoked its opposing journal, Arthur Mainwaring's *Medley*, to accuse *The Examiner* of working 'a World of Mischief'. Swift went on to write more propaganda, THE CONDUCT OF THE ALLIES, DELARIVIÈRE MANLEY replaced him as editor. *The Examiner* survived until 1716, though issued sporadically towards the end of its life.

Examiner, The A radical weekly magazine founded in 1808 by LEIGH HUNT and his brother John. It played an important role in bringing the poetry of KEATS and SHELLEY before the public, thus identifying Hunt and his friends in the eyes of their detractors as the COCKNEY SCHOOL of poetry. A libel against the Prince Regent was punished with a heavy fine and two years' imprisonment for the brothers; Leigh Hunt continued to edit the journal from his prison cell. *The Examiner* survived until 1881.

Excursion, The A poem in nine books by WILLIAM WORDSWORTH, published in 1814. As early as 1798 Wordsworth had planned what he describes in his preface as a 'philosophical poem, containing views of man, nature, and society, and to be entitled *The Recluse*, as having for its principal subject the sensations and opinions of a poet living in retirement'. THE PRELUDE was originally conceived as a 'sort of portico' to *The Recluse*. Though *The Excursion* was the only part of the main poem that Wordsworth completed, it is still his longest work.

The poet travels with a Wanderer; through him he meets the Solitary, a recent enthusiast for the French

Revolution and now dispirited by events in France. The Solitary is reproved for his lack of faith and loss of confidence in man. A Pastor enters the scene, offering the consolations of virtue and faith and illustrating his sermon with accounts of the lives of those buried in his churchyard. At the Pastor's house the Wanderer offers his conclusions, philosophical and political. The last two books present Wordsworth's thoughts on the Industrial Revolution and the havoc it played with the lives of the poor. He makes a strong plea for the education of children.

exemplum A short narrative tale illustrating a moral point. Exempla frequently appear in medieval didactic works (such as *HANDLYNGE SYNNE*) and in homilies or sermons. They are sometimes employed in secular works, like GOWER'S *CONFESSIO AMANTIS*.

Exeter Book, The A collection of Old English poems compiled *c.* 975 and donated by Bishop Leofric (d. 1072) to Exeter Cathedral, where it remains. It includes some of the most important surviving poems from the period: *CHRIST, DEOR, JULIANA, THE PHOENIX, THE SEAFARER, THE WANDERER, WIDSITH, THE WHALE, WULF AND EADWACER, THE HUSBAND'S MESSAGE, THE WIFE'S COMPLAINT*, and a collection of riddles.

Exodus An Old English poem preserved in the Junius manuscript (see JUNIUS, FRANCIS) which retells the story of the Exodus from Egypt. The biblical narrative is transformed into a vivid and evocative account which does not follow the source in all its details. It was at one time incorrectly attributed to CAEDMON.

Expedition of Humphry Clinker, The See *HUMPHRY CLINKER, THE EXPEDITION OF*.

expressionism A term coined by the French painter Julien-Auguste Hervé in 1901 to distinguish his painting from impressionism, and later applied to movements in the other arts. The first English dictionary definition was 'a style of painting in which the artist seeks to express emotional experience rather than impressions of the physical world; hence a similar style or movement in literature, drama, music, etc.'. That definition points to one widespread use of expressionism, as the antithesis of REALISM. In painting it usefully distinguished painters such as Van Gogh and Matisse, who forcefully conveyed their private experience, from the early impressionists who tried to paint external reality. Edvard Munch's *The Scream* is perhaps the most readily identifiable expressionist painting.

As a literary term expressionism has most often been applied to the theatre, describing Central European, especially German, productions between 1907 (the date of Oskar Kokoschka's *Murder, the Hope of Women*) and the mid 1920s. These plays, by Reinhard Sorge, Walter Hasenclever, Georg Kaiser, Ernst Toller and others, were marked by their non-realistic form and highly personal, idiosyncratic view of life. The plays often feature an autobiographical protagonist involved in a quest for his essential identity, other characters being reduced to stereotypes or nameless designations, The Man, The Father, etc. Short, often static scenes without causal links and staccato, telegrammatic dialogue interspersed with long rhapsodies characterize the formal structure. In Germany it was a drama of protest, young men rebelling against the proprieties of family life in the pre-war empire, boldly tackling taboo subjects like incest and parricide. Expressionist plays demanded a highly visual production style and a new generation of actors specializing in broad gesture and strident voice. Retrospectively, the term expressionist was applied to the plays of Buchner, Strindberg and Wedekind. In Germany expressionism soon developed a politically radical and Marxist temper and evolved into the 'epic' theatre of Brecht. German expressionist novelists included Franz Werfel, Max Brod and Karl Kraus.

It was mainly through the theatre that expressionism travelled from Germany. Its most successful exponents in America were EUGENE O'NEILL, particularly in *THE EMPEROR JONES* (1920) and *The Hairy Ape* (1922), and ELMER RICE in *THE ADDING MACHINE* (1923), although the experiments of THORNTON WILDER, TENNESSEE WILLIAMS and ARTHUR MILLER also owe something to expressionism. The second act of SEAN O'CASEY'S *THE SILVER TASSIE* (1929), set at the front during World War I, is overtly expressionist in style, while the rest of the play, set in Ireland, is realist. O'Casey's later plays make use of expressionist method.

The term has also been applied to film, music and architecture as well as poetry (such as parts of T. S. ELIOT'S *THE WASTE LAND*, for example) and some fiction (such as the Nighttown episode of JOYCE'S *ULYSSES*).

extravaganza A form of 19th-century theatrical spectacle. The finest exponent, J. R. PLANCHÉ, based his work on well-known myths or fairy-tales, embellishing them with punning rhyming couplets and frequent songs. They were travesties rather than satires, good-humoured to the point of blandness. In subject-matter and reliance on lavish visual effects they shadow the rise of the English PANTOMIME.

Eyeless in Gaza A novel by ALDOUS HUXLEY, published in 1936. The title and epigraph are from MILTON'S *SAMSON AGONISTES*: 'Eyeless in Gaza at the Mill with slaves'.

Largely autobiographical, it charts the career of Anthony Beavis from early childhood in 1902 to his discovery of mysticism in 1935. Through a series of flashbacks, which occupy entire chapters ('August 30th 1933', 'November 6th 1902', 'June 17th 1912', etc.) key moments in his life are interwoven. Several secondary characters are similarly observed as their relationships with Beavis change over the years, including Brian Foxe (a sensitive and intellectual schoolfriend who later commits suicide), Hugh Ledwidge and his wife Helen (who becomes Beavis's lover), and Mark Staithes (who in adulthood turns to Marxism).

The main burden of the novel is to reveal Beavis's increasing sense of the futility and meaninglessness of his life – and by extension, the meaninglessness of contemporary Western society. Accompanying Staithes to Mexico to join a revolution ('Simply to be shaken out of negativity') Beavis's whole life is changed. Staithes loses a leg after a minor wound becomes infected, and the doctor who treats him, an anthropologist named James Miller, introduces Beavis to mysticism and pacifism: 'Frenzy of evil and separation. In peace there is unity. Unity with other lives. Unity with all being.'

Ezekiel, Nissim 1924– Indian poet. He was born in Bombay. He and A. K. RAMANUJAN are probably the finest Indian poets in English. Both are quietly explorative, speculative and meditative, yet in both there is a wholly undogmatic religious strain, Ezekiel's Judaic, Ramanujan's Hindu. Reacting deliberately against the oratorical transcendentalism of the verse of Aurobindo Ghose (1872–1950), Ezekiel cultivated a direct, often conversational English to convey his predominant moods of questioning and scepticism. His early verse, in *A Time to Change* (1951), *Sixty Poems* (1953) and *The Third* (1958), is rational and reflective (even when the mode is passionate), much concerned with failures in human relationships and personal living, so that 'time is only meditation,/ Prayer and poetry, poetry and prayer'. Some poems express the desire for simple domestic happiness as the background to self-examination, but later verse declares that happiness impossible, even as the need for self-discovery intensifies. Restrained, tautly articulated confession of personal failure, even though apprehended as part of a whole generation's collapse of faiths, makes the poems in *The Unfinished Man* (1960) the most impressive he has written, though he continued to produce finely turned satirical and confessional poems in *The Exact Name* (1965) and *Hymns in Darkness* (1976). In *Latter-Day Psalms* (1982), which includes poems from earlier volumes, he acknowledges that a vestigial religious precipitate lies suspended within his low-key scepticism; nine Old Testament Psalms are ironically adapted to these times. University teacher, art critic, and literary editor, he has also published *Three Plays* (1969).

Faber, Frederick William 1814–63 Poet and hymn-writer. He was born at Calverley in the West Riding of Yorkshire and educated at Shrewsbury and Harrow schools and at Balliol College, Oxford. He became a scholar of University College, Oxford, in 1834 and a fellow in 1837. He was ordained in 1839 and appointed rector of Elton in Huntingdonshire in 1841. Having come under the powerful influence of J. H. NEWMAN, he was received into the Roman Catholic church in 1845 and joined the Oratorian order in 1848. Faber established the London Oratory in 1849. His volumes of verse include *The Styrian Lake and Other Poems* (1842), *The Rosary and Other Poems* (1845) and *Hymns* (1848). His 150 *Collected Hymns* was published in 1862.

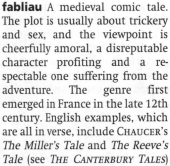

fable A short allegorical narrative relating the actions of anthropomorphized animals and objects and distinguished by a consciously derived moral. Traditionally the form is said to have originated with the work of Aesop, according to Herodotus a deformed Phrygian slave of the mid-6th century BC, but the earliest known fable is that of the hawk and the nightingale in the *Works and Days of Hesiod* (*c.* 8th century BC). The earliest attributable fables are the work of Phaedrus (*c.* AD 40) based on the lost collections of Demetrius Phalereus (4th century BC). The Latin fables of Phaedrus and the Greek Collection of Babritis (2nd or 3rd century AD) led to the works of Avianus (4th century) and Romulus (10th century) on which the medieval pseudo-Aesopian collections are based. The oldest of these is the work of Marie de France (12th century). Single fables appear in English in THE OWL AND THE NIGHTINGALE, PIERS PLOWMAN and CHAUCER's *Nun's Priest's Tale* (see THE CANTERBURY TALES). Fables were also used as religious EXEMPLA and collected as such. The Aesopian collections of ROBERT HENRYSON (*THE MORALL FABILLIS*) and WILLIAM CAXTON appeared at the end of the 15th century. Later writers of fables include JOHN DRYDEN, JOHN GAY, CHRISTOPHER SMART, WILLIAM COWPER, GEORGE ORWELL and JAMES THURBER.

Fable for Critics, A A verse SATIRE by JAMES RUSSELL LOWELL, first published anonymously in 1848. At a gathering on Olympus a critic is asked by Apollo to give an account of the state of letters in America. Those who come under his review are OLIVER WENDELL HOLMES, RALPH WALDO EMERSON, BRONSON ALCOTT, HENRY WADSWORTH LONGFELLOW, WILLIAM CULLEN BRYANT, MARGARET FULLER, WASHINGTON IRVING, JOHN GREENLEAF WHITTIER, EDGAR ALLAN POE, NATHANIEL HAWTHORNE and LOWELL himself. Among the most acute of the critical portraits are those of Emerson ('A Greek head on right Yankee shoulders, whose range/ Has Olympus for one pole, for t'other the Exchange'), Hawthorne ('There is Hawthorne, with genius so shrinking and rare/ That you hardly at first see the strength that is there'), and Poe ('There comes Poe, with his raven, like Barnaby Rudge,/ Three fifths of him genius and two fifths sheer fudge').

Fable of the Bees, The See MANDEVILLE, BERNARD DE.

fabliau A medieval comic tale. The plot is usually about trickery and sex, and the viewpoint is cheerfully amoral, a disreputable character profiting and a respectable one suffering from the adventure. The genre first emerged in France in the late 12th century. English examples, which are all in verse, include CHAUCER's *The Miller's Tale* and *The Reeve's Tale* (see THE CANTERBURY TALES) and the anonymous *DAME SIRITH*.

Faerie Queene, The EDMUND SPENSER's longest, most complex and greatest poem. The first three books appeared in 1590 with the author's epistle to his friend SIR WALTER RALEIGH, offering hints for interpretation of the work and indicating a plan of 12 books in all. The plan was apparently never completed. An edition of 1596 added Books IV–VI, while the first folio edition of the poem, published 10 years after Spenser's death, again added the two Mutability cantos, cautiously stating that they seemed to be part of some subsequent book of *The Faerie Queene*.

The main story is described in the letter to Raleigh as the quest of Arthur, who appears intermittently throughout, for Gloriana, who is one of the projections of Elizabeth in the poem as 'a most royal queen or empress'. The Queen also appears as Belphoebe, 'a most virtuous and beautiful lady', and in other guises.

Book I depicts the knight of holiness, Redcross, whose mission is to protect Una and free her besieged parents from a dragon. He is distracted by the magician Archimago and the disguised Duessa, imprisoned in the castle of the giant Orgoglio and freed by Arthur. As a penitent he is healed in the House of Celia, kills the dragon and finally marries Una. The book is concerned with the fate of the individual Christian seduced by false religion and finally triumphant with the assistance of truth. More topically it displays a Protestant bias against the falsehoods of Rome. Its incidents are heavily influenced by the Apocalypse and Protestant commentary on it.

In Book II Guyon is the patron of temperance. Having established a Christian framework of reference in Book I, Spenser draws some of the ideas in this book from classical sources. Guyon's adventures depict an Aristotelian definition of virtue as the mean between defect and excess, and his voyage to Acrasia's Bower of Bliss is strongly coloured by the story of Odysseus. Guyon's destruction of the Bower, which is a masterpiece of alluring sensuousness, has caused problems for those readers who see Spenser's poetic skill at odds with a moral intention.

In Book III both the narrative technique and the nature of the quest change. Britomart, the female knight of chastity, does not have the primary mission of destroying evil, but of finding Arthegall, her future husband. Interlaced with her story we find the beginnings of the stories of the estranged lovers, Amoret and Scudamour, Florimell and Marinell. Centrally placed in this book is the fruitful Garden of Adonis. At the end of the book Britomart frees Amoret from the enchanter Busirane, and in the 1590 edition Amoret and Scudamour were reunited. Spenser changed the ending in 1596, to delay the reunion until the next book.

Book IV is the book of friendship. It continues the stories of the separated lovers from the previous book and reunites most of them. Britomart and Arthegall pledge their love, but their story is not concluded until Book V. Book IV, meanwhile, is taken up with the story of Cambel and Triamond and their respective loves for Cambina and Canacee, a complicated quartet of relationships which suggests the book's theme of concord. Concord and union are embodied in the lovers of Book III finding each other and the magnificent description of the marriage of the Thames and the Medway which completes the book.

Book V is the most topical. It concerns the quest of Arthegall, the knight of justice, to destroy the giant Grantorto and to rescue Irena. Its incidents allude to Elizabeth's dealings with the Netherlands, France, Spain and Ireland. The trial of Duessa by Mercilla in canto ix provoked a complaint by James VI in 1596 that his mother, Mary Queen of Scots, was slandered in the person of Duessa. No action seems to have been taken, in spite of James's request that Spenser be tried and punished.

Book VI recounts the mission of Calidore, the knight of courtesy, to capture the Blatant Beast. Towards the end of the book, in a pastoral interlude, he stumbles across Colin Clout, the poet-shepherd of THE SHEPHEARDES CALENDER, piping to the three Graces dancing on Mount Acidale. Their triple movement of giving, receiving and giving again provides the pattern of courtesy for the book and its incidents. At the end of the book the Blatant Beast escapes from the world of the poem and threatens the poet's own work.

The Mutability cantos apparently contain no knight and no quest, and do not belong to the world of the preceding six books. They describe the threat of the giantess Mutability to claim the created universe

as being under her sway. She is arraigned on Arlo Hill before Nature herself who enigmatically pronounces that the giantess is herself evidence of constancy and stability, since change itself is a constant phenomenon. In the last two stanzas the poet finally turns from this 'state of life so tickle' to contemplate eternity. The poem reaches its tremendous climax in a prayer to 'the God of Sabaoth'.

No account of *The Faerie Queene* can do justice to its variety, complexity and richness, and any critical approach must be, in the words of one of Spenser's recent editors, 'only incomplete'. Even Spenser's letter to Raleigh 'expounding his whole intention' is not an infallible guide. In both its poetic style and thought *The Faerie Queene* is syncretic. Spenser blends heroic poetry with ALLEGORY. The heroic models for the poem are distantly the epics of Homer and Virgil, while Spenser's immediate Italian predecessors are Ariosto and Tasso, especially Ariosto's *Orlando Furioso*. Spenser's stanzaic form varies Ariosto's OTTAVA RIMA and adds a final ALEXANDRINE to produce the nine-lined Spenserian stanza which he bequeathed to later poets such as THOMSON and BYRON. The letter to Raleigh suggests an Aristotelian scheme of virtues, but the idealism of the poem and its assumption that the visible reflects abstractions has Platonic overtones. The poetic techniques include epic formulas, rhetorical devices and emblematic representations, and Spenser's sources for his imagery range from medieval descriptions of the virtues and vices to court pageants and MASQUES. Some 19th-century readers admired the visual element in *The Faerie Queene* but found its moralism distasteful. Spenser would not have understood, for the work is a sustained example of the speaking pictures intended to delight and instruct that SIDNEY talks of in his *APOLOGY FOR POETRY*.

Even so, the various meanings of the various pictures and narratives in *The Faerie Queene* are too dense to be easily unpacked. Thus Duessa may suggest falsehood, false religion, the Roman Catholic church, Mary Queen of Scots and many other meanings at different times, or more than one of those coexisting at one particular moment. As one medieval writer on allegory stated, the whole created world is a book and a picture and a mirror to mankind, offering divine truths. Spenser's imitation of a world offers images that multiply rather than delimit possible meanings.

Fainlight, Ruth 1931– Poet. Born to Anglo-Russian parents in New York, she has lived in Britain since she was 15. *A Forecast, A Fable* (1958) has been followed by, among other collections, *Cages* (1966), *Eighteen Poems from 1966*(1967), *To See the Matter Clearly and Other Poems* (1968), *The Region's Violence* (1976), *Another Full Moon* (1976), *Sybils and Others* (1980), *Two Wind Poems* (1980), *Climates* (1983), *Fifteen to Infinity* (1983), *Selected Poems* (1987) and *The Knot*

(1990). Determined to convey its meaning directly, her work is personal but not always introspective, returning repeatedly to the themes of isolation, the poet's role and the position of women. Fainlight has also translated the work of the Portuguese poet, Sophia de Mello Breyner Andresen, in *Navigaciones* (1988). She is married to ALAN SILLITOE.

Fair Em, the Miller's Daughter of Manchester
See SHAKESPEARE APOCRYPHA.

Fair Maid of Perth, The See *CHRONICLES OF THE CANONGATE.*

Fair Maid of the West, The A romantic comedy in two parts, of which the first may have been performed before 1610 and the second as late as 1630. The author was THOMAS HEYWOOD, whose best 'adventure' play it is.

The Earl of Essex's expedition is about to leave Plymouth for the Azores in 1597. Besse Bridges, 'the flower of Plymouth', is saved from molestation by Spencer; but he has the misfortune to kill the man while protecting Besse and has to flee the country. To provide for Besse he makes her the proprietress of the Windmill Tavern in Fowey. Spencer sails for the Azores, where his compulsive gallantry leads him to try and stop a quarrel; he is wounded and, apparently dying, sends a farewell to Besse, leaving all his property to her.

Besse fits out a ship to go to the Azores and bring Spencer's body back to England for burial. She finds him alive but a prisoner of the Spaniards. After many adventures, however, she rescues her gallant Spencer and they sail home to happiness.

Fair Penitent, The See *FATAL DOWRY*, THE.

Fair Quarrel, A A comedy by THOMAS MIDDLETON and WILLIAM ROWLEY, published in 1617 and probably performed a year or two earlier.

Captain Ager challenges a fellow officer to a duel; he regards a comment made by the other as an insult to his mother's virtue. Before the duel takes place Ager visits his mother and recounts the incident to her, wanting to be certain that his fight will be justified. His mother is indignant at first but when she realizes that a duel will follow she wants to avert the danger to her son and acknowledges the truth of the accusation.

Ager calls off the duel and his opponent brands him as a coward. He now has grounds for a confrontation and renews his challenge. He fights and wounds his opponent, who withdraws the charge of cowardice; the two are finally reconciled. The main story is supported by a bawdy sub-plot (probably the work of Rowley) but the principal interest of the drama lies in Ager's moral dilemma.

Fairburn, A(rthur) R(ex) D(ugard) 1904–57 New Zealand poet and personality. A journalist, radio scriptwriter and university tutor (in art history), he was a restless, ardent publicist for good causes (art galleries, New Zealand wine, good sewage) and a sharp satirist of small-minded prejudice. He began writing poems in the 1930s, sharing the determination of friends such as DENIS GLOVER and R. A. K. MASON to establish a distinctively local voice and form. He used some of Glover's BALLAD forms and much of Mason's IRONY, while establishing his own idiom in verse that ranged from the epigrammatic to the lyric. Longer poems, about New Zealand identity, are variable in quality but develop an intensity of mood and colour of phrase which his shorter poems can only occasionally match. His lyricism easily became sentimental, and his humour could be crude. His best writing, though, is coolly meditative, and offers memorable phrasings of gnomic power. It is found in *Dominion* (1938; reprinted in *Three Poems*, 1952) and *Strange Rendezvous* (1952). *Collected Poems* appeared posthumously in 1966, and a selection of his letters in 1984.

Fairfax, Edward ?1568–1635 Translator and poet. He was born in Leeds, the illegitimate son of Sir Thomas Fairfax of Denton, Yorkshire, and was probably educated at Clare Hall, Cambridge. He was acclaimed for his translation of Tasso's *Gerusalemme liberata*, retitled *Godfrey of Bulloigne* (1600). His other works, unpublished in his lifetime, include ECLOGUES, epitaphs and *Daemonologia*, an account of witchcraft as sensationally practised upon his own family in 1621–3.

Faithful Shepherdess, The A pastoral comedy by JOHN FLETCHER, first produced about 1608 and published about 1610. The play did not succeed on the stage and is generally regarded as too undramatic for revival, being lengthy and devoted to a formal theme too thin to be called a plot. Nevertheless, it is acknowledged as a poetic masterpiece and Fletcher's finest work in this vein.

The faithful shepherdess of the title is Clorin, who has vowed fidelity to her dead lover and lives by his grave. She is skilled in the use of herbs, which she gathers for the good of others. Thenot is attracted by her exemplary devotion. Amarillis loves Perigot, who loves Amoret. Repulsed by Perigot, Amarillis tries to seduce him by assuming the form of Amoret. Cloe, a wanton shepherdess, abandons the retiring Daphnis in favour of Alexis. The Sullen Shepherd is always ready to connive at the furtherance of lechery. Misunderstandings abound, while virtue and chastity are sorely tried.

Falconer, William 1732–69 Poet. Born in Edinburgh, the son of a barber, the young Falconer went to sea and was shipwrecked off the mainland of Greece. As a result, he wrote a narrative poem in rhyming couplets, *The Shipwreck*, published in 1762, which became popular and was admired by BURNS. It was reprinted in 1764 and 1769, the year in which Falconer first published *An Universal Dictionary of the Marine* and was then drowned when the frigate *Aurora*, on which he was serving, went down in a gale.

Falkland, Lucius Cary, 2nd Viscount 1610–43 Royalist. Falkland had a house at Great Tew, near Oxford, which became the meeting place for a circle of thinkers and writers including BEN JONSON, THOMAS CAREW and EDMUND WALLER. He entered Parliament in 1639, where he argued forcibly for the preservation of the reformed Anglican church, for moderation and for the ideal of a constitutional monarchy. He was Secretary of State in 1642 when the Civil War broke out, though his strong desire for peace had already led him into disagreement with Charles I. CLARENDON, who wrote a 'character' of Falkland, suggests that the outbreak of hostility left him permanently disillusioned. He was killed in the Battle of Newbury at the age of 33.

WILLIAM GODWIN, who probably learned of Falkland's career through Clarendon's account, borrowed his name for the flawed but noble character in his novel *CALEB WILLIAMS*.

Falkner, J(ohn) Meade 1858–1932 Writer of CHILDREN'S LITERATURE. Born in Wiltshire, the son of a clergyman, he was educated at Oxford before setting out on a successful career with the Armstrong Whitworth armaments company. He was a book collector as well as an author in his spare time. His first novel, *The Lost Stradivarius* (1895), was soon eclipsed by his extremely popular *Moonfleet* (1898), an adventure story about smuggling set in the 18th century and obviously indebted to STEVENSON's *TREASURE ISLAND*. Nothing Falkner wrote afterwards had the same power. The manuscript of his last novel was lost on a train journey.

Fall of Hyperion, The See *HYPERION*.

Fall of Princes, The A poem by JOHN LYDGATE in RHYME ROYAL and divided into nine books. Written between 1431 and 1439, it was the most popular and influential of his works. It tells the tragic stories of all the major historical and mythical figures from Adam to King John of France. The ultimate source is Boccaccio's *De casibus virorum illustrium* (1355–60) but Lydgate relied upon an expanded French prose version by Laurent de Premierfait, *Des Cas des nobles hommes et femmes* (1409). He adapted Premierfait, in particular adding 'envoys' apparently requested by his patron Humphrey, Duke of Gloucester, to offer a remedy to the ill fortune narrated. The philosophical

content of the poem is confused, especially in its varying portrayal of Fortune as indiscriminate and as the agent of divine retribution. The work constantly looks back to GEOFFREY CHAUCER, whose *Monk's Tale* (see *THE CANTERBURY TALES*) is its closest English analogue, mimicking the earlier poet's use of humour. The poem's value lies in its immense influence as a store of traditional and moral tales rather than in any intrinsic literary merit. It was also the inspiration for later works of a similar nature, most notably the *MIRROR FOR MAGISTRATES*.

Fallon, Padraic 1905–74 Irish poet and playwright. Born in Athenry, Co. Galway, and educated at St Joseph's College, Roscrea, he worked for many years as a customs official in Dublin and in Wexford. His verse plays for Radio Éireann, notably *Diarmuid and Grainne* (1950) and *The Vision of Mac Conglinne* (1953), treat legendary Gaelic material. They are considered among the most successful of their kind. Though Fallon published poems in a number of periodicals, he began to achieve recognition only with the collection *Poems* (1974) and remains unfairly overlooked. Neither his radio plays nor his writings for the stage have been published.

Fanny Hill *(The Memoirs of a Woman of Pleasure)* See CLELAND, JOHN.

Fanshawe, Sir **Richard** 1608–66 Translator and poet. The fifth son of Sir Henry Fanshawe of Ware Park, Hertfordshire, he was educated at Thomas Farnaby's renowned Cripplegate school and at Jesus College, Cambridge, where he showed promise as both classical scholar and poet. A staunch Royalist, Fanshawe was active in Charles I's service, was Secretary of War to the future Charles II and was taken prisoner at the battle of Worcester in 1651. After the Restoration, he was elected MP for Cambridge University and subsequently sent as ambassador to Portugal and then to Spain. In 1666, shortly after receiving news of his recall, he died of an ague in Madrid. His widow, Lady Ann Fanshawe (1625–80), piously recorded his adventurous life in her *Memoirs*, written in 1676 but not published in full until 1829.

Fanshawe's most important literary work consists of his translations, published in 1647 and 1655 respectively, of Guarini's *Il pastor fido*, the most important Renaissance pastoral drama, and of Camoens's *Lusiadas*, the great Portuguese national epic, of which Fanshawe's is the first English version. His versatility and resourcefulness as a translator can also be seen in *Selected Parts of Horace* (1652), Mendoza's *Querer por solo querer* and *Fiestas de Aranjuez* (1654, published 1671) and his version, in Spenserian stanzas, of the fourth book of Virgil's *Aeneid*, published in 1648, together with shorter poems and translations, in the second edition of *Il pastor fido. La fida pastora* (1658) is a Latin version of JOHN FLETCHER's play *THE FAITHFUL SHEPHERDESS*.

Far from the Madding Crowd A novel by THOMAS HARDY, first published serially in *THE CORNHILL MAGAZINE* between January and December 1874 and in volume form the same year. The first of Hardy's books to achieve popular success, it was also the first to use the name WESSEX. The title is taken from GRAY's *ELEGY WRITTEN IN A COUNTRY CHURCHYARD*.

Rejected by the capricious Bathsheba Everdene and financially ruined by his sheepdog driving his flock over a cliff, Gabriel Oak is forced off his land. Instrumental in quelling a fire at Bathsheba's farm, he is hired by her and soon rises from shepherd to bailiff. Unwisely, Bathsheba sends her neighbour, Farmer Boldwood, an anonymous valentine, which he takes so seriously as to fall in love with her. Meanwhile, the braggart Sergeant Troy has failed to marry the pregnant Fanny Robin because she went to the wrong church for the ceremony. Troy then courts Bathsheba and marries her secretly at Bath. But it is not a happy union and Troy, remorseful at Fanny's death in childbirth in the grim Casterbridge workhouse, leaves his wife and is mistakenly thought to be drowned; later he reappears as a member of a travelling circus in the West Country. However, believing him dead, Bathsheba accepts the frenetic attentions of Farmer Boldwood. Troy appears at their engagement party to claim his wife. This enrages Boldwood, who shoots Troy dead and then tries unsuccessfully to turn the gun on himself. Surrendering to the police, Boldwood is tried and condemned to execution, but his sentence is commuted to detention for life. Soon afterwards Oak, who has been overseeing the farms of Bathsheba and Boldwood, proposes for a second time and is accepted by her.

Farah, Nuruddin 1945– Somali novelist. Born in Baidoa, formerly part of Italian Somaliland, he has mastered at least five major languages as a consequence of his background and education: Somali, Amharic, Arabic, Italian and English. He went to school in Ethiopia and then attended the Istituto Magistrale di Mogadishu. His university education was in Chandigarh, India, and he then returned to Somalia where he taught in secondary schools and at the National University of Somalia. During this time he wrote in Somali as well as in English, following the creation of a written form of the Somali language in the early 1970s. He had already had published one novel in English, *From a Crooked Rib* (1970), the study of a girl's resistance to the traditional life she is expected to lead in a nomadic Somali community. It has been hailed as one of the best portrayals of a woman in African fiction. It has been followed by novels which present modern Somali society as a corrupt and repressive patriarchal tyranny: *A Naked Needle* (1976); *Sweet and Sour Milk* (1979), *Sardines* (1981) and *Close Sesame* (1983), which form a trilogy entitled *Variations on the Theme of an African Dictatorship*; and *Maps* (1984). Farah, who has not lived in Somalia since 1974, is increasingly seen as one of the major writers of Africa, as much for the quality of his characterization as for the acuity of his political and historical judgement.

farce A type of broad COMEDY in which extreme crisis for the characters is amusing for the audience. Although its techniques were familiar from folk-drama, from the popular jigs of the Elizabethan theatre and from the more literary INTERLUDES of such 16th-century exponents as JOHN HEYWOOD, the word 'farce' did not enter the English dramatic vocabulary until after the Restoration. It derives, by way of the French theatre, from the Latin *farcire*, 'to stuff', and must reflect, in part, the highbrow assumption that, while horseplay might enliven, it could be no more than spice to something more serious in its totality. The broad comic episodes of MARLOWE's *DOCTOR FAUSTUS* would be the model for this kind of farce, but the genre could not be so confined. It established an independent popularity with 18th- and 19th-century audiences, who relished the scope it gave to outstanding comic actors. But the lowly status of farce in the hierarchy of drama delayed its development in England, where it was conventionally expected to last for a single act and to provide a colourful after-piece to the long theatrical bill. It was the polish and artfulness of PINERO's farces, of Brandon Thomas's isolated masterpiece *CHARLEY'S AUNT* and of WILDE's *THE IMPORTANCE OF BEING EARNEST* that established new possibilities. A mode in which obedience to internal logic takes precedence over extra-theatrical plausibility permits an unusually direct challenge to conventional authority, and even to the prevailing morality. A study of farce in the 20th century must take account, not only of BEN TRAVERS, ALAN AYCKBOURN and NOËL COWARD, but also of GEORGE BERNARD SHAW, TOM STOPPARD, JOE ORTON, PETER BARNES and BECKETT's *WAITING FOR GODOT*.

Farewell to Arms, A A novel by ERNEST HEMINGWAY, published in 1929. Set mainly in war-torn Italy in 1917–18, the story focuses on Frederic Henry, an American ambulance driver for the Italian army. He meets a young English nurse, Catherine Barkley, at a military hospital and they begin a relationship which gradually becomes passionate. When Frederic is severely wounded in an enemy mortar attack and is sent to Milan for surgery and therapy, Catherine follows him and obtains a nursing position in the hospital where he is being treated. Shortly before he is to return to active duty Catherine informs him that she is pregnant. The two decide not to marry (as their private commitment is deemed bond enough), but look forward to the birth of their first child.

Frederic returns to active duty but, following disastrous engagements with Austrian forces, the Italians are compelled to retreat. Eventually, Frederic deserts and flees to neutral Switzerland with Catherine. In Montreux they enjoy an idyllic autumn and winter, remote from the direct impact of the war. In March 1918 Catherine gives birth, after a difficult labour and emergency surgery, to a stillborn son; she dies from complications soon after the birth. The story of the romance is set alongside a powerful portrayal of the horrors of war and its threat of the total destruction of civilization.

Farjeon, Eleanor 1881–1965 Writer of CHILDREN'S LITERATURE. Born in Hampstead, she led an intensely literary and imaginative existence as a child, memorably recorded in her autobiography, *A Nursery in the Nineties* (1935). Never going to school, she wrote numerous stories and poems, some of which eventually appeared in *Nursery Rhymes of London Town* (1916). Her first novel, *Martin Pippin in the Apple Orchard* (1921), mixed prose with verse, each story steeped in folksong and traditional country lore. Other successful publications for children included a play, *The Glass Slipper* (1944), written in conjunction with her brother Herbert. A collection of her best children's stories entitled *The Little Bookroom* (1955) won her both the Carnegie and the Hans Christian Andersen International Medal for services to children's literature. She was a close friend of EDWARD THOMAS, and her *Edward Thomas: The Last Four Years* (1958) includes selections from their correspondence.

Farmer, Beverley 1941– Australian novelist and short-story writer. Her work handles potentially feminist material with a compassion that is both sensitive and detached. In *Alone* (1980) the protagonist retreats into unsatisfactory lesbianism. Two collections of stories, *Milk* (1983) and *Hometime* (1985), draw on Farmer's marriage to a Greek and her experience of life in a Greek village. *A Body of Water* (1990) is a writer's diary from 1987 to 1988, setting newly written stories in the matrix of reading, thought and observation from which they emerged. *The Seal Woman* (1992) is about a woman's recovery from pain and loss.

Farnol, (John) Jeffery 1878–1952 Novelist. Born in Warwickshire, he was educated privately and at the Westminster School of Art. He married an American and lived in the USA from 1902, working as a scene painter. He had begun to write when he was 19 but his first novel, *The Broad Highway*, did not appear until 1910. Its success enabled him to return to England and make writing his career, producing romantic cloak-and-dagger novels often set in the Georgian or Regency period. He is probably best remembered for *The Amateur Gentleman* (1913); other works include *Our Admirable Betty* (1918), *The Crooked Furrow* (1939), *The Happy Harvest* (1939) and *The Glad Summer* (1951).

Farquhar, George c. 1677–1707 Playwright. He was born in Derry, attended Trinity College, Dublin, for a little over a year, worked for a Dublin bookseller and then as an actor at the Smock Alley Theatre, Dublin, and left for London in 1697. The last 10 years of his short life were spent in England, with the brief exception of a military campaign in Holland as a lieutenant in the militia (1700). He had been encouraged to make the move to London by his actor-friend, Robert Wilks, who was instrumental in the staging at DRURY LANE of Farquhar's first play, a derivative intrigue-comedy *Love and a Bottle* (1698). His second play, *The Constant Couple* (1699), brought the promise of fame. Contemporary audiences warmed particularly to Sir Harry Wildair, a Restoration libertine on the surface but in reality warmhearted and kindly. The part was created by Robert Wilks, but sustained a unique place in the theatrical repertoire for over a century as a breeches role for such outstanding actresses as Peg Woffington and Dorothy Jordan. Anxious to capitalize on the success of *The Constant Couple*, Farquhar wrote an untidy sequel, *Sir Harry Wildair* (1701), following it with an adaptation of JOHN FLETCHER's THE WILD GOOSE CHASE as *The Inconstant* (1702). With *The Twin-Rivals* (1702) he turned away from RESTORATION COMEDY towards the more demure morality of a theatre in retreat from JEREMY COLLIER and other reformists. The failure of this sentiment-laden comedy was only partially redeemed by the successful afterpiece, *The Stage Coach* (1704). Farquhar, who had married in 1703 only to find his wife not the heiress he had fondly hoped, joined the grenadiers to support his new family. Out of his experience in the Midlands he wrote the first of his great comedies, THE RECRUITING OFFICER (1706). The vitality of this play, as of its brilliant successor, THE BEAUX' STRATAGEM (1707), owes more to its vigorous pursuit of the values of romantic love than to its occasional exercises in epigrammatic cynicism. In both plays Farquhar extends the range of Restoration comedy by removing it from a fashionable London setting to the fresher air of the provinces. It is a context that allows the celebration of the boisterousness of low and middle life in early 18th-century England. The popularity of these last two works did not prevent Farquhar dying in poverty.

Farrar, Frederick William 1831–1905 Religious writer and author of CHILDREN'S LITERATURE. Farrar was born in Bombay and educated at London University and Trinity Hall, Cambridge. As headmaster of Marlborough (1871–6) he was influenced by THOMAS ARNOLD's pioneering example at Rugby. He finally became dean of Canterbury. Farrar published a large number of sermons and theological writings, including *The Life of Christ* (1874), but he was chiefly famous, and is now remembered, for his three heavily moralistic stories for children: *Eric: or, Little by Little* (1858), *Julian Home: A Tale of College Life* (1859) and *St Winifred's: or, The World of School* (1862).

Farrell, J(ames) G(ordon) 1935–79 Novelist. Born in Liverpool and brought up in Ireland, Farrell contracted polio while a student at Oxford – an experience he later recapitulated in his second novel, *The Lung* (1965). His major achievement is his 'Empire trilogy', dramatizing episodes in the history of the British Empire. *Troubles* (1969) is set in Northern Ireland during the civil disturbances of the 1920s; *The Siege of Krishnapur* (1973), which won the BOOKER PRIZE, covers the Indian Mutiny; and *The Singapore Grip* (1978) presents the fall of Singapore during World War II. Farrell's work combines a scrupulously researched historical verisimilitude with a Dickensian multiplicity of characters and exaggerated, quirky comedy. It is also richly symbolical, representing the progressive obsolescence and decline of the Empire through the protracted physical decay and destruction of an embattled English-run Grand Hotel in *Troubles*, or the Collector's Residency in *Siege*, or the rubber traders' godowns in *Singapore Grip*. A subsequent novel about British India, *The Hill Station* (1981), was left unfinished at Farrell's untimely and accidental death while fishing.

Farrell, James T(homas) 1904–79 American novelist. Born and educated in Chicago, he supported the Communist Party from 1932 to 1935 but was one of the first American intellectuals to break with it over the totalitarian character of Stalin's regime. The work for which he is best known, *The Studs Lonigan Trilogy*, began to appear in 1932 with the publication of *Young Lonigan: A Boyhood in Chicago Streets*. Set on the South Side of Chicago, the novel charts the effects of middle-class morality and adult corruption on the young protagonist, the son of an Irish housepainter, who soon learns the way of life of the street corner and the poolroom. *The Young Manhood of Studs Lonigan* (1934) and *Judgment Day* (1935) continue the story of Studs's violent and dissolute life until his death from a heart attack at the age of 29. The trilogy is a powerful indictment of the American Dream – the belief that it requires only individual initiative to achieve wealth, status and, above all, happiness – and it registers this indictment through a series of failures: the failure of urban industrialism to provide an adequate moral vision; the failure of the twin mythologies of Church and Nation to sustain an understanding of a hostile world; and the failure of

Studs, inculcated with these broken ideals, to develop his potential.

Farrell's second series of novels was in five volumes: *A World I Never Made* (1936), *No Star is Lost* (1938), *Father and Son* (1940), *My Days of Anger* (1943) and *The Face of Time* (1953). Linked thematically with those of the earlier trilogy, these novels revolve around the contrasted lives of two families, the middle-class O'Flahertys and the working-class O'Neills. A third series – *Bernard Clare* (1946), *The Road Between* (1949) and *Yet Other Waters* (1952) – chronicles the difficulties faced by radical literary intellectuals after World War II.

Farrell's subsequent work marked a new departure. Though he continued to believe in struggles for freedom, he rejected Marxist-Trotskyist politics. (In the 1950s he became associated with the anti-Communist American Committee for Cultural Freedom, but resigned when he learned that it was funded by the CIA.) A series from this period, known as *A Universe of Time*, offers an account of an aspiring young writer in the 1920s. Books in the series are *The Silence of History* (1963), *What Time Collects* (1964), *When Time was Born* (1966), *Lonely for the Future* (1966), *A Brand New Life* (1968), *Judith* (1969) and *Invisible Swords* (1970). Among the other books published by Farrell during his prolific career are *A Note on Literary Criticism* (1936), *Ellen Rogers* (1941), *The League of Frightened Philistines and Other Papers* (1945), *This Man and This Woman* (1951), *An Omnibus of Short Stories* (1956), *Boarding House Blues* (1961), *Selected Essays* (1964), *New Year's Eve/1929* (1967) and *The Dunne Family* (1976).

Fashion A comedy by ANNA CORA MOWATT, first performed in New York City in 1845. Mr and Mrs Tiffany, newly rich, have established themselves in an opulent house in New York, but Mrs Tiffany's remorseless pursuit of fashion outruns her husband's resources. He takes to forgery to cover his expenses, but is discovered and blackmailed by his clerk, Snobson, to whom he is forced to promise his daughter Seraphina, even though her fortune has attracted the affections of Count Jolimaitre. At the last minute Tiffany is saved by his honest friend, Adam Trueman, who sees that Snobson is packed off to the remoteness of California and who exposes Jolimaitre as a fraud, the lover of Mrs Tiffany's maid.

Fast, Howard 1914– American novelist. Born in New York, he became known during the 1940s and 1950s for novels reflecting his left-wing politics. Many were set during the American Revolution, and all displayed a strong sense of class consciousness: for example, *Conceived in Liberty* (1930), *The Unvanquished* (1942), *Citizen Tom Paine* (1943), *The Proud and the Free* (1950) and *April Morning* (1961). Other works which focus on particular moments in

American history include *The Last Frontier* (1941), about the 1878–9 campaign against the Cheyenne Indians; and *Freedom Road* (1944), dealing with black Southern legislators in the Reconstruction period. *The American* (1946) is about Illinois governor John Peter Altgeld, and *Clarkton* (1947) details the events of a recent strike in a Massachusetts mill-town. Fast is also the author of numerous historical novels set in ancient times, including *My Glorious Brothers* (1948), set in ancient Israel; *Spartacus* (1951), about a Roman slave revolt; *Moses, Prince of Egypt* (1958); and *Agrippa's Daughter* (1964). *The Naked God* (1957), a work of non-fiction, describes his disenchantment with the Communist Party during the Stalinist era. Later novels include *The Immigrants* (1977), *The Second Generation* (1978), *The Establishment* (1979), *The Outsider* (1984), *The Immigrant's Daughter* (1985) and *The Confession of Joe Cullen* (1989). Under the pseudonym E. V. Cunningham he also has written more than a dozen novels of suspense and mystery.

Fatal Curiosity, The A tragedy by GEORGE LILLO, first produced at the HAYMARKET THEATRE in May 1736 and published in the same year. Like his other better-known tragedy, THE LONDON MERCHANT, it deals with the lives of humble people, but is in BLANK VERSE rather than prose. The play is set in Jacobean England and is based on an old story of murder in Cornwall. The Wilmots are an elderly couple reduced to poverty; at the prompting of his wife, the old man murders a stranger who has left a casket with them. The dead man turns out to be their son, whom the couple had believed to be drowned at sea.

Lillo's play was the inspiration for the German dramatist Friedrich Werner in his *Die vierundzwanzigste Februar* (1810), and Albert Camus handled the same theme in *Le Malentendu* (1945).

Fatal Dowry, The A tragedy by PHILIP MASSINGER and NATHAN FIELD. It was first published in 1632 and only a corrupt text exists. The exact date of its first performance is not known.

Charalois's father, an old soldier distinguished for his service as marshal to the Duke of Burgundy, fell on hard times and died in a debtor's prison. Charalois cannot claim his father's body for burial until the debts are settled; but the creditors accept his offer to enter prison as succeeding debtor and release the old soldier's body for an honourable funeral. Charalois goes to prison with his friend, the soldier Romont. Charalois's loyalty to his father's memory and Romont's loyalty to his friend move Rochfort, former president of the Parliament, to help them; he procures their release and gives Charalois his daughter's hand in marriage.

The daughter, Beaumelle, is still attracted to a former suitor; one day Romont comes upon her and Novall embracing. Charalois is reluctant to believe his friend; but he surprises the lovers together, kills Novall in a duel, then calls on Rochfort to judge his daughter. Beaumelle is found guilty by her father whereupon Charalois kills her. Rochfort, shocked by Charalois's lack of mercy, hands him over to justice as a double murderer. Charalois is acquitted, but is killed in revenge by a friend of Novall.

NICHOLAS ROWE refashioned the play as *The Fair Penitent*; it was produced in May 1703 and first published in the same year. The characters have different names and the emphasis lies with the dilemma of Calista (Beaumelle), given to Altamont (Charalois) by her father Sciolto (Rochfort); she is unable to end her liaison with Lothario (Novall) and is observed by Horatio (Romont) in her guilt. The character of Lothario is completely different; he is still a libertine but Novall was no more than a mean-spirited dandy in the earlier play. Calista is the fair penitent of the title and the end of the play finds her both sorry and reconciled. DAVID GARRICK played Lothario with great success and Calista was one of Sara Siddons's famous roles. SAMUEL JOHNSON much admired Rowe's play, which held the stage for over a century.

Father and Son See GOSSE, SIR EDMUND.

Faulkner, William (Cuthbert) 1897–1962 American novelist. He was born in New Albany, Mississippi, into a family which had played a prominent role in the history of the South. His grandfather had served as a colonel in the Confederate army, and had come home to pursue a career as a lawyer, politician, railroad builder and civic benefactor. The strict family code of honour, its sense of white social status and its often violent exploits would provide a good deal of material for Faulkner's fiction.

When he was five the family moved to Oxford, Mississippi, which became his permanent home. He left high school in 1915 and took a clerical job at his grandfather's bank. In 1918, after being rejected by the US military because he was too short, he enlisted in the Royal Canadian Air Force, but the war ended while he was still in training, and he returned to Oxford. He enrolled as a special student at the University of Mississippi, and published poems and drawings in student magazines. His first book, a collection of poems entitled *The Marble Faun*, was published in 1924.

His first novel, *Soldiers' Pay*, was written in New Orleans in 1925 and published in the following year. The story centres on the return of a soldier who has been physically and psychologically disabled in World War I, and whose subsequent illness and death change the lives of his family and friends. Faulkner's second novel, *Mosquitoes* (1927), set in New Orleans, is a satirical tale about a group of Southern artists and intellectuals. His next novel was the first to be set in

William Faulkner

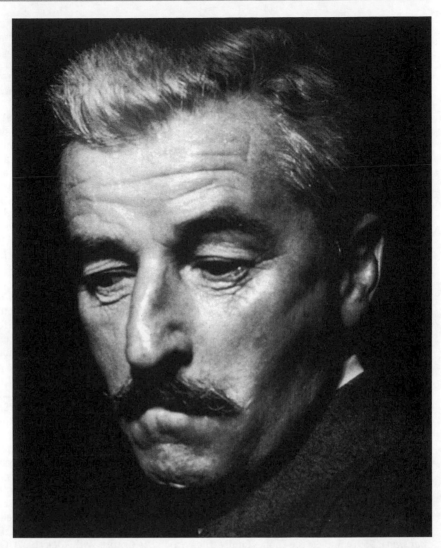

the fictional Mississippi county of Yoknapatawpha, which was to provide the setting for many of his best-known works. Originally called *Flags in the Dust*, it was rejected for publication but later accepted in an edited version retitled *Sartoris*, and published in 1929. (The uncut *Flags in the Dust* finally appeared in 1973.)

Faulkner's most productive period began with THE SOUND AND THE FURY (1929), about another Yoknapatawpha county family, in which he experimented with narrative technique by using multiple points of view. Perhaps due to its fragmented, non-chronological structure, it met with only limited success. AS I LAY DYING (1930) was still more splintered in form, being composed of 59 monologues by a variety of characters which gradually reveal the intricate ties that bind and frustrate the poor-white Bundren family of Yoknapatawpha county. In an effort to win a popular audience, Faulkner wrote *Sanctuary* (1931),

which was in fact an even more controversial work than its predecessors because of its graphic description of a horrific rape. With its more conventional form, however, it sold well amid the scandal it aroused. LIGHT IN AUGUST (1932) differs from his other early novels in that it does not concentrate on a single family, but it involves similar issues of human need, dissatisfaction, crisis and redemption through endurance. Also set in Yoknapatawpha county, it broadens the social scope of Faulkner's fiction through the attention it pays to the individual's sense of place in a racist society.

In 1929 Faulkner married Estelle Oldham Franklin, and in the following year purchased a traditional pillared house in Oxford which he named Rowan Oak. His fiction, however, enjoyed no more than mediocre sales, and he was frequently in financial straits. To earn money over the next 20 years he worked periodically as a scriptwriter in Hollywood. Among his more notable credits are versions of ERNEST HEMINGWAY's *To Have and Have Not* (1945) and RAYMOND CHANDLER's *The Big Sleep* (1946). His next novel, *Pylon* (1935), treats another of his strong interests, aviation, focusing on the lives of four adults and a child who travel nomadically from air show to air show to compete in races. He returned to Yoknapatawpha county with *ABSALOM, ABSALOM!* (1936), which concerns the frustrated attempts of Thomas Sutpen to found a Southern dynasty in 19th-century Mississippi. Sutpen's story is reconstructed by Quentin Compson, one of the characters in *The Sound and the Fury*, who is obsessed by the way in which the South's guilt in the matter of interracial relationships is embodied in the misfortunes of the Sutpen family. Following *The Unvanquished* (1938), *The Wild Palms* (1939) and *The Hamlet* (1940) – the first of three novels about the Snopes family – came *Go Down Moses* (1942), a novel composed of several interrelated stories about Southern blacks. One of these, 'The Bear', is among Faulkner's most frequently reprinted pieces. *Intruder in the Dust* (1948) tells the story of Lucas Beauchamp, a black man who is unjustly accused of murder but who is eventually acquitted despite the racial prejudice that permeates society. Faulkner was elected to the American Academy of Arts and Letters in 1949, and was awarded the Nobel Prize for literature in the following year. His *Collected Stories* (1950) received a National Book Award in 1951.

Requiem for a Nun (1951), a sequel to *Sanctuary*, offers a less brutal treatment of sexual themes than its horrifying predecessor. As his Nobel Prize address made clear, Faulkner wanted his new work to be more affirmative, more insistent on the power of humankind to endure and to prevail. The change of tone is reflected in *A Fable* (1954), an ALLEGORY of the story of Jesus in a World War I setting which won him a belated PULITZER PRIZE in 1955. *The Town* (1957) and *The Mansion* (1959) complete the Snopes family trilogy, a penetrating examination of the social fabric of the South. Faulkner's final novel, *The Reivers* (1962), which also won a Pulitzer Prize, is a mildly comic portrait of some of the characters introduced in his earlier books. He died in the year of its publication. His other works include *Knight's Gambit* (1949), a collection of DETECTIVE FICTION; *Uncollected Stories of William Faulkner* (1979); and a collection of poems originally written for his wife, *Vision in Spring* (1984). This last is one of several books which Faulkner wrote to present as gifts; another is the allegorical story *Mayday* (written 1926, published 1976), about the adventures of a medieval knight.

Fauset, Jessie R(edmon) 1882–1961 Black American novelist and editor. She was born in New Jersey and educated at Cornell and the Sorbonne. While editor of W. E. B. Du Bois's magazine *Crisis* she encouraged and published many of the new writers who constituted the HARLEM RENAISSANCE. She herself wrote four novels, all depicting the experience of black women, and all asserting the need to accept one's heritage rather than to escape it: *There is Confusion* (1924), *Plum Bun* (1929), *The Chinaberry Tree* (1931) and *Comedy: American Style* (1934).

Fearing, Kenneth (Flexner) 1902–61 American poet. He was born in Oak Park, Illinois, and educated at the University of Wisconsin. His first collection, *Angel Arms*, appeared in 1929 and defined the focus of much of his work: an urban and mechanized society lacking in human compassion. Among his other volumes are *Dead Reckoning: A Book of Poetry* (1938), *Afternoon of a Pawnbroker and Other Poems* (1943), *Stranger at Coney Island and Other Poems* (1948) and *New and Selected Poems* (1956). He also wrote several novels, including *The Hospital* (1939) and *The Big Clock* (1946).

Federal Theatre Project A branch of President Roosevelt's Works Project Administration, founded in 1935 to provide employment for out-of-work actors and theatrical workers and to create an uncensored forum for innovative productions. Under the directorship of Hallie Flanagan, the project mounted approximately 1000 shows in 30 states, varying from children's plays to dance productions to classic plays to a jazz version of GILBERT and Sullivan's *The Mikado* to a Voodoo *MACBETH*. Altogether it employed over 10,000 people, including E. G. Marshall, Burt Lancaster, Orson Welles, John Houseman, and LANGSTON HUGHES. Some of the most controversial offerings were the 'Living Newspapers', documentary-style dramas originated by ELMER RICE in New York. Despite the Project's aims censorship plagued many of its productions, such as Welles and Houseman's version of MARC BLITZSTEIN's leftist musical drama, *THE CRADLE WILL ROCK* (1937). Continuing conservative opposition to the radical nature of such productions brought about the abolition of the entire Project by Congress in 1939.

Feinstein, Elaine 1930– Novelist, poet and translator. Born in Bootle and brought up in Leicester, where she attended Wyggeston Grammar School, she read English at Newnham College, Cambridge. From 1960 to 1962 she worked for Cambridge University Press and from 1967 to 1970 she was assistant lecturer at the University of Essex.

Her first novel, *The Circle* (1970), examines a woman's attempt to reconcile her need for independence with her desire for everything that marriage might bring. Its successors include *The Amberstone Exit* (1972), in which dreams, images and memories pass through the mind of a woman about to give birth, and *The Survivors* (1982), an epic by comparison to her usually short fiction, which incorporates part of her own history into the story of two Jewish families who escaped from Russia at the turn of the century. Subsequent novels include *The Border* (1984), *Mother's Girl* (1988), *All You Need* (1989) and *Loving Brecht* (1992). Volumes of poetry include *The Celebrants and Other Poems* (1973), *Some Unease and Angels* (1977), *Feast of Eurydice* (1980) and *Cuty Music* (1989). Feinstein has also published highly acclaimed translations of the poems of Marina Tsvetayeva (1971) and of the work of Margaret Aliger, Yunna Moritz and Bella Akhmadulina (1978). A short biography of Bessie Smith (1985) was followed by a biography of Tsvetayeva, *A Captive Lion* (1987).

Felix Holt, the Radical A novel by GEORGE ELIOT, published in 1866.

Relinquishing thoughts of a materially rewarding life, the respectably educated Felix Holt returns to his native village in North Loamshire and pursues the humble trade of watch- and clock-keeping in order to maintain his needy mother. He is a forceful young man of honour and integrity, burning to participate in political life so that he may improve the lot of his fellow artisans and encourage them to assert themselves. Contrasted with Felix Holt is the intelligent, economically secure Harold Transome, just returned from the Middle East to assume responsibility for Transome Court, the local manor-house rapidly falling into decay. A good businessman and a widower with a small son, Transome intends to enter Parliament as a Liberal, thus taking up a political position contrary to the family's traditional Toryism. He is opposed to the questionable electioneering practices of the time – the early 1830s – and his growing disdain for his agent, the dishonest lawyer Jermyn, forms an important narrative line in the book. Much action in *Felix Holt* centres upon the hustings and the drunken behaviour of the mob, whose violent activities Felix Holt tries unsuccessfully to quell. For his efforts he receives a four-year prison sentence for alleged manslaughter. Both Felix Holt and Harold Transome vie for the hand of Esther, supposed daughter of the quixotic Dissenting minister, Rufus Lyon. A young woman of charm and virtue, Esther has a legitimate claim, through a long legal rigmarole, to the Transome estates, but she resigns it shortly before marrying Felix Holt. The narrative is enhanced by character studies of Harold Transome's mother and the corrupt political agent Johnson, as well as by the lesser figures of Mr Christian, Sir Maximus Debarry and the loyal servant Denner.

Female Quixote, The See LENNOX, CHARLOTTE.

feminist criticism Not a school, but a set of influential lines of enquiry encouraged by the growth of feminism since the 1960s. Firstly, forgotten women writers, whose work lacked a modern reprint or a properly informed readership, have been rediscovered. Publishers such as Virago, Pandora and The Women's Press have built up lists of such work and laid the ground for a major reassessment of the place of women writers in literary history. Critics have played their part by interpreting the texts, filling in the background detail and, not least, explaining how a dominant male tradition has managed effectively to write them out of its purview. It is no longer a question of admitting a few women (JANE AUSTEN, the BRONTËS, GEORGE ELIOT) as remarkable exceptions to the rule and otherwise tracing the 'rise of the novel' through a series of great male writers.

Women's experience as it is reflected in various kinds of writing has also been reinterpreted. This requires identifying explicitly with female characters, often against the grain of a dominant ideology which tends to distort, repress or simply ignore their experience. Thus feminist critics have proposed new readings of familiar texts, readings which challenge the established male idea of how women are supposed to think, feel or act. One result has been a revision of previously accepted views of 19th-century fiction, rejecting (for instance) the typecast notion of female 'hysteria' as a weakness peculiar to heroines like Maggie Tulliver in THE MILL ON THE FLOSS.

An obvious question arises: is there such a thing as 'feminine writing' marked by characteristic features of language or style? Some feminists argue that women have access to a realm of experience from which male language is effectively debarred. VIRGINIA WOOLF spoke of a 'woman's sentence', as yet barely glimpsed in occasional, fragmentary forms, but holding out the promise of deliverance from male habits of thought. Her novels support the idea by showing men often trapped in a grimly repressive, 'rational' way of thinking while women enjoy a much greater freedom of intuitive sympathy and grasp. Certain critics (e.g. Hélène Cixous) have developed this theory of an *écriture féminine* which shows women in touch with libidinal energies and drives outside the regimented discourse of male (patriarchal) reason. Men may perhaps gain access to such writing, and may even themselves produce it in rare instances. It could be argued, for instance, that Molly Bloom's soliloquy at the end of JOYCE's ULYSSES is a more striking example of *écriture féminine* than anything by Virginia Woolf.

Other feminists reject the very notion of some essential difference between male and female writing. In their view, culture establishes gender-roles which condition men and women to behave differently and accept a dominant patriarchal order. Any politics based on these roles will run the risk of simply inverting the old, hierarchical distinction between male and female, leaving its terms still securely in place. One function of criticism, therefore, is to examine the typecast, usually passive roles to which the conventional male view of female psychology has assigned women in fiction. Any reading of an author like ERNEST HEMINGWAY, for example, would concentrate on exposing the sexist assumptions apparent in his habit of casting women characters either as young, desirable and empty-headed or as archetypal earth-mother figures who no longer pose a seductive threat.

Another line of argument is represented by Judith Fetterly's *The Resisting Reader*. As its title suggests, it is most interested in the way women read and, more specifically, the way they read texts (like those of Hemingway or HENRY MILLER) which are drastically reductive of female 'nature' and experience. A feminist approach would interpret such texts deliberately against the grain, refusing to be a passive, unresisting reader. And such an approach would extend beyond literature to the whole domain of culture where women are often coerced into false or contradictory positions – as, for example, when they read a newspaper like *The Sun*, with its overtly sexist treatment of women as mere commodities or objects of mass-produced male fantasy. That such crude examples are not so remote from the high ground of literary culture is one of the main lessons to be learned from present-day feminist criticism.

Fenton, Sir **Geoffrey** ?1539–1608 Translator. He campaigned in Ulster and took an active part in the administration there. He had Elizabeth's confidence and she interceded personally on one occasion to release him from the debtors' prison in Dublin. His *Certain Tragical Discourses* (1567) were translations of stories, originally by Bandello, from Belleforest's French version. Fenton's version is loaded with rhetorical devices, proverbs and maxims. *Golden Epistles* (1575) is a similar work, a translation of pieces gathered from Guevara and other authors. His major work is a translation of the Italian historian Guicciardini's *La historia d'Italia*, again from a French version, as *The History of Guicciardin concerning the Wars of Italy* (1597).

Fenton, James 1949– Poet and journalist. Born in Lincoln and educated in Durham and at Magdalen College, Oxford, he won the Newdigate Prize for poetry. He worked as a journalist in England, Indo-China and Germany before becoming theatre critic for *The Sunday Times*. His first collection was *Terminal Moraine* (1972), but his reputation so far rests on *The Memory of War* (1982), poems based on his experience as a war reporter, which were compared to the early AUDEN. His journalism includes *All the Wrong Places: Adrift in the Politics of Asia* (1990).

Ferdinand Count Fathom, The Adventures of A novel by TOBIAS SMOLLETT, published in 1753. His third novel, it is by no means among his stronger works, but it is notable for moving away from the PICARESQUE and anticipating features of the GOTHIC NOVEL.

The child of a camp-follower to Marlborough's army, Ferdinand is an amoral, self-seeking villain. He adopts the title of Count Fathom and a benevolent German nobleman, Count de Melville, receives him into his family. Ferdinand hopes to marry the Count's daughter but fails. He turns to plundering the Count's house with the help of the daughter's maid. He cheats Renaldo, the Count's son, and tries to seduce his fiancée, Monimia. She escapes his attentions by feigning death. Eventually Ferdinand's wickedness is revealed and Monimia is restored to Renaldo. Ferdinand is saved from punishment when Renaldo relents towards him, and as a result he reforms.

Ferguson, Adam 1723–1816 Philosopher and historian. Born at Logierait in Perthshire and educated for the ministry at the universities of St Andrews and Edinburgh, Ferguson served in the Black Watch regiment before succeeding DAVID HUME in the library of the Faculty of Advocates. At Edinburgh University he was successively professor of natural philosophy, of moral philosophy and of mathematics. His *Essay on the History of Civil Society*, favourably noticed on its publication in 1767, attributed social decline to the failure of citizens to play their due part in public affairs. *The History of the Progress and Termination of the Roman Republic* (1783) provided a carefully designed introduction to GIBBON's great work on the Roman Empire.

Ferguson, Sir **Samuel** 1810–86 Irish poet and antiquary. The son of a Scots-Irish family, Ferguson was born in Belfast and educated at Trinity College, Dublin. Later he studied law and was called to the Bar in 1838; he became a Queen's Counsel in 1859. A scholar and antiquary, Ferguson became Deputy Keeper of the Irish Records in 1867; he had published his first poems in 1861 and more were to be published by his widow after his death. He was knighted in 1878.

Ferguson was not himself a poet of great distinction. His contribution to literature was his part in the restoration, from the original Irish, of the ancient literature which had been lost to generations brought up and taught in another language. *Lays of the Western Gael* (1864) contained 'The Tain-Quest', his version of the *Tain Bó Cúaigne* (The Cattle Raid of Cooley), and brought back to poetic circulation the myth of Cuchulain and the redoubtable Queen, Maev of Connaught. Other poems concerned Fergus, Conor, Deirdra and Dermid (in Ferguson's spelling). *Congal* (1872) is a poem on the last heroic stand of Celtic paganism against triumphant Christianity. Among other works by Ferguson were *Deirdra* (1880), *The Forging of the Anchor* (1883) and *Ogham Inscriptions* in *Ireland, Wales and Scotland* (1887). A collection of his prose tales was edited by Lady Ferguson and published as *Hibernian Nights' Entertainment* (1887).

Fergusson, Robert 1750–74 Scottish poet. Fergusson was born in Edinburgh, attended the High School for three years and then studied for two years at Dundee University on a bursary. He went to St Andrews University as a divinity student but had to leave after four years because of his father's money troubles. He succeeded in getting work as a copier in the Commissary Clerk's office, where he stayed for the rest of his short life.

His first poems were lyrics to Scots airs but they were written in imitation of English styles. Walter Ruddiman, proprietor of *The Weekly Magazine*, or *Edinburgh Amusement*, published 'The Daft Days' in January 1772 and became his patron. Fergusson did not find his true voice until he turned to the vernacular in works like 'The Farmer's Ingle'. A volume of his work appeared in 1773. Witty and sociable, he became sought after in Edinburgh literary circles but fell victim to religious mania, early in 1774. He died insane in October of that year, at the age of 24.

Fergusson was the poet of Edinburgh, the smoky city to which he gave a nickname in his most famous poem, 'Auld Reekie', which traces the progress of an Edinburgh day. He was the most notable Scots poet of the 18th century before Burns, who admired him, learned from his work and sometimes feared his own career might come to the same premature and unhappy end.

Ferlinghetti, Lawrence 1919– American poet, editor and publisher. Born in New York and educated at the University of North Carolina, Columbia University and the Sorbonne, he was a leading figure in the BEAT movement in the 1950s. With Peter D. Martin he founded City Lights in San Francisco, America's first all-paperback bookstore. His press, City Lights Books, has published many of the most important collections by GREGORY CORSO, ALLEN GINSBERG and DENISE LEVERTOV. Ferlinghetti's own work is experimental and often light or satiric in tone; underlying it, however, is a clear interest in social issues, and it frequently attacks American political policies. His first book of poetry was *Pictures from the Gone World* (1955); others include *A Coney Island of the Mind* (1958), *Starting from San Francisco* (1961; revised 1967), *The Secret Meaning of Things* (1969), *Open Eye, Open Heart* (1973), *Landscapes of Living and Dying* (1979), *The Populist Manifestos* (1981) and *Endless Life: The Selected Poems* (1981). *Her* (1960) is a novel. He has also written experimental drama and translations of work by Jacques Prévert.

Ferrar, Nicholas 1592–1637 Scholar and founder of the Little Gidding community. Born in London, Ferrar entered Clare College, Cambridge, in 1605 and became a fellow in 1610. A brilliant scholar, he travelled on the Continent for five years before entering Parliament in 1624. His religious aspirations led him to retire to Little Gidding, an estate near Huntingdon belonging to his mother, where he was joined by his brother and brother-in-law and their families, and they established a community life based on Church of England principles. In 1626 he was ordained a deacon by LAUD, and the community of some 30 people lived an ordered life of prayer and active good works. The Puritans denounced it as an attempt to reintroduce Catholic practices in England, and a Parliamentary raid in 1646 brought it to an end.

Ferrar's manuscripts were destroyed, so his only surviving writings are his published translations of Lessius' treatise *On Temperance* and Valdez's *Divine Considerations*, the latter with notes by GEORGE HERBERT, a close friend who entrusted Ferrar with the publication of his poems. For Little Gidding, see also *JOHN INGLESANT* and *FOUR QUARTETS*.

Ferrier, Susan (Edmonstone) 1782–1854 Novelist. The daughter of an Edinburgh official, who was a colleague of SIR WALTER SCOTT, Susan Ferrier led a quiet life, managing her father's household after her mother's death. She knew the literary society of Edinburgh through her father's friends and was warmly esteemed by Sir Walter Scott. Her three novels of Scottish life – *MARRIAGE* (1818), *THE INHERITANCE* (1824) and *Destiny* (1831) – mix comedy resembling JANE AUSTEN's with explicit didacticism.

Field, Nathan 1587–c. 1620 Elizabethan actor and playwright, the son of a Puritan clergyman who must have deplored his theatrical career. Field was educated at St Paul's School, and became a chorister in about 1600. It was as a boy actor in the early years of the 17th century that he made his reputation. Praised by BEN JONSON, in many of whose plays he acted, Field graduated to membership of adult companies, ending his acting career as a member of the KING'S MEN.

Field's two London comedies, *A Woman is a Weather-Cock* (c. 1609) and *Amends for Ladies* (c. 1610), are fashionably bawdy. He is known to have collaborated with MASSINGER in *THE FATAL DOWRY* (c. 1618) and with FLETCHER in several plays, including *The Honest Man's Fortune* (1613) and *The Knight of Malta* (c. 1618). That Field shared some of the soaring ambition of his most famous acting role, the hero of CHAPMAN's *BUSSY D'AMBOIS*, is suggested by his involvement with the Countess of Argyll, by whom he is supposed to have had a child.

Fielding, Henry 1707–54 Novelist and playwright. Born of aristocratic descent, at Sharpham Park, Somerset, Fielding was educated at Eton and went to

London to pursue legal studies during the late 1720s. Because of a disputed inheritance he was short of money, and his chief aspiration was to become a playwright. He briefly attended Leyden University but returned to London, where he wrote some 25 plays between 1728 and 1737. These were various and accomplished in nature, not depending upon the prevailing fashion for tired, Restoration-style dramas but embracing several forms, from the BALLAD OPERA to the conventional five-act comedy.

He had an early success with *Tom Thumb: A Tragedy*, produced at the HAYMARKET THEATRE in April 1730 and in a revised version the following year as *The Tragedy of Tragedies*, where it enjoyed a long run of almost 40 nights. It is a BURLESQUE of the traditions of heroic drama, set in an absurd court of King Arthur and humorously attacking Sir Robert Walpole. The density of contemporary allusions and classical echoes, here and in Fielding's other satirical plays, ensures that they are nowadays seldom revived. *Pasquin* (1736), though, is an entertaining 'Rehearsal' piece that offers some modern potential. *The Historical Register for the Year 1736*, another dramatic satire, was produced in 1737. In this year the authorities determined to stem the flow of political jibes appearing on stage and introduced the Licensing Act to impose censorship on the production of plays. So in 1737, at the age of 30, Fielding cast around to discover new outlets for his witty inventiveness. He had a wife to support, having married Charlotte Cradock, the model for two of his fictional heroines, in 1734. He resumed his legal studies (eventually being called to the Bar in 1740) and also applied himself to a spell of political journalism. As editor of the thrice-weekly *Champion* from November 1739 to June 1741 he used the pseudonym of Captain Hercules Vinegar to continue attacks on Walpole's government. After the latter's fall, Fielding edited *The True Patriot* (November 1745 to June 1746) and then the burlesque *Jacobite's Journal* from December 1747 until November 1748, a platform for his strongly Hanoverian views, following the Jacobite Rebellion of 1745.

Fielding was a good stylistic mimic, and adept at PARODY. The popularity of RICHARDSON's *PAMELA* (1740) prompted him in the following year to reply in print with a skilful parodic squib entitled *An Apology for the Life of Mrs Shamela Andrews* (1741), which makes the innocent virtue of Richardson's heroine appear scheming. Fielding followed up this idea with his first – and funniest – novel, *JOSEPH ANDREWS* (1742), in which the central character is Pamela's brother. The shapely narrative follows the mishaps of the innocent Joseph and his unworldly companion, Parson Adams, as they travel through the predatory world of Georgian England. Though suffering from the perennial problem of how to render virtue colourful, it is a most witty book with numerous comic episodes, and it was a popular success.

The third volume of his *Miscellanies* (1743) comprised THE LIFE OF JONATHAN WILD THE GREAT, a finely ironic fable which took as its basis the famous contemporary thief and thief-taker, pretending to equate goodness with greatness. *Miscellanies* also contained *A Journey from this World to the Next*, a spirited satire in the Lucianic mould which describes the progress of the soul. His beloved Charlotte died in 1744 and, to the sneers of his critics, Fielding in 1747 married her former maid, Mary Daniel. It was about this time that he began work on *THE HISTORY OF TOM JONES, A FOUNDLING* (1749), probably his greatest literary achievement. Ambitious in scope and scrupulous in design, it presents a refreshingly un-idealized hero and a narrator who is virtually a character in his own right. Less exuberant is his last novel, *AMELIA* (1751), reflecting his own grim experience of social hardships in the metropolis.

In 1748 Fielding had been appointed a Justice of the Peace for Westminster and for Middlesex. His serious concern at the social abuses and judicial corruption of the times is reflected in his essays: *A Charge Delivered to the Grand Jury* (1749), *An Enquiry into the Causes of the Late Increase of Robbers* (1751), *Examples of the Interposition of Providence in the Detection and Punishment of Murder* (1752) and *A Proposal for Making an Effectual Provision for the Poor* (1753). As a magistrate, Fielding was both dedicated and effective: together with his blind half-brother, John, he was responsible for Britain's first organized detective police force, the Bow Street Runners. In January 1752 he returned to journalism, editing *The Covent Garden Journal* under the pseudonym Sir Alexander Drawcansir. Among the essays he contributed were literary altercations with SMOLLETT. But his health was deteriorating – he suffered from asthma and gout – and on 26 June 1754 he set sail for the less inclement climate of Lisbon, with his wife and daughter. It was there that he died, on 8 October, and lies buried in the English cemetery. *The Journal of a Voyage to Lisbon*, published in 1755, is a sharply observed but unavoidably depressing account of his final travels.

Despite the legends of a rakish life-style, Fielding had a deserved reputation for generosity of spirit and natural sympathy for his fellow man. In religion he was a Broad Anglican (or Latitudinarian), believing in the principle of benevolence or 'good nature', which he defined in *The Champion* as 'a delight in the happiness of mankind'. The example of his later life shows this in practice; as a novelist, too, he is a committed critic of society's corruptions and hypocrisy. (In this, as in other ways, he is frequently compared to his friend HOGARTH.) He brought to the novel a new degree of psychological realism and a linear narrative strength, but the influences upon him were many and various, including the tradition of classical epic prose romances, the European PICARESQUE, and the learned fooling of the Scriblerian satirists. His own dramatic experience introduced a new sophistication in both structure and the representation of comic character through dialogue. Though the plays themselves are largely forgotten, SHAW considered him 'the greatest practising dramatist, with the single exception of SHAKESPEARE, produced by England between the Middle Ages and the nineteenth century'.

Fielding, Sarah 1710–68 Novelist and younger sister of HENRY FIELDING. Born in East Stour in Dorset, she went to live in Hammersmith and became the friend of SAMUEL RICHARDSON. *THE ADVENTURES OF DAVID SIMPLE* (1744) scored a considerable success; *Familiar Letters between the Principal Characters in David Simple* and a second edition of *The Adventures* appeared in 1747, both with prefaces by her brother. *The Governess: or, The Little Female Academy* (1749) preceded *David Simple: Volume the Last* (1753). Other works were *The Cry: A New Dramatic Fable* (with Jane Collier, 1754), *The Lives of Cleopatra and Octavia* (1757), *The History of the Countess of Dellwyn* (1759) and *The History of Ophelia* (1760). She published a translation of Xenophon's *Memorabilia* and *Apologia* in 1762.

Fiennes, Celia 1662–1741 Travel-writer. Born at the manor of Newton Toney, near Salisbury, she was granddaughter of the 1st Lord Saye and Sele. From 1685 until about 1703 she travelled extensively around England (initially for reasons of health, but also for a broadening of the mind) and began to record in journals what she saw. This account was primarily designed for her own family, but it constituted the most comprehensive impression of the countryside since the work of CAMDEN. However, it remained in manuscript form until it was roughly transcribed and published in 1888 as *Through England on a Side Saddle in the Time of William and Mary*. A fine scholarly edition, *The Journeys of Celia Fiennes*, by Christopher Morris, appeared in 1947, and divides the travels geographically into four parts.

As a document of period detail, this account is of interest and importance as social history, but it is also very readable. The style is natural and personal, opinionated and sometimes quirky, but full of enthusiastic observation and recording a wide variety of topics, from gardening to processes of manufacture. Her enquiring attitude decried insularity, observing that too many 'Gentlemen in general service of their country... are ignorant of anything but the name of the place for which they serve in Parliament'.

Fierstein, Harvey (Forbes) 1954– American playwright, actor and producer. Born in Brooklyn and educated at Pratt Institute, he is best known for his *Torch Song Trilogy*, first staged together in 1981,

which dramatizes different views of the gay experience. He has also written and starred in the film derived from it (1988) and written the book for the musical *La Cage aux folles* (1983).

Fiesta See SUN ALSO RISES, THE.

Figes, Eva 1932– Novelist. Born in Berlin, she left Germany with her family in 1939, and was educated at Kingsbury Grammar School and Queen Mary College, London. She worked as an editor at Longmans in 1955–7, Weidenfeld and Nicolson in 1962–3 and Blackie in 1964–7. Her first novel, *Equinox*, appeared in 1966; its successors include *Winter Journey* (winner of the Guardian Fiction Prize, 1968), *Nelly's Version* (1977), *Light* (1983), *The Seven Ages* (1986), *Ghosts* (1988) and *The Tree of Knowledge* (1990). She has also written several radio plays: *Time Regained* (1980), *Days* (1981; adapted from her own novel of the same name published in 1974) and *Between Friends* (1982). A lyrical writer whose prose flows smoothly, Figes has been compared to VIRGINIA WOOLF in her preoccupation with exploring the inner self. She acknowledges Kafka as a major influence. The darker elements in her work are the shadows cast by the Holocaust, and she remains very much part of a European tradition. She has also translated works by Martin Walser, Bernhard Grzimek and George Sand.

Fight at Finnsburh, The A fragment of 48 lines of Old English verse preserved in a corrupt 18th-century copy from a lost manuscript. The story the poem apparently told was well known and forms the subject of the minstrel's song in BEOWULF after the defeat of Grendel. The fragment describes the defence of the hall in which Hnaef and his men are under attack and the whole poem probably told of a feud between the Danes and Frisians. The relationship between the part of the tale preserved in the fragment and the section told in *Beowulf* has been a topic of controversy and research.

Findley, Timothy 1930– Canadian novelist. Born and educated in Toronto, he was an actor in Canada, Britain and the USA from 1950. He also worked in Canadian television and wrote dialogue in Hollywood. He began to write fiction in the 1950s and turned to writing full-time in 1962. With his collaborator William Whitehead he has won several awards for television scripts. His first novel, *The Last of the Crazy People* (1967), is a study of a decaying southern Ontario family, which serves as a social microcosm. *The Butterfly Plague* (1969) offers a similar perspective on a Hollywood family. Findley is best known for his novel *The Wars* (1977), the story of a young Canadian officer in World War I who reacts against the horror of the trenches with a treasonable act of heroism that is deemed 'mad'. Written by a narrator who investigates a variety of written, oral and pictorial sources, Ross's story also affords a vivid picture of the way notions of character and personal history are constructed. *Famous Last Words* (1981) is the fictional story of EZRA POUND's Hugh Selwyn Mauberley. Set at the end of World War II, it blends the conventions of the thriller with an exploration of the darker side of 20th-century history and mythologies, particularly the relationship of artistic elitism and fascism. *Not Wanted on the Voyage* (1984) is a highly imaginative account of the Great Flood. Findley has also published collections of short stories, *Dinner along the Amazon* (1984) and *Stones* (1988).

Finlay, George 1799–1875 Historian. Finlay was one of the enthusiasts for Greek freedom who was with BYRON in Missolonghi. He was born at Faversham in Kent and studied law at Glasgow University and at Göttingen. He went to Greece in 1823 and after the struggle for independence had succeeded he decided to settle there. He bought an estate in Attica and eventually died in Athens. His histories of Greece eventually covered the centuries that followed its subjugation by the Romans to its hard-wrested freedom from the Turks. *Greece under the Romans* (1844), *The History of Greece from its Conquest by the Crusaders to its Conquest by the Turks, and of the Empire of Trebizond* (1851), *The History of the Byzantine and Greek Empires 716–1453* (1853), *The History of Greece under Othman and Venetian Domination* (1856) and *A History of the Greek Revolution* (1861) supplemented the histories of GROTE and THIRLWALL and are pioneer works in their treatment of a continuous theme. They were published collectively as *A History of Greece from Its Conquest by the Romans to the Present Time: 146 BC to AD 1864* (1877). Many of Finlay's letters from Greece were published in *The Times* (1864–70). They are historically valuable but so far have not been collected.

Finlay, Ian Hamilton 1925– Poet and artist. Born in Nassau and brought up in Scotland, he became widely known as the leading British exponent of CONCRETE POETRY in the 1960s. In 1969 he moved to Stonypath, Lanarkshire, and began his work with inscriptions and landscape gardening, which uses imagery of the sea, the classical world and modern warfare and continues to cross over the traditional divisions between modes of artistic production. His work is represented in the Tate Gallery and the Scottish National Gallery of Modern Art, but is still primarily involved with the poetic use of language. *Selected Ponds* (1976) shows the landscape and inscription work to good effect. The best introduction to his complex and manifold art forms is Stephen Bann's pamphlet (1972) published by the Scottish National Gallery.

Finnegans Wake A novel by JAMES JOYCE, published in 1939. He began it in 1922 and published individual sections as *Work in Progress* during the 17 years of its composition. Joyce's last and most revolutionary work embodies his most extreme experiments with language and narrative. Puns, verbal compounds, and foreign words are combined with allusions from every conceivable source to create an obscure and densely structured text. Its aim is to relate the minimal central story to a much wider historical, psychological, religious and artistic cosmology, a procedure which has been likened to that of scholasticism and medieval ALLEGORY.

On a literal level, the novel presents the dreams and nightmares of Humphrey Chimpden Earwicker (a Dublin tavern-keeper) and his family (wife Anna, their sons Shem and Shaun, and daughter Isabel) as they lie asleep throughout one night. This, however, provides only a rationale for what is really a novel without narrative or plot, and in which all human experience is ultimately viewed as fragmentary. Major sources of influence have been identified in Vico's ideas of cyclical repetition, Freud's dream psychology, and Bruno's theory of the complementary but conflicting nature of opposites. The title is itself a compound of Finn MacCool, the Irish folk-hero who is supposed to return to life at some future date to become the saviour of Ireland, and Tim Finnegan, the hero of a music-hall BALLAD, who sprang to life in the middle of his own wake.

Firbank, (Arthur Annesley) Ronald 1886–1926 Novelist. Firbank was the son of a wealthy company director and was born in London. He was educated at Uppingham School and went on to Cambridge, but left in 1909 without graduating and travelled in the Mediterranean. He became a Roman Catholic while at Cambridge. Delicate in health and thoroughly eccentric, Firbank, whose character is described by his friend OSBERT SITWELL in *Noble Essences*, had wealth enough to indulge his own way of life. Witty, arch and meticulously, even artificially, written, his fiction carries what A. ALVAREZ has called as 'a sense of ominous unease'. A first book of stories, *Odette d'Antrevernes*, and *A Study in Temperament* appeared in 1905. The series of novels for which he is best known began with *Vainglory* (1915) and continued with *Inclinations* (1916), *Caprice* (1917), *Valmouth: A Romantic Novel* (1919), the short story *Santal* (1921), *The Flower beneath the Foot* (1923), *Prancing Nigger* (1924) and *Concerning the Eccentricities of Cardinal Pirelli* (1926). A play, *The Princess Zoubaroff: A Comedy* (1920), was not produced during his lifetime, and several short poems were published posthumously.

Firmilian: or, The Student of Badajoz A parody by WILLIAM EDMONSTONE AYTOUN of the poets he dubbed the SPASMODIC SCHOOL: SYDNEY DOBELL, PHILIP JAMES BAILEY and ALEXANDER SMITH. It was published in 1854. Firmilian, writing a poetic tragedy about Cain, decides that to do his subject justice he needs personal insight into the 'mental spasms of the tortured Cain'. He starts committing crimes, with ludicrous consequences.

Fisher, St John 1459–1535 Fisher was a humanist and Roman Catholic martyr who resisted Henry VIII's attempts to gain supremacy over the English church. He was ordained priest in 1491 and gained the patronage of Lady Margaret Beaufort whose confessor he became in 1497. He encouraged her patronage of the University of Cambridge where she founded a professorship in divinity in 1503 and Christ's College in 1505. The establishment of St John's, its sister college, was finally supervised by Fisher in 1511. Fisher was president of Queens' College in 1505–8 and became chancellor of the university and Bishop of Rochester in 1504. He encouraged Hebrew at the university and persuaded ERASMUS to lecture there on Greek in 1511–14.

A staunch supporter of the Roman Catholic church, Fisher was a controversialist against Lutheranism and preached against its heresies. He defended Catherine of Aragon in 1529 and opposed both the granting to Henry of the title Supreme Head of the Church in England and the Supremacy Act of 1534. He was condemned for not reporting the subversive prophecies of Elizabeth Barton and was imprisoned in the Tower with THOMAS MORE for refusing the oath consequent upon the 1534 Act of Succession. His position became even more dangerous when Paul III made him a cardinal in 1535. He was tricked into denying the King's headship of the church, condemned for treason and beheaded on Tower Hill, his head being afterward displayed on London Bridge. Fisher was beatified by Leo XIII in 1886 and canonized by Pius XI in 1935.

Fisher's complete Latin *Opera* were first published at Wurzburg in 1597.

His controversialist works against Luther, like *Assertionis lutheranae confutatio* (1523), were printed in England, as were some of his vernacular sermons, the sermon on the penitential psalms (1508) and an English sermon against Luther (1521).

Fisher, Roy 1930– Poet. Born in Handsworth, Birmingham, and educated locally and at Birmingham University, he worked as a teacher, becoming head of the English department at Bordesley College of Education in Birmingham (1963–71) and lecturer in American literature at the University of Keele (1971–82). Since 1982 he has been a freelance writer and jazz pianist. Although he is influenced by the American BLACK MOUNTAIN SCHOOL, his deliberately experimental approach makes his work hard to categorize or identify with a particular movement.

Poems 1955–1987 (1988) brings together new work and work from earlier volumes, including the prose poems of which he is a master. His best-known poem is probaby 'City', a study in urban desolation discussed by DONALD DAVIE in his study of THOMAS HARDY (1972).

Fitch, William Clyde 1865–1909 American playwright. Born in Elmira, New York, Fitch studied journalism at Amherst College before becoming a journalist in New York. His first play, *Beau Brummel* (1890), was a vehicle for the popular actor Richard Mansfield. Over the next 20 years he wrote nearly 60 plays, earning for himself a fortune and Broadway a new status as the home of American drama. The best are society MELODRAMAS combining superficial realism with emotional excess. They include *A Modern Match* (1892), *Barbara Frietchie* (1899), *The Climbers* (1901), *Captain Jinks of the Horse Marines* (1901), *The Girl with the Green Eyes* (1902), *The Truth* (1906) and *The Woman in the Case* (1909).

Fitzball, Edward 1793–1873 Playwright. Born plain Edward Ball in Cambridgeshire, he turned to writing when his Norwich printing house failed, and produced at least 150 plays as well as four novels, six volumes of bouncy verse and an informative autobiography, *Thirty-Five Years of a Dramatic Author's Life* (1859). Most famous for his spectacular MELODRAMAS, he wrote nothing better than *Jonathan Bradford* (1833), based on a recent murder. His quest for gallery-gripping effects can be read in his titles: *The Burning Bridge* (1824), *The Earthquake* (1828), *The Negro of Wapping* (1838), *The Wreck and the Reef* (1847). It was the bursts of red and blue fire rather than the skeletal text that brought *The Flying Dutchman* (1827) its phenomenal popularity. His output, in both quantity and quality, is typical of the journeyman dramatist's work in the busy London theatres. Adaptations of popular novels, thefts from the French stage, comic operas, BURLESQUES: whatever was wanted Fitzball provided at the rate of six a year.

FitzGerald, Edward 1809–83 Poet and translator. Born into a wealthy family at Bredfield, Suffolk, he was educated at the King Edward VI Grammar School in Bury St Edmunds and at Trinity College, Cambridge, where he encountered THACKERAY, TENNYSON and others soon to become eminent Victorians. FitzGerald pursued no career and passed almost his entire life in his native county. Its even tenor was disturbed only by an incautious marriage in 1856 to the daughter of the Quaker poet BERNARD BARTON, of whom he had written a striking *Memoir* in 1849. But FitzGerald's first separate volume was *Euphranor* (1851), a Platonic dialogue about the Victorian obsession with the rebirth of chivalry; next came *Polonius: A Collection of Wise Saws and Modern Instances*

(1852) and in 1853 his translation of *Six Dramas of Calderón* (he was to translate two more plays by the Spanish dramatist in the next decade). In the early 1850s FitzGerald took up Oriental studies in earnest and in 1856 came his translation *Salámán and Absal: An Allegory Translated from the Persian of Jami*. This was followed in 1859 by his major literary work, the anonymous pamphlet entitled THE RUBÁIYÁT OF OMAR KHAYYÁM. In later years FitzGerald translated the *Agamemnon*, *Oedipus Tyrannus* and *Oedipus Coloneus*, worked on a dictionary of the correspondence of Madame de Sévigné and assembled some readings from CRABBE, a poet he admired. His correspondence, marked by wit and sympathy, places him among the masters of epistolary art.

FitzGerald always loved the sea and maintained a yacht which he sailed off the Suffolk coast; he also enjoyed friendships among the local fisher-folk. An eccentric from a family of eccentrics, his marriage was a disaster and lasted less than a year. A shy, unobtrusive man given to melancholy introspection, FitzGerald was an undeniable influence on the late Victorian literature of pessimism mainly through his adaptation of the *Rubáiyát*, a poem whose extraordinary popularity survives even into our own time.

Fitzgerald, F(rancis) Scott (Key) 1896–1940 American novelist and short-story writer. He was born in St Paul, Minnesota, and entered Princeton University in 1913. In 1917 he left before graduating to take up a commission in the US Army. While stationed near Montgomery, Alabama, he courted and became engaged to Zelda Sayre, herself an aspiring writer. After his discharge from the army in 1919, he moved to New York and worked briefly for an advertising agency. That same year he sold his first story, 'Babes in the Wood', which appeared in *The Smart Set*. He returned to St Paul and rewrote a novel he had begun while in the army; originally entitled 'The Romantic Egotist', it appeared in 1920 as *This Side of Paradise* and was an almost immediate success. Its hero, Amory Blaine, like Fitzgerald himself goes to Princeton, where he becomes a member of the literary coterie. He serves in World War I (unlike Fitzgerald, he is sent to France and sees action) and then works in advertising. He has several romantic affairs, none of them lasting. At the end of the novel, aged 24, he recognizes that his own egotism has prevented his finding happiness.

Fitzgerald and Zelda Sayre were married in 1920, and in the same year his first collection of short stories, *Flappers and Philosophers*, was published. Fitzgerald's second novel, *The Beautiful and Damned*, appeared in 1922, and was less well received. Its main character, Anthony Patch, is an alcoholic whose goal in life is to inherit and spend his grandfather's money. Though he is eventually successful in contesting the will that has disinherited him, by the end of the novel he and his wife Gloria have declined both physically and spiritually because of their dissolute, alcoholic life-style. (For much of his life Fitzgerald was himself an alcoholic.) Another collection of short stories, *Tales of the Jazz Age*, which included 'The Diamond as Big as the Ritz', was published in 1922. 'The Jazz Age' is Fitzgerald's own descriptive phrase for the 1920s, and his early financial success as a writer enabled him and Zelda to lead the kind of decadent, boisterous existence it suggests.

In October 1922 the couple moved to Great Neck, New York. (Living in this affluent Long Island community provided Fitzgerald with material for his next novel, THE GREAT GATSBY.) While there he renewed his acquaintance with JOHN DOS PASSOS and became friendly with RING LARDNER. He also revised his play, *The Vegetable*, which had an unsuccessful one-week run in 1923, and continued to turn out stories for magazines in order to finance his extravagant lifestyle. Because they could live more cheaply in Europe than in the USA, the Fitzgeralds went to France in April 1924. There Fitzgerald met two other expatriate American writers, ERNEST HEMINGWAY, who became a close friend, and GERTRUDE STEIN. In 1925 he published what many consider his best novel, *The Great Gatsby*, and in 1926 a third collection of short stories, entitled *All the Sad Young Men*.

During the next five years the Fitzgeralds travelled back and forth between Europe and America several times. Zelda had the first of several nervous breakdowns in April 1930; she was hospitalized periodically, both in Europe and the USA, from then until her death in 1948. Fitzgerald published his fourth novel, TENDER IS THE NIGHT, in 1934; pressed for money, he was disappointed that it did not sell better, though it was generally well received by the critics. Another collection of stories, *Taps at Reveille*, followed in 1935. That same year he began to write confessional essays about his broken health and exhaustion as a writer. The essays – 'The Crack-Up', 'Pasting It Together' and 'Handle with Care' – were published in *Esquire* magazine in 1936, and were subsequently included in *The Crack-Up* (1945), a collection of Fitzgerald's essays, notes and letters edited by his friend EDMUND WILSON.

For a few months in 1927, and then again in 1931 and 1932, Fitzgerald worked in Hollywood as a screenwriter. In 1937 he returned to accept a lucrative contract with Metro-Goldwyn-Mayer. He worked on various screenplays, but completed only one (*Three Comrades*, 1938), and was eventually fired because of his drinking. Though he occasionally visited Zelda, who by this time was in a hospital in North Carolina, he became involved with another woman, the columnist Sheilah Graham, whom he met in Hollywood in 1937. He was to die in her apartment, of a heart attack, in December 1940. During his last months Fitzgerald returned to writing fiction, producing several short stories which were collected and published

Scott Fitzgerald

in 1962 as *The Pat Hobby Stories*. He also began a novel about a Hollywood producer, *The Last Tycoon*, which, though unfinished, was published in 1941.

Fitzgerald, Penelope 1916– Biographer and novelist. Educated at Wycombe Abbey and Somerville College, Oxford, she published nothing until 1975, when her biography of Edward Burne-Jones appeared. It has been followed by *The Knox Brothers* (1977), a portrait of her father Edmund Knox, editor of *PUNCH*, and his three eminent brothers, and a biography of CHARLOTTE MEW (1984). Her fiction, written in the same witty, economical style and showing the same gift for describing her subjects' working lives, includes: *The Golden Child* (1977); *The Bookshop* (1978); *Offshore* (1979), winner of the BOOKER PRIZE; *Human Voices* (1980), set in Broadcasting House during World War II; *At Freddie's* (1982); *Innocence* (1986); *The Beginning of Spring* (1988), about an English-run printworks in Moscow in 1913; and *The Gate of Angels* (1990). She has also edited WILLIAM MORRIS's *Novel on Blue Paper*.

Fitzgerald, Robert D(avid) 1902–87 Australian poet. Born in Hunter's Hill, Sydney, of Irish ancestry, he attended Sydney Grammar School and, briefly, studied science at the University of Sydney. He was articled to a firm of surveyors in 1922 and qualified in 1925. In 1926–36 he worked as a surveyor in Fiji, an experience which left its mark on his poetry. From 1939 until his retirement in 1965, he was employed by the Department of the Interior. He won many awards for his poetry, including an OBE for services to literature in 1951.

Concerned with philosophical issues, particularly free will, his work helped to bridge the gap between the 'difficult' poetry of CHRISTOPHER BRENNAN and the more accessible poetry of THOMAS SHAPCOTT or LES MURRAY. A strong humanitarian concern is always evident. His finest work includes 'The Hidden Bole', an ELEGY for Pavlova, which appeared in *Moonlight Acre* (1938) and which explores the nature of time and art. *Heemskerk Shoals* (1949) pursued the same ideas more colloquially. *Between Two Tides* (1952) is an account of a struggle between two Tongan chiefs and a meditation on how choices are made. His finest achievement was *The Wind at Your Door* (1959), a poetic attempt to come to terms with Australian ancestry, which is perceived as having two opposing strains: free settler and convict, victor and victim. Fitzgerald's other poetry includes *The Greater Apollo* (1927), *To Meet the Sun* (1929), *This Night's Orbit* (1953), *Southmost Twelve* (1962), *Forty Years' Poems* (1965) and *Product* (1978).

Fitzmaurice, George 1877–1963 Irish playwright. He was born in County Kerry to a Protestant clergyman and his Roman Catholic wife. His first published work, sketches of peasant life in Kerry, appeared in newspapers, and Irish peasants were the subject of his first play, *The Country Dressmaker* (1907), produced at the ABBEY THEATRE. The same theatre staged Fitzmaurice's idiosyncratic tragicomedies in one act, *The Pie-Dish* (1908) and *The Magic Glasses* (1913). Service in the British Army during World War I brought to an end Fitzmaurice's theatrical career. Increasingly reclusive, he resisted performance of his plays, and it was not until the posthumous publication of his *Collected Plays* (1967–70) that interest in this remarkable writer was revived. A tragedy, *The Moonlighter*, and such comic fantasies as *The Enchanted Land*, *The Ointment Blue* and *The Dandy Dolls*, show Fitzmaurice's range and originality.

Flatman, Thomas 1637–88 Poet and painter. A fellow of New College, Oxford, Flatman was much admired as a painter of miniatures. His *Poems and Songs* was published in 1674 and his verse occasionally appeared in anthologies; he also composed some hymns.

Flecker, James (Herman) Elroy 1884–1915 Poet and playwright. Born in Uppingham, he was educated at Trinity College, Oxford, and followed a career in the consular service, posted to Constantinople and Beirut. He contributed to *GEORGIAN POETRY* and published volumes of lyric poetry influenced by the last years of the AESTHETIC MOVEMENT: *The Bridge of Fire* (1907), *Forty-Two Poems* (1911) and *The Golden Journey to Samarkand* (1913). He wrote a dialogue on education, *The Grecians* (1910), and an experimental novel, *The King of Alsander* (1914). Two plays, *HASSAN* (1922) and *Don Juan* (1925), appeared after his early death from tuberculosis. His *Collected Poems*, edited by J. C. SQUIRE, appeared in 1947.

Flecknoe, Richard c. 1600–c. 1678 Poet and playwright. He was probably Irish but little is known of his youth beyond what he reveals in his *Relation of Ten Years Travels in Europe, Asia, Africa and America* (1654). He wrote: five plays, of which only *Love's Dominion* (1654) was ever performed; *Enigmatical Characters*, a collection of prose sketches (1658); and a book of verse, *Epigrams of All Sorts* (1670). His *Short Discourse on the English Stage* (1664) roused MARVELL to lampoon him (*An English Priest at Rome*) and DRYDEN to satirize him (*MAC FLECKNOE*).

Fleming, Ian (Lancaster) 1908–64 Novelist. Educated at Eton and Sandhurst, he worked as a journalist for Reuters and *The Times* (for both of which he served in Moscow) before writing the first of his 13 James Bond thrillers, *Casino Royale* (1952). The knowing exotic detail and the worldly wit of these books, and the glamorous, racy adventures of their protagonist, combined to make James Bond one of the most popular secret agents in the history of spy fiction. A parallel series of visually spectacular, and immensely successful, film adaptations starring first Sean Connery and then Roger Moore and Timothy Dalton further increased Fleming's and Bond's reputations. Since Fleming's death attempts have been made by KINGSLEY AMIS, in *Colonel Sun* (1968), and recently by John Gardner to extend the life of James Bond in pastiche thrillers.

Fletcher, Giles, the elder 1546–1611 Poet and diplomat. He was the father of the poets PHINEAS and GILES FLETCHER THE YOUNGER, and the uncle of the dramatist JOHN FLETCHER. At Eton he contributed Latin epigrams to a collection presented to Queen Elizabeth on her visit of 1563. He went as a scholar to King's College, Cambridge, in 1565 and graduated MA in 1573. He lectured at King's and to the university on Greek, became deputy Public Orator in 1577, and a senior fellow of King's in 1578. He became chancellor of the diocese of Sussex in 1582, an MP for Winchelsea in 1584 and, on the queen's recommendation, remembrancer (official letter-writer) of the City of London in 1585.

Of the Russe Commonwealth (1591), the most important description of Russia by a 16th-century Englishman, resulted from his mission as ambassador to Tsar Fyodor I in 1588. It remained popular long enough to include MILTON, as well as JONSON, among its readers. *Licia* (1593) is chiefly a collection of sonnets following in the wake of SIDNEY's *ASTROPHIL AND STELLA*, though it also contains an ode, a dia-

logue, some elegies and a monologue by Richard III on his rise to power. Fletcher's attempt to gain Burghley's patronage for a Latin history of the reign of Elizabeth was unsuccessful.

Fletcher, Giles, the younger 1585–1623 Poet. The younger son of GILES FLETCHER THE ELDER and brother of PHINEAS FLETCHER, he was educated at Westminster School and Trinity College, Cambridge, where he became reader in Greek. In 1619 he was appointed rector of Alderton in Suffolk, where he died at the age of 38. He is remembered for *Christ's Victory and Triumph in Heaven and Earth, over and after Death* (1610), a Baroque religious poem, influenced by SPENSER and popular in its day.

Fletcher, John 1579–1625 Playwright. He was the son of a bishop of London and a nephew of GILES FLETCHER THE ELDER. Little is known of his life after he left Cambridge, though he became more exclusively committed to the theatre than most contemporary writers of comparable standing. It was probably as one of BEN JONSON's circle that he met FRANCIS BEAUMONT in London. Together the two friends, who had provided the fashionable BOYS' COMPANIES with some marketable plays, took over as leading dramatists for the KING's MEN after that company began to perform in the indoor BLACKFRIARS. The extraordinary success of the partnership, most notably in *PHILASTER* (c. 1609), *THE MAID'S TRAGEDY* (c. 1610) and *A KING AND NO KING* (1611), encouraged their contemporaries and immediate successors to ascribe to them far more work (over 50 plays) than the seven or eight confidently allowed by modern scholars. See the entry about Beaumont for further details of the collaboration.

If, as is widely accepted, Fletcher was the sole author of *THE FAITHFUL SHEPHERDESS* (c. 1609), *Bonduca* (1609–?14), *VALENTINIAN* (1610–?14), *Monsieur Thomas* (1610–?15), *The Mad Lover* (c. 1616), *THE CHANCES* (c. 1617), *THE HUMOROUS LIEUTENANT* (c. 1619), *The Island Princess* (c. 1620), *Women Pleased* (1620–?23), *The Pilgrim* (c. 1621), *THE WILD-GOOSE CHASE* (c. 1621), *RULE A WIFE AND HAVE A WIFE* (1624) and *A Wife for a Month* (1624), then there is substance in the claim that Fletcher, although a subtle contriver of individual scenes, was less adept in the composition of whole plays. He was, however, a willing collaborator, most notably after the retirement and early death of Beaumont, with SHAKESPEARE in *HENRY VIII* (1613) and *THE TWO NOBLE KINSMEN* (1613), with FIELD in *The Honest Man's Fortune* (1613), *The Knight of Malta* (c. 1618) and other plays, and with MASSINGER in more than 20 plays. Effective products of this latter collaboration include: *The Tragedy of Sir John van Olden Barnavelt* (1619), about contemporary events in the Netherlands; *The Custom of the Country* (c. 1619), a bawdy tragicomedy; *The Beggar's Bush* (c.

1622), a romantic drama using thieves' and vagabonds' cant; and *The Spanish Curate* (c. 1622), a comedy of intrigue.

Fletcher's influence on the 17th-century development of a comedy of manners and his sophisticated treatment of tragicomedy are signs of his flexible talent and of the alertness with which he perceived the changing tastes of Stuart England.

Fletcher, John Gould 1886–1950 American poet. Born in Little Rock, Arkansas, and educated at Harvard, he went to live in England in 1900. He published his verse in five volumes, at his own expense, in 1913: *The Book of Nature, The Dominant City, Fire and Wine, Fool's Gold* and *Visions of the Evening.* Though critical reception was mixed, he did receive favourable notice from AMY LOWELL, who became his close friend. In 1914 he became associated with IMAGISM and contributed to Lowell's anthology *Some Imagist Poets. Irradiations: Sand and Spray* appeared in 1915, and *Goblins and Pagodas* in the following year. He remained in Europe until 1933, contributing to THE CRITERION (1923–7) and becoming friends with T. S. ELIOT, DONALD DAVIDSON and JOHN CROWE RANSOM. He returned to the USA in 1933, and his *Selected Poems* (1938) received the PULITZER PRIZE. His later works reflect his association with the FUGITIVES, and his continuing interest in Eastern mysticism (which had been evident in his early verse). His other works include *Japanese Prints* (1918), *The Tree of Life* (1918), *Parables* (1925), *Branches of Adam* (1926), *The Black Rock* (1928), *XXIV Elegies* (1935) and *South Star* (1941). His prose writings include *Paul Gauguin: His Life and Art* (1921), *John Smith – Also Pocahontas* (1928) and *The Two Frontiers: A Study in Historical Psychology* (1930). An autobiography, *Life is My Song*, appeared in 1937.

Fletcher, Phineas 1582–1650 Poet. The elder son of GILES FLETCHER THE ELDER and the brother of GILES FLETCHER THE YOUNGER, Phineas Fletcher was born at Cranbrook in Kent. He was educated at Eton and King's College, Cambridge, where he stayed for 11 years, writing some minor verse. He was ordained in 1615 and became chaplain to Sir Henry Willoghby; he was rector of Hilgay from 1621 until his death. Fletcher was the author of some vehemently anti-Catholic verse, of which *The Locusts or Apollyonists* (1627) is a typical piece. Like his brother, he wrote in imitation of SPENSER: his erotic narrative, *Britain's Ida* (1628), was ascribed to Spenser in order to safeguard the true author's ecclesiastical position. *The Purple Island* (1633) is a convoluted allegory examining the physical and mental nature of mankind, in which virtue and vice are interminably at war. Fletcher's pastoral play, *Sicelides: A Piscatory* (published in 1631), never received its intended performance before James I.

Flint, F(rank) S(tuart) 1885–1960 Poet. Born into appalling poverty in Islington, he left school at 13 and joined the civil service at 19. An autodidact, he mastered 10 languages and quickly became the leading authority on contemporary French poetry. His first collection, *In the Net of Stars* (1909), featured conventional love poems but *Cadences* (1915), published after he had met POUND and T. E. HULME and which appeared in Pound's *Des Imagistes* anthology (1914), made an important contribution to IMAGISM. It is written in accordance with Flint's theory of 'unrhymed cadence'. His final volume, *Otherworld: Cadences* (1920), reverted to his initial Romanticism, towards narrative rather than the juxtaposed images of imagism. After giving up writing he continued to work for the Ministry of Labour until 1951.

Flores and Blancheflour A VERSE ROMANCE in couplets composed c. 1250. One of the earliest English romances, it is based on a lost French version. Blanchefleur is a captive maiden brought up with Flores, son of the King of Spain. They fall in love, but the King disapproves and while Flores is absent Blanchefleur is sold as a slave. On his return Flores is told she is dead and tries to kill himself. At this his parents reveal the truth and he goes to seek her. He traces her to the harem of the Emir of Babylon and bribes his way into the harem concealed in a basket of flowers, but the reunited couple are discovered and condemned to death. Each is reluctant to use a magic ring which will save only one of them. This, and their story, move the Emir and he allows them to marry.

Florio, John ?1553–1625 Translator and lexicographer. The son of an Italian Protestant refugee, Florio studied at Oxford and, in 1604–19, was groom of the privy chamber to the queen. His greatest work was a translation of Montaigne's *Essais* (1603, revised 1613), free to the point of inaccuracy but still fertile reading for SHAKESPEARE among other contemporary writers. Florio's translation of Giovanni Battista Ramusio's account of the voyage of Jacques Cartier was printed in 1580 as *Navigations and Discoveries. Florio His First Fruits* (1578), a grammar and dialogues in English and Italian, was followed by *Florio's Second Fruits* (1591). His Italian–English dictionary, *A World of Words* (1598), was enlarged in a second edition as *Queen Anne's New World of Words* (1611). *Giardino di Ricreazione* (1591) is a collection of Italian proverbs.

Flower and the Leaf, The An anonymous poem written in the third quarter of the 15th century. It was at one time attributed to CHAUCER (see CHAUCERIAN APOCRYPHA) and has more recently, but improbably, been attributed to the author of THE ASSEMBLY OF LADIES. The narrator is female, but it is impossible to deduce the sex of the poet.

The lady observes the followers of the Flower and those of the Leaf jousting and singing on a summer day. The Flower's followers faint in the heat and are drenched by a storm, but those of the Leaf shelter and then comfort the others. The allegory is explained to the lady as demonstrating the contrast between those who are idle and pleasure-seeking and those who are faithful and chaste. Asked which side she favours, she opts for the Leaf.

folk revival, the The antiquarian researches of THOMAS PERCY, ALLAN RAMSAY, BURNS and SCOTT in the late 18th century and the folkloric researches of the German Grimm brothers in the early 19th century had become influential throughout the English-speaking world by the late 19th century. There was a flurry of activity by middle-class intellectuals anxious to preserve a traditional peasant culture which they saw as threatened by industrialization, urbanization and the spread of mechanical forms of entertainment.

Much of this energy was devoted to Celtic culture and forms part of the CELTIC REVIVAL. The folk revival in England was spearheaded by the work of SABINE BARING-GOULD, who collected and published folk songs in and around his Devon parish, and by Frank Kidson in Yorkshire; and in the USA by FRANCIS J. CHILD's collection, still regarded to a considerable extent as definitive, of *The English and Scottish Popular Ballads* (1882–98). In the early 20th century the work of collecting was continued and expanded by such influential young musicians as Ralph Vaughan Williams, Percy Grainger and E. J. Moeran, and by literary amateurs like George Gardiner and the Hammond brothers in Hampshire and the south, and Alfred Williams in the Upper Thames Valley. The most important and industrious of the collectors of this period was Cecil J. Sharp (1859–1924), who operated widely throughout England and the eastern USA, and after whom the London headquarters of the English Folk Dance and Song Society is named. His original interest was in folk dance; his song collecting was started by his having overheard a song in Somerset, sung at work by his clerical host's gardener, the felicitously named John England.

The second phase of the revival, following World War II, differed in that it was brought about largely by left-wing thinkers, often themselves of working-class origin, who saw folk song as a means of politicizing the working class through involvement in its own traditional artefacts. Ewan MacColl and A. L. Lloyd in England, Hamish Henderson in Scotland and Pete Seeger in the USA all come into this category: all were performers as well as writers and collectors. ARNOLD WESKER's Centre 42 project was also involved in the folk movement. Lloyd's *Folk Song in England* (1967) is an attempt to chart its subject's development in Marxist terms, and with Vaughan Williams he edited the influential *Penguin Book of English Folksongs* (1959).

Aesthetic appreciation of folk song spread across the social and political spectrum, but the left continued to predominate in the resultant folk-club movement. Performance took equal pride of place with scholarship in this phase. The bowdlerization of love-songs which their *zeitgeist* had forced on to the earlier collectors was despised and the songs were restored and republished. Many singers steeped in traditional song, such as MacColl, Cyril Tawney, Peter Bellamy, Bob Pegg and Peter Coe, were successful in creating new songs convincingly in the traditional idiom which the revival had brought to a wider audience.

The extent to which the working class has actually been involved in *any* phase of the revival, the most recent any more than the earlier manifestations in the 18th, 19th and early 20th centuries, has been cogently questioned by Dave Harker, a Trotskyist, in *Fakesong* (1985).

Fool of Quality, The A SENTIMENTAL NOVEL by HENRY BROOKE, published in five volumes (1766–72). Henry, second son of the Earl of Moreland, is called a 'fool of quality' because he seems dull and unintelligent in comparison with his elder brother. Rejected by his parents, he is reared by his foster-mother and educated by his uncle. He grows into a young man of strength, beauty and virtue who spends his time helping the unfortunate. On this slender framework Brooke hangs a number of discourses on various aspects of the human condition and, in the latter part, on Christian mysticism in the form of a discussion between the author and a friend. The device is cumbersome, but the book does raise issues that were soon to be taken up by Rousseau, WILLIAM GODWIN and THOMAS PAINE. JOHN WESLEY admired Brooke's ideas and made an edited version of the book for use by Methodists (1781), while CHARLES KINGSLEY wrote an admiring preface to the 1859 edition.

foot See METRE.

Foote, Horton 1916– American playwright and screenwriter. His best-known work has been for films such as *To Kill a Mockingbird* (based on the novel by HARPER LEE; 1962), *Tender Mercies* (1983) and *The Trip to Bountiful* (1985), based on one of his own plays. His *Orphans Home* cycle consists of nine plays – beginning with *Texas Town* (1942) and ending with *Dividing the Estate* (1989) – set in and around his Texas hometown of Wharton (renamed Harrison) and evoking the era 1902–28.

Foote, Samuel 1720–77 Playwright and actor. He was born into a wealthy Cornish family and educated in Truro and at Oxford, which he left without taking a degree. Foote lived extravagantly, and after a brief imprisonment for debt he decided to try his hand as an actor. His talent for mimicry brought him considerable notoriety, and it was this gift that he decided, opportunistically, to exploit in his own dramatic writing. Almost all his plays include satiric portraits of living individuals, most famously George Whitefield and his Methodist associates in *The Minor* (1760). Many of Foote's victims objected, and the Duchess of Kingston's fury at her portrait as Lady Kitty Crocodile in *A Trip to Calais* (1775) indirectly brought his theatrical career to an end. Tried on a trumped-up charge of homosexual rape, Foote was acquitted but effectively silenced.

During an adventurous life, he had been often in trouble. His evasion of the licensing laws – he would charge admission for 'tea' or 'chocolate' and provide satirical entertainment 'free' – offended the Lord Chamberlain in the 1740s and again in 1762–6. A riding accident, the result of a practical joke, led to his having a leg amputated in 1766, and, in compensation, some aristocratic friends procured for him a summer licence to perform plays at the HAYMARKET. Still determined to act, Foote wrote for himself a number of 'cripple' plays, including *The Devil upon Two Sticks* (1768) and *The Lame Lover* (1770). His last considerable play, *Piety in Pattens* (1773), was a vigorous attack on the fashion for sentimentalism. Like all his best work, including *The Author* (1757), *The Mayor of Garret* (1763), *The Patron* (1764), *The Commissary* (1765) and *The Nabob* (1772), it shows a talent for controversy and an ability to stretch the limits of the farcical 18th-century 'afterpiece'.

For the Term of His Natural Life See HIS NATURAL LIFE.

Ford, Ford Madox [Hueffer, Ford Hermann] 1873–1939 Novelist and literary journalist. He was the grandson of the painter Ford Madox Brown and the nephew of WILLIAM MICHAEL ROSSETTI, and changed his name from Hueffer in 1919. Brown illustrated Ford's first book, *The Brown Owl* (1892), though Ford later expressed mixed feelings about the PRE-RAPHAELITES in his art criticism. During the years of his early marriage to Elsie Martindale in 1894 he collaborated with CONRAD on *The Inheritors* (1901) and *Romance* (1903), and produced historical-topographical works, verse, SCIENCE FICTION and historical romance (*The Fifth Queen* trilogy, 1906–8). During his brief editorship of *THE ENGLISH REVIEW*, founded in 1908, he nevertheless managed to sponsor POUND, D. H. LAWRENCE and WYNDHAM LEWIS as well as publishing work by established figures such as JAMES, HARDY, BENNETT, GALSWORTHY and YEATS. He lost control of the *Review* in 1910, a time of crisis associated with his romance with VIOLET HUNT.

Ford published numerous works before World War I, including two novels, *A Call* (1910) and *THE*

GOOD SOLDIER (1915). A tetralogy, *PARADE'S END*, was published between 1924 and 1928, while he was living in France, the country which eventually became his homeland. In Paris, in 1924, he founded *The Transatlantic Review*; HEMINGWAY was deputy editor, and they published work by Pound, JOYCE, GERTRUDE STEIN, E E CUMMINGS and JEAN RHYS. Ford wrote about the Paris years in *It was the Nightingale* (1933), one of many works of personal recollection.

During his last years he lived frugally in the South of France with an American, Janice Biala, and expressed his liking for a self-sufficient life-style in *From Minstrels to the Machine* (1938) and other later works. He also gave support to many of the younger American Southern Agrarians such as ALLEN TATE, CAROLINE GORDON, KATHERINE ANNE PORTER and ROBERT LOWELL. He was briefly associated with a college in Michigan, and it was here that he planned his monumental last work, *The March of Literature* (1939), a survey of ancient literature and Mediterranean culture.

Ford, John c. 1586–c. 1640 Playwright. Little is known of his life. He was born in Devon, and probably educated at Oxford and the Middle Temple. He had published poems and prose some years before his first known involvement in the theatre, already displaying the interest in moral paradox that characterizes his best plays. The order and precise dating of his dramatic work is the subject of scholarly debate. He began, probably, as a collaborator with DEKKER and ROWLEY in *THE WITCH OF EDMONTON* (c. 1621), and was again associated with Dekker in *The Welsh Ambassador* (1623) and a masque, *The Sun's Darling* (1624). Of the work of which he was sole author, two comedies, *The Fancies, Chaste and Noble* (c. 1636) and *The Lady's Trial* (1638), are slight pieces. Ford's startling interest in morbid psychology and emotional excess belongs more readily to tragedy. *The Lover's Melancholy* (1628) is a comedy that edges towards tragedy. *Love's Sacrifice* (c. 1632) is a tragedy of almost unrelieved gloom, notable for its creation of a magnificent villain in D'Avalos. It is the two tragedies, *THE BROKEN HEART* (c. 1629) and *'TIS PITY SHE'S A WHORE* (c. 1625–33), together with the chronicle play *PERKIN WARBECK* (published 1634), that have established for Ford a unique place in the drama of Caroline England.

Ford, Richard 1944– American novelist and short-story writer. He was born in Jackson, Mississippi, and educated at Berkeley. Although the downbeat stories collected in *Rock Springs* (1988) can be classed with the work of RAYMOND CARVER as examples of DIRTY REALISM, his novels seek wider contexts. *A Piece of My Heart* (1976) is a Californian tale of brittle love and violence. *The Ultimate Good Luck* (1981), follows its hero, a Vietnam veteran, to Mexico. His most acclaimed work, *The Sportswriter* (1986), is an urbane account of a novelist who turns sportswriter because of his suspicion that 'there are no transcendent themes in life'. *Wildlife* (1990) was less well received.

Forest, The A collection of poems by BEN JONSON, published in the 1616 edition of his works. It includes some of his best-known pieces: the influential country-house poem 'To Penshurst', 'That Women are But Men's Shadows', 'Come My Celia, Let Us Prove' and the famous 'Song: To Celia' ('Drink to Me Only, with Thine Eyes').

Forester, C(ecil) S(cott) 1899–1966 Novelist. Born in Cairo, he was educated at Dulwich College, and studied medicine at Guy's Hospital before turning to writing. His first successful novel, *Payment Deferred* (1926), set during World War I, was made into a play (1931) and later a film. This was followed by *Brown on Resolution* (1929), then a biography of Nelson and two of his best-known novels of the Peninsular War: *Death to the French* (1932) and *The Gun* (1933). More popular historical fiction followed: *The African Queen* (1935; successfully filmed in 1952) and *The General* (1936) – both of which reworked the characteristic Forester theme of individual fortitude in war. He became a journalist during the Spanish Civil War and his novels continued with the immensely popular 'Hornblower' books, starting with *The Happy Return* (1937). Hero of the Napoleonic Wars, Hornblower was partly modelled on Nelson, and in a further dozen novels published over the next 25 years Forester charted his career from midshipman to admiral.

During World War II Forester devoted himself to writing propaganda for the Allied cause, much of it for American consumption. *The Ship* (1943) resulted from a mission in HMS *Penelope* which he undertook at the invitation of the Admiralty. He suffered from ill health for the latter half of his life, and settled in the United States at the end of the war. *Long before Forty*, an autobiography up to his 31st year, was published posthumously in 1967.

formalism A term applied both to a generalized tendency and to certain specific schools and movements within literary criticism. Aristotle was the greatest precursor of formalist method, with his emphasis on the structure and defining characteristics of TRAGEDY. Since then, criticism has tended to fluctuate from age to age between a broadly Aristotelian concern with systematic theory and a more subjective, less methodical style of approach. In the present century formalism has enjoyed a widespread revival of interest among critics determined to rescue their discipline from the vagaries of individual taste.

The Russian Formalists of the 1920s were the first to raise this doctrine into a high point of principle. Their efforts were concentrated on two main topics: the language of poetry and the structure of narrative discourse (folk-tales, novels and short stories). They saw poetry as a special kind of language, set apart from everyday prose by its use of certain devices – METAPHOR, METONYMY, RHYME, ALLITERATION, etc. – which focused attention on its formal or aesthetic attributes. The effect of such devices, so they argued, is to 'defamiliarize' the normal relation between language and reality, word and world, thus forcing us to break (momentarily at least) with our routine, jaded habits of perception. This power of 'making strange' – *ostranenie* in the Russian – is achieved through the 'foregrounding' of various stylistic features that emphasize the difference between poetry and prose, and thus prevent us reading straight 'through' the text to its mere paraphrasable content. In their work on narrative the Formalists again made a virtue of system and method. On the surface, it might seem impossible to achieve any unified general theory that would encompass all the myths, stories and elaborated plots that make up the corpus of world literature. But beneath this surface – so the Formalists argued – there exist certain deep regularities which amount to a 'grammar' of narrative types. Criticism is best, most usefully employed in deducing these deep-laid structures of the text, and not in the mere piling-up of endless new interpretations. It can then be placed on a truly scientific and co-operative footing, as well as being able to profit from advances in neighbouring disciplines like structural linguistics.

The practitioners of NEW CRITICISM in the 1930s and 1940s have also been described as formalists, since they read poetry with a keen attentiveness to its formal and rhetorical structure. They were, however, much less concerned with matters of theory and method, preferring to operate with a handful of non-technical terms ('ambiguity', 'irony', 'paradox', etc.) whose looseness of definition was compensated for by their flexibility in use. More recently, the proponents of French STRUCTURALISM have played an active role in reviving and developing the legacy of the Russian Formalists.

Fornés, Maria Irene 1930– American playwright and director. Born in Havana, she emigrated to the USA in 1945. Her greatest critical success, *Fefu and Her Friends* (1977), presents a feminist perspective on female friendship and women's roles in patriarchal society. Other plays and musicals which have established her reputation as an off-Broadway writer and director include *Tango Palace* (1964), *Promenade* (1965), *The Successful Life of Three* (1965), *Dr Kheal* (1968), *The Danube* (1984), *The Conduct of Life* (1985) and *Abingdon Square* (1987). They tackle serious indi-

E. M. Forster

vidual, national, and global problems with cinematic techniques and zany humour.

Fors Clavigera A compendium of some half-million words by JOHN RUSKIN, published as monthly letters to the workmen and labourers of England between January 1871 and March 1878 (when he became mentally ill) and intermittently thereafter. The enigmatic title suggests more than 'Fortune with the nail', as Ruskin himself informs the reader. 'Fors' he associates with 'Force' (the power of doing good work), with 'Fortitude' (the bearing of pain, if necessary, in the execution of that work) and with 'Fortune' (the 'necessary fate of man'). Similarly, 'Clavigera' is laden with meanings: the 'Club', the 'Key' and the

'Nail' – with Herculean strength, patience and the law, respectively. While *Fors Clavigera* includes many urgent messages on social issues, it moves into other discussions, often highly discursive. The most incongruous subjects jostle each other for attention, and the whole is a dazzling show of linguistic pyrotechnics. As autobiography, often cloaked in symbolism, the book is important in unlocking some of Ruskin's psychological complexities.

Forsaken Merman, The A poem by MATTHEW ARNOLD, published in *The Strayed Reveller and Other Poems* (1849). A merman laments his wife, a girl from the land; she bore him children and then felt the call of her own world in the sound of church bells at

Easter. She leaves her sea king and never returns. In its melancholy and its preoccupation with loss, *The Forsaken Merman* sounds a note that recurs throughout Arnold's poetry and, indeed, the poetry of many mid-Victorian contemporaries.

Forster, E(dward) M(organ) 1879–1970 Novelist, short-story writer and essayist. He was born in London and educated at Tonbridge School and King's College, Cambridge. His father died in 1880 and Forster's childhood was dominated by his mother and several adoring aunts. Tonbridge left him with an utter dislike of public-school values. Cambridge (1897–1901) proved more congenial, and in 1901 he was elected to the APOSTLES, through which he met members of what was to become the BLOOMSBURY GROUP. After graduating he travelled to Italy and Greece with his mother, and on his return began to contribute to the Cambridge-based journal, *The Independent Review*. His first short story, 'The Story of a Panic', appeared in 1904.

In 1905 Forster spent several months in Nassenheide, Germany, as tutor to the children of the Countess von Arnim. He returned to England (Weybridge) for the publication of his first novel, *WHERE ANGELS FEAR TO TREAD* (1905). The following year he lectured on Italian art and history for the Cambridge Local Lectures Board and became the tutor and close friend of an Indian Moslem, Syed Ross Masood. *THE LONGEST JOURNEY* (1907), his second novel, and *A ROOM WITH A VIEW* (1908) were widely reviewed, but it was with *HOWARDS END* (1910) that he fully established his reputation. However, a relatively minor volume of short stories, *The Celestial Omnibus* (1911), was followed by a period of silence which lasted for over a decade.

In 1912 Forster visited India with R. C. Trevelyan, G. Lowes Dickinson and G. H. Luce. After observing the British in India at close quarters, he developed an intense loathing for imperialism. Upon his return he wrote *MAURICE*, a novel depicting a successful homosexual relationship, which was circulated privately but not published until 1971, after his death.

Following the outbreak of World War I, Forster joined the International Red Cross and served in Alexandria until 1919. Copies of his *Alexandria: A History and a Guide* (1922) were destroyed in a fire before circulation, and the book was not revised and reprinted until 1938. During the war he met the Greek poet, C. P. Cavafy, a selection of whose poems he published in translation in his collection of Alexandrian essays, *Pharos and Pharillon* (1923).

In 1921–2 Forster returned to India as secretary and companion to the Maharajah of the native state of Dewas Senior and resumed work on a novel which he had begun, and then put aside, after his first visit. *A PASSAGE TO INDIA* (1924) was his most acclaimed novel; it was also his last, and for the remaining 46 years of his life he devoted himself to other activities. His Clark lectures were published as *Aspects of the Novel* (1927), and he was offered a three-year fellowship at King's College. *The Eternal Moment*, a volume of prewar short stories about the supernatural, appeared in 1928, and *ABINGER HARVEST* (1936) was a collection of the shorter essays and criticism.

Forster was an active member of PEN, arguing (in 1928) against the suppression of RADCLYFFE HALL's *The Well of Loneliness*, and later (in 1960) in defence of *LADY CHATTERLEY'S LOVER*. In 1934 he became first president of the National Council for Civil Liberties. After his mother's death in 1945 he was elected an honorary fellow of King's and lived there for the remainder of his life. *Billy Budd* (1949), based on MELVILLE's novel, was a libretto written with Eric Crozier for Benjamin Britten's opera; a collection of essays, reviews and broadcasts, *Two Cheers for Democracy* (1951), reflected his concern for individual liberty; and *The Hill of Devi* (1953) recalled his second visit to India and included letters sent from Dewas Senior.

In 1949 Forster refused a knighthood, but 20 years later, the year before his death, he was awarded the Order of Merit. *The Life to Come* (1972), a collection of earlier short stories which, like *Maurice*, treated the homosexual theme, had also to await posthumous publication.

Forster, John 1812–76 Essayist and biographer. Born in Newcastle, he attended the grammar school there before entering University College, London. He studied law and was called to the Bar in 1843, but was increasingly attracted to journalism and the literary life. A close friend of DICKENS, he succeeded the novelist as editor of *THE DAILY NEWS* in 1846. He also edited *The Foreign Quarterly Review* (1842–3) and *THE EXAMINER* (1847–55). Forster is remembered for his biographies of Dickens (1872–4) and another friend, WALTER SAVAGE LANDOR (1869). Among his other works were studies of GOLDSMITH (1848, enlarged 1854) and DEFOE and CHARLES CHURCHILL (1855), and *The Arrest of the Five Members by Charles the First* (1860). He completed only the first volume of a life of SWIFT (1876) before his death.

Forsyte Saga, The A sequence of novels by JOHN GALSWORTHY, comprising *The Man of Property* (1906), *In Chancery* (1920) and *To Let* (1921, with two interludes, 'Indian Summer of a Forsyte', 1918, and *Awakening*, 1920), published together in 1922.

It traces the fortunes of three generations of the Forsyte family, beginning in the prosperous upper middle class of Victorian London during the 1880s and ending in the early 1920s. Soames Forsyte, a successful solicitor, buys land at Robin Hill on which to build a house for his wife Irene and future family. Irene falls in love with its architect, Bosinney. Soames vindictively sues the latter for exceeding the estimates and Irene deserts him to live with her lover. Bosinney is run over and killed, and Irene is forced to return to her husband. The second novel, *In Chancery*, follows her love-affair with Soames's cousin, Jolyon. She divorces her husband and they marry. Soames himself marries Annette Lamotte, who gives birth to a daughter, Fleur. Irene and Jolyon produce a son, Jon.

To Let describes how Jon and Fleur, now both 19 years old, fall in love. However, when Jolyon informs his son of the past feud the latter finally decides that he cannot marry Fleur. Instead he travels to America. Fleur now throws herself at a long-standing admirer, Michael Mont, a fashionable baronet's son, and the two are married. After Jolyon's death, Irene joins Jon in America. Soames learns that Annette has been unfaithful to him and is left desolately contemplating the sale of Robin Hill. The Forsyte family begins to disintegrate when Timothy Forsyte, the last of the old generation, dies at the age of 100.

Fortescue, Sir John *c.* 1394–*c.* 1476 Author of legal treatises. Born in Norris in Somerset, Fortescue was admitted to Lincoln's Inn *c.* 1415 and by 1430 was a serjeant-at-law. He became a Member of Parliament in 1421, was appointed Chief Justice in 1442 and knighted the following year. He supported Henry VI against the Yorkists and fled into exile with the king in 1461. At the battle of Tewkesbury (1471) he was taken prisoner but he submitted to the new king, Edward IV, and was pardoned and admitted to the Council.

Fortescue wrote legal treatises in both English and Latin, his most famous being *De laudibus legum Angliae* (1468–70, published in 1546), written for the education of the young Prince Edward. His *De natura legis naturae* (1461–3) was rendered into English as *Monarchia: or, The Difference between an Absolute and a Limited Monarchy*. His formal retraction of his pro-Lancastrian arguments was written in English, *A Declaration upon Certain Writings* (1471–3), as was his most important work, *The Governance of England* (*c.* 1473). This is the earliest constitutional treatise in English, and shows an acute insight into the failure of the Lancastrian system of government. Fortescue's clear, straightforward use of the vernacular was an important early influence upon the development of English prose.

Fortnightly Review, The A periodical founded by ANTHONY TROLLOPE, Frederic Chapman the publisher and a number of friends and supporters to provide a platform for serious liberal opinion. The first number appeared in May 1865, edited by G. H. LEWES, with contributions from BAGEHOT, GEORGE ELIOT, FREDERIC HARRISON, HERSCHEL and Trollope. Its policy of printing the contributors' names was novel, and was later copied by many rival periodicals. It was not at first financially successful, and after November 1866 it was published once instead of twice a month. Its circulation recovered under its second editor, JOHN MORLEY (1867–82); his contributors included MEREDITH, MILL, HUXLEY, ARNOLD, SWINBURNE, SPENCER, Bagehot and LESLIE STEPHEN. Morley's agnostic temper and the doctrinaire positivism of his assistant, Frederic Harrison, gave the magazine its characteristic tone of opposition to traditional theology and eager support for humanitarian rationalism. FRANK HARRIS (editor 1886–94) rescued the *Fortnightly* from a period of decline by publishing much specifically creative literary work and by flouting respectable taste. Under W. L. Courtney (1894–1928) the *Fortnightly* was urbane, academic and distinguished. It ceased publication in 1954.

Fortune Theatre Built in 1600, just outside Cripplegate in the Liberty of Finsbury, the Fortune was the home of the Lord Admiral's Men (renamed Prince Henry's Men in 1603) and the main outdoor rival to the GLOBE during the first two decades of the 17th century. From the surviving building contract, we know that HENSLOWE wished it to incorporate many features of the Globe. The first Fortune was destroyed by fire in 1621. The second Fortune, opened in 1623, was the first brickbuilt outdoor theatre, but despite this costly innovation its reputation soon deteriorated. It was partially demolished in 1649.

Fortunes of Nigel, The A novel by SIR WALTER SCOTT, published in 1822, set in the reign of James I.

Nigel Oliphaunt, Lord Glenvarloch, is in desperate need of a large sum of money which his father advanced to the king during a crisis in his fortunes. Without it Nigel will lose his heavily mortgaged estates. He comes to London and is received by the king, who signs an order on his behalf on the treasury of Scotland. But Prince Charles and the Duke of Buckingham covet the Glenvarloch estates, and they send their favourite Lord Dalgarno, apparently to befriend Nigel but in fact to lead him into trouble and earn the king's displeasure. Margaret Ramsay, a London clockmaker's daughter, is uneasy about Nigel's friendship with Dalgarno: that gentleman's wronged wife, Hermione, is Margaret's patroness. Then Nigel discovers Dalgarno's true design and strikes him, an offence which, at the court of King James, could cost him his right hand. Nigel escapes to the underworld of Alsatia, while Margaret enlists the help of Lady Hermione and Richard Moniplies, Nigel's servant, on his behalf.

Nigel is taken, and sent to the Tower. Margaret tries to rescue him and at last disguises herself as a page to gain the king's attention. She succeeds, and at the same time secures reparation for Lady Hermione. Nigel marries Margaret and returns to Scotland.

Dalgarno pursues him but is killed by robbers on the way.

42nd Parallel, The See *USA*.

Foster, David (Manning) 1944– Australian novelist. Born in Sydney, he worked as a research biochemist before becoming a full-time writer. Impressively wide-ranging in their settings (Australian small-town life, America, 19th-century Scotland, the worlds of 14th-century alchemy, 18th-century comedy and a heavy metal rock band on tour), his novels can also intimidate by the complexity of their structure and linguistic play and by the vehemence of their SATIRE. They include *The Pure Land* (1974), *Moonlite* (1981), *Plumbum* (1983), *Dog Rock* (1985), *The Adventures of Christian Rosy Cross* (1986), *Testostero* (1987), *The Pale Blue Crotchet Coathanger* (1988) and *Mates of Mars* (1991).

Other work includes: a volume of poetry, *The Fleeing Atalanta* (1975); a SCIENCE-FICTION novel, *The Empathy Experiment* (with D. K. Lyall; 1977); a collection of stories, *Escape to Reality* (1977); two collections of novellas, *North South West* (1973) and *Hitting Wall* (1989); and a collection of *Self Portraits* (1991).

Four Georges, The Lectures by W. M. THACKERAY, first delivered in America in 1855, and published there in book form in 1860. Anecdotal and impressionistic, like his lectures on the ENGLISH HUMORISTS, his account of the Hanoverian kings comes to life in his contemptuous portrait of George IV, a 'fribble dancing in lace and spangles'.

Four Hymns SPENSER's *Four Hymns*, dedicated to the Countess of Cumberland and the Countess of Warwick, were printed together with the second edition of *Daphnaida* (1596). Their RHYME ROYAL stanzas show the formal influence of CHAUCER. They are in honour of Love, Beauty, Heavenly Love and Heavenly Beauty. Spenser's dedication, written from Greenwich, claims that the first two belong to 'the greener times of my youth' and that the hymns to Heavenly Love and Heavenly Beauty were written 'by way of retraction to reform' them. They are among Spenser's more difficult poems, part of the difficulty being their relationship to each other. They are at least intermittently influenced by Platonic and neo-Platonic theorizing about love, the notion in the *Symposium* that love is a desire for beauty partly explaining the double pairing of the poems. Platonic influence can also be detected in the parentage of Love in the first hymn and in its account of Love as the agent of creation. The second pair of poems is explicitly Christian in sentiment and tone, describing God's love in the Incarnation and the mysterious figure of Sapience enthroned in heaven. All four poems demonstrate a typically complex Renaissance synthesis of ideas about love, mingling Platonic philosophy and Renaissance commentaries on it with theological language and Protestant piety and, at least in the first poem, the pains of the suffering poet-lover.

Four Quartets Four long poems by T. S. ELIOT, published between 1935 and 1942 and collected in 1943. Together, they make a meditative or devotional sequence, linked by recurrent motifs and common themes: consciousness and memory, the individual's relation to time and the transcendent experience of timelessness. This unity contrasts with the deliberately fragmentary method of *THE WASTE LAND*, just as the openly religious character of *Four Quartets* contrasts with the apparently prevailing pessimism of the earlier work. Each of the four poems is firmly anchored in a place. 'Burnt Norton' (1935) meditates on a country house in the Cotswolds with a rose garden pervaded by children, or the memory of children. 'East Coker' (1940) takes its title from the Somerset village of Eliot's ancestors, where he himself chose to be buried, a fitting scene for meditation on transience and eternity. Like other poems in the sequence, it includes a moving consideration of the creative act itself. 'The Dry Salvages' (1941), named after a group of rocks off the Massachusetts coast, evokes memories of America, including Eliot's boyhood in St Louis. 'Little Gidding' (1942) refers to the religious community established near Huntingdon by NICHOLAS FERRAR in the 17th century, destroyed by Cromwell's troops and later rebuilt. It provides the setting for a meditation on war, destruction and reconciliation, and for a restrainedly jubilant ending which gathers together the arrivals and departures which have pervaded the sequence into an endless cycle of spiritual quest.

fourteeners See METRE.

Fowler, Henry Watson 1858–1933 Lexicographer and grammarian. Educated at Rugby and Balliol College, Oxford, he taught for a few years, first at Fettes and afterwards at Sedbergh. From 1899 he lived in London, reading, and writing literary essays, apart from brief volunteer service as a private in World War I. In collaboration with his brother Francis George Fowler (1870–1918) he produced a four-volume translation of Lucian (1905) and *The King's English* (1906). His *Concise Oxford Dictionary of Current English* (1911), an abridgement of *THE OXFORD ENGLISH DICTIONARY*, was the first of a series of Oxford dictionaries, the best known being the *Dictionary of Modern English Usage* (1926; re-edited by SIR ERNEST GOWERS, 1965), long consulted as authoritative for both word usage and grammar.

Fowler, Katherine 1632–64 Poet. Also known by her married name, Katherine Philips, she was the daughter of a London merchant and married James

Philips, a man of means from Cardigan, in 1647. A member of London's literary society, she organized a salon for the discussion of poetry and religion; VAUGHAN, COWLEY and JEREMY TAYLOR were part of the circle. She became known by the admiring title 'Matchless Orinda' and was made the subject of several verses. Her own work includes verses prefixed to Vaughan's *Poems* (1651), a translation of Corneille's *Pompée* (performed in 1663) and a posthumous collection of verses in 1667. Cowley wrote an ELEGY at her death.

Fowles, John (Robert) 1926– Novelist and essayist. After reading French at New College, Oxford, and serving in the Royal Marines, he became a teacher and spent some time working on the Greek island of Spetsai before the success of his first novel, *The Collector* (1963), enabled him to write full-time.

Fowles's fiction is characterized superficially by an extreme heterogeneity of subject-matter and treatment, and fundamentally by its preoccupation with the possibilities of genuinely free action. *The Collector* is a psychological thriller in which a girl, Miranda, is kidnapped by a psychotically possessive pools winner. *The Magus* (1966; revised, 1977) is a long, compulsive masquerade of sexual enticement and historical manipulation set on a Greek island. *THE FRENCH LIEUTENANT'S WOMAN* (1969) is a careful pastiche of a Victorian novel undercut by 20th-century literary and social insight. Its heroine, the governess Sarah Woodruff, is one version of the elusive, inscrutable woman who appears throughout Fowles's fiction, notably in the title novella of *The Ebony Tower* (1974), a collection of shorter fiction. *Daniel Martin* (1977) is a dense, realistic BILDUNGSROMAN rooted in postwar Britain and propounding 'an unfashionable philosophy, humanism'. *Mantissa* (1983) is a sexual *jeu d'esprit* and SATIRE of STRUCTURALISM, while *A Maggot* (1985), is a murder mystery set in the 18th century and written as a pastiche transcript of the subsequent interrogations.

The Aristos (1964; revised, 1980) is a 'self-portrait in ideas' setting forth the personal version of existentialism which underlies the novels, while *The Tree* (1979) is an autobiographical essay which attests to his interest in the natural world. Fowles's concern with the strategies of fictional narrative and the implications of conventional ways of writing fiction is explicated in the valuable 'Notes on an Unfinished Novel' in *The Novel Today*, edited by MALCOLM BRADBURY (1977).

Fox, George 1624–91 Founder of the Society of Friends. The son of a Leicestershire weaver, he was born at Fenny Drayton and apprenticed to a shoemaker. He abandoned churchgoing to preach his own belief that God spoke directly to the individual soul. Though he suffered imprisonment, Fox also attracted an increasing number of followers; from these beginnings the Society of Friends (or Quakers) was born. An organizer of genius, he made several missionary journeys to Ireland, Holland, America and the West Indies. He married Margaret Fell in 1669.

Fox is also remembered for his remarkable *Journal*, the story of his spiritual search told with simplicity and illustrated with vivid vignettes. It was prepared for publication by a committee of fellow Quakers in 1694. A *Collection of Epistles* was published in 1698, and *Gospel Truth* in 1706.

Fox, Paula 1923– American novelist and writer of CHILDREN'S LITERATURE. Born in New York, she worked in publishing and journalism before turning to writing. Her children's novels mark a distinct break with the more secure world described by earlier authors. Her small heroes and heroines often suffer from prolonged confusion, some of which will be shared by younger readers. In *How Many Miles to Babylon?* (1967) a small black boy is kidnapped by older children who want to use him for thieving; how much he ever understands about his adventures is never made clear. Other novels repeatedly take up the theme of youthful alienation, most memorably in *The Slave Dancer* (1973), about Jessie, a boy kidnapped into slavery in New Orleans in 1840, and his horrific experiences on a slave-ship. *The Lost Boy* (1987) is a troubling story set on a Greek island.

Fox and the Wolf, The A Middle English poem in couplets written *c.* 1250–75, probably in the South of England. It narrates an episode from the *Roman de Renart* in which the fox, after an unsuccessful raid on a poultry yard, is driven by thirst to jump into the bucket of a well and gets trapped at the bottom. He dupes the wolf Sigrim into believing he has gone to heaven and persuades Sigrim to make his confession and leap into the other bucket to join him. The fox escapes, leaving the wolf trapped, to be soundly beaten by the monks who own the well. The poem has features of both beast-epic and FABLE; it is the only piece of its kind extant from this period. The plot is handled with vigour and humour, and the anthropomorphism of the two animals is skilfully accomplished. Apart from CHAUCER's *The Nun's Priest's Tale* (see *CANTERBURY TALES*), it represents the only branch of the Renard cycle in Middle English before the appearance of CAXTON's translation, *REYNARD THE FOX*.

Foxe, John 1516–87 Martyrologist. Foxe went up to Oxford *c.* 1532 and became a fellow of Magdalen College in 1539. His radically Protestant views caused him to resign his fellowship in 1545 and move to London. There he became tutor to the children of the Earl of Surrey, who had been executed in 1547. To the years of this tutorship belong his early religious and moral tracts.

On the accession of Mary, the Roman Catholic Duke of Norfolk, the children's grandfather, was released from prison and Foxe lost his post. He fled from England, taking with him the beginnings of the work of Protestant history and propaganda published as ACTS AND MONUMENTS in 1563 but popularly known as 'Foxe's Book of Martyrs'. Latin versions of it appeared at Strasburg and Basle, which with Frankfurt made his places of refuge. His Latin play *Christus triumphans* was printed at Basle in 1556. It is a rather crude apocalyptic work which was later performed at Trinity College, Cambridge, and printed in an English translation in 1578. From exile Foxe also issued *Ad inclytos ac praepotentes Angliae proceres* (1557), an appeal to the English nobility to restrain Mary in her persecutions of Protestants.

He returned to England after Elizabeth's accession and was ordained priest by Grindal in 1560. He never gained high office in the Anglican Church because of his extreme Protestantism (he particularly objected to wearing a surplice). Among his later works are the anti-Catholic *A Sermon of Christ Crucified* (1570), which was preached at Paul's Cross, an edition of Anglo-Saxon texts of the Gospels (1571) and a Latin treatise on the Eucharist (?1580).

Fra Lippo Lippi A DRAMATIC MONOLOGUE by ROBERT BROWNING, published in *Men and Women* (1855). Filippo Lippi (*c.* 1406–69) was a painter of the Florentine school and a Carmelite monk. Taking hints from a passage in Vasari's *Lives of the Painters*, Browning makes him express his discontent with the constraints of monasticism and with the purely spiritual art his superiors want him to produce. Instead, he prefers a realism that attends to the fleshly details of the world around him.

Frame, Janet 1924– New Zealand novelist, short-story writer and poet. Born in Dunedin, she was brought up in Oamaru (the 'Waimaru' of her early novels) on the east coast of the South Island. Her father worked on the railways and the family lived in considerable poverty. She attended Dunedin Teacher's College and Otago University. As she was growing up two of her sisters were drowned in separate accidents. After a suicide attempt she was put into a psychiatric hospital and mistakenly diagnosed schizophrenic. Between 1947 and 1955 she spent most of her time in psychiatric hospitals receiving over 200 applications of unmodified ECT. She was saved by her writing: shortly before she was due to have a leucotomy her first collection of stories, *The Lagoon* (1951), won the Hubert Church award. Following her eventual release she was helped by FRANK SARGESON who gave her somewhere to live. Her first novel, *Owls Do Cry* (1957), was written in a hut in his garden. In 1957 she travelled to Europe on a grant from the New Zealand Literary Fund. After spending some time in Ibiza and Andorra she then lived in England for seven years, completing three more novels, written in six-monthly cycles to fit in with her guaranteed periods of National Assistance: *Faces in the Water* (1961), which fictionalized her experience of psychiatric hospitals, *The Edge of the Alphabet* (1962) and *Scented Gardens for the Blind* (1963). After returning to New Zealand, Frame spent long periods in the United States from the late 1960s. In the last decade she has once again lived in New Zealand.

She is generally regarded as New Zealand's finest novelist. One of her main themes is the clash of inner and outer worlds, often expressed through the figure of the misfit (epileptic, mental patient, artist). In *Owls Do Cry* the main protagonist has her imagination cut away by a leucotomy: her inner poetic voice dies and a drab world of everyday prose becomes the novel's sole voice. Though strongest in her earlier work, this theme recurs in her novel *The Carpathians* (1988). Frame's misfits depend on the power of language to express their difference and retain their identity, but in her fictional world language is the least stable element of all. This contradiction haunts most of her writing, from *The Adaptable Man* (1965) to the complex metafictional experiments with narrative and form in *Daughter Buffalo* (1972) and *Living in the Maniototo* (1979). An ambitious future-fiction, *Intensive Care* (1970), is another major novel. *To the Island* (1982), *An Angel at My Table* (1984) and *The Envoy from Mirror City* (1985), volumes of autobiography which uncover the sources of much of her writing, won her a wider reading public. She has also published five volumes of short stories, a collection of poetry, *The Pocket Mirror* (1967), and a children's book.

Framley Parsonage The fourth of ANTHONY TROLLOPE'S BARSETSHIRE NOVELS. It was published in THE CORNHILL MAGAZINE from January 1860 to April 1861.

The living of Framley is given to Mark Robarts by the widowed Lady Lufton; he is a close friend of her son, Lord Ludovic Lufton. Through Lord Lufton Mark meets Mr Sowerby and the Duke of Omnium, neither of them ideal companions for a young clergyman, since Sowerby is a spendthrift and Omnium is disreputable. After agreeing to support bills for Sowerby, Mark gains a prebendary at Barchester through his influence and the Duke, and proceeds to conduct himself in a way that annoys his patroness, Lady Lufton.

Lord Lufton falls in love with Lucy Robarts, Mark's sister, but his mother opposes the match. Lucy will not marry Ludovic without Lady Lufton's complete acceptance of her, and eventually her integrity and Ludovic's persistence carry the day. Mark, meanwhile, has been getting into deep water and is rescued by the generous Ludovic; he forswears the idle life which is really beyond his means. Sowerby himself is near ruin – his property is heavily mortgaged to the Duke – and hopes to marry the rich Miss Dunstable; but she refuses him and marries Dr Thorne. The novel features familiar Barsetshire characters: the Grantlys and their daughter Griselda, who marries Lord Dumbello; Bishop and Mrs Proudie; and the Rev. Josiah Crawley.

Francis, Sir **Philip** 1740–1818 Civil servant and politician. Born in Dublin and educated at St Paul's School in London, Francis held minor public offices before becoming a councillor to the Governor General of India in 1773. His disagreements with Warren Hastings led to bitter enmity and caused Francis, after his return to England in 1781, to join BURKE in the unsuccessful prosecution of Hastings on charges of corruption and cruelty. In 1784 Francis entered Parliament, giving up his seat in 1804; he owed his knighthood to his friendship with the Prince Regent.

There is evidence for identifying Francis as the JUNIUS of the famous letters which were published by his old schoolfellow Henry Sampson Woodfall in THE PUBLIC ADVERTISER between 1769 and 1771. However, Woodfall denied Francis's authorship and the letters treat some of Francis's friends harshly.

Frank, Waldo (David) 1889–1967 American novelist and critic. He was born in Long Branch, New Jersey, and educated at Yale. A member of *avant-garde* literary circles, he advocated social and political reform in his novels, which include *City Block* (1922); *Holiday* (1923), an examination of racial problems in the South; *The Death and Birth of David Markand* (1934), about an American businessman's decision to alter his life-style radically; and *The Bridegroom Cometh* (Britain, 1938; USA, 1939), which tells of a woman's discovery of faith while working for social reform. *Chalk Face* (1924) is a horror novel and *New Year's Eve* (1929) a play influenced by EXPRESSIONISM. He also wrote a good deal of historical and social criticism: *Our America* (1919), *Salvos* (1924), *The Re-Discovery of America* (1929) and *America Hispana* (1931); a study of industrial America, *In the American Jungle* (1937); *Birth of a World* (1951), about Simon Bolivar; a collection of sketches about Israel, *Bridgehead* (1957); and *The Prophetic Island: A Portrait of Cuba* (1961).

Frankenstein: or, The Modern Prometheus A GOTHIC NOVEL by MARY SHELLEY, published in 1818. She had begun it in 1816 when she, her husband SHELLEY, and BYRON wrote ghost stories to pass the time during a summer in Switzerland.

Frankenstein, a student of natural philosophy in Geneva, builds a creature in the semblance of a man and gives it life. Possessed of unnatural strength, the creature inspires horror in those who see it but is mis-erably eager to be loved. The unhappy Frankenstein deserts the creature but is pursued to Chamonix, where he agrees to make a mate. However, a wave of remorse makes him destroy the female he has been constructing, and the creature swears revenge on his creator. He kills Frankenstein's bride on their wedding night. Frankenstein's father dies of grief, and the scientist's mind gives way. Eventually he recovers and sets out to destroy his creation. After a chase across the world, the two at last confront each other in the Arctic wastes. Frankenstein dies and the creature, mourning the loss of the man who gave him life, disappears into the frozen wilderness, hoping for his own annihilation.

Franklin, Benjamin 1706–90 American politician and man of letters. Born in Boston, he received little formal education. At the age of 12 he was apprenticed to his half-brother, the printer James Franklin, to whose *New England Courant* he contributed the essays that were published anonymously in 1722 as *The Letters of Silence Dogood* and which are notable for their humorous commentary on COTTON MATHER's *BONIFACIUS*. He moved to Philadelphia in 1723, and then travelled to England to buy equipment for a press of his own. During a stay of two years he wrote and published *A Dissertation on Liberty and Necessity, Pleasure and Pain* (1725).

He returned to Philadelphia in 1726 and eventually succeeded in setting up his own press. In 1729 he published the first issue under his own proprietorship of *The Pennsylvania Gazette*, the newspaper which he managed and contributed to until 1766. Three years later he launched the widely read *POOR RICHARD'S ALMANAC* (1732–58) and *The General Magazine* (1741). He also became actively involved in the public affairs of Philadelphia: he was responsible for drawing up the plans for the lighting and maintenance of the city's streets, for a police force, and for a circulating library; he founded a city hospital, and an Academy for the Education of Youth which later became the University of Pennsylvania. Between 1751 and 1753 he published the results of his celebrated kite experiments in *Experiments and Observations on Electricity*.

He spent most of the 1760s in England, working to advance the cause of colonial representation in Parliament. He returned to Philadelphia in 1769 and founded the American Philosophical Society. He then went back to England, until, convinced that his efforts to promote the colonial cause had failed and that war was inevitable, he returned to America in 1775. He served in the Continental Congress and was part of the committee that ordered the drafting of the Declaration of Independence. While serving as Postmaster-General he was sent by the Congress to France, where he remained throughout the war and negotiated an economic and military alliance. When he returned to America in 1785, he was appointed president of the Executive Council of Pennsylvania, a post which he filled for three years, and participated in the Constitutional Convention; he signed the Constitution in 1787 and died three years later in Philadelphia.

Franklin produced numerous tracts on issues such as politics, legal theory, education, language and population control. Along with his large and varied correspondence, they constitute a witty and informative history of 18th-century America. His writings of note include *A Scheme for a New Alphabet and Reformed Mode of Spelling* (1768); *Edict of the King of Prussia* (1773) and *Rules by Which a Great Empire may be Reduced to a Small One* (1773), both of which oppose the Townshend Acts; *Remarks concerning the Savages of North America* (1784); 'On The Slave Trade' (1790), a memorandum to Congress which advocates the abolition of slavery; and his *Autobiography*, begun in 1771 and never completed.

Franklin, (Stella Maria Sarah) Miles 1879–1954 Australian novelist. Born near Tumut, New South Wales, she worked as a freelance writer in Sydney and Melbourne until 1905, when she travelled to the United States. She remained abroad, living in England and America, until 1927. Her best-known novel, *My Brilliant Career* (1901), was described as 'the very first Australian novel' on account of its original and distinctive Australian character. *My Brilliant Career* and its sequel *My Career Goes Bung* (published in 1946, some 40 years after it was written) describe the adventures and misadventures of Sybylla Melvyn, who aspires to the cultivated life of a writer but is hampered by the backwardness and rigid convention of bush society. The character of Sybylla, with her determined independence, fiery self-confidence and inopportune blundering, is curiously attractive, and was for some time thought to be an autobiographical portrait. In fact, Miles Franklin expressed astonishment at 'the literalness with which *My Brilliant Career* was taken'. Other novels include *Some Everyday Folk – and Dawn* (1909), *Old Blastus of Bandicoot* (1931), *Bring the Monkey* (1933) and *All That Swagger* (1936). A prestigious Australian award for fiction bears her name.

Franklin's Tale, The See CANTERBURY TALES, THE.

Fraser, George MacDonald 1925– Novelist and historian. He is best known for tracing the subsequent military career of Flashman, the bully from THOMAS HUGHES's *TOM BROWN'S SCHOOLDAYS*, in a series stretching from *Flashman* (1969) to novels such as *Flashman and the Dragon* (1985) and *Flashman and the Mountain of Light* (1990). Fraser has also written *The General Danced at Dawn* (1970) and *McAuslan in the Rough* (1974), stories of life in a Highland regi-

ment, and a work of history, *The Steel Bonnets: The Story of the Anglo-Scottish Border Reivers* (1971).

Fraser, G(eorge) S(utherland) 1915–80 Critic and poet. Born in Glasgow, Fraser was educated at Glasgow Academy, Aberdeen Grammar School and St Andrews University. After serving in the Middle East during the war, he became a critic, and from 1959 worked as a lecturer at Leicester University. His early poetry, in *The Fatal Landscape* (1941) and *Home Town Elegy* (1944), shows a neoclassical strain and lyrical clarity that has little to do with the excesses of the NEW APOCALYPSE movement, with which he was associated. A minor poet, his other collections include *The Traveller Has Regrets* (1948), *Conditions: Selected Recent Poetry* (1969), and the posthumous collected *Poems of G. S. Fraser* (1981). He is more important as the foremost journalistic critic of his era; his publications include *The Modern Writer and His World* (1953), a study of DYLAN THOMAS (1957), *Vision and Rhetoric: Studies in Modern Poetry* (1959) and *A Stranger and Afraid: Autobiography of an Intellectual* (1983).

Fraser's Magazine Founded by WILLIAM MAGINN and Hugh Fraser, this monthly magazine commenced publication in February 1830 and ceased in October 1882. Although it remained in the forefront of Victorian periodicals, it enjoyed its heyday under Maginn's editorship. Contributors included CARLYLE and THACKERAY, as well as JOHN GALT, CHARLES KINGSLEY, J. A. FROUDE and JAMES SPEDDING. Maginn was succeeded in the editorial chair by FRANCIS SYLVESTER MAHONY (Father Prout), Froude, WILLIAM ALLINGHAM and others.

Frayn, Michael 1933– Playwright, novelist and journalist. Born in London, he was educated at Kingston Grammar School and Emmanuel College, Cambridge. He first established his reputation with witty, gently satirical columns in *The Manchester Guardian* and *The Observer* and a series of novels in the same vein, including *The Russian Interpreter* (1966), *Towards the End of the Morning* (1967) and the fantasy, *A Very Private Life* (1968). While at Cambridge he had already contributed sketches to revues such as *Share My Lettuce* (1956). He turned again to the theatre with a quartet of short plays, *The Two of Us* (1970), and *The Sandboy* (1971), and established himself as a writer of intelligent comedy with: *Alphabetical Order* (1975), about mayhem in a newspaper cuttings library; *Donkeys' Years* (1976), about university lives and loves; and *Clouds* (1976), about journalists on a visit to Cuba. *Balmoral* (1978), re-titled *Liberty Hall* (1979), satirizes a writers' collective established by the state in Balmoral Castle. His first major commercial success came with *Noises Off* (1982), a backstage comedy about an appalling touring company. The less popular *Look, Look!* (1990) offers an equally jaundiced impression of audiences. Frayn has also made distinguished translations and adaptations of work by Chekhov and Tolstoy for the ROYAL NATIONAL THEATRE.

Frazer, Sir **James (George)** 1854–1941 Anthropologist and classical scholar. Born into a pious (Free Church of Scotland) middle-class family in Glasgow, Frazer was educated at the University of Glasgow and then at Trinity College, Cambridge. He was a fellow of Trinity from 1879 until his death. His best-known work is *The Golden Bough* (2 vols., 1890; 3 vols., 1900; 12 vols., 1911–15; abridged edition, 1922). In it he sifted the burgeoning ethnographic literature from a rationalistic, comparative and evolutionary point of view in describing the religious behaviour of the entire primitive world. To this encyclopaedic survey he added a discussion of the religions of classical antiquity to produce an attractive, if simplistic, thesis: that everywhere in human mental evolution a belief in magic preceded religion, which in turn was followed in the West by science. Although he employed the attitude and language of objective science, Frazer's analysis of the religions of the ancient eastern Mediterranean constituted an effective, because well-written, attack on what he regarded as the outworn absurdities and mistakes of religion in general and Christianity in particular. Between the wars he was widely read, and certain images drawn from his work (like that of the Fisher King) attained general intellectual currency: T. S. ELIOT's *THE WASTE LAND* (1922) is perhaps the best example of *The Golden Bough* literary influence. Frazer produced many other works in the history of religion, but as an 'armchair' anthropologist his standing today among students of religion is low; his more purely classical work, like his commentary on Pausanias (1898) and his edition of Ovid's *Fasti* (1929), has fared better among scholars.

Frederic, Harold 1856–98 American novelist. He was born in Utica, New York. As a young man he worked as a journalist, eventually as the London correspondent for *The New York Times.* He then gave up journalism for fiction, and became a pioneer of the American realist movement. His first novel, *Seth's Brother's Wife* (1886), portrays life on an American farm, and also examines the worlds of politics and journalism. *The Lawton Girl* (1890) and *The Return of the O'Mahoney* (1892) extended his reputation as a local colourist. *In the Valley* (1890) focuses on the American Revolution; *The Copperhead* (1893) and *Marsena and Other Stories* (1894) deal with the Civil War. His best-known novel, *THE DAMNATION OF THERON WARE* (1896), depicts the religious and psychological decline of a Methodist minister. His last three novels – *March Hares* (1896), and the posthu-

mously published *Gloria Mundi* (1898) and *The Market Place* (1899) – are historical tales set in England.

free verse See METRE.

Freeling, Nicolas 1927– Writer of DETECTIVE FICTION. Born in London, he worked throughout Europe as a hotel and restaurant chef before becoming a full-time writer in 1960. His immersion in European rather than British culture gives his work not just its characteristic locations but its wry, richly reflective prose style and its increasing indifference to generic labels. *Love in Amsterdam* (1962) began a series of novels featuring a Dutch detective, Van der Valk. *Double-Barrel* (1964), *Criminal Conversation* (1965), *The King of the Rainy Country* (1966) and *Tsing-Boum* (1969) were among the titles which showed Freeling outgrowing the model of Simenon's Maigret without leaving behind Simenon's sharp sense of place. *A Long Silence* (1972; as *Auprès de Ma Blonde* in USA) killed off Van der Valk, though he enjoyed a posthumous life on British TV and has been revived in *Sand Castles* (1989). *A Dressing of Diamonds* (1974) introduced a French PJ agent, Henri Castang, who has regularly appeared in subsequent novels, sometimes joined by Van der Valk's widow Arlette, herself the central character of *The Widow* (1979).

Freeman, Edward Augustus 1823–92 Historian. Born at Harborne in Staffordshire, he was privately educated before going to Trinity College, Oxford, where he became a fellow. He was appointed Regius Professor of Modern History in 1884. His best-known books are *The History of the Norman Conquest of England: Its Causes and Its Results* (1867–79) and *The Reign of William Rufus and the Accession of Henry I* (1882), eccentric in style and quickly superseded by more thorough research. Other works include *The History and Conquests of the Saracens* (1856), *The History of Federal Government* (1863), *A History of Europe* (1876), *The Turks in Europe* (1877), *The Historical Geography of Europe* (1881), *William the Conqueror* (1888) and *The History of Sicily from the Earliest Times* (1891–4). A fierce controversialist and regular contributor to periodicals, including *THE SATURDAY REVIEW*, he also published four collections of *Historical Essays* (1871, 1873, 1879 and 1892).

Freeman, Mary (Eleanor) Wilkins 1852–1930 American short-story writer and novelist. Born in Randolph, Massachusetts, Freeman began by writing stories for children, but soon devoted her attention to an adult audience. In 1887 she published her first collection, *A Humble Romance and Other Stories*, and followed this in 1891 with *A New England Nun and Other Stories*. Both volumes focus on the lives of women in small New England villages who are placed in situations where they must defend their own values against those of the community. *Pembroke* (1894), one of her more successful novels, is a fine study of the New England character and of conventional life there. Her other works include *Giles Corey, Yeoman: A Play* (1893), *Madelon* (a novel, 1896), *Silence and Other Stories* (1898), *The Heart's Highway: A Romance of Virginia* (1900), and *The Fair Lavinia and Others* (1907). With WILLIAM DEAN HOWELLS and HENRY JAMES among others, she was one of the contributors to *The Whole Family, A Novel by Twelve Authors* (1908).

French, David 1939– Canadian playwright. Born in Newfoundland and raised in Toronto, he began his career as an actor and writer for radio and television. *Leaving Home* (1972), his successful first stage play, and *Of the Fields Lately* (1973) explore archetypal family conflicts in the specific context of the Mercers, an 'immigrant' Newfoundland family in Toronto. French returned to the Mercers for a third work, *Salt-Walter Moon* (1984). The same autobiographical impulse, but in a very different genre, lies at the base of his most produced and praised play, *Jitters* (1979), a backstage comedy which offers an affectionate view of theatrical life as it is coloured by the specific problems and insecurities of producing theatre in Canada. His other plays include *One Crack Out* (1975), *The Riddle of the World* (1981) and *1949* (1989).

French, Marilyn 1929– American novelist and critic. Born in New York, she studied at Hofstra College, where she returned to lecture in 1964–8, and Harvard, where she was also a Mellon Fellow in 1976–7. She is best known for her first novel, *The Women's Room* (1977), hailed as a pioneering feminist text for its angry study of the continuing subjection of women. Further novels are *The Bleeding Heart* (1981) and *Her Mother's Daughter* (1987). She has also published *Beyond Power: On Women, Men and Morals* (1985), *The War against Women* (1992) and studies of JOYCE's *ULYSSES* (1976) and SHAKESPEARE (1981).

French Lieutenant's Woman, The A novel by JOHN FOWLES, published in 1969. It was widely praised for its attempt to combine the scope and solidity of Victorian fiction with experimental narrative devices.

At Lyme Regis on the Dorset coast Charles Smithson, a young Victorian palaeontologist, is struck by a solitary female figure standing at the far end of the Cob staring out to sea. She turns out to be Sarah Woodruff, an enigmatic governess ostracized by the community for her reported liaison with a French sailor who has since deserted her. Although he is already engaged to Ernestina Freeman, Charles is first beguiled and eventually infatuated by the woman, but on the single occasion when the affair is consummated he discovers Sarah to be a virgin. Charles and Ernestina's engagement is broken off, and the novel supplies alternative endings to Charles's story: both a happy and lasting reunion with Sarah and a bleak realization that they are irrevocably separated.

French Revolution, The A history by THOMAS CARLYLE, first published in 1837.

Carlyle's formidable warning to the British aristocracy, published half a century after the French Revolution, opens in 1774 with the death of Louis XV and closes a generation later in October 1795 with Bonaparte putting down the Insurrection of Vendémiaire. Thus the reign of the unfortunate Louis XVI occupies a central place in this sweeping prose work. Although Carlyle has been accused of bending history to his visionary philosophy, *The French Revolution* remains an epic work that traces with dramatic power the end of a long-established regime, the consequent Terror and the inevitable decline of insurrection. It is rich in portraits (of Robespierre and Mirabeau, for example) and descriptive set-pieces (of the murder of Marat, the flight to Varennes, the mutiny at Nancy). Carlyle alters his viewpoint effectively throughout the book, writing of some events as a moralist, of some as a detached observer and of some as a near-participant.

Freneau, Philip (Morin) 1752–1832 American poet. Of Huguenot ancestry, Freneau was born in New York and grew up in Monmouth, New Jersey. He attended the College of New Jersey (later Princeton University), where he met HUGH HENRY BRACKENRIDGE with whom he collaborated on *Father Bembo's Pilgrimage to Mecca* (1770), a prose SATIRE on American manners, and a patriotic poem, *The Rising Glory of America*, read at their graduation in 1771 and published the following year. A short collection of poems, *The American Village*, appeared in 1772 and was followed by 'Pictures of Columbus' in 1774. When the Revolution began he contributed patriotic poems in support of the American cause to the newspapers, but in 1776 he withdrew from politics and travelled to the West Indies.

The exotic settings of the Caribbean inspired him to write occasional poetry, some of which he published in Brackenridge's *United States Magazine* in 1779, together with poems on more patriotic themes, such as 'George the Third's Soliloquy', 'The Loyalists', and 'America Independent'. In 1780 he was captured by the British and held prisoner on the *Scorpion* in New York harbour. His brief but harsh captivity prompted him to write *The British Prison Ship*, published as a BROADSIDE in 1781. In 1781–2 he contributed essays and further Revolutionary War poems to the *Philadelphia Freeman's Journal*, celebrating

American heroes and attacking the British. He continued to express a passionate patriotism and hatred for the British in many of his later poems and journalistic writings – most notably in the *National Gazette* (1791–3), a Philadelphia journal that he founded and edited at THOMAS JEFFERSON's urging.

Between 1784 and 1790 he spent a good deal of time at sea, as captain of a trader. His poems during this period include *Journeys from Philadelphia to New York* (1787), which introduced the humorous persona of Robert Slender, weaver, one of the fictional voices which Freneau would use in later political essays. With the folding of the *National Gazette*, he returned to Monmouth, where he published an almanac, and founded and edited the *Jersey Chronicle. Letters on Various Interesting and Important Subjects*, a collection of some of the pro-Jefferson 'Robert Slender' letters that had appeared in the Philadelphia journal *Aurora*, was published in 1799. The 'Slender' series ended with Jefferson's election in 1801. *Poems on American Affairs* (1815) contained verses occasioned by the war of 1812, as well as poems influenced by DEISM, among them 'On the Universality and Other Attributes of the God of Nature'. Freneau spent his last years living in poverty in New Jersey. He died of exposure after being caught in a snowstorm.

Frere, John Hookham 1769–1846 Translator and poet. Born in London, he was educated at Eton and at Gonville and Caius College, Cambridge, and enjoyed a distinguished career as a diplomat. In the world of literature, he joined GEORGE CANNING (a lifelong friend whom he had first met at Eton) in publishing THE ANTI-JACOBIN and played a part in founding THE QUARTERLY REVIEW. His translations from the Spanish appended to SOUTHEY's *Chronicle of the Cid* (1808) were much admired. He also published translations of several plays by Aristophanes between 1839 and 1842. A witty MOCK-HEROIC poem, *Prospectus and Specimen of an Intended National Work by William and Robert Whistlecraft of Stowmarket in Suffolk, Harness and Collar Makers. Intended to Comprise the Most Interesting Particulars Relating to King Arthur and His Round Table* (1817), revived OTTAVA RIMA, the stanza form used by Pulci and other Italian poets, prompting BYRON to adopt it in *Beppo* and *Don Juan*. In 1819, however, Frere was one of the 'committee' of Byron's acquaintances who recommended against the publication of the first CANTO of *Don Juan* because of its indecency.

Freudian criticism See PSYCHOANALYTIC CRITICISM.

Friar Bacon and Friar Bungay, The Honourable History of A comedy in prose and verse by ROBERT GREENE, first printed in 1594 but probably produced a few years before. Friar Bacon and Friar Bungay are based on the 13th-century Franciscans of Oxford,

ROGER BACON and Thomas Bungay. Bacon makes a brass head with the help of Bungay; then, with the help of the Devil, he confers the power of speech on it. It will utter at some time in the course of a month but they must be present to hear it speak or all their labours will go for nothing. After a three-week vigil, day and night, Bacon hands the watch over to Miles, his servant, and falls into an exhausted sleep. When the head speaks it utters but two words, 'Time is', which Miles does not think important enough to justify waking his master. Next the head says, 'Time was' and then 'Time is past', before it falls on the floor, breaking into pieces. Bacon awakes, and the unfortunate Miles receives the full fury of his wrath. A subplot tells of the love of Lord Lacy and the Prince of Wales for the pretty Margaret, a gamekeeper's daughter. A notable scene has Bacon, Bungay and a German rival displaying their powers before the Kings of England and Castile and the Emperor of Germany.

Friar Daw's Reply See JACK UPLAND.

Friar's Tale, The See CANTERBURY TALES, THE.

Friel, Brian 1929– Irish playwright. He was born in Omagh and educated there and in Derry, where he taught in 1950–60. He is the best known, and in many ways the most accomplished of the playwrights who have emerged during recent years in both Northern and Southern Ireland. He began his writing career with short stories for magazines and radio plays for the BBC. *The Enemy Within* (1962) was staged at Dublin's ABBEY THEATRE, but he first achieved national and international recognition with *Philadelphia, Here I Come!* (1964), another Abbey production, a bitter-sweet comedy about dreams of emigration. Its wistfulness and traces of sentimentality also continue in *The Loves of Cass McGuire* (1966), *Lovers* (1967), *Crystal and Fox* (1968) and *Aristocrats* (1979). Plays tackling tougher themes include *The Freedom of the City* (1974) and *The Volunteers* (1975), about modern Ireland and the breakdown of its sense of community and social identity. *Faith Healer* (1979) is a compilation of monologues describing the life and death of a charlatan. With *Translations* (1980), set in 1833 when the English army was given the task of rationalizing Celtic place-names, and *The Communication Chord* (1984), about a farcical attempt to return the lost Irishness to the Irish, Friel emerged as the poet of the Troubles: able to trace the downward steps of an increasingly rocky path, but without the hostility of the committed underdog.

In 1980 Friel helped to found the theatre company Field Day in a town – Derry to Catholics and Londonderry to Protestants – whose name reveals the divisions of which he writes. The company receives public subsidies from both sides of the border and tours throughout Ireland. It staged Friel's adaptation of

Turgenev's *Fathers and Sons* (1987), but *Dancing at Lughnasa* (1990) was produced by the Abbey Theatre and transferred to the ROYAL NATIONAL THEATRE in London, and from there to the West End and Broadway. This tender evocation of his own boyhood in the 1930s has been compared to Chekhov in its lyrical naturalism.

Frost, Robert (Lee) 1874–1963 American poet. He was born and raised in San Francisco, but his father's death in 1885 forced the family to return to their native New England, where they settled in Lawrence, Massachusetts. Frost withdrew from Dartmouth College in his first term to return to Lawrence and support his family by teaching. He married in 1895 and applied to Harvard as a special student; he was accepted into a three-year programme but withdrew after two years. Following the deaths of his son Elliott, his mother and his daughter Elinor, he fell into a deep depression and seriously contemplated suicide. In 1912 he and his family moved to England, where he found a publisher for his first book of verse, *A Boy's Will* (1913). The collection was well received and was soon followed by a second, *North of Boston* (1914). These publications, along with his friendship with poets such as EZRA POUND and EDWARD THOMAS, increased his exposure in literary magazines. In 1915 he returned to the USA and settled on a farm in New Hampshire.

There Frost the poet was nurtured. Like that of many great national poets, his verse relies heavily on the language of the people. Many of his poems take the form of DRAMATIC MONOLOGUES or dialogues, using and transforming the New Englander's patterns of speech which he heard each day on his farm. His third collection, *Mountain Interval*, appeared in 1916, and he began to attract national attention. *New Hampshire* (1923) was awarded a PULITZER PRIZE. Following the publication of *West-Running Brook* (1928), his *Collected Poems* (1930) won him a second Pulitzer. The distinction was bestowed twice more, for *A Further Range* (1936) and for *A Witness Tree* (1942).

His work developed further with the production of *A Masque of Reason* (1945) and *A Masque of Mercy* (1947), dramatic poems in BLANK VERSE, portraying biblical characters and exploring the relation of man to God in the modern world. In 1947 he published *A Steeple Bush*, a collection of lyrics. Despite increasingly poor health, he wrote poetry to the end of his life; his last collection, *In the Clearing*, appeared in 1962. His poetry is among the most accessible of modern writers, given the central theme of all his collections: the quest of the solitary individual to make sense of the world.

Froude, James Anthony 1818–94 Historian. The younger brother of RICHARD HURRELL FROUDE, he was born at Totnes in Devon. He was educated at Westminster School and Oriel College, Oxford, where like his brother he came under the influence of JOHN HENRY NEWMAN. Newman's conversion to Rome weakened Froude's faith in Christianity; he wrote about this period of life in *Shadows in the Clouds* (1847) and *The Nemesis of Faith* (1848), two essays in semi-fictional autobiography. Two years later he met THOMAS CARLYLE and became his lifelong friend and disciple.

Like other 19th-century historians Froude wrote a great deal for journals, contributing essays, mainly historical, to THE WESTMINSTER REVIEW and to *FRASER'S MAGAZINE*, which he edited (1860–74). A notable essay, *England's Forgotten Worthies* (1852), printed in THE WESTMINSTER REVIEW attracted some attention. The first two volumes of *A History of England from the Fall of Wolsey to the Death of Elizabeth* were published in 1858 and the work was completed in 12 volumes in 1870. Froude was severely criticized for his presentation of history: he followed Carlyle in the belief that only extraordinary men initiate and control great events, and his approach was often polemical. In spite of that his history was highly successful, even while MACAULAY's work was still in progress. The reasons for its success were Froude's narrative gifts, his scrupulous research (he frequently paraphrases original documents and carefully identifies them), and his excellent prose style. *The English in Ireland in the Eighteenth Century* (1872–4) grew out of a series of lectures which Froude delivered in the USA. This book also became the centre of controversy and W. E. H. LECKY dealt with it very firmly in his *The History of England in the Eighteenth Century* (1878–92).

In 1874 Froude went on a government mission to South Africa to investigate the possibilities of federation; he also travelled in Australia (1884) and the West Indies (1886) and published *Oceana: or, England and Her Colonies* (1886) and *The English in the West Indies: or, The Bow of Ulysses* (1888), both readable and interesting for the contemporary view. As Thomas Carlyle's literary executor he was from 1881 engaged in the publication of the biographical remains of his friend and of JANE WELSH CARLYLE. He performed the task with commendable frankness. Froude's memoirs of Carlyle are published in *Thomas Carlyle: A History of the First Forty Years of His Life* (1882), *Thomas Carlyle: A History of His Life in London* (1884) and *My Relations with Carlyle* (1886).

Froude was appointed Regius Professor of Modern History at Oxford in 1892. Among his other works were the collections of his best essays, *Short Studies on Great Subjects* (four series, 1867, 1871, 1877 and 1883); *Bunyan* (1880), for the English Men of Letters series; *The Knights Templar* (1886); *Lord Beaconsfield* (1890); and *The Divorce of Catherine of Aragon: Being a Supplement to The History of England* (1891).

Froude, Richard Hurrell 1803–36 Religious controversialist. The elder brother of the historian JAMES ANTHONY FROUDE, and one of the early leaders of the OXFORD MOVEMENT, Froude was born near Totnes in Devon. He contributed to *TRACTS FOR THE TIMES* and was the intimate friend of JOHN HENRY NEWMAN; after his early death Newman wrote a preface to his friend's *Remains*. These were edited by J. B. Mozley (1838 and 1839) and were chiefly extracts from his private diary. They caused a disturbance in the Movement by their hostility to the leaders of the Reformation.

Fry, Christopher 1907– Playwright. Fry alternated teaching and acting until serving with the Non-Combatant Corps in 1940–4. His early plays attracted little attention, but the Bristol production of *A Phoenix Too Frequent* (1946), a lively version of the Widow of Ephesus story, proclaimed the arrival of a new contributor to the post-war revival of verse drama. Fry followed it with *The Firstborn* (1948), one of a number of plays in which he uses biblical themes to celebrate life's beauty and mystery. Fry's delight in language is shown at its best in *The Lady's Not for Burning* (1948), a comedy about the developing love between Jennet Jourdemayne, falsely accused of murder by witchcraft, and Thomas Mendip, impelled by world-weariness to confess to the murder. Fry later described it as the 'spring' piece in a seasonal cycle, completed by an 'autumn' play, *Venus Observed* (1950), the 'winter' *The Dark is Light Enough* (1954) and *A Yard of Sun: A Summer Comedy* (1970). *A Sleep of Prisoners* (1951) is among the best of his subsequent work, together with several effective adaptations of French plays, *Ring Round the Moon* (1950) and *The Lark* (1955) from Anouilh, *Tiger at the Gates* (1955), *Duel of Angels* (1958) and *Judith* (1962) from Giraudoux and *Cyrano de Bergerac* (1975) from Rostand.

Frye, (Herman) Northrop 1912–91 Canadian critic. He was born in Sherbrooke, Quebec and received an evangelical Methodist upbringing in Moncton, New Brunswick. He studied at the University of Toronto before being ordained to the ministry of the United Church of Canada in 1936. He had a brief period as a preacher in Saskatchewan, but soon decided that his real vocation was the academic study of literature. He attended Merton College, Oxford for two years and then returned to Canada to teach at Victoria College, University of Toronto, where he became professor of English in 1947 and principal in 1959. He later became the first University Professor of English at the University of Toronto in 1967 and chancellor of Victoria University, Toronto in 1978. His other activities included editing *Canadian Forum* and membership of broadcasting commissions.

The leading exponent of archetypal (or mythopoeic) criticism, he demonstrated his characteristic concern with the role of myth and SYMBOL in his first book, *Fearful Symmetry* (1947), a study of BLAKE. His most important work, *Anatomy of Criticism* (1957), elaborates an ambitiously comprehensive theory of literary models and genres which in his view reflect the processes of the human mind. It divides literature into four categories with a mythic or archetypal basis in the seasonal cycle: COMEDY (spring), romance (summer), TRAGEDY (autumn) and IRONY (winter). Frye applied his theories to SHAKESPEARE (*A Natural Perspective*, 1965; *Fools of Time*, 1967; *The Myth of Deliverance*, 1983), MILTON (*The Return of Eden*, 1965), T. S. ELIOT (1963), English ROMANTICISM (1968) and, controversially, the Bible (*The Great Code*, 1982; *Words with Power*, 1990). Much of his writing is concerned with the social and moral contexts of literature and culture. *The Bush Garden* (1971) and *Divisions on a Ground* (1982) are collections of his essays on Canadian literature, in which he identifies archetypal patterns in the nation's writing. His numerous other works include *The Well-Tempered Critic* (1963), *Fables of Identity: Studies in Poetic Mythology* (1963), *The Stubborn Structure* (1970), *The Critical Path* (1971), *The Secular Scripture: A Study of the Structure of Romance* (1976) and *On Education* (1988).

Fugard, Athol (Harold Lanigan) 1932– South African playwright, director and actor. Fugard was born in Middelburg, Cape Province. Despite periodic work in British and American theatre, his innovative drama has been forged under 'poor theatre' conditions with black-township groups. He deals compassionately with stunted, deprived lives, whether in black ghettos, as in *No-Good Friday* and *Nogogo* (both published with *Dimetos*, 1977), or amid the tensions of unfulfilled, white lower-middle-class households in *Hello and Goodbye* (1966) and *People are Living There* (1970). He directly confronts the apparatus of the apartheid state in *The Blood Knot* (1963), about brother exploiting brother; *Boesman and Lena* (1973), about dispossession and nonentity, perhaps his most powerful play; *SIZWE BANSI IS DEAD*, *The Island* and *Statements after an Arrest under the Immorality Act* (published together, 1974); and *My Children! My Africa!* (1990), set in a black South African classroom during the boycott of apartheid education. *Dimetos* (1977) and *A Lesson from Aloes* (1981) find gleams of hope even in tragic guilt and self-betrayal. '*Master Harold*'... *and the Boys* (1983) is a searing semi-autobiographical revelation of youthful racial arrogance. *The Road to Mecca* (1985) movingly presents an Afrikaner woman's rejection of conformity and spiritual darkness. *A Place with the Pigs* (1988) is a 'personal parable' based on the story of a deserter from the Russian army who hid in his own pigsty for 41

Henry Medwall's *Fulgens and Lucrece*, first performed in 1497. This engraving comes from the title-page of the text published *c*. 1515, believed to be the first time an English play appeared in print.

years. Fugard has also written a novel, *Tsotsi* (1981), and screenplays, and directed and acted in films, including *Marigolds in August* (1980). *Notebooks 1960–1977* (1983) contains autobiographical writings.

Fugitives, The A group of 20th-century American poets and writers committed to preserving both a distinctively Southern literature and the traditional rural economy of the South. It included JOHN GOULD FLETCHER, JOHN CROWE RANSOM, LAURA RIDING, ALLEN TATE, ROBERT PENN WARREN and DONALD DAVIDSON, who edited its magazine, *The Fugitive* (1922–5). Other notable publications include *Fugitives: An Anthology of Verse* (1928) and *I'll Take My Stand: The South and the Agrarian Tradition* (1930), a collection of essays edited by Ransom, who was mainly responsible for the 'Statement of Principles' summarizing the views of the group.

Fulgens and Lucrece A two-part play (or INTER-LUDE) written by HENRY MEDWALL for performance as a banquet entertainment. It was probably first performed in 1497 and published *c*. 1515, and is the first secular drama in English to have survived in full. The main plot of the play is predominantly in RHYME ROYAL stanzas. It takes the form of an illustrated debate as to whether the title of 'gentleman' is better earned by merit and service to the state than birth. The pretext is the choice before a Roman senator, Fulgens, and his daughter, Lucrece, of the more suitable of two potential husbands for Lucrece. The eventual choice falls on the worthy but low-born Flaminius.

If that were the whole story, *Fulgens and Lucrece* would be nothing more than a curiosity. What gives it interest is the sub-plot, in which two servants involuntarily parody their betters in their rivalry for Lucrece's waiting-maid.

Fuller, Henry Blake 1857–1929 American novelist and short-story writer. He was born in Chicago and, except for two years spent touring in Europe (1878–80), lived there all his life. His best-known novel is probably *THE CLIFF-DWELLERS* (1893), which satirizes the social ambitions of people living in a skyscraper apartment building. *WITH THE PROCESSION* (1895) also deals with social climbers, in this case a middle-class family. *Bertram Cope's Year* (1919) takes up the topic of homosexuality. In all three novels Fuller sought to deal in a realistic manner with social issues of his time. His other novels include *The Chatelaine of La Trinité* (1892), *The Last Refuge: A Sicilian Romance* (1900), *On the Stairs* (1918), *Gardens of This World* (1929) and *Not on the Screen* (1930). Among his collections of short stories are *The Chevalier of Pensieri-Vani* (1890), *Waldo Trench and Others: Stories of Americans in Italy* (1908) and *Lines Long and Short: Biographical Sketches in Various Rhythms* (1917). He also wrote plays, among them *O, That Way Madness Lies: A Play for Marionettes* (1895) and *The Red Carpet* (not published until 1939).

Fuller, John (Leopold) 1937– Poet and novelist. The son of ROY FULLER, he was born in Ashford, Kent, and educated at St Paul's School and New College, Oxford. He worked at the University of New York, Buffalo, and at Manchester University before becoming a fellow of Magdalen College, Oxford, in 1966. His many volumes of poetry include *Fairground Music* (1961), *Lies and Secrets* (1979), *Waiting for the Music* (1982), *The Beautiful Inventions* (1983) and *The Mechanical Body* (1991). A technically sophisticated writer, he often uses unexpected imagery, riddles and word-games in a poetry diverse in manner and subject. His novels include *Flying to Nowhere* (1983) and *Look Twice* (1991). He has also written a valuable guide to the SONNET (1972) and edited *The Chatto Book of Love Poetry* (1990).

Fuller, (Sarah) Margaret 1810–50 American writer. Born in Cambridgeport, she became a leading figure in TRANSCENDENTALISM and the BROOK FARM experiment, BRONSON ALCOTT's assistant and a friend of EMERSON. An early feminist, she wrote the monumental *Woman in the Nineteenth Century* (1845). After editing *THE DIAL* in 1840–2, she became literary critic of HORACE GREELEY's New York *Tribune*, by which in 1846 she was sent to Europe; her distinguished 'letters from abroad' appeared on the *Tribune's* front page. While in Italy she married the Marquis Angelo Ossoli. She was the inspiration for Zenobia in HAWTHORNE's *THE BLITHEDALE ROMANCE* and the heroine of HOLMES's *ELSIE VENNER*.

Fuller, Roy (Broadbent) 1912–91 Poet and novelist. Born in Failsworth, Lancashire, Fuller was educated at Blackpool High School, before qualifying as a solicitor and working for the Woolwich Building Society, becoming a director in 1969. During the war he served in the Royal Navy. His lectures as professor of poetry at Oxford in 1968–73 were published in *Owl and Artificers* (1971) and *Professors and Gods* (1974).

His first collection of verse, *Poems* (1939), showed the influence of AUDEN, but he found his own voice in *The Middle of a War* (1942) and *A Lost Season* (1944),

which reflect his wartime experience. *Epitaphs and Occasions* (1949) is his last volume in his early style, characterized by left-wing sympathies and an interest in man as a social animal. Later he became interested in outlining individual psychologies, and perhaps his best collections are *Counterparts* (1954), in which he started to experiment with syllabics, *Brutus's Orchard* (1957) and *Buff* (1965), coming after *Collected Poems 1936–1961* (1962). The poems, typically, are logical progressions from particular observation to general reflection. He was a master technician, but his interest in form, his detachment, and his urbane tone and easy use of IRONY laid him open him to criticisms of unadventurousness. His powers were undiminished, though, in later collections, which include *New Poems* (1968), *From the Joke Shop* (1971), *Tiny Tears* (1973), *The Reign of Sparrows* (1980) and *Consolations* (1987). *New and Collected Poems* appeared in 1985. His novels were more than an interesting sideline: after the MELODRAMA of *Fantasy and Fugue* (1954), *The Ruined Boys* (1959) achieves a subtle characterization and quiet evocation of the real world. Other novels include *Image of a Society* (1956), the ambitious but flawed *The Father's Comedy* (1961), *The Perfect Fool* (1963), the excellent *My Child My Sister* (1965) and *Stares* (1990). *Spanner and Pen* (1991) is an autobiography. His son is JOHN FULLER.

Fuller, Thomas 1608–61 Antiquarian and divine. Fuller was born at Aldwinkle St Peter's in Northamptonshire. He began his career as the youngest MA to come out of Cambridge University – he was 20 years old. He became a Bachelor of Divinity in 1635, and had by this time established himself as a preacher, and had been prebendary of Salisbury and rector of Broadwindsor. In 1641 he was appointed preacher to the Chapel Royal at the Savoy and during the Civil War was chaplain to the Royalist commander Sir Ralph Hopton. A Royalist and an Anglican, Fuller returned to London after the surrender of Exeter. He was allowed to preach but led an unsettled life until he secured the curacy of Waltham Abbey in 1649. He was reinstated at the Restoration, and became a royal chaplain.

Fuller was a prolific writer. His most celebrated book, *The History of the Worthies of England*, was unfinished but published posthumously in 1662. By no means as dull as its title suggests, it makes a county-by-county survey of England, describing the topography, characteristics, natural curiosities, local history and lore, and famous people associated with the different counties – all memorably treated in a frequently witty style. Fuller's first book of note was about the Crusades, *The History of the Holy War* (1639–40). *Good Thoughts in Bad Times* (1645), *Good Thoughts in Worse Times* (1647) and *The Cause and Cure of a Wounded Conscience* (1647) were topical tracts, later praised by COLERIDGE but less popular than *The Holy State and The Profane State* (1642), a book of 'characters' and essays on diverse subjects. Later works are *A Pisgah-Sight of Palestine* (1650) and *The Church History of Britain: From the Birth of Christ till 1648* (1655).

Furnivall, F(rederick) J(ames) 1825–1910 Philologist and scholar. The son of a wealthy doctor, Furnivall was born in Egham, Surrey, and educated at University College, London, and Trinity Hall, Cambridge, after which he practised as a barrister. He joined the Philological Society in 1847, becoming editor of the Society's *New English Dictionary* in 1861. This project, which he had first proposed and for which he dragooned many volunteers into collecting material, was later to become the OXFORD ENGLISH DICTIONARY. Furnivall was a passionate organizer: he founded the Early English Text Society (1864), the Chaucer Society (1868), the Ballad Society (1868), the New Shakspere Society (1873; one of its novelties being this spelling), and the Wyclif (1881), Browning (1881) and Shelley (1886) Societies. For the Chaucer and Early English Text Societies he edited a great number of editions, and he also edited SHAKESPEARE. Furnivall was a fervent vegetarian, socialist, teetotaller, agnostic and oarsman, and taught at the Working Men's College, which he helped to found in 1854.

Furphy, Joseph 1843–1912 Australian novelist. The son of Irish immigrant parents, Furphy was born near Melbourne, Victoria. After a sketchy education, and work on farms, roads, and goldfields, he became a teamster in the Riverina area of New South Wales. The failure of his business in 1884 obliged him to sell his bullock teams and find work in a foundry at Shepparton in north Victoria.

Furphy's first stories were published in *The Bulletin* in 1889 under the pseudonym of Tom Collins. In 1897 the literary editor of the paper, A. G. Stephens, was the recipient of a large unwieldy manuscript entitled *Such is Life: Being Certain Extracts from the Life of Tom Collins*. Revised and shortened, it was published in 1903. From the rich material trimmed from *Such is Life* two more books were published after Furphy's death: *Rigby's Romance* (1946) and *The Buln-Buln and the Brolga* (1948).

There is no formal plot in *Such is Life*, a picaresque novel of many digressions and reflections which one American critic, C. Hartley Grattan, described as 'a primary document for any student of Australian attitudes'. Furphy described his work as being of 'Temper democratic; bias offensively Australian'.

Gaddis, William 1922– American novelist. He was born in New York and educated at Harvard, though he left in 1945 without taking his degree. His first novel, *The Recognitions* (1955), focuses on a group of artists and poets in Greenwich Village during the late 1940s and early 1950s. Its dominant motifs of ruse and forgery are encountered on many levels – social, aesthetic, theological and sexual. A lengthy and complex work, it was not well received by the critics. His second novel, *JR* (1975), is written entirely in dialogue and takes place mostly at a school on Long Island. It enjoyed a more favourable critical reception, and better sales, than its predecessor, and received the National Book Award in 1976. *Carpenter's Gothic* (1985) examines the impact of the Vietnam war on those who endured it.

Gag, Wanda (Hazel) 1893–1946 American writer and illustrator of CHILDREN'S LITERATURE. Born in New Ulm, Minnesota, and educated at Minneapolis Art School, she became a schoolteacher before turning to commercial art. Her first children's book, *Millions of Cats* (1928), was soon recognized as a landmark in picture-books for its use of simple woodcuts and hand-lettered text. The story, about an old couple who wish for a pet and are inundated with cats, has become something of a 20th-century fable. None of her subsequent work rivalled this first masterpiece, although she did provide some fine illustrations for her *Tales from Grimm* (1937).

Gaines, Ernest J. 1933– Black American novelist and short-story writer. The son of a plantation worker in Oscar, Louisiana, he began working in the fields at an early age. In 1948 his family moved to Vallejo, California. After spending two years in the army, he attended San Francisco State College and then Stanford University. His fiction mostly treats black life in the bayou region of Louisiana. His first novel, *Catherine Carmier* (1964), tells of the difficulties encountered by a young black college graduate when he returns home to Louisiana. *Of Love and Dust* (1967) is set on a Louisiana plantation in the 1940s. *Bloodline* (1968) is a collection of five stories. His best-known novel, *The Autobiography of Miss Jane Pitman* (1971), consists of the recollections of a 110-year-old black woman whose experiences range from slavery to the civil rights movement of the 1960s. Gaines's concern with the effects of racism and the possibilities of social change is further revealed in *My Father's House* (1978), a novel which examines the conflict between a black preacher and his more radical son.

Gale, Zona 1874–1938 American novelist and short-story writer. Born in Wisconsin, she first rose to prominence as a writer in the 'local colour' vein. Among her early works are the novel *Romance Island* (1906) and a collection of short stories entitled *Friendship Village* (1908). After World War I her sentimental tendencies gave way to a sterner realism in novels such as *Birth* (1918), and her best-known book, *Miss Lulu Bett* (1920), a portrayal of bleak Midwestern life and the middle-aged woman who suffers it. *Faint Perfume* (1923) also centres on the stifled hopes and empty existence of a Midwestern spinster. In her later novels, however, Gale departed from the realism of her most highly acclaimed works. *Preface to a Life* (1926) and *Borgia* (1929) are representative of this later phase, during which she became interested in Eastern mysticism as a possible answer to the kind of suffering portrayed in her earlier novels. Her final works, *Papa La Fleur* (1933), *Light Woman* (1937), and the posthumously published *Magna* (1939), share a concern with the gap between the pre-war and post-war generations. Some of her best short stories are collected in *Yellow Gentians and Blue* (1927) and *Bridal Pond* (1930).

Gallant [née Young]**, Mavis** 1922– Canadian short-story writer and novelist. Born in Montreal and brought up bilingually till the age of 10, she then lived in Ontario and the USA, returning to Montreal in 1941 where she worked for the National Film Board and the *Montreal Standard*. Since 1950 she has lived abroad, mainly in Paris, returning to Canada for brief visits and as writer-in-residence at the University of Toronto (1983–4). As a regular contributor to THE NEW YORKER since the 1950s she has published over 100 stories, and her collections of short stories and two novels, *Green Water, Green Sky* (1959) and *A Fairly Good Time* (1970), have appeared in the USA and the UK. Her short-story collections include *The Other Paris* (1956), *My Heart is Broken* (1964; as *An Unmarried Man's Summer* in Britain), *The Pegnitz Junction* (1973) and *In Transit* (1988). Her first book to be published in Canada was *The End of the World and Other Stories* (1974) but only with *From the Fifteenth District* (1979), *Home Truths* (1981) and *Overhead in a Balloon* (1985) has she been widely read in Canada. She received the Governor General's Award for *Home Truths* and was awarded the Order of Canada in 1981. She has also written one play, *What is to be Done?* (1983). An expatriate writing with a mercilessly detached awareness about isolation and displacement in Paris, Montreal or in post-war Germany, Gallant is recognized as one of Canada's best short-story writers.

Galsworthy, John 1867–1933 Novelist and playwright. Born at Coombe, Surrey, and educated at Harrow and New College, Oxford, he studied law and was called to the Bar in 1890. He practised briefly, but could afford to travel and made a voyage to the Far East; on another journey he met and encouraged JOSEPH CONRAD, and the two became lifelong friends.

Galsworthy's career as a playwright began with the success of *The Silver Box* (produced 1906) which first employed his favourite device of presenting parallel and contrasted families – one rich, the other poor. In all he wrote over 31 full-length plays and a number of equally successful one-acters. Many commented on social injustices, and one of them, *Justice* (produced 1910), led to reform of the practice of solitary confinement in prisons. *Strife* (produced 1909) remains one of the most successful English plays about the effects of a strike. *The Skin Game* (produced 1920) is a trenchant commentary on jealously guarded privilege and social snobbery. His *Collected Plays* appeared in 1929.

His novels show him less uncomfortable with his own privileged background. His first success was *The Man of Property* (1906), which together with *In Chancery* (1920) and *To Let* (1921, with two interludes, 'Indian Summer of a Forsyte', 1918, and *Awakening*, 1920) made up his best-known work THE FORSYTE SAGA, published together in 1922. A second Forsyte chronicle, *A Modern Comedy* (1929), included *The White Monkey* (1924), *The Silver Spoon* (1926), *Swan Song* (1928) and two interludes, 'A Silent Wooing' and 'Passers By'. Other work included a trilogy, *End of the Chapter* (1925), on the family history of the Charwells (relatives of the Forsytes) and *Collected Poems* (1934).

Galsworthy was awarded the OM in 1929, and the Nobel Prize for Literature in 1932. Without remaining in critical favour, his writing has remained popular.

Galt, John 1779–1839 Novelist and essayist. The son of a sea captain, Galt was born in Irvine, Ayrshire, and spent his early life in Greenock. He went to London in 1804 and set up as a merchant, writing in his spare time and publishing verse and occasional prose pieces. His business failed in 1808 and he set off on a commercial journey to the Continent, where he made the acquaintance of BYRON. He continued in the poet's company to Greece and Turkey and subsequently published an account of his journeys in 1812 in *Voyages and Travels in the Years 1809, 1810 and 1811*. He also wrote a biography of the poet, *The Life of Lord Byron*, in 1830, but it was not well received. After 1813 he was back in London for various business posts.

He wrote a great deal, but it was not until his work was published in *BLACKWOOD'S EDINBURGH MAGAZINE* in 1820 that he achieved distinction. He dealt with his Scottish background in THE AYRSHIRE LEGATEES (1820), producing a successful novel about contemporary Lowland Scots. THE ANNALS OF THE PARISH (1821), THE PROVOST (1822), and THE ENTAIL (1823) are in the same vein and these are the books by which John Galt is best remembered. In 1826 he went to Canada as secretary to a company for development in what is now Ontario. He stayed for three years and then lost his post when the company's affairs went through a bad period. He returned to England but, short of money, was soon in debt and spent some months in prison. His straits were relieved by a gift of £200 from King William IV, but he wrote little of note in his remaining years.

Game at Chess, A A political allegory in the form of a comedy by THOMAS MIDDLETON. On its first performance in 1624 the play was a sensational success. The audience had no difficulty in recognizing that the Black Knight represented the hated Spanish Ambassador, Gondomar, who had given great offence by his attempts to secure an alliance between Protestant England and Catholic Spain through the marriage of the Prince of Wales to a Spanish princess. Diplomacy and confrontation are cleverly presented in terms of chess. The political detail may be obscure for a modern reader, but the lines of the play remain brilliantly clear. After nine successive performances at the GLOBE (an extraordinary number for the period) the play was banned and a warrant issued for Middleton's arrest.

The engraving on the title-page of Middleton's *A Game at Chess,* 1624, spelling out the references to contemporary politics

Gamelyn, The Tale of A VERSE ROMANCE in rhyming couplets, probably composed around 1350-70. It has been called *The Cook's Tale of Gamelyn*, and was at one time attributed to Chaucer (see CHAUCERIAN APOCRYPHA). It is one of the relatively few verse romances to have an English source. THOMAS LODGE used some of the story in his *ROSALYNDE* (1590), which formed the basis of SHAKESPEARE's *As You Like It*.

Sir John de Boundys leaves his property in equal parts to his three sons, of whom Gamelyn is the youngest. The eldest brother seizes Gamelyn's share and the romance tells how Gamelyn grows up to be very strong, reclaims his inheritance and defeats the elder brother, who is ultimately hanged. It is a vigorous and violent tale, with none of the courtly elements usually associated with verse romance. Criticism of the clergy is a recurrent theme in the poem.

Gamester, The A comedy by JAMES SHIRLEY, first performed in 1633 and published in 1637. Its hero, Wilding, is not only addicted to gambling but also in love with his wife's ward, Penelope. The play details the tricks by which his resourceful wife cures him of his adulterous love and exposes him to the dangers of his addiction. *The Gamester* is also the title of a tragedy (1753) by EDWARD MOORE.

Gammer Gurton's Needle A comedy that was possibly written in 1553 and vies with *RALPH ROISTER DOISTER* for the honour of being the first English comedy if the later date for UDALL's work is accepted. Authorship has been attributed to at least three people but the favourite is William Stevenson, identified by Henry Bradley from the 'Mr S. Mr. of Art' on the title-page of the printed edition of 1575, which also refers to the work as 'Played on Stage, not longe ago in Christes Colledge in Cambridge'. An earlier printed edition (c. 1563) has not survived, but Stevenson fulfils the requirements of the evidence: he was styled Master (Mr) of Arts in 1553-4 at Christ's College, where he produced plays from 1550 to 1554. The play is notable for its total Englishness; there is no trace whatever of the influence of Terence or Plautus, hitherto inescapable. It is written in rhymed doggerel.

The action turns on the losing of Gammer Gurton's needle, with which she mends the clothes of Hodge, her servant; the resolution is the finding of the needle in the seat of Hodge's breeches. The play is rich in character and the inventiveness never flags. Among the characters are: Diccon of Bedlam, who enjoys mischief-making; Gammer Gurton's enemy Dame Chat; Doctor Rat the curate; the servants Tib, Doll, and Spendthrift; and Gib the cat.

Garden of Proserpine, The A poem by ALGERNON CHARLES SWINBURNE, published in *Poems and Ballads* (1866). One of Swinburne's most anthologized pieces ('Here, where the world is quiet'), it is deliberately pagan in spirit. The poet's note says that it was intended to capture 'that brief total pause of passion and of thought, when the spirit, without fear or hope of good things or evil, hungers and thirsts only after the perfect sleep'.

Gardiner, Samuel Rawson 1829-1902 Historian. Born in Hampshire and educated at Christ Church, Oxford, he became professor of modern history at King's College, London and, in 1896, Ford Lecturer at Oxford. His main achievement was in chronicling the early Stuart and Commonwealth periods in *The History of England from the Accession of James I to the Outbreak of the Civil War* (1883-4), *The History of the Great Civil War* (1886-91) and *The History of the Commonwealth and Protectorate* (1894-1901), completed by C. H. Firth with *The Last Years of the Protectorate* (1909). Among his other works were *The Thirty Years War* (1874), *A School Atlas of English History* (1892) and his Ford Lectures, *Cromwell's Place in History* (1897).

Gardner, Dame Helen (Louise) 1908-86 Scholar and critic. Educated in London at the North London Collegiate School and at St Hilda's College, Oxford, she became Merton Professor of English Literature at Oxford (1966-75) after a distinguished tutorial career. Her two editions of JOHN DONNE, *Divine Poems* (1952) and *Elegies, and Songs and Sonnets* (1965), are important for both text and commentary; *The Art of T. S. Eliot* (1949) and her textual examination of ELIOT's *FOUR QUARTETS* (1978) are pioneering studies. As a critic she belonged to no 'school' but upheld traditional humane values (see, for example, her *The Business of Criticism*, 1960). She edited the *New Oxford Book of English Verse 1250-1950* (1972), providing a selection to replace QUILLER-COUCH's anthology. She was created a Dame of the British Empire in 1967.

Gardner, John 1933-82 American novelist, short-story writer and scholar. Born in Batavia, New York, he taught medieval literature and creative writing at various American universities. *The Wreckage of Agathon* (1970) – published after the critical failure of his first novel, *The Resurrection* (1966) – is set in ancient Sparta and presents a seer, Agathon, and his companion, Demodokos, who have been imprisoned and engage in a dialogue concerning individual freedom and civil restraint. His most highly praised book, *Grendel* (1971), retells *BEOWULF* from the monster's point of view and focuses on the potential meaninglessness of life, a theme also examined in *The Sunlight Dialogues* (1972). *Nickel Mountain* (1973), set in upstate New York, records the life of Henry Soames, a middle-aged motel proprietor who searches for a way of living in the face of intense lone-liness and fear of a fatal heart attack. Gardner's first collection of short fiction, *The King's Indian Stories and Tales*, was published in 1974. Two years later came the novel *October Light* (1976), an examination of the problems of ageing, which was awarded the National Book Critics Circle award in 1976. His other fiction includes the novels *Freddy's Book* (1980) and *Mickelsson's Ghosts* (1982), and a collection of stories entitled *The Art of Living and Other Stories* (1981). He also wrote an epic poem, *Jason and Medea* (1973); three libretti, *William Wilson*, *Frankenstein* and *Rumpelstiltskin* (collected in *Three Libretti*, 1979); and a volume of *Poems* (1978). His theories of fiction are developed in *The Forms of Fiction* (1962), *On Moral Fiction* (1978) and the posthumously published *The Art of Fiction: Notes on Craft for Young Writers* (1984).

Garfield, Leon 1921– Writer of CHILDREN'S LITERA-TURE. Born and educated in Brighton, Garfield went to Art College before serving in the Medical Corps during the war. After that he worked in the hospital service as a biochemical technician before turning to full-time writing in 1966. By then he had already pro-duced *Jack Holborn* (1964), a strongly imaginative, rambling adventure story written in a style owing something to FIELDING and DICKENS but perfectly in keeping with the stage-coaches, dark streets and candle-lit rooms of the 18th-century background in which this and most of his later novels are placed. Such dramatic settings are amply reflected in excit-ing plots that concern pickpockets (*Smith*, 1967), highwaymen (*Black Jack*, 1968), lost heirs, escape from prison, stolen wills, false accusations and all the other apparatus of traditional melodrama. Even so, the larger-than-life villains who populate Garfield's earlier books give way in later works to more ambigu-ous characterizations, where the unheroic often turn out to have hearts of gold and the initially plausible prove false friends. *The Strange Affair of Adelaide Harris* (1971) is a comic, fast-moving farce set in Regency Brighton. The constant moral battle that sur-faces in all his work is also memorably depicted in *Garfield's Apprentices* (1976–8), short stories about young people making their way in different trades but also having to decide upon important choices in their personal affairs. *The Empty Sleeve* (1982) in-volves another favourite theme in its story of a pair of twins who are spiritually opposite but also mutually dependent.

Garioch, (Sutherland) Robert 1909–81 Scottish poet and translator. Born in Edinburgh, he was edu-cated at the Royal High School and Edinburgh University before training as a teacher at Moray House College of Education. After service in World War II, including several years as a prisoner of war, he

taught in and around Edinburgh until his early re-tirement in the 1960s. He received a Scottish Arts Council award in 1968 and was writer-in-residence at Edinburgh University (1971–3) and with Radio Forth. His *Two Men and a Blanket: Memoirs of Captivity* ap-peared in 1975 and *Collected Poems* in 1977. Robin Fulton has edited his *Complete Poetical Works* (1983) and *A Garioch Miscellany* (1986).

Most of Garioch's poetry is written in a form of Scots which brings together contemporary colloquial speech and literary diction. He is predominantly an urban poet (taking ROBERT FERGUSSON rather than BURNS as his model), whose best-known work com-bines a gift for comic impersonation with satirical ob-servations of civic follies, hypocrisy and pretence. In 'At Robert Fergusson's Grave' and such longer medi-tations as 'The Wire' and 'The Muir', he shows that un-derlying his sense of the various comedies of urban discontent there is a more sombre vision and a broader ambition for the use of Scots in the modern world. He also translated into Scots the SONNETS of 19th-century Roman dialect poet Belli and the FREE VERSE of Apollinaire.

Garland, (Hannibal) Hamlin 1860–1940 Amer-ican short-story writer and novelist. He spent his youth on farms in Iowa, South Dakota and his native Wisconsin. In 1884 he moved to Boston, where he was befriended by WILLIAM DEAN HOWELLS, but he re-turned to the Midwest in 1887 and dedicated himself to depicting the life there and urging reforms to better it. His stories and sketches, written mostly before 1890, won acclaim when collected in MAIN-TRAVELLED ROADS (1891). Two further collections, *Prairie Folks* (1892) and *Wayside Courtships* (1897), were combined as *Other Main-Travelled Roads* (1910).

His writing often tended toward propaganda, espe-cially in his novels. *Jason Edwards, An Average Man* (1892) is a plea for the Single Tax Theory of HENRY GEORGE; *A Spoil of Office* (1892) campaigns for the Populist Party. Less political novels include two books about life in Dakota farm country, *A Little Norsk* (1892) and *Rose of Dutcher's Coolly* (1895). *The Captain of the Gray-Horse Troop* (1902) and *Cavanagh, Forest Ranger* (1910) are novels about the Far West. *A Son of the Middle Border* (1917) and *A Daughter of the Middle Border* (1921) are autobiographical narratives. His essays on his theory of realistic fiction, which he called 'veritism', appeared as *Crumbling Idols* (1894).

Garner, Alan 1934– Writer of CHILDREN'S LITERA-TURE. Born in Cheshire, the setting for many of his stories, Garner won a scholarship to Manchester Grammar School before going to Oxford University. Shortly after, he began writing his first children's book *The Weirdstone of Brisingamen* (1960), a power-ful mixture of fantasy and everyday reality. *Elidor* (1965) and, most memorably, *The Owl Service* (1967) concentrated on the role myth and legend can still play. Partly inspired by THE MABINOGION, *The Owl Service* looks at the way ancient hatreds erupt through the modern adolescent inhabitants of a Welsh valley. *Red Shift* (1973), another technically innovatory novel, presents three parallel stories of intolerance that have all occurred at the same place during different periods of history. *The Stone Book Quartet* (1976–8) is made up of four brief stories drawn from the author's own past family of local craftsmen and is told in Cheshire dialect.

Garner, Helen 1942– Australian novelist and short-story writer. Born in Geelong, Victoria, she was educated at the University of Melbourne. She worked as a secondary schoolteacher in Melbourne until she was dismissed for answering frankly her pupils' questions about sex. She subsequently became a freelance journalist before turning to fiction. Garner achieved overnight fame with the publication of her first novel, *Monkey Grip* (1977), made into a film in 1981. Written in the fragmentary post-modernist manner which typifies all her work, it compares the narrator-heroine's addiction to romantic love with her lover's addiction to hard drugs. She has secured her reputation in subsequent writing: *Honour and Other People's Children* (1980), two novellas; *The Children's Bach* (1984), a novel; *Postcards from Surfers* (1985), a collection of short stories; and *Cosmo Cosmolino* (1992), a novel. Her work chronicles contemporary Australian lifestyles, at home and abroad, in a highly evocative, elliptical style which lends itself both to comedy and to reflection on the processes of art.

Garner, Hugh 1913–79 Canadian novelist and short-story writer. Born in England in Batley, Yorkshire, he was taken to Toronto in 1919. After working briefly as a copy boy on *The Toronto Star*, he led an itinerant life in the Canadian West and was gaoled as a vagrant in West Virginia. He subsequently enlisted to fight for the Loyalists in the Spanish Civil War and served in the Canadian navy in World War II. After the war he embarked on his writing career and his first novel, *Storm Below*, which was based on his wartime experience, appeared in 1949. A butchered version of an earlier novel, *Cabbagetown*, followed in 1950, with the complete text not being published until 1968. *Cabbagetown* is a vivid account of the working-class district where Garner grew up in the 1930s and is his finest novel. His other novels include *The Silence on the Shore* (1962), *A Nice Place to Visit* (1970), *The Intruders* (1976) and three police novels, *The Sin Sniper* (1970), *Death in Don Mills* (1975) and *Murder Has Your Number* (1978). His short stories are collected in the volumes *The Yellow Sweater* (1952), *Hugh Garner's Best Stories* (1963), *Men and Women* (1966), *Violation of the Virgins* (1971) and *Hugh*

Garner Omnibus (1978). *One Damn Thing after Another* (1973) is his autobiography.

Garnett, David 1892–1981 Novelist. The son of Constance and EDWARD GARNETT, and grandson of RICHARD GARNETT, he was born in Brighton and educated privately, then at the Royal College of Science, where he studied botany. He married the illustrator Rachel Alice ('Ray') Marshall (d. 1940) who illustrated his early works, and after her death Angelica Bell, daughter of Vanessa. As a conscientious objector during World War I he worked as a farm labourer. After the war he started a bookshop in Soho with the journalist and drama critic Francis Birrell who, like Garnett, was associated with the BLOOMSBURY GROUP.

His first novel, *Lady into Fox* (1922), was a prose fantasy about a young wife, Sylvia Tebrick, who while out walking with her husband is suddenly changed into a vixen. This was followed by two more novels in the same genre, *A Man in the Zoo* (1924), about a man who donates himself as a specimen to the zoo, and *The Grasshoppers Come* (1931). Neither achieved the same success as his first. Garnett's subsequent novels relinquished fantasy, and *A Rabbit in the Air* (1932) drew on his early attempts to become an aviator. *Aspects of Love* (1955) was a delicate and bizarre love story. His later works included *A Shot in the Dark* (1958) and *A Net for Venus* (1962).

His non-fiction includes an edition of the letters of T. E. LAWRENCE (1938), a 10-volume edition of the novels of PEACOCK (1924–34) and his own correspondence with T. H. WHITE (1968). *The Golden Echo* (1953), *The Flowers of the Forest* (1955) and *The Familiar Faces* (1962) comprise his autobiography.

Garnett, Edward (William) 1868–1937 Man of letters. Born in London and educated privately, he was the son of RICHARD GARNETT and husband of Constance Garnett, a translator of the Russian classics. He is chiefly remembered as the influential publisher's reader (latterly with Jonathan Cape) who encouraged the talents of many leading contemporary writers, including JOSEPH CONRAD, D. H. LAWRENCE and E. M. FORSTER. His own works include critical biographies of HOGARTH (1911) and Turgenev (1917), a volume of essays, *Friday Nights* (1922), and *The Trial of Jeanne d'Arc and Other Plays* (1931).

Garnett, Eve 1900–91 Writer and illustrator of CHILDREN'S LITERATURE. She was born in Worcester and educated at art schools in London. *The Family from One End Street* (1937) describes the adventures of children from the poor but contented Ruggles family, vividly depicted in her rapid line drawings. Though its plot was traditional and its attitude to the Ruggles family sometimes patronizing, the book was one of the first 20th-century children's books to discuss the realities of domestic poverty. It was immediately popular and widely translated. Two sequels, *Further Adventures of the Family from One End Street* (1956) and *Holiday at the Dew Drop Inn: A One End Street Story* (1963), were less successful.

Garnett, Richard 1835–1906 Biographer, poet and short-story writer. Born at Lichfield, Garnett worked for the British Museum Library from the age of 16 until he retired in 1899. He was Superintendent of the Reading Room from 1875 to 1884, edited the library's first printed catalogue, and was responsible for the introduction of photography in the library. His knowledge of the classics and of international literature was reputed to be encyclopaedic – the result of a prodigious memory – and he published several short biographies, including works on MILTON, CARLYLE and EMERSON. He edited *Relics of Shelley* (1862), and wrote a *History of Italian Literature* (1897), but he is chiefly remembered for his collection of short stories, *The Twilight of the Gods* (1888), many of which had originally been published in THE YELLOW BOOK. Both his son, EDWARD GARNETT, and his grandson, DAVID GARNETT, became writers.

Garrick, David 1717–79 Actor, playwright and adapter of work by other playwrights. Born in Hereford and educated in Lichfield, where SAMUEL JOHNSON was one of his teachers, Garrick accompanied Johnson to London in 1737. For four years he took part in amateur theatricals while working in the wine trade, but his performance in CIBBER's version of SHAKESPEARE's *RICHARD III* in an unlicensed theatre in Goodman's Fields in 1741 caused a sensation and encouraged him to make the stage his career. From then until his retirement in 1776, above all during his 30 years as manager of DRURY LANE (1747–76), he was the leader of English theatrical taste and an actor whose superiority, though sporadically challenged, was never decisively defied.

Garrick's plays and adaptations have been too readily neglected. Prominent among his lively FARCES and afterpieces are *The Lying Valet* (1741), *Miss in Her Teens* (1747), *The Irish Widow* (1772) and *Bon Ton: or, High Life above Stairs* (1775). Of a dozen or so adaptations from Shakespeare, none of which say much for the 18th century's understanding of the original, *Florizel and Perdita* (1756), based on THE WINTER'S TALE, and a musical version of THE TEMPEST (1756) are of some interest. Above all his achievements in his own authorial right stands his collaboration with GEORGE COLMAN THE ELDER on THE CLANDESTINE MARRIAGE (1766). Garrick's letters, collected in three volumes (1963), give some indication of his wit and the uncertainty of his wisdom.

Garrison, William Lloyd 1805–79 American Abolitionist leader, editor and lecturer. Born in Newburyport, Massachusetts, he edited *The Genius of Universal Emancipation* with the Quaker Benjamin Lundy until his approach proved too radical for Lundy. Garrison then founded the Abolitionist newspaper THE LIBERATOR in 1831, and in the following year launched a vigorous attack on the American Colonization Society. He continued publishing the influential *Liberator* throughout the Civil War. His own books include *Thoughts on African Colonization* (1832), *Sonnets* (1843), and a collection of essays and speeches entitled *Selections* (1852).

Garth, Sir Samuel 1661–1719 Physician and poet. Garth was a member of the KIT-CAT CLUB, a Whig coterie centred on JACOB TONSON, the publisher. He wrote a burlesque poem *The Dispensary* (1699) which poked fun at the apothecaries who attempted to resist the supply of medicines to dispensaries beyond their control. The poem enjoyed a certain vogue and was praised by POPE.

Gascoigne, George ?1525–77 Poet, playwright and translator. He was educated at Cambridge and studied law at Gray's Inn, for which he translated two plays. He served with English troops in the Low Countries, where he was captured by the Spanish, and sat as MP for Bedford in the reigns of both Mary and Elizabeth (1557–9). The poet NICHOLAS BRETON became his stepson. Gascoigne's significance in Renaissance literature is that he did many things for the first time, or almost the first time, especially in the domestication of literary kinds and forms.

The Posies of George Gascoigne (1575) is an authorized printing of a miscellaneous collection which had previously appeared without his permission as *A Hundred Sundry Flowers* (1573). Its most important contents are two plays. *Supposes*, a prose play of mistaken identity based on Ariosto's *I suppositi*, is the first successful English adaptation of Italian comedy. It anticipated SHAKESPEARE's THE COMEDY OF ERRORS and provided the sub-plot of THE TAMING OF THE SHREW. *Jocasta* was the first Greek tragedy played on the English stage. Gascoigne also wrote *The Glass of Government* (1575), a CLOSET DRAMA in the form of a Roman comedy, and various court MASQUES. Other items in *The Posies* testify to a wide range of interests: *The Adventures of Master F. I.* is a very early example of an original English prose narrative, *Dan Bartholomew of Bath* a love poem, and *Certain Notes of Instruction in English Verse* a treatise on prosody.

The Steel Glass (1576) is a very early example of nondramatic blank verse in English. The honest and satirical steel glass reflects the state of the commonwealth and the work attacks worldliness and ends with praise of an ideal clergy. Another of Gascoigne's poems is *The Grief of Joy*. Until it was printed in 1869 this existed only in an unfinished text which was written by 1576. It is a RHYME ROYAL reflection, in imitation of Petrarch's *De remediis utriusque fortunae*, on the vanity of beauty and strength. *The Complaint of Philomene*, an Ovidian narrative, was printed with *The Steel Glass* (1576), although the preface to the latter work says that it was written some 12 years earlier. *The Spoil of Antwerp* (1576) is a piece of war journalism; *The Drum of Doomsday* (1576), treating the frailties and miseries of life, is a translation of part of a treatise by Innocent III.

Gascoyne, David (Emery) 1916– Poet. Born in Harrow and educated at Salisbury Cathedral Choir School and Regent Street Polytechnic in London, he published his first volume, *Roman Balcony* (1932), at the age of 16 and became a *habitué* of London's literary Fitzrovia. A critical survey (1935) established him as the leading British authority on surrealism, and *Man's Life is This Meat* (1936) as one of its leading British practitioners, with CHARLES MADGE, Hugh Sykes Davies and Roland Penrose. The remainder of his writing career, broken by long silences, has culminated in a revised edition of *Collected Poems* (1988), as well as *Three Translations* (1988) and *Hymns to the Night* (1989). His *Collected Journals 1936–42* (1991) is interesting for its portrait of Paris on the eve of World War II.

Gaskell, Elizabeth (Cleghorn) 1810–65 Novelist and biographer. Born in Chelsea, London, the daughter of William Stevenson, civil servant and sometime Unitarian minister, Elizabeth Gaskell was brought up in Knutsford, Cheshire, by an aunt. She was educated at the Avonbank School in Stratford-upon-Avon and subsequently spent two years in the family of a distant cousin, the Rev. William Turner, of Newcastle upon Tyne. In fact, her earlier years were peripatetic, a series of temporary sojourns, although at one of them she met her future husband, the Unitarian parson William Gaskell, author of many tracts and pamphlets relating to his calling, who held a chair of English history and literature at Manchester New College. They were married in August 1832 and henceforth Mrs Gaskell's life was in northern England.

Although she had early tried her hand at short-story writing, it was not until 1848 with the publication of her first novel, *MARY BARTON*, that Mrs Gaskell came upon the literary scene. This book, sub-titled *A Tale of Manchester Life*, was commenced shortly after the death of her little son, William, and its writing was suggested to her as a distraction from grief. It is a tale of industrial strife and unrest, touched by the melodramatic, and growing out of the Chartist movement of the 1840s.

Mary Barton earned Mrs Gaskell the friendship and respect of DICKENS, who encouraged her to continue to contribute to his magazine, *HOUSEHOLD WORDS*. *CRANFORD* appeared at irregular intervals in its pages from December 1851 until May 1853. Set in a thinly disguised Knutsford, it is a gentle understated tale of

Elizabeth Gaskell: a portrait by George Richmond

a retiring spinster and the little circle around her – a book that pronounces, if the word is not too strong, on the fundamental verities and decencies of the human condition. *RUTH* (1853) came next, boldly dealing with the concealment of an unmarried mother's problems. *NORTH AND SOUTH*, another industrial story of disquiet and confrontation, appeared in 1855. An eight-year interval in novel-writing closed with *SYLVIA'S LOVERS* (1863). *WIVES AND DAUGHTERS*, posthumously published in 1866, stands in striking contrast to her early work and is in the tradition and style of JANE AUSTEN.

Given her close friendship with CHARLOTTE BRONTË – the two writers first met in August 1850 – it was not surprising that she should have undertaken a biography after Charlotte's early death in 1855. *The Life of Charlotte Brontë* (1857) does not pretend to critical analysis; rather, it is a factual narrative, full in background and analytical of character, a book written out of sympathy and understanding for its subject. But just as Mrs Gaskell raised hackles over her treatment of illegitimacy in *Ruth* and of social strife in *North and South*, so she encountered antagonism over her account of the Brontë children at the Clergy Daughters' School at Cowan Bridge and, in particular, for her indiscreet allusions to Branwell Brontë's relations with a Mrs Edmund Robinson in whose household he was tutor. This last resulted in threats of legal action and, ultimately, withdrawal of questionable passages from the biography after its second edition. Yet, despite the problems surrounding *The Life of Charlotte Brontë*, the biography endures with acclamation.

Throughout her career Mrs Gaskell wrote longer short stories bordering on the novella. Several volumes were collected, among them *Life in Manchester* (1848), *Lizzie Leigh and Other Tales* (1855), *Round the Sofa* (1859) and *Cousin Phillis and Other Tales* (1865). Her control of the form appears in COUSIN PHILLIS, 'Lizzie Leigh', 'Lois the Witch' and in more than a handful of others as well.

In a century rich in women writers Mrs Gaskell stands to the forefront in her sympathy for the deprived, her evocations of nature, her gentle humour and her narrative pace. Of note is her exceptionally direct development as novelist from loosely structured melodramatic writing to the urbanity and balanced form of her later work, particularly *Wives and Daughters*.

Gass, William 1924– American novelist, short-story writer and scholar. Born in Fargo, North Dakota, he became a professor of philosophy at Washington University in St Louis. His fiction is notable for its experimental use of language. *Omensetter's Luck* (1966), his first novel, comprises three sections, each written in a different rhetorical style. It presents the conflict between Omensetter, who represents physicality and mindlessness, and Jethro Furber, who is intellectual and religious. A novella, *Willie Masters' Lonesome Wife* (1971) is still more experimental, containing unusual typography, parodies, footnotes, and authorial interruptions of the narrative. *In the Heart of the Heart of the Country and Other Stories* (1968), *The First Winter of My Married Life* (1979) and *Culp* (1985) are collections of short stories. His non-fiction includes *Fiction and the Figures of Life* (1970), *On Being Blue: A Philosophical Inquiry* (1975), *The World Within the Word* (1978) and *Habitations of the Word: Essays* (1985).

Gatty, Margaret 1809–73 Writer of CHILDREN'S LITERATURE. Born Margaret Scott, she married the Rev. Alfred Gatty. Mrs Gatty founded the enormously popular *Aunt Judy's Magazine* in 1866, editing and contributing to it until she died. She was best known for her *Parables from Nature*, published in a series of five books (1855–71). Other titles that enjoyed great popularity were *The Fairy Godmothers* (1851), *Aunt Judy's Tales* (1859) and *Aunt Judy's Letters* (1862).

Gawain-poet, The Author of SIR GAWAIN AND THE GREEN KNIGHT, to whom are attributed also the other poems in manuscript Cotton Nero A x, CLEANNESS, PATIENCE and PEARL. The theory of common authorship is based on similarities of style and diction. The poet's identity is not known; several names have been suggested, but none is conclusively supported by the evidence.

Gay, John 1685–1732 Poet and playwright. Born in Barnstaple, Devon, he was brought up by his uncle, educated at Barnstaple Grammar School and then apprenticed to a London silk-merchant in the Strand. Socially at ease from the start of his urban life, Gay befriended AARON HILL and began to move in literary circles. His first publication was *Wine* (1708), an anonymous BLANK-VERSE poem written to celebrate the Union of Scotland with England, a convivial piece overburdened by its echoes of MILTON. He met POPE and began to frequent the fashionable coffee-houses. His first attempt at drama, *The Mohocks* (1712), a 'Tragical-comical Farce' about a band of aristocratic thugs, was never acted.

Gay had contributed to Lintot's *Miscellany* and THE EXAMINER, and his essay *The Present State of Wit* (1711) drew attention to his presence in polite literary circles. In 1712 he was appointed secretary to the Duchess of Monmouth, which alleviated his immediate financial worries. 1713 saw the publication of *The Fan* (a pale imitation of THE RAPE OF THE LOCK) and the more accomplished *Rural Sports*, a GEORGIC poem dedicated to Pope, managing a genuine celebration of the English countryside combined with a characteristically comic dimension. Its use of animal parallelism anticipates his later *Fables*. Gay's first substantial success came with his wittiest poem, THE SHEPHERD'S WEEK (1714), a PASTORAL cycle that is partly PARODY and partly true to life, designed to support Pope's opposition to AMBROSE PHILIPS. Gay left the Duchess of Monmouth in 1714, and became secretary to Lord Clarendon on a mission to Hanover, but his hopes of advancement in public office collapsed with the death of Queen Anne in 1714, and the fall of Harley's Tory government.

The audience at the first night of his *What D'ye Call It* (1715) were so convinced by Gay's skill at BURLESQUE that they mistook it for tragedy and were moved to tears. One of his distinctive strengths as a writer was a quick ear for rhythms of speech and tones of voice, and this, combined with his lively interest in BALLADS and street literature, contributed much to the success of his poem TRIVIA: or, The Art of Walking the Streets of London (1716), an extended Juvenalian survey of the conditions of life in the capital, both realistic in atmosphere and parodic in style. His next work was a play, THREE HOURS AFTER MARRIAGE (1717), written with his fellow members of the SCRIBLERUS CLUB, Pope and ARBUTHNOT. SAMUEL JOHNSON, who regarded Gay as an idle dilettante, wrote approvingly 'it had the fate which such outrages deserve': the first night ended in fisticuffs between Gay and the leading actor COLLEY CIBBER, who had not realized his part was a lampoon of himself.

Poems on Several Occasions (1720), containing various ECLOGUES and songs, made him some money, which he promptly invested in the South Sea Company. Gay was ruined when the 'Bubble' burst, and his health had also begun to deteriorate. He stayed with Pope and Burlington, visited Bath for the 'waters', and, in a final attempt to secure preferment at court, began work in 1726 on his *Fables*, addressed to young Prince William. The first volume of these appeared in 1729 and proved popular, demonstrating the poet's gentle eye for detail and real affinity for natural topics; the second part, more serious, was published posthumously.

Since 1722, Gay had maintained a vigorous correspondence with his older friend SWIFT, and it was the latter who provided the idea for Gay's greatest work, *THE BEGGAR'S OPERA*. This BALLAD OPERA pokes fun at the imported fashion for opera, and inverts the heroic values of polite society by translating hypocrisy into the underworld of London's criminals. The Duchess of Queensberry – Gay's new patron – offered to back it, and the play was produced by John Rich at Lincoln's Inn Fields on 29 January 1728. It was prodigiously successful, running for an unprecedented 62 nights, and is reported to have made 'Gay rich, and Rich gay'. In a lean century for good drama, it was by far the most popular play, and contains some 69 songs. The sequel, *POLLY* (1729), was suppressed by Walpole, who was tired of being satirized, but this merely made it a *cause célèbre*, and the printed version sold quickly. It was finally produced in 1777. His friends started to worry at Gay's life-style, since he began to indulge freely in gambling and drinking, living a life of leisure at Bath or with the Queensberrys. He died in 1732 and is buried in Westminster Abbey. His refusal ever to be solemn about life is epitomized by the epitaph he composed for himself: 'Life is a jest, and all things show it;/ I thought so once – and now I know it.'

Gay's literary reputation has proved difficult to determine. As a dramatist he wrote some 13 pieces, all overshadowed by the runaway success of *The Beggar's Opera*. These include *The Wife of Bath* (1713) ('it received no applause' observed Johnson), *Dione* (1719), an impossible pastoral, and the libretto for Handel's *Acis and Galatea* (1732). As a poet, he was a master of the HEROIC COUPLET, and his songs and fables continued to be read after his death, for their sweetness of sound and neatness of phrase. Though his sybaritic life-style and lack of ambition perhaps prevented him from achieving more, Gay should not suffer by comparison to his more serious Scriblerian associates. He was intellectually acute, and a lively personality who made friends easily; Voltaire, for example, is said to have 'loved Gay vastly'.

Gee, Maggie [Mary] 1948– Novelist. Born in Dorset, she studied at Oxford and became a Creative Writing Fellow at the University of East Anglia in 1982. Her first novel, *Dying, in Other Words* (1981), is her most experimental and her second, *The Burning Book* (1983), about nuclear annihilation, her most substantial. Since *Light Years* (1985), an unsuccessful venture into whimsical comedy, she has produced *Grace* (1988), a psychological thriller inspired by the unsolved murder of the anti-nuclear campaigner Hilda Murrell, and *Where are the Snows* (1991), a chronicle of sexual ardour.

Gee, Maurice 1931– New Zealand novelist, short-story writer and writer of CHILDREN'S LITERATURE. He was born in Whakatane in the North Island. While working as a teacher and librarian he produced his early novels: *The Big Season* (1962), *A Special Flower* (1965) and *In My Father's Den* (1972). He became a full-time writer in 1975, the same year he published a volume of short stories, *A Glorious Morning, Comrade*. Gee secured his reputation as one of New Zealand's leading novelists with *Plumb* (1978), which marked a break with the traditional realism of his earlier work. It became the first volume of a trilogy, completed by *Meg* (1981) and *Sole Survivor* (1983), chronicling three generations of a family during this century and exploring the effects of New Zealand's Puritan inheritance on individual and social relations. Among his later novels are *Prowlers* (1987) and *The Burning Boy* (1990). His fine stories for children include *Under the Mountain* (1979) and *The Fire-Raiser* (1986).

Gelbart, Larry 1923– American writer for the stage, radio, television and film. Born in Chicago, he began writing sketches while still in his teens and has become one of America's most respected comic talents. His work for the theatre includes the highly successful musical *A Funny Thing Happened on the Way to the Forum* (with Burt Shevelove; 1961) as well as *Sly Fox* (1976), *Mastergate* (1989), *City of Angels* (1989), *Power Failure* (1990) and *Feats of Clay* (1991). For television he scripted the series *M*A*S*H* (1972–6). *The Wrong Box* (1966), *Oh, God* (1977) and *Tootsie* (1982) are among his film credits.

Gelber, Jack 1932– American playwright. Born in Chicago, he was educated at the University of Illinois. He is best known for *The Connection* (1959), about four heroin addicts waiting for a 'connection' to bring their drugs. Its use of improvisatory techniques to collapse the traditional distance between audience and actors also characterizes Gelber's other plays, which include *The Apple* (1961), *Square in the Eye* (1965), *The Cuban Thing* (1968), *Sleep* (1972) and *Jack Gelber's New Play: Rehearsal* (1976). He has written the screenplay for the film of *The Connection* (1961), adapted MAILER's *Barbary Shore* (1974) for the stage, and published a novel, *On Ice* (1964).

Gellhorn, Martha 1908– War correspondent and novelist. She was born in St Louis, Missouri, and educated at Bryn Mawr College. Since *The Trouble I've Seen* (1936), a collection of novellas about Americans in the Depression, she has published three more books of novellas, including *The Weather in Africa* (1978), as well as volumes of short stories and novels. But it is for her remarkable record as a war reporter that she is best known, a career which began when she travelled to Spain in 1937 and has since spanned World War II, Vietnam, the 1967 Six-Day War in the Middle East and the Sandinistas' defence of Nicaragua in the early 1980s. Her reports are collected in *The Face of War* (1959; third revised edition, 1986) and other journalism in *The View from the Ground* (1988). From 1940 to 1945 she was the third wife of ERNEST HEMINGWAY, the 'another' in her book of astringent travel pieces, *Travels with Myself and Another* (1978).

Generides A late 14th-century VERSE ROMANCE composed in the Midlands. It survives in two versions, one of 10,000 lines in couplets and the other 7000 lines in seven-line stanzas.

Knowing his wife is unfaithful with his steward, King Aufreus meets the Princess Sereyne on a hunt; he begets a son, Generides, whom she rears. When he is grown up he goes to Aufreus' court but leaves after the Queen tries to seduce him, travelling to Persia where he falls in love with the Sultan's daughter, Clarionas. He is betrayed and imprisoned but later released to fight as the Sultan's champion. Meanwhile Aufreus loses his kingdom and wife to the treacherous steward and marries Sereyne. Generides eventually marries Clarionas after defeating a rival who kidnaps her and despite the malicious attempts of the Queen, estranged from Aufreus, to separate them. The steward is defeated by Generides and the Queen also dies. The romance, well told and engaging, is a composite of many common themes and motifs. It has no known source; despite its Indian and Middle Eastern setting it is unlikely that it is of Eastern origin.

Genesis An Old English poem preserved in the Junius manuscript (see JUNIUS, FRANCIS). Once thought to be the work of CAEDMON, it is now known to be a composite of two works, neither of which can be attributed to Caedmon. The major part of the poem, known as *Genesis A*, was written in the 8th century by a northern monk. It begins with an account of the war in Heaven and then proceeds to relate the story of the Book of Genesis up to chapter 22. Interpolated are over 600 lines of a 9th-century poem, *Genesis B*, translated from a German source and telling the story of Satan. The subject matter is the same as that of MILTON's *PARADISE LOST*, and there are some striking resemblances between the two works.

Geneva Bible, The See BIBLE IN ENGLISH, THE.

genre fiction Novels written to prototypical formulations of plot and subject. WILKIE COLLINS's DETECTIVE FICTION, ALDOUS HUXLEY's SCIENCE FICTION and GRAHAM GREENE's spy thrillers all show that generic conformity does not prevent original and distinguished writing. But overwhelmingly genre fiction is prompted more by a sense of audience and market, and the commercial advantage in satisfying it, than by any attempt at individual self-expression. It is often published to visually recognizable, economically efficient specifications. Victor Gollancz gave all his crime and science fiction titles yellow jackets, and the romances issued by Mills and Boon are condensed or expanded at editorial stage to a uniform length.

As with detective and science fiction, popular fiction's other principal genres offer certain therapeutic and consolatory characteristics for the reader. The thriller is written to excite and enthral, through the diversion of a fast-moving adventure plot, perhaps comprehending political or financial intrigue, violence, military engagements, extended chase sequences and a cast matching colourful villains against a sympathetically virtuous hero. Early exponents include ROBERT LOUIS STEVENSON with *KIDNAPPED*, and JOHN BUCHAN with *The Thirty-Nine Steps* while IAN FLEMING's James Bond novels introduced a modish salaciousness, cynicism and penchant for high-tech weaponry. The complexity of modern current affairs, coupled with residual historical fears, offer modern thrillers an enormous range of contexts. World War II and the postulated resurgence of Nazism allow a British or American audience the consolatory affirmation of national integrity and heroism. Notable examples are Alistair Maclean's *HMS Ulysses* and the conspiracy narratives of Robert Ludlum. Thrillers tend to reduce the process of history to a linear sequence, pivoting on a single individual or event. The assassination of President de Gaulle, for example, was narrowly averted in Frederick Forsyth's *The Day of the Jackal* (1971). Similarly, genre fiction can both arouse and allay common social fears of disaster. Air crashes, ocean liner sinkings, financial crises and medical experimentation are all employed to tense effect, especially by spin-off feature films. Steven Spielberg's film of Peter Benchley's 1974 novel *Jaws*, about a shark terrorizing a seaside community, was a particularly lucrative instance. In order to authenticate their potentially overheated plot, and to ensure a democratic appeal to the widest possible audience, thrillers have increasingly affected an authority of saturated learning, as in Arthur Hailey's *Hotel* (1965) and *Airport* (1968). Topicality is opportunistically maintained. With the end of the Cold War, writers have turned to Israel's emergence as a nuclear power, the guerrilla war in Afghanistan, and the rise of Muslim fundamentalism.

Genre fiction is rarely subversive or radical. Indeed, its popular appeal depends on literary and political conservatism. Detective novels affirm that crimes will be solved and murderers punished, Cold War thrillers that the West will always outwit Communism, romances that the protagonists will always find true love. Occasionally the necessary accommodation to changing social trends can significantly transform a genre, particularly in its customarily stereotyped sexual politics. Ken Follett's thrillers use resourceful, courageous women in conventionally male-dominated heroic roles; the detective fiction of Joan Smith and Sara Paretsky sets female detectives to solving crime; Mike Phillips and the American John Edgar Wideman both offer black protagonists as private eyes. Romance has proved less adaptable. Aimed at a female audience, it has exhibited at most a decline in chastity and an increase in materialism in developing from the bloodless, virginal tales of Barbara Cartland and Mills and Boons novels to the 'bodice-ripper' or historical romance of Susan Howatch or Kathleen Woodiwiss, inspired belatedly by the example of GONE WITH THE WIND, and the equally lengthy sagas of Shirley Conran and Celia Brayfield. It has varied its appeal by offering either an aspirational glimpse of top people's high living, as in the novels of Jackie Collins or Barbara Taylor Bradford, or a consolatory empathy with working-class community and regional chauvinism, as in Catherine Cookson's tales of North Tyneside, or Maeve Binchy's Irish family sagas.

The most geographically specific genre of all, the Western, may have died out altogether, or at least transmuted its essential appeal into other genres. The classic cowboys-and-Indians fables of ZANE GREY, Louis L'Amour and J. T. Edson owed much of their success to Hollywood directors like John Ford. As Hollywood has moved on, so the Western's myths of the frontier spirit, and an embattled community defending a hard-won land against incursors and the threat of lawless chaos, can be seen surviving in many science fiction and disaster narratives. The horror novel, inherently reliant on and devoted to effect, has also found its continued survival linked to the feature-film business. Where early post-war writers such as Dennis Wheatley had established an adequate market for their narratives of diabolic possession, adaptations of William Peter Blatty's The Exorcist or Stephen King's The Shining offered a more graphic medium for horror's visceral stock-in-trade.

Sales for successful writers of genre fiction can be enormous. Jaws sold 10 million copies in the USA alone. Alistair Maclean's works have sold more than 150 million copies worldwide. Harold Robbins's bulky ROMANS À CLEF about tycoons and glitterati, like The Carpetbaggers (1961), exceed this with total sales of more than 200 million.

Gent, Thomas 1693–1778 Printer, poet and writer of topographical works. Born in Ireland, Gent was apprenticed to a Dublin printer who so ill-treated him that he ran away, eventually arriving in London. After various adventures he was admitted to the Stationers' Company in 1717, and shortly after was involved in illicit printing for ATTERBURY. In 1722 he produced an abridgement of ROBINSON CRUSOE with 30 rather crude woodcuts of his own design, and in that year or 1723 he set up in business for himself. Hearing that the woman he loved, Alice Guy, had married a former fellow apprentice, he wrote a highly successful poem, The Forsaken Lover's Letter to His Former Sweetheart, but on hearing of her widowhood shortly after he hastened to York and married her, thus acquiring the business of his now dead rival. He became the only master printer in York and, it is thought, in the North of England. He produced a number of topographical works, written and printed by himself, of which the most important are his History of York (1730) and History of Ripon (1734) which contains a poem in praise of Fountains Abbey by Peter Aram, father of the murderer Eugene Aram. His autobiography (1832) contains a considerable amount of interesting material about the printing trade and literary world in the early 18th century and also shows him to have been extraordinarily cantankerous. His topographical works, which were embellished with at times grotesque woodcuts, are now regarded as valuable both for their idiosyncratic printing practices and their detailed information.

Gentleman's Magazine, The A periodical founded by Edward Cave (1691–1754), the enterprising son of a cobbler in Rugby, who became a printer in London. He launched it in 1731 under the pseudonym of Sylvanus Urban. It began as a review of news, essays and comment from other journals but by January 1739 it was publishing original work and SAMUEL JOHNSON became a regular contributor. Johnson's suggestions to Cave influenced the character of the paper and it assumed a more serious tone, publishing parliamentary reports, maps, reviews of publications and music. The Gentleman's Magazine continued to be published until 1914.

Geoffrey of Monmouth d. ?1155 Chronicler. Probably born in Monmouth and having some connection with Caerleon-on-Usk, he was at Oxford from 1129 to 1151, perhaps a canon of the secular college of St George which was dissolved in 1149. He probably lived in London from 1148 to 1151, though maintaining his Oxford connections. In 1151 he became Bishop Elect of Asaph and was ordained a priest in 1152. Evidence of doubtful reliability alleges he died in 1155.

Three works of his survive, all written in Latin: Historia regum Britanniae (c. 1135), Propheti Merlini and *Vita Merlini. The Prophecies* and *Life* were conceived separately but finally incorporated into the *History*. Deriving from the work of BEDE, Gildas and Nennius, it traces events from the legendary founding of Britain by Brutus, grandson of Aeneas, to the death of the last British king, Cadwallader, in 689. Although some of the narrative bears a remote resemblance to actual events, the majority is pure invention. It relates the lives of among others, Kings Cole, Lear, Cymbeline and Arthur, Julius Caesar, Claudius, Vespasian and Gorboduc, and events such as the founding of London, the moving of Stonehenge to Salisbury Plain by Merlin, and the coming of St Augustine to Britain. But it is for the history of King Arthur that the work is best known. Occupying over a fifth of the work, Arthur's mythical life and deeds are reported for the first time. His marriage to Guinevere, Mordred's treason, his disappearance to Avalon and the exploits of Gawain, Bedevere, Cador and Kay are all related, though Lancelot does not appear. Geoffrey's *History* in turn formed the basis of Wace's *Roman de Brut* and of the vast ensuing body of ARTHURIAN LITERATURE.

Geoffrey of Vinsauf d. *c.* 1210–20 Rhetorician. Little is known of the life of Geoffrey, although hints in his work suggest he was an Englishman, flourishing in the second half of the 12th century. He was a teacher of the future Richard I and it is thought that he studied in Paris, and that he visited Rome on at least one occasion. Three major works survive: the *Documentum de modo et arte dictandi et versificandi*, the *Summa de coloribus rhetoricis*, and the influential handbook, the *Poetria nova*, which was cited by CHAUCER in *THE CANTERBURY TALES*. In the *Poetria nova*, poetry is studied as an aspect of rhetoric, and Geoffrey draws heavily on two main sources, the pseudo-Ciceronian *Ad Herennium* and Horace's *Ars poetica*. Geoffrey urges poets to improve their skills by acquiring a thorough knowledge of the rules of poetic composition (*ars*), studying and imitating the great poets of the past (*imitatio*) and practising steadily (*usus*). The *Poetria nova* is a valuable source of information on the rhetorical devices, techniques and methods of ornamentation prescribed by medieval theoreticians as necessary to polished and felicitous poetry.

George, Henry 1839–97 American journalist and political reformer. Born in Philadelphia, he moved to California in 1857 and worked as a ship's storekeeper, gold-digger and typesetter before settling down to a career as a crusading journalist and newspaper editor in San Francisco.

His first major political statement was an editorial in *OVERLAND MONTHLY* (October 1868) entitled 'What the Railroads Will Bring Us', in which he argued that the present organization of the railroad industry would serve only to make the rich richer and the poor poorer. His first two separate publications, both pamphlets, *The Subsidy Question and the Democratic Party* and *Our Land and Land Policy*, appeared in 1871. The latter contained the first statement of his Single Tax Theory; he developed this in his most important economic treatise, *Progress and Poverty* (published in 1879 at his own expense), arguing that the gap between the rich and the poor could be closed by replacing the various taxes levied on labour and capital with a single tax on the rental value of property. *Progress and Poverty* eventually sold more than two million copies. In four subsequent works he applied his Single Tax Theory to a number of social and economic issues: *Social Problems* (1883), *Protection or Free Trade* (1886), *Perplexed Philosopher* (1892) and *Science of Political Economy* (1897). During the last 16 years of his life he made six lecture tours in Europe, where his theories were even more influential than in the USA.

George Barnwell See *LONDON MERCHANT, THE*.

Georgian Poetry An anthology published in five volumes between 1912 and 1922, planned by its publisher HAROLD MONRO, RUPERT BROOKE and SIR EDWARD MARSH, the editor. The early, influential volumes included Brooke, LASCELLES ABERCROMBIE, GORDON BOTTOMLEY, W. H. DAVIES, WALTER DE LA MARE, JOHN DRINKWATER, RALPH HODGSON, D. H. LAWRENCE and JOHN MASEFIELD. Their poetry tended to be colloquial and lightly shocking in its realism, yet they were never a coherent movement. Later volumes included the work of BLUNDEN, GRAVES, ROSENBERG and SASSOON. Graves, in particular, rejected the early Georgians as 'principally concerned with Nature and love and leisure and old age and childhood and animals and sleep and similar uncontroversial subjects' and for having no experience of the 'grinding hardships of trench-service'. The group was also criticized by POUND, ELIOT and the SITWELLS, whose anthology *Wheels* was intended as a MODERNIST alternative.

georgic A poem offering instruction about some branch of skill or art, the most famous example being the *Georgics* of Virgil, which discussed the conditions of life in the countryside under Octavian (later Augustus Caesar), and various aspects of farming and husbandry. Numerous imitations were written during the 17th and 18th centuries, poems about sheep-shearing, cider-making, physical health and country sports; the subject was the occasion of an important essay by ADDISON, *Essay on the Georgic* (1697), in which he distinguishes it from the PASTORAL.

Gerard, John 1545–1612 Herbalist. Gerard was for some years apprenticed to a barber-surgeon in London before being granted leave to establish his own practice. He developed an interest in plants and in his garden in Holborn cultivated gifts of rare plants and seeds. His catalogue of the plants there was printed in 1596. Gerard also supervised Lord Burleigh's gardens in the Strand. His *Herbal* (1597) was in fact a completion of an unfinished translation by a Dr Priest of Dodoenus's *Stirpium historiae pemptades sex* (1583). The *Herbal* was illustrated with over 1800 woodcuts (including an early depiction of the potato), very few of which were original as they came from Tabernaemontanus, *Eicones plantarum.* The description of the plants includes their habitat and times of flowering. Gerard gives many of the plants their old English names, includes popular legends (the goose-tree which bears shells that eventually hatch into barnacle geese) and describes the 'virtues' of plants: the lettuce cools heartburn and causes sleep, narcissus root pounded with honey is good for burns. A second edition, revised by Thomas Johnson, was printed in 1633.

Gerhardie, William 1895–1977 Novelist. Originally 'Gerhardi', he changed the spelling of his name in old age on the grounds that Dante, SHAKESPEARE, Racine and Goethe all had an 'e' on the end of their names and he deserved one too. He was born into a family of English merchants in St Petersburg and studied at Worcester College, Oxford. He published the first non-Russian book on Chekhov (1923), a central influence on his own extravagantly plotted fiction, which disconcertingly juxtaposes the absurd and the profound, the comic and the tragic. *Futility: A Novel on Russian Themes* (1922), *The Polyglots* (1925) and their successors, notably *Pending Heaven* (1930), *Resurrection* (1934) and *Of Mortal Love* (1936), enjoyed brief critical success. Gerhardie also wrote the autobiographical *Memoirs of a Polyglot* (1931), *The Casanova Fable* (with HUGH KINGSMILL, 1934), a study of the Romanovs (1939) and *God's Fifth Column, A Biography of the Age: 1890–1940* (edited by MICHAEL HOLROYD and Robert Skidelsky, 1981). He published no more books after 1940 and the major novel on which he was rumoured to be working during the years of his obscurity never materialized.

Germ, The The literary magazine of the PRE-RAPHAELITES. It lasted for only four issues, published between January and April 1850, and contained poetry by DANTE GABRIEL ROSSETTI (*THE BLESSED DAMOZEL*), CHRISTINA ROSSETTI and COVENTRY PATMORE, Rossetti's short story *Hand and Soul* and reviews of contemporary verse by his brother, WILLIAM MICHAEL ROSSETTI, who was also the editor.

Gest Hystoriale of the Destruction of Troy A VERSE ROMANCE written in the second half of the 14th century. It is the longest of the Middle English poems in ALLITERATIVE VERSE, and is divided into a prologue

and 36 books. It treats the history of Troy from the story of Jason and the Golden Fleece and the destruction of the Old Troy to the destruction of the New Troy, the adventures of the Greeks after its fall and the death of Ulysses. It includes the story of Troilus and Briseida, invented by Benoît de Sainte-Maure and told in his *Roman de Troie* (*c.* 1160) and later told by CHAUCER in *TROILUS AND CRISEYDE*. While based on Guido's *Historia destructionis Troiae*, the poem treats the material of its source freely, adding, omitting and adapting episodes. Except for some moralizing digressions the story is vigorously told and the characters are vividly portrayed.

Gesta Romanorum A collection of tales from various sources which took shape in Europe during the 14th century. The title is misleading, since few of the stories are concerned with Rome and some are Eastern in origin. Each tale was designed to point a moral, though this is transparently contrived in many cases. Popular as a storybook, the collection was plundered for subjects by succeeding generations. Originally written in Latin, it appeared in several vernacular translations, including one in Middle English. The first printed version in English was issued by WYNKYN DE WORDE in 1510.

Ghose, Zulfikar 1935– Indian/Pakistani poet and novelist. Born in Sialkot (then India, now Pakistan), he emigrated to Britain and then the USA, inhabiting the interstices of an Indian-Pakistani-British-American network of allegiances, antipathies and doubts. *The Loss of India* (1964) contains verse nostalgic for a lost past, tentative in an uncertain present. *Jets of Orange* (1967) again laments loss, and records Indian subjects with a sensitive outsider's detachment – which operates also in the pungent satirical verse of *The Violent West* (1972). The stories in *Statement against Corpses* (1964), with B. S. JOHNSON, and the novels *Contradictions* (1966) and *The Murder of Aziz Khan* (1969) seek a 'still point' between, respectively, being alive and observing death, Western rationality and Eastern 'nothingness', outside physicality and interior sensibility. Two critical works, *Hamlet, Prufrock, and Language* (1978) and *The Fiction of Reality* (1984), point to the nature of Ghose's impressive output of sophisticated and challenging novels since 1972: a trilogy, *The Incredible Brazilian* (1972), *The Beautiful Empire* (1975), and *A Different World* (1979); *Hulme's Investigations into the Bogart Script* (1981); *A New History of Torments* (1982); and *Don Bueno* (1983). *Confessions of a Native-Alien* (1965) is an autobiography.

Gibbon, Edward 1737–94 Historian. The son of a family in comfortable circumstances, he was born at Putney and educated at Westminster School. He entered Magdalen College, Oxford, as a gentleman-commoner just before his 15th birthday but was disappointed in Oxford, finding it self-satisfied and outdated. He studied by himself and was received into the Roman Catholic church in June 1753. In alarm, Gibbon's father sent him to Lausanne and a tutor in the form of a Calvinist minister, Pavillar, who managed to reconvert him. At Lausanne, too, he formed an attachment to Suzanne Curchod, the only romantic attachment of his life, broken off because his father disapproved. She eventually married Jacques Necker.

Gibbon returned home in 1758, and in 1761 published his first work, *Essai sur l'étude de la littérature*; an English version appeared in 1764. He served in the Hampshire militia for four years and reached the rank of colonel (1759–63). After his service he toured Europe, spending some time in Paris and Lausanne, and proceeding to Rome intent on archaeological study. He reached the city in October 1764 and on the 15th of that month he found the historical subject he sought. 'It was at Rome... as I sat musing amidst the ruins of the Capitol, while barefoot friars were singing vespers in the Temple of Jupiter, that the idea of writing the decline and fall of the city first started to my mind.' He had, meanwhile, been producing a mass of miscellaneous reviews and exercises, including the *Observations of the Design of the VIth Book of the Aeneid* (1770). His father died in the same year, leaving financial problems for his son to clear up. Gibbon did, however, manage to salvage enough money to establish himself in London, with its libraries, intellectual stimulus and scholarly society.

Gibbon became an MP in 1774. The House of Commons was 'a school of civil prudence, the first and most essential virtue of an historian', as he wrote in his memoirs. He was a steadfast supporter of Lord North's government and was rewarded with the post of Commissioner of Trade and Plantations in 1779, holding it until its abolition in 1782. His political career amounted to little but his literary career had begun: the first volume of THE HISTORY OF THE DECLINE AND FALL OF THE ROMAN EMPIRE was published on 17 February 1776 and was greeted with general praise, except from orthodox Christians. In England certain theological critics, including RICHARD WATSON and Henry Edwards Davis, attacked Gibbon in print, and he replied eventually with *A Vindication of Some Passages in the Fifteenth and Sixteenth Chapters* (1779), in which he refuted completely their charges of plagiarism and misrepresentation. Similar attacks continued throughout his lifetime.

The second and third volumes of the *History* were published in 1783, when Gibbon resolved to extend it to cover the Eastern Empire, Byzantium, as well. Weary of London, he moved to Lausanne, where completed his *History* there in 1787 and took the three volumes to London in 1788 for the publisher. He then began *The Antiquities of the House of Brunswick* but,

lacking a knowledge of German, did not complete it. He left Lausanne in 1791 and returned to England, where his closest friend, John Baker Holroyd, now Earl of Sheffield, offered him the hospitality of Sheffield Park in Sussex and his London house. Lord Sheffield was to prepare his friend's *Memoirs of My Life and Writings* for publication (1796), as well as his (admirably edited) collections of *Miscellaneous Works*. Gibbon died in London and lies buried in the Sheffield family tomb in Fletching church in Sussex.

Gibbon, Lewis Grassic [Mitchell, James Leslie] 1901–35 Scottish writer. Born into a crofting family at Auchterless, Aberdeenshire, Mitchell was brought up in the Howe of Mearns, south of Stonehaven. He was educated at Arbuthnott School and briefly at Mackie Academy, Stonehaven, and became a journalist in Aberdeen and Glasgow. He was early a convert to socialism, his views reinforced by the urban poverty and unrest on Clydeside. Jobless, he served in the Royal Army Service Corps in Persia, India and Egypt, and later in the Royal Air Force until 1929. A packed and remarkable writing career was cut short when he died in Welwyn Garden City.

Lewis Grassic Gibbon was the name he used for his specifically Scottish undertakings, of which the best-known is *A Scots Quair*, a trilogy of novels set in the Howe of Mearns: *Sunset Song* (1932), *Cloud Howe* (1933) and *Grey Granite* (1934). It made a courageous, successful attempt to render the rhythms and cadences of North-East dialect, while using only a handful of local words. As Gibbon, he collaborated with HUGH MACDIARMID on *Scottish Scene: or, The Intelligent Man's Guide to Albyn* (1934), an important contribution to the SCOTTISH RENAISSANCE. Under his own name he published seven English novels, many short stories and works of history, archaeology and anthropology informed by his version of Diffusionist theory.

Gibbons, Stella See COLD COMFORT FARM.

Gibson, Graeme 1934– Canadian novelist. Born and educated in Ontario, he has travelled widely in Europe, the USA and Latin America. *Five Legs* (1969), *Communion* (1971) and *Perpetual Motion* (1982) are experimental but carefully constructed novels. All are set in southern Ontario, though the first two deal with private contemporary experience, conveyed in a STREAM-OF-CONSCIOUSNESS style, whereas *Perpetual Motion* is a historical novel leaning to MAGIC REALISM. All are concerned with man's relation to nature and spirit, though this is perhaps most evident in the last novel, where a 19th-century farmer's obsession with a mammoth bone and a machine serves to link past and future or earth and industrialism. Gibson has also published a collection of interviews, *Eleven Canadian Novelists* (1973). Prominent in Canadian cultural politics, he was an organizer and founding member of the Writers Union of Canada and its chairman in 1974–5, Canada's first exchange writer at the University of Edinburgh 1978–9, and president of PEN Canada (Anglophone) in 1987.

Gibson, Wilfred Wilson 1878–1962 Poet. He was born at Hexham in Northumberland and educated privately. He published his first collection of poems, *Urlyn the Harper and Other Songs*, in 1902, and thereafter his work appeared regularly in *New Numbers* and in EDWARD MARSH's *GEORGIAN POETRY*. His output was considerable, his commonest subject being the plight of the unfortunate, particularly the ordinary men and women at the mercy of industrial and political change. Gibson's *Collected Poems* (1926) was followed by another dozen collections before his death. *Within Four Walls* (1950) contains five verse plays.

Gibson, William 1948– American writer of SCIENCE FICTION. He was born in South Carolina and educated at the University of British Columbia. Most of his work – including the novels *Neuromancer* (1984), *Count Zero* (1985), *Mona Lisa Overdrive* (1988) and the short stories collected in *Burning Chrome* (1986) – is typical of so-called 'Cyberpunk' fiction, which deals with the intimate interaction of people and electronic machinery in an overpopulated, decadent near future. *Neuromancer* popularized the notion of 'cyberspace' as a medium in which computers store data and into which humans may ultimately be able to 'download' their personalities. *The Difference Engine* (with Bruce Sterling, 1990) is an alternative history novel in which Victorian England undergoes a technological revolution thanks to Charles Babbage's mechanical computer.

Gifford, William 1756–1826 Satirist and critic. Born at Ashburton in Devon, a glazier's son, Gifford was apprenticed to a shoemaker, but through the kindness of a local surgeon was able to enter Exeter College, Oxford, in 1782. He first came to notice with two SATIRES of the DELLA CRUSCANS, *The Baviad* (1791) and *The Maeviad* (1795). He became editor of *THE ANTI-JACOBIN* in 1797 and of *THE QUARTERLY REVIEW* in 1809. His criticism is sour and conservative. He was caricatured by THOMAS LOVE PEACOCK as Mr Vamp in *MELINCOURT* (1817) and rebuked by WILLIAM HAZLITT in *A Letter to Gifford* (1819). Gifford also translated the satires of Juvenal (1802) and Persius (1812), and prepared notable editions of several Jacobean dramatists: PHILIP MASSINGER (1805), BEN JONSON (1816), JOHN FORD (posthumously published, 1827) and JAMES SHIRLEY (completed by Alexander Dyce, 1833).

Gilbert, Sir Humphrey ?1539–83 A soldier and navigator, Gilbert was the stepbrother of SIR WALTER RALEIGH. His suggestions for voyages to discover the Northwest Passage, including those in *A Discourse of a Discovery for a New Passage to Cataia* (written in 1566 and printed in 1576), received only grudging support from Elizabeth, who eventually granted him a charter in 1578 to settle heathen lands not yet settled by any Christian ruler. In 1583 he claimed Newfoundland for the Queen but was lost at sea on the journey home. The scene is described in HAKLUYT's *Voyages*.

Gilbert, Kevin 1933–93 Australian part-Aboriginal poet, playwright and journalist. Orphaned and raised in institutions, he served 15 years of a life sentence for murdering his wife. Though he is not a prolific writer, his work pioneered the re-emergence of Aboriginal culture. *The Cherry Pickers*, which he wrote in prison, became in 1971 the first play by an Aborigine to be performed. It deals with the Aboriginal relation to the natural world and the failure of the white world to understand black culture. A volume of poetry, *End of Dreamtime* (1971), was so extensively changed by its white editor that Gilbert refused to acknowledge it; *People ARE Legends* (1977) is his own version. A collection of interviews, *Living Black: Blacks Talk to Kevin Gilbert* (1977), made a wide-ranging report on the state of Aboriginal cultural identity. *Inside Black Australia: An Anthology of Aboriginal Poetry* (1988) promotes his belief in direct representation of black writers. Other books are *Because a White Man Will Never Do It* (1973) and *Blackside* (1990).

Gilbert, William 1544–1603 Probably the most distinguished scientist of Elizabeth I's reign, although one who still lived in an animistic universe. He began to practise medicine in London in 1573, became physician to Elizabeth in 1601 and then JAMES I in 1603. His work *De magnete* (1600) was the first to use the term 'electrical force'. He agreed with Copernicus that the earth revolved on its axis. At his death he left manuscripts which were edited by his brother and published as *De mundo nostro sublunari philosophia nova* (1651).

Gilbert, Sir W(illiam) S(chwenck) 1836–1911 Playwright, librettist and lyricist. Born in London of a naval surgeon with literary leanings and a mother from whom both father and son became estranged, Gilbert was educated at Great Ealing School and University College, London. He had little success in his early career as a barrister and turned to journalism, contributing from 1861 humorous verse to *Fun* and other periodicals, much of it collected and published as *THE BAB BALLADS* (1868 and 1872). After considerable apprentice work for the theatre, particularly in the field of BURLESQUE, he achieved popularity with a verse-play, *The Palace of Truth* (1870), followed by *Pygmalion and Galatea* (1871), *The*

Wicked World (1873), *Sweethearts* (1874) and *Engaged* (1877). His career as a librettist was founded on his partnership with the composer Arthur Sullivan, beginning uncertainly with *Thespis* (1871), but flourishing from *Trial by Jury* (1875) onwards, and producing the series known as the SAVOY OPERAS, which proved enormously popular up to *The Gondoliers* (1889), though losing favour thereafter. Gilbert's prominence as a librettist reduced his output as a playwright, though he wrote several ambitious if less appreciated later plays, including *Broken Hearts* (1875) and *Gretchen* (1879).

Unlike his mentor T. W. ROBERTSON, he avoided REALISM and the contemporary scene, developing a style marked by formality and paradox. His profoundly pessimistic view of the selfishness of human nature (expressed in its purest form in *The Palace of Truth* and *Engaged*) was made more palatable in comic opera, and it is by his collaboration with Sullivan that his work continues to be represented in the theatre. His plays lacked the fashionable settings and social relevance which the Victorian audience hailed in the 'society' drama of WILDE, PINERO and JONES, who eclipsed his reputation in the 1890s. He remains nevertheless the most original writer for the Victorian stage. Gilbert was knighted in 1907, the first author to be so honoured specifically for services to the drama.

Gilchrist, Ellen 1935– American short-story writer and novelist. Born in Vicksburg, Mississippi, she was educated at Vanderbilt University, Millsap College in Jackson, Mississippi, and the University of Arkansas. Usually set in the South, her fiction maps the spoilt, anchorless lives of its upper classes, often with satirical wit but also lyrically and sensuously. *In the Land of Dreamy Dreams* (1981), *Victory over Japan* (1984), *Drunk with Love* (1986) and *Light Can be Both Wave and Particle* (1989) are volumes of stories. *The Blue-Eyed Buddhist and Other Stories* (1990) is Gilchrist's own selection from her shorter work. She has also published: novels, *The Annunciation* (1983), *The Anna Papers* (1988) and *Net of Jewels* (1993); a collection of three novellas, *I Cannot Get You Close Enough* (1990); a volume of poetry, *The Land-Surveyor's Daughter* (1979); and a personal journal, *Falling through Space* (1987).

Gildas See ARTHURIAN LITERATURE.

Gilded Age, The: *A Tale of Today* A satirical novel by MARK TWAIN and CHARLES DUDLEY WARNER, published in 1873 and dramatized by Twain and G. S. Densmore in the following year. The novel comments on greed, exploitation and economic speculation during the period of post-Civil War reconstruction (the era itself has been named after the book). Set in Missouri, New York and Washington, DC, the story

Charlotte Perkins Gilman

tells of various unscrupulous individuals, their personal relationships, and their rather dubious financial enterprises.

Gillette, William (Hooker) 1855–1937 American actor and playwright. Born in Connecticut, he was helped in his early career by MARK TWAIN, a family friend. Gillette gained a considerable reputation, writing parts for himself in which his restrained acting style could be exploited. *The Private Secretary* and *Esmeralda* (both 1881), the latter written in collaboration with FRANCES HODGSON BURNETT, launched his career as a dramatist. *All the Comforts of Home* (1890) and *Too Much Johnson* (1894) were adaptations of French FARCES. His best-known works are two MELODRAMAS about the Civil War, *Held by the Enemy* (1886) and *SECRET SERVICE* (1895); and *Sherlock Holmes* (1899), a dramatization of the SHERLOCK

HOLMES STORIES, in which he himself starred for over 30 years. A short comic sequel, *The Painful Predicament of Sherlock Holmes*, and a melodrama entitled *Clarice* were both produced in 1905.

Gilman, Charlotte Perkins 1860–1935 American feminist writer. She was born in Hartford, Connecticut. In *This Our World* (1893) is a collection of poems about 19th-century womanhood. *Women and Economics* (1898) is a strong indictment of patriarchal culture; other reforming works, including *Concerning Children* (1900) and *The Home: Its Work and Influence* (1903), discuss the detrimental effects that restrictions on women have on the family. *The Yellow Wallpaper*, written in 1890 and published in 1899, is a semi-autobiographical treatment of a woman writer's breakdown and the subsequent 'rest cure' prescribed by her physician husband; the cure forbids her to write and leads to true madness. From 1909 to 1916 Gilman edited *The Forerunner*, a magazine consisting entirely of her own articles and fiction dealing with women's issues. Two of her novels, *What Diana Did* (1910) and *The Crux* (1911), appeared in this periodical, as did *The Man-Made World*, which, with the independently published *His Religion and Hers* (1923), further developed her ideas about sexual relations and oppression in modern society. Her autobiography was published in 1935.

Gilmore, Dame **Mary** 1865–1962 Australian poet. Born Mary Jean Cameron in Goulburn, New South Wales, she worked as a teacher and journalist before joining William Lane's idealistic experimental community in Paraguay. Returning to Australia after the failure of the venture, she wrote for *The Sydney Worker*, conducting the women's page for 23 years. She published 10 books of verse including *Married and Other Verses* (1910), *The Passionate Heart* (1918) and *The Wild Swan* (1930), each typically enthusiastic and radical in tone. She was created a Dame of the Order of the British Empire in 1936. Her poems include 'Old Botany Bay', 'Eve-Song' and 'The Mopoke, Memory'.

Gilpin, William 1724–1804 Travel-writer. Educated at The Queen's College, Oxford, Gilpin became a schoolmaster and clergyman in Boldre, Hampshire. He achieved considerable success with accounts of tours through Britain and established himself as a leading authority on the PICTURESQUE. The books, all delicately illustrated by the author and all showing as great a concern for the abstract principles of beauty as for the particular scene, covered the following areas: the Wye Valley and South Wales (1782), the Lake District (1786), the Highlands (1789), the New Forest (1791), the West Country and the Isle of Wight (1789), the coasts of Hampshire, Sussex and Kent (1804), Cambridge, Norfolk, Suffolk, Essex and North Wales

(1809). Also notable is the collection *Three Essays: On Picturesque Beauty, On Picturesque Travel, On Sketching Landscape* (1792). The vogue for picturesque travel he helped encourage is satirized in WILLIAM COMBE'S *TOUR OF DR SYNTAX IN SEARCH OF THE PICTURESQUE*.

Ginsberg, Allen 1926– American poet. Born in Newark, New Jersey, he attended Columbia University, served in the US Military Sea Transport Service, and worked as a market researcher and book reviewer for *Newsweek* before establishing himself as a freelance writer. His first collection, *Howl and Other Poems* (1956), secured his reputation as a leader of the BEATS. His other collections include *Kaddish and Other Poems, 1958–1960* (1961), *Reality Sandwiches, 1953–1960* (1963), *Planet News* (1964), *Wichita Vortex Sutra* (1966), *Ankor Wat* (1968), *The Fall of America: Poems of These States, 1965–1971* (1972), *Mind Breaths: Poems 1972–1977* (1978), *Poems All Over the Place: Mostly Seventies* (1978), *Straight Hearts' Delight: Love Poems and Selected Letters* (1980), *Collected Poems 1947–1980* (1984) and *White Shroud: Poems 1980–1985* (1986). Ginsberg's verse derives its long-cadenced line from WILLIAM BLAKE and WALT WHITMAN, to whom 'A Supermarket in California' is a kind of comic tribute. He has also written two plays – *Kaddish* (1972) is the more important – and several volumes of prose miscellanies and

Allen Ginsberg

letters, including *Allen Verbatim: Lectures on Poetry, Politics, Consciousness* (1974) and *Journals, Early Fifties – Early Sixties* (1977), both edited by Gordon Ball.

Giovanni, Nikki (Yolande Cornelia) 1943– Black American poet. She was born in Knoxville, Tennessee, and educated at Fisk University. Her first two collections of poetry, *Black Feeling, Black Talk* (1968) and *Black Judgment* (1969), are set against the background of the civil rights movement and trace a young black woman's development into fiery militancy. In *Recreation* (1970) and *Spin a Soft Black Song* (1971) Giovanni's voice softened somewhat, and the expression of personal concerns is balanced with social and political statement. Her examination of the black experience is further developed in *My House* (1972), *Ego-Tripping and Other Poems for Young People* (1974), *The Women and the Men* (1975), *Cotton-Candy on a Rainy Day* (1983) and *Sacred Cows... and Other Edibles* (1988). *Gemini: An Extended Autobiographical Statement on My First Twenty-Five Years of Being a Black Poet* was published in 1971.

Gissing, George (Robert) 1857–1903 Novelist. Educated at a Quaker boarding school, Alderley Edge, Cheshire, and Owens College, Manchester (which later became the University of Manchester), he was expelled from the latter for stealing and spent a month in prison. Aged 19, he wandered for a year in America, then settled in London. A classical scholar, he survived by private coaching at just over a shilling (5p) an hour. He married two lower-class girls in succession and was disappointed when they were not grateful. He was a hardworking and prolific artist, obsessed with his vocation, proud and lonely because conscious of humble origins. His only friend was H. G. WELLS, from a similar background.

Gissing wrote, characteristically, about poverty and failure, but as a writer he was successful and respected as an exponent of NATURALISM in the French manner, though he never became rich. His first novel, *WORKERS IN THE DAWN* (1880), was published when he was 23. It was followed by *The Unclassed* (1884), *Eve's Ransom* (1885), *Isabel Clarendon* and *Demos* (both 1886), *Thyrza* (1887), *A Life's Morning* (1888), *The Nether World* (1889), *The Emancipated* (1890), *NEW GRUB STREET* (1891), *Born in Exile* (1892), *Denzil Quarrier* (1892), *THE ODD WOMEN* (1893), *Sleeping Fires* (1895), *The Whirlpool* (1897), *Human Odds and Ends* (short stories, 1897), *The Town Traveller* and a critical study of DICKENS (both 1898), *The Crown of Life* (1899), *Our Friend the Charlatan* (1901) and *By the Ionian Sea* (impressions of Italy, 1900). *THE PRIVATE PAPERS OF HENRY RYECROFT* (1903) is semi-autobiographical: the narrator is freed from financial anxiety by a legacy, as Gissing had been by his industry. After

his death came *Veranilda* (1904), a historical romance of 6th-century Italy, in which he used his knowledge of the late Latin historians and Italian antiquities, *Will Warburton* (1905), *The House of Cobwebs* (short stories, 1906), *The Sins of the Fathers* (1924), *The Immortal Dickens* (1925), *A Victim of Circumstances* (1927), *Brownie* (1931), *Notes on Social Democracy* (1968), *George Gissing's Commonplace Book* (edited by J. Korg, 1962) and *The Diary of George Gissing, Novelist* (edited by P. Coustillas, 1978). Since 1960 he has received increasing critical attention.

Glanvill, Joseph 1636–80 Philosopher and theologian. The son of a Puritan family in Plymouth, he became interested in Neoplatonism and science while at Oxford, took holy orders and ended his days with the living of the Abbey Church in Bath. He was 25 when he published *The Vanity of Dogmatizing* (1661), a pioneering work which argued for a scientific approach to learning. He published a new edition as *Scepsis scientifica* (1665), with some revisions. *The Vanity of Dogmatizing* contains the story which inspired MATTHEW ARNOLD's *THE SCHOLAR-GIPSY*. Glanvill's *Plus Ultra* (1668) emphasizes further the value of experimental science. Among his other works is *Saducismus triumphatus* (1681), an attempt to prove the existence of witchcraft.

Glasgow, Ellen 1874–1945 American novelist. She was born in Richmond, Virginia. She published her first novel, *The Descendant*, in 1897, and her only volume of poetry, *The Freeman, and Other Poems*, in 1902. The economic and social conditions of the old agrarian South form the subject of a series of historical novels, beginning with *The Voice of the People* (1900) and including *The Battle-Ground* (1902), *The Deliverance* (1904), *The Wheel of Life* (1906), *The Ancient Law* (1908), *The Romance of a Plain Man* (1909) and *The Miller of Old Church* (1911). Her next two novels, *Virginia* (1913) and *Life and Gabriella* (1916), examine the position of women in the modernization of the Old South. Her other novels include *The Builders* (1919), *One Man in His Time* (1922), *BARREN GROUND* (1925), *The Romantic Comedians* (1926), *They Stooped to Folly* (1929), *The Sheltered Life* (1932) and *VEIN OF IRON* (1935). In 1941 she was awarded a PULITZER PRIZE for *In This Our Life* (1941), a study of the decay of an aristocratic Virginia family. Two volumes of her stories have been issued: *The Shadowy Third* (1923) and *Collected Stories* (1963). A collection of the prefatory essays to her novels, *A Certain Measure*, was published in 1943, and an autobiographical reminiscence, *The Woman Within*, in 1954.

Glaspell, Susan 1882–1948 American playwright, novelist and short-story writer. She was born and educated in Iowa. With her husband, George Cram Cook, she was a founder of the Provincetown Players, later famous for promoting EUGENE O'NEILL's early plays. *Suppressed Desires* (1915), written in collaboration with Cook, was the inaugural piece for the Players. She followed it with a number of deft one-act plays, including *Trifles* (1916), *The People* (1917), *The Outside* (1917) and *Woman's Honor* (1918). Her concern that room should be maintained for broad personal and social exploration is also evident in full-length plays like *Inheritors* (1921), in which a Midwestern college struggles to maintain the liberal spirit of its foundation, *The Verge* (1921), in which a woman finds herself simultaneously on the verge of madness and of true discovery, and *Alison's House* (1930), a sensitive account of events and decisions in the quiet life of EMILY DICKINSON.

Her novels are unimpressive but her short stories, collected in *Lifted Masks* (1912) and *A Jury of Her Peers* (1927), display the intensity of her quest for a just society. *The Road to the Temple* (1927) is an evocative account of her life with George Cram Cook, written after his death in Greece in 1923.

Glass Menagerie, The A play by TENNESSEE WILLIAMS, first produced in 1944, and published in the following year. It was the play that established Williams in the American theatre.

Described by him as a 'memory play', it is framed by the recollections of Tom Wingfield, whose impressionistic narratives, accompanied by images projected on a screen, introduce a number of the scenes. Tom recalls his life in St Louis with his mother Amanda, a faded Southern belle who clings persistently to glamorous illusions about her past, and with his sister Laura, a crippled and painfully shy young woman whose intensely private world is centred on a treasured collection of small glass animals. Amanda, whose husband has long since deserted the family, has transferred her romantic hopes to Laura, continually asking her about her non-existent gentlemen callers. She persuades Tom, who has become a compulsive movie-goer to escape this intolerable situation at home, to invite his friend Jim O'Connor to dinner. Jim turns out to be the same young man with whom Laura was infatuated at high school; for a moment her sensitivity and reserve are eased by his warmth, but then, suddenly embarrassed, he tells her he is engaged to another girl, and leaves. Amanda is enraged with Tom for what she thinks was a deliberate practical joke. Finally pushed too far, Tom runs out of the house, never to return. The play ends with Amanda comforting Laura, and with Tom's final narration filled with pain for his sister.

Globe Theatre The home of the KING'S MEN, the leading Elizabethan and Jacobean theatre company, to which SHAKESPEARE and RICHARD BURBAGE belonged. They were among the shareholders who in 1599 supervised the salvage of timber from the company's old home, the THEATRE, to build the first Globe, on the south bank of the Thames, a short distance west of what is now Southwark Cathedral. It was here that most of the great plays of Shakespeare's maturity were first performed. Destroyed by fire in 1613, the Globe was reconstructed and reopened in 1614. It remained in use until the closing of the theatres under Cromwell, and was torn down in 1644.

Glover, Denis 1912–80 New Zealand poet. Born in Dunedin, he was educated at Auckland Grammar School and at the University of Canterbury, where he subsequently taught English between 1936 and 1938. He also taught typography at this time, and in 1936 in Christchurch founded Caxton Press, a significant outlet for New Zealand writers during the years of growth which followed. During World War II he was an officer in the Royal Navy and was awarded the DSC. After the war he worked as a journalist and publisher. A prominent figure in New Zealand letters, Glover was a president of New Zealand PEN.

He first achieved recognition as a poet in the 1930s when, with his close associate ALLEN CURNOW, he was a member of the Phoenix Group. His early poetry earned him a reputation as an *enfant terrible* and works like *Six Easy Ways of Dodging Debt Collectors* (1936) and his contributions to *A Caxton Miscellany* (1937) are wittily impudent reflections on the local cultural situation. Throughout his life he was a staunch champion of directness in verse but, despite their apparently rough-hewn quality, his poems exhibit considerable craftsmanship. Many can be seen as embodying a dialogue between the tough, supposedly unsentimental, male self-sufficiency that characterized the pioneer generation and a need for emotional liberation that is hard to acknowledge. In all, Glover published more than 20 volumes of verse, of which *Recent Poems* (1941), *Sings Harry* (1951), *Arawata Bill* (1953), a highly popular sequence about a wandering prospector, and *Since Then* (1957) are among the best-known. His *Selected Poems* was published in 1981.

Glover, Richard 1712–85 Poet and playwright. Born in London, where his father was a successful merchant, Glover followed the same career and was Member of Parliament for Weymouth (1761–8) in opposition to Pitt's administration. He wrote a great deal of poetry in indifferent BLANK VERSE, including *Leonidas* (1737) in nine books and *The Athenaid* in 30 books (posthumously published, 1787). He was the author of two tragedies, *Boadicea* (1753) and *Medea* (1767), both produced at DRURY LANE, and one, *Jason* (posthumously published, 1799), which was not produced. *Admiral Hosier's Ghost* (1740), a popular BALLAD on the misfortunes of Hosier and his fate in the West Indies, was included in THOMAS PERCY's *Reliques of Ancient English Poetry*.

Gluck, Louise 1943– American poet. Born in New York, she attended Sarah Lawrence College and Columbia University, where she studied under STANLEY KUNITZ. She taught for several years at Goddard College in Vermont before moving to Warren Wilson College in North Carolina. The influence of SYLVIA PLATH is strongly felt in her first volume, *Firstborn* (1969). Later verse, particularly that in *The House on Marshland* (1975) and *Descending Figures* (1983), establishes a more individualized, though still frequently confessional, voice. Other volumes are *The Triumph of Achilles* (1985), awarded the National Book Critics' Circle Award for poetry, *Ararat* (1990) and *The Wild Iris* (1992).

Glyn [*née* Sutherland], **Elinor** 1864–1943 Novelist. She was born in Jersey of Canadian parents and educated privately. Her 21 romantic novels were popular and controversial for their treatment of sex, particularly women's sexual feelings. *Three Weeks* (1907), the best known if only because of erotic scenes played out on a notorious tiger-skin, describes in purple prose the sensual awakening of Paul, a young English nobleman, in his affair with a Slavonic beauty of noble rank. As in Elinor Glyn's other novels, the ending punishes the lovers, thus upholding the moral code and averting the censor's wrath.

Go-Between, The A novel by L. P. HARTLEY, published in 1953. The narrator is an old man, Leo Colston, who in 1952 recalls events during the summer of 1900 while he was holidaying with a schoolfriend, Marcus Maudsley, at Brandham Hall near Norwich.

Besotted with Marcus's sister, Marian, the adolescent Leo confesses that he would do anything for her. Later he meets a local farmer, Ted Burgess, and agrees to deliver a clandestine message to Marian, so becoming their go-between. In his naivety, Leo imagines numerous innocent explanations for the letters he is asked to carry, but his curiosity to discover the truth leads him to read an unsealed note from Marian and he gradually begins to comprehend the relationship between the lovers. At the same time his own painful awakening into the adult world has begun.

Marian is to become engaged to Lord Hugh Trimingham. Leo, in a fit of conscience, refuses to deliver any more notes. He relents under Marian's scorn, but begins to feel exploited. On Leo's 13th birthday Mrs Maudsley, Marian's mother, intercepts him while he is carrying a message. He refuses to give it up, but later in the day she forces him to accompany her to a distant outhouse where they discover the couple making love. Leo learns afterwards that Ted Burgess has committed suicide. In an epilogue, Leo visits Marian 50 years later and she implores him to fulfil one last commission: to make contact with her grandson and explain to him the true nature of what happened so long ago.

Goblin Market A poem by CHRISTINA ROSSETTI, published in 1862. It tells the story of two sisters, Lizzie and Laura, who are tempted by goblins to eat their delicious but dangerous fruit. Laura succumbs and eats, but afterwards can no longer hear or see the goblins, though she grows ill with longing to taste their fruit again. Lizzie determines to buy fruit for her sister but the goblins, angered by her refusal to eat any herself, deny the request and pelt her with their wares. Thus Laura is saved and her craving satisfied, as she licks the juices with which Lizzie is covered. This cryptic fairy-tale is notable for its use of ALLITERATION and its metrical inventiveness.

Godber, John 1956– Playwright and director. He began his career at the age of 16 by writing for his local radio station, Radio Sheffield. He then turned to television, contributing to such series as *Crown Court* and *Brookside* before producing two works commissioned by the BBC: *Blood Sweat and Tears* (1986), adapted from his stage play, and *The Ritz* (1987). Since 1984 he has been artistic director of Hull Truck, for whom he has staged his best-known comedies: *Up'N'Under* (1984), which won the Laurence Olivier Comedy of the Year Award, *Bouncers* (1985), *Teechers* (1987), *Salt of the Earth* (1990), which transferred to London's West End in 1993. *Happy Families* (1991) had the privilege of being chosen for a group performance by 50 amateur companies throughout Britain. *April in Paris* (1992) describes the gloomy impressions a xenophobic British family forms of foreign parts. Often set in locations such as leisure centres and rugby clubs, Godber's work delights in physical and athletic gags and in jibes against the Establishment. Closely in touch with its northern audiences, it has yet to make its full impact in the South.

Godden, (Margaret) Rumer 1907– Novelist and writer of CHILDREN'S LITERATURE. Brought up in Bengal, she came to England at the age of 11 for her education but later returned to India. Beginning as an adult author, she won acclaim with a series of successful novels including *Black Narcissus* (1939), *Breakfast with the Nickolides* (1942) and *The Greengage Summer* (1958), a haunting story of first love set in France and now also considered a children's book. Her first book written expressly for children, *The Dolls' House* (1947), was followed by *The Mousewife* (1951), another typically original story, about the friendship between a mouse and a dove, based on a note found in DOROTHY WORDSWORTH's diary. Other successful books include the award-winning story *The Diddakoi* (1972) and *Peacock Spring* (1978), another tale of disappointed love, this time set in India and as before suitable for both old and young readers.

Godolphin, Sidney 1610–43 Poet and translator. Son of Sir William Godolphin of Godolphin, Cornwall, and educated at Exeter College, Oxford, Sidney Godolphin was a devoted Royalist, who entered Parliament in 1628, took up arms for the king in 1642 and was shot in a skirmish at Chagford. He is buried at Okehampton. A friend of LUCIUS FALKLAND and CLARENDON, he is characterized as 'little Sid' in SUCKLING's *Sessions of the Poets*. His translation of Book IV of Virgil's *Aeneid* was published in 1658, completed by WALLER. His occasional poems, both love lyrics and devotional work, were first collected in 1906.

Godric, St d. ?1170 Author of three fragments of verse written before 1170. Of slight literary merit, they are important as the earliest examples of native popular verse in Middle English. Godric was an uneducated pedlar before becoming a hermit at Finchdale, near Durham. A contemporary Latin life alleges that the words and music of the first and best-known of his poems, 'Cantus beati Godrici', were inspired by the Virgin as he knelt in prayer. The Virgin promised to succour him whenever he uttered the eight-line poem, a plea for help in obliterating sin and attaining the bliss of Heaven. A four-line hymn given to him by his dead sister in a vision consoled him in his bereavement. His third poem, 'Cantus Sancto Nicholao', was inspired by an Easter vision in which St Nicholas appeared to Godric. It asks the saint to bring the poet to bliss. The poems are metrically irregular but close to a four-stress line; they do not appear to have been influenced by foreign or Latin verse.

Godwin, William 1756–1836 Philosopher and novelist. He was born into a family that had produced three generations of Dissenting ministers and was educated at the famous Hoxton Dissenting Academy. In 1778 he became minister to a congregation at Ware in Hertfordshire. His Calvinist faith was progressively undermined by his reading of the French philosophers Rousseau, d'Holbach and Helvetius, however, and in 1783 he gave up his ministry and embraced atheism. He moved to London, where he was to spend the rest of his long life, initially contributing essays and reviews to various weekly literary and political journals. With the coming of the French Revolution he grew interested in political philosophy and emancipatory politics, and began to attend meetings of radical political groups and societies. He was present at the famous pro-revolutionary sermon, given in London on 4 November 1789, by the great Dissenting minister and political radical RICHARD PRICE. Godwin's own response to the debates and polemics of the revolutionary epoch, the celebrated *ENQUIRY CONCERNING POLITICAL JUSTICE*, conceived in 1791, was an immediate success on its publication in 1793. Among its young admirers were WORDSWORTH, SOUTHEY and COLERIDGE. The inner social and psychological drama masked by its elaborate philosophical method is impressively externalized in *CALEB WILLIAMS*, the novel which followed it in 1794. Somewhat ironically, in view of his stated antipathy to revolutionary violence, the loyalist reaction orchestrated by Pitt discovered its scapegoat in Godwin, and within two years he had been systematically defamed. It was a blow from which he never recovered intellectually, and which was to sour his personal relations and dealings in the decades ahead.

Godwin was the anarchist of the Age of Reason. Nothing if not consistent in his rationalistic individualism, he opposed both all existing institutions and all organized resistance to them. He never revised his model of reason, and jealously defended his system against the slightest imputation of activism. He insisted that differences and conflicts between men could be resolved only through sober and exhaustive discussion on a person-to-person basis. Such a proceeding presupposed the very rationality that was to be its outcome, and he was frequently accused of facile optimism by his radical opponents in the London Corresponding Society. Although he would continue to be alarmed by the Society's endorsement of agitational methods, his anonymously published *Cursory Strictures on the Charge Delivered by Lord Chief Justice Eyre to the Grand Jury* did much to persuade the jury to return a verdict of innocent in the trial of several of its members for treason in 1794.

In 1797 he wrote *The Enquirer*, another long essay in political philosophy which restates most of the themes of his earlier work. In the same year his wife MARY WOLLSTONECRAFT died a few days after the birth of their daughter, MARY SHELLEY, future wife of SHELLEY. His life of Wollstonecraft, *Memoirs of the Author of the Vindication of the Rights of Woman*, appeared in 1798. He also edited her *Posthumous Works* and portrayed her in his novel *St Leon* (1799). His subsequent remarriage to a Mrs Clairmont was largely an alliance of convenience.

Few of his many literary and publishing projects succeeded, and he had already become a relatively obscure and forgotten figure at the time of his discovery by the young Shelley in 1812. In 1814, however, Shelley – already married and the father of two small children – eloped abroad with his beloved daughter Mary and step-daughter Claire Clairmont, eventually marrying Mary in 1816 after the suicide of Harriet Shelley. Perhaps the best that can be said in summary of the relations between philosopher and poet is that Godwin managed to extract back in cash what Shelley had borne away in kind, though he responded with such coldness and moralistic insensitivity to the wave of family tragedies that fell upon the couple in Italy that Shelley was at one stage compelled to intercept his correspondence with Mary.

During the last two decades of his life Godwin repudiated many of the more radical aspects of *Political Justice*, and in the late 1820s spoke out against the increasingly powerful movement for parliamentary and suffrage reform. The only significant work of the period was his study *Of Population* (1820), an answer to MALTHUS's *Essay on the Principle of Population*, in which he argues that rational man would appreciate the madness of unlimited procreation, and voluntarily restrain his passions in order to curb population growth. His last years brought more financial distress, exacerbated by Shelley's death in 1822. Mary returned to England in 1823 and he saw a good deal of her in his declining years. His *Thoughts on Man*, which retreats from many of the positions taken in 1793, was published in 1831. His substantial literary output includes a life of CHAUCER (1803–4) and the novels *Fleetwood* (1805), *Mandeville* (1817), *Cloudesly* (1830) and *Deloraine* (1833). In 1833, with the Whigs in power for the first time since the French Revolution, he was awarded the sinecure of Yeoman Usher of the Exchequer at £200 a year. He died at the age of 80 and was buried next to Mary Wollstonecraft.

Gogarty, Oliver St John 1878–1957 Irish man of letters and poet. Born and educated in Dublin, he became a surgeon. His friend JAMES JOYCE portrayed him as Buck Mulligan in ULYSSES. His poetry in *An Offering of Swans* (1923), *Wild Apples* (1928) and *Selected Poems* (1933) was over-rated by YEATS in the *Oxford Book of Modern Verse* (1936). He also published several volumes of memoirs, *As I was Going Down Sackville Street* (1937), *Follow Saint Patrick* (1938) and *Tumbling in the Hay* (1939). Gogarty was appointed a senator of the Irish Free State in 1922. An attempt was made on his life and his country property, Renvyle House in County Galway, was burned. He left Ireland in 1939 for the USA, where he published three novels and an autobiography, *It isn't That Time of Year at All* (1954). *Collected Poems* appeared in 1950.

Golagros and Gawain A Middle Scots romance of the later 15th century in ALLITERATIVE VERSE written in 13-line stanzas. The story is freely adapted from the First Continuation of the *Conte du Graal* of Chrétien de Troyes. It exemplifies the contrast between Kay's churlishness and Gawain's courtesy that had become conventional in ARTHURIAN LITERATURE. The first episode tells how Kay's request for hospitality on behalf of Arthur and his knights is refused because of his rudeness, while Gawain's request is granted. In the second episode Arthur demands homage from the defiant Golagros, whom Gawain eventually defeats but treats with such generosity that the delighted Golagros yields to Arthur.

Gold, Herbert 1924– American novelist. Born in Cleveland, Ohio, he served in the US army during World War II and then attended Columbia University. Many of his novels are autobiographical: *Therefore be Bold* (1960) tells of the experience of a Jewish adolescent growing up in Cleveland; *Fathers: A Novel in the Form of a Memoir* (1967) draws on Gold's experiences as a father to his five children and as a son to his own father; *Family: A Novel in the Form of a Memoir* (1981) is about a Jewish immigrant family. His other novels are *Birth of a Hero* (1951); *The Prospect before Us* (1954); *The Man Who was Not with It* (1956), probably his best-known work, the story of a drug-addicted carnival barker and his world; *The Optimist* (1959); *Salt* (1963); *The Great American Jackpot* (1971) and *Waiting for Cordelia* (1977), two stories about a sociology student at Berkeley in the 1960s; *Swiftie the Magician* (1974); *He/She* (1980); *True Love* (1982); *Mister White Eyes* (1984), about a journalist's search for love and simple human feelings through, or despite, his profession; *A Girl of Forty* (1986); and *Dreaming* (1988). Gold's short stories and essays have been collected in *15 × 3* (1957), *Love and Like* (1960), *The Age of Happy Problems* (1962) and *The Magic Will: Stories and Essays of a Decade* (1971). *A Walk on the West Side: California on the Brink* (1981) has been followed by two more travel books, *Travels in San Francisco* (1990) and *The Best Nightmare on Earth: A Life in Haiti* (1991). *My Last Two Thousand Years* (1972) is his autobiography.

Gold, Michael 1894–1967 American journalist and novelist. Born Itzok Isaac Granich to Jewish immigrants, he was raised on the Lower East Side of New York. The major themes of his work are derived from this background. His best-known book, *Jews without Money* (1930), is a fictionalized autobiography which describes Jewish ghetto life and ends with a political rally in Union Square at which the protagonist is converted to the cause of Communist revolution.

During the years of radical ferment before World War I Gold published articles and stories in *The Masses* and in the Socialist *New York Call*, and had three of his one-act plays produced by the Provincetown Players. In 1920, after returning from Mexico, where he had evaded the draft, he became an editor of *The Liberator*, the successor of *The Masses*. THE NEW MASSES, which he founded as a successor to *The Liberator*, espoused under his editorship the cause of proletarian literature which sought to represent the working class as the saving grace of America – its last hope for true democracy. His fiery columns for *The New Masses*, notable for their polemical Communist views, have been collected in *The Mike Gold Reader* (1954) and *Mike Gold: A Literary Anthology* (1972), which also reprints articles from *120 Million* (1929) and *Change the World* (1937), his earlier collections of *New Masses* prose.

Goldbarth, Albert 1948– American poet. Born in Chicago, he attended the University of Illinois at Chicago Circle and the Writers' Workshop at the University of Iowa. He has taught at the universities of Utah and Cornell and is presently a professor of English at the University of Texas at Austin. His poetry, notable for its autobiographical preoccupation with Jewish family life in the USA, includes *Coprolites* (1973), *Different Fleshes: A Novel-Poem* (1977), *Faith* (1981), *Original Light: New and Selected Poems, 1978–1983* (1983), *Arts and Sciences* (1986), *A Sympathy of Souls* (1990), *Delft* (1991) and *Heaven and Earth, A Cosmology: Poems by Albert Goldbarth* (1991).

Golden Bough, The See FRAZER, SIR JAMES.

Golden Bowl, The A novel by HENRY JAMES, published in 1904. Adam Verver is an American millionaire living in Europe with his daughter Maggie and amassing an art collection. Maggie is of marriageable age, and her friend Fanny Assingham finds her an Italian prince, Amerigo. The beautiful Charlotte Stant comes to London to stay with Fanny, who knows that Charlotte and Amerigo had once been in love but could not marry since they were both penniless. Charlotte has no trouble persuading Amerigo to accompany her when she goes shopping in search of a wedding present for Maggie. At an antique dealer's she wants to give Amerigo a present also, a gilded crystal bowl. The presence of a flaw in the bowl brings it within the range of her purse; Amerigo, however, is disturbed that the bowl is flawed and declines the gift.

A year later, following the birth of a child to Maggie and Amerigo, Adam Verver, now a grandfather but not yet 50, proposes to and marries Charlotte. But Charlotte and Amerigo have not forgotten their original feelings for each other, and they meet in secret. For her father's birthday Maggie buys a gilded crystal bowl. She has not noticed that it is flawed, but the dealer feels compelled to point it out and calls on her. He recognizes the photographs of Amerigo and Charlotte and tells Maggie that the pair had visited his shop and rejected the bowl during the days of her engagement to Amerigo. Maggie sends for Fanny and makes clear that she knows the whole truth about Charlotte and Amerigo. She smashes the golden bowl just as Amerigo enters the room. Amerigo stops seeing Charlotte; Adam gives no hint to her that he knows of her liaison; Maggie conducts herself with unruffled serenity. Charlotte, wondering at her lover's withdrawal, cannot provoke Maggie to any kind of exchange. Adam finally resolves the situation by deciding to return to America with Charlotte.

Golden Legend, The A collection of biblical narratives and SAINTS' LIVES with some explanation of parts of the Mass and articles of faith. Originally a 13th-century Latin work, the *Legenda aurea* of Jacobus de Voragine, it was translated into French in the 14th century by Jean de Vignay and into English in the 15th century. The best-known English version is that printed by CAXTON *c.* 1487.

Golden Treasury, The See PALGRAVE, FRANCIS TURNER.

Golding, Arthur ?1536-1605 Translator. Golding produced very few original works: an account of a murder (1577) and the description of an earthquake (1580). His Puritan cast of mind is demonstrated by some of the texts he chose to translate: Calvin's commentary on Daniel (1570) and Calvin's sermons on Job (1574), on Ephesians (1576) and on Deuteronomy. He also completed SIR PHILIP SIDNEY's translation of de Mornay's *Trueness of the Christian Religion* (1587). Among classical texts, he produced translations of Caesar's *De bello gallico* (1565) and Seneca's *De beneficiis* (1578).

Golding's most important translation was of Ovid's *Metamorphoses*, the first four books appearing in 1565 and the complete work in 1567. One of the finest and most faithful of Elizabethan classical translations, the work was dedicated to Leicester. The dedicatory verse epistle, which talks of Ovid's 'dark philosophy of turned shapes', allies itself with the tradition of finding ALLEGORY in *Metamorphoses*: Phaethon signifies ambition, Arachne contest with our betters, and Midas covetousness. SHAKESPEARE certainly knew Golding's Ovid, as Prospero's speech 'Ye elves of hills...' (*THE TEMPEST*, Act V) draws on Golding's translation as well as Medea's original speech in *Metamorphoses*, Book VII.

Golding, Sir William (Gerald) 1911–93 Novelist. Born at St Columb Minor in Cornwall, he was educated at Marlborough and Brasenose College, Oxford. After working in the theatre as writer, actor and producer, he became a schoolteacher and served with the Royal Navy during World War II. He published a volume of *Poems* (1935) but it was with the publication of his first novel, *LORD OF THE FLIES* (1954), that he achieved success. It was followed by: *The Inheritors* (1955), about the ascendancy of brute force in primeval man; *Pincher Martin* (1956), in which a drowning man is tormented by the moral paradoxes of his past life; *Free Fall* (1959); *The Spire* (1964), a densely symbolic account of the building of Salisbury Cathedral spire; *The Pyramid* (1967); *The Scorpion God* (1971); *Darkness Visible* (1979); and *The Paper Men* (1984), an uncharacteristically comic account of a famous author, Wilfred Barclay, whose life is plagued by the unflagging attention of an American academic. *The Ends of the Earth* (1991) brings together a trilogy of powerful historical novels reflecting his abiding fascination with the sea and sailing: *Rites of Passage* (1980), which won the BOOKER PRIZE, *Close Quarters* (1987) and *Fire Down Below* (1989). Much of Golding's writing explores moral dilemmas at the centre of human existence, and he frequently places his characters in extreme situations to suggest a 'mythological' dimension to their lives. Preoccupied with evil and original sin, he treats these subjects in a way that transcends the boundaries of orthodox Christianity. Other works include a play, *The Brass Butterfly* (1958), and collections of essays, *The Hot Gates* (1965) and *A Moving Target* (1982). He was awarded the Nobel Prize for Literature in 1983 and knighted in 1988.

Goldsmith, Oliver ?1730–74 Playwright, poet, novelist and essayist. A son of the Irish Protestant clergy on both sides of the family, he was born at either Pallas, County Longford, or Elphin, Roscommon, and passed much of his childhood at Lissoy, Westmeath. After being miserable at various grammar schools, where he was beaten as a dunce and persecuted by his fellows, he went at the age of 16 to Trinity College, Dublin, as a sizar, performing menial jobs and living in a garret. After university he sought ordination, but arrived for interviews dressed in scarlet; applications for other jobs, and a plan to emigrate to America, were similarly unsuccessful, though he did work briefly as private tutor to a rich family. Given £50 to apprentice himself to the law, he gambled it all away. He spent a few months each at Edinburgh and Leiden Universities, but did not apply himself. The authenticity of the medical degree he later claimed has not been established. In 1755–6 he busked his way through France, Switzerland and Italy, playing Irish tunes on his flute and eking out his earnings with food distributed at convent gates. At this time he started the poem *THE TRAVELLER*, eventually published in 1764. On his arrival in England in 1756 he scraped a living as messenger, teacher and assistant to apothecaries and physicians.

In 1758 he translated Marteilhe's *Memoirs of a Protestant, Condemned to the Galleys of France for His Religion*. An *Enquiry into the Present State of Polite Learning in Europe* (1759), his first important work, attacked university education as inadequate, poetry as divorced from nature and stifled by pedantry, and drama as bound by the rules of current taste. It was still possible in those days for an educated man to make a meagre living as a GRUB STREET hack, and Goldsmith settled to writing reviews for SMOLLETT's *Critical Review* and contributing essays to *The Busy Body*, *The Weekly Magazine*, *The Royal Magazine* and *The Lady's Magazine*. His 'Chinese Letters' for NEWBERY's *The Public Ledger*, republished as *The Citizen of the World* (1762), gave a satirical view of contemporary English life and manners through the eyes of an imaginary foreigner.

In 1761 he moved to No. 6 Wine Office Court, off Fleet Street, and met SAMUEL JOHNSON, later becoming a member of the Club. Goldsmith's talents at this time seemed to be for gathering ideas and information from other people's books and reducing them to clarity. In 1762 he wrote essays for *Lloyd's Evening Post* and his biography of the arbiter of Bath society, *The Life of Richard Nash*. Goldsmith's finances were never stable, and he was about to be arrested for debt when Dr Johnson sold the manuscript of Goldsmith's sole novel, *THE VICAR OF WAKEFIELD*, for him. It was published in 1766 in Salisbury, a share having been sold by Newbery to a bookseller there.

In 1762 Goldsmith moved to Newbery's house in Islington. During the years that remained to him before his early death from a kidney infection he continued his diverse output with, among other work, *An History of England in a Series of Letters from a Nobleman to His Son* (1764); two anthologies, *Poems for Young Ladies* (1766, dated 1767) and *The Beauties of English Poesy* (1767); *The Roman History* (1769); and biographies of THOMAS PARNELL and BOLINGBROKE (1770). His *Grecian History* and his *History of the Earth and Animated Nature* both appeared posthumously in 1774.

Goldsmith had sold his oratorio libretto *The Captivity* in 1764. His first comedy, *THE GOOD-NATURED MAN*, was produced at COVENT GARDEN in 1768 after being rejected by GARRICK; its more famous successor, *SHE STOOPS TO CONQUER*, was staged in 1773. His most famous poem, *THE DESERTED VILLAGE*, which draws in part on his childhood memories of Ireland, appeared in 1770. *The Haunch of Venison*, posthumously published in 1776, is a lively expression in comic verse of gratitude for a gift from his friend Lord Clare.

Goldsmith's coffin was followed by BURKE and REYNOLDS, his bust in Westminster Abbey executed by Nollekens and his epitaph written by Johnson. The respect and affection which contemporaries felt for him was often mixed with exasperation at his gaucheness, vanity and habit of dwelling on imagined slights. Johnson said of him, 'No man was more foolish when he had not a pen in his hand, or more wise when he had', while Garrick's impromptu epitaph was, 'Here lies Molly Goldsmith, for shortness called Noll, / Who wrote like an angel, but talked like Poor Poll.' Subsequent critics, faced with the journeyman work by which Goldsmith earned his bread, have dismissed him as lightweight, inaccurate and superficial. Yet the diversity of his talent speaks for itself: he left a novel, *The Vicar of Wakefield*, which is still read, a poem, *The Deserted Village*, which has enriched the language with quotations, and a comedy, *She Stoops to Conquer*, which still holds the stage.

Gone with the Wind The only novel by the American writer Margaret Mitchell (1900–49), published in 1936 and awarded the PULITZER PRIZE in the following year. An immediate best-seller, it has sold more than 25 million copies, been translated into 27 languages and inspired an enduringly popular film (1939) starring Vivien Leigh and Clarke Gable.

The story opens, just before the outbreak of the Civil War, on a Georgia plantation, Tara, the home of Scarlett O'Hara, a spoilt and wilful 16-year-old Southern belle. Against the backdrop of the war, the defeat of the South, and reconstruction, the story follows the life and loves of Scarlett. Ashley Wilkes, with whom she is hopelessly infatuated, marries Melanie Hamilton; Scarlett marries Melanie's brother Charles out of spite, but soon becomes a young war widow. Having survived the siege and burning of Atlanta, she saves the lives of Melanie and her newborn child by leading them through the lines to the O'Hara plantation. Back at Tara, she finds her mother dead, her father demented, the slaves freed, and the plantation in ruins. The novel now focuses on Scarlett's determination to restore Tara. In need of money, she marries Frank Kennedy, her sister's fiancé, because he owns a profitable business. After he too is killed she marries Rhett Butler, a profiteer who has made a fortune from the war. Through him she acquires the wealth and power she craves, but throughout their marriage he struggles against her continuing passion for Ashley, and at the end of the novel, when Scarlett has finally come to realize her love for Rhett, he walks out on her with the words 'My dear, I don't give a damn.'

Good Soldier, The: *A Tale of Passion* A novel by FORD MADOX FORD, published in 1915.

The narrator, John Dowell, who has recently been made aware of the deception within his marriage, controls the reader's view of what he calls 'the saddest story'. For nine years he and his wife Florence, both American, have joined Edward Ashburnham, the good English soldier, and his Irish-Catholic wife Leonora at the German spa town of Nauheim. Using the pretence of having a bad heart, Florence has kept their marriage unconsummated, while conducting illicit affairs. Ashburnham has been her principal lover, while he has conducted his liaisons under the cold, watchful eye of Leonora. Edward is drawn into a tragic infatuation with Nancy Rufford, to whom he and Leonora are guardians. A sense of fatalism overtakes the characters and the story moves toward a DÉNOUEMENT at once melodramatic and formally ordered. Florence and Ashburnham commit suicide. Dowell buys Ashburnham's estate, where he looks after Nancy, reduced to invalidism by the adult world's hypocrisies.

Good-Natured Man, The A comedy by OLIVER GOLDSMITH, first produced at COVENT GARDEN in 1768 and published in the same year.

Sir William Honeywood despairs of his nephew, who is both generous and improvident. Young Honeywood is in love with the wealthy Miss Richland, but he is too wanting in self-confidence to propose. Sir William has him arrested for debt, to let him see who his true friends are and to stop him wasting his generosity on importuners. Young Honeywood believes that Lofty, a government official, is responsible for his release; Lofty is pressing his suit with Miss Richland and Honeywood, mistakenly grateful, recommends him to the lady. In fact it was Miss Richland who secured his release. The exasperated heroine and uncle between them expose Lofty's imposture and secure the marriage of Honeywood and Miss Richland.

The sub-plot concerns Croaker, Miss Richland's guardian, who wants his son Leontine to marry the heroine. Sent to Lyons to bring his sister home from school, Leontine returns with Olivia, a girl he has fallen in love with. He passes off Olivia as his sister and, in an effort to strengthen the pretence, proposes to Miss Richland; but the heroine knows the truth and mischievously accepts him. In desperation Leontine and Olivia try to elope but their plan is frustrated by Sir William. However, he persuades Croaker to consent to their marriage. Miss Richland, the heroine, indicates the departure from the SENTIMENTAL COMEDY fashionable at the time: she is the equal of most of the male characters and superior to some of them.

Goodbye to All That A memoir by ROBERT GRAVES, published in 1929 and revised in 1957. Covering his childhood, career at Charterhouse, World War I experiences and postwar life in Wales, Oxford and Egypt, it ends with a farewell to 'godawful' England, its characters and historical time. Highly controversial and successful when first published, it is organized in scenes of anecdote and caricature, and eschews historical fact in favour of deliberately anti-literary black FARCE and comedy.

Goodison, Lorna 1947– Jamaican poet. Born in Kingston, she studied art at the Jamaica School of Art and in New York. Now a freelance writer, she has worked as an artist, designer, illustrator and scriptwriter and writer-in-residence. Seeing many of her poems as attempts to deal with ideas that she has originally tackled in her painting, she writes with a strong consciousness of her identity as a Jamaican woman of African ancestry. The poems are notable for exploring women's family relationships and using a wide range of Jamaican voices, often within the compass of a single short piece. Her volumes include *Tamarind Season* (1980), *I am Becoming My Mother* (winner of the Americas section of the Commonwealth Poetry Prize; 1986) and *Heartease* (1988). Goodison is a fine performer of her work. She has also published a collection of short stories, *Baby Mother and the King of Swords* (1990).

Goodman, Paul 1911–72 American social critic and novelist. Born in New York, he wrote numerous books on a wide range of topics, including *Utopian Essays and Proposals* (1962), on political theory; *Gestalt Therapy* (1951), on psychology; *Communitas* with his brother Percival; 1947), on city planning; and *Compulsory Mis-Education* (1964), on education. *The Empire City* (1959), a novel set in New York from 1930 to 1950, first appeared as a series of shorter novels: *The Grand Piano* (1942), *The State of Nature* (1946) and *The Dead Spring* (1950). In 1960 he published an influential study of youth and delinquency, *Growing Up Absurd. Making Do* (1963), an autobiographical novel, was followed by a non-fictional work of autobiography, *Five Years: Thoughts during a Useless Time* (1966). He also wrote several volumes of literary criticism, and served as film editor for *PARTISAN REVIEW* and television critic for *THE NEW REPUBLIC*. *Collected Poems* appeared in 1974.

Googe, Barnabe 1505–94 Poet and translator. Googe was a long-lived kinsman of William Cecil, Elizabeth I's minister, who employed him in Ireland for 10 years. He was an industrious translator of Latin anti-Catholic pieces, and his Puritan nature is plainly apparent in his *Eclogues, Epitaphs and Sonnets* (1563), his chief claim to notice as a poet. They are among the earliest examples of PASTORAL poetry in English, though like those of his near-contemporary ALEXANDER BARCLAY they display little of the spirit of their classical originals.

Gorboduc: or, The Tragedy of Ferrex and Porrex A blank-verse tragedy by THOMAS NORTON (Acts 1–3) and THOMAS SACKVILLE (Acts 4 and 5) first acted in 1561 and printed in 1565. The origin of the story is found in GEOFFREY OF MONMOUTH's *Historia regum Britanniae*.

Gorboduc and Videna are King and Queen in legendary Britain and their sons are Ferrex and Porrex. The sons quarrel over the division of the kingdom and Porrex murders his brother. In revenge Videna kills Porrex and the Duke of Albany tries to seize the kingdom. Civil war ensues, and the people turn on Gorboduc and Videna and kill them. At the end of the play the royal line is extinguished and the country is in chaos.

The play adheres to the Senecan model and there is almost no action; it could be read as effectively as it could be played. But by departing from both the tradition of MORALITY PLAYS (there are no personifications, only characters) and the Aristotelian unities of time and place, it moved towards the flexible action of plays in the great age of English drama.

Gordimer, Nadine 1923– South African novelist and short-story writer. Born in Springs, Transvaal, she has consistently attacked apartheid while acknowledging that, as a white living within the system, she is also its unwilling beneficiary. She was awarded the Nobel Prize for Literature in 1991. Single instants, symptoms and symbols of the South African malaise are precisely captured by the short stories in *Face to Face* (1949), *The Soft Voice of the Serpent* (1952), *Six Feet of the Country* (1956), *Friday's Footprint* (1960), *Not for Publication* (1965) and their successors: *Livingstone's Companions* (1972), *Selected Stories* (1975), *Some Monday for Sure* (1976), *A Soldier's Embrace* (1980), *Something out There* (1984), *Why Haven't You Written?* (1990) and *Jump* (1991). Her first three novels – *The Lying Days* (1953), *A World of Strangers* (1958) and *Occasion for Loving* (1963) – chart a movement from underlying hope to disillusion in her view of South Africa, while a limited form of hope reappears in the tightly structured novel *The Late Bourgeois World* (1966). *A Guest of Honour* (1971) and *THE CONSERVATIONIST* (1974) announce the maturity of her fiction, successfully integrating the immediately personal with the panoramically political. The daughter of devout Afrikaner Marxists in *Burger's Daughter* (1979) painfully formulates her own creed before she too is imprisoned. In *July's People* (1981) psychological disintegration is pushed even further than in *The Conservationist*, as civil war bares the mutual falsity of supposedly enlightened personal relationships. In *A Sport of Nature* (1987) an attractive white girl becomes a political activist. *My Son's Story* (1990) is told by a young coloured man trying to come to terms with his father's tangled private and public life. Some of her essays have been gathered in *The Black Interpreters* (1973) and *The Essential Gesture – Writing, Politics and Places* (1988).

Gordon, Adam Lindsay 1833–70 Australian poet. The son of a retired Indian Army officer, Gordon was born in the Azores and educated at Worcester Royal Grammar School. A classical education and the background of a cultured home encouraged an interest in poetry which stayed with him throughout his short but adventurous life. When he was 20 Gordon's father sent him to Australia. He arrived in Adelaide in 1853 and worked as a mounted trooper, horse breaker, livery-stable keeper, and more notably as a steeplechase rider, a field in which he became famous. His first published work, *The Feud*, appeared in 1864 and he contributed regularly to *Bell's Life in Victoria* and *The Australasian*. A collection was published as *Sea Spray and Smoke Drift* (1867). *Ashtaroth, A Dramatic Lyric*, an unsuccessful exercise on the Faust theme, was published in the same year. Further poems were published in MARCUS CLARKE's paper *The Colonial Monthly*. He retired from steeplechasing in 1870 and his volume of poems *Bush Ballads and Galloping Rhymes* (1870) earned him praise but little else. He returned to steeplechasing and suffered a serious fall from which he never really recovered. He committed suicide at the age of 37.

Gordon, Caroline 1895–1981 American novelist and short-story writer. She was born in Trenton, Kentucky. Her first novel, *Penhally* (1931), contrasts the grandeur of the ante-bellum South with its diminished condition after the Civil War. *Aleck Maury Sportsman* (1934) has a hero based on her own father. *None Shall Look Back* (1937), modelled on Tolstoy's *War and Peace*, has as its hero an actual figure from the Civil War, General Nathan Bedford Forrest. Her other novels are *The Garden of Adonis* (1937), *Green Centuries* (1941), *The Women on the Porch* (1944), *The Strange Children* (1951), *The Malefactors* (1956) and *The Glory of Hera* (1972). In 1934 she was awarded the O. Henry Prize for her short story 'Old Red', which was later published in the collection *The Forest of the South* (1945), again in *Old Red and Other Stories* (1963) and in *The Collected Stories of Caroline Gordon* (1981).

Gore, Mrs Catherine Grace 1799–1861 Novelist and playwright. Born Catherine Moody, she produced 70 assorted works in under 40 years, including plays and occasional pieces. She was known best for SILVER-FORK NOVELS of fashionable life and high society. These include *Manners of the Day* (1830), *Mrs Armytage: or, Female Domination* (1836), *Cecil: or, The Adventures of a Coxcomb* (1841) and *The Banker's Wife* (1843). None is as memorable as THACKERAY'S PARODY of her work in PUNCH'S PRIZE NOVELISTS (1847).

Gorges, Sir Arthur 1557–1625 Poet and translator. Son of vice-admiral Sir William Gorges, he was born probably at Butshed Manor, near Plymouth, and educated at Oxford. He entered royal service in his early twenties. Closely involved with SIR WALTER RALEIGH, he fell from favour under JAMES I and spent the remainder of his life managing his family's property and many lawsuits. SPENSER praised him in the guise of 'Alcyon' for his love songs and sonnets, written in 1580–90, several of which appeared in Elizabethan poetical miscellanies. Gorges prepared a manuscript collection, 'his vanities and toys of youth'; also in manuscript is his chivalric narrative, *The Olympian Catastrophe* (1612), a memorial tribute to Prince Henry modelled on Spenser's FAERIE QUEENE. A complete edition of both was published in 1953. Gorges translated Lucan's *Pharsalia* in 1614 and, in 1619, BACON'S *DE SAPIENTIA VETERUM* and *ESSAYS*, the latter into French.

Gospel of Nicodemus, The An account of the events succeeding the accusation of the Jews including the death, Resurrection and Ascension of Christ, the acts of Joseph of Arimathea and of Pilate, and the Harrowing of Hell. It first appeared around AD 400, and exists in an Old English translation and a version in Middle English verse and prose. The work greatly influenced medieval art, theology and literature, providing the basis of the Harrowing of Hell episode in MIRACLE PLAYS.

Gosse, Sir Edmund (William) 1849–1928 Critic and essayist. He was born in London and brought up by his father, Philip H. Gosse, a distinguished zoologist and devout member of the Plymouth Brethren. Gosses's isolated, bleak childhood is finely evoked in his best-remembered work, *Father and Son* (1907), 'A Study of Two Temperaments' which blends sympathy and irony in its portrait of his father. He became an assistant librarian at the British Museum (1867), a translator at the Board of Trade (1874), lecturer in English literature at Trinity College, Cambridge (1884), and librarian of the House of Lords (1904). He published poems and plays, and was a central figure in London literary life, a friend of SWINBURNE, ROBERT LOUIS STEVENSON, THOMAS HARDY and HENRY JAMES. After World War I he became a contributor to *The Sunday Times* with a regular and influential essay on current books. He was knighted in 1925.

As a critic he also wrote studies of THOMAS GRAY (1882), JEREMY TAYLOR (1903) and SIR THOMAS BROWNE (1905) for the English Men of Letters series, as well as a biography of SWINBURNE (1917). These are less important than his interest in Scandinavian culture, expressed in *Studies in the Literature of Northern Europe* (1879), a study of Ibsen (1907) and influential translations of *Hedda Gabler* (1891) and *The Master Builder* (with WILLIAM ARCHER, 1893).

Gosson, Stephen 1554–1624 Pamphleteer. Born in Canterbury and educated at Oxford, he is known to have written some pastoral plays before the influence of Puritanism made him a leading opponent of the contemporary theatre. *The School of Abuse* (1579), attacking poets and actors, was dedicated without permission to SIR PHILIP SIDNEY, whose APOLOGY FOR POETRY was written partly to confute him. The controversy was still at its height when Gosson wrote *Plays Confuted in Five Actions* (1582). Never formally a Puritan, Gosson became an Anglican clergyman. His Paul's Cross sermon of 1598 was published as *The Trumpet of War*.

Gothic novel A type of romance popular in the late 18th and early 19th centuries. The word 'Gothic' had come to mean 'wild', 'barbarous' and 'crude', qualities which writers found it attractive to cultivate in reaction against the sedate NEOCLASSICISM of earlier 18th-century culture. Gothic novels were usually set in the past (most often the Middle Ages) and in foreign countries (particularly the Catholic countries of southern Europe); they took place in monasteries, castles, dungeons and mountainous landscapes. The plots hinged on suspense and mystery, involving the fantastic and the supernatural.

Horace Walpole's Gothic chapel in the grounds of Strawberry Hill: the Gothic was a theme used in architecture, the visual arts and the novel.

Elements of the form begin to appear as early as SMOLLETT'S *FERDINAND COUNT FATHOM* (1753), but the first Gothic novel proper is HORACE WALPOLE'S *THE CASTLE OF OTRANTO* (1764). Later novelists associated with the fashion for Gothic were CLARA REEVE, ANN RADCLIFFE, WILLIAM BECKFORD, M. G. ('MONK') LEWIS and C. R. MATURIN. Their influence can be felt in some Romantic poetry (for example, COLERIDGE'S *CHRISTABEL*), MARY SHELLEY'S *FRANKENSTEIN*, the stories of EDGAR ALLAN POE in America, and the novels of the BRONTË sisters.

Gould, Nathaniel (Nat) 1857–1919 Sporting novelist. He was born in Manchester and educated privately at Southport. In 1878 he joined the staff of the *Newark Advertiser* and in 1884 travelled to Australia, remaining there for 11 years as a journalist in several cities. His first novel, *The Double Event*, linking his interest in racing with his knowledge of Australia, appeared in 1891. He returned to England in 1895 and continued to write and publish prolifically. His later fiction includes *Banker and Broker* (1893), *The Famous Match* (1898) and *Left in the Lurch* (in *Nat Gould's Annual*, 1903). His other work includes *On and Off the Turf in Australia* (1895) and *Town and Bush* (1896).

Gower, John *c.* 1330–1408 Poet. Little is known of Gower's life. His family originated in Yorkshire, but he apparently lived in Kent and London, owning estates also in Suffolk and Norfolk. By 1398, and probably from 1377, he lived in the Priory of St Mary Overy in Southwark. He knew GEOFFREY CHAUCER, who dedicated *TROILUS AND CRISEYDE* to him.

He wrote in French, Latin and English, one major work in each language. The first of these, *Le Mirour de l'omme*, or *Speculum meditantis* (1376–9) is a moral poem in French. Its subject is the effects of sin upon the world, and it is divided into three unequal parts. The first is a schematic analysis of the seven deadly sins and their opposite virtues, the second part examines the effects of sin on different social ranks and the third outlines the way to redemption through repentance and the intercession of the Virgin. *Vox clamantis* (1379–82) again attacks man's sinfulness, analysing the corruption of Ricardian society. The first book, added after the Peasants Revolt of 1381, is an apocalyptic vision of political and social chaos.

Sometime after the deposing of Richard II in 1399 Gower added a sequel to *Vox clamantis*, the *Cronica tripertita*, finally condemning the king. CONFESSIO AMANTIS, written in 1386–90 and revised in 1393, is a notable contribution to the literature of COURTLY LOVE in English. It presents a collection of tales and EXEMPLA set within the framework of a lover's confession to Venus' priest. One of the tales supplied the source for SHAKESPEARE'S *PERICLES*, in which Gower appears as the Chorus.

Gower's only other work in English is the poem 'To King Henry IV, in Praise of Peace'; he also wrote some short Latin verses and, in French, the *Cinkante Balades*. During the 15th century he was lauded with Chaucer and LYDGATE as one of the greatest English poets.

Gowers, Sir Ernest (Arthur) 1880–1966 Writer on writing. Educated at Rugby and Clare College, Cambridge, Gowers was a distinguished civil servant. His rigorous insistence on simple clear English from his juniors led to an invitation from the head of the Civil Service to produce a brief paper on writing English: *Plain Words: A Guide to the Use of English* (1948). This was followed by his *ABC of Plain Words* (1951), and both were later published together as *The Complete Plain Words* (1954). He was responsible also for a second edition of HENRY FOWLER'S *A Dictionary of Modern English Usage* (1965). His influential *A Life for a Life? The Problem of Capital Punishment* (1956) grew out of his work as chairman of the Royal Commission of 1949–53.

Grace, Patricia 1937– New Zealand short-story writer and novelist. Born in Wellington, she has taught in schools in various parts of the North Island. *Waiariki* (1975) was the first collection of stories by a Maori woman writer. Since then she has published two further collections, *The Dream Sleepers* (1980) and *Electric City* (1987), and two novels, *Mutuwhenua: The Moon Sleeps* (1978) and *Potiki* (1986). Her writing explores the opposition of Maori and Pakeha (European) worlds from a point of view within contemporary Maori culture. *Potiki* is about a land dispute in which developers threaten a small Maori coastal community. Its theme of cultural antagonism is also expressed through its narrative method, and it blends realism and myth in its affirmation of Maori cultural identity. Like IHIMAERA, Grace emphasizes the Maori extended family (whanau). Her short stories are distinctive for their spare style based on the speech structures of Maori English. She has also collaborated with the Maori artist Robyn Kahukiwa in producing CHILDREN'S LITERATURE.

Graham, W(illiam) S(ydney) 1918–86 Poet. Born in Greenock, Renfrewshire, he left school at 14 but later took night-classes in literature and art appreciation at the University of Glasgow and won a bursary to Newbattle Abbey. He avoided conscription by going to Eire in 1939, returning to Scotland to work as a precision engineer in a torpedo factory. In 1954 he and his wife moved to the St Ives area of Cornwall, where he spent the rest of his life, coming in touch with many influential artists but also enduring considerable poverty. Although essentially a Scottish poet, he stood outside the tradition of his lifelong friend HUGH MACDIARMID and was conditioned by European and American influences, such as Rimbaud and HART CRANE. The early poems in *Cage without Grievance* (1942), *The Seven Journeys* (1944) and *The White Threshold* (1949), which brought him encouragement and support from T. S. ELIOT, are remarkable for their exotic mix of imagery drawn from industrial and rural scenes. In later work, such as his best-known single volume, *The Nightfishing* (1955), *Malcolm Mooney's Land* (1970) and *Implements in Their Place* (1977), he went on to produce a more developed poetry of considerable power which uses the extended metaphor of the voyage, inward and outward, to examine language and being. By the time *Collected Poems 1942–77* appeared in 1979 he had begun, at last, to receive a measure of the critical attention he deserved.

Grahame, Kenneth 1859–1932 Essayist and writer of CHILDREN'S LITERATURE. Born in Edinburgh, Grahame went to live with his grandmother in Berkshire as a child after the death of his mother. After attending school in Oxford he was forced to join the Bank of England instead of going to university as he wished.

His books of essays, *The Golden Age* (1895), and its sequel, *Dream Days* (1898), paint a convincingly unsentimental picture of childhood, with the adults in these sketches totally out of touch with the real concerns of the young people around them, including their griefs and rages. After marriage in 1899 Grahame took to telling stories to his young son Alastair, continued in a series of letters. These formed the basis for THE WIND IN THE WILLOWS (1908), which – after several rejections by publishers – came out to scant critical acclaim. However, its fame quickly grew and the addition of illustrations by E. H. SHEPARD and then ARTHUR RACKHAM helped it to its present classic status. Grahame produced no further written work of substance, becoming something of a recluse after the suicide of his son at the age of 19.

Grain of Wheat, A A novel by NGUGI WA THIONG'O, published in 1967. Set chiefly in the days just before Uhuru (Independence) celebrations in Kenya, it traces the experiences of four characters – Mugo, Gikenya, Karanga and Mumbi – in the struggle for independence and especially their relationship to Kihiga, a hero of the revolution hanged by the colonial authorities. The novel provides an authentic fictional record of the historical processes of the struggle through various devices: narration, interior monologue, dialogue, recollection and anecdote. Ngugi's political theme is balanced by a concern with the fragility of human life and of personal relationships. The influence of CONRAD, which Ngugi has acknowledged, is apparent in his preoccupation with the betrayal of people and ideals. The story gradually reveals the sources of individual guilt and follows the process of expiation.

Grammar of Assent, The A theological essay by JOHN HENRY NEWMAN, published in 1870. It argues that religious certainty comes not from logic, but from intuition, the conscience and the heart. Newman postulated the 'illative sense', which 'concerns itself with principles, doctrines, facts, memories, experiences, testimonies in order to attain insights too delicate and subtle for logical analysis'. The *Grammar* was an attempt to show that 'common sense' was as much a part of religious faith as it was of 'science and progress'. Newman's statement is Romantic in that it posits a 'religious imagination' and a 'whole man', not just the intellect.

Grand Guignol A particularly lurid and violent form of drama, in which the violence threatened but characteristically averted in MELODRAMA is carried through into performance. The name is derived, by ironic transference, from the 19th-century French marionette, Guignol. Immensely popular in Montmartre, Grand Guignol was confined, in 19th-century England, to the penny gaffs of London's East End. There are few notable examples in English. JAMES ELROY FLECKER's *HASSAN* has elements of the genre, as does Patrick Hamilton's proficient thriller, *Gaslight* (1938), but it is film that most insistently preserves the decadence of Grand Guignol.

Grandissimes, The: *A Story of Creole Life* A novel by GEORGE WASHINGTON CABLE, published in 1880, and set in New Orleans in the early 19th century. A feud between the Grandissimes and the De Grapions, aristocratic families of Louisiana, leads to a duel in which Mr Nancanou – related by marriage to the De Grapions – is killed. His widow, Aurora, the last survivor of the De Grapion family, goes to live with her daughter Clotilde in New Orleans. Impoverished, they live in seclusion. Through old Dr Keene, Honoré Grandissime meets Joseph Frowenfield, a young apothecary who is in love with Clotilde De Grapion. Through Joseph, Honoré meets Aurora and falls in love with her. Because Aurora is poor, and serves as a reminder of past hostilities between the two families, the Grandissimes oppose Honoré's marriage to her. However, family objections to the union are cleared

away in a deathbed scene: Honoré's uncle Agricola is dying from stab wounds inflicted by Honoré's quadroon half-brother. It was the arrogant Agricola who had killed Aurora's husband, but before he dies he reveals that 20 years earlier he had promised Aurora's father to allow the peace-engendering union between Aurora and Honoré. Obsessed with preserving the 'race', Agricola now finds the union desirable again because it will continue the French Creole 'aristocracy' to which the two families belong.

Granta A Cambridge University student magazine from 1889 until the mid-1970s, it published early work by E. M. FORSTER, A. A. MILNE, TED HUGHES and SYLVIA PLATH. After a period of moribundity it was resurrected in 1979 under the editorship of Bill Buford as a quarterly literary magazine. It has published work by MARTIN AMIS, IAN MCEWAN, A. N. WILSON, JAMES FENTON, SALMAN RUSHDIE, JOHN BERGER and GEORGE STEINER among others, and American writers such as RAYMOND CARVER and other exponents of what it has called DIRTY REALISM.

Granville-Barker, Harley 1877–1946 Actor, director, playwright and scholar. Born Harley Granville Barker, he hyphenated his name in 1918. His career was much affected by his contact with the eccentrically single-minded Shakespearean director, William Poel, who chose him as his Richard II in 1899. Poel's plain staging and pursuit of the original Elizabethan style affected Granville-Barker's own immensely influential productions of *THE WINTER'S TALE*, *TWELFTH NIGHT* and *A MIDSUMMER NIGHT'S DREAM* at the Savoy Theatre, London, in 1912–14 as well as his sensitive *Preface to Shakespeare* (1927–47). When GEORGE BERNARD SHAW chose him to play Marchbanks in the 1900 production of *Candida* by the Stage Society, a second major influence entered his life. The Barker-Vedrenne seasons at the ROYAL COURT THEATRE (1904–7) established Shaw as a major force in the British theatre, and Granville-Barker's own plays, particularly *The Voysey Inheritance* (1905), *Waste* (1907) and *The Madras House* (1910), show a Shavian commitment to intelligent debate.

Grapes of Wrath, The A novel by JOHN STEINBECK, published in 1939 and awarded a PULITZER PRIZE the following year.

The novel tells the story of Oklahoma farmers who are driven off their land by soil erosion. The Joad family drives to California, hoping to take advantage of what they imagine to be a land of plenty. The grandparents die on the way, and the Joads arrive only to be worn down by the impossibly hard life of migrant fruit-pickers. They find a temporary respite in a government labour camp, but when it closes they are forced to take work at a blacklisted orchard. There Tom Joad joins with Jim Casy, a minister turned labour organizer. During ensuing strike violence Casy is killed, and Tom, who had once served time for killing a man in Oklahoma, kills again to avenge Casy's death. In panic, the Joads flee and try to hide Tom, but they are exhausted by struggle and starvation. Finally Ma Joad decides that for the good of all the family Tom must leave. The rest of the family struggles on together, though to what end and in what direction nobody knows. At the controversial end of the novel, the eldest daughter, Rose of Sharon, who has just given birth to a stillborn child, nurses an anonymous starving man with her own milk.

Graves, A(lfred) P(ercival) 1846-1931 Irish essayist, songwriter, poet and editor. The son of the Rev. Charles Graves, FRS, mathematician and later protestant Bishop of Limerick, he was born in Dublin and educated at Trinity College. He was successively a clerk in the Home Office, a school inspector and an education official in London. Despite these responsibilities he quickly made a name for himself as an Irish writer and published three volumes of Irish songs (1873, 1882, 1892) including the rollicking 'Father O'Flynn', written in 1875 with music by C. V. Stanford. He also wrote the libretto for *The Postbag: A Lesson in Irish* (1902), a one-act opera with music arranged from old Irish airs. He was twice president of the London Irish Literary Society, which encouraged the Irish Literary Revival, and to this end he edited anthologies of Irish poetry and song, wrote *Irish Literary and Musical Studies* (1913) and contributed a valuable chapter on Anglo-Irish literature to the *Cambridge History of English Literature* (1916). Though he knew little Irish and no Welsh he made good use of translations from both languages in popular works such as *A Celtic Psaltery* (1917) and *Songs of the Gael* (1925). His own more serious poetry, lyrical and fluent, engaged increasingly with the heroic world of Irish myth and legend popularized by YEATS and LADY GREGORY, a development commended by DOUGLAS HYDE in his introduction to *Irish Poems* (1908). In 1930 Graves published his lively autobiography *To Return to All That*, in part a response to *GOODBYE TO ALL THAT* by his son ROBERT GRAVES, which had appeared the previous year.

Graves, Richard 1715-1804 Novelist. Born at Mickleton in Gloucestershire and educated at Pembroke College, Oxford, he became a fellow of All Souls and rector of Claverton, near Bath, in 1749. He is best remembered for his novel, *THE SPIRITUAL QUIXOTE* (1773), satirizing the Methodist preacher George Whitefield, whom he had known at Pembroke College. His other novels, interesting for their portrayal of social conditions, are *Columella: or, The Distressed Anchoret* (1779), *Eugenius: or, Anecdotes of the Golden Vale* (1785) and *Plexippus: or, The Aspiring Plebeian* (1790). A popular figure in Bath so-

ciety, he also corresponded with distinguished people and was a friend of WILLIAM SHENSTONE, whom he portrayed in *Columella* and made the subject of *Recollections* (1788).

Graves, Robert (von Ranke) 1895-1985 Poet, novelist and critic. The son of A. P. GRAVES, he was born in Wimbledon and educated at Charterhouse. After serving in World War I, during which he was severely injured and reported dead, he studied at St John's College, Oxford, where he became a close friend of T. E. LAWRENCE, whose biography he later wrote (1927). A controversial memoir, *GOODBYE TO ALL THAT* (1929), ends with his departure from England with his partner during this period, LAURA RIDING. He subsequently lived in Italy, France, Britain, the USA, and, most famously, Mallorca. He gave the Clark Lectures at Cambridge in 1954-5 and was professor of poetry at Oxford in 1961-6.

The early poems in *Over the Brazier* (1916), *David and Goliath* (1916), *Fairies and Fusiliers* (1917) and EDWARD MARSH's *GEORGIAN POETRY* were dominated by World War I. Subsequent work, gathered successively in *Poems 1914-26* (1927), *Poems 1926-30* (1931), *Poems 1938-45* (1946) and two editions of *Collected Poems* (1938 and 1975), records the development of a highly individual style, continually evolving yet always returning to tradition, classical literature and mythology for new inspiration. Many of the finest poems use a plain diction, refuse public themes and concentrate on love. His poetry went hand in hand with a mass of other work. Critical books include *On English Poetry* (1922), *The Meaning of Dreams* (1924), *Poetic Unreason* (1925) and *A Survey of Modernist Poetry* (with Laura Riding; 1928), highly critical both of popular attitudes to poetry and of MODERNISM in its more fashionable forms. *THE WHITE GODDESS* (1948) elaborated his mythology of poetic inspiration. His interest in myth, classical culture and biblical scholarship also prompted, among many other books, the two most famous of his 13 novels, *I, Claudius* (1934) and *Claudius the God* (1934), and a minor classic in *The Greek Myths* (1955). He also produced CHILDREN'S LITERATURE and translations from the classics, *The Anger of Achilles: Homer's Iliad* (1957) among them. Posthumous volumes have included a two-volume *Selected Letters* (1988-90), *Collected Short Stories* (1991) and *Selected Poems* (1992).

graveyard poets The common term for those 18th-century writers, never a formal school, who found inspiration in graveyards and the contemplation of mortality. They were especially fashionable in the 1740s and 1750s, but can be seen to feed the therapeutically melancholic side of ROMANTICISM. A generous collection of graveyard writing might include PARNELL's 'Night-Piece on Death' (1721); BLAIR's *The Grave* (1743); YOUNG's *NIGHT THOUGHTS* (1742-6);

JAMES HERVEY's prose *Meditations among the Tombs* (1746–7); GRAY's ELEGY WRITTEN IN A COUNTRY CHURCHYARD (1751), the *locus classicus* of its poetic kind; Beilby Porteus's 'Death', winner of the Seatonian Prize in 1759; and, as a late flower of the tradition, the forger William Dodd's *Thoughts in Prison* with all its attendant documents (1777).

Gravity's Rainbow A novel by THOMAS PYNCHON, published in 1973. A lengthy and extremely dense text, it involves more than 400 characters, and concerns itself with the historical trends identifiable in American society since World War II. It defies any summary statements, but can generally be said to treat scientific and technological discoveries as historical events and forces, and to explore the modes of consciousness which they generate. One of its central metaphors is the all-pervasive paranoia which has been crucial in other of Pynchon's works. Its allusions range from classical music theory to film and comic-strip characters. The literary figures evoked include WILLIAM FAULKNER, EMILY DICKINSON, Rainer Maria Rilke, Jorge Luis Borges, and JAMES JOYCE, to whose ULYSSES the novel has been frequently compared.

Gray, Alasdair 1934– Scottish novelist. A native of Glasgow, where he still lives, he worked as an artist and illustrator before turning to fiction in his forties. His home city provides the location for his first two novels, *Lanark* (1981) and *1982, Janine* (1984). Both are huge, sprawling PICARESQUE narratives that display a Sternian diffuseness, a Joycean eclecticism and hallucinatory, fantastic dimension, as well as reminders of Gray's graphic arts skills in their eccentric typology and marginal embellishments. His shorter fiction is collected in *Unlikely Stories, Mostly* (1983). Other works include: a slighter novel, *The Fall of Kelvin Walker* (1985), following the fortunes of a typically hapless, itinerant, dissipated protagonist during his sojourn in London; a short political SATIRE, *McGrotty and Ludmilla* (1990), issued by his own publishing imprint, the Dog and Bone Press; *Something Leather* (1990); and *Poor Things* (1992). Gray is the most prominent member of a new wave of Scottish writing, which also includes JAMES KELMAN and Agnes Owens.

Gray, Simon (James Holliday) 1936– Playwright. Publishing and university life make the setting for several of his plays, which sustain a flow of comedy while exploring the nature of suffering. *Wise Child* (1967), *Dutch Uncle* (1968) and *Spoiled* (1971) were followed by his first major success, *Butley* (1971), a wry view of his own career as a university lecturer in English. In *Otherwise Engaged* (1975) a publisher retreats into music from people whom he dislikes and distrusts. In *Close of Play* (1978) an academic stays silent during his last hours, while his family bickers

around him. In *Quartermain's Terms* (1981) a language teacher is left defenceless against the loss of his job and the friendships that apparently went with it. *The Common Pursuit* (1984) is an intricate study of a group of Cambridge graduates reaching middle age. In *Melon* (1987) a publisher suffers a nervous breakdown. *Hidden Laughter* (1990) describes a family whose affluent lifestyle conceals the utmost loneliness. *An Unnatural Pursuit* (1985), Gray's book about the production of *The Common Pursuit*, describes why it is easy to lose faith in the theatre.

Gray, Stephen 1941– South African poet and novelist. Born in Cape Town of Scottish and English parentage, he studied at the universities of Cape Town, Cambridge (where he was an editor of GRANTA) and Iowa, where he attended the Writers' Workshop. He has lectured in Johannesburg since 1969, publishing his doctorate as *Southern African Literature* (1979) and editing *The Penguin Book of Southern African Stories* (1985) and *The Penguin Book of Southern African Verse* (1989). His collections of poetry are *It's About Time* (1974), *Hottentot Venus* (1979), *Love Poems, Hate Poems* (1982), *Apollo Café* (1990) and *Season of Violence* (1992), with *Selected Poems* (1993). His novels are *Local Colour* (1975), *Visible People* (1977), *Caltrop's Desire* (1980), *John Ross: The True Story* (1987), *Time of Our Darkness* (1988) and *Born of Man* (1989). *War Child* (1991) is semi-autobiographical. His short stories and other short pieces have been collected as *Human Interest* (1993). *Accident of Birth* (1993) is his autobiography. He has also adapted South African authors for the stage, notably in *Schreiner: A One-Woman Play* (1983), and remains a resolute spokesman for the recognition of English-language values in the apartheid and post-apartheid society.

Gray, Thomas 1716–71 Poet. The only one to survive of the 12 children born to his parents, Gray was educated at Eton (where his two uncles were teaching) and there formed a friendship with HORACE WALPOLE, Richard West and Thomas Ashton which was nicknamed the 'Quadruple Alliance'. In 1734 he was admitted to Peterhouse, Cambridge, and considered embarking on a legal career, but was undecided. In 1739–41 he toured France and Italy with Walpole, taking down notes and maintaining a regular correspondence with his friends in England, but they quarrelled at Reggio and Gray returned to England with other friends. At this time he was working on some Latin verses.

The death of his father left Gray financially independent in 1741, and he began writing a tragedy *Agrippina* in 1742. On 1 June of that year West died, just after Gray (in one of the frequent letters they exchanged) had sent him his *Ode on the Spring*. The poet included a lament, *Liber quartus* (1742), in the

Latin poem on which he was working, a translation of LOCKE'S *ESSAY CONCERNING HUMAN UNDERSTANDING* entitled *De principiis cogitandi*. In October he returned to Peterhouse and, though he moved to Pembroke College in 1756, was based in Cambridge, with interludes away, for the rest of his life. At his mother's house in Stoke Poges he wrote the *Sonnet on the Death of Richard West*, his ode *On Adversity*, the *Ode on a Distant Prospect of Eton College* and the unfinished *Hymn to Ignorance*. Graduating as Bachelor of Laws in 1743, he became reconciled with Walpole the following year, and in 1747, on the death of Walpole's cat, Gray sent him the *Ode on the Death of a Favourite Cat, Drowned in a Tub of Gold Fishes*. His other friends at this time included CHRISTOPHER SMART, WILLIAM MASON and CONYERS MIDDLETON.

On 12 June 1750 Gray sent Walpole the completed manuscript of the poem that was to immortalize him, *ELEGY WRITTEN IN A COUNTRY CHURCHYARD*. Published by DODSLEY in 1751, it marked Gray's rise to fame as a poet. Apart from a small collection, *Designs by Mr R. Bentley for Six Poems by Mr T. Gray* (1753), which contained *A Long Story* and the *Ode to Adversity*, Gray published little more in the way of poetry. His two Pindaric odes, *Progress of Poesy* and *The Bard*, were printed by Walpole in 1757 at his Strawberry Hill press. In December of that year he was offered the post of POET LAUREATE, on the death of COLLEY CIBBER, but declined it.

Pursuing a plan to write the history of English poetry (for which he might have been ideally suited) Gray moved to London in 1759 and spent two years researching in the British Museum. Over the succeeding years he made several tours around England and Scotland, and recorded his impressions in his letters, a medium in which he positively excelled. He returned to Cambridge in 1761, having completed a number of imitations of Celtic and Norse verse, including *The Fatal Sisters* and *The Descent of Odin*. These appeared in a collected volume of his *Poems* published in 1768. Later that year he was appointed to the sinecure position of Regius Professor of Modern History at Cambridge, and in 1769 he wrote a masterful *Ode* at the installation of the Duke of Grafton as chancellor of the University. His second visit to the Lake District (1769), recorded in letters to THOMAS WARTON THE YOUNGER, had a major influence on the PICTURESQUE appreciation of landscape. He died in Cambridge but was buried next to his mother in the graveyard at Stoke Poges.

Polished and exact, Gray's verse bears witness to his wide reading, particularly in the classics. Yet his own voice is distinctive in its nice balance between introspection and sentiment, qualities which marked the shift from NEOCLASSICISM to the taste for the picturesque. His finest work, like the *Elegy Written in a Country Churchyard*, has a delicacy admired by the Romantic poets and still accessible today.

Great Expectations A novel by CHARLES DICKENS, serialized in *ALL THE YEAR ROUND* from December 1860 to August 1861 and published in volume form in 1861.

Narrated in the first person by Philip Pirrip (Pip) as he reflects on the three stages of his 'great expectations', the novel opens on the Kentish marshes where he lives an orphaned childhood under the harsh hand of his sister and her kindly blacksmith husband, Joe Gargery. One day Pip helps a starving convict, Abel Magwitch, who is soon recaptured and taken back to the nearby prison ship ('The Hulks'). Pip is later summoned to Satis House, home of the wealthy eccentric Miss Havisham, who has lived in seclusion since being jilted by her fiancé. He quickly becomes devoted to Miss Havisham's ward Estella, who treats his developing love only with deliberate coldheartedness. Pip is aided in his ambition of becoming a gentleman by a generous allowance, paid through the lawyer Jaggers, which he mistakenly assumes to come from Miss Havisham. He relinquishes his humble companions and goes to London to acquire polish, good manners and a smattering of education with the help of his room-mate Herbert Pocket. Urban life leads him into vain and extravagant ways. Magwitch reappears, having illegally returned to England after being transported, and reveals that he is Pip's benefactor, bent on using the fortune he has amassed in Australia to repay the boy's kindness. Pip plans to get Magwitch safely out of the country but the convict is mortally hurt, arrested and brought to trial; he dies before the sentence is carried out. Estella, dramatically revealed as Magwitch's daughter, marries an upper-class lout, Bentley Drummle, who gravely mistreats her before his early death. Pip, learning both loyalty and Christian humility from his experiences, returns to England after a successful career and meets Estella. In the book's original ending the two still remain separate, but at the urging of EDWARD BULWER LYTTON Dickens altered the conclusion to give *Great Expectations* a conventional happy ending.

Despite its neatly melodramatic plotting and its richly stocked gallery of comic minor characters – the histrionic Wopsle, the pompous Pumblechook, the eccentric Wemmick – *Great Expectations* is a book of sober and sustained purpose. The gradual discovery of human values Pip makes as he passes through the various stages of his 'great expectations' enacts a familiar Dickensian fable, enriched here by the presence of Pip's narrative voice to trace the processes of memory.

Great Gatsby, The A novel by F. SCOTT FITZGERALD, published in 1925.

The narrator, Nick Carraway, rents a cottage in West Egg, Long Island, next door to the mansion of Jay Gatsby and across the water from the home of Tom Buchanan and his wife Daisy, Carraway's cousin.

Gatsby's mansion is the scene of extravagant nightly parties, attended by many people who are uninvited and do not know their host. Carraway, both cynical and curious about Gatsby, soon becomes his confidant. He learns that Gatsby had met Daisy while he was in the army during World War I, and that they had fallen in love and planned to marry. Daisy, however, had grown impatient for him to return and had married Tom, a rich though boring man from Yale. Having risen from his lowly origins as Jimmy Gatz through dubious business deals, Gatsby is obsessed with winning Daisy back. He persuades Carraway to arrange a meeting between them, and Daisy, after initial resistance, succumbs to her former lover's generous attentions, impressed by his newly acquired wealth.

Tom, Daisy, Gatsby, Carraway and Carraway's girlfriend, Jordan Baker, spend a day together in New York. Tom, who himself has had a longstanding affair with Myrtle Wilson, the wife of a Long Island garage owner, becomes aware of Daisy's attentions to Gatsby. Gatsby tries to convince Daisy to leave Tom. Tom, in turn, tries to discredit Gatsby by revealing that he has made his money from bootlegging. Gatsby and Daisy leave in Tom's automobile, with Daisy driving. Myrtle Wilson, recognizing the car as it passes her husband's garage, runs out into the street and is hit and killed by Daisy, who drives on. Taking revenge on Gatsby, Tom tells Wilson it was Gatsby who killed his wife, and Gatsby, attempting to protect Daisy, lets the blame fall on himself. Wilson murders Gatsby and then commits suicide. Carraway is left to arrange Gatsby's funeral, which hardly anyone attends, and Tom and Daisy retreat 'back into their money, or their vast carelessness, or whatever it was that kept them together'.

Great Hoggarty Diamond, The A story by W. M. THACKERAY, published in FRASER'S MAGAZINE (September to December 1841). The Hoggarty Diamond, given to Samuel Titmarsh by his aunt, involves him with swindlers and shady dealings, from which he is rescued by his wife.

Greeley, Horace 1811–72 American journalist. Born in New Hampshire, he grew up in Vermont and in 1831 went to New York, where he worked as a printer before becoming editor of *The New Yorker* in 1834. In 1841 he founded *The Tribune*, the New York daily that he would edit until his death. Greeley was a consistent exponent of American democratic principles, and this was reflected in his editorial support of reform movements, of the new Republican party in the 1850s, of emancipation in the 1860s, and of amnesty and universal suffrage in the period of reconstruction. An opponent of the more radical Republicans in the 1870s, he was chosen as the Democratic presidential candidate in 1872; he was defeated by Ulysses S. Grant, however, and died within the month. Colourful, eccentric, independent, often controversial, Greeley's editorials were nevertheless influential throughout his career. Among his other writings were travel books: *Glances at Europe* (1851), and *An Overland Journey* (1860); *The American Conflict* (2 vols., 1864–6), an important contemporary history of the Civil War; and *Recollections of a Busy Life* (1868), an autobiography.

Green, Henry [Yorke, Henry Vincent] 1905–73 Novelist. Born in Tewkesbury, Gloucestershire, and educated at Eton College and Magdalen College, Oxford, he became an engineer and later managing director of his family's engineering company in Birmingham. While still at Oxford he attracted critical attention with his first novel, *Blindness* (1926). He also began but did not complete a second, *Mood. Living* (1929) is set in the sort of engineering works he knew very well (he worked as a foundryman). *Party Going* (1939) portrays an upper-class group who love wealth but have no sense of responsibility. Green's next book was a chapter of autobiography, *Pack My Bag: A Self Portrait* (1940). He resumed his career as a novelist with *Caught* (1943), a story of the Auxiliary Fire Service in World War II, and *Loving* (1945), which is of the same wartime period but set in a remote castle in Ireland. *Back* (1946), *Concluding* (1948), *Nothing* (1950) and *Doting* (1952) complete the list of his fiction.

Henry Green is distinguished as a novelist by his elegant impressionistic prose, his indirect and oblique dialogue, and his rapid cutting from scene to scene. His work displays a talent for observation, and a vein of poetry, in evidence most strongly, perhaps, in *Living*.

Green, John Richard 1837–83 Historian. Green was born in Oxford and educated at Magdalen College School and Jesus College, Oxford. He was ordained and served as a curate in various parts of London until ill health forced him to give up his duties; he became librarian of Lambeth Palace in 1869. This post gave him an opportunity for historical research; he became a frequent contributor to THE SATURDAY REVIEW and achieved a notable success with *A Short History of the English People* (1873), which proved the most popular history since MACAULAY'S. Green's narrative and descriptive powers are of a high order: they give life to his account of the literary and artistic events, as well as the political and economic ones, which make up the history of a nation. *Stray Studies from England and Italy* (1876) is a collection of essays; in the following year Green began publication of an extended version of his 'short' history as *A History of the English People* (4 vols., 1877–80). With the help of his wife, Alice Stopford Green, he expanded certain themes in *The Making of England* (1881) and *The Conquest of England* (1883).

Green, Matthew 1696–1737 Poet. Born in the City of London, Green was a civil servant who wrote a fluent poem in octosyllabics, *The Spleen* (1737), discussing boredom or depression and offering solutions for its prevention and cure.

Green, Paul (Eliot) 1894–1981 American playwright. Green was born in Lillington, North Carolina, and educated at the University of North Carolina, where he also taught from 1923 to 1924. His prolific dramatic output began with realistic folk-plays which portrayed the lives of blacks and poor whites in North Carolina. Outstanding among these is the one-act *White Dresses* (1923), one of the six plays for the black theatre published under the title *Lonesome Road* (1926). Another piece in the same collection was later expanded into the full-length *In Abraham's Bosom* (1926), for which Green won the PULITZER PRIZE in 1927. Staged in New York by the Provincetown Players, it is an angry story of the persecution and lynching of a black teacher. *The House of Connelly: A Drama of the Old South and the New* (1931), the first production of the GROUP THEATRE, deals with the deteriorating fortunes of a white landowning family in the South. *Tread the Green Grass* (1932) is one of a number of 'symphonic dramas', combining dance and music with dialogue. *Johnny Johnson* (1936), written for the Group Theatre, is a fiercely anti-war musical play with music written by Kurt Weill. Green's hatred of violence is again vividly expressed in *Hymn to the Rising Sun* (1936), which exposes the sadistic practices of state penitentiaries. He also dramatized RICHARD WRIGHT's novel *NATIVE SON* (1941), produced a new revival version of *Peer Gynt* (1951), and wrote 11 screenplays, among them an adaptation of John Howard Griffith's *Black Like Me* (1964).

After 1937, when he wrote *The Lost Colony* for a large-scale outdoor performance on the site of SIR WALTER RALEIGH's landing on Roanoke Island in North Carolina, Green devoted himself to writing and staging 'symphonic' pageant-dramas about American history, usually designed for outdoor performance in their appropriate geographical location. Other such productions include *The Common Glory* (1947) in Williamsburg, Virginia; *Faith of Our Fathers* (1950) in Washington, DC; *The Stephen Foster Story* (1959) in Bardstown, Kentucky; and *We the People* (1976) in Columbia, Maryland.

Green, Thomas Hill 1836–82 Philosopher. Green was educated at Rugby and Balliol College, Oxford, where he became White's Professor of Moral Philosophy in 1878. He made his first contribution to philosophy in 1874 with two extended introductions to an edition of DAVID HUME's *TREATISE OF HUMAN NATURE*; here he presented detailed criticisms of JOHN LOCKE, GEORGE BERKELEY and HUME, arguing that neither JOHN STUART MILL nor HERBERT SPENCER had advanced beyond the ideas presented by Hume in 1739. He suggested that students of philosophy should study the work of Kant and Hegel rather than that of the English empiricists. Green's principal work was *Prolegomena to Ethics* (1883).

Green Carnation, The See HICHENS, ROBERT.

Green Mansions: *A Romance of the Tropical Forest* A novel by W. H. HUDSON, published in 1904.

Abel Guevez de Argensola (Mr Abel) travels into the Venezuelan jungle (the 'green mansions') as a political refugee and eventually settles with the Indian tribe of his friend Runi. Exploring a forbidden part of the forest he hears and is enchanted by a beautiful voice, which he learns belongs to Rima, the daughter of an evil spirit called Didi. Abel meets Rima, who turns out to be a beautiful girl whose spirit has strong affinities with that of the forest itself. He also meets her grandfather, Nuflo, and he and the old man set out to try to locate Rima's mother. Abel and Rima are by now deeply in love.

After a long and arduous journey the two men return to the forest to discover that Rima's hut has been attacked and destroyed by the Indians. Rima herself has been trapped and burnt on a pyre surrounding a great tree in the forest. Abel is consumed by grief and revenges himself by attacking the Indians' village and slaying Runi. Afterwards he returns to civilization, bearing Rima's ashes in an urn, where he lives apart with his memories.

The Hudson Memorial in Hyde Park presents a sculpture of Rima by Sir Jacob Epstein, commissioned in 1925.

Greenaway, Kate 1846–1901 Illustrator and writer of CHILDREN'S LITERATURE. Born in London, the daughter of a successful wood-engraver, Kate eventually studied at the Slade School in London. Her first major success as a writer-illustrator was *Under the Window* (1879), printed in colour and selling over 100,000 copies. Her pictures here of demure little girls, accompanied by her own verses, helped popularize a particular fashion for high-waisted, frilly dresses and sun-bonnets. A friend of RUSKIN, she produced a large number of best-sellers, many of them in print today. Particularly good are her alphabet book, *A Apple Pie* (1886), and *Mother Goose: or, The Old Nursery Rhymes* (1881), although her essentially decorative style of drawing was not equal to the demands of the more vigorous nursery rhymes. But her charming characterizations of the young have always been appreciated by parents and teachers, even if children themselves may sometimes have found them a little too sweet and well-mannered.

Greene, (Henry) Graham 1904–91 Novelist, short-story writer, playwright, travel writer, essayist and critic. He was born in Hertfordshire and educated at Berkhamsted School, where his father was headmaster, and Balliol College, Oxford. He joined the staff of *The Times* in 1926 and married in 1927. A compulsive traveller, he made a journey through the interior of Liberia in 1935 which became the subject of a classic travel book, *Journey without Maps* (1936). On his return he was appointed film critic of *The Spectator*, of which he became literary editor in 1940. In 1938 he was commissioned to report on religious persecution in Mexico; the visit, which profoundly influenced his fiction, also prompted another travel book, *The Lawless Roads* (1939). During World War II he worked for the Foreign Office, mainly in Sierra Leone (1941–3). He was made a Companion of Honour in 1966, and a Chevalier de la Légion d'Honneur in 1969.

A key event in Greene's life was his conversion to Roman Catholicism in 1926. His first novel, *The Man Within* (1929), was a historical thriller which deployed many themes – pursuit, guilt, treachery and failure – which became the hallmark of his fiction. Popular success came with *Stamboul Train* (1932), a more topical thriller and the first of the novels which Greene termed 'entertainments'. These continued with *It's a Battlefield* (1934), *England Made Me* (1935), *A Gun for Sale* (1936), *The Confidential Agent* (1939), *Loser Takes All* (1955) and *Our Man in Havana* (1958). *BRIGHTON ROCK* (1938) was his first explicitly Catholic novel, taking up themes continued in *THE POWER AND THE GLORY* (1940), *THE HEART OF THE MATTER* (1948), *The End of the Affair* (1951) and *THE QUIET AMERICAN* (1955). Four more novels deal with the committed and the uncommitted caught up in places and events in which the 'comedians' are those who would never feel the need for commitment: *A Burnt-Out Case* (1961), set in the Belgian Congo; *The Comedians* (1966), set in Haiti; *The Honorary Consul* (1973), set in Argentina; and *The Human Factor* (1978), set in the London underworld of spies. Later novels include *Doctor Fischer of Geneva* (1980) and *The Captain and the Enemy* (1989). Two ventures into comedy are the PICARESQUE *Travels with My Aunt* (1969) and *Monsignor Quixote* (1982), a whimsical parable.

His short stories are collected in *The Basement Room and Other Stories* (1935), *Nineteen Stories* (1947), *Twenty-One Stories* (1954), *May We Borrow Your Husband?* (1967) and *The Last Word* (1990). His plays include *The Living Room* (1953), *The Potting Shed* (1957), *The Complaisant Lover* (1959) and *Carving a Statue* (1964), while his screenplay for Carol Reed's *The Third Man* (1949) remains his most memorable contribution to the cinema. His film criticism was gathered in *The Pleasure Dome* (1978). Essays and reviews, first collected in 1969, are also represented in *Reflections* (1990). *Getting to Know the General* (1984) marks his involvement in Third World politics. *A Sort of Life* (1971) and *Ways of Escape* (1980) are autobiographical.

Graham Greene

Greene, Robert *c.* 1558–92 Pamphleteer and playwright, born in Norwich and recipient of degrees from both Cambridge and Oxford. Greene married in 1585, but soon deserted his wife to lead a life of pleasure in London, where he associated with the UNIVERSITY WITS and particularly with PEELE. For many of the details of his dissipation we are reliant on his autobiographical pamphlets. These range from superior journalism to self-excoriating penitence. Of the first kind are his descriptions of low life in London in *The Art of Conny-Catching* (1591). 'Conny-catching' is the Elizabethan equivalent of confidence trickery, and Greene's treatment of it is racy, humorous and direct. Of the second kind is *Greene's Groatsworth of Wit, Bought with a Million of Repentance* (1592), famous for its attack on SHAKESPEARE as 'an upstart crow, beautified with our feathers'.

In order, perhaps, to buy his pleasures, Greene wrote prolifically. Early pamphlets in the style of LYLY culminated in his continuation of *EUPHUES* in *Euphues, His Censure of Philautus* (1587). A series of prose romances modelled on SIDNEY's *ARCADIA* included *Pandosto* (1588), on which Shakespeare based *THE WINTER'S TALE*, and *Menaphon* (1589), which contains the beautiful lyric, 'Weep not, my wanton'. Of his extant plays, the earliest is Alphonsus, King of Aragon (*c.* 1587), a shameless imitation of MARLOWE's rhetoric, and the best *FRIAR BACON AND FRIAR BUNGAY* (*c.* 1589). *A Looking-Glass for London and England* (*c.* 1590), written in collaboration with THOMAS LODGE, is a satirical dramatic treatment of material handled more lightheartedly in Greene's pamphlets. *James the Fourth* (*c.* 1591) interestingly combines the techniques of the chronicle play with fairy fantasy.

Greenwood, Walter 1903–74 Novelist. Born in Salford, Lancashire, of working-class parents, he was educated at a local council school and for many years after leaving school held a succession of ill-paid jobs, punctuated by long periods of unemployment. *Love on the Dole* (1933), his first novel and only commercial success, is a documentary work concentrating on the misfortunes of the Hardcastle family, particularly the daughter Sally, during the Depression of the 1930s. A stage version (with Ronald Gow) was produced in 1934 and a film in 1941. *There was a Time* (1967) is Greenwood's autobiography.

Greg, Sir W(alter) W(ilson) 1875–1959 Literary scholar. Born in Wimbledon, the son of a political journalist, he was educated at Harrow and at Trinity College, Cambridge, achieving only a pass degree in medieval and modern languages. His intellect was aroused, however, by the work of the Bibliographical Society, which he joined in 1898. A private income enabled him to devote the rest of his life to bibliography and textual criticism, although he did from 1907 to 1913 hold the post of librarian at Trinity College. In 1906 he founded the Malone Society for the reproduction of early (i.e. pre-1640) English plays, acting as its general editor from 1906 to 1939, when he succeeded E. K. CHAMBERS as president. After producing editions of *SIR THOMAS MORE* (1911) and other plays, Greg went on to publish *Dramatic Documents from the Elizabethan Playhouses* (1931) and *English Literary Autographs 1550–1650* (1925–32). The greatest task of his later years was *A Bibliography of the English Printed Drama to the Restoration* (1939–59), while his major editorial achievement of this period was the two texts of MARLOWE's *DOCTOR FAUSTUS* (1950). His other important works were *The Editorial Problem in Shakespeare* (1942), *The Shakespeare First Folio* (1955) and *Some Aspects and Problems of London Publishing 1550–1650* (1956). He was knighted in 1950.

Gregory, Lady (Isabella) Augusta 1852–1932 Playwright. The daughter of a wealthy Galway family, she married Sir William Gregory of Coole Park in 1880 and was widowed in 1892. Her friendship with YEATS, a frequent visitor to Coole Park, led to the foundation of the Irish Literary Theatre in 1899 and to the renaissance of Irish drama at the ABBEY THEATRE from 1904. She was one of the Abbey's most prolific playwrights, as well as director, occasional stage manager and frequent adviser. Her one-act plays about the Irish peasantry, which contain some of her best writing, include *Spreading the News* (1904), *The Rising of the Mood* (1906), the tragedy *The Gaol Gate* (1906) and *The Workhouse Ward* (1908). Of her Irish folk-history plays, the best are *The White Cockade* (1905), *The*

Canavans (1906) and *The Deliverer* (1911). *Hyacinth Halvey* (1906) is a contemporary comedy that shares the affectionate patriotism of her Irish adaptations of Molière, published in *The Kiltartan Molière* (1910). *Our Irish Theatre* (1913) and *Lady Gregory's Journals 1916–30* (1946) are important records.

Gregory, Horace (Victor) 1898–1982 American poet. He was born in Milwaukee, Wisconsin. His early verse – *Chelsea Rooming House* (1930), *A Wreath for Margery* (1933) and *No Retreat* (1933) – was strongly influenced by Marxist thought, but he later angered other left-wing writers by asserting that art should be apolitical. Throughout his career, however, he remained concerned with the plight of the poor and dispossessed in America's cities. His other volumes of poetry include *Chorus for Survival* (1935), *Poems 1930–1940* (1941), *Selected Poems* (1951), *Medusa in Gramercy Park* (1961), *Alphabet for Joanna: A Poem* (1963), *Collected Poems* (1964) and *Another Look* (1976). With his wife, the poet MARYA ZATURENSKA, he edited various poetry anthologies and wrote *A History of American Poetry 1900–1940* (1946).

Grenfell, Julian (Henry Francis) 1888–1915 Poet. The eldest son of Lord Desborough, he was educated at Eton and Balliol College, Oxford, and became a professional soldier. He is best known for 'Into Battle', published in *The Times* on the day he was killed in May 1915. His output was small and his work is usually to be found in anthologies, such as T. STURGE MOORE's *Some Soldier Poets* (1919).

Grenville, Kate [Catherine] **(Elizabeth)** 1950– Australian novelist and short-stort writer. Born in Sydney, she has worked as a teacher, journalist and film editor. *Bearded Ladies* (1984), a collection of stories, and *Lilian's Story* (1985), a novel, explore the ways in which women have been disadvantaged and manipulated. *Dreamhouse* (1986), using the structure of a thriller, reveals the misery of a woman in a one-sided relationship. *Joan Makes History* (1988) offers a feminist revision of Australian history which still finds room to register the 'comic poetry of suffering'. *Writing Book* (1990) is guidebook for novelists.

Greville, Charles Cavendish Fulke 1794–1865 Politician. Greville, who was born at Wilbury in Wiltshire, became Clerk to the Council in 1821 and held office until 1859. His brother Algernon Sidney Greville was Wellington's private secretary and Greville became the intimate friend of both Wellington and Palmerston; he knew every statesman of any account in his lifetime. He published anonymously *The Past and Present Policy of England to Ireland* (1845), in which he advocated a more liberal policy for religious endowments. But more interesting are his memoirs, which are probably the most rewarding of their kind; with Greville's portraits of the principal figures of the period they are indispensable to students of English history and politics from the accession of George IV to 1860. *The Greville Memoirs* appeared in three series: the first (1874) covers the reigns of George IV and William IV, the second (1885) the years 1837–52, and the third (1887) the years 1852–60. The second and third series were edited by Henry Reeve, who considered it advisable to suppress some of the contents. The complete text was eventually published in 1938.

Greville, Sir Fulke, 1st Baron Brooke 1554–1628 Courtier, poet and playwright. Greville's family were Warwickshire landowners and he was sent to Shrewsbury School in the same year as SIR PHILIP SIDNEY, his exact contemporary and later his close friend. After completing his education at Jesus College, Cambridge, he went to court and became a member of the AREOPAGUS club with Sidney, SPENSER and others. He represented Warwickshire in Parliament and enjoyed a long and distinguished public career under both Elizabeth and James I. He was knighted in 1597, served as Treasurer of the Navy from 1589 to 1604, and was Chancellor of the Exchequer from 1614 to 1622. James I made him first Baron Brooke in 1621, presenting him with Knowle Park and Warwick Castle. Greville was murdered by a servant who believed that his master had left him out of his will. Apart from Sir Philip Sidney, whose pallbearer he had been in 1586, he numbered among his friends SAMUEL DANIEL, FRANCIS BACON, WILLIAM CAMDEN and EDWARD COKE.

Greville's own writings were not published during his lifetime. The most famous is *The Life of the Renowned Sir Philip Sidney*, probably written between 1610 and 1614 and first published in 1652. The sequence of songs and sonnets called *Caelica* contains love poems as well as religious and philosophical verses. It was first published in 1633, together with Greville's two tragedies, *Alaham* and *Mustapha*, both showing his strong interest in political ideas. A third, on Antony and Cleopatra, reflected his feelings about the fall of his friend the Earl of Essex, but Greville destroyed it. He also wrote verse treatises on political subjects.

Grey, (Pearl) Zane 1872–1939 American novelist. Born in Zanesville, Ohio, Grey graduated from the University of Pennsylvania in 1896 with a degree in dentistry. He practised in New York City from 1898 to 1904, during which time he began to write fiction. His first novel, a romance entitled *Betty Sane*, was privately published by him in 1903 but received little public attention. In 1907 his wife convinced him to make his first trip to Arizona, in the company of C. J. 'Buffalo' Jones, a retired buffalo hunter. The journey proved to be the turning point in his career. He began

writing Western novels in the tradition of OWEN WISTER, and developed the conventions of the Western into a formula with enormous popular appeal. He wrote 60 books, which sold over 15 million copies in his lifetime, making him the single most popular author of the post-World War I era in America. Over 100 Western films were based on his stories. Novels such as *Riders of the Purple Sage* (1912), *To the Last Man* (1922), *Nevada* (1928), *Wild Horse Mesa* (1928) and *Code of the West* (1934) present the West as a moral landscape which destroys or redeems characters according to their response to its violent code.

Grierson, Sir Herbert J(ohn) C(lifford) 1866–1960 Scholar and critic. Born into a landowning family in Shetland, Grierson attended the Aberdeen Gymnasium and King's College, Aberdeen, before studying at Oxford University. From 1894 to 1915 he was the first professor of English at Aberdeen, where he established the canon of DONNE's poetry, producing a two-volume edition (1912); he also edited (with W. M. Dixon) *The English Parnassus: An Anthology of Longer Poems* (1909). In 1919 he moved to the University of Edinburgh, where he occupied the chair of rhetoric and English literature until 1935. Here he compiled the work for which he is best known, his anthology of *Metaphysical Lyrics and Poems of the Seventeenth Century* (1921). Its introduction prompted T. S. ELIOT and others to a major reassessment of the METAPHYSICAL POETS. Grierson also coedited SIR WALTER SCOTT's letters (1932–7) and wrote his biography (1938). He maintained his interest in 17th-century literature with *Cross Currents in English Literature of the XVII Century* (1929), and (with G. Bullough) *The Oxford Book of Seventeenth-Century Verse* (1934).

Grieve, Christopher Murray See MACDIARMID, HUGH.

Griffin, Gerald 1803–40 Novelist and poet. Born at Limerick, he came to London in 1823 but returned to Limerick in 1838 and joined the Christian Brothers. His novel, *The Collegians* (1829), was highly regarded, but Griffin's fame was eclipsed by DION BOUCICAULT, who dramatized it as THE COLLEEN BAWN in 1860 and scored one of the great successes of the Victorian theatre. The novel underwent a second transformation as *The Lily of Killarney*, a once popular opera by Julius Benedict, in 1863.

Griffiths, Trevor 1935– Playwright. He was born and educated in Manchester. His debate plays reveal his training in Marxist dialectic. *Occupations* (1970) sets left-wing pragmatism against the fervour of the Italian Marxist Gramsci. *Sam, Sam* (1972) contrasts two brothers, one loyal to his roots and the other who joins the new bourgeoisie. *Comedians* (1975) is a study of the social and class implications of popular comedy. *The Party* (1973) analyses why the events of May 1968 found so little response in Britain. *The Gulf between Us* (1992) looks at the Gulf War from the Arab point of view. His work for TV includes the series *Bill Brand* (1976) and *Fatherland* (1986).

Grigson, Geoffrey (Edward Harvey) 1905–85 Poet and man of letters. Born in Pelynt, Cornwall, he was educated at St Edmund Hall, Oxford, and worked as a journalist. His poetry is overshadowed by his achievements as a man of letters; he founded and edited the influential modernist periodical *New Verse* (1933–9), and he was an acerbic, controversial literary journalist, given to attacking inflated reputations – in particular, EDITH SITWELL – and championing excellent but little-known poets, such as E. J. SCOVELL and CLERE PARSONS. His early poetry, in *Several Observations: Thirty-Five Poems* (1939), *Under the Cliff* (1943) and *The Isles of Scilly* (1946), consists of precise, imagistic observations of the world. Later poems are less austere, more emotional, including the excellent sequence of love-poems *Legenda Suecana* (1953). After *Collected Poems* (1963), other volumes include *A Skull in Salop* (1967), *Ingestion of Ice Cream* (1969), *Discoveries of Bones and Stories* (1971), *Collected Poems 1963–1980* (1982) and *Montaigne's Tree* (1984). He wrote an autobiography, *The Crest on the Silver* (1950), and many books on nature, literature and art, as well as editing several Faber anthologies and selections of JOHN CLARE and WILLIAM BARNES which helped to restore them to common currency.

Grimald, Nicholas 1519–62 Translator and poet. After studying at Christ's College, Cambridge, Grimald became chaplain to Bishop Ridley and consequently fell under suspicion in Mary's reign, a suspicion he dispelled by abandoning Protestantism. The first extant edition of his translation of Cicero's *De officiis* is dated 1556, but there may have been an earlier one. His Latin paraphrase of Virgil's *Georgics* was printed in 1591. He wrote two plays, both in Latin and both printed at Cologne. *Christus redivivus* (1543), on the Resurrection, is subtitled a tragicomedy (*comoedia tragica*) and probably had performances in Germany. *Archipropheta* (1548) is a tragedy on the life and death of St John the Baptist. Grimald's main significance for English literature lies in his contribution of some 40 poems to TOTTEL'S MISCELLANY, which he may have edited.

Grocyn, William ?1446–1519 Humanist. Grocyn's significance lies in his introduction of the study of Greek at Oxford, and his connections with the circle surrounding ERASMUS and THOMAS MORE, his student. He was educated at Winchester School and New College, Oxford, which he entered in 1465, and afterwards held various ecclesiastical offices. He studied in Italy under Poliziano and learned Greek with the tutors of the children of Lorenzo de' Medici. In Italy he became acquainted with the Venetian printer Aldus Manutius. On his return to Oxford he taught Greek there, although according to one of Erasmus's letters he had taught Greek at Oxford even before his Italian visit of 1488. When JOHN COLET became Dean of St Paul's, Grocyn preached there at his invitation, notably on pseudo-Dionysius. The only known works of Grocyn are a letter of his to Aldus prefaced to LINACRE's *Sphaera Procli* (*c.* 1499) and an EPIGRAM on a lady who threw a snowball at him.

Grose, Francis ?1731–91 Antiquary and draughtsman. Grose was born in Greenford, Middlesex, the son of a Swiss jeweller. He did not attend a university, but studied art and became a member of the Incorporated Society of Artists. He was best known as a maker of 'tinted drawings, chiefly of architectural remains'. Grose was Richmond Herald in 1755–63, and then served in the army until his death. Between 1773 and 1787 he published the four folio volumes of his *Antiquities of England and Wales*; the text was not entirely his own but he was responsible for most of the drawings. In 1789–91 he published *The Antiquities of Scotland*; his *Antiquities of Ireland* appeared posthumously in 1791–5. *Essays on Gothic Architecture* (1800) contained work by, among others, Grose and THOMAS WARTON THE YOUNGER.

The art of caricature, military antiquarianism (especially armour), local proverbs and superstitions all caught the interest of this 'antiquarian Falstaff'. He was also a pioneer in the lexicography of slang and published *A Classical Dictionary of the Vulgar Tongue* in 1785. This was reissued in 1811 as *Lexicon Balatronicum: A Dictionary of Buckish Slang, University Wit and Pickpocket Eloquence*, and edited by PIERCE EGAN in 1823.

Grosseteste, Robert ?1167–1253 Churchman and scholar. Grosseteste was born in Stradbroke, Suffolk. His early years are poorly documented; he would seem to have studied at Oxford, then Paris, returning to Oxford to be the first chancellor of the university. When the Franciscans arrived in England in 1224, Grosseteste was appointed their lecturer. He maintained warm lifelong relations with them. He held several preferments between 1214 and 1232, all of which he resigned because of illness, except his Lincolnshire prebend. When Hugh de Wells died in 1235, Grosseteste was elected his successor as bishop of Lincoln. He was immediately active in the reform of abuses, beginning a series of 'visits' to monasteries, a much disliked practice. He was involved in disputes with Henry III over various church appointments, with Archbishop Boniface over the latter's right to 'visit', and with the Pope, again over church appointments. In 1252, shortly before his death, he withstood the King's appeal for money for a new crusade.

Grosseteste was an energetic writer, and regarded by contemporaries as one of 'the greatest clerics in the world'. The range of materials covered is immense. There are letters; sermons; biblical and Aristotelian commentaries; translations from the Greek (including John of Damascus, *The Testament of the Twelve Patriarchs*, Dionysius the Areopagite, and Aristotle); scientific treatises; and a long Anglo-Norman allegorical poem on the history of salvation from the Fall of Adam to the Resurrection of Christ. Matthew Paris's *Chronicle* contains fascinating anecdotes of Grosseteste's life.

Grossmith, George 1847–1912 and **Grossmith, Weedon** 1854–1919 Joint authors of THE DIARY OF A NOBODY (1892), which Weedon also illustrated, and for which they are now principally remembered. George started his career as a police court reporter for *The Times*, Weedon as an artist. Both brothers later became actors, George creating many of the most famous baritone *buffo* roles in GILBERT and Sullivan's SAVOY OPERAS, and Weedon eventually becoming manager of Terry's Theatre. Weedon also wrote a novel, *A Woman with a History* (1896), and several plays, of which the most successful was *The Night of the Party* (1901). George published two volumes of memoirs, *Reminiscences of a Clown* (1888) and *Piano and I* (1910).

Grote, George 1794–1871 Historian. The son of a banking family, Grote was born at Beckenham in Kent and educated at Charterhouse School. He was a follower of BENTHAM and JAMES MILL, publishing pamphlets in support of reform. He entered the family business in 1830, and in 1832 became MP for the City of London. From 1823 he worked intermittently on his *A History of Greece*, and after retiring from Parliament (1841) and banking (1843) he devoted himself to its completion. It was published in 12 volumes (1845–6) and surpassed the similar work (1835–44) by his friend from Charterhouse days, CONNOP THIRLWALL. Grote wrote two works on Greek philosophy: *Plato and the Other Companions of Sokrates* (1865) and *Aristotle* (published posthumously, 1872).

Group, The An informal circle of poets which flourished from the mid-1950s until 1965. Although it was initiated by PHILIP HOBSBAUM in Cambridge, the Group came to meet in EDWARD LUCIE-SMITH's home in London, once a week, to discuss and give unrestrained yet objective criticism of each other's poems. Those attending included PETER PORTER, GEORGE MACBETH, PETER REDGROVE and ALAN BROWNJOHN. The Group came to prominence with *A Group Anthology* (1963), edited by Hobsbaum and Lucie-Smith. The participants' critical perspective demanded poems that were immediately and easily understood, and poems were accordingly written to be read aloud, giving attention to the possibilities of the spoken voice. From 1965, under the influence of MARTIN BELL, the Group transmuted into the Poets' Workshop.

Group of Noble Dames, A Ten short stories by THOMAS HARDY, published in various periodicals in 1889 and 1890 and collected in 1891.

They derive from Dorset local history and particularly from Hardy's reading of John Hutchins's *History and Antiquities of the County of Dorset* (1861–73). Largely romantic and melodramatic, and set in various mansions and castles, they deal with such themes as 'the poor man and the lady', confusion (intentional or unintentional) of identity and sexual temptation. Hardy rewrote and bowdlerized a good deal in gathering them together.

Group Theatre, The A New York theatrical organization, founded in 1931 by a group formally associated with the Theatre Guild, including Lee Strasberg, Harold Clurman and Cheryl Crawford. In rebellion against the apolitical nature of the Guild's productions, the founders were committed to the stage as a forum for the open discussion of political and social issues. PAUL GREEN's *The House of Connelly* (1931) was their first production. The Group helped to launch the careers of the playwrights CLIFFORD ODETS and MARC BLITZSTEIN, and during its nine-year career produced some of the most enduring plays of the decade, including SIDNEY KINGSLEY's *Men in White* (1933), Paul Green and Kurt Weill's *Johnny Johnson* (1936), Irwin Shaw's *The Gentle People* (1939), WILLIAM SAROYAN's *My Heart's in the Highlands* (1939) and many plays by Clifford Odets, among them AWAKE AND SING! (1935), WAITING FOR LEFTY (1935), *Golden Boy* (1937), *Rocket to the Moon* (1938) and *Night Music* (1940). The Group ceased production in 1940.

Grove, Frederick Philip 1871–1948 Canadian novelist and essayist. Born in Russia, the son of a wealthy family, Grove spent his youth travelling Europe with his mother and attempting various careers in a dilettante fashion. While touring Canada he heard of his father's death and bankruptcy and thereafter spent many years working as an itinerant farm hand in the West. At 42 he became a teacher in Manitoba and worked at his writing, but the first book to be accepted, *Over Prairie Trails*, did not appear until 1922. It was followed by *The Turn of the Year* (1923) and *Settlers of the Marsh* (1925), a powerful and penetrating novel, condemned at the time as obscene. Persevering in spite of considerable hardship, Grove published *A Search for America*, a book he had been working at for many years, in 1927. His later works were *Our Daily Bread* (1928), *It Needs to be Said* (a volume of essays; 1929), *The Yoke of Life* (1930), *Fruits of the Earth* (1933), *Two Generations* (1939), *The Master of the Mill* (1944) and *Consider Her Ways* (1946). *In Search of Myself* (1946) is an autobiography. Regarded as Canada's first accomplished exponent of realistic fiction, Grove left 'Felix Powell's Career' and 'The Seasons', which he thought his best work, unfinished at his death.

Grub Street A term for busy hack writers and impoverished scribblers, journalists and word-peckers on the fringes of the professional literary industry, derived from an actual street in Moorfields which no longer exists. It is particularly applied to certain categories of minor Renaissance and Augustan literature – almanacs, verses, pamphlets, BROADSIDES – of indifferent literary quality. There is a definitive study of this subculture in *Grub Street* (1972) by Pat Rogers. See also GISSING, GEORGE.

Grundy, Sydney 1848–1914 Playwright. He was born and educated in Manchester, where he was working as a barrister when his first play, *A Little Change* (1872), was staged. Grundy's normal practice was to adapt, and if necessary clean up, French plays. Bowdlerized and reshaped versions of the works of Alexandre Dumas *père* – *A Marriage of Convenience* (1897), *The Silver Key* (1897), *The Musketeers* (1898), *The Black Tulip* (1899) – are typical, as is his best-known work, *A Pair of Spectacles* (1890), an adaptation from *Les Petits Oiseaux* by Labiche and Delacour. An outspoken opponent of the 'demoralizing' Ibsen, Grundy nevertheless provided Lillie Langtry with a *succès de scandale* in *The Degenerates* (1899), and enjoyed playing with fire in *A Fool's Paradise* (1889), a response to the Maybrick trial, and *Slaves of the Ring* (1894), in which he brushed with the adulterous passion of Tristan and Isolde. In the year of his death he published an outrageously reactionary booklet, *The Play of the Future: by a Playwright of the Past*.

Gryll Grange THOMAS LOVE PEACOCK's last novel, published in 1860–1. The setting is a house party held at the edge of the New Forest. The host, Mr Gryll, personifies the England of the immediate rosy past, as it exists in the minds of those who dislike the present. Taking part in the conversations which make up much of the book are: Dr Opimian, an amiable clergyman, comfortable and erudite; Mr Falconer, a romantic, though he has no delusions about reforming mankind; and Miss Ilex, an old maid of real charm.

Guardian, The A daily journal of essays, letters and news, founded and mainly edited by RICHARD STEELE during its short life from March to October 1713. ADDISON, who took over in the month of July, restored a measure of the political neutrality which in Steele's hands had given way to attacks on the Tory *EXAMINER*. The authorship of the 175 numbers has still not been satisfactorily established but, apart from Addison and Steele, contributors included: TICKELL, who wrote a series of papers on PASTORAL; POPE, who wrote at least eight issues, the most famous (No. 40) being an ironic paean on the pastorals of AMBROSE PHILIPS; BERKELEY; and GAY. Steele issued the first number of *The Englishman* five days after *The Guardian* came to an unexpectedly sudden end.

Guare, John 1938– American playwright. Born in New York, he attended Georgetown University and Yale and has taught at several universities. Major works since he first gained recognition with *Muzeeka* (1968) and *The House of Blue Leaves* (1970) include the adaptation and lyrics for *Two Gentlemen of Verona* (1971), *Rich and Famous* (1974), *The Landscape of the Body* (1977), *Bosoms and Neglect* (1979) and his most successful play, *Six Degrees of Separation* (1990). *Lydie Breeze* (1982), *Gardenia* (1982) and *Women and Water* (1984–5) belong to a projected tetralogy set in 19th-century New England. Though some critics have found his work too cerebral, few have failed to praise the lyrical and theatrical use of language. His distinguished screenplay for Louis Malle's *Atlantic City* (1981) shows his taste for SATIRE. *Moon over Miami* (1988) was originally meant as screenplay for the late John Belushi.

Gude and Godlie Ballatis A collection of Protestant hymns compiled and partly composed by the brothers James, John and Robert Wedderburn. The earliest surviving copy is 1567, but there must have been earlier editions. Many of the hymns are sacred versions of popular BALLADS, and some are anti-Catholic in sentiment.

Guest, Lady Charlotte See CELTIC REVIVAL and *MABINOGION, THE*.

Guest, Edwin 1800–80 Historian and philologist. Born at King's Norton in Worcestershire and educated at Gonville and Caius College, Cambridge, Guest became a fellow of the college in 1824 and master in 1852, a position he held until his death. With THOMAS ARNOLD, A. P. STANLEY and CONNOP THIRLWALL he was a founder of the Philological Society in 1842. Guest wrote *A History of English Rhythms* (1838) and various papers on philology and Romano-British history.

Guilpin, Everard *fl*. 1595–1600 Satirist. Little is known of Guilpin, save that he was educated at Emmanuel College, Cambridge, and Gray's Inn. His *Skialetheia* (1598), a collection of EPIGRAMS, displays intimate knowledge of contemporary theatre.

Gulliver's Travels (*Travels into Several Remote Nations of the World, in Four Parts, by Lemuel Gulliver...*) A prose SATIRE by JONATHAN SWIFT, first published anonymously in 1726 and subsequently one of the most reprinted books in the English language.

Swift probably began work on this book in 1721, and its original conception seems to have been as part of the MEMOIRS OF MARTINUS SCRIBLERUS. It is divided into four books, but the third was written last of all. Books I and II are the best known, but usually in an abridged form, since there is a degree of physical coarseness in the original, which has become misleadingly notorious.

In Book I Lemuel Gulliver, the ship's surgeon who narrates the story, is shipwrecked on the island of Lilliput, where he is taken prisoner by the population, who are only six inches tall. The Emperor and his diminutive court offer a physical counterpart to the small-minded attitudes shown as underlying human behaviour, for they are suspicious, deceitful and petty. There are several specific satires on contempo-

Gulliver meets the Houyhnhnms and the Yahoos: an illustration by Thomas Stothard to Book IV of *Gulliver's Travels* for *The Novelist's Magazine,* 1782

rary topics such as religious disputes (which end an egg should be opened) and in-fighting at court (rope-dancing).

In Book II Gulliver's next voyage sees him stranded in Brobdingnag, a kingdom where the gigantic inhabitants are twelve times taller than himself. His own attitudes and pomposity are exposed when, after a series of undignified adventures, he is interviewed by the King about European civilization. The swaggering description by Gulliver of the marvels of gunpowder and the splendours of the judicial system, to his surprise, fill the monarch with horror and he ends the audience with this verdict: 'I cannot but conclude the Bulk of your Natives, to be the most pernicious Race of little odious Vermin that Nature ever suffered to crawl upon the surface of the Earth.'

Book III is less unified, and has always held least appeal. Gulliver visits Laputa, a flying island where the nobles quite literally have their heads in the clouds. So immersed are they in impractical theories of knowledge that nothing works properly. He visits nearby Lagado and its Academy (a satire on the Royal Society), which is full of 'projectors' working on outlandish scientific schemes – breeding sheep with no wool, extracting sunbeams from cucumbers – several of which had real counterparts in Swift's age. Gulliver visits Glubbdubrib, the Island of Sorcerers, where famous historical figures are summoned from the past, to his disillusionment. He also meets the terrifying race of immortals, the Struldbruggs, whose fate is to become increasingly decrepit and despised.

Book IV is perhaps the most intellectual in concept, describing the country of the Houyhnhnms, coldly rational horse-like creatures who govern their nature dispassionately and keep in subservience the filthy brutes called Yahoos, in whom Gulliver distastefully finds a resemblance to himself. The two races represent the extremes of human potential, bestial physicality and remote rationality. Gulliver returns home thoroughly imbalanced in outlook, and passes most of his time in the stable, preferring the company of his horse to that of his family.

From the earliest days of its popularity, *Gulliver's Travels* has fooled readers into agreeing with attitudes it satirizes: one contemporary reader declared he didn't believe a word of it. It is a seriously reductive work, a satire on pride and folly; Gulliver himself is a human ambassador, gullible, snobbish and servile, and his opinions are often ridiculous, yet common. The book is also lastingly funny, the hero's antics arising entertainingly from the bizarre proportions of his various surroundings: there is an element of the fantastic, as well as the satirical, and it is this which has maintained its appeal for children in many languages. There is debate about whether the *Travels* counts as an early novel, or not. It is safest to label it a philosophical romance, largely because there is little structural unity, and no identification with a central character. Among other things it is also in part a PARODY of travel literature, then much in fashion with the work of DAMPIER and with DEFOE'S *ROBINSON CRUSOE*.

Gunn, Mrs Aeneas 1870–1961 Australian novelist. Born Jeanie Taylor, she was educated at the University of Melbourne and conducted a private school with her sister until her marriage in 1901. She accompanied her husband to the Northern Territory, where he was manager of Elsey cattle station until his death in 1903. Out of her brief exposure to the outback Mrs Gunn created *The Little Black Princess* (1905) and *We of the Never Never* (1908). Presenting an idealized picture of Aboriginal life and of relations between the white farmers and the native population, the two books attained widespread popularity both at home and abroad.

Gunn, Neil M(iller) 1891–1973 Scottish novelist. He was born in Dunbeath, Caithness, the setting of some of his best-known novels, *Morning Tide*, *Highland River* and *The Silver Darlings*. He passed by examination into the Civil Service, returned to Scotland in 1909 and entered the Customs and Excise service in 1911, working for various distilleries and publishing *Whisky and Scotland* in 1935. With the critical success of *Highland River* (1937) he became a full-time writer, interspersing his early novels with generally less successful plays. *Morning Tide* (1930) was his first financially successful book, and the first of his sensitive and symbolic accounts of a boy's growing up in the Highlands, the centre of many of the novels. He also attempted historical fiction. *Sun Circle* (1933) deals with the Viking invasion of Scotland, *Butcher's Broom* (1934) with the Highland Clearances in Sutherland, and *The Silver Darlings* (1941), widely considered his best novel, with the aftermath of the Clearances. During World War II, spurred on by the complaint of his friend NAOMI MITCHISON that the pastoral idyll of *Young Art and Old Hector* (1942) was an insufficient response to the dangers of fascism, he wrote *The Green Isle of the Great Deep* (1944), in which Art and Hector find their way to a dystopian world. The case against totalitarian rule and police states was repeated in later books. A friend of HUGH MACDIARMID, Gunn was also a socialist and involved in the politics of nationalism: although not himself a Gaelic speaker, he was concerned at the decline of Gaelic speech and culture. His later fiction culminates in the 'wise humour' of a more 'metaphysical' vision of existence in *The Well at the World's End* (1951). He produced essays, short stories, travel writings and *The Atom of Delight* (1956), his autobiography.

Gunn, Thom(son) (William) 1929– Poet. Born in Gravesend, he attended University College School,

London, and, after national service, read English at Trinity College, Cambridge. The tight verse forms and anti-romanticism of his first collection, *Fighting Terms* (1954), identified him with the MOVEMENT, though he lacked its reductive IRONY. In 1954 he moved permanently to the USA, where he has held a creative writing fellowship at Stanford University and come under the influence of YVOR WINTERS. Subsequent collections include: *The Sense of Movement* (1957), dominated by a Sartrean existentialism; *My Sad Captains* (1961), marking the start of his experiments with syllabics; *Touch* (1967); *Moly* (1971), a product of late-1960s hope; *Jack Straw's Castle* (1976); *Selected Poems 1950–1975* (1979); *The Passages of Joy* (1982), relaxed, anecdotal and open about his homosexuality; *The Man with the Night Sweats* (1992), ending with a series of poems about the death of friends from AIDS. Not always well received (Gunn has too often been written off by critics), they nevertheless testify to a relentless, unpredictable development. He has also published *The Occasions of Poetry: Essays in Criticism and Autobiography* (1982) and acknowledged his roots in the 16th and 17th centuries by his editions of FULKE GREVILLE (1968) and BEN JONSON (1974).

Gurney, Ivor (Bertie) 1890–1937 Poet and composer. Born in Gloucester, he attended the Royal College of Music from 1911, and served in the Gloucester Regiment on the Western Front as a private from 1915. After being gassed and wounded at Passchendaele in September 1917, he was sent to Bangor War Hospital, Edinburgh. He published two volumes of poetry, *Severn and Somme* (1917) and *War's Embers* (1919). The war damaged an already unstable mental condition, and he was committed in 1922. From December of that year until his death he stayed at the City of London Mental Hospital, Kent, where he continued to write and compose.

All his papers were preserved by Marion Scott. When preparing some texts for an issue of *Music and Letters* devoted to Gurney in 1938, Gerald Finzi wrote that 70 out of every 100 poems showed 'no sign of mental disturbance'. The first edition of the poems was by EDMUND BLUNDEN, whose selection of the post-war work appeared in 1954. A second by Leonard Clark in 1973 was followed by the *Collected Poems* edited by P. J. KAVANAGH (1982) – yet this, too, was a selection because Gurney often wrote several poems on one theme or idea, rather than drafts of a developing single poem. The poems in the two early volumes are either reflections on the Gloucestershire countryside (such as the song 'Only the Wanderer') or local incidents in the trenches. His best war poems, such as 'The Silent One', were written later and are modest and unrhetorical. The poems written in mental hospital are uneven, apparently lacking in control but often recovering vision and language to illuminate something anew. Gurney was impressed by the poetry and prose of EDWARD THOMAS, and set six of the poems to music in the sequence *Lights Out* (1918–25). He also composed two cycles on poems by A. E. HOUSMAN, *Ludlow and Teme* and *The Western Playland* (both 1919).

Gustafson, Ralph 1909– Canadian poet. Born in Lime Ridge, Quebec, he was educated at Bishop's University, Lennoxville, and Oxford University. After a brief period teaching school in Canada, he lived in England, where his first volumes of verse were published, from 1934 to 1938. He then settled in New York, working for the British Information Services between 1942 and 1946. He returned to Canada in 1960 and was poet-in-residence and professor of English at Bishop's University. For many years he was a music critic for the Canadian Broadcasting Corporation, and his poetry is characterized by an attempt to achieve the condition of music. Gustafson is one of the most prolific and accomplished Canadian poets of his generation. His career falls into several distinct phases. The conventional romantic verse of his English years yielded to the new sardonic style he found in New York, apparent in *Flight into Darkness* (1944). With his return to Canada, his poetic style changed again and his more recent work, especially that which deals with his experiences as a traveller, is frequently confessional. It includes *Rivers among Rocks* (1960), *Rocky Mountain Poems* (1960), *Sift in an Hourglass* (1966), *Ixion's Wheel* (1969), *Corners in the Glass* (1977), *Soviet Poems* (1978), *Conflicts of Spring* (1981) and *The Celestial Corkscrew and Other Strategies* (1988). *The Moment is All* (1983) is a selection of his verse from 1944 to 1983. Gustafson has also edited several anthologies, including *The Penguin Book of Canadian Verse* (1958, revised 1967).

Guthlac, St Two versions of Guthlac's life exist in Old English verse, known as *Guthlac A* and *Guthlac B*. The first was probably written during his lifetime or shortly after his death, while the second is based on the Latin *Vita Guthlaci* by Felix of Crowland. Both describe the life of the saint who became a monk and then a hermit (in 699) living a life of severe asceticism in the Lincolnshire Fens. He died in 714 or 715 and Crowland Abbey was later built on the site of his burial.

Guy Livingstone A novel by GEORGE ALFRED LAWRENCE, published in 1857. Guy is the true patrician hero, with the virtues and failings of his class: pride, courage, sportsmanship and readiness to fight. He starts by protecting a weaker boy (the narrator) at school, rescues him from police custody after an Oxford rag with a well-aimed blow, and defeats a professional boxer. In the hunting field none can match him. Guy becomes engaged to a gentle girl called Constance but his engagement is broken because of the machinations of heartless Flora. Guy and Constance are reconciled only on her deathbed. Eventually a fall on the hunting field cripples Guy and he dies. The author describes aristocratic violence with bloodthirsty gusto, and his moral stance is ambiguous.

Guy Mannering A novel by SIR WALTER SCOTT, published in 1815.

The action takes place in the 18th century. The title notwithstanding, it is the story of Harry Bertram, heir to Ellangowan, kidnapped as a child at the instigation of the lawyer Glossin, who hopes to gain the estate himself. Bertram grows up with the name of Brown, serves with the army in India, earns the good opinion of his colonel, Guy Mannering, and falls in love with the colonel's daughter Julia. A misunderstanding leads Mannering to believe that Harry is paying attentions to his wife. A duel follows and Harry is left for dead, but he recovers and returns to England. Finding that Julia is in Dumfries, in the neighbourhood of Ellangowan, he makes his way there.

On his journey he helps the Lowland farmer Dandy Dinmont beat off a gang of thieves, and on arrival at Ellangowan (now in the hands of Glossin) he is recognized by Meg Merrilies, a gypsy woman devoted to the Bertrams. Glossin is determined to have Bertram murdered before he can discover his true parentage. The plot is frustrated by Meg, with the help of Dandy, and Glossin meets his death at the hands of his henchman, Hatteraick. The novel ends happily, with Bertram regaining his inheritance and Guy Mannering's good opinion, thus leaving the way clear for his marriage to Julia.

Guy of Warwick An early 14th-century Middle English VERSE ROMANCE, ultimately derived from an Anglo-Norman romance composed *c.* 1232–42. There are several versions of the Middle English poem, the majority written in rhyming couplets; the complete romance runs to around 12,000 lines. In plot and style it resembles BEVIS OF HAMPTON.

The poem tells of Guy, spurned by his beloved Felice because of his low status. He fights in tournaments abroad and then undertakes various adventures for seven years. He returns to England and marries Felice, but after 50 days leaves England and his pregnant wife on a pilgrimage to atone for his earlier life as a warrior. After many adventures he returns incognito to live as a hermit, revealing himself to Felice shortly before his death; she dies soon afterwards. The story also describes the adventures of Guy's son Reinbrun, stolen by pirates at the age of seven, and the steward who searches for him. The poem is over-long and packed with spurious incident, but it enjoyed popularity for several centuries, first in its original form and later in adaptations.

H. D. See DOOLITTLE, HILDA.

Habington, William 1605–54 Poet. Habington was the son of a Roman Catholic gentleman of Worcester who suffered imprisonment for his involvement in the Gunpowder Plot. He published *Castara*, a book of verse celebrating his marriage to Lucy Herbert, anonymously in 1634. An edition of 1635 added elegies on the death of a friend, while a third (1640), in which Habington is identified as the author, included religious verse as well. Habington also wrote, with his father, Thomas, *The History of Edward the Fourth* (1640), *Observations upon History* (1641) and a play, *The Queen of Arragon* (1640).

Hadrian the Seventh See ROLFE, FREDERICK WILLIAM.

Haggard, Sir Henry Rider 1856–1925 Novelist and agricultural reformer. He was the eighth of the 10 children of William Haggard, a Norfolk squire, and his wife, Ella, herself an amateur author. Haggard was educated, not at a public school like his brothers, but privately at a London day-school, and at Ipswich Grammar School, since he was seen by his father as the family dunce. Because he failed the army entrance examination, he joined the Colonial Service as personal aide to Sir Henry Bulwer, the designated Lieutenant-Governor of Natal. His two periods of residence in South Africa (1875–9 and 1880–1) were the formative years of his life. He took part in Theophilus Shepstone's annexation of the Transvaal (1877) and for the rest of his life remained convinced of the British obligation to imperial responsibility – a view he shared with his close friend, RUDYARD KIPLING.

In 1881 he began to read law; he was called to the Bar in 1885. But the runaway success of *KING SOLOMON'S MINES* (1885), *ALLAN QUATERMAIN* (1887) and *SHE: A HISTORY OF ADVENTURE* (1887) meant that instead he became an established member of the literary scene of the 1880s, as a co-founder (with ROBERT LOUIS STEVENSON) of a new 'school of romance' which was seen by the literary journals of the period as a healthy antidote to both analytic fiction and NATURALISM. Haggard's romances develop a private myth of the heroic. His fascination with the Zulu culture can be seen in his portraits of Umbopa in *King Solomon's Mines* and Umslopogaas in *Allan Quatermain* and *Nada the Lily* (1892), as well as in his distinguished Zulu trilogy, *Marie* (1912), *Child of Storm* (1913) and *Finished* (1917). His versions of the 'primitive' are complex, by no means simply paternalist or racist, and his novels draw upon a considerable knowledge of history, tradition and mythographic theory, probably encouraged by his friendship with ANDREW LANG, with whom he collaborated in the writing of *The World's Desire* (1890). Apart from his African romances, his best works are *Eric Brighteyes* (1891), a recreation of the spirit of the Icelandic sagas, and *Montezuma's Daughter* (1893), a version of Cortes's conquest of Mexico which, in its sympathy for a martyred culture and its hostility to colonialism, anticipates CONRAD'S *HEART OF DARKNESS*.

Haggard's marriage in 1880 to Louise Margitson, heiress to the estate of Ditchingham House, Norfolk, led to his expertise in farming – an interest which produced *A Farmer's Year* (1899) and, more importantly, *Rural England* (1902). This vast survey of agricultural decline brought him into professional contact with THOMAS HARDY. Haggard served on many Royal Commissions, and it was for his public service that he was knighted in 1912. His autobiography, *The Days of My Life*, was published posthumously in 1926.

Hajji Baba of Ispahan, The Adventures of See MORIER, JAMES JUSTINIAN.

Hakluyt, Richard ?1552–1616 Historian and travel-writer. He was educated at Westminster School and Christ Church, Oxford. He was ordained some time before 1580 and held various ecclesiastical posts, including the chaplaincy to the English ambassador in Paris and the archdeaconry of Westminster, to which he was appointed in 1603. His interest in travel was aroused when, as a boy, he visited the Middle Temple and his imagination was stirred by being shown 'certain books of cosmography with an universal map'. He decided to dedicate himself to collecting, publishing and translating accounts of voyages. He was acquainted with sea-captains like SIR HUMPHREY GILBERT and Martin Frobisher, corresponded with the map-makers Ortelius and Mercator, and gave information to the newly founded East India Company. He also gave public lectures on exploration and is regarded as the first professor of modern geography at Oxford. His activities and campaigns for voyages of discovery gained the interest and approval of some of Elizabeth's most influential advisers: Lord Burghley, Sir Francis Walsingham and Sir Robert Cecil. His views on the foundation of a plantation in America are set out in a preface to JOHN FLORIO's translation of an account of the voyage of Jacques Cartier.

In publishing and collecting voyages Hakluyt deserved MICHAEL DRAYTON's epithet 'industrious'. *Divers Voyages Touching the Discovery of America* was published in 1582 and a translation from the

French, *A Notable History concerning Four Voyages Made by Certain French Captains into Florida*, in 1587. In support of RALEIGH's plan for colonizing Virginia he wrote *A Discourse concerning the Western Planting* in 1584, although this was not printed until 1831. His major work, *The Principal Navigations, Voyages and Discoveries of the English Nation* (1589), was enlarged and published in three volumes in 1598–1600. After his death SAMUEL PURCHAS continued his work with the aid of Hakluyt's manuscripts. As well as containing information that was useful to his contemporaries, Hakluyt's *Voyages* are full of adventurous stories: Cabot's discovery of Hudson Bay, Drake's raid on Cadiz and the last fight of the *Revenge* under Sir Richard Grenville.

Haldane, J(ohn) B(urdon) S(anderson)

1892–1964 Writer on science. He was born in Oxford and educated at Eton and New College, Oxford. During World War I he studied the effects of gas warfare and was involved in designing a more effective gas mask. In 1919 he became a Fellow of New College and taught physiology. Two years later he was appointed reader in biochemistry at Cambridge, and in 1933 he became professor of genetics at University College, London (later professor of biometry, 1937–57).

During the Spanish Civil War Haldane joined the Communist Party, and became chairman of the editorial board of *The Daily Worker* from 1940 to 1949. In 1957 he emigrated to India, where he established a genetics and biometry laboratory, and became a naturalized citizen in 1960.

Haldane's scientific works include *Enzymes* (1930) and *The Causes of Evolution* (1932), but it was as a popularizer of science that he became more widely known. His imaginative speculations about the future (see *Possible Worlds*, 1927) provided many of the scientific ideas to be found in the works of ALDOUS HUXLEY (see *BRAVE NEW WORLD*). *The Marxist Philosophy and the Sciences* (1938) was one of several works which emphasized the social and political context of science; others include *Science and Everyday Life* (1939) and *Everything Has a History* (1951). He also wrote a collection of children's stories, *My Friend Mr Leakey* (1937).

Hale, Sir Matthew

1609–76 Judicial writer. Educated at Magdalen Hall, Oxford, Hale became a judge in the Court of Common Pleas (1654), Baron of the Exchequer (1660) and Chief Justice of the King's Bench (1671). As a writer on law he is best known for his *History of the Common Law in England* (1713), published, like most of his work, after his death. He was the subject of a biography by GILBERT BURNET.

Hale, Sarah

1788–1879 American humanitarian. She edited *The Ladies' Magazine* from 1828 to 1837,

and *Godey's Lady's Book* for the next 40 years. Her novel *Northwood: A Tale of New England* (1827) is a didactic condemnation of slavery. Her short stories were collected in *Sketches of American Character* (1829). The later part of her career was dedicated to compiling her massive *Women's Record* (1853; expanded 1855 and 1870), an encyclopedic work that details the achievements of over 1500 distinguished women. By no means a radical feminist, Hale upheld a traditional view of women as bearers of spiritual and moral virtue. She was, however, a forceful advocate of education for women, as well as child welfare and the abolition of slavery.

Hales, John

1584–1656 Scholar and divine. Fellow of Merton College, Oxford, Regius Professor of Greek, canon of Windsor and fellow of Eton, Hales was, according to CLARENDON, 'one of the greatest scholars in Europe'. In religion, he contended that guidance of Scripture was the rightful way for each individual, and he opposed both the coercion of Rome and the extremism of Calvinism. His sermons and tracts were collected by JOHN PEARSON and published as *Golden Remains* (1659).

Haley, Russell

1934– New Zealand short-story writer and novelist. Born in Yorkshire, he emigrated first to Australia and then to New Zealand, where he has lived since the 1960s. As a mature student at Auckland University he was, with Murray Edmond, part of the group involved with the magazine *Freed*. After publishing two volumes of poetry he turned to fiction with a collection of stories, *The Sauna Bath Mysteries* (1978), one of the earliest examples of POST-MODERNISM in New Zealand writing. He has continued in this mode in another collection, *Real Illusions* (1985), and two novels, *The Settlement* (1986) and *Beside Myself* (1990). He has also co-edited *The Penguin Book of Contemporary New Zealand Short Stories* (1989) and written *Hanly* (1989), a study of the New Zealand painter.

Haliburton, Thomas Chandler

1796–1865 Canadian satirist and humorist. Born and educated in Windsor, Nova Scotia, he was called to the Bar in 1820 and eventually became a judge of the supreme court of the province. In 1829 he published *A Historical and Statistical Account of Nova Scotia* (the source of LONGFELLOW's *EVANGELINE*), and was persuaded by the publisher Joseph Howe to contribute to the latter's paper, *The Novascotian*, in 1835. Haliburton's contributions took the form of the 'Sam Slick' papers, observations by a shrewd itinerant clockmaker on life on the Eastern shore of America. The sketches were collected and published as *The Clockmaker: or, the Sayings and Doings of Samuel Slick* (1837). Further series followed, including *The Attaché: or, Sam Slick in England* (1843–4), which was, in effect, a reply to

DICKENS's *AMERICAN NOTES*. Among other titles by Haliburton are *The Letter Bag of the Great Western: or, Life in a Steamer* (1840) and *The Old Judge: or, Life in a Colony* (1849). Haliburton retired to England in 1856, where he held the parliamentary seat for Launceston for six years. ARTEMUS WARD declared that the American homespun philosophy and frontier humour practised by himself, MARK TWAIN and JOSH BILLINGS stemmed directly from Haliburton.

Hall [*née* Fielding], **Anna Maria** 1800–81 Irish novelist. Born in Dublin, she lived in England from the age of 15, marrying SAMUEL CARTER HALL in 1824. Her most successful works were delicate and humorous portraits of Irish life, among them *Sketches of Irish Character* (1829), *Lights and Shadows of Irish Life* (1838), *Marian* (1839) and *The White Boy* (1845). She also edited magazines and annuals, including *Finden's Tableaux* and *The Juvenile Forget-Me-Not*.

Hall, Edward ?1498–1547 A lawyer and historian, Hall went to school at Eton, graduated from King's College, Cambridge, in 1518 and then proceeded to Gray's Inn. He was a staunch supporter of Henry VIII and the Tudor dynasty. *The Union of the Two Noble and Illustre Families of Lancaster and York* (the first edition of 1542 is very rare, second edition 1548) traces a providential pattern in English history, beginning with the accession of Henry IV and ending, in Grafton's edition and continuation from Hall's notes (1550), with the death of Henry VIII. The work was prohibited in the reign of Queen Mary. It was a source for later historians, especially RAPHAEL HOLINSHED, and dramatists. Because Holinshed drew on Hall it is at times difficult to be certain which of them SHAKE-SPEARE is using in his history plays, but Hall seems to have directly contributed at least details to the *HENRY VI* and *HENRY IV* plays, *HENRY V*, *RICHARD II* and *RICHARD III*.

Hall, John 1627–56 Essayist, poet and translator. A member of the group of friends that included THOMAS STANLEY and William Hammond, John Hall earned praise from ROBERT HERRICK, HENRY MORE and THOMAS HOBBES in the course of his short career. His work included a book of lively essays, *Horae vacivae* (1646), *Poems* (1647) and the first English translation of Longinus. *An Humble Motion to the Parliament of England concerning the Advancement of Learning: and Reformation of the Universities* was written when he was 22.

Hall, Joseph 1574–1656 Satirist and divine. Born at Ashby-de-la-Zouch and educated at Emmanuel College, Cambridge, Hall took holy orders and was appointed chaplain to Prince Henry (1608); as Dean of Worcester he was one of King James's representatives at the Synod of Dort. He became Bishop of Exeter

(1627) and of Norwich (1641). A friend of JOHN DONNE and SIR THOMAS BROWNE, he was a versatile writer. The verse SATIRES in *Virgidemiarum* (1597 and 1598) are, with those of Donne, among the first in English to follow classical models. *Mundus alter et idem* (1605) is a prose satire, translated into English by J. Healey (1609). His religious writings include devotional works, notably *Meditations and Vows* (1605), and *Episcopacy by Divine Right, Asserted by J. H.* (1641), a reply to SMECTYMNUUS which brought him into conflict with MILTON. Hall was one of the 13 bishops imprisoned by Parliament in 1642 and was evicted from his palace in 1647.

Hall, (Marguerite) Radclyffe 1886–1943 Novelist and poet. Born in Bournemouth, she was educated at King's College, London, and in Germany. She published four volumes of verse – *'Twixt Earth and Stars* (1906), *Poems of the Past and Present* (1910), *Songs of Three Countries* (1913) and *The Forgotten Island* (1915) – before producing the novels for which she is known. *The Forge* (1924) was followed by *The Unlit Lamp* (1924) and *Adam's Breed* (1926), which won the Femina Vie Heureuse and Tait Black Memorial prizes. *The Well of Loneliness* (1928), a sympathetic study of lesbianism, became the object of a notorious obscenity trial and was for some years banned in England. It has since been frequently reprinted. Her later works include *The Master of the House* (1932), *The Sixth Beatitude* (1936) and a volume of short stories, *Miss Ogilvie Finds Herself* (1934).

Hall, Rodney 1935– Australian poet and novelist. Born in England, he lives in New South Wales. His novels include: *The Ship on the Coin* (1972), satirizing the American way of life; *A Place among the People* (1975) and *Just Relations* (winner of the Miles Franklin Award; 1982), satirizing small-town Australia; *Kisses of the Enemy* (1987), about an Australia of the future dominated by America; *Captivity Captive* (1988), re-opening an unsolved murder of 1898; and *The Colony Club* (1991), set in 1950s Brisbane. Since *Penniless till Doomsday* (1962), his poetry has included *Selected Poems* (1975), *Black Bagatelles* (1978) and *The Most Beautiful World* (1981). It experiments with a structure which he calls the 'Progression', in which as many as 60 short poems are organized to work together as one large one. He was poetry editor of the *Australian* in 1967–78 and has edited well-respected anthologies.

Hall, Roger 1939– New Zealand playwright. Born in Britain, he emigrated to New Zealand in the 1950s and has become the country's most commercially successful dramatist with works such as *Glide Time* (1976; also the basis for a TV series) and *Middle-Aged Spread* (1977; also filmed). Both take an enclosed setting – an office, a dinner party – and exploit it for mainly comic ends. Though social comedy and FARCE have remained his staple, later plays such as *The Rose* (1981) and *Dream of Sussex Downs* (1986) have tackled more serious subjects. He has also collaborated on a musical, *Footrot Flats* (1983).

Hall, Samuel Carter 1800–89 Journalist and art critic. He was founder and editor of *The Art Journal*, author of *A Book of Memoirs of Great Men and Women* (1871) and co-author (with his wife ANNA MARIA HALL) of several volumes, including *Ireland: Its Scenery, Character etc.* (1841-3).

Hallam, Arthur Henry 1811–33 Poet and essayist. After Eton, he went to Trinity College, Cambridge, where he was elected to the APOSTLES and became the close friend of ALFRED TENNYSON. Hallam's sudden and untimely death in Vienna prompted Tennyson's *IN MEMORIAM*. His *Remains in Verse and Prose* (1834) was edited by his father, HENRY HALLAM. His essay on Tennyson's early poems (*The Englishman's Magazine*, August 1831) proves him one of the poet's most discerning critics.

Hallam, Henry 1777–1859 Historian. Educated at Eton and Christ Church, Oxford, he obtained a sinecure appointment as Commissioner of Stamps and, on inheriting his father's estates in Lincolnshire, was able to devote himself to writing, first as a contributor to *THE EDINBURGH REVIEW. A View of the State of Europe during the Middle Ages* (1818) took 10 years to complete and was notable for its pioneering use of primary sources. It was followed by *The Constitutional History of England from the Accession of Henry VII to the Death of George II* (1827), and *An Introduction to the Literature of Europe in the 15th, 16th and 17th Centuries* (1837-9). He also edited the *Remains in Verse and Prose* (1834) of his son, ARTHUR HENRY HALLAM.

Halleck, Fitz-Greene 1790-1867 American poet and member of the KNICKERBOCKER GROUP. He was born in Guilford, Connecticut. He worked first in banking and then as personal secretary to John Jacob Astor. He collaborated with Joseph Rodman Drake on the satirical 'Croaker' poems, published anonymously in 1819 in the New York *Evening Post* and collected as *The Croaker Papers* in 1860. His long poem *Fanny* (1819) satirized New York society in the manner of BYRON. While travelling in Europe the following year he wrote 'Alnwick Castle', influenced by SCOTT as well as Byron. Other notable poems include 'Red Jacket' (1827), 'The Field of Grounded Arms' (1831), and 'Young America' (1865). His collected *Poetical Works* were published in 1847.

Halliwell [Halliwell-Phillipps], **J(ames) O(rchard)** 1820–89 Scholar of SHAKESPEARE. Born in Chelsea

and educated at Cambridge, he was elected a Fellow of the Royal Society in 1839. Of his numerous works the most important are the *Life of Shakespeare* (1848), *New Boke about Shakespeare and Stratford-on-Avon* (1850), a *Dictionary of Old English Plays* (1860) and an edition of Shakespeare (1853-65).

Halper, Albert 1904-84 American novelist. He was born in Chicago into a poor family of Jewish immigrants. His first books were *Union Square* (1933); *On the Shore* (1934); *The Foundry* (1934), which deals with electrotype workers in Chicago just before the 1929 crash; and *The Chute* (1937), about workers in a mail-order house. *Sons of the Fathers* (1940) is the story of a Jewish immigrant. His subsequent work includes *The Little People* (1942), short stories, and the novels *Only an Inch from Glory* (1943), *The Golden Watch* (1953), and *Atlantic Avenue* (1956). *Goodbye, Union Square*, his memoir of the 1930s, appeared in 1970.

hamartia From the Greek, 'error'. In Aristotle's theory of TRAGEDY, the mistake or failing which brings about the hero's downfall. 'Tragic flaw', the usual English translation, can mislead by its concentration on moral weakness – encouraging readers to view Hamlet's fate as a condemnation of his uncertainty, or Othello's as a condemnation of his jealousy – since hamartia can also be a matter of ignorance or mistaken judgement. Aristotle's term for the hero's realization of error is ANAGNORISIS.

Hamburger, Michael (Peter Leopold) 1924– Poet, translator and critic. Born in Berlin of a German family which emigrated to Edinburgh and then London in 1933, he was educated at St Paul's School and at Oxford. His first collection of poems, *Flowering Cactus* (1950), has been followed by many others, including *Travelling* (1969), *Ownerless Earth: New and Selected Poems* (1973), *Collected Poems* (1984), *Trees* (1988), *Selected Poems* (1988), *Testimonies* (1989) and *Roots in the Air* (1991). They are frequently concerned, as their titles suggest, with the experience of rootlessness. Hamburger draws on the European tradition as much as the English, and is also a distinguished translator of Hofmannsthal (1961), Grass (1966), Hölderlin (1966) and Paul Celan (1980). His critical books include a useful introduction to the themes of modern poetry from Baudelaire to the 1960s, *The Truth of Poetry* (1969), *After the Flood: Essays on Post-War German Literature* (1986) and *A Proliferation of Prophets: German Literature from Nietzsche to Brecht* (1986).

Hamilton, Charles (Harold St John) 1876–1961 Writer of CHILDREN'S LITERATURE. Born in London, the son of a journalist, he was probably educated at small private schools rather than the sort of major public school he later described in his fiction. He had stories accepted by boys' magazines and comics while still a schoolboy, and in 1906 he created a fictional public school called St Jim's for the boys' weekly *Pluck*. School stories followed in *The Gem*, *The Magnet* and other papers, with Hamilton producing about 70,000 words a week under various pseudonyms. As Frank Richards he created the enduring characters Harry Wharton and Billy Bunter of Greyfriars school for *The Magnet*. He made a well-argued reply to GEORGE ORWELL's criticism of such stories in the essay 'Boys' Weeklies' (1939). A Billy Bunter revival after World War II resulted in books about Bunter and about Tom Merry, and kept him fully occupied until his death. The more than 50 fictional schools he invented and the more than 72 million words he wrote make Hamilton the most prolific author in the history of juvenile fiction.

Hamilton, (Robert) Ian 1938– Poet, critic and editor. Born in King's Lynn, he was educated at Darlington Grammar School and Keble College, Oxford. He founded and edited *The Review* (1962–72), which was succeeded by the glossy and controversial *NEW REVIEW* (1974–9). His own poetry, distinctive in its density and compression but limited in bulk, has appeared in *The Visit* (1970) and *Fifty Poems* (1988). He is better known for his criticism: *A Poetry Chronicle: Essays and Reviews* (1963); *The Little Magazines: A Study of Six Editors* (1976); a sympathetic and informative biography of ROBERT LOWELL (1982); a study of J. D. SALINGER (1989); *Writers in Hollywood* (1990); and *Literary Estates and the Rise of Biography* (1992).

Hamilton, Mary Agnes 1884–1966 Novelist. Born Mary Agnes Adamson, she was educated at Newnham College, Cambridge, and in Germany; she later became Labour MP for Blackburn (1929–31) and a governor of the BBC (1933–7). Her novels include *Less Than the Dust* (1912), *Dead Yesterdays* (1916), *Special Providence* (1930) and *Life Sentence* (1935). She also wrote biographies of CARLYLE (1926), JOHN STUART MILL (1933) and SIDNEY and BEATRICE WEBB (1933). Her autobiography, *Uphill All the Way*, appeared in 1953.

Hamilton, Thomas 1789–1842 Scottish novelist. The younger brother of SIR WILLIAM HAMILTON, he was author of *Cyril Thornton* (1827), a lively account of university and military life which went through three editions in his lifetime.

Hamilton, Virginia (Esther) 1936– American writer of CHILDREN'S LITERATURE. Born in Yellow Springs, Ohio, the granddaughter of an escaped slave, she is a leading black author for children, with a constantly inventive, individual imagination that defies neat classification. Her most famous story, *M. C. Higgins the Great* (1974), concerns a boy who lives on top of a high steel pole set deep in the mountainside. Other novels include a SCIENCE-FICTION trilogy and *The Planet of Junior Brown* (1971), a moving story of homeless children trying to survive in a big city. *Sweet Whispers, Brother Rush* (1987) describes how a ghost explains the meaning of their past to two deprived children while their mother is out at work.

Hamilton, Sir William 1788–1856 Scottish philosopher. Born in Glasgow and educated at Balliol College, Oxford, he studied law and became an advocate in 1813. In 1816 he established his claim to the baronetcy of Hamilton of Preston. His reputation as a philosopher was secured by a series of contributions to THE EDINBURGH REVIEW (1829–36) and he was elected professor of logic and metaphysics at Edinburgh in 1836.

Hamilton's collected articles were published in *Discussions on Philosophy and Literature, Education and University Reform* (1852). *Lectures on Metaphysics and Logic* appeared posthumously (1859–60). He also prepared an edition of the works of THOMAS REID, completed by H. L. Mansel and published in 1846. Hamilton is notable for his contribution to the study of German philosophy, and for his influential theories concerning the association of ideas, unconscious mental modifications and the inverse relation of perception and sensation. J. S. MILL attacked him as a representative of the 'intuitional' school in his *Examination of Sir W. Hamilton's Philosophy* (1865).

Hamlet, Prince of Denmark A tragedy by WILLIAM SHAKESPEARE, first performed *c.* 1601. A bad, perhaps pirated, Quarto (Q1) was published in 1603. Modern editors use a second Quarto (Q2), published in 1604, and the text in the First Folio of 1623. Both are used by modern editors. Various sources have been proposed, among them a lost play, or *Ur-Hamlet*, perhaps by THOMAS KYD. We do not know whether Elizabethan audiences were familiar with the story before Shakespeare wrote his play.

The recent death of King Hamlet has brought his brother Claudius to the Danish throne. Claudius has also married the King's widow, Gertrude. Prince Hamlet, spectacularly mourning both his father's death and his mother's remarriage, learns from his friend Horatio that his father's ghost has appeared on the battlements of Elsinore. Hamlet decides to watch with him, encounters the ghost and learns that Claudius poisoned his father. Hamlet enjoins his friends to secrecy and swears vengeance, but defers it by alternating between self-doubting soliloquies and displays of feigned madness intended to confirm Claudius's guilt. He denounces Ophelia, whom he had loved, and succeeds in convincing her father, the court chamberlain Polonius, of his madness.

The arrival of a company of actors at the Danish court provides him with further opportunity. He persuades them to stage an old play whose story offers a persuasive parallel to Claudius's crime. Claudius gives himself away, and orders Hamlet to go to England, where he plans to have him killed. Hamlet escapes his pursuers, confronts Gertrude in her chamber and stabs to death the eavesdropping Polonius, apparently on the assumption that it is Claudius, not Polonius, behind the arras. Determined to avenge Polonius's death, his son Laertes returns to Denmark, where he finds Ophelia mad. News reaches Claudius that Hamlet is back in Denmark. He plots with Laertes a duel in which Hamlet's death will be assured by a poison-tipped sword. News of Ophelia's death by drowning strengthens Laertes's resolve. The duel takes place and culminates in the death of Gertrude, Laertes, Claudius and Hamlet. The play ends with Fortinbras of Norway, newly proclaimed King of Denmark, ordering a military funeral for Hamlet.

Because the figure of Hamlet has so fascinated successive generations, the play has provoked more discussion, more performances and more scholarship than any other in the whole history of world drama. It stands at the very centre of Shakespeare's dramatic career, on the one hand concluding a decade that had seen the composition of the mature comedies and English history plays, and on the other preceding the sequence of great tragedies. In no other play does Shakespeare subject to such detailed scrutiny the whole art of theatre itself. It is not an accident that the play-within-the-play holds a central position in the pattern of the drama; all the characters are affected by the compulsion to act a part. It is an aspect of the topsy-turvydom of Denmark under Claudius that real feeling should present itself as seeming. The histrionic temperament has never been so fully explored.

Hammett, (Samuel) Dashiell 1894–1961 American writer of DETECTIVE FICTION. Born in Maryland, he served in the US army during World War I and then went to work for the Pinkerton Agency in San Francisco as a private detective. His experiences served him well when he turned to writing. He published short stories in THE BLACK MASK, which were collected in *The Adventures of Sam Spade* (1944), *The Creeping Siamese and Other Stories* (1950) and *The Continental Op* (1974). His novels are *Red Harvest* (1929), *The Dain Curse* (1929), *The Maltese Falcon* (1930), *The Glass Key* (1931) and *The Thin Man* (1934). Hammett wrote in an unadorned, realistic manner – later christened the 'hard-boiled' style – that suited his material perfectly. His heroes are not merely tough; they often confront violence with full knowledge of its inherently corrupting potential. His longtime companion, the playwright LILLIAN HELLMAN, contributed a memoir to her selection of his short stories, *The Big Knockover* (1966), which also includes his unfinished autobiographical novel, *Tulip*.

Hammon, Jupiter 1720–1800 America's first published black poet. A slave in a Long Island household, he wrote *An Evening Thought* (1760). He is also known for his essay *An Address to the Negroes of the State of New York* (1787), in which he insisted that his fellow slaves be patient, and urged owners to free slave children. His work helped generate support for the Abolitionist movement growing in the northern states.

Hammond, Henry 1605–60 Theologian. Works like his *Paraphrase and Annotations on the New Testament* (1653) have led some to call him the father of English biblical criticism. His sermons are highly regarded for their clarity and tolerant spirit.

Hampton, Christopher (James) 1946– Playwright. Born on Fayal in the Azores, he was educated at Lancing College and at New College, Oxford. His first play, *When Did You Last See My Mother?* (1966), was produced while he was still an undergraduate. From 1968 to 1970 he was resident dramatist at the ROYAL COURT THEATRE, where his finely balanced study of the relationship between Rimbaud and Verlaine, *Total Eclipse* (1968), was staged, together with his comedy of linguistic errors, *The Philanthropist* (1970). Hampton was not a typical Royal Court playwright in that he disliked left-wing polemics: *Savages* (1973) portrays left-wing rebels as more hostile to the local Indians than a so-called Imperialist. He has also sought to provide modern, actable versions of European classics, including work by Chekhov, Ibsen, Molière, Laclos (whose *Les Liaisons Dangereuses*, 1986, was Hampton's greatest success) and the Austrian dramatist Odon von Horvath, barely known in Britain before Hampton adapted *Tales from the Vienna Woods* (1977), *Don Juan Comes Back from the War* (1978) and *Faith, Hope and Charity* (1989). Horvath appears with Thomas Mann, Heinrich Mann and Brecht in *Tales from Hollywood* (1983), set in the émigré community in California during World War II. He has also adapted GEORGE STEINER's *The Portage to San Cristobal of A.H.* (1982). The remembrance of his childhood in Egypt provides one of his most appealing (if slight) plays, *White Chameleon* (1991).

Hand of Ethelberta, The: *A Comedy in Chapters* A novel by THOMAS HARDY, serialized in THE CORNHILL MAGAZINE from July 1875 to May 1876 and published in volume form in 1876. His only venture into social comedy, it is among the least read of his works.

Despite being the daughter of a butler, the heroine Ethelberta Chickerel has married the son and heir of Sir Ralph and Lady Petherwin; he, however, has died on his honeymoon and a needless quarrel with her mother-in-law has deprived Ethelberta of a handsome bequest. Determined to make her way, she gives readings and achieves recognition as a 'Professed Story-

Teller'. Meanwhile, three suitors pay her court: the painter Eustace Lovell; Alfred Neigh, a rich young man; and the elderly, affluent Lord Mountclere, of dubious reputation. Ethelberta marries Mountclere over her family's protestations, while an earlier, faithful suitor, the organist Christopher Julian, secures the hand of her sister Picotee, who has loved him from the beginning of the story.

Handful of Dust, A A novel by EVELYN WAUGH, published in 1934.

Containing many of the qualities typical of Waugh's satirical novels (mainly written during the 1930s), it tells the story of Tony Last, proud owner of a Victorian gothic country house, Hetton. Frustrated by his old-fashioned ways, his wife, Lady Brenda, becomes infatuated with a young socialite, John Beaver, and deserts Tony and the family after their son, John Andrew, is killed in a hunting accident. Tony refuses to grant her a divorce, fearing the cost of alimony and the consequent loss of his beloved Hetton. He departs for an extended trip to Brazil and accompanies a casual acquaintance, Dr Messinger, up the Amazon. They run into trouble; Tony falls ill and Messinger is drowned. At the point of death Tony is rescued by a mad recluse, Mr Todd, who has lived in the jungle for nearly 60 years. Tony recovers but is forced to become Mr Todd's 'companion', spending the rest of his life reading aloud the works of Dickens. In England he is reported dead and Brenda marries a politician, Jock Grant-Menzies, her relationship with Beaver having faded. Hetton passes into the hands of Tony's cousin, Richard Last.

An 'Alternative Ending' offers a happier version of events. Tony returns to find Hetton entirely redecorated in his absence and to be met by a repentant Brenda.

Handley Cross A novel by R. S. SURTEES, first published in book form in 1843; an expanded version (1854) was illustrated by JOHN LEECH. It continues the adventures of John Jorrocks, the sporting grocer who appeared in *JORROCKS'S JAUNTS AND JOLLITIES* (1838) and returns in *HILLINGDON HALL* (1845). Master of the Handley Cross foxhounds, he recruits as huntsman the likeable and skilful, albeit drunken, James Pigg of Newcastle and makes a (pretty useless) whipper-in of his cockney servant Binjimin. He is assisted by Charlie Stubbs (Stobbs in the 1854 version) who is paying court to his gorgeous niece Belinda, although the appalling Mrs Jorrocks would rather she married the equally dreadful Captain Doleful. There are many hunting scenes described with Surtees's usual dash and authenticity, coupled with various ridiculous adventures; towards the end of the novel Jorrocks is certified insane but returns triumphant to the discomfiture of his wife and Doleful. Mr Jorrocks's public lectures on hunting, though delivered in the broadest cockney, are replete with technical knowledge and sound common sense.

Handling Sin See MANNYNG OF BRUNNE, ROBERT.

Handy Andy: *A Tale of Irish Life* A comic novel by SAMUEL LOVER, published in 1842. It tells of Andy Rooney, the hopelessly inefficient servant of Squire Egan, and Egan's rivalry with Squire O'Grady. After a succession of humorous incidents, Andy proves to be the heir of Lord Scatterbrain.

Hanley, James 1901–85 Novelist, short-story writer and playwright. Born into a Dublin working-class family, he went to sea at the age of 13 and finally became a journalist. *Drift* (1930), *A Passion before Death* (1930), *The Last Voyage* (1931), *Men in Darkness: Five Stories* (1931) and *Boy* (1931) established him as a novelist with a powerfully direct and painstaking style. *The Furys* (1935), *Secret Journey* (1936) and *Our Time is Gone* (1940) comprise a trilogy portraying the misery of life in the Dublin slums. Other titles include *Captain Bottell* (1933), *Quartermaster Clausen* (1934), *People are Curious* (short stories; 1938), *Hollow Sea* (1938), *The Ocean* (1941), *A Walk in the Wilderness* (short stories; 1950), *The Closed Harbour* (1952), *Another World* (1972), *A Woman in the Sky* (1973) and *A Kingdom* (1978). *Broken Water* (1937) is a volume of autobiography. Plays include *Say Nothing* (1962) and *The Inner Journey* (1965).

Hannay, James 1827–73 Novelist and journalist. Born at Dumfries, he served in the navy for five years before being dismissed for insubordination. He contributed to *PUNCH* and edited the Edinburgh *Evening Courant* in 1860–4. He published two novels of naval life, *Singleton Fontenoy* (1850) and *Eustace Conyers* (1855).

Hannay, James Owen See BIRMINGHAM, GEORGE A.

Hanrahan, Barbara 1939–91 Australian novelist and artist. Born and brought up in Adelaide, she lived in London for many years before returning to Adelaide. She first achieved recognition as an artist. Her paintings are displayed in the National Gallery of Australia. As a writer, she remains best known for *The Scent of Eucalyptus* (1973), an autobiographical first novel giving a sensitive and evocative account of an adolescent girl's growth. Her second, *Sea-Green* (1974), is another highly personal work, in which the heroine leaves suburban Australia for London. It was followed by a group of novels set in the 19th and early 20th centuries: *The Albatross Muff* (1977), *Where the Queens All Strayed* (1978), *The Peach Groves* (1979), *The Frangipani Gardens* (1980) and *Dove* (1982). They often include grotesque elements and use the perspective of a child with voyeuristic tendencies. In the course of her short but prolific career she also published *Kewpie Doll* (1984), a sequel to *The Scent of Eucalyptus*, as well as *Annie Magdalene* (1985), *Dream People* (1987), *Chelsea Girl* (1988), *Flawless Jade* (1989). *Good Night, Mr Moon* (1992) and *Michael and Me and the Sun* (1992) appeared posthumously.

Hansberry, Lorraine 1930–65 American playwright. Born in Chicago and educated at the University of Wisconsin, she was the first black woman to have a play produced on Broadway. Her best-known play, *A Raisin in the Sun* (1959), is a sympathetic examination of the economic, educational and racial concerns of a family of black Chicagoans who plan to move into a white neighbourhood. It was enormously successful, running for 530 consecutive performances, and winning a New York Drama Critics Circle Award. *The Sign in Sidney Brustein's Window* (1964) is the story of a group of Jews, other whites, and blacks in New York's Greenwich Village. In 1964, the year before her death, Hansberry wrote the captions for the photographs in *The Movement*, a documentary of the Civil Rights Movement. After her death her husband assembled *To be Young, Gifted and Black* (1969) from her letters, diaries and other unpublished material. *Raisin*, a musical adaptation of her best-known work, was produced in 1973.

Happy Days A play by SAMUEL BECKETT, first performed in English in New York in 1961, directed by Alan Schneider. The French version (*Oh! les beaux jours*) was distinguished by Madeleine Renaud's performance of the single speaking part.

Buried first to her waist and then to her neck in sand, Winnie joyfully itemizes the trivial details of her existence. Her only on-stage witness is her silent partner, Willie.

Hard Times: For These Times A novel by CHARLES DICKENS, published as a serial in *HOUSEHOLD WORDS* from April to August 1854.

Dickens's fable traces the life of the warm-hearted Sissy Jupe, a circus child deserted by her ailing father and adopted into the household of the fact-ridden retired hardware merchant Thomas Gradgrind, whose children Tom and Louisa are reared in ignorance of love and affection. The consequences of lovelessness are devastating for both. Louisa is driven to a miserable marriage with the boastful and wealthy Josiah Bounderby and then almost to an affair with the dandified James Harthouse. Tom descends to thieving, and is saved only through Sissy and the circus folk. Of comparable significance is the story of Stephen Blackpool, the honest worker in Bounderby's mill, who is burdened with a drunken wife and loved by the factory hand Rachel. Ostracized by his fellow workmen, Stephen is driven out of the community and sus-

pected in his absence of Tom Gradgrind's crime. He is exonerated only after death.

The novel depends on the opposition between Fact, Dickens's name for the cold and loveless attitude to life he associated with UTILITARIANISM, and Fancy, which represents all the warmth of the imagination – a contrast which gives it both tension and unity. Although compact and fast-moving, pressing its message home with persistence and conviction, *Hard Times* also presents several memorable minor characters. They include the fact-crammed Bitzer, ideal product of M'Choakumchild's school; the snobbish Mrs Sparsit, Bounderby's housekeeper; the windy trade union organizer Slackbridge; and the kindly members of Sleary's circus troupe.

Hardy, Thomas 1840–1928 Poet and novelist. The son of a builder and master mason, he was born in Higher Bockhampton near Dorchester, a town which remained the centre of his life and became the centre of his fictional WESSEX. He attended first a village school provided by Mrs Julia Martin, the local lady of the manor to whom he became closely attached; at the same time his mother encouraged him by giving him DRYDEN's *Aeneid* and JOHNSON's *RASSELAS* as reading matter. In 1850-6 he went to a school in nearby Dorchester conducted by the British and Foreign School Society, whose headmaster Isaac Last ensured his able pupil was well grounded in mathematics and Latin. During these schooldays the young Hardy absorbed much local folklore and became familiar with the grimmer facts of village life, of starvation and cruelty and of transportation for trivial offences. He joined his father as violinist in the village band which played at church services, weddings and other local occasions. Hardy's love of nature and sympathy for animals developed during these introspective and solitary years.

It was in the years 1856–62, when Hardy was apprenticed to a local architect, John Hicks, that he acquired the friendship of the poet, parson and antiquary WILLIAM BARNES and the brilliant but erratic Horace Moule (later to commit suicide), both of whom offered him intellectual stimulation. And although this was the time of DARWIN's *ORIGIN OF SPECIES* and *ESSAYS AND REVIEWS* Hardy the churchgoer remained unshaken in his faith. A five-year stint in London from 1862 to 1867 at the architectural offices of the celebrated Arthur Blomfield followed the apprenticeship with Hicks. While Hardy's innate morbidity responded to the seamy side of London, he also enjoyed the musical, theatrical and other artistic offerings of the capital. In 1865 he made an early appearance in print with 'How I Built Myself a House' and also won a couple of architectural prizes. By now, too, he was sending (and getting back) poems hopefully dispatched to periodicals. More significantly perhaps, he was failing to meet those challenges to his orthodoxy

Thomas Hardy, photograph by E. O. Hoppé

which resulted in a loss of faith and serious undermining of his health.

By 1867 Hardy was back again with Hicks and soon afterwards, his health restored, was writing the lost and partly cannibalized novel, *The Poor Man and the Lady*, in which GEORGE MEREDITH, then a reader for Chapman and Hall, saw merit although he advised against publication. In 1869 when Hicks died G. R. Crickmay, who had taken over the firm, offered Hardy a position in the Weymouth office and it was there he began to write *DESPERATE REMEDIES* (1871), his first published novel. That same year his employer sent him to survey the church at St Junot in Cornwall where he met his first wife, Emma Lavinia Gifford. Prior to this time Hardy appears to have experienced one or two disappointments in love, but shadow and speculation cloud this area of his life.

For a quarter-century following 1871 Hardy produced one novel after another. After *Desperate Remedies* came *UNDER THE GREENWOOD TREE* (1872) and a year later *A PAIR OF BLUE EYES*, followed in 1874 by *FAR FROM THE MADDING CROWD*, whose startling success enabled him to marry Emma Gifford. After a honeymoon at Brighton and on the Continent the couple stayed briefly in London but gravitated towards Hardy's rural roots in the West Country, living first at Swanage where he worked on *THE HAND OF ETHELBERTA* (1876); then they came to rest for a couple of years at Sturminster Newton – the time of the 'Sturminster Newton idyll' – where he wrote *THE*

RETURN OF THE NATIVE (1878). In March 1878 they moved to Upper Tooting in London, where they lived for three years while he wrote *THE TRUMPET-MAJOR* (1880) and *A LAODICEAN* (1881); although it was a time of illness and marital strain, Hardy met literary people, went to the theatre and dined at various clubs. By June 1881 he and Emma were back in Dorset living at Wimborne, where he wrote *TWO ON A TOWER* (1882). His next major work was *THE MAYOR OF CASTERBRIDGE* (1886). In June 1885 the Hardys had moved into Max Gate on the edge of Dorchester, where they were to spend the rest of their lives.

They maintained the habit of going to London for three months or so right after Easter for 'the season'. There are mixed impressions of their accommodation to a more sophisticated milieu but evidence suggests their provinciality rendered them ill at ease during such visits. Also, they travelled on the Continent in 1887 and visited Ireland in 1893. During these years, too, Hardy seemed to enjoy friendships with attractive, socially prominent women. All in all their lives appear active and full, even if their marital difficulties increased.

Yet the writing went on. And in those years Hardy showed interest in the short story by publishing *Wessex Tales* (1888), *A GROUP OF NOBLE DAMES* (1891), and *Life's Little Ironies* (1894), which, with the later volume *A Changed Man and Other Tales* (1913), round off his significant contributions to the genre. But as if this was not enough, novels of stature also appeared: *THE WOODLANDERS* (1887), *TESS OF THE D'URBERVILLES* (1891) and *THE WELL-BELOVED*, published in 1897 but written several years earlier. Above all, this was the time of *JUDE THE OBSCURE* (1895), a novel reflecting the distressing tensions of his married life. Its bizarre reception influenced his decision to give up writing novels.

Hardy had been writing poetry since his youth. He published a vast amount in the last 30 years of his life, after he ceased work as a novelist, beginning with *WESSEX POEMS AND OTHER VERSES* (1898) and *POEMS OF THE PAST AND PRESENT* (1902). The three parts of the epic verse-drama *THE DYNASTS* came in 1903, 1905 and 1908; in 1908 he also edited selections from the poetry of his old friend William Barnes. *TIME'S LAUGHINGSTOCKS AND OTHER VERSES* (1909) was followed by *SATIRES OF CIRCUMSTANCE, LYRICS AND REVERIES* (1914), a collection of particular interest for the elegiac 'Poems of 1912-13', written out of personal remorse and expiatory sadness at the sudden death of Emma Hardy in November 1912. The poetry continued: *MOMENTS OF VISION AND MISCELLANEOUS VERSES* (1917), *LATE LYRICS AND EARLIER* (1922), *HUMAN SHOWS, FAR PHANTASIES, SONGS AND TRIFLES* (1925) and the posthumous *WINTER WORDS IN VARIOUS MOODS AND METRES* (1928). *The Famous Tragedy of the Queen of Cornwall* (1923) is a verse-drama about Tristram and Iseult.

Increasingly the mantle of the Grand Old Man of English Letters tightened across Hardy's shoulders as distinctions and accolades – the Order of Merit and various honorary degrees – came to him. He continued to live simply in the melancholy twilight of Max Gate, and in 1914 married Florence Emily Dugdale (1879–1937). With her he destroyed many letters, notes and writings of a personal nature, received the inevitable admirers and receded into old age until death came peacefully to him in January 1928. *The Early Life of Thomas Hardy, 1840–1891* (1928) and *The Later Years of Thomas Hardy, 1892–1928* (1930), two sometimes misleading volumes which Hardy himself had compiled in his last years, were published under his wife's name.

Hare, David 1947– Playwright. His early work was written while he was a student at Cambridge. The university is the setting for one of his best plays, *Teeth 'n' Smiles* (1975), which follows the sordid progress of a pop group hired to play at a May Ball. The context allows Hare to analyse with some acerbity the operation of privilege in British society. *Fanshen* (1975) is a straightforward presentation of an alternative social system, that of Revolutionary China. Less sceptical and much less critical than his plays about British power politics, it is an unusual example of effective writing for an ensemble company (Hare wrote it with and for the Joint Stock Theatre). *Plenty* (1978), which Hare wrote and directed for the ROYAL NATIONAL THEATRE, is a bleak encounter with the moral bankruptcy of post-war Europe, more effective than the ambitious *Map of the World* (1983), also written and directed for the National. *Pravda* (1985), a study of the corruptions of newspaper ownership written in collaboration with HOWARD BRENTON, scored a striking success. Subsequent plays include the award-winning *Racing Demon* (1990). His work in other media includes *Licking Hitler* (TV, 1978) and two films of which he was writer-director, *Wetherby* (1985) and *Paris by Night* (1988).

Harington, Sir John ?1560–1612 Courtier, wit, epigrammatist and translator. The godson of Elizabeth I, he was educated at Eton and King's College, Cambridge. He is chiefly remembered for his EPIGRAMS and his translation of Ariosto's *Orlando furioso* (1591); the phrasing of its dedication to the Queen supports the tradition that she imposed the task on him as a penance after he had translated only the ribald 28th canto for the amusement of her maids of honour. *A New Discourse of a Stale Subject, Called the Metamorphosis of Ajax* (1596) – in fact three treatises published together – announced the invention of a water closet ('a jakes') with a display of erudition, indecency and satire that identifies Harington as an early English imitator of Rabelais. The satire, not the indecency, gave offence and he fell from royal favour.

Hariot [Harriot], **Thomas** 1560–1621 Mathematician and astronomer. Hariot was one of the circle around SIR WALTER RALEIGH, who sent him as scientific adviser on Sir Richard Grenville's expedition to Roanoake Island, 1585–6. Hariot's account of this journey was published as *A Brief and True Report of the New Found Land of Virginia* (1588). The famous 'Baines Note', reporting the shocking opinions of CHRISTOPHER MARLOWE, mentions Hariot's association with Raleigh. Marlowe is reported as saying that 'Moses was but a juggler and that one Heriots, being Sir W. Raleigh's man, can do more than he.' Hariot also contributed to the development of algebra in England, through his posthumously published treatise on equations, *Artis analyticae praxis ad aequationes algebraicas novo methodo resolvendas* (1631). This work also introduced the signs > (greater than) and < (less than). As an astronomer he observed sunspots and, independently of Galileo, the moons of Jupiter.

Harland, Henry 1861–1905 American novelist. Born in New York City, he studied at Harvard Divinity School before embarking on a literary career under the pseudonym of Sidney Luska. Pretending to be Jewish, he wrote several realistic novels about Jewish immigrants in New York: *As It was Written: A Jewish Musician's Story* (1885), *Mrs Peixada* (1886), *The Yoke of the Thorah* (1887) and *My Uncle Florimund* (1888). Migrating to Paris in 1889 and to London the following year, he dropped the pseudonym for his later short stories and novels, which included *A Latin Quarter Courtship and Other Stories* (1889), *Grandison Mather* (1889), *Two Women or One* (1890), *Two Voices* (1890), *Mea Culpa* (1891), *Mademoiselle Miss and Other Stories* (1893), *Grey Roses* (1895) and *Comedies and Errors* (1898). His most successful novels were *The Cardinal's Snuff Box* (1900) and *My Friend Prospero* (1904). He is best remembered as the first editor of THE YELLOW BOOK.

Harlem Renaissance A term (like the 'Black Renaissance' or 'New Negro') for the period of cultural activity by black American artists in the 1920s and 1930s. In his introduction to the anthology THE NEW NEGRO (1925), which served as a manifesto, ALAIN LOCKE noted a new spirit of opportunity for collective expression by black writers, in contrast to the solitary efforts of earlier figures. The Renaissance was also marked by its emphasis on the African heritage of American blacks.

Four major writers who established their reputation during this period were CLAUDE MCKAY, JEAN TOOMER, COUNTEE CULLEN and LANGSTON HUGHES. The publication of *Harlem Shadows* (1922) brought McKay recognition as a poet, and his novels *Home to Harlem* (1928) and *Banjo* (1929) were equally well received. Before going south in 1922 Jean Toomer spent time in

Harlem, and he remained in contact with New York intellectuals throughout his life. His *Cane* (1923), with its experimental style and form, and its complex examination of black heritage and culture, is a central text of the Renaissance. Cullen's *Color* (1925) is noted for its lyrical exploration of the writer's African heritage, and Hughes's *The Weary Blues* (1926) embodies the spirit of the Renaissance with its celebration of black culture and folk traditions. Other writers who came to prominence at this time were ZORA NEALE HURSTON, JESSIE REDMON FAUSET, ARNA BONTEMPS and STERLING A. BROWN. Lesser figures who contributed to the Renaissance include the novelists NELLA LARSEN, Walter White, George Schuyler, Wallace Thurman, Eric Walrond and Rudolf Fisher. Among the other poets connected with the movement were Waring Curney, Frank Horne, Gwendolyn B. Bennett and Helene Johnson.

Harley, Edward, 2nd Earl of Oxford 1689–1741 Patron of literature and book collector. The only son of ROBERT HARLEY, 1ST EARL OF OXFORD, he was educated at Westminster School. A close friend of POPE, with whom he corresponded in 1721–39, he was also friendly with SWIFT. MATTHEW PRIOR died at Harley's country seat at Wimpole, Cambridgeshire.

Harley was a manager of the Society for the Encouragement of Learning. In keeping with this position, having inherited a fine library from his father which he further improved at immense cost, he generously allowed scholars to publish its material, and often also gave financial aid. Among others, Pope published the poems of WYCHERLEY, William Oldys received material and money towards his *Life of Sir Walter Raleigh*, and Ames, the historian of printing, was given unlimited access to the library. On Harley's death most of the collection was sold. The printed material, 50,000 books, 41,000 prints and 350,000 pamphlets, was bought by Thomas Osborne, the bookseller, who then employed a number of scholars, including Oldys, to catalogue it as *Catalogus bibliothecae Harleianae*, published in five volumes (1743–5) with an introduction by JOHNSON. A selection of the material by Oldys appeared in eight volumes (1744–6), also prefaced by Johnson. The manuscripts, in 7639 volumes together with over 14,000 rolls, charters and similar legal material, were sold to the nation and now form the Harleian Collection in the British Library. Among these volumes are the HARLEY LYRICS, the finest extant collection of Middle English lyric poetry.

Harley, Robert, 1st Earl of Oxford 1661–1724 Politician. Son of Sir Edward Harley, he was educated at a private school near Burford, Oxfordshire. Gradually moving across the political spectrum, he became leader of the Tory Party and effectively Prime Minister under Queen Anne. On the accession of George I (1714) other notable Tories, including BOLINGBROKE, fled the country, but Harley remained and impeachment proceedings were started against him. These ground to a halt in 1717 as a result of procedural disagreement between the two Houses of Parliament, and he was acquitted. When in power he had been an effective manipulator of propaganda, employing the pens of DEFOE and STEELE among others, and helping to found *THE EXAMINER*, which SWIFT first edited. He was also a member of the SCRIBLERUS CLUB and an avid book collector, founding the excellent library enlarged by his son EDWARD HARLEY.

Harley Lyrics, The A collection of early Middle English lyrics, preserved in British Library MS 2253 and first assembled by ROBERT HARLEY, 1ST EARL OF OXFORD and his son EDWARD HARLEY. It is the earliest extant collection and contains more than half the secular lyrics surviving from before the 15th century. Apparently the work of several authors, the lyrics are of diverse types and treat both religious and secular topics. They range from the humorous 'Man in the Moon' to the justly famed love song 'Alysoun' and an evocative love song to Christ, 'Suete Iesu, King of Blysse'. (See also MEDIEVAL LYRIC.)

Harper, Frances E(llen) (Watkins) 1825–1911 Black American poet. She was born in Baltimore, Maryland. Her first volume of verse, *Poems on Miscellaneous Subjects* (1854), largely devoted to attacking slavery, proved extremely popular and went through 20 editions by 1874. Her other works include *Moses: A Story of the Nile* (1869), *Poems* (1871), *Iola Le Roy: or, Shadows Uplifted* (1892), about the tragic life of a young octoroon woman before and during the Civil War, and *Atlanta Offering: Poems* (1895).

Harper, Michael 1938– Black American poet. Born in Brooklyn, he moved with his family to Los Angeles in 1951 and attended Los Angeles State University (now California State University) and then the writers' workshop at the University of Iowa. Since 1970 he has taught at Brown University. Like many black writers of his generation, he is eager to emphasize the centrality of jazz to black culture: his first collection of verse, *Dear John, Dear Coltrane* (1970), takes its title from a poem in homage to the great saxophonist. Other volumes include *History is Your Own Heartbeat* (1971), *Song: I Want a Witness* (1972), *Debridement* (1973; a book-length poem), *Nightmare Begins Responsibility* (1975), *Rhode Island: Eight Poems* (1981) and *Healing Song for the Inner Ear* (1985). *Images of Kin* (1977) is a volume of selected poems. With Robert Stepto he has edited *Chants of Saints* (1976), a collection of black literature, art and scholarship.

Harper's New Monthly Magazine Founded in 1850 under the title *Harper's Monthly Magazine* by the publishing firm of Harper and Brothers in New York with Henry J. Raymond as editor, by 1860 its circulation had reached 200,000. It initially concentrated on publishing established British authors, such as DICKENS, THACKERAY, TROLLOPE and HARDY, but under the editorship of Henry M. Alden (1869-1919) it also drew regularly on American writers, among them JOHN DE FOREST, HAMLIN GARLAND, WILLIAM DEAN HOWELLS and SARAH ORNE JEWETT. Though fiction remained its main offering, after 1900 (and under its new title of *Harper's New Monthly Magazine*) it devoted more space to political and social issues, and featured articles by well-known public figures such as Woodrow Wilson, Calvin Coolidge and Theodore Roosevelt. In 1925 the shortened title of *Harper's Magazine* was adopted and it is now commonly known simply as *Harper's*.

Harpur, Charles 1813-68 Australian poet. His first volume, *Thoughts: A Series of Sonnets* (1845), was followed by *The Bushrangers: A Play and Other Poems* (1853), the first play by an Australian-born author to be printed in the colony. His later volumes were *A Poet's Home* (1862), *The Tower of the Dream* (1865) and *Poems* (edited by Henry Maydwell Martin; 1883). He has been called 'the grey forefather' of Australian poetry because of his early use of Australian subjects in such poems as 'The Creek of the Four Graves', 'The Bushfire' and 'Ned Connor'.

Harraden, Beatrice 1864-1936 Novelist and suffragette. Born in Hampstead, she was educated in Dresden, then at Cheltenham College, Queen's College, and Bedford College, London, where she graduated in 1883. She was an ardent suffragette and became a leader in the Women's Social and Political Union, selling newspapers and making numerous public speeches in support of feminist causes. Her extensive travels on the Continent were followed by a visit to the USA in 1894-5 to help foster international comity.

Her first published book, *Things Will Take a Turn*, appeared in 1891, but she had already contributed many short stories to BLACKWOOD'S EDINBURGH MAGAZINE. Success came with *Ships That Pass in the Night* (1893) which sold over a million copies. Set in a winter resort for consumptive patients in the Kurhaus at Petershof, its heroine, herself a consumptive, dies at the end of the novel in a street accident. It reflects many of her feminist beliefs and has been described as 'rhapsodical, elusive and deliberately parabolic'. *In Varying Moods* (1894) was a collection of short stories written in Sussex, Cannes and Menton. Other titles included *Hilda Strafford* (1897), *The Fowler* (1899), *Katharine Frensham* (1903), *Interplay* (1908), *Youth Calling* (1924) and *Search Will Find It*

Out (1928). She was awarded a Civil List pension in 1930 for her services to literature.

Harrington [Harington]**, James** 1611-77 Political theorist. Educated at Trinity College, Oxford, Harrington was a republican who had travelled extensively in Europe and was for a time in attendance to the Elector Palatine. In 1656 he published *The Commonwealth of Oceana*, a political romance in the manner of THOMAS MORE'S *UTOPIA*, presenting his idea of an ideal state; the features of this commonwealth include liberty, equality, restrictions on property, and a democratically elected 'Archon', or ruling Prince. These political ideas later influenced the early settlers of America, and are in sharp contrast to the scheme set down in THOMAS HOBBES'S *LEVIATHAN* (1651). Harrington was imprisoned for his views at the Restoration.

Harris, Frank (James Thomas) 1856-1931 Irish Journalist and literary editor. Born in Galway, he travelled to New York in his early teens and worked at a series of menial jobs before returning to Europe. As a journalist, he gained a considerable reputation on the London literary scene, editing *The Evening News* (1882-6), THE FORTNIGHTLY REVIEW (1886-94) and THE SATURDAY REVIEW (1894-8), which he transformed into the leading weekly with a new bias towards the arts. Regular contributors included G. B. SHAW, H. G. WELLS and MAX BEERBOHM, all of whom later testified to Harris's flair for controversial and often scandalous assaults on Victorian standards.

His notoriety as a braggart and liar was epitomized in *My Life and Loves* (4 vols., 1922-7), highly unreliable memoirs of his early life as a precocious intellectual and sexual buccaneer. His other publications included short stories (*Elder Conklin*, 1894; *Montes the Matador*, 1900), novels (*The Bomb*, 1908; *Great Days*, 1914) and two plays (*Mr and Mrs Daventry*, 1900; *Shakespeare and His Love*, 1910). His literary studies were enthusiastically received in some quarters, but never won scholarly acclaim. *The Man Shakespeare* (1909) was followed by *The Women of Shakespeare* (1911), and biographies of WILDE (1916) and Shaw (1931). His *Contemporary Portraits* (1915-23) met with the same kind of reception. A highly individual figure, Harris has continued to attract and frustrate readers, though many of his finer qualities as a writer have been overshadowed by an almost pathological boasting.

Harris, George Washington 1814-69 American short-story writer. Born in Pennsylvania, he worked as a Tennessee River steamboat captain before he turned to writing. His best-known work is *Sut Lovingood: Yarns spun by a 'Nat'ral Born Durn'd Fool'* (1867). A collection of tall tales and sketches, full of Southwestern frontier dialect and robust humour, it is a clear forerunner of some of MARK TWAIN's early writings.

Harris, Joel Chandler 1848–1908 American short-story writer, best known as the creator of Uncle Remus, Br'er Rabbit and Br'er Fox. He was born in Georgia, where from an early age he worked on plantations and imbibed the black folklore that was to inform the style and subject matter of his fiction. The first of the Uncle Remus stories, 'The Story of Mr Rabbit and Mr Fox, as Told by Uncle Remus', was published in 1879. *UNCLE REMUS: His Songs and Sayings* appeared in 1881 and was followed by *Nights with Uncle Remus* (1883), *Uncle Remus and His Friends* (1892), *Mr Rabbit at Home* (1895), *The Tar Baby and Other Short Rhymes of Uncle Remus* (1904) and *Uncle Remus and Br'er Rabbit* (1906). These stories offer traditional black folk-wisdom in what MARK TWAIN considered a flawless duplication of Southern black speech. His other works include *Mingo and Other Sketches in Black and White* (1884), and two novels, *Sister Jane: Her Friends and Acquaintances* (1896) and *Gabriel Tolliver: A Story of Reconstruction* (1902). *On the Plantation* (1892) recounts the childhood experiences that inspired so much of his work.

Harris, (Theodore) Wilson 1921– Guyanese novelist. Born in New Amsterdam, he was educated in Georgetown at Queen's College and worked as a government surveyor in the interior of Guyana. He published two volumes of verse, *Fetish* (1951) and *Eternity to Season* (1954), before moving to London in 1959. He has since become one of the most innovative novelists writing in English. His free-ranging, non-logical, highly metaphoric, associative techniques in prose derive from a poetic imagination fired intellectually by extensive reading (not least by Jung's use of the mythic), and visually by the savannahs, the powerful river currents, and the swirling rock strata of Guyana. In *PALACE OF THE PEACOCK* (1960), *The Far Journey of Oudin* (1961), *The Whole Armour* (1962) and *The Secret Ladder* (1963), published together as *The Guyana Quartet* (1985), he uses physical landscape as METAPHOR, even ALLEGORY, to dramatize the workings of the human psyche and establish its capacity to resist ossification by the categorical and static. The multi-racial Guyanese population also helped inspire his vision of the interpenetrability, rather than the antagonism, of different cultures. So, in his other 'Guyanese' novels, *Heartland* (1964), *The Eye of the Scarecrow* (1965), *The Waiting Room* (1967), *Tumatumari* (1968) and *Ascent to Omai* (1970), character is developed not towards stability, but fluidity, thus inducing new awarenesses and reinterpretations of experience. Since his volumes of salvaged or imagined pre-Columbian legends, *The Sleepers of Roraima* (1970) and *The Age of the Rainmakers* (1971), Harris has

written novels set in Scotland, South America, Mexico and London: *Black Marsden* (1972), *Companions of the Day and Night* (1975), *Da Silva da Silva's Cultivated Wilderness* with *Genesis of the Clowns* (1977), *The Tree of the Sun* (1978), *The Angel at the Gate* (1982) and his *Carnival* trilogy, *Carnival* (1985), *The Infinite Rehearsal* (1987) and *The Four Banks of the River of Space* (1990). In them his profound practical concern for human survival is even more intensely conveyed through the kaleidoscopic interacting of past and present, painting and literature, art and religion. His critical writings include *Tradition, the Writer and Society* (1967), *Explorations* (1981), *The Womb of Space: The Cross-Cultural Imagination* (1983) and *The Radical Imagination* (1992).

Harrison, Frederic 1831–1923 Philosopher and critic. He was educated at King's College, London, and Wadham College, Oxford. Called to the Bar in 1858, he was professor of jurisprudence and international law to the Inns of Court in 1877–89. Originally a member of the Church of England, Harrison became in 1870 a believer in Auguste Comte's creed of POSITIVISM and took a leading role in spreading its doctrines. His contemptuous remarks on culture stimulated MATTHEW ARNOLD to reply in *CULTURE AND ANARCHY* (1869). Harrison's own voluminous output included *Order and Progress* (1875), *Victorian Literature* (1895), *Carlyle and the London Library* (1907), *The Philosophy of Common Sense* (1907) and *The Positive Evolution of Religion* (1912). His *Autobiographical Memoirs* appeared in 1911.

Harrison, Tony 1937– Poet, translator and playwright. Born in Leeds and educated at Leeds Grammar School and Leeds University, he spent four years lecturing in West Africa and a year in Prague before returning to Britain to become the first Northern Arts Literary Fellow in 1967–8. One of Britain's most accomplished verse writers for the stage, he is perhaps best known for his translation and adaptation of *The Oresteia* (1981), performed, like much of his work, at the ROYAL NATIONAL THEATRE. Other texts have been *The Misanthrope* (1973), *Phaedra Britannica* (1975), *The Mysteries* (1985), *Trackers of Oxyrhyncus* (1990) and *A Common Chorus: A Version of Aristophanes' Lysistrata* (1992). *Theatre Works 1973–1985* (1986) is a collection. His disciplined but vernacular poetry has appeared in *The Loiners* (1970), *Palladas: Poems* (1975), *From 'The School of Eloquence' and Other Poems* (1978), *A Kumquat for John Keats* (1981), *US Martial* (1981), *Selected Poems* (1984) and *A Cold Coming* (1991). A 1987 television version of his poem *V.* (1985), about the desecration of his parents' grave and the social conditions which provoked such action, brought an overwhelming response.

Harrison, William 1534–93 Historian and topographer. Harrison was educated at St Paul's School, London, and Cambridge and Oxford, where he graduated in 1560. His *Description of England* was incorporated in HOLINSHED's *Chronicles*. It gives a vivid picture of social conditions in Elizabethan England with its food, institutions, customs, inns and fairs.

Harrower, Elizabeth 1928– Australian novelist. Born in Newcastle, New South Wales, she spent the first 12 years of her life there before moving to Sydney. In 1951 she went to Europe and lived in Scotland before settling in London. Her first two novels, *Down in the City* (1957) and *The Long Prospect* (1958), were published during this period in Britain. In 1959 she returned to Australia and worked briefly for the Australian Broadcasting Commission, and, for a longer period, in publishing. Most of her fiction deals with struggles in personal relationships and with conflicting moral issues. *The Catherine Wheel* (1960) describes the experiences of a young Australian law student in London, focusing on her infatuation for a self-centred and unreliable young man. Like *The Watch Tower* (1966), it sees female passivity as colluding with male egotism to perpetuate the subordinate role of women in relationships. In the latter novel the title refers to an elegant house in a respectable Sydney suburb, which appears to offer a haven for the heroine and her sister, but emerges as an emotional and intellectual prison for the two women. Her short stories remain uncollected.

Harry, Blind See BLIND HARRY.

Harry Richmond, The Adventures of A novel by GEORGE MEREDITH, published in 1871.

Richmond Roy is the son of a member of the royal family and an actress. Extravagant and charming, he teaches singing in the household of Beltham, a wealthy squire, and charms both his daughters. He elopes with one of them and she bears him a son but his unreliable character drives her to an early grave. Beltham, hating Roy, is determined to gain custody of his daughter's child, Harry Richmond. Roy, however, is obsessed with the idea of obtaining some exalted position for the boy. Harry loves his charming, irresponsible fool of a father, who eventually gets himself accepted at the courts of petty German princes. At one of these Harry and Princess Ottilia fall in love and Roy is determined to overcome all obstacles to the impossible marriage. Beltham, for his part, sees Harry's future in England, married to Janet Ilchester. Through his father Harry is exposed to embarrassment and humiliation, but he eventually marries Janet and the squire's plans are realized.

Hart, Moss 1904–61 American playwright and director. His first successes were written in witty partnership with GEORGE S. KAUFMAN: *Once in a Lifetime* (1930), *You Can't Take It with You* (1936) and *The Man Who Came to Dinner* (1939). On his own he wrote the book for a musical about psychoanalysis, *Lady in the Dark* (1941), and a comedy about the theatre, *Light Up the Sky* (1948).

Harte, (Francis) Bret [Brett] 1836–1902 American short-story writer. Born in Albany, New York, he went to California at the age of 18, working as a prospector, a teacher, a Wells Fargo expressman, and then as a journalist. In 1860 he settled in San Francisco, and began to contribute to the *Golden Era* and *The Californian*. As editor of the latter he commissioned weekly articles from his friend MARK TWAIN.

He was appointed secretary of the US Mint in San Francisco in 1863. He continued to write, however, and his first book of poems, *The Lost Galleon*, was published in 1867. *Condensed Novels and Other Papers*, PARODIES of distinguished authors, appeared in the same year. In 1868 he helped to establish OVERLAND MONTHLY as an outlet for Western writers, and edited it for its first two-and-a-half years. Among his own contributions to its pages was his most famous collection, THE LUCK OF ROARING CAMP AND OTHER SKETCHES (1868–70). He returned to the East, where he lived and wrote until 1878, when he was appointed US consul in Germany. He was consul at Glasgow from 1880 to 1885 and spent the rest of his life in London. His stories are collected in *Mrs Skaggs's Husbands* (1873), *Tales of the Argonauts* (1875), *An Heiress of Red Dog, and Other Sketches* (1878), *A Sappho of Green Springs, and Other Stories* (1891) and *Colonel Starbottle's Client, and Some Other People* (1892). He also published several novels, including *Gabriel Conroy* (1876) and *Jeff Briggs's Love Story* (1880); and two plays, *Two Men of Sandy Bar* (1876) and *Ah Sin* (1877), the latter in collaboration with Twain.

Hartford Wits See CONNECTICUT WITS.

Hartley, David 1705–57 Philosopher. He was born at Luddenden, near Halifax in Yorkshire, and was educated at Bradford Grammar School and Jesus College, Cambridge. He became a physician, was a Fellow of Jesus College, and is remembered for one of the earliest attempts at psychological enquiry in English. *Observations on Man: His Frame, His Duty and His Expectations* (1749) relates psychology to physiology, and contributed to the development of the 'association of ideas' theory. Its influence on COLERIDGE can be seen in his poetry and in his decision to name his eldest son HARTLEY COLERIDGE.

Hartley, L(eslie) P(oles) 1895–1972 Novelist and short-story writer. He was born at Whittlesey in Cambridgeshire and educated at Harrow and Balliol College, Oxford. During World War I he served in the

Norfolk Regiment, and afterwards spent much of his life in Venice.

His first short stories were published in a volume called *Night Fears* (1924). This was followed by numerous other collections, among them *The Killing Bottle* (1932), *The Travelling Grave* (1951), *The White Wand* (1954) and *Two for the River* (1961), which have established his reputation as a leading writer of the genre. His novels began with *Simonetta Perkins* (1925), which was set in Venice, but it was with his trilogy, *The Shrimp and the Anemone* (1944), *The Sixth Heaven* (1946) and the title volume, *Eustace and Hilda* (1947), that Hartley won his greatest critical accolade. The trilogy charts the relationship between Eustace and his elder sister Hilda, through childhood to adulthood in Oxford and Venice, and is indebted (without detriment) to the work of HENRY JAMES and the teachings of Freud about the influence of early childhood on the formation of character.

Hartley's best-known novel, THE GO-BETWEEN (1953), a beautifully observed portrayal of Edwardian England, won the Heinemann Foundation Award. His other novels include *A Perfect Woman* (1955), *The Hireling* (1957), *Facial Justice* (1960), *The Brickfield* (1964) and its sequel *The Betrayal* (1966), *Poor Clare* (1968) and *The Love Adept* (1969). He was also the author of a volume of critical essays, *The Novelist's Responsibility* (1968).

Harvey, Gabriel ?1550–1631 Scholar. Gabriel Harvey was educated at Christ's College, Cambridge, becoming a Fellow of Pembroke Hall in 1570 and of Trinity Hall in 1578. He pursued learned interests in rhetoric, neo-Aristotelian philosophy and law; his wide learning is also attested by the copious marginalia he left in his books. Harvey's earliest published work was *Smithus* (1578), an elegy on his patron Sir Thomas Smith. His friendship with SPENSER led to an exchange of letters, printed in 1580, partly dealing with metrics and referring to the coterie known as the AREOPAGUS. In it THE FAERIE QUEENE is mentioned for the first time, as are other poems by Spenser no longer extant and presumably since lost. With his brother, the astrologer Richard Harvey, he became embroiled in a bitter exchange of pamphlets with NASHE, described under the entry for that author. The last 30 years of Harvey's life were spent in Saffron Walden.

Harvey, William 1578–1657 Physician. Born in Folkestone, Kent, Harvey attended King's School in Canterbury. From Gonville and Caius College, Cambridge, he went on to take his medical degree at the University of Padua where Galileo was a teacher. In London he became a physician at St Bartholomew's Hospital and lecturer at the College of Physicians, where he expounded his theory of the circulation of the blood in 1616. He did not publish his treatise on the subject until 12 years later, in *Exercitatio anatom-ica de motu cordis et sanguinis in animalibus* (*On the Movement of the Heart and Blood in Animals*; 1628). Harvey's theories, the result of observation and experiment carried out without the help of a microscope, were substantiated only after 200 years of slow acceptance. Harvey also made considerable contributions to the knowledge of embryology and comparative anatomy. He was physician to Charles I, and was present with him at the Battle of Edgehill.

Harwood, Gwen(doline) [Nessie] 1920– Australian poet. Born in Taringa, Queensland, she did not publish her first book, *Poems*, until 1963. *Poems: Volume Two* (1968), *New and Selected Poems* (1975), *Lion's Bride* (1981), *Bone Scan* (1990) and *Collected Poems* (1991) have followed. Tense, controlled pieces like 'In the Park', 'Prize-Giving' and 'Cocktails at Seven', sketching scenes of middle-class despair and vacillating between rage and ELEGY, have made her one of Australia's foremost lyric poets. *Blessed City* (1990) contains the correspondence with Thomas Riddell at the start of the friendship which has inspired Harwood's work throughout her career.

Harwood, Lee (Travers Rafe) 1939– Poet. Born in Leicester and educated at Weybridge and Queen Mary College, London, he lives in Brighton and works for the Post Office. His first major collection, *The White Room* (1968), won praise from JOHN ASHBERY. Its successors include *Landscapes* (1969), *The Sinking Colony* (1970), *Monster Masks* (1985), *Rope Boy* (1988), *Crossing the Frozen River: Selected Poems* (1988) and translations from Tzara (1975).

Harwood, Ronald 1934– Playwright. Born in South Africa, he came to Britain and joined Sir Donald Wolfit's touring Shakespearean company, the inspiration for his first stage success, *The Dresser* (1980). His mixture of affection and despair is reflected in *J. J. Farr* (1987) and *Another Time* (1989). *Reflected Glory* (1992) describes the rivalry between a restaurant-owner and his more successful playwright-brother.

Hasluck, Nicholas (Paul) 1942– Australian novelist, short-story writer and poet. The son of a former Governor General, he was born in Canberra and is a practising barrister. His work is preoccupied with history, politics and moral confusion. *The Bellarmine Jug* (1984), his best-known novel, is about the efforts of a 20th-century historian to track down a mysteriously vanished document about a 17th-century massacre. *The Hand That Feeds You* (1982) is about corruption in a future Republican Australia and *Truant State* (1987) about financial chicanery in Western Australia at the time of secession. *The Country without Music* (1990) examines the corrupting effect of an imperialist Australia on imaginary French colonies. His first novels, *Quarantine* (1978) and *The Blue Guitar* (1980), were about moral pressures in, respectively, a Middle Eastern quarantine station and the world of pop music. *The Hat on the Letter O and Other Stories* (1978) demonstrates the variety of forms in which he works. The poetry in *Anchor and Other Poems* (1976) and *On the Edge* (with William Grono; 1980) is more conservative. He has also written *Chinese Journey* (with CHRISTOPHER KOCH; 1985), a collection of verse and prose.

Hassan A play by JAMES ELROY FLECKER, written in 1913–14, published in 1922 and first performed in German in Darmstadt in May 1923. For the first English performance, later in the same year, Delius provided music and Fokine a balletic choreography. It ran for eight months at His Majesty's Theatre, a spectacular successor to *Chu-Chin-Chow*. It is written in highly charged prose, with interspersed poems.

Hassan, a middle-aged confectioner in old Baghdad, becomes embroiled in the cruel and corrupt court of the Caliph as a result of his love for the courtesan, Yasmin. The Caliph takes sadistic revenge on Rafi, the King of the Beggars, who has tried to rescue his virginal lover, Pervaneh, from the Caliph's harem. Having been forced to watch the perverted execution of Rafi and Pervaneh, Hassan escapes with Ishak, the court poet, on the golden road to Samarkand. Influenced by GRAND GUIGNOL, the play contains enough voyeurism and sadism to explain the hesitation of Lord Cromer, the Lord Chamberlain of the time, to grant it a licence in 1923.

Haunted Man and the Ghost's Bargain, The A Christmas story by CHARLES DICKENS, published in 1848 and collected in *CHRISTMAS BOOKS* (1852).

The sadly reflective, learned Mr Redlaw is visited by an evil phantom who makes a compact with him to obliterate the sorrow, wrongs and troubles he has known. In return, Redlaw agrees to transmit this oblivion to others. But his influence is baleful upon everyone he encounters – the student Edmund Denham, the amiable Adolphus Tetterby and the goodnatured William Swidger. These and others fall away from their better selves, if only temporarily, when confronted by Redlaw. Ultimately, through the purity, goodness and gentleness embodied in William's wife, Milly, the unhappy man's bargain is terminated.

Hau'ofa, Epeli 1939– Tongan short-story writer and novelist. Born in Papua New Guinea to Tongan missionary parents, he went to school in Papua New Guinea, Tonga, Fiji and Australia, and to university in Australia and Canada, gaining a PhD in social anthropology from the Australian National University, Canberra. In 1978–81 he was deputy private secretary to the King of Tonga. He has taught at the University of Papua New Guinea and the University of the South

Pacific in Fiji where he is now head of the department of sociology. One of the most distinctive voices in South Pacific literature, Hau'ofa is unusual in his comic treatment of post-colonial themes. *Tales of the Tikongs* (1983), a collection of short stories, draws on the Tongan oral tradition of the tall tale to create a fictional world in which contemporary South Pacific society is gently ridiculed. Hau'ofa satirizes the traditional authorities and the new elites of the South Pacific, the effects of Christianity and the development programmes in the region. *Kisses in the Nederends* (1987), a novel, is a *tour de force* of comic-grotesque realism. The central character's search for a cure for his incurably fissured and ulcerated anus involves a satiric journey through all the region's problem-solving agencies and institutions. Some of Hau'ofa's poetry appeared in ALBERT WENDT's anthology of South Pacific literature, *Lali* (1980). He is also the author of works of social anthropology.

Havelok the Dane A VERSE ROMANCE composed *c.* 1280–1300, probably in the North-east Midlands.

The story, told in couplets, is English in character and while the romance apparently has an Anglo-Norman source – a similar tale features in Gaimar's *Histoire des engles* – no European romance of Havelok survives. All attempts to link the Havelok of the poem with a historical figure have proved inconclusive, though some of the characters live on in local folklore. The romance tells of Havelok, son of the Danish king, who is handed over by his guardian to the fisherman Grim to be killed. Magic tokens reveal his importance and lead Grim to flee with him to England. Havelok grows very strong and works as a scullion in the service of Godrich, evil guardian of the heir to the English throne, Goldborough. Godrich had promised her father he would marry Goldborough to the strongest man in the land, and hopes to gain the throne himself by marrying her to Havelok. Havelok's identity is revealed, by his magic tokens, to his wife and again when the couple have returned to Denmark. The two evil guardians are defeated and Havelok becomes king of Denmark and England.

Hawes, Stephen d. ?1523 Poet. Very little is known of Hawes's life except that, by his own account, he was groom of the chamber to Henry VII. His poetry belongs in spirit to the Middle Ages and shows the influence of CHAUCER, GOWER and especially LYDGATE. Hawes is medieval in his allegorizing, especially in the allegorical treatment of love, and in his reflections on the instability of fortune. However, his concern with the education of princes shows the influence of the 'New Learning'. The first editions of his works were printed by WYNKYN DE WORDE and are bibliographical rarities. *The Pastime of Pleasure* (the only copy of the first edition of 1509 is incomplete) deals with the education of the knight Graunde Amoure, by way of the seven liberal arts, to make him worthy of the lady La Belle Pucel. *The Example of Virtue* (earliest surviving edition, 1510) and *The Comfort of Lovers* (earliest surviving copy, ?1510) are also love-allegories. *The Conversion of Swearers* (1509) attacks blasphemy and *A Joyful Meditation* (a unique copy of the first edition of 1509 is at Cambridge) celebrates the coronation of Henry VIII.

Hawker, R(obert) S(tephen) 1803–75 Poet. The son of a doctor (later in holy orders), Hawker was born in Devon and educated at Cheltenham College and Pembroke College, Oxford, where he won the Newdigate Prize for poetry. Ordained priest in 1831 he became, three years later, vicar of Morwenstowe on the North Cornish coast. He described his parishioners as a 'mixed multitude of smugglers, wreckers and dissenters of various hues'. Twice married, a High Churchman who converted to Rome on his deathbed, 'Passon' Hawker was an eccentric and an antiquarian prone to superstition and addicted to the occult. He was a vigorous, irrepressible personality of ready wit, who affected the fisherman's jersey as emblematic of his calling and who is comparable to St Francis in his devotion to animals, many of whom accompanied him into his church.

By Victorian standards Hawker's output was modest, although his first volume, the anonymous *Tendrils by Reuben*, appeared when he was only 18. In 1826 a local newspaper published 'Song of the Western Men', his best-known poem. Other volumes include *Records of the Western Shore* (1832), *Poems* (1836), *Ecclesia* (1841), *Reeds Shaken with the Wind* (1st series, 1843; 2nd series, 1844) and *Cornish Ballads* (1869). *The Quest of the Sangraal* (1864) is generally acknowledged as his most ambitious work and often compared with TENNYSON'S *IDYLLS OF THE KING*, another Victorian treatment of Arthurian legend. Often cast as BALLADS, his poems deal with saints' legends, smuggling, village life and other motifs closely associated with Cornwall; there are also verses dedicated to the Christian life. Hawker wrote on antiquarian subjects, dabbled in translation and contributed to a number of prominent journals. His prose work, *Footprints of Former Men in Far Cornwall* (1870), is a rich source of the mysterious, the supernatural and the forbiddingly unusual that attaches to Cornish lore and legend.

Hawkes, John (Clendennin Burne, Jr**)** 1925– American novelist. Born in Connecticut and educated at Harvard, he has taught at Brown University since 1958. His first novel, *The Cannibal* (1949), is a bleak and formally complex work about the horrors of World War II. Subsequent novels, such as *The Beetle Leg* (1951), *The Goose on the Grave* (1954), *The Lime Twig* (1961) and *Second Skin* (1964), continued to evoke the extremes of violence he saw as characteris-

tic of the modern world. His more recent work includes a collection of stories called *Lunar Landscapes* (1969), and the novels *Death, Sleep and the Traveller* (1974), *Travesty* (1976), *The Owl* (1977), *The Passion Artist* (1979), *Virginie: Her Two Lives* (1981), *Innocence in Extremis* (1985), *Adventures in the Alaskan Skin Trade* (1985) and *Whistlejacket* (1989). His later fiction uses nightmarish surrealism to explore eroticism.

Hawkins, Sir **Anthony Hope** See HOPE, ANTHONY.

Hawkins, Sir **John** 1532–95 Sailor. A relative of Drake, Hawkins was a naval commander and, in his reconstruction of the fleet, the architect of the Elizabethan navy. His early career was as a slave-trader, running slaves from Guinea to the West Indies in 1562–9. The last voyage is described in *A True Declaration of the Troublesome Voyage of Mr John Hawkins* (1569). He was instrumental in discovering the Ridolfi Plot of 1571 to put Mary Queen of Scots on the English throne. He died on a raiding expedition with Drake to the Spanish West Indies.

Hawthorne, Nathaniel 1804–64 American novelist and short-story writer. He was born in Salem, Massachusetts, into a prominent family whose ancestors were among the earliest settlers of the colony. Later in life he was especially preoccupied, and troubled, by his descent from John Hathorne, a judge in the Salem witch trials of 1692. Hawthorne grew up in seclusion with his widowed mother, his father, a sea-captain, having died of yellow fever in 1808. When he was 11 they moved to Maine. There he attended Bowdoin College and made a number of important and lasting friends, including HENRY WADSWORTH LONGFELLOW and the future president Franklin Pierce.

After graduating in 1825 he returned to Salem and, determined to become a writer, worked on short stories and historical sketches. In 1828, anonymously and at his own expense, he published *Fanshawe*, a novel based on his college life. While the book itself received only slight critical attention and an ashamed author burned the unsold copies, it did initiate a long, productive friendship between Hawthorne and the publisher Samuel Goodrich. He returned to writing short fiction, and in historical and allegorical tales began to explore the impact of harsh Puritanism on the guilty conscience of New England. Many of these stories were published in Goodrich's *The Token*, an annual gift-book, and were later collected in *Twice-Told Tales* (1837; expanded 1842).

Hawthorne then worked for Goodrich as an editor and hack writer from 1836 to 1839, when he accepted a post as surveyor of the Boston Custom House. His involvement with the Boston literary circle led him to quit his post in 1841 and to invest in the communal experiment at BROOK FARM. That same year he mar-

Nathaniel Hawthorne

THE ATLANTIC MONTHLY. Four unfinished novels eventually appeared as *Septimius Felton: or, the Elixir of Life* (1872), *The Dolliver Romance* (1876), *Dr Grimshawe's Secret* (1882) and *The Ancestral Footstep* (1883). His wife edited his notebooks as *Passages from the American Notebooks* (1868), *Passages from the English Notebooks* (1870) and *Passages from the French and Italian Notebooks* (1871). Modern editions restore many sections which she cut or altered.

Hay, Ian [Beith, John Hay, Major-General] 1876–1952 Novelist and playwright. Hay was educated at Fettes and Cambridge. During World War I he served as a member of the British War Mission to the USA. *The First Hundred Thousand* (1915), an account of the enlisted men during the early stages of the war, achieved considerable contemporary popularity. Hay's novels, invariably written in a light-hearted vein, were frequently about life in English boys' boarding-schools. *A Safety Match* (1911) was the most famous; others included *A Man's Made* (1909), *The Middle Watch* (1930) and *The Housemaster* (1936).

As well as adapting many of his own novels to the stage, Hay dramatized stories by P. G. WODEHOUSE, a close friend, with whom he shares many literary qualities.

Hay Fever A comedy by NOËL COWARD, first performed at the Ambassadors Theatre, London, in 1925. It is a skilfully composed account of a weekend at the home of the eccentric Bliss family. The wife, a retired actress who continues to act in her private life, the husband and the two children have all invited guests to stay without telling each other. The bewildered guests, subjected to the Bliss version of bickering hospitality, creep away at breakfast on the second day, leaving the unnoticing family arguing about the exact topography of Paris.

Haydon, Benjamin Robert 1786–1846 Painter and diarist. The son of a printer and bookseller, Haydon was born in Plymouth and attended the Royal Academy before beginning a turbulent career as a painter of classical, biblical and historical subjects. After considerable initial success as a purveyor of large canvases in the Renaissance manner to the houses of the rich and great, he alienated his patrons and influential well-wishers with the often intemperate manner of his advocacy of otherwise sound and progressive schemes for the promotion of art education, the decoration of public buildings and the establishment of schools of design. He was among the first to appreciate the extraordinary merit of the Elgin Marbles, and was instrumental in securing their purchase for the British Museum. His friends included David Wilkie, KEATS, WORDSWORTH, HAZLITT (all of whom were portrayed in the crowd of his painting

ried Sophia Peabody, herself an active participant in TRANSCENDENTALISM. Soon, however, the retiring Hawthorne was disappointed by communal life; in 1842 he and his wife moved to Concord, where they lived in the Old Manse, a former home of RALPH WALDO EMERSON. He returned to serious writing, and in 1846 published *Mosses from an Old Manse*, which includes the famous story 'Young Goodman Brown'. After serving as customs surveyor at Salem for three years (1846–9), at the age of 45 he finally produced his first significant long work of fiction. THE SCARLET LETTER (1850), still considered the most important of his works, won almost immediate acclaim. It was rapidly followed by THE HOUSE OF THE SEVEN GABLES (1851) and THE BLITHEDALE ROMANCE (1852), which was based on his Brook Farm experience. Hawthorne was never again to equal the productivity of this three-year period, during which he also published *The Snow Image and Other Tales* (1851), which includes stories such as 'Ethan Brand' and 'My Kinsman Major Molineux'. The publication of *A Wonder Book* (1852), which retells Greek myths for children, and *Tanglewood Tales* (1853) marked the end of his most prolific period.

In 1853 Franklin Pierce became President and Hawthorne, who had written his campaign biography, was appointed US consul at Liverpool. He lived in England for four years and in Italy for two. On his return to the USA he published his final novel, THE MARBLE FAUN (1860), and *Our Old Home* (1863), a book of essays on England, as well as various pieces in

'Christ's Entry into Jerusalem'), LEIGH HUNT (in whose *EXAMINER* he virulently attacked the Academy), MARY RUSSELL MITFORD and ELIZABETH BARRETT BROWNING. Although consumed to the point of madness by the desire for glory with the brush, he was, in the event, a better writer and lecturer than painter, and is now best known for his posthumously published *Autobiography and Journals* (1853), a treasure-trove of anecdote and vivid observation of his famous contemporaries, and his *Lectures on Painting and Design* (1846), first given at the London Mechanics' Institution and subsequently to working-class audiences in the provinces. A courageous and soaringly idealistic figure, he was at length unable to surmount his many professional disappointments and committed suicide, the coroner's jury returning a verdict of insanity. His extravagant personality intrigued DICKENS, who used him, along with Leigh Hunt, as the model for the infantile egomaniac Harold Skimpole in *BLEAK HOUSE*.

Hayley, William 1745–1820 Poet and biographer. Born at Chichester and educated at Eton and Cambridge, Hayley spent most of his life at Eartham, Sussex. Although now of mainly antiquarian interest, his poetry, of which there is a great deal, was widely read in its day, and the considerable popular success of his two most ambitious works, *The Triumphs of Temper* (1781) and *The Triumphs of Music* (1805), earned him BYRON's ridicule ('Forever feeble, forever tame') in *English Bards and Scotch Reviewers*. His *Ballads Founded on Anecdotes of Animals* (1805) were written for and illustrated by BLAKE, whose patron Hayley was in 1800–3. Other literary friends included COWPER, of whom he wrote a *Life* (1803), and SOUTHEY, who thought him good in everything 'except his poetry'. The appearance of an article on Hayley by Southey for *THE QUARTERLY REVIEW* was long delayed by the editor on the grounds that he 'could not bear to see Hayley spoken of with decent respect'. Other biographical works by Hayley include lives of MILTON and the portrait painter Romney. In 1790 he declined the chance to become POET LAUREATE.

Haymarket Theatre Successively called the Little Theatre in the Haymarket, the Theatre Royal, Haymarket, and the Haymarket Theatre, it opened in 1720 as a speculative challenge to the monopoly of the PATENT THEATRES. HENRY FIELDING staged anti-Walpole satires there in 1735–7. During the management of SAMUEL FOOTE (1747–76) it acquired a licence for performing plays when the Patent Theatres were closed in the summer and thus became an important testing-ground for new work. On his death Foote's licence was acquired by GEORGE COLMAN THE ELDER, whose regime was continued by his son, GEORGE COLMAN THE YOUNGER, until 1817. The first building was replaced in 1820 by a larger theatre, designed by John Nash. The portico alone has survived subsequent improvements.

Hayward, Sir John ?1564–1627 Historian. Hayward graduated from Pembroke College, Cambridge, in 1584. *The First Part of the Life and Reign of King Henry IV* (1599), flatteringly dedicated to Essex, included an account of the deposition of Richard II which aroused the suspicion of Elizabeth I. Hayward was brought before the Star Chamber, imprisoned, and released only after Essex's execution. FRANCIS BACON, who found the book's politics unobjectionable, thought its borrowings from Tacitus felonious. In the reign of James, at the suggestion of his son Prince Henry, Hayward wrote *The Lives of the Three Normans, Kings of England* (i.e. William I, William II and Henry I) which was printed in 1613. *The Life and Reign of King Edward VI* was published posthumously in 1630. Another edition (1636) contains *The Beginning of the Reign of Queen Elizabeth*, part of a larger work which remained in manuscript until it was printed in 1840. *The Sanctuary of a Troubled Soul* (1616) is a collection of prayers and meditations; *David's Tears* (1622) is a commentary on three of the penitential psalms.

Haywood, Eliza c. 1693–1756 Hack. Little is known of Mrs Haywood's private life. She was an actress in Dublin around 1715 but shortly afterwards moved to London, where she wrote a few unsuccessful plays, and collaborated with William Hatchett on *Tom Thumb the Great* (1733), a comic opera with music by Arne, adapted from FIELDING's *Tragedy of Tragedies*. From 1744 to 1746 she edited *The Female Spectator*, a monthly collection of essays. In a career which spanned nearly 40 years she produced many novels, ranging from collaboration with DEFOE on *The Life of Mr Duncan Campbell* (1720), through the *ROMAN À CLEF Memoirs of a Certain Island Adjacent to Utopia* (1725), to *The History of Jemmy and Jenny Jessamy* (1753), which was praised by SCOTT for its pathos in *OLD MORTALITY*. She consistently asserted the didactic moral purpose of her work, both in prefaces and in the body of the texts, but was nevertheless condemned by POPE in *THE DUNCIAD* as 'the libellous Novelist' and by SWIFT as a 'stupid, infamous, scribbling woman'.

Hazard of New Fortunes, A A novel by WILLIAM DEAN HOWELLS, published in 1890. The title refers to Basil March's decision to move his family from Boston to New York and work for *Every Other Week*, a new magazine financed by Jacob Dryfoos. Dryfoos's son Conrad also works for the magazine but without interest, since he wants to become a minister; he has fallen in love with Margaret Vance, a young society woman he has met through his charitable work. March hires Lindau, an elderly socialist of German extraction who had taught him German when he was young, to translate pieces for the magazine. The idealistic Lindau interests young Conrad, but Jacob Dryfoos is enraged when he learns that Lindau is a socialist, and orders March to dismiss him. March refuses to do so, but Lindau – morally outraged at having received money (even if indirectly) from Dryfoos, a strike-breaking capitalist – resigns and returns all the money he has earned from the magazine. Near the end of the novel, both Conrad and Lindau appear on the scene of a streetcar-workers' strike. Conrad is killed by a stray bullet from a policeman's gun, and Lindau dies later from injuries inflicted by the police who are breaking the strike. Disheartened by his son's death, Jacob sells the magazine and travels to Europe with his wife and daughters to try their 'fortunes' in European society. Margaret Vance becomes an Episcopalian nun.

Hazlitt, William 1778–1830 Essayist, journalist and critic. Hazlitt was born at Maidstone, Kent, where his father, a friend of JOSEPH PRIESTLEY and RICHARD PRICE, was a Unitarian minister. After a period in America the family settled at the village of Wem, Shropshire, and here Hazlitt spent most of his youth, receiving his first education from his father. An intellectually precocious boy (his first essay, 'A Project for a New Theory of Criminal and Civil Legislation', appeared in 1792), he was intended for the ministry and attended the Unitarian college at Hackney in 1793–5. But he soon developed an 'extreme distaste' for the religious life and spent the next three years reading and painting. Through his father he became acquainted with COLERIDGE, who introduced him to WORDSWORTH, and although he was later to quarrel bitterly with them on politics and criticism, it was largely under the stimulus of their 'winged words', during the heady period of the LYRICAL BALLADS, that his 'understanding' found 'a language to express itself'. He continued to paint, however, producing portraits of his two friends, as well as LAMB, and it was not until 1804–5 that he decided his real talents lay in philosophy and literature. In London Lamb introduced him to GODWIN and other literary figures, and he began a long career as a prolific critic, journalist, essayist and lecturer.

Although his sympathies were radical and republican, his temperament precluded precisely defined loyalties, and he was always something of a one-man political party: he was strongly in support of the French Revolution, and deeply concerned about social conditions in England, yet his admiration for Napoleon lacked discrimination, and his attacks on opponents were often manifestly rancorous. In 1805 he published *An Essay on the Principles of Human Action*, a systematic defence of the unity of the mind against prevailing doctrines of sense impressions, which was followed in 1807 by his *Reply* to MALTHUS's

Essay on Population, in which he sides with Godwin, and *The Eloquence of the British Senate*, an annotated selection of parliamentary speeches by BURKE, Chatham, Fox, the younger Pitt and others. In 1808 he was married to Sarah Stoddard, with whom he settled first at Winterslow, near Salisbury, and then in London. In 1810 he lectured *On the Rise and Progress of Modern Philosophy* and published his *New and Improved Grammar of the English Language*, based on the linguistic theories of HORNE TOOKE.

He then exchanged philosophy for literature and journalism, and was a parliamentary reporter for THE MORNING CHRONICLE until 1814, when he became the paper's theatrical critic. He was by now also writing essays for *The Champion*, LEIGH HUNT's EXAMINER and THE EDINBURGH REVIEW. His *Characters of Shakespeare* appeared in 1817, and established him as a Shakespearean critic second only to Coleridge. The volume was dedicated to Lamb, with whom he enjoyed a long, if sometimes bumpy, friendship. It found an ardent admirer in KEATS, who was also deeply impressed, and influenced in his own writing, by *The Round Table* (with Leigh Hunt; 1817) and, above all, by the *Lectures on the English Poets* (1818), which immediately anticipate Keats's idea of the poet as an individual of NEGATIVE CAPABILITY. Hazlitt's next important critical work was the *Lectures on the English Comic Writers* (1819), which was followed in the same year by his *Political Essays* addressing the conditions of the poor.

In 1820 Hazlitt, who had been living apart from his wife, became passionately involved with Sarah Walker, his landlord's daughter. It was an attachment that was to bring him close to insanity over a period of three years. After divorcing his wife in Scotland, he returned to London to discover that the young lady had transferred her affections to another, if indeed she had not been deceiving him all along. His *Liber amoris* (1823) was, to his contemporaries, an embarrassingly transparent description of the whole affair, and was charitably described by DE QUINCEY as a kind of necessary exorcism, 'an explosion of frenzy... to empty his overburdened spirit'. His *Characteristics*, in imitation of La Rochefoucauld, appeared later in the same year.

Hazlitt had angered Leigh Hunt with a rather spiteful attack on SHELLEY in his *Table Talk* (1821–2), an action for which he made at least partial amends by contributing five pieces to THE LIBERAL (1823–4), a journal planned, with Hunt as editor, by BYRON and Shelley in Italy, shortly before the latter's death. In 1824 Hazlitt was married to a Mrs Bridgewater, a union which came to a mysteriously abrupt end in 1825, following his return from a European tour. Over the next two years he published two collections of essays containing some of his best work, THE SPIRIT OF THE AGE (1825) and *The Plain Speaker* (1826). One of his most unusual pieces is his account of his conversations with the painter Northcote, which appeared as *Boswell Redivivus* in 1827. The major project of his solitary last years was his *Life of Napoleon* (4 vols., 1828–30), a rather poorly researched and one-sided account which he considered his most important work.

Hazlitt's claim to literary fame is unusual in that it is founded almost exclusively on his work as a descriptive and critical essayist. Although he was often condemned as a hack, his ideas on art and creativity were highly regarded by later 19th-century writers and critics. Taken as a whole, his writing represents an early attempt at a critical history of English literature, and the establishment of the criteria of a canon. Whilst his judgements are based on conspicuously 'Romantic' ideas, he was hostile to Wordsworth's subjectivism and Coleridge's system-building, and fought against their tendency to exempt the artist from social and political responsibilities. On the other hand, his own lack of system prevented any bridging of the political and the aesthetic, and his appeal to well-tempered 'feeling' as a barometer of the good in art begs as many questions as it answers.

Hazzard, Shirley 1931– Australian novelist and short-story writer. Born and educated in Sydney, she went overseas with her parents in 1947. Her father was a trade commissioner whose postings took the family to Hong Kong and Wellington. In 1952–62 she worked in New York for the United Nations, about which she has written two works of non-fiction. She lives in Manhattan but pays frequent visits to Italy, the setting of *The Evening of the Holiday* (1966) and *The Bay of Noon* (1970), two early but formally assured works which follow the quests of their heroines in the tradition of Flaubert and HENRY JAMES. She first achieved recognition for her short stories, many of them published in THE NEW YORKER and subsequently collected in *Cliffs of Fall* (1963). *People in Glass Houses* (1967), a series of interconnected satirical portraits of people working for a dehumanizing institution, confirmed her stature. Her reputation further increased with *The Transit of Venus* (1980), winner of the US National Book Critics' Award for the best novel of the year, and a best-seller. Extending the themes of her earlier fiction, it encompasses a broad survey of the political and social movements of post-war society in its account of the odyssey of two sisters in Australia and England.

He Knew He was Right A novel by ANTHONY TROLLOPE, serialized in weekly numbers from October 1868 to May 1869, and published in two volumes in 1869.

Louis Trevelyan, a gentleman of education and secure private means, marries Emily Rowley, eldest of eight daughters of a colonial administrator. He becomes unreasonably jealous of the frequent visits made to their house by Colonel Osborne, a middle-aged friend of her father with the reputation of being a Lothario, and forbids Emily to receive him. She submits, but when Trevelyan vacillates and Osborne resumes his visits, her husband's jealousy becomes obsessive, hard words are exchanged, and they separate, she taking their young son with her. Sure that he is right in his suspicions, and insisting on a promise never to see Osborne again which Emily feels she cannot give, Trevelyan hires a private detective to watch her and with his help abducts the boy. They go to Italy where Trevelyan declines into a state of complete mental and physical breakdown. Emily follows him there and persuades him to return to England, where he dies. In one of several sub-plots Emily's sister Nora falls in love with Trevelyan's friend Hugh Stanbury, choosing him in preference to a wealthy aristocratic suitor, Mr Glascock. The novel's interest in the question of women's independence is reflected in the hostile portrait of an American feminist, Wallachia Petrie.

Head, Bessie 1937–86 South African novelist. Born in Pietermaritzburg, she lived in Botswana from the mid-1960s. In *When Rain Clouds Gather* (1968), *Maru* (1971) and *A Question of Power* (1974), her first three novels, she established connections between personal morality and political integrity; each investigates a lonely character's private problems within a corporate environment, so that the two intermesh. *Maru* and, especially, *A Question of Power* confront the nightmares of personal alienation and political tyranny through kaleidoscopic imagery of racism and sexism. *The Collector of Treasures* (1977) contains village tales that she collected and shaped. *Serowe:*

Bessie Head

Village of the Rain Wind (1981) recreates from oral tradition the history of the Bamangwato capital in Botswana, while *A Bewitched Crossroad* (1984) is a novel about peace and security under the benevolent Bamangwato king, Khama III (1875–1923), after the early 19th-century 'Wars of Calamity' in Central and Southern Africa. Posthumous publications include *A Woman Alone: Autobiographical Writings* (1990), *A Gesture of Belonging: Letters from Bessie Head, 1965–79* (1990) and *Tales of Tenderness and Power* (1990).

Head, Richard ?1637–?1686 Bookseller and hack. Of English parentage, Head was born in Ireland; his father, a domestic chaplain, was murdered in the rebellion of 1641, and the family escaped to England. Head was educated at Bridport Grammar School and was admitted to Oxford, but left before taking a degree, occupying himself initially in the bookselling trade and subsequently as a poorly paid publisher's hack. He was eventually drowned. His most famous work, often reprinted, is the licentious PICARESQUE fiction *The English Rogue: Described in the Life of Meriton Latroon, A Witty Extravagant* (1665), much of which is autobiographical. His many other productions include an eccentric comedy of Irish life, *Hic et ubique: or, The Humours of Dublin* (1663).

Headlong Hall The first of THOMAS LOVE PEACOCK's satirical novels, published in 1816. It reworks the themes of his two unpublished FARCES, 'The Dilettanti' and 'The Three Doctors'. Like most of his subsequent works it is cast in the form of a comic Platonic symposium.

The disputatious group of guests invited to spend Christmas at Squire Headlong's Welsh country house represents a broad spectrum of contemporary opinion on matters cultural, philosophical and scientific. The principal figures are Mr Foster the perfectibilian, Mr Escot the deteriorationist, Mr Jenkison the status quo-ite, and the Reverend Doctor Gaster, a gourmandizing cleric who has caught the Squire's eye with a learned treatise on the art of stuffing a turkey. They are joined by Dr Cranium, the phrenologist, and his daughter Cephalis; Mr Milestone, the landscape gardener; Mr Panscope the polymath; and assorted musicians, poets, and daughters of marriageable age.

The central debate addresses the question of civilization and progress. Foster rehearses the rational optimism of Condorcet and GODWIN, while the pessimist Escot is a blend of Rousseau, MALTHUS and the notes to SHELLEY's *QUEEN MAB*, and, though sometimes cranky, generally emerges ahead of his complacent opponent on points. In a finely worked comic episode Mr Milestone's expert comment on the unimproved appearance of his gardens causes his host to call immediately for explosives to blow away an offending rock, with near-fatal consequences for two of the guests. The Squire again proves true to his name during the DÉNOUEMENT, when in a matter of almost as many minutes he arranges no fewer than four marriages, including his own.

Heaney, Seamus (Justin) 1939– Irish poet. The son of a Roman Catholic farmer and cattle dealer, he was born in Mossbawn, County Derry, in Northern Ireland, and won scholarships to St Columb's College, Londonderry, and Queen's University, Belfast. After working as an English teacher at St Thomas's secondary school, Belfast, and at St Joseph's College, he was appointed a lecturer at Queen's University. In the 1960s he joined the regular meetings of Belfast poets organized by PHILIP HOBSBAUM and attended by MICHAEL LONGLEY, DEREK MAHON and James Simmons. After Hobsbaum's departure the group, meeting in Heaney's house, grew to include PAUL MULDOON, Frank Orsmby and Michael Foley. After working as guest lecturer at the University of California, Berkeley, in 1970–1, Heaney decided to leave Northern Ireland for the Republic, living first in County Wicklow and then moving to Dublin in 1976. He was appointed Boylston Professor of Rhetoric and Oratory at Harvard University in 1984 and professor of poetry at Oxford in 1989.

His early poetry, beginning with *Death of a Naturalist* (1966) and *Door into the Dark* (1969), is drawn from childhood experience as well as his strong – and enduring – sense of habitat and environment. The economic use of language never detracts from its value. *Wintering Out* (1972), *North* (1975) and *Field Work* (1979) are more political, beginning his intense concentration on the cultural and historical implications of words. They have been followed by: *Sweeney Astray* (1983), a version of the medieval Irish *Buile Suibhne*; *Station Island* (1984); *Haw Lantern* (1987), with its memorable first poem, 'Alphabets'; and *Seeing Things* (1991), which contains a sequel to the 'Glanmore Sonnets' in *Field Work*. *Selected Poems 1965–75* was published in 1980, *Selected Poems 1966–87* in 1990. His wide-ranging criticism includes *Preoccupations* (1980), *The Government of the Tongue and Other Critical Writings* (1988) and *The Redress of Poetry* (1990). Despite his connection with the USA and his growing reputation there, Heaney has underlined his commitment to the Republic of Ireland by his work (with TOM PAULIN and Seamus Deane) as a director of BRIAN FRIEL's theatre company, Field Day.

Hearn, (Patricio) Lafcadio (Tessima Carlos) 1850–1904 Journalist, travel-writer, novelist and writer about Japan. Born in Greece of Irish-Greek parentage, he was educated in France and England. In 1869 he emigrated to the USA but his progress in journalism was hampered by poverty and the scandal caused by his living with a black woman. His first successful newspaper articles were colourful descriptions of Creole life based on his experiences in New Orleans in 1877. *Gombo Zhebes*, published in 1885, was a collection of proverbs in French from Louisiana and the West Indies; this was followed in 1890 by *Two Years in the French West Indies*. Hearn then travelled to Japan to write a series of articles for HARPER'S NEW MONTHLY MAGAZINE, and in fact remained there for the rest of his life, becoming a Japanese citizen and adopting the name Yakimo Koizumi. His works describing the Japanese land, people and customs include *Gleanings in Buddha-Fields* (1897), *In Ghostly Japan* (1899), *A Japanese Miscellany* (1901) and *Japan: An Attempt at Interpretation* (1904). *Chita* (1889) is a novel set on the Gulf Coast of Louisiana.

Hearne, John 1926– Jamaican novelist. Born in Montreal, Canada, he saw wartime RAF service, and has taught and been an Arts Centre director. In his elegantly written novels articulate, middle-class characters respond generously to calls upon their humanity, but with disastrous personal consequences, as in *Voices under the Window* (1955), *Stranger at the Gate* (1956) and *The Autumn Equinox* (1959). The latter two novels and *The Faces of Love* (1957) and *Land of the Living* (1961), which both explore complex relationships between intellectual lovers, are about the fictional Caribbean island of Cayuna, a surrogate for Jamaica. Set on a slave-ship, *The Sure Salvation* (1981), his finest novel to date, is an ingenious treatment of racial conflict. As John Morris, he co-authored two thrillers with Morris Cargill.

Hearne, Thomas 1678–1735 Antiquary. He was born at Littlefield Green in Berkshire and educated at St Edmund Hall, Oxford. In 1712 he became keeper of the Bodleian Library but was deprived of his office as a NONJUROR in 1716, thereafter refusing invitations to political office of any kind and adhering to his Jacobite convictions.

Hearne was author of *Reliquiae Bodleianae: or, Some Genuine Remains of Sir Thomas Bodley* (1703) and *Ductor historicus: or, A Short System of Universal History and an Introduction to the Study of It* (1704–5); he was the editor of a valuable series of texts by English chroniclers and published editions of JOHN LELAND and WILLIAM CAMDEN. He appears as Wormius in POPE'S *THE DUNCIAD*.

Heart of Darkness A story by JOSEPH CONRAD, written in 1899 and published in 1902 in *Youth: A Narrative, with Two Other Stories*. This dark and riddling parable of imperialism, self-discovery and self-destruction is told mainly by Marlow to his friends as they wait on a yacht for the tide to turn in the Thames estuary. He had been employed by a European trading company to replace a steamship captain on a great African river (clearly the Congo).

The Westerners he meets at the trading post and the Central Station are interested only in extracting ivory and do not notice the suffering of the native workers. Marlow is sent upriver to rescue Kurtz, an agent, now seriously ill, whose commercial success is matched by his reputation for idealism. Expecting to meet an apostle of Western civilization, he finds a man who has made himself the natives' god. His depravity is signalled by the human heads which decorate the posts outside his hut. Marlow retains a paradoxical admiration for Kurtz, whose deathbed cry – 'The horror! The horror!' – intimates a kind of desperate self-knowledge. Having left a native woman grieving Kurtz's departure on the bank of the river, Marlow returns to the European city where the company has its headquarters and lies to Kurtz's 'Intended' by telling her that Kurtz had spoken her name as he died.

Heart of Midlothian, The A novel by SIR WALTER SCOTT, published in 1818 as the second series of *Tales of My Landlord*.

The heart of Midlothian is the Tolbooth prison in Edinburgh, and the story opens with the Porteous Riots of 1736. Porteous, commander of the city guard, had opened fire without reasonable provocation at the hanging of a robber named Wilson. Porteous was acquitted at his trial but the mob, led by Robertson (an associate of Wilson), stormed the prison. Robertson loves Effie Deans, imprisoned within on a charge of child murder, and the attack on the prison thus has a double motive for him. The mob drags Porteous from the prison and lynches him; Effie refuses to escape, preferring to face trial, knowing herself innocent. But at her trial her sister Jeanie, having taken the oath, cannot bring herself to lie and thus ensure Effie's acquittal. Effie is convicted and sentenced to death.

Jeanie sets out to walk to London to gain audience with Queen Caroline and is fortunate in having the help of the Duke of Argyle. The Queen is moved by Jeanie's honesty and a pardon is secured for Effie. Jeanie is enabled to marry her suitor, Reuben Butler. Robertson is now revealed as George Staunton, a rather wild son of good family and the father of Effie's child. He persuades Effie to marry him and, as Lady Staunton, she learns that the son whom she had been accused of murdering is alive. He had been stolen by a crazed girl, Madge Wildfire, and was eventually left with a band of robbers. Staunton is unwittingly killed by his own son when he tries to retrieve him from the robber band.

Modern readers and critics, who have on the whole reversed the judgement of earlier generations and allowed Scott's work to sink into neglect, have usually agreed that *Heart of Midlothian* is the finest of his novels and that Jeanie Deans is his best-realized character. The book is notable, too, for the lyric, 'Proud Maisie', sung by the dying Madge Wildfire.

Heart of the Matter, The A novel by GRAHAM GREENE, published in 1948.

The novel is located in typical Greene territory: a physical and moral wilderness in West Africa where the harsh climate and the still harsher struggle for survival furnish the back-drop to an intense moral drama. The story takes place during World War II. The deputy commissioner of police, Scobie, a Roman Catholic, becomes the victim of his own compassion for others: first for his unstable wife, Louise, then for a young widow, Helen, with whom he has an affair. Finding himself in debt, Scobie borrows money. This initiates a progressive descent into 'hell' which is observed throughout by a young intelligence agent, Wilson.

Increasingly, Scobie's attempts to retrieve his life only compromise him further, and he inadvertently causes the death of his servant Ali. He decides to commit suicide, a mortal sin in terms of his Catholic creed, and endeavours to conceal this from his wife by fabricating his diary. Wilson, who is in love with Louise but acts in his official capacity, uncovers the deceit after Scobie's death, thereby exposing the final tragic paradox in the latter's life.

Though many critics, including GEORGE ORWELL and WALTER ALLEN, have rejected the novel as sentimental and contrived, it epitomizes Greene's fiction and has continued to be one of his most-discussed works.

Heartbreak House: *A Fantasia in the Russian Manner on English Themes* A play by GEORGE BERNARD SHAW, begun before World War I, published in 1919 and produced in New York in 1920 and at the ROYAL COURT THEATRE in 1921.

The action ostensibly takes place during the war, since it closes during an air raid, but the war is not mentioned by any of the characters and the air raid has to be seen as a device to bring about a resolution. Shaw wrote that 'Heartbreak House... is cultured, leisured Europe before the war'; he presents a series of extraordinary encounters and mistaken identities in a crazy house (part of which has been rebuilt as the after-deck of a sailing ship) owned by the eccentric retired Captain Shotover, aged 88, and presided over by one of his daughters, Mrs Hector Hushabye. She invites her friend, Ellie Dunn, to stay. Ellie Dunn is engaged to Boss Mangan, an oaf of a millionaire, for the sake of her father Mazzini Dunn who, though clever and an idealist, has been outmanoeuvred by financiers. Ellie confides to Mrs Hushabye that she has fallen in love with Marcus Darnley, whom she met at a concert; but he turns out to be Hector Hushabye, a pathological liar and philanderer. Captain Shotover wonders if Ellie's father can be Billy Dunn, the boatswain and ex-pirate he once employed; but that Dunn turns up to burgle the house and is killed in the air raid with Boss Mangan. Another visitor to the house is Lady Utterword, another of the captain's daughters, whose husband has been governor of all the Crown Colonies in succession.

The great virtue of *Heartbreak House* lies in the exploration of motive in a very uncertain world, mostly through the conversations between Captain Shotover and Ellie. She seems able to focus his sympathy and intelligence better than anyone and provokes his comments on the present, which he observes from the eminence of old age.

Heath, Roy (Aubrey Kelvin) 1926– Guyanese novelist, who lives in London. His description of himself as 'a chronicler of Guyanese life in this century' is both accurate and understated, though his Guyana often has a gothic dimension. His novels range over slum poverty in *A Man Come Home* (1974), middle-class respectability in the trilogy, *From the Heat of the Day* (1979), *One Generation* (1981) and *Genetha* (1981), rural destitution in *Kwaku* (1982), and the clash between the values of 'civilization' and the hinterland in *Orealla* (1984). His fiction transcends the regional, however. Despite all the dissonances of Guyanese life that he faithfully records, he has developed a narrative technique that successfully blends social realism with the Amerindian, African and Indian folk legend and myth in Guyanese popular beliefs, in order to analyse modern problems like male-female relationships, personal liberty, and bourgeois ambitions in poverty-stricken communities. His treatment of psychotic behaviour in *The Murderer* (1978) constitutes original, ironical commentary on the 'normal'. Later novels include *Shadows round the Moon* (1991).

Heath-Stubbs, John (Francis Alexander) 1918– Poet. Born in London and educated at The Queen's College, Oxford, he worked as a teacher and in publishing before taking up fellowships and professorial posts at Leeds, Alexandria and Michigan. His first poems appeared with the work of KEITH DOUGLAS and SIDNEY KEYES in *Eight Oxford Poets* (1941). Later volumes, including *Wounded Thammuz* (1942), *Beauty and the Beast* (1943), *The Triumph of the Muse* (1958), *Selected Poems* (1965), the epic *Artorius* (1973), *The Watchman's Flute* (1975), *A Parliament of Birds* (1975), *Birds Reconvened* (1980), *Naming the Beasts* (1982), *Cats' Parnassus* (1987), *Collected Poems* (1988) and *Selected Poems* (1990), established him as a traditionalist with an interest in classical subjects and forms. His many translations include the poetry of Leopardi (1946) and Hafiz (1952) and a version of THE RUBÁIYÁT OF OMAR KHAYYÁM (1979). He has also edited *The Faber Book of Twentieth-Century Verse* (with DAVID WRIGHT; 1953), and written critical studies of BEDDOES, JOHN CLARE and GEORGE DARLEY, in *The Darkling Plain* (1950), and of CHARLES WILLIAMS (1955).

Heber, Reginald 1783–1826 Bishop and hymn-writer. Educated at Brasenose College, Oxford, where he won the Newdigate Prize with his poem 'Palestine', he was elected a Fellow of All Souls, and ordained in 1807. In 1822 he was appointed Bishop of Calcutta and he died in Trichinopoly four years later. He was the author of a *Narrative of a Journey through the Upper Provinces of India 1824–1825* and a few volumes of poetry, but he is best known for his hymns, which include: 'Brightest and Best of the Sons of the Morning!', 'From Greenland's Icy Mountains', 'The Son of God Goes Forth to War' and 'Holy, Holy, Holy! Lord God Almighty!'.

Hecht, Ben 1894–1964 American playwright, screenwriter and novelist. He was born in New York but his family later moved to Racine, Wisconsin, where he attended high school. After a brief period at the University of Wisconsin he moved to Chicago. He worked there for many years as a reporter, establishing a reputation as the most creative and energetic newsman in the city. In the early 1920s he began writing novels, the most successful of which was *Erik Dorn* (1921), a work inspired in part by his years in Germany as foreign correspondent for the Chicago *Daily News* after World War I. He did not achieve national prominence, however, until he began writing plays in the mid-1920s. He scored a huge success with *The Front Page* (co-written with CHARLES MACARTHUR; 1928), about Chicago newspapermen. He and MacArthur also co-wrote the popular comedy *Twentieth Century* (1932). From the early 1930s Hecht turned his attention to screenwriting, and he and MacArthur enjoyed further collaborative success. Their screenplays include *Nothing Sacred* (1937), *Wuthering Heights* (1939), *Spellbound* (1945) and *Notorious* (1946).

Heinlein, Robert A(nson) 1907–88 American writer of SCIENCE FICTION. His love of military life and his regret at not serving in World War II are obvious in the glorification of heroism which permeates his fiction. He began publishing science fiction stories in the pulp magazines in 1939, and was the first writer to fit a number of stories together into a coherent future history; they were assembled into the collection *The Past through Tomorrow* (1967) and that history features as an 'alternate world' in some of his subsequent novels. Heinlein's understanding of technology and enthusiasm for the myth of the conquest of space made him an outstanding pulp writer, and he was one of the first science fiction writers to break into more respectable markets. In the 1950s he wrote many novels aimed at teenagers, as well as the political fantasy *Double Star* (1956) and the future war story *Starship Troopers* (1959), but changed direction abruptly with *Stranger in a Strange Land* (1961), a best-selling novel with a messianic hero whose promotion of libertarian politics and morals managed to anticipate both the 1960s counter-culture and the right-wing backlash of the 1970s. His work grew increasingly idiosyncratic, extensive elaboration of his personal preoccupations largely displacing plot and invention. *The Cat Who Walked through Walls* (1985) and its sequel *To Sail beyond the Sunset* (1987) are typical examples.

Heir of Redclyffe, The A novel by CHARLOTTE M. YONGE, published in 1853. Sir Guy Morville, generous and impulsive, secretly pays the debts of his reprobate uncle but is consequently unable to explain his supposed extravagance to his guardian. His delicate and malicious cousin Philip accuses him of gambling, which prompts Guy's guardian to banish him from his house and the presence of his daughter Amy, whom he loves. Guy is later rehabilitated and married to Amy. Travelling to Italy, they encounter Philip dangerously ill with fever. Forgiving all injury, Guy nurses him back to health but catches the fever himself and dies. When Amy's child, a girl, is born, Philip becomes the heir of Redclyffe. The novel was immensely successful, passing through 17 editions in 15 years.

Heiress, The A comedy by JOHN BURGOYNE, first produced at DRURY LANE in 1786, and published in the same year. It was a great success, being quickly translated and played in France and Germany.

The plot concerns the wooing of Lady Emily Gayville by Clifford, her brother's close friend. Lord Gayville himself is expected to marry the vulgar Miss Alscrip, daughter of a newly rich family, because of her wealth. When Miss Alscrip is introduced to Emily, Gayville is made painfully aware of how silly and pretentious his fiancée is. Then he encounters a girl in the street, Miss Alton, and loses his heart to her. He follows her to her modest lodging and is so eager that he embarrasses her; to escape his attentions she goes into service, with Miss Alscrip. All ends well when she is discovered to be Clifford's long-lost sister, and the true heiress to the Alscrip fortune.

Heller, Joseph 1923– American novelist. He was born in Brooklyn, and educated at New York and Columbia universities. He is still best known for *CATCH-22* (1961), an anti-war SATIRE which drew on his own military experience, as he did again for his play *We Bombed in New Haven* (1968). Classed with NORMAN MAILER'S *THE NAKED AND THE DEAD* and KURT VONNEGUT'S *Slaughterhouse-Five*, *Catch-22* has given the language a term for self-contradicting illogic. His subsequent novels are *Something Happened* (1974), *Good as Gold* (1979), *God Knows* (1984) and *Picture This* (1988). His experience as a victim of Guillain-Barré syndrome, a debilitating virus, is described in *No Laughing Matter* (with Speed Vogel; 1986).

Hellman, Lillian (Florence) 1907–84 American playwright. Born in New Orleans, she started work as a publisher's reader while still a student at New York University and already had several years' experience as a reader of plays and filmscripts when she wrote her first play, *The Children's Hour* (1934), which tells of the havoc caused by a malicious schoolgirl's invention of a lesbian relationship between her two teachers. Though controversial, the play was an immediate success. She followed it with *Days to Come* (1936), which was a failure, and with several filmscripts. In 1937 her anti-fascist convictions led her to visit Spain. Her second successful play, THE LITTLE FOXES (1939), dealt with the breaking up of a Southern family, the Hubbards, through greed, cruelty and hunger for power; it was followed by two anti-Nazi dramas, *Watch on the Rhine* (1941) and *The Searching Wind* (1944). *Another Part of the Forest* (1946) took a second look at the Hubbard family, some 20 years earlier, revealing the sources of their cruelty and hatred for one another.

Called to testify in 1952 by the House Un-American Activities Committee, she agreed to talk about her own involvement with radical movements but refused to discuss the involvement of others. She was not sent to jail, but many friends were, including her companion, DASHIELL HAMMETT. One of her three autobiographical volumes, *Scoundrel Time* (1976), tells the story of this period of her life. The others, *An Unfinished Woman* (1969) and *Pentimento* (1973), are largely concerned with her childhood experiences and early political and personal involvements. She wrote two other plays, *The Autumn Garden* (1951) and *Toys in the Attic* (1960).

Helps, Sir Arthur 1813–75 Essayist, historian and novelist. Educated at Eton and Cambridge, he was appointed Clerk to the Privy Council in 1860, a post which led to his friendship with Queen Victoria. He edited *Speeches and Addresses of the Prince Consort* (1862) and Victoria's own *Leaves from the Journal of Our Life in the Highlands* (1868). He also published: three plays; three novels (including the popular *Realmah*, 1868); aphorisms (*Thoughts in the Cloister and the Crowd*, 1835); essays and dialogues (*Essays Written in the Intervals of Business*, 1841, and *Friends in Council*, four series, 1847–59); biography (*Columbus*, 1869, and *Hernando Cortes*, 1871); and history (*The Conquerors of the New World*, 1848–52, and *The Spanish Conquest in America*, 1855–61).

Helwig, David 1938– Canadian poet, novelist and short-story writer. Born in Toronto, he grew up there and in Hamilton and Niagara-on-the-Lake, Ontario. He attended the universities of Toronto and Liverpool, where he did postgraduate work between 1960 and 1962. Since then, apart from a period as a story editor for Canadian Broadcasting Corporation televi-sion, he has taught at Queen's University, Kingston, Ontario. Helwig's earliest poems, first collected in *Figures in a Landscape* (1967), deal mainly with everyday, domestic subjects, but in subsequent work he has tended to focus on the sinister and violent. It includes *The Sign of the Gunman* (1969), *The Best Name of Silence* (1972), *A Book of the Hours* (1979) and *Talking Prophet Blues* (1989). *Atlantic Crossings* (1974) – which describes journeys to the New World by St Brendan, a slave trader, Columbus and a Norse woman – attempts a reassessment of Canadian history. *The Glass Knight* (1976), *Jennifer* (1979), *It is Always Summer* (1982) and *A Sound like Laughter* (1983) form a tetralogy of novels set in Kingston. His other novels are *The Day before Tomorrow* (1971), *A Postcard from Rome* (1988), *Old Wars* (1989) and *Of Desire* (1990). *The Streets of Summer* (1969) is a collection of short stories. Helwig has also edited *A Book about Billie* (1972), from taped interviews with a habitual criminal, a work that demonstrates his fascination with the darker side of life, and has co-edited several short-story anthologies.

Hemans, Felicia Dorothea 1793–1835 Poet. Born in Liverpool, the daughter of George Browne, a merchant, and his first wife, Felicity Wagner, she was educated by her mother. Her parents encouraged her literary aspirations and arranged for the publication of her earliest volumes, *Poems* and *England and Spain; or, Valour and Patriotism*, in 1808. Her first important collection was *The Domestic Afflictions* (1812). In the same year she married Captain Alfred Hemans, but the marriage ended in separation in 1818. Working to support her five sons, Felicia Hemans produced numerous volumes of poetry, most notably, *The Forest Sanctuary* (1825), *Records of Woman* (1828) and *Songs of the Affections* (1830). Of her two plays, *The Siege of Valencia* and *The Vespers of Palermo* (both published in 1823), only the latter was produced on stage, with little success. An accomplished scholar and an acknowledged beauty, she was the friend of SCOTT and WORDSWORTH. Her best-known poems are 'The Better Land', 'The Landing of the Pilgrim Fathers in New England' and 'Casablanca' ('The boy stood on the burning deck').

Heminges, John d. 1630 Actor and theatre administrator, one of the original shareholders in the Lord Chamberlain's Men, later the KING'S MEN, when it was formed in 1594. Heminges acted little after 1611, devoting his time instead to the increasingly complex financial affairs of the company. With his friend, fellow actor and fellow administrator Henry Condell (d. 1627), he undertook editorial responsibility for the SHAKESPEARE folio of 1623, saving for posterity 20 plays which might otherwise have been lost. The two men were both churchwardens of St Mary's, Aldermanbury, and their careers illustrate the ready acceptance of professional actors in the busy commercial world of Elizabethan and Jacobean London.

Hemingway, Ernest (Miller) 1898–1961 American novelist and short-story writer. Born in Oak Park, Illinois, he spent much of his early life in the Great Lakes region, which provided the settings for his early stories. After graduating from high school he worked as a reporter for *The Kansas City Star*, and then volunteered for service in World War I. He served with an ambulance unit and was wounded in 1918. After the war he worked as a journalist in Chicago and Toronto, and in 1921 married Hadley Richardson, seven years his senior. The couple moved to Paris, and made frequent excursions to Spain and to the Austrian Alps.

Hemingway made friends easily; among those who encouraged him in his literary career were EZRA POUND, GERTRUDE STEIN and FORD MADOX FORD. His first collection of stories, IN OUR TIME (1925), consists of 15 tales, some relating the experiences of the young Nick Adams in the Great Lakes region and in Europe. His first novel was *The Torrents of Spring* (1926). His second, which first made him famous, was THE SUN ALSO RISES (1926; called *Fiesta* in Britain), about the disillusionment of the 'lost generation' – young British and American expatriates in France and Spain – in the aftermath of World War I.

In 1927 Hemingway and Hadley Richardson were divorced and he married Pauline Pfeiffer. Later that year he published the collection *Men without*

Ernest Hemingway

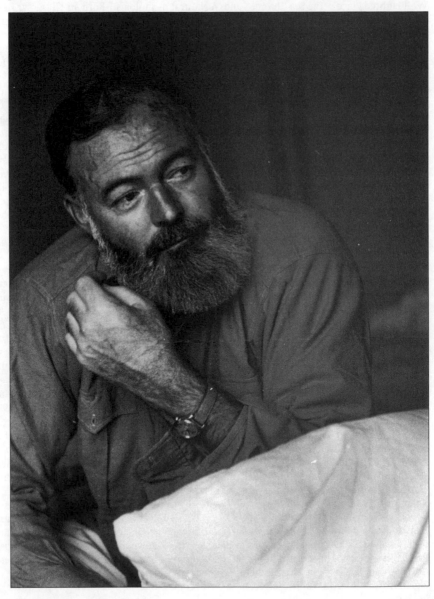

Women, which contains some of his most popular stories. 'The Killers' tells of Ole Andreson, whom two thugs have been hired to kill, and of his surrender to the fact that his death is inescapable. 'The Undefeated' depicts the pointless heroism of Garcia, an ageing bull-fighter facing his last fight. 'Fifty Grand' is a brutal and cynical tale of prizefighters, in which Jack Brennan bets money on his own defeat. Hemingway's next novel, *A FAREWELL TO ARMS* (1929), is the poignant story of Frederic Henry, an American lieutenant in the Italian ambulance corps during World War I, and Catherine Barkley, an English nurse on duty in Italy. *Death in the Afternoon* (1932), a study of bullfighting, was followed by *Winner Take Nothing* (1933), a collection of short stories including 'A Clean Well-Lighted Place', 'The Sea Change', and 'A Natural History of the Dead'. *Green Hills of Africa* (1935) is about big-game hunting. *To Have and Have Not* (1937) is a short novel about smuggling in the Key West-Havana region. The collection *The Fifth Column and the First Forty-Nine Stories* (1938) includes the story 'The Snows of Kilimanjaro'. *The Fifth Column*, a play about espionage in the Spanish Civil War, was subsequently produced in New York and in wartime England. The conflict in Spain, in which Hemingway was involved as a war reporter, also provided the background for *For Whom the Bell Tolls* (1940), an ambitious novel with the theme (implied in the title, with its quotation from JOHN DONNE) that the loss of freedom anywhere is a diminution of it everywhere. Hemingway was at the height of his fame and the book sold well: 270,000 copies in the first year.

In 1940 Hemingway was divorced from his second wife and married MARTHA GELLHORN. This marriage also ended in divorce, in December 1945, and he married his fourth wife, Mary Welsh, in March 1946. He spent World War II as a war correspondent, and in 1950 he published *Across the River and into the Trees*, his first novel in a decade. It was poorly received but he was awarded a belated PULITZER PRIZE for *The Old Man and the Sea* (1952), a parable of inner strength and courage about a Cuban fisherman's struggle to bring home a great marlin he has caught. Two years later he won the Nobel Prize for Literature. Still troubled by failing artistic and physical powers, he finally committed suicide. *A Moveable Feast*, a memoir of his years in Paris after World War I, was left completed but unrevised at his death. It was published in 1964. *Islands in the Stream* (1970) and *The Garden of Eden* (1986) are posthumously published novels; *The Dangerous Summer* (1985) is an account of his trip to Spain in 1959.

Henderson, Hamish 1919– Scottish poet, songwriter, folklorist and translator. Born in Blairgowrie, Perthshire, he read modern languages at Downing College, Cambridge, served in military intelligence in North Africa in World War II and became a lecturer in the School of Scottish Studies at Edinburgh University in 1951. His only volume of poetry, *Elegies for the Dead in Cyrenaica* (1948; reissued, 1977), is a tribute to 'the dead, the innocent' on both sides of the war in the 'brutish desert'. Henderson edited *Ballads of World War Two* in 1948 and in 1977 made a collection of songs on record, *Freedom Come All Ye*. His best-known songs – 'The John Maclean March' and 'Free Mandela' – show his strong socialist and republican sympathies. He is a distinguished translator of modern Italian poets such as Montale, Quasimodo and Ungaretti and has published an edition of Gramsci's *Letters from Prison* (1974).

Hendry, J(ames) F(indlay) 1912–86 Poet and anthologist. Born in Glasgow, Hendry studied French and Russian at Glasgow University, and German in London. After intelligence work during the war, he worked as a translator and interpreter before becoming professor of modern languages at Laurentian University, Ontario. He was a central figure in the NEW APOCALYPSE movement, introducing the first of its three major anthologies, *The New Apocalypse* (1939), and editing the other two, *The White Horseman* (1941) and *The Crown and the Sickle* (1943), with HENRY TREECE. Hendry's *Myth and Social Integration* (1940) is the major statement of the aims of the movement. Poems in *The Bombed Happiness* (1940) have tortuous, doom-laden imagery. *The Orchestral Mountain* (1943) attempts to connect the myth of Orpheus and Eurydice with the death of the poet's wife. A minor poet, he also published *Marimarusa* (1979), *A World Alien* (1980) and *Fernie Brae* (1987).

Henley, Beth 1952– American playwright and actress. Born in Jackson, Mississippi, she attended Southern Methodist University and the University of Illinois. Her first success, *Crimes of the Heart* (PULITZER PRIZE; 1981), is about three Mississippi sisters who rally round after one has shot her husband. It typifies her flair for witty, absurd comedy in the tradition of Southern Gothic. Other plays include: *The Wake of Jamey Foster* (1982); *Am I Blue?* (1982); *The Miss Firecracker Contest* (1984), another black comedy, about a woman's effort to redeem her life by winning a beauty contest; *The Debutante Ball* (1985); *The Lucky Spot* (1986); and *Abundance* (1990), about a 25-year friendship of mail-order brides in the Old West. She has also written screenplays for *Crimes* and *Miss Firecracker*.

Henley, W(illiam) E(rnest) 1849–1903 Poet, critic and editor. Born in Gloucester, he was struck down as a child with tuberculosis and consequently had a leg amputated. He was treated in Edinburgh by Joseph Lister and during a long convalescence began his 'In Hospital' poems (first published in 1875), which have been hailed as early examples of free verse. It was also in Edinburgh that he met ROBERT LOUIS STEVENSON (who used him as a model for Long John Silver in *TREASURE ISLAND*), and they formed a close friendship which was later to end in a bitter quarrel. He became editor of *The Magazine of Art* in 1882, and brought the work of Whistler and Rodin to a wider public. In 1889 he returned to Edinburgh to edit *The Scots Observer* (later *The National Observer*), an imperial review which aimed to increase Scottish cultural and political influence, and which introduced KIPLING. In 1894 he returned to England and edited the short-lived *New Review*, before settling to poetry in his last years.

Henley is best known for the poem 'Invictus' (1875), which contains the lines 'I am the master of my fate:/ I am the captain of my soul.' His poetry collections include *A Book of Verses* (1888), *The Song of the Sword* (1892), *London Voluntaries* (1893), *For England's Sake* (1900) and *Hawthorn and Lavender* (1901). There are two volumes of art and literary journalism: *Views and Reviews I* and *II* (1890 and 1892). Among many anthologies the best known is *Lyra heroica* (1891), a selection of verse for boys. There was an influential edition of BURNS (1896–7) and the *Tudor Translations* (1892–1903). He wrote four plays with Stevenson: *Deacon Brodie* (1882), *Admiral Guinea* (1884), *Beau Austin* (1884) and *Macaire* (1885).

Henri, Adrian See LIVERPOOL POETS.

Henrietta Temple A novel by BENJAMIN DISRAELI, published in 1837.

Ferdinand Armine, son of poor but noble parents, enters the army and is soon in debt; but he has hopes of a legacy from his grandfather. When this does not materialize, he proposes to his cousin, Katherine Grandison, because she is wealthy. But he falls in love with the penniless Henrietta Temple and becomes engaged to her, too. Ferdinand's treachery is exposed and Henrietta deserts him. In Italy Henrietta meets Lord Montfort, whom she consents to marry at her father's urging. Katherine, meanwhile, has forgiven Ferdinand and released him. She and Count Mirabel undertake to remedy Ferdinand's situation. He meets Henrietta again and her love for him is reawakened, while Lord Montfort is drawn to Katherine. Lord Montfort gives up Henrietta, who inherits a fortune and helps Ferdinand. Katherine marries Lord Montfort.

Henry, O. [Porter, William Sidney] 1862–1910 American short-story writer. He was born in North Carolina. He founded *The Rolling Stone*, a comic weekly magazine, in 1894. Five years later, while serving a three-year prison sentence for alleged embezzlement in Columbus, Ohio, he began to write short stories published under the pseudonym of O. Henry.

After his release from prison in 1902 he went to New York, where he became a popular and prolific writer of short stories for magazines. His stories are characteristically marked by a twist of plot which turns on an ironic or coincidental circumstance, and he is a master of the surprise ending. His first collection, *Cabbages and Kings* (1904), is set in South America; his second, *The Four Million* (1906), in New York. His other volumes are *Heart of the West* (1907), *The Trimmed Lamp* (1907), *The Gentle Grafter* (1908), *The Voice of the City* (1908), *Options* (1909), *Roads of Destiny* (1909), *Whirligigs* (1910) and *Strictly Business* (1910). Four more volumes were published posthumously: *Sixes and Sevens* (1911), *Rolling Stones* (1912), *Waifs and Strays* (1917) and *Postscripts* (1923).

Henry IV, King A history play in two parts by WILLIAM SHAKESPEARE. The shaping of the plot, drawn largely from HOLINSHED's *Chronicles*, suggests that he had the second part in mind when he prepared the first. Even so, they are distinct, and can be performed separately.

Part One. Probably first performed in 1597 and first published in Quarto (Q1) in 1598. Modern editors collate this text with that in the First Folio of 1623. The historical events described in the play begin with the uprising of Owen Glendower and the defeat of the invading Scots by Henry Percy (Hotspur) and culminate in the defeat and death of Hotspur at the Battle of Shrewsbury (1403). The decisive usurper, Bolingbroke of *RICHARD II*, has been transformed into a careworn king, thwarted in his desire to expiate his crime by leading a crusade by the threat of civil war. Henry IV is further troubled by his son's waywardness. Prince Hal beguiles the time in the company of the fat knight, Sir John Falstaff, drinking in taverns and plotting practical jokes. By comparison, Hotspur seems all the more a hero. But when Hotspur, angered by the King's refusal to ransom his brother-in-law Mortimer, joins forces with Glendower, it is Prince Hal who saves the day at Shrewsbury, fighting gallantly in defence of his father and killing Hotspur in single combat – a death for which Falstaff claims the credit.

Part Two. Probably first performed in 1598 and first published in a censored Quarto (Q1) in 1600. Modern editors collate this text with that in the First Folio of 1623. The play covers, in a highly compressed form, the period from the Battle of Shrewsbury to Henry IV's death in 1413. After his triumph at Shrewsbury, Prince Hal has returned to the riotous company of Falstaff and his cronies, but takes up arms when the rebel forces gather again. Falstaff, recruiting in the Cotswolds, finds a welcome with Justice Shallow, with whom, in his youth, he 'heard the chimes at midnight'. Prince John, younger son of Henry IV, persuades the rebels to disperse their army and then arrests the leaders for high treason. The dying King hears of this successful campaign. He falls asleep with the crown beside him, and Prince Hal, thinking him dead, holds the crown that will be his. They are reconciled, and the feeble King advises his son to unite England by undertaking a foreign campaign. Overjoyed to hear of Hal's succession, Falstaff boasts of his future under the new King, but the transformed Henry V spurns him in public during his coronation procession.

The two parts of *Henry IV* are an extraordinary achievement. The bare bones of the old-fashioned chronicle play are fleshed out with the riches of what is almost social history. Hotspur is a hero whose home-life is that of a benevolent merchant. Falstaff is both knight and vagabond, a vital link for the future king between the court he knows and the submerged life of London's back streets. Falstaff's trip into the Cotswolds introduces yet another layer of English life, that of rural culture. And Shakespeare has found a different language for each of the social strata he exhibits. So popular was the magnificent creation of Falstaff that he had to write THE MERRY WIVES OF WINDSOR to satisfy popular demand. This is fair evidence of the great contemporary popularity of *Henry IV*.

Henry V, The Life of A history play by SHAKESPEARE, concluding the sequence begun by *RICHARD II* and *HENRY IV*. It was first performed c.1599 and first published in a corrupt (probably pirated) Quarto (Q1) in 1600. The text in the First Folio of 1623 is probably taken from Q2 (1602). Shakespeare's main source was HOLINSHED's *Chronicles*, though he seems also to have consulted EDWARD HALL's *The Union of the Two Noble and Illustre Families of Lancastre and York*.

This most obviously patriotic of the English history plays is the only one that openly celebrates the achievements of a successful king. Mocked by the French, who revive memories of his frivolous youth, Henry displays his political astuteness by quelling a rebellion at home before going on to demonstrate his military prowess in a French campaign of which the Battle of Agincourt is the highlight. Magnanimous in victory, he charmingly woos the French princess, Katharine, and the play ends with their marriage plans sealed with a kiss.

A low-life sub-plot involves, first, the reported death of Falstaff and then the unruly conduct of various of his old associates, Pistol, Bardolph and Nym. Symbolizing the bonds of loyalty that hold Henry's united kingdom, but oddly ill at ease in both main and sub-plot, are four English, Welsh, Irish and Scottish commanders, Gower, Fluellen, Macmorris and Jamie.

Henry V is a slightly disappointing sequel to the splendid achievements of *HENRY IV*. The formula is similar, but the absence of Falstaff leaves Henry, even on his disguised trip around the Agincourt campfires, awkwardly isolated from the people he inspires and rules. Shakespeare seems sometimes overstretched in his attempt to win his audience's admiration for 'the mirror of all Christian kings'.

Henry VI A history play in three parts, of which SHAKESPEARE was the main, but almost certainly not the sole, author. It may contain his first surviving work for the stage. The first part may date from as early as 1590, and Elizabethan theatre practice would suggest that the second and third parts followed fairly closely; ROBERT GREENE's attack on Shakespeare as 'an upstart crow', which parodies a line from Part 3, was published in 1592. The only reliable text is that of the First Folio (1623).

Henry VI gives an episodic account of the king's reign, based largely on HOLINSHED's *Chronicles* and EDWARD HALL's *The Union of the Two Noble and Illustre Families of Lancastre and York*. It begins with Henry V's funeral and ends with Henry VI's murder by Richard, Duke of Gloucester, paving the way for Edward IV's accession to the throne and the events depicted in the altogether more inventive *RICHARD III*. Whereas Part I divides its attention between factional quarrels in England and the war in France, the last two parts confine themselves to the dynastic struggles between Yorkists and Lancastrians that have come to be known as the Wars of the Roses. The complex history of plot and counter-plot is uncertainly controlled, and the trilogy is less successful as a whole than it is memorable for a handful of episodes and characters (most notably perhaps Henry's wife Margaret of Anjou).

Henry VIII, The Life of King A historical play, probably written collaboratively by SHAKESPEARE and JOHN FLETCHER. It was apparently first performed in 1613, and it was first published in the First Folio of 1623. HOLINSHED's *Chronicles* is a main source. The play is at its most impressive in chronicling the guile of Wolsey and his sudden downfall, and the anguish of Queen Katharine over the question of the royal divorce. Its popularity on the 19th-century stage owed more to the taste for pictorial splendour and to its purple patches of rhetoric than to its intrinsic merit as a play. The history was perhaps too recent (the infant Elizabeth I is christened at the end) to allow the authors' imaginations sufficient freedom. If this was Shakespeare's last work for the theatre, it made a disappointingly half-hearted end.

Henry Esmond, The History of A novel by W. M. THACKERAY, published in three volumes in 1852. Set in the reign of Queen Anne, it is generally considered the finest Victorian historical novel, achieving Thackeray's stated aim to make 'history familiar rather than heroic' (Preface). The elegance of its historical pastiche is enriched by psychological undercurrents and a feeling for the secret life of memory.

Henry Esmond tells the story of his life, though predominantly in the third person. He grows up believing he is the illegitimate son of the 3rd Viscount Castlewood, who dies at the Battle of the Boyne. A lonely childhood in Jacobite circles is lightened when his cousin Francis Esmond inherits the title, and comes to live at Castlewood with his young wife Rachel and their two children, Frank and Beatrix. Their kindness to Henry wins his devotion, but when he unwittingly brings smallpox to the house, and Rachel's looks suffer as a result, husband and wife become estranged. She generously pays for Henry to go to Cambridge, and he returns to find the dissolute Lord Mohun a regular guest, gambling with Lord Castlewood and pursuing his wife. The two lords fight a duel in London and Castlewood is killed. At his death he gives Henry a written confession, which reveals him to be legitimate and the true heir of Castlewood, but Henry burns the document, refusing to disinherit his patron's son. He is imprisoned for his part in the duel, and rejected by Rachel, although the vehemence of her accusation is one of several signs in the novel of her hidden, guilty love for him.

On his release from prison Henry goes abroad to fight in the War of the Spanish Succession. He returns to an emotional reunion with Rachel at Winchester, and finding Beatrix grown into a proud and beautiful woman, falls in love with her. His pursuit of this worldly beauty at home alternates with his military service abroad in Marlborough's campaigns. He fights at Blenheim and Ramillies, and in Brussels learns of his Flemish mother and visits her grave. Beatrix is now established at court and becomes engaged to the Duke of Hamilton. But the Duke and Lord Mohun fight a duel, and both are killed. In a last effort to please Beatrix, Henry joins in a plot to restore James Edward Stuart, the Old Pretender, to the throne on the death of Queen Anne. The plot fails because of the Prince's reckless pursuit of Beatrix to Castlewood, when he should have been with his followers in London. Disillusioned with power and worldliness, Esmond marries Rachel, the woman he has always called his 'mistress', and retires with her to a life of domestic tranquillity in Virginia. THE VIRGINIANS continues the story of the Esmond family.

Henry the Minstrel See BLIND HARRY.

Henryson, Robert d. *c.*1508 Scottish poet. All that is known of Henryson's biography is that he lived in Dunfermline and died before the end of 1508, when WILLIAM DUNBAR wrote of him as already dead. It has been suggested that Henryson was a schoolmaster and that he studied medicine or law (or both), perhaps at Bologna, but none of this is certain. His poetry shows him well-read in the Church Fathers and the biblical commentaries, and familiar with the work of Aristotle and Boethius.

An important and influential Middle Scots poet, he is one of the group known as the SCOTTISH CHAUCERIANS. Despite the obvious influence of CHAUCER, Henryson's originality and skill are the most striking features of his work. His best-known poems are: THE TESTAMENT OF CRESSEID, an alternative ending to Chaucer's TROILUS AND CRISEYDE; THE MORALL FABILLIS OF ESOPE THE PHRYGIAN; ORPHEUS AND EURYDICE; and ROBENE AND MAKYNE, a version of pastoral. He also wrote a number of shorter works, several of them meditations on mortality, and two didactic allegories. *The Bludy Serk* is a brief narrative of a knight who rescues a maiden from a giant's castle but is killed in the process, leaving her a bloody shirt by which to remember him; it is interpreted in terms of Christ's sacrifice for the soul betrayed by the devil. *The Garmont of Gud Ladeis* is similar, describing an allegorical garment made up of various virtues.

Henslowe, Philip d. 1616 Theatre manager. Henslowe was the son of the master of the game in Ashdown Forest. He was probably born *c.*1550 and was certainly living in the Liberty of the Clink in London by 1577. Having been apprenticed to a dyer, he made himself rich by marrying his master's widow. The match brought Henslowe a step-daughter and, in 1592, a son-in-law through her marriage to the most famous actor of the day, EDWARD ALLEYN.

Henslowe's interest in theatrical property was well established by then. The ROSE, built in 1587 or 1588, was his, together perhaps with the theatre in Newington Butts. In partnership with Alleyn in 1604, he purchased the patent as Master of the Royal Game of Bears, Bulls and Mastiff Dogs, thereby crowning a decade of commercial interest in animal-baiting. Henslowe was the most consistently successful of all the Elizabethan speculators in entertainment. In 1600, when the Rose looked like losing out to the GLOBE THEATRE, he built the FORTUNE THEATRE north of the Thames, specifying in the building contract those features of the Globe he was keenest to have copied, and he may well have had some share in the management of the SWAN THEATRE as well. Finally, in 1614, he brought together his interests in animal-baiting and drama in the building of the HOPE THEATRE on Bankside. This was to be an adaptable arena, with a stage to be taken away when the business of the day was not drama.

That Henslowe took an interest in theatre is irrefutable evidence of its potential profitability in Elizabethan England. He was a businessman, and not an over-scrupulous one. Apart from maintaining some share in his brother's mines in Ashdown Forest, he was also involved in the manufacture of starch, in property, in pawnbroking and in money-lending. It was, in some part, by usury that he maintained his hold over actors and playwrights. It is the preservation of his *Diary* among the papers deposited in

Dulwich College by Edward Alleyn that gives Henslowe a peculiarly vital place in the study of the Elizabethan theatre. The *Diary* is less the systematic record of a fanatical book-keeper than fitful evidence of a wealthy man's attempt to keep his affairs in better order. The manuscript includes his brother's mining accounts, records of Henslowe's private affairs, three sets of pawn accounts, a list of unlikely cures for ailments and, crucially, records of theatrical income and expenditure at the Rose. It can be most conveniently read in the single-volume edition by R. A. Foakes and R. T. Rickert (1961).

Henty, G(eorge) A(lfred) 1832–1902 Writer of CHILDREN'S LITERATURE. Born near Cambridge, the son of a stockbroker, and educated at Cambridge University, Henty served first in the Crimean War and later covered other important armed conflicts as a war correspondent. Such background was to serve him well when he first started writing adventure stories for boys in 1868. Henty produced about 80 novels, sometimes at the rate of three per year, as often as not concentrating on action-packed episodes from British history. Typical titles include *Under Drake's Flag* (1883), *The Lion of the North* (1885) and his last book, *With the Allies in Pekin* (1904). Enjoying huge sales both in Britain and America, his books long remained popular, GEORGE ORWELL making several sardonic references to their unquestioning patriotism in his journalism. Today they are interesting only as period pieces.

heptameter See METRE.

Heraud, John Abraham 1799–1887 Poet. Born in London, educated privately. He made a career as a contributor and editor working for *FRASER'S MAGAZINE*, *THE ATHENAEUM* and the *Illustrated London News*. His powerful grandiose style is best represented in *The Descent into Hell* (1830) and *The Judgement of the Flood* (1834). He also wrote a successful play, *Videna: or, the Mother's Tragedy* (1854).

Herbert, A(lan) P(atrick) 1890–1971 Humorist and reformer. He was born at Ashstead in Surrey and educated at Winchester and New College, Oxford, where he studied law. After war service with the Royal Navy in Gallipoli and France, during which he was wounded, he became private secretary to an MP. His war experiences resulted in two volumes of poetry (1916 and 1918) and the novel *The Secret Battle* (1919), an account of the horrors of warfare. He was a regular contributor to *PUNCH* and joined the magazine's staff in 1924. His first stage play, a Christmas piece called *King of the Castle*, was written in the same year, as was the first of his mock law reports. These were later collected as *Misleading Cases in the Common Law* (1929) which ridiculed absurdities of court procedure. *Holy*

Deadlock (1934) was a novel which exposed the need for reform of the divorce law, a task which Herbert personally undertook as Independent MP for Oxford University (1935–50). The stormy battle over his Marriage Bill was related in *The Ayes Have It* (1937), while *Independent Member* (1950) described his years in Parliament, during which he continued to fight for a variety of legal reforms. His most popular novel, *The Water Gipsies* (1930), reflected his long-standing love for the English waterways. Herbert also wrote the libretti for a number of successful musicals, including a revue, *Riverside Nights* (1926), and several operas, *Tantivy Towers* (1930) and *Bless the Bride* (1947) among others. He was knighted in 1945. *APH: His Life and Times*, an autobiography, appeared in 1970.

Herbert, Edward, 1st Baron of Cherbury 1583–1648 Philosopher, poet and diplomat. The elder brother of GEORGE HERBERT, he was educated at University College, Oxford, and in 1606 moved to London to enter court circles. He was ambassador to France (1619–24) and travelled widely. His foremost work was *De veritate* (1625), a philosophical treatise in Latin which aligned him with the CAMBRIDGE PLATONISTS; the principles of natural religion he propounded have earned him the title the 'Father of DEISM'. He also published some spirited English verse.

In 1632 Charles I created him Baron Herbert of Cherbury, and he was appointed to the Council of War. Herbert was reluctantly active as a Royalist soldier until 1644, when he retired to Montgomery Castle, but submitted to Parliament the following year, and received a pension. His *The Life and Reign of Henry VIII* (1644) is not outstanding but, even though it stops short at 1624, his *Autobiography* (first published in 1764 by HORACE WALPOLE) is an interesting revelation of the times. Herbert's career was one of early promise but no ultimate greatness.

Herbert, Frank 1920–86 American writer of SCIENCE FICTION. He was born in Tacoma and educated at the University of Washington. His first novel was a thriller, *The Dragon in the Sea* (1956). He caught the mood of the day with the intense ecological mysticism of his epic novel *Dune* (1965), describing the advent of a messiah-figure in a desert world which produces a life-preserving spice. Five sequels were added to make a commercially successful series. *The Green Brain* (1966) and *Hellstrom's Hive* (1973) developed his interest in ecology. His fascination with religion continued in *The God Makers* (1972) as well as *The Jesus Incident* (1979), *The Lazarus Effect* (1983) and *The Ascension Factor* (1988), the sequels which he and Bill Ransom added to his solo novel *Destination: Void* (1966).

Herbert, George 1593–1633 Poet and divine. A member of the noble family that included the earldoms of Pembroke and Montgomery among their holdings, Herbert had an elder brother, Edward, later Baron Herbert of Cherbury (see HERBERT, EDWARD), and another who became Master of Revels, Sir Henry Herbert. Himself an outstanding scholar, he was educated at Westminster, and Trinity College, Cambridge, where he was a fellow at 22, and Public Orator to the University from 1619 to 1627. Before the death of James I, Herbert seems to have entertained aspirations for public advancement, acting as MP for Montgomery in 1624–5, but he became a deacon in the following year, which debarred him from civil office. His mother, who was a patron of JOHN DONNE, died in 1627, and Herbert married Jane Danvers in 1629.

During this period of professional indecision (he had resigned his oratorship) Herbert was working on the poems which were later published together as *The Temple*. He became a priest in 1630, obtained the living of Bemerton in Wiltshire, and continued

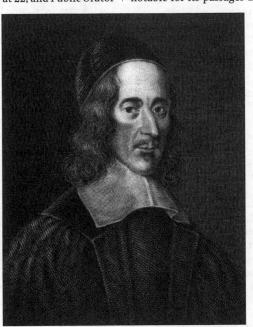

George Herbert: an engraving of 1674 by Robert White

there as a conscientious and benevolent rector until his wavering health gave out, and he realized he was dying. Early in 1633, therefore, he sent a consignment of verse to his friend NICHOLAS FERRAR, asking for his opinion. It appeared as *The Temple: Sacred Poems and Private Ejaculations* after his death that year and went through 13 editions by 1680. These 160 poems rank among the finest work produced by any of the METAPHYSICAL POETS, short but often exquisite, distinguished by their carefully wrought shapes, the ingenuity of their images, and their calm and subtle religious faith. They have found favour with many later poets, COWPER and COLERIDGE in particular. Herbert's short prose work, *A Priest to the Temple* (1652), offered guidance to country priests. IZAAK WALTON wrote his biography (1670).

Herbert, (Alfred Francis) Xavier 1901–84 Australian novelist. Born at Port Hedland in Western Australia, he trained as a pharmacist at the University of Melbourne, but abandoned a job as a hospital pharmacist at the age of 24 in favour of a career in literature. He served as Protector of Aborigines at Darwin from 1935 to 1936. In 1975 and 1976 he held appointments as writer-in-residence at the Universities of

Newcastle, NSW, and Queensland. His best-known work is a sprawling chronicle of Aborigines and white men set in the Northern outback, *Capricornia* (1938). Other novels are *Seven Emus* (1958) and *Soldiers' Women* (1960). In *Poor Fellow My Country* (1975) Herbert returned to the outback with a massive saga, notable for its passages dealing with Aboriginal life.

He is also the author of *Larger Than Life* (short stories, 1963) and *Disturbing Element* (autobiography, 1963).

Herbst, Josephine (Frey) 1897–1969 American novelist and journalist. She was born in Sioux City, Iowa, and educated at the University of California at Berkeley. Her first two novels, *Nothing is Sacred* (1928) and *Money for Love* (1929), were followed by *Pity is Not Enough* (1933), *The Executioner Waits* (1934) and *Rope of Gold* (1939), a trilogy dealing with the decay of capitalism and the emergence of a revolutionary movement which falters and fails to bring about the new Communist social order it seeks. A journalist of left-wing sympathies, she went to Germany as a special correspondent for the *New York Post* in 1935 and later covered the Spanish Civil War. Her other publications include two novels, *Satan's Sergeants* (1941) and *Somewhere the Tempest Fell* (1947). At the time of her death she was at work on *The Burning Bush*, a literary and personal history of the 1920s and 1930s, and *Hunter of Doves*, a collection of novelettes.

Herd, David 1732–1810 Scottish collector and anthologist of BALLADS. Born in Kincardineshire, he spent much of his life as a clerk in Edinburgh, where he moved in convivial literary circles. He accumulated a good deal of older Scottish traditional verse, notably in *Ancient and Modern Scottish Songs ... Collected from Memory, Tradition, and Ancient Authors* (1776).

Hermsprong See BAGE, ROBERT.

Herne, James A. 1839–1901 American playwright, manager and actor. He was born James Ahern in Cohoes, New York, to an immigrant Irish family. When he was 20 he joined a theatre group, through which he eventually met DAVID BELASCO, with whom he collaborated on many productions. Their first significant work was *Chums* (1879; retitled *Hearts of Oak*, 1880). This sentimental domestic MELODRAMA about an old sailor who adopts two orphans and falls in love with one of them is notable for its early indication of Herne's tendency towards REALISM in subject matter, dialogue, characterization and staging techniques. Herne later outlined his convictions about dramatic writing and presentation in the article 'Art for Truth's Sake in the Drama' (1896). His next play, *The Minute Men of 1774–75* (1886), was less successful, and in 1888 he wrote and produced the unconventional temperance drama, *Drifting Apart*. The most important of his contributions to American dramatic realism is *Margaret Fleming* (1891), the story of a woman's response to her husband's infidelity. Clearly influenced by Ibsen in both subject and style, the play was acclaimed by HAMLIN GARLAND and WILLIAM DEAN HOWELLS but relentlessly attacked by the critics. His next play, *Shore Acres* (1892), an equally realistic but happier story of life in New England, was very successful, and broke performance records in Boston. He wrote two more plays: *The Reverend Griffith Davenport* (1899), a Civil War story based on Helen H. Gardner's novel *An Unofficial Patriot* (1894); and *Sag Harbor* (1900), a reworking of the themes of *Hearts of Oak* in which two brothers are rivals for the love of the same woman.

Hero and Leander An erotic poem (or EPYLLION) left incomplete by CHRISTOPHER MARLOWE at his death in 1593 and finished by GEORGE CHAPMAN. Marlowe's share of the poem, published by itself in 1598, is its first two 'sestiads'. The word was coined by Chapman by analogy with 'Iliad'; it derives from Sestos, where the poem is set, and may also indicate Chapman's six-fold division. All six sestiads appeared later in 1598.

Marlowe's poem derives from the story by Musaeus, an Alexandrian poet of the 5th century. No English version of Musaeus' poem seems to have been available to Marlowe, but there were Latin, Italian and French translations. Marlowe's version is Ovidian in tone and manner: the digressive story of Mercury and the country maid and decorative mythological allusiveness show the influence of the *Metamorphoses*. The speaking voice of the narrator owes much to another Ovidian work, the *Amores*, which Marlowe translated. Marlowe's poem relates the meeting, wooing and eventual sexual consummation of the love of Hero and Leander. Having wooed Hero, 'Venus' nun', at Sestos, Leander swims to her turret, in the course of his swim naively rejecting the amorous advances of Neptune. It ends with the dawn breaking after a night of love. Chapman's continuation abandons the wry and detached narrative voice Marlowe had used to relate the passage of two lovers from innocence to experience, introduces conceit, ALLEGORY

and personified abstractions (notably the goddess Ceremony), and is in general more concerned with morality and decorum.

Heroes, Hero-Worship, and the Heroic in History, On A group of six lectures by THOMAS CARLYLE, delivered in May 1840 and published the following year. In the first lecture he said: 'The History of the World is but the Biography of great men... Could we see *them*, we should get some glimpses into the very marrow of the world's history.' His premise was that heroism could manifest itself in any field of human ability, and he proceeded to describe the different forms taken by the hero in different phases of human history: Divinity (Odin), Prophet (Mahomet), Poet (Dante and SHAKESPEARE), Priest (Luther and KNOX), Man of Letters (JOHNSON, Rousseau and BURNS) and King (Cromwell and Napoleon).

heroic couplet In English verse, a pair of rhyming iambic pentameters (see METRE and RHYME). The form was developed most notably by CHAUCER and championed by DRYDEN (especially in his *ESSAY OF DRAMATIC POESY*) against the BLANK VERSE of much English tragic drama. Dryden was also responsible for promoting its use in non-dramatic verse, cultivating the poised, epigrammatic effects which predecessors like BEN JONSON, DONNE and WALLER had occasionally managed and which 18th-century successors like POPE and JOHNSON emulated. The 'closed couplet' uses the END-STOPPED LINE, but the 'open couplet' uses ENJAMBEMENT.

Herr, Michael 1940– American journalist. After covering the Vietnam war for *Esquire* and *Rolling Stone*, he wrote his best-known book, *Dispatches* (1978), a vivid and shocking account of the war's glamour as well as its ferocity. It influenced a whole generation of Hollywood films about Vietnam, notably Coppola's *Apocalypse Now* (1979), for which he wrote the narration, and Kubrick's *Full Metal Jacket* (1987), for which he was consultant. *Walter Winchell* (1991) is a novel in the form of a screenplay.

Herrick, Robert 1591–1674 Poet. Apprenticed at the age of 16 to his uncle, a goldsmith named Sir William Herrick, he did not go up to Cambridge until 1613. He graduated with an MA in 1620, went to London, and began to mix in the artistic circles of the capital, where he became a friend of BEN JONSON, the writer with whom he is now most identified. Although he was beginning to write, none of Herrick's work was yet published; in 1623 he took holy orders, and acted as chaplain to Buckingham on the expedition to the Île de Ré. Herrick continued to write verse prolifically – during the course of his life he was responsible for some 2500 compositions, many dating from the 1620s – and in 1629 was appointed by Charles I to the living of Dean Prior in the diocese of Exeter. He enjoyed the calm parish life of Devon, but was ejected under the Commonwealth for refusing the Solemn League and Covenant, and returned to London, though he was reinstated in 1662. He died, a bachelor, at the age of 83, in his parish.

In 1648, the year after he was compelled to leave Dean Prior, Herrick published his major collection, *Hesperides*. This volume consists of 1200 poems, many of them short, and taking an impressive variety of forms including ELEGIES, epitaphs, EPIGRAMS, ANACREONTICS, hymns, songs (many later set to music) and imitations of Horace and Catullus. Some of the epigrams are positively vile, but elsewhere Herrick is capable of beautifully wrought lyrics which have invited analogies with his earlier craft as a goldsmith; 'The Funeral Rites of the Rose' and 'The Lily in a Crystal' demonstrate the intricate style of his more delicate lyrics. There is a whimsical grace in much of his love poetry – such as his classic exposition of the CARPE DIEM theme, 'To the Virgins, To Make Much of Time' – which allies him with the CAVALIER POETS as well as their common master, Jonson. 'Oberon's Feast' and 'Oberon's Palace' are two of his fantasy pieces about faeries. Included separately in *Hesperides* was the subsection *Noble Numbers*, a body of devotional verse which is less individual, and unlike his secular verses is not visually brilliant or embroidered with pretty CONCEITS. Although perhaps never a profound poet, Herrick was a distinguished verbal craftsman, and his erotic poems can be highly sensory. SWINBURNE praised him as 'the greatest song-writer ever born of English race'.

Herrick, Robert 1868–1938 American novelist. He was born in Cambridge, Massachusetts, and educated at Harvard. Many of his novels depict professionals or businessmen who struggle to achieve worldly success only to find that it leaves them unhappy and unfulfilled. In his first novel, *The Man Who Wins* (1897), the character who comes to this realization is a doctor who has given up research for a lucrative medical practice. *Web of Life* (1900) also has a doctor as its hero; *The Common Lot* (1904), an architect. *The Real World* (1901; republished as *Jock O'Dreams*, 1908), *A Life for a Life* (1910) and *Waste* (1924) all tell the stories of business executives who come to regret their material success. *Memoirs of an American Citizen* (1905), perhaps his best-known novel, is the story of Van Harrington, who makes a fortune and wins a seat in the Senate but, unlike Herrick's other leading characters, exhibits no regret. *Sometime* (1933) is a satirical Utopian novel. Herrick also published several collections of short stories: *Love's Dilemmas* (1898), *Their Child* (1903), *The Master of the Inn* (1908), *The Conscript Mother* (1916) and *Wanderings* (1925). He died in the Virgin Islands, where he had served for three years as secretary to the governor.

Herschel, Sir John Frederick William 1792–1871 Astronomer. The son of Sir William Herschel, born at Slough and educated at Cambridge, he was a founder of the Royal Astronomical Society and Secretary to the Royal Society 1824–7. He discovered many new stars, clusters and nebulae. His writings include *Outlines of Astronomy* (1841) and *Familiar Lectures on Scientific Subjects* (1867).

Hervey, James 1714–58 Essayist. A prominent member of early Methodist circles, Hervey was born at Hardingstone in Northamptonshire and completed his education at Lincoln College, Oxford. He became rector of Collingtree and Weston Favell in his native county. *Meditations among the Tombs* (1746–7), *Reflections on a Flower Garden* and *Contemplations on the Night* (both 1747) were popular in their day, appealing to the same tastes as the work of the GRAVEYARD POETS.

Hervey, John, Baron Hervey of Ickworth 1694–1743 Politician. Son of the Earl of Bristol, he was educated at Westminster School and Clare College, Cambridge, and went on a tour to Europe in 1716 when, in Hanover, he befriended the Prince Frederick (son of George II). In 1720 he married Molly Lepell, a London beauty who was maid of honour to the Princess of Wales. Hervey was a political supporter of Walpole and in 1730 he was appointed Vice-Chamberlain to George II; from 1733 until Walpole's fall in 1742 he was Lord Privy Seal and enjoyed the confidence of Queen Caroline.

As a friend of the accomplished LADY MARY WORTLEY MONTAGU, Hervey became a hated enemy of her admirer, ALEXANDER POPE, who penned a most withering verse-portrait of him as Sporus in the *Epistle to Dr Arbuthnot,* one of his keenest satires, and also in THE DUNCIAD. Hervey attempted to respond in kind, but Pope's representation of him as an unnatural, pernicious fop has had a lasting impression on Hervey's reputation. His own *Memoirs of the Reign of George the Second* (published in 1848) offer a satirical portrait of the times, remarkably frank about the motives and methods of his contemporaries seeking preferment.

Herzog A novel by SAUL BELLOW, published in 1964. It won the National Book Award for fiction in 1965 and became a best-seller. Moses Herzog, a 47-year-old scholar, undergoes an emotional, intellectual and moral crisis. From his summer home in the Berkshire Mountains he writes letters, in his head or on paper, to friends, relatives, his psychiatrist, politicians, philosophers (such as Heidegger and Nietzsche), the public (in letters to the editor), even God. Flashbacks provide the reader with information about Herzog's relations with his family, his two ex-wives (Daisy and Madeleine), his Japanese mistress Sono, and his current lover, Ramona. Herzog travels to Chicago, intent on avenging himself on Madeleine and her lover, Valentine Gersbach, but the expedition ends in humiliation when he is involved in a car accident and arrested for possessing a gun without a permit. He rejects his brother's suggestion that he go into a mental hospital, arranges to have his dilapidated summer place put to rights again, plans for a visit from his son Marco (his child by Daisy) and prepares for a dinner with Ramona. Herzog's excursions – physical and mental – have left him in relative peace, and for the time being he has 'no messages for anyone'.

Hewett, Dorothy (Coade) 1923– Australian playwright, poet and novelist. She was born in Perth and educated at Perth College and the University of Western Australia. She joined the Communist Party in 1945, working and writing energetically on its behalf until 1968 and the invasion of Czechoslovakia. In 1948 she had moved to Sydney, where her experience of factory work inspired her only novel, *Bobbin' Up* (1959). She returned to Perth in 1960. Her first play was a working-class drama, *This Old Man Comes Rolling Home* (1967). Mainly expressionistic works featuring music and poetry, her plays depict complex women characters trapped in ageing, domesticity and the stereotyped images of women, or evoke an idyllic pastoral world. They include *The Chapel Perilous* (1971), *Bon Bons and Roses for Dolly* (1972), *The Tatty Hollow Story* (1974), *Pandora's Cross* (1978), *The Man from Muckinupin* (1979) and *The Fields of Heaven* (1982). She has also published eight volumes of poetry: *What About the People* (with Merv Lilley, 1961), *Hidden Journey* (1967), *Windmill Country* (1968), *Rapunzel in Suburbia* (1975), *Greenhouse* (1979), *Journeys* (1982), *Alice in Wormland* (1985), *A Tremendous World in Her Head* (1989) and *Selected Poems* (1991). Structural weaknesses in most of her writing are overridden by a powerful Rabelaisian personality which cannot be ignored and is fully revealed in *Wild Card: An Autobiography* (1990). She was made a Member of the Order of Australia in 1986.

Hewitt, John (Harold) 1907–87 Irish poet. Born in Belfast of Nonconformist 'planter' stock, he was educated at the Methodist College and Queen's University, Belfast. He worked in museums and art galleries in Belfast and Coventry until his retirement in 1972. Hewitt first gained attention as a nature poet and celebrant of local landscapes, particularly the Glens of Antrim, but his inherited Nonconformity and his reading of PAINE, COBBETT and WILLIAM MORRIS made him a political dissenter. In his poetry this activated a stubbornly radical quest for an Ulster identity predicated on neither an increasingly strident Protestant unionism nor the traditions of Catholic and Celtic nationalism, but on the dialect and idiom generated by local history and environment. Hewitt's verse is characteristically 'mannerly', formally disciplined and understated but precisely observed, thoughtful and humane. MICHAEL LONGLEY has said of him that 'he made himself heard in a land of bellowers without raising his voice'. Frank Ormsby has edited the *Collected Poems* (1991), with a valuable introduction. Hewitt's lifelong concern with the art, poetry, speech and traditions of his native province – reflected in an anthology, *The Rhyming Weavers and Other Country Poets of Antrim and Down* (1974), and *Ancestral Voices: The Selected Prose of John Hewitt* (edited by Tom Clyde; 1987) – has influenced younger poets such as SEAMUS HEANEY and TOM PAULIN.

Hewlett, Maurice (Henry) 1861–1923 Novelist and poet. He studied law and was called to the Bar but never practised. In 1896–1900 he worked as Keeper of Land Revenue Records. His first novel, *The Forest Lovers* (1898), a medieval romance which became an immediate success, was followed by *Richard Yea and Nay* (1900) and *The Queen's Quair* (1904). A trilogy of modern life, *Halfway House* (1908), *Open Country* (1909) and *Rest Harrow* (1910), centred on John Maxwell Senhouse, a gentle itinerant scholar. *The Song of the Plow* (1916) is a narrative poem considering the lot of the agricultural labourer. Volumes of essays include *In a Green Shade* (1920), *Wiltshire Essays* (1921) and *Extemporary Essays* (1922).

hexameter See METRE.

Heylyn, Peter 1600–62 Religious controversialist. Educated at Magdalen College, Oxford, Heylyn was a supporter of Archbishop LAUD. His principal work was *Ecclesia Restaurata; or, The History of the Reformation of the Church of England* (1661). Two posthumously published works were *Cyprianus Anglicus; or, The History of the Life and Death of Archbishop Laud* (1668), which was a defence of the dead Archbishop against attacks by WILLIAM PRYNNE, and *Aerius Redivivus; or, The History of Presbyterianism* (1670), which sees Calvinism as the destructive force behind religious strife in England. Heylyn was also the author of a description of the known countries of the world, *Microcosmus: A Little Description of the Great World* (1621), enlarged and republished as *Cosmography* in 1652.

Heyward, Dorothy 1890–1961 and **Heyward, (Edwin) DuBose** 1885–1940 American playwrights. Their husband-and-wife partnership is remembered for *Porgy* (1927) and *Mamba's Daughters* (1929), both based on novels by DuBose Heyward and both notable for their vivid use of Southern black folklore. *Porgy* became enduringly famous in George Gershwin's operatic adaptation, *Porgy and Bess* (1935). DuBose Heyward also wrote *Peter Ashley* (1932), a chronicle of the Civil War, and *Star-Spangled Virgin* (1939), about the response of the Virgin Islanders to the New Deal, as well as several volumes of verse.

Heywood, John *c.* 1497–*c.* 1580 Playwright. Little is known about his early life beyond ANTHONY À WOOD's statement that he was educated at Broadgates Hall (later Pembroke College), Oxford, but found it 'not suiting with his airy genie'. His marriage to THOMAS MORE's niece helped his career at the court of Henry VIII, where he was a singer and player of the virginals from 1519 to 1528. He became a court pensioner in 1528 and held office in the City of London, later becoming a freeman. He remained in favour at court until 1544, when as a zealous Roman Catholic he was convicted of treason for his involvement in a conspiracy against THOMAS CRANMER. He later became a favourite of Queen Mary's but went into exile at Elizabeth's accession and was last heard of at Malines, in the Netherlands, in 1578. His daughter became JOHN DONNE's mother.

Heywood published several collections of EPIGRAMS and proverbs, and contributed to court MASQUES during the reigns of Edward VI and Mary. But his importance lies in his short dramatic INTERLUDES, which abandon allegory and instruction. Among them were *The Play of the Weather* (1533), *A Play of Love* (1533) and *A Dialogue concerning Witty and Witless* (first printed 1846). He moved nearer to true stage comedy with *The Play Called the Four PP* (*c.* 1544), in which Palmer, Pardoner and 'Pothecary dispute the value of their respective occupations. They are joined by Pedlar, who offers a prize to the one who shows the greatest capacity for lying. The palmer wins by declaring that he had never known 'any woman out of patience'. Heywood is plainly restoring the comedy of which CHAUCER, in narrative if not in drama, had been a master.

Heywood, Thomas 1573–1641 Playwright, actor, poet and pamphleteer. Much of his work has been lost and much that remains is ephemeral: interest in his mayoral pageants, for example, is likely to be confined to scholars. Of the 220 plays to which he claimed to have contributed, some 30 have survived. They include: an outstanding domestic tragedy, *A WOMAN KILLED WITH KINDNESS* (1603); a frolicsome adventure play in two parts, *THE FAIR MAID OF THE WEST* (published 1631); a chronicle history play, *If You Know Not Me, You Know Nobody* (1605); an ambitious but oddly perfunctory dramatization of Greek mythology in five plays, *The Golden Age*, *The Silver Age*, *The Brazen Age* and the two parts of *The Iron Age* (1611–13); and, in collaboration with RICHARD BROME, *The Late Lancashire Witches* (1634). The excesses of his chivalric romance, *The Four Prentices of London* (published 1615), are nicely satirized by FRANCIS BEAUMONT in *THE KNIGHT OF THE BURNING PESTLE*, but Heywood's

feeling for the theatre of his time should not be underrated. It is well represented in *An Apology for Actors* (1612), a spirited and informative defence of the theatre against Puritan attacks.

Hiawatha, The Song of A narrative poem by HENRY WADSWORTH LONGFELLOW, published in 1855. It tells how Hiawatha is reared by Nokomis, daughter of the moon, who helps him acquire the wisdom and power necessary for an Indian hero and leader. Upon reaching manhood, Hiawatha seeks to avenge his mother Wenonah, against his father, the West Wind. The combat ends in reconciliation, and Hiawatha becomes the leader of his people. Although his rule is marked by peace and prosperity, hard times come to his tribe; his wife, Minnehaha, dies, and he follows her to the land of the North Wind, having first advised his people to accept the white man, whose coming he has predicted. Longfellow based the METRE on that of a Finnish epic, *The Kalevala*. Its hypnotic effect has made it a frequent target for PARODY.

Hibberd, Jack 1940– Australian playwright and novelist. Born in Warracknabeal, Victoria, and brought up in Bendigo, he studied medicine at the University of Melbourne, graduating in 1964. He subsequently worked as a doctor until 1973, since when he has devoted himself to the theatre full-time, remaining in Melbourne, while several of his contemporaries have moved elsewhere. During the 1960s he was an important figure in the move to create a new Australian theatre. A Melbourne University group in which he was prominent took shape as the La Mama Theatre Company and later, in 1969, as the Australian Theatre Company. Hibberd was influential both as dramatist and director in this attempt to bring a more populist and experimental theatre into being, and was involved during this period with other innovatory figures in Australian drama, such as DAVID WILLIAMSON. His early plays, like *White with Wire Wheels* (1967), an examination of Australian male values, employ a rough vernacular style. *Dimboola* (1969), one of Australia's most performed plays, is an affectionately satirical treatment of a country wedding. *A Stretch of the Imagination* (1972), a monologue by an old man facing death, blends comedy and pathos and is widely regarded as his finest work to date. Its protagonist is a quintessentially Australian character, a teller of tall tales who brings together positive and negative aspects of the national legend. It is typical of Hibberd's attempt to create a popular theatre dealing with leading figures and events in Australian popular folklore. The same concerns inform his plays *Captain Midnite VC* (1972), *A Toast to Melba* (1974) and *The Les Darcy Show* (1975), in each of which a national figure is presented with a mixture of fondness and satire. Other plays by Hibberd include *Peggy Sue* (1974), *One of Nature's Gentlemen* (1976) and a number published in the left-wing Melbourne quarterly, *Meanjin*. Since abandoning the theatre he has published novels: *Memoirs of an Old Bastard* (1989), *The Life of Riley* (1991) and *Perdita* (1992), a companion to *Memoirs of an Old Bastard*.

Hichens, Robert (Smythe) 1864–1950 Journalist and novelist. Of his 66 books, the most famous is his first novel, *The Green Carnation* (1894), an amiable ROMAN À CLEF in which OSCAR WILDE appears as Esme Amarinth and LORD ALFRED DOUGLAS as Lord Reggie. The slight plot, which has Lord Reggie toying with the idea of marriage to Lady Locke but offering a green carnation to her son, is less memorable than Hichens's cunning PARODY of Wilde's style.

Higgins, Matthew 1810–68 Journalist. Born at Benown Castle, County Meath, and educated at Eton and at University College, Oxford, he spent some years managing his inherited estates in British Guiana. He showed his skill as a controversialist in his pamphlets and writings on the Irish question in 1847, often using the name or initials of 'Jacob Omnium, the Merchant Prince', the title of a SATIRE on mercantile dishonesty published in *THE NEW MONTHLY MAGAZINE* in 1845. He moved much in London society, sporting as well as literary, and was a friend of THACKERAY. His many pseudonymous letters to *The Times* (up to 1863) and his periodical contributions had a high reputation.

High Wind in Jamaica, A See HUGHES, RICHARD.

Higher Criticism, The The study of the Bible as literature, concentrating on literary technique and sources. Pioneered by 18th- and 19th-century German scholars, it grew out of the older textual criticism concerned with the establishment of the best texts. David Friedrich Strauss (1808–74) denied the historicity of all supernatural elements in the Gospels in his *Das Leben Jesu* (1835–6). He argued that they were 'myth', developed between the time of Christ and the writing of the Gospels in the 2nd century. GEORGE ELIOT translated Strauss in 1846, remarking that it made her ill 'dissecting the beautiful story of the Crucifixion'; the long-term effect was loss of her faith. Joseph Ernest Renan's *Vie de Jésus* (1863) also demythologized the life of Christ by portraying Jesus as an amiable rabbi.

The Higher Criticism implied that the Bible was not the directly inspired word of God but a human artifact; it was less a repository of incontrovertible truth than an anthology of literary beauties. This tendency in biblical studies was part symptom, part cause of the 19th-century decline in religious belief. It seemed that scholarship combined with Darwinian science and geological research to undermine the bases of Christian fundamentalism.

See also JOHN WILLIAM COLENSO and *ESSAYS AND REVIEWS*.

Highland Widow, The See *CHRONICLES OF THE CANONGATE*.

Highsmith, Patricia 1921– Novelist and short-story writer. Born in Fort Worth, Texas, she was brought up in New York and attended Barnard College. Since 1951 she has lived alternately in the USA and Europe. The ingenious symmetry of her first novel, *Strangers on a Train* (1950), successfully though not faithfully filmed by Alfred Hitchcock, encouraged reviewers to identify her work as DETECTIVE FICTION, a label which has not helped it find its best audience in the USA or Britain. Despite the advocacy of GRAHAM GREENE, she remains better and more widely read in France and Germany. Though her subject is usually crime and her treatment of it bleakly elegant, her real preoccupation is with guilt, unease and the refuges offered by obsession and fantasy. The last theme marks a particularly distinguished group of novels: *The Cry of the Owl* (1962), *The Glass Cell* (1964), *The Story-Teller* (1965; as *A Suspension of Mercy* in UK) and *The Tremor of Forgery* (1969). *Edith's Diary* (1977) is a powerful study of a woman's collapse into madness, *Found in the Street* (1986) of alienation in New York. Her unblinking and unjudging authorial stance generates IRONY and black comedy in several fine collections of short stories and the novels which follow the career of a likeable psychopath, Tom Ripley: *The Talented Mr Ripley* (1955), *Ripley under Ground* (1970), *Ripley's Game* (1974), *The Boy Who Followed Ripley* (1980) and *Ripley under Water* (1991).

Hill, Aaron 1685–1750 Theatre manager, playwright and versifier. Educated at Barnstaple Grammar School and Westminster, Hill travelled to Constantinople at the age of 15 and toured the area with a tutor for three years, publishing *A Full Account of the Ottoman Empire* in 1709. His first play, *Elfrid*, flopped in 1709 and was rewritten as *Athelwold* with only fractionally greater success in 1731. At the HAYMARKET THEATRE in 1710 he staged *Rinaldo*, his own translation of Rossi's libretto to music by Handel. He became friendly with SAMUEL RICHARDSON and on the appearance of *PAMELA* (1740) wrote him a sycophantic letter which Richardson printed in the preface to the second edition. Hill's astonishing belief in his own importance and ability led him to write letters advising GARRICK how to act, Walpole how to conduct political life, and POPE how to write. Pope retaliated by putting him in *THE DUNCIAD*. He died the night before the intended first performance of his translation of Voltaire's *Mérope*. Nearly all his writings are quite properly forgotten. His two lasting achievements were in stage scenery: a practicable mountain in *Rinaldo* and the first practicable bridge in his production of *HENRY V* at DRURY LANE in 1723.

Hill, Geoffrey 1932– Poet. Born in Bromsgrove, Worcestershire, and educated at the local grammar school and Keble College, Oxford, he began graduate work there before being appointed a lecturer at the University of Leeds. He then taught at Cambridge and, since 1988, at Boston University, Massachusetts. His first volume, *For the Unfallen* (1959), has been followed by *King Log* (1968), *Mercian Hymns* (1971), *Tenebrae* (1978), *The Mystery of the Charity of Charles Péguy* (1983) and *Collected Poems* (1986). Disciplined and rigorous, his poetry gives passionate voice to historical figures, both distant and recent. Although his attitude to Christianity is ambivalent, religious and moral themes play as prominent a role as his preoccupation with music. His precise use of language does not stifle the rich beauty of his verse, even if its resolute seriousness may disguise the melancholy, ironic humour. He has also published criticism: *Lords of Limit: Essays on Literature and Ideas* (1984), *Enemy's Country: Words, Contextures and Other Criticisms of Language* (1991) and *Illuminating the Shadows: Mythic Power of Film* (1992).

Hill, Susan 1942– Novelist, short-story writer and author of radio plays. Born in Scarborough, she studied at King's College, London. A frequent theme of her fiction is loneliness, which her best work treats with a lucid psychological precision and narrative composure: *In the Springtime of the Year* (1974) explores the aftermath of a woman's bereavement; *A Change for the Better* (1969) depicts a group of damaged, isolated people brought together in a hotel. *I'm the King of the Castle* (1970), probably her best-known book, won praise for its piercing fable of the brutality latent in childhood innocence. Her abandonment of fiction in order to look after a family (she is married to the Shakespeare scholar Stanley Wells) ended with the publication of *The Woman in Black* (1983) and *The Mist in the Mirror* (1992), both pseudo-Victorian ghost stories, and a novel, *Air and Angels* (1991).

Hillingdon Hall A novel by R. S. SURTEES, published in volume form in 1845. It is the third in the Jorrocks trilogy begun with *JORROCKS'S JAUNTS AND JOLLITIES* and *HANDLEY CROSS*, and it deals with his life in retirement, when he devotes himself largely to farming. Much of the humour lies in his enthusiastic but inexpert adoption of new 'scientific' ideas: he is brought back to earth by his former huntsman, James Pigg, who rapturously rejoins his establishment. There is little about hunting in the book and more than is usual with Surtees about human relationships and social intercourse. Jorrocks becomes a JP, a role which he fills with characteristically outrageous gusto; and we leave him at the point when he has been elected to Parliament. Mrs Jorrocks is as appalling as ever as 'grande dame' of the village.

Hillyer, Robert (Silliman) 1895–1961 American poet, novelist and critic. Born in East Orange, New Jersey, and educated at Harvard, he served in World War I and then returned to Harvard, where he taught from 1919 to 1945. His first volume, *Sonnets and Other Lyrics*, was published in 1917. *The Hills Give Promise* appeared in 1923. His novel *Riverhead* (1932) was followed in 1933 by *The Collected Verse of Robert Hillyer*, for which he won the PULITZER PRIZE. Subsequent publications include *First Principles of Verse* (1938, a critical work), *Pattern of a Day* (1940, poetry), *My Heart for Hostage* (1942, a novel), *Poems for Music, 1917–1947* (1947), *The Death of Captain Nemo, a Narrative Poem* (1949), *In Pursuit of Poetry* (1960, a critical work) and *Collected Poems* (1961). He generally wrote in traditional verse forms, most notably the SONNET and the HEROIC COUPLET.

Hilton, James 1900–54 Novelist. He was born at Leigh in Lancashire and educated at school and university in Cambridge. As a freelance journalist he contributed to many newspapers and journals. He first made his name with *Goodbye, Mr Chips* (1934; serialized in *The British Weekly* in 1933), a sentimental tale about an English public school master. His other bestselling novel was *Lost Horizon* (1933), which described 'Shangri-La', an imaginary land isolated in the heart of Asia where the inhabitants were liberated from the stresses of normal life. The name has since been used to signify any idyllic retreat from the world. Other novels include *Murder at School* (1931; written under the pseudonym Glen Trevor), *Contango* (1932), *Knight without Armour* (1933), *We are Not Alone* (1937) and *Random Harvest* (1941), about a man suffering from amnesia. Hilton became a Hollywood scriptwriter in the 1940s and died in California.

Hilton, Walter *c.* 1340–96 Author of *The Scale of Perfection* (or *The Ladder of Perfection*) and of several minor treatises and letters in English and Latin. After studying at Cambridge he became a hermit, but later became an Augustinian canon at Thurgaston priory, Nottingham, where he died. *The Scale of Perfection* is a devotional treatise in two parts, one written considerably later than the other. The first book aims to show how the soul must obliterate the image of sin, replace it with the image of Christ and practise virtue in the attempt to attain perfection. The second book explains the distinction between the active and contemplative lives of the religious and describes the beginnings of contemplation. Though familiar with *THE CLOUD OF UNKNOWING*, Hilton is unlikely to have been its author.

Himes, Chester (Bomar) 1909–84 Black American novelist and writer of DETECTIVE FICTION. Born in Jefferson City, Missouri, he was sentenced in 1928 to 20 years in the Ohio State Penitentiary for armed robbery. There he witnessed the prison fire of 1930 that killed 320 convicts, an event which became the subject of his first well-known story, 'To What Red Hell?' (1934). His novel *Cast the First Stone* (1952) is also based on his experiences in prison. He was paroled in 1936 and went to Cleveland, Ohio, where he became friends with LANGSTON HUGHES and LOUIS BROMFIELD before moving to Los Angeles, where he became involved in the Communist movement. His first novel, *If He Hollers Let Him Go* (1945), is a story about racial conflict in the defence plants of Los Angeles during World War II. *Lonely Crusade* (1947) examines racial discrimination and violence in the wartime labour unions of California. *The Third Generation* (1954), his first novel after moving to Paris, is a study of the middle-class black experience. *The Primitive* (1955) explores interracial sexuality, a topic taken up later in *Pinktoes* (Paris, 1961; USA, 1965).

His later work is dominated by richly detailed and extravagantly plotted detective novels, set in Harlem and usually following the exploits of two detectives, Coffin Ed Johnson and Gravedigger Jones. These include *For Love of Imabelle* (1957; reissued as *A Rage in Harlem*, 1965), *The Real Cool Killers* (1959), *All Shot Up* (1960), *Cotton Comes to Harlem* (1965), *The Heat's On* (1966), *Blind Man with a Pistol* (1969). His autobiographies are *The Quality of Hurt* (1972) and *My Life of Absurdity* (1976).

Hind and the Panther, The A poem in three parts by JOHN DRYDEN, published in 1687, two years after his conversion to Roman Catholicism. The first part characterizes various religious sects and identifies them with the emblems of specific animals, the chief pair being the 'milk-white Hind' of the Roman church, and the aggressive Panther, representing Anglicanism. In the second part, there is a theological argument between the two churches. The third and most notable part spills over into temporal satire and invokes two celebrated fables: the swallows and the martin (told by the Panther), and the pigeons and the poultry (told by the Hind).

The significant associations of the beast emblems are at times difficult to follow, but the doctrinal centre of this poem is Dryden's insistence on divine mystique, the belief that essential truth in things 'darkly writ' is accessible only through absolute faith. It is the poet's affirmation of his belief in the indefinable, and the infinite. Despite its earnestness of theme, this poem contains some of Dryden's most accessible verse – particularly the Hind's rebuke to her son, in Part 3 – as well as reflecting the practical and social difficulties involved in translating a faith from one affiliation to another.

Hindle Wakes A play by STANLEY HOUGHTON, first performed in London in 1912, when it was greeted with particular favour by supporters of the movement for women's emancipation.

Fanny Hawthorne, a weaver at Jeffcote's Lancashire cotton mill, and Alan Jeffcote, son of the owner, have spent a weekend together in Llandudno. Both sets of parents agree that they must marry, but Fanny ruins the plan by refusing to marry Alan just 'to turn him into an honest man'. She prefers to leave home and live on her earnings as a weaver.

His Natural Life A novel by MARCUS CLARKE, serialized in the *Australian Journal* from March 1870 to June 1872 and published in a thoroughly revised and shortened form in 1874. It was not until 1885, some four years after the author's early death, that the revised version was given the longer title of *For the Term of His Natural Life*.

In the original version, the dissolute son of the wealthy Sir Richard Devine is accused, while travelling in London under the pseudonym of Rufus Dawes, of the murder of his accomplice in a proposed fraud, Hans Blinzler. Though circumstantial evidence against him is strong, Dawes refuses to reveal the truth in an effort to protect his wife, Blinzler's daughter. His sentence of death is commuted to transportation. At the notorious Norfolk Island settlement in Australia he finds a sadistic persecutor in his cousin Maurice Frere, the commandant. Frere marries and destroys Dora, whom Dawes had saved while she was a child and loved faithfully ever since. After 30 years of suffering, all is finally resolved when Dawes reclaims his true identity and is reunited with his wife. His adopted daughter Dorcas, the child of Dora and Frere, marries his upright nephew Arthur Devine. The revised version shortens the prologue explaining Dawes's sentence, changes Dora's name to Sylvia, and ends as Dawes dies reunited with her while escaping from Norfolk Island.

The novel's authority and gloomy power stem partly from Clarke's extensive use of public records and recollections of the penal settlements, and partly from his own authentic and intense response to the harsh beauty of the Australian landscape and its contradictory society of the convicted and the free.

History of Great Britain, The DAVID HUME's most popular work, published in 1754–62. It extends from Caesar's invasion to the flight of James II in 1688.

Hume had originally begun with the Stuarts and worked backwards. The history of the 17th century best embodied his concern with the progress of society, by which he largely meant the development of political liberty. This interest leads him to concentrate less on the public history of wars and treaties than some earlier chroniclers and less on character studies of history's chief actors than some later ones. His analysis of the social and economic conditions which make 'liberty' possible, and of the relations between liberty and necessary authority, is conducted from a broadly Whig standpoint but without conspicuous partisan loyalties. The attempt at philosophical impartiality is matched by a prose style which is, according to BUCKLE, 'polished as marble, but cold as marble too'.

History of the Rebellion, The The title usually given to the EARL OF CLARENDON's history of his times, *The True Historical Narrative of the Rebellion and Civil Wars in England*. It was begun in 1646, when Edward Hyde (as he then was) accompanied Prince Charles into exile in the Scilly Isles, though not completed until the author's second exile, begun in 1667, and not published until 1702–4. The *History* is a landmark in English historical literature, as well as a valuable source of information about the political upheavals of the 17th century. Clarendon wrote as an eyewitness to events, aided by his lawyer's training in the making of considered judgements and, particularly, by a remarkable gift for characterization.

Histrio-Mastix See PRYNNE, WILLIAM.

Hoadly, Benjamin 1676–1761 Churchman and theologian. Hoadly was born at Westerham in Kent and educated at St Catharine's College, Cambridge. He became Bishop of Bangor, Hereford, Salisbury and Winchester successively. A serious illness in youth had left him so incapacitated that he usually preached on his knees. A sermon delivered before George I in 1717 argued that the Gospels afford no warrant for any visible church authority and provoked the 'Bangorian controversy', so called because both Hoadly and his main opponent, THOMAS SHERLOCK, had at different times held that see. Hoadly was the author of a number of religious works, including *A Plain Account of the Nature and End of the Lord's Supper* (1735), which maintained that the Last Supper was merely commemorative.

Hoadly, Benjamin 1706–57 Playwright. Son of Bishop BENJAMIN HOADLY, he was a physician in the royal household and became the friend of DAVID GARRICK. Like many others he owed such success as he was to enjoy as a playwright to the great actor, who staged Hoadly's comedy, *The Suspicious Husband*, at COVENT GARDEN in February 1747 and found an excellent part as Ranger, an audacious rake. Hoadly was the author of some medical textbooks; no other play of his was produced though he is believed to have written a total of three.

Hoban, Russell 1925– Novelist and writer of CHILDREN'S LITERATURE. Born in Pennsylvania, Hoban settled in London in 1960. For many years an illustrator,

he became a writer for children before turning to adult fiction as well. *The Mouse and His Child* (1969) is regarded as a modern children's classic. His first three novels – of which the third, *Turtle Diary* (1975), is considered the most substantial – are whimsical, wistful fables of loneliness and aspiration, which often break out in zany comedy. Hoban's fourth full-length fiction, *Riddley Walker* (1980), marked a major advance: ostensibly a scenario of a Britain reverted to primitivism after a late 20th-century holocaust, it is also a religious enquiry into the essence of knowledge, achieved through a broken-down phonetic diction that Hoban has formulated for his narrator, which is simultaneously halting and opaque, and capable of poetic precision. A further novel, *Pilgermann* (1983), set in the Holy Land, continues Hoban's metaphysical and mystical fabulation. *The Medusa Frequency* (1987) is a slighter, more anarchic fantasy preoccupied with word processors, Indian music and Greek myths. More children's books have included some lively picture-books, many of them illustrated by Quentin Blake.

Hobbes, John Oliver [Craigie (*née* Richards), Pearl Mary Teresa] 1867–1906 Novelist and playwright. Born in Boston, she was educated in America, England and France before finally settling in England. She contributed many articles to various newspapers and periodicals, but is chiefly remembered for her first novel, *Some Emotions and a Moral* (1891), and for her play *The Ambassador* (1898). Her other novels included *The Sinner's Comedy* (1892), *The Serious Wooing* (1901) and *The Flute of Pan* (1905). Another play, *The Wisdom of the Wise* (1900), achieved some contemporary success. She also published essays on GEORGE ELIOT (1901) and George Sand (1902).

Hobbes, Thomas 1588–1679 Philosopher. The son of a parson, Hobbes was born in Wiltshire. He graduated from Magdalen College, Oxford, in 1608 and became tutor to William Cavendish (later 1st Earl of Devonshire), remaining as secretary and companion. The connection proved invaluable to Hobbes: he enjoyed opportunities to travel (during which he met Galileo, Descartes and Père Mersenne), had access to fine libraries, and was able to spend five years (1621–6) working with FRANCIS BACON. He also made the acquaintance of BEN JONSON and LORD HERBERT OF CHERBURY. He left England in 1640 with the first group of Royalist émigrés and lived in Paris for the next 11 years. He was appointed tutor to the Prince of Wales (later Charles II) in 1647.

Hobbes had meanwhile discovered geometry and this, with the influence of Galileo, had helped clarify his ideas of philosophy as something that could be demonstrated in positive terms: 'the rules and infallibility of reason'. While in France he worked on a plan for an extensive treatise, beginning with matter as the first part, and going on to deal with human nature, society and government. Events in England, where the Civil War had begun in earnest in 1642, persuaded him to embark at once on the proposed third part, *De cive* (1642; translated as *Philosophical Rudiments concerning Government and Society*, 1651). The first part was *De corpore politico: or, the Elements of Law, Moral and Politic* (1650) and the second part *De homine* (1658).

LEVIATHAN: *or, The Matter, Form, and Power of a Commonwealth Ecclesiastical and Civil* (1651) caused offence in most religious and political quarters. Some Royalists mistook it as an argument in favour of Cromwell's kingship. Dismissed by the Prince of Wales, Hobbes returned to England, where he published *Questions concerning Liberty, Necessity and Chance* (1656). He had returned to the Cavendish family in 1653 and spent the rest of his life with them. Charles II granted his old tutor an annual pension, though he could do nothing to stop the Commons' bill against blasphemous books, among which *Leviathan* was listed. Hobbes was forbidden to publish any political and religious books and those already published were publicly burned. In his old age he embarked on a translation of Homer, publishing his *Odyssey* at the age of 85 and his *Iliad* in the following year, having previously translated Thucydides in 1629. He died at the age of 92 and posthumously published works include *Behemoth: The History of the Civil Wars of England* (1679–81) and *A Dialogue between a Philosopher and a Student of the Common Laws of England* (1681).

Hobbes was a materialist who argued from first principles: he refused to assume, because it was the habit of his time to proceed too easily from assumption. His dismissal of Christian terminology in his religious comments not only provoked a storm of abuse but obliged his contemporaries to argue with him in print. In the absolute precision of his language, Hobbes was the most impressive and influential philosopher of his time.

Hobsbaum, Philip (Dennis) 1932– Poet. Born in London, he was educated at Belle Vue Grammar School, at Downing College, Cambridge, under F. R. LEAVIS and at Sheffield University under WILLIAM EMPSON. He currently lectures in English at Glasgow University. He edited the magazine *Delta* (1954–5). The founder of the GROUP, he went on to edit *A Group Anthology* (1963) with EDWARD LUCIE-SMITH. His own poetry, which includes *The Place's Fault* (1964), *In Retreat* (1966), *Coming Out Fighting* (1969) and *Women and Animals* (1972), is influenced by ROBERT LOWELL and PHILIP LARKIN and characterized by tones of loss and regret.

Hobson's Choice A comedy by HAROLD BRIGHOUSE, first produced in 1915. Hobson is a hard-headed and

dominating cobbler, more dependent on his daughter Maggie than he cares to recognize. The play details the means by which Maggie breaks down her father's resistance to her marrying his downtrodden employee Will Mossop at the same time as she makes Will aware of his own potential.

Hoby, Sir **Thomas** See COURTIER, THE.

Hoccleve [Occleve], **Thomas** *c.*1368/9–*c.*1437 Poet. Born perhaps in Hockliffe, Bedfordshire, he trained at one of the Inns of Court, becoming a clerk in the office of the Privy Seal in 1387 or 1388. In 1395 he was granted a corrody at Hayling but resigned it after four years and remained at the Privy Seal until *c.* 1422–3. Details of his private life given in his poetry indicate that he suffered from eye-strain and backache, and found his work as a copyist unsatisfying. His claims to living in penury and having spent his youth in debauched and extravagant living beyond his means may be a literary pose; the debauched youth is a common topos. An ardent opponent of the LOLLARDS, he had hoped to become a priest but was unable to secure a benefice and instead married in 1410–11. He suffered a period of mental illness after 1416, but claims to have recovered by 1421. He was granted a minor benefice at Southwick priory in 1424 and probably remained there until his death.

Hoccleve was active as a poet from 1402 to 1422. Autobiographical or pseudo-autobiographical material is found in many of his best-known poems: *La Male Regle*, a confessional and begging poem relating the excesses of his youth and asking for payment of his annuity; *Hoccleve's Complaint*; *Dialogus cum amico*; and *De regimine principum*, where a description of his life and over 30 exempla are combined with political complaint and advice on good government. He also wrote: a poem in praise of women, *Lepistre de Cupide*, freely adapted from Christine de Pisan's *L'Epistre au Dieu d'Amours*; *Ars sciendi mori*, an adaptation from part of Heinrich Suso's *Horologium sapientiae* on the art of dying; the *Tale of the Emperor Jerelaus*, a version of the story of LE BONE FLORENCE OF ROME; and many short, mostly religious, pieces.

Hodgins, Jack 1938– Canadian novelist and short-story writer. Born and brought up in a logging and farming community on Vancouver Island, he attended the University of British Columbia, where he studied creative writing under EARLE BIRNEY. He returned to Vancouver Island and worked as a high-school teacher before becoming a full-time writer. During the 1970s Hodgins travelled to Ireland and Japan and his novel *The Invention of the World* (1977), which includes a quest for origins that takes some of the characters back to Ireland, is influenced by the oral storytelling traditions of Irish epic. *The Honorary Patron* (1987) examines the tensions felt by an elderly art historian when he returns, as patron of an arts festival, to his native Vancouver Island after an absence of 40 years. His other books are: the novels *The Resurrection of Joseph Bourne* (1979) and *Innocent Cities* (1990); two volumes of short stories, *Spit Delaney's Island* (1976) and *The Barclay Family Theatre* (1981); a children's book, *Left Behind in Squabble Bay* (1988); and an Australian travel journal, *Over Forty in Broken Hill* (1992). His early fiction deals with Vancouver Island; the seven daughters of the Barclay family provide points of contact between the different books. His later work is concerned with cross-cultural encounters. His strong regional flavour is combined with a post-modernist approach that has affinities with Latin American MAGIC REALISM. He lived in Ottawa for a number of years, but has now returned to Vancouver Island, where he teaches at the University of Victoria.

Hodgson, William Hope 1877–1918 Novelist. Hodgson escaped from an unhappy home by going to sea in his teens, but abandoned that career after eight years in 1899. He opened a school of physical culture but made more money by writing articles for the popular magazines. He diversified into fiction with short stories of the sea, many of them horror stories featuring monstrous life-forms. Two of his novels, *The Boats of the 'Glen Carrig'* (1907) and *The Ghost Pirates* (1909), are in the same vein, but *The House on the Borderland* (1908) is a visionary ALLEGORY extending over vast reaches of time and space and *The Night Land* (1912) is a bizarre far-future fantasy, difficult to read because of its mock-archaic style. Hodgson drew on his experience to bring a dramatic realism to his sea stories, making their fantastic elaborations all the more striking, and his poetry is affectively powerful when it draws on similar resources. The cosmic perspective of his more ambitious work is a remarkable, if eccentric, product of its age, even more humbling in its implications than that displayed by H. G. WELLS in *THE TIME MACHINE*. Hodgson was killed in action in World War I.

Hoffman, Charles Fenno 1806–84 American poet, novelist and travel-writer. He was born in New York. In 1833–4 he made a journey on horseback through the scarcely settled regions of Illinois and Michigan, and published an account of his experiences in *A Winter in the West* (1835). *Wild Scenes in the Forest and Prairie* followed in 1839. *Greyslaer*, a novel published in 1840, deals with a notorious Kentucky murder case and was a popular success. Three books of verse appeared between 1842 and 1847; many of the poems evoke the Hudson River setting of his New York home. A collection, *The Poems of Charles Fenno Hoffman*, was published in 1873.

Hofmann, Michael 1957– Poet. Son of the distinguished German novelist Gert Hofmann, he was born in Freiburg and was educated at Winchester and Magdalene College, Cambridge, where he read English, before pursuing postgraduate studies at Regensburg and Cambridge, on Rilke and ROBERT LOWELL. *Nights in the Iron Hotel* (1983) and *Acrimony* (1986) mark him out as an original, unusual talent. His poems are off-beat, anecdotal meditations on the detritus of contemporary urban society ('Mannequin' or 'From Kensal Rise to Heaven'), lonely, alienated people ('Boys' Own') or personal disappointment and failure ('A Brief Occupation'), told in a flat, laconic voice. 'The Nomad, My Father' and Part II of *Acrimony*, 'My Father's House', grew out of his feelings for his father and a childhood spent apart from his family.

Hogarth, William 1697–1764 Painter. The son of an unsuccessful schoolteacher, Hogarth was apprenticed to a silver-plate engraver, set up on his own as an engraver and began to design and execute book illustrations of which the most outstanding are his series to *HUDIBRAS*. In 1729 he clandestinely married the daughter of Sir James Thornhill, the Serjeant-Painter, and in 1757 was appointed to the same position, the intervening holder of the post having been his brother-in-law. His works were immensely popular, but disparaged by other artists for that very reason. His major literary work was *The Analysis of Beauty* (1753) in which he attempted to argue that it was possible to explicate beauty in geometric terms. The best paintings were constructed according to the principle of the pyramid – the major features of the painting being bounded by an isosceles triangle – and inside this triangle the eye was led by a serpentine 'line of beauty'. The argument foundered on Hogarth's failure to specify how serpentine the line should be. The idea was taken up by STERNE in *TRISTRAM SHANDY* in his description of Trim reading the sermon, and Hogarth provided a plate illustrating the scene, a composition not notable for its beauty. A close friend of FIELDING, Hogarth was praised in the preface to *JOSEPH ANDREWS* and produced in return a plate illustrating the essential differences between character and caricature that Fielding had laid down. From a literary point of view his main achievement was a legal victory in the matter of COPYRIGHT. The Act 8 Geo. II, *c*. 13 (1735), laying down the principle of copyright in engravings, went through Parliament mainly at his instigation and is sometimes known as Hogarth's Act.

Hogg, James 1770–1835 Poet, journalist and novelist. He was born at Ettrick Forest, Selkirkshire, the second of four sons of an impoverished farmer, and received only a smattering of formal education. In 1790–1800 he was shepherd to a farmer on the Douglas Burn, Yarrow, where he had access to books and began to write verse. His early collection, *Scottish Pastorals, Poems, Songs etc.* (1801), attracted the interest and friendship of SIR WALTER SCOTT, for whose collection *Minstrelsy of the Scottish Border* Hogg and his mother supplied BALLADS from their recollections of oral tradition. His first volume of original ballads, *The Mountain Bard*, appeared in 1807. After various misfortunes as a sheep-farmer he settled in Edinburgh, where he published *The Forest Minstrel* (1810), a miscellany padded with 'every ranting rhyme... that I ever made in my youth', and started *The Spy*, a critical weekly which folded after a year. THE QUEEN'S WAKE (1813) established his reputation as a poet, and led to friendships with BYRON, WORDSWORTH, SOUTHEY and JOHN MURRAY, who published an English edition of the work. He joined the editorial board of BLACKWOOD'S EDINBURGH MAGAZINE, to which he made many contributions and in which he appeared as the 'Ettrick Shepherd' in the regular editorial feature, *Noctes Ambrosianae*. It was he who later claimed credit for the initial conception of the notorious *Chaldee MS* of 1817, a scurrilous literary prank for which the journal was fined but which also considerably boosted its sales. In 1815 he published *Pilgrims of the Sun*, which was followed in 1816 by *The Poetic Mirror: or, the Living Bards of Great Britain*, a series of remarkably deft PARODIES of the Romantic poets. The two volumes comprising *The Jacobite Relics of Scotland* (1819) contain not only poems from the period before the fall of the Stuarts but also some of Hogg's own best lyric poetry. His chief works of fiction are *The Three Perils of Man* (1822) and its weaker sequel, *The Three Perils of Women* (1823), and THE PRIVATE MEMOIRS AND CONFESSIONS OF A JUSTIFIED SINNER (1824), for long neglected, but now recognized as his masterpiece. He also produced *The Domestic Manners and Private Life of Sir Walter Scott* (1834) and, with MOTHERWELL, an edition of BURNS (1834-5).

In 1816 Hogg's patroness, the Countess of Dalkeith, died, bequeathing him the farm of Eltrive Lake in Yarrow at a nominal rent. Here he lived for most of the rest of his life, combining farming with writing. Wordsworth's poem 'Extempore Effusion upon the Death of James Hogg' expresses a respect and an affection which were shared by many contemporaries.

Hoggart, Richard 1918– Critic of literature and contemporary culture. A Yorkshireman, Hoggart was educated at Cockburn High School and the University in his native Leeds. He returned from military service in 1946 to a tutorship at the University of Hull, and later lectured in English at the University of Leicester before becoming professor of English at the University of Birmingham in 1962; here he founded the Centre for Contemporary Cultural Studies in 1964. He was an Assistant Director-General of UNESCO from 1971 to 1975, and then Warden of Goldsmiths' College, University of London, from 1976 to 1984. He

has also held influential positions in broadcasting policy and on the Arts Council of Great Britain.

With the work of RAYMOND WILLIAMS, Hoggart's writings – especially *The Uses of Literacy* (1957) – have helped to broaden the scope of literary study to include questions of working-class culture, education and the communications media. His other books include *Auden* (1951), *The Critical Moment* (1964), *Speaking to Each Other* (2 vols., 1970), and his Reith Lectures, *Only Connect* (1972).

Holcroft, Thomas 1745–1809 Playwright and novelist. He was born in London, the son of a shoemaker. His *Memoirs* (posthumously published in 1816, edited by WILLIAM HAZLITT) give an account of his early struggles as pedlar, Newmarket stable-boy, tutor and strolling actor. His acting was unimpressive, but his experiences furnished the material for his first novel, *Alwyn: or, The Gentleman Comedian* (1780). The later novels, *Anna St Ives* (1792) and *Hugh Trevor* (1794), reflect his friendship with THOMAS PAINE and WILLIAM GODWIN. In the panic that afflicted England in the wake of the French Revolution, Holcroft was indicted for high treason in 1794. Despite his acquittal, he remained under suspicion as a freethinker for the rest of his life.

Holcroft's dramatic writing began with a comedy, *Duplicity* (1781), a solemn warning against gambling. The best of his subsequent plays include his resourceful adaptation of Beaumarchais's *The Marriage of Figaro* as *The Follies of a Day* (1784), *The School for Arrogance* (1791), the outstandingly successful THE ROAD TO RUIN (1792) and *Love's Frailties* (1794). *A Tale of Mystery* (1802), adapted from Pixérécourt's *Coelina*, was the first English play to be billed as a MELODRAMA.

Holden [*née* Gilbert], Molly (Winifred) 1927–81 Poet. Born in Peckham, South London, but brought up in the Wiltshire countryside, she was educated at Commonweal Grammar School, Swindon, and at King's College, London, where she read English. Writing was late in coming, and after the pamphlets *A Hill Like a Horse* (1963) and *The Bright Cloud* (1964), she was afflicted by multiple sclerosis, of which she eventually died. Her unflamboyant, fragile poems, which capture subtle details and movements in nature, belong to the tradition of JOHN CLARE, THOMAS HARDY and EDWARD THOMAS. Formally elegant, they show a stoical attitude to life. Her other collections include *To Make Me Grieve* (1968), *Air and Chill Earth* (1974) and *The Country Over* (1975). The posthumous *New and Selected Poems* (1987) includes 36 from more than 400 uncollected poems.

Hole in the Wall, The A novel by ARTHUR MORRISON, published in 1902. After his mother's death, Stephen Kemp goes to live with his grandfather,

Captain Nat Kemp, at a public house, The Hole in the Wall, in London's East End. The child is gradually drawn into the seedy world his grandfather inhabits. The plot revolves around the struggle for possession of illegal insurance money gained after the sinking of the *Juno*. Stephen quite innocently retrieves the money in a pocketbook, dropped after its unlawful owner is violently murdered; his grandfather wishes to keep it to buy Stephen's future. As pressure mounts on the Captain from other contenders for the money, he decides to surrender it and then bring the whole case before the authorities. However, his plan is frustrated and The Hole in the Wall is burned to the ground. At the end of the novel, Captain Kemp rebuilds his public house, but with another name, and turns to legitimate business. Stephen is sent to school at last. The novel is remarkable for its unsentimental portrayal of East End life during the 1890s, and, despite its debts to Zola, displays considerable originality.

Holinshed, Raphael d. ?1580 Chronicler. His *Chronicles* (1577) of British history up to 1575 made a favourite source-book for SHAKESPEARE, not just in his history plays but also in *MACBETH, KING LEAR* and *CYMBELINE*, and for MARLOWE in *EDWARD II*. Holinshed took the project over from the London printer Reginald Wolfe, whose universal history was left incomplete when he died in 1573. RICHARD STANIHURST was engaged to continue the description of Ireland and WILLIAM HARRISON to help with the description of England and Scotland. The description of Scotland draws on HECTOR BOECE's *Scotorum historiae*, that of England on EDWARD HALL's *Union of the Two Noble and Illustre Families of Lancaster and York*. On Holinshed's death the printers employed John Hooker, with the help of various assistants, to continue the work, and the 1587 edition inserted many new passages and continued the chronicles to 1586.

Holland, Philemon 1552–1637 Translator. He was educated at Trinity College, Cambridge, took a degree in medicine in 1597, and taught at Coventry for 20 years, becoming an usher at the Free School (1608) and a master there in 1628. In 1632 he was honoured with the freedom of the city. His mastery of Greek and Latin combined scholarship with a true feeling for antiquity, and he translated from Livy (*Roman History*, 1600), Pliny (*Pliny's Natural History of the World*, 1601), Plutarch (*The Philosophy, Commonly Called the Morals*, 1603) and Suetonius (*The History of the Twelve Caesars*, 1606). These were followed by a translation of Ammianus Marcellinus (1609), WILLIAM CAMDEN's *Britannia* (1610) and Xenophon's *Cyropaedia*, an account of Persia, in 1632. Acknowledged as one of the foremost translators of his age, Holland wrote in a style both lively and immediate – in his words, a 'meane and popular stile'.

Holland, Sir **Richard** *fl.* 1450 Scottish poet. Very little is known about his life except that he was a supporter of the Douglases in the court of James II; after their fall he may have retired to Shetland. His only extant work is *THE DUKE OF THE HOWLAT*, an allegorical alliterative poem into which he interpolated the history of the Douglas family's fate.

Hollander, John 1929– American poet and critic. He was born in New York and educated at Columbia and Indiana Universities. His verse, poignant and witty, formally strict and sometimes esoteric, has appeared in such volumes as *Movie-Going* (1962), *Visions from the Ramble* (1965), *The Night Mirror* (1971), *The Head of the Bed* (1974), *Tales Told of the Fathers* (1975), *Spectral Emanations: New and Selected Poems* (1978), *Powers of Thirteen* (1983), *In Time and Place* (1986), *Blue Wine and Other Poems* (1979) and *Harp Lake* (1988). Critical works, testifying both to scholarship and an engagement with contemporary poetry, include: *The Untuning of the Sky* (1961), *Rhyme's Reason* (1981), *Vision and Resonance: Two Senses of Poetic Form* (1985) and *Melodious Guile: Fictive Pattern in Poetic Language* (1988).

Hollo, Anselm (Paul Alexis) 1934– Poet and translator. Born in Helsinki, he was educated at the Universities of Helsinki and Tübingen, Germany. After living in Britain from 1958, where he worked for the BBC European Radio Services, he moved to America in 1967, where he has taught at many universities. His English poems, including *St Texts and Finnpoems* (1961), *History* (1964) and *The Coherences* (1968), were reprinted in *Maya: Works 1959–1969* (1970) and in *Sojourner Microcosms: New and Selected Poems 1959–1979* (1979). His poems, influenced by EZRA POUND and WILLIAM CARLOS WILLIAMS, are affirmations of all forms of life, and have strong ecological concerns; he is interested in language as it is spoken. American volumes include *Sensation* (1972), *Finite Continued* (1980) and *no complaints* (1983). He is also a translator to and from English; he has translated Yevtushenko, Vosnesensky and Kirsanov (in *Red Cats*, 1962), Brecht, Genet and Blok into English, ALLEN GINSBERG, GREGORY CORSO and Williams's *PATERSON* into German, and Ginsberg into Finnish.

Holman, Robert 1952– Playwright. Born in Yorkshire, he writes subtle studies of domestic and working lives which raise wide-ranging issues. *Coal* (1973), *Outside the Whale* (1976), *German Skerries* (1977), *Mucking Out* (1978), *Today* (1984), *The Overgrown Path* (1985) and three short plays, *Making Noise Quietly* (1986), are primarily naturalistic. *Across Oka* (1988), staged by the ROYAL SHAKESPEARE COMPANY, is about two contrasting families, English and Russian, while *Rafts and Dreams* (1990) is an oddly poetic play about a young woman's obsession with cleanliness. Holman was resident playwright at the ROYAL NATIONAL THEATRE in 1977–9.

Holme, Constance 1881–1955 Novelist. She was born in Milnthorpe, on the shores of Morecambe Bay. A true regional writer, she set many of her novels in her native area. Her most famous book, *The Lonely Plough* (1914), takes a landed estate and the relationship between landlord, agent and tenant as its subject, reflecting her own descent from a line of land agents. Her other books include *The Splendid Faring* (1916), which won the Femina Vie Heureuse Prize, *The Old Road from Spain* (1916), *Beautiful End* (1918), *The Trumpet in the Dust* (1921), *The Things Which Belong* (1925) and *He-Who-Came* (1930).

Holmes, John Clellon 1926–88 American novelist, essayist and poet. Born in Holyoke, Massachusetts, he was educated at Columbia University and the New School for Social Research in New York. A member of the BEATS, he recorded the lifestyle of his friends in his first novel, *Go* (1952; as *The Beat Boys* in Britain). *The Horn* (1958) describes the jazz scene of the day. *Nothing More to Declare* (1967) is a collection of essays chronicling the Beat movement. He published two collections of poems, *The Bowling Green Poems* (1977) and *Death Drag: Selected Poems* (1979). His memoir of JACK KEROUAC appeared in 1980.

Holmes, Oliver Wendell 1809–94 American essayist, novelist and poet. He was born in Cambridge, Massachusetts, and educated at Harvard, from which he received his MD in 1836. In the same year he published *Poems*, a collection of occasional and witty verses. He published two considerable medical works, *Homeopathy and Its Kindred Delusions* (1842) and *The Contagiousness of Puerperal Fever* (1843). In 1847 he became Parkman Professor of Anatomy and Physiology at Harvard, a chair he held until his retirement in 1882. A popular teacher and entertaining after-dinner speaker, he achieved considerable success with THE AUTOCRAT OF THE BREAKFAST TABLE (1858), a collection of humorous essays originally published in THE ATLANTIC MONTHLY, which he had co-founded with JAMES RUSSELL LOWELL in 1857. Later collections include *The Professor at the Breakfast Table* (1860), *The Poet at the Breakfast Table* (1872) and *Over the Teacups* (1891). Holmes also wrote light verse such as 'The Chambered Nautilus' and 'The Deacon's Masterpiece' and three novels exploring the biological and psychological factors determining human behaviour: ELSIE VENNER (1861), *The Guardian Angel* (1867) and *A Mortal Antipathy* (1885).

Holroyd, Michael 1935– Biographer. Born in London, he was educated at Eton, but claims his literary learning was gained entirely in Maidenhead

Oliver Wendell Holmes as seen by the cartoonist, Spy

Public Library. His work on behalf of the literary profession includes the Presidency of the English branch of PEN from 1985 to 1988, and spells of service on the Literature Panel of the Arts Council and with the Society of Authors and the National Book League. Though also the author of one work of fiction and a volume of critical essays, *Unreceived Opinions* (1973), he is best known for his lives of HUGH KINGSMILL (1964), LYTTON STRACHEY (1967–8; revised and reissued in one volume, 1971), Augustus John (1974–5; revised and reissued in one volume, 1976) and GEORGE BERNARD SHAW (1988–91). He has also edited a selection of Kingsmill's work (1970) and an anthology *The Shorter Strachey* (1980). In 1982 he married MARGARET DRABBLE.

Holtby, Winifred 1898-1935 Novelist. Born in the East Riding of Yorkshire, she was educated at Scarborough and Somerville College, Oxford, but gave up her studies to join the Women's Auxiliary Army Corps in France during World War I. After the war she became an ardent feminist and lecturer on politics, and joined the staff of *Time and Tide*. She was director from 1926 and made many contributions to other papers, including *The Manchester Guardian*.

Her original and pithy style is best savoured in her last novel, *South Riding* (1936), the portrait of a Yorkshire community, whose heroine, Sarah Burton, is a strong-willed headmistress. Most notable among her earlier works are: *The Crowded Street* (1924); *The Land of Green Ginger* (1927); *Poor Caroline* (1931), a subtle indictment of moribund charities; and *Mandoa! Mandoa!* (1933), set in Africa and satirizing the unfortunate effects of European civilization.

Other works include a critical study of VIRGINIA WOOLF (1932) and two volumes of short stories, *Truth is Not Sober* (1934) and *Pavements at Anderby* (1937). Her life and achievement are commemorated in VERA BRITTAIN's *Testament of Friendship* (1940).

Holy War, The: *Made by Shaddai upon Diabolus* The last major work by JOHN BUNYAN, published in 1682. It is a complex religious ALLEGORY, operating on an epic scale, which links the conversion of the individual soul to the early history of the world, to events in recent and contemporary English history, and to the forthcoming millennium described in the apocalyptic books of the Bible.

The City of Mansoul (man's soul) has been conquered by the wiles of Diabolus, and King Shaddai, the builder of the city, sends his captains to recover it. His son Emmanuel leads the besieging army. The city is regained and the King returns, but gradually it relapses into evil ways and Diabolus again takes possession. Emmanuel, however, holds the citadel and Diabolus is eventually defeated.

Holy Willie's Prayer A satirical poem by ROBERT BURNS, published in *Poems Chiefly in the Scottish Dialect* in 1786. It is a DRAMATIC MONOLOGUE, the reflections of Holy Willie, a bigoted elder of the Kirk who, with considerable eloquence and the conceit of the humourless, exposes himself as a canting hypocrite. He is based on William Fisher, an elder of the parish church of Mauchline, who fell from grace when he was accused of drunkenness in 1790 and eventually froze to death in a snow-filled ditch in 1809. He was also believed to have been guilty of pilfering from the almsbox, a charge Burns refers to in 'The Kirk's Alarm' (1790).

Homage to Catalonia An autobiographical work by GEORGE ORWELL, published in 1938.

During the Spanish Civil War Orwell fought in the militia of the far-left Workers' Party of Marxist Unity (POUM), and the book is an account of his time in Spain from December 1936 to July 1937. Having volunteered with no definite party allegiance, he had originally believed that he was fighting for 'common decency', 'the defence of civilization against a maniacal outbreak by an army of Colonel Blimps in the pay of Hitler'. However he rapidly discovers that as a militiaman 'one was also a pawn in an enormous struggle... between two political theories': that held by the Communist United Socialist Party of Catalonia (PSUC) ('The war first and the revolution afterwards') and that held by the more libertarian POUM and its anarchist allies ('The war and the revolution are inseparable'). Parts of the book record his personal experiences – of boredom and frustration and, occasionally, danger – and his general impressions of Spain and Spanish life. Other parts of the book analyse the politics of the struggle: the 'racket' of newspaper reports (except those by *The Manchester Guardian*), and the suppression of the POUM by the Soviet-backed forces. After the battle for Barcelona in May 1937, between anarchists and POUMists on one side and Communists and bourgeois loyalists on the other, the author returns to the front line. He is shot through the throat, hospitalized and nearly arrested as a member of the POUM before escaping from Spain and returning to England with his wife.

Home, Henry, Lord Kames 1696-1782 Scottish judge and philosopher. Born at Kames, Berwickshire, and educated in Edinburgh for the Scots Bar, he was admitted advocate in 1724 and raised to the bench (with the judicial title of Lord Kames) in 1752. Apart from writings on law, ethics, history and agricultural improvement, his works include the three-volume *Elements of Criticism* (1752), an influential analysis of literary style. He was a prominent figure of the Edinburgh enlightenment.

Home, John 1722-1808 Scottish playwright. Home was born in Leith and educated at Edinburgh University. He fought against the forces of Bonny Prince Charlie in 1745-6 and was briefly imprisoned at Falkirk in 1746. From 1747 to 1757 he was Presbyterian minister at Athelstaneford, but resigned his living in the wake of the scandal over his tragedy, *DOUGLAS* (1756). Moving to London as private secretary to the Earl of Bute, Home embarked on a moderately successful literary career. *Douglas* was followed by five more tragedies, of which the best is probably *The Siege of Aquileia* (1760), but none rivalled the extraordinary success of *Douglas*. Granted a pension by George III, whom he had tutored, he returned to Scotland in 1770, wrote his last two plays there,

Alonzo (1773) and *Alfred* (1778), and settled into silence, broken only in 1802 when he published his *History of the Rebellion of the Year 1745.*

Home, William Douglas 1912–92 Playwright. Born in Edinburgh, he was educated at Eton and Oxford. His comedies of upper middle-class and political life made him a natural successor to FREDERICK LONSDALE in the post-war West End theatre; they include *The Chiltern Hundreds* (1947), *The Manor of Northstead* (1954), *The Reluctant Peer* (1964), *The Jockey Club Stakes* (1970), *Lloyd George Knew My Father* (1972) and *The Dame of Sark* (1974). His skill in calculating what the stars of his generation could achieve was supported by a sound playwriting technique, whose main weakness lay in a facile sentimentality. *Now Barabbas...* (1947), however, showed his ability with a serious theme about prison life, while *The Secretary Bird* (1968) is a thoughtful comedy about a *ménage à trois.*

Homecoming, The A play by HAROLD PINTER, first performed in Cardiff by the Royal Shakespeare Company in 1965.

After six years in America, Teddy returns with his wife Ruth to the all-male household presided over by his cantankerous father, Max. Exacerbated by the presence of a woman, the rivalries and competitiveness of the household find alternately veiled and direct expression. At the end, Teddy returns alone to his university job in America, leaving Ruth as mother or whore to his family.

Homeric simile See EPIC SIMILE.

homily A didactic address or sermon, usually expounding a biblical text. See *BLICKLING HOMILIES* and *ORMULUM*.

Honest Whore, The A play by THOMAS DEKKER in two parts, the first published in 1604 and the second in 1630. PHILIP HENSLOWE's diary gives us the information that MIDDLETON contributed to the first part. The setting is apparently Italy but the atmosphere is Dekker's own London.

In the first part Count Hippolito is in love with Infelice, the Duke's daughter. The Duke is not in favour of the marriage and packs his daughter off to a convent, giving out the news that she is dead. His friends take Hippolito to the house of the beautiful Bellafront, but Hippolito discovers that she is a harlot and abuses her. Then he is brought news that Infelice is alive. He rescues and marries her. The angry Duke, arriving too late to prevent the marriage, is reconciled to it. Bellafront, meanwhile, has abandoned her old life, having fallen in love with Hippolito. The Duke arranges the marriage of Bellafront to Matheo, her first seducer.

In the second part Matheo, Bellafront's husband, is in prison. He is vicious and worthless but Bellafront is now a devoted wife; she goes to Hippolito to seek his help. Matheo is released, but Hippolito has now been married for some time and Bellafront's beauty arouses him. Matheo stops at nothing to find the means to support his pleasures and suggests that his wife resume her old way of life to supply him with money. But his servant, Orlando, is in fact Bellafront's father and he keeps a sharp eye on both Matheo and Hippolito. It is Orlando who saves his daughter when she is falsely accused of being a prostitute and ordered to a house of correction and who proves her innocent when Matheo accuses her of betraying him with Hippolito.

Hood, Hugh 1928– Canadian novelist and short-story writer. He was born in Toronto, the son of an English-Canadian father and a French-Canadian mother. Educated at Roman Catholic schools and at the University of Toronto, he has taught English at St Joseph's College, Hartford, Connecticut, and, since 1961, at the University of Montreal. Hood first achieved recognition as a writer of short stories, but has subsequently become better known as a novelist. His fiction describes specific occupations, physical objects and the workings of bureaucratic and other systems in a detailed and knowledgeable manner. Several of his early novels take an artist as their protagonist: *White Figure, White Ground* (1964) is centred on a painter, *The Camera Always Lies* (1967) on an actress, and *A Game of Touch* (1970) on a cartoonist. *You Can't Get There From Here* (1972) is a political novel set in a bilingual African state which evokes Canada. *The Swing in the Garden* (1975), *A New Athens* (1977), *Reservoir Ravine* (1979), *Black and White Keys* (1982), *The Scenic Art* (1984), *The Motor Boys in Ottawa* (1986) and *Tony's Book* (1988) belong to an ambitious projected sequence of 12 novels, entitled *The New Age/Le Nouveau Siècle*, which aims to survey Canadian life from the 1880s to the year 2000. Hood is essentially a novelist of ideas and his intellectual Catholicism frequently manifests itself in the form of religious allegory. His volumes of short stories include *Flying in a Red Kite* (1962), *Around the Mountain* (1967), *The Fruit Man, the Meat Man and the Manager* (1971), *Dark Glasses* (1976), *None Genuine without This Signature* (1980) and *August Nights* (1985). He has also published *The Governor's Bridge* (1973), a volume of social and personal essays.

Hood, Thomas 1799–1845 Poet. Son of a London bookseller and educated privately, he was apprenticed as an engraver, latterly to Le Keux, but ill health made him turn to writing. He worked for *THE LONDON MAGAZINE*, where he met DE QUINCEY, LAMB and HAZLITT, and in 1825 in collaboration with JOHN HAMILTON REYNOLDS produced *Odes and Addresses to*

Great People, a popular success. *Whims and Oddities* appeared in two series in 1826-7, the first series containing his two best-known comic poems: 'Faithless Nelly Gray' and 'The Ballad of Sally Brown and Ben the Carpenter', both of which demonstrate a remarkable skill in punning. In 1829 he became editor of *The Gem*, and published works by, among others, TENNYSON, and the following year started *The Comic Annual*. Among his hack works were various dramatic pieces and a three-decker novel, *Tylney Hall* (1834). After a financial disaster he spent 1835-40 on the Continent, though still producing *The Comic Annual*, returning to England to write for *The New Monthly Magazine*, becoming editor in 1841. In it he printed 'Miss Kilmansegg', a grotesque SATIRE on Victorian worship of money, in which the heroine is eventually murdered for her artificial gold leg. Hood's major serious poem, 'The Song of the Shirt', appeared anonymously in *PUNCH* in 1843. Based upon an account in *Punch* by DOUGLAS JERROLD of a woman accused of pawning articles belonging to her employer, it makes a powerful attack on exploitation. The poem was immediately reprinted by *The Times* and other newspapers, translated into French, German, Italian and Russian, dramatized by MARK LEMON as *The Sempstress*, printed on broadsheets and cotton handkerchiefs, and highly praised by many leading literary figures, including Dickens. Now principally known as a versifier with a penchant for puns, Hood has few rivals in English for his comic verbal dexterity.

Hook, Theodore Edward 1788-1841 Journalist, novelist, playwright and wit. Educated at Harrow, he was appointed Accountant General in Mauritius in 1813. He was recalled after four years because of a deficiency amounting to £12,000 (he described it as 'a disorder in his chest') and was subsequently imprisoned, though his worst crime was neglect of duty. In 1820 he became editor of the Tory *John Bull*. He moved in the fashionable society described in SILVER-FORK NOVELS such as *Maxwell* (1830), *Gilbert Gurney* (1836) and *Jack Brag* (1837). THACKERAY used him as the model for Mr Wagg in *PENDENNIS*.

Hooker, Richard, ?1554-1600 Anglican theologian. Born and educated in Exeter, he was sent (with Bishop Jewel as his patron) to Corpus Christi College, Oxford, graduating MA in 1577 and becoming a fellow of the college in the same year. He became assistant professor of Hebrew at the University and was Master of the Temple in 1585-91. He died at Bishopsbourne in Kent, where he had become vicar.

His great work, *Of the Laws of Ecclesiastical Polity*, is an apology for the Elizabethan religious and political settlement. Books I-IV were published in 1594 and Book V in 1597. Other books, VI and VIII (1648), and VII (1661), are of doubtful authority. *Ecclesiastical Polity* was partly his contribution to the controversy started by the Puritan *Admonition to Parliament* (1572). For Hooker the Anglican tradition relied on the Bible, the church and reason, which pronounced on those matters where the voices of the Bible and the church were silent or unclear. Natural law, which governs the universe, and whose voice is 'the harmony of the world', is an expression of God's reason. *Ecclesiastical Polity* also insists on the unity of church and state and suggests a contractual theory of political government. Some of Hooker's minor works were printed at Oxford in 1612 and 1614. IZAAK WALTON wrote his biography (1665).

As well as being an exceptional apologist, 'judicious' Hooker, as he is described on his monument in Kent, is a master of a prose style with long Latinate syntactical structures, discreetly adorned with rhetorical devices, which serve his purpose of careful distinction and qualification.

Hooker, Thomas 1586-1647 American Puritan minister. He was born in Leicestershire and educated at Emmanuel College, Cambridge, a Puritan stronghold. One of the first generation of emigrants to New England, he fled to Massachusetts in 1633 after being summoned by Archbishop LAUD to answer for his Nonconformism. Called to the church at Newton, he served as pastor there and then in 1636 migrated with his congregation to Hartford, in the Connecticut Valley.

Admired by his contemporaries as one of the most eloquent preachers in New England, Hooker was the most thorough exponent of the theory of preparation, or the set of steps that a Christian goes through during conversion; his *The Soul's Preparation for Christ* (1632) and the expanded *Application of Redemption, by the Effectual Work of the Word, and the Spirit of Christ, for the Bringing Home Lost Sinners to God* (published posthumously in 1656) are expositions of part of that process. His other works include *A Survey of the Sum of Church Discipline* (1648), an exposition of the independent Congregational church polity, and a defence of it against English Presbyterian critics. *The Poor Doubting Christian Drawn unto Christ* (1629) is a pastoral manual for dealing with religious melancholy or 'cases of conscience'.

Hope, A(lec) D(erwent) 1907- Australian poet. Born in Coona, New South Wales, he was educated at Sydney University and Oxford. Returning to Australia, he taught at Sydney Teachers' College and then at Melbourne University. He was professor of English (1951-8) at the Australian National University in Canberra. Hope's first poems appeared in magazines after World War II; his first collection was *The Wandering Islands* (1955) and he was welcomed as a poet who made skilful use of traditional verse forms for shrewd comment on modern values. *Poems* (1960),

New Poems 1965–1969 (1969), *Dunciad Minor: An Heroick Poem* (1970), *Collected Poems 1930–1970* (1972), *A Late Picking: Poems 1965–1974* (1975), *A Book of Answers* (1978), *The Drifting Continent* (1979), *The Age of Reason* (1985), *Ladies from the Sea* (1987) and *Orpheus* (1991) have given him a leading place in modern poetry. He has been awarded the Arts Council of Great Britain Poetry Award (1965), the Britannica Australia Award for Literature (1965), the Levinson Prize for Poetry (1968), the Ingram Merrill Award for Literature (1969) and the Robert Frost and Age Book Awards (1976). A prolific and influential critic, he has published *Australian Poetry* (1960), *Australian Literature 1950–1962* (1963), *The Cave and the Spring* (1965), *A Midsummer Eve's Dream: Variations on a Theme by William Dunbar* (1970), *Native Companions* (1974), a study of JUDITH WRIGHT (1975), *The Pack of Autolycus* (1978) and *The New Cratylus: Notes on the Craft of Poetry* (1979).

Hope, Anthony [Hawkins, Sir Anthony Hope] 1863–1933 Novelist. Educated at Balliol College, Oxford, he practised at the Bar until 1894. During this time he published a number of short stories and an unnoticed novel, *A Man of Mark* (1890). In 1894 he achieved success with *The Dolly Dialogues*, a series of witty sketches of the London season published in the *Westminster Gazette*, and a romance, THE PRISONER OF ZENDA, which earned high praise from ROBERT LOUIS STEVENSON and ANDREW LANG. A sequel, *Rupert of Hentzau* (1898), proved equally popular. Other novels include *Tristram of Blent* (1901), *Sophy of Kravonia* (1906) and *Lucinda* (1920). He was knighted for his services at the Ministry of Information during World War I. His reminiscences appeared as *Memories and Notes* (1927).

Hope, Christopher (David Tully) 1944– South African-born novelist and poet. Born Johannesburg into a Catholic family, he grew up in Pretoria, studied at the universities of Natal and the Witwatersrand, and worked in journalism in advertising. He has been based in London since 1975. His first poems appeared in Durban, where he edited a literary review, *Bolt*, in 1972–3. His first volume of poems published in Britain was *Cape Drives* (1974), dealing with his displaced and alienated English-speaking South African origins. It has been followed by *In the Country of the Black Pig* (1981) and a single poem, *Englishmen* (1985), subsequently dramatized by the BBC. But his main output has been fiction. His first novel, *A Separate Development* (1980), written in his characteristic burly satirical style, was briefly banned in South Africa. It has been followed by *Kruger's Alp* (1984), *The Hottentot Room* (1986), the novella *Black Swan* (1987), *My Chocolate Redeemer* (1989) and *Serenity House* (1992). His early stories, *Private Parts* (1981), have been reissued with additions as *Learning*

to Fly (1990). His play *Ducktails*, televised in 1977, deals with his youth in Pretoria, as does his semi-autobiographical *White Boy Running* (1988). His journalism includes *Moscow! Moscow!* (1990).

Hope, Thomas ?1770–1831 Novelist and art connoisseur. Using his fortune with discernment, Hope collected art and patronized major contemporary artists. He produced some notable works on ancient costume and an influential book on taste and design, *Household Furniture and Interior Decoration* (1807). His most important work, however, was *Anastasius: or, Memoirs of a Greek* (1819), a lively PICARESQUE novel which drew on his knowledge of the Near East to create the autobiography of an unscrupulous Greek of Chios in the 18th century. Published anonymously, it was once attributed to BYRON.

Hope Theatre Built in 1614 on the south bank of the Thames in London, the Hope was designed to accommodate animal-baiting as well as drama. Until his death in 1616 PHILIP HENSLOWE held a half-share in the lease. BEN JONSON's *BARTHOLOMEW FAIR* was performed there in 1614 but animal-baiting increasingly took precedence over plays. The building was closed in 1642 and demolished in 1656.

Hopkins, Gerard Manley 1844–89 Poet. He was born in Stratford, Essex, of well-to-do parents who encouraged him in drawing and music. At Highgate School he was taught by RICHARD WATSON DIXON and won the poetry prize in 1860. He read classics at Balliol College, Oxford, in 1863–7 and became known as the 'star of Balliol' after he got a First. He was taught by JOWETT and WALTER PATER, began a close friendship with ROBERT BRIDGES, and fell under the influence of the latter days of the OXFORD MOVEMENT. In 1866 he was received into the Roman Catholic Church by NEWMAN, at whose Oratory School in Birmingham he taught briefly during 1867. In 1868 he became a novitiate of the Society of Jesus, passing the years which followed at a succession of its foundations: Manresa House in Roehampton, Stonyhurst College in Lancashire and St Beuno's in North Wales. After his ordination in 1877 he ministered to parishes in Chesterfield, London, Oxford, Liverpool and Glasgow, before returning to Stonyhurst as teacher of Greek and Latin in 1882–4. His last, uncongenial post was as professor of classics at University College, Dublin, where he died of typhoid fever.

Doubting his ability to combine poetry with his vocation, Hopkins burned most of his early work when he became a Jesuit and resolved 'to write no more... unless by the wish of my superiors'. He remained silent until 1875, when the rector at St Beuno's encouraged him to write 'The Wreck of the *Deutschland*', dedicated to the memory of five Franciscan nuns drowned with the sinking of the *Deutschland* in the Thames estuary that year. An ODE of 35 stanzas, it is divided into two parts, which deal with the dramatic episodes of the wreck, Christ's Passion, and the poet's relation to both events and to God. It ends with a prayer for the conversion of England. The editor of *The Month*, a Jesuit periodical, accepted the poem before deciding that he 'dared not print it'. 'The Loss of the *Eurydice*' (1878) met a similar fate. Hopkins continued to write, producing 'God's Grandeur', 'The Windhover' and 'Pied Beauty' before his ordination, and ending his poetic career, during the bleak Dublin years, with the 'terrible' sonnets, 'Tom's Garland' and 'That Nature Is a Heraclitean Fire'. He circulated his poems in letters to Dixon and Bridges but made no attempt to publish them, believing that this could bring him only 'private notoriety'. A small selection appeared in anthologies after his death, but he did not gain an audience until Robert Bridges's edition in 1918. This late publication date effectively made the difficulties and idiosyncrasies of his work seem to anticipate modern poetry, and Hopkins's reputation eventually grew to make him a major influence on later writers.

His small body of work dwells chiefly on his spiritual relations with God, manifest not just in the agonized questioning of his later poems but also in the subtle yet ecstatic response to nature which is perhaps his most characteristic note. His view of the created world is controlled by what he called 'instress' and 'inscape', which mean, respectively, the animating energy in art, nature and God, and the distinctive organic form of a thing. His notebooks, journals and letters also clarify the principles behind his innovative use of language. Hopkins distinguished broadly between 'poetry proper, the language of inspiration' and 'Parnassian poetry', which was 'the language of poetry draping prose thought'. His own pursuit of a language of inspiration that would capture experience afresh led him to break with the conventional poetic diction of his time, reviving archaisms, borrowing dialect words and using coinages of his own. The emphatic or 'oratorical' rhythm of his poems (which were meant 'less to be read than heard') he called 'sprung rhythm' – an attempt to reconcile speech rhythms with the greatest possible poetic emphasis, which is scanned by stresses rather than by the number of syllables (see also METRE).

Hopkinson, Francis 1737–91 American essayist. Born in Philadelphia, he used the pseudonym of Peter Grievous for his pamphlet *A Pretty Story* (1774), a propagandistic but humorous ALLEGORY of a family of sons (the colonies) wronged by their wicked stepmother (Parliament). During the Revolution he wrote SATIRES for the *Pennsylvania Packet*, the *Pennsylvania Gazette* and the *Pennsylvania Magazine*, including, for the latter, essays in the persona of 'The Old Bachelor'. He also served in the Second Continental Congress (he signed the Declaration of Independence) and then in a variety of positions in the revolutionary government. Among his most popular political writings at this time was a BALLAD, 'The Battle of the Kegs' (1778), which ridiculed the British for overreacting to a colonial military ruse. In December 1781 *The Temple of Minerva*, a MASQUE with music celebrating the American cause, was performed for General Washington in Philadelphia. His next notable productions were further satires in support of the Constitution, including 'The New Roof' (an allegory referring to the proposed new government), which appeared in the *Pennsylvania Packet in* 1787. He spent his last years as a judge, and also published some volumes of songs. His revised *Miscellaneous Essays* appeared posthumously in 1792.

Horestes See PUCKERING, SIR JOHN.

Horne, Richard Henry [Hengist] 1803–84 Poet and essayist. Born in London, he was educated at Sandhurst. He led an adventurous early life, serving in the Mexican navy during the war of independence. His first work was a poem 'Hecatompylos', published in THE ATHENAEUM in 1828. He is chiefly known as the author of an EPIC poem, *Orion* (1843), which he priced at one farthing – according to ELIZABETH BARRETT BROWNING – as a satirical comment upon the contemporary valuation of poetry. He served as commissioner of enquiry into factories and his report on the employment of children in mines and factories provoked Elizabeth Barrett Browning to write 'The Cry of the Children'. His book of critical essays *A New Spirit of the Age* (1844) – ROBERT BROWNING and Elizabeth Barrett Browning being among the contributors – remains an illuminating account of notable contemporaries. In 1852 he joined the gold rush to Australia and held several official posts there before returning in 1869. His *Australian Autobiography and Australian Facts and Prospects* (1859) gives an account of his experiences.

Horner, Francis 1778–1817 Lawyer, politician and economist. Of mixed Scottish and English ancestry, Horner was born in Edinburgh where he was educated at the High School and the University. In 1795–7 he lived in England, apparently in order to tone down a strong Scottish accent, returning afterwards to Scotland, where, together with his friend BROUGHAM, he became a leading member of the Speculative Society. He was called to the Scottish Bar in 1800, and the English in 1807. A highly capable product and exponent of Scottish UTILITARIANISM, he was thrice elected to Parliament in the liberal Whig interest, and earned a distinguished reputation as a speaker on economic affairs and the slave trade, and as a member of select committees. With Brougham, FRANCIS JEFFREY and SYDNEY SMITH he founded THE EDINBURGH

REVIEW, contributing no fewer than four articles on politics and political economy to its first number in 1802, and numerous reviews and articles up to 1809. He died of consumption at Pisa. His *Memoirs* were edited by his brother, Leonard Horner, in 1843.

Hornung, E(rnest) W(illiam) 1866–1921 Novelist and short-story writer. Born in Middlesbrough, Yorkshire, he attended Uppingham School and lived in Australia (1884–6) before returning to England and marrying the sister of ARTHUR CONAN DOYLE. He is remembered as the creator of A. J. Raffles, the gentleman-burglar whose exploits are related by his faithful friend Bunny in several collections of short stories, *The Amateur Cracksman* (1899), *The Black Mask* (1901) and *A Thief in the Night* (1905), and a novel, *Mr Justice Raffles* (1909). Raffles was also popular on the stage and in the cinema, where he was portrayed successively by John Barrymore, Ronald Colman and David Niven. Several of Hornung's other books, notably *Stingaree* (1905), use an Australian background.

Horovitz, Frances 1938–83 Poet. Educated at Bristol University and RADA, she worked as a school-teacher and broadcaster until her death from cancer. Her books include *Poems* (1967), *The High Tower* (1970), *Water over Stone* (1980) and *Snow Light, Water Light* (1983). She is also represented in *Children of Albion* (1969) and its successor, *Grandchildren of Albion* (1992), edited by her husband MICHAEL HOROVITZ.

Horovitz, Israel (Arthur) 1939– American playwright. Born in Wakefield, Massachusetts, and educated at Harvard, he attracted critical attention with two one-act plays about urban violence, *It's Called the Sugar Plum* and *The Indian Wants the Bronx* (1968). Subsequent work, dealing with the *angst* of American life in realistic terms, has included: *The Wakefield Plays* (1974–9), a cycle set in his home town, consisting of *The Alfred Trilogy* and *The Quannapowitt Quartet*; *The Good Parts* (1982); *A Rosen by Any Other Name* (1987); *The Chopin Playoffs* (1988); and *Park Your Car in Harvard Yard* (1991).

Horovitz, Michael 1935– Poet and anthologist. Born in Frankfurt, he was educated in London and at Brasenose College, Oxford. Always anti-establishment, he has found a forum for his radical views in his magazine, *New Departures*, and two well-known anthologies, *Children of Albion: Poetry of the Underground in Britain* (1969) and *Grandchildren of Albion* (1992). In keeping the spirit of 1960s poetry alive, he also founded the Poetry Olympics, a series of public readings in which many poets took part. His own work includes *The Wolverhampton Wanderer* (1971) and *Growing Up: Selected Poems and Pictures 1951–79* (1979). He was married to FRANCES HOROVITZ.

Horse's Mouth, The A novel by JOYCE CARY published in 1944, the culminating volume of a trilogy which includes *Herself Surprised* (1941) and *To be a Pilgrim* (1942). Perhaps the best known of Cary's works, the novel traces the last stages in the career of Gulley Jimson, an amoral and egocentric artist endowed with a powerful genius and a grandiose conception of the artist's role which coincides uneasily with the values of modern society. An edition with illustrations by the author was published in 1957.

Horse-Shoe Robinson: *A Tale of the Tory Ascendancy* A historical novel by JOHN PENDLETON KENNEDY, published in 1835 and set in Virginia and the Carolinas during the last months of the American Revolutionary War. The characters include Mildred Lindsay, whose father is a Tory; Tyrrel, the British spy Mildred's father wants her to marry; Arthur Butler, a Revolutionary patriot whom Mildred loves; and the title character, Horse-Shoe Robinson, a blacksmith. Mildred and Arthur are secretly married. When Arthur is captured by the British, Horse-Shoe Robinson comes to the aid of Mildred, who undergoes several adventures before being reunited with her husband. Tyrrel is eventually hanged as a spy.

Hospital, Janette Turner 1942– Australian novelist. Born in Melbourne, she has lived in North America for many years, paying frequent return visits to her native country. She has travelled widely and taught at universities in North America and Australia. Her novels, variously set in India, Australia and North America, include *The Ivory Swing* (1982), *The Tiger in the Tiger Pit* (1983) and *Borderline* (1985). Hospital writes about nomads, whom she describes as 'characters who cross borders, who straddle cultures and countries, who live with a constant sense of dislocation'. *Charades* (1988), a complex post-modernist novel which draws on such disparate influences as the *Thousand and One Nights* and the new physics, is typical of her fiction's ability to cross national boundaries as well as borderlines between different categories of experience. *Dislocations* (1986) and *Isobars* (1990) are collections of short stories. She also writes DETECTIVE FICTION under the pseudonym of Alex Juniper.

Hostage, The A play by BRENDAN BEHAN, first staged in Gaelic in 1957 and given a famous production by Joan Littlewood at the Theatre Royal, Stratford East, in 1959. The plot is tragic in outline, but the treatment is predominantly comic, and the action interspersed with songs.

An English soldier is brought to an Irish brothel as a hostage. The play's interest is centred on the lives and attitudes of the people he encounters there and on the basic humanity that draws them together. The soldier is killed during a raid on the brothel by the forces of law during a clumsy attempt to rescue him, but is resurrected to lead the final chorus.

Houghton (William) Stanley 1881–1913 Playwright. He was a drama critic and book-reviewer for *The Manchester Guardian* when his first play, *The Dear Departed* (1908), was staged at the Gaiety Theatre. His lively opposition to the cant of respectability was further revealed in the excellent *HINDLE WAKES* (1912) and *The Younger Generation* (1910).

Hound of the Baskervilles, The See SHERLOCK HOLMES STORIES.

House at Pooh Corner, The See MILNE, A. A.

House for Mr Biswas, A A novel by V. S. NAIPAUL, published in 1961 and set in Trinidad's East Indian community. Mohun Biswas's life is centred on his quest to own a home of his own and his fortunes are closely related to the various houses in which he lives, alternating between dependence and freedom, between reliance on his in-laws, the Tulsis, and attempts to assert his independence. Finally he acquires his own house, a jerry-built property in Port of Spain, but dies soon afterwards. Generally regarded as Naipaul's masterpiece, the novel belongs to the tradition of DICKENS and H. G. WELLS and is particularly indebted to *THE HISTORY OF MR POLLY*. It is notable for its rich comic portraiture, its meticulously detailed representation of Caribbean East Indian life and above all its sympathetic rendition of its central character, like Mr Polly a tragi-comic 'little man'.

House of Fame, The An unfinished poem in octosyllabic couplets by GEOFFREY CHAUCER, written between 1374 and 1380. The poem is a DREAM-VISION in which the narrator is transported to a temple of glass where he sees images of famous warriors and lovers. He emerges into a desert and is carried off by a talking eagle which promises to take him where he may learn about love. He is dropped next to a tower of ice on which the engraved names of the famous are melting and unreadable. He enters a castle of beryl and sees Fame, a woman of indeterminate, varying height who has numerous eyes, ears and tongues. He watches petitioners being indiscriminately awarded or refused fame and notoriety, and learns of the arbitrary nature of fame. He then sees the house of Rumour built of sticks and is guided into it by the eagle; the poem breaks off as he is approached by an imposing figure. Attempts have been made to read the poem as an ALLEGORY of incidents in Chaucer's own life or events at court, but not enough parallels can be drawn to prove any particular interpretation correct.

House of Life, The A SONNET sequence by DANTE GABRIEL ROSSETTI, first published in full in *Ballads and Sonnets* (1881).

The 101 PETRARCHAN sonnets constituting the final form of *The House of Life* (the title derives from astrology) are a perplexing mixture of love, mysticism, Dantesque lore, exaltation, natural phenomena, deep despair and, in particular, autobiography. Groups of sonnets adhering to one motif or theme cluster together while others, especially in the second part of the sequence, tend to the miscellaneous and individual. As often with Rossetti, there are eccentric rhymes and arcane diction as well as obscure phraseology.

House of Mirth, The A novel by EDITH WHARTON published in 1905. Set in New York society during the first years of the 20th century, it records the disastrous social career of Lily Bart, a penniless orphan who is related to some of the city's prominent families. Supported by her wealthy aunt, she more or less makes a career of being a house guest in the homes of her more fashionable friends. Now that she is 29, she must secure a rich husband to ensure herself a place in society. She nearly captures Percy Gryce, a pious and somewhat stuffy heir to a large fortune, but loses him when she chooses to spend a Sunday with Lawrence Selden rather than go to church with Percy. Although she is attracted to Selden, she does not think of him as a potential husband: he is sufficiently genteel but not sufficiently rich, and has to earn his living as a lawyer. She also rejects Simon Rosedale, who is certainly rich enough but not yet accepted by genteel society. When she is unjustly accused of having an affair with another woman's husband, she is ostracized by society and her chance of finding a husband is ruined. Disinherited by her wealthy aunt, she is forced to take a job as a milliner to support herself. The novel concludes with her death from an overdose of a sedative.

House of the Seven Gables, The A novel by NATHANIEL HAWTHORNE, published in 1851 and inspired by the author's own family history. (According to legend, Hawthorne's great-grandfather, a judge at the Salem witch trials, was cursed by one of his victims.)

The story is set in the mid-19th century. Generations earlier, 'Wizard' Maule had pronounced a curse on Colonel Pyncheon just prior to being hanged for witchcraft. With Maule dead, Pyncheon was able to take possession of a plot of land, the ownership of which he and Maule had long disputed, and build the House of the Seven Gables on it. The current owner of the house is the hypocritical Judge Pyncheon, who does not occupy the decaying house himself but allows his poor cousin Hepzibah and her debilitated brother Clifford to live there. Clifford has just returned after spending 30 years in prison, a sentence he received from his cousin the Judge, having been wrongfully convicted of murdering their rich uncle. Clifford and Hepzibah are joined by Phoebe, a young cousin from the country, and Holgrave, a daguerreotypist who takes lodgings in the house. Believing that Clifford knows where the deeds to the 'murdered' uncle's property are, Judge Pyncheon threatens to have him put away as a lunatic, but the Judge then dies unexpectedly and Hepzibah and Clifford inherit his considerable wealth. Holgrave reveals that he is the last descendant of 'Wizard' Maule and explains how both the 'murdered' uncle and the Judge were victims, not of any human wrongdoing, but of the Maule curse. Holgrave and Phoebe plan to marry; their union will remove the curse.

House with the Green Shutters, The A novel by GEORGE DOUGLAS, published in 1901.

The story concerns the family of John Gourlay, a wealthy but arrogant and mean-spirited businessman in the small Scottish town of Barbie. His overweening pride leads him to insult and then to combat the humble but increasingly successful grocer, James Wilson. Disaster strikes when Gourlay's son, sensitive and intelligent, alternately ignored and petted, returns to his father's house in a drunken rage and murders him.

Household, Geoffrey (Edward West) 1900–88 Writer of thrillers and adventure novels. Born in Bristol, he was educated at Clifton and Magdalen College, Oxford. After working abroad as a businessman, he achieved fame with his second novel, *Rogue Male* (1939), in which the hero attempts to assassinate a foreign dictator (presumably Hitler) and is himself hunted through England by an enemy agent. Most of the 20 novels that followed drew on Household's interest in the psychology of the chase, notably *Watcher in the Shadows* (1960), *Dance of the Dwarfs* (1968) and *Rogue Justice* (1982), a belated sequel to his most famous book. *Against the Wind* (1958) is autobiographical.

Household Words A weekly magazine owned and edited by CHARLES DICKENS from 1850 until 1859, when it was superseded by ALL THE YEAR ROUND. The name (from SHAKESPEARE's HENRY V) announced its intention of providing family entertainment in the form of wholesome fiction and journalism. Dickens published his own novels in the journal and attracted contributions from BULWER LYTTON, WILKIE COLLINS, ELIZABETH GASKELL and CHARLES LEVER.

Housman, A(lfred) E(dward) 1859–1936 Poet and scholar. Born and brought up in the Bromsgrove area, he attended St John's College, Oxford, where, despite a reputation as a brilliant student, he managed to obtain only a pass degree. For the next 10 years he worked as a clerk at the Patent Office in London, publishing the scholarly work on Propertius, Ovid and Juvenal which earned him the professorship of Latin at London University in 1892. His definitive edition of the works of Manilius appeared in five volumes between 1902 and 1930. He became Kennedy Professor of Latin at Cambridge, and a fellow of Trinity College, in 1911.

A Shropshire Lad, Housman's collection of nature and love poems, was published at his own expense in 1896. Its idealized vision of the English countryside and its lyric pessimism made it extremely popular two decades later during World War I. Despite this success Housman largely turned away from poetry, though he did publish *Last Poems* (1922). *More Poems* appeared posthumously in 1936 and 18 additional poems were published in the memoir (1937) by LAURENCE HOUSMAN, his brother. *Collected Poems* appeared in 1939. Housman is also known for his lecture, *The Name and Nature of Poetry* (1933), less so for *Praefanda* (1931), an anthology of Latin passages on sex which he published, with an ironic preface, in Germany.

Housman, Laurence 1865–1959 Artist, art critic, poet and playwright. Brother of A. E. HOUSMAN, he was a protean figure, writing on feminism, socialism and pacifism, publishing volumes of light verse, popular novels (including *Thimblerigg*, 1924, a political SATIRE of Lloyd George) and the notorious and much-parodied *An English Woman's Love Letters* (1900). He is best known for his plays, which included *Bethlehem* (1902), *Angels and Ministers* (1921), *The Little Plays of St Francis* (1922) and *Victoria Regina* (1934). These 'royal playlets' remained unperformed until 1937 when the Lord Chamberlain's ban on the impersonation of the royal family was lifted. He also published an autobiography, *The Unexpected Years* (1937), and a memoir of his brother containing poems and letters (1937). His *Collected Poems* appeared in 1937.

Hove, Chenjerai 1956– Zimbabwean poet and novelist. After secondary education he gained his BA by private study from the University of South Africa. His poetry includes *And Now the Poets Speak* (1981), *Up in Arms* (1982) and *Red Hills of Home* (1983). *Matende Mashama* (1981) is a collection of stories. His novels are *Masimbo Evanhu* (in Shona; 1986) and *Bones* (1989), winner of a Noma award, widely acclaimed for its evocation of peasant life and the alienation between farmworkers and their white master. Hove agrees with CHINUA ACHEBE that the 'writer is the sensitive point in his community' and, though descriptive rather than proscriptive, his work seeks to suggest possibilities for greater freedom.

Chenjerai Hove

the shaping power of American society and convention upon human relationships. His epic Civil War drama, *Shenandoah* (1888), was one of the most successful of its kind. Its first staging in 1888 in Boston was a failure, but when it reopened in New York the following year it was a huge success, with a first run of 250 performances. His last popular work was *The Henrietta* (1887), a satiric comedy of Wall Street life that ran for 68 weeks and established his reputation as a pioneer in realist drama.

Howard, Edward See RATTLIN THE REEFER.

Howard, Sir Robert 1626–98 Playwright, courtier and politician. The son of the Earl of Berkshire and a fervent Royalist, Howard was imprisoned during the Commonwealth and honoured after the restoration of Charles II.

Howard's first play, *The Blind Lady* (1660), is a halfway house between Jacobean tragedy and the new heroic tragedy, but *The Indian Queen* (1664) is fully fledged heroic drama, the first of its kind. Of his four comedies, the best is *The Committee* (1662), notable for its creation of the comic Irish servant, Teague, and for the strength of its female characters. After 1668 Howard abandoned the theatre for a career in politics.

Hovey, Richard 1864–1900 American poet. He was born in Illinois and educated at Dartmouth College. In collaboration with the Canadian poet BLISS CARMAN, he wrote three volumes celebrating life on the open road: *Songs from Vagabondia* (1894), *More Songs from Vagabondia* (1896) and *Last Songs from Vagabondia* (1901). *Along the Trail* (1898) was published in the year of the Spanish-American War. *The Holy Graal* (1907) contains the fragments of an uncompleted cycle of poetic dramas drawn from ARTHURIAN LITERATURE. A posthumous collection, *To the End of the Trail*, appeared in 1908.

Howard, Sidney (Coe) 1891–1939 American playwright. Born in Oakland, California, he became a journalist in New York after serving in World War I. He began his career as a playwright in 1923 and had his first success in the following year with *They Knew What They Wanted*, based on the story of Paolo and Francesca. His most experimental play, *Yellow Jack* (written with Paul de Kruif, 1924), deals with the research which led to the identification of the cause of yellow fever. Other plays include *Lucky Sam McCarver* (1925), *The Silver Cord* (1926), *Salvation Nell* (with CHARLES MACARTHUR; 1928) and *The Late Christopher Bean* (1932).

How They Brought the Good News from Ghent to Aix A poem by ROBERT BROWNING published in *Dramatic Romances and Lyrics* (1845). Despite appearances, the narrative does not refer to any historical event. Browning admitted that he had simply wanted to evoke the rhythm of horses galloping; his success made the poem a favourite anthology piece.

Howards End A novel by E. M. FORSTER, published in 1910. It centres on the relationship between the cultivated and intellectual Schlegel sisters (Margaret and Helen) and the more practical and business-orientated Wilcox family (Henry, his sons Charles and Paul, and daughter Evie). Helen is briefly enamoured of Paul Wilcox, but immediately regrets her impulsiveness. Margaret meets a poor young married man, Leonard Bast, and establishes a friendship with Mrs Wilcox, the owner of Howards End. The latter, who is dying, bequeaths the house to Margaret in a note, but this is destroyed by the Wilcoxes before its contents are published. Leonard Bast, meanwhile, has become a close friend of the sisters, and they apply to Henry Wilcox for advice when the Basts' circumstances become straitened. Outraged by his indifference,

Howard, Bronson (Crocker) 1842–1908 American playwright. Born in Detroit, he had his first dramatic success with *Saratoga* (1870), a comedy of upper-class life which was produced by AUGUSTIN DALY and later adapted for the London stage as *Brighton* (1874). *The Banker's Daughter* (1878), a revised version of his *Lillian's Last Love* (1873), and *Young Mrs Winthrop* (1882) confirmed his reputation as a dramatist. In all his plays he was concerned with

Helen conducts Bast and his wife, Jacky, to the Wilcoxes' second home at Oniton during Evie's wedding celebrations. Wilcox and Jacky recognize each other as ex-lovers, but Margaret, who has by now become engaged to Wilcox, forgives his past adultery and they marry. Helen, carrying Leonard's child, retreats to the Continent, and Charles Wilcox thrashes Leonard to death for what he takes to be callous seduction. Charles goes to prison. Helen's child is born, and the sisters are reunited at Howards End. 'Only connect... ', the famous epigraph to the novel, expresses Forster's lifelong belief in salvation through fraternal sympathy.

Howe, E(dgar) W(atson) 1853–1937 American novelist and editor. Born in Indiana, Howe owned and edited the *Daily Globe of Atchison, Kansas* (1877–1911), and *E. W. Howe's Monthly* (1911–37). He also published novels and collections of editorials and aphorisms. Despite its melodramatic plot, his novel THE STORY OF A COUNTRY TOWN (1883) drew high praise from TWAIN among others when it first appeared and is widely regarded as a landmark of American realism.

Howe, Julia Ward 1819–1910 American poet and humanitarian. A tireless worker for women's suffrage, prison reform and the abolition of slavery, she edited the Abolitionist newspaper *Commonwealth* in Boston with her husband, Samuel Gridley Howe. Although she is probably best remembered as the author of THE BATTLE HYMN OF THE REPUBLIC (1861), she published several collections of poetry, including *Passion Flowers* (1854) and *Later Lyrics* (1866). She also wrote *Sex and Education* (1874), *Modern Society* (1881), a study of MARGARET FULLER (1883) and *Reminiscences* (1899).

Howell, James *c.* 1594–1666 A minor diplomat in the reign of Charles I, Howell was a much-travelled man and a fine linguist. He became an MP in 1627, and was imprisoned as a Royalist for eight years from 1643. At the Restoration he was appointed Historiographer Royal.

At the time of his arrest Howell was the author of two books, *Dodona's Grove* (1640), a political allegory, and *Instructions for Foreign Travel* (1642). He also wrote political pamphlets, and his years in prison saw the beginning of the work by which he is remembered, *Epistolae Ho-Elianae: Familiar Letters*, written to imaginary correspondents about a multitude of subjects. Its four books (1645, 1647, 1650 and 1655) are the most arresting source of detail about many contemporary events. Other books are his satiric *Perfect Description of the Country of Scotland* (1649) and *Londinopolis: An Historical Discourse or Perlustration of the City of London* (1657).

Howell, Thomas *fl.* 1560–80 Poet. Little is known of Howell, but he was probably a West Country man, educated at Oxford. His life was spent in service to the noble Herbert family, whom he celebrates in his poetry, *New Sonnets, and Pretty Pamphlets* (undated, licensed 1567–8), *The Arbour of Amity* (1568) and *H. His Devices* (1581); the last contains the first allusion to SIDNEY's ARCADIA (printed 1590).

Howells, William Dean 1837–1920 American novelist, journalist, editor and critic. He spent an itinerant childhood in Ohio and began to work as a typesetter for his father, a printer, when he was only nine years old. Between 1851 and 1861 he worked as a compositor, reporter and news editor of the *Ohio State Journal* (1860), correspondent of the Cincinnati *Gazette*, and contributor to his father's newspaper, *The Sentinel*. In 1860 he published *Poems of Two Friends* (with John J. Piatt) and a campaign biography of Abraham Lincoln for which he was rewarded with the US consulship in Venice (1861–5). *Venetian Life* (1866) and *Italian Journeys* (1867) drew on his experiences. On his return to the USA he settled in Boston, working briefly for *The Nation* before becoming assistant editor of THE ATLANTIC MONTHLY in 1866 and its editor-in-chief in 1871. From 1886 to 1892 he wrote an editorial column for *Harper's Monthly Magazine* (see HARPER'S NEW MONTHLY MAGAZINE), and in 1892 he served as co-editor of *Cosmopolitan* magazine.

Their Wedding Journey (1872) and *A Chance Acquaintance* (1873), the first of his 40 or so novels, make use of his travel experiences. *A Foregone Conclusion* (1874) and *The Lady of the Aroostook* (1879) deal with the contrast between Americans and Europeans. With *The Undiscovered Country* (1880), a novel about spiritualism and the Shakers, *Dr Breen's Practice* (1881) and *A MODERN INSTANCE* (1882), Howells moved beyond the comedy of manners to novels dealing with larger social issues. *A Woman's Reason* (1883) was followed by THE RISE OF SILAS LAPHAM (1885), which, like *A Modern Instance*, examines the effect of material success on the human soul. *INDIAN SUMMER* (1886), a delicately handled story of romance in middle age, was followed by *The Minister's Charge: or, The Apprenticeship of Lemuel Barker* (1886), and a scholarly work, *Modern Italian Poets: Essays and Versions* (1887).

In 1888, after completing *April Hopes* (1888) and *Annie Kilburn* (1889), Howells moved from Boston to New York. *A HAZARD OF NEW FORTUNES* (1890) announced a stronger political awareness while affirming his commitment to REALISM. *A Boy's Town* (1890) is autobiographical. His later fiction includes: *The Quality of Mercy* (1892), about embezzlement; *An Imperative Duty* (1892), which has a black heroine; *The World of Chance* (1893), examining the lack of causality in human affairs; *A Traveller from Altruria* (1894), a Utopian novel; *The Landlord at Lion's Head* (1897); *The Kentons* (1902); *The Son of Royal Langbrith*

(1904); *New Leaf Mills* (1913); *The Leatherwood God* (1916); and the posthumous *The Vacation of the Kelwyns: An Idyl of the Middle Eighteen-Seventies* (1920).

Among his critical works are *Criticism and Fiction* (1891) and *Life and Literature: Studies* (1902). His reminiscences in *Literary Friends and Acquaintance: A Personal Retrospect of American Authorship* (1900) and *My Mark Twain: Reminiscences and Criticism* (1910) document his wide-ranging friendships in the literary world, with OLIVER WENDELL HOLMES, JAMES RUSSELL LOWELL and HENRY JAMES as well as MARK TWAIN. HAMLIN GARLAND, PAUL DUNBAR, STEPHEN CRANE, FRANK NORRIS and ROBERT HERRICK all received encouragement from him, and contemporaries bestowed on him the title of the 'dean of American letters'.

Hoyt, Charles Hale 1860–1900 American playwright. He was born in Concord, New Hampshire. Between 1883 and 1899 he wrote and produced 17 FARCES and one comic opera. His early plays, like *A Bunch of Keys* (1883), the story of an incompetent hotel manager, are pure farce and slapstick comedy; his later works, like the comical MELODRAMA *A Midnight Bell* (1889) and the political SATIRE *A Texas Steer* (1890), are more socially aware. In 1892 he leased the Madison Square Theatre in New York, which later became known as Hoyt's Theatre. Among the plays he wrote and produced are: *A Trip to Chinatown* (1891), about down-and-out characters in the Bowery; *A Temperance Town* (1893), about the Prohibition movement; *A Milk White Flag* (1894), about home guard companies; *A Runaway Colt* (1895), about corruption in baseball teams; and *A Contented Woman* (1897), about the women's suffrage movement.

Huchown of the Awle Ryale He is mentioned in ANDREW OF WYNTOUN's *Cronykil* (*c.*1420) as the author of the *Geste of Arthure*, *Awntyre of Gawayn* and *Pistel of Swete Susan*. The first two have been dubiously identified as the alliterative *MORTE ARTHURE* and the *AWNTYRS OF ARTHURE*. The last is probably the extant *SUSANNA, OR, THE PISTIL OF SWETE SUSAN*. The identification of Huchown as the Hew of Eglinton mentioned in DUNBAR's *Lament for the Makaris* is no longer accepted.

Huckleberry Finn, The Adventures of A novel by MARK TWAIN, published in 1884. Conceived as a sequel to *THE ADVENTURES OF TOM SAWYER*, it achieves a moral dimension which its predecessor generally lacks through its harsh satire and its treatment of slavery.

Huck narrates the entire work in his native Missouri dialect. He has been adopted into the home of Widow Douglas and her sister Miss Watson. His blackguard father threatens his relative security by trying to claim the money that Huck and Tom had recovered from the cave of Injun Joe. Eventually Huck is kidnapped by his father and imprisoned in an isolated cabin. He frees himself by making it appear as if he has been murdered, and then flees to Jackson's Island.

While hiding out on the island Huck meets Jim, Miss Watson's goodhearted slave, who has decided to run away because he has overheard a plan to sell him. When Huck discovers that his own 'death' has been blamed on Jim and that a search party may be on its way to Jackson's Island, the two runaways resolve to travel down the Mississippi on a raft. Jim plans to leave the Mississippi at Cairo (the mouth of the Ohio River) and travel up the Ohio to freedom, but they miss Cairo in a dense fog, continue floating downstream, and undergo a series of encounters with feuding clans, murderers, lawless 'aristocrats' and numerous mobs, all of which they survive by luck, wit and determination. The casual cruelty of the river people is often presented, in all its grotesqueness, in an almost offhand manner for satirical effect. Finally, in Arkansas, the two scoundrels who have joined Huck and Jim on their raft, thinking that Jim belongs to Huck and not knowing that there really is a reward on him, tell a local farmer that he is a runaway and offer him to the farmer for a portion of a fictitious reward. By coincidence, this farmer and his wife are Tom Sawyer's Uncle Silas and Aunt Sally Phelps. Huck discovers Jim's whereabouts and tries to free him by posing as Tom. Tom himself happens to arrive and, catching on to Huck's game, poses as his own brother Sid. Tom and Huck free Jim, but only after making him suffer through an absurdly romantic rescue devised by the unsympathetic Tom. All the time Tom knows that Jim is actually a free man, having been freed by Miss Watson (who is now dead) in her will. The rescue goes awry and Tom is shot in the leg. Huck, after fetching a doctor for the injured Tom, becomes separated from him and Jim. Jim gives up his hard-won freedom, or so he thinks, to make sure that Tom receives the attention he needs. Shortly after Jim, Tom and the doctor return to Silas and Sally's farm, Tom's Aunt Polly arrives and sets matters straight. At the novel's end Huck decides to 'light out' for the territories rather than face life with Aunt Sally, who, Huck tells the reader, plans to 'sivilize' him.

Hudibras A satiric poem by SAMUEL BUTLER in three parts, published in 1663, 1664 and 1678. Its distinctive octosyllabic couplets and MOCK-HEROIC style gave rise to the term 'Hudibrastics'. It was immensely popular in its time for its satire (partly inspired by Cervantes and Rabelais) against Puritanism and the tyranny of the Commonwealth. The name 'Hudibras' comes from *THE FAERIE QUEENE* but his character was based on the zealous Sir Samuel Luke, whom Butler had served as secretary.

In Part 1 Hudibras, a Presbyterian, goes forth 'a-colonelling'. He rides a worn-out horse and bears rusty arms. His squire Ralpho is an Independent, and the two never cease from pedantic religious squabbling. They come upon a crowd preparing for a bear-baiting, a sport condemned by Puritans; they attack the bear-baiters and put their leader Crowdero in the stocks. The bear-baiters rally and counterattack; they capture Hudibras and Ralpho and release their leader. Hudibras and Ralpho are put in the stocks, where they continue to bicker with each other.

In Part 2 Hudibras is visited in the stocks by a widow whose property he covets. The widow exposes his mercenary motives, and requires him to undergo a whipping in order to regain her favour. Ralpho suggests that the penance could be accepted by proxy. His master is delighted and selects Ralpho as his substitute, to the latter's fury. After a quarrel they consult an astrologer, Sidrophel, to discover Hudibras's prospects with the widow. Hudibras learns that Sidrophel is a fraud; he beats him, robs him, and leaves him for dead, leaving Ralpho to face any charges. (Sidrophel is a satiric representation of Sir Paul Neale of the Royal Society.)

In Part 3 Hudibras visits the widow and gives her a fictitious account of all he has endured for her sake. But Ralpho has forestalled him and he is exposed once more. A loud knocking strikes terror into him; he believes supernatural agents are pursuing him and he hides under a table. The astrologer's friends, in fiendish disguises, haul him out and thrash him, and make him confess his many sins. On the advice of a lawyer, Hudibras starts to woo the widow by letter. At this point Hudibras is forgotten and the last two CANTOS turn to the activities of the Republicans just before the Restoration. Butler gives a notable study of the Earl of Shaftesbury, the Achitophel of DRYDEN's *ABSALOM AND ACHITOPHEL.*

Hudson, W(illiam) H(enry) 1841–1922 Novelist and naturalist. Born in Argentina of American parentage, he worked on his father's farm until he was 15, when his health gave way and he became unfit for outdoor work. He emigrated to England in 1869 and became an occasional contributor to various periodicals. *The Purple Land That England Lost* (1885), a series of stories set in South America, later became famous. Other stories and two novels, *A Crystal Age* (1887) and *Fan* (1892), followed but most of his writing during the 1890s was the work of a naturalist with an attractive, clear-cut style. He earned literary acclaim with *The Naturalist in La Plata* (1892), *Birds in a Village* and *Idle Days in Patagonia* (both 1893), *British Birds* (1895), *Birds in London* (1898), *Nature in Downland* (1900) and *Birds and Man* (1901).

In 1901 Hudson met RICHARD GARNETT, who was to give him much encouragement, and in the same year

he was awarded a Civil List pension, which enabled him to travel through England. *El Ombu and Other Tales* (1902) and *Hampshire Days* (1903) were followed by a romance, *GREEN MANSIONS* (1904), his first real success. He published 12 more books, of which *A SHEPHERD'S LIFE* (1910) and the autobiographical *Far Away and Long Ago* (1918) have established his place in literature. Other works included *A Little Boy Lost* (1905), *Afoot in England* (1909) and *The Birds of La Plata* (1920). His letters to Garnett were published in 1923.

Hueffer, Ford Madox See FORD, FORD MADOX.

Hughes, Langston 1902–67 Black American novelist, short-story writer, poet and playwright. Born in Joplin, Missouri, he attended Columbia University in 1921, but left to participate in the more lively activity in nearby Harlem. He was celebrated early on as a young poet of the HARLEM RENAISSANCE; his poetry appeared in *The Crisis* (1923–4) and was included in ALAIN LOCKE's important anthology *THE NEW NEGRO* (1925). With the support of CARL VAN VECHTEN, he published his first volume, *The Weary Blues*, in 1926, and in the same year wrote a critical essay for *THE NATION*, 'The Negro Artist and the Racial Mountain'. His second volume of poetry, *Fine Clothes to the Jew*, appeared in 1927, and his first novel, *Not Without Laughter*, in 1930.

During the 1930s Hughes embraced radical politics, publishing a collection of satiric short stories, *The Ways of White Folks* (1934). In two later collections, *Laughing to Keep from Crying* (1952) and *Something in Common* (1963), he again highlights the absurdities inherent in racial prejudice. His play, *The Mulatto,* was produced on Broadway in 1935, and he founded black theatre groups in Harlem, Chicago and Los Angeles. His drama is collected in *Five Plays* (1963). Other volumes of his poetry include *Shakespeare in Harlem* (1942), *Fields of Wonder* (1947), *Montage of a Dream Deferred* (1951), and *Ask Your Mama* (1961). He published two autobiographies: *The Big Sea* (1940) and *I Wonder As I Wander* (1956). He also wrote numerous books, essays and articles on social, historical and musical subjects, and edited collections of black folklore, poetry and stories. In the latter part of his life he devoted his creative energies to writing the 'Simple Stories', which involve a seemingly slow-witted black character who always outsmarts his antagonists: *Simple Speaks His Mind* (1950), *Simple Takes a Wife* (1953), *Simple Stakes a Claim* (1957) and *Simple's Uncle* (1965). His second novel, *Tambourines to Glory*, was published in 1958.

Hughes, Richard (Arthur Warren) 1900–76 Novelist and playwright. He was born in Weybridge, Surrey, and educated at Charterhouse and Oriel College, Oxford. After graduating in 1922 he helped to found the Portmadoc (Caernarvonshire) Players and directed the company until 1925; he was vice-president of the Welsh National Theatre from 1924 to 1936.

Hughes's first two works, a volume of poetry, *Gipsy Night*, and a one-act play called *The Sister's Tragedy* (produced at the ROYAL COURT THEATRE), both appeared in 1922. In 1924 he wrote the first radio drama, *Danger*, for the BBC, and his *A Comedy of Good and Evil* was performed at the Royal Court. *Confessio juvenis* (1926) was a volume of his collected poems.

In the 1920s Hughes travelled extensively in Europe and North America, though he did not visit Jamaica until after he had made it the setting for his first and most famous novel. *A High Wind in Jamaica* (1929; as *The Innocent Voyage* in USA) is a stirring tale about seven English schoolchildren who are kidnapped by Captain Jonsen and his crew of pirates during a voyage to England. In the course of their subsequent adventures one of the girls, Emily (aged 10), is panicked into killing another of the pirates' victims, a Dutch captain. When they eventually reach England the children – much to their amazement – are welcomed as heroes and heroines; and it is Emily's hysterical recollection of the murder which is mistakenly used to indict the pirates. The novel was unusual for its unsentimental portrayal of childhood, which broke with Victorian conventions and pioneered a new realism. *In Hazard: A Sea Story* (1938) tells of men whose lives are threatened first by a hurricane, powerfully described, and then by fears of a mutiny.

In 1961 Hughes broke a long silence with the first volume of an ambitious multi-volume novel (*The Human Predicament*), which was to include historical as well as fictional characters. Only two titles were published. The first, *The Fox in the Attic* (1961), opens in Wales at the end of World War I. *The Wooden Shepherdess* (1973), the second in the sequence, met with little critical enthusiasm.

Apart from early short stories (*A Moment of Time*, 1926; and *The Spider's Palace and Other Stories*, 1931) Hughes was the author (with J. D. Scott) of *The Administration of War Production* (1956), one of the official histories of World War II.

Hughes, Shirley 1929– Writer and illustrator of

CHILDREN'S LITERATURE. She was born in Lancashire and educated at art schools in Liverpool and Oxford. Her books include *Lucy and Tom's Day* (1960) and its many sequels, in which the plots arise from everyday situations and the adventures seldom go beyond mild mischief or the occasional misunderstanding. Her illustrations to her own and other writers' work specialize in distinctively realistic young children. She has also experimented with wordless picture-books, such as *Up and Up* (1979), and written full-length novels for slightly older readers, starting with *Here Comes Charlie Moon* (1980).

Hughes, Ted [Edward] (James) 1930– Poet. Born

in Mytholmroyd, Yorkshire, and educated at Mexborough Grammar School and Pembroke College, Cambridge, he began by studying English but later changed to archaeology and anthropology. At Cambridge he met SYLVIA PLATH, whom he married in 1956.

His first collection of poems, *Hawk in the Rain*, was published in 1957, the year that he went with Sylvia Plath to live in America, where they stayed until 1959. *Lupercal* (1960) was followed by two children's books: *Meet My Folks* (1961) and *Earth Owl* (1963). Hughes has written a great deal for the theatre, both for adults and for children. Subsequent poetry includes *Wodwo* (1967), *Crow* (1970), *Season Songs* (1974), *Gaudete* (1977), *Cave Birds* (1978), *Remains of Elmet* (1979), *Moortown* (1979) and *Selected Poems 1957–81* (1982). His forms owe something to D. H. LAWRENCE and HOPKINS but his version of the animal world is quite his own, isolating cruel and predatory instincts and projecting them on creatures of his own invention. He directs us to the distance of civilized society from its vital origins. *Wolfwatching* (1989) again approaches nature in a raw and vivid manner but also introduces a number of family poems which may signal a change in direction. Hughes succeeded SIR JOHN BETJEMAN as POET LAUREATE in 1984 and published his Laureate verse in *Rain Charm for the Duchy*

Ted Hughes

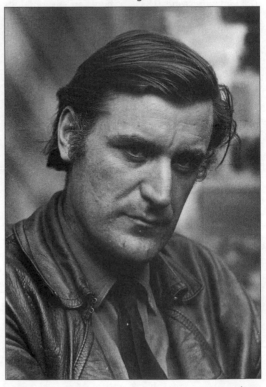

(1992). He has also edited selections from the work of KEITH DOUGLAS (1964) and EMILY DICKINSON (1968) and published criticism which includes *Dancer to God: Tributes to T. S. Eliot* (1992) and *Shakespeare and the Goddess of Complete Being* (1992).

Hughes, Thomas 1822–96 Miscellaneous writer and author of CHILDREN'S LITERATURE. Born the son of a country gentleman at Uffington in Berkshire, Hughes was educated at Rugby and Oriel College, Oxford. He was called to the Bar in 1848, served as a Liberal MP and ended his long and energetic career as a circuit judge in Chester. While studying for the Bar he became a supporter of CHRISTIAN SOCIALISM, with his friends F. D. MAURICE and CHARLES KINGSLEY. He helped to found the Working Men's College in London and acted as its principal in 1872–83.

Hughes's most famous work, *TOM BROWN'S SCHOOLDAYS* (1857), is a lightly fictionalized account of his old school under the headmastership of THOMAS ARNOLD. Its 'muscular Christianity', a code which stressed ethical behaviour and athleticism but neglected academic values, is tempered by a good humour that prompted Kingsley to call it 'the jolliest book ever written'. Hughes did not repeat the success in *Tom Brown at Oxford* (1861) or an intervening novel, *The Scouring of the White Horse* (1861), a slight compilation of the legends connected with the countryside of his birth. In later years he produced admiring biographies, *Alfred the Great* (1869) and *David Livingstone* (1889), a book on his religious views (*The Manliness of Christ*, 1879), and the touching *Memoir of a Brother* (1873) in tribute to George Hughes.

Hulme, Keri 1947– New Zealand novelist, short-story writer and poet. Born in Christchurch of mixed Maori, Scottish and English parentage, she has identified most strongly with her Maori origins. After working at many jobs she is now a full-time writer, painter and whitebait fisher on the west coast of New Zealand's South Island. Hulme had published stories and poems in magazines, and a volume of poetry *The Silences Between (Moeraki Conversations)* (1982), before becoming internationally famous with her novel *The Bone People* (1984). Originally published by a small feminist collective, the novel won the New Zealand Book Award for fiction and the Pegasus Award for Maori Literature before being published in Britain, where it won the 1985 BOOKER PRIZE. *The Bone People* was the most discussed New Zealand book of the 1980s, particularly because of its insistence on the hybrid nature of contemporary New Zealand society. Its exploration of Maori culture continues to be debated. Hulme has also published a collection of stories, *Te Kaihau: The Windeater* (1986), and two volumes of poetry, *Lost Possessions* (1985) and *Strands* (1992).

Hulme, T(homas) E(rnest) 1883–1917 Poet, essayist and 'philosophic amateur'. Born in Staffordshire and educated at Newcastle under Lyme and St John's College, Cambridge, he was killed in action in World War I. Only six of his poems were published during his lifetime, five of them as 'The Complete Poetical Works of T. E. Hulme' in Orage's *NEW AGE* (February 1912). He also published articles on 'Romanticism and Classicism' and Bergson in the same magazine in 1911, and translated Bergson's *Introduction to Metaphysics* and Georges Sorel's *Reflections on Violence* in 1913. Much of his work survived only in notebooks, which were edited by HERBERT READ in two volumes, *Speculations* (1924) and *Notes on Language and Style* (1929). Hulme's rejection of ROMANTICISM and his advocacy of the 'hard, dry image' influenced IMAGISM. T. S. ELIOT described him as 'classical, reactionary and revolutionary'.

Human Shows, Far Phantasies, Songs and Trifles The penultimate volume of verse by THOMAS HARDY, first published in 1925, when he was 85. It is a collection of older, revised, and recently written poems commemorating associations and affections of the past, among them his first wife Emma, his sister Mary, and his long-dead friend Horace Moule. Also gathered here are poems of philosophical reflection, of narrative (often in the BALLAD tradition), of love, of the poor man and the lady (even at this late date in the poet's life) and of contemporary events (the hanging of Edith Thompson in 1923). It is a distinctly heterogeneous collection.

Hume, David 1711–76 Philosopher and historian. He was born in Edinburgh, the second son of Joseph Hume, laird of Ninewells, near Berwick. Originally intended for the law, he left Edinburgh University without taking a degree to engage in private study at home and then in France (1734–7). At La Flèche he began *A TREATISE OF HUMAN NATURE*, publishing the first two volumes in 1739 and the third in 1740. It was received with indifference, despite Hume's addition of an abstract later in 1740.

The five volumes of his *Essays, Moral and Political* appeared between 1741 and 1748. By this time, his application for the chair of moral philosophy at Edinburgh University having failed, Hume had begun to combine the role of man of affairs with man of letters. In 1745 he became tutor to the Marquis of Annandale, in 1747 he accompanied General St Clair as judge advocate on a disastrous expedition to Port L'Orient, and in 1748 he went with the general on diplomatic missions to Vienna and Turin. *AN ENQUIRY CONCERNING HUMAN UNDERSTANDING* (originally called *Philosophical Essays concerning Human Understanding*, 1748; retitled 1758) included a sceptical discussion of miracles which profoundly damaged Hume's reputation in orthodox circles. *An*

Enquiry concerning the Principles of Morals appeared in 1751.

In 1752 Hume was appointed Advocates' Librarian in Edinburgh, a post he held until 1757. *Political Discourses* (1752) was translated into French and helped a growing reputation in Europe, consolidated by his most popular work, THE HISTORY OF GREAT BRITAIN (1754–62), which in its final form extended from Caesar's invasion to the flight of James II in 1688. *Four Dissertations* (1757) contained THE NATURAL HISTORY OF RELIGION, *Of the Passions, Of Tragedy* and *Of the Standard of Taste*; his dissertations on suicide and immortality were suppressed until after his death, when they appeared anonymously as *Two Essays* (1777).

Hume's sceptical stance, not always appreciated by his fellow countrymen, gave him much in common with French intellectual and literary life. His contact with France was deepened when he served, in 1763–5, as secretary to the Embassy in Paris. He returned to England with Rousseau, but the association led to a public quarrel and Hume published their correspondence in his own defence in 1766. He became Under-Secretary of State in 1767–8, but finally settled in Edinburgh, dying of cancer. His curiously detached autobiography, *The Life of David Hume, Written by Himself*, was published by his friend ADAM SMITH in 1777. DIALOGUES CONCERNING NATURAL RELIGION, written in the 1750s but reserved for posthumous publication, appeared in 1779.

Hume, Fergus (Wright) 1859–1932 New Zealand writer of DETECTIVE FICTION. He was educated at Otago and admitted to the New Zealand Bar in 1885. His first novel, *The Mystery of a Hansom Cab* (1886), gained immediate popularity, some half a million copies being sold in the author's lifetime. He was one of the first writers to concentrate on detective and mystery novels, producing some 140 books, none of which equalled the success of his first.

Humorous Lieutenant, The: *or, Generous Enemies* An eccentric comedy of intrigue by JOHN FLETCHER, first performed *c.* 1619 and published in 1647. The title character suffers from a mysterious infirmity that makes him courageous in battle. When he is cured, his courage deserts him; but it returns when he is convinced he is unwell again. The main plot concerns Celia who is held captive at the court of King Antigonus. Both the King and his son Demetrius fall in love with her and while Demetrius is at the wars Antigonus pursues his suit with Celia. She, however, loves Demetrius and resists him. Demetrius, returning victorious from the war, is greeted with the news that Celia is dead. Antigonus, leaving Demetrius to his despair, then tries to obtain a response from Celia with a love philtre. Unfortunately, the humorous lieutenant accidentally drinks the philtre and im-

mediately falls in love with the King. Celia eventually persuades Antigonus, by her loyalty and virtue, to restore her to Demetrius.

humour See WIT.

Humphrey, William 1924– American novelist and short-story writer. Born in Clarksville, Texas, he was educated at Southern Methodist University and the University of Texas. His novels are set primarily in the Red River country of north-east Texas. The first, *Home from the Hill* (1958), is a family tragedy emphasizing the continuance of early Southwestern mores and their conflict with modern values. It has been followed by *The Ordways* (1965), stressing the need for a quality of self-reliance tempered by forgiveness and understanding for others, *Proud Flesh* (1973), *Hostages to Fortune* (1984) and *No Resting Place* (1989). Two volumes of short stories, *The Last Husband and Other Stories* (1953) and *A Time and a Place: Stories* (1968), were incorporated into *The Collected Stories of William Humphrey* (1985). *Ah! Wilderness! The Frontier in American Literature* (1977) is a volume of criticism and *Open Season* (1986) is about sport.

Humphry Clinker, The Expedition of An EPISTOLARY NOVEL by TOBIAS SMOLLETT, published in 1771. Five characters write letters offering different views on the cavalcade of episodes which make up the book.

Matthew Bramble, a cranky but kind-hearted Welsh squire, travels through England and Scotland with his family: his unpleasant and domineering sister Tabitha, hungry for a husband; his amiable nephew Jerry, just down from Oxford; his teenage niece, Lydia; and Tabitha's maid, Winifred Jenkins. Humphry Clinker, an ostler, becomes their postilion and proves a resourceful and devoted servant. The family's travels take them to Bristol, Bath, Harrogate, York, Scarborough and Durham, where they are joined by Lieutenant Obadiah Lismahago, an eccentric and impecunious Scots soldier. Humphry, a Methodist, converts Tabitha; Tabitha succeeds in marrying Lismahago; Lydia falls in love with a handsome young actor who, fortunately, proves to be of good family; Humphry is falsely arrested and imprisoned; Winifred and Humphry fall in love, and Humphry proves to be Matthew Bramble's long-lost son.

His characters' adventures give Smollett an opportunity to comment on English life and manners in the 1760s, especially in the spa towns and resorts. Matthew Bramble, in particular, savagely criticizes much of what he sees – disliking equally the Palladian architecture of Bath and the Gothic architecture of York Minster, and being disgusted by the fashionable society he encounters. Despite his acerbic tone, and despite Smollett's predilection for violent or coarse descriptive episodes, *Humphry Clinker* is gentler in its humour than Smollett's earlier work. It has often been considered the finest of his novels.

Hunt, (James Henry) Leigh 1784–1859 Poet, journalist and critic. Hunt was born at Southgate, Middlesex, and educated at Christ's Hospital. His first book of poems appeared in 1801, when he was only 17. In 1805 Hunt began to write theatre criticism, publishing a collection entitled *Critical Essays on the Performers of the London Theatres* in 1807. In 1808 he and his brother John founded THE EXAMINER, a radical weekly journal. An uncomplimentary article about the Prince Regent led to Hunt and his brother suffering a heavy fine and two years' imprisonment. He continued the editorial work from his cell, where he was visited by BYRON, LAMB and CHARLES COWDEN CLARKE. Through *The Examiner* he introduced the work of KEATS and SHELLEY to the public. Meanwhile, he wrote *The Feast of the Poets* (1814), *The Story of Rimini* (1816), *Foliage* (1818) and *Hero and Leander* (1819). In 1819–21 he conducted another journal, *The Indicator*, in which Keats's *LA BELLE DAME SANS MERCI* first appeared.

In 1822 he travelled to Italy to join Byron and Shelley in setting up a new periodical, THE LIBERAL. Although Shelley's untimely death and Byron's departure for Greece brought *The Liberal* to an end after only four issues, it managed to publish Byron's *VISION OF JUDGEMENT* during its short life. Near destitute, Hunt returned with his family to England; his *Lord Byron and Some of His Contemporaries* (1828) offers a jaundiced view of Byron's part in the affair. He went on to edit – effectively, to write – *The Companion* (1828), the new *Tatler* (1830–2) and *Leigh Hunt's London Journal* (1834–5). His later works include: *Amyntas: A Tale of the Woods* (1820), translated from the Italian of Tasso; *Captain Sword and Captain Pen* (1835); *A Legend of Florence* (1840), a play produced with some success at COVENT GARDEN; *Imagination and Fancy* (1844); *A Jar of Honey from Mount Hybla* (1848) and *The Old Court Suburb* (1855). He published an entertaining autobiography in 1850.

Hunt's short poems 'Abou Ben Adhem' and 'Jenny Kissed Me' (about JANE WELSH CARLYLE) are favourite anthology pieces, but his most significant role was as a discerning and influential critic, recognizing the genius of Keats and Shelley. His personality is known to have given DICKENS the hint for his portrait of the romantic, effusive and unworldly Skimpole in *BLEAK HOUSE*, though Dickens insisted that Skimpole's selfish irresponsibility was not in Hunt's character.

Hunt, Violet 1866–1942 Novelist. The daughter of the painter Alfred William Hunt, she studied art, but turned to literature and produced her first book, *The Maiden's Progress: A Novel in Dialogue*, in 1894. Other novels include *Unkist, Unkind* (1897) and *The Tiger Skin* (1924). Her reminiscences of the PRE-

RAPHAELITES, *Those Flurried Years* (1926) and *The Wife of Rossetti* (1932), are interesting if unreliable.

Hunter, Evan [Lombino, Evan] 1926– American novelist. Born in New York, Lombino has also written under the pseudonyms of Ed McBain, Hunt Collins and Richard Marsten. His best-known novel is probably *The Blackboard Jungle* (1954), about an urban high school, drawing on his own teaching experiences. The novels he writes as Evan Hunter generally deal with social problems: *Second Ending* (1956) is concerned with drug addiction; *Mothers and Daughters* (1961) with the emptiness of middle-class life; *Sons* (1969) with the Vietnam War; *Love, Dad* (1981) with the hippie movement. He has also written plays and screenplays. As Ed McBain he has written DETECTIVE FICTION in a popular series of novels about the police of the 87th Precinct, among them *Cop Hater* (1956) and *Fuzz* (1968). A prolific writer, since the mid-1950s he has produced approximately one novel per year under each of his two main pseudonyms.

Hunting of the Snark, The A nonsense poem by LEWIS CARROLL, published in 1876. It describes the quest, led by the lugubrious Bellman, for a mysterious Snark who finally turns out to be a dangerous Boojum instead. Further précis is impossible, given the poem's deliberate lack of logic and its specially invented vocabulary ('Jub-jub', 'Bandersnatch' and of course the haunting figure of the Snark itself).

Huon of Bordeaux A translation by JOHN BOURCHIER, 2ND BARON BERNERS, of this 13th-century *chanson de geste*. It was printed after his death, apparently by WYNKYN DE WORDE in 1534. After Huon unwittingly kills Charlemagne's son, he is reprieved from execution and set apparently impossible tasks, for example to bring back some hair from the Emir of Babylon's beard and to kiss his daughter; he accomplishes them with the help of Oberon, king of the fairies. The story, and the character of Oberon whom it introduced to English readers, became popular.

Hurston, Zora Neale 1903–60 Black American novelist and folklorist. Born in Eatonville, Florida, the first incorporated black town in America, she won a scholarship to Barnard College and studied with the anthropologist Franz Boas. *Mules and Men* (1935) and *Tell My Horse* (1938) gather black traditions of the American South and the Caribbean. Her best-known novel, *THEIR EYES WERE WATCHING GOD* (1937), portrays the life of Janie Crawford, an independent black woman and folk heroine. She also published *Moses: Man of the Mountain* (1939), a novel which examines the figure of Moses as he appears both in the Old Testament and in black myth, and an autobiography entitled *Dust Tracks on a Road* (1942). Her popularity and critical reputation have grown since her death.

ALICE WALKER has edited a collection of her writings, *I Love Myself When I am Laughing* (1979). A volume of short stories, *Spunk*, appeared in 1984.

Husband's Message, The An Old English poem preserved in the EXETER BOOK. The message, apparently carved on a staff in runic letters, is to a woman of royal rank; her husband has been forced to flee because of a vendetta and he sends her assurances of his love, pleading with her to take ship for the south and join him in the spring. It is not clear whether the *Message* begins with Riddle 60, which immediately precedes it in the manuscript. The poem may be connected with THE WIFE'S LAMENT, also in the Exeter Book.

Hutchinson, Lucy b. 1620 Author of *The Memoirs of the Life of Colonel Hutchinson*, a biography of her husband John Hutchinson (1615-64), a prominent Parliamentarian soldier in the Civil War. Written for the interest of her descendants, it was not published until 1806, when it appeared together with a fragment of Lucy Hutchinson's autobiography. The book is valuable for its picture of the life of a distinguished Puritan family.

The colonel emerges as a quiet man who found himself swept along by the tide of events and did his conscientious best. He was a soldier on the rebel side, an MP, and a signatory of Charles I's death warrant (1649). At the Restoration he was in mortal danger. Lucy Hutchinson sent an eloquent letter of penitence to the Speaker of the House of Commons and the colonel was left in peace for two years, but was then arrested for alleged complicity in plots against Charles II and died in prison.

Hutchinson, R(ay) C(oryton) 1907-75 Novelist. He was born in Watford and educated at Monkton Combe School and at Oriel College, Oxford. *The Unforgotten Prisoner* (1933) deals with poverty and distress in post-war Germany, and *Testament* (1938) with the Russian Revolution; the latter established his stature as a novelist. Of his later novels, *A Child Possessed* (1964), on the love of a French *routier* for his idiot child, is the best. His finest work grappled with grand themes, often of tragedy in foreign countries he did not know well personally, but he deals skilfully with individual character as well as great historical movements. His writings were much praised and attracted a loyal but small readership.

Hutton, R(ichard) H(olt) 1826-97 Journalist, theologian and literary critic. Born in Leeds, he attended University College, London, where he first met WALTER BAGEHOT. He abandoned his original purpose of becoming a Unitarian minister, but never his preoccupation with religion and problems of faith. In 1855 he joined Bagehot in editing *The National*

Review, and in 1861 he became joint editor and part owner of *The Spectator*, contributing incisive reviews of contemporary literature to its pages. Hutton's books include: *Essays: Theological and Literary* (1871); *Essays on Some of the Modern Guides of English Thought in Matters of Faith* (1877), which considers CARLYLE, MATTHEW ARNOLD, GEORGE ELIOT, F. D. MAURICE and NEWMAN, later the subject of a full-length study (1891); *Criticisms on Contemporary Thought and Thinkers* (1894); and *Aspects of Scientific and Religious Thought* (1899).

Huxley, Aldous (Leonard) 1894-1963 Novelist and short-story writer. Huxley was born at Godalming, Surrey, of a distinguished family which included T. H. HUXLEY, his grandfather; MRS HUMPHRY WARD, his aunt; Leonard Huxley, his father, an editor of THE CORNHILL MAGAZINE; and SIR JULIAN HUXLEY, his elder brother. He was educated at Eton and Balliol College, Oxford.

After graduating in 1915 Huxley became a journalist, briefly joining the staff of THE ATHENAEUM and writing drama criticism for *The Westminster Gazette* (1920-1). Several volumes of poetry appeared before 1920 (*The Burning Wheel*, 1916; *Jonah*, 1917; *The Defeat of Youth*, 1918; and *Leda*, 1920) but it was with his fiction that Huxley made his name. A collection of short stories, *Limbo*, was published in 1920, and this was followed by *Crome Yellow* (1921), which launched his reputation as a witty and satirical commentator on contemporary events. Similar qualities were evident in *Antic Hay* (1923), *Those Barren Leaves* (1925) set in Italy, where Huxley and his wife lived during the 1920s, and *Point Counter Point* (1928), which contained thinly disguised portraits of D. H. LAWRENCE and JOHN MIDDLETON MURRY, both close friends of the author.

With BRAVE NEW WORLD (1932) Huxley turned his attention to the threat of world domination by scientific totalitarianism. His subsequent novels were equally marked by qualities of Swiftian despair and disgust. EYELESS IN GAZA (1936) was the last novel to be written in England. In 1937 Huxley moved to California and *After Many a Summer* (1939) is set in Los Angeles. Other novels during this period included *Time Must Have a Stop* (1944), *Ape and Essence* (1948) and *The Genius and the Goddess* (1955).

Island (1962) invokes a Utopian community with a new spiritual perspective and reflects Huxley's own search for an extension of awareness. His quest, which had begun with *The Perennial Philosophy* (1946), led him to experiment with altered states of consciousness through the use of mescalin, described in *The Doors of Perception* (1954) and its sequel, *Heaven and Hell* (1956).

Huxley's other works include *The Devils of Loudun* (1952), a study of demonic possession during the reign of Louis XIII (adopted by JOHN WHITING as the basis for

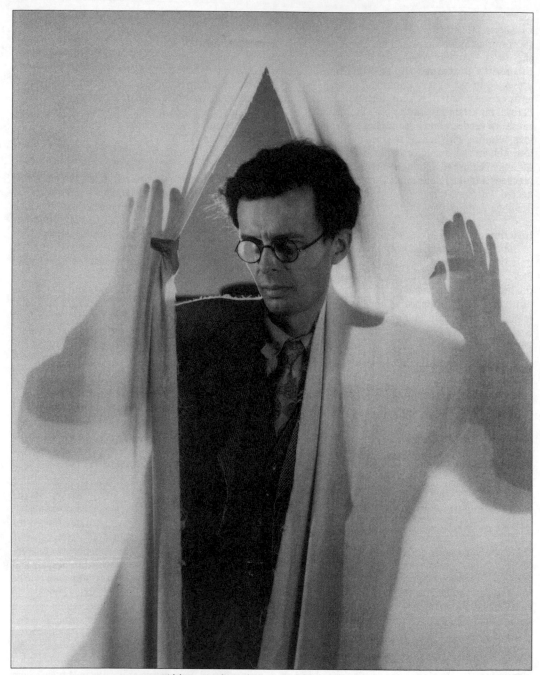

Aldous Huxley, photograph by Cecil Beaton

his play *The Devils*, 1961), and numerous essays (in *Collected Essays*, 1959). He also wrote two travel books (*Jesting Pilate*, 1926; and *Beyond the Mexique Bay*, 1943) and edited *The Letters of D. H. Lawrence* (1932), with an introductory essay which has been widely acclaimed. Huxley's short stories, also considered by many to be among his best work, were reprinted in *Collected Short Stories* (1957).

Huxley, Sir **Julian (Sorell)** 1887–1975 Biologist and writer. The elder brother of ALDOUS HUXLEY, he was educated at Eton and Oxford, where he won the Newdigate Prize for poetry. He held various academic posts in England and the USA. His books include *Essays of a Biologist* (1923), *Religion without Revelation* (1927), *The Captive Shrew and Other Poems* (1932), *Man in the Modern World* (1947),

Evolution in Action (1953) and *New Bottles for New Wine* (1957). He was Director-General of UNESCO in 1946–8 and was knighted in 1958.

Huxley, Thomas Henry 1825–95 Scientist. Born at Ealing, he was educated at his father's school and at London University, where he studied medicine. He continued his studies at Charing Cross Hospital and was particularly interested in comparative anatomy. In 1846 Huxley went to sea as assistant surgeon on HMS *Rattlesnake*, and became a Fellow of the Royal Society through his studies on marine organisms (1851). His lectures, essays and books cover natural science, philosophy and religion; his approach to religion is indicated by his invention of the word 'agnostic' to describe himself. He published *On the Educational Value of the Natural History Sciences* (1854), *On Races, Species and their Origin* (1860), *Evidence as to Man's Place in Nature* (1863), *On the Methods and Results of Ethnology* (1865), *The Evidence of the Miracle of Resurrection* (1876), *The Advance of Science in the Last Half-Century* (1887), *Social Diseases and Worse Remedies* (1891) and *Evolution and Ethics* (1893). His essays and lectures were published as *Collected Essays* (9 vols., 1893–4). Huxley was a powerful supporter of CHARLES DARWIN – arguing the case for evolution against Bishop Wilberforce at the famous Oxford meeting of the British Association in 1860 – and an advocate of free investigation and enquiry.

Hwang, David Henry 1957– American playwright. Born to immigrant Chinese parents in Los Angeles, he was educated at Stanford and Yale. He is best known for *M. Butterfly* (1988), a dazzling deconstruction of cross-cultural and sexual delusions. Other works include *F.O.B* (1980), *The Dance and the Railroad* (1981), *Family Devotions* (1981) and *The Sound of a Voice* (1983), mingling history, fantasy and naturalism. Though he links himself to the Asian-American theatre movement, his refusal to write only about his own ethnic milieu is witnessed by *Rich Relations* (1986), a satire of upper middle-class mores, and *1,000 Airplanes on the Roof* (1988), a SCIENCE-FICTION collaboration with composer Philip Glass.

Hyde, Douglas 1860–1949 Irish scholar, poet and translator. Born into a family of Irish Protestant clergymen in County Roscommon, he was a founder and, from 1893 to 1915, the first president of the Gaelic League, dedicated to preserving and spreading the Irish language, Irish games and Irish dancing. His most influential publication was *Love Songs of Connacht* (1893), printing the Irish originals alongside verse translations and carefully literal prose versions which revealed to YEATS and others the possibilities of an authentically Irish idiom in English. His *Literary History of Ireland* (1899) was deliberately confined to literature in Irish. He wrote verse and plays in Irish, including *Casadh an tSugain* (1901), later translated by LADY GREGORY as *The Twisting of the Rope*, as well as compiling volumes of folk-stories, songs and religious poems translated from the Irish. Hyde was professor of modern Irish at University College, Dublin, in 1905–32, and first president of the Irish Republic in 1938–44.

Hyde, Robin [Wilkinson, Iris Guiver] 1906–39 New Zealand novelist and poet. Born in Cape Town, she was taken to New Zealand as an infant. She was educated in Wellington, where she was regarded as a schoolgirl prodigy and later attended Victoria College. She worked on the Wellington *Dominion* from 1923 to 1926 and subsequently pursued a career as a freelance journalist and writer. From 1931 to 1933 she was editor of the *New Zealand Observer*. In 1938 she left New Zealand and travelled in China during the Sino-Japanese war, an experience she describes in *Dragon Rampant* (1939), before settling in England later in 1938. She committed suicide in 1939.

Her fiction includes *Passport to Hell* (1936), an account of the early life of Douglas Stark, a World War I bomber pilot, and its sequel, *Nor the Years Condemn* (1938), which give a vivid picture of New Zealand life in the opening years of this century. The interaction between private and public history is also the theme of her two best works, *Check to Your King* (1936), a fictionalized biography of Charles, Baron de Thierry, who attempted to establish a Utopian community for English settlers and Maoris in early 19th-century New Zealand, and the autobiographical *The Godwits Fly* (1938). *Persephone in Winter* (1937) is the most substantial volume of verse she published in her lifetime, but her best-known poetry is found in the posthumous *Houses by the Sea* (1952), a sequence begun in New Zealand and continued after she left, which recreates the natural and social environment of her youth in a style moving between lyrical retrospection and investigative irony.

Hyde Park A comedy by JAMES SHIRLEY, first produced in 1632 to celebrate the opening of Hyde Park as a place of recreation for the public. The play, first published in 1637, has the slightest of plots and comments on the fashionable life of Caroline London.

Hydriotaphia: or, Urn Burial A treatise by SIR THOMAS BROWNE, published with *The Garden of Cyrus* (1658) and taking as its point of departure the discovery of some ancient grave urns at Walsingham in Norfolk. Browne broadens his enquiry to consider the many ways mankind has disposed of its dead, and his zestful, idiosyncratic scholarship ranges over a wide field. His theme is brought to a close with an eloquent chapter expressing the Christian view of mortality.

Hymn to Proserpine A DRAMATIC MONOLOGUE by ALGERNON CHARLES SWINBURNE, published in *Poems and Ballads* (1866). Addressed to Proserpine, Queen of the Underworld, by a pagan Roman (possibly Julian the Apostate) of the 4th century of the Christian era, it sets forth the Heraclitan doctrine of flux and change as forcefully as it challenges fundamental Christian beliefs. The speaker denies Christianity while acknowledging its considerable power, mercy and compassion. But he sees it as swept away by forces of change, and hails the power of Proserpine with the conviction that 'Thou art more than the Gods who number the days of our temporal breath;/ For these give labour and slumber, but thou, Proserpine, death.' From death comes sleep, which contents the speaker. The poem ends on this note, deliberately at variance with Christian belief.

Hypatia: *or, New Foes with an Old Face* A historical novel by CHARLES KINGSLEY, published in *FRASER'S MAGAZINE* from January 1852 to April 1853 and in volume form in 1853.

The setting is Alexandria in the 5th century AD, a city governed ineffectually by the pagan prefect, Orestes, and threatened by the barbarian tribes advancing from the heart of Europe. The Christian church is the strongest power in Alexandria and, guided by the patriarch Cyril, it opposes the neo-Platonic philosophy expressed in the teachings of Hypatia, daughter of the mathematician Theon. Philammon, a young Christian monk, arrives from the desert and is repelled by the mindless fanaticism of his fellow monks. He is drawn to the beautiful Hypatia and the moderation and humanity of her doctrines. At the same time, he is discouraged by the weary scepticism of the intellectual, Raphael.

Violence explodes when the Christians are led to believe that Hypatia has set the prefect against them. Philammon witnesses a mob cut her to pieces outside the academy and returns, disillusioned, to the solitude of the desert.

hyperbole An exaggerated or extravagant statement designed to command attention or provoke reaction. A famous example is the question asked of Helen of Troy by the hero MARLOWE's *DR FAUSTUS*: 'Is this the face that launched a thousand ships/ And burned the topless towers of Ilium?'

Hyperion Two unfinished poems by JOHN KEATS, written in 1818–19. One version was published in 1820, the 'Advertisement' to the volume which contained it stating that it had been included at the publisher's wish, not the poet's. 'The poem was intended to have been of equal length with *ENDYMION*, but the reception given to that work discouraged the author from proceeding.' The second version is called *The Fall of Hyperion: A Dream* and was published by MONCKTON MILNES in 1856. It is also a draft, not a finished poem, and Keats gave it up (he said in a letter of 21 September 1819) because 'there were too many Miltonic inversions in it'.

The first version, called 'A Fragment' by Keats, tells the story of Hyperion from Greek mythology. Saturn and the other Titans, grieving over their fall and considering how they may regain their power, place their hopes in the only Titan who remains undeposed, the sun-god Hyperion. But with the advent of Apollo, god of knowledge, poetry and music, the Titans' rule is ended. The second version is a dream related by the poet. Because of his awareness of misery in the world, he is granted entry to a shrine. Moneta, the Titans' priestess, describes the fall of Hyperion and the coming of Apollo. An old order has gone, yielding place to a new.

iamb See METRE.

iambic pentameter See METRE.

Iceman Cometh, The A play by EUGENE O'NEILL, first performed in New York in 1946. The play was one of O'Neill's personal favourites, in which he attempted to portray man as a 'victim of the ironies of life and of himself'.

The men who gather in Jimmy-the-Priest's saloon, as well as its owner Harry Hope, are good-natured and trusting in the value of love and honour. When the salesman Hickey tries to persuade them to abandon their illusions and return to reality, the truths they discover and reveal cause them to despair. Only the cynical philosopher Larry Slade can stand up to Hickey, and it is he who eases the desperate Parritt's route to suicide. When, at the end of the play, it is revealed that Hickey too has been living a lie, the discovery gives Slade no pleasure; it merely confirms his belief in the necessity of pipedreams.

Idea A SONNET sequence by MICHAEL DRAYTON, first published as *Idea's Mirror* in 1594 but reissued with substantial changes and additions in 1599, 1600, 1602, 1605 and 1619, and also in collections of Drayton's poems.

It shows the influence particularly of SIR PHILIP SIDNEY's *ASTROPHIL AND STELLA*: Drayton's claim to originality in the prefatory sonnet to the 1594 version paradoxically quotes Sidney's 'I am no pickpurse of another's wit.' Echoes from SPENSER's *AMORETTI* and MARLOWE's *EDWARD II* can also be heard. Drayton was sensitive to comments from fellow poets and made revisions to accommodate their criticisms. His changes usually reject the extravagant CONCEITS of earlier versions and increase the clarity of logic and poetic structure, though later editions also contain sonnets that seem akin to the new metaphysical style (see METAPHYSICAL POETS). 'Since There's No Help' (added in 1619), which combines colloquial language in the octave with an allegorized deathbed scene in the sestet, is usually considered Drayton's finest.

Idea of a University, The Lectures by JOHN HENRY NEWMAN, dating from 1852 onwards and published in 1873, arising from his experience as rector of the new Roman Catholic university in Dublin, which he had sought to give the intellectual breadth of Protestant Oxford. The justification of a 'liberal education' is the 'enlargement of the mind'. Knowledge, despite having absolute value for Newman, is not the highest good. He argues that knowledge and reason are 'sure ministers to Faith' and that 'Right Reason... leads the mind to the Catholic Faith.' WALTER PATER said the book was 'the perfect handling of a theory'.

Ideal Husband, An A play by OSCAR WILDE (1895). The most strongly plotted of his earlier works for the theatre, it deals with political corruption, public and private honour, blackmail, repentance and forgiveness.

Idler, The A series of papers, largely by SAMUEL JOHNSON, contributed to *The Universal Chronicle or Weekly Gazette* from 15 April 1758 to 5 April 1760. The papers are similar in character to *THE RAMBLER* but shorter in length and generally lighter in tone. Representative characters are not given Latin names as they are in *The Rambler* but English ones: Tom Restless, Jack Whirler, Mr Sober, the author (Johnson himself) and the critic Dick Minim. Of the 12 papers not by Johnson, three are by JOSHUA REYNOLDS (Nos. 76, 79 and 82) and three by THOMAS WARTON THE YOUNGER (Nos. 33, 93 and 96).

A monthly journal edited by JEROME K. JEROME and Robert Barr, appearing from 1892 to 1911, was also called *The Idler*.

idyll From the Greek, 'little picture'. It is used of a descriptive piece of poetry or prose, usually with a PASTORAL or rural scene.

Idylls of the King, The A sequence of poems by ALFRED TENNYSON, his own most ambitious work as well as the most ambitious contribution to ARTHURIAN LITERATURE since MALORY's *LE MORTE DARTHUR*. The poems were written at different stages in his career. When he was 24 he wanted to compose a 'whole great poem' about Arthur and started with 'Morte d'Arthur', published in 1842. The reviews, however, were discouraging and Tennyson did not return to the subject until 1859, when he published a volume, *The Idylls of the King*, containing 'Vivien', 'Enid', 'Elaine' and 'Guinevere'. 'The Coming of Arthur', 'The Holy Grail', 'Pelleas and Ettarre' and 'The Passing of Arthur' appeared in 1869, 'The Last Tournament' in 1871 and 'Gareth and Lynette' in 1872. The Imperial Library edition gathered up all the *Idylls* and added the Epilogue, 'To the Queen'. 'Balin and Balan' was published in *Tiresias and Other Poems* (1885). 'Enid' was later divided into 'The Marriage of Geraint' and 'Geraint and Enid'. In its final order the sequence runs as follows:

The Coming of Arthur. Arthur, the newly crowned king, sets out to restore order to the kingdom and subdue the unruly barons. He falls in love with Guinevere, daughter of Leodegran, King of Cameliard. Successful in his campaigns, he seeks her hand but Leodegran hesitates because of Arthur's mysterious origins. He is persuaded by Bellicent, wife of King Lot of Orkney, who tells him the truth about Arthur's birth, upbringing and coronation and about Merlin and Excalibur. Arthur and Guinevere are married. The source is Malory's *Le Morte Darthur*.

Gareth and Lynette. Arthur's court, not long established, is the goal of all aspiring young men, one of whom is Gareth, son of King Lot of Orkney and his Queen, Bellicent. His mother reluctantly grants him permission to go to the court on condition that he present himself as a knave and serve in the kitchens for a year. Gareth works his allotted term under Kay, the Seneschal. Lynette, a noble lady, comes to Arthur's court to plead that Lancelot may rescue her sister, Lyonors, who is besieged in her castle by four knights. Gareth, the year over but still appearing as a kitchen scullion, claims the adventure and Arthur grants his wish. Lynette is disgusted and treats Gareth with elaborate discourtesy, addressing him as 'Sir Kitchen-Knave'. But he defeats the first three knights and then confronts the last, costumed as Death. Lancelot arrives and Lynette wants him to undertake the last combat. But Gareth fights and prevails, and finds the fourth knight is just a boy, brother of the other three, in hideous armour that strikes dread into the hearts of those who try to help Lyonors. The source of the poem is Malory's *Le Morte Darthur* in which Gareth marries Liones, the lady he rescues. Tennyson leaves the name of Gareth's partner undeclared, saying that tales vary as to Lyonors or Lynette.

The Marriage of Geraint and *Geraint and Enid.* The sources were the story of *Gereint and Enid* in THE MABINOGION (translated by Lady Charlotte Guest, 1838–49) and *Erec* by Chrétien de Troyes. Geraint, one of Arthur's knights, is married to Enid, daughter of Yniol. Uneasy about the character of the Queen, Guinevere, he decides to withdraw from the court and remove Enid from her influence. A remark of Enid's is misunderstood by him and he believes her faithless. He keeps her with him during his knightly encounters but forbids her to speak to him. But her devotion to him in all sorts of dangers reassures him of her love and fidelity.

Balin and Balan. The last of the *Idylls* to be written, it was intended to introduce the story of Merlin and Vivien. The source is Malory's *Le Morte Darthur*. Balin (Balin le Savage in Malory) is a violent and irascible but brave knight who is devoted to Queen Guinevere. His brother Balan, leaving to pursue a dangerous half-human forest demon, warns Balin to curb both his temper and his devotion. Disturbed by the Queen's friendship with Lancelot, Balin curses himself for a fool and leaves the court, then kills Sir Garlon, who dishonours the Queen's name. Garlon's father, King

Pellam, who is descended from Joseph of Arimathea, orders his knights to pursue Balin, who flees through Pellam's castle looking for a weapon. He finds a spear before an altar and uses it to vault through a casement to make his escape. Later he is found asleep in the forest by Vivien, the Queen's favour hanging on a tree above him. From pure malice, Vivien confirms Balin's unease about the Queen. In a fury he destroys the emblems of his devotion, but his wild cries are heard by Balan, who believes he has found his quarry and rides to the attack. Balan fails to recognize his brother and both die in combat. Vivien rides away, unconcerned.

Merlin and Vivien. Vivien, the child of a king whom Arthur defeated, dwells at the court of King Mark of Cornwall, where she hears a minstrel sing of the purity of the knights and ladies of Arthur's court. She goes to Camelot with a distressed and pleading countenance and begs, as an orphan, protection from the Queen. She tries to sow suspicion and to seduce the King but finally decides that Merlin, the master of all secret arts, will serve her purpose better. When Merlin leaves the court for Broceliande, Vivien follows him. She succeeds in extracting from him a charm which she uses to seal him up for ever in a giant oak tree. The story of Merlin's enchantment is in Malory's *Le Morte Darthur* but the character of Vivien is Tennyson's own invention.

Lancelot and Elaine. The story of Elaine, 'the lily maid of Astolat', and her hopeless love for Lancelot (which Tennyson had already used in THE LADY OF SHALOTT) follows closely the events related in the French prose *Lancelot* and the English MORTE ARTHUR (not to be confused with Malory's *Le Morte Darthur*), but does not continue to Agravain's betrayal of Lancelot and Guinevere.

The Holy Grail. The quest for the Holy Grail, in Tennyson's poem, is related by Sir Percivale, who has left the court to become a monk. The first vision of the Grail is conveyed to a holy nun, Percivale's sister, who tells her brother that 'all the world be healed' if a quest for the Grail succeeds. She recognizes in Galahad, the youngest of all the knights, the requisite purity of character and makes him a sword-belt of her hair. Galahad occupies the Siege Perilous, the vision of the Grail is seen by the knights of the Round Table, and the quest begins.

Pelleas and Ettarre. Pelleas, innocent and idealistic, sets out for Arthur's court to seek knighthood. On the way he encounters, and falls in love with, Ettarre, beautiful but vain. Pelleas is welcomed by Arthur, gains his knighthood, and wins the prize at a tournament, which he offers to Ettarre. But she, having obtained her desire, returns to her own castle and refuses to admit Pelleas. She sends her knights to kill him but he defeats them one by one. Then all three attack and bind him; he is taken before Ettarre, to whom he declares his continued loyalty. He is ejected, to be discovered by Gawain, who undertakes to further Pelleas's suit but betrays him with Ettarre. Pelleas, heartbroken, rides away. His feelings change from grief to bitterness after he encounters Percivale and learns from him that Lancelot and Guinevere, too, are false. When he meets Lancelot he attacks him furiously, telling him 'a scourge am I to lash the treasons of the Table Round'. Lancelot defeats him and the two return to Camelot. Pelleas scorns the Queen's gracious questioning and leaves the court. In gloomy silence Guinevere and Lancelot foresee 'the dolorous day to be', while Modred watches and waits.

The Last Tournament. The last tournament is held on a wintry day, when all glory is rapidly fading from Arthur's court. Lancelot rescues a baby girl from an eagle's nest and takes the child to Guinevere; but in spite of her loving care the baby dies. The Queen gives a ruby necklace found on the child to Arthur to use as a prize in a tournament: 'Perchance – who knows? – the purest of thy, knights/ May win them for the purest of my maids.' The Tournament of Dead Innocence is presided over by Lancelot, Arthur having departed with the younger knights to quell the growing disorder in the kingdom. Before leaving he tells Lancelot of his depressed state of mind. Lancelot knows too well that Arthur's depression is soundly based; he presides over the tournament with a heavy heart. The ruby necklace is won by Tristram, who does not want it for his wife but for his paramour, Isolt, the wife of King Mark. At Tintagel he offers his prize to Isolt but is surprised and executed by King Mark. Arthur's campaign has reinforced his depression. He encounters the hate-filled Pelleas as the Red Knight and returns to his castle to find that Guinevere has departed. He is greeted by his jester, Dagonet, in tears: 'I am thy fool,/ And I shall never make thee smile again.' Tennyson himself was pleased with his creation of the 'half-humorous half-pathetic fool Dagonet'.

Guinevere. Tennyson's account of the progress of Guinevere's remorse is his own invention. In Arthur's absence Guinevere, overwhelmed by guilt, implores Lancelot to leave the court and arranges a last meeting. The lovers are overheard by Vivien and surprised by Modred, whereupon Guinevere resolves to seek sanctuary in a nunnery at Almesbury while Lancelot returns to his own land. Among the novices she discovers that the names of Guinevere and Lancelot are notorious as faithless wife and false friend. Arthur comes to the nunnery and Guinevere begs his forgiveness. For three years, until her death, Guinevere remains with the nuns in penitent sorrow.

The Passing of Arthur. Bedivere tells the story of Arthur's last days. All the knights are slain in the great battle except Bedivere, Modred and Arthur. Arthur overcomes Modred in single combat but himself receives a mortal wound. He bids Bedivere throw Excalibur into the lake and the knight, overcoming his reluctance and fulfilling the command the third time it is given, sees 'an arm clothed in white samite, mystic, wonderful' receive the sword. Bedivere carries Arthur down to the water's edge to await the barge, with its three queens, which will bear the dying king to Avilion. He comforts Bedivere as best he can, in the famous lines beginning: 'The old order changeth, yielding place to new,/ And God fulfils himself in many ways...'.

Ieuan Brydydd Hir See CELTIC REVIVAL.

Ignoramus A farcical comedy by George Ruggle, produced at Cambridge University in 1615 during a visit by King James and Prince Charles. The King enjoyed the performance so much that he asked for it to be repeated on a subsequent visit. The play is a satire on lawyers and the title refers to the Recorder of Cambridge, Francis Brackyn, who is burlesqued as the foolish victim of various adventures. (Brackyn was also a target in THE PARNASSUS PLAYS.) Ruggle based his play on an Italian comedy by Giambattista della Porta (1538–1613) called *La trappolaria*.

George Ruggle (1575–1622) was a Fellow of Clare College who is believed to have written other plays, but *Ignoramus* is the only one to survive. It was published in 1630.

Ihimaera, Witi 1944– New Zealand novelist and short-story writer. Born in Gisborne in the North Island, he attended the universities of Auckland and Wellington and then worked in the New Zealand diplomatic corps. He currently holds a post in the Auckland University English department. Ihimaera was the first significant Maori writer in English to emerge. *Pounamu, Pounamu* (1972), a collection of short stories, was the first work of fiction published by a Maori. It was quickly followed by two novels, *Tangi* (1973) and *Whanau* (1974). These early works set out to represent what was most valuable and under threat in traditional Maori culture. They have mainly rural settings and celebrate the intense relation between Maori culture and the land. His second collection of stories, *The New Net Goes Fishing* (1977), shifts to an urban world but is still concerned with retrieving the cultural legacy of the past. Ihimaera broke almost a decade's silence with *The Matriarch* (1986), an ambitious attempt at a modern epic, and *The Whale Rider* (1987). He has also published *Dear Miss Mansfield* (1989), in which he rewrites several of KATHERINE MANSFIELD's stories, co-edited *Into the World of Light: An Anthology of Maori Writing* (1982), and written opera libretti.

Il Penseroso A poem by JOHN MILTON, written in 1632 and published with other early work in a volume of 1645. He had not then gained his later fluency in Italian and the title is a mistaken form of 'Il pensieroso', meaning 'the contemplative'. The poem invokes the goddess Melancholy and celebrates the delights of solitude, withdrawal, rumination, music, drama and epic poetry. Its companion piece, *L'ALLEGRO*, deals with happiness.

Imaginary Conversations of Literary Men and Statesmen

A series of dialogues by WALTER SAVAGE LANDOR. The first two volumes were published in 1824, the third in 1828 and the fourth in 1829. The dialogues range from classical times to Landor's own day, some containing action and incident. They cover a wide field of topics – dramatic, satirical, idyllic, social, political and literary. Among the best known are: 'Epicurus and Leantion and Ternissa', 'Leofric and Godiva', 'Dante and Beatrice', 'Leonora d'Este and Father Panigarola', 'Princess Mary and Princess Elizabeth', 'Lord Bacon and Richard Hooker', 'Calvin and Melancthon' and 'Aesop and Rhodope'.

Pericles and Aspasia (1836) and *Imaginary Conversations of Greeks and Romans* (1853) are in the same style. *Pericles and Aspasia* began as one of the conversations but outgrew the form and became a series of letters, covering the period from their first meeting at the theatre to the death of Pericles during the plague in Athens in 49 BC.

imagism

An early 20th-century movement in British and American poetry. Influenced by the aesthetic theories of T. E. HULME, it found its leading spokesman in EZRA POUND who, with F. S. FLINT, wrote an imagist 'manifesto' published in *POETRY* magazine in 1913. Among the tenets they put forth were a free choice of subject matter (often dealing with single, concentrated moments of experience), conciseness of expression, concreteness of imagery, and rhythm composed 'in sequence of the musical phrase, not in sequence of a metronome'. *Des Imagistes*, the first imagist anthology, was edited by Pound and published in 1914. Among the contributors were Pound himself, Flint, RICHARD ALDINGTON, HILDA DOOLITTLE, FORD MADOX FORD, JOYCE, AMY LOWELL and WILLIAM CARLOS WILLIAMS. After 1914 Amy Lowell assumed leadership of the movement, helping to publish three further anthologies, all entitled *Some Imagist Poets* (1915, 1916, 1917).

imitation

As a literary genre, the term signifies the attempt by one writer to rework the structure and theme of an earlier writer's work, recast in a contemporary mood. It is distinct from translation in allowing considerably more freedom. The most notable examples in English date from the late Renaissance, the Restoration and the AUGUSTAN AGE, when POPE produced his *Imitations of Horace* and SAMUEL JOHNSON his imitations of Juvenal in *LONDON* and *THE VANITY OF HUMAN WISHES*. Both poets, like many of their fellow imitators, wished to produce SATIRE that

was both contemporary in application and strengthened by its echo of an age long past.

The Latin *imitatio* and its Greek counterpart, *mimesis*, have a different connotation, referring to the whole process of representing reality through the written word.

Imlay, Gilbert

1754–1828 American novelist and radical. He was born in New Jersey and, though little is known about his life, seems to have been forced out of the USA in 1785 or 1786 after having become involved in dubious land speculation in Kentucky. During the 1790s he lived in London where he wrote and published two works. *A Topographical Description of the Western Territory of North America* (1792) portrays the post-Revolutionary West in a series of letters written to a friend in England. *The Emigrants* (1793), epistolary in form, is the first novel about the frontier area of Pennsylvania, which at the time extended from Pittsburgh west to the Mississippi; it envisages America as a promised land, and champions social reform, the rights of women and liberal divorce laws. In France Imlay frequented the radical circles of JOEL BARLOW and THOMAS PAINE, and for a time lived with MARY WOLLSTONECRAFT, who bore him a daughter.

Importance of Being Earnest, The: A Trivial Comedy for Serious People

A comedy by OSCAR WILDE, first produced in February 1895 at the St James's Theatre. His last play, it has proved his most enduringly popular. The slender but deftly worked plot concerns two fashionable young gentlemen, John Worthing (Jack) and Algernon Moncrieff (Algy), and their eventually successful courtship of Gwendolen Fairfax and Cecily Cardew. More important than the plot is the continual flow of witty, uncompromisingly artificial dialogue and the characterization, especially of Gwendolen's mother, Lady Bracknell, and also of Miss Prism and Canon Chasuble.

In a Glass Darkly

A book of short stories by SHERIDAN LE FANU, published in 1872. It is presented as a collection of cases investigated by Dr Martin Hesselius, who explores the supernatural in terms of psychopathology. With such stories as 'Green Tea', 'The Watcher', 'The Room in the Dragon Volant' and 'Carmilla' (about vampirism) the book has become a classic of mystery and occult literature.

In Memoriam A. H. H.

A poem by ALFRED TENNYSON, consisting of 132 connected lyrics, published in 1850. Though reaching out to consider many topics of contemporary intellectual debate, and everywhere tinged with the religious doubt characteristic of the age, it is essentially an ELEGY for Tennyson's close friend from Cambridge, ARTHUR HENRY HALLAM, who met an early death in 1833. Although some verses were written soon after Hallam's death, the poem took many years to gestate. The title was suggested by Emily Sellwood, the poet's future wife. An alternative title was 'Fragments of an Elegy', and Tennyson occasionally referred to the poem as 'The Way of the Soul'.

In Memoriam encompasses the fluctuating states of shock, despair, resignation and reconciliation as the poet explores his experience of bereavement. The three Christmas lyrics (XXVIII, LXXVIII and CIV) locate the process in a lengthy three-year cycle. Among the many remarkable passages is lyric CIII, which describes a symbolic voyage ending in a vision of Hallam as Tennyson's muse. The epilogue, in the form of a prothalamion on the marriage of the poet's sister Cecilia, was designed to bring the work to an optimistic close.

In many ways the cornerstone of Tennyson's reputation with his contemporaries, *In Memoriam* remains a highly original and influential work. T. S. ELIOT noted some part of the reason for this when he drew a parallel with 20th-century reaction to his own poem, THE WASTE LAND: 'It happens now and then that a poet by some strange accident expresses the mood of his generation, at the same time that he is expressing a mood of his own which is quite remote from that of his generation.'

In Our Time A collection of short stories by ERNEST HEMINGWAY, published in 1925 and expanded in 1930. Nick Adams is the hero of several stories. In 'Indian Camp' he is a young boy who goes with his father, a doctor, to help a pregnant Indian woman through a difficult delivery. 'Big Two-Hearted River', the two-part story with which the collection ends, is set several years later, when Nick, now an adult, is psychologically shattered by his experiences in World War I. Other notable stories are 'The Three-Day Blow', 'Mr and Mrs Elliot' (apparently a caricature of T. S. ELIOT and his wife), 'Cross-Country Snow', and 'My Old Man'. 'On the Quai at Smyrna' was added to the 1930 edition. The collection also includes vignettes about World War I and bullfighting.

In the Midst of Life A collection of stories by AMBROSE BIERCE, first published in 1891 as *Tales of Soldiers and Civilians*. More than half the stories derive from Bierce's disillusioning experience as a soldier in the American Civil War. Violence – particularly its psychological effect – and the macabre are dominant themes. Among the best-known stories are: 'The Middle Toe of the Right Foot', about a murderer who is haunted to death by his victim; 'A Horseman in the Sky', in which a young Union soldier is forced by circumstances to kill his own father, a Confederate officer; and 'An Occurrence at Owl Creek Bridge', presenting the fantasy which a man who is being hanged experiences in the last seconds of his life.

Inchbald, Elizabeth 1753–1821 Playwright and novelist. Born near Bury St Edmunds in Suffolk, she ran away from home in 1772, defying a speech impediment to become an actress. Little is known of her marriage to Joseph Inchbald (d. 1779), a minor actor. That she loved the much greater actor, John Philip Kemble, is well known, not least from the reasonable inference that he served as the model for Dorriforth in her novel *A SIMPLE STORY* (1791). Inchbald's acting career continued until 1789, after which time she devoted herself to writing. Her first play, *A Mogul Tale* (1784), cleverly exploited the current craze for hot-air balloons. It was followed by a number of comedies, of which the most successful were *I'll Tell You What* (1785), *Everyone Has His Fault* (1793), *Wives As They Were, and Maids As They Are* (1797) and *To Marry, or Not to Marry* (1805). *The Child of Nature* (1788) is a more ambitious piece, as was the adaptation of Kotzebue's *Lovers' Vows* (1798) whose rehearsal in the Bertram household causes such consternation in JANE AUSTEN's *MANSFIELD PARK*. Inchbald was also the editor of three collections of plays, *The British Theatre* (25 vols., 1808), *Farces* (7 vols., 1809) and *The Modern Theatre* (10 vols., 1809).

Indian Summer A novel by WILLIAM DEAN HOWELLS, published in 1886. It tells the story of a middle-aged American newspaper publisher, Theodore Colville, who travels to Florence to take up an interest in architecture he had abandoned years before. He encounters a friend from his childhood, Evalina Bowen, now a widow. Imogene Graham, Evalina's young friend and protégée, is attracted to Colville. Mrs Bowen tells her of an unhappy youthful romance of Colville's which had left him broken-hearted, and Imogene, her sympathy stirred, conceives a romantic attachment to him. The relationship comes to an end, however, when she experiences true love for the young clergyman Morton. This clears the way for the marriage of Colville and Evalina, who have secretly loved one another almost from the beginning of the novel.

Inge, William 1913–73 American playwright and novelist. He was born in Independence, Kansas. His first play, *Farther Off from Heaven* (1947), was followed by *Come Back, Little Sheba* (1950), about a married couple's fruitless battle with alcoholism. *Picnic* (1950), the story of a sexually attractive stranger's relationships with several lonely women in a small Kansas town, won both the PULITZER PRIZE and the New York Drama Critics Circle Award. Continuing his examination of the frustration of Midwestern life, he wrote *Bus Stop* (1955), the story of a love-affair between a nightclub singer and a lonely cowboy; and *The Dark at the Top of the Stairs* (1957), the semi-autobiographical psychological drama of the Flood family. Two studies of modern Oedipal situations, *A Loss of Roses* (1959) and *Natural Affection* (1963), and the domestic comedy *Where's Daddy?* (1966), were less successful. In 1961 he reworked his one-act play *Glory in the Flower* (1959) into the screenplay for *Splendor in the Grass*. His last play was *The Last Pad* (1970), about three men on death row. After 1970 he turned to writing novels. *Good Luck, Miss Wyckoff* (1971) relates the story of a white schoolteacher whose affair with the black janitor costs her her job and changes her life. His second novel, *My Son is a Splendid Driver* (1972), the first-person narrative of a lonely teacher, is clearly autobiographical. He committed suicide shortly after its publication.

Ingelow, Jean 1820–97 Poet, novelist and writer of CHILDREN'S LITERATURE. A native of Boston in Lincolnshire, she became a professional writer after moving to London. She enjoyed considerable success with 25 books of verse, children's stories, and novels. Her *Mopsa the Fairy* (1869) was a children's favourite for many years and some of her poems became popular anthology pieces. The most notable of these were 'The High Tide on the Coast of Lincolnshire, 1571' and 'Divided' from *Poems* (1863) and 'A Story of Doom' from the collection of that name (1867). Her novels are *Off the Skelligs* (1872), *Fated to be Free* (1875) and *Sarah de Beranger* (1879).

Ingoldsby Legends, The Humorous mock-medieval BALLADS by R. H. BARHAM, published in *BENTLEY'S MISCELLANY* and *The New Monthly Magazine* from 1837 onwards and in various collections from 1840. Their main interest is as a repository of early 19th-century slang and as precursor of the work of W. S. GILBERT in their outrageous rhymes and lively anapaestic rhythms.

Inheritance, The A novel by SUSAN FERRIER, published in 1824.

The Earl of Rossville repudiates his son when he marries beneath him, but admits his daughter-in-law and his granddaughter, Gertrude, to his presence after the son's death. Gertrude thus becomes heiress presumptive to Rossville. She falls in love with the profligate Colonel Delmour, and, after the death of the Earl, becomes engaged to him, to the despair of her cousin, Edward Lyndsay, who loves her. A coarse American stranger now appears on the scene claiming to be Gertrude's father – a claim which is eventually proved true. Gertrude's mother, despairing of children of her own, had adopted the child of a servant. Gertrude's 'inheritance' is therefore nullified. Colonel Delmour shows his true character and abandons her, but Edward Lyndsay remains faithful and eventually wins her.

Inn Album, The A dramatic poem by ROBERT BROWNING, published in 1875. The story concerns two couples who are never named, and whose fates are unavoidably intertwined. The visitors' book at the inn where the four are staying is used by the characters to convey messages, make assignations and record threats. Though it draws upon the career of a notorious Regency rake for its plot, the poem is given a contemporary setting and includes many specific allusions to events and preoccupations of the 1870s.

Innes, Michael See STEWART, J. I. M.

Innocent Voyage, The See HUGHES, RICHARD.

Innocents Abroad, The: or, *The New Pilgrim's Progress* A travel book by MARK TWAIN, published in 1869 and based on his visit to Europe and Palestine during the summer and autumn of 1867. It took shape from letters he wrote to the San Francisco *Alta California* and the New York *Herald* and *Tribune* while on his journey. Comprising the often humorous narrative of a shrewd American in the Old World for the first time, the book marked the beginning of the most productive and successful period of Twain's career.

inscape and **instress** See HOPKINS, GERARD MANLEY.

Instructions to a Painter A sub-genre in 17th-century verse. Several poems incorporate the formula in their titles, the most notable examples being by MARVELL, DENHAM, WALLER, JONSON and HERRICK. These poems offer a portrait or caricature of a contemporary figure, presented in the form of guidelines to an artist for a picture. The intent is usually satiric, and the subject made grotesque or ridiculous, though the form was sometimes used for Royalist panegyrics during the Restoration. The tradition is an ancient one, stretching back to the satirical thumbnail sketches of Martial, and was in vogue at Venice in the 17th century. In England, its popularity seems to have died out with the reign of Queen Anne; STEELE ridiculed such poems in the third number of his *TATLER* (14 April 1709). COWPER and ELIZABETH BARRETT BROWNING produced later examples.

Intelligencer, The A Dublin weekly paper started in 1728 by SWIFT and written with help from Thomas Sheridan. It ran to only 19 numbers, the contents ranging from discussion of the state of Ireland (particularly its poverty) to a famous defence of GAY's *THE BEGGAR'S OPERA* (in the third number). Swift's general aim was 'to inform, or divert or correct, or vex the Town'.

The Intelligencer was also the name of a newspaper published in the 1660s by ROGER L'ESTRANGE.

intentional fallacy A phrase from an essay in *The Verbal Icon* (1954) by W. K. Wimsatt and Monroe

Beardsley attacking romantic or expressive criticism. It summarizes their rejection of the view that it is the critic's job to search in the poem for the soul of the inspired poet or to consider the poem as personal statement, rather than as crafted fiction, assessed by such criteria as sincerity, spontaneity and originality. Instead Wimsatt and Beardsley argued for critical concentration on actual performance: what the poem really did say, regardless of the author's supposed intention.

Their argument has been much misunderstood. It was not meant to rule out external evidence but, rather, to ask what end external evidence should serve. If the business of literary criticism is to comprehend and appreciate the text rather than the author, all external evidence that is knowable and relevant will be admissible. If, however, the critic proceeds from the poem to the author or his society, then he is not acting as a literary critic but unwittingly as an amateur biographer, psychologist or sociologist. And even for that enterprise, the writer's intention will rarely be relevant, since it is normally unknowable and at best uncertain.

However, genuinely literary critics have argued that to judge a work as literature the critic needs to know the writer's intention. How can we judge the merit of a PARODY, for example, without knowing that the work was meant as parody? Once we do know, we have a standard of judgement and can measure the work's performance against its intention. This is true and important, for it indicates the main source of confusion about the intentional fallacy: the existence of two different but overlapping meanings of 'intention'.

The case against the relevance of author-intention as a standard seems to be overwhelming. We usually do not know the writer's intention, and if he or she is dead have few ways of finding it out. Scholarship can at best provide probability. Even the author's own statement might be misleading for political, legal or commercial reasons, or because he or she was influenced by an unconscious intention (whether for good or ill being a matter of literary judgement). Or the intention might be trivial or reprehensible but perfectly realized. Such a work could not reasonably be rated above one whose more admirable intention was not fully achieved. A hypothetical example can clarify the logical point underlying these practical ones. Imagine a computer programmed with the vocabulary and syntactical rules of SHAKESPEARE'S *SONNETS* and set to random sonneteering. Eventually, by chance, it produces an exact replica of one of them. By the intentional theory the critic would be obliged to say, nonsensically, when presented with two identical sheets of paper, that the one realizing the author's intention was valuable and the other unassessable, but that he could not tell which was which. To say, *faute de mieux*, that the writer's intention can be deduced from the work itself, is to concede that knowledge of it was not needed to perceive the meaning and qualities of the text in question.

This last point, however, does clarify the fact that there are two kinds of intention. The external intention, derived from the author or from scholarship, is theoretically irrelevant to literary criticism. This is all that the intentional fallacy maintains. The internal intention, implied by the work itself, is essential to critical appreciation. That it may in fact represent the intention in the writer's mind is, strictly speaking, beside the critical point. This intention is deduced from the words on the page, whose meaning, of course, may not be clear without relevant or knowable external evidence. Confusion might well be lessened if the term 'purport' were used for the work's, as against the writer's, intention.

interlude The name, from the Latin *interludium*, given to short dramatic sketches performed during intervals in banquets. The English origins cannot be exactly traced, though professional or semi-professional performers were active for many years before the first recorded reference to Players of the King's Interludes in 1493. The work of JOHN HEYWOOD, in particular, illustrates the importance of the 16th-century interlude in the evolution of English drama.

Invisible Man A novel by RALPH ELLISON, published in 1952. Widely regarded as one of the major works of recent American fiction, *Invisible Man* combines elements of realism, surrealism, and folklore. Set in the 1930s, the book details the often incoherent experiences of its nameless black narrator – as a bright high-school student in the South, as a disoriented college student who is eventually expelled from the Southern 'negro' college he attends, as a factory worker in New York, and as a rising figure in left-wing politics. His life is marked by various traumas of racial and individual identity, but it is through these experiences that he eventually achieves self-consciousness. This self-consciousness is inscribed in the title: he realizes that black skin in American society makes one 'invisible' to white eyes. The novel's climax recounts a race riot in Harlem, during which the narrator observes both the destructiveness of black nationalism and the failure of Communist attempts to reform society. He retreats, in his invisibility, to an underground sewer, which he furnishes and lives in while writing his book. At the end of the novel he is better off in one respect than when he began: his consciousness of the social phenomenon of 'invisibility' has provided him with the possibility for free personal action.

The Invisible Man is also the title of a novel (1897) by H. G. WELLS.

Iolo Morganwg See CELTIC REVIVAL.

Ipomadon A VERSE ROMANCE translated in the late 14th century from Hue de Rotelande's Anglo-Norman *Ipomédon* (c. 1190), unusual for an English romance of the period in retaining the preoccupation with the psychology and etiquette of COURTLY LOVE from its source. It is written in 12-line TAIL-RHYME stanzas in the North Midlands dialect. There are two other English versions: *Ipomedon,* in prose, and *The Lyfe of Ipomydon.*

The romance tells of Ipomadon's quest for the hand of the daughter of the Duke of Calabria, who has vowed to marry the most proficient knight in the world. In her court he devotes himself to hunting and shows no interest in arms. He leaves in disgrace and wins fame in foreign lands, later returning in disguise to win her in a tournament but leaving without claiming his prize. At this time he is attached to the court of Sicily where, again, he is known as a foolish and cowardly hunter. Ipomadon wins more glory abroad and becomes King of Apulia on his father's death. Hearing his beloved is besieged he returns to Sicily from where, disguised as a fool again, he is led to his lady's castle by a rude maiden and a dwarf. He defeats her suitor and the couple are eventually married.

The story is humorous and entertaining; it is packed with elaborate description and detail, the emotions of the lovers are sympathetically and realistically described (often in the form of soliloquies), and the courtly milieu is skilfully evoked. The lack of motivation for the hero's deception and delay does not detract significantly from the poem.

Ireland, David 1927– Australian novelist. Born in Lakemba in the suburbs of Sydney, he wrote plays and verse before turning to fiction. His novel *The Flesheaters* (1972) was adapted from his best-known play, *Image in the Clay* (1964). He uses discontinuous narrative, surrealism and a range of metafictive techniques, and is frequently highly political in his criticism of the status quo. His first novel, *The Chantic Bird* (1968), is the confession of a youthful outsider and has been called an Australian CATCHER IN THE RYE. *The Unknown Industrial Prisoner* (1971) attacks the dehumanizing pressures of working for a multinational oil company. *Burn* (1974) is a 'day in the life' of a half-caste Aborigine about to be evicted from his hut. *A Woman of the Future* (1979) presents a heroine, apparently representative of Australia, who remains innocent whatever degradations she superficially undergoes. Ireland's novels are frequently concerned with gender stereotypes and subcultures: *The Glass Canoe* (1976) is about a group of drinkers in a Sydney pub, who again represent an Australian microcosm; *City of Women* (1981), a novel set in a Sydney without men, follows the fortunes of a lesbian separatist. *Archimedes and the Seagle* (1984) is about a red setter and the trivia of life, while *Bloodfather* (1988) has

been called Joycean in its range of characters and structural invention.

Ireland, William Henry 1777–1835 Shakespearean forger. The possibly illegitimate offspring of the engraver Samuel Ireland (d. 1800), he was educated at private schools in Kensington, Ealing, Soho and France, and then articled to a conveyancer in New Inn. Taking advantage of both his access to old legal documents and his father's astonishing credulity, he began in 1794 to produce a whole series of forgeries, including a mortgage signed by SHAKESPEARE and HEMINGES, many books into which he copied Shakespeare's signature, the whole of *KING LEAR* and excerpts from *HAMLET* in the author's 'own hand'. In 1795 his naive father announced an exhibition of these items, and it is a reflection on the age that such personages as JOSEPH WARTON, BOSWELL (who went on his knees and kissed the relics) and HENRY PYE all accepted their authenticity. Ireland overreached himself when he offered his father two entirely new Shakespeare plays, *Vortigern and Rowena* and *Henry II.* The former was accepted by SHERIDAN for performance at DRURY LANE, for which Ireland received an initial payment of £250 and a share of profits. The play was denounced as a forgery by such genuine scholars as RITSON, STEEVENS and MALONE. The major performers, including Mrs Siddons, developed diplomatic illnesses, and at the only performance the audience made it clear that they did not expect to see the piece again. Though his son admitted the deception and published *An Authentic Account of the Shaksperian MSS,* Samuel Ireland refused to believe him and even published the two plays shortly before his death. William Henry, after an initial period of obloquy, set up a circulating library in Kennington, London, from which he sold copies of his famous forgeries, which he seems to have considered worthy of praise.

Irish Sketch Book, The A travel book by W. M. THACKERAY, with his own illustrations, published in two volumes in 1843. One of the best of Thackeray's travel writings, this account of a journey round Ireland made in 1842 paints a vivid picture of the country on the threshold of the Great Famine.

Iron Heel, The A novel by JACK LONDON, published in 1908. A socialist vision of capitalism's inevitable demise, it caused controversy and was banned in several parts of America. The story is presented as a manuscript written by Avis Cunningham Everhard in 1912–32 and edited 700 years later, in the fourth century of the Brotherhood of Man, by Anthony Meredith. Avis and her husband Ernest Everhard are socialists opposed to the Oligarchy, the Iron Heel of the title: a proto-fascist conglomeration of major trusts and their private militias defending capitalism. A socialist revolution is crushed and the manuscript breaks off on the eve of a second uprising, with Ernest already dead and Avis apparently about to be executed. Meredith's notes, which London uses throughout the book as a vehicle for his own opposition to capitalism, record the eventual defeat of the Iron Heel 300 years later.

irony A mode of discourse, whether lyric, narrative or dramatic, which purports to convey a latent meaning different from – indeed, usually opposite to – the ostensible one. The term has been stretched to cover understatement, naivety, HYPERBOLE, pun, paradox and in fact (especially in modern criticism) any contrast or ambiguity – in fact, to cover anything other than plain literal statement. But, on both etymological and practical grounds, these are better regarded as means of irony or, according to the literary circumstances, as overlapping concepts. If irony is thought of as a dissembling, in keeping with its origin in the *eiron* (a dissembler), then it becomes a term still broad but limited enough to be critically useful. Like Socrates, though, the *eiron* dissembles not to deceive but to enlighten. So irony, properly speaking, is a dissembling that is meant to be seen through.

The dissembling element, however, is not a husk to be discarded when the real meaning is perceived. The fact of opposition is as central to the ironic experience as the fact that it is overcome. Only then will there be the characteristic effect of inward amusement, smiling enlightenment, through the release of tension. The perception of irony thus involves both discernment and detachment – a fact which renders it the most effective weapon of SATIRE and (as tragic irony, a form of dramatic irony) the saving grace of TRAGEDY, distancing us from horror.

All irony is necessarily either textural or structural: inherent either in verbal constructions, making an immediate impression, or in the memory-dependent constructions of plot or story. These two kinds of irony are normally distinguished as verbal and dramatic irony, the one relying on treatment, the other on content. Sarcasm is verbal irony that is crude rather than clever; it is rightly regarded as inferior since it denies the reader the higher pleasures of discernment and detachment. JANE AUSTEN's description in *SENSE AND SENSIBILITY* of Robert Ferrars as having 'a person and face of strong, natural, sterling insignificance' provides an example of verbal (textural) irony. *Oedipus Rex* provides many examples of dramatic (structural) irony, such as the fact that his pursuit of the criminal leads Oedipus to himself, the fact that his vengeance falls on his own head, or the fact that in the end (like Tiresias whom he castigates at the beginning) he comes to 'see' only when blinded.

All irony can also be divided into two other broad categories: covert and overt. It would be convenient were these synonymous with the verbal and dramatic categories. But, though overt irony can always be brought within 'dramatic' boundaries and covert irony is usually verbal, the match is not exact.

Only covert irony is straightforwardly ironic in the sense given above, since it relies on a difference between ostensible and latent meaning, and thus requires of the reader or hearer some reconstruction. Overt irony, on the other hand, as the name implies is not a 'dissembling' statement or event – unless one postulates a benevolent deity, an idea of some built-in justice in nature. Colloquial speech provides many examples. The verbal irony, 'Lovely weather again!', said of pouring rain, requires a little reconstruction to find the real sense and is therefore a minimal example of covert irony. 'He went to help in the crash, phoned for an ambulance, and it knocked him down when it came – it was ironic' is an example of overt irony: it is not ironic at all, just a straight account of an absurd accident, unless we implicitly assume a world in which such 'injustice' is, or ought to be, ruled out.

Dramatic irony – a state of affairs very different from what the protagonists think – is normally overt. The audience usually sees this disparity throughout, and is thus more discerning and detached from the action than the protagonists. This state is similar to the experience of real, or covert irony; but it is not identical with it, since no reconstruction is required, no ostensible meaning is to be seen through – save in so far as the audience may partially identify itself with the protagonists. Even then, this form of irony is really near to being overt; at most it is pseudo-covert.

Other varieties of irony are all particular variants of the general categories, and may be briefly itemized. The term 'Socratic irony' refers to discrepancies between ostensible ignorance or simplicity and actual acuteness. It is verbal and covert. Romantic irony is also verbal, but perhaps more often pseudo-covert than strictly so, since it lies in discrepancies of tone and statement that result from an authorial detachment from the created characters and action, which allows unexpected moods or comments to be expressed; this is not necessarily a 'seeing through'. BYRON provides many examples, such as the following attitude to multiple rape of the elderly (in Canto 8 of *DON JUAN*): 'Some odd mistakes, too, happen'd in the dark,/ Which show'd a want of lanterns, or of taste –/ Indeed the smoke was such they scarce could mark/ Their friends from foes, – besides such things from haste/ Occur, though rarely, when there is a spark/ Of light to save the venerably chaste:/ But six old damsels, each of seventy years,/ Were all deflower'd by different grenadiers.' Tragic (or Sophoclean) irony lies in the distance between what the protagonists expect and the disastrous way things turn out; it is dramatic and usually overt or at most pseudo-covert, as the audience is usually in the know from the beginning. Irony of fate (or cosmic irony) lies in the difference between the just or orderly way the gods or fate or nature might be expected to behave and the cruel or random way they do in fact treat the protagonists; it is dramatic and overt. Witness the treatment meted out to HARDY's heroine in TESS OF THE D'URBERVILLES.

Finally, if irony is essentially a form of dissembling discourse, how is it recognizable as such? In literature, some contextual element must make recognition possible (whereas in conversation mere ironic intention and a tone of voice may suffice). In verbal irony, which is normally formal and covert, discrepancies in the immediate linguistic context usually give the clue (witness that 'insignificance' in the Jane Austen quotation above). Dramatic irony, which is normally contextual, and pseudo-covert or overt, is indicated either by discrepancies between what the character thinks and what the audience is shown to have reason to believe, or between what is shown to be the case and what, in the context of some metaphysical assumption, ought to be the case.

This gives us, so to speak, a basic ironic scale. If irony is taken to be essentially a dissembling mode of discourse whose discrepancies require some restructuring in order to bring about a smiling enlightenment as the ostensible is suffused by the latent, then at the top we have verbal irony, which is typically covert. In the middle is that dramatic irony which depends on the audience's knowing more than the characters – pseudo-covert because the author rarely dissembles the truth from the audience, so that any restructuring depends on a provisional identification with the characters. At the bottom is that kind of overt dramatic irony which, to be irony at all, depends on some extra-textual metaphysical assumption.

Irving, Edward 1792–1834 Minister and founder of the 'Catholic Apostolic Church'. Born in Annan and educated at Edinburgh, he formed an early friendship with THOMAS CARLYLE. After ordination as a minister of the Church of Scotland he preached at Hatton Garden and Regent Square in London, where he attracted a congregation of admirers and sightseers. His *Homilies on the Sacraments* (1828) were attacked as heretical and resulted in his expulsion from the church. He therefore founded his new 'Irvingite' sect, espousing the principles of the early Christian church and testifying to the revival of the gift of tongues, of which there was a high incidence among his adherents.

Irving, John 1942– American novelist. Born in Exeter, New Hampshire, he attended universities in Pittsburgh, Vienna, New Hampshire and Iowa. In 1967–72 and 1975–8 he was assistant professor of English at Mount Holyoke College. *Setting Free the Bears* (1969), *The Water-Method Man* (1972) and *The 158-Pound Marriage* (1974) found little attention but he made his name with *The World According to Garp*

(1978), a long, energetic *BILDUNGSROMAN*. It has been followed by *The Hotel New Hampshire* (1981), *The Cider House Rules* (1985) and *A Prayer for Owen Meany* (1989), the last two moving away from the comic exuberance and surreal invention of his earlier fiction. *Trying to Save Peggy Sneed* (1993) is a collection of short stories.

Irving, Washington 1783–1859 American essayist and short-story writer. Born in New York, he studied law. His letters to the *Morning Chronicle*, a newspaper edited by his brother Peter, were published as *The Letters of Jonathan Oldstyle, Gent.* in 1803. *SALMAGUNDI* (1807–8), a serial that ran through 20 numbers, was written in collaboration with his brother William and JAMES KIRKE PAULDING. His *History of New York* (1809) was an instant success. A BURLESQUE of contemporary historical narratives, it also lampooned THOMAS JEFFERSON and his policies; it was written under the pseudonym of Dietrich Knickerbocker, a name adopted by the KNICKERBOCKER GROUP, of which he was a leading member.

His arrival in England in 1815 to work in the family business began a 17-year stay in Europe. During these years he formed friendships with several writers – notably SIR WALTER SCOTT, MARY SHELLEY and LONGFELLOW – and himself became the first American writer to enjoy an international reputation. His success was largely due to *THE SKETCH BOOK OF GEOFFREY CRAYON, GENT.* (1820), a collection of tales and sketches which included 'Rip Van Winkle' and 'The Legend of Sleepy Hollow', and *BRACEBRIDGE HALL* (1822). *Tales of a Traveller* (1824) was less well received. His stay in Spain as diplomatic attaché to the American embassy in Madrid inspired several historical works: *Life and Voyages of Columbus* (1828), *Conquest of Granada* (1829), *Voyages and Discoveries of the Companions of Columbus* (1831) and *The Alhambra* (1832). He moved to London in 1829 to become secretary to the American legation under Martin Van Buren.

Irving was enthusiastically received on his return to America. *The Crayon Miscellany* (1835) combines memories of Europe in 'Abbotsford and Newstead Abbey' and 'Legends of the Conquest of Spain' with impressions of the far West in 'A Tour of the Prairies'. Later books include *Astoria* (1836), an ill-judged book about John Jacob Astor's fur-trade empire, *Adventures of Captain Bonneville, USA* (1837), *Mahomet and his Successors* (1850), *Wolfert's Roost* (1855) and a life of George Washington (1855–9).

Isabella: *or, the Pot of Basil* A poem in OTTAVA RIMA by JOHN KEATS, written in 1818–19 and published in 1820. The story is drawn from Boccaccio's *Decameron*. Isabella falls in love with Lorenzo, a young man employed by her family. Her proud brothers murder Lorenzo and conceal his body in a forest. But when

Rip Van Winkle's confusion on returning to his home in the Catskills is depicted by John Quidor in the painting, *The Return of Rip Van Winkle,* based on Washington Irving's tales.

Lorenzo appears to Isabella in a vision and relates the story of his fate, she finds the hidden grave, cuts off the head of her lover and, taking it home, places it in a pot which she plants with basil. While the basil flourishes, moistened by Isabella's tears, the girl herself wastes away. Their suspicions aroused, her brothers steal the pot of basil and, horrified at their discovery, flee from Florence. Isabella, bereft of Lorenzo and the pot of basil, loses her reason and dies.

Keats was never satisfied with the poem ('There is too much inexperience of life, and simplicity of knowledge in it') and said that if he were a reviewer, he would describe it as a 'weak-sided Poem'.

Isherwood, Christopher (William Bradshaw)

1904–86 Novelist, short-story writer and playwright. He was born at High Lane, Cheshire, and educated at St Edmund's preparatory school in Surrey (where he first met W. H. AUDEN), Repton (where he first met EDWARD UPWARD) and Corpus Christi, Cambridge. His first novels were *All the Conspirators* (1928) and *The Memorial* (1932). His life in Berlin, where he supported himself as a teacher of English from 1929 to 1933, led to the books by which he is usually remembered. *Mr Norris Changes Trains* (1935), set against the background of Hitler's rise to power, centres on the protagonist's intermittent encounters with the seedy and unsavoury Mr Norris. *Goodbye to Berlin* (1939) is another episodic and semi-autobiographical work which describes the Bohemian society of Berlin with wit and sympathy. The most famous sketch is 'Sally Bowles', about a cabaret artiste of extraordinary and idiosyncratic charm. It was later dramatized by John van Druten as *I am a Camera* (1951) and turned into a musical, *Cabaret* (1968). Isherwood collaborated with Auden on three plays, *The Dog beneath the Skin* (1935), *The Ascent of F6* (1936) and *On the Frontier* (1939), and on an account of their visit to China, *Journey to a War* (1938). The semi-autobiographical *Lions and Shadows* (1938) included portraits of his friends, Auden, Upward, STEPHEN SPENDER and VERNON WATKINS.

He emigrated to the United States with Auden in 1939, becoming an American citizen in 1946. In California he wrote screenplays and took an increasing interest in Indian philosophy and religion, shown by his translation of the *Bhagavadgita* (with Swami Prabhavananda, 1944) and a study, *Ramakrishna and*

His Disciples (1965). Later novels are *Prater Violet* (1945), *The World in the Evening* (1954), *Down There on a Visit* (1962) and *A Single Man* (1964). *The Condor and the Cows* (1949) is a travel book about South America, *Exhumations* (1966) a miscellany of stories, essays and verse, and *Christopher and His Kind* (1972), a frank account of his homosexuality.

Ishiguro, Kazuo 1954– Novelist. Born in Nagasaki, he came to Britain to study at the University of Kent before joining MALCOLM BRADBURY's creative writing course at the University of East Anglia. He began with two delicate, studied novels with Japanese themes: *A Pale View of Hills* (1981), about the aftermath of Nagasaki, and *An Artist of the Floating World* (1986), the reminiscences of a painter pondering an artistic career during the pre-war rise of Japanese militarism. *The Remains of the Day* (1990) won the BOOKER PRIZE and made his reputation. A deadpan first-person account of an ageing butler's motoring tour of England in the 1950s, it uses minute ironies to reveal a familiar English ferment of emotional starvation and reluctant but excessive servility beneath the narrator's brilliantined composure.

Israel Potter: *His Fifty Years of Exile* A novel by HERMAN MELVILLE, serialized in *Putnam's Monthly Magazine* in 1854–5 and published separately in 1855. It is loosely based on an obscure tract, *Life and Remarkable Adventures of Israel R. Potter*, which was published anonymously in 1824.

Israel Potter is a young Yankee from Massachusetts who leaves his home, works as a surveyor, hunter, fur trader and whale harpooner, and then enlists in the Revolutionary army in 1775. He serves at Bunker Hill, is taken prisoner by the British, and taken to England. After escaping, he adopts a series of disguises and meets George III. Falling in with clandestine friends of America, he is sent to Paris with messages for BENJAMIN FRANKLIN and meets John Paul Jones. Impressed into the British navy on his return to England, Israel contrives his ship's capture by Jones. He serves under Jones aboard the *Bon Homme Richard* in the raids on Scotland and in the capture of the *Serapis*. Later, he makes his way to London, where he marries and has a family. Owing to his poverty he is unable to return to America until 45 years have passed. Well past 80, he makes the voyage to Boston and revisits the scenes of his youth.

Ivanhoe SIR WALTER SCOTT's most popular novel, and the first of his works to be set in England, published in 1819. The period is the reign of Richard I.

Wilfred of Ivanhoe incurs the displeasure of his father Cedric because of his love for Rowena, his father's ward. Cedric, dedicated to the restoration of the Saxon line, plans to marry Rowena, a descendant of King Alfred, to Athelstane of Coningsburgh who is also of the royal Saxon race. Ivanhoe serves with King Richard in the crusades, while in England the King's brother John tries to usurp the throne, depending on the disloyal Norman barons for support. John is unexpectedly assisted in his plans when Richard is captured by Leopold of Austria on his way back from Palestine.

At length, arriving in England in disguise, Richard appears at the tournament at Ashby-de-la-Zouch, where he helps Ivanhoe defeat the knights of John's party, among them the Templar, Sir Brian de Bois-Guilbert. At the tournament Sir Brian falls in love with Rebecca, a beautiful and courageous Jewess, enamoured of Ivanhoe. Rebecca, her father Isaac, Rowena, Cedric and the wounded Ivanhoe are taken captive by the Norman barons and imprisoned in Torquilstone Castle. The King and a Saxon force, with the help of Locksley (ROBIN HOOD) and his band of outlaws, take the castle and release the prisoners – with the exception of Rebecca, who is carried off to the Preceptory of Templestowe by Bois-Guilbert.

Bois-Guilbert's designs on Rebecca are frustrated by the arrival of the Grand Master of the Order. But Rebecca is further imperilled by a charge of witchcraft. She demands trial by combat and Ivanhoe appears as her champion, opposing Bois-Guilbert, chosen as her reluctant accuser. In the conflict, Bois-Guilbert falls dead, untouched by Ivanhoe's lance, a victim to his own conflicting emotions. Rebecca, seeing Ivanhoe's love for Rowena, leaves England with her father.

Scott was severely criticized by historians for his inaccurate account of Saxon-Norman enmity persisting into the 12th century. But the success of his novel lies with its skilful blend of fact, myth and romance, combined with a vivid, if fanciful, interpretation of medieval life.

Iyayi, Festus 1947– Nigerian novelist. He was educated at Annunciation Catholic College, Irrua, Government College, Ughelli, the Kiev Institute of National Economy and the University of Bradford, where he took a doctorate. He now lectures in business administration at the University of Benin, Nigeria. Although his family background is rural, he has specialized in his fiction in presenting the poverty, corruption and alienation of city life, and can be regarded as being representative of the new generation of Nigerian novelists which has turned away from the anti-colonial and often village-based themes of earlier writers. His three novels are *Violence* (1979), *The Contract* (1982) and *Heroes* (1986), about the Nigerian Civil War, which won the Commonwealth Literature Prize in 1987.

Jack Juggler (*A New Interlude for Children to Play, Named Jack Juggler*) A comedy written in the late 1550s and first printed in 1562. It has been attributed to NICHOLAS UDALL without much evidence and the true authorship is unknown. It is based on the *Amphitruo* of Plautus but considerably toned down since it was written to be acted by schoolboys at Christmas. Jupiter and Amphitryon are removed from the plot entirely and Mercury becomes the trickster Jack Juggler, who takes over the identity of Jenkin Careaway. The other characters are as English as the London street in which the action takes place: the maid is Alison Tripandgo, the mistress and master are Dame Coy and Master Bongrace. The play ends with a cautionary epilogue on the times.

Jack Upland The first of a sequence of three pieces in a style somewhere between prose and rough ALLITERATIVE VERSE, tentatively dated 1390, 1420 and 1450 respectively. It is unlikely that they are the work of a single poet. *Jack Upland*, usually classified as prose, is a LOLLARD attack on the greed and hypocrisy of the friars, in particular the mendicant order of the Franciscans. The second piece, *Friar Daw's Reply*, answers the charges, defending in particular the Dominican order and condemning the Lollards as heretics. The third piece, *Jack Upland's Rejoinder*, is written in a coarser tone and attacks Friar Daw personally rather than answering his arguments.

Jackson, Helen (Maria) Hunt 1830–85 American novelist and poet. She was born in Amherst, Massachusetts. Her poetry is collected in *Verses by H. H.* (1870) and *Sonnets and Lyrics* (1886). Her concern with the US government's unjust treatment of the American Indians prompted her to write *A Century of Dishonor* (1881), a historical study, and *Ramona* (1884), a novel. Among her other publications are works for children, a travel book, and numerous magazine articles, some of which were written under the pseudonym Saxe Holm. She is also known as the friend of EMILY DICKINSON who most vehemently urged her to publish. Her novel *Mercy Philbrick's Choice* (1876) is probably a fictionalized portrait of Dickinson.

Jackson, Holbrook See NEW AGE, THE.

Jackson, Laura Riding See RIDING, LAURA.

Jackson, Shirley 1919–65 American novelist and short-story writer. She was born in San Francisco. Her first novel, *The Road through the Wall*, appeared in 1948, the year in which THE NEW YORKER published her best-known short story, 'The Lottery'. Although the novel escaped critical notice, the story – a depiction of a communal rite in which each year a person chosen by lot is stoned to death – established her reputation. Her next novel, *The Hangsaman* (1951), explores the schizophrenia of a young girl named Natalie Waite and typifies that portion of Jackson's *oeuvre* concerned with the dark side of human nature. She also produced a quantity of humorous stories and articles, some of which were collected in *Life among the Savages* (1953) and *Raising Demons* (1957). Her other works include *The Bird's Nest* (1954), *Witchcraft of Salem Village* (1956), *The Bad Children* (1959), *The Sundial* (1958), *The Haunting of Hill House* (1959), *Special Delivery* (1960), *We Have Always Lived in the Castle* (1962), *Nine Magic Wishes* (1963) and two collections edited by her husband, *The Magic of Shirley Jackson* (1966) and *Come Along with Me* (1968).

Jacob, Naomi (Ellington) 1889–1964 Novelist. Born at Ripon, Yorkshire, she followed her first novel, *Jacob Ussher* (1926), with numerous titles including *The Loaded Stick* (1935), *Straws in Amber* (1938), *Morning Will* (1953) and, most notably, *Four Generations* (1934). She also wrote a series of autobiographical volumes and a biography of Marie Lloyd (1936).

Jacob's Room A novel by VIRGINIA WOOLF, published in 1922. It was the first of her novels to be issued by the Hogarth Press, which she had founded with her husband, LEONARD WOOLF, in their home at Hogarth House in Richmond in 1917.

It is an episodic tale which attempts to evoke the inner life of Jacob Flanders (based upon the character of her brother Thoby) and his social milieu during the first decade and a half of the 20th century. At the beginning, Jacob is discovered wandering on a Cornish beach away from his recently widowed mother. As the novel proceeds, numerous impressionistic scenes – some involving STREAM OF CONSCIOUSNESS – capture the thoughts of surrounding characters, and there are many brief descriptions of the external landscape which have been noted for their poetic qualities. After Cambridge, Jacob is glimpsed at social gatherings in London, with his mistress, and abroad at Versailles and in Athens, including a visit to the Acropolis. The novel ends during World War I. Jacob has been killed and two friends are visiting his room in Bloomsbury to dispose of his possessions, the mundane and arbitrary record of a human life: odd bills, letters of invitation, a pair of old shoes. The novel was hailed by friends such as T. S. ELIOT, but attacked by others for its lack of plot. It represents its author's first move towards experimentation, for which she was later recognized.

Jacobs, W(illiam) W(ymark) 1863–1943. Author of some 20 volumes of humorous stories about barge crews, night-watchmen and other coastal workers. His first collection was *Many Cargoes* (1896); others are *The Skipper's Wooing* (1897), *Light Freights* (1901) and *Sea Whispers* (1926). He also wrote tales of horror, the best known being a gruesome story, 'The Monkey's Paw'.

Jacobson, Dan 1929– South African novelist and short-story writer. Born in Johannesburg, he spent a short spell on a kibbutz before settling in Britain in 1958. His novels examine uncontrolled states of mind in varying relationships with personal or political power. *The Trap* (1955) and *A Dance in the Sun* (1956), and even the more genial, though satirical, *The Price of Diamonds* (1957), hint at manic depths beneath apparently stable Northern Cape surfaces. After *Evidence of Love* (1960), about interracial love, he created a hero of conflicting loyalties in the accomplished, saga-like *The Beginners* (1966), before adapting, in *The Rape of Tamar* (1970), Old Testament material for a modern study in treacherous cynicism. *The Wonder-Worker* (1973) ventures into a schizophrenic mind, while *The Confessions of Joseph Baisz* (1977) moves between egocentricity and tyrannical dictatorship. *Her Story* (1987), comprising a series of notebooks, is set in the future. His volumes of short stories include *Beggar My Neighbour* (1964). *Time and Time Again* (1985) is an autobiography.

Jago, Richard 1715–81 Poet. Jago was born at Beaudesert near Henley-in-Arden in Warwickshire and was a friend of WILLIAM SOMERVILLE. He was admitted to Oxford as a servitor and ordained about 1739. He is remembered for his poem in four books, *Edge-hill: or, The Rural Prospect Delineated and Moralised* (1767), describing the view at various times of day from the ridge where the battle took place during the Civil War.

Jakobson, Roman See STRUCTURALISM.

James I of England 1566–1625 King of England and Scotland. James Stuart, son of Mary, Queen of Scots, and Henry, Lord Darnley, became James VI of Scotland in 1567, when barely a year old. Among his tutors was the scholar GEORGE BUCHANAN. Upon the death of Elizabeth I in 1603, he succeeded, at the age of 37, to the English crown and ruled both realms, styling himself (without parliamentary approval) 'King of Great Britain'.

A scholarly man, if exaggeratedly vain of his learning, he published several important works. *The Essays of a Prentice, in the Divine Art of Poesy* (1584) consists of original poems, translations of Du Bartas and Lucan, and, most significantly, the first Scots contribution to literary criticism in the Renaissance. *His Majesty's Poetical Exercises at Vacant Hours* (1591) includes further translations from Du Bartas. James expressed his philosophy of government in the anonymously published *The True Lawe of Free Monarchies* (1598) and *Basilikon Doron* (1599), both reissued and acknowledged in London in the year of his accession. His fascination with witchcraft bore fruit in *Daemonologie* (1597), which attacks REGINALD SCOT's sceptical *Discovery of Witchcraft* (1584). Perhaps his most enduring literary production is *A Counterblast to Tobacco*, issued anonymously in 1604, but acknowledged in the folio collection, *The Works of James I* (1616). Both as practitioner and as a patron, particularly of the development of the English MASQUE by BEN JONSON and Inigo Jones, James exercised a considerable influence on the culture of Stuart England.

James I of Scotland 1394–1437 Son of Robert III of Scotland, James was kidnapped by pirates in 1406 while on his way to France, given up to Henry IV of England and imprisoned until 1423. Robert died shortly after his son's capture, leaving James King of Scotland. On his release he married Joan Beaufort. He was assassinated at Perth.

The earliest reference to the King as a poet appeared in the 16th century, when THE KINGIS QUAIR was attributed to him, the poem being said to record his love for Joan Beaufort. There is little evidence to support the claim beyond the poem's autobiographical content and the manuscript colophon. It remains uncertain whether James was the author, whether indeed he was a poet at all, and which (if any) other surviving poems are his work.

James, Alice 1848–92 American diarist. The sister of HENRY JAMES and WILLIAM JAMES, she was born in New York. The family's life, and especially Alice's, was disrupted by the separations imposed by the Civil War, and she began to manifest the classic symptoms of neurasthenia. Like many women in the 19th century, and despite her intellectual acumen and curiosity, she was deprived of the formal education given her brothers. Her family, while respecting her abilities, coddled and protected her throughout her many illnesses. She suffered the first of several breakdowns at the age of 19.

Her letters and diary show that she was an astute critic of the work and careers of both her famous brothers and of the issues of her time. Her diary, which she seems to have intended for publication, was begun in December 1886, after she and her companion, Katherine Loring Peabody, had settled in England. Written over the next five years, the later portions were dictated to Peabody, as Alice was too ill to write herself. In March 1892 she died of breast cancer following a gradual decline. One of the major themes of her diary is her awareness of her approaching death, and her confrontation of that finality. Because of her brother Henry's belief that it would violate the family's privacy, the diary was not immediately published. In fact, it was not published until 1934, under the title *Alice James: Her Brothers – Her Journal*. It has since been republished as *The Diary of Alice James* (1964). A selection of her letters, *The Death and Letters of Alice James*, appeared in 1983.

James, C(yril) L(ionel) R(obert) 1901–89

Essayist and journalist. Born in Tunapuna, near Port of Spain, Trinidad, James came to England in 1933. He was assistant cricket correspondent of *The Manchester Guardian* under Neville Cardus in 1933–5, returning to the paper in 1953. His Marxist sympathies were developed during a prolonged stay in America between 1938 and 1953. His works include: a novel, *Minty Alley* (1936); *The Black Jacobins: Toussaint L'Ouverture and the San Domingo Revolution* (1938); and several volumes of political essays, among them *Mariners, Renegades and Castaways* (1953). But he is best known for a unique book on cricket, *Beyond a Boundary* (1963), which combines autobiography, cultural and social history, aesthetic appreciation and political polemics. Other writings on cricket were collected in 1986.

James, G(eorge) P(ayne) R(ainsford) 1799–1860

Author of over 100 historical novels. Born in London, he was a British consul for many years, holding office in the USA and Europe. His first novel was *Richelieu* (1829), followed by *The Huguenot* (1838), *The Man-at-Arms* (1840), *Arabella Stuart* (1844), *The Cavalier* (1859) and *The Man in Black* (1860). He also wrote historical and biographical works, including *Memoirs of Great Commanders* (1832) and a *Life of the Black Prince* (1836). His style was parodied by THACKERAY in *PUNCH'S PRIZE NOVELISTS*.

James, Henry 1843–1916

American novelist, short-story writer, playwright, critic and essayist. The brother of WILLIAM JAMES and ALICE JAMES, he was born in New York. He was educated by private tutors until the age of 12 and then at schools in Boulogne, Paris, Geneva, Bonn and – when the family returned to the USA – at Newport, Rhode Island. He entered Harvard Law School in 1862 but withdrew after a year and, with the encouragement of CHARLES ELIOT NORTON and WILLIAM DEAN HOWELLS, began to concentrate on writing. In the 1860s his early reviews and critical essays were published in *THE NORTH AMERICAN REVIEW* and *THE ATLANTIC MONTHLY*. *Pyramus and Thisbe* (1869) is a FARCE and *Watch and Ward*, serialized in *The Atlantic Monthly* in 1871, his

first novel. *A Passionate Pilgrim and Other Tales* (1875) and *Transatlantic Sketches* (1875) reflect his experiences of Europe on extended visits in 1869 and 1872–4. After spending 1875 in Paris he settled in England in 1876, making London his base for over 20 years before moving to Lamb House in Rye, Sussex. His remarkably wide range of acquaintance in the literary world came to include JOSEPH CONRAD, STEPHEN CRANE, H. G. WELLS, GEORGE GISSING and EDITH WHARTON, a particularly close friend during the last years of his life. He became a British subject in 1915.

Deeply influenced by Continental literature (he had met Turgenev, Daudet, Flaubert, the Goncourts and Zola in Paris), James took the American experience of Europe as the theme of his first important works: *RODERICK HUDSON* (1876), *THE AMERICAN* (1877), *THE EUROPEANS* (1878), *DAISY MILLER* (1879), *An International Episode* (1879) and, his masterpiece of this period, *THE PORTRAIT OF A LADY* (1881). *WASHINGTON SQUARE* (1880) and *THE BOSTONIANS* (1886) use an American setting and *THE PRINCESS CASAMASSIMA* (1886) studies the political underworld of London, while *THE ASPERN PAPERS* (1888) returns to his 'international theme'. In addition to short stories (*The Madonna of the Future and Other Tales*, 1879; *The Siege of London*, 1883), essays (*Partial Portraits*, 1888) and travel writings (*Portraits of Places*, 1883; *A Little Tour in France*, 1884), he also published three significant critical studies: of French poets and novelists (1878), of HAWTHORNE (1879) and of 'The Art of Fiction' (1884).

In 1890 he turned his attention to drama, writing several drawing-room comedies and adapting *The American* before becoming discouraged by the failure of *Guy Domville* (1895). The collections of short stories belonging to this period are: *The Lesson of the Master* (1892), which includes 'The Pupil', 'The Solution', and 'Sir Edmund Orme'; *The Real Thing and Other Tales* (1893); *Terminations* (1895), which includes 'The Altar of the Dead'; and *Embarrassments* (1896), which includes 'The Figure in the Carpet'. The novels which followed – notably *THE SPOILS OF POYNTON* (1897), *WHAT MAISIE KNEW* (1897), *THE AWKWARD AGE* (1899) and *THE SACRED FOUNT* (1901) – abandon his 'international theme', though it returns in his last three major works: *THE WINGS OF THE DOVE* (1902), *THE AMBASSADORS* (1903) and *THE GOLDEN BOWL* (1904). *THE TURN OF THE SCREW* (1898) is his most famous venture into the uncanny.

James first returned to the USA after a 21-year absence in 1904, staying with HENRY ADAMS and meeting President Theodore Roosevelt. His often unfavourable impressions of his native country make *The American Scene* (1907) an altogether less enjoyable travel book than either *English Hours* (1905) or *Italian Hours* (1910). The New York Edition of his works (1907–9) revised their texts and contributed 18 new prefaces which together amount to a major state-

Henry James

ment of his approach to fiction. His last completed novel was *The Outcry* (1911); *The Ivory Tower* and *The Sense of the Past* were left unfinished. *A Small Boy and Others* (1913) and *Notes of a Son and Brother* (1914) are autobiographical; a third volume, *The Middle Years*, appeared posthumously in 1917.

James, M(ontague) R(hodes) 1862–1936 Scholar and writer of ghost stories. He was educated at Eton College and King's College, Cambridge, and elected a fellow of King's in 1887. In the course of his distinguished career he became Provost of King's in 1905 and Provost of Eton in 1918, serving also as director of the Fitzwilliam Museum (1893–1908) and Vice-Chancellor of the University of Cambridge (1913–15). His broad scholarly interests embraced biblical studies, palaeography (he made pioneering descriptive catalogues of Western manuscripts in Cambridge and elsewhere) and the art and literature of the Middle Ages (he gave expert advice on the restoration of the stained glass in King's College chapel and Great Malvern priory church). Beyond the scholarly world James is best remembered for the recreations embodied in *Ghost Stories of an Antiquary* (1904), *More Ghost Stories of an Antiquary* (1911), *A Thin Ghost, and Others* (1919), *The Five Jars* (1922) and *A Warning to the Curious, and Other Ghost Stories* (1925). His *Collected Ghost Stories* appeared in 1931. The first volume contained the famous and much-anthologized 'Oh, Whistle and I'll Come to You, My Lad'. With their effective use of understatement and scholarly detail, his tales of the supernatural strongly influenced later practitioners of the genre.

James [White], **P(hyllis) D(orothy),** Baroness James of Holland Park 1920– Writer of DETECTIVE FICTION. Born in Oxford, she worked as an administrator in the National Health Service (1949–68) and as a civil servant with the Home Office (1968–79). Her work experience is clearly reflected in the settings of her novels, which have featured two recurrent detectives: the policeman Adam Dalgliesh (*Cover Her Face*, 1962; *A Mind to Murder*, 1963; *Unnatural Causes*, 1967; *Shroud for a Nightingale*, 1971; *The Black Tower*, 1975; *Death of an Expert Witness*, 1977; *A Taste for Death*, 1986; *Devices and Desires*, 1989) and the private detective Cordelia Gray (*An Unsuitable Job for a Woman*, 1972; *The Skull beneath the Skin*, 1982). By comparison with the classic efficiency of her early work, the Gothic elaboration of *The Skull beneath the Skin* marks a dissatisfaction with the conventional boundaries of detective fiction, though the result – particularly in *Innocent Blood* (1980), in which neither Dalgliesh nor Cordelia Gray appear – has been to expand circumstantial detail without finding new territory. Highly acclaimed for her novels and active in the Arts Council, British Council, Society of Authors and BBC (of which she became a governor in 1988), P. D. James was elevated to a life peerage in 1991.

**James,	William** 1842–1910 American philosopher. The elder brother of HENRY JAMES, he was born in New York. He received his MD from Harvard Medical School in 1869 and became an instructor in physiology at Harvard in 1872. As his interest shifted to psychology, in a pioneering venture he opened a laboratory of psychology at Harvard in 1876.

For the next 12 years he spent his spare time working on *THE PRINCIPLES OF PSYCHOLOGY*, which was published in 1890. It remains a classic in its field, even if later investigations – many of which it inspired – have superseded it. In 1897 he published a collection of essays, *THE WILL TO BELIEVE*, in which he defined his position as that of a 'radical empiricist'. His international reputation increased when he was appointed Gifford Lecturer on Natural Religion at Edinburgh University from 1901 to 1902. His two sets of lectures

there were published as *THE VARIETIES OF RELIGIOUS EXPERIENCE* (1902). In 1907 he published *PRAGMATISM*, whose thesis that an idea has meaning only in relation to its consequences in feeling and action won him new followers, but was also attacked in some quarters. *The Meaning of Truth* (1909) was his answer to these critics. Though he retired from Harvard in 1907, where he had been professor of psychology (1889–97) and philosophy (1897–1907), he continued to write and lecture; indeed, during this time he was probably the most honoured philosopher in America. He explained his metaphysical principles in *A Pluralistic Universe* (1909), a series of lectures he had delivered in Oxford in 1908. Posthumous publications were *Some Problems of Philosophy: A Beginning of an Introduction to Philosophy* (1911), *Memoirs and Studies* (1911) and *Essays in Radical Empiricism* (1912).

Jameson, Anna Brownell 1794–1860 Art and literary critic. Born Anna Murphy in Dublin, she moved to England and became a governess. Her experiences touring Europe in this capacity gave her the material for her first book, *Diary of an Ennuyée* (1826). After separating from her husband, Robert Jameson, whom she had married in 1825, she began to earn a reputation as a critic, with *Loves of the Poets* (1829) and *Characteristics of Women* (1832; later called *Shakespeare's Heroines*). Her books on art include *Memoir of the Early Italian Painters* (1845) and *Sacred and Legendary Art* (1848). Of her travel books, *Winter Studies and Summer Rambles* (1838) gives an interesting account of the lives and customs of the Canadian Indian tribes.

**Jameson,	(Margaret)	Storm** 1891–1986 Novelist. Born in Whitby, where her family were shipbuilders, she went to Leeds University. Her many novels include sagas depicting English life between the wars, notably two trilogies about a family of Yorkshire shipbuilders: *The Triumph of Time*, comprising *The Lovely Ship* (1927), *The Voyage Home* (1930) and *A Richer Dust* (1931), and *The Mirror in Darkness*, comprising *Company Parade* (1934), *Love in Winter* (1935) and *None Turn Back* (1936). She also wrote poetry, essays, criticism and biography. Her wartime work as president of PEN, assisting European refugee intellectuals, is related in one of her several substantial volumes of autobiography, *Journey from the North* (1969).

Jane Eyre A novel by CHARLOTTE BRONTË, published in 1847.

An orphan living with her unpleasant aunt, Mrs Reed, and cousins, Jane is too independent-minded to fit in to the household. As pupil and then teacher at Lowood Asylum she suffers appalling physical conditions, palliated by the friendship of the gentle, long-suffering Helen Burns and Maria Temple, the mistress. Helen dies of consumption, but not before Jane has learned from her that self-control is the surest means of retaining self-respect in adversity. She leaves Lowood to become a governess at Thornfield Hall. Her pupil is Adele Varens, the ward of Edward Rochester. Soon she finds herself drawn to him and he, attracted by her wit and self-possession, finally asks her to become his wife. Their wedding is interrupted by the unexpected arrival of Richard Mason, who reveals that Rochester is already married to his sister Bertha, a raving lunatic secretly confined at Thornfield Hall. Jane leaves the Hall and wanders, destitute, until she is finally taken in by a clergyman, St John Rivers, and his sisters Diana and Mary. Though she has assumed the name of Jane Elliott, a slip discloses her true name and leads to the revelation that the Riverses are her cousins and she sole heir to a fortune which she joyfully shares with them. St John, dedicated but narrow-minded, proposes that Jane should accompany him as his wife in his mission to India. She is nearly brought to consent when a voice, recognizably Rochester's, calls to her out of the air. Resolved to discover his fate, she returns to Thornfield to find it a blackened ruin and the master maimed and blind – the result of his vain efforts to save his mad wife from the flames. At last she can contract a marriage which includes spiritual equality, intellectual companionship and sexual passion.

Jane Eyre attracted immediate attention, but praise for its narrative force and the vivid way Jane's feelings are rendered was mixed with criticism. The merciless portrait of Lowood and its headmaster, Brocklehurst, offended Evangelicals. Above all, contemporaries were made uneasy by the book's morality: though Jane's actions observe the conventional code of female behaviour they still embody a powerful statement of woman's claim to independence.

Jane Shore, The Tragedy of A play by ROWE, first produced and published in 1714. It traces the fall from favour of Edward IV's mistress Jane Shore, daughter of a Cheapside mercer and a goldsmith's wife, who died in poverty. Rowe made his heroine an unlikely image of domestic virtue and provided her jealous friend, Alicia, with a conclusion in eloquent madness after the fashion of Belvidera in OTWAY's *VENICE PRESERVED*.

Janet's Repentance See *SCENES OF CLERICAL LIFE*.

Jarrell, Randall 1914–65 American poet and critic. He was born in Nashville, Tennessee, and educated at Vanderbilt University. After serving in the US Army Air Corps in 1942–6, he taught English literature and creative writing at various universities. His volumes of poetry are: *Blood for a Stranger* (1942); *Little*

Friend, Little Friend (1945); *Losses* (1948); *The Seven-League Crutches* (1951); *Selected Poems* (1955); *Uncollected Poems* (1958); *The Woman at the Washington Zoo* (1960), which consists of poems and translations, and for which he received the National Book Award in 1961; a second edition of *Selected Poems* (1964); and *The Lost World* (1965). Published posthumously were *Complete Poems* (1969) and *Jerome: The Biography of a Poem* (1971), which uses works by Albrecht Dürer as illustrations. His verse is characterized by a particular colloquial quality, a modern plainness. It emphasizes the grotesqueness of a reality made more, not less, chaotic by modern science. War is an important theme in several of his poems, including one of his best known, 'The Death of the Ball Turret Gunner'.

His critical writings include *Poetry and the Age* (1953), *The Third Book of Criticism* (1969) and *Kipling, Auden, & Co.: Essays and Reviews 1935–1964* (1979). *A Sad Heart at the Supermarket* (1962) includes both fables and essays. He held editorial positions on several periodicals: THE NATION (1946), PARTISAN REVIEW (1949–51), the *Yale Review* (1955–7) and the *American Scholar* (1957–65). He translated, among other works, Chekhov's short stories, Grimm's fairy tales, and Part I of Goethe's *Faust*. *Pictures from an Institution*, his only novel, was published in 1954. He also wrote CHILDREN'S LITERATURE.

Jason, The Life and Death of A narrative poem in heroic couplets by WILLIAM MORRIS, published in 1867. The story follows the classical myths and the *Argonautica* of Apollonius Rhodius. Morris's version begins with the birth of Jason, his education by Chiron the centaur, his confrontation with the usurper Pelias and his embarkation for Colchis in the *Argo*. The poem then describes the familiar adventures of his voyage, his encounter with King Aeëtes and Medea, his theft of the Golden Fleece and his flight with Medea. After numerous disasters, Jason's life ends in melancholy loneliness as he muses in the shadow of the rotten timbers of his once glorious ship.

Jebb, Richard Claverhouse 1841–1905 Greek scholar. Born in Dundee, and educated at Charterhouse and Trinity College, Cambridge, Jebb became professor of Greek at Glasgow University (1875–89) and then at Cambridge (1889–1905). He also served as MP for Cambridge University in 1891–1900. His works include *The Attic Orators from Antiphon to Isaeus* (1876–80), editions and translations of Theophrastus (1870), Sophocles (1883–96) and Bacchylides (1905), and a biography of RICHARD BENTLEY for the English Men of Letters series (1882).

Jefferies, (John) Richard 1848–87 Journalist and novelist. He was born at Coate Farm, Liddington, near

Swindon. Memorialized by a monument in Salisbury Cathedral and a bust in Taunton Shire Hall, he is mostly remembered for a body of novels and essays celebrating the countryside of southern England in a remarkably detailed but unsentimental way. He knew all country matters intimately, having the knack, acquired at an early age, of writing about them in an unpretentious, economical plain prose that was consistent both with his farming background and his early training as a reporter. From 1864 he worked for *The North Wiltshire Herald*, issuing the locally printed *Reporting, Editing and Authorship* in 1873.

He established himself in the public view during the early 1870s with his articles on wild life for *THE PALL MALL GAZETTE* and also by a long letter to *The Times* on the plight of the agricultural labourer in Wiltshire. After his marriage in 1874 he began to supplement his journalism by fiction, starting with a series of melodramatic and for the most part unsuccessful novels: *The Scarlet Shawl* (1874), *Restless Human Hearts* (1875) and *The World's End* (1877). In these books neither the aristocratic characters nor the sensational plots quite ring true. More convincing are his last novel, *Amaryllis at the Fair* (1887), with its portrait of his father in the character Iden, and, among earlier works, the autobiographical *Bevis, the Story of a Boy* (1882) and his actual autobiography, *The Story of My Heart* (1883), books which still await biographical and critical analysis. Jefferies's reputation chiefly depends, however, not on fiction or autobiography but on books, written in the style of the essayist, reflecting his close engagement with and knowledge of rural England. These include *The Amateur Poacher* (1879), *The Gamekeeper at Home* (1880), *Hodge and His Masters* (1880), *Greene Ferne Farm* (1880), *The Open Air* (1885) and the posthumous *Field and Hedgerow* (1889), in which detailed descriptions of natural scenes and objects are not complicated by irony, rhetoric or the type of authorial comment that goes beyond the author's exact knowledge. Within this narrow range, Jefferies came to be recognized as a master of straightforward descriptive prose. The vaguely poetic nostalgia for rural innocence that, for many urban and suburban readers, was and is part of the pleasure of reading these books was probably not shared by Jefferies, whose cast of mind was more pessimistic, or at least more practical than romantic. Few 'could long remain poetical', he once said, 'upon bread and cheese'.

Present but not precisely visible in the opaque documents of the naturalist is the thoroughgoing distaste for 19th-century industrial civilization implicit in *After London* (1885). Presenting, like other novels of the time, a vision of future disaster, it suggests that the individual must trust for his survival in his knowledge of the earth, and the animals and plants from which, without any other human being's help, he can gain sustenance. The vision is not just pre-industrial, but also pre-agricultural. If the attempt of the main character in *After London* to slip secretly away in a canoe from the world of other people is a fantasy expressing a fear of people that is the corollary of Jefferies's love of nature, it is nonetheless a fantasy with disturbing personal and social implications, something underlined by the story's ambivalent ending (or endings). Though his last years, and his last books, were tragically darkened by the long suffering of tuberculosis, *After London* is not just a consequence of that suffering but reaches back imaginatively to his beginnings, spanning much of his career in mood and effect.

Jeffers, (John) Robinson 1887–1962 American poet. Born in Pittsburgh, the son of a theologian and classical scholar, Jeffers spent most of his life in Carmel, on the Monterey coast of California. He called for a poetry of 'dangerous images' which would 'reclaim substance and sense, and psychological reality'. Many of his poems are based on biblical stories or Greek and Roman myths, and their language has a classical directness and clarity. His first two volumes, *Flagons and Apples* (1912) and *Californians* (1916), were relatively conventional; it was not until the publication of *Tamar and Other Poems* (1924) that his particular dramatic and rhetorical power became clear. The title poem is based on the Old Testament figure, and exhibits Jeffers's preoccupation with the themes of lust, incest and the corrupt nature of man. His many other volumes include *Roan Stallion* (1924), *The Woman at Point Sur* (1927), *Cawdor and Other Poems* (1928), *Dear Judas and Other Poems* (1929), *Give Your Heart to the Hawks and Other Poems* (1933), *Be Angry at the Sun* (1941), *The Double Axe* (1948) and *Hungerfield, and Other Poems* (1954). His best-known play, *Medea*, was staged in New York in 1947 and 1965.

Jefferson, Thomas 1743–1826 Third president of the USA. He was born in Virginia, and educated at the College of William and Mary. *A Summary View of the Rights of British America* (1774) established him as a leading voice of the colonies' grievances against the king. He went on, as a member of the Second Continental Congress, to draft the Declaration of Independence in 1776. During the American Revolution he served in the Virginia legislature (1776–9) and then as the state's governor (1779–81). A landed and wealthy slaveowner himself, he espoused a vision of an agrarian society based on an independent yeomanry, defended the principle of individual freedom against entrenched privilege and government encroachment, and supported the gradual abolition of slavery. *NOTES ON THE STATE OF VIRGINIA* (1785) is a clear expression of his ideals. After serving as American minister to Paris (1785–9), he became

George Washington's Secretary of State (1789–93), Adams's Vice-President (1797–1801) and then President (1801–9). In 1803 he approved the Louisiana Purchase from France, which doubled the size of the USA at the cost of four cents per acre.

Jefferson had lifelong interests in science, architecture and education. He served as president of the American Philosophical Society from 1797 to 1814. After leaving the presidency, he founded and helped to draw up plans for the University of Virginia, chartered in 1819. The Library of Congress was begun when he sold his personal library to the national government in 1815. He was also the author of *Observations on the Whale-Fishery* (1788), *A Manual of Parliamentary Practice* (1801) and a *Life of Captain Lewis* (1814). Among the papers unpublished at his death were his *Autobiography*, the *Anas* (political memoirs), and 'The Morals of Jesus of Nazareth', extracts from the Bible which reflected his DEISM.

Jeffrey, Francis 1773–1850 Lawyer, editor and critic. Born in Edinburgh, Jeffrey attended Edinburgh High School before studying at Glasgow and Oxford Universities. Called to the Bar in 1794, he was one of a group of Edinburgh lawyers who strongly supported Whig ideas of reform. He became MP for Edinburgh in 1832 and Lord of Session in 1834, as Lord Jeffrey. His contribution to literature was to found THE EDIN-BURGH REVIEW with SYDNEY SMITH, HENRY BROUGHAM and FRANCIS HORNER in 1802. He became its editor in 1803 and held the post for 25 years, establishing himself as an influential critic who (despite his dislike of WORDSWORTH's poetry) raised the standard of public taste. He published a selection from his papers in 1844.

Jellicoe, Ann 1927– Playwright. *The Sport of My Mad Mother* (1958) may owe some of its improvisational energy to the workshops at the ROYAL COURT THEATRE, of which Jellicoe was a leader. *The Knack* (1961) is a small-scale comedy, which was made into a successful film. Jellicoe directed both plays for their original performances, as she did the less successful but oddly impressive *Shelley* (1965). Having moved from London to Lyme Regis, she began a second career with the Colway Theatre Trust, writing and directing community plays based on local history and staged in small towns in the south-west of England, using up to 100 actors, musicians, etc. They include *The Reckoning* (1978), *The Tide* (1980), *The Western Women* (with FAY WELDON and JOHN FOWLES; 1984) and *Under the God* (1989).

Jenkins, (John) Robin 1912– Scottish novelist. Born in Flemington, Lanarkshire, he was educated at Hamilton Academy and Glasgow University, and became an English teacher in Glasgow and later Dunoon, with lengthy spells of teaching abroad. One of the most prolific post-war Scottish writers, he has often been neglected, perhaps because of his distance from both the SCOTTISH RENAISSANCE and MODERNISM. His novels, often autobiographical in origin, include *Happy for the Child* (1953), *The Cone-Gatherers* (1955), *The Changeling* (1958), *Guests of War* (1956), *A Would-be Saint* (1978) and a comic masterpiece, *Fergus Lamont* (1979). His spells abroad prompted *Dust on the Paw* (1961), *The Sardana Dancers* (1964), *The Holy Tree* (1969) and *A Figure of Fun* (1974). His short stories were collected in *A Far Cry from Bowmore* (1973).

Jennie Gerhardt A novel by THEODORE DREISER, published in 1911. Jennie, pretty but poor, helps her mother scrub floors in a fine hotel in Columbus, Ohio. There she meets Senator George Brander, and when her brother is arrested for stealing coal and Brander arranges his release, she gives herself to him out of gratitude. She becomes pregnant and her father, a rigid Lutheran, forces her to leave home. Her situation worsens when Brander dies.

After the birth of her daughter, Vesta, Jennie goes to work as a maid for the Bracebridges, a wealthy Cleveland family. She meets Lester Kane, who is attracted to her and, by being kind to her family, eventually persuades her to live with him. His family, socially prominent in Cincinnati, disapproves of the relationship. His father dies and leaves his inheritance in the trust of his brother Robert, stipulating that Lester can have it only if he abandons Jennie. Though he suffers pangs of conscience, he does indeed leave her, and eventually marries Letty Pace Gerald, a widowed socialite. Vesta dies and Jennie fights against despair by adopting two orphans. Lester falls ill and summons Jennie to his deathbed, declaring that he was wrong to leave her and that he has not found greater happiness by doing so. Jennie is with him when he dies but leaves before the arrival of his wife. She attends his funeral, masked behind a heavy veil, and watches his coffin being loaded on to the train for the trip to Cincinnati.

Jennings, Elizabeth (Joan) 1926– Poet. Born in Boston, Lincolnshire, she was educated at Oxford High School and at St Anne's College, Oxford, where she read English. After working as a librarian and a publisher's reader, she became a freelance writer in 1961. The restraint and clarity of diction of her first collection, *Poems* (1955), marked her out as a member of the MOVEMENT, but her Roman Catholicism gave her work a quiet vulnerability and made faith rather than reductive IRONY its dominant quality. Her early work, in *A Way of Looking* (1955) and *A Sense of the World* (1958), culminated in *Song for a Birth or a Death and Other Poems* (1961). Showing simplicity and a belief in traditional formal properties, she writes with correctness and good manners. *Re-*

coveries (1964) and *The Mind Has Mountains* (1966) come from a period of severe mental illness, and although they achieved popularity in the 1960s, are not her best work. Similarly, Jennings has chosen to reprint very little from the subsequent collections, *Lucidities* (1970) and *Relationships* (1972). More recent volumes have returned to more typical subject matter: love, friendship, childhood, places, religion and works of art, where painting, her 'second favourite art', is well represented. Her later work, in *Growing Points* (1975), *Consequently I Rejoice* (1977), *Moments of Grace* (1977), *Celebrations and Elegies* (1982), *Extending the Territory* (1985), a second *Collected Poems* (1986), *Tributes* (1989) and *Times and Seasons* (1992), gains power from the sense of triumph over disruptive mental forces and has the quiet authority of someone who has survived. Jennings has also written studies of religion and poetry, *Every Changing Shape* (1961) and *Christianity and Poetry* (1965).

Jenny A DRAMATIC MONOLOGUE by DANTE GABRIEL ROSSETTI, begun in 1847 and eventually published in 1870. Jenny is a prostitute. The poet regards her with sympathy as a victim of her time and circumstances, scorned by her virtuous sisters and, more tellingly, by the men who use her. Rossetti's only poem with a contemporary subject, it has a close connection with his only painting on a contemporary theme, the unfinished 'Found'.

Jerome, Jerome K(lapka) 1859-1927 Humorist and novelist. The son of an ironmonger, he was born at Walsall in Staffordshire and brought up in east London, where he became an actor and a reporter for various newspapers. *On Stage and Off* (1885) and *Idle Thoughts of an Idle Fellow* (1886) were lighthearted essays which set the tone for his most enduring work, *Three Men in a Boat* (1889), about an accident-prone rowing holiday on the Thames. *Three Men on the Bummel* (1900) took the same characters on a tour of Germany. Jerome founded *The Idler*, a humorous periodical, in 1892, and wrote many plays with some contemporary success. Best known of these was *The Passing of the Third Floor Back* (1907). His own favourite work was *Paul Kelver* (1902), an autobiographical novel. *My Life and Times* (1926) was autobiographical.

Jerrold, (William) Blanchard 1826-84 Journalist. The son of DOUGLAS JERROLD, he was educated in London and France and planned a career as an artist before his sight failed. He wrote four plays, including *Beau Brummel*, and succeeded his father as editor of *Lloyd's Weekly Newspaper*. He wrote a biography of his father (1859) and provided the text for Gustave Doré's famous volume of illustrations, *London: A Pilgrimage* (1872).

Jerrold, Douglas (William) 1803-57 Playwright and journalist. He was born in London and spent part of his youth as a sailor before starting a successful career in literature. In 1827 his FARCE *Paul Pry* was staged at the Coburg, London, and he became resident playwright there. A MELODRAMA, *Fifteen Years of a Drunkard's Life* (1828), did equally well and he had a major success in *Black-Eyed Susan* (1829). His next play was the melodrama *The Mutiny at the Nore* (1830), and *The Rent Day* (1832) was a drama, but he generally wrote comedy: *The Bride of Ludgate* (1831), *Beau Nash* (1834) and *Time Works Wonders* (1845).

In 1841 Jerrold joined the staff of a new weekly called PUNCH and from that date devoted most of his time to journalism. He was equally successful in his new role, signing his contributions 'Q'. His *Mrs Caudle's Curtain Lectures* (1845) helped to establish the paper's popularity and were published in book form (1846). Mrs Caudle is a nagging wife who always gets into her stride at bedtime when her suffering husband is hoping to sleep. From 1852 until his death Jerrold edited *Lloyd's Weekly Newspaper*.

Jew of Malta, The Famous Tragedy of the Rich A tragedy, with comic elements, by CHRISTOPHER MARLOWE. It was first produced in about 1590 but not published until 1633. The published text is believed to contain a number of alterations made during production and these are usually attributed to THOMAS HEYWOOD. The play was very popular and gave EDWARD ALLEYN, the creator of Tamburlaine and Doctor Faustus, another great opportunity as an actor.

Barabas, a successful Jewish merchant of Malta, counts his riches and ponders on the Christians' envy of his success, and their persecution of his people. He knows them for hypocrites who use their religion as their excuse. Barabas longs for the power that would enable him to deal with his enemies.

The Turks demand tribute from Malta and the governor of the island decides to extract the money from the Jews. Barabas resists but his wealth is taken by force and his house confiscated – the governor turns it into a nunnery. He decides to avenge himself on those who have wronged him and embarks on a campaign of destruction. Abigail, his daughter, has a Christian lover and he disposes of both of them. He poisons wells and destroys the entire nunnery, his former house, with poisoned porridge. But his plan to destroy the Turkish commander and his retinue at a banquet by means of a collapsible floor goes awry. He is betrayed and meets his death in a cauldron under the same floor.

Jewett, Sarah Orne 1849-1909 American novelist and short-story writer. She was born and raised in South Berwick, Maine, where her father was a doctor. She often travelled with him to outlying farms and fishing towns, and observed at first hand the decay and depopulation that afflicted them. (Deephaven, the harbour town of her early stories, was modelled on that of York, near her own home town.) Her observation of this desolation, coupled with her reading of HARRIET BEECHER STOWE's stories of New England life, provided the stimulus for her own first efforts at fiction; she decided to record the life of her own state and succeeded in getting a story accepted by THE ATLANTIC MONTHLY when she was 19. A collection of such pieces was published as *Deephaven* in 1877 and established her at once as a writer of considerable talent.

She then published two novels, *A Country Doctor* (1884) and *A Marsh Island* (1885), and further collections of stories – *A White Heron* (1886), *The King of Folly Island* (1888), *A Native of Winby* (1893) and *The Life of Nancy* (1895). In 1896 came the book that gave her a lasting place in American literature, *THE COUNTRY OF THE POINTED FIRS*. Her later work included two books for children; a historical romance, *The Tory Lover* (1901); and poems posthumously published as *Verses* (1916).

Jewsbury, Geraldine Endsor 1812–80 Novelist. Born in Derbyshire, she became the intimate friend of THOMAS and JANE CARLYLE. Her desire to work as a journalist was frustrated by ill health, but she produced several notable and unjustly neglected novels: *Zoe: The History of Two Lives* (1845), *The Half-Sisters* (1848), *Marian Withers* (1851), *Constance Herbert* (1855), *The Sorrows of Gentility* (1856) and *Right or Wrong* (1859).

Jhabvala, Ruth Prawer 1927– Indian novelist. Born in Cologne of Polish parents and educated in Britain, she migrated to India after marriage in 1951 and to the USA 30 years later. Though a satirically minded outsider, she has also experienced Indian joint family life, and skilfully exploits this duality in her fiction. *To Whom She Will* (1956), *The Nature of Passion* (1957) and *The Householder* (1960) deal with personality clashes and 'Westernized' attitudes within urban families. *Esmond in India* (1958) and *Heat and Dust* (1975) are about Westerners trying to understand India and Indians. The technically adventurous *A New Dominion* (1973; as *The Travelers* in the USA) and *A Backward Place* (1963) are about the interaction of Indians and expatriate Westerners. Satire flares brightly in *In Search of Love and Beauty* (1983), about European exiles in New York. *Like Birds, Like Fishes* (1963), *A Stronger Climate* (1968), *An Experience of India* (1971) and *How I Became a Holy Mother* (1976) are collections of stories. Part of the Merchant-Ivory film-making team, she has written several scripts, of which *Autobiography of a Princess* and *Shakespeare Wallah* were outstanding international successes.

Jocelin of Brakelond *fl*. 1173–1215 Monk and chronicler. Jocelin, whose name derives from a street in his native Bury St Edmunds, Suffolk, entered monastic life in 1173, holding an increasingly important series of posts in the great abbey at Bury until 1215, when his name disappears from the records. The subject of his Latin *Chronicle* is the life of the monastery, particularly under the rule of Abbot Samson, elected in 1182, whom Jocelin served as chaplain and of whom he paints an extraordinarily vivid and telling portrait. For six years Jocelin was 'constantly' with the Abbot 'night and day', and his narrative, striking for its human informality, describes a religious magnate, 'more remarkable for counsel than for piety' perhaps, who ruled the abbey's human and material resources with an iron will. He recounts Samson's vicissitudinous early career, his beautification of the abbey church and his sermons to the local people, delivered in his native Norfolk dialect. The chronicle ends eight years before Samson's death in 1211 at the age of 77. No other work by Jocelin survives, although he records composing an account of the martyrdom of St Robert, a child allegedly murdered in 1181 by the Jews of Bury and buried in the abbey church.

Jocelin's *Chronicle*, first published in 1840, won fame in the pages of CARLYLE's *PAST AND PRESENT* (1843), in which Book Two is wholly devoted to the Abbot and his 'Boswell', the latter sentimentally characterized as 'a learned, grown man, yet with the heart of a child'. As a result of Carlyle's enthusiasm, an English translation appeared in 1844.

John Bull, The History of The collective title of a group of pamphlets by JOHN ARBUTHNOT, first published in 1712 and rearranged for publication in POPE and SWIFT's *Miscellanies* of 1727. A satire directed against the war with France, it marks the first appearance of the typical Englishman, John Bull.

John Bull (England) and Nicholas Frog (Holland) are engaged in a lawsuit with Lewis Baboon (Louis XIV, Bourbon). Their case is fought and won by the attorney Humphrey Hocus (Marlborough). Then John Bull discovers an intrigue between Hocus and Mrs Bull (the Whig Parliament). Mrs Bull dies during the ensuing rumpus and John Bull marries again; the new Mrs Bull is the Tory Parliament and John Bull has spent a great deal in litigation, thereby losing the 'Plumbs' he had acquired by 'plain and fair dealing'. John Bull is 'an honest plain-dealing Fellow' who honours his mother (the Church of England) but is easily deceived by partners, apprentices and servants.

John Gilpin, The Diverting History of A comic BALLAD by WILLIAM COWPER, published anonymously in *The Public Advertiser* in 1782 and later in the same volume as *THE TASK* (1785). The real John Gilpin was a linen draper of Cheapside who owned land at Olney in

Buckinghamshire, where Cowper lived for some years. He heard the story of Gilpin's misadventure from his friend Lady Austen and wrote his poem the next day. It tells how Gilpin and his wife decide to celebrate their wedding anniversary at The Bell, Edmonton. She and the children travel by chaise and pair, while he proceeds on a borrowed horse which runs out of control, carrying him 10 miles further, to Ware, and back again.

John Halifax, Gentleman A novel by DINAH MULOCK, published in 1856. It is set in Tewkesbury (called Norton Bury). The hero is a poor, friendless orphan sustained by a proud consciousness of independence and integrity. He is given work by the tanner Abel Fletcher and befriended by his son Phineas. Through industry and perseverance he eventually succeeds in the world – becoming a 'gentleman' by merit rather than birth – and marries Ursula March. See also the CONDITION OF ENGLAND NOVEL.

John Inglesant A historical novel by JOSEPH HENRY SHORTHOUSE, privately printed in 1880 and published in 1881. It is set in the early 17th century and gives a skilful portrait of the age's religious and political tensions.

Inglesant comes under the influence of a Jesuit emissary, who sees in the highly wrought, sensuous young man excellent material for service in the religious intrigues of the later years of Charles I. Inglesant is strongly influenced by the community of Little Gidding (see NICHOLAS FERRAR) and the King's approval of it is a factor in his decision to undertake dangerous service in the Royalist cause. When secret negotiations to bring an Irish army into England come to light, the King repudiates him. Inglesant refuses to expose the King, even though his own life is in peril.

After Charles's execution, Inglesant goes to Italy where he hopes to find the Italian who murdered his brother. The author now moves his story of religious tensions to Rome, where Inglesant witnesses the drawn-out intrigues that attend the election of a successor to Innocent X. He meets Molinos, the Spanish mystic who was ultimately condemned for the influence of his doctrine of Quietism, and is temporarily drawn to the idea that human endeavour is futile except in devotion to God. The climax of the story comes with Inglesant's encounter with the murderer, now in his power. He renounces vengeance, believing it God's prerogative.

John of Salisbury *c.* 1115–80 Philosopher. After a failed boyhood apprenticeship to a necromancer, John of Salisbury went on to study under Peter Abelard and to work for the papal curia at Rome. He became treasurer of Exeter Cathedral and, in 1176, Bishop of Chartres. His writings reveal a broad educa-

tion not only in the classics, philosophy and the Bible, but also in canon law. His *Policraticus*, a major medieval work, deals, often satirically, with the ethics of politics and the state. The *Metalogicus* combines the studies of logic and metaphysics, while the *Historia pontificalis* is a delightful account of life in Rome, full of anecdotes and vignettes of the characters whom John had met while at the curia. A close friend of Cardinal Nicholas Brakespear (the future Pope Adrian IV), John was at the centre of medieval church and intellectual life. Two of his biographies of leading churchmen, Anselm and Thomas Becket, survive, as does a collection of his letters, witty, polished and erudite.

Johns, W(illiam) E(arle) 1893–1968 Writer of CHILDREN'S LITERATURE. Born in Hertford and educated at the local grammar school, Johns trained as a surveyor before enlisting in World War I, first as a trooper and later in the Royal Flying Corps. After various sorties as a pilot he was shot down and imprisoned, managing to escape despite his wounds before final recapture. After the war he stayed in the RAF as an officer, becoming founder-editor of the monthly *Popular Flying* in 1932. It was in those pages that his hero Biggles (Captain James Bigglesworth) first made an appearance in a series of short stories. Along with his inseparable companions Ginger, Algy and Bertie, Biggles provided young readers with an idealized image of toughness, honesty and stoicism. Johns went on to write over 70 Biggles novels, many of which remain in print today. In his undemanding but entertaining style, he also wrote about the adventures of the only slightly less popular commando hero, Gimlet, and created a female Biggles, Worrals of the WAAF.

Johnson, B(rian) S(tanley) 1933–73 Novelist. Born in London, he campaigned vigorously through his short writing life (he committed suicide at the age of 39) for a renaissance of technical innovation and experimentation in the English novel. His own fiction demonstrates admiration for JOYCE, BECKETT and FLANN O'BRIEN in its deliberate abjuration of realistic homogeneity, and for STERNE in its playfulness with the physical form of the novel. *Albert Angelo* (1964) contains a hole in page 149 which is later revealed to represent the knife-cut which killed CHRISTOPHER MARLOWE, and is also offered as the chance to read the future (on a subsequent page) through the past (a previous page). Johnson himself intrudes into *Christie Malry's Own Double Entry* (1973) to converse with the book's hero, while *The Unfortunates* (1969) is notorious for being published in a box of 27 loose-leaf sections, to be shuffled and read in any order, to embody in literal reading terms the haphazard, unreliable recollections of the narrator. Other novels include *Travelling People* (1963), *Trawl* (1966) and *See the Old*

Lady Decently (1975). The extremity of Johnson's technical adventures, which occasionally earned him the charge of gimmickry, may be seen as acknowledgement of the immense task of reversing the realistic bias of post-war British fiction.

Johnson, Colin See MUDROOROO.

Johnson, Edward 1598-1672 American historian. Born in Canterbury, he left his wife and seven children to travel to New England with JOHN WINTHROP aboard the *Arbella* in 1630, returning home the following year. In 1636 he and his family emigrated to Massachusetts, where he held many influential civic positions. He is best remembered, however, for his history, THE WONDER-WORKING PROVIDENCE OF SION'S SAVIOUR IN NEW-ENGLAND (1654).

Johnson, Emily Pauline 1862-1913 Canadian poet. The daughter of an Indian chief and an Englishwoman, she earned a living as a contributor to periodicals and by reciting her own verse under her Indian name of Tekahionwake. Her best works demonstrate a keen sympathy for, and understanding of, Indian life: *White Wampum* (1895), *Canadian Born* (1903) and *Flint and Feathers* (1913).

Johnson, James Weldon 1871-1938 American novelist and poet. Born and educated in Florida, he was one of the most influential black figures of his day. While practising law in Florida (he was the first black admitted to the state Bar after the Civil War), he collaborated with his brother in writing popular songs and spirituals. One of these, 'Lift Every Voice and Sing', became known as the black anthem. In 1912 he anonymously published his first novel, *Autobiography of an Ex-Colored Man*, about a light-skinned black man who poses as a white. It was reissued in his own name in 1927, the year he published *God's Trombones: Seven Negro Sermons in Verse*. *Black Manhattan* (1930) is a black history of New York. His autobiography, *Along This Way* (1933), tells of his political activities as US consul in Nicaragua and Venezuela (1906-12), and of his role as a major figure in the National Association for the Advancement of Colored People. Other volumes of his poetry are *Fifty Years and Other Poems* (1917), *Saint Peter Relates an Incident at the Resurrection Day* (1930) and *Selected Poems* (1935). He also edited a pioneering anthology, *The Book of American Negro Poetry* (1922).

Johnson, Linton Kwesi 1952- Poet. Born in Chapeltown in rural Jamaica, he came to Britain in 1963. He was educated in London at Tulse Hill Comprehensive School and Goldsmiths' College. His work, mostly DUB POETRY, has a huge popular following, particularly among young black people. It is often urban in theme and filled with street-wise aggression. Johnson can, however, be quietly lyrical and always shows himself in command of sound effects and METRE. His recorded poems give a better idea of his talents, but Johnson has also published several collections: *Voices of the Living and the Dead* (1974), *Dread Beat and Blood* (1975), *Inglan is a Bitch* (1980) and *Tings and Times* (1991). His records include *Dread Beat An' Blood* (1978), *Forces of Victory* (1979), *Bass Culture* (1980) and *Making History* (1984). His is one of the major talents in black British literature and almost certainly the best known, with many imitators who share his interest in matching words to music.

Johnson, Lionel (Pigot) 1867-1902 Poet and critic. Born in Kent, he grew up in Wales, and had a very successful academic career at Winchester and, from 1886, at New College, Oxford. After graduating, he began to publish reviews and articles in several London newspapers and periodicals. He was received into the Roman Catholic church in 1891. A member of the RHYMERS' CLUB and a close friend of W. B. YEATS, he began to explore his Irish ancestry in 1893, when he visited Dublin. He jointly edited *The Irish Home Reading Magazine* during 1894, and was an active member of the Irish Literary Society in London. His early full-length study of THOMAS HARDY (1894) was followed by *Poems* (1895) and *Ireland with Other Poems* (1897) which included 'Ways of War' (dedicated to John O'Leary). *Posliminium*, a posthumous collection of essays, appeared in 1912, and his *Complete Poems* edited by I. Fletcher in 1953. Although his Irish poems are rhetorical, his other work 'conveys an emotion of joy, of intellectual clearness, of hard energy', as Yeats wrote. Johnson influenced Yeats's early work, especially *The Wind among the Reeds* (1899), and he appears in 'In Memory of Major Robert Gregory' as a man of learning who 'brooded upon sanctity'. He acknowledged his alcoholism in 'Mystic and Cavalier': 'Go from me, I am one of those who fall.'

Johnson, Louis 1924-88 New Zealand poet and editor. He worked as a teacher, copywriter and educational journalist and was an important influence on New Zealand poetry in the 1950s. In 1951 he founded *Poetry Yearbook*, which he edited until it ceased publication in 1964. The journal was based in Wellington and there grew up around it a 'Wellington school', including JAMES K. BAXTER and ALISTAIR CAMPBELL, hostile to ALLEN CURNOW's insistence that New Zealand poetry should engage with local reality. Against Curnow's modernist-nationalist poetic they propounded a romantic-universalist theory and practice. Johnson's own poetry from this period includes *The Sun among the Ruins* (1951), *New Worlds for Old* (1957) and *Bread and a Pension* (1964). Apart from his characteristic Romantic mode, Johnson also wrote poems satirizing the Puritan ethos of New Zealand social life. From the late 1960s he lived in Australia and New Guinea, returning to New Zealand in 1980. His later work, especially the posthumous *Last Poems* (1990), is sparser in diction and tighter in form than his earlier work.

Johnson, Pamela Hansford 1912–81 Novelist and critic. Born and educated in London, she married C. P. SNOW in 1950. Her first novel, *This Bed Thy Centre* (1935), was followed by many others including *The Trojan Brothers* (1944), *An Avenue of Stone* (1947) and *Catherine Carter* (1952). Her talent for light SATIRE of literary life is best revealed in the 'Dorothy Merlin' trilogy: *The Unspeakable Skipton* (1959), *Night and Silence, Who is Here* (1962), and *Cork Street, Next to the Hatter's* (1965). Later titles include *The Honours Board* (1970), about the close relationships between the staff at a traditional English public school, *The Good Listener* (1975) and *The Good Husband* (1978). Her non-fictional works include critical studies of IVY COMPTON-BURNETT, Proust and THOMAS WOLFE, and *On Iniquity* (1967), a book about the Moors Murders based on her experiences as a reporter at the trial. She wrote one play, *Corinth House* (1948).

Johnson, Samuel 1709–84 Critic, scholar, lexicographer, poet and man of letters. Born the son of a bookseller in Lichfield, Johnson was throughout his life prone to ill health. At the age of three he was taken to London to be 'touched' for scrofula. He entered Pembroke College, Oxford, in October 1728 as an impoverished commoner and is said to have been hounded for his threadbare appearance. He left after only 14 months without taking a degree. He was awarded an MA in 1755 and an honorary doctorate of civil law in 1775, though Oxford was anticipated by Trinity College, Dublin, in entitling him to the 'Dr' by which the world came to know him but he himself rarely used.

Whilst an undergraduate he prepared a Latin version of *Messiah*, a collection of prayers and hymns by ALEXANDER POPE, published in 1731. His father's death in that year left the family in penury. Johnson taught at the grammar school in Market Bosworth during 1732, and then lived for three years in Birmingham, his first essays appearing in the *Birmingham Journal*. There he completed *A Voyage to Abyssinia* (1735), a translation from the French version of the travels of Father Jerome Lobo, a Portuguese missionary. In 1735 he married Mrs Elizabeth Porter ('Tetty'), a widow 20 years his senior; the couple harboured an enduring affection for each other. They started a school at Edial, near Lichfield, but the project was unsuccessful, so they moved down to London

Samuel Johnson and James Boswell (recovering from a hangover) in Scotland, as depicted by Thomas Rowlandson in *The Picturesque Beauties of Boswell*, 1786

in 1737, accompanied by one of their former pupils, DAVID GARRICK. Johnson began earning a steady living in the employ of Edward Cave, who had founded *THE GENTLEMAN'S MAGAZINE* in 1731. To this he contributed copious and varied work: essays, Latin verses, biographies and political commentaries on parliamentary proceedings. In 1738 he published his poem *LONDON*, a Juvenalian IMITATION approved by Pope.

The death in 1743 of his erstwhile friend, the poet RICHARD SAVAGE, prompted the first of Johnson's biographical pieces, published in 1744. The publisher ROBERT DODSLEY then persuaded him to address to the EARL OF CHESTERFIELD his *Plan of a Dictionary of the English Language* in 1747; little help was forthcoming but for the next eight years Johnson laboured intermittently with the project. In 1749 he published *THE VANITY OF HUMAN WISHES*, his longest and most enduring poem, and his loyal friend Garrick kept his promise by staging Johnson's indifferent, moralistic tragedy *Irene*, completed 12 years previously. The production at DRURY LANE earned its author a welcome £300. In 1750 Johnson undertook another enterprise for Cave, *THE RAMBLER*, a twice-weekly periodical of moral essays and commentaries. It ran until 1752, with Johnson writing, anonymously, all but four of its 208 numbers himself. His grief at the death of his wife Tetty in this year became an additional factor in provoking the bouts of depression from which Johnson suffered throughout his life.

A DICTIONARY OF THE ENGLISH LANGUAGE, his most substantial scholarly achievement and still a milestone in English lexicography, finally appeared in 1755. It was greeted with acclaim and belated endorsement from Chesterfield, whom Johnson rebuffed in terms echoing the definition of 'patron' in the *Dictionary* itself: 'Commonly a wretch who supports with insolence, and is paid with flattery'. He was still struggling to earn his bread, having to pen numerous political articles, reviews and essays for various periodicals, including the *Universal Visitor* and the *Literary Magazine*. He wrote lives of SIR THOMAS BROWNE (1756) and ROGER ASCHAM (1761), and from 1758 to 1760 contributed *THE IDLER* series of papers to the *Universal Chronicle*. A philosophical romance, *The Prince of Abyssinia: A Tale*, later known as *RASSELAS*, appeared shortly after his mother's death in 1759.

At the behest of Lord Bute, the new monarch George III awarded Johnson in 1762 an annual pension of £300, which somewhat relaxed his straitened circumstances. On 16 May the following year he first met the young Scot JAMES BOSWELL, who was later to become his biographer. In 1764 – along with JOSHUA REYNOLDS, the painter – Johnson founded 'the Club', an artistic coterie whose meetings at the Turk's Head in Gerrard Street, London, were attended by BURKE, GOLDSMITH, Garrick, Boswell and Charles James Fox. In this year he made the acquaintance of Henry

Thrale, a prosperous and cultured brewer, and his wife Hester, who offered generous hospitality during a period when depression continued to hover over him. After considerable delay, his eight-volume edition of SHAKESPEARE appeared in 1765; subsequent scholarship may have superseded most of the editorial work, but Johnson's *Preface* remains a model of critical good sense.

By now a deservedly famous literary figure whose opinions on a variety of subjects were eagerly noted in metropolitan circles, Johnson finally agreed to Boswell's proposal that they tour Scotland together. Johnson's observations appeared as *A JOURNEY TO THE WESTERN ISLANDS OF SCOTLAND* (1775), his friend's as *THE JOURNAL OF A TOUR TO THE HEBRIDES* (1785). At the suggestion of a number of London booksellers, Johnson began work in the spring of 1777 on a series of 'little prefaces' for a planned edition of the works of certain English poets, and these penetrating biographical essays were published separately in 1781 as *THE LIVES OF THE POETS*, 52 compelling studies which show him both informed and opinionated as a literary critic. Henry Thrale died in 1781 and Hester sold off the brewery; Johnson's outrage at her subsequent marriage to Gabriele Piozzi, a music teacher, completed their sad estrangement. He spent the summer of 1784 touring England, visiting Lichfield, Birmingham and Oxford, and returning to London in mid-November, dropsical and depressed. He died during the night of 13 December and is buried in Westminster Abbey.

He was also the author of: an introduction to the *Harleian Miscellany* (1744; see HARLEY LYRICS); *Miscellaneous Observations on the Tragedy of Macbeth* (1745); several prologues, the most notable being for Garrick on his management of Drury Lane, and the indignant prologue to *COMUS*. His political writings include various tracts – *The False Alarm* (1770), *Thoughts... respecting Falkland's Islands* (1771), *The Patriot* (1774), *Taxation no Tyranny* (1775) – and *Considerations on the Corn Laws* (1776), a parliamentary speech for General Hamilton. In addition to hymns, prayers and sermons, Johnson wrote English and Latin poems throughout his life, ranging from the stately to the personal, including excellent imitations from the classics. Though his verse lacks the verbal agility of Pope (to whom he is frequently compared), several memorable poems perhaps reveal more about his charitable, even passionate, nature than the public mode of his more familiar prose; 'Old Age' and 'On the Death of Dr Robert Levet' have a particular place in the line of 18th-century verse.

Johnson's reputation as the greatest man of letters England has produced was assisted by Boswell's *LIFE OF SAMUEL JOHNSON LL.D.* (1791), which fused its subject's personality with his writings and raised him to legendary status. A pioneering scholar, famous conversationalist in an age when conversation was considered a minor art form, and eloquent sage, Johnson is sometimes wrongly considered a reactionary embodying the High Tory principles of the dwindling AUGUSTAN AGE. Though famous in later life, he kept both his humility and his scepticism, and never forgot the real hardships of his early years as a struggling hack. He was not a philosopher who discovered an original system of thought, but his wisdom shaped a stern and practical critique of both human behaviour and literature. Pathologically lazy himself, he chastised idleness in others; fearful of insanity, he was fascinated by irrationality in others. He applauded originality, clarity, honesty and the perception of general truths, demonstrating these values in his life as well as his writings.

Boswell's biography is the main, but not the only, source of detail; Mrs Piozzi's *Anecdotes* (1786), for example, also contains informative insights. The *Correspondence* was edited by R. W. Chapman in 1952.

Johnston, Sir Charles (Hepburn) 1912– 86 Poet and translator. Educated at Winchester and Balliol College, Oxford, Johnston entered the diplomatic service in 1936, serving in Tokyo (where he was interned when Japan entered the war), Cairo, Madrid, Bonn, Amman and Aden, before becoming British High Commissioner in Australia (1965–71). Although he had already published two volumes of verse, *Towards Mozambique* (1947) and *Estuary in Scotland* (1974), his first major success was his translation of Pushkin's *Eugene Onegin* (1977). This was followed by annual privately printed volumes, *Poems and Journeys* (1979), *Rivers and Fireworks* (1980), *Talk about the Last Poet* (1981), *Choiseul and Talleyrand* (1982) and *The Irish Lights* (1983), which mixed new and old poems with translations from Latin and Russian, especially Pushkin and Lermontov. His wide range includes EPIGRAMS, autobiographical poems, DRAMATIC MONOLOGUES and narrative verse.

Johnston, (William) Denis 1901–84 Irish playwright. He was born in Dublin and educated at Cambridge and Harvard, where he trained for the law. Associated with both the ABBEY THEATRE and the Gate Theatre in Dublin from 1927 to 1936, Johnston had his first play, an expressionistic satire called *The Old Lady Says 'No!'* (1929), produced at the Gate. *The Moon in the Yellow River* (1931), his most popular play, is a powerful portrait of political and moral divisions in post-Civil War Ireland. Together with *The Scythe and the Sunset* (1958), a play about the Easter Rising written in conscious recollection of O'CASEY's THE PLOUGH AND THE STARS, it showed Johnston's ability to write realistic drama that is easy of access. More experimental plays, like *A Bride for the Unicorn* (1933), *Storm Song* (1934) and *The Golden Cuckoo* (1938), troubled critics and public. Johnston wrote both a play about SWIFT, *The Dreaming Dust* (1940), and a contentious study in

critical biography, *In Search of Swift* (1959). *Nine Rivers from Jordan* (1953) is an impressionistic account of his wartime experiences. *The Brazen Horn* (1977) proposes a personal mystical philosophy.

Johnston, George (Henry) 1912–70 Australian novelist. He was born in Melbourne and educated at Caulfield State School, Brighton Technical College and the National Gallery Arts School in his home city. He was a journalist who in 1942 became a war correspondent in New Guinea, Italy, Burma and China. He drew from this period of his life in many of his writings. He later lived for 10 years on the Greek island of Hydra, where he wrote his most famous work and also achieved success as a thriller writer under the pseudonym of Shane Martin. Although he is the author under his own name of several other works of fiction, among them *The Darkness Outside* (1959) and *The Far Face of the Moon* (1964), his fame rests today on a trilogy of self-examining novels: *My Brother Jack* (1964), *Clean Straw for Nothing* (1969) and *A Cartload of Clay* (1971). The first two books in the trilogy both won the Miles Franklin Award; the third was incomplete at his death. Together they brilliantly present aspects of 20th-century Australian life, depicting archetypal qualities in the Australian male character.

Johnston, Jennifer 1930– Irish novelist. She was born in Dublin, the daughter of DENIS JOHNSTON and the actress Shelagh Richards, and educated at Park House School and Trinity College, Dublin. She lives in Northern Ireland, near Derry. Her best work – *The Captains and the Kings* (1972), *How Many Miles to Babylon?* (1974) and *The Invisible Worm* (1991) – continues the tradition of the Irish 'Big House' novel, centring on the decay of the Protestant gentry and their embattled position in modern Ireland. The less successful *Shadows on Our Skin* (1977) and *Fool's Sanctuary* (1987) move beyond her customary range to depict the pressure of divided loyalties on families caught up in the Northern Irish troubles.

Johnstone, Charles c. 1719–1800 Journalist and satirist. Born in Ireland and educated at Trinity College, Dublin, Johnstone practised as a lawyer before going to Calcutta in 1782, where he became a journalist and newspaper proprietor. He was the author of *Chrysal: or, The Adventures of a Guinea* (1760–5), satirical episodes from the life of the times, told by a guinea as it is passed from hand to hand. Most notable are the scenes at the Hellfire Club and the successful manoeuvres of an ambitious wife on behalf of her clergyman husband.

Jolley, Elizabeth 1923– Australian novelist, short-story writer and radio playwright. Born in Birmingham to an English father and a Viennese mother who was the daughter of an Austrian general, she was brought up in a German-speaking household and educated at a Quaker boarding-school. During World War II she worked as a nurse. In 1959 she migrated to Western Australia and regards herself as a writer from this region. In 1974 she began attending classes at Fremantle Arts Centre, whose highly successful small press subsequently published her fiction. Though she has been writing since childhood, her habit of tinkering with several projects simultaneously for a number of years has resulted in an apparently late start followed by a rush of publications which belies the concentrated care bestowed on her work. She was first recognized for radio plays such as *Night Report* (1975), *The Performance* (1976), *The Shepherd on the Roof* (1977) and the award-winning *Two Men Running* (1982). Her next success came with the short stories in *Five Acre Virgin* (1976), *The Travelling Entertainer* (1979) and *Woman in a Lampshade* (1983). The first two volumes were combined in *Stories* (1984). A lesbian novel, *Palomino* (1980), was followed by *The Newspaper of Claremont Street* (1981) and *Mr Scobie's Riddle* (1983), bleakly comic investigations of old age. *Miss Peabody's Inheritance* (1983) and *Foxybaby* (1985) both feature women novelists; the play between different kinds of textual reality in the latter makes it a classic of post-modernism. Play with reality and illusion in *The Well* (1986) was followed by oddball social realism in *The Sugar Mother* (1988), a novel about surrogacy. *My Father's Moon* (1989) and *Cabin Fever* (1990) belatedly turn to autobiographical sources. *Central Mischief* (1992) is a collection of essays.

Jolly Beggars, The A verse cantata by ROBERT BURNS, first published in a Glasgow chapbook in 1799. An assortment of wretched folk are described enjoying themselves singing and drinking an evening away, despite the low quality of their daily lives. Each character sings a song in turn, and these are linked by descriptions of the singer, so evocative and precise that it is thought Burns was prompted to write the poem by a visit he paid to Poosie Nansie's tavern in Mauchline.

Jonathan Wild the Great, The Life of A novel by HENRY FIELDING, published in 1743 as part of his *Miscellanies*. It gives a fictionalized version of the life of the infamous criminal executed in 1725, ironically presenting him as an example of heroism and greatness. Wild's success in the underworld is offered as a parallel to the values at work in polite society and government, where, Fielding implies, greatness and influence are sanctioned irrespective of motive or morals. Sir Robert Walpole is the chief target for this aspect of the SATIRE.

Wild is baptized by Titus Oates, and shows an early propensity for underhand behaviour; he goes to work for Snap, warden of a sponginghouse (where arrested debtors were detained before being imprisoned) and is tutored in the arts of extortion and exploitation. He becomes chief of a gang of thieves, taking the lion's share of the profits and safeguarding himself by turning over to the law any subordinates who question his leadership. He marries Laetitia Snap, his former employer's amusingly hypocritical daughter, and concentrates on ruining his virtuous former schoolfellow, the jeweller Heartfree. Wild robs him and then gets him imprisoned for bankruptcy; he tricks Mrs Heartfree into fleeing the country and accuses her innocent husband of having murdered her. The jeweller is rescued from the scaffold by the exposure of Wild, who is hanged in his stead, a 'hero' and 'great man' to the last.

Jones, (Walter) David (Michael) 1895–1974 Poet and artist. Born of a Welsh father in Brockley, Kent, he studied at Camberwell Art School in 1909–14, joined the Royal Welsh Fusiliers and served as a private on the Western Front in 1915–18. He was profoundly affected by the war landscape, describing it as 'a place of enchantment'. In 1919 he studied at Westminster Art School, and was received into the Roman Catholic church in 1921. In the same year he began to learn carpentry and engraving under Eric Gill at Ditchling, Sussex, and lived with Gill's family in Capel-y-Ffin, South Wales, during 1925. He joined the Society of Wood Engravers in 1927, producing illustrations for a number of private presses. Following a breakdown in 1933, he visited Jerusalem and Cairo, landscapes which became crucial to his work. *In Parenthesis* (1937) was followed by *The Anathemata* (1952), *The Sleeping Lord and Other Fragments* (1974), *The Kensington Mass* (1975) and *The Roman Quarry and Other Sequences* (1981). *Epoch and Artist* (1959) and *The Dying Gaul* (1978) are collections of essays and articles.

Combining prose, verse, illustration and lettering, Jones's work makes highly allusive and associative use of a variety of sources of ritual and romance. A central theme is the need to connect a consciousness of the remote and recent past with the post-war world, and to re-establish traditional meanings and symbols. *In Parenthesis* relates the war experience of Private John Ball to chivalric antecedents, and the modern waste land to MALORY's *MORTE DARTHUR*. It avoids the 'wholesale slaughter' of the later war years. *The Anathemata*, divided into eight sections, is a much wider chronicle of the 'Western Christian *res*' and was much admired by W. H. AUDEN, KATHLEEN RAINE and EDWIN MUIR. It has an important preface which explores succinctly the problems of the 'sign maker' in the modern world. The later works are complete fragments relating to the Crucifixion.

Jones, Diana Wynne 1934– Writer of CHILDREN'S LITERATURE. She started writing for children at the age of 39. Her particular strength lies in her capacity to integrate magic with the normal realities of late 20th-century existence. In *The Ogre Downstairs* (1974) the magic derives from a pair of chemistry sets given by a desperate stepfather to the warring children of his second marriage. In *Power of Three* (1977) two children find themselves cast as giant and witch by a race of Little People threatened with drowning by a new reservoir. Although *Charmed Life* (1977) and its sequels take place in a completely magical world, the child characters still have to solve their own essentially human problems for themselves.

Jones, Henry Arthur 1851–1929 Playwright. Jones was born at Grandborough in Buckinghamshire, the eldest son of a farmer. He began work at the age of 12 in drapers' shops; he then worked in a London warehouse and as a commercial traveller, using his leisure to extend his reading and further his education. He wrote a novel and some one-act plays, none of which were accepted; he eventually achieved a modest success with a domestic drama, *It's Only round the Corner*, performed at the Theatre Royal, Exeter, in 1878, and later in London as *Harmony* (1884).

Jones made the drama his profession after 1878, and 45 full-length plays by him were staged in London and New York between 1878 and 1917. *A Clerical Error* (1879) was produced by Wilson Barrett, for whom Jones and Henry Herman devised a spectacular MELO-DRAMA called *THE SILVER KING* (1882). This was one of Barrett's most successful parts and the long run established Jones's reputation. He then turned to more serious theatre; he was interested in the drama of ideas and the drama as a vehicle for social criticism. With Herman he adapted Ibsen's *A Doll's House* as *Breaking a Butterfly* (1884) and in his own work displayed a talent for naturalistic dialogue and portrayal of character. However, it is now generally agreed that his drama lacked the firm philosophical basis that would have given his social and moral criticism a permanent place in the English theatre. His most notable plays were *Saints and Sinners* (1884), *The Dancing Girl* (1891), *The Case of Rebellious Susan* (1894) and *The Triumph of the Philistines* (1895). *Michael and His Lost Angel* (1896) was severely criticized because one of the central scenes contained a public confession of adultery by a priest. The star, Mrs Patrick Campbell, left the cast during rehearsals and the play was taken off after 10 performances. But Jones went on to further success with *THE LIARS* (1897) and *Mrs Dane's Defence* (1900). The last two plays are occasionally revived.

Jones, James 1921–77 American novelist. Born in Robinson, Illinois, he served in the US Army in the Pacific from 1939 to 1944. *From Here to Eternity* (1951), his first and best-known novel, is a realistic story of army life in Hawaii on the eve of the attack on Pearl Harbor; it won him the National Book Award and became a best-seller. His career continued with *Some Came Running* (1957), *The Pistol* (1959), *The Thin Red Line* (1962), *Go to the Widow-Maker* (1967) and *A Touch of Danger* (1973). His short stories are collected in *The Ice Cream Headache* (1968) and *The Merry Month of May* (1971). *Viet Journal* (1974) describes a visit to Vietnam.

Jones, LeRoi See BARAKA, AMIRI.

Jones, Sir William 1746–94 Jurist and orientalist. Educated at Harrow School and University College, Oxford, Jones was judge of the High Court at Calcutta from 1783 until his death. He published several books on law and oriental languages but is best remembered for his mastery of Sanskrit and his insistence, in his essay in *Asiatic Researches* (1786), on its study as the common source of Greek and Latin. Jones's work, together with JOHN HORNE TOOKE's advocacy of the study of Gothic and Anglo-Saxon (published in the same year), brought the science of comparative philology into being.

Jonson, Ben(jamin) 1572–1637 Playwright and poet. Probably born in Westminster and educated at Westminster School, Jonson may have worked with his stepfather, a master bricklayer. He is identified as an actor and playwright in 1597 by references in the papers of PHILIP HENSLOWE. Before that he had probably served as a soldier in Flanders, was certainly married and had fathered the first of several children. If as seems likely, he was one of the actors imprisoned after the performance of *The Isle of Dogs* in 1597, he had good reason to tread warily. The fact that he never did so is evidence of an unusually combative temperament. The following year he killed a fellow actor, Gabriel Spencer, in a duel but had the wit to escape execution by pleading benefit of clergy. The reputation for fearless speaking of his mind has clung to him ever since.

The presentation of his second known play, *EVERY MAN IN HIS HUMOUR*, in 1598 turned Jonson into a celebrity and created a brief fashion for 'humours' comedy. He followed it, less successfully, with *EVERY MAN OUT OF HIS HUMOUR* (1599) and *CYNTHIA'S REVELS* (1600), satirical comedies which displayed Jonson's classical scholarship and his delight in formal experiment. His quickness to take offence and a stubborn belief in his own superior talent made him a leading participant in the war of the theatres, in which MARSTON and DEKKER were his chief adversaries and to which *THE POETASTER* (1601) was his unattractive major contribution. His decision to portray himself in that play as Horace is indicative of his early admiration for the poet whose *Art of Poetry* he translated. (The translation was published posthumously in the revised *Works* of 1640.)

Jonson's next play, SEJANUS, HIS FALL (1603), brought further trouble. He was summoned before the Privy Council to answer charges of 'popery and treason'. He had converted to Roman Catholicism in 1598, and it has to be admitted that a play by a Catholic detailing conspiracy and assassination at court was a supremely tactless contribution to the first winter season of the KING'S MEN under their new patron, JAMES I. Like his later Roman tragedy, CATILINE HIS CONSPIRACY (1611), Sejanus is too ponderous to stand comparison with SHAKESPEARE'S Roman plays. Together with his contributions to EASTWARD HO (1604), for which he was once again briefly imprisoned, it put in jeopardy his emerging role as court poet and MASQUE writer to James I. The Masque of Blackness (1605) was the first of many collaborations with Inigo Jones, a collaboration threatened and finally destroyed by rivalry. Jonson's status as a writer of masques remains almost as secure as his status as a writer of comedies.

The plays on which his enduring reputation rests are all comedies and all written between 1605 and 1614. They are VOLPONE (1605), EPICOENE: OR, THE SILENT WOMAN (1609), THE ALCHEMIST (1610) and BARTHOLOMEW FAIR (1614). It is here that Jonson's stagecraft is at its most ingenious. The incidents and episodes are artfully controlled and yet preserve an air of improvisatory spontaneity. The characters, though strictly defined by their names, seem willing to command the freedom of the stage. The cutting edge of Jonson's comedies is sharp. They are peopled with deceivers and dupes, leaving the virtuous and intelligent an unusually small part to play. The 'image of the times', promised in the Prologue to the revised Every Man in His Humour (1616), is an uncomfortable one. It is an age of usury, in which human folly gives living room to moral outrage. Pug, a junior devil permitted a day of malpractice on earth in THE DEVIL IS AN ASS (1616), finds himself out of his depth among humans more devious than he.

The comparative failure of The Devil is an Ass may have discouraged Jonson. It was nine years before his next comedy, The Staple of News (1625), was staged and his effective dramatic output was completed by The New Inn (1629) and A Tale of a Tub (1633). But Jonson was never inactive. His vivid sense of his own stature is represented by the unprecedented publication, in folio, of his dramatic and poetic Works (1616) and by his continuing provision of masques at court. He was rewarded with a royal pension and appointment as POET LAUREATE. The songs and poems in the masques, together with the collected verse of EPIGRAMS and THE FOREST (both 1616) and UNDERWOODS (1640), explain his contemporary influence among younger poets, the self-styled 'tribe' or 'sons' of Ben. His prose style, founded like his poems on classical precedent, is memorably sketched in the published notes of WILLIAM DRUMMOND OF HAW-THORNDEN (1632), which record conversations held during Jonson's visit to Scotland in 1618–19, and in the posthumously published TIMBER (1640).

Jonson's profound knowledge of London life was aptly rewarded by his appointment as City Chronologer in 1628, the year in which he suffered a severe stroke. Many of the friends who remained loyal to him in his last years attended his funeral in 1637 in Westminster Abbey and contributed to the collection of memorial elegies, Jonsonus virbius (1638). One of them, the forgotten Jack Young, inscribed the words 'O rare Ben Jonson' on his gravestone.

Jorrocks's Jaunts and Jollities A collection of 10 stories by R. S. SURTEES, drawn from the pages of the New Sporting Magazine and published in book form, with illustrations by HABLOT K. BROWNE, in 1838. Other editions, illustrated by Henry Alken, appeared in 1843 and 1869, the latter including three extra episodes. Full of humour and crude life, the stories describe the adventures of John Jorrocks, a sporting London grocer, in the hunting field as well as racing, shooting, fishing, eating, drinking and driving. There is a fantastic jaunt to France. Besides Jorrocks, we meet his marvellously vulgar wife, his young Yorkshire friend Charlie Stubbs (modelled on Surtees himself) and his scapegrace servant Binjimin. Surtees's friend and rival C. J. APPERLEY is lampooned, as he is in HANDLEY CROSS (1843) which, with HILLINGDON HALL (1845), continues Jorrocks's adventures.

Joseph Andrews (The History of the Adventures of Joseph Andrews, and of his Friend Mr Abraham Adams. Written in Imitation of Cervantes, Author of Don Quixote) A novel by HENRY FIELDING, first published in 1742.

Joseph is the brother of Pamela Andrews, the heroine of RICHARDSON's PAMELA. He works as a footman in the London household of Lady Booby, a lascivious lady who (along with her unprepossessing companion Mrs Slipslop) has designs upon his chastity. Joseph resists these enticements and resolves to take to the road and return to his sweetheart, Fanny. He is accompanied by Parson Adams, a comically absent-minded and gullible curate from the vicinity of Sir Thomas Booby's country seat, who is intent on getting his sermons published. The pair suffer a long series of near-scrapes, embarrassments and exploitation. Life on the road brings them into contact with a rich cast of hypocritical and dishonest figures: clergy, squirearchy and criminals alike. True to comic convention, the main characters all converge for a final show-down at the Boobys' country seat, through a series of humorous coincidences. Squire Booby has meanwhile married Pamela (Joseph's sister) and the novel ends by revealing that Joseph is in fact the son of a respectable couple, and not Pamela's brother.

Joseph Andrews is often considered the author's happiest work. Initially a lampoon on Richardson's over-virtuous characters, it rapidly develops an original shape of its own, and extends the range of the novel form by its refusal to depend on exclusive and extensive identification with the sensibility of any central character. Fielding widens the social forms of the novel, setting his characters at large in the 'theatre of the road', the action of the novel more public and more dramatic than ever before. In his 'Preface to the Reader', the author claims to be 'the founder of a new province of writing', but the achievement is in large part a synthesis, a timely conflation of earlier forms of literary narrative with contemporary realism and a trenchant eye for telling detail. Such influences include the classical EPIC (and its MOCK-HEROIC application), the biblical epic (which echoes through the moralistic themes of the book), the questing features of medieval romances (also reflected in the names of certain characters) and, perhaps most importantly, the influence of the PICARESQUE tradition of Cervantes and Lesage. Despite this interweaving, the novel is an early masterpiece of the genre – comic in its characterization, yet seriously enquiring in its vignettes of contemporary behaviour.

Joshi, Arun 1939– Indian novelist and short-story writer. He has never established a major reputation outside India but within the country his English-language fiction is regarded as both humane and modestly innovative. *The Foreigner* (1968) and *The Strange Case of Billy Biswas* (1971), early novels combining the cosmopolitan and the local, are still his most widely read. Later novels include *The Apprentice* (1974), *The Last Labyrinth* (1981) and *The City and the River* (1990), in which, characteristically, private themes predominate over public ones.

Journal of a Tour to the Hebrides with Samuel Johnson, The A narrative by JAMES BOSWELL, published in 1785, describing the journey he had undertaken with his friend in 1773. In *A JOURNEY TO THE WESTERN ISLANDS OF SCOTLAND* JOHNSON himself gave a formal account of their itinerary, using its main stages as an opportunity to reflect on life and manners. Boswell, by contrast, writes informally about the discomforts, hazards and passing incidents of the journey, and concentrates in particular on bringing the character of his travelling companion vividly to life. The original manuscript, which was seen by Johnson and prepared for publication by Boswell with the help of EDMOND MALONE, was edited by Frederick A. Pottle and C.H. Bennett and published in 1936. This edition restored a previously unpublished third of Boswell's original.

Journal of a Voyage to Lisbon, The See FIELDING, HENRY.

Journal of the Plague Year, A An imaginatively reworked account, part fact and part fiction, of the Great Plague in 1664–5, written by DANIEL DEFOE and published in 1722. It was prompted by a recent outbreak of plague in Marseilles and partly intended as a warning for the future. The narrator is 'H.F.', a Whitechapel saddler who remains in London throughout the epidemic and provides a graphic commentary on its rise, the public reaction, the precautions taken by the authorities and the drastically changing atmosphere in the capital as it becomes depopulated.

For this, his most realistic and evocative work, Defoe probably had to invent relatively little; he skilfully weaves together plague bills of mortality, statistics, historical accounts, anecdotes and hearsay. The narrative is full of highly concentrated effects and vignettes of behaviour described with Defoe's finest colloquial energy. The result is both a study in human isolation and a life-affirming work that examines a city under threat. SIR WALTER SCOTT wrote in 1834: 'Had he not been the author of *ROBINSON CRUSOE*, De Foe would have deserved immortality for the genius he has displayed in this work.'

Journal to Stella A collection of private letters sent by JONATHAN SWIFT from London between September 1710 and June 1713 to his close friend Esther Johnson (later nicknamed Stella) and her companion Rebecca Dingley in Dublin. He was in London on an official commission to plead a case for the Irish clergy, and his letters give an intriguing inside view of the teeming metropolitan world of political intrigue, party wrangling, gossip and literary chitchat. Already a man of some reputation, Swift had many powerful acquaintances, but gradually he becomes anxious and disillusioned, longing for the quieter and more civilized company in Ireland, as his health deteriorates and his affections become complicated. The letters are written partly in a teasing form of baby-talk (the 'little language') which shows the formidable satirist's softer side. Though they were not designed for publication, a selection appeared in 1766 and an edition was prepared by his cousin, Deane Swift, in 1768.

Journey to the Western Islands of Scotland, A SAMUEL JOHNSON's description, published in 1775, of the three-month tour he made with JAMES BOSWELL in 1773.

After welcoming him at Edinburgh, Boswell took his friend north to St Andrews and Aberdeen, where Johnson was given the freedom of the city. They paid a visit to Lord Monboddo, an eccentric law lord, and then travelled west to Inverness. From here they went on horseback to Glenelg and took a boat to Skye, where they visited Flora MacDonald. They set out for Mull but a storm drove them to the island of Coll, where they were obliged to stay for two weeks. After Mull, their journey took them to Iona and thence to Oban. At Inverary they were guests of the Duke of Argyll, who provided them with good horses and made their journey much easier. At Glasgow University the faculty entertained Johnson, and at the family seat Boswell's father, Lord Auchinleck, clashed with his famous guest. (Boswell later declined to record the details of the quarrel.) Johnson left for London from Edinburgh.

Where Boswell's account, *THE JOURNAL OF A TOUR TO THE HEBRIDES WITH SAMUEL JOHNSON*, is casual and anecdotal, Johnson offers a formal survey. He went to Scotland not to see 'fine places, of which there were enough in England; but wild objects, – mountains, – peculiar manners; in short, things which he had not seen before'. His interest lay in exploring the variety and extent of nature, particularly of human nature. His aim was to record local differences in a scientific spirit and universal truths in a philosophical one. Apart from being more sympathetic to Scotland than the popular legend of Johnson's opinions on the subject would admit, the book is one of the finest achievements of 18th-century travel literature.

Journey's End A play by R. C. SHERRIFF, first performed in London in 1928. Perhaps the best-known play about World War I, set in a dugout in the British trenches in 1918, it is a powerful study of bravery and cowardice under fire. The part of Stanhope, a brave man broken by battle fatigue and threatened by hero-worship from Raleigh, a new arrival who had been a junior at the public school of which Stanhope had been a star pupil, was created by the then unknown Laurence Olivier.

Jowett, Benjamin 1817–93 Scholar and divine. Educated at St Paul's School and Balliol College, Oxford, Jowett became a fellow of his college in 1838, Regius Professor of Greek in 1855 and Master of Balliol in 1870. He taught WALTER PATER and GERARD MANLEY HOPKINS, and showed a sympathetic interest in the wayward undergraduate career of SWINBURNE.

The influence of Greek studies and his interest in German philosophy made Jowett a theological liberal, and his *Epistles of Paul to the Thessalonians, Galatians and Romans* (1835; revised 1855 and 1859) was notable for its fresh and original approach. 'The Interpretation of Scripture', Jowett's contribution to *ESSAYS AND REVIEWS* (1860), caused angry debate and cast grave suspicion on his orthodoxy. In the field of classical studies his translation of Plato (1871) became a standard work; his Thucydides followed in 1881 and the *Politics* of Aristotle in 1885.

Joyce, James (Augustine Aloysius) 1882–1941 Irish novelist, short-story writer, poet and playwright. Born in Dublin, he was educated at two Jesuit schools,

Clongowes Wood College in Kildare and Belvedere College in Dublin, which left a lasting mark on his sensibility even after he had abandoned youthful thoughts of becoming a priest and decided instead to study modern languages at University College, Dublin. While an undergraduate he cultivated the acquaintance of YEATS, SYNGE, LADY GREGORY and GEORGE WILLIAM RUSSELL (A. E.) and others fostering the Irish cultural renaissance but, eager to escape his depressed family circumstances and dissatisfied with the narrowness of Irish cultural life, he went to Paris after graduating in 1902. His mother's terminal illness obliged him to return to Dublin the following year. During this visit he met Nora Barnacle, who became his permanent companion (they finally married in 1931) in a life of exile, wandering and poverty dictated by his unwavering dedication to his art. They left Ireland together in 1904 and eventually settled in Trieste, where he taught English at the Berlitz School and made friends with the novelist Italo Svevo. He moved to Zurich during World War I and to Paris in 1920. During the 1930s he was increasingly beset by family worries – his daughter Lucia was diagnosed schizophrenic in 1932 – and by health problems, chiefly his deteriorating eyesight. The outbreak of World War II forced him to return to Zurich, where he died after an operation on a duodenal ulcer.

Apprentice work included an essay on 'Ibsen's New Drama', published by the *THE FORTNIGHTLY REVIEW* while he was still an undergraduate in 1900, and a volume of poetry, *Chamber Music* (1907). His first significant work was *DUBLINERS* (1914), a collection of scrupulously naturalistic short stories, whose very title announced a central if paradoxical feature of Joyce's mature work: for all his Continental wanderings and cosmopolitan sensibility, the subject of his art would always remain the city he had resolutely left behind him. The objections by the original publishers which transferred its place of publication from Dublin to London also anticipated his lifelong problems with censorship. *A PORTRAIT OF THE ARTIST AS A YOUNG MAN*, begun as *Stephen Hero* in 1904, was serialized in *THE EGOIST* from February 1914 to September 1915 and published in volume form in 1916. An autobiographical novel which follows his own life from infancy until his first departure for Paris, it used the technique of STREAM OF CONSCIOUSNESS which he had first encountered in Edouard Dujardin's novel *Les Lauriers sont coupés* (1888). Joyce's connection with EZRA POUND, the dominating influence on *The Egoist*, and with Harriet Shaw Weaver, its editor, gave him valuable sustenance in future years.

Joyce subsequently wrote an unsuccessful play, *Exiles* (published in 1918; performed in Munich in 1919), and a slight volume of verses, *Pomes Penyeach* (1927), but these were mere asides during the creation of the two great works which occupied his remaining

James Joyce in Zurich

life. *ULYSSES*, begun in 1914 and finished in 1921, used the character of Stephen Dedalus and the technique of stream of consciousness from the *Portrait*, while subduing both to a more radically ambitious purpose: nothing less than to recreate a day in the life of Dublin in painstaking detail while also locating it in the widest possible context of history and myth. The novel was serialized in *THE LITTLE REVIEW* from April 1918 until December 1920, when a prosecution for obscenity cut short its progress, and was first published in volume form in Paris by Harriet Shaw Weaver's Egoist Press on 2 February 1922, his 40th birthday. It was banned in the USA until 1933 and in Britain until 1937. *FINNEGANS WAKE*, begun in 1923, was serialized in 12 parts as *Work in Progress* between 1928 and 1937 and published complete in 1939.

Its radical experimentalism which dissolves narrative into dream and the English language into polyglot puns has given it an exaggerated reputation for inaccessibility, yet it takes its place with *Ulysses*, not just as a central text of MODERNISM, but as a work which can outlive fluctuating critical judgements of modernism. Both novels remain a living challenge to scholars, critics, readers and writers.

Jude the Obscure A novel by THOMAS HARDY, published in its complete form in October 1895. An abridged version appeared in *HARPER'S NEW MONTHLY MAGAZINE* from December 1894 to November 1895.

Jude Fawley, a stonemason with a talent and passion for scholarship, is trapped into marriage by Arabella Donn. It is only after Arabella deserts him that Jude, resurrecting his old love of learning, makes his way to Christminster (Oxford), where he earns his living as a labourer while aspiring to be a student. He meets and is attracted to his intelligent, unstable cousin Sue Bridehead. She marries Phillotson, Jude's former schoolmaster, but, finding the sexual aspects of her marriage repellent, flees her husband and lives with Jude. Two children are born to them and they also take care of Jude's son by Arabella, the uncannily adult 'Father Time'. As social outcasts living in abject poverty, they are bitterly unhappy: she retreats into morbid Christianity and he moves towards atheism. When Sue tells 'Father Time' that she is expecting another baby he kills the two children and himself, 'because we are too menny'. In a misguided attempt at expiation Sue returns to Phillotson. Jude declines, resentfully cared for by Arabella, and eventually dies alone, neglected both by her and the city of learning which had once epitomized the scope of his ambition.

Many contemporary readers and reviewers were outraged by the pessimism of the novel and its depiction of the 'deadly war waged between flesh and spirit'. Hardy wrote no more fiction afterwards.

Judith An Old English poem preserved in the same manuscript as *BEOWULF*. It is incomplete, but it is not certain how much has been lost; the surviving fragment is 350 lines long. The poem, based on the biblical story, describes Judith's execution of Holofernes, her flight and the Hebrew defeat of the Assyrians. It does not follow its source closely but adapts it into a compelling narrative, most notably in the description of the battle.

Julian and Maddalo: *A Conversation* A poem by PERCY BYSSHE SHELLEY, written during his visit to Venice in 1818 but not published until 1824. The conversation, presented as a dialogue in couplets, is between Shelley (Julian) and BYRON (Maddalo). Wandering through Venice and its environs (a scene which gives Shelley opportunity to introduce some highly effective descriptive passages), the two poets discuss religion, progress and freedom. They visit an incarcerated maniac whose bitter and profound effusions become in some sense the summary of their debate. Through the intervention of a child, innocence and virtue are proposed as lasting values, but the poem retains its presiding cynicism.

Julian of Norwich 1342–after 1429 Mystic. Little is known about her life besides the information she gives in her single work, *A REVELATION OF DIVINE LOVE*, which, being illiterate, she dictated to a scribe some time after 1393. It describes 16 revelations concerned with God's love for mankind and how the Christian should love God, though one is a diabolical vision. The first 15 occurred during a period of sickness and hysteria in 1373; the last, many years later, confirmed that her experience had been a token and manifestation of Christ's love. By 1394 she had become a recluse, living as an anchorite attached to St Julian's Conesford in Norwich. She was visited there by MARGERY KEMPE in about 1413. See MYSTICAL WRITING.

Juliana A short poem in Old English by CYNEWULF, preserved (except for a few missing pages) in the EXETER BOOK. Its subject is the martyrdom of Juliana, a Christian virgin persecuted in AD 303. She is tortured and imprisoned after refusing marriage and paganism. A devil disguised as an angel visits her in prison, but she realizes his true identity and forces him to tell her of the Devil's evil works. The first attempts to martyr her fail, and her executioners are converted and also martyred. The poem follows its Latin source closely.

Julius Caesar A tragedy by WILLIAM SHAKESPEARE, first performed in 1599 and published in the First Folio of 1623. For the story and much of the language, Shakespeare relied on SIR THOMAS NORTH's translation of Plutarch.

Having defeated Pompey, Julius Caesar represents, for the majority of the Roman people, the promise of a new prosperity. But he is mistrusted by Pompey's former supporters and a group of variously motivated patricians led by Cassius, who share a belief that Caesar wishes to be crowned. The shrewd Cassius manages to persuade Brutus, the most respected of republicans, to join the conspiracy. Ignoring the warning of a soothsayer, Caesar decides to go to the Capitol and is assassinated. After explaining the reasons for the murder to the crowd, Brutus allows Mark Antony to speak. His skilful rhetoric turns the people against the conspirators, and civil war is again inevitable. Brutus and Cassius flee the city and gather their forces, while Antony, Lepidus and Caesar's great-nephew Octavius form a triumvirate, organize a brutal proscription and prepare for war.

After quarrelling with Brutus, Cassius learns that Brutus' wife, Portia, has committed suicide. Partly out of remorse, he accepts Brutus' decision to march on Philippi and confront Antony's army, though he does not agree with it. The battle is lost, and Brutus and Cassius kill themselves. The play ends with Octavius' ominously ambiguous proposal that he and Antony should 'part the glories of this happy day'.

The unusual structure of the play has been often observed. To some it has seemed like two tragedies in one, first Caesar's and then Brutus'; but it is equally possible to see it as a sophisticated REVENGE TRAGEDY, in which Antony takes on the role of Caesar's avenger, and the second half of the play completes the true tragedy of Julius Caesar. For Shakespeare, the shift from English history in the recently completed *HENRY V* to Roman history released a new confidence.

Jungle, The A novel by UPTON SINCLAIR, published serially in the socialist weekly *Appeal to Reason* in 1905, and in book form in 1906. It portrays the appalling labour and sanitary conditions in the Chicago stockyards and slums, as seen through the eyes of Jurgis Rudkus, a young Lithuanian immigrant. Sinclair chronicles the exploitation and victimization of Jurgis and his family, who live and work in Packington, the stockyard district. Jurgis experiences successive changes of fortune and employment. He works in a fertilizer plant after being injured in the slaughterhouse, and serves time in jail for attacking a foreman who has taken advantage of his wife, Ona. The Rudkus family is plagued by ill fortune and sickness, culminating in the deaths of Ona and both the children.

After his incarceration, Jurgis is blacklisted in Packington; finds work in a harvester plant and then in the steelworks; escapes from the city briefly to lead the life of a tramp in the open country; survives as a thief upon his return to Chicago; works as a scab during a meat-packers' strike; serves as the tool of a corrupt politician; then ends up back on the street, outcast and unemployable. Finally, Jurgis is introduced to socialist thought at a political meeting which he attends in order to escape the cold. The novel ends with an affirmation of the need for socialist reform by the workers of Chicago.

Jungle Book, The and **Second Jungle Book, The** Collections of short stories and poems by RUDYARD KIPLING, published in 1894 and 1895 respectively. The sequence of stories about the boy Mowgli, accidentally thrust out of the human community into the jungle, forms the core of these collections. His growth from jungle boyhood to dominance over the animals, and his eventual return to human service as a forest ranger, provide the basic framework. The code of conduct in the animal world is severe and requires a high level of responsibility; this is demonstrated in 'Letting in the Jungle', where retribution is brought on the village which sought to destroy Mowgli. In comparison with the jungle law and the stoic social duty of the animals, humanity is unruly and undignified.

Mowgli's discovery of his inner nature takes the *Jungle Books* close to the conventions of the *BILDUNGSROMAN*. There are strong elements of myth, too, in the recurring *leitmotif* of a fallen Eden: Mowgli is effectively shut out from his boyhood paradise when the blood-tie with humanity reclaims him. The theme of a divided emotional and cultural allegiance is present in the stories outside the Mowgli group, notably in 'The Miracle of Purun Bhagat', about a man who has to adjust from Western codes of conduct to the life of a Hindu holy man.

Junius The pseudonym adopted by the author of a series of letters which appeared in *THE PUBLIC ADVERTISER* in 1769–71, making shrewd and unsparing political attacks from a Whig viewpoint. The Duke of Grafton, Lord North, Lord Mansfield and George III were all targets; Junius entered the lists on behalf of JOHN WILKES and later attacked the Earl of Chatham and Barrington, the War Secretary. His identity has never been discovered, though SIR PHILIP FRANCIS has for long been a favourite candidate. An edition of the letters was published by Henry Sampson Woodfall, editor of *The Public Advertiser*, in 1772.

Junius, Francis [Dujon, François] 1589–1677 Antiquary. Born in Heidelberg, he became librarian to Thomas Howard, 2nd Earl of Arundel, tutor to Howard's son and a friend of JOHN MILTON. As well as helping Oxford University Press with the printing of Gothic, Anglo-Saxon and runic material, Junius collected Anglo-Saxon manuscripts which, with his philological collections, he presented to the Bodleian Library. The Junius Manuscript contains Old English scriptural poems he optimistically believed to be the work of CAEDMON: see *GENESIS*, *EXODUS*, *DANIEL*, and *CHRIST AND SATAN*. He published *De pictura veterum* (1637) and an edition of Caedmon (Amsterdam, 1655), and wrote an *Etymologicum anglicanum* (first printed in 1743) which helped JOHNSON in preparing his *DICTIONARY OF THE ENGLISH LANGUAGE*.

Juno and the Paycock A play by SEAN O'CASEY, first performed at the ABBEY THEATRE in 1924. Its topicality – it is set in Dublin at the height of the civil war of 1922 – added to its controversial popularity.

It centres on the Boyle family, inhabitants of a Dublin tenement. Jack Boyle, known as 'Captain' because he was once at sea, is an idler who leaves the care of home and family to his wife Juno. Their daughter Mary is intelligent, their son Johnny a maimed and neurotic victim of Irish violence. When Jack Boyle learns that he has inherited a large sum of money, he borrows money from friends and neighbours and spends it in loquacious drinking bouts with his equally incorrigible crony, Joxer Daly. But that would be his way of life whatever his circumstances. He remains comically and horrifyingly unaffected by the domestic tragedies that surround him. Mary, courted by the attractive Charles Bentham, rejects Jerry Devine, a leader of the local labour movement. But Bentham is after Mary's money and, having seduced and impregnated her, leaves her when it is discovered that Boyle will, after all, inherit nothing. Even the faithful Jerry abandons her when he discovers that she is pregnant. Johnny, having suffered nightmares, is finally revealed as an informer whose betrayal led to the death in an ambush of his neighbour, Robbie Tancred. He is taken off to be executed by the Republican Army. Only now does Juno abandon her feckless husband, who is still talking with Joxer in the empty flat when the play ends.

Jurgen: *A Comedy of Justice* A romance by JAMES BRANCH CABELL published in 1919, part of his 18-volume 'Biography of the Life of Manuel'. It was suppressed on grounds of obscenity from 1920 to 1922. Like others in the cycle, it is set in the mythical kingdom of Poictesme. The pawnbroker Jurgen is married to the voluble Dame Lisa. He says some sympathetic things about the Devil, who overhears him and rewards him by making Lisa disappear into a dark cave. Feeling obliged to seek his wife, Jurgen also enters the cave and has several adventures – some of them ama-

tory – with various mythical figures. He encounters the Centaur Nessus, Guenevere, Thragnar, Merlin, Dame Anaitis (The Lady of the Lake), Queen Helen and others. He lives for a while in Hell, where he encounters Grandfather Satan. He then goes to Heaven, where he assumes the identity of Pope John XX. Finally he meets Koshchei, a powerful being who tempts him with beautiful women. After Jurgen has rejected them all, Lisa is returned to him and they resume their normal life. His adventures take exactly a year, extending from one Walpurgis Night to the next.

Just So Stories A collection of 12 stories and 12 poems by RUDYARD KIPLING, published in 1902.

This is the only book for which Kipling supplied his own illustrations. It was written to be read aloud by adults to children. The interplay between the human and the animal worlds in the first seven stories is a simpler and more playful device than in the earlier JUNGLE BOOK. The language made 'appropriate' for the animals veers between the childlike and the (usually pompous) diction of a grown-up world. An element of teasing is most obviously apparent in such stories as 'How the Leopard Got Its Spots', where Kipling travesties the Darwinian notion of evolutionary progression; the humour can satisfy both children and adults.

kailyard school A group of Scottish writers who flourished during the last decade of the 19th century. 'Kailyard', meaning 'cabbage patch', was used by Ian Maclaren (born John Watson, 1850–1907) as the motto for a collection of his stories, *Beside the Bonnie Briar Bush* (1894). Apart from Maclaren, the group included J. M. BARRIE and S. R. Crockett (1860–1914), author of *The Stickit Minister* (1893). Their books about humble, homespun topics, often written in the vernacular, promoted a sentimental image of small-town life in Scotland and were, briefly, extremely popular.

Kanga, Firdaus 1959– Indian novelist. *Trying to Grow* (1989) is an autobiographical novel dealing with his Parsee childhood in Bombay and his disability (he was born with brittle bones). *Heaven on Wheels* (1991) is an account of his journeys round Britain, where he now lives, and *A Kind of Immigrant* (1992) is a play about homosexual love.

Kangaroo A novel by D. H. LAWRENCE, published in 1923. Set in Australia, where he and his wife, Frieda, had spent four months in 1922, it is principally a vehicle for Lawrence's own passionate observations about politics and life in the post-World War I years.

The central characters are Richard Lovat Somers, a writer, and his wife, Harriet. Jack Calcott, a neighbour, introduces Somers to Benjamin Cooley (nicknamed 'Kangaroo'), a Jewish barrister and leader of a radical political party. Cooley tries unsuccessfully to enlist Somers's support for his programme, a combination of fascism and Lawrentian 'blood consciousness'. After a political meeting in Canberra Hall has been violently disrupted, the couple leave for America. The novel includes a vivid chapter, 'The Nightmare', which details Lawrence's reactions to World War I.

Katiyo, Wilson 1947– Zimbabwean novelist. *A Son the Soil* (1976) and *Going to Heaven* (1979) follow the unhappy story of Alexio's life in white-dominated Rhodesia. The first describes his father's death and his schooldays in Salisbury. The second describes the death of his wife and child when their village is razed and the political persecution which causes him to flee to London, the ironic 'heaven' of the title.

Kaufman, George S(imon) 1889–1961 American playwright and director. All but one of his 40 plays, half of them Broadway hits, were written in collaboration: with MARC CONNELLY (*Dulcy*,1921; *Merton of the Movies*, 1922; *Beggar on Horseback*, 1924); Edna Ferber (*The Royal Family*, 1927; *Dinner at Eight*, 1932; *Stage Door*, 1936); Morris Ryskind (*The Cocoanuts*, 1925, and *Animal Crackers*, 1928, two Marx Brothers vehicles, and *Of Thee I Sing*, PULITZER PRIZE, 1931); and MOSS HART (*Once in a Lifetime*, 1930; *You Can't Take It with You*, Pulitzer Prize, 1936; *The Man Who Came to Dinner*, 1939). Kaufman's distinctive contribution was the wisecrack, timed with the same precision he brought to his work as a director.

Kavanagh, Julia 1824–77 Novelist. Born in Thurles, County Tipperary, and educated at home. Much of her early life was spent in France, which provided the setting for many of her novels. She earned her living at literary work by snatching spare hours from the task of caring for an invalid mother. Her works include *Madeleine* (1848), *Nathalie* (1850), *Daisy Burns* (1853), *Adele* (1858), *Bessie* (1872) and *Woman in France during the Eighteenth Century* (1850).

Kavanagh, Patrick (Joseph) 1904–67 Irish poet. Born at Mucker near Inniskeen, County Monaghan, he had little formal education and followed his father into peasant farming. An interest in poetry led him to write and study privately and in 1928 his poems began to appear in Dublin newspapers. *Ploughman and Other Poems*, his first book, was published in 1936. His early life formed the basis for an autobiography, *The Green Fool* (1938), and a more cynical novel, *Tarry Flynn* (1948). In 1937 he left his farm, and thereafter worked as a freelance writer in Dublin, where he became a controversial figure, admired for his poetry but often disliked for his scathing criticism of the city's literary society. Kavanagh resented what he saw as YEATS's romanticized view of the Irish peasantry, and his major poem, *The Great Hunger* (1942), is a grimly compassionate account of the cultural and emotional poverty of Irish rural life, written in partially rhymed free verse influenced by the early T. S. ELIOT. A costly and unsuccessful libel action against a Dublin magazine and a period of serious illness damaged Kavanagh's later work but in 1955, after major surgery for lung cancer, he experienced a renewal of poetic power, shown in *Come Dance with Kitty Stobling* (1960). His *Complete Poems* appeared in 1972. Kavanagh is now generally recognized as the major Irish poet of the mid-20th century. His realistic treatment of rural life and his confidence (expressed in a SONNET entitled, with characteristic IRONY, 'Epic') that the 'parochial' or local subject need not entail a narrowly 'provincial' treatment influenced R. S. THOMAS and subsequent Irish poets, such as

SEAMUS HEANEY, who introduced Kavanagh as a character in *Station Island.*

Kavanagh, P(atrick) J(oseph) (Gregory) 1931–
Poet and novelist. Born in Worthing, Sussex, he was educated at schools in North Wales and Switzerland, and after drama school in Paris and national service, at Merton College, Oxford. Subsequently he worked for the BBC and the British Council and as an actor. Formally traditional and influenced by WORDSWORTH, YEATS and EDWARD THOMAS, his poems are preoccupied with the pains and joys of life, the hope given by love, and death – particularly the death of his wife, which is also the informing event behind his autobiography, *The Perfect Stranger* (1966). His collections include *One and One* (1959), *On the Way to the Depot* (1966), *About Time* (1970), *Edward Thomas in Heaven* (1974) and *Life before Death* (1979), all well represented in *Selected Poems* (1982), *Presences: New and Selected Poems* (1987) and *Collected Poems* (1988). His novels include *A Song and Dance* (1968) and *A Happy Man* (1973).

Kay, Jackie 1961–
Poet and playwright. Born in Edinburgh and brought up in Glasgow, she has worked as a touring officer for the Arts Council. Though she has published two plays, *Chiaroscuro* (1987) and *Twice Over* (1988), she is so far best known for her collection of poetry, *The Adoption Papers* (1992). The title-poem deals with her own history as a black girl adopted by a white Scottish couple. Her work has appeared in several anthologies, including *A Dangerous Knowing: Four Black Women Poets* (1984), edited by Prathiba Parmar.

Kaye-Smith, Sheila 1887–1956
Novelist. Born in Sussex and educated privately, she became a Roman Catholic in 1929. Her first novel, *The Tramping Methodist* (1908), started a series of rural novels focusing on a Sussex family, the Alards; the best known are *Sussex Gorse* (1916), *Tamarisk Town* (1919), *Green Apple Harvest* (1920), *Joanna Godden* (1921) and *The End of the House of Alard* (1923). *The History of Susan Spray* (1931), *Ember Lane* (1940) and *Mrs Gailey* (1951) are among her later novels. *Three Ways Home* (1937) is an autobiography.

Keary, Annie 1825–79
Novelist and writer of CHILDREN'S LITERATURE. She wrote two notable children's books, *The Heroes of Asgard* (with her sister Eliza Keary; 1857) and *Sidney Grey* (1857). Her novels for adults include *Oldbury* (1869), *Castle Daly* (1875) and *A Doubting Heart* (1879), unfinished at her death.

Keats, John 1795–1821
Poet. He was born at Moorfields, London, where his father was the manager of large livery stables belonging to his father-in-law. John was the oldest of four children who remained deeply devoted and intensely loyal to each other: George (b. 1797), Tom (b. 1799) and Frances, or Fanny (b. 1803). After their father's death in 1804 their mother remarried, but was soon separated from her second husband and went with the children to live with her mother at Edmonton, where she died of tuberculosis in 1810. From the age of 10 to 14 John divided his time between his grandmother's home and Clarke's School at Enfield. Here he was noted more for his love of cricket and boxing than for any studiousness until his final two years, when he began to read voraciously, particularly books on Greek mythology, and started a translation of Virgil's *Aeneid.* At the end of 1810 he was taken out of school and apprenticed to a surgeon-apothecary at Enfield, but continued to visit the school to pursue his friendship with CHARLES COWDEN CLARKE, the headmaster's son – some years his senior – who encouraged his interest in literature.

His ambition to become a poet was fired by his first acquaintance with SPENSER'S *FAERIE QUEENE,* which, according to Clarke, 'he ramped through... like a young horse turned into a Spring meadow'. His first poem, 'Lines in Imitation of Spenser', was written in 1814, but was not immediately followed by work of the same high promise. In 1814 he quarrelled with his master, Hammond, and went to live on his own in London, resuming his surgical studies in 1815 as a student at Guy's Hospital. To this year belong the ODES 'To Hope', 'To Apollo', the 'Sonnet Written on the Day after Mr Leigh Hunt Left Prison', and three SONNETS on Woman. In the autumn of the same year he began to read WORDSWORTH, whose new influence is discernible in the sonnet 'O Solitude', and with whom he, in common with other second-generation Romantic poets, developed a literary love–hate relationship. In 1816 he became a licentiate of the Society of Apothecaries but had, by the end of the year, effectively abandoned all thought of pursuing his profession, despite precarious financial circumstances. 'O Solitude' appeared in the May number of the liberal journal, *THE EXAMINER,* and through Cowden Clarke he met its editor, LEIGH HUNT, who instantly took him under his wing and helped to broaden his literary acquaintance. New friends included JOHN HAMILTON REYNOLDS and the painter BENJAMIN HAYDON, to whom he addressed the sonnet 'Great Spirits Now on Earth are Sojourning'. He also met SHELLEY, from whom he was, however, always careful to preserve a certain distance, sensing in the slightly older poet's dominating personality a potential threat to his own 'unfettered scope'. In the 'Young Poets' issue of *The Examiner* in November 1816 Hunt hailed Keats, Shelley and Reynolds as the most promising writers of their generation, and printed Keats's sonnet 'On First Looking into Chapman's Homer'. To 1816 belong also the important poems 'I Stood Tiptoe upon a Little Hill' and 'Sleep and Poetry' which appeared, together with sonnets, rhymed epistles and miscellaneous poems, in his first volume of poetry, *Poems*, published in March 1817. Sales of the book were poor and, apart from some flattering reviews by friends, its appearance passed unnoticed, though, ominously for Keats, his name was linked with that of Hunt as a member of the COCKNEY SCHOOL in the autumn number of *BLACKWOOD'S EDINBURGH MAGAZINE*.

Keats was a good deal out of London in 1817, spending the spring at Shanklin, on the Isle of Wight, and Margate, where he was joined by his brother Tom. In the summer he joined his friend Bailey at Oxford. It was at about this time that he first began to use his letters to his brothers, sister and friends as the vehicle of his most considered thoughts on poetry, love, philosophy, his own personality and the people and events surrounding him. Vivid, witty and revealing, they were published in 1848 and 1878, and have come to be almost as highly regarded as his poetry, to which many of them supply valuable commentaries. The year also brought new acquaintances such as CHARLES WENTWORTH DILKE and Charles Armitage Brown, who were his neighbours at Hampstead, and saw the completion, in November, of *ENDYMION*, his most ambitious poetic project to date; it was supposedly undertaken in friendly rivalry with Shelley, who was writing *Laon and Cythna* (later called *THE REVOLT OF ISLAM*) at the same time. During the winter of 1817–18 he was frequently in the society of his friends, and towards Christmas briefly stood in for Reynolds as theatrical critic for *The Champion*, producing a fascinating article on the Shakespearean actor Kean. At some point in December he read passages of *Endymion* to Wordsworth, who frostily complimented him on 'a pretty piece of paganism'. On 28 December he was present at Haydon's 'immortal dinner' which was attended by CHARLES LAMB and Wordsworth, and he regularly attended HAZLITT's lectures on English poetry, which greatly helped him to shape his own ideas on poetry and on the poet as an individual of NEGATIVE CAPABILITY. Many of his most interesting ideas are contained in his correspondence with Reynolds, with whom he also planned a volume of verse tales drawn from Boccaccio, for which his *ISABELLA: OR, THE POT OF BASIL* was written. It marks a great advance in his poetic technique. Tom Keats was now seriously ill with tuberculosis, and he was devoting much of his time to nursing him, first at Teignmouth and then in London. *Endymion*, which he dedicated to CHATTERTON, was published in the spring of 1818.

In June his brother George, one of his closest confidants, married and emigrated to America. Accompanied by Brown, he spent the summer touring the Lakes, Scotland and Northern Ireland. His impressions of the scenery, which was of a kind entirely new to him, are reflected in passages of *HYPERION*. The fatigue and exposure of West Highland travel, however, brought on a throat infection from which he was never afterwards free. Returning to London, he spent the next three months attending Tom. To the pains of the permanent departure of one brother, and the imminent death of another, were added the withering attacks on *Endymion* and his earlier poems in the autumn numbers of *Blackwood's*, and THE QUARTERLY REVIEW. Deeply wounded, he thought of giving up poetry, but rallied himself to write to George that, despite the reviews, 'I think I shall be among the English poets after my death', and began work on *Hyperion*. After Tom's death in December he moved to Brown's house at Hampstead, which was close to the home of Fanny Brawne, with whom he fell deeply and jealously in love. It was a relationship that seems to have brought him little real happiness, and was undoubtedly complicated by his lack of means to support a wife and, above all, by the morbid turn given to his thoughts by the development of his illness.

Keats's astonishing poetic development and productivity during the next year is comparable to Shelley's in Italy at roughly the same time. In the winter of 1818–19 he worked mainly on *Hyperion*. *THE EVE OF ST AGNES* and the fragmentary *Eve of St Mark* were composed during a visit to Dilke's parents and relatives in Sussex at the end of January. Returning to Hampstead in early February, he idled for a while and then, between March and May, wrote several of the reflective odes which have done more than anything else to secure him his place among the English poets: 'On Indolence', 'On a Grecian Urn', 'To Psyche', 'To a Nightingale' and 'On Melancholy'. The enigmatic BALLAD *LA BELLE DAME SANS MERCI* was copied for dispatch to George in April. Other poems of the spring are the two sonnets on 'Fame', and 'Why Did I Laugh Tonight?'. In the second half of 1819 he wrote (with Charles Brown) the tragedy *Otho the Great*, began another play on the subject of King Stephen, and finished *LAMIA*, which was followed by the beautiful 'Ode to Autumn' and the second version of *Hyperion*, called *The Fall of Hyperion*.

It was, however, also a year of unhappy love and increasing financial difficulties, his slender private means now exhausted, and the existence of a legacy from his maternal grandfather now having apparently been forgotten by both his family and his former guardian. Returning from America on a flying visit, George found him ill and dejected, 'not the same being'. He began the unfinished 'Cap and Bells', but in February 1820 he became seriously ill with tuberculosis, and, after seeing his second volume of poems through the press, was soon too weak to write. This volume was published under the title *Lamia, Isabella, The Eve of St Agnes and Other Poems* in July 1820, and included most of the great odes, *Hyperion*, *Fancy* and other works. The reviewers were this time generous in their praise, with even *Blackwood's* toning down its criticism of a poet it had so recently attempted to discredit as a mere imitator of Leigh Hunt. But this was now rather beside the point: Keats was nursed by the Hunts and then by Fanny and Mrs Brawne, but his condition gradually worsened and, in a last desperate bid for recovery, he put his affairs in order and sailed for Italy with his friend, the painter Joseph Severn, in September 1820. He declined Shelley's generous, but typically lordly, invitation to join him at Pisa, and went instead to Rome, where he died the following February.

Keats's reputation continued to grow during the 19th century, when his admirers included TENNYSON, MATTHEW ARNOLD and the PRE-RAPHAELITES. In the 20th century he is, together with Wordsworth, perhaps the most widely read and familiar of the English Romantic poets, and some of his odes ('To Autumn', for example, or 'On a Grecian Urn') are as well-known as anything by SHAKESPEARE, to whom he has, indeed, often been compared. Recent biographical studies have, in many respects, deepened the tragedy of his life by showing him to have been, while still in health, in many ways the precise opposite of the overburdened, sensitive soul of the posthumous legends which were fostered by, for example, Shelley's ELEGY ADONAIS.

Keble, John 1792–1866 Poet and clergyman. Born at Fairford in Gloucestershire, the son of a High Church clergyman, he studied at Corpus Christi College, Oxford. A brilliant scholar, Keble was elected a fellow of Oriel College at the age of 19. While acting as his father's curate at Fairford, he published *The Christian Year* (1827), a collection of poems for the Sundays and holy days of the church calendar which became perhaps the most popular religious verse of the 19th century. Its success led to his appointment as professor of poetry at Oxford in 1831.

A leading figure in the OXFORD MOVEMENT, Keble contributed nine of the *TRACTS FOR THE TIMES*, which affirmed the principles of the Movement and gave it its early name, Tractarianism. He published an edition of the works of RICHARD HOOKER (1836) and contributed a translation of St Irenaeus to the *Library of the Fathers* (posthumously published, 1872). His later sacred poetry included *Lyra apostolica* (with NEWMAN and ISAAC WILLIAMS; 1836), an English *Psalter* (1839) and *Lyra innocentium* (1846). Keble became parish priest at Hursley, near Winchester, in 1836 and never sought preferment. Keble College, Oxford, was founded in his memory in 1870.

Keeping, Charles (William James) 1924–88 Writer and illustrator of CHILDREN'S LITERATURE. Born and educated in London, he was always proud of his Cockney background and many of his picture-books feature the streets, yards and river banks of the city he knew so well. His vision of life was never cosy or nostalgic, and he did not hesitate to set young readers visual problems to be solved by their own imaginative efforts. *Through the Window* (1970), a wordless sequence of pictures, only hints at what the young hero has actually seen. *Inter-City* (1977), another wordless sequence, depicts a child's experience when travelling by train. Keeping's illustrations for ALFRED NOYES's poem 'The Highwayman' (1981) sometimes out-do the original text in suggestions of cruelty.

Keillor, Garrison 1942– American short-story writer, novelist and humorist. Educated at the University of Minnesota, he hosted a national public radio programme, 'A Prairie Home Companion', in 1974–87. It introduced a long-running series of tales, gently comic and confidentially anecdotal, about the fictional Minnesota town of Lake Wobegon. These have been collected in *Happy to be Here* (1985), *Lake Wobegon Days* (1985), *Leaving Home* (1987) and, with other short fiction, essays and verse, *We are Still Married* (1989). A novel, *WLT: A Radio Romance* (1992; as *Radio Romance* in Britain), shows a harder tone and an unexpected sexual frankness.

Kelly, George (Edward) 1887–1974 American playwright. He was born into a prominent Philadelphia family. His first successful full-length play, *The Torchbearers* (1922), presents a satiric account of a stagestruck woman's involvement with a 'little theatre' movement. His second play, *The Show-Off* (1924), a comedy about a braggart, was developed from his earlier one-act play *Poor Aubrey* (1922). *Craig's Wife* (1925), which won the PULITZER PRIZE in 1926, is a character study of a grasping and self-centred woman that shows the influence of Strindberg. *Daisy Mayme* (1926) and *Behold the Bridegroom* (1927) are domestic stories of rich and wilful women. Kelly's next two plays focused on conflict between generations: the unsuccessful *Maggie, the Magnificent* (1929) tells of a daughter's rebellion against her domineering mother; *Philip Goes Forth* (1931), which was better received, describes a son's conflict with his father over the choice between a theatrical career and a career in the family business. *Reflected Glory* (1936) further examines the conflict between the theatre and family responsibilities. His last two plays, *The Deep Mrs Sykes* (1945) and *The Fatal Weakness* (1946), are about suspicion and self-deception in marriage.

Kelly, Hugh 1739–77 Playwright. Born in Killarney and apprenticed to a staymaker in Dublin, Kelly moved to London in 1760 and struggled for a living as a writer. He was, at various times, editor of the *Court Magazine*, *The Lady's Museum* and *The Public Ledger*, winning more enemies than friends by his time-serving support of the government against JOHN WILKES. His *Thespis* (1766), written in emulation of CHARLES CHURCHILL's *The Rosciad*, is a gossipy account of DRURY LANE's leading actors and actresses, the very people who made his reputation by their performance of his mildly satiric SENTIMENTAL COMEDY *False Delicacy* (1768). *A Word to the Wise* (1770) and *The Man of Reason* (1776) were unsuccessful, and Kelly owes his brief reputation as a leading writer of comedies to *False Delicacy* and his version of Molière's *The School for Wives* (1773). His finances were not much helped by his theatrical fame and he died in poverty.

Kelman, James 1946– Novelist and short-story writer. He was born in Glasgow, where he lived and worked until moving to Edinburgh in the late 1980s. *Not Not While the Giro* (1983), his first short-story collection, blends a Beckettian deadpan humour with the authentic demotic of urban Scottish working-class life. Subsequent work, like the collection *Greyhound for Breakfast* (1987), has become more serious in tone. His novels include *The Busconductor Hines* (1984), a conscientious, occasionally wistful biography of a public servant, and *A Disaffection* (1989), an intense STREAM-OF-CONSCIOUSNESS account of a drink-sodden teacher. *How Late It Was, How Late* (1994), a monologue by a Glaswegian ex-convict, won the BOOKER PRIZE.

Kemble, Fanny [Frances] **(Anne)** 1809–93 Actress, playwright, poet and autobiographer. Born into a distinguished theatrical family, the daughter of Charles Kemble and the niece of Sarah Siddons and John Philip Kemble, she was more ambitious to write than to act. She made her stage début in 1829 in a bid to rescue her father from financial disaster at COVENT GARDEN and succeeded in parts from SHAKESPEARE and as Lady Teazle in SHERIDAN's *THE SCHOOL FOR SCANDAL*. She also acted in her own tragedy, *Francis I* (1832), which required the audience's indulgence as well as her father's. After an American tour (1832–3) she stayed behind in Philadelphia to marry Pierce Butler in 1834. She left him in 1845 after disagreements over slavery – she being an ardent Abolitionist and he a slave-owner – and he divorced her in 1849. After a year in Rome she reluctantly returned to the English stage, at first reduced to provincial tours but then supporting herself for many years (1848–74) by public readings from Shakespeare. Her *Poems* appeared in 1844 and her *Plays* in 1863. In retirement she supplemented her *Journal* (also called *Journal of a Residence in America*; 1835) and *Journal of a Residence on a Georgian Plantation in 1838–39* (1863) with several frank and discerning volumes of reminiscence, *Record of a Girlhood* (1878), *Records of Later Life* (1882) and *Further Records* (1890), and a novel, *Far Away and Long Ago* (1889).

Kemble, John Mitchell 1807–57 Philologist and historian. The son of the actor Charles Kemble and the elder brother of FANNY KEMBLE, he was born in London and educated at Trinity College, Cambridge. His interest in philology was developed by further study at Göttingen with Jakob Grimm, who became his friend. He published *The Anglo-Saxon Poems of Beowulf* (1833–7) and a scholarly work on the early history of England, *Codex diplomaticus aevi saxonici* (1839–48). His *The Saxons in England* (1849) argued that England's stability in a Europe racked by disturbance was owing to the principles and institutions inherited from Teutonic invaders.

Kemp [Kempe], **Will** c. 1560–c. 1603 Famous as a clown in the Elizabethan theatre, Kemp was a member of the Lord Chamberlain's men at the time when the decision was made to build the GLOBE on the south bank of the Thames in 1597–8. He is known to have played Peter in *ROMEO AND JULIET* and Dogberry in *MUCH ADO ABOUT NOTHING*. What is not known is the reason for his decision to leave SHAKESPEARE and his colleagues before they began operations at their new theatre. Whether or not it was a result of a dispute over the relative merits of plays and the post-play jigs in which Kemp specialized, the actor took his genius for self-advertisement elsewhere, most notably to Norwich on the famous morris dance of which he wrote an account in *Kemp's Nine Days' Wonder, Performed in a Dance from London to Norwich* (1600).

Kempe, Margery Mystic and autobiographer active in the early 15th century. All that is known of her life is recorded in her single work, *The Book of Margery Kempe*. After an early life devoted to pride and worldliness, Margery was converted to a life of worship. She abandoned her brewing business in her native King's Lynn and eventually succeeded in persuading her husband to allow her to live in chastity. Dressed in white, she went on pilgrimages in England, Europe and the Holy Land, relating her mystical experiences and offering divinely inspired advice. She claimed that all her actions were dictated by God, though often God's will seems happily to have coincided with momentary convenience and she was sometimes accused of being a charlatan and a hypocrite. She records a visit to JULIAN OF NORWICH in her travels. Valuable as autobiography, her book is disappointing as MYSTICAL WRITING.

Kempinski, Tom 1938– Playwright. Born of Jewish parents in London, he began his career as an actor. Success as a writer came with his first major production, *Duet for One* (1980), about a concert violinist stricken with multiple sclerosis and attempting to cope with her illness through therapy. Psychoanalysis and Freudian theory are prominent features of his work, notably *When the Past is Still to Come* (1992), an account of his own ten years in analysis and his 'struggle against the fear which kills', including family memories of the Holocaust. His gift for intimate conversations between stricken individuals distinguishes *Self-Inflicted Wounds* (1985) and *Separation* (1987), in which a reclusive writer in London conducts a long-distance relationship by phone with a sick, perhaps dying actress in New York. *Sex Please, We're Italian* (1991) makes an unconvincing venture into popular comedy.

Ken, Thomas 1637–1711 Poet and prelate. Born at Berkhamsted, Hertfordshire, Ken was orphaned while young, and lived with IZAAK WALTON, a relation by marriage. He was educated at Winchester and New College, Oxford, taking holy orders in 1661–2. He was chaplain to Charles II from 1680, and sailed with the English expedition to Tangier (1683–4), when he conversed frequently with SAMUEL PEPYS. In 1684, he was appointed Bishop of Bath and Wells, reputedly at the King's wish to have no one but 'the little black fellow that refused his lodging to poor Nelly', an allusion to Ken's having declined to allow Nell Gwynne to lodge at his prebendal house in Winchester. Ken attended Charles's deathbed, and absolved him. During James II's reign he was one of the famous group of seven bishops confined to the Tower for opposition to the King's pro-Catholic policies, but at the Glorious Revolution of 1688 he became a prominent NONJUROR, refusing to swear allegiance to William and Mary. In 1691 he was deprived of his see and he spent the remainder of his life in retirement, mostly at Lord Weymouth's seat at Longleat, Wiltshire, where he died. In his lifetime Ken was renowned for his piety, charity and asceticism, and it was widely believed that DRYDEN modelled his 'Character of a Good Parson' (1700) on him; he wrote several devotional works, in both prose and verse, most notably his *Hymns on the Christian Festivals* (published 1721) and the famous 'Morning, Evening and Midnight Hymns', composed for the use of Winchester scholars, and first published in 1695.

Kendall, Henry (Clarence) 1839–82 Australian poet. Born near Ulladulla in New South Wales, he worked in a solicitor's office and later for the State Survey Department. His first poems were sent to Henry (later Sir Henry) Parkes, who published them in his paper, *The Empire*; Kendall's first collection, *Poems and Songs*, appeared in 1862. Some new poems were published by THE ATHENAEUM on 27 September of the same year – the first recognition of an Australian poet by an English journal. At its best Kendall's work is a vivid realization of Australia and of the natural beauty which appealed to his lyric gifts. After 1862 his published volumes were *The Bronze Trumpet: A Satirical Poem* (1866), *Leaves from Australian Forests* (1869), *Songs from the Mountains* (1880), *Orara: A Tale* (1881) and *Poems* (1886).

Keneally, Thomas (Michael) 1935– Australian novelist. He trained as a priest but was not ordained, studied for the New South Wales Bar and began writing while working as a schoolteacher in Sydney. Three early Catholic novels, *The Place at Whitton* (1964), *The Fear* (1965) and *Three Cheers for the Paraclete* (1968), were followed by several novels with typically Australian subjects: convicts in *Bring Larks and Heroes* (1967), bush life in *A Dutiful Daughter* (1971) and Aborigines in *The Chant of Jimmie Blacksmith* (1972). A couple of Arctic adventures – *The Survivor* (1969) and *A Victim of the Aurora* (1978) – and an experimental novel, *The Passenger* (1979), are workmanlike explorations. His typical strengths lie in journalistic research and competent storytelling, applied to wartime settings in: *Blood Red, Sister Rose* (1974), about Joan of Arc; *Gossip from the Forest* (1975) and *Season in Purgatory* (1976), about World War I; *Confederates* (1979), about the American Civil War; and *Cut-Rate Kingdom* (1980), about the effects of World War II. His best-known work, *Schindler's Ark* (1982), about a German Catholic factory owner rescuing Jews in World War II, was conceived and written as a documentary but read sufficiently like a novel to receive the BOOKER PRIZE. Subsequent books include: *A Family Madness* (1986), again about the effects of World War II; *The Playmaker* (1987); *Towards Asmara* (1989), about Eritrean resistance in Ethiopia; *Flying Hero Class* (1991), about an international hijack; and

Thomas Keneally

Woman of the Inner Sea (1992). He has also written many plays and two travel books, *Now and In Time to Be: Ireland and the Irish* (1991) and *The Place Where Souls are Born: A Journey to the American Southwest* (1992).

Kenilworth A novel set in Elizabethan England, by SIR WALTER SCOTT, published in 1821. The story is Scott's interpretation of the events which led to the mysterious death of Amy Robsart in 1560.

Amy has been persuaded to contract a secret marriage with the Earl of Leicester, favourite of the Queen. She is kept at Cumnor Place, near Oxford, by the villainous Richard Varney and she is believed to be Varney's mistress by her rejected suitor Edmund Tressilian. Failing to persuade her to return to her father's house, Tressilian goes to the Queen and charges Varney with seduction. To protect Leicester, Varney declares that Amy is his wife, and Elizabeth orders Amy to appear before her at Kenilworth, where she will stay in the course of a royal progress. Varney and Leicester suggest that Amy should present herself as the wife of the former, but Amy indignantly refuses and, aided by Tressilian, makes her own way to Kenilworth where she is discovered by the Queen who finally extracts a confession of the truth from Leicester. Meanwhile he, suspecting the relation between Tressilian and his wife, orders Varney to carry her back to Cumnor Place and murder her. Tressilian arrives too late to prevent the 'accident'.

Kennedy, Adrienne (Lita) 1931– Black American playwright. Born in Pittsburgh, and educated at Ohio State University and Columbia, she has taught at several American universities. Her work blends symbols, historical figures, racial images and myths to surreal, highly personal effect. *Funnyhouse of a Negro* (1964) depicts the final moments before the suicide of Sarah, a mulatta unable to cope with her mixed racial heritage. *The Owl Answers* (1969) portrays another mulatta caught in a hallucinatory nightmare of confused racial identity. Other plays include *A Rat's Mass* (1966), a fantasy of war and prejudice; *The Lennon Play: In His Own Write* (1967); and *A Lancashire Lad* (1980), a children's play based on the early life of Charlie Chaplin.

Kennedy, John Pendleton 1795–1870 American novelist and essayist. While practising law in his native Baltimore, Kennedy took to writing and produced *The Red Book* (1818–19), which – like WASHINGTON IRVING's *SALMAGUNDI* – included sketches, satirical essays and poems. Under the pseudonym of Mark Littleton he then published *Swallow Barn* (1832), a collection of sketches set in Virginia. His first and best-known novel, *HORSE-SHOE ROBINSON*, appeared in 1835, and was followed by *Rob of the Bowl*

in 1838. He was a friend of Irving and OLIVER WENDELL HOLMES, and the American host to THACKERAY. He was also one of the first to recognize POE, to whom he awarded first prize in a short-story contest he judged.

Kennedy, Margaret (Moore) 1896–1967 Novelist. She was educated at Cheltenham and Somerville College, Oxford. Her first book, *A Century of Revolution* (1922), was a work of history. Her first novel, *The Ladies of Lyndon* (1923), was well received but it was *The Constant Nymph* (1924) that made her famous. Margaret Kennedy's poised style, cool wit and skilful characterization kept her novels welcome for three decades: *Red Sky at Morning* (1927), *The Fool of the Family* (1930), *Return I Dare Not* (1931), *A Long Time Ago* (1932), *Together and Apart* (1936), *The Midas Touch* (1938), *The Feast* (1950), *Lucy Carmichael* (1951), *Troy Chimneys* (James Tait Black Memorial Prize; 1953), *The Oracle* (1955), *The Heroes of Clone* (1957), *A Night in Cold Harbour* (1960), *The Forgotten Smile* (1961) and *Not in the Calendar* (1964). For the theatre she wrote *Come with Me* (with Basil Dean; 1928), *Escape Me Never* (1933), *Autumn* (with Gregory Ratoff; 1937) and *Happy with Either* (1948). *Jane Austen* (1950) is a critical biography and *The Outlaws on Parnassus* (1958) a study of the art of fiction.

Kentucky Cardinal, A A short novel by JAMES LANE ALLEN, published in 1894. Adam Moss is an amiable but reclusive nature lover who prefers his garden and the migrating birds it harbours to human society. The Cobb family moves into the house next door and disturbs his seclusion, but he soon feels himself drawn to the eldest daughter, Georgiana, who also loves birds. He falls in love with her, but she is hesitant. As proof of his love, she asks him to capture and cage a cardinal, a bird that lives in his garden and whose trust he has slowly gained. He does as she asks, thinking that his gesture will show her that he is ready to put aside animal attachments for human. The bird soon dies in captivity, and Adam and Georgiana quarrel about the meaning of the incident. Eventually, however, they forgive each other and plan to marry.

Aftermath (1895), the sequel, tells of their marriage. Adam tries to become more involved in town life and pays less attention to nature, but he finds only that human behaviour, especially with pre-Civil War tensions rising, is violent and foolish. Georgiana dies after giving birth to their first child, and Adam consoles himself by returning his attention to his first love, nature.

Kenyon Review, The A literary magazine founded by JOHN CROWE RANSOM in 1939. It soon became a leading organ for the NEW CRITICISM. Contributors of nonfiction have included ALLEN TATE, CLEANTH BROOKS, R. P. Blackmur, ROBERT PENN WARREN, WILLIAM EMPSON, PAUL GOODMAN, KENNETH BURKE, Leslie

Fiedler, NORTHROP FRYE, MARSHALL MCLUHAN, LIONEL TRILLING, Harry Levin and STEPHEN SPENDER. The emphasis shifted from criticism to poetry and fiction when Robie Macauley became editor in 1958. Contributors during this period included JOHN BARTH, FLANNERY O'CONNOR and THOMAS PYNCHON.

Ker, W(illiam) P(aton) 1855–1923 Critic and scholar. He was born in Glasgow, where he attended the Academy before going on to Glasgow University. Later he went to Balliol College, Oxford, and became a fellow of All Souls College in 1879. He was professor of English literature and history at Cardiff from 1883 to 1889, when he accepted the chair of English language and literature at University College, London. Later he directed the University of London's School of Scandinavian Studies, and was elected professor of poetry at Oxford in 1920. His high reputation as an authority on medieval literature was established by his works *Epic and Romance* (1897), *The Dark Ages* (1904) and *Essays on Medieval Literature* (1905). His *Collected Essays* (edited by C. Whibley) appeared in 1925.

Kerouac, Jack 1922–69 American novelist. He was born Jean-Louis Kerouac in Lowell, Massachusetts, and educated at Columbia University. After spending some time as a merchant seaman and wandering around the USA he published the first of his semi-autobiographical novels, *The Town and the City* (1950), about a family in his home town. ON THE ROAD (1957), his best-known book, describes the lifestyle and the often aimless search for significant experience of the BEATS. The book established Kerouac as the novelist of the Beats just as *Howl* had identified ALLEN GINSBERG as their poet. *The Subterraneans* and *The Dharma Bums* (both 1958), *Tristessa* (1960), *Big Sur* (1962) and *Desolation Angels* (1965) are all products of the Beat consciousness; *Doctor Sax* and *Maggie Cassidy* (both 1959) and *Visions of Gerard* (1963) are evocations of Kerouac's boyhood. *Satori in Paris* (1966) is an account of his quest for his Breton ancestors. Among his other books are *Lonesome Traveller* (1960; travel sketches), *Mexico City Blues* (1959; verse) and *Book of Dreams* (1961). *Visions of Cody*, written in 1951–2, was published posthumously in 1972.

Kesey, Ken 1935– American novelist. He was born in Colorado and educated at the University of Oregon. He volunteered for government drug experiments in the early 1960s and subsequently became an aide on a psychiatric ward in a veterans' hospital. ONE FLEW OVER THE CUCKOO'S NEST (1962) makes use of his experiences. *Sometimes a Great Notion* (1964) focuses on the lives of a logging family in the Northwest and *Sailor Song* (1993) is set in Alaska in the near future. *Kesey's Garage Sale* (1973) and *Demon Box* (1986) are collections of essays, letters, interviews, stories and

drawings. TOM WOLFE's *The Electric Kool-Aid Acid Test* (1968) records his wild lifestyle in the 1960s.

Keyes, Sidney (Arthur Kilworth) 1922–43 Poet. Born in Dartford, Kent, he was educated there, at Tonbridge School and at Oxford, where he read history. While an undergraduate he edited *The Cherwell* and introduced *Eight Oxford Poets* (1942), which included work by himself, JOHN HEATH-STUBBS and KEITH DOUGLAS. He enlisted in 1942 and was killed in Tunisia. In his first volume, *The Iron Laurel* (1942), his eye for dramatic detail is apparent in the most successful poems, 'The Buzzard' and 'William Wordsworth'; the symbols in the long 'The Foreign Gate' deprive the writing of immediacy and pressure. *The Cruel Solstice* (1943) included poems which brought symbolism more urgently near to the realities of wartime life ('War Poet' and 'To Keep off Fears'). Michael Meyer edited *Collected Poems* (1945); *Minos of Crete: Plays and Stories* appeared in 1948. As the reputations of other poets of World War II like Douglas and ALUN LEWIS continue to grow, it remains to be seen whether Keyes can excite as he did in the 1940s. His most enduring poems ('The Migrant', 'The Kestrels') are those in which landscapes, seascapes and birds appear in their least symbolically forced settings.

Keynes, J(ohn) M(aynard), 1st Baron Keynes of Tilton 1883–1946 Economist. He was born in Cambridge, and educated at Eton and King's College, Cambridge, where he subsequently lectured on economics. In 1906 he entered the Civil Service and was a member of the Royal Commission on Indian Finance and Currency. During the inter-war years Keynes published numerous works, including *A Treatise on Probability* (1921), *A Tract on Monetary Reform* (1923), *The End of Laissez-Faire* (1926) and *A Treatise on Money* (2 vols., 1930). However, *A General Theory of Employment, Interest, and Money* (1936) was by far his greatest and most influential work. It revolutionized the approach to unemployment by arguing for greater government spending on public works, and became the major framework in the formation of the Welfare State.

While at Cambridge Keynes was influenced by the teaching of G. E. MOORE, the philosopher whose ideas provided the BLOOMSBURY GROUP with many of its aesthetic and intellectual theories. Keynes became a central member of the Group, and Keynesian economics was based upon the assumption that prosperity would provide the foundation for cultural progress. Keynes founded and endowed the Arts Theatre at Cambridge and became first chairman of the Arts Council of Great Britain in 1945. Among his more general contributions to literature were *Essays in Persuasion* (1931), *Essays in Biography* (1933) and *Two Memoirs* (posthumously published 1949), which revealed an original and lively prose style combined with novelistic powers of character drawing.

Kickham, Charles J(oseph) 1828–82 Irish novelist. He was born in County Tipperary, the son of a prosperous farmer and shopkeeper, and ended his rather desultory education at the hands of private tutors after an accident with gunpowder left him deaf and disfigured. He was strongly influenced in his youth by the nationalism of the Young Ireland movement, and joined the revolutionary Fenian organization in 1860. One of the editors of the Fenian newspaper *The Irish People*, he was arrested in a police raid on the paper's offices in Dublin in 1865 and sentenced to 14 years' penal servitude, but was released after four years in English prisons, his health broken. He remained politically involved and was a leading member of the IRB, the Irish Republican Brotherhood. He wrote the novel *Sally Cavanagh* (1869) while in prison but his true fame as a novelist depends upon *Knocknagow: or, The Homes of Tipperary* (1879), one of the most popular novels in Irish literary history. Essentially a tale of the depopulation of the village of the title through the workings of the land-laws and landlord greed, its appeal lies in its reconstruction of the detail of Irish country life. Kickham's achievement as a novelist cannot be separated from his career as an Irish nationalist rebel.

Kidman, Fiona 1940– New Zealand novelist and short-story writer. Her first novel, the best-selling *A Breed of Women* (1979), seemed to articulate the experience of several generations of women in its story of a woman's struggle to find a life and career for herself in New Zealand society after World War II. Kidman has remained a popular and prolific voice of mainstream feminism in New Zealand writing. *Paddy's Puzzle* (1983; as *In the Clear Light* in USA, 1985) is set in wartime Auckland, while *The Book of Secrets* (1987) is a family saga. *Mrs Dixon and Friend* (1982) and *True Stars* (1990) are collections of stories. She has also published several volumes of poetry.

Kidnapped and ***Catriona*** A novel and its sequel by ROBERT LOUIS STEVENSON. *Kidnapped* was published in 1886 and *Catriona* in 1893.

After the death of his father, David Balfour goes for help to his miserly uncle, Ebenezer. But Ebenezer, who has unlawfully seized David's estate, first attempts to kill him and then, when this fails, has him kidnapped and put aboard a ship bound for the Carolinas. During the voyage Alan Breck, a Jacobite rebel homesick for his native country, is rescued from a sinking boat. When the ship is wrecked off the coast of Mull, David and Alan travel together and accidentally witness the murder of Colin Campbell, the king's factor on the forfeited estate of Ardshiel. Suspicion falls on them and they are forced to take flight across

the Highlands. The story ends with their safe escape, Ebenezer's exposure and the restoration of David's estate.

In the sequel David is in love with Catriona, daughter of the renegade James More. When James Stewart of the Glens is falsely accused of the murder of Colin Campbell, David comes forward on his behalf and finds his own life threatened. He manages to survive the plot against him, and Alan Breck finally escapes to safety in France.

Killigrew, Thomas 1612–83 Playwright and theatre manager. Born in London, Killigrew became page to King Charles I and went into exile with the future Charles II, a lifelong friend. At the Restoration Charles granted him Letters Patent to form a company of players (see PATENT THEATRES). Killigrew established the reconstituted KING'S MEN at DRURY LANE in 1662. His coarse and uninhibited comedy, *The Parson's Wedding*, based on the Spanish of Calderón, had originally been staged before the closing of the theatres in 1642. Published and revived in 1664, it contributed to the emergence of RESTORATION COMEDY. Killigrew also founded one of the first training-schools for actors, at the Barbican, and became Master of the Revels to Charles II in 1673. His brother William, and his son Thomas, both wrote plays; another son, Charles, took over the management of the Theatre Royal in 1671, supervising its rebuilding and reopening in 1674, after a fire had destroyed the first building.

Kilroy, Thomas 1934– Irish playwright and novelist. Born in Callan, County Kilkenny, and educated at University College, Dublin, he has been Professor of English at University College, Galway, since 1978. His novel *The Big Chapel* (1971) won a number of English and Irish awards, but outside his academic pursuits Kilroy has been primarily a dramatist, with *The Death and Resurrection of Mr Roche* (1968), in which otherworldly anticipations undermine an all-male drinking party; *The O'Neill* (1969); *Tea and Sex and Shakespeare* (1976); *Talbot's Box* (1977), in which kaleidoscopic, stylized scenes enact the life and death of the Dublin 'worker's saint', Matt Talbot; and *Double Cross* (1986).

Kilvert, (Robert) Francis 1840–79 Clergyman and diarist. The son of a country clergyman, Kilvert was born in Hardenuish, Wiltshire. Educated at home and at Wadham College, Oxford, he was ordained and served as a curate at Langley Burrell, Clyro, from 1865 to 1872. He became vicar of Bredwardine in Herefordshire in 1877.

On Kilvert's sudden death of peritonitis five weeks after his marriage to Elizabeth Anne Rowland in 1879, his wife destroyed two large sections of his extensive diary, probably for personal reasons (they are believed to have held an account of his courtship of her); a further 19 volumes were later destroyed by his niece. The remaining three volumes, covering the period 1870–9, were discovered by WILLIAM PLOMER and published separately in 1938–40, and in one abridged volume in 1944. Kilvert's *Diary* is a sensitive document of life in the Welsh border country at that time, depicting in vivid detail the local landscape in which he delighted, and the pains and pleasures of rural parish society. The clear and unaffected style of the diary reflects the author's gentle and attractively unworldly personality.

Kim A novel by RUDYARD KIPLING, published in 1901. Exploiting many of his childhood memories of India, it is generally considered his most successful full-length novel. His father supplied the illustrations and advised him on the Buddhist elements in the story.

Kim (Kimball O'Hara) is the orphan son of an Irish colour-sergeant and a nursemaid in a colonel's family. In his early life in the streets of Lahore, he shows self-reliance and resourcefulness, running errands for Mahbub Ali, who works for the British Secret Service. He also meets a Tibetan lama who is on a quest to be freed from the Wheel of Life and becomes his chela, or disciple. Mahbub uses Kim to carry a vital message to Colonel Creighton in Umballa; his journey with the lama on the Grand Trunk Road is rich with PICARESQUE incident and encounters. Kim's education takes a different turn when he is recognized by the chaplain of his father's old regiment and sent to the school for Anglo-Indian children at Lucknow. But he rejoins the lama during the holidays and is taken by Mahbub to Simla, where another agent, Lurgan, acts as a kind of benign Fagin in instructing Kim in the arts of spying and disguise. He plays his most active role in the great game of imperial espionage against the Russians when he joins the lama in an expedition to the hill country of the North. Kim's resourcefulness and worldliness are exercised in capturing documents from enemy spies. At the same time, Kim is united with the lama at the end of the latter's quest for the sacred River of the Arrow. Kim's destiny is left undecided, with the antithetical values of contemplation and the life of action both exerting their attractions upon him.

Kincaid, Jamaica 1949– Caribbean/American novelist and short-story writer. Born and brought up in St John's, Antigua, she went to the United States in her teens. There she worked as a freelance writer, publishing articles in *Rolling Stone, The Paris Review* and *THE NEW YORKER* for which she became a staff writer in 1976. Her novel *Annie John* (1985) is an account of Caribbean girlhood and coming of age which has affinities with the work of JEAN RHYS, ZEE EDGELL and ERNA BRODBER. It provides a particularly vivid account of the protagonist's relationship with her mother and the sense of trauma she experiences in growing away

from her and the Edenic world of childhood. Other works include: *Lucy* (1991), a novel; *At the Bottom of the River* (1983), a collection of sketches and short stories, each realizing a brief moment of experience in a spare, luminous style; and *A Small Place* (1988), a passionate essay attacking the exploitation of Antigua by colonialism in the past and tourism in the present.

King, Francis (Henry) 1923– Novelist and short-story writer. Born and initially brought up in Switzerland, he also spent part of his childhood in India, the setting for his graphic murder mystery, *Acts of Darkness* (1983). He wrote his first three novels while still an undergraduate at Balliol College, Oxford. Subsequently he worked for the British Council in Italy, Greece, Egypt, Finland and Japan, before starting to write full-time in 1964. His fiction displays a careful, sensitive concern with the impulses of human action, a fluent narrative skill and a preoccupation with decadent, sometimes horrific, aberrations of behaviour. Novels include *To the Dark Tower* (1946), *The Dividing Stream* (1951), *The Widow* (1957), *The Custom House* (1961), *Flights* (1973) and *The Action* (1979). *Voices in an Empty Room* (1984) investigates the world of the paranormal, while *The Ant Colony* (1991) deals with young love. Collections of short stories include *The Brighton Belle and Other Stories* (1968) and *Hard Feelings and Other Stories* (1976). He has also published an exemplary short biography of E. M. FORSTER (1978) and edited LAFCADIO HEARN's *Writings from Japan* and the diaries of J. R. ACKERLEY. He is president of the British division of the writers' organization, PEN.

King, Henry 1592–1669 Poet. Son of the Bishop of London who ordained JOHN DONNE, King became an acquaintance of the poet and eventually his executor. Educated at Westminster School and Christ Church, Oxford, he took his DD in 1625, and became Bishop of Chichester in 1642. An impressive preacher and resolute opponent of Puritanism, he was ejected from his see by the forces of Parliament in 1643, taking refuge with friends until he was reappointed at the Restoration. His occasional verses include ELEGIES on Donne, JONSON, RALEIGH and, most memorably, his first wife in *The Exequy*. His work first appeared in book form in 1657.

King, William 1663–1712 Poet and polemicist. He was educated at Westminster School and Christ Church, Oxford, and became a lawyer. After holding various minor posts in Ireland in 1702–8, he returned to England and was appointed gazetteer in 1711. A High-Church Tory, he contributed to the 'Battle of the Books' with *Dialogues of the Dead* (1699), an attack on RICHARD BENTLEY written with Charles Boyle. His first considerable piece was *Dialogue Showing the Way to Modern Preferment* (1690). King is often praised by scholars of the period for his urbane and witty poem *The Art of Cookery, in Imitation of Horace's Art of Poetry* (1708), and for the BURLESQUES and light verse collected in *Miscellanies in Prose and Verse* (1709) and *Useful Miscellanies* (1712).

King Alisaunder An anonymous VERSE ROMANCE of the early 14th century, written in octosyllabic couplets, probably in or near London.

The poem tells the mythical history of Alexander the Great, from the magical circumstances surrounding his conception to his death. The early part of Alisaunder's life to his defeat of Darius occupies the first half of the romance, while the second half deals with his travels and conquests in the East, with many pseudo-geographical descriptions of the lands visited and the marvels encountered there. The poem was intended for oral delivery. Prose and alliterative treatments of the story also exist, some only as fragments. A Scottish version, *The Alexander Buik*, was once attributed to JOHN BARBOUR.

King and No King, A An intrigue-laden tragicomedy by BEAUMONT and FLETCHER, first performed by the KING'S MEN in 1611 and published in 1619.

After a long war between Iberia and Armenia victory goes to Arbaces, King of Iberia, in single combat against Tigranes of Armenia. Arbaces offers Tigranes his liberty and continued peace if he will marry Panthea, his sister. Tigranes declines, for he loves Spaconia. He sends her to Panthea; he hopes that Spaconia will enlighten Panthea and enlist her help in opposing the marriage. Panthea has grown up during Arbaces' absence at the war and when she appears her beauty disturbs not only Tigranes but her brother too. Arbaces tries to smother his incestuous passion; then he discovers that his feelings are reciprocated. Gobrias, Lord Protector of the kingdom, resolves matters by disclosing that he is Arbaces' real father. The Queen Mother had despaired of bearing children and Gobrias had given her his infant son; Panthea was born to the late king and his queen six years later. There is no impediment to their union now, and Tigranes is also free to marry Spaconia.

King Hart [*King Heart*] See DOUGLAS, GAVIN.

King Horn A Middle English VERSE ROMANCE in couplets. Written *c.* 1225 in the South Midlands, the romance follows an Anglo-Norman source but has its origins in Old English storytelling. The poem recounts the life of Horn, the King of England's son, set adrift as a child by the pirates who killed his father. He is brought up by King Aylmer of Westnesse, whose daughter Rymenhild falls in love with him. They enjoy a clandestine affair until they are betrayed and slandered and Horn is consequently exiled. He avenges his father's death and lives abroad for seven years before Rymenhild, forcibly betrothed to King Mody, recalls him. He attends the wedding disguised as a beggar, making himself known to Rymenhild by puns and tokens. He kills Mody, denounces and eventually kills the slanderer, regains his kingdom and marries Rymenhild.

The vigorous narrative is devoid of the spurious incidents which so often mar romances. The treatment of the central couple is sensitive and has a certain degree of psychological realism. Two related poems, *Horn Child* and the *Ballad of Hind Horn*, are less successful.

King James Version, The See BIBLE IN ENGLISH, THE.

King John, The Life and Death of An early history play by WILLIAM SHAKESPEARE. Its relationship to the anonymous *The Troublesome Reign of John, King of England* has given rise to much speculation. That play was first published in 1591, and it may be that Shakespeare's text, first published in the First Folio of 1623, is a playhouse revision of the older text, prepared for a performance in *c.* 1595. It is certainly tempting to explain away the defects of Shakespeare's version by supposing it to be a piece of theatrical cobbling.

The King is determined to keep his throne despite the better claims of his young nephew, Arthur, who has the support of the King of France as well as a legitimate succession from John's older brother, Geoffrey. Harassed not only by the French, but also by Arthur's mother Constance and by Cardinal Pandulph, the papal legate, John bribes Hubert de Burgh to blind Arthur. In a memorable scene, the boy's pleas so move Hubert that he spares him. But Arthur later jumps to his death while trying to escape. The French invade and defeat John, who takes refuge in Swinstead Abbey. There he dies, believed poisoned by a monk. The French troops return home, leaving Cardinal Pandulph to negotiate an honourable peace.

The rantings of Constance attracted many notable 19th-century actresses, but the chief splendour of the play is the loyal but outspoken Bastard, Faulconbridge, under whose guidance the new king, Henry III, must try to restore England after the ravages of King John's reign.

King Lear A tragedy by WILLIAM SHAKESPEARE, first performed *c.* 1605. The text of the First Folio edition (1623) differs considerably from the 1608 Quarto. Shakespeare turned to various sources, including HOLINSHED's *Chronicles* for the outline of Lear's story and SIR PHILIP SIDNEY's *ARCADIA* for the Gloucester sub-plot.

The aged British King decides to share his kingdom between his three daughters and spend his remaining years as a regular guest at their courts. The plan goes awry when his youngest (and favourite) daughter, Cordelia, refuses to earn her share by joining her older sisters, Goneril and Regan, in exaggerated public declarations of love for her father. The angry King banishes the Duke of Kent when he defends Cordelia, and divides his kingdom between Goneril and Regan. The despised Cordelia is taken, without dowry, as wife by the King of France and leaves the country. Lear finds Goneril's grudging hospitality an outrage and leaves for Regan's castle, but she puts even greater restrictions on his entertainment. The incredulous King rants against his cruel daughters and is finally driven out to brave the hardships of the heath during a storm. Only his Fool and the loyal Kent, serving him in disguise, go with him. They meet 'poor Tom', apparently a mad beggar but really Edgar, son of the Duke of Gloucester, who has fallen from his father's favour through the plotting of his illegitimate brother Edmund. Tried beyond his strength, Lear goes mad, and, in his madness, encounters his own unprotected humanity.

When Goneril, Regan, Edmund and Regan's husband the Duke of Cornwall hear that a French army has landed, and that Lear is being taken to Dover to be reunited with Cordelia, they blind Gloucester, whose pity for the King has led him to assist his escape to Dover. Edgar, still posing as poor Tom, tends his father until death. Lear finds Cordelia at Dover and is restored to sanity; but the French lose the battle and Cordelia and Lear are captured. Edmund, powerful because he is the lover of both Regan and Goneril, gives orders that they should be put to death. He is defeated in single combat by Edgar but his dying confession comes too late to save Cordelia. Lear dies cradling her body and insisting she is still alive.

King Lear can be read in various ways: as a domestic tragedy of parents and children; as a public tragedy in which the king's sufferings make him discover a common humanity with the most despised of his subjects; as a theological or philosophical drama which probes the various meanings of 'nature'. On any reading, it is the most titanic of Shakespeare's great tragedies.

King Solomon's Mines A novel by Sir Henry Rider Haggard, published in 1885, his first successful work, although *Dawn* (1884) and *The Witch's Head* (1884) had already appeared.

The novel was inspired by Robert Louis Stevenson's *Treasure Island* and makes use of Stevenson's framework of a treasure-map and a perilous quest. Three European heroes, Sir Henry Curtis, Captain John Good RN and the narrator, Allan Quatermain, accompanied by their native servant, Umbopa, set off to find Curtis's missing brother, George, who has gone to look for the treasure of King Solomon's mines in the lost land of the Kukuanas. After an archetypally perilous journey over waterless desert and freezing mountains, they encounter the villainous King Twala and the horrific witch-doctor, Gagool. Umbopa turns out to be the rightful king, and civil war breaks out. Umbopa is victorious in the decisive battle, and Twala is killed in single combat with Curtis. Guided by Gagool, the heroes set off to find Solomon's diamond mine, but are tricked by Gagool and left to die in an underground vault. They escape and return to life and, finally, to civilization; on their return journey the missing brother is found.

Although Haggard's attitude to the 'savage' is ambivalently divided between the evil Twala and the heroic Umbopa, the final abdication of European influence and the sealing-off of the lost land to its own separate development show Haggard's uneasiness about the impact of intrusive European culture on 'primitive' peoples.

King's Men, The The finest of Elizabethan theatre companies, it was formed in 1594 as the Lord Chamberlain's Men, taken into his personal patronage by James I in 1603 and renamed the King's Men. Four of the original shareholders were still with the company at that time, Richard Burbage, Augustine Phillips, John Heminges and William Shakespeare. They had overseen the move from the Theatre to the Globe in 1599, losing Will Kemp, whom they replaced with Robert Armin, on the way. It was at the Globe that the company confirmed its supremacy, duly rewarded by the new king. As well as Shakespeare's plays, the repertoire of the King's Men included work by Jonson, Webster, Tourneur, Middleton, Marston, Beaumont and Fletcher. In 1608 they added the indoor Blackfriars Theatre to the outdoor Globe, continuing to perform at both until the closure of the theatres in 1642. After Shakespeare's retirement, Fletcher became the 'attached' playwright of the King's Men, to be succeeded in turn by Massinger. Evidence of the bonds of loyalty and friendship that united the company survives in wills and in the decision to assemble the plays of their late colleague in the priceless Shakespeare Folio of 1623. Like all of London's professional groups, the King's Men were disbanded during the Interregnum, and it was a quite different and less remarkable company that assembled at Drury Lane in 1662, under the nominal leadership of Thomas Killigrew and the patronage of Charles II.

King's Tragedy, The A poem by Dante Gabriel Rossetti published in *Ballads and Sonnets* (1881), in which Catherine Douglas (Kate Barlass) tells the story of the murder of James I of Scotland and her own vain attempt to save him.

Kingis Quair, The An early 15th-century poem written in a northern dialect. James I of Scotland has been proposed as its author but the attribution rests largely on the supposed autobiographical content of the poem. It tells how an imprisoned king falls in love with a woman he sees from the window of his tower. The central part of the poem is a DREAM-VISION in which the king learns about love and fortune. On waking he receives a message carried by a dove foretelling his fortune in love and he eventually weds the lady. While notable for its description, the poem has a very weak plot serving principally to support the moral allegory of the dream-vision. The verse is strongly influenced by CHAUCER and its philosophical content derived from Boethius. RHYME-ROYAL stanzas are probably so called because of their use in this poem.

Kinglake, Alexander William 1809–91 Historian and travel-writer. Born at Taunton in Somerset and educated at Eton and Trinity College, Cambridge, Kinglake was called to the Bar in 1837 and maintained a successful practice until 1856. He is best remembered as the author of *Eothen: or, Traces of Travel Brought Home from the Near East* (1844), a brilliant and evocative account of his adventures. He followed the British army to the Crimea and at the request of Lady Raglan, widow of the commander-in-chief, wrote a meticulous history, *The Invasion of the Crimea* (1863–87).

Kingsley, Charles 1819–75 Clergyman, novelist and writer of CHILDREN'S LITERATURE. Son of the vicar of Holne in Devon, he was educated at King's College, London, and Magdalene College, Cambridge. In 1842 he became curate, and two years later the vicar, of Eversley in Hampshire; he held the living until his death, combining his parochial duties with the many other activities of his restless, combative life. He served as professor of modern history at Cambridge in 1860–9, and was appointed Canon of Chester in 1869 and of Westminster in 1873.

The Saint's Tragedy, a drama about the life of St Elizabeth of Hungary, appeared in 1848. Other writings of this period show the influence of THOMAS CARLYLE and F. D. MAURICE, leader of the movement for CHRISTIAN SOCIALISM. Kingsley contributed to *Politics for the People* (1848) and *The Christian Socialist* (1850–1) under the pseudonym of Parson Lot. YEAST, serialized in FRASER'S MAGAZINE in 1848 and issued in book form in 1850, was followed by ALTON LOCKE (1850). With passionate and emphatic realism they expose the social injustice suffered by agricultural labourers and workers in the clothing trade. *Alton Locke* also deals memorably with the scandal of London's inadequate sanitation, as well as describing the Chartist agitation of the 1840s. HYPATIA (1843), a historical novel about the conflicts of early Christianity, is regarded by many as his finest work. WESTWARD HO! (1855), another historical novel, turned to the Elizabethan era and the landscape of Kingsley's West Country childhood. *Two Years Ago* (1857) has a contemporary setting.

Other works include: *Glaucus: or, The Wonders of the Shore* (1855), a volume of natural history; *The Heroes* (1856), retelling the legends of Perseus, Theseus and Jason, and THE WATER BABIES (1863), a didactic fantasy, both for children; *The Roman and the Teuton* (1864), a course of lectures given at Cambridge; *Hereward the Wake* (1866), a historical novel about the 'Last of the English' and his defeat by William the Conqueror at Ely; *At Last* (1871), an account of his journey to the West Indies; and *Prose Idylls* (1873), a volume of accomplished essays.

Kingsley was notable for his application of Christian ethics to the social problems of the age and for a commitment to change that stopped well short of radicalism. His own brand of athletic, hearty Protestantism, popularly dubbed 'muscular Christianity', frequently led him into conflict. His review of JAMES ANTHONY FROUDE's *History of England* in 1864 angered NEWMAN and prompted his APOLOGIA PRO VITA SUA.

Kingsley, Henry 1830–76 Novelist and younger brother of CHARLES KINGSLEY. He was an undergraduate at Worcester College, Oxford, but left under a cloud to spend five years (1853–8) in Australia, serving for a time in the Sydney mounted police. *Geoffrey Hamlyn* (1859), the novel he published on his return to England, took Australia as its setting. It was followed by a romance, RAVENSHOE (1862), *Austin Elliott* (1863) and *The Hillyars and the Burtons* (1865), another Australian novel. Kingsley became editor of *The Edinburgh Daily Review* in 1869 but left that post to become a reporter with the German armies during the Franco-Prussian War. Among his 16 other novels were *Leighton Court* (1866), *The Boy in Grey* (1871) and *Reginald Hetherege* (1874).

Kingsley, Mary 1852–1931 See MALET, LUCAS.

Kingsley, Mary (Henrietta) 1862–1900 Travel-writer. She was born in Islington, London, the niece of CHARLES KINGSLEY. In 1893 she travelled to West Africa in order to study primitive religion and published an original and informative account of the journey in *Travels in West Africa* (1897).

Kingsley, Sidney 1906– American playwright. He was born Sidney Kirschner in New York, and was educated at Cornell. He made his name with *Men in White* (produced by the GROUP THEATRE; 1933), about a young doctor's experiences in a hospital, and *Dead End* (1935), about young people in the slums. Subsequent work includes: *The Patriots* (1943), about the conflict between JEFFERSON and Alexander Hamilton; *Detective Story* (1949), about police brutality; an adaptation (1951) of KOESTLER's *Darkness at*

Noon; *Lunatics and Lovers* (1954), a FARCE; and *Night Life* (1962), a grim portrait of New York nightclub life.

Kingsmill, Hugh 1889–1949 Man of letters. He was educated at Harrow, Oxford (where he failed to get a degree) and Dublin (where he succeeded). The second son of Sir Henry Lunn, the travel agent, he worked for his father's firm until he was 38. Thereafter he supported himself precariously on literary earnings.

His first novel, *A Will to Love*, was published in 1919, shortly after his release from prisoner-of-war camp in Germany. This was followed by *The Dawn's Delay* (1924) and *Blondel* (1927). Biographies of MATTHEW ARNOLD (1928), FRANK HARRIS (1932), SAMUEL JOHNSON (1933), DICKENS (1934) and D. H. LAWRENCE (1938) gained him a reputation for irreverence. Better received was *The Return of William Shakespeare* (1929), in which SHAKESPEARE returns from the dead for six weeks, reads what the critics have said about him and delivers a long oration on the meaning of his works. Among Kingsmill's anthologies are *Invective and Abuse* (1929), *Made on Earth* (on marriage; 1937) and *The High Hill of the Muses* (studies of Johnson 'without Boswell'), published posthumously in 1955. He collaborated with WILLIAM GERHARDIE on *The Casanova Fable* (1934), with Malcolm Muggeridge on two books of PARODIES, *Brave Old World* (1936) and *Next Year's News* (1938), and with Hesketh Pearson produced a series of 'conversational travel books', *Skye High* (1937), *This Blessed Plot* (1942) and *Talking of Dick Whittington* (1947). Kingsmill wrote articles and book reviews for a number of periodicals and was literary editor of PUNCH and *The New English Review*. A collection of his essays published in 1949 as *The Progress of a Biographer* contains much of his best work. A critic of deep perception and sensibility, he is scarcely known by the general reading public today.

Kingston, Maxine Hong 1940– American novelist. Born in Stockton, California, she lives in Hawaii, where she has worked as a schoolteacher. *The Woman Warrior* (1976) and *China Men* (1980) are partly fictionalized memoirs dealing, respectively, with her childhood and the ancestors who emigrated from China to the USA. *Tripmaster Monkey* (1989) is an intricate PICARESQUE novel set in San Francisco in the 1960s.

Kinnell, Galway 1927– American poet. Born in Providence, Rhode Island, he was educated at Princeton, where W. S. MERWIN was among his classmates, and the University of Rochester. He has worked as director of an adult education programme in Chicago, field worker for the Congress of Racial Equality, journalist in Teheran and teacher at, among other institutions, Reed College in Oregon and the University of California at Irvine. His first books of

poetry, *What a Kingdom It Was* (1960), *Flower Herding on Mount Monadnock* (1964) and *Body Rags* (1968), established him as a contemporary master of free verse. *The Book of Nightmares* (1971) confirmed the sacramental dimension apparent in all his work with poems approximating a personalized chant which accepts death as part of the primal rhythm of existence. His other collections are *First Poems, 1946–54* (1970), *The Shoes of Wandering* (1971), *The Avenue Bearing the Initial of Christ into the New World: 1946–1964* (1974), *Mortal Acts, Mortal Words* (1980), *Selected Poems* (1982, PULITZER PRIZE) and *When One Has Lived a Long Time* (1990). He has also published: a novel, *Black Light* (1966); a collection of interviews, *Walking Down the Stairs* (1978); translations of French writers, including Villon; and a selection of WALT WHITMAN's work (1987).

Kinsella, Thomas 1928– Irish poet and translator. Born in Dublin, he abandoned a science course at University College, Dublin, for a career in the Irish Civil Service (1946–65). He subsequently taught English at the University of Southern Illinois and, since 1970, at Temple University, Philadelphia, though he continues to spend time in Dublin. One of the most prolific and respected of contemporary Irish poets, his published volumes range from *Poems* (1956) to *Songs of the Psyche* (1985) and *One Fond Embrace* (1988). The characteristic themes of his calmly objective earlier poetry are personal: love's difficulty, nightmare and illness, the sometimes ominous unpeopled serenities of the countryside. *Nightwalker* (1968), influenced by T.S. ELIOT and (self-consciously) by JOYCE, signalled a new departure, recording a sense of personal and cultural disarray. Some poems, such as the ELEGIES in *Fifteen Dead* (1979), have directly confronted the social and political realities of contemporary Ireland and its heritage of political violence. His later works have largely abandoned formal elegance and accessibility for ambitiously experimental explorations of psychic, historical and cultural origins and evolution. His translations from the Irish include *An Duanaire: Poems of the Dispossessed* (with Sean O'Tuama; 1981), a version of the ancient *Cattle Raid of Cooley* (*The Tain*, 1985) and items in his edition of *The Oxford Book of Irish Verse* (1986).

Kipling, Rudyard 1865–1936 Poet, short-story writer and novelist. He was born in Bombay, where his father, John Lockwood Kipling, taught at a school of art before becoming director of the Lahore museum. The family connections on his mother's side were distinguished: one of her sisters married the painter Edward Burne-Jones, a second was the mother of the politician Stanley Baldwin. When Kipling and his sister were sent to Southsea, England, in 1871, the boy's unhappiness – recalled in the story 'Baa, Baa, Black

Rudyard Kipling

Sheep' (1888) – was alleviated by visits to Burne-Jones, who along with WILLIAM MORRIS inspired his move in 1878 to the United Services College at Westward Ho! in Devon. Kipling's relatively happy years at school underlie the popular STALKY & CO. (1899).

Moving back to India in 1882, he began his early career as a journalist in Lahore on *The Civil and Military Gazette* and later as an editor for *The Pioneer* of Allahabad. His familiarity with all ranks of the Anglo-Indian community contributed to the freshness of the poems and tales he wrote for the *Gazette*. Many of these were subsequently published as *Departmental Ditties* (1886) and *Plain Tales from the Hills* (1888). Other tales which established his reputation in India were published in booklet form by the Indian Railway Library. The stories of SOLDIERS THREE (1892) began in this form, along with *The Phantom Rickshaw* and *Wee Willie Winkie* (both 1888).

After his return to England in 1889 he rapidly established himself in literary London, winning friendship as well as praise from HENRY JAMES, RIDER HAGGARD and W. E. HENLEY. Henley published Kipling's poems in his *Scots Observer*; these were later collected as *BARRACK-ROOM BALLADS AND OTHER VERSES* (1892). With the collections of short stories, *LIFE'S HANDICAP* (1891) and *MANY INVENTIONS* (1893), Kipling set a pattern for his major writings. The novels of this period, *The Light That Failed* (1891) and *The Naulahka* (in collaboration with Wolcott Balestier; 1892), were relative failures. In 1892 Kipling married Balestier's sister, Caroline, and they spent the years 1892–6 near her family in Vermont, USA. The stories in *THE JUNGLE BOOK* (1894) and *The Second Jungle Book* (1895) were written here. The elder of Kipling's daughters died in 1899 on a return visit to the USA. By the time his son John was born in 1897, the family had moved back to England, settling in Sussex in 1902. His best-known novel, *KIM*, was published in 1901.

Kipling began to visit South Africa regularly after 1898, including a period during the Boer War. Here he began the *JUST SO STORIES* (1902). This collection, along with *PUCK OF POOK'S HILL* (1906) and *Rewards and Fairies* (1910), shows an unusual sympathy with children. He continued to publish collections of short stories for adults throughout the rest of his life, including *TRAFFICS AND DISCOVERIES* (1904), *Actions and Reactions* (1909) and *A Diversity of Creatures* (1917), containing the famous 'Mary Postgate'. This story is only one example of his ability to reflect on empire and warfare with an eye to the personal bitterness and the cost of sustaining imperial ideals. To the late collections, *Debits and Credits* (1926) and *Limits and Renewals* (1932), there was added his posthumous work of autobiographical fragments, *Something of Myself* (1937).

Kipling's high reputation, as 'Poet of Empire' and the first English writer to receive the Nobel Prize for Literature (1907), had begun to wane before his death. It has been left to later generations to rediscover the craft of his poetry and the stern realism of his short stories.

Kipps: The Story of a Simple Soul A novel by H. G. WELLS, published in 1905.

Arthur Kipps remembers little of his mother, who left him to be raised by an uncle and aunt, shopkeepers in New Romney. George Woodrow, schoolmaster at the genteel Cavendish Academy, and others who also pose as social mentors to the inarticulate Kipps, are of little service. Kipps's natural feelings for Ann Pornick, a childhood sweetheart, prove a saving grace in the years of deadening apprenticeship to Mr Shalford the draper, in Folkestone. More particularly, Ann's influence contrasts with that of Helen Walshingham, Kipps's wood-carving teacher, who changes her attitude to him when she hears that he has inherited a fortune from his grandfather. Kipps's legacy leads to a bitterly comic process of social initiation, with Helen taking a leading part in his loss of self-esteem.

Kipps again meets Ann, now a servant at the house where he is a dinner guest. They decide to marry but Kipps soon learns that his money has been embezzled by Helen's brother. Kipps's social misfortunes are discussed by his friends, the impoverished, drunken playwright Chitterlow and the bitter working-class intellectual, Masterman. The unexpected success of Chitterlow's play, in which Kipps has invested, restores the fortunes of Kipps, Ann and their child.

Kit-Cat Club A coterie of 18th-century writers with Whig sympathies, including JOSEPH ADDISON, WILLIAM CONGREVE, RICHARD STEELE, SIR JOHN VANBRUGH and the physician SIR SAMUEL GARTH. The club originally met at the London house of a pastry-cook, Christopher Katt (or Catling), whose mutton pies were called kit-cats, but later moved to the home of the club's secretary, JACOB TONSON the publisher. Many of the members were painted by Sir Godfrey Kneller in portraits slightly less than half-length but including the hands, a size of canvas now termed *kit-cat*.

Kizer, Carolyn (Ashley) 1925– American poet. Born in Spokane, Washington, she was educated at Sarah Lawrence College and the University of Washington, where she studied under THEODORE ROETHKE. In 1959 she founded the magazine *Poetry Northwest*, which she edited until 1965. Her first volume, entitled simply *Poems*, appeared in 1959. Her work is notable for its exploration of feminist issues, continued in collections such as *The Ungrateful Garden* (1961), *Knock upon Silence* (1965), *Midnight was My City: New and Selected Poems* (1971), *Mermaids in the Basement: Poems for Women* (1984), *Yin: New Poems* (1984, PULITZER PRIZE) and *Carrying Over* (1992). *Proses: Selected Essays, Reviews, and Conversations* appeared in 1992.

Klein, A(braham) M(oses) 1909–72 Canadian poet. Born in Montreal of an orthodox Jewish family, he practised as a barrister from 1933–54. As a poet, one of the so-called 'Montreal group', he is highly regarded. Among his books of verse are *Hath Not a Jew* (1940) and his best-known collection, *The Rocking Chair* (1948). *The Second Scroll* (1951) is a short novel accompanied by poems and brief scenes of verse drama.

Knickerbocker Group, The Early 19th-century school of American writers, mainly living in New York. Deriving its name from WASHINGTON IRVING's pseudonym, Diedrich Knickerbocker, it tended towards sophistication in style and conservatism in politics. Members included Irving himself, WILLIAM CULLEN BRYANT, JAMES KIRKE PAULDING, FITZ-GREENE HALLECK and Joseph Rodman Drake. Much of their work appeared in THE KNICKERBOCKER MAGAZINE.

Knickerbocker Magazine, The A monthly magazine founded in New York by Lewis G. and Willis G. Clark in 1833. It survived until 1865. Although dominated by the KNICKERBOCKER GROUP, it published most living American writers of distinction – WASHINGTON IRVING, HENRY WADSWORTH LONGFELLOW, NATHANIEL HAWTHORNE, JOHN GREENLEAF WHITTIER, WILLIAM DEAN HOWELLS, OLIVER WENDELL HOLMES and WILLIAM CULLEN BRYANT among them.

Knight, Ellis Cornelia 1757–1837 Miscellaneous writer. The daughter of Admiral Knight, she became an associate of SAMUEL JOHNSON and his circle. *Dinarbas* (1790) is a romantic continuation of *RASSELAS*. After spending many years on the Continent, some of them as companion to Nelson's mistress, Lady Hamilton, she became a companion to Queen Charlotte in 1805, incautiously abandoning this dull job to become companion to Princess Charlotte in 1813. From 1816 onwards she lived mainly on the Continent, dying at Paris. Her *Autobiography*, posthumously edited from her diaries and published in 1861, is discreet about Nelson and Lady Hamilton but notable for its portrait of court life.

Knight, G(eorge) (Richard) Wilson 1897–1985 Critic. Born in Sutton, Surrey, and educated at Dulwich College and at St Edmund Hall, Oxford, Knight served in the Royal Engineers from 1916 to 1920, then worked as a schoolteacher in Kent and Cheltenham before becoming professor of English at the University of Toronto in 1931, where he also undertook and performed in productions of SHAKESPEARE's plays. After another spell of schoolteaching during the war, he returned to university life at Leeds in 1946, becoming professor of English literature from 1956 until his retirement to Exeter in 1962.

Although he also wrote critical books on Ibsen, BYRON and JOHN COWPER POWYS, Knight's life's work was devoted to Shakespeare, about whom he wrote 13 books. The most important of them, *The Wheel of Fire* (1930), pioneered a major new movement in Shakespearean interpretation, which concentrated on the 'spatial' dimension of the plays: Knight replaced the traditional reading of plot and character with a view of Shakespeare's plays as expanded poetic metaphors. This approach was taken up by L. C. KNIGHTS and other Shakespearean critics, and applied to prose fiction by F. R. LEAVIS and Q. D. LEAVIS. Knight's other principal works of Shakespearean interpretation are *The*

Imperial Theme (1931), *The Shakespearean Tempest* (1932), *The Crown of Life* (1947) and *The Mutual Flame* (1955). He also wrote *Principles of Shakespearean Production* (1936).

Knight, Richard Payne See PICTURESQUE.

Knight of the Burning Pestle, The A comedy, formerly attributed to the partnership of FRANCIS BEAUMONT and JOHN FLETCHER, but now believed to be the work of Beaumont alone. It was first produced, without great success, by a BOYS' COMPANY in 1607. It affords a precious glimpse of stage practices in the PRIVATE THEATRES of the time, and a wittily critical view of both contemporary drama and the attitudes of London's merchant class.

At a performance of 'The London Merchant' a grocer and his wife in the audience interrupt the play with a demand that their apprentice, Ralph, shall have a part in it. To fit Ralph's aspirations the play is interspersed with scenes written by the grocer himself and renamed 'The Knight of the Burning Pestle'. Ralph becomes a grocer errant, with a burning pestle as his device, and has wild adventures that include the defeat of Barbaroso, a villainous barber. His scenes are a BURLESQUE of the romantic knight errantry found in such works as HEYWOOD's *The Four Prentices of London*. Interspersed with Ralph's histrionic pretensions is the main plot concerning another apprentice, Jasper, who is in love with Luce, daughter of the merchant who is his master. The merchant favours Humphrey, but Jasper carries off Luce when she is about to be married to his rival. Luce is brought back by her furious parents and locked up, so Jasper feigns death and gets himself taken to the house in a coffin. He appears to the merchant as a ghost and succeeds in gaining his consent to the marriage by frightening him.

Knight's Tale, The See CANTERBURY TALES, THE.

Knights, L(ionel) C(harles) 1906– Critic. Born in Grantham and educated at Cambridge University, Knights began lecturing in English at the University of Manchester in 1933 before becoming professor of English at Sheffield University from 1947 and at Bristol University from 1953, returning to Cambridge as Edward VII Professor of English Literature from 1965 to 1973. He founded SCRUTINY in 1932, and as co-editor until 1953 he led that journal's work on SHAKESPEARE and 17th-century literature. His best-known work is the essay 'How Many Children Had Lady Macbeth?' (1933), a milestone in Shakespeare criticism, which attacked the literal-mindedness of A. C. BRADLEY's work on Shakespearean characters, thus clearing the ground for new methods of metaphorical interpretation led by G. WILSON KNIGHT and exemplified by Knights himself in *Some Shakespearian*

Themes (1959) and *An Approach to Hamlet* (1961). Knights's criticism, particularly in *Drama and Society in the Age of Jonson* (1937), shows a strong sociological interest. His essays were published as *Explorations* (1946), *Further Explorations* (1965) and *Explorations 3* (1976).

Knolles, Richard ?1550–1610 Historian. Knolles studied at Oxford, became a fellow there and then master of the grammar school at Sandwich. His *General History of the Turks* (1603) was one of the earliest English examinations of the Ottoman Empire. It gave WILLIAM D'AVENANT the basis for his spectacular entertainment, THE SIEGE OF RHODES, and in a later century influenced the poetry of BYRON.

Knowles, James Sheridan 1784–1862 Playwright. Knowles was born in Cork, the son of a lexicographer, but moved with his family to London in 1793 and studied medicine at the University of Aberdeen. After early practice as a doctor, he became an actor in 1808, a schoolmaster in 1811, an actor again from 1832 to 1843 and an evangelical preacher after 1844. His decidedly sanctimonious *Lectures on Dramatic Literature* (2 vols., 1873) are pulpit pieces, written with the brief authority of a former playwright considered in his time a rival to SHAKESPEARE. Almost forgotten today, Knowles is a victim of his own inflated reputation. Much of that reputation was owed to the actor, William Macready, whose moving portrayal of suffering fatherhood in Knowles's *Virginius* (1820) brought the playwright into prominence. Later paternal tragedies included *William Tell* (1825) and *John of Procida* (1840). Written, like all his 23 plays, in overregular blank verse they are too mawkish to survive 20th-century appraisal. The romances, modelled on JOHN FLETCHER rather than Shakespeare, are more successful. They include *The Beggar's Daughter of Bethnal Green* (1828), revised as *The Beggar of Bethnal Green* (1834), and the understandably popular *The Hunchback* (1832). Best of all, though entirely neglected because of Knowles's claims as a writer of tragedies, are the comedies, *The Love-Chase* (1837) and *Old Maids* (1841).

Knox, John ?1514–72 Knox was the most important and the most vehement of the Scottish Reformers. He was born in East Lothian and trained for the priesthood. His conversion to Protest-antism was influenced by the religious leader George Wishart, who was subsequently burned as a heretic. Knox was preaching the reformed religion by 1547. During the reign of the Protestant English king Edward VI he was licensed as a preacher in England, had an itinerant ministry in the South of England and was even offered the bishopric of Rochester.

On the accession of Mary he fled abroad, becoming pastor of an English congregation in Frankfurt am Main and then minister to Protestant exiles in Geneva, where he met Calvin. He regarded his years in Geneva as his happiest. From abroad he published *A Faithful Admonition* (1554) to the English Protestants and the famous *The First Blast of the Trumpet against the Monstrous Regiment of Women* (1558). It argued that women in authority are contrary to religion and natural law, and was directed against the three female Catholic rulers of France, Scotland and England (Catherine de' Medici, the regent Mary of Guise and Mary Tudor). Knox's belief that magistrates and the nobility may resist a ruler endangering true religion did not endear him to Queen Elizabeth, who banned him from England.

He was recalled by the Protestant party to Scotland in 1559, during the troubled times after the death of Mary of Guise. Knox was instrumental in organizing and establishing a liturgy for the Scottish Reformed Church, with its moderately Calvinist faith, elected ministry and prohibition of the mass. His *First Book of Discipline* (1559) advocated a national system of education. Mary Queen of Scots arrived in Scotland in 1561 and Knox was granted a famous series of audiences which culminated in Mary accusing him of treason, a charge which her Privy Council refused to uphold. These encounters are described in the fourth book of his major work, *The History of the Reformation of Religion within the Realm of Scotland* (1587). Knox died in Edinburgh after managing, despite illness, to preach a fiery sermon in St Giles's Cathedral on the St Bartholomew's Day Massacre.

Koch, Christopher 1932– Australian novelist. Born in Hobart, Tasmania, he was partly educated at a Christian Brothers' school, an experience on which sections of his novel *The Doubleman* (1985) are based. While an undergraduate at the University of Tasmania, he began writing his first novel, *The Boys in the Island*, subsequently published in 1958. In 1955 he travelled to Europe, spending time in India, which provided the inspiration for his second novel, *Across the Sea Wall* (1965), on the way. He subsequently lived in London for two years, before returning to Australia in 1957 and joining the Australian Broadcasting Commission where he worked as a radio producer and eventually became Federal Head of Radio for Schools. In the early 1970s he left the ABC to become a full-time writer. His third novel, *The Year of Living Dangerously* (1978), generally regarded as his finest work, is set in Sukarno's Indonesia, where he also lived and worked briefly. Koch now lives in Sydney.

He first came to the fore, with PATRICK WHITE and RANDOLPH STOW, in challenging the NATURALISM which dominated Australian fiction until the 1950s. A meticulous stylist, he writes prose aiming towards poetry in its symbolic density. His themes are an encounter with a romantic 'otherland' and an exploration of the dualities he finds at the heart of the human condition. Brought up as a Roman Catholic, he became interested in Gnosticism after spending time in Asia, and in *Across the Sea Wall* and *The Year of Living Dangerously* he explores the alternative spiritual possibilities which Eastern religions and cultures offer the Australian psyche. *The Boys in the Island* and *The Doubleman* are notable for graphic evocations of his native Tasmania. He has also written: *Chinese Journey* (with NICHOLAS HASLUCK; 1985), a collection of verse and prose; the screenplay for the film of *The Year of Living Dangerously* (1985), with Peter Weir and DAVID WILLIAMSON; and a collection of essays, *Crossing the Gap* (1987).

Koch, Kenneth 1925– American poet. Born in Cincinnati, Ohio, he served in the US Army in the Pacific and was educated at Harvard and Columbia universities. With FRANK O'HARA and JOHN ASHBERY, he emerged as a leading poet of the NEW YORK SCHOOL in the 1950s. Much of his early work in particular was influenced by the French surrealist Jacques Prévert, whom he discovered during three years spent in Europe. Like others of the New York School, Koch makes frequent use of urban settings and metaphors. His volumes include: *Poems* (1953); *Ko: or a Season on Earth* (1959), a comic EPIC in verse which simultaneously approximates to being a novel; *Permanently* (1960); *Thank You and Other Poems* (1962); *Sleeping with Women* (1969); *The Art of Love* (1975); *The Duplications* (1977); *Sleeping on the Wing* (1981); *Selected Poems, 1952–1982* (1985); *On the Edge* (1986); and *Seasons on Earth; Ko: or a Season on Earth; and The Duplications* (1987). As well as teaching poetry at Columbia University, he has taught the writing of poetry to children and the elderly, and published two books on the subject: *Rose, Where Did You Get That Red? Teaching Great Poetry to Children* (1973) and *I Never Told Anybody: Teaching Poetry in a Nursing Home* (1977). He has also written several off-Broadway plays, collected in *Bertha and Other Plays* (1969) and *One Thousand Avant-Garde Plays* (1988). *The Red Robins* (1975) is his only novel proper.

John Knox: an engraving of 1798

Koestler, Arthur 1905–83 Novelist and thinker. His early life was essentially a paradigm of the turmoil Europe suffered in the years before World War II, and his writings were essentially a commentary, always engaged but increasingly oblique and reflective, on the nature and roots of that turmoil. Born in Budapest and educated in Vienna, he lived in a Zionist settlement in Palestine, worked as a journalist in Berlin, joined the Communist Party and visited the Soviet Union, reported the Spanish Civil War, and suffered imprisonment in Spain, Paris and again after his escape to Britain. His first book in English, *The Scum of the Earth* (1941), recounts these experiences, while *Arrow in the Blue* (1952) and *The Invisible Writing* (1954) continue the autobiographical process. His most widely read book, *Darkness at Noon* (1940), a novel written in German and translated into English by Daphne Hardy, condemns Stalin's totalitarianism in its account of a political prisoner, N. S. Rubasov. *Arrival and Departure* (1943) examines the motives of those dealing with resistance groups, and *The Yogi and the Commissar* (1945) is a volume of essays on the contemporary political scene. *Thieves in the Night* (1946) is a novel concerning hopes for a Jewish state, and *Promise and Fulfilment* (1949) is a historical account of the Jews in Palestine from 1917 to 1949. *The Age of Longing* (1951) is a novel set in the immediate future when all societies are threatened by nuclear extermination. *The Sleepwalkers* (1959), *The Act of Creation* (1964) and *The Ghost in the Machine* (1967) are about the nature of mind. *The Roots of Coincidence* (1972) and *The Challenge of Chance* (with Sir Alister Hardy and Robert Harvie; 1973) investigate ESP. Suffering from leukaemia and Parkinson's disease, Koestler chose to die in a suicide pact with his wife and left a bequest in his will to promote academic study of psychic phenomena.

Kogawa, Joy 1935– Canadian poet and novelist. Born in Vancouver, a third-generation Japanese-Canadian, she and her family were interned and then sent as workers to the beet-fields in Alberta under the Canadian government's dispersal policy for citizens of Japanese origin during World War II. She did not return to British Columbia but attended university in Saskatchewan and Alberta, the Royal Conservatory of Music and the Anglican Women's Training College in Toronto. She has worked as a schoolteacher and now lives in Toronto. She has published three collections of poetry – *The Splintered Moon* (1967), *A Choice of Dreams* (1974) and *Jericho Road* (1977) – though she is known best for her novel *Obasan* (1981). The first novel about the Japanese-Canadian experience, it is a combination of documentary realism and lyrical protest against the silences of official history. Kogawa speaks out of her own double inheritance as a strongly individual voice within the Canadian multi-cultural tradition.

Kolatkar, Arun 1932– Indian poet. He was born in Kolhapur and works as a graphic artist in Bombay. His reputation as a poet in English is based mainly on his short volume, *Jejuri* (1976), which won the Commonwealth Poetry Prize in 1977. These pithy and sharply observed poems convey a true sense of Indian regional life. Kolatkar also writes in Marathi and translates between his two languages of expression. As well as being the leading poet of Maharashtra, he is regarded as one of the outstanding poets in English in India, though this claim is based upon a comparatively small and limited range of work.

Kopit, Arthur L(ee) 1937– American playwright. He was born in New York and educated at Harvard. His best-known work, *Oh Dad, Poor Dad, Mama's Hung You in the Closet and I'm Feelin' So Sad* (1960), is a PARODY of the THEATRE OF THE ABSURD in its style and of the Oedipal complex in its subject. Other plays have included: *The Day the Whores Came Out to Play Tennis* (1965), about social-climbing country-clubbers; *Indians* (1968), about the genocide of the Indians by white Americans; *Wings* (1978), about a stroke victim; *The End of the World* (1984), a dark comedy about nuclear proliferation; and *The Road to Nirvana* (1990), a scatalogical comedy about Hollywood. Kopit also wrote the book for the musical *Nine* (1982) and a version of *Phantom of the Opera* (1991).

Kroetsch, Robert 1927– Canadian novelist, poet and critic. Born in Heisler, Alberta, he attended the University of Alberta and then worked for six years in the Canadian North and Labrador. He subsequently attended McGill and the University of Iowa, and taught at the Binghamton campus of the State University of New York, where he co-edited the influential post-modernist journal *Boundary 2*. He moved back to Canada as professor of English at the University of Manitoba in the mid-1970s.

Virtually all his fiction is located in his native Alberta and is concerned with the specifics of Western Canadian place and identity. Drawing heav-

ily on classical and native Canadian myths, it frequently involves quests. Perhaps the most notable examples are *The Studhorse Man* (1969), *Gone Indian* (1973), *Badlands* (1975) and *Alibi* (1983). Other novels are *But We are Exiles* (1965), *The Words of My Roaring* (1966) and *What the Crow Said* (1978). His many volumes of verse have been gathered into a poetic autobiography, *Field Notes* (vol. I, 1981; vol. 2, 1985; 'completed' version, 1989). A leading critic, strongly influenced by American post-modernist theory, he has published his essays in *The Lovely Treachery of Words* (1989). Other works include: *Alberta* (1988), a travel book; *The Crow Journals* (1980), a literary diary; *Labyrinths of Voice* (1982), a book-length conversation with two interviewers; and *Excerpts from the Real World* (1986), a prose poem.

Kubla Khan: *or, A Vision in a Dream* A 54-line fragment of an unfinished poem by SAMUEL TAYLOR COLERIDGE, published in *Christabel and Other Poems* (1816). Vaguely oriental in its setting, it presents a sequence of suggestive but cryptic images. In the preface Coleridge gave a famous account of how he came to write it and why it was never completed: 'In the summer of the year 1797, the author then in ill health, retired to a lonely farmhouse between Porlock and Lynton... In consequence of a slight indisposition, an anodyne [probably laudanum] had been prescribed, from the effects of which he fell asleep in his chair at the moment he was reading the following sentence, or words of the same substance in PURCHAS's Pilgrimage: "Here the Khan Kubla commanded a palace to be built, and a stately garden thereunto. And thus ten miles of fertile ground were enclosed with a wall." The author continued for about three hours in a profound sleep.' Coleridge goes on to say that he composed between 200 and 300 lines in his sleep, and hastened to write them down when he woke. 'At this moment he was unfortunately called out by a person on business from Porlock, and detained by him above an hour.' On returning to his room Coleridge found that the rest of the poem had passed from his memory.

Kumin, Maxine 1925– American poet, novelist and short-story writer. Born in Philadelphia and educated at Radcliffe College, she has taught at Brandeis, Columbia and Tufts and served as consultant in poetry to the Library of Congress in 1981–2. Her volumes of poetry include *Halfway* (1961), *The Privilege* (1965), *The Nightmare Factory* (1970), *Up Country: Poems of New England* (PULITZER PRIZE, 1972), *House, Bridge, Fountain, Gate* (1975), *The Retrieval System* (1978), *Our Ground Time Here Will be Brief* (1982) and *The Long Approach* (1985); the best introduction is *New and Selected Poems* (1982). Largely CONFESSIONAL POETRY, her work focuses on loss and survival, and frequently emphasizes the importance of family bonds. Recent writing has stressed the role of the poet and dealt with the threat of Armageddon that seems to hover over contemporary society. Kumin's fiction includes novels – *Through Dooms of Love* (1965), *The Passions of Uxport* (1968), *The Abduction* (1971) and *The Designated Heir* (1974) – and a collection of short stories, *Why Can't We Live Together Like Civilized Human Beings?* (1982).*To Make a Prairie: Essays on Poets, Poetry, and Country Living* appeared in 1979. She was a close friend of ANNE SEXTON, with whom she wrote two books for children; 'How It Was', her preface to *The Collected Poems of Anne Sexton* (1981), is among the most sensitive essays on the poet's work.

Kunene, Mazisi 1930– South African poet. Of Zulu inheritance, he is a graduate of the University of Natal, though he later studied Zulu literature at the School of Oriental and African studies in London. He was in charge of African Studies at the University College of Lesotho from 1958 to 1962 and has subsequently held other university positions outside South Africa. He has been an active representative of the African National Congress in Europe and the USA. Kunene writes in Zulu and then makes his own English version. *Zulu Poems* (1970) and *The Ancestors and the Sacred Mountain* (1982) are both steeped in the Zulu oral tradition while at the same time sounding a strong note of political dissent. His major achievements, identifying him as probably the most ambitious poet in modern Africa, are two long epic works, *Emperor Shaka the Great* (1979) and *Anthem of the Decades* (1981), both of which help to dignify the modern African by extolling the Zulu cultural and historical inheritance. *Anthem of the Decades* tells of the origin of life as conceived by an African community, and by taking such a perspective of time spells out great hope for the future.

Kunitz, Stanley 1905– American poet. Born in Worcester, Massachusetts, and educated at Harvard, he served with the US Army Air Transport Command in 1943–5. His first volume, *Intellectual Things*, appeared as early as 1930. A second, *Passport to the War: A Selection of Poems* (1944), brought him to a wider audience but it was not until the appearance of *Selected Poems: 1928–58* (1958), which won the PULITZER PRIZE, that he began to command general esteem. His poetry is admired for the frequently extravagant lyricism of its language. Other volumes include *The Testing Tree* (1971), *The Coat without a Seam: Sixty Poems, 1930–1972* (1974), *The Lincoln Relics* (1978), *The Wellfleet Whale and Companion Poems* (1983) and *Next to Last Things* (1985). The

Frontispiece to the 1615 edition of THOMAS KYD's *The Spanish Tragedy,* depicting Hieronimo and Bel-imperia with the murdered Horatio

Poems, 1928–1978 (1979) introduces the full range of his work. He has edited literary anthologies and translated from the Russian of Anna Akhmatova, Andrei Voznesensky and Yevgeny Yevtushenko. *A Kind of Order, A Kind of Folly: Essays and Conversations* appeared in 1975.

Kuppner, Frank 1951– Poet. Born in Glasgow, he read English and German at Glasgow University, later qualifying as an engineer. He earned a living by typing theses and theatre reviewing. His first volume, *A Bad Day for the Sung Dynasty* (1984), consists of 511 quatrains, or one long poem of 511 stanzas, based on Chinese paintings. It is remarkable for its variety: the formality of Chinese landscape mixes with playfulness, bizarre humour alternates with lyricism and SATIRE, modes veer from BATHOS to obscenity. His second collection, *The Intelligent Observation of Naked Women* (1987), features five sequences, including 'An Old Guide-Book to Prague', which attempts elegiac tones. Other work includes: *A Very Quiet Street* (1985), which transforms the story of a notorious Glasgow murder into a series of surreal images; *Ridiculous, Absurd, Disgusting* (1989); and *A Concussed History of Scotland* (1990). Kuppner remains an eccentric, unpredictable talent.

Kyd, Thomas 1558–94 Playwright. Born in London and educated at the Merchant Taylors' School, Kyd practised as a scrivener, was for some years in the service of an unknown lord, was arrested for heresy in 1593 because of his association with CHRISTOPHER MARLOWE, was probably tortured, and died soon after his release. That is almost all we know about him. Even our belief in his authorship of the brilliantly original THE SPANISH TRAGEDY (c. 1589) rests on a reference in THOMAS HEYWOOD's *Apology for Actors* (1612). *The Spanish Tragedy* was an influential adaptation of Senecan tragedy to the English stage. It displays Kyd's inventiveness and his sense of theatre, lending credibility to the view that he wrote a lost *Hamlet* of which SHAKESPEARE made use. The only other surviving play of which we can be fairly certain Kyd was the author is *Cornelia* (1594), a version of Robert Garnier's Senecan tragedy, *Cornélie*.

Kynaston, Sir Francis 1587–1642 Kynaston was the author of a romance in verse, *Leoline and Sydanis* (1642), and the translator into Latin of CHAUCER's *TROILUS AND CRISEYDE*. He opened an academy for young gentlemen and the sons of noblemen, the Museum Minervae, where they could learn the basics of science, languages and courtly accomplishments.

La Belle Dame sans Merci A poem of 100 eight-line stanzas translated from the French of Alain Chartier (*c.* 1424) by Richard Ros of Leicestershire about 1450. It consists of a debate about COURTLY LOVE between a lover and his cruel lady. She consistently refuses him, and he eventually dies. Except for changing the metre from tetrameter to pentameter and adding a brief introduction and conclusion, the translator follows the French source closely. The work was at one time attributed to CHAUCER, being first printed as his in 1526. See CHAUCERIAN APOCRYPHA and also next entry.

La Belle Dame sans Merci A BALLAD by KEATS, written in 1819 and first published in LEIGH HUNT's *The Indicator* the following year. The title derives from Alain Chartier's *La Belle Dame sans Merci* (*c.* 1424), which Keats probably read in Middle English translation (see previous entry). A deceptively slight and self-ironizing work, it tells of a knight's fatal enthralment by a beautiful 'lady', who appears partly as a witch and partly as some 'fairy's child'. It contains what must be one of the most succinct poetic rehearsals of the morbid aspect of Romantic love, though its unconscious profundities are, in turn, often emphasized at the expense of the prevailingly playful tone. Keats did not consider it a major piece, but it was later taken very seriously by the PRE-RAPHAELITES, and WILLIAM MORRIS considered it to be 'the germ from which all the poetry of his group had sprung'.

La Guma, Alex 1925–85 South African novelist. Born in Cape Town, he worked as a clerk, labourer and journalist. One of the 156 successful defendants in the notorious Treason Trial (1956–61), he was detained in 1960, under house arrest in 1962–6, and twice in solitary confinement before the family emigrated to London in 1966. He represented the African National Congress in Havana (1978–85). *A Walk in the Night* (1962) is his first novel, a short, accomplished story about the Cape Town slum, District Six, which it evokes vividly in terse, spare descriptions. While La Guma's novels engrave the iniquities of apartheid in the scrupulously detailed language of realism, they also assert a romantic faith in his characters' potential for compassion. *And a Threefold Cord* (1964) counters miserable, deprived, shantytown living with the inhabitants' sense of community. Within the prison in *The Stone Country* (1967), a precise metaphor for South Africa itself, some humane responses miraculously survive. *In the Fog of the Season's End* (1972) evokes the sufferings and heroism, large and small, of those involved in underground resistance. *Time of*

the *Butcherbird* (1979), set in a tribal area, succeeds in correlating the pursuit and punishment of a private atrocity with communal resistance to the enforced removal of villagers from their ancestral lands. *A Soviet Journey* (1978) is a travel book.

La Ramée, Louise de See OUIDA.

Lady Anna A novel by ANTHONY TROLLOPE, serialized in THE FORTNIGHTLY REVIEW from April 1873 to April 1874. The spirited heiress Lady Anna, daughter of an earl, is successfully wooed by Daniel Thwaite, a hard-working tailor from Cumberland. In spite of opposition and the advice of artistic and aristocratic friends, Anna marries Daniel and they leave for Australia.

Lady Audley's Secret A SENSATION NOVEL by MARY ELIZABETH BRADDON, published in volume form in 1862 after being serialized in *Robin Goodfellow* from September 1861 and then, after the failure of that journal, in *The Sixpenny Magazine* from March 1862.

George Talboys returns from Australia to learn that the wife he had abandoned is now dead. His friend Robert Audley takes him for a holiday near Audley Court, the seat of Robert's uncle, Sir Michael, and his beautiful young wife. When Talboys disappears, Robert investigates the mystery, becoming transformed from an idle dandy into a man of serious purpose. His enquiries show that Talboys's wife is Lady Audley; she had faked her death and married Sir Michael bigamously. Lady Audley tries to kill Robert by burning down the inn where he is staying, but he survives to make her confess that she had pushed Talboys down the well at Audley Court when he confronted her. Her crimes are the result of hereditary insanity and she is permanently committed to a private asylum. In a final twist to the story, Talboys turns out to be alive, having secretly left the country after surviving the attempted murder.

Written in great haste but with a breathlessly readable plot and a striking central character in Lady Audley, the work became the most famous sensation novel, reviled by critics and moralists but loved by the public. It was successfully adapted for the stage in 1863.

Lady Chatterley's Lover A novel by D. H. LAWRENCE, written and privately printed in Florence in 1928.

Constance (Connie) Chatterley is married to Sir Clifford, a wealthy and cultured mineowner in Derbyshire. A war wound has left him paralysed and impotent, and he increasingly devotes all his energy to the management of his mines and to himself. Constance grows restless within the confines of their marriage. She has a brief and superficial affair with Michaelis, a young playwright, then enters into a passionate relationship with Sir Clifford's gamekeeper, Oliver Mellors. He is an ex-officer who rose from the ranks, a forthright, individualistic man uncontaminated by industrial society. Connie becomes pregnant and attempts to conceal the father's identity from her husband. She later confesses and asks him for a divorce. Sir Clifford considers Mellors his social inferior, therefore not worthy, and refuses to release her. The lovers depart and, though separated, wait hopefully for a time when the obstacles between them will have been surmounted and they can be united.

The novel was denied full publication in England for over 30 years because of its sexual explicitness. An expurgated version, released in 1932, contained none of Lawrence's detailed descriptions of the sexual act and eliminated all four-letter words. The unexpurgated text became freely available in 1960 after Penguin Books survived a prosecution under the Obscene Publications Act in 1959. Defence witnesses at the trial included E. M. FORSTER, HELEN GARDNER and RICHARD HOGGART, and the verdict marked a major victory against literary censorship. Lawrence's two earlier versions of the novel have been published independently as *The First Lady Chatterley* (1944) and *John Thomas and Lady Jane* (1972).

Lady of Shalott, The A poem by ALFRED TENNYSON, published in 1832 and revised for the 1842 edition of his *Poems*. The setting is Arthurian. The lady of the title leads an isolated life on an island, never looking out of her window but instead weaving pictures from a mirror's reflection of the scene. When Sir Lancelot passes by, she is tempted to gaze directly on reality and dies. Like many of Tennyson's early poems, the work displays a ripe luxury of imagery and language, both manipulated with extraordinary skill. On a figurative level, the main interest of the poem lies in its consideration of the relationship between life and art.

The theme was suggested by an Italian story, *Donna di Scalotta*, in *Cento novelle antiche* of the 14th century. Tennyson gave the story a different treatment in 'Lancelot and Elaine', one of the *IDYLLS OF THE KING*.

Lady of the Lake, The A poem in six CANTOS by SIR WALTER SCOTT, published in 1810. The lake is Loch Katrine, the Lady is Ellen, daughter of the outlawed James of Douglas, and the period is the early 16th century.

Roderick Dhu, a Highland chief, gives hospitality to a mysterious knight, James Fitz-James. Roderick loves Ellen, but she has given her heart to Malcolm Graeme.

Threatened by the royal armies, Roderick summons his clan, but James of Douglas, believing himself to be the cause of the royal army's approach, decides to go to Stirling to surrender to the king. Fitz-James returns to offer refuge to Ellen, but withdraws when Ellen declines, confessing her love for Malcolm. Fitz-James gives her a ring which will secure the king's favour in an emergency. On the road to Stirling Fitz-James meets Roderick with whom he quarrels and fights. Roderick is worsted, and taken to Stirling as Fitz-James's prisoner. When Ellen arrives in Stirling to plead for her father, using the ring to gain an audience, Fitz-James proves to be none other than the king himself. Roderick dies of his wounds, but Douglas is pardoned and Ellen marries Malcolm. The poem includes Ellen's memorable song 'Rest, Warrior, Rest', and the beautiful funeral lament, 'He is Gone on the Mountain'.

Lady Windermere's Fan A play by OSCAR WILDE, performed in 1892. His first theatrical success, it deals with a blackmailing divorcée driven to self-sacrifice by maternal love. The dialogue has the paradoxical, witty comments on society that made Wilde famous.

Lai le Freine A fragment of a VERSE ROMANCE in couplets, written in the early 14th century in the southeast. One of the better Middle English BRETON LAYS, it is derived from one of MARIE DE FRANCE's *Lais*, *Lai le Fresne*, but does not follow its source closely. The poet – perhaps the author of *SIR ORFEO* – adds a lengthy prologue, alters the setting, adds, omits and adapts sections, increases dramatic effect and adds concrete detail to the story.

The wife of a knight slanders her neighbour, who has borne twins, as unfaithful. When she then bears twin girls herself she avoids embarrassment by having one taken away and abandoned, with a robe and a ring, in an ash tree near a convent. The nuns who bring the girl up christen her Freine, 'ash'. When mature, she lives as the mistress of a knight, Guroun, who is eventually persuaded to marry and weds Freine's sister. The fragment ends here, but in the source Freine covers the bridal bed with her robe and it is recognized by her mother who confesses her crime. Guroun's marriage is dissolved and he weds Freine. The story contains several common medieval motifs which are not specifically Breton. Analogues, written over several centuries, are found in other European languages.

Laing, B(ernard) Kojo 1946– Ghanaian novelist and poet. Born in Kumasi, he was educated at schools in both Ghana and Scotland, before taking his degree at the University of Glasgow. He has worked in government administration and as secretary to the Institute of African Studies at the University of Ghana, but now runs a private school in Accra. His fiction is surreal, inventive and technically accomplished. *Search Sweet Country* (1986) is set in Accra in the mid-1970s, while *Woman of the Aeroplanes* (1988) and *Major Gentl and the Achimota Wars* (1992) take place in the near future. The poems in *Godhorse* (1989) also display startling, witty combinations of imagery and formal invention.

Laing, R(onald) D(avid) 1927–89 Psychiatrist. Born and brought up in Glasgow, where he attended the university, he practised as a psychiatrist in Scotland and England. Early works – *The Divided Self* (1959), *The Self and Others* (1961), *Reason and Violence* (with D. Cooper; 1964) and *Sanity, Madness and the Family* (with E. Esterson; 1965) – argued that madness was less a biological disorder than a maladjustment induced by the stresses of familial living. His fashionable polemics on free relationships made him a cult figure, particularly in the USA. In the 1970s he became attracted to Zen Buddhism, composed poetry and published transcripts of conversations with his children. His major later works include *Knots* (1970), *The Facts of Life* (1976), *Sonnets* (1979) and *Do You Love Me?* (1977).

Lake Poets [Lake School], **The** A term applied to WORDSWORTH, COLERIDGE and SOUTHEY because of their close association with the Lake District. It was apparently first used by THE EDINBURGH REVIEW in 1817.

Lalla Rookh: *An Oriental Romance* Four narrative poems, with a connecting tale in prose, by THOMAS MOORE, published in 1817. In its day it was one of the most popular examples of the Orientalism which Moore's friend BYRON also helped to make fashionable.

Lalla Rookh, the daughter of the Emperor Aurungzebe, journeys from Delhi to Cashmere, where she is to be married to the King of Bucharia. The journey is enlivened by stories told by Feramorz, a young poet from Cashmere, who joins her retinue. 'The Veiled Prophet of Khorassan' tells of the tragic love affair of Zelica and Azim. In 'Paradise and the Peri' a *peri*, or child of a fallen angel, finally gains admission to paradise by bringing the tear of a repentant criminal to its gates. 'The Fire-Worshippers' tells another tragic love story, about Hafed, a young Gheber or fire-worshiper, and Hinda, daughter of the emir Al Hassan of Arabia, who crushes the Ghebers. In 'The Light of the Haram' Nourmahal wins back the love of her husband, Selim, with a magic song she learns from the enchantress Namouna. The self-important chamberlain Fadladeen vents his irritation at the mishaps of the journey by criticizing the stories told by Feramorz, but Lalla Rookh falls in love with him and eventually discovers that he is none other than her prospective husband, the King of Bucharia.

L'Allegro A poem by JOHN MILTON, written in 1632 and published with other early work in a volume of 1645. Its title means 'the cheerful man' and the work is the young poet's celebration of mirth, in the delights of rustic scenery and also in the busy city. Its companion piece, IL PENSEROSO, celebrates the qualities of meditative retirement.

Lamb, Charles 1775–1834 Essayist and poet. The youngest child of Elizabeth and John Lamb, a lawyer's clerk, he went to school in Fetter Lane, London, and later entered Christ's Hospital, where he formed a lifelong friendship with COLERIDGE. In his youth Lamb spent some time at Blakesware in Hertfordshire where Mary Field, his grandmother, was housekeeper. After 1789 Lamb was employed in the South Sea House and later at the East India House where he worked until his retirement in 1825. In 1796 his sister Mary Ann Lamb (1764–1847) murdered their mother in a fit of insanity and was confined to an asylum, at length being released into her brother's care. Lamb himself suffered a period of insanity in 1795–6.

He contributed four SONNETS to Coleridge's *Poems on Various Subjects* (1796). In 1798, with Charles Lloyd, he published *Blank Verse* which included 'The Old Familiar Faces'. *A Tale of Rosamund Gray and Old Blind Margaret* also appeared in 1798, followed by *John Woodvil* (1802; initially entitled 'Pride's Cure'), a tragedy, and *Mr H* (1806), a FARCE. Lamb established a reputation in literary circles as a contributor to *The Albion*, THE MORNING CHRONICLE and *The Morning Post,* and as the popular host to intellectual gatherings which included Coleridge, SOUTHEY, LEIGH HUNT, BENJAMIN HAYDON, CRABB ROBINSON, THOMAS TALFOURD and the mathematician Thomas Manning. WILLIAM GODWIN, another acquaintance, suggested that Lamb contribute to his 'Juvenile Library' and so, with his sister, he produced the well-known TALES FROM SHAKESPEARE (1807). Other books for children were: *The Adventures of Ulysses* (1808); *Mrs Leicester's School* (1809), written with Mary and containing reminiscences of their childhood; *Poetry for Children* (1809); and *Prince Dorus* (1811), a fairy-tale in verse.

Lamb's contributions to journals included his essay 'On the Character and Genius of Hogarth' (published by Leigh Hunt's *Reflector* in 1811), 'On the Tragedies of Shakespeare', and a review of WORDSWORTH'S THE EXCURSION (published with editorial alterations by THE QUARTERLY REVIEW in 1814). He is best remembered for THE ESSAYS OF ELIA, pseudonymously contributed to THE LONDON MAGAZINE from 1820 to 1823. They were collected in 1823, and a second series, *The Last Essays of Elia*, appeared in 1833. Deliberately good-humoured, they had a lasting influence on the tradition of essay-writing in England.

In 1827 Lamb, his sister and Emma Isola, an orphan whom they had adopted, moved to Enfield and later to Edmonton, where he died and was buried. Talfourd published a volume of his letters with a biographical sketch in 1834 and *Memorials of Charles Lamb* in 1848. Lamb's gentle and engaging personality, his debilitating stammer, his burden of responsibility and his whimsical humour attracted many friends whose memoirs record their lasting admiration.

Lamb, Mary Ann See LAMB, CHARLES.

Lamia A poem by JOHN KEATS, written in 1819 and published the following year. The serpent Lamia is transformed by Hermes into a beautiful maiden. She loves a young man of Corinth, Lycius, who, though a serious student, is enchanted by her beauty and retires with her to an exquisite but mysterious and secret palace. After some time in blissful union, Lycius overrules Lamia's fears and insists on inviting his friends to a sumptuous feast. Among the guests comes Apollonius, the sage philosopher, who recognizes Lamia's true nature. She vanishes with a 'frightful scream' and Lycius dies.

The subject is borrowed from ROBERT BURTON's THE ANATOMY OF MELANCHOLY (III, ii, 1, 1), which quotes Philostratus' *De vita Apollonii*. The poem's central theme – the tension between appearance and reality – occurs elsewhere in Romantic poetry, most notably in COLERIDGE's CHRISTABEL and THOMAS LOVE PEACOCK's *Rhododaphne*, which both portray dissembling woman. Keats's poem regards Apollonius' coldly scientific attitude with ambivalence.

Lamming, George 1927– Caribbean novelist. He was born in a village in Barbados and went on to attend the island's leading secondary school, Harrison College. His first novel, *In the Castle of My Skin* (1953), which draws upon his boyhood there, is a finely wrought account of growing up in poverty in a community undergoing fundamental social change. Its immediate success opened literary London to Lamming. *The Emigrants*, about West Indian disillusion with life in Britain, appeared in 1954. *Of Age and Innocence* (1958) contrasts peasant wisdom and youthful tolerance with violent, Caribbean, pre-Independence politicking, while in *Season of Adventure* (1960) the heroine painfully achieves Caribbean identity by accepting what she had previously despised. Rather less accessible with their tumbling, swirling issues are two ambitious novels: *Water with Berries* (1971) and his masterpiece, *Natives of My Person* (1972). Set aboard a 17th-century slave ship, *Natives of My Person* offers a powerful allegory of political and sexual domination, which Lamming has said can be applied to the contemporary Caribbean as well as its past. *The Pleasures of Exile* (1960) consists of Lamming's essays. He edited an anthology of black writing, *Cannon Shots and Glass Beads* (1974). Though reputedly working on new fiction, he has produced no new novel in the last two decades.

Lampman, Archibald 1861–99 Canadian poet. Educated at Trinity College, Toronto, he graduated in 1882. He worked as a teacher for a time and later joined the Post Office Department in Ottawa. His reputation rests upon two small collections published in his lifetime, *Among the Millet* (1888) and *Lyrics of Earth* (1893). *Alcyone* (1899), which includes 'The City of the End of Things', was in preparation at the time of his death. His emphasis is upon natural themes, and his setting is Canadian; a broadening of interest is seen in *At the Long Sault* (1943), a collection of hitherto unpublished poems edited by Lampman's friend DUNCAN CAMPBELL SCOTT in collaboration with E. K. BROWN.

Lancelot of the Laik A Middle Scots romance written in the last quarter of the 15th century. The poem is a clumsily managed DREAM-VISION in which the poet, inspired by the God of Love to write a work for his lady, decides to translate part of a French Lancelot story. The poem, a paraphrase of part of the Vulgate *Lancelot*, is incomplete, and includes an incongruous digression on the political duties of a king, usually thought to have been intended for James III (1460–88).

Land of Cockaygne, The A Middle English poem written in Ireland during the second half of the 13th century. It presents a lively parody of the Christian Paradise and of the Earthly Paradise of European tradition, describing a land devoid of all unpleasant things where the buildings are edible, the monks and nuns enjoy a guiltless, licentious life and geese fly ready-roasted. It can be reached only by wading through the filth of swine for seven years.

Landon, Letitia Elizabeth 1802–38 Poet and novelist, who generally used the initials L. E. L. She was among the most popular and prolific authors of her time. Her first volume, *The Fate of Adelaide* (1821), was followed by *The Improvisatrice* (1824), *The Troubadour* (1825), *The Venetian Bracelet* (1829) and *The Vow of the Peacock* (1835), among others. She also contributed to numerous periodicals and her poems were collected in 1850 and 1873. She married George Maclean, governor of Cape Coast Castle in West Africa, in 1838, and died there shortly afterwards. Her most successful novel was *Ethel Churchill* (1837); others were *Romance and Reality* (1831), *Francesca Carrara* (1834) and *Duty and Inclination* (1838).

Landor, Walter Savage 1775–1864 Poet and essayist. Born at Ipsley Court, Warwickshire, the son of a doctor, he was educated at Rugby School and Trinity College, Oxford. He was sent down in 1794 and published his first collection of poems in the following year, but suppressed the work soon after. It was followed by *Gebir* (1798), an exotic poem in seven books, and *Count Julian* (1811), a tragedy. Subject to an inflammable temper which made his residence in Monmouthshire untenable, he left England in 1814, living abroad in Como, Pisa and Florence. He did not return to England until 1835 when he separated from his wife, Julia Thuillier, whom he had married in 1811. From 1824 to 1829 he published *IMAGINARY CONVERSATIONS OF LITERARY MEN AND STATESMEN*. Other works include: *Citation and Examination of William Shakespeare Touching Deer-Stealing* (1834); *Pericles and Aspasia* (1836), which began as one of his imaginary conversations; *Pentameron* (1837); the trilogy *Andrea of Hungary, Giovanna of Naples* and *Fra Rupert* (1839–40); *The Hellenics* (1847); *Poemata et inscriptiones* (1847); and *Imaginary Conversations of Greeks and Romans* (1853).

In 1858 Landor again departed for the Continent on account of an action for libel arising out of a lampoon included in *Dry Sticks Fagoted* (1858). He returned to Florence, an extraordinary and irascible old man, where ROBERT BROWNING, who had long admired his work, attempted to protect and care for him. Landor's boisterous manner and short temper were tolerantly caricatured by DICKENS in the character of Boythorn in *BLEAK HOUSE*.

An accomplished writer of prose, Landor is not remembered for his poetry, but much of it displays a distinguished simplicity: 'Lately Our Poets Loitered in Green Lanes', 'Dying Speech of an Old Philosopher', 'Mother I Cannot Mind My Wheel', 'Rose Aylmer' and 'To Ianthe'.

Lane, Edward William 1801–76 Arabic scholar. Born at Hereford and educated at Bath and Hereford grammar schools, he published his classic *Account of the Mariners and Customs of the Modern Egyptians* in 1836. Other works were a translation of the *Arabian Nights' Entertainments* (1838–40) and *Selections from the Kur-an* (1843). His *Arabic Lexicon* was left unfinished at his death, and was completed by his nephew S. Lane Poole.

Lang, Andrew 1844–1912 Poet, scholar and man of letters. Born in Selkirk, he was educated at St Andrews, Glasgow and Balliol College, Oxford. Lang became a fellow of Merton College but settled in London as a journalist and man of letters in 1875. There was almost no type of writing that he did not touch: essays, reviews, literary controversy, plays, novels and biographies all form part of his collected works.

His first volume of poetry, *Ballads and Lyrics of Old France*, had appeared in 1872, before he left Oxford; it was followed by *Ballades in Blue China* (1880 and 1881), *Helen of Troy*, a narrative poem in six books (1882), *Rhymes à la Mode* (1885), *Grass of Parnassus* (1888), *Ban and Arrière Ban* (1894) and *New Collected Rhymes* (1905). As a classical scholar he worked

mostly on Homer. As a historian he was chiefly concerned with Scotland, though he also wrote a book on Joan of Arc, *The Maid of France* (1908). As a biographer he wrote lives of Sir Stafford Northcote (1890) and J. G. LOCKHART (1896). As an anthropologist he published *Custom and Myth* (1884), *Myth, Ritual and Religion* (1887) and *The Making of Religion* (1898).

Lang's involvement in scholarly controversy about folk-tales led to his best-remembered work. In contrast to Max Müller, professor of philology at Oxford, he did not believe that all fairy tales originated in Central Asia and were spread by travellers over the rest of the world. Instead, he thought such tales to be relics of savage customs and thoughts common to early man – such as the belief that animals can understand and speak in human language. He began his famous collections with *The Blue Fairy Book* in 1889; 11 more volumes known by the colours in their titles enjoyed great popularity, the last appearing in 1910. Taken from many different sources, these stories were rewritten by Lang's wife and a committee of ladies in the same spirit that they altered his *Arabian Nights' Entertainments* (1898) to 'omit pieces suitable for Arabs and old gentlemen'. Lang also edited one of the best and most inclusive of nursery rhyme anthologies still in print today, *The Nursery Rhyme Book* (1897).

Langland, William Author of the religious poem *PIERS PLOWMAN*, surviving in three versions (known as the A-, B- and C-texts) which together span the period 1360–87. Nothing is known of his life beyond what can be deduced from the poem and a few details from notes in a 15th-century manuscript of the C-text. Traditionally, he is supposed to have been the son, perhaps illegitimate, of Stacy de Rokayle, an Oxfordshire gentleman, and to have been educated at the priory of Great Malvern until the death of his father curtailed his education. The poem implies a knowledge of the Malvern Hills and suggests that Langland lived in London. His connection with the church is not known. His familiarity with the Scriptures is abundantly clear, although his knowledge of biblical commentaries, the patristic writers and other areas of scholarship was patchy. Though he was passionately concerned with the corruption of the regular clergy and the mendicant orders, he seems to have sought reformation within the church in its established form rather than being the herald of the Reformation his successors sometimes claimed. SKEAT's attribution of *Richard the Redeless* (see *MUM AND THE SOTHSEGGER*) to Langland is no longer accepted and no other poem is now associated with his name.

Lanier, Sidney 1842–81 American poet and critic. Born in Macon, Georgia, Lanier graduated from Oglethorpe University in 1860. After writing his only novel, *Tiger Lilies* (1867), he turned to poetry, greatly influenced by his work as a professional musician. Two years after the publication of his first book of poetry, *Poems* (1877), he became a lecturer at Johns Hopkins University in Baltimore. His *The Science of English Verse* (1880) remains an important study of prosody. Most of his other works were published posthumously. His collected *Poems* appeared in 1884 and was reissued with additions in 1891 and 1916. *Poem Outlines* – also verse – was published in 1908. Among his critical works are *The English Novel and the Principles of its Development* (1883), *Music and Poetry: Essays upon Some Aspects and Interrelations of the Two Arts* (1898) and *Shakespeare and his Forerunners: Studies in Elizabethan Poetry and its Development from Early English* (1902).

Laodicean, A: *A Story of Today* A novel by THOMAS HARDY, first published serially in the European edition of HARPER'S NEW MONTHLY MAGAZINE between December 1880 and December 1881 and in book form in 1881.

Paula Power, the Laodicean or vacillator, is left Stancy Castle in Somerset by her wealthy father. She and George Somerset, a young architect, fall in love but by virtue of her nature she will not agree to an engagement. Then Captain de Stancy, a member of the family who once owned the castle, seeks her hand and, after procrastination, is accepted. He is assisted in his quest for Paula by his illegitimate son, Will Dare, a conniving villain who blackens Somerset's character. Upon discovery of Dare's knavery Paula breaks her engagement and follows Somerset to Normandy, where they are reconciled and married. But their intention of living in the restored castle is thwarted when Dare contrives to burn it to the ground, leaving only the stout walls.

Lardner, Ring(gold) (Wilmer) 1885–1933 American short-story writer. Born in Michigan, he worked as a sports reporter for various newspapers and eventually as a syndicated columnist. The letters he wrote in the guise of 'Jack Keefe', a newcomer to a professional baseball team, made him famous. They first appeared in *The Chicago Tribune* and were collected as *You Know Me, Al: A Busher's Letters* (1914). Lardner had a sharp-edged sense of humour and a remarkable ear for vernacular speech. Americans of every walk of life appeared in his stories, their utterances establishing their characters. He demonstrated a talent for verse in the *Bib Ballads* (1915). *Gullible's Travels* (1917) and *Treat 'em Rough* (1918) consist of satirical stories. His only novel, *The Big Town*, was published in 1921. By the time he published *How to Write Short Stories (with Samples)* (1924) he already had a large and enthusiastic following. His later works are the collections *What of It?* (1925), *The Love Nest* (1926), *Round Up* (1929) and *First and Last* (1934).

Larkin, Philip (Arthur) 1922–85 Poet, novelist and essayist. He was born in Coventry and educated locally at the King Henry VIII Grammar School before reading English at St John's College, Oxford. After graduating in 1943, he took a post in the library at Wellington in Shropshire and remained a librarian throughout his career, working at universities in Leicester and Belfast before moving to the University of Hull in 1955.

In the 1940s he had published two finely understated novels, *Jill* (1946) and *A Girl in Winter* (1947). Conversely, the early poems collected in *The North Ship* (1945) give little indication of his future distinction as a poet: written under the pervasive influence of the early YEATS, they are uncharacteristically rhapsodic and rhetorical. A privately printed pamphlet, *XX Poems* (1951), marked the emergence of his true poetic voice, but it was the publication of *The Less Deceived* (1955) which brought Larkin's mature work before the public for the first time. His reputation rests on what PETER LEVI has called '85 perfect poems', the contents of this volume and its two successors, *The Whitsun Weddings* (1964) and *High Windows* (1964). Working with traditional, often ingeniously constructed poetic forms, he simultaneously extended the territory of poetry in his generous, wry and emotionally complex treatment of contemporary English life. The magnificent title-poem of *The Whitsun Weddings*, describing the poet's journey by train from Hull to London, is his best-known work. At the heart of *High Windows* are 'The Old Fools' and 'The Building', two substantial poems about ageing, illness and death in which the stance is one of clear-eyed endurance. The arrangement of his work in *The Collected Poems* (1988), edited by ANTHONY THWAITE, did not please all readers.

In 1961–71 he reviewed jazz records for *The Daily Telegraph*, work collected in *All What Jazz?* (1970). Its introduction shows the same dislike of MODERNISM which informs his edition of *The Oxford Book of Twentieth-Century English Verse* (1973). *Required Writing* (1983) is a witty and engaging selection of occasional articles and reviews. *Collected Letters 1940–1985* (1992), edited by Anthony Thwaite, has prompted less admiring estimates of his personality.

Larsen, Nella 1891–1964 Black American novelist. She was born in Chicago to a Danish mother and Caribbean father. After teaching in the South, she went to New York, where she qualified and worked as both nurse and librarian. With the encouragement of CARL VAN VECHTEN, she published two novels which were hailed for their contribution to the HARLEM RENAISSANCE but were later overlooked. *Quicksand* (1928) follows the search for identity by a heroine, Helga Crane, who shares her own mixed ancestry. *Passing* (1929) contrasts the lives of two childhood friends from Chicago: Irene Redfield, who (like Larsen herself) joins the Harlem middle class through marriage, and Clare Kendry, who marries a white man and passes as white.

Laski, Marghanita 1915–88 Novelist, critic and broadcaster. The niece of Harold Laski, she was educated in Manchester and then at Somerville College, Oxford. She is now probably best remembered for her dedication to public funding of the arts, as vice-chairman of the Arts Council in 1982–6 and chairman of its literature panel in 1980–4. She was also a frequent radio broadcaster, compiled several literary anthologies, wrote biographies of JANE AUSTEN and GEORGE ELIOT, and produced six well-regarded novels between 1944 and 1953. The last, *The Victorian Chaise-Longue* (1953), was the most popular but *Love on the Supertax* (1944), *To Bed with Grand Music* (1946) and *Tory Heaven* (1948) also struck a chord with their portrayal of middle- and upper-class women's subordinated, morally directionless lives in a male-dominated society.

Last Chronicle of Barset, The The final volume in ANTHONY TROLLOPE'S BARSETSHIRE NOVELS, published in 1867. In his *Autobiography* Trollope named it as his own favourite in the series.

The story is mainly concerned with Josiah Crawley, the poor but righteous and intractable curate of Hogglestock. When Lord Lufton's agent, Mr Soames, loses his wallet in Crawley's house and Crawley later cashes a cheque for £20, the clergyman falls under suspicion of theft. His explanation that the money was a gift from Dean Arabin is inadequate and he is committed for trial. The bishop's wife, Mrs Proudie, plays a leading part in the persecution which now focuses on Crawley. Archdeacon Grantly's son, Major Henry Grantly, is in love with Crawley's daughter Grace and insists on becoming engaged despite his father's opposition; a serious breach between them is the result. When the whole affair reaches a crisis, it is resolved by Mrs Arabin (the former Eleanor Harding), who reveals that she had slipped the cheque into a letter from her husband to Crawley. His innocence established, Crawley is appointed to the parish of the late Mr Harding. Archdeacon Grantly is won over when he meets Grace Crawley, and welcomes her as his daughter-in-law. The novel also contains the death of the dreadful Mrs Proudie and follows Johnny Eames's ever-hopeful pursuit of Lily Dale.

Last Days of Pompeii, The A novel by EDWARD BULWER LYTTON, published in 1834. The action takes place just before and during the catastrophic eruption of Vesuvius in AD 79. The book has some lively pictures of 1st-century Roman life (including an early Christian sect), and a particularly memorable villain, Arbaces, the Priest of Isis.

Last of the Barons, The A novel by EDWARD BULWER LYTTON, published in 1843, and set during the Wars of the Roses. The hero of the title is the Earl of Warwick, known as 'the kingmaker'. The book was intended as a political ALLEGORY: Warwick's defeat at the Battle of Barnet represents the overthrow of the hereditary feudal order by the new commercial classes, and prefigures the Reform Bill's eclipse of the landowning Tory aristocracy by Whig industrialists.

Last of the Mohicans, The See LEATHERSTOCKING TALES, THE.

Last Puritan, The: *A Memoir in the Form of a Novel* A novel by GEORGE SANTAYANA, published in 1935. Oliver Alden, the 'Last Puritan', is the heir of a wealthy, established New England family. He and his mother are abandoned by his drug-addict father, who has rebelled against the puritanical values of New England and sails about the world in his yacht, employing Jim Darnley to accompany him on his travels. Oliver is raised by his mother. At the age of 17 he joins his father for a cruise and becomes Jim Darnley's friend. He then enrolls at Williams College where he is both studious and athletic. His father commits suicide. Oliver becomes friendly with a European cousin, Mario, whom his father has supported, and courts another cousin, Edith. After graduation Oliver visits the Darnleys in England, where he meets and falls in love with Jim's sister Rose. But Rose falls in love with Mario (who does not love her in return) when he in turn visits Oliver at the Darnleys. World War I having begun, Oliver follows Mario's example and enters the army. Rose refuses Oliver's proposal of marriage. He leaves for France, and is killed there. His estate goes to the Darnleys.

Late Lyrics and Earlier A collection of poems by THOMAS HARDY, first published in 1922. Music is the main theme of this volume, a number of whose lyrics have been set by various composers. As in other collections of Hardy's verse, there is the characteristic subject matter – mismatings, dramatic moments, misunderstandings, sardonic memories, grotesque happenings – together with technical virtuosity of a singular order. But a lyric presence predominates in this volume, which is replete with impressions of earlier times frequently recalled and evoked through the rhythms of the BALLAD or the folksong.

Latimer, Hugh ?1485–1555 Preacher and Protestant martyr. Latimer was ordained c. 1510 and gained a great reputation as a preacher at Cambridge, where he was educated; in 1522 the university licensed him to preach anywhere in the country. He preached before both Henry VIII (the annulment of whose marriage to Catherine he supported) and Edward VI. However, some of his sermons, which attacked purgatory and the veneration of saints, led to a charge of heresy and he was excommunicated until he made his submission in April 1532. In 1535 he became Bishop of Worcester but resigned his see when he refused to subscribe to the Act of Six Articles (1539), which were designed to halt the further spread of reforming ideas. He was confined to the Tower in 1546 but released on the accession of Edward VI. On the accession of Mary he was again committed to the Tower in 1553 and sent to Oxford with Ridley and CRANMER to defend his views before divines from both universities. He was condemned as a heretic, excommunicated and burned with Ridley in 1555.

Latimer's vernacular sermons are vividly graphic, engaging and anecdotal. 'Sermon on the Card' was preached c. 1529 and disparages 'voluntary' works (e.g. pilgrimages) and encourages 'necessary' ones (e.g. mercy). It develops an extended metaphor of card-playing: 'Now turn up your trump, your heart (hearts is trump, as I said before)'. His most famous sermon 'Of the Plough' was preached on New Year's Day 1548 at Paul's Cross. It envisages the preacher as God's ploughman and urges London to repent of its covetousness: 'Charity is waxen cold, none helpeth the scholar nor yet the poor.' Collections of Latimer's sermons were printed in Elizabeth's reign: *Twenty-Seven Sermons* in 1562 and *Fruitful Sermons* in 1571, with many reprintings in the 16th century.

Laud, William 1573–1645 Divine. The son of a Reading clothier, he was educated at St John's College, Oxford, and enjoyed a distinguished career as a cleric before becoming Charles I's Archbishop of Canterbury. His defence of order and ceremonial against Puritan demands for change, and his allegiance to the king in his conflict with Parliament, led finally to his impeachment. He was tried in 1644 and executed the following year. Some of his sermons were published in 1651 and a collection of his writings in 1695–1700. Their literary value is slight, but *The History of the Troubles and Trial of William Laud*, written by himself in the Tower and published with his diary in 1695, has some historical interest.

Lauder, William d. 1771 Schoolteacher and literary hoaxer. Educated at Edinburgh University, he was an excellent classical scholar who translated Grotius' *Eucharista* and edited a collection of Scots neo-Latin religious poetry. He is principally renowned, however, for his fraudulent attempt to convict MILTON of plagiarizing from Masenius' poem *Sarcotis* and Grotius' *Adamus exil* in PARADISE LOST. He first made the allegations in a series of articles for THE GENTLEMAN'S MAGAZINE beginning in February 1747. Interest being aroused, Lauder issued an extended version of these pieces as *An Essay on Milton's Use and Imitation of the Moderns in his 'Paradise Lost'* (1749). SAMUEL JOHNSON, who had first introduced Lauder to

the editor of *The Gentleman's Magazine*, Edward Cave, contributed a prospectus for the proposed publication of *Adamus exil*. The works of Masenius and Grotius were not readily available in England, and Lauder had simply inserted extracts from William Hog's Latin translation of *Paradise Lost* into genuine passages from their writing. The scale and brazenness of the forgery was exposed by John Douglas in 1750. An apology, dictated by Johnson and signed by Lauder, appeared as *A Letter to the Reverend Mr Douglas, Occasioned by his Vindication of Milton* (1751), though Lauder subsequently retracted it. His reputation never recovered and he emigrated to Barbados, where he died in poverty. Johnson's opponents attempted, with little success, to implicate him in the fraud.

Launfalus Miles See SIR LAUNFAL.

Laurence, (Jean) Margaret 1926–87 Canadian novelist. She was born, to parents of Scots ancestry who died while she was young, in Neepawa, Manitoba, and grew up there, subsequently attending the University of Manitoba in Winnipeg. She later lived in Somaliland (1950–2), Ghana (1952–7), Vancouver (1957–62) and England (1949–50 and 1962–9) before settling in Ontario. Her most important achievement is her 'Manawaka' sequence, five works set in a fictional version of Neepawa which becomes a quintessential Canadian small town to vie with those created by STEPHEN LEACOCK, ROBERTSON DAVIES and ALICE MUNRO. It consists of *The Stone Angel* (1964), *A Jest of God* (1966), *The Fire-Dwellers* (1969), *A Bird in the House* (short stories, 1970) and *The Diviners* (1974), the most impressive volume. The Manawaka novels deal with the lives of women: housewives, spinsters, widows and girls. They belong primarily to a social realist mode, though *The Diviners* is indebted to post-modernist developments and is more overtly feminist. It establishes a broader context for its representation of Western Canadian identity, demonstrating how 'official' versions of Canadian history have been biased against the inhabitants of the Prairie provinces, particularly those of Scots and Métis (mixed French and native Canadian) descent. Laurence also published several works about Africa: *This Side Jordan* (1960), a novel set at the time of Ghanaian independence; *The Tomorrow-Tamer* (1963), short stories; *The Prophet's Camel Bell* (1963), a non-fictional account of her life in Somaliland; and *Drums and Cannons* (1968), a study of Nigerian novelists and playwrights. *Heart of a Stranger* (1976) is a collection of her personal essays. *Dance of the Earth* (1989) is a posthumously published autobiographical memoir.

Laus Veneris A poem by ALGERNON CHARLES SWINBURNE, published in *Poems and Ballads* (1866).

Both a peroration on physical love and a treatment of the Tannhäuser legend, *Laus Veneris* ('Praise of Venus') is a reworking of the medieval tale to stress the tragedy of the knight's return to Venus. He depicts Tannhäuser in thrall to the goddess in whose lair, the Horselberg, he is ensnared. Tannhäuser's vain remonstrations and struggles, his pilgrimage to Rome, his confession to the Pope and the papal response are related in elaborate and luxuriant language. The poem follows the metrical scheme of *THE RUBÁIYÁT OF OMAR KHAYYÁM*.

Lavengro: *The Scholar – The Gypsy – The Priest*
A fictionalized autobiography by GEORGE BORROW, published in 1851. 'Lavengro' is the gypsy name for a philologist.

The book which for many generations of readers established Borrow as the master of vigorous but unaffected prose narrative was at first intended to be an autobiography which would build on the success of *THE BIBLE IN SPAIN* through accounts of Borrow's other travels and adventures, notably in Russia. However, Borrow discovered while writing the book that he was unwilling to present his life straightforwardly in a coherent, chronological narrative. By a quirk of genius he seemed to perceive that the avoidance of the literal truth, frustrating though that might be to readers who knew part of his actual life story, would create imaginative space for a set of episodes of the open road that expressed his narrative self in a convincing manner. He said nothing of Russia, though he had lived there for two years (1833–5). He concealed his early family life behind irresistibly romantic portraits of his father and mother. He drew a veil over the seven-year period (1825–32) which preceded his employment with the British and Foreign Bible Society. Written episodically and with disregard for chronology, *Lavengro* consists of a series of brilliantly conceived episodes concerning the adventures of an almost penniless young man who, leaving London in 1825, wanders about England for a year or more, consorting with tinkers, innkeepers, Nonconformist ministers, eccentric old gentlemen, chaste young women and gypsies. Though many of Borrow's contemporaries distrusted the book, it was soon recognized as a narrative masterpiece. *THE ROMANY RYE* (1857) is a sequel.

Lavin, Mary 1912– Irish short-story writer and novelist. Born in Walpole, Massachusetts, she was brought to Ireland when she was 11. Her work provides a sharp view of the small tensions of Irish middle-class life: children, widows and young people of marked sensitivity living in a comfortable, stifling environment, their loneliness enhanced by the intensity with which they experience love in a society dominated by pragmatic considerations. Although she has published novels, *The House in Clewe Street* (1945)

and *Mary O'Grady* (1950), her preferred form is the short story. Volumes include *Tales from Bective Bridge* (1942), *The Long Ago and Other Stories* (1944), *The Becker Wives and Other Stories* (1946), *At Sallygap and Other Stories* (1947) and *In the Middle of the Fields* (1967). *Collected Stories* appeared in 1971.

Law, William 1686–1761 Religious writer. Born at King's Cliffe, Northamptonshire, and educated at Emmanuel College, Cambridge, he became a fellow of Emmanuel in 1711, after being ordained. Law was a NONJUROR, refusing to take the Oath of Allegiance to George I, and was deprived of his fellowship and forbidden to take up any church appointment. In 1717 he published the first of *Three Letters to the Bishop of Bangor*, a reply to Bishop HOADLY's defence of the church's submission of loyalty to George I (*Preservative against the Principles and Practices of the Nonjurors*, 1716). *Remarks on a Late Book Entitled The Fable of the Bees* (1723) is a reply to the satire of BERNARD DE MANDEVILLE; and in 1726 he wrote *The Absolute Unlawfulness of the Stage Entertainment*, which attacked the contemporary theatre.

In 1726 Law also published *A Practical Treatise on Christian Perfection* and in 1728 came *A Serious Call to a Devout and Holy Life*, the two books by which he is best known. They constitute a guide to the full practice of Christian ideals in everyday life, are written in vigorous prose, and carried a strong appeal in the simplicity of their teaching. *A Serious Call* had great influence: SAMUEL JOHNSON admired it and JOHN WESLEY declared that the beginnings of Methodism were to be found in it. *The Case of Reason* (1731) was Law's answer to the Deists (see DEISM); he saw reliance on reason as a fundamental error, since both man and the universe are mysteries that admit of no explanation.

In middle life Law became interested in the writings of the German Lutheran mystic, Jakob Boehme, but as a mystic he lost the loyalty of some of his former disciples and Wesley became estranged from him. Among his mystical writings are *The Spirit of Prayer* (written in two parts, 1749 and 1750), *The Way to Divine Knowledge* (1752), and *The Spirit of Love* (again in two parts, 1752 and 1754).

Law was tutor to EDWARD GIBBON's father from 1727 to 1737 and remained the family's spiritual guide until 1740.

Lawler, Ray(mond) (Evenor) 1921– Australian playwright. Born in Footscray, Melbourne, he left school at 13 and worked in a factory before becoming an actor. His first play, *Cradle of Thunder* (1949), was given an amateur production, but his second, *SUMMER OF THE SEVENTEENTH DOLL* (1955), was selected as the first native Australian play to be performed by the Australian Elizabethan Theatre Trust in Sydney. It stands unchallenged as the first sign of a new movement in the Australian theatre. Later, less successful works have included: *The Piccadilly Bushman* (1959), written during his long residence in Ireland but still preoccupied with Australian themes; *Breach in the Wall* (1967); and *Godsend* (1982). He departed from his normally realistic style in *The Unshaven Cheek* (1963), an exercise in flashbacks, and the more accomplished *The Man Who Shot the Albatross* (1972), an experimental play about Captain Bligh's two years as governor of New South Wales (1806–8). *Kid Stakes* (1975) and *Other Times* (1976) treat earlier years in the lives of the characters in *Summer of the Seventeenth Doll*.

Lawless, Emily 1845–1913 Irish poet and novelist. Born in County Kildare, the daughter of the 3rd Baron Cloncurry, she was educated privately and led a retired life, producing several novels, generally serious and thorough studies of the Irish peasantry. They include *A Millionaire's Cousin* (1885), *Hurrish* (1886) and *Grania* (1892). *With the Wild Geese* (1902), a volume of poetry, was well received by contemporary critics.

Lawrence, D(avid) H(erbert) (Richards) 1885–1930 Novelist, short-story writer, poet, critic, playwright and essayist. He was born at Eastwood, Nottinghamshire. His father was a coal-miner, his mother from a family with genteel aspirations; emotional friction between the parents, and Lawrence's close relationship with his mother, left important traces in his later writing. He was subject to illness, including lung infections, from a very early age and ill health dogged him throughout his life. For a brief period after leaving Nottingham High School in 1901 Lawrence became a junior clerk in a surgical appliance factory. From the following year until 1906 he worked as a pupil-teacher, at Eastwood and then at Ilkeston, while saving the money necessary to take a training-course at University College, Nottingham. He matriculated at 22 and joined the staff of Davidson Road School in Croydon, an important move towards emotional and financial independence and the prelude to his literary career.

In 1909 a number of his poems were submitted by his friend from youth, Jessie Chambers, to FORD MADOX FORD of THE ENGLISH REVIEW and these were published in the November issue. Ford also read his first novel, THE WHITE PEACOCK (1911), and successfully recommended it to William Heinemann, who subjected it to some censorship. Lawrence gave up teaching after a serious illness and his second novel, THE TRESPASSER, followed in 1912. Early in the same year he met Frieda Weekley (*née* von Richthofen), daughter of a German baron and wife of a professor at Nottingham whom Lawrence knew. They went to Germany together and were married after Frieda's divorce in 1914. SONS AND LOVERS (1913), which draws on Lawrence's childhood and contains a portrayal of Jessie Chambers (the Miriam of the novel), has always been one of his most popular books.

During World War I the Lawrences at first lived in London, then moved to Cornwall; they developed close friendships with many of the leading literary figures of the period. DAVID GARNETT was already a friend; others included ALDOUS HUXLEY, BERTRAND RUSSELL, LADY OTTOLINE MORRELL, KATHERINE MANSFIELD, JOHN MIDDLETON MURRY and RICHARD ALDINGTON. THE RAINBOW (1915), considered by many critics to be his best novel, was prosecuted by the authorities and banned on grounds of obscenity. Further harassment occurred when the Lawrences were accused of spying for the Germans; they were officially expelled from Cornwall in October 1917. He had completed another novel, WOMEN IN LOVE, but was unable to find a publisher. Two volumes of poems appeared, *Look! We Have Come Through!* (1917) and the misnamed *New Poems* (1918), but in 1919 he and Frieda left England for Italy. *Women in Love* was published privately in 1920 in New York, defeating court action there in 1922; an English edition followed in 1921 with changes dictated by censorship and a threatened libel suit. With *The Lost Girl* (1920), which won the James Tait Black Memorial Prize, and AARON'S ROD (1922), Lawrence at last had the financial security to travel. An incomplete novel written in 1920–1, *Mr Noon*, carrying forward his life following *Sons and Lovers*, was published in 1984.

Between 1922 and 1926 he and Frieda left Italy to live intermittently in Ceylon, Australia, New Mexico and Mexico, and these provided the settings for several of his subsequent novels and stories. KANGAROO (1923) was written during a four-month stay in Australia, where Lawrence met M. L. Skinner (with whom he collaborated on *The Boy in the Bush*, 1924); THE PLUMED SERPENT (1926) was inspired by his stays in Mexico. His last novel, LADY CHATTERLEY'S LOVER, was published in Florence in 1928 and an expurgated edition in England and USA in 1932, but had to await favourable court verdicts in 1959 and 1960 respectively before it became freely available in its original form. The first two versions of the novel were published independently as *The First Lady Chatterley* (1944) and *John Thomas and Lady Jane* (1972).

In 1925, after a severe illness in Mexico, it was discovered that Lawrence was suffering from tuberculosis, and he was given a year or two to live; there is contradictory testimony about whether he was told what his disease was, but he never called it by name. He and Frieda returned to Europe, but his health continued to decline and he died at Vence in France at the age of 44.

Although his literary career spanned only two decades, the body of work is considerable. His short stories, which include some of his finest work, appeared in *The Prussian Officer* (1914), *England, My*

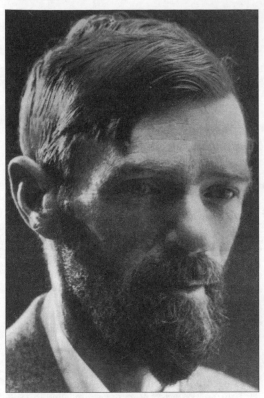

D. H. Lawrence

England (1922), The Woman Who Rode Away (1928), Love among the Haystacks (1930) and The Lovely Lady (1933). His novellas, also among his best work, include The Ladybird, The Fox, The Captain's Doll (1923); St Mawr together with The Princess (1925); Sun (1926); The Escaped Cock (1929; also known as The Man Who Died), and The Virgin and the Gipsy (1930). His poetry, first collected in a two-volume edition in 1928, includes Love Poems (1913), Amores (1916), Look! We Have Come Through! (1917), New Poems (1918), Bay (1919), Birds, Beasts and Flowers (1923), Pansies (1929), Nettles (1930) and Last Poems (1932). In addition Lawrence wrote plays, several about mining families, collected in The Complete Plays (1965).

His non-fictional prose covers a broad spectrum. Psychoanalysis and the Unconscious (1921) and Fantasia of the Unconscious (1922) stand in intimate relationship to the thinking which informs his major novels. His literary criticism includes the groundbreaking Studies in Classic American Literature (1923) and a study of HARDY (first published in Phoenix). Reflections on the Death of a Porcupine (1925) and Assorted Articles (1930) are collections of essays. His travel books include Twilight in Italy (1916), Sea and Sardinia (1921), Etruscan Places (1932) and Mornings in Mexico (1927). Movements in European History (1921) is a school history book written under the pseudonym of Lawrence H.

Davison. Many of his uncollected stories, essays, reviews and introductions were included in Phoenix: The Posthumous Papers (1936) and Phoenix II: Uncollected, Unpublished and Other Prose Works (1968). Most of his pictures – like his novels, victims of the censor – were reproduced in The Paintings of D. H. Lawrence (1929). The Cambridge edition of his complete works and letters promises to be definitive.

Lawrence, George Alfred 1827–76 Novelist. Educated at Rugby and Balliol College, Oxford, he was called to the Bar in 1852. His popular novel GUY LIVINGSTONE (1857) introduced 'muscular blackguardism' (as opposed to CHARLES KINGSLEY's 'muscular Christianity') in the character of its brutally strong and unprincipled hero. Eight other novels followed, including Sword and Gown (1859), Barren Honour (1862), Breaking a Butterfly (1869) and Hagarene (1874).

Lawrence, T(homas) E(dward) 1888–1935 Soldier and author, commonly known as 'Lawrence of Arabia'. He was born at Tremadoc in Caernarvonshire, the illegitimate son of Sir Robert Chapman. Educated at Oxford High School and Jesus College, Oxford, he travelled to the Middle East in 1911 as an archaeologist. In World War I he worked in the intelligence section of the Arab Bureau, and in 1916 organized the revolt of the Arab tribesmen against the Turks, acquiring a tenacious reputation as a legendary hero, enhanced by his appearance with the Arab delegation at the Versailles conference. Refusing numerous honours, and dissatisfied with British policy, he enlisted in the Royal Air Force under the name of Ross, and later, Shaw.

His Oxford thesis was eventually published as Crusader Castles (1936). The Seven Pillars of Wisdom: A Triumph (privately printed, 1926; abbreviated as Revolt in the Desert, 1927), his account of his war years, has alternately been praised as a masterpiece and condemned as an exercise in self-aggrandizement. Apart from contributions to early archaeological reports and occasional introductory essays, Lawrence also published a translation, The Odyssey of Homer (1932), and The Mint (limited edition, 1936), a curiously uncertain and ambiguous account of his experience of life in the ranks, subtitled 'Notes made in the RAF depot between August and December 1922, and at Cadet College in 1925'. DAVID GARNETT edited his letters (1938).

Lawson, Henry 1867–1922 Australian poet and short-story writer. The son of a Norwegian sailor who became a gold prospector, Lawson was born at Grenfell in New South Wales. He had only a rudimentary education, restricted by deafness from the age of 10, and started to earn his living when he was 13. After his parents separated he went to Sydney with his mother, who launched a socialist periodical, *The Republican*, to which Lawson contributed his first writings. He also wrote for *The Boomerang* (a radical Brisbane weekly) and *The Sydney Worker* but, like his contemporary A. B. PATERSON, he found his best form and outlet in *The Bulletin*. He went to live in the outback in the north of New South Wales in 1892 and the bush ballads and stories that resulted from his stay there became a popular feature of *The Bulletin* in the 1890s. He married in 1896 and travelled to Europe and New Zealand, returning to Australia in 1902. The best of Lawson's work was written by the turn of the century; after 1901 he seemed unable to recapture his laconic humour and fine balance of style, and his later work is marred by sentimentality. Lawson's first collection was *Stories in Prose and Verse* (1894), followed by *While the Billy Boils* (1896), *On the Track* (1900) and *Joe Wilson and His Mates* (1901). A collection in three volumes, *The Stories of Henry Lawson*, was edited by Cecil Mann (1965).

Lawson, John Howard 1894–1977 American playwright. Born in New York and educated at Williams College, he helped to shape the theatre of social consciousness in the 1920s and 1930s. His first play, *Processional* (1925), is a protest against the harshness of life during a coal strike in West Virginia. Lawson was among the first playwrights to move to Hollywood, where he became active as a leader of the Communist faction. *Marching Song* (1937) showed the triumph of labour's solidarity over the persecutions of an uncaring management. His career was cut short when he was summoned before the House Un-American Activities Committee. As one of the 'Hollywood Ten', he served a one-year sentence (1950–1) for contempt of the House. *Parlor Magic* (1963) was the only play he produced after the effective blacklisting of his name. His other plays include *Roger Boomer* (1923), *Nirvana* (1926), *Loudspeaker* (1927), *The International* (1928), *Success Story* (1932), *Gentlewoman* (1934) and *The Pure in Heart* (1937).

Lay of the Last Minstrel, The A poem in six CANTOS by SIR WALTER SCOTT, published in 1805. It was the first of Scott's romances in this form. The story is told by an ancient minstrel, the last of his race, and set in the 16th century.

The widowed lady of Branksome Hall blames her husband's death on Lord Cranstoun, who is in love with her daughter Margaret. Margaret returns his love but the feud between the two families prevents a marriage. Margaret's mother resorts to sorcery to avenge herself on Cranstoun, commissioning the dubious Sir William Deloraine to steal a magic book from the tomb of the alchemist Michael Scott in Melrose Abbey. Deloraine's encounter with Cranstoun after the theft serves to introduce the character of Gilpin Horner, Cranstoun's goblin page. This legendary Border character was the real inspiration of the poem (suggested to Scott by the Countess of Dalkeith); in spite of his wilful pranks, he is the agent for the reconciliation of the two families and the union of Margaret and Lord Cranstoun.

Layamon All that is known of Layamon comes from an early version of his sole surviving work, *BRUT*, written in the late 12th century. He was, he says, a priest at Areley Kings in the Severn valley and there decided to write a history of England from its foundation by the legendary Brutus. The poem, based on Wace's *Roman de Brut* (1155), is notable for its contribution to the development of ARTHURIAN LITERATURE.

Layard, Sir **Austen Henry** 1817–94 Archaeologist and excavator of Nineveh. After working for some years in the office of a London solicitor he became, almost accidentally, interested in the excavations in western Asia which resulted in the publication of his famous works, *Nineveh and Its Remains* (1848–9) and *The Ruins of Nineveh and Babylon* (1853). In 1861–6 he held the office of Under-Secretary for Foreign Affairs and was later ambassador to Madrid and Constantinople. He was a close friend of CHARLES DICKENS.

Lays of Ancient Rome, The A sequence of poems by THOMAS BABINGTON MACAULAY, published in 1842. Prompted by Barthold Niebuhr's suggestion that Livy's narrative was based on traditional BALLADS, he produced simple, vigorous verses which for long remained favourites of the anthology and the classroom. 'Horatius' tells of the defence of the Sublician Bridge against the Etruscans by Horatius Cocles; 'The Battle of Lake Regilius' describes the Romans' defeat of the Latins (*c.* 496 BC) with the divine aid of Castor and Pollux; 'Virginia' concerns the maiden killed by her father, Virginius, to save her from the lust of Appius Claudius; and 'The Prophecy of Capys' looks forward to the future greatness of Rome.

Layton, Irving 1912– Canadian poet. He was born in Romania but his family emigrated to Canada in 1913 and settled in Montreal, where he studied agriculture before entering McGill University. He graduated in 1936 and served with the Royal Canadian Air Force during World War II. After the war he became a teacher and editor of *First Statement*, a literary magazine which later merged with *Preview* to become *Northern Review*. With LOUIS DUDEK and RAYMOND SOUSTER he founded Contact Press, the leading publisher of Canadian poetry, in 1952. He was also lecturer in modern poetry at Sir George William's University and professor of English at York University, Ontario. Layton's career as a poet began with *Here and Now* (1945). *In the Midst of My Fever* (1954), *The Bull Calf and Other Poems* (1956), *A Red Carpet* for the Sun (1959), The Swinging Flesh (1961), The Shattered Plinths (1968) and Droppings from Heaven (1979) are among his many volumes. A Wild Peculiar Joy (1982) is a collection of his verse from 1945 to 1982. Layton's early work was designed to oppose the austerity of the poetry being published in Canada at the time. His later work discloses his increasing resentment of social inequality and a deepening sensitivity. Wild Gooseberries (1989) is a selection of his letters.

Le Bone Florence of Rome An anonymous VERSE ROMANCE of the late 14th century written in the north Midlands. Florence, wooed by an aged emperor, is eventually married to Esmere, whom she sends to destroy him. In his absence she is wooed by her brother-in-law and imprisoned for adultery when she refuses him. She flees, and in the ensuing years is falsely accused of murder, sold into slavery and shipwrecked. She eventually becomes a famous healer and all her wrong-doers come to her for aid. They confess, she cures them and is reunited with her husband. The romance is notable for its vivid descriptions and attention to detail, and for its portrayal of the heroine. Florence's patience and kindness recall the popular story of the 'constant' Constance (see EMARE); her goodness and the moralizing tone of the end of the poem recall the SAINT'S LIFE.

Le Carré, John [Cornwell, David John Moore] 1931– Novelist. After a public-school education, he attended the universities of Berne and Oxford, taught briefly at Eton and then spent five years in the British Foreign Service. His novels about the grey, duplicitous underworld of the secret service have increasingly come to be regarded less as thrillers than as perceptive documentations of the post-1945 Cold War climate. His third novel, The Spy Who Came In from the Cold (1963), made his reputation and remains his most concentrated study. A previous novel, Call for the Dead (1961), introduced his best-known character, George Smiley, who has reappeared several times, notably in Tinker, Tailor, Soldier, Spy (1974) and Smiley's People (1980). Other novels include: The Looking-Glass War (1965); A Small Town in Germany (1968); The Honourable Schoolboy (1977); The Perfect Spy (1986), drawing on his own relations with his domineering and raffish father; The Naive and Sentimental Lover (1971), unsuccessfully forsaking espionage; The Little Drummer Girl (1983), about the cause of Palestinian liberation; The Russia House (1989), in response to the end of the Cold War; and The Secret Pilgrim (1991).

Le Fanu, (Joseph) Sheridan 1814–73 Novelist. Born in Dublin of a family related to RICHARD BRINSLEY SHERIDAN, he was educated at Trinity College and called to the Bar in 1839, though he did not practise. He contributed to the Dublin University Magazine and became well known with the publication of his Irish ballads, 'Phaudrig Croohoore' and 'Shamus O'Brien' (1837). His first novel, The Cock and Anchor, appeared in 1845. He became proprietor and editor of the Dublin University Magazine in 1869. In all, he published some 20 books including novels, stories and verse, the latter including a drama 'Beatrice', 'The Legend of the Glaive' and 'Song of the Bottle'. He is best known, however, for ingenious and skilfully constructed tales of mystery and terror, notably The House by the Churchyard (1863), UNCLE SILAS (1864) and a volume of short stories, IN A GLASS DARKLY (1872).

Le Gallienne, Richard (Thomas) 1866–1947 Poet and essayist. Born and educated in Liverpool, he worked as a chartered accountant before the publication of My Lady's Sonnets in 1887. His best-known book of verse, The Lonely Dancer, was published in 1913. His style is characteristic of the 1890s, being uncompromisingly mannered and artificial. The Romantic Nineties (1926) gives a valuable account of the circle which included WILDE, ARTHUR SYMONS and AUBREY BEARDSLEY. Other volumes of reminiscences are Quest for the Golden Girl (1896) and From a Paris Garret (1936).

Le Guin, Ursula K(roeber) 1929– American novelist, poet and critic. The daughter of the anthropologist Alfred Kroeber, she was born in Berkeley, California, and educated at Radcliffe College and Columbia University. Most of her SCIENCE-FICTION novels are painstaking and elegant thought-experiments in human science. The Left Hand of Darkness (1969) imagines a society of human hermaphrodites where there can be no discrimination on sexual grounds. The Lathe of Heaven (1971) is a metaphysical fantasy about dreams which alter reality. The Word for World is Forest (1972) is a heartfelt condemnation of colonialism and imperialism. The Dispossessed (1974) contrasts the quasi-Utopian anarchist society of an arid moon with the capitalist system of its technologically developed parent world. Always Coming Home (1986) describes in great detail the folkways, myths and artwork of the 'post-technological' society of the Kesh, future inhabitants of northern California. Her short science fiction stories are collected in The Wind's Twelve Quarters (1975) and The Compass Rose (1982).

Her CHILDREN'S LITERATURE includes the much-acclaimed 'Earthsea' fantasy series: A Wizard of Earthsea (1968), The Tombs of Atuan (1971), The Farthest Shore (1972) and Tehanu (1990). Her non-fantastic fiction, including Orsinian Tales (1976) and Malafrena (1979), is usually set in imaginary kingdoms of the past. Her critical essays are collected in The Language of the Night (1979; revised 1989) and

Dancing at the Edge of the World (1989). Her poetry includes Wild Angels (1975), Hard Words and Other Poems (1981) and In the Red Zone (1983). Buffalo Gals and Other Animal Presences (1987) is a curious mélange of prose and verse about animals.

Le Sueur, Meridel 1900– American radical and feminist writer. Born in Murray, Iowa, she spent her childhood in Texas, Oklahoma and Kansas. Her father was a socialist lawyer and participated in various reform movements on behalf of farmers and workers. After a period in New York, where she studied at the American Academy of Dramatic Art and lived in an anarchist commune with Emma Goldman, among others, she moved to Hollywood and began to write articles and stories for radical publications such as The Daily Worker and THE NEW MASSES. Her first novel, The Girl (1939), examines the lives of various women whom she had known and observed in the 1930s. Salute to Spring (1940) is a collection of short stories describing the struggle of ordinary women's lives during the Depression. North Star Country (1945) is a history of the Midwest in which she grew up. She continued to write radical journalism throughout the 1950s and 1960s. Harvest Song (edited by John F. Crawford; 1990) collects her essays and stories up until 1958. A volume of her poetry, Rites of Ancient Ripening, was published in 1975. Her other works include Conquistadors (1973), The Mound Builders (1974) and CHILDREN'S LITERATURE. Her writings helped to establish a tradition of feminist dissent on which the women's movement of today is partly based.

Leacock, Stephen 1869–1944 Canadian humorist. Born at Swanmore, Hampshire, he was taken to Canada when he was six. He grew up in the Lake Simcoe region of Ontario and was educated at Toronto's leading secondary school, Upper Canada College, the University of Toronto and the University of Chicago. A political economist, he taught at McGill University from 1901 until his retirement in 1936. Elements of Political Science (1906) became a standard college textbook.

Beginning with Literary Lapses (1910), he published an average of one humorous book a year for the remainder of his life. These include Nonsense Novels (1911), Sunshine Sketches of a Little Town (1912), Arcadian Adventures with the Idle Rich (1914), Moonbeams from the Larger Lunacy (1915), Further Foolishness (1916), Frenzied Fiction (1918), Winnowed Wisdom (1926), My Remarkable Uncle (1942) and Last Leaves (1945). My Discovery of England (1922) and My Discovery of the West (1937) grew out of highly successful lecture tours. A master of the short sketch or extended anecdote with a strong oral flavour, Leacock belongs in the tradition of such North American humorists as ARTEMUS WARD, MARK TWAIN and, in Canada, THOMAS CHANDLER HALIBURTON.

Leader, The A weekly periodical founded by G. H. LEWES and Thornton Leigh Hunt, published from 1850 to 1866.

Lear, Edward 1812–88 Artist, traveller and nonsense poet. Born in London, the son of a stockbroker and the youngest of 20 children, he was educated at home, chiefly by his sister Anne, but was obliged to start earning his living at the age of 15. He was commissioned to make drawings of the parrots in the Zoological Gardens, and this led to his being engaged as an artist by the Earl of Derby, who kept a menagerie at Knowsley Hall. Lear's task was to produce illustrations for a description of the inhabitants. Successfully establishing himself as an accomplished artist, Lear was eventually engaged to give drawing lessons to Queen Victoria. He travelled extensively in the Mediterranean and visited India and Ceylon, finally settling at San Remo in Italy.

While working at Knowsley Hall, Lear wrote nonsense poetry for the Earl of Derby's children; later he made nonsense drawings to accompany them. This singular talent produced some of his most enduring work. Lear's verse was published as A Book of Nonsense (1845; enlarged 1861, 1863, 1870), A Book of Nonsense and More Nonsense (1862), Nonsense Songs, Stories, Botany and Alphabets (1871), More Nonsense, Pictures, Rhymes, Botany, Etc. (1872) and Laughable Lyrics, a Fresh Book of Nonsense Poems

'Manypeeplia Upsidownia': one of Edward Lear's botanical sketches of 1871

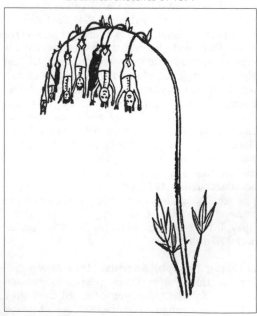

(1877). *Queery Leary Nonsense* (1911) contained new material and was compiled by Lady Strachey; *Teapots and Quails* (1953) contained unpublished fragments and was edited by P. Hofer and A. Davidson. *The Complete Nonsense of Edward Lear* (1947) was edited by Holbrook Jackson. Lear's many well-known poems include 'The Owl and the Pussycat', 'The Jumblies' and 'The Courtship of the Yongy-Bonghy-Bo'. He was also an accomplished exponent of the limerick form, and did much to popularize such verse jingles.

Lear's travel books include *Illustrated Excursions in Italy* (1846), *A Tour in Sicily* (1847), *Journal of a Landscape Painter in Albania, Illyria etc.* (1851), *Journal of a Landscape Painter in Southern Calabria* (1852), *Journal of a Landscape Painter in Corsica* (1870) and *Italian Journal* (1873-5). *The Letters of Edward Lear* (1907) and *Later Letters* (1911) were edited by Lady Strachey, and are valued for their discerning pictures of his times. TENNYSON's poem 'To E. L. on his Travels' was addressed to Lear.

Although at the centre of a wide circle of gifted literary and artistic friends, Lear suffered throughout his life from loneliness, depression and melancholy, conditions partly attributable to his subjection to epilepsy. In some sense all the isolated and marked creatures of his fantasy, the Yongy-Bonghy-Bo, the Dong with the Luminous Nose and the Pobble Who Has No Toes, are partial self-portraits.

Leatherstocking Tales, The A series of novels by JAMES FENIMORE COOPER, consisting of *The Pioneers: or, The Sources of the Susquehanna* (1823), *The Last of the Mohicans: A Tale of 1757* (1826), *The Prairie: A Tale* (1827), *The Pathfinder: or, The Inland Sea* (1840) and *The Deerslayer: or, The First War Path* (1841).

Set in the early frontier period of American history, they take their name from the protagonist, Natty Bumppo, variously called Leatherstocking, Deerslayer, Hawkeye and Pathfinder. The chronological sequence differs from the dates of composition.

The Deerslayer, the first novel in order of events but the last to be written, relates Bumppo's experiences as a young man, and takes place in upstate New York in the early 1740s. The action begins as Deerslayer and his friend Hurry Harry approach Lake Glimmerglass, or Oswego, where the trapper Thomas Hutter lives with his daughters, the beautiful Judith and the feeble-minded Hetty. Hutter's floating log fort is attacked by Iroquois Indians, and the two frontiersmen join in the fight. Harry and Hutter are captured. Deerslayer is joined by his Mohican friend, Chingachgook, whose bride Hist is being held by the Iroquois, and they eventually manage to ransom the two men. They then try to rescue Hist, but Hutter is killed and Deerslayer is captured in the attempt. The frontiersman is released on parole so that he may see his friends for the last time and, keeping his word, he returns to the Indian camp to await his death. Judith,

however, manages to delay the proceedings long enough for Chingachgook to arrive with a troop of English soldiers and save Deerslayer's life.

The next novel in the series, *The Last of the Mohicans*, presents Bumppo in his maturity, and is set in 1757 during the Seven Years' War between the French and the British. (In this novel he is known as Hawkeye.) Cora and Alice Munro are on their way to Fort William Henry to join their father, the commander. They are accompanied by Major Duncan Heyward and a singing teacher, David Gamut. Their Indian guide, Magua, plans to betray the group to the Iroquois, who are fighting on the side of the French. Magua's plan, however, is frustrated by Hawkeye and his friends Chingachgook and Uncas, who are the last Mohican chieftains. The group arrives at the fort, but Munro is forced to surrender to the French commander Montcalm. Although supposedly given safe conduct, the English are attacked and the girls captured by Delawares and Hurons. The former take Cora; the latter, Alice. Alice and Uncas, also a prisoner, manage to escape. Uncas is then welcomed at the camp of the Delawares and named successor to the old chief. Magua, however, has laid claim to the captive Cora, and he eventually kills both the young woman and Uncas. Hawkeye avenges the death of his friend and kills Magua.

The Pathfinder takes place soon after *The Last of the Mohicans*, in the same conflict between French and Indians and the British colonials. Mabel Dunham is making her way to Oswego, the British fort on Lake Ontario, to join her father. She is accompanied by a group consisting of her uncle, Charles Cap, a Tuscarora Indian named Arrowhead and his wife Dew-in-June, the scout Pathfinder (Natty Bumppo), Chingachgook the Mohican chief and Jasper Western, sailor. The party is harassed by Iroquois, and Arrowhead and his wife disappear. The rest of the company arrives safely at the fort, then proceeds with Mabel's father on Jasper Western's boat to relieve a post in the Thousand Islands. But Jasper is suspected of being disloyal to the English and is sent back to Oswego, while Dunham and his force set out to attack French supply boats. Dew-in-June then arrives, with the warning that Arrowhead, at the head of an Iroquois force, is leading an attack on the post. The Iroquois are eventually routed by Pathfinder and Chingachgook, and Jasper is arrested as a traitor, to the despair of Mabel who, in spite of a promise to Pathfinder, is in love with Jasper. Muir – the lieutenant who had accused Jasper – is unmasked as the real traitor, and Arrowhead kills him. Dunham dies and Pathfinder, realizing the truth, relinquishes Mabel to Jasper.

The next novel in the series, *The Pioneers*, is set in 1793 in Otsego County in the recently settled region of New York state. While hunting deer, Judge Temple, one of the principal landowners in the area, wounds

Oliver Edwards, the companion of the ageing Natty Bumppo, now known as Leatherstocking. The judge and his daughter Elizabeth befriend Edwards, who becomes their overseer, meanwhile maintaining his friendship with Bumppo and with old John Mohegan, whom everyone knows to be the Mohican chief Chingachgook. It is suspected that Edwards is the chief's son and soon Elizabeth and her friends are disdaining his company. Bumppo is arrested for shooting deer out of season and spends a short time in prison. Elizabeth goes to visit him upon his release but is caught in a forest fire on her return, and is saved by Edwards. Chingachgook is also caught in the fire, and dies in spite of Bumppo's efforts to save him. A party searching for Elizabeth comes upon a demented old man. It is discovered that he is Major Effingham, the Loyalist who had once owned Judge Temple's estate, but who was lost in the war and had his lands confiscated. It is revealed that Oliver Edwards is his grandson. Temple relinquishes half of his estate to Oliver, and he and Elizabeth are betrothed at the end.

The Prairie is set in 1804 on the frontier of the great plains. Natty Bumppo – now in his 80s and known simply as the trapper – has joined the western movement. He meets a wagon train, gains an unpleasant impression of its leaders, Ishmael Bush and his brother-in-law Abiram White, and is puzzled by the confinement of a woman in a covered wagon. The trapper's wisdom enables the train to evade an Indian raiding party, and he guides it to a safe camp. A young soldier then joins the camp and Bumppo is overjoyed to recognize Duncan Uncas Middleton, a descendant of his friend Duncan Heyward. Duncan is on a mission for the army but is also seeking his betrothed, Inez de Certavallos, who has been kidnapped and is being held for ransom. The trapper remembers the confined woman, who proves to be Inez, and the two proceed to rescue her. The travellers endure a prairie fire, a buffalo stampede, and capture by the Sioux. A Pawnee raid on the Sioux frees them, but Ishmael Bush catches up with them and accuses Bumppo of the murder of one of his men. There has indeed been a murder, but the guilty man proves to be Abiram White. The arrival of Duncan's soldiers finally provides the party with safety, with the trapper's Pawnee friends watching quietly. The end of the tale brings the frontiersman's life to a close. He dies peacefully on the prairie, surrounded by his friends of both races.

Leaves of Grass A volume of poems by WALT WHITMAN, first published in 1855 and expanded until the 'Deathbed' edition of 1891–2. Its elaboration was the masterwork of his career as a poet. The first edition included the poems eventually titled 'Song of Myself', 'I Sing the Body Electric', and 'The Sleepers'. 'Song of Myself', over 1300 lines long in its final version, celebrates the poet's self and its relation to common men and women, announcing the presence of the cosmic 'I' who sings the poem. The second edition (1856) omitted the original preface but added 20 new poems, among them 'Sun Down Poem' (later renamed 'Crossing Brooklyn Ferry') and 'Poem of the Open Road' (renamed 'Song of the Open Road'). The third edition (1860) added 'Out of the Cradle Endlessly Rocking', the 'Calamus' poems, extolling friendship among men, and 'Enfants d'Adam' (later titled 'Children of Adam'), about procreative love. The fourth edition (1867) was bound with *Drum-Taps*, a series of poems inspired by Whitman's experiences nursing the wounded during the Civil War, separately published in 1865, and *Sequel*, containing his elegies for Lincoln: 'When Lilacs Last in the Dooryard Bloom'd' and 'O Captain! My Captain!'. The fifth edition (1871) added a new 'annex', 'Passage to India', incorporated into the body of the work for the sixth edition (1881), which also added the prose pamphlet *Democractic Vistas*. The 1876 reissue is sometimes referred to as the 'Centennial' edition. For the 1889 reissue of the 1881 edition, Whitman added another annex, which included a group of new poems entitled 'Sands at Seventy' and a prose piece called 'A Backward Glance o'er Travel'd Roads', both of which had previously appeared in *November Boughs* (1888). The final version, sometimes called the 'Deathbed' edition (1891–2), is simply a reissue of the 1881 edition supplemented with 'Sands at Seventy' and 'Goodbye My Fancy'.

Both the form and content of the poems in *Leaves of Grass* were revolutionary; Whitman's sprawling lines and cataloguing technique, as well as his belief that poetry should include the lowly, the profane, even the obscene, have had enormous influence. His intention in writing *Leaves of Grass*, he said, was to create a truly American poem, one 'proportionate to our continent, with its powerful races of men, its tremendous historic events, its great oceans, its mountains, and its illimitable prairies'. In fact, the poem goes beyond its specifically American subject to deal with the universal themes of nature, fertility and mortality.

Leavis, F(rank) R(aymond) 1895–1978 Critic. He was born in Cambridge and educated at the Perse School and Emmanuel College, where he abandoned history in favour of English. After serving as a stretcher-bearer in World War I he returned to his studies and absorbed the critical teachings of I. A. RICHARDS, whose Practical Criticism lectures he attended. He lived by part-time teaching, and during a period as a probationary lecturer married his former pupil Q. D. Roth (see Q. D. LEAVIS) in 1929; but he had to wait until 1936 for a fellowship at Downing College, and 1937 for a university lectureship.

In the early 1930s he wrote a series of cultural manifestos – *Mass Civilization and Minority Culture* (1933), *For Continuity* (1933), and *Culture and*

Environment (with Denys Thompson; 1933) – which propose the study of English literature as a base from which to rally the discriminating educated minority against the threats to cultural continuity posed by the processes of industrialism, especially by the cinema, advertising and the spread of 'mass' culture. These arguments formed the basis of the critical campaign undertaken by SCRUTINY, which Leavis guided as co-editor from 1932 to 1953. His *New Bearings in English Poetry* (1932) began a thorough revision of the English literary tradition, championing GERARD MANLEY HOPKINS, T. S. ELIOT, POUND and YEATS as the creators of a modernist tradition after the post-Swinburne 'arrest' (see MODERNISM). The implicit recasting of the poetic tradition (based on the theories of Eliot and I. A. Richards) was defined in *Revaluation* (1936), where Leavis opposed a 'line of WIT' from DONNE to Eliot to the line, with its emphasis on melody and special poetic diction, running from MILTON to SWINBURNE. In *The Great Tradition* (1948) he brought the same kind of historical and critical discrimination to the English novel. The 'great' novelists (JANE AUSTEN, GEORGE ELIOT, HENRY JAMES, JOSEPH CONRAD) were admired for their life-enhancing moral seriousness. The subsequent rehabilitation of DICKENS in *Dickens the Novelist* (with Q. D. Leavis, 1970) identified a complementary tradition linking BLAKE and D. H. LAWRENCE, whose work he had defended in *D. H. Lawrence: Novelist* (1955). This shift accompanied his increasingly embattled response to 'technologico-Benthamite' trends in British culture.

Leavis refused to define the theoretical basis of his judgements, though it can be inferred from numerous asides. Historically considered, he belongs to the tradition of ARNOLD, RUSKIN and other writers on 'the condition of England'. The almost religious seriousness which he introduced to criticism inspired a generation of followers ('Leavisites') with a sense of vocation in teaching a subject deemed central to civilization. His revaluation, not just of the canon of English literature, but of the status of criticism, established him as the most important English-speaking critic of his time.

Leavis, Q(ueenie) D(orothy) 1906–81 Critic. Born in London, the daughter of a draper, she was educated at Girton College, Cambridge, studying English under I. A. RICHARDS. While researching into the history of the English reading public, she married F. R. LEAVIS in 1929. Her only book, *Fiction and the Reading Public* (1932), offered a sociological diagnosis of trends in English popular culture since the 17th century, tracing how the readership of fiction had progressively split into the 'highbrow' minority interested in the art of the novel and a mass audience consuming popular romances, with best-sellers tending to confuse standards. This early attempt at a sociological approach to literature influenced her husband's critical work and the ethos of SCRUTINY, to which she was a regular contributor while bringing up her family. She wrote important critical reassessments of DICKENS in *Dickens the Novelist* (with F. R. Leavis; 1970) and of JANE AUSTEN, CHARLOTTE and EMILY BRONTË, NATHANIEL HAWTHORNE and EDITH WHARTON in essays gathered posthumously, with other work, in three volumes (1983–89). She had a special interest in women writers.

Lecky, William Edward Hartpole 1838–1903 Historian. Born near Dublin, he was educated at Cheltenham College and Trinity College, Dublin. Influenced by HENRY THOMAS BUCKLE's approach to history, he published *The Religious Tendencies of the Age* (1860) and *The Leaders of Public Opinion in Ireland* (1861) anonymously. *The Declining Sense of the Miraculous* (1863) became the first two chapters of *A History of the Rise and Influence of the Spirit of Rationalism in Europe* (1865), which argued with considerable force that progress is due to the spirit of rationalism and the tolerance demanded by reason, and is always impeded by theological dogmatism and bigotry. The book made Lecky famous and he followed it with *The History of European Morals from Augustus to Charlemagne* (1869). *A History of England in the Eighteenth Century* (1878–90) was published in eight volumes, which were extended to 12 (1892). Lecky also published some historical essays and two later volumes, *Democracy and Liberty* (1896) and *The Map of Life: Conduct and Character* (1899). From 1895 he sat in Parliament as MP for Dublin University; he opposed Home Rule for Ireland though his sympathies lay with the welfare and interests of that country.

Lee, Dennis 1939– Canadian poet and writer of CHILDREN'S LITERATURE. Born in Toronto, he attended the University of Toronto and subsequently taught there and at York University, Toronto. He has played an important part in Canadian publishing, helping to found the House of Anansi Press, an outlet for Canadian writers, and working for Macmillan and McClelland and Stewart. Far from prolific, he is essentially an elegiac poet. *Civil Elegies* (1968, expanded 1972) and *The Gods* (1979) are about various kinds of loss, including his country's loss of vision and, more generally, the erosion of spiritual values. *The Death of Harold Ladoo* (1976) moves from its ostensible subject, the murder of a Trinidadian friend and fellow-writer, to become an elegy for cultural and spiritual impoverishment. *Alligator Pie* (1974) is a collection of nonsense rhymes for small children. Other children's verse includes *Nicholas Knock* (1974), *Garbage Delight* (1977), *Jelly Belly* (1983) and song lyrics for the popular television programme *Fraggle Rock*. *Savage Fields* (1977) is a study of LEONARD COHEN and MICHAEL ONDAATJE.

Lee, (Nelle) Harper 1926– American novelist. Born in Monroeville, Alabama, she attended the University of Alabama and studied for a year at Oxford before becoming a full-time writer. Her first and only novel is *To Kill a Mockingbird* (1960), a story of racial prejudice set in a Southern town like Monroeville, in which a white lawyer, Atticus Finch, defends a black man, Tom Robinson, falsely accused of raping a white girl. The action is presented from the viewpoint of Finch's six-year-old daughter, Jean Louise ('Scout'). *To Kill a Mockingbird* received a PULITZER PRIZE and was filmed (1962) with a screenplay by HORTON FOOTE.

Lee, Laurie 1914– Autobiographer and poet. Born in Gloucestershire, he was educated locally at Slad Village School and Stroud Central School. He served as publications editor at the Ministry of Information during World War II and later worked for the Festival of Britain. He is best known for *Cider with Rosie* (1959), a lyrical and nostalgic memoir of his Gloucestershire childhood. It was followed by *As I Walked Out One Midsummer Morning* (1969), about his youthful adventures on the road to London and in Spain, and, belatedly completing the trilogy, *A Moment of War* (1991), about his experiences in the Spanish Civil War. *The Sun My Monument* (1944), *The Bloom of Candles* (1947) and *My Many Coated Man* (1955) are among many volumes of poetry showing his love of the countryside. He has also written screenplays and travel books.

Lee, Nathaniel *c*. 1653–92 Playwright and actor. Lee's theatrical career began when he turned actor after graduating from Trinity College, Cambridge. His first plays, *Nero* (1674), *Sophonisba* (1675) and *Gloriana* (1676), were tragedies written in HEROIC COUPLETS and showing an appetite for rhetoric and sensation. His masterpiece, *The Rival Queens* (1677), led the return to BLANK VERSE as the poetic style for tragedy. It reveals, as does *Lucius Junius Brutus* (1680), an ability to create complex characters and a recognition of political motives sufficiently acute to lead to the banning of the later play.

Lee was drawn into the dissipated circle of friends surrounding the EARL OF ROCHESTER, whom he portrays without flattery as Nemours in the satiric sex-comedy, *The Princess of Cleve* (1681). Lee's physical and mental health declined so far that he was confined to Bedlam from 1684 to 1689.

Lee, Sir Sidney 1859–1926 Shakespearean scholar and biographer. Born in London, the son of a Jewish merchant, he was educated at the City of London School and at Balliol College, Oxford, where the Master, BENJAMIN JOWETT, recognized his promise. In 1882 he became assistant to LESLIE STEPHEN, then planning the *Dictionary of National Biography*, suc-ceeded Stephen as editor in 1891 and saw the main project to its conclusion in 1900, working later on supplementary volumes. His principal separate work, a biography of SHAKESPEARE (1898), grew from his main *DNB* contributions. Several times revised, it was in its time the fullest statement of the sparse biographical facts, set in a wide literary and historical context with full attention to foreign influences. Having written on the Queen for the *DNB* he prepared a prompt and frank *Queen Victoria, a Biography* (1902) and was later commissioned to write a two-volume *Life of King Edward VII* (1925–7). Neither is as successful as his work on the Elizabethan period, on which he wrote many books and articles. He was knighted in 1911.

Leech, John 1817–64 Comic artist and illustrator. Born in London, he attended Charterhouse – where he first met THACKERAY – and studied medicine at St Bartholomew's Hospital. In 1841 he became a founding member of *PUNCH*, acting as its chief artist until his death. Outstanding among the 50 books Leech illustrated are DICKENS's *A CHRISTMAS CAROL* (1844), the sporting novels of R. S. SURTEES and GILBERT À BECKETT's *The Comic History of England* (1847) and *The Comic History of Rome* (1852).

Left Book Club A London-based publishing venture launched early in 1936 by Victor Gollancz, the Labour MP John Strachey and Harold Laski, professor of political science at the London School of Economics. Its editorial director was John Lewis, co-founder and first president of the Welsh Nationalist Party. The Club's aim was to combat the rise of fascism by fostering a united front, providing its members with books with a socialist bias, most of which were specifically commissioned. Beginning with a membership of 10,000, numbers rapidly rose to 50,000 by 1939, but then suffered an equally rapid decline after the Nazi-Soviet Pact. The Pact was denounced by many of the Club's leaders, including Gollancz (see *The Betrayal of the Left*, 1941, which he edited), whose earlier pro-Soviet stance had precluded criticism of Stalin's Great Purge and of the Moscow trials (1936–8). The Club never recovered from its great slump after 1939, and it was dissolved in 1948.

The majority of the Club's publications were factual, and few achieved lasting success. Two exceptions were GEORGE ORWELL's *THE ROAD TO WIGAN PIER* (1937), ironically enough a book about which Gollancz had misgivings, and CLIFFORD ODETS's play *WAITING FOR LEFTY* (1937).

Legend of Good Women, The An unfinished poem by GEOFFREY CHAUCER, immediately preceding *THE CANTERBURY TALES* and making the earliest known use of the HEROIC COUPLET in English. A prologue in the form of an allegorical DREAM-VISION uses a debate about the supremacy of the flower or the leaf (see also *THE FLOWER AND THE LEAF*) to proclaim allegiance to the daisy, which the poet says is a transformation of Alceste, the leader of 'Good Women'. The prologue goes on to explain the main body of the poem by saying that Chaucer, after having defamed women in *TROILUS AND CRISEYDE* and his translation, *THE ROMAUNT OF THE ROSE*, has now been required by the God of Love to write in their praise. (It is not known whether *The Legend of Good Women* was written in response to genuine criticism of his earlier works.) The work is a 'Legend', or legendary, narrating the lives of women who suffered or died as a result of their faithful love. The stories are drawn from Virgil and Ovid, and tell of classical heroines: Cleopatra, Thisbe, Dido, Hypsipyle and Medea, Lucrece, Ariadne, Philomela, Phyllis and Hypermnestra. The legends do not share the fresh and lively poetry of the prologue, and the uniformity of their tone and intention makes them less appealing to the modern reader than many other works by Chaucer. The prologue exists in two versions; the second (perhaps written as late as 1394) is apparently an attempt to make the structure more consistent, but omits several of the most beautiful passages of the earlier version.

Legend of Montrose, The

A novel by SIR WALTER SCOTT, in the third series of *Tales of My Landlord*, published in 1819. Its setting is the rising of the Highland clans against the Covenanters and in support of Charles I in 1644.

Interwoven in the plot is the story of Allan M'Aulay, nephew of a man murdered by Highland raiders calling themselves Children of the Mist. Passionate and vengeful, he falls in love with Annot Lyle, whom he has rescued from the raiders, but she loves the young Earl of Menteith. The Earl returns her affection, though they cannot marry because of an unresolved mystery surrounding her birth. She is eventually revealed to be the daughter of Sir Duncan Campbell, but Allan interrupts her wedding to Menteith to stab his rival and disappear.

The novel is more successful in its portrait of history, particularly the opposing characters of Montrose, the Royalist, and Argyle, than in its account of the lovers' problems.

Lehmann, (Rudolph) John (Frederick)

1907–87 Poet and man of letters. The brother of ROSAMOND LEHMANN and the actress Beatrix Lehmann, he was born at Bourne End in the Thames Valley and educated at Eton and Trinity College, Cambridge. He edited *New Writing* (1936–9), *New Writing and Daylight* (1942–6) and, most importantly, *Penguin New Writing* (1940–50), which ran for 40 numbers and featured the work of ROY FULLER, LAURIE LEE and HENRY REED. He was also editor of *THE LONDON MAGAZINE* in 1954–61. His eponymous publishing imprint issued more than 200 titles between 1946 and 1951, including Sartre's *La Nausée* and SAUL BELLOW's *Dangling Man*. Lehmann's verse, including *A Garden Revisited and Other Poems* (1931), *The Noise of History* (1934), *The Sphere of Glass* (1944) and *Poems New and Selected* (1986), came only intermittently, between major publishing and editorial ventures. Marked by unostentatious rhythms and direct treatment of experience, it is now neglected.

Lehmann, Rosamond (Nina)

1903–90 Novelist. She was born in London, the sister of JOHN LEHMANN and the actress Beatrix Lehmann. She was taught at home before going to Girton College, Cambridge, the background for her first novel, *Dusty Answer* (1927). Its themes, developing womanhood and the subtle shades of emotional relationships, served the author well in a successful career which included: *A Note in Music* (1930), *Invitation to the Waltz* (1932) and its sequel *The Weather in the Streets* (1936), *The Ballad and the Source* (1944) and *The Echoing Grove* (1953). She also wrote a play, *No More Music* (1939), a volume of short stories, *The Gypsy's Baby* (1946), and an autobiography, *The Swan in the Evening* (1967).

Leland [Leyland], John

?1506–52 Antiquary and poet. The earliest of the 16th-century antiquarians, Leland was educated at St Paul's School, London, Christ's College, Cambridge (where he graduated in 1522), and Paris. He became Keeper of Libraries to Henry VIII sometime before 1530 and the king's antiquary in 1533. He was granted permission by the king to search the libraries of monasteries and colleges for ancient documents and in 1534–43 toured the country in his researches, intending to write a work called 'History and Antiquities of this Nation'. An English version of the account he presented to Henry was published by his friend JOHN BALE as *The Laborious Journey and Search of John Leland* (1549). In 1547, in Bale's words, 'a most pitiful occasion fell besides his wits' and Leland became insane. He was given into his brother's care in 1551 and died the next year, his great work still in notes.

Leland's notes were used by later topographers and historians like WILLIAM HARRISON, RAPHAEL HOLINSHED and WILLIAM CAMDEN, as well as MICHAEL DRAYTON in writing *POLY-OLBION*, before being published as the nine-volume *Itinerary* (1710–12). Leland also wrote a defence of the Arthurian legends, *Assertio inclytissimi Arthuri* (1544), which was translated as *A Learned and True Assertion of the Original Life, Acts and Death of... Arthur* (1582). He wrote a few Latin poems: on the death of SIR THOMAS WYATT (1542) and the birth of Prince Edward (1543); *Cygnea cantio* (1545), which has been suggested as a model for SPENSER's *PROTHALAMION*; and *Laudatio pacis* ('Praise of Peace',1546).

Lemon, Mark 1809–70 Co-founder, with HENRY MAYHEW, of *PUNCH* in 1841. The new journal did not at first succeed, and was subsidized by Lemon's earnings as a playwright. Over 60 of his pieces were performed in London. Meanwhile, he contributed to other journals, and was a founder-editor of *The Field*. He wrote over 100 songs, lyrics, novels, Christmas fairy-stories and a joke-book. He collaborated with DICKENS in 1851 in a one-act FARCE, *Mr Nightingale's Diary*, in which they both acted. Eventually *Punch*, which had originally belonged to Lemon, Mayhew and the printer and engraver, was sold to a new proprietor, and Lemon stayed on as editor until he died. He nursed it to success and by the time of his death *Punch* had become a national institution.

Lennox, Charlotte (Ramsay) 1720–1804 Novelist. She was born in New York, the daughter of the lieutenant governor, and moved to England at the age of 15. She worked as an actress for a short time and then became a professional writer and novelist. *The Life of Harriot Stuart* (1750) was a SENTIMENTAL NOVEL of manners but she achieved success with a SATIRE, *The Female Quixote: or, The Adventures of Arabella* (1752). It depicts a heroine whose world is conjured up from French romances of the previous century – a far more satisfying one for her than the real world. But reality keeps intruding, and Mrs Lennox makes some successful comedy out of Arabella's conviction that all men are either suitors or ravishers. She dramatized the novel as *Angelica: or, Quixote in Petticoats* (1758). *The History of Henrietta*

(1758) was followed by *Sophia* (1762) and *Euphemia* (1790). *The Sister* (1769) is a play.

Leonard, Hugh [Byrne, John Keyes] 1926– Irish playwright. He was born in Dalkey, County Dublin. The ABBEY THEATRE produced his first two long plays, *The Birthday Party* (1956) and *A Leap in the Dark* (1958). Shortly afterwards he joined Granada television, writing original plays, adaptations and a farcical series, *Me Mammy*. Leonard, who has adapted Labiche's *Célimare* , is knowledgeable in FARCE. *The Patrick Pearse Motel* (1971) and *Time Was* (1976) use the genre to satirize Dublin's fashionable outer suburbs. *Da* (1973) is a serio-comic treatment of the same location. *A Life* (1976) retraces its main character's path to his desiccated marriage, accounting for and perhaps disturbing his defensive reserve.

Lessing, Doris (May) 1919– Novelist. Born to British parents in Khermanshah in Persia, she grew up on a farm in Southern Rhodesia and moved to England in 1949. *The Grass is Singing* (1950), a powerful study of a white woman's obsession with her black servant, announced the interest in the private action of the mind which distinguishes many of her later novels. *Martha Quest* (1952), *A Proper Marriage* (1954), *A Ripple from the Storm* (1958), *Landlocked* (1965) and *The Four-Gated City* (1969) make up a sequence collectively entitled *The Children of Violence*, reflecting her enduring commitment to radical politics and challenging literary conventions in their exploration of mental processes and breakdown. *The Golden*

Doris Lessing

Notebook (1962), hailed if not conceived as the expression of feminist politics, examines the experience of a woman writer. The narrative is split into a conventional novel, ironically entitled 'Free Women', and a series of lyrical and exploratory asides represented by the four notebooks kept by the protagonist, Anna Wulf.

Later work concentrated on the 'space within'. Two experimental novels, *Briefing for a Descent into Hell* (1971) and *The Memoirs of a Survivor* (1974), were followed by a 'space fiction' series, *Canopus in Argos: Archives*, consisting of *Re: Colonised Planet 5, Shikasta* (1979), *The Marriages between Zones Three, Four and Five* (1980), *The Sirian Experiments* (1981), *The Making of the Representative for Planet 8* (1982) and *Documents Relating to the Sentimental Agents in the Volyen Empire* (1983). She has since returned to realistic narrative with: *The Diary of a Good Neighbour* (1983), an unsparing study of the privations of old age, and *If the Old Could* (1984), originally published under the pseudonym of Jane Somers; *The Good Terrorist* (1985), about urban terrorism; and *The Fifth Child* (1988), a bleak novella about a couple's unexpectedly malevolent progeny. In addition to volumes of short stories, beginning with *This Was the Old Chief's Country* (1951), she has also published autobiographical works, *Going Home* (1957) and *In Pursuit of the English* (1960), poetry and travel books.

L'Estrange, Sir **Roger** 1616–1704 Journalist and translator. The son of Norfolk landowners, L'Estrange was an active Royalist during the Civil War, taking part in an abortive Royalist rising in Kent in 1648. He escaped to the Continent, where he first used his talents as a writer with political pamphlets against the army leaders and the Presbyterians. He contributed to the climate of opinion that made the Restoration possible and in 1663 was appointed Surveyor of the Press. From 1663 to 1666 L'Estrange published two newspapers, *The Intelligencer* and *The News*, but he had less success than HENRY MUDDIMAN, whose *London Gazette* ousted all rivals. Another paper published by L'Estrange was the *City Mercury*, founded in 1675. His supposed connection with the Popish Plot forced him to leave England, but he was able to return in 1680, and published *The Observator* (1681– 7), attacking Titus Oates particularly and Dissenters and Whigs generally. He earned a knighthood from James II in 1685.

The Revolution and the accession of William and Mary ended L'Estrange's career as a journalist; he was deprived of his office as Surveyor and imprisoned several times. In later life he supported himself by translations, a field in which he had already enjoyed some success: among them were ERASMUS' *Colloquies* (1680 and 1689), *The Fables of Aesop and Other Eminent Mythologies* (1692) and the works of Josephus (1702).

See also NEWSPAPER, THE RISE OF THE ENGLISH.

Letters concerning Toleration The first of JOHN LOCKE's *Letters* was published in Latin as *Epistola de tolerantia* in Holland in 1689. The English version and *A Second Letter concerning Toleration* appeared in 1690. *A Third Letter for Toleration* followed in 1692. A convinced Christian and an empiricist, Locke was a powerful advocate of free enquiry. He favoured religious liberty for all except atheists and Catholics, and a national church that made possible the freedom of individual opinion which was every man's right.

Letters from an American Farmer A collection of 12 essays by J. HECTOR ST JEAN DE CRÈVECOEUR describing rural life in 18th-century America. They were first published in London in 1782, though they were probably written several years earlier. The first American edition appeared in Philadelphia in 1793.

Addressing his letters to a British correspondent, Crèvecoeur, in the person of 'Farmer James', writes glowingly of the conditions of American agrarian life and of the virtue, independence, industry, and prosperity of the American farmer. In the third essay, 'What is an American?', he speculates on the roles that the experience of immigration and of working the American land play in the 'Americanization' process that produces this singular breed. He also observes the relationship between the geography of different regions and the typical character and activities of their people, discussing on the one hand Quaker simplicity and the whale fishery on Nantucket, and on the other the luxuries of Charleston and the slave system Southerners depend upon. Though extolling the virtues of stable, agrarian life throughout, Farmer James ends with a disillusioned essay, 'Distresses of a Frontier Man', describing his realization that the agrarian idyll is not possible in the midst of frontier raids and Revolutionary violence. Reluctantly he resolves to join the Indians on the frontier, leaving his farm and the political conflict that white, European-American society imposes upon him.

Lever, Charles (James) 1806–72 Novelist. Born in Dublin, he studied medicine at Trinity College and made his name with a succession of lively novels about Ireland and the army: *The Confessions of Harry Lorrequer* (1837), *Charles O'Malley* (1840), *Jack Hinton the Guardsman* (1842), *Tom Burke of Ours* (1844), *Arthur O'Leary* (1844) and *The O'Donoghe* (1845). Their tone was well parodied by THACKERAY in PUNCH'S PRIZE NOVELISTS. In 1845 Lever toured the Continent in extravagant style, settling in Italy, where he held two consulships as sinecures, at Spezzia (1865) and then Trieste (1867). His later novels were more subdued, partly through an attempt at greater realism and partly through fatigue; they include *Roland Cashel* (1850), *Sir Jasper Carew* (1855),

The Fortunes of Glencore (1857), *Luttrell of Arran* (1865) and *Lord Kilgobbin* (1872). The failure of *A Day's Ride* (1863) in its original serialization in ALL THE YEAR ROUND prompted DICKENS to begin GREAT EXPECTATIONS.

Leverson, Ada 1865–1936 Novelist. Born Ada Beddington in London, she was educated privately. She became a member of the circle which included WILDE, GEORGE MOORE and MAX BEERBOHM, and contributed to THE YELLOW BOOK. Her six novels are *The Twelfth Hour* (1907), *Love's Shadow* (1908), *The Limit* (1911), *Tenterhooks* (1912), *Bird of Paradise* (1914) and *Love at Second Sight* (1916).

Levertov, Denise 1923– American poet. Born in Ilford (England), she served as a civilian nurse in London during World War II, married the American writer Mitchell Goodman and moved to the USA in 1948. Her first volume, *The Double Image* (1946), was written and published in Britain. Subsequent work has been associated with the BLACK MOUNTAIN SCHOOL and the influence of WILLIAM CARLOS WILLIAMS, with whom she shares a preference for sparing use of METAPHOR and allusion. Written in the rhythms of speech, her poems are full of sensory detail and often concern the nature of the creative process itself. *Here and Now* (1957) and *Overland to the Islands* (1958) belong to her years living in Mexico; *With Eyes at the Back of Our Heads* (1959) reflects her decision to return to New York. *The Jacob's Ladder* (1961) appeared in the same year she became poetry editor of THE NATION. Since then she has concentrated increasingly on political and feminist themes, in volumes such as *O Taste and See: New Poems* (1964), *A Tree Telling of Orpheus* (1968), *To Stay Alive* (1971), *The Freeing of the Dust* (1975), *Pig Dreams: Scenes from the Life of Sylvia* (1979), *Wanderer's Daysong* (1981) and *Candles in Babylon* (1982). Other volumes include *Collected Earlier Poems, 1940–1960* (1979), *Poems 1960–1967* (1983), *The Menaced World* (1984) and *Selected Poems* (1986). *In the Night* (1968) is a work of fiction, and *The Poet in the World* (1973) and *Light up the Cave* (1981) are volumes of essays. After teaching at Vassar College, Tufts University and the Massachusetts Institute of Technology, she became professor of English at Stanford University in 1982. A recipient of the Shelley Award for poetry, she was elected to the American Academy in 1980.

Levi, Peter (Chad Tigar) 1931– Poet, critic and translator. Born in Ruislip, and educated at Beaumont and Oxford, Levi trained as a Jesuit and taught at Stonyhurst, the Catholic public school, before being ordained as a priest in 1964. Thereafter he taught classics at Campion Hall, Oxford, and pursued archaeological work in Greece. His translation of Pausanias' *Guide to Greece* appeared in 1971. He left the priesthood, married and became a fellow of St Catherine's College, Oxford, in 1977. He was elected professor of poetry at Oxford in 1984.

Levi's poetry is characterized by tranquillity and indirectness. *The Gravel Ponds* (1960) shows elements of social concern, combined with a decorative use of nature-imagery. The mature poetry gathered in his *Collected Poems* (1976), *The Echoing Green* (a volume of ELEGIES; 1983) and *Shadow and Bone* (1989) represents a merging of PASTORAL with SYMBOLISM. Aspects of landscape and the seasons are presented in a cryptic, subtly disjunctive manner to evoke elusive states of mind or a mood of philosophical questioning. The formal elegance and inconspicuous originality of Levi's work has won him a steadily growing reputation. He has also published: translations of several Eastern European poets; criticism in *The Noise Made by Poems* (1977) and *The Art of Poetry* (1991), based on his lectures as professor of poetry at Oxford; an autobiography, *The Flutes of Autumn* (1983); DETECTIVE FICTION; and travel books, including a classic, *The Light Garden of the Angel King: Journeys in Afghanistan* (1983).

Lévi-Strauss, Claude See SEMIOTICS and STRUCTURALISM.

Leviathan: *or, The Matter, Form, and Power of a Commonwealth Ecclesiastical and Civil* A treatise on political philosophy by THOMAS HOBBES, written during the Interregnum while he was in Paris as tutor to the future Charles II, and published in 1651.

The title of Hobbes's work refers to the principle of sovereign rule, and the fundamental tenet of his philosophy is that the basis of government must be practical consent, since man is not inherently peaceful, nor prone to communal society in any stable fashion. To preserve man from self-destruction resulting from individual competition, a series of 'articles of peace' needs to be assembled. Hobbes depicted society as a necessary contract whereby voluntary adherence to such articles would result in a 'commonwealth' in which each individual acknowledged his obligation to the peaceful liberty of others on an equal basis to his own. Communal security would be vested in a person or assembly – the sovereign and indivisible power – ruling under a covenant between each individual governed, and subordinating all other potential power (such as the church) to its absolute influence.

Hobbes attracted the criticism of both Royalist and Parliamentarian camps by his proviso that a failure on the part of the sovereign to honour the covenant and preserve the electors of office might constitute a case for insubordination to authority. Without this cohesive contract, he memorably contended, 'the life of man is solitary, poor, nasty, brutish and short'.

Levine, Norman 1923– Canadian short-story writer and novelist. Born in Ottawa of Polish-Jewish parents, he served in the Canadian Air Force in World War II. After studying at Cambridge and McGill universities, he settled in England in 1949 and lived mainly at St Ives, Cornwall. He returned to Canada in 1980 and settled in Toronto. In tight, economic prose, his fiction evokes place vividly and often concentrates on social outsiders, the problems of the writer's life and his Jewish-Canadian upbringing. His volumes of short stories include *One Way Ticket* (1961), *I Don't Want to Know Anyone Too Well* (1971), *Thin Ice* (1979), *Why Do You Live So Far Away?* (1984) and *Something Happened Here* (1991). *Champagne Barn* (1984) is a collection drawn mainly from his earlier volumes. Levine has written two novels, *The Angled Road* (1952), about war, and *From a Seaside Town* (1970). Although he is best known for his fiction, he has also published poetry, much of it about St Ives, and an autobiographical memoir, *Canada Made Me* (1958), a consideration of Canadian life on 'the other side of the tracks' which attacks the complacency of conservative attitudes in Canada.

Levine, Philip 1928– American poet. He was born to a Jewish family in Detroit and, after going to work in a factory at the age of 14, attended Wayne (now Wayne State) University, the University of Iowa (where JOHN BERRYMAN and ROBERT LOWELL were among his teachers) and California State University at Fresno, where he has subsequently taught. His first books of poetry, *On the Edge* (1961), *Silent in America: Vivas for Those Who Failed* (1965) and *Not This Pig* (1968), established him as a bitter and ironic chronicler of the working classes of Detroit and southern California. Subsequent volumes include *Pili's Wall* (1971), *They Feed They Lion* (1972), *1933* (1974), *The Names of the Lost* (1976), *7 Years from Somewhere* (1976), *Ashes: Poems New and Old* (1979), *One for the Rose* (1981), *Selected Poems* (1984), *Sweet Will* (1985), *A Walk with Thomas Jefferson* (1988) and *What Work Is* (1991). *New Selected Poems* (1991) introduces the full range of his work. *Don't Ask* (1981) is a collection of essays and interviews. Levine has also translated contemporary Spanish poetry.

Lewes, George Henry 1817–78 Journalist, critic, philosopher and scientist. Born in London, he flirted with business, the law, medicine and the theatre before becoming a journalist, writing for THE MORNING CHRONICLE and *The Penny Encyclopedia*. In 1850 he founded and edited THE LEADER with Thornton Leigh Hunt, and later helped to found THE FORTNIGHTLY REVIEW, of which he was the first editor. In 1851 Lewes met GEORGE ELIOT with whom he lived from 1854 until his death. The couple were unable to marry, although Lewes's wife Agnes was involved in a long-standing liaison with Hunt.

Lewes is probably best remembered today as the supporter and encourager of George Eliot's first efforts in fiction, but his own talents also claim attention and exerted an influence on her work. He wrote two novels, *Ranthorpe* (1847) and *Rose, Blanche and Violet* (1848), ten plays, a *Life of Robespierre* (1849) and a number of books on the contemporary theatre, most notably *Actors and the Art of Acting* (1875). His most important work was *The Life and Works of Goethe* (1855). His writings on philosophy include *A Biographical History of Philosophy* (1845), and *Comte's Philosophy of the Sciences* (1853). *Problems of Life and Mind* (1873–9) was completed after his death by George Eliot. Among his scientific writings are *Seaside Studies* (1858) and *Studies of Animal Life* (1862).

Lewis, Alun 1915–44 Poet and short-story writer. Born in Cwmaman, South Wales, he was educated at the University College of Wales, Aberystwyth, and at the University of Manchester. After working as a journalist and teacher he joined the army in 1940, despite pacifist leanings. He died during action in Burma from a gunshot wound which may have been self-inflicted. *Raiders' Dawn* (1942) contained important poems concerned with the identity and environment of industrial Wales, with love and with wartime Britain. *The Last Inspection* (1942) contains 23 wry and observant stories. Poems, stories and letters from India were collected in *Ha! Ha! Among the Trumpets* (1945), with a foreword by ROBERT GRAVES, and *In the Green Tree* (1948). Confronting the people and ideas of the East gave Lewis a context for his views on the war, just as the Western Desert did for KEITH DOUGLAS; he emerges, not as a minor 'war poet', but as a mature, wide-ranging writer with a coherent pattern of themes.

Lewis, C(live) S(taples) 1898–1963 Critic, theologian, writer of SCIENCE FICTION and CHILDREN'S LITERATURE. Born in Belfast, he read voraciously as a child and started writing early. The death of his mother when he was 10 destroyed a happy and secure childhood and plunged him into education at all-male schools. At these Lewis discovered Wagner, and Norse, classical and Celtic mythology with delight, lost his Christianity, and continued to write. His abilities won him a classical scholarship to Malvern College in 1913, but he disliked it so much that he was soon placed with a private tutor in Surrey, who coached him for a scholarship to Oxford (1916). After war service (1917–18), and a published collection of poems, *Spirits in Bondage* (1918), he entered University College to read classics and philosophy, turning to English for a fourth year, and winning Firsts throughout.

After his first year at Oxford, Lewis set up a joint home with a Mrs Moore, mother of a friend killed in the trenches. His generosity imposed a financial and emotional burden on him which lasted over 30 years. Lewis became a Fellow of Magdalen College in 1925, where he soon was noted as an excellent lecturer and incomparable teacher. A group of his friends ('The Inklings'), including J. R. R. TOLKIEN, Hugo Dyson and CHARLES WILLIAMS, began to meet regularly in his rooms to read their own work to each other.

Between 1929 and 1931 Lewis was converted back to Christianity, an experience charted in his spiritual autobiography, *Surprised by Joy* (1955), and the mainspring of all his subsequent writing, starting with *The Pilgrim's Regress* (1933) and then his science-fiction trilogy, *Out of the Silent Planet* (1938), *Perelandra* (1939) and *That Hideous Strength* (1945). The first and still the most famous of his scholarly books is *The Allegory of Love* (1936), a study of COURTLY LOVE, but others remain influential: *A Preface to Paradise Lost* (1942), the third volume of the Oxford History of English Literature, *English Literature in the Sixteenth Century, Excluding Drama* (1954), *Studies in Words* (1960) and *The Discarded Image* (1963). What brought him wide popularity, however, were his radio talks on Christianity during World War II (collected as *Mere Christianity*) and *The Screwtape Letters* (1942). The seven 'Narnia' stories for children, combining strong imagination and lively adventure with artfully concealed Christian parable, secured him another large audience; they began with *The Lion, the Witch and the Wardrobe* (1950) and closed with *The Last Battle* (1956). In 1954 Lewis moved to Cambridge to occupy the first chair of medieval and Renaissance English. In 1956 he married Joy Davidman, who brought him much happiness before her death from cancer in 1960, when Lewis was already suffering from the osteoporosis which would cause his own death.

Lewis, Leopold 1828–90 Playwright. His single claim to fame was his adaptation of *Le Juif polonais* by Erckmann and Chatrian as *THE BELLS*. The role of the guilt-stricken Mathias was superbly played by Sir Henry Irving in 1871. Lewis was a solicitor, volatile to the point of instability. Of three later plays staged in London, none succeeded.

Lewis, M(atthew) G(regory) 1775–1818 Novelist, playwright and poet. Born into a wealthy family, he was educated at Westminster School and Christ Church, Oxford, before entering the diplomatic service. He wrote *THE MONK* (1796), a sensationally successful GOTHIC NOVEL, at the age of 19 during a period as attaché at the British Embassy at The Hague. It earned him the nickname of 'Monk' Lewis. Although it is almost the only work by which he is now remembered, he wrote other novels (*The Bravo of Venice*, 1804; *Feudal Tyrants*, 1806) and plays (*The Castle Spectre*, 1796; *The East Indian*, 1799; *Alphonso, King of Castile*, 1801; *The Wood Demon*, 1807). He also published several volumes of verse, but his best poem, 'Alonzo the Brave and the Fair Imogine', appeared in *The Monk*. HAZLITT considered that he was, after ANN RADCLIFFE, 'the greatest master in the art of freezing the blood', and he is credited with introducing English readers to popular German Romantic literature. Passionately addicted to the company of the rich, the titled and the famous, he dined everywhere and spent much time at ducal country residences. He visited Goethe and Wieland in Weimar, and was on friendly terms with BYRON ('Lewis was a good man, a clever man, but a bore') and SCOTT. He held a seat in the House of Commons in 1796–1802. After his father's death in 1812 he gave up writing to devote himself to the improvement of the West Indian sugar plantations where most of his money came from, incurring the displeasure of his neighbours by his efforts to better the condition of his slaves. He visited Jamaica twice in the last three years of his life, and died of yellow fever on his way back to England in 1818. He left behind his *Journal of a West Indian Proprietor*, published in 1834, a highly respected work and certainly his most important since *The Monk*.

Lewis, Norman 1908– Travel writer and novelist. He owes his literary standing to his non-fiction, his novels being unpretentious thrillers marked by an unusually sure sense of place in their many foreign locations. One of the least egotistical travel writers, he has sought out countries and communities on the brink of radical, irreversible change and tried to chronicle their last years of peaceful cultural authenticity. *A Dragon Apparent* (1951) records a journey through Cambodia, Laos and Vietnam in the final years of the French administration. *Golden Earth* (1952) is an equally judicious portrait of Burma. His best books, perhaps, are *Naples '44* (1978), the compassionate war diary of his service with the Intelligence Corps in Italy, and *Voices of the Old Sea* (1984), a limpid account of summers spent among the ancient fishing community at Farol in southern Spain. Lewis has also written: *The Honoured Society* (1964), praised as the most authoritative history of the Sicilian Mafia; *Jackdaw Cake* (1985), a characteristically quirky autobiography; and *The Missionaries* (1988), an attack on the genocidal activities of Christian evangelists among the tribes of the Amazon. *A View of the World* (1986) collects shorter travel pieces.

Lewis, (Harry) Sinclair 1885–1951 American novelist. Born in Sauk Center, Minnesota, he entered Yale in 1903 but left in 1906 to join UPTON SINCLAIR's socialist colony in Englewood, New Jersey. He then became a freelance writer and editor in New York before returning to Yale and graduating in 1908. Four years later he published his first novel, a boys' book entitled *Hike and the Aeroplane* (1912), under the pseudonym of Tom Graham.

In 1914 he published *Our Mr Wrenn*, which was followed by *The Trail of the Hawk* (1915) and three more novels before the successful MAIN STREET (1920), a satirical portrayal of smalltown life in the Midwest. He continued his critique of provincial American life in BABBITT (1922). In 1926 he was awarded but declined a PULITZER PRIZE for *Arrowsmith* (1925), the story of an altruistic doctor who struggles to resist the temptations of a fashionable and profitable practice in order to pursue a scientific career. His next novel, *Elmer Gantry* (1927), is the story of a sham revivalist minister. *DODSWORTH* (1929), about a retired car manufacturer travelling in Europe, appeared a year before Lewis was awarded the Nobel Prize, the first American to be so honoured.

His commitment to social and political change is evident also in his novels of the 1930s and 1940s. *Ann Vickers* (1933) is about a discontented Midwestern girl who goes east to college and becomes a social worker; she becomes involved in the women's movement and works for prison reform. *Work of Art* (1934) is about the American hotel industry. During the late 1930s and the 1940s Lewis began a career as an actor. *It Can't Happen Here* (1935), a warning about the possibility of fascism in the USA, was dramatized and produced by the FEDERAL THEATRE PROJECT in cities throughout the country with Lewis himself playing the lead. The revolt of children against their parents is the subject of *The Prodigal Parents* (1938). *Bethel Merriday* (1940) deals with the career of a young actress. *Gideon Planish* (1943) is about a speech professor who marries a student and then finds himself manipulated into the lucrative advertising profession by his wife. Lewis's next three novels return to the Minnesota setting of *Main Street*. *Cass Timberlane* (1945) is another story of a middle-aged man, a judge, who marries a young girl; *Kingsblood Royal* (1947) deals with race relations; *The God-Seeker* (1949) treats the American-Indian question. His last novel, *World So Wide*, was published posthumously in 1951.

Lewis, (Percy) Wyndham 1882–1957 Artist, novelist and critic. He was born on his father's yacht off the coast of Maine (his father was American, his mother British). He was educated at Rugby School, then at the Slade School of Art, after which he lived and studied in Paris for several years. He earned a reputation as a painter, mainly among the *avant-garde*, and with the help of EZRA POUND edited the experimental publication *BLAST: The Review of the Great English Vortex* (1914–15). Originally intended as a periodical, it lasted for only two issues, but the excitement of VORTICISM had considerable impact.

Lewis's novels began with *Tarr* (1918), set in pre-war Paris; it is an intellectual comedy of art, life and

Teutonic romanticism embodied in Kreisler, a would-be artist with no talent. *The Childermass* (1928) was the first novel of a trilogy called *The Human Age*; the other two novels, *Monstre Gai* and *Malign Fiesta*, did not appear until 1955. This remarkable fantasy is located in a waste land outside heaven's gate where the remnants of mankind await inquisition by the Bailiff.

The Apes of God (1930) is a SATIRE mocking the fashionable racket of art and literature in the London of the 1920s. Many consider it Lewis's best work, but his next, *The Revenge for Love* (1937), also has its admirers. It is a political satire of the 1930s, set against the background of the Spanish Civil War. *Self Condemned* (1954) was Lewis's last major novel and is semi-autobiographical. Professor Harding, a figure with many of Lewis's characteristics, finds himself unable to bear the insanity and cowardice engulfing Europe in the immediate pre-World War II period. He resigns his post and retreats to Canada with his wife, eventually emerging, alone, as no more than a shell of a man.

Lewis brought a painter's eye to his writing, but he rejected many of the techniques of MODERNISM practised by his contemporaries. As a critic, he made enemies everywhere: VIRGINIA WOOLF, JAMES JOYCE, D. H. LAWRENCE, ERNEST HEMINGWAY, WILLIAM FAULKNER and T. S. ELIOT were all his targets at different times. Eliot, however, wrote a complimentary preface to the 1960 edition of Lewis's verse satire *One-Way Song* (1933). This celebration of individual will and consciousness opposed the surrender to inwardness and subjectivism, so much an element in the art of the 1920s and 1930s.

Lewis's political and critical essays include *The Art of Being Ruled* (1925), *Time and Western Man* (1927), *Men without Art* (1934), *The Mysterious Mr Bull* (1938) and *The Writer and the Absolute* (1952). His short stories were collected in *The Wild Body* (1927) and *Rotting Hill* (1951). Chapters of his autobiography were published in *Blasting and Bombardiering* (1937) and *Rude Assignment* (1950).

Leyden, John 1775–1811 Polymath. He was born at Denholm, Roxburghshire, and educated at Kirktown and Edinburgh University, where he took all knowledge as his province. Leyden was an early champion of THOMAS CAMPBELL and was himself encouraged by Richard Heber. The breadth of his interests is extraordinary: he moved easily from composing a discourse on the colonization of North Africa to contributing 'The Elf King', a BALLAD, to M. G. LEWIS's *Tales of Wonder* (1801). A passion for ancient Scottish literature enabled him to help SIR WALTER SCOTT with *The Minstrelsy of the Scottish Border* (1802). He edited *The Scots Magazine* during part of 1802 and in 1803 prepared his *Scenes of Infancy* for publication.

Meanwhile, this unstoppable figure had qualified as a doctor in order to take up the post of assistant-surgeon in Madras. His hospital was not allowed to monopolize his time. On an official mission into the Mysore provinces in 1804 Leyden concerned himself with the area's agriculture, geology, public health and languages. He succumbed to fever on this exercise: his method of convalescence was to study Sanskrit and translate from Persian and Hindustani. He extended his growing knowledge of Asiatic languages on a trip to Penang in 1805, finding a moment during a brush with a French privateer to eulogize his Malay dagger in verse. Back in Calcutta, Leyden became not only a professor of Hindustani (1807) but also Judge of the Twenty-four Pergunnahs and Commissioner of the Court of Requests. In 1811 he accompanied his patron, Lord Minto, on an expedition to annex Java, but three weeks after the fall of Batavia caught a fever while foraging in an airless library and died aged 35.

Leyden served both Scotland and Asia well. Scott wrote an appreciative memoir of him for *The Edinburgh Annual Register* of 1811; and he further commemorated him in *The Lord of the Isles* (1815). William Erskine, who completed Leyden's *Commentaries of Baber* for publication in 1826, praised the thoroughness of his classification of Asiatic languages and dialects. Leyden's *Poetical Remains* appeared in 1819 and his translation of *Malay Annals* in 1821. A collection, *Poems and Ballads*, was published in 1858.

Liars, The A social comedy by HENRY ARTHUR JONES, first performed in London in 1897. It elaborates on the need to lie in a hypocritical society, which turns an innocent friendship into a serious threat to the marriage of Lady Jessica Nepean. The play is expertly crafted and the ice it skates on thin enough to demand all its author's dexterity.

Libeaus Desconus (*'The Fair Unknown'*) A VERSE ROMANCE of the mid-14th century written in the South of England, perhaps by THOMAS CHESTRE.

The poem is an uninspired treatment of the story of the Fair Unknown, Gawain's son Gingelein (or Gauinglain), current in several European languages in the Middle Ages. The illegitimate son of Gawain is brought up by his mother in ignorance of his identity and in isolation in the forest. He steals the armour of a dead knight and goes to Arthur's court where he is knighted as Libeaus Desconus. Despite the initially contemptuous attitude of the court, he soon proves his prowess in various adventures. At one point he is bewitched and lives in idleness and luxury for a year, but resumes his career as a knight and undertakes more adventures. Finally he enters a magic hall where a serpent with a woman's face encircles him. Having been bewitched until she should kiss Gawain or one of his line, she is transformed into a beautiful woman; she weds Libeaus Desconus.

Libel of English Policy, The A Middle English poem provoked by the attack on Calais in 1436 and written in that year or 1437. Divided into a prologue and 12 chapters, the *Libel* ('little book') stresses the importance of maritime trade and the need to control Dover and Calais in order to maintain it. It advocates a powerful navy to ensure peace and prosperity for England. The poem was important in its time, and appeared in two later versions. It provides detailed information on contemporary political and commercial conditions.

Liberal, The A periodical founded by SHELLEY and BYRON in 1822, when they were both in Pisa; LEIGH HUNT was brought from England as its editor. Only four issues appeared, between September 1822 and June 1823, before the venture succumbed to a series of problems: the death of Shelley in July 1822, the growing hostility between Byron and Hunt, Byron's departure for Greece and the legal difficulties arising from the journal's publication of Byron's THE VISION OF JUDGEMENT.

Liberator, The An American Abolitionist weekly journal founded by WILLIAM LLOYD GARRISON in Boston in 1831 and edited by him for the next 34 years. From its first issue, *The Liberator*'s editorial policy was unequivocally opposed to slavery, calling for immediate emancipation of the slave population. Its circulation was never higher than 3000, but its radical stance aroused vocal and violent antagonism in South and North alike. A law was passed forbidding its distribution among free blacks, and a reward was offered in South Carolina for information leading to the arrest of anyone who circulated it. The Georgia Senate passed a resolution offering another reward for the arrest of Garrison himself. The last issue was published on 29 December 1865, shortly after the Thirteenth Amendment, abolishing slavery, was ratified.

Liberty, On An essay by JOHN STUART MILL, first published in 1859. He regarded it as the most important of his works. One of his earliest articles had been in support of the freedom of speech and publication which was a Benthamite prerequisite for good government. By 1859 Mill had realized, partly as a result of reading de Tocqueville's DEMOCRACY IN AMERICA, that democracy did not of itself guarantee freedom; public opinion might be as repressive of minority rights as any other form of dictatorship. He therefore sought to devise a principle by which individual liberty might be legitimated and interference with this liberty limited only to those occasions where its exercise might involve harm to others.

libraries Organized collections of books belonging to an individual, a group or an institution have existed since early classical times. They both serve their own times and also, either in their surviving stocks or in their catalogues, provide records of the tastes, preoccupations, achievements and thought of past generations. Thus they have both a current and a historic value. Naturally these functions have resulted in a variety of different kinds of libraries, for different people and in different subjects. The following summary concentrates on those perhaps most obviously of interest to users of this *Guide*.

1 *British Isles*
(a) Monastic and collegiate libraries
The earliest libraries known to have existed in England are those connected with religious houses. At Canterbury an abbey was established within 10 years of the arrival of St Augustine in 596; Winchester Cathedral priory was founded *c.* 604, and Peterborough Abbey *c.* 655. Though each eventually accumulated sizeable libraries, little evidence survives of their earliest collections. At Wearmouth-Jarrow, Benedict Biscop (*c.* 628–89), one of the most active bibliophiles of pre-Conquest England, accumulated an outstanding library thanks largely to connections with the Continent (chiefly Italy and Gaul), and the collection was used thoroughly by BEDE for his treatises and for his *Ecclesiastical History*. At York there was a library attached to the cathedral school by the mid-8th century, and its contents were recalled in verse by ALCUIN in his 'Carmen de pontificibus et sanctis ecclesiae eboracensis', composed at the end of the century. The libraries at both Lindisfarne and York were sacked by the Danes, in 793 and 866–7 respectively. Partly no doubt because of the Viking invasions, and despite the literary revival under KING ALFRED, monastic life (and with it the production of books) did not return generally to normal until the 10th century. The major monastic libraries of which substantial portions survive (very often elsewhere) today include Bury St Edmunds, Christ Church and St Augustine's, Canterbury, Durham, Norwich, Reading, Rochester, St Albans and Worcester (all Benedictine houses) and the secular cathedrals of Exeter, Hereford, Lincoln and Salisbury. Yet apart from these, books are recognizable as having survived in smaller quantities from over 400 other libraries, not including those at Oxford and Cambridge.

The establishment of these two universities in the 13th century brought further developments. At Cambridge, Peterhouse (founded 1284) still preserves much of its medieval library, as do Gonville and Caius (founded 1349) and Pembroke (1347) Colleges. Little is known of the university library before the first years of the 15th century: its earliest catalogue dates from 1424. At Oxford, Merton College (founded 1263–4), Balliol (1261–6), New College (1379), Oriel (1324),

Lincoln (1429), All Souls (1438) and Magdalen (1448) likewise preserve notable portions of their old libraries; but the old university library, greatly enriched by the humanist influence of Humfrey, Duke of Gloucester (1390–1447), was dispersed completely at the Reformation. Among other educational establishments, manuscripts survive both from Eton College and from Winchester. In Scotland catalogues survive for Glasgow University Library from 1475 onwards, and Aberdeen University Library possesses three books known to have belonged to King's College, Aberdeen.

These medieval libraries were generally chained, at least in part, and sometimes remained so until years later. The chains were removed at Eton in 1719, at Merton and Magdalen Colleges only in the 1790s. The most celebrated chained library now extant is at Hereford Cathedral, but there are major collections of chained books, dating from the 16th and 17th centuries, in parochial or school libraries at (among other places) Grantham, Wimborne and All Saints', Hereford, as well as the grammar schools at Guildford and Bolton.

The suppression of the monasteries in the 1530s, and the accompanying upheavals of the Reformation, resulted in the dispersal or destruction of most books from medieval libraries. Many, however, found their way as groups into other libraries: from Exeter Cathedral into the Bodleian, from Norwich Cathedral into Cambridge University Library, from Bury St Edmunds into Pembroke College, Cambridge. The dispersal encouraged a new generation of private collectors: the antiquary JOHN LELAND (?1506–52) was already prospecting among ecclesiastical libraries in the 1520s, noting their most important holdings for his master Henry VIII; and MATTHEW PARKER, Archbishop of Canterbury (1504–75), amassed a collection especially valuable for its Anglo-Saxon manuscripts, now divided by gift and bequest respectively between Cambridge University Library and Corpus Christi College, Cambridge. Parker's collection included the 6th-century Gospels believed to have been brought to England by St Augustine in 596, and the best manuscript of the *ANGLO-SAXON CHRONICLE*. In the next generations the mathematician John Dee (1527–1608) and the politician SIR ROBERT COTTON (1571-1631) were only the most important among many who took advantage of the relative wealth of medieval manuscripts on the market, and assembled major collections of their own: Dee's is now dispersed, but Cotton's descended in his family until 1702, when it passed to the state, and then, in 1753, became one of the foundation collections of the British Museum.

Cathedral libraries did not really recover until after the Restoration in 1660, when some of the collections were virtually refounded by men such as Michael Honywood (1597–1681) at Lincoln, George Morley (1597–1684) at Winchester, Henry King (1592–1669) at

Chichester, and Henry Compton (1632–1713) at St Paul's Cathedral, London.

At Oxford and Cambridge, the libraries seem to have suffered in the mid-16th century more from neglect than deliberate destruction, as the Catholic reaction to the Protestant Reformation was in turn replaced by the reign of Queen Elizabeth. Their post-Reformation recovery came at the end of the century. At Cambridge, Andrew Perne, Master of Peterhouse, engaged the interest of Matthew Parker, Sir Nicholas Bacon (Lord Keeper) and others in the 1570s. At Oxford, SIR THOMAS BODLEY (1545–1613), a London diplomat and businessman, announced his intention of refounding the university library in 1598: his new library was opened in 1602 and grew quickly, fortified by the gifts elicited by Bodley, the income from the estate of Bodley himself, and an agreement with the London Stationers' Company (concluded in 1611) whereby one copy of every new book printed in London was to be given to Oxford. The gifts of collections of manuscripts by the Earl of Pembroke (1629), WILLIAM LAUD (1635–40), SIR KENELM DIGBY (1634), and, among printed books, the bequests of ROBERT BURTON (1640) and the arrival of JOHN SELDEN's books in 1659 meant that by 1700 the library was the greatest in the country.

(b) Copyright libraries
Under the Licensing Act of 1662 Cambridge University Library, the Bodleian and the Royal Library were each to receive one copy of every new book published in England. This right was embodied in the Copyright Act (1709) and has been repeated in subsequent legislation, the Royal Library being replaced by the British Museum from the mid-18th century. Between 1710 and 1836 the right was shared with Sion College in London, the Faculty of Advocates in Edinburgh, the Universities of Edinburgh, Glasgow, St Andrews and Aberdeen, and from 1801 to 1836 the King's Inns and Trinity College, Dublin. In 1836 these deposit libraries were reduced to five (British Museum; Oxford; Cambridge; Trinity College, Dublin; and the Faculty of Advocates), the last being succeeded by the National Library of Scotland on its foundation in 1925 and the National Library of Wales (founded in 1907) in 1911. Until 1814 deposit depended on entry in the Stationers' Register, and was therefore irregular; but efforts to improve it during the 19th century were increasingly successful, thanks particularly to Sir Anthony Panizzi (1797–1879) at the British Museum. This long history of deposit has been a principal factor in the emergence of the British Museum (since 1973 the British Library), the Bodleian and Cambridge University Library as the three largest in the country.

In 1753 the British Museum was established by Act of Parliament. Its foundation collections included those of Sir Robert Cotton (including the unique manuscripts of BEOWULF and SIR GAWAIN AND THE GREEN KNIGHT), Sir Hans Sloane (1660–1753), and ROBERT HARLEY and EDWARD HARLEY, Earls of Oxford. In 1757 these were increased by the gift of George II of the Old Royal Library, dating back to the reign of Edward IV and including the Codex Alexandrinus (a 5th-century Greek manuscript of the Bible). This gift was followed by George III with the collection of Civil War pamphlets known (after the bookseller who collected them) as the Thomason Tracts, and by the bequest (1799) of C. M. Cracherode (notable for its collection of classical texts and fine printing), as well as by smaller collections such as DAVID GARRICK's English plays. The great library assembled by George III and the Prince Regent between 1760 and 1820 was given by George IV. Other collections acquired in the 19th century included the Arundel Manuscripts, assembled by Thomas Howard, Earl of Arundel (1592–1646) and containing the unique manuscript of the AYENBITE OF INWIT; the library of the naturalist Sir Joseph Banks (1743–1820); Charles Burney's collection, including both classics and a unique collection of early English newspapers; the collection of Thomas Grenville (1755–1846), outstanding for its Italian and Spanish books; the manuscripts of F. H. Egerton, 8th Earl of Bridgewater (d. 1829); and the Stowe manuscripts, collected by the 1st Duke of Buckingham (d. 1839) but bought only in 1883. In the mid-19th century the British Museum was established as the greatest library in the world, buying in all subjects and in most languages under the auspices of an outstanding series of keepers including (in printed books) Thomas Watts (1811–69) and Sir Anthony Panizzi, and (in manuscripts) Sir Frederic Madden (1801–73). Some important collections, however, went elsewhere, such as that of JOHN FORSTER, biographer of DICKENS, and ALEXANDER DYCE, editor of SHAKESPEARE, which went to the South Kensington Museum (now the Victoria and Albert Museum), and much of the working library of GEORGE ELIOT, which is now in Dr Williams's Library, Gordon Square.

The gradual publication of authoritative catalogues of the British Museum's printed books – of early English books in 1884, of 15th-century books from 1908 (still in progress), and of successive editions of the general catalogue itself – emphasized the Museum's leading position, and has contributed profoundly to bibliographical studies: the most recent edition of the General Catalogue (known as GK4) began publication in 1979.

Accessions in the last hundred years have generally been less wholesale than previously, but they include the library of the bibliographer and forger T. J. WISE (1859–1937), especially rich in 16th- and 17th-century literature and in 19th-century poetry, collections of illuminated manuscripts from Henry Yates Thompson and Eric George Millar, and bookbindings from Henry Davis (d. 1977). The music collection was transformed by the gift in 1957 of the Royal Music Library, by

Right: The Bodleian Library, Oxford

Below: A Jacobean bookcase and chained book in Trinity Hall Library, Cambridge, England

The Round Reading Room of the British Library, built between 1854 and 1857

Queen Elizabeth II, and the acquisition of Paul Hirsch's music collection in 1946. In 1973, by Act of Parliament, the British Library was established, composed of the British Museum Library, the National Reference Library of Science and Invention, the National Lending Library for Science and Technology, the National Central Library and the British National Bibliography.

In the 18th and 19th centuries, both the Bodleian Library and Cambridge University Library consolidated their positions as the major national libraries outside the British Museum. Cambridge University Library was trebled by the gift (by King George I) of the library of John Moore, Bishop of Ely (d. 1714), the finest of its generation and celebrated for its books printed by CAXTON and as containing the earliest extant manuscript then known of Bede's *Ecclesiastical History*. However, Oxford in particular attracted a long series of benefactions, most notably Richard Rawlinson's manuscripts (1755), Richard Gough's collection (rich especially in topography) in 1809, EDMOND MALONE's library in 1821, and FRANCIS DOUCE's in 1834. More recently the Bodleian has acquired the John Johnson collection of printed ephemera and (by bequest) the considerable collection of Walter N. H. Harding (1883–1973), a Chicago popular musician, devoted partly at least to the history of popular song. Following his death in 1982, Cambridge University Library acquired the collection of Sir Geoffrey Keynes, with its renowned series of author collections including DONNE, EVELYN, SIR THOMAS BROWNE, WILLIAM BLAKE, JANE AUSTEN, RUPERT BROOKE and SIEGFRIED SASSOON. Among the college libraries, that at Trinity College, Cambridge (built to the design of Sir Christopher Wren from 1676 onwards), is the richest in either university; its printed books alone include most of the surviving portion of SIR ISAAC NEWTON's library, the Shakespeare collection of EDWARD CAPELL, and the collection of 18th-century English literature formed by Lord Rothschild. Colleges at both Oxford and Cambridge house private libraries of unusual distinction: that of SAMUEL PEPYS is at Magdalene College, Cambridge, many of the books of Robert Burton (other than those in the Bodleian) are in Christ Church, Oxford, and those of the economist MALTHUS are at Jesus College, Cambridge.

(c) University libraries

Apart from the university libraries at Oxford and Cambridge with quasi-national status, and apart from the libraries of the ancient Scottish universities already mentioned, the libraries attached to the universities founded in the 19th and 20th centuries have usually come in some way to serve research well beyond their own localities. Of these the most important is the John Rylands University Library of Manchester, founded by the merger in 1972 of the University of Manchester Library with the John Rylands Library. The latter was founded by Mrs John Rylands in 1900 as an independent collection; it includes the library of the 2nd Earl Spencer (d. 1834), one of the greatest bibliophiles of his age, as well as the manuscripts assembled by the Earls of Crawford in the 19th century. Leeds University, founded in 1875, is remarkable in its library not least for the Brotherton collection (presented 1935). The University of London Library, which includes the Sir Louis Sterling (1879–1958) collection of English literature and the Goldsmiths' Company library of economic literature, has been housed in the Senate House, just to the north of the British Museum, since 1937–8, though the University itself was founded in 1836. All university-connected libraries grew rapidly in the wake of the Robbins Report on higher education (1963), and the 1960s and 1970s also saw considerable changes in their housing, as new buildings were erected. The subsequent revision of university grants has placed increasing pressure on inter-library co-operation, principally in loans of books: as in the public library sector, this is heavily dependent on the British Library Lending Division at Boston Spa, Yorkshire.

(d) Circulating libraries

The 18th century witnessed a widespread development of circulating libraries, commercially run and charging a small subscription for the loan of books. These paid especial attention to fiction, poetry, travel, biography and periodicals, and were satirized by (among others) SHERIDAN and Jane Austen. By the end of the century they had become immensely fashionable and, because of their buying power, became in the 19th century of crucial importance to publishers of novels especially: the lasting popularity of the 'three-decker' novel was due largely to the most successful of all circulating libraries, that of Charles Edward Mudie (1818–90). Vestiges of these libraries survived until the mid-20th century, either on a small scale or in those run by the chain stores Boots the Chemists and W. H. Smith, stationers and booksellers. These libraries are to be distinguished from those founded in the 19th century by Mechanics' Institutes (in which self-improvement and education played a prominent part) and from the major subscription libraries, of which the most notable are the Leeds Library (founded in 1768) and the London Library (founded in 1841 by THOMAS CARLYLE and others), the latter of which is the largest of its kind in the world.

(e) Public libraries

The earliest English public library to be established was at Norwich in 1608; another was opened at Bristol in 1613. In Manchester, a chained library was founded by the will of Humphrey Chetham (1580–1653). But in London, though a library had been established in

1423–5, the modern Guildhall Library dates only from 1824–8 and as a public library from 1872; the most important early public library there was that founded by Thomas Tenison, Archbishop of Canterbury (1636–1715), whose foundation (attached to St Martin-in-the-Fields) survived from 1684 to 1861.

Modern public library services date from the Museums Act (1845) and, especially, the Public Libraries Act (1850) and its successor of 1919. Among the first free public libraries to be established after the 1850 legislation were Winchester (1851), Manchester (1852) and Ipswich (1853). Birmingham Public Library (founded in 1861) contains the Shakespeare library founded in 1864, and many other public libraries have special collections relating to well-known local authors. In many towns public libraries owed their foundation or improvement to the Carnegie United Kingdom Trust, founded in 1913 by Andrew Carnegie (1835–1919), an American steel magnate who was the son of a Scottish handloom weaver. By 1919 Carnegie and his trust had given over 2800 public libraries, not only in Britain but in most of the English-speaking world as well. During the 1930s the trust took a leading part in making possible organized inter-library loans, by the establishment of regional catalogues. Local authority spending, particularly by county authorities, increased notably after World War II, and by the 1960s encouraged a proliferation of activities sometimes only indirectly related to books. Besides this, special attention has been given generally to improvements in provision for children's reading, and in some parts of Britain an increasingly multiracial society has been met with the provision, gradually improving, of foreign-language materials. On the other hand, in both public and university libraries, the information revolution of the early 1980s, and the advent of generally available computerized databases, have further challenged traditional librarianship and have brought often unexpected costs.

2 USA

In America virtually the earliest known library dates from the bequest in 1638 of John Harvard to what became Harvard College, later Harvard University. Yale University Library was founded in 1701, and New Jersey College Library, Princeton, was founded in 1746. Outside the college and university community, William Bray gave a library to Annapolis in Maryland in 1696, so beginning a campaign for parochial libraries in both the American colonies and England. As in England, the 18th century saw the growth of subscription libraries, among which the Library Company of Philadelphia (founded 1731 by a group headed by BENJAMIN FRANKLIN) soon incorporated the library of James Logan (1674–1751), the finest to be thus far assembled in North America. At Newport, Rhode Island, the Redwood Library was founded in 1747, using money given to a local literary and philosophical society by Abraham Redwood.

National library provision dates from the foundation of the Library of Congress, established by Act of Congress in 1800; the infant library was destroyed by British troops in 1814, and the present collections are based on the library of THOMAS JEFFERSON (1743–1826), purchased subsequently that year. Thanks to its position as a copyright deposit library, its world-wide collecting policy, and its role as provider of catalogue records to other libraries (for which cards were first made available in 1901), it is now the most influential, as well as the largest, library in the world. Among many special collections, notable acquisitions include the Lessing J. Rosenwald collection of illustrated books dating from the 15th century, the John Boyd Thacher collection (including incunables, Americana, and materials relevant to the French Revolution), and outstanding assemblages, both printed and manuscript, relating to WALT WHITMAN. Here, as in many other libraries in North America especially, the traditional collecting areas of books, manuscripts, maps and music have been extended to include photographs, sound and video recordings, globes and musical instruments.

The establishment of free public libraries in America depended at first in the 19th century on town or state, rather than federal, legislation. The first state law was passed in New Hampshire in 1849, followed by Massachusetts in 1851. Among the most important are Boston Public Library (founded 1852), Chicago (whose modern history dates from 1872, after the burning of the city in 1871), and, largest of all, New York Public Library. The last was created, in its modern form, in 1895 from a merger of three collections: the Astor Library, a general reference library founded in 1848 under the terms of the will of a fur-trader and capitalist, John Jacob Astor (1763–1848); the Lenox Library, amassed by the wealthy bibliophile James Lenox (1800–80) and especially rich in Americana, early printed books, and Bibles; and the estate of Samuel J. Tilden (d. 1886).

The libraries of the new American universities founded in the latter part of the 19th century developed slowly at first. Among the most important are now Cornell (founded 1868), the University of California (1869), Texas (1883) and Chicago (1891). Their growth this century has been rapid, like those of the older universities. It has been greatly helped by American tax law and the generosity of private benefactors, quite apart from the imagination and determination of successive librarians. These libraries have also often been more able, as well as more ready, than their English counterparts to buy entire collections, such as Sir Michael Sadleir's 19th-century three-decker novels at the University of California, Los Angeles, or the entire stock of the 19th-century Berlin bookseller S. Calvary at Chicago. At Austin, Texas, the

Harry Ransom Center bears witness to inspired and aggressive buying in English literature in the late 1950s and early 1960s; the Latin American collections here are however hardly less outstanding. In 1986 the University of Texas announced the acquisition, thanks to a private benefactor, of the Carl H. Pforzheimer collection of early English literature, assembled originally in the 1920s and 1930s.

The major independent research collections in America have likewise often benefited in this manner. In Chicago, the Newberry Library (founded 1887) contains rich collections on (among others) MELVILLE, the history of printing and the American Indian. The Huntington Library, San Marino, California (opened 1920), was founded by the railway entrepreneur Henry E. Huntington (1850–1927), and contains one of the richest collections anywhere of Americana, English literature and incunables. The Pierpont Morgan Library, New York, is likewise still housed in the building erected by its founder, the banker John Pierpont Morgan (1837–1913). In 1924 his son established it as a public reference library, and it owes much of its present character to its formidable first librarian, Belle da Costa Greene. A reminder that neither this kind of collection nor this kind of collecting is a thing of the past came in 1983, when the J. Paul Getty Trust of Malibu, California, negotiated the purchase of the princely collection of medieval manuscripts assembled by the West German book-collector Peter Ludwig.

3 Canada

In Canada Toronto University (founded in 1827 as King's College) dominates the retrospective collections with, in the Thomas Fisher Library, outstanding collections in the history of science and a unique collection of the 17th-century illustrator Wenceslaus Hollar. McGill University Library, an older foundation (1821), is celebrated for the Sir William Osler collection, principally but not entirely on the history of medicine. McMaster University Library, Hamilton, Ontario, was established in 1887, and its library houses the BERTRAND RUSSELL Archives. Public libraries were founded at Toronto in 1883 and at Ottawa in 1906, though both were long preceded by the Bibliothèque de Québec, founded in 1848. The national libraries at Ottawa and (for Quebec) at Montreal were established in 1953 and 1967 respectively.

4 Australia and New Zealand

The different services offered by circulating, subscription, public, university and national libraries naturally developed more quickly in Australia and New Zealand, keeping pace with the rapid expansion of the two countries. Sydney had a subscription library by 1826, which has since developed into the State Library of New South Wales. Each state now has its own state library, which acts also as a copyright deposit collection. The University of Sydney was founded in 1850, its library a year later, and 1853 witnessed the foundation of both Melbourne Public Library and the University of Melbourne. Under the National Library Act (1960) the National Library of Australia was established at Canberra: among its holdings are the D. Nichol Smith collection of English literature, the C. T. Onions collection of English philology, and the Clifford family library from Ugbrooke Park, Devon, England.

In New Zealand, the two most notable libraries are those of the University of Auckland (founded in 1884) and the Alexander Turnbull Library (since 1966 part of the National Library), which had its origins in the bequest of Alexander Horsburgh Turnbull (1868–1918). The latter has outstanding collections relating to MILTON as well as to the Pacific. The first Public Libraries Act was passed in 1869, and the public library system has always depended, to an extent matched in few other places, on the postal service for the transport of books between library and borrower.

5 Africa and Asia

By the end of the 19th century, only a few of what were to prove to be major international libraries had been established elsewhere in the English-speaking world. The South African Library, Cape Town, was founded in 1818 from money raised by a tax on wine. (The Pretoria State Library was founded in 1887 by Paul Kruger.) In Singapore, the present National Library traces its history back to the Singapore Institution founded by Sir Stamford Raffles in 1823. The National Library of India, in Calcutta, is founded on a public library established in 1836, and was given its modern name in 1953 on removing to a former winter residence of the Viceroys.

With the important exception of Makerere University Library in Uganda, founded as Makerere College in 1922, most changes came after World War II. In Ghana, the Balme Library, University of Accra, was originally founded in 1948. In India, Delhi Public Library was founded in 1951, as part of a UNESCO plan for developing countries. In Jamaica, the University of the West Indies Library opened in 1948. In Kenya, the University of Nairobi Library can be traced from 1956. In Nigeria, Ibadan University Library was founded in 1948. In Pakistan, the University of Karachi Library was founded in 1952 (Punjab University College, later Punjab University, had, however, been established in 1882). In Zimbabwe, the University of Zimbabwe (formerly Rhodesia) Library was founded in 1956. In many of these countries, both university and public libraries often reflect British practices, thanks partly to the efforts of the British Council.

Life in London: *or, The Day and Night Scenes of Jerry Hawthorn Esq. and His Elegant Friend*

Corinthian Tom, Accompanied by Bob Logic, The Oxonian, in Their Rambles and Sprees through the Metropolis A boisterously comic description of life in Regency London by PIERCE EGAN THE ELDER. It appeared in 20 one-shilling parts (1820–1) and in book form (1821), with illustrations by Robert and GEORGE CRUIKSHANK.

Corinthian Tom, helped by his friend Bob Logic, shows the sights of the capital to his country cousin, Jerry Hawthorn. Tom is a Regency rake, Bob a man of facetious wit and continual good humour, and Jerry Hawthorn an amiable rustic eager for adventure. In a series of cheerfully coarse episodes the book gives a revealing picture of the manners of the age and an interesting record of fashionable slang.

It was enormously popular with young men who aspired to a dashing life. THACKERAY confessed that when he read it in youth he believed the three principals 'to be types of the most elegant, fashionable young fellows the town afforded' and their activities 'those of all highbred English gentlemen'. Twenty years later he could find nothing to say in its favour. Egan himself seems to have had second thoughts about his characters as time passed. *The Finish to the Adventures of Tom, Jerry and Logic, in Their Pursuits through Life in and out of London* (1828) has Tom breaking his neck while hunting, his mistress Kate dying of drink, Logic succumbing to his excesses, and Jerry settling down to a quiet life in the country.

Life of Samuel Johnson LL.D., The JAMES BOSWELL's biography of his friend SAMUEL JOHNSON, published in 1791. The seventh life of Johnson to appear, it gave the fullest treatment of its subject and remains by common consent the greatest biography in the language.

The 22-year-old Boswell first met Johnson, then aged 54, in Tom Davies's bookshop on 16 May 1763. In his journal for 31 March 1772, Boswell writes of his 'constant plan to write the life of Mr. Johnson', though he was at first nervous of divulging the plan to Johnson. Six months later he refers to a 'store of materials' for the *Life*. Johnson became certain of the scheme after reading the manuscript of Boswell's *JOURNAL OF A TOUR TO THE HEBRIDES*, and it had his blessing. Boswell's methods and emphases as biographer coincided with Johnson's own as expressed in *THE RAMBLER* (No. 60).

Working always with a master-plan in mind, Boswell was tireless in his search for authenticated truth. His training as a lawyer helped him sift the evidence of friends and to operate forensically on Johnson himself: he was able to draw him out as no one else could. Johnson was actually made more 'Johnsonian' by Boswell's transformation of his conversation and doings into the scenic forms and polished prose of the published *Life*. Boswell certainly kept immediate rough notes of many of his encounters with Johnson, but when writing up the *Life* he relied mainly upon a prodigious memory and what he called 'a mind impregnated with the Johnsonian aether'.

Because of the date of their first meeting, Boswell's treatment of the last 20 years of his subject's life occupies three-quarters of the book; but his skill in reconstructing the early years is quite remarkable. Another important aspect of the *Life*'s greatness is pointed at by part of its full title: 'The whole exhibiting a view of literature and literary men in Great-Britain, for near half a century, during which he flourished'. Johnson's centrality in 18th-century letters is established not only by Boswell's record of his life and conversation, but also by the success of the work in placing him in a literary and cultural context.

Life on the Mississippi A book by MARK TWAIN published in 1883, part history, part geography, part memoir and part travelogue. It opens with a brief history of the Mississippi River from its discovery by Hernando de Soto in 1541 to the early 19th century, which is more or less factual except for a famous passage in chapter 3 in which Twain offers as 'historical' an episode experienced by his fictional character Huck Finn (the passage had originally been intended for inclusion in the novel *ADVENTURES OF HUCKLEBERRY FINN*). Twain then turns to a more personal form of history, and for the next 19 chapters describes his own childhood and youth, and his life as a river pilot during the antebellum era.

Some seven years later Twain added the second half of *Life on the Mississippi*, which recounts his experiences during a return trip to the scenes of his youth. He travels from St Louis to New Orleans, observing the changes wrought by, among other things, the railways. He reminisces about friends from that earlier period of his life, and ruminates on the detrimental effects of Southern romanticism, which he links to the historical romances of SIR WALTER SCOTT that were so popular in the antebellum South. In his opinion it was this self-conscious romanticism that prevented social and economic progress in the South and made the Civil War inevitable.

Life's Handicap: Being Stories of Mine Own People A collection of 27 stories by RUDYARD KIPLING, published in 1891. They helped to establish him as a literary figure in London.

Almost all reflect his experiences of India. One group deals with the characters who also appear in *SOLDIERS THREE*; it includes 'The Courting of Dinah Shadd' and 'On Greenhow Hill', which have been particularly admired. 'On Greenhow Hill' is unusual in that the setting for the soldier's reminiscences, and his passion for a dying woman, is green Yorkshire valleys. The atmosphere of a group of horror stories permeates the collection as a whole, with its air of haunted lives. The mood of 'The End of the Passage', in which Hummil, the victim of terrifying nightmares, is literally scared to death, is also felt in 'The Limitations of Pambe Serang'. Here the consequences of an obsession are played out in a story of vengeance. At the story's climax, the Negro Nureed, who has been pursued across the globe by Pambe for no more than a few lightly traded insults, shows compassion for his sick and poverty-stricken pursuer. The pathos of this moment of reconciliation is violently destroyed: Pambe knifes Nureed, and the tale ends with the murderer being restored to health in order that he may go to the gallows.

Light in August A novel by WILLIAM FAULKNER, published in 1932. Set in the imaginary Yoknapatawpha County, Mississippi, it has three main characters: Lena Grove, Joe Christmas, an orphan unsure of his racial origins, and the Reverend Gail Hightower, a disgraced and reclusive minister. Pregnant and unwed, Lena arrives in Jefferson, Mississippi, in search of Lucas Burch, her baby's father. Instead she finds Byron Bunch, a hardworking, dependable bachelor who immediately falls in love with her. Flashback scenes provide an account of Joe Christmas's early life and the circumstances which drove him to kill his lover Joanna Burden. He is denounced by Lucas Burch, his partner in bootlegging, and captured. He escapes and takes refuge in Hightower's home where, despite the minister's frantic efforts to protect him, he is shot by Percy Grimm of the National Guard. Hightower withdraws once more into private reverie. Lena, now accompanied by her baby and Byron Bunch, continues her search for Burch, who has once again fled town.

Lilliburlero An anti-Catholic song popular with the army. In January 1686 the Earl of Tyrconnel was sent to Ireland as Lieutenant to James II, and a song with the catchy refrain 'Lero, lero, lilli-burlero; lilli-burlero bullen-ala!' became familiar among the troops. Lord Thomas Wharton was probably the author of the words, and was said to have composed the music, though this is doubtful; the tune was also once attributed to Purcell. Because of its popularity, the song is said to have sung the Catholic James II out of his kingdom. It is a favourite of Uncle Toby's in LAURENCE STERNE'S TRISTRAM SHANDY, and is included in THOMAS PERCY'S Reliques of Ancient English Poetry (1786). Radio listeners know it as the identifying tune of the BBC World Service.

Lillo, George c. 1693–1739 Playwright. Believed to have been of Flemish and English parentage, he was born in London. His most important works, THE LONDON MERCHANT: or, The History of George Barnwell (1731) and THE FATAL CURIOSITY (1736), were pioneering examples of bourgeois or domestic TRAGEDY, abandoning the world of kings and courtiers to insist on the seriousness of high emotion in ordinary people lower down the social ladder. In this respect they express the same trend in art and society during the 18th century that produced the engravings of HOGARTH and the novels of SAMUEL RICHARDSON. Lillo also wrote: Sylvia: or, The Country Burial (1730), a BALLAD OPERA; The Christian Hero (1735); Marina (1738), based on SHAKESPEARE'S PERICLES; Elmerick: or, Justice Triumphant (1740); and an adaptation of the Elizabethan tragedy, ARDEN OF FEVERSHAM (1759). Britannia and Batavia, a MASQUE, was not performed.

Lilly, William 1602–81 Astrologer. Lilly wrote a number of pamphlets containing 'Prophesies' and published an annual almanac from the year 1644. He was the author of Monarchy, or No Monarchy, in England (1651), the second part of which is called Secret Observations on the Life and Death of Charles King of England. He claimed to have foretold the execution of the king.

limerick A form of nonsense verse with a strict rhyme scheme (aabba). The name is said to derive from parties where each guest contributed a verse followed by the chorus 'Will you come up to Limerick?' The form was first used in the 1820s and made popular by EDWARD LEAR. An example is: 'There was a young lady of Clyde/ 'Twas of eating green apples she died/ The apples fermented/ Inside the lamented/ And made cider inside her inside.'

Linacre, Thomas ?1460–1524 Scholar and founder of the Royal College of Physicians. He was educated at the Cathedral School at Canterbury and at Oxford, where he became a Fellow of All Souls. In 1485–97 he travelled extensively in Italy, studied under Poliziano and was awarded an MD from Padua in 1496. On his return he became tutor to Prince Arthur in 1500. He was a friend of ERASMUS and THOMAS MORE who, together with Henry VIII and Cardinal Wolsey, were also his patients. He was granted letters patent by the king to set up the Royal College of Physicians in 1518, and ordained priest in 1520. One of the first English scholars to cultivate the study of Greek, Linacre translated many of Galen's works into Latin, including De sanitate tuenda (1517), which was dedicated to Wolsey, and De morbis et symptomatibus (1524). His Latin grammar, Rudimenta graminatices, was originally written for the future Queen Mary, to whom he was Latin tutor.

Lincoln Center for the Performing Arts A cultural centre on New York's West 65th Street, incorporated in 1956. Its first auditorium, the Philharmonic Hall, was opened in 1962 and the Vivian Beaumont Theater, designed by Eero Saarinen and Jo Mielziner, in 1965. The Center also contains a much smaller 300-seat auditorium, originally called the Forum, but renamed the Mitzi E. Newhouse Theater in 1973, when Joseph Papp began his five-year directorship. The original intention to establish a repertory theatre in the heart of New York has been pursued, with mixed fortunes, by successive directors.

Lindsay, Lady **Anne** 1750–1825 Scottish poet and diarist. The daughter of the Earl of Balcarres, Anne Lindsay became Lady Anne Barnard by marriage and accompanied her husband to South Africa. Her journals were edited by D. Fairbridge in 1924 as *Lady Anne Barnard at the Cape, 1797–1802* and are a valuable source of information on the first English occupation of the Cape. She is also known as the author of the BALLAD 'Auld Robin Gray' (1771) and the poem 'Why Tarries My Love?' (1805).

Lindsay, David 1876–1945 Novelist. Though now classed as an authentically Scottish writer, he was born in London and spent much of his life in Cornwall and on the Sussex coast. He is best remembered for *A Voyage to Arcturus* (1920). Ostensibly SCIENCE FICTION, it is more precisely a symbolic morality tale grounded in the Calvinist theology he had imbibed from his father. Its innovative synthesis of space fantasy and religious ALLEGORY influenced C. S. LEWIS. *The Violet Apple* and *The Witch* appeared posthumously in 1976.

Lindsay, Sir **David** See LYNDSAY, SIR DAVID.

Lindsay, Jack 1900–90 Australian writer, editor and publisher. The son of NORMAN LINDSAY, he was born in Melbourne, spent his early years in Sydney and studied at Brisbane University. Before emigrating to Britain in 1926, he published *Fauns and Ladies* (1924), a celebration of Aphrodite, and was a founding editor of *Vision*, a seminal literary magazine. In England he edited various journals, of which *The London Aphrodite* was the most significant, and founded the Fanfrolico Press, which between 1927 and 1930 published fine limited editions of classical works. A prolific writer, often too little noticed, he published over 120 books, including translations of Aristophanes, Petronius and other classical authors, historical novels and verse plays. *The Roaring Twenties* (1960) is of particular interest for its portrait of Sydney literary life in the early 1920s. It was reissued as the second part of an autobiographical trilogy, *Life Rarely Tells* (1982).

Lindsay, Norman (Alfred William) 1879–1969 Australian artist, novelist and writer of CHILDREN'S LITERATURE. Born in Victoria, he first became known as an illustrator and cartoonist. His first novel, *A Curate in Bohemia* (1913), was followed by an endur-

ing fantasy for children, *The Magic Pudding* (1918). *Redheap* (1930), *Saturdee* (1933) and *Halfway to Anywhere* (1947) form a trilogy about boyhood and adolescence in the Ballarat district of Victoria. The first volume was banned in Australia for some years. Lindsay also published three volumes of essays which express his philosophy of life: *Creative Effort* (1920), *Hyperborea: Two Fantastic Travel Essays* (1928) and *Madam Life's Lovers* (1929).

Lindsay, (Nicholas) Vachel 1879–1931 American poet. Born in Springfield, Illinois, he studied art in Chicago and New York, then tramped across much of the USA and began to write verse, which he would often barter for food and lodging. His third collection of poetry, and the first to bring him recognition, was *General William Booth Enters into Heaven and Other Poems* (1913), the title-piece of which had originally been published in HARRIET MONROE's *POETRY* magazine. He was welcomed as a new poet whose work was dramatic and full of incisive rhythms, and one whose vivid imagery was drawn from a broad American background. *The Congo and Other Poems* appeared in 1914, and *The Chinese Nightingale and Other Poems* in 1917.

As a reader of his own poetry Lindsay became a popular figure; indeed, he tried to extend the popularity of poetry in general by presenting it in what he liked to call 'the higher vaudeville'. The method enjoyed only limited success but he retained the hope that he might become the great singer of everyman; he wanted above all to 'reconcile culture and manliness'. This idealism is evident in his *Golden Book of Springfield* (1920), in which he depicts a Utopia based on the 'Gospel of Beauty'. As his audience dwindled and he could no longer support himself by his poetry readings, he suffered from depression and killed himself. His last published work was a book of political essays, *The Litany of Washington Street* (1929). His *Collected Poems* appeared in 1923 and a revised edition in 1925. A volume of *Letters* was published in 1979.

Lindsay of Pittscottie, Robert ?1500–?65 Author of *The History and Chronicles of Scotland*, or at least of that part from the accession of James II in 1437 until 1565. The continuation of the narrative up to 1604 is by another hand. The work is Protestant in sympathy, and shows considerable inaccuracy and confusion over dates. It exists in several early manuscript copies and was first printed in Robert Freebairn's edition (Edinburgh, 1728). It was one of SIR WALTER SCOTT's favourite sources: he draws on it in *MARMION*.

Lingard, John 1771–1851 Historian. Lingard was born in Winchester, the son of a Roman Catholic family, and educated at the English College at Douai, which he entered in 1782. The Revolutionary wars forced him to leave in 1793 and he completed his training for the priesthood at Crook Hall, near Durham, taking holy orders in 1795. He taught natural and moral philosophy there, and published *The Antiquities of the Anglo-Saxon Church* (1806, enlarged 1845). After 1811, he spent most of his life at Hornby, near Lancaster, making a successful journey to Rome in 1817 to negotiate the reopening of the English College. *The History of England from the First Invasion of the Romans to the Accession of William and Mary* (8 vols., 1819–30) enjoyed considerable success; it was praised for its objectivity, its careful use of original documents and its balanced view of the Reformation. Lingard was also the author of A *New Version of the Four Gospels* (1836).

Linklater, Eric 1899–1974 Novelist and writer for radio. He was born in Penarth, Wales, of a family from Orkney, where he spent much of his childhood and later life. He studied medicine and then English literature at the University of Aberdeen. After serving in World War I, he became assistant editor of *The Times of India* from 1925 to 1927. From 1928 to 1930 he held a Commonwealth Fellowship in the United States, and published a satirical novel, *Juan in America* (1931). Other novels of this period, *White Maa's Saga* and *Poet's Pub* (both 1929), were set in the Orkney Islands.

During World War II he commanded a fortress in the Orkneys and then worked for the War Office. He wrote various 'conversation' pieces for radio, including *The Great Ship* and *Rabelais Replies*, and a radio play, *Crisis in Heaven* (all in 1944). The following year he became Rector of Aberdeen University (until 1948) and wrote his most successful novel, *Private Angelo* (1946), a comic account of post-war reorganization in Italy. *Husband of Delilah* (1962) is the best known of his later works. *The Man on My Back* (1941) and *A Year of Space* (1953) are autobiographical.

Linton, Eliza Lynn 1822–98 Novelist. Born Eliza Lynn, the daughter of a clergyman in Keswick, she left home in 1845 determined to earn a living by her pen and published her first novel, *Azeth the Egyptian*, in the following year. From 1848 to 1851 she was on the staff of THE MORNING CHRONICLE and later worked for THE SATURDAY REVIEW and ALL THE YEAR ROUND. *Amymone* (1848) and *Realities* (1851) having failed, she settled for a time in Paris before marrying William James Linton, the engraver and poet, in 1858. They separated shortly afterward. Her best novels are *The True History of Joshua Davidson* (1872), *Patricia Kemball* (1874) and *The Autobiography of Christopher Kirkland* (1885). In spite of her own success in an independent life, she was a vehement anti-feminist, as *The Girl of the Period and Other Essays* (1883) shows.

Lippard, George 1822–54 American novelist. Born in Pennsylvania, he was best known for his sensational books about the immorality of large cities. The most famous is *The Quaker City: or, The Monks of Monk Hall* (1844), which went through 27 printings in five years and enjoyed lively sales abroad. Like *New York: Its Upper Ten and Lower Million* (1854), it is lurid in plot but reformist in intention, portraying the corruption of the ruling classes and their sexual, political and financial exploitation of the poor. Lippard also wrote romantic historical novels, including *Blanche of Brandywine* (1846) and *Legends of Mexico* (1847).

Lippmann, Walter 1889–1974 American journalist and political commentator. He was born in New York, and educated at Harvard, where he taught philosophy under GEORGE SANTAYANA. After serving as an assistant to the Secretary of War in 1917–19, he returned to THE NEW REPUBLIC, a journal he had helped to found, and established himself as an important spokesman for liberalism. He soon became editorial commentator for the New York *World* (1921–31) and then for the *Herald Tribune* (1931–62). *A Preface to Politics* (1913), *Drift and Mastery* (1914), *The Stakes of Diplomacy* (1915), *The Political Scene* (1919), *Public Opinion* (1922), *The Phantom Public* (1925), *A Preface to Morals* (1929), *The Method of Freedom* (1934) and *The Good Society* (1937) represent his attempts to promote a mature liberalism that would depend upon public virtue, individual freedom, and *laissez-faire* economics. His later books include *Some Notes on War and Peace* (1940), *US Foreign Policy* (1943), *US War Arms* (1944), *The Cold War* (1947), *Isolation and Alliances* (1952), *The Public Philosophy* (1955), *The Communist World and Ours* (1959) and *The Coming Tests with Russia* (1961). He was awarded PULITZER PRIZES for reporting in 1958 and 1962.

Listener, The A weekly magazine of general interest published by the BBC from 1929 until 1991. *The Listener* had a strong literary bias, printing occasional articles, broadcast talks and poems by many established writers, particularly during the editorship of J. R. ACKERLEY in 1935–59.

litotes A figure of speech which uses understatement for rhetorical effect, a positive being expressed by the negative of an opposite, e. g. 'Shakespeare's was no mean achievement.'

Little Dorrit A novel by CHARLES DICKENS, published in 20 monthly parts from December 1855 to June 1857 and in volume form in 1857. Its working title, 'Nobody's Fault', emphasizes the theme of individual responsibility in all areas of life, commercial, political and personal.

Amy, or 'Little Dorrit', is born in the debtors' prison where her father William Dorrit has spent so many years that he is called 'the father of the Marshalsea'. They are befriended by Arthur Clennam who has recently returned from a long period abroad, and whose mother employs Little Dorrit as a seamstress. William Dorrit escapes the Marshalsea when he inherits a fortune, and the family, assuming a station befitting their wealth, travel to Italy. There Dorrit dies, unable at the last to remember anything but his past years in the prison.

In England, Arthur Clennam, fighting his own battles with the bureaucracy of the Circumlocution Office, is himself victim of a gigantic fraud perpetrated by the eminent financier, Merdle, and is sentenced to the Marshalsea. There he is found by Little Dorrit whose resilient optimism, generosity and humility are unaffected by the social aspirations of her sister and brother. Arthur now recognizes Amy's enduring love for him, but only when the Dorrit fortune is once more lost can the couple be united, to go 'quietly down into the roaring streets, inseparable and blessed'.

A sub-plot centres on Arthur Clennam's mother, a gloomy and bigoted paralytic who, symbolically, lives in a crumbling and mysterious house. This part of the plot involves two villains, the Frenchman Rigaud, alias Blandois, and Jeremiah Flintwich. The latter's wife Affery is a memorable character, much put upon by her husband and mistress, Mrs Clennam, and haunted by extraordinary 'dreams' which turn out to be true events.

The novel includes some of Dickens's most memorable comic creations, among them 'Mr F's aunt' ('There's milestones on the Dover road'), Flora Finching (apparently a satirical portrait of Dickens's early love, Maria Beadnell, in middle age), John Chivery, a despairing suitor of Amy's, and the highly correct governess-companion Mrs General. The brief appearance of the self-tormenting Miss Wade strikes a deliberately disturbing note.

Little Foxes, The A play by LILLIAN HELLMAN, first performed in New York in 1939. It is an angry study of the voracious capitalism that Hellman believed to have swept aside the older values and traditions of the Southern states. Like the later and less impressive *Another Part of the Forest* (1946), it concentrates on the complex of loyalties and rivalries that bind and divide the newly wealthy Hubbard family. Ben is a bachelor, Oscar has entered into an alliance with the old aristocracy by marrying Birdie, whom he has proceeded to destroy as systematically as the new rapacity has destroyed the old nobility, and Regina has married a liberal financier. The three Hubbards need each to provide a large sum to complete a lucrative deal. The play details the processes by which Regina's portion is provided, and concludes when she has

proved herself stronger than the whining Oscar and more merciless even than the bullying Ben. It is a vigorous and disturbing study of corruption, cruelty and blackmail in a family community that expels any humanity that it cannot silence.

Little Lord Fauntleroy See BURNETT, FRANCES HODGSON.

Little Review, The A literary periodical published from 1914 to 1929, edited by Margaret Anderson and Jane Heap. Begun in Chicago, it moved to New York in 1917 and to Paris in 1924. Many writers from both sides of the Atlantic were represented in its pages, among them RICHARD ALDINGTON, SHERWOOD ANDERSON, Apollinaire, DJUNA BARNES, HART CRANE, T. S. ELIOT, ERNEST HEMINGWAY, WYNDHAM LEWIS, VACHEL LINDSAY, AMY LOWELL, MARIANNE MOORE, EZRA POUND (who also served as the periodical's foreign editor), GERTRUDE STEIN, WALLACE STEVENS, Tristan Tzara, WILLIAM CARLOS WILLIAMS and WILLIAM BUTLER YEATS. *The Little Review* gained notoriety when its editors were tried and found guilty of obscenity in 1920 for publishing a portion of JOYCE's *ULYSSES*.

Little Women A novel by LOUISA MAY ALCOTT, originally published in two parts. The first part, *Little Women: or, Meg, Jo, Beth, and Amy*, appeared in 1868; the second, under the title *Good Wives*, in 1869. In 1871 the two appeared as a single volume, *Little Women and Good Wives*. Subsequent editions have generally included both sections and have been entitled simply *Little Women*.

The March sisters, Meg, Jo, Beth and Amy, are the daughters of an army chaplain in the Civil War who live with their mother (Marmee) in a small town in New England. The story follows the girls' lives and their efforts to increase the family's small income. Jo, the independent and unconventional sister, wants to be a writer and is on the verge of success at the end of the first part. The second part relates the girls' emergence into womanhood. Meg and Amy marry; Beth falls ill and dies. Jo becomes a successful novelist and later marries a professor, Dr Bhaer. Together Jo and Dr Bhaer establish a school for boys, the subject of Alcott's later novels *Little Men* (1871) and *Jo's Boys* (1886).

Lively [*née* Greer], **Penelope (Margaret)** 1933– Novelist and writer of CHILDREN'S LITERATURE. Born in Cairo, she grew up in Egypt, settled in Britain after World War II and took a degree in history from St Hilda's College, Oxford. A preoccupation with the effect of the past on the present, often manifested in a supernatural manner, is the hallmark of her books. She began as a writer for children. *Astercote* (1970), *The Wild Hunt of Hagworthy* (1971) and *The Whispering Knights* (1971) are pleasant if unexcep-

Roger McGough, one of
the Liverpool poets

tional adventure stories. Her first work of note was
The Ghost of Thomas Kempe (1973), winner of the
Carnegie Medal. A witty vision of the clash between
the centuries, it concerns the ghost of a 17th-century
sorcerer who returns to haunt a present-day family. In
A Stitch in Time (1976), which won the Whitbread
Award, the heroine becomes obsessed with a sampler
embroidered by a girl who lived in the house more
than 100 years before. Her first adult novel, *The Road
To Lichfield* (1977), was followed by *Judgement Day*
(1980), *According to Mark* (1984) and *Moon Tiger*
(1987), which won the BOOKER PRIZE. Stories for
younger children include *A House Inside Out* (1987),
about humanized animals.

Liverpool poets A group of poets, Adrian Henri
(1932–), Roger McGough (1937–) and Brian Patten
(1946–), committed to reviving poetry as a public, performed art. They flourished particularly during the
1960s in Liverpool, strongly influenced by the pop
music and culture for which the city was then known.
The Mersey Sound (1967), in the Penguin Modern
Poets series, is an anthology of their work. All three
poets have developed separately, while maintaining
their belief in poetry as entertainment worthy of
public performance.

Lives of Girls and Women A collection of short
stories by ALICE MUNRO, published in 1971. It presents

episodes from the girlhood and adolescence of Del Jordan in the fictional town of Jubilee, Ontario. Taken together, the stories come close to forming a BILDUNGSROMAN. Most involve an initiation or rite of passage, as Del comes to terms with mortality, sexuality and the mutability of personal relationships. An artist in the making, she differs from the other women – her conventional schoolfriend Naomi, her mother and her aunts – in being able to see below the surface of Jubilee life and to realize that the most mundane events can conceal Gothic depths. Her perception confirms the central theme of the stories: the presence of the extraordinary within the ordinary and the lack of clear demarcation between the 'abnormal' and the 'normal'.

Lives of the Poets, The A series of succinct critical biographies by SAMUEL JOHNSON, published between 1779 and 1781. Already the author of several literary 'profiles' or 'lives', Johnson was asked in 1777 by a number of London booksellers to prepare introductory essays for an edition of selected poetry. He originally proposed to begin with CHAUCER, though in the event the Lives started several centuries later with ABRAHAM COWLEY. Even so, they ran to 52 in all and amounted to a comprehensive review of the previous century of verse – a major undertaking for a writer then in his seventies. Of differing lengths, they offer a combination of biographical sketch, analysis of character and subjective opinion which make lively reading. Johnson was an unrelenting, though honest, critic of people and writing, and his comments are sometimes lasting, sometimes just of historical interest, but never dull. There is an unmistakable tendency to chastise those failings in others which resemble his own: indolence, for example, or (as in the case of SWIFT) derangement. But many of the pieces, however subjective, have become landmarks of literary criticism: the lives of DRYDEN and GAY, for example, and the dissection of metaphysical poetry in the life of Cowley (see METAPHYSICAL POETS). Others, like the life of SOMERVILLE, are masterly achievements in Johnson's inimitable style of prose.

Livesay, Dorothy 1909– Canadian poet. Born in Winnipeg, she moved to Toronto in 1920 and was educated at the University of Toronto and the Sorbonne, working later as a social worker in Montreal and New Jersey during the Depression. She has also been a newspaper reporter, teacher of English and writer in residence at many Canadian universities. She now lives on Galiano Island in British Columbia. Her first collection of poems, Green Pitcher (1928), appeared before she was 19. Works like Day and Night (1944) reflect her left-wing activism during the 1930s and 1940s. Collected Poems: The Two Seasons (1972) provides the most comprehensive sample of her work up to this date. She continued to explore the interaction

of individual and political experience in volumes like Ice Age (1975) and The Woman I Am (1977). The Phases of Love (1983) is a retrospective collection of previously unpublished love poems, while Feeling the Worlds (1985) was published for her seventy-fifth birthday. The Self-Completing Tree (1986) is her selection from almost 60 years of writing. She has also published a volume of autobiographical short stories, A Winnipeg Childhood (1973), a memoir, Right Hand, Left Hand (1977) and a novel, The Husband (1989), as well as editing several anthologies of women's poetry. A writer of wide stylistic range, she is regarded as the first major feminist poet in Canada, and is particularly admired for her love poems.

Livings, Henry 1929– Playwright. He was born and educated in Lancashire. A prolific writer, he has television and radio plays to his credit as well as more than 30 works for the stage. These include Stop It, Whoever You Are (1961), Big Soft Nellie (1961), Nil Carborundum (1962), Kelly's Eye (1963), Eh? (1964) and Stop the Children's Laughter (1992). Anarchically cheerful, they show special sympathy for the underdog and a feeling for North Country life.

Livingstone, Douglas 1932– South African poet. Born of Scottish parents in Malaysia, he went to South Africa when he was ten. He attended the Pasteur Institute in Harare, Zimbabwe, and works in marine bacteriological research in Durban. Some of his most memorable poems focus on animals and other aspects of the natural universe; always tightly woven, they are ironic and astringent, even at their most passionate. His first important volume, Sjambok and Other Poems (1964), has been followed by Eyes Closed against the Sun (1970), A Rosary of Bone (1975; enlarged 1983), The Anvil's Undertone (1978) and A Littoral Zone (1991). At a time when the main surge of creative energy in South Africa was centred in the struggle against apartheid, he has offered – by example and sometimes good-humoured argument – the case for an older and less politicized art.

Liyong, Taban lo 1939– Ugandan essayist and poet. He was born in northern Uganda and educated at Gulu High School, Sir Samuel Baker School, the National Teachers College, Kampala, and several American colleges, including Howard University. His first book, paradoxically entitled The Last Word (1969), was the first indigenously published East African literary criticism. The essays are wide-ranging in setting and subject, conveying the notion of what Liyong terms 'cultural synthesism', an attempt to make sense out of the uniquely fragmented age in which he believes we live. Liyong is no respecter of literary form and in Eating Chiefs: Lwo Culture from Lolwe to Malkal (1970) he attempts to create a new medium which can call upon African traditional culture and yet be appropriate to the modern world. He has also written a collection of short stories, *Fixions* (1969), and several volumes of poetry, among which the best known are *Frantz Fanon's Uneven Ribs* (1971), *Another Nigger Dead* (1972) and *Ballads of Underdevelopment* (1976). His 'funeral dirge', *Meditations of Taban lo Liyong* (1978), was composed after working with a writers' workshop at the University of Iowa. Liyong now lives in Sudan, where he teaches at the University of Juba. His is regarded as an individual voice in African literature, verging at times on the bizarre and eccentric, but his ability to yoke together the principles of traditional culture with modern trends in Western intellectual life has made him a force to be reckoned with.

Llewellyn, Richard [Lloyd, Richard Dafydd Vivian Llewellyn] 1907–83 Novelist and playwright. Born in St David's, Pembrokeshire, he was educated in Cardiff and London. At the age of 16 he went to Italy to learn hotel management, and while in Venice he began to study painting and sculpture. In 1926 he enlisted in the regular army. Throughout the 1930s he lived in England, working in film studios as a director. During the war he served as a captain in the Welsh Guards, and for much of his life thereafter he lived abroad. A gifted linguist and avid traveller, he described himself as 'an expatriate Welshman who now lives in the world and will stay there'. Based in North America, he spent several years in Argentina tracing the descendants of Welsh colonists who had settled in Patagonia in the 18th century.

Llewellyn achieved early success with his stage plays, some of which were later filmed. *Poison Pen* (1937) and *Noose* (1947) were popular, but it was with his novel *How Green was My Valley* (1939), set in a Welsh mining community, that he gained more lasting recognition. It became the first and most famous best-seller of the war years, and its blend of lyricism, realism and humour has represented something quintessentially 'Welsh' for many readers. Other novels included *None But the Lonely Heart* (1943) and *A Few Flowers for Shiner* (1950), about cockney characters in the London slums. A sequence of spy novels, *The End of the Rug* (1968), *But We Didn't Get the Fox* (1969), *White Horse to Banbury Cross* (1971) and *The Night is a Child* (1972), concerned a British agent-turned-industrialist called Edmund Trothe. *A Night of Bright Stars* (1979), about a Brazilian pioneer aviator, was set in *fin-de-siècle* Paris.

Lochhead, Liz 1947– Poet and playwright. Born in Motherwell, she studied at the Glasgow School of Art and has taught art in various schools. As well as a highly visual eye, she brings a preoccupation with the condition of woman to her individual and occasionally controversial work. The mainly domestic, localized poems in *Memo for Spring* (1972) have been

followed by volumes developing her skills in narrative and characterization, and showing her interest in BALLAD and fairy-tale: *Islands* (1978), *The Grimm Sisters* (1981), *Dreaming Frankenstein and Collected Poems* (1984), *True Confessions and New Clichés* (1985), which includes songs, sketches and monologues from her revues and plays, and *Bagpipe Muzak* (1991), which brings together poetry and prose. Her plays include *Blood and Ice* (1982), *Silver Service* (1984), a rhyming adaptation of Molière's *Tartuffe* (1985), *The Big Picture* (1988) and *Mary Queen of Scots Got Her Head Chopped Off* (1989). Her dual role as playwright and poet underlines her aim of reaching a wide audience and her ability to construct dramatic situations within her poems.

Locke, Alain (Leroy) 1886–1954 Black American editor, critic, philosopher, art historian and educator. Born in Philadelphia, he was educated at Harvard, Oxford (where he was the first black Rhodes Scholar) and the University of Berlin. From 1918 to 1953 he was professor of philosophy at Howard University.

His influential career as critic and editor began with the March 1925 publication of a special illustrated edition of *The Survey* magazine, entitled 'Harlem, Mecca of the New Negro'. Locke edited the issue and wrote an introductory essay which announced the arrival of the HARLEM RENAISSANCE. Contributors to the volume included such young writers and poets as CLAUDE MCKAY, JEAN TOOMER, COUNTEE CULLEN and LANGSTON HUGHES. Later in the same year Locke published *THE NEW NEGRO*, the first literary anthology of the Renaissance. The volume consisted of material from *The Survey* with additional essays, stories, poems and extensive bibliographies. Locke's other publications include a volume edited with Montgomery Gregory, *Plays of Negro Life* (1927), as well as *The Negro and His Music* (1936), *Negro Art: Past and Present* (1936) and *The Negro in Art: A Pictorial Record of the Negro Artist and of the Negro Theme in Art* (1940). He also wrote numerous reviews and essays on black literature and culture, many of which were published in the magazines *Opportunity* and *Phylon* from the 1930s to the early 1950s.

Locke, John 1632–1704 Philosopher. Born at Wrington in Somerset, and educated at Westminster School and Christ Church, Oxford, Locke remained at the university to teach Greek and rhetoric. He also studied medicine, though he did not take a degree until 1674, and was interested in the new experimental science being developed by NEWTON, BOYLE, HARVEY and others. In 1667 he became physician to the household of Anthony Ashley Cooper, Lord Ashley, later 1st Earl of Shaftesbury, a position from which he gained a considerable knowledge of trade, politics and the role of the monarchy. Meanwhile, he received several minor government appointments and kept up his connection with Oxford. Between 1675 and 1679 he was in France, and was dismissed by the university for suspected complicity in Shaftesbury's plots. Shaftesbury's fall came in 1682 and Locke fled to Holland the following year, staying there until the accession of William and Mary. From 1691 until 1700 he was adviser on coinage to William's government and a member of the Council of Trade. He resigned when his health failed, and died at his manor house in Kent.

Locke's earliest published work, LETTERS CONCERNING TOLERATION (1689–92), argued the case for religious freedom. TWO TREATISES ON GOVERNMENT (1690) was followed by a book begun as a proposed reply, on a single sheet of paper, to the question of 'what objects our understandings were, or were not, fitted to deal with'. It was published in 1690 as the ESSAY CONCERNING HUMAN UNDERSTANDING. Four essays on money (1692, 1695 and 1699) showed Locke's wide-ranging knowledge of economics; the future of learning was examined in Some Thoughts concerning Education (1693) and the problems of faith in The Reasonableness of Christianity As Delivered in the Scriptures (1695), a book which contributed to the development of DEISM. He published two replies to attacks on his work in Vindications (1695 and 1697). His last years found him increasingly preoccupied with religion; two posthumous publications were A Paraphrase and Notes on the Epistle of St Paul to the Galatians (1705) and A Discourse on Miracles (1716).

Locke's view of society was based on his belief in religious toleration, parliamentary democracy and the laissez-faire system of commerce and trade. In religion, he was an analytical but convinced Christian whose contempt for traditional theological argument earned him the wrath of the church. As befitted a man who had become a Fellow of the Royal Society in 1666, he followed the principles of the new experimental science in his investigation of the mind, rooting his ideas in evidence. Though he stimulated later metaphysics, he was not concerned with metaphysical speculation: he appealed constantly to experience, from which reason and knowledge proceed.

Locker [Locker-Lampson], **Frederick** 1821–95 Poet. Born in Greenwich, he worked for a time at Somerset House and at the Admiralty. After he left government service he wrote 'society verse' and published London Lyrics (1857), an anthology called Lyra Elegantiarum (1867) and a miscellany of verse and prose, Patchwork (1879). His reminiscences were published as My Confidences (1896).

Lockhart, John Gibson 1794–1854 Biographer, critic and novelist. Born at Cambusnethan, Lanarkshire, he was educated at Glasgow and Oxford and called to the Scottish Bar in 1816. As a shaping influence on BLACKWOOD'S EDINBURGH MAGAZINE during its early years and as editor of THE QUARTERLY REVIEW from 1824 to 1853, he earned himself the nickname of 'The Scorpion' by his savage and uncompromising criticism, most notoriously of the so-called COCKNEY SCHOOL of writers. He translated Schlegel's Lectures on the History of Literature and published sketches of Edinburgh society in 1819 as Peter's Letters to his Kinsfolk. In 1820 he married Sophia, SIR WALTER SCOTT's eldest daughter. His Life of Scott (1838) is one of the finest biographies in the language. He also published a life of BURNS (1828) and four novels, Valerius (1821), Adam Blair (1822), Reginald Dalton (1824) and Matthew Wald (1824).

Locksley Hall A poem by ALFRED TENNYSON, first published in Poems (1842), written in the unusual form of eight-stress trochaic couplets. According to Tennyson, Locksley Hall 'represents young life, its good side, its deficiencies, and its yearnings'. But beyond its narrative of the hero's frustrated love for his cousin Amy, the poem is invested with ideas and concepts contributing to the formation of the Victorian frame of mind. Much that is contemporary – ballooning, the middle-class intellectual's fear of encroaching democracy, material optimism, emigration, a touch of Carlylean thought implicit in the doctrine of active participation – informs Locksley Hall. Biographically the poem may refer to Tennyson's own frustrated love for Rosa Baring in the 1830s or to the breaking of his engagement in 1840 to Emily Sellwood.

Locrine, The Lamentable Tragedy of A play first published in 1595 and once attributed to SHAKESPEARE (see SHAKESPEARE APOCRYPHA). Modern scholarship has named GEORGE CHAPMAN as a likely author but definite attribution is not possible.

The Locrine of the title is Logrin, King of Britain, mentioned by GEOFFREY OF MONMOUTH and EDMUND SPENSER (THE FAERIE QUEENE, Book I). Locrine's queen is Gwendolen, who watches with growing rage the king's infatuation with Estrildis, a German maiden. Estrildis had come to England with the invasion by the Huns under King Humber, defeated at the battle of the river Albus (called the Humber thereafter). Estrildis bears Locrine a daughter, and Gwendolen has mother and daughter drowned in the Severn.

Lodge, David (John) 1935– Novelist and critic. Educated at University College, London, he was professor of modern English literature at the University of Birmingham from 1976 to 1987. His literary criticism is concerned with the nature of and current possibilities for fiction. The Language of Fiction (1966) looks at the variety of verbal modes open to the novelist. The Novelist at the Crossroads (1971) assesses the state of contemporary British fiction. Working with

Structuralism (1981) applies current structuralist analysis to 19th-and 20th-century novels. *After Bakhtin* (1990) formulates a working critical response to the theories of STRUCTURALISM.

His novels themselves frequently test and exploit the assumptions and conventions of fictional narrative. *The British Museum is Falling Down* (1965) contains parodies of modernist writers like JOYCE and VIRGINIA WOOLF. The plot of *Small World* (1983) mimics the structure of an Arthurian romance. But Lodge's fiction is also grounded solidly in the experience of his own time: *Ginger, You're Barmy* (1962) is an early, vigorous evocation of post-war National Service; *Changing Places* (1975), to which *Small World* is the sequel, is a satirical 'campus' novel much in the school of KINGSLEY AMIS's *LUCKY JIM* or the early work of MALCOLM BRADBURY; *How Far Can You Go?* (1978) looks at the problems of Roman Catholic faith in Britain in the 1970s. *Nice Work* (1988) is an industrial novel self-consciously in the tradition of ELIZABETH GASKELL. *Paradise News* (1991) contrasts wordly pleasure and heavenly hopes in a Hawaiian setting. *The Writing Game* (1991) is his only play.

Lodge, Thomas ?1557–1625 Pamphleteer, poet, playwright and author of prose romances. His life seems to have been as adventurously miscellaneous as his writings. The son of a Lord Mayor of London, he attended Merchant Taylor's School and Trinity College, Oxford, briefly studied law, took part in privateering expeditions to the Canaries (1588) and South America (1591), qualified and practised as a doctor, converted to Catholicism and spent strategic periods of exile on the Continent, particularly after the Gunpowder Plot in 1605.

His earliest work is a short pamphlet, *A Defence of Poetry, Music and Stage Plays* (1580), in reply to GOSSON's *The School of Abuse*. It was followed by various pamphlets and sermons on moral and religious themes, less significant than his poetry: an erotic EPYLLION, *Scillae's Metamorphosis* (1589; republished as *Glaucus and Scilla*, 1610); a sonnet cycle, *Phillis* (1593); and a collection of Horatian satires, *A Fig for Momus* (1595). His most successful prose romance is *ROSALYNDE* (1590), the main source for *As You Like It*. It was preceded by *The Delectable History of Frobonius and Prisceria* (1584) and followed by *Robert Second Duke of Normandy* (1591), *William Longbeard* (1593) and *A Margarite of America* (1596), a story he claimed to have found in a Jesuit library on his South American trip. Lodge wrote two plays, neither of them distinguished: *The Wounds of Civil War* (printed in 1594 but probably performed *c.* 1586), about Roman history, and *A Looking Glass for London and England* (1594), a morality play in collaboration with GREENE. Though he apparently wrote little after 1600, he did translate the historian Josephus (1602) and Seneca (1614) and produce two medical works, *A Treatise of the Plague* (1603) and *A Poor Man's Talent* (not printed until 1883).

Lofting, Hugh (John) 1886–1947 Writer of CHILDREN'S LITERATURE. Born in Berkshire and educated at a Jesuit boarding school in Derbyshire, he went on to train first as an architect and later as a civil engineer. His children's stories originated in the illustrated letters he sent to his family from the front in World War I, describing how army horses managed to fare and how much better off they would be if they had the services of a doctor who could speak their language. This idea was incorporated into *The Story of Dr Dolittle* (1920), where the vague, benign hero learns how to address the many animals who share his home and dominate his surgery. They all sail to Africa to cure a deadly monkey disease. Further adventures are described in many other books, all illustrated with simple drawings by the author. Sometimes attacked today for his occasionally patronizing attitudes to race, Lofting nevertheless created, in the endearingly absent-minded Dr Dolittle, one of the most famous characters in children's fiction.

Logue, Christopher 1926– Poet, translator and playwright. Born in Portsmouth, he attended Portsmouth Grammar School. He served in the Commandos in the Middle East and has lived in London and Paris, working on *Private Eye* and as a film actor. His early poems, *Wand and Quadrant* (1953), are influenced by POUND. *Devil, Maggot and Son* (1958) was followed by *Songs* (1959), which revealed his conversion to radical socialism and his debt to Brecht, also apparent in stage plays like *Jazzetry* (1959) and *Antigone* (1960). Selections from his earlier books appear in *Ode to the Dodo: Poems 1953–78* (1981), confirming Logue as a writer of populist lyric and SATIRE with a strong sense of the possibilities of the voice. *War Music* (1981) is a free adaptation of Books 16–19 of Homer's *Iliad* and *Kings* (1991) of Books 1–2.

Lolita A novel by VLADIMIR NABOKOV, published in France by Maurice Girodias in 1955 and in the USA in 1958. Between these dates it had begun its rise from the status of underground pornography to that of a work exploring the discrepancies of texts, languages and cultures and belonging more to the literature of COURTLY LOVE than to any other defined category. It is presented as a document ('Lolita: or, The Confession of a White Widowed Male'), edited and introduced by an unhelpful Freudian psychiatrist, written by the pseudonymous Humbert Humbert before his death in prison while awaiting trial for murder.

Its avowed focus is the fascination Humbert Humbert feels with 'nymphets', or young girls. An Englishman teaching in New England, he lodges with the widowed Charlotte Haze and marries her to remain near her 12-year-old daughter Lolita.

Charlotte dies in a car accident in distraction after discovering his private diaries. Humbert and Lolita embark on a year-long journey together across America, before she seduces and leaves him, apparently for Clare Quilty. After tracking her down to an unsatisfactory meeting, Humbert locates Quilty and kills him.

Lollards, The Originally a group of Oxford adherents to the unorthodox doctrines of JOHN WYCLIF (c. 1320–84), they were led by Nicholas of Hereford. The movement gained in strength and numbers despite continual persecution, as well as recantations by several early supporters, but was driven underground after suffering military defeat at the hands of Henry V in 1414. It resurfaced several times well into the 16th century. The main demands of the Lollards were for freely available vernacular translations of the Bible (see also THE BIBLE IN ENGLISH), and a reduction in the materialism and powers of the Catholic Church. They denied the value of pilgrimages and prayers for the dead, the necessity of confession and the validity of the doctrine of transubstantiation.

By far the most important Lollard writings are the two translations of the Bible (c. 1375–96), though Wyclif's own contribution seems to have been limited to an unfinished version of the New Testament. Many sermons, tracts and commentaries attributed to Wyclif are apparently the work of followers like his secretary, John Purvey, drawing partly on Wyclif's Latin writings. They are concerned principally with attacking the worldliness and corruption of the friars and the orthodox Roman Church. See also the satiric *JACK UPLAND*.

London A poem by SAMUEL JOHNSON in IMITATION of Juvenal's Third Satire, published in 1738. The Latin original, a popular model for Augustan poets, presents a dialogue with a friend leaving the metropolis for the country. In Johnson's version the poet Thales, about to leave London for Wales, delivers an eloquent tirade against the 'thoughtless age' in which he lives, denouncing courtiers and flatterers as well as fashion and other general characteristics of the time. Robustly constructed, the poem contains some memorably contemptuous lines, a spirited description of the streets of the capital and a rousing defence of poverty.

London, Jack [Chaney, John Griffith] 1876–1916 American novelist. Born in San Francisco, he grew up on the tough Oakland waterfront, spending much of his youth on the wrong side of the law. At the age of 17 he signed on a sealing ship which took him to the Arctic and Japan. Depression had struck the USA when he returned, and he was unable to find work. In 1894 he joined a march on Washington to petition for relief for the poor. The petition was not successful,

Jack London

but London, who had just won first prize in a newspaper competition, added the event to his rapidly expanding store of experience. The aspiring writer became also an aspiring reformer. He discovered the *Communist Manifesto*, and from then on was an active socialist. He enrolled in the University of California in 1896, but dropped out after one semester. He continued his education on his own, reading sociology and political science intensively. In 1897 he joined the Klondike gold rush, carrying the works of CHARLES DARWIN and MILTON in his backpack. He returned to Oakland in 1898 and began to write about his various experiences.

His early stories were accepted by *OVERLAND MONTHLY* in the West and *THE ATLANTIC MONTHLY* in the East, and in 1900 were collected in a volume entitled *The Son of the Wolf*. Like his first novel, *A Daughter of the Snows* (1902), they drew on his experiences in the Klondike. Subsequent collections of his short stories include *Love of Life* (1907), *Lost Face* (1910), *South Sea Tales* (1911), and *The Red One* (1918). His second novel, *The Cruise of the Dazzler* (1902), was based on his own teenage experiences as an oyster pirate. His next novel, the hugely successful *THE CALL OF THE WILD* (1903), is the story of a sledge dog in the Klondike who eventually becomes the leader of a pack of wolves. *The People of the Abyss*, also published in 1903, draws on his observation of the slums of London made during a visit to England in the previous year. *THE SEA-WOLF* (1904) chronicles the voyage of a ship run by a ruthless captain. In 1905 he published a socialist treatise called *The War of the Classes* and a novel, *The Game*, about a man's fatal fascination with prizefighting. *Before Adam* (1906) attempts to recreate a prehistoric community, and *White Fang* (1906) deals with the taming of a wild dog in the Klondike. *THE IRON HEEL* (1908), set in the near future, tells of socialist struggles against the totalitarian consolidation of capitalist power. *MARTIN EDEN* (1909), more directly autobiographical than most of London's work, is concerned with his attempts to become a successful writer, and then to come to terms with that success. *Burning Daylight* (1910) is set in the Klondike, *Smoke Bellew* (1912) in the Yukon. *The Valley of the Moon* (1912), another socialist novel, is about a working-class couple who escape from the harshness of industrial life in Oakland to an idyllic life on the land. *John Barleycorn* (1913), an autobiographical memoir, deals with the debilitating effects of alcohol. *The Star Rover* (1915) is the story of a San Quentin lifer's spiritual struggles.

With the success of his fiction, London was also in demand on the lecture circuit. He visited Korea, Japan and Mexico as a foreign correspondent and travelled for two years in the South Seas. But for one so celebrated and so rich (during his career he earned over a million dollars) he was an unhappy man who could not reconcile his own success with the things he had seen and endured. He died at the age of 40, perhaps by suicide. *The Human Drift*, a socialist treatise, was published posthumously in 1917.

London Assurance A five-act comedy by DION BOUCICAULT, first staged at COVENT GARDEN in 1841 and effectively revived by the Royal Shakespeare Company at the Aldwych Theatre in 1970.

Sir Harcourt Courtly, a vain widower who believes himself irresistibly attractive, plans to marry Grace Harkaway, a country heiress 45 years his junior. He arrives at Oak Hall to meet her, but is anticipated by his son Charles, driven out of London by debts and taking refuge under a pseudonym at an address conveniently discovered by his confidence-trickster friend Dazzle. Charles has already fallen in love with Grace, who finds him a challenge to her belief that love is an unnecessary passion. With the help of the sporting Lady Gay Spanker, Charles eventually wins both Grace and his father's forgiveness.

London Labour and the London Poor See MAYHEW, HENRY.

London Lickpenny A satirical poem from the first half of the 14th century; it exists in two versions, one in eight-line stanzas and the other in RHYME ROYAL. It was at one time wrongly attributed to JOHN LYDGATE. A countryman coming to London in search of justice finds he cannot be heard without bribing the legal officials. Abandoning his case, he leaves for home and the second half of the poem consists of a series of vividly described scenes from London street life.

London Magazine, The The earliest periodical to be called *The London Magazine* was published from 1732 to 1785 but the more famous monthly of the same name appeared between January 1820 and June 1829. Edited by John Scott, it appealed to the readership created by the success of *BLACKWOOD'S EDINBURGH MAGAZINE* and rivalled its circulation. It published THOMAS DE QUINCEY'S *CONFESSIONS OF AN ENGLISH OPIUM-EATER* and CHARLES LAMB'S *ESSAYS OF ELIA*, as well as poems by JOHN KEATS and JOHN CLARE. Apart from Scott, Lamb and De Quincey, the staff of the magazine consisted of WILLIAM HAZLITT, THOMAS HOOD and MARY RUSSELL MITFORD. Rivalry between *The London Magazine* and *Blackwood's* was fierce, and Scott successfully exposed the careless libels of his competitor. A duel resulted, in which Scott was mortally wounded.

The London Magazine is also the name of a monthly literary journal founded in 1954 by JOHN LEHMANN, who was succeeded as editor in 1961 by Alan Ross, a poet, travel-writer and cricket reporter. The magazine has shown an interest in international rather than narrowly English literature. Two recent examples of writers whose work it has discovered and propagated are TONY HARRISON and the Nobel Prize-winning Czech poet Jaroslav Seifert.

London Merchant, The: *or, The History of George Barnwell* A tragedy by GEORGE LILLO, first produced at DRURY LANE in 1731 and published the same year. It is often called *George Barnwell*, the title of the BALLAD from which its plot is taken. It follows the downward path of an apprentice seduced into evil ways by a courtesan, Millwood. Barnwell becomes her creature and even robs his employer, the honest merchant Thorowgood, whose moral probity is expressed in his observations to the upright apprentice, Trueman. Eventually Millwood persuades Barnwell to rob and murder his uncle; the two of them are hanged for the crime. Written in prose and dealing with the fortunes of ordinary people, *The London Merchant* was a pioneering example of bourgeois or domestic tragedy (see TRAGEDY). It enjoyed a long history of popularity on the boards, as the references to it in the opening chapters of DICKENS's *GREAT EXPECTATIONS* show.

London Prodigal, The A play of unknown authorship, published in 1605 and of interest only because it was once attributed to SHAKESPEARE (see SHAKESPEARE APOCRYPHA). A comedy, it is concerned with the wayward young Flowerdale, the prodigal of the title, and how his constant and loving wife reclaims him.

London Review of Books, The A fortnightly paper devoted to literature, the arts and political philosophy, modelled on the prestigious NEW YORK REVIEW OF BOOKS and founded by Karl Miller in 1979. It filled a gap left by a prolonged industrial dispute which had closed THE TIMES LITERARY SUPPLEMENT, and has survived as an important journal, publishing reviews by Frank Kermode, John Bayley and other leading critics, and poems by SEAMUS HEANEY, TOM PAULIN, DOUGLAS DUNN, CRAIG RAINE and others. Its letters page is a forum for literary controversy.

Long Day's Journey into Night A semi-autobiographical play in four acts by EUGENE O'NEILL, written in 1940 and first performed in the USA in 1956, three years after the author's death. The action takes place during a single day in August 1912 at the summer home of the Tyrone family (which to some extent is a dramatic recreation of O'Neill's own family). The members of the family are the father, James Tyrone, an actor, the drug-addicted mother, Mary, the elder brother, the alcoholic James Jr, and the younger brother, Edmund (based on O'Neill himself), who is stricken with tuberculosis. The play explores the tragic nature of family relations, and questions the possibility of forgiveness and redemption. It was awarded a PULITZER PRIZE in 1957.

Longest Journey, The A novel by E. M. FORSTER, published in 1907.

Frederick Elliot, nicknamed Rickie, was a lame and delicate child who hated his father and gave all his affection to his cold and reticent mother. While an undergraduate at Cambridge he is visited by his friend Agnes Pembroke and her brother Herbert with news of her engagement to Gerald Dawes, an 'athletic marvel'. Shortly afterwards Dawes dies of a sporting injury, and Rickie and Agnes marry. Thwarted in his attempts to become a writer, Rickie accepts a teaching post offered by Herbert, who is housemaster at Sawston, a minor public school. On a visit to his father's sister, Mrs Failing, Rickie discovers that her drunken but amiable scapegrace of a nephew, Stephen Wonham, is in fact his half-brother, and Rickie assumes that Stephen is his father's illegitimate son. Agnes tries, without Rickie's knowledge, to persuade Mrs Failing to send Stephen away as a remittance man, and the discovery of her action coincides with Rickie's growing disillusionment with Herbert.

Stewart Ansell, Rickie's Cambridge friend, condemns the selfish preoccupations of the Pembrokes, and eventually reveals that Stephen is in fact the son of Rickie's mother. Leaving his wife, Rickie resolves to assist his half-brother, who promises to reform. However, becoming helplessly drunk soon afterward, Stephen falls on the railway tracks at a level crossing and, in attempting to save him, Rickie is fatally injured.

The title of the novel is drawn from SHELLEY's *Epipsychidion*: 'Who travel to their home among the dead.../ With one chained friend.../ The dreariest and the longest journey go.'

Longfellow, Henry Wadsworth 1807–82 American poet. Born in Portland, Maine, he was educated at private schools and at Bowdoin College. After travelling in Europe in 1826–9 he returned to Bowdoin as a professor of languages and married Mary Potter. She died during a second visit to Europe in 1835. The following year he took up a professorship at Harvard, which he resigned in 1854, while continuing to live in Cambridge, Massachusetts, and remaining a major figure in its intellectual circles. His later life was overshadowed by the loss of his second wife, Frances Appleton, in 1861.

His early work included *Outre-Mer: A Pilgrimage beyond the Sea* (1833–5), a series of travel sketches, and *Hyperion* (1839), a prose romance reflecting his grief at the death of his first wife. *Voices of the Night* (1839), his first volume of poems, was followed by *Ballads and Other Poems* (1842). Such pieces as 'A Psalm of Life', 'Footsteps of Angels' and 'The Reaper and the Flowers' in the former volume, and, particularly, 'The Wreck of the Hesperus' and 'The Village Blacksmith' in the latter helped to establish Longfellow as one of the most popular poets of his day. Finely attuned to contemporary taste in Britain as well as America, the mixture of sentiment and didacticism in his verse perfectly expressed the atmosphere of the Victorian parlour and fireside. His later work reflects his reading of European epics and his interest in establishing an American mythology. It includes EVANGELINE (1847); THE SONG OF HIAWATHA (1855); *The Courtship of Miles Standish* (1858); three series of *Tales of a Wayside Inn*, modelled on CHAUCER's CANTERBURY TALES, the first (1863) containing the famous 'Paul Revere's Ride'; and a trilogy, *Christus* (1872). His translation of Dante appeared in 1867.

Longley, Michael 1939– Irish poet. He was born in Belfast and attended the Royal Belfast Academical Institution before studying classics at Trinity College, Dublin. After schoolteaching in Dublin, London and Belfast he joined the Northern Ireland Arts Council in 1970 and is now Combined Arts Director. His relatively slender output includes *Poems 1963–1983* (1985), combining earlier collections and new work, and *Gorse Fires* (1991). Since the appearance of his first collection, *No Continuing City* (1969), he has been praised for the sharp clarity of his visual imagery and his immaculate diction. A versatile lyric poet, he explores strange moments of fulfilment or misgiving, describing love, grief, visited landscapes, country lore, birds and animals. In his imaginative recoil from contemporary political violence and celebration of nature's permanencies he seeks identification not only with other Ulster poets such as his friends SEAMUS HEANEY and DEREK MAHON but also with the lyric poets of Greece and Rome and the poets of World War I. Many of his more recent poems have distilled a laconic tenderness from vividly rendered experiences of sexuality and bereavement, isolation and horror, family memories and mythic history. His *Selected Poems* appeared in 1981. He has also edited a symposium on the arts in Ulster (*Causeway*, 1971) and an anthology of children's verse.

Longstreet, Augustus Baldwin 1790–1870 American writer. Born in Georgia and educated at Yale, he was at various times a college president, newspaper editor, clergyman and jurist. He founded and edited the *States Rights Sentinel* in Augusta in 1834. He is best remembered for his *Georgia Scenes, Characters and Incidents, &c., in the First Half Century of the Republic* (1835), a collection of 18 humorous sketches which record Georgian customs and language. A pioneering regionalist, he also wrote a series of short stories and a novel, *Master William Mitten* (1864).

Lonsdale, Frederick 1881–1954 Playwright. He began his career with a series of libretti for musical comedy, including *The Maid of the Mountains* (1917). After *Madame Pompadour* in 1923 he turned to social comedies dealing ironically with polite manners and modern marriage, which at the time were compared to MAUGHAM. Epigrammatic wit and neatly constructed, near-farcical situations made his work highly successful, and the best of his 11 plays, *The Last of Mrs Cheney* (1925), in which the maid in a gang of burglar-servants gives up her criminal career to marry into the aristocracy, still retains its popularity.

Look Back in Anger A play by JOHN OSBORNE, first performed at the ROYAL COURT THEATRE in 1956, when it spearheaded the post-war revival of the British theatre.

Jimmy Porter, graduate of a redbrick university, runs a sweet stall in a London market and lives in squalor with a middle-class wife, whom he persistently abuses. When she leaves him, he sets up home with her middle-class actress friend, subjecting her to exactly the same treatment. The play ends with Jimmy and his wife reconciled in a scene which many critics have found falsely sentimental. The play's contemporary importance was not dependent on its flimsy plot, but on the articulate anger of Jimmy Porter, whose tirades against the complacency of the English establishment won Osborne a reputation as leader of the ANGRY YOUNG MEN.

Looking Backward: 2000–1887 A Utopian novel by EDWARD BELLAMY, published in 1888. It is narrated by Julian West, a Bostonian, who falls asleep in 1887 and wakes in the year 2000. He finds himself in a brilliant new society in which the lot of man has been drastically transformed. Dr Leete, who revives Julian and takes him into his home, explains how American society came – through peaceful means – to adopt a rigorous socialist programme under which labour is performed according to a system similar to military service. With all basic human needs accounted for and happiness ensured, human ills once thought to be inevitable have simply vanished. Great political, technological and sociological achievements are described in vivid detail. At the end of the novel Julian dreams of a nightmarish return to 19th-century Boston but wakes again in the year 2000 to find that Edith Leete, a descendant of his former fiancée, returns his love. The effect of *Looking Backward* was enormous, comparable perhaps only to that of UNCLE TOM'S CABIN. Numerous Bellamy clubs were founded; political journals and even a Nationalist party all advocated the changes represented in the book.

Lord Chamberlain's Men See KING'S MEN.

Lord Jim A novel by JOSEPH CONRAD, published in 1900.

Jim is chief mate on the steamship *Patna*. During a voyage towards Mecca with a cargo of pilgrims the ship strikes a submerged object. Watching the small crew lowering a lifeboat to save their own skins, Jim appears to be an idealistic onlooker but then, impulsively, he jumps. The significance of his action is the crux of the novel. In Aden the narrator, Marlow, observes Jim at the Court of Inquiry. Ironically, the *Patna* had not sunk, but only Jim has elected to face the official consequences of his action. Marlow is interested in Jim's private consciousness of disgrace: being stripped of his master's certificate proves a public but not a spiritual atonement. With Marlow's assistance Jim moves through a variety of jobs ashore, but the promise of real freedom from 'talkers' (those who know of his sullied reputation) is provided only by a position as agent at the remote trading post of Patusan.

Jim's life at Patusan, recalled by Marlow, has an active and practical character: to the people, including the elderly chief Doramin, he is Tuan, or Lord Jim. His relationship with the woman he calls Jewel, stepdaughter of his corrupt predecessor, contributes to his partial serenity. This is violently disrupted by the arrival of Gentleman Brown and his fellow thieves. Jim pledges to Doramin that Brown will leave the island without bloodshed; he is proved horribly wrong. Doramin's son is killed as a result of Jim's misplaced trust. Taking responsibility for his action, Jim allows himself to be shot by an angry and grieving Doramin.

Lord of the Flies A novel by WILLIAM GOLDING, published in 1954. His first published novel, it is an inverted Victorian boys' adventure story, whose regular allusions to R. M. BALLANTYNE's *CORAL ISLAND* stress Golding's choice of savage knowledge rather than blithe innocence as the conclusion of his fable.

Marooned on a desert island after a plane crash, a party of schoolboys quickly degenerates into vindictive barbarism. The roguish Jack emerges as a calculating and ruthless dictator, while the fat and clumsy Piggy is taunted, tortured and eventually killed with the Christlike Simon. It is only when the boys are rescued by a British destroyer that Piggy's well-meaning friend Ralph realizes the true extent of their depravity.

Golding has said that the genesis of his novel lay in the brutalities he witnessed during his service at sea in World War II and in his experiences teaching small boys for 13 years. His use of an obvious but effective symbolism throughout the story allows it to work as an ALLEGORY of humanity's fallen nature as well as a graphically realistic scenario.

Lord of the Rings, The See TOLKIEN, J. R. R.

Lord Ormont and His Aminta A novel by GEORGE MEREDITH, published in 1894.

The elderly and disappointed Lord Ormont meets Aminta Farrell in Madrid. Although she is of lowly birth, Lord Ormont proposes to Aminta, who accepts him in spite of his age. After a period of travel, the couple return to London, where Ormont refuses to present his wife in society.

She becomes involved with a disreputable set, one of whom, the profligate Morsfield, is particularly spiteful and importunate. Meanwhile Ormont acquires a secretary, Matie Weyburn, who proves to be a youthful admirer of Aminta. Matie disposes of Morsfield, and his obvious liking for Aminta persuades her husband that Aminta should be accorded her appropriate status in society. Nevertheless, Aminta leaves Ormont and later acknowledges her love for Matie. The couple depart for Switzerland in defiance of convention and open a school there. Ormont forgives them before he dies.

Lorna Doone: A Romance of Exmoor A novel by R. D. BLACKMORE, published in 1869. It is set on Exmoor during the late 17th century; Monmouth's rebellion, the Battle of Sedgemoor, and Judge Jeffreys form part of the background to the story. Young John Ridd, a yeoman, is determined to avenge his father's death at the hands of the Doones, an evil clan which pursues a career of murder and theft from a nearby valley. The progress of the story has a further impulse in his love for Lorna, daughter of the head of the clan. John Ridd and his friends bring the Doones to account and he rescues the girl from them. It is then revealed that Lorna was stolen; she proves to be the daughter of a noble house. John is acutely aware of the difference in their positions but Lorna's love and faith in him do not waver. Later he is able to render valuable service both to the king and to a kinsman of Lorna; his reluctance is overcome and the story ends happily for the young lovers.

Lothair A novel by BENJAMIN DISRAELI, published in 1870.

Lothair is an orphaned nobleman of enormous wealth. His guardians are Lord Culloden and Grandison, a clergyman who embraces Roman Catholicism and rises so rapidly that he becomes a cardinal. Lothair reaches manhood after a Scots Protestant upbringing and joins Garibaldi's campaign in Italy. His wealth makes him a target for the Catholics: Cardinal Grandison, Clare Arundel and Monsignor Catesby combine to try and convert him. Lord Culloden, Lady Corisande and Theodora, the Italian girl who supports Garibaldi, resist their influence. In the campaign against the papal forces Theodora is killed. Lothair promises the dying girl that he will never enter the Roman Church. When Lothair himself is wounded at Mentana the cardinal renews his attempts at persuasion. Lothair, however, eventually returns to England, unconverted, and marries Lady Corisande. The cardinal is probably Disraeli's best-realized character, his persuasive powers well served by the author's wit.

Lotos-Eaters, The A poem by ALFRED TENNYSON, first published in 1832 and revised for the 1842 *Poems.* Its subject comes from Book IX of the *Odyssey,* where the sailors returning home after the fall of Troy land on a strange island inhabited by people who eat only the fruit of the lotos plant. Some of the sailors sample it and are filled with a languorous content that makes them reluctant to continue their journey. Tennyson uses all his skill with verbal music in evoking the desire, commonly expressed in his early poetry, to withdraw from the world of work and competitive struggle.

Love, Nicholas *fl.* 1410 Translator. The scanty records which survive suggest that he came to prominence in 1409–10, when he was made rector, and then prior, of Mount Grace, a Carthusian house recently established in Yorkshire. At about the same time his translation of the *Meditationes vitae Christi,* once attributed to Bonaventura, was approved for copying. The translation, known as the *Mirror of the Blessed Life of Jesu Christ,* omits some of the doctrinal material of its source, and is striking for its concentration on the nature of Christ's humanity, dealing with the events of the Gospels with simple realism and emotional intensity. The *Mirror* was one of many texts which the late medieval church used to combat the perceived heresies of the LOLLARDS and the general demand for the translation of the Bible. Love concentrated on orthodox views of the sacraments, offering a detailed and sympathetic interpretation of the significance of Christ's life which could be read by members of the clergy and the laity alike. In the years after the publication of the *Mirror*, Love became preoccupied with the difficulties of running the monastery of Mount Grace and it appears that he had no further time for writing.

Love and Mr Lewisham A novel by H. G. WELLS, published in 1900.

The novel's title suggests the symmetry with which its underlying themes are explored. As a young schoolmaster at Whortley Preparatory School, Sussex, Lewisham dreams of his coming greatness as a scholar and man of influence. His ambition is matched, and appears threatened by, his attraction to the more experienced Ethel Henderson, a young visitor from town. Lewisham's idealism is also offset by inadequate figures of authority in the adult world: Bonover, the shallow headmaster who dismisses him, and particularly Ethel's father, Chaffery, an exponent of deviousness and intelligence in the modern world. Chaffery's ambitions are satisfied by the misuse of spiritualism and science; posing as a medium, he draws from the wealth of his victim, the weak-minded Mr Lagune.

Later, Lewisham follows a principled pathway as a gifted student in London, although distracted by the attentions of the bluestocking, Miss Heydinger. When he meets Ethel again after a three-year gap, his strength of purpose is dominant. He perceives that she is a victim of her unscrupulous father. Their courtship, Ethel's pregnancy and their marriage are all traced with sympathy for the pains as well as the pleasures of married life. Lewisham's ambitious individualism and his desires for a settled life and fatherhood are reconciled.

Love for Love A comedy by WILLIAM CONGREVE, produced and published in 1695. Thomas Betterton and Anne Bracegirdle played the parts of Valentine and Angelica.

Valentine is a fashionable man-about-town whose extravagance has led him into debt. His father, Sir Sampson Legend, agrees to pay the debts only if Valentine will sign his inheritance away to his younger brother, Ben, a sailor. Valentine has to agree but, realizing that he faces ruin, pleads and even feigns madness to avoid signing the bond. Angelica, whom he has been unsuccessfully courting, intervenes. She uses her charms to extract a proposal of marriage from Sir Sampson, and gets possession of

the bond. Valentine, believing that she will marry his father, despairs and declares himself willing to sign. Angelica then reveals her plot, declares her love for Valentine and tears up the bond. Meanwhile, the independent-minded Ben has baulked at Sir Sampson's plan to marry him to Miss Prue, a foolish country girl. The plot involves some diverting minor characters, including Valentine's resourceful servant Jeremy and the amorous Mrs Frail.

Love Song of J. Alfred Prufrock, The A poem by T. S. ELIOT, published in the American magazine *POETRY* in 1915 and reprinted in his first collection, *Prufrock and Other Observations* (1917). The title is ironic, for the middle-aged Prufrock, the speaker of the poem, shows himself too nervously timid to make the significant gesture that might redeem or free him from the empty social rituals of his genteel world. He remains trapped in a state of wan hopelessness as his social habits and consideration of his futility overwhelm him. Both the use of the DRAMATIC MONOLOGUE and the setting, with the seamier side of urban life glimpsed at the edges of Prufrock's bourgeois existence, anticipate THE WASTE LAND.

Love's Labour's Lost A comedy by WILLIAM SHAKESPEARE, first performed c. 1594. The text of the 1623 Folio is based on that of a Quarto edition published in 1598. No precise source has been identified, so the story may be one of the few Shakespeare invented.

Having forsworn the company of women for three years, Ferdinand, King of Navarre, and his three lords, Berowne, Dumain and Longaville, are sorely tried and eventually overcome by the embassy of the Princess of France with her three ladies, Rosaline, Katharine and Maria. The news that the princess's father has died forestalls the expected ending, for the ladies require their suitors to wait a year, and the play concludes with the delightful song 'When Icicles Hang by the Wall'. The complications of the plot are wittily prolonged and the language the most ornate that Shakespeare wrote. This is a play that has been understandably called Mozartian, though LYLY's *EUPHUES* and the fashion it created were the immediate influence and the object of Shakespeare's affectionate SATIRE. The extravagant conceits of the courtly lovers are a feature of the play, but Shakespeare has also created a gallery of minor characters, the fantastical Spaniard Armado, the pedantic schoolteacher Holofernes, Dull the constable and Costard the clown being the most notable. They are of the kind that BEN JONSON would later develop into 'humours'.

Love's Last Shift A comedy by COLLEY CIBBER, first performed in 1696.

Loveless, having deserted his wife Amanda after a mere six months of marriage, returns from abroad penniless to resume his rakish life in London. Amanda wins him back by disguising herself as a stranger, conducting an intrigue with him and then, by appealing to his better nature, persuading him to mend his ways.

Provoked by the popularity of Cibber's play, VANBRUGH provided in *THE RELAPSE* an immediate sequel, in which Loveless reverts to type. The two plays are a fascinating part of the growing argument about the morality of the English theatre of the period.

Lovecraft, H(oward) P(hillips) 1890–1937 American writer of fantasy, horror and SCIENCE FIC-TION. He was born in Providence, Rhode Island, where he lived all his life except for a short married interlude in New York. A frail and often solitary man, he wrote popular scientific journalism and contributed to pulp magazines. Written in highly charged prose, his stories were influenced by EDGAR ALLAN POE and preoccupied with the history of New England. The various collections which have appeared after his death, such as *Beyond the Wall of Sleep* (1943) and *The Dunwich Horror* (1945), and his novel, *The Case of Charles Dexter Ward* (1951), have earned him a cult reputation.

Lovel the Widower A story by W. M. THACKERAY, first published in *THE CORNHILL MAGAZINE* (1860). Lovel lives with his overbearing mother-in-law, Lady Baker, and a charming governess, Miss Prior, who was once a dancer. Lady Baker uncovers the truth of Miss Prior's past and high-handedly orders her out of the house, but Lovel takes Miss Prior's side and asks her to marry him.

Lovelace, Earl 1935– Trinidadian novelist. His fluent narrative gift and mastery of varieties of Trinidadian speech enable his fiction attractively to penetrate serious contemporary issues, especially the unexpected outcome of social change. In *The Schoolmaster* (1968) the new village school brings seduction and catastrophe. In his two finest novels, *The Dragon Can't Dance* (1979) and *The Wine of Astonishment* (1984), the status of formerly admired stick-fighters and despised steel-band players is reversed. Narrated by a Trinidadian countrywoman, the latter is a *tour de force* in the use of Creole. From his first novel, *While Gods are Falling* (1966), to the most recent Lovelace's central preoccupation is whether people have something to live by. *Jestina's Calypso and Other Plays* appeared in 1984. He has also published *A Brief Conversion and Other Stories* (1988) and a dramatized version of *The Dragon Can't Dance* (1989).

Lovelace, Richard 1618–58 CAVALIER POET. The handsome and dashing son of a wealthy Kentish knight, Lovelace gained a romantic reputation in the eyes of contemporaries. He was granted an honorary MA from Oxford at the age of 18, and adorned the courtly and artistic life of London until, in 1639–40, he took up arms for his king in the Bishops' Wars. The victory of the Covenanters made Parliament's will in the matter absolute, and Lovelace defiantly presented a petition for the retention of the bishops in 1642, earning himself seven weeks in the Gatehouse Prison at Westminster. Enforcedly idle, Lovelace spent his money on the king's behalf and his time among the poets and wits of the day. He travelled abroad but returned to England in 1648, when he was imprisoned again, for ten months, probably because of his family's efforts on behalf of the king, which he had financed. He was freed after Charles I's execution and spent the rest of his life in relative poverty. During his second imprisonment he had prepared for publication the collection of verses called *Lucasta: Epodes, Odes, Sonnets, Songs, etc.*, which includes 'On Going to the Wars'. Another volume, *Lucasta: Posthume Poems*, was published by his brother a year after Lovelace's death. Lucasta was his fiancée, Lucy Sacheverell. His work was almost forgotten until 1765, when THOMAS PERCY included the lovely 'To Althea from Prison' in his *Reliques of Ancient English Poetry*. Lovelace was not prolific, and his poetic reputation depends on a handful of elegant lyrics. His personal reputation may have prompted SAMUEL RICHARDSON to use his name for the dare-devil rake in *CLARISSA*.

Lover, Samuel 1796–1868 Novelist and songwriter. A Protestant Irishman, born in Dublin. As a songwriter, he is best remembered for 'Rory O'More', a BALLAD developed into a novel in 1836 and a play the following year. Lover's *Songs and Ballads* appeared in 1839. As a humorous novelist working in the same vein as CHARLES LEVER, he scored his greatest success with *HANDY ANDY* (1842), which remained popular long after his death. Lover also wrote several plays, successful in their time, and a number of stories about Irish life.

Loves of the Angels, The A poem by THOMAS MOORE, published in 1823. The source was the Koran, and the tradition of the angels Harut and Marut, whose purpose is to tempt men and teach them sorcery. Moore elaborated this into the story of three fallen angels who loved mortal women. One loves Lea, but loses her when he reveals the word which will open the gates of heaven. Lea speaks the word and rises to the skies. Another loves Lilis, but when he comes to her in all the glory at his command she is consumed. The third loves Nama, and for her sake lives among mortals. Their happiness on earth is imperfect but they look forward to immortality.

Lowell, Amy 1874–1925 American poet. Born in Brookline, Massachusetts, into a prominent New England intellectual family, she was a champion of modern poetry, introducing IMAGISM to America in what many of her critics felt was a bastardized form. Her first volume of verse, *A Dome of Many-Colored Glass*, appeared in 1912; *The Complete Poetical Works of Amy Lowell* in 1955. She is best remembered for individual poems such as 'Lilacs' and 'Patterns'. Her idiosyncratic masculine appearance and her vigorous sponsorship of modern poetry have invested her with almost legendary status within the American poetic tradition.

Lowell, James Russell 1819–91 American poet and man of letters. He was born in Cambridge, Massachusetts, and educated at Harvard. His first publications were two volumes of verse: *A Year's Life* (1841) and *Poems* (1842). A critic, humorist, and political satirist, in a single year (1848) he published *Poems: Second Series*, *A FABLE FOR CRITICS*, *The Vision of Sir Lanufal*, and the first series of THE BIGLOW PAPERS.

In 1855 he succeeded LONGFELLOW as professor of French and Spanish at Harvard, a position he held until 1886, though he taught very little during the last ten years of his tenure. He did, however, publish seven books of essays. During this period he was also editor of *THE ATLANTIC MONTHLY* (1857–61) – which he co-founded with OLIVER WENDELL HOLMES in 1857 – and, jointly with CHARLES ELIOT NORTON, of *THE NORTH AMERICAN REVIEW* (1864). He also produced the second series of *The Biglow Papers* (1867), which criticized England's part in the American Civil War, and a reflective poem called *The Cathedral* (1869). He was the US minister in Spain (1877–80), and then in England (1880–5), where he was received as a cultured and charming man who did much to interpret American aspirations and ideals to the Old World.

Lowell, Robert 1917–77 American poet. The great-grandnephew of JAMES RUSSELL LOWELL, he was born in Boston and educated at Harvard and Kenyon College. He served a prison term (1943–4) as a conscientious objector during World War II. In 1970 he moved to England, where he spent a good deal of time until his death in 1977.

His early work, which was formal and highly symbolic, often focused on the history of New England and of his own family, subjects which continued to interest him throughout his life. *Land of Unlikeness* (1944), his first book, dealt especially with his temporary conversion to Catholicism; *Lord Weary's Castle* (1946) was awarded the PULITZER PRIZE. *Life Studies* (1959) introduced the loose form and sharp IRONY which characterize his mature style. It is also usually identified as a major example of CONFESSIONAL

Robert Lowell

POETRY, though Lowell did not confine himself to purely personal subjects. *Imitations* (1961) included translations of classical and European poets, while later volumes, such as *For the Union Dead* (1964) and *Near the Ocean* (1967), linked an understanding of the self to an understanding of politics and history. His other collections are *The Mills of the Kavanaughs* (1951), *The Voyage, and Other Versions of Poems by Baudelaire* (1968), *Notebook 1967–68* (1969), *Notebooks* (1970), *History* (1973), *For Lizzie and Harriet* (1973) and *The Dolphin* (1973). *Selected Poems* was published in 1976 and a final volume, *Day by Day*, in 1977. His other work includes a number of plays: *Phaedra* (1961), a translation; *The Old Glory* (1965); and versions of *Prometheus Bound* (1969) and *The Oresteia* (1978). *Collected Prose* appeared in 1987.

Lowndes, Marie (Adelaide) Belloc 1868–1947 Novelist, short-story writer and playwright. The sister of HILAIRE BELLOC and wife of the journalist Frederic Sawrey Lowndes, she published over 40 novels. Most are skilfully plotted and observed stories of crime or mystery, and several derive from real-life criminal cases. Her most famous book, *The Lodger* (1913), describes how landlady Mrs Bunting comes to realize that her genteel lodger is in fact Jack the Ripper; its highly effective ending finds her incapable of summoning the will to denounce him to the police. *The*

Lodger inspired several early film versions, including one by Alfred Hitchcock (1926).

Lowry, (Clarence) Malcolm 1909–57 Novelist. He was born at Wallasey in Cheshire, the son of a wealthy Liverpool stockbroker against whom he rebelled while still at public school. He left school and sailed to China as a deckhand on a merchant ship, but was persuaded to complete his education at St Catharine's College, Cambridge. *Ultramarine*, a novel of seafaring, was published in 1933. An alcoholic and a wanderer, Lowry lived in Mexico and then British Columbia for some years. His second novel, UNDER THE VOLCANO, widely regarded as his masterpiece, appeared in 1947. He spent his last years with his second wife at Ripe, near Lewes in East Sussex. The volume of short stories *Hear Us, O Lord, from Heaven Thy Dwelling Place* (1961), *Selected Poems* (1962), *Lunar Caustic* (1968), *Dark as the Grave Wherein My Friend is Laid* (1968) and *October Ferry to Gabriola* (1971) have been published from the mass of work he left behind.

Lubbock, Percy 1879–1965 Critic. Born in London, the son of a merchant banker, Lubbock was educated at Eton and at King's College, Cambridge. He worked briefly as a journalist and as a librarian before taking up writing full-time: an occupation interrupted by his service with the Red Cross during World War I. He lived in Italy from 1926 until his death. His writings range from autobiography (*Earlham*, 1922) to fictional travelogue (*Roman Pictures*, 1923) and biography (*Samuel Pepys*, 1909, and *Portrait of Edith Wharton*, 1947). A friend and disciple of HENRY JAMES, Lubbock edited the novelist's *Letters* (1920) and the 35 volumes of his *Novels and Stories* (1921–3) while working on his own best-known book, which is also his fullest homage to James: *The Craft of Fiction* (1920). This work, which became an essential point of reference in subsequent discussions of the novelist's technique, is a distillation of the lessons of the master on artistic form and dramatic presentation in fiction, although Lubbock saw more merit than James could in the 'loose, baggy monsters' of Tolstoy and other European writers.

Lucie, Doug 1953– Playwright. *John Clare's Mad Nuncle* (1975), *Rough Trade* (1977), *We Love You* (1978), *The New Garbo* (1978), *Heroes* (1979), *Strangers in the Night* (1981) and *Progress* (1984) are hard-bitten comedies satirizing Mrs Thatcher's Yuppies. *Hard Feelings* (1983), about a group of Oxford graduates living in the Brixton of the 1981 riots, belongs to a sequence about the seamier sides of privilege, which also includes *Strangers in the Night* (1981) and *Progress* (1984). *Fashion* (1988), produced by the ROYAL SHAKESPEARE COMPANY, turns its attention to the world of advertising, while *Grace* (1992) attacks American evangelism.

Lucie-Smith, (John) Edward (McKenzie) 1933– Poet, art critic and anthologist. Born in Kingston, Jamaica, he came to England in 1946, and was educated at King's School, Canterbury, and Merton College, Oxford, before national service in the RAF. Between 1959 and 1965 he was chairman of the GROUP, who met in his Chelsea home, and he edited *A Group Anthology* (1963) with PHILIP HOBSBAUM. His first collection of verse, though, *A Tropical Childhood* (1961), an evocation of childhood memories, demonstrates MOVEMENT virtues of clarity and tight literary forms. His involvement with the Group led to an interest in DRAMATIC MONOLOGUE and ROBERT BROWNING's work – he edited *A Choice of Browning's Verse* (1967) – which is evident in *Confessions and Histories* (1964). An interest in syllabics, the BLACK MOUNTAIN SCHOOL and Elizabethan experiments with classical metres – he edited *The Penguin Book of Elizabethan Verse* (1965) – resulted in the complicated prosodic experiments of *Towards Silence* (1968) and *The Well Wishers* (1974). His interest in *avant-garde* poetry is shown not only in this later work but in his *Primer of Experimental Poetry* (1971). *Beasts with Bad Morals* (1984) contains comic poems. A prolific art critic, his publications also include *Movements in Art since 1945* (1969), *Work and Struggle: The Painter as Witness 1870–1914* (1977), *Super Realism* (1979), *Art Today* (1989), *Impressionist Women* (1989), *Art Deco Painting* (1990), *Art in the Eighties* (1990), *Sexuality in British Art* (1991) and *The Faber Book of Art Anecdotes* (1992). Other anthologies of poetry include *British Poetry since 1945* (1970; sensibly revised in 1985).

Luck of Roaring Camp and Other Sketches, The

A collection of stories and sketches by BRET HARTE published in 1870. The stories originally appeared between 1868 and 1870 in issues of *OVERLAND MONTHLY*, a journal which Harte himself helped initiate as a forum for Western writers. Harte's popular reputation was established with the appearance of this volume, which is known for its sharply naturalistic depiction of frontier life in the American West. As well as the famous title piece, the collection includes 'The Outcasts of Poker Flat', 'Tennessee's Partner' and 'Miggles'. Most of the stories explore the nature of the individual in frontier society, focusing on human relationships in difficult or even tragic circumstances.

Lucky Jim

The first novel by KINGSLEY AMIS, published in 1954. It is the story of Jim Dixon, an assistant lecturer in history in his first term of employment at a provincial university. The plot is a catalogue of Jim's hapless misadventures and disasters as he attempts to settle into his new job and make a good impression. Virtuoso sequences of comic catastrophe include Jim setting his bed on fire with his cigarette while staying at the home of the professor of English, and a crucial lecture to the faculty at the end of term which turns somehow into a blatant parody of the university principal and Dixon's own professor. As well as being a work of sustained, often farcical comedy, the novel also derives a scornful, satirical humour at the expense of 'phoniness' and pretension – a characteristic which links it to other contemporaneous fiction such as JOHN WAIN's *Hurry On Down*.

Ludlow, Edmund 1617–92 Author of memoirs. An MP for Wiltshire, and staunch anti-Royalist, Ludlow rose to become a lieutenant-general in Cromwell's army, though later an opponent of his Protectorship. One of the signatories of Charles I's death warrant, he fled England at the Restoration and settled in Switzerland, where he wrote his *Memoirs* (published 1698–9). These offer a unique first-hand account of the major events of the Civil Wars and the changes of allegiance during the Interregnum.

Ludlow, John Malcolm See CHRISTIAN SOCIALISM.

Ludus Coventriae See MIRACLE PLAYS.

Lurie, Alison 1926– American novelist. Born in Chicago and educated at Radcliffe College, she has taught since 1968 at Cornell University, where she now specializes in CHILDREN'S LITERATURE – the subject of her study, *Don't Tell the Grown-Ups* (1990). Her poised, witty novels explore the subversive effects of change on comfortable, middle-class Americans, often academics exposed to the world outside the campus. In *Imaginary Friends* (1967) a sociologist is drawn into the millenarian Christian cult which he sets out to investigate. *Foreign Affairs* (1985, PULITZER PRIZE) translates an American academic to London for a Jamesian examination of mores on both sides of the Atlantic. In *The Truth about Lorin Jones* (1988) an art historian's researches into the life of a woman painter force her to re-examine her own sexual identity. Other novels are *Love and Friendship* (1962), *The Nowhere City* (1965), *Real People* (1970), *The War between the Tates* (1974) and *Only Children* (1979).

Luska, Sidney See HARLAND, HENRY.

Luttrell, Narcissus 1657–1732 Diarist, historian and collector. He was born in London and educated at Sheen, St John's College, Cambridge, and Gray's Inn. He appears to have practised law and held a number of significant public and legal appointments. He served as Member of Parliament for Bossiney (1679–80) and Saltash (1690–5). He was a Whig at heart – JACOB TONSON was one of his friends – but he was also on terms with Tories such as ROBERT HARLEY.

He published nothing during his lifetime, but began early to collect the books and ephemera upon which he based his two *Popish Plot Catalogues* (published 1956) and *A Brief Historical Relation of State Affairs from September 1678 to April 1714* (6 vols., 1857). The latter compilation and what he called *An Abstract...* (edited by Henry Horwitz in 1972 as *The Parliamentary Diary of Narcissus Luttrell 1691–1693*) are now appreciated as indispensable source books for the parliamentary and political history of the period. Luttrell also kept a diary of 'private transactions' between November 1722 and January 1725.

His collection, which was much admired by THOMAS HEARNE and to which he devoted himself during his last years, was dispersed, in stages, after 1786.

Lyall, Sir Alfred Comyn 1835–1911 Poet. Lyall was born at Coulsdon in Surrey and entered the Indian Civil Service in 1856. He became Lieutenant-Governor of the North-West Provinces and a member of the India Council, and founded the University of Allahabad in 1885. He was the author of *Asiatic Studies* (two series, 1882 and 1899, dealing chiefly with Hinduism), a biography of Warren Hastings (1889), *The Rise of the British Dominion in India* (1893) and a study of TENNYSON for the English Men of Letters series (1902). *Verses Written in India* (1889), revised, enlarged and reprinted as *Poems* in 1907, enjoyed some success.

Lyceum Theatre Of the several theatres on the Lyceum site, just off London's Strand, the first was opened in 1772. A second, built in 1816, was destroyed by fire in 1830. The third Lyceum opened in 1834 and became famous in the last 30 years of the 19th century as the 'temple' of Sir Henry Irving, its manager from 1878 to 1902. Irving staged SHAKESPEARE and indifferent MELODRAMAS, while resisting the new movement in drama initiated by TOM ROBERTSON. Irving's Lyceum was demolished in 1904.

Lycidas An ELEGY by JOHN MILTON on the death of Edward King, a Cambridge contemporary – but not, apparently, close friend – drowned in the Irish Sea while returning to Dublin in August 1637. It first appeared in a volume of memorial verses to King published in 1638. The poem moves from personal grief at the loss of a promising man to a larger consideration of the meaning of death, eventually achieving consolation and affirming belief in the immortality and resurrection of the soul. It prefigures later works like *PARADISE LOST* in its skilful union of classical and Christian traditions (of PASTORAL as well as elegy) and its pointed contemporary references (to the sad state of the church). The closing line in which the shepherd-poet contemplates his own life with renewed hope ('Tomorrow to fresh woods, and pastures new') is one of several which have permanently entered the language.

Lydgate, John c. 1370–1449 Poet. Born in the village of Lidgate, Suffolk, from which he took his name, he entered the nearby Benedictine abbey at Bury St Edmunds in or before 1382, and was ordained a priest in 1397. He remained in the abbey for most of his life, although he is known to have spent some time in London, Oxford and Paris, and was prior of Hatfield Broad Oak, Essex, from 1421 to 1432.

Lydgate's works vary considerably in content and style, ranging from brief occasional poems to the long translations from French and Latin by which he is best known. THE TROY BOOK (1412–20), a version in decasyllabic couplets of Guido delle Colonne's *Historia troiana*, was followed by THE SIEGE OF THEBES, largely drawn from a lost French work but also indebted to Boccaccio and CHAUCER. In it Lydgate presents himself as a Canterbury pilgrim invited by Chaucer's pilgrims to tell his tale (see THE CANTERBURY TALES). In 1426 he began a translation of *Le Pèlerinage de la vie humaine* by Guillaume de Deguileville, a long and mediocre moral allegory (though with some humorous touches) which describes the Christian's quest for salvation. THE FALL OF PRINCES (1431–9) is a RHYME-ROYAL translation of a French version of Boccaccio's *De casibus virorum illustrium*. An allegory on chastity translated from French, *Reason and Sensuality* (c. 1408), is a less austere and more pleasing work, as are the love-allegories THE TEMPLE OF GLASS and THE COMPLAINT OF THE BLACK KNIGHT. He also wrote lyrics, specially commissioned occasional pieces, SAINTS' LIVES (including a life of St Edmund), versions of Aesop's fables and a short prose work about Julius Caesar, *The Serpent of Division* (1422). Although Lydgate's immediate successors considered him the equal of Chaucer and GOWER, his work has never returned to popularity, damned by its uneven metre, its fondness for clichés and aureate diction, and its verbosity.

Lyly, John ?1554–1606 Playwright and author of prose romances. He was brought up in Canterbury and probably attended the King's School there, when MARLOWE was also a pupil. He graduated from Magdalen College, Oxford, in 1575 and vainly petitioned Burghley's support for a fellowship.

EUPHUES: OR, THE ANATOMY OF WIT (?1578) and its sequel *Euphues and His England* (1580), the prose romances that began his writing career, were instantly successful: EUPHUISM, as prose modelled on his own elaborate and elegant style was called, became the fashionable mode of the 1580s. In 1583, the year of his marriage to the Yorkshire heiress Beatrice Browne, Lyly gained control of the first BLACKFRIARS THEATRE. The stage comedies that followed, all written for BOYS' COMPANIES and aimed at a courtly audience, achieve a patterned artifice combining Italian pastoralism with intrigue derived from Plautus and Terence. *CAMPASPE* (early 1580s), *Sapho and Phao* (early 1580s),

Gallathea (1584), *ENDYMION: THE MAN IN THE MOON* (1586–7), *Love's Metamorphosis* (1589), *Midas* (1589) and *Mother Bombie* (1589) helped establish prose as a medium for comedy. *The Woman in the Moon* (?1594) is his only play in verse. Their influence is felt in SHAKESPEARE's comedies, where Moth in *LOVE'S LABOUR'S LOST* is a notably witty and precocious Lylian page and Beatrice and Benedick's prose fencing in *MUCH ADO ABOUT NOTHING* echoes Lyly.

Despite encouragement from Elizabeth I, Lyly never succeeded in becoming Master of the Revels, though he did serve as an MP: in 1589 he was elected MP for Hindon in Wiltshire, the first of three constituencies he was to represent. Most of the years 1592–6 were spent at his wife's home in Mexborough, Yorkshire. *Pap with a Hatchet* (1589) is Lyly's contribution, on the side of the bishops, to the Marprelate controversy (see MARPRELATE, MARTIN).

Lyndsay [Lindsay], **Sir David** 1490–1555 A poet, dramatist, diplomat and herald, Lyndsay was one of the 'makaris' of early 16th-century Scottish poetry. He was companion, playfellow and story-teller to the young prince James (later James V), and continued in the office of usher to the king until 1522. He was dismissed from office when James fell under the influence of Douglas but returned to the king's service in 1528. Not later than 1529 he became Lyon King of Arms. Lyndsay represented the king on an embassy to Charles V in 1531 and other diplomatic missions. After James's death in 1542 Lyndsay continued as a diplomat and was sent to the court of Henry VIII in 1544 and to that of Christian III of Denmark in 1548.

His literary career started late. *The Dreme*, finished in 1528 and printed in Paris (1558), is a DREAM-VISION in which Dame Remembrance shows the poet hell, purgatory and heaven from where he sees the kingdoms of the earth, including Scotland. *The Testament and Complaynt of Our Soverane Lordis Papingo* (finished 1530, printed 1538) has advice to the king and SATIRE against ecclesiastics put into the mouth of a dying 'papyngo' (popinjay or parrot). Lyndsay's frequent satire on ecclesiastical corruption manifests his reforming sympathies. *An Answer Quhilk Schir David Lyndsay Maid to the Kingis Flyting* (1536) is an example of 'flyting', or poetic abuse, of which WILLIAM DUNBAR is the most famous exponent. *The Complaynt and Publict Confessioun of the King is Auld Hound* (c. 1536) is another satirical poem put into an animal's mouth. For Epiphany 1540 Lyndsay produced a play, *SATIRE OF THE THREE ESTATES*. He had shown an early interest in drama by acting before James and Margaret Tudor at Holyrood in 1511. His other poems are: *The Tragedy of the Cardinal* (1547), in which the lately dead Cardinal Beaton offers his fall as a warning to princes and prelates; *The History and Testament of Squire Meldrum* (?1550, first printed 1582), a romance about the exploits of a Scottish laird;

The Monarchie (1554), a long work of over 6000 lines, describing four ancient empires which are succeeded by the anti-Christian papacy and attacking veneration of images and pilgrimages; and *Kitteis Confessioun*, satirizing the confessional. Lyndsay's *Works* were printed at Edinburgh in 1574.

lyric Originally from the Greek ('for the lyre'), the term is now commonly used to describe any short poem, especially one expressing the poet's personal sentiments. The lyric mode covers a wide range of topics ranging from the experience of love, to pastoral description and praise of God. See also MEDIEVAL LYRIC.

***Lyrical Ballads,** with a Few Other Poems* A collection by WORDSWORTH and COLERIDGE, first published by Cottle at Bristol in 1798. A second edition in two volumes, containing a preface by Wordsworth in place of his original short 'Advertisement', appeared in January 1801 (though it is usually dated 1800), and a third in 1802.

The book has become one of the abiding reference points of English ROMANTICISM. The idea for it was conceived when the two poets were living as close neighbours in Somerset, and was nurtured by their shared sense of the emotional artificiality of 18th-century poetry and the petrifaction of its conventions. Of the original 23 anonymous poems, only four are by Coleridge: THE RIME OF THE ANCIENT MARINER, 'The Nightingale', 'The Foster-Mother's Tale' and 'The Dungeon', the two last taken from his tragedy *Osirio*. Wordsworth's contribution includes BALLADS, songs and narratives such as 'Goody Blake and Harry Gill', 'The Idiot Boy', 'The Thorn', 'The Mad Mother', 'Simon Lee', as well as other lyrical and personal poems: 'The Tables Turned', 'Lines Written in Early Spring' and 'Lines Composed a Few Miles above Tintern Abbey'. The 'Advertisement' characterizes these works as 'experiments... written chiefly with a view to ascertain how far the language of conversation in the middle and lower classes of society is adapted to the purposes of poetic pleasure', and challenges readers 'accustomed to the gaudiness and inane phraseology of many modern writers' to rethink their criteria of poetic decorum. Some of the early reviews were far from flattering: SOUTHEY considered that the author

of 'The Thorn' 'should recollect that he who personates tiresome loquacity, becomes tiresome himself', and Dr Burney judged the 'Mariner' to be 'the strangest story of a cock and a bull that we ever saw on paper', conceding, however, that 'there are in it poetical touches of an exquisite kind'.

The second edition includes a further poem by Coleridge, 'Love', but omits his name from the title-page. Wordsworth's claim to effective sole authorship receives additional support from the relegation of the 'Mariner' from first to twenty-third position; from the long new preface, in which he expounds his ideas on poetic diction and the origin of poetry in 'emotion recollected in tranquillity'; and from the second volume, which consists entirely of his own new poems, including important works such as the 'Lucy' poems, 'The Old Cumberland Beggar', and 'Michael, a Pastoral Poem'. In the expanded version prepared for the 1802 edition, he managed to accommodate some of his collaborator's reservations concerning aspects of the preface, but Coleridge later became dissatisfied with the Hartleian, or 'associationist', premises of Wordsworth's poetic theory as a whole, and explicitly distanced himself from the ideas in *BIOGRAPHIA LITERARIA*. *Lyrical Ballads* paved the way for Wordsworth's later fame as a poet. Its preference for subjects drawn from 'low and rustic life', and the self-mythologizing poetic persona, were often ridiculed and lampooned, yet no poet of the Romantic generation was to escape the underlying force of its call for a poetic reinterpretation of the world.

Lyttelton, George, 1st Baron 1709–73 Poet and patron. Born at Hagley, Worcestershire, the country seat of his father, he was educated at Eton and Christ Church, Oxford, made the Grand Tour, and entered political life as Member of Parliament for Okehampton in 1735. In literature he is remembered as a minor poet and as a generous patron, the friend of POPE, THOMSON, HENRY FIELDING and WILLIAM SHENSTONE. His poetry includes *Monody* (1747) to the memory of his wife, and *Dialogues of the Dead* (1760). He published *The History of the Life of Henry the Second* in four volumes between 1767 and 1771.

Lytton, Edward Bulwer See BULWER LYTTON, EDWARD.

Mabbe, James 1572–*c.* 1642 Translator from the Spanish. Educated at Magdalen College, Oxford, he became a fellow there and later a lay prebendary of Wells Cathedral. His first work was *The Rogue: or, The Life of Guzman de Alfarache* (1622), from Mateo Alemán (see PICARESQUE). He is best remembered for *The Spanish Bawd* (1631), from Fernando de Rojas's *Celestina* , which had already served as the basis for the play CALISTO AND MELIBEA, and his translation of Cervantes's *Novelas ejemplares* as *Exemplary Novels* (1640), the most famous of which is *The Spanish Lady*.

Mabinogion, The The collective name for a group of 11 medieval Welsh prose tales first published in an English translation by Lady Charlotte Guest (1812–95) between 1838 and 1849. The complete *Mabinogion* is found in the Red Book of Hergest (*c.* 1400), although fragments in the White Book of Rhydderch (*c.* 1350) suggest this was an earlier complete version. The tales were composed during the late 11th and 12th centuries, and there may have been a written version as early as 1200. The word *mabinogion* occurs once in the manuscripts but is clearly an error for *mabinogi*. In modern scholarship, *Mabinogi* is used to refer to a group of four of the tales known as 'Pedair Cainc y Mabinogi' (*The Four Branches of the Mabinogi*). The word is apparently derived from the Welsh *mab*, 'boy' or 'youth', but in what sense it describes the 'Four Branches' has not been conclusively established.

The 'Four Branches' are the tales of 'Pwyll', 'Branwen', 'Manawydan' and 'Math', loosely connected stories commemorating ancient strata of Celtic myth and history. Located in a remote pre-Norman past where independent Welsh rulers vie for power, the tales create a strong sense of 11th-century Welsh society and early Norman influence on the material life of the nobility. At the same time, the pervasive presence of the Celtic otherworld recalls the mythological significance of the tales. Lacking a coherent narrative structure by modern standards, the tales possess a powerful unity of style and technique.

Of the other stories, 'Culhwch ac Olwen' (*Culhwch and Olwen*) is the longest and the oldest, possibly antedating the Norman Conquest. The tale is set at Arthur's court and describes a sequence of feats which the hero, Culhwch, must accomplish in order to win Olwen, daughter of the giant Ysbaddaden. Since the story was composed before GEOFFREY OF MONMOUTH's *Historia regum Britanniae*, it is a crucial text in ARTHURIAN LITERATURE, preserving early Welsh traditions about Arthur and his men. The most notable feature of the tale is a long list of all the knights

present at Arthur's court, indicating a lost wealth of oral legends and folk-tales.

The *Tair Rhamant* (*Three Romances*) of 'Owain', 'Peredur' and 'Geraint' also have a native Arthurian context but are strongly influenced by Continental Arthurian literature. The heroes are depicted as chivalric knights and Arthur himself is the passive king of French romance rather than the active war-leader of the native tradition. The Welsh romances correspond to the 12th-century French romances of 'Yvain', 'Perceval' and 'Erec et Enide' by Chrétien de Troyes, and it is likely that both groups derive from French or Breton versions of original Welsh material.

The remaining tales, 'Breuddwyd Rhonabwy' (*The Dream of Rhonabwy*), 'Breuddwyd Macsen' (*The Dream of Maxen*) and 'Cyfranc Lludd a Llefelys' (*The Tale of Lludd and Llevelys*), are 12th-century versions of native historical legends. Arthur and Owain appear in 'Breuddwyd Rhonabwy', which has a contemporary setting and clearly belongs to Welsh rather than French Arthurian tradition. The other two tales, using material found in Geoffrey of Monmouth's *Historia* and its Welsh translations, hark back to the achievements of British Celts in the pre-Saxon era.

At a time when literature in England was dominated by French, the Welsh tales testify to a rich and continuing native prose tradition in Britain. Taken together, the tales illuminate centuries of oral story material as well as contemporary social practice in the immediate post-Norman period. Stories from *The Mabinogion* have inspired several modern English texts, including *The Virgin and the Swine* by Evangeline Walton (1936; reprinted in 4 vols., 1970–4) and *The Owl Service* by ALAN GARNER (1967). *The Mabinogion* has been translated by Gwyn Jones and Thomas Jones (1948), Jeffrey Gantz (1976) and Patrick Ford (1977). See also CELTIC REVIVAL, THE.

Mac Flecknoe: *or, A Satire upon the True-Blue-Protestant Poet T.S.* A satirical poem by JOHN DRYDEN, written about 1678, pirated in 1682 and officially published in 1684. Its target is THOMAS SHADWELL, who had attacked Dryden, the POET LAUREATE, in *The Medal of John Bayes*. Dryden's poem describes how Shadwell assumes the mantle of literary dullness from its previous possessor, RICHARD FLECKNOE, and makes him into the epitome of the absurdly untalented poet with a pretentious and empty style. The climax is a comic coronation scene which influenced POPE in *THE DUNCIAD*. Characterized by its MOCK-HEROIC manner and its wide allusiveness, Dryden's verse compares the anti-hero Shadwell to Arion, Christ, Romulus, Elijah and a piece of excrement.

McAlpine, Rachel 1940– New Zealand poet, novelist and playwright. Her first volume of poetry, *Lament for Ariadne* (1975), appeared in the same year as the first collections of LAURIS EDMOND and ELIZABETH SMITHER. Her exuberant, strongly feminist lyrics are seen to best advantage in *Recording Angel* (1983). *Selected Poems* appeared in 1988. Her novels include *The Limits of Green* (1985), about ecological issues, and *Farewell Speech* (1990), about the suffragette movement in New Zealand. She has also written plays for secondary school students and for radio, as well as for the stage. These include *The Stationary Sixth Form Poetry Trip* (1980), *The Life Fantastic* (1982) and *Paper Towers* (1986).

MacArthur, Charles 1895–1956 American playwright. Born in Scranton, Pennsylvania, the son of a Unitarian clergyman, he studied for two years in a theological seminary, then joined the Hearst Press in Chicago as a journalist and eventually became a popular feature writer. His first play, *Lulu Belle* (1926), was written with his uncle, Edward Sheldon. In 1927 he collaborated with SIDNEY HOWARD on *Salvation*, an exposé of a female revivalist, produced in the following year as *Salvation Nell*. MacArthur's long collaboration with BEN HECHT began with *The Front Page* (1928), a play about Chicago newspapermen, and continued with a comedy, *Twentieth Century* (1932), as well as various screenplays, including *Nothing Sacred* (1937), *Wuthering Heights* (1939), *Spellbound* (1945) and *Notorious* (1946).

Macaulay, Dame **(Emilie) Rose** 1881–1958 Novelist, essayist and travel-writer. Born in Cambridge, where her father was a lecturer in classics, she was educated at Somerville College, Oxford. Her writing career began with *Abbots Verney* (1906) but it was not until *Potterism* (1920), several novels and two books of verse later, that she attracted popular and critical interest. Its satirical view of modern journalism and commercialization was also her view of modern humanity in general. Before World War II she completed 12 further novels, mixing a tart intelligence with compassion and humour; the best known are *Told by an Idiot* (1923), *Orphan Island* (1924), *Crewe Train* (1926), *They were Defeated* (a historical novel about the poet ROBERT HERRICK, 1932), *I Would be Private* (1937) and *No Man's Wit* (1940). Her two post-war novels were *The World My Wilderness* (1950) and *The Towers of Trebizond* (1956). She was made a DBE in the year of her death.

Her non-fiction included collections of essays: *A Casual Commentary* (1925), *Catchwords and Claptrap* (1926) and *The Writings of E. M Forster* (1938); and the travel books *They Went to Portugal* (1946), *Fabled Shore: From the Pyrenees to Portugal* (1949) and *The Pleasure of Ruins* (1953). Constance Babington Smith edited her correspondence with her religious adviser as *Letters to a Friend* (two volumes, 1961–2), as well as *Letters to a Sister* (1964), which includes the fragment of a novel, *Venice Besieged*.

Macaulay, Thomas Babington 1800–59 Historian and essayist. The son of Zachary Macaulay, an anti-slavery campaigner and leading 'Clapham Sect' Evangelical, he was educated at private schools and at Trinity College, Cambridge, where he twice won the Chancellor's Medal for poetry. He was elected a Fellow of Trinity in 1824 but made a wider reputation with his articles for the Whig EDINBURGH REVIEW, notably his essays on MILTON (1825) and UTILITARIANISM (1829), and his attack on SOUTHEY's *Colloquies* (1830), a classic expression of the Whig faith in 'the natural tendency of society to improvement'. These articles attracted the attention of Lord Lansdowne, through whose influence Macaulay was elected to Parliament as member for Calne. There he threw himself enthusiastically into the campaign for reform, and his speeches in support of the 1831–2 Reform Bill made him famous.

Political rewards followed. In 1832 Macaulay became secretary to the Board of Control for India and gained entry to the Holland House circle of influential Whigs. After further success in the House, now as a member for Leeds, he was appointed to the new Supreme Council for India with responsibility for drafting legislation. During his four years in India he initiated major reforms in education and the penal code, as well as writing his essay on FRANCIS BACON and most of the *LAYS OF ANCIENT ROME* (1842). He returned home in 1838 and next year became MP for Edinburgh, entering the Cabinet as the Secretary-at-War. His contributions to *The Edinburgh Review* included essays on Clive (1840), Warren Hastings (1841) and ADDISON (1843). The first collected edition of his *Critical and Historical Essays* appeared in 1843.

In 1849 the first two volumes of his *History of England* scored an immediate and spectacular success, selling 3000 copies within 10 days and 13,000 in four months. On the strength of it Macaulay decided to devote himself mainly to writing, though he sat in the Commons again in 1852–5. The third and fourth volumes of his *History* appeared in 1855 and a posthumous volume, edited by his sister, in 1861. His original plan was to pursue the narrative from 1685 to the threshold of the First Reform Bill, thus dealing with the development of Britain 'between the revolution, which brought the crown into harmony with the parliament, and the revolution which brought the parliament into harmony with the nation'. Though the final work deals only with the period 1685–1702, its progressive thrust and conviction of the rightness and adaptability of the English constitution survive.

The epic sweep of Macaulay's narrative and his eye for pictorial and dramatic effects enrich the work and save it from the callow buoyancy which often mars his earlier essays.

McAuley, James Phillip 1917–76 Australian poet. Born at Lakemba, New South Wales, McAuley was appointed senior lecturer in colonial administration at the Australian School of Pacific Administration after World War II. Later he held the chair of English literature at the University of Tasmania. He published two books of verse, *Under Aldebaran* (1946) and *A Vision of Ceremony* (1956), and edited the literary quarterly *Quadrant*. His work exhibited a commitment to control, formality and sophistication. His poetic theories were further shown by the hoax he concocted with Harold Stewart in 1944, publishing the 'posthumous' works of 'Ern Malley' in the modernist journal *Angry Penguins*. The verses were in fact deliberately concocted nonsense, a PARODY of contemporary verse, particularly that of DYLAN THOMAS and HENRY TREECE.

McBain, Ed See HUNTER, EVAN.

Macbeth A tragedy by WILLIAM SHAKESPEARE, first performed *c.* 1606 and published, in an imperfect text, in the First Folio of 1623. The main source is HOLINSHED's *Chronicles*. In turning to Scottish history and particularly in presenting a sympathetic portrait of Banquo, legendary ancestor of the Stuart kings, Shakespeare clearly intended some flattery to JAMES I; the play also appealed to the king's well-known interest in witchcraft.

Macbeth begins with Scotland torn by rebellion. King Duncan's threatened army is rescued by the gallantry of his two generals, Macbeth and Banquo. On their way back to the king, they are confronted by three witches, who prophesy that Macbeth will become Thane of Cawdor and King of Scotland and that Banquo's heirs will be kings. Almost at once Macbeth learns that his bravery has been rewarded by his proclamation as Thane of Cawdor. His thoughts are conveyed to his wife in a letter, which also reports Duncan's intention to visit Macbeth in his castle at Inverness. Lady Macbeth immediately resolves to have Duncan killed. She overrides Macbeth's hesitation and helps him in the aftermath of the murder. Suspicion falls immediately on Duncan's sons, Malcolm and Donalbain, and grows stronger when they flee from Scotland.

Having become king, Macbeth feels no safety. Remembering the witches' prophecy, he resolves to kill Banquo and one of his sons, but the murderers botch their task and the son escapes. Banquo's ghost haunts him at a banquet. Weighed down by guilt and sleeplessness, he seeks out the witches and takes comfort from their assurance that he will not be defeated until Birnam Wood comes to Dunsinane Castle and

that no man born of woman can harm him. But Scotland is suffering under his guilty reign and Macduff, the powerful Thane of Fife, seeks out Malcolm in England. The angry Macbeth orders the slaughter of Macduff's family.

The play's last movement begins as Malcolm's army advances on Macbeth's castle. Lady Macbeth walks and talks in her sleep, distraught with guilt over Duncan's murder. Macbeth is now so isolated that he hardly reacts to the news of her death. When Malcolm instructs his army to cut branches from Birnam Wood to camouflage their attack on Dunsinane, Macbeth is deprived of one part of the reassurance he had taken from the witches' words. The rest goes when he learns that Macduff was not 'born' but 'untimely ripped' from his mother's womb. Macduff kills Macbeth in combat and establishes Malcolm on the Scottish throne.

Only at the very end of the play does Macbeth's behaviour recall the heroism of his defence of Duncan. Attaining the throne brings him no joy, nor even contentment. For the original audience, his passage towards damnation would have been clear, and there is contemporary evidence that the appearance of the witches and of Banquo's ghost was theatrically impressive. The play certainly provides scope for spectacular staging, and is outstanding among the great tragedies for the vigour of its story-telling and the splendour of its famous soliloquies.

MacBeth, George (Mann) 1932–92 Poet. Born in Shotts, Lanarkshire, he was educated at King Edward VII School, Sheffield, and New College, Oxford. From 1955 to 1976 he was a BBC producer responsible for poetry programmes. A central figure in the GROUP in the 1950s, and involved in performance poetry in the 1960s, he published many volumes. They include *The Broken Places* (1963), *The Colour of Blood* (1967), *Collected Poems 1958–70* (1971), *Shrapnel* (1973), *The Long Darkness* (1983), *Anatomy of a Divorce* (1988) and *Trespassing: Poems from Ireland* (1991). His main themes are suffering, death, war and violence, though later work is quieter, simpler, and more genuinely moving. *Another Love* (1990) is a novel.

MacCaig, Norman (Alexander) 1910– Scottish poet. Son of an Edinburgh chemist, but proud of a Gaelic-speaking mother from Scalpay and a majority of Gaelic-speaking grandparents, MacCaig was educated at the Royal High School, Edinburgh, and read classics at Edinburgh University. He was a primary teacher and headmaster in 1934–67, except for the war years, when he was a conscientious objector. He was creative writing fellow at Edinburgh University 1967–9, and lecturer in English and eventually reader in poetry at Stirling University until 1977. Widely regarded as Scotland's finest contemporary poet, he has received many awards and honours, including FRSL

(1965), OBE (1979) and the Queen's Gold Medal for Poetry (1986). In two early volumes MacCaig dabbled with the influence of the New Apocalypse before starting on what he calls 'the long haul towards lucidity' with *Riding Lights* (1955). Since then he has published a succession of slim volumes and his prize-winning *Collected Poems* (1985, revised 1990). His close friend Hugh MacDiarmid described MacCaig as apolitical by nature, and he declares himself both a born atheist and a born pacifist. His poems tend to centre on Edinburgh, or on north-west Sutherland, where he spends time each summer. His poetry has moved from tight traditionality to more open forms, characterized by sharp wit and playfulness; much of it is 'metaphysical', concerned with the nature of perception. The deaths of Hugh MacDiarmid and Sydney Goodsir Smith affected him strongly, and in *Equal Skies* (1980) there is a sequence of poems for another dead friend, Angus MacLeod, which achieves a new depth of emotion. *As I Say It* (1971) is a recording of MacCaig reading his own poems.

MacCarthy, Sir (Charles Otto) Desmond 1877–1952 Literary and dramatic critic. He was educated at Eton and Trinity College, Cambridge, where he was a member of the Apostles, and became a close friend of the philosopher G. E. Moore, G. M. Trevelyan and Thoby Stephen, brother of Vanessa Bell and Virginia Woolf. By 1903 he was writing reviews and dramatic criticism for *The Speaker*. In 1907–10 he edited *The New Quarterly*, and in 1913 joined *The New Statesman* as dramatic critic, later becoming literary editor (1920–7), where he wrote under the pen-name 'Affable Hawk'. In 1928 he succeeded Sir Edmund Gosse as senior literary critic of *The Sunday Times*, continuing to write weekly articles for that paper until his death. He was knighted in 1951.

A brilliant conversationalist of whom great things were expected by his friends in the Bloomsbury Group, he never produced any major works, though his critical essays were published in some 10 volumes. His criticism always preserved the precise thought and an element of the philosophic interest that he had learned at Cambridge. Portraits of Samuel Butler, Meredith, Henry James, Shaw, Conrad, Ruskin and Asquith are among his most admired pieces and he was among the first to recognize the significance of Ibsen and Chekhov.

McCarthy, Justin 1830–1912 Irish journalist, novelist, historian and politician. Born near Cork, the son of a magistrates' clerk, he was brought up in genteel poverty. As a young journalist on *The Cork Examiner* he imbibed the political and literary enthusiasms of Thomas Davis and the Young Ireland movement, reporting the Irish famine and the treason trials of the Young Ireland leaders in 1848. He moved to Liverpool in 1854 and joined *The Morning Star* in London in

1859. In the 1860s he embarked on a successful career in fiction, publishing some 20 now-forgotten novels. The best is probably *Mononia: A Love-Story of 'Forty-Eight'* (1901), reflecting the country life and political enthusiasms of his Munster youth, though *Dear Lady Disdain* (1875) and *Miss Misanthrope* (1878) were also very popular. He entered Parliament in 1879, becoming vice-chairman of the Irish parliamentary party under Parnell and after 1890 chairman of the anti-Parnellite majority of the Irish members. His immensely popular *History of Our Own Times* was eventually completed in seven volumes (1879–1905), covering the whole of Queen Victoria's reign. To this he added *The Reign of Queen Anne* (1905) and *The History of the Four Georges and William IV* (1884–1901) as well as shorter studies of Sir Robert Peel (1891) and Gladstone (1898). Despite the failure of his health and eyesight in 1897 he continued to write, publishing works such as his good-humoured *Reminiscences* (1899), *The Story of an Irishman* (1904) and *Irish Recollections* (1912).

McCarthy, Mary 1912–89 American novelist, short-story writer, essayist and critic. Born in Seattle, Washington, she attended Vassar and moved to New York, writing book reviews for *The New Republic*, *The Nation* and *Partisan Review*. She began to write fiction at the urging of her second husband, Edmund Wilson, whom she married in 1938. Her first collection of stories, *The Company She Keeps*, appeared in 1942. She then transformed much of her life into fiction: *The Groves of Academe* (1952) draws on her experiences as a university teacher, and *Memories of a Catholic Girlhood* (1957) describes her childhood. Her best-selling novel *The Group* (1963) follows the lives of eight Vassar women of the class of 1933 for seven years after their graduation. Her political interests are evident in all her writing, including her travel books *Venice Observed* (1956) and *The Stones of Florence* (1959). After a visit to Vietnam in the 1960s she published critical accounts of the war in *Vietnam* (1967) and *Hanoi* (1968). She also produced works of literary criticism (*The Writing on the Wall*, 1970, *Ideas and the Novel*, 1981) and many more novels, short stories and essays, including *Birds of America* (1971), *The Mask of State: Watergate Portrait* (1974), *Cannibals and Missionaries* (1979), *The Hounds of Summer and Other Stories* (1981) and *Occasional Prose: Essays* (1985). *How I Grew* (1987) is autobiographical.

McClure's Magazine An American literary and political magazine founded by Samuel Sydney McClure and John Sanborn Phillips in June 1893; its last issue appeared in March 1929, after which it merged with *New Smart Set*. In its first period it ranked as one of the three great illustrated ten-cent monthlies. In its second period, beginning in 1902, it pioneered reformist non-fiction, which was later called muckraking journalism. After 1919 the magazine declined, and despite efforts by people such as William Randolph Hearst to infuse new life and money into it, it lost its prestige. Contributors of fiction included RUDYARD KIPLING, O. HENRY, WILLA CATHER and JACK LONDON.

McCrae, Hugh Raymond 1876–1958 Australian poet. Born in Melbourne of a literary family, McCrae was articled to an architect, but went to Sydney to work as a freelance writer. He also pursued a brief career as an actor in New York and Australia. Seeing the poet's task as 'to live in making others live', McCrae created a vivid mythological world in the volumes *Satyrs and Sunlight* (1909), *Columbine* (1920), *Idyllia* (1922) and *The Mimshi Maiden* (1938). The *Dr Poissey Anecdotes* (1922) are fictional revelations in the 18th-century manner, and *My Father and My Father's Friends* (1935) is a biography of George Gordon McCrae and his friends MARCUS CLARKE, HENRY KENDALL and ADAM LINDSAY GORDON.

McCullers, Carson (Smith) 1917–67 American novelist. She was born in Georgia and educated at Columbia and the Juilliard School of Music. Her work often deals with spiritual isolation and the attempt to overcome it through love. She was also one of the first American writers to deal openly with homosexual relationships. Her first novel, *The Heart is a Lonely Hunter* (1940), won immediate recognition. *Reflections in a Golden Eye* (1941) was followed by *The Ballad of the Sad Café* (1951), *Clock without Hands* (1961) and *The Mortgaged Heart* (1971), a collection of stories. EDWARD ALBEE dramatized *The Ballad of the Sad Café* and she herself dramatized *The Member of the Wedding* (1946), as well as writing another play, *The Square Root of Wonderful* (1958).

MacDiarmid, Hugh [Grieve, Christopher Murray] 1892–1978 Scottish poet and critic. Born in Langholm in the Scottish Borders, he attended Langholm Academy and trained as a teacher in Edinburgh before becoming a journalist in 1912. After serving in World War I, he married in 1915 and returned to journalism in 1920. He published his first book, *Annals of the Five Senses*, under his own name in 1923, but in 1922–3 began to publish poems in Scots and thereafter, as Hugh MacDiarmid, became the central figure of the 20th-century SCOTTISH RENAISSANCE. A Communist and nationalist, he became a founder-member of the Scottish National Party in 1928 and was involved in political controversy throughout his life. He was expelled from both the SNP and the Communist Party during the 1930s and rejoined the Communist Party in 1956 after the Hungarian uprising. In 1931 he met his second wife Valda Trevlyn (his first marriage ended in divorce)

and in 1933–42 they lived through a period of troubled but in many ways productive 'exile' on Whalsay in the Shetlands. In 1950 he received a Civil List pension and in 1951 he finally settled at Brownsbank, near Biggar. From the early 1960s he began to enjoy growing recognition as a major modern poet. In the last two decades of his life he received many literary honours and travelled extensively throughout Europe and to North America and China.

He had already written a good deal in English before he established his reputation with poems like 'The Watergaw' and 'The Eemis Stane', which demonstrated new potentialities for the use of Scots as a modern literary language. MacDiarmid's revived or synthetic Scots drew on dictionaries, dialect glossaries and literary diction as well as contemporary speech. Two collections of lyrics, *Sangschaw* (1925) and *Penny Wheep* (1926), were followed by *A Drunk Man Looks at the Thistle* (1926), a sequence regarded by many as his masterpiece and certainly the most important single poem in 20th-century Scottish literature. He continued to extend the use of Scots throughout the 1920s and 1930s in such works as *To Circumjack Cencrastus* (1930) and in styles ranging from the political polemic of *First Hymn to Lenin* (1931) to the meditation of 'By Wauchopeside', 'Whuchulls' and 'Depth and the Chthonian Image'. By the mid 1930s, however, his desire to create a modern EPIC led him to experiment with what he called 'synthetic English', a poetic idiom created from a variety of esoteric vocabularies and scientific terminologies, particularly geology and modern linguistics. 'On a Raised Beach' (in *Stony Limits*, 1934) is his most impressive achievement in this mode, but he continued the experiment in two major works, *In Memoriam James Joyce* (1954) and *The Kind of Poetry I Want* (1961).

MacDiarmid's two-volume *Complete Poems 1920–76*, edited by Michael Grieve and W. R. Aitken, appeared after his death in 1978 and was reissued, with minor amendments and additions, in 1982. He was a notable translator of Scottish Gaelic and modern European poetry, and edited several literary magazines and poetry anthologies. He also wrote short stories, critical and political essays and the prose autobiography *Lucky Poet: A Self-Study in Literature and Political Ideas* (1943, reissued in 1972). *The Letters of Hugh MacDiarmid*, edited by Alan Bold, appeared in 1984.

MacDonagh, Donagh 1912–68 Irish poet and playwright. Born in Dublin, the son of THOMAS MACDONAGH, he became a barrister and later a judge. He published *Twenty Poems* (1934), *Veterans and Other Poems* (1941), *The Hungry Grass* (1947) and *A Warning to Conquerors* (1968). In 1947 his play *Happy As Larry* was a considerable success in London and New York, and several others were performed on radio. He edited *The Oxford Book of Irish Verse* (1958) with LENNOX ROBINSON.

MacDonagh, Thomas 1878–1916 Irish poet. Born in Tipperary, he attended University College, Dublin, and was later appointed its professor of English literature. In his time he was a successful and well-regarded poet, publishing *Through the Ivory Gate* (1902), *April and May* (1903), *The Golden Toy* (1906), *Songs of Myself* (1910) and *Lyrical Poems* (1913). Other works were a tragedy, *When the Dawn is Come* (1908), *Thomas Campion and the Art of English Poetry* (1913) and *Literature in Ireland* (1916). Another play, *Pagans*, was published posthumously in 1920. He was executed for his part in the Easter Rising and mourned by YEATS in 'Easter 1916'. *Collected Poems* (1917) was introduced by JAMES STEPHENS.

MacDonald, George 1824–1905 Scottish novelist and writer of CHILDREN'S LITERATURE. The son of a Scottish weaver, he was educated at Aberdeen University before training as a Congregational minister. Finding his own individualistic views unacceptable to his parish, he gradually turned to literature, producing original fairy-stories shot through with an unmistakable blend of Christian symbolism and mystical imagination. His most famous story, *At the Back of the North Wind* (1871), describes a little cabdriver's son called Diamond who ventures forth each night from his bedroom in the company of the North Wind, pictured as a beautiful lady, to travel over the world. Subsequent classics include *The Princess and the Goblin* (1872), a powerful ALLEGORY of good and evil, and *The Princess and Curdie* (1883), where the miner's son Curdie once more braves dangers from goblins and other misshapen figures in order to save the princess to whom he owes allegiance. MacDonald's adult fiction – the allegorical *Phantastes* (1858) and *Lilith* (1895), and novels such as *David Elginbrod* (1863) – is less well remembered, but his vivid imagination has influenced G. K. CHESTERTON, C. S. LEWIS and J. R. R. TOLKIEN.

McEwan, Ian 1948– Novelist and short-story writer. A former student of MALCOLM BRADBURY's creative writing course at the University of East Anglia, he attracted immediate attention with two collections of short stories, *First Love, Last Rites* (1975) and *In between the Sheets* (1977), and a novella, *The Cement Garden* (1978). They combine a perfectly modulated prose style with sexual explicitness and a preoccupation with perversion and obsession. *The Comfort of Strangers* (1981) is a more substantial investigation of psychopathology, owing its location and claustrophobic concentration to Mann's *Death in Venice*. *The Child in Time* (1987) is an intense and sober study of the bereavement visited on young parents whose infant daughter is stolen and never found.

The Innocent (1990) is set against a background of espionage in Berlin during the 1950s, while *Black Dogs* (1992) uses the memory of Nazi atrocities in World War II for an investigation of evil. McEwan is also the author of a thoughtful television play, *The Imitation Game* (1981), about the Bletchley Park code-breaking centre in World War II; an oratorio, *Or Shall We Die?* (1983), which is a polemic against nuclear war; and the screenplay of *The Ploughman's Lunch* (1983), a film satirizing political complacency at the time of the Falklands campaign and the Greenham Common protests.

MacEwen, Gwendolyn 1941–87 Canadian poet, novelist and short-story writer. Born in Toronto, where she was raised and educated, she travelled in Egypt, Israel and Greece before returning to Canada. She was briefly married to MILTON ACORN. Her first work appeared in *Canadian Forum* before she was 15 and her first novel was completed by the age of 19. Her many volumes of poetry include *Selah* (1961), *The Drunken Clock* (1961), *The Shadow-Maker* (1969), which won the Governor General's Award, *The Armies of the Moon* (1972), *The T. E. Lawrence Poems* (1982) and *Earthlight: Selected Poems 1963–1982* (1982). A prolific writer in a wide range of forms, she also published: *Julian the Magician* (1963) and *King of Egypt, King of Dreams* (1971), novels; *Noman* (1972), *The Honey Drum: Seven Tales from Arab Lands* (1984) and *Noman's Land* (1985), collections of stories; *The Trojan Women* (1979), a version of Euripides' play; and translations from Y. Ritsos. Preoccupied with myth, magic and a sacrificial view of life, she was one of Canada's most intense and accomplished writers at the time of her early death.

McGahern, John 1934– Irish novelist and short-story writer. He writes out of and about Ireland in astringent, measured, often bleak fiction, psychologically acute and linguistically economical. *The Leavetaking* (1975) is about the love affair between an Irish Catholic schoolteacher and an American divorcée. *The Pornographer* (1979) contrasts the protagonist's efficiency at writing pornography with the gauche failures of his actual sexual encounters, but also with the tenderness he can summon up in caring for others. *Amongst Women* (1990) is about an ageing farmer. His other novels are *The Barracks* (1963) and *The Dark* (1965). The short stories to which his style is ideally suited are gathered in *Collected Stories* (1992).

McGee, Thomas D'Arcy 1825–68 Irish journalist and poet. McGee was born in Carlingford, County Louth, and emigrated to America in 1842. He quickly made his mark as a precocious orator and was editing a newspaper in Boston at the age of 19. He returned to Ireland in 1845 and became London correspondent of

The Freeman's Journal and the Young Ireland organ, *The Nation*. He neglected his official business to explore Irish history and literature in the British Museum and wrote hurried but valuable pioneering studies of *The Irish Writers of the Seventeenth Century* (1846) and *The Life and Conquest of Art McMurrough* (1847). The facile popular poetry he wrote for *The Nation*, chiefly on nationalist or historical themes, was admired by YEATS as technically superior to that of his colleague THOMAS DAVIS. He was actively involved in the Young Ireland rising of 1848 and escaped to America, where he continued to lecture and write indefatigably if controversially on Irish subjects. He concerned himself with the welfare and education of the growing Irish expatriate community both in the USA and later in Canada, where he represented Irish-Canadian interests in Parliament and held ministerial rank. He was assassinated in Ottawa in 1868, possibly by an Irish political extremist since he had become critical of the Fenian movement of the 1860s. His best-remembered poems are the dreamily nostalgic 'The Celts' and 'Salutation to the Celts' addressed to the 'sea-divided Gael' throughout the world. His several touching elegies for Irishmen include a tribute to THOMAS MOORE, to whose influence his own metrical virtuosity and lyric grace are largely attributable.

McGonagall, William 1830–1902 Scottish versifier, self-styled 'Poet and Tragedian'. A Dundee weaver aspiring to act SHAKESPEARE and write great poetry, McGonagall became and has remained a butt for audiences, with the unscanned doggerel and painful rhymes of his *Poetic Gems* (1890). This volume also contains a 'Brief Autobiography' and 'Reminiscences'. In his poetry he specialized in shipwrecks, battles and beauty spots, and perhaps his most frequently quoted work is 'The Tay Bridge Disaster'.

McGough, Roger See LIVERPOOL POETS.

McGrath, John (Peter) 1935– Playwright. *Events While Guarding the Bofors Gun* (1966) and *Bakke's Night of Fame* (1968) combine event-packed stories with a strong social message. Since 1971, when he founded the 7:84 Theatre Company (so called on the strength of an estimate that 7 per cent of Britain's population owned 84 per cent of its wealth), McGrath has written for the political fringe of the British theatre. Plays for the Scottish branch of 7:84 include *The Cheviot, the Stag and the Black, Black Oil* (1973), *Little Red Hen* (1975) and a trilogy of Scottish history plays concluding with *John Brown's Body* (1990). *Watching for Dolphins* (1991) is about an elderly revolutionary and *The Wicked Old Man* (1992) is a black FARCE.

McGuane, Thomas (Francis) 1939– American novelist. He was born in Michigan and educated at Michigan State University. Comic and energetic, his fiction is about the individual's attempt to find a workable set of values in the modern world. It includes *The Sporting Club* (1969), *The Bushwacked Piano* (1971), *Panama* (1978), *Nobody's Angel* (1979), *Something to be Desired* (1984) and *Nothing But Blue Skies* (1993). *Ninety-Two in the Shade* (1973) was filmed in 1975. *To Skin a Cat* (1986) is a volume of short stories. He has also written the screenplays for *Rancho Deluxe* (1973), *The Missouri Breaks* (1976) and *Tom Horn* (1980).

McGuckian, Medbh 1950– Poet. Born in Belfast and educated at Queen's University, she has taught English since 1975. Her first, slim collection, *Single Ladies: Sixteen Poems* (1980), was quickly followed by *Portrait of Joanna* (1980), *Trio Poetry* (1981) and her first major volume, *Flower Master* (1982), which signalled the future direction of her work in tapping the world of daydreams. *Venus and the Rain* (1984), *On Ballycastle Beach* (1988), *Two Women, Two Shores* (1989) and *Marconi's Cottage* (1992), consolidating her reputation as one of Ireland's foremost contemporary poets, have also emphasized her Celtic refusal to be intimidated by 'English' requirements for poetry. She chooses instead to concentrate on rich, complex and sometimes unashamedly obscure language.

Machen, Arthur (Llewellyn) 1863–1947 Novelist. Born in Caerleon, Monmouthshire, he was educated privately before moving to London in 1880. He was deeply influenced by and steeped in Welsh folklore, and worked for a time as a cataloguer of diabolistic and occult books. Later he joined the Order of the Golden Dawn, a group of theosophists involved in Cabbalistic magic, of which YEATS and Aleister Crowley also became members. After many years of neglect he joined the London *Evening News* in 1910 and was 'rediscovered', a process which culminated in the publication of the Caerleon Edition of his works in 1923.

He is chiefly remembered for his supernatural tales, of which the most notable are *The Great God Pan* (1894) and *The Hill of Dreams* (1907), about the aura of a terrifying past which surrounds a Roman fort. His other works include: translations of *The Heptameron* (1886) and *The Memoirs of Casanova* (1894); a volume of criticism, *Hieroglyphics* (1902); *Notes and Queries* (1926) and *Dreads and Drolls* (1926). *Far Off Things* (1922) and *Things Near and Far* (1923) were both autobiographical.

McIlvanney, William 1936– Scottish novelist, writer of DETECTIVE FICTION and poet. Born into a mining family at Kilmarnock, Ayrshire, he was educated at Kilmarnock Academy and read English at Glasgow University, becoming a teacher in 1960. The first of his prizewinning novels, *Remedy is None* (1966), tells how a student is confronted with his working-class origins through his father's death, and *A Gift from Nessus* (1968) is a strong tale of life crisis and marital breakdown. His reputation rests particularly on two novels examining the Scots tradition of the 'hard man': *Docherty* (1975), about an Ayshire miner in the early years of the century, and *The Big Man* (1985), about bare-knuckle fighting. *Laidlaw* (1978), *The Papers of Tony Veitch* (1983) and *Strange Loyalties* (1991) are equally tough and gritty detective novels. He has also published two books of poetry, *The Longships in Harbour* (1970) and *These Words: Weddings and After* (1984).

MacInnes, Colin 1914-76 Novelist and journalist. Son of the popular novelist Angela Thirkell and a descendant of RUDYARD KIPLING, he grew up in Australia, where his first novel, *June in Her Spring* (1952), is set. He is now remembered, and frequently idolized, for his 'London trilogy' of novels, which offer a vivid, jauntily enthusiastic and often prophetic evocation of a London just beginning to become multi-racial and develop, with the onset of popular music, a militant youth culture. The best of the three books, *City of Spades* (1957), explores London's nascent West Indian community and the alternate pleasures and crises of white–black race relations; *Absolute Beginners* (1959), while predominantly a celebration of youth and style, culminates in the Notting Hill race-riots of 1958. The third novel, *Mr Love and Justice* (1960), a morality fable about the relationship between a policeman and a pimp, is overly schematic. MacInnes is also notable for his essays, originally published in journals like *New Society* and subsequently collected in volumes such as *England, Half English* (1961), which apply incisive and iconoclastic cultural criticism to contemporary topics from the *Oz* pornography trial to cricket.

Mackay, Charles 1814-89 Scottish songwriter. Born in Perth, educated in London and Brussels, he was sub-editor of the Glasgow *Morning Chronicle*, editor of the Glasgow *Argus* and later of *The Illustrated London News*. He published several volumes of verse, beginning with *Songs and Poems* (1834). Many of his poems were set to music; it was said that 400,000 copies were sold of 'A Good Time Coming'. His daughter was the novelist MARIE CORELLI.

McKay, Claude 1890-1948 Black American poet and novelist. Born in Jamaica, he emigrated to the USA in 1912. His first two collections of poetry, *Songs of Jamaica* (1912) and *Spring in New Hampshire and Other Poems* (1920), attracted favourable critical attention, but it was not until *Harlem Shadows* (1922) that his popular reputation was established. His first

novel, *Home to Harlem* (1928), tells of a black soldier's return to the USA after serving in France. *Banjo: A Story without a Plot* (1929) is about a vagabond's life on the Marseilles waterfront. *Banana Bottom* (1933) examines the dilemma of a young black woman who has returned to Jamaica after an education in England, and explores the racial traditions and attitudes which make her readjustment a painful process. McKay's other publications include a collection of stories, *Gingertown* (1932); an autobiography, *A Long Way from Home* (1937); and a study of the black community, *Harlem* (1940). *Trial by Lynching: Stories about Negro Life in North America* was written in English but first appeared in Russian in 1925, and had to be translated back into English by Robert Winter in 1975.

MacKaye, Percy (Wallace) 1875-1956 American playwright. He was born in New York and educated at Harvard. His first play, *The Canterbury Pilgrims* (1903), was a blank verse drama about the Wife of Bath's amorous pursuit of CHAUCER. His later work includes *Jeanne d'Arc* (1906) and *Sappho and Phaon* (1907). His most successful play, *The Scarecrow*, was based on NATHANIEL HAWTHORNE's story 'Feathertop'. It was published in 1908, produced at the Harvard Dramatists' Club in 1909, and then opened at Garrick's Theatre in New York in 1911.

MacKaye also wrote about the theatre. *The Playhouse and the Play* (1909), *The Civic Theatre* (1912), and *Community Drama* (1917) all emphasize the communal functions of theatrical production. He wrote one community masque called *St Louis* (1914) for 7500 actors, and on the occasion of SHAKESPEARE's tercentenary wrote another, entitled *Caliban, by the Yellow Sands* (1916). His later work included an ambitious tetralogy of verse plays, *The Mystery of Hamlet, King of Denmark – or, What We Will* (1949), which depicts the major characters in *HAMLET* prior to that play's beginning.

Mackenzie, Sir (Edward Montague) Compton 1883-1972 Novelist. Educated at St Paul's School, London, and Magdalen College, Oxford, he studied law, but published *Poems* in 1907 and earned considerable praise with his first novels, *The Passionate Elopement* (1911) and *Carnival* (1912). The best of his many works include *Sinister Street* (2 vols., 1913-14), *Guy and Pauline* (1915), *Sylvia Scarlett* (1918), *Extraordinary Women* (1928), *Our Street* (1931), *The Four Winds of Love* (6 vols., 1937-45) and the well-known Scottish novels, *The Monarch of the Glen* (1941) and *Whisky Galore* (1947). He drew on his experience of serving in the Dardanelles during World War I for *Gallipoli Memories* (1929), *Athenian Memories* (1931) and *Greek Memories* (1932). His autobiography *My Life and Times* was issued in ten volumes in 1963-71.

Mackenzie, Henry 1745-1831 Novelist, playwright and man of letters. Mackenzie was an Edinburgh lawyer, born on the day Prince Charles Edward Stuart landed in Scotland, and educated at the High School and University of Edinburgh. In 1765 he went to London to further his law studies, and became Attorney for the Crown in Scotland and later Comptroller of Taxes. While in London he started his novel, THE MAN OF FEELING, published anonymously in 1771, about a man whose morality is too delicate for a harsh world. It was followed by *The Man of the World* (1773), about the selfish pursuit of happiness, and an EPISTOLARY NOVEL, *Julia de Roubigné* (1777). SIR WALTER SCOTT ranked him with STERNE as a practitioner of the SENTIMENTAL NOVEL.

Mackenzie's membership of an Edinburgh literary society led to his editing *The Mirror* (1779-80) and later *The Lounger* (1785-7). He also contributed to the Transactions of the Royal Society of Edinburgh and was one of the original members of the Highland Society. In 1792 he published tracts intended to calm the lower orders and prevent revolution. In 1793 he wrote *The Life of Dr Blacklock*. In 1805 a committee chaired by Mackenzie decided that JAMES MACPHERSON's *Ossian* was not the true Gaelic epic it claimed to be. In 1808 Mackenzie published his complete works, in eight volumes, including an unperformed tragedy, *The Spanish Father*, another tragedy, *The Prince of Tunis*, performed in Edinburgh (1763), and a comedy, *The White Hypocrite*, performed once at COVENT GARDEN. He was also the author of a political tract, *An Account of the Proceedings of the Parliament of 1784*, which brought him to the notice of Pitt. His *Anecdotes and Egotisms* were edited by his biographer, Harold William Thompson, in 1927. These jottings give a vivid picture of Edinburgh life, with gossip about the lordly and the famous, as observed by a civilized intelligence.

Mackenzie, Seaforth [Mackenzie, Kenneth Ivo] 1913-54 Australian novelist and poet. Born in Perth, Western Australia, he was a journalist and agricultural labourer. He published two novels, *The Young Desire It* (1937) and *Chosen People* (1938), and two volumes of poetry, *Our Earth* (1937) and *The Moonlit Doorway* (1944).

Mackintosh, Elizabeth 1897-1952 Author of DETECTIVE FICTION under the pseudonym of Josephine Tey and of plays and novels under the pseudonym of Gordon Daviot. Born in Inverness, she studied at the Royal Academy there and at the Anstey Physical Training College in Birmingham, going on to teach physical education in schools. Her first detective novel, *The Man in the Queue* (1929, first published as being by Gordon Daviot), introduced the genteel police detective Alan Grant who reappeared as the hero of *A Shilling for Candles* (1936), *To Love and be Wise* (1951), *The Daughter of Time* (1951) and *The Singing Sands* (1952). *Miss Pym Disposes* (1946), which used her background in physical education, *The Franchise Affair* (1948) and *Brat Farrar* (1949) belonged to no identifiable series. All enjoyed a reputation for their well-crafted stories, and the use of historical mysteries – an 18th-century *cause célèbre* in *The Franchise Affair* and the character of Richard III in *The Daughter of Time* – received high praise. Her career as Gordon Daviot showed the same interest in history, with *Richard of Bordeaux* (1932) and *Queen of Scots* (1934) among her best-known plays. Other work as Gordon Daviot included radio dramas and three novels, *Kif: An Unvarnished History* (1929), *The Expensive Halo* (1931) and *The Privateer* (1952).

Macklin, Charles 1699-1797 Irish actor and playwright. He was a notable figure in the London theatre from 1733 until his retirement in 1789. Of his ten plays, some are specifically about the stage, like *The New Play Criticized* (1747) and *Covent Garden Theatre* (1752), and all are clearly written from the viewpoint of an actor. *Love à-la-Mode* (1759) is a wittily satirical afterpiece, while *The True-Born Irishman* (1762) and *The Man of the World* (1781), a revised version of *The True-Born Scotsman* (1764), are comedies which provided Macklin with fine opportunities to act out and ridicule national characteristics.

Maclaren, Ian See KAILYARD SCHOOL.

MacLaverty, Bernard 1945- Irish novelist and short-story writer. Born in Belfast, MacLaverty took a degree in English at Queen's University. He left Ireland in the early 1970s to live on Islay, off the west coast of Scotland. His first book, *Secrets and Other Stories*, won a Scottish Arts Council award in 1977, as did the novel *Lamb* in 1980. *A Time to Dance and Other Stories* appeared in 1982, and the novel *Cal*, which deals directly with the political violence in Northern Ireland, was widely acclaimed on its publication in 1983. *Lamb* and *Cal* have been made into films.

Maclean, Sorley 1911- Gaelic poet. Born in Raasay, he graduated from Edinburgh University and became a schoolteacher, first in Edinburgh and later, as headmaster, in Plockton, Ross-shire. *Dain do Eimhir Agus Dain Eile* (1943), combining traditional and modern elements, had the effect of leading Gaelic poetry into the 20th century. It is chiefly a book of love poems, many written at the time of the Spanish Civil War and showing a clash between private needs and social responsibilities. Many of them reappeared in *Reothairt is Contraigh, Taghadh de Dhain 1932-72* (1977), rearranged in sections according to theme, with new work which included his most admired single poem, 'Hallaig', about a township depopulated at the time of the Highland Clearances. Later books are *Ris a' Bhruthaich* (1985), a collection of critical essays particularly concerned with the great 16th- and 17th-century Gaelic songs, and *From Wood to Ridge: Collected Poems in Gaelic and English* (1989). His work to promote the teaching of Gaelic in Scottish schools has done much to preserve the culture, history, poetry and song of the Gael.

MacLeish, Archibald 1892–1982 American poet and playwright. Born in Glencoe, Illinois, he graduated from Yale in 1915 and published his first book of poems, *Tower of Ivory*, in 1917. After serving in World War I he enrolled at Harvard and took a law degree. He practised briefly, but from 1923 to 1928 joined the group of Americans who had settled in Paris.

The early poetry in *The Happy Marriage* (1924), *The Pot of Earth* (1925), *Streets in the Moon* (1926) and *The Hamlet of A. MacLeish* (1928) was highly subjective and owed much to T. S. Eliot and Ezra Pound. *New Found Land* (1930) was written after his return to the USA. *Conquistador* (1932), an epic about the conquest of Mexico, was awarded the Pulitzer Prize in 1933. *Frescoes for Mr Rockefeller's City* appeared in 1933. He also wrote skilful and fluent verse plays: *Nobodaddy* (1926) and *Panic* (1935), which dealt with the Wall Street crash. *The Fall of the City* (1937), a denunciation of totalitarianism written for radio, reached a wide audience in the USA and England. *Air Raid* (1938) was also written for radio. His *Collected Poems* (1952) won him a second Pulitzer in 1953. Among his later works are three more verse plays: *The Trojan Horse* (for radio, 1952), reflecting the contemporary fear of Communist infiltration; *J. B.* (1958), about a modern Job, which brought him a third Pulitzer Prize in 1959; and *Herakles* (1967), which explores the conflict between human needs and reason and science.

Parallel with his career in letters, MacLeish led an active public and academic life. After editing *Fortune* from 1929 to 1938 he became Librarian of Congress (1939–44), Assistant Secretary of State (1944–5) and Boylston Professor of Rhetoric and Oratory at Harvard (1949–62). He also represented the USA in UNESCO.

MacLennan, (John) Hugh 1907–90 Canadian novelist and essayist. He was born at Glace Bay, Nova Scotia, and educated at Dalhousie University, Oxford and Princeton. He taught classics for some years, later becoming professor of English at McGill University (1967–79). His first (and best-known) novels, *Barometer Rising* (1941) and *Two Solitudes* (1945), employed a blend of realism and symbolism to examine perceptions of Canadian identity in the early 20th century. Other works are *The Precipice* (1948), *Each Man's Son* (1951), *The Watch That Ends the Night* (1959), *Return of the Sphinx* (1967) and *Voices in Time* (1981). An accomplished essayist, MacLennan frequently includes lengthy asides of didactic exposition and description in his novels. His work argues for a view of civilization in which classical humanist and contemporary materialist values are brought together.

MacLeod, Alistair 1936– Canadian short-story writer. Born in North Battleford, Saskatchewan, he lived in Alberta and Cape Breton, working as a miner and logger before attending St Francis Xavier University, Antigonish, the University of New Brunswick and Notre Dame University. He taught at the University of Indiana but returned to Canada as professor of English and creative writing at the University of Windsor. He is a meticulous stylist whose entire fictional *oeuvre* consists of less than 20 stories, collected in *The Lost Salt Gift of Blood* (1976) and *As Birds Bring Forth the Sun* (1986). A British collection, also called *The Lost Salt Gift of Blood* (1991), includes virtually all his best work. It deals almost exclusively with the fishermen, miners and farmers of Cape Breton, probing family relationships and examining the community's Celtic heritage. Mostly written in the first person, the stories often use the perspective of a narrator who has 'gone east' in adult life and now looks back at the rural world of his childhood, contrasting its elemental vitality and harshness with the comfortable lifestyle of his present-day existence.

Macleod, Fiona See Sharp, William.

McLuhan, (Herbert) Marshall 1911–80 Canadian critic and media theorist. Born in Edmonton and converted to Catholicism in the 1930s, he was educated at the Universities of Manitoba and Cambridge. He returned to Canada in 1944 and from 1946 taught at the University of Toronto, becoming director of its Centre for Culture and Technology in 1963. His first major work, *The Mechanical Bride: Folklore of Industrial Man* (1951), analyses how mass media affect consciousness, but it was *The Gutenberg Galaxy: The Making of Typographical Man* (1962) and *Understanding Media: The Extensions of Man* (1964) which made his name a household word in the 1960s. They explore various aspects of his famous aphorism, 'the medium is the message', *The Gutenberg Galaxy* by discussing the changes in culture and consciousness brought about by the spread of print technology, *Understanding Media* by dealing with the effect of electronic media. The form of McLuhan's books reflects their content by employing a mélange of elements drawn from various print and visual media. Other works include *The Medium is the Massage* [sic] (1967), *Peace and War in the Global Village* (1968), *The Interior Landscape: The Literary Criticism of Marshall McLuhan* (1969), *Culture is Our Business* (1970) and *The City as Classroom* (1977).

McNally, Terrence 1939– American playwright. Born in St Petersburg, Florida, he attended Columbia University. He began by expressing the outraged, turbulent mood of the late 1960s and early 1970s, but has since developed a more lyrical and positive style, offering unsentimental hope for intimacy in a time when fear and death rule. His plays include *And Things That Go Bump in the Night* (1964), *Where Has Tommy Flowers Gone?* (1971), *The Ritz* (1975), *Broadway* (1979), *It's Only a Play* (1982), *The Lisbon Traviata* (1985), *Frankie and Johnny in the Clair de Lune* (1987) and *Lips Together, Teeth Apart* (1991). He has also written for television and radio.

MacNeice, (Frederick) Louis 1907–63 Poet. The son of a Church of Ireland rector, he was born in Carrickfergus and schooled in England, first at Sherborne then at Marlborough. His Irish background – Northern by birth, Southern by parentage – was a lasting source of anger and pleasure to him. He read Greats at Merton College, Oxford, emerging with a first and a collection of poems, *Blind Fireworks* (1929). Teaching classics at Birmingham University, and later at Bedford College, London, did not engage him: he was writing a pseudonymous novel (*Roundabout Way*, 1932), critical essays (notably *Modern Poetry*, 1938), plays for the Group Theatre, and a widely praised translation of *The Agamemnon of Aeschylus* (1936). He also published *Poems* (1935), *Letters from Iceland* (with AUDEN; 1937), *The Earth Compels* (1938) and *Autumn Journal* (1938), superbly capturing the mood of the Munich weeks. It is a brilliant epitome of his own characterization of the poet as 'able-bodied, fond of talking, a reader of the newspapers, capable of pity and laughter, appreciative of women, susceptible to physical impressions' – a description that indicated his affinities with YEATS (see his 1941 study of the poet). From 1941 until his death he worked for BBC radio, writing dozens of feature programmes and plays, notably *Christopher Columbus* (1944) and *The Dark Tower* (1947). With a few exceptions, the radio work encouraged his tendency towards a fluent superficiality, what he called 'bloom or frill or floating image'. His poems of the 1940s and early 1950s are discursive, but he felt he had returned to 'syntax and bony feature' in his shorter lyrics. With *Solstices* (1961) and *The Burning Perch* (1963) his work achieved a taut intensity reaching beyond one man's experience to attain at times the resonance of myth and dreams. He has always been linked with Auden, DAY-LEWIS and SPENDER under the 'Macspaunday' umbrella, which does his work a disservice: his detachment can be defensive but also freed him from their need to recant. His debonair professionalism as a poet often disguises the pervasive sense of loss in the poems: loss of faith, of love, of belonging to one country. As a love poet, a poet of urban rhythms and delights, as a reporter

with an educated and sensuous intelligence, his reputation stands very high. His unfinished autobiography, *The Strings are False*, was published in 1965, his *Collected Poems* in 1966, and a volume of *Selected Literary Criticism* in 1987.

McNickle, D'Arcy 1904–77 American novelist. A half-blood Indian of the Flathead (or Salish) tribe, he was educated at the University of Montana and then at Oxford and Grenoble. His first novel, *The Surrounded* (1936), is about a youth facing an identity crisis: half Flathead Indian and half Spanish, he is torn between the two cultures. *Runner in the Sun: A Story of Indian Maize* (1954) is a novel for young people. His last novel, *Wind from an Enemy Sky*, published the year after his death, deals with the conflicts between Indian and non-Indian cultures. He also wrote *Indian Man: A Life of Oliver LaFarge* (1971), as well as several histories: *They Came Here First* (1949), *The Indian Tribes of the United States* (1962), *Native American Tribalism* (1973), and, with Harold E. Fey, *Indians and Other Americans* (1970).

Macpherson, James 1736–96 Scottish poet and translator. Born a farmer's son at Ruthven in Inverness, he studied at Marischal College in Aberdeen and at Edinburgh University before becoming a teacher. In 1758 he published *The Highlander*, a poem in HEROIC COUPLETS. Macpherson's knowledge of Gaelic poetry prompted the dramatist JOHN HOME to suggest he undertake some translations. *Fragments of Ancient Poetry Collected in the Highlands of Scotland and Translated from the Gaelic or Erse Language* (1760) was warmly received by JAMES BEATTIE, Hugh Blair, ADAM FERGUSON, WILLIAM ROBERTSON and the rest of Edinburgh literary society. Its preface spoke of a Gaelic epic which, given support and encouragement, Macpherson could recover for literature. The necessary money was found and he published the result of his labours as *Fingal: An Ancient Poem* (1762), closely followed by *Temora: An Ancient Epic Poem* (1763). A collection attributing the originals to Ossian, a legendary Gaelic bard, appeared in 1765.

Some critics were sceptical of the Ossianic poems. SAMUEL JOHNSON and DAVID HUME challenged their authenticity, and doubts were strengthened by Macpherson's failure to produce the originals. After his death a committee of inquiry headed by the novelist HENRY MACKENZIE concluded that he had treated the Gaelic poems in a free and selective fashion, adding much verse of his own invention. But such considerations did not check the enormous success and the wide influence of Macpherson's Ossianic poems. Their popularity spread beyond Britain to include Napoleon, Goethe and Herder among admirers. By turning attention to wild nature, the mythic past and folk culture, the poems played a crucial role in the emergence of ROMANTICISM and, in particular, of the CELTIC REVIVAL.

After his Ossianic poems, Macpherson published mainly historical works: *An Introduction to the History of Great Britain and Ireland* (1771); *The History of Great Britain from the Restoration to the Accession of the House of Hanover* (1775); and *Original Papers: Containing the Secret History of Great Britain from the Restoration to the Accession of the House of Hanover* (also 1775), for which he was paid £3000. A prose version of the *Iliad* appeared in 1773. Macpherson entered Parliament in 1780, acquired the estate of Belville in Inverness, where he died, and was buried in Westminster Abbey.

Macpherson, Jay 1931– Canadian poet. Born in Britain, she went to Canada at the age of nine. She was an undergraduate in Ottawa and took her MA and PhD at the University of Toronto during the 1950s and early 1960s. She is a professor of English at Victoria College, Toronto. Her first poems were published in 1949 and as a graduate student she was the publisher of a Canadian poetry series, Emblem Books, which included the work of DOROTHY LIVESAY, ALDEN NOWLAN and AL PURDY. *Nineteen Poems* (1952) and *O Earth Return* (1954) were collected in her poetic cycle, *The Boatman* (1957), which won a Governor General's award for poetry. This was expanded by another collection, *Welcoming Disaster* (1974), and republished as *Poems Twice Told* (1981). Her concentrated, allusive lyrics swing confidently within the tradition of English poetry, supplemented by the oral tradition of BALLAD and nursery rhyme. Her fascination with biblical and classical myth and its continuities as realized through the poetic imagination suggests her double affinities with European MODERNISM and the Canadian mythopoeic tradition exemplified by NORTHROP FRYE. Her idiosyncratic voice with its elusive mixture of the comic and the sinister and its evocation of duplicitous female archetypes has been an important influence on contemporary Canadian poets, especially MARGARET ATWOOD. Macpherson's Canadianness is eclectic, and her imaginative response to landscape finds its overt expression not in her poetry but in her scholarly study, *The Spirit of Solitude: Conventions and Continuities in Late Romance* (1982), which in its epilogue explores Canadian PASTORAL with the same subtle sense of transformations to be found in her poetry.

McTeague: *A Story of San Francisco* A novel by FRANK NORRIS, published in 1899. McTeague (Mac) practises dentistry, though he has never attended dental college or obtained a licence. He is a bear-like man who appreciates little beyond the physical pleasures of eating, drinking and smoking. When his friend Marcus Schouler brings Trina Sieppe to have her tooth fixed, Mac experiences another physical desire – the sexual – which he accommodates by courting and marrying her.

Shortly before the wedding Trina learns that she has won $5000 in a lottery. Marcus, who had previously entertained notions of marrying Trina himself, now becomes jealous of Mac's good fortune. The newlyweds live happily enough for a while, though Trina becomes miserly. The tension between Mac and Marcus erupts at a picnic; they wrestle like animals, and Mac breaks Marcus's arm. Marcus takes his revenge by informing on Mac that he is practising dentistry without a licence. Forced to give up his trade, Mac works for a while making dental instruments. When he loses that job also, he has to get money for tobacco, beer and food from Trina, who jealously guards her hoard. Theirs is now a sado-masochistic relationship: Mac beats Trina or bites her fingers to get her to give him the money, and she takes a perverse pleasure in this treatment. Eventually, he beats her to death and runs off with her hoard of gold coins.

He flees to the gold mines in the hills where he grew up, but is easily recognizable because he takes his canary and its gold cage with him. Having abandoned his job in a mine, he encounters a prospector and together they discover a rich vein of gold, but he senses that he is being pursued and moves on towards Death Valley. Marcus, who has joined the posse searching for him, tracks him down there. They fight and Mac kills him, but not before Marcus has handcuffed himself to Mac. The novel ends with him handcuffed to the corpse, still with his canary but without water.

Madame Delphine A short novel by GEORGE WASHINGTON CABLE, published in 1881, which tells the story of Delphine Carraze, a quadroon, who lives in 19th-century New Orleans with her daughter Olive. Olive's father, who was white, had left his wife and daughter his property when he died, which was against Louisiana law. Olive falls in love with the banker Ursin Lemaitre, a white man who associates with the pirate Jean Lafitte. A marriage is arranged through Père Jerome, but Lemaitre's affairs come under investigation and he goes into hiding. His friends seize the opportunity to break off what they regard as his disastrous commitment to the daughter of the quadroon. Madame Delphine then declares that Olive is not her daughter, but rather a white woman's child she was given to foster. The marriage takes place. The story ends as Madame Delphine confesses to Père Jerome that she lied for her daughter's sake; she dies as the priest grants her absolution.

Madge, Charles (Henry) 1912– Poet and sociologist. Born in Johannesburg, he was educated at Winchester and Magdalene College, Cambridge, and worked as a reporter for *The Daily Mirror* in 1935–6. With Humphrey Jennings he founded Mass Observation in 1937. After social and economic research and planning during World War II, he became a social development officer (1947–50) and then professor of sociology at Birmingham University (1950–70). A Marxist influenced by both AUDEN and surrealism, he produced two notable collections of poetry, *The Disappearing Castle* (1937) and *The Father Found* (1941). Some of his prose-poems, such as 'Bourgeois News', and longer lyrics, such as 'The Storming of the Brain', are imaginatively original. He has published a number of sociological studies, including Mass Observation surveys and *Inner City Poverty in Paris and London* (with P. Willmott; 1981).

***Maggie:** A Girl of the Streets* A novel by STEPHEN CRANE, privately printed in 1893 under the pseudonym Johnston Smith and entitled *A Girl of the Streets*. A pioneer work of American NATURALISM, it describes the sordid and almost hopeless existence of Maggie Johnson in the Bowery area of New York. She and her brothers are alternately neglected and abused by their drunkard parents, and her baby brother Tommie dies as a result of maltreatment. Her other brother, Jimmie, grows up to be a truck driver, but like his parents he is coarse, cynical, and drinks too much. Her father dies and her mother becomes known to the police for her frequent bouts of drunkenness. Maggie, who dreams of a better life, works in a collar-and-cuff factory and falls in love with a bartender friend of her brother's called Pete. After he seduces and abandons her, her mother and brother disown her. She tries to survive by becoming a prostitute, but eventually drowns herself.

magic realism The exact provenance of the term is disputed, but it probably originated in the question posed by the Cuban novelist Alejo Carpentier: 'What is the story of Latin America if not a chronicle of the marvellous in the real?' It was first employed as a literary definition by the American critic Alastair Reid, and referred then to the large body of spectacular, fantastic fiction produced in South American countries after World War II. This powerful and fecund outpouring of a nascent literary autonomy paralleled such nations' newly-won political independence, and came to be known as 'el boum'. Major exponents of 'lo real maravilloso' included Miguel Angel Asturias, Alejo Carpentier, Carlos Fuentes, Julio Cortázar, Mario Vargas Llosa and Gabriel Garcia Márquez, whose novel *One Hundred Years of Solitude* (trans. G. Rabassa; 1970) is generally regarded as the paradigm of magic realism.

Essentially a manifestation of POST-MODERNISM, the genre is characterized by the juxtaposition of apparently reliable, realistic reportage and extravagant fantasy: Márquez's novel will at one moment narrate the building of a new banana-processing plant, at another describe a woman visibly ascending to heaven. While there is a certain inscrutable playfulness to

magic realism (Márquez is recorded as proposing that 'you can get people to believe anything if you tell it convincingly enough'), its method was first conceived, more importantly, as a response to the nature of South American reality. In countries previously ruled despotically as colonies and subsequently negotiating independence with no long-established institutions or freedoms, the fact that information can easily be manipulated or even commandeered by power groups makes truth a far more provisional, relative entity. Magic realism both mimics and exploits this phenomenon through its own merging of realism and fantasy. Indeed, the genre's further assumption – demonstrated well in Márquez's later fable about the responsibility for a mysterious crime, *Chronicle of a Death Foretold* (trans. G. Rabassa; 1982) – is that truth is best viewed as a communal, collaborative construct, rather than as residing in the integrity of individual perceptions, whose authority tends merely to that of caprice and rumour. Such emphasis, implying the limitation of individual responsibility and the quixotic unpredictability of fate, makes magic realism an essentially comic genre.

Magic realism has since been identified in other literatures, such as in the work of the Czech novelist Milan Kundera, and the Italian Italo Calvino. The principal examples in British fiction are the novels of the Anglo-Indian writer SALMAN RUSHDIE. In Kundera's *The Book of Laughter and Forgetting* (trans. M. H. Heim; 1982) and *The Unbearable Lightness of Being* (trans. M. H. Heim; 1984), or Rushdie's MIDNIGHT'S CHILDREN (1981) and *Shame* (1983), the authors use magic realism for sharp political SATIRE in protest at the restrictions placed on information and truth after the Prague Spring or during India's 1977 Emergency, but also for wilful tall-story-telling, in a celebration of the imaginative freedom available in writing.

In the European tradition, it is possible to see Rabelais and Kafka as precursors of the magic realist idiom, while Rushdie's work points back through the English novel to STERNE's *TRISTRAM SHANDY*, KIPLING's *KIM* and the major novels of DICKENS. Other examples of magic realism in recent fiction are GRAHAM SWIFT's novel *Waterland* (1983), ANGELA CARTER's *Nights at the Circus* (1984) and the Australian writer PETER CAREY's *Illywhacker* (1985).

Maginn, William 1793–1842 Journalist. Born in Cork, he attended Trinity College, Dublin, and worked as a schoolmaster before joining the staff of *BLACKWOOD'S EDINBURGH MAGAZINE* to form one of a gifted trio with JOHN GIBSON LOCKHART and JOHN WILSON. He is believed to have suggested the idea for the *NOCTES AMBROSIANAE* dialogues which became so popular a feature of *Blackwood's*. His own contributions to the journal were under the pseudonym of Ensign O'Doherty. A lively and witty journalist, Maginn went to London in 1823 and in 1830 helped

Hugh Fraser to launch *FRASER'S MAGAZINE*, in which his *Homeric Ballads* and *Illustrious Literary Characters* appeared. He was the model for Captain Shandon in THACKERAY's *THE HISTORY OF PENDENNIS*.

Magnalia Christi Americana COTTON MATHER's ecclesiastical history of New England, *The Great Works of Christ in America*, was published in London in 1702. Mather began planning his history in 1693 and worked on it throughout the 1690s, during which time some chapters were published separately. It is divided into seven parts: a history of New England's settlement; biographies of governors; biographies of ministers; a history of Harvard College, including biographies of eminent graduates; a description of New England church practices; a collection of instances of special providences in New England; and an account of New England's 'Wars of the Lord', or conflicts with heretics, Indians, and other 'subversives'. Mather's General Introduction, with its Virgilian echoes, announces his epic subject: the work is intended to be a comprehensive and (especially for its European audience) celebratory account, a vision of a providentially guided, Christian New England. Mather consulted and cited numerous original documents for he had access to the papers of many of the actors in his history; as such, the *Magnalia* is a doubly valuable historical document.

Magnyficence A MORALITY PLAY by JOHN SKELTON, first published in 1530 but probably performed in *c.* 1516. It owes something to Skelton's experience as tutor to the future Henry VIII and more to his perception of himself as *orator regius*. The central character, tempted by such characters as Cloaked Collusion and Crafty Conveyance, must learn from Adversity, Poverty and Despair to trust more in the advice of Sad Circumspection and Perseverance how best to regulate both himself and those who depend on him. The play is very long and too infrequently relieved by lively encounters.

Mahapatra, Jayanta 1928– Indian poet. He was born in Cuttack, Orissa, and has lived there all his life, working as a teacher of physics. He writes both in English and Oriya, but it is as an outstanding writer in English that he has received international recognition. His best collections of poetry include *A Rain of Rites* (1976), *Waiting* (1979), *The False Start* (1980), *Relationship* (1980), *Life Signs* (1983) and *Burden of Waves and Fruit* (1988). His poems are wide-ranging in style but all have a close response to the landscape and smells of Mahapatra's part of India.

Mahon, Derek 1941– Irish poet. Born in Belfast, he was educated at the Royal Belfast Academical Institution and Trinity College, Dublin, graduating in 1965. He has worked as a schoolteacher, a journalist, scriptwriter and reviewer. He was Visiting Writer at the New University of Ulster at Coleraine in 1977 and held the same position in Trinity College, Dublin, in 1985–6. He now lives in County Cork.

Mahon first came to prominence as one of the leading members of the 'Northern Poets', along with SEAMUS HEANEY and MICHAEL LONGLEY, in Belfast in the 1960s. Urban and urbane, his poetry is deeply influenced by LOUIS MACNEICE, although perhaps stricter in its formality and bleaker in its implications than MacNeice's work. The Northern Irish crisis has deepened its native sense of estrangement and doom, goading him to question the relationship between poetry and public troubles. His chief collections are *Night-Crossing* (1968), *Lives* (1972) and *The Snow Party* (1975), gathered with revisions in *Poems 1962–1978* (1979), and *The Hunt by Night* (1982), *Antarctica* (1985) and *Selected Poems* (1991). His translations include Molière's *The School for Wives* (1986), *The Selected Poems of Philippe Jacottet* (1988) and *The Bacchae of Euripides* (1991).

Mahony, Francis Sylvester 1804–62 Poet under the pseudonym of 'Father Prout'. Born in County Cork, Ireland, he was educated at Jesuit centres in Amiens, Paris and Rome. A scandal at Clongoweswood, Ireland, where he had a teaching position, forced his resignation. However, he eventually acquired priestly orders and briefly exercised spiritual functions in London. In the 1830s a friendship with WILLIAM MAGINN led to contributions to *FRASER'S MAGAZINE*, the most famous being *The Reliques of Father Prout*, a pot-pourri of writings about the life of a parish priest interspersed with literary dialogues, verse translations, prose and the supposed discovery of original stanzas in French, Latin and Greek of the songs and verses of such popular melodists as THOMAS MOORE – all showing the quirky, capricious nature of Father Prout's gifts. Witty, well-informed classically, a literary jester who once described himself as 'an Irish potato seasoned with Attic salt', Father Prout had a sentimental side as well. His last years were passed in Paris as correspondent for *The Globe*. This eccentric man is perhaps best remembered for his poem 'The Bells of Shandon'.

Mahy, Margaret 1936– New Zealand writer of CHILDREN's LITERATURE. Born in Whakatane and educated at the University of Auckland, she worked in the School Library Service before turning to writing. Starting with picture-books, she created a series of improbable eccentrics who battle with pirates, thieves and wild animals, as well as traditional fairy-tale villains like witches, wizards and dragons. Refreshingly, the young heroines are as tough and resourceful as their male counterparts. Her stories for older readers, vividly original in their language and plotting, combine fantasy and magic with psychological realism. In

The Haunting (1982) a shy young boy has to coexist with the real world and the ghosts which continue to haunt him. *The Changeover* (1985) describes how a schoolboy becomes supernaturally possessed.

Maid Marian A novel by THOMAS LOVE PEACOCK, published in 1822. In contrast to his earlier novels, it uses the framework of historical romance, introducing the characters of ROBIN HOOD and Richard I into a SATIRE of oppression and extreme doctrines of social order. Coming hard on the heels of SIR WALTER SCOTT's *IVANHOE* (1819), which had introduced Robin Hood as Robin of Locksley, Peacock's novel confirmed the Romantics' interest in the legendary outlaw and contributed much to his present image in popular culture.

Maid's Tragedy, The A tragedy by BEAUMONT and FLETCHER, performed by the KING'S MEN in c. 1610 and published in 1619. It is a sensational piece, bordering in at least one scene on the pornographic.

Amintor, betrothed to the Lord Chamberlain's daughter Aspatia, is ordered by the king to marry Evadne, sister of Amintor's friend Melantius. On the wedding night, Evadne reveals to Amintor that she is the king's mistress. Shattered but loyal, Amintor conceals the fact, but Melantius discovers the truth, compels Evadne to kill the king and takes possession of the citadel. The rejected Aspatia, disguised as her own brother, provokes Amintor into killing her in a duel. With the king dead, Evadne hopes to persuade Amintor to accept her. When he refuses, she kills herself, as does Amintor on discovering that he has killed Aspatia. Melantius, who has himself contemplated suicide, is pardoned by the new king.

Mailer, Norman 1923– American novelist and journalist. He was born in Long Branch, New Jersey, raised in Brooklyn, and educated at Harvard. His war service in the Pacific provided the basis for *THE NAKED AND THE DEAD* (1948), an uncompromisingly harsh war novel which also makes bitter commentary on American society. The book made Mailer famous on both sides of the Atlantic. His critical view of society also informed *Barbary Shore* (1951) and *The Deer Park* (1955; dramatized in 1967). *Advertisements for Myself* (1959) is a collection of stories and essays linked by autobiographical sketches. He excels at what has been called 'the new journalism', a form which he helped to create, taking actual events and submitting them to imaginative transformation. In this mode he registered changes in the American sensibility in *An American Dream* (1965), *Why are We in Vietnam?* (1967) and *Armies of the Night* (1968). The last of these, sub-titled 'History as a Novel, The Novel as History', takes the 1967 protest march on the Pentagon as its subject; it won a National Book Award and a PULITZER PRIZE in 1969. Subsequent non-fiction – loquacious, foregrounding its author as a quizzical protagonist and always alive to the mythical possibilities of its subjects – includes *Miami and the Siege of Chicago* (1969), *Of a Fire on the Moon* (about the Apollo 11 moon landing; 1969), *The Prisoner of Sex* (1971), *Marilyn: A Biography* (a study of Marilyn Monroe; 1973) and *The Fight* (1975), about Muhammad Ali's recapture of the heavyweight boxing championship of the world in Zaire. *The Executioner's Song* (1979, Pulitzer Prize), recreates events surrounding the execution of the murderer Gary Gilmore. Though versatile, his later fiction has found less favour. *Ancient Evenings* (1983) is an intractably esoteric disquisition on ancient Egypt, *Tough Guys Don't Dance* (1984) a routine thriller and *Harlot's Ghost* (1991) a byzantine conspiracy narrative about the CIA.

Main Street A novel by SINCLAIR LEWIS, published in 1920, and his first great success. Carol Milford, after working as a librarian in St Paul for three years, marries Dr Will Kennicott and moves to the small town of Gopher Prairie, Minnesota. She attempts to start an experimental theatre and a discussion group on the appreciation of poetry, but meets only resistance and is finally ostracized by the residents. Her growing sense of discontent is exacerbated by her unsophisticated husband. The story ends with her abandonment of her progressive aspirations and her submission to the complacent values of the small Midwestern town.

Main-Travelled Roads A collection of short stories by HAMLIN GARLAND, it comprised just six stories when it first appeared in 1891. Three more were added to the 1899 edition, and a further two to the final edition of 1922. All of them depict life in the rural Midwest as something drab and monotonous which crushes the spirit out of many of those who live it. 'Under the Lion's Paw', one of the original six stories, is a naturalistic tale about the economic survival of the fittest, or (as the narrator makes clear) of the most ruthless. In 'Up the Coulee' an actor returns to the Midwestern farm where he grew up, and sees with fresh eyes the brutality of the life his family leads. Contrasted with the harshness and squalid poverty are the 'silent heroism' of some of the characters and the panoramic beauty of the prairies.

Mais, Roger 1905–55 Jamaican novelist. Born in the Blue Mountains area and variously employed after leaving school, he was politically awakened by the Kingston riots of 1938. All his writings concentrate on what he called 'the dreadful condition of the working classes'. Social-realist accounts of human despair in the Kingston slums thus characterize his collections, *Face and Other Stores* (1942) and *And Most of All Man* (1943), and the novels, *The Hills were Joyful Together* (1953) and *Brother Man* (1954);

without ideological compromise, the more fluid, non-realist *Black Lightning* (1955) suggests that poverty and suffering do not totally preclude fulfilment.

Maitland, Sir Richard 1496–1586 Scottish lawyer, statesman and poet. Maitland studied at St Andrews and Paris, served under James V and was Keeper of the Great Seal to Mary Queen of Scots (1562-7). He collected examples of Scottish poetry in the Maitland Folio (begun *c*. 1570), continued by his daughter in the Maitland Quarto. These collections, second in importance only to those made by GEORGE BANNATYNE, contain Maitland's own poems (mainly SATIRE and reflections on the disturbed state of Scotland) as well as poems by WILLIAM DUNBAR, GAVIN DOUGLAS and ROBERT HENRYSON. The manuscripts passed into several hands, including those of PEPYS, and are now in Magdalene College, Cambridge. A selection was printed in 1786.

Maja-Pearce, Adewale 1953– Nigerian/British essayist and editor. Born of Nigerian parents in London, he received his BA from University College, Swansea, in 1975 and his doctorate from the School of African and Oriental Studies at the University of London in 1986. He works as a consultant for Heinemann Educational Books in Oxford. As well as editing the *Collected Poems* of CHRISTOPHER OKIGBO (1986), he has published two collections of extended essays, *In My Father's Country: A Nigerian Journey* (1987), exploring his double identity as Nigerian and Englishman, and *How Many Miles to Babylon?* (1989).

Major Barbara A play by GEORGE BERNARD SHAW, first performed at the ROYAL COURT THEATRE in 1905.

Major Barbara, daughter of the armaments manufacturer Andrew Undershaft, has joined the Salvation Army in revolt against her father's profession. Quite as much a rebel as Barbara against the conventions of society (represented by his wife and son), Undershaft weakens her faith, not only by argument, but also by showing her the model conditions in which his workers live. Barbara is forced to realize that her own fight against poverty is less successful than her father's.

Makculloch manuscript One of the earliest Scottish manuscripts extant, containing readings of three poems by ROBERT HENRYSON and one by WILLIAM DUNBAR. It was written in 1477 in Louvain by Magnus Makculloch.

Malamud, Bernard 1914–86 American novelist. The son of immigrant Russian parents, he was born and educated in New York. His first novel, *The Natural* (1952), deals with baseball as a realm of American heroism and myth. *The Assistant* (1957) is about a poor New York Jewish shopkeeper who takes on a delinquent Italian-American youth as a helper; the young man comes to look on his employer as a father, but the powerful emotional bonds between them are complicated by cultural barriers. His next novels, *A New Life* (1961), *The Fixer* (1966) and *Pictures of Fidelman* (1969), all explore aspects of the personal struggle involved in the Jewish experience. *The Fixer*, the story of a Russian Jew falsely accused of murder, won the National Book Award and a PULITZER PRIZE. Later novels are *The Tenants* (1971), *Dubin's Lives* (1979) and *God's Grace* (1982). Malamud's short stories are collected in *The Magic Barrel* (1958), *Idiots First* (1963) and *Rembrandt's Hat* (1973).

Malcontent, The A tragicomedy by JOHN MARSTON, commonly regarded as his most accomplished play. It was published (with revisions probably by JOHN WEBSTER) and performed (with RICHARD BURBAGE as Altofronto/Malevole) in 1604, but may originally have been produced a few years earlier.

Altofronto, Duke of Genoa, has lost his throne to the usurper, Pietro, but has returned to court disguised as Malevole, a philosopher–buffoon licensed to speak his mind. His ally in the deception is Mendoza, Pietro's first minister. But Mendoza is an ambitious rogue, who has seduced Pietro's willing wife Aurelia and now has his eyes on Altofronto/Malevole's wife Maria. Malevole warns Pietro that Mendoza is plotting against him and persuades him to go into hiding. He then announces that Pietro is dead. Mendoza seizes the throne, banishes Aurelia and plans to rid himself of Malevole. The usurped Duke outwits Mendoza by revealing himself to Pietro in his true guise as Altofronto, and Mendoza's duplicity is exposed during a ball at the ducal palace.

Malet, Lucas [Kingsley, Mary] 1852–1931 Novelist. Mary Kingsley was the daughter of CHARLES KINGSLEY. Among her novels, *The Wages of Sin* (1891) and *The History of Sir Richard Calmady* (1901) were highly popular.

Mallet, David *c*. 1705–65 Poet. A Scot who went to London and anglicized his name from 'Malloch', he succeeded in gaining entrance to ALEXANDER POPE's circle. He collaborated with JAMES THOMSON on a MASQUE, *Alfred* (1740), which is now remembered only for 'Rule Britannia', in fact contributed by Thomson but claimed by Mallet. Mallet himself is remembered for *William and Margaret* (1724), a forerunner of Gothic and Romantic verse in which Margaret's ghost visits the faithless William and induces him to join her in death. It was developed from the fragment of an old BALLAD, 'Margaret's Ghost', which was later included in THOMAS PERCY's *Reliques of Ancient English Poetry*. Mallet was also literary executor to HENRY ST JOHN, VISCOUNT BOLINGBROKE.

Mallock, W(illiam) H(urrell) 1849–1923 Conservative thinker. The nephew of J. A. FROUDE and RICHARD HURRELL FROUDE, he was born at Cheriton Bishop in Devon and educated at Balliol College, Oxford, where he won the Newdigate Prize for Poetry. His output of essays, political studies, poetry and fiction was united by his defence of traditional values against liberal theology, the progress of science and new political ideologies. He is chiefly remembered for two satirical works which, in a manner reminiscent of THOMAS LOVE PEACOCK, bring together fictional characters based on famous contemporaries to debate the issues of the day. *The New Republic: or, Culture, Faith, and Philosophy in an English Country House* (1877) pits the views of RUSKIN, with which Mallock sympathized, against those of T. H. HUXLEY, BENJAMIN JOWETT, MATTHEW ARNOLD and WALTER PATER. *The New Paul and Virginia: or, Positivism on an Island* (1878–9) – its title referring to Bernardin de Saint-Pierre's novel *Paul et Virginie* (1787) – takes Huxley, JOHN TYNDALL, FREDERIC HARRISON and HARRIET MARTINEAU as its particular targets.

Malone, Edmond 1741–1812 Scholar. Born in Dublin and educated at Trinity College, he entered the Middle Temple in 1763. He met JOHNSON, who became a lifelong friend, in 1765. GEORGE STEEVENS, who gave him early encouragement, later dropped him. Malone spent some years on the Continent and back in Ireland before inheriting sufficient money to be able to settle in London in 1776. He then moved in high literary circles. He was a friend of REYNOLDS, who had painted him in 1774 and whose writings he was to publish with a biographical memoir in 1797; of BURKE, who dedicated his *REFLECTIONS ON THE REVOLUTION IN FRANCE* to him; and of HORACE WALPOLE. He published an edition of GOLDSMITH in 1780.

Malone was devoted to the methodical study of SHAKESPEARE. His *An Attempt to Ascertain the Order in Which the Plays of Shakespeare were Written* was published by Steevens in the second volume of his own edition of Shakespeare in 1778. In 1780 Malone published a two-volume *Supplement* to the Johnson-Steevens edition of 1778, with the first critical edition of SHAKESPEARE's SONNETS together with editions of the poems and items from the SHAKESPEARE APOCRYPHA. He added two appendixes to his *Supplement* (1783) and new annotations to Isaac Reed's third edition of the Johnson–Steevens *Shakespeare* (1785). A dispute about these annotations led to a break with Steevens. Meanwhile, Malone was at work on his great edition of Shakespeare, which appeared in 10 volumes (or 11, since the first volume is in two parts) in 1790. It is important bibliographically and for its abundance of information about Shakespeare's life and the theatre of his time. Its 'Historical Account of the English Stage'

laid the foundations of English stage history.

Shakespeare did not monopolize Malone's efforts. He played an important part in exposing the forgeries of THOMAS CHATTERTON and, later, WILLIAM HENRY IRELAND. In 1785 he assisted BOSWELL with *THE JOURNAL OF A TOUR TO THE HEBRIDES* and over the following six years he helped with the preparation of *THE LIFE OF SAMUEL JOHNSON*, later editing it from its third (1799) to its sixth (1811) edition.

Despite the information he had amassed in his earlier work, Malone had still not produced the biography of Shakespeare which EDWARD CAPELL had longed for. He resumed research in 1793, but found himself diverted by work on the AUBREY manuscripts in Oxford, his duties as Reynolds's executor and the preparation of a four-volume edition of DRYDEN's prose (1800), which included an important life of the poet. His sight failed in the early 1800s and he died without finishing his biography of Shakespeare. Boswell's son made some order out of Malone's completed work, notes and revisions: the 21-volume *Plays and Poems of William Shakespeare* appeared in 1821. See also SHAKESPEARE: PERFORMANCE AND CRITICISM.

Malory, Sir Thomas d. ?1471 Author of *LE MORTE DARTHUR*, a title taken from the epilogue of CAXTON's edition (1485). Malory's identity is uncertain and several possible figures have been suggested. The author himself provides the following information: that his name was Thomas Malory, that he was a knight, and that he wrote most if not all of his work while imprisoned in Newgate, where he completed it in 1469–70. *Le Morte Darthur* is divided into eight tales in 21 books, but is usually taken as a single work. It is the greatest of the medieval prose romances, distilling both English and French sources. It has inspired many later translations and adaptations, such as TENNYSON's *IDYLLS OF THE KING*. See also ARTHURIAN LITERATURE.

Malouf, David 1934– Australian novelist and poet. Born in Brisbane of Lebanese and English parents, he was educated at Brisbane grammar school and the University of Queensland, where he taught for two years after graduating. He spent the next decade in England and Italy. In 1968 he returned to Australia and lectured in English at the University of Sydney before once again leaving for Europe and settling in Tuscany. His movement between the two continents is reflected in similar oppositions in his writings. From his technically assured early poems onwards, his work has shown a habitual concern with juxtaposing opposed modes of existence and perception. He first achieved recognition as a poet with *Bicycle and Other Poems* (1970), *Neighbours in a Thicket* (1974), *The Year of the Foxes* (1979), *First Things Last* (1980), *Wild Lemons* (1981), *Selected Poems* (1981) and *New and Collected Poems* (1991). He has, however, become better known as a novelist. All his fiction is concerned with artistic process and transformations of identity. *Johnno* (1975), his most conventional novel, explores the hero's rebellion against the constrictions of Brisbane society in the 1940s and 1950s in a comparatively straightforward autobiographical structure, though even here there is emphasis on multiple possibilities. *12 Edmonstone Street* (1985) contains four more autobiographical explorations. *An Imaginary Life* (1978), about Ovid in exile, reflects on the artist's role. *Harland's Half Acre* (1984) is an account of an artist's attempt to regain the land lost by his ancestors, realized through his painting rather than actual posession. The title-novella of *Child's Play* (1982), about an Italian terrorist planning to assassinate a famous writer, becomes a study of consciousness in transition. *Fly Away Peter* (1982) and *The Great World* (1990), opposing the calm of Australia with the horrors of World War I, explore the imagination's capacity to transform experience and perception. *Antipodes* (1985) is a collection of stories and *Blood Relations* (1988) is his only play.

Malthus, Thomas Robert 1766–1834 Economist. Born near Guildford in Surrey, he was educated at Jesus College, Cambridge, became a fellow of his college, was ordained and appointed curate of Albury, Surrey, in 1798. In the same year he published his famous essay, *On the Principle of Population as it Affects the Future Improvement of Society*. Its central proposition was that population increases geometrically while food supply increases mathematically; population levels would outgrow the means of subsistence. After a period of research on the Continent, he published a second edition in 1803. His theory provoked a storm of controversy, largely because of his apparent acceptance (in the first edition) of poverty and disease as necessary checks on population growth, but exerted a lasting influence on 19th-century thought. Malthus's later writings were directly concerned with economics, notably *An Investigation of the Cause of the Present High Price of Provisions* (1800), *Observations on the Effect of the Corn Laws* (1814) and *The Principles of Political Economy* (1820).

Mamet, David 1947– American playwright. Born in Flossmoor, Illinois, he was educated at Goddard College. He first attracted attention with one-acters, such as *Duck Variations* (1972) and *Sexual Perversity in Chicago* (1974), and made his name with the Broadway production in 1977 of *American Buffalo*, a witty but scathing attack on the decline of American values from the perspective of a Vietnam War veteran. Like all his work, it is minimally plotted and concentrates on character development. Other plays include: *A Life in the Theatre* (1977), contrasting an elderly and a youthful actor onstage and backstage; *The Woods* (1977); *All Men are Whores* (1977); *Dark Pony* (1977);

Shoeshine (1979); *Glengarry Glen Ross* (1983; PULITZER PRIZE 1984; filmed, 1992), about the world of real-estate salesmen; and *Speed-the-Plow* (1988). Subsequently much of his attention has been devoted to filmwriting, directing, and adapting Chekhov.

Man and Superman A comedy by GEORGE BERNARD SHAW, first performed in 1905 and published in 1908. His ideas about the 'life force' are embodied in the characters of the battling lovers, Ann Whitefield and John Tanner.

Under her father's will, Ann has two guardians, the respectable Roebuck Ramsden and the shockingly progressive John Tanner. She decides to marry Tanner and the decision, however Tanner may struggle to evade it, proves irresistible. Some of the play's liveliest encounters occur in Spain, where he flees to escape her. It is in the Sierra Nevada that he dreams the scene, sometimes omitted and certainly separable from the play in performance, 'Don Juan in Hell'.

Man of Feeling, The A novel by HENRY MACKENZIE, published anonymously in 1771. Despite being labelled a SENTIMENTAL NOVEL, it has a pervasive, gentle IRONY. The quixotic hero, 'rather eccentric', leaves home to seek his fortune and is educated in the harsh realities of the world. His good heart and ready sympathies are no protection against its cheats. The novel is a critique of acquisitive society and a warning against being taken in by appearances. Harley is an innocent abroad. He is robbed by a pair of professional cardsharpers and befriends a prostitute who has known happier days. She and the lower-class characters, including a fortune-telling beggar, all speak with the same antithetical orotundity, the diction of 18th-century moral discourse. In Bedlam Harley meets a girl who has gone mad for love. The narrative is distanced by the use to which poor Harley's papers are put: a clergyman is using them as wadding for his gun. SIR WALTER SCOTT admired the book's 'tone of moral pathos' and its representation of those 'finer feelings to which ordinary hearts are callous'.

Man of Law's Tale, The See CANTERBURY TALES, THE.

Man of Mode, The: *or, Sir Fopling Flutter* The third and last comedy by SIR GEORGE ETHEREGE, produced and published in 1676. One of the first great examples of RESTORATION COMEDY, it reflects society as seen through the brilliant personification of its types, who come together and separate, forming new pictures and dissolving into further pictures. It is not concerned only with the fashionable, for even the shoemaker and the orange-woman are sharply observed.

Among those present are: the poet Young Bellair and his love Emilia; the old-fashioned Lady Woodvill and the fashionable and wise Lady Townley; Dorimant, the finest of fine gentlemen (perhaps the EARL OF ROCHESTER), and his follower Medley; Harriet, beautiful and intelligent, who has the measure of Dorimant perfectly; Sir Fopling Flutter, a remarkable creation who, in DRYDEN's words, is a 'Fool so nicely writ,/ The Ladies wou'd mistake him for a Wit'. Dorimant's formidable wit makes him the major character in this passing parade, but he by no means has his own way entirely and in one scene the shoemaker makes short work of his attitudes. He has already discarded Loveit and Bellinda; Harriet is next on his list but this delightful heroine (if the play has a heroine at all) is more than a match for Dorimant, who falls in love with her.

Manciple's Tale, The See CANTERBURY TALES, THE.

Mandeville, Bernard de 1670–1733 Satirist. A Dutchman, he was born at Dort and educated at the Erasmus School in Rotterdam and the University of Leyden, but came to England to practise medicine. His most famous work was a SATIRE in doggerel verse, first published as *The Grumbling Hive: or, Knaves Turned Honest* (1705) and reissued with prose commentaries as *The Fable of the Bees: or, Private Vices, Public Benefits* (1714 and 1723). A second part was added in 1728, and both parts appeared together in 1734. Its mordant view of society as a hive in which mankind flourished through mutual greed, advanced in deliberate contradiction to the optimistic philosophers of the age, provoked replies from WILLIAM LAW in *Remarks on a Late Book Entitled The Fable of the Bees* (1723) and GEORGE BERKELEY in *Alciphron* (1732). Mandeville's other writings include *A Modest Defence of Public Stews: or, An Essay upon Whoring, as it is Now Practised in These Kingdoms* (1724), *An Enquiry into the Causes of the Frequent Executions at Tyburn* (1725) and *An Enquiry into the Origin of Honour, and the Usefulness of Christianity in War* (1732).

Mandeville's Travels: *or, The Travels of Sir John Mandeville* An account in Middle English prose of travels through Europe and the Near East, purporting to be the work of Sir John Mandeville; the identity of the real author is unknown. Originally written in French, possibly at Liege, *c.* 1357, it became immensely popular and was translated into many European languages. Its chief source is a series of itineraries translated into French by Jean de Long of St Omer completed in 1351, which included accounts of the Holy Land by William of Boldensele (1336), of the East by Odoric of Pordenone (1330) and Haiton's *Fleurs des histoires d'Orient* (before 1308). 'Mandeville' also used the encyclopedia of Vincent de Beauvais (*c.* 1250).

The narrator gives to his account a fictitious framework made up from details from the sources, saying he was born in St Albans and left on his travels on 29 September 1322, and that he wrote his account from memory when suffering from arthritic gout. The figure of Mandeville, one of the earliest fictitious narrators in English literature, gives the work some structural cohesion; it is otherwise a delightful and simply told series of unconnected descriptions and pieces of information. Mandeville describes interesting features of the terrain, flora and fauna and the customs of the inhabitants of countries in Europe and the East together with some traditional stories and legends. Descriptions of legendary creatures appear alongside accounts containing a surprising proportion of accurate observation and scientific fact.

Manfred A dramatic poem by BYRON, published in 1817, in temporary interruption of work on the third canto of *CHILDE HAROLD'S PILGRIMAGE*. He later explained that it had been inspired by the Alps, where his hero Manfred leads a solitary life as an outcast guilty of some mysterious crime. Neither the spirits of the universe nor the Witch of the Alps relieve his misery, though the spirits of Evil summon the shade of Astarte, the sister whom he loved and whose death is the cause of his guilt. She tells him that he will die the next day. When the evil spirits come to claim him, Manfred rejects his compact and they disappear. Though he dies at the time Astarte foretold, his resolution to remain master of his fate never falters.

Mangan, James Clarence 1803–49 Poet. Born in Dublin of a poor family, Mangan was educated by a priest who instructed him in languages. He worked as a lawyer's clerk and later in the library of Trinity College while he contributed poems and translations to *The Dublin University Magazine*. Later he contributed verse to *The Nation*, the patriotic paper founded by Charles Gavan Duffy and Thomas Osborne Davis, and published *Anthologia Germanica* (1845), translations from German poets. *The Poets and Poetry of Munster* (1849) was called translations but is more correctly versions in English. He contributed to *Romances and Ballads of Ireland* (edited by E. Ellis; 1850) and left a version of the Irish satire *The Tribes of Ireland* by Aenghus O'Daly (1852). His best-known poems, 'Dark Rosaleen' and 'The Nameless One', are often found in collections of Irish verse.

Manhattan Transfer A novel by JOHN DOS PASSOS, published in 1925. It was here that he first employed the themes and techniques that came to characterize his fiction. The novel tells the stories of numerous characters who have in common only their status as New Yorkers, and who come together randomly and impersonally. Each chapter begins with passages comprising observations of city life, slogans, snatches of dialogue, phrases from advertisements, and newspaper headlines. These passages further emphasize that *Manhattan Transfer* is a 'collective' novel about the city of New York – about the shallowness, immorality, and mechanization of urban life – not simply the story of a few characters' lives.

The two most prominent figures are Ellen Thatcher and Jimmy Herf. The novel opens with Ellen's birth; it ends with a scene in which Jimmy, having left his job with the *Times* (a job that never fulfilled him) and having left Ellen (whom he married and with whom he has had a child), hitches a ride out of New York and thus makes his escape. At 18 Ellen marries John Oglethorpe, a bisexual whom she eventually divorces. She then falls in love with Stanwood Emery, an alcoholic playboy who marries someone else while drunk (he eventually dies in a fire); pregnant with Emery's child, she has an abortion. She then achieves success on the stage and marries Jimmy Herf. At the end of the novel she agrees to marry the self-serving lawyer George Baldwin, even though she does not love him.

Manhire, Bill 1946– New Zealand poet, short-story writer, critic and editor. Educated at the University of Otago and University College, London, where he studied Old Norse sagas, he now lectures in English at Victoria University of Wellington. One of the best of the important generation of poets which emerged in the late 1960s, he was influenced by contemporary American poetry, particularly ROBERT CREELEY. Early poems published in the influential Auckland journal *Freed* (1969–72) were followed by *The Elaboration* (1972) and *How to Take Off Your Clothes at the Picnic* (1977). Typically using a short line and combining clarity of diction with ambiguity of meaning, his poetry explores the possibilities of mixing different idioms and registers of language. It also demonstrates considerable lyric gifts. Later volumes include *Good Looks* (1982), *Zoetropes: Poems 1972–82* (1984) and *Milky Way Bar* (1991). *The New Land* (1990) is an inventive, offbeat collection of stories. Manhire has also written a critical study of MAURICE GEE (1986) and co-edited several collections of short stories.

Manley, Delarivière (Mary) 1663–1724 Novelist, playwright and political journalist. Born in the Channel Islands, she was trapped into a bigamous marriage by her cousin, who then deserted her. In 1696 a comedy, *The Lost Lover*, and a tragedy, *The Royal Mischief*, were performed, the latter with rather more success. Her first ROMAN À CLEF, and the earliest example of such a work in English, is *The Secret History of Queen Sarah and the Sarazians* (1705; second part, 1711). Her most notorious work is *Secret Memoirs and Manners of Several Persons of Quality, of Both Sexes*, more usually known as *The New Atalantis* (2 vols., 1709). The scurrilous nature of this work was such that Mrs Manley, the publishers and the printer were all arrested, but throughout her examination she steadfastly asserted that the correspondence between real persons and the characters in her writings was entirely fortuitous. She was finally discharged. The following year she brought out two more volumes under the title *Memoirs of Europe towards the Close of the Eighth Century*. In 1711 she took over the editorship of THE EXAMINER from SWIFT, with whom she collaborated in a number of polemic pamphlets: *A Learned Comment upon Dr Hare's Excellent Sermon* (1711), *A True Narrative of What Pass'd at the Examination of the Marquis de Guiscard* (1711) and *A Modest Enquiry into the Reasons of the Joy Expressed by a Certain Set of People, upon the Spreading of a Report of Her Majesty's Death* (1714). *The Power of Love, in Seven Novels* (1720) is a collection of conventional romances.

Manning, Olivia 1908–80 Novelist. Born in Portsmouth, she spent much of her childhood in Ireland, making Dublin the setting of her first novel, *The Wind Changes* (1937). She married a British Council lecturer, R. D. Smith, in 1939 and joined him in Bucharest just as World War II broke out. Her wartime experiences there and in Athens, Egypt and Jerusalem form the basis of her major fictional achievement, six novels grouped into *The Balkan Trilogy* (1960–5) and *The Levant Trilogy* (1977–80). They trace the fate of a newly married English couple, Harriet and Guy Pringle. *The Great Fortune* (1960) and *The Spoilt City* (1962) show the gradual subordination of Bucharest to the Nazis, and *Friends and Heroes* (1965) describes the Pringles' flight to Egypt. The second trilogy (*The Danger Tree*, 1977; *The Battle Lost and Won*, 1978; *The Sum of Things*, 1980) deals with the desert war in Egypt. While they are notable for their compassionate portrayal of Guy and Harriet's developing marriage, their multitudinous cast of often vivid minor characters and their understated tragicomedy, their major significance resides in the scope of historical event and detail which the whole sequence accumulates. Her other novels include *School for Love* (1951) and *The Doves of Venus* (1955); she also published two collections of short stories.

Mannyng of Brunne, Robert c. 1283–1338 Author of *Handling Sin* and the *Story of England*. Born at Bourne in Lincolnshire in or before 1283, he was at Cambridge University in c. 1300 and spent 15 years as a Gilbertine canon at Sempringham Priory, Lincolnshire (c. 1302–17). *Handling Sin*, begun in 1303, translates the Anglo-Norman *Manuel des péchés* (c. 1250–70) usually ascribed to William of Wadington. The Ten Commandments, the seven deadly sins, sacrilege, the 12 requisites of penance and the 12 graces of shrift are all discussed, and illustrated with skilfully told EXEMPLA which are the work's chief interest. Thirteen of them were added to his source by Mannyng. The *Story of England*, compiled in 1338, is a verse CHRONICLE in two parts covering the periods from the Flood to the death of Caedwalla (689) and from then until the death of Edward I (1307). The first part is based on *Le Roman de Brut* of Wace, but also draws on Wace's source, GEOFFREY OF MONMOUTH's *Historia regum Britanniae*, on BEDE and on the Anglo-Norman *Chronicle* of Peter Langtoft. The second section relies principally upon Langtoft's *Chronicle*, again with some additions from other sources, including VERSE ROMANCES.

Mansfield, Katherine [Beauchamp, Kathleen Mansfield] 1888–1923 Short-story writer. Born in Wellington, New Zealand, she was sent to London in 1903 to complete her education at Queen's College. Returning to New Zealand in 1906 she became a wide-ranging reader and began to write. Several 'Vignettes' were accepted in the Australian monthly *Native Companion* in 1907, and in 1908 she returned to London determined on a literary career. She married George Bowden in 1909 but left him soon afterwards. At Bowden's suggestion she submitted some of her short pieces to A. R. Orage, editor of THE NEW AGE. These were accepted and Mansfield's relationship with the periodical continued.

After meeting JOHN MIDDLETON MURRY in 1911 she began to publish in *Rhythm*, an *avant-garde* quarterly founded by Murry and Michael Sadleir in that year. Mansfield's health was poor, and like D. H. LAWRENCE

Katherine Mansfield

(near whom she and Murry lived in Cornwall for some weeks in 1915) she discovered that she was suffering from tuberculosis. Despite periods of recuperation in the South of France, her health continued to decline. She and Murry were married in 1918. She died at Fontainebleau.

Critics have praised her penetrating and relentless intelligence, which is balanced by a delicate sense of form – qualities ideally suited to her chosen genre, the short story. Her first collection, *In a German Pension* (1911), was followed by *Prelude*, a story published singly in 1918, which like much of her best work drew on her childhood in New Zealand and showed the influence of Chekhov. Others appeared in *Bliss and Other Stories* (1919), *The Garden Party and Other Stories* (1920) and *Other Stories* (1922), the last work published during her lifetime. Posthumous works included *Poems* (1923; edited by Murry), *Something Childish and Other Stories* (1924) and *A Fairy Story* (1932). *The Collected Stories of Katherine Mansfield* (1945) was an omnibus volume. Murry also edited *The Letters of Katherine Mansfield* (1928) and *Katherine Mansfield's Letters to John Middleton Murry: 1913–1922* (1951).

Mansfield Park A novel by JANE AUSTEN, begun in 1811 and published in 1814.

Sir Thomas and Lady Bertram of Mansfield Park have two daughters, Maria and Julia, and two sons, Tom and Edmund. Fanny Price, niece of Lady Bertram and one of a large improvident family, is brought to live at Mansfield Park where she is patronized by three of her cousins, but finds a friend in Edmund.

When Sir Thomas leaves for the West Indies to look after his interests there, his children, on whom he has always impressed the need for manners and social (rather than moral) accomplishments, demonstrate the deficiencies in their upbringing. Though private theatricals are forbidden, they plan to stage a play, ELIZABETH INCHBALD's *Lovers' Vows*, and engage in self-indulgent flirtations from which Fanny alone stays aloof. Maria Bertram, though engaged to Mr Rushworth, is attracted to Henry Crawford; his sister Mary fascinates Edmund Bertram. But Maria decides after all to marry Rushworth, whereupon Henry turns his attention to Fanny. When she refuses his proposal, Sir Thomas, now back at Mansfield, is highly displeased at her apparent foolishness.

The unhappy Fanny goes to visit her own family in Portsmouth and, distressed by the noise and disorder of her father's house, longs to be back at Mansfield Park. Meanwhile Maria, now Mrs Rushworth, runs off with Henry Crawford. Julia elopes with a Mr Yates. Edmund, who has taken orders, is rejected by Mary Crawford because she has no wish to be a clergyman's wife, and he at last begins to see her character in a clear light. Edmund and Fanny eventually find happiness together.

Many Inventions A collection of 14 stories by RUDYARD KIPLING, published in 1893. It includes six Indian tales, of which two concern characters who also appear in *SOLDIERS THREE*. In 'His Private Honour' Ortheris's conduct is dictated by a code which transcends the army rule book. Other notable stories are: 'The Disturber of Traffic', about the delusions and growing obsession of Dowse, a lighthouse keeper in the Java Straits; 'The Finest Story in the World' in which Charlie begins to recall moments of previous lives as a Roman galley slave and on a Viking ship; and 'The Record of Badalia Herodsfoot', a realistic account of the heroine's struggle for survival in the London slums of the 1890s.

Mapanje, Jack 1945– Malawian poet. A single volume, *Of Chameleons and Gods* (1981), established him as one of Africa's most accomplished and distinctive poets. It draws on a wide range of subjects and techniques, including traditional forms and symbols, colloquial monologues, and satires on African politicians and intellectuals. He was head of the department of English at Chancellor College, University of Malawi, until 1987 when he was imprisoned for four years without charge or trial. His case became an international *cause célèbre*. He now lives in Britain.

Marble Faun, The: or, *The Romance of Monte Beni* A novel by NATHANIEL HAWTHORNE, published in 1860. In Britain it was entitled *Transformation*. Kenyon and Hilda are two Americans studying art in Rome. With their friend Miriam, an artist, they meet an Italian nobleman named Donatello and notice that he resembles the Marble Faun sculpted by Praxiteles. Handsome, innocent and warm-hearted, Donatello falls in love with Miriam, but realizes that she is troubled by some secret from the past. There are various unproven rumours circulating about Miriam: she may be the heiress of a Jewish banker fleeing from an unwanted marriage, or a German princess, or the mulatta daughter of a South American planter, or the mistress of an English nobleman come to Italy to pursue her interest in art. Whatever the truth, she is tormented by a mysterious Capuchin monk. One night, when the four friends are walking among the hills of Rome, Donatello is enraged to find the Capuchin following them and, perhaps encouraged by a gesture from Miriam, pushes him off a precipice. Hilda witnesses the scene.

Donatello, horrified by what he has done, flees to his ancestral estate of Monte Beni. Miriam, sharing his guilt, follows him; they agree that they must both bear the consequences. He returns to Rome, gives himself up, and goes to prison; she embarks on a penitential pilgrimage. Hilda also remains troubled, feeling tainted by what she has witnessed; setting aside her Puritan training, she finds relief in a Catholic confessional and marries Kenyon. The secret of Miriam's past is never revealed. In the Postscript to the novel, the narrator claims that to seek to know whether Donatello really is a faun, and who Miriam really is, would destroy the poetry and beauty of the story.

Mardi and a Voyage Thither A novel by HERMAN MELVILLE, published in 1849. The narrator, Taji, and Jarl, an older seaman, desert their ship in a whaleboat. They encounter the brigantine *Parki*, which has been abandoned by all except a Polynesian couple, Samoa and Annatoo. The four live a contented life on board until the ship sinks during a storm and Annatoo is drowned. The three survivors take to the whaleboat and reach the islands of Mardi, where the adventure tale gives way to a kind of ALLEGORY. The islands represent a mythical or transcendental realm. Taji lives happily with Yillah, a young woman he and his companions rescue from a priest who had intended to sacrifice her. In saving her Taji killed the priest, whose sons take their revenge by kidnapping her again. Taji sets out to find his lost love, accompanied by a king, a historian, a philosopher, and a poet. Their search takes them to many lands, whose societies are closely observed and discussed. The voyage is now generally seen as an allegorical exploration of the world of 1848, in which Dominora stands for Great Britain, Porpheero for Europe, and Vivenza for the USA. The travellers eventually reach the land of Serenia, which is ruled by Alma (Christ). The philosopher declares that Alma's doctrine of love is the ultimate wisdom, but Taji observes that man ignores the doctrine. Although his companions try to convince him to give it up, Taji continues his voyage – alone, still in search of what he has lost, still pursued by the priest's sons.

Marechera, Dambudzo 1952–87 Zimbabwean novelist and short-story writer. Educated in a mission school, he was expelled from the University of Rhodesia and had an equally chequered career at New College, Oxford. *The House of Hunger* (1978), consisting of a novella and short stories, aroused great interest as a cry of distress from one of the new generation of African writers brought up against a background of war and injustice. It won the *Guardian* Fiction Award in 1979. *Black Sunlight* (1980), an intense postmodernist novel, deals with the violent world of urban guerrillas. *An Articulate Anger: Dambudzo Marechera, 1952–87* (1988) contains interviews with and statements by him shortly before his death, while *The Black Insider* (1990) is a selection from his previously unpublished, and sometimes unfinished, writings.

Marie de France Late 12th-century French poet who probably lived in England, writing in ANGLO-NORMAN. Conjecture plausibly identifies her as the illegitimate daughter of Godefroy d'Anjou, who was abbess of Shaftesbury by 1181 and died *c.* 1216. Her works are the oldest definitely attributed to a woman writer in England or France. The *Lais*, probably her first work and written before 1189, are a collection of 12 BRETON LAYS, preceded by a prologue defending literary activity, varying from a mere snippet of the Tristan legend ('Le Chevrefoil') to the long and involved 'Eliduc'. They exercised a powerful influence over the spread of ideas associated with COURTLY LOVE in England. The *Fables* are a collection of 102 Aesopic fables which she claims are based on an English translation by 'Alvrez' of a Latin collection. Neither the English nor Latin source survives, though the fables can be traced to various collections. They are introduced by a prologue and are in octosyllabic couplets. The *Espurgatoire Saint Patrice*, written after 1189 and apparently the last of the three, is a retelling of the popular legend of St Patrick's vision of purgatory.

Marino Faliero A tragedy by BYRON, published and produced (against his wishes) at DRURY LANE in 1821. Like *THE TWO FOSCARI*, it is set in Venice. Marino Faliero, a 14th-century Doge, slights Michele Steno, a gentleman of poor but distinguished family. Steno writes a gross lampoon on the Doge's chair of state; he is tried and punished by the Council of Forty but Faliero is furious at what he regards as a mild sentence. Faliero plots with malcontents to overthrow the constitution of Venice and take his revenge on the council. But the plot is exposed and Marino Faliero is beheaded on the staircase of the Doge's Palace.

Marino Faliero is also the title of a tragedy by SWINBURNE (1885) in which the old Doge is presented as a symbol of liberty.

Marius the Epicurean A philosophical romance by WALTER PATER, published in 1885. The story is set in ancient Rome during the time of the Antonine emperors, the zenith of the empire's greatness. The life of Marius is followed from his childhood to his education at Pisa and his adult life in Rome. Pater examines Marius' response to the philosophical influences of his time, to the Roman religion, to the brutal spectacles of the amphitheatre, finally to the growing power of Christianity. Although Marius does not become a Christian, he is strongly attracted by the high principles and commitment of his Christian friend Cornelius. He dies to save his friend's life and the Christian church regards him as a martyr.

Mark, Jan(et) (Marjorie) 1943– Writer of CHILDREN'S LITERATURE. She was born in Welwyn Garden City after the evacuation of the City of London Maternity Hospital during World War II, and educated in Ashford and at the Canterbury College of Art. The RAF base near her Norfolk home furnished the setting for her first novel, *Thunder and Lightnings* (1976), a finely observed and gently humorous story which won the Penguin-*Guardian* competition and the Carnegie Medal. *Handles* (1983), which won a second Carnegie Medal, also has a Norfolk setting. *Nothing to be Afraid Of* (1980) and *Feet* (1983) are collections of short stories. Her SCIENCE-FICTION trilogy for older children, *The Ennead* (1978), *Divide and Rule* (1979) and *Aquarius* (1982), provides a bleak and despairing vision of a corrupt society and its victims. A lighter note is evident in *Dream House* (1987) and *Man in Motion* (1989), which describes how a boy makes friends in a new neighbourhood.

Markandaya, Kamala 1924– Novelist. Born and educated in South India, she has lived in Britain since her marriage. She is an impressive explorer of human consciousness and of the convolutions of intimate relationships. *Nectar in a Sieve* (1954) elevates peasant subsistence to tragic stoicism. The heroine in *Some Inner Fury* (1955) renounces her English lover in the 1940s Independence agitation; the artist in *Possession* (1963) deserts an English patroness to seek his Indian roots; *A Silence of Desire* (1960) probes the tensions between religious wife and agnostic husband, and in *The Coffer Dams* (1969) an English marriage is strained because the engineer husband and his wife hold opposed attitudes to Indians. In *A Handful of Rice* (1966) urban poverty utterly overwhelms individual effort, while a village forms the setting for the unfolding of young female consciousness in *Two Virgins* (1974). *The Golden Honeycomb* (1977), about a minor princely court, is marred by over-ambitious structuring and some prolixity, but *Pleasure City* (1982) admirably presents a sensitive Britisher and ingenious Indian villager coping with some on-the-spot effects of the historical process of neo-colonialism.

Markham, E(dward) A(rchibald) 1939– Caribbean/British poet. Born in Montserrat, he migrated to Britain in 1956 and studied English and philosophy at the University of Wales in Lampeter. He has taught in a London polytechnic, held several writing fellowships and edited a number of magazines, including *Artrage*. Although best known as a poet, he has written several plays, worked with semi-professional theatrical troupes, directed the Caribbean Theatre Workshop and worked as a media co-ordinator in Papua, New Guinea, in 1983–5. Reacting against simple oppositions between British and Caribbean experience, he prefers to see himself as a resourceful traveller, concerned with the survival of his own culture but also offering something to his host society. Both to reflect the diversity of the Caribbean language and to accommodate different forms of consciousness, his poetry uses a broad spectrum of voices and personae, ranging from the young black Paul Vincent to Sally Goodman, a white feminist. Volumes include *Crossfire* (1972), *Human Rites* (1984), *Living in*

Disguise (1986) and *Towards the End of the Century* (1989). He has also published a collection of short stories, *Something Unusual* (1986), and edited an anthology, *Hinterland: Caribbean Poetry from the West Indies and Britain* (1989).

Markham, Edwin 1852–1940 American poet. Born in Oregon City, he had little formal education but became a schoolteacher and, inspired by the poets he read, began to write verse himself. His first poem, 'The Gulf of Night', appeared in 1880. His most famous piece, the title-poem of his 1899 volume, *The Man with the Hoe and Other Poems*, was inspired by Millet's painting. This collection and *Lincoln and Other Poems* (1901) are largely concerned with the degrading conditions of the working classes. Other, less popular volumes include *California the Wonderful* (1915), *Gates of Paradise* (1920), *Ballad of the Gallows Bird* (1926), *New Poems: Eighty Poems at Eighty* (1932) and *Collected Poems* (1940).

Markham, Gervase c. 1568–1637 Miscellaneous writer. A soldier and horseman, he returned to England after some years of fighting in the Netherlands, and wrote prolifically for a popular audience. *A Discourse on Horsemanship* (1593) and *Cavelarice: or, The English Horseman* (1610) were supplemented by a veterinary work, *Markham's Masterpiece: or, What Doth a Horseman Lack* (1610), and books about husbandry and the art of war, as well as plays and poems. The performing horse mentioned by Markham in the title of *Cavelarice* was Marocco, famous throughout Europe: SHAKESPEARE refers to him in the first act of *LOVE'S LABOUR'S LOST* as 'the dancing horse' of Armado's conversation with his page.

Marlatt, Daphne 1942– Canadian poet and novelist. Born in Melbourne of English parents, she lived in Malaysia for six years as a child before moving with her family to Vancouver in 1951. She attended the University of British Columbia, where she studied English and was an editor of the *avant-garde* magazine *TISH*. She subsequently obtained her MA in comparative literature at the University of Indiana and has since worked in Vancouver as a writer and researcher in oral history. Her poetry is concerned with the perceptual process and with attempting to render this in language. She frequently relates mental states to exterior surroundings. *Rings* (1971), a long poem which describes the situation of a pregnant woman enclosed in a room with her husband during a snowstorm, offers a vivid picture of the isolation of the individual. *Vancouver Poems* (1972) documents a personal response to the external phenomena of the city. *Steveston* (1974), generally regarded as her most important work to date, is a meditation on the history of a Japanese-Canadian fishing town, which intersperses sociological material about the community with personal reflection. Other volumes include *Frames* (1968), *Our Lives* (1975), *Net Work* (1980), *Here and There* (1981), *How Hug a Stone* (1983) and *Double Negative* (1988). *Zocalo* (1977) and *Ana Historic* (1988) are novels.

Marlowe, Christopher 1564–93 Playwright and poet. Born in Canterbury, the son of a shoemaker, Marlowe was awarded a scholarship at Corpus Christi College, Cambridge. Possibly while still at the university, he became an agent of Francis Walsingham and a favourite of Walsingham's brother, Thomas. The detail of any missions Marlowe undertook in the secret service of Elizabeth I's great schemer is unknown, and it is no more than intelligent speculation that links his activities as an agent with his death by violence in a Deptford tavern. What is known is that Marlowe took his BA in 1584, his MA (after some hesitation by the university authorities) in 1587, and almost at once presented the London theatre with the startling success of the first part of *TAMBURLAINE THE GREAT* (1587). The play's rhetoric, its self-proclaimed 'high astounding terms', was superbly delivered by the actor EDWARD ALLEYN, leading performer of the Lord Admiral's Men. The second part of *Tamburlaine* (1587) rivalled the success of the first. The notoriety of Marlowe's private life, which led to accusations of atheism, blasphemy, subversion and homosexuality, added spice to his reputation. Certainly he was free-thinking and indiscreet. Marlowe may already have written *Dido, Queen of Carthage*, whose first edition (1594) named NASHE as co-author: the chronological order of his work cannot be precisely established. For all its shortcomings, *Dido* gives evidence of a serious application to the playwright's craft. Like the translation of Lucan's *Pharsalia* (published in 1600, but possibly completed at Cambridge) and of Ovid's *Elegies* into HEROIC COUPLETS (published in 1595, but probably also student work), it shows a careful apprenticeship in the classics. Whilst the play is drawn mainly from Book Four of Virgil's *Aeneid*, it reveals a confident familiarity with the whole poem.

After *Tamburlaine*, Marlowe continued to dramatize the careers and aspirations of overreaching heroes whose bold defiance of social, political and religious morality invites admiration at the same time as it deserves condemnation. *THE JEW OF MALTA* (c. 1590), described as a tragedy, is equally well read as a grotesque comedy in which murderous excess and inflated rhetoric parody statesmanship and the posturings of Christian authority. As in *Tamburlaine*, interest – and most of the best lines – belongs to the utterly unscrupulous villain-hero, Barabas. *The Massacre at Paris* (c.1589), which has survived in a manifestly corrupt text, is not unlike *The Jew of Malta* in tone. Its central figure, the Duke of Guise, adopts with similar gusto the self-confessed villainy of Barabas. That the horrific St Bartholomew massacre of 1572 should be treated so sardonically is, of course, disturbing still. In Protestant England, so soon after the event, it must have been risky.

So, in a different way, was Marlowe's most accomplished play, *EDWARD II* (c. 1592), in which the defeat and eventual murder of a homosexual king by powerful barons are depicted with a new and unexpected plainness of style. *Edward II* carried the crude chronicle play a long step towards its sophistication in the mature history plays of SHAKESPEARE. It is a character tragedy, in which the focus shifts subtly from Edward to his lover Gaveston, to his Queen, Isabella, and to her lover, Mortimer.

The Marlovian overreacher comes to what, in retrospect, seems a logical conclusion in *DOCTOR FAUSTUS*, and it may be that this sense of logic has contributed to the scholarly claims that this is the last of Marlowe's plays. It survives in two unsatisfactory texts (1604 and 1616), each of which shows the marks of playhouse accretion and adaptation, but Faustus himself and his increasingly symbiotic relationship with Mephistopheles are magnificently unaffected. No one can say what plays Marlowe might have gone on to write. In plague-affected London, he spent the last months before his murder writing the narrative poem *HERO AND LEANDER* (published in 1598), which, together with the lyrical *THE PASSIONATE SHEPHERD*, is his poetic monument.

Marmion: *A Tale of Flodden Field* A poem by SIR WALTER SCOTT, published in 1808. Like its predecessor, *THE LAY OF THE LAST MINSTREL*, it is divided into six CANTOS.

The Marmion of the title is a fictitious favourite of Henry VIII who wants to marry the rich and beautiful Lady Clare in spite of his entanglement with Constance de Beverley, a nun who has broken her vows and followed him disguised as a page. Clare herself is betrothed to Sir Ralph de Wilton. Conspiring to accuse de Wilton of treason, Marmion forges an incriminating letter and is helped by Constance, who hopes to recover her influence over him. However, she is betrayed, returned to her convent and walled up alive.

When Ralph and Marmion fight in the lists, Ralph is defeated and left for dead. Clare flees to a convent to escape from Marmion. Ralph survives, goes to Scotland disguised as a palmer and consults the Abbess of St Hilda, who is attended by Clare. The Abbess has proof of Marmion's crime, which she received from Constance before her death, and she entrusts it to the palmer, who can now reveal his true identity to Clare. The climax takes place at the battle of Flodden, where Marmion is killed.

The poem includes the songs 'Where Shall the Lover Rest?' and 'Lochinvar'.

Marmion, Shakerley 1603–39 Poet, playwright and Royalist. Marmion was born near Brackley, Northamptonshire, and educated at Oxford. He enjoyed the patronage of BEN JONSON and the friendship of SIR JOHN SUCKLING. Of his three plays, *Holland's Leaguer* (1631) is notable for its depiction of the famous Southwark brothel run by Elizabeth Holland. *A Fine Companion* (1633) is a Jonsonian 'humours' comedy. *The Antiquary* (*c.* 1635), which mocks the foolishness of old age, is Marmion's best play. His long poem, *Cupid and Psyche* (1637), based on Apuleius' *The Golden Ass*, is among the best examples of Caroline narrative poetry.

Marprelate, Martin The name assumed by the author of a series of pamphlets issued in 1588–9 and printed on secret presses in various parts of the country (e.g. Kingston, Coventry, Manchester). They were extreme Puritan attacks on the bishops, part of a war originally occasioned by Whitgift's 1586 Star Chamber decree attempting to suppress Puritan pamphlets. The identity of Marprelate is in doubt, though John Penry and John Udall were arrested. Penry was executed in 1593 and Udall probably died in prison. Job Throckmorton denied complicity at Penry's trial and escaped punishment. Seven tracts survive: *The Epistle* (October 1588), *The Epitome* (November 1588), *Certain Mineral and Metaphysical Schoolpoints* (February 1589), *Hay* [i.e. have you] *Any Work for Cooper* (March 1589), *Martin Junior* (July 1589), *Martin Senior* (July 1589) and *The Protestation of Martin Marprelate* (September 1589). The bishops replied in *An Admonition to the People of England* (1589) by the Thomas Cooper alluded to in one of the tracts. Richard Bancroft preached a sermon against false prophets and the tracts at St Paul's Cross in February 1589; it was printed the next month. At Bancroft's suggestion the bishops also employed professional writers on their side. JOHN LYLY wrote *Pap with a Hatchet* (1589); *A Whip for an Ape* and *Mar-Martin* (both 1589) have also been attributed, although doubtfully, to him. Various pamphlets have been attributed to THOMAS NASHE, but only *An Almond for a Parrot* (1590) with certainty. Richard Harvey wrote *Plain Percival* (1589) and *A Theological Discourse of the Lamb of God* (1590). But the professional writers could not match the force of Marprelate's scandalous ridicule and railing against 'swinish rabble... petty Antichrists, petty popes, proud prelates, intolerable withstanders of reformation'. The SATIRE in the tracts is some of the best produced in Elizabeth's reign.

Marriage A novel by SUSAN FERRIER, published in 1818.

Lady Juliana, daughter of the Earl of Courtland, elopes with Henry Douglas, a penniless young officer. Her romantic illusions are stripped away quickly: Douglas's Highland home is a cheerless place, containing grim-faced aunts and five dull sisters. Then her expected child proves to be twin daughters. The couple move to London where Henry falls into debt and is imprisoned. Upon his release he joins the army and goes to India.

Lady Juliana's daughters, and their future, are now her main preoccupation: she is convinced that all her troubles are the result of an 'imprudent' marriage. One daughter, Mary, has been brought up in Scotland while the other, Adelaide, grows up in the Earl of Courtland's London home. Mary rejects the ambitious marriage Lady Juliana wants her to make; Adelaide allows herself to be pushed into marriage with an elderly duke. Mary gives her heart to the man of her choice and returns to Scotland with him to settle down contentedly. Adelaide, after less than a year of her prudent marriage, deserts the duke and runs off with a worthless man.

Marriage à la Mode A comedy by JOHN DRYDEN, first produced in 1672 and published in 1673. There are two, unrelated plots. One, written in 'heroic' verse, concerns Leonidas and Palmyra, daughter of the usurping King of Sicily; Leonidas is in fact the rightful heir and all ends satisfactorily for them. The other, in a contrasting 'comedy of manners' style, concerns Rhodophil and Doralice, married for two years and bored with each other. Rhodophil's friend Palamede has been ordered to marry Melantha but has meanwhile fallen in love with Doralice, not knowing that she is married to Rhodophil. Rhodophil pursues Melantha, not knowing that she is intended for Palamede. The quadrille is played out until the characters discover they want their original partners after all.

Marriage of Heaven and Hell, The A prose work by WILLIAM BLAKE, usually dated 1790, expressing his revolt against the accepted values of his age. It is prefaced by a poem, 'The Argument', declaring that the paths of truth have been corrupted by false religion. Of the six sections that follow, 'The Voice of the Devil' attacks the conventional religious distinction between body and soul, proclaims that 'Energy is Eternal Delight' and sides with Satan in MILTON's *PARADISE LOST*. 'Proverbs of Hell' explores this Romantic doctrine in a series of aphorisms, sometimes deliberately shocking.

Marryat, Captain Frederick 1792–1848 Novelist and writer of CHILDREN'S LITERATURE. Born in London, the son of a Member of Parliament, he joined the navy at 14 and was a Commander by the age of 23. After an adventurous career, during which he won the Royal Humane Society's Gold Medal for bravery, he resigned in 1830 to concentrate on writing. He had already published his first novel, *The*

Naval Officer: or, Scenes and Adventures in the Life of Frank Mildmay (1829). His first great success, *Peter Simple* (1834), was followed by *Jacob Faithful* (1834) and *Mr Midshipman Easy* (1836), all likewise drawing on Marryat's experience of the sea. After *Japhet in Search of a Father* (1836) and *Snarleyyow* (1837) he turned to children's fiction with *Masterman Ready* (1841). Written as a form of rebuke to the romanticism of Johann Wyss's *The Swiss Family Robinson*, the book concentrates on the toughness of life for his marooned Seagrave family, not least in the way it has to fight marauding savages. It is in one such final encounter that the faithful family friend and retainer Ready dies, doing his duty to the last. Although this and other moments in the story are heavily weighed down with moral didacticism, Marryat provided children with one of their best adventure stories for years to come. His other great success as children's writer, *The Children of the New Forest* (1847), left the sea in favour of a story set in the Civil War, with heroic Royalist children hiding from their Roundhead oppressors in the shelter of the forest. There they also learn how to live off the land, before finally claiming their inheritance at the Restoration. One of the first – and most exciting – historical novels written for a young audience, it passed its particular prejudices about English history on to many succeeding children's books.

Marsh, Sir **Edward (Howard)** 1872–1953 Civil servant and patron of the arts. Educated at Trinity College, Cambridge, he became a clerk in the Colonial Office (1896) and private secretary to SIR WINSTON CHURCHILL (1906), a post he retained in various guises for 23 years, following Churchill to the Board of Trade, the Home Office, the Admiralty, the War Office and the Treasury. He retired and was knighted in 1937. Marsh was a connoisseur and influential collector of English painting; Mark Gertler, John and Paul Nash, Stanley Spencer and many others owed him uncountable friendly acts of help and advice. He assisted several generations of poets with money and intelligent kindness, including FLECKER, DE LA MARE, D. H. LAWRENCE, GRAVES and BLUNDEN; the five volumes of Marsh's anthology, *GEORGIAN POETRY* (1912–22), first brought many of them to public notice. He edited the *Collected Poems* (1918) of his friend RUPERT BROOKE, whose literary executor he was. The habit of elaborate scholarly proof-correction which he exercised on behalf of Churchill, SOMERSET MAUGHAM, HUGH WALPOLE, Sir Ronald Storrs and other writers was a precise, valuable form of literary surgery. Much mocked for his treble voice and fussy manner, he was a painstaking translator of Horace and La Fontaine and a fine gossiping letter-writer.

Marsh, Dame **Ngaio** 1899–1982 New Zealand writer of DETECTIVE FICTION and playwright. Born and

brought up in Christchurch, she attended Canterbury University College School of Art in 1915–20 and worked in the theatre, first as an actress and later as a producer. Her first novel, *A Man Lay Dead* (1934), introduced Superintendent Roderick Alleyn of Scotland Yard, her equivalent of CHRISTIE's Hercule Poirot and SAYERS's Lord Peter Wimsey. The settings are often theatrical and her plots show a tight dramatic construction. More than 30 in all, her novels include *Artists in Crime* (1938), *Died in the Wool* (1945), *Opening Night* (1951), *Killer Dolphin* (1966) and *Black as He's Painted* (1974). Her plays include *A Surfeit of Lampreys* (1950) and *False Scent* (1961), both adapted from her own novels. She also wrote travel books and two works on play production. Her autobiography, *Black Beech and Honeydew* (1966), is primarily about her life in the theatre.

Marston, John 1576–1634 Playwright and poet. Born in Oxfordshire and educated at Brasenose College, Oxford, Marston first studied and then wrote in lodgings in the Middle Temple. His verse SATIRE, collected in *The Metamorphosis of Pygmalion's Image* and *The Scourge of Villainy* (both 1598), earned him a reputation for bitter invective, further reinforced by his disputes with BEN JONSON in the 'war of the theatres', to which parts of *Histriomastix* (1599) refer. Marston had already written, for a BOYS' COMPANY, the dark comedy *ANTONIO AND MELLIDA* and its sequel *ANTONIO'S REVENGE*, a REVENGE TRAGEDY (both 1599 or 1600). The satiric comedies *Jack Drum's Entertainment* (1600) and *What You Will* (c. 1601) were followed by Marston's best plays, *THE DUTCH COURTESAN* (before 1603), *THE MALCONTENT* (1604) and *Parasitaster: or, The Fawn* (c. 1605). These are all comedies, though *The Malcontent* in particular touches on tragedy in its exploration of moral complexities. *The Wonder of Women: or, The Tragedy of Sophonisba* (1606) is an austere Roman tragedy, uneasily accommodating spectacle and sensation of the kind expected in the Jacobean theatre. An unfinished tragedy, *The Insatiate Countess*, was completed by William Barksted and published in 1613.

Marston's volatile temperament is well illustrated by his decision to dedicate *The Malcontent* to his former adversary, Ben Jonson, and by his collaboration with Jonson and CHAPMAN on *EASTWARD HO* (1605), a parody of the newly fashionable CITIZEN COMEDY. The whole of the first act is Marston's and his hand is detectable elsewhere in the play, whose references to the Scots so offended James I that Chapman and Jonson were briefly imprisoned. Marston seems to have gone unpunished, but he was imprisoned, for unknown reasons, in 1608, abandoned the theatre after his release, and took holy orders in 1609. From 1616 to 1631, he was rector of Christchurch in Hampshire.

Marston, John Westland 1819–90 Playwright and dramatic critic. His best-known play, *The Patrician's Daughter* (1842), was one of many verse tragedies promoted and performed by the actor William Macready. Marston's intelligent theatrical reviews for THE ATHENAEUM in the 1860s and his retrospective book, *Our Recent Actors* (1888), are substantial contributions to theatrical literature.

Marston, Philip Bourke 1850–87 Poet. The son of JOHN WESTLAND MARSTON, he was born in London and lost his sight as a child. He published *Song-Tide and Other Poems* (1871), *All in All: Poems and Sonnets* (1875) and *Wind-Voices* (1883). *Garden Secrets* (1887), *For a Song's Sake and Other Stories* (1887) and *A Last Harvest* (1891) appeared posthumously.

Martian poets, the A term coined by JAMES FENTON to describe the school or group of poets, first coming to prominence in the late 1970s, whose work presents familiar objects in unfamiliar ways. The leading figure is CRAIG RAINE. The title poem of his collection, *A Martian Sends a Postcard Home* (1979), which purports to be a Martian's uncomprehending reaction to everyday things, typifies the technique and suggested the label for the group. Disciples include CHRISTOPHER REID and David Sweetman.

Martin, Violet Florence See SOMERVILLE AND ROSS.

Martin Chuzzlewit A novel by CHARLES DICKENS, published in 20 parts from January 1843 to July 1844 as *The Life and Adventures of Martin Chuzzlewit, His Relatives, Friends and Enemies. Comprising All His Wills and His Ways, with an Historical Record of What He Did and What He Didn't; Shewing Moreover Who Inherited the Family Plate; Who Came in for the Silver Spoons, and Who for the Wooden Ladles. The Whole Forming a Complete Key to the House of Chuzzlewit.*

Martin Chuzzlewit is a selfish young man, the despair of his grandfather and namesake, the head of the family. When Martin is articled to Pecksniff the architect, a hypocrite of beatific appearance, old Martin, in an excess of misanthropy, has Pecksniff dismiss the boy. Old Martin's nephew, Jonas Chuzzlewit, engineers the death of his own father and marries Mercy, one of Pecksniffs two daughters. Although warned by the elder Martin Chuzzlewit of the probable consequences of marriage to Jonas, Mercy had gone her own way, and reaps the results of her thoughtlessness as Jonas treats her with brutal cruelty. Jonas becomes involved in the crooked schemes of Montague Tigg, and succeeds in drawing Pecksniff into their dubious enterprise.

Meanwhile, young Martin has sought his fortune in America with his irrepressible servant Mark Tapley. He is defrauded by the Eden Land Corporation and nearly dies of fever. His convalescence is cut short by the serious illness of Mark, and Martin learns some valuable lessons about the nature of true generosity. Returning to England, resolved to make peace with his grandfather, Martin finds him living in Pecksniff's house, apparently entirely subject to him. Eventually old Martin's purpose of testing both Pecksniff and his grandson is revealed, and Martin is able to marry Mary Graham, Chuzzlewit's companion and adopted daughter. Pecksniff is exposed and Jonas, when arrested for the murder of Montague Tigg, who had blackmailed him over the death of his father, poisons himself. Tom Pinch, at one time Pecksniff's loyal assistant and adherent, being so innocent and open himself that he was unable to believe the warnings of young Martin and a sensible young friend, John Westlock, is suitably employed by old Martin. Although he cherished an unrequited and untold passion for Mary Graham, Tom's unassuming ideals of happiness are fulfilled when his beloved sister Ruth marries John Westlock, and the three settle down together.

Dickens's energetic wit and inventive characterization are displayed to their full effect in *Martin Chuzzlewit*, even though the famous character of Mrs Gamp, the midwife 'dispoged' to the not altogether occasional glass of gin, and the American episodes, had not been part of his original intention. When concluding the work, the novelist thought it 'in a hundred points immeasurably the best of my stories'.

Martin Eden A novel by JACK LONDON, published in 1909. Martin Eden, a labourer who was once a sailor, has a questioning mind and has undertaken a programme of self-education. He aspires to a higher sort of life, such as that personified by Ruth Morse, a college graduate and the daughter of a wealthy family. He works hard to succeed as a writer, and his work reflects the influence of HERBERT SPENCER's ethical theories. Although his friend Russ Brissenden, a socialist poet, believes in his work, he has no success. When a newspaper calls him a socialist Ruth deserts him. Then one of his books brings him both fame and money. Ruth seeks him out, but he realizes her true nature and turns away from her. He becomes depressed, and Russ's suicide makes matters worse. He grows to despise the society that has finally honoured him, and he commits suicide on a sea voyage.

Martineau, Harriet 1802–76 Writer on religion and economics, and novelist. She was born in Norwich the daughter of a manufacturer and the sister of JAMES MARTINEAU. A Unitarian, she began her writing career with religious subjects, in *Devotional Exercises for the Use of Young Persons* (1823) and *Addresses with Prayers and Additional Hymns for the Use of Families* (1826). She subsequently became interested in economics and earned a reputation as a lively expositor of UTILITARIANISM, using fiction to advance her theories and proposals for social reform: *Illustrations of Political Economy* (1832–4), *Poor Law and Paupers Illustrated* (1833) and *Illustrations of Taxation* (1834). A visit to the USA prompted *Society in America* (1837), which contains her comments on slavery, and *Retrospect of Western Travel* (1838). Later she wrote two novels, *Deerbrook* (1839) and *The Hour and the Man* (1841), which takes Toussaint L'Ouverture as its subject. An active journalist, she contributed regularly to THE DAILY NEWS and THE EDINBURGH REVIEW, and in 1841 published a book of stories for young people, *The Playfellow*. She had moved steadily away from her religious beliefs, and in 1853 produced a condensed version of Auguste Comte's *Cours de philosophie positive*. *A History of the Thirty Years' Peace, 1815–45* appeared in 1849. Her *Autobiographical Memoir*, posthumously published in 1877, is valuable for its first-hand comments on her contemporaries in literature.

Martineau, James 1805–1900 Theologian. The brother of HARRIET MARTINEAU, he studied as an engineer, but was ordained in the Unitarian ministry in 1828. In 1840 he was appointed professor of mental and moral philosophy at Manchester New College. His highly influential works of philosophy include *Ideal Substitutes for God* (1879), *Study of Spinoza* (1882), *Types of Ethical Theory* (1885), *A Study of Religion* (1888) and *The Seat of Authority in Religion* (1888). He also composed poems and hymns and contributed regularly to the *National Review*.

Martyn, Edward 1859–1923 Irish playwright. He was born in Galway and attended schools in Dublin and Windsor before going to Oxford. A prominent figure in the Irish cultural revival, he became one of the founders of the Irish Literary Theatre (see ABBEY THEATRE). *The Heather Field* (1899) and *Maeve* (1900) were among its earliest productions. *Romulus and Remus* (1907) and *The Dream Physician* (1914) reflect his later disagreement with YEATS and his circle. *Grangecolman* (1912) was written for the Independent Theatre Company. In 1914 Martyn founded the Irish Theatre to present plays in Gaelic.

Martyrs, Foxe's Book of See ACTS AND MONUMENTS.

Marvell, Andrew 1621–78 METAPHYSICAL POET and satirist. Born the son of a vicar at Winestead-in-Holderness, Yorkshire, Marvell moved with his family to Hull in 1624, where he was educated at the grammar school. He went to Trinity College, Cambridge, in 1633, and received a wide linguistic training, reading intently the Roman poets such as Juvenal and Horace, whose work was to influence the form of his later poems. His father died in 1641, and Marvell left for the Continent the following year, returning in 1647 after visits to Holland, France, Italy and Spain. While in Rome he visited RICHARD FLECKNOE, whom he lampooned in a poem. Marvell's travels and broad cultural interests contributed much to the civilized, urbane tone of his verse.

In 1648, he wrote some commendatory verses for LOVELACE's *Lucasta*. In 1649 his ELEGY for Lord Hastings appeared, and in 1650 Marvell's sometimes equivocal political affiliations expressed themselves in favour of Cromwell in 'An Horatian Ode upon Cromwell's Return from Ireland', which voices approval but stresses the conditions upon which such a leadership must be maintained. In 1651 he moved to Yorkshire to act as tutor to the daughter of Lord Fairfax, the Parliamentary general, and during the two years of his residence at Nun Appleton House Marvell probably composed his finest poetry, including his magnificently sustained 'Upon Appleton House', which celebrates the civilized retirement of Fairfax from the world of public affairs.

Marvell became a friend of MILTON, by whom he was recommended in 1653 for the post of Assistant Latin Secretary to the Council of State, a post he finally secured in 1657. In the interim he acted as tutor to William Dutton, later a ward of Cromwell's. He became MP for Hull in 1659, holding the seat for the rest of his life. With the Restoration, Marvell's moderate eulogies of Cromwell's regime were converted into a reasonable acceptance of monarchical stability, but he rapidly became an outspoken opponent of Charles II's government, its failure to promote religious toleration and its inefficiency in military matters. He travelled to Holland for eleven months (1662–3) and later acted as Secretary to the Earl of Carlisle in an embassy to Russia, Sweden and Denmark, returning in 1665. During the naval wars with the Dutch, Marvell was, therefore, in a strong position to be critical of the political mismanagement of the campaign, and in 1667 wrote his comprehensively withering SATIRE *The Last Instructions to a Painter* (not published until 1689), a catalogue of verse-portraits criticizing and pillorying those who had influence on affairs of state. He wrote several other political and religious satires, for which at the time of his death he was well known; these include 'Clarindon's House Warming', 'The Loyal Scot', 'The Statue in Stocks-Market' and a powerful prose satire, *The Rehearsal Transprosed* (published in two parts, 1672–3), a denunciation of the opinions of Samuel Parker, Archdeacon of Canterbury. On 16 August 1678, Marvell died of a tertian ague and his housekeeper, Mary Palmer, later claimed that they had been married.

Before 1681, little of his poetry had been published, but in that year appeared *Miscellaneous Poems by Andrew Marvell, Esq...* which omitted his 'Horatian Ode'. Known at his death as a formidable satirist, Marvell was 'discovered' in the 19th century (by

TENNYSON, for instance) as the writer of some beautifully accomplished pastoral poetry about gardens and flowers, and was celebrated as 'the green poet'. These poems probably belong to the period before 1653, and include 'The Garden' (a complicated contemplation on sophistication and innocence), 'The Picture of Little T.C. in a Prospect of Flowers', and 'The Nymph Complaining for the Death of Her Fawn'. As a lyric poet, Marvell was both dramatic and visually exact, and his fascination for small natural detail seems peculiarly representative of the age of the microscope, the miniature and intricate floral horticulture. His chief influence was DONNE whose metaphysical CONCEITS clearly impressed Marvell, though he is stylistically less brittle than his predecessor. His most famous poem is 'To His Coy Mistress', a seductive love poem of the CARPE DIEM mode, precisely constructed and erotically pitched. In style and finesse, Marvell's best poetry properly belongs to the earlier years of his century, but his political satires, though coarser in their effects, are also of contemporary interest, and show the diversity of verse genres available at that time.

Marxist criticism During the 19th century Marx and Engels developed explanations of the historical development of the capitalist mode of production, but had little time to elaborate a cultural theory to explain how literature and art were conditioned or determined by the social and economic forces which constitute the 'base' of a particular historical system. Their asides on this problem varied from rather mechanical statements about culture and ideology being the 'reflexes' in men's brains of real life-processes to more subtle statements (Engels) about the 'relative autonomy' of 'superstructures' (which rest on the base).

After a liberal phase the Soviet Union, during the early 1930s, adopted Socialist Realism as its official doctrine. It demanded that artists should be committed to the working-class cause of the Party, that literature should reflect a progressive outlook on society, provide a sense of the ideal possibilities of social development, and should be accessible to the masses. Modernist tendencies in Western literature were regarded as decadent, subjective and pessimistic in outlook (see MODERNISM), while the 19th-century realist novel was praised as a precursor of the 20th-century socialist-realist novel.

From within Socialist Realism Georg Lukács evolved a sophisticated theory of 'reflection', according to which a novel gives us a structural understanding of social development. In marked contrast, Bertolt Brecht favoured the experimental techniques of modernism (reportage, photo-montage, etc.) and other devices from Elizabethan and Chinese acting, which prevented the theatre audience from adopting a passive and empathic attitude to the actors on stage. His technique of ALIENATION aimed to preserve critical engagement between actor and audience.

The Frankfurt School, which flourished in Germany and the United States, developed a Hegelian strain of cultural theory, in response to the threats from totalitarianism in the 1930s. Adorno, Horkheimer and others believed that *avant-garde* literature and art played a special role in giving us a 'negative' knowledge of a hostile social world, reflecting the alienated existence of humanity in late capitalist societies. The writings of Walter Benjamin, an associate of Adorno, developed a highly personal mixture of fundamentalist Marxism and Cabbalistic lore.

In the 1960s Marxist criticism entered a new phase of sophistication under the influence of STRUCTURALISM. Lucien Goldmann's 'genetic structuralism' revealed the 'homologies' (structural parallels) between literature, ideas and social groups. In contrast, Louis Althusser argued that the different levels within the social formation have no overall unity but possess their own 'specific effectivity', while the economic level is determinant only 'in the last instance' (Engels's phrase). His disciple Pierre Macherey developed the literary implications of these views.

RAYMOND WILLIAMS and Terry Eagleton are the best-known English Marxist critics. The former developed late as a Marxist from an early socialist reinterpretation of F. R. LEAVIS, while Eagleton was influenced by Althusser's theories of ideology and then by the tradition of Brecht and Benjamin. In the USA Fredric Jameson wrote under the influence of the Frankfurt School and, later, POST-STRUCTURALISM.

***Mary Barton:** A Tale of Manchester Life* A novel by ELIZABETH GASKELL, published in 1848. The background to the story is the 'hungry forties' of the 19th century, when a series of bad harvests, beginning in 1837, coupled with taxation on imports of wheat, placed a heavy burden on the lower-paid workers. The Chartist movement and the Anti-Corn Law agitation arose out of these conditions. (See also the CONDITION OF ENGLAND NOVEL.)

One of the sufferers is John Barton, an upright man and a good worker. He is an active trade unionist. His daughter, Mary, has attracted the attention of Henry Carson, her father's employer. Flattered, she discourages the attentions of Jem Wilson, a young engineer. John Barton's fellow workers, in despair at their condition, which the employers will do nothing to ease, decide to kill Henry Carson as a warning to his class and the lot falls to John Barton to commit the murder.

In the meantime Mary Barton, realizing her foolishness, determines to break with Carson. At this point Carson is murdered and suspicion falls on Jem, his rival for Mary. Mary, discovering that it was her father who shot Carson, is faced with a terrible choice. Since she cannot betray her father's guilt, she has to prove Jem's innocence; her father, meanwhile, is enduring acute mental anguish which Jem's acquittal does nothing to allay. At the end of the book John Barton, on the verge of death, confesses his crime to Henry Carson's father and succeeds in obtaining his forgiveness.

In her Preface to *Mary Barton*, Elizabeth Gaskell explained that she knew nothing 'of Political Economy, or the theories of trade', but that her work grew out of her own observation of the poor and uneducated factory-workers of Manchester. Her merciless descriptions of poverty, her sense of outrage and her boundless sympathy remain a powerful combination, and *Mary Barton* is one of the most important works to have been written in a decade which produced many remarkable novels.

Masefield, John (Edward) 1878–1967 Poet, novelist, playwright, journalist and writer of CHILDREN'S LITERATURE. After an idyllic childhood in Ledbury, Herefordshire, he joined the merchant navy at the age of 13. He suffered from seasickness on his first voyage, to Chile. On a second voyage in 1895 he deserted in New York, reading, writing and taking various jobs in America before returning to England and joining the staff of *The Manchester Guardian*.

His career as a poet began with *Salt-Water Ballads* (1902), which included 'Sea Fever' ('I must go down to the sea again'), later set to music by John Ireland. *Ballads and Poems* (1910) was followed by *The Everlasting Mercy* (1911), the long narrative poem for which he is best known. It tells the realistic story of the sin and redemption of Saul Kane in colloquial, sometimes profane, language. *The Widow in the Bye Street* (1912) and *The Daffodil Fields* (1913) were followed by *Dauber* (1913), perhaps the best of his narrative poems, in which an artist is mocked by the crew on a long sea-voyage. *Reynard the Fox* (1919) is a Chaucerian narrative of a fox-hunt told by a man who dislikes hunting. *Collected Poems* (1923) proved a great success, and in 1930 Masefield became POET LAUREATE. His critical reputation waned in later years, but recently he has again been admired for his wide range, encompassing ballads, lyrics, nature poetry and mythological narrative, and for his attempt to make poetry a popular art. A close friend and admirer of YEATS, whom he first met in London in 1900, he published *Some Memories of W. B. Yeats* (1940) and an ELEGY, 'Oh What He Was'.

In all, Masefield published more than 50 books. His novels include *Sard Harker* (1924), *The Bird of Dawning* (1933), *Dead Ned* (1938) and *Live and Kicking Ned* (1939). His plays include *The Trial of Jesus* (1926) and *The Coming of Christ* (1928). *The Midnight Folk* (1927) and *The Box of Delights* (1933) were written for children. *So Long to Learn* (1952) and a further fragment, *Grace before Ploughing* (1966), are autobiographical.

Mason, A(lfred) E(dward) W(oodley) 1865–1948 Novelist. He was educated at Dulwich College and Oxford, and became an actor before turning to writing. The best known of his many popular historical novels and adventure stories is *The Four Feathers* (1902). He is also remembered for his contribution to DETECTIVE FICTION in creating Inspector Hanaud of the Sûreté, who appeared in *At the Villa Rose* (1910), *The House of the Arrow* (1924), *No Other Tiger* (1927) and *The Prisoner in the Opal* (1929).

Mason, R(onald) A(lison) K(ells) 1905–71 New Zealand poet and playwright. Born and educated in Auckland, he attended the university there in the late 1920s and again in the late 1930s, graduating with a BA in classics in 1939. In the 1920s he worked as a part-time tutor and in the 1930s as a company secretary and public works foreman. About this time he turned to Marxism and for many years he wrote left-wing political journalism for the magazines *People's Voice* and *Challenge*, which he edited from 1943 to 1954. During this period he was an active trade-unionist and also wrote a number of political plays, including *Squire Speaks* (1938), *China* (1943) and *Refugee* (1945). In later life he worked as a landscape gardener and part-time teacher.

Mason's poetry is strongly influenced by his classical education, but also contains a strong religious element, characterized by an emphasis on suffering and an ironic treatment of the Passion. BLAKE, Horace and Catullus are major influences. His best work belongs to his early life; most of the poems in *The Beggar* (1924) were written before he was 18, but already display considerable technical control. *No New Thing* (1934), which brought together poems written between 1924 and 1929, introduced a new concern for craftsmanship into New Zealand verse. After 1934 Mason wrote comparatively little poetry. His other volumes include *In the Manner of Men* (1923), sometimes seen as marking the beginnings of modern New Zealand verse, *End of Day* (1936), *This Dark Will Lighten: Selected Poems 1923–1941* (1941) and *Collected Poems* (1962). A modern Romantic, whose best poetry appears to be an urgent expression of spontaneous feeling, Mason is highly regarded, though seldom imitated, in his native New Zealand.

Mason, William 1725–97 Poet, playwright, gardener and musician. Son of the Rev. William Mason, Vicar of Holy Trinity, Hull, he was educated at Hull Grammar School and St John's College, Cambridge, subsequently being elected, with the help of THOMAS GRAY, fellow of Pembroke Hall. Ordained in 1754, he rose to be canon and precentor of York in 1762. He died from an injury to his shin while stepping out of his carriage. His plays adopted old-fashioned forms: *Elfrida* (1752) and *Caractacus* (1759) were both historical tragedies in the classical mode. As a poet he pro-

William Mason's poem *Caractacus* inspired this engraving in Francis Grose's *The Antiquities of England and Wales* (1773–6), showing a druid and an imaginary version of Stonehenge

duced rather plodding couplets, though the didactic *The English Garden* (1772–82) is in BLANK VERSE. It advocates the informality which he put into practice in his own designs; his garden at Nuneham for the 2nd Earl of Harcourt still exists. An equally avid musician, he invented the celestinette, wrote essays on cathedral music and was a friend of Thomas Arne. He painted, badly, and translated Du Fresnoy's *Art of Painting* (1782). On the death of Gray, Mason became the poet's literary executor and published Gray's *Life and Letters* in 1774. He is principally remarkable for his friendships, which, besides Arne and Gray, included JOSHUA REYNOLDS, HORACE WALPOLE, MARY DELANY and GARRICK. Mason was living proof of the fact that in the 18th century the gentleman amateur could always gain access to the genuinely able. His achievements were second-rate: his friends were first-rate.

masque At its height in the court of JAMES I and Charles I, the English masque was a spectacular entertainment, involving dance, drama, music, lavish costumes and splendidly inventive scenery devised by Inigo Jones. The uneasy collaboration of BEN JONSON with Inigo Jones lasted from 1605 to 1634 and produced many of the finest court masques. It was the Civil War that brought to an end the vogue for this costly form of entertainment.

The precise origins of the masque are uncertain. In primitive folk ritual, disguised guests would present gifts to their wealthy host (king or nobleman) before joining him and his household in a ceremonial dance, and the fashion for 'disguisings' was revived in Tudor England. The entertainments provided for Queen Elizabeth I during her 'progresses', whilst retaining some of the features of the simple disguising, pointed the way to the vastly more elaborate Jacobean masques, through which Inigo Jones introduced Italian perspective scenery to the English audience.

Massacre at Paris, The See MARLOWE, CHRISTOPHER.

Massinger, Philip 1583–1640 Playwright. Philip Massinger was born in Salisbury and educated at Oxford. By 1606 he had settled in London, where he is first identified as a playwright in a 1613 reference in PHILIP HENSLOWE's *Diary*. He was one of the busiest of Jacobean and Caroline dramatists. That he was highly esteemed as a professional writer is strongly suggested by his long association (1613–40, almost without a break) with the leading theatre company, the KING'S MEN. Much of his work was collaborative, and much has been lost. Among his collaborators in plays that survive are NATHAN FIELD in *THE FATAL DOWRY* (c. 1618), THOMAS DEKKER in *THE VIRGIN MARTYR* (1620) and JOHN FLETCHER in more than 20 plays. These include: *The Tragedy of Sir John van Olden Barnavelt* (1619), about contemporary events in the Netherlands; *The Custom of the Country* (c. 1619), a bawdy tragicomedy; *The Beggar's Bush* (c. 1622), a romantic drama using thieves' and vagabonds' cant; and *The Spanish Curate* (c. 1622), a comedy of intrigue. Massinger was buried in Fletcher's tomb in Southwark Cathedral.

In the work of which he is generally supposed to have been sole author, Massinger's independent, satirical temperament is unmistakable. *The Maid of Honour* (c. 1621) dared to attack the Elector Palatine and *The Bondman* (1623) criticized the powerful Duke of Buckingham. In *The Renegado* (1624), Massinger risked offending anti-Catholic London by presenting a sympathetic portrait of a Jesuit priest, and the anti-Spanish bias of *Believe As You List* (1631) led to its being banned from performance in its original version. Massinger believed his tragedy about the Emperor Domitian, THE ROMAN ACTOR (1626), to be his best work, but it is the bitter comedies *A NEW WAY TO PAY OLD DEBTS* (c. 1622) and THE CITY MADAM (c. 1632), with their monstrously energetic central characters, Sir Giles Overreach and Luke Frugal, that have lasted best.

Masson, David 1822–1907 Biographer. Born in Aberdeen, the son of a stonecutter, he was educated at the universities of Aberdeen and Edinburgh and became professor of rhetoric and English literature at Edinburgh (1865–95).

In 1859 he founded *Macmillan's Magazine*, which he edited until 1867. Masson's principal work is his exhaustive life of MILTON (1859–94). Other works include studies of DRUMMOND OF HAWTHORNDEN (1873), CHATTERTON (1874), and DE QUINCEY (1881); *Essays Biographical and Critical, Chiefly on English Poets* was published in 1856. *Edinburgh Sketches and Memories* (1892), *Memories of London in the Forties* (1908) and *Memories of Two Cities, Edinburgh and Aberdeen* (1911) offer interesting pictures of Masson's career and the circles in which he moved. He was made Historiographer Royal for Scotland in 1893.

Master Humphrey's Clock A weekly miscellany by CHARLES DICKENS, begun in 1840. It reintroduced the characters of Mr Pickwick and the Wellers, and served as a framework for the publication of THE OLD CURIOSITY SHOP, but was never in itself the commercial success Dickens had hoped. He dropped the title when *BARNABY RUDGE* began to appear in weekly numbers in 1841.

Master of Ballantrae, The: *A Winter's Tale* A novel by ROBERT LOUIS STEVENSON, published in 1889. Set in Jacobite Scotland in the period immediately following the 1745 Rebellion, it is based on the story of the Marquis of Tullibardine. Stevenson saw it as a chronicle of domestic animosity, 'a drama in a nutshell'.

The story is told by Ephraim Mackellar, one of Stevenson's most successfully characterized first-person narrators. It follows the lifelong feud between two brothers: James Durie, the Master of Ballantrae, violent, charming and unscrupulous, and the younger Henry, quiet, dutiful and dull. The Master goes off to support the Young Pretender and is reported killed at Culloden. Henry succeeds to the title and the estate, and marries his brother's sweetheart, Alison Graeme. The Master returns, embittered by his exclusion, and proceeds to milk the estate of its revenues. The brothers' enmity culminates in a moonlit duel, and the Master is left for dead. When he reappears a second time the family flee to their estates in America. The Master follows them and Henry's reason gives way when he hears the rumour that the Master will be pardoned and reinstated. The Master evades Henry's murderous attack on him by having his servant bury him alive. When he reappears from the dead for a third time, or appears to do so for a few seconds, Henry dies from the shock and the brothers are buried in a common grave. The novel is complex and subtle, and the reader's sympathies are divided between the two brothers.

Master of Game, The A hunting treatise by Edward Plantagenet, 2nd Duke of York, written c. 1410. Largely a translation of parts of the *Livre de chasse* of Gaston Phoebus, Comte de Foix, it includes additional chapters on details of the hunts for the hare and hart. The work deals with the natural history of the prey, the types and care of hounds and how to find a hart, as well as details of the hunt itself. It follows its source faithfully in the translated passages and, while not notable for any literary qualities, it was popular and widely copied during the 15th century.

Masterman Ready See MARRYAT, CAPTAIN FREDERICK.

Masters, Edgar Lee 1868–1950 American poet and novelist. Born in Kansas, he practised law in Chicago from 1891 to 1920. His first publications were *A Book of Verses* (1898) and a blank-verse drama entitled *Maximilian* (1902). He became famous in 1915 with the publication of SPOON RIVER ANTHOLOGY, a book of epitaphs in free verse about the lives of those buried in a cemetery in rural Illinois. He was never to repeat its success, perhaps because he never again found a subject so perfectly suited to his free-verse style and his vein of irony. He did command attention, however, and published several more collections; three dramatic poems, *Lee* (1926), *Jack Kelso* (1928) and *Godbey* (1931); three novels based on his own youth, *Mitch Miller* (1920), *Skeeters Kirby* (1923) and *Mirage* (1924); and a hostile biographical study of Abraham Lincoln, *Lincoln the Man* (1931). In 1924 he returned to the scene of his initial success with *The*

New Spoon River, which applies the same technique to the urban life that was beginning to prevail in America. *Across Spoon River*, an autobiography, appeared in 1924.

Masters, John 1914–83 Novelist. Born in Calcutta and educated at Wellington and Sandhurst, Masters joined a regiment in India in 1934, subsequently commanded a brigade of the Chindits in Burma, and was a member of the 19th Indian Division at the taking of Mandalay. He turned to writing after retiring from the army in 1948. His novels are works of fast-moving, epic adventure on a wide canvas, and divide into two groups. The first (for which he is best known) is a series of books about British India, of which notable examples are *Nightrunners of Bengal* (1951), a historical fiction set during the Indian Mutiny, and *Bhowani Junction* (1954), about the post-war strife immediately preceding Indian independence. The second phase of his work is a trilogy, *Loss of Eden*, about World War I, comprising *Now, God be Thanked* (1979), *Heart of War* (1980) and *By the Green of the Spring* (1981).

Masters, Olga 1919–86 Australian novelist, short-story writer and journalist. The fiction which she began to write when she was nearly 60 orchestrates 'the violence in the human heart', offering a quiet record of malice and pain in domestic life and unremarkable places. A collection of stories, *The Home Girls* (1982), was followed by a novel, *Loving Daughters* (1984), and a collection of linked stories, *A Long Time Dying* (1985). Posthumously published works are: *Amy's Children* (1987), another novel; *The Rose Fancier* (1988), more stories; *A Working Man's Castle* (1988), a play; and *Olga Masters: Reporting Home: Her Writings as a Journalist* (1991).

Mather, Cotton 1663–1728 American Puritan minister, the eldest son of INCREASE MATHER and grandson of JOHN COTTON and RICHARD MATHER. A prodigy, he entered Harvard at the age of 12 and prepared for the ministry. He was ordained in 1685 and soon after became co-minister with his father of the Second Church of Boston. In 1689 he took some 'possessed' Boston girls into his home to observe and treat them, and then wrote about the cases in *Memorable Providences, relating to Witchcrafts and Possessions* (1689). He later published an account of the Salem witch trials and other instances of what he believed to be the operation of evil spirits in *The Wonders of the Invisible World* (1693).

During the 1690s he worked on his history of New England, *MAGNALIA CHRISTI AMERICANA* (published in London in 1702); he also published numerous sermons expounding Puritan doctrine, and was regarded by many as the pre-eminent spokesman for Puritan culture. *BONIFACIUS*, published anonymously

in 1710, was an attempt to give Puritan piety a social component, explaining how a true Christian acts in an increasingly secular world of complex business and family relations. Like his father, Mather was interested in science, and he was elected to the Royal Society in 1714. *The Christian Philosopher* (1721) includes scientific observations of the natural world with suggestions of their spiritual significance. *The Angel of Bethesda* (1722) was a medical work. With his prominent family and his own political activism and intense religious involvement, in many ways Cotton Mather epitomized his culture; his extensive diary is a massive record of the American Puritan experience.

Among his other works were *Parentator* (1724), a biography of his father, 'Paterna', an unpublished autobiography written for his children, *Psalterium Americanum* (1718) and *Manuductio ad ministerium* (1726), a handbook for ministers. His lifelong project, *Biblia Americana*, a systematic commentary on the Bible, remained unpublished at his death.

Mather, Increase 1639-1723 American Puritan minister. The son of RICHARD MATHER, he was born in Dorchester, Massachusetts, and educated at Harvard and later at Trinity College, Dublin. He married the daughter of JOHN COTTON, the prominent Puritan minister, and himself became the minister of the Second Church of Boston, which he served for the rest of his life, latterly with his son, COTTON MATHER. He also became a Fellow of Harvard and eventually its president.

A leading figure in the affairs of Massachusetts, Mather frequently wrote on matters of public import. His election sermon, *The Day of Trouble is Near* (1674), was sometimes interpreted as a prophecy of the Indian wars that followed. *A Relation of the Troubles Which Have Happened in New England, by Reason of the Indians There* (1677) is a narrative of Indian relations starting with the first Massachusetts settlements, and *A Brief History of the War with the Indians* (1676) is about King Philip's War (1674–6). Both histories interpret the Indian wars as contests between the saints and the forces of the devil; the Indian attacks are seen as judgements on the colonists for apostasy, colonial victories as signs of God's providence.

Mather also wrote frequently on scientific subjects, though his curiosity about natural phenomena was motivated less by an empirical scientific spirit than by a desire to see the glory of God's works in the world. His *Kometographia* (1683) and other works on comets, as well as his *Essay for the Recording of Illustrious Providences* (1685), include detailed observations which point to the mysterious ways of God rather than to rational understanding. No stranger to physical explanations (albeit they were of secondary importance), he was an early champion of inoculation against smallpox, writing in defence of the practice during the epidemic of 1721.

In 1688, he headed a mission to England that obtained a new charter for the colony, and a new governor in the person of Sir William Phips. Mather and Phips returned to Massachusetts, just as the Salem witch trials were beginning. Although Mather believed in the possibility of witches and witchcraft, he later censured the court in his *Cases of Conscience concerning Evil Spirits* (1693) for basing convictions on 'spectral evidence', which he said could be deceptive. His other writings, which exemplify the Puritan mentality of his time, include sermons on conversion and church membership policy, speculations on the millennium, and his 'Autobiography'.

Mather, Richard 1596–1669 Puritan minister and father of INCREASE MATHER. Born in Lancashire, he spent a year at Oxford before being ordained in 1619. Because of his nonconformity, he was suspended by Archbishop LAUD in 1633, and emigrated to New England in 1635. There he was called by the Dorchester church, which he served from 1636 to the end of his life. He became one of the leading ministers in the Bay Colony, contributing to the translations of the Psalms in the *BAY PSALM BOOK* (1640). In the 1630s and 1640s he produced a series of treatises defending the New England congregational system against Presbyterian opponents, the most significant of which is *Church Government and Church Covenant Discussed* (1643). He took part in the two major synods of his time in 1648 and in 1662. He was one of the main architects of the 1648 Cambridge Synod's *Platform of Church Discipline* (1649), which set out the main principles of New England church polity. His *Journal*, which includes an account of his Atlantic crossing, was published for the first time in the 19th century.

Mathers, Peter 1931– Australian novelist and playwright. Born in England, he has worked in agriculture and public service and as an adviser to students of theatre. His underlying belief in anarchy gives his work a comic ebullience which survives even the most dreadful events. *Trap* (1966), a winner of the Miles Franklin Award, anticipated THOMAS KENEALLY's *The Chant of Jimmy Blacksmith* in its study of the relationship between a part-Aboriginal and the society which seeks to understand and control him. Equally loose in structure, *The Wort Papers* (1972) takes up similar themes of persecution and hardship in the history of a family's relationships. After a collection of short stories, *A Change for the Better* (1984), Mathers turned to drama with *Mountain King* (1985), *Shirt Tales* (1985), *Bats* (1986), *Grigori Two* (1987), *Caught* (1987), *Urbiculture* (1987), *Travelling* (1988), *More Urbiculture* (1988), *Real McCoy* (1988) and *Caught: or, In the Name of the Rose* (1988).

Mathews, John Joseph *c.* 1894-1979 An Osage Indian born in Pawhuska, Oklahoma, and educated at the University of Oklahoma and at Oxford. His first work, *Wah 'Kon-Tah: The Osage and the White Man's Road*, a historical study of the Osage Indians from 1878 to 1931, appeared in 1932. His other books include *Sundown* (1934), a novel, and *The Osages: Children of the Middle Waters* (1961).

Matthiessen, Peter 1927– American novelist and travel writer. Born in New York, he was educated at the Sorbonne and at Yale. He returned in the 1950s to Paris, where he founded the *Paris Review* and wrote his first novel, *Race Rock* (1954). Other novels include: *Partisans* (1955); *Raditzer* (1960); *At Play in the Fields of the Lord* (1965), about a threatened Amazonian tribe; *Far Tortuga* (1975), a seafaring narrative based on his own experiences; and *Killing Master Watson* (1990), a murder mystery. He has travelled widely on expeditions of zoological research and anthropological observation. His works of natural history include *Wildlife in America* (1959), *The Shore Birds of North America* (1967) and *The Wind Birds* (1973). His travel books include: *Under the Mountain* (1963), about New Guinea; *The Tree Where Man was Born* (1972), the journal of a safari in Africa; *The Snow Leopard* (1978), about Nepal and Buddhism; *Blue Meridian* (1971); *In the Spirit of Crazy Horse* (1983); *Indian Country* (1984); and *African Silences* (1991).

Matura, Mustapha 1939– Playwright. He was born in Trinidad and settled in Britain in 1960. A co-founder of the Black Theatre Co-operative, he has written about both Trinidad and the West Indian communities in Britain. *Play Mas* (1974) is about a carnival, *Independence* (1979) contrasts kinds of independence, and *Meetings* (1981) deals with the differing values of two generations. Matura has also written for television and produced West Indian versions of European classics, such as *The Playboy of the West Indies* (1984) from SYNGE and *Trinidad Sisters* (1988) from Chekhov's *Three Sisters*.

Maturin, Charles Robert 1782–1824 Novelist and playwright. Of Huguenot descent, Maturin was born in Dublin and took holy orders after studying at Trinity College. He is remembered for *MELMOTH THE WANDERER* (1820), a powerful GOTHIC NOVEL. His other novels were *The Fatal Revenge* (1807), *The Wild Irish Boy* (1808), *The Milesian Chief* (1811), *Women: or, Pour et Contre* (1818) and *The Albigenses* (1824). His tragedy *Bertram* was produced with great success at DRURY LANE by Edmund Kean in 1816, but two other tragedies, *Manuel* (1817) and *Fredolfo* (1819), failed.

Maud A poem by ALFRED TENNYSON, published in 1855. It grew out of the lyric 'Oh! That 'Twere Possible', written in 1833–4 after the death of ARTHUR

HENRY HALLAM. The original title was *Maud: or, The Madness*, but Tennyson retitled it *Maud: A Monodrama* in 1875.

The narrator recounts the melancholy history of his life: his father's death and the ruin of his family, his love for Maud and the duel in which he killed her brother, his flight from home, his descent into insanity and his recovery through patriotic commitment to the Crimean War. Tennyson described the work as 'a little *HAMLET*, the history of a morbid, poetic soul, under the blighting influence of a recklessly speculative age ... The peculiarity of this poem is that different phases of passion in one person take the place of different characters.' It is outstanding for the virtuosity with which Tennyson uses a variety of metres to convey the hero's different moods.

Maugham, (William) Somerset 1874–1965 Novelist, short-story writer and playwright. He was born at the British Embassy in Paris, where his father was a solicitor, but orphaned at the age of ten and brought up in Whitstable, Kent, by his uncle and aunt. After an unhappy time at King's School, Canterbury, he studied philosophy at Heidelberg and then trained as a doctor at St Thomas's Hospital, Lambeth, qualifying in 1897. A small private income allowed him to settle as a writer in Paris the following year. After World War I he travelled widely with his secretary and companion, Gerald Haxton, before making his permanent home at Cap Ferrat in the South of France in 1926.

His first novel, *Liza of Lambeth* (1897), was an experiment in NATURALISM based on his observation of the slums and cockney life. In Paris he wrote seven more novels, short stories, a travel book about Andalusia and plays. He first achieved success as a playwright with *Lady Frederick* (1907). It was followed by a FARCE, *Jack Straw* (1908), and several pieces which gained him wide popularity; they include *The Tenth Man* (1910), *Our Betters* (1917), *The Circle* (1921), *The Letter* (1927) and *For Services Rendered* (1932). After *Sheppey* (1933) he gave up writing for the theatre.

His first really successful novel was *Of Human Bondage* (1915), a semi-autobiographical work charting the life and adventures of a young man in 'Blackstable' (Whitstable) and 'Tercanbury' (Canterbury). *The Moon and Sixpence* (1919), set in Tahiti, is about a Gauguinesque artist, Charles Strickland. Other novels were: *The Painted Veil* (1925), *Cakes and Ale* (1930), a light-hearted comedy which contains a fictionalized portrait of HARDY, *The Razor's Edge* (1945) and *Catalina* (1948). His short stories, including

Somerset Maugham

some that have been considered among the best in the language, appeared in collections beginning with *Orientations* (1899) and ending with *Creatures of Circumstance* (1947). Particularly notable volumes are *The Trembling of a Leaf* (1921), *Ashenden: or, The British Agent* (1928) and *Six Stories in the First Person Singular* (1931). Many were adapted for the stage and screen.

Maugham's travels are the subject of *On a Chinese Screen* (1922) and *Don Fernando* (1935). His personal views on life and art can be found in *The Summing Up* (1938), *Strictly Personal* (1942), *A Writer's Notebook* (1949) and *Points of View* (1958). In his own judgement he was one of the leading 'second-raters'. Critics have praised his narrative skill and his merciless, anti-romantic powers of observation.

Maupin, Armistead 1944– American novelist. Born in Washington DC, he grew up in Ralegh, North Carolina, and attended the University of North Carolina. After serving as a naval officer in Vietnam, he settled in California in 1971. The six volumes of his *Tales of the City* sequence – *Tales of the City* (1978), *More Tales of the City* (1980), *Further Tales of the City* (1982), *Babycakes* (1984), *Significant Others* (1988) and *Sure of You* (1990) – have been praised for their Dickensian narrative multiplicity, their unsentimental portrait of the gay lifestyle on the West Coast and their light WIT.

Maurice A novel by E. M. FORSTER, written in 1913–14 and circulated privately but not published until 1971, after his death.

Maurice Hall, aged 14, is to attend public school. The senior prep school master acquaints the boy with 'the mystery of sex', an evasive idealization of relations between the sexes. Maturing, Maurice experiences homosexual tendencies but represses them to avoid conflict with the prevailing sexual ethos. Cambridge too is 'hell', but Maurice, now entering his twenties, meets Clive Durham. After an agonizing and protracted flirtation, first Clive and then Maurice declare their love and a clandestine relationship ensues. Maurice leaves Cambridge for clerical work, and Clive qualifies as a barrister.

Whilst convalescing in Greece, Clive decides to become 'normal' and breaks off their relationship. Maurice is heartbroken when Clive marries, and suffers acute isolation. However, during a visit to the newly-weds he meets Alec Scudder, Clive's gamekeeper. Alec is about to emigrate, but approaches Maurice in search of love. The latter responds, then is suspicious of Alec's motives and inhibited by class prejudice. They reach an understanding and spend Alec's last night in England together. Alec leaves for Southampton. Maurice, watching the boat sail, learns that Alec has decided to stay and proceeds triumphantly to join his lover.

In a 'Terminal Note', added after the final revision in 1960, Forster explains the inspiration behind the novel – his visit to EDWARD CARPENTER, the 'Whitmannic poet' and primitive socialist, in 1913 – and defends its 'happy ending'. He concludes with an impassioned indictment of the persecution of homosexuals in England in the absence of legal reform.

Maurice, (John) Frederick Denison 1805–72 Clergyman and leader of CHRISTIAN SOCIALISM. He was born at Normanstone, near Lowestoft, the son of a Unitarian minister. In 1823 he entered Trinity College, Cambridge; with his friend John Sterling he moved to Trinity Hall in 1825, but was excluded from both a degree and a fellowship because of his refusal to subscribe to the Thirty-Nine Articles. In 1830, however, he joined the Church of England, studied at Oxford and was ordained in 1834. He was appointed chaplain to Guy's Hospital in 1836, and while there he wrote *The Kingdom of Christ* (1838), a plea for religious unity that was generally misunderstood. In 1840 he became professor of English literature and history at King's College, London, and six years later professor of theology in the college's new Theological School.

Associating Christian practice with the need for social reform, Maurice held that 'a true socialism is the necessary result of a sound Christianity'. The belief led to the formation of the Christian Socialist group and his connection with J. M. F. Ludlow, THOMAS HUGHES and CHARLES KINGSLEY. *Theological Essays* (1853) brought Maurice into conflict with authority once more by questioning the accepted doctrine of eternal punishment. He was dismissed from King's College, an event which prompted TENNYSON's lyric, 'To the Rev. F. D. Maurice' (1855). In 1866 he became professor of moral philosophy at Cambridge. Maurice's lasting memorial is the Working Men's College, London, which arose from the organization of evening classes and was firmly established in 1854.

His views are expressed in *The Religions of the World* (1847), *Social Morality* (1869) and *Moral and Metaphysical Philosophy* (1871–2).

Maurice, Furnley [Wilmot, Frank] 1881–1942 Australian poet. Most of his working life was spent as a bookseller and publisher, though he wrote verse from an early age. His first important book, *Unconditioned Songs*, was published anonymously in 1913. His vivacious poetry draws on the Australian vernacular and is fresh, engaging and playful. Other works are *To God: From the Weary Nations* (1917), *The Bay and Padie Book* (1917), *Eyes of Vigilance* (1920), *Ways and Means* (1920), *The Gully and Other Verses* (1929), *Odes for a Curse Speaking Choir!* (1933) and *Melbourne Odes* (1934). *Poems by Furnley Maurice* was published in 1944.

Mavor, Osborne Henry See BRIDIE, JAMES.

Maxwell, Gavin 1914–69 Writer, conservationist and traveller. Born at the family home of Monreith, Wigtownshire, he developed an early interest in the wildlife around him, a boyhood described in *The House of Elrig* (1966). Educated at Stowe and Hertford College, Oxford, he later described his degree in land management as 'a useless achievement'. Invalided out of the army with the rank of major in 1944, he bought the island of Soay, off Skye, with the aim of setting up a shark fishing industry. The ultimate failure of this project gave him the material for his first autobiographical book, *Harpoon at a Venture* (1952). After trying his hand at journalism and portrait painting, Maxwell travelled in Sicily and Iraq, and produced three further books, including *A Reed Shaken by the Wind* (1956), an award-winning study of the Marsh Arabs of Southern Iraq.

Returning to Britain, Maxwell brought with him an otter cub, starting a relationship which was to dominate much of the rest of his life. The idyllic story of life with this and succeeding otters on the west coast of Scotland was related to great popular response and considerable critical acclaim in *Ring of Bright Water* (1960). It struck a note of innocence and joy which Maxwell failed to recover in the bitter sequels *The Rocks Remain* (1963) and *Raven Seek Thy Brother* (1968), as he was increasingly overtaken by personal and financial insecurities. He died in 1969, a year after the world of 'Camusfearna' was destroyed by fire.

May, Thomas 1595–1650 Translator, playwright and poet. Born in Sussex, May was educated at Sidney Sussex College, Cambridge. He was one of the many admirers of BEN JONSON and Jonson himself praised May's translations of Lucan's *Pharsalia* (1627) and Virgil's *Georgics* (1628). Two earlier efforts by May, *The Heir* and *The Old Couple* (both c. 1621), were undistinguished comedies; he also wrote three undistinguished tragedies, *Antigone, the Theban Princess* (c. 1626), *Cleopatra* (1626) and *Julia Agrippina* (1628). His translations from the Latin, which are regarded as his best work, continued with *Selected Epigrams of Martial* (1629) and a further instalment of Lucan, *Continuation* (1630). *The Mirror of Minds* (1631) is a translation of *Icon animorum* (1614) by JOHN BARCLAY. But his next works were very long and practically unread historical narrative poems, *The Reign of King Henry the Second* (1633) and *The Victorious Reign of King Edward the Third* (1635).

May was a Puritan and embraced the Parliamentary cause during the Civil War. He became secretary to the Long Parliament and his *History of the Parliament in England Which Began November the Third, 1640, with a Short and Necessary View of Some Precedent Years* (1647) is a valuable historical document.

Mayhew, Henry 1812–87 Journalist. Born in London, the son of a solicitor, and educated at Westminster School, Mayhew worked for a while in his father's office before joining his friend GILBERT À BECKETT on the illustrated comic weekly, *Figaro in London*. His farce, *The Wandering Minstrel*, was produced in 1834. In 1841 he was one of the original founders of *PUNCH*, but a change in the financial control of the magazine caused him to leave it in 1846.

In 1849 Mayhew began to publish *London Labour and the London Poor*, the ambitious, detailed and compassionate survey for which he is remembered. Its first instalments appeared as 'Labour and the Poor' in *THE MORNING CHRONICLE* and were continued independently in weekly parts. A collection was gathered together in book form in 1851, and the work was at last completed in four volumes in 1861–2. The fourth volume, dealing entirely with those who lived outside the law, was enlarged and republished in 1864.

In 1856 Mayhew began to issue a concurrent series called *The Great World of London* in monthly instalments, nine of which were brought together in a volume at the end of the year. It was incorporated with *The Criminal Prisons of London*, which Mayhew himself considered his most important work of social criticism, to form *The Criminal Prisons of London and Scenes of Prison Life* (1862).

Apart from these great achievements, Mayhew's busy career produced only ephemeral journalism. Among more than a score of other books, two works of travel are worth mention: *The Rhine and Its Picturesque Scenery* (1856) and *German Life and Manners As Seen in Saxony* (1864).

Mayne, Rutherford [Waddell, Samuel J.] 1878–1967 Irish actor and playwright. The brother of HELEN WADDELL, he was a leading force in the ULSTER LITERARY THEATRE from its foundation in 1902. His plays include *The Turn of the Road* (1906), *The Drone* (1908) and two one-act tragedies, *The Troth* (1908) and *Red Turf* (1911), in which the Irish experience of eviction and land-grabbing is tersely recreated. Mayne had served in the Irish Land Commission after 1909, and his last play, *Bridge Head* (1934), is about the efforts of the Commission to apportion land more equitably. Like its immediate predecessor, the comedy *Peter* (1930), it was written for the ABBEY THEATRE.

Mayne, William (Cyril) 1928– Writer of CHILDREN'S LITERATURE. Born in Hull, the son of a doctor, he was educated at Canterbury Cathedral Choir School before working intermittently for the BBC. *A Swarm in May* (1955) is a gentle adventure story set in a choir school. His subsequent works favoured understatement and left readers to draw their own inferences, a characteristic which has led to objections that Mayne's work is sometimes too difficult for most children. *Earthfasts* (1966), his first break with strict realism, used one of his favourite themes: the appearance of a figure from the past in modern life. The ambitious *A Game of Dark* (1971) parallels a consuming illness in a family with a fantasy dragon that has to be slain. *The Jersey Shore* (1973), perhaps his most difficult book, conveys an overwhelming sense of place, however fragmentary the story. Later works have continued to explore new settings and ideas, in particular the interdependence between humans and animals.

Mayor of Casterbridge, The Life and Death of the: *A Story of a Man of Character* A novel by THOMAS HARDY, serialized in *The Graphic* from January to May 1886 and published in book form the same year. It endows the rise and fall in its hero's fortunes with the inevitability of tragic process.

Michael Henchard, an out-of-work hay trusser, gets drunk at Weydon Priors fair and sells his wife, Susan, and child for five guineas to a sailor named Newson. Sober the next morning, Henchard swears an oath to abstain from alcohol for 21 years. After 18 years Mrs Newson, believing her sailor-husband drowned at sea, comes with her daughter, Elizabeth-Jane, to seek out Henchard, now a prosperous grain merchant and mayor of Casterbridge. He receives them generously and, at a clandestine meeting with Susan, arranges to court and marry her anew so that respectability may be maintained. A complicating factor, however, is his commitment to Lucetta Le Sueur, a woman of means he was supposed to be marrying; but upon hearing the mayor's true explanation of affairs their engagement is terminated, although Lucetta comes to Casterbridge to live.

Meanwhile, Henchard has engaged as his manager the newly-arrived Scotsman, Donald Farfrae, an energetic young man of commercial acumen. Henchard marries Susan, who soon dies but leaves a letter telling him Elizabeth-Jane is really Newson's daughter; this alienates him from Elizabeth-Jane and his bitterness rises to such a point that she leaves home to live as housekeeper-companion with Lucetta. And now Farfrae, who has shown an interest in Elizabeth-Jane, marries Lucetta. Because of Henchard's pigheadedness a rift opens between him and the Scotsman who, going into business for himself, thrives as Henchard declines to the point of bankruptcy. The old liaison between Henchard and Lucetta is publicized and she dies of shame. Newson returns, Elizabeth-Jane and Farfrae marry, and the lonely, embittered Henchard, reduced even below itinerant labour, dies on Egdon Heath cared for by the loyal but simple Able Whittle.

Mazeppa A poem by BYRON, published in 1819. It is based on a story told by Voltaire in his *Histoire de Charles XII* (1731). The Swedish king and his officers are resting after their defeat at Pultowa in 1719. They listen to Ivan Stepanovitch Mazeppa telling the story of his life. Born of a noble Polish family, he becomes page to the king of Poland, Casimir V. When his affair with the wife of a wealthy merchant is discovered, he is punished by being bound naked across the back of a horse, which is whipped into madness and gallops away with him. The poor animal races across rivers and through forests with its semiconscious burden and eventually falls dead on the plains of the Ukraine. Mazeppa is rescued and restored to health by the local people, and he becomes their leader. He seizes the opportunity presented by the Swedish invasion to desert and make his way west.

Mazeppa is also the subject of Pushkin's *Pultowa*.

Mazrui, Ali 1933– Kenyan political economist, cultural historian and novelist. Born in Mombasa, he attended the universities of Manchester, Columbia and Oxford, and has held various academic posts in Africa and abroad. He is best known for his political writings and his BBC TV series on the evolution of African culture. His one novel, *The Trial of Christopher Okigbo* (1971), arraigns the Nigerian poet posthumously for sacrificing his art to public and political interests in the Nigerian Civil War.

Measure for Measure A play by WILLIAM SHAKESPEARE, formally a comedy but so dark in tone that it is more often classed among the PROBLEM PLAYS. It was first performed *c.* 1604 and published in the First Folio of 1623. The main source is the story of Promos and Cassandra which WHETSTONE had borrowed from Cinthio's *Hecatommithi* in a play (1578) and a collection of romances (1582).

Disturbed by the unruliness of Vienna, Duke Vincentio resolves to absent himself from rule and entrusts law-enforcement to his puritanical deputy, Angelo. Disguised as a friar, the duke remains in Vienna to observe the consequences of his decision. Angelo orders the destruction of the brothels and, invoking a law against lechery, imprisons Claudio for impregnating the woman to whom he is betrothed. Knowing that the penalty is death, Claudio asks his sister, Isabella, a novice in a nunnery, to intercede. Confronted by Isabella, the unyielding Angelo experiences his own lust. He offers Claudio's life as an exchange for Isabella's body. Outraged when Claudio begs her to accept the offer, Isabella abandons him, but is persuaded by the disguised duke to play a trick on Angelo. The duke reveals that Angelo had broken a marriage-contract with a certain Mariana when Mariana's dowry was lost. Mourning her lost love, Mariana now lives in isolation. She would willingly take Isabella's place in Angelo's bed. The substitution is arranged, but the duke's scheme is ruined by Angelo's decision to have Claudio killed despite his promise to Isabella. The fortunate death in prison of a pirate with some physical resemblance to Claudio gives the duke another opportunity to thwart Angelo, whose villainy is unmasked when the duke makes his unexpected 'return' to Vienna. Claudio can now marry the pregnant Juliet, Angelo's punishment is to marry Mariana, and the duke declares his love for the chaste Isabella.

Measure for Measure raises more enduring issues than can be resolved by its conventional comic ending. After Isabella's two finely written encounters with Angelo, in which issues of justice and mercy, morality and the law, sin and grace are raised, the hurried plotting of the bed-trick and Claudio's escape seem perfunctory. It may be that Shakespeare was forced, through theatrical exigency, to finish in haste what he had begun in comparative leisure.

medieval lyric A short poem originally written for musical accompaniment, or written as if to be sung. It is usually characterized by a repeated stanza form, with a forceful METRE, simple RHYME and a refrain. More religious than secular lyrics survive, largely because they were often recorded in the margins of manuscripts containing other material – legal and historical records, theological works, and so forth – and these were most often executed in religious houses. Penitential lyrics, prayers to the Virgin and meditations upon Christ's Passion predominate, but are expressed in a wide variety of styles and poetic forms. Amongst the secular lyrics, love is the most frequent theme. The poems record lovers' pleas, bitter recriminations, celebrations of the beauty of the beloved and complaints at fickleness. The voice of the poem is usually, but not invariably, masculine. Some humorous and satiric lyrics survive, a particularly common form being the description of an ugly woman, a parody of the lover's description of a beautiful mistress. Many lyrics survive independently, but the most famous collection is the HARLEY LYRICS. The authors are generally not known.

Medwall, Henry *c.* 1462–1502 Playwright. Little is known about Medwall beyond his work – much of which is now lost – and the fact that he was chaplain to Cardinal Morton. He was ordained an acolyte in 1490, and is thought to have been a member or connection of a noble family since various livings were granted to him by the Crown. The last was at Calais after Morton's death in 1500. His surviving works are a MORALITY PLAY, *Nature* (printed in 1530), and *FULGENS AND LUCRECE*, an INTERLUDE and the first completely secular play in English. It was first performed about 1497 and first printed *c.* 1515.

Mehta, Ved 1934– Indian essayist and autobiographer. Born in Lahore, Punjab, he was partly educated in the USA and Britain, and as a young man worked for *THE NEW YORKER*, where many of his essays have first appeared. Although he has written a short satirical novel, *Delinquent Chacha* (1967), he is best known

as a shrewd and observant commentator on Indian society. His most distinguished work is highly autobiographical. *Face to Face* (1957) describes his childhood and his early struggle with blindness. *Walking the Indian Streets* (1963) deals with a journey round India after his years abroad. A more ambitious journey resulted in *Portrait of India* (1970), an epic travelogue in which public figures such as Indira Gandhi appear alongside ordinary people. Mehta explores the intellectual life not only of India but also of Europe and the USA in *Fly and the Fly Bottle* (1963) and *John is Easy to Please: Encounters with the Written and Spoken Word* (1971). *Daddyji* (1972) and *Mamaji* (1979), touching studies of his parents, have been followed by more volumes of autobiography, now collectively titled *Continents of Exile: The Ledge between the Streams* (1977), *Sound Shadows of the New World* (1986) and *The Stolen Light* (1989). He has also published a study of Gandhi (1977). Though some critics have dismissed Mehta as a high-class journalist, it is likely that his work will survive as a testament to the human spirit as well as a penetrating account of contemporary Indian life.

Melibeus, The Tale of See *CANTERBURY TALES, THE*.

Melincourt: or, Sir Oran Haut-Ton The second novel by THOMAS LOVE PEACOCK, published in 1817. Generally regarded as more ambitious and less successful than his first, *HEADLONG HALL*, it satirizes both the enthusiasms and the reactions of the period after Waterloo, including the current belief in progress. Rich Mr Sylvan Forester has educated the orangoutang of the title so that he appears to be a charming gentleman who plays the flute, and has bought a baronetcy and a seat in Parliament for him. The portrait of Forester himself owes something to Peacock's friend, SHELLEY. Among the book's targets are WORDSWORTH (Mr Paperstamp), COLERIDGE (Mr Mystic), SOUTHEY (Mr Feather-nest) and WILLIAM GIFFORD (Mr Vamp).

Melmoth the Wanderer A GOTHIC NOVEL by CHARLES ROBERT MATURIN, published in 1820. The hero has made a pact with Satan to prolong his life, but the debt can be transferred if he can find someone else willing to assume it. The situation provides a framework for a series of episodes in which Melmoth approaches various desperate people and tries to persuade them to take on his dreadful debt: one possibility is a man in a lunatic's cell, another is a victim of the Inquisition and a third sees his children dying of hunger. Nobody will change places with Melmoth and he is doomed.

OSCAR WILDE, a descendant of Maturin, adopted the name of Melmoth in Paris after his release from prison; Sebastian, the Christian name he used, was suggested by the arrows of his convict garb.

melodrama A type of play, popular in the Victorian theatre, which exposed the uncommonly virtuous to the threat of defeat by the uncompromisingly vicious, allowing good to win only after sensational risks had been taken or fearsome adventures undergone. Constant peril sustained the tension, and disaster for the good characters was almost always averted in the nick of time. Outstanding examples included DOUGLAS JERROLD's *Black-Ey'd Susan* (1829), TOM TAYLOR's *THE TICKET-OF-LEAVE MAN* (1863), BOUCI-CAULT's *THE SHAUGHRAUN* (1874) and HENRY ARTHUR JONES's *THE SILVER KING* (1882). Their influence can be felt in popular Victorian fiction, notably the NEWGATE NOVEL and the SENSATION NOVEL. The first English play to be advertised as a melodrama was THOMAS HOLCROFT's *A Tale of Mystery* (1802). It borrowed the term from France, where *mélo-dramas* – like Rousseau's *Pygmalion* (1770) – were works combining spoken words and music. In opera the term 'melodrama' defines passages spoken to musical accompaniment.

Melville, Herman 1819–91 American novelist, short-story writer and poet. He was born in New York into an established merchant family. His father became bankrupt and then insane, and died when he was 12. At the age of 15 he left school and began working to support his family, first as a bank clerk, then as a teacher, and as a farm labourer. At the age of 19 he sailed on a merchant ship to Liverpool. This was followed by several other sea voyages, one of them a whaling trip during which he jumped ship and lived briefly among the Typee cannibals in the Marquesas.

Although he had no early designs as a writer, he was encouraged to set down some of his more exotic experiences, and the result was *TYPEE* (1846), loosely based on his encounter with the cannibals. *OMOO* (1847), *MARDI* (1849), *REDBURN* (1849), and *WHITE-JACKET* (1850) also treat themes involving life on the sea. These early works won Melville a good deal of popular acclaim; they also stirred controversy because of their sympathy with pagan societies, sometimes to the point of contempt for Western attitudes and practices. During this time Melville began to read widely, acquainting himself with a broad range of writers and philosophers. In 1850 he and his wife moved to Pittsfield, Massachusetts, where they became neighbours and friends of Sophia and NATHANIEL HAWTHORNE. Inspired by Hawthorne and by his reading, Melville entered into his most ambitious phase. In 1851 he published *MOBY-DICK*, the whaling adventure dedicated to Hawthorne that is considered by many to be the greatest work of American fiction. To his intense disappointment the novel was not well received, and from relative popularity he began to fade into obscurity. *PIERRE* (1852), a psychological and moral study based on his childhood, and thus removed from the ocean setting of most of his other fiction, was hardly read at all in the 19th century. At odds with his public, and deprived of the company of Hawthorne, who had moved to Concord, Melville turned increasingly to shorter fiction. After the short novel *ISRAEL POTTER* (1855) he published *THE PIAZZA TALES* (1856), a collection of stories which includes 'Bartleby the Scrivener', 'Benito Cereno' and 'The Encantadas'. His last novel, *THE CONFIDENCE-MAN* (1857), a harsh satire of American life set on a Mississippi River steamboat, represented his most radical innovation in narrative form since *Mardi*.

At the age of 40 he turned almost exclusively to poetry. *BATTLE-PIECES AND ASPECTS OF THE WAR* was issued in 1866, *John Marr and Other Sailors* in 1888, and *Timoleon* in 1891. *CLAREL* (1876) is a long poem about religious crisis, based on Melville's trip to the Holy Land in 1857. It was the last of his published works; the later volumes were privately printed and distributed among a very small circle of acquaintances. Additional material was published from manuscript long after his death, when his reputation was beginning to revive. Most notably, the unfinished tale *BILLY BUDD* appeared in 1924. *Journal up the Straits* (1935), *Journal of a Visit to London and the Continent* (1948), and *Journal of a Visit to Europe and the Levant* (1955), all record his travels in the 1850s. *Weeds and Wildings* (1924) is a collection of previously unpublished poetry; his letters were published in 1960.

Melville, James 1556–1614 Poet and diarist. A Scottish Presbyterian minister and educator, Melville graduated from St Andrews in 1571 and received additional instruction in Greek and Hebrew from his uncle. In 1575 he became one of the regents of Glasgow University, in 1580 professor of Hebrew at St Andrews and in 1589 Moderator of the General Assembly of the Church of Scotland. His strongly Presbyterian views and his opposition to episcopacy in Scotland meant that he had a troubled career, especially after the accession of James VI as JAMES I of England. He wrote poems, some on ecclesiastical affairs in Scotland. *The Diary of Mr James Melville, 1556–1601*, was first published in 1829.

Memoirs of a Cavalier: or, *A Military Journal of the Wars in Germany, and the Wars in England, from the Year 1632 to the Year 1648* A novel by DANIEL DEFOE, published in 1720.

The cavalier who tells the story is Andrew Newport, an English gentleman who travels to Europe in 1630. His travels take him to Vienna, and he accompanies the imperial army during the Thirty Years War. He is present at the sack of Magdeburg (a remarkable piece of 'reporting' by Defoe) and after it joins the army of the opposing forces led by Gustavus Adolphus, King of Sweden. After the king's death at the Battle of Lutzen in 1632 he returns to England and as a Royalist colonel serves King Charles I, taking the narrative to the Battle of Naseby and the end of the Civil War.

Memoirs of a Woman of Pleasure *[Fanny Hill]* See CLELAND, JOHN.

Men at Arms See SWORD OF HONOUR.

Mencken, H(enry) L(ouis) 1880–1956 American essayist, editor and critic. He was born in Baltimore, Maryland. With GEORGE JEAN NATHAN he edited the New York periodical *Smart Set* (1914–23), as well as founding the detective magazine THE BLACK MASK (1920) and THE AMERICAN MERCURY (1924), which he edited until 1933. He became famous with the publication of *The American Language* (1919), a study of English as developed and used in the USA. It went through three revised editions, and supplementary volumes were also added, the last in 1948. His essays, with their characteristically caustic and often vulgar tone, were collected in six volumes called *Prejudices* (1919–27). Though known primarily as entertainments for middle-class America, they were often sharply critical of what Mencken himself termed the 'booboisie'. He also published plays, several critical works, including studies of GEORGE BERNARD SHAW and Nietzsche, and three volumes of autobiography, *Happy Days* (1940), *Newspaper Days* (1941) and *Heathen Days* (1943).

Menologium A poetical calendar in Old English prefixed to one version of the ANGLO-SAXON CHRONICLE. It follows the progression of the year, combining sensitive descriptions of nature with an account of the saints' days observed by the church. Although predominantly Christian, it shows the influence of some pre-Christian elements.

Mercer, David 1928–80 Playwright. Born in Wakefield, Yorkshire, he wrote prolifically for the stage, TV and films. He established his reputation with a TV trilogy later published as *The Generations* (1964). A later TV play, *A Suitable Case for Treatment* (1962), was filmed as *Morgan* (1965). His first West End stage play, *Ride a Cock Horse* (1965), was followed by *In Two Minds* (1967), *Flint* (1970), *After Haggerty* (1970) and *Cousin Vladimir* (1978). As a writer from the working-class North, he frequently took class conflicts and loyalties as his theme, showing their pressures in a series of protagonists who are eccentric, rebellious or in retreat from society. Mercer's dialogue is usually witty, handling profound ideas and complicated themes with energy and grace; his more abstract style of writing, as in *Duck Song* (1974), worked less well in the theatre.

Merchant of Venice, The A comedy by WILLIAM SHAKESPEARE, first performed *c.* 1596, and published in Quarto (Q1) in 1600 as well as in the First Folio of 1623. A main source was a story by Giovanni Fiorentino. The casket episode is from GESTA ROMANORUM, and Shakespeare may also have had in mind MARLOWE's THE JEW OF MALTA and the scandalous contemporary reputation of Roderigo Lopez, a Jewish physician executed in 1594 on suspicion of attempting to poison Queen Elizabeth I.

When Bassanio needs money to woo the heiress Portia, his friend Antonio borrows it from the Jewish moneylender Shylock. Shylock hates Antonio and proposes that a pound of his flesh be the bond for failure to repay within three months. Confident that his ships will return from their trading, Antonio accepts. Bassanio wins Portia by choosing the right casket in a test stipulated in Portia's father's will, but their marriage celebrations are interrupted by the news that Antonio's fleet has foundered and Shylock has demanded his bond. Shylock's hatred of Christians has been sharpened by the elopement of his daughter Jessica with Bassanio's friend, Lorenzo. In court before the Duke of Venice, Antonio is represented by an unknown advocate and his clerk (Portia and her maid Nerissa in male disguise). Shylock rejects Portia's plea for mercy and demands his bond. But Portia insists that it mentions flesh only, no blood, and the Duke upholds the point. Shylock is pardoned on condition he give half his wealth to Antonio and become a Christian. The celebrations in Belmont are completed with news that Antonio's ships have, after all, returned safely.

The qualities of *The Merchant of Venice* have been, in some ways, distorted by the theatrical impact of Shylock. For almost two centuries (1680–1880), it was normal to perform the play without its final act, so that the curtain-calls could follow Shylock's final exit. In fact the play shows Shakespeare's increasing maturity in the handling of comic form, and is often grouped with A MIDSUMMER NIGHT'S DREAM among the 'middle comedies'.

Merchant's Tale, The See CANTERBURY TALES, THE.

Meredith, George 1828–1909 Novelist and poet. The son of a naval outfitter in Portsmouth, he received part of his education in Germany at the Moravian School at Neuwied. He was articled to a London solicitor at the age of 17, but, more interested in writing than in the law, he published poetry in magazines, beginning with a poem on the Battle of Chillianwallah, which appeared in *Chamber's Journal*. In 1849 he married Mary Ellen Nicholls, the widowed daughter of THOMAS LOVE PEACOCK. She deserted him for the painter Henry Wallis in 1857. In 1860 Meredith settled down to weekly journalism for the *Ipswich Journal* and to reading for Chapman and Hall, the publishers; in the latter capacity he gave encouragement to the young THOMAS HARDY and

GEORGE GISSING. His wife died in 1861, leaving him free to marry Marie Vulliamy. The Merediths moved to Flint Cottage at Box Hill in Surrey in 1864; it was to be his home for the rest of his life.

His first published book was *Poems* (1851), which contained the first version of 'Love in the Valley'. After two fantasies, *The Shaving of Shagpat* (1856) and *Farina* (1857), came *THE ORDEAL OF RICHARD FEVEREL* (1859) and *EVAN HARRINGTON* (1861), the novels which established his distinctive voice, at once wryly questioning and exuberant. *MODERN LOVE* (1862), a sequence partly reflecting the failure of his first marriage, earned him a permanent place as a poet. Over the next 20 years Meredith published a steady flow of novels: *SANDRA BELLONI* (first called *Emilia in England*; 1864); *RHODA FLEMING* (1865); *VITTORIA* (1867), a sequel to *Sandra Belloni*; *THE ADVENTURES OF HARRY RICHMOND* (1871); *BEAUCHAMP'S CAREER* (1876); *THE EGOIST* (1879), probably his masterpiece; *THE TRAGIC COMEDIANS* (1880); and *DIANA OF THE CROSSWAYS* (1885). *Poems and Lyrics of the Joy of Earth* appeared in 1883.

OSCAR WILDE, with good reason, described Meredith as 'a prose BROWNING'. His condensed and loaded prose, discovered in all his novels, is particularly notable in later works: *ONE OF OUR CONQUERORS* (1891), *LORD ORMONT AND HIS AMINTA* (1894) and *THE AMAZING MARRIAGE* (1895). His critical essay *On Comedy and the Uses of the Comic Spirit* (1897) is a highly regarded study of the function of comedy in literature. Further volumes of poetry included *Poems and Ballads of Tragic Life* (1887), *A Reading of Life* (1909) and *Last Poems* (1909).

Meredith, Owen See BULWER LYTTON, EDWARD ROBERT.

Meres, Francis 1565–1647 The clergyman Meres published a sermon and two translations of Spanish religious works, but his importance for Renaissance literature lies in his contribution to a series of apophthegms and *sententiae* inaugurated by the publication of *Politeuphuia* (1598). Meres's contribution, *Palladis Tamia: Wit's Treasury* (1598), written mainly in euphuistic prose (see EUPHUISM), has a section entitled 'A Comparative Discourse of our English Poets with the Greek, Latin and Italian Poets'. It offers rapid estimations of mainly contemporary English authors and is important for the dating of SHAKESPEARE's earlier plays. CHAUCER, 'the god of English poets', is compared to Homer; *PIERS PLOWMAN* and SKELTON are also mentioned. MICHAEL DRAYTON comes out particularly well among the Renaissance poets. The soul of Ovid lives in Shakespeare in his *VENUS AND ADONIS, THE RAPE OF LUCRECE* and 'sugared sonnets'. As Plautus and Seneca were the best for Roman comedy and tragedy so Shakespeare 'is the most excellent in both kinds', as witnessed by the comedies he had written by 1598 (*THE TWO GENTLEMEN OF VERONA, THE COMEDY OF ERRORS, LOVE'S LABOUR'S LOST*, the problematic *Love's Labour's Won, A MIDSUMMER NIGHT'S DREAM* and *THE MERCHANT OF VENICE*), and his 'tragedies' (*RICHARD II, RICHARD III, HENRY IV, TITUS ANDRONICUS* and *ROMEO AND JULIET*). Meres also mentions MARLOWE, who 'for his epicurism and atheism had a tragical death'.

Merrill, James 1926– American poet. Born in New York, he served with the US Army during the last years of World War II and attended Amherst College in Massachusetts. His earliest volume, *Jim's Book: A Collection of Poems and Short Stories* (1942), appeared while he was still in his teens but it was *First Poems* (1950) that gained the attention of the poetry-reading public. His reputation was secured by volumes such as *The Country of a Thousand Years of Peace and Other Poems* (1959, revised edition 1970), *Selected Poems* (1961) and *Water Street* (1962). In *Nights and Days* (1966) and *The Fire Screen* (1969) he became increasingly concerned with the visionary and esoteric. *Braving the Elements* (1972) is autobiographical and confessional, a development confirmed in subsequent volumes: *The Yellow Pages: 59 Poems* (1974); *The Divine Comedies* (PULITZER PRIZE, 1976), which attempts to mythologize the self in relation to a cosmic order; and *Metamorphosis of 741* (1977). In *Mirabell: Books of Number* (1978) and *The Changing Light at Sandover* (1982) he again creates 'sacred' books, turning to the ouija board as a source of divine intervention. Recent volumes include: *Marbled Paper* (1982); *Santorini: Stopping the Leak* (1982), which completes the project begun with *The Divine Comedies*; *From the First Nine: Poems, 1947–1976* (1982), a selection; *Souvenirs* (1984); *Bronze* (1984); *Late Settings* (1985); *The Inner Room* (1988); and *New Selected Poems* (1993). He has also written two novels, *The Seraglio* (1957) and *The (Diblos) Notebook* (1965), and *Recitative: Prose* (1986), a collection edited by J. D. McClatchy. In addition to the Pulitzer Prize he has been awarded the Bollingen Prize and the National Book Award. He was elected to the American Academy in 1971.

Merry, Robert See DELLA CRUSCANS, THE.

Merry Devil of Edmonton, The An anonymous comedy, first performed at the GLOBE THEATRE in 1602, and published in 1608. It was found in a volume of SHAKESPEARE in the library of Charles II and for a time was assumed to be one of his plays (see SHAKESPEARE APOCRYPHA). CHARLES LAMB attributed it to MICHAEL DRAYTON but it is now acknowledged to be of unknown authorship. The play has a rural setting (Edmonton in those days lay some eight miles from the urban centre of London) and is chiefly concerned with Sir Arthur Clare's objections to the marriage of his daughter Millicent to Raymond Mounchensey. The young couple are helped in their elopement by the kind magician of Edmonton, Peter Fabel. The only part magic has in the play actually takes place in the prologue. Peter Fabel has made a compact with the Devil and his time is up; the Devil comes to collect, but Fabel tricks him into a magic chair, which holds him fast until he agrees to a new deal.

Merry Tales of the Mad Men of Gotham A collection of jests of the proverbially wise fools of Gotham by 'A. B.', possibly ANDREW BOORDE (d. 1549). The first extant edition is 1630. The foolishness of the men of Gotham was known in the 15th century, when it is mentioned in the Towneley *Shepherds' Play* (see MIRACLE PLAYS). The traditional explanation is that it was a trick to outwit King John who was intending to pass through Gotham, in Nottinghamshire, and perhaps claim the land. By such actions as linking hands around a cuckoo on a bush in order to catch it, the men of Gotham persuaded John that the land was not worth having. There were numerous collections of the jests of the men of Gotham in the 17th century and after.

Merry Wives of Windsor, The A comedy by WILLIAM SHAKESPEARE, first published in an unreliable Quarto (Q1) in 1602 and later in the First Folio of 1623. JOHN DENNIS claimed, in 1702, that the play was written at the Queen's command, and NICHOLAS ROWE embellished the claim in his 1709 edition: 'She was so well pleas'd with that admirable Character of *Falstaff* in the two Parts of *Henry* the Fourth, that she commanded him to continue it for one Play more, and to shew him in Love.' However attractive the story, it is no more certain than the more recent proposal that it was first performed at the Garter feast of 1597. An equally likely date for the first performance is 1600. The source of the play is unknown, and it may be one of the few examples of a story invented by Shakespeare.

The impoverished Falstaff is lodging at the Garter Inn in Windsor. He decides to woo Mistress Ford and Mistress Page, for money not for love, because he knows that they have control of their husbands' purses. But his scheming is revealed to Ford and Page by Falstaff's disgruntled followers, and the exaggeratedly jealous Ford takes revenge by thrashing Falstaff. To add to the humiliation, the two women play a series of practical jokes on Falstaff, culminating in his being pinched and punched by fairies (the Page family in disguise) in Windsor Forest, to which he has gone, disguised as Herne the Hunter, for an assignation with Mistress Ford. A much subdued Falstaff is finally forgiven and taken home to a fireside and a hot posset. A slightly more serious plot involves the Pages' daughter Anne in an ultimately successful attempt to marry Fenton, the impoverished gentleman she loves, rather than the suitors her parents prefer.

The Merry Wives of Windsor is a play written to a well-established comic formula. There seems no reason to doubt that Shakespeare was primarily interested in exploiting the theatrical popularity of Falstaff.

Merwin, W(illiam) S(tanley) 1927– American poet. The son of a Presbyterian minister, he was born in New York and educated at Princeton. After graduation he worked briefly as a tutor to ROBERT GRAVES's son in Mallorca and as a freelance translator in London between 1951 and 1954. His poetry often reflects his concern with contemporary loss of belief in traditional myths and the sense of emptiness which follows it. *A Mask for Janus* (1952), his first volume, was followed by *The Dancing Bears* (1954), *Green with Beasts* (1956), *The Drunk in the Furnace* (1960) and *The Moving Target* (1963). In 1962 he became poetry editor for THE NATION. The traditional, rather formal structures of his early work are loosened in volumes such as *The Lice* (1967), *The Carrier of Ladders* (1970, PULITZER PRIZE) and *Signs: A Poem* (1971). Later volumes include *The First Four Books of Poems* (1975), *Three Poems* (1975), *The Compass Flower* (1977), *Feathers from the Hill* (1978), *Opening the Hands* (1983), *Selected Poems* (1988), *The Rain in the Trees* (1988), *The Lost Upland* (1992) and *Travels: Poems* (1993). He has also produced several plays and many translations (particularly from French and Spanish), including *The Poem of the Cid* (1959), Marivaux's *The False Confession* (1963) and *Selected Poems of Osip Mandelstam* (with Clarence E. Brown; 1973). Some of his prose appears in *Unframed Originals: Recollections* (1982) and *Regions of Memory: Uncollected Prose, 1949–1982* (1987). In addition to the Pulitzer Prize, he has received the International PEN prize for translation, the Shelley Memorial Award and the Bollingen Prize.

mesostich See ACROSTIC.

metaphor Where SIMILE asserts the likeness of one thing to another, metaphor asserts their identity. Usually, though not always, something relatively abstract is identified with something relatively concrete, making it more vivid or accessible. Since the mind seems better able to understand a new concept through concrete illustration than abstract explanation, the language is full of dead metaphors, in which illustration has been fully absorbed into concept. 'Metaphor' itself (literally 'a carrying over') is one, and so are 'abstract' and 'explanation'. Certain metaphors, like 'head of State' and 'table leg', seem to inhabit the borderline between death and life.

The terms commonly used nowadays for the figurative or concrete element of a metaphor and its literal or conceptual element are those suggested by I. A. RICHARDS: 'vehicle' and 'tenor' respectively. In a good metaphor the two should have enough in common to avoid absurdity while being different enough for the vehicle to enrich the tenor as well as illustrating it. Where tenor and vehicle are particularly difficult to distinguish – as in BLAKE's 'The Sick Rose' – it is customary to speak of SYMBOL, or at least symbolic metaphor.

As might be expected, creative literature uses more live metaphors than ordinary language does. These are distinguished from dead metaphors by the fact that the figurative element has not been absorbed into the conceptual, but it should be emphasized that the specific images conveyed (which may differ somewhat from reader to reader anyway) are less important than the vehicle's ability to make the idea in the tenor powerfully connotative. Thus, in order to appreciate SHAKESPEARE's 'Bare ruin'd choirs where late the sweet birds sang', it is not necessary to create a mental picture of choir stalls superimposed on winter trees, and choir boys on blackbirds or thrushes. On the contrary, what is required is an openness to a common idea and an aura of suggestion and implication. Indeed, what normally characterizes the mixed metaphor is not so much an exaggerated unlikeness between tenor and vehicle as excessively vivid but incongruous images: 'Let us not be afraid to dive in at the deep end, now we have them on the run!'

metaphysical poets A term used to group together certain 17th-century poets, usually DONNE, HERBERT, MARVELL, VAUGHAN and TRAHERNE, though other figures like ABRAHAM COWLEY are sometimes included in the list. Although in no sense a school or movement proper, they share common characteristics of WIT, inventiveness and a love of elaborate stylistic manoeuvres.

Metaphysical concerns are the common subject of their poetry, which investigates the world by rational discussion of its phenomena rather than by intuition or mysticism. DRYDEN was the first to apply the term to 17th-century poetry when, in 1693, he criticized Donne: 'He affects the Metaphysics... in his amorous verses, where nature only should reign; and perplexes the minds of the fair sex with nice speculations of philosophy, when he should engage their hearts.' He disapproved of Donne's stylistic excesses, particularly his extravagant conceits (or witty comparisons) and his tendency towards hyperbolic abstractions. JOHNSON consolidated the argument in THE LIVES OF THE POETS, where he noted (with reference to Cowley) that 'about the beginning of the seventeenth century appeared a race of writers that may be termed the metaphysical poets'. He went on to describe the farfetched nature of their comparisons as 'a kind of *discordia concors*; a combination of dissimilar images, or discovery of occult resemblances in things appar-

ently unlike'. Examples of the practice Johnson condemned would include the extended comparison of love with astrology (by Donne) and of the soul with a drop of dew (by Marvell).

Reacting against the deliberately smooth and sweet tones of much 16th-century verse, the metaphysical poets adopted a style that is energetic, uneven and vigorous. (Johnson decried its roughness and violation of decorum, the deliberate mixture of different styles.) It has also been labelled the 'poetry of strong lines'. In his important essay, 'The Metaphysical Poets' (1921), which helped bring the poetry of Donne and his contemporaries back into favour, T. S. ELIOT argued that their work fuses reason with passion; it shows a unification of thought and feeling which later became separated into a 'DISSOCIATION OF SENSIBILITY'.

Metcalf, John 1938– Canadian novelist, short-story writer and critic. Born in Carlisle, England, he graduated from the University of Bristol and, in 1962, emigrated to Canada where he has held a variety of teaching positions and writer-in-residence posts, and is currently living in Ottawa, Ontario. In his fiction Metcalf brings a disciplined, sometimes spare poetic style to capture the beauty and the absurdity of modern life; traditional in format and technique, his stories are hauntingly evocative in their depiction of the human condition. His collections of stories include *The Lady Who Sold Furniture* (1970), *The Teeth of My Father* (1975), *Selected Stories* (1982), and *Adult Entertainment* (1986). His two novels, *Going Down Slow* (1972) and *General Ludd* (1980), satirize the pretentiousness of academic life. Metcalf has edited many anthologies of new fiction and a series of high school and college textbooks. Increasingly outspoken in his irritation at the Canadian literary establishment, he published some of his literary criticism in *Kicking against the Pricks* (1982) and renewed his attack in *Writers in Aspic* (1988), an edition of short stories and accompanying critical essays.

metonymy A figure of speech which replaces the name of an object by the name of an attribute or something closely connected with it. It is common not just in literary language but in everyday speech, when we use 'the Crown' for the monarchy, 'the pen' for writing or 'the Press' for journalism. See also SYNECDOCHE.

metre Language 'measured', usually by the foot, into line-lengths of patterned verse. Such measuring can be of four kinds: quantitative (by long and short sounds); syllabic (by syllable count); accentual (by stress count); and accentual/syllabic (by both stress and syllable count).

Since both sense and implication in English rely considerably on stress, quantitative and syllabic metre have never become naturalized, though the influence of classical poetry and French poetry, respectively, has encouraged a number of attempts. Accentual metre, with feet made up of one stressed syllable and a varying number of unstressed ones, was used in Anglo-Saxon and much pre-Chaucerian poetry and is still common in nursery rhymes, jingles and popular ballads. GERARD MANLEY HOPKINS, who revived it, calls it sprung rhythm (and its unstressed syllables 'hangers' or 'outrides'); 'strong rhythm' is another, more recent name.

Accentual/syllabic metre, however, is by far the most common kind in English poetry – with good reason, for it accommodates itself easily to natural speech rhythms, as syllabic metre does not, and is less prone than accentual metre to lapse into jingle or singsong. The most common type of foot (or component unit of metre) is the iamb, consisting of one unstressed syllable followed by a stressed one: 'The cūr|fĕw tōlls|thĕ knēll|ŏf pārt|ĭng dāy.' The trochee is the reverse: 'Brīght thĕ|vīsion... '. The anapaest has two unstressed syllables followed by a stressed one: 'Ănd hĭs cō|hŏrts wĕre gleām|ĭng wĭth pūrp|lĕ ănd gōld'. The dactyl is the reverse of the anapaest: 'Ō fŏr thĕ|wīngs ŏf ă... '. The feet often used to vary these metres are the spondee (––), the pyrrhic (ᵕᵕ) and two so-called 'rocking feet', the amphimacer (–ᵕ–) and the amphibrach (ᵕ–ᵕ).

The four-foot line (tetrameter) and the five-foot line (pentameter) seem to provide the best setting for poetry's blend of formality and freedom, and are in fact by far the commonest verse lines. The iambic pentameter, in particular, has come close to dominating English poetry, used without rhymes in everything from Elizabethan drama and MILTON's PARADISE LOST to WORDSWORTH's THE PRELUDE and TENNYSON's IDYLLS OF THE KING, and rhymed in the Renaissance SONNET and the satirical verse of DRYDEN and POPE. The dimeter, trimeter and hexameter (two-, three- and six-foot lines) are less common. The iambic hexameter is usually known as an alexandrine, and Pope vividly demonstrated the reasons for its relative unpopularity among English poets: 'A needless Alexandrine ends the song/ That like a wounded snake drags its slow length along.' The monometer (one-foot line) is rare, like the heptameter (seven-foot line), also called a 'fourteener' when its feet are iambic.

Perhaps surprisingly, these patterns are not restrictive. Indeed, they may offer the poet possibilities lacking in innovations designed to free him from the shackles of metre – like free verse (prose rhythm moderated only by line-length). Accentual/syllabic metre has both rhythm and arithmetic at its service; free verse, only rhythm. It can play off freedom against order, emphasize by reinforcing sense with metrical stress or undercut by doing the opposite; it can add a musical or a hypnotic element by modulating or by

formalizing its basic regularities; and it can structure the unorganized as in life we must structure the raw sense-experience presented to us. In fact, accentual/syllabic metre not only may but must make some accommodation with the rhythms of natural speech; otherwise it lapses into doggerel, in which sense is subordinated to and trivialized by a mechanical metre. In good verse, then, absolutely regular lines are probably rather less common than those where at least one foot departs from the norm. And in those lines that are entirely regular not all the stresses will be equal. What determines whether a syllable counts as stressed is not the actual amount of breath used but the amount used in relation to the adjoining syllables; the emphases of sense might even result in an unstressed syllable at one point of the line requiring more effort than a stressed one elsewhere. This is probably the main way in which metre makes its accommodation with the rhythms of prose.

Rhythm, however, is more than the organization of sense-groups centred on meaningful stresses, though this is its most obvious feature. Just as the rhythm of a good games player involves the smooth co-ordination of many movements and a sense of timing, so dictional rhythm involves the co-ordination of stress with pitch and tone, pause and speed. Thus it will be affected not only by the emphases required but also by consonantal clusters, word-length and purpose (e.g. introducing, climaxing, coming to a conclusion). For such reasons, lines that are metrically identical may be rhythmically diverse. Consider these two lines, for instance, both in perfectly regular iambic pentameter but utterly different in effect:

(lust) Ĭs pēr|jŭr'd, mūrd'|rŏus, blood|ў, fūll |
of blāme
(SHAKESPEARE, Sonnet 129)

(the weary weight) Ŏf āll|thĭs ūn|ĭntēllĭgĭb|lĕ
world
(WORDSWORTH, 'Tintern Abbey Re-Visited')

The rhythm of the first, conditioned by its extreme content, is a series of pounding body blows, each accented syllable (with the partial exception of 'full') being heavily stressed. The rhythm of the second, mediating a philosophical sense and contemplative mood, is murmurous. Aided by the relative rapidity of three feet being encompassed by one word, 'unintelligible', and the fact that only 'world' is heavily stressed, it passes easily and mildly into consciousness. The interplay of rhythm, metre and meaning, then, is infinitely subtle in the accentual/syllabic system.

Just why poetry at all times and in all places should have adopted some form of metre is not a question that lends itself to simple and certain answer. There is probably some truth in all of the following explanations. In conjunction with rhyme, metre contributes to the heightening of language that poetry seeks. It becomes part of meaning (in its widest sense) as an element of tone and mood. Like rhyme, it acts in the same way as a picture frame, creating aesthetic distance by signalling that the work is an art-object to be contemplated rather than a statement to be acted on. Or, rather contradictorily, it is an aid to rhetoric. Its order may add authority, its repetitions hypnotize or, modulated, bring a music into meaning. In its varying tension with rhythm there may be a liberating sense of play. But more importantly, it seems to share something of our basic physical being. Our whole body is a system of rhythms accommodated to such regularities as heartbeat, breathing, walking, running, and to certain work activities like threshing, hauling, passing objects along a human chain. And singing – perhaps the earliest poetry – hovers between instinctive bodily activity and the activities of work and play. One thing is sure: the patterning of language required by metre is not the arbitrary requirement it might at first seem.

metrical romance See VERSE ROMANCE.

Mew, Charlotte 1869–1928 Poet and short-story writer. The daughter of an architect, she was born and lived in London. Championed by HAROLD MONRO, she published two volumes of verse, *The Farmer's Bride* (1916) and *The Rambling Boy* (1929). Their colloquial diction and restrained expression of romantic passion (mostly for women) was admired by VIRGINIA WOOLF, who thought her 'unlike anyone else', and by THOMAS HARDY, who became a close friend, secured her a Civil List pension and called her 'far and away the best living woman poet'. Her *Collected Poems and Prose*, edited by V. Warner, appeared in 1981.

Meynell, Alice (Christiana Gertrude) 1847–1922 Poet, essayist and critic. Born in Barnes, Middlesex, she spent much of her childhood in Italy and became a Roman Catholic in 1868. She married the journalist and poet Wilfrid Meynell (1852–1948) in 1877, helping him with his periodical, *Merry England* (founded in 1883), to which she contributed a number of critical essays, and joining him in the rescue of FRANCIS THOMPSON from destitution. Literary gatherings at her Bayswater home attracted other writers, notably GEORGE MEREDITH and COVENTRY PATMORE. Her poetry, the best of which takes religious mystery as its theme, appeared in *Preludes* (1875), *Poems* (1893), *Other Poems* (1896), *Later Poems* (1902), *A Father of Women* (1917) and *Last Poems* (1923), together with a *Collected Poems* of 1912. Among several volumes of perceptive and original essays were *The Rhythm of Life* (1893), *The Colour of Life* (1896), *The Spirit of Place* (1899), *Ceres' Runaway* (1909) and *The Second Person Singular* (1921). A centennial volume of *Poetry and Prose* (1947) was introduced by V. SACKVILLE-WEST.

Michaelmas Term A comedy by THOMAS MIDDLETON performed by a BOYS' COMPANY c. 1606 and published in 1607. It satirizes materialism and mercantile affluence by portraying the self-defeating acquisitiveness of a London woollen-draper, Ephestian Quomodo.

Quomodo tricks Easy, an amiable gentleman from Essex, out of his estates. Gloating over his prospects as a gentleman landowner, he feigns death to determine whether his wife and son deserve their new status. But his 'widow' falls in love with Easy and his son is unmoved by his father's 'death'. To complete Quomodo's downfall, he is tricked into signing a document that returns Easy's land to him.

Middlemarch: *A Study of Provincial Life* A novel by GEORGE ELIOT, published in 1871–2.

Initially the narrative concentrates on the blighted marriage of the wealthy young Puritanical idealist, Dorothea Brooke, to the middle-aged pedant, Dr Edward Casaubon, labouring fruitlessly on his *Key to All Mythologies*. Upon his death, affection develops between Dorothea and her former husband's cousin, Will Ladislaw, whom she eventually marries. Another strand traces the career of the equally idealistic Dr Tertius Lydgate, devotee of scientific progress and the new medicine, and his marriage to the local mayor's daughter, Rosamund Vincy, whose foolish social ambitions ruin his life. A third narrative depicts the down-to-earth relationship between Rosamund's brother Fred and Mary Garth, daughter of the honest estate manager, Caleb Garth. The affairs of Bulstrode, the rich hypocritical banker who harbours a grim secret, are also followed to their humiliating end. These narratives involve many sharply observed minor characters: Dorothea's uncle Mr Brooke, a characteristic early 19th-century landowner and source of much unintentional humour; Mrs Cadwallader, the witty wife of the Rector, himself hardly a fisher of souls; Sir James Chettam, a stolid local squire who marries Dorothea's sister, Celia; Mrs Bulstrode, a woman of dignity and integrity, and the billiard-playing vicar, Camden Farebrother. Beyond them is a huge gallery of briefer portraits of servants, auctioneers, clergymen, businessmen, housewives, labourers, tenants, medical men, schoolmistresses, children and apothecaries. Even those who appear fleetingly are fused into a portrait of English economic, social, and religious life during the pre-Reform years 1829–32.

All the characters and the narrative strands in which they play their part serve George Eliot's purpose of examining the 'web of society' and asking whether it merely destroys or is eventually improved by ardent but flawed souls like Dorothea and Lydgate.

Middleton, Christopher 1926– Poet. Born in Truro, he read German and French at Oxford. He has lectured at the universities of London and Zurich and, since the mid-1960s, has been professor of Germanic languages and literature at the University of Texas at Austin.

Torse 3 (1962) and *Woden Dog* (1962) marked the beginning of a poetic journey of experimentation, innovation and delight unattached to any particular school or movement. *Nonsequences/Selfpoems* (1965), *Our Flowers and Nice Bones* (1969), *Briefcase History* (1972), *The Lonely Suppers of WV Balloon* (1975) and *Carminalenia* (1980) contain poetry which demands that the reader share the poet's complete absorption in language, places, people and real or metaphorical journeys. *111 Poems* (1983), a selection from previous volumes, has been followed by *Two Horse Wagon Going By* (1986), which contains Middleton's most 'American' poems, and *The Balcony Tree* (1992). *Pataxanadu and Other Prose* (1977) is a collection of prose poems, fables and fantasies on journeys or parts of journeys.

His translations include Robert Walser's *Jakob von Gunten* (1969), Canetti's *Kafka's Other Trial* (1974), Goethe's *Selected Poems* (1983), Gert Hofmann's *The Spectacle in the Tower* (1985), Balzac's *Horse and Other Stories* (1988) and *Andalusian Poems* (with Leticia Garza-Falcón; 1992). The essays in *Bolshevism in Art* (1978) and *The Pursuit of the Kingfisher* (1983) develop his own poetic and his wide range of literary, political and cultural interests.

Middleton, Conyers 1683–1750 Theologian. The son of the rector of Hinderwell, near Whitby in Yorkshire, Middleton became a fellow of Trinity College, Cambridge, and head of the University Library in 1721. He published a *Life of Cicero* in 1741 but is best remembered for *A Free Inquiry into the Miraculous Powers Which are Supposed to Have Existed in the Christian Church through Several Successive Ages* (1748), which examined and rejected the evidence for post-apostolic miracles. The book caused a considerable disturbance and showed that some of the principles of DEISM could find a sympathetic response in the ranks of the established church.

Middleton, Stanley 1919– Novelist. During a career as a Nottingham schoolmaster, he has produced a succession of quietly observed, 'implacably domestic' novels set in his native Potteries. They include *Holiday* (1974), a joint winner of the BOOKER PRIZE, *Entry into Jerusalem* (1982), *Valley of Decision* (1985), *Beginning to End* (1991) and *A Place to Stand* (1992).

Middleton, Thomas *c.* 1580–1627 Playwright. The son of a master bricklayer, Middleton was probably born in London. He may have spent some time at Gray's Inn after leaving Oxford, and is identified as a working playwright in PHILIP HENSLOWE's *Diary* in

1602. His literary ambitions were already evident – he had published three volumes of verse by 1600 – and his industry is attested by the plays he wrote for the BOYS' COMPANY of St Paul's at the same time as he was providing material for the adult Admiral's Men. The CITIZEN COMEDIES written for boy actors from 1602 to 1607 include some of his best plays: *A Mad World, My Masters* (*c.* 1605), *A TRICK TO CATCH THE OLD ONE* (*c.* 1605) and *MICHAELMAS TERM* (*c.* 1606). For adult companies, he wrote, with DEKKER, *THE HONEST WHORE* (1604) and *THE ROARING GIRL* (1610), and his own comic masterpiece, *A CHASTE MAID IN CHEAPSIDE* (1611). Like all Middleton's plays, these comedies combine several plots, sharing themes and, sometimes, characters. They make moral, but strangely uncorrective, observations on mercantile values and manners.

After 1613, Middleton was responsible for many City of London pageants, serving as City Chronologer from 1620 until his death; but he continued to write plays. Three collaborations with WILLIAM ROWLEY, in which critics have detected a sharp division between their work, are notable: *A FAIR QUARREL* (published 1617), *The World Tossed at Tennis* (published 1620) and the outstanding tragicomedy *THE CHANGELING* (1622), in which Middleton's fluency and craftsmanship are unerring. He is an unfussy poet, with a fine ear for dialogue. That he was also tough-minded is suggested by the sombre perceptions of his insistently unsentimental plays, as well as by the vigour of his boldly anti-Spanish satire in *A GAME AT CHESS* (1624) and the almost mischievous conclusion to his tragedy, *WOMEN BEWARE WOMEN* (*c.* 1625), a scene of slaughter verging on comedy which has reinforced the argument of those critics who believe Middleton wrote *THE REVENGER'S TRAGEDY*.

Midnight's Children A novel by SALMAN RUSHDIE, published in 1981 and awarded the BOOKER PRIZE. Its garrulous and unreliable narrator, Saleem Sinai, is one of a thousand and one children born in India at midnight on the moment of its declaration of independence and thereby endowed with magical powers. The novel extends the CONCEIT of a country born without a history, and therefore fated to make it up as it goes along, into a fabulous and teeming display of tall-story-telling. A major example of MAGIC REALISM, *Midnight's Children* is also Rushdie's literary homage to India's ancient art of oral story-telling, and equally to the lurid and melodramatic tenor of Bombay's feature films. Above all, as the book of an Indian exile whose personal displacement prompted his synthesis of many literary traditions, it resists reductive classification as merely English, Indian or Commonwealth writing, and justifies the recently coined term 'international English literature'.

Midsummer Night's Dream, A A comedy by WILLIAM SHAKESPEARE, first performed *c.* 1596 and published in Quarto (Ql) in 1600 as well as in the First Folio of 1623. The story is gathered from a number of sources and amplified by Shakespeare's own invention.

Theseus, Duke of Athens, is to wed the Amazon queen, Hippolyta. Egeus asks for his judgement on his daughter Hermia, who has refused his order to marry Demetrius. Theseus upholds Egeus and the law, which requires that Hermia should obey her father or choose between death and a nunnery. Hermia decides to elope with the man she loves, Lysander, and confides her plans to Helena. Helena, who loves Demetrius, in turn tells him, and the four young people arrive at various points of a wood near Athens.

In this fairy wood, Oberon, king of the fairies, quarrels with his queen, Titania, over the care of a changeling boy. He punishes her by dropping in her eyes the juice of a magic flower, which will make her love the first person she sees on waking. Later, having overheard Helena pleading with Demetrius to love her, he instructs his servant Puck to drop the juice into

Midsummer Night's Dream: Bottom and his fellow 'mechanicals' in an 18th century engraving

Demetrius's eyes. But Puck confuses Lysander with Demetrius, with the result that Lysander falls in love with Helena, as does Demetrius when Oberon tries to correct Puck's error.

Also in the wood are several Athenian artisans, rehearsing the play of 'Pyramus and Thisbe', which they hope to present at the wedding of Theseus and Hippolyta. The dominant one, a weaver called Bottom, is mischievously given an ass's head by Puck, and it is the ass-headed Bottom whom Titania first sees (and falls in love with) when she wakes. Oberon's magic eventually unravels all and, at the wedding celebrations of Theseus and Hippolyta, Hermia is matched with her Lysander and Helena with her Demetrius, while Bottom and his fellow actors perform their play to the assembled nobles.

The most persistently popular of all Shakespeare's comedies, *A Midsummer Night's Dream* is much more than a piece of gentle fairy-fun. Its concern with

illusion and reality has been amply demonstrated by many critics as has its profound exploration of the whole art of theatre.

Miles, Josephine 1911– American poet and literary critic. Born in Chicago, she was educated at the University of California, Los Angeles, and the University of California at Berkeley, and has been associated with Berkeley's English department since 1940. Her early work was published in 'little magazines' and *Lines at Intersection* (1939). Later volumes include *Prefabrications* (1955), *Poems 1930–1960* (1960), *Civil Poems* (1966), *Kinds of Affection* (1967), *Fields of Learning* (1968) and *Coming to Terms* (1979). *Collected Poems, 1930–1983* (1983) is a valuable conspectus of her work. Her critical works include *The Vocabulary of Poetry* (1946), *The Continuity of Poetic Vocabulary* (1951) and *Poetry and Change* (1974). Among her many academic honours are awards from the American Council of Learned Societies, the American Academy of Arts and Sciences, the Guggenheim Foundation and the National Institute of Arts and Letters.

Mill, James 1773–1836 Philosopher, economist and historian. Born the son of a shoemaker in the Scottish village of Forfar, Mill was a boarder at Montrose Academy before being sent by patrons to train for the ministry at Edinburgh University. In 1802, however, Mill left for London and earned his living as a freelance journalist, editing two periodicals and contributing to others, including THE EDINBURGH REVIEW. His marriage in 1805 resulted in a family of nine children, including JOHN STUART MILL. In 1806 Mill began the lengthy project of writing *The History of India*, published in 1817, in which he concentrated not on wars and the lives of the country's successive rulers, but upon social analysis. Despite his reputation as a radical, the work won him a position with the East India Company.

In 1808 he met JEREMY BENTHAM and became a warm disciple of UTILITARIANISM. Bentham's reclusive nature facilitated Mill's emergence as leader of the 'philosophical radicals'. He encouraged the work of other disciples, notably that of the economist DAVID RICARDO, took an active part in founding the Benthamite organ, THE WESTMINSTER REVIEW, and, in his own writings, such as *Elements of Political Economy* (1821), *Analysis of the Human Mind* (1829) and *Fragment on Mackintosh* (1835), applied Benthamite principles to a wide range of subjects. His psychological justification of Utilitarian theory, found in the *Analysis*, was derived from HARTLEY's theory of association. J. S. Mill's *Autobiography* (1873) provides a lasting testament to the way in which Mill put theory into practice by beginning the rigorous education, intended to fit his son for future leadership of the Benthamite cause, at the tender age of three when the first important associations are formed.

Mill, John Stuart 1806–73 Philosopher, economist and administrator. He was born in London, the eldest son of JAMES MILL, who gave him a formidably rigorous education designed to equip him as leader of the next generation of UTILITARIANISM. Mill's *Autobiography* (1873) tells how he started Greek at three, and at eight, Latin, history, geometry, logic, mathematics and political economy as taught by ADAM SMITH and DAVID RICARDO. The duty of weighing the evidence for himself, combined with the task of teaching his siblings, prevented his education from being merely mechanical. A year spent in France (1820–1) left Mill with a keen interest in French society and politics and enabled him to pursue further studies in chemistry, botany, mathematics, psychology, Roman law and Aristotle.

In 1823 his father's influence obtained for him a clerkship in the East India Company where he worked until 1858. His spare time was spent editing the papers of JEREMY BENTHAM, writing articles for periodicals, notably the Utilitarian *WESTMINSTER REVIEW*, and in discussion with like-minded contemporaries at meetings of the Utilitarian Society (1823–6) and the London Debating Society, where he first encountered COLERIDGE's views. In 1826 Mill suffered an acute attack of depression which led him to re-evaluate the Benthamite doctrines of his upbringing and to judge that they had wholly neglected the cultivation of the emotions in favour of developing the intellect. The poetry of WORDSWORTH, with its emphasis upon the morally educative role of emotional association, played a restorative part in redressing the balance. By 1830 Mill had begun to revise his philosophical and economic thinking in the light of those aspects of St Simonian, Positivist and Coleridgean ideas which seemed to offer truths neglected by Benthamism (see POSITIVISM). The strength of his initial reaction against 'sectarian Benthamism' was tempered by the constructive eclecticism which was to characterize his thought. As the essays on Bentham (1838) and Coleridge (1840) reveal, Mill saw the moral and mental improvement of mankind, to which he was dedicated, emerging, not from one set of assumptions superseding and defeating another, but from toleration of diversity and the achievement of a synthesis of the elements of truth from competing or apparently outmoded philosophies.

In 1830 he met Mrs Harriet Taylor, whom he claimed to be the dominant intellectual influence in his life, and continued an intense but platonic relationship with her until their marriage in 1851, two years after her first husband's death. In 1858 Mill retired from the East India Company shortly after his promotion to Chief of the Examiner's Office, and declined government service. After his wife's unexpected death at Avignon in 1858 he bought a house there so that he might be near her grave, returning to London only for short visits every year. In 1865–8 he served as independent MP for Westminster, a seat which he won despite his refusal either to campaign or pay any contributions towards the expenses of a campaign. In Parliament he made notable contributions to debates on Irish land reform and women's suffrage.

His influence, as the voice of 19th-century liberalism, sprang in part from his deep-seated conviction of the connection between theory and practice. He was able to deploy his immense learning and capacity for logical analysis in such a way that the central thread of argument always emerged clearly. His major works, therefore, often gained a readership far wider than their apparent subject matter would invite. In books such as *THE SYSTEM OF LOGIC* (1843) or *Principles of Political Economy* (1848) Mill was able to use the platform of theoretical discussion to present his unconventional views on contemporary society. He published a plethora of essays and reviews from his early twenties, amongst which the most noteworthy are *ON LIBERTY* (1859), *Utilitarianism* (1861), 'Auguste Comte and Positivism' (1865), *THE SUBJECTION OF WOMEN* (1869) and *Three Essays on Religion* (1874).

Mill on the Floss, The A novel by GEORGE ELIOT, published in 1860.

The story concerns Maggie Tulliver and her brother Tom, the children of the miller of Dorlcote, an honest but ignorant and unimaginative man. His wife is weak and foolish. Tom himself, in spite of being dearly loved by Maggie, is resourceful but insensitive. In this oppressive environment Maggie's intelligence, scholarly competence and wide-ranging imagination become liabilities, especially in a woman. She responds to Philip Wakem, the deformed son of the leading lawyer in the nearby town of St Ogg's, as the only person who can appreciate her intellectual life

An illustration by W. J. Allen for George Eliot's *The Mill on the Floss* (1860). Maggie and Tom meet their deaths in the flood

and sympathize with her interests. But Tulliver regards the lawyer Wakem as his enemy and Tom, blindly supporting his father's cause, makes Maggie give up Philip's friendship.

After Tulliver's death Maggie goes to St Ogg's to stay with her cousin Lucy, who is to marry Stephen Guest. He is attracted to Maggie and his irresponsible behaviour on a boating expedition compromises her reputation. Tom turns her out of his house and she is ostracized by local society, except for Lucy, Philip and the rector, Dr Kenn. Autumn brings a flood which threatens the mill, and Maggie attempts to rescue Tom. She fails, and brother and sister are drowned together, but not before they have briefly recaptured the affection they felt for each other as children.

Response to *The Mill on the Floss* has, since its first publication, been divided between admiration of the skill with which George Eliot evokes rural life as a background to Maggie and Tom's childhood and criticism of the novel's rushed and arbitrary ending.

Millay, Edna St Vincent 1892–1950 American poet. She was born in Rockland, Maine. Her first collection, *Renascence and Other Poems* (1917), consisted of pieces she had written as an undergraduate at Vassar. The poems in a second volume, *A Few Figs from Thistles* (1920), established her as a representative voice of her generation in their freshness, gaiety, and implied rebellion against established moral standards. Her popularity continued to grow with the publication of her third volume, *The Harp-Weaver and Other Poems* (1923), which exhibited her mature style and mastery of traditional verse forms; it received the PULITZER PRIZE in 1923. She wrote less as time went on, but her later works showed a new political and social consciousness. They include: *Distressing Dialogues* (1924), a book of satirical sketches written under the pseudonym of Nancy Boyd; *Three Plays* (1926); *The King's Henchman* (1927), a libretto; *The Buck in the Snow and Other Poems* (1928); and *Fatal Interview* (1931), a SONNET sequence. Subsequent volumes of verse are *Wine from These Grapes* (1934), *Conversation at Midnight* (1937), *Huntsman, What Quarry?* (1939) and *Make Bright the Arrow* (1940).

Miller, Arthur 1915– American playwright. Born in New York, the son of a Jewish manufacturer whose business failed during the Depression, he studied journalism at the University of Michigan. His first Broadway play, *The Man Who Had All the Luck* (1944), closed after only four performances but his next four plays were enthusiastically received. His concern with conflict between the generations informed *All My Sons* (1947), about a veteran who discovers that his father sold faulty aeroplane parts to the government, and *DEATH OF A SALESMAN* (1949), still his most famous play, about the unsuccessful salesman Willy Loman. Like Ibsen, whose *An Enemy of the People* he translated in 1950, Miller often explores the origins and consequences of shameful actions. *THE CRUCIBLE* (1953) connects the Salem witch trials with the McCarthyite era. (Miller himself was one of the many who refused to give names when summoned before the House Un-American Activities Committee in 1956 because of his left-wing politics.) *A View from the Bridge* (1955, revised 1956) examines the tragic consequences of Sicilian-American longshoreman Eddie Carbone's passion for his niece Catherine.

After an eight-year absence Miller returned to the New York stage with *After the Fall* (1964), a semi-autobiographical play with obvious references to his marriage to Marilyn Monroe. *Incident at Vichy* (1964) deals directly with the Nazi persecution of the Jews, an undercurrent in much of his work. *The Price* (1968), his last international success, again examines the issues of family conflict and filial disloyalty. Subsequent plays include *The Creation of the World and Other Business* (1972), *Up from Paradise* (1974),

The Archbishop's Ceiling (1977) and *The American Clock* (1980). His *Theatre Essays* (1971) contain the well-known 'Tragedy and the Common Man' (1949). Other work includes a novel about anti-semitism, *Focus* (1945), and the screenplay for *The Misfits* (1961).

Miller, Henry (Valentine) 1891–1980 American writer. Born in New York, he left college after just two months and took various jobs before moving to Paris in 1930. He lived there until 1939, recording his promiscuous lifestyle in the autobiographical *Tropic of Cancer* (1934), his most famous work. Because of its sexual frankness, the book was suppressed in both the USA and England. (It was not in fact published in the USA until 1961.) *Black Spring* (1936), which consists of ten autobiographical stories, and *Tropic of Capricorn* (1939), an account of his years with the Western Union telegraph company, were also suppressed.

Following a trip to Greece in 1939, he produced what some consider his best work, *The Colossus of Maroussi* (1941), a travel book more about people than places. He returned to the USA in 1940. *The Plight of the Creative Artist in the United States of America* (1944), *The Air-Conditioned Nightmare* (1945) and *Remember to Remember* (1947) all decry the materialism of his native land. Miller was also a painter, and with Hilaire Hiler and WILLIAM SAROYAN he wrote *Why Abstract?* (1945), a discussion of modern painting. Among his other notable works are *The World of Sex* (1940), *Books in My Life* (1951), *The Time of the Assassins: A Study of Rimbaud* (1956) and a trilogy – *Sexus* (1949), *Plexus* (1953; first published in French, 1952) and *Nexus* (1960) – collectively titled *The Rosy Crucifixion*. *My Life and Times*, a heavily illustrated volume, appeared in 1971.

Miller, Joaquin [Miller, Cincinnatus Hiner (Heine)] 1839–1913. American poet. Born in Liberty, Indiana, he moved to the Oregon frontier and later lived with Digger Indians in northern California. He published his first collection of poems, *Specimens*, in 1868. In the following year came *Joaquin et al.*, a defence of the Mexican bandit, Joaquin Murietta, from whom he derived his nickname. In 1870 he went to London and there published *Pacific Poems* (1871), which won acclaim from the PRE-RAPHAELITES, especially DANTE GABRIEL ROSSETTI, who took an active interest in this 'BYRON of Oregon' and helped him revise his next book of poetry, *Songs of the Sierras* (1871), which made him famous. He produced numerous other volumes of poetry, novels and plays, including the successful *The Danites of the Sierras* (1877) about Mormons, and an autobiography, *Life amongst the Modocs* (1873).

Miller's Tale, The See CANTERBURY TALES, THE.

Millin, Sarah Gertrude 1889–1968 South African novelist. Born Sarah Liebson, she was educated in Kimberley, and published her first novel, *The Dark River*, in 1920. She was the author of several novels which are generally regarded as a major contribution to South African fiction during the inter-war period. Among them are *Adam's Rest* (1922), *God's Stepchildren* (1924), *Mary Glenn* (1925) and *The Sons of Mrs Aab* (1931). Her novels have been praised for the awareness they display of the realities and complexities of racial conflict, a subject she explored further in a study entitled *The South Africans* (1926, revised 1934). She also published biographies of Rhodes (1933) and Smuts (1936).

Milman, Henry Hart 1791–1868 Historian and poet. The son of a fashionable physician, Milman was born in London and educated at Eton College, and Brasenose College, Oxford. He won the Newdigate Prize for Poetry and the Chancellor's Essay Prize, and was made a fellow of his college in 1814. His career as a poet began with *Fazio: A Tragedy* (1815) and *Samor: Lord of the Bright City* (1818). Milman was ordained in 1816 and appointed rector of St Mary's, Reading, in 1818. He continued to write dramatic poetry: *The Fall of Jerusalem* (1820), *The Martyr of Antioch and Belshazzar* (1822), *Anne Boleyn* (1826) and *Nala and Damayanti and Other Poems* (translations from the Sanskrit; 1835). He became professor of poetry at Oxford in 1821.

Milman is better remembered as a historian. His *History of the Jews* (1830), *History of Christianity* (1840) and *History of Latin Christianity* (1854–5) reflect his admiration for the work of EDWARD GIBBON, whose *DECLINE AND FALL OF THE ROMAN EMPIRE* he edited (1838–9) and whose biography he wrote (1839).

He became rector of St Margaret's, Westminster, in 1835 and dean of St Paul's in 1849. His later publications included *The Life of Thomas à Becket* (1860), *The Annals of St Paul's Cathedral* (1868) and versions of *The Agamemnon* of Aeschylus and *The Bacchae* of Euripides (1865).

Milne, A(lan) A(lexander) 1882–1956 Novelist, playwright, humorist and writer of CHILDREN'S LITERATURE. The son of a Scottish schoolmaster, Milne won a scholarship to Westminster School and later read mathematics at Cambridge. His real interest was in light-hearted writing and at the age of 24 he became assistant editor of *PUNCH*. After serving as a signals officer in World War I he won additional good opinions as a playwright, with *Wurzel-Flummery* (1917), *Mr Pim Passes By* (1919; published, 1922), *The Truth about Blayds* (1921; published, 1922) and *The Dover Road* (1921; published, 1922). His great success, however, came with children's books. *When we were Very Young* (1924) and *Now we are Six* (1927) were verses about his young son Christopher Robin. The works by which he will always be remembered are *Winnie-the-Pooh* (1926) and *The House at Pooh Corner* (1928). Both were based on the imaginary conversations and adventures of Christopher Robin's toys, with the boy making an occasional, masterful appearance to sort out some minor crisis or muddle. While each toy has one distinctive characteristic – Pooh's greediness, Eeyore's misanthropy, Tigger's bounciness or Piglet's timidity – they also emerge as individuals in their own right, talking very much in character and occasionally with an underlying humour more meaningful to adults than to children. But the stories in which they feature are perfectly adapted to young readers' interests, concentrating on topics such as birthday presents, the quest for food and mini-adventures involving unexpected bouts of bad weather, mysterious footprints or getting lost. The little verses sung by Pooh and E. H. SHEPARD's illustrations are also memorable.

After these little books Milne turned away from children's writing, coming to resent his success in this area at the expense of his other, adult work. This includes: DETECTIVE FICTION; two novels, *Two People* (1931) and *Chloë Marr* (1946); a plea against war, *Peace with Honour* (1934); and an autobiography, *It's Too Late Now* (1939). His last triumph was a stage adaptation of KENNETH GRAHAME's THE WIND IN THE WILLOWS as *Toad of Toad Hall* (1929), which – apart from introducing a talking horse – stays close to the original. It is still revived every Christmas.

Milnes, Richard Monckton, 1st Baron Houghton 1809–85 Man of letters and poet. The son of a wealthy Yorkshire family, he was educated at Trinity College, Cambridge, where he was a member of the APOSTLES, which also included TENNYSON and ARTHUR HALLAM. He became MP for Pontefract in 1837 and a peer in 1863.

During an active life he published five volumes of verse but was less important as a poet than as a patron of letters and generous host to writers at his home, Fryston Hall, in Yorkshire. In THE EDUCATION OF HENRY ADAMS his American secretary left a vivid account of these gatherings and of guests like SWINBURNE, whose poetry Milnes defended against hostile criticism. Milnes was also notable for helping to secure the reputation of KEATS, by his *Life, Letters and Literary Remains of John Keats* (1848).

Milton, John 1608–74 Poet. Born in Bread Street, Cheapside, he lived with few intermissions in London for the rest of his life. His father, a Puritan convert from a Catholic Oxfordshire family, had set up as a scrivener (a kind of stockbroker) but also composed music. His prosperity facilitated his son's education and granted him the financial independence necessary to pursue, in adult life, a private programme of study. Having attended St Paul's School Milton was admitted to Christ's College, Cambridge, in 1625 but found university life disappointing. Not only does he seem to have quarrelled with his tutor (possibly he was rusticated in 1626, if this was the occasion for his *Elegia Prima*), but he was pejoratively known as 'the Lady of Christ's' by his contemporaries. While at Cambridge he began to write poems in Latin, Italian and English, including 'At a Vacation Exercise'.

Although he had intended to join the clergy, after taking his BA in 1629 and MA in 1632 he showed no anxiety to commit himself to a career, defending his studious leisure and poetic interests to his perhaps impatient father in 'Ad Patrem' (c. 1634). His family had moved first to Hammersmith in 1631/2 and then in 1635 to Horton, Buckinghamshire, where he continued his private programme of study in European, classical and patristic literature, publishing a few occasional poems. Already, in 1629, he had written his first great lyric in English, the 'Ode upon the Morning of Christ's Nativity'. *L'ALLEGRO* and *IL PENSEROSO* were written in 1632, the same year as 'On Shakespeare' was published in the Second Folio of SHAKESPEARE's plays. Milton's musical interests, no doubt encouraged by his father, had already found expression in collaboration with the musician Henry Lawes on two masques: *Arcades* (1633), commissioned by the Dowager Countess of Derby, and that which is now known as *COMUS*, performed at Ludlow in 1634 to celebrate the institution of her son-in-law, the Earl of Bridgewater, as Lord Lieutenant of Wales, and published anonymously in 1637. *LYCIDAS* (1638) appeared in a volume of memorial verses to Edward King, a Cambridge contemporary who had drowned while crossing the Irish Sea.

Evidently Milton's poetic career was not yet established in England, but in 1638 he undertook a Continental tour, finding in Italy both intellectual delight and an appreciative audience for his Italian verses. There he met Galileo, and, in France, the distinguished Dutchman Hugo Grotius. Meanwhile his closest friend, Charles Diodati (himself an Italian resident in England), died. Written shortly after Milton's return to England in 1639, *Epitaphium*

John Milton: a drawing by Jonathan Richardson after Faithorne

Damonis memorializes his friend in his most sustained Latin poem.

Milton's return was prompted, he said, by news of ecclesiastical controversies in England, although he took no part until the 'second Bishops' War' which prompted five anti-episcopal pamphlets in 1641–2: *Of Reformation*, *Of Prelatical Episcopacy*, *The Reason of Church Government* and, defending the Presbyterian SMECTYMNUUS against bishops JOSEPH HALL and USSHER, *Animadversions* and *An Apology against a Pamphlet*. Probably he had already abandoned the notion of an ecclesiastical career. For the better part of the 1640s he acted as a private tutor, a pursuit which seems to have followed adventitiously from the educational needs of his nephews, Edward and John Phillips (Edward left a brief biography of his uncle, and in 1694 printed some of his unpublished poems).

In 1642 Milton married Mary Powell, his junior by 16 years, but within a mere six weeks she returned to her Royalist relatives. Her desertion provoked Milton's four pamphlets arguing for the legitimacy of divorce on the grounds of incompatibility (*The Doctrine and Discipline of Divorce*, *The Judgement of Martin Bucer*, *Tetrachordon* and *Colasterion*; 1643–5). He urged the novel view that a mismatch of mind and spirit was a better ground for separation than sexual incompatibility or adultery. Despite the public storm aroused by these pamphlets (which blackened his reputation for the rest of his life) he also found time for a treatise *Of Education* (1644), addressed to his friend Hartlib. Inspired by the wide humanist curriculum he had studied at St Paul's and his own experience as a teacher, he advocated a remarkably extensive regimen for the religious, intellectual and physical training of boys as responsible citizens. By this date the question of a new form of church organization was being widely debated, and Milton's career as a public controversialist now found its most impassioned expression in *AREOPAGITICA* (1644), a classical oration pleading for freedom of the press. In the following year he also published a volume of his early poems, but they caused no great stir. He was reconciled with his wife in 1645, and their first child, Anne, was born in 1646, followed by Mary (1648), John (1651) and

Deborah (1652), but 1652 also saw the death of his son and his wife. The family now lived in Petty France, Westminster.

Meanwhile Milton had pursued his defence of individual liberties, in the conviction that 'all men naturally were born free, being the image... of God himself'. His public role in the forging of the English Commonwealth was confirmed in 1649 by his pamphlets attacking monarchy and justifying the regicide of Charles I, *The Tenure of Kings and Magistrates* and *Eikonoklastes* (or 'Image Breaker'), a riposte to a work attributed to the king, *EIKON BASILIKE* ('The Royal Image'). In the same year he was appointed Secretary of Foreign Tongues to the Council of State, a post which required him to translate diplomatic documents and correspondence. In 1657 MARVELL was appointed as one of his assistants; by then assistance was the more necessary because after 1651 Milton was effectively blind.

Despite the signs that his sight was deteriorating, he had continued to write political pamphlets in an official capacity, answering the Royalist propagandist Salmasius in *Pro populo anglicano defensio* (1651). When this produced a storm of controversy on the Continent he returned to the fray in *Defensio secunda* (1654), against Du Moulin's *Clamor* (which he wrongly attributed to Alexander More). Here and in the *Defence of Himself* (1655) the personal vilifications of his opponents evoke autobiographical digressions of great interest. Although he considered *Pro populo* his most significant work to date, he also believed that it had required the final sacrifice of his sight, a conviction reflected in one of his sonnets to Cyriack Skinner (1654/5). Such sonnets are among the few poems Milton wrote in the intervals of prose controversy during the late 1640s and 1650s, and several of these – to Fairfax, Cromwell and Vane, and 'On the New Forcers of Conscience' – share the same public themes. In 1655 the massacre of Waldensian Protestants aroused all of Milton's apocalyptic fervour, so strong in his pamphlets, in 'On the Late Massacre in Piedmont'; the same event required his drafting Cromwell's letters of protest to European rulers. The sonnets on personal topics include another on his blindness, 'When I consider how my light is spent', and one mourning his wife; possibly his second wife, since in 1656 he had married Katherine Woodcock. She and their daughter Katherine both died in 1658.

To these personal distresses was added bitter political disappointment, as the Protectorate crumbled after Cromwell's death. Defiantly, Milton published his republican protest, *The Ready and Easy Way to Establish a Free Commonwealth*, even as the restoration of the monarchy loomed in 1660. After the Restoration copies of his works were publicly burned. In danger of execution, he was initially a fugitive, then a prisoner, though after payment of a massive fine he was finally released into a life of relative retirement – owing partly, it is said, to the intercession of Marvell (who spoke for him in Parliament) and D'AVENANT. In 1663 he married Elizabeth Minshull; apart from a retreat to Chalfont St Giles from the plague of 1665, they settled in Bunhill Row, London. With renewed leisure for poetry, he completed *PARADISE LOST*, which he had probably begun before the Restoration. Its publication in 1667 was followed in 1671 by the joint publication of *PARADISE REGAINED* and the verse drama *SAMSON AGONISTES*. This, too, it has been suggested, had been written much earlier, although most scholars remain convinced that it is his last major poem. He also published a revised edition of his first poetic collection (1673), and some pamphlets written at an earlier date: on grammar (1669), on Ramist logic (1672), on *The History of Britain* (1670) and *Of True Religion* (1673). Milton died of gout on 8 November 1674, before the second edition of *Paradise Lost* – divided now into 12 books rather than 10 – was published, prefaced with a commendatory poem by Marvell. *The History of Moscovia* was also published posthumously, in 1682.

Even by Renaissance standards, Milton was a polymath. Although he had asserted, publicly in *Defensio secunda* and privately in letters, his conviction that his life should be dedicated to a great literary work, his early poems and letters show signs of self-doubt stemming from what he saw as his own dilatoriness. Immersed in controversy during the 1640s and 50s, he considered his pamphlets the work of his 'left hand' merely. Published towards the end of a life which had, superficially regarded, been spent in disparate, if distinguished, literary activity, *Paradise Lost* won Milton a reputation that was largely posthumous. His eminence was confirmed by ADDISON's *SPECTATOR* papers (1712), the first substantial contribution to Milton criticism. Throughout the 18th century his style was considered a model for the 'Sublime' mode in English poetry, though JOHNSON's complaint that Milton's language was 'harsh and barbarous' anticipated 20th-century attacks by T. S. ELIOT and LEAVIS. In the Romantic period his radical politics, as well as his achievement in producing an English EPIC, attracted admiration. For KEATS he was 'an active friend to Man all his Life, and has been since his death'. BLAKE's contention that in *Paradise Lost* Milton 'was of the Devil's party without knowing it' has exerted considerable influence on critics and readers in this century.

Mimic Men, The A novel by V. S. NAIPAUL, published in 1967. It is written in the form of a first-person memoir by its central character, Ralph Singh, a former Caribbean politician now living in a suburban London hotel. His unchronological narrative reviews his life: as a student in England, when he married the

English Sandra; as a child on the (fictional) island of Isabella; as one of a new generation of Caribbean politicians and, after his fall from power, as an exile in London. Singh sees displacement and disorder as central to his existence and describes his frustrated search for order, which he believes he has at last found in writing his memoir. The reader is left to judge whether this is in fact so.

Minot, Laurence The author of 11 fervently nationalist poems, all short and most in ALLITERATIVE VERSE, written during the 14th century, probably in Lincolnshire. Nothing is known of Minot's life. The poems describe battles and political events which took place between 1328 and 1352, and include accounts of Crécy (1346), Halidon Hill (1333), Sluys (1340), Neville's Cross (1346) and the defeat of the Spanish fleet at Winchelsea (1350).

miracle [mystery] **plays** Dramatized versions of biblical stories from the Creation to the Resurrection, popular in the Middle Ages. Their early history cannot be confidently outlined, though it is widely accepted that the movement towards dramatizing Christian doctrine and biblical history outgrew the church in which it began. The medieval church approved the elaboration of the liturgy into dialogue, in order to make its central doctrine of man's redemption plainer. The establishment in 1311 of the Feast of Corpus Christi provided a focus for a form of worship that was moving further from liturgy and further towards performance. By the middle of the 14th century, sequences of biblical plays were being performed all over England. Responsibility for their production was increasingly entrusted to the trade guilds, each working on individual episodes under the overall control of the corporation.

The survival of certain sequences (or, as they are more commonly known, cycles) of miracle plays seems to be largely haphazard. The Chester cycle is probably the earliest. It consists of 25 plays, in rhyming verse. The York cycle contains 48 plays, in verse forms of varying sophistication. A surviving roll lists the guilds responsible for each play. The Wakefield cycle (or Towneley cycle, after the family to whom the manuscript belonged) has 32 plays, five of them in the nine-line stanza associated with the anonymous Wakefield Master, who was the finest exponent of the form. His work, especially in the *Second Shepherds' Play*, exemplifies the secularization of the stories that may have contributed to church hostility during the 15th and 16th centuries. The *Ludus Conventriae* (or Coventry or N-town cycle), of uncertain provenance but believed by many scholars to be East Anglian, relies on the richness of ALLITERATIVE VERSE for many of its most forceful effects.

Debate about the staging of the miracle cycles continues. Pageant wagons were certainly used in York,

Chester and Wakefield, but that does not license the romantic but impractical assumption that the plays were in continuous performance as the wagons bounced and banged along cobbled streets. We must assume that a fixed site, or a few fixed sites, were designated for presentation of the plays to a festive audience as well as to local dignitaries. It was an occasion for the whole community to take stock of itself, to contribute and, no doubt, to compete. During the religious onslaught of the Reformation, and in its aftermath, the miracle plays lost their communal centrality. The fact that some at least survived is further evidence of a growing secularity. By 1550 they were already relics.

Mirror for Magistrates, A A 16th-century collection of didactic poetry illustrating the instability of fortune, the fall of the great and the punishment of the vicious. Its complicated publishing history began with the first edition in 1559, commissioned by the printer John Wayland as a continuation of JOHN LYDGATE's *FALL OF PRINCES* (itself an English version of Boccaccio's *De casibus virorum illustrium*). An earlier attempt to publish the book during Queen Mary's reign had been prevented by her chancellor Stephen Gardiner. The authors – the title-page named William Baldwin and George Ferrers as chief collaborators – drew on chronicle sources to provide 19 examples of the fall of famous men from the reigns of Richard II to Edward IV. The poems are connected by prose links and many deal with characters later made familiar by MARLOWE and SHAKESPEARE's history plays: the Mortimers, Richard II, Owen Glendower, Henry VI ('a virtuous prince'), George, Duke of Clarence, and Edward IV (who dies through 'surfeiting and untemperate life').

The 1563 edition added eight more stories, including that of Jane Shore by THOMAS CHURCHYARD and that of Buckingham by THOMAS SACKVILLE. The volume makes an interesting comparison with Shakespeare's *RICHARD III*, containing poems on Richard himself, Hastings and Rivers as well as Sackville's poem. The edition of 1578 added the legends of two characters also found in *HENRY VI*, *Part Two*, Humphrey, Duke of Gloucester, and Elinor Cobham, Duchess of Gloucester.

In 1574 *The First Part of the Mirror for Magistrates* appeared. This was not the Baldwin-Sackville work but one by John Higgins, the 'first part' of the *Mirror* in the sense that it gives 16 legends from early British history. *The Second Part of the Mirror for Magistrates* (1578) is by yet another hand, Richard Blennerhassett, and gives 12 legends of early British and Saxon characters.

In 1587 another edition appeared. This was the work of Higgins, and contains an enlarged version of his early British histories and a Sackville-Baldwin *Mirror* which is itself enlarged (for example, by the addition of poems about James IV, Flodden and Cardinal Wolsey). The last reshaping was that of Richard Niccols (1610). It includes material from previous versions, shuffles some of it around, omits the prose links and adds MICHAEL DRAYTON's legend of Thomas Cromwell.

C. S. LEWIS said that nobody laid down the *Mirror* without a sense of relief but SIDNEY's *APOLOGY FOR POETRY* calls it 'meetly furnished of beautiful parts' and finds it the only poetry, apart from the work of the EARL OF SURREY, worth mentioning between CHAUCER and SPENSER's *THE SHEPHEARDES CALENDER*.

Misfortunes of Arthur, The A tragedy by Thomas Hughes, first published in 1587 and performed by the Gentlemen of Gray's Inn for Elizabeth I at Greenwich in 1588. Fully titled *The Misfortunes of Arthur (Uther Pendragon's Son) Reduced in to Tragical Notes*, it shows the interest in ARTHURIAN LITERATURE crossing the bridge from medieval romance to Elizabethan drama. Thomas Hughes of Gray's Inn had been a fellow of Queens' College, Cambridge.

Misfortunes of Elphin, The A romance by THOMAS LOVE PEACOCK, published in 1829. Peacock used the Welsh Arthurian legends to parody the literary affectations of his day and to satirize contemporary political movements. When Elphin succeeds to the kingdom of Ceredigion, much of his territory has been lost through the negligence of Seithenyn, a drunkard who has failed to keep the walls of the kingdom in good repair and allowed the sea to flood the land. Elphin is imprisoned by a neighbouring prince, Maelgon, but the bard Taliesin secures his release by appealing to King Arthur. The book contains many songs and set-piece speeches; some of them adapt or translate Peacock's Welsh sources, while others, like 'The War-Song of Dinas Vawr', are his own.

Misogonus A comedy acted at Trinity College, Cambridge, between 1568 and 1574 and printed in 1577. It varies the theme of the prodigal son, popular with playwrights of the time, by making the prodigal the one who stays at home. Misogonus is vicious and debauched, and wastes the fortune of his father Philogonus. The return of the long-lost elder son, the virtuous Eugonus, brings about Misogonus's repentance. The play is notorious for its coarseness and for the elaborate scenes of Misogonus's dissipation. The author's identity is not known with certainty but evidence points to Anthony Rudd (c. 1549–1615), who became Bishop of St David's in 1594.

Miss Ravenel's Conversion from Secession to Loyalty A novel by JOHN DE FOREST, published in 1867. Dr Ravenel is a New Orleans physician who is forced to move north because of his Abolitionist beliefs. The sympathies of his daughter Lillie, however, are with the Confederates. Her conversion begins when she and her father settle in New Boston (based on New Haven, where De Forest lived). There she is wooed by two Union officers, Colbourne and Carter. The more dashing and aristocratic Carter better suits Lillie's Southern sensibility. She marries him and for his sake supports the Northern cause. Although his habits of drinking and womanizing seem to have abated, he begins a secret affair with Lillie's young aunt, Mrs Larue. He breaks off the affair after Lillie gives birth to a child, but Dr Ravenel learns of it and informs his daughter. Lillie eventually leaves her husband and later he is killed in battle; she returns to New Boston and finally marries the virtuous Colbourne. Her conversion to Abolitionism is by now complete. In spite of his preference for the Union cause, De Forest – with his customary harshness – satirizes New England society as well as that of New Orleans. The novel is also memorable for its grimly realistic battle scenes, which anticipate those of STEPHEN CRANE.

Mistry, Rohinton 1952– Indian short-story writer and novelist. Born in Bombay, he emigrated to Canada in 1975. Some of his stories have been collected in *Tales from Firozsha Baag* (1987). *Such a Long Journey* (1991), a novel, intertwines the political events which led to the creation of Bangladesh with a study of thwarted aspirations in the person of Gustad Noble, one of the most powerfully realized protagonists in modern Indian fiction.

Mitchel, John 1815–75 Irish patriotic writer. Born near Dungiven, County Londonderry, he qualified as a solicitor in 1843. After meeting THOMAS DAVIS, he joined O'Connell's Repeal Association, wrote for the Young Ireland paper *The Nation*, and founded his own more extreme paper, *The United Irishman*, in 1848. Soon afterwards he was arrested and convicted of treason. Sentenced to transportation, he was taken to Bermuda, South Africa and finally Tasmania, whence he escaped to the USA in 1853. All these experiences were recorded in his most famous work, the *Jail Journal* (1854), which registers his quarrel not merely with British policy but with the economic triumphalism, as he saw it, of British civilization, well represented by MACAULAY. He became notorious in America for his defence of slavery before and after the Civil War. His other writings include *The Life and Times of Aodh O'Neill* (1846), an edition of pamphlets on the Irish economy by SWIFT and BERKELEY (1847), a series of *Letters to the Protestant Farmers... of the North of Ireland* (1848; republished as a book, 1917) and a *History of Ireland* (1868). His savage and sardonic account of the Irish famine and the Young Ireland insurrection of 1848, *The Last Conquest of Ireland (Perhaps)* (1861), assumes a more or less efficient British strategy of systematic extermination and dispersion of the Irish people and shows his familiarity with the polemical techniques of Swift, to whom he has often been compared. PATRICK PEARSE venerated him as one of the four evangelists of Irish nationality.

Mitchell, Adrian 1932– Poet, novelist and playwright. Born in London, he was educated at private schools and Christ Church, Oxford. From the start his poetry was populist, rhetorical and overtly political. Accessible forms, popular idioms and immediacy of image and WIT are deployed in polemic against bad government and the threat of nuclear war and in celebration of New Jerusalems. He frequently gives public performances of his work, and it has appeared in two widely read anthologies, MICHAEL HOROVITZ's *Children of Albion* and *The Penguin Book of Socialist Verse*. *For Beauty Douglas* (1982) brings together poems from earlier volumes, including *Out Loud* (1966) and *The Apeman Cometh* (1975). New poems appeared in *On the Beach at Cambridge* (1986), *Love Songs of World War II* (1989) and *Greatest Hits* (1991). Mitchell's novels include *If You See Me Comin'* (1962) and *The Bodyguard* (1970). Of his work for the stage, the best known is his adaptation of Peter Weiss's *Marat/Sade* (1966).

Mitchell, James Leslie See GIBBON, LEWIS GRASSIC.

Mitchell, Julian 1935– Playwright and novelist. He was educated at Winchester and Wadham College, Oxford. He began his career by writing novels, including *Imaginary Toys* (1961), *A Disturbing Influence* (1962), *As Far As You Can Go* (1963), *The White Father* (1964), *A Circle of Friends* (1966) and, most notably, *An Undiscovered Country* (1968). Since then he has concentrated on drama, working for the stage and television. As well as adaptations of IVY COMPTON-BURNETT, his stage plays include *Half-Life* (1977), *The Enemy Within* (1980), *Francis* (1983) and *After Aida* (1986), but he is perhaps best known for *Another Country* (1981; filmed 1984), about the making of a traitor.

Mitchell, Ken 1940– Canadian playwright, novelist and short-story writer. Born in Moose Jaw, Saskatchewan, he began writing radio plays and publishing fiction while attending the University of Saskatchewan. He has taught English at the University of Regina since 1967 and has been a visiting lecturer in Edinburgh and Nanking. Firmly rooted in the prairie environment, his plays focus on eccentric, nonconformist protagonists. *Cruel Tears* (1976), based on OTHELLO, is a 'country opera' about Saskatchewan truck-drivers. *Davin: The Politician* (1979) is about an early Western politician and his unconventional lover. *The Great Cultural Revolution* (with the Chinese-Canadian composer David Liang;

1980) inserts a Chinese opera into a play about its staging in contemporary China. Other plays include *The Medicine Line* (1976), *The Shipbuilder* (1979), *The Promised Land* (1983) and *Gone the Burning Sun* (1985). *Rebel in Time: Three Plays* (1991) brings together *Davin, The Great Cultural Revolution* and *Gone the Burning Sun*. Mitchell's fiction includes: *Wandering Rafferty* (1972), a PICARESQUE novel; *The Con Man* (1979), in which the title character fulfils a necessary social role; and *Everybody Gets Something Here* (1977), short stories.

Mitchell, Langdon (Elwyn) 1862–1935 American playwright. He was born in Philadelphia, the son of the novelist S. Weir Mitchell. He began his career with a romantic tragedy, *Sylvian* (1885). His best-known play is *The New York Idea* (1906), a satirical examination of contemporary attitudes to love and marriage. He also wrote stage adaptations of novels, including *The Adventures of François* (1900), from his father's novel of 1898, and *Becky Sharp* (1899) and *Major Pendennis* (1916), from THACKERAY's *VANITY FAIR* and *PENDENNIS* respectively. A collection of essays, *Understanding America*, was published in 1927.

Mitchell, Margaret See GONE WITH THE WIND.

Mitchell, W(illiam) O(rmond) 1914– Canadian novelist, raconteur and playwright. He was born in Weyburn, Saskatchewan, and spent part of his youth in Florida. After his return to Canada in 1931 he studied at the University of Manitoba, did various odd jobs, travelled in North America and Europe, completed his BA at the University of Alberta and became a rural schoolteacher. In 1944 he gave up teaching to become a full-time writer. Mitchell's first novel, *Who Has Seen the Wind*, a classic account of a Prairie boyhood, was published in 1947. From 1948 to 1951 he was fiction editor for the news magazine *Maclean's* and lived in Toronto. Since then, apart from periods as writer-in-residence at various Canadian universities, he has mainly lived in Alberta. Between 1950 and 1958 he wrote over 300 scripts for his popular 'Jake and the Kid' series on Canadian Broadcasting Corporation radio. Thirteen of the original stories for these are collected in *Jake and the Kid* (1961). Mitchell is a seminal figure in the development of recent western Canadian writing. He is popular as a raconteur and humorist and much of his work has its origins in oral story-telling. His fiction stresses the value of the organic, natural life. His other works include *The Kite* (1962), *The Vanishing Point* (1973), *How I Spent My Summer Holidays* (1981), *Ladybug, Ladybug* (1988), *According to James and the Kid* (1989), *Roses are Difficult* (1990), and the plays *The Devil's Instrument* (1973) and *Back to Beulah*, published in *Dramatic W. O. Mitchell* (1982).

Mitchison, Naomi (Mary Margaret) 1897–
Novelist and short-story writer. Daughter of the physiologist J. S. Haldane and sister of the biologist J. B. S. HALDANE, she published some 70 books during a long career. The best are generally acknowledged to be the novels and stories of the 1920s and 1930s which evoke classical Greece and Rome: *The Conquered* (1923), *When the Bough Breaks* (short stories; 1924), *Cloud Cuckoo Land* (1925), *Barbarian Stories* (1929), *Black Sparta* (short stories; 1928), *The Corn King and the Spring Queen* (1931) and *The Delicate Fire* (short stories; 1933). *The Blood of the Martyrs* (1939) is a novel about early Christians in Rome. *Anna Comnena* (1928) is a biography of the Byzantine princess and historian of the 12th century AD.

Mitford, Mary Russell 1787–1855 Author of sketches and short stories, novelist and playwright. The daughter of a country doctor in Alresford, Hampshire, who ruined his family through extravagance, she supported her father by her earnings as a writer. The charming *Our Village: Sketches of Rural Life, Character and Scenery* began as a series of contributions to *The Lady's Magazine* in 1819 and appeared in five volumes between 1824 and 1832. The village is Three Mile Cross, near Reading, which itself was made the subject of *Belford Regis: Sketches of a Country Town* (1835). A novel, *Atherton and Other Tales* (1854), was less successful. Miss Mitford's plays include *The Foscari* (1826), *Rienzi* (1828) and *Charles I* (1834). *Recollections of a Literary Life* (1852) offers bright and gossipy comment on her contemporaries.

Mitford, Nancy (Freeman) 1904–73 Novelist and biographer. The daughter of the 2nd Baron Redesdale, she was born in London and educated privately. Her younger sister, Jessica, wrote an account of their family life in *Hons and Rebels* (1960). Nancy Mitford's novels generally describe Bohemian life in upper-class society and combine a witty and satiric tone with a sharp ear for dialogue. *Highland Fling* (1931), *Christmas Pudding* (1932), *Wigs on the Green* (1935) and *Pigeon Pie* (1940) were followed by *The Pursuit of Love* (1945), her first real success. Other successful novels included *Love in a Cold Climate* (1949) and *The Blessing* (1951), which follow the same range of characters through numerous affairs of the heart, and are closely observed studies of English class mores. Her biographies include *Madame de Pompadour* (1954), *Voltaire in Love* (1957), *The Sun King* (1966), and *Frederick the Great* (1970).

With A. S. C. Ross she edited and contributed to *Noblesse Oblige: An Enquiry into the Identifiable Characteristics of the English Aristocracy* (1956), a collection of satirical essays on snobbery which gave the terms 'U' and 'non-U' to the language. She also edited volumes of revealing family correspondence, *The Ladies of Alderley* (1938) and *The Stanleys of Alderley* (1939).

Mitford, William 1744–1827 Historian. Educated at The Queen's College, Oxford, he served in the Hampshire militia at the same time as EDWARD GIBBON and published a treatise on England's military strength. His *History of Greece*, published in five volumes between 1784 and 1818, was suggested by Gibbon and praised by MACAULAY.

Mittelholzer, Edgar 1909–65 Guyanese novelist, born in New Amsterdam. Under his mother's rigid Puritanism, he grew up passionate for absolute personal freedom. Veerings between order and licence produce many unresolved contradictions in both his moral vision and fictional design, but his 23 novels helped to create a genuine Caribbean consciousness that incorporates Guyanese history and landscape. The first novel, *Corentyne Thunder* (1941), uneasily shackles the authentic realism with which Mittelholzer depicts Indian peasantry in Guyana with overwritten, romantic description, while *A Morning at the Office* (1950), his second novel, is a polished handling of Jamaican race relations, exemplified in personal interactions within a single office on a single day. Much research went into the Kaywana novels, a Guyanese family saga covering the years 1612–1953: *Children of Kaywana* (1952; including *Kaywana Heritage*, separately published from 1976), *The Harrowing of Hubertus* (1954; later published as *Kaywana Stock*) and *Kaywana Blood* (1958). Here vigorous writing and imaginative sweep are weakened by melodrama, and sexual frankness by titillation. *Shadows Move among Them* (1952) and *The Mad MacMullochs* (1959) figure free, sexually liberated communities, yet both are under authoritarian leaders.

Mittelholzer's attack on race prejudice in *A Morning at the Office* seems undermined by the hero's inadequately distanced anti-black sentiments in *Latticed Echoes* (1960). In *The Life and Death of Sylvia* (1953), faith in human resilience, and despair over its failure, seem equally weighted. His last novel, *The Pilkington Drama* (1965), ends with a suicide by fire. So did Mittelholzer's own life.

Mo, Timothy 1950– Novelist. Born in Hong Kong of English and Cantonese parents, he attracted attention with *The Monkey King* (1978), set in Hong Kong, and *Sour Sweet* (1982), a densely realistic portrait of London's Chinese community, remarkable for its wealth of detail and also its spry, bizarre comedy. *An Insular Possession* (1986), a historical novel about the Opium Wars, forsakes Mo's previous gingery wit for a more studied comedy of manners. *The Redundancy of Courage* (1991) is about a political guerrilla movement in a fictional country modelled on the Philippines.

Moby-Dick: *or, The Whale* A novel by HERMAN MELVILLE, published in New York and London in 1851. The British title was *The Whale*.

The highly complex story begins with the narrator Ishmael's decision to go to sea. On his way to Nantucket he meets and befriends Queequeg, a harpooner from the South Sea Islands who is the image of the noble savage – a 'George Washington cannibalistically developed'. The two friends sign aboard the whaler *Pequod*, named after the first Indian tribe exterminated by white Americans. Before they set sail, a man named Elijah delivers mysterious warnings about a disastrous voyage and Father Mapple delivers a symbolic sermon about the prophet Jonah who was swallowed by a whale.

The *Pequod*'s mysterious Captain Ahab appears after several days at sea. He reveals to the crew the purpose (as he conceives it) of the voyage: to hunt and kill the white sperm whale, known among whalers as Moby-Dick, which took off his leg on a previous voyage. Ahab's eloquence convinces the crew to pledge themselves to his monomaniacal plan for vengeance. Only Starbuck, the first mate, demurs, feeling that Ahab's mission is a sacrilege and a threat to the financial investment the ship's owners have made. Stubb, the second mate, and Flask, the third, are easily drawn into Ahab's plan. The crew, castoffs and refugees of all races and lands, is a microcosm of humanity. The harpooners are Queequeg, Tashtego (a Gay Head Indian) and Daggoo (an African). On the first encounter with whales, they find that Ahab has kept hidden his own boat's crew, which is led by Fedallah, a Parsee and fortune-teller.

The narrative is sometimes naturalistic, sometimes fantastic and shaped into obscure parables. Large sections dwell upon the science of whales or upon the intricacies of the whaling business and its history. Amid the often turbulent complexity of the narrative form, the dramatic events unfold slowly. As the men of the *Pequod* sail the open sea in search of a single whale, they still occupy themselves with the regular business of whale hunting. Occasional chases after whales, storms, or meetings with other ships punctuate the long voyage. The crew captures and processes a sperm whale; Pip, a young black cabin boy, becomes caught in a harpoon line and is nearly drowned, whereupon he becomes insane; the *Pequod* nearly founders when Ishmael drowses at the helm; a meeting with the British whaler, the *Samuel Enderby*, provides Ahab with news that Moby-Dick has been sighted recently; and Queequeg has a coffin made when he nearly dies of fever.

When a lightning storm sets the mastheads ablaze with St Elmo's fire, Ahab delivers a speech to his crew that confirms his mad devotion to the quest; the crew is panic-stricken and Starbuck warns Ahab that God is against him. These ominous events lead up to the eventual sighting of Moby-Dick and the three-day chase with which the novel culminates. On the first day the great whale crushes one of the boats and nearly kills Fedallah. On the second day it drags Fedallah down in Ahab's harpoon line, and Ahab's artificial leg is snapped off as the whaleboat is wrecked. Finally, on the third day, a stricken Moby-Dick charges the *Pequod* and smashes her sides. Ahab, in the whaling boat, manages to strike a final blow but is himself caught in the harpoon line and drowned, tied to the whale. The *Pequod* sinks, taking all of the whaling boats and their crews down in the suction. The only survivor is Ishmael, who is shot back up, clinging to the coffin that had been made for Queequeg.

mock-heroic The use for comic effect of a high or epic style out of all proportion to its low or trivial subject matter (compare BURLESQUE). Late 17th- and 18th-century literature, in particular, offers many examples, including DRYDEN's *MAC FLECKNOE* and POPE's *THE RAPE OF THE LOCK* and *THE DUNCIAD*.

Modern Chivalry A novel in seven volumes by HUGH HENRY BRACKENRIDGE, published in instalments between 1792 and 1815. Captain John Farrago and his Irish servant, Teague O'Regan, American versions of Don Quixote and Sancho Panza, travel around the Pennsylvania countryside, their adventures providing the occasion for satirical observations about post-Revolutionary American life and manners.

Farrago is a stuffy, aristocratic landowner; Teague, a stereotypical Irishman – irresponsible, untrained, uneducated, one of the men who have been newly placed in positions of power by the Revolution and the institution of democracy. Much of the book consists of a series of incidents in which Teague is given opportunities – as preacher, Indian treaty maker, potential husband for a well-bred young lady, pupil to a French dancing master – for which, according to an earlier set of values, he is socially unqualified. (He is, in fact, unqualified by any standard.) Farrago's unprincipled attempts to discourage and prevent him from exploiting these opportunities derive from his own desire to keep the old aristocratic system in place, thereby retaining Teague as his servant and preserving his own class's exclusive prerogative to fill these roles. The tensions between them thus dramatize the problem of authority and leadership in a democracy.

Modern Instance, A A novel by WILLIAM DEAN HOWELLS, serialized in *THE CENTURY MAGAZINE* in 1881 and published in volume form in 1882.

Bartley Hubbard, a young Boston journalist, is married to Marcia Gaylord. The marriage quickly deteriorates, however, because of his unscrupulous business practices and moral decline. Despite her love for her husband, Marcia leaves him. Hubbard sues for divorce but his suit is defeated and the divorce is granted to

Marcia. After the divorce he moves to Arizona where he is killed by someone about whom he has published personal details in his newspaper. Marcia, meanwhile, is courted by Ben Halleck, a highly principled man who cannot decide whether or not to leave the ministry for her. The novel ends without giving his final decision. Howells developed the idea of the divorce theme after seeing a performance of the *Medea*. He referred to the novel as his 'New Medea', a 'modern instance' of what would happen to a gradually estranged couple.

Modern Love A sequence of poems by GEORGE MEREDITH, published in 1862. There are 50 poems, unconventional SONNETS of 16 lines. Obliquely inspired by the failure of his first marriage, but not literally depicting it, the sequence traces the decline of passion and the disintegration of a marriage, with the wife dying and the husband taking a mistress. The narrative serves chiefly as framework for a psychological study of romantic expectation and disillusionment.

Modern Painters A five-volume treatise on art by JOHN RUSKIN, published intermittently between 1843 and 1860.

The full title of the first volume was *Modern Painters: Their Superiority in the Art of Landscape Painting to All the Ancient Masters Proved by Examples of the True, the Beautiful and the Intellectual, from the Works of Modern Artists, Especially from those of J. M. W. Turner, Esq., R.A.* On one level it is a defence of Turner, whose recent contributions to Royal Academy exhibitions had been widely attacked. But it quickly transcends that goal to advocate Truth and Beauty, whose elusive qualities Ruskin finds best exemplified in Turner's work, to consider art as a social force and to praise Nature. All this is expressed in prose both persuasive and grandiloquent. The second volume (1846) is a more formidable treatise on ideas of beauty and the imaginative faculty.

A decade then elapsed while Ruskin developed theories of architecture, morality and society. The third volume (1856) is appropriately subtitled 'Of Many Things', for it seems, initially, a bewildering mass of diverse topics. The reader is swept through commentary on painting and poetry, on landscape modern, medieval and classical – all enlivened with proliferating references to Homer, Dante, WORDSWORTH, BYRON, SCOTT and hosts of others. Chapters such as 'Touching the "Grand Style" ' and 'Of the Pathetic Fallacy', as well as discussions of the true and the false ideal and of the teachers of Turner, nevertheless give cohesion and unity to this impressive discourse. With the fourth volume (also 1856), whose five opening chapters interpret Turner's art in the light of the theories advanced earlier, came such memorable chapters as 'The Mountain Gloom' and 'The Mountain

Glory', relating these natural phenomena to spiritual, social and aesthetic temperaments. The final volume (1860) is marked by its author's conviction that the entire series reveals Turner as the supreme landscape painter. Yet it is also suffused with disappointment and futility, for Ruskin was by now becoming hopeless in the face of the amount of work remaining to be done in art criticism. There is also a growing desire to speak on social questions, clearly shown in 'The Two Boyhoods' with its malediction on industrial England.

Modern Painters, then, is large in its ambition and diverse in its accomplishment. The volumes are born of different moods, varying perspectives and shifting purposes. Yet Ruskin's idealism – be it aesthetic or social – does not waver, and the book at least succeeds in embodying (in the words of one critic) 'Ruskin's comprehensive theory of art criticism'.

modernism The term for an international tendency in the arts brought about by a creative renaissance during the last decade of the 19th century and lasting into the post-war years. Strictly speaking, modernism cannot be described as a 'movement' or reliably characterized by a uniform style. Indeed it may be said to have embraced a wide range of artistic movements (including SYMBOLISM, impressionism, post-impressionism, futurism, constructivism, IMAGISM, VORTICISM, EXPRESSIONISM, dada and surrealism) and to have originated in cosmopolitan circles in Berlin, Vienna, Munich, Prague, Moscow, London and Paris. At a slightly later period it spread to New York and Chicago, and became synonymous with a worldwide reaction against positivism and representational art. Its most notable landmarks in English literature are commonly understood to include HENRY JAMES's *THE AMBASSADORS* (1903), CONRAD's *NOSTROMO* (1904), T. S. ELIOT's *THE WASTE LAND* (1922), and JOYCE's *ULYSSES* (1922). One might add the work of POUND, YEATS, FORD MADOX FORD, VIRGINIA WOOLF and, in America, FAULKNER, to a list which is by no means exhaustive.

Technically, modernism was distinguished by its opposition to traditional forms and to the aesthetic perceptions associated with those forms. It was persistently experimental. A common quality was the highly self-conscious manipulation of form, together with an awareness of pioneering studies which were contemporaneous in other disciplines. These included, in psychology, WILLIAM JAMES's *PRINCIPLES OF PSYCHOLOGY* (1890) and Freud's *The Interpretation of Dreams* (1899); in physics, Einstein's *General Principles of Relativity* (1915); and in anthropology, SIR JAMES FRAZER's *The Golden Bough* (1890–1915).

HERBERT READ suggested that modernism 'is not so much a revolution, which implies a turning over, even a turning back, but rather a break-up, a devolution, some would say a dissolution. Its character is catastrophic.' Much of the difficulty of modernist texts, which has intimidated some readers, stems from this attempt to 'break up' or re-create the experience of reading. STREAM OF CONSCIOUSNESS, the use of myth as a structural principle, and the primary status given to the poetic image, all challenged traditional representation.

Modest Proposal, A: *for Preventing the Children of Poor People from being a Burden to Their Parents, or the Country, and for Making Them Beneficial to the Public* A satirical pamphlet by JONATHAN SWIFT, first published in 1729.

Despite his repeated claims to dislike Ireland, Swift was a patriotic defender of the cause of the repressed Irish nation, the conditions of poverty and the carelessness of absentee English landlords moving him to indignant outrage. The central 'proposal' of this satire is that it would make sound economic sense if the offspring of the Irish poor were farmed for the table of the rich English. With the scrupulous reasoning of an economic 'projector', Swift brilliantly imitates the shape and method of such arguments, adopting a dispassionate, even benevolent tone as he sets down the appallingly plausible plan. As with much of his SATIRE, the basic strategy is the literalization of an idea: since the greedy landlords are metaphorically devouring the profits of the country, they might as well literally eat up the inhabitants. The several advantages of this proposal, which it is suggested will benefit everyone, include the reduction of beggars, the year-round availability of tasty meat, profit to the mothers (or 'dams') and the certainty that husbands would look after their women for a change, as a source of their livelihood. Swift by implication suggests that cannibalism on a commercial scale would be no less justifiable than the economic system which allows England to exploit Irish labour and trade. As a rhetorical performance in satiric impersonation the *Modest Proposal* is probably unrivalled in English prose.

Moir, David Macbeth 1798–1851 Scots novelist. A doctor in Musselburgh, he contributed regularly to *BLACKWOOD'S EDINBURGH MAGAZINE* and other periodicals, signing his name with the Greek capital delta. *The Life of Mansie Wauch, Tailor in Dalkeith*, his best-remembered book, first appeared in parts in *Blackwood's* and was published in volume form in 1828. Dedicated to JOHN GALT, a friend whose novels influenced Moir, it is the imaginary autobiography of a small-town tailor and contains much wryly humorous observation.

Molesworth, Mary Louisa 1839–1921 Writer of CHILDREN'S LITERATURE. Born Mary Louisa Stewart in Rotterdam, she was educated in Switzerland. *Lover and Husband* (1869) and several other novels ap-

peared under the pseudonym Ennis Graham before she turned to children's books with great popular success. Macmillan made a practice of issuing a book by Mrs Molesworth every Christmas, sometimes illustrated by WALTER CRANE. Among the more than 100 titles are *The Cuckoo Clock* (1877), *The Tapestry Room* (1879), *The Adventures of Herr Baby* (1881), *The Children of the Castle* (1890), *The Carved Lions* (1895), *Peterkin* (1902), *The Little Guest* (1907) and *The Story of a Year* (1910).

Moll Flanders: *The Fortunes and Misfortunes of the Famous* A novel by DANIEL DEFOE, published in 1722.

Moll Flanders is born in Newgate, where her mother is under sentence of death for theft. The hanging is delayed because 'being found quick with child, she was respited for about seven months' and then her sentence is commuted to transportation to Virginia. The abandoned child is taken in by the mayoress of Colchester, from whom she passes to another gentlewoman who gives her an education; but the son of the house seduces her. She leads an adventurous love life and eventually marries. In Virginia with her husband, she finds her mother and discovers that her husband is in fact her brother. She leaves him and her children and goes back to England, where she falls into bad company and finds herself destitute. She becomes a successful thief but is caught and, like her mother before her, transported to Virginia. On the ship is one of her former husbands, who had been a highwayman, and they renew their liaison. Moll inherits her mother's plantation and prospers. When their sentence runs out, she and her husband return to England, where in comfort and serenity Moll looks back from the age of 70 over 'the wicked lives we have lived'.

Moll Flanders owes much of its continuing popularity and its importance in the development of English fiction to the fact that it is a novel of character, as opposed to an adventurous romance. The book may not be neat or shapely in structure – indeed, it is riddled with inconsistencies and contradictions – but Moll herself is made an identifiable personality, and her autobiography continually poses questions about the motives for human conduct. The familiar themes of domestic allegiance and self-sufficiency link *Moll Flanders* with Defoe's other fiction, together with his love of portraying urban low life and foreign travel.

Molloy, Michael (Joseph) 1917– Irish playwright. Born in Milltown, County Galway, he abandoned training for the priesthood because of illness, then farmed near his birthplace. His chief works are *The Old Road* (1943), *The Visiting House* (1946), *The King of Friday's Men* (1948), *The Wood of the Whispering* and *The Paddy Pedlar* (1953). Set in Western Ireland in 1817, *The King of Friday's Men* mourns the passing of a feudal way of life. Molloy deals less certainly with the contemporary residue of those folkways, but *The Visiting House* effectively dramatizes the dying institution where country districts were regaled with songs and stories. Molloy's dialect speech at its fluent best carries his often knotty plots. Though more restricted by his region than SYNGE or FITZMAURICE, Molloy is the last remarkable exponent of their folk-drama.

Momaday, N(atachee) [Navarre] **Scott** 1934– American-Indian novelist, poet and scholar. Born on a Kiowa reservation in Oklahoma and educated at Stanford, he first became known as editor of the poems of FREDERICK GODDARD TUCKERMAN (1965). He was awarded a PULITZER PRIZE for his first novel, *House Made of Dawn* (1968), the story of Abel, an Indian who leaves the reservation when he is drafted and is forced to confront the non-Indian world. Momaday has since published: a collection of Kiowa folk-tales, *The Way to Rainy Mountain* (1969); a volume of poetry, *Angle of Geese and Other Poems* (1974); *The Gourd Dancer* (1976); *The Names: A Memoir* (1976); and a second novel, *The Ancient Child* (1989).

Moments of Vision and Miscellaneous Verses Poems by THOMAS HARDY, first published in 1917. A short poem, 'Moments of Vision', gives the volume its title and also evokes its ambience and tenor, for there is much of Wordsworthian introspection, of inner searching, in the collection. Yet whilst the older Hardy (he was 77 at the time of publication) harks back for subject matter, much of the verse is contemporary in composition and one group of poems is given to war and patriotism. But strong human feelings, the pulsations of the heart and the reverberations of folk-song and rural life create a sustained emotional unity unique in collections of Hardy's poetry. The volume includes 'The Last Signal' (about WILLIAM BARNES), 'The Blinded Bird', 'During Wind and Rain', and 'Near Lanivet' (the latter two among those about Emma, his first wife) and 'Afterwards'.

Monastery, The A novel by SIR WALTER SCOTT, published in 1820. The setting is the monastery of Kennaquhair (based on Melrose Abbey) in the time of Elizabeth I.

An English adherent of the Catholic cause, Sir Piercie Shafton, takes refuge in Scotland, where the Abbot of Kennaquhair lodges him with his tenants, the Glendinnings. Years before, Simon Glendinning had given a home to an orphan girl, Mary Avenel, with whom both his sons have fallen in love. Edward is quiet and studious and Mary prefers the spirited and gallant Halbert. Halbert falls into conflict with the arrogant Sir Piercie and leaves him for dead after a duel. The White Lady of Avenel, a beneficent ghost, restores

the English knight to life. Halbert enters the service of the Earl of Murray, prospers and marries Mary. Edward enters the monastery.

The Abbot (1820), set in the reign of Mary, Queen of Scots, was intended as a sequel.

Moncrieff, William Thomas 1794–1857 Playwright and theatre manager. He was born in London, where he worked from boyhood as a solicitor's clerk before risking a theatrical career. Lessee at various times of the Queen's, Astley's Amphitheatre, the Coburg, Vauxhall Gardens and the City Theatre, Moncrieff was a hack writer who turned out plays to suit the time. Adaptations of popular novels were entrusted to him by managers eager to cash in on the latest vogue. *The Lear of Private Life* (1820), from a novel by AMELIA OPIE, has some interest as a 19th-century domestication of SHAKESPEARE. *The Shipwreck of the Medusa* (1820) exploited the excitement created by Géricault's picture. *Tom and Jerry* (1821) was a particularly zestful adaptation of PIERCE EGAN'S *LIFE IN LONDON*. *The Cataract of the Ganges* (1823) was the sensation of its season at DRURY LANE, less for the text than for the use of a horse troupe and the lavish sets of Clarkson Stanfield and David Roberts. Moncrieff, who wrote over 100 plays, was evidently willing to accept the modest standing of contemporary playwrights.

Money A comedy by EDWARD BULWER LYTTON, first produced at the Theatre Royal, HAYMARKET, in 1840 by William Charles Macready, who had suggested the plot to the author.

Alfred Evelyn is a nobody until he suddenly, and entirely unexpectedly, inherits a fortune. Determined to sort out which of his friends are true and which of two women he should marry, Evelyn pretends to have lost all his money through gambling (and the collapse of a bank). The reading of the will in Act One and the gambling scene at Crockford's in Act Three are the outstanding sequences in this socially alert play.

Monk, The A GOTHIC NOVEL by M. G. LEWIS, published in 1796, at the height of the craze stimulated by ANN RADCLIFFE'S *MYSTERIES OF UDOLPHO* (1794). It is more sensational than her work, and relies on horror rather than terror; it also allows supernatural events to remain without natural explanation.

The theme of the story is the sexual repression at the heart of asceticism. A young monk, Ambrosio, famous for his religious devotion, is tempted by Matilda, the model for his own much beloved portrait of the Virgin Mary. Initially she comes to him dressed as a boy entering the monastery as a novice. She initiates him into sexual depravity and he proves insatiable. Matilda helps him to pursue a young girl living with her mother; he ends by destroying both women, who are later revealed to be his mother and sister. He is unmasked and sentenced to death, but believes that the Devil, with whom he has made a pact, will save him. Just as he is hurled to damnation he learns that Matilda is the Devil's emissary. Sub-plots compound the horror of the tale which was considered both ridiculous and indecent by many, though it also enjoyed considerable popularity.

Monk's Tale, The See CANTERBURY TALES, THE.

monometer See METRE.

Monro, Harold (Edward) 1879–1932 Publisher and poet. Born in Brussels, he came to England at the age of seven and was educated at Radley and Gonville and Caius College, Cambridge. He is best remembered for the Poetry Bookshop, which he established in 1913 to publish and sell work by contemporary poets and organize public readings. He published EDWARD MARSH's GEORGIAN POETRY anthologies, founded *The Poetry Review* and its short-lived successor, *Poetry and Drama*, and issued pamphlets by W. W. GIBSON and JOHN DRINKWATER from his Samuria Press. His *Chronicle of a Pilgrimage: Paris to Milan on Foot* appeared in 1909 and his *Collected Poems* in 1933. This was introduced by T. S. ELIOT, who saw Monro's work as isolated between the Georgians and the Moderns.

Monroe, Harriet 1860–1936 American editor and poet. Born in Chicago, she first attracted attention with her *Columbian Ode*, a poem written for the dedication ceremony of the World's Columbian Exposition, held in the city in 1892. Her other poetry was published in *Valeria and Other Poems* (1891), *You and I* (1914), *The Difference* (1924) and *Chosen Poems* (1935). She also wrote several verse dramas, five of which were published in 1903 as *The Passing Show*.

She founded POETRY: A Magazine of Verse to encourage and publish the 'new poetry' in 1912 and edited it until her death. The magazine played a prominent role in the Chicago Renaissance in literature, publishing work by EZRA POUND, T. S. ELIOT (THE LOVE SONG OF J. ALFRED PRUFROCK) and many other distinguished figures. Monroe's autobiography, *A Poet's Life: Seventy Years in a Changing World* (1937), provides an informative account of the changes in the American literary scene during the late 19th and early 20th centuries. *Poets and Their Art* (1932) is a collection of critical essays.

Monsarrat, Nicholas (John Turney) 1910–79 Novelist. Born in Liverpool, he was educated at Winchester and Trinity College, Cambridge. He is chiefly remembered for his novel of World War II, *The Cruel Sea* (1951), also made into a successful film. It was preceded by *Think of Tomorrow* (1934), *At First Sight* (1935) and *The Whipping Boy* (1936), and followed by *The Story of Esther Costello* (1953), *The White Rajah* (1961), *A Fair Day's Work* (1964), *The Tribe That Lost Its Head* (1965), *Richer Than All His Tribe* (1968) and *The Kappillan of Malta* (1973). Monsarrat died before completing what he considered his major work, *The Master Mariner*, a projected three-volume novel of seafaring life from Napoleonic times to the present; the first part appeared in 1978 and the second (unfinished) after his death. The first volume of his autobiography, *Life is a Four-Letter Word*, was published in 1966, the second in 1970.

Mont-Saint-Michel and Chartres: *A Study of Thirteenth-Century Unity* A work of history by HENRY ADAMS, printed privately for distribution among family and friends in 1904 and published by the American Institute of Architects in 1913. Adams identifies the dominant cultural power of the Middle Ages as the Catholic faith which informed and unified all artistic and intellectual endeavour, as well as religious and moral thought. In particular, he sees the unifying symbolic 'force' of the Virgin as having provided the spiritual impulse for the arts of the time, which he discusses in separate chapters devoted to architecture, sculpture, stained-glass windows, literature and historical and religious figures. The book's investigation of medieval culture is complemented by the discussion of modernity in THE EDUCATION OF HENRY ADAMS, subtitled 'A Study of Twentieth-Century Multiplicity'.

Montagu, Elizabeth 1720–1800 Leading member of the BLUESTOCKING circle. Born Elizabeth Robinson, she spent several childhood years at the Cambridge home of her maternal grandmother and her grandmother's second husband, CONYERS MIDDLETON. There she was trained to listen to the conversation of divines, scholars, philosophers, travellers and men of the world. Her father also encouraged her conversational powers, and the brothers and sisters used to debate. In 1742 she married Charles Montagu, cousin of Edward Wortley Montagu (see LADY MARY WORTLEY MONTAGU). She held regular assemblies for intellectual and literary conversation at her house in Hill Street, near Park Lane. Members of her 'Blue Stocking Society' included HANNAH MORE, FANNY BURNEY, HESTER CHAPONE and HORACE WALPOLE. SAMUEL JOHNSON christened her 'Queen of the Blues' and thought that 'Mrs Montagu is *par pluribus*. With her, you may find *variety in one*.' They quarrelled, however, in 1781, when she criticized the manuscript of his 'Life of Lyttelton' for THE LIVES OF THE ENGLISH POETS. She was author of the *Essay on the Writings and Genius of Shakespeare* (1769), defending SHAKESPEARE against the attacks of Voltaire.

Montagu, Lady Mary Wortley 1689–1762 Poet and letter-writer. Born in London the eldest daughter of the 1st Duke of Kingston, Lady Mary Pierrepoint was well educated and an accomplished 'belle let-triste'. In 1712, against her father's wishes, she married Edward Wortley Montagu, an MP who became ambassador to Constantinople in 1716. The couple became well known in literary circles, associating with ADDISON and POPE. Lady Mary stayed in Turkey for two years, returning to London in 1718; while abroad she maintained a lively correspondence, the letters giving a sharp account of life in the Ottoman Court. She introduced the practice of inoculation against smallpox. Pope had an unhappy disagreement of some sort with Lady Mary in 1723, and was thereafter malicious to her in print on several occasions, although there was still a portrait of her in his room when he died. She went to live abroad in 1738, living in France and Italy and returning to England in 1762, where she died while staying with her daughter, Lady Bute. Lady Mary's publications included *Court Poems* (1716) and *Court Poems by a Lady of Quality* (1716), spirited *vers de société* that are witty and perceptive, and a collection of *Letters* published in 1763-7. *The Complete Letters* were published in three volumes in 1965-7, edited by Robert Halsband.

Montague, John 1929- Irish poet. Born in New York, he grew up in County Tyrone in Northern Ireland. He was educated at University College, Dublin, and at the University of Iowa. Between 1956 and 1959 he worked for the Irish Tourist Board and was Paris correspondent for *The Irish Times*. He taught widely in the USA and Canada, and lived for the most part in Paris until 1974, when he returned to Ireland to teach at University College, Cork.

His work is contained in *Poisoned Lands* (1961; revised edition, 1976), *A Chosen Light* (1967), *Tides* (1970), *The Rough Field* (1972), *A Slow Dance* (1975), *The Great Cloak* (1978), *Mount Eagle* (1989) and *New Selected Poems* (1990). A contemporary and friend of THOMAS KINSELLA, he introduced American and French influences into Irish poetry at a time when it was becoming introverted and provincial. He and Kinsella were the leading poets with the Dolmen Press, founded by Liam Miller. Deeply affected by the crisis in Northern Ireland, his poetry – most notably in *The Rough Field* – has always sought for a reconciliation between the intimacies of private life and the brutalities of historical and public experience. He has also published a volume of short stories, *Death of a Chieftain* (1964), and edited an important anthology, *The Faber Book of Irish Verse* (1974).

Montgomerie, Alexander ?1556-?1610 Scottish poet. Montgomerie held office in the Scottish court, first under the regent Morton and then under James VI, who quotes from his verse in *Rewlis and Cautelis of Scottis Poesie* (1584). He fell from favour in 1594 after being implicated in a popish plot. His principal work is *The Cherrie and the Slae* (1597), an allegorical work

about the choice between the noble and virtuous cherry and the lowly sloe. It contains debates between such personified abstractions as Hope, Experience, Reason and Cupid. *The Flyting betwixt Montgomerie and Polwart* (1621) is an example of the exchanged invective used by earlier Scottish poets such as DUNBAR. Montgomerie also wrote versions of the psalms, lyrics and songs.

Montgomery, L(ucy) M(aud) 1874-1942 Canadian novelist and writer of CHILDREN'S LITERATURE. Born on Prince Edward Island where she spent her youth, she became a teacher and enjoyed a modest success with contributions to periodicals. Later she married Ewen Macdonald, a Presbyterian minister, and settled in Toronto. *ANNE OF GREEN GABLES* (1908), which began as a serial for a Sunday-school paper, was an immediate success. She followed it with *Anne of Avonlea* (1909) and numerous other titles centring on the life of her scapegrace heroine, Anne Shirley. Other novels include *The Blue Castle* (1926), *Kilmeny of the Orchard* (1910) and the melancholy, semi-autobiographical *Emily of New Moon* (1923), *Emily Climbs* (1925) and *Emily's Quest* (1927).

Moodie, Susanna 1803-85 Poet, novelist and essayist. She was born Susanna Strickland at Reydon Hall in Suffolk, the sister of CATHARINE PARR TRAILL and AGNES STRICKLAND. She married John Dunbar Moodie in 1831 and emigrated to Canada in 1832, where they made a precarious living near Cobourg and later at Rice Lake and Belleville. A book of verse, *Enthusiasm and Other Poems*, was published in 1831 and other volumes were written in Canada to contribute to the family finances, including the novels *Mark Hurdlestone and the Gold Worshipper* (1853), *Geoffrey Monckton* (1853) and *Flora Lyndsay* (1854). Her most enduring works are two books based on her experiences in Canada, *Roughing It in the Bush: or, Life in Canada* (1852) and *Life in the Clearings versus the Bush* (1853).

Moody, William Vaughn 1869-1910 American playwright and poet. He was born in Indiana, and educated at Harvard. His first published work was *Class Poem* (1894). *The Masque of Judgment* (1900) was the first part of a verse drama trilogy continued by *The Fire Bringer* (1904) and the uncompleted *The Death of Eve* (1912). *Poems* (1901) contains the often-anthologized pieces 'Gloucester Moors' and 'An Ode in Time of Hesitation'.

Although only two of his plays were produced during his lifetime, Moody's brief career as a dramatist was of considerable importance to the development of the American theatre. Unlike many dramatists of his time, he chose distinctively American subjects for his plays. His enormously popular *A Sabine Woman* (1906), which was later produced and published under the title *The Great Divide* (1909), treats the conflict between the values of established Eastern culture and the realities of free-spirited frontier life, describing the abduction of a woman from Massachusetts by a man from Arizona and the events that lead to their eventual marriage. Its realism challenged the melodramatic conventions of the contemporary American stage. Moody's final play, *The Faith Healer*, appeared in 1909.

Moonstone, The A novel by WILKIE COLLINS, published serially in *ALL THE YEAR ROUND* from January to August 1868 and in volume form the same year.

The story is told in Collins's customary manner, through eyewitness accounts by various characters. The prologue describes how Colonel John Herncastle stole the Moonstone diamond from a Hindu holy place at the siege of Seringapatam. He leaves it to his niece, Rachel Verinder, and Franklin Blake brings it to her Yorkshire home for presentation on her eighteenth birthday. By the next morning the stone has disappeared, and the mystery is investigated first by the slow-witted Superintendent Seegrave and then by the shrewd, melancholy Sergeant Cuff from London. Suspicion falls variously on three Hindus who have been seen in the neighbourhood, the servant Rosanna Spearman and Rachel herself. She inexplicably turns against Franklin Blake and becomes engaged to Godfrey Ablewhite, a pious philanthropist also staying in the house.

With Cuff unable to advance the matter further, Franklin Blake takes over the investigation. To his surprise, he discovers that he himself is the thief: Ezra Jennings, the local doctor's assistant, demonstrates that Blake unknowingly removed the diamond while under the influence of opium. The diamond, meanwhile, is traced to a London bank and Sergeant Cuff re-enters the story to expose Ablewhite as the real villain – but not before Ablewhite has been killed and the diamond retrieved by the mysterious Hindus.

Carefully paced and sharply characterized, *The Moonstone* uses features of the SENSATION NOVEL to create a pioneering example of DETECTIVE FICTION. T. S. ELIOT called it 'the first, the longest, and the best of modern English detective novels'.

Moorcock, Michael 1939– Writer of SCIENCE FICTION. He became editor of *New Worlds* in 1964 and transformed it into an *avant-garde* periodical. His 'Jerry Cornelius' stories – including a tetralogy of novels, *The Final Programme* (1968), *A Cure for Cancer* (1971), *The English Assassin* (1972) and *The Condition of Muzak* (1977) – are key examples of the surreal, modernist science fiction which he promoted. In *Behold the Man* (1969) a guilt-ridden time-traveller goes in search of Christ and is forced to assume the role himself. In the 'Dancers at the End of Time' series, including *An Alien Heat* (1972), *The*

Hollow Lands (1974) and *The End of All Songs* (1976), bored immortals with infinite technological resources search for the means to maintain their interest in life. Moorcock has also been a prolific writer of 'sword and sorcery' novels. Many, such as *The Stealer of Souls* (1963), *The Fortress of the Pearl* (1989) and *The Revenge of the Rose* (1991), feature the albino anti-hero Elric. His most substantial work in this vein is the baroque alternate-world fantasy *Gloriana* (1978). His mildly surrealistic non-fantasy novels include *The Brothel in Rosenstrasse* (1982), *Byzantium Endures* (1983), *The Laughter of Carthage* (1984), and an exuberantly vivid study of the city where he spent his childhood, *Mother London* (1988). Much of his recent work, including *Casablanca* (1989), has been set in North Africa.

Moore, Brian 1921– Irish novelist. Born in Belfast, he emigrated to Canada in 1928, working as a journalist in Montreal, and then to the USA in 1959, living in New York and California. The unflinchingly realistic surfaces of his novels, usually reflecting contemporary life as he has encountered it in Ireland, Canada and the USA, belie an underlying engagement with the phantasmagoric, the atavisms of myth and ritual and the ordeals of disturbed sexual consciousness, both male and female, sensitively conveyed through internal monologue. His own experience of Catholicism and a divided Ireland has issued in themes of guilt, isolation, ancestral memory and religious unease. His first novel, *Judith Hearne* (1955; later retitled *The Lonely Passion of Judith Hearne*), recounts the descent into delusion of a Belfast spinster. Its successors include: *The Feast of Lupercal* (1957); *The Luck of Ginger Coffey* (1960); *An Answer from Limbo* (1962); *The Emperor of Ice Cream* (1965); *I Am Mary Dunne* (1968), perhaps his best book, a study of imperilled identity; *Catholics* (1972); *The Great Victorian Collection* (1975); *The Mangan Inheritance* (1979); *Cold Heaven* (1983), about earthly reincarnation; *Black Robe* (1985), about 17th-century Jesuits and Canadian Indians, a paradigm of sectarian intolerance and mutual incomprehension in contemporary Ulster; *The Colour of Blood* (1987), about the conflict between politics and priesthood in Communist Poland; and *Lies of Silence* (1990), a thriller about Ireland.

Moore, Edward 1712–57 Playwright and poet. Born in Abingdon and trained as a linen draper, he turned to literature when his London business failed, and became one of the many writers who enjoyed LYTTELTON's patronage. Of his three plays, *The Foundling* (1748), *Gil Blas* (1751) and *The Gamester* (1753), only the last is of any enduring significance. A bourgeois or domestic TRAGEDY, it describes the destruction of Beverley through the lure of gambling and the machinations of the villainous Stukeley. Its heightened prose and eager pursuit of virtue carried the influence of GEORGE LILLO, profoundly affecting the development of drama in Germany and easing the passage of MELODRAMA into the English theatre. Moore was editor of *The World* magazine in 1753-6.

Moore, George (Augustus) 1852-1933 Anglo-Irish novelist and playwright. The son of an Irish MP, he was born at Ballyglass in Mayo and educated at Oscott College in Birmingham. He spent ten years in Paris, studying painting and publishing two books of verse, *Flowers of Passion* (1878) and *Pagan Poems* (1881). After his arrival in London in 1880 he published poems, plays, essays, *Modern Painting* (1893), *Confessions of a Young Man* (1888; autobiography) and novels which clearly showed the influence of Zola's NATURALISM: *A Modern Lover* (1883), *A Mummer's Wife* (1885), *A Drama in Muslin* (1886), *A Mere Accident* (1887), *Spring Days* (1888), *Mike Fletcher* (1889) and *Vain Fortune* (1891). He achieved a major success with *ESTHER WATERS* (1894), generally acknowledged as his finest work.

He opposed the Boer War and returned to Ireland in 1899-1911. His involvement in the Irish cultural revival, whose leading figures were W. B. YEATS and LADY GREGORY and whose collective achievement was the establishment of the ABBEY THEATRE, is the subject of a trilogy of reminiscence, *Hail and Farewell* (1911-14), originally published as *Ave* (1911), *Salve* (1912) and *Vale* (1914). Other works from this period include two collections of stories, *Celibates* (1895) and *The Untilled Field* (1903); the novel *Evelyn Innes* (1898) and its sequel *Sister Theresa* (1901); and *Reminiscences of the Impressionist Painters* (1906).

In London Moore went to live in Ebury Street, and made it his home for the rest of his life, acquiring a reputation as a literary sage. His later stage as a writer began with *The Brook Kerith* (1916), a novel about Jesus. Other works include: *A Story-teller's Holiday* (1918), short stories; *Conversations in Ebury Street* (1924), essays; *Daphnis and Chloé* (1924), a translation from the Greek; *Héloïse and Abelard* (1921) and *Aphrodite in Aulis* (1930), novels; and *The Making of an Immortal* (1927) and *The Passing of the Essenes* (1930; a revised version of *The Apostle*, 1911), plays.

Moore, G(eorge) E(dward) 1873-1958 Philosopher. Born in London, he was educated at Dulwich College and Trinity College, Cambridge, where he was a contemporary of BERTRAND RUSSELL. He was professor of philosophy at Cambridge in 1925-39.

Moore broke away from the prevailing idealistic philosophy which held the universe to be an all-inclusive mind, and defended the independent reality of material objects, minds and their states, and such abstract items as concepts and propositions. His first major essay, 'The Refutation of Idealism' (1903; reprinted in *Philosophical Studies*, 1922), argued against the idea that we really perceive nothing but our own sensations. His major work, *Principia ethica* (1903), rejected the view that moral properties such as goodness can be reduced to 'naturalistic properties' such as happiness or evolutionary success. He argued for 'direct moral awareness' and claimed that the contemplation of beauty and affectionate personal relations are the only supremely good states of mind.

His ideas were profoundly influential on the BLOOMSBURY GROUP, many of whom had studied under him at Cambridge and were also members of the APOSTLES. Other works include two important essays, 'A Defence of Common Sense' (1923) and 'A Proof of an External World' (1939), and *Some Main Problems of Philosophy* (1953). He was the brother of T. STURGE MOORE and the father of NICHOLAS MOORE.

Moore, Marianne (Craig) 1887-1972 American poet. She was born near St Louis, Missouri, and educated at Bryn Mawr College. *Poems* (1921) was followed by *Observations* (1924), *Selected Poems* (1935), *The Pangolin and Other Verse* (1936), *What are Years* (1941), *Nevertheless* (1944), *A Face* (1949), the PULITZER PRIZE-winning *Collected Poems* (1951), *Like a Bulwark* (1956), *O, to be a Dragon* (1959) and *Tell Me, Tell Me: Granite, Steel, and Other Topics* (1966). Her poetry is marked by an unconventional but disciplined use of METRE and a witty, often ironic tone. Known for its eclectic subject matter, it contains references to scientific and historical works and to current affairs; it also reveals an abiding interest in aesthetic and philosophical issues. Many poems are about exotic animals. Other works include a volume of critical essays, *Predilections* (1955), and two volumes of translations, *The Fables of La Fontaine* (1954) and *Selected Fables of La Fontaine* (1955). *The Complete Poems of Marianne Moore* was published in 1967, and *The Complete Prose of Marianne Moore* in 1986.

Moore, Nicholas 1918-86 Poet. The son of G. E. MOORE, he was born in Cambridge, went to school in Oxford and Reading, and studied at Trinity College, Cambridge. The editor of *Seven* (1938-40) and *New Poetry* (1944-5) and a prolific poet in the 1940s, he was a central figure in the NEW APOCALYPSE movement, appearing in two of its anthologies: *The New Apocalypse* (1939), introduced by J. F. HENDRY, and *The White Horseman* (1941), edited by Hendry and HENRY TREECE. Indebted to AUDEN, WALLACE STEVENS and BLAKE, his poetry has a visual clarity and lyrical fluency: surrealism mixes with effects from popular songs. His principal volumes are *A Wish in Season* (1941), *A Book for Priscilla* (1941), *The Cabaret, the Dancer, the Gentleman* (1942), *The Glass Tower* (1944) and *Recollections of the Gala: Selected Poems 1943-48* (1950).

Moore, Thomas 1779–1852 Poet. Born in Dublin, he began writing verse while studying at Trinity College. He migrated to London to study law at the Middle Temple in 1799, and in 1803 was appointed Admiralty Registrar in Bermuda. His lighthearted attitude to this post embarrassed him when his deputy misappropriated £6000 in 1819. Moore left England for the Continent and did not return until 1822, when he had repaid the debt.

His first work, *Odes of Anacreon Translated into English Verse, with Notes* (1801), earned him the nickname 'Anacreon Moore'. It was followed in the same year by a volume of amorous verses, *The Poetical Works of the Late Thomas Little, Esq.*, and *Epistles, Odes and Other Poems* (1806), savaged by FRANCIS JEFFREY in THE EDINBURGH REVIEW. After *Corruption and Intolerance: Two Poems with Notes, Addressed to an Englishman by an Irishman* (1808) he turned, more successfully, to light satire in *Intercepted Letters: or, The Twopenny Post Bag, by Thomas Brown the Younger* (1813) and *The Fudge Family in Paris, Edited by Thomas Brown the Younger* (1818). A sequel, *The Fudges in England*, appeared in 1835. Meanwhile, he was preparing the work which secured his reputation during his lifetime and would prove his most enduring. *A Selection of Irish Melodies* (in ten parts, with musical arrangements chiefly by Sir John Stevenson; 1808–34) offered a reassuringly sentimental view of Ireland and included 'The Last Rose of Summer'. LALLA ROOKH: *An Oriental Romance* (1817) and THE LOVES OF THE ANGELS (1823) were not only romantic but exotic, a combination for which the poetry of his friend BYRON had already created a large public.

On his death Byron left his manuscript 'Memoirs' to Moore, who destroyed the original but used some material from it to compile his controversial *Letters and Journals of Lord Byron, with Notices of His Life* (1830). MACAULAY declared that 'it deserves to be classed among the best specimens of English prose which our age has produced'. Other works include lives of SHERIDAN (1825) and Lord Edward Fitzgerald (1831), *The Epicurean* (1827), a novel about the 3rd-century philosopher Alciphron, and *The History of Ireland* (1835–46).

Moore, T(homas) Sturge 1870–1944 Poet and art historian. Brother of the Cambridge philosopher G. E. MOORE, he was born at Hastings in Sussex. Indifferent health brought his schooling to an early end but he succeeded as a wood engraver and later as an art historian, publishing studies of Altdorfer (1900), Dürer (1905), Correggio (1906) and Charles Ricketts (1933). He was a close friend of YEATS and designed the covers for several volumes of his poetry. Moore's own poetry, often classical in theme, was cordially received by the critics but neglected by the public; it includes *The Vinedresser* (1899), *Danae* (1903), *The Gazelles* (1904),

Marianne (1911), *Medea* (1920) and *Judas* (1923). His collected poems were issued in four volumes in 1931–3.

Moorhouse, Frank 1938– Australian short-story writer. Born and educated in Nowra, New South Wales, he attended Wollongong Technical Institute and subsequently worked as a journalist in Sydney and in country areas. He is now a full-time writer and lives in the Sydney suburb of Balmain, an area he has celebrated in his fiction. As co-founder (with MICHAEL WILDING) and editor of the alternative fiction magazine *Tabloid Story*, he has had an influence on the contemporary Australian short story beyond that of his own writing. Moorhouse described his early work as 'discontinuous narrative', though he has now dropped the term. While more traditional than some Australian post-modernists, he uses forms reflecting the fragmentation of contemporary urban life. All his work shows a strong interest in social and cultural issues. His books, clearly developing connections which suggest a continuing *Comédie Humaine*, include *Futility and Other Animals* (1969), *The Americans, Baby* (1972), *The Electrical Experience* (1974), *Conference-Ville* (1976), *Tales of Mystery and Romance* (1977), *The Everlasting Secret Family and Other Secrets* (1980), *Room Service* (1986), *Forty Seventeen* (1988) and *Lateshows* (1990). He has also edited an important anthology of Australian contemporary fiction, *The State of the Art: The Mood of Contemporary Australia in Short Fiction* (1983). *Days of Wine and Rage* (1980) collates material documenting the literary, cultural and social world of the 1970s. Moorhouse's work shows a strong interest in breaking down the barriers between contemporary media and he has written the scripts for several films, including *Between Wars* (1974) and *The Disappearance of Azaria Chamberlain* (1983).

Moral Essays Four poems by ALEXANDER POPE, each taking the form of a verse epistle addressed directly to one of his acquaintances. Epistle I, *Of the Knowledge and Characters of Men*, is addressed to Viscount Cobham and sets out the poet's belief that each individual has a key to his particular behaviour, a 'Ruling Passion', which dictates his perspective on life. Epistle II, *Of the Characters of Women*, is addressed to Pope's friend Martha Blount and includes waspish verse-portraits, such as 'Atossa' (the Duchess of Marlborough), and SATIRE of other contemporary females. Epistle III, *Of the Use of Riches*, to Lord Bathurst, takes the form of a dialogue praising his well-disposed house and gardens; it contains descriptions of the benevolent 'Man of Ross' (John Kyrle, the philanthropist) and the death of Buckingham. Epistle IV, to Lord Burlington, the cultivated patron of art, also considers the uses of wealth, equating good taste with good sense (morality) and contrasting the architectural 'finesse' of Burlington with the ghastly uselessness of 'Timon's villa', the embodiment of opulent vulgarity.

morality plays Where the MIRACLE PLAYS of the late Middle Ages derived from the liturgy and celebrated God as manifest in the life and death of Jesus, the morality plays took their inspiration from the sermon and treated the problems and dilemmas confronting Man. Their form was usually allegorical, with abstractions such as Mercy or Justice and Envy or Lust representing the opposed forces which accompany Man in his progress through life.

The earliest morality play of which any record survives is the *Pater Noster*, which may have been the work of JOHN WYCLIF and was performed at York. The earliest manuscript to survive, *The Pride of Life*, is imperfect and may date back as far as the end of the 14th century. The most remarkable collection is *The Macro Plays* (named after the former owner of the manuscripts), which may have come from the abbey at Bury St Edmunds. The three plays in this collection are *Mankind* (c. 1473), *Wisdom, Who is Christ* (c. 1460) and the earliest and most elaborate, THE CASTLE OF PERSEVERANCE (c. 1425). The most famous morality play belongs to the whole of Western Europe: EVERYMAN was probably an English version of the Dutch *Elckerlijk* (1495). It enjoyed a new fame in the German verse translation *Jedermann* by Hugo von Hofmannsthal (1911), which became the opening item of the Salzburg Festival each year in Max Reinhardt's celebrated production. The morality play did not die with the Middle Ages, for examples abound in England up to 1550. But by then the form had become flexible enough to be used for SATIRE and COMEDY, and for abstraction to give way to character.

Morall Fabillis of Esope the Phrygian, The Twelve verse FABLES, derived from Aesop and drawing on a long European tradition of Aesopic writing, by the 15th-century Scottish poet ROBERT HENRYSON. The fables are allegorical, lightheartedly using animal characters to convey observations and criticisms of human society. Henryson makes original use of his material, often describing animal life in sympathetic detail, and sometimes creating a deliberate discrepancy between the moral given at the end of the tale and the moral suggested by the tale itself.

Mordaunt, Elinor [Mordaunt, Evelyn May] 1877–1942 Novelist and traveller. Her first published work, *The Garden of Contentment* (1902), was written in Mauritius and drew on English memories. She later travelled to Australia and all over the world, recounting her experiences in *The Venture Book* (1926), *Purely for Pleasure* (1932) and *Traveller's Pack* (1933).

Her many novels include *The Rose of Youth* (1915) and *Reputation* (1923). Her autobiography appeared in 1937 as *Sinabada*.

More, Hannah 1745–1833 Playwright and religious writer. The youngest of five sisters, she was born at Stapleton in Gloucestershire and educated at her sisters' boarding school in Bristol, where she learned French, Italian, Spanish and Latin. At the age of 22 she became engaged to a Mr Turner, who never married her but eventually settled a small income on her. Her first publication was a pastoral play, *The Search after Happiness* (1773), and she went to London the following year. There she was fortunate in making an impression on JOSHUA REYNOLDS and his sister and in gaining through them the entrée to London society. She became the friend of JOHNSON, GARRICK, HORACE WALPOLE and the circle of BLUESTOCKING ladies surrounding ELIZABETH MONTAGU. Her play, *Inflexible Captive*, was published in 1774 and her tragedies, *Percy* and *The Fatal Falsehood*, were produced by Garrick in 1777 and 1779.

In later life her strong Evangelical convictions caused her to abandon the theatre (she refused to allow her plays to be reprinted) and devote herself to religious and didactic writing, aimed largely at the poorer classes perceived as vulnerable to the dangerous ideas put in circulation by the French Revolution. *Village Politics* (1793) was followed by the popular series of *Cheap Repository Tracts* (1795–8), which included an enduringly famous story, 'The Shepherd of Salisbury Plain'. The Religious Tract Society was formed to continue her work, while she herself went on to support William Wilberforce in his campaign against slavery, to play a pioneer role in the Sunday School movement and to write a didactic novel, *Coelebs in Search of a Wife* (1809). Her *Letters*, many to distinguished correspondents, were published in 1834.

More, Henry 1614–87 A prominent CAMBRIDGE PLATONIST, he was born at Grantham, Lincolnshire, and educated at Eton College and Christ's College, Cambridge. He became a fellow of his college in 1639, and stayed there for the rest of his life, refusing the offers of rich preferments. Although his family tended to Calvinism, More himself remained a steadfast supporter of the Church of England and was Royalist in sympathy during the Civil Wars. Like his fellow Platonist RALPH CUDWORTH he was opposed to the materialism of THOMAS HOBBES, and eventually rejected the philosophy of René Descartes for the same reason. More was an industrious writer, expounding his ideas in both verse and prose. *Psychozoia Platonica* (1642) was enlarged and incorporated in *Philosophical Poems* (1647). His later works include *Enthusiasmus Triumphatus* (1656), an effective denunciation of Puritan 'enthusiasms' (extravagant claims for their faith and inspiration) and *The Immortality of the Soul* (1659).

More, St Thomas 1477–1535 England's foremost Christian humanist and sometime Lord Chancellor, More was a martyr to Catholics and a traitor to extreme Protestants in the 16th century who, like FOXE in *ACTS AND MONUMENTS*, saw him as an enemy to the Gospel. The son of the judge Sir John More, Thomas was educated at St Anthony's School in Threadneedle Street, London. He spent his youth at the house of Cardinal Morton, who predicted that he would be a 'marvellous man', and, with Morton as his patron, went to Oxford, where he was a pupil of THOMAS LINACRE and WILLIAM GROCYN. He was back in London to study common law in c. 1494, being admitted to Lincoln's Inn in 1496 and becoming a barrister in 1501. While at Lincoln's Inn he was testing a vocation for the priesthood by living at a nearby Carthusian monastery and sharing some of the monastic life; the habits of prayer, fasting and penance stayed with him for the rest of his life. He married for the first time in 1504 or 1505, and in 1504 entered Parliament.

He met ERASMUS on the latter's first visit to England in 1499 and their friendship and correspondence began in that year. During Erasmus' second visit they both produced Latin translations of some of Lucian's works which were printed at Paris in 1506. On Erasmus' third visit to England in 1509 he wrote *Encomium Moriae* (*Praise of Folly*), whose title quibbles with More's name, at the house of his friend.

From 1510 to 1518 More was one of the two undersheriffs in London where he gained a reputation for impartiality and patronage of the poor. In 1511 his first wife died in childbirth and very soon More was married again, this time to the redoubtable Dame Alice. In 1515 he was part of a delegation to Flanders to sort out disputes about the wool trade; it is with a reference to this delegation that *UTOPIA* opens. In 1517 a London mob rose against foreign residents and More's quelling of this mob is reflected in a scene, possibly by SHAKESPEARE, in *SIR THOMAS MORE*. He was present at the Field of the Cloth of Gold in 1520–1, participated in trade talks at Calais and Bruges and was knighted in 1521.

More helped Henry VIII to write his *Defence of the Seven Sacraments* in answer to Luther, and in response to Luther's reply More, under a pseudonym, wrote *Epistola ad Pomeranum* (1568). With Henry's favour More's career prospered as he became Speaker of the Commons in 1523, Chancellor of the Duchy of Lancaster in 1525 and Wolsey's successor as Lord Chancellor in 1529. His fall came rapidly. He refused to attend the coronation of Anne Boleyn and in 1534 was one of those accused of complicity with Elizabeth Barton, the visionary nun of Kent who opposed Henry's break with Rome. The Lords passed the bill for attainting those accused only when More's name had been deleted. In April 1534 he found himself unable to swear to the Act of Succession and on 17 April he was committed to the Tower. Richard Rich, the Solicitor-General, acted as prosecutor at More's trial in July. More was sentenced as a traitor and executed on 6 July 1535 claiming that he was dying for his faith. He was beatified in 1886 and canonized by Pius XI in 1935.

Many lives of More were written in the 16th century. That by his son-in-law William Roper, with its famous exchanges between More and Dame Alice in the Tower, was not printed until 1626. Nicholas Harpsfield's biography was written in the reign of Mary but not printed until 1932 and Thomas Stapleton's Latin work on the three Thomases (the Apostle, Becket and More) was printed in 1588. Others exist in manuscript, while some are lost.

More's first published work was the Lucian translations in collaboration with Erasmus (1506). His English translation of a Latin life of the Italian humanist Giovanni Pico della Mirandola was printed by WYNKYN DE WORDE in 1510. *Utopia* was published at Louvain in 1516 and in an English translation by Ralph Robinson in 1551. More's controversialist defences of the Catholic faith against the criticisms of TYNDALE, written in the late 1520s and early 1530s, include *The Confutation of Tyndale's Answer* (1532). His predictably hostile *History of Richard III*, written c. 1513–18 but left unfinished, exists in both Latin and English versions. It was imperfectly printed in English in Grafton's *Chronicle* (1543), while the Latin text first appeared in the Louvain edition of his Latin works (1565). It was used by JOHN STOW, EDWARD HALL and HOLINSHED, thus transmitting material to Shakespeare for *RICHARD III*. While in the Tower More wrote *A Dialogue of Comfort against Tribulation* (printed in 1553), a supposed English translation of a French version of a Latin dialogue between two Hungarians, Anthony and Vincent. More's English *Works* appeared in the edition by William Rastell in 1557.

Morgan, Charles (Langbridge) 1894–1958 Novelist and playwright. Born in Kent, he studied at the naval colleges of Osborne and Dartmouth from 1907 to 1913. He then resigned, intending to go up to Oxford, but rejoined the Royal Navy during World War I. He was captured and interned in Holland until 1917, spending some of this time on parole at Rosendaal Castle. In 1919 he went up to Brasenose College, Oxford, and published his first novel, *The Gunroom*, about his unhappy experiences as a young midshipman.

In 1921 he joined *The Times*, working as its drama critic from 1926 to 1939 and contributing to *THE TIMES LITERARY SUPPLEMENT* under the pseudonym 'Menander'. His 11 novels include: *Portrait in a Mirror* (1929); *The Fountain* (1932), set in Rosendaal Castle and sometimes considered his most successful work;

The Voyage (1940); *The Judge's Story* (1947), a fable about the struggle between spiritual and material values, echoed in a collection of essays, *Liberties of the Mind* (1951); and *Challenge to Venus* (1957), his last novel. His plays are: *The Flashing Stream* (1938); *The River Line* (1952), dramatized from his 1949 novel of the same title; and *The Burning Glass* (1954). He also wrote a publishing history of *The House of Macmillan* (1943), *Epitaph on George Moore* (1935), a close friend, and *Ode to France* (1942), a country where his work was much admired. He was made a member of the Institut de France in 1957.

Morgan, Edwin (George) 1920- Scottish poet, translator and critic. Born in Glasgow, he has lived there all his life, apart from a period of military service during World War II, studying and then teaching at the University. He was Titular Professor of English in 1975-80. His poetic career stretches from *The Vision of Cathkin Braes* (1952) to *A Second Life* (1968), *Glasgow Sonnets* (1972), *Sonnets from Scotland* (1984) and *From the Video Box* (1986) and *You: Anti-War Poetry* (1991). *Collected Poems* appeared in 1990. Although essentially a poet of Glasgow, his interests are wide-ranging. He has experimented with sound and CONCRETE POETRY and embraced both the social observation of the *Glasgow Sonnets* and the playfulness of 'The Computer's First Christmas Card'. He has translated literature from several languages into Scots and English, showing a particular affinity with modern Italian poets such as Montale and Quasimodo. *Rites of Passage: Selected Translations* appeared in 1976. *Crossing the Border* (1990) is among the works which have established him as a notable critic of HUGH MACDIARMID and contemporary Scottish literature.

Morgan, Lady Sydney ?1783-1859 Novelist. Born Sydney Owenson in Dublin, she married Sir Thomas Morgan in 1812. She was well known as a writer of Irish romances, the best being *The Wild Irish Girl* (1806), *O'Donnel* (1814) and *The O'Briens and the O'Flaherties* (1827). She also wrote two lively books on France and Italy, and a life of Salvator Rosa.

Morier, James Justinian *c.* 1780-1849 Traveller and novelist. The son of the Consul General of the Levant Company, Morier was born at Smyrna and returned to Turkey after being educated at Harrow. He entered the diplomatic service in 1807 and went with Sir Hartford Jones's mission to Persia. In 1812 he published his *Journey through Persia, Armenia and Asia Minor*, and in 1818 the more notable *Second Journey through Persia*. After his retirement he used his experiences in several Oriental romances, of which the most successful is *The Adventures of Hajji Baba of Ispahan* (1824), a PICARESQUE novel which presents real people in a setting both exotic and authentic. Its

hero rises from being a barber, doctor and executioner's assistant to become adviser to the Shah. Morier's uncomplimentary account of Persian society drew a protest from the Persian minister in London which was later printed in a sequel, *The Adventures of Hajji Baba of Ispahan in England* (1828).

Morley, Henry 1822-94 Journalist and critic. Born in London, he studied medicine at King's College, London, and practised for a time before turning to journalism. He contributed to DICKENS's *HOUSEHOLD WORDS* and *ALL THE YEAR ROUND*, edited *THE EXAMINER* and published translations, biographies and miscellanies. Morley, who became professor of English at University College, London, was active in the field of adult education and produced valuable editions of English classics in cheap format: Cassell's Library of English Literature (1875-81) and Cassell's National Library (begun in 1886). In 1887 he started his ambitious history of English literature, *English Writers*: 11 of a projected 20 volumes were completed, taking his subject as far as SHAKESPEARE before he died.

Morley, John, 1st Viscount 1838-1923 Statesman, biographer and journalist. Born at Blackburn in Lancashire, he was educated at Cheltenham College and Lincoln College, Oxford. He studied law and was called to the Bar, but did not practise. He contributed to *The Saturday Review*, and later became editor of *THE FORTNIGHTLY REVIEW* (1867) and *THE PALL MALL GAZETTE* (1881). Morley entered politics in 1883, when he was elected Liberal MP for Newcastle. A staunch supporter of Gladstone, he held office as Chief Secretary for Ireland (1886 and 1892), Secretary of State for India (1905) and Lord President of the Council (1910). His chief contribution to literature was *The Life of William Ewart Gladstone* (1903). He also edited the English Men of Letters series, to which he contributed the volume on EDMUND BURKE (1879). Among his other works were *Voltaire* (1872), *Rousseau* (1873), *Diderot and the Encyclopaedists* (1878), *Richard Cobden* (1881), *Machiavelli* (1897) and *Oliver Cromwell* (1900). He also published two collections of speeches on Indian affairs (1908 and 1909) and *Critical Miscellanies* (1871-1908), four collections of essays written for *The Fortnightly Review*.

Morning Chronicle, The A Whig journal founded in 1769 by William Woodfall. It became prominent at the turn of the century under the editorship of James Perry and John Black. Famous contributors included SHERIDAN, CHARLES LAMB, THOMAS MOORE, DAVID RICARDO, JOHN STUART MILL, W. M. THACKERAY and HENRY MAYHEW. As a young man, CHARLES DICKENS was employed by the paper as a reporter and part of *SKETCHES BY BOZ* first appeared in its pages. *The Morning Chronicle* ceased publication in 1862.

Morrell, Lady **Ottoline** 1873–1938 Literary patron and socialite. Born Ottoline Violet Anne Cavendish-Bentinck, she lived at Welbeck Abbey before her marriage to the Liberal MP Philip Morrell. From 1908 she entertained a wide circle of political and literary celebrities at 44 Bedford Square, London, and then, during the post-World War I decade, at her country house, Garsington Manor, near Oxford. The circle included BERTRAND RUSSELL, VIRGINIA WOOLF, T. S. ELIOT, W. B. YEATS, D. H. LAWRENCE and ALDOUS HUXLEY. Lawrence (in *WOMEN IN LOVE*) and Huxley (in *Crome Yellow*) both used her as the model for striking but eccentric fictional characters. In the late 1920s the Morrells returned to London where she remained until her death. Her *Memoirs*, edited by Robert Gathorne Hardy, appeared in two volumes in 1963 and 1974.

Morris, Sir **Lewis** 1833–1907 Poet. Born in Carmarthen, educated at Sherborne and Oxford, he was called to the Bar and practised until 1880. He assisted in the foundation of the University of Wales and was knighted in 1895. His cheerful and musical collection, *Songs of Two Worlds* (1871), was well received by the reading public. Still more popular was *The Epic of Hades* (1876–7). Other works included *Gwen* (1879), *Songs Unsung* (1883), *Gycia: A Tragedy* (1886) and *A Vision of Saints* (1890). *The New Rambler* (1905) is a volume of essays.

Morris, **Mervyn** 1937– Jamaican poet. He was born in Kingston and educated at Munro College, the University of the West Indies, and as a Rhodes scholar at the University of Oxford. Although he has been both a schoolteacher and a university administrator, his main career has been as a lecturer in English at the Jamaica campus of the University of the West Indies. He has published several collections of verse, among them *The Pond* (1973), *On Holy Week* (1976) and *Shadowboxing* (1979). His poems deal with precisely wrought moments of feeling or observation. They are sometimes said to lack commitment – 'Another friend arraigns me:/ too detached, he says' – but as personal statements they are deeply felt and well crafted, showing that Caribbean poetry can be about private pains as well as about public causes. He has also played an important part in encouraging a younger generations of oral poets. He has edited volumes by MICHAEL SMITH and Jean Minta Breeze, as well as a number of anthologies.

Morris, **William** 1834–96 Writer, artisan and socialist. Born at Walthamstow in Essex, he was educated at Marlborough College and Exeter College, Oxford, where he first met his lifelong friends Edward Burne-Jones and Charles Faulkner and fell under the influence of the PRE-RAPHAELITES. After briefly working for the Oxford architect G. E. Street, he lodged in London with Burne-Jones, began to design furniture and, with encouragement from DANTE GABRIEL ROSSETTI, abandoned architecture for painting. In 1857 he worked with Rossetti and Burne-Jones on frescoes at the Oxford Union Society and met Jane Burden, whom he married in 1859. One of the most famous Pre-Raphaelite models, she appears as Queen Guinevere in his only extant oil painting, one of many examples of his fascination with ARTHURIAN LITERATURE. His experience furnishing his new home, The Red House, prompted him in 1861 to found Morris, Marshall, Faulkner and Co. (reconstituted as Morris and Co. in 1875) and thus begin a major revival of decorative arts and crafts. His own talents lay in designing pattern for wallpapers, chintzes, damasks, embroideries, tapestries and carpets; the firm is also famous for its stained glass, stencilled mural decoration, painted tiles and furniture.

Morris published his first collection of verse, *THE DEFENCE OF GUENEVERE AND OTHER POEMS*, in 1858. Only one further collection followed, *Poems by the Way* (1891), as his interest turned increasingly to ambitious narrative poetry. He scored a public success with *THE LIFE AND DEATH OF JASON* (1867), a greatly enlarged version of a tale originally intended for the epic *THE EARTHLY PARADISE* (1868–70), which secured his reputation as a leading poet of his day. Though he returned to classical poetry, translating *The Aeneids of Virgil* (1875) and *The Odyssey of Homer* (1887), his literary career was profoundly affected by his meeting with the Icelandic scholar Eirikr Magnússon in 1868. He studied Icelandic, visited Iceland in 1871 and 1873, and collaborated with Magnússon on prose translations from the sagas – preparatory work for *SIGURD THE VOLSUNG AND THE FALL OF THE NIBLUNGS* (1876), his great poetic version of the *Volsunga Saga*. Other writings show his interest in Norwegian stories, medieval French literature and *BEOWULF*, which he translated with A. J. Wyatt (1895).

The unhappiness of his personal life during the 1870s is reflected in his first attempt at a novel, *The Novel on Blue Paper* (written in 1872, but not published until 1982). In 1876 his life was dramatically changed by his outraged response to the Bulgarian atrocities, beginning a political pilgrimage that culminated in the foundation of the Socialist League in 1884 and the Hammersmith Socialist Society in 1890. Much of his writing was now devoted to political polemic and his contiguous theories of art (as in *Hopes and Fears for Art* , 1882). Though he wrote political poems and even tried his hand at a political play, *The Tables Turned: or Nupkins Awakened* (1887), his most important socialist works were the prose pieces *A DREAM OF JOHN BALL* (1886–7) and *NEWS FROM NOWHERE* (1890).

Though he suffered from ill health in later years, Morris could never be idle. The Kelmscott Press, which began printing in 1891, aimed to produce books characterized by beauty rather than economy. To this end he designed two typefaces, 'Golden' and 'Troy', and collaborated with Burne-Jones in designing books which include the great folio CHAUCER (1896). Writings include *A Tale of the House of the Wolfings and All the Kindreds of the Mark Written in Prose and Verse* (1888), which set the tone for his late romances: *The Roots of the Mountains* (1889), *The Story of the Glittering Plain* (1890), *The Wood beyond the World* (1894), *THE WELL AT THE WORLD'S END* (1896) and the posthumously published *The Water of the Wondrous Isles* and *The Sundering Flood* (both 1897). When he died at the age of 63 one doctor described the cause of death as simply being William Morris and having done more work than most ten men.

Morris's importance both in the Arts and Crafts movement and in the history of British socialism is not in doubt. However, little of his vast literary corpus is now read, with the exception of the still popular *News from Nowhere*. This is due partly to the variable quality of his work and partly to his unfashionable interest in epic narrative and Teutonic mythology. In the 20th century the influence of the prose romances has been greatest on YEATS, while in recent years they have acquired a new readership among devotees of TOLKIEN and C. S. LEWIS.

Morris, Wright 1910– American novelist, short-story writer and critic. He was born in Central City, Nebraska, a town which figures prominently in his fiction. His principal concerns have always been with a definition of the American character, with the American Edenic myth, and with the uses and influences of American history. His narratives are often fragmented and his novels many-voiced and subtly ironic. They include *My Uncle Dudley* (1942), *The Man Who was There* (1945), *The World in the Attic* (1949), *The Works of Love* (1952), *A Field of Vision* (1956, National Book Award), *Love among the Cannibals* (1957), *Ceremony in Lone Tree* (1960), *Cause for Wonder* (1963), *In Orbit* (1967), *Fire Sermon* (1971), *A Life* (1973), *The Fork River Space Project* (1977) and *Plains Song* (1980). *Collected Stories: 1948–1986* appeared in 1986. He has published three volumes of memoirs: *Will's Boy: A Memoir* (1981), *Solo: An American Dreamer in Europe, 1933–34* (1983) and *A Cloak of Light: Writing My Life* (1985). His literary criticism includes *The Territory Ahead* (1958), *About Fiction* (1975) and a study of American writers, *Earthly Delights, Unearthly Adornments* (1978).

Morrison, Arthur 1863–1945 Novelist, short-story writer and writer of DETECTIVE FICTION. Born in Poplar, he spent most of his life in the East End of London where his best stories are set. He became clerk to the trustees administering the People's Palace in Mile End Road, where he met WALTER BESANT, proba-

bly responsible for appointing him sub-editor of *The Palace Journal*. Morrison afterwards became a free-lance journalist, and in 1891 an article in *Macmillan's Magazine* brought him to the notice of W. E. HENLEY, who invited him to write a series for *The National Observer*. The series was published as *Tales of Mean Streets* (1894), which – together with *A CHILD OF THE JAGO* (1894) and *THE HOLE IN THE WALL* (1902) – is his best-known work. In these books Morrison described a world he knew at first hand, and presented the working people and criminals of the slums in terms of their own values and attitudes, without imposing his own moral standards.

His detective stories – *Martin Hewitt, Investigator* (1894), *Chronicles of Martin Hewitt* (1895) and *Hewitt: Third Series* (1896) – enjoyed a brief popularity in the wake of the SHERLOCK HOLMES STORIES. More interesting, and now equally little known, is a novel of witchcraft and smuggling in Napoleonic times, *Cunning Murrell* (1900), set on the Essex shore of the Thames estuary. Morrison also collected Japanese prints and paintings, bequeathed to the British Museum at his death. *The Painters of Japan* (2 vols., 1911) was an early and influential study.

Morrison, Blake 1950– Poet, anthologist and critic. Born in Skipton, Yorkshire, he read English at Nottingham University before pursuing postgraduate studies in Canada and at University College, London. He has published a scholarly and informative study of the MOVEMENT (1980) and a monograph on SEAMUS HEANEY (1982). With ANDREW MOTION he edited the controversial *Penguin Book of Contemporary British Poetry* (1982). Morrison's work as a critic precedes and outweighs his poetry, which includes *Dark Glasses* (1984), winner of a Somerset Maugham Award, and *The Ballad of the Yorkshire Ripper* (1987).

Morrison, John (Gordon) 1904– Australian short-story writer and novelist. Born in England, he emigrated in 1923 and worked as a gardener. His polished, realistic stories bridge the gap between HENRY LAWSON and 20th-century Australian fiction. 'The Incense Burner' and 'North Wind' are touchstones in the development of Australian writing. Collections are *Sailors Belong Ships* (1947), *Black Cargo* (1955), *Twenty-Three* (1962) and *North Wind* (1982). His novels are *The Creeping City* (1947) and *Port of Call* (1949).

Morrison, Toni 1931– Black American novelist. She was born in Ohio and educated at Howard and Cornell universities. Her first novel, *The Bluest Eye* (1970), is the story of a year in the life of Pecola Breedlove, a young black girl in Ohio who comes to believe that she has blue eyes. She endures degradations, including incest with her father and subse-

Toni Morrison

quent pregnancy, until her fixation with a doll's blue eyes degenerates into insanity. *Sula* (1973), also set in Ohio, focuses on the friendship between two black women as they mature during the 1920s and 1930s. Their friendship is based on a shared sense of alienation from community and family values, and a similar experience of emptiness in their other relationships – especially with men. *Song of Solomon* (1977) is an intricate narrative about Milkman Dead's exploration of his family history, his quest for a place as an individual within a heritage of slavery and violence. *Tar Baby* (1981) is about motherhood and the relationships between black and white cultures in the Caribbean and America. *Beloved* (1987, PULITZER PRIZE) chronicles the ghostly and redemptive return of a dead daughter to the mother who killed her when faced with a renewed term of slavery. She won the Nobel Prize for Literature in 1993.

Morte Arthur A Middle English poem written in the north-west Midlands *c.*1400. Derived from a version of the French prose *Mort Artu*, it tells the same story as the last two tales of THOMAS MALORY'S LE MORTE DARTHUR, on which it had an important influence. Guinevere mistakenly believes Lancelot returns the Maid of Astolat's love and causes him to leave court. She is accused of poisoning a knight and when she learns of Lancelot's innocence he returns to defend her successfully. Agravain, Gawain's brother, betrays Lancelot and Guinevere to Arthur and is killed

by Lancelot. Arthur and Gawain besiege Lancelot and Guinevere, and pursue him to Brittany even after the queen has been restored. Arthur and Gawain return to England to deal with Mordred's uprising, but both armies and their leaders are destroyed in the ensuing battle, and Arthur's body is borne to Avalon. Lancelot lives as a hermit-priest and Guinevere as a nun until their deaths. The poem is remarkable amongst medieval ARTHURIAN LITERATURE in that the powerful, yet simple and concise, narrative moves towards the inexorable destruction of the society of the Round Table without digression or spurious incident.

Morte Arthure An alliterative poem (*c.* 1360) by an unknown author, at one time thought to be HUCHOWN OF THE AWLE RYALE. The principal source was probably a version of Wace's *Roman de Brut*, but it follows none of its sources closely. It relates in epic style Arthur's early victories, his defeat of Lucius, and the revolt led by Mordred in Arthur's absence and the battle culminating in Arthur's death. Arthur, vividly portrayed as a warrior-hero, dominates the narrative; the removal of his body to Avalon is replaced by an account of a solemn, grand burial ceremony at Glastonbury. The poem was used by THOMAS MALORY in LE MORTE DARTHUR; see also ARTHURIAN LITERATURE.

Morte Darthur, Le A prose version of the Arthurian legends by SIR THOMAS MALORY, completed in 1469–70. It survives in CAXTON's printed text of 1485 and in a manuscript discovered at Winchester in 1934. The most ambitious and comprehensive contribution to ARTHURIAN LITERATURE in English, it derives from three French texts, the prose *Tristan*, the Vulgate Cycle and the *Roman du Graal*, and two English works, the alliterative MORTE ARTHURE and the stanzaic MORTE ARTHUR. Malory unravelled intertwined narratives and made the Arthuriad more compact by cutting extraneous material, but the extent to which he also created a unified narrative – or had this as his main purpose – has been a matter of debate.

The work is divided into eight tales and 21 books. The first tale (Books 1–4) relates Arthur's birth, accession and marriage to Guinevere, his begetting of Mordred by his half-sister Morgan and the establishment of the Round Table. The stories of Merlin and of various knights of the Round Table also appear. The second (Book 5) tells of Arthur's defeat of the Roman emperor Lucius and his coronation by the Pope. The third and fourth tales (Books 6 and 7) are concerned with the stories of Lancelot du Lake and Sir Gareth of Orkney respectively. The fifth tale (Books 8-12), which occupies almost half of the work, relates the life of Sir Tristram de Lyones. An accident with a love-potion causes Tristram to fall in love with Isode, the wife of his king and uncle, Mark. The history of the love and jealousy of the three characters is adapted and combined with other exploits including Lancelot's begetting of Galahad, but Malory omits the tragic end of the story of Tristram and Isode. In the 'Tale of the Sankgreall' (Books 13–17) Malory deals with the fragmentation of the Round Table and the quests by all the knights for the Holy Grail. They are successful according to their spiritual purity, only Galahad, Perceval and Bors succeeding completely and taking the Grail to Sarras. The seventh tale (Books 18–19) deals with the adulterous affair of Lancelot and Guinevere, while the final tale (Books 20–21) tells of the destruction of the Round Table through Arthur's discovery of Guinevere's adultery with Lancelot, the war between Lancelot and Arthur, and Mordred's revolt against the king. After his death in the final battle with Mordred, Arthur's body is carried to the Isle of Avalon, and Malory mentions the legend that the king still lives, awaiting the time for his return.

Mortimer, John (Clifford) 1923– Playwright and journalist. Educated at Harrow and Brasenose College, Oxford, he served with the Crown Film Unit during World War II. He was called to the Bar in 1948 and became a QC in 1966; aside from his writing, he is well known for his work as a barrister on behalf of liberal causes. His one-act plays for radio in the 1950s include *The Dock Brief*, staged with *What Shall We Tell Caroline?* in 1958. Although his theatrical career began during the era of the ANGRY YOUNG MEN, he maintained a cool, witty and professional tone in comedies such as *The Wrong Side of the Park* (1960) and *Two Stars for Comfort* (1962). His adaptations for the ROYAL NATIONAL THEATRE include *A Flea in Her Ear* (1966), from Feydeau, and *The Captain of Kopenick* (1971), from Zuckmayer, while his evenings of one-acters include *Come As You Are* (1970) and *Heaven and Hell* (1976). The full-length *A Voyage round My Father* (1970), still his greatest critical success, is a semi-autobiographical study of his father revealing an emotional warmth and understanding which could not have been predicted from his other work. Mortimer's highly successful career for TV has included: *I, Claudius* (1972), adapted from ROBERT GRAVES's novels; *Rumpole of the Bailey*, featuring a splendidly disreputable barrister introduced in a volume of short stories (1978); an adaptation of EVELYN WAUGH's *BRIDESHEAD REVISITED* (1981); and his own *Paradise Postponed* (1986). He was created a CBE in 1986.

Morton, H(enry) V(ollam) 1892–1979 Travel-writer. Born and educated in Birmingham, he began his career as a journalist working for various London newspapers, but after the success of *The Heart of London* (1925) and *In Search of England* (1927) devoted himself to his travel-writing. During his career Morton visited and wrote about numerous countries. A volume on Scotland appeared in 1929, on Ireland in 1930, and on Wales in 1932. He then moved further afield, and his other travel books include one about South Africa (1948), where he finally settled, as well as volumes on the Middle East (1941), Spain (1954), Rome (1957) and the Holy Land (1961).

Morton, Nathaniel 1612–85 American colonial historian. Born in the pilgrim community in Leyden, Holland, Morton emigrated to Plymouth Colony in 1623, and went to live with his uncle, Governor WILLIAM BRADFORD. In 1647 he was appointed secretary of Plymouth Colony, a post which he occupied until his death and which gave him responsibility for keeping the colony's political records. His history of the colony, published in 1669, was entitled *New England's Memorial: or, A Brief Relation of the Most Memorable and Remarkable Passages of the Providences of God, Manifested to the Planters of New England, in America: With Special Reference to the First Colony Thereof Called New Plymouth*. The book relied on and elaborated Bradford's *History of Plymouth Plantation*, and provided a source for COTTON MATHER's *MAGNALIA CHRISTI AMERICANA*.

Morton, Thomas 1764–1838 Playwright. Born in County Durham, he was sent to study at Lincoln's Inn, but showed no interest in the law, preferring cricket – he was a senior member of the MCC – and the theatre, in which he won his first success with a musical play, *The Children in the Wood* (1793). There followed a succession of comedies, written for COVENT GARDEN, of which the best are *The Way to Get Married* (1796), *A Cure for the Heart Ache* (1797), *Secrets Worth Knowing* (1798), *SPEED THE PLOUGH* (1800) and *The School of Reform* (1805). The character of Tyke in the last play was as famous in its time as that of Mrs Grundy in *Speed the Plough*.

Mosley, Nicholas, Lord Ravensdale 1923– Novelist. Born in London, he was educated at Eton and Balliol College, Oxford. His early novels, *Spaces of the Dark* (1951), *The Rainbearers* (1955) and *Corruption* (1958), deriving from World War II, are essentially realistic, influenced by HENRY JAMES and WILLIAM FAULKNER. *Accident* (1966), filmed by Joseph Losey, and *Natalie, Natalia* (1971) adopt a simpler style. More abstract and experimental is the sequence consisting of *Catastrophe Practice: Plays Not for Acting, and Cypher: A Novel* (1979), *Imago Bird* (1980), *Serpent* (1981), *Judith* (1986, revised 1992) and *Hopeful Monsters* (1990). His other works include a study of JULIAN GRENFELL (1976) and a biography of his parents, Sir Oswald and Lady Cynthia Mosley (1982–3).

Motherwell, William 1797–1835 Poet. Born in Glasgow and educated at Glasgow University, Motherwell published a collection of Scottish ballads, *Minstrelsy Ancient and Modern* (1827), and a collection of his own work, *Poems Narrative and Lyrical*

(1832). His BALLAD 'Jeanie Morison' was widely popular. He collaborated with JAMES HOGG in editing the poetry of ROBERT BURNS (5 vols., 1834–6).

Motion, Andrew (Peter) 1952– Poet. Born in London, he was educated at Radley and University College, Oxford. He has been a lecturer in English at the University of Hull, editor of *Poetry Review* and poetry editor at Chatto and Windus. His volumes are: *The Pleasure Steamers* (1978), containing work which owes a good deal to the benign influence of EDWARD THOMAS, as well as poems about his invalid mother; *Independence* (1981), a retrospective narrative spoken by a retired colonial businessman and centred on the year of Indian independence, 1947; *Secret Narratives* (1983); *Dangerous Play* (1984); *Natural Causes* (1987); and *Love in a Life* (1991), preoccupied with marriage, children and death. With BLAKE MORRISON he edited the controversial *Penguin Book of Contemporary British Poetry* (1982). He has also published critical books on Edward Thomas (1980) and PHILIP LARKIN (1982), whose official biographer he is, and a group biography of George, Constant and Kit Lambert (1986). *Pale Companion* (1990) is a novel.

Motley, John Lathrop c. 1814–77 American historian. He was born in Dorchester, Massachusetts, into a prosperous New England family, and educated at Harvard. He published two novels, *Morton's Hope: or, The Memoirs of a Young Provincial* (1839) and *Merry-Mount: A Romance of the Massachusetts Colony* (1849). He also spent time in the diplomatic service in Russia, Austria and England. *The Rise of the Dutch Republic: A History* was published in three volumes in 1856 after ten years' work in the USA, Holland and Germany. The history, which ends with the death of William of Orange, was well received and soon translated into the principal European languages. Motley followed it with *The History of the United Netherlands*, which examines the years up to the truce of 1609; two volumes were published in 1861 and a further two in 1867. Another history, *The Life and Death of John of Barneveld, Advocate of Holland* (2 vols., 1874), spans the period from 1609 to the Thirty Years War. Motley planned another instalment, which would carry the history to the year 1848, but died before the project was realized.

Motley, Willard 1912–65 American novelist. Born in Chicago, he had a diverse career which included working as a ranch hand, cook, migrant labourer and photographer. His observation of the slums of Chicago in the 1940s served as material for his first novel, *Knock on any Door* (1947). *We Fished All Night* (1951) and *Let No Man Write My Epitaph* (1958) are also critical examinations of the urban environment. He lived in Mexico for the last 12 years of his life; *Let Noon be Fair*, published posthumously in 1966, traces the gradual corruption and cultural decline of a Mexican tourist town.

Motteux, Peter Anthony 1663–1718 Journalist, translator and playwright. A Huguenot brought up in Rouen, he fled to England at the Revocation of the Edict of Nantes in 1685. His early years in England are obscure, but in January 1692 he produced the first number of *The Gentleman's Journal: or, The Monthly Miscellany... Consisting of News, Philosophy, Poetry, Music, &c.* This sophisticated literary periodical adopted the epistolary form of the French *Mercure galant* and ran until November 1694. Largely a clever amalgam drawing on the *Mercure* and a host of unusual sources, the *Journal* includes contributions from Henry Purcell, SIR CHARLES SEDLEY, JOHN DENNIS, Tom Brown and MATTHEW PRIOR. Motteux seems to have brought the word 'journalist' into English, and his *Journal*, coming almost twenty years before ADDISON and STEELE'S *TATLER*, can claim an important place in the history of English literary journalism.

Motteux completed the translation of Rabelais left unfinished by SIR THOMAS URQUHART; and he published a translation of *Don Quixote* which, in the version revised by John Ozell, was, like the Rabelais, to remain standard for many years.

Motteux's involvement with the theatre began with his *Love's a Jest* in 1696. Thereafter he composed a multitude of entertainments. His more significant pieces include the tragedy *Beauty in Distress* (1698) and the libretto for *Arsinoë, Queen of Cyprus* (1705). *Arsinoë*, though sung in English, gave the London audience its first hint of the Italian opera which was to become so dominant as to be satirized by JOHN GAY's *THE BEGGAR'S OPERA* (1728).

In his later years, as his letter to *THE SPECTATOR* (Number 288) reveals, Motteux ran a China warehouse in Leadenhall Street. He also dealt in pictures and kept up lively contacts with foreign artists working in England: there is a sketch of Motteux and his family by Pellegrini in the British Museum. Motteux died in exquisitely unfortunate circumstances in a City brothel on his birthday in 1718.

Mottram, R(alph) H(ale) 1883–1971 Novelist. He was born in Norwich and educated there and in Lausanne. GALSWORTHY, with whom he became friends in 1904, encouraged him to write but he did not achieve recognition until *The Spanish Farm* (1924), the first part of *The Spanish Farm Trilogy* continued in *Sixty-four, Ninety-four* (1925) and *The Crime at Vanderlynden's* (1926). Set on a farm near the Front during World War I, it is the story of the owner, Vanderlynden, his youngest child, Madeleine, and the men who pass through in search of peace and serenity. Mottram wrote 60 books altogether, and many of his later novels are set in East Anglia, where he spent most of his life. He was awarded the honorary degree of Doctor of Letters by the University of East Anglia in 1966.

Mourning Becomes Electra A trilogy of plays by EUGENE O'NEILL, based on the *Oresteia* of Aeschylus, and first produced in New York in 1931. The 13-act trilogy is set in a small New England coastal town at the close of the Civil War. During General Mannon's absence in the war his wife Christine takes Captain Adam Brant as her lover. The grim Mannon house, built in the style of a Greek temple, becomes the setting for the first death, that of General Mannon, poisoned by Christine. Their daughter Lavinia hates her mother as fervently as she loved her father, and finding the remains of the poison, she urges her brother Orin to exact revenge. Orin kills Brant and Christine commits suicide. Driven towards madness by the consciousness of his crime, Orin is taken on a voyage by the unrepentant Lavinia. On their return to the Mannon house, he is still ill but she is transformed into a beauty exactly like her mother (the play was originally intended for performance with masks). Orin's passionate attachment to his mother is now incestuously transferred to Lavinia, and remorse leads him to suicide. Lavinia accepts the punishment of shutting herself away in the decaying mansion of the doomed Mannons.

Mourning Bride, The A tragedy by WILLIAM CONGREVE, his only essay in the form, first produced in February 1697 and published the same year. A considerable success, it provided a fine part for a tragic actress in the character of Sara, created by Elizabeth Barry. The play has not been revived, but two quotations from it are remembered: 'Music has charms to soothe a savage breast' and 'Heav'n has no rage, like love to hatred turn'd,/ Nor Hell a fury, like a woman scorn'd.'

Movement, The A loose grouping of poets who made their names during the 1950s. The term derives from an unsigned article by J. D. Scott, 'In the Movement', published in *The Spectator* on 1 October 1954. Although it can be extended to include novelists and playwrights, it has come to identify essentially those poets included in ROBERT CONQUEST's anthology *New Lines* (1956): Conquest himself, KINGSLEY AMIS, DONALD DAVIE, D. J. ENRIGHT, THOM GUNN, JOHN HOLLOWAY, ELIZABETH JENNINGS, PHILIP LARKIN and JOHN WAIN. Conquest's introduction claimed that they shared a 'negative determination to avoid bad principles'. In practice, this meant a determination to re-establish the values of rational intelligence and skilful craftsmanship in English poetry. Their stance was ironic and anti-romantic, their manner at times literary, and, to some tastes, academic: detractors have not failed to point out how many Movement poets earned their living in universities. Yet no post-war anthology of new writers has included such an impressive proportion of subsequently distinguished poets as *New Lines*.

Mowat, Farley 1921– Canadian essayist, story-teller and writer of CHILDREN'S LITERATURE. Born in Belleville, Ontario, and raised in Saskatoon, Saskatchewan, he interrupted his education at the University of Toronto for military service in World War II. After the war he spent two years in the Arctic before finishing his university degree and embarking on his highly successful career as a freelance writer. Mowat's first book, *People of the Deer* (1952), denounced the treatment of the Inuit by government officials and missionaries. Its impassioned prose created an immense readership and very considerable controversy, both of which have stayed with him throughout his career. More than 30 books document his interest in the north, the wilderness, the animal kingdom and the disadvantaged peoples. *The Desperate People* (1959), *Canada North* (1967), and *Canada North Now: The Great Betrayal* (1976) study the Canadian north. *Never Cry Wolf* (1963) and *A Whale for the Killing* (1972) are his most famous animal books. His children's books include *The Dog Who Wouldn't Be* (1957), *Owls in the Family* (1961), *Lost in the Barrens* (1965) and *The Boat Who Wouldn't Float* (1968). His military service provides the background for his autobiographical *And No Birds Sang* (1979). He has also edited many journals of early Canadian explorers. Translated into 23 languages and published in more than 40 countries, his 'subjective non-fiction', as he himself describes his writings, has raised public awareness, both in Canada and throughout the world, of mankind's inhumanity to man, to animal life and to the environment. His ecological concerns are to the fore in *Rescue the Earth: Conversations with the Green Crusaders* (1990).

Mowatt, Anna Cora 1819–70 American playwright, novelist and actress. She was the ninth of 16 children born in a wealthy American family living in Bordeaux, France, where she spent her early years before the family returned to settle in New York. She was 15 when she married James Mowatt, a respected lawyer much older than herself. He encouraged her to write, and she published a verse romance, *Pelayo* (1836), and a verse SATIRE, *Reviewers Reviewed* (1837), before turning her hand to novels of New York social life, including *The Fortune Hunter* (1844) and *Evelyn: or, A Heart Unmasked* (1845).

As a figure in New York society, she risked ridicule for her literary aspirations. To turn to the theatre was considered even worse, but when her comic social satire, *FASHION*, opened in 1845 and became widely popular, she was encouraged to take to the stage herself. For nine years she toured as an actress, retiring in

1854 to live in Richmond, Virginia, and after 1861 in Florence, Italy. She spent the rest of her life writing romantic narratives of life in the theatre, *Mimic Life* (1856) and *Twin Roses* (1857), her own *Autobiography of an Actress* (1854) and various historical sketches.

Mphahlele, Es'kia [Ezekiel] 1919– South African novelist, short-story writer, autobiographer and critic. Born in a Pretoria township, he worked at menial jobs before becoming a teacher and journalist. In 1957–78 he lived in Nigeria, France, Kenya, Zambia and the USA, returning to a professorship in Johannesburg in 1978. The stories of the ghetto and the black experience in *Man Must Live* (1947), *The Living and the Dead* (1961) and *In Corner B* (1967) sound a rising note of political protest. *The Unbroken Song* (1981) draws on these volumes, while *The Wanderers* (1971), *Chirundu* (1979) and *Father Come Home* (1984) are novels, the last an affecting tale of dispossessed and scattered African families. However, his narrative skill is seen at its best in his autobiography, *Down Second Avenue* (1959), a vivid, candid, angry, life-affirming account of a humane personality maturing under grinding poverty and racial oppression. *Afrika My Music: An Autobiography 1957–1983* (1984) is less compelling. Mphahlele's influential criticism includes *The African Image* (1962, revised edition 1974), a pioneering study of African literature and its politico-cultural context, and a collection of essays, *Voices in the Whirlwind* (1972).

Mr Badman, The Life and Death of A religious ALLEGORY by JOHN BUNYAN, published in 1680. It consists of a dialogue between Mr Wiseman and Mr Attentive, who relate and comment on the life of Mr Badman, an utterly immoral character who has recently passed over into damnation. Selfish and deceitful, he courts a rich woman and maltreats her after their marriage, is a swindler in business, behaves drunkenly, and degenerates physically, though he pretends to repent. His wife dies in despair, whereupon he remarries – this time a woman of similar disposition to his own – and at last expires peacefully.

The book shows a considerable degree of realism, especially in its vivid representation of a 17th-century market town, and through the lively credibility of Mr Badman's own character, making an unmistakable contribution to the development of the novel.

Mr Britling Sees It Through A novel by H. G. WELLS, published in 1916. Strongly autobiographical, it captured the national mood of growing disillusionment with World War I. The story centres on the household circle of Matching's Easy, undoubtedly based on Wells's Essex household, Easton Glebe. Through Britling, a mature and successful writer, we are given a picture of Wells's public and private worlds. Britling's early enthusiasm for the war, gen-

erally endorsed by the detached narrator, is destroyed when Hugh, his son by a first marriage, dies in battle. The depiction of Britling's boredom with his wife and children, and his marital infidelities, is generally considered among the novelist's less discreet reflections on his life.

Mr Gilfil's Love Story See SCENES OF CLERICAL LIFE.

Mr Midshipman Easy See MARRYAT, CAPTAIN FREDERICK.

Mr Polly, The History of A novel by H. G. WELLS, published in 1910.

Alfred Polly, now 37 years old, has always lived half in an impeding world of real misfortunes and half in a joyous imaginative world, often associated with the past. He has suffered from an appalling education followed by several years apprenticed, unsuitably, to a low-class draper. A legacy from his father has worsened his lot: his own shop is unprofitable, and marriage to his cousin Miriam has been loathsome, and produced severe indigestion for 15 years.

Polly escapes after a comically abortive attempt at suicide, when he starts a fire and fails to cut his throat. As a result of his actions during this 'great Fishbourne fire', bundling his neighbour's mother-in-law across the rooftops, Polly is proclaimed a hero. In his fat, romantic way, he tends to achieve his weak ambitions by accident.

When Polly abandons his home for a life on the road, the novel endorses his Utopian dreams of escape. The landscapes of rural England, around the Potwell Inn and its plump landlady, are a haven from the pressures of his class and its failed commercial prospects. But Polly is able to settle at the Inn only after proving his manhood in a fight with the criminal Uncle Jim, and after Miriam has been awarded life insurance for the husband that she imagines to be dead.

Mr Scarborough's Family A novel by ANTHONY TROLLOPE, serialized in *ALL THE YEAR ROUND* from May 1882 to June 1883 and published in volume form in 1883.

The plot concerns the disappointment of Mr Scarborough who, after the birth of a son, Mountjoy, marries his wife again before the birth of a second son, Augustus, to ensure that he can declare the latter his heir, should Mountjoy not prove of responsible character. The novel is enlivened by the characters of Mr Grey, Scarborough's gentle, long-suffering attorney, and his daughter, Dolly, who refuses to marry because all the men she meets compare unfavourably with her father.

Mr Sponge's Sporting Tour A novel by R. S. SURTEES, published in 1853 with illustrations by JOHN

LEECH. Probably Surtees's best novel, it has more form and balance than the others and the central character is convincingly developed. Sponge lives up to his name by forcing himself upon rich men and making up to their daughters. He is, however, redeemed by enormous courage and skill on horseback and a genuine love of hunting. His peregrinations take us into the company of such extraordinary folk as Lord Scamperdale and Sir Harry Scattercash; and there are some marvellous low-life characters from horsedealers' yards and hunting stables. A sequel, *Mr Facey Romford's Hounds*, was published in 1865, the year after Surtees died.

Mrs Dalloway A novel by VIRGINIA WOOLF, published in 1925.

Clarissa Dalloway, the wife of Richard Dalloway MP and a fashionable London hostess, is to give an important party. Her character is gradually revealed through her thoughts on that day and through her memories of the past, rendered by interior monologue and STREAM OF CONSCIOUSNESS. The other people who have touched her life are: her one-time suitor Peter Walsh, lately returned from India after five years' absence; her childhood friend Sally Seton; her daughter Elizabeth and spinster tutor Miss Kilman; and a political hostess, Lady Bruton. A complementary character is Septimus Warren Smith, a shell-shock victim who has retreated into a private world and ends the day by committing suicide. He and Clarissa Dalloway never meet, but their lives are connected by external events and news of his death is casually mentioned by a guest at Clarissa's party. It provokes in her thoughts of her own isolation and loneliness: 'Death was defiance. Death was an attempt to communicate, people feeling the impossibility of reaching the centre which, mystically, evaded them; closeness drew apart; rapture faded; one was alone.'

Mrs Warren's Profession A play by GEORGE BERNARD SHAW, written in 1893, but denied performance by the Examiner of Plays, who considered it immoral. It was given a private performance by the Independent Theatre Club in 1902 and its first public performance in 1925.

Mrs Warren's profession is prostitution. She runs a chain of brothels in the capitals of Europe. She cannot be certain who is the father of her brilliant and independent daughter, Vivie. Shaken by the discovery of the truth about her mother, Vivie rejects both her suitors in favour of continuing actuarial work with her friend Honoria. The conflict between mother and daughter is the dramatic centre of the play. Vivie is not prepared to learn what Mrs Warren is prepared to teach – that prostitution is economically determined by a society which only pretends to outlaw it.

Mtshali, Oswald Mbuyiseni 1940– South African poet. He was born in Vryheid. With *Sounds of a Cowhide Drum* (1971) he led the creative outburst of black 'township' poetry which broke a decade of post-Sharpeville silence and found voice in the work of MONGANE WALLY SEROTE, SIPHO SEPAMLA and the other poets in the anthology, *Black Poets in South Africa* (1974). Mtshali's conversational, free-flowing verse often expresses communal ghetto emotions – frustration, anger, bitterness, pathos, pity – though *Fireflames* (1980) also looks forward to a time 'long/ after the fiendish ideology has been reduced to rubble'.

Mucedorus, The Comedy of A play of unknown authorship first published in 1598. Discovered in a volume of SHAKESPEARE in the library of Charles II, it was once regarded as an early work of the poet, though this possibility has now been rejected. (See SHAKESPEARE APOCRYPHA.) The story concerns the efforts of Mucedorus, Prince of Valencia, to discover the virtues of Amadine, daughter of the King of Aragon. In the process he falls in love with her, saves her life on two occasions, and successfully overturns the king's objections to him as a husband for his daughter.

Much Ado about Nothing A comedy by WILLIAM SHAKESPEARE, first performed *c.* 1598 and published in Quarto (Q1) in 1600 as well as in the First Folio of 1623. The Claudio/Hero plot was already a familiar story and could have been taken from any number of sources. More original is the invention and elaboration of the unwilling love of Beatrice and Benedick.

Claudio, in the service of the Prince of Aragon, Don Pedro, falls in love with Hero, daughter of Leonato, Governor of Messina. The match is welcomed by all but Don Pedro's discontented brother, Don John, who determines to destroy it. With the aid of his henchman, Borachio, he convinces Claudio that Hero is unfaithful, and Claudio waits till the marriage service itself to reject his intended bride. Hero faints away, and Leonato is persuaded to challenge assumptions of her guilt by announcing that she is dead. When the garrulous Borachio is overheard boasting of Don John's trick, Claudio's horror is relieved by Leonato's forgiveness and by Hero's return to life.

In what is formally a sub-plot, but one which attracts more attention than the conventional main plot, Claudio's friend Benedick and Leonato's niece Beatrice fight a duel of wit which, through the manoeuvres of their friends, is exposed as a disguise of their real love for each other. That love is tested when Beatrice, outraged by Claudio's treatment of Hero, demands that Benedick kill him. Benedick challenges Claudio to a duel, but the timely discovery of Don John's duplicity spares the two friends that confrontation. It is characteristic of Shakespeare's inventiveness that the real villainy of Don John should be exposed by a fumbling and incompetent constable, Dogberry. A surviving reference makes it almost certain that the part of Dogberry was written for the famous comic actor, WILL KEMP, who left Shakespeare's company shortly after the play's first production.

Much Ado about Nothing is a mature comedy with a long history of success in the British theatre. The influence of Beatrice and Benedick was felt in the Restoration comedy of manners, whose competitive loving couples similarly disguise their true affection by verbal combat. Millamant and Mirabell in CONGREVE'S *THE WAY OF THE WORLD* are the most famous of a number of examples.

Muddiman, Henry b. 1629 Journalist. Almost nothing is known of his personal life. A pensioner at St John's College, Cambridge, and later a schoolteacher, he was licensed through the influence of General Monk and the patronage of Sir John Williamson to write a news-sheet under the Long Parliament in 1659. *The Oxford Gazette*, which he began to publish in 1665, quickly became *The London Gazette* and enjoyed a monopoly of printed news until 1678. See also NEWSPAPER, THE RISE OF THE ENGLISH.

Mudrooroo [Johnson, Colin] 1939– Australian Aboriginal novelist, poet and critic. He changed his name in protest against the bicentennial celebrations. He is still best known for his first novel, *Wild Cat Falling* (1965), a brief but intense book focusing on a 19-year-old half-Aboriginal, half-white 'antihero'. *Doin Wildcat* (1988) describes the filming of the novel. Some of its philosophical elements anticipate Mudrooroo's own conversion to Buddhism, which has taken him to remote parts of Asia. He has, however, been an active supporter of Aboriginal rights in his native country. His other fiction includes *Long Live Sandawara* (1979), which switches between northwest Australia in the 1890s and the slums of modern Perth, and *Doctor Wooreddy's Prescription for Enduring the Ending of the World* (1983), set in the Australian states of Tasmania and Victoria at the time of the first contact between Aboriginals and white men. *Master of the Ghost Dreaming* (1990) uses MAGIC REALISM to contrast Aboriginal 'human' imagination and that of 'ghosts' (white men). His verse includes *The Song Circle of Jacky and Selected Poems* (1986) and *Dalwurra: A Poem Cycle* (1988). He has written the first theorizing account of Aboriginal literature, *Writing from the Fringe* (1990), and co-edited *Paperbark* (1990), the main collection of Aboriginal writings.

Muggleton, Lodowicke 1609–98 and **Reeve, John** 1608–58 Founders of the sect known as the Muggletonians. They were cousins, both London tailors, who in 1651 claimed to be the 'Two Last Witnesses' foretold in Revelation 11.3–6; they were to prepare the elect for the coming of Judgement Day. They preached complete freedom of conscience in matters of religion, and their beliefs included the special inspiration of the elect, the mortalism of the soul, and the conviction that matter was composed of the substance of God. They were pacifists and quietists. The sect survived obscurely until the present century, and the recent discovery of a large archive of Muggletonian material has provided historians with an exceptional amount of information about the workings of a radical 17th-century sect.

Muir, Edwin 1887–1959 Poet, novelist, translator and critic. Born in Orkney, he moved to Glasgow with his family, worked as a clerk, and began to contribute to A. R. Orage's *NEW AGE*. He married in 1919, moved to London and, at Orage's suggestion, began psychoanalysis. This released the 'mythological dreams' which were to become important for his poetry. He travelled to Prague with his wife Willa, and between 1930 and 1949 they published translations of Kafka's novels. After the war he returned to Prague to work for the British Council, and then became director of the British Institute in Rome in 1949. He was professor of poetry at Harvard University in 1955–6.

His volumes of poetry include *First Poems* (1925), *Chorus of the Newly Dead* (1926), *Journeys and Places* (1937), *The Narrow Place* (1943), *The Voyage* (1946), *The Labyrinth* (1949) and *One Foot in Eden* (1956). *Collected Poems 1921–1958* was published in 1960. His poetry became increasingly allegorical and philosophical, though he is perhaps best represented by the often-anthologized 'The Horses'. His prose work includes three novels, *The Marionette* (1927), *The Three Brothers* (1931) and *Poor Tom* (1932), and several critical studies, *Transition: Essays on Contemporary Literature* (1926), *The Structure of the Novel* (1928), *Scott and Scotland* (1936), *Essays on Literature and Society* (1949) and *The Estate of Poetry* (1962). His autobiography, *The Story and the Fable* (1940), was revised as *An Autobiography* (1954).

Mulcaster, Richard ?1530–1611 Writer on education. Mulcaster was educated at Eton and Christ Church, Oxford, where he graduated (1556) with a reputation as one of the best Hebrew scholars of his age. In 1561 he became the first headmaster of Merchant Taylors' School where he remained until 1586. SPENSER may have been one of his pupils. In 1596 he became high master of St Paul's School. His two works on education, *Positions* (1581) and *The First Part of the Elementary* (1582), show that he held advanced views, advocating university education and adequate salaries for teachers, close contact between teachers and parents, and music in schools. He wrote some Latin verse including an elegy on the death of Elizabeth (1603).

Muldoon, Paul 1951– Irish poet. He was born in Moy, County Armagh, Northern Ireland and educated at Queen's University, Belfast, where SEAMUS HEANEY was among his teachers. He worked as a producer for the BBC for many years before resigning in 1985 and now lives in the USA. His verse is adroit, developing its peculiar rhetoric in stages to a fine point of sophisticated eloquence. After the first volumes, *New Weather* (1973) and *Mules* (1977), he intensified his humour and broadened his range in *Why Brownlee Left* (1980), *Quoof* (1984) and *Madoc: A Mystery* (1990), his most ambitious work. *Selected Poems* appeared in 1986. He has edited a controversial anthology, *Contemporary Irish Poetry* (1986), and translated contemporary Gaelic poetry.

Mulock, Dinah Maria [Mrs Craik] 1826–87 Novelist. Born near Stoke-on-Trent, where her father was a minister, she helped her mother in conducting a school. In 1846 she settled in London, starting her writing career with stories for children. Her first novel, *The Ogilvies*, appeared in 1849 and was followed by *Olive* (1850), *The Head of the Family* (dedicated to ELIZABETH BARRETT BROWNING; 1852) and *Agatha's Husband* (1853). In 1857 she published her most popular work, *JOHN HALIFAX, GENTLEMAN*. Later novels included her own favourite, *A Life for a Life* (1859), as well as *Christian's Mistake* (1865), *The Woman's Kingdom* (1869) and *Young Mrs Jardine* (1879). She also published volumes of poetry in 1859, 1875, 1880 and 1881. Of a number of sensible and penetrating essays, 'A Woman's Thoughts about Women' (1853) is most interesting.

Mum and the Sothsegger Two anonymous fragments of ALLITERATIVE VERSE from the first decade of the 15th century, generally assumed to belong to a single work. The first, once known as *Richard the Redeless* and attributed by SKEAT to LANGLAND, is divided into four sections and a prologue. They deal with the events surrounding Richard II's deposition in 1399 and criticize the king for his unwise behaviour. The second fragment refers to events after 1402 and is not divided into sections. It takes the form of a debate between Mum and the soothsayer (or truth-teller), the former advocating discreet silence and the second adamant that criticism should be voiced. In a dream the narrator is told by a gardener that truth-telling is best, and so he writes the poem. Verbal similarities between the second fragment and the A-text of *PIERS PLOWMAN* suggest that the author was familiar with the text.

mummers' play The mummers' play, with its central theme of death and resurrection, belongs less to literature than to anthropology. Associated with the death of winter and the new birth of spring, it is presumed to have survived from the folk festivals of agricultural communities. More than 3000 texts have been recovered by 19th- and 20th-century researchers, who have divided them into three main groups: the Hero-Combat Play, the Sword Play (mainly from the north-east of England), and the Wooing Ceremony (mainly from the east Midlands). Adapted over the centuries, the texts can accommodate heroes from St George to Winston Churchill and villains from the Turkish Knight to Adolf Hitler. Whoever dies can be revived by a remedy of the Doctor's, and the play ends with a procession and the taking of a collection. HARDY described the performance of a mummers' play in *THE RETURN OF THE NATIVE* and borrowed from the form in *The Famous Tragedy of the Queen of Cornwall*.

Munby, A(rthur) J(oseph) 1828–1910 Poet and diarist. He was born near York and educated at Trinity College, Cambridge, writing most of his first volume of poetry, *Benoni* (1852), while still an undergraduate. A reluctant lawyer who always preferred the literary life, he entered Lincoln's Inn, was called to the Bar and worked from 1860 onwards as a clerk with the Ecclesiastical Commission. His subsequent volumes included *Verses New and Old* (1865), *Vestigia retrorsum* (1891), *Vulgar Verses* (under the pseudonym of Jones Brown; 1891), *Poems: Chiefly Lyric and Elegiac* (1901), *Relicta* (1909) and several verse romances, notably *Susan* (1893). Their recurrent preoccupation with working women and the frequent theme of the gentleman who falls in love with a servant have an autobiographical counterpart in Munby's love for Hannah Cullwick, a maid of all work whom he met in 1854 and secretly married in 1873. This side to his life, first glimpsed by friends and contemporaries on the publication of his will, is recorded in the diaries he kept from 1859 onwards, and used by Derek Hudson as the basis for his account in *Munby: Man of Two Worlds* (1972).

Munday, Anthony 1560–1633 Playwright. Born in London, Munday may have been a boy actor before being apprenticed to a stationer. He was engaged in anti-Catholic espionage from early in his adulthood. There are even suspicions that he was a double agent, though his religious pamphlets are vigorously and unequivocally Protestant. Munday was certainly capable of changing his mind. Within a few years of writing *A Second and Third Blast of Retreat from Plays and Theatres* (1580), an anti-theatrical tract, he was engaged in writing plays for the public theatre. Not many have survived. *Fedele and Fortunio* (c. 1584), a piece for court performance, is now believed to be mostly Munday's work, as is *John a Kent and John a Cumber* (1594). His is one of many hands at work in

Charles Mungoshi

the revision of SIR THOMAS MORE (c. 1593–5) and in Part One of *Sir John Oldcastle* (1599). By 1598 he was well enough known to be referred to by FRANCIS MERES in *Palladis Tamia* as 'the best for comedy' and 'our best plotter'. The latter skill suggests a journeyman's useful talent for dividing a given story into suitable dramatic episodes. It is certainly arguable that the plotting is better than the writing in the two-part play, written in collaboration with HENRY CHETTLE, on the ROBIN HOOD legends, *The Downfall of Robert, Earl of Huntingdon* and its sequel *The Death of Robert, Earl of Huntingdon* (both 1598), which completes the list of extant plays known to have been Munday's in whole or in part. In addition, there are several pageants for the City of London, dating from the period 1592–1623 when he was keeper of the pageant properties and the city's official poet.

As translator of many French and Spanish prose romances, Munday made a widely acknowledged contribution to the growth of Arthurian and semi-Arthurian stories in England. There, and in his own *Zelauto* (1580) and *A True and Admirable History of a Maiden of Consolens in Poitiers* (1603), he was also advancing the development of the English novel.

Munera Pulveris Essays by JOHN RUSKIN, first published in *FRASER'S MAGAZINE* as 'Essays On Political Economy' in 1862–3 and then in book form as *Munera Pulveris* in 1872.

In *Munera Pulveris* Ruskin attempts to analyse the salient aspects of political economy which he sees as 'a system of conduct' that cannot be achieved 'except under certain conditions of moral culture'. He defines the commercial cornerstones of Wealth, Money and Riches and in each case his definitions assume life-giving qualities, assert human principles and demonstrate adherence to a moral standard – an approach very different from that of Victorian *laissez-faire* capitalism. Many familiar Ruskinian motifs – treatment of the worker, relations between rich and poor, between the powerful and the weak, and the 'national store' of wealth – come under consideration. Although lacking the pungency of UNTO THIS LAST, *Munera Pulveris* is a noble statement of Ruskin's idealism.

Mungoshi, Charles 1947– Zimbabwean novelist and short-story writer. He has worked as a research assistant for the Forestry Commission and for a firm in Harare. His best-known novel, *Waiting for the Rain* (1975), is set in rural, pre-independence Zimbabwe and draws on both Shona and Christian traditions for its portrait of spiritual, political and material drought. It concentrates on the ambivalent relationships between the older generations and two brothers: Lucifer, about to depart for England, and Gabhara, a drummer sympathetic to the visionary experience of his grandfather. Mungoshi's other work in English includes the stories in *Coming of the Dry Season* (1972), banned before Zimbabwe became independent, and *Some Kinds of Wounds and Other Short Stories* (1980), and the poetry in *The Milkman Doesn't Only Deliver Milk*. His work in Shona includes three novels and a play.

Munro, Alice 1931– Canadian short-story writer. Born in Wingham, Ontario, she studied at the University of Western Ontario. She has lived in British Columbia but once again lives in small-town southwestern Ontario, the territory she explores in all her work. Her low-key, understated stories gradually reveal levels of human behaviour which question notions of 'normality' and make her provincial towns mythical places in which universal dramas are enacted. She is both an acute observer of small-town Canadian cultural codes – and in particular how women are socialized through the forces of family upbringing, gender expectations, education and popular culture – and a writer who describes patterns of growing up and behaviour that are common across cultures. Her superficially naturalistic narrative mode is deceptive, frequently concealing Gothic and fabulist layers. Two books, LIVES OF GIRLS AND WOMEN (1971) and *Who Do You Think You Are?* (1978; as *The Beggar Maid* in Britain), are collections of short stories with common protagonists who provide a sense of novelistic unity. Other collections – *Dance of the Happy Shades* (1968), *Something I've Been Meaning to Tell You* (1974), *The Moons of Jupiter* (1982), *The Progress of Love* (1987) and *Friend of My Youth* (1990) – are unified by recurrent themes and motifs.

Munro, Hector Hugh See SAKI.

Murder Considered as One of the Fine Arts, On An essay in black humour by THOMAS DE QUINCEY, published in *BLACKWOOD'S EDINBURGH MAGAZINE* in 1827, and followed by a *Supplementary Paper* in the same periodical in 1839.

It purports to be the text of a lecture given in London at a meeting of the Society of Connoisseurs in Murder. After surveying the history of murder since Cain, the speaker addresses the 'Augustan Age of Murder' in the 17th and 18th centuries, before subjecting a number of recently committed murders to detailed aesthetic criticism, based absurdly but logically on BURKE's conceptions of the 'sublime'. In defending himself against the charge that his remarks could be taken as an incitement to murder, the speaker argues his purpose to oppose it: 'For once a man indulges in murder, very soon he comes to think little of robbing, and from robbing he comes next to drinking and Sabbath-breaking, and from that to incivility and procrastination.' The sustained poker-faced seriousness of the piece invites comparison with SWIFT, though its sequel featuring the Society's celebration dinner degenerates into rather laboured buffoonery.

Murder in the Cathedral A verse drama by T. S. ELIOT, first produced at the Chapter House of Canterbury Cathedral during the Canterbury Festival of 1935 and published in the same year. It follows the events at Canterbury after Archbishop Thomas à Becket's return from exile in 1170.

A Chorus of Women lament the absence of their archbishop and the people's helplessness in the schism between church and state. A herald announces to them, and to the priests, that Becket is returning; the news is welcome but all, except the second priest, distrust Henry II's reconciliation with Becket. Becket enters, determined to resolve the crisis, though he knows it may cost him his life. In a long scene, the Four Tempters illustrate the conflict his decision provokes within himself; the temptation to seek martyrdom is powerful. Becket realizes that the only course he can follow is to offer his life to 'the Law of God above the Law of Man'. The Christmas morning sermon of 1170 makes his position clear. Four days later the King's Four Knights arrive and charge Becket with rebellion; he is ordered to depart from England. He refuses, and the abusive knights warn him they will come again. The priests try to persuade Becket to barricade himself in the cathedral. He refuses, and orders them to unbar the door and open it. The knights return, half drunk, and murder him; then they address the audience in turn with a justification of their deed. After they withdraw the stage is left to the priests, who offer thanks to God for having given another saint to Canterbury.

Murdoch, Dame **Iris (Jean)** 1919– Novelist and philosopher. Born in Dublin of Anglo-Irish parents, she was educated at Badminton and at Somerville College, Oxford. She lectured in philosophy at Oxford and then at the Royal College of Art in London. Her philosophical works include *Sartre: Romantic Rationalist* (1953), *The Sovereignty of Good* (1970) and *The Fire and the Sun: Why Plato Banned the Artists* (1977).

Her first novel, *Under the Net* (1954), used a first-person male narrator and displayed her gift for humour. It was followed by *The Flight from the Enchanter* (1955), *The Sandcastle* (1957) and *The Bell* (1958), widely considered her most successful novel, about a declining religious community. Her prolific output has continued with *A Severed Head* (1961), *An Unofficial Rose* (1962), *The Unicorn* (1963), *The Italian Girl* (1964), *The Red and the Green* (1965), *The Time of the Angels* (1966), *The Nice and the Good* (1968), *Bruno's Dream* (1969), *A Fairly Honourable Defeat* (1970), *An Accidental Man* (1971), *The Black Prince* (1972), *The Sacred and Profane Love Machine* (1974), *A Word Child* (1975), *Henry and Cato* (1977), *The Sea, the Sea* (BOOKER PRIZE; 1978), *The Philosopher's Pupil* (1983), *The Book and the Brotherhood* (1987) and *Message to the Planet* (1989). With their blend of realism and symbolism, they reflect her interest in psychological patterns and myths in human relationships. Their narrative skill and talent for irony has also helped attract a wide readership. Her plays include an adaptation of *A Severed Head* (with J. B. PRIESTLEY; 1963), *Servants and the Snow* (1970), *The Three Arrows* (1972) and *Art and Eros* (1980).

Iris Murdoch

Murnane, Gerald 1939– Australian novelist and short-story writer. He was born in Melbourne, where he lives and lectures. His fiction draws on autobiographical experience, distanced and made objective by the novelist's craft, which itself becomes the object of passionate attention. Novels include *Tamarisk Row* (1974), *A Lifetime on Clouds* (1976), *The Plains* (1982), *Landscape with Landscape* (1985) and *Inland* (1988). *Velvet Waters* (1990) is a collection of finely controlled stories.

Murphy, Arthur 1727–1805 Playwright, editor and critic. An Irishman born in Roscommon, he had unusually broad interests. Educated at the English Jesuit College in St Omer, France, he began his adult life as a clerk and book-keeper, but by 1752 was submitting contributions to FIELDING's *Covent Garden Journal* and the *New Craftsman*. From 1753 to 1754 he was editor of the *Gray's Inn Journal* and from 1756 to 1757 of the political weekly *The Test*, through which he supported Henry Fox's attacks on the militarism of the elder Pitt. A committed Tory, Murphy alienated progressive Londoners by his defence of Lord Bute's government in articles submitted to *The Auditor* in 1762, protesting against JOHN WILKES and *THE NORTH BRITON*. His appointment as commissioner of bankruptcies came in recognition of the journalistic support he had lent to an often unpopular administration.

Remembered primarily as a playwright, Murphy was also an actor from 1754 to 1756, during which time he played Othello at COVENT GARDEN. *The Apprentice* (1756) was the first of several accomplished FARCES that were among the most popular 18th-century afterpieces. Others were *The Upholsterer* (1758), *The Citizen* (1761) and the excellent *Three Weeks after Marriage* (1776), a revised version of *What We Must All Come To* (1764), which had been damned by the public during the furore caused by the prosecution of John Wilkes.

The unpopularity of Murphy's politics has disguised from many critics the talent as a writer of unsentimental comedies which ought to have earned him comparison with GOLDSMITH and SHERIDAN. *The Way to Keep Him* (three-act version 1760, five-act version 1761), *All in the Wrong* (1761) and particularly *Know Your Own Mind* (1777) have been unfairly neglected in the theatre. Murphy's tragedies, even the best of them, *The Grecian Daughter* (1772), are less effective.

When it is remembered that Murphy sustained an active career as a barrister from 1763 to 1787, his literary output is prodigious. It includes the first edition of Fielding's works, in four volumes with a biographical and critical introduction (1762), *An Essay on the Life and Genius of Samuel Johnson* (1792), *The Life of David Garrick* (2 vols., 1801) and a translation of *The Works of Tacitus* (4 vols., 1793).

Murphy, Richard 1927– Irish poet. Born in County Galway, he spent part of his childhood in Ceylon, where his father was posted as a colonial official, before going to Wellington College, followed by Oxford and the Sorbonne. He has taught at various schools and universities. His first small collection, *The Archaeology of Love* (1955) has been followed by *Sailing to an Island* (1963), *The Battle of Aughrim* (1968), *High Island* (1974), *Selected Poems* (1979), *The Price of Stone* (1985), *New Selected Poems* (1989) and *Mirror Wall* (1989). In a sense he is the last of the Anglo-Irish poets, dwelling on a heritage similar to that of YEATS but also ranging beyond it in search of the other Ireland of hovels, famine and disaster. This double allegiance is reflected in a technique which borrows from both Anglo-Saxon and Gaelic poetry. His most ambitious poem, 'The Battle of Aughrim', commissioned and broadcast by the BBC, coolly explores 'the last decisive battle in Irish history' fought between 'planters' and 'mere Irish' in 1691.

Murphy, Thomas (Bernard) 1935– Irish playwright. He was born in Tuam, County Galway. His first play, *A Whistle in the Dark* (1961), concerns an Irish immigrant family in Coventry whose despairs find outlet in brutal violence. After writing television and radio scripts in London, he returned to Ireland in 1970. He has explored various modifications of the realism of his first work in: *Famine* (1968); *A Crucial Week in the Life of a Grocer's Assistant* (1969), with a tight, surrealistic structure and Joycean wordplay; *The Morning after Optimism* (1971), in which a whore and a pimp are the shadows and finally the murderers of two idealized lovers in a debased Forest of Arden; *The Sanctuary Lamp* (1975), about three grotesque derelicts; *The Blue Macushla* (1980), a SATIRE of Irish politics set in a night club; *The Gigli Concert* (1983), about an Irish businessman who aspires to sing like Gigli; and *Bailegangaire* (1986).

Murray, Sir James A(ugustus) H(enry) 1837–1915 Lexicographer. A tailor's son from Hawick, he left school before he was 15 and worked locally as a casual labourer while continuing to read up many subjects avidly. From the age of 17 he was a highly successful assistant master at Hawick United School, his zest for learning astonishing all who met him. His move to London, where he at first worked as a bank clerk, was to get his wife into a better climate. Through membership of the Philological Society he met F. J. FURNIVALL, who involved him in preparing medieval texts for the Early English Text Society series, and the headmaster of Mill Hill School, who gave him a teaching job (1870). Despite widespread recognition of his scholarship he schooled himself through a University of London external degree (1874). In 1878 he was appointed editor of THE OXFORD ENGLISH DICTIONARY, becoming the driving force behind that formidable project and continuing to pour his enthusiasm and compulsively hard work into it even in his seventies. His achievement brought him many honorary doctorates as well as the award of a Civil List pension (1884) and a knighthood (1908).

Murray, John 1778-1843 Publisher. Born in London, and educated at private schools in Edinburgh, Margate and London, Murray was the son of John Murray I (born MacMurray, 1745-93), who founded the publishing house that still exists today. Assuming control of the business after his father's death, he built it up into one of the most prestigious and successful houses of the 19th century. Combining considerable commercial talent with cultivated literary taste, he was one of the new breed of highly professionalized patron-entrepreneurs that emerged at the end of the 18th century. His house at Albemarle Street became a meeting place for many of the leading literary figures of the day, and he held a reputation for liberality towards his authors, occasionally burning his fingers (COLERIDGE appears not to have produced a line of his translation of Goethe's *Faust*), but in general reaping the rewards of finely judged advances. In 1808 he discontinued his part interest in *THE EDINBURGH REVIEW* and, with the encouragement and support of SCOTT, founded the Tory *QUARTERLY REVIEW* in 1809, installing WILLIAM GIFFORD as editor and securing the services of SOUTHEY as his star contributor. He took an active interest in its management, and its influence, both literary and political, was for almost a century rivalled only by that of the *Edinburgh* itself. He was also for a time joint publisher of *BLACKWOOD'S EDINBURGH MAGAZINE* but pulled out in 1818, in protest at the tone of its attacks on LEIGH HUNT and KEATS in the famous COCKNEY SCHOOL articles. His single most important author was his friend BYRON, who awoke to find himself among the immortals after the publication of the first two cantos of *CHILDE HAROLD'S PILGRIMAGE*. *THE CORSAIR* reputedly sold 10,000 copies on the first day of its publication alone. Their alliance continued for some time after Byron's departure for the Continent, and only broke down under the strains of *DON JUAN*. Murray published, but withheld his imprint on, Cantos I to V, but thereafter his Tory instincts rose in rebellion, and the later cantos, as well as the anti-establishment SATIRE *THE VISION OF JUDGEMENT*, were gratefully snapped up by Leigh Hunt for his *EXAMINER*. In the complicated controversy relating to Byron's *Memoirs*, which he had bought from THOMAS MOORE in 1821, Murray was compelled to resell them to Moore who then burned them in the grate at Albemarle Street.

Murray's other authors included JANE AUSTEN (on whose novels he later sold the copyright), CRABBE, Southey, Coleridge, BORROW and the historian Napier. The famous series of guidebooks was inaugurated by Mariana Starke's *Guide for Travellers on the Continent* (1820), and continued by the third John Murray (1808-92). In the mid-1820s Murray suffered his only major financial catastrophe with the discontinuation, after only six months, of the daily newspaper *The Representative* which he had been persuaded to launch by the young BENJAMIN DISRAELI.

Murray, Les(lie) A(llan) 1938- Australian poet. Born in Bunyah, New South Wales, he attended Sydney University. 'The Powerline Incantation' and 'An Absolutely Ordinary Rainbow' typify the adventurous and commanding poetry which has won him an international reputation. The much-anthologized 'Noonday Axeman' epitomizes his role as sage and as mythologizer of Australian landscape and culture. His controversial 'Buladelah-Taree Holiday Song Cycle' blends Aboriginal poetic forms with an account of holidaying Australians. Volumes include *The Ilex Tree* (with Geoffrey Lehmann; 1965), *The Weatherboard Cathedral* (1969), *Poems against Economics* (1972), *Lunch and Counter Lunch* (1974), *Ethnic Radio* (1977), *Daylight Moon* (1980), *Dog Fox Field* (1990) and a verse novel, *The Boys Who Stole the Funeral* (1979). The continually expanded *Selected Poems: The Vernacular Republic* (1976, 1982, 1988) preserves what he regards as his essential canon. His articles and reviews are gathered in *The Peasant Mandarin* (1978), *Persistence in Folly* (1984) and *Blocks and Tackles: Articles and Essays 1982-1990* (1990). He is co-editor of *Poetry Australia*.

Murray, Thomas Cornelius 1873-1959 Irish playwright. Born at Macroom, County Cork, he was headmaster of a County Dublin model school from 1915 to 1932. With LENNOX ROBINSON, he was one of the 'Cork realists' whose work determined the characteristic style of the ABBEY THEATRE. In *Birthright* (1910), his first play, a father's jealous care for his land becomes a mortal issue between his two sons. His most successful later plays are *Aftermath* (1922), *Autumn Fire* (1924), and *Michaelmas Eve* (1932). They present a sombre vision of a small-farming society bound by Catholic teaching and obsessed by ownership of their harsh land.

Murry, John Middleton 1889-1957 Critic. Born in Peckham, London, the son of an Internal Revenue clerk, he was educated at Christ's Hospital and at Brasenose College, Oxford, where he edited the magazine *Rhythm*. In 1912 he met the writer KATHERINE MANSFIELD, with whom he lived (as her husband from 1918) until her death in 1923, and whose letters and stories he later edited. His close but often troubled association with D. H. LAWRENCE began in 1914, when they drew up an abortive plan for a Utopian community called 'Rananim'. Murry worked in the political intelligence department of the War Office from 1916 to 1919, before becoming editor of *THE ATHENAEUM* from 1919 to 1921. In this post, and as editor of *THE ADELPHI*, which he founded in 1923, Murry was an energetic force behind the new wave of post-war literature, encouraging and publishing the work of T. S. ELIOT, VIRGINIA WOOLF and other modernist writers (see MODERNISM). His influence subsequently waned as his strongly mystical disposition came to the fore in his work, but he is still remembered for *The Problem of Style* (1922) and particularly for *Son of Woman* (1931), an analysis of Lawrence's struggles with the female element in his nature. He wrote an autobiography, *Between Two Worlds* (1935), as well as studies of Dostoevsky (1916), KEATS and SHAKESPEARE (1925) and SWIFT (1954).

Muses' Looking-Glass, The A play by THOMAS RANDOLPH, first performed in 1632 and published in 1638. It is a defence of the dramatist's art and is considered Randolph's best work by scholars of the period. Two Puritans, Bird and Flowerdew, sell posies and feathers in the Blackfriars playhouse; but at the same time proclaim their abhorrence of theatres. Roscius joins them, persuades them to attend the play with him, explains the action of the piece as it proceeds, and eventually converts them to a more tolerant view.

Mwangi, Meja (David) 1948– Kenyan novelist. Born in Nanyuki, he is part of the generation of Kenyan writers to be deeply affected by the Mau Mau emergency of the early 1950s and by the struggle for independence. He was educated at Nanyuki Secondary School and at Kenyatta College, Nairobi. The first book he wrote, though not the first to be published, is *Taste of Death* (1975), which presents the Mau Mau in a heroic light. Most of his later fiction has been concerned with the social conditions of life in post-independence Kenya, the most famous of these being *Going down River Road* (1976), a novel which despite its comic touch gives a graphic portrait of life in the industrial areas and nightspots of Nairobi. His other books include: *Kill Me Quick!* (1973); *Carcase for Hounds* (1974), another novel about the Mau Mau, filmed as *Cry Freedom*; *The Cockroach Dance* (1979); *The Bushtrackers* (1979); *Bread of Sorrow* (1987); *Weapon for Hunger* (1989); *The Return of Shaka* (1990); and *Striving for the Wind* (1992). Mwangi is sometimes felt to have compromised too much with the standards of popular fiction, yet he remains an astute observer of modern Kenyan life.

My Ántonia A novel by WILLA CATHER, published in 1918. It takes the form of a memoir by Jim Burden, recounting the life of his childhood friend Ántonia Shimerda, the eldest daughter of an immigrant Bohemian family of farmers in Black Hawk, Nebraska.

When Ántonia's father commits suicide, she is forced to work in the fields like a man though she is still in her early teens. Later she goes to work as a hired girl for the Harling family. She remains in this position for some years, leaving only when she refuses to accede to Mr Harling's demand that she cease attending the town's Saturday night dances lest she lose her reputation. She takes up a similar position with Wick Cutter and his wife until Wick's amorous attentions drive her away. Jim enters college in Lincoln, Nebraska, and then moves East to attend Harvard. When he returns to Black Hawk two years later, he learns that Ántonia has been duped by Larry Donovan, a flashy railroad man she had sporadically dated years before, and who had pretended he wanted to marry her. Abandoned by him in Denver, Colorado, pregnant and unwed, she returns to her mother's farm outside Black Hawk and resumes her hardworking routine. In due course she gives birth to a daughter. After a reunion with Ántonia Jim goes East again to attend Harvard Law School. While he is away Ántonia marries a fellow Bohemian, Anton Cuzak, and has a large family. When Jim comes home 20 years later he visits Ántonia and her husband on the farm they have built. He finds her worn down but thoroughly satisfied with her lot.

My Last Duchess A DRAMATIC MONOLOGUE by ROBERT BROWNING, published in *Dramatic Lyrics* (1842). Although the poem is apparently based on an incident in the life of Alfonso II, Duke of Ferarra, and set in the 16th century, the historical background takes second place to Browning's interest in the psychology of the speaker. On the point of marrying again, the duke displays a strikingly life-like portrait of his previous wife. It soon becomes obvious that, in his jealous obsession with the duchess, he had resented her vivacity and arranged her murder.

Myers, F(rederic) W(illiam) H(enry) 1843–1901 Poet, critic and psychical researcher. He was born at Keswick and educated at Trinity College, Cambridge, where his academic achievements were exceptionally high. A classics lecturer and fellow of Trinity in 1865, he gave up university teaching to become a school inspector in 1869. His most famous poem, *St Paul* (1867), an exclamatory meditation on the life of the saint, was published in an unusual though not original metre, and was widely parodied. He wrote much ardent, emotional verse on a note of unrest and baffled enquiry, in particular *The Renewal of Youth* (1882). His monograph on WORDSWORTH appeared in 1881 and *Essays, Classical and Modern* in 1883. Myers shared with HENRY SIDGWICK a deep practical interest in the education of women, but his dominant passion was the scientific study of paranormal phenomena and the evidence of life after death. A founder of the Society for Psychical Research in 1882, he contributed to *Phantasms of the Living* (1886) on the nature of apparitions, and his papers on hallucination, mediumship and double personality were the first of their kind. He married Eveleen Tennant in 1880 and was the first Englishman to swim the river below Niagara Falls.

Myers, L(eopold) H(amilton) 1881–1944 Novelist. He was born in Cambridge, and educated at Eton and Cambridge, which he left upon the death of his father, F. W. H. MYERS. A legacy in 1906 gave him financial independence and, except for service at the Board of Trade in World War I, he devoted his life to writing and travel. His first published work was a verse play, *Arvat* (1908), but it was 13 years before he managed to complete his first novel, *The Orissers* (1921). It was followed by *The Clio* (1925). *The Near and the Far* (1929) began a tetralogy set in 16th-century India at the court of the Mogul emperor Akbar. The other volumes are *Prince Jali* (1931), *The Root and the Flower* (1935) and *The Pool of Vishnu* (1940), and the sequence was republished in one volume as *The Near and the Far* in 1943. With profound moral imagination, it uses the setting of a past and idealized society to explore the poverty of contemporary existence, particularly its failure to reconcile material and spiritual values. Myers committed suicide at the age of 63.

Mysteries of Udolpho, The A GOTHIC NOVEL by ANN RADCLIFFE, published in 1794.

The setting is Gascony and the Italian Apennines at the end of the 16th century. Emily de St Aubert is a beautiful girl of Gascon family; after losing her parents, she becomes the ward of her tyrannical aunt, Madame Cheron. Madame Cheron marries Montoni, a sinister character, and disapproves of Emily's attachment to the Chevalier de Valancourt, whose means are too moderate for the aunt's ambitions. Emily is carried off to Montoni's castle, Udolpho, in the Apennines, where frightening and apparently supernatural occurrences are frequent. Montoni's cruelty brings about the aunt's death and he then turns his attentions to Emily. She manages to escape, however, and returns to Gascony, where she is eventually united with her chevalier. The evil Montoni, who has been pillaging the countryside from his sinister castle, is captured and brought to justice.

The combination of terrifying incidents which befall the heroine and lavishly PICTURESQUE settings made for a potent and distinctive formula. In its own age *The Mysteries of Udolpho* was one of the most popular of all Gothic novels, and it has never entirely lost its appeal.

Mystery of Edwin Drood, The CHARLES DICKENS's last novel, left unfinished at his death in June 1870. Only six of the projected 12 monthly numbers were written.

Dickens had planned to write a mystery story, set chiefly in the cathedral city of Cloisterham (closely modelled on Rochester). John Jasper leads a double life as cathedral choirmaster and opium addict, travelling secretly to a London opium den to satisfy his craving. Edwin Drood, on whose mysterious disappearance the story was to have centred, is Jasper's nephew; he was betrothed as a child to Rosa Bud, but the couple are not in love and their engagement is dissolved. Jasper nurses a passion for Rosa. Edwin vanishes on Christmas Eve after a ferocious thunderstorm.

There have been many attempts to complete the novel and much speculation as to its DÉNOUEMENT. Most commentators have presumed that Drood has been murdered by Jasper. Other matters are less clear, notably the role which would have been played by Neville and Helena Landless, the orphaned twins who have come to live with Mr Crisparkle in Cloisterham, and the true identity of Dick Datchery, the obviously disguised detective who arrives in Cloisterham to investigate Drood's disappearance just as Dickens's fragment breaks off.

mystery plays See MIRACLE PLAYS.

mystical writing Medieval religious prose dealing with personal spiritual experiences. The 12th century saw an introspective and individual approach to religion, in reaction against the absolute authority of the church and its role as an essential mediator between man and God at a time when it had become corrupt and embroiled in secular politics. The mystical writers describe widely different experiences and attitudes, but in general they were wholly orthodox. They did not seek doctrinal or social change in any form, and although a tension between the teachings of the church and the writings of the mystics may sometimes be discerned their allegiance to the church is usually emphasized. Mystical writing is the only genre in which the work of women authors was prominent in the Middle Ages. See also *THE CLOUD OF UNKNOWING*, WALTER HILTON, JULIAN OF NORWICH, MARGERY KEMPE, RICHARD ROLLE.

mythopoeic criticism See FRYE, NORTHROP.

N-town cycle See MIRACLE PLAYS.

Nabokov, Vladimir 1899–1977 American novelist, short-story writer and poet. He was born into a wealthy and prominent family in St Petersburg. His father, a member of the Russian Constituent Assembly, moved the family to exile in 1919, following the start of the Bolshevik Revolution and the White army's defeat in the Crimea. Nabokov studied modern languages at Trinity College, Cambridge, in 1919–22 and, while living in Berlin and Paris, produced a critically acclaimed canon of poems, short stories and novels written in Russian and published under the pseudonym of V. Sirin: *Mashen'ka* (1926), *Korol', Dama, Valet* (1928), *Zashchita Luzhina* (1930), *Soglyadatay* (1930), *Podvig* (1932), *Kamera Obskura* (1932–3), *Otchayanie* (1936), *Priglashenie na Kazn'* (1938) and *Dar* (1937–8).

The second phase of his career began in 1940 when he emigrated to America and settled in Boston. While teaching Russian literature at Wellesley College, he published his first novel in English, *The Real Life of Sebastian Knight* (1941), and wrote many of his short stories and poems, which appeared in periodicals

Vladimir Nabokov

such as *THE NEW YORKER*. His second novel was *Bend Sinister* (1947). In 1948 he became professor of Russian literature at Cornell and during his tenure there published his first memoir, *Conclusive Evidence* (1951; expanded and revised as *Speak, Memory*, 1966). The success of *LOLITA* (1955), which grew from the underground cult status of a book which might be prosecuted on its publication in the USA to the crititical acclaim of a serious masterpiece, enabled him to move to Switzerland. While working steadily on his translation of Pushkin's *Eugene Onegin* (1964), he wrote three more novels: *Pnin* (1957), about an émigré teacher as baffled by the USA as the hero of *Lolita*; *Pale Fire* (1962), which ingeniously explores the discrepancies between John Shade's autobiographical poem and the commentary by its posthumous editor, Charles Kinbote; and *Ada, or Ardor: A Family Chronicle* (1969), another 'edited' text of maze-like design, set in Amerussia on the planet Antiterra. *Nabokov's Dozen* (1958) and *Nabokov's Quartet* (1966) are collections of short stories. He also supervised the translation of his Russian novels by his son Dimitri. *The Enchanter*, a novella showing links with *Lolita*, was lost for 30 years and published in 1987.

Nahal, Chaman 1927– Indian novelist. He is best known for a sequence of novels dealing with Partition and its aftermath, using historical figures such as Gandhi as well as fictional creations. *Azadi* (1975) describes Hindus, Muslims and Sikhs living peacefully together in the Punjab until Partition turned neighbours into enemies. *The Crown and the Loincloth* (1981) and *The Salt of Life* (1990) show Gandhi's movement in action. *The Last of the Tricolour* will complete the quartet. Nahal has also written a satirical novel, *The English Queens* (1979), and a volume of stories, *The Weird Dance* (1965).

Naipaul, Shiva(dhar) (Srinivasa) 1945–85 Trinidadian novelist and journalist. The younger brother of V. S. NAIPAUL, he was born in Port of Spain. *Fireflies* (1970) and *The Chip-Chip Gatherers* (1973) satirize the wilting of Hindu culture among Trinidadians of Indian origin, though with compassion for the deracinated; chilling despair characterizes *A Hot Country* (1983), about a corrosive colonialist past producing an 'independent' future of nullity. *North of South* (1978) reports sardonically on travel in Africa, *Black and White* (1980) on American subcultures and the People's Temple mass suicides in Guyana in 1978. *Beyond the Dragon's Mouth* (1984) collects journalism, autobiography and stories.

Naipaul, Sir **V(idiadhar) S(urajprasad)** 1932–
Trinidadian novelist and travel writer, of Indian descent. Born in Chaguanas, he was educated at the Queen's Royal College, Trinidad, and University College, Oxford. He has lived in Britain since 1950 but travelled widely. His fastidious, sardonic novels express a profound concern with 20th-century uncertainties and the damaging effects of imperialism. His first three books are satirical but genial: *The Mystic Masseur* (1957), *The Suffrage of Elvira* (1958) and *Miguel Street* (1959) mock and delight in, respectively, a colonial politician's career, the running of a Trinidadian election and the antics of neighbourhood characters. *A HOUSE FOR MR BISWAS* (1961) portrays a nonentity, simultaneously absurd and heroic, barely establishing a distinctive personality for himself. *Mr Stone and the Knights Companion* (1963), set in England, is a study of human potential blighted by commercial, urban influences. *THE MIMIC MEN* (1967) shows a growing interest in larger political themes. *In a Free State* (1971), which won the BOOKER PRIZE, suggests that all modern notions of 'freedom' are illusions, while the main characters of *Guerrillas* (1975) are rootless. On an extensive, tragic scale, *A Bend in the River* (1979) proclaims the corruptibility of mankind, the fallibility of most 20th-century shibboleths, yet also the human ability to survive. *The Enigma of Arrival* (1987) is a slow-moving, forensically observed dramatization of the English countryside. *A Flag on the Island* (1967) collects his short stories.

Much of his non-fiction is closely related to his novels. *The Middle Passage* (1962) is about a return journey to the Caribbean and *The Loss of El Dorado* (1969) about the history of the West Indies. His travels in India have produced *An Area of Darkness* (1964), about an anguished and ultimately fruitless search for roots, and *India: A Wounded Civilization* (1977), prompted by the state of emergency. The place of religion in modern societies also exercises his sceptical consideration in *Among the Believers* (1981), about the Islamic cultures of Iran, Pakistan, Malaysia and Indonesia, and *A Turn in the South* (1989), about evangelical Christianity in the American South. *Finding the Centre* (1984) contains a memoir of his father, while *The Overcrowded Barracoon* (1972) and *The Return of Eva Perón* (1980) collect shorter pieces of non-fiction. He was knighted in 1990.

Nairne, Carolina, Baroness 1766–1845 Scottish poet. Carolina Oliphant was the daughter of a Jacobite family of Perthshire and married Major William Nairne, who became 5th Baron Nairne in 1824. She is remembered as a songwriter and song collector. In the former activity her Jacobite sympathies are plain, in the latter her tendency was to refine the robust lyrical strength of Scotland which remained intact in the hands of ROBERT BURNS. Most of her work was contributed anonymously to *The Scottish Minstrel* (1821–4); it was collected after her death and published as *Lays from Strathearn* (1846). Among her songs are 'Will Ye No Come Back Again?', 'The Auld Hoose', 'The Rowan Tree', 'The Land o' the Leal', 'The Laird of Cockpen', 'Caller Herrin' and 'Charlie is My Darling'.

Naked and the Dead, The A novel by NORMAN MAILER, published in 1948 when the author was 25. Set on a Pacific island during World War II, the story reflects in numerous brutally naturalistic combat scenes Mailer's own army experiences; it won quick acclaim as one of the best personal accounts to emerge from the war. But the major concern of the book centres not on the campaign against the Japanese but on the disparate and often desperate political and moral philosophies of the fighting men – on the problems of the pluralistic American society from which they have emerged. Mailer focuses on 13 characters, whose civilian lives are recalled through flashbacks. The men are thus characterized as carrying not only the weapons of war but also the weight of their pasts – of economic, radical and religious tensions. Mailer's cynicism about America's past and his doubts about its post-war future are expressed largely through the clash between General Cummings, who holds that enlisted men must be made into automatons, and Lieutenant Hearn, a rich, educated and confused liberal who finds that he cannot argue with true conviction his hope for the survival of a democratic spirit. Rough in language, violent in action, and hostile towards mainstream American values, the novel foreshadows much of Mailer's later writings.

Narayan, R(asipuram) K(rishnaswami) 1907–
Indian novelist. He was born in Madras. His deceptively simple English and ironic outlook make him particularly accessible to Western readers, though the unobtrusive, wry moral thrust of his fiction also aligns it with traditional Indian story-telling. *Swami and Friends* (1935) and *The Bachelor of Arts* (1937) are episodic novels about boyhood and youthful self-exploration. While *The Dark Room* (1938) treats Hindu marriage sombrely, *The English Teacher* (1945; as *Grateful to Life and Death* in the USA, 1953) celebrates fulfilled union, psychically extended after the wife's death. Malgudi, Narayan's fictional South Indian town, provides a solid, realistic setting for his tragicomedy of human aberration and attainments – with locals overreaching themselves, like the printer in *Mr Sampath* (1949; as *The Printer of Malgudi* in the USA, 1955) and the pavement moneylender in *The Financial Expert* (1952), or cyclonic outsiders causing havoc, like the demonic taxidermist in *The Man-Eater of Malgudi* (1962) and the family-planning woman official in *The Painter of Signs* (1976). *Waiting for the Mahatma* (1955) tolerantly exposes the mixed motives of some of Gandhi's followers. Narayan's irony is

R. K. Narayan

at its best in *The Guide* (1958), as a loquacious trick-ster is 'tricked' into becoming a holy man, and *The Sweet Vendor* (1967; as *The Vendor of Sweets* in the USA), in which a sweet manufacturer seeks self-con-trol by conquering taste. Transparently clear narra-tive itself becomes a device for satirizing human follies in a tiger's 'autobiography', *A Tiger for Malgudi* (1983). Narayan has also published numerous vol-umes of short stories, a genial autobiography, *My Days* (1975), and *The World of Nagaraj* (1990).

Nasby, Petroleum V(esuvius) [Locke, David Ross] 1833–88 American humorist and journalist. In the style of ARTEMUS WARD and BILLINGS, he specialized in facetious letters-to-the-editor and achieved a wide audience with the series first published in the *Jeffersonian* of Findlay, Ohio, and collected as *The Nasby Papers* (1864). It ridiculed the Confederate cause in the Civil War by loudly proclaiming its right-eousness in the silliest way possible. Locke became editor and later owner of the Toledo *Blade*, in which he continued to publish letters under his pseudonym. He also wrote a political novel, *The Demagogue* (1881).

Nash, Ogden 1902–71 American poet. He was born in Rye, New York, and educated at Harvard. His light verse shows him a master of IRONY, adept at question-ing the commonplace in American life and finding humour in social assumptions, domestic problems,

even the nature of grammar and prosody itself. Though critics often neglect Nash, other 20th-century poets have frequently admired and been influenced by him. His books include *Cricket of Cavador* (1925), *Free Wheeling* (1931), *The Bad Parents' Garden of Verse* (1936), *I'm a Stranger Here Myself* (1938), *Good Intentions* (1942), *Versus* (1949), *Family Reunion* (1950), *Everyone But Thee and Me* (1962), *Marriage Lines* (1964), *Merrill Lynch We Roll Along* (1965), *Bed Riddance: A Posy for the Indisposed* (1970) and the posthumous *A Penny Saved is Impossible* (1981).

Nashe [Nash]**, Thomas** 1567–1601 Satirist, pam-phleteer and playwright. Nashe graduated from St John's College, Cambridge, in 1586. After a tour through France and Italy he settled in London in 1588 and joined the circle of writers that included ROBERT GREENE. His first published work was a stern review of recent literature prefaced to Greene's *Menaphon* (1589), which attacks plagiarism from classical au-thors and ranting tragedies, and praises SPENSER and PEELE as well as Greene. *The Anatomy of Absurdity* (1589) is another piece of SATIRE on contemporary lit-erature, attacking artificiality in romances. These early works display a fashionable EUPHUISM and Nashe confessed in a later work: '*Euphues* I read when I was a little ape in Cambridge.'

Various anti-Puritan pamphlets in the Marprelate controversy have been assigned to him (see MARPRELATE, MARTIN), but only *An Almond for a Parrot* (1590) with any certainty. Nashe was also in-volved in a personal controversy with GABRIEL HARVEY and his brother Richard. Richard attacked Nashe for presumption in the preface to *Menaphon* and Nashe replied in *PIERCE PENNILESS HIS SUPPLICATION TO THE DEVIL* (1592). Gabriel Harvey gave a bitter account of the last days of Greene in *Four Letters* (1592), prompt-ing Nashe's defence of his dead friend in *Four Letters Confuted* (also known as *Strange News of the Intercepting of Certain Letters*; 1593). An attempt at peace-making is to be found in *Christ's Tears over Jerusalem* (1593), his most serious prose work, which offers the fall of Jerusalem as a warning to Londoners. Harvey contributed *Pierce's Supererogation* (1593) and Nashe replied in *Have with You to Saffron Walden* (1596), which added Wrinkle de Crinkledum to the splendid list of absurd names he found for his adversary. The pamphlet war was eventually brought to an end by the decree of Archbishop Whitgift and Bishop Bancroft in 1599 ordering confiscation of books by the two men.

Nashe's prose writings manifest a racy and collo-quial diction, grotesque characterizations, fantasy and a dislike of foreigners and Puritans. They are often brilliantly inventive linguistically, but there is a general lack of coherence. The loose PICARESQUE struc-ture of *THE UNFORTUNATE TRAVELLER* (1594) suited him best and has helped make this proto-novel his most admired work. *The Terrors of the Night* (1594) is a series of visions and an account of demons, spirits and superstitions. *Nashe's Lenten Stuff* (1599), a mock panegyric of a red herring, contains a vivid description of Yarmouth and a splendid burlesque of the story of Hero and Leander.

Summer's Last Will and Testament was written for private performance at Croydon, perhaps for Whitgift's household, in the late summer of 1592. It has motifs from folk drama. Summer, attended by the seasons, classical deities and Harvest, makes his will. Among the characters is Will Summers, Henry VIII's fool who died in 1560, who opens the play and comments on its action. The play contains the poignant lament on transcience, 'Adieu, farewell earth's bliss'. The title-page of *The Tragedy of Dido Queen of Carthage* (1594) makes Nashe co-author with CHRISTOPHER MARLOWE. *The Isle of Dogs*, performed in 1597, is lost. The Privy Council suppressed it as lewd and seditious, searched Nashe's lodgings and arrested several of the suspected authors, including BEN JONSON.

Nathan, George Jean 1882–1958 American editor and critic. He was born in Fort Wayne, Indiana, and educated at Cornell. In 1908 he began contributing to *Smart Set*, and in 1914 became its editor in partnership with H. L. MENCKEN, with whom he founded the detective magazine THE BLACK MASK in 1920 and THE AMERICAN MERCURY in 1924 and contributed to it from 1924 to 1930 and from 1940 to 1951. In 1934 he helped to found the New York Drama Critics' Circle, and was president of the group from 1937 to 1939. His works include plays, *The Eternal Mystery* (1913), *Heliogabalus* (with Mencken, 1920) and *The Avon Flows* (1937), and the annual record of the New York stage, *The Theatre Book of the Year* (1943–51).

Nation, The An American weekly magazine, first published in 1865. Those who sponsored it were concerned with securing full rights for the newly freed American blacks, a concern recorded prominently in the early issues. The National Association for the Advancement of Colored People was first housed in *The Nation*'s office in New York. In its early years it consisted almost entirely of political commentary and literary reviews, but by the 1920s it came to include original works of literature. The first editor was E. L. Godkin, an Anglo-Irish journalist. Subsequent editors have included WILLIAM LLOYD GARRISON, Paul Elmer More, Oswald Garrison Villard, Freda Kirchway, Carey McWilliams and Victor Navasky.

National Theatre See ROYAL NATIONAL THEATRE.

Native Son A novel by RICHARD WRIGHT, published in 1940. It recounts the story of Bigger Thomas, a black ghetto dweller on the south side of Chicago, who is hired by a wealthy family as their chauffeur. The family's spoiled, liberal-leaning daughter, Mary, and her Communist boyfriend, Jan, befriend him. One night, after Mary has had too much to drink, and while Bigger with the best of intentions is getting her back to her room, he accidentally smothers her with a pillow. A black man with a white woman's death on his hands, he knows that it matters little that his act was not intended, and tries to escape. He goes to his girlfriend for help, but realizing that she is too distraught by the murder to trust him, he kills her too and is soon caught. Waiting in jail for his trial, he feels for the first time a sense of freedom in having successfully carried out an act he was impelled to do by the social conditions from which he arose. His Communist lawyer, Max, shows him what real emotional connection with a white person can be. Max tries to make him talk about the social conditions which led to his acts, but Bigger is too proud to do anything more than affirm that 'what I killed for, I am!'

Natural History of Religion, The One of the *Four Dissertations* by DAVID HUME, published in 1757.

Hume examines the theoretical argument that leads to theism and the mental processes from which religion arises. In primitive societies, religious beliefs spring not from any specific instinct, but from the fear of death or pain and the desire for security and pleasure: God is simply a particular providence, not the author of nature. By further insisting that polytheism preceded monotheism in the development of religious beliefs, he concludes that the existence of God cannot be proved by reason.

naturalism A term generally applied to art which seeks to adhere to nature. More strictly, it refers to the scientifically based extension of REALISM propounded by Émile Zola in the 1870s and 1880s in essays such as 'Naturalism in the Theatre' and 'The Experimental Novel', and exemplified in his hugely popular cycle of *Rougon-Macquart* novels, which chart the social and genetic development of a single family through several generations of legitimate and illegitimate descendants. In naturalist writing, medical and evolutionary theories of 19th-century science inform readings of human character and social interactions, which are seen as being genetically and historically determined. The struggle of the individual to adapt to environment, the fight for the spouse and the Darwinian idea of the survival of the fittest become central concerns of naturalist fiction and drama.

Inspired by Zola's writing, André Antoine founded the Théâtre Libre in Paris in 1887 and staged plays, including Tolstoy's *Powers of Darkness*, Strindberg's *Miss Julie*, Ibsen's *Ghosts* and Hauptmann's *The Weavers*, which were informed by naturalist ideas and which subsequently became standard works in the new European independent theatres. Plays in

English which invoke naturalist ideas about social and genetic inheritance and the struggle for survival include SYNGE's *RIDERS TO THE SEA* (1904) and GALSWORTHY's *Strife* (1909). Naturalist ideas occur in HARDY's novels and underpin GISSING's *NEW GRUB STREET* (1891) and GEORGE MOORE's *ESTHER WATERS* (1894) but are less evident in Britain than in America, where THEODORE DREISER, JACK LONDON and STEPHEN CRANE in *MAGGIE* (1893) are the notable naturalist writers.

Nature A book by RALPH WALDO EMERSON, developed from his early lectures, and published in 1836. In it he sets forth the main principles of TRANSCENDENTALISM, postulating the need for 'an original relation to the universe' and rejecting timeworn attitudes to God and Nature. He elaborates on his conception of Nature as the expression of a divine will, asserting the need for man to establish a relationship with Nature that will allow him to take advantage of its spiritual self-governance, and thereby to reunite himself with his own spiritual source. An expanded second edition was published in 1849.

Naughton, Bill 1910– Playwright. After working as a lorry driver and weaver in Lancashire, he started to write novels and short stories in the 1940s. His upbringing in Bolton provided the background for two gentle, ironic comedies, *All in Good Time* (1963) and *Spring and Port Wine* (1964), making him the natural successor to the dramatists of the Manchester School, STANLEY HOUGHTON, HAROLD BRIGHOUSE and later WALTER GREENWOOD. But his range was wider than that of Lancashire comedy. *Alfie* (1963) concerned a Cockney 'wide boy' with a gift for 'pulling the birds'. His philandering was presented with a cool sense of tragic waste, in sobering retort to ANN JELLICOE's *The Knack*, which made a similar philandering parable for the Swinging Sixties. Naughton also attempted Orwellian SATIRE, *He was Gone When We Got There* (1966), and wrote his autobiography, *Pony Boy*, in 1966.

Nazareth, Peter 1940– Ugandan novelist, playwright and literary critic. Born to Goan parents in Kampala, he studied at Makerere University College and in Britain at the University of Leeds. He worked in Entebbe from 1965 until 1973, when his first novel, *In a Brown Mantle* (1972), won him a Seymour Lustman Fellowship at Yale. A second novel, *The General is Up* (1984) has appeared in Canada. He currently teaches at the University of Iowa. *Brave New World*, a play dramatizing the confusions of the elite in modern Africa, was included in *Origin East Africa* (1965). It became the first East African play to be produced by the BBC African Theatre, which went on to broadcast *The Hospital* and *X*, published in 1976. Nazareth's view of the role of literature in Africa and the Third World as

a reflection of the hopes, fears and tensions of the ex-colonial experience is made clear in his literary criticism: *Literature and Society in Modern Africa* (1972), *The Third World Writer: His Social Responsibility* (1978) and *A Fene Fele* (1984).

Ndebele, Njabulo S(imakahle) 1949– South African short-story writer, critic and poet. Born in Western Native Township, Johannesburg, and brought up in Charterston Location near Nigel in the Transvaal (the setting for most of his stories), he attended the universities of Botswana, Cambridge and Denver, Colorado. He is currently vice-rector of the University of the Western Cape. In both his critical work, collected in *Rediscovery of the Ordinary* (1991), and his stories, some of which are collected in *Fools and Other Stories* (1983), he shows a desire to move beyond the representation of what he calls the 'spectacular' aspects of life under apartheid to depict the 'ordinary', by which he means the daily routines, individual experiences and inner feelings which survive despite deprivation and horror. Both his fiction and criticism have been greeted as a landmark in South African writing.

Neale, John Mason 1818–66 Church historian and hymn writer. Born in London, Neale was educated at Sherborne School and Trinity College, Cambridge. A convinced High Churchman, he was in

Njabulo Ndebele

sympathy with the Oxford Movement and opposed to liberal tendencies in the Church of England. With his friend Benjamin Webb he founded the Cambridge Camden Society for the study of ecclesiastical art in 1839. He was the author of *A History of the Holy Eastern Church* (1847–50) and a number of hymns, some translated from Greek and Latin originals, which were eventually edited by M. S. Lawson as *Collected Hymns, Sequences and Carols* (1914). They include 'O Happy Band of Pilgrims', 'Art Thou Weary?', 'Good Christian Men, Rejoice', 'Good King Wenceslaus' and 'Jerusalem the Golden'. A novel, *Theodora Pranza*, recounts the fall of Christian Constantinople; it was serialized in 1853–4 and published in volume form in 1857.

negative capability A term coined by John Keats to describe the quality he thought essential to the poet: 'when man is capable of being in uncertainties, Mysteries, doubts, without any irritable reaching after fact & reason' (letter to George and Tom Keats, 21–27 December 1817). The same letter goes on to cite Shakespeare as the supreme example of negative capability and to note its absence in Coleridge, who 'would let go by a fine isolated verisimilitude caught from the penetralium of Mystery, from being incapable of remaining content with half-knowledge'. Milton and Wordsworth are elsewhere classed with Coleridge, while Keats's original discussion concludes: 'with a great poet the sense of Beauty overcomes every other consideration, or rather obliterates all consideration'.

Neilson, John Shaw 1872–1942 Australian poet. Born at Penola, South Australia, Neilson received little formal education and worked as a manual labourer. After the publication of his first two volumes, *Old Granny Sullivan* (1916) and *Heart of Spring* (1919), he was awarded a small literary pension (1922). Poor health and bad eyesight dogged him in later life, but his poetry reflected his dreary circumstances only in displaying an enhanced pity and tenderness for suffering. Later volumes were *Ballad and Lyrical Poems* (1923), *New Poems* (1927), *Collected Poems* (1934), *Beauty Imposes* (1938) and the posthumous edition, *Unpublished Poems of Shaw Neilson* (1947).

Nemerov, Howard 1920– American poet, novelist, short-story writer and critic. He was born in New York and educated at Harvard. After graduation he joined the Royal Canadian Air Force and, in 1944, the US Army Air Force. His first volume, *The Image and the Law* (1947), established many of the preoccupations which characterize his work, notably an interest in moral and philosophical complexities. Subsequent volumes such as *Guide to the Ruins* (1950), *The Salt Garden* (1955), *Small Moment* (1957), *Mirrors and Windows* (1958) and *New and Selected Poems* (1960)

helped to secure his growing reputation. His fiction, which often explores moral problems in modern society, includes *Commodity of Dreams and Other Stories* (1959), *Stories, Fables and Other Diversions* (1971) and three novels: *The Melodramatists* (1949), *Federigo: or, The Power of Love* (1954) and *The Homecoming Game* (1957). His criticism appears in *Poetry and Fiction: Essays* (1963), *Reflexions on Poetry and Poetics* (1972), *Figures of Thought: Speculations on the Meaning of Poetry and Other Essays* (1978) and *New and Selected Essays* (1985). *Journal of the Fictive Life* (1965) is a novelistic, autobiographical self-examination throwing light on his own work and the creative process. Later volumes of poetry include *Departure of the Ships* (1966), *The Blue Swallows* (1967), *A Sequence of Seven* (1967), *The Winter Lightning: Selected Poems* (1968), *Gnomes and Occasions* (1972), *The Western Approaches: Poems 1973–1975* (1975), *The Collected Poems* (1977, Pulitzer Prize), *Sentences* (1980), *Inside the Onion* (1984), *War Stories: Poems about Long Ago and Now* (1987) and *Trying Conclusions: New and Selected Poems, 1961–1991* (1991). He has also written plays, including *Endor* (1962). A recipient of the National Book Award and the Bollingen Prize, Nemerov was made chancellor of the American Academy of Poets in 1977 and served as US Poet Laureate in 1988–90. He is presently Distinguished Professor of English at Washington University in St Louis.

Nennius See Arthurian literature.

neoclassicism A term for the ideas about art and literature which evolved during the 17th and 18th centuries under the influence of the classical (i.e. Graeco-Roman) tradition.

The survival of classical texts and their transmission to the Renaissance was often haphazard and fortuitous. The satirist Horace (65–8 BC) and the Latin theorists of rhetoric arrived fairly intact but the *Poetics* of Aristotle (384–322 BC), with its discussion of tragedy, survived only in a fragment. It was not until a gradual revival of interest among Italian scholars in the 15th and 16th centuries that many works were recovered. An interest in oratory and education in rhetoric progressively led Renaissance critics to the matter of poetry *per se*. By the end of the 16th century, on the Continent at least, Aristotle was established as the presiding genius of classical criticism, while the philosophy of Plato (427–347 BC) was beginning to attract new commentaries.

In England the classical theory of literature made itself felt in Sir Philip Sidney's *Apology for Poetry* (1595), but it was not until the beginning of the 17th century that such harking-back became current. Ben Jonson was an early and erudite poet in the classical mode, imitating Martial and Juvenal, and taking an interest in the theories of dramatic action derived from Aristotle. He was followed in this respect by DRYDEN, both in his criticism – notably his *ESSAY OF DRAMATIC POESY* (1668) – and in his plays, which show him as one of the first (and very few) major dramatists in English to temper SHAKESPEARE's abundance by observing the strict neoclassical unities of time, place and action.

Although there was never any concerted body of neoclassical principles as such, writers of the AUGUSTAN AGE shared a common ground in their response to the writings of the various ancients. They agreed in admiring the concision, elegance, good taste and WIT of their classical predecessors. Their poetry emulated the intelligent articulacy of Horace's verse epistles, or the vituperative energy of Juvenal's SATIRE, or the heroic elevation of Homer's EPIC. Their theory of literature was shaped by a composite classical influence in which the names of Aristotle and Horace stand out. It followed Aristotle's *Poetics* in making the classification of genres a foremost consideration and agreed with Horace's *Ars poetica* in several vital tenets: the need to discipline the creative impulse by practice and self-control, the usefulness of imitating past models of excellence, the desirability of a literary decorum that matches content to style, and the aim of combining pleasure with instruction. POPE's *ESSAY ON CRITICISM* (1711) is representative of neoclassical concern with artistry and structure; as are FIELDING's Preface to *JOSEPH ANDREWS* (1742), several of JOHNSON's *RAMBLER* papers (1750–2) and his superlative *Preface to Shakespeare* (1765).

Such theoretical enquiry into the methods and rules of composition stimulated wider interests derived to some extent from the Graeco-Roman tradition: in the connection between nature and art and between the various sister arts, for example, and in the various relations of imagination and reason, taste and sense, originality and imitation, beauty and pleasure. These manifested themselves in discussion of several topics: the merit of ancient versus modern literature (typified by SIR WILLIAM TEMPLE's essay *Upon Ancient and Modern Learning*, 1690); the functions of satire (Dryden's *Discourse*, 1693); the pleasures of the imagination (ADDISON in *THE SPECTATOR*, 1712, and, later, MARK AKENSIDE); and the *ut pictura poesis*, as exemplified in Dryden's *Parallel betwixt Poetry and Painting* (1695).

Behind such theorizing there lay an essential fascination with the systematic principles of art, but as the 18th century progressed an interest in the universal aspects of nature itself came to predominate over any notion of artistic rules. BURKE's essay on the *Sublime and the Beautiful* (1757) is just one text which shows less concern for artistic systems than for the spirit or quality of an individual work: 'truth', 'wit' or 'beauty' were more important than the technical correlation of stylistic components. In this way, in fits and starts over the course of several decades, European sensibility shifted its attention to the human faculties involved in art: the workings of the mind and the imagination, and the nature of genius. By the middle of the 18th century poetry written by recipe and formulaic regulations had become stale and outworn. The formal stimulus of the classical revival weakened. By concentrating attention on the poet rather than his audience, his mind rather than his medium, and the nature that was his matter rather than the art which manifested his genius, the later decades of the 18th century moved away from the general body of inherited classical principles towards the poetic which is usually labelled ROMANTICISM.

Nesbit, E(dith) 1858–1924 Writer of CHILDREN's LITERATURE. Born in London, the youngest daughter of an agricultural chemist, Edith had an unsettled childhood, receiving her education in Britain, France and Germany. Turning to hack literary work after marrying young and in poverty, she eventually discovered her true talent for writing lively family stories unburdened with the heavy moralizing of earlier writers. Her first great success, *The Story of the Treasure Seekers* (1899), concerned the Bastable children and their mini-adventures, often in search of extra pocket money. Succeeding books (written at a great rate but always with a sensitive ear for children's dialogue) mix fantasy with reality, most successfully in *The Phoenix and the Carpet* (1904) and *The Story of the Amulet* (1906). Both involve time-travel, later a staple ingredient of children's literature. But her most famous novel, *The Railway Children* (1906), has a more realistic setting. The title characters are forced to retreat to the countryside after the arrest of their father on a trumped-up charge. There they make friends with the local railway porter Perks, a character whom Nesbit, as a Fabian socialist, treats sympathetically rather than as a figure of fun. The story also involves a political refugee, theft, misplaced charity and fierce family loyalty – powerful ingredients for young readers, though always balanced by romantic adventures, fortunate coincidences and happy endings. Towards the end of her life her writing lost popularity but made a triumphant comeback for later generations, still selling well today and popular in film and television adaptations.

New Age, The A journal founded in 1907 by two members of the Fabian Arts Group, Holbrook Jackson (1874–1948) and A. R. Orage (1873–1934), with financial support from GEORGE BERNARD SHAW. Under Orage's editorship until 1922 it published regular contributions from Shaw, ARNOLD BENNETT and J. C. SQUIRE but also lived up to its name by welcoming MODERNISM and recruiting new talents like EZRA POUND, KATHERINE MANSFIELD, T. E. HULME and EDWIN MUIR. It was *The New Age* which introduced Freud's psychoanalytic theories to the British reading public.

New Apocalypse, The A literary movement which flourished in Britain just before and during World War II in reaction against the committed rationalism of AUDEN's generation. Responding to what they saw as a crisis in European civilization, writers of the New Apocalypse reinterpreted Freud and Marx in the light of D. H. LAWRENCE's *Apocalypse* (1931) and accommodated diverse strands of a European non-rational impulse, principally EXPRESSIONISM and surrealism, within British literary culture. Key figures were J. F. HENDRY, who introduced *The New Apocalypse* (1939), an anthology of verse, prose and criticism, and HENRY TREECE, who joined Hendry as editor of two further anthologies, *The White Horseman* (1941) and *The Crown and the Sickle* (1943). Poems by G. S. FRASER, NICHOLAS MOORE, NORMAN MACCAIG and VERNON WATKINS appeared in their pages. Hendry published a major statement of the movement's aims in *Myth and Social Integration* (1940), while Treece contributed a collection of essays, *How I See Apocalypse* (1946). DYLAN THOMAS was also associated with the movement.

New Atlantis, The An unfinished Utopian fiction by FRANCIS BACON, posthumously published in 1627. It recounts the discovery by English mariners of an island in the Pacific called Bensalem. Bacon describes a high civilization of great antiquity, coeval with Plato's lost Atlantis, that has long isolated itself from the world in order to preserve its integrity. The island has, however, received the gospel of Christianity by miraculous means. Bacon's chief intention in devising this fiction is to introduce his ideal design for a college of sciences, here given the name of Salomon's House or the College of the Six Days' Works, for its purpose is the study of the entire physical creation. The College is publicly financed, and its members engage in cooperative research. The scope of its activities includes physics, chemistry, mechanics, astronomy, agriculture and medicine; the work is experimental, and the results advance the knowledge and enhance the life of the people of Bensalem. 'The end of our foundation is the knowledge of causes, and secret motions of things, and the enlarging of the bounds of human empire, to the effecting of all things possible.' Salomon's House represents the kind of institution that Bacon hoped JAMES I would establish – James liked to be regarded as the British Solomon – in which the programme of experiments that Bacon had suggested in *Sylva Sylvarum* would be carried out, following the methods of scientific enquiry he had laid out in THE ADVANCEMENT OF LEARNING and the *NOVUM ORGANUM*. Nothing came of his proposals in his lifetime, but in the 1650s there were several schemes to realize his design put forward by Samuel Hartlib, ABRAHAM COWLEY and JOHN EVELYN, amongst others. Eventually, Bacon's hopes were in some measure fulfilled by the foundation of the Royal Society in 1660; the Society's programme of research was undoubtedly inspired by the model provided by Salomon's House.

New Bath Guide, The See ANSTEY, CHRISTOPHER.

New Criticism A term first used by the American critic, Joel Spingarn, in an address at Columbia University in 1910 ('The New Criticism') which anticipated the New Criticism of the 1930s and 1940s. Spingarn employed it to describe a modern trend towards scholarship and the application of extra-literary, statistical, stylometric devices. The term was not generally known until JOHN CROWE RANSOM used it (in *The New Criticism*, 1941) to prescribe a new 'ontological' approach to literary studies, as distinct from traditional criticism which had generalized broadly from biographical data and influences. His qualified recognition of the contributions of I. A. RICHARDS, T. S. ELIOT, WILLIAM EMPSON and YVOR WINTERS had the (largely unintentional) effect of promoting them as a new 'movement'. Other critics (including ROBERT PENN WARREN, ALLEN TATE, R. P. Blackmur and CLEANTH BROOKS) were later conscripted, though the group always differed widely in its individual aims. Winters, for instance, had been concerned with the moral aspects of form and style (*In Defence of Reason*, 1947), Brooks with the ambiguity of poetic statement (*The Well-Wrought Urn*, 1947), Blackmur with the larger meanings of language (*Language as Gesture*, 1932).

I. A. Richards (*Practical Criticism*, 1929) and Eliot (*The Use of Poetry and the Use of Criticism*, 1933) were formative influences on F. R. LEAVIS, who applied many of the principles of New Criticism and made an enormous impact on the development of literary studies in England during the same period.

As a general rule, the New Critics may be said to have initiated a view of the text as an autonomous whole, an object with its own inherent structure, which invited rigorous scrutiny. They encouraged an awareness of verbal nuance and thematic organization. Although widely rejected as too limited by many more recent schools, New Criticism still has influence; close reading of the text remains a dominant principle in most literary criticism.

New Grub Street A novel by GEORGE GISSING, published in 1891. Its bleak portrait of the literary world, obviously drawn from Gissing's own years of discouraging struggle, concludes that self-advertisement is a better route to success than any amount of artistic endeavour.

Edward Reardon, the author of two fine books, is hampered by poverty and an unsympathetic wife. Jasper Milvain is a facile and self-interested reviewer. Alfred Yule is a sarcastic, embittered scholar whose learning goes unappreciated. Yule's daughter Marian falls in love with Jasper and, on learning that she has expectations of a legacy, he decides to marry her. When the legacy does not materialize, he withdraws from the engagement. Reardon's wife, Amy, deserts him and this, coupled with his failure to make his mark as a writer, sends him to the grave. Jasper marries the widowed Amy and becomes, in worldly terms, a success.

Other representatives of the literary life are Harold Biffen, earnestly polishing a novel of absolute realism called 'Mr Bailey, Grocer', and Whelpdale, a literary failure who becomes an 'adviser to literary aspirants' and achieves success by thinking up the best name for a magazine full of scraps – a reference to *Tit-Bits*, which had begun publication in 1881.

New Masses, The An American journal founded in 1926 by MICHAEL GOLD, who edited it with Egmont Arens, Joseph Freeman, Hugo Gellert, James Rorty and John Sloan before becoming its sole editor in 1928. Until it ceased publication in 1948 *The New Masses* served as a forum for writers and intellectuals involved with left-wing politics and the Communist party. Among its contributing editors were SHERWOOD ANDERSON, Van Wyck Brooks, MAX EASTMAN, WALDO FRANK, Lewis Mumford, EUGENE O'NEILL, Lola Ridge and CARL SANDBURG. Contributors of fiction, poetry and critical essays included ROBINSON JEFFERS, HORACE GREGORY and KENNETH FEARING.

New Negro, The An anthology of essays, stories, a play, and extensive bibliographies of black American writers, edited by ALAIN LOCKE and published in 1925. It served as a manifesto of the HARLEM RENAISSANCE and gave it an alternative label, the 'New Negro'. In his preface Locke argued that blacks were making progress against prejudice, and that they possessed a new spirit of 'group expression and self-determination' which would in turn enrich American culture as a whole.

New Republic, The An American literary and political journal founded by Herbert Croly in 1914. Its literary editors have included EDMUND WILSON, Malcolm Cowley, Richard Gilman and Reed Whittemore. Though markedly liberal in its politics, it has published literary and critical pieces by writers of various political orientations, including ROBERT FROST, GEORGE SANTAYANA, H. L. MENCKEN, JOHN DOS PASSOS, JOHN CROWE RANSOM, ALLEN TATE, ARCHIBALD MACLEISH, WILLA CATHER, ERNEST HEMINGWAY, EUDORA WELTY, MICHAEL GOLD and WALTER LIPPMAN. From the 1950s the magazine began to print more political commentary and less fiction and poetry.

New Review, The A monthly literary magazine published from 1974 to 1979 under the editorship of IAN HAMILTON, who had founded and edited its prede-cessor, *The Review*. During its short but controversial life, *The New Review* was notable for its consistency of editorial policy and its preference for short, minimalist poems. It published the verse of JAMES FENTON and CRAIG RAINE, the irreverent prose of JULIAN BARNES and Clive James, and the fiction of IAN McEWAN. Typical work can be sampled in *The New Review Anthology* (1985).

New Way to Pay Old Debts, A A comedy by PHILIP MASSINGER, based on THOMAS MIDDLETON's *A TRICK TO CATCH THE OLD ONE*, first performed c.1622 and published in 1633.

Sir Giles Overreach, a monster of greed, has succeeded in gaining possession of the property belonging to his prodigal nephew, Frank Wellborn. The destitute Wellborn is helped by Lady Allworth, who makes out that she intends to marry him. On the promise of so good a match, Sir Giles is prepared to advance money to Wellborn. Sir Giles's daughter, Margaret, is less fortunate. Her love for Lady Allworth's stepson, Tom, is frowned on by Sir Giles, because Tom is no more than a page in the service of Lord Lovell. However, Lord Lovell enters into the plot to outwit Sir Giles, who, believing that his daughter is marrying the lord, finds she has married the page. His unbalanced rage is toppled into madness when he learns that his claim on Wellborn's estate cannot be upheld, and he is carried off to Newgate. Lady Allworth marries Lord Lovell, and Wellborn takes a commission in Lovell's regiment.

The character of Overreach was based on that of a contemporary extortioner, Sir Giles Mompesson. It is a famous actor's part (BYRON experienced a kind of fit as a result of Kean's powerful playing of it in 1815), and in the 18th and 19th centuries was often allowed to dominate the play in performance.

New York Review of Books, The An American magazine founded by Robert Silvers and Barbara Epstein to provide book reviews during the New York newspaper strike of 1963. It was financed initially only by revenue from publishers' advertisements. Publishing 22 issues a year in newspaper format, the magazine immediately established itself as a viable addition to the range of review media, specializing in extended essay reviews, often by writers of the left. The *Review* also publishes articles on politics and has been active in protesting against the Vietnam war, the Watergate scandal and, more recently, government policy in Central America. Among its contributors have been Hannah Arendt, J. K. Galbraith, Elizabeth Hardwick, MARY MCCARTHY, NORMAN MAILER, V. S. PRITCHETT, SUSAN SONTAG, I. F. Stone, H. R. Trevor-Roper, GORE VIDAL and EDMUND WILSON. The *Review* has received the compliment of having THE LONDON REVIEW OF BOOKS modelled on it.

New York School A group of American poets, including JOHN ASHBERY, KENNETH KOCH and FRANK O'HARA, which flourished in the 1950s in reaction against the academic austerity of mid-century American poetry. The name acknowledged its connection with the New York abstract-expressionist painters.

New Yorker, The An American weekly magazine founded in 1925 by Harold W. Ross. Many of his contributors, who included Alexander Woolcott, JAMES THURBER, DOROTHY PARKER, ROBERT BENCHLEY, E. B. WHITE, Peter Arno and Charles Addams, were given the security of salaried employment and allowed to develop their gifts at their own pace. The result was a light, witty style which epitomized literary New York in the 1930s. Ross was succeeded in 1951 by William Shawn, who published much notable short fiction, poetry, criticism and non-fiction, as well as maintaining *The New Yorker*'s reputation for sophisticated cartoons. Recent contributors have included TRUMAN CAPOTE, Saul Steinberg, JOHN UPDIKE, DONALD BARTHELME, ALICE MUNRO, John McPhee and Jeremy Bernstein. Robert Gottlieb in 1987 and then Tina Brown have succeeded Shawn as editor.

Newbery, John 1713–67 Publisher specializing in CHILDREN'S LITERATURE. Born in Waltham St Lawrence, Berkshire, Newbery acquired *The Reading Mercury* by marrying the previous owner's widow. In 1744 he moved to London, where he set up shop as a vendor of patent medicines and a publisher. Most of his large output was designed for children, consisting of moral tales with copious woodcut illustrations. His policy of cheap, visually interesting and overtly didactic works was a major influence in educational publishing. He also issued many works by CHRISTOPHER SMART, who married his step-daughter. In 1759 he began to publish *The Public Ledger*, a periodical to which his friends JOHNSON and GOLDSMITH contributed.

Newbolt, Sir Henry (John) 1862–1938 Poet. He was educated at Clifton and Corpus Christi College, Oxford. His many volumes of patriotic BALLADS and lyrics include *The Island Race* (1899), *Admiral's All and Other Verses* (1907), *Clifton Chapel and Other School Poems* (1908), *Songs of Memory and Hope* (1909) and *Drake's Drum and Other Sea Songs* (1919), the title poem of which was set to music by Charles Stanford in *Songs of the Sea*. His *A Naval History of the War, 1914–18* appeared in 1920, and his memoirs, *My World as in My Time*, in 1932.

Newcastle, Margaret Cavendish, Duchess of 1623–74 Biographer, poet and playwright. Born Margaret Lucas, she was an indefatigable writer but is remembered only for her biography of William Cavendish (1592–1676), whom she married in 1645 when he was Marquis of Newcastle. One of the wealthiest peers in England, he served the king faithfully as governor of the Prince of Wales but was dismissed and eventually went to Paris with the queen's suite when she left England at the king's insistence. He was made Duke of Newcastle at the Restoration. His wife's biography (1667) was dismissed as ridiculous by PEPYS but highly praised in later centuries by CHARLES LAMB and VIRGINIA WOOLF. It remains a notable document of its age.

Newcomes, The: *Memoirs of a Most Respectable Family* A novel by W. M. THACKERAY, published in 24 parts between October 1853 and August 1855. The story is told by Arthur Pendennis, the hero of *PENDENNIS*.

Colonel Thomas Newcome is a simple gentleman of the highest honour. His son Clive is in love with his cousin Ethel, daughter of the wealthy banker, Sir Brian Newcome. The union of Clive and Ethel is opposed by most of her relatives – chiefly her mean-minded and snobbish brother Barnes and her grandmother, the Countess of Kew. Yielding to the pressure of her family, Ethel becomes engaged to her cousin, Lord Kew, and then to the spineless and callow Lord Farintosh, but her own character asserts itself and she eventually rejects both of them. Despairing of Ethel, Clive allows himself to be manoeuvred into marrying the daughter of Mrs Mackenzie, a scheming widow. Rosey Mackenzie proves empty-headed and the household is dominated by her mother. When Colonel Newcome loses his fortune he is so bullied and reproached by the vindictive Mrs Mackenzie that he takes refuge in the Greyfriars almshouse, where he dies. Clive's fortunes are restored by the discovery of a will and, with his wife's death, he is presumably free to marry Ethel.

Newgate Calendar, The The title, or generic label, of various 18th- and 19th-century collections describing the careers of notorious criminals. Although they usually claimed to have a moral purpose in recording the downfall of lawbreakers, and sometimes alleged a political purpose in advocating reform of the criminal law, their main interest was always salacious and sensational. The first *Newgate Calendar*, running to five volumes and dealing with crimes from 1700 onwards, appeared in 1774. The lawyers Andrew Knapp and William Baldwin published a second *Newgate Calendar* in four volumes in 1824 and the six-volume *New Newgate Calendar* in 1826, on which GEORGE BORROW worked. The last of the series was C. Pelham's *Chronicles of Crime: or, The New Newgate Calendar* (1886).

Newgate novel A school of crime fiction popular in the 1830s, chiefly associated with the names of

EDWARD BULWER LYTTON and WILLIAM HARRISON AINSWORTH. The Newgate novelists took real-life cases (often from THE NEWGATE CALENDAR) as the source for their plots and pointed to the treatment of crime in the work of FIELDING, GAY and HOGARTH as a respectable precedent. According to their many detractors, however, they portrayed the criminal in a dangerously sympathetic manner. In Bulwer Lytton's *Paul Clifford* (1830) he is the victim of social circumstances, while in the same author's *EUGENE ARAM* (1832) he is a conscience-stricken philosopher. In Ainsworth's *Rookwood* (1834) and *Jack Sheppard* (1839) he becomes a glamorous outlaw. DICKENS's *OLIVER TWIST* (1837-8) and THACKERAY's *CATHERINE* (1839-40) rejected Newgate fiction by offering a harshly realistic view of criminal life.

Newman, John Henry 1801-90 Theologian. Of Huguenot and Jewish descent, Newman was educated privately at Ealing and went, aged 16, to Trinity College, Oxford. In 1822 he was elected to a fellowship at Oriel College and in 1826 became tutor there. The following year he became vicar of St Mary's, Oxford, and in 1832 he resigned his tutorship at the college.

With KEBLE and PUSEY he played a leading part in the OXFORD MOVEMENT, preaching influential sermons at St Mary's in the late 1830s. Afterwards Newman regretted that his influence had been on undergraduates rather than on his parishioners. During this period he defended the Anglican church as the *via media* or middle way between Romanism and popular Protestantism. His researches into early church history led to his publishing, in *TRACTS FOR THE TIMES*, the famous *Tract XC* (1841), which argued that the 39 Articles of the Anglican church were compatible with Catholicism. It was condemned by the Bishop of Oxford, and Newman ceased publishing tracts and gave up being editor of *The British Critic*. In 1842 he set up a monastic community at Littlemore, where he continued his studies of the early church. In 1845 he became the most celebrated of the 19th-century converts from the Church of England to Rome. Many clergy followed him. His effect on the Anglican church was eventually to bring the study of patristics into the Anglican purview.

In 1854 Newman went to Dublin as rector of a new Catholic university, work which occupied him for four disappointing years and prompted an eloquent statement of his view of education in *THE IDEA OF A UNIVERSITY* (1873). CHARLES KINGSLEY's attack on his honesty provoked his *APOLOGIA PRO VITA SUA* (1864; revised 1865), describing the changing convictions which had led him to become a Catholic. In 1870 he published *THE GRAMMAR OF ASSENT*, an argument for religious belief. Newman became a cardinal in 1879.

Newman's poem, *THE DREAM OF GERONTIUS*, and the hymn, 'Lead, Kindly Light', were written in 1832. The latter was first collected in the volume *Lyra*

Apostolica (with KEBLE and ISAAC WILLIAMS; 1836). He also wrote two novels, *Loss and Gain* (1848) and *Callista* (1856).

***News from Nowhere:** or, An Epoch of Rest, being Some Chapters from a Utopian Romance* A prose work by WILLIAM MORRIS, serialized in *The Commonweal* between 11 January and 4 October 1890 and first published in book form later that year in Boston.

The story falls into three sections. Morris dreams of waking in his Hammersmith house amid a Communist society in the early 21st century. He travels through a London so changed that the Houses of Parliament are used as a 'dung market'. The central chapters comprise a detailed discussion with an aged historian, in which the course of history from the 19th century through violent socialist revolution and up to the Utopian present is described. In the concluding chapters Morris journeys up the Thames beyond Oxford to Kelmscott for the hay-making season.

As in *A DREAM OF JOHN BALL* the central dialogue enables Morris to give a critique of his own time, though here his vision of human social potential is more fully developed. The non-industrial society Morris describes draws upon his beloved medieval period in many details. However, the lack of any central government, legal structure and monetary system is part of a classless non-materialist future. The society envisaged is based on 'the religion of humanity', the sanctity of labour and its inseparability from art. *News from Nowhere* proved a seminal work, reappearing nine times (including in Italian translation) before Morris's death in 1896.

newspaper, the rise of the English The early growth of the press was episodic. The first news publications printed in English date from 1620 and came from the Netherlands. Known as corantos (or 'currents' of news), these consisted of a single unfolded sheet carrying two columns of print on each side. They concentrated on international events, a feature of the news section of the press that was to remain true for over two centuries. Both JAMES I and Charles I regarded the development of the press as dangerous and sought to restrict it: in 1632 the Star Chamber prohibited all unauthorized news publications. Stuart suspicion was to some extent justified by the massive expansion of the press that accompanied the English Civil War, when radical opinion was widely disseminated. The response after the Restoration was restraint, the Printing Act of 1662 being based on the theory that the freedom to print was hazardous to the community and dangerous to its ruler, a threat to faith, loyalty and morality.

This restrictive legislation, which limited the number of printers and established a licensing system to enable pre-publication censorship, remained in force until 1695. It did not, however, completely prevent the appearance of newspapers. In 1663 SIR ROGER L'ESTRANGE was appointed Surveyor of the Press, a position he exploited to produce a newsbook entitled *The Intelligencer*. L'Estrange's monopoly was breached two years later by HENRY MUDDIMAN's *Oxford Gazette*, which rapidly became *The London Gazette*, a half-sheet folio that enjoyed a monopoly of printed news until 1678. The Exclusion Crisis, which began in that year, both raised public interest in political news and made government regulation more difficult. By the end of 1679 more papers were being published than at any time since 1649. Many of the features and devices that were to characterize the 18th-century press, such as a paranoid mentality, rigid convictions and a style that exploited humour, offering mock-advertisements, fictional creeds and fake prophecies, were already present. Ministerial papers were founded to challenge the opposition Whig press, but Charles II wished to end a propaganda war rather than to conduct one: the Whig press was stamped out by prosecutions for seditious libel, and the Licensing Act, which had expired in 1679, was revived in 1685. James II continued the policy of regulation, *The Gazette* regaining its monopoly.

The Glorious Revolution of 1688 was not followed by any immediate freeing of the press. William III, no supporter of press liberty in the Netherlands, maintained the machinery of press control and unlicensed works were seized. However, difficulties in the enforcement of the Licensing Act in the early 1690s led to increased doubts about the existing regulatory system. The Act expired in 1695 without any agreement as to how to replace it, and, despite considerable support for the idea of press censorship, successive attempts to revive it over the next two decades failed.

The lapsing of the Licensing Act spurred considerable growth. There were 12 London newspapers by 1712 and 52 by 1811 – a number swelled by Sunday papers, the first of which, *The British Gazette and Sunday Monitor*, was begun in about 1779, and all of which were illegal due to sabbatarian legislation. Circulation also increased rapidly, reaching about 44,000 copies a week in 1704. By 1801, 16 million newspaper stamps were being issued annually, and in 1851 the comparable figure was 85 million. This growth was accompanied by an expansion in the number of types of newspaper, in no way restricted to London. In 1702 the first daily paper, *The Daily Courant*, appeared. However, in the first half of the century most newspapers were weeklies or evening tri-weeklies. Though the earliest extant copy of a provincial newspaper, *The Bristol Post-Boy*, dates from 1704, it is probable that the first provincial paper was *The Norwich Post*, starting in 1701. By 1748

there were 43 provincial papers, a figure that had more than doubled by the end of the century.

Newspapers were of course not the only type of printed material whose sale rose markedly during the 18th century: CHAPBOOKS, almanacs and ballad sheets were increasingly popular too. It was not until the 19th century that the press significantly sought to expand into the popular literary market catered for by these other products. If a distinction between polite and popular culture is to be adopted, then the press was clearly a facet of the former. An examination of the literary or theatrical news or the bulk of the advertisements in the London and provincial press does not suggest much of an effort to create or cater for a mass, and the bulk of the claims made for its existence relate to London, the only place where unstamped and cheap papers were produced in the 18th century. Newspapers were expensive and their readership was limited by comparison with that of the Victorian period. News and opinion were rapidly disseminated among an appreciable portion of the community, but this hardly amounts to the national political culture whose creation has sometimes been alleged.

A striking feature of the 18th-century press was the active participation of most of the leading men of letters. Writers such as ADDISON, BOLINGBROKE, DEFOE, FIELDING, GOLDSMITH, JOHNSON, SMOLLETT, STEELE and SWIFT did not simply contribute items: they also played a major role in founding and running newspapers, and often in conducting press campaigns. Though certain journals, such as *THE SPECTATOR* of Addison and Steele, were largely concerned with matters of social conduct and can be understood in terms of the literature of social behaviour, many prominent writers were actively involved in the political press. Swift defended the Tory ministry of ROBERT HARLEY, and his *EXAMINER* competed with Mainwaring's Whig *Medley*. Steele was a leading Whig critic of the Harley ministry. Defoe followed an ambiguous course in the political press of the early 18th century. Many prominent literary figures used the press as a vehicle in the criticism of the Walpole ministry. Bolingbroke was one of the joint founders of *The Craftsman* and wrote numerous articles for this influential weekly. Fielding wrote *The Champion* for the opposition before producing *The True Patriot* and *The Jacobite's Journal* for the government of the Pelhamite Whigs. Such intervention by writers could result from political patronage (Lord North, for example, persuaded Johnson to write pamphlets against the supporters of JOHN WILKES and in defence of the government's policy in the Falkland Islands crisis) but it also reflects the heavily politicized nature of English society and literary life. The age made no attempt to separate literature from the social sphere, and the press simply provided another opportunity for writers to advance their arguments.

The didactic function of the press was not restricted to political opinion. Although political news, particularly that of foreign lands, was the dominant element of the British press, both metropolitan and provincial, English and non-English, instruction was also a recurrent theme. It took many forms, ranging from social manners to religious issues. Much of it was contributed by unpaid correspondents, necessarily so in light of the absence of any reporting staff in the newspapers of the period, and thus provided a significant opportunity for literary enterprise. Unfortunately, as the vast bulk of such material was anonymous or pseudonymous, it is rarely possible to establish the authorship of these pieces. The characteristic form of such contributions was the essay, itself a significant development of the early 18th-century press, and these were sometimes written by leading literary figures such as BOSWELL, BURKE, Goldsmith and Johnson. The essay proved ideally suited both to the press and to the magazines. THE GENTLEMAN'S MAGAZINE, founded in 1731 by Edward Cave, was a monthly deliberately designed to be of general interest which achieved a circulation of 10,000 within a decade and acquired a number of rivals, particularly THE LONDON MAGAZINE (1732–85). The rise of such magazines influenced the newspapers, particularly the weeklies, whose readers appear to have expected reflective essays or shorter pieces. The increased number of words per paper, achieved by means of smaller print and more columns per page, ensured that instructive material was not sacrificed to the pressure of more advertising or economic, sport and theatrical reports.

In the 19th century technical innovations, such as the spread of the iron press and the introduction of steam printing, facilitated the mass production of newspapers. This, in combination with the ending of newspaper duties, helped to produce a cheap press and papers such as The Daily Mail were printed in quantities and at a price that would have been inconceivable in the Georgian period. The provincial press ceased to be a vehicle for the reprinting of material in the London newspapers. However, the 19th-century press conformed in many ways to the patterns laid down in the earlier period, understandably so as many of the problems of reporting were identical. In assessing its significance it is necessary to guard against the tendency to treat the press as a fourth estate. It was not an autonomous agency or force. Instead, in the literary field as in so much else, the press reflected and sought to meet social changes. It did so within the context of competition, but also in a fashion that reflected the conservative nature of the newspaper world, in which well-tried methods that produced successful results were maintained by men whose conception of the potentialities of print was based on experience. The press was arguably less influential and autonomous than is commonly believed.

Newton, Sir Isaac 1642–1727 Scientist and philosopher. Born at Woolsthorpe near Grantham in Lincolnshire, and educated at Grantham grammar school and Trinity College, Cambridge, he succeeded his teacher, ISAAC BARROW, as Lucasian Professor of Mathematics in 1669. The preceding years (1664–6) had been spent at Woolsthorpe, beginning the scientific enquiries that led to his theories of gravitation and the spectrum, and the development of the calculus – the instrument he used to discover the results published in *Philosophiac Naturalis Principia Mathematica* ('The Mathematical Principles of Natural Philosophy'; 1687). A milestone in the history of science, Newton's *Principia* demonstrated the principle of gravitation. His first communications to the Royal Society on light and colour here made in 1672; his *Opticks* (1704) established him as the founder of the modern science of optics. To this book was attached *Method of Fluxions* – the Newtonian calculus which anticipated Leibniz in the same field and caused a bitter dispute between them over priority of invention.

Newton has been called the greatest English scientist. He was honoured generously during his lifetime: he was twice Cambridge University's representative in Parliament (1689 and 1701), president of the Royal Society (1703 until his death), Warden of the Mint (1696) and Master in 1699. He was knighted by Queen Anne in 1705.

Ngugi wa Thiong'o [Ngugi, James] 1938– Kenyan playwright, novelist and critic. Born in Limuru, he helped establish the Kamiriithu Cultural and Community Centre, where the successful performance of *Nhaahika Ndeenda*, which he co-authored with Ngugi wa Mirii, was banned in December 1977 (English version, *I Will Marry When I Want*, 1982). *Detained* (1981) describes his year-long detention in 1978. He has lived in exile since 1982.

Weep Not, Child (1964) projects a sensitive Kikuyu youth's perspective of the Mau Mau War. *The River Between* (1965), written first, covers white settlers' and Christian missionaries' incursions into Kikuyuland. Both are lucid, freshly written novels of youthful idealism and disillusion. *A GRAIN OF WHEAT* (1967) is structurally and thematically more complex, exploring various characters' painful confrontation of their own acts of betrayal during the Mau Mau struggle. His plays, *The Black Hermit* (1968), *This Time Tomorrow*, with *The Rebels* and *The Wound in the Heart* (1970), and *The Trial of Dedan Kimathi* (with Micere Mugo; 1976), dramatize the peasant, proletarian and national struggles. The powerful, boldly designed novels *Petals of Blood* (1977) and *Devil on the Cross* (originally written and published in Gikuyu, the language of the Kikuyu; 1982) expose, in Marxist terms, the exploitation of ordinary Africans by international neocolonialism. *Matigari*

Ngugi wa Thiong'o

(originally written and published in Gikuyu; 1987) is about a Kenyan freedom fighter. *Secret Lives* (1975) is a collection of short stories. Essays in *Homecoming* (1972) and *The Writer and Politics* (1981) discuss the social and political functions of literature, those in *Barrel of a Pen* (1983) Kenyan education, culture and politics.

nichol, b p 1944–88 Canadian poet and writer of fiction. Born in Vancouver, he spent his youth there and in Winnipeg and Port Arthur, Ontario. He attended the University of British Columbia, where he was influenced by the *TISH* group of poets, a counter-culture movement that stressed the importance of the spoken idiom. From 1964 until the early 1980s he worked in Toronto as a therapist. Nichol first attracted recognition in the mid-1960s with his CONCRETE POETRY. In the latter years of that decade he published numerous volumes of poetry, all concerned with the visual or, by using exploratory new forms, with foregrounding the way language operates. *The Year of the Frog* (1967) uses comic-strip techniques. *Ballads of the Restless Are* (1968) and *Dada Lama* (1968) are attempts to reach the oral roots of poetry and language. After 1970 he worked in a wide variety of modes – publicly performed sound-poetry, free verse and STREAM OF CONSCIOUSNESS prose among them – always challenging commonly held assumptions about language and the creative process. His best-known work is *The Martyrology*, a continuing

poem in several parts, of which the first two books appeared in 1972 and the last book, as *gIFTS*, in 1990. It is an investigation of the nature of the poetic process, in which the artist is presented as a saint or martyr. Other works include *Two Novels* (1969), *Still Water* (1970), *ABC: The Aleph Beth Book* (1971), *Love: A Book of Remembrances* (1974), *Craft Dinner* (1978), *Journal* (1978) and *extreme positions* (1981).

Nicholas Nickleby A novel by CHARLES DICKENS, published in 20 monthly parts from April 1838 to October 1839, and in volume form in 1839, as *The Life and Adventures of Nicholas Nickleby, Containing a Faithful Account of the Fortunes, Misfortunes, Uprisings, Downfallings and Complete Career of the Nickleby Family*.

After the death of the improvident Nicholas Nickleby senior, his widow and children Nicholas and Kate turn for help to his brother Ralph, who has made a fortune as an unscrupulous financier. Kate is apprenticed to a dressmaker, Madame Mantalini, and Nicholas is sent to teach at Dotheboys Hall in Yorkshire. He finds the school a miserable place where the master, Wackford Squeers, starves and ill-treats his pupils, secure in the knowledge that their relieved and uncaring parents will not interfere. Horrified by his discovery, and particularly by the treatment of the half-witted orphan Smike, Nicholas rebels, thrashes Squeers into insensibility and runs away with Smike. They work where they can, travelling in the pleasant company of Vincent Crummles and his band of actors.

Kate, meanwhile, is exposed to the unwelcome attentions of Ralph Nickleby's friends and business associates, among them the vicious Sir Mulberry Hawk. But they are no match for her and she treats Sir Mulberry with contempt. Alerted to her danger by Newman Noggs, Ralph's eccentric clerk, Nicholas returns to London with Smike and obtains a post in the business of the amiable Cheeryble brothers. Overhearing a conversation in which Kate's name is mentioned with disrespectful insinuation, he thrashes Sir Mulberry. Squeers and Ralph Nickleby conspire to injure Nicholas through Smike, but their plan fails when the ill-used and frail Smike dies with Nicholas at his side. Newman Noggs and the Cheeryble brothers help frustrate the villains' designs completely, and when they disclose that Smike was his son, Ralph Nickleby hangs himself.

Loosely structured, and taking frequent advantage of its looseness for excursions into sentiment and MELODRAMA, *Nicholas Nickleby* is nevertheless informed by the joyful energy that typifies Dickens's early work. The scenes at Dotheboys Hall and on the road with Vincent Crummles's strolling players are particularly memorable, and Dickens himself was sufficiently proud of his portrait of the garrulous Mrs Nickleby to revive her for his public readings in later life.

Nichols, Grace 1950– Guyanese/British poet and novelist. Born in Georgetown, she worked as a journalist before coming to Britain in 1977. She first established herself as a writer of CHILDREN'S LITERATURE, but it was the award of the Commonwealth Poetry Prize in 1983 for *i is a long memoried woman* which brought her to the attention of a wider audience. Concern with race and gender are key topics in her poems, but she treats both with a measure of comedy, particularly apparent in *The Fat Black Woman's Poems* (1984) and *Lazy Thoughts of a Lazy Woman* (1989). However, some poems show a strong sense of the historic injustices perpetrated against black people and against women. Her poetry has a vigorously oral quality, as a result of which both she and her fellow Guyanese poet, John Agard, with whom she lives, are in great demand for public recitals. She has also written a novel, *Whole of a Morning Sky* (1986), apparently based on her own growing-up in Guyana.

Nichols, Peter (Richard) 1927– Playwright. Born and brought up in Bristol, he worked as an actor and schoolteacher before starting to write television plays in the early 1960s. His first stage success came with *A Day in the Death of Joe Egg* (1967), about the parents of a spastic child. Subsequent works fall, perhaps deceptively, into two categories. There are broad, expansive plays about social or historical themes, written in a spacious manner; these include *The National Health* (1969), *The Freeway* (1974), *Privates on Parade* (1977) and *Poppy* (1983). The second category consists of domestic plays, tightly written, naturalistic and exact in their details, such as *Down Forget-Me-Not Lane* (1971), *Chez Nous* (1974), *Born in the Gardens* (1980), *Passion Play* (1981) and *A Piece of My Mind* (1986). *A Piece of My Mind* is a *cri de coeur* against directors' theatre.

Nichols, Robert (Malise Bowter) 1893–1944 Poet and playwright. Educated at Winchester and Trinity College, Oxford, he enlisted in the Royal Field Artillery in World War I, but was sent back to England suffering from neurasthenia after three weeks in the line. Encouraged by EDWARD MARSH, he contributed to GEORGIAN POETRY and published two volumes, *Invocations* (1915) and *Ardours and Endurances* (1917). Both were extremely popular for their celebration of the 'loved, living, dying heroic soldier', and he was compared to RUPERT BROOKE. He toured the United States giving lectures and readings, published *Aurelia* (1920), and became professor of English literature in Tokyo in 1921–4. His plays include *Guilty Souls* (1922) and *Wings over Europe* (1930). His only further volumes of poetry were the satirical *Fisbo* (1934) and *Such was My Singing* (1942), a selection of his work with an introduction outlining his ideas about poetry and extracts from two long works in progress. WILFRED OWEN described Nichols's poetry as 'deplorably self-concerned and *vaniteux*', and it is not now critically admired. He was a close friend of ROBERT GRAVES, who wrote 'To Robert Nichols' in reply to his 'Faun's Holiday'.

Nicholson, Norman 1914–87 Poet, playwright and critic. He was born in Millom, on the fringe of the Lake District, a region on which he draws in books such as *The Lakes* (1977) as well as in a poetry informed by the tradition of COWPER and WORDSWORTH, locating morality, metaphysics and imaginative vision in particular places and communities and in people's relationships with the natural world. Volumes include *The Pot Geranium* (1954), *Wednesday Early Closing* (1975), *A Local Habitation* (1972), *Sea to the West* (1981) and *Selected Poems, 1940–1982* (1982). *The Old Man of the Mountains* (1946) and two other verse dramas have a biblical basis; a fourth, *Prophesy to the Wind* (1950), concerns survival after a nuclear holocaust. They and the critical writing – principally *Man and Literature* (1943) – owe much to his interest in T. S. ELIOT's work and to his own Anglicanism.

Nicolson, Sir Harold (George) 1886–1968 Diplomat, politician and man of letters. Born in Teheran, where his father was the English chargé d'affaires, he was educated at Wellington College and

Oxford. In 1909 he joined the diplomatic service and was posted to Madrid, Constantinople, Teheran and Berlin. He married VITA SACKVILLE-WEST in 1913. After his resignation from the diplomatic service he entered politics in later life, serving as MP for West Leicester (1939–45) and receiving a knighthood in 1953.

Nicolson began his literary career in 1921 with a study of Verlaine and a novel, *Sweet Waters*. There followed biographical and critical studies of TENNYSON (1923), BYRON (1924) and SWINBURNE (in the English Men of Letters series, 1926), as well as *The Development of English Biography* (1927) and *Some People* (1927). Later works included another novel, *Public Faces* (1932), *The Congress of Vienna: A Study in Allied Unity 1812–1822* (1946), a highly praised official biography of King George V (1952) and a biography of the French critic Sainte-Beuve (1957). His *Diaries and Letters* (3 vols., 1966–8), edited by his son Nigel Nicolson, give an interesting picture of political life between the two world wars.

Nigger of the 'Narcissus', The A novel by JOSEPH CONRAD, published in 1897. Narrated by an anonymous seaman, the action concentrates on the human community of the ship, the *Narcissus*, on its way from Bombay to London. The tensions within that small number are as perilous as the weather itself and are produced partly by two different generations of seamen. Captain Alistoun and the veteran Singleton have the reticence of men primarily concerned with their duties as seamen. Conversely, the detachment from the working community of the younger Donkin and of Wait, the Negro of the book's title, comes to represent a powerful, if less practical, set of interests.

The illness and confinement of Wait claim the humanitarian sympathies of the remaining crew. At the height of a storm five men chance their lives to save the trapped Wait from his deck cabin; as Singleton and Alistoun are uneasily aware, the safety of the entire ship is meanwhile at risk. Confrontation between the captain and Donkin (who supports Wait's demands to go back on duty) comes to a head. After Donkin has hurled a belaying pin in his direction, the captain calmly reasserts a seaman-like authority, with the remaining crew looking on. More strangely, Singleton's superstition that Wait will die at the first sight of land comes true.

Conrad's Preface is frequently cited as a manifesto of literary Impressionism and of its chief aim: 'it is, before all, to make you see'.

Night Thoughts The usual abbreviation by which EDWARD YOUNG's lengthy didactic poem, *The Complaint: or, Night-Thoughts on Life, Death and Immortality* (1742–6), is known. The first of its nine books is devoted to reflections by the poet. The following seven take the form of a soliloquy rebuking the worldly Lorenzo, who is exhorted to turn to faith and the virtuous life. The final book, called 'The Consolation', includes a vision of the Day of Judgement, a contemplation of eternity, a survey of the firmament, a last exhortation to Lorenzo and an invocation to God. The solemn subject and diffuse manner appealed to the taste of the age, and *Night Thoughts* made Young one of the most popular of the so-called GRAVEYARD POETS.

Nightmare Abbey A satirical novel by THOMAS LOVE PEACOCK, published in 1818.

Perhaps the most popular of Peacock's topical SATIRES, its principal target is the contemporary literary intelligentsia, with its predilection for morbid subjects and unworldly philosophical systems. The most persistently foregrounded figure of fun is COLERIDGE, whom Peacock is at pains to unmask as a cultural reactionary, but BYRON's misanthropy and SHELLEY's illuminist politics are also mocked. As usual with Peacock, there is little in the way of plot, and the narrative frequently makes way for fully dramatic exchanges between the figures.

Mr Glowry, once a very harassed husband, now 'a very consolate widower', is the master of Nightmare Abbey on the edge of the Lincolnshire Fens, where he lives with his philosophical son Scythrop (Shelley). Taking his cue from the opening of GODWIN's *Mandeville*, Peacock has Glowry surround himself with domestics chosen for a depressive appearance or a dismal name: his butler is Raven, his steward Crow, and his grooms are called Mattocks and Graves. He keeps open house for his fellow spirits and relatives who include Mr Toobad, a 'Manichean Millenarian' pessimist, Mr Flosky (Coleridge), Mr Cypress (Byron), and Mr Listless, representing the 'common reader' and currently prostrate with the 'blue devils' of Romantic *ennui*. Their modish melancholy is offset by the unquenchable enthusiasm of the scientist Mr Asterias, whose life is committed to the capture of a mermaid and, in a more serious vein, by Mr Hilary, whose protests against the prevailing 'conspiracy against cheerfulness', and advocacy of nature, Mozart and the life-affirming wisdom of the ancient Greeks, appear to have the author on their side. Scythrop is hopelessly divided in his affections between his conventionally feminine cousin Marionetta and Toobad's philosophical daughter, Celinda. Refusing to relinquish either, he ends by losing both, the former to Listless, the latter to Flosky; he thinks of a suicide in the manner of Goethe's Werther, but calls instead for a bottle of Madeira.

Nin, Anaïs 1903–77 American diarist, novelist and critic. Her father was a Spanish composer, her mother half-French and half-Danish. She was born in Neuilly, just outside Paris, and moved in 1914 with her mother to New York, where she lived until returning to Paris in 1923, where she became a friend of LAWRENCE DURRELL and HENRY MILLER. She returned to the USA at the start of World War II. In her early life she was a model, dancer, teacher and lecturer; she later became a practising psychoanalyst under the tutelage of Otto Rank.

In 1931 she began the *Diary* (1966–83), her most enduring work, in which Miller is a central figure. Its elegant sparsity is as much at odds with Miller's writings as it is with her volumes of erotica, *Delta of Venus: Erotica* (1977) and *Little Birds* (1979), and other fiction. Influenced by D. H. LAWRENCE (of whom she wrote a study in 1932) and psychoanalysis, this includes: *House of Incest* (Paris, 1936; USA, 1947); *The Winter of Artifice* (Paris, 1939; USA, 1942), a collection of three novelettes; *Under a Glass Bell* (1944), a volume of short stories; *Cities of Interior*, a five-part sequence which appeared as *Ladders to Fire* (1946), *Children of the Albatross* (1947), *The Four-Chambered Heart* (1950), *A Spy in the House of Love* (1954) and *Solar Barque* (1958); and *Collages* (1964). Her critical studies are *Realism and Reality* (1946), *On Writing* (1947) and *The Novel of the Future* (1968).

Nine Worthies, The A group of nine great historical and mythical figures frequently mentioned in medieval and early Renaissance literature. It consists of three pagans (Alexander, Hector and Julius Caesar), three Jews (Joshua, David and Maccabeus) and three Christians (Arthur, Charlemagne and Godfrey of Bouillon). There is some variation, with the occasional addition of a tenth or the substitution of a different name for one of the original nine, but the list remains fairly constant. Occasionally an equivalent list of worthy women was also given. The earliest surviving treatment of the group is in Jacques de Longuyon's *Voeux du paon* (c. 1312).

Nineteen Eighty-Four A novel by GEORGE ORWELL, first published in 1949.

In 1984 Britain has become Airstrip One in the superstate Oceania, which is perpetually at odds with the other superstates Eurasia and Eastasia. It is ruled by the Party, under the aegis of the possibly non-existent Big Brother, whose image is ever present. The Party's agents constantly rewrite history and are redesigning the language, with the aim of controlling people's thoughts absolutely. A minor Party operative, Winston Smith, commits thought-crimes by keeping a secret diary and loving a girl named Julia, but is seduced into self-betrayal by his superior, O'Brien. His interrogation ultimately leads him to Room 101, where resides every man's ultimate horror. There, his spirit is so utterly broken that he surrenders his identity to the state and learns to love Big Brother.

This brilliant, bitter novel marks the culmination of the loss of faith in mankind which affected British futuristic fiction in the 1930s and was intensified by World War II. It provides a heavily ironic commentary on the state of the world in 1948, exaggerating all its worst traits to a nightmarish extreme. The development of world politics from 1948 to 1984 did nothing to soothe the anxieties with which it plays.

1919 See *USA*.

Njau, Rebeka 1934– Kenyan novelist, short-story writer and playwright. Born at Kanyariri in the Kiambu district, she attended Makerere University College before becoming a schoolteacher and founding headmistress of Nairobi Girls' Secondary School. Her husband, Elimo Njau, is a leading artist and cultural entrepreneur in East Africa. She has published: *The Scar* (1965), a play; *Ripples in the Pool* (1975), a novel dealing with the conflict between traditional values and the quest for affluence and power in the post-independent state; and *The Hypocrite* (1980), a collection of stories.

Nkosi, Lewis 1936– South African novelist, playwright and critic. Born in Durban, he began his career as a journalist on the Zulu-English weekly, *Ilanga Lase Natal* (*Natal Sun*), before joining the staff of *DRUM*. He left South Africa in 1961 for the USA, Britain and Zambia, where he became professor of literature. His eloquent and often provocative essays about township life, the generation of 1950s writers in South Africa, apartheid, exile and African literature appeared in journals and papers such as *THE NEW YORKER*, *The Observer*, *The New Statesman* and *The Spectator* before being collected in *Home and Exile* (1964), which was awarded a prize at the 1965 Dakar Festival of Negro Arts. A later collection, *Tasks and Masks* (1981), is concerned with contemporary African writing. *Rhythm of Violence* (1965), set in Johannesburg, was one of the first English-language plays written by a black South African. *Mating Birds* (1986), a novel, portrays the violent consequences of the interaction between sexual and racial politics in South Africa.

Noah, Mordecai Manuel 1785–1851 American playwright. He was born into a Portuguese-Jewish family in Philadelphia. The first of his plays to be produced was *Paul and Alexis: or, The Orphans of the Rhine* (1812), a melodrama later retitled *The Wandering Boys*. This was followed by his best-known work, *She would be a Soldier: or, The Plains of Chippewa* (1819), a patriotic comedy about a young woman who disguises herself as a soldier in order to follow her lover who is fighting in the War of 1812. His other plays include *The Siege of Tripoli* (1820), *Marion: or, The Hero of Lake George* (1821), *The Grecian Captive: or, The Fall of Athens* (1822) and *The Siege of Yorktown* (1824). Whether his subject was ancient or contemporary, Noah always wrote what he himself termed 'national plays', plays that self-consciously recalled and represented the course of the nation's history.

Noctes Ambrosianae See BLACKWOOD'S EDINBURGH MAGAZINE.

Nonjurors The name given to those Church of England clergymen who refused to take the Oath of Allegiance to William and Mary in 1689 on the grounds that they could not lawfully break the oath they had given to the deposed James II. Among them were the Archbishop of Canterbury, William Bancroft, and seven bishops.

Noonuccal [Nunukul], **Oodgeroo** See OODGEROO.

Norman, Marsha 1947– American playwright. Born in Louisville, Kentucky, and educated at Agnes Scott College and the University of Louisville, she has taught and worked with disturbed children. Characters in her plays confront some devastation in their past to determine whether and how to survive. *Getting Out* (1978) dramatizes the internal conflict of a woman parolee and *'night, Mother* (1983) enacts the last night of a hopeless young woman as she prepares herself and her mother for her suicide. Other works include *Third and Oak, The Laundromat (and) The Pool Hall* (1978), *The Holdup* (1983), *Traveler in the Dark* (1984), *Winter Shakers* (1983), *Sarah and Abraham* (1988), a musical with Norman L. Berman, and *The Secret Garden* (1991), a musical based on FRANCES HODGSON BURNETT's novel.

Norris, (Benjamin) Frank(lin) 1870–1902 American novelist. Born in Chicago, he moved with his family to San Francisco at the age of 14, studied in Paris and then attended the University of California 1890–4. In 1895 he visited South Africa, hoping to find material for travel sketches; instead he reported the conflict between the English and the Boers for the San Francisco *Chronicle*. After being captured by the Boer forces he was deported, and returned to San Francisco where he joined the staff of a magazine called *The Wave. Moran of the Lady Letty*, a sea story set off the California coast, was serialized in the magazine and published in book form in 1898. *A Man's Woman*, a romantic adventure story, appeared in 1900. Other contributions to *The Wave* were published in later years: *The Joyous Miracle* (a novelette, 1906), and the short-story collections *A Deal in Wheat* (1903) and *The Third Circle* (1909).

After reporting from Cuba on the Spanish-American War for MCCLURE'S MAGAZINE, Norris took a job with Doubleday, who published *Blix* (1899), a love story, and *McTEAGUE*, his first major contribution to American NATURALISM. *THE OCTOPUS* (1901) and *THE PIT* (1903), two volumes of a projected trilogy, *The Epic of the Wheat*, were completed before his early death from an appendix operation. The third part, *The Wolf*, which would have told of a wheat famine in Europe, was never written. Also published posthumously were *The Responsibilities of the Novelist* (1903), describing the type of naturalistic writing he had derived from Zola, and *Vandover and the Brute* (1914), a novel which he had started in 1895.

Norris, John 1657–1711 Philosopher. The last of the CAMBRIDGE PLATONISTS, Norris was educated at Winchester and Exeter College, Oxford, and became a Fellow of All Souls. He was a follower of Nicholas Malebranche, the French philosopher who combined the ideas of Descartes with a Platonic mysticism. Norris's chief work was the elaborate two-part *Essay towards the Theory of the Ideal or Intelligible World* (1701 and 1704), which criticizes the empiricist JOHN LOCKE's *ESSAY CONCERNING HUMAN UNDERSTANDING*. Norris also wrote devotional verses.

North, Christopher See WILSON, JOHN.

North, Sir Thomas ?1535–?1601 Translator. North may have been educated at Peterhouse, Cambridge. He entered Lincoln's Inn in 1557 and accompanied his brother on a diplomatic mission to France in 1574. He was knighted *c.* 1591, and was also a Justice of the Peace for Cambridge.

His translation of Guevara's *El relox de príncipes* as *The Dial of Princes* (1557) anticipated the EUPHUISM of the 1580s. *The Moral Philosophy of Doni*, a translation from Italian of beast FABLES of eastern origin, was printed in 1570. His most important translation was of Plutarch's *Lives* as *The Lives of the Noble Grecians and Romans* (1579), from a French version by Amyot. The second edition appeared in 1595 and the third (1603), which added new lives, was dedicated to Queen Elizabeth. This was an important source for SHAKESPEARE's knowledge of the ancient world and its great men. Shakespeare seems to have read it by the time he wrote *A MIDSUMMER NIGHT'S DREAM*, and his Roman plays all draw heavily on North. Enobarbus' description of Cleopatra on the river Cydnus in *ANTONY AND CLEOPATRA* is a reworking of North's prose.

North American Review, The A New England quarterly first published in Boston in 1815 under the editorship of William Tudor. Later, as a monthly publication, its editors included CHARLES ELIOT NORTON, JAMES RUSSELL LOWELL, HENRY ADAMS and Henry Cabot Lodge. Although founded as a literary journal, it began to publish articles on political and social matters when it was moved to New York in 1878. After World War I it reverted to quarterly publication and continued until 1940. Writers published in the

Review include RALPH WALDO EMERSON, WASHINGTON IRVING, HENRY WADSWORTH LONGFELLOW, FRANCIS PARKMAN, WALT WHITMAN, MARK TWAIN, HENRY JAMES, Leo Tolstoy, Gabriele D'Annunzio, H. G. WELLS, Maurice Maeterlinck and ALAN SEEGER.

North and South A novel by ELIZABETH GASKELL, published serially in *HOUSEHOLD WORDS* from September 1854 to January 1855 and in volume form in 1855. Its portrait of the contrast between the comfortable south and industrial north makes it an important CONDITION OF ENGLAND NOVEL.

Mr Hale, prompted by his conscience, leaves his living in the village of Helstone to go to the grim industrial city of Milton-Northern, where he teaches aspiring millowners. His wife and daughter, Margaret, accompany him. Margaret detests trade of any kind but soon discovers that the reality behind it all arrests and challenges her: her true character begins to emerge. She takes the side of the mill workers and confronts John Thornton, the millowner who is the employers' leader. Although he has little sympathy with Margaret's argument for a humane approach to his workers' problems, Thornton is nevertheless strongly drawn to her. When he is attacked by a mob of strikers, Margaret's courage in protecting him convinces him that his feelings are returned. He proposes to her but Margaret rejects him so coldly and firmly that he is deeply hurt. He later sees her with another man and is shocked by her apparent lie when she denies that she has a lover. In fact, the man was her brother Frederick, who had sought her out secretly while in danger of arrest. Thornton's attitude to the workers causes problems in his business and he is made to realize the need for the warmer approach Margaret had advocated. For her part, Margaret has been deeply affected by her fall in Thornton's estimation and begins to appreciate how much his regard matters to her. The two come together at the end of the novel.

Mrs Gaskell originally planned to call *North and South* 'Margaret' or 'Margaret Hale', and her portrait of the heroine – tough, wilful and self-confidently proud – owes much to her admiration of the work of her friend CHARLOTTE BRONTË.

North Briton, The A political weekly founded by JOHN WILKES in June 1762 and run with the help of CHARLES CHURCHILL. Its chief aim was to oppose the Earl of Bute's paper, *The Briton*, edited by SMOLLETT. Ironically named, *The North Briton* was supposed to be edited by a Scot who rejoiced to see his fellow countrymen in powerful positions. Wilkes risked prosecution by publishing the 'obscene' *Essay on Woman* and also for No. 45, which alleged that a speech from the throne had contained a lie about the Peace of Paris. *The North Briton* was suppressed in April 1763 and Wilkes, able to escape prosecution by claiming parliamentary privilege, was expelled from the House of Commons and banished.

Northanger Abbey A novel by JANE AUSTEN, published posthumously in 1818, though it had been begun in 1798 and accepted by a publisher in 1803. Her shortest major work, it makes fun of the prevailing fashion for the GOTHIC NOVEL, particularly the work of ANN RADCLIFFE.

Catherine Morland goes to Bath for the season as the guest of Mr and Mrs Allen, and there she meets the eccentric General Tilney, his son Henry and his daughter Eleanor. She is invited to the Tilneys' home, the Northanger Abbey of the title, where she imagines numerous gruesome secrets surrounding the General and his house. Henry proves that her suspicions have no substance but, while she is still recovering from the humiliation, she finds herself ordered out of the house by the General. She returns home and is followed by Henry. He explains that the General, mistakenly believing her to be penniless, had been anxious to keep her away from his son. Restored to a sensible humour by the truth, the General finally gives his blessing to Henry's marriage to Catherine.

Northward Ho A comedy by THOMAS DEKKER and JOHN WEBSTER, produced about 1605 and published in 1607. The plot concerns the efforts of Greenshield to seduce Mistress Maybury, who rejects him. He tries to convince her husband that she is unfaithful by producing a ring he has stolen from her. Maybury, convinced of her innocence, takes his revenge upon Greenshield with the help of the old poet Bellamont. The character of Bellamont is an amiable caricature of the authors' fellow playwright, GEORGE CHAPMAN.

Nortje, Arthur 1942–70 South African poet. Born in Oudtshoorn, Cape Province, he came to England in 1966. His death from a drug overdose in Oxford, where he was working for a doctorate, was seen by many as a tragic consequence of the psychic wounds inflicted by apartheid and exile, and the sad loss of one of Africa's most promising poets. His one volume, *Dead Roots*, posthumously published in 1973, contains supple free verse using a range of tones and images; it contrasts South African prison and township life with British life to express the consciousness of an African in exile.

Norton, Caroline Elizabeth Sarah 1808–77 Poet, novelist and pamphleteer. Born Caroline Sheridan, the granddaughter of RICHARD BRINSLEY SHERIDAN, she married George Chapple Norton in 1827 but the union was unhappy. Needing to earn money, she published a book of poetry, *The Sorrows of Rosalie* (1829), followed by a romance, *The Undying One* (1830), and a novel, *The Wife and Woman's Reward* (1835), all with considerable success. She also edited *La Belle Assemblée* and *The English Annual*. In 1836 Norton brought a suit against Lord Melbourne for alienating her affections which, though unsuccessful, brought their marriage to an end. Her marital wrongs prompted her to publish *English Laws for Women* (1853) and other powerful, eventually influential pamphlets on women's rights. She continued to publish poetry – *A Voice from the Factories* (1836) and *The Lady of La Garaye* (1861) – while her novels include *Stuart of Dunleath* (1851), *Lost and Saved* (1863) and *Old Sir Douglas* (1867). *The Martyn* (1849) is a play. In 1877 she married Sir William Stirling-Maxwell. Her beauty, talent and determination earned Caroline Norton much abuse and much admiration. Her character was said to have provided the model for the heroine of MEREDITH's *DIANA OF THE CROSSWAYS*.

Norton, Charles Eliot 1827–1908 American man of letters, and professor of the history of fine art at Harvard from 1875 to 1898. A regular contributor to THE ATLANTIC MONTHLY and co-editor of THE NORTH AMERICAN REVIEW, he also helped to found THE NATION in 1865. Frequent visits to Europe gave him a wide acquaintance among British as well as American writers. He published discreet editions of CARLYLE's early letters (1886) and *Reminiscences* (1887) and of RUSKIN's letters to him (1904). Other works include a prose translation of Dante's *The Divine Comedy* (1891–2), an edition of DONNE's poetry (1895) and *Notes of Travel and Study in Italy* (1859). His *Letters*, published in 1913, are a valuable document of intellectual life in Massachusetts in the latter half of the 19th century.

Norton, Mary 1903– Writer of CHILDREN'S LITERATURE. Educated in a convent school, she spent much of her childhood in the Georgian manor house in Bedfordshire which became Firbank Hall in *The Borrowers*. After a brief career as an actress she married and went to live in Portugal. She first turned to writing as a means of support in the USA during World War II. Her first novels, *The Magic Bedknob* (1943) and *Bonfires and Broomsticks* (1947), since reissued together as *Bedknob and Broomstick* (1970), concern the adventures of three children and Miss Price, a village spinster who is also studying to be a witch. *The Borrowers* (1952), awarded the Carnegie Medal, was the first in a series of five books about a family of tiny people who flee when they are discovered by the 'human beans' and embark on an epic journey across the countryside to a new home.

Norton, Thomas 1532–84 Poet and playwright. Norton was co-author with THOMAS SACKVILLE of *GORBODUC* (first acted in 1561 and printed in 1565) which has claim to be the first proper English tragedy. He also translated Calvin's *Institutes* (1561), wrote Latin verses and contributed a poem to TOTTEL'S MISCELLANY. Probably educated at Cambridge, Norton became amanuensis to Protector Somerset, married Archbishop CRANMER's daughter and, as a lawyer, took an active part in the examination of Catholics during the reign of Elizabeth.

Nostromo: A Tale of the Seaboard A novel by JOSEPH CONRAD, published in 1904. A turbulent political history is part of the background of the coastal province of Sulaco, the wealthiest region of the South American republic of Costaguana. Along with the San Tomé silver mine, the Englishman Charles Gould has inherited the instability of a civil war between the legal government of Ribiera and the populist party of his military chief Montero. In order to prevent the confiscation of silver by the rebels, Gould is persuaded to entrust it to Martin Decoud, a journalist with ambiguous commitments to the Ribiera government. Decoud is joined by the Italian Nostromo ('our man'), the Capataz de Cargadores and a local hero, in smuggling the silver out into the gulf. In the darkness, their loaded lighter is hit and damaged by a rebel troopship; forced to run aground on nearby islands, the Isabels, they conceal the silver and Nostromo returns to Sulaco.

Shocked into awareness by their near-disaster, Nostromo considers how far he has been exploited by his allies, who are aware of his appetite for adventure and glory. Decoud's dilemma is more extreme: his usual scepticism turns to near-madness, and he drowns himself weighted with silver. At this point Nostromo is persuaded to further, desperate heroism by another bearer of disillusionment: Dr Monygham, who was tortured under the previous political regime, and who is in love with Charles Gould's wife, the humane and wise Emilia. Owing to Nostromo's actions in summoning loyal forces, Sulaco and the Goulds are saved from the violence of the rebels.

The ensuing peace proves to be superficial for most characters. Nostromo, who is betrothed to Linda, the daughter of Giorgio Viola, fosters the belief that the silver has been sunk. But he makes clandestine visits to the Isabels, where Giorgio is appointed lighthouse keeper; here, he steals back portions of the silver and finds himself in love with Giselle, the sister of his betrothed. When he is mistaken for an intruder and shot by Giorgio, the secret of the silver is lost for ever.

Notes of a Journey from Cornhill to Grand Cairo A travel book by W. M. THACKERAY, with his own illustrations, published in 1846.

This account of a steamer journey round the Mediterranean, made in 1844 at the invitation of the Peninsular and Oriental Company, describes Thackeray's honest and often irreverent response to such landmarks of the ancient world as Athens, Constantinople, Jerusalem and Cairo.

Notes on the State of Virginia A book by THOMAS JEFFERSON, published in 1785. He first drafted it, while Governor of Virginia, to answer a set of questions about American landscape, customs and institutions circulated among American statesmen by François Marbois, a French representative in Philadelphia during the Revolutionary War. In its final form, it goes well beyond its original purpose and is perhaps the best single expression of Jefferson's ideas. The programme he advocates for America includes religious toleration, the emancipation of the slaves and a society based on an agrarian ideal. Jefferson also describes the legal history of the colonies, especially Virginia, including the events leading up to the Declaration of Independence.

novel of sensibility See SENTIMENTAL NOVEL.

Novels by Eminent Hands See PUNCH'S PRIZE NOVELISTS.

Novum organum A Latin treatise by FRANCIS BACON, published in 1620, which forms the second part of the great programme of intellectual and scientific reform that he proposed under the title of *Instauratio magna* ('Great Instauration'). THE ADVANCEMENT OF LEARNING constituted the preliminary section to this scheme, with its attack on the Aristotelian structures of knowledge that were still dominant in the universities of Europe, coupled with an appeal to develop new, systematic and profitable methods of enquiry into all areas of research. The *novum organum* of the title means 'the new instrument' that will be employed to advance learning, *Organon* being the name given to Aristotle's logical treatises as instruments of reasoning.

In the work Bacon deplores the limited understanding that men have of the operations of the natural world, their ignorance of the causes of natural phenomena, and their inability to control the forces of nature for the benefit of mankind. The fault lies principally in the sterile methods of intellectual enquiry that scholastic teachers, weakly imitating Aristotle, employ. In addition, there are various kinds of prejudice that prevent men thinking clearly and objectively. These Bacon characterizes as the Idols of the Mind (which he also describes in *The Advancement*, Book V). He identifies four notable 'fallacies of the mind of man': the Idols of the Tribe, the commonly received beliefs and superstitions of one's society; the Idols of the Cave, the particular foibles of an individual's mind; the Idols of the Market Place, by which phrase Bacon describes the loose meanings of words in common usage, and the lack of a precise and defined relationship between words and things; and the Idols of the Theatre, the various false philosophic systems that present an attractive but misleading view to the mind, in the manner of a stage play that pleases but deceives as it conjures up an imaginary world.

The method of enquiry that Bacon recommends in *Novum organum*, the reliable new instrument of discovery, is induction: the method of inferring a general law or principle from the observation of particular instances. Induction forms the basis of Bacon's experimental technique, and Book II of his treatise is given over to a practical application of the method in an investigation of the nature of heat.

Nowlan, Alden 1933–83 Canadian poet. Though he grew up in the impoverished community of Stanley, Nova Scotia, during the Depression and World War II, he spoke of himself as having enjoyed a Huckleberry Finn-like freedom from middle-class respectability. After working as road maintenance man, tree-cutter and nightwatchman, he became a journalist and newspaper editor in New Brunswick. Early volumes include *The Rose and the Puritan* (1958), *A Darkness in the Earth* (1959), *Under the Ice* (1961) and *The Things Which Are* (1962), all notable for their realistic rendition of Canadian maritime life and examination of the damage wrought by Puritanism. Subsequent work is more varied, both formally and thematically. *Various Persons Named Kevin O'Brien* (1973), a novel treating his own life, raises basic questions about the stability of identity. Similar notions of multiple consciousness and alternative conceptions of reality inform later verse collections, which include *Bread, Wine and Salt* (1967), *The Mysterious Naked Man* (1969), *Playing the Jesus Game* (1970), *I'm a Stranger Here Myself* (1974), *Smoked Glass* (1977) and *An Exchange of Gifts* (1985). *Miracle at Indian River* (1968) is a collection of short stories and *The Wanton Troopers* (1988) a posthumously published novel.

Nowra, Louis 1950– Australian playwright. His plays, often with exotic or historical settings, depict the private worlds of illusion, obsession and madness under pressure from external power structures, and are characterized by episodic construction, heightened language and powerful, even lurid, theatrical effects. They include four radio plays and four television plays, including *Displaced Persons* (1985). Plays for the theatre are *Albert Names Edward* (1975), *The Golden Age* (1975), *Inner Voices* (1977), *Visions* (1978), *The Song Room* (1980), *Inside the Island* (1980), *The Precious Woman* (1980), *Sunrise* (1983), *Capricornia* (based on the novel by XAVIER HERBERT; 1988), *Byzantine Flowers* (1990) and *Summer of the Aliens* (1992).

Noyes, Alfred 1880–1958 Poet, novelist, short-story writer and playwright. Born in Wolverhampton and educated in Wales, he attended Exeter College, Oxford, but concentrated on producing his first volume of poetry, *The Loom of Years* (1902), and left without a degree. Noyes's first wife was American and he spent many of the years before her death in 1926 in the USA, lecturing on 'The Sea in English Poetry' (a favourite topic) at Harvard University in 1913 and teaching F. SCOTT FITZGERALD and EDMUND WILSON among others at Princeton between 1914 and 1923. His own poetry – which includes the EPIC in BLANK VERSE *Drake* (1906–8) and famous shorter poems like 'The Barrel Organ' ('Come down to Kew in lilac time') and 'The Highwayman' – was vigorously traditional and increasingly out of tune with his contemporaries.

The *Torch-Bearers*, an ambitious trilogy about science and Christianity consisting of *The Watchers of the Sky* (1922), *The Book of Earth* (1925) and *The Last Voyage* (1930), reflected a growing preoccupation with religion; he converted to Roman Catholicism in 1926. Notable among his fiction are the ventures into fantasy in *Walking Shadows* (1918), *The Hidden Player* (1924) and *The Last Man* (1940). *Two Worlds for Memory* (1953) is autobiographical.

Nun's Priest's Tale, The See CANTERBURY TALES, THE.

Nunukul [Noonuccal], **Oodgeroo** See OODGEROO.

Nwapa, Flora (Nwanzuruahal) 1931– Nigerian novelist. Born in Eastern Nigeria, she attended school in Port Harcourt and Lagos before studying at Ibadan University College and Edinburgh University. She has taught, held administrative posts and toured abroad, speaking on behalf of the Biafran cause during the Nigerian Civil War. She now runs a publishing house, Tana Press, in Enugu. *Efuru* (1966) and *Idu* (1969) established her as Nigeria's first woman novelist. Both study the lives of women in rural society and seek to portray the particular flavour of Igbo culture. Nwapa has adopted a mode closer to popular romance in later books such as *This Is Lagos and Other Stories* (1971), *Wives at War and Other Stories* (1981), *One is Enough* (1981), *Never Again* (1984) and *Women are Different* (1986), which often deal with urban women who have rejected traditional mores. She has also written CHILDREN'S LITERATURE.

O Pioneers! A novel by WILLA CATHER, published in 1913. Alexandra Bergson, the eldest daughter of Swedish immigrants living on the Nebraska Divide, manages the farm and homestead after her father's death. Her innovative farming ideas meet resistance from her conservative brothers Oscar and Lou, but after the division of the land upon their marriages, Alexandra's fields flourish, and she becomes rich enough to send her youngest brother Emil to college. She develops a close relationship with a young Bohemian woman, Marie Tovesky, who lives with her husband on a neighbouring farm, once the home of Alexandra's childhood sweetheart, Carl Linstrum. Carl, who had left the Divide years ago when he moved east with his parents, returns to visit Alexandra and then travels west to California. Emil graduates from the University of Nebraska and decides to visit Mexico. Back from his travels, he becomes romantically involved with Marie Tovesky. One day Marie's husband finds the two lovers together in a field, and shoots them in a rage. Hearing of the tragedy, Carl returns and marries Alexandra.

Oakley, Barry (Kingham) 1931– Australian playwright, novelist and short-story writer. Born in Melbourne, he has worked as a journalist, copywriter and teacher, and now lives in Sydney. His many plays, often distinctly literary in their bias, range through vaudeville, buffoonery, NATURALISM, REALISM, dream and SATIRE. *The Ship's Whistle* (1978) is about R. H. HORNE, *The Hollow Tombola* (1980) satirizes PATRICK WHITE's *The Solid Mandala*, and *Scanlan* (1980) parodies a conference paper on HENRY KENDALL. Satire is also a recurrent mode in his stories, *Walking through Tiger Land* (1977), while *picaro* characters (see PI-CARESQUE) are often used to criticize contemporary society in his novels. They include *A Wild Ass of a Man* (1967), *A Salute to the Great McCarthy* (1969), *Let's Hear it for Prendergast* (1970) and *Craziplane* (1989). Other books are *How They Caught Kevin Farrelly* (1972), *Letter from Hospital* (1975) and *Scribbling in the Dark* (1985).

Oates, Joyce Carol 1938– American novelist, short-story writer, poet and critic. She was born at Lockport, New York, in the 'Eden County' of many of her novels, and educated at Syracuse University and the University of Wisconsin. Her intense, often violent vision, sustained throughout a prolific writing career, is perhaps most powerfully expressed in *Wonderland* (1971), based on LEWIS CARROLL's Alice stories, and in the loosely arranged trilogy, *A Garden of Earthly Delights* (1967), *Expensive People* (1968)

and *Them* (1969; National Book Award). Other novels include *With Shuddering Fall* (1964), *The Assassins: A Book of Hours* (1975), *Bellefleur* (1980), *A Bloodsmoor Romance* (1982) and a trilogy of pastiche Gothic romances, *Mysteries of Winterhurn* (1984), *Solstice* (1985) and *Marya: A Life* (1986). She has explored the incursion of random violence into suburban lives in *American Appetites* (1989) and *Because It is Bitter, Because It is My Heart* (1990). *Black Water* (1992) is a novella recognizably based on Senator Edward Kennedy's accident at Chappaquiddick. Her short-story collections are *By the North Gate* (1963), *The Wheel of Love* (1970) which includes the often anthologized 'Where are You Going, Where have You Been' and 'The Region of Ice', *The Goddess and Other Women* (1974), *The Seduction and Other Stories* (1975), *Last Days* (1984) and *Raven's Wing* (1987). Her essays and criticism include *The Edge of Impossibility: Tragic Forms in Literature* (1972), *The Hostile Sun: The Poetry of D. H. Lawrence* (1973), *Contraries: Essays* (1981). *On Boxing* (1987) is a monograph, sometimes tendentious and sometimes trenchant, further evidencing her fascination with violence. Volumes of poetry include *Women in Love, and Other Poems* (1968) and *Anonymous Sins, and Other Poems* (1969).

objective correlative A term coined by T. S. ELIOT in his essay on *HAMLET* (1919): 'The only way of expressing emotion in the form of art is by finding an "objective correlative"; in other words, a set of objects, a situation, a chain of events which shall be the formula of that *particular* emotion; such that when the external facts, which must terminate in sensory experience, are given, the emotion is immediately evoked.'

objectivism An American poetic movement of the 1930s, in reaction against IMAGISM. The poets concerned – GEORGE OPPEN, LOUIS ZUKOFSKY, CHARLES REZNIKOFF and WILLIAM CARLOS WILLIAMS – believed that the principles of imagism were too vague, being applicable to almost any conceivable idea. Instead, they emphasized the importance of the poem as a physical object, and this led to an increased attention to typography as well as to the use of more conventional poetic devices. *An 'Objectivists' Anthology* appeared in 1932, but the movement disbanded soon afterwards.

O'Brien, Edna 1932– Novelist and short-story writer. Born in Tuamgraney in County Clare, Ireland, she was educated locally at Scarriff and at Loughrea in

Edna O'Brien

Galway. Later she studied pharmacy in Dublin and became a Licentiate of the Pharmaceutical College of Ireland. Her first novel, *The Country Girls* (1960), introduces 'Kate' Brady and 'Baba' Brennan, two Irish girls who leave their restrictive backgrounds for the excitement of Dublin. They appear again in *The Lonely Girl* (1962) and *Girls in Their Married Bliss* (1963), in which their quest for 'life' eventually leads them to London. Other novels include; *August is a Wicked Month* (1965); *Casualties of Peace* (1966); *A Pagan Place* (1971), about rural Ireland; *Night* (1972), narrated by a middle-aged woman as she lies alone in bed; *Johnny I Hardly Knew You* (1977); and *The High Road* (1988).

Much of her writing is concerned with the position of women in society: their lack of fulfillment and the repressive nature of their upbringing. The bleakness of tone, especially in the later novels, is lightened by a lyrical quality associated with nostalgia for Ireland, and by odd moments of joy in which O'Brien's heroines achieve temporary happiness. Her collections of short stories include *The Love Object* (1968), *A Scandalous Woman and Other Stories* (1974), *Mrs Reinhardt and Other Stories* (1978; as *A Rose in the Heart* in USA) and *Lantern Slides* (1990).

O'Brien, Fitz-James *c.* 1828–62 Short-story writer. Born in Ireland, O'Brien was already an experienced journalist when he emigrated to the USA in 1852. There he established a popular reputation as a writer of short stories in the fantastic vein, of which his most famous, 'The Diamond Lens', was published in THE ATLANTIC MONTHLY in 1858. It tells of an inventor who creates a powerful microscope, becomes obsessed with the vision of a human-like figure in a drop of liquid, and goes mad when the creature dies. O'Brien also published a play, *A Gentleman from Ireland* (1858). He fought in the Civil War and died at the battle of Bloomery Gap. The posthumous collection *Poems and Stories* appeared in 1881.

O'Brien, Flann [O'Nolan, Brian] 1911–66 Irish novelist. Born in Strabane, he studied Irish, German and philosophy at University College, Dublin. As 'Myles na Gopaleen' he contributed a column to *The Irish Times* from 1940, in which he constantly argued against the use of clichés about Ireland. A collection, *The Best of Myles*, was published in 1968.

His first and most important novel, *At Swim-Two-Birds* (1939), stands in a direct line of descent from JOYCE'S *ULYSSES* in the mixture of REALISM and fantasy which embraces a description of his everyday life by the narrator, a Dublin student, an account of the Irish folk hero Finn MacCool in a novel-within-a-novel by 'Dermot Trellis', and a cheerfully farcical representation of Irish folklore. Like *Ulysses*, it may also be read as a sustained exploration of the fictional process. O'Brien's other novels include *The Hard Life* (1961), *The Dalkey Archive* (1964), and *The Third Policeman* (1967). A novel in Gaelic, *An Béal Bocht* (1941), was translated by P. C. Power as *The Poor Mouth* (1973).

O'Brien, Sean 1952– Poet. Born in London, he grew up in Hull and was educated at Selwyn College, Cambridge, as well as the universities of Birmingham, Hull and Leeds. Though he taught in Sussex for much of the 1980s, his roots are in the North, particularly Hull. Without aligning himself with any group or style, he is receptive to the influence of poets like DOUGLAS DUNN, TONY HARRISON and, more remotely, AUDEN who forcefully address social problems. His preoccupation with place is apparent in *Indoor Park* (1983), about Pearson Park in Hull, and *Boundary* (1989), about the beach at Brighton. *The Frighteners* (1987) blends SATIRE and historical observation, as well as introducing the dark and nihilistic Ryan, 'a liar who means what he says'. *HMS Glasshouse* (1991), confirming O'Brien's socio-political interests and his suspicion of post-war Britain, also develops his talent for portrayal through images.

O'Casey, Sean 1880–1964 Irish playwright. Born in Dublin, the youngest of an impoverished Protestant family, he suffered from poor health during his boyhood. Trachoma permanently damaged his eyesight and interrupted his education. Unable to read properly until he was 13, he read avidly from then on. During years of physical hardship as a roadbreaker, docker and hod-carrier he fell increasingly under the influence of the Irish labour leader Jim Larkin. Nationalism took him into the Irish Citizen Army, but his greater concern for the welfare of the proletariat made him resign from it in 1914 to protest against its anti-Union attitudes.

O'Casey's first publication was a broadside, *The Story of Thomas Ashe* (1917), about a friend in the Citizen Army who died on hunger strike, but he was already interested in the work of the ABBEY THEATRE. After rejecting at least three of his plays, the Abbey staged *THE SHADOW OF A GUNMAN* (1923), following it in regular succession with the one-act *Kathleen Listens In* (1923), O'Casey's first experiment with EXPRESSIONISM, and *JUNO AND THE PAYCOCK* (1924). Another one-act piece, *Nannie's Night Out* (1924), brought him his first experience of hissing from the intensely nationalistic Abbey audience, and *THE PLOUGH AND THE STARS* (1926) provoked a full-scale riot led by objectors to its unheroic portrait of participants in the Easter Rising. Feeling rejected by the theatre whose fortunes his plays had sustained, O'Casey left Dublin for London. Against his expectations, and perhaps against his own dramatic interests, he never lived in Ireland again.

The decisive break came when YEATS and his fellow directors at the Abbey decided against staging O'Casey's next play, *THE SILVER TASSIE*, in 1928 (it was first staged in London in 1929 and, in an atmosphere of protest, at the Abbey in 1935). The particular stumbling-block for Yeats was the expressionistic second act, embedded in a play that otherwise closely resembled O'Casey's Abbey successes in the tragicomic realism with which it viewed the urban poor of Dublin. O'Casey had never wished to be limited by the tenets of dramatic realism. *Within the Gates* (1943), his next play, is wholly expressionistic. Set in Hyde Park, and reliant on the careful interweaving of music, dance and stylized dialogue, it explores the conflicting claims made on the Young Woman by her urge for joy and her hope for religious salvation.

O'Casey's later plays never rivalled the popularity of his Dublin tragicomedies. They include several overtly Communist pieces, like *The Star Turns Red* (1940) and *Red Roses for Me* (1943), which is set against a background with which O'Casey was personally familiar – the Irish Transport Workers' strike of 1913. An ambitious play, its expressionistic third act presents poetically a vision of Dublin as it might be. That O'Casey's preoccupation with Ireland remained with him in exile is further illustrated by *Purple Dust* (1943), *Cock-a-Doodle Dandy* (1949), *The Bishop's Bonfire* (1955), *The Drums of Father Ned* (1959) and *Behind the Green Curtains* (1962). Many of these Irish plays press home the point that the constraints of a joy-denying church obstruct the Irish instinct for happiness. It is a theme often referred to in the six volumes of his compelling but not literal autobiography, beginning with *I Knock on the Door* (1939) and ending with *Sunset and Evening Star* (1954).

Occleve, Thomas See HOCCLEVE, THOMAS.

O'Connor, Flannery 1925–64 American short-story writer and novelist. Born in Savannah, Georgia, and educated at Georgia State College for Women, she suffered from a terminal illness, lupus, for much of her adult life and was frequently hospitalized and in great pain until her death at the age of 39.

Despite the brevity of her career, she made a strong impression on the American literary scene, and exerted considerable influence on the development of the American short story. Her own Southern origins and devout Roman Catholic faith are evident throughout her fiction, in which she often uses poor, disabled, or socially marginal characters involved in absurd and violent situations to convey the spiritual poverty and crippled intellect of the modern world. Her vision of violent spiritual struggle in the rural South is marked by a grotesque humour and unnerving IRONY. Her first novel, *WISE BLOOD* (1952), tells the story of Hazel Motes, the lonely prophet of a 'church without Christ, where the blind stay blind, the lame stay lame, and them that's dead stays that way'. Another novel, *The Violent Bear It Away*, was published in 1960. Her short stories are collected in *A Good Man is Hard to Find* (1955; as *The Artificial Nigger and Other Stories* in Britain, 1959) and the posthumously published *Everything That Rises Must Converge* (1965).

O'Connor, Frank [O'Donovan, Michael Francis] 1903–66 Irish short-story writer. Born and educated in Cork, he worked in Dublin and eventually emigrated to the USA. He first began to write in Gaelic. When he turned to English he produced translations from Irish verse, novels, plays for the ABBEY THEATRE (of which he was a director), and literary criticism. However, his reputation depends on the scrupulously realistic short stories, often about his native Cork, which were first published by AE (GEORGE WILLIAM RUSSELL) in *The Irish Statesman* and thereafter appeared in regular collections: *Guests of the Nation* (1931), *The Saint and Mary Kate* (1932), *Bones of Contention* (1936), *Three Old Brothers* (1937), *The Big Fellow* (1937), *Crab Apple Jelly* (1944), *The Common Chord* (1947), *Traveller's Samples* (1950), *Domestic Relations* (1957) and *My Oedipus Complex* (1963). *An Only Child* (1961) and the unfinished *My Father's Son* (1968) are autobiographical.

Octavian A VERSE ROMANCE written in the mid-14th century and existing in two versions, one from the North and the other from the South-east. Both were derived from a French version, though the story is extant in several other European and Nordic languages. Florence, wife of the Emperor Octavian, bears twin sons, Octavian and Florentyn. Her jealous mother-in-law (in the northern version, her father) contrives to have the mother and children driven out into the forest. The children are stolen by an ape and a tiger; Octavian is brought up by a lioness, and Florentyn by a Parisian butcher. Florence, sailing to the Holy Land, recovers the young Octavian with his lioness step-mother and lives in Jerusalem. Florentyn becomes a local champion, then defeats a Saracen sultan's giant champion and marries the sultan's daughter. In a battle with the sultan he and the Emperor Octavian are captured with others. The young Octavian and his lioness fight the pagans and free the prisoners. The family is reunited and the mother-in-law burned.

Octopus, The: *A Story of California* A novel by FRANK NORRIS, published in 1901, the first part of his uncompleted trilogy *The Epic of the Wheat*. The second volume is *THE PIT* (1903); the third volume was never written.

The octopus is the Pacific and Southwestern Railroad, which in the course of the story economically strangles the wheat farmers of California, who are led by Magnus Derrick, the owner of a large ranch near the town of Bonneville. The railroad is the most powerful vested interest in the state; it dominates the government, gains total control of Bonneville, and is behind the movement of all prices and interest rates. Many of the farmers hold their land on option from the railroad, and it dispossesses them at will; it also manipulates freight charges to lower the price of wheat and thereby ruin other farmers when it wants their land too. Derrick's direct opponent is the railroad agent Behrman, who is eventually suffocated when he falls into the wheat he has plundered from the ruined and dispossessed farmers, wheat that he was intending to sell at a huge profit. Derrick himself is ruined when the railroad succeeds in bribing his son Lyman, a lawyer on the state commission, to act against the farmers' interests. Other leading characters are Dyke, a railroad engineer who wants to be a farmer, and Shelgrim, the railroad president, who blandly tells the protesting poet, Presley, that what has happened has nothing to do with the people: it is all a matter of economic forces and the law of supply and demand.

Octoroon, The A MELODRAMA by DION BOUCICAULT, first performed at the Winter Garden, New York, in 1859, a few days after the execution of the abolitionist John Brown. The play was adapted from *The Quadroon*, a novel by CAPTAIN MAYNE REID.

The octoroon of the title is Zoe, a freed slave on the impoverished Southern plantation of the late Judge

Peyton, whose daughter by a quadroon slave she is. The play deals with the attempts of the Judge's widow, his nephew George and the virtuous Yankee Salem Scudder to save both Zoe and the plantation from the villainous M'Closky. Exposed as a murderer by Scudder's camera, M'Closky is hunted and killed by the Indian chief Wahnotee, but too late to save Zoe, who kills herself rather than give pain to George Peyton. When English audiences objected to this ending, Boucicault grudgingly provided an alternative in which Zoe survives.

O'Curry, Eugene 1796–1862 Irish scholar. Born in County Clare and self-educated, he was employed in the topographical and historical section of the Ordnance Survey Office in Dublin in 1834. Like his colleagues GEORGE PETRIE and JOHN O'DONOVAN, he made pioneering contributions to the scholarly aspect of the CELTIC REVIVAL. He set to work on the collections of Irish folk material, establishing the British Museum catalogue in the field. In 1850 he became professor of Irish history and archaeology at the new Catholic University in Dublin. His famous lectures of 1855 were published in 1861 as *Lectures on the Manuscript Materials of Ancient Irish History*.

Odd Women, The A novel by GEORGE GISSING, published in 1893.

The death of the improvident Dr Madden leaves his three daughters stranded with very little money and no training of any kind. Their loneliness and poverty in London lodgings and their desperate maintenance of middle-class respectability – Virginia has found a secret consolation in gin – are conveyed with considerable pathos. In contrast to the Madden sisters is Rhoda Nunn, an active feminist who proposes to prepare women for some fate other than marriage.

ode A lyric poem in rhymed stanzas, generally in the form of an address and exalted in feeling and expression. Famous examples include KEATS's 'To a Nightingale' and 'On a Grecian Urn' and WORDSWORTH's 'Intimations of Immortality from Recollections of Early Childhood'. The Pindaric ode takes its name from the Greek poet Pindar (522–442 BC) whose work, designed to honour victors in the Greek games, used an elaborate stanzaic pattern of strophe, antistrophe and epode. ABRAHAM COWLEY introduced it into English, though he and successors like DRYDEN and POPE loosened the stanzaic pattern while keeping the poem's public function. TENNYSON's 'Ode on the Death of the Duke of Wellington' is a fine late example.

O'Dell, Scott 1903–89 American writer of CHILDREN'S LITERATURE. Born in Los Angeles and educated at Stanford University, California, O'Dell worked in films and journalism before writing successfully for adults and, later, for children. His most celebrated work, *Island of the Blue Dolphin* (1960), tells how Karana, an Indian girl, survives for 18 years alone on a tiny island, gradually coming to terms with the animal life around her. The whole story is also a form of parable stressing mankind's need to coexist peaceably with his environment. O'Dell's next children's novel, *The King's Fifth* (1966), describes how ruthless foreign adventurers looted South America.

Odets, Clifford 1906–63 American playwright. Born in Philadelphia, the son of middle-class Jewish immigrants, he left school at the age of 17 to become an actor, working in radio and playing small parts in stock companies and then in Theatre Guild productions. In 1931 he helped found the GROUP THEATRE, in which he initially participated simply as an actor. One act of his play *AWAKE AND SING!* was given a trial reading in 1933 but was rejected for production. Then in 1935 he wrote *WAITING FOR LEFTY* in response to a New Theatre League contest for one-act plays. He won the contest and was rewarded with a production. It was an instant success; the Group Theatre reconsidered and produced *Awake and Sing!* (1935), followed by a double bill of *Waiting for Lefty* and *Till the Day I Die*, a short anti-Nazi play Odets wrote quickly for the purpose. His career as playwright and champion of the underprivileged was launched.

He joined the Communist Party in 1934, but soon resigned; he later told the House Un-American Activities Committee that he had found it impossible to write in line with a party programme, and that his sympathy for the working classes was due to family experience rather than party ideology. His second full-length play, *Paradise Lost* (1935), dealt with the disintegration of a middle-class family as a result of the Depression. He then accepted a lucrative offer to become a Hollywood screenwriter, but returned to New York to see a new play, *Golden Boy* (1937), through production by the Group Theatre. This play, which was to be his greatest commercial success, is the story of Joe Bonaparte, a talented young Italian violinist who chooses to become a prizefighter, thereby destroying his talent, his integrity and finally himself and the woman he loves. Of Odets's later plays, *Rocket to the Moon* (1938) explores a dentist's mid-life crisis; *Night Music* (1940) is a story of distrustful love between alienated people in Hollywood; *Clash by Night* (1941) depicts a love triangle which ends in murder. *The Big Knife* (1949) concerns Charlie Castle, a Hollywood actor who has compromised his ideals; in *The Country Girl* (1950), another love triangle centres on a self-pitying, alcoholic actor struggling to make a comeback. Odets's last play, *The Flowering Peach* (1954), retells the story of Noah's ark.

O'Donovan, John 1809–61 Irish scholar and topographer. Born in County Kilkenny, O'Donovan was appointed to the Ordnance Survey Office in 1829, where he worked with EUGENE O'CURRY and GEORGE PETRIE. Like them he made an important contribution to the CELTIC REVIVAL by his pioneering researches into ancient Irish civilization. He published *A Grammar of the Irish Language* in 1845, but his masterwork was his edition of *Annala Rioghacta Eireann: Annals of the Kingdom of Ireland by the Four Masters* (7 vols., 1848–51).

O'Dowd, Bernard 1866–1953 Australian poet. Educated at the University of Melbourne, O'Dowd was assistant librarian at the Supreme Court, Melbourne (1887–1913) and State Parliamentary Draughtsman (1931–5). He corresponded with WALT WHITMAN, whose sense of the poet's duty as an 'answerer', dealing with the most useful and interesting questions of the age, influenced his work. His volumes of verse included *Dawnward?* (1903), *The Silent Land* (1906), *Dominions of the Boundary* (1907), *The Seven Deadly Sins* (1909), *The Bush* (1912) and *Alma Venus!* (1921). His poetic technique is discussed in the address *Poetry Militant: An Australian Plea for the Poetry of Purpose* (1909).

O'Faolain, Sean 1900–91 Irish novelist, short-story writer and biographer. Born in Cork, he was educated at the National University, Dublin, and at Harvard. During the 1920s he was a member of the Irish Republican Army, and from 1929 to 1933 he lectured in English at St Mary's College, Middlesex. In the 1940s he was editor of *The Bell*, and in 1957 became director of the Arts Council of Ireland.

O'Faolain's first book of short stories, *Midsummer Night Madness* (1932), was followed by a novel, *A Nest of Simple Folk* (1933), about the spirit of Irish rebellion. Other short stories followed, and he was encouraged by the support of EDWARD GARNETT. *Bird Alone* (1936) and *Come Back to Erin* (1940), like his earlier novel, deal with the tyranny and pathos of Irish life and politics, particularly the oppression of Irish Catholicism. Other writing included biographies of Constance Markiewicz (1934), Daniel O'Connell (1938), De Valera (1939) and *Hugh O'Neill* (1942). *The Short Story* (1948) and *The Vanishing Hero* (1956) are works of literary criticism, and *Vive-moi!* (1964) is his autobiography.

Ofeimum, Odia 1950– Nigerian poet. Born at Pruekpon, he overcame interruptions in his early education to study political science at the University of Ibadan. After serving on the Lagos *Guardian* and as general secretary of the Association of Nigerian Authors, he moved to Oxford in 1989 to work with Adzido, the leading African dance company in Britain. His poetry has appeared in journals such as *OKIKE* and collections such as WOLE SOYINKA's *Poems from Black Africa* (1975). Volumes include *The Poet Lied* (1980, enlarged edition 1989), which brought him considerable notoriety, and *A Handle for the Flutist and Other Poems* (1986).

Officers and Gentlemen See SWORD OF HONOUR.

O'Flaherty, Liam 1897–1984 Irish novelist and short-story writer. Born at Inishmore in the Aran Islands, he abandoned his training for the priesthood to study at University College, Dublin. In 1922 he joined the militant demonstrations against unemployment in Dublin and was forced to leave the country. He finally settled in Aran.

He is best known for his unsentimental short stories, many of them about his native Aran Islands and reflecting his interest in the patterns of Gaelic speech. Volumes include *Spring Sowing* (1926) and *The Fairy Goose* (1929), collected in *The Short Stories of Liam O'Flaherty* (1956). His first novel was *The Neighbour's Wife* (1923), published with the support of EDWARD GARNETT. *The Informer* (1925), generally considered his best novel, is about the last day of Gypo Nolan, a destitute Irish revolutionary who turns in a comrade. *The Martyr* (1927), *The Assassin* (1928), *The Puritan* (1931) and *Famine* (1937) are equally uncompromising and realistic accounts of the Irish condition. *Two Years* (1930), *I Went to Russia* (1931) and *Shame the Devil* (1934) are autobiographies which document O'Flaherty's wide travels.

Ogot, Grace 1930– Kenyan novelist and short-story writer. Born in Central Nyanza, she trained as a nurse in Uganda and Britain before embarking on a varied career – largely in Kenya – as nurse, scriptwriter and broadcaster for the BBC Overseas Service, community development officer, public relations officer for Air India and, in 1975, delegate to the General Assembly of the United Nations. She was a founder member of the Writers' Association of Kenya. Her stories have appeared in journals such as *Black Orpheus*, *TRANSITION*, *Présence Africaine* and *East Africa Journal*, and in three collections: *Land without Thunder* (1968), *The Other Woman and Other Stories* (1976) and *The Island of Tears* (1980). *The Promised Land* (1970) and *The Graduate* (1980) are novels. Her writing reflects her wide-ranging experience of contemporary social, political and economic problems, and also her interest in her Luo ancestors, whose pre-colonial culture she came to understand through assisting her husband, Bethwell Ogot, in his historical researches.

O'Grady, Standish James 1846–1928 Irish historian. Born at Castletown Berehaven in Cork, and educated at Tipperary Grammar School and Trinity College, Dublin, he was called to the Bar in 1872 but never practised, preferring the world of letters. An interest in his country's epic past led to the two-volume *History of Ireland* (1878–80), which aroused considerable interest and had great influence on Irish poets. *The Early Bardic Literature of Ireland* (1879) also helped inspire the CELTIC REVIVAL by popularizing ancient legends. *Red Hugh's Captivity* (1889) and its sequel, *The Flight of the Eagle* (1897), are novels about Ireland in the days of Elizabeth I. Irish myth is the matter of *Cuculain: An Epic* (1882), *Finn and His Companions* (1892), *The Coming of Cuculain* (1894) and *The Departure of Dermot*, *The Triumph of Cuculain* and *The Passing of Cuculain* (all 1917). *The Bog of Stars* (1893) is a collection of stories about Ireland in the 16th century; *Hugh Roe O'Donnell* (1902) is a play set in the same period.

O'Hara, Frank 1926–66 American poet and playwright. He was born in Baltimore, Maryland, and educated at Harvard and the University of Michigan. A leading figure in the NEW YORK SCHOOL, he assimilated a wide variety of influences – from painting as well as literature – to create a deceptively casual poetry in an American idiom. It appeared in *A City Winter and Other Poems* (1952), *Meditations in an Emergency* (1957), *Odes* (1960), *Lunch Poems* (1964), *Love Poems* (1965) and two posthumous volumes, *Collected Poems* (edited by Donald Allen; 1971) and *Poems Retrieved* (1977). His plays are *Try, Try!* (1951), *Changing Your Bedding* (1952), *Awake in Spain* (1960), *Love's Labor* (1960) and *The General Returns from One Place to Another* (1964). *Selected Plays* was published in 1978.

O'Hara, John 1905–70 American novelist and short-story writer. He was born in Pottsville, Pennsylvania, a town which later figured as the 'Gibbsville' of his fiction. His first novel, *Appointment in Samarra* (1934), is set in Gibbsville and is a naturalistic account of three days that culminate in the suicide of Julian English, the victim of a stratified society and of his own reckless sexual appetite. The book was well received, and in the same year O'Hara embarked on a career as a screenwriter in Hollywood which lasted until the mid 1940s. *Butterfield 8* (1935) is a novel about the experiences of a Manhattan newspaperman. *Pal Joey* (1940), which he adapted as a musical in the same year, consists of a comic series of letters from a nightclub entertainer to a friend. Other novels include *A Rage to Live* (1949), *Ten North Frederick* (1955, National Book Award), *From the Terrace* (1959), *Ourselves to Know* (1960), *The Big Laugh* (1962) and *The Lockwood Concern* (1965). *Sermons and Soda Water*, a collection of three novellas, was published in 1960. His short stories, like his novels, often focus on questions of class and social privilege. His collections include *The Doctor's Son* (1935), *Files on Parade* (1939), *Pipe Night* (1945), *Hellbox* (1947), *Assembly* (1961), *The Cape Cod Lighter*

(1962), *The Horse Knows the Way* (1964) and *Waiting for Winter* (1967). His dramatic work was published in *Five Plays* (1961).

Okai, Atukwei [John] 1941– Ghanaian poet. He was born in Accra and was educated at Gambaga Native Authority Primary School, Nalerigu Middle Boys' School, Methodist Middle Boys' School and Accra High School, before studying for degrees at the Gorky Institute in Moscow and the University of London. He has based his academic career at the University of Ghana, where he teaches Russian language and literature, but he was for a brief time a minister in the first Rawlings government in Ghana. His poetry is little known outside Ghana, both because it incorporates many local references and words and because it relies for a full appreciation upon an element of performance, sometimes accompanied by drums. His collections of poetry include *Flowerfall* (1969), which was published in typescript, *Fontonfrom, and Other Poems* (1971) and *Lorgorligi Logarithms, and Other Poems* (1974). His *Selected Poems* came out in 1979. He frequently reads publicly from unpublished collections such as 'Calabash Chorus' or from long unpublished sequences such as 'Rhododendrons in Donkeydom'. He is one of the most metrically inventive African poets, always aware of the aural quality of a poem. He has very effectively amalgamated the traditions of African orality with innovatory modern poetic techniques, while at the same time stretching the possibilities of the English language in Africa.

Okara, Gabriel (Imomotimi Gbaingbain) 1921– Nigerian poet and novelist. The son of an Ijaw chief, he was born at Bumoundi in the Niger delta and educated at Government College, Umuahia, Yaba Higher College and, as a mature student, at Northwestern University in the USA. He has followed careers in publishing and in government information services. During the Nigerian Civil War he was director of the Cultural Affairs Division of the Biafran Ministry of Education and acted with CHINUA ACHEBE as a roving ambassador for the Biafran cause. Though he has published little and did not issue his first collection, *The Fisherman's Invocation*, until 1978, he enjoys a high reputation for lyric poetry rooted in the oral tradition. Many of his best-known poems, such as 'The Snowflakes Sail Gently Down', are frequently included in anthologies. A novel, *The Voice* (1964), has been widely noticed for its attempt at a form of English which incorporates the structural principles of the Ijaw language.

O'Keeffe, John 1747–1833 Irish playwright, born in Dublin. Of the 60 plays and operas he refers to in his *Recollections* (2 vols., 1826), most were written after he had settled in London in *c.* 1780. Only one, *Wild Oats* (1791), has achieved lasting fame. It is an artificial but quick-moving comedy, whose leading character, a strolling player called Rover, has a dramatic quotation to suit every occasion. O'Keeffe had been blind for several years when he wrote it.

Okigbo,   Christopher 1932–67 Nigerian poet. Born in Ojoto village, he graduated in classics (1956) before working first in business and then as civil servant, teacher, librarian and publisher. A Biafran major in the Nigerian Civil War, he was killed in action near Nsukka. Most of his poetry was posthumously collected in *Labyrinths* (1971), with an introduction he wrote in 1965; *Collected Poems* (1986), edited by ADEWALE MAJA-PEARCE, is fuller. Among anglophone African writers, Okigbo has possibly the most fertile, and most mythopoeic, poetic imagination; he always rejoiced in unexpected correspondences among apparently disparate cultural references. In his own life he could reconcile his Catholicism with his being hereditary priest of a traditional Igbo village deity, and this priesthood is subsumed in his function as a modern poet in English open to influences from the classics, the Bible, Catholic liturgy, and poets like HOPKINS and T. S. ELIOT. To Okigbo poetry is offering, ceremony and ritual, with the celebrant (the speaking voice of the persona in the poem) seeking to break through the mufflings of normality, to reach a truer definition of self and a larger reality, of which snatches of music and gleams of light are revealed to him as intimations. Moreover, 'Heavensgate' (1962) and 'Limits' (1964) are structured like musical compositions with *leitmotifs*, rather than through logical progression. Okigbo the individualist seeking elusive other-worldly revelation is never wholly self-centred, and in his last, 'drum' poems, the poet-prophet, 'I, Okigbo, town-crier', warns of the storm about to break over his people, leaving 'barren farmlands', 'homesteads abandoned', 'corn cobs in burning barns'. He is the subject of a novel, *The Trial of Christopher Okigbo* (1971), by ALI MAZRUI, and a commemorative volume, *Don't Let Him Die* (1978), by his friend CHINUA ACHEBE.

Okike: An African Journal of New Writing A journal founded by CHINUA ACHEBE in 1971 and edited by him for its first decade. *Okike* (the Igbo word for 'creation') provides a forum for poets, novelists, playwrights, artists and literary critics, encouraging them to create and discuss works which are distinctively African. The special Educational Supplement introduced in 1979 seeks to promote a greater interest in African writing in the school and university systems. The current editor is Ossie Onnara Enekwe and the journal is published in Nsukka, Anambra State, Nigeria.

Okpewho, Isadore 1941– Nigerian novelist and

critic. Born in Abraka in the former Mid-West state, he was educated at St Patrick's College, Asaba, the University of Ibadan and the University of Denver, Colorado. He has worked as a publisher and editor in Lagos and as a teacher of oral literature and creative writing at the University of Ibadan. In addition to a critical study, *The Epic in Africa* (1979), he has published two novels. *The Victims* (1970) presents a family consumed by guilt and hatred and ground down into poverty without the institution of polygamy to provide economic and psychological support. *The Last Duty* (1981) studies the effects of the Nigerian Civil War on six characters who interpret their duty in different ways.

Okri, Ben 1959– Nigerian novelist and short-story writer. Born in Lagos, he was educated there privately after a period at Urhobo College, Warri. He also studied at the University of Essex in England. He belongs a small group of younger writers who have largely abandoned the historical and political subjects, the interest in rural life and the attempt to 'Africanize' English which characterize the work of CHINUA ACHEBE's generation in favour of a more personal and introspective mode. His prodigious if slightly unwieldy talent was announced in two apparently autobiographical novels, *Flowers and Shadows* (1980) and *The Landscapes Within* (1981), and two collections of short stories, *Incidents at the Shrine* (1986) and *Stars of the New Curfew* (1988), ranging more widely to include sharply realistic tales set at the time of the Nigerian Civil War as well as surreal evocations of urban and village life. *The Famished Road* (1991), which won the BOOKER PRIZE,

Ben Okri

views urban Nigeria through the eyes of an *abiku*, or child returned from the dead. The result is vivid, hallucinatory and sometimes brutal, mingling Yoruba myth and tradition with the harsh realities of life in the shanty towns.

Old Bachelor, The WILLIAM CONGREVE's first play, a comedy, produced and published in 1693. Its success was helped considerably by the performances of Anne Bracegirdle and Thomas Betterton.

The old bachelor of the title is Heartwell, who maintains a pose of despising women. But he falls in love with Silvia and is persuaded to marry her, only to discover that she is Vainlove's discarded mistress. He is later intensely relieved to discover that the parson who married them is Vainlove's friend Belmour, in disguise to pursue an intrigue with Laetitia Fondlewife, already married to an uxorious old banker. Heartwell is still a bachelor, and a husband is found for Silvia in the person of Sir Joseph Wittol, a foolish old man deceived into believing he is marrying the wealthy Araminta. His companion, the bully Captain Bluffe, is similarly deceived into marrying Silvia's maid.

Old Creole Days A collection of seven stories of life in 19th-century Louisiana by GEORGE WASHINGTON CABLE, published in 1879. (A short novel, *MADAME DELPHINE*, was added in later editions.) The chief setting is the old French section of New Orleans populated by Creoles, Cubans, Spaniards and Santo Domingan refugees, as well as by incoming groups of Germans, Irish and Sicilians. Cable was especially adept in transcribing the varied dialects of the region, but his plots often take a sentimental or melodramatic turn.

A typical tale, 'Jean-ah Poquelin', set in the first decade of the century, deals with a once wealthy indigo planter, who now lives a secluded life on his decayed estate near the edge of the burgeoning settlement. Because of the unexplained disappearance of his half-brother and his militant refusal to let anyone trespass on his property, he has gained a reputation as an evil man who has some great wickedness to hide. After his death it is discovered that he has for many years concealed and cared for his half-brother, now an aged and helpless leper. The collection ends with the tale 'Madame Délicieuse'. It concerns a longstanding quarrel between Madame Délicieuse's fiancé, Dr Mossy, a forward-looking young man who champions scientific advances, and his father, General Villivicencio, who is waging a campaign for public office to restore old Bourbon values and to purge New Orleans of Yankee ideals. Madame Délicieuse, a Creole beauty, engineers a reconciliation between father and son, thus making her marriage possible. The other stories in the volume are 'Café des Exiles', 'Belle Demoiselle Plantation', 'Posson Jone', 'Tite Poulette' and 'Sieur George'.

Old Curiosity Shop, The A novel by CHARLES DICKENS, first published in the weekly miscellany *MASTER HUMPHREY'S CLOCK* from April 1840 to February 1841. It appeared in volume form in 1841.

Little Nell (Nell Trent) lives in the shop of the title with her grandfather, the proprietor. A gambler and a prey to grasping relatives, he falls into the clutches of the moneylender Daniel Quilp, an evil dwarf. Nell and her grandfather run away and roam the countryside, reduced to beggary. Quilp seizes the shop and sets out in pursuit. Kit Nubbles, the errand boy at the shop, does his best to find and help them; he becomes a victim of Quilp's hatred, which nearly succeeds in getting him framed and transported. Nell's great-uncle, returned from abroad, succeeds in tracing them only when it is too late. Exhausted by her troubles, Nell dies a lingering death, followed soon afterwards by her grandfather. Trying to evade arrest, Quilp drowns in the Thames. Although it is today among the least regarded of Dickens's novels, *The Old Curiosity Shop* was at the time an immediate success. Little Nell's prolonged deathbed scenes appealed powerfully to the 19th-century love of pathos and her death caused widespread mourning among Dickens's readers.

Old Fortunatus, The Pleasant Comedy of An allegorical play by THOMAS DEKKER, first performed before Elizabeth I on Christmas night, probably in 1598, and published in 1600. Its source is a story in the German *Volksbuch* (1509) which had been dramatized by Hans Sachs in 1553.

An old beggar, Fortunatus, meets the goddess Fortune and is offered the choice of long life, wisdom, strength, health, beauty or riches. He takes the last and is given a purse that will yield ten pieces of gold at any time. He goes on his travels with his sons and frequently encounters both Vice and Virtue. He gains possession of the miraculous hat of the Soldan of Turkey, which takes the wearer wherever he wants to go. But Death takes Fortunatus. The purse and hat go to his son, Andelocia, who follows the same way of life as his father and comes to grief when Fortune withdraws the purse and hat. He has learned nothing and without Fortune's favour can make nothing of his life.

Old Mortality A novel by SIR WALTER SCOTT, the second in the first series of his *Tales of My Landlord*, published in 1816 and for many years one of his most admired works. The title is the nickname of Robert Paterson who, at the end of the 18th century, wandered round Scotland caring for the graves of the Cameronians, or strict Covenanters. His stories of the 17th-century Covenanters persecuted by John Graham of Claverhouse form the basis of the novel.

The hero of the story is Henry Morton, who shelters

John Balfour of Burley, an old friend of his father, not knowing him to be guilty of having taken part in the murder of the Archbishop of St Andrews. Morton's narrow escape from execution, and his anger at the suppression of his countrymen, lead him to join the Covenanters, though he does not share their religious extremism.

Against this background are set the vicissitudes of Morton's love for Edith Bellenden of a royalist family. His rival is the honourable Lord Evandale, who helps save Morton's life, at Edith's plea, when Morton is arrested after the murder of the archbishop. Banished for some years after the defeat of the Covenanters at Bothwell Bridge, Morton returns to England on the accession of William III to find that Edith has given him up for dead and is about to marry Evandale. Preparations for the marriage are halted and shortly afterwards Evandale is attacked by a band of religious fanatics and killed in spite of Morton's desperate intervention.

Old Vic Theatre This theatre in the Waterloo Road, London, was called the Royal Coburg when it opened in 1818. By the time it was renamed the Royal Victoria in 1833 it was already a popular home of spectacular and often crude MELODRAMA. Soon referred to as the 'Old Vic', the theatre suffered a decline in fortune and was closed in 1880. From 1881 until 1912 it was owned and managed by Emma Cons, who dedicated herself to the provision of cheap but decent entertainment 'on strict temperance lines'. Her niece, Lilian Baylis, took over the management from 1912 until her death in 1937. It was under her idiosyncratic direction that the Old Vic established its reputation as a theatre for SHAKESPEARE. Bombed in 1941 and not fully rebuilt until 1950, the Old Vic, under the direction of Michael Benthall, presented all the plays in the Shakespeare First Folio between 1953 and 1958. It was the first home of the ROYAL NATIONAL THEATRE (then just the National Theatre) in 1962–76.

Old Wives' Tale, The A play by GEORGE PEELE, published in 1595. Usually regarded as his best work, it combines rhetoric, spectacle, robust humour and lyricism to satirize the romantic drama of the time. MILTON used the plot as the basis for his masque *COMUS*.

Delia has been stolen by the wicked magician Sacrapant and her two brothers are searching for her. But the brothers also fall victim and a gallant knight, Sir Eumenides, sets out to rescue them. Sir Eumenides is aided in his quest by the ghost of Jack, a poor man whose funeral he had paid for. The quest is successful, the magician defeated, and Delia and her brothers rescued.

Old Wives' Tale, The A novel by ARNOLD BENNETT, published in 1908.

The lives of two sisters, Constance and Sophia, are the focus of a study of the Baines family, prosperous drapers of Bursley in the Potteries. The story starts in 1860 and ends in about 1906 with the sisters' deaths. 'Mrs Baines', the first of four parts, shows the domestic and commercial struggles of a family in which the father is bedridden. Constance's restricted ambitions, her marriage to the Baines's apprentice, Samuel Povey, and motherhood, are densely elaborated through Parts One and Two. The parallelism between her life and Sophia's, whose ambition to become a teacher is frustrated, is one component of a highly structured novel.

Constance is left in lonely widowhood when her son Cyril departs to a London art college. Part Three recapitulates the life of Sophia. We are told of her elopement with Gerald Scales, a glamorous commercial traveller; his desertion of her in Paris; her survival of the Siege of Paris in the Franco-Prussian War; and her achievement of independence as proprietor of the Pension Frensham.

After an exchange of letters, an elderly Sophia returns to the same house in Bursley to live with her sister. Sophia's journey to Manchester, where she is too late to speak to the dying Gerald Scales, strikes a grim keynote to this concluding section, 'What Life Is'.

Oldham, John 1653–83 Satirical poet. The son of a Nonconformist minister, Oldham was born at Shipton-Moyne in Gloucestershire. He was educated at Tetbury Grammar School and St Edmund Hall, Oxford, earning his living as a teacher after graduating in 1674.

Oldham impressed contemporaries (DRYDEN among them) as a poet of great promise, and his early death from smallpox was mourned as a serious loss to literature. His chief works were *A Satire upon a Woman, Who by Her Falsehood and Scorn was the Death of My Friend* (1678), *A Satire against Virtue* (1679) and four *Satires upon the Jesuits* (1681), all written in the aftermath of the discovery of the 'Popish Plot' by Titus Oates. The manner is confident, the matter (especially in the attacks on the Jesuits) aggressive in the extreme. Oldham had a propensity for roughness of effect and for the stylistic excesses of his age. Perhaps Dryden's tribute was earned by Oldham's other works: an ODE *Upon the Works of Ben Jonson*, SATIRES in the manner of Horace and two translations from Juvenal. His *Poems and Translations*, which appeared in the year of his death, was widely read until the early 18th century.

Oldmixon, John 1673–1742 Historian. Born at Axbridge in Somerset, he was privately educated in the household of Admiral Blake and later succeeded to the manor of Oldmixon near Bridgwater. His career as a historian began with *A Complete History of*

England, with the Lives of All the Kings and Queens Thereof to the Death of William III, which he edited; it was published in 1706 and again, with additions, in 1716. More important was The British Empire in America (1708), the first history of that subject. The Secret History of Europe (4 vols., 1712–15) was unsparing in its criticism of the Tory party for its willingness to reach agreement with the French. To the third edition (1727) of the Critical History of England (2 vols., 1724–6) Oldmixon added an 'Essay on Criticism' that revealed his own fiercely anti-Tory bias and made him the target for POPE and other hostile wits. The History of England during the Reigns of the Royal House of Stuart (1730) is regarded by some scholars as his best work; it states at length the reason for believing that the Oxford editors of CLARENDON'S HISTORY OF THE REBELLION meddled with the text for political reasons.

Oldtown Folks A novel by HARRIET BEECHER STOWE, published in 1869, and set in the fictional Oldtown, Massachusetts, during the post-Revolutionary period. The young Horace Holyoke narrates a rather conventional romance plot about two runaway children who find happiness in spite of their oppressive upbringing in a leading Oldtown family. Holyoke's spiritual turn of mind makes him particularly attentive to the town's religious life. Both children are adopted into clerical families. The boy, Henry, becomes an Anglican minister. Tina marries Davenport, a dashing aristocratic officer, but when Davenport is killed in a duel she eventually marries Holyoke. Other memorable citizens are Parson and 'Lady' Lothrop, and Sam Lawson, whose offhanded commentary provides the novel's comic perspective.

Oliphant, Laurence 1829–88 Travel-writer and journalist. He was born in Cape Town and qualified as a barrister in Ceylon, where his father was Chief Justice, before embarking on an adventurous life which made him one of the most remarkable travellers of his day. He published Journey to Khatmandu (1852) and The Russian Shores of the Black Sea (1853); later he was consulted as an authority upon the outbreak of the Crimean War. He was Lord Elgin's secretary in the USA and Canada (1853–4) and published Minnesota and the Far West in 1855. As a correspondent for The Times he covered certain aspects of the Crimean War, the Indian Mutiny, and the Risorgimento. He accompanied Lord Elgin to the Far East, published a Narrative of the Earl of Elgin's Mission to China and Japan in the Years 1857, 58, 59 (1859), and sent dispatches to The Times from the Franco-Prussian War. To all this can be added a pleasantly satirical novel about London life, Piccadilly (1866).

In 1867 Oliphant became so besotted with the American 'prophet' Thomas Lake Harris that he surrendered his property to him. After this disillusioning experience he founded a community of Jewish immigrants at Haifa, where he wrote a second novel Altiora Peto (1883) and, with his wife, the curious Sympneumata (1885), which they believed to have been dictated by a spirit. The autobiographical Episodes of a Life of Adventure appeared in 1887, and his cousin MARGARET OLIPHANT wrote his biography (1892).

Oliphant, Margaret 1828–97 Novelist and biographer. Born near Musselburgh, she married her cousin, the artist Francis Wilson Oliphant. Her first novel, Mrs Margaret Maitland (1849), began a prolific career in literature extending to more than 100 books and some 200 contributions to BLACKWOOD'S EDINBURGH MAGAZINE. Of the Chronicles of Carlingford, a series of novels dealing with Scottish life, Salem Chapel (1863) and Miss Marjoribanks (1866) received particular praise. Her other Scottish novels included The Minister's Wife (1869), Effie Ogilvie (1886) and Kirsteen (1890). A Beleaguered City (1880) is a story of the occult. She also wrote histories and biographies, notably a Life of her cousin LAURENCE OLIPHANT (1892) and Annals of a Publishing House: William Blackwood and His Sons (1897). Her Autobiography (1899) records her efforts to support her own and her brother's children through writing.

Oliver Twist: or, The Parish Boy's Progress A novel by CHARLES DICKENS, first issued in monthly instalments in BENTLEY'S MISCELLANY between February 1837 and April 1839. It was published in book form in 1838.

Oliver Twist is born in the workhouse, where his mother has been brought after being found half-dead in the street. She dies giving birth to him and, until he is nine, Oliver is placed in the care of Mrs Mann at a branch workhouse; then he is taken back by Mr Bumble, the parish beadle, to the workhouse proper. After outraging the authorities by daring to 'ask for more', Oliver is apprenticed to an undertaker, where he is no better used than in the workhouse. He runs away and meets the Artful Dodger (Jack Dawkins), who takes him to Fagin's den in the London slums. Fagin has a stable of boys being trained to steal; his associates are the coarse and brutal burglar Bill Sikes and Nancy, a prostitute.

Oliver is rescued by the benevolent Mr Brownlow but the gang of thieves kidnaps him; prompted by the villainous Monks, they have a special interest in keeping him. They send him out with Bill Sikes to break into a house, but the thieves are surprised and Oliver is shot. The lady of the house, Mrs Maylie, is horrified to discover that the wounded burglar is only a child; she and her adopted daughter Rose take care of Oliver, nursing him back to health.

Nancy, meanwhile, has learned that there is something about Oliver's origins that Monks wants to suppress. She visits Rose Maylie and warns her that Fagin is being bribed by Monks to corrupt Oliver and that there is some relationship between Rose herself and Oliver. With the help of Mr Brownlow, enquiries are begun. Nancy's betrayal is discovered by the gang and Bill Sikes murders her. In the hue and cry that follows he hangs himself accidentally and Fagin and the rest are taken. Monks is investigated by Mr Brownlow and his motives at last revealed: he is Oliver's half-brother, greedily seeking the whole inheritance for himself. Rose Maylie is Oliver's aunt. Fagin is hanged at the end of the story and Oliver is adopted by Mr Brownlow.

Although Dickens wrote *Oliver Twist* while he was finishing THE PICKWICK PAPERS and editing *Bentley's Miscellany*, the novel is remarkable for its clarity of purpose and its sustained intensity. One aim, as the preface made clear, was to correct the glamorous portrayal of criminals in the popular NEWGATE FICTION of the day by showing the sordid reality of the London underworld. Another was to attack the harsh inhumanity of the New Poor Law of 1834. In later years Dickens used an edited version of the murder of Nancy and Sikes's flight from justice in his successful public readings.

Olsen, Tillie 1913– American short-story writer and novelist. Born in Nebraska, she published her first book, *Tell Me a Riddle* (1962), when she was nearly 50. The stories draw on her experience as a working-class wife, mother, wage-earner and labour activist in San Francisco. The title story, an often anthologized feminist classic, portrays a working-class grandmother reviewing her early political and personal aspirations and their gradual fragmentation and frustration by the competing claims of her role as wife and mother. *Yonnondio: From the Thirties* (1974) is the story, seen through the eyes of a young girl, of a poor family's journey from a mining town to a tenant farm to the slums of an industrial city in an unsuccessful search for a way out of poverty and despair. *Silences* (1978), a collection of essays, draws on personal and literary sources to explain how social and economic pressures prevent members of oppressed groups from becoming writers.

Olson, Charles 1910–70 American poet. He was born in Worcester, Massachusetts, and educated at Harvard, Yale and Wesleyan Universities. In 1948 he took a position at the experimental Black Mountain College in North Carolina, and from 1951 to 1956 was rector there. His essay 'Projective Verse' (1950), advocating 'open forms' and 'composition by field' which abandoned conventional METRE, was widely influential and attracted a number of poets to the college, including ROBERT CREELEY, DENISE LEVERTOV and ROBERT DUNCAN. They became known as the BLACK MOUNTAIN SCHOOL.

Olson's major poetic work, the *Maximus Poems*, began to appear in 1953. Like WILLIAM CARLOS WILLIAMS's *PATERSON*, it concentrates on a single town – in this case, Gloucester, Massachusetts – in which the central figure, Maximus, attempts to discover the energies shaping both personal and social history. Its various volumes are *The Maximus Poems 1–10* (1953), *The Maximus Poems 11–22* (1956), a single edition containing poems 1–22 and simply entitled *The Maximus Poems* (1960), *Maximus, from Dogtown I* (1961), *Maximus Poems IV, V, VI* (1968) and the posthumously published *The Maximus Poems: Volume Three* (1975). The first complete edition was published in 1983.

Olson's other books of verse include *To Corrado Cagli* (1947), *y & x* (1948), *Letter for Melville* (1951), *This* (1952), *In Cold Hell, in Thicket* (1953), *O'Ryan 1 2 3 4 5 6 7 8 9 10* (1965), *Selected Writings* (1967), *Archaeologist of Morning: The Collected Poems outside the Maximus Series* (1970). His prose works include *Mayan Letters* (1953), *Human Universe and Other Essays* (1965), *Causal Mythology* (1969) and *The Special View of History* (1970). *Projective Verse* (1959) and *Poetry and Truth: The Beloit Lectures and Poems* (1971) are books of criticism.

Omnium, Jacob See HIGGINS, MATTHEW.

Omoo: A Narrative of Adventures in the South Seas A novel by HERMAN MELVILLE, published in 1847. It was inspired by the author's second whaling voyage, beset by a dry whaling season, a sick captain, and an unsuccessful mutiny. A sequel to the controversial *TYPEE*, accepted only reluctantly by the publisher, it incited new attacks by critics who objected to Melville's depiction of the failure of missionary work in Tahiti.

The nameless narrator is rescued from the sea after his flight from the Marquesas and signs on the crew of the *Julia*, the ship whose boat has picked him up. The *Julia* proves to be unseaworthy and her captain ill and unstable, but the narrator makes friends with the mate, Jermin, and with the worldly and cheerful Dr Long Ghost. In Tahiti the crew members refuse to take the ship to sea again and are imprisoned. The narrator and the doctor are released and manage to find work on a plantation in Imeeo. Finding that fieldwork is not to their liking, they resort to beachcombing, at the same time exploring the island and observing the people. At the end the doctor stays on in Tahiti while the narrator ships out on the whaler *Leviathan*.

On the Road A semi-autobiographical novel by JACK KEROUAC, published in 1957. One of the most fundamental and popular statements by the BEATS, it tells of a group of friends travelling around America in search of new and intense experiences. The chaos, exhilaration and despair of the quest is conveyed by the headlong style of Sal Paradise's narration. Sal accompanies his friends on four separate trips as they travel the country, spending time in Colorado, California, Virginia, New York and Mexico. Several of the characters are modelled on Kerouac's friends: Dean Moriarty, the guiding spirit of the group, is Neal Cassady and Carlo Marx is ALLEN GINSBERG.

Ondaatje, Michael 1943– Canadian writer, born in Sri Lanka. He moved to England, where he was edu-

cated at Dulwich College, in 1954 and to Canada, where he studied at the University of Toronto and Queen's University, Kingston, in 1962. He has taught at the University of Western Ontario and York University, Toronto, and now lives in Toronto. He first received critical acclaim for *The Dainty Monsters* (1967), *The Man with Seven Toes* (1969) and *Rat Jelly* (1973), poetry characterized by a surreal vision in which macabre imagery and unexpected conjunctions force readers to reassess their habitual ways of

Michael Ondaatje

viewing the world. Later volumes are *There's a Trick with a Knife I'm Learning to Do* (1979) and *The Cinnamon Peeler* (1990), a collection which brings together much of the best of his earlier poetry. Ondaatje's exploration of cultural assumptions has led him to a new form combining prose, poetry and visual representation in discontinuous narratives. The first, *The Collected Works of Billy the Kid* (1970), is a collage of fictional and factual response to the outlaw, presented as an engaging psychopath. *Coming through Slaughter* (1979) deals with the life of the New Orleans jazz musician Billy Bolden. In *Running in the Family* (1982), based on a journey back to Sri Lanka, the exploration of personal and public mythologies is centred on the figure of the travelling author.

Two novels, *In the Skin of a Lion* (1987) and *The English Patient* (1992), co-winner of the BOOKER PRIZE, are considered his finest works to date. The former is set in Toronto during the 1920s and 1930s. The latter, set in war-torn Italy in 1945, brings together four characters, of different ages and backgrounds, whose lives have been affected by the larger forces of public history.

One Flew over the Cuckoo's Nest A novel by KEN KESEY, published in 1962, about the inmates of a psychiatric ward. The story is told from the viewpoint of an ex-reservation Indian named Bromden, who pretends to be deaf and dumb. The inmates are kept in place by their dread of Big Nurse. Into this scene comes the reckless, ingenious and defiant McMurphy. Under his leadership the inmates rebel against Big Nurse, the climax – and McMurphy's triumph – coming when they sneak out for a trip on a yacht. However, McMurphy has a lobotomy performed on him by the doctors. Bromden cannot bear to see him in this state. He smothers him out of rage and pity and then heaves a panel of medical equipment through a window to make his escape.

One of Our Conquerors A novel by GEORGE MEREDITH, published in 1891.

Nesta Victoria is the illegitimate daughter of Victor Radnor and Natalia Dreighton. Victor's wife, a rich elderly woman to whom Natalia was once companion, is still alive and his life with Natalia is haunted by the fear of exposure. Nesta's suitor, the Hon. Dudley Sowerby, is unenthusiastic when he learns the story of her birth and of her determination to continue her friendship with the hapless Mrs Marsett, the mistress of an army officer. Natalia, also unhappy about her daughter's friendship, falls ill during the crisis and dies. Victor receives news of his wife's death within a few hours of Natalia's passing. The cruel irony of this, and the loss of Natalia, unhinge his mind. Victor lives for a few years, while Nesta eventually marries a more worthy suitor, Dartrey Fenellan.

O'Neill,   Eugene   (Gladstone) 1888–1953 American playwright. He was born in New York, the younger son of James O'Neill, a popular actor. As a child he toured with his father, and attended a Catholic boarding school and a preparatory school in Connecticut. He enrolled at Princeton University for a year (1906–7), then held a series of jobs including prospecting for gold, several months as a seaman on a Norwegian freighter and a brief spell as a journalist in Connecticut. He then spent time in a tuberculosis sanatorium (1912–13), and his early one-act plays date from this period of confinement. His involvement with the Provincetown Players brought him, and the company, to the attention of the New York public, initially with a sequence of plays about the SS *Glencairn* and its crew: *Bound East for Cardiff* (1916), *In the Zone* (1917), *The Long Voyage Home* (1917) and *The Moon of the Caribees* (1918). Two other plays, not in the Glencairn cycle but drawing on his memories of life at sea, won the PULITZER PRIZE: *Beyond the Horizon* (1920) and *Anna Christie* (1921; first produced as *Chris* in 1920).

O'Neill went on to become a major influence on the development of the modern American theatre, exploring difficult subjects and experimenting with a variety of dramatic styles. Black Americans made up the cast of *The Dreamy Kid* (1919); an interracial marriage is the subject of *All God's Chillun Got Wings* (1924); and in *THE EMPEROR JONES* (1920) a black actor dominates the stage in the central role. The EXPRESSIONISM of *The Emperor Jones* is further developed in *The Hairy Ape* (1922), in which a ship's stoker's alienation from his peers causes him to embrace his own animality, and in the mask-drama *The Great God Brown* (1926). *STRANGE INTERLUDE* (1928), which won O'Neill a third Pulitzer Prize, portrays the life of its central character, Nina Leeds, through the juxtaposition of conventional dialogue with stylized internal monologue. O'Neill's interest in the familial patterns of Greek tragedy and in Nietzsche's opposition of the Apollonian and the Dionysian is evident in the grim New England tragedy *Desire under the Elms* (1924), and is the motive force behind *MOURNING BECOMES ELECTRA* (1931), a reworking of Aeschylus' *Oresteia* in the context of the American Civil War.

After the failure of *Days without End* (1934), O'Neill, suffering from increasing ill health which was eventually diagnosed as Parkinson's disease, maintained a long theatrical silence, unbroken by the award of the Nobel Prize in 1936. *THE ICEMAN COMETH* (1946), his first new play to be performed for 12 years, is set in a Bowery bar. *LONG DAY'S JOURNEY INTO NIGHT* (first performed 1956; Pulitzer Prize 1957) is a tortured but compassionate portrait of his own family, a subject he had treated more lightly and with nostalgia in the comedy *Ah, Wilderness!* (1933). *A Moon for the Misbegotten* (first performed 1957) continues the story of the alcoholic elder brother of *Long Day's*

Journey into Night, describing the process of his self-destruction on a Connecticut farm following his mother's death. Of a projected 11-play cycle which was to trace the fortunes of an American family from the 18th to the 20th centuries, only *A Touch of the Poet* (first performed 1957) and the incomplete *More Stately Mansions* (first performed 1962) were actually written. *Hughie*, the single play of another projected series, was first performed in 1958.

onomatopoeia The formation of a word by imitation of a sound associated with the thing described; for example, 'hurlyburly', 'lullabye', and many of our words for animal calls.

Oodgeroo [Walker, Kath] 1920–93 Australian Aboriginal poet, of the tribe Noonuccal or Nunukul. She grew up on Stradbroke Island, Moreton Bay, Queensland, where many of the old Aboriginal customs survived. *We are Going* (1964) swiftly gained popularity with a white Australian audience. Its title-poem is a moving ELEGY on the dispossession of the Aboriginal people; other poems, such as 'Municipal Gum', call attention to their plight. Later collections are *Dawn is at Hand* (1966) and *My People* (1970). *Stradbroke Dreamtime* (1972) combines traditional Aboriginal stories with stories from her childhood. *Father Sky and Mother Earth* (1981) and *Australian Legends and Landscapes* (1990) also seek to make the Aboriginal view of the world accessible.

Opie, Amelia 1769–1853 Novelist and poet. Born Amelia Alderson in Norwich, she inherited radical opinions from her father and in youth became a friend and admirer of WILLIAM GODWIN and MARY WOLLSTONECRAFT. She turned to writing in earnest after her marriage to the painter John Opie in 1798, producing much popular fiction and poetry. Her novels included *Father and Daughter* (1801), *Adeline Mowbray* (suggested by Mary Wollstonecraft's life; 1802) and *Simple Tales* (1806). Their subject is usually domestic, their tone moral and sentimental. After her husband's death in 1807 she returned to Norwich, continuing her career with *Valentine's Eve* (1816) and *Madeline* (1822). She stopped writing novels after her conversion to Quakerism in 1825, but continued to find the lure of literary society irresistible and remained a friend of many leading figures of the day. In later life she devoted much of her energy to the Bible Society and the Anti-Slavery Society. Her last book, a volume of poetry, was *Lays for the Dead* (1833).

Opie, Peter (Mason) 1918–82 and **Opie, Iona (Margaret Balfour)** 1923– British folklorists and anthologists. Peter Opie was born in Cairo but educated in England. He married Iona Archibald in 1943. After the birth of their first child in 1944 the couple decided to concentrate on the culture of childhood,

producing *I Saw Esau* (1947), a collection of children's skipping and singing rhymes. Their next project was *The Oxford Dictionary of Nursery Rhymes* (1951), an annotated collection that singlehandedly demolished the various false historical interpretations that Mother Goose has always managed to attract over the years. Next, for children alone, came *The Oxford Nursery Rhyme Book* (1955) and *The Puffin Book of Nursery Rhymes* (1963). Meanwhile, their *The Lore and Language of Schoolchildren* (1959) recorded the rhymes, chants and teases popular all over Britain, with *Children's Games in Street and Playground* (1969) doing the same for various non-verbal favourites. *The Oxford Book of Children's Verse* (1973) collected poems written about rather than by children, and *The Classic Fairy Tales* (1974) reissued some of the most famous of these stories as they first appeared, with a discussion of how and why they were often to change so radically over time. *The Singing Game* (1985) is a masterly survey of another aspect of children's oral culture, completed by Mrs Opie after her husband's death. She collaborated with Moira Tatem on *A Dictionary of Superstitions* (1989).

Oppen, George 1908–84 American poet. Born in New Rochelle, New York, he operated a poetry publishing house, called 'To Publishers', with his wife in 1930–3. Having joined the Communist Party in 1935, he moved to Mexico in 1950 to escape the pressure of McCarthyism. His first volume, *Discrete Series* (1934), was not followed by a second until *The Materials* (1962). *Of Being Numerous* (Pulitzer Prize, 1968) contains his two best-known works, the title poem and 'Route'. His work is gathered in *The Collected Poems of George Oppen, 1929–1975* (1975) and sampled in a selection by CHARLES TOMLINSON (1990). Closely associated with OBJECTIVISM, Oppen's work is concerned to realize concrete objects without drawing attention to itself formally; it uses clear images and lean, precise diction.

Orage, A. R. See NEW AGE, THE.

Orczy, Baroness **(Emma Magdalena Rosalia Marie Josefa Barbara)** 1865–1947 Novelist, short-story writer and playwright. Born in Hungary, she was educated in Brussels and Paris and arrived in London with her parents at the age of 15. She studied art and married a fellow student, Montagu Barstow, in 1894. Her fame as a writer of historical romance was established with *The Scarlet Pimpernel*, which introduced her hero, Sir Percy Blakeney, and his exploits rescuing victims from the guillotine during the French Revolution. Written in 1902, the novel was rejected by several publishers and Baroness Orczy had already dramatized it successfully in collaboration with her husband before its first publication in 1905. Its many popular sequels included *I Will Repay* (1906) and *The Elusive Pimpernel* (1908). Baroness Orczy also wrote DETECTIVE FICTION, notably in her ingenious stories about 'The Old Man in the Corner' (*The Case of Miss Elliott*, 1905; *The Old Man in the Corner*, 1909; *Unravelled Knots*, 1925) and less successfully in *Lady Molly of Scotland Yard* (1910).

Ordeal of Richard Feverel, The A novel by GEORGE MEREDITH, published in 1859.

Deserted by his wife, Sir Austin Feverel brings up his son Richard in his own way. Believing all schools to be corrupt, he educates the boy at home. But when Richard reaches adolescence be confounds his father by falling in love with Lucy Desborough, niece of a local farmer. Sir Austin acknowledges her quality but opposes the match because of her humble birth, and the two young people marry in secret.

Richard is devoted to his father, who now ruthlessly manipulates the boy's feelings to separate him from Lucy. Sir Austin sends Richard to London, where his friend Lord Mountfalcon, who has designs on Lucy, puts Richard in the path of a 'fallen' woman of considerable allure. Thinking to redeem her, Richard is easily seduced. He prolongs his absence from home and goes abroad, ashamed of his infidelity. He then learns that he is a father; moreover, Sir Austin is at last reconciled to Lucy as his daughter-in-law through the good offices of Richard's uncle, Wentworth. Richard hurries home. But just when happiness seems to be within his grasp, he discovers Lord Mountfalcon's villainy, challenges him to a duel and is seriously wounded. Lucy loses her reason and dies.

Oregon Trail, The FRANCIS PARKMAN's account of the journey he made with his cousin Quincy Adams Shaw in April–Sept 1846. It was serialized in *THE KNICKERBOCKER MAGAZINE* in 1847–9 and published in volume form as *The California and Oregon Trail* in 1849; the 1872 edition restored the original title.

Parkman and Shaw set out from St Louis to explore the northern Great Plains and Rocky Mountains. Travelling along both the Mormon and Oregon trails as far west as Fort Laramie, Wyoming, they encountered wagon trains of emigrants, Indians, Mormons, hunters, trappers, traders and buffalo. Excited by rumours that a Sioux chief, 'The Whirlwind' (Tunica), was planning to make war against the Snake Indians, Parkman planned to witness the event and was disappointed when the attack was called off. Leaving Shaw behind, he joined a band of 'Ogillallah' (Oglala) Sioux for a hunting excursion and lived among them for several weeks. He rejoined Shaw at Fort Laramie for the return trip. They travelled south through Colorado to the Arkansas River and then east to Missouri.

Origin of Species, The A work of natural history by CHARLES DARWIN, published in 1859 as *On the Origin of Species by Means of Natural Selection: or,*

The Preservation of Favoured Races in the Struggle for Life.

With Marx's *Capital*, it is probably the work which has most transformed the explanatory systems of the past hundred years. Darwin's theory of 'descent with modification' challenged the assumption that species are fixed and eternal. Rather, in the long history of the physical world many forms have passed away and their offspring have diverged more and more widely from the parent-type. Darwin argues for a 'single progenitor' of life on earth, an irrecoverable form far removed from any current type; he also argues that few current types will survive far into the future. Several mechanisms of change have been at work, including sexual selection and natural selection. 'Artificial selection', or husbandry, demonstrates that it is possible within a few generations to breed plants and creatures whose selected characteristics have advantages for the breeder. 'Natural selection', on the contrary, works unconsciously and to the advantage only of the individual and its progeny within a species, never in order to benefit other species. It operates through descent and relies on variation: individual organisms vary in differing degrees and across a spectrum of characteristics from the parent-generation. Those variations most apt to current physical conditions will prosper and produce offspring, which will in turn vary one from another and in some cases will intensify advantageous characteristics. By this slow means the highly specialized skills of current species have evolved: 'from so simple a beginning endless forms most beautiful and most wonderful have been, and are being evolved' concludes the sixth edition (1872).

Most commentators have represented Darwin's argument as a theory of competition, though it is now clearly recognized also as an ecological theory. It has been extrapolated into many fields, sometimes in contradictory ways. We meet it in race-theory, musical history and politics, though Darwin always insisted on its entirely biological reference. Darwin's name, and mutated forms of his theory, are inescapable in late 19th- and 20th-century literature ranging from THOMAS HARDY to DORIS LESSING's *Canopus in Argos* sequence of science-fiction novels.

Orlando: *A Biography* A novel by VIRGINIA WOOLF, published in 1928 and dedicated to V. SACKVILLE-WEST.

The deliberately fanciful story traces the career of the androgynous Orlando from the late 16th century to the present day, and contains a great many well-observed literary and historical insights into the ages through which it sweeps. As a handsome boy of 16, Orlando turns to poetry and completes 'Æthelbert: A Tragedy in Five Acts'. He becomes a favourite of Queen Elizabeth 1, who confers on him the Order of the Garter, and the lover of a Muscovite princess. Later he retires from society, writes 'forty-seven plays, histories, romances, poems', and enjoys the company of the irreverent English poet, Nicholas Greene. Under Charles II, Orlando becomes Ambassador Extraordinary to Constantinople and is rewarded with a dukedom. Then, after spending one night with a dancer, Rosina Pepita, he sleeps for a week and wakes to find that his sex has changed. Lady Orlando now pursues a career in high society through Queen Anne's reign, meeting POPE, ADDISON and SWIFT, until (as a Victorian) she eventually marries a sailor, Marmaduke Bonthrop Shelmerdine. Nicholas Greene reappears as the most influential critic of the Victorian age and arranges for the publication of Orlando's centuries-old poem 'The Oak Tree', which subsequently wins her 200 guineas. She gives birth to a baby, and the novel reaches the present day; as at the beginning, Orlando is a young poet, but this time a female one. The novel ends with her driving back from town to her ancestral home in Kent.

Orley Farm A novel by ANTHONY TROLLOPE, issued in 20 monthly parts from March 1861 to October 1862.

Sir Joseph Mason's will leaves his estate to Joseph, his son by his first wife, and in a codicil reserves Orley Farm for Lucius, his son by his second wife. Joseph contests the validity of the codicil but the law upholds it, and the widowed Lady Mason and her son Lucius live there in comfortable circumstances for 20 years. Then one of Lady Mason's tenants, Dockwrath, an attorney of dubious character, is given notice to quit. Feeling unjustly used, Dockwrath reopens the matter of the codicil. Everything points to forgery but Lady Mason's friends rally round to support her and her elderly lover, Sir Peregrine Orme, does not swerve from his belief in her probity. Mr Chaffanbrass appears in the case for Lady Mason and all goes in her favour. But her apparently unshakeable resolution breaks down afterwards and she confesses everything to Sir Peregrine. Orley Farm reverts to Joseph Mason.

The characters of Joseph Mason and his stepmother Lady Mason, so sharply contrasted, are consistent and totally believable; so are the former's resentment, smouldering for 20 years, and the strain on the latter, held at bay for the same period until her resolution is exhausted.

Ormulum A series of verse HOMILIES written in the early 13th century in the North-east Midlands. In a dedication the author identifies himself as Orm, saying that he is an Augustinian canon writing at the request of his brother Walter, also an Augustinian canon. He says that he will give in English the gospels of the mass book for the entire year, each accompanied by its interpretations and applications. The table of contents lists 242 homilies of which only 32 are extant; the series was probably never finished. The work has no literary merit, but is remarkable for its orthography, the most striking feature of which is the consistent doubling of consonants after a short vowel.

Oroonoko: *or, The Royal Slave* A novel by APHRA BEHN, published *c.* 1678 and included in *Three Histories* (1688). It was adapted for the stage by THOMAS SOUTHERNE in 1695 and enjoyed considerable further success.

Oroonoko, the grandson and heir of an African king, loves the beautiful Imoinda, daughter of the king's general. But the old king himself falls in love with Imoinda and commands that she be taken to his harem. When he discovers that she loves his grandson, he instead has her sold as a slave. The grieving Oroonoko is captured by an English slaver and sold in Surinam, where he finds Imoinda, also a slave. Oroonoko rouses the other slaves and inspires them to make an escape. They are hunted, and eventually induced to surrender to Byam, the deputy governor, on promise of a pardon. But Byam, once he has Oroonoko in his hands, has him flogged. Determined to exact retribution from Byam, Oroonoko realizes that he will not escape the consequences of killing him. At the same time he knows what will happen to Imoinda when he is no longer there to protect her. She understands and surrenders her life to Oroonoko, who is discovered near her body; he is prevented from taking his own life and executed with savage cruelty.

In Southerne's dramatized version Byam is motivated by his passion for Imoinda, and there is a comic sub-plot.

Mrs Behn's novel was the first expression in English literature of sympathy for the plight of slaves, and the author is thought to have had some first-hand experience of Surinam.

Orphan, The: *or, The Unhappy Marriage* A tragedy by THOMAS OTWAY, produced and published in 1680. The principal parts were played by Thomas Betterton and Elizabeth Barry.

Acasto has brought up Monimia, the orphan daughter of a friend, with his own twin sons, Castalio and Polydore. Monimia's brother, Chamont, is a soldier. The twin brothers have both fallen in love with Monimia; she loves Castalio, but from consideration of Polydore's feelings Castalio pretends indifference. Visiting his sister, Chamont believes that her disturbed emotions can be blamed on one of the twins, but his questions annoy her. Castalio declares his love, and he and Monimia are secretly married. Polydore does not know of the secret marriage; he overhears his brother arranging to meet Monimia during the night and contrives to take his brother's place. Monimia accepts him and Castalio, arriving later, finds himself barred from his wife's room. The deception is eventually revealed by Chamont, and the three unhappy lovers kill themselves.

Orpheus and Eurydice A Middle Scots poem by ROBERT HENRYSON. It adapts the classical story of Orpheus and Eurydice as a moral allegory of the vulnerability of affection and the relationship between reason and affection. The juxtaposition of narrative and moral is in places discordant, as in THE MORALL FABILLIS. The poem has some affinities with both classical and medieval renderings of the story of Orpheus, but is not closely dependent on either. Although there are some powerful lyric and descriptive passages, characterization is minimal, the narrative being subordinated to the moral allegory.

Ortiz, Simon 1941– Native American poet and short-story writer. He was born in Albuquerque, New Mexico, raised in the Acoma Pueblo community and educated at Fort Lewis College, the University of New Mexico and the University of Iowa. All his work reflects a strong concern for Native American civil rights. His volumes of poetry include *Naked in the Wind* (1970), *Going for the Rain* (1976), *Fight Back: For the Sake of the People, For the Sake of the Land* (1980), *From Sand Creek* (1981) and *Woven Stone* (1992). His stories include *Howbah Indians* (1977) and *Fightin': New and Collected Stories* (1983).

Orton, Joe (Kingsley) 1933–67 Playwright and actor. Born in Leicester, he trained at the Royal Academy of Dramatic Art. His exuberant tastelessness established him as a pioneer of a style of black FARCE. His first plays, *The Ruffian on the Stair* (1964) and *Entertaining Mr Sloane* (1964), derived from PINTER the idea of showing how the familiar inhabitants of a room can be menaced by a stranger's intrusion, but Orton's language was already distinct from the studied naturalness of Pinter. He admired the combination of elegance and crudity that he found in the work of the French playwright, Jean Genet, and it was this combination that characterized his best work. In *Loot* (1966), a mother's corpse becomes a comic property. In *The Erpingham Camp* (1967) Orton's malice towards professed religion culminates in an orgy of ritual destruction. In *What the Butler Saw* (1969) polished wit and artful mischief carry the farce tradition of threatened adultery into forbidden realms of incest and violence. Two years before this last play's performance, Orton was murdered by his male lover, who subsequently took his own life.

Orwell, George [Blair, Eric Arthur] 1903–50 Novelist, essayist and journalist. He was born in Bengal and educated in England at St Cyprian's and Eton. In 1922 he joined the Imperial Police in Burma, serving for five years before his mounting dislike of imperialism induced him to resign. He returned to a series of ill-paid jobs in Paris, then London, living in a state of 'fairly severe poverty' before becoming a regular contributor to THE ADELPHI from 1930. His first

book, *Down and Out in Paris and London* (1933), described these early experiences and was followed by *Burmese Days* (1934), a novel which continued to reflect his indignation over political injustice. Orwell's second novel, *A Clergyman's Daughter* (1935), about a middle-class woman's brief period of freedom among the tramps and hop-pickers, was followed by *Keep the Aspidistra Flying* (1936), the story of a young bookseller's assistant, Gordon Comstock, whose aspirations and humiliations closely paralleled the author's.

In 1936 Orwell was commissioned by the publisher Victor Gollancz to produce a documentary account of unemployment in the north of England for the LEFT BOOK CLUB. The result was THE ROAD TO WIGAN PIER (1937), a milestone in modern literary journalism which has become a classic of its kind. It established Orwell's political outlook as an unaligned democratic socialist, a position which he underlined in HOMAGE TO CATALONIA (1938), about his experiences as a volunteer with the Republican army during the Spanish Civil War.

Under the threat of World War II Orwell wrote *Coming Up For Air* (1939), a novel which reflected in the person of George Bowling, an insurance clerk, many of the frustrations and political concerns which preoccupied Orwell throughout his life. From 1943 to 1945 he was literary editor of *Tribune* and contributed many articles to it and other papers, including *The Observer* and *The Manchester Evening News*. His lucid and colloquial style was ideally suited to journalism, and it was as a pamphleteer that his talents were most in evidence. As he himself admitted, he was not really a novelist: 'One has masses of experience which one passionately wants to write about... and no way of using them except by disguising them as a novel.' However, ANIMAL FARM (1945) and NINETEEN EIGHTY-FOUR (1949), pessimistic SATIRES about the threat of political tyranny, have remained his most popular works.

His essays (including *Inside the Whale*, 1940; *Critical Essays*, 1946; and *Shooting an Elephant*, 1950) are gathered in the four volumes of *Collected Essays, Journalism and Letters*, edited by Sonia Orwell and Ian Angus (1968) and contain over 200 pieces on literature, politics and English life. Orwell's first wife, Eileen, died in 1945. He remarried in 1949, a year before he died of tuberculosis.

Osborne, Dorothy See TEMPLE, SIR WILLIAM.

Osborne, John (James) 1929– Playwright. Born in London and educated at a public school in Devon, Osborne wrote his first plays while working as an actor in English repertory theatres. LOOK BACK IN ANGER (1956), seen as the harbinger of a revolution in English drama, established him as the leader of the ANGRY YOUNG MEN. Those who viewed it, on its first

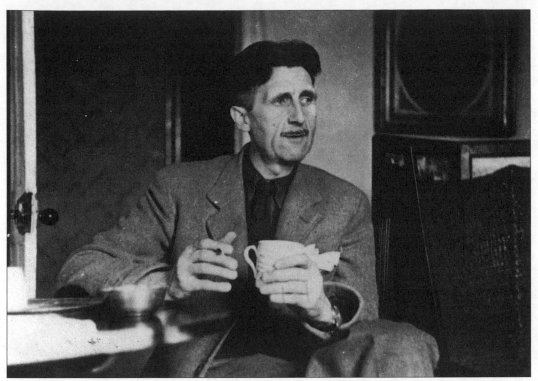

George Orwell

staging at the ROYAL COURT THEATRE in London, as an attack on British complacency have been disappointed by Osborne's subsequent plays, in which he is more often nostalgically disgruntled than angry. *The Entertainer* (1957) reflects the death of Edwardian values in the declining career of a music-hall comedian. *Luther* (1961) is a character study rather than a social thesis-play. *Inadmissible Evidence* (1964) takes its solicitor-hero through a draining process of self-recognition. *A Patriot for Me* (1966) is as much a spy-story as a study of decadence in the Austro-Hungarian Empire at the beginning of the 20th century. Later work has included *The Hotel in Amsterdam* (1968), *Time Present* (1968), *West of Suez* (1971), *A Sense of Detachment* (1972), *The End of Me Old Cigar* (1975), *Watch It Come Down* (1976) and *Déjàvu* (1992), returning to Jimmy Porter, the hero of *Look Back in Anger*. He is the author of a vigorous autobiography, *A Better Class of Person* (1981).

O'Shaughnessy, Arthur William Edgar 1844–81 Poet. Born in London and educated privately, he spent his working life in the British Museum and the Natural History Museum, where his subjects were fish and reptiles. ROSSETTI and other members of the PRE-RAPHAELITE BROTHERHOOD were both friends and influences on his poetry. He published *An Epic of Women* (1870), *Lays of France* (1872), *Music and Moonlight* (1874) and, with his

wife, a volume of verse for children, *Toyland* (1875). Today he is usually remembered only for the delicate 'Ode' in *Music and Moonlight* beginning 'We are the music-makers'.

Osofisan, Femi 1946– Nigerian playwright and novelist. Arguably the most talented and productive figure in the Nigerian theatre after WOLE SOYINKA, he uses his writing as an ideological weapon, treating social and political issues both seriously and satirically. His plays include: *The Chattering and the Song* (1977), a play within a play, which explores the attempt by a group of artists and intellectuals to remake the world; *Who's Afraid of Solarin?* (1978), a study of mistaken identity reminiscent of Gogol's *The Inspector General*, written to honour Tai Solarin, journalist and retired Commissioner of Public Complaints for Ogun, Oyo and Ondo States in western Nigeria; *Once Upon Four Robbers* (1978); *Farewell to a Cannibal Rage* (1986); *Oriki of a Grasshopper* (1987); *Birthdays Are Not For Dying* (together with *Fires Burn and Die Hard* and *The Inspector and the Hero* (1990); *Eshu and the Vagabond Minstrels* (1991); *Arigindin and the Nightwatchman* (1991); and *Yungba Yungba and the Dance Contest* (1993). Osofisan's novel *Kolera Kolej* (1975) is a SATIRE of political machinations in a post-independent African country; it was later adapted for staging by the department of theatre arts at the University of Ibadan, where he now teaches.

Ossian See MACPHERSON, JAMES.

O'Sullivan, Vincent 1937– New Zealand poet, short-story writer, novelist, playwright and critic. Educated at Auckland University and Oxford, he has taught at the University of Waikato and Victoria University of Wellington, where he is professor of English. Primarily a poet and short-story writer, O'Sullivan is one of New Zealand's most versatile writers. His early volumes of poetry, *Our Burning Time* (1965), *Revenants* (1969) and *Bearings* (1973), are predominantly lyric, repeatedly turning to myth for shape and meaning. *Butcher and Co.* (1977) and *The Butcher Papers* (1982) use a persona, the butcher, and show his flair for drama and SATIRE, as well as his keen ear for New Zealand vernacular. These qualities are also apparent in his short stories, *The Boy, The Bridge, The River* (1978) and *Dandy Edison for Lunch* (1981), which typically dramatize the awkward position of the outsider or nonconformist, a common theme in New Zealand writing. Subsequent volumes include poetry (*The Pilate Tapes*, 1986) and short stories (*Survivals*, 1985; *The Snow in Spain*, 1990). O'Sullivan has also written: *Miracle* (1976), a satirical novel; plays, including *Shuriken* (1985) and *Billy* (1990); and a critical study of JAMES K. BAXTER (1976). He has edited *The Oxford Anthology of Twentieth-Century New Zealand Poetry* (1970, 1976, 1987).

Osundare, Niyi 1947– Nigerian poet. Born in Ikere Ekiti, he was educated in Nigeria, Britain and Canada. A university lecturer and freelance journalist, he has helped to popularize poetry in Nigeria through his newspaper column in *Newswatch*. Reminiscent of the African oral tradition, his work is distinguished by its sustained lyricism and predominantly dramatic tone. It is best appreciated in performance and within the larger context which embraces the DUB POETRY of the Caribbean and Britain. Allying himself with the tradition of using poetry to chastize wrongdoers and advocate a just society, Osundare highlights the absurd, the humorous and the grotesque, and caricatures the ruling class while encouraging the audience to embrace his sympathetic portrayal of the people. Published collections include: *Songs of the Marketplace* (1983); *Village Voices* (1984); *A Nib in the Pond* (1986); *The Eye of the Earth* (1986), winner of the Association of Nigerian Authors' Poetry Prize and the Commonwealth Poetry Prize; *Moonsongs* (1988); *Songs of the Seasons* (1990); and *Waiting Laughters* (1990), winner of the 1991 Noma Award.

Othello, the Moor of Venice A tragedy by WILLIAM SHAKESPEARE, first performed *c.* 1604 and published in Quarto (Q1) in 1622 as well as in the First Folio of 1623. The source is a story in the *Hecatommithi* of Giraldo Cinthio (1565).

Othello, a Moor who has become a trusted general

Niyi Osundare

of the Venetian army, has secretly married Desdemona, daughter of a senator, Brabantio. It is immediately revealed to the audience that Othello's ensign Iago, whom Othello believes to be utterly loyal and 'honest', is scheming against him, ostensibly but perhaps no more than partially, because Othello chose Michael Cassio as his lieutenant in preference to him. At Iago's prompting Roderigo, a foolish suitor for Desdemona's hand, reports the marriage to Brabantio. The outraged father demands Othello's arrest, but has to accept the whole-heartedness of Desdemona's love when she appears before the senate. The news that the Turks are planning an attack on Cyprus requires Othello's immediate departure. He is joined in Cyprus by Desdemona, Iago, Cassio and Roderigo.

The dispersal of the Turkish fleet leaves Iago free to pursue his schemes in Cyprus. He contrives to discredit Cassio, whom Othello dismisses. Iago advises Cassio to appeal to Desdemona, and implants in Othello's mind a suspicion that Desdemona is more than friendly with Cassio. Her support of Cassio, together with Iago's torrent of innuendo, deepens the suspicion. Iago takes full advantage of Desdemona's accidental dropping of a handkerchief, the very one that Othello gave her as the first token of his love. He secretes it among Cassio's possessions, and the luckless Cassio gives it to his mistress, Bianca. When Othello sees the handkerchief in Bianca's possession, he is convinced of Desdemona's infidelity and humiliates her in public, to the dismay not least of Iago's increasingly troubled wife, Emilia.

Iago incites Roderigo to kill Cassio, but Roderigo manages only to wound him. Iago kills Roderigo to ensure his silence, and Othello, overwhelmed by the horror of a tarnished love, kills Desdemona. In the presence of Venetian emissaries, Emilia now tells the details that reveal Iago's guilt. Iago kills her, is wounded by Othello and escapes. The remorseful Othello stabs himself, the recaptured Iago is condemned to torture and prison, and Cassio is appointed to take command in Cyprus.

Whilst affairs of state are prominent in *Othello*, the domestic tragedy of a fine marriage vindictively destroyed is the play's dominant concern. This narrow focus makes the play unique among Shakespeare's great tragedies, but the towering achievement of both craft and imagination is the plotting and portrayal of the relationship between Iago and Othello. No attempt to explain the motives for Iago's malice can adequately account for its impact. An antagonism that masquerades as friendship is embodied even in the language of the two men. The manner in which Othello's rhetoric is mocked by the prosaic Iago has been the basis of many famous stage rivalries. Very few actors of Othello have been able to hold their own against the undermining thrusts of clever Iagos.

ottava rima A verse form using stanzas of eight lines, each with 11 syllables, rhyming abababcc (see also RHYME). Italian in origin, it was much used by Tasso, Ariosto, Luigi Pulci and other Italian masters. The *ottava rima* entered English poetry in the Renaissance but did not fully come into its own until the Romantic period, when JOHN HOOKHAM FRERE revived it and BYRON found it ideally suited to his needs. In his adaptation, the verse line is shortened to 10 syllables.

Otuel and Roland A Middle English VERSE ROMANCE in TAIL-RHYME STANZAS, written before *c*. 1330–40 in the East Midlands. It is based on the French romance *Otinel* and forms the second part of the compound romance *Charlemagne and Roland*, of which *ROLAND AND VERNAGU* is the first fragment. A Saracen emissary Otuel delivers an insulting ultimatum to Charlemagne and is challenged by Roland. During the duel a dove alights on Otuel's helmet and he submits, becoming a Christian. He fights as a knight of Charlemagne's in the invasion of Lombardy. The last third of the romance continues the story of *Roland and Vernagu*. Charlemagne defeats the Saracens at Cordova and Navarre, and the story ends with the ambush at Roncesvalles and the emperor's subsequent defeat of the Saracens which form the subject matter of the Old French *chanson de geste*, *La Chanson de Roland*.

Otway, Thomas 1652–85 Playwright. Born in Sussex and educated at Winchester and Oxford, Otway failed as an actor some years before he succeeded as a playwright. His first two plays, *Alcibiades* (1675) and *Don Carlos* (1676), are tragedies in the then-dominant style of HEROIC COUPLETS and elevated rhetoric, but there are signs, particularly in *Don Carlos*, of a more delicate and intimate approach to the creation of character under duress. It is Otway's emotional honesty, together with his satiric denial of hope, that distinguishes his finest tragedies, *THE ORPHAN* (1680) and *VENICE PRESERVED* (1682). Written in sensitive response to their Jacobean models, and benefiting from Otway's encounter with the work of Racine (whose *Bérénice* he had adapted as *Titus and Berenice* in 1676), they are among the finest English BLANK-VERSE tragedies. Otway's comedies have not lasted so well, though his adaptation of Molière's *The Cheats of Scapin* (1676) was popular in its time. The plots of *The Soldier's Fortune* (1680) and its sequel, *The Atheist* (1683), are too flimsy to carry the burden of Otway's cynicism. Unable to secure a patron, despite the esteem in which he was held, Otway died in poverty. His unrequited love for the actress, Elizabeth Barry, for whom he wrote several of his finest female characters, is recorded among the *Familiar Letters* collected by Tom Brown and Charles Gildon (2 vols., 1697), which also show the independence of Otway's opposition to the ascendant Whigs.

Ouida [de la Ramée, Marie Louise] 1839–1908 Novelist. The pseudonym was taken from a childish corruption of her Christian name 'Louise'. Born at Bury St Edmunds, where her father taught French, she was encouraged by HARRISON AINSWORTH and her first published works were short stories contributed to *BENTLEY'S MISCELLANY* in 1859–60. Her first novel, *Held in Bondage* (1863), was followed by *Strathmore* (1865) and *Chandos* (1866). *Under Two Flags* (1867), her most famous work, is a story of the Foreign Legion. Among the rest of her 45 novels were *Tricotin* (1869), *Puck* (1870), *Two Little Wooden Shoes* (1874), *Moths* (1880) and *In Maremma* (1882). Her vivid, artificial brand of hot-house romanticism kept her novels popular until about 1890. Afterwards, she lived in poverty for some years before she was awarded a Civil List pension.

Our Mutual Friend A novel by CHARLES DICKENS, published in monthly parts from May 1864 to November 1865 and in volume form in 1865.

The chief of its several plots centres on John Harmon. He returns to England as his father's heir after many years' absence and is thought drowned under suspicious circumstances, a situation convenient to his wish for anonymity until he can evaluate Bella Wilfer who, by a quirk in the paternal will, he must marry to secure his inheritance. Assuming the name of Julius Handford and then that of John Rokesmith, he becomes secretary to Mr Boffin (also known as Noddy and the Golden Dustman) to whom Harmon senior, himself a wealthy dust contractor, has left his property if his son does not marry Bella. The worthy Boffin asks the lawyer Mortimer Lightwood to offer a reward for the discovery of John Harmon's murderer, whilst he and his wife take Bella under their wing. Harmon falls in love with her, proposes and is scornfully rejected. Boffin and his wife concoct a plan to change her flighty attitude. He affects a miserly unpleasantness and calumniates Harmon, finally discharging him from his post. Distressed by Boffin's conduct, Bella returns to her parents' home and is finally reconciled with Harmon. Soon afterwards, his real identity is established.

A second narrative concerns Lizzie Hexam, daughter of the dishonest waterman Gaffer Hexam, who makes a living by recovering bodies from the Thames and is wrongfully accused of murdering Harmon. She is passionately loved by Bradley Headstone, schoolmaster of her brother Charley, but she loves the indolent barrister Eugene Wrayburn, a friend of Lightwood. So acute is Headstone's jealousy that he tries to kill his rival; Lizzie saves her lover's life, nurses him back to health and, by marriage, redeems him. Headstone is blackmailed by Rogue Riderhood, and they kill each other in a fight.

Dickens's last complete novel, *Our Mutual Friend* gives one of his densest and most comprehensive accounts of contemporary society, as well as perhaps his bleakest. Its vision of a culture almost stifled by materialistic values emerges not just through its central narratives but through its apparently incidental characters and scenes: the faded aristocrats and parvenus gathered at the Veneerings' dinner table, or Betty Higden and her terror of the workhouse, or the greedy plotting of Silas Wegg.

Our Town A play by THORNTON WILDER, performed in New York in 1938 and awarded a PULITZER PRIZE. Its three acts treat Daily Life, Love and Marriage, and Death, respectively, in the small New Hampshire town of Grover's Corners and focus on two families in particular: the Gibbses and the Webbs. Each act is played without curtain or scenery and is introduced by the Stage Manager in a direct address to the audience.

The first act takes place on 7 May 1901; as it begins, the Stage Manager describes the town and introduces the first characters as they appear on stage and go about the business of starting a new day in Grover's Corners. Act Two, set three years later, traces the courtship and marriage of George Gibbs and Emily Webb and the reaction to this of the older generation. By the third act, which is set in the town cemetery, a further nine years have passed, and the Stage Manager begins by describing the changes they have

brought to the town. The central event of the act is Emily's funeral, which is followed by the reactions of both the living and the dead. The occupants of the cemetery are present on stage but remain invisible to the living characters. The voices of the dead are the last heard, as they comment on man's foolishness, his inability to understand the events which structure his life and his ignorance of the nature and meaning of death.

Overland Monthly An American literary journal, founded in San Francisco in 1868, intended to give California and the West a serious magazine and review of the quality of those of New England and the Atlantic states. For the first two-and-a-half years it was edited by BRET HARTE. It continued in its original form until 1875; then, after a hiatus, was revived in 1883, absorbing *The Californian* at the same time. It published the work of writers such as JACK LONDON, EDWIN MARKHAM and FRANK NORRIS, and lasted until 1935.

Owen, Robert 1771–1858 Socialist and philanthropist. Born at Newtown in Wales, the son of a saddler and ironmonger, he had become by the age of 19 the wealthy owner of cotton-spinning mills in Manchester. In 1799 he purchased the New Lanark mills in Scotland and set up there a model community and village, with a workforce of 2000 people, organized on principles of mutual co-operation. New Lanark became a place of pilgrimage for social reformers, statesmen and royal personages, and its example was instrumental in bringing about the Factory Act of 1817. His ideas of philanthropic education and social improvement were embodied in *A New View of Society*, published in 1813.

In 1821, disappointed with the slowness of reform, Owen left Britain for America to set up another model community at New Harmony, Indiana. On his return to Britain after the failure of the New Harmony experiment he headed a vigorous propaganda campaign and became the pioneer of co-operation between workers and consumers, his ideas strengthening the growing co-operative movement. His *The Revolution in Mind and Practice of the Human Race* appeared in 1849.

Owen, Wilfred (Edward Salter) 1893–1918 Poet. Born in Plas Wilmot, Oswestry, he studied at the Birkenhead Institute and the Shrewsbury Technical College, matriculating in 1911 but without the honours necessary to enter university. His mother, to whom he was particularly close, was an evangelical Anglican, and may have influenced his decision to take an unpaid post as lay assistant to the vicar of Dunsden, teaching Bible classes, leading prayer meetings and attending missionary gatherings. His letters of the period anticipate the social and moral insights of his later war poems. He left Dunsden in 1913, soon afterwards falling seriously ill with congestion of the lungs. In the summer he failed to win a scholarship to read English literature at University College, Reading, and went instead to Bordeaux to teach at the Berlitz School of Languages. He became private tutor to a family through whom he met the poet and pacifist Laurent Tailhade. It is likely that Tailhade's definition of poetry in *Pour la paix* (1909) as a call to generosity and brotherhood influenced his own.

Owen stayed in France after August 1914 and enlisted in the Artists' Rifles in late October 1915. Commissioned into the Manchester Regiment, then stationed at the Somme, he endured the worst winter of the war, suffering trench fever and concussion. He was diagnosed 'shell-shocked' in May 1917 and sent to Craiglockhart Hospital, Edinburgh, where he edited the hospital magazine, *Hydra*, and in August met SIEGFRIED SASSOON. Sassoon's account of the meeting appeared in *Siegfried's Journey* (1945). Discharged in late October, Owen was posted to Ripon before rejoining the 5th Manchesters at Scarborough in June 1918. It was during the period from his convalescence at Craiglockhart until his decision to return to the trenches (rather than take the option of an officer-training post) in August that he drafted and revised his best poems. This return was, he felt, necessary if he were to write poetry 'in no sense consolatory'. He was killed on 4 November on the Sambre Canal, one week before the armistice.

Only four of his poems were published during his lifetime – 'Song of Songs', anonymously, in *Hydra* and three others in THE NATION. A handful more appeared soon after his death (notably seven in EDITH SITWELL's *Wheels* in 1919), but the bulk awaited publication in successively enlarged editions by Sassoon (1920), EDMUND BLUNDEN (1931) and C. DAY-LEWIS (1963). *The Complete Poems and Fragments* (1983) was edited by Jon Stallworthy. In a draft preface Owen wrote: 'My subject is War, and the pity of War. The Poetry is in the pity.' His best poems, such as 'Strange Meeting', 'Anthem for Doomed Youth', 'Dulce et Decorum Est', 'Futility' and 'Mental Cases', achieve a remarkable nightmare vision which becomes, by virtue of its power and detail, also a protest. ROBERT GRAVES commented that 'the poetry is not, of course, in the propaganda, but in spite of the propaganda'. YEATS, on the other hand, excluded Owen's work from his *Oxford Book of Modern Verse* (1936) because 'passive suffering is not a subject for poetry' and described it, still more dismissively, in a letter as 'all blood and dirt and sucked sugar-stick'. While just possibly an appropriate description of Owen's early derivative poetic diction, it is inadequate to the forceful language and psychic horror of his war poems.

Herbert Owen, the poet's brother, published a three-volume memoir in *Journey from Obscurity* (1960–5). Benjamin Britten combined several of the poems with the Latin mass for the dead in his *War Requiem* (1962).

Owl and the Nightingale, The An anonymous DEBATE POEM in octosyllabic couplets, written between 1189 and 1216, probably in the South-east. The narrator overhears a dispute between a sombre owl and a lighthearted nightingale covering topics from theology to the different characteristics of their species. The debate is inconclusive, the birds leaving to consult the mysterious Nicholas of Guildford – perhaps the poet's patron – for an answer to their quarrel. The masterly evocation of the two 'characters' gives the debate an additional dimension and is the main source of its charm. Although the poem has been interpreted as allegorical, its tone is comic and gently satiric, the serious topics of discussion serving mainly to illustrate the folly and contentiousness of man.

Oxford English Dictionary, The The generic label (often abbreviated to OED) for the most ambitious of all ENGLISH DICTIONARIES. It has appeared under more than one title as well as in several editions. The first, originally called a *New English Dictionary on Historical Principles* (hence the abbreviations NED and HED), appeared in 125 parts between 1884 and 1928. It fulfilled a project begun by the Philological Society in 1857. Editors and co-editors included Herbert Coleridge, F. J. FURNIVALL, Henry Bradley, William Craigie and C. T. Onions, though the nickname 'Murray's dictionary' acknowledges the unique contribution of JAMES MURRAY. *The Oxford English Dictionary*, a 12-volume edition, appeared together with the first supplements in 1933. A 20-volume second edition or *New Oxford English Dictionary* (1989) is known as the NOED, though it may also be nicknamed 'Burchfield's dictionary' in tribute to R. W. Burchfield's 4-volume *Supplement* (1972–86), which it incorporates.

Since its first publication the OED has been uniquely important in providing a full survey of the English vocabulary from 1150 and looking back to the earlier history of words in use at that date. Full dialect coverage is given into the 15th century. Each main entry identifies spelling, variant forms and pronunciation, and provides etymological information. Senses are listed according to their chronological emergence, illustrated by at least one or two quotations per century of usage. Conceived as an aid to reading English literature, the OED's bias has made it a valued quarry for writers and literary scholars.

The most notable of many abridgements and adaptations is the two-volume *Shorter Oxford English Dictionary*, retaining the most essential historical information, first published in 1933.

Oxford Movement, The A 19th-century religious

movement, so called because its leaders – JOHN KEBLE, E. B. PUSEY and JOHN HENRY NEWMAN – and many of its followers were connected with Oxford. Alternative names were the High Church Movement and the Tractarian Movement, the latter referring to TRACTS FOR THE TIMES (1833–41), the series of pamphlets which announced its doctrines. These included belief in the Church of England as a divinely inspired institution, in the validity of the Apostolic succession and in the importance of the BOOK OF COMMON PRAYER. The Movement reintroduced ritual, vestments and incense into Anglican practice, and stirred young men to 'earnestness', which had originated in 18th-century Methodist 'seriousness' and the Evangelical doctrines which had gained ground early in the 19th century. Its interest in the church of the 17th century and earlier stimulated Victorian medievalism. Always controversial, the Movement was attacked by the bishops and liberal clergy. Tracts for the Times came to an end after Newman's Tract XC, which found the 39 Articles of the Church of England compatible with Catholic theology. Pusey was suspended from the office of university preacher after his 1843 sermon, 'The Holy Eucharist, a Comfort to the Penitent', declared his belief in the Real Presence. He hoped for a reunion of the English and Roman churches and did his best to prevent conversions to Rome, of which Newman's in 1845 was the most famous.

oxymoron A rhetorical device which deliberately joins apparently contradictory words. Oxymoron is a particularly notable feature of PETRARCHAN verse – for example, 'sweet enemy' and 'I burn and freeze like ice'.

Ozick, Cynthia 1928– American short-story writer and novelist. She was born in New York and educated at New York and Ohio State universities. Her first novel, *Trust*, was published in 1966. Written in the first person, it is the story of the unnamed daughter of Allegra Vand, who searches for the father whom her mother has prevented her from knowing; she no sooner finds him than he dies. *The Pagan Rabbi and Other Stories* followed in 1971. Both this volume and *Bloodshed and Three Novellas* (1976) reflect Ozick's interest in mysticism and the supernatural. In 1981 she published another collection of short works, *Levitation: Five Fictions. The Cannibal Galaxy* (1983) and *The Messiah of Stockholm* (1987) are novels and *The Shawl* (1991) brings together a novella and a short story about the ordeal in later life of a Holocaust survivor. She has twice received the O. Henry Award (1975 and 1980). *Art and Ardor* (1983) and *Metaphor and Memory* (1989) are collections of essays.

Page, P(atricia) K(athleen) 1916– Canadian poet, novelist and painter. Born in Swanage, Dorset, she moved with her family to Alberta in 1919. She worked at a variety of occupations, including those of shop assistant, clerk and historical researcher before coming into contact with writers in Montreal, where her first poems were published in the early 1940s and collected in *As Ten As Twenty* (1946). Her early work demonstrates a strong political commitment and a concern with psychoanalytic themes. Her novel *The Sun and the Moon* (1944), published under the pseudonym Judith Cape and not issued under her own name until 1973, is about a young woman in touch with strange Gothic forces. After the war she worked for the National Film Board of Canada. The poems of *The Metal and the Flower* (1954) deal with the plight of those on the fringes of society. From 1953 to 1964, when her husband served as Canadian ambassador in Australia, Brazil and Mexico, she lived abroad, writing comparatively little, but developing a talent as an artist. Since returning to Canada she has held numerous solo exhibitions of her paintings. Other volumes include *A Flask of Sea Water* (1989), a children's book, and several poetry collections, *Cry Ararat!* (1967), *Evening Dance of the Grey Flies* (1981) and *The Glass Air* (1985), in which she turns to a spare economic verse that represents a marked departure from the style of her earlier poetry and an interest in spiritual self-liberation. All her poetry uses METAPHOR and SYMBOL to suggest possibilities of human transformation.

Page, Thomas Nelson 1853–1922 American novelist and short-story writer. He was born in Virginia and his work is characterized by its preoccupation with the Old South, whose aristocratic ideals he sentimentalized in much of his writing. *In Ole Virginia: or, Marse Chan and Other Stories*, a collection of short stories, was published in 1887. It was followed by two novels, *On Newfound River* (1891) and *Red Rock: A Chronicle of Reconstruction* (1898). The latter focused on the hardship the Reconstruction period caused to southerners, and became a bestseller. Others of his works are: *Two Little Confederates* (1888), a children's story, *The Old South: Essays, Social and Political* (1892), *Social Life in Old Virginia before the War* (1897), essays; *Gordon Keith* (1902) and *John Marvel, Assistant* (1909), two novels; and *Robert E. Lee, Man and Soldier* (1911), a biography. Page became the US ambassador to Italy in 1913. His last works were *The Land of Spirit* (1913), *Life of Thomas Jefferson* (1918) and *Italy and the World War* (1920).

Paine, Thomas 1737–1809 Radical politician and writer. Born in Thetford to an Anglican mother and a Quaker father who ran a small farm and made corsets, Paine attended school until the age of 13, when he became an apprentice in his father's shop. Following an unsuccessful attempt to run away to sea in 1756, he began work as a staymaker in 1757 and two years later opened his own shop in Sandwich, Kent. He became a customs officer in 1764, but was dismissed in the following year because of his attempts to organize the workers. He then moved to London and worked as a schoolteacher until 1768, when he was reappointed to excise service in Lewes. The publication of his first pamphlet, *The Case of the Officers of Excise* (1772), and his continued activity as a labour agitator led to his dismissal from the post in 1774. He returned to London immediately, and there met BENJAMIN FRANKLIN, who in the same year sent him to America with letters of introduction.

Paine arrived in Philadelphia already a confirmed radical. As editor of *The Pennsylvania Magazine* he attacked slavery and advocated independence. *COMMON SENSE* (1776), his most influential pamphlet, demanded an immediate declaration of independence. During the Revolutionary War he served in Washington's army and continued his political writing; *THE AMERICAN CRISIS*, a series of pamphlets in defence of the war, appeared between December 1776 and April 1783. In 1780 he published *Public Good*, a reiteration of the case for federal union made in *Common Sense* and an objection to the Virginia Plan. After successfully executing a diplomatic mission to France in 1781, he withdrew to his farm in New Rochelle (which the State of New York had given him), where he wrote *Dissertations on Government*, an attack on paper money and a warning against the dangers of inflation.

He returned to England in 1787 and replied to BURKE'S *REFLECTIONS ON THE REVOLUTION IN FRANCE* with *THE RIGHTS OF MAN*, published in two parts in 1791 and 1792. The tract prompted Pitt's government to introduce a law against seditious publication, and Paine, who had fled to France, was convicted of sedition in his absence and outlawed. In Paris the revolutionary Assembly made him a citizen of France (1792) and a member of the Convention; but he was a moderate republican – a Girondist, not a Jacobin – and when he opposed the King's execution he nearly went to the guillotine himself. Instead, he was deprived of citizenship and arrested. Assuming that he was safer in prison, Gouverneur Morris, the American minister, did not assist him – a decision which Paine viewed as a plot against him and criticized in *A Letter to George Washington* (1796). Following the Reign of Terror James Monroe secured his release. The years he spent in prison (1793–5) saw the completion of his most famous work, *THE AGE OF REASON* (1794–6), a stark critique of accepted religious beliefs and practices.

Paine, the patriot in 1776, returned to the USA an infidel in 1802. Former friends such as John Quincy Adams ostracized him for his 'atheism'. Refused burial in consecrated ground, he was interred on his New Rochelle farm at a funeral which nobody of note attended. COBBETT exhumed his bones 10 years later and brought them back to England; he was not allowed to bury them and they eventually disappeared.

Painter, William ?1540–94 Translator. Painter was educated at St John's College, Cambridge, ordained in 1560 and became master of Sevenoaks School in Kent. His *Palace of Pleasure* is a collection of tales based on originals from classical writers, such as Herodotus and Livy, and the *novelle* of Italian authors, such as Boccaccio and Bandello. First published in 1566, it contained some 60 tales. A second volume, printed in 1567, contained another 34 stories, and all the tales were printed again in 1575, when another seven new stories were added. It was a source for plots for Renaissance English dramatists: WEBSTER, BEAUMONT and FLETCHER and SHIRLEY all found stories in it. It also probably provided the version of the story of Giletta of Narbonne that SHAKESPEARE used in *ALL'S WELL THAT ENDS WELL*.

Pair of Blue Eyes, A A novel by THOMAS HARDY, first published in *Tinsley's Magazine* from September 1872 to July 1873.

Stephen Smith, a young architect, comes to Endelstow on the north Cornish coast to work on the restoration of the church. There he falls in love with Elfride Swancourt, the daughter of the vicar who, learning that Stephen is of humble origin, opposes the marriage. Elfride, at first agreeable to the idea that they run away to marry, later vacillates and their plans come to nothing. Stephen goes to India in the hope of making his fortune. In his absence Elfride saves the life of Henry Knight, formerly Stephen's friend and patron. Henry and Elfride become engaged. But he proves a stern and rigidly idealistic man: on learning of Elfride's earlier involvement with Stephen he abandons Elfride with harsh words, leaving her heartbroken.

Later, Stephen and Knight meet again. Their conversation reveals to Stephen that Elfride is still free and to Knight that he has behaved cruelly. They both hurry down to Cornwall but the train they take also carries the corpse of Elfride, being transported home for burial. She had married Lord Luxellian, a widowed nobleman, but neither his devotion nor his children's affection could prevent her decline.

Hardy's third published novel, *A Pair of Blue Eyes* has often been overshadowed by the popularity of its successor, *FAR FROM THE MADDING CROWD*. Yet it remains notable, not merely for showing the full emergence of those ironies of plot which characterize his later and better-known work but also for its autobiographical qualities. The setting, Stephen Smith's profession, his reasons for going to Cornwall, and even his embarrassment about his class origins: all these echo the circumstances of Hardy's courtship of Emma Gifford only shortly before he began writing the novel. The portrait of Elfride herself is perhaps the most interesting of Hardy's several attempts to capture the charm he found in Emma at their first meeting.

Palace of Honour, The See DOUGLAS, GAVIN.

Palace of Pleasure, The See PAINTER, WILLIAM.

Palace of the Peacock A novel by WILSON HARRIS, published in 1960. Like CONRAD's *HEART OF DARKNESS* and PATRICK WHITE's *VOSS*, it uses a journey into a physical interior as a metaphor for a voyage of psychic discovery. The complex narrative method makes extensive use of religious imagery, fusing Christian and Amerindian myth. A multi-racial crew travels upriver into the heartland of Guyana (then British Guiana), led by the imperialist Donne, who is seeking Amerindian labour for his plantation. Their journey retraces that of an earlier crew, all of whom died, and more generally the conquest of the country by colonizers. It leads, on a literal level, to death and disaster but also to rebirth and a sense of mystical fulfilment in the attainment of an Eldorado of the spirit which provides liberation from the materialistic exploitation in which they have hitherto been trapped. The title alludes to the final stage in the alchemical process, where, in Jungian interpretations, a psychic change accompanies the physical transmutation of base metal into gold.

Paley, William 1743–1805 Theologian and philosopher. Born at Peterborough, he completed his education at Christ's College, Cambridge, where he became a lecturer, a senior wrangler at the age of 20, and a fellow in 1766. His lectures on ethics, much indebted to the theories of ABRAHAM TUCKER, were expanded and published as *THE PRINCIPLES OF MORAL AND POLITICAL PHILOSOPHY* (1785). *Horae Paulinae* (1790) sought to demonstrate the historical truth of the New Testament by a close examination of the life and epistles of St Paul. Like much of Paley's work, *A View of the Evidences of Christianity* (1794) earned its wide popularity more by clear presentation and lucid style than by originality of argument. *Natural Theology* (1802) made a more intensive examination of the same issues.

Despite his ability, Paley's advance as an 18th-century churchman was hindered by the latitudinarianism of his younger days. He became rector of Musgrave in Westmorland in 1776 and archdeacon of Carlisle in 1782.

Palgrave, Sir **Francis** 1788–1861 Historian. Born in London, the son of a Jewish stockbroker, he converted to Christianity on his marriage in 1823 and changed his name from Cohen to Palgrave. He studied law, was called to the Bar in 1827, and from 1838 to 1861 served as Deputy Keeper of the Records. *A History of the Anglo-Saxons* (1831) was the first of several works of medieval history, followed by *The Rise and Progress of the English Commonwealth* (1832), *An Essay on the Original Authority of the King's Council* (1834), *Truths and Fictions of the Middle Ages* (1837) and *The History of Normandy and England* (1851–64).

Palgrave, Francis Turner 1824–97 Poet and anthologist. The son of SIR FRANCIS PALGRAVE, he was born at Great Yarmouth and educated at Charterhouse and Balliol College, Oxford. He was made a fellow of Exeter College and became a civil servant when he left Oxford, serving as vice-principal of Kneller Hall Training College (1850–5) and later as assistant secretary in the Education Department. Palgrave published several books of verse, among them *Idylls and Songs* (1854), *Hymns* (1867), *Lyrical Poems* (1871), *The Visions of England* (1881) and *Amenophis* (1892). But he is chiefly remembered as an anthologist. *The Golden Treasury* (1861), compiled with the help and advice of his friend TENNYSON, was a classic statement of Victorian taste in poems and lyrics; it was reprinted many times and a second series appeared in 1896. In 1895 Palgrave became professor of poetry at Oxford. His other works include: autobiographical reflections, *The Passionate Pilgrim* (1858), *Essays on Art* (1866) and a volume of lectures, *Landscape in Poetry* (1897).

palindrome From the Greek, 'running back again'. A word, phrase or verse which reads the same both forwards and backwards. 'Rotor' is such a word, 'Madam I'm Adam' such a phrase. Like the ACROSTIC, palindromic verse is occasionally used as an exercise of writer and reader's ingenuity. An ancient example which combines both the acrostic and the palindrome is the word square. The Roman word square from Cirencester is one of several variants to survive:

ROTAS
OPERA
TENET
AREPO
SATOR

Pall Mall Gazette, The An evening newspaper founded by GEORGE SMITH and Frederick Greenwood, its first editor, in 1865. The name was taken from the journal 'written by gentlemen for gentlemen' in THACKERAY'S *PENDENNIS*. Its purpose was to digest the news from the morning papers and to publish substantial articles on political and social questions in competition with the weekly magazines. Among its most distinguished editors were JOHN MORLEY (1880–3), W. T. STEAD (1883–90), Henry Cust (1892–6) and J. L. Garvin (1911–15). Contributors and reviewers included RUSKIN, ARNOLD, PATMORE, WILDE, PATER, WELLS and KIPLING. The political complexion of the paper changed sharply under Morley from conservative to radical and under Cust from radical to independent conservative. The phrase 'the New Journalism' was coined by Arnold in 1887 to describe Stead's brash editorship, and the paper achieved its greatest notoriety with Stead's crusade against child prostitution. As a social and literary influence, its most brilliant success was under Cust. After a long decline it was incorporated in *The Evening Standard* in 1923.

Palladis Tamia See MERES, FRANCIS.

Palliser Novels, The A sequence of novels by ANTHONY TROLLOPE, about political and Parliamentary life. Plantagenet Palliser – the Liberal politician who first appeared in a BARSETSHIRE NOVEL, *THE SMALL HOUSE AT ALLINGTON* – and his wife Glencora are central presences. The sequence consists of *CAN YOU FORGIVE HER?* (1864–5), *PHINEAS FINN* (1867–9), *THE EUSTACE DIAMONDS* (1871–3), *PHINEAS REDUX* (1873–4), *THE PRIME MINISTER* (1875–6) and *THE DUKE'S CHILDREN* (1879–80).

Palmer, Nettie 1885–1964 Australian critic and woman of letters. Born Janet Gertrude Higgins in Bendigo, she attended the Presbyterian Ladies' College in Melbourne and the University of Melbourne, from which she graduated in 1909. Her next few years were divided between Melbourne and Europe, where she studied languages. In London in 1914 she married the writer VANCE PALMER, whom she had met in Melbourne. They returned to Australia and settled there the following year. She published two volumes of her early poetry, *The South Wind* (1914) and *Shadowy Paths* (1915). As socialists and promulgators of a national Australian culture, the Palmers became two of the most influential figures in Australian intellectual life in the years to come and Nettie's influence was comparable with her husband's, even though her work, which was mainly literary journalism, has not received the same recognition as her husband's more creative output. Nettie's contribution to Australian social and literary life included work for migrants, acting as a spokeswoman for writers and anti-fascist activity in the 1930s. She also did a great deal to establish the reputation of HENRY HANDEL RICHARDSON, of whose work she wrote the first major Australian study in 1950. Her most significant literary work was *Modern Australian Literature, 1900–1923* (1924), a pioneering essay which, besides providing a survey of the field in a comparatively small compass, emphasized the difficulties faced by Australian writers, while arguing for the development of an organic local literature. Her other books include a volume of essays, *Talking It Over* (1932), and *Fourteen Years: Extracts from a Private Journal, 1925–1939* (1948), but it is impossible to measure her achievement from her full-length works. It lies rather in her prolific journalism, in which she helped establish the reputation of many of Australia's finest writers.

Palmer, Vance (Edward Vivian) 1885–1959 Australian novelist and critic. Born in Bundaberg, Queensland, he spent much of his youth in England and travelling in Europe. He married NETTIE PALMER in London in 1914. Eager to promote and contribute to a national literature, he attempted to establish himself as a popular writer, producing plays for LOUIS ESSON's Pioneer Players and fiction for the NSW Bookstall Company. It was not until *The Man Hamilton* (1928) that he began to shape a career as a serious novelist. It was followed by *Men are Human* (1930), *The Passage* (1930), *Daybreak* (1932) and *The Swayne Family* (1934). His later work included a trilogy based on the mining community of Mount Isa, *Golconda* (1948), *Seedtime* (1957) and *The Big Fellow* (1959). Palmer also published poetry, essays, criticism and collections of short stories, among them *Let the Birds Fly* (1955) and *The Rainbow-Bird* (1957).

Paltock, Robert 1697–1767 Novelist. Paltock was born in London and became a lawyer. He is remembered for his novel of fantasy, *The Life and Adventures of Peter Wilkins* (1751). The hero is shipwrecked in the far south and reaches a country inhabited by people who can fly by means of an outer silk-like skin which spreads out to enable them to become airborne. One of these, the beautiful Youwarkee, falls out of the sky by Wilkins's hut and he falls in love with her. He marries her and rises to importance in the kingdom. The book was much admired by ROBERT SOUTHEY and LEIGH HUNT.

Pamela: or, Virtue Rewarded An EPISTOLARY NOVEL by SAMUEL RICHARDSON, its first part published in 1740 and its second part in 1741.

Pamela Andrews, the heroine, is a teenage maidservant in a household where her mistress has just died. The lady's son, Mr B., conceives a lustful passion for Pamela and, helped by his servants Mrs Jewkes and Monsieur Calbrand, tries to take advantage of her position. Pamela is partly revolted and partly attracted by the amorous Mr B. but at length his persistence causes her to leave the house. Part of Pamela's journal, which has been stolen by Mrs Jewkes, enables Mr B. better to understand her character. He writes asking her to return and at length, to her delight, proposes marriage. The second, less inspiring part of the book depicts Pamela's acclimatization to her new position, the changing attitudes of Mr B.'s family, her husband's wayward behaviour and the dignified way she handles married life.

Pamela was the 18th-century equivalent of a runaway bestseller, attracting a particularly strong following among female and clerical readers. It was translated into several languages. An early example of the unified novel of character, it owed its success largely to the plight of the heroine and the strongly evocative atmosphere of domestic tension which Richardson creates. HENRY FIELDING was the most memorable of the contemporary parodists of Richardson, both in *An Apology for the Life of Mrs Shamela Andrews* (1741), a skilful BURLESQUE on the values and mannerisms of the first part of *Pamela*, and in his adaptation of Pamela's brother Joseph as the central character in *JOSEPH ANDREWS*.

pantomime The English pantomime developed from two sources: delight in spectacular scenery and costume, and popular interest in storytelling dances. By 1723, particularly at the theatre in Lincoln's Inn Fields managed by John Rich, entertainments known as 'pantomimes' were regular features of the London stage. By the end of the 18th century, stories from British folklore and nursery tales were nudging out the previously established mish-mash of Greek and Roman myths, and the dumb Harlequin, whose danced adventures had been the fanciful centre of the spectacle, was being permitted to talk and sing. Under the influence of Joseph Grimaldi (1778–1837), attention was shifted from Harlequin to the figure of the Clown. It was during this period that the transvestite roles of dame and principal 'boy' became established. The fashion for outrageous punning in rhymed couplets, exemplified in the work of J. R. PLANCHÉ and H. J. BYRON, combined with a continuing love of spectacle. By mid-century, pantomimes were increasingly associated with Christmas, and the involvement of music-hall stars in the latter half of the 19th century confirmed their hold on popular culture.

Paracelsus A dramatic poem by ROBERT BROWNING, published in 1835. Like many of Browning's works, it portrays an imaginary character based on a historical figure – in this case the Swiss doctor, alchemist and philosopher (1493–1541) – and describes the 'incidents in the development of a soul'. In Browning's poem Paracelsus is a man single-mindedly bent on searching out true knowledge. Eventually, when he is discredited and dying, he sees why he ultimately failed. His great learning was inadequate without the secret now known to him: love becomes the means of knowledge and intelligence the instrument of love.

Though not a commercial success, the poem was praised by a number of thoughtful critics and for many years it was primarily as the author of *Paracelsus* that Browning was known.

Parade's End A tetralogy of novels by FORD MADOX FORD, consisting of *Some Do Not...* (1924), *No More Parades* (1925), *A Man Could Stand Up* (1926) and *Last Post* (1928). It describes the struggle for survival by Christopher Tietjens in pre-war London and in action during World War I. Events enter into Christopher's consciousness impressionistically and the impersonal narrator, using many time-shifts, is faithful to the characters' inner constructions of reality.

Paradise Lost Poem by JOHN MILTON, published in 1667. A revised edition (1674) rearranged the 10 books as 12. *Paradise Lost* was begun in 1658 and completed in 1663, its appearance being delayed by both the Great Plague and the Great Fire. Milton had announced his ambition of writing an EPIC nearly 30 years before. He named Samson and Macbeth as possible subjects and sketched plans for an Arthurian epic as well as for biblical dramas including 'Adam Unparadized', a dramatization of Genesis probably influenced by Grotius' *Adamus Exil* (1601).

Book I. The argument of the poem concerns the Fall of Man, the origins of his disobedience to God's laws being traced to Satan's efforts to exact revenge for his expulsion from Heaven. Satan and the rebel angels are first shown lying in the burning lake. He rouses his followers and tells them there is hope of regaining Heaven. He orders them into legions, naming the leaders and telling them of a new world being created somewhere in the utter darkness of Chaos. Then he summons a council and the palace of Satan, Pandemonium, is built.

Book II. Satan and his followers debate whether or not to wage another war at once to regain Heaven. They finally decide to investigate the new world: Satan himself will go. He passes through Hell Gates past the twin sentinels, Death and Sin, and journeys through the realm of Chaos.

Book III. God observes Satan's journey to the newly created world and foretells how Satan will succeed in bringing about the Fall of Man and how God will punish Man for yielding to temptation. The Son of God offers himself as a ransom for Man, to answer for the offence and undergo his punishment. To rejoicing in Heaven, God accepts and ordains his incarnation on a future day. Satan meanwhile has reached the outer rim of the universe; he passes the Limbo of Vanity and arrives at the Gate of Heaven, where he changes his form to deceive Uriel, Guardian of the Sun. From him he learns the where-abouts of the new world, and about Man, the creature God has placed there.

Book IV. Satan arrives on earth and finds the Garden of Eden, where he observes Adam and Eve. They speak of the Tree of Knowledge and Satan decides to concentrate his temptation on this. Meanwhile Uriel has heard that one of the fallen has escaped from Hell, and warns Gabriel, who in Eden finds Satan at Eve's bower, trying to tempt her in a dream. The tempter is ejected.

Book V. Eve awakens, troubled by her dream of temptation, and is comforted by Adam. God sends Raphael to Adam: so that Man may know the nature of his enemy and the need for obedience to God, Raphael tells him of Satan's revolt in Heaven. Satan had gathered many to hear him and had proclaimed his resistance to the supreme authority of God.

Book VI. Raphael continues his narrative. Michael and Gabriel command the hosts of Heaven but it is the Son of God who decides the outcome. He orders his angels to hold, then from the centre he charges straight into Satan and his legions, driving them to the wall of Heaven, and down from there into the Deep of Hell. The passage where the Son mounts his attack on the rebels is the literal and thematic centre of the poem, Man's future disgrace being the indirect consequence.

Book VII. The archangel tells Adam that God, after the defeat of Satan, decided on another world, from which Man may aspire to Heaven. He sends his Son to perform the Creation in six days.

Book VIII. Adam asks for knowledge of the celestial bodies but Raphael tells him that his first need is for knowledge of his own world. Adam then talks to him of Eve and of the passion she arouses in him. The archangel warns him to attend also to his higher instincts, lest he subordinate these to his love for Eve. Then Raphael departs.

Book IX. Satan meanwhile has returned to Eden as a mist by night and has entered into a sleeping serpent. He finds Eve working alone and speaks flatteringly to her, extolling her beauty. Eve is curious that the creature has the gift of speech. He tells her he gained it by eating the fruit of a certain tree in the Garden which he shows her, the Tree of Knowledge. At length he weakens her resolve and she eats the fruit. Satan slips out of the Garden and Eve, feeling transformed in awareness, takes more of the fruit and goes with it to Adam who sees at once that she is lost. He eats the fruit also in order to share her transgression: they will fall together. Their innocence departs: they look for cover from their nakedness and the seeds of dissension are shown.

Book X. After the transgression, the guardian angels return to Heaven. The Son of God goes to Eden to deliver the judgement on Adam and Eve (as known from the Book of Genesis). Before he leaves the Garden he clothes them, out of pity for their shame in their nakedness. Satan has returned triumphant to Hell; henceforth a path is open for Sin and Death to enter the world of Man. Adam and Eve approach the Son of God in repentance and supplication, begging for mitigation of the doom pronounced upon their children.

Book XI. The Son of God intercedes with the Father, but God declares that Adam and Eve must be expelled from Paradise. Michael descends to the Garden and tells them they must go out into the world, which he shows Adam from the summit of a hill. Adam is also shown what will happen in the world until the time of the Flood.

Book XII. Michael continues his account of the world, telling of Abraham and of the Messiah promised in the Son's intercession. Adam is comforted by these revelations; he wakes the sleeping Eve and Michael leads them from the Garden.

The poem's greatness is partly a function of its sheer sustained length, but also the visual immediacy with which Milton realizes the imagined scenes. Both Adam and Eve are archetypes with whom a reader can identify as humans, and the network of abstract influences surrounding their central transgression rarely threatens to obscure their essential characteristics. As an embodiment of malicious cunning, Satan is a dramatic and almost recognizable character. Milton has been criticized for glossing over certain contemporary developments in scientific and intellectual thought (the astronomical ambiguities in Book VIII, for example) but the poem's realism is that of myth, and its credibility dependent on the shapes of Christian belief rather than any specific historical details. As a long poem it is a monumental achievement, both intellectually as a work of the literary imagination and for the powerful expanses of its verse which, with the strength of classical precedents behind it, proved inimitable.

Paradise of Dainty Devices, The One of the most popular of the Elizabethan miscellanies, it includes verse by minor 16th-century poets such as THOMAS CHURCHYARD, Jasper Heywood, William Hunnis and THOMAS VAUX, the Earl of Oxford. It was originally compiled by Richard Edwards, who also contributed some poems, and published in 1576; there were several later editions, with enlargements.

Paradise Regained A poem by JOHN MILTON, published in 1671. The title suggests it is a sequel to *PARADISE LOST* and the subject – Satan's unsuccessful temptation of Christ, closely derived from the Gospel – is clearly a counterpart to Satan's successful temptation of Man. But *Paradise Regained* is shorter and prefers debate to epic splendour.

Book I. Jesus hears the call of John the Baptist and goes to Bethabara on the Jordan. He is baptized, and the Father's voice from Heaven proclaims his beloved Son. Satan is alarmed, seeing his dominion over Man threatened, and resolves to outwit the Son of God. In the guise of an aged countryman he approaches Jesus, who is fasting in the desert, and asks him why, if he is the Son of God, he does not make bread of the stones in that desert place? But Jesus recognizes the tempter and resists him; Satan disappears as night falls.

Book II. Mary awaits her son's return from the Jordan, unaware that he is in the desert. Satan returns to confer with his diabolical colleagues. Jesus wakes, hunger heavy upon him, and is confronted by the tempter, now in the guise of a man of wealth. He entices him, this time with a richly laden table and the finest wine; waiting to serve are comely youths and maidens and 'all the while Harmonious Airs were heard'. All this is rejected, and disappears. Satan then tells him that all the riches of the world will be at his disposal if Jesus will listen to him. Jesus refutes him: the empires of the earth have come and gone 'In height of all their flowing wealth dissolved'.

Book III. Satan persists: he tells Jesus he is born to the kingdom of David, now under the Roman yoke. Will he not perform his duty and free his country? Jesus answers that he is under his Father's rule and knows the tempter seeks his destruction: Satan retorts that Jesus knows nothing but the meanest aspects of life; he takes him to a high mountain to show him the eastern kingdoms of the earth. He will ally any of these, he says, to Jesus and will restore to him the kingdom of David.

Book IV. Satan takes Jesus to the other side of the mountain, and looks west towards the seat of Roman imperialism with the evil Tiberius in power. Satan will help Jesus overthrow him. But who, asks Jesus, made him evil? He rejects the argument of Satan, and also turns his back on the brilliant society of Athens. Satan, having failed, returns Jesus to the desert as the second night falls. On the third day Satan makes his last try, tempting Jesus (as in the Gospel narrative) to prove his godhead. He takes him to the Temple, and sets him on the pinnacle, exhorting him 'Cast thyself down.' Jesus tells him he shall not 'tempt the Lord thy God'. Satan, defeated, falls back into the pit and angels come to bear Jesus away.

Pardoner's Tale, The See *CANTERBURY TALES, THE*.

Paris Sketch Book, The A travel book by W. M. THACKERAY, with his own illustrations, published in 1840. A miscellaneous collection of travel essays, stories, art and literary criticism, interspersed with comment on French manners and society, it was the first book of Thackeray's to be published in England, and appeared under the pseudonym 'Michael Angelo Titmarsh'.

Parker [Rothschild], **Dorothy** 1893–1967 American poet, short-story writer and critic. Born in West

End, New Jersey, she was raised in New York, where she was educated at a convent, later moving to an exclusive girls' school in Morristown, New Jersey.

Her first poetry appeared in *Vogue* magazine in 1916. That same year she went to work for *Vogue*, and in 1917 moved on to *VANITY FAIR*, where she later served as drama critic (1919–20). In an active career she contributed reviews, articles, columns, poems and short stories to magazines such as *Esquire*, THE *NEW YORKER*, THE *NATION*, THE *NEW REPUBLIC*, *Cosmopolitan*, *The Saturday Evening Post* and THE *AMERICAN MERCURY*. Her writings are characterized above all by a sardonic wit and irreverent sophistication. Her first collection of poems, *Enough Rope* (1926), was a best-seller. It was followed by two other books of verse, *Sunset Gun* (1928) and *Death and Taxes* (1931). Her collected poems, *Not So Deep As a Well*, were published in 1936. *Laments for the Living* (1930) and *After Such Pleasure* (1933) are collections of short stories. *Here Lies*, published in 1939, contains all her fiction written up to that time. She collaborated with ELMER RICE on the play *Close Harmony* (1929) and with Arnaud d'Usseau on *Ladies of the Corridor* (1953).

Parker, Matthew 1504–75 Elizabeth's first Archbishop of Canterbury was educated at Corpus Christi College, Cambridge, of which he was elected a Fellow in 1527 (the same year as his ordination as priest) and Master in 1544. He was licensed to preach by CRANMER in 1533, became chaplain to Anne Boleyn in 1535 and was appointed Dean of Lincoln in 1552. In the reign of Mary his preferments were removed and he fled to Frankfurt. On Elizabeth's accession he was consecrated Archbishop of Canterbury at Lambeth Palace in 1559. As a churchman he was moderate, and had to face the opposition of more radical reformers. He concerned himself with the issuing of the 39 Articles and the translation of the Bible in 1568 that became known as the Bishops' Bible (see THE BIBLE IN ENGLISH). In 1648 his remains were disinterred by revolutionary Puritans and buried in a dunghill.

He was a scholarly man, and produced editions of early chroniclers – Gildas, ASSER and AELFRIC – and of Matthew of Westminster (1567–70), Matthew Paris (1571) and Thomas of Walsingham (1574). His most substantial work was a history of the early English church, *De antiquitate ecclesiae et privilegiis ecclesiae cantuarensis* (1572). Parker left his collection of books and manuscripts to Corpus Christi (see LIBRARIES) and founded scholarships there, one of which was held by CHRISTOPHER MARLOWE.

Parker, Theodore 1810–60 American theologian and social reformer. One of the leading figures of the generation prior to the Civil War, he was born in Lexington, Massachusetts, and educated at Harvard.

His sermon *The Transient and Permanent in Christianity*, delivered in 1841, denied the authority of the Bible and the supernatural origin of Christ. Christian theological dogma was transient, Christian moral truths permanent. These beliefs were more fully elucidated in *A Discourse of Matters Pertaining to Religion* (1842). In 1845 he became pastor of the new Twenty-Eighth Congregational Society of Boston, and for the next 14 years he sought to apply Christian morality to contemporary problems, championing before large crowds such causes as prison reform, temperance and women's education. His great passion, though, was the abolition of slavery. He delivered strident and moving denunciations of slavery, was part of the secret committee supporting John Brown and sheltered and encouraged fugitive slaves. His views on the matter were detailed in *A Letter to the People of the United States Touching the Matter of Slavery* (1848).

Parkes, Sir Henry 1815–96 Australian politician, journalist and poet. Born in Warwickshire, he emigrated to Australia at the age of 24. Success enabled him to found a liberal newspaper, *The Empire*, and he made a successful career in politics also, becoming Premier of New South Wales. He was one of the moving spirits behind the Australian Federal Commonwealth, which finally came into being in 1901, five years after his death. Parkes also encouraged the art of poetry in Australia and wrote poetry himself as a recreation, *Murmurs of the Stream* (1857) being the most highly regarded of the five volumes he published. Other books were *Australian Views of England: Eleven Letters, 1861 and 1862* (1869) and *Fifty Years in the Making of Australian History* (1892).

Parkinson, John 1567–1650 Botanist and herbalist of the royal gardens. Parkinson published *Paradisi in Sole Paradisus Terrestris: or, A Garden of All Sorts of Pleasant Flowers Which Our English Air Will Permitt to be Nursed up* (1629) and a massive herbal, *Theatrum Botanicum* (1640), which dealt with nearly 4000 plants and contained 2600 illustrations.

Parkman, Francis, Jr 1823–93 American historian. He was born in Boston and educated at Harvard. During the summer of 1846 he and his cousin Quincy Adams Shaw undertook a 1700-mile trek across the prairies and into the Rocky Mountains of the American West. THE *OREGON TRAIL* (1847–9) records their journey. In spite of a chronic nervous disorder Parkman continued to travel extensively in the wilds of America, researching the great histories known collectively as *France and England in North America*: *Pioneers of France in the New World* (1865), *Jesuits in North America in the Seventeenth Century* (1867), *The Discovery of the Great West* (1869; revised and published as *LaSalle and the Discovery of the Great*

West in 1878), *The Old Regime in Canada* (1874), *Count Frontenac and New France under Louis XIV* (1877), *Montcalm and Wolfe* (1884) and *A Half-Century of Conflict* (1892). Though Parkman greatly admired the courage and stamina of the French, these works still betray his bias against what he perceived as Catholic despotism and in favour of Protestant democracy, represented by the English. He also published a *History of the Conspiracy of Pontiac* (1851; revised and retitled as *The Conspiracy of Pontiac and the Indian War after the Conquest of Canada*, 1870) and a single novel, *Vassall Morton* (1856).

Parlement of Foules, The A poem in RHYME ROYAL by GEOFFREY CHAUCER, probably written between 1374 and 1381. The negotiations for a marriage between Richard II and Anne of Bohemia (1381) and Princess Marie of France (1376–7), and even the poet's own marriage (1366?), have all been suggested as its occasion. The form is a DREAM-VISION. The narrator describes the *Somnium Scipionis*, which he has been reading, and falls asleep. Following the pattern of the work he has read in which Africanus appeared to the younger Scipio in a dream and showed him heaven and the mysteries of the future, the Chaucerian dreamer is led by Africanus to a garden where he first visits the temple of Venus and then witnesses a congregation of birds of all varieties gathered before the goddess Nature. It is St Valentine's Day, and they are there to choose their mates. A tercel (i.e. male) eagle claims the formel (female) eagle on Nature's wrist but the claim is contested by two other tercels of lower rank. All the birds debate the issue and finally Nature rules that the formel herself shall choose between her suitors. She asks for a delay of a year before making her choice, and the other birds choose their mates and all sing a roundel in praise of St Valentine and the summer. The debate between the birds, which is both delightful and comic, has elements of social SATIRE, the hierarchy of birds reflecting distinctions of social class and their debate at times mocking the stylized ideals of COURTLY LOVE. It is not clear whether any more specific allegorical reference is intended.

Parliament of the Three Ages, The A poem in AL-LITERATIVE VERSE written in the North Midlands between 1370 and 1390. After a poaching expedition which gives a detailed account of the butchering of a dead deer, the narrator falls asleep and witnesses a debate between Youth, Middle Age and Old Age. It is not a lively exchange: Old Age dominates, asserting the inevitability of death and the transience of worldly bliss, common themes of medieval literature, and giving an account of the NINE WORTHIES. The latter is longer than the argument demands and was clearly thought to have intrinsic interest. The poem is perhaps the work of the author of *WYNNERE AND WASTOURE*.

Parnassus Plays, The A group of plays produced at St John's College, Cambridge, in about 1600. It consists of *The Pilgrimage to Parnassus* and *The Return from Parnassus*; the second play is in two parts and its second part is called *The Scourge of Simony*. Their authorship is not known, though they have been attributed to JOHN DAY.

The Pilgrimage traces the allegorical journey of Philomusus and his cousin Studioso to Parnassus by way of the Trivium (logic, grammar and rhetoric) and Philosophy. They encounter Madido, the votary of wine, Amoretto, the voluptuary, and Ingenioso, who has forsaken the struggle and burned his books. The cousins resist temptation and diversion, and reach their goal. *The Return* is satirical and shows the characters on their way back to London, learning how difficult it is to survive. They are obliged to take humble jobs, though they try the accepted forms of attempting to secure a patron or gull the tradesmen. Eventually they are reduced to being shepherds. The satire continues in *The Scourge of Simony*, which surveys the literary and academic scenes. The separation of town and gown is considered and Brackyn, the Recorder of Cambridge, is subjected to a fair amount of abuse (he also suffers in *IGNORAMUS*). The merits of contemporary poets are satirically examined, SHAKESPEARE and BEN JONSON among them; WILL KEMP and RICHARD BURBAGE appear as characters.

Parnell, Thomas 1679–1718 Poet. Born in Dublin, and educated at Trinity College, Dublin, he became a canon of St Patrick's Cathedral in 1702 and Archdeacon of Clogher in 1706. After moving to London in 1712, he contributed to *THE SPECTATOR*, thereby attracting the attention of SWIFT and POPE and joining the SCRIBLERUS CLUB. Pope, denied a university education because of his Catholicism, was particularly impressed by Parnell's formal training in the classics and Parnell contributed *An Essay on the Life of Homer* to Pope's translation of the *Iliad*.

During his lifetime, he published relatively little, apart from *An Essay on the Different Styles of Poetry* (1713), and after his return to Ireland in 1716 he descended into a state of melancholia from which he died. Pope was responsible for the publication of a posthumous selection of his friend's verse, which appeared as *Poems on Several Occasions* (1721) and included his only outstanding verse: 'A Night-Piece on Death' (which anticipates the work of the GRAVE-YARD POETS) and the 'Hymn to Contentment', another ode in octosyllabics. 'The Hermit', his narrative poem in HEROIC COUPLETS, was based on a story in the *GESTA ROMANORUM*. Parnell remains rather an elusive figure, a minor poet with sufficient affinities with his more illustrious contemporaries to suggest he might have gone on to produce verse of a higher order.

parody A form of literary mimicry that holds up a glass in which writers may see their own worst potentialities realized, and take heed. For the reader, it is literary criticism of a particularly palatable kind.

Since outright bad literature may itself resemble a parody of better literature, parody usually mimics the mighty rather than the humble, and often mingles admiration with mockery. However, this is not always the case: witness the parodies of advertisements, newspaper styles, novelettes and so forth in JOYCE's *ULYSSES*.

At its best, parody remains close to the original and is fairly good-natured; it warns rather than demeans. At one end of its spectrum, however, parody may approximate to BURLESQUE by exaggerating mimicry into caricature. At the other end, it may approximate to SATIRE by permitting moral criticism to usurp its central function as literary criticism.

Since literary structures tend to be generic, and thus common to writings of very varying quality, parody normally mimics the victim's style or content but merely uses his structure. Exceptionally, however, when some generic type of highly conventionalized structure is mimicked (such as DETECTIVE FICTION or the heroic romance), structure as well as style and content may be said to be parodied. In general, though, such cases would be thought of rather as travesties or burlesques.

Parr, Samuel 1747–1825 Latin scholar. Educated at Harrow and Emmanuel College, Cambridge, he became the perpetual curate of Hatton in Warwickshire and assembled a library of 10,000 volumes. Parr's scholarship gained him considerable distinction and the nickname of the 'Whig Johnson'; he wrote the Latin epitaph on JOHNSON in St Paul's Cathedral. His writings were collected and published in eight volumes in 1828, and he is the subject of THOMAS DE QUINCEY's essay, 'Dr Samuel Parr, or Whiggism in Relation to Literature'.

Parson's Tale, The See *CANTERBURY TALES, THE*.

Parsons, Clere (Trevor James Herbert) 1908–31 Poet. Educated at Oxford, he produced only one slender volume, *Poems*, published posthumously by Faber in 1932. His early death, and the promise shown in his slender *oeuvre*, can only point to what he might have achieved. Despite the occasional archaic phrase, his poems have a graceful elegance and a distinctive, original voice. Such impressive poems as 'Introduction', 'Suburban Nature Piece' and 'Garden Goddess', which show the influence of W. H. AUDEN and LAURA RIDING, do not deserve the obscurity into which they have fallen. Parsons has been championed by GEOFFREY GRIGSON, who believed that his early death 'probably extinguished a talent as considerable as any', and by C. H. SISSON, who refers to his 'few remarkable lyrics'.

Partisan Review An American literary and political journal, founded in 1934, with Philip Rahv and William Phillips as co-editors. Although its founders intended it to maintain an independent Marxist position, it has long since modified its political complexion. Distinguished contributors have included Gide, Trotsky, W. H. AUDEN, WALLACE STEVENS, WILLIAM CARLOS WILLIAMS, DYLAN THOMAS, T. S. ELIOT, GEORGE ORWELL, VLADIMIR NABOKOV, Camus, Malraux, STEPHEN SPENDER, ROBERT PENN WARREN, SAUL BELLOW, F. R. LEAVIS and Borges.

Partonope of Blois A 15th-century VERSE ROMANCE in couplets; a fragment of a stanzaic version also survives. After becoming lost on a hunt Partonope is carried by a magic ship to a city which is apparently uninhabited. He becomes the lover of an invisible empress, Melior, who promises to wed him if he does not attempt to see her for two and a half years. On return visits to his native France he achieves military glory and is persuaded by his mother to break his promise to Melior. She casts him out and he lives in suicidal despair and near-madness until found by Melior's sister and nursed back to health. He defeats rivals for Melior's hand and eventually regains her love. The poem is based on a French romance, but is not a direct translation of any extant version.

Partridge, Eric (Honeywood) 1894–1979 Philologist and lexicographer. Born in Gisborne, New Zealand, he was educated at the University of Queensland and at Oxford. He worked for three years as a schoolmaster before service as a private in the Australian infantry during World War I. University teaching at Oxford, Manchester and London was followed by four years in which he ran his own small publishing business. The 1931 slump brought this to an end, and for the rest of his life he depended on his writing. Partridge specialized in slang and bawdy, areas of the English vocabulary not covered by *THE OXFORD ENGLISH DICTIONARY*. His most popular publications include the *Dictionary of Slang and Unconventional English* (1937), *Usage and Abusage* (1942), *Dictionary of the Underworld* (1950), *Origins* (1958) and *Shakespeare's Bawdy* (1947).

Passage to India, A A novel by E. M. FORSTER, published in 1924.

Adela Quested visits Chandrapore with Mrs Moore in order to make up her mind whether to marry the latter's son, Ronny. He is a city magistrate who exemplifies the narrow anti-Indian prejudices of the imperial bureaucrat. Adela's desire to understand the 'real India', an interest shared by Mrs Moore, annoys the whole white community apart from Cyril Fielding, principal of the government college. Fielding's liberal views have set him apart from his compatriots, and he has nurtured a close relationship with Dr Aziz, assistant to the British Civil Surgeon. Visiting a mosque, Mrs Moore encounters Aziz and a friendship is established. She and Adela accept his invitation to visit the renowned and mysterious Marabar Caves, but Fielding, who was to have escorted them, misses the train and the party proceeds without him. The expedition proves to be an unmitigated disaster. Mrs Moore undergoes a traumatic and nihilistic psychic experience from which she never recovers, and Adela believes herself to have been the victim of a sexual assault by Aziz. He is arrested and committed to prison to await trial, and the entire community at Chandrapore is sharply divided into opposing racial factions. Only Fielding amongst the British continues to assert Aziz's innocence, but their friendship is irrevocably compromised.

Mrs Moore dies on the voyage home, and Adela, under extreme psychological pressure, admits that she was mistaken. Some time afterwards, Aziz and Fielding meet for the last time and discuss the future of India. Aziz, who has now adopted an entrenched radical stance, insists that only when the British are driven out of India can he and Fielding be friends.

Passionate Pilgrim, The A slim volume of poems, the earliest surviving complete edition of which is the second (1599), whose title-page bears the ascription 'By W. Shakespeare... Printed for W. Iaggard'. Of the 20 poems, five are certainly by SHAKESPEARE (three pieces from LOVE'S LABOUR'S LOST and versions of Sonnets 138 and 144), one by MARLOWE (THE PASSIONATE SHEPHERD TO HIS LOVE), two by RICHARD BARNFIELD, and the remainder still unattributed. Jaggard was undoubtedly trading on Shakespeare's popularity in attributing the whole collection to him, and in his *Apologie for Actors* (1612) the playwright THOMAS HEYWOOD describes Shakespeare as being 'much offended with M. *Jaggard* that (altogether unknowne to him) presumed to make so bold with his name'. No other of Shakespeare's *Sonnets* appeared in print until 1609. There is no reason to think Shakespeare the author of any of the unattributed poems, although claims have been made for the charming lyric 'Crabbed Age and Youth Cannot Live Together.' By a fine irony, the great Folio edition of Shakespeare, published in 1623, was printed by the piratical William Jaggard's son Isaac.

Passionate Shepherd to His Love, The CHRISTOPHER MARLOWE's poem, an invitation to the loved one to share life in an idyllic world, was first published in an anthology, THE PASSIONATE PILGRIM (1599), but the text that appeared in ENGLAND'S HELICON (1600) is the commonly accepted one. SIR WALTER RALEIGH's witty counter, *The Nymph's Reply to the Shepherd*, is almost as well known. Together they constitute a classic pairing of romantic extravagance and romantic realism.

Past and Present A prose work by THOMAS CARLYLE, first published in 1843.

Its first two books contrast medieval and Victorian England. To that end Carlyle made use of the recently published *Chronicle* of JOCELIN OF BRAKELOND, an account of life in the 12th-century abbey of St Edmund under the shrewd and sagacious Abbot Samson. Setting this beside Victorian England, Carlyle asks if the medieval peasant, secure in his place in the social order, is not happier and better off than his 19th-century counterpart. The third book, 'The Modern Worker', is in the main a satirical attack on Mammonism, Benthamism, politicians and similar forces that Carlyle considers anathema to society. The final book, 'Horoscope', is an urgent, apocalyptic plea for putting things to rights.

Past and Present is notable for Carlyle's concept of the Hero. Through Abbot Samson, the firm, efficient, kindly, astute man of God, Carlyle pleads for a renewal of society, a healthier, abler ordering of human life through good leadership. Thus he suggests Victorian England encourage 'Captains of Industry' as well as a more compassionate understanding among members of society. Also, visionary though he may be, in the last part of *Past and Present* Carlyle makes a number of surprisingly practical suggestions for improvements. As a whole, the book is an arresting combination of the idealistic and the pragmatic; it is laced with humour, rife with fantastic metaphors, and populated by grotesquely named characters such as Sir Jabesh Windbag, Plugson of Undershot and Bobus Higgins. An energetic, explosive and provocative book, *Past and Present* exercised considerable influence over contemporaries' view of their society; see THE CONDITION OF ENGLAND NOVEL.

Paston letters, The The collected correspondence and documents of the Paston family of Norfolk from the period 1425–95. The letters record the daily lives of three generations of the family and reveal the personalities of individuals as well as many domestic details of the life of a wealthy provincial family in the 15th century. They are a valuable record for both social and literary historians.

pastoral Literature about an idealized rural life, concentrating especially on the loves and laments of shepherds and shepherdesses. The kind is established by Theocritus' *Idylls* in the 3rd century BC. Virgil's *Eclogues* provide the major Roman example. A pastoral poem therefore can also be called an IDYLL or an ECLOGUE (or a bucolic). The GEORGIC also deals with rural life, but more realistically, concerning itself with farming and its labours rather than with the singing, dancing and loving of shepherds.

The chief example of pastoral romance in English is SIDNEY's ARCADIA, SPENSER's SHEPHEARDES CALENDER being the chief poetic example. As these examples suggest, there is little pastoral of merit after the Elizabethan period (unless, dubiously, some of WORDSWORTH and KEATS may count as such). However, WILLIAM EMPSON's *Some Versions of Pastoral* seizes on the moral implication of pastoral – that rural life provides a model of a simpler, more wholesome way of life than court or city – and extends the definition to include any such moral world, whether set in the country or not. Hence a Western and a gangster movie alike might count as pastoral.

Patchen, Kenneth 1911–72 American poet and novelist. He was born in Niles, Ohio. His experimental verse, with its proletarian stance, anticipated and influenced the work of the BEATS. It appeared in *Before the Brave* (1936), *First Will and Testament* (1939), *The Teeth of the Lion* (1942), *Cloth of the Tempest* (1943), *Pictures of Life and Death* (1946), *To Say if You Love Someone* (1948), *Hurrah for Anything* (1957), *Because It Is* (1960) and *Collected Poems* (1968). His fiction includes: *The Journal of Albion Moonlight* (1941), a surrealist ALLEGORY; *Memoirs of a Shy Pornographer* (1945), a SATIRE; *Sleepers Awake* (1946); and *See You in the Morning* (1948). *Panels for the Walls of Heaven* (1947) and *The Famous Boating Party* (1954) are prose poems.

Patent Theatres The Letters Patent issued by Charles II to THOMAS KILLIGREW and WILLIAM D'AVENANT in 1662 gave them the sole legal right to arrange performances of plays in the City of Westminster. Killigrew established his company of players at DRURY LANE, which has remained a Patent Theatre ever since. D'Avenant's patent was invested initially in Lincoln's Inn Fields, then in Dorset Garden, and finally, in 1732, in COVENT GARDEN. Despite challenge from the HAYMARKET THEATRE in the 18th century, the monopoly of Drury Lane and Covent Garden over the performance of legitimate drama in London effectively survived until 1843, when an Act of Parliament ended it.

Pater, Walter (Horatio) 1839–94 Essayist, critic and novelist. Born in London, educated at King's School, Canterbury, and The Queen's College, Oxford, Pater lived an uneventful life at the latter place, becoming a fellow of Brasenose in 1864. Shy and remote in personality, he occasionally ventured forth on Continental tours with his sisters, but preferred the bachelor obscurity of Oxford where he was the diffident centre of a small group of followers. In the 1860s and 1870s he began publishing articles on literature, philosophy and the fine arts in the burgeoning journals of the time, but it was his *STUDIES IN THE HISTORY OF THE RENAISSANCE* (1873) that secured his reputation as a leader of the AESTHETIC MOVEMENT. It was followed by a novel, *MARIUS THE EPICUREAN* (1885),

Imaginary Portraits (1887), the unfinished *Gaston de Latour* (1888), *Appreciations with an Essay on Style* (1889), *Plato and Platonism* (1893), *The Child in the House* (1894) and several posthumous publications, *Miscellaneous Studies* (1895), *Greek Studies* (1895) and *Essays from 'The Guardian'* (1896). An edition of his collected works came out in 1900–1.

'Appreciation' was a byword with Pater, who rarely if ever took an opposing stance. To him an understanding and an apprehension of beauty were paramount, as was a melancholy recognition of the brevity of human life. Disciples often misrepresented him as a hedonistic voice of 'Art for Art's sake' but he never wholly relinquished the ethical implications of aestheticism. The morbid side to his work, most evident in *Gaston de Latour*, was seized on by followers in the 1890s.

Paterson A long poem in free verse by WILLIAM CARLOS WILLIAMS, published in five volumes from 1946 to 1958. The name refers both to a city on the Passaic River near Williams's home town of Rutherford, New Jersey, and to a character in the poem who merges the details of the poet's private life with the public history of the region. Williams said that 'all art begins in the local', and in *Paterson* he combines historical documents, newspaper stories, geological surveys, and personal letters in an attempt to localize his material. The dominant image of the poem is that of the Passaic River, which in its fluid, continual movement unites the particulars of human experience with time. Fragments of a sixth book were published posthumously in 1963 as an appendix to the poem.

Paterson, A(ndrew) B(arton) 1864–1941 Australian poet, journalist and novelist. Born near Orange in New South Wales, Paterson was educated in Sydney and later trained for the law. He practised as a solicitor in Sydney until 1899, when he became a war correspondent in South Africa. He edited the Sydney *Evening News* in 1904 and the Sydney *Town and Country Journal* in 1907–8.

Apart from his journalism Paterson also wrote novels, including *The Outback Marriage* (1906), but is famous for the ballads he contributed to *The Bulletin*, the widely read Sydney paper founded in 1880 by J. F. Archibald and John Haynes, while still practising as a solicitor. His collection, *The Man from Snowy River* (1895), became a best-seller. He also gathered authentic bush ballads and published an anthology, *Old Bush Songs*, in 1905. Their slangy idiom and infectious rhythms make Paterson's own poems, and the ones he collected, immediately memorable; everyone in the English-speaking world knows 'Waltzing Matilda', which he adapted from a traditional source. Paterson's ballads create a vivid picture of early Australian life, capturing its hardships, recklessness and grim, matter-of-fact humour. His nickname, 'Banjo', comes from the pseudonym he used in *The Bulletin*. Paterson's *Collected Verse* was published in 1921. His *Happy Dispatches* (1934) is a volume of reminiscences.

pathetic fallacy A term coined by JOHN RUSKIN, in the third volume of *MODERN PAINTERS* (1856), for the practice of attributing human emotions to the inanimate or unintelligent world. The opening lines of ROBERT BROWNING's 'Porphyria's Lover' provide an example:

> The rain set early in tonight,
> Sullen wind was soon awake,
> Tore the elm-tops down for spite,
> And did its worst to vex the lake.

Pathfinder, The See LEATHERSTOCKING TALES, THE.

Patience A late-14th-century poem in ALLITERATIVE VERSE and the West Midlands dialect. Preserved in the same manuscript as *SIR GAWAIN AND THE GREEN KNIGHT*, *PEARL* and *CLEANNESS*, it is grouped with them as the work of the same, unidentified author, known as the *GAWAIN*-POET. It is homiletic in intention, aiming to teach the virtue of patience and illustrating it with the story of Jonah, taken from the Vulgate Bible. The skilful, humorous characterization of the surly and disobedient Jonah and the vivid realization of the scenes with a particularly medieval aspect are characteristic of the art of the *Gawain*-poet.

Patient Grissel, The Pleasant Comedy of A play by THOMAS DEKKER, written in collaboration with HENRY CHETTLE and William Haughton and first published in 1603. The story is based on CHAUCER's *The Clerk's Tale*, in *THE CANTERBURY TALES*, which comes in turn from Boccaccio. The play is remembered for Dekker's beautiful songs, 'Art Thou Poor Yet Hast Thou Golden Slumbers? O Sweet Content!' and 'Golden Slumbers Kiss Your Eyes'.

Patmore, Coventry (Kersey Dighton) 1823–96 Poet and critic. Born at Woodford in Essex, he was educated at home by an eccentric father, apart from a brief interlude in Paris. In 1846, sponsored by MONCKTON MILNES, he secured an assistant librarianship in the British Museum, where he worked nearly 20 years, and in 1847 he married Emily Andrews.

Soon after his *Poems* (1844) appeared Patmore became associated with the PRE-RAPHAELITE BROTHERHOOD, contributing to their short-lived journal, *THE GERM*, in 1850 and interceding successfully with RUSKIN to support the Brotherhood when it was attacked in the early 1850s. Millais took one of his early verses, 'The Woodman's Daughter', as the subject for a painting. *Tamerton Church-Tower and Other Poems* (1853) was followed by his most popular work, *THE*

ANGEL IN THE HOUSE, a loosely constructed sequence of poems in praise of married love which originally appeared in four parts: *The Betrothal* (1854), *The Espousals* (1856), *Faithful for Ever* (1860) and *The Victories of Love* (1863).

His wife Emily died in 1862, though Patmore went on to marry twice more, in 1864 and in 1881. He became a Roman Catholic in the year of his second marriage, and the 42 odes of *The Unknown Eros* (1877) show him entering a new – and to contemporaries, less accessible – literary phase. Their theme once again is love, but now the earthly conception is harmonized with the transcendental. These post-conversion verses apotheosize divine love, complementing and contrasting with *The Angel in the House*. Afterwards Patmore turned chiefly to prose, beginning with the study of METRE which introduced his next volume of poems (1878) and continuing with such critical, philosophical and aphoristic studies as *Principle in Art* (1879), *Religio Poetae* (1893) and *The Rod, the Root and the Flower* (1895).

Chiefly identified in his own day as the author of *The Angel in the House*, Patmore had passed from the public view before the end of his career and is now largely forgotten. The very exactitude with which his most successful work captured mid-Victorian values, with its glorification of marriage and domesticity, guaranteed its neglect by later generations. Yet his narrative ability – apparent in his own favourite poem, 'Amelia' – as well as his melodic sense and his occasional delicacy of phrase cannot be denied.

Paton, Alan (Stewart) 1903–88 South African novelist and short-story writer. Born in Pietermaritzburg, he became principal of Diepkloof Reformatory, Johannesburg (1935–48) and gained the insights into segregated black living conditions which illumine his first novel, *Cry, the Beloved Country* (1948) and *Debbie Go Home: Stories* (1961; as *Tales from a Troubled Land* in USA, 1965). The novel pricked white South African Christian consciences and alerted world opinion to the country's long-established racial inequalities. Altogether more accomplished, *Too Late the Phalarope* (1953) explores the tragedy of Afrikaner racial and political inflexibility. Other publications include: two substantial biographies, *Hofmeyr* (1964) and *Apartheid and the Archbishop* (1973); *Knocking on the Door: Shorter Writings* (1975); *Towards the Mountain* (1981), an autobiography; and *Ah, But Your Land is Beautiful* (1981), an uneasy combination of 'experimental' fiction and 1950s history. He was president of the Liberal Party in 1958–68.

Patten, Brian See LIVERPOOL POETS.

Pattison, Mark 1813–84 Scholar. Born at Hornby in Yorkshire, he went to Oriel College, Oxford, where the Evangelical faith of his childhood was altered by contact with NEWMAN and the OXFORD MOVEMENT. He became a fellow of Lincoln College in 1839 and its Rector in 1861, having suffered a decade of disappointment after missing election to the post in 1851. He held liberal views on University affairs and, in later years, on theology, as his contribution to ESSAYS AND REVIEWS (1860) demonstrated. In literary studies, he edited poems by POPE (1869 and 1872) and MILTON's sonnets (1883) and wrote the volume on Milton for the English Men of Letters series (1879). But his chief interest was in the Renaissance scholars Isaac Casaubon and Joseph Scaliger; his biography of Casaubon appeared in 1875 but his work on Scaliger was left incomplete at his death. His wife, the art historian Emilia Francis Strong, was many years younger than himself; she later married the politician Sir Charles Dilke. Pattison's marriage, among other circumstances, has prompted the suggestion that he was the model for Casaubon in GEORGE ELIOT's MIDDLEMARCH. His memoirs were published by his widow in 1885.

Paulding, James Kirke 1778–1860 American man of letters. He grew up in Tarrytown, New York, where his contemporary WASHINGTON IRVING also lived. His sister Julia married Washington's brother William. With the Irving brothers he founded and contributed to SALMAGUNDI (1807–8), producing a second series of Salmagundi single-handedly in 1819–20. A staunch defender of his native country in the Anglo-American literary dispute, he wrote The Diverting History of John Bull and Brother Jonathan (1812), The Lay of the Scottish Fiddle (1813; a PARODY of SIR WALTER SCOTT's narrative poems) and The United States and England (1815). The Backwoodsman (1818), a long poem written in couplets, celebrates the American frontier spirit. He also produced over 70 tales and five novels: Konigsmarke (1823), The Dutchman's Fireside (1831), Westward Ho! (1832), The Old Continental (1846) and The Puritan and His Daughter (1849).

Paulin, Tom 1949– Poet and critic. He was born in Leeds but grew up in Belfast. He studied English at the Universities of Hull and Oxford and is currently a lecturer in English at the University of Nottingham. His poems have been collected in A Sense of Justice (1977), The Strange Museum (1980) and The Liberty Tree (1983). His work is bleaker and more urban than that of other contemporary Ulster poets. It is often informed by a brooding political awareness responding to violence and injustice in Northern Ireland but invoking a more cosmopolitan post-imperial frame of reference. His poetry has paid homage to the radical dissenting tradition of late 18th-century Belfast and the resonances of Ulster dialect verse first explored by JOHN HEWITT. His version of Sophocles' Antigone, The

Riot Act (1985), incorporates traces of Ulster dialect to draw attention to Ulster parallels with the tangle of power politics, religion and personal responsibility in the original. Seize the Fire (1990) is a version of Aeschylus' Prometheus Bound, and in Fivemiletown (1987) Paulin again returns to his central themes, the Irish predicament and, in particular, the matter of Protestant identity. He has also published a critical study of HARDY's poetry (1975) and Ireland and the English Crisis (1984), a collection of critical essays, as well as editing two anthologies, The Faber Book of Political Verse (1986) and The Faber Book of Vernacular Verse (1990).

Payne, John Howard 1791–1852 American playwright and actor. He was born in New York, where his first play, Julia: or, The Wanderer (1806), was staged when he was only 14. It was followed by a successful adaptation of August von Kotzebue's Lover's Vows (1809). In 1813 Payne went to England, where Trial without Jury (1815), an adaptation from the French, better known by its alternative title The Maid and the Magpie, was followed by several other adaptations, and then by Brutus: or, The Fall of Tarquin (1818), a clever compilation from several sources, which provided Edmund Kean with one of his more notable roles. In 1820, having failed as manager of Sadler's Wells Theatre, he was imprisoned for debt. The successful production of Thérèse: The Orphan of Geneva (1821), which he wrote in prison, bought his release, and he settled in Paris. The success of Clari: or, The Maid of Milan (1823), which contained the famous 'Home Sweet Home', set to music by Henry Bishop, encouraged him to return to London, where he collaborated on a number of plays with WASHINGTON IRVING, including Charles the Second (1824). He wrote little more for the theatre after his return to New York in 1832, but collected voluminous notes on the Cherokee Indians, unpublished during his lifetime; Grant Foreman edited Indian Justice: A Cherokee Murder Trial in 1934.

p'Bitek, Okot 1931–82 Ugandan poet. He was born in Gulu. His writings were seminal to the East African search for cultural identity in the 1970s. In Song of Lawino (1966), his spirited poem in the manner of Acoli oral verse, the persona of Lawino vigorously defends traditional culture, and scathingly attacks her husband's westernized ways. Song of Ocul (1970) is his reply. Two Songs ('Song of Prisoner', 'Song of Malaya', i.e. prostitute; 1971) lament the post-Independence penury of most Africans, though he always argued, as in African Religions in Western Scholarship (1971) and Africa's Cultural Revolution (1973), that neo-colonialism was cultural rather than economic.

Peabody, Elizabeth 1804–94 American educator. One of the leading literary women of her day, she was born in Massachusetts. At 18 she opened a school in Boston and began to meet many of the influential New England literati, including RALPH WALDO EMERSON and WILLIAM ELLERY CHANNING. After serving for many years as Channing's close assistant, in 1834 she began to assist BRONSON ALCOTT at his experimental Temple School. The following year she anonymously published *Record of a School*. In 1839 she opened the bookshop in Boston that established her as an important member of the TRANSCENDENTALIST movement; the only source of foreign books in the city, her shop became a centre of intellectual life. (The planning of the BROOK FARM experiment took place there.) From the printing press in the back of her shop, she published three books by NATHANIEL HAWTHORNE (her brother-in-law), several of MARGARET FULLER's translations of German works, and from 1842 to 1843 the Transcendentalist journal *THE DIAL*. She contributed several articles to *The Dial*, but devoted most of her writing to textbooks of grammar and history, including her *Chronological History of the United States* (1856). In 1860 she opened the first American kindergarten, and later published the *Kindergarten Messenger* (1873–7). From 1879 to 1894 she was a member and lecturer at Bronson Alcott's Concord School of Philosophy. Her final days were spent in support of Indian education, and in putting together *A Last Evening with Allston* (1886), which combines memoirs with her early articles for *The Dial*. Her impact on the Boston literary community is reflected in HENRY JAMES's characterization of her as Miss Birdseye in *THE BOSTONIANS*.

Peacham, Henry *c.* 1576–*c.* 1643 Author of essays and 'characters'. Peacham is best remembered for *The Complete Gentleman* (1622), a book of advice to young men about to enter the world, which contained instructions on art, poetry and heraldry as well as manners. The heraldic definitions in the 1661 edition helped SAMUEL JOHNSON when he came to compile his *DICTIONARY OF THE ENGLISH LANGUAGE*. Other works by Peacham were *Coach and Sedan* (1636), *The Truth of Our Times* (1638) and *The Art of Living in London* (1642). His treatise on art, *Graphice*, was first published in 1606 and appeared in many subsequent editions as *The Gentleman's Exercise*.

Peacock, Thomas Love 1785–1866 Novelist, poet and essayist. The only son of a London glass merchant, Peacock was born at Weymouth and after his father's early death was brought up by his mother at Chertsey, receiving his only formal schooling at a private school in Englefield Green which he left at the age of 13. A modest inheritance from his father allowed him to live as private scholar and man of letters, and he was not obliged to seek regular employment until he was in his thirties, when he obtained a senior post at the East India Company. He remained at India House

until his retirement in 1856, succeeding JAMES MILL as Examiner in 1837. In 1820 Peacock married Jane Gryffydh, with whom he appears to have lived happily until she suffered a complete breakdown at the death of their third child, a three-year-old daughter, and continued a mental invalid until her death in 1851. He was also to survive his remaining daughters, Jane (d. 1851) and his favourite Mary Ellen, who died at Capri in 1861, following her disastrous marriage to GEORGE MEREDITH, who revenged himself with the unkindly portrait of Peacock as Dr Middleton in *THE EGOIST*.

In many ways Peacock's development as a writer was inseparable from his close friendship with SHELLEY, whom he first met in 1812. Despite differences of temperament, each man discovered in the other a kindred radical spirit, and if Peacock became something of a literary adviser to Shelley, particularly in respect of the classical literatures in which he was exceptionally well read, it was largely through the younger poet that he acquired greater confidence in his own distinctive creative powers, and was for the first time drawn into a wider literary circle. By the time he made his debut as a satirical novelist Peacock's authorial *persona* is already that of the informed insider. His prose satires *HEADLONG HALL* (1816), *MELINCOURT* (1817) and *NIGHTMARE ABBEY* (1818) all presuppose a reader intimately versed in British intellectual controversy during the years following the end of the Napoleonic wars. Although some of their figures are clearly intended to be identified with real-life counterparts, the primary target of Peacock's urbane ridicule is the particular philosophical, social and political attitudes and ideologies they typify. His most characteristic formal device is the suspension of narrative for a kind of wickedly parodied Socratic dialogue or Platonic symposium, in which the representative minds of the nation argue each other under the well-laden tables of their country hosts. The satiric disputations are leavened by FARCE, witty songs and romantic love-plots ending in incongruous marital alliances. In *MAID MARIAN* (1822) and *THE MISFORTUNES OF ELPHIN* (1829) Peacock combines topical satire with historical romance, but returns to his earlier, and perhaps more congenial, form in *CROTCHET CASTLE* (1831). Thirty years were to elapse before the appearance of his last novel *GRYLL GRANGE* (1860–1), a satire on the mid-Victorian age, and regarded by many readers as his masterpiece.

Peacock's most important poetical writings include *Rhododaphne* (1818), a celebration of natural religion based on Apuleius' treatment of the myth of Cupid and Psyche, which anticipates KEATS's *LAMIA*; lyrical pieces such as 'Long Night Succeeds the Little Day' (1826) and 'Newark Abbey' (1842); and, perhaps most famously, *The Paper Money Lyrics*, a satirical assault on political economy and the banking fraternity, written in the 1820s, but withheld from publication until the death of JAMES MILL, Peacock's immediate superior at India House, in 1837. The fragmentary *Essay on Fashionable Literature* (1818) and *The Four Ages of Poetry* (1820) are Peacock's most systematic critical writings, and the scepticism expressed in the latter concerning the social value and utility of art and literature in an age of philosophy and science provoked Shelley, who perhaps overlooked his friend's tongue-in-cheek manner, to write his *A DEFENCE OF POETRY*. The two-part *Memoirs of Shelley* appeared in 1858–60.

Peake, Mervyn (Laurence) 1911–68 Novelist, artist and poet. Born at Kuling in China, the son of a medical missionary, he was educated at Tiensin until the age of 11, then at Eltham College in Kent. Later he studied at the Royal Academy School and worked as an artist on the island of Sark in 1934–7. On his return to London he held several exhibitions and published illustrated verse and short stories for children. During World War II he suffered a nervous breakdown and was invalided out of the army. However, he became a war artist, notably for *The Leader*, in which capacity he visited Belsen at the close of the war.

He showed himself a master of the grotesque with his first novel, *Titus Groan* (1946), a minutely detailed Gothic fantasy about the Earl of Groan, the incumbent of Gormenghast, an ancient castle peopled by monumental and bizarre figures. *Gormenghast* (1950) and *Titus Alone* (1959) followed; all were reissued as a trilogy in 1967. Peake's verse includes *Rhymes without Reason* (1944), *The Glassblowers* (1950) and *The Rime of the Flying Bomb* (1962), a BALLAD of the blitz. There is one play, *The Wit to Woo* (1957). Most of his work he illustrated himself; he also provided drawings for editions of COLERIDGE's *THE RIME OF THE ANCIENT MARINER* in 1943, and STEVENSON's *TREASURE ISLAND* in 1949. In *A World Away* (1970) his wife Maeve Gilmore provides an insight into his life, tragically marred by Parkinson's disease in the later years. *A Book of Nonsense* was published posthumously in 1972.

Pearce, (Ann) Philippa 1920– Writer of CHILDREN'S LITERATURE. Born in Cambridgeshire, the daughter of a flour miller, she grew up in the countryside, finishing her education at Cambridge. She then worked in the BBC and in publishing, meanwhile producing her first novel, *Minnow on the Say* (1955). This is a charming, understated adventure story involving the search for a lost will, but it was her next novel, *Tom's Midnight Garden* (1958), that made her reputation and won her the Carnegie Medal for the most outstanding children's book of the year. It describes the visit of a solitary child, Tom, to an old house where each succeeding night he travels into the past, always meeting an equally lonely Edwardian little girl. Only at the end of the story does he realize that the girl is in fact the present owner of the house in which he is staying, but now turned into a crabbed old lady. Since then Philippa Pearce has written some excellent short stories and another minor classic, *A Dog So Small* (1962), about the clash in a child's mind between fantasy and reality. Stories for younger readers include *The Tooth Ball* (1987) and *Freddy* (1988).

Pearl A late-14th-century poem in ALLITERATIVE VERSE and the West Midlands dialect. The influence of *MANDEVILLE'S TRAVELS* sets *c.* 1357 as the earliest possible date of composition. Preserved in the same manuscript as *SIR GAWAIN AND THE GREEN KNIGHT*, *PATIENCE* and *CLEANNESS*, it is grouped with them as the work of the same, unidentified author, known as the *GAWAIN*-POET.

Pearl has a complex and very tight structure. It is divided into 20 sets of five stanzas, each stanza having 12 octosyllabic lines; the last line of each is a variation on the last line of the first stanza in the group and acts as a refrain. The stanzas rhyme abababababbcbc, c remaining the same throughout each group. The first line of each stanza echoes the last line of the previous stanza. Despite the extreme restrictions of the form, the verse flows easily and realistically reproduces direct speech.

The poem is an allegorical DREAM-VISION and an ELEGY on the death of a young child, probably the poet's daughter. The authenticity of the autobiographical situation cannot be determined and is not relevant. The grieving narrator falls asleep and in a vision visits a beautiful and strange land where he sees, across a stream, the Pearl-maiden, the dead child as a young woman dressed in pearl-encrusted clothing. He questions her and she teaches him points of doctrine, answering his ignorant and impudent comments born of outraged grief with arguments from biblical texts delivered with little sympathy. The Dreamer is naive and obstinate, unable to see that his understanding of human society has no relevance in the Kingdom of God. He is shown the Heavenly City, the procession of the 144,000 virgin brides of Christ and the Lamb of God bleeding. Overcome by longing, he attempts to cross the stream and awakens to his grief with a better understanding of how to cope with it. The poem draws extensively on the Vulgate Bible, most importantly the parable of the vineyard (*Matthew* 20: 1–16), the vision of the Heavenly City (*Revelation* 21 and 22) and the procession of the 144,000 virgins (*Revelation* 14). The symbol of the pearl, central to the poem, is introduced as the narrator mourns his loss in the form of a metaphor: he has lost a precious pearl in the grass. The symbol's meaning is cumulative and complex, involving the biblical pearl of great price (*Matthew* 13: 45–6), concepts of spiritual purity and perfection, the state of salvation and divine grace, and the Kingdom of Heaven.

The poem, one of the greatest medieval allegories, is concerned with grief and spiritual crisis; it shows, in the contrast of the emotional dryness of rational argument and doctrine with the overwhelming love and pity the Dreamer feels for the Lamb, how both reason and love are necessary to faith. *Pearl* combines austerity in the maiden's teaching with humour in the sympathetic portrayal of the Dreamer and, in the parable of the vineyard in particular, makes biblical stories contemporary and familiar in the same manner as *Patience* and *Cleanness*.

Pearse, Patrick [Padraig] 1879–1916 Irish poet. Born in Dublin, he was educated by the Christian Brothers and at University College. Although he studied for the Bar, his main work was as a publicist for DOUGLAS HYDE's Gaelic League and for a revival of Gaelic literature and culture in education and society. His execution for his part in the Easter Rising, mourned by YEATS in 'Easter 1916', drew greater attention to his poems and plays of patriotic dedication, chiefly in Gaelic but including some poems in English, such as 'The Fool', 'The Rebel' and 'The Mother'. While remaining a devout Roman Catholic, Pearse developed the cult of the Irish nation into an alternative religion. His *Plays, Stories and Poems* were collected and published (in English) in 1917.

Pearson, John 1613–86 Divine. Pearson was born at Great Snoring in Norfolk, educated at Eton and Queens' College, Cambridge, and ordained in 1639. He lived quietly in London during the Commonwealth and after the Restoration became Master of Jesus College, Cambridge (1660), Lady Margaret Professor of Divinity (1661), Master of Trinity College, Cambridge (1662), and Bishop of Chester (1673). Pearson is acknowledged as the most learned and profound divine of an age rich in contenders. His *Exposition of the Creed* (1659), developed from a series of sermons delivered at St Clement's, Eastcheap, was for long a standard work in English divinity studies. He also collected the sermons and tracts of JOHN HALES as *Golden Remains* (1659).

Pecock, Reginald *c.* 1395–*c.* 1460 Religious writer. He was born in or near St David's in Wales and educated at Oxford, becoming a fellow of Oriel College in October 1417. He was ordained a sub-deacon in 1420, and deacon and priest in 1421. He became Master of Whittington College, London, in 1431 and Bishop of St Asaph in 1444. An anti-Lollardist, he concentrated on the points at dispute between the Lollards and the orthodox Church. After a sermon preached at St Paul's Cross in 1447 offending both radicals and reformers he moderated his teachings a little. He became Bishop of Chichester in 1450 and in 1455 completed his most important work, *Repressor of Over Much Blaming of the Clergy*. In this he proposes to examine 11 Lollard objections to the clergy but only actually considers the first six, referring his reader to other works for the remaining five. He anticipated HOOKER in arguing in favour of moral law based on natural reason illustrated by the Scriptures rather than defined or declared by them. In 1456 he issued his *Book of Faith* analysing faith and the roles of reason and Scriptural authority.

Throughout his career he provoked all sections of theological opinion by his writings. In 1457 he was expelled from the Privy Council for denying the authority of the patristic writers, having set natural law above that of the Scriptures and for writing on important theological matters in the vernacular. Given the choice of recanting or being burned, he recanted, first privately and then in public. He resigned his bishopric in exchange for a pension at Thorney Abbey in Cambridgeshire; there is further record of him, but he probably died soon after his move. Besides *Repressor* and the *Book of Faith*, his surviving works are *The Book of Christian Religion, The Donet* and *The Follower to the Donet*, the last two in the form of dialogues, all written before 1454. His prose style is clear and forceful, his works well-argued and rational.

Peele, George 1558–96 Playwright. The son of a London salter, Peele was educated at Christ's Hospital and Oxford. One of the UNIVERSITY WITS, he seems to have lived in London after 1581, earning what he could by writing plays, poems and pageants. His later years were spent in sickness and poverty.

Peele's first surviving play, *The Arraignment of Paris* (published in 1584), is a combination of debate and PASTORAL written for performance before Elizabeth I. Like much of his work, it is dramatically slight but notable for the beauty of its songs, which include 'Fair and Fair, and Twice So Fair'. *The Battle of Alcazar* (*c.* 1589), a fanciful account of a recent Moroccan encounter, owes its style to MARLOWE's TAMBURLAINE. *King Edward the First* (published in 1593), despite its historical characters, is more a romance than a history play. *The Love of King David and Fair Bathsheba* (*c.*1594, published in 1599) – which contains Bathsheba's song, 'Hot Sun, Cool Fire, Tempered with Sweet Air' – is better constructed. Peele's best play is THE OLD WIVES' TALE (published 1595), a highly original work whose mockery of romantic drama anticipates THE KNIGHT OF THE BURNING PESTLE.

The songs from Peele's plays have been much anthologized. Among his poems are *Polyhymnia* (1590), *The Honour of the Garter* (1593), and *Anglorum Feriae* (1595), all of which seem to have been written for ceremonial recitation at court.

***Pelham:** or, The Adventures of a Gentleman* A novel by EDWARD BULWER LYTTON, published in 1828. Henry Pelham is a fashionable dandy, whose habit of wearing black for dinner started a trend which has persisted to the present day, but who, for all his apparent foppishness, succeeds in clearing a friend from suspicion of a vicious murder (based on the notorious Thurtell case of 1824). Bulwer Lytton's first full-length novel, and a prime example of the SILVER-FORK NOVEL of high society, it was enormously popular in its day and remains one of his most enjoyable productions.

Pendennis, The History of A novel by W. M. THACKERAY, with illustrations by him, published in monthly parts from November 1848 to December 1850.

Arthur Pendennis's father, a medical man turned country squire, dies while his son is at school, and he is brought up by his unworldly widowed mother, who lives at Fairoaks with her adopted daughter Laura Bell. The young Pen falls in love with a travelling actress, Miss Fotheringay, but is saved from an imprudent marriage by his worldly uncle, Major Pendennis, who persuades the girl and her father, the tipsy Captain Costigan, to break off the engagement. Pen then goes to Oxbridge, where he becomes idle and extravagant, fails his exams and gets into debt; his mother and Laura pay his debts and he takes his degree. Back at Fairoaks he flirts with Blanche Amory, the shallow and coquettish daughter of the second wife of Sir Francis Clavering, the local baronet, and dutifully proposes to Laura, who rejects him. Pen goes to London to study law, but through his friendship with George Warrington, whose chambers he shares, he starts to write for the *Pall Mall Gazette* and publishes a successful fashionable novel, *Walter Lorraine*.

Introduced to London society by his uncle, Pen meets Blanche again, and in turn introduces her to his friend Harry Foker, who falls in love with her. Pen becomes attracted to a porter's daughter, Fanny Bolton, but resolves not to seduce her. He falls ill and is nursed by Fanny, but unknown to him she is dismissed by his mother, who wrongly suspects her of being his mistress. When he subsequently challenges Mrs Pendennis with suppressing Fanny's letters, his own innocence becomes apparent, and mother and son are reconciled before her sudden death. Major Pendennis tries to arrange a worldly marriage between Pen and Blanche, using his knowledge of scandal in the Clavering family to persuade Sir Francis to give up his seat in Parliament to Pen, and they become engaged. When Pen discovers the scandal, that Blanche's father is alive and a criminal, he repudiates the arrangement but decides to honour his engagement. Blanche, however, has transferred her affections to Foker, now the wealthy inheritor of the family fortune. Pen is now free to propose to Laura, whom he has come to love, and she accepts him.

This leisurely *BILDUNGSROMAN*, often compared to DICKENS's contemporaneous *DAVID COPPERFIELD*, was Thackeray's attempt to portray a representative gentleman of the age, 'no better nor worse than most educated men' (Preface). It has autobiographical elements, especially in the portrayal of London literary life and the fashionable novel industry.

Penguin New Writing See LEHMANN, JOHN.

Penn, William 1644–1718 Quaker and founder of Pennsylvania. The son of Admiral Sir William Penn, who captured Jamaica from the Dutch, he was born in London, and was sent down from Christ Church, Oxford, in 1661 for refusing to conform to the rules of the restored Anglican Church. He entered Lincoln's Inn (1665), but was soon a convinced Quaker and published a defence of his new faith in *The Sandy Foundation Shaken* (1668). This attacked both orthodox and Calvinistic doctrines and resulted in his imprisonment in the Tower, where he wrote *No Cross, No Crown* (1669), now a recognized classic of Quaker literature. He had meanwhile become interested in the foundation of a colony in America. The death of his father left him financially secure, and a debt to his father by the Crown was settled by a grant of land in the New World. Penn named it Pennsylvania and hoped to establish liberty of conscience for all settlers, whether Quakers or not. After establishing the colony, Penn returned to England in 1684, and wrote a loyal address to James II and a pamphlet (1687) expressing gratitude for the Declaration of Indulgence.

When James II lost his throne Penn continued their lifelong friendship; he was accused of treason and deprived of the governorship of Pennsylvania. He wrote *Some Fruits of Solitude* (1692), a collection of aphorisms of some literary interest. Pennsylvania was annexed to New York until 1694, and Penn spent his remaining years in England preaching and writing, except for his spell of retirement to the Colonies in 1699–1701. His last years were troubled: Penn was imprisoned for debt (1707–8) after his steward had successfully swindled him, and he became alienated from his eldest son. He suffered a stroke in 1712 and took no further part in public life.

Penn wrote a great deal, being a man of tireless energy. An advocate of tolerance, a courageous and stubborn upholder of human rights, he was noted for his gentleness and was a worthy representative of the movement he espoused.

Pennant, Thomas 1726–98 Naturalist, antiquary and travel-writer. Born near Holywell and educated at Wrexham, he was an undergraduate at The Queen's College, Oxford, but left without taking a degree. He was elected a Fellow of the Society of Antiquaries in 1754 and of the Royal Society in 1767. His most important works of natural history were *The British Zoology* (1766; revised 1768–70) and a *Synopsis of Quadrupeds* (1771), expanded as the *History of*

Quadrupeds (1781). Pennant was in touch with Linnaeus, Sir Joseph Banks, Buffon (whom he visited in Burgundy) and GILBERT WHITE, who addressed some of the letters which make up *The Natural History of Selborne* to him. The most influential of his many learned and detailed travel books were *A Tour in Scotland* (1771), revised in 1772 and again as *A Tour in Scotland and Voyage to the Hebrides* (1774–6), and *A Tour in Wales* (1778–81). SAMUEL JOHNSON defended Pennant's account of Scotland against THOMAS PERCY's criticisms: 'He's a Whig, sir; a sad dog. But he's the best traveller I ever read; he observes more things than any one else does.'

pentameter See METRE.

Pepys, Samuel 1633–1703 Diarist and naval reformer. The son of a London tailor, John Pepys, he was educated at St Paul's School and Magdalene College, Cambridge, graduating in 1654. He entered the employ of a relation, Sir Edward Montagu (later the 1st Earl of Sandwich), as secretary in his household, and in 1655 married Elizabeth St Michel, the teenage daughter of a Huguenot family. Pepys was from the start fortunate in his connections. Montagu's patronage coincided with the great Royalist opportunity of the Restoration, and he was commander of the fleet that escorted the monarch back to England – a voyage at which the young Pepys assisted, recording a vivid account of Charles II's fortunes after the battle of Worcester.

On 1 January 1660 (the year of the Restoration) Pepys began his now famous *Diary*, when he was living in Axe Yard, Westminster, in conditions of hardship. Enterprising and fastidious, he managed to secure preferment within the Navy Office, becoming Clerk of the King's Ships, Clerk of the Privy Seal, Surveyor-General of the Victualling Service (1665) and finally Secretary to the Admiralty (1672). In an age when the efficient official was still a rarity, Pepys (though initially preferred through nepotism) became a first-rate civil servant and bureaucrat to whose reforms in supply and administration the Navy was subsequently indebted. He was also a JP, an MP, and a Fellow of the Royal Society, as well as being a man about town and a figure in court circles. His sybaritic personality attracted the attention of both the monarch and the Duke of York, his brother (later James II).

In 1679 Pepys was imprisoned in the Tower of London on the charge of involvement in the 'Popish Plot' and deprived of office. In 1683 he went to Tangier with Lord Dartmouth, and made a record of his experiences there in a journal. He was reinstated as Secretary to the Admiralty in 1684, but had to resign in 1688 with the ousting of James II. He was imprisoned by the new government but released, and in 1700 retired to his house in Clapham, which he shared with his faithful confidant and factotum, William Hewer (who features strongly in the *Diary*).

Pepys was a personal friend of JOHN EVELYN, like him an early fellow of the newly established Royal Society, and a man of lively and enquiring intelligence; it was the publication in the 19th century of Evelyn's *Memoirs* (1818) which led to the rediscovery of the manuscript version of the work for which Pepys is now known across the English-speaking world. Along with a sizeable bequest of contemporary pamphlets, broadsides, ballads and manuscripts, Pepys left to the library at Magdalene six volumes of encoded diaries which were approximately deciphered by a Cambridge undergraduate, John Smith, and shortly thereafter published under the auspices of Lord Braybrooke in 1815. The *Diary* covered the period of Pepys's life from the beginning of 1660 until 31 May 1669, when he was compelled to abandon his minute record, due to the apparent onset of blindness. (John Smith, his earliest transcriber, suffered the same consequence.) The text appeared in varying stages of completeness (both the obscurity of the cipher and the explicit nature of the revelations contributing to a certain caution on the part of publishers) until finally reaching the reading public in the full annotated edition by R. Latham and W. Matthews (Bell and Hyman, 11 volumes) completed in 1983, a masterpiece of lively scholarship.

The *Diary* was never designed for publication during the author's lifetime and, despite its length, it covers a short period of his extraordinarily eventful public and private life. It is a phenomenon of literature, practically a household name. As the private, first-hand record of a historical personality it can

Samuel Pepys

scarcely be rivalled, and the decade which is so evocatively chronicled could hardly have been a more colourful one into which an ambitious, self-interested, and passionately enthusiastic young man could have launched himself. More neatly perhaps than any other individual contemporary (bar the monarch himself) Pepys seems to embody the more youthful attributes of the Restoration era – indeed, much of the colourful detail which has reached us has filtered through the very medium of his clandestine document. Pepys's record catches exactly that balance of civility and coarseness, *laissez-faire* and rationalism which typified his age.

Apart from its historical interest, which is unequalled, the *Diary* is a fine, quirky achievement of literature – the literature of privacy, self-conscious, voyeuristic, intimate and unique. There is the perceptive analysis of the professional, and the biased aside of the rival. In everything, Pepys is outspoken: the Duchess of Albemarle is 'a damned ill-looking woman', and a production of SHAKESPEARE's *A MIDSUMMER NIGHT'S DREAM* is said to be 'the most insipid ridiculous play that ever I saw in my life'. The whole document is wonderfully enlivened by the comedy of the diarist's own frank descriptions of himself (set upon by a dog, spotted with a mistress, terrified by a pillow) and his constantly shifting attention, a mind which was 'with child to see any strange thing'.

Percy, Thomas 1729–1811 Antiquarian. The son of a Shropshire grocer, he was educated at Bridgnorth grammar school and Christ Church, Oxford. He became vicar of Easton Maudit in Northamptonshire, then chaplain to the king and the Duke of Northumberland, and later Dean of Carlisle (1778) and Bishop of Dromore in Ireland (1782). His enquiring mind pleased SAMUEL JOHNSON, who declared that Percy was a man 'out of whose company I never go without having learnt something'.

His interest in ancient and foreign poetry was first expressed in works from the Chinese, which he found in European translations: *Hau Kiou Choaan, or The Pleasing History* (1761) was the first English version of a Chinese novel. The great success of MACPHERSON's Ossianic poetry stimulated him to publish *Five Pieces of Runic Poetry Translated from the Islandic Language* (1763) and to begin his collection of early and traditional poetry. His most important acquisition was the Percy Folio (as it became known), a 17th-century manuscript of BALLADS and other material, including a 14th-century allegorical poem, 'Death and Life'. The Folio was the main source for the ballads in his *Reliques of Ancient English Poetry* (1765; expanded in 1767, 1775 and 1794). Though Percy followed the custom of his age in adapting the original texts freely, *The Reliques* was an important step in reviving the ballad tradition and an acknowledged in-

fluence on the Romantic poets. The Percy Folio, now in the British Library, was edited for publication by F. J. FURNIVALL and J. W. Hales (1867–8).

Percy, Walker 1916–90 American novelist. Born in Alabama, he attended the University of North Carolina and received an MD from Columbia. Most of his novels are about Southerners, usually alienated individuals in search of fulfilment. His first book, *The Moviegoer* (1961), portrays a New Orleans stockbroker who insulates himself from the real world by going to movies until eventually, during Mardi Gras, a complicated involvement with his neurotic cousin Kate restores him to real life. *The Last Gentleman* (1966) is about a transplanted Southerner who returns home for a visit; in the sequel, *Second Coming* (1980), the same character seeks to affirm the value of his own life in a world which he sees as disintegrating. Percy's novels are often comic, even as they deal with fundamental problems of human experience. *Love in the Ruins* (1971) is a satire about a scientist who seeks to redeem America's mechanistic culture. *Lancelot* (1977) is a darker work, about a man whose quest for self-fulfilment leads him to a murderous arson. *The Thanatos Syndrome* appeared in 1987. Percy's essays on language were collected in *The Message in the Bottle* (1975).

Percy Folio, The See PERCY, THOMAS.

Peregrine Pickle, The Adventures of The second novel by TOBIAS SMOLLETT, published in 1751. The story is farcical and violent, and it pilloried well-known people. Its reception was mixed and in 1758 Smollett published an expurgated version, softening some of the attacks and removing some of the 'low' passages.

Peregrine is a PICARESQUE hero, an ungovernable youth who goes from bad to worse before being tamed by disillusion and imprisonment. He is released by the good offices of those to whom he has formerly been generous and is rewarded by the hand of Emilia, whom he has treated badly, despite their mutual love. The story was considered on the whole improving, but not to be put into the hands of young persons. It has two unusual features: one is the interpolated story of the widowed Lady Vane's remarriage and subsequent adulteries, which she is believed to have paid Smollett to publish; the other is chapter 95, which deals with Peregrine's purchase of a beggar girl. He proceeds to turn her into a fine lady, by means of lessons in dancing and French and a smattering of polite literature. The only difficulty is her inveterate habit of swearing, but she learns to be on her guard. Her social success is considerable, until in a quarrel at cards, she opens 'the floodgates of her own natural repartee'. She elopes with Peregrine's valet and Peregrine gives them a wedding present of £500. The parallels with

SHAW's *PYGMALION* have been noted. DICKENS preferred *Peregrine Pickle* to FIELDING's *TOM JONES*.

Perelman, S(idney) J(oseph) 1904–79 American humorist, born in Brooklyn, and educated at Brown University. In 1931 he published the first of hundreds of articles for *THE NEW YORKER*. The success of his first book, *Dawn Ginsbergh's Revenge* (1929), a collection of prose and cartoons, introduced him to Hollywood, where he wrote scripts for the Marx brothers and the screenplays *Ambush* (1939) and *The Golden Fleecing* (1940), both with his wife Laura Weinstein, the sister of his friend NATHANAEL WEST. A sharp and humorous observer and critic of contemporary American society, Perelman published some 20 books, mostly collections of his journalistic pieces. He also wrote travel books, including *Westward Ha! or Around the World in Eighty Clichés* (1948) and *Eastward Ha!* (1977).

Pericles, Prince of Tyre A play of which WILLIAM SHAKESPEARE wrote a substantial part; the first two acts have been often ascribed to George Wilkins. It was first performed *c.* 1608, published in Quarto (Q1) in 1609 but not included in the First Folio of 1623. It is based on a story in GOWER's *CONFESSIO AMANTIS* and Gower himself appears as Chorus.

While in Antioch, Pericles guesses that King Antiochus has an incestuous love for his daughter, for whose hand Pericles is a suitor. Afraid of Antiochus, Pericles leaves Tyre and is shipwrecked in Pentapolis. There he wins the hand of the king's daughter, Thaisa, in a tournament. They are married and set sail for Tyre, where the king and his daughter have died, leaving Pericles as rightful heir to the throne. But the sea intervenes again. Thaisa gives birth to a daughter, is herself believed dead and her body placed in a chest and put to sea. Pericles entrusts his aptly named infant daughter Marina to the care of Cleon, governor of Tarsus, and returns to Tyre.

The Chorus now explains how 16 years have passed, with Pericles in Tyre and Marina in Tarsus, where her grace and beauty arouse the jealousy of Cleon's wife Dionyza. A plan to kill Marina is foiled when she is kidnapped by pirates and sold to a brothel in Mytilene. Cleon and Dionyza publish it abroad that Marina is dead. Protected from contamination by her purity, Marina attracts the love of Lysimachus, governor of Mytilene. When the despairing Pericles arrives there, it is Lysimachus who accidentally brings about the reunion of father and daughter. Impelled by a dream, Pericles sets sail for Ephesus and is there united with his long-lost wife, who has become a priestess of Diana. Pericles decides that Lysimachus and Marina shall rule in Tyre and he and Thaisa in Pentapolis.

Pericles followed the contemporary fashion for extravagant adventure and pictorial staging, but the untidy plotting that accompanies these effects has been a leading cause of its comparative unpopularity.

It has often been grouped with *CYMBELINE*, *THE WINTER'S TALE* and *THE TEMPEST* and, whatever its defects, its mixture of romance, tragedy and comedy has much in common with these remarkably experimental late plays.

Perkin Warbeck A tragedy by JOHN FORD. It was published in 1634 but there is no record of its first production.

It closely follows the historical facts about Warbeck (de Werbecque), the son of a burgess of Tournai, who briefly succeeded in gaining support for his claim to be Richard, Duke of York, younger son of Edward IV and hence true heir to the throne occupied by Henry VII. The play deals with Warbeck's arrival at the court of James IV of Scotland, his marriage to Lady Katherine Gordon, and the events surrounding the treason and execution of the disaffected Sir William Stanley in London. James IV leads an expedition to England in support of Warbeck, but deserts him when the Tudor king offers forceful resistance. Warbeck makes a last attempt by landing in Cornwall but the support he had hoped for is not forthcoming. He is captured and executed, maintaining his royal origins to the end. The love and loyalty of Lady Katherine are movingly portrayed.

Persuasion JANE AUSTEN's last completed novel, published in 1818. Though written when her health was rapidly failing, it shows no loss of power: the social comedy is deftly handled and the overriding tone is one of serious and profound reflection.

Sir Walter Elliot of Kellynch Hall – whose favourite reading is his own entry in *The Baronetage* – has three daughters: Elizabeth, who shares his haughty vanity and, at 28, has found no one quite good enough to marry; Mary, who has, with some condescension, married Charles Musgrove, the son of the local squire; and the admirable but neglected Anne. Unable to keep up a style of living appropriate to his status, Sir Walter is forced to let Kellynch to Admiral and Mrs Croft. Anne re-encounters Captain Frederick Wentworth, a brother of Mrs Croft's, whom she had known, loved – and refused – eight years previously when she had yielded to the persuasion of her godmother and friend, the excellent but cautious Lady Russell. Anne, who still loves Wentworth, is at once disappointed and relieved when he appears to care for her no longer. Wentworth becomes a favourite with the Musgrove family, particularly Charles's two high-spirited sisters, Louisa and Henrietta, and Anne suspects that he is attracted to Louisa. A cheerful jaunt to Lyme Regis is cut disastrously short when Louisa falls on the steps of the Cobb and suffers a severe head injury. Wentworth's concern seems to confirm Anne's suspicions.

On arriving in Bath, where her father and sister have settled, Anne meets William Elliot, her cousin and father's heir. Elliot pays her marked attention, but Anne, who has renewed an old acquaintance with Mrs Smith, a school-friend, now a widow and an invalid, learns from her of Elliot's past misdeeds and his present schemes. Unexpected news arrives of Louisa Musgrove's engagement to Captain Benwick, and soon afterward Wentworth appears in Bath, by now anxious to renew his addresses to Anne but uncertain of his reception. Hearing Anne, in a conversation on the quality of love, declare that woman's love is more enduring than man's, especially where the object seems lost for ever, Wentworth understands her remark to refer to her own experience. Leaving Anne an ardent declaration, hastily scribbled, he later overtakes her in the town, and all is at last settled between them before they reach the top of Milsom Street.

Peter Grimes See BOROUGH, THE.

Peter Pan: *or, The Boy Who Would Not Grow Up* A play by J. M. BARRIE, first performed at the Duke of York's Theatre, London, in 1904 and now established as an annual Christmas favourite, with a long succession of well-known actresses in the title role. *Peter Pan* occupies blurred ground between drama and PANTOMIME, though it began its life quite simply as a play for children, and its subsequent history owes more to its theatrical than its literary qualities.

The play begins in the Bloomsbury flat of the Darlings, which is visited by Peter Pan, a boy who ran away on the day he was born when he heard his parents talking about what might happen to him when he grew up. The Darlings' dog frightened Peter, and he flew away, leaving his shadow behind him. Unreasonably jealous of the dog's hold on his children, Mr Darling chains her in the yard before taking his wife out to dinner, with the result that Peter can return to find his shadow without intervention. After Wendy Darling has sewn his shadow back on, he teaches the three Darling children to fly. They accompany him to the Never Land, where he lives with all the lost boys, protected by a tribe of Red Indians. A pirate gang led by Captain Hook overcomes the Red Indians while Peter is away, and Wendy, who has become mother to the lost boys, is captured along with all her 'family'. Peter arrives just in time to prevent Captain Hook from making them walk the plank, defeats the villainous pirate in a duel and sees him eaten by the crocodile that has stalked him for years. He then takes Wendy and her brothers back home, declines Mrs Darling's offer to adopt him and is partly compensated for the loss of his beloved Wendy when Mrs Darling promises to let her return to the Never Land each year to do the spring cleaning.

Peters, Lenrie 1932– Gambian poet and novelist. Born in Bathurst (now Banjul), The Gambia, he received his secondary education at Prince of Wales School in Freetown, Sierra Leone. He qualified as a doctor in Cambridge and for a time was a surgeon at a hospital in Northampton, England. Returning to The Gambia, he has for many years practised privately as a doctor. His collections of poetry include *Poems* (1964), *Satellites* (1967), *Katchikali* (1971) and *Selected Poetry* (1981). His poems are easily accessible to people brought up in the English literary tradition, seldom calling upon the traditional oral techniques of African poetry. The need to be pan-African in outlook is a central interest of all Peters's writings and, with an unfashionable lack of doctrine, he expresses great fear for the future of his continent: 'madness and infirmity/ threaten all who hope for better things'. His novel, *The Second Round* (1965), portrays a young doctor returning to Sierra Leone to be faced with the difficulty of fulfilling people's expectations of him. Peters is the most prominent Gambian writer and one of the calmest voices in contemporary African literature.

Petrarchan After Petrarch, the anglicization of the surname of Francesco Petrarca (1304–74), a major humanist scholar and poet of the Italian Renaissance chiefly remembered for his collection of lyric poems and sonnets, *Rime sparse* (or *Canzoniere*). The term is sometimes used for the style of his poetry, particularly its use of antithesis, paradox, OXYMORON and the CONCEIT. More usually it distinguishes what might be regarded as the standard form of the SONNET from the Shakespearean sonnet.

Petrie, George 1790–1866 Irish antiquarian, musicologist and scholar. Born in Dublin and educated at Trinity College, Petrie edited the short-lived but important *Irish Penny Journal* (1840–1) and was a central figure in the Ordnance Survey Office, where EUGENE O'CURRY and JOHN O'DONOVAN were his assistants. Like them he made a pioneering contribution to the scholarly aspect of the CELTIC REVIVAL. His studies of the Round Towers of Ireland and of the Hill of Tara led to his archaeological work, *The Ecclesiastical Architecture of Ireland* (1845). He is best remembered for his continuation of EDWARD BUNTING's work in preserving traditional music in *The Petrie Collection of the Ancient Music of Ireland* (2 vols., 1855–82).

Pettie, George 1548–89 Very little is known of his life, except that he graduated from Christ Church, Oxford, and subsequently travelled abroad. Influenced by both the popularity and the name of WILLIAM PAINTER's collection of stories, *The Palace of Pleasure* (1566), he issued *A Petite Palace of Pettie His Pleasure*, licensed in 1576 and published soon after, although the first edition is not dated. It consists of 12 stories, which the preface says are intended for gentlewomen, including those of Alcestis, Tereus and Pygmalion. Pettie also translated Guazzo from a

French version as *Civil Conversation* (1581). His prose style anticipates EUPHUISM.

Peveril of the Peak A novel by Sir WALTER SCOTT, first published in 1823.

The novel concerns religious strife in the reign of Charles II. Two neighbouring Derbyshire gentlemen, the Royalist Sir Geoffrey Peveril and the Puritan Major Bridgenorth, quarrel after having managed to live through the Civil War as friends. Julian Peveril, son of Sir Geoffrey and a trusted member of the Catholic Countess of Derby's household on the Isle of Man, falls in love with Bridgenorth's daughter Alice. The machinations of Bridgenorth, his brother-in-law Edward Christian and the licentious Duke of Buckingham threaten the lovers. Julian and his father are arrested for complicity in the Popish plot, but are acquitted thanks to the intervention of Charles II.

Peyton [*née* Herald], **K. M.** [Kathleen Wendy] 1929– Writer of CHILDREN'S LITERATURE. Born in Birmingham and brought up in Surbiton, she went to Wimbledon High School and later to Art College. Already writing children's stories while at school, she published her first book, *Sabre, the Horse from the Sea* (1948), when she was still 19. Several subsequent pony or adventure books were followed by *Windfall* (1963), a more original tale of danger at sea written with meticulous accuracy reminiscent of ARTHUR RANSOME at his best. Other successes culminated in *Flambards*(1967), the first of a trilogy about a decayed Edwardian landed family and its various intrigues for restoring its fortunes. High drama is much in evidence throughout, together with a strong feeling for history, particularly in regard to changing ideas about social class. Since then she has written another trilogy about a brilliant but disturbed schoolboy musician first encountered in *Pennington's Seventeenth Summer*(1970), and has also produced a ghost story, *A Pattern of Roses* (1973). Stories about humanized animals include *Plain Jack* (1988).

Phalaris controversy See TEMPLE, SIR WILLIAM.

Philaster: or, Love Lies A-Bleeding A tragicomedy by BEAUMONT and FLETCHER, first performed *c*.1609, probably at the BLACKFRIARS, and published in 1620. It was a popular success. Philaster has often been compared with SHAKESPEARE'S *CYMBELINE*, written at much the same time and for the same company of actors.

Philaster is the rightful heir to the throne of Sicily but the kingdom has been taken by the King of Calabria. He is obliged to live in the usurper's court. He and Arethusa, the usurper's daughter, are in love and Philaster places his page, Bellario, in Arethusa's service as his go-between. A marriage is arranged between Arethusa and the Spanish prince, Pharamond;

but Arethusa is able to reveal that Pharamond has been amusing himself with Megra, a lady of the court, and the marriage is called off. Pharamond gets his revenge with the accusation that Arethusa has been conducting an affair with Bellario. Philaster believes the story and, distracted, alters his intention to kill himself to an intention to kill the 'guilty' pair. He is arrested and entrusted to the custody of Arethusa, who promptly marries him, thereby saving his life. Her honour is shown to be intact when it is revealed that Bellario is a girl, daughter of a Sicilian nobleman who, infatuated with Philaster, had disguised herself as a boy to be his page. The usurper is overthrown and Philaster is restored to his inheritance.

Philip, The Adventures of A novel by W. M. THACKERAY, with illustrations by him and Frederick Walker, serialized in *THE CORNHILL MAGAZINE* from January 1861 to August 1862, and published in three volumes in 1862. Narrated by Arthur Pendennis, it completes the trio of interconnected and semi-autobiographical novels begun in *THE HISTORY OF PENDENNIS* and *THE NEWCOMES*.

Philip Firmin is the son of Dr Brand Firmin, the 'Brandon' of *A SHABBY GENTEEL STORY*, who has since made a runaway match with a wealthy woman, Lord Ringwood's niece, and become a fashionable London physician. Philip's mother, now dead, has left him a fortune, and his independent spirit wins him the approval of Lord Ringwood, to the chagrin of his aunt's family, the toadying Twysdens. He suspects his father's shady past, and discovers that he is being blackmailed by Tufton Hunt, the dissolute clergyman who had performed the sham marriage ceremony between Brandon and Caroline Gann in the earlier story. Hunt tries to persuade Caroline, now a nurse, to claim her legal rights, but she refuses to disinherit Philip, to whom she has become devoted after nursing him through a childhood illness.

Meanwhile Dr Firmin has speculated with Philip's fortune and lost it, fleeing to America; and the now penniless Philip is rejected by his cousin Agnes Twysden for a wealthy suitor. The rest of the novel deals with Philip's struggles against his misfortunes, his engagement to Charlotte Baynes, whom he marries despite her mother's opposition, and his early career as a journalist. His father's debts continue to plague him, and his hot temper gets him into trouble, but through the kindness of Arthur and Laura Pendennis, and the unselfish devotion of Caroline Brandon, he and his family survive until the discovery of a lost will of Lord Ringwood's restores him to prosperity.

Philips, Ambrose *c*. 1675–1749 Poet and the original 'Namby-Pamby'. Educated at Shrewsbury School, Philips became a Fellow of St John's College, Cambridge, and a friend of ADDISON. He wrote a version of Racine's *Andromaque* under the somewhat understated title of *The Distrest Mother*, published in 1712, and *A Collection of Old Ballads* (1723). But his chief claim to fame is the degree of contempt he earned from distinguished contemporaries after his *Pastorals* appeared in JACOB TONSON's *Miscellany* of 1709 beside the undoubtedly superior examples by POPE (written, he claimed, when he was only 16). Pope elegantly demolished Philips's poetic reputation in *THE GUARDIAN* and a 'pastoral war' in print ensued, with JOHN GAY parodying Philips in his sequence *THE SHEPHERD'S WEEK*. Philips's verses for children were praised by SAMUEL JOHNSON but earned him the nickname 'Namby-Pamby' from HENRY CAREY.

Philips, John 1676–1709 Poet. Educated at Winchester and Christ Church, Oxford, Philips is remembered as a poet who wrote BLANK VERSE during a period when the couplet was the fashionable form. *The Splendid Shilling* (1701) is in BURLESQUE Miltonic verse and contrasts the well-being of the man who possesses a shilling with the privation of being a poet. A Tory, Philips was persuaded by ROBERT HARLEY, EARL OF OXFORD and HENRY ST JOHN, VISCOUNT BOLINGBROKE to write a blank-verse poem, *Blenheim* (1705), as a counter to ADDISON's *The Campaign* (1704) on the same subject. The piece was not a success but *Cider: A Poem in Two Books* (1708) is a notable performance in blank verse in the manner of Virgil's *Georgics*.

Philips, Katherine See FOWLER, KATHERINE.

Phillips, Caryl 1958– Caribbean/British novelist and playwright. Born in St Kitts, he was brought to Britain when he was a year old and lived in Leeds until he went to Oxford, where he read English and was active in student theatre. His plays include *Strange Fruit* (1980), a powerful naturalistic drama about generational conflicts in a family, and *Where There is Darkness* (1982). Since the mid-1980s he has mainly written fiction: *The Final Passage* (1985), about a small islander who migrates to Britain and increasingly becomes a victim of her sense of alienation; *A State of Independence* (1986), about a West Indian's return home at the time of his country's independence; *Higher Ground* (1989), a panoramic account of the black diaspora which spans two hundred years and moves between Africa, the USA and Britain; and *Cambridge* (1991), about Caribbean plantation society in the last years of the slave era. He has also published a work of non-fiction, *The European Tribe* (1987), and *Playing Away* (1987), one of several screenplays.

Phillips, John 1631–1706 Poet, journalist and translator. Although educated by his uncle, JOHN MILTON, he wrote one of the most extreme anti-

Puritan poems of any literary quality, *The Satire against Hypocrites*, in 1655. Characteristic of a certain breed of professional writer surviving on his wits and a shoestring, he was also the translator of *Pharamond* (by La Calprenède) and *Almahide* (by Madeleine de Scudéry). As well as writing a number of burlesques, he was responsible for editing the periodical *The Present State of Europe* from 1690 until his death.

Phillips, Stephen 1864–1915 Playwright and poet. Born near Oxford, Phillips was an actor in his cousin F. R. Benson's company in 1885–92, but was working as a schoolteacher when his *Poems* (1898) earned him the prestige of a literary award. There followed a short-lived vogue for his sonorous poetic dramas, of which Herbert Beerbohm Tree produced four, *Herod* (1900), *Ulysses* (1902), *Nero* (1906) and *Faust* (1908), and George Alexander staged the best, *Paolo and Francesca* (1902). Success and self-doubt affected Phillips's stability. Unprotected by the theatrical flair of Tree and Alexander, *Iole* (1913) and *The Sin of David* (1914) failed, and the man who had been so recently celebrated as the great reviver of poetic drama died destitute.

Phillpotts, Eden 1862–1960 Novelist and playwright. Born in India, he was educated in Devon and remained associated with the county for most of his long, secluded life. He was the author of well over 200 books, the best of them being novels about Dartmoor, like *Children in the Mist* (1898), *The Secret Woman* (1905), *The Thief of Virtue* (1910) and *Widecombe Fair* (1913). He collaborated with his daughter Adelaide on two successful comedies, *The Farmer's Wife* (1924), which was a revision of his own earlier version, and *Yellow Sands* (1926), as well as on several shorter pieces.

Philotus A play of unknown authorship probably written about 1600. The earliest known text was printed by Robert Charteris (Edinburgh, 1603), and it represents the only complete survival of Scottish drama apart from the *SATIRE OF THE THREE ESTATES* by SIR DAVID LYNDSAY. The theme is the attempt of two old men, Philotus and Alberto, to marry young and pretty girls, and how their plans are frustrated by the girls, Emilie and Brisilla, with the aid of their lovers.

Phineas Finn: The Irish Member A novel by ANTHONY TROLLOPE, serialized in *St Paul's Magazine* from October 1867 to May 1869, and published in two volumes in 1869. The second of his PALLISER NOVELS, it is the first in the series to deal with the workings of Parliament itself.

Phineas Finn, a young Irish barrister, is elected to Parliament for his local borough of Loughshane. In London his charm and good looks win him the love of Lady Laura Standish, a politically astute and ambitious woman whom he pursues despite his commitment to an Irish sweetheart, Mary Jones. Forced by family debt to make a wealthy match with the gloomy Scots laird Robert Kennedy, she continues to use her influence to help Phineas to the family pocket-borough, after he rescues Kennedy from a street assault. Phineas turns his attention to another eligible girl, Violet Effingham, and clashes with her fiery suitor Lord Chiltern. The two men fight a duel abroad, which leads to their reconciliation, and Violet marries Lord Chiltern. The background to these amorous intrigues is the new reform bill which Phineas's party, the Liberals, are trying to steer through Parliament. Phineas becomes a junior minister but is forced to resign his post when he votes in support of Irish tenant rights. He attracts the attention of Madame Max Goesler, a wealthy widow and companion of the elderly Duke of Omnium, who offers him her hand and fortune to pursue his political career. But the now discouraged Phineas refuses and returns to Ireland, where he marries Mary Jones and becomes Inspector of the Cork Poor Houses.

Written at the time of the Second Reform Bill debates, the novel is thought to portray aspects of DISRAELI in Mr Daubeny and of Gladstone in Mr Gresham.

Phineas Redux A novel by ANTHONY TROLLOPE, the fourth of his PALLISER NOVELS, serialized in *The Graphic* from July 1873 to January 1874, and published in two volumes in 1873.

Now a widower, Phineas Finn returns to England and contests the borough of Tankerville, successfully. Lady Laura Kennedy, living apart from her increasingly insane husband, still loves Phineas, but his efforts to mediate between husband and wife only inflame Mr Kennedy's jealousy, who attempts to shoot Phineas but misses. The incident is publicized in its worst light by his old enemy Quintus Slide, a radical journalist, and more scandal ensues when Phineas quarrels publicly with a cabinet minister, Mr Bonteen, who is afterwards found murdered. Phineas is arrested and brought to trial, but the skill of the lawyer Chaffanbrass, and the perseverance of Madame Max Goesler in unearthing new evidence, results in his acquittal. Suspicion falls on Mr Emilius, the estranged husband of Lady Eustace, who escapes prosecution through lack of sufficient evidence. Phineas is re-elected for Tankerville and offered a post in the government, but his sufferings have disillusioned him with public life, and he refuses the post. Meanwhile the old Duke of Omnium has died, attended to the end by Madame Max, who shows her disinterestedness by refusing a legacy left her by the duke. This comes to Plantagenet Palliser's cousin Adelaide, enabling her to marry her penniless suitor Gerard Maule. The novel ends with the marriage of Phineas and Madame Max.

The political pessimism of *Phineas Redux* reflects Trollope's disillusioning experience at the Beverley election of 1868, but is balanced in the novel by the rise of Plantagenet Palliser, the new Duke of Omnium, as his ideal statesman.

Phiz See BROWNE, HABLOT K.

Phoenix, The An Old English poem preserved in the EXETER BOOK. It tells the myth of the phoenix and develops it as a Christian symbol. The first part of the poem describes the Earthly Paradise, the phoenix, its flight to Syria and its death and rebirth. It is derived from the Latin poem *De ave phoenice* attributed to Lactantius, but adapts this source freely; the version of the myth used is that given in Pliny's *Natural History*. The second part of the poem introduces a Christian significance not found in *De ave phoenice* and makes the bird a symbol of Christ and the Christian life.

Phoenix and the Turtle, The This 67-line poem by SHAKESPEARE appeared, in the company of verse by BEN JONSON, GEORGE CHAPMAN and JOHN MARSTON, as an occasional poem appended to Robert Chester's *Love's Martyr* (1601). Chester's long, poor poem tells ramblingly of the love of the phoenix and the turtle (i.e. turtledove) and digresses on matters from King Arthur to beast lore and the properties of precious stones. Shakespeare's obscure and enigmatic poem is an ELEGY for the two birds, and ends with Reason's threnody celebrating their married chastity.

Phoenix Nest, The A poetic miscellany published in 1593. It was a gentlemanly enterprise, edited by one R. S. of the Inner Temple, and the contributors as well as the editor are usually identified by discreet initials; they include THOMAS LODGE, GEORGE PEELE, NICHOLAS BRETON, THOMAS WATSON and, perhaps, SIR WALTER RALEIGH. The phoenix of the title is clearly SIDNEY, whose death in 1586 is lamented in several poems.

Physician's Tale, The See CANTERBURY TALES, THE.

Piazza Tales, The A volume of six stories by HERMAN MELVILLE, published in 1856. Except for the title piece, they had all previously been published individually in *Putnam's Monthly* or in *HARPER'S NEW MONTHLY* in the early 1850s. The volume is introduced by 'The Piazza', Melville's descriptive recollection of his Massachusetts farmhouse, to the north side of which he added a piazza. 'The Bell Tower' is about an ambitious artist named Bannadonna, who attempts to rival God by creating a mechanical man, and is destroyed by his own creation. 'The Lightning-Rod Man' is the story of a man who refuses an insistent lightning-rod salesman because he believes that man should not fear the acts of God. 'The Encantadas: or, Enchanted Isles' contains 10 separate sketches, all concerning the Galapagos Islands.

'Benito Cereno' is set in 1799. The narrator, Amasa Delano, is a sea captain who puts in to an uninhabited island off the coast of Chile to take on water, and encounters a Spanish ship commanded by a seriously ill Benito Cereno. He listens to Cereno's story of the ship's recent misfortunes at Cape Horn, but suspects something amiss in the unruly and insubordinate behaviour of the crew, Cereno's strange relationship with his Senegalese valet Babo, and his ingratitude when Delano offers him aid. As Delano prepares to return to his ship, Cereno suddenly follows him. The crew attack them, but the two captains escape. Cereno then confesses that the apparent crew were in fact slaves, who, led by Babo, had mutinied and demanded that Cereno take them to Africa. When Cereno had succumbed to fever, the mutineers had planned to seize Delano's ship instead. Delano later succeeds in capturing the slave ship, and takes it to Lima, where Babo is executed. Cereno enters a monastery and dies soon after.

The last of the *Piazza Tales* is 'Bartleby the Scrivener'. A Wall Street lawyer hires Bartleby as a copyist. Bartleby is pale, quiet and strange, but extremely diligent in his single task of copying legal documents. To the lawyer's consternation, when Bartleby is asked to do anything other than copy, he replies only, 'I would prefer not to.' Soon, he would prefer not to leave, and begins to live in the office. Baffled, the lawyer moves his office to another building. The new tenant has Bartleby arrested as a vagrant. He dies in prison within days, resisting the attempts of his former employer to help him. The lawyer later hears that Bartleby had previously worked in the Dead Letter Office in Washington, and ponders on the relevance of this fact to his strange behaviour.

picaresque The Spanish *pícaro* was a character from low life, living on his wits and often a scoundrel, but the term came to be applied to anyone at odds with society. The *pícaro* first appeared in fiction in the anonymous *Lazarillo de Tormes* (1554). *Guzmán de Alfarache* (1559) by Mateo Alemán was widely read and translated – into English by JAMES MABBE – and the *pícaro* eventually appeared in the literature of all western Europe. The picaresque novel is the episodic narrative describing the progress of the *pícaro*, but the term is rather loosely used: *Don Quixote*, for example, is told in the picaresque form while being a satirical romance. Le Sage's *Gil Blas* (1715–35) and Hans Jacob Christoph von Grimmelshausen's *Der abentheurliche Simplicissimus Teutsch* (1669) are picaresque novels in a narrower sense. In English literature the tradition begins with THOMAS NASHE's *THE UNFORTUNATE TRAVELLER* (1594) and continues in the

work of DEFOE (*MOLL FLANDERS*), FIELDING, SMOLLETT and DICKENS. By the 19th century the English picaresque novel has on the whole forgotten its origin in the literature of roguery and is usually an episodic story involving a journey. In America, the picaresque novel has an obvious influence on TWAIN's *THE ADVENTURES OF HUCKLEBERRY FINN* and many later works chronicling the adventures of the open road.

Pickering, John See PUCKERING, SIR JOHN.

Pickwick Papers, The CHARLES DICKENS's first novel, published in monthly parts from April 1836 to November 1837 as *The Posthumous Papers of the Pickwick Club, Containing a Faithful Record of the Perambulations, Perils, Travels, Adventures and Sporting Transactions of the Corresponding Members*.

It takes its loose, easy structure from the travels to Ipswich, Rochester, Bath and elsewhere of Samuel Pickwick and his three fellow members of the Pickwick Club, Tracy Tupman, Augustus Snodgrass and Nathaniel Winkle. Mr Pickwick's innocent and trusting nature repeatedly makes him the butt of comic adventures: struggling with a recalcitrant horse on the way to Dingley Dell; over-imbibing in punch; tenuously disporting himself on the ice; making an untoward appearance in the wrong hotel bedroom; and, in the book's most prolonged episode, unintentionally making his landlady Mrs Bardell think he wishes to marry her, and so provoking her into suing him for breach of promise. Interspersed among these and many other similar adventures are moral and melodramatic stories – 'The Bagman's Story', 'The Convict's Return', 'The Stroller's Tale' and others – which counterbalance the prevailing comedy of the book.

The bustling scenes of *Pickwick Papers* introduce a wide variety of characters: Sam Weller, Pickwick's sharp-witted Cockney servant, and his coachman father Tony; the glib strolling player Alfred Jingle, who lives by his wits and his cool nerve, and his rascally servant Job Trotter; the medical student Bob Sawyer ('Nothing like dissecting, to give one an appetite'); the good-natured Wardles; the duel-hungry Dr Slammer of the 97th; the poetical Mrs Leo Hunter; and a host of watermen, lawyers, clerks, fashionable women, military men, footmen, and others. Most heighten the sheer humour of the book, but some strike a deeper note and hint at the force of Dickensian satire and anger against social injustice in later novels. The antics of the Parliamentary candidates Slumkey and Fizkin show Dickens's awareness of corrupt electioneering practices, just as the canting hypocrite Mr Stiggins shows his dislike of evangelical religion. Above all, the characters connected with the lawsuit of Bardell versus Pickwick – the rapacious Dodson and Fogg, the pompous Serjeant

Buzfuz – and Pickwick's own experiences in prison near the end of the novel hint at that darker vision which Dickens's later work would explore.

Picture of Dorian Gray, The A novel by OSCAR WILDE, serialized by *Lippincott's Magazine* in 1890 and expanded in book form the same year. Once regarded as daringly modern in its portrayal of *fin-de-siècle* decadence, it draws on traditional motifs to create a powerful GOTHIC NOVEL. In an updated version of the Faust story, Dorian sells his soul to keep his youth and beauty. The tempter is Lord Henry Wotton, who lives selfishly for amoral pleasure; Dorian's good angel or conscience is Basil Hallward, the portrait painter, whom Dorian murders. The book highlights the tension between the polished surface of high life and the life of secret vice. Although sin is punished in the end, the book has a strong flavour of the elegantly perverse. The preface asserts: 'There is no such thing as a moral or an immoral book. Books are well written or badly written. That is all.'

Pictures from Italy A travel book by CHARLES DICKENS, published in *THE DAILY NEWS* in 1845.

It is based on travels beginning in Paris in the summer of 1844 and lasting until the next year. Dickens entered Italy at Genoa, renting a house for some months in the nearby suburb of Albaro. The local fiestas, gambling, bowls, puppetry, shops, food and wine-drinking are described in compelling detail. Restless as ever, he visits Rome, Pisa, Ferrara, Parma, Florence, Bologna and Venice, which he sees as if in a dream, and goes as far south as Pompeii, Paestum and Naples. He vividly depicts a gory execution in Rome but, above all, he animates every person or scene his pen touches, giving individuality to the work of couriers, the life of inns, the stench of byways, the quarrying of marble, the economy of a palazzo and the ways of Neapolitans. Little is remarked about art or religion, although the activities of Holy Week are drily observed. His experience with AMERICAN NOTES may have taught Dickens to deal discreetly with national customs and habits, but *Pictures from Italy* also shows a genuine warmth and friendliness towards its subject markedly absent from the earlier travel book.

picturesque The term for an ideal of beauty which flourished, to the point of becoming a cult, during the 18th and early 19th centuries, principally in relation to landscape and gardens and the depiction of these scenes in painting and literature. It signified a departure from NEOCLASSICISM in its admiration for what was irregular, disordered or decayed, but stopped short of ROMANTICISM by admiring these effects in a spirit of judicious connoisseurship (or taste) rather than exalted feeling. The beginnings of the cult may be found as early as ADDISON's *Remarks on Several Parts of Italy* (1705) and Pope's *Eloisa to Abelard* (1717). It was developed, but never precisely or with complete agreement, by a later generation: WILLIAM MASON in his poem *The English Garden* (1771–81); THOMAS GRAY in his travel journal (published 1775); Richard Payne Knight (1750–1824) in *The Landscape: A Didactic Poem* (1794) and his *Analytical Enquiry into the Principles of Taste* (1805); Sir Uvedale Price (1747–1829) in his *Essay on the Picturesque* (1794); and the landscape gardener Humphry Repton (1752–1818) in various essays published between 1795 and 1816. Probably the most influential figure was WILLIAM GILPIN, in his *Three Essays: On Picturesque Beauty; on Picturesque Travel; on Sketching Landscape* (1792) and his various travel books.

The chief manifestations were a tradition of landscape gardening which stretched from William Kent (1685–1748) to Repton and beyond; an increased interest by travellers in the wilder scenery of Wales, the Wye Valley and the Lake District and in Gothic ruins; and the widespread popularity in England of paintings by Gaspard Poussin (1615–75), Claude (Claude Lorrain, 1600–82) and Salvator Rosa (1615–73). Literary references to the picturesque occur for the most part from the end of the 18th century onwards. ANN RADCLIFFE and SIR WALTER SCOTT described scenery in conventional picturesque terms in their novels. Writers such as JANE AUSTEN, in *NORTHANGER ABBEY* and *PRIDE AND PREJUDICE*, and THOMAS LOVE PEACOCK, in *HEADLONG HALL*, adopted a sceptical attitude, and the cult is satirized by WILLIAM COMBE in his very popular *TOUR OF DOCTOR SYNTAX IN SEARCH OF THE PICTURESQUE*.

Pied Piper of Hamelin, The A poem for children by ROBERT BROWNING, published in *Dramatic Lyrics* (1842). The story of the piper whose music lures away first the rats and then the children of Hamelin is based on what was apparently a common legend of the Middle Ages, though Browning encountered it in the prose compilation, *The Wonders of the Little World* (1678), by NATHANIEL WANLEY. It is now generally believed that the story is connected with the Children's Crusade, when 20,000 children left their homes to follow Nicholas of Cologne and, for the most part, perished without ever reaching the Holy Land.

Pierce Penniless His Supplication to the Devil A pamphlet by NASHE, printed in 1592. Prevented by society from using his talents, Pierce asks the Devil for a loan. The SATIRE attacks foreigners, Nashe's enemy Richard Harvey, and the Puritans for the MARPRELATE tracts and their criticism of the theatre. A grotesque characterization of the Seven Deadly Sins demonstrates Nashe's talent for fantasy: Greed has shoes made of 'crabshells... toothed at the toes with two sharp sixpenny nails'.

Pierce the Ploughman's Crede A Middle English poem in ALLITERATIVE VERSE, written in the South-west Midlands *c.* 1394. An early and competent imitation of *PIERS PLOWMAN*, it follows the same basic plan as the first part of LANGLAND's poem. The narrator, ignorant of his Creed, questions friars of various orders but hears only abuse of the others' orders and evidence of corruption. Eventually he meets the poor ploughman Pierce and his family; Pierce offers him comfort, exposes the sins of the friars and teaches him his Creed. The poem is remarkable for its detailed descriptions and accounts of contemporary life.

Piercy, Marge 1937– American novelist and poet. Born in Detroit, she has been active in the women's movement for many years. Most of her work deals with women's assigned place in a male-dominated society and the relationships which result. *Woman on the Edge of Time* (1976) is a dystopian feminist fantasy which inaugurated a fertile subversion of SCIENCE FICTION exploited by works like MARGARET ATWOOD's *The Handmaid's Tale*. Other novels include *Going Down Fast* (1969), *Dance the Eagle to Sleep* (1970), *Small Changes* (1973), *Vida* (1979), *Braided Lives* (1982) and *Fly Away Home* (1984). *Gone to Soldiers* (1987), about World War II, is a departure from her customary idiom, returned to in *Body of Glass* (1992). Among her volumes of poetry are *Breaking Camp* (1968), *Hard Loving* (1969), *4-Telling* (1971), *To be of Use* (1973), *Living in the Open* (1976), *The Twelve-Spoked Wheel Flashing* (1978), *The Moon is Always Female* (1980), *Circles on the Water: Selected Poems* (1982) and *Stone, Paper, Knife* (1983).

Pierre: or, The Ambiguities A novel by HERMAN MELVILLE, published in 1852.

Pierre Glendinning is the 19-year-old son of a wealthy widow in upstate New York. He is engaged to Lucy Tartan, a young woman from a prominent family, but he then meets Isabel, who claims to be his illegitimate half-sister. He knows that his mother will never accept a girl whose very existence exposes her husband's immoral behaviour. To give Isabel some measure of protection, he takes her to New York, allowing everyone to believe that he has married her. He confides in his cousin, Glen, who rejects his boyhood companion on hearing the truth. Impoverished, Pierre turns to writing to earn a living, but the novel which results from his exhaustive efforts is turned down for publication. Lucy, meanwhile, has followed Pierre to New York. Isabel shows jealousy at her appearance, and Pierre begins to realize his true feelings about his half-sister. During a confrontation with Glen and Lucy's brother, Pierre kills his cousin. He is arrested, and Lucy and his mother die of grief. Tormented by conflicting emotions about their forbidden love, Pierre and Isabel commit suicide in his prison cell.

Piers Plowman An allegorical poem in ALLITERATIVE VERSE by WILLIAM LANGLAND written in the West Midlands during the second half of the 14th century. It survives in three versions, known as the A-, B- and C-texts, representing different stages of revision almost certainly carried out by Langland himself. The A-text, 2500 lines long, dates from the 1360s and was probably complete by 1369–70. The B-text was written in the following decade and makes repeated reference to the events of 1376–9. It expands and develops the material of the A-text, trebling its length. The C-text was complete by 1387; THOMAS USK (d. 1388) borrowed from its unique sections in his *Testament of Love*. The same length as the B-text, it seems intended to elucidate the earlier version and to incorporate the significance of recent events; the result is not always superior. The B-text is the version most commonly read and discussed.

The poem is divided into passus of unequal length, 12 in the A-text, 20 in the B-text and 23 in the C-text. It falls into two parts, known as the *Visio* and the *Vita* after the Latin rubric dividing the B- and C-texts into the *Visio Willilmi de Petrus Plowman* and the *Vita de Dowel, Dobet et Dobest*. The basic format of the poem is a DREAM-VISION but in its progress it moves in and out of dream and does not employ consistently the characteristic features of the form. Through a series of allegorical narratives the *Visio* reveals the corrupt state of the world, of secular government, society and the established Church, and makes an attempt to remedy it by creating an ideal society in which each individual exercises humility and submits to the common good. Social reform is inadequate and soon the order breaks down as selfishness and disobedience undermine the structure. The *Visio* initiates the search for Truth and the quests for the means to salvation and for Charity which provide the impetus for the remainder of the poem.

The *Vita* is more introspective, exploring the reasons for the failure in the *Visio* by intellectual enquiry. Allegorical narrative is largely replaced by a series of interviews with personified abstractions representing facets of the Dreamer's psyche (Wit, Thought, Conscience) and concepts or ways of life (Study, Clergy, Reason). The Dreamer's search for Dowel, Dobet and Dobest, the various stages of good Christian life and understanding, is beset with problems of incomprehension, backsliding and confusion. At one stage he disappears, to be replaced by Rechelesnesse, representing his wallowing in worldliness and temporary abandonment of the quest in favour of easy and superficial answers. The Dreamer returns to continue his search through more interviews and a vision of the history of Christianity, the progress of which must be echoed in the spiritual progress of the individual. The Devil's undermining of man's attempts is revealed and the individual's consequent need for divine grace is stressed. After a vision of the Crucifixion and the harrowing of Hell the Dreamer sees the establishment of the Church and returns to its state of decay in the 14th century with an ultimate realization that the search must begin again.

The figure of Piers Plowman is part of the shifting allegorical fabric of the poem. His first appearance is as a humble servant of God who organizes society into an ideal structure in the allegorical episode of the Ploughing of the Half Acre. After the failure of the social experiment he leads his followers in the search for Truth, disappearing after the reading of an enigmatic pardon from Truth which states only that those who live well shall be saved. During the first stages of the Dreamer's search for the meaning of living well Piers is absent, but he reappears towards the end of the *Vita* as the Good Samaritan and as the incarnated form of Christ, demonstrating the ideal progression of the Christian soul to an imitation of Christ (*imitatio Christi*).

The poem's use of ALLEGORY is complex, often confusing and unconventional. Its various modes include the personification of abstract concepts, fully developed narrative episodes, EXEMPLA and tableaux; the whole work has a substructure of biblical reference and exegesis. The poem shifts in and out of allegory, mingling it with the literal, varying and developing its symbols. The meaning of an argument or symbol at any one time is dictated and limited by the Dreamer's capacity for understanding and so changes with the poem's progress. The reader follows the Dreamer's path towards understanding, restricted by and sharing his difficulties. The very impenetrability of the poem, its allegory and its meandering path, is a part of its meaning, mirroring the difficult process of apprehending its critical issues.

Apart from its allegorical content, *Piers Plowman* provides a detailed record of late 14th-century life, covering all aspects of political and theological debate and echoing common sentiments in its satire of the corrupt church and especially the friars. It is packed with details of contemporary life, often portrayed with extraordinary vividness and sympathy, as in the confessions of the Seven Deadly Sins, and the poet's portrayal of common humanity is characterized by deep compassion and astute observation. While the aim of the work was not principally poetic, and it is frequently difficult and daunting for the modern reader, *Piers Plowman* remains one of the greatest literary works of the Middle Ages.

Pilgrim's Progress, The: *From this World to That Which is to Come* A religious ALLEGORY by JOHN BUNYAN, Part I published in 1678, Part II in 1684. It is presented as a dream by the author, in which he sees a man called Christian with a book in his hand and a burden on his back, in great distress of mind because the book tells him that he lives in the City of

Destruction, and is condemned to death and judgement. Advised by Evangelist to flee towards a Wicket Gate, he sets out forthwith, leaving behind his wife and children who refuse to accompany him. The course of his subsequent pilgrimage takes him through the Slough of Despond, past the Burning Mount, thence to the Wicket Gate, the Interpreter's House, the Cross (where his burden rolls away), the Hill Difficulty, the House Beautiful, the Valley of Humiliation, the Valley of the Shadow of Death, Vanity Fair, Lucre Hill, the River of the Water of Life, By-Path Meadow, Doubting Castle, the Delectable Mountains, the Enchanted Ground and the country of Beulah, until at length he passes over the River and into the Celestial City. On the way Christian has been helped by trusty companions, first Faithful, who is put to death in Vanity Fair, and then Hopeful, who accompanies him into the Celestial City. Both separately and together they encounter a great number of allegorical characters. Some are hostile, like the foul fiend Apollyon who is slain by Christian, Lord Hategood who presides over their trial in Vanity Fair, and Giant Despair who imprisons them in Doubting Castle. Others are seemingly friendly but give the pilgrims dangerous advice; these include Mr Worldly Wise-man, Ignorance, Talkative and By-ends.

In Part II Christian's wife Christiana follows him on pilgrimage, together with her children and their neighbour Mercy. At the Interpreter's House the party is joined by Great-heart, who subsequently slays Giant Despair and various other giants and monsters. They meet with many fellow pilgrims on the way, such as Mr Feeble-mind, Mr Ready-to-halt, Mr Honest, Valiant-for-truth, Mr Stand-fast, Mr Despondency and his daughter Much-afraid, and at the end they all pass over the River one by one.

In Part I Bunyan is drawing on his own experience of conversion which, according to his view of it, is no instantaneous event or abrupt redirection of the spiritual life, but a long and arduous progression. But whereas his earlier autobiographical GRACE ABOUNDING is notable for its inward-turning, isolated and agonized preoccupation with his individual experience, here the process is given flesh in figurative terms: his own temptation to despair is transmuted into a Giant who locks the pilgrims up; the scriptural texts which had threatened him become demons with which Christian must contend. Part II, by contrast, is much more relaxed in tone, and leisurely in pace: the pilgrims enjoy fellowship together, and they have met to get married and entertain one another. The greater number and variety of pilgrims, perhaps reflecting Bunyan's increased responsibilities as a nonconformist pastor, make this part of the book more like a social novel.

From the moment of its publication, Bunyan's allegory of the Christian life has appealed to an extraordinarily wide readership. It has been published in

A scene from Pinero's *The Second Mrs Tanqueray* with Mrs Patrick Campbell as Paula: cover illustration from *Black & White*, 10 June 1893

innumerable editions, and has been translated into well over 100 languages. The book's popularity in languages other than English undoubtedly owes something to the folk-tale elements in its structure – the story of a man in search of the truth is one which crosses cultural boundaries. But the book is solidly rooted in Bunyan's own time, and owes a great deal to his experiences as an itinerant sectarian preacher, and prisoner of conscience. Much of its attraction lies in the beauty and simplicity of Bunyan's prose, and in the vividness with which he brings his allegorical characters to life, acutely catching the rhythms of colloquial speech. Though allegorical in form, the work is also profoundly realistic, particularly in its portrayal of the pilgrims as they strive to hold on to their beliefs in a hostile and uncomprehending world.

Pindar, Peter [Wolcot, John] 1738–1819 Satirist. Born at Dodbrooke, near Kingsbridge in Devon, Wolcot studied medicine in London and at Aberdeen University, where he took his MD in 1767. In the same year he became physician to Sir William Trelawny, Governor of Jamaica. After two years he took holy orders, and returned to Cornwall to practise medicine. He abandoned it in 1778 and went to London with his protégé, the painter John Opie. He began his own career as a satirist, using the name of Peter Pindar, with *Lyric Odes to the Royal Academicians* (1782–5) in *The Weekly Review*. *The Lousiad* (1785–95), a MOCK-HEROIC poem, took the Royal Family as its target, *Ode upon Ode* (1787) the yearly official ODES to the king. *Bozzy and Piozzi* (1786) satirized BOSWELL and Mrs Thrale, the friends of DR JOHNSON. Peter Pindar elsewhere turned his attention to JAMES BRUCE, William Pitt and EDMUND BURKE. His verse was collected in 1812.

Pindaric ode See ODE.

Pinero, Sir **Arthur Wing** 1855–1934 Playwright. Born in London and frugally educated there, Pinero left his father's law office to become an actor in 1874. He was the author of 15 plays by 1884, when he abandoned the stage to commit himself to writing, and his best work post-dates his acting career. He was the leading dramatist of his age in two distinct fields, FARCE and the PROBLEM PLAY. *The Magistrate* (1885), *The Schoolmistress* (1886) and *Dandy Dick* (1887) are all among the finest English farces. *The Cabinet Minister* (1890) is less secure. Pinero had, by the time he wrote it, established a reputation as a writer of comedy with the sentimental *Sweet Lavender* (1888) and risked that reputation with *The Profligate* (1889), controversial in its time simply because its plot hinged on seduction. Without radically criticizing contemporary moral values, Pinero proceeded to write a succession of social dramas highlighting the plight of women in an unforgiving world. They include THE SECOND MRS TANQUERAY (1893), *The Notorious Mrs Ebbsmith* (1895), *The Benefit of the Doubt* (1895), *Iris* (1901), *Letty* (1903), *His House in Order* (1906), *The Thunderbolt* (1908) and *Mid-Channel* (1909). A readiness to examine, if not quite to challenge, convention also distinguishes two effective comedies, *The Princess and the Butterfly* (1897) and *The Gay Lord Quex* (1899). Pinero's best comedy, TRELAWNY OF THE 'WELLS' (1898), is a nostalgic celebration of the mid-Victorian theatre, already lost in the era of the long run. Pinero was knighted in 1909. He continued to write plays for the rest of his life, seeking to maintain a hold in a theatre that changed too fast for him.

Pinter, Harold 1930– Playwright. Born and educated in Hackney, London, he trained as an actor at the Royal Academy of Dramatic Art and worked under the stage name of David Baron. Although influenced by BECKETT and associated with him in the THEATRE OF THE ABSURD, he is better appreciated as the inventor of a new kind of comedy, sometimes called the 'comedy of menace'. The majority of his plays are set in a single room, whose occupants are threatened by forces or people whose precise intentions neither the characters nor the audience can define. *The Room* (1957) and THE BIRTHDAY PARTY (1957) were the first to be produced. *The Dumb Waiter* (1960), a brilliantly crafted one-act piece, and THE CARETAKER (1960) established him as a major playwright in the suddenly adventurous British theatre. Four more short plays, *A Slight Ache* (1961), *The Collection* (1962), *The Dwarfs* (1963) and *The Lover* (1963), were followed by THE HOMECOMING (1965), perhaps his most enigmatic play. His long association with Sir Peter Hall, begun with the ROYAL SHAKESPEARE COMPANY's production of *The Homecoming* and continued at the ROYAL NATIONAL THEATRE, includes *No Man's Land* (1975), *Betrayal* (1978) and *A Kind of Alaska* (1982), about a patient suffering from sleeping sickness who recovers her memory with the help of the drug L-Dopa. *One for the Road* (1984), *Mountain Language* (1988) and *Party Time* (1991) mark a renewed political urgency.

Pioneers, The See LEATHERSTOCKING TALES, THE.

Pippa Passes A dramatic poem by ROBERT BROWNING, the first of the series called *Bells and Pomegranates*, published in 1841. Pippa is a silk winder who spends her holiday wandering through the small Italian town of Asolo, singing songs and thinking of the local people whom she considers the most blessed: Ottima, Phene, Luigi and the Bishop. In reality, the lives and characters of these four are entirely different from Pippa's innocent imaginings.

Pirate, The A novel by SIR WALTER SCOTT, published in 1822. It is set in the 17th century in a remote part of Zetland (Shetland).

The amiable and attractive Mordaunt, son of the misanthropic Basil Mertoun, is a close friend of Minna and Brenda, daughters of his father's landlord, the wealthy Magnus Troil. When a buccaneer, Cleveland, is wrecked on the coast Mordaunt rescues him and Minna falls in love with him. Mordaunt and Cleveland develop a hatred for each other and Mordaunt finds himself unwelcome at his landlord's house. Brenda, however, remains true to their friendship and he grows to love her. Eventually the pirates and Cleveland attempt to capture Magnus and his daughters but Mordaunt raises the alarm and they are rescued by a frigate. Minna and Cleveland (who proves to be half-brother to Mordaunt) are thus parted for ever. Mordaunt and Brenda find a happy ending.

Pirsig, Robert (Maynard) 1928– American novelist. He was born in Minneapolis and educated at the University of Minnesota. *Zen and the Art of Motorcycle Maintenance* (1974) is an account of a cross-country trip with his son which combines autobiography, fiction and philosophical reflection. It caught the mood of its time and earned Pirsig a cult reputation, not renewed by his only subsequent work, *Lila: An Inquiry into Morals* (1991).

Pistil of Swete Susan, The See SUSANNA: OR, THE PISTIL OF SWETE SUSAN.

Pit, The: *A Story of Chicago* A novel by FRANK NORRIS, posthumously published in 1903. It is the second part of his uncompleted trilogy, *The Epic of the Wheat*, begun with THE OCTOPUS (1901); the third volume was never written.

The 'pit' of the title is the Chicago stock exchange, where Curtis Jadwin is a leading speculator in the wheat market. By the time he gains a monopoly of the wheat stocks, Jadwin's obsession with money and the operations of the pit has driven him almost to madness. In the meantime, however, the growth of farming in the West has increased the supply of grain, devaluing his investment. With a glut of wheat on the market, Jadwin, already in poor health, loses all his money. His rise in the wheat market is paralleled by the decline of his marriage to the attractive Laura Dearborn. Neglected by her husband, she begins to return to the flirtations which had characterized her behaviour prior to their marriage and resumes her relationship with the aesthete Sheldon Corthell. At the end of the novel, however, she returns to Jadwin; they renew their commitment to each other and are able to look towards the future with hope.

Pitt-Kethley, (Mary) Fiona 1954– Poet. Born in Edgware, she was educated at Haberdashers' Aske's School and the Chelsea College of Art. Witty, outrageous and relentlessly self-advertising, she describes herself as a satirist bent on demolishing contemporary hypocrisies, particularly by tilting at men and the Establishment, though her taste for flippancy and easy effects usually prevents her work achieving its goal. *London* (1984), *Rome* (1985) and *The Tower of Glass* (1985) have been followed by more substantial collections: *Sky Ray Lolly* (1986), *Gesta* (1986), *Private Parts* (1987) and *The Perfect Man* (1989). She has also published: *Journeys to the Underworld* (1988), a travel book; *The Misfortunes of Nigel* (1991), a novel; and a *Literary Companion to Sex* (1992).

Plaatje, Solomon Tshekisho 1877–1932 South African politician and writer. He was born near Boshof. Court interpreter during the Mafeking siege, he wrote a posthumously discovered *Boer War Diary* (1972). Newspaper editor and first Secretary of the African National Congress (1912), he attacked in his *Native Life in South Africa* (1916) the 1913 Natives Land Act for turning blacks into pariahs in their own country. *Mhudi* (1930), written about 1917, was the first novel to present pre-colonial African society as having humane religious, social, and legal institutions. Other works include *Sechuana Proverbs and Their... Equivalents* (1916) and, with Daniel Jones, *Sechuana Reader in International Phonetic Orthography (with English Translations)* (1916).

Plain Dealer, The A comedy by WILLIAM WYCHERLEY, produced in December 1676 and published in 1677. Its source is Molière's *Le Misanthrope*. The most mordant of Wycherley's four plays, it is regarded by many as his finest. His friend JOHN DRYDEN described it as 'one of the most bold, most general, and most useful satires which has ever been presented on the English theatre'. The plain dealer of the title is the misanthropic Manly, a sea-captain who believes that only his betrothed Olivia and his friend Vernish are sincere. He returns from the Dutch wars to find that Olivia has married another and has no intention of returning the money he left in her care. Manly uses his page as a go-between in his vengeance on Olivia. Part of his plan is to dishonour her, but he does not know that his page is a girl, Fidelia, who has always loved him and has followed him to the war in disguise. Olivia is charmed by the page and makes an assignation with him; Manly accompanies Fidelia thinking his plan successful and intending to expose Olivia. But Olivia's husband, none other than the supposed friend Vernish, arrives on the scene. In the scuffle that follows Fidelia is wounded and her disguise discovered. Manly is touched by her devotion and sees the worthlessness of his obsession with Olivia. Fidelia wins her man.

Planché, James Robinson 1796–1880 Playwright, musician, historian of costume, herald and antiquarian. He wrote well over 150 plays and libretti, the best known being *The Vampyre: or, The Bride of the Isles* (1820). His crucial role in the development of the English PANTOMIME is widely recognized, as is the contribution he made to the thoughtful costuming of SHAKESPEARE by his designs for a revival of *KING JOHN* at DRURY LANE in 1823. *Recollections and Reflections* (2 vols., 1872) is a lively and informative autobiography.

Plater, Alan (Frederick) 1935– Playwright. He is best known for his long career of writing for television, which has ranged from scripts for *Z Cars* and *Softly, Softly* to adaptations of TROLLOPE and of OLIVIA MANNING's *Balkan Trilogy* and *Levant Trilogy* (as *Fortunes of War*). He has also adapted several of his own TV plays for the stage. *A Smashing Day* (1965) is about a confused young man; *See the Pretty Lights* (1970) is a tender love-story between a middle-aged man and a teenage girl. His true vitality emerged only when he started to work in a style of regional 'epic', combining songs, music-hall sketches and comedy gags into what were often serious social themes. The most successful of these local documentaries was *Close the Coalhouse Door* (1968), which described the history of coal-mining as seen through the eyes of the Milburn family.

Plath, Sylvia 1932–63 American poet. Born in Boston, and educated at Smith College, she won a Fulbright to Cambridge, receiving her MA in 1957, the same year she married the English poet TED HUGHES. She studied with ROBERT LOWELL and her work has clear affinities with CONFESSIONAL POETRY. However, she often distances herself from her personal subject matter by assuming a sharply ironic tone. Whether writing about tulips and elm trees, her experiences as a daughter and a wife, or her suicide attempts, there is always an undercurrent of terror in her poems. *The Colossus and Other Poems* (Britain, 1960; USA, 1962) was the only one of her books of poetry to be published before her suicide. Posthumous volumes include *Ariel* (1965), *Crossing the Water* (Britain, 1971; USA, 1972), and *Winter Trees* (Britain, 1971; USA, 1972). *The Bell Jar* (Britain, 1963; USA, 1971) is a partly autobiographical novel. Her prose is collected in *Johnny Panic and the Bible of Dreams: Short Stories, Prose, and Diary Excerpts* (1979). *The Journals of Sylvia Plath* appeared in 1982. Her life and death, as much as her poetry, continue to fascinate critics and biographers (see, for example, A. ALVAREZ and ANNE STEVENSON).

Playboy of the Western World, The A comedy by J. M. SYNGE, first performed at the ABBEY THEATRE, Dublin, in 1907, when the mere mention of an undergarment prompted a riot. It is one of the masterpieces of the Irish theatre.

The action takes place near a village on the coast of County Mayo during two autumn days. On the first, a stranger called Christy Mahon arrives, confessing himself a fugitive because he has killed his tyrannical father. Overwhelmed by the boldness of the deed, the villagers lionize him. Pegeen Mike, daughter of the owner of the local shebeen, and Widow Quinn give him his first experience of female admiration. Flourishing in the atmosphere of adulation, Christy wins a mule race and is rewarded with a promise of marriage to Pegeen Mike. But his triumph is cut short by the return of his father, bandaged but not dead, to reclaim his errant son. For the second time Christy 'kills' his father with a spade and for the second time old Mahon rises from the dead. Christy goes with him in the end, but no longer into servitude. Mahon respects him now, and Pegeen grieves over the loss of her playboy from the west.

Plomer, William (Charles Franklyn) 1903–73 Poet and novelist. Born in South Africa, he was educated in England at Rugby. After working as a farmer he founded the literary magazine *Voorslag* with ROY CAMPBELL in 1926. Plomer's first, angry novel, *Turbott Wolfe* (1926), precociously treats racism. He travelled widely, living in Japan (1926-9) before settling in England. He worked as a publisher's reader and served in Naval Intelligence (1940–6). Plomer's poems, including *Notes for Poems* (1927), *The Family Tree* (1929), *The Fivefold Screen* (1932), *Visiting the Caves* (1936) and *Celebrations* (1972), fall into two categories. His serious verse, exemplified by 'The Taste of the Fruit', is often moving and elegiac; his light verse, including the satirical balladry of *The Dorking Thigh* (1945), is comparable in stature to that of BETJEMAN. After *Collected Poems* (1960), he received wide recognition, including the CBE and the Queen's Gold Medal for Literature. Besides editing the diaries of FRANCIS KILVERT (1938–40) and MELVILLE's poems, he collaborated with Benjamin Britten as librettist for *Gloriana* (1953) and his three 'church operas'.

Plough and the Stars, The A play by SEAN O'CASEY, first performed at the ABBEY THEATRE, Dublin, in 1926, where it was the occasion of a famous riot. The action covers one day in November 1915 and the week of the Easter Rising in 1916. It was O'Casey's blunt and often humorous treatment of the behaviour of ordinary people involved in great events that offended many Irish people. The play is set in the Dublin slums and the title refers to the banner of the Irish Citizen Army, to which O'Casey had once belonged.

The occupants of a Dublin tenement are a cross-section of Irish social and political attitudes. Jack Clitheroe is a member of the Irish Citizen Army. His wife Nora is concerned only for Jack's safety. Nora's uncle, Peter Flynn, supports the independence movement from a safe distance. Jack's cousin, Covey, hopes for social revolution but does nothing to further it. Fluther Good does nothing but talks a lot. Mrs Gogan is ghoulishly fascinated by death, not only because her daughter Mollser is dying of consumption. Bessie Burgess, finest of them all, is a fruit-vendor with a son in the British army, a taste for drink and a heart of gold. The first act ends with Jack Clitheroe angrily brushing off his wife's protests and going to a gathering of the Citizen Army. The extraordinary second act brings some of the occupants together in a Dublin pub, where they hear and respond to the inflammatory speeches of Irish patriots addressing a crowd outside. The last two acts take place during Easter Week 1916. Nora's frantic attempts to keep Jack at home fail and he is killed. Fluther, Covey and others take their chances to loot shops. Bessie Burgess, trying to protect the demented Nora, is shot by a sniper.

Plowman's Tale, The: or, The Complaint of the Plowman A Middle English poem in ALLITERATIVE VERSE, probably written in the early 15th century. It is likely that the main part of the poem was written by one, or perhaps two, LOLLARD sympathizers, the prologue being added in the 16th century. In the form of a debate between a pelican and a griffin, the poem attacks the Church and supports Lollard ideals; the Griffin, proponent of the established Church, is defeated. The prologue introduces the tale as that of the ploughman mentioned in the General Prologue to THE CANTERBURY TALES; as a consequence the poem was included in early editions of CHAUCER's works. (See CHAUCERIAN APOCRYPHA.)

Plumed Serpent, The A novel by D. H. LAWRENCE, published in 1926.

Kate Leslie, an Irish widow, visits Mexico in search of some quality that will renew her life. She attends a bullfight and is revolted by what she considers the degeneration of modern Mexico. Then she meets General Don Cipriano Viedma, a pure-bred Indian whose primitive sexual energy she finds mysterious but attractive. Cipriano introduces her to Don Ramón Carrasco, scholar and political leader, whose mission is to dispose of Christianity and revive the old gods of Mexico. Quetzalcoatl, the plumed serpent, will preside and Don Ramón will represent him. This cult is characterized by an actual and symbolic reawakening of primeval sexuality marked by the dominance of the male over the female and of the political leader over the masses.

As Don Ramón rises to lead the people Kate witnesses violent blood sacrifices by Cipriano, but is fascinated by the cult's elemental power. She herself is reborn as Malintzi, a fertility goddess and bride of Cipriano, now elevated by Ramón to the status of war god, Huitzilopochtli. Possessed by the man-god, Kate seems about to become wholly subservient to his will – thereby fulfilling the emotional and symbolic sacrifice demanded of the female in the cult and in Lawrence's own quasi-mystical scheme – but the novel ends with her continued expression of doubt.

Plumptre, Anne 1760–1818 Translator, novelist and traveller. The daughter of the President of Queens' College, Cambridge, and the older sister of JAMES PLUMPTRE, she spent most of an industrious literary life in Norwich and London. Novels like *Antoinette* (1796), *The Rector's Son* (1798), *The Western Mail* (1801), *Something New* (1801) and *The History of Myself and a Friend* (1813) were largely unnoticed, while her most ambitious translations, from the work of the German playwright Kotzebue in the 1790s, were overshadowed by the rival translations of ELIZABETH INCHBALD and SHERIDAN. She attracted more attention, much of it unfavourable, with two travel books: *Narrative of Three Years' Residence in France* (1810), based on a trip of 1802–5 begun in the company of AMELIA OPIE and John Opie, and *Narrative of a Residence in Ireland* (1817), derived from her experiences in 1814–15. The former book is remembered for its spirited defence of Napoleon, though it also contains sharp and independent-minded comments on fellow radicals, like THOMAS HOLCROFT, who had recorded their impressions of post-Revolutionary France. *Tales of Wonder, of Honour and of Sentiment* (1818) is a moralistic work for children written jointly with her younger sister Annabella, who pursued a similar career to her own.

Plumptre, James 1771–1832 Playwright, critic, editor and traveller. He was born in Cambridge, son of the President of Queens' College and younger brother of ANNE PLUMPTRE. Whilst an undergraduate he changed from Queens' to Clare College, of which he became a fellow in 1794. From 1816 until his death he was vicar of nearby Great Gransden. Of several plays he wrote in youth the most notable are two comedies, *The Coventry Act* (produced and published in 1793) and *The Lakers* (unproduced but published in 1798), a genial SATIRE of PICTURESQUE tourism. His Evangelical bias in later years prompted him to produced censored editions, in the manner of BOWDLER, of popular airs in a *Collection of Songs* (1805) and English stage classics in *The English Drama Purified* (3 vols., 1812). Unlike many Evangelicals, however, Plumptre still believed that the drama could be purified, a case he argued in a steady stream of pamphlets and essays beginning with *Four Discourses on Subjects Relating to the Amusement of the Stage* (1809) and ending with *A Letter on the Subject of a Dramatic Institution* (1820), and attempted to illustrate in a last collection of his own work, *Original Dramas* (1816). None of these achievements was as significant as the journals in which he recorded his tours, usually walking tours, round England, Wales and Scotland between 1790 and 1800. A selection has been published as *James Plumptre's Britain: The Journals of a Tourist in the 1790s* (1992).

Poe, Edgar Allan 1809–49 American poet, short-story writer, writer of DETECTIVE FICTION and critic. Born in Boston, Poe was raised by the Richmond merchant, John Allan, after the early death of his parents. Later, by choice, he took Allan as his middle name. The Allans moved to England, and Poe attended school in Stoke Newington from 1815 to 1820. He completed his schooling in the USA and entered the University of Virginia in 1826, but left soon after in order to pursue a literary career. He published *Tamerlane and Other Poems* anonymously and at his own expense in 1827 and a second volume of poetry, *Al Araaf*, in 1829. Neither was successful. Using an assumed name and giving an incorrect age to enlist in the army, he entered West Point in 1830. He was dismissed for neglect of duty the following year.

After a brief stay in New York he published *Poems* (1831) and then went to Baltimore, where he began to write short stories for magazines. 'MS Found in a Bottle' (1833) won first prize in a contest judged by JOHN PENDLETON KENNEDY, who found him an editorial position on *THE SOUTHERN LITERARY MESSENGER* in 1835. The next year he married his 13-year-old cousin, Virginia Clemm, and moved to Richmond, Virginia. On being dismissed from *The Messenger*, he went to New York and then to Philadelphia, where he worked as assistant editor of *Burton's Gentleman's Magazine* (1839–40) and literary editor of *Graham's Magazine* (1841–2). Returning to New York again, he worked for *The New York Mirror* and in 1845 bought the *Broadway Journal*, though it closed the following year. After the death of his young wife in 1847 he returned to Richmond, undertook lecture tours and died, in squalid and partly unexplained circumstances, at Baltimore.

In the course of this makeshift and itinerant career, increasingly complicated by poverty, nervous disorder and alcoholism, Poe neverthless managed to produce a steady stream of reviews, critical essays, poems and short stories. The title work of *The Raven and Other Poems* (1845), his chief popular success as a poet, prompted him to write an explanatory essay, 'The Philosophy of Composition' (1846), which – together with his lecture, 'The Poetic Principle' (posthumously published, 1850) – constitutes his chief aesthetic statement. The emphasis on calculated craftsmanship and intensity of effect is reflected in the short stories partly collected in *Tales of the Grotesque and Arabesque* (1840) and *Tales* (1845). Leading titles include 'Ligeia', 'The Fall of the House of Usher', 'William Wilson', 'A Descent into the Maelström', 'Eleanora', 'The Masque of the Red

Death', 'The Pit and the Pendulum', 'The Tell-Tale Heart', 'The Gold-Bug', 'The Black Cat', and 'The Cask of Amontillado'. Three stories about Dupin, 'The Murders in the Rue Morgue', 'The Purloined Letter' and 'The Mystery of Marie Roget', had a decisive influence on the development of the detective story. All of this work begins by borrowing the conventions, and usually the European settings, of the GOTHIC NOVEL but creates its own distinctive milieu of private horror, psychological rather than physical. Obsession shading into madness and morbid terror approaching mental disintegration are his recurrent preoccupations. They are presented with the same clinical, even grimly humorous detachment that makes Poe interested in hoaxes and mathematical puzzles. His only novel, *The Narrative of Arthur Gordon Pym* (1838), belongs to the same world as the stories, while *Eureka* (1848), an ambitious treatise which is among his least-read work, attempts to explore its philosophical implications.

Poema Morale: *or, Moral Ode* A striking and powerful poem of religious warning, dating from *c.* 1150. It treats the common theme of the consequences of wrongdoing, and admonishes the reader to work towards salvation through virtuous living.

Poems of the Past and Present A volume by THOMAS HARDY, first published in 1902. Much of it was written in the 1880s and 1890s, although some goes back as far as the 1860s. Some, too, had already appeared in *The Tatler*, THE ACADEMY, *The Westminster Gazette* and other publications. Divided into several parts – 'War Poems', 'Poems of Pilgrimage', 'Miscellaneous Poems', 'Imitations', and 'Retrospect' – this richly variegated collection includes some of Hardy's most enduring verse. Beginning with a reverie on Queen Victoria, published in *The Times* a week after her death, Hardy next offers poems on the Boer War which include the finely wrought 'Drummer Hodge'. 'Poems of Pilgrimage' evoke literary and historical memories of SHELLEY, of GIBBON, of Rome, of Genoa and of Fiesole. 'Miscellaneous Poems' dwells – often sardonically, sometimes lyrically – on the timeless themes of doom and sadness, of nature and female beauty, of marital and emotional complexities, and they include 'To an Unborn Pauper Child', 'Lizbie Brown', 'The Darkling Thrush', 'The Ruined Maid', 'In Tenebris' (I–III) and 'The Lost Pyx'.

Poet Laureate Originally a title given generally to British poets in recognition of their achievement, it became in later times an official post awarded to a poet who received a stipend as an officer of the Royal Household. The formal duty of writing occasional verses and appropriate odes for public occasions is no longer demanded, and the title is largely honorific.

The stipend, similarly, is nominal. BEN JONSON and D'AVENANT first performed the duties of Poet Laureate, though the post was first bestowed officially on DRYDEN, who was followed by SHADWELL, TATE, ROWE, EUSDEN, CIBBER, WHITEHEAD, THOMAS WARTON THE YOUNGER, PYE, SOUTHEY, WORDSWORTH, TENNYSON, AUSTIN, BRIDGES, MASEFIELD, DAY-LEWIS, BETJEMAN and TED HUGHES.

Several US states have a tradition of nominating writers of local reputation as poets laureate. The post of national laureate (formally Poet Laureate Consultant to the Library of Congress), created in 1986, has been held by ROBERT PENN WARREN, RICHARD WILBUR, HOWARD NEMEROV, MARK STRAND and JOSEPH BRODSKY.

Poetaster, The: *or, The Arraignment* A satirical comedy by BEN JONSON, directed at contemporary writers. It was produced in 1601 and published the following year. The thin storyline, set at the court of the Emperor Augustus, concerns the efforts of Crispinus (MARSTON) and Demetrius (DEKKER) to defame Horace (Jonson). Dekker, perhaps helped by Marston, replied with *SATIROMASTIX*.

Poetical Rhapsody, A A collection of Elizabethan verse published by Francis Davison and his brother Walter in 1602. It includes 'The Lie', attributed to SIR WALTER RALEIGH, and poems by SIR PHILIP SIDNEY, SPENSER, DONNE, GREENE, WOTTON and THOMAS WATSON.

Poetry: *A Magazine of Verse* An American monthly journal, founded in 1912 by HARRIET MONROE, who edited it until her death in 1936. Since the days when she published early work by EZRA POUND and T. S. ELIOT (*THE LOVE SONG OF J. ALFRED PRUFROCK*), most major American 20th-century poets and many foreign poets have appeared in its pages.

Poetry Bookshop See MONRO, HAROLD.

Pohl, Frederik 1919– American writer of SCIENCE FICTION. Born in New York, he worked as an editor before and after World War II. *The Space Merchants* (1953), one of several novels he wrote with C. M. Kornbluth, is an unfortunately prophetic SATIRE about a future society in which advertising agencies employ all possible methods to maintain consumer spending. His extensive collaboration with Jack Williamson produced *The Singers of Time* (1991), one of the few science-fiction novels to dramatize modern cosmological theories. His many solo novels include: *Man Plus* (1976), about the adaptation of a man for life on Mars; the 'Heechee' series begun with *Gateway* (1977); and *Chernobyl* (1987), a drama-documentary account. Notable collections of short stories include *The Case against Tomorrow* (1957), *The Man*

Who Ate the World (1960), Day Million (1970) and In the Problem Pit (1976). The Years of the City (1984) gathers stories chronicling the future history of New York. The Day the Martians Came (1988) combines a sharply satirical series about a benign alien 'invasion'.

Poliakoff, Stephen 1952– Playwright. Born in London, he studied at Cambridge and started to write plays as a teenager, contributing to Lay-By (1971), a group play about pornography and rape. The Carnation Gang (1973), Hitting Town (1975), City Sugar (1975) and Heroes (1975) established him as a prolific writer with an instinct for depicting the urban deserts of modern Britain. Strawberry Fields (1977) was written while he was writer-in-residence at the ROYAL NATIONAL THEATRE, but Shout across the River (1978) was more telling in its account of an agoraphobic mother who fails to protect her daughter from city life but manages to cure herself. Subsequent work has included: American Days (1979); Favourite Nights (1981); Breaking the Silence (1984), about his grandfather's experience as an inventor on the run with his family from the Russian Revolution; Coming in to Land (1987); Playing with Trains (1989); and Sienna Red (1992).

Pollock, Sharon 1936– Canadian playwright. Born in Fredericton, New Brunswick, she grew up in the Eastern Townships of Quebec and returned to Fredericton to attend the University of New Brunswick for two years. Subsequently she worked in amateur theatre, first in New Brunswick and later in Alberta as a member of a touring company, Prairie Players. She won a Dominion Drama Best Actress Award in 1966. She began to write for radio and the stage in the early 1970s. She has held various posts in theatrical centres and at the University of Alberta and has lived in Vancouver, Edmonton and Calgary. Her first play, A Compulsory Option (1972), a black comedy, was followed by a series of works which focus on political and social issues in both present and past, often using the historical to cast light on the contemporary. Walsh (1974), which first attracted national attention to her work, examines the treatment meted out to Sitting Bull and his followers when they fled to Canada after their victory at Little Big Horn. Out You Go (1975) satirizes contemporary politics in British Columbia, while The Komagata Maru Incident (1978) finds a parallel for contemporary racism in a 1914 episode, when 400 Sikh immigrants were prevented from entering Canada by a gang of Vancouver hooligans. One Tiger to a Hill (1980) attacks the complacency of Canadian attitudes to prison reform. Pollock's best-known play, Blood Relations (1980), is about Lizzie Borden, the New England spinster charged with and acquitted of the axe murder of her parents in 1892. It is a tightly constructed family

drama which represents a departure from her previous work. It exploits the possibilities for ambiguity inherent in dramatic production and leaves the central issue of the protagonist's guilt open, but suggests a revisionist feminist perspective. Pollock has also written Generations (1979), Whiskey Six (1983), Doc (1984) and a number of children's plays.

Polly A BALLAD OPERA by JOHN GAY, written as a sequel to THE BEGGAR'S OPERA. It follows Polly Peachum to the West Indies in search of the transported Macheath, where she unintentionally delivers him to justice on the scaffold. Walpole's government refused it a performing license in 1729 and it was eventually produced, in an adaptation by GEORGE COLMAN THE ELDER, in 1777.

Poly-Olbion An enormous poem by MICHAEL DRAYTON, published in 1612 and 1622, running to some 30,000 alexandrines in rhyming couplets. Its 'Chorographical Description' (that is, a description of a country or locality) embraces both England and Wales: their landscapes, notable sights, ancient history and beliefs. Its chief source was the BRITANNIA by the antiquary WILLIAM CAMDEN, who also sub-titled his work 'chorographica descriptio'. The result is both a versified map and a vast storehouse of information, much of it of great antiquarian interest. Some of the finest verse is to be found in Drayton's descriptions of landscapes and the countryside.

Drayton was planning this 'Herculean labour' (as one of his friends called it) by 1598 but the first part did not appear until 1612. The splendid title-page of this edition shows Britannia on her throne holding a sceptre and a cornucopia – the latter alluding to the meaning of the title, 'many blessings'. On her garments are rivers and hills of the British Isles. This first part has 18 songs and is annotated with great learning and remarkable accuracy by the antiquary JOHN SELDEN. The remaining 12 songs were finished by 1619 but not added to a new edition until 1622, because of Drayton's difficulty in finding a printer willing to undertake so vast (and apparently unprofitable) a project.

Pomfret, John 1667–1702 Poet. The son of Thomas Pomfret, vicar of Luton, the poet was educated at Bedford grammar school and Queens' College, Cambridge. He followed his father's calling, becoming rector of two Bedfordshire parishes. In 1699 he published Poems on Several Occasions, but it was to The Choice, which appeared the following year, that he owed his immense contemporary popularity. A civilized and elegant account of a life at once genteel and epicurean, it was perfectly suited to the taste of the time. Pomfret's other works include moral reflections, Pindaric essays and the disappointingly unexciting Cruelty and Lust. His popularity endured for more than a century, and led JOHNSON to suggest to the publishers of LIVES OF THE POETS that he be included (one of only four such additions to the original scheme). 'Perhaps no composition in our language has been oftener perused than Pomfret's *Choice*', he wrote, adding in judicious bafflement, 'He pleases many, and he who pleases many must have some species of merit.' ROBERT SOUTHEY, in 1807, seems moved by a similar sentiment: 'Why is Pomfret the most popular of the English Poets? The fact is certain, and the solution would be useful.'

Poole, John 1786–1872 Playwright. His first dramatic work, the *Hamlet Travestie* (1811), set a fashion for BURLESQUE versions of SHAKESPEARE. Only with *Paul Pry* (1825) did Poole again rise above the journeyman level.

Poor Richard's Almanac An almanac published and written by BENJAMIN FRANKLIN under the pseudonym of Richard Saunders from 1732 to 1758. From 1747 onwards it was entitled *Poor Richard Improved*. As well as calendars and astronomical data, it contained many of Franklin's well-known maxims recommending homely wisdom, virtue, and frugality. Its fictional author, Richard, and his wife Bridget became popular literary characters. Franklin sold the almanac in 1758, but it continued publication until 1796.

Poor White A novel by SHERWOOD ANDERSON, published in 1920. It tells how late-19th-century technology changes the lives of the inhabitants of Bidwell, Ohio, and particularly that of Hugh McVey, a telegraph operator, who at the beginning of the novel is the shy, inhibited 'poor white' of the title.

McVey invents a mechanical planter which he hopes will improve the life of the local farmers. He is exploited by the enterprising speculator Steve Hunter, who convinces the townspeople to invest in a company which, like the invention, is a failure. Hugh's next inventions, however, a corn-cutter and a device to help load coal on to trains, are extremely profitable. Hunter becomes a millionaire and Bidwell gradually changes into a bustling industrial town. McVey too becomes rich and famous, but is lonely and isolated in his prosperity. He then marries Clara Butterworth, the daughter of a wealthy farmer, and though their marriage is unhappy initially they are reconciled at the end of the novel. Anderson traces Bidwell's economic development from a craftsman's town to an industrial centre and the troubles faced by the inhabitants as a result. Social distinctions based on wealth emerge, and the town's former peaceful existence is marred by outbreaks of violence, strikes, and company lock-outs. Disillusioned, McVey finally realizes the negative effects of industrial progress.

Pope, Alexander 1688–1744 Poet and satirist. Born the son of a Roman Catholic linen-draper in London in the year of the Protestant Revolution, he had an uneven education and was debarred by his religion from attending university. Precociously bright, he was largely self-taught, learning Latin and Greek from a local priest at eight, and later acquiring knowledge of French and Italian. He is said to have been whipped for satirizing a master at Twyford School. In 1700, the year his family moved to Binfield in Windsor Forest, he contracted tuberculosis, which permanently damaged his health. During his life the poet got progressively weaker (he also suffered from asthma), and physically dependent on others; in middle age, no more than 4ft 6in tall, he was unable to dress without assistance and needed to wear a stiffened canvas bodice to support his spine. Half-jokingly he later referred to 'this long disease, my life'. While still at school Pope embarked on his poetic apprenticeship, writing paraphrases and IMITATIONS of classical poets, the Psalms, CHAUCER and COWLEY. He claimed to have written his first significant work, *The Pastorals*, at 16; published in 1709, they display an extraordinary degree of technical control and a sensitive awareness of the genre, derived from his reading of Virgil and SPENSER.

Pope moved to London and began to move in literary circles. His *ESSAY ON CRITICISM* was published in 1711 and its accomplished tone drew the attention of ADDISON, with whose powerful Whig friends the young poet began to associate. In May 1712 he published his religious eclogue *Messiah*, in *THE SPECTATOR*, and also the first version of *THE RAPE OF THE LOCK* (expanded in 1714), the witty feminized epic which established his reputation in London society. He was a friend of WYCHERLEY and CONGREVE, but by 1713 had drifted away from Addison's circle (the Whigs were anti-Catholic) towards the Tory coterie presided over by SWIFT. In 1713 Pope became one of the SCRIBLERUS CLUB. *Windsor Forest* (begun in 1704 and published in 1713), a Royalist PASTORAL that combines a celebration of rural Albion with a political affirmation of the peace under Queen Anne, confirmed his allegiance with the Tories.

At this time Pope was also working on an ambitious translation of Homer into HEROIC COUPLETS. The first volume of the *Iliad* appeared in 1715 and the project was completed in 1720. It strays considerably from the original but has its own merits, chiefly the visually arresting descriptions. The translation (and its less fortunate successor, *The Odyssey*, which appeared in 1725–6) freed Pope from both booksellers and patrons by giving him financial independence. He became one of the first professional poets to be self-sufficient as a result of his non-dramatic writings. The publication in 1717 of his collected works, in a handsome volume, established Pope as the leading man of letters of his day. It included an adaptation of

Chaucer's *THE HOUSE OF FAME*, the 'Ode for Music on St Cecilia's Day' and two new love poems: *Eloisa to Abelard* is a bleak study in the self-imposed loneliness of the legendary female whose love has been blighted, while his *Elegy to the Memory of an Unfortunate Lady* is another melancholy piece, about a suicide. These expressions of dejection and rejection are haunting, and are perhaps occasioned by the two affectionate relationships that belong to this period of his life. He formed an attachment with LADY MARY WORTLEY MONTAGU, the sophisticated wife of the ambassador to Turkey, but the friendship soured and led to unpleasantness after 1723. More successful was the lifelong relationship with Martha Blount, to whom Pope addressed some epistles that are among his most attractive works. In the same year he collaborated with ARBUTHNOT and GAY, his fellow Scriblerians, on the play *THREE HOURS AFTER MARRIAGE*, his only venture into drama proper.

Despite the rising accolade with which he was greeted, Pope now seems to have entered a period of doubt about his achievements, and became tired of the literary business. The stricter measures taken against Roman Catholics following the Jacobite rebellion of 1715 meant he could no longer reside in central London, and in 1719 he moved out to Twickenham, to a villa with a garden that was to be his home for the rest of his life. He began to be fascinated by horticulture and landscape gardening – he was later consulted by Bathurst and Burlington on these subjects – and constructed for himself a shell-lined grotto on the far side of the London road which ran through the end of his garden. Pope was happy at Twickenham, where Lady Mary was a neighbour, and entertained numerous visitors including Swift, whom he helped with the publication of *GULLIVER'S TRAVELS*.

The Odyssey, completed in 1726 with the help of Elizabeth Fenton and William Broome, followed one of his less distinguished projects, an edition of SHAKESPEARE (1725) commissioned by the bookseller JACOB TONSON. It prompted a pamphlet by LEWIS THEOBALD, *Shakespeare Restored* (1726), pointing out Pope's scholarly deficiencies. The three-volume *Miscellany* of pieces by the Scriblerian group (1727–8) contained an early version of the masterful *Epistle to Dr Arbuthnot* and a prose piece, *Martinus Scriblerus peri Bathous; or, The Art of Sinking in Poetry*, which ridiculed the literary capabilities of his former collaborator William Broome, together with Theobald (who was to come in for further antagonism), AMBROSE PHILIPS (with whom Pope had disagreed over the *Pastorals*) and JOHN DENNIS, the opinionated critic. A comic inversion of Longinus' treatise on the sublime (*Peri Hupsous*), Pope's essay illustrates the lowest qualities in contemporary verse, the tendency for BATHOS and anticlimax, drawing upon his enemies as examples.

Pope had for some time planned an elaborate 'Opus Magnum' which would comprise four parts. The first was his *ESSAY ON MAN* (1733–4), four epistles mapping out the intellectual plan for the larger work. The second part was to be *THE DUNCIAD*, his all-embracing satire of Dullness in contemporary culture. Its first version (1728), consisting of three books, was enlarged in 1729 and a fourth book added in 1742; these appeared in a revised version in 1743. In the process Pope transferred his malignant displeasure from Theobald, the original anti-hero of the piece, to COLLEY CIBBER, the POET LAUREATE. The epic conceived as the third part of his 'Opus Magnum' was never finished but its final part appeared as his four *MORAL ESSAYS* or *Ethics* (1731–5). Though their philosophical content is hardly original, the poems epitomize the highly developed intellectual concerns with which he was preoccupied.

In 1733 he began to produce his miscellaneous *Imitations of Horace* (an idea of BOLINGBROKE'S), 11 translations and adaptations of Horace's *Odes, Satires* and *Epistles*. These are probably his easiest verses to enjoy, and demonstrate the fundamental affinity between Pope's genius and the foremost poets of the classical age. Effectively a 'Prologue' to these satires was *An Epistle from Mr Pope to Dr Arbuthnot* (1735), the most brilliantly sustained rhetorical performance that the poet ever achieved. Addressed to his dying friend, the erudite physician who had in turn looked after the poet, these verses embody the ideals of civilized friendship, good sense and honesty as well as offering blistering verse-portraits of, among others, Addison and Lady Mary Wortley Montagu. As an example of ironic autobiography versified, it has no equal. *One Thousand Seven Hundred and Thirty Eight*, named for the year of its publication, consists of two satirical dialogues modelled on Horace. Pope also prepared an edition of his correspondence, doctored to his own advantage, and had it published by Edmund Curll in 1735, though he subsequently pretended the edition was piratical.

Pope's reputation did not long outlive the AUGUSTAN AGE. Drastic changes of taste later in the 18th century made his sophistication appear merely a lack of 'feeling' and his satire merely an expression of malice. He did not appeal to writers or readers again until this century, when he has come once more to be highly regarded. Pope is perhaps our foremost poet of culture; the audience to whom he addressed his shapely poems is urban, urbane and civilized. He himself was interested in all the arts except music – he was virtually tone-deaf though his verse is far from tuneless. He studied painting under Charles Jervas, and was for part of his life almost as much preoccupied with architecture and landscape gardening as with poetry. A sense of proportion and an awareness of contrasting effects within the 'correctness' of a design are consequently features of much of his verse. They do not, however, make it impersonal or unemotional. Pope's writing is continually informed by his own personality, especially in the outstanding verse epistles, and by an exciting, even baroque, sense of performance which is both lively and articulate.

Porson, Richard 1759–1808 Classical scholar. Humbly born, he attended the village school at East Rushton in Norfolk, but found a patron in Sir George Baker, the physician, who sent him to Eton and Trinity College, Cambridge. He became a Fellow of Trinity College in 1782 and Regius Professor of Greek in the university in 1792. Expert in Greek metres and idiomatic usage, he produced notable editions of Euripides and Aeschylus, annotated Pausanias, and worked on the lexicons of Suidas, Hesychius and Photius. He also contributed to THE MORNING CHRONICLE and THE GENTLEMAN'S MAGAZINE, including three letters on Sir John Hawkins's biography of SAMUEL JOHNSON. Contemporaries considered he wasted his brilliant talents on journalism, as well as the heavy drinking and habit of procrastination which grew on him with age. The Greek typeface called 'Porson' is supposedly based on his hand. He is buried in the chapel of his old college, near the statue of SIR ISAAC NEWTON.

Porter, Anne Maria 1780–1832 Novelist and younger sister of the more successful JANE PORTER. The most popular of her many novels was The Hungarian Brothers (1807), about the French Revolutionary war.

Porter, Hal 1911–84 Australian short-story writer, novelist, poet and playwright. Born in Melbourne and brought up in Bairnsdale, a country town in western Victoria, he worked briefly as a cub reporter before becoming a teacher of English and modern languages at schools in Victoria, South Australia, Tasmania and New South Wales. In 1949–50 he taught the children of Australian army personnel in Japan. After returning to Australia, he was director of the National Theatre in Hobart for three years. In 1953 his varied career took another turn, when he became chief librarian of Bairnsdale and Shepparton. From 1961 he devoted himself to full-time writing.

Although he worked in many genres, he is best known for his short stories and his three volumes of autobiography, The Watcher on the Cast-Iron Balcony (1963), The Paper Chase (1966) and The Extra (1975). As the title of the first suggests, he adopts a detached, spectatorial stance. He is both one of Australia's finest prose stylists and a chronicler of many uncelebrated aspects of the country's social life. His novels – A Handful of Pennies (1958), set in occupied Japan; The Tilted Cross (1961), which deals with Tasmania's convict past; and The Right Thing (1971) – are sympa-

thetic towards loners and eccentrics. Cosmopolitan in range, Porter's stories are precise and carefully crafted works which extended the scope and style of the Australian short story. They are collected in Short Stories (1942), A Bachelor's Children (1962), The Cats of Venice (1965), Mr Butterfry and Other Tales of New Japan (1970), Fredo Fuss Love Life (1974) and The Clairvoyant Goat (1981). His other works include: three plays The Tower (1963), The Professor (1966) and Eden House (1969); volumes of poetry, The Hexagon (1956), Elijah's Ravens (1968) and In an Australian Country Graveyard (1974); and the non-fictional Stars of Australian Stage and Screen (1965) and The Actors: An Image of the New Japan (1968).

Porter, Jane 1776–1850 Novelist and sister of ANNE MARIA PORTER. Her historical romances, amongst the earliest examples of the form, were highly successful in their day. Thaddeus of Warsaw (1803) is more romantic in its setting than its date, which was not far removed from the author's time. The hero, Thaddeus, apparently a member of the Sobieski family, accompanies the Polish patriot army against the occupying Russians. The Poles are defeated, the Sobieski castle is destroyed, and Thaddeus, an exile, arrives in England. There he suffers hardship and deprivation, until he proves to be none less than the long lost son of an English gentleman. The Scottish Chiefs (1810) is more ambitious. The story opens with the murder of William Wallace's wife by Heselrigge, the English governor of Lanark, when he tries to make her divulge her husband's whereabouts. It continues with the career of the ill-fated Wallace and his barbarous execution by the English, and closes with the triumph of Bruce at Bannockburn.

Porter, Katherine Anne 1890–1980 American short-story writer and novelist. She was born in Indian Creek, Texas. Her first collection of stories, Flowering Judas, and Other Stories, was published in 1930. Hacienda: A Story of Mexico appeared in 1934. She received widespread critical acclaim for the volume Pale Horse, Pale Rider (1939), which consists of three short novels: 'Old Mortality', 'Noon Wine', and the title-piece, which tells of a short-lived love affair between a soldier and a young Southern newspaperwoman during the influenza epidemic of World War I.

She published two further collections of stories, The Leaning Tower, and Other Stories (1944) and The Old Order: Stories of the South (1944), as well as two volumes of essays, The Days Before (1952) and A Defense of Circe (1954). Her best-known work, Ship of Fools, appeared in 1962 after 20 years in the writing. A bitterly ironic novel, it is set on a German passenger ship sailing from Mexico to Germany in 1931, and explores the origin and potential of human evil through the allegorical use of characters as almost one-dimensional representatives of various national and moral types. *The Collected Stories of Katherine Anne Porter* (1965) received both the PULITZER PRIZE and the National Book Award. *Collected Essays and Occasional Writings* appeared in 1970. *The Never-Ending Wrong* (1977) is an account of the infamous Sacco-Vanzetti trial and execution. Her other works include *The Itching Parrot* (1942), *Holiday* (1962) and *A Christmas Story* (1967).

Porter, Peter (Neville Frederick) 1929– Poet. He was born and educated in Brisbane, Australia, where he worked as a reporter before emigrating to Britain in 1951. He became an advertising copywriter in 1959, and since 1968 has earned his living as a freelance broadcaster and journalist.

It is possible to distinguish three main poetic identities in Porter's work. The social satirist dominates his first three collections, *Once Bitten, Twice Bitten* (1961), *Poems Ancient and Modern* (1964) and *A Porter Folio* (1969). They include 'Annotations of Auschwitz' and 'Your Attention Please', both dealing with appalling events in a disarmingly matter-of-fact tone. The cultural conservationist dominates *The Last of England* (1970), *Preaching to the Converted* (1972) and *Living in a Calm Country* (1975), wryly and uneasily aware of his own detachment, as in 'The Sanitized Sonnets'. *The Cost of Seriousness* (1978), both shadowed and inspired by his wife's death, introduced a moving elegist in the title-poem, 'An Angel at Blythburgh Church' and 'An Exequy', widely acclaimed as his finest poems. Subsequent work has included *English Subtitles* (1981), *Fast Forward* (1984), *Automatic Oracle* (1987), *Chair of Babel* (1992). *Complete Poems* appeared in 1988 and *Porter Selected* in 1989. *After Martial* (1972) is a volume of translations.

Portnoy's Complaint A novel by PHILIP ROTH, published in 1969. It takes the form of an account by Alexander Portnoy to his analyst of his relationship with his suburban Jewish family: his domineering, guilt-inducing mother who dotes on him and yet waves a knife over his head when he won't eat; his perpetually constipated, weak-spirited insurance salesman father; and his pathetic, conformist sister. Portnoy's guilty responses to his family's needs alternate with self-conscious rebellions against them: as an adolescent he performs brilliantly in school, but he seeks relief and revenge through constant masturbation; as an adult he has a respected job as the Assistant Commissioner for the City of New York Commission on Human Opportunity, but he refuses to get married and instead has affairs with gentile women. Toward the end of the novel, having abandoned his latest lover in Greece, he travels to Israel and meets an Israeli girl. For the first time in his life he is impotent. The girl confronts him with the contradictions of his existence, and embodies for him a noble, self-sacrificing model of Jewishness.

Portrait of a Lady, The A novel by HENRY JAMES, first published serially in THE ATLANTIC MONTHLY (1880–1), and then in volume form in 1881.

Isabel Archer, of Albany, New York, a penniless orphan, becomes the protégée of her wealthy aunt, Lydia Touchett. She goes to England to stay with her aunt and uncle, a retired American banker, and their tubercular son, Ralph, who persuades her father to provide for Isabel in his will. When Mr Touchett dies, Isabel finds herself rich and goes to the Continent with Mrs Touchett and her friend, Madame Merle. In Florence, Madame Merle introduces her to Gilbert Osmond, a middle-aged widower with a young daughter, Pansy. To preserve her freedom, Isabel has previously turned down proposals of marriage from Casper Goodwood, a rich young American, and from Lord Warburton, an English neighbour of the Touchetts. Now, however, impressed with Osmond's taste and intellectual detachment, she accepts his proposal, only to discover him to be a selfish and sterile dilettante who has married her for her money. When she hears that Ralph is dying she prepares to depart for England to be with him, but Osmond forbids her to go. It is at this point that she discovers that Madame Merle is Pansy's mother, and she at last understands the woman's part in her marriage to Osmond. She goes to England after a final confrontation with Madame Merle and is at Ralph's side when he dies. Casper Goodwood makes a last attempt to gain Isabel, but though she feels an attraction for him she rejects him and returns to Osmond and Pansy in Italy.

Portrait of the Artist as a Young Man, A An autobiographical novel by JAMES JOYCE, serialized by THE EGOIST in 1914–15 and published in volume form in 1916.

Stephen Dedalus (representing Joyce), an intelligent but frail child, struggles towards maturity in Ireland at the turn of the century. The novel traces his intellectual, moral, and artistic development from babyhood to the completion of his education at University College, Dublin. His individuality is stifled by many levels of convention, dictated by the family, Catholicism and Irish nationalism. As a child he witnesses a fiery political dispute between supporters of Parnell and anti-Parnellites, and suffers unjust punishment at the hands of a stupid and brutal priest, Father Dolan. Adolescent sexuality causes him moral torment, and this is exacerbated at a school 'retreat' where he hears a sermon on 'hellfire' from Father Arnall. Rejecting the call to the priesthood, Stephen begins to assert his own identity. At University College he embraces the wider and more rewarding world of literature, philosophy and aesthetics, and by the end of the novel he has freed himself from the claims of family, church and state. He resolves to leave Ireland for Paris to encounter 'the reality of experience' and to forge 'the uncreated conscience' of his race.

The novel was developed from *Stephen Hero*, begun in 1904. Part of the earlier work survived and was edited by T. Spencer in 1944. Stephen Dedalus reappears in *ULYSSES*.

Positivism A creed deriving from Auguste Comte (1798–1857). Comte believed that humanity, both the individual and the race, progressed by three stages: the theological, the metaphysical and the positive. This cultural maturity was evinced by confining intellectual enquiry to observable facts: philosophy and theology were treated as illegitimate. Women's role was to safeguard the emotions. FREDERIC HARRISON was a leading English advocate of Positivism, GEORGE ELIOT embraced its doctrines for a while, and HARRIET MARTINEAU produced a condensed version of Comte's *Cours de philosophie positive*. Positivism has links with the scientific attitude and led to the 20th-century school of 'Logical Positivists' who deny the existence of metaphysics.

post-modernism An international movement, affecting all the contemporary arts, which has succeeded MODERNISM. Opinions vary as to whether it is entirely distinct from modernism or differs from it only in degree. In literature, it has its origins in the rejection of traditional mimetic fiction in favour of a heightened sense of artifice, a delight in games and verbal pyrotechnics, a suspicion of absolute truth and a resulting inclination to stress the fictionality of fiction. All these traits, of course, are already present in modernist works like JOYCE's *FINNEGANS WAKE*. Key American texts of early post-modernism include NABOKOV's *Pale Fire* (1962), THOMAS PYNCHON's *V* (1963) and KURT VONNEGUT's *Slaughterhouse 5* (1969).

Various reasons have been offered for these departures, including the belated availability of Kafka's work in English and the influence of SAMUEL BECKETT and the THEATRE OF THE ABSURD. Stressing socio-historical and political conditions, the critic Larry McCaffrey has identified 22 November 1963 – the day Kennedy was shot – as the beginning of post-modernism. Later events (the Vietnam War, the proliferation of nuclear weapons) encouraged the fantasies of WILLIAM BURROUGHS, the reclusive abstractions of DONALD BARTHELME and the intricate structures favoured by JOHN BARTH. Elsewhere, the incipient independence of nations like Colombia catalysed the emergence of MAGIC REALISM, a central subset of post-modernism. Márquez's *One Hundred Years of Solitude* is often celebrated as the key post-modernist text. In Germany the suspicion of linguistic structures inherited from Nazism prompted the work of Gunter

Grass. Literature in English outside the USA has seen post-modernist strategies most commonly adopted by writers confronting a post-colonial experience, like SALMAN RUSHDIE in *MIDNIGHT'S CHILDREN* (1981).

The distrust of traditional mimetic genres, allied to the philosophical climate of STRUCTURALISM and DECONSTRUCTION, has encouraged post-modernism to embrace popular forms, such as DETECTIVE FICTION (Umberto Eco's *The Name of the Rose*, 1983), SCIENCE FICTION (DORIS LESSING's *Canopus in Argos* sequence) and fairy tale (a recurrent source in the work of ANGELA CARTER). Equally post-modernist is the blurring of boundaries between the novel and journalism in TRUMAN CAPOTE's *In Cold Blood* (1966), the New Journalism of TOM WOLFE and others, and ROBERT PIRSIG's *Zen and the Art of Motorcycle Maintenance* (1974). Recent observers have noted an abandonment of the extravagance of authors like Pynchon and the emergence – in the work of RAYMOND CARVER or Nicholson Baker, for example – of a kind of 'experimental realism' which ostensibly returns to mimetic structures while retaining a distinctly post-modernist bewilderment. Perhaps the most typical recent practitioner is DON DELILLO, who, by returning to the Kennedy assassination in *Libra* (1989), links post-modernism's latest phase to what is arguably its first cause.

post-structuralism A modern critical theory which begins by asserting the unstable relationship between signifier and signified (see STRUCTURALISM and SEMIOTICS). The signifier refuses to be tied to a single signified, as is evident in jokes, dreams and poetry. This theory of signification is expressed in a number of characteristic post-structuralist positions: (1) the author should not be regarded as the origin of his text or the authority for its meaning (see Roland Barthes's 'The Death of the Author'); (2) there are no objective 'scientific' discourses. Our metalanguages (discourses used to explain other discourses) are always capable of being subjected to other metalinguistic operations *ad infinitum*; (3) literature cannot be isolated as a separate discourse but is always contaminated with the entire universe of discourses.

Barthes's *S/Z* (1970) examines a Balzac short story by cutting it into fragments (lexias) and dispersing them in the infinite sea of the 'already written'. He attacks the structuralist attempt to find *the* structure of narrative, arguing that narrative draws upon the 'codes' which form a grid of possible meanings which permit no ultimate 'closure'. Even though 'readerly' texts try to limit the possibilities of meaning, they can always be read, against the grain, for a certain plurality. The 'writerly' text actually celebrates its openness and encourages the reader's productive activity, which resembles the writer's own in its deployment of the codes. Barthes names five codes: 'hermeneutic', 'semic', 'symbolic', 'proairetic' and 'cultural'.

Under the influence of Nietzsche, who believed that all knowledge is the 'will to power', Michel Foucault examined the historical construction of knowledge. What is considered rational and scholarly is determined not by absolute standards of reason but by unspoken rules, institutional constraints and the power of particular discursive practices. Edward Said takes up Foucault's historical kind of post-structuralism and emphasizes the pressures of reality which constrain the possibilities of knowledge. Literary critics, he argues, can grasp a past text only within the discursive 'archive' of the present.

Potter, (Helen) Beatrix 1866–1943 Writer and illustrator of CHILDREN'S LITERATURE. Born the only daughter of well-to-do parents in Kensington, she was taught at home by a governess. To enliven her otherwise dull and sheltered life, she kept a journal in code (deciphered and published by Leslie Linder in 1966) and drew and painted, often using specimens from the nearby Natural History and Victoria & Albert museums.

In 1893 she sent a letter to a young friend illustrated with drawings of animals; with much encouragement from several quarters, she turned this into *The Tale of Peter Rabbit*, privately printed in 1901 and followed the next year by *The Tailor of Gloucester*. Subsequent picture-books for the very young, issued during a long and profitable association with the publisher Frederick Warne, include: *The Tale of Squirrel Nutkin* (1903), *The Tale of Benjamin Bunny* (1904), *The Tale of Two Bad Mice* (1904), *The Tale of Mrs Tiggy-Winkle* (1905), *The Tale of Jeremy Fisher* (1906), *The Story of a Fierce Bad Rabbit* (1906), *The Story of Miss Moppet* (1906), *The Tale of Tom Kitten* (1907), *The Tale of Jemima Puddle-Duck* (1908), *The Tale of the Flopsy Bunnies* (1909), *The Tale of Mrs Tittlemouse* (1910), *The Tale of Timmy Tiptoes* (1911) and *The Tale of Pigling Bland* (1913). Her tales range from stories of escape from near-death to charming, eventless catalogues of animal domesticity. Each one, however, was written with a natural ear for what she described as 'fine-sounding words'. Her illustrations usually showed animal characters wearing human clothes but otherwise treated without sentimentality.

After her marriage to a solicitor, William Heelis, in 1913 Beatrix Potter went to live in the Lake District, which she had learned to love during childhood holidays and which she made the setting for many of her books. She put most of her energies into sheep farming and conservation, leaving 4000 acres of land to the National Trust. *The Tale of Little Pig Robinson* (1930) was the only story of note to appear in her declining years.

Potter, Dennis (Christopher George) 1935–94 Playwright. Born into a mining family in the Forest of Dean and educated at Oxford, he started his career as a journalist and was a member of the BBC's Current Affairs Staff in 1959–61. His first TV play, *Vote, Vote, Vote for Nigel Barton* (1965; staged in 1968), is about a miner's son who stands for Parliament. *Stand Up, Nigel Barton* (1965) is a sequel. *Son of Man*, staged and screened in 1969, is a bold portrayal of Christ as human and self-doubting. Later TV series, rich in their feeling for popular culture and the music which expresses it, included *Pennies from Heaven* (1978), *Blue Remembered Hills* (1979), *The Singing Detective* (1986), the poorly received *Blackeyes* (1989) and, a welcome return to form, *Lipstick on Your Collar* (1993). Potter also adapted work by THOMAS HARDY, ANGUS WILSON and EDMUND GOSSE for TV and published a novel, *Hide and Seek* (1973).

Pound, Ezra (Weston Loomis) 1885–1972 American poet. He was born in Hailey, Idaho, and educated at the University of Pennsylvania and at Hamilton College in New York State. In 1906 he took up a fellowship at the University of Pennsylvania, and then taught briefly at Wabash College in Crawfordsville, Indiana. His academic career, however, was short-lived; he sailed for Europe in February 1908 and went to live in Venice.

His first volume of poetry, *A Lume Spento*, was published in Venice in June 1908. In September of that year he travelled to London, where he renewed his acquaintance with W. B. YEATS, whom he had first met during Yeats's visit to the USA in 1903. While in London he also became friendly with FORD MADOX FORD, T. E. HULME, JAMES JOYCE and WYNDHAM LEWIS. Ford published Pound's 'Sestina Altaforte' in *THE ENGLISH REVIEW* in 1909. Two collections of his poems, *Personae* and *Exultations*, appeared in the same year. *The Spirit of Romance* (1910), a volume of critical essays adapted from lectures he gave in London, further demonstrated the literary erudition that had been evident in his early poetry. His next two collections of poems, *Provença* (1910) and *Canzoni* (1911), again showed the influence of medieval literature, Provençal poetry, troubadour ballads and ROBERT BROWNING.

His translation of *The Sonnets and Ballate of Guido Cavalcanti* and his volume of poems entitled *Ripostes* (both 1912) marked the beginning of his association with the movement known as IMAGISM, which encouraged experimentation with verse forms, the economic use of language, brevity of treatment, and concreteness of detail. The movement, with Pound as its central figure, was at its peak between 1912 and 1914. During these years he also established his association with HARRIET MONROE, and through her magazine *POETRY* promoted the work of fellow imagists, as well as that of T. S. ELIOT and ROBERT FROST. In 1914 he published an anthology of imagist poetry, *Des Imagistes*, which included contributions by HILDA

Ezra Pound, photograph by E. O. Hoppé

DOOLITTLE, RICHARD ALDINGTON, James Joyce, AMY LOWELL, and WILLIAM CARLOS WILLIAMS, as well as by Pound himself. Another influence on him at this time was the sculptor Henri Gaudier-Brzeska, and from their association came the short-lived movement called VORTICISM, which opposed representational art in favour of abstract forms and structures. The movement's journal, *BLAST*, to which Pound contributed, survived for just two issues (1914–15).

Pound's next volumes of poetry were *Lustra* (1916) and *Quia Pauper Amavi* (1919). During the course of World War I he became increasingly disillusioned with what he saw as a decayed civilization, and this sense of living in a world of false values found its clearest expression in his 1920 volume, *Hugh Selwyn Mauberly*. Late that year he and his wife Dorothy, whom he had married in 1914, went to live in Paris; there he worked through the first draft of THE WASTE LAND with T. S. Eliot. He moved from Paris to Italy in 1924, and made a home in Rapallo. An epic poem had been one of his ambitions since his student days, but the form had taken 10 years to evolve. He had begun THE CANTOS before the vorticist period and had worked on them intermittently. The first collection, *A Draft of XVI Cantos*, was published in 1925. He continued to work on this, his modern epic, for the rest of his life; eventually it consisted of 117 Cantos.

Personae: The Collected Poems of Ezra Pound was published in 1926; *Selected Poems*, edited by T. S. Eliot, appeared in 1928. *A Draft of XXX Cantos* (1930) continued the sequence, which was further extended by *Eleven New Cantos* (1934), *The Fifth Decad of Cantos* (1937), and *Cantos LII–LXXI* (1940). In 1933 Pound had met Mussolini and been impressed by the dictator's imposition of order on Italy. In 1939 he visited the USA, where his new political beliefs and his anti-semitism alienated many of his friends. When he wanted to return in 1941 he was denied permission. In the same year he began to broadcast for the Axis in Rome. In April 1945 he was arrested by partisans and handed over to the American authorities. He was held under harsh conditions in an American disciplinary centre at Pisa and then transferred to the USA; in November 1945, in Washington, he was declared unfit to stand trial for treason on grounds of insanity, and was confined to St Elizabeth's Hospital. While incarcerated at Pisa he had begun an additional volume of Cantos; *The Pisan Cantos* were completed at St Elizabeth's in January 1946 and published in 1948. (Their receipt of the Bollingen Prize for poetry in 1948 caused an uproar which led to the Library of Congress's relinquishing the administration of the prize, which thereafter passed to Yale University.) Pound added to the Cantos with the publication of *Section: Rock-Drill: 85–95 de los Cantares* (1956) and *Thrones: 96–109 de los Cantares* (1959). *The Cantos of Ezra Pound* (I–CXVII) appeared in 1970. *Collected Early Poems* was published posthumously in 1976.

Pound's confinement in St Elizabeth's finally came to an end in 1958, and he returned to Italy. He died in Venice at the age of 87. He himself was uncertain of his achievements, but he is widely recognized as one of the makers of modern poetry. Among his volumes of criticism are *Pavannes and Division* (1918), *Instigations* (1920), *Indiscretions* (1923), *How to Read* (1931), *ABC of Reading* (1934), *Polite Essays* (1937), and *A Guide to Kulchur* (1938). *Gaudier-Brzeska: A Memoir* was published in 1916; his adaptation from the Chinese, *The Classic Anthology Defined by Confucius*, in 1954; and his translation of Sophocles' *The Women of Trachis* in 1956.

Powell, Anthony (Dymoke) 1905– Novelist. The son of a serving army officer, he was born in London but spent much of his childhood at army bases. He was educated at Eton and Balliol College, Oxford. Before serving in World War II, he worked for a publishing firm and as a book reviewer and film scenario writer.

Powell's first novel was *Afternoon Men* (1931), a precisely judged SATIRE of the Bohemian world and the futile foolishness of those inhabitants of Chelsea and Bloomsbury who felt their existence justified by mere aspiration. Powell's characteristically polished style makes for incisive social comedy. It was followed, in similar vein, by *Venusberg* (1932), *From a View to a Death* (1933), *Caledonia: A Fragment* (a privately printed verse satire; 1934), *Agents and Patients* (1936) and *What's Become of Waring?* (1939). After World War II Powell published a biographical study, *John Aubrey and His Friends* (1948), and edited a selection of AUBREY's *Brief Lives* in the following year. He also began work on an ambitious sequence of 12 novels, *A DANCE TO THE MUSIC OF TIME*, which began with *A Question of Upbringing* (1951) and ended with *Hearing Secret Harmonies* (1975), amounting to a leisurely survey of English society as Powell has experienced it. Later, more eccentric novels are *O, How the Wheel Becomes It!* (1983) and *The Fisher King* (1986).

Powell's memoirs were published in four volumes as *To Keep the Ball Rolling* (1976–82) and his book reviews, mostly written for *The Daily Telegraph* in a spirit of defiant pedantry, collected in two volumes, *Miscellaneous Verdicts* (1990) and *Under Review* (1992).

Power and the Glory, The A novel by GRAHAM GREENE, published in 1940.

The novel arose out of Greene's visit to Mexico in 1937, after he had been commissioned to report on religious persecution there. It is set in the violent context of a new revolutionary republic where the Church is outlawed and priests are banned, and traces the 'martyrdom' of a lapsed priest, guilty of drunkenness and lechery. Despite being outlawed (or perhaps because of it) he rediscovers the integrity of his original commitment and determines to perform his duties until physically prevented by the authorities. His life is contrasted to that of several other characters: a fellow priest, Padre Jose, who has capitulated to the regime, and a 'gringo' thief and murderer, hunted by the police. His opponent, a police lieutenant, represents the non-religious humanist viewpoint. He is described as a good and honourable man, and is acknowledged as such by the priest when, at the end of the novel, the latter is cornered at the bedside of the dying 'gringo'. The priest's execution is imbued with Christlike implications, and the novel closes on a subdued note of triumph about the Church's survival in the face of religious intolerance.

As in so many of Greene's novels, the thriller element is employed to dramatize an ambiguous moral drama.

Power of Sympathy, The An EPISTOLARY NOVEL by WILLIAM HILL BROWN, published anonymously in 1789 and generally considered to be the first American novel. Based in part on an actual scandal in Boston society, it warns young women of the danger from would-be seducers by telling the tragic tale of an attempted seduction which, if it had been successful, would also have been incestuous.

Harrington is determined to win Harriot Fawcet, unaware that she is the illegitimate child of the elder Harrington and hence his half-sister. He confides his plans – which to start with are simply to seduce Harriot, but change quickly to marrying her without his father's permission – to his friend Mr Worthy, who sensibly counsels against this course. When the truth of Harriot's parentage is revealed, she collapses and dies soon afterwards. The grief-stricken Harrington becomes increasingly unstable and eventually commits suicide.

Powys, John Cowper 1872–1963 Novelist. The brother of LLEWELYN POWYS and T. F. POWYS, he was born in Derbyshire and educated at Sherborne and Corpus Christi College, Cambridge. His boyhood was spent in the West Country, which provided the setting for many of his later novels, but for much of his life he lived and worked as a lecturer in the USA. He returned to Great Britain in his 60s and lived at Blaenau-Festiniog in North Wales for the remainder of his life.

His career began with poetry and essays. *Odes and Other Poems* (1896) was followed by *Poems* (1899) and *Visions and Revisions: A Book of Literary Devotions* (1915). *Suspended Judgements*, a collection of essays, appeared the following year, and there were many other essays on subjects ranging from literature to religion and philosophy. He also published a group of romances – *Wood and Stone* (1915), *Rodmoor* (1916), and *Ducdame* (1925) – but his reputation as the author of highly individual and immensely long novels with an esoteric interest began with *Wolf Solent* (1929). Like *A Glastonbury Romance* (1932), it blends elements of folklore and the supernatural with elements of the epic. *Weymouth Sands* (1934; republished as *Jobber Skald* in 1935 because of a libel suit, but restored to its original form in 1963) is cast in the same mould and centres upon the unfolding of an intense love-hate relationship between its major protagonists: Jobber, his lover Perdita, and enemy Dog Cattistock. *Maiden Castle* (1936) is set among the excavations of the Dorchester fort and, like much of Powys's work, celebrates the power of human fortitude in the face of disillusionment. *Morwy: or The Vengeance of God* (1937), about man's inhumanity to man, was followed by two more historical romances: *Owen Glendower* (1940) and *Porius: A Romance of the Dark Ages* (1951). Other novels include: *The Inmates* (1952), about madness, *Atlantis* (1954), a fantastic tale about Homer's Odysseus which ends with the discovery of America, and *The Brazen Head* (1956), about ROGER BACON.

Powys, Llewelyn 1884-1939 Essayist, journalist and novelist. The brother of JOHN COWPER POWYS and T. F. POWYS, he was born in Dorchester and educated at Sherborne and Corpus Christi College, Cambridge. Like his brother, John Cowper, he worked in the

United States, but on his return in 1909 discovered that he was suffering from tuberculosis. From 1914–19 he farmed in Kenya with his brother William. He spent another five years in the United States as a journalist, and then travelled in Palestine and the West Indies. For the remainder of his life he lived in Switzerland.

Powys wrote many essays and sketches, including *Ebony and Ivory* (1923), based on his experiences in Kenya, and *Skin for Skin* (1925), an account of his illness set in Swiss sanatoria, in Israel, the United States and Dorset. Newspaper serialization made *Earth Memories* (1934) and *Dorset Essays* (1935) perhaps his best-known volumes. His novels included *Black Laughter* (1924) and *Apples be Ripe* (1930).

Confessions of Two Brothers (1916) was written in collaboration with John Cowper Powys, while *Damnable Opinions* (1935) shows the independent-mindedness that characterized all three brothers. His other autobiographical writings included *The Verdict of Bridlegoose* (1926) and *Love and Death: An Imaginary Autobiography* (1939).

Powys, T(heodore) F(rancis) 1875–1953 Novelist and short-story writer. The brother of JOHN COWPER POWYS and LLEWELYN POWYS, he was born in Dorchester and educated at schools in East Anglia. In 1902 he returned to East Chaldon in Dorset, the setting for most of his novels and short stories. His first published work was *An Interpretation of Genesis* (1907), and this was followed by *Soliloquies of a Hermit* (1916), a series of meditations; both works indicated his preoccupation with religious themes. His first fiction appeared in two collections of stories, *The Left Leg* and *Black Bryony* (both 1923), which revealed him to be a master of the short form. *Mr Tasker's Gods* appeared the following year, a highly individual work which introduced many strange and grotesque figures who were to reappear in his subsequent books.

Powys is best known for *Mr Weston's Good Wine* (1927), an allegorical fantasy of love and death in which God and the archangel Michael visit the village of Folly Down in the person of Mr Weston, wine merchant, and his junior partner. In *Unclay* (1931), Powys's other major novel, John Death visits the village of Dodder with orders from God to kill various of its inhabitants. Like *Mr Weston's Good Wine* the book defies classification but is imbued with profoundly moral paradoxes about good and evil. Other works include *Feed My Swine* (1926; short stories), *The House with the Echo* (1928), *Fables* (1929; also published as *No Painted Plumage*, 1934), *The White Paternoster and Other Stories* (1930), *Captain's Patch* (1935) and *Bottle's Path* (1946), one of a very few books to appear after 1940.

practical criticism See RICHARDS, I. A.

Praed, Mrs Campbell 1851–1935 Australian novelist. She was born Rosa-Caroline Murray-Prior at Bromelton in Queensland. She grew up in Queensland, where her father was Postmaster-General, and received some education at Brisbane. *My Australian Girlhood* (1902) is the story of those years. After marrying Arthur Campbell Mackworth Praed in 1872, she lived on his station on Curtis Island until 1876, when the couple settled permanently in England. Of some 40 novels at least half draw on her experience of Australia and often revolve around a contrast between the refined English gentleman and the crude, spiky Australian whose qualities prove more enduring. Her novels include *An Australian Heroine* (1880), *Policy and Passion* (1881), *Miss Jacobsen's Chance* (1886), *The Romance of a Station* (1889), *Mrs Tregaskiss* (1895), *Nulma* (1897), *The Maid of the River* (1905), *Opal Fire* (1910) and *Sister Sorrow* (1916).

Praed, William Mackworth 1802–39 Poet. Born in London and educated at Eton and Trinity College, Cambridge, he was called to the Bar in 1829 but soon turned to politics and sat for several constituencies. In 1835 he was appointed Secretary to the Board of Control under Peel but such work was more the foundation for the future political career denied him by early death than a realization of any achievement. At its best his verse is humorous, light, unforced, and of a social inclination redolent of the order to which he belonged. He also wrote some romantic poetry, a mode he often touched with mockery. He had a turn for the grotesquely amusing, as well as a taste for SATIRE, frequently expressed in 'squibs' directed against prominent figures like BROUGHAM and Palmerston. His *Poems* appeared in 1864.

Praeterita The unfinished autobiography of JOHN RUSKIN first appeared intermittently in 28 parts between July 1885 and July 1889. Although written between bouts of madness, it contains some of its author's most lucid and carefully formulated prose. It is selective in detail, and concentrates on the first half of Ruskin's long life. But *Praeterita* is replete with character sketches of painters, teachers, literary folk, servants and friends, and it is rich in descriptions of nature remembered by Ruskin from his ceaseless travels. Above all, perhaps, *Praeterita* engages as an absorbing portrait of the household of a middle-class 19th-century merchant on the way up, for at times Ruskin's parents seem as much to the fore as their son himself.

Pragmatism: A New Name for Some Old Ways of Thinking A book by WILLIAM JAMES, published in 1907 and based on lectures delivered in Boston and repeated at Columbia University. It is considered by some to be the most significant work of American philosophy. As he describes it, pragmatism is not so much a theory as a method of choosing among theories – a means of mediating between rationalist absolutism and empiricist materialism. Although James distrusts the abstract manipulation of words (rationalism), he does not reject abstraction altogether (as perhaps a rigid empiricist would); rather, he accepts abstractions insofar as they redirect one profitably into experience. Ideals are 'real' because they have results. James argues that truth, an abstraction, does not reside innately within any proposition; rather, one can call a proposition truthful if it has practical consequences. For the pragmatist, therefore, truth is relative.

Prairie, The See LEATHERSTOCKING TALES, THE.

Pratt, E(dwin) J(ohn) 1882–1964 Canadian poet. Born in Western Bay, Newfoundland, the son of an itinerant Methodist minister, he attended St John's Methodist College and, after working as a preacher and schoolteacher in remote island communities, went to Victoria College, University of Toronto, where he took four degrees, culminating in a doctorate in theology. He was a demonstrator-lecturer in psychology at Victoria College from 1913 to 1920, and from 1920 to 1953 worked in the Department of English there.

His work, generally regarded as Canada's most important narrative poetry, embodies central Victorian themes such as the conflict between man and nature and within nature itself. *The Witches' Brew* (1925), in which three sea-witches attempt to discover what effect alcohol has on fish, is a comic ALLEGORY about Prohibition. *The Iron Door* (1927) is an ode written to commemorate his mother's death, which reflects on death more generally and concludes with an ambivalent affirmation of faith. *The Titanic* (1935) places the ship and the iceberg which destroyed it in contrast as an ironic commentary on man's belief in technological progress.

Pratt's best-known works raise subjects from Canadian history to epic status: *Brébeuf and His Brethren* (1940) is about a group of missionaries massacred by the Iroquois in the 17th century, while *Towards the Last Spike* (1952) deals with the building of the transcontinental railroad in Canada, and national unity and communication more generally. Pratt was a meticulous craftsman who worked in a variety of metrical forms. His other volumes include *Newfoundland Verse* (1923), *Titans* (1926), *The Roosevelt and the Antinoe* (1930), *Verses of the Sea* (1930), *Many Moods* (1932), *The Fable of the Goats* (1937), *Still Life* (1943), *Behind the Log* (1947) and *Collected Poems* (1958).

Prayer Book, The See BOOK OF COMMON PRAYER, THE.

Pre-Raphaelites A mid 19th-century school of painters and poets. Its nucleus was the Pre-Raphaelite Brotherhood, or PRB, founded in 1848 by Holman Hunt, John Everett Millais, DANTE GABRIEL ROSSETTI, WILLIAM MICHAEL ROSSETTI, F. G. Stephens, James Collinson and Thomas Woolner. The PRB was in youthful revolt against the canons of the Royal Academy and, thanks to the influence of RUSKIN, dedicated to recovering the purity of medieval art which Raphael and the Renaissance had destroyed. Though the original PRB was almost as short-lived as its journal, *THE GERM*, its principles found later recruits in, for example, WILLIAM MORRIS and Edward Burne-Jones. Pre-Raphaelitism in the wider sense became one of the most influential tendencies in Victorian art. In painting it is distinguished by its love of bright colour, vividly naturalistic detail and subjects drawn from religion or literature (Dante, SHAKESPEARE, KEATS and ARTHURIAN LITERATURE). In poetry, where it is most clearly represented by the work of Dante Gabriel Rossetti, CHRISTINA ROSSETTI, COVENTRY PATMORE and Morris, Pre-Raphaelitism found congenial precedents in Keats's *LA BELLE DAME SANS MERCI* and the work of TENNYSON. Such examples encouraged, not just the choice of medieval subjects or the use of medieval forms like the BALLAD, but the cultivation of a mood of dreamy melancholy. Despite its use of naturalistic detail, Pre-Raphaelitism in both painting and poetry turned decisively away from REALISM – as indeed it deliberately turned its back on the realities of 19th-century industrial society – and occasionally anticipated SYMBOLISM.

Prelude, The: *or, Growth of a Poet's Mind* An autobiographical poem in BLANK VERSE by WILLIAM WORDSWORTH, begun at Goslar in Germany in the autumn of 1798. Unpublished during Wordsworth's life, and known to his circle simply as 'the Poem to COLERIDGE', the work is available to modern readers in three versions: a two-part text completed in 1799, first published in 1973; the earliest full-length *Prelude* of 1805, edited from the manuscripts by Ernest de Selincourt in 1926; and the poet's own definitive version in 14 books, put aside in 1839, and published after his death in 1850, with its present title, suggested by Mary, his widow. The 1850 text irons away some of the infelicities and clarifies the syntax of the 13-book 1805 version, but late 20th-century critics are generally agreed that it also weakens its poetic force. The work was originally intended to be a 'sort of portico' to *The Recluse*, an ambitious philosophical poem on 'Nature, Man and Society' which Wordsworth began but never completed (see *THE EXCURSION*).

The Prelude is a poetic reflection on poetry itself, although this does not become fully evident until the final three books. In the course of the poem the imagination is progressively distanced from, and finally raised above, all other modes of understanding and acting upon man and the world, becoming 'but another name for absolute strength/ And clearest insight, amplitude of mind,/ And Reason in her most exalted mood'. The authority for this derives less from any generalizable aesthetic philosophy than from the poet's (i.e. Wordsworth's) own personal experiences and the exemplary significance of his intellectual development. The fortunes of Wordsworth and the fate of poetry are thus essentially one. Wordsworth was not insensitive to the 'self-conceit' implicit in his undertaking, and tried to rectify matters by insisting on the 'real humility', and even 'diffidence', with which he had approached it. The chosen confessional form, however, necessarily places the 'I' of the narrator in the position of principal subject of the narrative. Wordsworth's encompassing claims for his craft are grounded in a comprehensive critique of the negativity of modern civilization. The deadening equation of knowledge with book-learning and writing; the debased conception of human community inscribed upon the streets and buildings of the London metropolis (Book VIII); the bloodless abstractions of the rationalistic philosophy of WILLIAM GODWIN; and, above all else, the catastrophic degeneration of the French Revolution into 'domestic carnage' and wars of foreign conquest (IX, X, XI) are all, in the final analysis, both causes and symptoms of an estrangement of man from his true purpose and being. Only the poetic imagination, the repository of truths anterior to, and immeasurably larger than, the fragile constructions of the rational understanding, is capable of restoring him to wholeness. The poet's privileged purchase upon truth is the reward of his intuitive intimacies with Nature, who teaches him to avoid the enthralments of 'sensible impressions' and to 'hold communion with the invisible world'. Yet Wordsworth is not a nature mystic: enhanced by vision though it may be, the model for his lost totality is a recognizable social order. Significantly, *The Prelude* begins in, revisits and finally returns in spirit to the world of his Cumberland childhood and youth, with its undisturbed beauty and stillness and the timeless patriarchal simplicity of its social and economic relations. The poem is Wordsworth's greatest work, and it is astonishing that his fame in his own lifetime as the architect of conservative ROMANTICISM was actually achieved without it.

Prescott, William Hickling 1796–1859 American historian. He was born in Salem, Massachusetts, and educated at Harvard. His *History of the Reign of Ferdinand and Isabella, the Catholic* was published in three volumes in 1838. He was encouraged by its reception and in the following year began to prepare *History of the Conquest of Mexico*, which was published in three volumes in 1843 and brought him widespread acclaim. Prescott was careful to indicate

the tragedy inherent in the advance of the conquistadors; his careful examination of sources and his adventurous narrative method provided a model for a younger generation of historians. *History of the Conquest of Peru* followed in 1847, and the cycle was completed with the publication of three volumes of *History of the Reign of Philip the Second* (1855–8).

Preston, Thomas *fl.* 1570 Nothing is known of the life of the author of *CAMBISES, KING OF PERSIA* (1569), though he has often been confused with his namesake, the Vice-Chancellor of Cambridge University. Preston may also have been the author of the heroical romance *Sir Clyomon and Sir Clamydes*.

Price, Richard 1723–91 Writer on philosophy and politics. Born at Tynton in Glamorgan, he became a Unitarian minister in London. In 1756 he published *A Review of the Principal Questions in Morals*, arguing that the rightness and wrongness of any action belonged to that action intrinsically and opposing the 'moral sense' view of ethics taken by the EARL OF SHAFTESBURY and Francis Hutcheson. Price advocated the reduction of the national debt in *An Appeal to the Public on the Subject of the National Debt* (1772) and strongly supported American independence in *Observations on the Nature of Civil Liberty, the Principles of Government and the Justice and Policy of the War with America* (1776; supplemented in 1777 and 1778). He became a friend of BENJAMIN FRANKLIN and in 1778 was invited by Congress to live in America. The French Revolution was the occasion for a famous sermon and *A Discourse on the Love of our Country* (1789): 'After sharing in the benefits of one Revolution, I have been spared to be a witness to two other Revolutions, both glorious.' Price's *Discourse* provoked BURKE to write his *REFLECTIONS ON THE REVOLUTION IN FRANCE*, published the following year.

Price, Sir Uvedale See PICTURESQUE.

Prichard, Katherine Susannah 1883–1969 Novelist and poet. Born in Fiji, she spent her childhood in Tasmania, and was educated in Melbourne. She worked as a journalist in Melbourne and then went to London, where she spent six years as a freelance journalist and published her first novel, *The Pioneers* (1915). In Australia she took pains to familiarize herself with the background of her novels, travelling the continent and observing the life she depicts with considerate care. The life of teamsters is featured in *Working Bullocks* (1926); the life of a cattle station and a relationship with an Aboriginal girl in *Coonardoo* (1929), her best novel; and circus life in *Haxby's Circus* (1930). Her trilogy of novels about the goldfields, *The Roaring Nineties* (1946), *Golden Miles* (1948), and *Winged Seeds* (1950), is set in Western Australia, where she eventually made her home. She also wrote verse, including *Clovelly Verses* (1913) and *The Earth Lover and Other Verses* (1932).

Prick of Conscience, The Northern Middle English poem of the first half of the 14th century, surviving in many versions; the best has 9000 lines in couplets. It is divided into seven parts and a prologue and deals with man's miserable state, the world and worldly life, death, Purgatory, the signs of Doomsday, the torments of Hell and the joys of Heaven. It is drawn from many sources, Latin and English, amongst the most notable being Pope Innocent III's *De contemptu mundi*, Bartholomew's *De proprietatibus rerum* (see JOHN DE TREVISA), Honorius d'Autun's *Elucidarium* and Aquinas's *Compendium theologicae veritatis*. It concentrates on spiritual experience and is more introspective than works with similar intentions, such as *HANDLYNGE SYNNE*. Its title expresses the author's hope that reading the poem will stir men to repentance. The work was immensely popular and is preserved in a very large number of manuscripts.

Pride and Prejudice A novel by JANE AUSTEN. It was begun in 1796 and completed the following year under the title 'First Impressions', but rejected by a publisher in this form. It finally appeared in 1813, after careful revision and with a new title.

Mr and Mrs Bennet of Longbourn are an ill-matched couple, he detached and ironic, she vulgar, gossipy and mainly engaged in seeking husbands for their five daughters. Netherfield, a house near Longbourn, is leased by the wealthy Charles Bingley, who stays there with his sisters and his friend, the still wealthier FitzWilliam Darcy. To Mrs Bennet's delight, Bingley falls in love with her eldest daughter, Jane. But the witty and high-spirited Elizabeth Bennet, next in age of the Bennet children, frankly dislikes Mr Darcy for his cold and superior manner; her prejudice against him is increased by the story she hears from George Wickham, an engaging young militia officer, of the unjust treatment he has received from Darcy. For their part the Bingley sisters and Darcy find Mrs Bennet and the younger Bennet sisters impossibly vulgar, and prevail on Bingley to detach himself from Jane.

The Bennet family is visited by William Collins, a rector under the patronage of Lady Catherine de Bourgh, who will inherit Mr Bennet's entailed property on his death. With great pomposity Mr Collins proposes to Elizabeth but she refuses him, despite the financial convenience of such a marriage. Mr Collins transfers his attentions to Elizabeth's friend, Charlotte Lucas, who accepts him out of expediency. Elizabeth goes to visit the newly married couple and finds that Darcy is in the neighbourhood visiting Lady Catherine, his aunt. He falls in love with Elizabeth but phrases his proposal in so condescending a manner

that she refuses, taking the opportunity to upbraid him for his treatment of Wickham and for his role in separating Jane and Bingley. In a letter, Darcy exposes Wickham as an adventurer who had once cherished designs on Darcy's 15-year-old sister Georgiana, and protests that he had never been convinced of Jane's love for Bingley.

Elizabeth leaves on a tour of Derbyshire with her aunt and uncle, the Gardiners. They visit Pemberley, Darcy's seat, in the belief he is absent but accidentally meet him. He welcomes them, and his charm and grace begin to impress Elizabeth. Then comes the news that her sister Lydia has eloped with Wickham. Darcy helps trace the runaways and makes sure that they marry. Bingley renews his courtship of Jane and, despite insolent attempts at interference from Lady Catherine, Darcy persists in his courtship of Elizabeth. Both couples are finally united.

Priestley, J(ohn) B(oynton) 1894–1984 Novelist, playwright, critic and broadcaster. He was born in Bradford and educated locally and, after infantry service during World War I, at Trinity Hall, Cambridge. He wrote over 60 books and more than 40 plays. His wide-ranging interest in England and the English character, and his appeal to 'the man in the street', made him one of the most popular 'middlebrow' authors of his day.

His early publications include *The Chapman of Rhymes* (1918) and *Brief Diversions* (occasional pieces for *The Cambridge Review*, 1922). *Papers from Lilliput* also appeared in 1922, the year in which he became a journalist in London. During the 1920s Priestley wrote several volumes of criticism, including studies of MEREDITH (1926) and PEACOCK (1927), and several novels. His first popular success was *The Good Companions* (1929), a high-spirited novel about three people who, at crises in their lives, join a concert party. *Angel Pavement* (1930), a more sombre tale of London life, consolidated his reputation but was less popular.

Priestley made his debut as a playwright in 1931 with a dramatization of *The Good Companions* (with Edward Knoblock). His best-known works for the stage are *Dangerous Corner* (1932), *I Have been Here Before* (1937) and *Time and the Conways* (1937), known collectively as the 'Time' plays because of the use they made of theories from J. W. Dunne's *An Experiment with Time* (1927).

Postscripts (1940), *Britain Speaks* (1940) and *All England Listened* (1968) are selections from his popular wartime broadcasts. Post-war publications include novels (*Festival at Farbridge*, 1951; *Saturn over the Water*, 1961; *It's an Old Country*, 1967) and many volumes of criticism, including *The Art of the Dramatist* (1957) and *Literature and Western Man* (1960), influenced by Jung. *Martin Released* (1962) and *Instead of the Trees* (1977) are autobiographical.

Priestley, Joseph 1733–1804 Writer on science, religion and politics. A native of Fieldhead in Yorkshire, he was educated at Batley Grammar School and at Heckmondwike. He trained for the Presbyterian ministry at Daventry and became minister at Needham Market, Suffolk, in 1755 and at Nantwich in Cheshire in 1758, where he opened a school. His views became increasingly controversial and he accepted the ministry of Mill Hill Chapel, an unorthodox church in Leeds, in 1767. In his magazine, *Theological Repository*, he argued for the autonomy of the individual congregation and the proliferation of sects, attacked the principle of an Established Church and demanded complete toleration for Roman Catholics. *A History of the Corruptions of Christianity* (1782), published soon after he had become a minister of the New Meeting Society in Birmingham, was widely read and widely resented, while *A History of Early Opinions concerning Jesus Christ* (1786) provoked an attack from Samuel Horsley, Bishop of St Asaph. Priestley denied the infallibility of Christ, though throughout his life he held to a belief in Christ as the Messiah. In 1791 he became one of the founders of the Unitarian Society.

His politics were as radical as his theology. *An Essay of the First Principles of Government* (1768) first stated the idea, later developed by JEREMY BENTHAM and the UTILITARIANS, that the happiness of the majority is 'the great standard by which everything relating to that state must finally be determined'. His support for the French Revolution, expressed in his *Letters to Edmund Burke* (1791), earned him the nickname 'Gunpowder' Priestley and provoked a Church and King mob to wreck his house in Birmingham. After an interval in London, Priestley went to America in 1794 and spent his remaining years in Northumberland, Pennsylvania.

His scientific work was of lasting importance. After publishing *The History and Present State of Electricity* (1767) and conducting a series of groundbreaking experiments with electricity, he turned his attention to chemistry. The years 1772–80 when his appointment as librarian to Lord Shelburne gave him additional leisure to pursue his experiments with gases were particularly fruitful. Priestley discovered oxygen (1774), hydrochloric acid, nitric oxide, sulphur dioxide, silicone tetrafluoride and other gases.

Prime Minister, The A novel BY ANTHONY TROLLOPE, the fifth of his PALLISER NOVELS, serialized in monthly parts from November 1875 to June 1876 and published in four volumes in 1876.

Ferdinand Lopez, an adventurer of doubtful ancestry and profession, wants to marry Emily Wharton. Her crusty but honest father objects to their marriage on the grounds that Lopez is not a 'gentleman', preferring instead the well-bred Arthur Fletcher, a hardworking barrister. Emily and Lopez marry, but his true nature emerges when he gets her to extract money from her father to finance his shady speculations. In a parallel plot Plantagenet Palliser, now Duke of Omnium, becomes Prime Minister at the head of an insecure coalition government, which Lady Glencora helps to sustain with lavish entertaining at Gatherum Castle. There she meets Lopez and foolishly encourages him to stand in the Silverbridge by-election. Although the duke will have nothing to do with it, he is embarrassed when Lopez loses and accuses the duchess of treachery. To protect his wife the duke pays the election expenses demanded by Lopez, and this becomes a source of scandal until Phineas Finn silences the gossip with an effective speech in the House of Commons. Meanwhile the financial affairs of Lopez and his partner deteriorate, and he commits suicide by throwing himself in front of a train. In due course Emily marries Arthur Fletcher and the duke's coalition government falls.

In *The Prime Minister* Plantagenet Palliser is revealed as a man too thin-skinned for party politics but remarkable for his honesty and integrity, Trollope's 'perfect gentleman'.

Prime of Miss Jean Brodie, The A novel by MURIEL SPARK, published in 1961.

Miss Jean Brodie is a schoolmistress in Edinburgh during the 1930s. Her ideas about the education of her pupils and about her own role at the Marcia Blaines School for Girls are out of place but representative of 'those women who from the age of thirty and upwards... crowned their war-bereaved spinsterhood with voyages of discovery into new ideas and energetic practices in art or social welfare, education or religion'. The 'Brodie set', as her five 16-year-old charges are scornfully nicknamed, are tutored in Renaissance painting, the advantages of cleansing cream over 'honest soap', and the love life of CHARLOTTE BRONTË and of Miss Brodie herself. She becomes the subject of intense fascination for the girls, and they are increasingly drawn into her emotional life and her relationships with the art master, Teddy Lloyd, and the singing master, Gordon Lowther. The girls too are famous for different things: Monica Douglas for mathematics, Rose Stanley for sex, Eunice Gardiner for gymnastics and 'glamorous swimming', Mary Macgregor for being a scapegoat, and Sandy Stranger for her 'vowel sounds' in recitation. Sandy has an affair with Teddy Lloyd during the summer of 1938 and the effects of Miss Brodie's teaching concern the headmistress, Miss Mackay. Betrayed by Sandy, Miss Brodie is eventually forced to retire at the end of 1939 on the grounds that she has been teaching Fascism. The 'Brodie set' leave school to meet very different and in some cases tragic fates but the colourful and morally ambiguous influence of 'Miss Jean Brodie in her prime' endures long after her death.

Prince, F(rank) T(empleton) 1912– Poet and scholar. Born in South Africa, he was educated there, at Balliol College, Oxford, and at Princeton University. During World War II he served in the Intelligence Corps. From 1954 to 1974 he was professor of English at Southampton University; in 1973 he delivered the Clark lectures at Cambridge. His first book, *Poems*, appeared in 1938 but he established his reputation with the widely anthologized 'Soldiers Bathing', which became the title poem of a later collection (1954). Subsequent volumes include *The Doors of Stone* (1963), *Collected Poems* (1979), *Later On* (1983) and *Walls in Rome: Poems* (1987). Many poems derive from imaginary confrontations with past events and people, including Michelangelo, BYRON, SHELLEY and RUPERT BROOKE. Scholarly works include the Arden edition of SHAKESPEARE's *Poems* (1960).

Prince and the Pauper, The: *A Tale for Young People of All Ages* A novel by MARK TWAIN, published in England in 1881 and in the USA in 1882. It is set during the last years of Henry VIII's reign and tells how Prince Edward and a pauper boy exchange places by mistake.

The Prince encounters the poor Tom Canty, and is fascinated to see that they appear to be exact twins. They exchange clothes, and the Prince is chased from the palace by guards. He is abused by Tom's family, and then wanders through London in rags until a disinherited knight, Miles Hendson, takes pity on the boy, whom he believes – from his repeated claim to royal birth – to be unbalanced. In Miles's company Edward sees at first hand the wretchedness of the poor and the cruelty of the law. Meanwhile, Tom has been treated as a prince, and when the king dies he is prepared for coronation. Edward makes his way to Westminster Abbey and manages to establish his identity by revealing the whereabouts of the Great Seal. The Prince becomes Edward VI, and during his brief reign does his best to keep in mind the lessons of his own days as a pauper.

Prince's Progress, The An allegorical poem by CHRISTINA ROSSETTI, published in 1866. A prince sets out confidently and happily to claim his bride. In the course of his long and arduous journey he yields to temptation, seeking mere comfort at first but then turning to one pleasing distraction after another. When he arrives he finds that the princess who had been awaiting him has died of despair.

Princess, The: *A Medley* A poem by ALFRED TENNYSON, first published in 1847.

Framed by its setting of the typically English estate of Sir Walter Vivian, who 'all in a summer's day/ Gave his broad lawns until the set of sun/ Up to the people', *The Princess* consists of a Prologue, Conclusion, and seven parts. They tell the story of a Prince, subject to

'weird seizures', whose betrothed, Princess Ida, daughter of King Gama, rejects marriage, preferring 'to live alone/ Among her women' and to found a centre of learning devoted to feminists. The Prince, accompanied by two friends Florian and Cyril, gain admittance to this fortress disguised as women but their identities are soon revealed, although not before the Prince has rescued the Princess from drowning. Further complications of an amatory nature involve Cyril and Florian. The kingly fathers of the Prince and Princess almost do battle; Arac, the Princess's brother, appears, and ultimately his forces and those of the Prince engage in combat. Arac is victorious, the Prince, Cyril and Florian are all wounded, the Princess modifies her feminism, her college is transformed into a hospital, and all parties are happily reconciled.

It is perhaps unnecessary to add that the narrative of *The Princess* is not its principal strength. But the poem is a characteristically Tennysonian work in its dichotomy between the pragmatic and the lyrical. On the one hand, the poem manifests the growing Victorian concern for geology, astronomy, mathematics, evolutionary theory, feminism, domesticity, paternalism, and other aspects of the social hierarchy; on the other, *The Princess* is a poem transformed by some of the finest lyrics in the language. At the end of each section – interpolated in the third edition of 1850 – are such enduring songs as 'Sweet and Low, Sweet and Low' and 'The Splendour Falls on Castle Walls'. Within the body of the work are 'Tears, Idle Tears' and 'Now Sleeps the Crimson Petal'.

Princess Casamassima, The A novel by HENRY JAMES, published serially in *THE ATLANTIC MONTHLY* from September 1885 to October 1886, and then in volume form in 1886.

Set in London in the 1880s, it portrays a range of characters from all social classes. The hero is an orphan boy, Hyacinth Robinson, who has been brought up by Miss Pynsent, a quiet little spinster who makes a living as a dressmaker and lives in a lower-class district of London. Hyacinth has seen his mother only once, when she was dying in prison, condemned for the murder of his father, 'Lord Frederick'. He becomes apprenticed to the book-binder Eustache Poupin, a French Communist in exile. While learning his trade he meets Paul Muniment, a proletarian revolutionary, joins a secret society, and commits himself to the movement. He also comes into contact with Christina, the Princess Casamassima, who, separated from her Italian husband (see *RODERICK HUDSON*), finds the revolutionary movement an outlet for her energies. After Miss Pynsent dies, Hyacinth travels to Europe and returns with a somewhat altered social vision. Though he no longer supports the society, he receives a summons from it to carry out the assassination of a duke. The Princess Casamassima goes to his apartment, planning to offer to substitute for him, but she arrives too late. He has given up in despair and killed himself.

Principles of Moral and Political Philosophy, The

A theological treatise by WILLIAM PALEY, published in 1785. Its argument is heavily indebted to ABRAHAM TUCKER'S *The Light of Nature Pursued* (1768–78) but presented with greater system and clarity. Paley's version of theological utilitarianism is firmly grounded in Christianity, and his ethical system requires the acknowledgement of rewards and penalties after death. Paley's skill as an expositor kept his book widely read in academic circles for a number of years.

Principles of Psychology, The

A book by WILLIAM JAMES, published in 1890. The text, 12 years in the making, was based in part on James's observations at the psychological laboratory he established at Harvard in 1876. In this laboratory, the first of its kind in the USA, James developed his functional approach to psychology. His findings indicated that the mind operates as a part of the body, and that an individual's mental adjustments are in fact environmental responses. In *Principles* he defines the mind as an instrument which, by controlling choice, effort, and will, makes adjustments which are modified by deterministic factors such as heredity and biology. The book is also notable for coining the term STREAM OF CONSCIOUSNESS.

Pringle, Thomas 1789–1834 Poet. Born at Kelso in Scotland, he completed his education at the University of Edinburgh. He published *The Institute: A Heroic Poem* (1811) and became editor of *The Edinburgh Monthly Magazine* in 1817. *The Autumnal Excursion* (1819) was published the same year that financial difficulties led him to accept the post of government librarian in Cape Town. He spent six years in South Africa, where he opened a school and founded a periodical, *The South African Journal*. This led to his dismissal by the governor, who objected to Pringle's politics and rejected his hopes of bringing the country's various cultural groups together. Pringle left South Africa in 1826 and settled in London with his family. He devoted his energies to the Anti-Slavery Society, working closely with Wilberforce and Clarkson, and to giving the first authentic breath of South Africa to English literature. His poems were published in *Ephemerides* (1828) and *African Sketches* (1834). *The History of Mary Prince, a West Indian Slave* (1831) and *Narrative of a Residence in South Africa* (1835) reinforce the humanitarian tone of his poems, which were admired by COLERIDGE and TENNYSON.

Prior, Matthew 1664–1721 Poet and diplomat. Of a humble but respectable Dorset family, Prior was born in Stephen's Alley, Westminster, and sent to nearby Westminster School. His father's death forced his withdrawal for financial reasons but he was 'discovered' by CHARLES SACKVILLE, EARL OF DORSET, who financed his return, a generosity warmly acknowledged by Prior in the dedication to his first collection of poems in 1709. He went on to St John's College, Cambridge, being elected a fellow in 1688 and retaining the position until his death.

Prior's diplomatic career began in 1690, as secretary to the British ambassador at The Hague, where he remained for seven years, for much of the time as his country's sole representative. In a series of complex negotiations he won William III's confidence, acting as a trusted itinerant diplomat. The accession of Queen Anne initially brought a reversal of fortunes, but the Tory ministry of ROBERT HARLEY, EARL OF OXFORD, revived his career and in 1711 he was secretly dispatched to France to negotiate peace. The officiousness of a British customs official resulted in a public fiasco, as recounted in SWIFT'S *A Journey to Paris* (1711).

Prior remained instrumental in Franco-British peace negotiations, both secret and public, being named Minister Plenipotentiary in 1712. His star reached its zenith when, after the signing of the Treaty of Utrecht in 1713 (popularly known as 'Matt's Peace'), he was Louis XIV's personal guest at Fontainebleau in the autumn. The death of Queen Anne in 1714 brought a new administration, hostile to Prior; returning to England the following year, he was arrested, interrogated and imprisoned for more than a year. He retired to private life, occupied in the preparation of the great subscription edition of his works, a massively handsome folio published in 1718, and in the beautification of the country house, Down Hall, which he had bought with EDWARD HARLEY's aid. On 18 September 1721, Prior, whose health had always been delicate, died of cholera. At his request, he was buried in Westminster Abbey at the feet of his favourite poet, SPENSER.

Prior first achieved fame as a poet with SATIRES on DRYDEN, particularly with his lively, good-humoured BURLESQUE of *THE HIND AND THE PANTHER* as *The Hind and the Panther Transversed to the Story of the Country Mouse and the City Mouse* (1687), written in collaboration with his friend Charles Montague. The bulk of his work consists of occasional pieces: burlesques, epistles, lyrics, patriotic ODES, BALLADS and imitations of CHAUCER and Spenser. His comic writing is made particularly vivid by his wry self-characterization (as Matt). Serious works include *Carmen Seculare* (1700), eulogizing his master William III, and the weighty *Solomon on the Vanity of the World* (1718), in three books. *Alma: or, the Progress of the Mind* (1718), written in prison, is a witty mock-scholastic conversation between Matt and a friend, a burlesque counterpart to *Solomon*. These were the two works Prior himself most valued. In his last years he began work on the superlative *Dialogues of the Dead*, a sequence of imaginary conversations – that between Montaigne and JOHN LOCKE is the most brilliant. Prior's voice, vivacious and well-mannered, conforms to his own ideal: 'a style close, distinct, and familiar; and in your writing easy and civil'.

Prioress's Tale, The See CANTERBURY TALES, THE.

Prisoner of Zenda, The A novel by ANTHONY HOPE, published in 1894. It follows the swashbuckling adventures of Rudolf Rassendyll, an Englishman who bears a striking resemblance to the King of Ruritania. When the monarch is kidnapped by his enemies Black Michael and Rupert of Hentzau, Rassendyll impersonates him and helps thwart the plot to usurp the throne. A sequel, *Rupert of Hentzau*, appeared in 1898.

Pritchett, Sir **V(ictor) S(awdon)** 1900– Man of letters. Born in Ipswich and educated at Dulwich College, he became a journalist in 1923, serving as literary critic of *The New Statesman* for 20 years and as director from 1946 to 1978. Although he has also published novels, travel books and biographies, he is best known as a critic and short-story writer. His collections of stories include *The Spanish Virgin and Other Stories* (1932), *You Make Your Own Life* (1938), *It May Never Happen* (1945), *When My Girl Comes Home* (1961) and *The Camberwell Beauty* (1974). His criticism includes studies of GEORGE MEREDITH (1970), Balzac (1973) and Turgenev (1977). *Dead Man Leading* (1937) and *Mr Beluncle* (1951) are among his novels. *A Cab at the Door* (1968) is a notable autobiography. He was knighted in 1975.

Private Lives A comedy by NOËL COWARD, first performed at the Phoenix Theatre, London, in 1930, with the author, Gertrude Lawrence and Laurence Olivier in the cast.

A divorced couple, Elyot and Amanda, meet while honeymooning at Deauville after their marriage to

A scene from Act II of Coward's *Private Lives* with Noël Coward as Elyot and Gertrude Lawrence as Amanda

new partners. Still powerfully attracted to each other, they run off to Paris together, only to rediscover the reasons for the original separation. Their deserted spouses catch up with them just as their quarrels edge towards violence; but the following morning they sneak off again, leaving their partners squabbling. Whatever Elyot and Amanda may do to each other, they always prefer each other's company.

Private Memoirs and Confessions of a Justified Sinner, The A novel by JAMES HOGG, published in 1824. Chilling, psychologically challenging and grimly humorous, it is the most ambitious, and now most widely read, of Hogg's prose works. Set against the background of the violent religious and political divisions of late-17th-century Scotland, the story is divided into two main parts, the first of which contains the 'editor's narrative' of the strife-torn marriage of the Lord of Dalcastle and the mysteriously contrived murder of his son and heir, George Colwan, in circumstances pointing to the complicity of his half-brother Robert Wringhim, a Calvinist bigot. The second part consists of Wringhim's own memoir which is discovered in his grave a century after his presumed suicide. In it he reveals how, with the aid of the uncanny skills of a malign *alter ego*, or *Doppelgänger*, he murdered first a preacher, then his brother, and then apparently his mother, having been persuaded by his helper's antinomian sophistry that he was thereby doing God's work, and that no act he might commit could affect his predestined salvation. He gradually realizes that the companion is in fact the Devil, who appears to have claimed him in the end, for the body found beside the memoir is still firmly covered with flesh and the skull appears to have grown a tiny pair of horns.

Private Papers of Henry Ryecroft, The A novel by GEORGE GISSING, published in 1903. It takes the form of a journal kept by a recluse who has been helped by a legacy from a friend to withdraw from the London literary world where he had failed as a writer.

private theatres The indoor playhouses of Elizabethan, Jacobean and Caroline London were, and still are, sometimes called 'private theatres' to distinguish them from the open-air PUBLIC THEATRES. They were, in fact, open to the public on payment of an admission charge, generally higher than at the public theatres, but the fiction that they were private made a useful defence against interference from the civic authorities. The first actors to use private playhouses were choristers (see BOY'S COMPANIES), and it was convenient for their managers to claim that what the public witnessed were private rehearsals of plays for presentation at court. The main private theatres were the unknown home of the Boys of St Paul's (c. 1575), the first BLACKFRIARS (1576), the second Blackfriars (1600), the Whitefriars (1605-8), the Cockpit or Phoenix (1616) and the Salisbury Court (1629). More genuinely private were the COURT THEATRES.

problem play A term in common use by the end of the 19th century to describe plays dealing with contemporary social and moral issues. Even in England and the USA, where he was frequently denounced, Ibsen was the major inspiration of a new seriousness, and his influence lies behind the problem plays of PINERO, HENRY ARTHUR JONES, GALSWORTHY and GRANVILLE-BARKER, as it does behind the more openly subversive early plays of SHAW.

It was F. S. Boas who, in 1896, first applied the term to a group of plays by SHAKESPEARE, and it has kept some critical currency as a group title for the three tragicomedies, *ALL'S WELL THAT ENDS WELL, MEASURE FOR MEASURE* and *TROILUS AND CRESSIDA*. Each of these plays addresses with a harshness untypical of Shakespeare's comedies the interrelationship of private and public morality. Some critics have proposed the advantage of associating *JULIUS CAESAR* and *HAMLET* with Shakespeare's problem plays.

Procter, Adelaide Anne 1825-64 Poet. The daughter of B. W. Procter (BARRY CORNWALL), she published sentimental verse: *Legends and Lyrics* (two series, 1858 and 1861), *A Chaplet of Verses* (1862) and *The Message* (1892). Her work was popular in its day, and admirers included CHARLES DICKENS.

Professor, The CHARLOTTE BRONTË's first completed novel, written in 1846 but not published until 1857, two years after her death. It draws on the same experiences that she was later to use more successfully in *VILLETTE*. An Englishman, William Crimsworth, goes to Brussels as a schoolmaster and falls in love with Frances Henri, a fellow teacher and Anglo-Swiss girl.

Prometheus Unbound A CLOSET DRAMA by SHELLEY, written in 1818-19 and published in 1820.

The action is drawn from Aeschylus' *Prometheus Bound* and what is known of its lost sequel *Prometheus Unbound*, though, as he explains in his preface, Shelley felt obliged to depart from the Greek dramatist's 'feeble' idea of 'reconciling the Champion with the Oppressor of mankind'. A second, more positive, source of inspiration was MILTON's Satan, whom Shelley considered to be the real hero of *PARADISE LOST*, with God occupying the role of tyrant. Combining, rewriting and updating these two myths, he creates a Prometheus of beauty, energy and moral perfection, who suffers the persecution of a jealous, irrational and wholly vindictive God. His liberation by the personified forces of Hope, Love and 'Necessity' brings about the triumph of mankind over tyranny, and the transfiguration of the world in a new golden age. Partly mythical drama, partly political ALLEGORY, the work blends Shelley's preoccupations as poet, philosopher and radical into a sequence of powerful symbolic tableaux, cast in a bewildering variety of forms: dreams, visions, epic narrative, rhetorical soliloquies, songs, choruses and dramatic dialogues.

Act I opens with Prometheus chained to a precipice in the Indian Caucasus, where his heart is daily consumed by Jupiter's eagle. Aided by his mother, the Earth, he recalls his curse of Jupiter, and his hatred for his adversary turns to pity. Mercury is sent by Jupiter with a vast chorus of Furies who tempt him to despair with visions of human inadequacy: he is made to relive the failure of the French Revolution, and sees Christ eternally crucified, and 'Wailing for the faith he kindled'. Panthea (Hope) reminds him of her sister Asia (Love), whom he has forgotten. In Act II Panthea tells Asia of her dream of Prometheus rejuvenated by love, and together they follow the mysterious echo of a second dream to the dark underworld realm of Demogorgon, the 'people-monster', an inscrutable ultimate source of revolutionary power, whom Asia rouses into action with her passionate declaration of love for suffering humanity. Jupiter is summarily overthrown by Demogorgon at the beginning of Act III, and the unchained Prometheus is reunited with Asia. The Spirit of the Hour describes the universal liberation consequent upon the fall of kings, and the end of social classes, nations and racial distinctions. Act IV, which Shelley added as an afterthought, is a kind of coda or epithalamion, sung first by a chorus of Spirits of the Hour and another chorus of the Spirits of the Human Mind; then by the Spirit of the Earth (male) and the Spirit of the Moon (female).

The first two acts of the drama must count among Shelley's poetic masterpieces, though there are considerable differences of opinion on Acts III and IV, which some consider anticlimactic. The centrality of the theme of liberation is clear but Shelley's magic-wand approach to revolutionary processes has been variously commented upon, and the figure of Demogorgon remains open to conflicting readings.

Proposal for the Universal Use of Irish Manufacture The first of JONATHAN SWIFT's pamphlets about Ireland, published in 1720. It protests against the exploitation of the Irish economy by England, proposing that the home-produced cloth of Ireland – devalued because the English in Ireland regarded it without justification as inferior – should be promoted as an industry and that imported fabrics from England should be boycotted.

Prothalamion The word was invented by SPENSER to entitle his poem to celebrate the double betrothal of Katherine and Elizabeth, daughters of the Earl of Worcester. They were married in November 1596, the same year in which the poem was published. 'Prothalamion' is glossed in the poem's title as 'a spousal verse' and Spenser formed the word by analogy with 'epithalamion' (marriage-song). His own EPITHALAMION had appeared in 1595. The poem's ten stanzas, modelled on Italian *canzoni*, offer a description by a discontented courtier of sights along the Thames, the most important being 'two swans of goodly hue' (Katherine and Elizabeth Somerset). Stanza nine makes complimentary reference to Essex. The poem has been praised for its graceful movement and music. Its famous refrain 'Sweet Thames run softly, till I end my song' is echoed by T. S. ELIOT in THE WASTE LAND.

Prout, Father See MAHONY, FRANCIS SYLVESTER.

Proverbial Philosophy See TUPPER, MARTIN.

Provincetown Players See GLASPELL, SUSAN and O'NEILL, EUGENE.

Provoked Wife, The A comedy by SIR JOHN VANBRUGH, produced and published in 1697.

Sir John Brute is a coward and a bully whose wife suffers greatly. Lady Brute has a devoted admirer, Constant, but she has remained true to her marriage vows. Constant's friend Heartfree has always declared his indifference to women, but falls in love with Bellinda, Lady Brute's niece. Bellinda persuades her aunt to join her in a lighthearted frolic, a meeting with Heartfree and Constant in Spring Garden whilst Sir John is out drinking. Lady Brute finds Constant's attentions persuasive and is about to yield when the jealous and spiteful Lady Fancyfull intrudes upon them. The two couples hurry away from the garden and repair to Lady Brute's house, where they sit down to cards. Sir John Brute, meanwhile, has been indulging in drunken and vulgar behaviour with Lord Rake and Colonel Bully, and has taken a parson's gown from a poor tailor. He is wearing it when he is arrested for brawling; the magistrate dismisses him and he lurches off home unexpectedly early. Constant and Heartfree hide in a closet, where he discovers them. But he is outfaced by Constant and accepts that the two men are present because of Heartfree's forthcoming marriage to Bellinda, though he is sure in his own mind that he has been cuckolded. Lady Fancyfull does her best to make mischief but fails because her fellow conspirator Rasor, Sir John Brute's valet, baulks at the extent of her spite. The play ends with Bellinda's marriage to Heartfree.

COLLEY CIBBER later completed and staged Vanbrugh's unfinished *A Journey to London* as *The Provoked Husband* (1728). It does not involve the same characters.

Provost, The A novel by JOHN GALT, published in 1822. An essay in sustained irony, it displays his rich humour, ready sympathy and fine command of the Scots vernacular in all its shades. The story is narrated by Mr Pawkie, who has three times reached the office of provost (mayor). He unwittingly reveals his own canny nature as he reflects on his progress through public life and contrasts the sophistication of the wider world of business and politics with the manners and speech of provincial Scotland.

Prynne, J(eremy) H(alward) 1936– Poet. Born in Kent and educated at St Dunstan's College and at Jesus College, Cambridge, where he read English, he spent a year in the USA before returning to Cambridge to become a Fellow of Gonville and Caius College in 1962. He is the leading British exponent of a post-modernist, experimental poetry which has its origins in the later work of EZRA POUND and in the 'projective verse' of CHARLES OLSON. His work avoids concentration on an identifiable subject matter and instead uses enigmatic imagery and disorientating twists and fractures of syntax to force the reader into a self-conscious awareness of the processes of reading and writing. His volumes include *Kitchen Poems* (1968), *Brass* (1971), *Into the Day* (1972), *High Pink on Chrome* (1975), *Down Where Change* (1979), *Poems* (1982) and *The Oval Window* (1983). Seen as a difficult poet, he has nevertheless attracted a considerable following and influenced younger writers.

Prynne, William 1600–69 Puritan pamphleteer. Born in Somerset, he attended Bath Grammar School and Oriel College, Oxford, and then studied law at Lincoln's Inn; he was called to the Bar in 1628. A fanatical Puritan, Prynne published a 'pamphlet' of over 1000 pages, *Histrio-Mastix* (1632), attacking the playhouses. Archbishop LAUD decided that the work contained veiled attacks on Henrietta Maria and King Charles, and Prynne was sentenced by the Star Chamber in 1634 to life imprisonment, a huge fine, loss of his law and university degrees, and the pillory, where his ears were 'cropped'. He was later branded for sedition.

Prynne was freed by the Long Parliament in 1640 and emerged as a hero. In 1648 he became MP for Newport and, surprisingly, opposed the trial and execution of Charles I. He became therefore a victim of Pride's Purge and suffered imprisonment again. However, he continued as an MP, opposing the Commonwealth Army and the Rump Parliament until in 1660 he brought in the bill dissolving Parliament for the restoration of the monarchy. Charles II made him Keeper of the Tower Records and Prynne continued writing busily until the end of his days. He was the author of no fewer than 200 miscellaneous works.

Psalters The book of 150 psalms in the Old Testament, traditionally ascribed to King David, was the basis for the liturgy of the medieval church. There is a long tradition of Old and Middle English Psalters. The version in the BOOK OF COMMON PRAYER is largely based on the translation by MILES COVERDALE in his first complete Bible of 1535 (see BIBLE IN ENGLISH). Coverdale's metrical version of 13 psalms, *Ghostly Psalms and Spiritual Songs*, with words and tunes mainly adapted from Lutheran sources, was printed *c.* 1539.

Frequently reprinted – even annually after 1549 – was the *Whole Books of Psalms Collected into English Metre*, by T. Sternhold and J. Hopkins, a version with tunes adapted from the Genevan Psalter. This was the Old Version (hence 'Old Hundredth' as the name of the hymn tune for 'All People That on Earth Do Dwell'). *The Bay Psalm Book* (1640), a translation by RICHARD MATHER, JOHN ELIOT and Thomas Weld which replaced the Sternhold and Hopkins version in the Massachusetts Bay Colony, was the first book printed in America; revised by Henry Dunster and Richard Lyon as *The Psalms, Hymns and Scriptural Songs of the Old and New Testament* (1651), it was reissued several times in the following century.

In England there were many publications of metrical psalms in various arrangements between the Old Version and the New Version by Nicholas Brady and NAHUM TATE (1696). The whole Psalter was translated into metrical forms by MATTHEW PARKER, SIR PHILIP SIDNEY and JAMES I, and parts by JOHN MILTON, FRANCIS BACON, GEORGE HERBERT, RICHARD CRASHAW, HENRY VAUGHAN and others. For over a thousand years the Psalter has been one of the greatest influences on English lyric poetry.

Pseudodoxia Epidemica: or, Enquiries into Very Many Received Tenents and Commonly Presumed Truths Often known as *Vulgar Errors*. SIR THOMAS BROWNE's second work, published in 1646; revised and expanded editions appeared in 1650, 1658 and 1672. It investigates credulity and popular hearsay, analysing the reasons for mistaken beliefs and tracing their origins in the susceptibility of humans to the dictates of others, as well as the ultimate agency of Satan. Browne enquires widely into instances of such mistakes, wittily and vivaciously rummaging through legends and cherished beliefs which result from gullibility, deceit, custom and superstition.

psychoanalytic criticism A loose label for the various methods or theories of criticism ultimately derived from Freud's therapeutic technique for uncovering the unconscious repressions of childhood emotions. His analytic methods have sometimes been applied to literary texts on the assumption that the author's repressed emotions were at work in the text's affective patterns – that texts are shaped by unconscious desire. The unconscious often expresses itself in dreams, jokes and ambiguous uses of language, and especially in figurative language. Freud discovered that forbidden thoughts are retold by patients under the influences of certain mental processes, including displacement (of an emotional focus from one object to another) and condensation (of several ideas into one), which correspond (as Roman Jakobson shows) to two figures of speech – METAPHOR and METONYMY (see also STRUCTURALISM).

Among modern critical uses of psychoanalysis is the development of 'ego-psychology' in the work of Norman Holland, who concentrates on the relations between reader and text. He argues that readers use texts in order to satisfy unconscious wishes. In recent studies he sees reading as the re-creation of the reader's identity: the text's challenging nature requires some adjustment of identity but also is matched by the self-confirming ruses of the reader.

Jacques Lacan (1901–81) has reinterpreted Freud in the light of structuralism and POST-STRUCTURALISM. He questions the static concepts of ego-psychology, and produces a new theory of the 'subject' by inserting a structural linguistics into Freud's theory of the unconscious processes. The 'I' is a signifier which takes on meaning (substantial identity etc.) only within a language system. Sexual identity and position within the family system are a product of this entry into the symbolic system of language. Before this stage there is only the rule of the 'pleasure principle'. Part of the process of identity formation is the repression of desire following the Oedipal phase. However, the desire will not go away, and, remaining in the unconscious, produces a split subject, which never possesses full 'presence'.

Lacan's theories have encouraged a criticism which focuses not on the author but on the linguistic processes of the text. He himself in his celebrated study of POE's 'The Purloined Letter', shows that the text reduplicates the processes of the unconscious: the letter represents the unconscious and its (dis)placements in the story determine the positions of the characters. He reads the story as an allegory of psychoanalyis itself: the letter (signifier) lures both the writer and the reader, for it embodies their unconscious drives. This means that meaning is nothing more than the shifting chains of desire in language. Either the writer or the reader can try to impose his or her desire upon the letter. For Lacan art is never representation: even the most realistic novel involves fantasy and wish fulfilment.

Jung's theory of a collective unconscious manifested in certain recurring images, stories and forms, which he called 'archetypes', has also left its imprint on criticism. MAUD BODKIN, NORTHROP FRYE, Leslie Fiedler and others have traced in literary texts the presence of the archetypal patterns which express the most profound and universal experiences of human existence.

Public Advertiser, The A newspaper founded in 1752 as *The London Daily Post and General Advertiser*; it ceased publication in 1798, when it was amalgamated with JOHN NEWBERY's *The Public Ledger*. The paper carried home and foreign news as well as a great deal of political correspondence, including a dispute between JOHN WILKES and JOHN HORNE TOOKE. The letters of JUNIUS were published in its pages by Henry Sampson Woodfall, editor from 1758 to 1793.

public theatres The open-air theatres of Elizabethan, Jacobean and Caroline London were, and still are, sometimes called 'public' playhouses to distinguish them from the equally public but more exclusive indoor PRIVATE THEATRES. They are, in approximate chronological order, the THEATRE (1576), the Curtain (1577), a theatre of unknown name in Newington Butts (c. 1580), the ROSE (c. 1587), the SWAN (1595), the GLOBE (1599), the Boar's Head (c. 1599), the FORTUNE (1600), the Red Bull (1605), the second Globe (1614), the HOPE (1614) and the second Fortune (1623).

Puck of Pook's Hill A collection of 10 stories and accompanying poems by RUDYARD KIPLING, published in 1906. The stories were intended for both adults and children.

The meeting of two children, Dan and Una (loosely modelled on Kipling's own children), with the nature spirit Puck provides the framework for tales reaching back in English history, past the Normans and Saxons to the Roman invaders. Most show individuals who are able to illuminate their historical predicaments, such as the centurion, Parnesius, whose unorthodox handling of his Imperial duties – in co-operating with the Picts – shows an insight which is absent from the higher echelons of the declining Roman Empire. The stories also point to the capacity of civilization to renew itself. The God Weland, in 'Weland's Sword', is freed from an unwanted heathen immortality by a novice monk, Hugh. While Weland adapts to the Christian world, Hugh becomes a warrior. Along with one of the Norman invaders, Sir Richard Dalyngridge, he brings leadership and good management to the land. The figure of Old Hobden, known to Dan and Una as someone who had instinctive understanding of local traditions and the ways of the world, is also a representative of a stoical spirit in the common man which can endure historical change.

A sequel to the collection, *Rewards and Fairies* (1910), followed a similar format. Both volumes contain some of Kipling's best-known verse. In the latter volume particularly, 'A St Helena's Lullaby', 'The Way through the Woods' and 'If' have been much admired.

Puckering, Sir John 1544–96 Sir John Puckering is identified as the 'John Pickering' who wrote *Horestes*, a play which is itself identified as the *Orestes* acted at court in 1567 or 1568 and published just before it was produced. Puckering was a lawyer of Lincoln's Inn who later became Lord Keeper of the Seal and who was an implacable enemy of Mary of Scotland.

Horestes was a distinct advance on the bombastic clumsiness of contemporary works such as *CAMBISES* and *Appius and Virginia*. There are still hangovers from the MORALITY PLAYS in the characters who personify Vice, Revenge and Nature; but the action develops steadily and the speeches by the principal characters mix credibility and poetry.

Pudd'nhead Wilson, The Tragedy of A novel by MARK TWAIN, published in 1894. The title character of this story of confused identities is a lawyer, David Wilson, called 'Pudd'nhead' by a community which ridicules his eccentric ideas and practices.

The story takes place in the Missouri town of Dawson's Landing in the 1830s. Tom, the son of the prosperous slave-owner Percy Driscoll, is born on the same day as Chambers, the son of one of Driscoll's slaves, a light-skinned woman named Roxana, and a Virginian gentleman. The children closely resemble each other. Roxy is afraid that Chambers might eventually be sold down the river, so she switches the two babies to protect her son. When Percy Driscoll dies, his brother Judge Driscoll adopts Chambers, thinking him to be Tom. The boy grows up to be a bully, a gambler, and an arrogant coward. To pay his gambling debts he decides to sell Roxy, but she escapes from her new owners and blackmails him with the secret of his true birth. He resorts to stealing to help pay his various debts, and, during a robbery attempt, murders the Judge with a knife he had stolen from Luigi, one of a pair of aristocratic Italian twins who have recently arrived in town. Although the twins were initially well received, the false Tom had caused a series of disturbances which led to enmity between them and Judge Driscoll. It is therefore supposed by all that Luigi committed the murder. The unpractised attorney 'Pudd'nhead' Wilson successfully proves Luigi's innocence by showing that the fingerprints on the knife belong to the false Tom. He also establishes the true identities of Tom and Chambers. Wilson becomes a town celebrity, the disgraced Chambers is sold down the river as a slave and Roxy is supported by her surrogate son, the true Tom.

Pulitzer Prizes A group of American literary prizes awarded annually to works in the following categories: fiction, drama, poetry, history, biography and general non-fiction (or journalism). They were founded in 1917 as part of the bequest with which the newspaper proprietor Joseph Pulitzer (1847–1911) established the Columbia University School of Journalism. The prizes for poetry and for journalism were added to the original categories in 1921 and 1962 respectively. The terms of the fiction prize,

which originally specified that the work should have an American subject, were relaxed in 1932 to allow the award to go to PEARL BUCK's *The Good Earth* and in 1947 to allow collections of short stories as well as novels to be considered.

From the earliest days an impressive number of major writers have featured in the lists of prize-winners. Novelists have included EDITH WHARTON (for *THE AGE OF INNOCENCE* in 1921), WILLA CATHER (for *One of Ours* in 1923) and JOHN STEINBECK (for *THE GRAPES OF WRATH* in 1940). EUGENE O'NEILL was honoured in 1920, 1922, 1928 (for *STRANGE INTERLUDE*) and posthumously in 1957 (for *LONG DAY'S JOURNEY INTO NIGHT*). THORNTON WILDER received the prize for *OUR TOWN* in 1938 and *The Skin of Our Teeth* in 1943 as well as for his novel *The Bridge of San Luis Rey* in 1928. EDWIN ARLINGTON ROBINSON, first winner of the poetry prize in 1922, went on to win it twice more, while ROBERT FROST, first honoured in 1924, again won the prize in 1931, 1937 and 1943. Any list of prescient choices would certainly mention the awards to ROBERT PENN WARREN for *All the King's Men* in 1947, TENNESSEE WILLIAMS for *A STREETCAR NAMED DESIRE* in 1948 and *CAT ON A HOT TIN ROOF* in 1955, and ARTHUR MILLER for *DEATH OF A SALESMAN* in 1949.

These examples take their place among the many forgotten items, like Ernest Poole's *Our Family*, the first novel to be honoured, and Jesse L. Williams's *Why Marry?*, the first play. Major writers have sometimes been acknowledged only late in their career or, as in the case of WALLACE STEVENS and WILLIAM CARLOS WILLIAMS, in the year of their death. No award was given to HEMINGWAY until 1953 (for *The Old Man and the Sea*) or to FAULKNER until 1955 (for *A Fable*). The fiction category, in particular, was for many years tainted with insularity and conservatism even though it had shed the terms of its original rubric, which spoke embarrassingly of 'the American novel published during the year which shall best present the wholesome atmosphere of American life and the highest standard of American manners and manhood'. One result was a liking for safe best-sellers. In 1937 Margaret Mitchell's *GONE WITH THE WIND* was preferred to Faulkner's *ABSALOM, ABSALOM!* and the concluding part of JOHN DOS PASSOS's *USA*, and in 1952 Herman Wouk's *The Caine Mutiny* was preferred to Faulkner's *Requiem for a Nun* and J. D. SALINGER's *CATCHER IN THE RYE*. The most extraordinary omission from the list of prize-winners is F. SCOTT FITZGERALD. In 1926 *THE GREAT GATSBY* was passed over in favour of SINCLAIR LEWIS's *Arrowsmith* and in 1935 the panel judged Pauline Johnson's *Now in November* a more distinguished work than *TENDER IS THE NIGHT*.

Punch: or, The London Charivari A weekly comic magazine founded in 1841, partly through the efforts of HENRY MAYHEW, with MARK LEMON and Joseph

Stirling Coyne (1803–68), his joint editors, and a circle of contributors which included GILBERT À BECKETT, THOMAS HOOD, DOUGLAS JERROLD and THACKERAY. JOHN LEECH was the chief artist and RICHARD DOYLE drew the famous cover. Originally noted for its radical abrasiveness, *Punch* soon settled for a more comfortable style of humour that came to be seen as typically English. Shirley Brooks (1816–74) and TOM TAYLOR were among later editors; its artists included SIR JOHN TENNIEL (1820–1914), Charles Keene (1823–91), GEORGE DU MAURIER and Linley Sambourne (1845–1910). It ceased publication in 1992.

Punch's Prize Novelists A series of PARODIES of contemporary novelists by W. M. THACKERAY, published in *PUNCH* from April to October 1847, with his own illustrations, and later retitled *Novels by Eminent Hands*. The targets include BULWER LYTTON, FENIMORE COOPER, G. P. R. JAMES, CHARLES LEVER and DISRAELI, whose *CONINGSBY* is devastatingly mocked in 'Codlingsby'. Thackeray's playful critique of fashionable fiction throws light on his intentions and achievements in *VANITY FAIR*, written at the same time.

Purchas, Samuel c. 1575–1626 Historian and travel-writer. Born at Thaxted in Essex and educated at St John's College, Cambridge, Purchas was vicar of a parish on the Thames estuary for ten years and then became rector of St Martin's, Ludgate. He published *Purchas His Pilgrimage: or, Relations of the World and the Religions Observed in All Ages* in 1613 and *Purchas His Pilgrim: Microcosmus: or, the Histories of Man* in 1619. An assistant to RICHARD HAKLUYT in his later years, Purchas inherited the maritime historian's manuscripts and compiled the extensive *Hakluyt Posthumous: or, Purchas His Pilgrims: Containing a History of the World, in Sea Voyages and Land Travels by Englishmen and Others* (1625). Of the book's two parts, the first deals with the Mediterranean and the East, the second with the Northwest Passage, Russia (Muscovy), the West Indies and Florida. Although generally considered inferior to Hakluyt's work, it contains some notable accounts, particularly William Adams's description of his journey to Japan and his residence there.

Purdy, Al(fred) (Wellington) 1918– Canadian poet. Born in Wooller, Ontario, he left school at 16 and embarked on a wandering life before settling at Roblin Lake at Ameliasburgh. One of his country's finest contemporary poets, he presents the people of modern Canada against a vivid background of allusion and imagery drawn from mythological and historical sources. His verse is firmly rooted in the landscapes and idioms of Eastern Ontario. Numerous volumes include *Poems for All the Annettes* (1962), *The Cariboo Horses* (1965), *North of Summer: Poems*

from Baffin Island (1967), *Wild Grape Wine* (1968), *Love in a Burning Building* (1970), *Hiroshima Poems* (1972), *In Search of Owen Roblin* (1974), *To Feed the Sun* (1976), *A Handful of Earth* (1977), *Moths in the Iron Curtain* (1979), *The Stone Bird* (1981), *Piling Blood* (1984) and *The Woman on the Shore* (1990). His verse is gathered in *Being Alive* (1978) and *The Collected Poems of Al Purdy* (1986). *A Splinter in the Heart* (1990) is a novel.

Purdy, James 1923– American novelist. Born in Ohio, he was educated at the universities of Chicago and Puebla, Mexico. His first book, a collection of short stories entitled *Color of Darkness*, appeared in 1957. Much of his fiction focuses on small-town provincial America; sometimes a character from a small town is transplanted to a large urban setting and the values of each are juxtaposed. His first novel, *Malcolm*, was published in 1959. Other books are: *The Nephew* (1960); *Cabot Wright Begins* (1964); *Eustace Chisholm and the Works* (1967); *I am Elijah Thrush* (1972); a trilogy, *Sleepers in Moon-Crowned Valleys*, comprising *Jeremy's Version* (1970), *The House of the Solitary Maggot* (1974) and *Mourners Below* (1981); *In the Hollow of His Hand* (1986); and *Garments the Living Wear* (1989). He has also published collections of poetry, including *The Running Sun* (1971); some plays are included with short stories in *Children is All* (1962). His short stories have been collected as *The Candle of Your Eyes* (1987).

Purity See CLEANNESS.

Pusey, Edward Bouverie 1800–82 Theologian and leading member of the OXFORD MOVEMENT. Educated at Eton and Christ Church, Oxford, he became a Fellow of Oriel College in 1822. After studying Hebrew and Arabic at Göttingen and Berlin, he returned to Oxford, where he was ordained in 1828 and became Regius Professor of Hebrew and canon of Christ Church. A close associate of JOHN HENRY NEWMAN and JOHN KEBLE in the Oxford Movement, he contributed essays on the holy eucharist and baptism to *TRACTS FOR THE TIMES*. He defended Newman's analysis of the Thirty-Nine Articles in the controversial 'Tract 90' and was suspended from the office of university preacher in 1843, but remained firm in his allegiance to High Church Anglicanism after Newman's conversion to Roman Catholicism. His *Doctrine of the Real Presence* was published in 1856.

Puttenham, George 1529–90 It was probably George rather than his brother Richard (?1520–?1601) who was the author of *The Art of English Poesy* (1589), although each has, at various times, seemed the likelier candidate. Both were nephews of SIR THOMAS ELYOT. George was educated at Cambridge and admitted to the Middle Temple in 1556. The apparent claim of the author of *The Art of English Poesy* to have been at Oxford is one of the details that has cast doubt on George Puttenham's authorship.

The work is a critical discussion of poetry, mainly from the formal aspect. Its three books are concerned respectively, as its title-page announces, with 'poets and poesy', 'proportion' and 'ornament'. Book I defines poetry and claims, as does SIR PHILIP SIDNEY's *APOLOGY FOR POETRY*, that in ancient times poets were priests, prophets and lawgivers. It also makes the same claim as the *Apology* for the antiquity and dignity of poetry, and the educative and reprehensive powers of fiction. Book I also gives major divisions of fiction (e.g. epic, tragedy, comedy) and minor divisions of poems (e.g. of praise, lamentation, marriage). Book II is concerned with METRE, pattern poems appealing to the eye (like those later written by GEORGE HERBERT), anagrams and devices. Book III is largely concerned with figures of speech; Puttenham gives English equivalents for the Greek terms of rhetoric: *ironia* is 'the dry mock', *sarcasmus* 'the bitter taunt', *antiphrasis* 'the broad flout' and *charientismus* 'the privy nip'.

Pye, Henry James 1745–1813 POET LAUREATE from the death of THOMAS WARTON THE YOUNGER in 1790 until his own death, when ROBERT SOUTHEY was appointed to the office. Pye's work – which includes plays, translations from the classics and critical essays as well as poetry – was not highly regarded during his lifetime and has not been reprinted since 1822.

Pygmalion A romantic comedy by GEORGE BERNARD SHAW, first produced in German at Vienna in 1913. The first English production was staged the following year with Mrs Patrick Campbell, for whom the part was written, as Eliza Doolittle.

The play turns on the claim made by Professor Higgins, a professor of phonetics, to his friend Colonel Pickering that he could pass off a Cockney flower girl, Eliza Doolittle, as a duchess by teaching her to speak properly. She asks Higgins for lessons and he takes her as his pupil. In the course of her education she emerges not merely as a presentable lady but as a beautiful woman of increasing sensitivity. To Higgins, however, she is just a successful experiment. The play, as originally written, ends with Eliza asserting herself as a human being and rejecting Higgins. The film adaptation of 1938, which Shaw approved, brought Eliza and Higgins together at the end. This version was made into the musical comedy, *My Fair Lady* (1956).

Shaw based the character of Higgins on the phonetician and scholar of Old English, HENRY SWEET.

Pyle, Howard 1853–1911 American author and illustrator of CHILDREN'S LITERATURE. Born in Delaware, the son of a Quaker businessman, Pyle studied draw-ing before travelling to New York in the hope of making good as an artist. After some success contributing to children's magazines, he became famous with his version of *The Merry Adventures of Robin Hood of Great Renown in Nottinghamshire* (1883). There followed a succession of historical romances before he turned to writing and illustrating fairy-stories. His outstanding work, *King Arthur and His Knights* (1903), continued into three more volumes, ending with *The Story of the Grail and the Passing of Arthur* (1910). A perfectionist to the last detail, Pyle was always conscious of the total appearance of a page, at times adding his own decorative surrounds and always making sure text and illustration merged harmoniously together. His pictures abound in good humour and invention, with the busy movements of numerous characters introducing a new vigour that has lasted to this day.

Pym, Barbara (Mary Crampton) 1913–80 Novelist. Brought up in Shropshire in a solicitor's family, Pym attended St Hilda's College, Oxford, and later worked in London at the International Africa Institute. After success with novels such as *Excellent Women* (1952) and *A Glass of Blessings* (1958), she fell out of favour with her publishers and remained in obscurity until, with the publication of *Quartet in Autumn* in 1977, her work was championed and her reputation rescued by PHILIP LARKIN. *The Sweet Dove Died* followed in 1979, and four further novels, *A Few Green Leaves* (1980), *An Unsuitable Attachment* (1982), *Crampton Hodnet* (1985) and *An Academic Question* (1986), have appeared since her death. All Pym's books are wistful, delicate comedies with an unsparingly sad undertow; the frustration in love suffered by hapless spinsters is their common theme, and the intrigue-ridden world of middle-class church-going a distinctive milieu.

Pynchon, Thomas 1937– American novelist. Born in Glen Cove, New York, and educated at Cornell, he worked for a time at the Boeing Aircraft Corporation in Seattle, but little else is known about his life (he avoids interviews) beyond his liking for Mexico. His first novel, *V.* (1963), is a long, dark-toned fantasy – his preferred medium for depicting American life in the latter half of the 20th century. In *The Crying of Lot 49* (1966) he explores the attempts of the modern mind to organize an apparently chaotic universe, and juxtaposes various systems and ideologies that exist in contemporary society. *GRAVITY'S RAINBOW* (1973) received the National Book Award. The much-awaited *Vineland* (1990) is a shorter and more conventional narrative. He has also published a collection of his early short stories, *Slow Learner* (1984), which includes 'Lowlands' and 'Entropy'.

pyrrhic See METRE.

Q See QUILLER-COUCH, SIR ARTHUR.

Quality Street A comedy by J. M. BARRIE, first performed at the Vaudeville Theatre, London, in 1902. It is set at the beginning of the 19th century. Two sisters, Susan and Phoebe Throssel, considered a little too lively by their respectable lady visitors, pin their hopes on the likelihood that a young doctor, Valentine Brown, will propose to Phoebe. However, he enlists in the army and poverty forces the sisters to start a school 'for genteel children'. When Brown returns ten years later, having lost a hand in battle, he is shocked by Phoebe's drabness. Letting loose her ringlets, she masquerades as her own niece, first captivating Brown and finally driving him to prefer 'the schoolmistress in her old-maid's cap'.

quantitative metre See METRE.

Quarles, Francis 1592–1644 Poet. Born in Essex, the son of a surveyor-general of victualling for the Navy, he was educated at Christ's College, Cambridge, before entering Lincoln's Inn. Quarles found favour at court, travelling with the Princess Elizabeth's entourage to Germany for her marriage to the Elector Palatine and writing pamphlets in defence of Charles I. He suffered for his Royalist sympathies when the Parliamentary party came to power, having his property sequestered and his manuscripts destroyed. His wife and nine children were left in poverty at his death. Although he published a mass of work, he is remembered only for *Emblems* (1635), the most popular 17th-century EMBLEM BOOK and perhaps the most popular verse of its age. *Enchiridion* (1640–1), a book of aphorisms, was also highly regarded.

Quarterly Review, The A Tory rival of the Whig *EDINBURGH REVIEW*, founded in 1809 by JOHN MURRAY, the second John Murray of the distinguished publishing house. Its guiding principles were suggested by SIR WALTER SCOTT, and its early editors were WILLIAM GIFFORD, COLERIDGE's nephew Sir J. T. Coleridge, and J. G. LOCKHART, Scott's son-in-law. Scott himself contributed a discerning review of JANE AUSTEN's *EMMA* and a lighthearted review of his own *Tales of My Landlord*. JOHN WILSON CROKER wrote the savage attack on KEATS's *ENDYMION* in 1818 which friends alleged had contributed to the poet's early death. Other contributions came from GEORGE CANNING, JOHN HOOKHAM FRERE, ROBERT SOUTHEY, SAMUEL ROGERS, MATTHEW ARNOLD, Gladstone, Lord Salisbury and Sir John Barrow. *The Quarterly* survived until 1967.

quatrain A four-line STANZA usually but not necessarily in rhyme. The heroic (or elegiac) quatrain is in iambic pentameter (see METRE). For the ballad quatrain, see BALLAD.

Queen Mab A visionary philosophical and political poem in nine CANTOS, with prose notes, by SHELLEY, privately published and circulated in 1813.

Shelley's first major poem is prefaced by Voltaire's 'Écrasez l'infâme!', and quotations from Lucretius and Archimedes. The mixed heroic and descriptive blank verse form is indebted to MILTON's *SAMSON AGONISTES* and SOUTHEY's *Thalaba*. The spirit of the sleeping maiden Ianthe is transported by a spectral chariot to the Fairy Queen's 'etherial palace' in deep space. Here Mab rewards her for her personal virtue with a synoptic vision of historical and present humanity, and the new moral, social and economic order which will inevitably arise from the miseries of time. The Queen's speeches, to which most of the poem is devoted, attack conditions in contemporary England. The most impassioned assaults are reserved for the institutions of monarchy (canto III), law (III), warfare (IV), marriage and commerce (V), and established religion (VI and VII). Canto VIII contains a measured and beautiful evocation of the state of perpetual peace which will follow the work of 'Necessity'.

Of equal if not greater interest are the 17 prose notes, almost as long as the poem itself when taken together, and clearly intended to be read as part of it. Six are fully developed essays, dealing with the labour theory of value (note 7); the theory and practice of free love (particularly striking here is the influence of GODWIN and MARY WOLLSTONECRAFT) (9); necessity in the moral and material universe (12); atheism (13); Christianity (15); and vegetarianism (17).

Despite certain contradictions, the poem reveals the young Shelley as a poet of a considerably more radical turn of mind than other writers of the Romantic epoch, too radical in fact to be properly published. In 1821, however, *Queen Mab* was pirated by radical publishers, and by 1840 it had gone through no fewer than 14 cheap editions. The most widely read of all Shelley's works, it became known as the 'Chartist's Bible'.

Queen's Wake, The A poem by JAMES HOGG, published in 1813. The 'Introduction' describes Queen Mary's return from France to assume the Scottish throne and the announcement of her Christmas 'wake' at Holyrood Palace, during which 13 bards – including Rizzio, 'The gaudy minstrel from the south' –

compete in song for the glory of their clans and the prize of a jewelled harp. The songs are performed before the court over three nights, and take the form of ballad narrative in various styles. Although not among the winning entries, the story of 'Kilmeny', the rasping 'Witch of Fife' and 'The Fate of Macgregor' are particularly effective. The work was admired by BYRON and established Hogg's reputation.

Quennell, Peter 1905–93 Man of letters. He was born in Berkhamsted and educated at Berkhamsted School and Balliol College, Oxford. His early reputation as a poet (*Poems*, 1926) launched him on a literary career in which biographical writing has predominated. His books include studies of BYRON (1934–5), RUSKIN (1949) and HOGARTH (1955); *Four Portraits* (1945) deals with BOSWELL, GIBBON, STERNE and JOHN WILKES. *The Marble Foot* (1976) is autobiographical. He founded the monthly *History Today*, which he edited from 1951 to 1979.

Quentin Durward A novel by SIR WALTER SCOTT, published in 1823. Its background is the rivalry between Louis XI and Charles the Bold, Duke of Burgundy, in 15th-century France. Louis enlists the aid of William de la Marck, the Wild Boar of the Ardennes, to provoke a revolt against the duke in Liège. Quentin Durward, a young Scot in the king's guard, is sent to conduct the Burgundian heiress, Isabelle de Croye, to the protection of the Bishop of Liège to save her from marriage to Count Campo-Basso, an Italian in the service of the duke. Their journey is beset by dangers, many of them provoked by the duke but complicated by de la Marck's villainous nature. The murder of the Bishop of Liège threatens not only Isabelle's safety but also the king's careful plans for controlling the duke's ambitions. The story ends happily: Quentin Durward kills de la Marck and wins the hand of Isabelle, and Louis outwits the duke.

Quiet American, The A novel by GRAHAM GREENE, published in 1955.

The narrator is Thomas Fowler, a cynical, middle-aged English journalist working in Vietnam during the French war against the Vietminh. His story concerns the murder of Alden Pyle (the Quiet American), a naive and high-minded idealist. It alternates between the period immediately after Pyle's death and the events leading up to it. Pyle has stolen Fowler's mistress, Phuong, able to offer her the dream of marriage and a home in America. He has also become involved in subversive politics, directing funds to a small guerrilla army under the nationalist General Thé in the mistaken belief that it will help the struggle against Communism. When Fowler learns that the American has played a part in a bomb explosion in a local café, he lays information against him which prompts his murder. Vigot, a priest-like Sûreté officer, appears after the event to investigate. At the end of the novel Fowler has retrieved Phuong, and now finds himself in a position to marry her, but is left wishing that 'there existed someone to whom I could say that I was sorry'.

Quiller-Couch, Sir **Arthur** 1863–1944 Critic, novelist and poet, better known by his pen-name, Q. Born at Bodmin in Cornwall, he was educated at Clifton and Trinity College, Oxford. After working as a journalist he returned to Cornwall in 1892, living at Fowey for the next 20 years. Q used his Cornish background in his novels, among them *Dead Man's Rock* (1887), *Troy Town* (1888), *The Splendid Spur* (1889) and *The Ship of Stars* (1899). Volumes of poetry included *Verses and Parodies* (1893), *Poems and Ballads* (1896) and *The Vigil of Venus* (1912). In 1900 he edited *The Oxford Book of English Verse*, the first of several famous anthologies he compiled for Oxford University Press. He was knighted in 1910 for political services (he had been much involved with the Liberal *Leader*) and in 1912 he was appointed the first King Edward VII Professor of English Literature at Cambridge. Two volumes containing his lectures, *On the Art of Writing* (1916) and *On the Art of Reading* (1920), enjoyed great popularity.

Raban, Jonathan 1942– Travel writer and critic. He studied at Hull and then worked as a lecturer in English and American Literature at Aberystwyth (1965–7) and East Anglia (1967–9) before becoming a full-time writer. *The Technique of Modern Fiction* (1969) and *The Society of the Poem* (1971) are early works of literary criticism. *For Love and Money* (1987) collects his later book reviews. His reputation rests on his drily ruminative travel writing. *Arabia* (1979) is a topical investigation of the Arab Middle East states at the time of the oil price boom and the Sadat Peace Initiative. *Old Glory* (1981) describes a journey down the Mississippi by small boat. His interest in sailing is pursued in *Coasting* (1986), about his circumnavigation of the British Isles, and *The Oxford Book of the Sea* (1992). *Hunting Mr Heartbreak* (1990) takes the writings of JOHN BERRYMAN, HECTOR ST JOHN DE CRÈVECOEUR and others as inspiration for a travelling exploration of the American sensibility. Raban has also written a conscientious study of London, *Soft City* (1973), and a rather stolid CONDITION-OF-ENGLAND novel, *Foreign Land* (1985).

Rabe, David (William) 1940– American playwright. Born in Dubuque, Iowa, he attended Loras College and Villanova University before being drafted and sent to serve in Vietnam in 1965. The experience prompted his best-known work, the trilogy consisting of *The Basic Training of Pavlo Hummel* (1971), *Sticks and Bones* (1971) and *Streamers* (1976). Other plays include: *In the Boom Boom Room* (1973–4), about the victimization of a Philadelphia go-go dancer; *The Orphan* (1974), an adaptation of the *Orestia*; *Goose and Tomtom* (1982, 1986), an existential comedy about a bizarre robbery; and *Hurlyburly* (1984) and its prequel *These the River Keeps* (1991), about Hollywood image-making and failed dreams. Filled with violence, racism, betrayals, foolish heroism and male tribal customs, his work combines grotesque comedy, surreal fantasy and SATIRE. Screenplays include *I'm Dancing As Fast As I Can* (1982), *Streamers* (1983) and *Casualties of War* (1990).

Rackham, Arthur 1867–1939 Artist and illustrator of CHILDREN'S LITERATURE. Born in London, the son of a successful civil servant, Rackham studied art at the Slade as well as in Paris. He scored an early success with his illustrations for R. H. BARHAM'S *INGOLDSBY LEGENDS* (1898), where his talent for the grotesque first found true expression. Subsequent work included illustrations for *Fairy Tales by the Brothers Grimm* (1900), BARRIE'S *Peter Pan in Kensington Gardens* (1906) and *Mother Goose: The*

Old Nursery Rhymes (1913). There is no denying Rackham's brilliant use of light and shade, but his penchant for sinister detail was sometimes thought too frightening for very young audiences, even though much of his work appeared in limited editions to be treasured as gifts rather than used for casual reading. As he aged his style mellowed, most memorably in the illustrations for a new edition of THE WIND IN THE WILLOWS (1940), only half of which were completed at his death.

Radcliffe, Ann 1764–1823 Novelist. Ann Ward, the daughter of a London tradesman, grew up in an artistic and cultured circle. In 1786 she married William Radcliffe, who later became proprietor and editor of *The English Chronicle*. Her first novel, *The Castles of Athlin and Dunbayne* (1789), was followed by *A Sicilian Romance* (1790), which SIR WALTER SCOTT praised for its quality as a poetical novel, *The Romance of the Forest* (1791), THE MYSTERIES OF UDOLPHO (1794), *The Italian* (1797) and the posthumously published *Gaston de Blondeville* (1826). She was also a talented writer of romantic verse which was included in her novels and collected in two volumes (1834). *A Journey Made in the Summer of 1794 through Holland and the Western Frontier of Germany* (1795), to which an account of the Lake District is added, shows the same mastery of landscape description as her novels.

Although she did not originate the GOTHIC NOVEL, Mrs Radcliffe became its best-known exponent. Her persecuted heroines, wild and lonely settings, cliffhanging chapter endings and apparently supernatural events epitomize its conventions. Her importance is further acknowledged by the fun JANE AUSTEN pokes at the delicious terrors of *Udolpho* in NORTHANGER ABBEY.

Railway Children, The See NESBIT, E.

Rainbow, The A novel by D. H. LAWRENCE, published in 1915.

It chronicles the lives of three generations of the Brangwen family in Nottinghamshire during a period which spans the transition from rural to urban culture. After the death of his father, Tom Brangwen inherits Marsh Farm in the Erewash Valley and marries a Polish widow, Lydia, who already has a daughter, Anna, by her first marriage. Tom becomes devoted to Anna but estranged from his wife, even after the birth of two sons, Tom and Fred. Anna marries Will Brangwen, Tom's nephew, like his father (Alfred) a lace-designer and gifted craftsman. They move into a cottage nearby, leased them by Tom, where they spend a rapturous and passionate honeymoon. However, over the succeeding years Anna grows apart from her husband and devotes herself to her six children. The oldest of these, Ursula, 'a free, unabateable animal', becomes strongly attached to her father, and overshadows her more reserved and fanciful sister, Gudrun. Increasingly, the novel's focus shifts towards Ursula, following her development through adolescence and early womanhood. Her grandfather is drowned when she is eight years old and she grows close to her Polish grandmother, Lydia, whose foreign origins intrigue her. Later, as a young woman, she meets and is fascinated by Anton Skrebensky, a Polish connection of Lydia's. He and Ursula begin a passionate relationship, but Anton, an army engineer, departs for the Boer War leaving her sexually overwrought and frustrated. She enters into a brief lesbian relationship with her class mistress, Winifred Inger, who subsequently becomes lover and then wife of her uncle, Tom Brangwen, a colliery manager.

Ursula matriculates and struggles for two years as a schoolteacher in Ilkeston. The Brangwen family moves to Beldover and Ursula studies for a BA degree. Anton returns during her final year and they renew their passionate relationship. Largely as a result of this Ursula fails her degree, but Anton, now an officer, begs her to marry him and live in India. She declines, seeking something more lasting than sexual attraction, but when later she believes herself to be pregnant she writes to him changing her decision. Anton, however, has already settled his future and cables from India that he is married to his colonel's daughter. In the meantime, Ursula has fallen deliriously ill, after experiencing a symbolic charge of horses while out walking. She appears to suffer a miscarriage, but recovers finally to contemplate through her window a rainbow: 'the earth's new architecture' symbolically sweeping away 'the old, brittle corruption of houses and factories'. Ursula and Gudrun reappear in WOMEN IN LOVE.

Although Lawrence's publisher had forced him to make changes to his original text, *The Rainbow* was prosecuted and banned for obscenity; unsold copies were destroyed. A scene involving the pregnant Anna gave particular offence. The novel was reissued in 1926 from an American edition which had been further censored.

Raine, Craig 1944– Poet. He was born in Shildon, County Durham. The autobiographical prose section in his third collection, *Rich* (1984), describes the eccentricity of his upbringing. Raine was educated at Barnard Castle School and at Exeter College, Oxford, where he read English. He lectured at Oxford before becoming poetry editor at Faber and Faber in 1981–91. With its original, startling metaphors, his first book, *The Onion, Memory* (1978), set out to reawaken the reader's visual awareness. Presenting

domestic objects in unfamiliar ways, Raine celebrates the ordinary. The title poem of his second collection, *A Martian Sends a Postcard Home* (1979), which purports to be an alien's uncomprehending reaction to everyday objects, is typical of his technique. JAMES FENTON has dubbed him and his followers the MARTIAN POETS. Raine's libretto for Nigel Osborne's opera, *The Electrification of the Soviet Union* (1986), commissioned by Glyndebourne, is adapted from Pasternak's novella *The Last Summer*.

Raine, Kathleen (Jessie) 1908– Poet and critic. She was born at Ilford, Essex, and educated there, at Bavington, Northumberland, and at Girton College, Cambridge. Her first collection of poems, *Stone and Flower* (1943), was illustrated by Barbara Hepworth. Notable subsequent volumes include *The Year One* (1952), *The Hollow Hill* (1965), *The Lost Country* (1971), *The Oval Portrait* (1977), *Collected Poems* (1981), *To the Sun: Three Poems* (1988), *The Presence: Poems 1984–7* (1988) and *Living with Mystery: Poems 1987–91* (1992). Influenced by YEATS and EDWIN MUIR, her poetry is contemplative and lyrical, concerned mainly with the relationship between man and nature, with dreams, and with an inner spiritual quest. As well as an autobiography (*Farewell Happy Fields*, 1973; *The Land Unknown*, 1975; *The Lion's Mouth*, 1977), she has published much influential criticism, notably *Defending Ancient Springs* (1967), *Blake and Tradition* (1969) and *Yeats the Initiate* (1986). She founded *Temenos*, 'a review devoted to the arts of the imagination', in 1981.

Raleigh [Ralegh], Sir **Walter** 1554–1618 Courtier, adventurer, poet and historian. Born the younger son of a gentleman at Hayes Barton in Devon, he studied at Oriel College, Oxford, for about a year and later entered the Middle Temple. Before this time, in 1569, he had fought with a contingent of volunteers from Devon on the side of the Huguenots; later, in 1580, he fought against the Irish rebels in Munster. He came to the attention of Queen Elizabeth and by 1582 was established as her favourite, rewarded with monopolies, vast estates in Ireland and England, a knighthood, the Captaincy of her Guard and the Vice-Admiralship of Devon and Cornwall. His secret marriage to Elizabeth Throckmorton, one of the queen's attendants, became public with the birth of their son in 1592 and Raleigh was briefly committed to the Tower. The couple settled at Sherborne in Dorset. In 1595 Raleigh led an expedition up the Orinoco and in 1596 he took part in Essex's raid on Cadiz, though he quarrelled violently with Essex the following year.

As the queen's favourite Raleigh had not been popular. His pride and extravagance had excited dislike, and he had acquired a reputation for unorthodox thought. A Jesuit pamphlet of 1592 accused him of patronizing a 'school of atheism' and there were suspicions, too, about his connection with the mathematician THOMAS HARIOT. He was certainly interested in sceptical philosophy, chemistry and mathematics.

In 1603 he was again arrested, this time on suspicion of conspiracy to dethrone James I. After an unfair trial (although Raleigh was by no means entirely innocent) he was again committed to the Tower, where he lived with his wife until 1616. He was released to undertake an expedition to the Orinoco in search of gold, but again arrested after its failure. Raleigh was executed at Westminster in 1618, to become a martyred hero to the Parliamentarians of the next generation.

Very little of his verse appeared in print during his lifetime and some works are only dubiously attributed to him. Even the authenticity of the famous 'Passionate Man's Pilgrimage' (beginning 'Give me my scallop shell of quiet') is in doubt. Other famous anthology pieces attributed to Raleigh are the reply to MARLOWE's PASSIONATE SHEPHERD TO HIS LOVE and the poignant 'What is our life?', which appeared in a madrigal setting by Orlando Gibbons in 1612. Perhaps some of the poems in THE PHOENIX NEST are also by him. Undoubtedly in Raleigh's hand are 'The Eleventh and Twelfth Books of the Ocean to Cynthia', a formalized courtship devoted to Elizabeth, though it is not certain whether this formed part of a longer work.

Raleigh published accounts of his voyages and expeditions: *A Report of the Truth of the Fight about the Isles of the Azores* (1591) deals with Sir Richard Grenville's encounter with the Spanish fleet, and *A Discovery of the Empire of Guyana* (1596) describes his 1595 expedition. *The History of the World* (1614), written during his imprisonment, was published unfinished. Raleigh started with the creation and got as far as the 2nd century BC, including the history of the Jews and the Egyptians and some account of the myths of the Greeks. The work was designed for Prince Henry, who had shown some sympathy for his predicament and had visited him in the Tower.

Raleigh, Sir Walter Alexander 1861–1922 Critic. Born in London and educated at the universities of Edinburgh and Cambridge, he was professor of English at Aligarh in India, Liverpool and Glasgow. In 1904 he became the first professor of English literature at Oxford. A respected critic in his day, he was the author of among other books, *The English Novel: From the Earliest Times to the Appearance of Waverley* (1891), *Robert Louis Stevenson* (1895), *Milton* (1900), *Wordsworth* (1903), *Shakespeare* (for the English Men of Letters series; 1907), and *Six Essays on Johnson* (1910). He was knighted in 1911. After World War I Raleigh was chosen to write the official history of the RAF, but he died after completing only the first volume (1922).

Ralph Roister Doister A comedy by NICHOLAS UDALL, who probably intended it for performance by schoolboys. There is disagreement about its date of composition. Some scholars place it before 1541, when Udall was dismissed from Eton, and others as late as 1553. What is certain is that Udall based the contrasting characters of braggart lover (Ralph Roister Doister) and flattering parasite (Matthew Merrygreek) on the plays of Terence, particularly *Eunuchus* and *Miles gloriosus,* adding to his classical model such homely English figures as the servants, Meg Mumblecrust and Tib Talkapace, and combining them all in lively rhyming doggerel. The action takes place outside the house of Christian Custance, a widow betrothed to the absent merchant, Gawyn Goodluck. Needing little encouragement from Merrygreek, Ralph determines to woo and win Dame Custance. When his suit is unsuccessful, he determines to take the house by storm, but is routed by the widow and her loyal household. Gawyn Goodluck returns in time to deliver the widow from further harassment.

Ram Alley: or, Merry Tricks A coarse, popular comedy produced about 1609 and published in 1611. Nothing is known about its author, Lording Barry. The setting, Ram Alley, was a disreputable part of the City of London off Fleet Street, where Mitre Court now stands.

Ramanujan, A(ttipat) K(rishnaswami) 1929– Indian poet. Born in Mysore, he has taught linguistics at the University of Chicago since 1962, and writes in Kannada and English. A poet of delicate, thoughtful sensibility, he has always aimed at purity and translucence of expression. The title-poem of his first volume, *The Striders* (1966), refers to water-insects that can stand motionless upon 'the ripple skin/ of a stream'. It fittingly describes his preoccupation with the precarious moment of fixity upon an under-torrent of change, caught just long enough for a flash of understanding of experience. This preoccupation of his is not just as a poet but also as a professional analyst of language, as a Hindu of orthodox upbringing living in a largely rationalist Western ethos and as a 20th-century man earning his bread 'in exile'.

The title of *Relations* (1971) refers both to kin in India and to intimate connections between moments, incongruous yet illuminating, from different periods of his life. Correspondences, contrasts and contradictions successively turn much of Ramanujan's poetry into daring forays into a 20th-century mind that regards its external and interior environment questioningly. *Selected Poems* (1976) is a choice from the earlier volumes. In a new phase he has produced *Second Sight* (1986) and continued to translate from classical Tamil.

Rambler, The A twice-weekly periodical edited by SAMUEL JOHNSON, for 208 issues published between 20 March 1750 and 14 March 1752. All but four were written by Johnson himself: No. 30 was by Catherine Talbot, No. 97 by SAMUEL RICHARDSON, and Nos. 44 and 100 by ELIZABETH CARTER, while parts of three others, notably the second letter in No. 15 by GARRICK, were also from outside contributors. Consisting of essays on wide variety of topics, it was not initially a great commercial success, but extracts were frequently reprinted by such journals as *THE GENTLEMAN'S MAGAZINE* and the whole run was reprinted nine times in Johnson's lifetime. Though at first Johnson wished the work to be anonymous, his style was quickly recognized and the bi-weekly essays did more than any other work, except his *DICTIONARY*, to establish his reputation.

The quality of writing was uneven, as might be expected in a work produced to such a tight schedule, but Johnson's belief that this was more than an ephemeral periodical may be gauged from the fact that he extensively revised the text twice, for the collected edition of 1752, and for the fourth edition of 1756. *The Rambler* is a highly moral work and, with *RASSELAS* (1759), has been regarded as a prose companion to and explication of *THE VANITY OF HUMAN WISHES* (1749). Very different from *THE SPECTATOR*, Johnson's work is much more akin to the essays of Montaigne in tone and ethical approach. He is recorded as saying, 'My other works are wine and water; but my *Rambler* is pure wine.'

Ramsay, Allan 1686–1758 Scottish poet and anthologist. Born at Leadhills in Dumfriesshire, he went to Edinburgh and worked as a journeyman wigmaker. In 1712 he founded the Easy Club for the promotion of conversation and the exchange of ideas, and in 1718 he became a bookseller. In the same year he published *Christis Kirk on the Grene*, a poem attributed to JAMES I OF SCOTLAND, to which he had incautiously made additions of his own. *The Tea Table Miscellany* (1724–32) collected Scots songs and BALLADS; it was to give ROBERT BURNS and other later Scottish writers the impetus for their work. *The Ever Green, being a Collection of Scots Poems, Wrote by the Ingenious before 1600* (1724) presented the work of such poets as ROBERT HENRYSON and WILLIAM DUNBAR from the Bannatyne Manuscript (see GEORGE BANNATYNE) and so made another contribution to the revival of Scots secular poetry. Ramsay's readiness to 'improve' what he reprinted, later the object of criticism, was again apparent in his *Collection of Scots Proverbs* (1736), which modified originally coarse and vital expressions.

Ramsay began to publish occasional poems of his own in BROADSIDES and periodicals in 1713 and collections of his poetry in 1721; his most notable work is to be found in *Poems* (1728). A pastoral drama, *The Gentle Shepherd* (1725), was staged as a BALLAD OPERA with Scots airs. Ramsay founded the first circulating library in Great Britain in 1728, and succeeded in opening a playhouse in Edinburgh in 1736, though it was closed by Walpole's Licensing Act of the following year.

Rand, Ayn 1905–82 American novelist and social critic. Born and educated in St Petersburg, she emigrated to the USA in 1926. Her first publication was a mystery play, *The Night of January 16th* (1935). Her novel, *We the Living* (1936), was followed by *Anthem* (England 1938, USA 1946), a short novel which depicts the plight of an individual in the face of an oppressive, totalitarian society. With the publication of *The Fountainhead* (1943) she attracted a substantial popular audience. Her credo that humans are rational, self-interested and pledged to individualism was advocated in *The Objectivist*, a journal she founded in 1962, and in *The Ayn Rand Letter* (1971–82). The novel *Atlas Shrugged* (1957) portrays what she considered to be the inevitable results of altruism – socialism or, worse, anarchy. Her critical works include *For the New Intellectual* (1961), *The Virtue of Selfishness* (1965) and *The New Left: The Anti-Industrial Revolution* (1971).

Randolph, Thomas 1605–35 Playwright. Born near Daventry and educated at Westminster School and Trinity College, Cambridge, Randolph owed his contemporary reputation to the work he produced while at university. The facility with which he wrote is well illustrated by 'An Ode to Master Anthony Stafford', which is a charming poem in praise of country life. His pastoral play, *Amyntas* (1630), is enlivened by its comic scenes, but his other full-length piece, *The Jealous Lovers* (1632), is dramatically insipid. Randolph was better suited to the writing of dramatic sketches. *Aristippus: or, The Jovial Philosopher* (c. 1626) proposes that study of the philosophy of drinking should be added to the university syllabus, a theme pursued with variations in *The Drinking Academy* (c. 1626). *The Conceited Pedlar* (1627) is an ephemerally witty monologue. *THE MUSES' LOOKING-GLASS* (1630), in which an actor out-argues Puritan opposition to the theatre, is Randolph's most interesting work. It reflects the influence of BEN JONSON, of whom Randolph was a favoured 'son'.

Ransom, John Crowe 1888–1974 American poet and critic. Born in Tennessee, he was educated at Vanderbilt and Oxford universities and taught at Vanderbilt from 1914 until 1937. His first collections of verse were *Poems about God* (1919), *Chills and Fever* (1924), *Grace after Meat* (1924) and *Two Gentlemen in Bonds* (1927). While at Vanderbilt he became a member of the FUGITIVES, editing *I'll Take My Stand: The South and the Agrarian Tradition*

(1930), a collection of essays by 12 'Fugitive' writers: the poets DONALD DAVIDSON, ALLEN TATE, ROBERT PENN WARREN, JOHN GOULD FLETCHER and Ransom himself; the scholars Stark Young, John Donald Wade and Andrew Lytle; the historian Frank Owsley; the political scientist Herman Clarence Nixon; the psychologist Lyle Lanier; and the economist and journalist Henry Blue Kline. The 'Statement of Principles', written mainly by Ransom, maintained that the industrial way of life was causing unhappiness and unemployment among the work force and destroying the very roots of religion, culture and art. After leaving Vanderbilt, Ransom taught at Kenyon College, Ohio, where in 1939 he founded THE KENYON REVIEW, which became one of the most influential academic journals in America. Two years later he gave currency to the principles of the NEW CRITICISM in a book of that title. His other critical writings include *God without Thunder: An Orthodox Defense of Orthodoxy* (1930), *The World's Body* (1938) and *Poems and Essays* (1955).

Ransome, Arthur (Michell) 1884–1967 Journalist and writer of CHILDREN'S LITERATURE. Born in Leeds and educated at Rugby, he began his career as an office boy in a London publishing house before becoming a journalist for *The Daily News* in 1912, later for *The Manchester Guardian*. His work in Russia produced *Old Peter's Russian Tales* (1916) and an account of the Bolshevik Revolution, *Six Weeks in Russia* (1919). After extensive travel during the 1920s, including a visit to China, he wrote *Swallows and Amazons* (1931), the first in a series of children's adventure stories reflecting his enthusiasm for sailing, the outdoor life and those parts of England (the Lake District, the Norfolk Broads) which favour such activities. Other titles in this vein included *Pigeon Post* (1936), *We Didn't Mean to Go to Sea* (1938), *The Big Six* (1940), and *Great Northern?* (1947). He was also the author of *Racundra's First Cruise* (1923) and *Mainly about Fishing* (1959). *The Autobiography of Arthur Ransome*, edited by Rupert Hart-Davis, appeared in 1976.

Rao, Raja 1908– Indian novelist. Born in Hassan, he was professor of philosophy at the University of Texas, Austin in 1965–83. His early stories were in Kannada and English, the latter published as *The Cow of the Barricades* (1947); a second English collection appeared as *The Policeman and the Rose* (1978). His first novel, *Kanthapura* (1938), successfully attempted 'to convey in a language ... not one's own the spirit that is one's own'. In the ample manner of the *Mahabharata* and *Ramayana*, and using a purana-like episodic structure, a talkative villager tells how a village community obtains from daily life, with its millennia-old worship of the local deity, the strength for non-violent resistance to the British Raj. Whether

Hindu myth still has a viable place in modern, urban Indian life, is the major theme of *The Serpent and the Rope* (1960), Raja Rao's most important book, a taxing but immensely rewarding experience for non-Indian readers. About a spiritual quest in Europe and India, it is a modern rendering of the *Mahabharata* legend of Satyavan and Savithri, dramatizing also the relationships between India and the West, the earthly and the spiritual, the physical and the metaphysical, illusion (the serpent) and reality (the rope). *The Cat and Shakespeare* (1965), the story of a loquacious official helping the narrator receive divine grace (symbolized by the cat), is about self-surrender through love, enabling the human will not to surrender to, but unite with, God's will. *Comrade Kirillov* (1976; in French translation, 1965) chiefly satirizes communism, and argues that all foreign creeds gradually become Indianized. Later works, such as *The Chessmaker and His Moves* (1988) and *On the Ganga Ghat* (1989), a collection of stories, require stamina and patience.

Rape of Lucrece, The A narrative poem by SHAKESPEARE, entitled simply *Lucrece* on its first appearance in 1594. Like the slightly earlier *VENUS AND ADONIS*, it was dedicated to Henry Wriothesley, Earl of Southampton. The poem is in seven-line stanzas and describes the rape by Tarquinius, son of the King of Rome, of Lucretia, whose husband Collatinus had extolled her chastity. Shakespeare could have read the story in Livy, Ovid's *Fasti* and CHAUCER's *THE LEGEND OF GOOD WOMEN*.

The first section describes the furious ride of 'lust-breathed Tarquin' to Collatium, his entertainment there by an unsuspecting Lucrece, and his restlessness and night journey by torchlight through the house to her chamber, in the course of which he has an internal debate between 'frozen conscience and hot-burning will'. After Lucrece has been described in bed, she awakens to hear Tarquin's threats and pleads unavailingly with him. In the second section, after the rape, Lucrece rails at length against night, opportunity and 'misshapen time', all of which conspired in her violation. When day comes she sends her husband a letter and views a picture of the fall of Troy, which has poignant parallels with her own case. Collatinus returns with attendant lords and Lucrece, having identified Tarquin as her violator, stabs herself.

In *The Rape of Lucrece* Shakespeare turns from the mythic world of *Venus and Adonis* to a grim tragedy from Roman history. The ambiguous ethics of Lucretia's suicide had been debated from the time of St Augustine, but SIDNEY in the *APOLOGY FOR POETRY* describes a picture of Lucretia as depicting the outward beauty of virtue. Shakespeare's version is full of ornamented language and CONCEITS, and its obviously self-conscious delight in verbal artifice has led to accusations of lack of feeling in the treatment of so tragic a tale. HAZLITT described both this poem and

VENUS AND ADONIS as 'a couple of ice-houses' and COLERIDGE found *Lucrece* lacking in pathos. The story stayed in Shakespeare's imagination: in *TITUS ANDRONICUS* it is cited as a parallel to the rape of Lavinia, in *CYMBELINE* the villainous Iachimo remembers Tarquin as he approaches Imogen's bed, and, before he kills Duncan, Macbeth personifies murder as having 'Tarquin's ravishing strides'.

Rape of the Lock, The A poem by ALEXANDER POPE, published in a two-CANTO version in 1712 and expanded to five cantos in 1714. The occasion for this elegant comic piece was the forceful cutting by Lord Petre (a 20-year-old Catholic Peer) of a lock of hair from Lady Arabella Fermor's head, this apparently trivial event causing dissension between their two aristocratic families. Pope's avowed intention was 'a jest to laugh them together again', and the early version of his poem became something of a *cause célèbre* in the metropolitan Catholic circles in which they all moved.

One of the poet's most glittering performances, the *Rape* subjects this event to an extended MOCK-HEROIC treatment, playing upon the war between the sexes, feminizing EPIC conventions and satirizing the superficial concerns of society women while still celebrating their beauty – something to which the poet was especially attracted. The poem traces the course of the fateful day when Belinda the society beauty wakes up, glorifies her appearance at a ritualistic dressing table (the 'Toilette' scene is one of Pope's most celebrated set-pieces), plays cards, flirts, drinks coffee and has her hair ravaged. As in PASTORAL, this action is set within the wider cycle of time itself so that at the close, when the violated lock is transformed into a new constellation, the immortality of the story is seen to be a function of poetic artifice as well as of feminine charms. The enlarged version of the poem includes some elaborate 'machinery', or accompanying details of supernatural elements surrounding the mortal events, partly modelled on *Le Lutrin* of Boileau. Part love poem and part satire, the *Rape* is a virtuoso piece of writing, designed to demonstrate 'What mighty contests rise from trivial things.'

Rasselas: *Prince of Abyssinia, The History of* A philosophical romance by SAMUEL JOHNSON, published in 1759. It is said to have been written in the evenings of a single week to pay for his mother's funeral. Johnson was already familiar with much of the background material for such a project (he had translated *A Voyage to Abyssinia* by Father Jerome Lobo in 1735) and the exotic setting ensured the book instant success.

The book (which consists of three parts followed by a sort of 'coda') is concerned with Johnson's habitual theme of the 'choice of life' whereby Rasselas, son of the Abyssinian Emperor, determines to seek the world outside the luxurious 'happy valley' in which he has hitherto been living an insulated existence. Full of theoretical hopes and fruitless meditations, Rasselas escapes from his privileged confines along with his sister Nekayah and the elderly philosopher Imlac; they reach Egypt, where the prince's romantic notions about the conditions of human life are contradicted by the actual instances they encounter. The plot itself is slender, but the whole work is invigorated by Johnson's robust common sense, occasional glints of humour, and avoidance of the over-melancholy. Idealism and innocence, the pastoral values, are gently deflated but with ample opportunities for wide-eyed raillery. *Rasselas* displays some of the author's finest aphoristic writing (partly in imitation of oriental literary style) but its antithetical method is careful to leave unresolved the larger issues it handles. The Prince encounters apparent paradoxes which prevent him from formulating neat opinions – the monks of St Anthony can only be certain of hardship, the Sultan is tormented by suspicions, the philosopher's wisdom is useless in his grief. 'The Conclusion, in which Nothing is concluded' illustrates the book's deliberate structure, and affirms Johnson's conviction that action is superior to introspection. *Dinarbas* (1790) by ELLIS CORNELIA KNIGHT is a sequel to *Rasselas*.

Rattigan, Sir **Terence** 1911–77 Playwright. Born in London and educated at Harrow and Oxford, he committed himself to writing plays on leaving university. *French without Tears* (1936), a light comedy, established him as a West End favourite, and he is best remembered as the writer of carefully crafted plays and screenplays in which character and plot take precedence over social comment. Rattigan wrote several plays based on historical incidents and characters: *The Winslow Boy* (1946), *Ross* (a perceptive study of T. E. LAWRENCE; 1960) and *A Bequest to the Nation* (1970) exhibit his compassion for the humiliated and the ashamed. The same concern characterizes his serious plays, like *Flare Path* (1942), *The Browning Version* (1948), *The Deep Blue Sea* (1952) and *Separate Tables* (1954). Rattigan was knighted in 1971.

Rattlin the Reefer A novel by Edward Howard (?1791–1841), published in 1836. Howard was a shipmate of CAPTAIN MARRYAT and his story resembles Marryat's own more famous novels of the sea. Marryat himself thought enough of the work to prepare it for publication, describing it as 'Edited by the author of *Peter Simple*'.

Rauf Coilyear, The Tale of A late 15th-century Scottish poem in ALLITERATIVE VERSE. It relates the story of Rauf, a forthright and independent charcoal-burner who entertains Charlemagne (Charles) in his hut after the emperor has become lost in a storm.

Ignorant of his guest's identity, Rauf treats him politely and hospitably but as an equal. Charlemagne invites Rauf to court, reveals his true identity and knights his former host. Rauf fights a Saracen, Magog, and is made a Marshal of France.

Raven, Simon 1927– Novelist. Having attended Charterhouse, and then read classics at King's College, Cambridge, he joined the King's Shropshire Light Infantry, with which he served in Germany and Kenya. He resigned his commission as the commander of a rifle company in 1957 in order to become a book reviewer, and published his first novel, *The Feathers of Death*, in 1959. A prolific novelist, who also writes with enthusiasm about cricket and with malicious enthusiasm about public-school education, he has made his reputation for rakish, witty and satirical fiction with two ROMANS FLEUVES: the 10-volume *Alms for Oblivion*, beginning with *Fielding Gray* (1967) and ending with *The Survivors* (1976); and 7-volume *The First-born of Egypt*, beginning with *Morning Star* (1984) and ending with *The Troubadour* (1992).

Raverat, Gwen(dolen) (Mary) 1885–1957 Wood engraver and autobiographer. Born in Cambridge into the Darwin family (CHARLES DARWIN was her grandfather), she was educated privately and at the Slade School of Art. In 1911 she married the French artist Jacques Raverat (d. 1925). An accomplished pioneer in the revival of wood engraving, she also wrote *Period Piece: A Cambridge Childhood* (1952), originally conceived as a short narrative to accompany reminiscent drawings. Instead, though it is charmingly illustrated, this avowedly 'circular book' portrays her extended family of sisters, cousins, aunts and uncles (many of them people of academic or scientific consequence) in their full range of well-observed eccentricity. An important branch of the 'intellectual aristocracy' is shown in an endearingly domestic light.

Raworth, Tom 1938– Poet. He grew up in London and has studied and worked, as writer-in-residence, in Britain, Spain, Mexico and the USA. An important figure in the 'underground' poetry of the 1960s, he edited the magazine *Outburst* and ran the Matrix Press in 1961–3, and co-founded an important small press, Goliard, which published CHARLES OLSON and J. H. PRYNNE. His early work, in *The Relation Ship* (1966), *The Big Green Day* (1968) and *Lion, Lion* (1970), conformed to Olson's projectivist doctrine that one perception should lead instantly to another, without reflection, qualification or discrimination, though in Raworth's poetry the effect was often comic and surreal. Instants are recorded without editing in a poem such as 'Stag Skull Mounted', in *Moving* (1971). Such experiments, at the edge of what is recognizably

poetry, are related to contemporary developments in conceptual art. The text becomes increasingly minimal. Later work, such as *Ace* (1977), *Writing* (1982), *Tottering State: Selected and New Poems 1963–83* (1984), *Lazy Left Hand: Notes from 1970–1975* (1986) and *From External Sections* (1990), have tended to find an American audience more readily than a British one.

Read, Sir **Herbert (Edward)** 1893–1968 Critic and poet. Born in Yorkshire and educated at Leeds University, he served in France during World War I before becoming assistant keeper at the Victoria and Albert Museum (1922–31) and professor of fine art at Edinburgh University (1931–3). He edited *The Burlington Magazine* from 1933 to 1939. Read's critical work includes *Reason and Romanticism* (1926), *English Prose Style* (1928), *Form in Modern Poetry* (1932), *Art and Industry* (1934), *The True Voice of Feeling* (1953) and *The Literature of Sincerity* (1968). He also produced editions of T. E. HULME, Kropotkin, Orage and Jung, and several volumes of autobiographical prose, including *In Retreat* (1925), *Ambush* (1930) and *The Contrary Experience* (1963). His novel *The Green Child* (1945) is an allegorical fantasy. His poetry, which was much influenced by IMAGISM, included *Songs of Chaos* (1915), *Naked Warriors* (1919), *The End of a War* (1933) and several *Collected Poems*, the last of which appeared in 1966. He was knighted in 1953.

Read, Piers Paul 1941– Novelist. The son of SIR HERBERT READ, he was born in Beaconsfield and educated at Ampleforth and St John's College, Cambridge. Always coloured by his Catholicism, his novels are sternly moralistic and almost Victorian, not just in their assiduously realized social colour and probing of conscience but also in their propensity to extravagant plot contrivance. *A Married Man* (1979) is a sober, candid study of a barrister in mid-life crisis, while *The Upstart* (1973) is a BILDUNGSROMAN. An interest in Eastern Europe has prompted *Polonaise* (1976), about Nazi collaboration in Poland, and *A Season in the West* (1988), about a dissident Czech writer who seeks asylum in Britain.

Reade, Charles 1814–84 Novelist, playwright and journalist. Born at Ipsden House, Oxfordshire, he studied at Magdalen College, Oxford, qualified as a barrister without practising and abandoned medicine through squeamishness. The various offices he held at Magdalen College did not detain him in Oxford. His interest in theatre management led to collaboration with TOM TAYLOR in several plays, beginning with *Masks and Faces* (1852), which he turned into a novel, *Peg Woffington* (1853). His first success as a novelist came with *It is Never Too Late to Mend* (1856), intended to reform prisons. Other 'novels with a purpose' included: *Hard Cash* (1863), attacking abuses in private lunatic asylums; *Foul Play* (1868), about abuses at sea; *Put Yourself in His Place* (1870), attacking Trade Union closed shops; *A Terrible Temptation* (1871), returning to the attack on private asylums; and *A Woman-Hater* (1877), about the disadvantages of village life. Still involved in the theatre, he dramatized several of his novels, including *Griffith Gaunt* (1866), which he considered his best work, and collaborated with BOUCICAULT. Ill-health made him turn to short stories but did not prevent him writing *Hang in Haste, Repent at Leisure* (1877), a series of letters which led to the reprieve of four people condemned to death for murder, and adapting Zola's *L'Assommoir* for the English stage as *Drink*. Unflaggingly energetic, fiercely polemical and cannily commercial, Reade was ranked with DICKENS and GEORGE ELIOT in his day. Now he is remembered, if at all, for *THE CLOISTER AND THE HEARTH* (1861), his most carefully researched historical novel.

Reade, (William) Winwood 1838–75 Historian, novelist and travel-writer. He studied at Magdalen Hall, Oxford, but left without taking a degree to pursue his interest in the natural sciences, exploring Africa to study the habits of the gorilla and then entering St Mary's Hospital as a student. His travel books deal with his African experiences and his novels imitate the work of his uncle, CHARLES READE. He made his name with *The Martyrdom of Man* (1872), a history of civilization written from a standpoint frankly hostile to religion. The book remained popular for a number of years after his early death, being praised by H. G. WELLS and CONAN DOYLE's Sherlock Holmes among others.

Reading, Peter 1946– Poet. Born in Liverpool and educated at its College of Art, he has worked as a schoolteacher, lecturer in art history, labourer in an animal feed company and, since 1983, weighbridge operator. A maverick who has variously been judged offensive, contradictory and intense, he has never aligned himself with any group or school, though his early work was partly influenced by AUDEN. Since *For the Municipality's Elderly* (1974), his prolific output has continued with volumes designed as unified wholes rather than just collections of recent work. They include: *Nothing for Anyone* (1977); *Fiction* (1979); *Tom O'Bedlam's Beauties* (1981); *Diplopic* (1983); *C* (1984), a *tour de force* about terminal illness; *Ukelele Music* (1985), a study of violence in both prose and poetry; *The Essential Reading* (1986); *Perduta Gente* (1989); and *Evagatory* (1992), which can best be described as a testament to cruelty and those vulnerable to cruelty.

realism A term first used in France in the 1850s to characterize works concerned with representing the world as it is rather than as it ought to be, with description rather than invention. Champfleury and Duranty were among its earliest exponents but the term was applied retrospectively to Balzac's *La Comédie humaine*, begun in 1830, because of its authentic detail, its perceptions about the function of environment in shaping character and the setting of its constituent books in the present or the very recent past. Realism observes and documents contemporary life and everyday scenes as objectively as possible in low-key, unrhetorical prose, drawing its characters from all social levels and reproducing the flavour of their colloquial speech in its dialogue. Because they seek to explore areas of life customarily ignored by the arts, realist writers frequently look to the lowest social classes and to cruelty and suffering for their subject matter.

Realism became the dominant mode of the 19th-century European novel and also of the theatre, from the late 1880s, where it initiated a revival of serious drama and led to the development, by Antoine in Paris and Stanislavski in Moscow, of less histrionic, more natural-seeming acting styles.

The great works of European realist fiction include Flaubert's *Sentimental Education*, Tolstoy's *Anna Karenina* and Dostoevsky's *Crime and Punishment*. Accurate observation and attention to the structures of society make GEORGE ELIOT's *MIDDLEMARCH* and ELIZABETH GASKELL's *MARY BARTON* notable examples of English 19th-century realism. The chief American realists are WILLIAM DEAN HOWELLS and SINCLAIR LEWIS, while the line of English realist writing continues in the 20th century via H. G. WELLS (*TONO-BUNGAY*, 1909) and ARNOLD BENNETT (*CLAYHANGER*, 1910) to the post-World War II evocations of English middle-class life of ANGUS WILSON and the Northern working-class fiction of the 1950s, best exemplified by ALAN SILLITOE's *The Loneliness of the Long Distance Runner* (1959).

Realism played an important part in the revival of the English theatre in the first decade of this century (GRANVILLE-BARKER, ST JOHN ERVINE, GALSWORTHY, STANLEY HOUGHTON) and, again, in the 1950s (OSBORNE, WESKER, SHELAGH DELANEY). In Ireland O'CASEY recreated the texture of tenement life in the setting and language of his early Dublin plays, *JUNO AND THE PAYCOCK* (1925) and *THE PLOUGH AND THE STARS* (1926), while in America O'NEILL and ARTHUR MILLER developed native versions of the dramatic realism of Ibsen and Strindberg. See also NATURALISM.

Reaney, James (Crerar) 1926– Canadian poet and playwright. Born near Stratford, Ontario, he grew up on a farm in a Protestant fundamentalist atmosphere. He attended the University of Toronto between 1944 and 1948 and then taught English at the University of Manitoba until 1960, apart from the years 1956 to 1958, during which he completed his doctorate at the University of Toronto under the supervision of NORTHROP FRYE. Since 1960 he has lectured at the University of Western Ontario. While still in his early twenties, he achieved recognition as a poet with a powerful Gothic and regional voice. His first volume, *The Red Heart* (1949), which shows the attempts of a lonely southern Ontario boy to reconcile his reading with the environment around him, was seen as introducing a new strain into Canadian poetry. Subsequently he came to be regarded as a 'mythopoeic' poet writing under the influence of Frye, but far from aspiring towards the universalism favoured by the mythic approach, both *The Red Heart* and his finest volume, *Twelve Letters to a Small Town* (1962), are strongly regional. His other poetry includes *A Suit of Nettles* (1958), *The Dance of Death at London, Ontario* (1963) and *Performance Poems* (1990). He turned to the theatre with *The Killdeer*, *The Sun and the Moon, One-Man Masque* and *Night Blooming Cereus*, published in 1962. Like his poetry, these early plays show a world of fantasy and the macabre lurking beneath the surface of rural Ontario. All Reaney's plays use the conventions of MELODRAMA, but later work shows a more conscious awareness of theatrical artifice. Mime is combined with music, dance, puppets and magic lanterns in his dramatic masterpiece, a trilogy consisting of *Sticks and Stones* (1975), *The St Nicholas Hotel* (1976) and *Handcuffs* (1977). It tells the story of an Irish immigrant family mysteriously murdered in Lucan, Ontario, in 1880. Other plays include *Colours in the Dark* (1969), *Listen to the Wind* (1972), *The Dismissal* (1978) and *The Canadian Brothers* (1984). He has also written opera libretti, *Crazy to Kill: A Detective Opera* (1989) and *Serinette* (1990).

Rebecca of Sunnybrook Farm See WIGGIN, KATE DOUGLAS.

Rechy, John (Francisco) 1934– American novelist. Born in El Paso, Texas, he was educated there at the University of Texas and at the New School for Social Research in New York. His work usually concerns a search for love and identity in socially marginal settings; his leading characters tend to be homosexual or bisexual and are frequently associated with danger and violence. *City of Night* (1963), his first novel, has been followed by *Numbers* (1967), *This Day's Death* (1969), *The Vampires* (1971), *The Fourth Angel* (1973), *Rushes* (1979), *Bodies and Souls* (1983), *Marilyn's Daughter* (1988) and *The Miraculous Day of Amalia Gómez* (1991). His representations of urban life-styles are generally based on the homosexual communities of major cities such as New York and Los Angeles, and incorporate the crime and violence of the urban underworld. He has also published a study of urban homosexual lifestyles, *The Sexual Outlaw* (1977).

Recollections of the Lakes and the Lake Poets A series of autobiographical reflections and literary portraits by THOMAS DE QUINCEY, first published in *Tait's Magazine* 1834–9. Written some 20 years after the period of his association and intimacy with them, De Quincey's reminiscences of his Lakes-dwelling friends and former neighbours, WORDSWORTH, COLERIDGE, SOUTHEY and DOROTHY WORDSWORTH, are a revealing blend of fulsome admiration and praise for their literary and poetic achievements, and mischievous – occasionally malicious – gossip, unflattering personal description, and the carefully placed negative inference. Except in his rather cruel presentation of Mary and Dorothy Wordsworth, however, the wounded vanity which seems to have been the fruit of his relations with the self-consciously great is never allowed to blunt a fineness of moral and psychological perception. Coleridge is shown in all his intellectual grandeur and human weakness: simultaneously the most original English mind of his time and a compulsive plagiarist. Wordsworth's genius is fully honoured, but he is also the proud bibliophobe – sacrilegiously cutting open precious pages with a used butter-knife on the kitchen table – as well as the supremely competent manager of his own interests. (In a splendidly humorous passage De Quincey shows how the deaths of wealthy friends, benefactors and distributors of stamps are miraculously synchronous with the poet's ever-increasing material requirements.) Southey is effectively damned with faint praise for his moral integrity and love of books. All three have little understanding of political economy, the one area in which De Quincey may justly claim to have outshone them.

Recruiting Officer, The A comedy by GEORGE FARQUHAR, first performed in 1706. Farquhar's experience as a recruiting officer in Lichfield and Shrewsbury in 1705–6 inspired not only the plot but also the decision to set it in Shrewsbury, against the prevailing view that comedy required a London setting.

Captain Plume recruits men by courting their sweethearts. His sergeant, Kite, poses as an astrologer to persuade the gullible. Sylvia, daughter of Justice Ballance, loves Plume. Disguised as a man, she is handed over to the army by her deceived father. A secondary plot concerns the failure of a rival recruiting officer, Captain Brazen, to win the rich wife he had set his sights on.

Red Badge of Courage, The A novel by STEPHEN CRANE, published in 1895. In preparation for publication, the story was subject to considerable emendations and deletions. An edition of the original manuscript was published in 1982.

The Red Badge of Courage, though only his second novel, established Crane's reputation in critical and literary circles. It is set during the American Civil War, and the frightening realities of battle are violently contrasted with the heroic ideals of conventional war narrative. Eager for glory, Henry Fleming enlists in the Union army. His expectations are disappointed by his first encounter with the enemy, in which his fellow soldiers retreat and he receives a head wound from the butt of a gun when he grabs a deserter to ask for an explanation. He is temporarily proud of his own bravery, but during a second encounter with the enemy he is overcome by fear and flees from the battle into the forest. There he attempts to find solace in Nature, but fails to justify his desertion in his own eyes. After coming across the spectral figure of a dying soldier, he becomes enraged by the injustices of war. He returns to the lines with the wounded, marked by the 'red badge' of a soldier who has fought but does not tell anyone how he received his wound. Back with his regiment, in the heat of battle he automatically picks up the regiment's colours when they fall from another's hands. But he can no longer be proud of his own heroics. He is filled with guilt and haunted by the memory of the 'tattered' soldier, a wounded man who was deserted on the field.

Red Book of Hergest See MABINOGION, THE.

Redburn: *His First Voyage* A novel by HERMAN MELVILLE, published in 1849. He wrote the book in about ten weeks, drawing on the experiences of his first voyage as an apprentice seaman.

The son of an impoverished New York family, Wellingborough Redburn ships out on the *Highlander*, a trader bound for Liverpool. On this his first voyage, he must learn slowly and painfully not only the sailor's strenuous trade but also that he is the lowest in social standing among the crew. Captain Riga seems to treat him kindly at first, but then ignores him contemptuously; his attempts to approach crew members alternate with their rebuffs and his similarly contemptuous withdrawal. Feeling isolated and receiving few kindnesses, he is disturbed by the deaths of some of the seamen and still more by the torments of the evil and tubercular sailor Jackson.

When the ship reaches Liverpool, Redburn finds that a guidebook belonging to his dead father (who had made business trips abroad) is no longer accurate or useful; feeling dislocated and disillusioned, he explores the city and sees the appalling conditions among the poor. He encounters a spendthrift aristocrat, Harry Bolton, and the two go off to London together. London's glitter, however, only thinly disguises its corruption. Harry, who has run up a gambling debt, is obliged to run away and ship out on the *Highlander* with Redburn for the trip home. Emigrants to America accompany them on this return voyage, and the unhealthy conditions lead to an epidemic and more deaths. Jackson's treacheries continue, though he dies as they near New York;

Captain Riga cheats Harry and Redburn out of their wages, but Redburn is happy to be home with his family.

Redeemed Captive, Returning to Zion, The An account by John Williams (1664–1729), published in 1707, of his two-year captivity among the Mohawk Indians and French Jesuits in Quebec. A minister in the frontier town of Deerfield, Massachusetts, he was taken prisoner in a raid in 1704 during the French and Indian Wars. He describes how he saw his wife and two of his children killed, and how he himself was constantly threatened with death during the march with the Indians to Canada. He and the party were delivered to the Jesuits in Quebec and their physical hardships lessened, but the Jesuits tried to convert them to Catholicism, an experience which Williams found almost as harrowing as physical deprivation. The latter part of the narrative contains his exchange of letters with his son, also a captive, who had been separated from him and successfully converted by the Jesuits, but who soon reverted to Protestantism and, together with his father, was released from captivity in 1706. Williams's youngest daughter, however, was not released; in fact she later married an Indian, joined the Roman church, and refused to return to New England. Williams stresses that the afflictions of Indian raids and captivities have been visited on the colony for its sins.

Redgauntlet An EPISTOLARY NOVEL by SIR WALTER SCOTT, published in 1824. The background to the story is the supposed return of the Young Pretender after the defeat of the 1745 rebellion to make one more attempt on the throne.

Herries of Birrenswork (Sir Edward Redgauntlet) is a fanatical Jacobite. As part of his plan for helping the Pretender he kidnaps Sir Arthur Darsie Redgauntlet, his nephew and the head of the family. Alan Fairford sets out to rescue his friend Darsie, and their adventures form the substance of the novel. In the end Sir Edward is forced to flee abroad (where he becomes a prior) and Prince Charles Edward's hopes are again crushed. A famous feature of the book is 'Wandering Willie's Tale', a classic ghost story.

Redgrove, Peter (William) 1932– Poet and novelist. Educated at Taunton School in Somerset and at Queens' College, Cambridge. After a brief period in scientific journalism he became a resident author at Falmouth School of Art, where he subsequently taught for many years. In 1956 he became a founder member of the GROUP and his first volume of poems, *The Collector and Other Poems*, appeared in 1960. Subsequent collections include *At the White Monument* (1963), *Sons of My Skin: Selected Poems* (edited by Marie Peel; 1975), *The Weddings at Nether Powers* (1979) and *The Moon Disposes: Poems 1954–87*

(1987). They exhibit a densely packed and vivid visual imagery. The muscular power and rich language of his poems also marks his novels, which include *In the Country of the Skin* (1973) and *The Beekeepers* (1980). He has collaborated on several books with his wife, the novelist and poet Penelope Shuttle, including a documentary on the human fertility cycle, *The Wise Wound* (1978). His work has developed in a strongly mystical vein, repeatedly exploring the enduring religious and sexual mysteries of man.

Reed, Henry 1914–86 Poet and radio playwright. He was born in Birmingham and went to the King Edward VI School and Birmingham University. He worked as a teacher and freelance journalist before serving in the British Army (1941–2) and in the Foreign Office (1942–5). After the war, he worked as a broadcaster, journalist and radio playwright, being known for the verse plays collected in *The Streets of Pompeii* (1971) and for the satirical prose plays in *Hilda Tablet and Others* (1971). His only volume of poetry, *A Map of Verona* (1946), includes 'Lessons of the War', three poems that deal with army training; of these, the precise and poignant 'Naming of Parts' is often anthologized. The exploratory mode of 'The Place and the Person' calls to mind T. S. ELIOT's FOUR QUARTETS, though Reed is better known for his short, acute PARODY of Eliot in the same volume, 'Chard Whitlow'. *Collected Poems* appeared in 1991.

Reed, Ishmael (Scott) 1938– Black American novelist and poet. Born in Chattanooga, Tennessee, he was raised in Buffalo, New York. With their combination of radical surrealism and angry social satire, Reed's novels aspire to break the cycle of oppression of American minorities. The first of these experimental works, *The Free-Lance Pall-Bearers* (1967), represents a parodic departure from the autobiographical style of earlier black American narratives. *Yellow Back Radio Broke-Down* (1969) portrays the remarkable adventures of a black cowboy. *Mumbo-Jumbo* (1972) sets forth a pseudo-history of racial oppression. *The Last Days of Louisiana Red* (1974) is loosely based on the racial violence in Berkeley in the 1960s. *Flight to Canada* (1976) surrealistically merges the Civil War period with modern America. *The Terrible Twos* (1982) and *The Terrible Threes* (1989) are fantastic satires of corruption in present and future American society. *Reckless Eyeballing* appeared in 1986. Reed's volumes of poetry include *Catechism of D Neo-American HooDoo Church* (1970), *Chattanooga* (1973) and *A Secretary to the Spirits* (1978). *Shrovetide in New Orleans* (1978) and *God Made Alaska for the Indians* (1982) are collections of essays.

Reed, Talbot Baines 1852–93 Writer of CHILDREN'S LITERATURE. His popular boys' stories – *The Fifth Form at St Dominic's* (1887), *Cock House at Fellsgarth* (1891) and *The Master of the Shell* (1894) – glamorized the shibboleths and traditions of public-school life.

Reeve, Clara 1729–1807 Novelist. She was born at Ipswich in Suffolk. She earned herself an important place in the development of the GOTHIC NOVEL with *The Champion of Virtue: A Gothic Story*, first published in 1777 but revised and republished as *The Old English Baron* in 1778. Writing some 12 years after THE CASTLE OF OTRANTO had appeared, she acknowledged her debt to WALPOLE while criticizing his performance. Her other novels were *The Two Mentors* (1783), *The Exiles* (1788), *The School for Widows* (1791), *Memoirs of Sir Roger de Clarendon* (1793) and *Destination* (1799). She also published a critical dialogue, *The Progress of Romance through Times, Centuries and Manners* (1785).

Reeve, John See MUGGLETON, LODOWICKE.

Reeve's Tale, The See CANTERBURY TALES, THE.

Reeves, James 1909–78 Poet. Born in Middlesex, he was educated at Cambridge before becoming a schoolteacher as well as a widely regarded poet. His 12 volumes for adults include *Collected Poems 1927–74* (1974). His first collection for children, *The Wandering Moon* (1950), an instant success, was followed by volumes illustrated by EDWARD ARDIZZONE. In later life be took to retelling classics to a child audience, notably in *The Exploits of Don Quixote* (1959) and *Fables from Aesop* (1961). In 1973 he published his *Complete Poems for Children*. Virtually blind in old age, Reeves continued to work as author and editor, sensitive as always to the sound as well as the sense of what he was producing. The irreverent humour, lively imagination and occasional melancholy of his poetry helped make him a favourite with readers of all ages.

Reflections on the Revolution in France A treatise by EDMUND BURKE, published in 1790, the year after the outbreak of the French Revolution. Burke attacks revolutionary movements based on noble humanitarian ends because he believed that people are not at liberty to destroy the state and its institutions in the hope of some contingent improvement. He criticizes those who make an abstraction of liberty without real knowledge of what is meant by it. Equality is contrary to nature and therefore impossible to achieve, while fraternity is dismissed as 'cant and gibberish'. A memorable passage laments that with the destruction of the *ancien régime* 'the age of chivalry is gone... and the glory of Europe is extinguished forever'.

The seeming inconsistency of supporting the movement for Irish independence and the rebellion of the American colonists against the English government is justified, he argues, because these were actions on behalf of traditional rights and liberties, while the French Revolution was designed to produce a new social order based on a false rationalistic philosophy at the expense of personal property and the traditional class structure of a Christian kingdom.

Prompted by RICHARD PRICE's sermon and *Discourse* in praise of the Revolution, Burke's treatise in turn provoked notable replies from THOMAS PAINE in *THE RIGHTS OF MAN*, James Mackintosh in *Vindiciae Gallicae* and MARY WOLLSTONECRAFT in her two *Vindications*.

Rehearsal, The A BURLESQUE play by GEORGE VILLIERS, 2ND DUKE OF BUCKINGHAM, perhaps with the help of SAMUEL BUTLER and others, first performed in 1671. Its mockery of heroic tragedy probably contributed to the decline of the style.

Bayes brings his friends, Smith and Johnson, to watch the rehearsal of his heroic drama. Constantly providing ludicrous annotation to his overblown verse and tragic account of the attempted usurpation of the kingdom of Brentford, he emerges as a pompous fool. Buckingham's original target in the creation of Bayes was probably WILLIAM D'AVENANT, but the revised version was aimed at DRYDEN, who retaliated in *ABSALOM AND ACHITOPHEL*.

Reid, Christopher (John) 1949– Poet. Born in Hong Kong, he was educated at Tonbridge School and Exeter College, Oxford. He works as a literary journalist. His first two collections, *Arcadia* (1979) and *Pea Soup* (1982), concentrating on unusual perceptions of everyday reality and using a technique built on the deliberate misrecognition of signs, identified him with the MARTIAN POETS and made comparisons with CRAIG RAINE, his Oxford tutor, inevitable. Reid's taste for impersonality is emphasized by *Katerina Brac* (1985), which purports to be the translated work of its imaginary title character, and *In the Echoey Tunnel* (1991).

Reid, Forrest 1875–1947 Irish novelist. He was born and lived for most of his life in Belfast. At Cambridge he struck up a lifelong friendship with E. M. FORSTER who, with other Cambridge friends like EDWIN MUIR and WALTER DE LA MARE, was an admirer of his work. Most of his 16 novels are centred on childhood and set their values against those of the decaying commercial society of north-east Ulster in the early 20th century. *Peter Waring* (1937) is widely regarded as his best work, although the Tom Barber trilogy, *Uncle Stephen* (1931), *The Retreat* (1936) and *Young Tom* (1944), is almost as well known. His autobiographies, *Apostate* (1926) and *Private Road* (1940), are steeped in the nostalgia which characterizes the best of his fiction. Reid also wrote critical studies of YEATS and Walter de la Mare.

Reid, J. Graham 1945– Irish playwright. He was born in Belfast and educated at Queen's University. Reid's first two plays, *The Death of Humpty-Dumpty* (1979) and *The Closed Door* (1980), tell equally harrowing stories of victims on the periphery of terrorist violence and the widening circle of loss. He has also written a successful television trilogy, *Billy* (1982), and two stage plays, *The Hidden Curriculum* (1982) and *Remembrance* (1984).

Reid, Captain (Thomas) Mayne 1818–83 Anglo-American writer of CHILDREN'S LITERATURE. Born in Ballyroney, County Down, he was intended for the Presbyterian ministry but, at the age of 19, went to America, where he spent several adventurous years and acquired his captaincy in the Mexican-American war. After his return to Europe in 1849 he settled in England, though he returned to America for a further stay in 1867–70. Reid drew on his American experiences in his popular novels for boys, notably *The Rifle Rangers: or, Adventures in Southern Mexico* (1850), *The Scalp Hunters: or, Romantic Adventures in Northern Mexico* (1851), *The Boy Hunters* (1853), *The Maroon* (1862), *The Cliff-Climbers* (1864), *Afloat in the Forest* (1865), *The Headless Horseman* (1866), *The Castaways* (1870) and *Gwen-Wynne* (1877). The *Quadroon: or, A Lover's Adventure in Louisiana* (1856) was adapted for the stage by DION BOUCICAULT as *THE OCTOROON* (1859). Reid's later work showed signs of strain, for by this time he was in financial difficulties brought about by his extravagance and weakness for unsuccessful business ventures. He also wrote travel books, poetry, plays and a book on croquet.

Reid, Thomas 1710–96 Scottish philosopher. Born at Strachan in Kincardineshire, the parish minister's son, be completed his education at Marischal College, Aberdeen. He was professor of moral philosophy at King's College, Aberdeen, from 1752 to 1764, when he succeeded ADAM SMITH in the same chair at Glasgow University. Reid's first publication was *An Essay on Quantity* (1748) but he made his mark with *An Inquiry into the Human Mind on the Principles of Common Sense* (1764). *Essays on the Intellectual Powers of Man* (1785) and *Essays on the Active Powers of Man* (1788), his later works, confirmed him as the founder of the 'common-sense' school of philosophy, in ranging the principles common to the understanding of all rational men against the scepticism generated by philosophers like LOCKE, BERKELEY, and HUME who could not, he insisted, produce any evidence for their assumptions. Reid's rhetorical prose style has confined his readership to students of philosophy.

Reid, V(ictor) S(tafford) 1913–87 Jamaican novelist. Born and educated in Kingston, he was a journalist on the Jamaica *Daily Gleaner*, edited several magazines and was director of an advertising agency.

With ROGER MAIS and the sculptress Edna Manley, he was a member of the Focus group which helped to promote a sense of cultural nationalism in Jamaica in the 1940s. His first novel, *New Day* (1949), was a seminal work in the development of Caribbean fiction, anticipating the region's literary renaissance of the 1950s. The first Caribbean novel to use Creole as its narrative medium (albeit in a modified form), it describes changes in Jamaican society between 1865, the date of the Morant Bay rebellion, and 1944, when a new constitution was introduced. Told by an 87-year-old man, who as a boy was an eyewitness at Morant Bay and who links his family's fortunes with those of his country, the novel is also notable for its use of oral history, its vivid realization of landscape and folk customs and its use of a child's perspective as a way of discovering a place hitherto effectively unchronicled in literature. In this respect it anticipates GEORGE LAMMING's *In the Castle of My Skin*, MICHAEL ANTHONY's *The Year in San Fernando*, ZEE EDGELL's *Beka Lamb* and JAMAICA KINCAID's *Annie John*. Reid's other novels include: *The Leopard* (1958), a work set in Kenya at the time of the Mau Mau freedom fighters' struggle; *Sixty-Five* (1960), a children's novel about the Morant Bay rebellion; *Peter of Mount Ephraim* (1971); and *The Jamaicans* (1976). He also published *The Horses of the Morning* (1985), a biography of Norman Manley, with whom he was associated in the 1940s and who appears in a fictional guise in *New Day*.

Relapse, The: *or, Virtue in Danger* SIR JOHN VANBRUGH's first play (1696), a hastily written riposte to COLLEY CIBBER's *LOVE'S LAST SHIFT*. Cibber had shown the rakish Loveless resolved on reform and determined to live faithfully with his wife Amanda. Vanbrugh shows his immediate relapse when, on a visit to London, he becomes involved with the witty widow, Berinthia, while Amanda resists the advances of Berinthia's former lover, Worthy.

More substantial than the main plot is a sub-plot involving some of the most memorable characters in RESTORATION COMEDY. Having bought himself a title, Lord Foppington, the epitome of empty fashion, wishes to acquire a wife who can afford him. The choice falls on Miss Hoyden, a spirited girl brought up in rustic seclusion by her father, Sir Tunbelly Clumsy. Outwitted by his young brother, Fashion, who has secretly married Hoyden while claiming to be Lord Foppington, his lordship has to concede defeat. Ironically, Cibber himself scored a major success as Lord Foppington in the first production at DRURY LANE.

Religio Laici: *or, A Layman's Faith* A religious poem by JOHN DRYDEN, first published, to considerable acclaim, in 1682. The argument of the piece is in favour of the Christian religion over any belief in DEISM (the inference of a godlike presence from an examination of the created world), and an affirmation of the primary importance of the Bible as a guide to salvation. The second part of the poem strives to express the infinite preferability of the Anglican church over its Catholic counterpart (Dryden was later to become a convert to Rome), but is generally less successful.

Religio Medici The first published book by SIR THOMAS BROWNE, it was originally written for his 'private exercise and satisfaction'. The widely circulated manuscript was obtained by a printer and published in 1642 but reissued in an authorized edition in the following year.

The work affirms the author's Christian faith but refers to such a wide diversity of topical thought that the book transcends the normal barriers of devotional literature, becoming a fascinating and allusive investigation of the richness of God's creation. Browne is both sceptical and celebratory, erudite and fantastical in his attitudes, and the whole is realized in some of the century's finest prose, firm and yet idiosyncratic. The book includes two fine prayers in verse, and numerous sections on subjects ranging from the occult to the nature of sleep.

Reliques of Ancient English Poetry See PERCY, THOMAS.

Renaissance, The See *STUDIES IN THE HISTORY OF THE RENAISSANCE*.

Renault, Mary [Challans, Mary] 1905–83 Novelist. A doctor's daughter, born in London, she was educated at St Hugh's College, Oxford. Her work as a nurse provided the background for her early novels: *Purposes of Love* (1939; as *Promise of Love* in USA), *Kind are Her Answers* (1940), *The Friendly Young Ladies* (1944; as *The Middle Mist* in USA), *Return to Night* (1947), *North Face* (1948) and *The Charioteer* (1953), a story of servicemen and homosexuality during the war. Her reputation rests mainly on her historical novels about the ancient world, notable for combining liveliness with scholarly sophistication: *The Last of the Wine* (1956), *The King Must Die* (1958) and *The Bull from the Sea* (1962), about Theseus; *The Lion in the Gateway* (1964), for young people; *The Mask of Apollo* (1966), *Fire from Heaven* (1970), *The Persian Boy* (1972) and *Funeral Games* (1981), about Alexander; and *The Praise Singer* (1978). *The Nature of Alexander* (1975) is a historical study.

Rendell, Ruth 1930– Writer of DETECTIVE FICTION. Born in London, she worked as a reporter for an Essex local newspaper before establishing a reputation with talented and prolific writing which falls into several categories. Most popular is her series of novels about Detective Chief Inspector Reginald Wexford, and his colleague Mike Burden, of the Kingsmarkham police: *From Doon with Death* (1965), *A New Lease of Death* (1967; as *Sins of the Fathers* in USA), *Wolf to the Slaughter* (1967), *The Best Man to Die* (1969), *A Guilty Thing Surprised* (1970), *No More Dying Then* (1970), *Murder Being Once Done* (1972), *Some Lie and Some Die* (1973), *Shake Hands for Ever* (1975), *A Sleeping Life* (1978), *Put On by Cunning* (1981; as *Death Notes* in USA), *The Speaker of Mandarin* (1983), *An Unkindness of Ravens* (1985) and *The Veiled One* (1988). In contrast to their solid and conventional reliance on police procedure, other novels have treated crime in deliberately unsettling ways. Notable titles include *To Fear a Painted Devil* (1965), *One Across, Two Down* (1971), *The Face of Trespass* (1974), *A Demon in My View* (1976), *Make Death Love Me* (1979), *Master of the Moor* (1982) and *The Bridesmaid* (1989). Similar preoccupations, and particularly an interest in past crimes which cast their shadow over the present, inform the novels she has published under the pseudonym of Barbara Vine: *The Dark-Adapted Eye* (1986), *A Fatal Inversion* (1987), *The House of Stairs* (1989) and *Gallowglass* (1990).

Renee [Kahungunu, Ngati] 1929– New Zealand playwright. She left school at the age of 12 but completed a university degree as a mature part-time student. She worked as a director in community theatre for more than 20 years before writing her first play, *Setting the Table* (1981). Since then she has become the strongest influence on feminist theatre in New Zealand. Her early agit-prop style developed into an effective mixture of historical realism and musical revue in her best-known work, a trilogy about four generations of working-class women: *Wednesday to Come* (1984), *Pass It On* (1986) and *Jeannie Once* (1990). She has also published a collection of stories, *Finding Ruth* (1987), and a novel, *Willy Nilly* (1990).

Representative Men A book by RALPH WALDO EMERSON, published in 1850 and consisting of seven essays that were originally delivered as lectures in Boston between 11 December 1845 and 22 January 1846. The series was given again shortly afterwards in Concord, Massachusetts, and again, with various revisions, in England between May 1847 and November 1848. In the opening essay Emerson suggests that truly great men are representative of their time and place: the genius is not aloof from his society, but is the earliest and finest manifestation of that society's possibilities. The six representative men he discusses in the other essays are Plato, Swedenborg, Montaigne, SHAKESPEARE, Napoleon and Goethe.

Restoration comedy With the reopening of London's theatres after the Restoration of Charles II, there came a demand for new plays to fill out the na-

tional repertoire. Revivals of the comedies of BEN JONSON, BEAUMONT and FLETCHER and translations of Molière were increasingly replaced by colourless imitations of their work. The fashionable audiences of the period, aping the manners and aspiring to the taste of the new king's court, sought out stronger and more salacious material for the new sensations of the stage, actresses. A competitive comedy of wit and repartee, concluding in marriage only after extensive foreplay with adultery, was pioneered by such gentleman-writers as ETHEREGE and SEDLEY. The masterpieces of the genre are Etherege's *SHE WOULD IF SHE COULD* (1668) and *THE MAN OF MODE* (1676), WYCHERLEY's *THE COUNTRY WIFE* (1675) and *THE PLAIN DEALER* (1676), CONGREVE's *THE DOUBLE DEALER* (1693), *LOVE FOR LOVE* (1695) and *THE WAY OF THE WORLD* (1700) and VANBRUGH's *THE RELAPSE* (1696) and *THE PROVOKED WIFE* (1697). Plots are characteristically based on the deception of the witless and the would-be wits by the truly witty. Opposition to the immorality and decadence of Restoration comedy started early, and came to a head with the publication of JEREMY COLLIER's *Short View* (1698), in the wake of which Congreve abandoned the theatre. A new comedy of conscience and reformation was signalled by the success of COLLEY CIBBER's *LOVE'S LAST SHIFT* (1696) and immediately challenged by Vanbrugh's sparkling sequel, *The Relapse*. The plays of GEORGE FARQUHAR are the outstanding works of transition from the Restoration comedy of manners to 18th-century SENTIMENTAL COMEDY.

Return of the Native, The A novel by THOMAS HARDY, first published in 1878 in book form and as a serial in the magazine *Belgravia*.

Damon Wildeve, an engineer turned publican, is proprietor of 'The Quiet Woman' on Egdon Heath. He is engaged to the gentle Thomasin Yeobright but carrying on an affair with Eustacia Vye, who lives with her grandfather at nearby Mistover Knap and whose desire in life is 'to be loved to madness'. Wildeve, 'to wring the heart' of Eustacia, marries Thomasin. Meanwhile, Clym Yeobright, the latter's cousin, wearying of his meretricious life as a Parisian jeweller, returns to his native heath intending to become a schoolmaster. Greatly to his mother's disapproval he falls in love with and marries Eustacia, who has unwisely accepted him in the hope he will take her away to the more exciting life of a city, preferably Paris. But Clym's sight fails and he is reduced to furze-cutting for a livelihood, a catastrophe that drives his wife to despair. Then, out of her renewed association with Wildeve, Eustacia becomes partially, but unknowingly, responsible for Mrs Yeobright's death; a quarrel with Clym which arises from that tragedy causes her to leave home. In desperation Eustacia drowns herself in Shadwater Weir and Wildeve loses his life trying to save her. Some 18 months later Clym, remorseful over the deaths of Eustacia and his mother, becomes an open-air preacher and Thomasin marries Diggory Venn, the 'isolated and weird' reddleman who moves in and out of the narrative at psychologically suitable times.

Revelation of Divine Love, A See JULIAN OF NORWICH.

Revenge of Bussy D'Ambois, The A REVENGE TRAGEDY by GEORGE CHAPMAN, written for indoor theatre performance in *c.* 1610 and published in 1613. It is a sequel to *BUSSY D'AMBOIS.*

Clermont D'Ambois, close friend of the Duc de Guise, is a gentleman of honour and courage. The ghost of his murdered brother, Bussy, urges him to avenge the crime; Clermont intends to do so, but only by the honourable method of a formal duel. He sends a challenge to his brother's murderer, Montsurry, who proves himself a coward. When the ghost of Bussy renews his plea, Clermont forces Montsurry to fight and kills him. He then learns that his friend, the Duc de Guise, has been assassinated and, despairing of the vicious time in which he lives, he kills himself.

revenge tragedy A type of TRAGEDY derived from Seneca and made fashionable on the Elizabethan and Jacobean stage by KYD's *THE SPANISH TRAGEDY* (*c.* 1589). Revenge tragedies usually begin with the ghost of a wronged and/or murdered man appearing to a descendant or friend and demanding vengeance. In carrying it out, the avenger sometimes feigns madness and uses the device of the play-within-the-play. Rarely adherents of strict form, the playwrights incorporated those features that best suited them whilst re-ordering or abandoning others. SHAKESPEARE's two revenge tragedies, *TITUS ANDRONICUS* (*c.* 1592) and *HAMLET* (*c.* 1601), exhibit almost the full range of their kind. Other notable examples are *THE REVENGER'S TRAGEDY* (1607), WEBSTER's *THE WHITE DEVIL* (*c.* 1612) and *THE DUCHESS OF MALFI* (?before 1614), MIDDLETON's *THE CHANGELING* (1622) and *WOMEN BEWARE WOMEN* (*c.* 1625), MARSTON's *ANTONIO'S REVENGE* (1600) and SHIRLEY's *THE TRAITOR* (1631), but the theme of revenge so dominated the tragedies of the period that the list could be vastly prolonged.

Revenger's Tragedy, The A REVENGE TRAGEDY published in 1607 and generally, though not confidently, ascribed to CYRIL TOURNEUR. He was not named as its author until 1656, and the manifest inferiority of his other surviving play, *THE ATHEIST'S TRAGEDY*, has strengthened the critical case that THOMAS MIDDLETON is the author.

The complex plot centres on two families. The first consists of Gratiana, widow of an Italian nobleman impoverished by the chicanery of the reigning duke,

and her three children, Castiza, Hippolito and Vindice. The second consists of the conniving duke, his son Lussurioso, his bastard son Spurio, his second wife and her three sons, Ambitioso, Supervacuo and the unnamed Junior Brother. The primary link in the chain of revenge is established at once, when Vindice enters holding the skull of his loved one, poisoned by the lecherous duke because she would not yield to his lust. Sworn to revenge, Vindice finds opportunity in his employment by Lussurioso, for which he assumes disguise as the mercenary Piato. Lussurioso's object is the seduction of Vindice's sister, Castiza. She angrily rejects the suit, but 'Piato' is horrified to find his mother ready to persuade Castiza to surrender her virginity to Lussurioso. Junior Brother is imprisoned for raping the virtuous wife of the noble Antonio. Without much difficulty the duchess persuades Spurio, the duke's bastard son, to become her lover. The duke continues his career of lust. All the brothers and step-brothers conspire against each other to succeed to the dukedom. Methodically, Vindice, with some help from his brother Hippolito, plots their downfall, aided by their own rivalries. He contrives a startlingly apt death for the duke by applying poison to the skull of his dead lady and tricking the duke into kissing it in the belief that it is his procured new mistress. Junior Brother has already been executed as a direct result of confused orders issued by his elder brothers. The climax comes at the festivities to celebrate the inauguration of the new duke, Lussurioso. In the disguise of masquers, Vindice and Hippolito assassinate Lussurioso and his corrupt noblemen. They are followed by the 'real' masquers, Spurio, Ambitioso and Supervacuo, who, finding Lussurioso dead, turn on each other in a paroxysm of mutual murder. The restoration of the shattered dukedom rests with the virtuous Antonio, whose first act is to order the execution of Vindice and Hippolito, self-confessed murderers of the old duke.

Review, The A periodical founded by DANIEL DEFOE with the help of ROBERT HARLEY, EARL OF OXFORD, on 19 February 1704, upon Defoe's release from prison. It was first called *A Weekly Review of the Affairs of France, Purged from the Errors and Partiality of News-Writers and Petty-Statesmen, of All Sides.* It had become *The Review* by 11 June 1713, the year it closed, when Defoe went to prison for the second time. After the first six weekly issues it came out twice weekly and from 22 March 1705 was appearing thrice weekly. It was written almost entirely by Defoe himself, a remarkable feat since he was often in Scotland as Harley's clandestine agent during the paper's existence. *The Review* offered well-informed comment on the affairs of Europe (England was at war with France), dealt with aspects of the social life of the day, and kept its readers informed on commerce and trade. Non-partisan, Defoe gave his opinion on political topics and thus became the first leader writer of the English press.

Revolt of Islam, The A poem by PERCY BYSSHE SHELLEY, in SPENSERIAN STANZAS, published in 1818. Written in 1817, it was originally called 'Laon and Cythna'; the principal characters, who become lovers, are brother and sister. Charles Ollier, who published the revised poem, persuaded Shelley to change the relationship.

The poem is set in Islam where Cythna, a maiden dedicated to the freedom of her sex from harsh laws, joins forces with Laon, another revolutionary. They unite the people in revolt and for a time succeed; but the ruling tyrants, with reinforced armies, crush the revolt and lay waste the land. Famine and pestilence follow, and at the instigation of a priest Laon and Cythna are burned alive as a sacrifice. Its revolutionary significance lay in Shelley's response to contemporary conditions in England.

Rexroth, Kenneth 1905–82 American poet. Born in South Bend, Indiana, he led a Bohemian life-style in Chicago in the 1920s, and then moved to San Francisco, where he became active in leftist and union movements and eventually established himself as a central figure in the literary community. His work variously consists of elegiac, erotic, and political verse, and is often surreal and experimental in style. His early volumes of poetry are *In What Hour* (1940), *The Phoenix and the Tortoise* (1944), *The Art of Worldly Wisdom* (1949) and *The Signature of All Things* (1949). Although he later distanced himself from the movement, Rexroth was briefly associated with the BEATS. His other volumes of verse are *Poems* (1955), *Natural Numbers* (1963), *The Collected Shorter Poems* (1967), *The Collected Longer Poems* (1968), *New Poems* (1974), *The Silver Swan* (1976) and *The Morning Star: Poems and Translations* (1979). He also published a collection of four plays in verse entitled *Beyond the Mountains* (1951) and numerous translations, including *100 Poems from the Japanese* (1954), *100 Poems from the Chinese* (1956) and *100 Poems from the Greek and Latin* (1959). His critical essays are collected in *The Bird in the Bush* (1959) and *Assays* (1961). *An Autobiographical Novel* appeared in 1966.

Reynard the Fox A prose translation by WILLIAM CAXTON, published in 1481, of the Dutch *Hystorie van Reynaert die Vos*, a version of the composite Renard Cycle. This probably originated in Latin but is best known in its French form, the verse *Roman de Renart* largely produced in the 12th and early 13th centuries, where CHAUCER found the source for *The Nun's Priest's Tale* in THE CANTERBURY TALES. The whole cycle is dominated by the deceitful character of the fox, at first sympathetic but later simply evil, and by

an increasing tendency to satiric attack on the nobility and the Church.

The part of the cycle given by Caxton relates how the fox is called to court to answer for his misdeeds. By trickery and corruption he escapes death. On his second trial he is challenged to single combat by the wolf Isengrim, whom he defeats unfairly. He becomes a favourite at court. The story is a parable, showing how the evil are advanced and teaching avoidance of wickedness.

Reynolds, John Hamilton 1796–1852 Poet. The son of a schoolmaster, Reynolds was born at Shrewsbury, Shropshire, and educated at Shrewsbury and St Paul's Schools, and worked in a London insurance office before taking up law. In 1814 he published his first work, *Safie*, an oriental novel in the style of BYRON, and *The Eden of the Imagination*, which recalls the verse of the late 18th century. In 1815 he became a contributor to the periodical *The Champion*, and his collection *The Naiad: A Tale with Other Poems* appeared in 1816. LEIGH HUNT's 'Young Poets' issue of *THE EXAMINER* (November 1816) ranked him with his friend KEATS and SHELLEY as one of the most promising writers of the day, but Reynolds failed to find his own voice as a poet, and is now chiefly remembered for his friendship and correspondence with Keats. His most crafted serious work is *The Garden of Florence* (1821). A witty and mercurial figure, his real genius lay in imitation and PARODY, and his skit on WORDSWORTH's *PETER BELL*, *Peter Bell: A Lyrical Ballad* (1819), is one of the finest parodies in English literature; it inspired Shelley to try his own hand in *Peter Bell the Third*. *The Fancy* appeared in 1820, and in 1825 he collaborated with THOMAS HOOD in *Odes and Addresses to Great People*.

Reynolds, Sir Joshua 1723–92 Painter and writer on art. Son of the master of the grammar school at Plympton-Earl's, Devonshire, where he was educated, Reynolds was apprenticed to Thomas Hudson, the portrait painter, in 1740. He had a highly successful career, culminating in the foundation presidency of the Royal Academy in 1768. As president, Reynolds delivered the lectures (1769–90) published as *Discourses on Art*. The dedication to the King, prefacing the work, was written by SAMUEL JOHNSON, who also improved the text at various points. Philosophically, these pieces were based upon the theories of Aristotle and Plato in that notions of truth and beauty were the result of generalizing from particular examples, and these notions were inextricably linked with moral qualities. Reynolds also strongly advocated that the aspiring artist should build upon the achievements of his predecessors: copying the works of suitable masters was a key element in the education of the student. Creation was presented as an entirely rational process. The *Discourses* were vitriolically assailed by

BLAKE: they are more conventionally seen as perceptive discussions of 18th-century attitudes to art. Reynolds had earlier contributed three papers on art to THE IDLER (Nos. 76, 79 and 82) and provided the annotations to WILLIAM MASON's verse translation of Du Fresnoy's *Art of Painting*. In 1781 he toured Flanders and Holland and recorded the tour with detailed notes on all the pictures he had seen, advancing the then unfashionable opinion that Dutch paintings, particularly those of Rubens, were not inferior to the Italian School. Some of his notes on SHAKESPEARE were printed in the final volume of Johnson's edition and others in MALONE's supplement of 1780. He also left short descriptions of GARRICK, GOLDSMITH and Johnson which were published posthumously. Johnson described Reynolds as 'almost the only man whom I call a friend', and was encouraged by him to found the literary gathering known as the Club in the winter of 1763–4. Initially the Club had nine members: Johnson, Reynolds, Beauclerk, BURKE, Chamier, Goldsmith, Hawkins, Langton and Nugent. Others, including Garrick, Banks and Malone, were subsequently elected. BOSWELL dedicated *THE LIFE OF JOHNSON* (1791) to him, as had Goldsmith *THE DESERTED VILLAGE* (1770). In his long and highly successful career (he had 156 sitters in 1759) he painted many literary and theatrical figures, including: Mrs Abington, Baretti, Boswell, Burke, Charles Burney, Sir William Chambers, Kitty Fisher, FOOTE, Charles James Fox, Garrick (seven times), Warren Hastings, Johnson (five times), SHERIDAN, Mrs Siddons, STERNE and HORACE WALPOLE. Some 700 engraved plates were made of his works, and it has been through Reynolds's eyes that the public have come to see many of these figures.

Reznikoff, Charles 1894–1976 American poet. He was born in Brooklyn and educated at the University of Missouri and New York University. He is generally identified with OBJECTIVISM, and much of his work emphasizes the role of Judaism in his life. His first publication was a volume of poetry, *Rhythms* (1918). Other volumes include *Poems* (1920), *Uriel Acosta: A Play and a Fourth Group of Verse* (1921), *Chatterton, The Black Death, and Meriwether Lewis: Three Plays* (1922), *Coral and Captive Israel: Two Plays* (1923), *Five Groups of Verse* (1927), *Nine Plays* (1927), *Jerusalem the Golden* (1934) and *Inscriptions: 1944–1956* (1959). A poetic meditation on US history, *Testimony: The United States, 1885–1890*, appeared in 1965; its sequel, *Testimony: The United States, 1891–1900*, in 1968. He also wrote a historical novel, *The Lionhearted* (1944).

Rhoda Fleming A novel by George MEREDITH, first published in 1865.

Interested in metropolitan life, Rhoda and Dahlia, the two daughters of the widowed Farmer Fleming, come to London under the protection of their uncle, Anthony Hackbut, where they encounter the cousins Edward and Algernon Blancove. The former seduces and deserts Dahlia, whose shame is deepened by a miserable marriage to the bigamous and contemptible Sedgett, an alliance contracted in the hope of expiating her shame. After various melodramatic adventures, she attempts suicide whilst the hand of the self-willed, determined Rhoda is successfully sought by the ex-soldier and farm-assistant Robert Eccles.

Although *Rhoda Fleming* is a sombre novel, several down-to-earth characters – among them Master Gammon, Mrs Sumfit and Mrs Boulby – enliven the pages with their local humour and steadfastness.

rhyme [rime] The repetition of a sound or sounds, a common feature of linguistic usage put to organized and systematic effect in much, though not all, poetry. For repeated initial sounds only, usually called ALLITERATION, the term 'initial-' or 'head-' rhyme may also be used. Similarly, compound identical sounds such as *feet* and *feat* may count as rhyme. But the more interesting kind of repetition normally styled rhyme requires different initial sounds followed by the same final sound or sounds, the first of which must be an accented vowel: *bough/cow, acidity/quiddity*, but not *acidity/jollity*. This more demanding repetition is sometimes called 'full' or 'exact' rhyme, to distinguish it from less precise matchings normally classed as 'near-', 'half-' or 'para-rhyme'. Such full rhymes are further classified as 'masculine', if monosyllabic, or 'feminine' (or 'double', 'triple', etc.) if unstressed identical syllables follow the stressed one, as in *acidity/quiddity*. So-called 'eye-rhymes' (*love/move*) are not rhymes at all, only tenuous near-rhymes at best. But this can pose a problem. Many such eye-rhymes were once full rhymes: 'Here thou, great ANNA, whom three realms obey,/ Dost sometimes counsel take – and sometimes Tea.' (POPE, *THE RAPE OF THE LOCK*). If, like Pope, we read 'Tay', we risk sounding pedantic. But if we read 'Tea' instead, we risk spoiling a brilliant and exact effect. The question, clearly, is one of usage.

What is the point of rhyme? The example above suggests that its precise effects must be innumerable, each dependent on the particular context. The ideas of social order, for instance, which underlie *The Rape of the Lock* are clearly exemplified in the strict rhyme of its HEROIC COUPLETS. However, rhyming the trivial 'tea' with the triple-kingdomed 'obey' chimes in with the humorous juxtaposition of counsels of state and chit-chat over teacups, suggesting that minor disorders (such as the rape of a lock, merely) can be taken lightly as not disruptive of the larger order implied by the unflawed rhyming of the poem as a whole.

Some more general observations can help to indicate why so much verse is rhymed, even though rhyme is not a requirement of verse. One obvious use is to mark the measures of song or the repetitions of some communal dance or task. In a wider sense, rhyme, like METRE, seems to image the basic human need to structure experience, to make sense of sense-data, to organize emotions or to socialize them into play (as in certain children's games: 'I'm the king of the castle/ You're a dirty old arsehole'). More technically, the rhyme of discursive poems, such as those of Pope and the other Augustans, can underline cut and thrust, the presentation of parallel or antithetical ideas. In shorter poems, it may support the thematic structure: witness LARKIN's 'Talking in Bed', where the stanzas of the argument are linked (aba cac dcd) while the conclusion is separated (eee); or witness the Petrarchan SONNET, which uses the sestet for one purpose (to set a scene or recreate an experience) and the octet which follows it for another (to reflect or draw a conclusion). The rhyme-scheme of the Shakespearean sonnet implies a different movement, leading to a summary moral or a disconcerting twist in the tail in the concluding couplet. BYRON, a master of the deliberately forced rhyme which draws wry attention to itself, uses the couplet which finishes the stanza in OTTAVA RIMA to focus a joke or give extra punch to a sardonic aphorism. SHAKESPEARE's plays demonstrate many other uses of rhyme. A scene in blank verse may end with a rhymed couplet, summing up its import and discreetly moving the hearer/reader away from action and practicality to moral reflection, or even with a song, to mark a more pronounced shift in atmosphere.

Oddly enough, the constraints of rhyme can make it easier for a poet to write interesting verse. English may be poor in rhyming words by comparison to the romance languages and so the tight rhyme-schemes of TERZA RIMA, which flow so easily from Dante's pen, can merely frustrate. But the rhyme-schemes which English poets have preferred, usually looser than those of French or Italian poetry though no less demanding in terms of the resources offered by the language, still provide a stimulus that prevents the writer from resting content with first thoughts or words. Finding the proper rhyme, satisfying the chosen convention, can often generate originality. On a deeper level, the presence of rhyme must always enhance the formality inherent in verse, acting like the frame of a picture to suggest that this is a work of art to be contemplated, not a statement demanding action. In this way, and in helping to legitimize the linguistic heightening which is native to verse, it is the natural ally of metre.

rhyme royal Stanza form of seven decasyllabic lines rhyming ababbcc. Its name probably derives from its use in THE KINGIS QUAIR, attributed to JAMES I OF SCOTLAND. An alternative name, the Chaucerian stanza, pays tribute to its first appearance in

CHAUCER's 'Complaint unto Pity'; Chaucer went on to use it again in TROILUS AND CRISEYDE, THE PARLEMENT OF FOULES and some of THE CANTERBURY TALES. Later poets who wrote in rhyme royal include SIR THOMAS WYATT, EDMUND SPENSER, SHAKESPEARE (THE RAPE OF LUCRECE), MICHAEL DRAYTON and WILLIAM MORRIS.

Rhymers' Club, The A group of poets who met at the Cheshire Cheese in Fleet Street between 1891 and 1894. It included its founders, Ernest Rhys and W. B. YEATS, RICHARD LE GALLIENNE, ERNEST DOWSON, LIONEL JOHNSON, ARTHUR SYMONS, JOHN DAVIDSON, T. W. Rolleston, Selwyn Image and Edwin Ellis. According to Yeats's memoir Four Years: 1887–1891, WILLIAM WATSON joined but never came, FRANCIS THOMPSON came once but did not join, and OSCAR WILDE would only attend meetings in private houses. Yeats described the meetings as 'always decorous and often dull'. The group published two collections of verse, in 1892 and 1894. See also AESTHETIC MOVEMENT.

Rhys, Jean 1894–1979 Novelist and short-story writer. Born in Roseau, Dominica, she came to England in 1909 and spent most of the inter-war years in Paris. The painful clarity of her understanding of personal, sexual, or social exploitation gives her writings firm coherence. European, Bohemian, modernist, her stories in The Left Bank (1927), together with the novels Postures (1928; as Quartet in USA, 1929 and subsequently), After Leaving Mr Mackenzie (1930), Voyage in the Dark (1934) and Good Morning, Midnight (1939) all reveal single-minded craftsmanship in presenting female characters of intense vitality, but deracinated, lonely and directionless. A long period of silence and artistic oblivion preceded her finest novel, Wide Sargasso Sea (1966). It invents the tragic story of Rochester's mad wife in JANE EYRE, portraying her as a victim of commercial, decadent colonial society, reduced to the very insanity for which her individuality was mistaken. Tigers are Better-looking (1968) and the finely designed collection, Sleep It Off Lady (1976) contain stories that confirm the imaginative unity of Rhys's work. Smile Please: An Unfinished Autobiography appeared in 1979, Letters 1931–1966 in 1984.

rhythm See METRE.

Ricardo, David 1772–1823 Political economist. Born in the City of London into a Jewish family with strong Dutch connections, he had a 'common-school' education followed by two years in Amsterdam, probably at the Talmud Tora, where he was taught by rabbis. This developed the 'taste for abstract and general reasoning' which characterized his deductive method of economic enquiry and eventually dominated the field of economics. Introduced early to the

Jean Rhys

family stockbroking business, he established himself as a jobber in the Stock Exchange and quickly prospered. Between 1806 and 1815 he joined partnerships bidding for the government loans which financed the Napoleonic War, and the victory at Waterloo set the seal on his fortune. He restricted his business activities to concentrate on Parliament (which he entered in 1819 for the pocket borough of Portarlington), his estates (which included Gatcomb Park in Gloucestershire) and writing.

ADAM SMITH'S *WEALTH OF NATIONS* had first aroused his interest in political economy. Ricardo's earliest work is in the field of monetary economics, concerned with the high price of gold and the depreciation of paper money, the role of the Bank of England and monetary theory. His writing, never brilliant, is at its clearest in *The High Price of Bullion* (1810) and the *Reply to Mr Bosanquet's Practical Observations on the Report of the Bullion Committee* (1811). His *Proposals for an Economical and Secure Currency* (1816) are grounded in the Quantity Theory of Money, which demonstrates that inflation is caused by too much money in circulation. Ricardo's pamphlets brought him into contact with leading economists, including MALTHUS and JAMES MILL. Mill encouraged him to develop the ideas in the *Essay on the Low Price of Corn on the Profits of Stock* (1815) into his major work, *On the Principles of Political Economy and*

Taxation (1817; twice revised by 1821). It develops a theory of value which is used to explain how the proportions of the wages of labour and the profits of capital are determined, as well as the effects of taxes. Ricardo did not produce another book, although he wrote a critical commentary on Malthus's *Principles of Political Economy* not published until 1928. His article 'Funding System' appeared in the *Supplement to the Encyclopaedia Britannica* (1820). His interest in free trade led him to publish *On Protection to Agriculture* (1822). The *Plan for the Establishment of a National Bank* appeared posthumously.

Rice, Elmer 1892–1967 American playwright. Born Elmer Leopold Reizenstein in New York to German-Jewish immigrant parents, he left school at the age of 14. He worked for a time as a clerk in his cousin's law office, then studied law, and was admitted to the Bar in 1913, but shortly thereafter gave up this career to become a playwright. His first play, *On Trial* (1914), was a financial and critical success and effectively launched his career. He is often credited with inventing the technique later called flashback: in *On Trial*, a court-room drama, the action switches between testimony and flashbacks initiated by the testimony, moving progressively further back in time to exonerate the accused man. Despite its revolutionary construction, it deals with relatively conventional themes of honesty, infidelity and the preying of the immoral rich upon female innocence. In the course of the long and active career that followed, Rice wrote over 50 plays, of which the best known are THE ADDING MACHINE (1923) and STREET SCENE (1929), which won him the PULITZER PRIZE.

Though his drama ranges from EXPRESSIONISM to NATURALISM to light-hearted comedy, his devotion to social justice and liberal causes is apparent throughout his work. Two early plays, *The Home of the Free* (1917) and *The Iron Cross* (1917), took up pacifist themes at an unpopular time; *The Subway* (1929) told the story of a young working girl victimized by lecherous men; *See Naples and Die* (1929) and *The Left Bank* (1931) were light-hearted critiques of expatriate morality, for which Rice gathered material on trips abroad. Other plays include *We, the People* (1933), a vehement indictment of conditions during the Depression, including an attack on racial prejudice; *Judgement Day* (1934), a thinly fictionalized account of the trial which followed the Reichstag fire; *Between Two Worlds* (1934), in which characters on a transatlantic voyage debate and play out the contradictions between the American system and the Soviet, which Rice had observed on a long visit to Russia; *Dream Girl* (1945); *Love among the Ruins* (1963); and *Close Harmony* (1929; also called *The Lady Next Door*) written in collaboration with DOROTHY PARKER.

Rice wrote several novels, Hollywood screenplays, an autobiography (*Minority Report*, 1963), and a history of the theatre. He also worked as a producer and director, and in 1937, three years after a widely publicized 'retirement from the theatre' prompted by a battle with the critics, formed the Playwrights Company with MAXWELL ANDERSON, ROBERT SHERWOOD, SIDNEY HOWARD and S. N. BEHRMAN. He was a founding member of the American Civil Liberties Union and later of the FEDERAL THEATRE PROJECT.

Riceyman Steps A novel by ARNOLD BENNETT, published in 1923. The story of Henry Earlforward concentrates on his life in and around the antiquarian bookshop he has inherited in Clerkenwell. His courtship, in middle age, of Violet Arb, the widow who has moved into a neighbouring shop, leads to marriage. But Henry's main passion is with his money and possessions: the novel gives keen insight into the self-centred world of the miser, its glimpses of openheartedness and its gradual decline from the state of emotional under-nourishment to physical illness. Henry's grim calculations over the honeymoon outing to Madame Tussaud's, his gift to Violet of a second-hand safe, and his horrified reactions when Violet has the house vacuum-cleaned, are only part of a detailed narrative, generous in its human interest.

Violet's thwarted attempts to bring warmth into the marriage before her death of a wasting illness are echoed in the life of her maidservant Elsie – and with a note of triumph. Detailed attention is given to Elsie's past, including her marriage, the death of her soldier husband, and her life in cramped lodgings. Her romance with the shell-shocked Joe, whom she nurses through malarial illness, and marries, contrasts with the struggle of Henry with his own illness. Only when near to death does he begin to acknowledge that Violet and he have been victims of a life-denying passion and that he has been responsible for this end.

Rich, Adrienne (Cecile) 1929– American poet. She was born in Baltimore and educated at Radcliffe College. *A Change of World* (1951), in the Yale Series of Younger Poets, and *The Diamond Cutters and Other Poems* (1955) were followed by *Snapshots of a Daughter-in-Law: Poems 1954–1962* (1963), in which she turned increasingly innovative forms and a startlingly frank idiom to explore feminist themes. Subsequent volumes were *The Necessities of Life: Poems 1962–1965* (1966), *Focus* (1966), *Selected Poems* (Britain, 1966; USA, 1967), *Leaflets: Poems 1965–1968* (1969), *The Will to Change: Poems 1968–70* (1971), *Diving Into the Wreck: Poems 1971–72* (1973), *Poems: Selected and New, 1950–1974* (1975), *The Dream of a Common Language: Poems 1974–1977* (1978), *A Wild Patience Has Taken Me This Far: Poems 1978–1981* (1981), *Sources* (1983), *The Fact of A Doorframe: Poems Selected and New 1950–1984* (1984) and *Your Native Land, Your Life* (1986), *Time's Power: Poems 1985–1988* (1989), *An Atlas of the Difficult World: Poems 1988–1991* (1991) and *Collected Early Poems, 1950–1970* (1993). A prose work, *Of Woman Born: Motherhood as Experience and Institution* (1976), established Rich as an influential radical feminist critic. She has also published *On Lies, Secrets, and Silence: Selected Prose 1966–1978* (1979), *Compulsory Heterosexuality and Lesbian Existence* (1981), *Blood, Bread, and Poetry: Selected Prose 1979–1985* (1986) and *Women and Honor: Some Notes on Lying* (1990). She has taught at many institutions and received the Shelley Memorial Award for Poetry and the National Book Award.

Rich, Barnabe 1542–1617 Author of romances and pamphlets. Rich entered military service in 1562, serving in France, the Low Countries and Ireland, where he spent most of the time between 1572 and 1582. During this time he rose to the rank of captain. His literary career consisted of the production of some 25 books: romances in the popular style of EUPHUISM, tracts on military affairs and the state of government in Ireland, some anti-Catholic works (including an account of a girl's false visions) and satires. His earliest publication was a dialogue on military affairs, *A Right Excellent and Pleasant Dialogue between Mercury and an English Soldier* (1574). His most important work is *Rich his Farewell to the*

Military Profession (1581), a collection of eight romances, including 'Apolonius and Silla' which is the source of the plot for *TWELFTH NIGHT*. This was followed by a series of euphuistic romances in 1581, 1584 and 1592. His later works were mainly satirical.

Richard II, The Life and Death of

A historical tragedy by WILLIAM SHAKESPEARE, first performed *c.* 1595 and published in two good Quartos in 1597 (Q1) and 1608 (Q4) before the First Folio of 1623. The main source is HOLINSHED's *Chronicles.*

The play opens with the conflict of two powerful noblemen, Thomas Mowbray, Duke of Norfolk and Henry Bolingbroke, Earl of Hereford. Richard II orders them to settle their differences in a duel at Coventry. With all preparations made, the king suddenly intervenes and banishes both men. Bolingbroke's resentment is exacerbated when Richard takes advantage of John of Gaunt's death to confiscate Bolingbroke's inheritance. He needs the money to finance his Irish wars. But the confiscation gives the calculating Bolingbroke a pretext for bringing an invading force to England. He receives sufficient support from English lords, overtaxed to gratify Richard's extravagance, to encourage him to claim the throne. In a famous scene, the histrionic Richard stages his own deposition. He is then confined to Pomfret Castle, where he reflects on the divine right of kings. Threatened by conspiracies, Bolingbroke exercises a diplomacy and discipline that distinguish him from the deposed king. Sir Pierce of Exton, interpreting Bolingbroke's secret wishes, kills Richard II at Pomfret, but is repudiated by Bolingbroke, now firmly enthroned as Henry IV. The play ends with the new king's expressed intention to expiate the regicide by making a pilgrimage to the Holy Land.

Richard II, because it deals with the deposition of an anointed king, was a controversial play. Shakespeare's company earned the queen's displeasure by performing it on the eve of the Earl of Essex's rebellion in 1601. Shakespeare, conscious of the notoriety of MARLOWE's *EDWARD II*, wrote it as the tragedy of a misguided king. Although it stands as the first of a sequence of English history plays, to be completed by the two parts of *HENRY IV* and by *HENRY V*, it was written as a single tragedy.

Richard III, The Life and Death of

A historical tragedy by WILLIAM SHAKESPEARE, first performed *c.* 1594 and published in Quarto (Q1) in 1597 as well as in the First Folio of 1623. Although continuing the story told in the three *HENRY VI* plays (and based like them on HOLINSHED's *Chronicles*), it is entirely self-sufficient. Its vigorous portrait of the deformed, ambitious and maliciously intelligent Richard, Duke of Gloucester, his pursuit of the throne and his final downfall assured the play a lasting place in the English theatre.

Richard woos Anne, widow and daughter-in-law of his previous victims, and arranges the death of his brother, George, Duke of Clarence. With the connivance of the Duke of Buckingham, he eliminates Hastings, Rivers and Grey, further rivals. Once on the throne he makes his position secure by ordering the deaths of his young nephews, the sons of the dead Edward IV, and insisting on marrying their sister. Opposition to his tyrannies hardens, and Richard is troubled by the prophecy that the Earl of Richmond will become king. Buckingham, now alienated by Richard's ingratitude, raises an army but is captured and executed. Richard's isolation increases when Richmond invades. Disquieted by dreams on the eve of the Battle of Bosworth, Richard rallies his strength in a desperate fight, but is eventually killed in single combat by the Earl of Richmond, who, as Henry VII, ends the cycle of bloodshed begun in the *Henry VI* trilogy by establishing the Tudor dynasty on the throne of England.

Richard Coeur de Lyon

A VERSE ROMANCE written soon after 1300, probably in south-east England. Combining history with romance, it tells the story of Richard the Lionheart: his parentage, his triumph over a lion sent to devour him and the Crusade during which he dined on Saracens' heads before eventually capturing Babylon and Jaffa. The central episode of the Crusade includes detailed accounts of military campaigns. Richard's exuberant and dominating personality, which the poem celebrates with patriotic pride, is explained by his having a supernatural mother. Sir WALTER SCOTT drew on the poem for *THE TALISMAN.*

Richard Mahony, The Fortunes of

A trilogy of novels by HENRY HANDEL RICHARDSON, consisting of *Australia Felix* (1917), *The Way Home* (1925) and *Ultima Thule* (1929), first published together in 1930. The novel is unhurried and covers a broad canvas of events and characters. Its closing chapters draw heavily on the fate suffered by the author's father.

Richard Townshend Mahony, a brilliant young doctor, is fascinated by the accounts of Australia and the gold rush which he reads in the English press. He gives up his practice and emigrates, arriving in Melbourne in the 1850s. Six months of prospecting at Ballarat finds him doing very badly and he uses his last resources to buy a barrow-load of sundries. With these he opens a 'Diggers Emporium'. A friend, Purdy Smith, who followed his example and emigrated to Australia, introduces him to the Beamish family in Melbourne; at their hotel he meets Mary Turnbull, a girl from England whom he marries. The emporium at Ballarat prospers until Mahony refuses to support the diggers in militant action against the authorities. They boycott his store and he is forced to sell up. Mary persuades Mahony to return to medicine, but in spite of his ability he lacks sympathy for his patients. He also becomes morbidly sensitive to patronage, real or imagined, and alienates patients at all levels of society. He retreats into himself, preoccupied by books, and turns first to religion and then to spiritualism. When things seem at their lowest ebb some shares in a dubious mine soar in value and the Mahony fortunes are reversed. He and Mary return to Europe and he spends lavishly. The crash comes when Richard's agent absconds. He returns to Australia and learns that he is ruined, but hides the full truth from Mary, who has joined him with their children. The strain of trying to get his affairs back in order takes severe toll of Richard, who eventually suffers mental and physical collapse. At the end of the tale Mary, resolute and uncomplaining, works as a postmistress in a remote settlement, nursing her husband in the last weeks of his life.

Richard the Redeless See MUM AND THE SOTHSEGGER.

Richards, David Adams 1950- Canadian novelist. Born and raised in New Brunswick, he writes exclusively about Maritime Canada and the tightly knit, often intense lives of its inhabitants. After studying at St Thomas University in Fredericton, he moved back to his native Newcastle. His first novel, *The Coming of Winter* (1974), is a vividly realistic account of the life of a young New Brunswick mill-worker and is notable for its rendition of the local idiom. *Blood Ties* (1976) employs a slow-paced narrative style, almost entirely reliant on dialogue and deadpan accounts of action and remarkable for its ability to evoke intense emotions without explicitly describing inner feelings. *Lives of Short Duration* (1981) is a more wide-ranging novel which examines the history of a deprived Maritime community through a complex interior monologue technique. *Nights below Station Street* (1988) is another study of a laconic Maritime community in which feelings speak louder than words. Recent work includes *Evening Snow* (1990). *Dancers at Night* (1978) is a volume of short stories.

Richards, Frank See HAMILTON, CHARLES.

Richards, (Franklin Thomas) Grant 1872-1948 Publisher. The son of an Oxford don, he left school at 16 and joined a wholesale publishing firm. On the staff of *The Review of Reviews* between 1890 and 1896 he made literary friendships which proved valuable when he set up his own publishing firm in 1897. Despite habitual irresponsibility in finance (he twice went bankrupt), Richards developed a strong literary list which included SAMUEL BUTLER'S *THE WAY OF ALL FLESH*, JOYCE'S *DUBLINERS* and the poetry and scholarly writings of A. E. HOUSMAN. His light-hearted autobiography, *Author Hunting* (1934), owes much to the correspondence with SHAW that animates it. He also wrote well on Housman (1941), the austere poet having unexpectedly been a close friend of his rapscallion publisher.

Richards, I(vor) A(rmstrong) 1893-1979 Critic. Born the son of a factory manager in Cheshire, Richards was educated at Clifton College and at Magdalene College, Cambridge, where he studied moral sciences before becoming a lecturer in the recently founded school of English in 1919. In his early writings, *The Foundations of Aesthetics* (with C. K. Ogden and J. Wood, 1922) and *The Meaning of Meaning* (with C. K. Ogden, 1923), he began to use methods of Positivist philosophy to clarify problems of language and art. In the much more influential *Principles of Literary Criticism* (1924) and in *Science and Poetry* (1926) he presented an almost clinical view of poetry as a kind of mental hygiene which reconciles conflicting impulses in the mind. He distinguished the scientific or referential use of language from the 'emotive' uses of language found in the 'pseudo-statements' of poetry, attributing a variety of evils – from bad taste to violent patriotism – to the illegitimate mixture of the two.

Richards's best-known work, *Practical Criticism* (1929) was the result of an experiment in which he gave his Cambridge students a series of unsigned poems for comment. Analysing the written responses, he catalogued the various kinds of misreading to which poems can be subjected. His argument displaced the uncritical notions of poetry inherited from the late Victorian age, and it prompted a new 'close reading' of poetry for verbal ambiguities, ironies and other complexities in the work of his pupil WILLIAM EMPSON, F. R. LEAVIS and the SCRUTINY group, and the proponents of NEW CRITICISM. 'Practical criticism' became a standard classroom exercise throughout the English-speaking world.

In 1931 after a year spent teaching in China, Richards moved to Harvard University, where he taught until 1963. These years were devoted to the promotion of Basic English, which he had formulated with C. K. Ogden as a simplified system for learners of the language, with a vocabulary of only 850 words. His important works of literary interest in this period were *Coleridge on the Imagination* (1934), *The Philosophy of Rhetoric* (1936), and *Interpretation in Teaching* (1938). *Goodbye Earth, and Other Poems* appeared in 1959, to be followed by three more volumes of verse. His life's work was dedicated to clarity of communication, which he felt vital in an age of world wars.

Richardson, Dorothy M(iller) 1873-1957 Novelist. She was born in Abingdon and attended local schools before working as a teacher and a clerk. She married a painter, Alan Odle. After publishing

The Quakers Past and Present and *Gleanings from the Works of George Fox* (both 1914) she embarked on *Pilgrimage*, the sequence of 12 novels for which she is remembered. Making an early use of STREAM OF CONSCIOUSNESS, it deals with the life of Miriam Henderson. The individual volumes are: *Pointed Roofs* (1915), *Backwater* (1916), *Honeycomb* (1917), *Interim* (1919), *The Tunnel* (1919), *Deadlock* (1921), *Revolving Lights* (1923), *The Trap* (1925), *Oberland* (1927), *Dawn's Left Hand* (1931), *Clear Horizon* (1935) and *Dimple Hill* (1938).

Richardson, Henry Handel [Ethel Florence] 1870–1946 Australian novelist. Born in Melbourne, she was educated at the Melbourne Presbyterian Ladies' College, where she showed a talent for music that led to further study at the Leipzig Conservatorium. At Leipzig she met her future husband, John George Robertson, who became lecturer in English at Strasbourg (1896–1903), and professor of German language and literature at the University of London in 1904.

She successfully used music as the theme for her novel *Maurice Guest* (1908) and for *The Young Cosima* (1939). Her own adolescence provided the background for *The Getting of Wisdom* (1910). She revisited Australia only once, to ensure the authenticity of the background of *Australia Felix* (1917), the first part of a trilogy completed in *The Way Home* (1925) and *Ultima Thule* (1929) and published as THE FORTUNES OF RICHARD MAHONY (1930). She left an autobiography, *Myself When Young* (1948), which appeared after her death.

Richardson, Samuel 1689–1761 Novelist and printer. Although Richardson was born in Derbyshire, his father was a London joiner and the family had returned to the capital by 1700. His father could not afford the classical education needed to make him a clergyman, and he was bound apprentice to a printer in 1706. He proved diligent, and his reward was the hand of his master's daughter, Allington Wilde. He married in 1721, the year he set up in business by himself as master printer. By this first wife he had five sons and one daughter, all of whom died young. After her death he married Elizabeth Leake, daughter of a fellow printer and sister of a bookseller, who survived him. They had five girls and a boy, of whom four girls survived.

As a boy, Richardson – whose nicknames were 'Serious' and 'Gravity' – entertained his schoolfellows with tales remembered from his reading, and all his tales, according to him, 'carried with them... an useful moral'. He served an unofficial apprenticeship as a writer of love-letters for servant girls from the age of 13, and before that as author of a reproving letter to a lady who professed religion but practised slander and backbiting, and by providing prefaces and dedica-

Henry Handel Richardson

tions for booksellers. In 1733, he published *The Apprentice's Vade Mecum*, which urged the ambitious youth to diligence, sobriety, self-denial and morality, an ethic of deferred gratification; this was followed by his own didactic version of *Aesop's Fables*. He also edited *The Negotiations of Sir Thomas Roe in his Embassy to the Ottoman Port for the years 1621 to 1628 Inclusive* (1740) and continued DEFOE's *A Tour through the Whole Island of Great Britain*, which was completed anonymously.

Richardson prospered, and as well as his business address off Fleet Street, had second homes, first near Hammersmith, and later near Parsons Green. In 1754 he was elected Master of the Stationers' Company, and in 1760 he purchased a share of the patent of the printer to the king. In later life he suffered from ill health which he considered nervous in origin. His virtues were those of the industrious apprentice; his weakness was agreed to be his vanity. However, he was a self-made man, who started life with few advantages, and his achievement was distinguished. Among his circle of friends and admirers were two sisters, LADY BRADSHAIGH and Lady Echlin, both of whose correspondence with Richardson survives.

He wrote three novels. PAMELA (first part 1740; second part 1741) made him famous and CLARISSA (1747–8), his masterpiece, consolidated his reputation as both a celebrant of female virtue and a subtle psychologist. *THE HISTORY OF SIR CHARLES GRANDISON* (1753–4), a portrait of male virtue, was influential in its day but is now less well remembered. Taking up a hint from his friend SAMUEL JOHNSON, he also published *A Collection of the Moral and Instructive Sentiments, Maxims, Cautions and Reflections, Contained in the Histories of Pamela, Clarissa and Sir Charles Grandison, Digested under Proper Heads* (1755). His three major works are all EPISTOLARY NOVELS, a form he did not invent but brought to a new height of sophistication, as he did the novel of common life, avoiding 'the improbable and the marvellous'.

HENRY FIELDING's mockery was expressed in *An Apology for the Life of Mrs Shamela Andrews* and *JOSEPH ANDREWS*, but otherwise Richardson's reputation stood high during his lifetime. Mrs Thrale wrote in her commonplace book: 'Were I to make a scale of novel writers I should put Richardson first, then Rousseau; after them, but at an immeasurable distance–CHARLOTTE LENNOX, SMOLLETT and Fielding.' She thought both Fielding and Smollett 'knew the Husk of Life perfectly well', yet 'for the Kernel – you must go to either Richardson or Rousseau'. Johnson, though admitting that 'if you were to read Richardson for the story your impatience would be so much fretted that you would hang yourself', believed 'there is more knowledge of the human heart in one letter of Richardson's than in all of *TOM JONES*'. Yet his reputation was in decline even by 1797, when Mary Hay, writing in *The Monthly Magazine*, while admitting Richardson was 'a sovereign genius', complained of his 'false and pernicious principles, the violation of truth and nature,... absurd superstitions and ludicrous prejudices' and compared him unfavourably with Fielding and Smollett. During the 19th century, Richardson's supposedly effeminate preoccupations were denigrated by comparison with Fielding's manliness, but his greatness has been once more acknowledged in the second half of the present century.

Richler, Mordecai 1931– Canadian novelist. Born into a working-class Jewish milieu in Montreal, he attended the well-known predominantly Jewish Baron Byng High School. After dropping out of Sir George Williams University, he travelled to Europe where he spent the next two years, mainly in Paris. He returned to Canada and worked for the Canadian Broadcasting Company before settling in England in 1959, where he lived for many years supporting himself as a freelance journalist. He eventually moved back to Canada in 1972 and now lives in Montreal and a cottage in Quebec's Eastern Townships. Richler's early work – notably *The Apprenticeship of Duddy Kravitz* (1959) – is broadly comic, satirizing Canadian sacred cows and showing an ambivalent attitude to his Jewish heritage. *St Urbain's Horseman* (1971), a product of his years in England, is centred on the experi-

ence of a Jewish-Canadian in London. His finest work to date, *Solomon Gursky was Here* (1989), won the 1990 Commonwealth Writers Prize. Peopled by a rich gallery of comic characters, it moves between 19th-century London, Franklin's Arctic expedition, the Prairie during the years of Prohibition and contemporary Quebec to provide an unconventional view of Canadian history. Richler's other novels are *The Acrobats* (1954), *Son of a Smaller Hero* (1955), *A Choice of Enemies* (1957), *The Incomparable Atuk* (1963), *Cocksure* (1968) and *Joshua Then and Now* (1980). He has also published: volumes of essays, including *Hunting Tigers under Glass* (1968) and *Shovelling Trouble* (1972); a collection of sketches, *The Street* (1969); and CHILDREN'S LITERATURE, including *Jacob Two-Two Meets the Hooded Fang* (1975) and *Jacob Two-Two and the Dinosaur* (1988). He has also written screenplays for films.

Rickword, (John) Edgell 1898–1982 Critic. The son of a librarian from Colchester, where he attended the grammar school, Rickword fought in World War I before studying at Pembroke College, Oxford. He was a reviewer for *The New Statesman* and *THE TIMES LITERARY SUPPLEMENT* (in which he reviewed T. S. ELIOT's *THE WASTE LAND*), before acting as editor of the short-lived *CALENDAR OF MODERN LETTERS* (1925–7). This journal was admired for its exacting critical standards and for its uncompromising 'Scrutinies' of established literary reputations, by (among others) F. R. LEAVIS, who edited a selection of *Calendar* articles in 1933, and who saw his own periodical *SCRUTINY* as a continuation of Rickword's efforts. After adopting Marxism in the early 1930s, Rickword became associate editor of *Left Review* in 1934–6 and editor until 1938, and later edited CHRISTOPHER CAUDWELL's *Further Studies in a Dying Culture* (1949). He published six volumes of poetry and a short study of Rimbaud, but his most important work is collected in *Essays and Opinions 1921–1931* (1974) and *Literature and Society: Essays and Opinions 1931–1978* (1978).

Riders to the Sea A one-act tragedy by J. M. SYNGE, first performed at the ABBEY THEATRE, Dublin, in 1904. Within its very limited length, the play achieves extraordinary emotional intensity.

The single scene is the kitchen of a cottage on one of the Aran Islands. The whole life of the community is centred on the sea. When the play opens Maurya has already lost four sons and a husband to the sea. A fifth son is missing. Only the youngest, Bartley, remains to help his mother and his two sisters. By the end of the play, the missing son's death has been confirmed and Bartley is dead too, drowned on his way to the horse fair in Connemara.

Ridge, Lola 1871–1941 American poet. Born in Dublin, she spent her childhood in Australia and New

Mordecai Richler

Zealand, emigrated to San Francisco in 1907, and moved to New York in 1908. In 1918 she published *The Ghetto and Other Poems*, a collection which focuses on immigrant life in New York and shows the influence of IMAGISM on her work. Her next publication, *Sun-Up* (1920), contains poems which explore both the nature of artistic vision and the realities of working-class experience. The collection *Red Flag* (1927) includes tributes to those who lost their lives in revolutionary struggles, as does *Firehead* (1929), which was written in response to the executions of Sacco and Vanzetti in 1927. Her last volume of verse, *Dance of Fire* (1935), reflects her lifelong concern with the exploitation and martyrdom of the working class.

Riding, Laura 1901– American poet, novelist, short-story writer and critic. Born Laura Reichenthal

in New York, she was educated at Cornell University. She married the writer Louis Gottschalk in 1920 and published her work as Laura Riding Gottschalk until she adopted the surname of Riding in 1926. During a stay in Europe (1926–39) she lived with ROBERT GRAVES on Mallorca; together they founded the Seizin Press and edited the influential *A Survey of Modernist Poetry* (1927). Her own early poetry associated her with the FUGITIVES. *The Close Chaplet* (1926), her first volume, was followed by a steady stream of work throughout the late 1920s and the 1930s, culminating in *Collected Poems* (1938; reprinted with a new introduction in 1980). She wrote less and less verse after 1938, and her early work, expressing private feeling in strikingly concrete imagery, is usually considered her best. Other works of criticism include *Contemporaries and Snobs* (1928) and *Anarchism is Not*

Enough (1928). She also wrote novels, including *Description of Life* (1980), and three volumes of short stories.

Ridler, Anne (Barbara) 1912– Poet. Born in Rugby, she went to Downe House School and King's College, London. Her poetic output has been relatively small: among her collections are *The Nine Bright Shiners* (1943), *The Golden Bird and Other Poems* (1951), *A Matter of Life and Death* (1959), *Selected Poems* (1961) and *Some Time After and Other Poems* (1972). She has also written verse dramas such as *Cain* (1943). A devotional poet, not only in her explicit concern with faith but in her receptivity to transcendental intimations outside formal religious contexts, she brings a quiet, traditional craft to the evocation of religious experience, married love, children, the sense of mortality, and the feelings aroused by places and paintings. She has affinities with WYATT and HERBERT, as well as T. S. ELIOT and LARKIN.

Ridley, James 1736–65 Novelist. Born in London, and educated at Winchester and University College, Oxford, he served as a chaplain with the East India Company and then with the army. He is remembered for *The Tales of the Genii: or, the Delightful Lessons of Horan, the Son of Asmar* (1764), originally presented as a translation from the Persian by 'Sir Charles Morrell', supposedly a former ambassador to the court of the Great Mogul, but in fact an exercise in Orientalism modelled on *The Arabian Nights*. This lively and occasionally satirical work includes a portrait of Ridley's friend JOSEPH SPENCE as Phesoi Enceps. It proved immensely popular and was many times reprinted, sometimes in censored versions intended for children.

Rienzi: The Last of the Tribunes A novel by EDWARD BULWER LYTTON, published in 1835. The hero is Cola di Rienzo, a visionary idealist who briefly succeeded in subduing the warring baronial factions of 14th-century Rome and in establishing a republic with himself as tribune. He was eventually turned on by the ungrateful people and torn to pieces in the streets. The story thus had a message for post-Reform Bill England: that liberty cannot be imposed upon a nation which is not politically or morally ready to accept its responsibilities.

Rights of Man, The A tract by THOMAS PAINE, published in two parts, in 1791 and 1792. Written to defend the ideals of the French Revolution against BURKE's attack in *REFLECTIONS ON THE REVOLUTION IN FRANCE* (1790), it prompted Pitt's government to introduce a law against seditious publication. Paine fled to France but was convicted of sedition in his absence and outlawed.

The first part advocates the theory of a social contract. Sovereignty is inherent in the will of the majority and should be reaffirmed by each generation; no generation has any right to bind its successors to its own order. The social contract should be embodied in a formal constitution; where that did not exist, authority – and therefore tyranny – prevailed. The purpose of government should be the freedom and security of the individual; the rights of man include the maximum freedom of thought and action compatible with the rights of others. In the second part Paine compares the constitutions of the United States and the new France with British institutions, to the latter's disadvantage. But the work is most interesting in the radical social policy which it outlines. Paine advocated, among other measures, a tax on income above a certain level, old-age pensions, free education for the poor, family allowances and the limitation of armaments by treaty.

Riley, James Whitcomb 1849–1916 American poet. He began his career in 1877 as a writer for the Indianapolis *Journal*. The poems he published in the paper established him as a regional writer of light and sentimental verse. He became known especially for his dialect poems, which include 'Little Orphant Annie', 'The Raggedy Man', and 'When the Frost is on the Punkin'. His great popularity as a poet and lecturer made him one of the wealthiest writers of his time. His most famous collection was *The Old Swimmin'-Hole and 'Leven More Poems* (1883). Other volumes include *Afterwhiles* (1888), *Pipes o' Pan at Zekesbury* (1889) and *Poems Here at Home* (1893).

Riley, John 1937–78 Poet. Born into a Methodist, working-class family in Leeds, he read English at Cambridge and became a teacher. He was killed by muggers after his return to Leeds. Founder of the Grosseteste Press and *The Grosseteste Review*, he was also a leading experimental poet. His work owed little to any native tradition but was influenced instead by POUND, OLSON and OPPEN, and by Hölderlin and Mandelstam, whom he translated. Marked by an increasingly religious perspective and an unparochial sense of place, his poems treat moments of illumination and dislocation with, at times, elegant lyricism and subtly changing rhythms. Volumes include *Ancient and Modern* (1967), *What Reason Was* (1970), *Ways of Approaching* (1973) and *That is Today* (1978), gathered with other poems in the posthumous *Collected Poems* (1981), which contains the important long poem 'Czargrad'. Ignored by the literary establishment, Riley's work – produced during only 15 years – deserves a wider readership.

Rime of the Ancient Mariner, The A poem by SAMUEL TAYLOR COLERIDGE, published in *LYRICAL BALLADS* (1798).

The poem tells of the 'ancient mariner' who meets three gallants on the way to a wedding feast and recounts to one of them the story of his ship, driven south by a storm into the ice of the South Pole. An albatross, which appears as a bird of good omen when the ship escapes from the ice, is wilfully shot down by the mariner. His shipmates at first upbraid him but are willing to condone the crime when they seem to have a clear passage, which they attribute to the death of the bird. The ship is carried north into tropic seas where it is becalmed. Water runs out and the crew blame the mariner; they hang the dead albatross around his neck. After a ghost ship passes the crew begin to die. The mariner's redemption starts with a vision of the creatures of God and the beauty of His world, seen by moonlight. When he is at last able to pray, the dead bird falls from his neck into the sea and the Virgin Mary sends life-giving rain. The mariner is eventually rescued and confesses to a hermit, who shrives him; but he knows his penance will continue throughout his life. He must go on relating his story.

Coleridge wrote *The Ancient Mariner* as a BALLAD, a form the Romantics brought back into poetic currency. The elaborate prose gloss accompanying the poem in most modern editions was added by Coleridge when he included it in his collection *Sybilline Leaves* (1817).

The Rime of the Ancient Mariner: illustration by Mervyn Peake

Ring and the Book, The A poem by ROBERT BROWNING, published in four monthly instalments between November 1868 and February 1869. Divided into 12 books and running to 21,000 lines of blank verse, it is his most ambitious and complex work.

The story comes from a *cause célèbre* in Rome towards the end of the 17th century. Count Guido Franceschini, an impoverished nobleman of Arezzo in search of an advantageous marriage, discovered the Comparinis, an elderly Roman couple who had only one daughter, Pompilia, to inherit their property. A match was arranged and the girl delivered to Arezzo. Pompilia led a wretched life, finding her husband cruel and his younger brother frankly lustful.

Her appeals to the archbishop and the governor of the province did nothing for her. Her only help came from a young canon, Giuseppe Caponsacchi, whom she persuaded to take her back to her parents in Rome. Franceschini pursued and caught them, accusing them of adultery and confining Pompilia to a convent. When she was taken to her parents' house to await the birth of her child, Pompilia learned that she had in fact been adopted from the slums of Rome. The enraged Franceschini hired four accomplices and, using Caponsacchi's name to gain entrance to the house, murdered the Comparinis. Pompilia died later of her wounds. Franceschini was arrested and brought to trial with his accomplices. Taking advantage of the fact he had been in minor orders earlier in life, he appealed to Pope Innocent XII for special privilege as a cleric. His plea was rejected. Franceschini was beheaded and his accomplices hanged on 22 February 1698.

The title of Browning's poem is founded on a number of allusions. The 'Book' is 'the Old Yellow Book', the collection of documents about the case he had found on a bookstall in Florence in 1860. The 'Ring' represents the 'pure gold' of fact found in the book, shaped and given form by the 'alloy' of the poet's imagination. The poem begins with Browning's account of his sources and his well-known invocation to the Muse, a tribute to his wife, ELIZABETH BARRETT BROWNING, who had died in 1861. Succeeding books narrate the story from different points of view: gossips in Rome favourable to Count Guido, those favourable to the hapless Pompilia, an impartial observer (Tertium Quid), Guido himself, Giuseppe Caponsacchi, and Pompilia on her deathbed. These are followed by statements for the defence and for the prosecution, and Pope Innocent's soliloquy on the nature of evil and the fallibility of human judgement, and his decision to let the sentence stand. The closing books are occupied by Guido's expression of abject cowardice when he realizes he is doomed, and the Pope's declaration of Pompilia's innocence.

Ringwood, Gwen Pharis 1910–84 Canadian playwright, born in the USA. She wrote her first play, *The Dragon of Kent* (produced in 1935), while studying at the University of Alberta. Four more plays – including her classic one-act folk drama *Still Stands the House* (1938) – belong to the years 1937–9, when she attended the University of North Carolina. From 1939 she taught playwriting at the University of Alberta. Like many of her plays, her prairie tragedy *Dark Harvest* (1945) is based on local history. Her later works became more socially conscious but still dealt with local concerns. However, her move in 1953 to Williams Lake, a remote town in British Columbia, distanced her from the mainstream of Canadian drama, though she continued to write and work in community theatre. The theatre in Williams Lake was named after her in 1968. Her other plays include *The Rainmaker* (1945), *Widger's Way* (1952), *Mirage* (1979) and *Garage Sale* (1981). She also wrote short stories and a novel, *Younger Brother* (1959).

Ripley, George 1802–80 American philosopher and man of letters. He was born in Greenfield, Massachusetts, and educated at Harvard. His sermon, *Jesus Christ, the Same Yesterday, Today, and Forever*, delivered on 14 May 1834 at the ordination of ORESTES BROWNSON, is considered an exemplary pronouncement of TRANSCENDENTALISM. In 1836 he helped to found the Transcendental Club and also published *Discourses on the Philosophy of Religion Addressed to Doubters Who Wish to Believe*. This was followed by *The Temptations of the Times* (1837) and *Philosophical Miscellanies* (1838). He then edited 14 volumes of translations of European idealistic philosophy, *Specimens of Foreign Standard Literature* (1838–42).

Ripley handled the business affairs of the Transcendentalist magazine *THE DIAL* (1840–4) and also assisted MARGARET FULLER in editing it. He left the ministry in 1841 and established BROOK FARM, a Transcendentalist experiment in communal living which continued until 1847. From 1845 to 1849 he edited *The Harbinger*, a socialist weekly published by the Brook Farm Community. He became literary critic for the *New York Tribune* in 1849, and continued as critic, philosopher, and political commentator for the *Tribune* and other periodicals until his death. In 1850 he helped to found *HARPER'S NEW MONTHLY MAGAZINE*. With Charles A. Dana he edited a 16-volume work entitled *The New American Cyclopedia* (1858–63).

Rippingale, C(uthbert) E(dward) 1825–97 Novelist. The son of a wealthy and strongly Nonconformist manufacturing family in Bradford, he studied at Lincoln's Inn before abandoning the law in favour of writing. His first novels rejected both aspects of his background, *Robert Higden: or, The Sweat*

Shop (1851) attacking conditions in the clothing trade and *The Lion Yard Meeting* (1852) the hypocrisies of evangelical religion. Several years of silence followed, and Rippingale's only other novel of the 1850s – *Can These Bones Live?* (1859) – would seem to confirm that the decade was for him a period of spiritual crisis. Later novels combined High Anglican fervour with a love of medieval chivalry. *The Testing of Sir Richard Fortescue* (1865) and *The Trials of Sir Clarence* (1872) are typical of the books which enjoyed a modest success in appropriate circles and won him praise from KENELM HENRY DIGBY and, more reservedly, CHARLOTTE M. YONGE. Toward the end of his life Rippingale devoted his energies to a campaign for standards of purity in stained-glass windows, contributing much of his inherited fortune and many of his own designs to this cause.

Rise of Silas Lapham, The A novel by WILLIAM DEAN HOWELLS, serialized in *CENTURY MAGAZINE* in 1884–5 and published in volume form in 1885.

Colonel Silas Lapham, originally a Vermont farmer, makes a fortune manufacturing paint. He moves his family to Boston, and urges his wife and daughters to enter fashionable society. He looks forward to a new life, but thinks back on his old business practices with increasing moral discomfort. The family does not fit in well with Boston society, though one of its representatives, Tom Corey, falls in love with Lapham's older daughter, Penelope. The younger daughter, Irene, convinces herself and Penelope that Tom is really in love with her; Penelope refuses his proposal and does not attend the Coreys' dinner party. Her father does, however, and gets drunk. Meanwhile his business speculations have been unsuccessful and he is threatened with bankruptcy. His partner urges him to save himself by selling some property to a British firm, even though he knows it to be worthless. After a struggle with himself he decides not to make the sale. Economically bankrupt, socially disgraced, but morally restored, he returns to Vermont. Penelope and Tom run away to Mexico to escape the rigid social barriers that have created such unhappiness for them in New England.

Ritchie, Anne (Isabella) Thackeray, Lady 1837–1919 Novelist and biographer. The elder daughter of THACKERAY, she received an unconventional upbringing as a result of her mother's confinement in a mental asylum, spending her formative years with her grandparents in Paris, and subsequently in her father's bachelor home in London. Paris is the setting of her first novel, *The Story of Elizabeth* (1863). Of the seven others which followed, *Old Kensington* (1873) and *Mrs Dymond* (1885) are still remembered. Although VIRGINIA WOOLF and others have paid tribute to their impressionistic charm Lady Ritchie's most enduring work was as a memorialist of the Victorian writers she had known, notably in her *Records of Tennyson, Ruskin and Robert and Elizabeth Browning* (1892) and *Chapters from Some Memoirs* (1894), and in the introductions she wrote to the 13-volume 'Biographical Edition' of her father's works (1894–8). She is portrayed as Mrs Hilbery in Woolf's *Night and Day*.

Ritson, Joseph 1753–1803 Antiquary. Trained as a conveyancer, Ritson early adopted a strict vegetarian diet after reading BERNARD DE MANDEVILLE's *Fable of the Bees*, and to this diet has been ascribed his remarkable acerbity in literary disputes and his eventual insanity. His own excessively punctilious scholarship is best seen in his two-volume accumulation of allusions to ROBIN HOOD in popular literature which appeared in 1795 with woodcuts by BEWICK. He issued numerous similar anthologies of popular literature. Most of his literary productions were vitriolic attacks on what he saw as the shortcomings of other editions: THOMAS WARTON's *History of English Poetry*, THOMAS PERCY's *Reliques of Ancient English Poetry* and the SHAKESPEARE edition of JOHNSON and STEEVENS. His aggressive behaviour was such that he appears to have retained the friendship only of SURTEES and SIR WALTER SCOTT.

Rivals, The A comedy by RICHARD BRINSLEY SHERIDAN, first performed at COVENT GARDEN in 1775. It was a failure on its opening night and Sheridan rewrote parts of it before its successful second performance 11 days later.

Among the fashionable visitors to Bath is Captain Jack Absolute, humbly disguised as Ensign Beverley to suit the romantic yearnings for love and poverty of his beloved Lydia Languish. Lydia's friend Julia, much more robust, is loved by the self-tormenting man of feeling, Faulkland. The play brings the lovers to a happy agreement, after many adventures, and despite the obstacles erected by Lydia's aunt, Mrs Malaprop, and the impecunious Irish knight, Sir Lucius O'Trigger.

Mrs Malaprop achieved a fame beyond the play in which she appears, and her uncertain grasp of long words ('No caparisons, miss, if you please') has given the term 'malapropism' to the language.

Road, The A play by WOLE SOYINKA, published in 1965. A complex work, it is at once a meditation on death, a sardonic comedy about life on the fringes of society and a comment on the brutality of the Nigerian road. The chief characters who gather at Professor's 'Aksident Store' are: Professor himself; his deaf and dumb, and recently dead, palm-wine tapper Murano; Kotonu, the driver who has killed Murano on the road; Kotonu's mate Samson; and a mercenary leader of a gang of thugs. They test their understanding by contemplating Murano, who is in the *agemo*

state, a phase of gradual withdrawal from the physical world and of growing apprehension of the spiritual realm he will eventually enter.

Road to Ruin, The A comedy by THOMAS HOLCROFT, first produced at COVENT GARDEN in 1792 and published the same year. It was translated and played in Holland, Denmark and Germany.

Harry Dornton's extravagance causes a run on his father's bank and brings it close to ruin. In love with Miss Warren, he resolves to save the house by marrying the girl's wealthy mother, an unpleasant woman who surrounds herself with sycophantic admirers. Among them is Goldfinch, heavily in debt from his idle fashionable way of life, who is determined to marry Mrs Warren himself. In the end the bank is saved by the genius of Old Dornton's chief clerk, the grim old Mr Sulky. Harry, a reformed character, is able to marry Miss Warren, while her odious mother is disinherited by the discovery of a new will.

Road to Wigan Pier, The A work by GEORGE ORWELL, commissioned and published by the LEFT BOOK CLUB in 1937.

Orwell's account of 'the great industrial wastelands' of Yorkshire and Lancashire began as an attempt to write the urban equivalent of COBBETT's *RURAL RIDES*. His mission, as he states it at the beginning of Part Two, is twofold: 'partly... to see what mass-unemployment is like at its worst, partly in order to see the most typical section of the English working class at close quarters'. The first prompts a damning record of poverty, apathy, malnutrition, and overcrowding; the second leads him to confront his own class prejudices ('When I was fourteen or fifteen I was an odious little snob, but no worse than other boys of my own age and class'). Fashionable 'bourgeois socialism' provokes his scorn, and there are excellent analyses of middle-class prejudices about 'the lower classes'. The book concludes with an impassioned exhortation to the Socialist movement to unite lower-middle and working classes, whose interests Orwell believes are essentially the same. This line of polemic did not please his sponsors but, despite Victor Gollancz's reservations, the work proved successful and has remained a classic of literary journalism.

Roaring Girl, The: *or, Moll Cutpurse* A comedy by THOMAS MIDDLETON and THOMAS DEKKER, first produced in 1610 and published in 1611. The play is a comment on the notoriety of Moll Cutpurse, a thief and forger whose real name was Mary Frith; she was not apprehended until 1612, when she was sentenced to public penance at St Paul's Cross as part of her punishment.

Sebastian Wentgrave and Mary Fitzallard are betrothed but Sebastian's father, the mean and mean-spirited Sir Alexander, forbids the match. To force his hand Sebastian pays court to the notorious Moll Cutpurse. Moll herself is touched by the young lovers' plight; she agrees to follow Sebastian's scheme and also to be his means of contact with Mary. Sebastian announces that he has fallen in love with Moll Cutpurse and must marry her. The distracted old villain, Sir Alexander, sends his unpleasant servant Trapdoor to worm his way into Moll's confidence and then betray her. But Trapdoor is unequal to the task, and Moll and Sebastian extract Sir Alexander's consent by a carefully staged wedding.

Rob Roy A novel by SIR WALTER SCOTT, published in 1817. It is set in the north of England and Scotland in the early 18th century.

The story follows the adventures of Francis Osbaldistone, banished from London by his father, a successful merchant. At the house of his uncle, Sir Hildebrand, he meets Rashleigh, the greedy and malicious youngest son, and Diana Vernon, Rashleigh's cousin on whom he has designs. When Francis is favourably received by Diana, Rashleigh determines to destroy him. He is already plotting to ruin Francis's father. At the prompting of Diana, Francis goes to the Highlands, accompanied by Bailie Nicol Jarvie, to seek the help of Rob Roy MacGregor, the outlaw. In the Highlands Francis witnesses a clash between clansmen and the king's troops and Rob Roy's escape. With the help of the spirited Diana and Rob Roy, Francis is able to unmask Rashleigh's villainy and regain the money which the latter has embezzled from Francis's father. Rashleigh betrays them to the government and Rob Roy kills him.

The historical Rob Roy (1671–1734), a drover, became a powerful and dangerous outlaw when he and his clan were proscribed as Jacobite sympathizers. He was a ruthless opponent of the government but famous for disinterested kindness and sympathy with the oppressed. In 1716 he came under the protection of the Duke of Argyll and assumed the name of Campbell.

Robene and Makyne A Middle Scots poem by ROBERT HENRYSON. Owing something to the traditions of both the *pastourelle* and the debate poem, it tells how the shepherd Robene refuses Makyne's love but is scorned in turn when he later falls in love with her.

Robert Elsmere A novel by MRS HUMPHRY WARD, published in 1888.

Robert Elsmere is a young Anglican parson whose faith is untroubled during undergraduate days at Oxford despite encountering two characteristic strains of 19th-century unorthodoxy in the morbidly critical spiritual paralysis of Edward Langham and the philosophic idealism of the Hegelian Grey. After his marriage to a girl of the strictest Anglican Evangelical piety, 'the Thirty-nine Articles in the flesh', Elsmere takes a country living where he combines a life of practical parochial work in the style of CHARLES KINGSLEY with scientific interests and historical studies. The local squire, Roger Wendover, places at his disposal an extensive library which covers all the main movements of modern thought from the OXFORD MOVEMENT and the HIGHER CRITICISM to works of more general philosophical and historical enquiry. The squire, a dry rationalist, is the notorious author of a book attacking religious orthodoxy and is engaged on a work on the nature and value of historical testimony. Elsmere's studies gradually lead him to abandon his faith in miracles and in Christ as anything more than a symbol of the divine spirit at work in humanity. His conscience demands that he leave the Anglican church and find a new way of expressing a deeply religious, but undogmatic, piety. Eventually he founds the New Brotherhood of Christianity, an educational settlement in the London slums.

The drama of the novel derives from the emotional anguish experienced by Elsmere as he makes a spiritual pilgrimage which inevitably opens a chasm between the honest doubter and his orthodox wife. In this respect the novel undoubtedly draws upon the strain imposed on Mrs Ward's own parents by her father's changing religious allegiances. The tenor of the novel's discussion of 19th-century religious and sceptical thought is in general closer to the mid than the late 19th-century atmosphere, but the portraits the novel was commonly supposed to offer of T. H. GREEN, WALTER PATER and MARK PATTISON ensured its topical success. Gladstone's lengthy review in the *Nineteenth Century* boosted its sales yet further.

Robert of Gloucester *fl*. 1250–1300 A monk at Gloucester abbey involved in the writing of a Middle English verse CHRONICLE, 12,000 lines long in its earliest version. He was probably the principal author, revising the early part of the work and writing the last section; two other writers apparently worked on the chronicle at some stage.

The chronicle covers the history of England from the beginning of the reign of Stephen to the death of Henry III. It combines historical fact and legend, a large part of it being devoted to King Arthur (see ARTHURIAN LITERATURE). The sources are diverse, ranging from the pseudo-historical GEOFFREY OF MONMOUTH to more reliable records such as the Annals of Winchester. The most valued portion of the chronicle, apparently reliable and probably first-hand, is the account of the last part of the reign of Henry III, including the battle of Evesham (1265), the death of Simon de Montfort and the town and gown riots of Oxford (1263). The work conveys an enthusiasm for accurate representation and a love of England. It is characterized by sincerity and directness of style, and the author's generosity of feeling.

Robert the Devil A popular story of the Middle Ages found in a variety of forms – EXEMPLUM, romance, drama, BALLAD – throughout western Europe. The story is the basis of the Middle English romance, *SIR GOWTHER*.

Roberts, Sir Charles G(eorge) D(ouglas) 1860–1943 Canadian poet, short-story writer and novelist, called 'the father of Canadian literature'. Born near Fredericton, he was educated at the University of New Brunswick. He taught for some years before becoming editor of *The Week* in Toronto, where he met and encouraged many young writers. He was professor at King's College in Nova Scotia and later lived in New York, Paris and London, returning to Canada in 1925. He was a prolific writer, producing ten books of poetry – the first being *Orion and Other Poems* (1880) – several romances, and 18 collections of short stories, including *Earth's Enigmas* (1896), *The Kindred of the Wild* (1902), *The Watchers of the Trails* (1904) and *Kings in Exile* (1909). His earlier poetry, found in volumes such as *In Divers Tones* (1886) and *Songs of the Common Day* (1893), is generally thought his best. His *Selected Poems* were published in 1936. He was knighted in 1935.

Roberts, Michael (William Edward) 1902–48 Anthologist, poet and critic. Born in Bournemouth, he was educated at King's College, London, and Trinity College, Cambridge. He worked as a teacher, as a wartime propagandist and as a college principal. Roberts's first successes were the Marxist anthologies *New Signatures* (1932) and *New Country* (1933), which featured new poets such as W. H. AUDEN, C. DAY-LEWIS, WILLIAM EMPSON, JOHN LEHMANN and CHARLES MADGE. His reputation as anthologist was confirmed by the influential *Faber Book of Modern Verse* (1936), which introduced GEORGE BARKER, DAVID GASCOYNE and DYLAN THOMAS and omitted the Georgians (see GEORGIAN POETRY). Roberts's poetry, published in *These Our Matins* (1930), *Poems* (1936), *Orion Marches* (1939) and the posthumous *Collected Poems* (1958), is now neglected, despite the appearance of a *Selected Poems and Prose* (1980). The poems evoke bleak, mountain landscapes, and explore man's need to accept responsibility for his own life. His diverse prose writings include a fine study of T. E. HULME (1938), *The Recovery of the West* (1941), and the unfinished *The Estate of Man* (1951), which can now be seen as a pioneering ecological work.

Robertson, Thomas William 1829–71 Playwright. Born in Newark, the eldest of 22 children in a theatrical family, Robertson worked on and behind the stage from his childhood to his death. Only a few of the 50 or so plays and adaptations for which he was responsible are of lasting value, but those few are of enormous significance in the development of English drama during the 19th century. It is no exaggeration to say that the six comedies by Robertson, presented at the Prince of Wales's Theatre in 1865–70, set a standard for realistic attention to domestic detail that prepared the way for a revival of serious drama. Their effect on acting styles was more immediate and quite as profound. The best are *Society* (1865), *Ours* (1866), *CASTE* (1867) and *School* (1869). *Play* (1868) and *M. P.* (1870) were and are less successful. The term 'cup-and-saucer drama' was applied to Robertson and his imitators. PINERO's warm portrait of him as Tom Wrench in *TRELAWNY OF THE 'WELLS'* invites more serious attention to a writer who was one of the first to combine the vision of the director and the art of the playwright.

Robertson, William 1721–93 Historian. Born at Borthwick, Midlothian, and educated at the common school there, Dalkeith grammar school and Edinburgh University, Robertson was licensed as a preacher in the Church of Scotland in 1741. His *History of Scotland* (1759) was described by HORACE WALPOLE as 'what all the world now allows to be the best modern history', and was also praised by BURKE, CHESTERFIELD, GIBBON and MALLET. Its success was such he was elected principal of Edinburgh University in 1762 and the following year Moderator of the General Assembly of the Church of Scotland, in which capacity he established the independence of the Church from government interference. His *History of Charles V* (1769) was praised by Voltaire and said by Catherine the Great to be '*le compagnon constant de tous mes voyages*', while the *History of America* (1777), a work of great popular appeal as a result of the almost simultaneous American War of Independence, is believed to have influenced KEATS's view of Cortez. Robertson was a major force in the Scottish Enlightenment.

Robin Hood An outlaw hero of English folktale. Several historical figures have been identified as the 'real' Robin Hood, but there is little evidence to support any particular claim or, indeed, to show that he was ever anything but legendary. The first reference suggests that he was already a famous figure by the last quarter of the 14th century. The extant parts of the medieval legend are preserved in five poems and a fragment of a play. The stories attached to him and his band of outlaws have changed considerably over the centuries, his continuing struggle against the sheriff of Nottingham and his poaching of the king's deer being their only constant features. Robin Hood's most famous characteristic, his practice of robbing from the rich to give to the poor, is a later addition to the legend and does not feature in the medieval stories. His companions Little John and Will Scarlet (or Scarlok) appear in the earliest versions, but Maid Marian was not introduced until the 16th century.

Her character and that of Friar Tuck owe something to THOMAS LOVE PEACOCK's *MAID MARIAN* (1822) which, with SIR WALTER SCOTT's *IVANHOE* (1819), assured the survival of the Robin Hood legend in the Romantic period and laid the basis for its continuing popularity in the age of film and television.

Robinson, Edwin Arlington 1869–1935 American poet. He was born in Head Tide, Maine, and educated at Harvard. Deeply influenced by Victorian poetry, ROBERT BROWNING and THOMAS HARDY in particular, he began his poetic career with a bleak portrayal of New England life in character sketches of, or DRAMATIC MONOLOGUES by, the inhabitants of the fictional Tilbury Town, based on his childhood home of Gardiner. His reputation was established in *The Torrent and the Night Before* (1896; expanded, and reissued as *The Children of the Night*, 1897), which contained 'Richard Cory', and in *Captain Craig* (1902) and *The Town down the River* (1910), which contained 'Miniver Cheevy'. His mature style – direct, ironic but never abandoning traditional forms – emerged in *The Man against the Sky* (1916) and *Collected Poems* (1921), which added another Tilbury poem, 'Mr Flood's Party', and two more favourite anthology pieces, 'The Tree in Pamela's Garden' and 'Rembrandt to Rembrandt'. His many later volumes, written when the MODERNISM he refused to embrace was increasingly fashionable, enjoyed a mixed reception which never completely reduced him to the margins of 20th-century poetry. They include several long poems, most notably a trilogy based on ARTHURIAN LITERATURE, *Merlin* (1917), *Lancelot* (1920) and *Tristram* (1927), and *The Man Who Died Twice* (1924), about a musician's betrayal of his talent. Robinson was three times awarded the PULITZER PRIZE.

Robinson, Henry Crabb 1775–1867 Lawyer, journalist and diarist. Born in Bury St Edmunds, Robinson was a solicitor at Colchester, and from 1813 to 1828 a barrister on the Norfolk circuit. In 1800–5 he lived in Germany, where he matriculated as a student at the University of Jena in 1802. During this period he met many of the leading German poets and thinkers, including Goethe, Schiller and Herder, and on his return to England was influential in making German literature and philosophy more widely known to British readers. In 1807 he was appointed foreign editor of *The Times*, and was its first war correspondent during the Spanish Peninsular War in 1808–9. A Liberal and Dissenter, he was active in the anti-slavery campaign, and was one of the founders of both University College, London, and the Athenaeum Club. He is, however, now chiefly remembered for his voluminous diaries and letters, first published in 1869, which are a valuable source for the early Romantic period. His friends included BLAKE (of whose last years his is the only first-hand account), WORDSWORTH,

LAMB, HAZLITT and COLERIDGE, of whose public lectures he made careful notes. A renowned conversationalist, Robinson was noted for his Sunday breakfast parties which brought together poets and men of affairs.

Robinson, (Esmé Stuart) Lennox 1886–1958 Irish playwright, actor, director and critic. Born in County Cork, he was associated with Dublin's ABBEY THEATRE from 1908 – when his first play, *The Clancy Name*, was produced there – until his death. His work includes serious plays about Irish politics like *Patriots* (1912), *The Dreamers* (1913), *The Lost Leader* (1918) and *The Big House* (1926) and comedies, like *The White-Headed Boy* (1916), the one-act *Crabbed Youth and Age* (1922), *The Far-Off Hills* (1928) and the more experimental *Church Street* (1934). His commitment to the Irish theatre is adroitly illustrated in *Drama at Inish* (1933), also known by the title *Is Life Worth Living?* Robinson wrote *A History of the Abbey Theatre* (1951) and an autobiographical memoir, *Curtain Up* (1942), and edited a useful collection of lectures under the title *The Irish Theatre* (1939). With DONAGH MACDONAGH he edited *The Oxford Book of Irish Verse* (1958).

Robinson, 'Perdita' (Mary) 1758–1800 Novelist, poet and playwright. Born in Bristol, she attended the school run by HANNAH MORE and her sisters in the course of a childhood made turbulent by the eccentricities of her father, a whaling captain. Her adult life was equally eventful. Discovered by DAVID GARRICK, she enjoyed fame as an actress and notoriety as the mistress of the future George IV, who addressed his amorous letters to 'Perdita' and signed them 'Florizel'. Her reputation helped the popularity of the writing to which she turned in earnest after she was paralysed. It included: poems, notably a collection of SONNETS, *Sappho and Phaon* (1796); several insignificant plays; and a succession of romances beginning with a GOTHIC NOVEL, *Vancenza* (1792). She was a friend of WILLIAM GODWIN and MARY WOLLSTONE-CRAFT, who encouraged her to write *Thoughts on the Condition of Women* (1798).

Robinson, Peter 1953– Poet and critic. Born in Salford, he was educated at the universities of York and Cambridge. Since gaining attention with early pamphlets, he has published *This Other Life* (1988), *More about the Weather* (1989), *Leaf-Viewing* (1992) and *Entertaining Fates* (1992), increasingly confident volumes which have established his reputation and announced his preoccupation with the visual arts. The last two volumes also record the influence of Japan, where he has lived and taught since 1989. His affection for Italy and Italian literature is expressed in two volumes of translations from Vittorio Sereni, *The Disease of the Elm and Other Poems* (1983) and

Selected Poems (1990), both in collaboration with Marcus Perryman. Other publications include an edition of the poetry of ADRIAN STOKES (1981), a collection of essays on GEOFFREY HILL (1985) and In the Circumstances: About Poems and Poets (1991).

Robinson Crusoe *(The Life and Strange Surprising Adventures of Robinson Crusoe, of York, Mariner. Written by himself)* A novel by DANIEL DEFOE, published in 1719 when the author was practically 60, and the most enduring of his many works. Although it subsequently assumed a near-mythological status, the story is based squarely upon the true account published by Alexander Selkirk, a fugitive sailor who went to sea in 1704 under WILLIAM DAMPIER and was put ashore (at his own request) on an uninhabited island in the Pacific, where he survived until his rescue in 1709 by WOODES ROGERS. An unsubstantiated rumour has Defoe meeting Selkirk in person in 1711.

In Defoe's imaginative reworking of the story, Crusoe is a mariner who takes to the sea despite parental warnings, and suffers a number of misfortunes at the hands of Barbary pirates and the elements, finally being shipwrecked off South America. A combination of systematic salvaging, resourcefulness and good fortune enables him to exist on his island for some 28 years, two months and 19 days (according to the painstaking journal in which the adventures are recorded). During this time he needs to adapt to his alien environment, demonstrate the self-sufficiency so admired by Defoe himself, and come to terms with his own spiritual listlessness. If as a psychological study in isolation, the book now seems inconsistent and even unconvincing, it should be remembered that the novel was then barely in its infancy, and Robinson Crusoe owes more to the previous literary pedigree of Puritan spiritual autobiographies and allegories (BUNYAN's Grace Abounding was a strong influence). It is at any rate a deliberate amalgam of the specific and the general. The narrative interest combines typical characteristics of the adventure story (for instance, Crusoe's horrified discovery of a strange footprint in the sand) and the exotic fascination of travel literature with a fable more widely representative of human behaviour under conditions of difficulty and pressure.

Robinson Crusoe enjoyed instant and permanent success, and has become one of those classics of English literature which (like GULLIVER'S TRAVELS, perhaps, or PILGRIM'S PROGRESS) appeal at various levels to adults and children alike. It draws its strength from a combination of disparate echoes and shapes: Jonah, Job, Everyman, the Prodigal Son, the colonial explorer and the proto-industrialist are all elements in Crusoe's character. Defoe continued the story in The Farther Adventures of Robinson Crusoe (1719), in which he revisits the island and loses Friday in an attack by savages, and The Serious Reflections... of Robinson Crusoe (1720), neither of which has achieved wide recognition.

Roche, Billy 1949– Irish playwright. His Wexford trilogy, Handful of Stars (1988), Poor Beast in the Rain (1989) and Belfry (1991), won him immediate critical acclaim for his ear for dialect, knack of condensing large dilemmas into small incidents and sympathy for the characters. The hero of Handful of Stars, which won the John Whiting Award, has affinities with the ANGRY YOUNG MEN of the 1950s. Poor Beast in the Rain, which won the Thames Television Best Play Award, is set in a betting office on the eve of the All-Ireland final, while Belfry tells of a sacristan's brief fling with a married woman. Perhaps the most impressive feature of the trilogy was Roche's development in confidence from play to play. Amphibians (1992), produced by the ROYAL SHAKESPEARE COMPANY, is set in a fishing village near Wexford whose inhabitants are suffering hard times.

Rochester, [Wilmot, John] **Earl of** 1647–80 Poet and wit. Born at Ditchley, near Woodstock, and educated briefly at Wadham College, Oxford, Rochester became one of the most dashing and notorious personalities of the Restoration, a peculiar combination of libertine and intellectual, a favourite of Charles II, who continually fell into disrepute. He distinguished himself by gallant action in the second Dutch War (1665) and was involved in a number of subsequent civil 'imbroglios' for which he was duly banished from court. He once claimed not to have been sober for five years at a stretch. He kidnapped Elizabeth Malet (a wealthy heiress) whom he married in 1667, and then surprised by becoming a relatively attentive husband according to the standards of his day. It was no coincidence for such an inveterately posturing personality that one of his mistresses should have been Elizabeth Barry, one of the first really celebrated English actresses. He was intermittently the patron of several poets, and was rumoured to have been responsible for the vicious attack on DRYDEN in Covent Garden (1679), when the poet was severely beaten. The subject of rumour and legend, Rochester's exuberant life-style caused his health to collapse in 1679, alcohol and venereal disease having taken their toll; though he died a reformed character after the religious instruction of GILBERT BURNET during his final months persuaded him to renounce HOBBES and scepticism and embrace the Christian faith.

Little of Rochester's poetic output was actually published during his lifetime, but much of it was evidently designed for clandestine circulation in manuscript form, being scurrilous or pornographic in nature ('Signior Dildo', 'The Imperfect Enjoyment', 'A Ramble in St James's Park' and 'The Maim'd Debauchee'). As a satirical poet Rochester was more accomplished than his 'minor' status now suggests; he was later an influence on POPE ('Upon Nothing' is recognizably in the paradoxical style of Augustan wit) but his best-known poem is 'A Satire against Reason and Mankind' (1675), which ranges the sensualist against the rationalist attitude towards the capabilities of the human mind. His other two substantial achievements are the 'Letter from Artemisia in the Town to Chloe in the Country', a pungent social satire on dissembling and gullibility, and the superbly contemptuous 'Allusion to Horace: The 10th Satire of the First Book', both of which establish Rochester as an intelligent and skilful versifier. His inclination for physical self-indulgence cut short one of the most vivacious poetic imaginations of the Restoration years.

rocking feet See METRE.

Roderick Hudson A novel by HENRY JAMES, first published as a serial in *THE ATLANTIC MONTHLY* in 1875, and then in volume form in 1876. The author revised it for publication in England in 1879.

Roderick Hudson, an amateur sculptor, is taken to Europe by Rowland Mallet, a wealthy connoisseur who is impressed by his talent. In Rome he introduces Roderick to his circle, which includes the French sculptor, Gloriani, who is certain that the young American's talent will never develop. Roderick meets Christina Light, the daughter of an expatriate American widow; he is fascinated by her and deserts his work. In order to force him back into reality, Rowland brings his mother and fiancée, Mary Garland, from New England. Their arrival seems to have its desired effect, and Roderick executes a fine bust of his mother. But then Christina, urged on by her ambitious mother, marries Prince Casamassima (see *THE PRINCESS CASAMASSIMA*), and Roderick's work comes to a complete halt. Once again Rowland attempts to rekindle Roderick's interest by arranging a visit to Switzerland for Mary, Mrs Hudson, Roderick, and himself. Unfortunately Christina is there too and Roderick borrows money from Mary so that he can follow her. This provokes Rowland to a furious outburst and he condemns Roderick as an ungrateful egoist. Roderick walks off into the mountains where he is caught in a thunderstorm. He is found dead, and it is unclear whether or not he committed suicide.

Roderick Random, The Adventures of The first novel by TOBIAS SMOLLETT, published in 1748.

Roderick Random's father disappears and the boy is left in the care of his grandfather, who ill-treats him and leaves him penniless when he dies. Roderick is befriended by his uncle, Tom Bowling, a lieutenant in the navy, and decides to go to London to make his fortune; an old school-friend, Hugh Strap, accompanies him as valet. The journey bristles with crude adventures. In London, Roderick qualifies as a surgeon's mate but discovers that a bribe, not qualifications, is necessary to secure a commission. He becomes assistant to a French apothecary, but is seized by the press gang.

Forced into service as a common sailor on the man o'war *Thunder*, Roderick proves his qualifications and becomes a surgeon's mate, after all. The *Thunder* takes part in the siege of Cartagena (1741) and Roderick suffers many humiliations and misadventures. While returning to England he is shipwrecked and robbed and, lying naked on the shore, is found and taken care of by a middle-aged woman poet, whose footman he becomes. He falls in love with the poet's niece, Narcissa, but the presence of suitors of considerable means obliges him to leave. He is kidnapped by smugglers and taken to France, where he finds his uncle Tom Bowling and a 'Monsieur d'Estrapes' – his old friend Strap. The two return to London in their original partnership: Strap sets up Roderick, acts as his valet, and is going to aid and abet Roderick's design to marry an heiress.

Melinda Goosetrap is a likely quarry, but her mother is not impressed. At Bath, Roderick meets Narcissa again. He loses all he has at the gaming tables and, returning to London, is thrown into a debtors' prison. Tom Bowling obtains his release, and takes him aboard his own ship as a surgeon for a trading trip. During the voyage they encounter a wealthy trader, Don Roderigo; he proves to be Roderick's father, who had been disinherited by the evil grandfather and had left the country to make his fortune. They return to England and Roderick marries Narcissa. Strap marries her maid, Miss Williams. Roderick repurchases the family estate and has a rewarding time snubbing those relatives who, formerly, had scorned him as an impecunious dependant.

Modelled on Le Sage's *Gil Blas*, *Roderick Random* has the savage energy of true PICARESQUE. Unlike later novelists in the English tradition – including those whom he strongly influenced, like DICKENS – Smollett saw no need to soften the roguery of his villains or temper the coarseness of their adventures. It is not a book which can engage the reader's sympathy or moral approval, for there is hardly a pleasant episode in the whole narrative; there is, moreover, a marked obsession with filth and violence. What commands attention is the unabashed vitality of the writing and the vivid portrayal of life in London, at sea and, in later chapters, in fashionable society.

Roethke, Theodore (Huebner) 1908–63 American poet. He was born in Saginaw, Michigan, and educated at the University of Michigan and at Harvard. His first volume of poetry, *Open House*, was published in 1941. In it, as in much of his early work, he returns to the landscapes of his childhood as a means of reconstructing transcendent moments of 'waking'. His second volume, *The Lost Son and Other Poems*, appeared in 1948. In 1954 he received the PULITZER PRIZE for *The Waking: Poems, 1933-1953* (1953). *Words for the Wind: The Collected Verse of Theodore Roethke* (1957) won him the 1958 Bollingen Prize and the 1959 National Book Award. His later volumes, which include a good deal of love poetry, are *I am! Says the Lamb* (1961), *Sequence, Sometimes Metaphysical, Poems* (1963) and *The Far Field* (1964). Two collections of prose pieces appeared posthumously: *The Contemporary Poet as Artist and Critic* (1964) and *On the Poet and His Craft: Selected Prose* (1965).

Rogers, Samuel 1763-1855 Poet. The son of a banker, Rogers was born at Stoke Newington, then just north of London. He succeeded to his father's fortune and took the opportunity to indulge his fancy for writing poetry. A generous patron at whose table the cultured society of London was always welcome, he commissioned Turner as illustrator for an edition of his *Italy* (1822-8), for which he had followed Childe Harold's footsteps as a tribute to BYRON. The volume enjoyed considerable popular success. He declined the office of POET LAUREATE on the death of WORDSWORTH. Among his volumes of verse are *Ode to Superstition* (1786), *The Pleasures of Memory* (1792), *Columbus* (1810) and *Jacqueline* (1814). *Recollections of the Table-Talk of Samuel Rogers* (edited by Alexander Dyce: 1856) and *Recollections* (edited by William Sharpe; 1859) are valuable sources of information on the artistic life of the period.

Rogers, Will(iam) (Penn Adair) 1879-1935 American actor and humorist. Of Cherokee ancestry, he was born in Oologh Indian territory in what is now Oklahoma. As a young man he travelled the world, and during the Boer War worked as a horse-breaker for the British in South Africa. On his return to the USA he worked as a rodeo cowboy in vaudeville shows, and for several years, starting in 1913, performed in the *Ziegfield Follies*. In 1919 he became an actor, first in silent films and later in the 'talkies'. In 1926 he began writing newspaper articles which commented humorously on American politics and society; eventually his column was syndicated and reached an estimated 40 million readers. His books include *The Cowboy Philosopher on Prohibition* (1919), *The Illiterate Digest* (1924), *Letters of a Self-Made Diplomat to His President* (1927) and *There's Not a Bathing Suit in Russia* (1927). He died in a plane crash in Alaska. *The Autobiography of Will Rogers* appeared in 1949, and a collection of his newspaper pieces, *Sanity is Where You Find It*, in 1955.

Rogers, Woodes d. 1732 A captain in command of two privateering ships, the *Duke* and *Duchess*, during an expedition to the Pacific (1708-11), Rogers wrote a vivid account in his journal, published as *A Cruising Voyage round the World* (1712). His pilot was WILLIAM DAMPIER, and Rogers tells of the seizure of Guayaquil in Ecuador from the Spaniards, who were forced to ransom the city, and the captain of a galleon from Manila. Also described is Rogers's visit to the island of Juan Fernández, where they found 'a man clothed in goat-skins, who seemed wilder than the original owners of his apparel'; his name was Alexander Selkirk, whose strange adventures gave DEFOE the idea for *ROBINSON CRUSOE*. Rogers became governor of the Bahamas (1718-21 and 1729-32), where he was chiefly responsible for the suppression of piracy.

Roget's Thesaurus A reference book originated by Peter Mark Roget (1779-1869), a doctor who spent most of his life in medical and scientific research, and first published as *Thesaurus of English Words and Phrases, Classified and Arranged So As to Facilitate the Expression of Ideas and Assist in Literary Composition* (1852). After going through 28 editions in his lifetime, it was edited by his son and grandson, being many times revised, abridged and modernized. Despite its elaborate taxonomic arrangement of vocabulary into six major classes of 'Ideas' and about 1000 subdivisions, 'Roget' is more often than not viewed as a collection of synonyms. Users generally consult the alphabetically arranged index of common words at the back as a way of finding their way to a topic appropriate to their needs.

Roland and Vernagu A VERSE ROMANCE in TAIL-RHYME stanzas written before 1330-40, probably in the east Midlands. It is the first part of the composite romance *Charlemagne and Roland*, the second fragment of which is *OTUEL AND ROLAND*. Its source is the Old French prose *Estoire de Charlemagne* (1206), a translation of the Latin prose *Chronicle of the Pseudo-Turpin* (c. 1140). *Roland and Vernagu* relates Charlemagne's journey to Constantinople and return with the relics of the Passion, followed by his conquest of Spain and a long episode in which Roland defeats the Saracen giant Vernagu in a duel after showing him charity and explaining the Christian faith to him. The structure is episodic, with lengthy descriptions of the relics and miracles connected with them or independent of them. The romance is incomplete, breaking off as Otuel hears of Vernagu's death.

Rolfe, Frederick William 1860-1913 Novelist and short-story writer, who also styled himself Baron Corvo and Fr. (i.e. Father) Rolfe. A Londoner, born in Cheapside and educated in Camden Town, he turned to teaching after he failed to get into Oxford. He became a Roman Catholic convert in 1886 and spent the next few years training for the priesthood, first at Oscott and then at Scots College in Rome, before being finally rejected in 1890. He remained in Rome, calling himself Baron Corvo, but returned to England before the end of the decade to begin his career as a writer. *Stories Toto Told Me* (1898), which first appeared in *THE YELLOW BOOK*, was followed by the expanded collection, *In His Own Image* (1901). Rolfe's fascination with late medieval and Renaissance Italy was expressed in *Chronicles of the House of Borgia* (1901), a collection of essays defending the Papal family, and informed two romances, *Don Tarquinio* (1905) and *Don Renato* (1909). His paranoid sensibility and ornate prose style were best displayed in *Hadrian the Seventh* (1904), the story of how George Arthur Rose, a failed priest clearly modelled on the author, is elected Pope. His most famous book, it was successfully adapted for the stage by Peter Luke in 1968. Two posthumously published works belong to the same category of extravagantly fictionalized autobiography: *The Desire and Pursuit of the Whole* (1934), which takes a characteristically savage revenge on Rolfe's friends and patrons, and *Nicholas Crabbe* (1958), based on the unhappy years at the start of his career as a writer. A. J. A. Symons's *The Quest for Corvo* (1934) is a classic account of the biographer's difficulty in separating the reality of Rolfe's life from the lies, fantasy and mystery in which he delighted to shroud it.

Rolle of Hampole, Richard *c.* 1300–49 Religious writer and poet, in English and Latin. Born in Thornton, Yorkshire, he was apparently educated at Oxford, though be never graduated. He was not ordained and there is no evidence to suggest he entered orders, but he became a hermit while still young, living in various parts of Yorkshire, finally near a Cistercian convent in Hampole, where he died. His best-known and principal mystical work, *De incendio amoris*, was a product of his youth and is marred by attacks on his opponents and by preciosity. He taught that the contemplative must renounce the world and the self in total love of God to receive divine inspiration and revelation, and that knowledge would come in Heaven but love must be exercised on earth. His best writing is to be found in his lyrics on God's love and the crucified Christ, characterized by fervour and sincerity and devoid of the egocentricity of his prose.

Rolliad, Criticism on The A series of Whig political SATIRES which appeared in *The Morning Herald* and *The Daily Advertiser* after the victory of William Pitt and his followers in the election of 1784. The authors belonged to a Whig club, the Esto Perpetua, and included General Richard Fitzpatrick, Lord John Townshend, the antiquary George Ellis, and French Laurence, Regius Professor of Civil Law at Oxford. The satires took the form of reviews of an imaginary epic, *The Rolliad*, narrating the adventures of the Norman Duke Rollo, heroic ancestor of Pitt's supporter John Rolle. The *Rolliad* satires were followed by *Political Eclogues*, in which Pitt and his followers appeared as Virgilian shepherds. The death of WILLIAM WHITEHEAD, the POET LAUREATE, in 1785 prompted further satire against the Tories from the same group in the form of *Probationary Odes* for the vacant laureateship.

roman à clef A 'novel with a key', in which real people appear under fictitious names, lightly disguised but still recognizable. The purpose is often satiric, if only mildly so, as the novels of THOMAS LOVE PEACOCK and ALDOUS HUXLEY's *Crome Yellow* demonstrate; but the portrait of D. H. LAWRENCE as Mark Rampion in Huxley's *Point Counter Point* shows that the form can also express admiration.

roman à thèse A 'thesis novel', intended to popularize or propagate an idea or cause. The political novels of DISRAELI and KINGSLEY's *ALTON LOCKE* are examples.

Roman Actor, The A tragedy by PHILIP MASSINGER, first produced in 1626 and published in 1629. Although it has not been revived in the modern theatre, Massinger considered it his best work and it was highly regarded in its time. The plot comes from Suetonius, whom Massinger could have read in the translation by PHILEMON HOLLAND.

The Emperor Domitian conceives a passion for Domitia Longina, wife of the senator Aelius Lamia; Domitia is taken from her husband and is made empress. Domitian is intensely jealous, but Domitia does not care for the emperor and falls in love with an actor, Paris. Unfortunately she betrays herself at a performance in which Paris plays a character who threatens suicide when his love rejects him. Domitian is brought information by his wife's enemies; he surprises her with Paris and kills the actor with his own hands. Domitia heaps contempt on the emperor and abuses him for his subservience to his passions, but he cannot bring himself to harm her. However, he adds her name to a list of the proscribed – thus ensuring that someone else will attempt her life. Domitia discovers the proscription while he sleeps and hastily summons those named along with her. Domitian is tricked into leaving the protection of his tribunes by one of the conspirators, Parthenius, with the promise of news of a victory in the east. Among the six who strike him down are Domitia, his niece Julia, and his cousin Domitilla.

roman fleuve A sequence of novels, in which the individual books are linked by recurrent characters. It may describe a family (as in GALSWORTHY's *FORSYTE SAGA*) or a social milieu (as in TROLLOPE's BARSETSHIRE NOVELS and ANTHONY POWELL's *DANCE TO THE MUSIC OF TIME*).

romance See VERSE ROMANCE.

Romans of Partenay, The (Lusignan) A VERSE RO-
MANCE of 6600 lines of RHYME ROYAL translated in the
north-east Midlands c. 1500 from a French version by
La Coudrette (c. 1400). Raymond meets Melusine by a
fountain after becoming lost on a disastrous hunt and
agrees to marry her. Melusine demands that
Raymond never try to discover what she does on
Saturday nights, but he is persuaded by his brother to
break the vow and, spying on her, finds that she turns
into a serpent from the waist down. When he reveals
his knowledge in an argument she turns into a serpent and leaves him. Her metamorphosis is the result
of her mother's revenge on her three daughters for
imprisoning their father, who had broken a vow
never to visit his wife in childbirth. The other two
daughters, Melior and Palestine, are respectively
exiled in Armenia and forced to guard the mother's
treasure on a mountain in Aragon. The second half of
the romance is concerned with the stories of these
two and of Melior's ten sons, all deformed in some respect, and in particular of Geoffrey of the Great Tooth,
who becomes something of a central figure in a tale
without a proper focal point.

Romanticism A comprehensive term for all the various tendencies towards change observable in
European literature, art and culture in the later 18th
and early 19th centuries. Although it manifested
itself everywhere in the form of a pronounced shift in
sensibility, Romanticism was not a unified movement with a clearly agreed agenda, and its emphases
varied widely according to time, place and individual
author. Intellectually it pulled away from the philosophical rationalism and NEOCLASSICISM of the
Enlightenment, developing an alternative aesthetic
of freedom from the 'dead' letter of formal rules and
conventions, and of uninhibited self-expression, of
which the German Sturm und Drang movement of
the 1770s, which included the early writings of
Herder, Schiller (Die Räuber) and Goethe (Werther),
was an important precursor. A corresponding sense of
strong feeling, but also of original, fresh and, above
all, authentic feeling was also important, and the development of natural, unforced poetic diction
became an essential qualification for the standing of
the poet (as in the LYRICAL BALLADS). The most typical
Romantic attitude is individualism. Underlying the
Romantic epoch as a whole is a pervasive sense of the
collapse within the individual subject of those intricate systems of moral, religious and psychic control,
constraint and limitation which were being shaken
apart at the public or institutional level by the
American and French Revolutions. Whatever the
colour of his politics, the Romantic poet assumes the
mantle of prophet, seer and legislator. The Romantic
hero is either a solitary dreamer, or an egocentric

plagued by guilt and remorse but, in either case, a
figure who has kicked the world away from beneath
his feet. In their explicitly 'reactionary' phase, writers
such as WORDSWORTH and COLERIDGE tended to look
back on their earlier revolutionary radicalism as a
transgression against an unheeded sense of the
proper truth of things, for which they were punished
with a kind of existential vertigo. A similar derangement of the official political economy of the emotions
seems to have been the effect, if not the conscious intention, of the GOTHIC NOVELS of HORACE WALPOLE,
'MONK' LEWIS and ANN RADCLIFFE, which anticipate
and to some extent overlap with Romanticism proper.
Other important harbingers of Romanticism were
introspective 18th-century poets such as BLAIR,
CHATTERTON, YOUNG, GRAY and COWPER, as well as the
cult of the primitive in the Celtic bardic verse of
MACPHERSON's Ossianic poetry, and the folk ballads
collected by PERCY. The Romantic valorization of personal experience was accompanied by a deepening
sense of history which found its expression in the
novels of SIR WALTER SCOTT. Another general feature
of the period was the fascination for the private lives
of individuals reflected in countless 'memoirs', 'recollections', 'lives', and in the adoption by writers such
as DE QUINCEY, LAMB and HAZLITT of autobiography as
a literary form. The invasion of the inner recesses of
the personality was continued in the analysis of
dreams and the irrational, and in drug-taking and
dabblings in the occult.

'Romanticism' seems to have assumed its present
connotations around the mid-19th century, when the
phenomenon to which it referred was already regarded as belonging to a completed past. Except in
Germany, the principal protagonists of literary
Romanticism were not, themselves, self-consciously
'romantic', nor were they perceived by their contemporaries as belonging to a particular school. The
English Romantic poets – BLAKE, Coleridge, Wordsworth, KEATS, SHELLEY and BYRON – divided into two
distinct generations, came from disparate backgrounds, differed sharply in their theory and practice,
held conflicting political views, and in some cases cordially disliked each other. Friedrich Schlegel's characterization of Romantic writing as medieval, Christian
and transcendental as opposed to classical, pagan and
worldly was part of a specifically German polemic
which was taken up by Madame de Staël in her De
l'Allemagne, published in England in 1813. It may
have fitted Coleridge, appropriately the only English
poet with an extensive knowledge of the German theorists, but it seems quite wide of the mark in the case
of Byron, Keats and Shelley, who were neo-pagan in
their inclinations, liberal-to-radical in their politics
and a long way from any idealization of medieval
social systems. What the English Romantics did share
was a belief in the poet's mission. Perhaps the most
lasting achievement of Romanticism, in England and

Germany, and later on in France (where writers such as Chateaubriand, Hugo, and De Vigny were strongly influenced by the English poets), was what might be called the institutionalization of the Imagination: the emergence of the poet as a person possessing a special kind of faculty which sets him apart from his fellow men.

Romany Rye, The GEORGE BORROW'S sequel to *LAVENGRO*, published in 1857.

Though intended to provide the facts omitted from the earlier book, *The Romany Rye* instead sustains the original narrative in the unchronological, episodic, open-ended way that had already puzzled and irritated literal-minded readers. Yet despite its irony and ambivalence, the book contains some of Borrow's best writing, not least the enigmatic conclusion to the Isopel Berners episode, a tale which soon established itself as a classic of prose romance. But instead of giving the book a conventional structure, Borrow abruptly broke off the account of his life in mid-career and added the 'Appendix', one of the most powerfully written pieces of invective in the English language. To some, the violent attacks on identifiable people seemed tasteless and inappropriate, yet Borrow had hit upon a means by which his interior life could be recoded in psychological rather than documentary terms. The notoriously unsettling 'Appendix' is in fact all of a piece with the narrative that preceded it. Thus the savage attacks on 'gentility nonsense' become the exposition of his suppressed radical self, while his vitriolic dismissal of the critics of *Lavengro* permitted the indirect expression of his own unconventional, anti-bourgeois attitude to life.

Romaunt of the Rose, The A fragmentary translation of the French *Roman de la rose* (begun *c.* 1327 by Guillaume de Lorris and continued some 40 years later by Jean de Meun), a DREAM-VISION and ALLEGORY which played an important role in developing the medieval ideal of COURTLY LOVE. The dreamer visits a delightful garden in which he sees a rosebud and is pierced by one of Cupid's arrows. With the aid and hindrance of various allegorical personifications he attempts to win the rosebud. The first of the three English fragments has been attributed to CHAUCER. 'Thou hast translated the Romaunce of the Rose', says the God of Love to the poet in *THE LEGEND OF GOOD WOMEN*. The God's claim that the translation was a crime against women is not supported by the extant fragments, which do not include Jean de Meun's antifeminist satire but give half of Guillaume de Lorris's account, Jean de Meun's discussion of love and his account of hypocrisy. Though the style is Chaucerian throughout, Chaucer cannot have been the only translator; the second fragment shows the influence of a northern dialect.

Romeo and Juliet A tragedy by WILLIAM SHAKESPEARE, first performed *c.* 1595 and published in a corrupt Quarto (Q1) in 1597 and an authentic one (Q2) in 1599 as well as in the First Folio of 1623. The source was a poem by Arthur Brooke, *The Tragical History of Romeus and Juliet* (1562), but the story was, in its main outlines, well known.

The enmity of two great families, the Capulets and the Montagues, is a blight on the city of Verona. After a street brawl, the Prince orders the families to keep the peace on pain of death. Capulet, partly to demonstrate his willingness for Count Paris to marry his daughter Juliet, plans a masqued ball. Romeo, the lovesick son of Montague, decides to attend, effectively masked, in pursuit of his beloved Rosalind. At the ball, he and Juliet meet and immediately fall in love, but Tybalt, recognizing Romeo as a Montague, has to be restrained from fighting him. Romeo waits under Juliet's balcony, and they arrange a secret marriage, with the collusion of their mutual confessor, Friar Lawrence, and Juliet's Nurse.

The marriage takes place, and is immediately followed by disaster, when Romeo tries to prevent a duel between his mercurial friend Mercutio and the angry Tybalt. Mercutio is fatally wounded as a result of Romeo's intervention, and Romeo kills Tybalt as a reprisal. Banished from Verona, he leaves for Mantua after a single night with his new wife. Before Friar Lawrence can find a way of making the marriage public, Capulet decides that Juliet must marry Paris immediately. Friar Lawrence advises Juliet to acquiesce, but gives her a potion to take on the eve of the bigamous wedding. He explains that the potion will give her the appearance of death for 42 hours. She will be taken to the family vault, where the friar will arrange for Romeo to greet her when she wakes.

In plague-torn Mantua, Friar Lawrence's message fails to reach Romeo. Desperate at the news of Juliet's death, Romeo buys poison, goes to the Capulet vault for a last sight of Juliet and, encountering Paris there, kills him and drinks the fatal draught. Juliet wakes, finds Romeo dead and stabs herself with his dagger. The sequence of events, related by Friar Lawrence, serves to reconcile the two warring families.

The achievements of *Romeo and Juliet* have been so long recognized as to threaten the play with overfamiliarity. Theatrical popularity has been assured by its clear plotting and the lyrical heights of its love poetry, together with the vivid creation of its minor characters, particularly Mercutio and the Nurse. That Shakespeare could write a tragedy of 'star-crossed' love at much the same time as he was parodying one in the Pyramus and Thisbe play of *A MIDSUMMER NIGHT'S DREAM* is an indication of his extraordinary range as a writer.

Romer, Stephen 1957– Poet and journalist. He was born in London and educated at Cambridge. *Islay*

Romeo and Juliet: Dorothy Tutin and Brian Murray in the Royal Shakespeare Company production, 1961

(1985) was followed by his first major collection, *Idols* (1985), and *Plato's Ladder* (1992), a Poetry Book Society choice. Praised for its 'emotional candour and intellectual clarity', his verse combines tightly controlled forms with an ability to luxuriate in language and colour. Although obviously influenced by French literature and France, it has steadily broadened its horizons. *Plato's Ladder* contains poems influenced by Italy, Spain and the Hebrides as well as a section about Poland, where he spent a momentous year in 1989–90. Romer has also translated Jacques Dupin and Jean Follain.

Romola A novel by GEORGE ELIOT, published in *THE CORNHILL MAGAZINE* in 1862–3 and in book form in 1863. It is set in Florence during the 1490s, a period of intense political strife and religious upheaval following the death of Lorenzo de' Medici, the invasion of Italy by the French, and the rise and fall of the fundamentalist Dominican friar Girolamo Savonarola.

Tito Melema, a handsome young Greek, ingratiates himself with the blind scholar Bardo de' Bardi and then marries his high-minded daughter Romola. Though superficially charming, Tito turns out to be utterly unscrupulous; he has robbed and abandoned his adoptive father, Baldassare, and duped a peasant girl, Tessa, into a mock marriage. When his self-seeking leads him to betray Bardo's solemn trust, and to indulge in unprincipled political duplicity, Romola's love for him is replaced by contempt. She turns for spiritual guidance to Savonarola and for a time becomes his disciple, but rejects him too when his vision of establishing God's kingdom on earth degenerates into religious tyranny. As the several strands of the novel are drawn to a climax, Tito is killed by the demented Baldassare who has found his way to

Florence; Romola finds fulfilment through self-sacrifice, in caring for the sick during an outbreak of plague and in looking after Tessa and her children by Tito; while Savonarola, undone by his own fanaticism, is tried for heresy and burned at the stake.

Besides Savonarola, the dramatis personae include Machiavelli, the artist Piero di Cosimo, and 50 or more lesser figures of the time. George Eliot spent months researching the historical background to the story, which abounds with details of almost every aspect of life in Renaissance Florence. *Romola* always held a special place in George Eliot's own affections; in 1877 she wrote, 'there is no book of mine about which I more thoroughly feel that I could swear by every sentence as having been written with my best blood'.

rondeau Sometimes distinguished from and sometimes taken to be synonymous with the rondel; the English 'roundel' is used for either or both. One could say that the rondeau is a poem of 13 lines in iambic pentameter or tetrameter (see METRE), divided into two unequal STANZAS, using only two rhymes throughout and repeating the opening phrase as a refrain at the end of each stanza. The rondel may be 14 lines long and occasionally has a third rhyme. However, poetic practice – in England mostly confined to the late 19th century – varies considerably. SWINBURNE's roundels, for instance, have three stanzas but only 11 lines, including the refrains; CHAUCER's three roundels all have 13 lines and, instead of a refrain, repeat the first three lines at the end, as well as including other repetitions. Perhaps, in the light of these variations – in which the idea of 'rounding' seems most prominent – a looser definition might serve: a short poem, using only two rhymes and repeating some part of the beginning at the end and also, normally, at the end of each stanza.

Room of One's Own, A An essay by VIRGINIA WOOLF based upon two papers read to the Arts Society at Newnham College and the Odtaa at Girton College, Cambridge, in October 1928. It was published in 1929.

It has become a feminist classic. Woolf begins by announcing her basic thesis: that 'a woman must have money and a room of her own if she is to write fiction'. In answer to the rhetorical question about why there were no famous Elizabethan women writers, Woolf employs the conceit that SHAKESPEARE had a talented sister called Judith who was driven to suicide by artistic frustration. She then examines the educational, social, and financial disadvantages and prejudices which have thwarted women writers throughout (English) history. Special tribute is paid to APHRA BEHN, DOROTHY OSBORNE, JANE AUSTEN and the BRONTË sisters.

In the last chapter Woolf discusses 'the androgynous mind' ('If one is a man, still the woman part of the brain must have effect; and a woman also must

have intercourse with the man in her') and deplores the male-centred perspective of 'some of the finest works of our greatest living writers' which makes them incomprehensible to women. The essay concludes by exhorting women to struggle to help realize a world in which 'the dead poet who was Shakespeare's sister will put on the body which she has so often laid down'.

Room with a View, A A novel by E. M. FORSTER, published in 1908.

Lucy Honeychurch and her chaperone, the genteel Miss Bartlett, are frustrated in their hopes of obtaining a room with a view at the Pensione Bertolini in Florence. Offered an exchange by Mr Emerson and his son, George, Miss Bartlett's sense of social propriety is offended. She graciously accepts the proposal, however, after being reassured by a respectable acquaintance, the Rev. Mr Beebe. Lucy, innocent and impressionable, is shown around Florence by the lady novelist, Miss Lavish, one of the novel's many English 'characters' about whom Forster is gently satirical.

Venturing out alone, Lucy witnesses a quarrel between two Italians, one of whom is stabbed and dies in front of her. She faints, and recovers to find herself in the arms of George Emerson. Later, a party from the pensione joins an excursion to Fiesole. During the trip Lucy is again rescued, after a fall, by George and impulsively embraced. She and Miss Bartlett are affronted and take themselves off to Rome, then back to Surrey.

Lucy becomes engaged to the cultured, but shallow and over-protective Cecil Vyse. Her independent spirit is aroused and she eventually rebels. The Emersons, meanwhile, arrive to take up residence nearby. Lucy realizes with some perturbation that she loves George, not Cecil. She extricates herself from the relationship with Cecil, aided by Miss Bartlett, and marries George. The close of the novel finds George and Lucy on their honeymoon in the Pensione Bertolini.

Rosalynde A prose romance written by THOMAS LODGE during his voyage to the Canaries and first printed in 1590. A second edition appeared in 1592, and the eight subsequent editions up to 1642 testify to its popularity. It catered to a popular taste for PASTORAL, EUPHUISM (its sub-title is *Euphues Golden Legacy Found after his Death at Selexidra*) and Arcadian romance.

Based on the 14th-century *TALE OF GAMELYN*, *Rosalynde* tells the story of the usurper Torismond, which is paralleled by that of Saladyne who dispossesses his brother Rosader. Rosader falls in love with Rosalynde at a wrestling match and the subsequently banished Rosalynde and her cousin Alinda meet him in the forest of Arden. *Rosalynde* provided the basic narrative, main characters and some incidents for SHAKESPEARE's *As You Like It*.

Roscommon, 4th Earl of See DILLON, WENTWORTH.

Rose Theatre Situated on the south bank of the Thames at Southwark, in the Liberty of the Clink, the Rose was leased by PHILIP HENSLOWE and became the preferred home of the Lord Admiral's Men during the last decade of the 16th century. It was there that the plays of MARLOWE were probably first performed. Built in about 1587, it was old-fashioned by 1600, when Henslowe largely replaced it with the FORTUNE, and probably demolished c. 1605.

Rosenberg, Isaac 1890–1918 Poet and artist. Born in Bristol of Russian-Jewish émigré parents, he grew up in Whitechapel in the East End of London, where his father earned a living as a market trader. He became an apprentice engraver in 1911, until a wealthy Jewish family supported him to study at the Slade School. Encouraged by GORDON BOTTOMLEY and EZRA POUND, he published at his own expense two collections of poems, *Night and Day* (1912) and *Youth* (1915), and *Moses: A Play* (1916). Despite his family's pacifism, he joined the army in 1915 and went to France early the following year. Many of his best poems, including 'Break of Day in the Trenches' and 'Louse Hunting', were written at the front, where he also began a second play, *The Unicorn*, which survives only in fragments. He was killed in battle near Arras, on the Somme, in April 1918. In 1922 Bottomley edited a selection of his poems and letters, introduced by LAURENCE BINYON. *Collected Works* (1937), edited by Bottomley and D. W. Harding, gained him a wider recognition. A foreword by SIEGFRIED SASSOON praised Rosenberg's experimentation and his 'fruitful fusion between English and Hebrew culture'. A new *Collected Works* (1979), including paintings, drawings and letters and reprinting Sassoon's essay, was edited by Ian Parsons.

Rosencrantz and Guildenstern are Dead A play by TOM STOPPARD, first performed at the Edinburgh Festival in 1966, and in revised form by the ROYAL NATIONAL THEATRE in London in 1967. It is a wittily resourceful cross-fertilizing of artistic and philosophical themes, in which the eponymous heroes puzzle over their own identities, their relationship to the great events at Elsinore, the possibility of making decisions and the extent to which their roles have already been determined (in *HAMLET*). The dovetailing with SHAKESPEARE is attractively neat.

Ross, (James) Sinclair 1908– Canadian novelist and short-story writer. Born at Shellbrook, Saskatchewan, he left school at 16, joined the Royal Bank of Canada in Abbey, Saskatchewan, in 1924 and spent his entire working career in banking. After his retirement he travelled to Europe, living in Athens, Barcelona and Malaga. His first story was published in

1934 but it was not until the publication of his first novel, *As for Me and My House* (1941), that Ross achieved wide recognition. A classic of Western Canadian fiction, it vividly portrays the repressive nature of prairie life from the point of view of a small-town minister's wife. It was followed by *The Well* (1957) and *Whir of Gold* (1970). Between 1934 and 1952 he published several short stories, many of them in *Queen's Quarterly*; some were collected in *The Lamp at Noon and Other Stories* (1968). Other works are *Sawbones Memorial* (1974) and *The Race and Other Stories* (1982).

Rossetti, Christina (Georgina) 1830–94 Poet. The sister of DANTE GABRIEL ROSSETTI and WILLIAM MICHAEL ROSSETTI, she was born in London and educated at home by her mother. She showed early promise as a poet, and her grandfather had small collections printed when she was 12 and 15. She was a delicate and religious girl, her devotion to High Anglicanism later moulding much of her finest verse. Her religious convictions seem also to have caused the eventual collapse of her prolonged engagement to the PRE-RAPHAELITE painter James Collinson.

Christina Rossetti's lyrics 'An End' and 'Dream Lane' were published in the first number of *THE GERM* (1850) under the pseudonym Ellen Alleyne. She contributed further poems to this and other journals. Her first major collection was *GOBLIN MARKET and Other Poems* (1862), followed in 1866 by *THE PRINCE'S PROGRESS and Other Poems*. *Sing Song: A Nursery Rhyme Book* (1872) was illustrated by Arthur Hughes. By the 1880s bouts of ill health had made her an invalid, but she continued to write and publish. *A Pageant and Other Poems* (1881) contained the SONNET sequence 'Monna Innominata', celebrating the superiority of divine love over human passion, while *Time Flies: A Reading Diary* (1885) consisted of 130 poems and thoughts for each day. The last original work published in her lifetime was *The Face of the Deep: A Devotional Commentary on the Apocalypse* (1892). Her brother, William Michael, edited her complete works (1904).

Her verse is remarkable for its love of verbal invention and of metrical experiment. In both her religious and her secular poetry she shows a keen interest in natural, pictorial imagery, while her addresses to an unnamed lover or suitor suggest both a determination and a carefully controlled ambiguity. Her delicate, frank meditations on death and Heaven are balanced by the imaginative vigour of poems like *Goblin Market*.

Rossetti, Dante Gabriel 1828–82 Poet, painter and translator. He was born in London, the son of Gabriele Pasquale Giuseppe Rossetti, a Neapolitan political exile and sometime professor of Italian at King's College, London, and of Frances Mary Lavinia

The Rossetti family in 1863, photographed by Lewis Carroll. Left to right: Dante Gabriel Rossetti, Christina Rossetti, Frances Rossetti (mother), and William Michael Rossetti

Polidori Rossetti, daughter of Gaetano Polidori and sister of Byron's physician, Dr John Polidori, and was christened Gabriel Charles Dante. Thus Rossetti's background and heritage were essentially Italian and the London household far more Italian than English. Rossetti was educated in 1836–43 at King's College School, London, where he was well prepared in Latin and French; Italian was of course spoken at home. In 1843–6 he attended Cary's Art Academy in Bloomsbury Street, by which time his inclination toward painting and poetry was apparent. Soon after leaving he spent a brief unfruitful period at the Antique School of the Royal Academy and persuaded Ford Madox Brown to take him as a pupil; his mentor demanded the young aspirant paint picklejars, medicine bottles and other still-lifes, so the association was short-lived. Meanwhile, Rossetti had come to know Holman Hunt and John Everett Millais, and these friendships in turn led in the autumn of 1848 to the formation of the Pre-Raphaelite Brotherhood (PRB), the first generation of Pre-Raphaelites, whose other members were Thomas Woolner, Frederick George Stephens, William Michael Rossetti and James Collinson.

A dominant figure in the early stages of the Pre-Raphaelite attempt to revolutionize Victorian art, he worked with unusual consistency in the late 1840s and throughout the 1850s both as painter and poet. In the former capacity he produced 'The Girlhood of Mary Virgin', 'How They Met Themselves', 'Ecce Ancilla Domini' and other works inspired by the Bible, Dante and Arthurian literature. Except for 'Found', a study of the evils of modern city life, his paintings are highly symbolic, spiritually charged and redolent of other, remote, worlds. His poetry included an early draft of Jenny, a dramatic monologue about a London prostitute, and a second version of his best-known poem The Blessed Damozel, which appeared in The Germ, as well as early studies of 'Dante at Verona', 'The Bride's Prelude' and the pseudo-medieval Sister Helen. Rossetti's poetry, like his painting, was detailed, symbolic, concerned with the remote and sometimes erotic; it was often cast in ballad form and sometimes archaic in language.

The 1850s were also notable in Rossetti's life for the drawings he made for Poems by Alfred Tennyson (1857) in which Millais and Holman Hunt also participated. He also engaged to undertake some decorations for the Oxford Union with several of his friends as assistants, among them Burne-Jones, WILLIAM MORRIS and Arthur Hughes. As the walls were unprepared the subject matter, Arthurian legend, soon deteriorated and later restoration did little to evoke the originals. In Oxford he met Jane Burden, who later married Morris but continued to play an important role in Rossetti's private life. She was one of the many 'stunners', to use the PRB term, whom the poets and painters made their subject: beautiful women with red-gold hair, attenuated fingers, faintly sulky mouths and swan-like necks.

Another stunner was Elizabeth Siddal, whom Rossetti had met and fallen in love with in 1850. They were unable to marry until 1860, and Lizzie died from an overdose of laudanum in 1862. Although Rossetti had not been a faithful husband or lover, her loss affected him deeply and an increasing morbidity became apparent in his work. However, he published *The Early Italian Poets* (1861; revised as *Dante and His Circle*, 1874), translations from some 60 writers which demonstrate another side of his gifts. Passages from Dante, Guido Cavalcanti, Fazio degli Uberti and others appear with succinct biographical notes, critical introductions and editorial apparatus. In the 1860s, too, Rossetti's painting yielded to decorative art – he produced designs in stained glass, furniture, and tiles for William Morris's firm – and then, as eye strain developed, he turned increasingly to poetry. *Poems* (1870) drew on the manuscripts he had first, in a fit of remorse, interred with Lizzie Siddal but later exhumed. Shortly thereafter he was attacked by ROBERT BUCHANAN in a scurrilous pamphlet, 'The Fleshly School of Poetry' (1872), to which he replied with 'The Stealthy School of Criticism'. By now increasing illness, morbidity and paranoia beset him, and in 1872 he attempted suicide. Yet he published *Ballads and Sonnets* (1881), which included a SONNET sequence, THE HOUSE OF LIFE, and THE KING'S TRAGEDY as well as 'The White Ship'. Chloral, imagined treacheries and groundless suspicions took their toll and, a near-recluse, he died shortly before his fifty-fourth birthday.

Rossetti, William Michael 1829–1919 Man of letters. Born in London, the brother of DANTE GABRIEL ROSSETTI and CHRISTINA ROSSETTI, he was educated at King's College School and worked for almost half a century in the Internal Revenue as the main support of his family. One of the founders of the PRE-RAPHAELITES, he edited THE GERM and wrote about the movement in *Ruskin, Rossetti, Praeraphaelitism* [*sic*] (1899) and *Praeraphaelite Diaries and Letters* (1900). He also contributed countless articles on literature and art to journals, translated Dante's *Inferno*, wrote a life of KEATS (1887), produced editions of SHELLEY, BLAKE and WHITMAN, edited the collected works of his

brother (1911) and the poetry of his sister (1904), and published *Some Reminiscences* (1906). He was married to Lucy Madox Brown, daughter of the painter Ford Madox Brown.

Roth, Henry 1906– American novelist. He was born in Austria-Hungary to Jewish parents who emigrated to the USA when he was an infant. His reputation is based primarily on the novel *Call It Sleep*. Though it went relatively unnoticed at its initial publication in 1934, it was reissued in 1960 and received widespread critical acclaim. It portrays the mind of David Schearl, the only child of Jewish immigrants who settle in New York, and centres on his relationship with his family and his experiences in the streets of New York between the ages of six and eight. David has a troubled relationship with his stern father, who sees his son as soft and pampered, and the boy's only security lies in his affection for his sympathetic but socially isolated mother. At the climax of the book he slips a milk ladle into a slot in the live rail of a trolley car line and almost electrocutes himself, causing a blinding flash and a blackout in the neighbourhood. He awakens to a new sense of self-knowledge. Roth's use of dialect and ethnic speech patterns in the book, his vivid descriptions of the diverse streets of New York, and his sensitivity to the processes of David's growth, combine into a powerfully illuminating story. His output since *Call It Sleep* has been modest, but he has published his memoirs, *Nature's First Green* (1979) and a collection of shorter writings, *Shifting Landscapes* (1987).

Roth, Philip 1933– American novelist. Born in Newark, New Jersey, he was educated at Bucknell and the University of Chicago. His first book, *Goodbye, Columbus* (1959), consisted of a novella and five short stories and won him the National Book Award in 1960. Jewish-American life in particular, and modern American society in general, are the subjects of his subsequent comedies of manners, which include *Letting Go* (1962), *When She was Good* (1967), *PORTNOY'S COMPLAINT* (1969), *The Breast* (1972), *The Great American Novel* (1973), *My Life as a Man* (1974) and *The Professor of Desire* (1977). *Our Gang* (1971) is a satire on the Nixon administration. *Reading Myself and Others* (1975) is a collection of essays. Later work has elided the boundaries between fiction and autobiography. *The Ghost Writer* (1979), *Zuckerman Unbound* (1981), *The Anatomy Lesson* (1983) and *The Counterlife* (1986) form a semi-autobiographical sequence of novels about the education, sudden fame, and subsequent disillusion of a writer. Recent work includes two volumes: of memoirs, *The Facts* (1988) and *Patrimony: A True Story* (1991), an essay about his father; and *Deception* (1990), combining fiction and self-revelation.

roundel See RONDEAU.

Roughing It An early book of autobiographical episodes by MARK TWAIN, published in 1872. It tells the story of his journey from St Louis to Nevada, including visits to a Mormon community in Utah and to Virginia City. He also describes his stay in San Francisco and his visit to the Sandwich Islands (Hawaii). At the outset Twain portrays himself as an Eastern greenhorn, amused and comically befuddled by strange Western ways. As the story progresses, however, the narrator begins to adjust to the life-style he portrays and to speak from a Western perspective. Though hardly a coherent picture of life in the American West in the 1860s, the book is held together by the vivid personality and wit of its author.

Rowe, Nicholas 1674–1718 Playwright, poet and editor. Born in Bedfordshire and educated at Westminster School, he trained for the law but abandoned it on inheriting the family estate in 1692. Rowe held various official appointments during the later years of his life, serving as Secretary of State for Scotland in 1709–11 and POET LAUREATE from 1715 until his death. His best plays held a prominent place in the English repertoire well into the 19th century. *Tamerlane* (1701) is an even more vivid example of the domestication of Elizabethan tragedy than DRYDEN'S *ALL FOR LOVE*. It transforms the hero of MARLOWE'S *TAMBURLAINE* to represent the values of William III in contrast to those of a villainous Bajazet (Louis XIV). It was less popular than Rowe's three 'she-tragedies', *The Fair Penitent* (1703), *JANE SHORE* (1714) and *Lady Jane Gray* (1715), the first two of which provided Mrs Siddons with famous roles. *The Fair Penitent* is derived from MASSINGER and FIELD'S *THE FATAL DOWRY*, from which it deviates into pathos. *Lady Jane Gray* portrays its heroine as a Protestant martyr, who rejects a pardon from the Catholic Queen Mary. Rowe's competent handling of blank verse was extravagantly admired by some contemporaries and temperately praised by DR JOHNSON. His edition of SHAKESPEARE (1709) is rightly seen as innovatory. Rowe established his text by comparing copies, made generally thoughtful emendations and supplied logical act and scene divisions. Some of these divisions, like certain of his added stage directions and detailed exits and entrances, reflect and are limited by the regularizing spirit of his age, and such limitations are fully displayed in his scrupulous Preface.

Rowlands, Samuel 1570–*c.* 1630 Satirist. Nothing is known of Rowlands's life, though he may have been a cooper and churchwarden of east Smithfield in London. Although he is remembered as a writer of verse and prose satires, he also wrote religious poems, notably *The Betraying of Christ: Judas in Despair* (1598), *A Sacred Memory of the Miracles Wrought by Jesus Christ* (1618), and *Heavens Glory, Seek It; Hearts Vanity, Fly It; Hells Horror, Fear It* (1628). Among his satires are the spirited *The Letting of Humours Blood in the Head-vein* (1600), *'Tis Merry when Gossips Meet* (1602), *Look to It, For I'll Stab Ye* (1604), *Hell's Broke Loose* (1605) and *Democritus: or, Doctor Merry-Man His Medicines against Melancholy Humours* (1607). *A Terrible Battle between the Two Consumers of the Whole World; Time and Death* (1606) is a dialogue in verse and *The Famous History of Guy Earl of Warwick* (1608) a comic ballad. *The Melancholy Knight* (1615) is a verse monologue which ridicules nostalgia for a romantic past.

Rowlandson, Mary White *c.* 1635–*c.* 1678 The wife of an American Puritan minister, Rowlandson lived in the frontier town of Lancaster, Massachusetts. During King Philip's War (1674–6), the Narragansett Indians raided the town, killed some of her family, and took her and two children captive; she was ransomed three months later through the efforts of her husband. Her account of her experiences, *The Sovereignty and Goodness of God, Together with the Faithfulness of His Promises Displayed; being a Narrative of the Captivity and Restoration of Mrs Mary Rowlandson*, was published in 1682 in Cambridge, Massachusetts. Likening her captivity to a spiritual affliction, she tells how she was taken around the countryside by the Indians, and how she gradually learned how to survive with them. The book went through many editions, becoming a classic of the American captivity genre.

Rowley, Samuel *c.* 1575–1624 Actor and playwright. A leading member of the Admiral's Men and an 'attached playwright' to his company, Rowley probably agreed not to publish his work. The only known survival, *When You See Me, You Know Me* (1603), is a rambling chronicle play about Henry VIII. His name is associated with the lost *The Taming of a Shrew* (*c.* 1589), which SHAKESPEARE knew, and HENSLOWE records a payment to him in 1602 for 'additions' to MARLOWE'S *DOCTOR FAUSTUS*.

Rowley, William *c.* 1585–1626 Actor and playwright. Nothing is known of Rowley's life beyond the fact that he was an actor noted for his playing of fat clowns. He collaborated with a number of other dramatists, most notably with THOMAS MIDDLETON on *A FAIR QUARREL* (published in 1617) and *THE CHANGELING* (1622), but also with DEKKER and FORD on *THE WITCH OF EDMONTON* (*c.* 1621), and probably with WEBSTER and FLETCHER as well. *The Birth of Merlin* (published in 1662) was attributed to Rowley and Shakespeare (see SHAKESPEARE APOCRYPHA). His unaided plays include a muddled tragedy, *All's Lost by Lust* (*c.* 1620), and two CITIZEN COMEDIES, *A New*

Wonder: A Woman Never Vexed (published in 1632) and *A Match at Midnight* (published in 1633).

Rowson, Susanna Haswell c. 1768–1824 American novelist, poet and playwright. Born in England, she went to America with her family as a child; her father was a naval lieutenant stationed in Massachusetts. She returned to England in 1777 and later began to write, producing several SENTIMENTAL NOVELS and books of verse, including *Victoria* (1786), *The Inquisitor: or Invisible Rambler* (1788, US publication 1793), *Poems on Various Subjects* (1788), a collection of poems entitled *A Trip to Parnassus* (1788) and *Mary: or, The Test of Honour* (1789). *CHARLOTTE TEMPLE: A Tale of Truth* (1791, US publication 1794) became the first American best-seller. Rowson and her husband returned to the USA in 1793 to pursue careers in the theatre. Following *Mentoria: or, The Young Lady's Friend* (1791), a collection of essays and tales on education, and *Rebecca: or, The Fille de Chambre* (1792; US publication 1794), Rowson wrote social comedies and romances for the stage: *Slaves in Algiers* (1794), *The Female Patriot* (1794), *The Volunteers* (1795), *A Kick for a Bite* (1795), *Trials of the Human Heart* (1795), and *Americans in England* (1796). She founded a girls' boarding school and left the stage in 1797, devoting her time to more didactic works for youth, including *Reuben and Rachel: or, Tales of Old Times* (1798), *Miscellaneous Poems* (1804), *Sarah: or, The Exemplary Wife* (1813) and *Charlotte's Daughter: or, The Three Orphans* (1828), a sequel to *Charlotte Temple*.

Roxana: *or, the Fortunate Mistress* A novel by DANIEL DEFOE, published in 1724. It is presented as the autobiography of the beautiful Mlle Beleau, the daughter of Huguenot refugees in England.

Ambitious for a more exciting life, she parts company with her husband, a London brewer, after squandering his fortune and producing five children. She becomes a high-class kept woman, moving between 'protectors' across England, Holland and France and earning the nickname 'Roxana' after her dancing in the manner of Alexander the Great's widow. Her faithful maid Amy accompanies her progress. After amassing a considerable fortune, Roxana marries a wealthy Dutch merchant but he discovers her deviousness. She receives only a pittance from his will and is left in penury and penitence. Despite the sometimes unconvincing psychology and the anticlimactic ending, the book has unmistakable energy and narrative strength.

Royal Court Theatre This small theatre in London's Sloane Square, opened in 1888, has twice made a major contribution to the development of English drama. In 1904–7, under the joint management of J. E. Vedrenne and HARLEY GRANVILLE-BARKER,

it established SHAW as a force in the British theatre, as well as introducing several socially relevant new plays to a sluggish public. After 1956 it spearheaded the revival of serious drama in England, under the aegis of the English Stage Company. JOHN OSBORNE's *LOOK BACK IN ANGER* was the first of a remarkable succession of new plays at the Royal Court, and many dramatists, including ARDEN, JELLICOE, BOND, BRENTON and HARE, were given their first significant opportunities there.

Royal National Theatre Britain's National Theatre was established only after a long struggle. This began with calls from DAVID GARRICK in the 18th century, gained widespread support from MATTHEW ARNOLD among others in the 19th century and was given further impetus with the publication of a detailed scheme by WILLIAM ARCHER and HARLEY GRANVILLE-BARKER in 1907. Delays resulting from two world wars, a lack of funds and opposition even within the theatre community were followed by the token laying of a foundation-stone in 1951; even then matters did not advance further until Sir Laurence (later Lord) Olivier lent his support to the cause. He served as director of the National Theatre from its opening at the OLD VIC in 1962 with a production of *HAMLET* until 1973, when he was succeeded by Sir Peter Hall. In 1976–7 the company moved to a new complex, designed by Denys Lasdun, on the South Bank. It consists of three theatres: the open-stage Olivier, the proscenium arch Lyttelton and the experimental Cottesloe. Despite a decline in public subsidy and some loss of its original idealism, the National Theatre has kept its foremost place among British companies, rivalled only by the ROYAL SHAKESPEARE COMPANY.

Royal Shakespeare Company The title adopted by the Shakespeare Theatre Company in 1961, following the revision of its Royal Charter and its acquisition of a London base at the Aldwych Theatre. Based in Stratford-upon-Avon, the Company already ran a distinguished seasonal festival of SHAKESPEARE's plays in the Shakespeare Memorial Theatre, built in 1932 as successor to the building opened in 1879 but destroyed by fire in 1926. Under its new name and the directorship of Sir Peter Hall, the RSC further acquired an annual public subsidy, and, through its work at the Aldwych Theatre, a reputation for performing modern plays as well as Shakespeare and the classics which placed it beside (and sometimes in rivalry with) the ROYAL NATIONAL THEATRE. Under the artistic directorship of Trevor Nunn (1968–86) two further theatres were opened in Stratford: The Other Place (1974), for studio productions, and the Swan (1986), for the production of plays by Shakespeare and his contemporaries in an environment resembling an Elizabethan theatre. In 1982 the RSC moved its London headquarters to the Barbican Arts Centre, with its smaller studio theatre, the Pit, as well as a main auditorium. Adrian Noble is current director.

Rubáiyát of Omar Khayyám of Naishápúr, The

A free translation by EDWARD FITZGERALD from the Persian, first published as an anonymous pamphlet in 1859. Omar Khayyám was a 12th-century astronomer and poet; *Rubáiyát* is the plural of the Persian for 'a poem of four lines'. In the original the quatrains were placed in alphabetical order, a procedure not followed by FitzGerald who, however, arranged the epigrammatic stanzas to follow the course of the day. FitzGerald's version distils the spirit rather than extracting the specific meaning from its original.

The *Rubáiyát* crept on to the market; only 250 copies of the pamphlet were printed, and a mere two journals (one in a review of one sentence) noted its appearance. Seemingly sunk without trace, it was praised by DANTE GABRIEL ROSSETTI, MONCKTON MILNES, SWINBURNE, RUSKIN and MORRIS among others, and slowly achieved a recognition it has never forfeited. In its own time its colourful, exotic and remote imagery appealed greatly to the Victorian interest in the Oriental and its hedonistic philosophy offered escape from a world fast surrendering to scientific determinism. In the poem FitzGerald, albeit unwittingly, offers a luxurious sensual warmth to counter the despair so many saw in the heartless doctrine of the survival of the fittest. The poem also suggests withdrawal from 'this sorry scheme of things', from the dreary responsibilities of a mundane middle-class existence. Its romantic melancholy anticipates the pessimistic poetry of MATTHEW ARNOLD, JAMES THOMSON and HARDY, while its Epicurean motifs link it with the AESTHETIC MOVEMENT.

Rubens, Bernice (Ruth)

1928– Novelist. Born in Cardiff, she studied at the University of Wales (later becoming a Fellow of University College, Cardiff), and briefly taught English in Birmingham. Before settling to a full-time writing career, she was a distinguished film-maker. Her novels customarily treat themes of loneliness and rejection. The context is social and domestic in *Go Tell the Lemming* (1973) and *Birds of Passage* (1981). *Spring Sonata* (1979), the monologue of a soon-to-be stillborn baby, moves toward ALLEGORY. With *The Elected Member* (BOOKER PRIZE, 1970) and *Our Father* (1987), the context is explicitly metaphysical.

Rudd, Steele

[Davis, Arthur Hoey] 1868–1935 Australian humorist. Born near Toowoomba in Queensland, Davis had a rudimentary education, leaving school at the age of 11 and working as an odd-job man before obtaining a post in Brisbane, eventually becoming Under-Sheriff. In 1895 he began to contribute to *The Bulletin* a series of broad comic sketches about the Rudd family, set in the Darling Downs. They were published in 1899 as *On Our Selection*, and Davis followed the fortunes of his extended and hapless family – Mum, Dan, Dave, Nora, Kate and Sarah, all guided by Dad Rudd – in other volumes: *Sandy's Selection* (1904), *Back at Our Selection* (1906), *Dad in Politics* (1908), *On an Australian Farm* (1910), *We Kaytons* (1921) and *Me an' th' Son* (1924).

Rudkin, (James) David

1936– Playwright. He was born in London and educated at King Edward's Grammar School, Birmingham, and St Catherine's College, Oxford. His first play, *Afore Night Come* (1960), revealed an instinct for high tragedy and myth. It concerns an Irish tramp who is murdered by a gang of fruit-pickers, but the heightened language evoked themes of ritual slaughter, infertility and the suppression of the imagination (and Ireland) by British imperialism. The relationship between Ireland and England is the subject of *Cries from Casement as his Bones are Brought to Dublin* (1973) and *Ashes* (1974), about a Belfast couple whose infertility is mysteriously linked to the struggle in Northern Ireland. *Sons of Light* (1976) moves away from a specific political situation towards an allegorical assessment of contemporary man. Later work includes *The Triumph of Death* (1981), *Space Invaders* (1983), *Will's Way* (1984) and *The Saxon Shore* (1986). Rudkin has also written extensively for radio and television. An accomplished linguist and musician, he has translated the libretto to Schoenberg's *Moses and Aaron* (1965) and adapted Euripides' *Hippolytus* (1978).

Ruggle, George

See IGNORAMUS.

Ruin, The

A fragment (45 lines) of an Old English poem preserved in the EXETER BOOK. It gives a descriptive and reflective account of a decaying Roman city, probably Bath since much attention is paid to the springs and baths of the city. In its imaginative evocation of the city's past splendour and its description of current decay the poem is powerful and striking. It owes something to the classical tradition of the poem in praise of a city (*encomium urbis*) exemplified in DURHAM.

Rukeyser, Muriel

1913–80 American poet. She was born in New York City. Her concern with the Spanish Civil War, women's rights, and the Vietnam War is evident in her many volumes of verse, the first of which, *Theory of Flight*, was published in 1935. Others include *U.S.1.* (1938), *The Turning Wind* (1939), *The Green Wave* (1948), *Body of Waking* (1958) and *The Gates* (1976). She also produced one work of fiction, *The Orgy* (1965), and wrote two biographies, *One Life* (1957), about Wendell Wilkie, and *Willard Gibbs* (1942).

Rule, Jane 1931– Canadian novelist and short-story writer. Born in Plainfield, New Jersey, she was educated mainly in California; she moved to Vancouver in 1956 and now lives on Galiano Island in British Columbia. She has taught English at Concord Academy, Massachusetts, and the University of British Columbia. Canada's best-known lesbian writer, she has written the novels *Desert of the Heart* (1964), *This is Not for You* (1970), *Against the Season* (1971), *The Young in One Another's Arms* (1977), *Contract with the World* (1980) and *After the Fire* (1989). Her books of short stories include *Theme for Divers Instruments* (1975) and *Inland Passage* (1985). She has also written *Lesbian Images* (1975), a psychological study of 12 women writers including GERTRUDE STEIN, Colette and V. SACKVILLE-WEST, and *Outlander* (1980), a collection of essays on lesbianism. Her sense of the importance of women's issues is combined with her ideals of human community and art as celebration.

Rule a Wife and Have a Wife A comedy by JOHN FLETCHER, first performed in 1624 and published in 1640. It is one of several works by Fletcher that had an influence on the development of RESTORATION COMEDY.

Margarita, a rich heiress from Seville, wishes to marry only in order to give a cover of respectability to her amorous intrigues. Her companion Altea, knowing that she wants a fool for a husband, persuades her brother Leon to court her in the guise of a simpleton. Once married, Leon turns the tables on Margarita, eventually winning her admiring agreement to remain faithful.

Rumens, Carol 1944– Poet. Born in Lewisham, South London, she attended convent schools before reading philosophy at Bedford College, London. She has worked in advertising and publishing, and as poetry editor for *Quarto* and *The Literary Review*. Her early collections, *Strange Girl in Bright Colours* (1973), *A Necklace of Mirrors* (1979) and *Unplayed Music* (1981), are characterized by detailed observation and accurate descriptions of domesticity and female experience. Later work – *Star Whisper* (1983), *Direct Dialling* (1985), *The Greening of Snow Beach* (1989) and *From Berlin to Heaven* (1989) – has developed her preoccupation with suffering, persecution and the sense or loss or exile. *Selected Poems* appeared in 1987. She has also published a novel, *Plato Park* (1988), and edited *Making for the Open: The Chatto Book of Post-Feminist Poetry 1964–1984* (1985).

Runyon, (Alfred) Damon 1884–1946 American short-story writer and humorist. Born in Manhattan, Kansas, he grew up in Pueblo, Colorado, and began contributing pieces to local newspapers while still at school. He enlisted for the Spanish-American War at the age of 14 and then returned to journalism. During World War I he became a war correspondent for the Hearst papers, and stayed on there as a columnist after the war. The New York scene provided the material for his unique vernacular humour: athletes, show people, gamblers, hustlers, crooks and their women are transformed into recognizable types. His volumes of stories include *Guys and Dolls* (1931), *Blue Plate Special* (1934), *Take It Easy* (1938), *Furthermore* (Britain 1938, USA 1941), *Runyon à la Carte* (1944), *Short Takes* (1946) and *Runyon on Broadway* (1950). In collaboration with Howard Lindsay, he wrote a FARCE, *A Slight Case of Murder* (1940), which had a successful run on Broadway.

Rural Rides An anthology of essays by WILLIAM COBBETT, selected from pieces composed for his newspaper, *The Political Register*, between September 1822 and October 1826, and published together in 1830 under the full title *Rural Rides in the Counties of Surrey, Kent, Sussex, Hampshire, Wiltshire, Gloucestershire, Herefordshire, Worcestershire, Somersetshire, Oxfordshire, Berkshire, Essex, Suffolk, Norfolk, and Hertfordshire: With Economical and Political Observations Relative to Matters Applicable to, and Illustrated by, the State of those Counties Respectively*. In 1853 Cobbett's son James Paul added further material from *The Political Register*, dealing with his father's eastern and northern tours of 1830 and 1832, to make the version of *Rural Rides* that has been most frequently read in the 20th century.

When Cobbett travelled about southern England by coach and on horseback in the 1820s, his immediate purpose was to gather material for *The Political Register*. He wished his campaign for Parliamentary reform to be based on up-to-date, first-hand observation of living conditions in rural England, so that his strictures of corrupt and ineffective government would be well-founded. 'My object was, not to see inns and turnpike roads, but to see the country; to see the farmers at home, and to see the labourers In the fields.' The power of his writing comes from its immediacy. The reader sees with Cobbett's eyes, hears Cobbett's voice. Through page after page of keen observation spiced with indignation and acerbity, the social concerns of the convinced democrat are expressed in witty, flowing, energetic prose that soon established *Rural Rides* as the classic it is still recognized to be. Throughout the book, moreover, Cobbett's radical purposes are never in conflict with his unfeigned patriotism.

Rushdie, (Ahmed) Salman 1947– Novelist. Born in Bombay, he emigrated to Britain in 1965. Fostered by JAMES JOYCE and Günter Grass among others, Rushdie's interests are in reshaping the history of his time to make it congruent with identities fractured by imperialism, and in questioning how fiction dare undertake so colossal a task. His novels are important examples of MAGIC REALISM. *Grimus* (1975), a richly entertaining story about a truism, is grandly conceived as an extravagant fable about man's need for myths in a demythologized age. Rushdie's volcanic imagination and narrative gifts come together in *MIDNIGHT'S CHILDREN* (1981), a winner of the BOOKER PRIZE, where he succeeds in matching a grand subject, the multitudinousness of India itself, with a narrator's microcosmic personal history and in fashioning out of the absurd incongruity a novel about the creative process in a world under constant threat. In *Shame* (1983) he is again concerned with the creative process, more than with the wretched of Pakistan, rewriting the history of a country founded in the year of his birth and scarifying its elitist class so that a major character is allegorized into Shame itself. *The Jaguar Smile* (1987) is a concise and pertinent travel book about Nicaragua under the Sandinista régime.

Nothing in his previous critical success prepared Rushdie or his publishers, Viking/Penguin, for the reception which awaited his next novel, *THE SATANIC VERSES* (1988), making it an *affaire* that raised questions of censorsip and freedom of expression. From its abrupt opening, when Gibreel Farishta and Saladin Chamcha suffer their 'angelicdevilish fall' to earth as their hijacked aircraft explodes, *The Satanic Verses* announces its purpose of addressing religion – particularly Islam – not directly but with intense, proliferating and often comic energy. Its kaleidoscopic structure seems designed both to mock and confirm faith. Islamic protest against the novel's 'blasphemy' began with demonstrations and book burnings in England, a publication ban in India, and disturbances in Pakistan, Saudi Arabia, Egypt and South Africa. In February 1989 the Ayatollah Khomeini of Iran proclaimed a *fatwa*, or death sentence, against the author. Rushdie was forced into hiding, from which he has given occasional interviews and published: a children's story, *Haroun and the Sea of Stories* (1990); a volume of essays, *Imaginary Homelands* (1991); and a monograph on the film version of *The Wizard of Oz* (1992).

Ruskin, John 1819–1900 Critic of art, architecture and society. He was born in London, the only child of a prosperous wine merchant, John James Ruskin, and his wife Margaret. These overly protective parents educated him at home and at small private schools, and his mother accompanied him when he went to Christ Church, Oxford, where he won the Newdigate Prize for Poetry but took a bad degree. He was accustomed to travel from early boyhood, for his father took his son and wife with him when touring England in search of orders for his business; Ruskin was barely six

when the family ventured abroad to savour Continental life. Steeped in the classics (in the original), the Bible and the works of SIR WALTER SCOTT, he also studied drawing and in 1832, with the gift of SAMUEL ROGERS's *Italy* illustrated by Turner, began his lifelong devotion to that painter.

Although Ruskin wrote poems and articles for various magazines before he was 20, he first gained public attention with the first volume of *MODERN PAINTERS* in 1843. Originally conceived as a defence of Turner, the book had outgrown its original purpose long before its digressive course was brought to a close with the publication of the fifth volume in 1860. *THE SEVEN LAMPS OF ARCHITECTURE* (1849) was followed by *THE STONES OF VENICE* (1851–3), an epic of detailed research which includes the famous essay on 'The Nature of Gothic'. By now Ruskin was without dispute England's most prominent art critic, and however much he might be resented by more orthodox and less gifted practitioners (particularly architects), his forceful prose, keen eye and revolutionary courage in judgement rendered his position unassailable. By now, too, thanks to generous allowances from his father, he had become an eager collector of Turner's drawings. He was also a champion of the PRE-RAPHAELITES, a student of geology and botany and (like almost all the major Victorians) a victim of spiritual problems and religious doubts. Having survived two love affairs, he had in 1848 married Euphemia (Effie) Chalmers Gray; the marriage was annulled in 1854 on the grounds of non-consummation, and the next year Effie married the painter John Everett Millais.

In 1855 Ruskin began his *Academy Notes*, a beacon in Victorian art criticism, and in 1856 he published *The Harbours of England*, a commentary on marine drawings by Turner. He was also busily engaged in writing notes on the artist and cataloguing his drawings, in an attempt to fulfil the troublesome position of executor to which he had been appointed in Turner's will. Furthermore, in the mid- and late 1850s he frequently appeared on the lecture platform; like his work for the Working Men's College in 1854–8, his addresses showed increasing interest in social and economic problems. But his social concerns are most effectively and directly shown by *UNTO THIS LAST*, appearing in *THE CORNHILL MAGAZINE* in 1860 and published as a book in 1862. Of similar importance were the 'Essays on Political Economy' that appeared in *FRASER'S MAGAZINE* in 1862–3, subsequently revised and republished as *MUNERA PULVERIS* (1872). The lectures continued and were collected under such arresting titles as *Sesame and Lilies* (1865) and *The Crown of Wild Olive* (1866); in the latter year he also published *The Ethics of the Dust*, dialogues deriving from his interest in Miss Bell's school for girls at Winnington. By this time Ruskin was also in love with the young Irish girl Rose La Touche, some 30 years his junior. The sufferings and perplexities of this relationship were not brought to an end by her death in 1875 at the age of 27, for Rose's memory was to Ruskin a source of deep emotion and turbulence.

The death of his father in 1864 left Ruskin a wealthy man, yet his frenetic activity continued. He published *Time and Tide, by Weare and Tyne*, a series of letters on social problems, in 1867 and *The Queen of the Air*, a study of Greek myths, in 1869. Between the two he sandwiched one of his most humane pronouncements, 'The Mystery of Life and Its Arts' (1868). He became the first Slade Professor of Fine Arts at Oxford in 1870, and in January 1871 he began that vast and remarkable miscellany, *FORS CLAVIGERA*, continued monthly until 1878 and irregularly after that. Two further things of significance happened to Ruskin in 1871: he fell dangerously ill at Matlock in Derbyshire, and he bought Brantwood, the Lake District home where he was to spend his later years cared for by his cousin, Joan Severn. In this same year he was instrumental in founding the Guild of St George, a Utopian organization.

Now, too, he published his Oxford lectures: *Aratra Pentelici*, on sculpture, and *The Eagle's Nest*, on science and art, both in 1872; *Love's Meinie*, on ornithology, in 1873–81; *Val d'Arno*, on Tuscan art, and *Ariadne Florentina*, on wood and metal engraving, in 1876. In 1875 (the year of Rose's death) he began publishing *Mornings in Florence*, the botanical series *Proserpina* and the geological lectures entitled *Deucalion*, all in parts. Further writings – on drawing, on Venice and on fiction – cascaded forth. But Ruskin's mind was seriously disturbed, and in the late 1870s and 1880s he suffered severe breakdowns; indeed, his condition in 1878 was so bad that he could not testify at the notorious libel suit brought against him by the artist Whistler. He managed in February 1884 to deliver the prophetic masterpiece 'The Storm Cloud of the Nineteenth Century' and in 1885 to begin his last enduring work, the autobiographical *PRAETERITA*, which ran intermittently in parts until July 1889. Under ever-increasing pressure, he deteriorated steadily until, in 1888, he collapsed during a Continental trip and was taken home to Brantwood, where he lived a tragically disturbed life until his death on 20 January 1900.

A man of large and restless mind who alternately impressed and exasperated his contemporaries, Ruskin remains one of the most vital of the great Victorians made formidable to the modern reader by the sheer bulk and diversity of his writings. As an art critic, his importance goes far beyond his decisive impact on the reputations of Turner, the Pre-Raphaelites and the Italian painters, significant though that is in itself. Works like *Modern Painters* are key documents in the development of the aesthetics of ROMANTICISM. As a critic of architecture, Ruskin did far more than praise the Gothic style and so confirm the fashion for medievalism. His discovery in the medieval churches and cathedrals of moral and social values – the freedom of the individual craftsman, the superiority of hand over machine – paved the way for the work of WILLIAM MORRIS and the Arts and Crafts Movement. Made explicit in his writings on political economy and in his later books, Ruskin's vision of society exerted a powerful influence over those later thinkers who have sought to resist the dehumanizing effects of industrial culture.

Russell, Bertrand (Arthur William), 3rd Earl 1872–1970 Philosopher and mathematician. He was born at Trelleck in Wales and educated privately and at Trinity College, Cambridge, of which he became a fellow in 1895. His first book, *German Social Democracy* (1896), was followed by *An Essay on the Foundations of Geometry* (1897), demonstrating his skill as an exponent in his two chosen fields. He was to become famous for his application of mathematical reasoning to the solution of ethical and political problems. Russell's work in the field of mathematics and logic began with *The Principles of Mathematics* (1903) which led him to the central insight that 'mathematics and logic are identical'. The paradoxes discovered during his research prompted him to embark on a project (with his former tutor A. N. Whitehead) which resulted in *Principia Mathematica* (3 vols., 1910–13).

After the publication of this, his major academic work, Russell turned to more traditional philosophical problems, and he became increasingly involved in political campaigns. His pacifism led to internment during World War I and the temporary deprivation of his fellowship. His other important philosophical works included *The Analysis of Mind* (1921), *An Inquiry into Meaning and Truth* (1940) and *Human Knowledge: Its Scope and Limits* (1948).

Russell was also the author of many controversial works aimed at a wider audience, including *The Practice and Theory of Bolshevism* (1920), *Power: A New Social Analysis* (1938), *Human Society in Ethics and Politics* (1954) and *Why I am Not a Christian* (1957). He also wrote two collections of short stories, *Satan in the Suburbs* (1953) and *Nightmares of Eminent Persons* (1954).

He was awarded the Order of Merit in 1949, and the Nobel Prize for Literature in 1950. *The Autobiography of Russell* came out in three volumes in 1967–9.

Russell, George William 1867–1935 Irish poet, playwright and painter. An Ulsterman who became a fellow student of YEATS at the Metropolitan School of Art, he was a poet and painter of mystical landscapes, incidents and figures owing much to Theosophy. His pseudonym, ΑΕ (or Λ. E.), started as a printer's error for AEON (an eternal being in gnostic belief) on the title-page of his first book, *Homeward: Songs by the Way* (1894). It was followed by *The Divine Vision*

(1904), *Gods of War* (1915), *The Interpreters* (1922), *Song and Its Fountains* (1932), *The Avatars* (1933), *The House of the Titans* (1934) and *Selected Poems* (1935). In 1902 his poetic drama *Deirdre* was presented with Yeats's CATHLEEN NI HOULIHAN by the Irish National Theatre (see the ABBEY THEATRE), which he helped to form. Russell also edited *The Irish Homestead* (1905–23) and *The Irish Statesman* (1923–30) and worked for the Department of Agriculture, organizing dairy co-operatives. His friend JOHN EGLINTON published a memoir of him (1937).

Russell, Willy 1947– Playwright. He was born near Liverpool and his career was supported in its early days by the local Everyman Theatre, which commissioned several works. These included his first hit, *John, Paul, George, Ringo and... Bert* (1974), a musical based on the Beatles. Other early plays include *Breezeblock Park* (1975), *One for the Road* (1976) and *Stags and Hens* (1978). *Blood Brothers* (1981), a modernized version of BOUCICAULT's *The Corsican Brothers*, was written as a straight play but Russell added his own songs and it became better known, and more successful, as a musical (1983). Russell's directness in good-humoured, straightforward and usually very funny chronicles is one of his best assets. *Educating Rita* (1979) is about a working-class girl seeking education from, and then outgrowing, her male mentor. In *Shirley Valentine* (1986) a woman approaching middle age succeeds in breaking away from her humdrum life. Both were successful on film as well as the stage.

Ruth A novel by ELIZABETH GASKELL, first published in 1853.

Ruth Hilton, an innocent young seamstress, is seduced and abandoned in Wales during her pregnancy by Henry Bellingham, a country gentleman. Thurstan Benson, a dissenting parson, and his sister Faith take her to his northern parish of Eccleston, where she lives as their widowed relative, Mrs Denbigh, gives birth to a son, Leonard, and works as governess to the Bradshaws. Bellingham (now calling himself Donne) reappears in Ruth's life as parliamentary candidate for Eccleston. He offers marriage but she refuses. Soon afterwards Bradshaw senior learns her secret and dismisses her; she and the Bensons are treated as pariahs and Leonard falls ill. Ruth qualifies as matron in a fever-ward and rehabilitates herself with brave deeds during a cholera epidemic. The kindly family physician, Dr Davis, ensures Leonard's future by offering to bring him up to medicine. In a last gesture Ruth nurses Bellingham back to health before falling ill and dying herself, deeply mourned by the local people. The sub-plot describes the attachment between Bradshaw's daughter Jemima and his partner Walter Farquhar, while lesser figures like old Sally the housekeeper give substance to the book.

Rutherford, Mark See WHITE, WILLIAM HALE.

Ryga, George 1932– Canadian playwright. Born in Deep Creek, Alberta, of Ukrainian parents, he spent his early years on a marginal homestead farm. He left school at the age of 12 and worked at a variety of casual jobs, while continuing to educate himself. He briefly attended the University of Texas in 1949, after which he worked as a farm labourer, in the construction industry and at a radio station in Edmonton. Since 1962 he has been a full-time writer. As a young man he was a Communist Party member and was heavily involved in the Canadian Peace Movement. Much of his work as a dramatist has pleaded the case of oppressed minorities. *The Ecstasy of Rita Joe* (1967, first published 1970) is the story of an Indian torn between the traditional ways of her people and the contemporary Canadian urban world. *Grass and Wild Strawberries* (1969, first published 1971) dramatizes another conflict between cultures, in this case between the hippie movement of the late 1960s and middle-class society. Ryga's dramatic technique attempts to recapture the quality of the BALLAD and he frequently incorporates elements from other media into his plays. These include film projection, recorded sound, dance and song. His other stage plays include *Indian* (1962, first published 1971), *Captives of the Faceless Drummer* (1971), *Sunrise on Sarah* (1973), *Ploughmen of the Glacier* (1977), *Seven Hours to Sundown* (1977) and *Paracelsus* (1982). He has also written many radio and television plays, as well as publishing novels, poetry and *The Athabasca Ryga* (1990), a selection from his early writing in various genres.

Rymer, Thomas 1641–1713 Critic and historian. The son of a Puritan country gentleman executed for treason in 1664, Rymer was born at Yafforth in Yorkshire. Educated at Sidney Sussex College, Cambridge, he later studied law and was called to the Bar at Gray's Inn. As a dramatist, he was not successful: his tragedy, *Edgar: or, The English Monarch* (1678), was never performed. As a critic, he championed extreme NEOCLASSICISM. His first essay was a preface to a translation of René Rapin's *Réflexions sur la poétique d'Aristote* (1674). *The Tragedies of the Last Age Consider'd* (1678) was praised by DRYDEN but *A Short View of Tragedy* (1693), notorious for its attack on SHAKESPEARE – particularly *Othello* – has earned him ridicule. Rymer was appointed Historiographer Royal in 1692 and undertook the task of collecting English treaties, covenants and similar documents in the 20-volume *Foedera* (1704–35).

Sackville, Charles, 6th Earl of Dorset 1638–1706
Poet and courtier. A dissolute young roisterer like his fellow wits, ROCHESTER and SEDLEY, he later led a more responsible life, leaving England during the reign of James II (with whose sober attitudes he was not in keeping) and playing a role in the Revolution of 1688. He served as Lord Chamberlain to King William and was the longest-lived of the clique of Restoration literary blades. His reputation now rests on a handful of lyrics. He was a patron to DRYDEN and PRIOR, who admired his work in return, and POPE later regarded him as one of the wittiest poets of the day. Much of his verse was designed to be circulated in manuscript form, but in 1664 he collaborated with Sedley and others in translating Corneille's *Pompey the Great*, and in 1665 he wrote his celebrated 'To All You Ladies Now at Land', a song composed at sea during the naval campaign of the Second Dutch War, which enjoyed great popularity. Rochester rated him highly as a satirist ('The best good man, with the worst-natured muse') and verses such as 'On Mr Howard' are certainly lively, with an imaginative line in simile and invective. His four poems to Katherine Sedley (later James II's mistress) are also remarkable for their expression of contemporary attitudes to women and the city.

Sackville, Thomas, 1st Earl of Dorset 1536–1608
Playwright and poet. With THOMAS NORTON he wrote *GORBODUC*, which has some claim to be the first proper English tragedy (acted in 1561 and printed in 1565). He also contributed the 'Induction' and the 'Complaint of Buckingham' to the 1563 edition of *A MIRROR FOR MAGISTRATES*. Sackville was educated at Oxford, became a barrister at the Inner Temple and was elected an MP in 1558. He was a successful statesman, becoming a member of the Privy Council and being sent on diplomatic missions to France and the Low Countries. He had the task of announcing her death sentence to Mary Queen of Scots. He was rewarded by Elizabeth with a knighthood and with the title Lord Buckhurst, both in 1567. He became Chancellor of the University of Oxford in 1591, and Lord High Treasurer in 1599, an office in which he was confirmed for life by James I in 1603. The king made him Earl of Dorset in 1604.

Sackville-West, Vita [Victoria] **(Mary)** 1892–1962 Novelist, poet, biographer and gardener. Born at Knole in Kent, the seat of the Sackvilles since the 16th century, she married the diplomat HAROLD NICOLSON in 1913, travelling with him to Persia and many other countries. Her first published work was a collection of verse, *Poems of West and East* (1917). It was followed by a novel, *Heritage* (1919), then another volume of poetry, *Orchard and Vineyard* (1921). Other novels, short stories and miscellaneous prose works followed, but she achieved recognition with her long poem *The Land* (1926), awarded the Hawthornden Prize. A realistic PASTORAL set in the Weald of Kent, it details the progress of the seasons and acknowledges the struggle of man with nature.

She produced a total of some 50 books. *Knole and the Sackvilles* (1922, revised 1958) is an account of her family and the family home. *The Eagle and the Dove: A Study in Contrasts* (1943) examines two saints, Teresa of Avila, the Spanish mystic, and Thérèse of Lisieux, the 'Little Flower' of France. *Daughter of France* (1959) is a biography of 'La Grande Mademoiselle'. Among her novels, *The Edwardians* (1930) and *All Passion Spent* (1931) have been rated most highly. Victoria Sackville-West was an expert and passionate gardener, an art which she practised at Sissinghurst, her home with Harold Nicolson, and about which she wrote with great success in a weekly column in *The Observer*. Her contributions were published in several collections (1951, 1953, 1955, and 1958). She was a close friend of VIRGINIA WOOLF for whom she was the model for the androgynous hero of *ORLANDO*.

Vita Sackville-West, photograph by E. O. Hoppé

Sacred Fount, The A short novel by HENRY JAMES, published in 1901. The story takes place at a weekend party at Newmarch, an English country house. The nameless narrator develops the theory of the 'sacred fount' when he observes that his hostess, Grace Brissenden, is much older than her husband, Guy, yet after a few years of marriage seems to be the more youthful and energetic of the two. The narrator speculates that Guy is the 'fount' from which his wife draws her new vitality, leaving him correspondingly devitalized. He then applies this theory to another pair of guests, Gilbert Long and May Server. He posits the passage of vital force from May, who appears to be emotionally disturbed, to Gilbert, who once seemed dull but is now a witty man of the world. He further decides that Gilbert and Grace, the dominant partners of their respective marriages, are drawing closer together, and that so are May and Guy, the weaker partners. But Grace, whom the narrator has taken into his confidence, eventually tells him that he has imagined the whole thing. The reader is left uncertain whether Grace is lying or the narrator has merely invented the idea.

Sad Fortunes of the Reverend Amos Barton, The See SCENES OF CLERICAL LIFE.

Sahgal, Nayantara 1927– Indian novelist and journalist. Born in Allahabad, she graduated from Wellesley College, Massachusetts, in 1947. As Nehru's niece she was very close to Gandhian idealism before Independence and political in-fighting thereafter. Respect for Gandhi's principles and concern with political morality among the elite inform her elegantly written novels: *A Time to be Happy* (1958), *This Time of Morning* (1965), *Storm in Chandigarh* (1969), *The Day in Shadow* (1971), *A Situation in New Delhi* (1977), *Rich Like Us* (1985), and, with a new imaginative sweep, *Plans for Departure* (1986) and *Mistaken Identity* (1988). *Prison and Chocolate Cake* (1954) and *From Fear Set Free* (1962) are autobiographical. Her biography of her cousin Indira Gandhi (1982) is highly critical.

Saint Joan A play by GEORGE BERNARD SHAW, first produced in New York in 1923 and in London in 1924, when it was also published. Its popularity has been assured by a central part which has attracted distinguished actresses from Sybil Thorndike onwards.

The action follows Joan of Arc's career from her first encounter with Robert de Baudricourt, to her meeting with the Dauphin at Chinon, and her fortunes after she leads the assault on the English and raises the siege of Orleans. After the victory her faith in her inspiration raises the suspicion of heresy, which the Earl of Warwick exploits. The Bishop of Beauvais and John de Stogumber see her as a girl who may be in error but whose soul can be saved; Warwick sees her as a dangerous enemy to be extinguished. When Joan is taken by the Burgundians she is sold to Warwick, who hands her over to the Church. She is tried for heresy and, terrified by the threat of burning, signs a recantation of her belief in the voices that inspired her. But the alternative sentence, perpetual imprisonment, is worse. Joan destroys her recantation and they hurry her out to the stake. The witty Epilogue deals with the nullification of the Church's verdict of 1431 and her canonization.

St Ronan's Well A novel by SIR WALTER SCOTT, published in 1824. It departs from his usual historical settings and takes place at a fashionable Scottish spa in the early 19th century. The story concerns two half-brothers, sons of the late Earl of Etherington, whose enmity is inflamed by their vexed and tragic relationship with Clara Mowbray, daughter of the laird of St Ronan's. The plot is heavily burdened with improbabilities but Scott's portrait of Meg Dods, a down-to-earth landlady, has been praised.

saint's life Prose and verse accounts of saints' lives flourished during the Middle Ages. They are preserved both independently and in collections such as THE GOLDEN LEGEND and THE SOUTH ENGLISH LEGENDARY. Usually taken from Latin *Vitae*, the stories often included fanciful as well as miraculous episodes. Their main purpose is didactic, but clearly they were often felt to be entertaining also. Some saints' lives have features of the VERSE ROMANCE and, conversely, there are verse romances (EMARE, for example) which include features of the saint's life.

Saintsbury, George (Edward Bateman) 1845–1933 Critic and literary historian. Born at Southampton, he was educated at King's College School, London, and Merton College, Oxford. He taught for a number of years and wrote reviews for THE ACADEMY, gaining attention with his notices of the work of French writers, especially Baudelaire, in 1875.

Saintsbury's first book was *A Primer of French Literature* (1880). *A Short History of French Literature* (1882), a standard book for students for decades, and *Specimens of French Literature from Villon to Hugo* (1883) were followed by *Essays on French Novelists* (1891), and *A History of the French Novel to the Close of the Nineteenth Century* (1917–19). His books on English literature and on the history of criticism extend from 1881 to the year of his death. Among them were a study of DRYDEN in the English Men of Letters series (1881), *Essays in English Literature 1780–1860* (two series, 1890 and 1895), *A Short History of English Literature* (1898), *A History of Criticism* (1900–4), *Minor Poets of the Caroline Period* (1905–21), *A History of English Prosody* (1906–10), *The English Novel* (1913), *The Peace of the Augustans* (1915) and the Oxford edition of the works of

THACKERAY (1907). Saintsbury contributed 21 chapters to *The Cambridge History of English Literature* and was professor of rhetoric and English literature at the University of Edinburgh (1895–1915). He was also a wine connoisseur and his *Notes on a Cellar Book* (1920) is an acknowledged classic of its kind.

Saki [Munro, Hector Hugh] 1870–1916. Short-story writer and novelist. He was born in Akyab, the son of an officer in the Burma police, and brought up by two maiden aunts in Devon. After being educated at a school in Exmouth and at Bedford grammar school, he followed his father into the Burma police but was invalided home. In 1896 he settled in London, contributing political SATIRES to *The Westminster Gazette* (collected in *The Westminster Alice*, 1902). Between 1902 and 1908 he acted as correspondent for *The Morning Post* in Poland, Russia and Paris.

His first book, *The Rise of the Russian Empire* (1899), was the only one written in a serious vein. Thereafter he adopted the name of the cup-bearer in the last stanza of THE RUBÁIYÁT OF OMAR KHAYYÁM for his collections of short stories: *Reginald* (1904), *Reginald in Russia and Other Sketches* (1910), *The Chronicles of Clovis* (1912) and *Beasts and Superbeasts* (1914). Whimsical in their plots and light-heartedly cynical in their tone, these stories are also given a darker side by Munro's memories of his unhappy childhood with his aunts. He also published two novels, *The Unbearable Bassington* (1912) and *When William Came* (1913), the latter a satirical fantasy subtitled 'A Story of London under the Hohenzollerns'.

Munro served with the Royal Fusiliers in World War I and was killed on the Western Front. Two collections of stories and sketches appeared posthumously, *The Toys of Peace and Other Papers* (1919) and *The Square Egg and Other Sketches* (1924).

Sala, G(eorge) A(ugustus) 1828–96 Journalist and travel-writer. Born in London, and educated there and in Paris, Sala trained as a miniature painter and worked as a scene painter and book illustrator before turning to journalism and becoming a contributor to DICKENS's *HOUSEHOLD WORDS*. *A Journey Due North* (1858), about Russia, was derived from articles for ALL THE YEAR ROUND. *My Diary in the Midst of the War* (1865) was based on his work as correspondent for *The Daily Telegraph* during the American Civil War. His most successful book was *Twice Around the Clock: or, The Hours of the Day and Night in London* (1859), a series of social sketches which had originally appeared in *The Welcome Guest*, a journal he himself edited. Sala also wrote a volume of reminiscences, *Things I Have Seen and People I Have Known* (1894).

Salinger, J(erome) D(avid) 1919– American novelist and short-story writer. He was born in New York and educated at Valley Forge Military Academy, and at New York and Columbia universities. He published short stories in *The Saturday Evening Post* and other magazines during the early 1940s and served in the US infantry during World War II. His only novel has been the highly successful THE CATCHER IN THE RYE (1951), narrated by a teenage schoolboy in rebellion against the dubious values of the adult world. *Nine Stories* (as *For Esmé – With Love and Squalor* in Britain; 1953) introduces the Glass family, who reappear in *Franny and Zooey* (1961), *Raise High the Roofbeam, Carpenters* (1963) and *Seymour: An Introduction* (1963). Further brief instalments in their history have appeared in magazines but Salinger has since announced that he now writes only for personal diversion. The desire to preserve his privacy led him into a lengthy legal battle against IAN HAMILTON's biography (1987).

Salkey, (Felix) Andrew (Alexander) 1928– Jamaican novelist, poet and writer of CHILDREN'S LITERATURE. Born in Colon, Panama, he worked in London from 1952 to 1976 and has lived since then in the USA, teaching at Hampshire College, Massachusetts. His children's novels include *Hurricane* (1964), *Earthquake* (1965), *Drought* (1966) and *Riot* (1967). Adult novels stress the aridity of Caribbean experience: in a drought-stricken Jamaican parish in *A Quality of Violence* (1959), in the colonial futility of politics in *The Late Emancipation of Jerry Stover* (1968). English society proves no less bleak and inhospitable to West Indians in *Escape to an Autumn Pavement* (1960), *The Adventures of Catullus Kelly* (1969) and *Come Home, Michael Heartland* (1976). *Havana Journal* (1971) and *Georgetown Journal* (1972) are travel books. Salkey has also published volumes of poetry, including *Jamaica* (1973) and *In the Hills Where Her Dreams Live* (1981), and edited anthologies of Caribbean writing.

Salmagundi: or, The Whim-Whams of Opinions of Launcelot Langstaff Esq. and Others A series of satirical essays and poems by WASHINGTON IRVING, his brother William, and JAMES KIRKE PAULDING, issued in 20 periodical pamphlets and then in two volumes in 1807–8. Somewhat in the manner of THE SPECTATOR, the authors used a variety of pseudonyms to represent members of an imaginary club. The essays cover aspects of life in New York, their political stance favouring aristocratic federalism in opposition to Jeffersonian democracy. Paulding was the sole author of a further series of *Salmagundi* papers published in 1819–20.

Salome A play by OSCAR WILDE, written in 1891 in French, with grammatical help from Pierre Loüys. It deals with Salome's destructive love for John the Baptist. An English translation by LORD ALFRED DOUGLAS, with illustrations by AUBREY BEARDSLEY, appeared in 1894. Although published translations still bear Lord Alfred's name, the one in current use is not believed to be his. The play went into rehearsal in 1893, but was banned by the Lord Chamberlain for its depiction of biblical characters; the first production, with Sarah Bernhardt, took place in Paris in 1896, when Wilde was in prison. It was not performed in Britain until 1931. *Salome* inspired Richard Strauss's opera, first performed at Dresden in 1905.

Samson Agonistes: *A Dramatic Poem* A CLOSET DRAMA by JOHN MILTON, published in 1671. Its subject is the biblical Samson, blind (like the poet himself) and a prisoner of the Philistines: 'Eyeless in Gaza at the mill with slaves'. 'Agonistes' refers to Samson as an athlete or wrestler. The poem is cast in the form of a Greek tragedy, using a Chorus, confining the action to one place and compressing its narrative into the last hours of the hero's life. Although Milton never intended it for the stage, it has been successfully performed and Handel used it as the basis for an oratorio.

On a festival day Samson is brought into the open air, where he reflects on his fate: 'Dark, dark, dark, amid the blaze of noon'. The men of Dan, his tribe, find him and try to comfort him; his aged father Manoa also comes and tells him he will attempt to ransom him from the Philistines. The news torments Samson, who feels that his fate is deserved. Manoa, nevertheless, goes ahead to treat with the Philistines for his son's freedom. Dalila is the next character to appear. She pleads for forgiveness for her part in Samson's downfall but he treats her with scorn. She replies that she is like all women and feared that he would abandon her. He still rejects her with contempt, not even allowing her to touch him. She leaves declaring that she is now honoured above all women for her part in his defeat and that she will leave him to his lot. The Chorus watches her go and observes that her new pride is assumed. Next comes Harapha the Philistine, a bully who taunts the fallen Samson. He is disposed of by Samson's furious defiance.

The Chorus praises the hero's unquenchable spirit but is disturbed to see a Philistine officer approaching. His news is that the Philistines want a demonstration of Samson's superhuman strength at the festival to their god Dagon. Samson dismisses him and the Chorus voices unease at what may happen. Samson realizes he has regained all his old strength now that his hair has regrown and, when the officer returns, agrees to go with him. The Chorus watches him depart and at once Manoa hurries in seeking his son: the Philistines have relented, he says, and will accept a ransom. His words are interrupted by the great shouting in the streets as the Philistines see their enemy in chains. The poem ends with the Messenger's arrival and his description of the destruction of the temple and Samson's death.

Sandburg, Carl 1878–1967 American poet. Born to Swedish immigrant parents in Galesburg, Illinois, he left school at the age of 13 and worked as an itinerant labourer, then served in the Spanish-American War, and later found work as a journalist and advertising copywriter. His career as a poet began with the privately printed *In Reckless Ecstasy* (1904), which failed to attract critical attention. From 1910–12 he served as secretary to the socialist mayor of Milwaukee, Wisconsin.

In 1914 some of his work was published by HARRIET MONROE in *POETRY* magazine, and his reputation as a major poet of the Midwest was finally established in 1916 with the publication of *Chicago Poems*, a volume of free verse on 20th-century urban themes. Other collections of poetry followed: *Cornhuskers* (1918), *Smoke and Steel* (1920), *Slabs of the Sunburnt West* (1922), *Good Morning, America* (1928) and *The People, Yes* (1936). *Complete Poems* (1950) was awarded the PULITZER PRIZE. Though his later verse reveals a darker poetic vision, tempered by the experience of the Depression, Sandburg always kept his optimism about the enduring qualities of ordinary working people. In addition to his poetry, he is known for his two-part biography of Abraham Lincoln: *Abraham Lincoln: The Prairie Years* (2 vols., 1926) and *Abraham Lincoln: The War Years* (4 vols., 1939). He also published CHILDREN'S LITERATURE, including *Rootabaga Stories* (1922), *Rootabaga Pigeons* (1923) and *Potato Face* (1930); a novel, *Remembrance Rock* (1948); and an autobiography, *Always the Young Strangers* (1952).

Sanditon An unfinished novel which JANE AUSTEN worked on during the early months of 1817, the year of her death. It was first published in 1925. Charlotte Heywood is a guest of the Parker family at Sanditon, a seaside village rapidly developing into a fashionable resort. There she meets Lady Denham and her nephew and niece, Sir Edward and Miss Denham.

Sandra Belloni A novel by GEORGE MEREDITH, published in 1864 as *Emilia in England*.

Emilia Sandra Belloni, an Italian girl with a fine singing voice, leaves her disreputable father and is taken up by the Pole family. Pole is a city merchant with three aspiring daughters and a spineless son, Wilfred. Pericles, a wealthy Greek and business ally of Pole, tries to persuade Emilia into taking musical training in Italy under his direction. But she and Wilfred have fallen in love, and she resists Pericles's persuasions. Pole, involved in speculation by Pericles and brought to the verge of ruin, tries to marry Wilfred to the rich Lady Charlotte Chillingworth. The wretched young man is more than willing but Lady Charlotte sees him for what he is, as do Merthyr Powys and his sister, who have taken a liking to Emilia. Charlotte exposes Wilfred to the girl and the Powyses take Emilia under their wing. To save the Poles – to whom, in spite of everything, she owes much – Emilia persuades Pericles to part with a large sum of money by agreeing to go to the conservatory at Milan. She departs, and both she and Merthyr look forward to her return and their probable marriage. The story continues in Meredith's later novel, VITTORIA.

Sandys, George 1578–1644 Translator, poet and travel-writer. Educated at St Mary Hall, Oxford, Sandys travelled in Italy and the Levant, publishing a widely read account in *A Relation of a Journey Begun An. Dom. 1610: Four Books Containing a Description of the Turkish Empire, of Egypt, of the Holy Land, of the Remote Parts of Italy, and Islands Adjoining* (1615). In 1621 he went to America as treasurer of the Virginia Company for five years and began the translations from Latin for which he was best known. His version of Ovid's *Metamorphoses* appeared in 1626, its trim and regular couplets being much admired by younger poets. A later edition of 1632 added the first book of *The Aeneid*, rendered in the same style, and *Christ's Passion: A Tragedy*, from the Latin of Hugo Grotius, was published in 1640. Sandys also undertook verse translations from the Bible: *A Paraphrase upon the Psalms of David, and upon the Hymns Dispersed throughout the Old and New Testaments* (1636) and *A Paraphrase upon the Song of Solomon* (1641).

Sansom, William 1912–76 Short-story writer, novelist and travel-writer. Born in London, he was educated at Uppingham School and then studied German in Bonn. He travelled widely in Europe, worked in a City bank and an advertising agency, as well as in radio and films. Throughout World War II he served as a full-time fireman. He began writing when he was very young but was unpublished until he was 30. In 1942 his work appeared in *Penguin New Writing* and *Horizon*. His first collection of short stories, *Fireman Flower*, appeared in 1944. *South* (1948), *Something Terrible, Something Lovely* (1948), *The Passionate North* (1950), *A Touch of the Sun* (1952), *Lord Love Us* (1954), *A Contest of Ladies* (1956), and *Among the Dahlias* (1957) followed. Sansom also wrote film scripts, television plays and lyrics. In 1946 and 1947 he was awarded two literary prizes by the Society of Authors; he was elected a Fellow of the Royal Society of Literature in 1951.

Santayana, George 1863–1952 American philosopher. Born Jorge Ruiz de Santayana y Borrais in Madrid, he was taken to Boston by his family in 1871 and educated at Harvard, where he was professor of philosophy from 1889 to 1912. He then returned to live in Europe. *The Life of Reason* (1905–6) is a five-volume study of reason in everyday life, science, art, and literature. He offers the conclusion that the only

reality is matter itself and that all else arises from man's experience of, and response to, matter. He took this idea further in *The Realms of Being*, which began with the introductory volume *Scepticism and Animal Faith* in 1923, and was eventually published in four volumes (1927–40). His work also includes three studies of American life: *Philosophical Opinion in America* (1918), *Character and Opinion in the United States* (1920), on the conflict of idealism and materialism, and *The Genteel Tradition at Bay* (1931), a criticism of the 'new humanism'. His one novel, THE LAST PURITAN, appeared in 1935. His memoirs, *Persons and Places*, were published in three volumes: *The Backgrounds of My Life* (1944), *The Middle Span* (1945) and *My Host the World* (1953).

Sapphics A verse form named after Sappho, Greek poetess of 7th–6th century BC. It consists of four-line STANZAS, the first three lines being long (⁻ ˇ | ⁻ ⁻ | ⁻ ˇ ˇ | ⁻ ˇ | ⁻ ⁻), the fourth short (⁻ ˇ ˇ | ⁻ ⁻). Attempts to reproduce classical quantities in English inevitably seem unnatural, since English is a stressed language, yet if stresses are made to substitute for the long syllables some compromise with sense seems almost unavoidable. There are, however, a number of Sapphic imitations to be found, especially in the Victorian period. (See also METRE.)

Sardanapalus A tragedy by BYRON, written at Ravenna in 1820 and published in 1821. Charles Kean produced it at DRURY LANE in 1834. The action is set about 640 BC and based on the history of Diodorus Siculus. Beleses, a Chaldean soothsayer, and Arbaces, a governor of Medea, organize a revolt against the extravagantly spendthrift king of Assyria, Sardanapalus. The revolt rouses him to action and, with the encouragement of the beautiful Myrrha, a Greek slave whom he loves, he leads his army into battle. But in spite of his valour the fighting goes against him and Sardanapalus has to retreat to his palace. He makes provision for the safe withdrawal of Zarina, his queen, prepares a funeral pyre around his throne and dies on it with Myrrha and his supporters.

Sargeson, Frank 1903–82 New Zealand short-story writer and novelist. Born at Hamilton in North Island, he qualified as a solicitor but worked at a number of jobs, becoming familiar with all levels of society and reacting sharply against bourgeois values. The Depression sharpened his sympathies with society's victims. His first stories were published in the 1930s in the Auckland periodical *Tomorrow*. His first collection, *Conversations with My Uncle* (1936), showed his skill at using the language of the ill-educated and semi-literate. Sargeson's *Collected Stories* was published in 1965; he is also the author of *I Saw in My Dream* (1949), *I for One* (1956) and *Joy of the Worm* (1969).

Saroyan, William 1908–81 American playwright, novelist and short-story writer. Born in Fresno, California, of Armenian parents, he spent most of his youth in San Francisco. He left school at 15, worked for a telegraph company, and began writing short stories in the late 1920s. His first collection of short stories, *The Daring Young Man on the Flying Trapeze* (1934), which attracted considerable critical and popular attention, typifies the rather genial vision which characterized his work as a whole. Other volumes of short fiction include *Inhale and Exhale* (1936), *Three Times Three* (1936), *The Trouble with Tigers* (1938), *My Name is Aram* (1940) and *Dear Baby* (1944). His first novel, *The Human Comedy*, appeared in 1943, and was followed by *The Adventures of Wesley Jackson* (1946), *Rock Wagram* (1951), *Mama, I Love You* (1956), *Papa, You're Crazy* (1957) and a story about an ageing author, *One Day in the Afternoon of the World* (1964).

He perhaps achieved his greatest fame as a playwright. The one-act play, *My Heart's in the Highlands*, was produced in 1939 and published in 1941. *The Time of Your Life* (1939), set in a San Francisco waterfront saloon, was awarded a PULITZER PRIZE which he refused. His other plays include *Love's Old Sweet Song* (1941), *The Beautiful People* (1942), *Across the Board on Tomorrow Morning* (1942), *Hello Out There* (1943), *Don't Go Away Mad* (1949) and *The Cave Dwellers* (1957). He published three autobiographical works: *The Bicycle Rider in Beverly Hills* (1952), *Here Comes, There Goes, You Know Who* (1961) and *Obituaries* (1979).

Sarton, May 1912– American novelist and poet. Born in Belgium, she emigrated to the USA in 1916 and became a citizen in 1924. Her first publication was a collection of lyrics entitled *Encounter in April* (1937). Other volumes of verse include *Inner Landscape* (1939), *The Lion and the Rose* (1948), *The Land of Silence* (1953), *In Time Like Air* (1957) and *Cloud, Stone, Sun, Vine* (1961). *Collected Poems* appeared in 1974. Her novels and poetry address moral and political issues in a controlled and crafted manner, using a distinct and localized idiom. Her novels include *The Single Hound* (1938), about a young English poet, *The Birth of Grandfather* (1957), *The Small Room* (1961), about a young female teacher and a student at a New England college, *Mrs Stevens Hears the Mermaids Singing* (1965), *Kinds of Love* (1970), *As We are Now* (1973), *Anger* (1982) and *The Education of Harriet Hatfield* (1990). Her autobiographical writings include *I Knew a Phoenix* (1959), *Plant Dreaming Deep* (1968), *Journal of Solitude* (1973), *Recovering* (1980) and *Honey in the Hive* (1988).

Sartor Resartus A prose work by THOMAS CARLYLE. It was first published in *FRASER'S MAGAZINE* from November 1833 to August 1834 and in book form in the United States in 1836. The first English edition appeared in 1838.

Written under the influence of German Romantic thought, *Sartor Resartus* ('The Tailor Re-patched') is in three parts, the first of which satirically examines the philosophy of clothes, their importance as symbols and as coverings of an inner reality. The enquiry is made through the papers and memoranda of the idealistic Professor Diogenes Teufelsdröckh ('God sent Devil's-dung') as set forth by a down-to-earth editor. The second movement is largely Carlyle's spiritual autobiography in the guise of Teufelsdröckh's romantic wanderings and peregrinations. These come to a spiritual climax, like one experienced by the author himself in the chapters 'The Everlasting Nay', 'The Centre of Indifference' and 'The Everlasting Yea'. The final part is a poetic hymn to the romantic aspirant toward a nobler universe.

Sartor Resartus is a strangely complex book. Rich in SYMBOL and ALLEGORY, frequently rough in humour, bizarre in style, it stands outside the accepted movement of prose writing of its own or any other time. The polarization of light and dark, hot and cold, night and day, as well as the employment of countless poetical figures – cut across by Germanic puns, satirical commentary on contemporary literary figures and hosts of linguistic whims and crotchets – combine to render a unique and often perplexing text. Over all hovers the Divine Spirit whose presence supports the convictions of the romantically intuitive man.

Sassoon, Siegfried (Louvain) 1886–1967 Poet and autobiographer. Educated at Marlborough and Clare College, Cambridge, he joined the Royal Welch Fusiliers in World War I and went to France, where he met ROBERT GRAVES. He was wounded twice and awarded the MC, which he later threw away. Encouraged by BERTRAND RUSSELL, he protested in 'A Soldier's Declaration' (July 1917) that the war was 'being deliberately prolonged by those who have the power to end it'. Graves persuaded the War Office not to treat the matter as a disciplinary case. A medical board sent Sassoon to W. H. R. Rivers, a neurologist specializing in neurasthenia, at Craiglockhart Hospital, Edinburgh, where he met WILFRED OWEN, whose poems he edited in 1920. His own realistic, savagely ironic anti-war poems were published with little critical success in *The Old Huntsman* (1917) and *Counter-Attack* (1918).

After the war he was involved in Labour politics, and became literary editor of *The Daily Herald*. He later returned to his pre-war life of a country gentleman, writing *Satirical Poems* (1926) and the semi-autobiographical trilogy *Complete Memoirs of George Sherston* (1937), consisting of *Memoirs of a Fox-Hunting Man* (1928), *Memoirs of an Infantry Officer*

Siegfried Sassoon

and another dream sequence boldly dramatizing the controversial question of whether certain disputed verses in *The Koran* may have been the work of the Devil rather than God.

Such criticism, however, chooses to ignore both Rushdie's deliberately combative IRONY and the ostentatious fictiveness of his whole project. *The Satanic Verses* is anything but a polemical or categorical novel. Aside from its religious notoriety, it is remarkable for its imaginative rendering of the experience of exile, for its politically charged depiction of London's multi-cultural society and, above all, for its bewildering narrative energy.

Satchell, William 1860–1942 New Zealand novelist. He was born in London and completed his education at Heidelberg. He emigrated to New Zealand in the 1880s, settling near Auckland, and published his first novel of New Zealand life, *The Land of the Lost*, in 1902. Others were *The Toll of the Bush* (1905), *The Elixir of Life* (1907) and the highly praised *The Greenstone Door* (1914), a novel about Anglo-Maori relations.

(1930) and *Sherston's Progress* (1936), all published anonymously. He then continued with three volumes of childhood autobiography, *The Old Century and Seven More Years* (1938), *The Weald of Youth* (1942) and *Siegfried's Journey* (1945). His later volumes of poetry included *Vigils* (1935) and *Sequences* (1956). Both were predominantly spiritual in content, and Sassoon became a Roman Catholic in 1957. He published an important biography of MEREDITH in 1948 and his *Collected Poems* in 1961.

Satanic Verses, The novel by SALMAN RUSHDIE, published in 1988. It announces its robustly iconoclastic assault on certainty in the opening image of Gibreel Farishta, a glamorous Indian film star, and Saladin Chamcha, a film extra, plummeting earthwards after their airliner has been blown apart by a terrorist bomb. The byzantine plot follows their fortunes once they have safely landed in England. Farishta's charismatic amorality suggests that he is destined for a diabolic role but in fact it is Chamcha, cuckold and victim of police racism, who soon grows horns and tail. Rushdie transmutes his modern protagonists into other identities, notably the exiled Imam waiting to return to his decadent homeland of Sodom (a fictional version of the Ayatollah Khomeini's Islamic revolution in Iran) and the prophet-figure Mahound (an ancient Western term of abuse for Muhammad), founding a new faith in the mythical City of Sand, Jahilia. Violent Islamic outrage was also provoked by an imaginary brothel scene in which the girls are named after the prophet's 12 wives

satire Defined by SAMUEL JOHNSON as 'a poem in which wickedness or folly is censured'. Provided we amend 'a poem' to 'literature' the definition is adequate, for though the main weapons of European satire are IRONY and WIT, it is not necessarily a form of COMEDY. ORWELL's *ANIMAL FARM* is certainly a comic satire, but *NINETEEN EIGHTY-FOUR* is equally certainly a horrific one.

Satire seems to have begun as magical abuse purporting, like a curse, to wreak effective harm on the victim. Such attacking literature, using invective as its main weapon, would now be styled 'lampoon' rather than satire. On the other hand, when methods of stylistic caricature and farcical content so predominate that malice and morality tend to melt away in the mockery, BURLESQUE or MOCK HEROIC would be preferred.

Since the satirist tends to assume some moral or social norms by which degrees of wickedness or folly can be measured, satire is more frequent in classical periods. Where Romantic satire does exist it needs a higher proportion of wit in order to succeed (witness BYRON's *VISION OF JUDGEMENT* and *DON JUAN*), since the writer cannot take it for granted that all his readers share his norms; he must jolly them along, slipping in his punches when he can.

Satire is usually designated as either Juvenalian or Horatian, the former indignantly attacking wickedness, the latter suavely attacking folly. Elizabethan satire is almost entirely Juvenalian, partly because it inherits a morality tradition and partly because of a belief that satire should be rough (the result of an etymological mistake deriving the word from the shaggy satyr of mythology). The satire of the AUGUSTAN AGE, on the other hand, as befits a 'polite' society, more often follows Horace; its major exemplar is POPE.

Satire of the Three Estates, Ane Pleasant

A MORALITY PLAY by SIR DAVID LYNDSAY, first performed before the Scottish king, James V, in 1540. A surviving manuscript, dated 1568, records the text of a second performance in 1552, and the printed text (1602) of a third in 1554. The play is written in a variety of metres and mingles couplets with eight- and six-line stanzas. It contains nearly 5000 lines. Part I dramatizes the temptations of Rex Humanitas, beset by evil counsellors and falling prey to Sensuality. Good Counsel, returning to Scotland, is refused access to the court, Verity is clapped into the stocks and Chastity ignored. Only when Divine Correction arrives to reform the Three Estates does moral order return to the court of Rex Humanitas. An interlude details the misfortunes of an impoverished farmer and the chicanery of a pardoner. Part II brings the Three Estates before the King, to be denounced by John the Commonweill. Lords and Commons confess their faults and promise reform, but the Lords Spiritual defy the complainants and are forcibly dispossessed. The play ends with a stringent sermon from Folly.

Lyndsay's intention was to attack corruption wherever he saw it, but it was his vivid attack on the Lords Spiritual that made the play a favourite source for the advocates of reform in the Scottish Church. Modern revivals have found the lively language and the scenes of common life stronger than the lengthy debates.

Satires of Circumstance, Lyrics and Reveries

Poems by THOMAS HARDY, first published in 1914. Consisting of some poems already published and a number never before in print, *Satires of Circumstance* (misleadingly titled by Hardy's publisher) contains an impressive amount of the poet's finest work. Foremost are the deeply felt 'Poems of 1912–13', which are recollections of travelling in March of the latter year to Cornish scenes he had known over 40 years previously when courting his first wife, Emma Lavinia Gifford. These are poems of sadness and meditation upon a flawed, complex marriage; they constitute a chapter of emotional autobiography and, to use Hardy's own term, 'an expiation'. The 1912–13 verses are skilfully wrought, impressively unsentimental and marked by profound regret. Hardy idealizes Emma's youthful beauty ('Beeny Cliff'), laments her sudden death ('The Going'), recalls visiting her at Tintagel ('I Found Her Out There') and replies to her dead spirit ('The Voice'). They are among the great achievements of English elegiac verse.

The volume also contains philosophic and religious ruminations, as well as poems on contemporary events and spectral imaginings. Among the finest are 'Channel Firing', 'Wessex Heights', 'When I Set Out for Lyonnesse', 'Ah, are You Digging on My Grave' and 'Under the Waterfall'.

Satiromastix

A play by THOMAS DEKKER, perhaps with contributions from JOHN MARSTON, first produced by a BOYS' COMPANY in 1601 as a rejoinder to JONSON's *POETASTER* and revived later the same year by the Lord Chamberlain's Men (see KING's MEN).

The play is an unsatisfactory mixture, its archaic plot (virgin takes poison rather than lose her honour to a lustful king) largely hidden behind its abuse of Ben Jonson. Dekker and Marston, in the disguise of Demetrius and Crispinus, ridicule Horace, representing Jonson, as vain. Like so much of the writing that grew out of the war of the theatres, the satire is unattractively splenetic now that the quarrel is dead.

Saturday Review, The

A periodical founded in 1855 by A. J. B. Beresford Hope (1820–87) with John Douglas Cook as its first editor. For many years the periodical maintained an exceptional position in London journalism. With *The Spectator*, it became the most influential paper of the period and published contributions from most of the leading figures in public life.

Politically, it was at first Peelite but rapidly moved towards a Conservative view. Under the editorship of FRANK HARRIS (1894–8) its literary interests broadened and there were contributions from THOMAS HARDY, H. G. WELLS, MAX BEERBOHM and others. BERNARD SHAW was its drama critic from 1895 to 1898. In 1899 it was sold to Lord Hardwicke, and was edited by Harold Hodge. It survived until 1938 but, despite some bright periods, it never regained its earlier influence.

Saunders, James

1925– Playwright. Born in London, and educated at Wembley County School and the University of Southampton, he began his career as a chemistry teacher. His early plays were influenced both by poetic drama and the THEATRE OF THE ABSURD. *Next Time I'll Sing to You* (1963), his first stage success, was suggested by the life of an Essex hermit; loneliness is also a theme in *A Scent of Flowers* (1964), about a young girl who dies from lack of love. *Bodies* (1978), the most successful of his later work, is about two middle-aged couples facing various crises. *Making It Better* (1992) is an intelligent comedy about a World Service radio producer at the time of the 'velvet revolution' in Czechoslovakia. Saunders has also collaborated with IRIS MURDOCH in adapting *The Italian Girl* (1968) for the stage.

Savage, Marmion

1803–72 Anglo-Irish novelist. He was the author of six novels, among them a satire on the Young Ireland party, *Falcon Family* (1845). Most of his work was written in London, where he was editor of *THE EXAMINER*.

Savage, Richard c. 1696–1743 Poet and playwright. He claimed to be the illegitimate son of the 4th Earl Rivers and the Countess of Macclesfield, and wrote a poem, *The Bastard* (1728), censuring his supposed mother. The story convinced his friend SAMUEL JOHNSON, who wrote a sympathetic biography in his *LIVES OF THE POETS*, but is no longer accepted. Savage's first work was a poem, *The Convocation* (1717), followed by a comedy, *Love in a Veil* (1718), and *The Tragedy of Sir Thomas Overbury* (1723). Although Queen Anne paid him a pension for celebrating her birthday with an annual ODE, his poetry is forgotten except for *The Wanderer* (1729), a rambling contemplation of the nature of existence which Johnson called 'a heap of shining materials thrown together by accident'. In 1727 Savage was found guilty of killing a man in a tavern brawl but pardoned; he eventually died in a debtors' prison in Bristol.

Savile, George, Marquess of Halifax 1633–95 Politician and writer on politics. Savile was the son of a Yorkshire baronet and entered Parliament in 1660. A man of independent politics, he became Viscount Halifax in 1668, Earl in 1679 and Marquess in 1682. He led the opposition to Shaftesbury and the Exclusion Bill in the House of Lords and carried the house with him. (See *ABSALOM AND ACHITOPHEL.*) His influence at court waned with the accession of James II, whom he had criticized freely. As chairman of the committee of peers it fell to Halifax to ask William and Mary to accept the throne of England in 1689. The last office he held before retirement was Lord Privy Seal.

In literature Halifax is remembered for his political tracts and essays, most notably *The Character of a Trimmer* (1688), a bold and seminal pamphlet which contains a famous passage in praise of truth. The main body of his work is to be found in *Miscellanies* (1700) and *A Character of King Charles the Second: And Political, Moral and Miscellaneous Thoughts and Reflections* (1750), both published after his death.

Savile, Sir Henry 1549–1622 Scholar and translator. Educated at Brasenose College, Oxford, Savile became a fellow of Merton College and eventually its Warden in 1585. He served both as Greek tutor and Latin secretary to Queen Elizabeth, whom he importuned successfully for the provostship of Eton, which he obtained in 1596. Savile was one of the scholars commissioned by JAMES I to produce the Authorized Version of the Bible (see BIBLE IN ENGLISH). James knighted him in 1604. Savile assisted SIR THOMAS BODLEY in founding his great library and also endowed Oxford with two professorships, in geometry and astronomy, in 1619. Savile translated four books of Tacitus' *Histories* (1619), and edited St John Chrysostom (1610–13) and Xenophon's *Cyropaedia* (1613).

Savoy Operas, The A group of 13 comic operas, excluding the early *Thespis* (1871), by W. S. GILBERT (librettist) and Arthur Sullivan (composer): *Trial by Jury* (1875), *The Sorcerer* (1877), *H.M.S. Pinafore* (1878), *The Pirates of Penzance* (1879), *Patience* (1881), *Iolanthe* (1882), *Princess Ida* (1884), *The Mikado* (1885), *Ruddigore* (1887), *The Yeomen of the Guard* (1888), *The Gondoliers* (1889), *Utopia Limited* (1893) and *The Grand Duke* (1896). Although the first five were originally produced elsewhere, the series is always called after the Savoy Theatre, London, built for their performance by the impresario Richard D'Oyly Carte. They established new standards of writing and presentation for the English musical theatre, proved immensely popular throughout the English-speaking world, and have been widely performed ever since. Gilbert's libretti are characterized by a strong satirical streak allied to a personal vein of fantasy. His lyrics are deftly contrived, often shrewdly pointed, and at their strongest in humorous and patter songs; his sentimental songs tend to be commonplace. The dialogue is marked by an elaborate command of paradox and a profound cynicism sometimes verging on the callous, as in his much criticized presentation of the ageing spinster. This flavour is idiosyncratic enough to justify the term 'Gilbertian', subsequently applied in extra-theatrical contexts. Sullivan's scores admirably complement the libretti, providing in their melody and harmony the warmth which Gilbert's work lacks, and heightening his wit and satire by their vivacity. Like Gilbert, Sullivan did not always avoid the sentimental commonplace. The Savoy Operas represent the main legacy of the Victorian stage to the modern repertory.

Sawles Warde A homiletic prose ALLEGORY written in the late 12th century near the Welsh border. It freely adapts chapters 13–15 in Book IV of *De anima*, attributed to Hugh of St Victor; these chapters represent a separate work, *De custodia interioris hominis*, circulated in the Middle Ages as the work of St Anselm. *Sawles Warde* uses the common allegorical figures of the body as the house of the soul, the senses as the wards of the heart and the Four Daughters of God (Righteousness, Prudence, Temperance and Ghostly or Spiritual Strength). Wit must rule Will and, with the help of the Daughters of God, guard the house of the soul against the assaults of the Devil. Fear, the messenger of Death, enters and delivers a speech on the horrors of Hell, a catalogue of vividly realized physical torments. The Daughters of God protect the household from fear of death after a period of deliberation and another messenger, that of Mirth, arrives and describes Heaven, giving hope and joy to the soul. The meaning of the allegory is clearly explained and the evocative descriptions of Heaven and Hell add power to the work's message.

Sayers, Dorothy L(eigh) 1893–1957 Writer of DETECTIVE FICTION, playwright and translator. Born in Oxford, she spent much of her childhood in the Fens (where her father was vicar of Bluntisham-cum-Earith) and returned to Oxford in 1912–15 to study at Somerville College. After working variously as a schoolteacher, publisher's reader and copywriter in an advertising agency, she became a full-time writer in 1931. By this time she had begun her series of detective novels about the elegant and apparently light-hearted Lord Peter Wimsey, eventually to make her one of the most popular writers of the day: *Whose Body?* (1923), *Clouds of Witness* (1926), *Unnatural Death* (1927), *The Unpleasantness at the Bellona Club* (1928), *Strong Poison* (1930), which also introduced Harriet Vane, *The Five Red Herrings* (1931), *Have His Carcase* (1932), *Murder Must Advertise* (1932), set in an advertising agency, *The Nine Tailors* (1934), set in the Fens, *Gaudy Night* (1935), with Wimsey and Vane in Oxford and *Busman's Honeymoon* (1937), in which Wimsey and Vane are married. The later novels in the series determinedly introduce a new note of seriousness. Her only detective novel without Wimsey is *The Documents in the Case* (with Robert Eustace; 1930). She also wrote 11 short stories with the commercial traveller Montague Egg as detective, and contributed thoughtful introductions to two collections of *Detection, Mystery and Horror* (1928 and 1931, as *The Omnibus of Crime* in the USA).

Although she served as president of the Detection Club from 1949 until her death, she had by then abandoned detective fiction for a sequence of radio plays about the life of Christ, *The Man Born to be King* (broadcast 1941–2) and for translations of Dante's *Inferno* (1949), *Purgatorio* (1955) and *Paradiso* (completed by Barbara Reynolds; 1962) and of *The Song of Roland* (1957).

Scannell, Vernon 1922– Poet. Born in Spilsby, Lincolnshire, he was educated at Queen's Park School, Aylesbury, and Leeds University. His unconventional career embraced army service, professional boxing and work in a fairground boxing booth, and teaching before he became a freelance writer and broadcaster. Scannell's many volumes of verse include *Graves and Resurrections* (1948), *A Sense of Danger* (1962), *Epithets of War: Poems 1965–1969* (1969), *Selected Poems* (1971), *The Winter Man* (1973), *The Loving Game* (1975), *New and Collected Poems 1950–1980* (1980), *Winterlude* (1982), *Funeral Games* (1987), *Dangerous Ones* (1991) and *A Time for Fire* (1991). His poems are formally traditional and rooted in recognizable human experience; they are acute observations of the 20th-century, with its disillusionments, daydreams and underlying violence. His novels include *The Fight* (1953), *The Wound and the Scar* (1953) and *Ring of Truth* (1983). *The Tiger and the Rose* (1971)

and *Drums of Morning: Growing Up in the 1930s* (1992) are autobiographical.

Scarlet Letter, The A novel by NATHANIEL HAWTHORNE, published in 1850 and developed from an incident described by him in the story 'Endicott and the Red Cross' (1837).

An introductory section describes Hawthorne's work in the Custom House at Salem. The novel itself is set in 17th-century Boston, and opens as a young woman named Hester Prynne emerges from prison with her illegitimate baby in her arms. Charged with adultery, she must stand exposed on the public scaffold for three hours, and must thereafter wear a scarlet letter 'A' on her breast as a lifelong sign of her sin. Her husband is an elderly English scholar who two years earlier had sent her to Boston to prepare a home for them, but had failed to follow her at the appointed time. Unknown to Hester, he had been captured by Indians, and in fact arrives just in time to see his wife publicly condemned. Hester will not reveal the identity of her lover, try as the community does to draw out the secret. Ironically, the guilty man is one of that community's most respected figures, the young minister, Arthur Dimmesdale. A highly conscientious man, he escapes outward condemnation, but is inwardly tormented by sin.

Years pass and Hester settles into her new life. She proves to be a strong-minded and capable woman and, in spite of her humiliation, finds a place in Boston society by helping other unfortunates and outcasts. Her daughter, Pearl, has developed into a mischievous 'elfin' child who reminds Hester of her guilt by asking rather acute questions about the minister and the letter. Meanwhile, Hester's husband has taken the name Roger Chillingworth and has settled in Boston as a doctor. He makes Hester swear to keep his identity secret, and indulges his private obsession with finding the identity of her lover. Happening upon Hester, Pearl, and Dimmesdale speaking together one midnight, he guesses correctly at Dimmesdale's guilt. Aware that the minister's failing health is related to his unconfessed sin, Chillingworth pretends to help him medically, while torturing him spiritually with veiled allusions to his crime. Hester intercepts Arthur one day on a walk through the forest and begs him to escape with her to Europe. He would like to do so, and Hester even removes the letter from her breast, but he sees flight as yielding to further temptation. He returns to town, his mind filled with evil thoughts, to finish writing his Election Day Sermon. Hester learns that Chillingworth has blocked her plan of escape by booking passage on the same ship. Having delivered a powerful sermon, Dimmesdale leaves the church and bids Hester and Pearl to join him on the pillory, where at last he publicly confesses his sin. As Dimmesdale dies in his lover's arms, Chillingworth cries out in agony at having lost the sole object of his perverse life. Hester and Pearl, now free from the restraints of the mortified community, leave Boston. The book ends with Hester's return to Boston and her voluntary decision to resume wearing the scarlet letter. While Pearl settles in Europe, Hester continues her life of penance, a model of endurance, goodness and victory over sin.

scène à faire The scene of crucial confrontation between two adversaries whose meeting or recognition has been delayed. In the WELL-MADE PLAY it is the prelude to the DÉNOUEMENT.

Scenes of Clerical Life Three tales by GEORGE ELIOT, marking her début as a writer of fiction. They first appeared in BLACKWOOD'S EDINBURGH MAGAZINE in 1857 and were published in volume form under their collective title in 1858.

'The Sad Fortunes of the Reverend Amos Barton' concerns the well-meaning but maladroit curate of Shepperton, who acquires the sympathy and understanding of his parishioners only after the death of his wife, Milly. Sadly, his curacy is terminated and he has to take a parish in an ugly manufacturing town. 'Mr Gilfil's Love-Story' centres on the tragic life of an earlier clergyman of the same parish, Shepperton. Maynard Gilfil falls in love with a talented singer, Caterina Sarti (Tina), but she loves the feckless Captain Anthony Wybrow and becomes dangerously unbalanced when he dies. Gilfil seeks her out, restores her to health and marries her, but her spirit is so broken that she dies soon afterwards, leaving him to a lonely old age. 'Janet's Repentance', the last and longest tale, tells the tragic story of the hostility of the drunken, braggard lawyer, Robert Dempster, towards the conscientious Reverend Edgar Tryan of Milby. Dempster is joined in the hostility by his wife, Janet, also addicted to drink. But Tryan helps her when she is forced to flee her home and, now able to resist the temptation of alcohol, she is at his bedside when he dies, exhausted by his work for the parish.

Scholar-Gipsy, The A poem by MATTHEW ARNOLD, published in *Poems: A New Edition* (1853). It derives from a legend, told by JOSEPH GLANVILL in *The Vanity of Dogmatizing* (1661), about an Oxford student who left the university to live with gipsies. In Arnold's poem the speaker has Glanvill's book beside him and envies the scholar-gipsy's escape into the pastoral charms of the countryside around Oxford. For himself and his generation, however, he acknowledges that no such escape is possible from 'this strange disease of modern life,/ With its sick hurry, its divided aims,/ Its heads o'ertaxed, its palsied hearts'.

School for Scandal, The A comedy by RICHARD BRINSLEY SHERIDAN, first performed at DRURY LANE in 1777. Sheridan, who was the leading partner in the management of the theatre, wrote the play in a hurry and under pressure, but even so it is the most accomplished comedy of manners to have been written in the 18th century.

The ageing Sir Peter Teazle has married a young and ingenuous wife, fresh to London and dazzled by its social excitements. Among those she meets are the brothers, Charles and Joseph Surface. Charles is dissolute but good-hearted; Joseph is decorous but hypocritical. Each of them would like to marry Sir Peter's ward, Maria, who is also being courted by Sir Benjamin Backbite, one of the malicious circle headed by Lady Sneerwell. The plot is complex and ingeniously handled. It hinges on the return of Sir Oliver Surface from Bengal, his discovery of the true characters of his nephews, and the eventual unmasking of Joseph Surface in a justly famous 'screen scene'. The end sees Charles Surface united with Maria and the much-tried Teazles reconciled.

Schreiner, Olive 1855–1920 South African novelist. Born at Wittebergen Mission Station, Cape Colony, she was largely self-educated. Her unconventional thinking was coloured by HERBERT SPENCER's *First Principles* and EMERSON's *Essays*. She started writing while a governess from 1874 until she first went to England in 1881. The success of *The Story of an African Farm* (1883), originally published under the pseudonym of Ralph Iron, made her the first colonial writer to be clasped to the bosom of literary London. The bleak farm is an unromantic metaphor that undermines the imperial, heroical image of the frontier, while the passionate authority that shapes the heroine's role made the novel an important document for feminists. The allegory and pulpit rhetoric of the novel *Trooper Peter Halket of Mashonaland* (1897) contribute much to the moral impact of its attack upon Cecil Rhodes and his Chartered Company's barbarous treatment of blacks in 'Rhodesia'. Two novels she often re-worked were posthumously published by her husband S. C. Cronwright: *From Man to Man* (1926) and *Undine* (1929).

Olive Schreiner saw herself less as a novelist than a writer trying to transform an uncaring society, hence such works as *Dreams* (1891) and *Dream Life and Real Life* (1893). Her polemical writings consistently championed the victims of injustice: the Boer republics soon to be invaded by Britain in *A South African's View of the Situation* (1898), unfranchised black South Africans in the prescient, still relevant *A Letter on the South African Union and the Principles of Government* (1909) and women in *Woman and Labour* (1911).

Schulberg, Budd (Wilson) 1914– American novelist. The son of the film pioneer B. P. Schulberg, he was born in New York and brought up in Hollywood, to which he returned after attending Dartmouth College. His most famous screenplay is *On the Waterfront* (1954). His novels cultivate a fast filmic pace. *What Makes Sammy Run?* (1941) is the story of a Hollywood mogul's rise to power. *The Harder They Fall* (1947) is an exposé of the boxing business based on the career of Primo Carnera. *The Disenchanted* (1951) is a disguised portrait of F. SCOTT FITZGERALD. Later novels are *Sanctuary* (1970) and *Everything That Moves* (1981). His short stories are collected in *Some Faces in the Crowd* (1954) and *Love, Action, Laughter and Other Sad Tales* (1989). He has also written a biography of Muhammad Ali (1972) and a volume of memoirs, *Moving Picture Memoirs of a Hollywood Prince* (1982).

Schwartz, Delmore 1913–66 American poet, short-story writer and critic. He was born in Brooklyn and educated at New York University. The principal concern of much of his work is the complex relationship between the private self and the outside world. The intellectual energy of his writing was reflected also in his career as a teacher at Harvard, Princeton, New York and Syracuse universities, and in his influential position in the group of Jewish writers who emerged after World War II, particularly as a member of the editorial board of *PARTISAN REVIEW* from 1943 to 1955.

His first book of stories and poems, *In Dreams Begin Responsibilities*, was published in 1938. Other collections which combine prose and poetry are *Genesis, Book One* (1943) and *Vaudeville for a Princess, and Other Poems* (1950). In 1941 he published a verse-play, *Shenandoah*, and a collection of essays, *The Imitation of Life*. His collection of short stories, *The World is a Wedding* (1948), deals with the problems of Jewish life in America. *Summer Knowledge: New and Selected Poems 1938–58* appeared in 1959 and *Successful Love, and Other Stories* in 1961.

science fiction Stories which are set in the future, or in which the contemporary setting is disrupted by an imaginary device such as a new invention or the introduction of an alien being. They were first labelled 'science fiction' in American magazines of the 1920s; a term previously used in Britain was 'scientific romance', and many contemporary writers and critics prefer the term 'speculative fiction'. Stories of this kind are distinguished from other kinds of fantastic narrative by the claim that they respect the limits of scientific possibility, and that their innovations are plausible extrapolations from modern theory and technology, though relatively few examples are genuinely conscientious in this respect.

Although elements of science fiction appear in many stories of imaginary voyages, it was not until the 19th century that the advancement of science

began to inspire a good deal of work in this vein. MARY SHELLEY's *FRANKENSTEIN* (1818) is a notable early example, and science-fictional themes play a significant part in the work of EDGAR ALLAN POE and NATHANIEL HAWTHORNE. Following George Chesney's account of an imaginary invasion of England, 'The Battle of Dorking' (1871), there was a spate of future war stories in Britain, and the influence of Jules Verne helped to popularize tales of imaginary tourism involving hypothetical flying machines, submarines and spaceships. Speculation about the future was also encouraged by movements for political reform and by ideas drawn from the theory of evolution. These various threads were drawn together when scientific romance came briefly into vogue in the British popular periodicals of the 1890s. By far the most ambitious and successful author of this period was H. G. WELLS, whose fertile imagination was fired by THOMAS HENRY HUXLEY's lectures on biology and by his fervent socialism. He produced a series of classic scientific romances, including *THE TIME MACHINE* (1895), *The Island of Dr Moreau* (1896), *The Invisible Man* (1897), *THE WAR OF THE WORLDS* (1898), *When the Sleeper Wakes* (1899), *The First Men in the Moon* (1901) and *The War in the Air* (1908).

This was a time when the entire world-view of traditional religion seemed to have crumbled away, to be replaced by a scientific perspective in which the earth was a tiny atom in an infinite universe and man's dominion but a brief moment in an earthly history extending over billions of years. Many of Wells's contemporaries in the genre were sons of clergymen converted to free thought, who often used fiction to work out or display details of the revelation associated with their conversion; they included M. P. SHIEL, WILLIAM HOPE HODGSON, J. D. BERESFORD and GRANT ALLEN. Even some of the writers who were attracted to scientific romance by the opportunities which it offered for writing exotic adventure stories were the free-thinking sons of clergymen; examples include George Griffith, Fred T. Jane and C. J. Cutcliffe Hyne. Apart from the work of Wells, the most important scientific romances produced before World War I were Shiel's *The Purple Cloud* (1901), Hodgson's *The House on the Borderland* (1908), Beresford's *The Hampdenshire Wonder* (1912) and *The Lost World* (1912) by SIR ARTHUR CONAN DOYLE. The most important American writer who contributed to the genre in this period was JACK LONDON, in such works as *THE IRON HEEL* (1907) and 'The Scarlet Plague' (1912).

World War I had a profound effect on British futuristic fiction, and in the period between the wars British scientific romance was dominated by the idea that a new war could and probably would obliterate civilization, plunging mankind into a new Dark Age. This idea can be seen in *People of the Ruins* (1920) by Edward Shanks and *Theodore Savage* (1922) by Cicely Hamilton, and in the work of the new writers who were to be the most prolific producers of scientific romance between the wars: OLAF STAPLEDON, S. Fowler Wright, Neil Bell and John Gloag. Wells's *The Shape of Things to Come* (1933) reaches an optimistic conclusion, but only after describing the devastation of the world by war and plague. A frequent corollary of this notion that man was living on the brink of catastrophe was that he must ultimately be replaced by a new species which had transcended his innate brutality. This preoccupation with the supersession of *homo sapiens* is at its most extravagant in Stapledon's *Last and First Men* (1930) and *Odd John* (1935) but can also be seen in *The Clockwork Man* (1923) by E. V. Odle, in Gloag's *Tomorrow's Yesterday* (1930), in Shiel's *The Young Men are Coming!* (1937) and in Beresford's *'What Dreams May Come...'* (1941). Utopian speculation in this period was not entirely stifled, but was undermined and opposed by a determined cynicism seen most comprehensively in *The Question Mark* (1923) by Muriel Jaeger and *BRAVE NEW WORLD* (1932) by ALDOUS HUXLEY.

The USA, by contrast, was relatively untouched by World War I, and its futuristic fictions were haunted by no such anxieties. Interplanetary fiction, which played a very minor role in British scientific romance, enjoyed something of a vogue in America, largely due to the example of EDGAR RICE BURROUGHS, who used other planets as settings for gaudy adventure stories like *A Princess of Mars* (1912). Such stories became part of the staple diet of the pulp magazines, and helped pave the way for Hugo Gernsback to introduce magazines specializing in futuristic and interplanetary fiction in the late 1920s; it was he who first popularized the term 'science fiction'. Critics of these exuberant but preposterous space adventure stories contemptuously dubbed them 'space operas', but they embodied a mood of buoyant self-confidence that was current in America at the time. Gernsback's writers were not in the least anxious about the possible destruction of civilization and had no need to imagine new species to replace mankind: in their futures the powers of human creativity, deployed in new technologies, would make men equal to all possible challenges if only they were careful enough, and would enable *homo sapiens* to conquer the universe. American science fiction remained naïve in tone until the mid-1930s, but anxieties bred by the Depression combined with the influence of magazine editor John W. Campbell Jr to encourage a more sober and realistic approach. A new generation of writers recruited by Campbell included ISAAC ASIMOV, ROBERT A. HEINLEIN, Clifford D. Simak, Theodore Sturgeon, A. E. VAN VOGT and Fritz Leiber. These writers brought a measure of intellectual sophistication to science fiction while retaining its imaginative fertility and adventurousness. In the 1940s science fiction remained virtually confined to popular magazines, and the most notable American works of the period were often story series subsequently assembled into book form; they include Asimov's robot stories (*I, Robot*, 1950) and *Foundation* trilogy (1951–3), Heinlein's 'Future History' series, and the series collected in Simak's *City* (1952).

After World War II the British tradition of scientific romance petered out, its last notable practitioners being C. S. LEWIS and Gerald Heard. Its pessimistic tone, further encouraged by Hiroshima, culminated in such bleak works as GEORGE ORWELL'S *NINETEEN EIGHTY-FOUR* (1949) and Aldous Huxley's *Ape and Essence* (1949). Works owing their allegiance to this tradition have occasionally been produced since, but scientific romance was almost entirely displaced by and absorbed into American science fiction, which became established in Britain in the late 1940s as part of the more general 'coca-colonization' of British culture. The best of the British writers of futuristic fiction who came to prominence after the war, however, combined the serious and anxious concerns of scientific romance with the greater imaginative scope and ideative playfulness of science fiction. They included JOHN WYNDHAM, BRIAN ALDISS, John Brunner and J. G. BALLARD, all of whom retained a strong interest in the catastrophist tradition and exemplified it in their best works: Wyndham's *The Day of the Triffids* (1951), Ballard's *The Drowned World* (1962), Aldiss's *Greybeard* (1964) and Brunner's *Stand on Zanzibar* (1968). The most successful of the British post-war writers of science fiction, ARTHUR C. CLARKE, is more strongly affiliated to the American optimistic tradition, but shows marked Stapledonian influences in some of his most famous work, including *Childhood's End* (1953) and *The City and the Stars* (1956).

In the USA the popularity of science fiction increased dramatically with the advent of paperbacks, and there was a gradual shift from the short-story form towards novels and, eventually, novel series. Most of the best writers of the 1950s, though, made their names as writers of slick and clever short stories, and some of the apologists for the genre who helped it to gain respectability – notably KINGSLEY AMIS – argued that science fiction works best in short-story form because its strengths lie with the ingenious development of ideas rather than with the elaborate characterization that longer works require. The most important new writers to emerge in America in the 1950s and early 1960s were FREDERIK POHL, Cyril M. Kornbluth, James Blish, Robert Sheckley, Poul Anderson, ROBERT SILVERBERG and RAY BRADBURY. Significant works include Bradbury's *The Martian Chronicles* (1950) and *Fahrenheit 451* (1953), Pohl and Kornbluth's *The Space Merchants* (1953), Alfred Bester's *The Demolished Man* (1953) and *The Stars My Destination* (1956), Blish's *A Case of Conscience* (1958) and Walter M. Miller's *A Canticle for Leibowitz* (1960). The last two show a preoccupation with religion which has – rather paradoxically and perhaps surprisingly – become noticeable in modern science fiction. Even where religious ideas are not explicitly evoked there is still a fascination with the relationship between moral and metaphysical issues – in Sturgeon's *More than Human* (1953) and Simak's *Time and Again* (1951), for example.

The mid-1960s saw in both Britain and the USA a modish experimental phase in the development of science fiction. In Britain a 'new wave' was promoted by MICHAEL MOORCOCK, who converted the magazine *New Worlds* into an Arts Council-supported *avant-garde* periodical. In America Harlan Ellison promoted a series of 'taboo-breaking' anthologies begun with *Dangerous Visions* (1967). Moorcock's tetralogy of novels featuring Jerry Cornelius (1968–77) exemplified his new approach, while Ellison's graphic short fictions are best displayed in *I Have No Mouth and Must Scream* (1967). The best of the experimental new writers were Roger Zelazny, SAMUEL R. DELANY, Barry Malzberg, John Sladek and THOMAS M. DISCH – all American, though the last two were first received more enthusiastically in Britain. Their most impressive works include Delany's *Dhalgren* (1975) and Disch's *Camp Concentration* (1968). Alongside this *avant-garde*, however, great commercial success was achieved by many more conventional science-fiction writers. Writers like Pohl and Silverberg found new success as novelists, having previously been better known as short-story writers. Asimov, Clarke and Heinlein all attained best-seller status, as did FRANK HERBERT with *Dune* (1965) and KURT VONNEGUT with *Slaughterhouse–5* (1969). Following Vonnegut's capture of a cult following on American campuses the American academic establishment began to pay serious attention to science fiction, helping to boost the reputations of PHILIP K. DICK and URSULA LE GUIN. The former attracted attention because of his ingenuity in presenting images of artificial and hallucinatory worlds which dissolve into confusion, the latter because of her moral earnestness and purity of style. Dick's most important works include *The Man in the High Castle* (1962) and *Do Androids Dream of Electric Sheep?* (1968); Le Guin's two classic novels are *The Left Hand of Darkness* (1969) and *The Dispossessed* (1974).

Before 1965 science fiction was read mostly by young men, but the feminist movement in America generated a new interest in the possibilities of reform in the area of sexual politics, and several new female writers became prominent in the genre in the 1970s, including Joanna Russ and the pseudonymous James Tiptree Jr (Alice Sheldon). In recent years science fiction has been partly displaced in the marketplace by 'sword and sorcery' fantasies, following the extraordinary success of US paperback editions of J. R. R. TOLKIEN's *The Lord of the Rings*. The two genres have overlapped in the work of recent best-selling writers like Anne McCaffrey and Piers Anthony. The situation has been further complicated by a resurgence of interest in horror fiction, with writers like Stephen King frequently borrowing science-fictional ideas to mingle and blend with traditional supernatural motifs.

The boundaries of the genre are now more difficult to outline than ever before. Some American 'mainstream' novelists have also begun to use science-fictional elements in their work; examples include THOMAS PYNCHON's *GRAVITY'S RAINBOW* (1973), GORE VIDAL's *Kalki* (1978) and Jeremy Leven's *Creator* (1980). This reflects a considerable evolution of science fiction from the days when it was virtually an esoteric literary cult; its imagery has now diffused throughout contemporary culture to become familiar in some measure to everyone. This familiarity has not entirely eroded the contempt in which science fiction was held when it was an absurdly gaudy species of pulp fiction (much of it, in fact, remains both absurd and gaudy, especially in its film and TV manifestations) but it has enabled some writers and individual works to escape stigmatization, and has helped make the products of the scientific imagination available to reputable writers. The difficulty of achieving elaborate characterization and density of environmental detail in futuristic and hypothetical settings still prevents even the best science-fiction novels from living up to the expectations of traditionally minded literary critics, but the excellence of modern fabulists like Vonnegut and Disch is helping to change hidebound expectations of what novels can and ought to be.

Scot [Scott], Reginald ?1538–99 Writer on witchcraft. Scot was educated at Hart Hall, Oxford, and was MP for New Romney in Kent. *A Perfect Platform of a Hop Garden* (1574) was the first practical treatise on the subject in English, while *The Discovery of Witchcraft* (1584) was remarkably rational and sceptical for its time. Scot, who was influenced by the sceptical German writer and doctor, Johann Weyer, does not portray witches as malevolent hags armed with terrific powers to kill and maim. Instead, his witches are 'old, lame, blear-eyed, pale, foul and full of wrinkles; poor, sullen superstitious and papists, or such as know no religion'. They are ignorant, credulous and prone to melancholy and victimization. His scepticism about the supposed activities of witches and spirits was so strong that it laid him open to the charge of sadducism (or disbelief in the existence of spirits). There is a tradition that the *Discovery* was burned by the public hangman at the order of JAMES I, who attacks it in the preface to his *Demonology*. SHAKESPEARE and THOMAS MIDDLETON were among its readers.

Scott, Dennis 1939– Jamaican poet and playwright. He has worked as actor, dancer and director, an edited the journal *Caribbean Quarterly*. His first collection was *Journeys and Ceremonies* (1969). He came to the attention of readers outside the Caribbean when his American-published collection of poems, *Uncle Time*, won the Commonwealth Poetry Prize in 1974, a year after its publication. He confirmed his technical assurance and his ability to mix Caribbean subject matter with wider concerns in a second collection of poems, *Dreadwalk* (1982). Scott, who was Principal of the Jamaica School of Drama from 1978 to 1982, and who has been Jamaica's leading theatre critic, is the author of several plays. *An Echo in the Bone* (1974), written for the silver jubilee of the University Drama Society in Jamaica, is the best known: ritualistic and violent in parts, it ambitiously links together different phases in the historical development of black people. Others include *Dog* (1981), an ALLEGORY of human viciousness, and *Terminus* (1966). Scott's dramatic talent is innovative in terms of stage technique and seeks to make fundamental statements about man's historical behaviour. His poetry is at times more intimate and personal.

Scott, Duncan Campbell 1862–1947 Canadian poet and short-story writer. Scott was born in Ottawa. His father was a Methodist minister and his family lived in various places in Ontario and Quebec. He worked for the Department of Indian Affairs in Ottawa from 1879 until his retirement in 1935. Scott's friend ARCHIBALD LAMPMAN encouraged him to write and his first book of verse, *The Magic House*, appeared in 1893. He published seven more volumes of poetry, including *New World Lyrics and Ballads* (1905), *Beauty and Life* (1921), *The Green Cloister* (1935) and *The Circle of Affection* (1947). *In the Village of Viger* (1896) and *The Witching of Elspie* (1923) are collections of short stories.

Scott, F(rancis) R(eginald) 1899–1985 Canadian poet and lawyer. Born in Quebec and educated at Bishop's College, Lennoxville, Magdalen College, Oxford, and McGill University, he was called to the Canadian Bar in 1927. He became a lecturer at McGill University, where he remained until his retirement. His poetry, beginning with *Overture* (1945), demonstrates the same sense of social responsibility that made him a champion of civil rights and a leading authority on constitutional law. His later volumes include *Selected Poems* (1966), *Trouvailles* (1967), *The Dance is One* (1973) and *Collected Poems* (1981). *Essays on the Constitution* (1977) was the last of his many legal works.

Scott, Paul (Mark) 1920–78 Novelist. Born in London, he spent his army service during World War II in India and Malaya, the only time (apart from a return visit in 1964) he ever went to the subcontinent. He was subsequently a publisher and then a literary agent before devoting his time to writing.

His principal achievement is the *Raj Quartet* and its coda, *Staying On* (1977), which won the BOOKER PRIZE. Like the Quartet, his eight earlier novels show a dense, painstaking realism and are all set in either India or Malaya, except for *The Bender* (1963), which has a London setting and opts for a picaresque manner. The best of them is generally taken to be *The Birds of Paradise* (1962), which illustrates Scott's preoccupation with the process of history and the shifting perspectives of the past, seen to greatest effect in the long, slow movement of the Quartet. *The Corrida at San Feliu* (1964) prefigures the Quartet in its complex, fragmentary narrative structure composed of multiple points of view, a technique Scott learned from CONRAD.

The *Raj Quartet* consists of *The Jewel in the Crown* (1966), *The Day of the Scorpion* (1968), *The Towers of Silence* (1972) and *A Division of the Spoils* (1974), covering the final five years of British India (1942–7). From a variety of standpoints, ranging from the ostracized Anglo-Indian Hari Kumar to the sadistic disciplinarian Ronald Merrick, Scott explores his theme. This is not just the actual loosening of the British hold on India but, more importantly, the gradual, retrospective change in the moral climate among the British community in India, as they are progressively shown to be governing (and then bequeathing to a troubled, uncertain future) an alien, often violently antagonistic land. The final novel in the sequence introduces an element of humour absent from its sober, even solemn precursors, a tendency more marked in the spry, sanguine comedy of *Staying On*, which returns to two minor characters from the Quartet, Tusker and Lucy Smalley, living out a bleak and isolated retirement in India long after independence.

Scott, Sir Walter 1771–1832 Novelist, poet, editor and critic. Son of a Writer to the Signet, Scott was born in Edinburgh, the ninth of 12 children, and was early lamed by infantile paralysis, a handicap that was rarely to inhibit his activities. He was educated at Edinburgh High School and at Edinburgh University, where his major study was law. He was admitted to the Bar in 1792. Possessed of an astonishingly retentive memory, he read voraciously and devoured antiquarian lore, ballads, fairy-tales, chivalric romances and exotic tales of distant places; further education came from architectural observation and from tales and legends told him by the peasantry with whom he talked in his travels on horseback whilst executing legal business. In 1795 Scott married Margaret Charlotte Carpenter (Charpentier) and briefly, in 1797, he acted as paymaster, quartermaster and secretary to the Edinburgh Light Dragoons. By 1799 he was Deputy-Sheriff of Selkirk and just on the edge of literary life.

Scott entered literature through poetry and, absorbed as he was in folklore and the supernatural, he started his literary career by anonymously publishing in 1796 an adaptation of BALLADS by G. A. Burger, which he followed in 1801 by contributions to M. G. LEWIS's 'hobgoblin repast', better known as *Tales of Wonder*. About this time, too, he translated Goethe's *Goetz von Berlichingen* and, in 1802–3, put out the *Minstrelsy of the Scottish Border*, an edition of old and new ballads. A metrical version of the romance of *Sir Tristrem* appeared in 1804. Scott's poetic writing so far was dominated by a blend of Gothic-Germanic sorcery and antiquarian enthusiasm.

It was in 1805, with the publication of *THE LAY OF THE LAST MINSTREL*, based on an old border narrative, that his name became more widely known. This was followed by a number of longer poems, among them *MARMION* (1808), *THE LADY OF THE LAKE* (1810), *The Vision of Don Roderick* (1811), *Rokeby* and *THE BRIDAL OF TRIERMAIN* (both 1813), *The Lord of the Isles* and *The Field of Waterloo*

Sir Walter Scott: an engraving by H. T. Ryall after J. P. Knight

(both 1815), and *Harold the Dauntless* (1817). In addition there were, of course, other shorter poems dating from this period but, ironically perhaps, some of Scott's more memorable verses are found in the novels.

During these years Scott was also involved in prose writing and editorial work on a grand scale, much of it relating to criticism, antiquarianism, and history. Among such works were: *Original Memoirs Written during the Great Civil War* (1806), an edition of DRYDEN with biographical material (1808), *Memoirs of Captain George Carleton* (1808), *The State Papers of Sir Ralph Sadler* (1809), *The Secret History of James I* (1811), as well as numerous book reviews for the Whig *EDINBURGH REVIEW*, then edited by the fierce FRANCIS JEFFREY. In 1809 Scott took a prominent force in establishing the Tory *QUARTERLY REVIEW*.

The magnitude of these enterprises is prodigious. Writing aside, Scott's energy appears in his printing and publishing agreements with the Ballantyne brothers, James and John. These unfortunately led him towards a position verging on bankruptcy in 1811, the year he purchased Abbotsford. But he was rescued by Archibald Constable, 'the grand Napoleon of the realms of print', who was eager to have the prolific author under his wing. During this time of muddled business interests Scott also embarked on his

career as a novelist with the highly acclaimed *WAVERLEY*, some of which had been drafted as early as 1805 and which appeared with the Constable imprint in 1814.

One reason for attempting fiction was the astonishing success in 1810 of the first two CANTOS of BYRON's *CHILDE HAROLD'S PILGRIMAGE*, whose sophistication quite eclipsed the once successful romance narratives in which he excelled. The fact that Scott issued *Waverley* anonymously implies caution, but its immediate and enormous popularity decisively turned his career from poetry to fiction. A torrent of novels, merely identified as being by 'the author of *Waverley*', poured forth: *GUY MANNERING* (1815), *THE ANTIQUARY* (1816), *The Black Dwarf* and *OLD MORTALITY* (both 1816 and constituting the first series of *Tales of My Landlord*), *ROB ROY* (1817), *THE HEART OF MIDLOTHIAN* (1818; second series of *Tales of My Landlord*), *THE BRIDE OF LAMMERMOOR* and *THE LEGEND OF MONTROSE* (1819; third series of *Tales of My Landlord*), *IVANHOE* (1819), *THE MONASTERY* and *The Abbot* (both 1820), *KENILWORTH* and *THE PIRATE* (both 1821), *THE FORTUNES OF NIGEL* (1822), *PEVERIL OF THE PEAK*, *QUENTIN DURWARD* and *ST RONAN'S WELL* (all 1823), *REDGAUNTLET* (1824), *The Betrothed* and *THE TALISMAN* (as *Tales of the Crusaders*, 1825) and *WOODSTOCK* (1826).

Beyond his novel writing Scott was, throughout these years, again busy with editions, antiquarian studies and literary criticism. A significant monument of the time is his edition of SWIFT (1814), complete with biographical data. This was followed by *Memories of the Somervilles* (1815), *The Border Antiquities of England and Scotland* (1814–17), *Lives of the Novelists* contributed to Ballantyne's Novelists' Library (1821–4) as well as other writings of a dramatic and historical character. The output beggars belief. Furthermore, Scott was entertaining on a baronial scale at Abbotsford, enjoying the role of laird, and functioning as a man of law as well as of letters, so it is not surprising that his health was considerably undermined. From 1817 on he experienced attacks of jaundice, bowel trouble, vomiting and stomach cramp, which culminated in 1819 in agonizingly painful seizures and a narrow escape from death.

Nevertheless, he continued writing in improved but still impaired health and then, in 1825–6, a financial crisis involving Ballantyne and Co. and Archibald Constable left Scott with a debt of £130,000. Honourably disdaining bankruptcy, he set to work at an even more furious pace and in the next five years came CHRONICLES OF THE CANONGATE, with *The Two Drovers*, *The Highland Widow* and *The Surgeon's Daughter* in its first series (1827) and *St Valentine's Day: or, The Fair Maid of Perth* in the second (1828), *Anne of Geierstein* (1829), and *Count Robert of Paris* and *Castle Dangerous* (1832) in the fourth series of *Tales of My Landlord*. But the merciless toil overwhelmed him and he was brought home from Italy, where he had been vainly seeking health, to die at his beloved Abbotsford in September 1832.

Few authors have enjoyed a higher reputation than Scott once did. In his lifetime and for nearly a century after his death he was not merely an immensely popular writer – acclaimed as a poet and often regarded as the greatest novelist in the language – but a major cultural force. His Scottish novels, particularly *Waverley* and *Rob Roy*, did much to rescue that country from the low esteem it had acquired after the 1745 rebellion and to make it at once respectable and romantic. The descriptions of landscape and ruins with which his books abound helped to shape ROMANTICISM. Above all, his use of history confirmed the taste for medievalism which lasted throughout the 19th century and the conduct of his historical figures served as the model of the chivalric code by which Victorian gentlemen attempted to live. Yet today Scott is forgotten as a poet and neglected as a novelist. The immense bulk of his writing and the sheer length of his individual works intimidate. His characters are dismissed as artificial, and his plots as stilted and melodramatic; his fascination with history can appear a mere love of fancy dress. These charges carry enough force to prevent any revival of his reputation to its former heights, but they overlook his undoubted merits: his humour, his gift for memorably eccentric characters, his erudite and down-to-earth mastery of folklore and, most important, the underlying seriousness of his preoccupation with history and the processes of social and political change.

Scottish Chaucerians, The The name given to the 15th- and 16th-century Scottish poets influenced by GEOFFREY CHAUCER, principally ROBERT HENRYSON, GAVIN DOUGLAS, WILLIAM DUNBAR and the author of the *KINGIS QUAIR*. Although all these poets were openly indebted to Chaucer, the label can mislead by obscuring the original and innovative aspects of their style.

Scottish renaissance A movement in Scottish literature which flourished between 1920 and 1940. It was originally applied to the work of several minor poets (Marion Angus, Violet Jacob, Sir Alexander Gray and Lewis Spence) dedicated to the revival of Scots as a literary language, through its regional dialects or the revival of the language and traditions of Scottish poets of the 15th and 16th centuries. In 1924, however, the term was given a new meaning and force when the French critic Denis Saurat used it to mark the emergence of HUGH MACDIARMID, whose poems in revived or synthetic Scots, especially *A Drunk Man Looks at the Thistle* (1926), transformed Scottish poetry. MacDiarmid committed himself to a vigorous revaluation of Scottish literary traditions, and his definition of a renaissance broadened to include not only the recreation of Scots as a national language but also the revival of Gaelic and the re-establishment of separate Scottish social and political institutions. The example of Irish writers, particularly YEATS, supported his belief in the need to reverse what he called the 'English ascendancy'. A strong antipathy to the English and towards anglicized Scots became – along with a frequent depreciation of BURNS in favour of DUNBAR and HENRYSON – a permanent feature of his literary-political polemic. Although MacDiarmid was the major figure in the renaissance, appropriating and expanding its purposes to meet his own ambitions, at least some of his aims were shared by other writers, notably LEWIS GRASSIC GIBBON, WILLIAM SOUTAR and SORLEY MACLEAN. In the 1940s and 1950s a number of younger poets writing in Lallans (as they now called Scots) attempted a second phase of the renaissance, even though MacDiarmid himself was by then writing most of his work in English.

Scovell, E(dith) J(oy) 1907– Poet. Born in Sheffield, she was educated in Westmorland and read English at Oxford. She worked as a secretary and a journalist in London before marrying the biologist Charles Elton and working as his field assistant in northern Brazil and Panama. Although she has written since the 1920s, her first collection was *Shadows of Chrysanthemums* (1944). Other collections include *The Midsummer Meadow* (1946), *The River Steamer* (1956) and *The Space Between* (1982). Her quiet, meditative work, with its exact perceptions of nature, childhood and old age, was neglected in the neo-Romantic atmosphere of the post-war period, but she has been championed by GEOFFREY GRIGSON, CAROL RUMENS and John Mole, who called her 'a visionary in sensible shoes'. *Collected Poems* (1988) introduced her to a wider readership.

Scriblerus Club, The An association of Tory intellectuals and writers, which flourished in about 1713. Its purpose was to discuss topics of contemporary interest, enjoy the conviviality of witty conversation and ridicule 'all the false tastes in learning'. The members were SWIFT, POPE, ARBUTHNOT, GAY, PARNELL, ATTERBURY, CONGREVE and ROBERT HARLEY. Collectively they invented a character named Martinus Scriblerus, a pedantic hack whose intellectual shortcomings they recorded in the *Memoirs of Martinus Scriblerus* (published in the second volume of Pope's *Works*, 1741). Gay, Pope and Arbuthnot also collaborated on the comedy, THREE HOURS AFTER MARRIAGE, unsuccessfully performed in 1717. SATIRE directed at false taste, irrational thinking or political exploitation was common to the independent writings by many of the club's distinguished members, giving rise to the term 'Scriblerian' for such literature.

Scrutiny The most influential English critical journal of its time, founded in Cambridge by L. C. KNIGHTS and Donald Culver in 1932 and mainly edited until its closure in 1953 by F. R. LEAVIS and Q. D. LEAVIS. It focused on the study of literature, starting from the practice of close critical analysis advocated in Cambridge by I. A. RICHARDS, and from the sociological and historical account of English cultural history implicit in Q. D. Leavis's *Fiction and the Reading Public* (1932). The main contributor was F. R. Leavis himself: *Revaluation* (an account of trends in English poetry, 1936), *The Great Tradition* (the English novel, 1948), and *D. H. Lawrence – Novelist* (1955) were among the books based on articles in *Scrutiny*. Other important contributions were D. A. Traversi's and L. C. Knights's work on Elizabethan drama, D. W. Harding's essays on literature written from the point of view of a psychologist, Martin Turnell on French literature, D. J. ENRIGHT on German literature and Denys Thompson on English in the secondary school. The stance was that in the secular change from a pre-industrial to an industrial society, and with the rise of mass literacy, popular literature had become the manipulative product of entrepreneurs who could be philistine or unscrupulous. The maintenance of critical standards must become the role of an elite, and the university English school was its natural communications centre. Importantly, in the 1930s it offered a middle ground between Marxism and the right-wing literary politics of T. S. ELIOT. *Scrutiny* questioned current reputations as well as proposing its own view of literary and cultural history: those whom it thought 'middle-brow' retorted that it was 'puritanical'. Many of the contributors were pupils or colleagues of the Leavises: in the 1950s this began to seem like an orthodoxy. The journal was reprinted as a bound set in 1963; F. R. Leavis edited a two-volume selection in 1968.

Scupham, (John) Peter 1933– Poet. Born in Liverpool, he was educated at the Perse School, Cambridge, St George's, Harpenden, and, after national service, at Emmanuel College, Cambridge, where he read English. He works as a teacher and runs the Mandeville Press. A latecomer to poetry, he published his first book, *The Snowing Globe*, in 1972.

Subsequent volumes have been *The Gift* (1973), *Prehistories* (1975), *The Hinterland* (1977), *Summer Palaces* (1980), *Winter Quarters* (1983), *Out Late* (1986), *Selected Poems* (1991) and *Watching the Perseids* (1991). Much of his poetry is domestic: places, objects and heirlooms are his subject matter, examined in great detail and filtered through his deepening sense of history, geology and geography. Together with an elegant, spare lucidity of language, he is a formalist, interested in regular METRE and strict RHYME. His major work is the title-sequence of *The Hinterland*, 15 interlocking SONNETS.

Sea-Wolf, The A novel by JACK LONDON, published in 1904. Humphrey Van Weyden is thrown overboard when two ferry boats collide in the fog on San Francisco Bay. He is saved by a sealing schooner, the *Ghost*, whose captain, Wolf Larsen, presses him into service. He is at once fascinated by Larsen's brute power and repelled by his ruthlessness. They reach the sealing grounds off Japan, where Maude Brewster, a castaway from a shipwreck, is rescued by the *Ghost* and almost at once becomes the object of Larsen's attentions. She finds a sympathetic response in Van Weyden, but the struggle between the two men is hopelessly unequal and she and Van Weyden flee from the ship. They reach a deserted island, but the *Ghost* is driven ashore there. Larsen has been deserted by his crew, and, suffering from cerebral cancer, is blind. Van Weyden and Miss Brewster manage to make the *Ghost* seaworthy again and set out for civilization; Larsen, defiant to the last, dies on the island.

Seafarer, The An Old English poem preserved in the EXETER BOOK. It falls into two halves not connected by their subject matter. The first 64 lines present a monologue by a seafarer about the hardships and dangers of his life and about his love for the sea. The second half of the poem is a homiletic discourse, perhaps intended to draw a general moral from the seafarer's description; it considers the transience of worldly bliss and praises humble, honest living.

Seasons, The A poem in BLANK VERSE by JAMES THOMSON, consisting of one book for each season and a final Hymn to Nature. The first three books were originally published separately: *Winter* in 1726, *Summer* in 1727 and *Spring* in 1728. *Autumn* appeared in the first collective edition of *The Seasons* in 1730. From 1738 onwards, aided perhaps by POPE and GEORGE LYTTELTON, Thomson made extensive revisions and a much enlarged edition appeared in 1744.

The poem presents a vision of the world progressing amid much change through the cycle of the seasons, each book assembling landscape descriptions, anecdotes and vignettes that show the effect of Nature on human beings. *Winter* describes the bitterness of the elements, the death of a wayfarer in a snowdrift, the comfort of life indoors and the Arctic circle. *Summer* presents outdoor scenes of pastoral industry, and the mythical stories of Celadon and Amelia, and Damon and Musidora. *Spring* gives glowing and verdant descriptions of the season's effect on the whole of Nature, including man, who is seen in the charmingly idealized image of the contented angler. In *Autumn* there is a vigorous account of shooting and hunting, a denunciation of the barbarity of these pastimes, and an episode narrating the love affair of Palemon and Lavinia. The poem as a whole is distinguished by fine, evocative descriptions of rural life.

Thomson's most recent editor, James Sambrook, has pointed out that *The Seasons* cannot easily be assigned to any single genre and looks unmethodical. He suggests that it can profitably be considered as devotional, scientific, GEORGIC, geographical, historical, narrative, descriptive and subjective writing, but that it shows above all the power of landscape as a poetic subject. We find in Thomson the influence of Poussin and Claude, just as we find the influence of Thomson in Turner. *The Seasons* has its roots in Virgil's *Georgics* and in MILTON; at the same time it marks a shift in taste and sensibility, anticipating elements of the PICTURESQUE and of ROMANTICISM. WORDSWORTH and COWPER, in particular, owe a debt to Thomson. *The Seasons* was much translated (especially into German) in the 18th and early 19th centuries. There are even versions in Polish and Hebrew.

Second Jungle Book, The See *JUNGLE BOOK, THE*.

Second Mrs Tanqueray, The A play by ARTHUR WING PINERO, first performed at the St James's Theatre, London, in 1893 with Mrs Patrick Campbell in the title role.

Paula Tanqueray has concealed her past from her respectable husband, Aubrey, but it catches up with her when her step-daughter becomes engaged to her seducer. In opposing the marriage, Paula is forced to confess her own history, and she commits suicide to save herself and those she loves from shame.

Second Nun's Tale, The See *CANTERBURY TALES, THE*.

Secret Agent, The: A Simple Tale A novel by JOSEPH CONRAD, published in 1907. The ironic sub-title establishes the tone of this novel about revolutionary politics in turn-of-the-century London.

Mr Verloc's run-down Soho shop and his marriage to Winnie provide cover for his work as a double agent, infiltrating the underworld of anarchists to supply information to Inspector Heat of Scotland Yard and the Russian *agent provocateur*, Vladimir. Frustrated by English complacency, Vladimir orders Verloc to blow up the Greenwich Observatory. He equips himself with explosives from a sinister American 'Professor' and recruits his weak-witted stepson Stevie as his innocent accomplice. Stevie's horrifying accidental death in Greenwich Park prompts investigation by Heat and the Assistant Commissioner, a man whose colonial service predisposes him to look for the savagery of the jungle beneath the veneer of civilization. It also destroys the banal domesticity which Winnie has selflessly created for Verloc. When he admits to his role in Stevie's death, she stabs him with a carving knife. She plans to leave the country with the anarchist Ossipon, but he deserts her on learning of Verloc's murder. Driven to madness, she jumps overboard from a Channel ferry.

Secret Garden, The See BURNETT, FRANCES HODGSON.

Secret Service A MELODRAMA by WILLIAM GILLETTE, first performed in Philadelphia in 1895. In its New York production the following year, Gillette himself replaced Maurice Barrymore in the leading role. In a series of fast-moving scenes, the play describes the ruses and eventual unmasking of a gallant Union spy, Captain Thorne, in the Confederate city of Richmond, Virginia. At the last moment his death sentence is commuted, and the audience is left with the prospect of a post-war marriage between him and Edith Varney, the daughter of a Confederate general, for love of whom Thorne had failed to carry out a crucial act of espionage.

Sedgwick, Catharine Maria 1789–1867 American novelist. She was born into a wealthy Calvinist family at Stockbridge, Massachusetts. Her first novel, *A New England Tale* (1822), became one of America's first best-sellers. It tells the story of the orphaned Jane Elton who, after a difficult adolescence of restrictions imposed by poverty, dependence on others, and Calvinist orthodoxy, finally achieves the emotional maturity to assume the responsibilities of marriage and a family. Sedgwick's second novel, *Redwood* (1824), brought its author a popularity equal to that of her contemporaries JAMES FENIMORE COOPER and WASHINGTON IRVING. It tells the story of Ellen Bruce, another orphan, who competes with Caroline Redwood for the attentions of Charles Westall. Eventually, Caroline reveals her petty nature and Charles marries Ellen. It is then revealed that Ellen is in fact Caroline's half-sister by their father's secret first marriage, and is thus entitled to a share of the family fortune. The novel envisages a society in which women's influence will produce an age of virtue, family harmony and love. Sedgwick's third novel, *Hope Leslie* (1827), is about relations between whites and Indians in 17th-century New England; it introduces the theme of miscegenation that was common in subsequent American fiction. Her other

works include *Clarence* (1830), *The Linwoods* (1835) and a trilogy consisting of *Home* (1835), *The Poor Man and the Rich Man* (1836), and *Live and Let Live* (1837). Her last novel, *Married or Single?* (1857), reflects her awareness of the social difficulties faced by unmarried women.

Sedley, Sir Charles c. 1639–1701 Playwright and poet. The younger son of a baronet, Sedley inherited the title on the death of his elder brother. He spent some time at Wadham College, Oxford, but left without taking a degree. In London he settled down to a dissolute life like that of his friend the EARL OF ROCHESTER. Later, as MP for Romney, he was an active parliamentary speaker and became something of a patron of men of letters. Sedley was the author of some lyrics, two forgotten tragedies and three comedies, of which the best are *The Mulberry Garden* (1668), influenced by both Molière and ETHEREGE, and the ribald *Bellamira: or, The Mistress* (1687), based on the *Eunuchus* of Terence.

Seeger, Alan 1888–1916 American poet. He was born in New York into an old New England family and educated at Harvard. Two years after completing his education he made France his home. During World War I he served with distinction in the Foreign Legion, dying in the Battle of the Somme. He was posthumously awarded the Croix de Guerre and the Médaille Militaire. His volume entitled *Poems* was published in the year of his death; his famous 'I Have a Rendezvous with Death' had originally appeared in THE NORTH AMERICAN REVIEW in October 1916. His *Letters and Diary* was published in 1917.

Seeley, Sir J(ohn) R(obert) 1803–95 Historian and essayist. He was born in London and educated at the City of London School and Christ's College, Cambridge, where the poet CALVERLEY and the novelist WALTER BESANT were his contemporaries. He held a fellowship at his own college and was appointed professor of Latin at University College, London, before succeeding CHARLES KINGSLEY as professor of modern history at Cambridge in 1869. His most famous book, *Ecce Homo* (published anonymously in 1865), was an account of the life and work of Christ made controversial by its failure to acknowledge Christ's divinity. Seeley's historical works include *The Life and Times of Stein: or, Germany and Prussia in the Napoleonic Age* (1878) and two books justifying British imperialism, *The Expansion of England in the Eighteenth Century* (1883) and *The Growth of British Policy* (1895).

Sejanus, His Fall A tragedy by BEN JONSON, produced in 1603 and published in 1605. The first performance was given by the KING'S MEN at the GLOBE THEATRE with RICHARD BURBAGE and SHAKESPEARE in the cast. The play, which is rarely revived, follows the career of Lucius Aelius Sejanus, favourite of the Roman Emperor Tiberius, who leaves him in charge of Rome while he spends more and more time on his island, Capri. Sejanus aspires to the purple and poisons the emperor's son, Drusus; he has seduced and hopes to marry his widow, Livia. He also succeeds in discrediting Agrippina, widow of the great soldier Germanicus. But Tiberius grows suspicious and Naevius Sertorius Macro, the ambitious commander of the Praetorian Guard, is more than willing to supplant Sejanus. Eventually Tiberius denounces Sejanus to the Senate; he is killed by the mob.

Selborne, The Natural History of See WHITE, GILBERT.

Selby, Hubert Jr 1928– American novelist and short-story writer. Born and educated in New York, he drew upon personal experiences for his stories of life in the lowest circles of society. His best-known work, the collection of stories entitled *Last Exit to Brooklyn* (1964), was the subject of a much-publicized obscenity trial in Britain. It deals with homosexuality, prostitution and brutality, while exploring human isolation in an urban environment. He followed it with three novels – *The Room* (1971), the story of a nameless psychopath awaiting trial, *The Demon* (1976), about a man possessed by lust, ambition and violence, and *Requiem for a Dream* (1978), an examination of drug addiction – and a volume of short stories, *Song of the Silent Snow* (1986).

Selden, John 1584–1654 Lawyer and scholar. The son of a Sussex yeoman, Selden became a lawyer and was keeper of the records at the Inner Temple. He entered Parliament in 1623, having acquired meanwhile a certain fame as the author of a *History of Tithes* (1618), which angered the Church authorities. No lover of the episcopacy, Selden was a sharp opponent of the crown's prerogative. His clear, detached criticism often earned him the ill will of both sides and he had no patience with parliamentarians who fought to displace princes, only to assume princely powers. He withdrew from public affairs before the trial of Charles I.

His most notable work is the posthumous *Table Talk: Being the Discourses of John Selden Esq... Relating Especially to Religion and State*, which was collected by his amanuensis Richard Milward and published in 1689. In it Selden pronounces upon matters of law, personal freedom, and the motives of authority in crisp, direct English. He contributed notes ('illustrations') to the first 18 cantos of DRAYTON's POLY-OLBION and was also the author of books on antiquities and on law. In *Mare Clausum* (1635) he disputed the principle of sovereignty on the high seas with Hugo Grotius. Selden was a friend of BEN JONSON and admired by MILTON.

Selvon, Samuel (Dickson) 1923– Trinidadian novelist, short-story writer and playwright, of Indian and Scottish descent. After serving in the RNVR (1940–5), he worked on *The Trinidad Guardian* until 1950, when he migrated to London. He lived there until he moved to Canada some 30 years later. His first, briskly written novel, *A Brighter Sun* (1952), is about an Indian couple of tradition-bound, rural background, married at 16, yet growing into love of each other and understanding of their urban creole neighbours. The sequel, *Turn Again, Tiger* (1958), follows the process of their creolization and arrival at a mature acceptance of their Indian origins. *An Island is a World* (1955), *I Hear Thunder* (1963), *The Plains of Caroni* (1970) and *Those Who Eat the Cascadura* (1973), also set in Trinidad, involve the central characters' discovery that individuals within different socio-racial communities seldom correspond with group stereotypes of them. Selvon pioneered the use of Caribbean Creole dialect for other than merely comic effects; he makes it a flexible instrument capable of farce, comedy, satire, and even irony and pathos. All these modes operate in his sharp-edged interpretation of West Indian settlement in Britain in *The Lonely Londoners* (1956), with its jaunty Creole narrator Moses, and *The Housing Lark* (1965), with such comic episodes as a West Indian Bank Holiday picnic at Hampton Court. Widespread British racism and its concomitant Black Power protests are the major satirical targets in the more pungent *Moses Ascending* (1975) and *Moses Migrating* (1983). Selvon has also written short stories, collected in *Ways of Sunlight* (1958), and numerous radio plays from *Lost Property* (1965) to *Zeppi's Machine* (1977). *Eldorado West One* (1988) is a collection of seven one-act plays about characters who first appeared in *The Lonely Londoners*. *Highway in the Sun* (1988) brings together four of his longer plays. *Foreday Morning* (1989) is a selection of his prose.

semiotics (semiology) The science of 'signs'. The two influential early theorists were C. S. Peirce (1839–1914) and Ferdinand de Saussure (1857–1913). The former made two important contributions to semiology. First, he showed that a sign never arrives at a definite meaning; any definition is always subject to a further definition (rather as in a dictionary any definition can itself be looked up for a further definition). Secondly, he distinguished between three types of sign: the 'iconic' (where sign resembles referent, as in a road-sign for falling rocks), the 'indexical' (where the sign is associated with its referent; smoke equals fire), and the 'symbolic' (where the sign and its referent bear an arbitrary relationship, as in language).

Saussure's writings are devoted to linguistics, but he believed that behind and beyond language lay a whole range of sign systems, the study of which he called 'semiology'. His theory of the divided nature of the sign is fundamental to developments not only in semiology but in STRUCTURALISM, POST-STRUCTURALISM and Lacanian PSYCHOANALYTIC CRITICISM. Having made the primary distinction between language as a system (*langue*) and language as individual utterance (*parole*) he went on to reject the view of language as a system of symbols corresponding to referents (things in the world). Words are 'signs' which have two sides (like a sheet of paper): a mark, either written or spoken, called a 'signifier', and a concept, called a 'signified'. In this model of language, 'things' have no place; words acquire meaning only in so far as they enter a system of relations.

In France under the influence of Claude Lévi-Strauss (1908–), Roland Barthes (1915–80) and A. J. Greimas (1917–), semiology has examined social forms (kinship systems, myths, fashions, etc.) as if they were languages. In Greimas, narrative discourse itself is studied as if it were language writ large (see STRUCTURALISM).

Sendak, Maurice (Bernard) 1928– American writer and illustrator of CHILDREN'S LITERATURE. Born in New York, the son of poor Jewish immigrants, he went to work as a window-dresser after leaving school at the earliest opportunity. His talents as an artist were soon noticed. After illustrating the books of others he began supplying his own texts, first in *Kenny's Window* (1956) and more memorably in *The Sign on Rosie's Door* (1958), about a small child putting on a show for her friends. His most famous work, *Where the Wild Things Are* (1963), was also highly controversial, dividing critics between those who thought it too frightening and those who championed its imaginative brilliance. The book itself is about Max, a naughty boy sent in disgrace to his room, where he invents a host of monsters; despite their gargoyle faces and menacing claws, they all agree that Max himself is the wildest thing of all. Subsequent books have included the surreal adventures of *In the Night Kitchen* (1970) and *Outside Over There* (1981), both illustrated with Sendak's characteristic blend of pastel colours, stunted, tough children and dream-like imagery.

Senior, Olive 1941– Jamaican short-story writer and poet. Born in rural Jamaica, she grew up moving between impoverished and wealthy households, in which she was respectively one of ten children and an only child, and in so doing experiencing opposite extremes of the Jamaican social and racial hierarchy. She attended Montego Bay High School and subsequently studied journalism at Carleton University in Ottawa. She has edited the University of the West Indies' *Social and Economic Studies* and *Jamaica Journal* and was managing director of the Institute of Jamaica's publications section. After winning the first Commonwealth Writers' Prize in 1987 for her collection of short stories, *Summer Lightning* (1986), she turned to full-time writing and has since lived in England, Portugal and Canada. The stories in *Summer Lightning* draw on her own broad experience of Jamaican social life, examining issues of race, class, colour and gender in a variety of styles that span the full range of the Jamaican linguistic continuum. Written in a subtle and usually understated manner, they focus particularly on the experience of children being initiated into the differences between the island's folk culture and middle-class experience. Her second collection, *Arrival of the Snake Woman* (1989), again contains stories written from a child's perspective, as well as pieces which reflect the discontent of adults who look nostalgically back to their childhood. Senior has also published: *The Message is Change* (1972), about the 1972 Jamaican General Elections; *A–Z of Jamaican Heritage* (1983), a valuable source of information about folk customs and traditions; *Talking of Trees* (1985), a collection of verse; and *Working Miracles: Women's Lives in the English-Speaking Caribbean* (1991), a sociological study.

sensation novel A type of Victorian novel which took mystery and crime as its subject and suspense as its narrative method. Like the GOTHIC NOVEL of the late 18th and early 19th centuries, it appealed directly to the reader's sensations by seeking to induce fear, excitement and curiosity. Unlike the Gothic novel, it preferred a modern setting and sometimes included criticism of current social abuses. The sensation novel enjoyed its heyday in the 1860s, with the work of WILKIE COLLINS, particularly his hugely successful *THE WOMAN IN WHITE* (1860), and with MARY ELIZABETH BRADDON's *LADY AUDLEY'S SECRET* (1862). DICKENS was influenced by the form, most obviously in his unfinished *THE MYSTERY OF EDWIN DROOD* (1870), and HARDY chose it for his first published novel, *DESPERATE REMEDIES* (1871). RUSKIN was the most thoughtful of contemporary moralists who condemned the form, in 'Fiction – Fair and Foul'.

Sense and Sensibility JANE AUSTEN's first published novel (1811). It began as a story, 'Elinor and Marianne', which the novelist read to her family in 1795. She began to rewrite it in 1797, when she was also drafting the first sketches for *PRIDE AND PREJUDICE* and *NORTHANGER ABBEY* and working on a story, 'The Watsons', which was never completed.

The Dashwoods of Norland Park, in Sussex, have a life interest in the estate while Henry Dashwood lives; on his death it passes to John Dashwood, his son by his first marriage. Henry Dashwood recommends his second wife and his daughters to John when he dies. But John and his wife are selfish and, encouraged by Mrs Ferrars, John's mother-in-law, defeat his father's wish. Mrs Henry Dashwood and her daughters retire to a cottage in Devonshire. Elinor Dashwood and Mrs

John Dashwood's brother, Edward Ferrars, feel a mutual attraction but Elinor feels an odd constraint in Edward's relations with her.

In Devonshire, Marianne Dashwood falls passionately in love with the charming and penniless John Willoughby and is deeply distressed when he suddenly leaves for London. Elinor and Marianne go to London, too, at the invitation of their friend Mrs Jennings, and Marianne now finds Willoughby indifferent to her. Her importunities finally provoke an insolent letter from him, announcing his forthcoming marriage to an heiress. Elinor, meanwhile, has learned that Edward Ferrars has been secretly engaged to Lucy Steele for four years. Elinor's self-control enables her to conceal her distress. It is Edward's dependence on his mother that made him conceal his engagement and now Mrs Ferrars, learning of it, dismisses him and settles her property on his silly young brother Robert. Edward, who intends taking orders, has a small living offered him by Colonel Brandon, a quiet worthy man who has long been an admirer of Marianne. But now Lucy transfers her attention to Robert and marries him instead. At last free of a commitment he deeply regretted, Edward proposes to Elinor and she accepts him. The staunch and generous Colonel Brandon wins Marianne, who is brought to see that her passionate sensibility would hardly make for happiness.

sentimental comedy Often loosely applied to the plays by writers like GEORGE FARQUHAR and COLLEY CIBBER that replaced RESTORATION COMEDY on the English stage, the term properly refers to works of a slightly later date, when mere variety of emotion had become an object of fascination. Plots rewarded benevolence and relied on a timely change of heart to bring about a happy ending. The arrival of sentimental comedy as a popular form was announced by the extravagant success of HUGH KELLY's *False Delicacy* at DRURY LANE in 1768, eclipsing OLIVER GOLDSMITH's less bland *THE GOOD-NATURED MAN*. Kelly never repeated his triumph, and the most consistently successful purveyor of sentimental comedy was RICHARD CUMBERLAND, particularly with *The Brothers* (1769) and *The West Indian* (1771). It was against sentimental comedy in general and Cumberland in particular that RICHARD BRINSLEY SHERIDAN sought to revive a more astringent comedy of manners. See also the SENTIMENTAL NOVEL.

Sentimental Journey through France and Italy, by Mr Yorick, A The second and last novel by LAURENCE STERNE, published shortly before his death in 1768. Sterne himself had travelled through France and Italy from 1765–6 to help his tuberculosis. Converting his experiences into fiction, he adopted the character of Yorick from his previous novel, *TRISTRAM SHANDY*. Hastily undertaken, Yorick's journey whisks the reader across the Channel to France on the first page but never reaches Italy: the narrative breaks off with memorable suddenness when he is still short of Lyons. Indifferent to tourist sights, Yorick is a virtuoso of emotion, continually finding experiences that affect his delicate sensibilities, stimulate his benevolence, arouse his libido or cause comic confusion. TOBIAS SMOLLETT, whom Sterne met in Italy, is caricatured as the learned Smelfungus.

sentimental novel (novel of sensibility) A style of fiction, fashionable from the middle of the 18th century onwards, reflecting a belief that the natural emotions were good, kindly and innocent, and that society, law and civilization were to blame for corrupting man. The highly charged emotional world of SAMUEL RICHARDSON'S *PAMELA* (1740), *CLARISSA* (1747–8) and *SIR CHARLES GRANDISON* (1753–4) contributed to its rise, though the sentimental novel reached its full expression in works such as HENRY BROOKE'S *THE FOOL OF QUALITY* (1766–72), STERNE'S *A SENTIMENTAL JOURNEY* (1768) and HENRY MACKENZIE'S *THE MAN OF FEELING* (1771), in all of which lively and effusive emotion is celebrated as evidence of a good heart. GOLDSMITH'S *THE VICAR OF WAKEFIELD* (1776), a tragicomedy of clerical life, is frequently included among the hundreds of sentimental novels produced in the period, though it is arguably an early PARODY.

The reaction against the uncontrolled excesses of sentimentalism is apparent in later writers as diverse as MARY WOLLSTONECRAFT, HANNAH MORE and JANE AUSTEN (notably in *SENSE AND SENSIBILITY*, 1811, and *NORTHANGER ABBEY*, 1818.) The word 'sentimental' came to mean 'false and self-indulgent feeling' after Schiller's division (1795) of poets into two classes, the 'naive' and the 'sentimental': 'naive' writers are natural and instinctive; 'sentimental' ones are forced and artificial.

Sepamla, Sipho 1932– South African poet and novelist. He was born in Krugersdorp. His poetry belongs to the creative outburst of black 'township' poetry which broke a decade of post-Sharpeville silence and found voice in the work of OSWALD MBUYISENI MTSHALI, MONGANE WALLY SEROTE and the other poets in the anthology, *Black Poets in South Africa* (1974). It includes *Hurry Up to It* (1975), *The Blues is You in Me* (1976), *The Soweto I Love* (1977) and *Children of the Earth* (1983). *The Root is One* (1979) and *A Ride on the Whirlwind* (1981) are novels; the second, like Serote's *To Every Birth Its Blood*, celebrates the schoolchildren of the 1976 Soweto uprising.

Serjeant Musgrave's Dance: *An Unhistorical Parable* A play by JOHN ARDEN, first performed at the ROYAL COURT THEATRE, London, in 1959, when its enigmatic treatment of its title character's peculiarly violent pacifism puzzled and intrigued critics.

To a northern town, strike-bound and snow-covered, come four uniformed soldiers. Are they strikebreakers? Or are they, as they allow to appear, recruiters? Musgrave himself is strong, brooding and dutiful, outraged when an encounter with a local barmaid causes the accidental death of one of his men. He goes ahead, none the less, with his planned meeting in the market-place, dancing his macabre dance of vengeance as a gatling-gun is unveiled and pointed at the crowd – and the audience.

Serote, Mongane Wally 1944– South African poet and novelist. He was born in Sophiatown. Imprisoned without trial in 1969, he lived in exile in Botswana and Britain, serving as a spokesman for the African National Congress. Volumes such as *Yakhal'inkomo* (1972), *Tsetlo* (1974), *No Baby Must Weep* (1975), *Behold Mama, Flowers* (1978) and *The Night Keeps Winking* (1983) belong to the creative outburst of black 'township' poetry which broke a decade of post-Sharpeville silence and found voice in the work of OSWALD MBUYISENI MTSHALI, SIPHO SEPAMLA and the other poets in the anthology, *Black Poets in South Africa* (1974). *To Every Birth Its Blood* (1981) is a novel which, like Sepamla's *A Ride on the Whirlwind*, celebrates the schoolchildren of the 1976 Soweto uprising.

Service, Robert W(illiam) 1876–1958 Canadian poet and novelist. Born in Preston, Lancashire, he grew up in Scotland, where he worked for the Commercial Bank of Scotland in Glasgow, before emigrating to Canada in 1897. He worked on a farm and later on a ranch in Vancouver Island and then, in 1903, resumed his banking career. In 1904 he was transferred to the Yukon, where the Klondike gold rush had recently taken place, and this provided the impetus for his best-known verse. In rapid succession he published *Songs of a Sourdough* (1907), *The Spell of the Yukon* (1907) and *Ballads of a Cheechako* (1909). The success of the popular BALLADS in these early volumes enabled him to give up banking and write his first novel, *The Trail of '98* (1910). Service subsequently left Canada and worked as a newspaper correspondent and stretcher-bearer with the Canadian army between 1912 and 1916. *Rhymes of a Red-Cross Man* (1916) came out of this experience. He was a reporter for Canadian Army Intelligence during the last two years of World War I. After the war he settled in France. Service's essentially melodramatic verse is considered of comparatively little literary merit, but his witty ballads of Yukon life, such as 'The Shooting of Dan McGrew', 'The Cremation of Sam McGee' and 'The Law of the Yukon', were immensely popular in his own day. His work shows the influence of BRET HARTE and RUDYARD KIPLING. Other books include *Rhymes of a Rolling Stone* (1912), *Ballads of a Bohemian* (1921), *Bar-Room Ballads* (1940), the novels

The Pretender (1914) and *The Roughneck* (1923), and two volumes of autobiography, *Ploughman of the Moon* (1945) and *Harper of Heaven* (1948).

Seth, Vikram 1952– Poet, novelist and travel-writer. Born in Calcutta, he went to Corpus Christi, Oxford, before studying Chinese economic demography at Stanford and Nanjing Universities. In 1983 he won the Thomas Cook Travel Book award for *From Heaven Lake*, an account of his journey through Sinkiang and Tibet to Nepal. His collections are: *The Humble Administrator's Garden* (1985), quiet, graceful pieces, influenced by THOMAS HARDY, PHILIP LARKIN and Timothy Steele, and reflecting his encounters with his own and alien cultures; *The Golden Gate* (1986), a novel in verse about Californian life, using the Pushkin sonnet stanza inspired by CHARLES JOHNSTON's translation of *Eugene Onegin*; and *All You Who Sleep Tonight* (1990). *A Suitable Boy* (1993), which claims to be the longest serious 20th-century novel in English, examines the lives of four families against the background of a turbulent post-Independence India.

Seton, Ernest Thompson 1860–1946 Canadian naturalist. He was born Ernest Thompson in South Shields, County Durham, but later adopted the surname Seton; his family emigrated to Canada and he was educated in Toronto. Later he studied art in London at the Royal Academy and wildlife in Manitoba, where he became Government Naturalist. He founded the Boy Scouts of America and the Woodcraft League, and wrote a great number of books on wildlife (illustrated by himself) which enjoyed considerable success. Best known are *Wild Animals I Have Known* (1898), *Biography of a Grizzly* (1900), *Lives of the Hunted* (1901), *Biography of a Silver Fox* (1909), *The Arctic Prairies* (1911), *Wild Animals at Home* (1913) and *Woodland Tales* (1921). Apart from several books on scouting and woodcraft, he wrote an autobiography, *The Trail of an Artist-Naturalist*, published in 1940.

Settle, Elkanah 1648–1724 Playwright. Born in Dunstable and educated at Westminster School and at Oxford, which he left within a year, Settle lived in London from 1666. His first play, *Cambyses, King of Persia* (1667), was a grandiloquent heroic tragedy. It was successful enough to encourage him to keep on writing in the same style. *The Empress of Morocco* (c. 1671), performed at court and sponsored by the EARL OF ROCHESTER, is Settle's best-known play. *The Female Prelate, Pope Joan* (1680) was considered offensive by some of his former supporters. He had, by then, joined in the pamphlet wars on the side of the Earl of Shaftesbury, and his *Absalom Senior* (1682) was a poem written as a counter to DRYDEN's *ABSALOM AND ACHITOPHEL*. Settle's reward was Dryden's wicked por-

trait of him as Doeg in the second part of *Absalom and Achitophel*. It is to this portrait, more than to his own work, that Settle owes his place in literary history.

Settle was appointed Official Poet to the City of London in 1691 and wrote Lord Mayor's pageants from then until 1708. He achieved some theatrical success with musical pieces, particularly with his adaptation of *A MIDSUMMER NIGHT'S DREAM* as *The Fairy Queen* (1692), for which Henry Purcell wrote the music. When he fell out of theatrical favour, he wrote drolls (short comic pieces often based on scenes from well-known plays) for Bartholomew Fair. The text of one, *The Siege of Troy* (1707), survives. Settle was taken into the Charterhouse as a poor brother in 1718 and died there.

Seuss, Dr [Giesel, Theodor] 1904–91 American writer and illustrator of CHILDREN'S LITERATURE. Born in Massachusetts, he was educated at Dartmouth College and later attended Oxford University before losing patience with the academic life. Returning to America, he worked in films and advertising before producing his first children's book, *And To Think That I Saw It on Mulberry Street* (1937). It established his distinctive style, marrying catchy, doggerel verse to energetic, sometimes outlandish illustrations. Such a combination also lent itself well to books for early readers, with *The Cat in the Hat* (1957) achieving wonders of surreal humour with only a limited vocabulary. There followed more than 50 such 'Beginner' books, many written and designed by Seuss himself and the rest produced by a company of which he was president. Never a favourite with critics, who complain about occasional violence in his drawings and careless rhyming in his verses, Seuss has always been appreciated by children who usually respond positively to his raw energy and hectic good humour.

Seven Lamps of Architecture, The A treatise on architecture by JOHN RUSKIN, first published in 1849.

In Ruskin's words, the purpose of *The Seven Lamps* was 'to show that certain right states of temper and moral feeling were the powers by which all good architecture, without exception, had been produced'. To that end Ruskin claims that architecture should be informed by seven lamps (or spirits): Sacrifice, Truth, Power, Memory, Beauty, Obedience and Life. Each lamp illuminates the author's vision of the heights to which all architecture should aspire. Into his discourse Ruskin weaves problems involving the exertion of the worker, the bearing of labour upon architecture, the matter of ornamentation (its truth or falsity), the significance of colour and the contemporary habit of building houses to last but one generation. The book is a plea for the building as a holy place consecrated in love and affection, stability and contentment. There is, Ruskin avers, a moral duty upon man to build in patience, care and diligence, and where historical building is concerned the Gothic style should prevail because it 'admits of a richness of record altogether unlimited'. His idealism moves him to claim that the earth is an entail rather than a possession and that it belongs as much to those who precede us as to those who will follow and therefore when we build 'let us think we build forever'.

Seven Sages of Rome, The A collection of 15 tales set within a narrative framework and surviving in several versions, of which the earliest was written *c.* 1300-25 in Kent. It is based on a French original, *Les Sept Sages de Rome* (before 1150), but its ultimate source is the western collection analogous to *The Book of Sinbad*.

Diocletian, emperor of Rome, sends his son to be educated by seven sages. The emperor marries a wife who is jealous that the son will succeed and sends for him and his tutors, determined that he should die. One of the sages uncovers the plot and tells the boy not to speak for seven days. The queen tries to seduce him to break his silence and then accuses him to the emperor of trying to rape her. The queen tells seven stories, one each night, to convince her husband of the boy's guilt and the sages tell a tale each morning to persuade him of the queen's duplicity. Each day the king condemns and frees his son. On the eighth day the boy tells a tale after which the queen confesses and is burned. The structural device of a series of tales within a framework was common in the Middle Ages; notable examples are CHAUCER's CANTERBURY TALES and GOWER's CONFESSIO AMANTIS.

Sewall, Samuel 1652-1730 American Puritan writer. The son of New England settlers, Sewall was born in England and returned with his family to Boston in 1661. He received his BA from Harvard in 1671. He served as special commissioner at the witchcraft trials in 1692, but soon regretted the proceedings and, in fact, was the only one of the nine judges to make a public confession of error.

Sewall distinguished himself as a humane and liberal jurist, most notably while he was chief justice of the Superior Judicature (1718-28). His writings testify to that reputation. *The Revolution in New-England Justified* (1691), written in conjunction with Edward Rawson, justifies the uprising of 1689 which deposed Royal Governor Andros. Having produced a text which typically conceives of New England as the eventual seat of the New Jerusalem, *Phaenomena Quaedam Apocalyptica* (1697), Sewall went on to write one of the earliest published arguments against slavery, *The Selling of Joseph* (1700). In 1713 he produced another theological treatise, *Proposals Touching the Accomplishment of Prophesies* (1713). Finally came two tracts that most clearly reveal his kind heart and innovative judgement: *A Memorial Relating to the Kennebeck Indians* (1721), an argument for the humane treatment of the Indians; and *'Talitha Cumi'* (Massachusetts Historical Society, 1873), a rebuttal of a theological position which denied the resurrection to women (the work's Arabic title translates as 'maiden arise' and is taken from *Mark* 5:41). As a historical document, Sewall's *Diary* is his greatest contribution to colonial literature. Published 1878-82 by the Massachusetts Historical Society, it covers the years 1674-7 and 1685-1729, and offers an intimate and detailed account of day-to-day life in Puritan New England.

Sewanee Review, The An American literary journal, affiliated with the University of the South (Sewanee, Tennessee) and published continuously since 1892. Although essentially a critical journal, concentrating in particular on modern English and American literature, it also publishes some poetry and fiction. It exerted great influence as a journal of the NEW CRITICISM, particularly under the editorship of ALLEN TATE (1944-6).

Seward, Anna 1747-1809 Poet. She was born at Eyam in Derbyshire but spent most of her life in Lichfield, Staffordshire, where she was the centre of a literary circle and was known as the Swan of Lichfield. She met SAMUEL JOHNSON on his visits to his home town and, though not an admirer, supplied BOSWELL with information for his biography. She bequeathed her poems to SIR WALTER SCOTT, who published them with a memoir in 1810. Her letters, carefully written with an eye to publication, appeared in six volumes (1811).

Sewell, Anna 1820-78 Writer of CHILDREN'S LITERATURE. She was born into a family of Norfolk Quakers and sometimes assisted her mother, who wrote verses and stories for children. Not until she was 50, when a childhood accident that had long disabled her at last made her a complete invalid, did she begin writing her only novel, *BLACK BEAUTY*. This enduringly popular story of a horse was published in 1877, only a few months before her death.

Sewell, Stephen (John) 1953- Australian playwright. He was born in New South Wales. With *The Father We Loved on a Beach by the Sea* (1977), *Traitors* (1979), *Welcome the Bright World* (1982), *The Blind Giant is Dancing* (1983), *Dreams in an Empty City* (1986) and *Hate* (1988) he established himself as a leader of an 'internationalist' phase which has shed the domestic bias of much previous Australian drama. He believes that public and private are inevitably entwined and that all things are therefore political. His work has been called Marxist, but this does not fully account for its sombre and universal vision.

Sexton, Anne 1928–74 American poet. She was born in Newton, Massachusetts. Her work (like that of Robert Lowell, with whom she studied) is CONFESSIONAL POETRY in its use of ordinary events from daily life to explore the self and its relation to the world. Among her main subjects were the loneliness and depression which finally led to her suicide, her experiences as a daughter, wife, and mother, and the natural world, specifically that of the Massachusetts coastline and Maine. Her first volume was *To Bedlam and Part Way Back* (1960). Subsequent books include *All My Pretty Ones* (1962), *Selected Poems* (1964), *Live or Die* (1966), *Love Poems* (1969), *Transformations* (1971), *The Book of Folly* (1972), *The Death Notebooks* (1974) and *The Awful Rowing towards God* (1975). *45 Mercy Street* (1976) and *Words for Dr Y: Uncollected Poems with Three Stories* (1978) were edited by Linda Gray Sexton. Maxine Kumin, who wrote two childrens' books with Anne Sexton, contributed a sensitive preface to her *Collected Poems* (1981).

Seymour, Alan 1927– Australian playwright. Born in Perth, where he was educated in state schools, Seymour was orphaned at a young age. He worked for the Australian Broadcasting Corporation and as a film and theatre critic in Sydney in the 1940s and 1950s. In the early 1960s he went to London for the production of his best known play, *The One Day of the Year*, which had first been performed in Adelaide in 1960, and has since mainly lived abroad. Between 1963 and 1965 he was theatre critic for *The London Magazine*. More recently he has lived in Turkey. Seymour first attracted attention as a dramatist with the performance of his play, *Swamp Creatures* (1957), a surrealist ALLEGORY set in a Gothic house, in which experiments to create monster-insects serve as a metaphor for expressing fears of a nuclear holocaust. Experimental in its time, it is a play which is far more typical of Seymour's work than the comparatively naturalistic *The One Day of the Year*, which has come to be regarded as a classic of the Australian theatre. The 'one day' referred to in this title is Anzac Day (25 April), which is used as a focal point for the exploration of issues of national identity. The play's main theme is the conflict between generations in a time of rapid social change. Its appeal can be attributed to its vivid use of the Australian vernacular, careful construction and themes such as the conflict between mateship and individualism which, while quintessentially Australian, have broad resonances which cross cultural boundaries. Seymour's many other plays include *The Gaiety of Nations* (1965), *A Break in the Music* (1966), *The Pope and the Pill* (1968), *The Shattering* (1973), *Structures* (1973) and *The Float* (1980). He has also published *The Coming Self-Destruction of the United States of America* (1980), a novel, and has adapted *The One Day of the Year* into a novel. His television adaptations of L. P. Hartley's *Eustace and Hilda*, John Masefield's *The Box of Delights* and Antonia Fraser's *Frost in May* have won acclaim.

Shabby Genteel Story, A A story by W. M. Thackeray, published in *Fraser's Magazine* from June to October 1840, and in book form in 1852.

'George Brandon', a fashionable young gentleman fleeing his creditors, comes to lodge at Margate with the shabby genteel Gann family. Piqued that the two older daughters are unimpressed by his aristocratic airs, he sets out to seduce the youngest, Caroline, who loves him. Jealousy of a rival leads to love, and he plans to marry her, but his fashionable friends persuade him to go through a mock ceremony. The unfinished story is developed in *The Adventures of Philip*, where 'Brandon' reappears under his real name, Firmin.

Shadbolt, Maurice 1932– New Zealand novelist and short-story writer. Born in Auckland, where he attended university, he subsequently worked as a journalist and as a scriptwriter for the New Zealand National Film Unit. A prolific but uneven writer, he has frequently tackled large public themes. His collections of short stories include *The New Zealanders* (1959), *Summer Fires and Winter Country* (1963) and *Figures in Light* (1978). His novels include: *Among the Cinders* (1965); *Strangers and Journeys* (1972), a solidly realistic work taking in events such as the Depression and the 1951 waterfront strike; *A Touch of Clay* (1974); *Danger Zone* (1976), about French nuclear testing in the Pacific; *The Lovelock Version* (1980), using a broad chronological sweep but breaking with realistic narrative conventions; *Season of the Jew* (1986), a historical novel about the rebellion of the 19th-century Maori leader Te Kooti (treated, rather differently, in Witi Ihimaera's *The Matriarch*); and *Monday's Warriors* (1990).

Shadow of a Gunman, The A two-act play by Sean O'Casey, produced in 1923, the first of his plays to be staged at the Abbey Theatre, Dublin.

In a Dublin tenement in 1920, when the Black and Tans are making their reprisal raids, Donal Davoren, a poet who is believed by fellow lodgers to be on the run from the British, shares a room with Seumas Shields, a feckless pedlar. Donal is, in fact, no kind of gunman or hero, and the play's bitter conclusion (much of its conduct is comic) sees the admiring and admirable Minnie Powell, a girl who lives in the same tenement, killed in an ambush as a result of her attempts to shield Donal.

Shadwell, Thomas c. 1642–92 Playwright and poet. Born in Norfolk, Shadwell was at Cambridge University from 1654–6 and studied law (he was a lawyer's son) at the Middle Temple from 1658 until he determined on a literary career. His earliest published work was a play, *The Sullen Lovers* (1668), written on the model of BEN JONSON's comedy of humours. It was a mode that suited Shadwell's firm moral orthodoxy, and he never wholly abandoned it. But Shadwell had a professional preparedness to adapt to changing theatrical fashions. After the comparative failure of *The Humorists* (1670), he incorporated into *Epsom Wells* (1672) the new techniques of the witty society comedy pioneered by ETHEREGE. His best plays, *Epsom Wells*, *The Virtuoso* (1676), *The Squire of Alsatia* (1688) and *Bury Fair* (1689), helped to assimilate the Jonsonian urge to instruct through satire into the developing style of English comedy. Not all of Shadwell's successful work is so estimable. His adaptation of *THE TEMPEST* (1674) owed more to the fashion for spectacular opera than to SHAKESPEARE. A second opera, *Psyche* (1675), was a tame exploitation of the popularity of the first. *The Libertine* (1675) and an adaptation of *TIMON OF ATHENS* (1678) are weak examples of the heroic tragedy brought into vogue by JOHN DRYDEN.

Even so, the punishment inflicted on Shadwell's subsequent reputation by the magnificent satire of Dryden's *MAC FLECKNOE* (1678) is excessive. He was by no means as dull a writer as Dryden encourages us to believe. That he should have succeeded Dryden as POET LAUREATE in 1689 is an irony that has done Shadwell no posthumous favours. His best verse is contained either in his plays or in the satirical prologues and epilogues that accompanied them in the theatre. The Juvenalian satire of *The Medal of John Bayes* (1682) and the version of Juvenal's *Tenth Satire* (1687) has lost its bite and the panegyric of his 'Laureate' poems is predictably empty.

Shaffer, Peter 1926– Playwright. Born in Liverpool and educated in London and at Cambridge, Shaffer first published three novels in collaboration with his twin brother Anthony, but it was the play *Five Finger Exercise* (1958) that first brought him acclaim. It showed his command of drawing-room drama, while his TV scripts, *The Salt Land* (1955) and *Balance of Terror* (1957), expressed a preoccupation with religious and philosophical subjects. The first stage play to combine his craftsmanship and wider preoccupations was *The Royal Hunt of the Sun* (1964), about the Spanish destruction of the Inca civilization of Peru. Subsequent work has included: *Black Comedy* (1965), later matched in a double bill with *White Lies* (1968); *Equus* (1973), in which a psychoanalyst grapples with the mysterious Dionysiac faiths of a delinquent youth; *Amadeus* (1979), about the rivalry between Salieri and Mozart; *Lettice and Lovage* (1987), about a romantic tour guide; and *The Gift of the Gorgon* (1992).

Shaftesbury, Earl of [Cooper, Anthony Ashley] 1671–1713 Philosopher. He was the grandson of the 1st Earl of Shaftesbury, politician, champion of the Duke of Monmouth's cause and the Achitophel of DRYDEN's *ABSALOM AND ACHITOPHEL*. Born in London, he was educated at Winchester College under the supervision of JOHN LOCKE, who had been physician and secretary to his grandfather. After travelling in Europe Shaftesbury entered Parliament, inheriting the title in 1700; he retired from public life because of ill health and in 1711 went to live in Naples, where he died.

After withdrawing into private life Shaftesbury devoted himself to moral philosophy. He rejected the bleakness of HOBBES and Locke but at the same time questioned religious dogma; the CAMBRIDGE PLATONISTS were his philosophical ancestors. His works include *An Inquiry concerning Virtue* (1699), *A Letter concerning Enthusiasm* (1708), *The Moralist* (1709) and *Soliloquy: or, Advice to an Author* (1710). He collected his writings in *Characteristics of Men, Manners, Opinions, Times* (1711), which contained further reflections and essays on new subjects. A carefully revised text was published in 1714; his unfinished *Second Characters: or, The Language of Forms* was published in 1914.

Shaftesbury's prose is uncomplicated and his moral philosophy has no need of technicalities. He disliked religious controversy and regarded it as valueless; he used ridicule against superstition, but thought the use of ridicule as the sole weapon for argument detestable. At a time when many people were dismayed by the rival – and sometimes stridently argued – claims of DEISTS, philosophers and religious dogmatists, Shaftesbury's 'moral sense' (the innate capacity to distinguish right and wrong) had strong appeal and his work was widely read.

Shakespeare, William 1564–1616 In a flamboyant age and a notoriously flamboyant profession – he was an active member of a theatre company for at least 20 years – Shakespeare was notably reticent. As a result, scholars have had painstakingly to piece together the story of his life from surviving scraps of evidence, and there remains ample room for speculation.

He was born in Stratford-upon-Avon, where his father was a prosperous glover and one of the town's 14 principal burgesses. In 1565 John Shakespeare was promoted to the rank of alderman and in 1571 was appointed Chief Alderman. It is a reasonable assumption that such a man would send his son to the grammar school in Stratford. The evident decline in John Shakespeare's fortunes after 1576 has allowed speculation that his son did not complete his education. He is known to have married Anne Hathaway in 1582. A daughter was born to the couple within six months. She was the Susanna who later married the physician John Hall and lived prosperously in Stratford. The family was completed with the birth of

Shakespeare's birthplace: the earliest known engraving, published in *The Gentleman's Magazine,* July 1769, from a drawing by Richard Greene

the twins, Judith and Hamnet, in 1585: Hamnet died in 1596 and Judith lived until 1662.

Virtually nothing is known of Shakespeare's life from 1585 to 1592. Tradition and conjecture have filled these 'seven lost years' with various activities – schoolmastering, soldiering or working in the law – designed to explain the expert knowledge of these branches of life which some readers have detected in the plays. One of the many possibilities is that Shakespeare left Stratford with a group of London actors. Certainly his name was sufficiently well known in the London theatre by 1592 to invite GREENE's jibe at him as an 'upstart Crow'. Greene had in mind Shakespeare's part in writing *HENRY VI.* This early collaboration suggests that his apprenticeship as a playwright was served alongside the growing number of aspiring writers, seeking to benefit from the demand for plays in the emergent professional theatre. The texts that survive from the 1590s imply that Shakespeare preferred to work alone, though there is no means of telling what may have been lost. Only in *SIR THOMAS MORE* (*c.* 1593–5) of the works outside the early canon has his hand been confidently detected. By 1594, when he found the money and professional commitment to purchase a share in the newly formed Lord Chamberlain's Men, Shakespeare had probably written his three early comedies, *THE COMEDY OF ERRORS, THE TWO GENTLEMEN OF VERONA* and *THE TAMING OF THE SHREW,* and two corpse-laden tragedies, *TITUS ANDRONICUS* and *RICHARD III,* the latter bringing the three *Henry VI* plays to a brilliantly original conclusion. He had also reached a fashionable audience with the two narrative poems, *VENUS AND ADONIS* (1593) and *THE RAPE OF LUCRECE* (1594). It

was enough to encourage the mature actors who formed the Lord Chamberlain's Men to accept him, not merely as an actor, but also as a potential resident writer for their proposed London home, the THEATRE in Shoreditch.

Living in the region of Bishopsgate, not far from the Theatre, Shakespeare continued to write plays at the rate of approximately two a year. The period 1594–8 may have seen the first productions of *KING JOHN* (sometimes dated as early as 1589), the middle comedies *LOVE'S LABOUR'S LOST* (scholars continue to argue about *Love's Labour's Won,* ascribed to Shakespeare by MERES), *A MIDSUMMER NIGHT'S DREAM* and *THE MERCHANT OF VENICE,* the outstandingly popular tragedy *ROMEO AND JULIET* and the cycle of English history plays, *RICHARD II,* the two parts of *HENRY IV* and *HENRY V.* That he also had aspirations as a gentleman, and the means to support them, is apparent in the application, on his father's behalf, for a coat of arms in 1596; it was granted. The following year Shakespeare bought one of Stratford's finest houses, New Place. Early in 1598 he made a small investment in malt (malting was Stratford's principal industry). The London theatres were experiencing hardship at this time, and it is possible that he was contemplating the life of a country gentleman with his wife and daughters in Stratford. If so, he changed his mind. With other shareholders of the Lord Chamberlain's Men, he met the landlord's threat of eviction from the Theatre by moving its timbers to the south bank of the Thames and re-erecting them as the GLOBE.

Shakespeare wrote his greatest plays during the first decade of his company's occupation of the Globe. They include the mature comedies, *MUCH ADO ABOUT*

NOTHING (more probably dating from 1598), *As You Like It* and *Twelfth Night*; the darker comedies, sometimes called PROBLEM PLAYS, *ALL'S WELL THAT ENDS WELL*, *MEASURE FOR MEASURE* and *TROILUS AND CRESSIDA*; a pot-boiler, *THE MERRY WIVES OF WINDSOR*, bringing Falstaff back to life from *Henry IV*; and the succession of great tragedies, *JULIUS CAESAR*, *HAMLET*, *OTHELLO*, *KING LEAR*, *MACBETH*, *ANTONY AND CLEOPATRA*, *CORIOLANUS* and *TIMON OF ATHENS*. It was a period that saw the Lord Chamberlain's Men honoured by the new monarch with the title of the KING'S MEN and confirmed in their ascendancy at court. Shakespeare had moved his London lodgings to Southwark, but maintained his financial interests in Stratford. A small investment in land in 1602 was followed by a larger one in 1605. But theatrical fashions were changing. The faddish interest in BOYS' COMPANIES, playing in indoor theatres, had attracted the interest of some of the best playwrights of the age. As the interest in the boys waned, these playwrights began to write for the adult companies. BEAUMONT and FLETCHER were particularly adept at suiting the new fashions almost before they declared themselves. Shakespeare was probably feeling the need to look to his well-established laurels. When the King's Men decided to invest in an indoor playhouse of their own, at the BLACKFRIARS, he joined them, perhaps recognizing the greater scenic scope offered by indoor playing. His last plays, *PERICLES, PRINCE OF TYRE* (written in collaboration, probably with George Wilkins), *CYMBELINE*, *THE WINTER'S TALE* and *THE TEMPEST*, are romances, which acknowledge even as they transcend the growing interest in spectacle, magic and improbable resolutions. The collaborations with Fletcher on *HENRY VIII*, *THE TWO NOBLE KINSMEN* and the lost *Cardenio* (see also SHAKESPEARE APOCRYPHA) suggest a dulling of his own creativity. It was at a performance of *HENRY VIII* in 1613 that the Globe was burned down. Shakespeare had just bought the upper floor of one of the Blackfriars gatehouses and may not have wished to pay out more money for the rebuilding of the Globe. The probability is that he spent his last years in Stratford, dying there in 1616.

It was as a poet as well as a playwright that Shakespeare was honoured by his contemporaries. *THE PHOENIX AND THE TURTLE* had appeared in Robert Chester's *Love's Martyr* (1601). *SONNETS* (1609), written probably many years before they were published with an enigmatic dedication to Mr 'W. H.', confirmed his genius, if confirmation were needed. Two fellow actors, JOHN HEMINGES and Henry Condell, produced the posthumous collection of his plays known as the First Folio in 1623. It was a vast undertaking, without which 20 of Shakespeare's plays may have been lost to posterity. Plays were not highly prized as literature. SIR THOMAS BODLEY had classed most of them among the 'idle books, and riff-raffs' he did not wish to have catalogued in his library in 1612, so that the decision to publish so many by one man, and in the exalted folio form, is evidence of the esteem in which Shakespeare was held, not only by the public, but also by his fellow professionals. The Folio was republished three times in the course of the seventeenth century, and the first scholarly edition of his work followed in 1709, edited by the playwright NICHOLAS ROWE.

Shakespeare apocrypha JOHN HEMINGES and Henry Condell, in their epistle 'to the great variety of readers' prefaced to the 1623 Folio collection of SHAKESPEARE's plays, claimed to have included all those previously printed together with 'all the rest'. In fact, they nearly left out *TROILUS AND CRESSIDA*, which is missing from the list of contents. Since his lifetime, Shakespeare has been named as the author of other plays which they did not include. *PERICLES* (1609) is now admitted to the canon. *THE TWO NOBLE KINSMEN* (1634) continues to provoke debate, but is probably his work, in collaboration with JOHN FLETCHER. *Pericles* together with six plays printed between 1595 and 1619 as his (or at least as the work of 'W.S.') were added in 1664 as a supplement to the Third Folio (1663). None of the others is now accepted as his, but they provide the basis for what modern scholarship has christened the 'Shakespeare apocrypha'. They are: *LOCRINE* (1595); Part I of *Sir John Oldcastle* (1600), by ANTHONY MUNDAY and others; *THOMAS, LORD CROMWELL* (1602); *THE LONDON PRODIGAL* (1605); *The Puritan* (1607) and *A YORKSHIRE TRAGEDY* (1608), both possibly by THOMAS MIDDLETON.

Two further attributions have seemed plausible enough to receive serious attention. Three pages of the late Elizabethan manuscript of *SIR THOMAS MORE* (c. 1593–5) are widely accepted as Shakespeare's own revision of a rejected scene. Since EDWARD CAPELL first suggested it in 1760, many have found reason to entertain his view that *EDWARD III* (1596) may be wholly or in part the work of Shakespeare; at least he would appear to have been very well acquainted with it. The rest of the conventional group is an anthology of popular drama attributed to Shakespeare on various and tenuous grounds. The plays are *ARDEN OF FEVERSHAM* (1592); *Fair Em, the Miller's Daughter of Manchester* (1593); *MUCEDORUS* (1598); *THE MERRY DEVIL OF EDMONTON* (1608); and *The Birth of Merlin*, printed as late as 1662 and attributed to WILLIAM ROWLEY and Shakespeare.

Attempts are still occasionally made to attach Shakespeare's name to further unassigned plays of the period, but they rarely achieve much conviction and are more often rationalizations of preconceived conclusions than impartial enquiries. *The Double Falsehood, or, The Distressed Lovers* (1728) should probably be added to the core of plays whose attribution is more than fanciful. It is either what it claims to be, namely a thorough reworking for the 18th-century theatre, undertaken by LEWIS THEOBALD, of a play by Shakespeare and Fletcher known to us only by its title, *Cardenio*, or an entire fabrication by Theobald himself. Sufficient grounds exist for believing that the play is of Jacobean origin.

Shakespeare: performance and criticism After the Restoration in 1660 Shakespeare's plays were altered to suit new tastes and performance methods. Actresses superseded young men and boys in female roles, perspective scenery was used on stage. The interests of a more exclusive clientele were served. Some plays were radically revised: *The Tempest* acquired new characters, including Miranda's sister and a prince who has never seen a woman, together with more music and grander spectacular effects. In some plays, adaptation was less wholesale, achieved by omission rather than alteration. Critical response to Shakespeare valued energy in language and character but censured what were considered breaches of decorum in plots, imagery and characterization. DRYDEN, in *AN ESSAY OF DRAMATIC POESY* (1668) and other writings, expressed this mingled dispraise and celebration, crediting Shakespeare with the 'largest and most comprehensive soul' among the moderns. Less willing to admit extenuation was THOMAS RYMER, whose account of *Othello* insisted on standards of ideal, dignified discourse: the 'tragical part' of the play appeared 'plainly none other than a bloody farce without salt or savour'. The theatre still offered compromise. NAHUM TATE, having found *King Lear* 'a heap of jewels, unstrung and unpolished', restrung the dazzling disorder to provide a happy ending in which Lear and Gloucester are reprieved and Cordelia is united with Edgar. This denouement, and Tate's omission of the Fool, survived in stage practice up to the early 19th century.

The notion of Shakespeare as a natural genius with more or less pardonable faults was developed in the next century. The works were presented to readers in a succession of handsome and scholarly editions by POPE (1725), Hanmer (1743–4), Warburton (1747), JOHNSON (1765), CAPELL (1767–8), STEEVENS (1773 etc.), MALONE (1790, augmented by James Boswell the younger in 1821). These encouraged attention to Shakespeare's own (rather than his adapters') words. Pope, in the preface to his edition of the *Works*, describes him as 'not so much an imitator as an instrument of Nature'. In Johnson's preface he is the 'poet of nature' who 'holds up to his readers a faithful mirror of manners and life' and whose artistic failings should be forgiven if not imitated.

This confidence in Shakespeare's mimetic powers was reflected in a renewed emphasis on his characters. In the 1740s the actors DAVID GARRICK and Charles Macklin broke with an oppressively 'formal' manner of playing the tragic roles (represented in the Restoration period by Thomas Betterton and in the early 1700s by James Quin). At the same time the lan-

guage and structure of the plays gradually returned to the stage, although Garrick's acting texts included a *Romeo and Juliet* in which Juliet awakes in the tomb before Romeo expires (allowing a prolonged pathetic death-scene for both lovers) and a truncated *Taming of the Shrew*. Explorations of psychology – the display of the symptoms of the 'passions' – resulted in performances which impressed audiences as startlingly 'real', for example Macklin's new, serious (and villainous) Shylock and the jarred sensibilities of Garrick's Hamlet. The critic Maurice Morgann, defending his subject against charges of cowardice in an *Essay on the Dramatick Character of Falstaff* (1777), established a precedent for elaborate reconstructions of a dramatic character's personality.

Romantic criticism confirmed Shakespeare's preeminence in modern literary culture. In various lectures between 1808 and 1819, in *BIOGRAPHIA LITERARIA* (1817) and elsewhere, COLERIDGE proclaimed his discovery of the characters as vividly individualized examples of human types. The 'organic regularity' of Shakespeare's characters and plots, distinguished from the 'mechanic regularity' of neoclassical drama, corresponded to the order of nature in exhibiting 'a law in which all the parts obey, conforming themselves to the outward symbols and manifestations of the essential principle'. Obscurities and compression in poetic language were beginning to be valued rather than condemned or merely condoned. WILLIAM HAZLITT's *Characters of Shakespeare's Plays* (1817), informed by experience of stage performances, described forcefully the aesthetic impact of dramatic characters. *TALES FROM SHAKESPEARE* (1807) by CHARLES LAMB and his sister Mary and THOMAS BOWDLER's notorious expurgation, *The Family Shakespeare* (1807 in 4 vols., 1818 in 10 vols.), helped to make the plays current in education and in middle-class family reading.

In the theatre of the early 1800s the actress Sarah Siddons and her brother John Philip Kemble imbued tragic roles with neoclassical grace and dignity, inspiring sensations of awe rather than intimacy. Kemble often achieved dignity at the expense of emotional power, but some of Siddons's performances were remarkable for psychological complexity. Her Lady Macbeth was both alluring and evil. In contrast with the statuesque effect of Kemble and Siddons, Edmund Kean's acting startled by its carefully prepared effects of sudden and intense emotion. Coleridge compared the audience's experience to that of reading Shakespeare 'by flashes of lightning'. Hazlitt described the 'fresh shocks of delight and surprise' afforded by the rapid transitions in his Shylock (1814). The more measured emotionalism of Kean's contemporary and successor William Charles Macready marked a transition to a recognizably Victorian cultivation of private, domestic feelings. Kemble's acting versions were closer than Garrick's to

The Shakespeare Monument in Poets' Corner, Westminster Abbey, London

the original texts, although they were still cut to remove indecencies and suit pictorial staging. Public taste now required costumes and settings that rendered the historical milieu of each play as accurately as possible. Satisfying the taste for historical pageantry was an expensive business, and the actor-managers who presented these shows were expected to dominate them with personal performances of great vigour into the bargain. In the 1840s to 1860s Shakespearean production in London was led by Charles Kean's management at the Princess's Theatre in Oxford Street and the more modest but energetic and idealistic enterprise of Samuel Phelps at Sadler's Wells in Islington. In the 1880s and up to World War I the providers of such 'traditional' Shakespeare were Henry Irving and Herbert Beerbohm Tree. Both were famous for their ability to make characters part of a striking stage-picture: one of the best examples of this was the moonlit scene in Irving's *Merchant of Venice* when Shylock returned alone to the house from which his daughter had just eloped.

In the 19th century editions began to cater for a variety of tastes and pockets: Charles Knight issued a *Pictorial Shakespeare* in parts between 1839 and 1842, providing a wealth of historical material and illustrations at a popular price; one-volume editions of the works were edited by Clark and Wright (the Globe, 1864), FURNIVALL (the Leopold, 1877) and Craig, whose 1891 Oxford edition remained in print well into the 1980s. More august scholarly enterprises were the edition by HALLIWELL, or Halliwell-Phillipps, (1853–65) and the New Variorum, begun by Furness in 1874. Cheap reprints of the plays proliferated, and the introduction of Shakespeare into the curriculum of the Board Schools created a market for editions annotated (and expurgated) for the use of pupils.

Victorian criticism focused mainly on character and dramatic effect. ANNA JAMESON's *Shakespeare's Heroines* (originally called *Characteristics of Women*, 1832) and the writings of the actress Helen Faucit offered sentimental accounts of the female characters. CARLYLE's *HEROES, HERO-WORSHIP AND THE HEROIC IN HISTORY* (1841) included a eulogy of Shakespeare as a type of the 'poet as hero', confirming him in the Romantic tradition of poets-as-legislators. Against this sentiment and celebration should be set a growth of interest in matters of chronology and attempts to find the dramatist's life in his art. SWINBURNE's *A Study of Shakespeare* (1880), which attempts to combine biography with hero-worship, has the distinction of being the worst book on Shakespeare by a major poet. Furnivall's energetic work as an editor and as founder of the New Shakspere [*sic*] Society was the basis of much scholarly and critical thinking in the later decades of the century. EDWARD DOWDEN, in *Shakspere: A Critical Study of his Mind and Art* (1875), traced the playwright's career as a struggle for self-mastery. His *Primer* (1877) made this construction of the biography current at all levels of education. The reverential manner that prevailed in Victorian writing on Shakespeare was challenged by GEORGE BERNARD SHAW, whose dramatic criticism for the *Saturday Review* includes several spirited hatchet-jobs on Shakespearean productions.

A. C. BRADLEY's *Shakespearean Tragedy* (1904), in some respects a culmination of Romantic preoccupations, also marks a change of attitude in its proposal of a secular, intellectually consistent tragic vision: it has been accused of turning the heroes into Victorian idealists. Although it centres the tragic ethos on individual characters, Bradley's work sets out a world-view bleaker and less sentimental than any offered in earlier criticism. The plays are treated as dramas in the manner of later 19th-century naturalism. Theatrical interpretation was moving away from what had come to seem cluttered scenic realism. William Poel's experiments with Elizabethan staging conventions, and the growth of scholarly interest in theatrical history joined the generally felt impulse to discover non-naturalistic modes of theatre. In HARLEY GRANVILLE-BARKER's productions of *Winter's Tale*, *Twelfth Night* and *A Midsummer Night's Dream* (1912–14) open staging, simplified stylized settings and full texts rapidly delivered revealed Shakespeare as a dramatist whose techniques had little in common with the quasi-operatic spectacle of most Victorian and Edwardian productions. Granville-Barker's example and the principles enunciated in his subsequent series of *Prefaces to Shakespeare* (1927–47) set standards for a new generation of interpreters working in the brisker schedules, tighter budgets and integrated ensembles of the repertory theatres. The new, non-commercial companies in the provincial cities and at the OLD VIC in London offered a greater variety of plays in simpler stagings and quicker succession than had been possible in the commercial actor-managers' theatre.

Criticism in the decades after Bradley extended awareness of Elizabethan literary as well as theatrical conventions. L. L. Schücking's *Character Problems in Shakespeare's Plays* (1919, translated 1922) and E. E. Stoll's *Art and Artfice in Shakespeare* (1933) were influential in displacing Romantic notions of characterization and dramatic method. Bernard Spivack's *Shakespeare and the Allegory of Evil* (1958) reached back into earlier dramatic and literary works to establish a non-naturalistic system of significance underlying such characters as Iago and Richard III. Bradley's mode of speculation on character had been challenged on other grounds by F. R. LEAVIS and by L. C. KNIGHTS, whose 'How Many Children Had Lady Macbeth?' (1933; reprinted in *Explorations*, 1946) provided a catch-phrase for anti-Bradleyans. The discipline of editorial experience informed JOHN DOVER WILSON's teasing out of plot and characterization in *What Happens in Hamlet* (1935). The poetic texture of the plays was investigated by Caroline Spurgeon (*Shakespeare's Imagery*, 1935) and, more subtly, Wolfgang Clemen (*The Development of Shakespeare's Imagery*, 1936; revised and translated, 1951). Studies by G. WILSON KNIGHT (notably *The Wheel of Fire*, 1930, on the tragedies) focused on verbal imagery and patterning. This important shift of emphasis, together with the example of the NEW CRITICISM and WILLIAM EMPSON's explorations of ambiguity and wordplay, helped to establish a way of reading the plays as poems that characterized much post-1945 criticism. A parallel development was the historical study of 'background', exemplified in Hardin Craig's *The Enchanted Glass* (1936) and E. M. W. TILLYARD's construction of a 'world picture' which the plays (especially the histories) were held to set forth. Tillyard's *Shakespeare's History Plays* (1944), although rejected by many as proposing a simplified, conservative intention in the works, mapped out a field of study that would relate the plays to other, non-literary discourses of the period. A. P. Rossiter's essays, collected in *Angel with Horns* (1961), challenge the notion that the plays endorse the 'Tudor myth'.

Thinking on the comedies was given a new impetus by NORTHROP FRYE's formulation of an archetypal comic structure in *An Anatomy of Criticism* (1957) and the complementary thesis of C. L. Barber's *Shakespeare's Festive Comedy* (1959). The bleak outlook in Jan Kott's *Shakespeare, Our Contemporary* (1967) has influenced theatrical directors as well as readers; less abrasive, reflecting the more optimistic liberalism of the humanities in the 1960s, was Norman Rabkin's *Shakespeare and the Common*

Understanding (1967). A dominant feature of criticism in the 1970s – working alongside MARXIST CRITICISM and STRUCTURALISM – has been a renewed feminist interrogation of the texts, of which the work of Marilyn French, Coppelia Kahn and Irene Dash is representative.

Research into the conditions of Shakespeare's theatre, consolidated by the documentary labours of E. K. CHAMBERS, has resulted in work on the theatrical language of the plays (by J. L. Styan, Nevill Coghill, Bernard Beckerman and others). The use of the play metaphor in Shakespeare, set out concisely in Anne Barton's *Shakespeare and the Idea of the Play* (1969), has been pursued by many critics and directors. Another kind of stage-centred scholarship concentrates on the plays' stage-life in the centuries since Shakespeare: A. C. Sprague's *Shakespeare and the Actors* (1944) described points of interpretation using prompt-books and reports of performances in a manner that set the standard for many later studies. Investigations of the biographical evidence, although no longer widely accepted as a route into the interpretation of the plays, were set in order by Chambers's magisterial *William Shakespeare: A Study of the Facts and Problems* (1930) and have been brought up to date by Samuel Schoenbaum, in *William Shakespeare: A Documentary Life* (1975). The same author's *Shakespeare's Lives* (1971) provides an amusing and comprehensive account of the history of Shakespeare biography.

Editions of the plays published since the turn of the century have reflected changes in bibliographical theory and the development of English studies in higher education. The Arden edition (1899–1924) was superseded by the New Arden (1951–) and a Cambridge edition known as the New Shakespeare (1921–62) is being replaced by a New Cambridge (1984–). Paperback editions have included the original Penguin series (1937–59), a breakthrough in popular publishing followed by the Pelican (1956–67), the American Signet (1963–) and the New Penguin (1967–). Oxford University Press's editions of individual plays (1982–), the New Cambridge Shakespeare and the New Arden editions have also appeared in paperback. Important one-volume editions of the complete *Works* are Peter Alexander's (1951), and the American Riverside (1974). A new Oxford edition (1986) offers two versions (rather than a conflated text) of *Lear* and includes the newly attributed poem 'Shall I Die...?'.

After Granville-Barker, Shakespearean production in Britain has been characterized by diversity of style: it would be hard to identify a 'tradition'. Directorial practice ranged from the scholarly but enterprising Elizabethanism of Robert Atkins to the cheery, trenchant iconoclasm of Tyrone Guthrie. Between the wars a number of leading Shakespearean actors and actresses established themselves, but their personal styles were diverse: John Gielgud, Laurence Olivier, Ralph Richardson and Peggy Ashcroft worked on occasion with each other, with various directors and in a number of different companies. In the 1940s an actor-manager of the old kind emerged in Donald Wolfit. The parallel institutions of the Old Vic in London and the Memorial Theatre in Stratford were developed (with the advent of state subsidy) into the ROYAL NATIONAL THEATRE and the ROYAL SHAKESPEARE COMPANY. Laurence Olivier's management of the National (Old Vic, 1964–74) began with an unexciting *Hamlet*, but went on to achieve critical acclaim with an all-male *As You Like It* and Franco Zeffirelli's *Romeo and Juliet*. Olivier himself appeared in *Othello* and in Jonathan Miller's production of *The Merchant of Venice*. Neither company can be said currently to offer a 'house style' for Shakespeare, although the RSC's cycle *The Wars of the Roses* (1963–4) set new standards in the presentation of the history plays. A marriage of sorts was arranged between Brechtian epic theatre and a renewed awareness of Elizabethan staging conditions. The scale and breadth of mainstage Stratford productions has been challenged lately by more intimate stagings by other companies. The RSC's own studio work has contributed to this movement: a powerful impression was made by Trevor Nunn's *Macbeth* (1974) and Buzz Goodbody's *Hamlet* (1975). Peter Brook, a *Wunderkind* in the late 1940s and 1950s and now more of a guru, achieved world-wide success with his *Titus Andronicus* (with Olivier, 1956) and *A Midsummer Night's Dream* (RSC, 1970). Mention should also be made of the 'offshoots' in which modern dramatists have reworked Shakespearean material, either in direct confrontation with the originals (e. g. Charles Marowitz's *Hamlet* and other plays) or in order to capitalize on received ideas about characters and circumstances (ARNOLD WESKER's *The Merchant*; EDWARD BOND's *Lear*). Some stage versions have hovered between interpreting and revising the plays: Brecht's *Coriolanus* is a famous example.

Shakespeare's plays attracted film-makers from the earliest days of commercial cinema. The first 'talkie' based on Shakespeare was *The Taming of the Shrew* with Douglas Fairbanks and Mary Pickford (1929). In 1936 Max Reinhardt, who had staged the play many times in Europe and America, directed a Hollywood film version of *A Midsummer Night's Dream* with a cast including James Cagney as Bottom and Mickey Rooney as Puck. Olivier, as actor and director, made popular movies of *Henry V* (1944), *Hamlet* (1947) and *Richard III* (1955); Orson Welles filmed idiosyncratic versions of *Macbeth* (1948) and *Othello* (1950) and an epic compilation of Falstaffian episodes, *The Chimes at Midnight* (1965). Franco Zeffirelli's *The Taming of the Shrew* (1966), *Romeo and Juliet* (1968) and *Hamlet* (1990), Roman Polanski's *Macbeth* (1971) and Kenneth Branagh's *Henry V* (1989) have enjoyed great popularity. *Hamlet* (1964) and *King Lear* (1971) by the Russian director Grigori Kozintsev and Akira Kurosawa's Japanese versions of *Macbeth* (as *Throne of Blood*, 1957) and *Lear* (as *Ran*, 1984) have been widely acclaimed. Shakespeare's plays have been a regular feature of British radio broadcasting since the 1920s, although these productions have never enjoyed the attention lavished on such television adaptations as those included in the BBC's series covering the whole canon (1978–84).

A full survey of the transpositions of Shakespeare's work into the other arts would have to include graphic representations (especially the Shakespearean paintings so popular in the 19th century), music and writings inspired by the plays and poems. It seems prudent to restrict the present account to works offering to perform the plays in a new medium. Shakespearean operas may be said to date from the Restoration versions of *The Tempest* and, particularly, *A Midsummer Night's Dream* (as *The Fairy Queen*, 1692, with music by Purcell and a libretto by SETTLE). Incidental music – by, for example, Berlioz, Liszt, Tchaikovsky and Elgar – has sometimes been provided on such a scale as to turn the plays into semi-operatic entertainments, while Mendelssohn's *Dream* music was for long almost inseparable from the play. Verdi's *Macbeth* (1847 and 1865) and *Otello* (1887) are vigorous, perceptive readings of the plays, and his last opera, *Falstaff* (1893), has a poetic quality not usually found in *The Merry Wives of Windsor*. A popular and likeable adaptation of the same work is Otto Nicolai's *Die lustigen Weiber von Windsor* (1849). Benjamin Britten's *A Midsummer Night's Dream* (1960) is considered by many to be the best Shakespeare opera since Verdi. Shakespeare has also been put to good account in musical comedy: Rodgers and Hart made *Comedy of Errors* into *The Boys from Syracuse* (1938); Cole Porter's *Kiss Me, Kate* (1948) is about the tribulations of actors touring with *The Taming of the Shrew*; and in *West Side Story* (1957) Leonard Bernstein and Jerome Robbins transposed the story of *Romeo and Juliet* to New York. Choreographers as well as composers have found inspiration in the plays, with results that range from the brief psychodramas of Robert Helpmann's *Hamlet* (1948) and Jose Limon's *The Moor's Pavane* (1949) to the lavish full-length *Romeo and Juliet* ballets using Sergei Prokofiev's score (1938). *The Taming of the Shrew* was made into a ballet by John Cranko (1969).

Shakespeare's *Sonnets* They were first printed in 1609 by George Eld for Thomas Thorpe. At least some were written earlier, for FRANCIS MERES's *Palladis Tamia* (1598) spoke of Shakespeare's 'sugared sonnets' circulating among his friends, and versions of 138 and 144 appeared in *THE PASSIONATE PILGRIM* (?1599). Since the 1590s saw a great English vogue for the sonnet, initiated by SIDNEY's sequence *ASTROPHIL*

AND STELLA, it is likely that Shakespeare wrote most of his sonnets before 1600. They are dedicated to 'Mr W. H.', the 'only begetter' of the poems. His identity and whether he is to be identified with the youth addressed in the sonnets is still a matter for debate, which is sometimes only tangentially relevant to the sonnets themselves. Henry Wriothesley, Earl of Southampton, and William Herbert, Earl of Pembroke, have long been popular as candidates for Mr W. H. and also for the youth in the sonnets, who is apparently aristocratic. Similar, and even less successful, attempts have been made to identify the so-called 'Dark Lady' who is the troublesome and unfaithful mistress of the later sonnets, and the 'Rival Poet' of such poems as sonnet 86.

It is uncertain whether the order of the 1609 quarto is authorial. Attempts have been made at rearrangement, but Thomas Thorpe's order remains the usual one. As the sequence of sonnets stands, it falls into two sections: 1–126 are concerned mainly with the youth and 127–154 mainly with the mistress. Shakespeare's sonnets do not even have the barely suggested narrative lines of *Astrophil and Stella* and SPENSER's *AMORETTI*, but it is just possible to glimpse the poet's love for a young man, whom he initially persuades to marry and beget children, and promises to immortalize, and who is then seduced by the poet's mistress. Within the larger divisions of poems to the youth and to the mistress smaller groups of poems can be identified. Sonnets 1–7 urge the youth to marry as a means of immortality. Their theme and poetic imagery may be summed up by a line from ERASMUS's *Education of the Christian Prince:* 'He does not die who leaves behind a living image of himself.' This image, even in the later poems of this first section, becomes the image created by poetry, and the theme is fully expressed at the end of sonnet 18, the famous 'Shall I Compare Thee to a Summer's Day', in the triumphant assertion 'So long as men can breathe or eyes can see,/ So long lives this, and this gives life to thee.' The poet offers his poetry as a means of immortality for both the youth and himself. The sonnets up to 126 record the oscillations in the relationship between poet and youth: 33–42 tell of a temporary estrangement and then reconciliation. The promises of immortality have to contend with the threat of change and time and 65 is one of the many poems dwelling on 'sad mortality'. Others speak of the discrepancy between the poet's age and the friend's youth. In some poems from 97 onwards we hear of the poet's absence from the youth. The poems to the youth dwell on the great Renaissance themes of friendship, love, death, change and immortality and the relationship of the poet's art to all of these. Sonnet 116, 'Let Me Not to the Marriage of True Minds', bravely asserts that 'Love's not Time's fool', but it is untypical in its unshaken faith in the permanence of affection. 126, a truncated sonnet of only 12 lines, may be intended as a conclusion to the first group.

The rest of the sonnets are mainly about the poet's relationship with the mistress. Sonnet 130, 'My Mistress' Eyes are Nothing Like the Sun', parodies the excessive hyperbole of sonneteering conventions. Many of these poems are bitter about the mistress's infidelity and some express disgust at sexual activity with bawdy quibbles (135 puns relentlessly on 'will' and 129 describes lust as 'Th'expense of spirit in a waste of shame').

WORDSWORTH in a sonnet about sonnets thought that 'with this key/ Shakespeare unlocked his heart' and LYTTON STRACHEY talked of the mystery of the sonnets, both anticipating the desire of many readers to find a biographical key to the poems. Wordsworth elsewhere found the sonnets to the lady 'abominably harsh, obscure and worthless', but COLERIDGE thought better of the sonnets as a whole and enthusiastically recommended them to his son. This century has been more attentive to the poetry than the supposed biography and few now could agree with HAZLITT that if we had only Shakespeare's poems he would be regarded as a cold and artificial writer. Although, as W. H. AUDEN observed, not all the sonnets are of the same excellence, the very finest of them would alone have assured Shakespeare of that immortality which is one of the sonnets' constant themes.

Shamela Andrews, An Apology for the Life of Mrs See PAMELA and FIELDING, HENRY.

Shange, Ntozake 1948– Black American playwright, novelist and poet. She was born Paulette Williams in Trenton, New Jersey, and educated at Barnard College. She is best known for her first play, *For Colored Girls Who Have Considered Suicide/ When the Rainbow is Enuf*(1976), in which women recount their life experiences in individual recitations. Subsequent works, showing her interest in merging poetry, music and dancing, include *A Photograph: A Still Life with Shadows/A Photograph: A Study of Cruelty* (1977; revised as *A Photograph: Lovers-in-Motion*, 1979), *Spell #7* (1978), *From Okra to Greens* (1978), *Boogie Woogie Landscapes* (1980) and *Betsey Brown* (with Emily Mann and Baikida Carroll; 1991), a rhythm-and-blues musical based on her 1985 novel. Other fiction includes *Sassafrass: A Novella*(1977) and her first novel, *Sassafrass, Cypress and Indigo* (1982). *Nappy Edges* (1978) and *A Daughter's Geography* (1983) are volumes of poems.

Shapcott, Thomas (William) 1935– Australian poet, novelist, writer of CHILDREN'S LITERATURE and critic. Born in Brisbane, he served as director of the Literature Board from 1983 to 1990. An early commitment to poetry produced several award-winning vol-

umes, *Time on Fire*(1961), *A Taste of Salt Water*(1967) and *Inward towards the Sun*(1969), as well as *Sonnets 1960–1963*(1964), *The Mankind Thing*(1964), *Fingers at the Air*(1969), *The Seven Deadly Sins*(1970), *Begin with Walking*(1972), *Shabby Town Calendar*(1975), *Seventh Avenue Poems*(1976), *Turning Full Circle* (1979), *Welcome!*(1983) and *Travel Dice*(1987). *Selected Poems 1956–1988*(1989) is the best introduction to the range of a poet committed both to traditional and experimental forms. In the 1980s he turned to fiction. *Flood Children*(1981) and *The Birthday Gift*(1982) are novels, *Limestone and Lemon Wine*(1988) is a volume of stories, while *The White Stag of Exile*(1984) and *The Search for Galina*(1989) are experimental narratives, the latter combining poetry with prose. *Holiday of the Icon*(1984), *Mr Edmund*(1990) and *His Master's Ghost*(1990) are for children. As an editor, he has tried to define the direction of Australian verse in a succession of influential anthologies stretching from *New Impulses in Australian Poetry* (with Rodney Hall; 1968) to *Consolidation: The Second Paperback Poets Anthology* (1981). He has also published *Biting the Bullet: A Literary Memoir*(1990).

Shapiro, Karl 1913– American poet and critic. Born in Baltimore and educated at the University of Virginia and Johns Hopkins, he served in the US Army in 1941–5. After publishing *Poems* (1935) he was anthologized in *Five Young American Poets*(1941), but it was *Person, Place, and Thing* (1942) which brought him to the attention of a wider public. *V-Letter and Other Poems* (PULITZER PRIZE, 1944) treats his war-time experiences, while later volumes such as *Poems 1940–1953*(1953), *The House*(1957) and *Poems of a Jew* (1958) are often caustic and iconoclastic in tone and written in tight, disciplined verse. The Whitmanesque prose paragraphs of *The Bourgeois Poet* (1964) announced a change, though *White-Haired Lover* (1968) and *Adult Bookstore* (1976) returned to more traditional forms, notably the SONNET. He has also written two plays and a work of fiction, *Edsel* (1971), and embarked on a projected three-volume autobiography with *The Younger Son* (1988) and *Reports of My Death* (1990). His critical works include *English Prosody and Modern Poetry* (1947), *Beyond Criticism* (1953; reissued in 1965 as *A Primer for Poets*), *In Defense of Ignorance* (1960), *The Writer's Experience* (with RALPH ELLISON; 1964), a study of RANDALL JARRELL (1967), *To Abolish Children and Other Essays* (1968) and *The Poetry Wreck: Selected Essays 1950–1970* (1975); with Louis Untermeyer and RICHARD WILBUR he edited *Modern American and Modern British Poetry*(1955). He edited the magazine *POETRY* from 1950 to 1956 and has taught at the universities of Wisconsin, California at Berkeley, Nebraska and Illinois at Chicago Circle, among other institutions. In addition to the Pulitzer

Prize, he has also won the Shelley Memorial Award for Poetry and the Bollingen Prize.

Sharp, Cecil J. See FOLK REVIVAL.

Sharp, William 1855–1905 Scottish poet, novelist and biographer, and author of works as Fiona Macleod. Born in Paisley, he attended Glasgow University but left without a degree, travelling to Australia instead. After his arrival in London in 1878 he soon became a member of the circle of artists and writers centred on DANTE GABRIEL ROSSETTI and a regular contributor to literary journals. He published hack biographies of Rossetti (1882), SHELLEY (1887), Heine (1888) and ROBERT BROWNING (1890) and introduced popular editions of poetry. His novels included *The Sport of Chance* (1888) and *The Children of Tomorrow* (1889) and his volumes of poetry *The Human Inheritance, The New Hope, Motherhood and Other Poems* (1882), *Earth's Voices* (1884), *Romantic Ballads and Poems of Phantasy* (1888) and *Sospiri di Roma* (1891). In later years he also wrote rhapsodic verse and prose romances on Celtic themes, represented as being by Fiona Macleod (see also CELTIC REVIVAL). They include *Pharais* (1894), *The Mountain Lovers* (1895), *The Sin-Eater and Other Tales* (1895), *The Washer of the Ford* (1895) and a collection of articles, *The Winged Destiny* (1904). More than a pseudonym, Fiona Macleod was a second literary personality whose identity with himself he kept a closely guarded secret. A much-travelled man, Sharp died in Sicily.

Shaughraun, The A MELODRAMA by DION BOUCICAULT, first performed at Wallack's Theatre, New York, in 1874 with Boucicault in the title-role of Conn the Shaughraun.

Robert Ffolliott, a convicted Fenian, has escaped from Australia with the help of the feckless but charming Conn. He returns to Ireland to visit his sweetheart Arte O'Neal before embarking for America. Betrayed by his villainous 'friend' Kinchela, Robert is regretfully arrested by the English officer, Captain Molyneux, who has fallen in love with Robert's sister Claire. Once again Conn arranges his escape, but is shot during it. Conn's wake, hilariously observed by Conn himself, is a finely conceived scene, which leads to the final exposing of the villains. Robert Ffolliott is freed under a general pardon to Fenians, and the play ends with the promise of three weddings, Robert's to Arte, Molyneux's to Claire and Conn's to his sorely tried sweetheart Moya.

Shaw, George Bernard 1856–1950 Playwright, critic and novelist. Born in Dublin, where he worked for an estate agent after leaving school at 15, he went with his mother, a singer, to London in 1876. There he began a programme of voracious reading. An active interest in socialism was added to his love of music. He became a socialist in 1882 and in 1884 joined the Fabian Society, on whose Executive Committee he served for many years.

With the generous aid of WILLIAM ARCHER, whose interest in Ibsen he shared, Shaw obtained work as a journalist, becoming, as 'Corno di Bassetto', an outstanding music critic on *The Star* (1888–90) and then drama critic for THE SATURDAY REVIEW (1895–8). His trenchant articles on the contemporary theatre are collected in *Our Theatre in the Nineties* (3 vols., 1932). His first publications were novels, *Cashel Byron's Profession* (1886) and *An Unsocial Socialist* (1887); he returned to the form several times, most notably in the socio-political parable, *The Adventures of the Black Girl in Her Search for God* (1932).

From Shaw's friendship with William Archer came the suggestion that they should collaborate on writing a play. They never did, but *The Quintessence of Ibsenism* (1891) is as much a manifesto for Shaw's future work as a playwright as it is an advocacy of Ibsen's genius. WIDOWERS' HOUSES (1892), a vigorous attack on slum landlordism, was produced by J. T. Grein for the Independent Theatre Club. Like MRS WARREN'S PROFESSION (written 1893, first produced 1902) and *The Philanderer* (written 1893, first produced 1905), it was considered too strong to pass the censor and confined to private performance. *Arms and the Man* (1894), which wittily subverts the conventional view of male gallantry, was the first of Shaw's plays to be presented publicly. It was followed by *Candida* (1897), *The Devil's Disciple* (1897), *The Man of Destiny* (1897), *You Never Can Tell* (1899) and *Captain Brassbound's Conversion* (1900).

Known to the theatrical public as an *enfant terrible*, Shaw owed his emergence into fame to the seasons organized by HARLEY GRANVILLE-BARKER and J. E. Vedrenne at the ROYAL COURT THEATRE in 1904–7. They presented the first performances of *John Bull's Other Island* (1904), a provocative thrust at the Irish question, *How He Lied to Her Husband* (1904), MAN AND SUPERMAN (1905), MAJOR BARBARA (1905) and *Doctor's Dilemma* (1906). It was an unfamiliar experience for the theatre-going public to be drawn into intelligent debate and to encounter unpalatable truths, however beguilingly dressed. *Caesar and Cleopatra* (1907) maintained Shaw's growing reputation for mischief and iconoclasm, as did *Getting Married* (1908), *The Shewing Up of Blanco Posnet* (1909) – censured for blasphemy – *Misalliance* (1910), *Fanny's First Play* (1911), *Androcles and the Lion* (1913) and PYGMALION (1913). He contributed four of his most serious plays to the new theatre of the 1920s: HEARTBREAK HOUSE (1920), BACK TO METHUSELAH (1922), SAINT JOAN (1923) and *The Apple Cart* (1929). Of his later plays, the best include *Too True to be Good* (1932), *The Millionairess* (1936) and *In Good King Charles's Golden Days* (1939).

George Bernard
Shaw

His social, political and ethical opinions are on display in the wonderfully lively *Prefaces* to his published plays (collected in a single volume in 1934, with revisions and additions in 1938 and 1965), as well as in such studiously and vivaciously controversial works as *Common Sense about the War* (1914), *How to Settle the Irish Question* (1917), *The Intelligent Woman's Guide to Socialism and Capitalism* (1928, revised 1937) and *Everybody's Political What's What* (1944). His voluminous correspondence includes separately published exchanges with Ellen Terry (edited by C. St John, 1931), Mrs Patrick Campbell (edited by A. Dent, 1952), Granville-Barker (edited by C. B. Purdom, 1957) and the actress Molly Tompkins (edited by P. Tompkins, 1960). MICHAEL HOLROYD has written the authorized biography (1988–91).

She: *A History of Adventure* A novel by SIR HENRY RIDER HAGGARD, published in 1887.

Horace Holly, a Cambridge scholar who narrates the story, goes to Africa with his ward, Leo Vincey, on a quest to fulfil Leo's inherited duty to avenge his first ancestor, Kallikrates ('the beautiful-in-strength'), murdered by an unknown woman. After a brush with the dangerous Amahaggar tribe, they are conducted to the underground tombs of Kôr, ruled over by a mysterious queen who has the secret of eternal life: She-Who-Must-Be-Obeyed, or Ayesha. She cures Leo of fever and recognizes him as the reincarnation of Kallikrates, whom she murdered because he would not accept her love. She takes Leo and Holly to the Place of Life, an underground cavern where they may step into the Fire of Life and be made immortal. When Ayesha herself enters the Fire she becomes immeasurably old and then monkey-like before dying. The heroes regain the upper world of ordinary life, shattered and transformed by what they have experienced. They set out for Thibet (*sic*), where they hope to encounter Ayesha again.

The story has been interpreted mythically many times, notably by Jung, who cites it as the primary example of an 'extraverted' or ignorantly intuitive myth. In fact, it has close connections with the Cambridge school of mythography summed up in SIR JAMES FRAZER's *The Golden Bough*. Haggard wrote two sequels, *Ayesha* (1905) and *Wisdom's Daughter* (1923), both lacking the haunting power of the original.

She Stoops to Conquer: or, The Mistakes of a Night A comedy by OLIVER GOLDSMITH, first produced at COVENT GARDEN in 1773 and published the same year.

Mr and Mrs Hardcastle have a daughter, Kate, and Mrs Hardcastle has a son by a previous marriage, the oafish and dissolute Tony Lumpkin. Sir Charles Marlow has proposed a match between his son and Kate Hardcastle. Young Marlow and his friend Hastings accordingly make the journey to the Hardcastles' home in the country but, thanks to Tony Lumpkin's misdirections, arrive there believing it to be an inn. The scene is thus expertly laid for the comedy that follows. Young Marlow takes Kate to be a servant and falls in love with her; his mistake frees him of the inhibitions he normally feels in the presence of ladies. Kate's friend Constance Neville falls in love with Hastings; Mrs Hardcastle, who dotes on her son Tony and had intended him to marry Constance, is thoroughly displeased. Sir Charles Marlow's arrival puts everything to rights.

She Would If She Could The second of SIR GEORGE ETHEREGE's three comedies, first staged in 1668. Unlike his first, *THE COMICAL REVENGE* (1664), it has no heroic plot to contrast with the comic plot of sexual misadventures. It is, thus, a better model of what has come to be known as RESTORATION COMEDY. The characters divide into two groups, with the older trio showing less social and moral perception than the younger quartet. Sir Oliver Cockwood, his wife and Sir Joslin Jolley come to London, bringing with them Sir Joslin's two nieces, Ariana and Gatty, whose charms attract the attention of Courtall and Freeman, two young men-about-town. Determined to taste London's pleasures, the country visitors find their way to the Bear in Drury Lane, where they can both drink and dance. Assignations made there lead to the comic crises of the final act, which are resolved by the pairing up of the young lovers but no more than partially resolved for their elders, who return, not much wiser, to the country.

Sheffield, John, 3rd Earl of Mulgrave and 1st Duke of Buckingham and Normandy 1648–1721 Politician and poet. He was born in London and spent most of his flamboyant social and political life at court. His literary works include the *Essay on Satire* (?1680) and *Essay on Poetry* (1682), both published anonymously, a number of love lyrics, and several prose pieces. His reworking of SHAKESPEARE's *JULIUS CAESAR* into two plays, *Julius Caesar* and *Marcus*

Brutus, with additional love interest and diminished plebeian presence, was printed in the authorized edition of his *Works* (1723) prepared by his friend ALEXANDER POPE. He was a generous patron to DRYDEN, whose monument in Westminster Abbey he financed.

Shelley, Mary (Wollstonecraft) 1797–1851 Novelist and editor. The only daughter of WILLIAM GODWIN and MARY WOLLSTONECRAFT, who died a few days after her birth, she was brought up by her father and stepmother. At 16 she ran away to France and Switzerland with SHELLEY, marrying him in 1816 on the death of his wife Harriet. Her most famous work, *FRANKENSTEIN: or, The Modern Prometheus* (1818), was begun on Lake Geneva in the summer of 1816 as her contribution to a ghost-story competition devised by BYRON, Shelley and Byron's friend Polidori. In 1818 the Shelleys left England for Italy, where they remained until Shelley's death in 1822. Of their children only one, Percy Florence, survived infancy, and in 1823 Mary returned with him to England, where she devoted herself to his welfare and education and to her career as a writer. None of her later novels matched the power, originality, and mythical sweep of her legendary first work – both *Lodore* (1835) and *Faulkner* (1837) are little more than romantic pot-boilers – and when public taste began to move away from Byronic heroes and Trelawnyesque adventurers to the new realism of the young DICKENS, she gave up writing long fictions. Of more abiding interest, however, are: *Mathilde*, an unfinished novel begun in 1819 (published in 1959), which draws strongly on her relations with Godwin and Shelley; *Valperga* (1823), a romance set in 14th-century Italy which portrays the lovelessness and destructiveness of personal political ambition; and *The Last Man* (1826), a politically disillusioned and conservative vision of the end of human civilization, set in the 21st century. The image of Mary Shelley presented by the biographers suggests an intensely private, imaginatively exuberant, yet also emotionally withdrawn figure, whose political melancholy and strong religious faith are intriguingly at odds with the optimistic rationalism of her famous parents, and her poet husband's atheistic radicalism.

In addition to numerous short stories for popular periodicals, particularly *The Keepsake*, she produced several volumes of *Lives* for Lardner's *Cabinet Cyclopedia*, and the first authoritative edition of Shelley's poems, with a preface and valuable notes (4 vols., 1839). Her travelogue, *Rambles in Germany and Italy, in 1840, 1842 and 1843* (1844), was well received.

Shelley, Percy Bysshe 1792–1822 Poet. The elder son of Timothy (later Sir Timothy) Shelley, he was born at Field Place, near Horsham in Sussex. He attended Syon House Academy and Eton, where his independence of spirit eventually won him respect and the nickname 'Mad Shelley' was promoted to 'Eton Atheist'. While still at Eton, he privately published a GOTHIC NOVEL, *Zastrozzi* (1810). This was followed by poems written with his sister Elizabeth, published anonymously as *Original Poetry by Victor and Cazire* (1810) and another Gothic tale, *St Irvine: or, The Rosicrucian* (1811). At University College, Oxford, Shelley continued to read radical authors and adopted provocatively eccentric dress and behaviour. With Thomas Jefferson Hogg in spring 1811 he wrote and circulated a pamphlet, *The Necessity of Atheism*, almost the first open profession of atheism to be printed in England. Their refusal to answer questions from the college authorities resulted in their summary expulsion. This affair, and his elopement to Scotland in August 1811 with the 16-year-old Harriet Westbrook, caused a permanent break with his family. Shelley refused his father's demand for a public retraction of the pamphlet, solemnized his 'misalliance' in Edinburgh and renounced his inheritance in favour of a small annuity.

Three years of nomadic living followed. In York Shelley attempted to bring Harriet together with Hogg, and from time to time supplemented the household with other female friends. In the Lakes he found only SOUTHEY in residence, with whom he argued politics. He corresponded with WILLIAM GODWIN, alarming him by the revolutionary rhetoric of *An Address to the Irish People* (1812) and his *Proposals* for new kinds of reform associations. In Dublin he made speeches on the repeal of the Union and Catholic emancipation. *A Letter to Lord Ellenborough* (1812) defended the radical publisher Daniel Eaton. At Lynmouth in Devon, where he tried to set up a small community of free spirits, copies of the democratic broadsheet *A Declaration of Rights* were launched on the sea in bottles and flown across the Bristol Channel in patent Shelley fire balloons. The Shelleys left abruptly on discovering they were being watched by Home Office spies, and briefly set up house in Tremadoc, Wales, where he observed the labourers' living conditions during the harsh winter of 1812. The poetic harvest of this political and philosophical education was *QUEEN MAB* (1813), a work that brought him no immediate recognition.

In London the Shelleys became frequent visitors to Godwin, who became the poet's philosophical mentor and, before Shelley tired of him in 1820, received in return 'the amount of a considerable fortune'. THOMAS LOVE PEACOCK also became a close friend. The birth of a daughter, Ianthe, did not prevent the failure of Shelley's marriage in autumn 1813. The next year he fell in love with Mary (MARY SHELLEY), Godwin's 16-year-old daughter by MARY WOLLSTONECRAFT, and they eloped, accompanied at Shelley's invitation by Jane 'Claire' Clairmont, who was 15. A triangular relationship developed which endured

Percy Bysshe Shelley

until Shelley's death. The literary fruit of their Continental journey was an unfinished novella, *The Assassins* (1814), and their combined journal, later reworked by Mary Shelley and published as *History of a Six Weeks' Tour* (1817).

Back in England Shelley fell into financial difficulties, resolved in negotiations following his grandfather's death. Harriet gave birth to their second child, Charles, in November 1814 and the following spring Mary gave birth to a daughter, who died prematurely. Shelley and Mary took a cottage on the edge of Windsor Great Park where, in a more stable period, he wrote *ALASTOR* (1816). Its publication coincided with the birth of his favourite son, William. The summer of 1816 was spent with BYRON at Lake Geneva. Mary began *FRANKENSTEIN* and Shelley wrote two philosophical poems, the 'Hymn to Intellectual Beauty' and 'Mont Blanc'.

Shelley married Mary immediately after Harriet drowned herself in autumn 1816. He was taken up by LEIGH HUNT, who had given him his first favourable notice in *THE EXAMINER* and now introduced him to KEATS, HAZLITT and other members of their circle. At Marlow, where the family settled near Peacock in 1817, he wrote *An Address to the People on the Death of Princess Charlotte*, perhaps his finest political pamphlet, and worked on 'Laon and Cythna', published as *REVOLT OF ISLAM* (1818).

He left England in spring 1818 and spent the rest of his life in Italy, staying first at Lucca, Venice and Este, where he wrote *JULIAN AND MADDALO*, an exploration of his relations with Byron. The 'Stanzas Written in Dejection' belong to the winter at Naples; the 'Roman spring' of 1819 saw completion of the major part of *PROMETHEUS UNBOUND*. His registration in Naples as father of an illegitimate baby, Elena Adelaide Shelley, still puzzles his biographers. The death in Rome of his adored son 'Will-mouse' was a devastating blow. The now childless household settled in Tuscany, first near Livorno, then Florence and finally Pisa, which became more or less their permanent base until 1822.

Despite these difficulties the year from summer 1819 to summer 1820 was Shelley's most creative period. He completed the fourth act of *Prometheus Unbound* and wrote another drama, *THE CENCI* (August 1819). News of the Peterloo massacre inspired *The Mask of Anarchy* (September 1819), still perhaps the greatest poem of political protest in the language, though unpublished in his lifetime. The 'Ode to the West Wind' was written at a single sitting on 25 October 1819, shortly followed by his SATIRE on WORDSWORTH, *Peter Bell the Third*. The political ODES 'To Liberty' and 'To Naples' came in the spring of 1820, the vivid, personal *Letter to Maria Gisborne* in July and *The Witch of Atlas* in August, interspersed with smaller-scale propaganda poems, 'Young Parson Richards', 'Song to the Men of England' and 'Sonnet: England 1819', and such lyric poems as 'To a Skylark' and 'The Cloud'. Percy Florence Shelley was born in November 1819.

During the Pisan period (1820–1) he completed his remarkable political document, *A Philosophical View of Reform* (1820), the entertaining *Essay on the Devil*, *THE DEFENCE OF POETRY* and a sequence of exquisite short poems: 'To the Moon', 'The Two Spirits', 'The Aziola' and 'Evening: Ponte Al Mare, Pisa'. His BURLESQUE, *Swellfoot the Tyrant*, was published in 1820. News of Keats's death produced *ADONAIS* in spring 1821. The absence of Claire left him susceptible to a platonic affair with Teresa Viviani, an heiress immured in a convent by her father. *Epipsychidion* (1821) was the reward of Shelley's self-restraint on this occasion.

At Shelley's encouragement Byron moved to Pisa in winter 1821. Together they formed the centre of a circle which included Jane and Edward Williams, EDWARD TRELAWNY and a colourful assortment of exiles, expatriates and adventurers. Shelley translated scenes from Goethe's *Faust* and wrote his last completed verse drama, *Hellas*, to raise money in England for the Greek war of independence. It was published in 1822. March saw the abandonment of *Charles I*, a drama of the Civil War.

After the breakup of the Pisa group the Shelleys moved to the village of Lerici on the Bay of Spezia. Shelley assumed responsibility for Claire, distraught at Byron's news of the death of their daughter, Allegra. He began his last major poem, *The Triumph of Life*, and composed a sequence of short lyrics for Jane Williams: 'The Keen Stars are Twinkling', 'When the Lamp is Shattered' and the sad 'Lines Written in the Bay of Lerici'. It was also a time of nightmares and premonitory visions. In July 1822 Leigh Hunt reached Livorno to assume editorship of a new journal, *THE LIBERAL*. On the way back from meeting him, Shelley, Edward Williams and their boatboy were drowned in the Bay of Spezia. Shelley's body was cremated on the beach at Viareggio in the presence of Byron, Trelawny and Hunt.

Two collections appeared after his death: *Poetical Pieces* (1823) and *Posthumous Poems* (1824). Mary Shelley's four-volume edition of *The Poetical Works* was published in 1839, an undertaking whose criteria of inclusion were partly influenced by Sir Timothy Shelley, who began the family's attempt to repair his son's tarnished image.

Shelley's colourful life and his achievements as a lyric poet have until recently obscured the central aspects of his art. He drew no essential distinction between poetry and politics. His work continues and revitalizes the radical tendencies of earlier Romantic writing, expanding its critique of social injustice into an attack on specific institutions of oppression. Anticipating the early Marx, Shelley portrayed law and religion as ideological functions of the state, and imaged the growth of capitalist relations of production in terms of its mechanical suppression of the spontaneous growth of human personality. The revolutionary optimism of his great visionary poems is wrung from a painful consciousness of the moral, psychological and historical dimensions of social and political bondage. Taken as a whole, his work represents a decidedly materialist inflection of the Romantic dream of the fusion of poetry and life. He was fascinated by the emancipatory potential of science, and his mythical dramas abound in images of space travel, flight and technologically achieved leisure.

The infelicities of his lesser writing have been carefully rehearsed: excessive rhetoric, abstractionism and the lurking arrogance and emotional chilliness of the poetic voice. Of increasing interest to modern Shelleyans are what might be called the creative contradictions of his work: the tantalizing ambiguity of certain key myths, ideas and images, and the persistence of philosophical idealism in his political thought. Recent criticism has produced a more differentiated view of Shelley, for so long perhaps the least read of English Romantic poets.

Shenstone, William 1714–63 Landscape gardener and poet. Born at Halesowen, Worcestershire, Shenstone was educated at a dame school, Halesowen Grammar School and then by a tutor, proceeding to Pembroke College, Oxford, where he was a contemporary of SAMUEL JOHNSON. He did not take a degree. Much of his verse has been properly forgotten; his best-known work, described by THOMAS GRAY as 'excellent of its kind and masterly', was *The Schoolmistress* (1742), a revised version of a poem which had appeared in a privately published collection when he had been at Oxford and which he had made every effort to suppress. His major achievement was as a landscape gardener. On the death of his guardian in 1745 he bought the Leasowes and thereafter spent most of his income in efforts to beautify the site. It became a famous showpiece of the PICTURESQUE style, enthusiastically described by DODSLEY in the three-volume posthumous collection of Shenstone's works (1764–9). Johnson's account in his *LIVES OF THE POETS* is disdainful and HORACE WALPOLE summed Shenstone up as a man who 'had much more fame than his talents entitled him to'. His friend RICHARD GRAVES edited a volume of *Recollections* (1788).

Shepard, E(rnest) H(oward) 1879–1976 Illustrator. Born in London, the son of an architect, he studied at the Royal Academy, having begun drawing and painting as a small child. He started contributing cartoons to *PUNCH* in 1907 and maintained the association for the next 50 years. His fame as a children's illustrator was established by his work for A. A. MILNE's quartet of Christopher Robin and Winnie-the-Pooh books (1924–8). Even more successful were his illustrations for a new edition of KENNETH GRAHAME's *WIND IN THE WILLOWS* in 1931, his fine line, liberal use of space and telling eye for detail doing much to make this classic even more accessible to young readers. In later life Shepard was persuaded to add colour to some of these illustrations, but he is best remembered for the original black-and-white drawings.

Shepard, Sam 1943– American playwright, screenwriter and film actor. He was born Samuel Shepard Rogers in Sheridan, Illinois, and raised and educated in California. The more than 40 plays he has produced since *Cowboys* (1964) have established him as a leader of the *avant-garde* theatre as well as perhaps the most critically acclaimed contemporary American playwright. His work has dealt with the myth of the West, the death and betrayal of the American dream, the travail of the family and the search for roots in an eclectic, volatile, sometimes undisciplined fashion which makes it hard to classify but uniquely American and contemporary. Major works include: *La Turista* (1966); *The Tooth of Crime* (1972), a rock-drama written during his four years' residence in London; *Curse of the Starving Class* (1976), *Buried Child* (1979) and *True West* (1980), a trilogy exploring the relationship of Americans to their land, their family and their history; *Fool for Love* (1979); *A Lie of the Mind* (1985); and, after a theatrical silence of several years, *The States of Shock* (1991), an ambiguous look at post-Vietnam America. His screenplay for *Paris, Texas* won the Golden Palm Award at the 1985 Cannes Film Festival. The films in which he has appeared as an actor include his own *Fool for Love*.

Shepard, Thomas 1605–49 American Puritan minister. He was born in Towcester and educated at Emmanuel College, Cambridge. Following his ordination he served as occasional lecturer at Earles-Colne in Essex until 1630, when he was silenced by Archbishop LAUD for his Puritan leanings and accepted a position as private tutor and chaplain to Sir Richard Darley of Buttercrambe. In 1632 he moved to Hedden, where Bishop Morton of Durham denied him the privilege of public preaching, which drove him to Massachusetts Bay in 1635.

Although Shepard lived only 14 years in New England, he exerted a powerful influence on the Puritan experiment. Between 1636 and 1637 alone, he was appointed pastor of the prestigious church at Newton (Cambridge), convinced his friend John Harvard to locate his college there, married the daughter of THOMAS HOOKER, and played a key role in the Cambridge Synod of 1637 which condemned Antinomianism. His exploration of the stages leading to conversion, *The Sincere Convert* (1641), soon became the most widely read formulation of the theory of preparation. Two of his other tracts, *Theses Sabbaticae* (1649) and *Church Membership of Children and Their Right to Baptism* (1663), demonstrate his contribution to the central ecclesiastical debates of American Congregationalism. Although known as a rigorous theologian and ardent pastor, Shepard tempered his religious conviction with empathy for the common Puritan's struggle with spiritual truths, as is testified to by his sermons, most notably those collected in *The Parable of the Ten Virgins Opened and Applied* (1660) and by his autobiography (first published in 1747 as *Three Valuable Pieces, Viz., Select Cases Resolved; First Principles of the Oracles of God;... ; And a Private Diary; Containing Meditations and Experiences Never Before Published*).

Shepheardes Calender, The EDMUND SPENSER's first important work was published pseudonymously as by Immerito (unworthy) in 1579. Subsequent editions in 1581, 1586, 1591 and 1597 testify to its great popularity. Its importance was hailed by E. K. (perhaps Edward Kirke), the author of a commentary accompanying the poems. It is one of the few significant works of 16th-century English poetry that SIDNEY can point to in his *APOLOGY FOR POETRY*, written at about the same time as the publication of *The Shepheardes Calender*. The classic models for Spenser were the *Idylls* of Theocritus and Virgil's *Eclogues:* more recent Continental models were provided by the French poet Marot and the Italian Mantuan. *The Shepheardes Calender* expresses a typically pastoral constant regret for lost golden ages – of purity in love, poetry, morality and religion – and a consequent 'satirical bitterness' about contemporary failings. It consists of twelve poems, one for each month of the year, beginning and ending in winter, with Colin Clout's complaints in January and December. The other months contain dialogues between shepherds concerning love, poetry and religious affairs; April contains a panegyric of Eliza, queen of shepherds (Elizabeth I), November is an elegy on Dido ('some maiden of great blood'), and October contemplates the profession and responsibilities of the poet. In October Piers encourages Cuddie to turn from pastoral poetry to sing of wars, jousts and knights. As E. K. points out in his introduction, pastoral was regarded as a literary genre where, following the example of Virgil, poets might test their 'tender wings' before the higher flights of epic: thus, in some sense, *The Shepheardes Calender* is a prologue to Spenser's FAERIE QUEENE.

Shepherd's Calendar, The A cycle of poems by JOHN CLARE, completed in 1823, first published in 1827, and republished from the original manuscripts in 1964 (ed. E. Robinson and G. Summerfield). Perhaps the most widely read of his longer poems, it is the work in which Clare first succeeded in developing his own distinctive PASTORAL idiom, ignoring the well-meaning but misplaced advice of LAMB to aim for the 'true rustic style' of THOMSON and GOLDSMITH. Clare's rural 'realism' – his use of dialect words and the peasant vernacular of his native parish of Helpston, the proliferating detail and extraordinary concreteness of his observation of seasonal changes in nature, his insider's eye for the unromantic harshness of agricultural labour, and his criticism of enclosing farmers and 'tyrant justice' on the land – failed to win the approval of his London publisher, who pruned the text as a whole to half its original length, corrected Clare's idiosyncratic grammar, and introduced punctuation.

Shepherd's Life, A: *Impressions of the South Wiltshire Downs* W. H. HUDSON's account of life around Salisbury Plain before the automobile age, published in 1910.

Hudson's observations of the wildlife of the country, both flora and fauna, together with his arresting stories about dogs, in themselves make the book worth reading; but the recollections of a shepherd in addition make it a classic of country life from about 1840 to the first years of the 20th century. The shepherd, Caleb Bawcombe, is in his eighties and from early boyhood has tended his master's flocks on the downs; he would not wish for a different life if one were offered him. He trained his sheepdogs, his only company, to the level of almost human response. It is chiefly from Caleb's memories that the vivid parade of human characters is drawn – the villagers and gyp-

sies, employers of every quality from good to tyrannical and greedy, and deer stealers, poachers, and machine wreckers. The author's wrath is aroused most by gamekeepers, to whom everything is subordinate to the care of pheasants and game birds, which are reared with extravagant care so that they may be destroyed.

Shepherd's Week, The A series of six poems by JOHN GAY, published in 1714. Partly designed to parody the work of AMBROSE PHILIPS, these witty pieces are at once mock-classical and realistic. In Gay's version of PASTORAL, rustic conditions are grubby, superstitious, fractious and exhausting as well as endearing and amorous; the myth of the Golden Age of past innocence is replaced instead by real, sunburnt, lustful, sweating peasants.

Sheridan, Frances 1724–66 Novelist and playwright. The mother of RICHARD BRINSLEY SHERIDAN, she was born Frances Chamberlaine in Dublin and married the actor-manager Thomas Sheridan in 1747. They went to London in 1754 when his enterprises failed and she met SAMUEL RICHARDSON, at the height of his success; he read her unpublished novel *Eugenia Adelaide* (it finally appeared posthumously in 1791) and encouraged her to continue writing. She launched her career as a novelist with the popular *Memoirs of Miss Sidney Biddulph: Extracted from Her Own Journal* (1761), heavily influenced by Richardson's PAMELA. The narrator endures such agonies of love and jealousy that SAMUEL JOHNSON questioned the author's right to make her readers suffer so much. A sequel recounting Miss Biddulph's further tribulations, *Continuation of the Memoirs*, appeared in 1767, the same year that another novel, *The History of Nourjahad*, was published. Three plays, *The Discovery* (1763), *The Dupe* (1764) and *A Trip to Bath* (1765), were produced at DRURY LANE (*The Discovery* by DAVID GARRICK) but were not published until 1902.

Sheridan, Richard Brinsley 1751–1816 Playwright. He was born in Dublin, where his father, Thomas, was manager of the Smock Alley Theatre. His mother, FRANCES SHERIDAN, achieved fame as a novelist and playwright, and Thomas himself was the author of one of the age's most influential books on rhetoric and acting, *Lectures on Elocution* (1762). They sent their son to Harrow, intending him for the law, but Sheridan became romantically and gallantly involved with the young singer Elizabeth Linley, on whose behalf he fought two duels. The couple married, to the accompaniment of scandalous interest, in 1773, and set up home in London. They had met in Bath, the setting for Sheridan's first play, THE RIVALS (1775). After its stumbling opening night at COVENT GARDEN, Sheridan rewrote sections of the play, and it became a favourite with contemporary audiences. Its success loosened Sheridan's pen, and two other pieces were produced in 1775, a FARCE called *St Patrick's Day: or, The Scheming Lieutenant* and a comic opera, with music by his father-in-law Thomas Linley, *THE DUENNA*.

Impulsively committed to the theatre, Sheridan bought a share in DRURY LANE in 1776, and wrote all his remaining work for performance there. The best of it appeared before the end of 1779: *A Trip to Scarborough* (1777), a softening of VANBRUGH's *THE RELAPSE*; *THE SCHOOL FOR SCANDAL* (1777), perhaps the finest of all 18th-century comedies; and *THE CRITIC* (1779), modelled on the DUKE OF BUCKINGHAM's *THE REHEARSAL*. Of his later work only *Pizarro* (1799), a bombastic version of the German play by the modish Kotzebue, matched the success of the work Sheridan produced in his twenties. The second half of his life, after his election to Parliament in 1780 and until his failure to secure a seat in 1812, was more notable politically than theatrically, although he maintained a major share in the management of Drury Lane until its burning in 1809. As a parliamentary speaker, he rivalled EDMUND BURKE and took a famous part in the impeachment of Warren Hastings in 1788–94.

Sherlock Holmes stories A total of four novels and 56 short stories by SIR ARTHUR CONAN DOYLE. They are not just the most famous and enduring contribution to DETECTIVE FICTION by any single writer, but also probably the most imitated, parodied and adapted literary works in the language.

Holmes and his colleague Dr Watson first appeared in a novel, *A Study in Scarlet*, published in *Beeton's Christmas Annual* for 1887. A second novel, *The Sign of Four* (1890), was commissioned by the American publisher Lippincott but Holmes did not reach a wide readership until Doyle began his short stories for *THE STRAND MAGAZINE* in July 1891, collected as *The Adventures of Sherlock Holmes* (1892) and *The Memoirs of Sherlock Holmes* (1894). In an attempt to free himself from his creation Doyle used the arch-villain Moriarty to kill Holmes off in the last story, 'The Final Problem', but the resulting public outcry eventually forced him to return to a subject which he increasingly saw as a distraction from his serious work. *The Hound of the Baskervilles* (1902) narrates an early case of the dead detective's, but 'The Adventure of the Empty House', at the beginning of *The Return of Sherlock Holmes* (1905), reveals how Holmes had in fact survived apparent death. Gratitude made readers willing to swallow the implausibility, and Holmes appeared in a further novel, *The Valley of Fear* (1915), and two more collections, *His Last Bow* (1917) and *The Case-Book of Sherlock Holmes* (1927).

Some of Holmes's idiosyncrasies and his scentific method were borrowed from Dr Joseph Bell, one of Doyle's teachers at Edinburgh University, but the literary model was EDGAR ALLAN POE's stories of Dupin. The brilliant but eccentric detective, the admiring friend who narrates the story, the cases which are puzzling and fantastic as much as sensationally criminal, the dramatically revealed solution at the end: all these are elaborated from the earlier writer. To them Doyle added distinctive touches of his own: a strong feeling for the atmosphere of late Victorian and Edwardian London; witty, comic dialogue between the leading figures; a subtle sense of the macabre; and a chivalric concern for justice and the unjustly oppressed. Such qualities are perhaps best displayed in the early short stories, particularly 'A Scandal in Bohemia', 'The Red-Headed League' and 'The Adventure of the Speckled Band'. Of the novels, *The Hound of the Baskervilles*, mainly set on Dartmoor, is the most firmly constructed.

In England the success of Sherlock Holmes owed something to Sidney Paget's illustrations, which firmly established in the public mind attributes of the great detective (the deerstalker hat, the meerschaum pipe) absent from or rarely mentioned in the text. In America the artist Frederic Dorr Steele took as his model WILLIAM GILLETTE, author of a MELODRAMA loosely derived from the stories, *Sherlock Holmes* (first performed in Buffalo in 1899). Gillette toured in the play for more than 30 years, the first of many actors to be identified with Holmes in various media – Basil Rathbone on film, Carleton Hobbs on radio and Peter Cushing, Douglas Wilmer and Simon Brett on television, being only a few of the most memorable examples.

Sherlock, Thomas 1678–1761 Churchman and theologian. Son of WILLIAM SHERLOCK, he was born in London and became Bishop of London in 1748 after having previously held the sees of Bangor and Salisbury. He made a reputation as a preacher and, while Master of the Temple (1704–53), opposed BENJAMIN HOADLY in the 'Bangorian controversy' (so called because both men had at different times occupied that bishopric). His exercise in Christian apologetics, *The Trial of the Witnesses of the Resurrection of Jesus* (1729), is his most notable published work. Sherlock was known for being athletic as well as studious, and his prowess at swimming made him the 'plunging prelate' of POPE's *DUNCIAD*.

Sherlock, William 1641–1707 Churchman and theologian. Born in Southwark and educated at Eton and Peterhouse, Cambridge, he became Master of the Temple, a post in which he was succeeded by his son, THOMAS SHERLOCK. He published *A Practical Discourse concerning Death* in 1689. During the Revolution which forced the abdication of James II he was a NONJUROR, but he took the oath to William and Mary in 1690. This change of mind and the book he published the same year, *A Vindication of the*

Doctrine of the Trinity and of the Incarnation, made him a target of criticism and his appointment as Dean of St Paul's in 1691 exposed him further. Sherlock suffered most from the witty attacks of ROBERT SOUTH, rector of Islip. MACAULAY admired his published sermons (1719).

Sherriff, R(obert) C(harles) 1896–1975 Playwright and screenwriter. Sherriff was born and educated at Kingston upon Thames and at New College, Oxford. His war service in the East Surrey Regiment provided some of the background for his most famous play, *JOURNEY'S END* (1928). Of Sherriff's other plays, only *Badger's Green* (1930) and the radio drama *The Long Sunset* (1955) have earned critical attention. His film credits include *The Invisible Man* (1933), *Goodbye Mr Chips* (1939), *Odd Man Out* (1947) and *The Dam Busters* (1955).

Sherwood, Mary Martha 1775–1851 Writer of CHILDREN'S LITERATURE. The daughter of a country clergyman, she taught religion to the poor before writing devotional stories and tracts for children. In 1803 she went out to India, where she began her celebrated novel *The History of the Fairchild Family* (1818), described on its title-page as 'A child's manual, being a collection of stories calculated to show the importance and effects of religious education'. But despite this pious intention, the three Fairchild children Lucy, Emily and Henry all quarrel, get into mischief and disobey their parents in quite human (and sometimes unintentionally entertaining) ways. In the most famous passage, where Mr Fairchild shows them a rotting corpse hanging on a gibbet as a warning against family disputes, flesh-creeping suspense mingles with the solemn warning in a way that many young readers found not unagreeable. Later Victorian editions played down this section, and today Mrs Sherwood is unread.

Sherwood, Robert E(mmet) 1896–1955 American playwright. He was born in New Rochelle, New York, and educated at Harvard. After graduating, he joined the Canadian army and was wounded in action in 1918. His war experiences led him to adopt an outspoken pacifist stance, evident in his first play, *The Road to Rome* (1927), a comedy about Hannibal's deferred march to Rome. *Idiot's Delight* (1936) won him the first of four PULITZER PRIZES. The advocacy of participation in a virtuous war in the late play, *There Shall be No Night* (1940; Pulitzer Prize 1941), marked a change of heart in a man who was by then serving as special assistant to the Secretary of War as well as writing many of President Roosevelt's speeches. His other plays include *The Queen's Husband* (1928), *Reunion in Vienna* (1931), *The Petrified Forest* (1935), *Abe Lincoln in Illinois* (1938; Pulitzer Prize 1939), *The Rugged Path* (1945) and *Small War on Murray Hill*

(1957). He also wrote screenplays, receiving an Academy Award for his screenplay for *The Best Years of Our Lives* (1946). *Roosevelt and Hopkins: An Intimate History* (1948; Pulitzer Prize 1949) is a political memoir.

Shiel, M(atthew) P(hipps) 1865–1947 Writer of DETECTIVE FICTION, fantasy and SCIENCE FICTION. Shiel was born in Montserrat in the West Indies; he went to London to study medicine but was absorbed instead into the literary world of the yellow 1890s. He wrote grotesque detective and horror stories in the collections *Prince Zaleski* (1895) and *Shapes in the Fire* (1896), before cashing in on the boom in future war stories with *The Yellow Danger* (1898). He was a fervent believer in social and evolutionary progress, combining a quasi-Nietzschean interest in 'overmen' with a fierce insistence on the necessity of altruism. His literary masterpiece is *The Purple Cloud* (1901), an allegorical fantasy which visits world-wide catastrophe upon the earth to test the faith of a modern Job. Other early futuristic works like *The Lord of the Sea* (1901) and *The Last Miracle* (1906) develop Shiel's philosophy further, as do non-fantasy novels like *The Weird o'It* (1902) and *The Evil That Men Do* (1904), but his ideas are more comprehensively and coherently displayed in later novels like *How the Old Woman Got Home* (1928) and *Dr Krasinski's Secret* (1929) and in his last scientific romance, *The Young Men are Coming!* (1937). Shiel's luxuriant prose style and feverishly flamboyant plotting alienate some readers, but he is a fascinating and challenging writer who has been unjustly neglected.

Shiels, George 1881–1949 Irish playwright. Born in Ballymoney, County Antrim, he emigrated to Canada and worked there for seven years before being permanently disabled in an accident whilst working for a railroad company. Back in Ballymoney, Shiels wrote articles and short stories for Ulster newspapers before turning to playwriting. After some success in Ulster theatres, he began writing for the ABBEY THEATRE, Dublin, in 1921 (*Bedmates* and *Insurance Money*), achieving his first major success with the characteristically sardonic comedy *Paul Twyning* (1922).

Shiels was the most consistently effective of the Abbey dramatists in the years that followed O'CASEY's departure to England. Among his best work, unrelentingly realistic in its presentation of acquisitive and unscrupulous 'decent' people, is *Cartney and Kevney* (1927), *Mountain Dew* (1929), the challenging comedy *The New Gossoon* (1930), *The Passing Day* (1936), *Give Him a House* (1939), *The Rugged Path* (1940) and its sequel *The Summit* (1941), *The Fort Field* (1942) and *The Caretakers* (1948).

Shipman's Tale, The See CANTERBURY TALES, THE.

Shirley A novel by CHARLOTTE BRONTË, published in 1849. A CONDITION OF ENGLAND NOVEL, it is set in Yorkshire during the Luddite riots and the last stages of the Napoleonic war.

Robert Gérard Moore, a millowner, is determined to install new machinery and is undeterred by the opposition of his workers, who attempt first to destroy the mill in protest and then to kill him. Robert's brother, Louis, is tutor to the wealthy Keeldar family and, even though he loves Caroline Helstone, the rector's niece, Robert sees that marriage to Shirley Keeldar would enable him to weather the financial difficulties caused by the troubled times. Shirley rejects him with contempt. The end of the war frees Robert from his difficulties and the devoted Caroline accepts him. Shirley, meanwhile, is drawn to Louis.

The novelist's father, Patrick Brontë, had once been appointed to the parish of Hartshead-cum-Clifton, near Dewsbury, where a riot at Rawfold's Mill resulted in 14 men being hanged. Robert Moore was based on William Cartwright, who was decorated for his part in the defence of the mill. The character of Shirley, which made the Christian name popular, is believed to have been modelled on EMILY BRONTË.

Shirley, James 1596–1666 Playwright. Born in London and educated at the Merchant Taylors' School and both Oxford and Cambridge, Shirley took holy orders after graduating and was headmaster of the grammar school in St Albans in 1623–5. After his conversion to Roman Catholicism in 1625 and the consequent loss of his post, he settled in London and began writing for the stage. The 36 plays he wrote between 1625 and the closing of the theatres in 1642 establish him as the leading dramatist of the Caroline theatre.

Shirley's avowed admiration for the work of BEAUMONT and FLETCHER is evident in the cleverly contrived multiple plots of his comedies and tragicomedies. These include his first play, *The School of Compliment* (1625; later renamed *Love Tricks*), *HYDE PARK* (1632), *THE GAMESTER* (1633), *The Young Admiral* (1633), *The Lady of Pleasure* (1635), *The Imposture* (1640) and *THE SISTERS* (1642). His tragedies also reflect the influence of Beaumont and Fletcher in their vivid opposition of good and evil, uncomplicated by the moral shading of characterization associated with the best of Jacobean tragedy. They include *THE TRAITOR* (1631), *Love's Cruelty* (1631), *The Politician* (c. 1639) and *THE CARDINAL* (1641).

Various of Shirley's masques, including the spectacular *The Triumph of Peace* (1634) and *Cupid and Death* (1653), survive, as well as a modest volume of *Poems* (1646). His famous dirge, 'The Glories of Our Blood and State', concludes a dramatization from Ovid of *The Contention of Ajax and Ulysses for the Armour of Achilles* (published 1658).

Having fought with the Royalists during the Civil War, Shirley was probably lucky to obtain employ-

ment as a schoolteacher during the Commonwealth. His death was caused by exposure and privation during the Great Fire of 1666.

Shoemaker's Holiday, The: *or, The Gentle Craft* A comedy by THOMAS DEKKER, first performed at the ROSE THEATRE in 1599. The sub-title apparently acknowledges its source in DELONEY's prose fiction, *The Gentle Craft*. One of the finest CITIZEN COMEDIES, the play is less remarkable for its various interrelated plots than for the gallery of characters it creates.

At the centre is Simon Eyre, a high-spirited shoemaker, whose bustling household of journeymen and apprentices is barely controlled by his comfortable and loving wife, Margery. One employee is a nobleman, Rowland Lacy, who has adopted the disguise of a Dutch shoemaker in order to pursue his love for Simon Eyre's daughter, Rose. Another is Ralph, loving husband of Jane, whose departure for the wars leaves Jane under threat from the attentions of the wealthy Hamond. Another is Firk, salt of the London earth and quite as good as his betters. The lovers triumph and Simon becomes Lord Mayor.

Shorthouse, Joseph Henry 1834–1903 Novelist. Born into a Quaker family in Birmingham, he became a chemist in his father's business. *JOHN INGLESANT* (privately printed, 1880; published, 1881), the one novel by which his name is remembered, reflects his preoccupation with the tensions between Anglicans and Catholics in the aftermath of the OXFORD MOVEMENT. Apart from other novels, he also wrote *The Platonism of Wordsworth* (1882) and edited GEORGE HERBERT's *The Temple* in 1882.

Showalter, Elaine 1941– American critic. Born in Cambridge, Massachusetts, and educated at Bryn Mawr College and the University of California, she has taught at Rutgers University and Princeton. One of the leading proponents of FEMINIST CRITICISM, she is best known for *A Literature of Their Own* (1977), studying the work of women novelists from 1800 to the present. It aims both to rescue individual writers from obscurity and to trace the evolution of a specific women's consciousness in the history of the novel. She has also published: *The New Feminist Criticism* (1986), an anthology; *The Female Malady: Women, Madness and English Culture 1830–1930* (1987); *Speaking of Gender* (1989); *The Modern Women* (1989), a collection of women's autobiographical writings from the 1920s; and *Sexual Anarchy* (1991).

Shropshire Lad, A See HOUSMAN, A. E.

Shute, Nevil [Norway, Nevil Shute] 1899–1960 Novelist. Educated at Shrewsbury and Oxford, he served in both world wars. He worked as an engineer at Howden Airship Works, and later became managing director of an aeroplane factory. His practical expertise was often skilfully worked into his novels: *No Highway*(1948) deals with the subject of metal fatigue in a manner which turns a technical subject into the stuff of mystery and suspense. He eventually settled at Langwarria in Victoria, Australia. Other novels include *Marazan* (1926), *So Disdained* (1928), *Lonely Road* (1932), *Ruined City* (1938), *What Happened to the Corbetts* (1939), *Pied Piper* (1942), *Pastoral* (1944), *The Far Country* (1952), *In the Wet* (1953), *The Breaking Wave* (1955), *On the Beach* (1957) and *The Trustee from the Toolroom* (1960). *A Town Like Alice* (1949), his best-known novel, invests its bleak Australian setting with romance and adventure. *Slide Rule* (1954) is an autobiography.

Sidgwick, Henry 1838–1900 Philosopher. Born at Skipton in Yorkshire, he was educated at Rugby and Trinity College, Cambridge, where he became a fellow. A leading advocate of reform in Cambridge (he opposed the religious test and supported women's education), he was appointed Knightbridge Professor of Moral Philosophy in 1883. A follower of JOHN STUART MILL, Sidgwick made ethics his special study, in *The Ethics of Conformity and Subscription* (1870), *The Methods of Ethics* (1874), *An Outline of the History of Ethics* (1886) and *The Scope and Limits of the Work of an Ethical Society* (1900). Other works include *The Principles of Political Economy* (1883) and *The Elements of Politics* (1891).

Sidney, Sir **Philip** 1554–86 Courtier, poet, critic and author of prose romance. Born at Penshurst in Kent, he was the eldest son of Sir Henry Sidney, Elizabeth's Lord Deputy in Ireland from 1559 onwards. Philip II of Spain, for whom he was named, was his godfather. After some private tutoring he went to school in Shrewsbury in 1564, entering it the same day as his life-long friend and future biographer, SIR FULKE GREVILLE. In 1568 he entered Christ Church, Oxford, left without taking a degree and was licensed to travel abroad to learn foreign languages in 1572. He stayed at the embassy in Paris, leaving after the St Bartholomew's Day Massacre. At Frankfurt he met the scholar Languet with whom he was to exchange a long correspondence and who influenced him not a little. In Venice he studied music and astronomy. Before his return to England in 1575 he also visited Genoa, Padua, Vienna, Prague and Antwerp. In his journeys he greatly impressed those who met him ('wheresoever he went he was beloved and obeyed', according to Greville) and left behind a trail of books dedicated to him.

In 1577 he was given the formal mission of condoling with some German princes on the death of their fathers; in reality he was sounding out the possibilities of a Protestant league. This promising start to a public career was never fulfilled. His relations with the queen were chequered, his ardent Protestantism not finding favour with Elizabeth's more cautious religious policies. His suggestion that Elizabeth enter into an alliance to protect Holland received a cool reception, and his letter of 1579 advising the queen against marriage to the Duke of Anjou endeared him to Elizabeth even less. He seems to have chafed for lack of employment and his clandestine attempt to join Drake's expedition to the Spanish coast in 1585 resulted in Elizabeth's summoning him to court. He was finally given a minor appointment in the Low Countries as governor of Flushing and left England in 1585. In 1586 he was involved in an unimportant skirmish at Zutphen and wounded in the thigh. The wound did not heal and within 22 days he was dead, not having reached his 32nd birthday. The grief felt in England and in Europe was as profound as the long funeral progress from the Low Countries to St Paul's Cathedral was spectacular. The London crowds are said to have cried out 'Farewell, the worthiest knight that lived' as the funeral passed, and Sidney's death was generally mourned. His friend Fulke Greville was desolate ('The only question I now study is whether weeping sorrow or speaking sorrow may most honour his memory') and expressed the general sense of loss and Sidney's worth: 'What he was to God, his friends and country, fame hath told.' Lord Buckhurst noted that 'even Her Majesty and the whole realm besides do suffer no small loss'. England felt the loss of a man who had seemed to embody all the qualities and graces of the perfect courtier of Castiglione's *THE COURTIER*. ARTHUR GOLDING lamented the death of a Protestant knight in the field, THOMAS NASHE the death of a 'Maecenas of learning' and the patron of virtue and wit. In *Astrophel* (1595) EDMUND SPENSER mourned the passing of 'a gentle shepherd' and poet. Soon after his death Sidney became the idealized representative of an idealized Elizabethan age. For SAMUEL DANIEL, Sidney's eternal songs could show 'what great Eliza's reign hath bred'. The legend continued into the Romantic period and beyond. For SHELLEY in *ADONAIS*, Sidney fought and fell as he lived, 'Sublimely mild, a spirit without spot', and W. B. YEATS's 'In Memory of Major Robert Gregory' paid Gregory the consummate compliment of comparison with Sidney: 'Our Sidney and our perfect man'.

Sidney's references to his literary works are the self-deprecating remarks of a Renaissance courtier. He speaks in the *APOLOGY FOR POETRY* of 'having slipped into the title of a poet'. His massive prose romance, *ARCADIA*, is this 'idle work of mine' and 'but a trifle'. Yet the debt of English literature to Sidney is enormous. *ASTROPHIL AND STELLA* is the first English sonnet sequence, the *Apology* is the most important and best-written critical work of its period in English, and the *Arcadia*, as well as being the finest work of English prose fiction of the period, has also been seen as the ancestor of the English novel. His minor works include the playlet *The Lady of May*, composed in 1578 for the entertainment of Elizabeth; a translation of a work on the truth of the Christian religion by du Plessis Mornay, which was completed by Arthur Golding; and a metaphrase of the first 43 Psalms. Sidney was interested in metrical experimentation and his poems display an astonishing variety of stanzaic and metrical forms, some used for the first time in English. None of his works was published in his lifetime (the folio containing his major works appeared in 1598) but were circulated in manuscript.

Sidney, Sir **Robert** 1563-1626 Poet and courtier. Younger brother to SIR PHILIP SIDNEY, Robert accompanied him to Flushing in Holland in 1585; the following year he was knighted for his gallantry on the field of Zutphen 10 days before his brother's death from wounds sustained in the same battle. From 1589 until 1616, when the town was returned to the Dutch, he was governor of Flushing, and enjoyed a long and honourable career in public life. His poetry, which disappeared in the early 19th century, was never printed in his lifetime; it was rediscovered and edited by Peter Croft (1983). Consisting of a planned sequence of songs, sonnets and pastorals, it shows the influence of his elder brother's verse at every turn, and is chiefly remarkable for the form in which it survives: a manuscript notebook, in the poet's own hand, showing his alterations and corrections. It is the largest body of original verse to have descended to us from the Elizabethan period in a text entirely set down by the poet himself. A patron as well as a practitioner of poetry, Robert Sidney is paid noble tribute as the lord of the manor to whom BEN JONSON's great poem *To Penshurst* is addressed.

Siege of Jerusalem, The A poem in ALLITERATIVE VERSE written in the North-west Midlands between 1390 and 1400. Although the subject is mainly religious, it is given the courtly and chivalric setting of VERSE ROMANCE. The Roman Titus, hearing that belief in Christ and his miracles may cure his cancer, grieves over the Passion and is healed. He is baptized and travels to Rome where his leprous father Vespasian is cured by touching the veil of St Veronica. The remainder of the poem describes Vespasian and Titus' attack on Jerusalem. The Jews are eventually defeated and Vespasian becomes emperor of Rome. The greater part of the poem is concerned with describing the battles and chivalrous deeds of the siege. The principal sources are the *Legenda aurea*, Higden's *Polychronicon* and the *Vindicta salvatoris*. An inferior version in couplets written in or near London *c.* 1400 is known as *Titus and Vespasian*.

Siege of Rhodes, The A spectacular entertainment by WILLIAM D'AVENANT, staged at Rutland House in 1656. It combined heroic drama with opera, both newcomers to the English stage. The music, which is lost, was by Henry Lawes and various collaborators. The text, in rhymed dialogue with frequent songs and choruses, is based on the account of the siege of Rhodes in RICHARD KNOLLES's *General History of the Turks* (1603). The perspective scenes were designed for the first production by John Webb.

Siege of Thebes, The A poem by JOHN LYDGATE presented as an addition to CHAUCER's *THE CANTERBURY TALES*, a tale told by the poet after meeting the pilgrims at Canterbury. At 9400 lines, however, it is longer than any of Chaucer's tales. It narrates the history of Thebes from the story of Oedipus to the war between Polyneices and Eteocles and the destruction of the city by Theseus. The poem acknowledges the influence of Boccaccio as well as Chaucer, and Lydgate also apparently used Martianus Capella, Seneca and a French version of the story of Thebes.

Sigurd the Volsung and the Fall of the Niblungs, The Story of An epic poem by WILLIAM MORRIS, published in November 1876.

The poem is in four books, the first telling the story of Sigmund and the other three of his son Sigurd. Morris drew his material from the fuller Scandinavian rather than the German version of the Niblung legend. He eliminated Latin and Romance language words as far as possible and continued to use the long anapaestic line he had developed for his *Aeneid of Virgil* (1875).

In August 1869 Eiríkr Magnússon sent a translation of the Icelandic *Volsunga Saga* to Morris in Germany. Morris initially thought it 'of the monstrous order' but by 1870, when he and Magnússon jointly published a prose translation, he had come to regard it as 'the Great Story of the North, which should be to all our race what the Tale of Troy was to the Greeks'. At the same time Richard Wagner was working to complete his opera epic *Der Ring des Nibelungen* and in 1873 Morris complained: 'the idea of a sandy-haired German tenor tweedledeeing over the unspeakable woes of Sigurd, which even the simplest words are not typical enough to express!... I wish to see Wagner uprooted!' In October 1875 Morris began work on his own poetic version of the legend and the book appeared within three months of the first performances of the entire *Ring* at Bayreuth, news of which he took 'as a personal outrage'. Clearly Morris regarded the Icelandic saga as legitimate Teutonic material for a poem in the English language, and *Sigurd* is an important milestone in the 19th-century revival of northern European values. 'It is the central work of my father's life', wrote May Morris, which 'he held most highly and wished to be remembered by'.

Silas Marner: *The Weaver of Raveloe* A novel by GEORGE ELIOT, first published in 1861.

Falsely judged guilty of theft, Silas Marner leaves his dissenting community and, as the novel opens, has been living for 15 years as a linen-weaver in the village of Raveloe where, an alien figure, he has worked hard to accumulate a goodly sum of gold. Squire Cass, 'the greatest man in Raveloe', has two sons: Godfrey, attracted to Nancy Lammeter but secretly married to the opium-ridden Molly Farren, and the good-for-nothing Dunstan (Dunsey) who blackmails him. Dunstan steals Marner's gold and promptly disappears. Molly dies in the snow-covered fields of Raveloe trying to reach the squire's residence to disclose her marriage, thus avenging Godfrey's refusal to acknowledge her. Their little girl, Eppie, toddles away from her dying mother to the threshold of Marner's cottage, where she is cared for by the lonely weaver. In his eyes she becomes more precious than his lost gold. The narrative moves forward 16 years to the discovery of the skeleton of Dunstan Cass with Silas's gold in a newly drained stone-pit. This revelation and his belief that 'everything comes to light' prompts Godfrey Cass to admit to Nancy, now his wife but childless, that Eppie is his daughter. They try to adopt the young girl, but neither Eppie nor Silas wish to be separated, and the novel concludes with her marriage to the worthy Aaron Winthrop who is more than willing to accept the weaver as part of the household. The story is spiced with rustic humour and forceful village characters.

Silkin, Jon 1930– Poet and editor. Born into a Jewish family in London, he was educated at Dulwich College. After national service and a series of manual jobs, he became Gregory Fellow in Poetry at Leeds University in 1958, staying on to read English. From 1952 to 1957 and from 1960 to the present day, he has edited the important literary magazine *Stand*. His first volume, *The Peaceable Kingdom* (1954), contained the excellent and much-anthologized 'Death of a Son'. After the over-grandiloquence of *The Two Freedoms* (1958), the three-beat line of *The Re-ordering of the Stones* (1961) and, especially, 'Flower Poems' in *Nature with Man* (1965) are more successful. A poet of commitment, Silkin writes of persecuted minorities; his main theme is growth through the experience of pain, and the parallel existence of joy. Later poems, in *Amana Grass* (1971), *The Principle of Water* (1974), *The Psalms with their Spoils* (1980), *Selected Poems* (1980) and *Autobiographical Stanzas* (1984), are often obscure. Other publications include *Out of Battle: Poetry of the Great War* (1972), *The Penguin Anthology of First World War Poetry* (1979) and *Poetry of the Committed Individual: A Stand Anthology* (1973).

Silko, Leslie Marmon 1948– American poet, novelist and short-story writer. Born of mixed ancestry (Laguna Pueblo, Mexican, and Anglo-American), she was raised in traditional Laguna ways but educated in white schools, notably the University of New Mexico at Albuquerque. Her work uses material and techniques from traditional Laguna sources to explore contemporary issues and dilemmas. Her best-known work remains *Ceremony* (1977), a novel about Tayo, a half-breed Laguna haunted by his experiences in the Pacific during World War II. Silko has also published: *Laguna Woman* (1974), a collection of poems; *Storyteller* (1981), a collection of poetry and short fiction; and a screenplay, *Black Elks. The Delicacy and the Strength of Lace* (edited by Anne Wright; 1985) collects the correspondence between Silko and JAMES WRIGHT.

Sillitoe, Alan 1928– Novelist. Born and brought up in Nottingham, he served in Malaya with the RAF and began to write after demobilization when tuberculosis forced him to spend a year and a half convalescing. His first novel, *Saturday Night and Sunday Morning* (1958), remains his best known. Its anti-hero, Arthur Seaton, a young, anti-social, hedonistic Nottingham factory-worker, belonged to a fictional type found also in the work of other provincial realists of the late 1950s and early 1960s such as JOHN BRAINE and STAN BARSTOW. Sillitoe's attachment to the anarchic outsider is further illustrated by the title story of his first collection of short stories, *The Loneliness of the Long-Distance Runner* (1959), which is narrated by a borstal boy who refuses to win the races he has been entered for. Subsequent novels include: *The General* (1960), a political fable; and *Travels in Nihilon* (1971), a dystopian fantasy; *The Death of William Posters* (1965), *A Tree on Fire* (1967) and *The Flame of Life* (1974), a trilogy about working-class revolution in the context of a modern industrialized provincial society; *The Lost Flying Boat* (1983), an adventure narrative about flying; *The Open Door* (1989), whose protagonist, Brian Seaton, is brother of the hero of *Saturday Night and Sunday Morning*; and *Leonard's War* (1991).

Silver King, The A MELODRAMA by HENRY ARTHUR JONES, first performed in London in 1882. Its success established Jones as a leading dramatist.

Wilfred Denver, dissipated but kindly, is persuaded that he has committed a murder. He is forced to abandon his family and flee to America. There he makes a fortune and is known as the Silver King. When he hears that his family is starving in England, he returns to save them. But he cannot reveal himself until he discovers both his own innocence and the identity of the murderer.

Silver Tassie, The A tragicomedy by SEAN O'CASEY, first staged in London in 1929 after its rejection by the directors of Dublin's ABBEY THEATRE.

The first act, set in the familiar O'Casey world of Dublin's tenements, shows Harry Heegan, on leave from World War I, leading his football team to victory and the trophy of the silver tassie. It was Act Two, originally performed in a startling stage-setting designed by Augustus John, that upset those who expected from O'Casey nothing but urban realism. It is a macabre theatrical poem, expressionist in technique and enacted in a battle-scarred landscape, which abandons the exploration of character in order to expose the futility of a foolish war. The remaining two acts return Harry Heegan to Ireland. Maimed and bitter, he cannot reconcile himself to his changed circumstances. The climactic final act, which takes place at the football club's dance, forces a recognition of how much has been lost and how little gained.

silver-fork novel A mocking name for early 19th-century novels of fashionable life and manners, derived from the description by FRASER'S MAGAZINE of EDWARD BULWER LYTTON as a 'silver-fork polisher'. Although Lytton claimed his intent was satirical, the genre offered the reader a vicarious experience of high life. Other authors included Lady Charlotte Bury (1775–1861), THEODORE HOOK, LADY BLESSINGTON, Lady Caroline Lamb (1785–1828), BENJAMIN DISRAELI, FRANCES TROLLOPE, Thomas Henry Lister (1800–42), Robert Plumer Ward (1765–1846), CATHERINE GORE and SUSAN FERRIER.

Silverberg, Robert 1935– American novelist and short-story writer. He was born in New York and educated at Columbia. He has been extremely prolific, producing more than 100 works of SCIENCE FICTION, more than 60 non-fiction books, and various works in other genres. His most careful and accomplished work is a series of novels using the science-fictional vocabulary of ideas to model situations of extreme psychological alienation; it includes *Thorns* (1967), *The Man in the Maze* (1969), *A Time of Changes* (1971), *Dying Inside* (1972) and *Shadrach in the Furnace* (1976). His other novels include *Downward to the Earth* (1970), about a man's quest for redemption in an alien world; *Son of Man* (1971), an allegorical romance of the far future; and the historical novels *Gilgamesh the King* (1984) and *Lord of Darkness* (1985). *The Reality Trip and Other Implausibilities* (1972), *Born with the Dead* (1974) and *The Conglomeroid Cocktail Party* (1984) are among his many collections of short stories.

Simic, Charles 1938– American poet. Born in Belgrade, he emigrated to the USA in 1949, settling in Chicago and attending the University of Chicago. He served briefly in the US Army before completing his BA at New York University. Since 1974 he has taught at the University of New Hampshire. *What the Grass Says* (1967) has been followed by many volumes, of which the most distinguished are *Dismantling the Silence* (1971), *Return to a Place Lit by a Glass of Milk*

(1974), *Charon's Cosmology* (1977), *Austerities* (1982), *Unending Blues* (1986) and *The World Doesn't End: Prose Poems* (1989). *Selected Poems: Nineteen Sixty-Three to Nineteen Eighty-Three* (1985) is the ideal introduction to his poetry. *Dime-Store Alchemy: The Art of Joseph Cornell* (1992) is a literary response to montages by the American artist, showing Simic's indebtedness to the parallel traditions of MODERNISM and surrealism. He has also devoted much of his energy to translating the work of other Yugoslav poets, notably I. Lalic and Vasko Popa, in volumes such as *Four Modern Yugoslav Poets* (1970) and *Horse Has Six Legs: Contemporary Serbian Poetry* (1992). Arguably the most important of his other editions and translations (from Serbo-Croat, French and Russian) is *Another Republic: 17 European and South American Writers* (1976), which he co-edited with MARK STRAND.

simile Where METAPHOR asserts the identity of unlike things, simile asserts their similarity: 'My love is like a red, red rose' (BURNS). The concrete element of a simile, therefore, has to be taken figuratively not literally. Burns's love is not to be envisaged as suffering from some skin disease that renders her prickly and bright red, but as sweet, natural and voluptuous. Cognition, in fact, plays at least as large a part as visualization in the appreciation of simile.

Simile naturally lends itself to expansion – a process reaching its peak in the EPIC SIMILE – while metaphor tends to condensation. The parallelism of simile has led some critics to see it as a paradigm of ALLEGORY, metaphor being more akin to a symbolic work, particularly one based on a central ramifying SYMBOL.

Considering the deep-rooted involvement of metaphor in the development of language and its presence in almost every kind of expression, it is somewhat surprising to find how small a part it plays in literature before SHAKESPEARE. In the earlier periods simile predominates.

Simms, William Gilmore 1806–70 American novelist, short-story writer and poet. He was born in Charleston, South Carolina. In 1825 he published his first book of verse and began contributing to *The Album*, a Charleston periodical. In 1827 he was admitted to the Bar. Between 1827 and 1830, in addition to practising law, he published four more volumes of poetry. From 1830 to 1832 he edited the Charleston *City Gazette*. His sixth book of verse, *Atalantis: A Story of the Sea*, appeared in 1832. In the following year he published his first novel, *Martin Faber*, a study of a murderer, and a collection of short stories entitled *The Book of My Lady: A Melange. Guy Rivers: A Tale of Georgia* (1834) is a romance of the Southern frontier. It was followed by his best-known novel, THE *YEMASSEE: A Romance of Carolina* (1835), the fictional account of an actual uprising by the Yemassee Indians against British colonists. In the same year he published *The Partisan: A Tale of the Revolution*. A second Revolutionary War romance, *Mellichampe: A Legend of the Santee*, followed in 1836.

Simms continued to write historical romances – another 22 novels published in book form between 1838 and 1859, plus at least three more published serially (appearing in volume form only after his death). Perhaps the most notable of these later novels is *Woodcraft: or, Hawks about the Dovecote* (1854), which originally appeared in 1852 under the title of *The Sword and the Distaff: or, 'Fair, Fat, and Forty'*. During this period he also published three collections of short stories and 12 books of verse. His non-fiction works include the essay 'Slavery in America' (1837), *The History of South Carolina* (1840), *The Geography of South Carolina* (1843) and *The Life of Francis Marion* (1844). He was also connected with several periodicals, among them the *Southern Quarterly Review*, which he edited from 1849 to 1854. From 1844 to 1846 he served as a member of South Carolina's legislature. The Civil War broke him financially and spiritually. An extremely successful novelist in his own lifetime, Simms not only depicted the Old South in its essence but also helped to propagate the Southern myth of perfectibility – the myth that God had given the land to the Southern whites so that they could form an ideal society which would include benevolent enslavement of the blacks.

Simon, (Marvin) Neil 1927– American playwright. Born in the Bronx, New York, he began by writing comic material for radio and television personalities and, with his brother Danny, sketches for Broadway shows. *Come Blow Your Horn*, his first play, was written with his brother in 1961. Since then he has enjoyed more Broadway hits than any other American playwright, though critical acclaim has been tempered by his reputation for writing gags and wisecracks which appease rather than challenge his audiences. His major successes, interspersed with only a few failures and fallow periods, are *Barefoot in the Park* (1963), *The Odd Couple* (1965), *The Star Spangled Girl* (1966), *Plaza Suite* (1968), *The Last of the Red Hot Lovers* (1969), *The Prisoner of Second Avenue* (1971), *The Sunshine Boys* (1972), *California Suite* (1976), *Chapter Two* (1977), *Brighton Beach Memoirs* (1983), *Biloxi Blues* (1984), *Broadway Bound* (1986) and *Lost in Yonkers* (1991).

Simple Cobbler of Aggawam, The A satire by NATHANIEL WARD, written in America in 1645 and published in London in 1647. It is an appeal, in the midst of the English Civil War, for an end to hostilities and a return to national stability. Ward chides the king for having overreached his authority and supports the Parliamentary cause against the Royalists,

but warns the radical Independents that their decentralizing, tolerationist policies will bring instability to England. He takes the side of the Presbyterians, urging the Parliamentarians to end the war and, in the interests of national unity, 'rather to compose than to tolerate differences in Religion'. Although orthodox, Ward's *Cobbler* is unusual among Puritan texts for its ebullient style. Ward develops the 'simplicity' of his persona, the cobbler Theodore de la Guard, in terms of his living on the American frontier (Aggawam was the Indian name for Ipswich), quite removed from the London scene. Mixing a colloquial style with elaborate word play, puns and analogies and doggerel verses, *The Simple Cobbler* is perhaps more reminiscent of Elizabethan than of Puritan literature.

Simple Story, A A novel by ELIZABETH INCHBALD, published in 1791. The story concerns Dorriforth, a priest, and his ward, the worldly and flirtatious Miss Milner, who falls in love with him. He loves her, but because of his calling they both conceal their feelings. Dorriforth inherits a peerage, is released from his vows, and, as Lord Elmwood, marries Miss Milner. However, her basic weakness of character leads to an affair with a former suitor, Sir Frederick Lawnley, and Elmwood banishes her from his house with their daughter, Matilda. Lady Elmwood dies of remorse and Matilda is left unprotected. Elmwood's feelings are brought back to life when Matilda is abducted by a reckless libertine and he restores her to her home and position. Another priest, Father Sandford, who succeeds Dorriforth as a spiritual guide, plays an important part in the course of the novel, which is frankly didactic, but notable for the author's attempt to portray emotions honestly.

Simpson, Louis 1923– American poet, playwright, novelist and critic. Born in Jamaica, he emigrated to the USA in 1940 and served with the US Army in 1943–5, completing his bachelor's degree at Columbia University after his discharge. He has taught at Columbia, the University of California at Berkeley and, since 1967, the State University of New York at Stony Brook. His poetry combines a mythical, dream-like quality with a colloquial, often ironic tone. His first volume, *The Arrivistes: Poems 1940–1949*, was published in Paris in 1949. Subsequent publications include: *The Father out of the Machine: A Masque*, which appeared in *The Chicago Review* in 1950; *Good News of Death and Other Poems* (1955); *Andromeda*, a play (1956); *A Dream of Governors* (1959); and *Riverside Drive* (1962), his one work of fiction. *At the End of the Open Road* (PULITZER PRIZE, 1963) was followed by *Selected Poems* (1965), *Adventures of the Letter I* (1971), *The Mexican Woman* (1973), *Searching for the Ox: New Poems and a Preface* (1976), *Caviare at the Funeral: Poems* (1980), *The Best Hour of the Night* (1983), *People Live Here: Selected*

Poems 1948–1983(1983), *In the Room We Share*(1990) and *Wei Wei and Other Friends* (1990). *Collected Poems* appeared in 1988 and *Selected Prose* in 1989. Simpson's criticism includes: a study of JAMES HOGG (1962); *An Introduction to Poetry* (1967, revised edition 1973); *Three on the Tower* (1975), essays on EZRA POUND, T. S. ELIOT and WILLIAM CARLOS WILLIAMS; *A Revolution in Taste* (1978), studies of DYLAN THOMAS, ALLEN GINSBERG, SYLVIA PLATH and ROBERT LOWELL; and *A Company of Poets*(1981). With Donald Hall and Robert Pack he edited an influential anthology, *The New Poets of England and America*(1957).

Simpson, N(orman) F(rederick) 1919– Playwright. Born in London, he worked in a bank and served in the Intelligence Corps in World War II before becoming an adult education lecturer. The success of *A Resounding Tinkle* in a competition organized by *The Observer* in 1957 brought him to prominence. Like his other successful piece, *One-Way Pendulum* (1959), it is a zany disruption of middle-class normality. Written during the brief popularity of the THEATRE OF THE ABSURD in Britain, Simpson's work also belongs to a comic tradition that links Will Hay to *The Goon Show* and *Monty Python*.

Sinclair, May [Mary] **(Amelia St Clair)** 1863–1946 Novelist. Born in Cheshire, she was educated at Cheltenham Ladies' College. Her first novel, *Audrey Craven* (1896), was followed by *Divine Fire* (1904). At this time she was involved in the suffragette movement. She later served with the Red Cross in Belgium during World War I. But before the outbreak of war she published *The Three Sisters*(1914), a study of middle-class women in the repressive society of Victorian and Edwardian Britain. The first of her 'psychological' novels, it showed the influence of Freud, Jung and HAVELOCK ELLIS. Sinclair was also an admirer of DOROTHY RICHARDSON'S *Pilgrimage*, the first volume of which appeared in 1915, and became a leading exponent of STREAM OF CONSCIOUSNESS. Her next psychological novel, *Mary Oliver* (1919), was an intense study of a mother–daughter relationship; it was followed by a third, *The Life and Death of Harriet Frean* (1922). In all, Sinclair wrote 24 novels as well as short stories and literary criticism.

Sinclair, Upton 1878–1968 American novelist. Born in Baltimore, Maryland, and educated at the City College of New York and Columbia, he began writing dime novels at the age of 15 and won international reputation with *THE JUNGLE* (1906). An exposé of the meat-packing industry in Chicago, it remains his best-known work and perhaps the most famous of all 'muckraking novels'. Sinclair went on to publish more than 100 books, including a series of pamphlets on American life: *The Profits of Religion* (1918); *The Brass Check* (1919), on journalism; *The Goslings*

(1924), on education; *Money Writes!*(1927), on art and literature; and *The Flivver King* (1937) on the motor industry.

By 1953 he had completed 11 volumes of an immense ROMAN FLEUVE, *World's End*. Its hero, Lanny Budd, the illegitimate son of a munitions tycoon, travels the world and becomes involved in international political intrigues. The first novel in the series, also entitled *World's End*, was published in 1940 and narrates the events of Budd's life between 1913 and 1919; *Between Two Worlds* (1941) covers the period from the Treaty of Versailles to the 1929 stock-market crash; *Dragon's Teeth* (1942), which won the PULITZER PRIZE, concerns Budd's encounters with anti-Nazi sentiment in Europe in the early 1930s; *Wide is the Gate* (1943) also deals with anti-Nazi sentiment, in Spain and France; *The Presidential Agent* (1944) recounts Budd's relationship with President Roosevelt; *Dragon Harvest*(1945) carries his history through to the fall of Paris; *A World to Win* (1946) and *A Presidential Mission* (1947) cover his experiences in Europe, North Africa, and the Orient during the early years of World War II; *One Clear Call* (1948) and *O Shepherd, Speak!* (1949) recount the last years of the war and the subsequent peace plans; the final novel in the series, *The Return of Lanny Budd* (1953) deals with hostile sentiment in the USA towards post-war Soviet Russia. Sinclair published a selection from his correspondence, *My Lifetime in Letters*(1960), and an autobiography (1962).

Singer, Burns (James Hyman) 1928–64 Poet. He was born in New York, but his Scottish parents brought him back to their native land when he was four. After reading English and biology at Glasgow University he worked as a marine biologist before becoming a freelance writer. Only one volume of poems, *Still and All*(1957), appeared in his lifetime. An inadequate *Collected Poems* (1970) left much of his work unpublished and he remains largely unread. Influenced by W. S. GRAHAM, HUGH MACDIARMID and Wittgenstein, his poetry explores personal and public language and identity, and humanity's place in the complex and beautiful processes revealed by science; rhythmically subtle and intellectually complex, it is never merely cerebral.

Sinners in the Hands of an Angry God A sermon preached by JONATHAN EDWARDS at Enfield, Connecticut, on 8 July 1741, at the height of the Great Awakening, and printed soon after its delivery. Developing the theme of the precariousness of the sinner's position and the imagery of the fire of damnation (invoking a famous image of a spider held over the fire by a slender thread), Edwards tried to move his hearers to feel the force of the Calvinist doctrine and to experience the first stirrings of a religious conversion.

Sir Charles Grandison, The History of An EPIS-
TOLARY NOVEL by SAMUEL RICHARDSON, published in
1753–4.

Harriet Byron, an attractive young lady, arrives in
London society and excites the desires of Sir Hargrave
Pollexfen, a wealthy, dishonourable swaggerer who is
unused to being rebuffed. Harriet repeatedly refuses
his insolent proposals of marriage until in a rage he
has her abducted from a masked ball and, still failing
to bully her into a secret marriage, packs her off to his
country estate in a carriage. She is fortunate enough
to be saved by the intervention of the wealthy and gallant Sir Charles Grandison, and the pair become enamoured of each other.

While in Italy, though, Sir Charles had previously
become attached to Clementina della Porretta,
daughter of a noble family which was indebted to him
for his services; the two had not actually married due
to the differences in their religions. Clementina,
more distraught than he at the prospect of their being
apart, now suffers a mental breakdown and her parents beg Sir Charles to return urgently to Italy, to save
her at any price. The lady recovers when he arrives,
and the hero's honour is saved from a difficult
dilemma by Clementina's decision that their religions constitute too great an impediment after all. So,
with a clear conscience Sir Charles returns to England
and happily marries the lovely Harriet.

Throughout this long novel the portrayal of sustained virtue threatens to become incredible, but
there are many touches of delicate sensibility and
feeling, and a sureness in domestic description that
won the book the admiration of JANE AUSTEN.

Sir Cleges A VERSE ROMANCE in TAIL-RHYME stanzas
written in the late 14th century in the north
Midlands. Its source is unknown. Sir Cleges's generosity leads him into poverty. Praying in his garden at
Christmas, he sees a cherry tree richly laden with fruit
and determines to take the fruit to court for the king.
Three officials demand a third each of his reward
before they will admit him, so when he is asked to
name his reward he requests 12 blows to be administered to the officials. The king is delighted to learn
Cleges's identity, since he had supposed him dead. He
is made a steward and given property.

Sir Degare A Middle English VERSE ROMANCE in cou-
plets, written before 1325, probably in the south-west
Midlands. Degare is conceived when his mother is
raped in the forest by a fairy knight who leaves her a
broken sword. He is abandoned at birth with his
mother's glove and is brought up by a hermit. The
adult Degare leaves to search for his parents, developing from an untrained and crude fighter into a proficient knight. He unwittingly marries his mother, who
is revealed when the glove fits her. She gives him the
sword and he goes to seek his father. He acquires a

wife but puts off the wedding until after his quest. He
eventually fights with his father who recognizes the
sword and reveals himself. Degare's parents marry
and he marries the lady he has won.

The romance sustains interest by its treatment of
events rather than character, creating suspense and
expectation through Degare's search. Its setting is
Brittany, and it shows many of the features associated
with the BRETON LAY.

Sir Degrevant An alliterative VERSE ROMANCE in
TAIL-RHYME stanzas, composed in the north or north-
east Midlands in the late 14th century.

Degrevant is recalled from a Crusade because his
neighbour is persistently despoiling his forests. The
earl will not make amends, and the two live in a state
of hostility. Degrevant falls in love with the earl's
daughter Melidor and defeats a suitor for her hand.
She secretly entertains him every night but they
remain chaste. When Degrevant is detected by the
steward an ambush is prepared, but he escapes.
Finally the earl relents and the couple are allowed to
marry.

The poem contains various motifs common
amongst the verse romances, but is distinguished
by its vivid and realistic descriptions and its portrayal
of feudal society.

Sir Eglamour of Artois A Middle English VERSE RO-
MANCE of the mid-14th century composed in the north
of England. The poem is written in 12-line TAIL-RHYME
stanzas. It contains motifs common to much romance
and folk literature of the period, most notably the
wife set adrift and the child stolen by animals.

Eglamour, in love with Christabelle, is set tasks by
her father. These he accomplishes, killing a famous
deer and boar and the giants who keep them. On his
return he finds that Christabelle and her new-born
son have been set adrift and leaves to seek them. The
child, Degrebelle, is stolen by a griffin and later marries his own mother; she, however, recognizes him
before the marriage is consummated. Eglamour recognizes his son when fighting in a tournament for
Christabelle's hand and the family is reunited.

Sir Firumbras (Sir Ferumbras) A Middle English
VERSE ROMANCE of the late 14th century, based on an
Old French source. The story begins after the capture
of Rome by the Saracens and the city is in the hands of
the Sultan of Babylon. Charlemagne comes to Rome's
aid and his champion, Oliver, fights and overcomes
Firumbras, the Sultan's son. Firumbras is baptized.
Roland and Oliver are captured and imprisoned by
the Sultan but Floripas, his daughter, falls in love
with another of the French prisoners, Guy, and
arranges their escape and the Sultan's defeat. She
marries Guy, and he and Firumbras are rewarded by
Charlemagne. The story is substantially the same as

the second half of *THE SOWDON OF BABYLON.* The METRE changes from septenary couplets to TAIL-RHYME stanzas (aabccb).

Sir Gawain and the Carle of Carlisle

A VERSE ROMANCE composed *c.* 1400 near Shropshire; it is in 12-line TAIL-RHYME stanzas.

After a hunting trip Gawain, Kay and Bishop Baldwin seek shelter in the castle of the giant Carle of Carlisle. Baldwin and Kay behave rudely and disobediently, but Gawain is polite and obeys all his host's requests. He goes to bed with the Carle's wife at his bidding, but only kisses her and spends the night with the Carle's daughter instead. In the morning he reluctantly agrees to behead his host, who regains the shape of a normal knight, confesses and renounces his vow to kill any knight who disobeys him. The Carle becomes a knight of the Round Table and Gawain marries his daughter. The romance centres on the traditional courtesy of Gawain and rudeness of Kay.

Sir Gawain and the Green Knight

A late-14th-century VERSE ROMANCE preserved in the same manuscript as *PEARL, PATIENCE* and *CLEANNESS.* Although these are explicitly religious and *Sir Gawain* is not, all four are linked by similarities of dialect (west Midlands), diction and style. They are usually taken to be the work of the same, unidentified author, known for convenience as the *GAWAIN*-POET. *Sir Gawain* comprises 2500 lines of ALLITERATIVE VERSE disposed into stanzas of unequal length and ending with a BOB AND WHEEL, a line of two syllables followed by four lines of seven syllables (three stresses) rhyming abab. The whole poem is divided into four fitts (or sections) of approximately equal length.

The story is set in the early days of Arthur's court. It is Christmas time and the court is about to dine when a huge, bright green knight rides into the hall and demands a game. He challenges any member of the court to borrow his axe and deal him a blow, to be returned the following year at his own home, the Green Chapel. Gawain accepts the challenge and beheads the knight, who promptly recovers his head, reminds Gawain of the bargain and rides out, leaving the dismayed court to resume its revelry.

The second fitt follows the course of the year and deals with Gawain's preparation for his departure in search of the Green Chapel, and his journey through the winter landscape from Camelot towards the North of England. The poet deals at length with the pentangle blazoned on Gawain's shield, an emblem of the interlocking scheme of virtues to which he is dedicated. Gawain arrives at a castle where he is offered hospitality for Christmas. The castle, he is told, is very close to the Green Chapel and he is persuaded to stay until New Year's Day, the time appointed for his meeting.

The third fitt describes the last three days of Gawain's stay in the castle, during which time he and his host agree to exchange at dinner whatever they have gained during the day. While the host hunts (first deer, then a boar, and on the third day a fox), his beautiful wife attempts unsuccessfully to seduce Gawain. On the first two days Gawain exchanges successively one and two kisses for his host's game. On the third day the lady begs a gift of him and, when he refuses to give her one, offers him first a ring and then her green girdle. Gawain at first refuses, but is persuaded to accept it when told that the wearer cannot suffer violent death. However, he surrenders to his host only the three kisses he has received.

Gawain rides to the Green Chapel in the fourth fitt, accompanied at first by a guide who tries to persuade him to abandon his mission. The Green Knight swings at Gawain's exposed neck twice, and stops short each time. The third time he nicks the skin and Gawain leaps up, defiant and ready for battle. The Green Knight laughs and reveals that he is in fact Gawain's host, Sir Bertilak de Hautdesert. He knew of his wife's actions and gave Gawain the nick in the neck for his failure to keep the bargain of the third day by concealing the green girdle. He explains that the whole episode was planned by Morgan le Fay with the purpose of frightening Guinevere to death. He invites Gawain to return to his castle, but Gawain refuses and returns to Arthur's court wearing his green girdle as a badge of shame. The court, however, are delighted at his return and all adopt the girdle as a badge of honour.

Sir Gawain and the Green Knight is the best of the surviving Middle English romances, characterized by passages of beautiful poetry, moments of gentle comedy and keenly observed psychology. The vigorous narrative includes sustained and detailed description conveying the poet's joy in the sensory world. The poem follows Gawain's psychological processes during the course of his testing and concentrates on the moral dilemmas he has to face in trying to live by the scheme of values he adopted at Arthur's court. The Green Knight's testing of Gawain and, by extension, of the Arthurian court, pits this idealistic scheme against man's natural urges, in particular his instinct to preserve his life. Critical controversy over a number of aspects of the poem remains unresolved; the 'identity' of the Green Knight and the adequacy of his explanation of the adventure's purpose are two such points.

The poem has no single known source, though it shares several episodes and motifs with earlier works and traditions of both French and Celtic origins. See also ARTHURIAN LITERATURE.

Sir Gowther

A VERSE ROMANCE in 12-line TAIL-RHYME stanzas composed *c.* 1400 in the north-east Midlands; it is one of the Middle English BRETON LAYS. The poem tells the popular story of ROBERT THE DEVIL, and its source is a 12th-century French version, *Robert le Diable*.

Gowther, born after his mother was raped by a devil disguised as her husband, grows up to be very strong and violent. He leads an unremittingly evil life until he learns of his true parentage. At this he goes to Rome and confesses, then to Almayne where he eats food from the mouths of hounds as penance and is known as a fool. In disguise he defeats a Saracen suitor of the emperor's dumb daughter, with whom he has been having a chaste affair. After thinking him wounded and falling from a tower, she miraculously recovers her speech. The couple marry, and Gowther works miracles and is held as a saint. The poem has some features of the SAINT'S LIFE.

Sir Harry Hotspur of Humblethwaite A novel by ANTHONY TROLLOPE, serialized in *Macmillan's Magazine* from May to December 1870, and published in a single volume in 1871.

Sir Harry Hotspur is a wealthy Cumberland squire whose only son and heir has died two years before the novel opens. He has a daughter, Emily, and the next male heir is a distant cousin, George Hotspur, charming but untrustworthy and a gambler. Rather than make George his heir, Sir Harry resolves that Emily shall have the property in the hope that when she marries her husband will take the family name. But the suitor favoured by her parents fails to win her heart, and her cousin George does, despite evidence which emerges of his lying, gambling debts, and liaison with an actress. Emily believes she can redeem him but promises not to marry without her father's consent, which Sir Harry refuses to give. It transpires that George has cheated at cards and, pressed by creditors and the threat of the law, he undertakes never to see Emily again in return for payment of his debts and an annuity. Emily is taken to Italy by her parents, where she learns of George's marriage to his mistress and dies broken-hearted.

A study in ancestral pride and the stubbornness born of high breeding and noble feelings, *Sir Harry Hotspur* has a tragic power and concentration unique in Trollope's work and rare in Victorian fiction.

Sir Launcelot Greaves, The Life and Adventures of A novel by TOBIAS SMOLLETT, published in volume form in 1762. His fourth novel, it is generally regarded as one of his weakest. Sir Launcelot Greaves is an 18th-century Don Quixote, riding about England in armour with his ludicrous squire, Timothy Crabshaw. The humour is harsh and the main interest of the book lies in its picture of England before the Industrial Revolution and in a few of its characters: the rogue Ferret, Mrs Gobble, a justice's wife and Captain Crowe, a naval knight-errant.

Sir Launfal *(Launfalus Miles)* A late-14th-century VERSE ROMANCE written in south-east England. It is the only known work of THOMAS CHESTRE (although he perhaps also wrote LIBEAUS DESCONUS), and is an adaptation of one of the 12th-century *Lais* of MARIE DE FRANCE, *Lanval*.

Launfal, a proud and generous knight, leaves Arthur's court because of his dislike of Guinevere and goes to Caerleon where his generosity leads him into poverty. When out riding he is summoned by two maidens to the pavilion of Tryamour, the daughter of a faery king. She becomes his mistress, gives him riches and comes at his command as long as their love remains secret. For a while Launfal prospers, then he returns to Arthur's court and annoys Guinevere by refusing her advances and telling her of Tryamour's beauty. He loses his mistress and his riches and is challenged to produce Tryamour within a year. She arrives at the last moment, blinds Guinevere, and takes Launfal to Olyroun where they still live.

Another translation of *Lanval*, in couplets, survives in three versions, *Sir Landeval*, *Sir Lambewell* and *Sir Lamwell*, which generally follow the Anglo-Norman source more closely than does *Sir Launfal*.

Sir Orfeo A Middle English VERSE ROMANCE probably written in the south of England early in the 14th century. The best of the English BRETON LAYS, it is based loosely on the story of Orpheus and Eurydice told by Ovid and Virgil. No medieval source has been identified, though Celtic and French features can be discerned.

Orfeo loses his wife Herodis when she is abducted from beneath a tree by the king of faery. He entrusts his kingdom to his steward and wanders in the forest with his harp for years before eventually gaining access to the faery otherworld and winning back his wife as a reward for his harp-playing. The tragic ending of the legend is omitted, Orfeo and his queen regaining their own kingdom.

It is possible that the poet also wrote LAI LE FREINE, although the evidence – the appearance of the same prologue in *Le Freine* and two of the manuscripts of SIR ORFEO – is inconclusive.

Sir Thomas More A play that has been dated c. 1593–5, but for which there is no evidence of production. It was first printed in 1844. The incomplete manuscript is preserved in the British Museum, its great interest lying in the identification of SHAKESPEARE's handwriting and the proof of his contribution to a work by many hands. The other contributors are ANTHONY MUNDAY, HENRY CHETTLE, THOMAS HEYWOOD and THOMAS DEKKER.

The play is based on the main events of MORE's life (already well chronicled by this date) from his rise to favour, through his friendship with ERASMUS and opposition to the king, to his fall and death on the scaffold. Henry VIII does not appear. The scene attributed to Shakespeare shows More confronting the rebellious apprentices of London.

Sir Thomas Wyatt, The Famous History of A historical drama by THOMAS DEKKER and JOHN WEBSTER, published in 1607 and probably produced a few years before. The Wyatt of the title is the son of the poet SIR THOMAS WYATT. He raised an unsuccessful rebellion in 1554 against the accession and marriage of the Catholic Mary Tudor. Its failure led to his own execution and endangered the lives of those who might have been regarded as the focus for a new revolt.

Sir Thopas, The Tale of See CANTERBURY TALES, THE.

Sir Torrent of Portyngale A VERSE ROMANCE in 12-line TAIL-RHYME stanzas, written in the late 14th or early 15th century in the east Midlands. It has no known source but is poorly constructed from a series of very familiar motifs (compare OCTAVIAN and SIR EGLAMOUR OF ARTOIS).

The cruel king of Portugal forces Torrent to undertake apparently impossible tasks before allowing him to marry his daughter, Desonell. Torrent is betrayed by the king who promises her to the prince of Aragon while he is absent on the appointed quests. Torrent defeats the prince and his champion and agrees to wait six months before marrying Desonell, then goes to Norway. Desonell meanwhile bears twins and is set adrift with them by her father. On his return Torrent sets the king adrift in a leaky boat and spends 15 years in battles before being reunited with his sons, each of whom he defeats unrecognized in tournaments. His armour is recognized by Desonell and they are married.

Sir Triamour A late-14th-century VERSE ROMANCE in 12-line TAIL-RHYME stanzas, written in the north or north-east Midlands.

King Ardus of Aragon leaves his wife, Margaret, to go on a pilgrimage to pray for an heir, unaware that she is already pregnant. The steward Marrok makes advances to her which she rejects. After Ardus's return Marrok tells him he had found Margaret with a lover; she is banished, accompanied by an old knight, Roger, and a dog. Marrock attacks them, killing Roger, but Margaret escapes and bears a son, Triamour. After guarding Roger's grave for 12 years (seven in one version), the dog returns to court, kills Marrok and leads the courtiers to the grave. Ardus seeks Margaret and is defeated by Triamour in a tournament for the hand of the daughter of the Hungarian king. He rescues Triamour from a rival whose father in turn besieges Ardus and is defeated by Triamour. The family is reunited and Triamour married.

The romance is notable for the number of conventional motifs incorporated in the plot: false steward, exiled wife, faithful hound, birth in the forest and combat between father and son.

Sir Tristrem A VERSE ROMANCE of the late 13th century, written in the north of England. Apart from SIR THOMAS MALORY's prose treatment in LE MORTE DARTHUR, it is the only rendering in Middle English of the story of Tristan and Iseult. Though based on the same Anglo-Norman source (Le Roman de Tristan by Thomas of Britain) used by Gottfried von Strassburg, it offers only an incomplete, condensed and disappointing version of one of the great stories associated with COURTLY LOVE, and is less interested in the hero's relationship with his beloved than in his other adventures.

Tristrem is born to the sister of King Mark of Cornwall after her husband has been killed; she dies in childbirth and he is brought up in Parmenie by a tutor. At the age of 15 he is abducted by pirates and abandoned on the Cornish shore where he educates Mark's hunters in proper hunting procedure and is taken into the court. He defeats the Irish champion who has come to collect a tribute, but is wounded. The wound does not heal and he eventually goes to Ireland where, known as Tramtris, he is healed by the queen, sister of the champion Moraunt. A year later he returns to claim the queen's daughter, Ysonde, as Mark's bride; he is recognized as Moraunt's killer but escapes death. He and Ysonde accidentally drink a love-potion intended for her and Mark and are compelled to conduct a secret affair after her marriage. Mark discovers their relationship and, despite trial by an ambiguous oath, Tristrem is eventually banished. He goes to Brittany where he marries Ysonde of the White Hands on account of her name, but the union is not consummated. On a return trip to England he is wounded again, but here the narrative breaks off. It is possible to supply the ending from other treatments of the same version: Tristrem sends for Ysonde to heal him in Brittany, demanding that the ship bear white sails if she is aboard and black if she is not. The ship returns but his jealous wife deceitfully tells him it has black sails and he dies of grief before Ysonde arrives; she dies beside him.

Sisson, C(harles) H(ubert) 1914– Poet, novelist, translator and essayist. Born in Bristol, he read English at Bristol University before pursuing his studies at the Universities of Berlin and Freiberg (1934–5) and at the Sorbonne (1935–6). Apart from active service in India (1942–5) – where his first novel, *An Asiatic Romance* (1953), is set – he worked from 1936 in the Civil Service, rising to Under-Secretary in the Ministry of Labour before his retirement in 1971. His dissatisfaction with the Civil Service is registered in *The Spirit of British Administration* (1959). Although he had published *Poems* (1959), *London Zoo* (1961), *Numbers* (1965) and *Metamorphoses* (1968), he achieved a wider recognition only with *In the Trojan Ditch: Collected Poems and Selected Translations* (1974). His themes are age, decline and death. His early work is a quest towards 'plain statement', but his belief in the unconsidered nature of poetic utterance has led to a 'softening' process, where dream states are reflected, meaning is unparaphrasable and syntax is ambiguous. He rejects whatever appears 'with the face of familiarity', and subtle, fluid rhythms are an outstanding feature of his work. An Anglican and a conservative, he is also a classicist – both in his pervading pessimism and rejection of Romantic possibilities, and in the influence of Roman literature. His range of translations is wide: they include Heine (1953), Catullus (1966), Horace's *Ars poetica* (1975), Lucretius' *De rerum natura* (1976), La Fontaine (1979), Dante's *The Divine Comedy* (1979), *The Song of Roland* (1983), Du Bellay's *The Regrets* (1984) and Virgil's *The Aeneid* (1986). Later collections of verse include *Anchises* (1976), *Exactions* (1980), *Collected Poems 1943–1983* (1984) and *God Bless Karl Marx!* (1987). His critical works, *English Poetry 1900–1950: An Assessment* (1971) and *The Avoidance of Literature: Collected Essays* (1978), are characterized by a desire to debunk received opinion and a forceful independence of mind. His second novel, *Christopher Homm* (1965), told in reverse chronology, is a pessimistic masterpiece. His large *oeuvre* combines to make Sisson one of the handful of leading poets since the war.

Sister Carrie A novel by THEODORE DREISER, published in 1900.

It tells the story of Carrie Meeber, a Midwestern country girl who moves to Chicago. She meets a salesman called Charles Drouet, and after a period of unemployment becomes his mistress. Soon, however, she becomes disillusioned with him and takes up with his friend George Hurstwood, a middle-aged, married restaurant manager. He embezzles money and elopes with Carrie to New York, where he opens a saloon which proves a failure. Their liaison continues for some three years, until Carrie is forced by their impoverishment to work as a chorus girl to support them. Though she makes an impression in a small part and begins what is to become a successful career, she fails to find happiness. She deserts Hurstwood, who ends up a drunken beggar on Skid Row. Eventually, and unknown to Carrie, he commits suicide.

Sister Helen A BALLAD by DANTE GABRIEL ROSSETTI, first published in 1870. It derives from the medieval superstition that revenge may be obtained by melting a waxen image of one's enemy. The narrative exchanges between Sister Helen and her younger brother reveal that Keith of Ewern has violated his troth and is to die in pain and fear, despite successive pleas from his relations. The poem is carefully wrought (Rossetti laboured on it over many years) and relies on IRONY, a subtly employed refrain, pointedly economical language and a pervading sense of doom for its striking effects.

Sisters, The A comedy by JAMES SHIRLEY, produced in 1642 and published in 1652.

The sisters are the presumptuous and haughty Paulina and the unassuming and modest Angellina. Frapolo, a bandit chief, comes to their house masquerading as a fortune teller and persuades Paulina that she is destined to marry a prince. He next appears as the Prince of Parma, and Paulina accepts him without hesitation. Then the real prince arrives on the scene and falls in love with Angellina. Frapolo is exposed and Paulina is discovered to be a changeling, the daughter of a peasant.

Sistren Theatre Collective, The A Jamaican theatre group founded ln Kingston in 1977 to promote awareness of women's issues, particularly the problems of working-class Caribbean women, through popular drama. It has enjoyed great success both in Jamaica and on foreign tours. Its first production, *Downpression Get a Blow* (1977), was followed by annual part-time productions until 1979, after which the collective was established on a full-time basis. Sistren uses agit-prop techniques to try to bring about social change and encourage those who take part in their workshops to contribute personal testimony. It also holds workshops and produces books, textiles and a magazine. *Lionheart Gal* (edited by Honor Ford Smith, 1986) gives the life-histories of several women involved with the collective.

Sitwell, Dame Edith (Louisa) 1887–1964 Poet and critic. The older sister of OSBERT SITWELL and SACHEVERELL SITWELL, she was born in Scarborough and brought up at Renishaw Hall, Derbyshire. Her first volume of verse, *The Mother and Other Poems* (1915), was a slim pamphlet of 10 pages published at her own expense. Between 1916 and 1921 she edited *Wheels*, an annual anthology intended as a radical alternative to EDWARD MARSH's *GEORGIAN POETRY*, which she and her brothers despised. The seven poems by WILFRED OWEN it published in 1919 were among the first of his work to appear in print. Her poetic career continued prolifically throughout the 1920s, notably with *Façade* (1922), *Troy Park* (1925), which contained 'Colonel Fantock' and other poems about her family background, and *Gold Coast Customs* (1929). *Façade*, a suite of 'abstract poems' or 'patterns in sound' (as she later called them), typified her taste for experimentation, just as the controversy surrounding its performance to musical accompani-

Edith Sitwell, photograph by
Cecil Beaton

ment by William Walton in 1923 typified her highly publicized role in literary life.

During the 1930s she turned to prose, publishing a study of POPE (1930), *English Eccentrics* (1933) and a biography of Queen Victoria (1936). *Aspects of Modern Poetry* (1934) examined the work of HOPKINS, YEATS, ELIOT, POUND, JOYCE and GERTRUDE STEIN; an ironic promise in the preface of a similar volume on the Georgian poets was never fulfilled. Her only novel, *I Live under a Black Sun* (1937), was based on the affairs of SWIFT, Vanessa and Stella.

A preoccupation with war and suffering marked her later poetry, notably *Street Songs* (1942), which included the famous 'Still Falls the Rain', and *The Shadow of Cain* (1947), provoked by an eye-witness account of the first nuclear bomb on Hiroshima. *Collected Poems* appeared in the USA in 1954 and in an enlarged edition in Britain in 1957. Later prose work includes two books on Elizabeth I, *Fanfare for Elizabeth* (1946) and *The Queens and the Hive* (1962); an appreciation of American poetry, *The American Genius* (1951); and a volume of autobiography, *Taken Care Of* published posthumously in 1965. Her popularity was increased by lecture tours in America

during the 1950s, and the eccentricities of her dress and appearance were made famous by Cecil Beaton's photographs. She was created a Dame of the British Empire in 1954, and entered the Roman Catholic Church in 1955.

Sitwell, Sir **(Francis) Osbert (Sacheverell)**
1892–1969 Novelist, critic and poet. He was born in London and educated at Eton, spending much of his youth at the family home, Renishaw Hall in Derbyshire. Like his sister EDITH SITWELL and his brother SACHEVERELL SITWELL, he was an enemy of the Georgian poets, producing political and pacifist satires in *The Winstonburg Line* (1919). He wrote the text for William Walton's choral work, *Belshazzar's Feast*, first performed in 1931, and his *Collected Satires and Poems* (1931) was followed by *Demos the Emperor* (1949), a 'Secular Oratorio'. Other work included several novels, the best known of which is *Before the Bombardment* (1926); travel writing in *Winters of Content* (1932), set in Italy, and *Escape with Me* (1939), about China and the Far East; and a collection of journalism, *Penny Foolish* (1935). His best-regarded work is his autobiography, which ap-

peared in five volumes: *Left Hand, Right Hand* (1945), *The Scarlet Tree* (1946), *Great Morning!* (1948), *Laughter in the Next Room* (1949) and *Noble Essences* (1950). A later volume was *Tales My Father Taught Me* (1962).

Sitwell, Sacheverell 1897–1988 Poet and art historian. Brother of EDITH SITWELL and OSBERT SITWELL, he published over 40 books on a wide variety of subjects. His poetry, more traditional than his sister's, first appeared in *The People's Palace* (1918). He described *Dr Donne and Gargantua* (1930), a long poem which took 10 years to write, as 'a contest between Good and Evil'. His *Collected Poems* (1936), introduced by Edith, was followed by *The Dance of the Quick and the Dead* (1936). Sub-titled 'An Entertainment of the Imagination', it consisted of interrelated prose reflections and fantasias on art, literature, life and death. The similar but more despairing *Journey to the End of Time* (1959) was based on his belief that 'I have informed myself of nearly all works of art in the known world.' He published *Southern Baroque Art* (1924) and *German Baroque Art* (1927) at a time when these subjects had been little studied, and wrote biographies of Mozart (1932) and Liszt (1934). He also published *British Architects and Craftsmen* (1945) and a study of Japanese art, *The Bridge of the Brocade Sash* (1959). *A Retrospect of Poems* appeared in 1979.

Sizwe Bansi is Dead A play by ATHOL FUGARD, written in collaboration with Kani and Ntshona, the black actors who first performed in it in 1972. It was published together with *Statements after an Arrest under the Immorality Act* and *The Island* in 1974. A SATIRE of the South African 'pass laws', it recounts how a migratory worker lacking an identity card steals one from the corpse of Sizwe Bansi and thus loses his dignity and sense of identity.

Skeat, W(alter) W(illiam) 1835–1912 Literary scholar and philologist. An architect's son, Skeat was born in London and educated at King's College School, Highgate School and Christ's College, Cambridge, where he became a fellow in 1860. He entered the ministry and practised as a curate for a time, but ill health obliged him to give up and return to Christ's College as a lecturer in mathematics.

His interest in early English texts, pursued privately, was the basis of his reputation. He edited texts for the Early English Text Society, the Chaucer Society, the Scottish Text Society and the English Dialect Society (which he founded in 1873). His editions of PIERS PLOWMAN (1867–85) and the works of CHAUCER (1894–7) were standard authorities for a number of years. He was appointed Elrington and Bosworth Professor of Anglo-Saxon at Cambridge in 1878.

Skeat's study of the English language was scientific with a historical bias; his published works include *An Etymological Dictionary of the English Language* (1882), *A Concise Dictionary of Middle English* (1888), *A Primer of Classical and English Philology* (1905) and *The Science of Etymology* (1912). Skeat was also the author of numerous essays and editor of the poetry of THOMAS CHATTERTON (1871).

Skeffington, Sir **Lumley St George** 1771–1850 Playwright. The son of a rich London merchant, he was a fashionable dandy, a member of the Carlton House circle and a lover of the theatre. Two comedies, *The Word of Honour* (1802) and *The High Road to Marriage* (1803), and a MELODRAMA, *The Sleeping Beauty* (1805), were among the slight pieces he produced – 'skeletons of plays', BYRON called them – before squandering his fortune and sinking into chronic poverty.

Skelton, John ?1460–1529 Poet and satirist. Skelton may have been educated at Cambridge. Oxford conferred on him the title of laureate (a higher degree in rhetoric) in 1488, and Louvain and Cambridge also made him laureate in 1492 and 1493 respectively. In 1489 he was appointed court poet to Henry VII, by which time he had completed his translation of Diodorus Siculus (from a Latin version by Poggio) into English. From 1496 to 1501 he was tutor to the young prince Henry and was ordained priest in 1498. He obtained the rectorship of Diss in Norfolk *c.* 1503, a post he held until his death. In 1512 he received the title 'Orator Regius' from Henry VIII. He died in 1529, although the tradition that it was in sanctuary at Westminster, where he had taken refuge from Cardinal Wolsey, cannot be proved. Indeed, after the satirical attacks he made on Wolsey in the early 1520s in *Speak Parrot, Colin Clout* and *Why Came Ye Not to Court* he seems to have been reconciled with the Cardinal in the later 1520s, for Skelton's *How the Doughty Duke of Albany* was written at Wolsey's suggestion in 1523.

The Bowge [rations] *of Court* was written in the autumn of 1498 and printed by WYNKYN DE WORDE in the following year. It is a satirical dream-allegory about the court of Henry VII. *Philip Sparrow*, a lament by Jane Scroupe for her sparrow which was killed by Gib the cat, and which is also a requiem for the bird, was probably composed in 1505. *A Ballad of the Scottish King*, celebrating the English victory at Flodden, was printed in 1513. Skelton's huge secular MORALITY PLAY *MAGNYFICENCE* belongs to *c.* 1516. *The Tunning of Elinor Rumming*, probably written in 1517 and probably printed in 1521, portrays a drunken woman and the customers at her ale-house; it is largely responsible for POPE's description of Skelton's subject matter as 'beastly'. 1521-2 saw the writing of his satirical attacks on Cardinal Wolsey. In

The Garland of Laurel Skelton presents himself among the great poets, and if we are to believe the list of his works he gives there, many have been lost. A fairly complete collected edition of Skelton's poems was printed in 1568.

Skelton was highly regarded by most of his contemporaries: ERASMUS called him 'the light and glory of English letters', CAXTON praised him for his classical learning and his 'polished and ornate terms'. However, ALEXANDER BARCLAY described him as 'devoid of wisdom' and attacked one of his poems for its 'wantonness' and William Lily described him as 'neither learned nor a poet'. Later readers have often been deterred by his 'Skeltonics': headlong, irregular lines with no apparent metre or rhyme scheme.

Sketch Book of Geoffrey Crayon, Gent., The A book of essays and tales by WASHINGTON IRVING, serialized in 1819-20. Most of the pieces are descriptive and thoughtful essays on England, where Irving had been living for some years. Six sketches are set in America, among them Irving's most celebrated tales, 'The Legend of Sleepy Hollow' and 'Rip Van Winkle'. *The Sketch Book* made Irving the first American author to receive international recognition.

Sketches by Boz: Illustrative of Every-Day Life and Every-Day People Essays, stories and sketches by CHARLES DICKENS, contributed mainly to periodicals in 1833-6 and collected in 1836-7, with illustrations by GEORGE CRUIKSHANK.

The collection, Dickens's first published book, shows the variety of interest and the acuteness of observation fostered by his youthful training as a reporter. Whether driving home the moral lesson implicit in 'The Drunkard's Death', parodying middle-class pretensions in 'The Tuggses at Ramsgate' or simply visiting Astley's Circus, he shows a vivid eye for the pertinent detail. Casting his net widely, the author gives kindly accounts of the schoolmaster, the beadle, the curate and other timeless inhabitants of the local parish, and he records with sympathetic insight the events of a rural election or a dispossession. In comic vein, he writes of amateur theatricals in Clapham Rise. For grimmer subjects he turns to the city life of Seven Dials, the gin shop, the criminal court and, above all, Newgate. Occasionally turgid and sometimes forced, *Sketches by Boz* nevertheless anticipates the literary achievement to come.

Slessor, Kenneth 1901-71 Australian poet. Born at Orange and educated in Sydney, he became a reporter on the Sydney *Sun*, and after serving in World War II was appointed literary editor. His earliest work, *The Thief of the Moon* (1924), was reprinted with illustrations by NORMAN LINDSAY as *Earth-Visitors* (1926). Other works were 'Five Visions of Captain Cook' (in *Trio: A Book of Poems*, 1931),

Darlinghurst Nights and Morning Glories (a volume also including verse by Virgil Gavan Reilly; 1933), *Five Bells: XX Poems* (a moving ELEGY for a drowned friend; 1939) and *One Hundred Poems: 1919-1939* (1944). Slessor's verse, while controlled and formal, is elaborately decorative and highly visual.

Small House at Allington, The A novel by ANTHONY TROLLOPE, the fifth of his BARSETSHIRE NOVELS, serialized in *THE CORNHILL MAGAZINE* from September 1862 to April 1864 and published in two volumes in 1864.

The widowed Mrs Dale lives with her daughters Lily and Bell at the Small House at Allington, as family tenants of her brother-in-law Squire Dale, the unmarried proprietor of the adjacent Great House. Lily falls in love with a London civil servant, Adolphus Crosbie, but their engagement does not survive his visit to Courcy Castle and the attractions of rank in the person of Lady Alexandrina De Courcy. He jilts Lily and marries Lady Alexandrina, but the marriage is unhappy and they soon separate. Lily is deeply hurt and struggles to recover, but her continuing love for Crosbie prevents her marrying her honest and devoted local suitor Johnny Eames. Her more cautious sister resists a financially advantageous marriage with her cousin Bernard, the suitor favoured by her uncle the squire, and marries instead a local physician, Dr Crofts. A related plot deals with Johnny Eames and the romantic and financial entanglements brought on by his lonely life in London. He administers a public thrashing to Crosbie, which makes him a local hero at Allington.

Plantagenet Palliser, a central character in the PALLISER NOVELS, first appears in *A Small House at Allington*. The saddest of the Barsetshire novels, it is notable for the sympathetic power Trollope brings to the portrayal of Lily's loss and Crosbie's remorse. Lily Dale was his favourite heroine with the Victorian reading public.

Smart, Christopher 1722-71 Poet. Born at Shipborne in Kent, he moved to Durham on the death of his father in 1733, and was educated at Pembroke College, Cambridge, where he was elected a Fellow in 1745. A classical scholar of considerable standing, he also learned Hebrew, and was known as a writer of Latin verse. Around 1747, however, he began to display signs of erratic and obsessive behaviour – they were to intensify as he grew older – and he was arrested for debt. Rescued by friends, he returned to Pembroke in 1748 but went to London the following year and worked as a journalist for the publisher JOHN NEWBERY, whose stepdaughter he married in 1752.

Between 1750 and 1755 Smart won the prestigious Seatonian Prize for sacred poetry on five occasions, with his verses on 'the Supreme Being'; his *Poems on Several Occasions* appeared in 1752, and *The Hilliad*, a rather weak SATIRE on the quack doctor John Hill, was published in 1753. In 1756 there appeared a *Hymn to the Supreme Being* in thanks for his recovery from illness, but he was already teetering on the brink of what friends regarded as insanity. During the next seven years the poet was forcibly incarcerated in St Luke's Hospital for intermittent periods, during which time he busied himself with his writing, his gardening, and his cat Jeffrey.

His particular affliction was a religious mania which in his poetry manifests itself in convoluted patterns, puns, echoes and numerology, but which in his life gave rise to sudden and impassioned bouts of prayer and extravagant incantation. He was befriended by SAMUEL JOHNSON, a fellow contributor to *The Universal Visitor* (1756), who loyally declared: 'I'd as lief pray with Kit Smart as anyone else. Another charge was that he did not love clean linen; and I have no passion for it.' Legend has it that Smart, when not enthusiastically addressing the flowers or his cat, scratched certain of his verses with a key on the wainscot of his cell; whatever the means, he composed two quite exceptional poems during his confinement. The first, *A Song to David* (1763), is now his best-known poem though it was largely disregarded by his contemporaries; it is a hymn of praise to the author of the Psalms, an alliterative ecstasy which combines the compression of lyric with the splendour of religious language. The second, *Jubilate Agno* (not published until 1939), was more unconventional. It demonstrates the poet's extraordinary linguistic range, and is unique in the history of 18th-century verse, an extended incantation on the divinely designed patterns in the natural world with catalogues of rousing, irregular stanzas in praise of the significative variety of Creation. A blend of biblical and Renaissance archaisms and exotic vocabulary, this remarkable poem also assumes a strangely prophetic note ('The English tongue shall be the language of the west') and appears to anticipate some of the verbal effects of more recent verse – 'the great flabber dabber flat clapping fish with hands' – though its obscurity seems at points to shade off into absurdity.

For a writer with such an idiosyncratic concept of the effects of language (he considered the bull and the mouse to be most important among the English fauna in view of the incidence of '-ble' and '-mus' suffixes), he was notably precise in his classical scholarship. He was much influenced by Horace's *Ars poetica*, and translated the Latin poet's work into prose (1756) and verse (1767), including the notoriously difficult SAPPHICS in the complex variety of metrical schemes he imitated. Among his other work was *A Translation of the Psalms of David* (1765), *The Parables... Done into Familiar Verse* (1768) and *Hymns for the Amusement of Children*, written in 1770 during his final imprisonment for debt. His more complicated work is only now attracting careful attention.

Smart, Elizabeth 1913–86 Canadian novelist and poet. Born into a wealthy Ottawa family, she was educated at private schools in Canada and finished her education by making 22 transatlantic trips during her teens. After working briefly as a journalist in Ottawa in 1938, she travelled to New York, Mexico and California. A long liaison with the poet GEORGE BARKER began in 1940. She returned to England in 1943 where she lived for the rest of her life, only once going back to Canada in 1982–3 as writer-in-residence at the University of Edmonton. Her best-known novel is *By Grand Central Station I Sat Down and Wept* (1945). Based on her affair with Barker, it is a passionate love-poem in prose, infused with the language of the Song of Solomon and literary discourses about love, and structured in a formal arrangement of movements like a symphony. It became popular in England and New York during the 1950s and 1960s but was not available in Canada till 1975. Smart published two collections of poems, *A Bonus* (1977) and *Eleven Poems* (1982), as well as a second short novel, *The Assumption of the Rogues and Rascals* (1978), and a collection of poetry and prose, *In the Mean Time* (1984). As an expatriate writer, Smart's closest affinities are with English poetry; she was closely involved with the activities of the London little poetry magazines during the late 1930s and 1940s.

Smectymnuus The name adopted by five Presbyterian writers (Stephen Marshall, Edward Calamy, Thomas Young, Matthew Newcomen and William Spurstow) for a pamphlet against episcopacy in 1641. It was attacked by bishops JOSEPH HALL and USSHER and defended by MILTON.

Smedley, Francis Edward 1818–64 Novelist. Crippled from childhood, he achieved some success as the author of novels blending romance with sport and adventure. The most popular was *Frank Fairleigh: or, Scenes from the Life of a Private Pupil* (1850); others were *Lewis Arundel* (1852) and *Harry Coverdale's Courtship* (1855).

Smiles, Samuel 1812–1904 Biographer and essayist. Born in East Lothian, near Edinburgh, he was educated at Haddington High School and Edinburgh University. He became a doctor and later a journalist and company secretary in the expanding railway business. He held definite ideas on social and political reform, combined with a strong belief in work and self-improvement. These views emerge clearly in his biographies of successful men of the industrial age: *George Stephenson* (1857), *The Lives of the Engineers* (1867, expanded 1874) and *Josiah Wedgwood* (1894). He is best known for *Self-Help: With Illustrations of Character and Conduct* (1859), which sold in enormous numbers and was translated into several languages. Smiles continued his work as a popular moralist in *Character* (1871), *Thrift* (1875) and *Duty* (1880).

Smith, A(rthur) J(ames) M(arshall) 1902–80

Canadian poet. Born in Montreal and educated at McGill University and the University of Edinburgh, he taught at Michigan State University 1936–72. *News of the Phoenix and Other Poems* (1943), *A Sort of Ecstasy* (1954), *Collected Poems* (1962), *Poems: New and Collected* (1967) and *The Classic Shade* (1978) demonstrate his sharp and finely controlled style. He published a number of anthologies of Canadian verse as well as works of criticism: *Towards a View of Canadian Letters: Selected Essays 1928–72* (1973) and *On Poetry and Poets* (1977).

Smith, Adam 1723–90 Philosopher and political

economist. The posthumous son of the local comptroller of customs, he was brought up in Kirkcaldy, Fife. He went to Glasgow University and as a Snell exhibitioner to Balliol College, Oxford, where his interest in DAVID HUME'S *TREATISE OF HUMAN NATURE* brought him into conflict with the college authorities. In 1748 he was invited to Edinburgh under the auspices of HENRY HOME, LORD KAMES, to give courses of lectures, which covered rhetoric and *belles-lettres*, jurisprudence and, probably, the history of philosophy. He also edited the poems of the Jacobite William Hamilton of Bangour (1748). Smith took up the chair of logic at Glasgow University in 1751 and the following year that of moral philosophy, a post he held until 1763. The foundations of his system of thought were laid down in this period. His lectures on ethics became *THE THEORY OF MORAL SENTIMENTS* (1759). He published *On the First Formation of Languages* in *The Philological Miscellany* in 1761. His work on jurisprudence and government appeared posthumously as *Lectures on Jurisprudence* (1896).

Smith's international reputation was made by *The Theory of Moral Sentiments*. In 1766 he was elected a Fellow of the Royal Society and in 1764–6 he toured the Continent as tutor to the young Duke of Buccleuch, meeting Voltaire in Geneva and the Physiocrats in Paris. His major work, *THE WEALTH OF NATIONS* (1776), was begun during the tour and was continued in Kirkcaldy, Edinburgh and London. In London he spent time at the Club with GIBBON, BURKE, JOSHUA REYNOLDS, JOHNSON (with whom he was not on good terms), BOSWELL and GARRICK. He read a draft of parts of *The Wealth of Nations* to BENJAMIN FRANKLIN. He was also intimate with the major figures of the Scottish Enlightenment, notably John Millar, WILLIAM ROBERTSON, ADAM FERGUSON, Joseph Black, James Hutton, Hugh Blair and DUGALD STEWART. Smith showed his loyalty to Hume by publishing a controversial edition of his friend's autobiography in 1777.

He moved to Edinburgh in 1778 as Commissioner of Customs for Scotland and of Salt Duties, taking an active part in the intellectual life of the city and becoming a founder-member of the Royal Society of Edinburgh in 1783. He was elected Lord Rector of Glasgow University in 1787, serving until 1789. His last major work was a revised, sixth edition of *The Theory of Moral Sentiments*. His literary executors were instructed to burn 16 folios of his unpublished writings, perhaps containing an unfinished version of a projected book on jurisprudence. Some essays, including the 'History of Astronomy', were spared and published in 1795 as *Essays on Philosophical Subjects*.

Smith, Alexander 1830–67 Poet. Born in Kilmarn-

ock, Ayrshire, he earned his living as a lace-pattern designer in Glasgow. *Poems* (1853) contained 'A Life Drama', praised by the reviewers but ridiculed by WILLIAM AYTOUN as part of the SPASMODIC SCHOOL OF POETRY. *Sonnets on the War*, with SYDNEY DOBELL, appeared during the Crimean War in 1855. *City Poems* (1857) contained what is usually regarded as his best poem, 'Glasgow'. *Edwin of Deira* (1861) helped Smith live down his reputation as a Spasmodic but provoked the accusation that he had plagiarized from TENNYSON'S *IDYLLS OF THE KING*. Smith turned to prose. *Dreamthorpe* (1863) and *Last Leaves* (published posthumously, 1868) are collections of essays, *Alfred Hagart's Household* (1865) is a novel and *A Summer in Skye* (1865) is a description of the island and its people.

Smith, Charlotte 1749–1806 Novelist and poet.

Born Charlotte Turner in London, she married a merchant in the West Indies trade in 1765. After the ruin of his business in 1782 he was imprisoned for debt and she turned industriously to writing. Her first published work was a translation of Prévost's *Manon Lescaut* (1785), though she became known as a poet and, chiefly, as a novelist. *Emmeline: or, The Orphan of the Castle* (1788) and *The Old Manor House* (1793) were widely admired by contemporaries.

Smith, Dave 1942– American poet. Born in Ports-

mouth, Virginia, he studied at the University of Virginia and then served in the US Air Force before completing his MA and Ph.D at the universities of Southern Illinois and Ohio respectively. He has taught at the University of Utah and is now a professor of English at Virginia Commonwealth University in Richmond. His early poems about the lives of Chesapeake Bay oyster fishermen appeared in *The Fisherman's Whore* (1974). Later poems, showing the development of a strong moral sensibility, are to be found in volumes such as *Goshawk, Antelope: Poems* (1979), *Dream Flights: Poems* (1981), *Homage to Edgar Allan Poe* (1981), *Gray Soldiers: Poems* (1983), *In the House of the Judge* (1983), *Southern Delights* (1984) and *Cuba Night: Poetry* (1990). *The Roundhouse Voices: Selected and New Poems* (1985) makes an excellent introduction to his work. He has also written *Onliness: A Novel* (1981) and a collection of essays, *Local Assays: On Contemporary American Poetry* (1985).

Smith, George (Murray) 1824–1901 Publisher. Born of Scottish parents in London, he started work in his father's publishing firm, Smith Elder, at the age of 14 and took charge of the business in 1843. An enormously energetic publisher, Smith was particularly good at recognizing authors. The BRONTË sisters were his most famous discovery, but he added many great Victorians to his list: RUSKIN, THACKERAY, HARRIET MARTINEAU, ELIZABETH GASKELL, ROSSETTI, WILKIE COLLINS, CHARLES READE, ROBERT BROWNING, DARWIN, MEREDITH and MRS HUMPHRY WARD. He founded *THE CORNHILL MAGAZINE* in 1860, with Thackeray and later LESLIE STEPHEN as editor, and, in collaboration with Frederick Greenwood, *THE PALL MALL GAZETTE* in 1865. In 1882 he started to publish *The Dictionary of National Biography*, with Leslie Stephen as its first editor. His authors were his friends, and so were LEIGH HUNT, John Everett Millais, Lord Leighton and JOHN LEECH.

Smith, Goldwin 1823–1910 Historian, literary critic and liberal reformer. Born in Reading, he was educated at Eton and Christ Church, Oxford, becoming Stowell Law Professor at University College in 1846 and Regius Professor of Modern History in 1859. Rejecting the OXFORD MOVEMENT, Smith identified himself with the cause of liberal reform in Oxford and beyond, serving on the commission which led to the Oxford University Reform Act (1854), taking a sceptical position about religion in a disagreement with Bishop Wilberforce, attacking imperialism in *The Empire* (1863), supporting the North in the American Civil War, and joining JOHN STUART MILL on the committee urging the impeachment of Governor Eyre of Jamaica in 1867. An extended visit to America led to his appointment as the first professor of English and constitutional history at Cornell University in 1868. He settled in Toronto in 1871, at first advocating Canada's independence from Great Britain and then favouring its commercial union with the United States. His later works include political histories of the United States (1893) and the United Kingdom (1899), a volume on COWPER for the English Men of Letters series (1880) and a life of JANE AUSTEN (1892).

Smith, Iain Crichton 1928– Scottish poet, translator, playwright, novelist and short-story writer. Born on the island of Lewis and educated at Aberdeen University, he worked as a schoolteacher in Clydebank from 1955 until 1977, when he became a full-time writer. He writes in English and Gaelic

and translates his own work and that of other Scottish Gaelic poets, such as SORLEY MACLEAN. The Gaelic language and the landscape and people of the Scottish islands and Highlands figure prominently in his writing. His fiction includes: *Consider the Lilies* (1968), a moving account of the Highland Clearances; *The Dream* (1990); *Selected Stories* (1990); and *An Honourable Death* (1992). The verse, gathered in *Collected Poems* (1992), includes 'Shall Gaelic Die?', a sequence showing his concern for the survival of the language, and the much-anthologized 'Old Woman'.

Smith, John Thomas 1766–1833 Artist, engraver and, after 1816, Keeper of Prints and Drawings at the British Museum. As well as the many antiquarian and topographical books which he wrote and illustrated, Smith published a maliciously candid biography of Joseph Nollekens (1828), the sculptor who had been his father's employer and his own teacher. *A Book for a Rainy Day: or, Recollections of the Events of the Years 1766–1833* (1845) is a mine of information on literary and artistic life.

Smith, Ken(neth) (John) 1938– Poet. Born in East Rudston, Yorkshire, he escaped the isolation of his childhood when he was called up for national service. After reading English at Leeds University, he taught at Dewsbury and Exeter Art Colleges. He writes visionary poetry which is populist, humorous and subversive. Despite the success of *The Pity* (1967) and his co-editorship, with JON SILKIN, of *Stand* magazine, he moved to America in 1967, where he learned from JAMES WRIGHT, ROBERT BLY and William Stafford and from oral poetry. *Work, distances/poems* (1972), *Tristan Crazy* (1978) and *Fox Running* (1980) are featured in *The Poet Reclining: Selected Poems 1962–1980* (1982), which marked Smith's re-establishment as a poet in Britain. Other works are: *Abel Baker* (1981); *Burned Books* (1981); *Terra* (1985); *A Book of Chinese Whispers* (1987), in prose; *Inside Time* (1989), prompted by his work as writer-in-residence in Wormwood Scrubs; and *Berlin: Coming in from the Cold* (1990), prompted by the destruction of the Berlin Wall.

Smith, Michael 1954–83 Jamaican poet. Associated with the Rastafarian movement in Jamaica, Smith was also radically influenced by the writings of Marcus Garvey and by the teachings of the Guyanese political theorist Walter Rodney. He was stoned to death by unknown murderers. Although some of his work is available in anthologies, he never brought out a printed collection and relied almost entirely on public performance. As a result his poems are now best heard on records such as *Word* (1978), *Me Cyaan Believe It* (1980) and *Roots* (1980). Among the new generation of poets in the Caribbean and 'black' Britain he has been, with Bob Marley and LINTON KWESI JOHNSON, much the most influential.

Smith, Pauline (Janet) 1882–1959 South African short-story writer and novelist. Born in Oudtshoorn, she was educated and lived mostly in Britain, yet the austere, rigorously crafted short stories in *The Little Karoo* (1925), and also the novel *The Beadle* (1926), about late 19th-century Boer peasant life, superbly demonstrate how a sensitive and sympathetic writer of one culture can penetrate the psychological hinterlands of another. To simulate Afrikaans speech in English sentences, she skilfully incorporates Afrikaans words and phrases into 'un-English' cadences with inverted word-order and unusual rhythms. *A.B.* (1933) is a modest, remarkably understanding tribute to ARNOLD BENNETT, who first encouraged her.

Smith, Stevie [Florence Margaret] 1902–71 Poet and novelist. Born in Hull, she moved to an aunt's house in Palmers Green, London, at the age of three and lived there for the rest of her life. She was educated at North London Collegiate School. Her lifelong employment was with the magazine publishers Newnes-Pearson, where she became private secretary to Sir George Newnes and Sir Neville Pearson. She made her reputation with her first novel, *Novel on Yellow Paper* (1936), and her first volume of poems, *A Good Time was Had by All* (1937). She published two more novels, *Over the Frontier* (1938) and *The Holiday* (1949), and seven more collections of poetry, including *Not Waving But Drowning* (1957). Her wittily barbed verse found a wide and enthusiastic audience, promoted by her distinctive public readings and recordings. It was often illustrated with naive line drawings in the manner of EDWARD LEAR, with whom she shared an often sad but irrepressible love of life. *Collected Poems* appeared posthumously in 1975.

Smith, Sydney 1771–1845 Essayist, parson and wit. 'The wisest of witty men, and the wittiest of wise men' was born at Woodford, Essex, educated at Winchester and New College, Oxford, and ordained in 1796. After a brief curacy in the West Country, Smith spent several years in Edinburgh where he was of the circle of WALTER SCOTT, DUGALD STEWART and FRANCIS HORNER. In company with FRANCIS JEFFREY, HENRY BROUGHAM, John Allen and other intellectuals Smith founded *THE EDINBURGH REVIEW*, one of the most eminent journals of the century, in 1802.

Removing with his wife to London in 1804, Smith soon became a popular preacher, a lecturer in moral philosophy and, because of his brilliant wit, a familiar among the Whigs of Holland House. In 1808 he 'was suddenly caught up by the Archbishop of York and transported' to the living of Foston-le-Clay in Yorkshire where, 'not knowing a turnip from a

carrot', he had to farm several hundred acres. Meanwhile, he had written for *The Edinburgh Review*, and in 1807 he began to publish *The Letters of Peter Plymley*, on Catholic Emancipation. After two decades in Yorkshire, Smith became a prebend in Bristol cathedral in 1828 and soon thereafter exchanged Foston for the living of Combe Florey in Somerset. A conscientious clergyman, Smith never achieved a bishopric, although in 1831 he was appointed Canon Residentiary at St Paul's. He died a wealthy man.

Charming and blessed with common sense, Sydney Smith is rare among divines of any age. He published volumes of sermons as well as pamphlets, reviews and essays on matters as remote from each other as Dissent, alehouse licensing, vice and female education.

Smith, Sydney Goodsir 1915–75 Scottish poet. The son of a celebrated Edinburgh professor of forensic medicine, he was born, despite the resolute Scottishness of his thinking and writing, in Wellington, New Zealand. He was educated at Edinburgh and Oxford universities. Several minor books of verse appeared before *Under the Eildon Tree* (1948) showed his full power and established his reputation. These 24 elegies on the unhappy loves of poets have a wide range of literary reference to reinforce the autobiographical element. For all its background in earlier texts, his fluent and effective Scots has the suppleness of spoken language. His other major works are a play, *The Wallace* (Edinburgh Festival, 1960), patriotic but weak in structure, and a novel, *Carotid Cornucopius* (1947, revised 1964), an ambitious fantasy which owes something to JOYCE but more to the Scottish Rabelaisian tradition of SIR THOMAS URQUHART. Smith was in many ways the principal successor to HUGH MACDIARMID, with whom his linguistic affinities are strong.

Smith, William Robertson 1846–94 Biblical scholar. Born at Keig in Aberdeenshire, he studied at New College in Edinburgh and the universities of Bonn and Göttingen, and was appointed professor of oriental languages and Old Testament exegesis at Free College, Aberdeen, in 1870. His contributions to the ninth edition of the *Encyclopaedia Britannica*, which began publication in 1875, were influenced by the HIGHER CRITICISM and angered the General Assembly of the Free Church of Scotland by their failure to present the Bible as the authoritative word of God. He was dismissed from his post in 1881. After working as joint editor of the *Encyclopaedia Britannica*, he was appointed professor of Arabic at Cambridge in 1883 and spent the rest of his career there.

Smither, Elizabeth 1941– New Zealand poet and novelist. She has spent most of her life in New

Plymouth, working as a librarian, journalist and editor. EMILY DICKINSON, WALLACE STEVENS and WILLIAM EMPSON are acknowledged influences on the spare, often witty lyrics, informal in tone and seemingly impersonal in subject, which have appeared in such volumes as *Here Come the Clouds* (1975), *You're Very Seductive William Carlos Williams* (1978), *Casanova's Ankle* (1981), *Professor Musgrove's Canary* (1986) and *A Pattern of Marching* (1989). *First Blood* (1983) and *Brother-love Sister-love* (1986) are novels.

Smithyman, Kendrick 1922– New Zealand poet and critic. First a school-teacher and then a university tutor in English, he has spent most of his life in Auckland. Although associated with ALLEN CURNOW, who singled him out for praise in his 1960 Penguin anthology, he has always been less interested in a poetry of national identity. On one hand, his poetry is intensely local, rooted in particular histories and geographies; on the other it is fluently international, drawing adroitly and innovatively on different traditions of MODERNISM. Much of his early work in *The Blind Mountain* (1950) and other volumes published during the 1950s and early 1960s is tortuously difficult. *Earthquake Weather* (1972) and *The Seal in the Dolphin Pool* (1974) continue earlier preoccupations with place, history and language, but their style is more relaxed and their forms are more open. *Dwarf with a Billiard Cue* (1978) and *Stories about Wooden Keyboards* (1985) have more pronounced social and comic elements. *A Way of Saying* (1965) remains the only full-length critical study of New Zealand poetry.

Smollett, Tobias (George) 1721–71 Novelist, travel-writer, critic, political controversialist, unsuccessful playwright and poet. Smollett was the first of the Scots novelists, from the village of Leven, near Loch Lomond. While still at Dumbarton grammar school he wrote verses to the memory of the national hero, Wallace, and at 18 wrote a play, *The Regicide*, about James I of Scotland and his queen. Smollett wanted an army career, but was apprenticed to a surgeon in Glasgow, having at Glasgow University studied Greek, mathematics and natural philosophy. He studied medicine at Edinburgh University but left without taking a degree. Aged 19, he went to London, and became a surgeon's mate in the navy, under Admiral Vernon, at the siege of Cartagena in 1741.

His youthful writing included poetry, notably *The Tears of Scotland* (1746), about the Duke of Cumberland's reprisals after the 1745 rebellion, and the satirical *Advice* (1746) and *Reproof* (1747). In his first novel, *THE ADVENTURES OF RODERICK RANDOM* (1748), he used his naval experience and theatrical disappointments. Most of the characters, in particular Crab, Potion and Squire Gawkey, were recognized as living portraits. It also contained an attack on GARRICK (Marmoset). Smollett then wrote an opera,

Alceste, to music by Handel, but when the piece was not staged, Handel adapted the music to DRYDEN's 'Song for St Cecilia's Day'. Smollett worked tirelessly to get *The Regicide* performed, but without success. In 1749 it was published by subscription, with a preface attacking the duplicity of theatrical managers. *THE ADVENTURES OF PEREGRINE PICKLE* (1751) continued the vein of violent, hard-bitten PICARESQUE for which his novels are known.

In 1752 Smollett obtained the degree of Doctor of Physic and settled in Bath, writing *An Essay on the External Use of Water, in a Letter to Dr––, with Particular Remarks upon the Present Method of Using the Mineral Waters at Bath in Somersetshire, and a Plan for Rendering Them More Safe, Agreeable and Efficacious*, his only professional publication. He soon gave up medicine and moved to Chelsea, where he made a living writing for booksellers, who commissioned him for prefaces, translations and other hack work. He remained chronically short of money, and his wife, Anne Lascelles, was extravagant. In 1753 he published *THE ADVENTURES OF FERDINAND COUNT FATHOM* and in 1755 a translation of *Don Quixote*, with explanatory notes. This was judged inadequate, as he lacked the requisite knowledge of Spanish language and culture. In 1756 appeared *A Compendium of Authentic Voyages, Digested in a Chronological Series* in seven volumes. Smollett was believed to be the editor, partly because the work included 'A Short Narrative of the Expedition to Carthagena, 1741' written 'with great spirit, but abounding with acrimony'. In 1757 his comedy, *The Reprisal: or, The Tars of Old England* was staged at DRURY LANE by Garrick. From 1756 to 1763 he edited the *Critical Review or Annals of Literature*, in which he pursued quarrels with other authors. As a result of a libel on Admiral Knowles's conduct in the expedition to Rochford, 1758 ('an engineer without knowledge, an officer without resolution, and a man without veracity'), Smollett was fined £100 and served three months in prison. While there, he wrote *THE LIFE AND ADVENTURES OF SIR LAUNCELOT GREAVES*, later printed in *The British Magazine* (which he edited 1760–1) and in volume form in 1762. He published his *Complete History of England Deduced from the Defeat of Julius Caesar to the Treaty of Aix-la-Chapelle, 1748 in 1758*. Written in 14 months, it made him £2000. *The Briton*, the journal he started in 1762 to defend the Earl of Bute, the prime minister, prompted JOHN WILKES to reply with *THE NORTH BRITON*. The controversy dissolved their friendship, without preventing Bute's resignation or earning Smollett his gratitude.

Smollett, who complained most of his life of ill health (constant rheumatism and a neglected ulcer), went in June 1764 to France and Italy. *TRAVELS THROUGH FRANCE AND ITALY* was published in 1766. Smollett, who considered himself 'traduced by malice, persecuted by fashion, and overwhelmed by...

domestic calamity', was satirized by STERNE in *A Sentimental Journey* as 'the learned Smelfungus', who 'set out with the spleen and jaundice, and every object he passed by was discoloured and distorted'. In 1769 Smollett published *Adventures of an Atom*, a political satire supposed to have been written in 1748 and showing, under Japanese names, the British political parties. In 1770 he went, again in search of health, to Edinburgh and Inverary. In 1771 *THE EXPEDITION OF HUMPHRY CLINKER* appeared, in which, under the character of Matthew Bramble, he inserted the observations he made on revisiting his native country. He died at Leghorn .

Snodgrass, W(illiam) D(eWitt) 1926- American poet. Born in Wilkinsburg, Pennsylvania, he was educated at Geneva College in Pennsylvania and the University of Iowa. Usually autobiographical, his poetry uses traditional forms and a sensitive, often delicate tone. His first volume, *Heart's Needle* (PULITZER PRIZE, 1959), centred on his divorce from his first wife and the resulting separation from his daughter. Other volumes include *After Experience: Poems and Translations* (1968), *Remains* (1970), *The Fuhrer Bunker: A Cycle of Poems in Progress* (1977), *If Birds Build with Your Hair* (1979), *The Boy Made of Meat* (1983), *Owls: A Poem* (1983), *Heinrich Himmler: Platoons and Flies* (1985) and *The Death of Cock Robin* (1989). *Selected Poems 1957-1987* appeared in 1987. His translations include Christian Morgenstern's *Gallows Songs* (1967), *Six Troubadour Songs* (1977) and *Six Minnesinger Songs* (1983). *Radical Pursuit: Critical Essays and Lectures* appeared in 1975.

Snow, C(harles) P(ercy), Baron Snow of Leicester 1905-80 Novelist. Born in Leicester, he was educated at Alderman Newton's School and Leicester University College, where he studied science. At Cambridge he took a PhD for research in physics, became a Fellow of Christ's College in 1930 and taught science in 1935-45. He served as a scientific adviser during World War II and was a Civil Service Commissioner in 1945-60. He married the novelist PAMELA HANSFORD JOHNSON in 1950. He became Parliamentary Secretary to the Ministry of Science and Technology in 1964.

His first novel, *Death under Sail* (1932), was a conventional piece of DETECTIVE FICTION. *The Search* (1934) looked forward to his later work in its concern with power and the ethics of science. Snow is best known for the *ROMAN FLEUVE*, *Strangers and Brothers*, which began in 1940 with a novel of that name (subsequently retitled *George Passant*) and continued with *The Light and the Dark* (1947), *Time of Hope* (1949), *The Masters* (winner of the James Tait Black Memorial Prize, 1951), *The New Men* (1954), *Homecomings* (1956), *The Conscience of the Rich* (1958), *The Affair* (1959), *Corridors of Power* (1963), *The Sleep of*

Reason (1968) and *Last Things* (1970). The protagonist, Lewis Eliot, achieves fame and fortune after an inauspicious start; the various stages of his career permit Snow to offer a wide, leisurely survey of academic, scientific and political life. He also published critical studies, including a biography of TROLLOPE (1975), but gained most impact with his Rede Lecture on *The Two Cultures and the Scientific Revolution* (1959). In this he contrasted the culture of 'literary intellectuals' and that of 'scientists', and argued that the two had ceased to communicate. His suggested remedy, involving a radical change in educational attitudes, was savagely attacked by F. R. LEAVIS for its utilitarian approach to the study of the humanities. *Science and Government* (1961, originally the Godkin Lectures at Harvard) examined the scientist's vocation and the factor of power involved in government-sponsored research. *Public Affairs* (1971) warned of the dangers and assessed the benefits of advanced technology, and *A Variety of Men* (1967) was a group of biographical studies.

Snyder, Gary 1930- American poet. He was born in San Francisco and educated at Reed College, the University of Indiana and the University of California at Berkeley. In San Francisco he met JACK KEROUAC, ALLEN GINSBERG and other members of the BEATS, with whom he shared a rejection of mainstream American values and an interest in experimental poetic forms. His work also reflects his experiences as a seaman, logger and Forest Service trailman, and his preoccupation with Buddhism, which he studied in Japan. Meditative or philosophical in tone, it often presents his views of nature, religion, and Western culture. His first book, *Riprap* (1959), has been followed by *Myths and Texts* (1960), *Riprap, and Cold Mountain Poems* (1965), *Six Sections from Mountains and Rivers without End* (1965, revised edition 1970), *A Range of Poems* (1966), *The Back Country* (1968), *Regarding Wave* (1969 enlarged edition 1970), *Turtle Island* (including both prose and poetry, 1974; PULITZER PRIZE), *Axe Handles* (1983), *Left Out in the Rain: Poems 1947-1984* (1986), *The Practice of the Wild* (1990) and *No Nature: New and Selected Poems* (1992). *Earth House Hold* (1969), *The Old Ways: Six Essays* (1977) and *The Real Work: Interviews and Talks 1964-1979* (edited by Scott McLean; 1980) are among his prose collections.

Sohrab and Rustum: *An Episode* A poem by MATTHEW ARNOLD, published in *Poems: A New Edition* (1853). The story comes from Firdousi's *Shah Nameh*, a Persian epic, which Arnold encountered in an essay by the French critic Sainte-Beuve and Sir John Malcolm's *History of Persia* (1815).

Sohrab, son of the Persian hero Rustum, was born while his father was away at war. His mother, fearing that he would spend his life in fighting, gave out that she had borne a girl and returned to her own country with her son. Nevertheless, he grew up to be a warrior in the Tartar armies. When the Tartars attack Persia Sohrab challenges their bravest soldier to meet him in single combat. During the struggle the Persian champion calls out his own name, 'Rustum!', and Sohrab realizes that he is fighting his father. He recoils and his opponent strikes him down. Sohrab reveals his identity, by the seal pricked on his arm, but dies at his father's feet. With its heroic subject and its frequent use of the EPIC SIMILE, *Sohrab and Rustum* deliberately sets out to avoid that melancholy subjectivity which the preface to the volume where the poem first appeared had diagnosed as one of the ills of contemporary poetry. Arnold told his friend CLOUGH in a letter: 'Homer *animates* – Shakespeare *animates* – in its poor way I think Sohrab and Rustum animates.'

Soldiers Three A collection of 13 stories by RUDYARD KIPLING, first published separately in 1888 alongside the booklets entitled *Under the Deodars*, *The Phantom Rickshaw* and *Wee Willie Winkie*. They were included in a two-volume collection published in 1892.

Kipling depicts the soldierly virtues necessary to sustain the Empire. It is for his creation of the daily life of the British fighting man and of an army on the alert against potential invaders from Afghanistan that the stories are chiefly admired. Through the taxing ordeals of action and drilling, Mulvaney, one of the 'soldiers three', learns the stoical virtues. His rule-breaking individualism and imagination, qualities which are central to the later *STALKY & Co.*, finally reinforce the army system of values. Elements of FARCE and MELODRAMA are often seen most strongly in the short episodes of battle and skirmish; in these Kipling has been seen as a forerunner of cinematic vision. But the strongest ingredients are the atmosphere of the brooding landscape and the men's stoicism, companionship and ability to survive a tedious, emotionally cheerless routine.

soliloquy The convention permitting an actor, alone on the stage, to address the audience directly. Although it dates from the earliest years of English drama, the use of the soliloquy to allow an actor to talk revealingly to himself was largely an invention of the Elizabethan playwrights. The opening speech of MARLOWE's *DOCTOR FAUSTUS* is a flamboyant early example.

Soliloquy of the Spanish Cloister A poem by ROBERT BROWNING, published in *Dramatic Lyrics* (1842). It takes the form of a DRAMATIC MONOLOGUE by a spiteful monk who envies the innocent happiness of his fellow, Brother Lawrence.

Somerville, Edith See SOMERVILLE AND ROSS.

Somerville, William 1675–1742 Poet. A country gentleman from Edstone near Henley-in-Arden, Warwickshire, he was educated at Winchester and at New College, Oxford, where he became a Fellow. His pastime was to compose poetry, and in 1727 he published *Occasional Poems, Translations, Fables, Tales, etc.* His slender reputation depends on *The Chace* (1735), a poem in four books of Miltonic BLANK VERSE describing the pleasures of hunting and the variety of dogs, hounds, terrain and quarry. The work enjoyed a certain circulation and became the preferred poem of Mr Jorrocks in SURTEES's novel *HANDLEY CROSS*, though it prompted a scathing treatment of its author in JOHNSON's *LIVES OF THE POETS*. *Field Sports* (1742) is a less extended work, on hawking, and *Hobbinol* (1740) is a MOCK-HEROIC PASTORAL describing rustic May games in the Vale of Evesham.

Somerville and Ross [Somerville, Edith Anna Oenone (1858–1949) and Martin, Violet Florence (1862–1915)] Novelists, short-story writers and travel-writers. Edith Somerville was born in County Cork and studied art in London and Paris. Her cousin Violet Martin was born in County Galway and educated in Dublin. Edith Somerville enjoyed some success as an artist, exhibiting from 1920 to 1938, but her literary career began as early as 1889, when the first book by Somerville and Ross, *An Irish Cousin*, was published. The best of the cousins' work represents the Anglo-Irish tradition of exploiting the humours of the true Irish in relation to the owners of the big houses and estates.

Other novels were *Naboth's Vineyard* (1891) and *The Real Charlotte* (1894). *In the Vine Country* (1893) related travels in France, and *Through Connemara in a Governess Cart* (1893) travels in the west of Ireland. *The Silver Fox* (1898) is a novel about hunting. The enormously popular *Some Experiences of an Irish RM* (1899) contains stories about a resident magistrate, continued in *Further Experiences of an Irish RM* (1908). *Beggars on Horseback* (1895) told of a riding tour of North Wales. *A Patrick's Day Hunt* (1902) and *All on the Irish Shore* (1903) continued the short stories of Irish life. *Dan Russell the Fox* (1911) is a novel, the last collaboration before Violet Martin died. Edith Somerville's later works, published under the familiar pseudonym, included *In Mr Knox's Country* (1915), *Mount Music* (1919), *The Big House of Inver* (1925), *The Sweet Cry of Hounds* (1936) and *Sarah's Youth* (1938).

Songs of Innocence and of Experience *Shewing the Two Contrary States of the Human Soul* A collection of combined poems and etchings by WILLIAM BLAKE, issued in 1794 but incorporating his *Songs of Innocence* (1789).

In the 'Introduction' a spirit child weeps with delight at the poet-piper's songs of 'happy chear' and commands him to 'sit thee down and write/ In a book that all may read'. Some of the poems indeed appear to issue directly from the mouths of children (e.g. 'Little Lamb, Who Made Thee?', 'The Little Black Boy', 'The Chimney Sweeper'); others view the state of infancy through the eyes of mothers and nurses ('Infant Joy', 'A Cradle Song', 'Nurse's Song'). Poems such as 'The Divine Image', 'Night' and 'On Another's Sorrow', on the other hand, quietly suggest an opposite world of sorrow and violence of which the child is necessarily unaware.

The *Songs of Experience* – including 'The Tyger' and 'The Sick Rose', Blake's most frequently quoted and interpreted poems – contain a number of poems whose titles echo the *Songs of Innocence*. They show how the experiences of adult life corrupt and finally destroy innocence. The two Nurse's songs are a striking instance of Blake's antithetical procedure: where the children of the first song are encouraged to play on uninhibitedly, the soured and disillusioned nurse of the second undermines their play with thoughts of the transience of life and the fraudulence of adult sexual relations. Similarly, the innocent anarchy of 'The Echoing Green' contrasts with the religious prohibitions of 'The Garden of Love'. Blake's angry attack on institutionalized coercion and enslavement embraces the ecclesiastical swindle of deferred gratification ('The Little Vagabond'), the creation of poverty in the midst of plenty ('Holy Thursday', 'Infant Sorrow'), and the moral and psychological devastations of early English capitalism ('London'). Only the Bard, who summons the Earth to awake from her materialist slumber and to return to the free life of the imagination, is able to envisage a healing of the grievous split between innocence and experience ('Introduction').

sonnet COLERIDGE defined the sonnet as 'a small poem, in which some lonely [i.e. single and coherent] feeling is developed'. Traditionally it is a short single-stanza lyric poem in iambic pentameters, usually consisting of 14 lines, rhyming in various patterns (see METRE and RHYME). The PETRARCHAN sonnet has an octave (8 lines) rhyming abba abba and a sestet (6 lines) rhyming cde cde (or some variation such as ccd ccd). SIR THOMAS WYATT was an early imitator of Petrarchan sonnets in England. There was also the so-called English or Shakespearean sonnet, developed by the EARL OF SURREY and others in the 16th century, which consisted of three quatrains and a concluding couplet: Shakespeare's rhyme abab cdcd efef gg. The late 16th century saw a vogue for sonnet sequences, such as SHAKESPEARE's *SONNETS*, SIDNEY's *ASTROPHIL AND STELLA* and SPENSER's *AMORETTI*. The latter has a different rhyme scheme for its sonnet: three quatrains with interlinked rhymes abab bcbc cdcd ee. In the 17th century JOHN DONNE and JOHN MILTON expanded the sonnet's range from love poetry to include religious feelings and serious contemplation. Most of the Romantic poets wrote sonnets. The form was used by W. H. AUDEN and is still used by practising poets. WORDSWORTH's sonnet beginning 'Scorn not the Sonnet' at once gives an example of his own use of the form and a brief history of the sonnet up to Milton.

Sonnets from the Portuguese A sequence of SONNETS by ELIZABETH BARRETT BROWNING, published in *Poems* (1850). The deliberately misleading title – there are no Portuguese originals – veils the intensely personal nature of these love poems, written before her marriage to ROBERT BROWNING in 1846. The volume was the object of a notorious bibliographical fraud, the so-called 'Reading edition' of 1847 fabricated by T. J. WISE.

Sonnets of Shakespeare See SHAKESPEARE'S *SONNETS*.

Sons and Lovers A novel by D. H. LAWRENCE, published in 1913. Largely autobiographical, it is based on his childhood and youth in Eastwood, Nottinghamshire.

Gertrude Coppard becomes a schoolteacher to escape her harsh and overbearing father. She is fascinated by the miner, Walter Morel, whose earthy liveliness is in stark contrast to the Puritan atmosphere of her home. She and Morel are married and live happily for a time; but he is a heavy drinker and resists her efforts to change him. Mrs Morel concentrates all her energies on her children, three sons and a daughter, and seeks some stimulus for her mind at the Co-operative Women's Guild. Her eldest son, William, goes to work and brings in a little more money for the family. Later he moves to London and dies there. Mrs Morel is stunned by William's untimely death, but when Paul, her second son, also falls ill she nurses him back to health and transfers her emotions and aspirations to him. Walter Morel is scorned and excluded by his wife and children. Paul starts work as a junior clerk in Nottingham. He falls in love with Miriam Leivers, an intense, reserved and 'spiritual' girl (a character based on Lawrence's friend Jessie Chambers). Mrs Morel becomes possessive and jealous of Paul's relationship with Miriam. Eventually Paul meets and has an affair with Clara Dawes, a married woman, and is also powerfully drawn to her husband Baxter. Mrs Morel suffers a long and painful illness, which Paul relieves by administering morphia. After her death, at the end of the novel, he determines to set out and make his own life.

Sontag, Susan 1933– American critic. Born in New York, she was educated at the University of Chicago and at Harvard. Two novels, *The Benefactor* (1963) and *Death Kit* (1967), and a collection of short fiction, *I, etcetera* (1978), share an intense preoccupation with dreams and the unconscious. A later novel, *The Volcano Lover* (1992), is about Nelson and Sir William and Lady (Emma) Hamilton. She is probably best known, however, for her essays on *avant-garde* film and for her literary criticism, much of which was first published in *PARTISAN REVIEW* and *THE NEW YORK REVIEW OF BOOKS*, and later collected in *Against Interpretation* (1966). Another collection of essays, *Styles of Radical Will* (1969), includes the autobiographical 'Trip to Hanoi'. The influence of Roland Barthes is evident in a monograph, *On Photography* (1977). When she contracted cancer she wrote *Illness as Metaphor* (1977), a study of the stereotypical thinking that surrounds disease in general, and cancer in particular; *AIDS and its Metaphors* (1989) adopts a similar approach to its subject. Another collection of essays, *Under the Sign of Saturn*, appeared in 1980. She has written two filmscripts, *Duet for Cannibals* (1969) and *Brother Carl* (1971).

Sordello A poem by ROBERT BROWNING, published in 1840. The action takes place in the early 13th century against the background of the struggles between Guelphs and Ghibellines, and concerns the troubadour Sordello, torn between his vocation as a poet and the duties of his birthright. Criticized by contemporary reviewers for its obscurity (a charge which dogged the poet throughout his career), *Sordello* remains the most challenging and impenetrable of Browning's works.

Sorley, Charles (Hamilton) 1895–1915 Poet. Born in Aberdeen, he grew up in Cambridge, where his father was Knightbridge Professor of Moral Philosophy, and Marlborough, where he gave remarkable talks to the school literary society on JOHN MASEFIELD and A. E. HOUSMAN. In 1913 he went to Germany and studied briefly at the University of Jena, before returning home in August 1914. He joined the Suffolk Regiment and was killed at the Battle of Loos in October 1915. 'What waste!' wrote ROBERT GRAVES, his exact contemporary and admirer.

Marlborough *and Other Poems* (1916) contained, as well as much juvenilia, several SONNETS which anticipate the anti-romanticism of the later war poets, notably those beginning 'When you see millions of the mouthless dead' and 'Such, such is death; no triumph: no defeat.' *The Letters of Charles Sorley* (1919) contain some of his best writing, including his acute criticism of RUPERT BROOKE's '1914' sequence: 'He has clothed his attitude in fine words; but he has taken the sentimental attitude.' *Collected Poems* was edited by Jean Moorcroft Wilson (1985).

Sound and the Fury, The A novel by WILLIAM FAULKNER, published in 1929. A complex account of the history of the Compson family, it is divided into four sections, largely reliant on STREAM OF CONSCIOUSNESS. The first (7 April 1928) is narrated by Benjy, the youngest member and an 'idiot'. Like his brothers Quentin and Jason, he is chiefly preoccupied with his sister Caddy. For Benjy, her disappearance amounts to the loss of the centre of his universe. The second section is told by Quentin, a Harvard freshman, on the day (2 June 1910) he commits suicide. In the third section (6 April 1928) Jason, the eldest son, reveals his bitterness and anger at the opportunities he has lost because of the irresponsibility and selfishness which he feels predominate in his family. The final section (8 April 1928, Easter Sunday) concentrates on the Compsons' black servant, Dilsey, and her grandson, Luster. An appendix which Faulkner added in 1946 reviews the history of the Compson family from 1699 to 1945 and ends with this assessment of the blacks who served the Compsons: 'They endured.'

Souster, Raymond 1921– Canadian poet. Born in Toronto, he has lived there all his life, apart from a period in World War II, when he served in the Canadian Air Force and spent time in Nova Scotia, Newfoundland and England. He has worked for the Canadian Imperial Bank of Commerce since leaving school at the age of 18. Above all a poet of Toronto, he is a prolific writer of short lyrics describing ordinary and often overlooked aspects of the urban experience in an economical, understated manner. The colloquialism of his style stands in marked contrast to the academicism of much modern Canadian verse. In 1952 he joined LOUIS DUDEK and IRVING LAYTON in founding Contact Press, the leading publisher of Canadian poetry in the 1950s, and has been active throughout his career in editing, anthologizing and promoting the work of other poets. His many volumes of poetry include *When We are Young* (1946), *Go to Sleep World* (1947), *Shake Hands with the Hangman* (1953), *Crêpe-Hanger's Carnival* (1958), *A Local Pride* (1962), *Place of Meeting* (1962), *The Colour of the Times* (1964), *As Is* (1967), *Change-Up* (1974), *Hanging In* (1979), *Collected Poems, 1940–80* (4 vols., 1980–3), *Going the Distance* (1983) and *Asking for More* (1988). He has also published two novels.

Soutar, William 1898–1943 Scottish poet. Born in Perth, he served in the Navy during World War I and contracted a spinal infection which made him an invalid. He graduated from Edinburgh University in 1923. He worked in the same vein as HUGH MACDIARMID to establish a distinctively contemporary Scots poetry (see SCOTTISH RENAISSANCE). His first publication was *Gleanings by an Undergraduate* (1923), his last the posthumous *The Expectant Silence* (1944). Most of his work is brought together in *Collected Poems* (1948), edited with an introductory essay by Hugh MacDiarmid, and *Poems in Scots and English* (1961), edited by W. R. Aitken. An autobiographical volume, *Diaries of a Dying Man* (1954), was edited by A. Scott.

South, Robert 1634–1716 Preacher and theologian. Born in London, the son of a merchant, he attended Westminster School and Christ Church, Oxford. In 1660 he became chaplain to the EARL OF CLARENDON, who procured for him the degrees of BD and DD in 1663. Famous for his sermons, South was Public Orator to the University of Oxford from 1660 to 1667 and used his considerable wit to excellent effect. ('Piety', he declared, 'engages no Man to be dull.') After serving as chaplain to the English ambassador in Poland, he became rector of Islip in Oxfordshire in 1678. South opposed the Toleration Act of William and Mary (1689), which gave freedom of worship to Dissenters. He delivered a brilliant attack on WILLIAM SHERLOCK in *Animadversions on Mr Sherlock's Book* (1693) and *Tritheism Charged* (1695). His sermons were collected and published in seven volumes in 1823.

South English Legendary, The A collection of narrative EXEMPLA incorporating biblical history and SAINTS' LIVES, which developed by accretion through the 13th to 15th centuries. It survives in over 50 manuscripts, each in effect a different version as material was rearranged, omitted or expanded. The title reflects the belief based on the dialect of the earliest versions, that the collection originated in the south. It was apparently written by friars for a secular audience, but no more precise details of the work's authorship or intention are known. A similar, earlier collection, the *Legenda aurea* (translated as the *GOLDEN LEGEND*), probably influenced the *South English Legendary* but the English collection is not directly dependent upon it.

South Wind A novel by NORMAN DOUGLAS, published in 1917. Considered very *risqué* at the time, it became his most popular work.

It is set on the island of Nepenthe in the Mediterranean (based upon the island of Capri where Douglas was living at the time). The Bishop of Bambopo, Thomas Heard, is visiting his cousin Mrs Meadows during the season of the sirocco (the south wind) which has a degenerative effect upon the populace's religious and moral standards. The bishop comes into contact with many of the island's exotic inhabitants, including the Duchess of San Martino (an aspiring Catholic), Don Francesco ('a thoroughgoing pagan'), Mr Keith (a heretical eccentric) and Freddy Parker, the Commissioner. The plot revolves around a series of Rabelaisian conversation pieces in which various unorthodox moral and sexual opinions and practices are exposed. It is ironic in tone and contains many erudite passages about the legends and topography of the island. The bishop himself is caught under the pagan spell of the south wind and finds himself condoning much that he should not (including a murder).

Southall, Ivan (Francis) 1921– Australian writer of CHILDREN'S LITERATURE. Born and educated in Melbourne, Southall first trained as a journalist before serving with distinction in the Royal Australian Air Force. After the war he turned to children's fiction, producing orthodox adventure stories featuring Squadron Leader Simon Black, in many ways the Australian equivalent to CAPTAIN W. E. JOHNS's flying hero Biggles. But Southall first found his true talents in *Hills End* (1962), a tough, realistic story about country children cut off by serious flooding. Something of the same formula also appears in subsequent novels such as *Ash Road* (1965), which has as its main disaster a ferocious bush fire, and *To the Wild Sky* (1967), which describes an air crash and its aftermath. *Finn's Folly* (1969) also deals in sudden danger, but, more controversially, with a central plot involving a road crash. Southall afterwards turned to novels concentrating more on inner conflict than external threat, a process already beginning with *Let the Balloon Go* (1968), which describes in meticulous detail a spastic boy's attempts to climb an 80-foot tree. Equally memorable is *Josh* (1971), a painful story of one child's social isolation. Subsequent books include *What about Tomorrow?* (1976) and *A City out of Sight* (1985), which continues the earlier story of *To the Wild Sky*.

Southern Literary Messenger, The The longest-lived of American antebellum Southern literary magazines, founded in Richmond in 1834 by T. W. White, and intended to publish and promote Southern letters. Until it folded in 1864 it printed fiction, poetry, travel accounts, and sketches of Southern life and manners by such writers as JOHN ESTEN COOKE, WILLIAM GILMORE SIMMS, JOSEPH G. BALDWIN and AUGUSTUS BALDWIN LONGSTREET. One of its most prominent contributors was EDGAR ALLAN POE, many of whose tales and poems appeared for the first time in the *Messenger*'s pages; he also served as editor from December 1835 to January 1837, during which period his criticism and book reviews often sparked controversy. White wanted his magazine to promote Southern regional pride and achievement, and in the first few years of its existence he attempted to remain neutral on the question of slavery. But he and his successors were to adopt an increasingly defensive and sectional tone in their editorial statements as the Civil War approached, eventually identifying Southern literary regionalism with a defence of slavery.

Southerne, Thomas 1660–1746 Playwright. Born near Dublin and educated at Trinity College, Dublin,

Southerne went to London to study law in 1678. His first play, *The Loyal Brother* (1682), was a panegyric to the Duke of York. Of the remaining nine, the best are the comedies, *Sir Anthony Love* (1690) and the extraordinarily mixed *The Maid's Last Prayer* (1693), and the two sentimental tragedies adapted from stories by APHRA BEHN, *The Fatal Marriage* (1694) and *Oroonoko* (1695). *The Wives' Excuse* (1691) is of interest as a transitional piece between the earlier comedy of ETHEREGE and WYCHERLEY and the more elegant comedy of CONGREVE and VANBRUGH. Southerne's last performed play was an unsuccessful comedy, *Money the Mistress* (1726).

Southey, Robert 1774–1843 Poet, historian and man of letters. The son of a Bristol linen draper, Southey spent a large part of his childhood in the care of an eccentric aunt, at whose home he acquired his insatiable appetite for books. He was educated at Westminster School, from which he was expelled for an attack on corporal punishment in his magazine, *The Flagellant*. A decidedly rebellious figure in his early years, he went on to Oxford, where he wrote the poem *Joan of Arc* (1792, published 1796) in support of the French Revolution, and the republican play *Wat Tyler* (first published 1817). In 1794 he became friendly with COLERIDGE, with whom he collaborated on another play, *The Fall of Robespierre*, and planned to set up a 'Pantisocratic' community in the United States. It was to have put into practice GODWIN's ideas of human perfectibility, but his enthusiasm soon waned, causing a break with Coleridge.

Following his secret marriage to Elizabeth Fricker (he also played a significant role as matchmaker in Coleridge's marriage to her sister, Sara), he travelled to Portugal at the end of 1795, an experience which appears to have taught him to 'thank God for having made [him] an Englishman'. His poetry of this period includes many of the lyrics and BALLADS by which he is now chiefly remembered, and which in their own way contributed to the dismantling of the formal constrictions of late 18th-century verse: 'My Days among the Dead are Past', 'The Inchcape Rock', 'The Battle of Blenheim', as well as 'The Holly Tree', perhaps his best-known poem. The change from radical to Tory, which was to make him the *bête noire* of the next generation of poets, was consolidated by a further visit to Portugal and Spain in 1800–1.

Returned to England, he settled at Greta Hall in Keswick and was thus misleadingly classed with WORDSWORTH and Coleridge as one of the LAKE POETS. His oriental verse epic, *Thalaba the Destroyer*, was indifferently received upon its appearance in 1801, though SHELLEY later borrowed its irregular verse form for *QUEEN MAB* (1813). It was followed by *Madoc* (1805), another exotic narrative, featuring the somewhat unlikely South American adventures of the son of the medieval Welsh king, Owen Gwyneth. Between 1804 and 1810 the Southeys had six children, and after Coleridge abandoned his family to go to Malta, Southey assumed for a while the additional responsibility of caring for his household.

He was henceforth obliged to write virtually without pause: poetry, history, biography, translations and editions of earlier writers. His abridgement of *Amadis of Gaul* (1803) was followed in 1807 by a revised translation of *Palmerin of England*. In the same year he was awarded a government pension, and published *Letters from England by Don Manuel Alvarez Espriella*, a series of observations on English manners and society by a fictitious Spaniard. His translation of the *Chronicle of the Cid* appeared in 1808, and in 1809 he commenced his long association with the recently founded Tory *QUARTERLY REVIEW*, which provided him with his first regular income, and for which he had, by 1838, written nearly a hundred political articles. His long poem, *The Curse of Kehama*, another tale in the fashionable oriental mode, appeared in 1810.

In 1813 Southey succeeded the abysmal HENRY JAMES PYE as POET LAUREATE, a post he did not particularly relish, but which inevitably set the seal on his reputation as a radical who had prostituted himself to the Establishment. His short and still very readable *Life of Nelson* appeared in the same year, and was followed in 1814 by his Christian romance *Roderick the Last of the Goths*. During the next three years he completed his three-volume *History of Brazil* (1810–19), and his *Life of Wesley* (1820). The poems of his laureateship include 'The Poet's Pilgrimage to Waterloo' (1816), 'Princess Charlotte's Epithalamium and her Elegy' (1817), and 10 ODES on various public events. In 1817 he tried in vain to secure an injunction from chancery to stop the publication, by his liberal enemies, of *Wat Tyler*, the play of his Jacobinical youth. He was repeatedly attacked and lampooned during these politically tense years, notably by PEACOCK, who caricatures him as Mr Feathernest in *MELINCOURT* (1817). In no way a shrinking violet, he typically responded with provocations of his own. *A VISION OF JUDGEMENT* (1821), an apotheosis of the recently deceased King George III, is prefaced by a violent attack on BYRON, whose rejoinder, *THE VISION OF JUDGEMENT*, is one of the great satirical parodies of English literature. Southey's prolific output continued with the publication of *The Book of the Church* (1824), his poem *A Tale of Paraguay* (1825), *Sir Thomas More* (1829) – a conversation between the author and More's ghost – and the long ballads *All for Love* and *The Pilgrim to Compostella* (1829). *Essays Moral and Political* came out in 1832, and the same year saw the completion of his *History of the Peninsular War* (1823–32), which was followed in 1833 by the *Lives of the British Admirals*. A miscellany of anecdote, quotation and comment, *The Doctor*, appeared in 1834–7. In 1835 he was awarded a pension of £300 by Peel, but declined a baronetcy. His wife died in 1837, following a period of insanity, and in 1839 he married Caroline Bowles. His own mind was to become clouded during his last years.

Southwell, Robert ?1561–95 Poet and Catholic martyr. Southwell was sent abroad for his education, the usual practice in recusant families. He entered the Jesuit School at Douai in 1576 and was afterwards accepted for the Jesuit novitiate at Rome. He was ordained priest in 1585, and in 1586 went with Henry Garnett as part of the Jesuit mission to England. Southwell probably had to re-learn English in preparation, having forgotten his native tongue. Captured in 1592 while saying mass, he was tortured, imprisoned in the Tower, and finally executed in 1595. He was beatified along with other English martyrs by Pius XI in 1929.

His best-known poem, 'The Burning Babe' (published with other devotional poems in the collection *Maeoniae*, 1595), uses PETRARCHAN language to meditate on the details of Christ's Passion. It was much admired by BEN JONSON, who told WILLIAM DRUMMOND OF HAWTHORNDEN that he would have been content to destroy many of his own poems if he had written it. *St Peter's Complaint* (1595) is a lengthy narrative about the life of Christ, put into the mouth of the repentant saint. A prose work, *An Epistle of Comfort*, was secretly printed in 1587 and his letters were circulated in manuscript. His *Fourfold Meditation on the Four Last Things* was printed in 1606.

Sowdon of Babylon, The A VERSE ROMANCE written *c.* 1400 in the east Midlands. The Sowdon (Sultan) attacks Rome and captures it before the arrival of Charlemagne's troops. He takes the holy relics back to his homeland; Charlemagne follows him and attacks his army there. The Sowdon's son, Ferumbras, is taken and submits to baptism (see *SIR FIRUMBRAS*), but the Saracens capture Roland and Oliver. The remainder of the 12 peers are sent to demand their release but they too are captured. The Sowdon's daughter, Floripas, is in love with one of them and succeeds in releasing them to expel the Sowdon from the city. He lays siege to it but is defeated by Charlemagne and eventually executed.

Soyinka, Wole 1934– Nigerian playwright, novelist and poet. Born in Abeokuta, he taught for many years at Obafemi Awolowo University (formerly University of Ife) and has also taught in the USA. His verbal inventiveness and ebullient imagination are linked with an uncompromising sense of justice and humanity. His basic dramatic mode is comedy: genial in *The Trials of Brother Jero* (in *Three Plays*, 1963), *The Lion and the Jewel* (1963) and *Requiem for a Futurologist* (1985), satirical in *Kongi's Harvest* (1967), pungent in the anti-militarist *Madmen and Specialists* (1971) and *Jero's Metamorphosis* (1973),

and angrily farcical in *A Play of Giants* (1984). While trying to habilitate traditional African (in his case Yoruba) beliefs in modern life, as in his first novel, *The Interpreters* (1965), and the long title-poem of *Idanre and Other Poems* (1968), Soyinka also satirizes pre-colonial African regimes, as in the complex but life-affirming play *A Dance of the Forests* (1963). In *Myth, Literature and the African World* (1976) he explicates Yoruba cosmography and culture, using them as dramatic themes, questioningly in *The Swamp Dwellers* and *The Strong Breed* (both in *Three Plays*, 1963), cryptically in *THE ROAD* (1965) and with tragic profundity in *DEATH AND THE KING'S HORSEMAN* (1975). *Season of Anomy* (1973), a novel, makes a powerful attempt to resolve modern civil violence in terms of Yoruba beliefs. In *The Bacchae* (1973) he successfully adapts Euripides, in *Opera Wonyosi* (1981) GAY and Brecht. He writes about his political imprisonment (1967–9) during the Nigerian Civil War eloquently in his prose journal *The Man Died* (1973) and more meditatively in the verse collections *Poems from Prison* (1969) and *A Shuttle in the Crypt* (1972). His long poem *Ogun Abibiman* (1976) and some of the poems in *Mandela's Earth* (1988) call for the liberation of South Africa. *Aké: The Years of Childhood* (1981) recreates his experience of growing up with a dual inheritance of Yoruba and Western traditions and *Isara: A Voyage Around 'Essay'* (1990) lovingly remembers his father. He has also edited *Poems from Black Africa* (1975) and collected many of his essays in *Art, Dialogue and*

Wole Soyinka

Outrage: Essays on Literature and Culture (1988). He received the Nobel Prize for Literature in 1986.

Spanish Gypsy, The A poem by GEORGE ELIOT, first published in 1868. Cast in pseudo-dramatic form and running to considerable length, it takes duty, happiness, love, race and loyalty as its themes. But these preoccupations overshadow the dramatic action, which is often unconvincing, and the characterization, which is weak. Although well received when it first appeared, *The Spanish Gypsy* is no longer ranked among George Eliot's distinguished writings.

Spanish Tragedy, The: *or, Hieronimo is Mad Again* A play by THOMAS KYD, produced *c.* 1589 and published in 1592. The first English REVENGE TRAGEDY, it proved popular with Renaissance audiences, being revised for later productions. SHAKESPEARE'S *HAMLET* is among its many successors.

Hieronimo is a marshal of Spain at the time of his country's victory over Portugal in 1580. His son Horatio and his nephew Lorenzo captured Balthazar, son of the Viceroy of Portugal, during the war and now Balthazar is courting Bel-imperia, Lorenzo's sister. Lorenzo favours the match and so does the King of Spain for political reasons but Bel-imperia loves Horatio. Lorenzo and Balthazar surprise the two lovers in Hieronimo's arbour at night: they murder Horatio and hang his body to a tree. Bel-imperia escapes but Hieronimo, hearing the disturbance, finds his son's body and is beside himself with grief. He ascertains the murderers' identity and plots their destruction with Bel-imperia. To accomplish this he engages them to take part in a play, with himself and Bel-imperia, to be acted before the court. Revenge on Lorenzo and Balthazar is carried out successfully in the play within the play; Hieronimo and Bel-imperia then take their own lives.

Spark, Muriel (Sarah) 1918– Novelist, short-story writer and poet. Born Muriel Sarah Camberg in Edinburgh, she was educated there at Gillespie's School for Girls. After some years in Africa (1936–44) she returned to Britain and worked in political intelligence at the Foreign Office. She married S. O. Spark in 1938. From 1947 to 1949 she edited *Poetry Review*, publishing a volume of poems, *The Fanfarlo*, in 1952. After various works of literary criticism and biography, she published her well-received first novel, *The Comforters* (1957), which displayed her talent for IRONY and black humour. It was followed by *Memento Mori* (1959), about old age, and *The Ballad of Peckham Rye* (1960), about underworld life, which established her reputation as a satirical novelist with a sharp, oblique humour and a detached, elegant style. She is perhaps best known for *THE PRIME OF MISS JEAN BRODIE* (1961), which was successfully filmed, and *Girls of Slender Means* (1963), set in Kensington at the close of the war. Other novels include *The Mandelbaum Gate* (1965), *The Public Image* (1968), *The Driver's Seat* (1970), *The Take-Over* (1976), *Loitering with Intent* (1981), *A Far Cry From Kensington* (1988) and *Symposium* (1990). *Collected Stories* and *Collected Poems* both appeared in 1967. *Curriculum Vitae* (1992) is an autobiography.

Spasmodic School of Poetry, The A term coined by WILLIAM AYTOUN to ridicule the extravagance of feeling and language in the work of PHILIP JAMES BAILEY, SYDNEY DOBELL and ALEXANDER SMITH.

Spectator, The A periodical founded and jointly conducted by RICHARD STEELE and JOSEPH ADDISON, appearing daily from 1 March 1711 to 6 December 1712 (a total of 555 issues). Addison revived it in 1714 for a further 80 issues. Among other contributors were ALEXANDER POPE, AMBROSE PHILIPS, LADY MARY WORTLEY MONTAGU, THOMAS TICKELL, LAURENCE EUSDEN, and THOMAS PARNELL.

The Spectator was presented as the work of a small club of representative gentlemen from different walks of life: Sir Andrew Freeport (commerce), Captain Sentry (the army), Will Honeycombe (the townsman), and a lawyer and a clergyman, both anonymous. Sir Roger de Coverley, the periodical's most enduringly famous creation, was the country gentleman. Mr Spectator himself was the detached observer who took no 'practical part in life'. The papers addressed cultural, moral and topical concerns, and carried a series of entertaining character sketches.

Speed, John ?1552–1629 Map-maker and historian. By 1598 he had presented several maps to Queen Elizabeth, and from 1608 to 1611 he published a series of 44 maps of England and Wales, collected in 1611 as *The Theatre of the Empire of Great Britain*. He became a member of the Society of Antiquaries and was encouraged by WILLIAM CAMDEN and SIR ROBERT BRUCE COTTON (who loaned him manuscripts) to begin the work published in 1611 as a continuation of the *Theatre of Great Britain* and entitled *The History of Great Britain*. The popularity of his biblical genealogies is attested by their numerous editions.

Speed the Plough A melodramatic comedy by THOMAS MORTON, first performed at COVENT GARDEN in 1800. The play has a variety of plots. The 'main' one is a mawkish story of quarrelling brothers brought to reconciliation at the final curtain. Much better is a sub-plot in which the simple goodness of Farmer Ashfield is convincingly and humorously displayed. The play has been given a deserved place in cultural history by its author's invention of Mrs Grundy, a character who never appears but is constantly referred to by Farmer Ashfield's wife as an arbiter of acceptable behaviour.

Speke, John Hanning 1827–64 Explorer. Speke was SIR RICHARD BURTON's companion on two expeditions to explore East Africa. They went to Somaliland (1854) and to the interior (1857–9), discovering Lake Tanganyika in 1858. Speke continued after Burton's physical condition obliged him to withdraw to Tabora, and discovered Lake Victoria. His belief that this was the source of the Nile had no supporting evidence, but was proved right. Speke's *Journal of the Discovery of the Source of the Nile* was published in 1863.

Spencer, Elizabeth 1921– American novelist and short-story writer. She was born in rural Mississippi, and her Southern experience is evident in many of her short stories, as well as in her first three novels, *Fire in the Morning* (1948), *This Crooked Way* (1952) and *The Voice at the Back Door* (1956). These show how the effort to preserve the ways of the antebellum South can sometimes overwhelm the sensitive members of the Mississippi upper-middle class. Other novels include: two set in Italy, *The Light in the Piazza* (1960) and *Knights and Dragons* (1965); two set in New Orleans, *No Place for an Angel* (1968) and *The Snare* (1972); *The Salt Lines* (1984), set in Mississippi; and *The Night Travellers* (1991). Her stories have been collected as *Ship Island and Other Stories* (1968), *The Stories of Elizabeth Spencer* (1981), *Jack of Diamonds and Other Stories* (1988) and *On the Gulf* (1991).

Spencer, Herbert 1820–1903 Philosopher and social scientist. Born to a Nonconformist family in Derby, he failed to thrive with the orthodox classical curriculum at the local day school, though his knowledge of science and other subjects was already advanced. He moved to the educational care of his radical uncle, Thomas Spencer, and left school at 16. He started a promising career as a railway engineer but then in 1848 became sub-editor of *The Economist*. His speculative and synthesizing bent of mind began to declare itself in powerful writing in the 1850s. His first book was the later much-admired *Social Statics: or, The Conditions Essential to Human Happiness Specified* (1851). His 1852 essay on the 'Development Hypothesis' sets forth a general theory of evolution before DARWIN, though without Darwin's concept of natural selection and his compelling variety of evidence. Spencer's polymathism was uneven in depth. The determination to work from *First Principles* (1862) through to a 'synthetic philosophy' dominated his writing career. *Education* (1861) and *The Principles of Sociology* (1876–96) in particular caused great interest and controversy among his contemporaries. In *Education* he insisted on the importance of scientific study. Spencer's early writings seem to provide a model for the programme of upbringing invented by Sir Austin Feverel for his son in GEORGE MEREDITH's *THE ORDEAL OF RICHARD FEVEREL* (1859).

Spencer insisted on individualism as the basis both of a free society and of ethics. This insistence created methodological problems for his classificatory systems within his syncretic philosophy. It also created difficulties in his personal life, since he was notoriously assertive about his intellectual property. Spencer was an intimate early friend of GEORGE ELIOT, who loved him before she became a novelist. He maintained a difficult friendship with her and G. H. LEWES throughout their life together. He has been suggested as one model for Mr Casaubon in *MIDDLEMARCH* (1872).

Spencer's intellectual ordering power and his stamina and range of enquiry are remarkable, as can be seen from his works, *The Principles of Psychology* (1855–72), *The Principles of Biology* (1864–7, enlarged 1898–9) and *The Principles of Sociology*. He was a productive influence on both THOMAS HARDY and H. G. WELLS.

Spender, Sir Stephen (Harold) 1909– Poet and man of letters. Born in London, he was educated at University College School, London, and at University College, Oxford, where he first met W. H. AUDEN and the other young writers of Auden's circle. Leaving Oxford without taking a degree, he went to Berlin in 1930, and was in Spain during the Civil War. He served as a fireman in London during World War II. Since 1948 he has split his time between England and the USA, holding many academic posts, including a professorship of English at University College, London, in 1970–5. He was co-editor of the magazine *Horizon* (1939–41), with CYRIL CONNOLLY, and of *ENCOUNTER* (1953–66). Many honours culminated in a knighthood in 1983.

His best work as a poet appeared in his first major collection, *Poems* (1933). 'I Think Continually of Those Who are Truly Great' displays a natural lyric gift unfulfilled in later writing but, under Auden's influence, muted by a sense of obligation to include the detritus of contemporary life (as in the often anthologized 'The Express' and 'The Pylons'). His work is dominated by an unsuccessful search for a faith and a quest to integrate the private and the political. *Vienna* (1934) is an unsuccessful long poem. *The Still Centre* (1939) contains effective poems about Spain but generally marks a movement towards more personal work. Although *Poems of Dedication* (1947), *The Edge of Being* (1949) and *The Generous Days* (1969) have appeared, Spender seems to have written little verse since the war. Instead, he has concentrated on critical works, which include *The Creative Element* (1953), *The Struggle of the Modern* (1963) and *Love-Hate Relations: A Study of Anglo-American Sensibilities* (1974). His brief flirtation with Communism, really an opposition to fascism, is analysed in his chapter in Richard H. Crossman's *The God That Failed* (1950). *World within World* (1951) is a revealing account of himself and his generation. 1987 saw the publication of *Journals 1939–1983*, and his poetic career can be surveyed in *Collected Poems 1928–1985* (1985).

Spenser, Edmund ?1552–99 Poet. Spenser was born in London, perhaps in Smithfield, although the family may have come from Lancashire. He entered Merchant Taylors' School in 1561, where the headmaster was the humanist RICHARD MULCASTER and fellow pupils included THOMAS KYD, LANCELOT ANDREWES and THOMAS LODGE. In May 1569 he entered Pembroke Hall, Cambridge, as a sizar, graduating BA in 1573 and MA in 1576. At Cambridge he began his friendship with GABRIEL HARVEY. 1569 saw his first publication, anonymous translations, mainly of sonnets, of Petrarch and Du Bellay, in *A Theatre Wherein be Represented As Well the Miseries and Calamities That Follow the Voluptuous Worldlings*, an apocalyptic and anti-Catholic compilation by the Dutch Calvinist Jan van der Noodt. In 1578 he became secretary to John Young, Bishop of Rochester, and in 1579 entered Leicester's service where he became familiar with SIR PHILIP SIDNEY and SIR EDWARD DYER. In the same year he married Maccabeus Chylde, of whom virtually nothing is known. In 1580 he became secretary to Lord Grey de Wilton, Lord Deputy of Ireland, arriving in Dublin in August of that year. Spenser lived in Ireland, apart from intermittent visits to England including an audience with the queen in 1589, until his return to London at the end of 1598. In Ireland Spenser held a succession of official posts such as commissioner for musters and deputy to the Clerk of the Council in Munster. He lived in a succession of houses, at Enniscorthy in Wexford, Dublin and the ruined castle of Kilcolman in Cork, which he leased in 1588. Kilcolman was sacked and burned during Tyrone's rebellion in October 1598, causing Spenser to take refuge in Cork and afterwards to return to England.

THE SHEPHEARDES CALENDER, dedicated to Sidney, was published anonymously in 1579, and Spenser's correspondence with Harvey a year later. In 1591 appeared a volume of nine of his poems entitled *Complaints*. This included revisions of his 1569

Edmund Spenser: an engraving by J. Thomson from an original painting

poems with other minor works such as *Virgil's Gnat* (a translation of the pseudo-Virgilian *Culex*) and *Muiopotmos* on the fate of a butterfly. In the same year *Daphnaida* was published, an ELEGY on the death of Lady Howard in imitation of CHAUCER'S BOOK OF THE DUCHESS. In 1595 AMORETTI and EPITHALAMION appeared together in one volume. The sonnet sequence and marriage hymn may in some way record respectively Spenser's courtship of and marriage (in June 1594) to his second wife, Elizabeth Boyle. They had one son, Peregrine. COLIN CLOUT'S COME HOME AGAIN (1595) is an autobiographical PASTORAL. FOUR HYMNS (1596) are platonizing reflections on human and divine love, and PROTHALAMION (1596) celebrates the double betrothal of Katherine and Elizabeth, daughters of the Earl of Worcester. The prose dialogue, *A View of the Present State of Ireland*, was entered in the Stationers' Register in 1598 but not published until 1633. A translation of the pseudo-Platonic *Axiochus* is also attributed, very doubtfully, to him. The first three books of Spenser's great poem THE FAERIE QUEENE came out 1590 and these were published again in 1596 with the addition of Books IV–VI. The six completed books with the addition of the 'Mutability Cantos' appeared in folio in 1609, ten years after Spenser's death.

Spenser died at Westminster on 13 January 1599, 'for lack of bread' according to BEN JONSON. This assertion, although supported by the antiquary WILLIAM CAMDEN, is of doubtful authority. He was buried in Westminster Abbey and his hearse, according to Camden, was 'attended by poets, and mournful elegies and poems, with the pens that wrote them, thrown into the tomb'. The queen's order for a memorial to Spenser was never carried out, although a funeral memorial to 'the Prince of Poets in his time' was erected in Westminster Abbey in 1620 and restored in marble in 1778. His collected works were first published in 1611.

The Shepheardes Calender provided English literature with a series of pastorals that could stand comparison with European examples; *The Faerie Queene* with a great heroic romance that could justly claim to outshine the continental chivalric romances of Ariosto and Tasso. E. K.'s enthusiasm in *The*

Shepheardes Calender for the emergence of an English Virgil was echoed by WILLIAM WEBBE in *Of English Poetry* (1586). Sidney's complaints about Spenser's archaisms were repeated by Ben Jonson, who claimed that he 'writ no language', and by EVERARD GUILPIN, who objected to Spenser's 'grandam words'. But Jonson would still have him read for his 'matter', thus anticipating MILTON's commendation of the moral earnestness of the 'sage and serious' Spenser, whom he found a better teacher than either Thomas Aquinas or DUNS SCOTUS. The 18th century was a great period of Spenser scholarship, with THOMAS WARTON's *Observations on the Faerie Queene* (1754) and Upton's annotated edition of the poem. The AUGUSTAN AGE liked the pictorial quality of Spenser and saw *The Faerie Queene* as a poem of the imagination, although it found its allegory distasteful and its form disquieting. For the Romantics, Spenser was the poet's poet, a poet of dreams, beauty and sensuous appeal, but HAZLITT was not alone in not wishing to meddle with the allegory. WORDSWORTH's *The White Doe of Rylstone* shows him to have liked the first book of *The Faerie Queene*, and Book III of *THE PRELUDE* describes Wordsworth at Cambridge reading 'Sweet Spenser, moving through his clouded heaven/ With the moon's beauty and the moon's soft pace'. W. B. YEATS liked the 'charmed sleep' of Spenser's poetry but found his morality official and impersonal: he was for Yeats 'the first salaried moralist'. In 1932 T. S. ELIOT doubted that any except scholars had read the whole of *The Faerie Queene* with delight. Fortunately in recent years, thanks partly to the championship of C. S. LEWIS, readers and scholars on both sides of the Atlantic have found that Milton's didactic Spenser and the Romantics' recorder of charmed dreams are happily the same man, one whose speaking pictures both teach and delight.

Spenserian stanza A stanzaic form first used by SPENSER in *THE FAERIE QUEENE*. It varies OTTAVA RIMA, and adds a final alexandrine to eight iambic pentameters to produce a nine-line stanza rhyming ababbcbcc. BYRON used it in *CHILDE HAROLD'S PILGRIMAGE*, KEATS in *THE EVE OF ST AGNES* and SHELLEY in *ADONAIS*.

Spirit of the Age, The A volume of essays by WILLIAM HAZLITT, published in 1825. Widely regarded as Hazlitt's critical masterpiece, it attempts to synthesize the intellectual life of the Romantic age and the period preceding it. Incisive and authoritative essays deal with the work and personalities of many contemporaries, and contain some of his most mature and balanced criticism of GODWIN, COLERIDGE, WORDSWORTH, BYRON, LAMB and SIR WALTER SCOTT.

Spiritual Quixote, The: or, The Summer's Ramble of Mr Geoffry Wildgoose: A Comic Romance A novel by RICHARD GRAVES, published in 1773.

Geoffry Wildgoose, a young man of property in the Cotswolds, is enthusiastic about Methodism. He sets forth with the village cobbler, Jerry Tugwell, on a summer tour to preach the Gospel and meet his hero, George Whitefield. With Tugwell as his Sancho Panza, Wildgoose encounters life on the road in 18th-century England. The Methodists generally, and Whitefield in particular, are satirized.

Spoils of Poynton, The A short novel by HENRY JAMES, serialized in *THE ATLANTIC MONTHLY* from April to June 1896 under the title of *The Old Things*, and published in volume form as *The Spoils of Poynton* in the following year.

Poynton Park is the home of Owen Gereth, and the 'spoils' are the antiques and *objets d'art* with which his mother has filled it. When Mrs Gereth discovers that Owen has decided to marry the tasteless Mona Brigstock, she tries to interest him instead in Fleda Vetch, a kindred spirit who shares her own aesthetic taste. As Fleda secretly falls in love with Owen, he enlists her help in persuading his mother to vacate Poynton, which will now be the home of his bride. Mrs Gereth moves out, but takes the most prized possessions with her. Mona threatens to break off the engagement unless the spoils are returned. All the while Owen is becoming more and more attracted to Fleda; Mrs Gereth, certain that he has now transferred his affections to Fleda and will not marry Mona, returns the spoils to Poynton. Owen attempts to break his engagement with Mona, but, hearing of the replenishment of Poynton, she forces him to marry her. Fleda receives a letter from Owen, travelling abroad with Mona, asking her to choose from Poynton whatever object she would like to possess. She arrives at Poynton Park just as the house and its contents inexplicably go up in flames.

spondee See METRE.

Spoon River Anthology A collection of 245 epitaphs in free verse by EDGAR LEE MASTERS, published in 1915. The speakers, from a small town in rural Illinois, reveal their secret ambitions, transgressions and miseries, as well as the interconnectedness of their lives. The volume was extremely popular and somewhat scandalous at the time, exploding as it did the myth of small-town respectability.

Spoonerism The popular name for metathesis, the transposition of the initial letters of two or more words, usually to comic effect. The name derives from the Rev. W. A. Spooner (1844–1930) of New College, Oxford, whose own accidental utterances are said to have included 'Kinquering congs their titles take'.

Sprigg, Christopher St John See CAUDWELL, CHRISTOPHER.

sprung rhythm See HOPKINS, GERARD MANLEY and METRE.

Spy, The: *A Tale of the Neutral Ground* A novel by JAMES FENIMORE COOPER, published in 1821, His first successful book, it is set during the American Revolution. The complicated story centres on the activities of Harvey Birch, a supposed loyalist who is actually a spy for George Washington, in the 'neutral ground' of Westchester County, New York. Washington appears several times disguised as 'Mr Harper'.

Squire, Sir **J(ohn) C(ollings)** 1884–1958 Critic and poet. The son of a veterinary surgeon, Squire was born in Plymouth, and attended Blundell's School, Tiverton, before studying history at St John's College, Cambridge. After a spell as a journalist, he began contributing to THE NEW AGE, and became literary editor of both *The New Statesman* (1913–19) and *Land and Water* (1914–20). As a regular reviewer for *The Observer* and as editor of *The London Mercury*, which he founded in 1919, Squire was a powerful influence in the literary world of the 1920s, leading a clique of Georgian writers (known to its enemies as the 'Squirearchy') in a critical campaign against MODERNISM. He published several volumes of PARODIES and edited some successful anthologies of modern verse, as well as *The Comic Muse* (1925). He was knighted in 1933. His *Collected Poems*, edited by JOHN BETJEMAN, appeared in 1959.

Squire of Low Degree, The A VERSE ROMANCE in couplets written *c.* 1500 in the east Midlands. Apparently built up from a series of motifs familiar from other romances, it tells of a poor squire's love for a princess. She imposes a seven-year period of trial, but they are betrayed by the steward to the king, who nevertheless trusts the squire. The squire is ambushed by the steward on his way to take leave of the princess; he kills the steward and is himself captured. The disfigured body is dressed in the squire's clothing and the princess, finding it, embalms it and treasures it for seven years. The king meanwhile releases the squire to go abroad for seven years. He returns as the princess is about to become an anchoress and they are married. The poem is notable for its extravagant and picturesque descriptions of courtly life, though its use of the romance form is largely nostalgic and artificial.

Squire's Tale, The See CANTERBURY TALES, The.

Stacpoole, Henry de Vere 1863–1951 Novelist and short-story writer. Born in Kingstown, County Dublin, he was educated at an Irish public school, Portalington, and then at Malvern. He studied medicine at St George's and St Mary's hospitals, qualifying in 1891. Stacpoole subsequently made several voyages as a ship's doctor which provided the background for much of his writing. His friends included OSCAR WILDE, Lillie Langtry, WARWICK DEEPING, A. J. CRONIN and AUBREY BEARDSLEY. The influence of Beardsley and the other writers and artists associated with THE YELLOW BOOK is evident in his early novels, *The Intended* (1894) and *Pierrot!* (1896).

His first commercial successes were *The Crimson Azaleas* (1907) and *The Blue Lagoon* (1908). The latter is a romantic story of a boy and girl shipwrecked on a Pacific island and has been compared to BARRIE's PETER PAN and Maeterlinck's *The Blue Bird*. It was later filmed. Stacpoole wrote four more 'Blue Lagoon' novels: *The Beach of Dreams* (1919), *The Garden of God* (1923), *The Gates of Morning* (1925) and *The Girl of the Golden Reef* (1929). *The Street of the Flute Player* (1912) is set in Athens, *Monsieur de Rochefort* (1914) in 18th-century France and *Goblin Market* (1927) in the Isle of Wight. Stacpoole wrote well over 50 novels in lively descriptive prose, and deserves more recognition than he now enjoys. He was also a poet and the translator of Sappho and Villon.

Stafford, Jean 1915–79 American novelist and short-story writer. She was born in Covina, California. Her first novel, *Boston Adventure* (1944), deals with the social and economic barriers in Boston society in the early 20th century. Her second novel, *The Mountain Lion*, appeared in 1947, and her third, *The Catherine Wheel*, in 1952. She was associated with the literary circle which included ROBERT LOWELL (her former husband), DELMORE SCHWARTZ and RANDALL JARRELL. She also published volumes of highly crafted short stories, including *Children are Bored on Sunday* (1953) and *Bad Characters* (1964). *The Collected Stories of Jean Stafford* (1969) received a PULITZER PRIZE.

Staffrider A South African literary journal, first published in 1978. Its title, the colloquial word for someone who rides illegally on the outside of a suburban train, was intended to suggest the flair and courage of the mainly young black writers who expressed their feelings of anguish and defiance at a time when the government, shaken by the 1976 Soweto uprising, had fallen back into repressiveness. Edited by a collective, and both praised and criticized for its openness, *Staffrider* was largely distributed in the townships by a popular network.

Stalky & Co. A collection of nine stories by RUDYARD KIPLING, first published in 1899. Five other Stalky tales appeared in separate collections; the 14 tales were brought together in *The Complete Stalky & Co.* (1929).

Kipling drew on his boyhood experiences at the United Services College at Westward Ho! in Devon, a school founded by retired army officers largely to fit its pupils for an army career. Stalky, M'Turk and

Beetle (the last a loose self-portrait of Kipling) are a schoolboy trio who conduct a battle of wits with the masters and other boys. Stalky's cunning and self-reliance, his willingness to infringe the minor social rules of the school and to take his punishment when his transgressions are discovered come to represent a highly practical ethic. It is notable that the authority of the headmaster, 'Prooshian' Bates, is never seriously questioned, and that the laws of social responsibility and self-discipline are affirmed by the trio. Kipling's didactic intention in writing about the education of the young is clearly signalled in the final story, where the ex-schoolboys continue their exploits in India at the frontiers of the Empire they have implicitly been learning to defend.

Standing Bear, Luther 1868–1939 American Indian writer of Sioux extraction. Unhappy with reservation life, he joined Buffalo Bill's Wild West Show. After one tour, he returned to the reservation but decided to sell his allotment and become a US citizen. He then moved to California and became active in Indian affairs. In 1928 he published his autobiography, *My People, My Sioux*. His next book, *My Indian Boyhood* (1931), was written for children. This was followed by *The Land of the Spotted Eagle* (1933) and *Stories of the Sioux* (1934). His writings deal with Sioux customs and beliefs as well as the life of adjustment in white America, and are often critical of government Indian policy.

Stanihurst, Richard 1547–1604 Scholar and historian. Born in Dublin, he was educated at Oxford and later studied law at Furnival's and Lincoln's Inns. Stanihurst went to Leiden and took holy orders, becoming chaplain to the Governor of the Spanish Netherlands. One of the most important of the Roman Catholic 'Old English' writers in Ireland, he is best remembered for the *Description of Ireland* he contributed to the 1577 edition of HOLINSHED's *Chronicles* and for his friendship with SIR PHILIP SIDNEY. Most of his writings are in Latin.

Stanley, Arthur Penrhyn 1815–81 Broad Churchman. The second son of a clergyman of aristocratic background, later created Bishop of Norwich in 1837, Stanley was born at Alderley, Cheshire, and educated at Rugby under THOMAS ARNOLD, whose favourite pupil and subsequent biographer he became. He entered Balliol College, Oxford, in 1833 and was elected a Fellow of University College in 1838. Ecclesiastical preferment made him in turn a canon of Canterbury Cathedral and of Christ Church, Oxford, and finally, in 1864, Dean of Westminster.

Stanley's conciliatory, anti-dogmatic position won him admiration well beyond the bounds of the Anglican Church, but made him enemies within it, where those of an extreme High or Low Church persuasion believed his views to be tainted with German rationalism. He was the strong champion of those in danger of being pilloried for their theological views and defended the right of such men to express the most widely divergent views within the confines of the Anglican communion. *The Life of Dr Arnold* (1844) remained his most substantial work, whilst *Essays, Chiefly on Questions of Church and State from 1850 to 1870* (1870) provides the best guide to his views on many topical controversies. His determination to celebrate uncontroversial absolutes such as Truth and Unity made the hymns he wrote blandly unremarkable.

Stanley, Sir **Henry Morton** 1841–1904 Journalist and explorer. He was born John Rowlands at Denbigh in Wales, and after the early death of his father spent most of his childhood in the workhouse. At the age of 15 he went as a cabin boy to New Orleans, where he was adopted by an English cotton merchant whose name, Henry Stanley, he took. (The 'Morton' was his own invention.) After an adventurous youth, he finally turned to journalism.

Stanley became world famous in 1871, when he successfully carried out his assignment for *The New York Daily Herald* to find the Scottish missionary and explorer, David Livingstone, in Africa. His own remarkable career as an explorer included the tracing of the Congo (Zaire) river from its source to its mouth. His experiences are recorded in *How I Found Livingstone* (1872), *Through the Dark Continent* (1878), *In Darkest Africa* (1890) and the autobiography posthumously edited by his widow in 1909. Stanley was knighted in 1899.

Stanley, Thomas 1625–78 A descendant of the Stanley family who rose to prominence with the accession of Henry VII, Thomas Stanley wrote a *History of Philosophy* (1655 62), an early and commendable effort at popularization. He prepared an edition of Aeschylus (1663) and translated the work of Anacreon, Moschus, Bion, and other classical poets. Stanley was also the author of some little-known original poems, which were collected in 1650.

stanza A group of lines of verse, making up a unit repeated throughout a poem. It is often referred to as a 'verse', but strictly speaking a verse (from Latin, 'furrow' or 'turning') is a single line. Since that strict sense accords with such uses as 'rhymed verse', 'free verse' and 'blank verse', stanza is to be preferred for a repeated group of lines. (See also RHYME.)

Stapledon, W(illiam) Olaf 1886–1950 Writer of SCIENCE FICTION. Although his early years were spent in the Middle East, Stapledon lived most of his life near Liverpool, supplementing a small private income mainly by teaching philosophy for the WEA.

His novels are painstaking exemplary fictions displaying his ideas about ethics and evolution. The most famous are *Last and First Men* (1930), a history of man's descendants extending over billions of years, and *Star Maker* (1937), a spectacular vision of the whole universe and its creator. His more orthodox scientific romances – *Odd John* (1935), *Sirius* (1944), *The Flames* (1947) and *A Man Divided* (1950) – deal with exceptional individuals enabled by nature or artifice to catch glimpses of glorious possibility but doomed to frustrating personal failure. The combination of cosmic perspective and despairing anxiety gives Stapledon's work a poignant grandeur.

Stark, Dame **Freya** 1893–1993 Travel-writer. She was born at Chagford, Devon, and educated at Bedford College, London University. A long lifetime of courageous solitary expeditions in Arabia, Turkey, etc., has provided material for her many travel books from *Bagdad Sketches* (1933) onwards. Vividly written, with a strong sense both of history and topography, they owe much to their author's indomitable personality, which also suffuses her six-volume collected *Letters* (1974–81). She was created a Dame of the British Empire in 1972.

Stead, C(hristian) K(arlson) 1932– New Zealand critic, poet, short-story writer and novelist. Born in Auckland and educated at the University of Auckland and the University of Bristol, he spent most of his academic career at the University of Auckland. He is now New Zealand's leading writer-critic. He has published two well-known studies of MODERNISM, *The New Poetic* (1964) and *Pound, Yeats, Eliot and the Modernist Movement* (1986). *In the Glass Case* (1981) is a collection of critical writing on New Zealand literature, while *Answering to the Language* (1989) includes essays on English and Australian writers as well. Stead's poetry has followed a similar path to his criticism, influenced first by T. S. ELIOT and then by POUND and later American modernists. Collections include *Whether the Will is Free* (1962), *Crossing the Bar* (1972), *Walking Westward* (1979), *Poems of a Decade* (1983) and *Voices* (1990). His novels, often demonstrating his political concerns, include: *Smith's Dream* (1971), set in a future fascist New Zealand; *All Visitors Ashore* (1984), set against the background of the 1951 waterfront strike; *The Death of the Body* (1986); and *Sister Hollywood* (1989). *Five for the Symbol* (1981) is a collection of stories. He has also edited a selection of KATHERINE MANSFIELD's letters and journals (1977).

Stead, Christina (Ellen) 1902–83 Australian novelist and short-story writer. Born in New South Wales and educated in Sydney, she lived abroad between 1928 and 1974, chiefly in Britain and the USA. The only novel in her main corpus to be set in Australia is *Seven Poor Men of Sydney* (1934), faithfully recreating the place and generation of her youth. As a result, though internationally recognized, she was at first not seen as an Australian writer and not properly acknowledged in her own country.

Her particular gift was for minute, objective observation of subjective experience, located in fully registered social and political environments. Her first book, *The Salzburg Tales* (1934), a collection of stories modelled on *The Decameron*, was followed by *The Beauties and Furies* (1936) and *The House of All Nations* (1938), about life in Paris. *The Man Who Loved Children* (1940) and *For Love Alone* (1944) provide a picture of the artist very close to her own development, the former (though set in America) dealing with her early struggles against a domineering father, the latter portraying her fight to get to England and the different kinds of love she experienced there. *Letty Fox: Her Luck* (1946), *A Little Tea, A Little Chat* (1948) and *The People with the Dogs* (1952) have American settings, while *The Dark Places of the Heart* (1966; as *Cotter's England* in UK, 1967) is a study of England during the Cold War. The last, with her two autobiographical novels, constitute her major achievement. Subsequent works include *The Little Hotel* (1973), *Miss Herbert (The Suburban Wife)* (1976), *The Puzzleheaded Girl* (four novellas; 1967) and the posthumous *Ocean of Story* (1985), gathering her uncollected stories, generally less successful than her novels. Also posthumously published were the unfinished *I'm Dying Laughing* (1986) and two volumes of letters, *A Web of Friendship: Selected Letters (1928–73)* (1992) and *Talking into the Typewriter: Selected Letters (1973–83)* (1992).

Stead, W(illiam) T(homas) 1849–1912 Journalist. Born at Embleton, Northumberland, he began his career on *The Northern Echo*, but by 1880 he had moved to London to work on THE PALL MALL GAZETTE. His editorship of this vigorous London paper (1883–90) initiated the 'new journalism' of the 1880s: strident, courageous and itself influential in shaping political events. 'The Maiden Tribute of Modern Babylon', articles on procuring a female child for sexual purposes, led to his imprisonment in 1889, but also to a change in the age of consent. He later edited *The Review of Reviews*, became a spiritualist, and died in the *Titanic* disaster.

Steele, Sir **Richard** 1672–1729 Essayist and playwright. Born in Dublin, the son of an attorney, he was educated at Charterhouse (where he first met ADDISON) and matriculated at Christ Church, Oxford, from which he migrated to Merton, leaving without a degree in order to join the Life Guards. In 1700 he successfully fought a duel, seriously wounding his adversary, an experience which led to a lifelong campaign against duelling which first became clear in *The*

Christian Hero (1701), a popular guide to conduct. The same year saw the first performance of a comedy, *The Funeral*, which was followed by two unsuccessful dramatic pieces, derived from French originals by Corneille and Molière, in which Steele attempted to put into practice the advice of JEREMY COLLIER in his *Short View of the Immorality and Profaneness of the English Stage*. He was at this time attempting to discover the philosopher's stone, and these pseudo-scientific interests remained with him, as witness his 1718 patent for a 'Fish-pool', a fishing boat built like a water tank which transported its catch live. In 1707 he was appointed by ROBERT HARLEY to write the government-sponsored *Gazette*, which post he held till the change of government in October 1710. In 1709 he founded THE TATLER, which he edited under the pseudonym of ISAAC BICKERSTAFF. Two months after it came to a sudden, unexplained end in January 1711 Addison, who had contributed to *The Tatler*, joined him in founding THE SPECTATOR. This was followed by THE GUARDIAN (March–October 1713) and the more political *Englishman* (1713–14). During the run of *The Spectator* Steele engaged in polemical pamphleteering, the most notable examples being *The Importance of Dunkirk Considered* (1713), which provoked a strong reply from SWIFT, and *The Crisis* (1714), a consideration of the Hanoverian succession so ill-timed as to result in Steele being charged with issuing a seditious libel and being deprived of his seat as MP for Stockbridge.

With the accession of George I this expulsion was palliated by a number of official appointments, the most important being patentee of the Theatre Royal, DRURY LANE. This patent was lost after a political difference with the Duke of Newcastle, thus eliciting from Steele *The Theatre*, a periodical which ran from January to April 1720, full of details of the contemporary theatrical world. The following year Walpole arranged for the patent to be restored, and in November 1722 Steele produced THE CONSCIOUS LOVERS, derived from Terence's *Andria*. Its instant success was in part due to the publicity and acrimonious reactions provoked by *The Theatre*. Steele's only important dramatic piece, it influenced the development of SENTIMENTAL COMEDY by its high moral tone.

Steevens, George 1736–1800 Shakespearean scholar. He was born in Poplar and educated at Eton and King's College, Cambridge, which he left without a degree. After a brief spell in the Temple he settled in Hampstead, where he built up a fine library and an impressive collection of HOGARTH's engravings. He did important bibliographical work on Hogarth, which was used in *The Genuine Works of Hogarth* (1803–17).

His greatest passion was SHAKESPEARE. In 1766 he published reprints of the Shakespeare quartos which

he had borrowed from GARRICK's library. JOHNSON agreed to Steevens's plan for a more fully annotated version of his own edition of 1765. The 10-volume Johnson–Steevens edition appeared in 1773; a revised edition (1778) included EDMOND MALONE's account of the plays' chronology and a further revision (1785) was prepared by Isaac Reed. Three variorum editions appeared after Steevens's death, incorporating his unpublished notes, though the last, edited by James Boswell the younger in 1821, was based largely on Malone's work. In life Steevens had quarrelled with Malone and set out to displace his 1790 edition of Shakespeare with his own 15-volume edition (1793). Designed to differ from Malone as much as possible, it took emendation to ridiculous lengths; some notes bore witness to the spite for which Steevens was also known. He knew most of literary London, was one of Johnson's circle – helping him with THE LIVES OF THE POETS – and became a member of the Club in 1774. Something of a journalist as well as a scholar, he revelled in epigrams and parodies. His interest in forgery was shown by his role in the controversies surrounding CHATTERTON and WILLIAM HENRY IRELAND, as well as the tombstone of King Hardecanute which he fabricated in 1789 as a hoax against Richard Gough of the Society of Antiquaries. See also SHAKESPEARE: PERFORMANCE AND CRITICISM.

Stein, Gertrude 1874–1946 American woman of letters. Born in Allegheny, Pennsylvania, she spent her early childhood in Vienna and Paris and then moved with her family to Oakland, California. She was educated at Radcliffe College (1893–7), where she studied philosophy with WILLIAM JAMES, and then enrolled at the Johns Hopkins Medical School (1897–1901), but failed several courses in her fourth year and did not take a degree. From 1903 until her death she lived in France, remaining in Paris except for the period of Nazi occupation, when she moved to the south. A lesbian, she lived with another expatriate American, Alice B. Toklas, from 1907 onwards. Friends of painters such as Picasso, Braque, Matisse, and Juan Gris, Stein and Toklas found themselves at the centre of an art movement. During the 1920s Stein became a famous literary figure; her salon was a gathering place for both European artists and expatriate Americans such as ERNEST HEMINGWAY, SHERWOOD ANDERSON and F. SCOTT FITZGERALD. Her first books – *Fernhurst* and *Q.E.D.* (later retitled *Things as They are: A Novel in Three Parts*) – were written during the period 1903–5 but were not published until much later. Her first published work, which she claimed to have written under the influence of Flaubert's *Trois Contes* and Cézanne's painting, was *Three Lives: Stories of the Good Anna, Melanctha, and the Gentle Lena* (1909). Its prose style is highly unconventional: she periodically repeats phrases, sentences, even whole paragraphs, and more or less

Gertrude Stein: photograph by Cecil Beaton

dispenses with normal punctuation. Subsequent works, even more experimental, were considered exciting by some and merely eccentric by others. *Tender Buttons* (1914) uses words so idiosyncratically that many sentences literally make no sense. *The Making of Americans, being a History of a Family's Progress* (1925) is an extremely long novel in which she again employs her technique of repetition.

Altogether, Stein produced over 500 titles – novels, poems, plays, articles, portraits of famous people and memoirs. Among the most notable are: *Composition as Explanation* (1926), a critical work; *Lucy Church Amiably* (1930), a novel; *Four Saints in Three Acts* (1929), a lyric drama staged as an opera (with music by Virgil Thompson) in 1934; *Lectures in America* (1935); *Everybody's Autobiography* (1937), which is her own autobiography; *Wars I Have Seen* (1945), a memoir; and *Brewsie and Willie* (1946), a novel about the lives of American soldiers in France during and immediately after World War II. One of her best-known works from the later period is THE AUTOBIOGRAPHY OF ALICE B. TOKLAS (1933), a fictionalized account of her own life from her companion's point of view.

Steinbeck, John 1902–68 American novelist. Born in Salinas, California, he studied marine biology at Stanford. His literary career began in 1929 with a romantic novel, *Cup of Gold*, about the buccaneer Sir Henry Morgan. His next book was a collection of short stories portraying the people in a farm community, *The Pastures of Heaven* (1932). *To a God Unknown* (1933), his second novel, is about a California farmer whose religion is a pagan belief in fertility and who sacrifices himself on a primitive altar to bring an end to drought. It was *Tortilla Flat* (1935), however, with its vivid picture of life among the *paisanos* in Monterey, that brought Steinbeck to prominence. The tone of his work changed with *In Dubious Battle* (1936), a powerful novel about a strike among migratory workers in the California fruit orchards, and with *Of Mice and Men* (1937), the story of two itinerant farm workers who yearn for some sort of home.

The Long Valley (1938), which consists of 13 stories set in Salinas Valley, was followed by THE GRAPES OF WRATH (1939), about a family fleeing from the dust bowl of Oklahoma to what they hope will be a better life in California. His best-known work and the high point of his career, it won a PULITZER PRIZE and became a classic American film in 1940. It was followed by *The Moon is Down* (1942), a short novel about Norwegian resistance to the Nazi occupation, *Cannery Row* (1945), in which he returned to the *paisanos* of Monterey, and *The Wayward Bus* (1947), in which the passengers on a stranded bus in California become a microcosm of contemporary American frustrations. Among his other novels are *The Pearl* (1947), *East of Eden* (1952), *Sweet Thursday* (1954) and *The Winter of Our Discontent* (1961). His non-fiction includes *Bombs Away: The Story of a Bomber Team* (1942), *The Log of the Sea of Cortez* (1951), a selection of his dispatches as a war correspondent, *Once There was a War* (1958), and *Travels with Charley* (1962), about his personal rediscovery of America. He was awarded the Nobel Prize for literature in 1962.

Steiner, (Francis) George 1929– Critic. Born in Paris, to Austrian Jewish parents, he fled with his family to the United States in 1940. Here he was educated at the universities of Chicago and Harvard. In the 1950s he studied at Oxford as a Rhodes Scholar and worked on the staff of *The Economist*, then returned to the United States to research and teach at Princeton. He has been a Fellow of Churchill College, Cambridge, since 1961, and professor of English and comparative literature at Geneva since 1974.

Steiner's writings are those of a *Kulturkritik* in the humanist traditions of Central European Jewry, showing a truly international range of learning. Over all his work – especially *Language and Silence* (1967), *In Bluebeard's Castle* (1971), and the novel *The Portage to San Cristobal of A. H.* (1981) – falls the shadow of the Holocaust. A later venture into fiction, *Proofs and Three Parables* (1992), takes the collapse of Marxism in Eastern Europe as its subject. His characteristic concern is with the status of language and the literary imagination in a century of barbarism and political terror. His other principal works are *Tolstoy or Dostoevsky* (1959), *The Death of Tragedy* (1961), *After Babel* (1975), *Antigones* (1984) and *Real Presences: Is There Anything in What We Say?* (1989), his most complete and eloquent statement of his critical stance. Steiner has also written on chess, and edited *The Penguin Book of Modern Verse in Translation* (1966). A varied selection of his writings has been published as *George Steiner: A Reader* (1984).

Stephen, Sir Leslie 1832–1904 Critic and scholar. He came from a family involved in the Evangelical group known as the 'Clapham Sect', whose leading member was William Wilberforce. His father Sir James Stephen, Under-Secretary of State for the Colonies, played a role in the campaign to abolish slavery. His older brother was Sir James Fitzjames Stephen, a distinguished jurist. Stephen himself was educated at Eton, King's College in London and

Trinity Hall, Cambridge, where he was ordained and became a college tutor. His reading of Kant, JOHN STUART MILL and HERBERT SPENCER made him resign his orders in 1870 and adopt the agnosticism set forth in *Essays on Free Thinking and Plain Speaking* (1873) and the *Agnostic's Apology* (first published in 1876).

By this time he was already well established as a literary journalist, contributing to THE SATURDAY REVIEW, FRASER'S MAGAZINE and THE FORTNIGHTLY REVIEW and, from 1871 to 1882, editing THE CORNHILL MAGAZINE. In this capacity he published the serial version of HARDY'S FAR FROM THE MADDING CROWD. His own lively essays were gathered in *Hours in a Library* (1874, 1876 and 1879). *A History of English Thought in the Eighteenth Century* (1876) is generally regarded as his most important work, though he also wrote studies of JOHNSON (1878), POPE (1880), SWIFT (1882), GEORGE ELIOT (1902) and HOBBES (1904) for the English Men of Letters series. *The Playground of Europe* (1871) reflects his love of mountaineering. Stephen's best monument is his work for GEORGE SMITH of Smith & Elder as the first editor of *The Dictionary of National Biography* in 1882–91. He oversaw its first 26 volumes, writing many entries himself and continuing as a contributor after he resigned the editorship.

Stephen was the model for Vernon Whitford in MEREDITH'S *THE EGOIST*. His first wife was THACKERAY'S daughter Harriet Marian ('Minny'), and his youngest daughter by his marriage to Julia Duckworth was VIRGINIA WOOLF, who used him as the basis for the character of Mr Ramsay in *TO THE LIGHTHOUSE*.

Stephen Hero See PORTRAIT OF THE ARTIST AS A YOUNG MAN, A.

Stephens, James 1882–1950 Irish poet and novelist. He became famous with THE CROCK OF GOLD (1912) a prose fantasy which weaves Irish folk traditions and ancient legends into a tale of whimsical charm. *The Demi-Gods* (1914) is in the same vein, while *Deirdre* (1923) again took Celtic legend for its subject. Born into poverty in the Dublin slums, Stephens had received his first encouragement from GEORGE WILLIAM RUSSELL (AE), who helped with the publication of *Insurrections* (1909), the first of several volumes of verse later gathered in *Collected Poems* (1926, enlarged 1954). Collections of stories include *Here are Ladies* (with poems, 1913), *In the Land of Youth* (1924), *Etched in Moonlight* (1928) and *Irish Fairy Tales* (1920). An active Sinn Feiner, Stephens also edited the poems of his friend and colleague THOMAS MACDONAGH, executed in the Easter Rising of 1916, and published *The Insurrection in Dublin* (1916).

Sterne, Laurence 1713–68 Novelist. The son of an army subaltern, Sterne was born in Clonmel, Tipperary, spent his earliest years in various garrison towns, and was educated for eight years in Halifax until his father's death in 1731 left the family penniless. A cousin helped him to enter Jesus College, Cambridge, as a 'sizar' (poor scholar). He received his degree in 1737 and then took orders, becoming vicar of Sutton-on-the-Forrest in Yorkshire in 1738 and later prebendary of York Minster. After his marriage to Elizabeth Lumley in 1741 Sterne moved to Stillington, another Yorkshire parish. His wife suffered an emotional breakdown in 1758, when he was involved in a number of 'sentimental' dalliances with local ladies.

The restricted social environment of Yorkshire had furnished him with a mass of minutely observed details. He began work on his novel TRISTRAM SHANDY in 1759, reading excerpts to a circle of friends at Skelton Hall, the home of a Cambridge contemporary, John Hall-Stevenson. The first two volumes were published in 1760, and their author was at once catapulted to literary fame; further volumes appeared in 1761, 1762, 1765 and 1767. In London Sterne was lionized by fashionable society, an experience he relished after the parochial surroundings of Yorkshire. Taking a flamboyant delight in playing the parts of his own characters in real life, he became a cult figure, the subject of outlandish anecdotes and, to some, the object of disapproval.

His new recognition brought him the perpetual curacy of Coxwold, near his other Yorkshire parishes, where he named his home Shandy Hall. He adopted the persona of the parson in Tristram Shandy for The Sermons of Mr Yorick, of which successive volumes appeared in 1760, 1766 and 1769. They were extremely well subscribed, despite their lack of doctrinal content and infrequent attention to such devotional topics as faith. In his oratory as well as his fiction, Sterne was a master of shock tactics, while at the same time remaining capable of powerful emotion. (Tolstoy is said to have been influenced by the sermons, which he read as a young man.) In 1762–4 Sterne lived abroad at Toulouse, with his depressed wife and his daughter Lydia, spending much of his remaining life in Continental travel intended to relieve his tuberculosis. A seven-month tour of France and Italy during 1765 resulted in A SENTIMENTAL JOURNEY (1768), a second novel as arresting and fragmentary as his first. It takes an incidental swipe at SMOLLETT (the learned Smelfungus) of whose more caustic travel writing Sterne disapproved.

During 1767 Sterne formed an attachment to Mrs Eliza Draper, the wife of an East India Company officer for whose eyes he kept a journal from April to August, published after his death, with Mrs Draper's consent, as Letters from Yorick to Eliza (1775). Shortly after the appearance of A Sentimental Journey in 1768 he died of pleurisy at his lodgings in Old Bond Street, leaving his family insolvent. They were helped by John Hall-Stevenson and Mrs Draper, who raised subscriptions on his posthumous publications.

Despite the immense popularity of Tristram Shandy, in particular, during Sterne's lifetime, his full importance has been acknowledged only since his death. JOHNSON, RICHARDSON and GOLDSMITH were among contemporaries to denounce his whirling, anarchic method or take offence at his playful indecency. Yet Sterne's oddity is neither accidental nor perverse; it is the strategy of an inventive, thoughtful comic talent. His work points the way to later experiments (by JOYCE and his successors, for example), though not all of these would be conducted with that vein of good humour, delicate yet often dark, which runs so riddlingly through his work.

Steuart [Steuart-Denham], **Sir James** 1712–80 Political economist. Born in Edinburgh, Steuart was a Jacobite who returned from a long exile in 1763. In 1767 he published An Inquiry into the Principles of Political Economy, which in some respects anticipated the work of ADAM SMITH (who knew Steuart and his book), not least in its view of man as 'acting uniformly in all ages, in all countries, and in all climates, from the principles of self-interest, expediency, duty and passion'.

Stevens, Wallace 1879–1955 American poet. He was born in Reading, Pennsylvania, and educated at Harvard. In 1900 he got a job on the editorial staff of The New York Tribune and then on the periodical The World's Work. He was unhappy with journalism, though, and in 1901 he entered New York Law School. He was admitted to the Bar in New York in 1904. He joined the legal staff of the Hartford Accident and Indemnity Company in 1916 and remained with the firm until his death.

His early verse appeared in Trend and in HARRIET MONROE's magazine POETRY (which published one of his most famous poems, 'Sunday Morning', in 1915). 'Three Travelers Watch a Sunrise', which won the Poetry magazine prize for a verse play in 1916, was produced in the following year at New York's Provincetown Playhouse. Stevens's first collection of verse, Harmonium (1923), sold fewer than 100 copies but was well received by reviewers such as MARIANNE MOORE. For the next few years he wrote very little, concentrating on his career in the business world (he became vice-president of his company in 1934). His second volume of poetry, Ideas of Order, appeared in 1935 and was followed in 1936 by Owl's Clover. The latter collection included poems written in response to charges that he was unconcerned with social issues. Another of his most famous poems provided the title piece of his fourth collection, The Man with the Blue Guitar and Other Poems (1937). Two further collections, Parts of a World and Notes toward a Supreme Fiction, appeared in 1942, Esthétique du Mal in 1945 and Transport to Summer in 1947. The Auroras of Autumn was published in 1950, the year after he was awarded the Bollingen Prize. *Collected Poems* (1954) won Stevens a belated PULITZER PRIZE. *The Necessary Angel: Essays on Reality and the Imagination* (1951), a collection of essays and addresses on poetry and art, received the National Book Award. *Opus Posthumous* (1957) contains poems, essays and plays, many hitherto unpublished. *The Letters of Wallace Stevens* appeared in 1966.

Poetry for Stevens was 'a part of the structure of reality'. Throughout his poetic career he worked with the joint awareness of his Romantic heritage and his distinctively modern sensibility. His poetry reveals, on the one hand, an effort to reconcile the product of his imagination with fundamental reality, and on the other his disbelief in the possibility of any such reconciliation. His use of language is meticulous, though frequently exotic.

Stevenson, Anne (Katherine) 1933– Poet. Born in Cambridge to American parents, she was educated at the University of Michigan, Ann Arbor. Subsequently she has worked in publishing, as a tutor at Glasgow University and as the proprietor of a poetry bookshop, and she has held many posts as writer-in-residence and writing fellow. The central theme of her work is an attempt to 'rationally' communicate 'the reality of the a-rational', to use finite language to express the infinite. This dilemma is often mirrored in a landscape, be it the Sierra Nevada in *Reversals* (1969), the flat, unassuming Fenlands, or the stark grandeur of the north-east coast of Scotland in *Enough of Green* (1977). Other collections have been *Living in America* (1965), *Correspondences: A Family History in Letters* (1974), *Minute by Glass Minute* (1982), *The Fiction Makers* (1985), *Selected Poems 1965–1986* (1987) and *The Other House* (1990). Her admission of the limits of language – she speaks of being unable to capture 'the mudness of mud' – makes her poems poignant and courageous. She has also written a study of ELIZABETH BISHOP (1966) and a biography of SYLVIA PLATH (1990).

Stevenson, Robert Louis 1850–94 Novelist, poet, playwright, essayist, travel-writer and writer of CHILDREN'S LITERATURE. He was born in Edinburgh, the son of Thomas Stevenson, joint-engineer to the Board of Northern Lighthouses. He entered Edinburgh University in 1867 to study engineering but, since he had no interest in his father's profession, changed to law and was admitted advocate in 1875. He showed his interest in a literary career by student contributions to *The Edinburgh University Magazine* in 1871 and *The Portfolio* in 1873. Even in his childhood his health was extremely poor; as an adult, there were times when he could not even wear a jacket for fear of bringing on a haemorrhage of the lungs. In spite of this, he was all his life an enthusiastic traveller: an account of his canoe tour of France

and Belgium was published in 1878 as *An Inland Voyage*, and *Travels with a Donkey in the Cevennes* followed in 1879. In this year he travelled to California by emigrant ship and train: his account of these experiences was published posthumously in 1895 as *The Amateur Emigrant*. In America he married Mrs Fanny Osbourne, whom he had previously met in France. TREASURE ISLAND (1883) was originally devised for her young son, Lloyd, who later collaborated with him on two unfairly neglected novels, *The Wrong Box* (1889) and *The Wrecker* (1892). After a brief stay at Calistoga – recorded in *The Silverado Squatters* (1883) – he returned to England, determined to stand or fall by his ability to earn a living by writing.

Stevenson contributed to various periodicals, including THE CORNHILL MAGAZINE and *Longman's Magazine*, where his best-known article, 'A Humble Remonstrance', was published in 1884, in reply to HENRY JAMES's 'The Art of Fiction'. This friendly controversy about the relationship between life and art led to a lifelong friendship. Stevenson's essays and short stories were collected in *Virginibus Puerisque* (1881), *Familiar Studies of Men and Books* (1882), *New Arabian Nights* (1882), *The Merry Men* (1887), *Memories and Portraits* (1887), *Across the Plains* (1892) and *Island Nights' Entertainments* (1893). The list of his novels mixes glib popular romances and works of steadily developing psychological intensity. In addition to works already mentioned, it includes *Prince Otto* (1885), THE STRANGE CASE OF DR JEKYLL AND MR HYDE (1886), KIDNAPPED (1886) and its sequel, *Catriona* (1893), THE BLACK ARROW (1888) and THE MASTER OF BALLANTRAE (1889). He left unfinished WEIR OF HERMISTON (1896) and *St Ives* (1897 and 1898), which was completed by SIR ARTHUR QUILLER-COUCH. Minor works include his charming books of poems, *A Child's Garden of Verses* (1885) and *Underwords* (1887), and his fustian dramas, *Deacon Brodie* (1880), *Admiral Guinea* (1884), *Beau Austin* (1885) and *Macaire* (1885), written in collaboration with W. E. HENLEY.

Stevenson left England in search of health in 1888 and never returned. After sailing for a while among the Pacific islands, he settled in Samoa and bought the Vailima estate. Here he enjoyed a period of comparative good health and literary productivity. He died suddenly from a cerebral haemorrhage and was buried on the island where he had been known as 'Tusitala' or 'The Teller of Tales'. During his residence in Samoa, Stevenson had become fascinated by the Polynesian culture and incensed at the European exploitation of the islands, engaging in various letters to *The Times* in London on the islanders' behalf. *In the South Seas* (1896) and *A Footnote to History* (1892) document his indignation; even more important are his two South Sea novellas, *The Beach of Falesá* (1893) and *The Ebb-Tide* (1894). *The Ebb-Tide* is a condemnation of colonial exploitation which prefigures CONRAD's *Heart of Darkness*, while *The Beach of Falesá* was so inimical to his readers that though a version was included in *The Island Nights' Entertainments*, its full text was not published until 1984.

Long categorized merely as a belletrist and children's writer, Stevenson is now being widely revalued. It is unlikely that his essays, poems and plays will ever revive, but his novels are beginning to take their rightful place in the adult tradition of early MODERNISM. His interest in the romance, which he explores in 'Victor Hugo's Romances' (1874), 'A Gossip on Romance' (1883) and 'A Humble Remonstrance' (1884), shows his search for a fiction which would avoid the trap of representationalism, his focus on 'incident' as a type of narrative epiphany, and his use of old forms for new purposes.

Stewart, Douglas 1913–85 Playwright and poet. Born in Eltham, New Zealand, and educated at university in Wellington, Stewart crossed to Australia in 1938 and made Sydney his home. He was literary editor of the Sydney *Bulletin* in 1940–61; *The Flesh and the Spirit* (1948), *The Broad Stream* (1975) and *Writers of the Bulletin* (1977) represent his critical writing which, though valuable, remains notorious for its early dismissal of *Voss*. His interest in the Australian bush BALLAD is evident in his own poem *Glencoe* (1947) and several editions with Nancy Keesing (1955, 1957, 1967 and 1968). Besides *Glencoe*, he published eight other volumes of verse which, though experimenting with narrative forms, remain memorable for their shorter lyrics. The *Collected Poems, 1936–1967* was published in 1967. His high reputation as a writer of verse plays rests on three written for radio – *The Fire on the Snow* (1941), about Captain Scott's expedition, *The Golden Lover* (1943), a Maori love story, and *The Earthquake Shakes the Land* (1944) – and three written for the stage – *Ned Kelly* (1944), *Shipwreck* (1948) and *Fisher's Ghost* (1961). A volume of stories, *A Girl with Red Hair* (1944), and his autobiography, *A Springtime in Taranaki* (1983) are set in New Zealand. *Garden of Friends* (1988) was published posthumously.

Stewart, Dugald 1753–1828 Philosopher. Born in Edinburgh, he completed his education at Edinburgh and Glasgow Universities, becoming professor of moral philosophy at Edinburgh in 1785 and remaining there until 1810. A disciple of THOMAS REID, he did much to encourage a distinguished generation of Scottish writers and philosophers. Among his pupils were JAMES MILL, SIR WALTER SCOTT, HENRY BROUGHAM and SYDNEY SMITH. His philosophical works include *The Elements of the Philosophy of the Human Mind* (1792–1827), *Outlines of Moral Philosophy* (1794), and *The Philosophy of the Active and Moral Powers* (1828).

Stewart, J(ohn) I(nnes) M(ackintosh) 1906–94 Critic, novelist and, as Michael Innes, author of DETECTIVE FICTION. Born in Edinburgh, he studied at Oriel College, Oxford, and taught English at Leeds, Adelaide and Belfast before returning to Oxford in 1949 as Student (i.e. Fellow) of Christ Church. Under his own name Stewart wrote a number of novels and critical studies, notably *Eight Modern Writers* (1963). But he was better known for his long and prolific career as Michael Innes, beginning with *Death at the President's Lodging* (1936; as *Seven Suspects* in USA), *Hamlet, Revenge!* (1937), *Lament for a Maker* (1938) and *Stop Press* (1939). Ingenious, urbane and donnishly playful, packed with casual erudition and witty talk, these books remain classics of their form. Their policeman hero, John (later Sir John) Appleby, subsequently featured in other, more heterogeneous types of adventure. *The Secret Vanguard* (1940), *From London Far* (1946), *The Journeying Boy* (1949) and *Operation Pax* (1951; as *The Paper Thunderbolt* in USA) are chase novels in the tradition of JOHN BUCHAN. *Appleby on Ararat* (1941), *The Daffodil Affair* (1942) and *Appleby's End* (1945) are frankly fantastic. *A Private View* (1952), *Silence Observed* (1961) and *A Family Affair* (1969) deal with the world of art. A later attempt to replace Appleby by his son Bobby – in, for example, *An Awkward Lie* (1971) – was not successful. More promising was the introduction of the painter and reluctant detective Honeybath, who first appears in *The Mysterious Commission* (1975).

stichomythia Dialogue in alternating lines of verse, usually signifying conflict or quarrel. It is a common device in classical drama. The exchange between Richard and Elizabeth in SHAKESPEARE's *RICHARD III* (Act 4, Scene iv) provides a famous example from the English theatre.

Stoddard, Solomon 1643–1729 American Puritan minister. Born in Boston and educated at Harvard, he became pastor of the church at Northampton, Massachusetts, in 1670.

His appointment marked a major turning-point in colonial American history. At first a proponent of the Half-Way Covenant, which granted partial church membership to children of regenerate parents, in 1677 he ceased to distinguish between full and Half-Way church members because of his conviction that the sacraments were vehicles for God's grace and thus should be available to all seeking Christian salvation. This view, referred to as 'Stoddardeanism', secured for him not only the title of 'Pope' but also the wrath of the orthodox Ministry of Massachusetts Bay. At the synod held in 1679 he defended his theory and practice in 'Nine Arguments against Examinations concerning a Work of Grace before Admission to the Lord's Supper', a paper attacked by INCREASE MATHER.

The exchange initiated a pamphlet war with the Mathers in which Stoddard defended himself with *The Doctrine of Instituted Churches* (1700), *The Inexcusableness of Neglecting the Worship of God, under the Pretence of Being in an Unconverted Condition* (1708) and *An Appeal to the Learned* (1709). Most of the churches throughout western Massachusetts accepted Stoddard's admission policy, which laid the theological groundwork for the Great Awakening. JONATHAN EDWARDS was Stoddard's grandson.

Stoker, Bram [Abraham] 1847–1912 Novelist. Born in Dublin and educated at Trinity College, he became a civil servant, as well as drama critic of *The Dublin Mail* and editor of *The Penny Press*, before settling in London and working as personal manager to Sir Henry Irving. His first publication, *The Duties of Clerks of Petty Sessions in Ireland* (1879), was followed by 15 works of fiction. *DRACULA* (1897) is the most famous. Stoker also wrote the two-volume *Personal Reminiscences of Henry Irving* (1906).

Stokes, Adrian 1902–72 Art critic, painter and poet. Born in London, he was educated at Rugby and Magdalen College, Oxford. During visits to Italy in the 1920s he met EZRA POUND, a significant influence later joined by that of the psychoanalyst Melanie Klein, whose patient he was in 1930–7. *Quattro Cento* (1932), *Stones of Rimini* (1934) and *Colour and Form* (1937) distinguish between carving, which seeks to discover what already exists in the material, and modelling, which impresses the artist's imagination on the material. Later works, which include *Reflections on the Nude* (1967), elaborate and modify the distinction, particularly in light of his interest in psychology. Stokes's critical writings have been edited by Lawrence Gowing (1978) and his poetry, which belongs largely to the last years of his life, by PETER ROBINSON as *With All the Views* (1981).

Stone, Louis 1871–1935 Australian novelist. Born in Leicester, he was taken to Australia by his parents in 1884. After attending classes at the University of Sydney and training as a primary schoolteacher, he taught in country areas of New South Wales and the Sydney suburbs. His best-known novel, *Jonah* (1911), is a realistic account of the life of a working-class larrikin ('street rowdy' or 'Jack the lad') in Sydney. Today it is highly regarded, as the first classic novel of Sydney life and an important work in the naturalist tradition, which has suffered from neglect in Australia until comparatively recently, but at the time of its publication it failed to bring Stone the recognition he had hoped for. Lack of critical or financial success and a progressive nervous illness, which ultimately led to his early retirement from teaching, prevented him from realizing the promise suggested in *Jonah* and he produced only one further novel, *Betty Wayside* (1915), which describes the fortunes of a woman pianist in Sydney. Stone subsequently became interested in drama and in the 1920s travelled to London in the hope of getting his only play *The Last of the Gods* (1923) staged.

Stone, Robert (Anthony) 1937– American novelist. Born in Brooklyn, he attended university in New York and at Stanford. *A Hall of Mirrors* (1968) follows three shiftless people to New Orleans, where a right-wing political rally explodes into violence. *Dog Soldiers* (1975) is about heroin smuggling on the Californian border. *A Flag for Sunrise* (1981), his most praised and also his most Conradian novel, chronicles a popular uprising in Central America. *Children of Light* (1986) is a SATIRE on Hollywood.

Stones of Venice, The A three-volume study of architecture, history and society by JOHN RUSKIN, published in 1851–3. The first volume (1851) is an architectural essay of authoritative dryness and stylistic restraint whose initial chapter, 'The Quarry', is a panoramic anticipation of the entire work. But it is with the publication in 1853 of the last two volumes that the work assumes epic scope with Ruskin's praise of Venetian Gothic architecture as an expression of the feelings and aspirations of those who laboured to form it. By contrast with earlier Greek, Egyptian or Ninevite workmen – slaves all – the Gothic workman, a child of Christianity, enjoyed freedom because his faith recognized the liberality of the individual soul. Then, bringing his argument up to his own time, Ruskin envisages the Victorian workman as dehumanized and enslaved. In a well-known passage he compares the Venetian glass-blower, whose work may be clumsily cut and imperfect in form, with his 19th-century counterpart who is compelled to be 'accurate' and 'perfect'. He concludes that the Gothic is superior and that the Victorian worker should be delivered from commercial slavery. The last part of *The Stones of Venice* – 'The Fall' – records the debasement and corruption of the state, a decline traced by Ruskin through Early, Roman, and Grotesque Renaissance architecture. Pride, Luxury, Self-adulation, Infidelity – these degradations resound in the pages of the last volume as the immense work reaches a 'Conclusion' recapitulating the controlling motifs and warning the reader of similar contemporary tendencies.

The Stones of Venice states a compelling (if debatable) thesis and – despite some digression, sweeping generalization and over-confident claims – the innate power of the work and the magisterial sweep of the prose bear the reader along. In its scope and magnanimity, its humanitarianism, and its belief in imperfection under divine law, the book remains a central Victorian document.

Stonor letters, The The correspondence and papers of the Stonor family, from Stonor in Oxfordshire. The earliest piece is a Latin charter of *c.* 1290 and the latest is from 1483. In between are personal letters, legal and official documents and household accounts written by or to various members of the family in English, Latin and ANGLO-NORMAN. Some of the letters provide a valuable insight into everyday affairs and domestic details of the Middle Ages.

Stoppard [Straussler], **Tom** 1937– Playwright. Born in Czechoslovakia, he emigrated via Singapore to Britain, where he completed his education at Pocklington School. He was a journalist in Bristol and then London, where he worked as a freelance while writing plays. The modest success of some early radio and television pieces, which included *A Walk on the Water* (TV, 1963; later adapted for the stage as *Enter a Free Man*, 1968), preceded the startling popularity of *ROSENCRANTZ AND GUILDENSTERN ARE DEAD* (1966). Stoppard's highly intelligent and quizzical investigation of artistic conventions and cultural assumptions is characteristic, not only of this play, but also of subsequent work: *The Real Inspector Hound* (1968); the short farce *After Magritte* (1970); *Jumpers* (1972), in which a variety of philosophical perceptions occupy all the dialogue while the murder story that constitutes the plot is almost completely ignored; and *Travesties* (1974), in which ideas that mattered intensely to such of its characters as Tristan Tzara, JAMES JOYCE and Lenin are made to matter very little. Some of his later work suggests a greater engagement with social and political realities. *Every Good Boy Deserves Favour* (1977), written for performance by actors and a symphony orchestra, the short *Cahoot's Macbeth* (1979) and *Night and Day* (1979) raise issues about freedom and totalitarianism. A preoccupation with the farcical aspects of espionage enlivens *Neutral Ground* (TV, 1968), *Professional Foul* (TV, 1977), *The Dog It was That Died* (radio, 1982) and *Hapgood* (1988). *The Real Thing* (1982) is a neat boulevard play, and *Artist Descending a Staircase* (1988) pays comic homage to the surrealists.

Storey, David 1933– Novelist and playwright. Born into a mining family in Wakefield, he studied at the Slade School of Art and worked as a professional Rugby League footballer, teacher, farmer and tent erector. His rugby-playing days gave him the subject for *This Sporting Life* (1960), a grim, rawly realistic portrait of a Rugby League footballer. Though the novel is often classed with the ANGRY YOUNG MEN fiction of ALAN SILLITOE and JOHN BRAINE, its particularly harsh and hapless vision prefigures Storey's later, more extreme depictions of isolated male protagonists in mental and emotional crisis, of which *Radcliffe* (1963) and *Pasmore* (1972) are prominent examples. In *Radcliffe* the self-division and conflict generated by a tense homosexual affair build to a climax of horrifying breakdown and violence. Storey's subsequent novels, *Saville* (1976), which won the BOOKER PRIZE, *A Prodigal Child* (1982) and *Present Times* (1985), continue his two major themes: the loss of working-class roots through upward social movement, and the crises of marriage and career arising out of mid-life stasis and the narrowing of future opportunity. His realistically set but tangentially plotted plays include: *The Contractor* (1970), about the putting-up of a marquee at a wedding; *Home* (1970), set in a mental home; and *The Changing Room* (1972), about football. *Collected Poems* appeared in 1992.

Story of a Country Town, The A novel by E. W. HOWE, published in 1883. The story is told by Ned Westlock, the son of a stern, Bible-quoting minister-farmer. John Westlock's religious gatherings each Sunday are the only social occasions for the neighbours in the Midwestern farming community, and their severity of doctrine is commonly accepted. The important people in young Ned's life are Jo Erring, his mother's younger brother, who works on the Westlock farm, the young schoolteacher Agnes Deming, and the miller Damon Barker, to whom Jo is later apprenticed. It is Damon who makes Ned aware that there is a rich and varied world outside.

Jo falls in love with Mateel Shepherd and develops an increasing dislike for Clinton Bragg, a friend of the Shepherd family. Then, to everyone's surprise, John Westlock leaves the land and moves his family to the country town of Twin Mounds. He trades in land and buys the local newspaper, which Ned helps him to edit. Jo builds a mill and a home of his own and is accepted by Mateel Shepherd. John Westlock runs off with Damon's sister; Ned's mother becomes ill with worry, and Ned keeps the paper going on his own. Damon himself turns out to be the father whom Agnes Deming never knew and she goes to live with him at the mill. Ned's mother dies just before his father comes back, alone. The return is brief. John Westlock is now a man without resolution or purpose and he soon disappears again. Jo has been prospering but now he discovers that Mateel and the hated Clinton Bragg were once lovers. His insane jealousy leads to Mateel's death, and he then murders Bragg. He surrenders to the police but commits suicide. Ned and Agnes marry and settle down happily. Thus the life of the country town continues.

Stow, John 1525–1605 Historian and antiquary. A tailor for many years, he was collecting and transcribing manuscripts and writing histories from 1560 onwards. His annotated edition of CHAUCER (1561) was followed by a summary of English CHRONICLES (1565), and then, with the encouragement of MATTHEW PARKER, Matthew of Westminster's *Flores Historiarum* (1567), Matthew Paris's *Chronicle* (1571),

Thomas of Walsingham's *Chronicle* (1574), and *Chronicles of England* (1580), known as *Annals* in later editions. His most famous work is *A Survey of London* (1598), which contains information about both the city and its customs. It was revised and enlarged in 1603, and then again by JOHN STRYPE.

Stow, Randolph 1935– Australian novelist, poet and writer of CHILDREN'S LITERATURE. Born in Geraldton, Western Australia, Stow was educated at the University of Western Australia. He graduated with an arts degree in 1956 and has subsequently held brief appointments as a lecturer at the universities of Adelaide, Western Australia and Leeds. He has also studied anthropology and worked on a mission station for Aborigines in north-west Australia and as a patrol officer in Papua New Guinea. Since 1960 he has lived in England, mainly in East Anglia, but has travelled widely.

Stow has won the Miles Franklin Award (1958) and the Patrick White Award (1979). His reputation was established by five novels published between 1956 and 1965. The first two, *A Haunted Land* (1956) and *The Bystander* (1957), link a poetic feeling for landscape with an account of turbulent, emotional lives determined by family origins. Reminiscent of PATRICK WHITE's *Voss*, *To the Islands* (1958, revised edition 1982) is a symbolic fable about an old missionary who experiences a spiritual crisis and journeys into a desolate inner landscape which takes him 'to the islands', an Aboriginal expression for death. *Tourmaline* (1963), Stow's densest symbolic novel, and the more realistic *The Merry-Go-Round in the Sea* (1965) are also concerned with self-exploration. After these novels he wrote a popular children's book, *Midnite: Stories of a Wild Colonial Boy* (1967), and then continued to write poetry, a field in which he is best known for his technically assured lyrics. His verse is collected in *A Counterfeit Silence* (1969). From 1971 to 1981 he wrote for musical theatre with the composer Peter Maxwell Davies. He returned to the novel with one of his finest books, *Visitants* (1979), an account of a confrontation between developed and primitive culture in Papua. *Girl Green as Elderflower* (1980) is set in Suffolk and *The Suburbs of Hell* (1984) deals with a series of murders in a town on the East Anglian coast.

Stowe, Harriet Beecher 1811–96 American novelist. She was born in Litchfield, Connecticut, where her father, Lyman Beecher, was rector of the First Church. Her brother, HENRY WARD BEECHER, became an influential preacher and her sister Catharine a prominent writer and ideologue of domesticity, female education and woman's separate sphere. Harriet was a student and then a teacher at Catharine's Hartford Female Seminary until 1832, when the whole family accompanied Lyman to Cincinnati, where he became president of the new Lane Theological Seminary and took up the mission of converting the West. In 1834 Harriet began to write sketches and short fiction for the *Western Monthly* and other, mostly evangelical, periodicals. Her first book, *The Mayflower: Sketches and Scenes and Characters among the Descendants of the Puritans*, appeared in 1843. In 1836 she married Calvin E. Stowe, a professor at Lane, with whom she would eventually have seven children. The Cincinnati years were marked by poverty, isolation, and a cholera epidemic in which the Stowes lost a young son. In 1850 Calvin Stowe was offered a professorship at Bowdoin, and they moved to Brunswick, Maine.

There, amid household cares, Harriet wrote her first novel, UNCLE TOM'S CABIN, prompted by the passage of the Fugitive Slave Law. Like most of her subsequent novels, it was written as a serial, and began appearing in the *National Era* magazine in 1851. It was an immediate and scandalous best-seller, both in the USA and abroad. Stowe made three triumphal tours of Europe (1853, 1856 and 1859), where she formed important friendships with GEORGE ELIOT, ELIZABETH BARRETT BROWNING and Lady Byron, among others, and gathered material for *Sunny Memories of Foreign Lands* (1854). Meanwhile, attacks on the veracity of her portrayal of the South led her to publish *The Key to Uncle Tom's Cabin* (1853), a book of source material. A second anti-slavery novel, *Dred: A Tale of the Great Dismal Swamp* (1856), told the story of a dramatic attempt at a slave rebellion, while attacking ministers who had failed to take a strong anti-slavery stand and demonstrating again the redemptive powers of Christian womanhood, white and black.

After this, however, Stowe turned away from the political sphere. *The Minister's Wooing* (1859), set in New England, is a novel of love and marriage in the context of Calvinist uncertainty about salvation and the dread of seeing a loved one die unconverted. (She drew on the experiences of her sister, whose fiancé had been lost at sea, and of her own grief at the drowning of her son Henry in 1837.) *Agnes of Sorrento* (1862) took up similar theological themes but was set in the Catholic Italy of Savonarola. *The Pearl of Orr's Island* (1862), another treatment of the redemption of wayward youth by female piety and example, drew heavily on the local colour of the New England shore; SARAH ORNE JEWETT credited this book with inspiring her own career. Stowe wrote three more works in a similar vein: OLDTOWN FOLKS (1869) and *Oldtown Fireside Stories* (1871) drew on her husband's childhood memories, and *Poganuc People* (1878), her last novel, on her own. She also wrote three novels of New York society: *Pink and White Tyranny* (1871), which attacks female frivolity, the French, and divorce, and *My Wife and I* (1871) and its sequel, *We and Our Neighbours* (1875), in which she shows how rural values can be brought to the city.

She was a remarkably prolific writer of both books and articles in many genres and styles. She wrote children's books, travelogues, purely theological works, such as *In the Footsteps of the Master* (1877) and *Bible Heroines* (1878), temperance tracts and practical articles about housekeeping, decoration and the 'servant problem', including the highly influential *The American Woman's Home* (1869, co-written with her sister Catharine).

Strachey, (Giles) Lytton 1880–1932 Biographer and essayist. The son of a distinguished soldier and Indian administrator, Sir Richard Strachey, he was born in London and educated at Leamington College and Liverpool University (1897–9). Then he went up to Trinity College, Cambridge, where his friends included JOHN MAYNARD KEYNES, LEONARD WOOLF, E. M. FORSTER and Saxon Sydney-Turner. He was elected to the APOSTLES in 1902. Later, in London, he became a prominent member of the BLOOMSBURY GROUP.

In 1904 Strachey became a reviewer for *The Spectator*; he was also to contribute to *The Edinburgh Review*, *The Nation*, THE ATHENAEUM and *Life and Letters*. He published two collections of verse, *Prolusiones Academicae* (1902) and *Euphrosyne* (1905), and won the Chancellor's Medal for 'Ely: An Ode'. His first book, *Landmarks in French Literature*, was published in 1912 for the Home University Library series.

Strachey was a conscientious objector during World War I, and he gave up his attempt to make an academic career. *Eminent Victorians* (1918), containing controversial essays on Florence Nightingale, Cardinal Manning, THOMAS ARNOLD, and General Gordon, illustrated his contention that the biographer should 'attack his subject in unexpected places' and 'shoot a sudden, revealing searchlight into obscure recesses'. It was highly iconoclastic and, with *Queen Victoria* (1921), *Books and Characters, French and English* (1922), *Elizabeth and Essex: A Tragic History* (1928), *Portraits in Miniature* (1931) and *Characters and Commentaries* (1933), has been cited as originating the art of modern biography. Strachey was, perhaps, the first biographer to use Freudian insights, accompanied by sharp but affectionate satire and fine narrative skill. Throughout his life suffered from poor health. His close friend, the painter Dora Carrington (Mrs Ralph Partridge), who nursed him throughout his last illness, committed suicide shortly afterwards. *Spectatorial Essays*, a collection of reviews published in *The Spectator* (1904–14), appeared in 1964. Strachey himself is the subject of a widely admired biography (1967–8) by MICHAEL HOLROYD.

Strand Magazine, The A periodical founded by George Newnes in 1891, it survived until 1950. Perhaps best known for publishing SIR ARTHUR CONAN DOYLE'S SHERLOCK HOLMES STORIES, it also included fiction by RUDYARD KIPLING, H. G. WELLS, W. W. JACOBS, SOMERSET MAUGHAM, ARTHUR MORRISON, STANLEY WEYMAN, ANTHONY HOPE, JEROME K. JEROME and P. G. WODEHOUSE, among others.

Strand, Mark 1934– American poet. Born on Prince Edward Island, Canada, he was educated in the USA at Antioch College and the Yale Art School. US POET LAUREATE in 1990–1, he has taught at Iowa, Yale, Brandeis and Columbia universities and then became writer-in-residence at the University of Utah in Salt Lake City. His volumes of verse include *Reasons for Moving* (1968), *Darker* (1970), *The Story of Our Lives* (1973), *The Late Hour* (1978), *Selected Poems* (1980), *Rembrandt Takes a Walk* (1987) and *Dark Harbor: A Poem* (1993). One of his finest poems is the frequently anthologized 'Elegy for My Father'. An active advocate of the work of other poets, he has edited *The Contemporary American Poets: American Poetry since 1940* (1969) and, with CHARLES SIMIC, *Another Republic: 17 European and South American Writers* (1976); other translations include *Owl's Insomnia: Selected Poems of Rafael Alberti* (1973) and *Souvenir of the Ancient World: Carlos Drummond de Andrade* (1976). *Mr and Mrs Baby* (1985) is a collection of short stories and *The Monument* (1978) a collection of assorted prose.

Strange Case of Dr Jekyll and Mr Hyde, The See DR JEKYLL AND MR HYDE, THE STRANGE CASE OF.

Strange Interlude A play in nine acts by EUGENE O'NEILL, first performed in New York in 1928. Its extreme length is largely the result of O'Neill's decision to have his characters articulate the sub-text of their speeches as well as the text, to say what they are thinking as well as what they actually voice. With this rather daring and unconventional use of dramatic 'asides', the play received a mixed critical reception, but won a PULITZER PRIZE. Nina Leeds, the daughter of a New England professor, has been prevented by her father from marrying the man she loves before he goes to war. His death in the war turns her against her father, and she leaves home to become a nurse. In homage to her dead lover, she offers herself as mistress to any war-wounded man who wants her, and is saved from this promiscuity by a fond but loveless marriage to Sam Evans, motivated by her wish for a child. When she discovers that there is madness in her husband's family she obtains a secret abortion and asks her husband's friend, Dr Edmund Darrell, to impregnate her. Darrell's life is destroyed by his love for her, and Nina's possessiveness for their son almost leads her to destroy that son's own hopes of marriage.

stream of consciousness A technique used by novelists to represent a character's thoughts and sense impressions without syntax or logical sequence. Four main types have been identified: soliloquy, omniscient narration of mental processes, and both direct and indirect interior monologue.

The phrase 'stream of consciousness' was first used by WILLIAM JAMES in his PRINCIPLES OF PSYCHOLOGY (1890) to describe the random flux of conscious and sub-conscious thoughts and impressions in the mind. A parallel description can be found in Bergson's account (1889) of the élan vital, popularized in England by GEORGE BERNARD SHAW. Literature can show many examples before both James and Bergson of the attempt to capture inner consciousness, notably LAURENCE STERNE's TRISTRAM SHANDY (1767). But stream of consciousness becomes important as a technique with the rise of MODERNISM in the 20th century. It can be seen in the works of JOYCE (who claimed to have inherited it from Edouard Dujardin's Les Lauriers sont soupés, 1888), DOROTHY RICHARDSON, VIRGINIA WOOLF and, among Americans, WILLIAM FAULKNER.

Streatfeild, Noel 1895–1986 Writer of CHILDREN'S LITERATURE. The daughter of a Sussex clergyman, she studied acting at RADA after a somewhat rebellious childhood. Her career on the stage was not greatly successful and by 1929 she gave it up in favour of writing. There followed some undistinguished novels for adults, beginning with The Whicharts (1931), and then her first and best book for children, Ballet Shoes (1936). Drawing freely on her own experience, it describes a family of orphans who eventually make good in the ballet and theatre world. Its success was instant, young readers relishing its blend of hard fact about auditions, drudgery and stage fright with the romance of final artistic triumph. Noel Streatfeild wrote a number of other 'career' novels, including Tennis Shoes (1937) and a novel about skating, White Boots (1951). The Bell Family (1954) chronicles the more domestic adventures of a gently idealized middle-class family that first featured in radio plays written for the BBC's programme Children's Hour.

Street Scene A play by ELMER RICE, first produced in 1929. Despite many previous successes in the theatre, Rice had difficulty finding a producer for this ground-breaking drama, which required over 50 actors and an innovative and elaborate set to present a day in the life of a New York tenement. It proved a critical and popular success, running for 601 performances and winning a PULITZER PRIZE. In 1947 Rice worked with LANGSTON HUGHES and the composer Kurt Weill on a successful musical adaptation.

In the course of one extremely hot day, the tenants, drawn from many ethnic groups, converse, complain, quarrel, and gossip, mostly about one of their number, Mrs Maurrant. A baby is born; a poor family is evicted after a visit from an unsympathetic social worker; the relative merits of socialism and capitalism are discussed; Mr Maurrant comes home to find his wife in bed with another man, shoots them both, and is captured by the police; and Rose Maurrant, the heroine, rejects the attentions both of her boss, the flashy Harry Easter, and of Sam Kaplan, the earnest young law student who lives in the building, and strikes out on her own.

Streetcar Named Desire, A A play by TENNESSEE WILLIAMS, first performed in New York in 1947. It ran for 855 performances and received both a New York Drama Critics Circle Award and a PULITZER PRIZE.

The action revolves around the visit of Blanche Du Bois to her sister Stella, who lives in New Orleans, near the stop of the streetcar named Desire, with her brutish husband Stanley Kowalski. Blanche has an appearance of ladylike grace, and constantly refers to her early life at the family estate of Belle Reve. Bewildered by her new environment and by the antagonism of her brother-in-law, she turns to his friend Mitch for consolation and company. Stanley, however, learns that Blanche is not the Southern belle she purports to be, and tells Mitch that she is in fact a lonely alcoholic who has been forced into bankruptcy and who has lost her job because of an affair with a young boy who reminded her of her dead husband. Blanche's antagonistic relationship with Stanley culminates in his raping her. She tells Stella but Stella does not believe her, and at the end of the play she is taken into psychiatric care.

Strickland, Agnes 1796–1874 Writer of miscellaneous works. She was born in London, the sister of SUSANNA MOODIE and CATHARINE PARR TRAILL. She wrote poetry and CHILDREN'S LITERATURE before turning eventually to the short popular biographies for which she is remembered: The Lives of the Queens of England from the Norman Conquest (1840–8) and The Lives of the Queens of Scotland, and English Princesses (1850–9).

Strong, L(eonard) A(lfred) G(eorge) 1896–1958 Novelist, playwright and man of letters. Born in Plymouth, of mainly Irish stock, he was educated at Brighton College and at Wadham College, Oxford. He worked as a preparatory schoolmaster before becoming a full-time writer in 1930. The successful Dewer Rides (1929), a novel of Dartmoor, was followed by a great deal of fiction from his pen, some of it with Irish backgrounds. Travellers (1945) won the James Tait Black Prize. Extremely versatile and fluent, he wrote plays and radio scripts, compiled anthologies, and produced several biographies and autobiographies. His lyric verse, collected as The Body's Imperfection (1957), shows him pausing more reflectively than his vast output usually allowed.

structuralism A movement of thought affecting a number of intellectual disciplines, including anthropology, philosophy, history and literary criticism. The common element derives from linguistics and especially the writings of Ferdinand de Saussure (see SEMIOTICS). He argued that linguistics should study the 'synchronic' dimension of language (the system of relations within language operating at a given moment) rather than its 'diachrony' (temporal dimension). Speakers are able to use the system by registering the differences between possible elements within it. For example, at the level of the phoneme (minimum unit of sound) we distinguish between 'bus' and 'buzz' on the basis of a difference between a voiced (s) and an unvoiced (z) sibilant. Structuralists have applied the patterns of 'binary oppositions' derived from phonemics, syntax or grammar to human sign-systems of various kinds.

Claude Lévi-Strauss (1908–) developed 'phonemic' analyses of kinship relations, myths, rites, and so on. Roland Barthes (1915–80) examined *haute cuisine*, narrative discourse, garments and all kinds of social artefacts. The underlying idea is that all human performances (*paroles*) presuppose a system (*langue*) of differential relations.

Structuralist narratology is especially well advanced. Tzvetan Todorov, Gérard Genette and A. J. Greimas are the key theorists. Greimas developed the theories of the Russian Formalist Vladimir Propp, fitting them more closely to the linguistic model. The basic syntactical functions of subject and predicate have their equivalent functions in narrative: actor and action. In *The Morphology of the Folktale* (1968) Propp found 35 'functions' (basic narrative actions) and seven 'spheres of action' in the Russian folk-tale. Greimas's universal 'grammar' of narrative proposes three binary oppositions which include the six roles (*actants*) he requires: (1) subject/ object; (2) sender/receiver; (3) helper/opponent. The pairs allow a description of all the fundamental patterns governing narrative: (1) aiming at something, (2) communicating, (3) helping or hindering. Lévi-Strauss developed a phonemic analysis of the Oedipus story; he aimed to establish the structural pattern which gives the myth its meaning. Todorov outlined a comprehensive application of the linguistic model, discovering the rules of agency, adjectival and verbal functions, mood, aspect and so on. Genette divided narrative into three levels: story, discourse and narration. These levels are related to one another through three aspects derived from three verbal qualities: tense, mood and voice.

The most influential theorist on modern criticism is probably Roman Jakobson (1896–1982) whose essays 'Linguistics and Poetics' and 'Two Aspects of Language' are especially important. The latter develops a theory of the binary structure of language which is typified in the opposition between metaphor and metonymy. DAVID LODGE has applied the theory to develop a complete structural study of modern literature. Jonathan Culler, using the mentalistic linguistics of NOAM CHOMSKY, argued for a reader-oriented structuralist poetics which sought the rules governing the reader's construction of a text's meaning. Culler has subsequently adopted and developed the theories of Jacques Derrida (see DECONSTRUCTION).

Strutt, Joseph 1749–1802 Antiquary. Apprenticed as an engraver, Strutt was awarded both silver and gold medals at the Royal Academy. He devoted himself to antiquarian researches and published a number of important illustrated works which were often the first in their field, including: *The Regal and Ecclesiastical Antiquities of England* (1773), *Manners, Customs, Arms, Habits, &c. of the People of England* (3 vols., 1774–6), and his *Biographical Dictionary of Engravers* (2 vols., 1785–6), upon which all subsequent such dictionaries have been based. His best-known work is the curiously titled *Glig Gamena Angel Deod* (1801), a history of popular sports and pastimes. SIR WALTER SCOTT acknowledged Strutt's unfinished romance 'Queenhoo Hall' as the original impetus for his Waverley novels.

Strype, John 1643–1737 Church historian. Born in London, he attended St Paul's School and went on to Jesus College, Cambridge, but transferred to St Catharine's Hall. After Cambridge he became curate and lecturer at Leyton in Essex (1669) and from 1689 to 1724 added a lectureship at Hackney to his activities. He was given the sinecure of West Tarring in Sussex in 1711.

Strype made a remarkable collection of Tudor documents that are now in the British Library. The first of his documentary works was *Memorials of Thomas Cranmer* (1694). Works on the lives of Sir Thomas Smith (1698), John Aylmer (1701), and Sir John Cheke (1705) were followed by his magnum opus, *Annals of the Reformation and Establishment of Religion, and other Occurrences in the Church of England, during the First Twelve Years of Queen Elizabeth's Reign* (4 vols., 1709–31). Lives of Edmund Grindal (1710) and John Whitgift (1718) were also written while work proceeded on the *Annals*. Strype's *Ecclesiastical Memorials relating Chiefly to Religion and the Reformation of It under Henry VIII, Edward VI and Mary* was published in 1721. He also edited and extended JOHN STOW's *Survey* as *A Survey of the Cities of London and Westminster*, adding a life of Stow (1720, with a much enlarged edition in 1754).

Stuart, Francis 1902– Irish novelist. A lifelong Republican, he married Iseult, daughter of Maud Gonne, the Irish nationalist loved by YEATS. His experience in Germany during World War II is reflected in

The Pillar of Cloud (1948), Redemption (1949) and The Flowering Cross (1950), a trilogy balanced by three novels dealing variously with the Irish political crisis, Memorial (1973), A Hole in the Head (1977) and The High Consistory (1981). Black List, Section H (1971), an autobiographical novel, brought him wider acclaim.

Stubbes, Philip ?1555-1610 Puritan pamphleteer. He is best known for The Anatomy of Abuses (1583), a denunciation of sinful customs and fashions, which includes a section on stage plays. His earlier works had been BROADSIDE ballads, usually demonstrating God's vengeance on sin. A Christal Glass for Christian Women (1591), a biographical account of his wife Katherine, was extremely popular.

Stubbs, William 1825-1901 Historian. Born at Knaresborough in Yorkshire, he was educated at Ripon grammar school and Christ Church, Oxford, where he fell lastingly under the influence of the OXFORD MOVEMENT. He became a Fellow of Trinity College in 1848, rector of Navestock in Essex in 1850, and Regius Professor of Modern History at Oxford in 1866. In later years he was a canon of St Paul's (1879), Bishop of Chester (1884) and Bishop of Oxford (1889). As a historian, he made major contributions to the medieval Rolls Series, beginning with Registrum Sacrum Anglicanum (1858). He is best remembered for Select Charters and Other Illustrations of English Constitutional History from the Earliest Times to the Reign of Edward I (1870) and The Constitutional History of England (1873-8), which takes his subject up to the accession of the Tudors.

Studies in the History of the Renaissance Essays by WALTER PATER, first published in 1873 and later retitled The Renaissance: Studies in Art and Poetry.

Pater extends the chronology of the Renaissance from the Middle Ages to the 18th century. Although he includes an early essay on Winckelmann (the 'last fruit of the Renaissance'), one on Du Bellay and an opening essay on 'Two Early French Stories', he is mainly concerned with Italy. With grace and simplicity, elegance and disciplined fluency, he advances his own aesthetic theories in discussions of Pico della Mirandola, Botticelli, Leonardo, della Robbia and others. The 'Conclusion', excised from the second edition of The Renaissance for fear it might 'mislead' young men, became the manifesto of the AESTHETIC MOVEMENT. It stresses that the intensity of the moment, the profundity of experience and the necessity of one's presence 'at the focus where the greatest number of vital forces unite in their purest energy' are central to self-realization and fullness of life. In Pater's memorable phrasing, 'To burn always with this hard, gemlike flame, to maintain this ecstasy, is success in life.'

Stukeley, William 1687-1765 Antiquary. Born at Holbeach, Lincolnshire, Stukeley left the free school there when he was 13 to join his father's legal business. Dissatisfied with the law, he persuaded his father to send him to Cambridge and he was admitted to Corpus Christi College in 1703. After Cambridge he practised medicine, first in Lincolnshire, then, from 1717, in London. At this time he was made a Fellow of the Royal Society and helped establish the Society of Antiquaries, whose first secretary he became in 1718. He cultivated connections with painters, engravers and intellectual noblemen. He was interested in astronomy and was an early enthusiast of Gothic architecture.

Though indebted to previous scholars such as AUBREY, his early work on Stonehenge and Avebury was remarkable; and in his sense of nature Stukeley anticipates such figures as RICHARD JEFFERIES and W. H. HUDSON. After 1729 an obsession with the Druids as builders of the stone circles took hold of him: he produced Stonehenge: A Temple Restored to the British Druids (1740) and Abury: A Temple of the British Druids (1743). Eccentric as this Druidism may now appear, poets such as WILLIAM COLLINS, WILLIAM MASON, THOMAS GRAY and the WILLIAM BLAKE of the Prophetic Books stand clearly in his debt. Stukeley's particular kind of primitivism provides an interesting link between the early British antiquaries and the first Romantics.

Sturt, George 1863-1927 Essayist and historian of rural society. Sturt, whose early works were published under the pseudonym of George Bourne, was born at Farnham in Surrey and educated at Farnham grammar school, where he taught from 1878 to 1884. On the death of his father in 1884 Sturt inherited the family wheelwright business and, under RUSKIN's influence, advocated the traditions of local craftsmanship. He gave up business for writing in 1900. His books included The Bettesworth Book (1901) and its sequel, Memoirs of a Surrey Labourer (1907). Change in the Village (1912) was followed by A Farmer's Life (1922). The Wheelwright's Shop (1923), published under his own name, chronicles the family business which had begun at Farnham in 1706. It describes the stages in the construction of farm waggons before the advent of the tractor and notes that 'the provincial wheelwright could hardly help reading, from the waggon-lines, tales of haymaking and upland fields, of hilly roads and lonely woods and noble horses'.

Styron, William 1925- American novelist. He was born in Newport News, Virginia, and educated at Davidson College and Duke University. His first novel, Lie Down in Darkness, was published in 1951. Other novels include The Long March (1952), Set This House on Fire (1960), The Confessions of Nat Turner (1967), and Sophie's Choice (1979). His work generally concerns forms of oppression, ranging from that of the family to the wider social issues of racism and politics. His account of Nat Turner's rebellion met with considerable protest from the black community; *William Styron's Nat Turner: Ten Black Writers Respond* (1968) contains essays which reflect the animosity toward his 'white' approach to race relations. In *Sophie's Choice*, his most commercially successful novel to date, he deals with the horrors of the Holocaust as it affects the lives of those who survived the concentration camps and Nazi persecution. *This Quiet Dust* (1982) is a collection of essays and *Darkness Visible* (1990) an account of his battle with depression.

Subjection of Women, The An essay by JOHN STUART MILL, published in 1869. 'The purpose of that book', Mill declared, 'was to maintain the claim of women, whether in marriage or out of it, to perfect equality in all rights with the male sex'.

In the last published work of his life Mill drew together the political, moral and social ideas diffused throughout the rest of his work in pungent rhetorical form. Twentieth-century feminism has drawn attention to the essay again. It remains an advanced piece of criticism, historically speaking, but is flawed by Mill undervaluing and therefore neglecting the sexual aspect of this political struggle.

Suckling, Sir John 1609–41 CAVALIER POET and playwright. Born into a well-established Norfolk family (his father served as Comptroller of James I's household), he was educated at Trinity College, Cambridge, and at Gray's Inn. His early manhood was spent in military and ambassadorial adventures in Europe, and he was knighted in 1630. Suckling returned to England in 1632 and embarked on a career of less honourable if not less public activity: the prodigal dissipation of his patrimony. His reputation for both wit and extravagance led AUBREY to characterize him as 'the greatest gallant of his time, and the greatest Gamester, both for Bowling and Cards ... [he] invented the game of Cribbidge'. By the late 1630s Suckling's literary reputation was fully fledged. His SATIRE, *The Wits* (or *Sessions of the Poets*), a mock-BALLAD in which contemporary writers contend for the laurel and are discomfited (Suckling himself refuses the summons, preferring bowls to the Muses), had been sung before the king in 1637, and his tragedy *Aglaura* was staged twice the next year, to great applause, the second time with a re-written fifth act, in which the catastrophe was averted. A magnificent folio text (1638) was a popular subject for lampoon. In 1639 Suckling resumed soldiership, ingloriously participating in Charles I's defeat by the Scots; in 1641, he levied troops as part of the 'Army Plot' to free the imprisoned Earl of Strafford. The plot was discovered, and Suckling fled to France, where (according to Aubrey) he committed suicide by taking poison.

Apart from *Aglaura*, Suckling's plays comprise the unfinished *The Sad One* (a first draft of *Aglaura*), *The Goblins*, a musical comedy-romance indebted to THE TEMPEST, and *Brennoralt*, a tragedy whose protagonist has often been considered a self-portrait (*The Discontented Colonel* is an alternative title). *The Goblins* and *Brennoralt*, both in the repertory of the KING'S MEN by 1641, were printed in *Fragmenta Aurea* (1646), the collection which also includes Suckling's most famous poems, 'Ballade. Upon a Wedding' and 'Why So Pale and Wan, Fond Lover?' The influences of SHAKESPEARE, JONSON and DONNE can be variously felt throughout Suckling's work, and he shares many characteristics with his close friends CAREW and D'AVENANT; what ROCHESTER aptly described as 'Suckling's easy pen' makes him one of the most attractive of the Cavalier poets.

Summer of the Seventeenth Doll A play by RAY LAWLER, first performed in Melbourne, Australia, in 1955. It was the first Australian play to win an international audience. Its realistic appraisal of the Australian cult of 'mateship' and its reliance on female submissiveness administered a sharp shock to a theatre that had taken both for granted.

Roo and Barney are sugarcane cutters who work for half the year and return each summer to their waiting women, bringing always a kewpie doll among their gifts. Having failed to notice the needs of the women, they are unprepared for the discovery that the 17th summer cannot be the same as its predecessors.

Summoner's Tale, The See CANTERBURY TALES, THE.

Sun Also Rises, The A novel by ERNEST HEMINGWAY, published in 1926. The English edition which appeared the following year was entitled *Fiesta*. Set in the mid-1920s, it deals with the 'lost generation' of American and British expatriates who have settled in Paris, depicted here as a moral wasteland of drunkenness and promiscuity.

The story is narrated by Jake Barnes, an American journalist who has been rendered sexually impotent by a wound suffered during World War I. Jake is in love with the queen of the pleasure-seekers, Lady Brett Ashley. Brett returns his love but, knowing that consummation is impossible, agrees to marry Mike Campbell. Jake lives according to a self-taught emotional pragmatism, which is contrasted with the self-pitying sentimentalism of his acquaintance Robert Cohn. Robert, under Brett's spell, joins her, Mike, and Jake on a jaunt to Spain to witness the fiesta and bullfights at Pamplona. At the bullring Jake finds meaning and hope in the ritual which pits man against beast, and life against death; he especially admires the young matador Pedro Romero, whose skill, bravery, and moral earnestness characterize him as a true

Hemingway hero. The others in his group, however, remain true to form, and the fiesta degenerates into a series of brawls. Angered by Brett's seduction of the matador, Cohn beats up both Romero and Jake, and the party disintegrates. Brett runs off with Romero. Jake retreats to a seaside resort in an effort to regain moral stability, but his recovery is interrupted by a telegram from Brett pleading that he come to her aid in Madrid. There she tells him that she has sent Romero away because she does not want to corrupt him further. In a last taxi ride around the city, Brett and Jake face the hopelessness of their situation. Brett clings to the notion that they 'could have had such a damned good time together', but Jake responds that it would be 'pretty' to think so, his word for finally rejecting false hopes.

Surfacing A novel by MARGARET ATWOOD, published in 1972. The unnamed narrator-protagonist journeys with her lover Joe and two friends to northern Quebec in search of her missing father. It becomes clear that the novel is more centrally about a quest for her own past, particularly its repressed aspects, which she comes to terms with when she dives into a lake and discovers her father's drowned body. 'Surfacing' with a new-found awareness, both of the sanctity of life and of the importance of women's not allowing themselves to become victims, she regresses into an animal-like state of existence that enables her to free herself from the negative cultural influences of her past. The end sees her emerging from this state, possibly about to go back to the city with Joe. *Surfacing* exerts much of its force through its original narrative method, which involves a total immersion in the interior monologue of its alienated narrator. Readers are similarly compelled to share her sceptical response to facets of Western society that would normally be taken for granted.

Surgeon's Daughter, The See CHRONICLES OF THE CANONGATE.

Surrey, Earl of [Howard, Henry] ?1517–47 Poet and translator. Henry Howard received the courtesy title Earl of Surrey when his father became 3rd Duke of Norfolk in 1524. After some private tuition he became the companion of the Earl of Richmond, the bastard son of Henry VIII, at Windsor. At the same time came a suggestion from Anne Boleyn (who soon changed her mind) that Surrey should marry the Princess Mary. Norfolk affianced his son to the daughter of the Earl of Oxford and they were married in 1532. Surrey's fortunes declined in 1536, the year of the deaths of Anne Boleyn and of Richmond, and of Henry VIII's marriage to Jane Seymour. The Seymours schemed against the Howards and already in 1536 were accusing Surrey of secretly sympathizing with the Catholic Pilgrimage of Grace rebellion. On this

suspicion, Surrey was confined for a time at Windsor. In the 1540s Surrey campaigned successfully in Scotland and France. He was in favour again in the early 1540s, made Knight of the Garter in 1541, and became Commander of Boulogne in 1545-6. In 1546 Henry VIII's health was failing and Surrey made some ill-advised and public remarks about his father's obviously strong candidacy for the Protectorship of the young Prince Edward. He was arrested on the pretext of a heraldic nicety (he had been displaying royal quarterings in his shield), and after some damaging evidence from the Countess of Richmond (Surrey's sister) he was imprisoned in the Tower and executed on Tower Hill.

Even when Surrey was a child, his tutor had commended his translations from Latin and Italian. His translation of Books II and IV of the *Aeneid* introduced BLANK VERSE in English poetry. With SIR THOMAS WYATT, he is one of the early imitators of the Italian SONNET in English and his work represents one of the first flowerings of 16th-century poetry. Much of it was probably written during his confinement at Windsor and most (some 40 poems) was published for the first time in TOTTEL'S MISCELLANY (1557). SIR PHILIP SIDNEY found in Surrey's lyrics 'many things tasting of a noble birth, and worthy of a noble mind'.

Surtees, R(obert) S(mith) 1805-64 Sporting novelist and journalist. Surtees came of a long line of country gentlemen who had lived in and owned land in County Durham for centuries; he spent his early life on his father's estate of Hamsterley Hall. After attending Durham School he studied law in Newcastle and London, qualifying in 1828. He does not seem to have practised very seriously, spending much time foxhunting with packs in the London area. He started writing for the *Sporting Magazine* and in 1831 in partnership with Rudolph Ackermann, a London publisher and print-seller, founded the *New Sporting Magazine*, of which he became the first editor. In this capacity he made a number of hunting tours and paid summer visits to Brighton, indulging in various 'jaunts and jollities' which provided material for the doings of Mr Jorrocks, chronicled in the *NSM*. Surtees abandoned the law in 1835, continuing as editor of the *NSM* until the end of 1836. He returned to Hamsterley in 1837 and succeeded to the property on his father's death in 1838. He lived there for the rest of his life, hunting regularly and writing for pleasure rather than profit; he insisted that his books appeared anonymously. He married in 1841, became a JP and a Deputy Lieutenant for County Durham in 1842 and was created High Sheriff of Durham in 1856.

His major works were: his trilogy about John Jorrocks, the sporting grocer, *JORROCKS'S JAUNTS AND JOLLITIES* (1838; enlarged, posthumous version, 1869), *HANDLEY CROSS* (1843; enlarged version, 1854) and

HILLINGDON HALL (1845); *MR SPONGE'S SPORTING TOUR* (1853); *Ask Mamma* (1858); *Plain or Ringlets?* (1860); and *Mr Facey Romford's Hounds*, a sequel to *Mr Sponge's Sporting Tour* which was being serialized when he died and appeared in book form in 1865. They are loosely, sometimes carelessly, constructed. What gives them life are the hard-bitten, talkative, closely observed characters taken from the whole spectrum of country life from dukes to 'chawbacons'. (One of KIPLING's characters describes his people as 'Dickens-and-horsedung', but changes his mind later when the books start to grip him.) There is much about foxhunting and the material rings true, being written by an expert. The notation of speech, especially North Country dialect, is masterly.

Susanna: or, The Pistil of Swete Susan A poem in ALLITERATIVE VERSE written between 1350 and 1380 in the north or north-west Midlands. It tells the story of Susanna and the Elders from an apocryphal addition to the Book of Daniel in the Vulgate Bible: Susanna, wife of a rich Babylonian, is accused of unchastity by two elders whose advances she had rebuffed but their dishonesty is discovered by Daniel and they are executed. The poem follows its source closely but has some additions and divergences including a description of a garden which draws on the 12th-century *Roman de la rose* of Guillaume de Lorris and Jean de Meun. It has been dubiously identified with the *Pistil of Swete Susan* mentioned in ANDREW OF WYNTOUN's *Cronykil* (*c.* 1420) as the work of HUCHOWN OF THE AWLE RYALE.

Sutcliff, Rosemary 1920– Children's historical novelist. Born in Surrey, the daughter of a naval officer, she started school only at the age of nine because of poor health. On leaving school at 14 she trained as an artist, specializing in miniatures, but soon gave this up in favour of writing. Her first book, *The Chronicles of Robin Hood* (1950), established her as a fine historical novelist: she has since gone on to write over 30 such books, including some that have become classics. Her favourite era is the Roman occupation of Britain, which also gives her the opportunity to write about the divided loyalties so often experienced by the characters in her books. Adding this type of psychological dilemma to stories of action was something new in the development of historical fiction for children, and is perhaps most memorably achieved in *The Eagle of the Ninth* (1954). The story of King Arthur offered another opportunity to explore character as well as events, the whole cycle beginning with *The Light beyond the Forest* (1979). She has also reconstructed the story of Boadicea in *Songs for a Dark Queen* (1978), a savage novel which never falsifies the horrors of the time. *Blue Remembered Hills* (1983) tells the story of her own early life.

Sutherland, Efua (Theodora Morguel) 1924– Ghanaian playwright and writer of CHILDREN'S LITERATURE. Born in the Cape Coast area, she was educated in Ghana and Britain. Since the late 1950s and early 1960s she has made a career of promoting traditional dramatic forms in her work for the Experimental Theatre and the Ghana Drama Studio, which she established, and the magazine *Okyeame*, which she also helped to found. The Drama Studio has subsequently been attached to the University of Ghana's Institute of African Studies and the School of Drama in Legon. The conflict between traditional Ghanaian and contemporary Western values and customs is dramatized tragically in *Edufa* (1969) and comically in *The Marriage of Anansewa* (1975). Other published plays include *You Swore an Oath* (1964), *Foriwa* (1967), *Odasini* (1967) and *The Original Bob* (1969). *Vulture! Vulture!* (1968) is among the most frequently performed of her many children's plays in both Akan and English. *Playtime in Africa* (photographs by Willis Bell; 1962) is a pictorial essay for older children. Her poetry and short stories appear in several anthologies.

Swan Theatre Built in *c.* 1595, the Swan's importance in the history of English theatre architecture is assured by the chance survival of a drawing by the Dutchman De Witt of its interior in 1596. It is the only reliable evidence we have of the auditoria of the open-air theatres of the Elizabethan period. The history of the Swan, which survived until *c.*1637, is unimpressive. It seems never to have recovered from the scandal surrounding the 1597 performance of *The Isle of Dogs*.

Sweet, Henry 1845–1912 Scholar. The son of a London solicitor, Sweet was educated at King's College School, London, and studied at Heidelberg before going on to Balliol College, Oxford. Here he invented his own system of phonetics and published an edition of ALFRED's version of the *Cura pastoralis*, but graduated with only a fourth-class degree in 1873. His *History of English Sounds* (1874) became a standard textbook, as did the *Anglo-Saxon Reader* (1876). These works were followed by his *Handbook of Phonetics* in 1877, the year in which Sweet persuaded the Oxford University Press to consider publishing the Philological Society's new dictionary, which became the OXFORD ENGLISH DICTIONARY. Sweet's leading position in the study of Old English and phonetics was not rewarded by the University until he was appointed to a Readership in 1901. His later works included *A New English Grammar* (1892), *The History of Language* (1900) and *The Sounds of English: An Introduction to Phonetics* (1908). It was on Sweet that SHAW based the character of the phonetician Professor Higgins in *PYGMALION*.

Swift, Graham 1949– Novelist and short-story writer. The preoccupation with history and memory in his first two novels, *The Sweet-Shop Owner* (1980) and *Shuttlecock* (1981), has continued in subsequent work: *Waterland* (1983), an ambitious saga set in the Fens which has much in common with MAGIC REALISM and the early fiction of Günter Grass; *Out of This World* (1987), a slighter and less successful meditation, activated through the reminiscences of a famous war photographer; and *Ever After* (1992), again using first-person testimonial to explore inheritance and family history. *Learning to Swim* (1982) is a varied collection of short stories.

Swift, Jonathan 1667–1745 Satirist and poet. He was born in Dublin, the posthumous child of Jonathan Swift, an expatriate English lawyer, and Abigail Erick. His mother returned to her native Leicestershire when he was three, so from an early age Swift was looked after by his Uncle Godwin, who sent him to Kilkenny School in 1673, where CONGREVE was a fellow pupil. In April 1682 he entered Trinity College, Dublin, but his academic career there was not distinguished and he only managed to graduate *speciale gratia* in 1686. Swift seems in retrospect to have regarded the education he received as second-rate, though this is perhaps merely one of several instances of resentment on his part during the course of a long and disappointing life which he saw as characterized by the ingratitude of others.

Early in 1689 an outbreak of troubles in Ireland – the result of the arrival of James II – led Swift to visit his mother in England. He entered the household of SIR WILLIAM TEMPLE as his secretary, and settled at Moor Park, Surrey. From such a position the young Swift might reasonably have expected influential introductions that would lead to preferment, but neither a visit to William III nor an errand to Ireland on his patron's behalf advanced his ambitions for a public post. In July 1692, having already completed most of the required work, Swift took an MA from Hart Hall, Oxford, a qualification which would at least enable him to enter the Church.

Swift remained at Moor Park until May 1694, reading voraciously through Temple's library, and composing his largely unsuccessful Pindaric ODES, one of which was published in *The Athenian Mercury* in 1692, his first appearance in print. During this period he acted as tutor to the eight-year-old Esther Johnson (Stella), the daughter of the companion to Temple's sister. Impatient for advancement, Swift was ordained in 1694 and returned to Ireland where he was granted the prebend of Kilroot, near Belfast, the following year.

Returning to Moor Park in 1696, he there edited Temple's correspondence and wrote THE BATTLE OF THE BOOKS in 1697, which further identified him with his patron's affairs. He was perhaps over-dependent on Temple's influence, for when the latter died in 1699 Swift found himself in effect 'unprovided both of friend and living', since he had resigned his prebend a year previously. He returned to Dublin as chaplain to Lord Berkeley, the new Lord Justice, managed to obtain the living of Laracor, and was granted a prebend in St Patrick's, Dublin, where Stella and her companion Rebecca Dingley were to join him.

Jonathan Swift

He visited London with Lord Berkeley in 1701, and published his *Discourse of the Contests and Dissensions in Athens and Rome*, a political pamphlet concerning the impeachment of certain Whig lords. During his several trips to England during the period 1702–4 he made the acquaintance of ADDISON and STEELE, and, with the anonymous publication in 1704 of his *TALE OF A TUB*, a vehement and comprehensive SATIRE on contemporary intellectual abuses, Swift began to gain notoriety and a certain popularity in Whig literary circles.

A period of writing on religious matters began in 1707, when he again visited England on a mission to obtain Queen Anne's Bounty for the Irish clergy. In 1708 he wrote his ironic ARGUMENT AGAINST ABOLISHING CHRISTIANITY (published 1711), *The Sentiments of a Church of England Man* (published 1711), *A Letter concerning the Sacramental Test* (1708) and his *Project for the Advancement of Religion* (1709), which identify him as a staunch Anglican and strong supporter of the terms of the Revolutionary settlement, intolerant of Dissent and especially those factions associated with 'enthusiasm', or a fanatical belief in inspiration. This attitude was one reason for his moving away from his former Whig associates and inclining towards the Tory circle of wits by 1710. In 1708 he invented the character of ISAAC BICKERSTAFF for *Predictions for the Ensuing Year*, his *jeu d'esprit* at the expense of the astrologer John Partridge, and in 1709 he published two of his more celebrated short poems in *THE TATLER*.

Allegiance to the Tory ministry of ROBERT HARLEY, EARL OF OXFORD, was sealed by Swift's acceptance in 1710 of the editorship of *THE EXAMINER*, a post he relinquished in June 1711 in order to concentrate on *THE CONDUCT OF THE ALLIES*, his outstanding political pamphlet in support of the proposals for peace in the Continental campaign. He was by now on terms of close familiarity with Harley and enjoying an increasingly bright reputation in London, where he befriended POPE, ARBUTHNOT and GAY. Their association was formalized in the SCRIBLERUS CLUB. The intimate, playful letters Swift addressed to Stella in Dublin, posthumously published as the *JOURNAL TO STELLA* (selection, 1766; edition, 1768), tell us much about his movements during these years. Meanwhile, he was also seeing Esther Vanhomrigh (whom he nicknamed Vanessa), a young London lady whose love he first encouraged but then rebuffed. His poem, *CADENUS AND VANESSA* (written 1713; published 1726), represents the equivocal nature of the affair. Indeed, his exact relationship with Stella has also been the cause of much speculation, one theory holding that they were secretly married in 1716, another that they were already related illegitimately by blood. The extent of his involvement with any of the women in his life remains unclear, but his reputation as a misogynist is patently unfounded, as his charming 'Birthday Poems' to Stella indicate.

Made Dean of St Patrick's Cathedral in 1713 (he had taken his DD in 1701), Swift's official appointments now reached a peak, but until the collapse of the Tory ministry with which he was socially and intellectually identified his literary stature in London continued to grow with the publication of various poems and pamphlets. But the death of Queen Anne in 1714 signalled for the dean a period of self-imposed exile in Ireland, where he prudently retreated to avoid the recrimination of the new Whig administration. Swift realized that his hopes for preferment, both secular and ecclesiastical, were now to be thwarted for ever, and he based himself busily in Dublin where, despite persistent claims of loathing for the country, he proceeded to involve himself in championing the rights of Ireland. He defended the cause of the Irish economy, in particular, with his *PROPOSAL FOR THE UNIVERSAL USE OF IRISH MANUFACTURE* (1720) and the *DRAPIER'S LETTERS* (1724), which effectively prevented the exploitation of Ireland through the issuing of debased coinage. He succeeded, ironically, in establishing himself as one of the leading Irish patriots of the century.

Despite his many protests to the contrary, Swift seemed fairly content with his new circle of friends in Dublin and its environs. He exchanged bantering correspondence with DELANY and SHERIDAN, and maintained his contact with those friends in England whom he missed. As well as writing a good deal of satirical verse, it was probably around 1720 that he began work on his best-known book, *GULLIVER'S TRAVELS*, published in 1726 to great acclaim and the only piece of writing for which he was ever paid. He saw his old Scriblerian friends for the last time in the following year when, after a stay in England to remonstrate with Walpole, whom he detested, Swift had to return to Ireland, as Stella was desperately ill. She died in 1728, leaving him to an intermittently lonely existence, though there is certainly no evidence that his mental powers were fading until much later in life. His writings prove the contrary. As well as maintaining a vigorous correspondence with his many friends and founding a short-lived weekly paper, *THE INTELLIGENCER*, in 1728, he produced a diverse and talented body of work, including his notoriously powerful *A MODEST PROPOSAL* (1729), poems such as 'The Grand Question Debated' (1729), 'On Poetry: A Rhapsody' (1733) and *VERSES ON THE DEATH OF DR SWIFT* (1739), and the delightful dialogues of his *Polite and Ingenious Conversation* (1738).

Swift was both a prolific and a versatile writer, and, though his reputation has suffered many fluctuations, the originality of his imagination has never seriously been in question. The close and constant proximity of his complex personality and his writings has often caused Swift to be severely misrepresented. The myth that he was eventually driven insane by misanthropy persists, though in fact the senility of his last years was largely the result of physical causes such as Ménière's syndrome from which he had long suffered. The tenacity with which he held his views, his fierce dislike of injustice and his intolerance of folly, which combine to make the satirist's *saeva indignatio* (fierce indignation), were tempered by his charitable concern for the ordinary people of Ireland, his love of pranks and spoofs, and his devotion to the cause of common sense.

Swinburne, Algernon Charles 1837–1909 Poet, playwright, novelist and critic. The son of an admiral, he was born in London but spent his childhood on the Isle of Wight. He was educated in France and at Eton and Balliol College, Oxford, which he left without a degree. From the start, his eclectic interests ensured that his vast literary output would reflect a wide variety of influences. Mastery of Greek and Latin, as well as French and Italian, gave him a strong classical bias and an abiding fascination with the intricacies of poetic form, particularly the lyrical. Admiration for LANDOR, Mazzini, Victor Hugo and later WHITMAN encouraged his own defiant individualism, political and literary. His stay at Oxford coincided with the ill-starred efforts of DANTE GABRIEL ROSSETTI, Edward Burne-Jones, WILLIAM MORRIS and Holman Hunt to decorate the walls of the Oxford Union with frescoes. Later Swinburne was briefly an inmate, with Rossetti and GEORGE MEREDITH, of their bizarre wombat-ridden household at Cheyne Walk, Chelsea.

In 1860 Swinburne published two plays, *The Queen-Mother* and *Rosamund*. They were followed by *Chastelard* (1865), the first of a trilogy about Mary Queen of Scots, continued in *Bothwell* (1874) and *Mary Stuart* (1881). *ATALANTA IN CALYDON* (1865) is a verse drama containing lyrics that later became favourite anthology pieces. But it was in 1866 with the publication of the notorious *Poems and Ballads* (including *THE GARDEN OF PROSERPINE*, *HYMN TO PROSERPINE* and *LAUS VENERIS*) that Swinburne's name truly reverberated through literary circles. With their themes of moral, spiritual and political rebellion, and their sometimes sadistic or blasphemous subject matter, the poems of this volume goaded the middle-class Victorian reading public to fury. JOHN MORLEY's review castigated Swinburne as the 'libidinous laureate of a pack of satyrs'. Revolutionary in both form and content, *Poems and Ballads* broke with contemporary taste and pointed to the *fin-de-siècle* and beyond.

From the mid-1860s to the late 1870s Swinburne's pen barely stopped. *Poems and Ballads* was followed by the lyrically and politically charged *A Song of Italy* (1867) and *Songs before Sunrise* (1871). *Under the Microscope* (1872) defended Rossetti against ROBERT BUCHANAN's attack in 'The Fleshly School of Poetry'. Returning to his Greek models, he published another drama, *Erechtheus* (1876), and *Poems and Ballads: Second Series* (1876), still touched by paganism despite its elegiac tone. It included 'The Forsaken Garden' and a tribute to Baudelaire in *AVE ATQUE VALE*. One novel, *Love's Cross-Currents: A Year's Letters* (1877), belongs to this period; another, *Lesbia Brandon*, was not published until 1952.

By the 1870s Swinburne had sunk into alcoholism. With the consent of his family THEODORE WATTS-DUNTON carried him off in 1879 to The Pines, in Putney where, for the rest of his life, the *enfant terrible* of Victorian letters lived a passive, conventional suburban existence under his friend's solicitous eye. His talent tamed but not extinguished, Swinburne continued to write prodigiously. A highly successful venture into PARODY, *The Heptalogia: or, The Seven against Sense*, appeared in 1880, with *Songs of the Springtides* and *Studies in Song*. They were followed by *Tristram of Lyonnesse* (1882), *A Century of Roundels* (1883), *A Midsummer Holiday* (1884) and, in 1889, *Poems and Ballads: Third Series*. *Astrophel*

appeared in 1894, followed by *The Tale of Balen* (1896) and *A Channel Passage* (1904).

His verse plays included *Marino Faliero* (in rivalry with BYRON's *MARINO FALIERO*; 1885), *Locrine* (1887), *The Sisters* (1892), *Rosamund Queen of the Lombards* (1899) and *The Duke of Gandia* (1908). Swinburne was also a discerning if at times erratic and impetuous critic of literature and over the years cast his net widely by writing on Baudelaire, BLAKE (whose genius he was early to note), Hugo, WEBSTER, SHAKESPEARE, BYRON, Rossetti, DICKENS and others. Swinburne's criticism could reach the heights of enthusiasm and erudition, frequently displaying a mastery of technical analysis; on the other hand, his praise could be exaggerated and his ferocity of attack so uncontrollable, particularly with a pedant in his sights, as to preclude serious consideration of what he had written.

A child of both the romantic and classical traditions, Swinburne used old forms imaginatively and experimented boldly with new ones. His poetry is chiefly notable for its verbal cascades, luxurious imagery and metrical pyrotechnics, for it would be difficult to make a case for its spiritual, philosophical or political profundity. Perhaps above all, Swinburne deserves to be remembered as one of the more courageous spirits to survive Victorian England, taking arms against the prudery of the age, reinvigorating its poetic language and fearlessly, if sometimes misguidedly, pronouncing on new currents of ideas that would be shaped and deepened by later literary men and women.

Swinnerton, Frank (Arthur) 1884–1982 Novelist and critic. Born in north London, he left school at 14 to become an office boy. He worked in 1902–7 as a confidential clerk at J. M. Dent, the publishers, and in 1907–26 as a reader at Chatto and Windus, reading manuscripts by ALDOUS HUXLEY and LYTTON STRACHEY among others and 'discovering' DAISY ASHFORD's *The Young Visiters*. He began his career as a novelist with *The Merry Heart* (1909) and *The Casement* (1911). *Nocturne* (1917) was a critical and commercial success which Swinnerton felt overshadowed his subsequent work. This consisted of nearly 40 more novels, including *Young Felix* (1923), *The Georgian House* (1932) and *A Woman in Sunshine* (1944), and 20 books of criticism. Through his work as a publisher, and as a literary critic for *The Evening News* and *The Observer*, he knew and befriended the leading writers of his time, ARNOLD BENNETT and H. G. WELLS among them. A man of kindness and perception, he added the dimension of close personal contact to his criticism. Living to the age of 98, he became an important link between the Georgian literary scene and later writing.

Sword of Honour A trilogy by EVELYN WAUGH, comprising *Men at Arms* (1952), *Officers and Gentlemen*

(1955) and *Unconditional Surrender*(1961), published as a single work in 1965.

Guy Crouchback, an honourable man, has no place in the modern world. He receives no consolation from personal relationships or from his Catholicism, but World War II gives him the opportunity to establish his identity. He enlists in the Royal Corps of Halberdiers and much of the first volume, *Men at Arms*, is concerned with an eccentric fellow officer, Apthorpe, who eventually dies of a tropical disease in West Africa. Through the characters of Virginia Troy, Guy's beautiful but empty-headed ex-wife, her current husband, Tommy Blackhouse, and the extraordinary Brigadier Ritchie-Hook, Waugh blends nostalgia with a satirical portrait of upper-class English life.

At the end of the second volume, *Officers and Gentlemen*, Guy has been stripped of his illusions about the army. He has an affair with Virginia and departs for action in Alexandria. The novel ends with the withdrawal from Crete and Guy's capture by the enemy.

In the last volume, *Unconditional Surrender*, Guy volunteers for service in Italy with the military government, and he eventually goes to Yugoslavia as a liaison officer with the Partisans. Virginia gives birth to a son (not Guy's) and is killed in an air raid. At the end of the book Guy has again asserted himself in the rescue of a group of Jewish refugees, and realizes what kind of man he used to be: one who believed that his private honour would be satisfied by war. In the Epilogue we learn that he has remarried and surrounded himself with a family.

Sybil: or, The Two Nations A novel by BENJAMIN DISRAELI, published in 1845. About Chartist agitation, it was the earliest and in some ways the best CONDITION OF ENGLAND NOVEL, famous for its description of the miserable living and working conditions of the poor. With numerous historical disquisitions, the novel contrasts the lives of a spurious aristocracy, ennobled by monastic plunder and commercial greed, living in affluence and political selfishness, with the noble aspirations of the journalist, Stephen Morley, and his friend, Walter Gerard, thoughtful representatives of the working class. Walter's daughter, Sybil, is a Catholic who wishes to take the veil but eventually marries a member of the 'aristocracy'. Disraeli shows a keen, humane sympathy with the sufferings of England's oppressed working class but, like other novelists who tackled these themes, his view was paternalistic. With his deeply-entrenched prejudice in favour of 'ancient blood', he makes his 'daughter of the people' (who seems to be a lady of leisure, with no visible means of support), the heir to an ancient title and so fit to rule.

Sydney Opera House Designed by Jorn Utzon and opened in 1973, this remarkable building houses four separate auditoria, of which one is specifically for drama. Since 1979, it has been the home of the Sydney Theatre Company.

syllabic metre See METRE.

syllepsis The application of one word to two semantically different parts of a sentence: 'Here, thou, great Anna! whom three realms obey,/ Dost sometimes counsel take – and sometimes tea' (POPE, *THE RAPE OF THE LOCK*). Zeugma is the same thing, save that one of the applications is, strictly speaking, incorrect. Fluellen's 'Kill the boys and the luggage' in SHAKESPEARE'S *HENRY V* is the most famous example. Syllepsis, therefore, shares something with punning, zeugma with METAPHOR.

Sylvester, Joshua ?1562–1618 Poet and translator. Born in Kent of comfortable bourgeois stock, Sylvester was educated at Southampton grammar school, notable for the excellence of its instruction in French, until 1576, when he embarked on a career in the guild of Merchant Adventurers. A member of Prince Henry's circle, he was friendly with the poet and cleric JOSEPH HALL. Among voluminous translations from French and Latin, his version of Du Bartas (*The Divine Weeks and Works*, 1592–1608) brought him fame but little fortune. Original poems include the entertaining *Tobacco Battered; and the Pipes Shattered* (1617) and the allegorically autobiographical *The Wood-man's Bear*, written in 1587 but published posthumously in 1620. Folio editions of Sylvester's works appeared in 1621, 1633 and 1641.

Sylvia's Lovers A novel by ELIZABETH GASKELL, published in 1863.

Set in Monkshaven (Whitby) during the late 18th century, it combines a realistic portrait of whaling and the cruelties of the press gangs with an increasingly melodramatic plot. Sylvia is the daughter of Daniel Robson, a former sailor and smuggler turned farmer. She loves Charley Kinraid, a 'spectioneer' (harpooner), and is loved by her earnest Quaker cousin Philip. When Kinraid is taken by the press gang Philip fails to deliver his parting message of constancy to Sylvia and allows her to suppose him dead. Daniel Robson is hanged for his part in a riot against the press gangs. Sylvia contracts a loveless marriage with Philip. When Kinraid returns three years later, she refuses to go away with him but disdains her husband for his dishonesty. Philip leaves in disgrace, enlists in the navy and encounters Kinraid, whose life he saves. Eventually Philip returns to Monkshaven, sick and friendless, and is reconciled with Sylvia before his death. Kinraid, it is revealed, has conveniently married an heiress. Other characters include: Kester, an honourable family servant;

the Foster brothers, Quaker shopkeepers; and Hester Rose, whose love for Philip remains unrequited throughout.

symbol A word that has been, and still is, used in very different ways. For literary purposes, as opposed to those of the mathematician, grammarian, or computer programmer, it may profitably be distinguished from sign and SIMILE to give an imprecise but usable meaning. Signs are purely conventional: green stands for Go, red for Stop, by agreement not by nature. In a simile some natural affinity between the two parts is presupposed but the difference is equally important, and the figurative part is not meant to be 'really' like its referent. The symbol, however, draws together different worlds, usually tangible and intangible, into a unity that purports to be more real than either. It tends to be less precise than a sign and more pretentious than a simile – and more powerful when the pretensions turn out to be justified. The symbol, therefore, may be thought of as a METAPHOR that purports to be more than 'merely metaphorical'. In practice, this means that metaphors apparently having a number of referents and an indefinite reverberation of suggestions tend to be distinguished as symbols. Thus BLAKE's 'Sick Rose' seems to be a rose, a vulva, jealousy and corruption at least, but, rather than inviting translation into any or all of these, it offers itself as a complex unity of which they are all inseparable parts.

Symbolism A term specifically applied to the work of late-19th-century French writers who reacted against the descriptive precision and objectivity of REALISM and the scientific determinism of NATURALISM. It was first used in this sense by Jean Moréas in *Le Figaro* in 1886. Baudelaire's sonnet 'Correspondances' and the work of EDGAR ALLAN POE were important precursors of the movement, which emerged with Verlaine's *Romances sans paroles* (1874) and Mallarmé's *L'Après-midi d'un faune* (1876). Other Symbolist writers included the poets Rimbaud and Laforgue, the novelists Joris-Karl Huysmans (*A Rebours*, 1884) and Edouard Dujarin, the dramatists Maurice Maeterlinck and Villiers de l'Isle Adam (*Axël*, 1890) and the critics Rémy de Gourmont and Marcel Schwob. Its influence on the other arts can be seen in the music of Debussy (who wrote many settings of Mallarmé's poems, notably '*Prélude à l'après-midi d'un faune*') and the paintings of Odilon Redon, Gustave Moreau, Van Gogh and Gauguin.

Symbolism emphasized the primary importance of suggestion and evocation in the expression of a private mood or reverie. The symbol was held to evoke subtle relations and affinities, especially between sound, sense and colour, and between the material and spiritual worlds (although in the works themselves these were often antagonistic). The notion of affinities led to an interest in esoteric and occult writings (notably Swedenborg and the cabbala) and to ideas about the 'musicality' of poetry which, combined with the Wagner cult, stressed the possibility of orchestrating the theme of a poem through the evocative power of words.

Outside France T. S. ELIOT, YEATS, POUND, JOYCE, VIRGINIA WOOLF and WALLACE STEVENS were all variously interested in Symbolism. The most significant work was ARTHUR SYMONS's *The Symbolist Movement in Literature* (1899), an introduction to the French literature which Eliot found 'a revelation'. It characterized Symbolism as a reaction against naturalism and realism, and as an 'attempt to spiritualise literature'. It was to be a reflection, not merely a sign, of spiritual reality: 'a kind of religion, with all the duties and responsibilities of the sacred ritual'. Yeats, the dedicatee of the book and himself a poet using symbols of the occult, agreed that Symbolism was 'the recoil from scientific materialism'. His essay, 'The Symbolism of Poetry', emphasized the importance of rhythm. In their poetry, however, both Yeats and Eliot returned to what the latter called the 'music latent in the common speech of its time'.

Symonds, John Addington 1840–93 Poet, translator and art historian. Born in Bristol, he was educated at Harrow and Balliol College, Oxford, where he studied under BENJAMIN JOWETT. His poem 'The Escorial' won the Newdigate Prize, and he was made a Fellow of Magdalen College in 1862, but following a nervous and physical breakdown he spent much of the following year in Italy and Switzerland. In an attempt to repress his homosexuality he married in 1864, and returned to Bristol where he studied law and began to publish criticism, reviews, studies in the Hellenism of the Renaissance and volumes of lyric verse. His circle of friends included EDWARD LEAR, SWINBURNE, LESLIE STEPHEN and ROBERT LOUIS STEVENSON. Completion of the three-volume *The Renaissance in Italy* (1875–86) led to another breakdown, and he then settled at Davos Platz, Switzerland. He was buried near SHELLEY's grave in the Protestant Cemetery in Rome.

His publications include studies of Dante (1872), the Greek poets (1873), WHITMAN (1893) and Michelangelo (1892); translations of Michelangelo and Campanella (1878) and of Goliardic songs in *Wine, Women and Song* (1884), and the *Life of Cellini* (1888). His essays were collected in *Essays Speculative and Suggestive* (2 vols., 1890) and *In the Key of Blue* (1892). He published two privately printed pamphlets in a discreet campaign for legal reforms and recognition of 'inversion', *A Problem in Greek Ethics* (1883) and *A Problem in Modern Ethics* (1891), and he anonymously contributed his own case history to HAVELOCK ELLIS's *Sexual Inversion* (1897). His volumes of poetry include the privately printed *Verses* (1871), followed by *Many Moods* (1878), *New and Old* (1880) and two SONNET sequences dealing obliquely with *'l'amour de l'impossible': Anima Figura* (1882) and *Vagabundulis Libellus* (1884).

Symons, Arthur (William) 1865–1945 Critic and poet. He was born in Milford Haven of Cornish parents, his father being a Wesleyan minister. He was privately educated, became fluent in French and Italian, and, on taking up residence in London, frequented the RHYMERS' CLUB, where he became the friend of ERNEST DOWSON, LIONEL JOHNSON and OSCAR WILDE. For a time he shared lodgings with W. B. YEATS.

A leading light of the Decadence in the 1890s, Symons contributed to *THE YELLOW BOOK* and in 1896 became editor of *The Savoy*. His own poetry, published in *Days and Nights* (1889), *Silhouettes* (1892), *London Nights* (1895) and *Images of Good and Evil* (1899), is forgotten now, but Symons is still remembered for *The Symbolist Movement in Literature* (1899), an influential study which introduced French SYMBOLISM to English readers. He wrote several other critical studies, including *An Introduction to the Study of Robert Browning* (1886), *William Blake* (1907), *Charles Baudelaire* (1920), and *Studies in Elizabethan Drama* (1920), and translated Baudelaire's *Les Fleurs du mal* and Zola's *L'Assommoir*.

synecdoche A figure of speech which replaces the whole by the part, or *vice versa*. Thus a newly arrived person becomes a 'new face'.

Synge, J(ohn) M(illington) 1871–1909 Irish playwright. Born into a moderately affluent Protestant family in Rathfarnham, near Dublin, he was educated privately and at Trinity College, Dublin. His boyhood interest in music was allowed to flourish after his graduation, and he studied piano and violin at the Royal Irish Academy before travelling and studying music in Germany, Italy and France. It was while he was living in Paris that he met W. B. YEATS in 1896 and accepted his advice to develop his growing interest in the Irish language and traditions. Five summers in the Aran Islands between 1898 and 1902 excited his interest in the durability and humour of this isolated community. The notebooks he filled during these visits, and out of which he culled his commentary *The Aran Islands* (1907), show his developing ear for the music of speech. The posthumously published *In Wicklow, West Kerry and Connemara* (1911) is similarly observant, and the two books are the authentic background material of the group of plays, written in 1903–9, which made Synge the first great writer of the Irish Literary Theatre.

Involved with Yeats and LADY GREGORY in the dramatic movement which would culminate in the opening of the ABBEY THEATRE in 1904 (he was one of its directors until his death), Synge wrote his first play,

the one-act *In the Shadow of the Glen* (1903), as a conscious celebration of the independent spirit of the Irish. Set in a cottage in Wicklow, it shows Nora Burke choosing to forsake her ageing and suspicious husband in favour of the freedom of the open road. The prudish section of the Dublin audience declared its opposition to Synge's view of Ireland, as it would continue to declare it throughout Synge's brief dramatic career. The one-act tragedy *RIDERS TO THE SEA* (1904) is both a threnody and a song of praise to the indomitable spirit of the Aran islanders. *The Well of the Saints* (1905), set in the east of Ireland 'one or more centuries ago', is a bitter comedy, in which Synge's ironic pessimism finds expression in the decision of the blind beggars, Martin and Mary Doul, to reject the gift of sight because it has destroyed their illusions. *The Tinker's Wedding*, first performed in 1909, was written and revised between 1903 and 1907. It is a comedy which confronts Sarah Casey, a tinker, with the problem of reconciling her wandering life with the urge to be properly married by a priest. More inevitably even than Synge's masterpiece *THE PLAYBOY OF THE WESTERN WORLD* (1907), it offended the vocally pious of Dublin, who did not like to see a priest bundled into a sack. After the riots that had greeted *The Playboy of the Western World* at the Abbey, it was thought prudent to stage *The Tinker's Wedding* in London rather than Dublin.

DEIRDRE OF THE SORROWS (1910), his only dramatization of Irish mythology, was written during the late stages of Hodgkin's disease and never subjected to the rigorous revision that was his habit. The *Poems and Translations* (1909) give some indication of Synge's range, from the spiritual delicacy of Petrarch to the earthiness of Villon, from nature mysticism to the acute observation of Irish people in an Irish landscape.

System of Logic, The A treatise by JOHN STUART MILL, published in 1843. It lays the groundwork for his re-evaluation of UTILITARIANISM. His attack on all forms in which an assumption of *a priori* knowledge of the external world manifested itself led him first to an analysis of meaning and then to a discussion of inferential knowledge derived from the data of experience. He drew his proofs first from mathematics and then, by extension, from the world of the moral sciences of psychology and sociology. In this latter part Mill's tolerant liberalism is justified by asserting that human behaviour is both causally explicable and still free, and that society can never be greater than the sum of its constituent parts. The book's sociopolitical implications ensured a wide readership beyond the universities, but its adoption as a textbook by Oxford and Cambridge ensured that its discussion of the philosophy of logic created the agenda for much of the work in this field in the latter half of the 19th century.

Tagore, Rabindranath 1861–1941 Bengali mystic, poet and novelist. The 14th child of Debendranath Tagore, the Maharishi or 'great sage', he had little formal education but helped to inspire the Bengali literary revival with the poems, short stories and popular songs he began to publish at the age of 20. From 1891 he managed family estates in East Bengal, founding a school at Shantiniketan ('abode of peace') which by 1921 had become a Vishva-Bharati ('all-India') university. After his wife's death in 1902 Tagore spent much of his time in overseas travel.

To the wider world his appeal came through his own translations of his work into English. In 1912 Tagore showed the artist Sir William Rothenstein his first attempt in this direction: *Gitanjali* ('song offerings'), 103 short poems on the love of God, stripped of Bengali ornament and clothed in simple English dress, amounting to virtually a new creation. It was published, with an enthusiastic introduction by YEATS, for the India Society in 1912 and for the general public in 1913. In that year, on the recommendation of T. STURGE MOORE, Tagore became the first Asian to receive the Nobel Prize for Literature. He was knighted in 1915 but renounced the title after a massacre by British troops in Amritsar in 1919.

Rabindranath Tagore: a sketch by Satyajit Ray

Further translations included: poems like *Fruit Gathering* (1916) and *The Crescent Moon* (1918); philosophical plays such as *Chitra* (1913) and *The King of the Dark Chamber* (1914); *The Home and the World* (1919) and *Gora* (1924), both novels; *Nationalism* (1917), a political tract; and the Hibbert Lectures on *The Religion of Man* (1930). European and American interest in Tagore had declined by the 1930s, though *Gitanjali* and some other works remain in print. His reputation remains high in Bengali poetry and fiction.

tail-rhyme A verse form which uses a short line followed by two or more long lines and then another short line rhyming with the first. The tail-rhyme stanza thus has various forms. It is common in medieval VERSE ROMANCE, but also features in the work of later poets, as in SHELLEY's 'To Night'.

Tale of a Tub, A A prose SATIRE by JONATHAN SWIFT, his first major work, written in about 1696 but published in 1704. The principal narrative is the 'fable of the coats', an ALLEGORY following the fortunes of three brothers each left a coat by their father with strict instructions never to alter it. Peter (the Catholic Church), Martin (the Anglican) and Jack (the Calvinist) all exercise their utmost ingenuity in treating what they have inherited as they please, and the fable traces the squabbling that ensues.

The fable is of less interest, though, than the numerous formal digressions with which it is interspersed (on critics, madness and digressions, for example) which, ironically, are designed to carry the main satiric force of the book. The title itself (as well as meaning 'flim-flam') refers to the nautical practice of throwing tubs off the back of ships to distract the attention of whales; the digressions act in similar fashion. The chief targets of this most complex and accomplished of Swift's early works include religious fanaticism (he was no advocate of Dissent), pedantry, scientific credulity, quackery and self-delusion. Swift frequently imitates the thought processes of those he is attacking, which gives rise to deliberate confusion in the reader. Although complicated, the book enjoys an intellectual symmetry in the 'tradition of learned wit', finding several precedents in the prose of BROWNE, BURTON and MARVELL. Its apparently chaotic nature, its paradoxes and contradictions, are similarly part of authorial design: with its clumsy paraphernalia of prefaces and notes, non-sequiturs and gaps, the *Tale* is, like *THE DUNCIAD*, partly a PARODY of a bad book. The work made Swift notorious, and was widely misunderstood, especially by Queen Anne herself who mistook its purpose for profanity. It effectively disbarred its author from proper preferment within the church, but is often considered his most extraordinary work. Swift himself was certainly pleased with its imaginative flow; he is supposed to have remarked in later life, 'Good God, what a genius I had when I wrote that book.'

Tale of Mystery, A The first English play to be advertised as a MELODRAMA, *A Tale of Mystery* is a perfunctory adaptation by THOMAS HOLCROFT of a French original by Pixerécourt. It was first performed as an afterpiece at COVENT GARDEN in 1802.

Tale of Two Cities, A A novel by CHARLES DICKENS, published as a serial in *ALL THE YEAR ROUND* from April to November 1859.

The novel is set in London and Paris at the time of the French Revolution, and was written in the shadow of CARLYLE's *THE FRENCH REVOLUTION*. Dr Manette is released after being imprisoned for 18 years in the Bastille for his innocent involvement in a discreditable secret of the aristocratic Evrémonde family. He comes to England, where his daughter Lucy has been brought up. She loves Charles Darnay, an honourable man cursed by his descent from the Evrémondes, and is hopelessly loved by the noble-minded wastrel, Sydney Carton. After his marriage to Lucy, Darnay finds that he must return to France to help a family servant imprisoned by the Revolutionaries. Because of his heritage he is immediately arrested and imprisoned, but the intercession of Manette secures his release. Soon afterwards he is arrested again and this time, ironically, the evidence against him is a long denunciatory account of the Evrémonde family written by Manette during his imprisonment. Darnay is condemned to death but saved at the last moment by the heroic self-sacrifice of Sydney Carton, who exploits his strong physical resemblance to Darnay and takes his place at the guillotine.

The narrative includes several striking minor characters – among them the fanatical Madame Defarge, the upright Miss Pross and Jerry Cruncher, the odd-job man and part-time grave robber – but contemporaries were disappointed by the novel's lack of humour. Like *BARNABY RUDGE*, Dickens's only other venture into historical fiction, it is most alive in its descriptions of mob violence.

Tales from Shakespeare A prose summary of 20 plays by SHAKESPEARE, prepared by CHARLES LAMB and his sister Mary and published in 1807. Mary Lamb's name did not appear on the title-page until the edition of 1838, although she was responsible for 14 of the plays in the book. None of the history plays is included and the selection favours the comedies at the expense of the tragedies. The preface explained that the work was 'submitted to the young reader as an introduction to the study of Shakespeare'; it succeeded in becoming a classic for several generations.

Talfourd, Sir **Thomas Noon** 1785–1854 Judge, playwright and literary critic. The son of a brewer, Talfourd was born at Reading and educated privately and then at Mill Hill Dissenting School and Reading Grammar School. After many years at the Bar he was elevated to the bench in the Court of Common Pleas in 1849, and was also thrice elected MP for Reading between 1835 and 1847. Comfortably dividing his time between law and literature, he was acquainted with most of the leading literary figures of the early 19th century, and his numerous contributions to *The New Monthly Magazine* included articles on SCOTT, GODWIN and MATURIN and a long and influential essay on WORDSWORTH. His vapid blank-verse tragedies, *Ion* (1836), *The Athenian Captive* (1838) and *Glencoe* (1840), have mercifully failed to withstand the passage of time, although they enjoyed brief fame as vehicles of the acting and directorial genius of Macready. Talfourd's most enduring work is his reverent edition of the letters of his friend CHARLES LAMB (1834 and 1848), and he is additionally remembered for his introduction of the Copyright Bill in 1837, which earned him the dedication of DICKENS's *PICKWICK PAPERS* and which was eventually passed in 1842.

Talisman, The A novel by SIR WALTER SCOTT, the second of his *Tales of the Crusades*, published in 1825. The talisman of the title has a historical basis in the amulet, known as the Lee-penny, brought back from the Crusades by Sir Simon Lockhart and kept in the possession of his heirs, the Lockharts of the Lee. In Scott's novel the talisman is given to the hero, Sir Kenneth, the Knight of the Leopard, during his adventures in the Holy Land at the time of Richard I. The book was once enormously popular, rivalling Scott's more famous historical romance, *IVANHOE*.

Tam O'Shanter A narrative poem by ROBERT BURNS, first published in *The Edinburgh Magazine* in March 1791. Burns had asked the antiquary FRANCIS GROSE to include an engraving of Alloway Kirk, where the poet's father was buried, in his *Antiquities of Scotland*. Grose agreed, provided that Burns would supply an account of one of the witch legends surrounding the kirk to accompany the picture. Burns gave him three accounts, one of which told the story of Tam O'Shanter. After a satirical prologue, the drunken Tam is found in a tavern with his crony, Souter Johnnie. He lurches out, mounts his mare and starts for home. Passing Alloway Kirk, he sees a witches' celebration in progress and watches in fascination. The witches pour out of the kirk with Auld Nick himself and pursue Tam. He is barely able to make it across the bridge over the Doon, one of the witches seizing his mare's tail at the last moment. Once on the other side he is safe, since witches will not cross water.

Tamburlaine the Great A tragedy by CHRISTOPHER MARLOWE, written in two parts and probably first performed in 1587. It was this play, more than any other, that determined the literary status of Elizabethan drama and drew into the public theatre the best writers of the age. Its towering central role, the first and most rhetorical of Marlowe's overreachers, was created by the actor EDWARD ALLEYN.

Part I shows Tamburlaine's irresistible rise through military conquest from his Scythian origins as a shepherd-robber to unrivalled power. Having helped Cosroe to overthrow his brother, the Persian king Mycetes, Tamburlaine ousts Cosroe as King of Persia. He next conquers the forces of the Turkish Emperor Bajazet, whom he imprisons and humiliates until Bajazet and his Empress Zabina kill themselves by beating their heads against the bars of the cage in which Tamburlaine exhibits them. The only sign of tenderness in the cruel conqueror is his love for Zenocrate, at whose pleading he spares the life of the Soldan of Egypt, her father, when he captures Damascus. *Part II* continues the story of Tamburlaine's conquests, which reach their peak when he has his carriage drawn to Babylon by the captured kings of Trebizond and Soria, in relay with the kings of Anatolia and Jerusalem. But Zenocrate's death precipitates his raging against mortality, whose victory over Tamburlaine ends the play. It is *Tamburlaine the Great* that best exhibits the 'mighty line' of Marlowe.

Taming of the Shrew, The A comedy by WILLIAM SHAKESPEARE, first performed c. 1594. The First Folio of 1623 provides the accepted text, though this is still defective; a quarto, *The Taming of a Shrew* (1594), is usually taken to be a corrupt or pirated version. The source for the main plot is GASCOIGNE's *Supposes*, a translation from Ariosto.

In the Induction a lord plays a practical joke on the drunken tinker Christopher Sly, treating him as a lord and inviting him to the performance of a comedy, *The Taming of the Shrew*, in his honour. In the Folio text Sly then disappears from the action, which continues with the play within the play. Baptista, a rich Paduan, has two daughters but will not allow the younger, Bianca, to marry until a husband has been found for the notoriously ill-tempered Katharina. Petruchio, a visitor from Verona in search of a rich wife, decides to take her on. Oblivious of her rudeness and evidently delighting in what others find offensive, he succeeds in getting a marriage arranged. He arrives late at the wedding, wearing rags and riding an old nag, rushes Katharina off before the wedding feast and embarks on a programme of systematic humiliation. When he takes her back to Baptista's house, Petruchio can present her, in a not entirely jocular competition, as the most docile wife in the whole company. Even Bianca, who has married her Lucentio, cannot rival Katharina.

The Taming of the Shrew is an early comedy whose particular strength is the vigorous control of its central relationship. Modern audiences must accept an Elizabethan argument that Katharina is not the loser by her taming, though arguments about the possible ironies of her dutiful final speech will continue.

Tan, Amy 1952– American novelist. Born of Chinese immigrant parents in Oakland, she studied at San José State University and worked as a reporter, editor and administrator of a home for disabled children. Her novels are *The Joy Luck Club* (1989) and the more ambitious *The Kitchen God's Wife* (1991), about the relations between Chinese and American women.

Tancred: *or, The New Crusade* A novel by BENJAMIN DISRAELI, published in 1847. The third in the trilogy begun by *CONINGSBY* and *SYBIL*, it draws together characters from the earlier books and reintroduces the enigmatic Sidonia, who is revealed to be an international negotiator. Tancred, Lord Montacute, a thoughtful young man, retraces the journey made by his Crusader ancestors to Jerusalem, to find the roots of his Christian religion. There he becomes an unwitting pawn in political machinations, is kidnapped for ransom, discovers a community who worship the old Greek gods, and falls in love with Eva, daughter of the Jewish financier Besso. Eva is an acute theologian and lectures the willing Tancred on the history of Mediterranean civilization, which was ripe when 'flat-nosed Franks' were living as savages in the northern forests. In the final pages, Tancred declares his love for Eva, but she refuses him and swoons at the moment his parents come from England to claim him. The book is a piece of special pleading for Jewish culture, despite the disclaimer that Christianity is the 'perfection' of Judaism, but Tancred cannot fulfil the desire indicated by the drive of the narrative: like Disraeli, he is a 19th-century Christian, who cannot revert to Judaism, however deep his nostalgia.

Tancred and Gismund A tragedy by Robert Wilmot, Christopher Hatton, Henry Noel and others, based on a story by Boccaccio. The version presented before Elizabeth I at Greenwich, probably in 1568, as *Gismond of Salerne* was in rhyming verse. The published version of 1591 changes the title and is in blank verse.

Tannahill, Robert 1774–1810 Poet. Tannahill was a weaver of Paisley whose lyrics achieved a brief contemporary success. 'Jessie the Flower of Dunblane' was set to music by R. A. Smith, the editor of *The Scottish Minstrel. Poems and Songs* was published in 1807. Tannahill drowned himself after burning his manuscripts when Constable, the publisher, rejected a collection of his poems.

Tarkington, (Newton) Booth 1869–1946 American novelist, writer of CHILDREN'S LITERATURE and playwright. He was born in Indianapolis, Indiana, and educated at Purdue and Princeton. His first two novels, *The Gentleman from Indiana* (1899) and *Monsieur Beaucaire* (1900), were accepted for publication on the advice of HAMLIN GARLAND; the former is an example of literary realism in the manner of WILLIAM DEAN HOWELLS, the latter a historical romance.

In all, Tarkington went on to write over 40 volumes of fiction. Among his nostalgic novels of boyhood and adolescence for juvenile readers are *Penrod* (1914), *Seventeen* (1916), *Penrod and Sam* (1916) and *Penrod Jashber* (1929). His novels for adults include three – *The Turmoil* (1915), *The Magnificent Ambersons* (1918, PULITZER PRIZE) and *The Midlander* (1924) – which in 1927 were published as a trilogy entitled *Growth*, and which treat the effects on society of the rise in social prominence of the *nouveau riche* businessman. *Alice Adams*, published in 1921 and awarded the Pulitzer Prize in the following year, is an ironic novel of manners about a middle-class American girl who seeks but fails to marry a rich man.

Tarkington's plays include an adaptation of his novel *Monsieur Beaucaire* (1901), *The Man from Home* (1908), *The Country Cousin* (1921), *The Intimate Strangers* (1921), *The Wren* (1922) and *Bimbo, the Pirate* (1926). In 1928 he published a volume of reminiscences, *The World Does Move*. He continued to write prolifically until his death at the age of 76; among his notable later works are the novels *The Heritage of Hatcher Ide* (1941), *Kate Fennigate* (1943) and *The Image of Josephine* (1945).

Tarlton [Tarleton], **Richard** d. 1588 Clown. He is first heard of in 1570 as the supposed author of a ballad, and the Stationers' Register lists among his lost work *Tarlton's Toys* and *Tarlton's Tragical Treatises* (both 1576) and *Tarlton's Device upon this Unlooked for Great Snow* (1579). The manuscript of *Tarlton's Jig of a Horse Load of Fools* is now assumed to be a forgery by JOHN PAYNE COLLIER, but Tarlton was almost certainly author of the popular play, *The Seven Deadly Sins* (1585), of whose second part an outline plot survives. It was performed by Queen Elizabeth's Men, which he joined on the company's formation in 1583; prior to that date he had probably been one of Leicester's Men. There is every indication that he was more suited to solo or extempore performance than to the faithful recitation of other men's lines. The spirit, though not the letter, of his comic routines is probably present in the posthumously published *Tarlton's Jests* (1611), an important source of biographical information. The well-known drawing by John Scottowe shows him as a rustic clown, with curly hair and broad nose, wearing a simple suit, buttoned cap and short boots, playing a pipe while beating a tabor. That Tarlton's fame outlived him is not surprising. He was the finest popular entertainer of his generation as well as a favourite at court. It is something more than sentiment that reinforces claims that SHAKESPEARE had him in mind when he wrote Hamlet's reminiscence of Yorick.

Task, The A poem in BLANK VERSE by WILLIAM COWPER, published in 1785. The title comes from the task that his friend Lady Austen set him, to write a poem about his sofa, which provides the title for the first of its six books. Those that follow are 'The Timepiece', 'The Garden', 'The Winter Evening', 'The Winter Morning Walk' and 'The Winter Walk at Noon'. Their purpose, Cowper stated, was 'to recommend rural ease and leisure as friendly to the cause of piety and virtue'. His delight in the pleasures he found in country life is rendered with exactitude; so is his anger at the failings of the clergy and the cruelty of blood sports. Generally acknowledged as Cowper's masterpiece, *The Task* earned the praise of BURNS and COLERIDGE.

Tate, (John Orley) Allen 1899–1979 American poet and critic. He was born in Winchester, Kentucky, and educated at Vanderbilt University. His first publication was the privately printed volume *The Golden Mean and Other Poems* (with Ridley Wills; 1923). A leading member of the FUGITIVES, he contributed one of his most famous pieces, 'Ode to the Confederate Dead', to *Fugitives: An Anthology of Verse* (1928), and an essay to JOHN CROWE RANSOM's *I'll Take My Stand* (1930). His volumes of poetry include *Mr Pope and Other Poems* (1928), *Poems: 1928–1931* (1932), *The Mediterranean and Other Poems* (1936), *Selected Poems* (1937), *Poems: 1922–1947* (1948), *Poems* (1960) and *Collected Poems* (1977). They frequently reflect his interest in the history of the South, which also prompted biographies of Stonewall Jackson (1928) and Jefferson Davis (1929). He received the Bollingen Prize for poetry in 1956.

His critical works include *Reactionary Essays on Poetry and Ideas* (1936), *Reason in Madness, Critical Essays* (1941), *On the Limits of Poetry, Selected Essays 1928–1948* (1948), *The Forlorn Demon: Didactic and Critical Essays* (1953), *Collected Essays* (1959) and *Essays of Four Decades* (1968). A leading proponent of the NEW CRITICISM, Tate also served as the editor of THE KENYON REVIEW (1938) and THE SEWANEE REVIEW (1944–6). His only novel, *The Fathers* (1938), is a first-person narrative in which the 65-year-old Lacy Buchan recalls his past, which spans the demise of the Old South and the stability it represented.

Tate, James 1943– American poet. He was born in Kansas City and educated at the Iowa Writers' Workshop, from which he received an MA in 1967. Since 1970 he has taught at the University of

Massachusetts at Amherst. His early volumes, *The Lost Pilot* (1967) and *The Oblivion Ha-Ha* (1970), reveal an essentially comic and often sardonic voice within structures that are loosely surrealistic. Later work, progressively tempered by a contemplative intelligence, has appeared in *Hints to Pilgrims* (1971), *Absences* (1972), *Hottentot Ossuary* (1974), *Viper Jazz* (1976), *Riven Doggeries* (1979), *Constant Defender* (1983), *Reckoner* (1986), *Distance from Loved Ones* (1990) and *Selected Poems* (1991).

Tate, Nahum 1652–1715 Poet, translator and playwright. Born and educated in Dublin, Tate settled in London in 1672 and began a busy career in literature. He was appointed POET LAUREATE in 1692 and Historiographer Royal in 1702. His reputation as a poet is sustained by his collaboration with DRYDEN in the second part of *ABSALOM AND ACHITOPHEL* and by the carol 'While Shepherds Watched Their Flocks by Night', as a translator by his *New Version of the Psalms of David* (1696), undertaken with Nicholas Brady (see PSALTERS), and his version from Fracastoro of *Syphilus: A Poetical History of the French Disease* (1686). He is best remembered for his work in the theatre, particularly his libretto for Purcell's *Dido and Aeneas* (1689) and his scaled-down and immensely popular version of *KING LEAR* (1681), which spares Cordelia's life and betrothes her to Edgar in a happy ending.

Tatler, The A periodical founded by RICHARD STEELE, appearing three times a week from April 1709 until January 1711. It presented its reports on various subjects as coming from different coffee and chocolate houses, the newly fashionable meeting places of the age: entertainment from White's, politics and foreign news from St James's, poetry from Will's. As it grew successful, *The Tatler* developed into an arbiter of conduct and taste, and the editor ISAAC BICKERSTAFF (a pseudonym Steele borrowed from SWIFT) introduced the marriage of his sister Jenny Distaff to make it a family magazine. Of 271 numbers Steele wrote the entire contents of nearly 190, JOSEPH ADDISON wrote 42, and 36 were written in collaboration. *The Tatler* was succeeded by *THE SPECTATOR*.

Taylor, Bayard 1825–78 American travel-writer, poet and novelist. Born to Quaker parents in Kennett Square, Pennsylvania, he published his first collection of verse as *Ximena* (1844) in the same year he travelled to Europe, the subject of his second book, *Views A-Foot* (1846), and a series of letters published in the *New York Tribune*. When he returned to America, the *Tribune* appointed him manager of their literary section and sent him to California to cover the Gold Rush of 1849. His account appeared in book form as *Eldorado: or, Adventures in the Path of Empire* (2 vols., 1850). The following year he set off on an exten-

sive journey which took him to Egypt, Abyssinia, Turkey, India and China, before he joined Commodore Perry in the Pacific. On his return to New York In 1853, Taylor began a series of lectures and wrote several accounts of travels and adventures, including *A Journey to Central Africa* (1854), *The Lands of the Saracen* (1855) and *A Visit to India, China and Japan in the Year 1853* (1855). In 1856 he travelled .extensively in Europe and Russia and again published several accounts of the journey: *Northern Travel* (1857), *Travels in Greece and Russia* (1859) and *At Home and Abroad* (1860).

He also wrote several novels, all set in America. They include: *Hannah Thurston* (1863), *John Godfrey's Fortunes* (1864), *Joseph and His Friend* (1870) and *Beauty and the Beast and Tales of Home* (1872). Throughout his life, he published numerous volumes of verse, a body of work which reflects his wide, international experience and varied tastes: *Rhymes of Travel, Ballads and Poems* (1849), *Lars: A Pastoral of Norway* (1873) and *The Echo Club and Other Literary Diversions* (1876).

Taylor, Cecil P(hilip) 1928–81 Playwright. Throughout his life he kept faith with the socialism of his Glasgow Jewish childhood, but the revolutionary tone of his early plays, such as his first, *Aa Went to Blaydon Races* (1962), gave way to the warm humour of such works as *The Black and White Minstrels* (1972). His most successful play, *Good* (1981), is about a liberal German professor whose moral cowardice leads to a military career and a job in Auschwitz. A prolific dramatist whose energy and charm were present in all his work, Taylor also adapted plays by Sternheim and Ibsen, as well as writing for television.

Taylor, Edward *c.* 1645–1729 American poet. Born in Leicestershire, England, Taylor emigrated to Massachusetts in 1668. He graduated from Harvard in 1671 and served as minister to the church in the frontier town of Westfield, Massachusetts, for the rest of his life. A friend of INCREASE MATHER, COTTON MATHER and SAMUEL SEWALL, he was a conservative in matters of church polity; he corresponded with SOLOMON STODDARD, his frontier neighbour, on the subject of the latter's open communion policy.

Today Taylor is considered the pre-eminent poet of early New England, but his poetry was not known in his own day; his manuscripts remained undiscovered in the Yale University library until 1937. Thomas H. Johnson edited the *Poetical Works* in 1939. In addition to a few occasional poems, he wrote the long series *God's Determinations touching His Elect; and the Elects' Combat in Their Conversion, and Coming Up to God in Christ: Together with the Comfortable Effects Thereof*, a poetic treatment of Puritan dogma; and the devotional *Meditations*, each exploring the imagery of a biblical text.

Taylor, Elizabeth 1912–75 Novelist and short-story writer. Born Elizabeth Coles in Reading, she was educated there and worked as a teacher and librarian until her marriage in 1936. Her first novel, *At Mrs Lippincote's* (1946), a gentle study of bourgeois life written with simplicity and precision, was followed by many others of similar quality: *Palladian* (1947), *A Wreath of Roses* (1950), about a middle-aged woman's emotional involvement with a younger man, *The Soul of Kindness* (1963), *Mrs Palfrey at the Claremont* (1972), about old age, and *Blaming* (1976), about a young woman whose life is thrown into emotional turmoil after her husband's death on their holiday in Istanbul. She is also the author of collections of short stories – *Hester Lilly* (1954), *The Blush* (1958), *A Dedicated Man* (1965) and *The Devastating Boys* (1962) – and a book for children, *Mossy Trotter* (1967).

Taylor, Sir Henry 1800–86 Playwright. He was born at Bishop-Middleham, Durham, and educated at home. He earned his knighthood for his long service in the Colonial Office. Taylor's verse dramas were never produced but one of them, *Philip van Artevelde* (1834), was much admired as a study of character. Others were *Isaac Comnenus* (1827), *Edwin the Fair* (1842), *The Virgin Widow* (1850) and *St Clement's Eve* (1862). Taylor was also the author of *The Statesman* (1836), a satirical essay on the art of succeeding as a civil servant, and *Autobiography (1800–75)* (1885). His *Collected Works* were published in 1877 and his *Correspondence* in 1888.

Taylor, Jeremy 1613–67 Devotional writer. The son of a Cambridge barber, Taylor was educated at Gonville and Caius College and became a substitute preacher at St Paul's. He came to the notice of LAUD, Archbishop of Canterbury, who gave him a fellowship at All Souls, Oxford. He became rector of Uppingham in 1638 and chaplain to both Charles I and the archbishop, leaving his rectorship in 1642 to join the king's personal attendants. He was at Cardigan Castle when it surrendered to the Parliamentary army, but found shelter as teacher and chaplain to the Earl of Carbery at Golden Grove in Carmarthenshire. Taylor spent ten years at Golden Grove and the best of his writing dates from this period. He moved next to London and Lord Conway, another friend, secured him a chaplaincy in Northern Ireland in 1658. He resumed his writing, and was given the see of Down and Connor at the Restoration, and later of Dromore, where he is buried in the cathedral.

Taylor's work did much to shape the Church of England. He wrote clear unadorned prose to set forth his plea for tolerance: men should be allowed to differ in opinion when they plainly agreed on Christian fundamentals. His principal works are *A Discourse on the Liberty of Prophesying* (1647), *The Golden Grove* (1655), *Discourse of the Nature, Offices and Measures*

of *Friendship* (1657), *The Worthy Communicant* (1660) and, best known of all, *The Rule and Exercises of Holy Living* (1650) and *The Rule and Exercises of Holy Dying* (1651). The last was written in a period of deep personal grief following the deaths of his wife and of his patroness, Lady Carbery.

Taylor, John 1580–1653 The 'Water Poet'. Born in Gloucester and educated locally at the grammar school, he was apprenticed to a London waterman before being pressed into the navy. He was present at the siege of Cadiz in 1596, and, according to his own account, completed 16 voyages before retiring with a lame leg. He returned to working as a Thames waterman but found the trade damaged by excess of competition. He hit on the expedient of collecting sponsors for whimsical journeys, on foot or by water, and writing up his experiences in lively prose and doggerel. In this fashion he travelled to the Continent and Bohemia, and made water journeys from London to York, Salisbury and Queenborough, reaching the last destination in a brown-paper boat. *The Penniless Pilgrimage* (1618) describes a walk from London to Edinburgh and Braemar without money; when some of his sponsors complained that he had cheated, Taylor upbraided them in *A Kicksey Winsey* (1619). He eventually became an innkeeper, in Oxford from 1642 and in London from 1645.

Taylor, Peter 1917– American short-story writer. Born in Trenton, Tennessee, he spent his youth in Nashville, St Louis and Memphis. These cities, as well as the fictional town of Thornton, Tennessee, are the setting of many of his works, which frequently centre on the conflict between the values of small-town Southern life and those of an urban culture. He has published a novella, *A Woman of Means* (1950), a novel, *A Summons to Memphis* (1987), and several collections of stories: *A Long Fourth and Other Stories* (1948), *The Widows of Thornton* (1954), *Happy Families are All Alike* (1959), *Miss Leonora When Last Seen* (1963), *The Collected Stories of Peter Taylor* (1969), *In the Miro District and Other Stories* (1977), and *The Old Forest and Other Stories* (1985).

Taylor, Tom 1817–80 Playwright, editor and critic. Born near Sunderland, Taylor attended the universities of Glasgow and Cambridge, where he taught in 1842–4. He was professor of English in the University of London in 1845–7, during which time he qualified for the Bar. He practised law on the northern circuit in 1847–50, was assistant secretary and then secretary to the London Board of Health in 1850–71 and editor of *PUNCH* from 1874 until his death. His phenomenal industry allowed him, during this time, to write 80 plays, leaders for THE MORNING CHRONICLE and THE DAILY NEWS, art criticism for *The Times* and *The Graphic* and numerous contributions to *Punch*. He was house dramatist at the Olympic Theatre, 1853–60, and at the HAYMARKET 1857–70.

During his long theatrical career, Taylor wrote in almost all the current dramatic styles. His first play, *A Trip to Kissingen* (1844), was a FARCE. His PANTOMIMES included such popular favourites as *Cinderella* (1845) and *Little Red Riding Hood* (1851). There was even a hippodrama, *Garibaldi* (1859), and a series of historical verse dramas, of which the best is *The Fool's Revenge* (1859), adapted from Hugo's *Le Roi s'amuse*. Most of his work is derivative, as was typical of working Victorian playwrights, but there is merit in such MELODRAMAS as *Plot and Passion* (with John Lang; 1853) and particularly THE TICKET-OF-LEAVE MAN (1863), and in the comedies, conventionally theatrical but not without social perception, *Masks and Faces* (with CHARLES READE; 1852), *To Oblige Benson* (1854), *Still Waters Run Deep* (1855), *Contested Election* (1859), *Victims* (1857), *The Overland Route* (1860) and *New Men and Old Acres* (with A. W. Dubourg; 1869). It is unjust that Taylor should be best remembered as the author of *Our American Cousin* (1858), whose success owed more to the actor E. A. Sothern's inventiveness as Lord Dundreary and whose notoriety was a result of Abraham Lincoln's being assassinated at a performance in Washington DC.

telestic See ACROSTIC.

Tempest, The A play by WILLIAM SHAKESPEARE, first performed *c.* 1611 and published in the First Folio of 1623. It draws on accounts of a shipwreck off the Bermudas in 1609 and Montaigne's essay 'Of the Cannibals' (as translated by FLORIO), but no single main source has been identified. This very eclecticism has given strength to those who argue that, in writing what he felt might be his last work for the stage, Shakespeare was consciously summarizing his theatrical art.

Prospero, exiled Duke of Milan, has taken up a 12-year residence on a remote island, previously inhabited only by the airy spirit, Ariel, and the earthy Caliban, deformed son of the dead witch, Sycorax. With Prospero is his innocent daughter, Miranda, together with the books and the staff that enable him to practise magic. It is by magic that he brings about a storm and arranges for the arrival on the island of a group of shipwrecked figures from his past. From Milan come his usurping brother Antonio and the loyal counsellor Gonzalo, who gave Prospero what help he could when he was cast adrift 12 years before; and from Naples come King Alonso, his son Ferdinand and Sebastian, the king's scheming brother. The play recounts the various adventures of these characters, all overseen by Prospero and organized by Ariel. The outcome is that Miranda, who could recall no man save Caliban and her father, falls in love with Ferdinand, that Sebastian's malice is exposed to

Alonso, and that Antonio restores the dukedom of Milan to Prospero. At the play's end, Prospero releases Ariel from his service, returns the island to a chastened Caliban, breaks his staff and buries his books. All will sail for home, guided by the gentle winds Ariel has conjured up.

Although formally a comedy, *The Tempest* is more aptly associated with the group of tragicomic romances with which Shakespeare greeted his company's move into the indoor BLACKFRIARS THEATRE: PERICLES, CYMBELINE and THE WINTER'S TALE. It is a complex poetic work, whose mechanical plotting serves to draw attention to wider aesthetic and philosophical themes.

Temple, Sir **William** 1628–99 Diplomat and essayist. The son of Sir John Temple, Master of the Rolls in Ireland, Temple was born in London and completed his education at Emmanuel College, Cambridge. In 1648 he met Dorothy Osborne (1627–95), whom he married in 1655 despite the opposition of her father, a severe Royalist. She wrote regularly to him in the years 1652–4; her letters were first published in 1888. Temple became an envoy at Brussels in 1666, and in 1668 negotiated the Triple Alliance of England, Holland and Sweden to counterbalance the power of France and her ambitions in Spain. His work was negated, however, by Charles II's secret treaty with Louis XIV. Temple returned to Holland in 1674 and arranged the marriage of Princess Mary to William of Orange. He retired soon after and lived first at Sheen and then at Moor Park in Surrey, where JONATHAN SWIFT worked as his secretary.

In literature Temple is remembered for his essays, his *Memoirs* (1692) and his letters, which were edited by Swift (1701). Apart from *Essay upon the Present State of Ireland* (1668), *Observations upon the United Provinces of the Netherlands* (1672) and *The Advancement of Trade in Ireland* (1673), the essays are brought together in three volumes of *Miscellanea* (1680, 1690 and 1701). Its second volume contains the *Essay upon the Ancient and Modern Learning*, in which he compared modern writers and philosophers unfavourably with their classical counterparts and lavishly praised the epistles of Phalaris, the tyrant of Agrigentum in the 6th century BC. However, the scholar RICHARD BENTLEY showed the epistles to be forgeries and the result was a lively controversy which produced Swift's THE BATTLE OF THE BOOKS. MACAULAY found Temple 'a man of the world among men of letters, a man of letters among men of the world'. He was an informed and opinionated amateur, whose best essays – on gardening or poetry, for example – still have at least historical interest.

Temple of Glass, The A poem by JOHN LYDGATE in RHYME ROYAL and couplets, written between 1400 and 1420. The form is an allegorical DREAM-VISION and the poem draws extensively on the work of GEOFFREY CHAUCER, in particular THE HOUSE OF FAME, THE PARLEMENT OF FOULES and The Knight's Tale (see THE CANTERBURY TALES), as well as earlier poems in the tradition. The dreamer is transported to a temple of glass where he sees depicted famous lovers complaining to Venus. He then sees a woman complain that she is bound to a man she does not love and separated from her beloved. Venus promises her aid and a knight enters complaining of his unrequited love for the woman. They are united and blessed by Venus. The poem may refer to a historical event, but no specific references are found and it cannot be identified. The allegory is barely sustained and there is none of the philosophical and psychological complexity, or the humour, which characterize the poem's models.

Tenant of Wildfell Hall, The ANNE BRONTË'S second novel, published in 1848. A much more ambitious work than *AGNES GREY*, it has a male narrator, Gilbert Markham.

Helen Graham, the tenant of Wildfell Hall, is young, beautiful and said to be a widow. Her reticence about herself provokes local gossip. Markham, a neighbouring farmer who has fallen in love with her, defends Helen's reputation until he overhears her in affectionate conversation with her landlord, Frederick Lawrence. Markham and Lawrence quarrel violently.

Helen Graham is in fact in love with Markham, and writes of this in her diary, which also records the secret of her life. She was married young to Arthur Huntingdon and is the mother of his son. Huntingdon proved to be a drunkard and, despite her attempts to reclaim him, she led a life of misery and humiliation. Finally, afraid of the effect of his way of life on their son, she appealed to Lawrence, who is in fact her brother, and who provided her with the refuge of Wildfell Hall. She tells Markham the truth, and then has to go back to her husband, who is dangerously ill. Huntingdon dies of his excesses and Helen is free. Markham is dismayed to learn that she is now a wealthy woman but is encouraged by Lawrence to win her hand.

Although the novel was a popular success, its frank portrait of Huntingdon's alcoholism and of Helen's struggle to free herself from such a husband struck some contemporaries as offensive and inappropriate subjects for a woman author. Even her sister CHARLOTTE BRONTË was disturbed, doubtless by the echoes of their brother Branwell's fate in the portrait of Huntingdon. Anne Brontë was unrepentant, defending herself in the preface to the second edition: 'I wished to tell the truth, for truth always conveys its own moral... To represent a bad thing in its least offensive light is doubtless the most agreeable course for a writer of fiction to pursue; but is it the most honest?'

Tender is the Night A novel by F. SCOTT FITZGERALD, published in 1934. Adverse criticism led Fitzgerald to believe that the story's time scheme was faulty, and a revised edition (based on his notes), which reorganized the action into chronological order, was published posthumously in 1948. However, most modern editions follow the original version, which begins on the Riviera.

It is a novel about the squandering of creative promise. It is the story of Dick Diver, a young American psychiatrist studying in Zurich in 1917. He becomes interested in the case of Nicole Warren, a beautiful and wealthy American suffering from schizophrenia. As she recovers, she comes to depend on Dick, and eventually they marry. The doctor-patient relationship, however, carries over to their marriage; caring for Nicole prevents Dick both from loving her and from pursuing his intellectual career. They have two children and lead a leisurely life on the Riviera. Their friends include Abe North, a composer who has become an alcoholic and, like Dick, failed to fulfil the creative promise of his youth. His failure is consummated when he is killed in a Paris bar. Dick's life as the impeccable host on the Riviera gradually deteriorates. He becomes infatuated with Rosemary Hoyt, an American actress much younger than himself; he begins to drink heavily; he is involved in a brawl in Rome; and his medical career is on the verge of ruin. Nicole falls in love with Tommy Barban, a French mercenary and member of their Riviera circle, and eventually divorces Dick, whose own failure is complete when he returns to a small-town medical practice in America.

Tennant, Emma 1937– Novelist. Born in London and brought up in Scotland, she founded the literary newspaper *Bananas*, which during its short life in the early 1970s established a reputation for publishing quirky and adventurous fiction. Her most original novels explore extreme psychological states and alternative notions of reality through fantasy and the use of dreams and STREAM OF CONSCIOUSNESS. The most virtuoso performances are perhaps *The Bad Sister* (1978) and *Wild Nights* (1980). Later novels such as *Queen of Stories* (1982) and *Woman Beware Woman* (1983) tended towards more realistic narrative and incorporated a strong element of mystery and suspense, while continuing to explore the imprecise borders of reality. *The House of Hospitalities* (1987) and *A Wedding of Curiosity* (1988) began a surprisingly conventional projected sequence, *Cycle of the Sun. Faustine* (1992) signalled a return to more fantastic narrative.

Tennant, Kylie 1912–88 Australian novelist and writer of CHILDREN'S LITERATURE. Born in Manly and educated at the University of Sydney, she worked for the Australian Broadcasting Commission for a time.

Her first novel, *Tiburon* (1935), was well received. It concerns the fate of an impoverished community in a small country town during the Depression years, a setting to which Tennant returned in later novels. *Foveaux* (1939) was followed by *The Battlers* (1941), *Ride on Stranger* (1943), *Time Enough Later* (1945), *Lost Haven* (1946), *The Joyful Condemned* (1953), *The Honey Flow* (1956), *Tell Morning This* (1967) and *Tantavallon* (1983). IRONY, humour, a talent for the swift evocation of atmosphere and an inclination to value the country more than the city characterize her novels. Her work for children includes *All the Proud Tribesmen* (1959) and several plays. She also wrote: a history, *Australia: Her Story* (1953); a study of Aborigines, *Speak You So Gently* (1959); and an autobiography, *The Missing Heir* (1986).

Tennant, William 1784–1848 Poet. Born in Anstruther, Fifeshire, he completed his education at St Andrews University, where he later became professor of oriental languages. His poem, *Anster Fair* (1812), is a MOCK-HEROIC description of a rural fair in the reign of James V of Scotland.

Tenniel, Sir John 1820–1914 Cartoonist and illustrator. Born in London, he studied art at the Royal Academy. After the success of his illustrations for *Aesop's Fables* (1848) he was invited to join PUNCH as leading cartoonist with JOHN LEECH. There followed over 50 years of political cartoons on all the great issues of the day, yet he is now remembered for his illustrations to LEWIS CARROLL's *ALICE'S ADVENTURES IN WONDERLAND* (1865) and *THROUGH THE LOOKING-GLASS* (1871). In all, he submitted over 90 drawings, of which only one was accepted without reservation by the author. The final result was extremely successful, with many of the details that Tenniel suggested in his pictures (such as the price label stuck in the Mad Hatter's top hat) now virtually a standard part of any new illustrator's reaction to Carroll's text. Tenniel agreed to illustrate the second Alice book only after much hesitation, and afterwards abandoned book illustration altogether.

Tennyson, Alfred Lord 1809–92 Poet. He was born in Somersby, Lincolnshire, one of eight children in the gloomy and neurotic household of the local vicar, George Clayton Tennyson, and his wife, Elizabeth Fytche Tennyson. He was educated at Louth grammar school and privately by his father. As early as 1823–4 he had written *The Devil and the Lady*, a precocious fragment in the Elizabethan manner which remained unprinted until 1930. He entered Trinity College, Cambridge, in November 1827, becoming a member of the APOSTLES, winning the Chancellor's Gold Medal for poetry with 'Timbuctoo', and forming a close friendship with ARTHUR HENRY HALLAM. The misnamed *Poems by Two Brothers* (1827), unobtrusively published in Louth and including work by his brothers Frederick and CHARLES TENNYSON TURNER, marked his debut. It was followed by *Poems, Chiefly Lyrical* (1830). The next year his father, a past victim of severe physical and mental breakdown, died, and the young Tennyson left the university without a degree. *Poems* (published in December 1832 but dated 1833) received a savage mauling from JOHN WILSON CROKER in THE QUARTERLY REVIEW.

There followed the 'Ten Years' Silence', a period of neurotic refusal to publish, when Tennyson's life lacked direction and his emotional instability seemed unusually apparent. He suffered the shock of Hallam's death in 1833 and the lesser shock of a family move to Epping, fell briefly in love with Rosa Baring, began his long and interrupted engagement to Emily Sellwood and made a disastrous investment in the woodcarving scheme of his friend Dr Allen. Had it not been for American pressures over copyright, the silence might well have continued, but Tennyson felt compelled to publish. The result was the masterly *Poems* of 1842, its first volume composed of earlier, revised work (*THE LADY OF SHALOTT*, *THE LOTOS-EATERS*) and the second containing new poems (*LOCKSLEY HALL*, *ULYSSES*). It was followed by *THE PRINCESS* (1847), an amorous polemic on the rights of women. 1850 was Tennyson's *annus mirabilis*. He published his most enduring work, *IN MEMORIAM A. H. H.*, an ELEGY for Hallam begun as early as 1834, succeeded WORDSWORTH as POET LAUREATE and, finally, married Emily Sellwood.

Henceforth Tennyson trod the leonine, bardic path and, like many abnormally shy people, he trod it somewhat roughly. In 1853 he and Emily moved to Farringford on the Isle of Wight, where his privacy was constantly invaded. He became a member of the Athenaeum and was invited to join 'the Club', founded a century before by JOHNSON and REYNOLDS; but because of his obsessive shyness Tennyson invariably resigned or withdrew from such organizations. The poetry continued to pour forth. *MAUD and Other Poems* (1855) included 'The Charge of the Light Brigade' and the magnificent 'Ode on the Death of the Duke of Wellington'. In 1859 'Enid' (already privately printed in 1857), 'Vivien', 'Elaine' and 'Guinevere' began *THE IDYLLS OF THE KING*. In 1862 the Laureate had his first of several audiences with Queen Victoria. In 1864 he published *ENOCH ARDEN* in a volume which also included *TITHONUS*, and in 1865 (as on several other occasions) he refused a baronetcy, though he did eventually agree to a title and took his seat in the Lords in 1883. Also in the 1860s the Tennysons built another home, in Aldworth near Haslemere, and he developed an interest in the Metaphysical Society. At the end of the decade he published *The Holy Grail and Other Poems* (1869, dated 1870). In 1872 came *Gareth and Lynette*, followed in 1872–3 by the Imperial Library edition of

Tennyson reading
Maud, sketched by
D. G. Rossetti in
1855

the works which gathered up the *Idylls* (except *Balin and Balan* of 1885), added the Epilogue ('To the Queen') and rounded off his astonishing contribution to ARTHURIAN LITERATURE.

In 1875 Tennyson published his first play, *Queen Mary,* which was produced a year later; a clutch of dramatic works followed, among them *Harold* (1876), *Becket* (1884), and *The Cup* (1881), though not even the combined talents of Henry Irving and Ellen Terry could save the last from oblivion. His muse occasionally nodding, Tennyson nevertheless continued to publish volumes of poetry in old age: *Ballads and Other Poems* (1880), *Tiresias and Other Poems* (1885), *Locksley Hall Sixty Years After* (1886) and *Demeter and Other Poems* (1889), which contained CROSSING

THE BAR. *The Death of Oenone, Akbar's Dream, and Other Poems* appeared posthumously in 1892.

Perhaps no poet's reputation has received – and withstood – so severe a buffeting since his death. Always highly neurotic, often roughly eccentric, a poet of twilight and half-shadows marked by his delicate poignancy and controlled sadness, yet also the trumpeter of Empire and exponent of a higher morality, Tennyson remained a supreme technician torn between the bardic voice and the solitary lyric.

Tennyson Turner, Charles 1808–79 Poet. Like his younger brother, ALFRED TENNYSON, he was born at Somersby in Lincolnshire and educated at Louth grammar school and Trinity College, Cambridge. He became vicar of Grasby, Lincolnshire, and changed his name to Turner on succeeding to his great-uncle's property in 1830. With Frederick and Alfred Tennyson he contributed to the misnamed *Poems by Two Brothers* (1827), and later produced four volumes of restrained but distinguished SONNETS (1830, 1864, 1868, 1874).

tercet See TRIPLET.

Terkel, Studs (Louis) 1912– American broadcaster and social historian. Born in New York, he graduated from the University of Chicago and worked as an actor before establishing his reputation as a radio and TV interviewer. As a writer he is best known for his oral histories of 20th-century American experience, skilfully compiled from interviews and conversations with ordinary people. They include *Division Street America* (1966), *Hard Times* (about the Depression; 1970), *Working* (1974), *American Dreams: Lost and Found* (1980), *The Good War: An Oral History of World War II* (1985, PULITZER PRIZE) and *The Great Divide: Second Thoughts on the American Dream* (1988). *Talking to Myself* (1977) is a memoir.

Terson, Peter [Patterson, Peter] 1932– Playwright. He was born and brought up on Tyneside, where he worked as a teacher for 10 years before his first play, *A Night to Make the Angels Weep*, was produced in 1964. With *The Mighty Reservoy* (1964), it showed him an amusing observer of life in the Midlands and the North, able to seize on an idea which raised naturalism toward myth. *Mooney and His Caravans* was seen on TV in 1966 before its stage production in 1968. Terson's association with the National Youth Theatre began with *Zigger Zagger* (1967), about football fans and hooligans, and continued with *The Apprentices* (1968), *Spring-Heeled Jack* (1970) and *Good Lads at Heart* (1971). *Strippers* (1984) describes the life of women in areas of high unemployment who take to stripping in pubs for pocket money.

terza rima A series of three-line STANZAS interlocked by RHYME, as follows: aba bcb cdc ded. The form was originally Italian, used by Dante in *The Divine Comedy*. The relative difficulty of rhyming in English makes it a less suitable form for English literature, but poets from CHAUCER to W. H. AUDEN have used it successfully; SHELLEY's 'Ode to the West Wind' is a famous example.

Tess of the d'Urbervilles: *A Pure Woman Faithfully Presented* A novel by THOMAS HARDY, serialized in a bowdlerized form in *The Graphic* from July to December 1891 and in book form the same year. Its rejection of the conventional Victorian heroine pro-

voked a controversy, continued by *JUDE THE OBSCURE*, which encouraged Hardy to abandon fiction for poetry.

Unwisely, Parson Tringham tells John Durbeyfield, a haggler (local carrier) of Marlott, that he is descended from the Norman family of d'Urbervilles. Fortified by this information, he and his wife Joan encourage their daughter Tess to seek the kinship of the parvenu Stoke d'Urbervilles who have adopted the ancient name. She is seduced by their son, the vulgar rake Alec, and bears a child that mercifully dies. To make a fresh start, Tess goes to work in southern Wessex at the fertile Talbothays farm. There she meets Angel Clare, younger son of a parson, and after a struggle within herself accepts his offer of marriage. On their wedding night Tess confesses her unhappy past to Angel, who recoils in puritanical horror. He goes off to Brazil and Tess seeks employment at the grim upland farm, Flintcomb Ash, belonging to the tyrannical Farmer Groby. There she is again afflicted by the advances of Alec d'Urberville, now an itinerant preacher. He is insistent that Tess is more his wife than Angel's and relentless in his pursuit of her. Angel returns to England a wiser man and traces Tess to Sandbourne, where she is living as Alec's wife. She considers it too late for reconciliation and sends him away. In her despair and entrapment she kills Alec and, after a brief idyllic period with Angel, is arrested at Stonehenge, tried, and hanged in Wintoncester (Winchester) jail.

Testament of Cresseid, The A poem by ROBERT HENRYSON, continuing the story of CHAUCER's *TROILUS AND CRISEYDE*. The first printed version to survive is in Thynne's 1532 edition of Chaucer, and the poem regularly appeared in editions of Chaucer for some time after.

Abandoned by Diomede, Cresseid becomes promiscuous. She is taken in by her father, Calchas, and blasphemes against Cupid and Venus. The planetary gods in session depute Saturn and the Moon to punish her with leprosy (which, for Henryson's readers, would be identified with syphilis). Troilus, riding back to Troy, takes pity on the lepers and in a scene of exquisite pathos he and Cresseid meet, but 'not ane ane uther knew', although the meeting provokes in Troilus a faint memory of 'fair Cresseid sumtyme his awin darling'. Told by a leper that her benefactor was Troilus, Cresseid makes her 'testament' (will), bequeathing her wealth to the lepers and returning a ring given her by Troilus. The poem has many echoes of Chaucer's *Troilus*, but alters Chaucer's story in which Diomede killed Troilus. Henryson introduces elaborate astrological machinery and gives Cresseid a fine complaint on the familiar theme of the transitoriness of beauty and security in this world.

tetrameter See METRE.

Tey, Josephine See MACKINTOSH, ELIZABETH.

Thackeray, William Makepeace 1811–63 Novelist. Born in Calcutta of Anglo-Indian parents, he came to England in 1817, and was educated at private schools and, from 1822 to 1828, at Charterhouse, the 'Slaughterhouse' and 'Grey Friars' of his fiction. He spent two dissolute years at Trinity College, Cambridge, where he fell in with a fast set and lost heavily at cards, leaving in 1830 without taking a degree. A holiday visit to Paris in 1829 gave him a lifelong love of the city, and in 1830-1 he travelled to Germany and spent six months at Weimar, where he met Goethe. This was followed by spells as a law student in London and as Paris correspondent of the *National Standard* newspaper, which failed in 1834. The prospect of a life of gentlemanly ease was shattered when Thackeray lost most of his patrimony in the Indian bank failures of 1833, and he decided to make his living as a painter, for which he had some apti-

William Makepeace Thackeray: an engraving from the portrait by Samuel Laurence, *c. 1850*

tude, studying art in London and, from 1834 to 1837, in Paris. In 1836 he published his first book, lithograph caricatures of the ballet 'La Sylphide' entitled *Flore et Zéphyr*, and on the strength of his post as Paris correspondent of *The Constitutional*, a short-lived radical newspaper set up by his stepfather, he married Isabella Shawe, the young and mentally unstable daughter of an expatriate Anglo-Irish family.

Thackeray returned to London in 1837, where his daughter (later to attain some literary fame as ANNE THACKERAY RITCHIE) was born in June. A second daughter followed in 1838, but died eight months later, and in 1840 Harriet Marian ('Minny'), future wife of LESLIE STEPHEN, was born. By 1840 signs of his wife's incipient insanity were unmistakable, and she had to be confined. Forced to write for a living, Thackeray contributed a stream of reviews, comic sketches, PARODIES and SATIRES to a number of periodicals, most notably FRASER'S MAGAZINE and, from 1842, PUNCH. For *Fraser's* he wrote THE YELLOWPLUSH PAPERS (1837-8), the comic memoirs of a footman, CATHERINE (1839–40), a pastiche of the NEWGATE NOVEL, *A SHABBY GENTEEL STORY* (1840) and *THE GREAT*

HOGGARTY DIAMOND (1841). Many of his early works appeared under such pseudonyms as Charles James Yellowplush, a footman, Michael Angelo Titmarsh (after Thackeray's sketching talent and broken nose), and George Savage Fitz-Boodle, the heavy, tobacco-addicted clubman who is the autobiographical subject of *The Fitz-Boodle Papers* (1842-3) and the editor of Thackeray's first real novel, *BARRY LYNDON*, serialized in *Fraser's* in 1844. At this period Thackeray also published three travel books: THE PARIS SKETCH BOOK (1840), THE IRISH SKETCH BOOK (1843) and NOTES OF A JOURNEY FROM CORNHILL TO GRAND CAIRO (1846).

Thackeray's growing reputation in the 1840s was consolidated by his writings for *Punch*, especially the highly successful BOOK OF SNOBS (1846-7), which anatomized the class-consciousness of the early Victorian age. This concern, and the discontent with contemporary fictional stereotypes evident in his masterly parody, PUNCH'S PRIZE NOVELISTS (1847), are reflected in the satirical, anti-heroic vision of his first major novel, VANITY FAIR (1847-8), published in the monthly-part form which DICKENS had revived. An immediate popular and critical success, *Vanity Fair* was followed by THE HISTORY OF PENDENNIS (1848–50), a semi-autobiographical BILDUNGSROMAN portraying one of 'the gentlemen of our age'. In 1848 Thackeray became attached to Jane Brookfield, the wife of a college friend, but their platonic relationship was brought to an end by her in 1851, and some of the melancholy of unfulfilled love enters THE HISTORY OF HENRY ESMOND (1852), the most carefully planned of his novels and the only one to be published originally in the three-volume format. A historical novel, *Esmond* also reflects Thackeray's growing interest in the reign of Queen Anne. In 1851 he gave a series of lectures on THE ENGLISH HUMORISTS OF THE EIGHTEENTH CENTURY (published 1853), and made them the basis of his first lecture tour of the United States in 1852-3. THE NEWCOMES (1853-5), a panoramic novel of English social life during the first half of the 19th century, was followed by *The Rose and the Ring* (1855), the last and best of his six Christmas Books. On a second visit to the United States in 1855–6 he lectured on *THE FOUR GEORGES* (1860). *THE VIRGINIANS*, another historical novel continuing the Esmond family saga in 18th-century England and America, was published in monthly parts in 1857–9.

In 1859 Thackeray became the founding editor of *THE CORNHILL MAGAZINE*, a monthly literary journal set up by the publisher GEORGE SMITH and launched with great success in January 1860. Now plagued by recurrent ill health, he found editorial duties irksome, and resigned in 1862. His last works were published in the *Cornhill*: a short novel, *LOVEL THE WIDOWER* (1860), the discursive essays gathered as *The Roundabout Papers* (1860–3), and his last complete novel, *THE ADVENTURES OF PHILIP* (1861–2). *DENIS DUVAL* (1864) was left unfinished.

Thackeray's reputation rests on *Vanity Fair, Henry Esmond* and, less securely, *Pendennis* and *The Newcomes*. The authorial garrulity of his later fiction and essays, his sense of the novel as 'a sort of confidential talk between writer and reader', has not always been congenial to modern taste, but recent critics have rediscovered the keen satirical eye and comic irreverence of his early stories and travel books, which have the robust energy of the 18th-century writers he admired. Thackeray remains a central figure in the history of Victorian REALISM, and his sceptical, ironic but compassionate vision of human conduct in a society dominated by the power of money and class gives his best work the authority of major art.

Theatre, The The first purpose-built public playhouse in England. Situated in Shoreditch, London, it was opened in 1576 as a commercial speculation by James Burbage, actor and master carpenter. It became the favourite home of the Lord Chamberlain's Men, to which SHAKESPEARE belonged. When Burbage's lease ran out in 1597, his sons, together with other members of the acting company, dismantled it and carried its timbers over the Thames as building material for the GLOBE THEATRE.

Theatre of Cruelty See CRUELTY, THEATRE OF.

Theatre of the Absurd See ABSURD, THEATRE OF THE.

Their Eyes were Watching God A novel by ZORA NEALE HURSTON, published in 1937. The story centres on Janie Crawford, a strong-willed seeker of beauty who is unwilling to lead an existence of drudgery and deprivation like that of the grandmother who raised her. She suffers through a marriage of convenience, finally leaving her husband for the smooth-talking and handsome visionary, Joe Starks. Janie and Joe establish Florida's first all-black town and Joe becomes its mayor. Following Joe's death Janie is left financially secure, fortyish, and sexually, romantically and spiri-

tually oppressed. Rather than settle into comfortable widowhood, she falls passionately in love with Vergible Woods (known to everyone as Tea Cake), who is several years younger and penniless. Against friends' advice, she goes off with Tea Cake and marries him. Their marriage provides her with the idyllic love she had dreamed of but it ends tragically. Following a violent hurricane, Tea Cake is bitten by a rabid dog and contracts the disease. When, in his frenzy, he attacks Janie, she is forced to shoot him in self-defence. She is charged with murder, but quickly exonerated. She returns, saddened but victorious, to the town she and Joe Starks had founded. The novel openly confronts the issues of civil and social rights in both a racial and a feminist context.

Theobald, Lewis 1688–1744 Scholar and playwright. An exact contemporary of ALEXANDER POPE, he was born at Sittingbourne, Kent, and became an attorney before turning to literature.

Theobald's earliest work was a Pindaric ode on the Union of England and Scotland in 1707. He then turned to translation as the readiest way to make money, producing versions of Plato's *Phaedo* (1713), plays by Sophocles and Aristophanes (1714–15) and the first Book of the *Odyssey* (1716). He wrote 'The Censor' for *Mist's Journal*, which brought him into conflict with JOHN DENNIS. Between 1715 and 1720 Theobald turned his hand to many forms: tragedy (*The Persian Princess* and *The Perfidious Brother*, 1715), prose romance (*The Loves of Antiochus and Stratonice*, 1717), opera (*Pan and Syrinx*, 1717; *The Lady's Triumph*, 1718), MASQUE (*Decius and Paulina*, 1718), biography (*A Memoir of Sir Walter Raleigh*, 1719) and Shakespearean adaptation (of *RICHARD II*, 1720). He also played an important role in the history of the PANTOMIME, writing several for John Rich, manager of DRURY LANE: *The Rape of Proserpine, Harlequin a Sorcerer* (both 1725), *Perseus and Andromache* (1730) and *Merlin: or, The Devil at Stonehenge* (1734). Irritated by Pope's 1725 edition of SHAKESPEARE, Theobald published *Shakespeare Restored: or, A Specimen of the Many Errors As Well Committed As Unamended by Mr Pope in his Late Edition of This Poet* (1726). This contains a number of fine emendations, which Pope incorporated in the second edition of 1728. Pope had not let this debt prevent him from satirizing Theobald as eel and swallow in *Peri Bathous* or from making him hero of the first *DUNCIAD* (1728). One of the works satirized in *Peri Bathous* was *The Double Falsehood* (produced 1727, published 1728), which Theobald claimed was by Shakespeare and derived from an old manuscript in his possession. Theobald never published his 'original', and the play may anticipate that tradition of Shakespearean forgery which became so strong later in the 18th century. (See also SHAKESPEARE APOCRYPHA.)

In 1728 Theobald published the first volume of the posthumous works of Pope's early friend WILLIAM WYCHERLEY; Pope pre-empted Theobald's second volume by publishing one himself. He failed to succeed EUSDEN as POET LAUREATE in 1730. In 1731 he wrote *Orestes*, a tragedy, and contracted with TONSON to produce an edition of Shakespeare, which appeared in seven volumes in 1734. It went through three editions between 1734 and 1757 and was reprinted four times between 1757 and 1773. Lack of funds drove him back to writing for the stage: GEORGE STEEVENS suggested that Theobald is the subject of HOGARTH's *The Distressed Poet* (1737). Theobald announced an edition of BEAUMONT and FLETCHER in 1742 and was working on this when he died. His efforts formed the basis of the 10-volume Beaumont and Fletcher published in 1750.

Theory of Moral Sentiments, The A treatise on ethics by ADAM SMITH, published in 1759 and derived from lectures at Glasgow University, where he was professor of moral philosophy. It investigates the forms and objects of moral consciousness. Smith recognizes the social factor in morality, and identifies sympathy as a source of moral sentiments. Sympathy can have real value only when it comes from an 'impartial and well-informed spectator' and such a spectator is an ideal, not an actual person. In ordinary life self-interest or imperfect understanding frequently affects our attitudes.

Theron Ware, The Damnation of A novel by HAROLD FREDERIC, published in 1896. Its British title was *Illumination*. It tells the story of a talented young Methodist minister's growing disillusionment with conservative, small-town life in upstate New York, and his attraction for exotic, sophisticated ideas which in the end prove disastrous for him.

Through his friendships with Dr Ledsmar, a scientist, Father Forbes, a Catholic priest, and Celia Madden, the beautiful Catholic church organist, Theron Ware becomes fascinated with experimental science, biblical criticism and aesthetics, which, together with the lifestyles of his new acquaintances, represent for him a new sort of intellectual and personal freedom outside his narrow Methodist experience. He becomes increasingly detached from his wife and congregation, and increasingly drawn to the beautiful and free-spirited Celia; a series of exciting encounters between the two culminate in a kiss at a church picnic. Elated, Theron follows Celia to New York and calls on her in her hotel room, but she upbraids him for spying on her and taking a prurient interest in her affairs. Devastated by her rejection and by the realization that he has misunderstood her apparent freedom – it rests on a tradition of spirituality and church institutions that are foreign to him – Theron falls ill. When he eventually recovers, he and his wife go west to Seattle, where he will try to go into business and perhaps into politics.

Theroux, Paul 1941– Novelist, short-story writer and travel writer. Born in Massachusetts, he wrote his first novel, *Waldo* (1967), in the USA before beginning an extended stay as a university lecturer in East Africa. He now lives in Britain. He first captured attention with vivid, opinionated travel books about train journeys: *The Great Railway Bazaar* (1975), an account of a ride across Europe and Russia to Japan; *The Old Patagonian Express* (1978), about South America; and *Riding the Iron Rooster* (1988), about China. *The Kingdom by the Sea* (1983) tours the coast of the British Isles and *The Happy Isles of Oceania* (1992) explores the South Pacific. His witty, stylish fiction essays many genres. *Girls at Play* (1969) and *Jungle Lovers* (1971) are tales of naive Westerners in Africa; *Saint Jack* (1973) is a vigorous PICARESQUE about a Singapore pimp; *The Family Arsenal* (1976) is an atmospheric London thriller; and *The Consul's File* (1977) and *The London Embassy* (1982) are collections of linked stories about expatriate communities in Malaya and London. *The Mosquito Coast* (1981), set in the Honduran jungle, is a graphic parable of civilization courting barbarism and *My Secret History* (1989) is an ambitious BILDUNGSROMAN. Other fiction includes *Doctor Slaughter* (1985), the dystopian fantasy *O-Zone* (1986) and *Chicago Loop* (1990). *Sinning with Annie* (1975) and *World's End* (1980) are among his collections of short stories.

Thersites A comedy sometimes attributed to NICHOLAS UDALL, first acted in 1537 and printed *c.* 1562. It was adapted from the Latin of Ravisins Textor, a French scholar whose text was acted at Queens' College, Cambridge, in 1543. The setting is the siege of Troy. The English version introduces allusions to ROBIN HOOD into the story of Thersites, who persuades Mulciber (Vulcan) to make him a suit of armour that will render him invulnerable. Thersites puts the armour on and immediately begins to defy young and old, heaven and hell – but runs to his mother for protection when threatened by another soldier and is completely demoralized by a snail. Eventually he abandons his splendid armour and deserts the field.

Things Fall Apart CHINUA ACHEBE's first novel, published in 1958. He began it in reaction to the African novels of JOSEPH CONRAD and JOYCE CARY, seeking to tell the story of Nigeria from the inside. It depicts the coming of British missionaries and colonial administrators to Umuofia, an Igbo village in Eastern Nigeria, in the last decade of the 19th century and concentrates particularly on the fall of Okonkwo. Originally a wealthy elder, he becomes progressively discredited until he is imprisoned for his role in burning the new church. He kills a messenger sent by the new District Commissioner and commits suicide. Achebe's depiction of an intricate, finely balanced social structure based on oral traditions, his use of proverbs, folk tales, anecdotes and local imagery to convey a non-literary agrarian culture, and his ironic portrayal of the colonial encounter set an influential new pattern for African writing. *Things Fall Apart* has sold millions of copies on the African continent and been translated into more than 50 languages.

Thirlwall, Connop 1797–1875 Historian. He was born in London and educated at Charterhouse and Trinity College, Cambridge, of which he became a Fellow in 1818. He studied law at Lincoln's Inn, but eventually decided on the church and became Bishop of St David's in 1840. With J. C. Hare he translated Barthold Niebuhr's *History of Rome* (1828–42). His principal work was *A History of Greece* (8 vols., 1835–44), overshadowed by the work of his former schoolfellow, GEORGE GROTE.

Thomas, Audrey 1935– Canadian novelist and short-story writer. Born in New York State and educated at Smith College, Massachusetts, she moved to England before emigrating to Canada in 1959. In 1964–6 she lived in Ghana, returning to British Columbia in 1967, where she has lived since. She has travelled extensively in Mexico and Europe, and was the first Canadian woman writer-in-residence at the University of Edinburgh in 1985-6. Her first short story was published in 1965 in THE ATLANTIC MONTHLY and her first collection, *Ten Green Bottles*, in New York in 1967. She has since published several more collections, including *Real Mothers* (1981), *Goodbye Harold, Good Luck* (1986) and *The Wide Blue Yonder* (1990). Her novels include *Mrs Blood* (1970), *Songs My Mother Taught Me* (1973) and *Blown Figures* (1975), which form a trilogy centred on one female protagonist; *Latakia* (1979), set in Crete, Greece and Syria; and *Intertidal Life* (1985), set on Galiano Island, British Columbia. Her fiction is eclectic and influenced by POST-MODERNISM; it is also strongly feminist in its exploration of women's ambitions and self-contradictions as they seek to redefine relationships between men and women.

Thomas, Augustus 1857–1934 American playwright. He was born in St Louis, Missouri. Much of his work depends on a specific locality for its effect: *Alabama* (1891), *In Mizzoura* (1893), *Arizona* (1899), *Colorado* (1901) and *Rio Grande* (1916). His greatest success, *The Copperhead* (1918), is about an Illinois farmer who helps President Lincoln by pretending to be a supporter of the Confederacy. *The Witching Hour* (1907) and *The Harvest Moon* (1909) reflect his interest in mindreading and hypnotism. He also dramatized FRANCES HODGSON BURNETT's *Editha's Burglar* as *The*

Burglar (1899) and RICHARD HARDING DAVIS's *Soldiers of Fortune* (in collaboration with the author; 1902). *The Print of My Remembrance* (1922) is his autobiography.

Thomas, (Walter) Brandon 1856–1914 Actor and playwright. He made his stage debut in 1879, supplementing his income by writing and singing 'coon-songs' in London music halls. Of the many plays he wrote, mainly in collaboration, only the eighth is remembered. This was the immensely popular FARCE, *CHARLEY'S AUNT* (1892), which opened in Bury St Edmunds before running for four years at London's Royalty Theatre.

Thomas, D(onald) M(ichael) 1935– Novelist, poet and translator. Born in Redruth, Cornwall, he read English at New College, Oxford, and has worked as a teacher and lecturer. His early collections, *Personal and Possessive* (1964), *Two Voices* (1968) and *Logan Stone* (1971), feature erotic poems, science-fiction ballads and Cornish lyrics. Later collections, such as the autobiographical *The Shaft* (1973), *Love and Other Deaths* (1975), *The Honeymoon Voyage* (1978) and *Dreaming in Bronze* (1981) develop greater depth and range. *Selected Poems* appeared in 1983. He has also published translations from the Russian of Anna Akhmatova, Yevtushenko and Pushkin.

His preoccupation with the Freudian concepts of 'Eros' and 'Thanatos' gained him a wide public in his controversial novel *The White Hotel* (1981), a pastiche of a Freudian case history in which the protagonist's neuroses are shown to have been premonitory of her eventual mutilation and death in the Babi Yar massacre. Other novels include *The Flute Player* (1979), *Birthstone* (1980), a *Russian Quartet* consisting of *Ararat* (1983), *Swallow* (1984), *Sphinx* (1986) and *Summit* (1987), *Lying Together* (1990) and *Flying into Love* (1992), which meditates on the assassination of John F. Kennedy. *Memories and Hallucinations* (1988) is a sexually candid autobiography.

Thomas, Dylan (Marlais) 1914–53 Poet. Born in Swansea, South Wales, and educated at Swansea Grammar School, where his father taught English, he began writing poetry during childhood. He left school in 1931 and worked as a reporter, writing prolifically in his spare time. He moved to London in 1934 and his first book, *18 Poems*, appeared the same year. *Twenty-five Poems* (1936) attracted the attention of EDITH SITWELL and other poets and critics. Thomas married Caitlin Macnamara in 1937. Rejected as unfit for military service, he spent the war years in London, working as a scriptwriter and broadcaster for the BBC. He published two volumes of stories, *The Map of Love* (1939) and *Portrait of the Artist as a Young Dog* (1940), as well as *New Poems* (1943), which, together with his broadcast work, established his popular reputation.

Dylan Thomas

Two further volumes, *Deaths and Entrances* (1946) and *In Country Sleep* (1952), were followed by *Collected Poems* (1953), which was received rapturously by both critics and the public. Thomas undertook extensive reading-tours of the USA, mainly for financial reasons, in 1950, 1952 and 1953. His readings drew large audiences and the tours confirmed Thomas's reputation both as an extraordinarily charismatic reader of poetry and as a charming but disruptive and hard-drinking Bohemian. They also took a severe toll of his already fragile health. None the less, he wrote his 'play for voices', UNDER MILK WOOD, in 1952 and revised it for performance during his final tour in 1953. He also met Stravinsky, for whom he hoped to write a libretto. In October 1953 he returned, ill and exhausted, for a fourth visit to the USA, and died of alcoholic poisoning in New York the following month.

Overpraised during his lifetime, Thomas's work has since suffered critical disparagement. His elaborate and frequently obscure style, influenced centrally by HOPKINS and more marginally by psychoanalysis and surrealism, deploys religious, archetypal and biological imagery in rhetorical patterns to evoke an exuberant, pantheistic mysticism. The poems are romantic in their idiosyncratic individualism, their delight in emotion, and their ideal-

ization of natural energies. Many of them offer interesting verbal textures, and though some critics have found them sentimental or pretentious they retain a wide popular readership. A few at least of his poems – among them 'The Force that through the Green Fuse Drives the Flower', 'And Death Shall Have No Dominion', 'Do Not Go Gentle into That Good Night' and 'Fern Hill' – seem likely to remain popular, as does *Under Milk Wood*.

Thomas, Edward (Philip) 1878–1917 Poet, critic, biographer and writer on nature. Born in London soon after his parents had moved from Tredegar, Wales, he was educated at St Paul's School and Lincoln College, Oxford. Beginning with *The Woodland Life* (1897), he established himself as a full-time writer with a voluminous output, producing more than 40 books before his early death and regarding much of what he published as hackwork. His prose identified him as a nature writer in the tradition of RICHARD JEFFERIES and GEORGE BORROW, of whom he wrote critical biographies (1909 and 1912 respectively). He turned his walking tours into *The Heart of England* (1906), *The South Country* (1909), *The Icknield Way* (1913) and *In Pursuit of Spring* (1914). These travel narratives combine natural observation with passages of reflective description and an allegorical search for the spirit of England, which became one of the central themes of his poetry. He produced editions of GEORGE HERBERT (1908), CHRISTOPHER MARLOWE (1909), *Celtic Stories* (1911) and *Norse Tales* (1912). His studies of Maurice Maeterlinck (1911) and LAFCADIO HEARN (1912) included some acute criticism of SYMBOLISM, while his books on SWINBURNE (1912) and WALTER PATER (1913) argue against what he called these 'modern English half-martyrs, half-heroes of style'. He also wrote widely as a reviewer, and became part of a circle of friends which included W. H. DAVIES, WALTER DE LA MARE, JOSEPH CONRAD, ARTHUR RANSOME and ROBERT FROST. After the outbreak of World War I he joined the Artists' Rifles in 1915 and was killed two years later.

All his poetry belongs to the last two and a half years of his life. Two prose experiments, *The Happy-Go-Lucky Morgans* (1913) and *The Childhood of Edward Thomas* (1938), preceded his discovery of a poetic form without 'the exaggerations of rhetoric'. Following a breakdown in 1911, the consequent elucidation of his own ideas about poetry in his criticism, and conversations with Robert Frost, he began in November 1914 to convert prose notes into the blank verse of 'Up in the Wind'. His characteristically subtle, quizzical poetry frequently used material from his nature writings, but with World War I providing a dark, metaphorical counterpart to the Kent and Wiltshire countryside. His landscapes become, like the past, something elusive and vulnerable to destruction. EDWARD GARNETT thought the plain diction and irregular rhythm 'puzzling', and Thomas had much difficulty in finding a publisher. Twenty-seven poems appeared under the pseudonym of Edward Eastaway in *An Anthology of New Verse* in early 1917. *Poems* 'by E. E.' appeared posthumously in October 1917, followed by *Last Poems* (1918). The definitive *Collected Poems of Edward Thomas* (1978), edited by R. George Thomas, is the fullest of several collections which progressively established his reputation as a poet. His wife Helen Thomas wrote two memoirs, *As It Was* (1926) and *World without End* (1931).

Thomas, Lord Cromwell *(The True Chronicle History of the Whole Life and Death of Thomas, Lord Cromwell)* A chronicle play published in 1602. Because its title-page gave the author as 'W.S.', it was for a time proposed as the work of SHAKESPEARE but scholarship has rejected the attribution. See also SHAKESPEARE APOCRYPHA.

Thomas, R(onald) S(tuart) 1913- Poet. Born in Cardiff, he was educated at the University College of North Wales, Bangor, where he read classics, and St Michael's College, Llandaff, where he studied theology. He was ordained a clergyman in the Church of Wales in 1937, and has subsequently worked in rural parishes. His first major book, *Song at the Year's Turning: Poems 1942–54* (1955), which collected earlier volumes, contains the first of his 'Iago Prytherch' poems. *Poetry for Supper* (1958), *Tares* (1961), *The Bread of Truth* (1963), *Pietà* (1966) and *Not That He Brought Flowers* (1968) display his rich early style, with its straightforward yet unexpected images. *H'm* (1972) is the major flowering of his later style, increasingly economical in language and vulnerable because its fragility risks more. He has developed away from rootedness in a particular landscape towards ALLEGORY and prophecy. Subsequent volumes – *Young and Old* (1972), *Laboratories of the Spirit* (1975), *The Way of It* (1977), *Frequencies* (1978), *Between Here and Now* (1981) and *Counterpoint* (1990) – have disappointed many admirers of his early work. Honesty is Thomas's strength. His typically Welsh eschewal of the easy comforts of church polity gives much of his work a granitic vein. He attacks the hypocrisy with which people surround their lives, believing that the poet's task is to make them see a certain amount of reality. At the same time, he sets their pattern of life against a created world which, for all its grimness, is still 'stubborn with beauty'. The regular and traditional forms he prefers allow that beauty to emerge unromanticized and unmolested by showmanship. He remains the leading Anglo-Welsh poet since the death of DAVID JONES. There are two selections: *Selected Poems 1946–1968* (1973; reissued 1986) and *Later Poems: A Selection* (1983). *Selected Prose* appeared in 1986.

Thompson, Edward 1886-1946 Poet and critic. Born and educated at Bath, he entered the Wesleyan Methodist ministry in 1909 and served in Bengal as a missionary teacher (1910–23) except for an interval as an army chaplain during World War I. He became a lecturer in Bengali at Oxford (1923–33) and was later made research Fellow in Indian history (1936–46). He had some reputation as a poet (his *Collected Poems* appeared in 1930) and as an interpreter of India. Among his books were *A History of India* and *An Indian Day* (both 1927), *A Farewell to India* (1930) and a study of TAGORE (1926).

Thompson, Flora (Jane) 1876-1947 Writer on rural life. Born Flora Timms at Juniper Hill, near Brackley, on the boundary between Oxfordshire and Northamptonshire, she went to school in nearby Cottisford and began work at the age of 14 as a Post Office clerk in Fringford. She later worked at Grayshott in Hampshire, and, after her marriage to another Post Office worker, John Thompson, worked in Bournemouth (1903–16), Liphook (1916–28) and Dartmouth. She began writing in Bournemouth, contributing essays and poems to magazines and later publishing a volume of verse, *Bog Myrtle and Peat* (1921). She is famous, though, for the subtle and unsentimentally precise evocation of the rural culture of her childhood in *Lark Rise to Candleford* (1945), a trilogy originally issued as *Lark Rise* (1939), *Over to Candleford* (1941) and *Candleford Green* (1943). *Still Glides the Stream*, posthumously published in 1948, weaves memories again drawn from childhood into a fictional story.

Thompson, Francis 1859-1907 Poet. Born in Preston, Lancashire, and educated at Ushaw College, he abandoned his first ambition of becoming a Roman Catholic priest and spent six years at Owens College (now the University of Manchester) in an unsuccessful attempt to become a doctor. In 1885 he went to London, rapidly sinking into opium addiction and destitution. He was rescued by ALICE MEYNELL and her husband Wilfred, the editor of *Merry England*, to which Thompson first submitted his poems on ragged scraps of paper in 1887. After meeting him in 1888, they took charge of his life and work: finding him lodgings, introducing him to other writers, encouraging and publishing his poetry, and placing his literary criticism in *The Academy* and THE ATHENAEUM. Despite their care and despite retreats at monasteries in Sussex and Wales, Thompson never fully recovered, dying from the combined effects of opium addiction and tuberculosis.

He published three volumes of poetry, *Poems* (1893), *Sister Songs* (1895) and *New Poems* (1897). The best-known example of his ornate, densely metaphorical style is 'The Hound of Heaven', which appeared in the first volume; it describes his flight from and recapture by God. Thompson's prose writings include 'Health and Holiness' (1905) and an essay on SHELLEY (1909). A three-volume *Works* (1913) was edited by Wilfred Meynell.

Thompson, Hunter S(tockton) 1937– American journalist. Born in Louisville, Kentucky, he attended Columbia University and became a sports reporter in Florida. He has written for *Esquire* and *THE NATION* but is best known for his writing for *Rolling Stone*. An iconoclast and commentator on the wilder fringes of American culture, he joined JOAN DIDION and TOM WOLFE in pioneering the New Journalism in works such as *Hell's Angels* (1966), *Fear and Loathing in Las Vegas* (1971), *Fear and Loathing on the Campaign Trail* (1973), *The Great Shark Hunt* (1979), *Generations of Swine* (1988), *Songs of the Doomed* (1990) and *The Curse of Lono* (1991), one of several collaborations with the British cartoonist Ralph Steadman.

Thompson, Mervyn 1936–92 New Zealand playwright, producer, actor and teacher. He developed his own form, the 'song-play', in which song was at least as important as dialogue, and used it to dramatize aspects of New Zealand's social history. Early examples include *O! Temperance* (1974) and *A Night at the Races* (1977). *Songs to the Judges* (1980) turned the theatre into a courtroom for an ironic treatment of racism. *Coaltown Blues* (1986), about labour history, and *Passing Through* (1991) are solo works which he himself performed. *Selected Plays* appeared in 1984. Thompson also published an autobiography, *All My Lives* (1980).

Thomson, James 1700–48 Poet and playwright. He was born at Ednam, Roxburghshire, and educated at schools in Southdean and Jedburgh. In 1715 he entered Edinburgh University, where he joined a literary club, the Grotesques, and published pieces in *The Edinburgh Miscellany*. After his arrival in London in 1725 he acquired Lord Minto and Duncan Forbes of Culloden as patrons; the latter introduced him to ARBUTHNOT, POPE and GAY. He was also taken up by DAVID MALLET and became tutor to Thomas Hamilton, the son of Charles, Lord Binning. Thomson established his reputation with *THE SEASONS*, still the poem for which he is best remembered. It was originally published in separate parts: *Winter* in 1726, *Summer* in 1727 and *Spring* in 1728. *Autumn* appeared in the first collective edition of *The Seasons* in 1730, for which Arbuthnot, BOLINGBROKE, Pope, Spence and YOUNG subscribed. From 1738 onwards, aided perhaps by Pope and GEORGE LYTTELTON, Thomson made extensive revisions to the poem. A corrected and much enlarged edition appeared in 1744.

In 1730 Thomson produced his tragedy *Sophonisba* (with its famous line, 'Oh! Sophonisba, Sophonisba, Oh!'). He then became tutor to Charles Talbot and es-

corted him around Europe. After Talbot's untimely death his father gave Thomson the first of his sinecures, the Secretaryship of Briefs. He retired to live at Richmond, where he is said to have grown so sybaritic that he ate 'the sunny side off the peaches in his garden with his hands in his pockets'. *Liberty*, a lengthy patriotic poem published in instalments between 1734 and 1736, was remarkable for its HYPERBOLE and its failure to sell. After Talbot's death in 1737, Thomson turned again to the stage with a series of tragedies. Pope attended the first night of *Agamemnon* in 1738, but *Edward and Eleanora* was never acted. *Tancred and Sigismunda* enjoyed a vogue in 1745, and *Coriolanus* was performed posthumously in 1749 with his old friend James Quin in the leading role. Lyttelton, Thomson's new patron, secured him a pension of £100 a year from the Prince of Wales and he responded suitably by collaborating with Mallet on a MASQUE, *Alfred* (1740), which included 'Rule Britannia'. (Mallet later laid claim to the ODE but it was in fact by Thomson.) In 1748 he published the poem he had been working on for 15 years: *THE CASTLE OF INDOLENCE*, an ALLEGORY written in SPENSERIAN STANZAS and admired by GRAY. He died after catching a chill in a rowing-boat and was buried in Richmond parish church. WILLIAM COLLINS commemorated him in his ode 'In Yonder Grave a Druid Lies'.

Thomson, James 1834–82 Poet and essayist. Born in Port Glasgow, the son of an Irvingite mother and a merchant seaman, Thomson was educated at the Royal Caledonian Asylum, Hertfordshire, in 1842–50 and at the 'model school' of the Royal Military Asylum, Chelsea, in 1850–1, where he prepared to qualify as an army schoolmaster. Shortly afterwards he was sent to Ballincollig, Cork, as a student teacher in a garrison school. Here he fell deeply in love with Matilda Weller whose early death in 1853 accentuated his melancholia and influenced the writing of his poem *The Doom of a City* (1857). During his Irish period he also formed a friendship with the rationalist Charles Bradlaugh, whose atheistic ideas coloured Thomson's thought and work. A schoolmaster from 1854 to 1862, Thomson was dismissed from the service for a trifling breach of discipline and subsequently served briefly as a solicitor's clerk. In 1872 secretaryship to a wildcat gold and silvermine company took him to the western United States and 1873 found him correspondent in Spain for *The New York World*.

Despite his psychological handicaps, Thomson was surprisingly prolific both in poetry and prose. In the 1860s and early 1870s he wrote for Bradlaugh's *National Reformer*, often under the pseudonym B. V. (Bysshe Vanolis), and it was in that magazine that his masterpiece, *THE CITY OF DREADFUL NIGHT*, first appeared in 1874. It appeared in book form in 1880, followed by *Vane's Story, Weddah and Om-el-Bonain and Other Poems* (also 1880), *Essays and Phantasies*(1881) and *A Voice from the Nile and Other Poems* and *Satires and Profanities* (both 1884). There were also many reviews, translations from Heine, and essays on divers subjects, for Thomson wrote for *The Secularist, The London Investigator, The Liberal* and many other publications.

Thomson had a vein of realistic humour, apparent in 'Sunday at Hampstead' and 'Sunday up the River'; other verses show romantic yearnings after beauty, autobiographical glimpses, speculations on faith and atheism, and satirical barbs. But he was above all a poet of despair. His vision of life as futile and man as trapped in loneliness and desolation makes him an expressive voice of late Victorian pessimism.

Thoreau, Henry David 1817–62 American man of letters. Born in Concord, Massachusetts, he spent most of his life in the area as a writer, teacher, essayist and orator, earning extra income by working as a gardener, pencil-maker and surveyor.

While attending Concord Academy and Harvard, he became known as an individualist who was often scornful of authority. Nevertheless, he was much influenced by many of the men he encountered during those years: EDWARD CHANNING, ORESTES BROWNSON, and especially RALPH WALDO EMERSON. Shortly after his graduation from Harvard in 1837, he and his brother John opened their own school in Concord, and operated it according to the principles of TRANSCENDENTALISM. When John became fatally ill in 1841, Henry was unable to find another position, whereupon he lived in Emerson's home as a handyman. It was Emerson who encouraged him to keep the journals which form the basis of most of his major writings.

By this time Thoreau had already contributed several pieces to the Transcendentalist journal, THE DIAL; and he was also an occasional speaker at the Concord Lyceum, which he had started in 1838. His mature writing, however, dates from the two-year period (1845–7) when he lived at Walden Pond. There he put into final form *A WEEK ON THE CONCORD AND MERRIMACK RIVERS*(1849), based on a trip he took with his brother John in 1839. The experience at Walden itself, and the journal he kept there, became the source of *WALDEN* (1854), a lengthy autobiographical essay which sets forth many of his ideas on how the individual should live life to the best advantage of his nature and principles. Another of his best-known works, *ON THE DUTY OF CIVIL DISOBEDIENCE* (1849), reflects similar values: Thoreau was arrested in the summer of 1846 for refusing to pay his poll tax, and the night he spent in jail prompted his reflections on a man's moral right passively to resist an unjust law.

Most of his work was published after his death. Aware that he was dying of tuberculosis, he cut short

his therapeutic travels and returned to Concord, where he prepared some of his journals for publication. Selections from his manuscripts were edited and posthumously published as *The Maine Woods* (1864), *Cape Cod* (1865) and *A Yankee in Canada* (1866), all based on his various journeys. *Excursions* (1863) is a collection of pieces previously published in magazines. His letters were edited by Emerson and published in 1865 (enlarged 1894). *Poems of Nature* appeared in 1895, *Collected Poems* in 1943. Thoreau's immense collection of journals was published in 1906.

Three Clerks, The A novel by ANTHONY TROLLOPE, published in three volumes in 1858. It offers a lively picture of the Civil Service undergoing the Victorian reforms and also a self-portrait of the young Trollope in Charley Tudor.

Harry Norman and Alaric Tudor, of the prestigious Weights and Measures office, and Alaric's cousin Charley Tudor are regular visitors at the home of the widowed Mrs Woodward and her three daughters. Harry loves the eldest, Gertrude, but is supplanted by the ambitious Alaric, who is also promoted above him through success in the new system of competitive examination which has been introduced in the Civil Service. Alaric and Gertrude marry, but desire to succeed leads him to speculate in shares and then to embezzle a trust fund, for which he is tried and imprisoned. Alaric's rise and fall contrasts with the struggles of Charley, an honest scapegrace, to extricate himself from debt and an imprudent entanglement with an Irish barmaid, Norah Geraghty. Harry marries the second Woodward girl, Linda, and settles down as a country squire. Charley marries the third, Katie, and wins promotion to the Weights and Measures office. Alaric and his family emigrate to Australia.

Three Hours after Marriage A comedy in three acts written collectively by GAY, POPE and ARBUTHNOT and performed with no great success in 1717. Partly a FARCE and partly a dramatized Varronian SATIRE, the play takes as targets for its humour the characteristic concerns of the SCRIBLERUS CLUB: pedantry, credulity and intellectual pretensions. It is densely written (the three playwrights observing the three unities of the three hours of action in three acts) and the plot turns on a number of elaborate metamorphoses and disguises. A jealous old man, Fossile, marries a younger wife, Townley, in secret at the start of the play; his moonstruck niece, Phoebe the poetess, reads her newest play to Sir Tremendous (the critic, JOHN DENNIS); Fossile intercepts amorous notes to his new wife from Plotwell (played by COLLEY CIBBER) and decides to adopt various disguises to discover the fidelity of his spouse, posing as a footman, and then as Dr Lubomirski, a projector full of scientific gibberish.

His suspicion and jealousy lead him to absurd contrivances that culminate in two amorous beaux hiding in his private museum, Plotwell in a mummy and Underplot in an alligator. The satire being no longer topical, the chief interest of the play is that it contains the only formal dramatic writing by Pope, and that its production prompted backstage fisticuffs between Gay and Cibber, the latter having discovered his part of Plotwell to be a lampoon on himself.

Through the Looking-Glass and What Alice Found There A fantasy (1871) by LEWIS CARROLL, as successful as its predecessor, *ALICE'S ADVENTURES IN WONDERLAND*. Alice enters the back-to-front land behind the mirror, where she meets characters caught up like herself in a cosmic chess game. Favourites among them include the Red Queen, the White Queen, Tweedledum and Tweedledee, the White Knight and the Walrus and the Carpenter. Humpty Dumpty also makes an appearance, with his oft-quoted remark 'When I use a word it means just what I choose it to mean – neither more nor less.' Poems include the memorable, slightly sinister 'Jabberwocky'. The book was illustrated by SIR JOHN TENNIEL, despite his previous determination to have nothing further to do with so temperamental an author.

Thurber, James (Grover) 1894–1961 American humorist and cartoonist. He was born in Columbus, Ohio, and educated at Ohio State University. After working as a government clerk in Washington, he joined the embassy staff in Paris, and then became foreign correspondent for a Chicago newspaper. On his return to the USA he worked on the staff of *THE NEW YORKER* (1927–33) and continued after that as a regular contributor. In both his drawings and writings Thurber expressed the dilemma of the moral innocent in a complex modern world. A direct and disarming humorist, he frequently satirized such subjects as psychoanalysis, sexual awareness, the search for identity and the problem of communication.

Probably his most famous short story is 'The Secret Life of Walter Mitty' (1932), about the escapist dreams of an average man. His collections of stories and sketches include *The Owl in the Attic, and Other Perplexities* (1931), *The Seal in My Bedroom, and Other Predicaments* (1932), *Let Your Mind Alone* (1937), *My World – And Welcome to It!* (1942) and *The Beast in Me, and Other Animals* (1948). With E. B. WHITE, his colleague on *The New Yorker*, he wrote *Is Sex Necessary?* (1929), and with Elliot Nugent he produced a successful comedy, *The Male Animal* (1940). *My Life and Hard Times* (1933) is autobiographical, and *The Years with Ross* (1959) a memoir of his years on the staff of *The New Yorker*. He also wrote several books for children, including *The Thirteen Clocks* (1950).

Thwaite, Anthony (Simon) 1930– Poet. Born in Chester, he was educated at Kingswood School, Bath, and, after national service, at Christ Church, Oxford. As well as having been the literary editor of *The New Statesman* and the co-editor of *ENCOUNTER*, he has taught in Japan and Libya and lectured abroad extensively for the British Council. His early work, in no. 17 of the Fantasy Poets series (1953), and in *Home Truths* (1957), is impersonal and aphoristic. His second collection, *The Owl in the Trees* (1963), captures items of everyday experience in tones of desolation and resignation. Like PHILIP LARKIN, Thwaite adopts a man-in-the-street persona and uses intricate stanzas and RHYME schemes. Later volumes, including *The Stones of Emptiness* (1967), *Inscriptions* (1973) and *New Confessions* (1974), based on St Augustine, develop towards the DRAMATIC MONOLOGUE. *A Portion for Foxes* (1977) is mainly lyric but *Victorian Voices* (1980) contains 14 monologues by 19th-century literary and historical figures which also have a strong confessional, autobiographical element. *Poems 1953–1983* (1984) sums up his poetic career. Thwaite has edited Larkin's collected poems (1988) and letters (1992).

Thyrsis: A Monody, to Commemorate the Author's Friend, Arthur Hugh Clough, Who Died at Florence, 1861 A poem by MATTHEW ARNOLD, published in *New Poems* (1867). In the form of a PASTORAL lament for CLOUGH, it recalls the Oxford countryside known to both men in their undergraduate days, a territory Arnold had earlier described in *THE SCHOLAR-GIPSY*.

Tickell, Thomas 1686–1740 Poet. A protégé of JOSEPH ADDISON, Tickell was educated at The Queen's College, Oxford, where he became a fellow. His poem, *On the Prospect of Peace* (1712), was widely read in the period leading to the Treaty of Utrecht in 1713. Tickell contributed to *THE GUARDIAN* and *THE SPECTATOR* and published a translation of the first book of the *Iliad* at the same time as POPE published his. Pope believed that Addison had prompted Tickell and quarrelled with him. Tickell went to Ireland with Addison in 1709 and became Secretary to the Lords Justice in Ireland. He held this post for the rest of his life and edited Addison's works when his patron died. His work is largely forgotten, though his elegy on Addison (1721) is sometimes remembered.

Ticket-of-Leave Man, The A MELODRAMA by TOM TAYLOR, first performed at the Olympic Theatre, London, in 1863. It is notable for its introduction of a stage detective, Hawkshaw, adept at disguise and more than a match for the leaders of London's underworld. His persistence exonerates the hero, Bob Brierly, a convict released on ticket-of-leave.

Till Eulenspiegel Eulenspiegel (Owlglass) was the name of a German peasant prankster, supposedly born *c.* 1300 in Brunswick. A collection of tales and jests grew up around his name, mainly of a farcical, broad and bawdy kind. In them Eulenspiegel is a cunning peasant who outwits the nobility, churchmen and townspeople. Stories connected with his name were probably first printed in German *c.* 1500; the earliest extant text is 1515. An English translation of some stories was printed at Antwerp *c.* 1510. The printer William Copland produced three editions, none of them dated: *Here Beginneth a Merry Jest of a Man that was Called Owlglass* was published *c.*1528.

Tillotson, John 1630–94 Archbishop of Canterbury. He achieved the position in 1691, after a career in which his latitudinarian views had frequently put him in conflict with his superiors. His literary importance lies in his sermons, the copyright of which his widow sold for the immense sum of 2500 guineas. They were frequently reprinted during the 18th century and had considerable influence on both theological thought and English prose style, not only in their own right but through borrowings by other sermon writers (such as STERNE). Rather than deliver their own work, some clergymen would simply read one of Tillotson's sermons, which in 1742–4 were published weekly, presumably with this trade in mind.

Tillyard, E(ustace) M(andeville) W(etenhall) 1889–1962 Critic. A Cambridge man by birth and lifelong residence, Tillyard was educated at the Perse School and studied classics at Jesus College, where he returned to a fellowship in 1913 after studying archaeology in Athens. After serving in France and Greece in World War I, he helped to establish the new school of English at Cambridge University, devoting his work to MILTON and SHAKESPEARE. He published five books on Milton, of which the best known are *Milton* (1930) and *The Miltonic Setting* (1938), and three on Shakespeare: *Shakespeare's Last Plays* (1938), *Shakespeare's History Plays* (1944) and *Shakespeare's Problem Plays* (1950). His best-known work, *The Elizabethan World-Picture* (1943), is a brief explanation of the late medieval concept of a 'chain of being' as the harmonious design of the universe. Tillyard became Master of Jesus College in 1945, and later wrote *The Muse Unchained* (1958), an account of the early days of the Cambridge English school. His other works include *The Personal Heresy* (with C. S. LEWIS; 1939) and *The English Epic and Its Tradition* (1954).

Timber: *or, Discoveries Made upon Men and Matter* The commonplace book of BEN JONSON, published in the posthumous folio edition of 1640, a fascinating collection of notes, mordant observations on human behaviour and morality, aphorisms, short essays on a variety of subjects, and adaptations of Latin originals. It is a valuable repository of the learning and wisdom of England's first great neoclassical critic and poet, continually demonstrating the breadth of his reading.

Time Machine, The A short novel by H. G. WELLS, developed by degrees from a series of speculative articles which he wrote in 1888 for *The Science Schools Journal*. The story appeared in two serial versions before book publication in 1895.

The central character, referred to throughout as the Time Traveller, tells a group of friends that he has invented a machine which can travel through time, enabling him to investigate the destiny of the human species. In the year 802,701, where he is temporarily stranded, he finds the meek and beautiful Eloi living in apparently idyllic circumstances, but discovers that they are the prey of the degenerate Morlocks, descendants of labourers who have lived underground for centuries. In later eras he sees the life-forms which survive the extinction of man, and 30 million years hence he is witness to the world's final decline as the sun cools. In his later writings Wells remained preoccupied with the need to save mankind from the kind of failure represented by the divided world of the Eloi and the Morlocks.

Time's Laughingstocks and Other Verses Poems by THOMAS HARDY, first published in 1909. Divided into four parts – 'Time's Laughingstocks', 'More Love Lyrics', 'A Set of Country Songs' and 'Pieces Occasional and Various' – this third volume of Hardy's verse, some of which had already appeared in British and American publications, is stamped with many personal associations and recollections of rural and family life. There are short poems about his parents and grandparents set beside love lyrics written during his young manhood; there are country songs celebrating Casterbridge Fair as well as a small handful of Dorset dialect poems. Several are BALLADS, including Hardy's own favourite, the powerful 'Trampwoman's Tragedy'. As in preceding volumes, the isolated incident, the minor key, the ironical flick, the robustly humorous and the poignancy of the unrealized in life inform one poem after another in these verses of bucolic memory and meditation.

Times Literary Supplement, The Originally, as its name suggests, a weekly section of *The Times* newspaper begun in 1902, the *TLS* became a separate paper in 1914. Its character and reputation were shaped by Bruce Richmond, the editor from 1903 to 1937, who commissioned reviews and articles from, among others, T. S. ELIOT, HERBERT READ, EDGELL RICKWORD and VIRGINIA WOOLF. Reviews were anonymous until John Gross abolished the practice on assuming the editorship in 1974. The *TLS* publishes poems by established writers, but is devoted chiefly to reviewing books across a wide range from fiction to science, politics, music and the other arts.

Timon of Athens

Timon of Athens A tragedy by WILLIAM SHAKESPEARE, first performed *c.* 1607 and published in the First Folio of 1623. Shakespeare probably found the story during his reading of Plutarch's life of Alcibiades, though he may also have known Lucian's satiric dialogue, *Timon misanthropus*.

Timon is a rich and noble Athenian whose generosity leaves him penniless. When he asks his rich friends for help he is denied, and he finds that those who formerly sought his company now avoid him. He invites them all to a banquet, where he serves them with dishes of water, which he throws in their faces. He curses the city of Athens, and leaves it, followed only by his faithful servant Flavius.

Now a committed misanthrope, Timon lives in a cave, where, digging for roots, he uncovers a hoard of gold. He is visited by the exiled Athenian general, Alcibiades, who is on the way to Athens with an avenging army. Timon gives him gold to pay his soldiers. He also rewards the loyalty of Flavius, whom he swears to silence as he gives him all that remains of his treasure. It is the bitter philosopher Apemantus who spreads news of Timon's sudden riches, but the Athenian senators who come to seek his help against Alcibiades are spurned. The victorious Alcibiades promises to destroy only those who are his own or Timon's enemies, but a soldier brings him news that Timon is dead, and Alcibiades decides to offer peace with mercy.

Timon of Athens is the least loved of Shakespeare's great tragedies, perhaps because the bitter pride which Timon shares with Coriolanus is too readily justified by his experience. Recent criticism has sought to establish for the play a quality which it has still to prove in the theatre.

Timrod, Henry 1828–67 American poet. He was born in Charleston, South Carolina, and educated at Franklin College (now the University of Georgia). Though he published a volume of poems in 1860, he was best known for his verse during the Civil War, which earned him the title of the 'Laureate of the Confederacy'; it was collected by his friend Paul Hamilton Hayne in 1872. *Katie*, a love poem addressed to his wife, was published in 1884 and *Complete Poems of Henry Timrod* in 1899. With Hayne, Basil Gildersleeve and WILLIAM GILMORE SIMMS he founded *Russell's Magazine* in Charleston in 1867, modelling it on *BLACKWOOD'S EDINBURGH MAGAZINE*.

Tindal, Matthew 1655–1733 Religious writer. Born in Devon and educated at Lincoln College and Exeter College, Oxford, he became a fellow of All Souls in 1678. After a brief period as a Catholic during the reign of James II, he returned to the Church of England in 1688 and thereafter became a leading proponent of DEISM. His most influential work, *Christianity as Old as the Creation: or, The Gospel a Republication of the Religion of Nature* (1730), argued that the Gospels neither added to nor detracted from the perfect and unchanging law of reason, but freed man from superstition. His other writings include *The Rights of the Christian Church Asserted against the Romish and All Other Priests Who Claim an Independent Power over It* (1706) and *A Defence of the Rights of the Christian Church* (1709).

'Tis Pity She's a Whore A tragedy by JOHN FORD, the finest example of his psychological intensity. There is no certainty of the date of its first performance, though it probably took place between 1625 and the year of the play's first printing, 1633. The central theme is the incestuous love of Giovanni and Annabella, a pure thing in the enveloping context of corruption. Only when she discovers that she is pregnant does Annabella agree to marry, in the vain hope of shielding her brother. But Soranzo, whom she selects from a trio of unsatisfactory suitors, is the most tainted. He interrupts his adulterous affair with Hippolita to court Annabella and rejects Hippolita, despite earlier assurances, when the death of her husband is announced. But the husband, Richardetto, is not dead. Suspecting his wife's faithlessness, he has disguised himself as a physician, and he now plans the murder of Soranzo. He enlists the help of the second of Annabella's suitors, the jealous Grimaldi, but they bungle the attempt on Soranzo's life, killing the third suitor, the harmlessly idiotic Bergetto, instead. At the feast to celebrate the wedding of Annabella and Soranzo, Hippolita's plan to poison him is foiled by Soranzo's clever servant, Vasques, who contrives that Hippolita drink the poison herself. It is again Vasques who discovers the identity of Annabella's lover and reveals it to Soranzo. The play's climax is the banquet at which Soranzo intends to expose his wife and Giovanni. Forewarned of Soranzo's scheme, Giovanni kills Annabella and arrives at the banquet carrying her heart. Defiantly proclaiming their love, he kills Soranzo and is, in turn, killed by Vasques.

Tithonus A DRAMATIC MONOLOGUE in BLANK VERSE by ALFRED TENNYSON, published by THACKERAY in *THE CORNHILL MAGAZINE* in 1860 and in a volume with *ENOCH ARDEN* in 1864. Its original form was the poem 'Tithon', which Tennyson wrote in 1833 as a companion piece to *ULYSSES* but did not publish. In Greek myth Tithonus was loved by Aurora (Eos), goddess of the dawn, who begged her father Zeus to grant him eternal life. Zeus agreed, but Aurora had neglected to ask for eternal youth as well and so Tithonus grew ever older without dying.

Titus Andronicus A tragedy by William SHAKESPEARE, perhaps written collaboratively. It was one of the earliest works with which his name was associated. Some critics have argued for a staging as early as 1590. It was published in Quarto (Q1) in 1594 and in the First Folio of 1623, where there is an additional scene. No certain source has been identified, although the influence of Seneca is manifest. The play is set in ancient Rome under the empire but is not related to any known emperor or historical event.

Titus Andronicus returns to Rome in triumph after defeating the Goths, whose queen Tamora and her three sons are among his prisoners. A chain of revenge is started when he sacrifices Tamora's eldest son to appease the spirits of his own dead sons. There follow, in relentless succession, acts of murder and violence which include the kidnapping of Titus's daughter Lavinia, the death of his son Mutius, the murder of the late emperor's son Bassianus, the rape and mutilation of Lavinia, the self-mutilation of Titus, the beheading of two more of his sons, the murder of Tamora's remaining sons and the use of their blood to make pies containing their severed heads, Titus's mercy-killing of Lavinia, his murder of Tamora after she has eaten the pies containing her sons' heads, the killing of Titus by the Emperor Saturninus and of Saturninus by Titus's remaining son, Lucius. Lucius is elected emperor by the people of Rome, and he decrees honourable burial for Saturninus, Titus and Lavinia. He also orders that the body of Tamora be thrown to the birds and beasts of prey and that her black-skinned and black-hearted lover Aaron be buried up to his neck and left to starve to death.

Titus Andronicus gives notice of Shakespeare's later achievements only at rare moments and in the gathering bewilderment and madness of Titus himself.

Tlali, Miriam (Masoli) 1933– South African novelist, short-story writer and essayist. Born into a working-class family in Doornfontein, Transvaal, she grew up in Sophiatown, attended the universities of Witwatersrand and Lesotho, and now lives in Soweto. She has published two novels: *Muriel at Metropolitan* (edited version 1975, fuller version 1979), about the daily experiences of a hire-purchase clerk who becomes aware of white racism and capitalist exploitation, and *Amandla* (1981), about the Soweto schoolchildren's rebellion of 1976 and its aftermath. Both books were banned in South Africa, as was 'The Point of No Return', one of her stories in *STAFFRIDER*. It was reprinted in *Mihloti* (1984), which otherwise contains journalism, interviews and travel pieces about the lives of black women under apartheid. *Footprints in the Quag: Stories and Dialogues from Soweto* (1989; as *Soweto Stories* in Britain) moves away from her earlier documentary mode.

To Kill a Mockingbird See LEE, HARPER.

To the Lighthouse A novel by VIRGINIA WOOLF, published in 1927.

There is little action. The novel works through STREAM OF CONSCIOUSNESS and imagery to create an atmospheric and impressionistic record of the characters' moment-by-moment experiences, tracing the conflict between male and female principles (see *A ROOM OF ONE'S OWN*) and making a statement about time, death and artistic transcendence.

Mr Ramsay is a tragic and self-pitying philosopher whose mind is rational but rather cold; Mrs Ramsay is a warm, creative and intuitive woman, the centre of the household. The first section, called 'The Window', describes a day during their summer holiday on the west coast of Scotland, where their guests include: a painter, Lily Briscoe; an ageing poet, Augustus Carmichael; a scientist, William Bankes; and a priggish young academic, Charles Tansley. The novel focuses on the conflict arising from young James Ramsay's desire to visit the lighthouse, and his father's quenching of this hope. The expedition takes on symbolic qualities and epitomizes the underlying tensions and differences of perspective between Mrs Ramsay and her husband.

In the second section, 'Time Passes', Mrs Ramsay has died, her eldest son, Andrew, has been killed in World War I, and the daughter, Prue, has died in childbirth. The Ramsays' seaside house lies deserted and desolate, but at the end of the section Lily Briscoe and Augustus Carmichael arrive to reawaken life.

Lily Briscoe assumes the 'visionary' mantle left by Mrs Ramsay, and during the final section ('The Lighthouse') Ramsay and his son, James, at last make the long-delayed voyage to the lighthouse. James, now 16 years old, is able to forgive his father and Lily Briscoe completes a painting which had been inspired by Mrs Ramsay. The mood at the end of the novel is one of muted optimism and triumph in which the two events, the visit to the lighthouse and the completion of the painting, are linked in Lily's mind: ' "He has landed," she said aloud. "It is finished." '

Toccata of Galuppi's, A A poem by ROBERT BROWNING in *Men and Women* (1855). The composer Baldassare Galuppi (1706–85) was organist of St Mark's Cathedral in Venice during the last years of his life; a toccata is a light piece of music displaying the musician's virtuosity. Browning's poem is designed to capture the rhythms of Galuppi's music, finding in them the decadent gaiety of Venice under Austrian rule in the 18th century.

Tocqueville, Comte Alexis de See *DEMOCRACY IN AMERICA*.

Toland, John 1670–1722 Philosopher and religious controversialist. Born in Donegal, he abandoned Roman Catholicism at the age of 16 and studied successively at the universities of Glasgow, Leiden and Oxford. His *Christianity Not Mysterious* (1696) made a vital contribution to DEISM by dismissing the 'mysteries' of Christianity as pagan intrusions maintained by the priesthood and arguing that God and his revelation were within the comprehension of all. Toland's subsequent writings showed the same gift for controversy and moved further away from orthodoxy. His biography of MILTON (1698) contained a passage thought to question the authenticity of the New Testament; he replied with *Amyntor: or, A Defence of Milton's Life*, published the following year. *Nazarenus: or, Jewish, Gentile and Mahometan Christianity* (1718) displayed his remarkable knowledge of the apocryphal literature of the early church. *Tetradymus* (1720) is a collection of essays on the natural explanation of biblical miracles. Toland coined the term 'pantheism', expressing the creed in *Pantheisticon* (1720).

Tolkien, J(ohn) R(onald) R(euel) 1892–1973 Scholar and writer of fantasy. Born in South Africa, where his father was a bank manager, Tolkien came to England at the age of three. Educated first in Birmingham then at Oxford University, he went on to have a distinguished academic career at Leeds University and from 1925 at Oxford, where he was Merton Professor of English (1945–59).

His expertise in Anglo-Saxon literature, particularly EPIC and folklore, and his fluency in medieval languages formed a natural background to his imaginative writing. *The Hobbit* (1937), developed from the stories he told his children at bedtime, is about an amiable type of gnome called Bilbo Baggins, unwillingly required to destroy a menacing dragon who preys on the idealized, rural community in which the story is set. On his journeys he meets both friends and foes drawn from folklore, epic poetry and the author's own richly-stocked imagination. Best-known among these characters are the Orcs, a dangerous breed of goblins, and Gandalf the benign wizard who helps Bilbo through his worst trials. The same characters and a similar quest to destroy evil – this time reluctantly undertaken by the hobbit Frodo – appear in *The Lord of the Rings* (3 vols., 1954–5), a much longer and more ambitious work which seeks to create a history and mythology for an unspecified period of the past which Tolkien calls 'Middle Earth'. Opposed at every turn by supernatural obstacles and almost let down at the last moment by his own essentially human vulnerability to temptation, Frodo finally accomplishes his mission only to find that things also need to be put right back at home.

Tolkien's underlying pessimism about the destruction of rural England struck a chord with new generations of readers concerned about conservation and the threat of nuclear extinction, helping his novel to achieve cult status. A posthumous sequel, *The Silmarillion* (1977), did not enjoy the same popularity.

Tom Brown's Schooldays A novel by THOMAS HUGHES, published in 1857. The first great school story, *Tom Brown's Schooldays* set a pattern for future writing in the genre. Written when its author was still young enough to remember his own days at Rugby, the novel describes the experiences of an upper middle-class boy going to boarding school for the first time. Shy at first, he learns how to put up with teasing from the older boys while carrying out various menial duties as their 'fag'. His two best friends represent opposite poles in behaviour and attitude, with Arthur gentle, law-abiding and idealistic and East mischievous and irreverent. But when some younger boys are picked on by the notorious school bully Flashman, it is East and Tom who bravely stand up to him, despite their still small size. The story ends with Tom as Head Boy under the kindly tutelage of THOMAS ARNOLD himself. Hughes's affection for his own schooldays is never in doubt, and his story helped to found a long tradition of uncritical acceptance for public-school values and practices in CHILDREN'S LITERATURE.

Tom Jones, A Foundling, The History of A novel by HENRY FIELDING, published in 1749.

Mr Allworthy, a rich and benevolent country gentleman, finds a baby in his bed one night. He becomes the baby's guardian, names him Tom and gives him a home, later shared with Blifil, Mr Allworthy's nephew and heir. The mean-spirited Blifil is supported in his resentment of Tom by Thwackum the tutor and his friend Square, the philosopher. As he grows up, Tom enjoys the favours of Molly Seagrim, the gamekeeper's daughter, but falls in love with Sophia Western, the squire's daughter, who is intended for Blifil. Sophia detests Blifil and wants to marry Tom, who is confounded by Molly's declaration that she is pregnant. He is prepared to do the honourable thing in the face of Mr Allworthy's displeasure; fortunately, he learns that Molly has been free with her favours. But Blifil's malice succeeds and Mr Allworthy closes his house to Tom.

He sets out with the schoolmaster, Partridge, unsure where he is going but believing the army to be his best hope. He encounters Sophia, who has run away from her father because he insists that she marry Blifil. With her maid, Mrs Honour, she is going to London to shelter with a relative. Tom finds a pocket book belonging to Sophia and follows her to London in order to return it. His adventures on the way are an opportunity for Fielding to portray a rich gallery of characters.

In London Tom drifts into an affair with Lady Bellaston, who keeps him. She tries to procure Sophia for her friend Lord Fellamar; the outraged girl also discovers Tom's relationship with Lady Bellaston and turns her back on him. Tom is forced into a duel and apparently kills his opponent. Lady Bellaston, furious at being left by Tom, and Lord Fellamar, furious at being rejected by Sophia, instigate Tom's arrest and imprisonment. Fortunately, Tom's opponent does not die, and it is revealed that Blifil knows the truth of Tom's birth and has concealed it. Tom is the son of Mr Allworthy's sister Bridget and as such is Mr Allworthy's proper heir. Sophia forgives him for his infidelities, and they are married.

The novel is Fielding's masterpiece. The introductory chapters that preface each of the novel's 18 books cultivate the reader in a way that was then unprecedented in English fiction; they establish a narrative voice satisfying the contemporary reader's fondness for moral commentary. The tangled comedies of coincidence are offset by the neat, architectonic structure of this most shapely novel. The portrait of the virtuous Sophia is triumphantly free from stereotypes while Tom Jones himself is both a vital and a fallible hero, generous and imprudent but ultimately happy in his pursuit of Sophia, or wisdom.

Tom Sawyer, The Adventures of A novel by MARK TWAIN, published in 1876. Tom is an intelligent and imaginative boy, who is nevertheless careless and mischievous. In one of the book's most famous episodes he is forced to whitewash the front-yard fence as a punishment for playing truant. He evades the task by pretending it is a great privilege, and then allowing other boys to take over from him – for a considerable price.

Tom lives in the respectable home of his Aunt Polly in the Mississippi River town of St Petersburg, Missouri. His preferred world, however, is the outdoor and parentless life of his friend Huck Finn. When Tom is rebuffed by his sweetheart, Becky Thatcher, he and Huck take to the diversion of playing pirates. By coincidence, they are in the graveyard on the night that Injun Joe murders the town doctor and frames the drunkard, Muff Potter, by placing the knife in his hands. Tom, Huck, and a third boy hide out on a river island in fear of the mestizo murderer, and are believed dead. They finally return to witness their own passionate eulogies, and with much uproar they are discovered in the funeral audience. Later Tom becomes a hero, when at the trial of Muff Potter he stands up and accuses the true murderer. Injun Joe rushes from the room and thus proves his own guilt. Subsequently Tom and Becky abandon a school picnic and get themselves lost for several days in the very cave where Injun Joe is hiding. They make good their escape, and Tom then returns to the cave with Huck. They find Injun Joe dead, and also find his buried treasure. The two boys return to town as heroic as ever, and the riches are divided between them. Their story

is continued in *The Adventures of Huckleberry Finn* (1884).

Tomlinson, (Alfred) Charles 1927– Poet, translator and painter. Born in Stoke-on-Trent, he was educated at Longton High School, Queens' College, Cambridge – where his tutor was DONALD DAVIE – and London University. He has taught at the University of Bristol since 1968, since 1982 as professor of English. His first collection, *The Necklace* (1955), received wider recognition in the USA than in Britain, and his links with American literature are strong: his precursors are POUND, ELIOT, WILLIAM CARLOS WILLIAMS, WALLACE STEVENS and LOUIS ZUKOFSKY. His prose book, *Some Americans: A Personal Record* (1981), casts light on these debts and his intellectual development. In attempting to accord 'objects their own existence', Tomlinson's poems are often imagistic, visual responses to landscapes, experiences and events. The title of his second collection, *Seeing is Believing* (1960), is apposite, and it should be remembered that Tomlinson is a visual artist of considerable originality and talent; *In Black and White* (1975) is a collection of his graphic work. His work has been criticized for being cold, humourless and without human interest – charges which led to the ironic title of his next book, *A Peopled Landscape* (1963). His best collection, *The Way of a World* (1969), contains the cinematic 'Swimming Chenango Lake' and the political poem 'Prometheus'. Later collections have been *Written on Water* (1972), *The Way In* (1974), *The Shaft* (1978), *The Flood* (1981), *Notes from New York and Other Poems* (1984), *The Return* (1987), *Annunciations* (1989) and *Boot in the Wall* (1992). *Selected Poems 1951–1974* appeared in 1978 and *Collected Poems* in 1985. One source of originality in his work is the influence of Spanish-American writers. He has collaborated with Octavio Paz on a SONNET sequence, *Airborn/Hijos del Aire* (1981), and produced translations from the work of Paz and Antonio Machado, gathered in *Translations* (1983). He has also edited *The Oxford Book of Verse in Translation* (1980).

Tomlinson, H(enry) M(ajor) 1873–1958 Novelist and journalist. Born in the dockland area of East London, he entered a shipping office at the age of 12 but left to join the staff of *The Morning Leader* in 1904. In 1912 he went to South America, and *The Sea and the Jungle* (1912) was based on his experiences on the Amazon. During World War I he became a war correspondent in France for *The Daily News*, and he was literary editor of *The Nation* from 1917 to 1923.

His novels continued with *Old Junk* (1918), *London River* (1921) and *Waiting for Daylight* (1922), but he is chiefly remembered for *Gallions Reach* (1927) and the powerful anti-war novel *All Our Yesterdays* (1930), a quasi-historical account of British domestic and foreign affairs from 1900 to the Armistice in 1918. Its descriptions of the horrors of trench warfare were backed by Tomlinson's own experiences in Flanders and gave the novel considerable authority.

His other works include the novels *The Snows of Helicon* (1933), *All Hands* (1937) and *Morning Light* (1946), and the travel books *South to Cadiz* (1934) and *Malay Waters* (1950). *A Mingled Yarn* (1953) was a collection of autobiographical essays.

Tono-Bungay A novel by H. G. WELLS, published in 1909.

Often regarded as a CONDITION OF ENGLAND NOVEL, it follows George Ponderevo's quest for moral and intellectual certainties. As first-person narrator, Ponderevo reviews his childhood at Bladesover, a country house where his mother worked as housekeeper. His admiration for the aristocratic order is overruled by his awareness of its obsolescence. After being sent as baker's apprentice to the narrow-minded Evangelist, Nicodemus Frapp, George is entered into the commercial world by his uncle Edward Ponderevo. He is required to be the salesman for 'Tono-Bungay', the quack medicine emanating from Teddy Ponderevo's chemist's shop. Tono-Bungay, the panacea of an irreligious age, brings prosperity to George's uncle and kindly Aunt Susan. George, less contented, can now marry Marion Ramboat.

Marriage, like his experiences of religion and commerce, is a failure for George. His real destiny is with the progress of science, and he becomes a student of aeronautics. Meanwhile Uncle Edward's fortunes decline, with his financial speculations and his ill-judged purchase of Lady Grove, a venerable estate. He appears less a country gentleman than a vulgar philanderer; his bankruptcy ensues. George undertakes an expedition to an island off Africa to collect 'quap', a radioactive material which will redeem the Ponderevo fortunes. The project fails, with 'quap' rotting the timbers of the ship. George's perpetual quest continues amid recurring disillusions. He flies his dying uncle to France to save him from imprisonment; a love affair with the Hon. Beatrice Normandy fails. Despite the presiding motif of decay in the nation, George is finally perceived as the producer of inexorable changes as he passes along the Thames on board a destroyer, his latest invention.

Tonson, Jacob the elder 1655–1736 Publisher. The second son of a shoemaker who was, nonetheless, a member of the Barber-Surgeons' Company, Tonson was apprenticed to Thomas Basset, a bookseller in Fleet Street, London, in 1670 and became a freeman of the Stationers' Company in December 1677. In 1679 he published DRYDEN's version of *Troilus and Cressida*, and in 1684 started to publish the *Miscellany Poems*, which were edited and, in the earlier volumes, to a large extent written by Dryden, and are commonly referred to as *Tonson's Miscellany*. In

two instalments, 1683 and 1690, he acquired the copyright of *PARADISE LOST*, and in 1688, when still only owning half the copyright, published an edition of the poem by subscription. This was the first of a series of major publications issued in this fashion which Tonson, though not initiating, made popular. In 1705 he published ADDISON's *Remarks on Several Parts of Italy*, and in 1713 the same author's *CATO*. The sixth volume of his *Miscellany* included POPE's *Pastorals*. He also actively encouraged and published works by such figures as APHRA BEHN, CONGREVE, NATHANIEL LEE, OTWAY, AMBROSE PHILIPS, PRIOR, ROWE, STEELE, SWIFT and TATE, and took over the publication of both *THE TATLER* and *THE SPECTATOR*. His business was continued, after 1720, by his nephew, Jacob the younger. Tonson was secretary of the KIT-CAT CLUB, a coterie of Whig writers.

Tooke, John Horne 1736–1812 Radical politician and philologist. The son of a well-to-do poulterer named Horne, he was educated at Westminster School, Eton and St John's College, Cambridge. In 1782 he assumed the additional surname of Tooke, his wealthy friend William Tooke of Purley having apparently made him his heir. He was ordained and became vicar of New Brentford, Middlesex, in 1760, but resigned his living in 1773. Although he held a lifelong respect for things 'established', he had no religious calling and later bitterly regretted that he had not chosen the law. In 1765 he became friendly with JOHN WILKES, to whom he lent vigorous support in the Middlesex election of 1768. A skilled and witty speaker and pugnacious campaigner for constitutional reform, he was involved in numerous legal battles and skirmishes: his support for the American colonists against the King led to conviction and one year's imprisonment for blasphemous libel in 1777–8, but he was acquitted (with HOLCROFT and Thelwall) in the treason trials of 1794. Tooke represented an older type of British radicalism, appealing to Magna Carta and the revolution of 1688, and he treated the 'rights of man' generation of the 1790s with some scorn. In 1801 he was elected to the House of Commons, but immediately afterwards an Act (which is still in force) excluding the Anglican clergy from membership was passed, and he was disqualified. His literary reputation was established by *Epea Pteroenta: or, the Diversions of Purley* (1786–1805; two volumes of a projected three), which launched the science of comparative philology. He was among the first to see languages as historical developments rather than fixed structures, and stressed the importance of the study of Gothic and Anglo-Saxon. The work was extremely popular and greatly admired by JAMES MILL and other exponents of UTILITARIANISM. Tooke's friends and acquaintances included BOSWELL, BENTHAM, COLERIDGE, GODWIN and THOMAS PAINE.

Toole, John Kennedy 1937–69 American novelist. He was born in New Orleans and educated at Tulane and Columbia universities. *A Confederacy of Dunces* is a satirical comedy about a depraved New Orleans society. It did not appear until 1980, 11 years after he had committed suicide, when WALKER PERCY read the manuscript. It quickly won acclaim and received a PULITZER PRIZE. *The Neon Bible*, a slighter work, appeared in 1990.

Toomer, Jean (Nathan Eugene) 1894–1967 Black American writer and central figure in the HARLEM RENAISSANCE. Born in Washington DC, he attended the University of Wisconsin and the City College of New York. In 1921 he worked as superintendent of a black rural school in Sparta, Georgia, an experience which provided the source for some of the material in his most widely read work, *Cane* (1923), composed of stories and poems. It attracted the attention of a number of prominent editors, critics and authors, including WALDO FRANK and WILLIAM STANLEY BRAITHWAITE. During the 1920s Toomer contributed poetry to the black journals *Opportunity* and *Crisis*, as well as to *avant-garde* magazines such as *Broom* and THE LITTLE REVIEW. In 1924 he studied in France under the mystic Georges Gurdjieff, whose influence is apparent in Toomer's later work. *Essentials*, a collection of aphorisms on philosophical subjects, appeared in 1931. He experimented with dramatic conventions in two unpublished plays, 'Natalie Mann' (1922) and 'The Sacred Factory' (1927). He also wrote numerous poems, stories, and autobiographical sketches which remained unpublished in his lifetime and were subsequently collected in *The Wayward and the Seeking* (1980), edited by Darwin T. Turner.

Toplady, Augustus 1740–78 Hymn writer and theologian. Born at Farnham in Surrey, he attended Westminster School and completed his education at Trinity College, Dublin. He was ordained in 1764 and became vicar of Broad Hembury in Devon in 1768. He is remembered for his hymns ('Rock of Ages' is the most famous) and for his violent reaction to the teaching of JOHN WESLEY, whom he had once admired. Toplady regressed into Calvinism and wrote *The Historic Proof of the Doctrinal Calvinism of the Church of England* (1774).

Torrington, 5th Viscount See BYNG, THE HONOURABLE JOHN, 5TH VISCOUNT TORRINGTON.

Tottel's Miscellany The first of the poetic miscellanies popular in the later 16th century, brought out in 1557 by the printer Richard Tottel in collaboration with NICHOLAS GRIMALD. Its formal title was *Songs and Sonnets Written by the Right Honourable Lord Henry Howard Late Earl of Surrey and Other* (i.e.

others). SIR THOMAS WYATT is generously represented as well as SURREY, the first time that the work of either poet had appeared in print. Other writers include Grimald himself, THOMAS NORTON and THOMAS VAUX. There was a second edition in 1557 and many subsequent editions with additions and deletions in the 16th century.

Tour of Dr Syntax in Search of the Picturesque, The See DR SYNTAX IN SEARCH OF THE PICTURESQUE, THE TOUR OF.

Tourgée, Albion W(inegar) 1838–1905 American novelist. Born in Williamsfield, Ohio, and educated at the University of Rochester, he served with the Union forces during the Civil War and was seriously wounded. In 1864 he was admitted to the Bar and in the following year moved to North Carolina. A transplanted Northerner who disapproved of all the Old South stood for, he was labelled a carpetbagger. In 1868 he was elected a judge of North Carolina's Supreme Court, in which capacity he served for six years.

Tourgée's commitment to Reconstruction ideology and to the reform of the South is reflected in the novels he wrote there. *Toinette: A Novel* (1874; republished as *A Royal Gentleman*, 1881) is the story of a near-white slave girl who is freed but left in a tragic position when her lover, a white Southerner who has fathered her child, refuses to marry her. *A Fool's Errand* (1879) portrays the conflict between a former Confederate general and a former Union colonel who sides with the freed blacks and fights both the Ku Klux Klan and the carpetbaggers. The novel was republished in 1880 incorporating *The Invisible Empire*, a factual enquiry into the history of the Ku Klux Klan. *Bricks without Straw* (1880) tells of a black's struggle to establish himself as a free and independent man; terrorized by the Klan, he is forced to move with his family to the North. After leaving the South in 1879, Tourgée continued to write fiction, producing a further 17 novels, among which are *Hot Plowshares* (1882), *Black Ice* (1888) and *Eighty-Nine: or, The Grand Master's Story* (1891), in which he returned to the theme of Republican reform of the South after the Civil War. From 1882 to 1884 he edited *Our Continent*, a weekly publication in which he continued to champion the rights of blacks and to expose the evil of the Ku Klux Klan. He served as US consul in Bordeaux from 1897 until his death.

Tourneur, Cyril c. 1575–1626 Playwright. Virtually nothing is known of Tourneur's life before 1613, though he seems to have been at various times in the service of the Cecils, the Veres and the Earl of Essex, and probably combined military and diplomatic work both before and after 1613, when he was a government courier to Brussels. As secretary to Sir Edward Cecil he was involved in the 1625 raid on Cadiz, and put ashore in Ireland after the raid's failure. He died there early in 1626, perhaps as a result of wounds suffered in the expedition.

Tourneur's first published work was an obscure poetic SATIRE, *The Transformed Metamorphosis* (1600), but he is remembered as the author of two plays, the magnificent THE REVENGER'S TRAGEDY (1607) and the greatly inferior THE ATHEIST'S TRAGEDY (published 1611). Tourneur is named as the author of the latter play on the title-page of 1611, but the attribution of *The Revenger's Tragedy* to him has no stronger basis than the word of a certain Edward Archer in 1656. The disparity in quality between the two has helped the case for assigning *The Revenger's Tragedy* to THOMAS MIDDLETON.

Tourneur is known, from a reference in the Stationers' Register, to have written a play called *The Nobleman* (1612–13), and was also asked to write one act of *The Arraignment of London* (1613). Neither work has survived. In effect, Tourneur's reputation rests on the splendours of a play he may not have written.

Tourtel, Mary 1874–1948 Writer and illustrator of CHILDREN'S LITERATURE. Born in Kent and educated at Canterbury Art School, she began her career as an illustrator of animal stories for children. Married to a sub-editor of *The Daily Express*, she twice tried to develop a comic strip story about an animal hero before creating Rupert Bear in 1920. Unfailingly turned out in check trousers, jumper and scarf, Rupert lives in the quiet suburb of Nutwood. Nevertheless, he and his friends Algy Pug, Bill Badger, Podgy Pig and Edward Trunk regularly fall into alarming adventures involving magic castles, ogres, malevolent dwarfs and witches. The regular appearance of a balloon, giant bird or small aeroplane to rescue Rupert from danger reflects Tourtel's own interest in flying. She and her husband had made a record-breaking flight from London to Belgium in 1919. By the time she handed over her strip to ALFRED BESTALL in 1935 Rupert's daily adventures were enjoying equal success collected in book form.

Towneley cycle See MIRACLE PLAYS.

Townshend, Aurelian ?1583–?1643 Poet. Little is known of Townshend's life. His family home was in Norfolk, and he entered Sir Robert Cecil's service at an early age, travelling to France and Italy. The linguistic proficiency he acquired is manifest in his letters (in both languages) to his patron. He made, however, undesirable connections, was recalled and was probably with Cecil when he died in 1612. Apart from registering his children, Townshend disappears until early in 1632, when he is found supplanting

BEN JONSON as collaborator with Inigo Jones on two court MASQUES, *Albion's Triumph* and *Tempe Restored*. These, and a handful of lyrics and occasional poems, uncollected in his lifetime, constitute his literary work.

Toynbee, Arnold (Joseph) 1889–1975 Historian. The nephew and namesake of the social reformer Arnold Toynbee, he was born in London and educated at Winchester and Balliol College, Oxford, of which he became a fellow and tutor (1912–15). After Oxford he served at the Foreign Office until 1919, when he was appointed Koraes Professor of Byzantine and Modern Greek Language, Literature and History at King's College, London. He was director of studies at the Royal Institute of International Affairs from 1925 to 1955. During World War II he directed the Foreign Office Research Department (1943–6) and at its conclusion was a member of the British delegation at the peace conference in Paris.

Toynbee's first work was a pamphlet, *Greek Policy since 1882* (1914), and many of his subsequent works were concerned with European politics and ancient Greek culture. The first part of *A Study of History* appeared in 1934; it was completed in 12 volumes in 1961. A philosophy of world history from earliest to contemporary times, it views the history of mankind as a recurring cycle of growth, breakdown and eventual dissolution, and advances the proposition that a 'spiritual initiative' by a new universal church would provide the chrysalis from which a new civilization could emerge. The work proved highly controversial, but a two-volume condensation by D. C. Somervell (1946 and 1957) enjoyed a remarkable popular success.

Among other works by Toynbee were the texts of his notable Reith Lectures, *The World and the West* (1952), *Hellenism: The History of a Civilization* (1959) and *Hannibal's Legacy* (1965). An enthusiastic traveller, he was also the author of several travel books, *Between Oxus and Jumna* (1961), *Between Niger and Nile* (1965) and *Between Maule and Amazon* (1967). *Comparing Notes: A Dialogue across a Generation* (1963) was written with his son, the critic and novelist Philip Toynbee (1916–81).

Tracts for the Times An offshoot of the OXFORD MOVEMENT, *Tracts for the Times* appeared from 1833 until 1841, providing another label for the ferment: the Tractarian Movement. JOHN HENRY NEWMAN wrote the first tract; others were contributed by JOHN KEBLE, E. B. PUSEY and ISAAC WILLIAMS. Originally brief leaflets, the tracts developed into learned theological treatises. In 1841 Newman's *Tract XC*, which argued that the 39 Articles of the Anglican Church were compatible with Catholic theology, caused an outcry which made it the last of the series. The Tractarians were officially banned, and in 1845 the group was further weakened by Newman's conversion to Catholicism.

Traffics and Discoveries A collection of 11 stories and 11 poems by RUDYARD KIPLING, first published in 1904. The stories range in subject matter from the supernatural to the Boer War. Recent critical opinion has been divided on the best-known, 'They' and 'Mrs Bathurst'. 'They' – which hints at Kipling's feelings for his daughter Josephine, who died as a child in 1899 – describes the narrator's visits to an other-worldly house where he finds elusive but charming children. 'Mrs Bathurst' has a strong element of unexplained mystery, but not of the supernatural, in its account of the effect that Mrs Bathurst, a New Zealand hotel-keeper, has on Vickery, a naval warrant-officer. Vickery's desertion and violent death in a thunderstorm are unexplained; tantalizingly, the story associates Mrs Bathurst with the terrible retribution of an otherwise random universe. 'Below the Mill Dam' and 'Wireless', in which mystery and the supernatural figure prominently, have attracted favourable attention but the Boer War stories – notably 'A Sahibs' War' – have often been found muddled and disappointing, reflecting the more jingoistic Kipling.

tragedy There is no satisfactory explanation of the process by which a Greek word meaning 'goat song' came to be applied to the poetic dramas of ancient Greece, in which the kings and heroes of Greek mythology were displayed in the crisis of confrontation with their gods. The mature Greek tragedy of 5th-century BC Athens was analysed in Aristotle's influential *Poetics*, and the greater exactness of his neoclassical interpreters, particularly in Renaissance France, established the responsibility of tragedy to deal with the fall of great men (or, exceptionally, great women).

By an accident of scholarship, it was the Roman poet Seneca (c. 4 BC–AD 65), rather than the greater Greek writers Aeschylus, Sophocles and Euripides, who influenced the form of the earliest English tragedies. The Senecan atrocities of, for example, *TITUS ANDRONICUS*, were a readily acceptable part of Elizabethan tragedy, and the formal conventions of REVENGE TRAGEDY, a distinctive sub-genre for 50 years after the first performance of KYD's *THE SPANISH TRAGEDY* (c. 1589), were originally adopted from Seneca. But English dramatists rejected the restrictions of their classical models. Their corpse-strewn stages owed much to Seneca, but their preparedness to use prose as well as verse, and to spread the action over comic as well as tragic characters and episodes, gave a unique emotional breadth to English tragedy. Beside the colour of MARLOWE and SHAKESPEARE, the Senecan severity of BEN JONSON's two Roman tragedies is unattractive. While Elizabethan and

Jacobean tragedies were, with very few exceptions, obedient to the expectation that rulers or noblemen were the proper protagonists, their authors were more concerned to write popular plays than great literature.

English tragedy has suffered from the subsequent elevation of the genre. Whereas COMEDY thrived in the reopened post-Restoration theatres, the rhymed bombast of heroic tragedy led to dwindling popularity. Increasingly, through the 18th and 19th centuries, great tragic actors made their names in revivals, much altered, of Shakespeare. The most successful tragedies of LEE, OTWAY, DRYDEN and ROWE owed their attraction to their ability, however sporadically, to recall Shakespeare. It has been argued often that the increasing disunity of society, its loss of common spiritual values, was inimical to tragedy, which relies on the representative nature of individual disaster. Domestic or bourgeois tragedy, already present on the Elizabethan and Jacobean stage in works like *ARDEN OF FEVERSHAM* and THOMAS HEYWOOD's *A WOMAN KILLED WITH KINDNESS*, was made fashionable in the 18th century by LILLO with *THE LONDON MERCHANT*. But Lillo's moral directives, which push the audience towards thrift and industry, were absorbed into MELODRAMA, and the further intrusion of tragedy into the lives of the middle classes had to await the emergence of Ibsen. Meanwhile, the conviction that tragedy was the proper preserve of poets continued to tempt most of the greatest from Dryden to T. S. ELIOT. Some, like COLERIDGE, BYRON, BROWNING and TENNYSON, had fleeting success in the theatre, but few of their plays have lasted well. With the arguable exception of Byron, their model was Shakespeare, and the artistic outcome analogous to the reproduction of antique furniture.

Those who argue that the 20th-century English-speaking theatre has witnessed a revival of tragedy are more likely to base their claims on domestic and social dramas than on such historical works as the more conventionally tragic *MURDER IN THE CATHEDRAL*. O'NEILL and ARTHUR MILLER in the USA, O'CASEY in Ireland and BOND in England have their adherents, but their determined emphasis on the world of Everyman removes them from the Aristotelian world of high tragedy.

Tragic Comedians, The A novel by GEORGE MEREDITH, published in 1880. It was based on Helene von Donniges's account of her love affair with the German socialist, Ferdinand Lassalle, who appears in the novel as Alvan. Helene von Donniges is represented as the character Clotilde, a nobleman's daughter who is prepared to marry Alvan in the face of her family's wrath. Quixotically honourable, Alvan insists that she gain their full consent. Clotilde returns to her family, who bully her mercilessly and in the end deceive her into accepting the suitor of their choice, Marko. When he learns what has happened, Alvan writes a furious and insulting letter to Clotilde's father. Marko challenges him, and in the ensuing fight Alvan is killed. Clotilde marries Marko after the tragedy.

Traherne, Thomas 1637–74 Religious poet and essayist. Born in Hereford, the son of a shoemaker, he studied at Brasenose College, Oxford, in 1653–6. Appointed by the Parliamentary Commissioners as rector of Credenhill near Hereford in 1657, he was ordained by the restored Church of England in 1660 and reappointed to Credenhill. There he became part of a devotional circle around Mrs Susanna Hopton, for whom he is thought to have composed his *Centuries of Meditations*. He became chaplain to Sir Orlando Bridgeman, the Lord Keeper of the Great Seal, in 1667 and was buried in Teddington church, Middlesex, near Bridgeman's seat. In his lifetime, he published *Roman Forgeries* (1673), an account of the fabrication of false documents in the medieval church. *Christian Ethics* appeared in 1675, 'opening the way to blessedness by the rules of virtue and reason'. His *Thanksgivings* were published anonymously in 1699.

Traherne remained an unregarded writer until early this century when the discovery of his poems and the *Centuries of Meditations* revealed him as a man of outstanding religious sensibility. The *Centuries* transmit Traherne's childhood sense of living in an earthly paradise, surrounded by the beauty of the creation. He had no sense of property, division or limit; he felt, like Adam, that the world had been created entirely for his delight. His natural response was praise of the creator. Later, his spirit was clouded by a darkening sense of sin and of the sorrow of the world, but the experience of spiritual regeneration enabled him to recover the former intensity of delight in the world and its creator. This condition of spiritual elevation and joy he termed 'Felicity'. The *Centuries* are written in lucid metrical prose; they have a psalm-like quality of praise and thanksgiving, and they express a kind of luminous spirituality that is quite exceptional. Traherne sets himself apart from most of his contemporaries by his rejection of the doctrine of original sin; sin, he was inclined to believe, was a habit acquired by contact with society. His poems complement the experience of the *Centuries*, with much recall of the wonder of his childhood, and with a visionary sense of the divinity that permeates the creation.

Traill, Catharine Parr 1802–99 Canadian writer on emigrant life. The sister of AGNES STRICKLAND and SUSANNA MOODIE, she was born in London and moved to Canada in 1832, soon after her marriage. She published her first book, *The Blind Highland Piper and Other Tales*, at the age of sixteen and produced several popular books for children. In spite of a difficult life in Canada, marked by financial troubles, her most enduring works grew out of her pioneering days: *The Backwoods of Canada* (subtitled 'Letters from the Wife of an Emigrant Officer, Illustrative of the Domestic Economy of North America', 1836) and *The Female Emigrant's Guide* (1854). She was also an accomplished naturalist and published several books on Canadian wildlife.

Traitor, The A tragedy by JAMES SHIRLEY, first produced in 1631 and published in 1635. The play has some basis in the history of the Medici family of Florence. The Duke is enamoured of Amidea, the sister of Sciarrha, one of his nobles. His kinsman, Lorenzo, plotting to seize power, does his best to further the Duke's desires, while at the same time arousing Sciarrha's wrath at the threat to his sister's honour. Sciarrha kills Amidea to save her from dishonour and lays out her body where the Duke will find her. When the Duke comes upon the body he calls for Lorenzo, who seizes the opportunity to murder him. Lorenzo is killed by Sciarrha in the last moments of accusation and recrimination; Sciarrha dies of his wounds.

Transcendentalism A literary and philosophical movement in New England in the early and middle part of the 19th century. Its most notable voices were those of RALPH WALDO EMERSON, HENRY DAVID THOREAU, MARGARET FULLER and BRONSON ALCOTT. GEORGE RIPLEY founded the BROOK FARM community in practical application of its ideals. Transcendentalism opposed the idea that man needs an intercessor for reaching the divine and was critical of formalized religion. Like the physical universe itself, all constructive practical activity, all great literature, all forms of spiritual awareness were viewed as an expression of the divine spirit. The often-expressed ambition was to achieve vivid perception of the divine as it operates in common life, an awareness seen as leading at once to personal cultivation and to a sense of history as a potentially, progressive movement.

Transition The most influential cultural journal in black Africa during its 15-year life from 1961 to 1976. Rajat Neogy, its founder, conceived it as a forum for all topics of general cultural interest: literature, poetry, criticism, politics, business and racial issues. Contributors included writers such as CHINUA ACHEBE, WOLE SOYINKA, J. P. CLARK BEKEDEREMO and OKOT P'BITEK and statesmen such as Kenneth Kaunda of Zambia, Julius Nyerere of Tanzania and Milton Obote of Uganda, where *Transition* was published. It ceased publication when Obote banned it and imprisoned Neogy in 1968 but resumed when Neogy moved to Ghana. Soyinka became editor in 1974 and *Transition*'s name changed to *Ch'indaba*, combining

'Cha', the Swahili word for 'to dawn', and 'indaba', the Matabele word for 'a great council'.

Tranter, John (Ernest) 1943– Australian poet. Born in New South Wales, he attended the University of Sydney and has worked as a freelance editor and writer-in-residence at several universities. At the head of a group of young writers credited with bringing MODERNISM into Australian poetry in the 1970s, he believes that poetry is about language itself. A succession of volumes have experimented with different linguistic approaches to perception and the poetic process: *Parallax* (1970), *Red Movie* (1972), *The Blast Area* (1974), *The Alphabet Murders* (1976), *Crying in Early Infancy* (1977), *Dazed in the Ladies Lounge* (1979), *Gloria* (1986) and *Under Berlin: New Poems* (1988). *Selected Poems* appeared in 1982. He has also advanced his view of Australian poetry through influential anthologies: *Poetry Australia's Preface to the 70s* (1970), *The New Australian Poetry* (1979), *The Tin Wash Dish* (1989) and *The Penguin Book of Modern Australian Poetry* (with Philip Mead; 1991).

Traveller, The: *or, A Prospect of Society* A poem by OLIVER GOLDSMITH, published in 1764 and the first work to appear under his own name. It was dedicated to his brother Henry, to whom he had sent the rough draft from Switzerland during his own travels 10 years before. The traveller – or compulsive wanderer – is the poet himself. From a peak in the Alps he ponders the lessons of his travels and notes the faults and virtues of the countries he has visited. Happiness, he realizes, may be found in any place, as well as discontent. The poem is written in fluent rhyming couplets which encompass description and philosophy with apparent ease.

Travels through France and Italy A memoir of his travels from June 1764 to June 1765 by TOBIAS SMOLLETT, published in 1766.

Smollett's health broke down in 1763, and in April of that year he was distressed by the death of his daughter Elizabeth at the age of 15. He set out for Europe with his wife in June of the following year and journeyed across France. After Nice, the Smolletts proceeded to Genoa and then through Italy, visiting Florence and continuing as far south as Rome. They returned to Nice in the winter and then made their way back to England. The book takes the form of letters to imaginary correspondents and gives a remarkable picture of mid-18th-century life on the Continent. Though his attitude may frequently be quarrelsome and resentful, Smollett remains a sharp and perceptive observer. LAURENCE STERNE met him during his wanderings and included him in *A SENTIMENTAL JOURNEY* as Smelfungus: 'he set out with spleen and jaundice, and every object he passed by was discoloured or distorted'.

Traven, B. Pseudonym of the novelist and short-story writer best remembered for *The Treasure of the Sierra Madre*. An elusive and shadowy figure, he claimed to be an American born in Chicago but is now usually identified with Otto Fiege, born in 1882 at Zwiebodzin (then in Germany and now in Poland). Traven seems to have used several *noms de guerre*, including Traven Torsvan, Ret Marut and Hal Croves, under which name he died in Mexico in 1969. His works were first published in German and then translated into English, often by himself with assistance from his publisher's editor. *The Treasure of the Sierra Madre* (1934; originally *Der Schatz der Sierra Madre*, 1927) is an adventure story of greed and desperation which declares his debt to JACK LONDON and the American school of NATURALISM. It was successfully filmed by John Huston in 1947. Other works include *Die Baumwollpflücker* (1926; *The Cottonpickers*, 1956), *Das Totenschiff* (1926; *The Death Ship*, 1934), *Die Brücke im Dschungel* (1929; *The Bridge in the Jungle*, 1938) and *Die Rebellion der Gehenkten* (1936; *The Rebellion of the Hanged*, 1952), about the exploitation of Indian workers in Mexico at the turn of the century.

Travers, Ben 1886–1980 Playwright. Born in Hendon and educated at Charterhouse, Travers worked for the family firm before joining the Royal Naval Air Service in 1914 and the Royal Air Force in 1918. Between 1922 and 1933 he wrote custom-made FARCES for the talented Aldwych company under the supervision of Tom Walls. The best include *A Cuckoo in the Nest* (1925), *Rookery Nook* (1926), *Thark* (1927) and *Plunder* (1928). Away from the Aldwych after 1933, Travers had less theatrical success, though his last play, *The Bed before Yesterday* (1975), is a touching retrospect on the younger world of 1930.

Travers, P(amela) L(yndon) 1906– Writer of CHILDREN'S LITERATURE. Born in Australia, she came to England in 1923 and worked as an actress-dancer until 1936. She based her first novel for children, *Mary Poppins* (1934), on stories she had originally told to children of her acquaintance. It was memorably illustrated by Mary Shepard (wife of E. H. SHEPARD). Its mixture of strong nursery discipline with exciting magic made it an immediate success and led to four sequels as well as a Walt Disney musical in 1964. Other novels for children include *The Fox at the Manger* (1963) and *Friend Monkey* (1971), a moving story about the adoption of an untamed animal. She is also a talented poet.

Trease, (Robert) Geoffrey 1909– Writer of CHILDREN'S LITERATURE. Born in Nottingham and educated at Oxford University, he began writing fiction after a short career in journalism and schoolteaching. His challenge to the conservative values then ruling historical novels for children attracted the approval of GEORGE ORWELL among others. *Bows against the Barons* (1934) portrayed ROBIN HOOD as a working-class hero fighting against the oppression of the rich. *Comrades of the Charter* (1934) offered a left-wing interpretation of more recent history. His many subsequent books, less politically motivated but still ahead of their time in the determination to write for and about ordinary children, include *No Boats on Bannermere* (1949), *Follow My Black Plume* (1963) and *Song for a Tattered Flag* (1992).

Treasure Island An adventure novel for children by ROBERT LOUIS STEVENSON, serialized as *The Sea Cook: or, Treasure Island*, by 'Captain George North', in *Young Folks* from October 1881 to January 1882 and published in book form in 1883. Although Stevenson himself did not take it seriously, it has always been his most popular work.

Jim Hawkins, the landlady's son at the Admiral Benbow inn near the coast in the West Country, tells the story. Billy Bones arrives, an old pirate dogged by his former confederates. Jim outwits them and secures Bones's map showing where Captain Flint's treasure is buried. Squire Trelawney and his old friend Dr Livesey charter a schooner, the *Hispaniola*, commanded by Captain Smollett, and set sail for Treasure Island with Jim on board. He discovers that the crew includes the pirates, led by the ship's one-legged cook, Long John Silver. The rest of the story, telling how the pirates are defeated and the treasure found, takes second place to the interest Stevenson finds in Silver, charming, comic, swaggering and villainous by turns, embodying every young boy's image of what a pirate should be. The character is said to have been modelled on Stevenson's friend W. E. HENLEY.

Treatise of Human Nature, A A philosophical essay by DAVID HUME, the first two volumes published in 1739 and the third in 1740.

Hume acknowledges his debt to LOCKE and earlier philosophers who had used experimental reasoning in the examination of moral subjects. Book I, on understanding, examines man's process of knowing, tracing the origin of ideas – of space, time, causality, and so forth – in experience and the data of the senses. Book II, on the 'passions', provides an elaborate psychological machinery to explain the affective order in man, assigning a subordinate role to reason. Book III, on morals, describes 'moral goodness' in terms of 'feelings' of approval or disapproval generated by the agreeable or disagreeable consequences of human behaviour.

The *Treatise* is Hume's first and most comprehensive attempt to formulate his philosophical position. Its varying aspects are separately developed in *AN ENQUIRY CONCERNING HUMAN UNDERSTANDING* (1748), *An Enquiry concerning the Principles of Morals* (1751)

and the discussion on the passions in *Four Dissertations* (1757).

Treatise on the Astrolabe, A A prose translation by GEOFFREY CHAUCER from Latin texts. Dedicated to his young son, Lewis, it offers a simplified account of the astrolabe, a mechanical device for making various astronomical and astrological measurements and calculations. Most of the work is translated from the 8th-century *Compositio et operatio astrolabii* of the Arabian Messahala, but some passages are apparently derived from John de Sacrobosco's *De spaera* and others have not been traced to a source. The introduction is interesting as the only substantial piece of Chaucer's prose which is not a close translation from another author, but otherwise the work is of little literary interest. The *Treatise* is apparently the earliest complex scientific work to have been written in English. It is possible but not yet proven that Chaucer also wrote the more erudite astronomical treatise *The Equatorie of the Planets*.

Treece, Henry 1911–66 Poet and writer of CHILDREN'S LITERATURE. Born in Staffordshire and educated at Wednesbury Grammar School and Birmingham University, he became a schoolteacher before enlisting with the RAF during World War II. One of the founders of the NEW APOCALYPSE movement, he published several volumes of poetry, including *The Black Seasons* (1945) and *The Exiles* (1952). His critical works include *How I See Apocalypse* (1946) and the first book on DYLAN THOMAS (1949). His first children's book, *The Legion of the Eagle* (1954), describes battles between the Romans and the Celts. The many other novels which followed, dealing mostly with the Viking and Roman periods of British history, are distinguished by a feeling for the past that goes beyond mere accuracy of detail. He also produced a series of thrillers for children and a fine novel about one of the most baffling episodes of medieval history, *The Children's Crusade* (1958), widely translated and probably his best book.

Trelawny, Edward (John) 1792–1881 Author and adventurer. The son of a senior army officer from an old Cornish family, he was born and brought up in London, and sent to a school in Bristol, from which he ran away. At the age of 13 he entered the Royal Navy, receiving his discharge in 1812. His experiences as a midshipman form the basis of his autobiographical novel, *Adventures of a Younger Son* (1831), in which he claims to have deserted in India and assumed command of a French privateer. In 1822 he surfaced in Pisa where he became a member of the circle round BYRON and SHELLEY. He was acutely distressed by the news of Shelley's drowning in the Bay of Spezia, and it was he who supervised the recovery and cremation of the body, designed the tomb, and raised the money for MARY SHELLEY (to whom he some years later made a half-serious proposal of marriage) to return to England. In 1823 he accompanied Byron to Greece to take part in the struggle for national independence, where he got embroiled in the dissensions of the Greek leaders and survived an attempt on his life. He was married, for the second time, to a Greek girl in 1824. In 1833–5 he travelled in the United States, where, among other exploits, he swam the Niagara River just above the Falls and demonstrated his solidarity with the abolitionists by purchasing the freedom of a slave. His elopement in 1841 with the married Lady Augusta Goring caused a major social scandal and led to his third unsuccessful marriage. The second instalment of his autobiography appeared in 1858 under the title *Recollections of the Last Days of Byron and Shelley* (later altered to *Records of Byron, Shelley and the Author*, 1878), an extremely lively and readable account, though none too scrupulous with the facts. A larger-than-life figure of striking appearance and enormous social charm, Trelawny had become a monument of the Byronic age by the end of his long life. His ashes were buried next to Shelley's in the Protestant Cemetery in Rome.

Trelawny of the 'Wells' A comedy by ARTHUR WING PINERO, first performed at the ROYAL COURT THEATRE, London, in 1898.

The play is a nostalgic recollection of theatrical conditions in 1860, before the realism of TOM ROBERTSON (alluded to in the character of Tom Wrench) had challenged the hold of melodrama. Rose Trelawny, star of Bagnigge Wells Theatre, is to quit the stage and marry. Her theatrical friends give her a farewell party, but she finds her fiancé's respectable family too unattractive, and returns to the theatre, determined to help stage the 'new' plays of Tom Wrench. All ends happily when her fiancé, having renounced his family, turns up as her leading man.

Trench, Richard Chenevix 1807–86 Philologist, theologian and poet. He first made his name as a poet with *The Story of Justin Martyr, and Other Poems* (1835), but, although he published other collections, few of his poems are read today. Fame came to him with *Notes on the Parables of Our Lord* (1841) and *Notes on the Miracles of Our Lord* (1846), written while he was a country clergyman. His most popular book, *On the Study of Words* (1851), grew out of lectures given at the Winchester Diocesan Training School and was followed by *English Past and Present* (1855) from teaching at King's College, London. He played a part in launching THE OXFORD ENGLISH DICTIONARY by reading two papers before the Philological Society, his *On Some Deficiencies in Our English Dictionaries*, in 1857 and proposing to the so-

ciety in 1858 that a new dictionary be undertaken. Dean of Westminster from 1856, he returned to his birthplace as Archbishop of Dublin in 1864.

Trespasser, The A novel by D. H. LAWRENCE, first published in 1912. It was based on the experiences of Lawrence's friend Helen Corke, as revealed in her diaries. The story follows Helena Verden's intense, though largely non-sexual, affair with her ex-violin teacher, Siegmund MacNair. She cannot give herself to him completely and he cannot bring himself to desert his wife and children for her. He finally commits suicide. The novel ends a year after his death, with Helena turning to her would-be suitor Cecil Byrne for 'rest and warmth'.

Trevelyan, G(eorge) M(acaulay) 1876–1962 Historian. Trevelyan was the third son of the statesman and historian SIR GEORGE OTTO TREVELYAN. He was born at Stratford-upon-Avon and educated at Harrow and Trinity College, Cambridge. His dissertation, published as *England in the Age of Wycliffe* (1899), won him a fellowship at Trinity, where he taught until moving to London in 1903. During World War I he commanded an ambulance unit on the Italian front. He became Regius Professor of Modern History at Cambridge in 1927. An influential conservationist and keen walker, he was also a supporter of the National Trust and in 1931 became president of the newly founded Youth Hostels Association.

England under the Stuarts (1904) confirmed Trevelyan's reputation as a scholarly but popular writer, but his academic stature was established with the trilogy on Garibaldi: *Garibaldi's Defence of the Roman Republic* (1907), *Garibaldi and the Thousand* (1909) and *Garibaldi and the Making of Italy* (1911), published as a single work in 1933. *British History in the Nineteenth Century* (1922) and *History of England* (1926) were both popular successes, and his nostalgic *English Social History* (1944) became his most widely read book, though it was not considered his best. Other publications include a three-volume history of *England under Queen Anne* (1930–4) and *Grey of Falloden* (1937), a biography. *A Layman's Love of Letters* (1954), based on his 1953 Clark Lectures, expressed admiration for BROWNING, SCOTT, MEREDITH and HOUSMAN. His *Autobiography and Other Essays* was published in 1949.

Trevelyan, Sir George Otto 1838–1928 Historian. Born in Leicestershire and educated at Harrow and Trinity College, Cambridge, he entered Parliament in 1865 and held a variety of public appointments. His early writings, *The Dwak Bungalow* (1863), *The Competition Wallah* (1864) and *Cawnpore* (1865), are about India; his humorous work was collected in *The Ladies of Parliament* (1869). A later, non-historical work, *Interludes in Prose and Verse*, appeared in 1905.

His first major historical writing was the *Life and Letters* of his uncle, MACAULAY (1876). This was followed by *The Early History of Charles James Fox* (1880), intended as the first part of an exhaustive biography of the Whig politician; it is notable for its vivid presentation of social and political life in the late 18th century. However, his next work, *The American Revolution* (4 vols., 1899–1907), suggests that his intentions had changed, and *George III and Charles Fox* (1912–14) completed his study of the American Revolution.

Trevisa, John de 1326–1412 Born at Crocadon in St Mellion, Cornwall, he was a Fellow of Exeter College, Oxford, in 1362–9. He became a Fellow of The Queen's College in 1369 but was expelled in 1379 with others. Before 1387 he became chaplain to Lord Berkeley and vicar of Berkeley; he was also a canon of Westbury-on-Severn. He translated and augmented Higden's *Polychronicon* in 1387 and *De proprietatibus rerum* by Bartholomew de Glanville (or Bartholomaeus Anglicus) in 1398. The former is a CHRONICLE, the latter an encyclopedia. Several other works of lesser significance have been attributed to Trevisa, and CAXTON credited him with a translation of the Bible. His work is notable as an example of early English prose treatment of secular topics.

Trevor, William [Cox, William Trevor] 1928– Novelist and short-story writer. He was born in Mitcheldown, County Cork, and went to Trinity College, Dublin. Much of his fiction, which is divided equally into novels and short stories, is set in Ireland, where he has continued to live for extended periods. His work frequently deals with the corruption or destruction of innocence, for which childhood and old age are recurrent prototypes, and shows a penchant for settings of shabby, faded gentility. Novels include *The Old Boys* (1964); *Mrs Eckdorf in O'Neill's Hotel* (1969), which, like *Fools of Fortune* (1983), treats the civil struggle in Northern Ireland; *Elizabeth Alone* (1973); *The Children of Dynmouth* (1976), about a psychopathic teenager menacing a quiet English retirement resort; and *The Silence in the Garden* (1988). His prolific output of shorter fiction includes *The Day We Got Drunk on Cake* (1969), *The Ballroom of Romance* (1972), *Angels at the Ritz* (1975), *Lovers of Their Time* (1978), *Beyond the Pale* (1981), a collected volume (1983), *The News from Ireland* (1986), *Family Sins* (1989) and a pair of novellas, *Two Lives* (1991).

Trick to Catch the Old One, A A comedy by THOMAS MIDDLETON, performed by a BOYS' COMPANY *c.* 1605 and published in 1608. The plot gave MASSINGER the basis for *A NEW WAY TO PAY OLD DEBTS*.

Theophilus Witgood, a young ne'er-do-well, wishes to get money from his miserly uncle, Pecunius Lucre.

His former mistress, a courtesan known as the Widow Medler, agrees to pose as his wealthy 'intended'. In fact, Witgood is in love with Joyce, niece of the usurer Walkadine Hoard, Pecunius Lucre's sworn enemy. Scenting a good match for himself, Hoard courts and wins the Widow Medler. Thus disappointed of the money promised by his uncle on the prospect of a wealthy marriage, Witgood is arrested for debt, but persuades Hoard to pay off his debts by alluding to a breach of promise by the Widow. Witgood marries Joyce in secret. His uncle is delighted when Hoard learns, at the wedding feast, that he has married a courtesan, and, partly from malicious glee, agrees to forgive and finance his nephew. As for Hoard, he is consoled by the Widow's promise to be a good wife.

Trilby A novel by GEORGE DU MAURIER, published in 1894 and illustrated by himself. Originally, Du Maurier offered the outline to HENRY JAMES, suggesting that he should write it, but finally wrote it himself, to follow up the success of his first novel, *Peter Ibbetson*. Trilby is an artist's model who, manipulated by Svengali, becomes a famous singer. But at the moment of his death during a performance, her voice cracks and fails her. The novel was immediately and enduringly popular, because it combined the Victorian fascination with 'animal magnetism', hypnotism and occult powers with an archetypal story of demonic possession. Svengali, who has given his name to the language, was a German-Polish Jew, and the anti-semitism of the narrative jars on the modern reader. In 1895 the novel was adapted for the stage, Beerbohm Tree playing Svengali. A century later, Trilby's name survives as that of a man's felt hat, dented across the crown.

Trilling, Lionel 1905–75 American critic. He was born in New York and educated at Columbia, where he taught for most of his life. His publications include studies of MATTHEW ARNOLD (1939) and E. M. FORSTER (1943) and essays collected in *The Liberal Imagination* (1950), *The Opposing Self* (1955), *A Gathering of Fugitives* (1956), *Beyond Culture: Essays on Literature and Learning* (1965) and *Sincerity and Authenticity* (1972). Trilling addressed the broadest cultural questions: the relation of morality to politics, and the aesthetic as well as the political meaning of liberalism. His single novel, *The Middle of the Journey* (1947), also reflects these concerns. A volume of his short stories, *Of This Time, of That Place and Other Stories*, was published posthumously in 1979.

trimeter See METRE.

triolet A verse form, derived from French poetry, which consists of eight lines and two RHYMES. The first, fourth and seventh lines, and the second and eighth lines, are the same or very similar. The few English poets who have attempted it include AUSTIN DOBSON and FRANCES CORNFORD (in 'To a Fat Lady Seen from a Train').

triplet A three-line STANZA, usually on a single RHYME, or a variation of three rhyming lines in a poem of HEROIC COUPLETS. As a stanza, it is also referred to as a tercet.

Tristram and Iseult A poem by MATTHEW ARNOLD, published in *Empedocles on Etna and Other Poems* (1852). In Brittany the dying Tristram remembers his happiness with Iseult of Ireland while her rival, Iseult of Brittany, watches over him. Iseult of Ireland arrives and there is one last passionate exchange between the lovers before he dies.

Tristram Shandy, Gentleman, The Life and Opinions of A novel by LAURENCE STERNE, published in instalments: Volumes I and II in 1760, III and IV in 1761, V and VI in 1762, VII and VIII in 1765 and Volume IX in 1767.

Immediately popular in England, it was soon translated into French and German – a surprising success for a novel which lacks a clear beginning, middle or end and defies convention at every turn. *Tristram Shandy* distributes its narrative content across a bafflingly idiosyncratic time-scheme interrupted by digressions, authorial comments and interferences with the printed fabric of the book. The comically fragmented storyline is a reaction against the linear narratives of HENRY FIELDING and the epistolary artifice of SAMUEL RICHARDSON; it aims instead at a realistic impressionism, a shape determined by association of ideas.

The story does manage to start *ab ovo*, with the narrator-hero describing his own conception. But he is not actually born for several volumes and disappears from the book in Volume VI. In the meantime, the circumstances surrounding his birth are described in an apparently random fashion. His father is Walter Shandy, the science-smitten but benevolent head of Shandy Hall, where he lives in continuous exasperation with his wife. He has elaborate theories about society, the education of his son, and such topics as baptism by injection. His brother, 'my uncle Toby', is an old soldier wounded in the groin at the siege of Namur. Toby's obsessional hobby is the recreation of various military sieges, a pastime in which he is assisted by the devoted Corporal Trim (who received a wound in the knee, at Carden) whose reflections on morality comprise Volume V. These are some of the characters whose behaviour can be understood in terms of their personal 'hobby-horses'. Dr Slop is the man-midwife delayed in delivering the infant Tristram by a complex knot on his bag, the Widow Wadman is the neighbour with amorous

designs on Uncle Toby, and Yorick is the amiable local parson. (Sterne published his own sermons and his journal to Eliza Draper under Yorick's name, and made him the fictional narrator of *A SENTIMENTAL JOURNEY*.)

After Tristram is born, Volume IV opens with the story of Slawkenbergius (a mock-ENCOMIUM on noses) and an account of how the baby came to be christened 'Tristram' instead of the intended 'Trismegistus'. After Trim's discourse there is a fine dialogue between Tristram's parents in Volume VI, about the 'breeching' (or dressing) of their child, and the story of Le Fevre (a 'sentimental' set-piece of great popularity), after which the novel arbitrarily abandons the English village setting and follows the author's travels to France, reverting to an account of the Widow Wadman's designs on Uncle Toby in Volume IX.

With its black pages, wiggly lines, misplaced chapters and other surprises, *Tristram Shandy* stands in part against the idea of literature as finished product, its surfaces capable of reflecting with accuracy the conditions of life. That is one reason why it has proved so fertile an influence on 20th-century fiction. Yet Sterne's achievement was not the act of revolutionary isolation or iconoclasm that is sometimes suggested. *Tristram Shandy* was also very much in keeping with the mood of an age caught up in the cults of 'sensibility' (see SENTIMENTAL NOVEL) and the PICTURESQUE, with its love of ruins, exciting fragments and the formally imprecise. Aside from his debt to LOCKE's theory of the association of ideas, Sterne was working in a long tradition of intellectual SATIRE embracing Montaigne, Rabelais, ERASMUS and SWIFT, as well as drawing on a mass of PICARESQUE and travel literature.

Trivia: *or, The Art of Walking the Streets of London* A poem in three parts by JOHN GAY, published in 1716. An ambitious and very popular work, it subjects the topography of the capital to a Juvenalian treatment, surveying its dangers and delights in a splendid combination of the heroic classical style and the reality of contemporary conditions. The peripatetic narrator gives the reader a conducted tour that remains unrivalled for its atmospheric detail: there is advice on reading the weather signs, escaping the filth, taking one's bearings, recognizing the street cries, avoiding criminals and so forth. The poem incorporates several notable set-pieces and digressions.

trochee See METRE.

Troilus and Cressida A play by WILLIAM SHAKESPEARE, first performed *c.* 1602 and published in Quarto (Q1) in 1609 as well as in the First Folio of 1623. Shakespeare's telling of the story owes something to oral tradition as well as to translations of Homer and, perhaps, to LYDGATE and to CHAUCER.

The story of the doomed love of Troilus and Cressida is interwoven with events in the Trojan war, in particular the death of Hector, the play's only consistently high-principled character. During a truce in the war, the weary Troilus confesses his love for Cressida to her uncle, Pandarus. True to his name, Pandarus contrives their meeting and oversees their love-making. The Greek generals are quite as jaded with the war as most of their Trojan counterparts. In particular, the effeminate and indulgent behaviour of Achilles has damaged morale. It is at Achilles that Hector's challenge to single combat is directed, and the devious Greek generals attempt to manoeuvre him into confrontation with Hector.

Cressida's father Calchas, a seer, has deserted to the Greek camp. Wishing to be reunited with his daughter, he persuades the Greeks to offer a captured Trojan general in exchange for Cressida, and Diomedes arrives in Troy to collect her. Having promised eternal love to Troilus, Cressida finds herself admired and flattered by the Greeks. She becomes Diomedes' mistress.

Hector fights Ajax, but withdraws at the point of victory because he will not harm anyone related to his father's family. Achilles offers Hector hospitality on the eve of renewed hostility between Greeks and Trojans. The next day Troilus, embittered by Cressida's faithlessness, fights fiercely. Hector, having killed Achilles' friend Patroclus, is deceitfully murdered by Achilles. As the Trojans prepare to continue the war, Pandarus leaves Troy, rejected by Troilus, whose abuse of Pandarus is an attack also on the concupiscent Cressida.

Troilus and Cressida is neither a comedy nor a tragedy. Often grouped with the PROBLEM PLAYS, *All's Well That Ends Well* and *Measure for Measure*, it is more accurately a tragicomedy than either of these associated pieces. It is not the least dispiriting feature of the play that the invective and cynicism of the scabrous Greek soldier Thersites should be truer to our experience of it than the nobility of Hector.

Troilus and Criseyde A poem by GEOFFREY CHAUCER. Displaying a fully matured control of verse, narrative and characterization, it was probably a late work, perhaps written *c.* 1385–90. Though the story has a Trojan setting it is not found in the Greek accounts of the war but first appears as an episode in the 12th-century *Roman de Troie* of Benoît de Sainte-Maure. This was translated into Latin prose by Guido delle Colonne as the *Historia destructionis Troiae* from which Boccaccio developed the incident into a complete story in its own right as *Il Filostrato*. This latter was Chaucer's source, but he adapted, expanded and greatly improved it.

The poem relates the love of Troilus, a noble young warrior second only to Hector, and Criseyde, the widowed daughter of Calchas, an astronomer who had foreseen the fall of Troy and defected to the Greek camp. Troilus sees and falls in love with Criseyde and through the agency of her uncle and guardian, Pandarus, they begin a secret affair. They live very happily until Calchas and the Greeks demand Criseyde in exchange for a prisoner of war. Afraid of public scorn the lovers neither flee nor negotiate, and Criseyde goes to the Greeks promising to return as soon as possible. When she does not come Troilus becomes desolate, consumed with grief. Meanwhile, Criseyde has – reluctantly at first – taken the Greek Diomede as a lover. Troilus sees his betrayal in a dream, sees a brooch he had given Criseyde worn by Diomede and, on creeping into the enemy camp, hears the two together. In despair he devotes himself to the battle and dies in glory. He ascends to the seventh sphere whence he looks down on earth and recognizes the vanity of worldly concerns.

The poem is remarkable in particular for its characterization. Chaucer developed the relatively simple lovers of Boccaccio's poem into complex individuals with a high degree of psychological realism in their behaviour and motivation. Troilus, perfectly noble and totally devoted to Criseyde, is at the same time incapable of decisive, assertive action and is prone to fatalism, passivity and self-pity. Criseyde, while genuinely loving Troilus, is fearful for her safety and her reputation, and lacks determination. Yet the characters are considerably more complex than any brief account can convey. Humour, coarseness, a sense of fun and boldness emerge in Criseyde's banter with her uncle, the character who is the main source of humour in the poem. The complexity and realism of the characterization has led some critics to argue that the poem approaches the form of a novel.

Characteristic of Chaucer is the subtle comedy maintained throughout, the articulate dialogue and the self-effacing narrator who is reluctant to speak ill of Criseyde. The poet's interest in Boethius' philosophy (which led to his translation *BOECE*) is shown in Criseyde's discussion of false felicity and in Troilus' long monologue on free-will and predestination (in which he misunderstands the lesson of Boethius). Dante also contributes to the philosophical fabric of the poem, and the influence of Machaut, Petrarch, Ovid and Joseph of Exeter may be found in its content. The poem's concern with love is central and has been variously interpreted as in praise and in bitter criticism of the code of COURTLY LOVE. More than a pair of courtly lovers, Troilus and Criseyde are fully developed individuals, and it is not with an artificial code but with the psychological realities of love that Chaucer is principally concerned.

Trollope, Anthony 1815–82 Novelist. Born in London, he was educated at Harrow and Winchester, where his family's poverty exposed him to humiliation and unhappiness vividly remembered in his

Autobiography (1883). The family fortunes, blighted by his father's unsuccessful business experiments, improved when his mother, FRANCES TROLLOPE, embarked on a successful literary career at the age of 50 with *Domestic Manners of the Americans* (1832). He left school, 'a hobbledehoy of nineteen, without any idea of a career' and was found a position in the Post Office through his mother's influence. He began inauspiciously as an unpunctual and debt-ridden junior clerk – a period of his life portrayed in his novel *THE THREE CLERKS* (1858) – but his career changed for the better when he was posted to Ireland in 1841–51, returning in 1853–9. There Trollope prospered: he organized the postal services, courted and married an English girl, Rose Heseltine, in 1844, wrote his first novel, *The Macdermotts of Ballycloran* (1847), and acquired a lifelong passion for hunting. Trollope resigned from the Post Office in 1867 after a distinguished career – he had introduced the pillar-box – which he felt had been insufficiently recognized by his superiors.

By this time he was already a successful and respected novelist. Recognition came with his fourth novel, *THE WARDEN* (1855), conceived, according to his *Autobiography*, while wandering round Salisbury cathedral on a summer evening, 'from whence came that series of novels of which Barchester, with its bishops, deans, and archdeacon, was the central site'. It was followed by *BARCHESTER TOWERS* (1857), *DOCTOR THORNE* (1858), *FRAMLEY PARSONAGE* (1860), *THE SMALL HOUSE AT ALLINGTON* (1862–4), and *THE LAST CHRONICLE OF BARSET* (1866–7), Trollope's favourite in the series. With their recurrent characters in a familiar, unfolding community, the BARSETSHIRE NOVELS marked a new departure for the English regional novel; their realistic presentation of middle-class domestic relationships proved highly congenial to the reading public. Trollope's other great sequence was the political or PALLISER NOVELS. Political interests are peripheral in the first, *CAN YOU FORGIVE HER?* (1864–5), and the third, *THE EUSTACE DIAMONDS* (1871–3), but *PHINEAS FINN* (1867–9), *PHINEAS REDUX* (1873–4), *THE PRIME MINISTER* (1875–6) and *THE DUKE'S CHILDREN* (1879–80) paint an unrivalled portrait of parliamentary political society in the high Victorian period. The series owes much to the steadily deepening presentation of Plantagenet Palliser and his wife Glencora, the characters on whom, with Mr Crawley of *The Last Chronicle*, Trollope believed his reputation with posterity would rest. The pessimistic vision of *Phineas Redux* reflects his own experience as unsuccessful Liberal candidate for Beverley in 1868, also treated in a separate novel, *Ralph the Heir* (1870–71). A broader pessimism informs *THE WAY WE LIVE NOW* (1874–5), a wide-ranging social SATIRE which many consider his masterpiece, though Trollope himself later declared that its 'accusations' were 'exaggerated'.

Though they are his best-known works, the Barsetshire Novels, the Palliser Novels and *The Way We Live Now* make up less than a quarter of his fictional output. It also includes: *THE BERTRAMS* (1859), *CASTLE RICHMOND* (1860), *ORLEY FARM* (1861–2), *THE BELTON ESTATE* (1865–6), *THE CLAVERINGS* (1866–7), *HE KNEW HE WAS RIGHT* (1868–9), *THE VICAR OF BULLHAMPTON* (1869–70), *SIR HARRY HOTSPUR OF HUMBLETHWAITE* (1870), *LADY ANNA* (1873–4), *THE AMERICAN SENATOR* (1876–7), *DR WORTLE'S SCHOOL* (1880), *AYALA'S ANGEL* (1881), and *MR SCARBOROUGH'S FAMILY* (1882–3). The indifferent reception of *Nina Balatka* (1866–7) and *Linda Tressel* (1867–8), which he published anonymously, confirmed his suspicion that 'a name once earned carried with it too much favour'. Trollope also produced travel books on *The West Indies and the Spanish Main* (1859), *North America* (1862), *Australia and New Zealand* (1873) and *South Africa* (1878); wrote biographies of Cicero (1880) and Lord Palmerston (1882), a politician congenial to his own position as an 'advanced conservative liberal'; and a study of THACKERAY (1879), the novelist he considered his master. Such an output was made possible by a legendary work-routine, which involved Trollope getting to his desk by 5.30 a.m. and writing 250 words each quarter of an hour for three hours, a rate of 10 pages a day, before leaving for a day's work at the Post Office.

Few of Trollope's novels are without interest. His prodigious productivity meant that he relied unduly on the conventional entanglements of romantic plot-making (for which he professed indifference) and cultivated an even professionalism of style which can lull the reader into ignoring the subtle and varied understanding of human nature on which his best work is based. He held, in his *Autobiography*, that the novelist's task was 'to make his readers so intimately acquainted with his characters that the creations of his brain should be to them speaking, moving, living, human creatures. This he can never do unless he know these fictitious personages himself, and he can never know them well unless he can live with them in the full reality of established intimacy.' To this 'intimacy' of portraiture should be added Trollope's understanding of the institutions of mid-Victorian England and the unobtrusive irony which informs his sympathetic vision of human fallibility.

Trollope, Mrs Frances 1780–1863 Novelist and travel-writer. Born into a clergyman's family in Hampshire, Fanny Milton moved to London in 1803 and married Thomas Anthony Trollope in 1809. They had six children, of whom two, ANTHONY TROLLOPE and THOMAS ADOLPHUS TROLLOPE, became novelists. Her husband's failure as a barrister and farmer led him to conceive a scheme to repair the family fortunes by sending her to Cincinnati to set up a fancy goods emporium. The scheme failed but the travel book she wrote about her American experiences, *Domestic Manners of the Americans* (1832), made her a best-selling author at the age of 52. Driven on by the family debts, she was to publish a further 40 volumes in the next 25 years, mainly novels but also several travel books based on the many spells she spent abroad during the remainder of her life. Her career is remarkable more for her heroic productivity in the face of illness and debt than for the intrinsic quality of her writing, although two novels have a place in the history of Victorian fiction: the anti-evangelical novel *Vicar of Wrexhill* (1837), an early contribution to the novel of religious controversy, and *The Life and Adventures of Michael Armstrong, the Factory Boy* (1840), one of the first Victorian 'industrial' novels.

Trollope, Thomas Adolphus 1810–92 Novelist and historian. Eldest son of FRANCES TROLLOPE and older brother of ANTHONY TROLLOPE, he was educated at Harrow and Winchester and, after some time in America, at Magdalen Hall, Oxford, where he took his degree in 1835. After a spell teaching at King Edward's School, Birmingham, he travelled abroad with his mother, settling in Florence in 1843. He married Theodosia Garrow in 1848 and their home in Florence became a centre of expatriate literary life. His first wife died in 1865 and he married the novelist Frances Eleanor Ternan, moving to Rome in 1873 as correspondent for the London *Standard*. He wrote some 60 volumes of history, fiction and travel, all now forgotten, although his autobiography, *What I Remember* (1887–9), is valuable for its picture of expatriate life in Italy in mid-Victorian times, and for its reminiscences of famous writers, including DICKENS, ELIZABETH BARRETT BROWNING, ROBERT BROWNING, GEORGE ELIOT and G. H. LEWES.

Troy Book, The A poem by JOHN LYDGATE, written in 1412–20. It narrates the history of Troy, beginning with Jason's search for the Golden Fleece and ending with the death of Ulysses. Its principal source is Guido delle Colonne's *Historia destructionis Troiae* (1287), a Latin prose translation of the *Roman de Troie* of Benoît de Sainte-Maure (*c.* 1160), but it also draws on the works of Ovid, Isidore of Seville and of medieval authors, and the influence of CHAUCER is evident throughout. The story is presented as historical fact (as it was believed to be) and Lydgate's expansion and elaboration of his source do not obscure that aim. Many of his additions are rhetorical or biographical, making the poem longer and more formal and complete than Guido's work. *The Troy Book* was very popular in the Middle Ages and influenced Renaissance writers such as CHRISTOPHER MARLOWE, THOMAS KYD and SHAKESPEARE.

Trumbull, John 1750–1831 American poet. He was born in Connecticut, and educated at Yale. His valedictory poem, *An Essay on the Uses and Advantages of the Fine Arts* (1770), condemns neo-classical aesthetics, and in its closing verses, entitled 'Prospect of the Future Glory of America', celebrates the potential of American literature. While teaching at Yale (1770–3), Trumbull also wrote a SATIRE on college education, *The Progress of Dulness: or, the Adventures of Tom Brainless* (1772). He left Yale to study law in Boston with John Adams, who inspired his patriotic poem *An Elegy on the Times* (1774). Practising law in New Haven and Hartford (1774–1825), he became associated with the CONNECTICUT WITS and with them fought to broaden Yale's curriculum to include the study of contemporary American literature, and to defend Federalist politics. After publishing *M'Fingal* (1775, 1776 and 1782), a mock EPIC which satirizes British conduct during the American Revolution, he collaborated with the other Connecticut Wits on *The Anarchiad* (1786–7) and *The Echo* (1791–1805).

Trumpet-Major, The A novel by THOMAS HARDY, first published as a serial in *Good Words* from January to December 1880 and as a book the same year. It is set during the Napoleonic wars.

Anne Garland and her mother, the widow of a landscape painter, live in one part of Overcombe Mill, the other being occupied by Miller Loveday who has two sons – Robert, a sailor, and John, trumpet-major of a regiment of Dragoons sent to the West Country to ward off a possible Napoleonic invasion. An honourable, unselfish man, John loves Anne but she does not return his affection. She, however, is irked by the unwanted attentions of the buffoonish Festus Derriman, nephew of the local squire. The lively narrative follows the fortunes of these varied individuals. Robert falls prey to Matilda Johnson, a woman of questionable reputation, and is rescued by his brother; he also narrowly escapes the press-gang but ultimately goes off to fight at Trafalgar on the *Victory*. Mrs Garland succumbs to the charms of Miller Loveday. John thrashes Festus, and Robert returns a lieutenant to marry Anne. Sadly, John leaves his family and village and goes off 'to blow his trumpet till silenced for ever upon one of the bloody battle-fields of Spain'.

Tucker, Abraham 1705–74 Amateur philosopher and country gentleman. His first work, *Free Will, Foreknowledge and Fate* (1763), was published under the pseudonym Edward Search; his second, *Man in Quest of Himself* (also 1763), appeared under the pseudonym Cuthbert Comment. His principal work was the seven-volume *The Light of Nature Pursued* (1768–78), so long and diffuse that its ideas were not recognized until systematized by WILLIAM PALEY in THE PRINCIPLES OF MORAL AND POLITICAL PHILOSOPHY. Tucker asserted that the principle of moral conduct was to be found in general happiness, while the motive of the individual could be found in his own content. The two do not always agree. Moral conduct demands self-sacrifice, which is justified by religion with its hope of a future life.

Tuckerman, Frederick Goddard 1821–73 American poet. Born in Boston and educated at Harvard, he is best known for his SONNETS, personal and often melancholy in tone. His only volume, *Poems*, appeared in 1860. NATHANIEL HAWTHORNE, RALPH WALDO EMERSON and HENRY WADSWORTH LONGFELLOW all praised his work, but he was generally forgotten until the poet Witter Bynner published a selection from *Poems* in 1931 along with three previously unpublished sonnets. All of his work was later collected, edited and introduced by N. SCOTT MOMADAY in *The Complete Poems of Frederick Tuckerman* (1965).

Tupper, Martin (Farquhar) 1810–89 Poet. Born in London, he was educated at Charterhouse, where THACKERAY was a contemporary, and Christ Church, Oxford, where Gladstone became a friend. His first volume, *Sacra Poesis* (1832), was religious; the second, *A Voice from the Cloister* (1835), warned undergraduates against vice. Tupper became famous with *Proverbial Philosophy: A Book of Thoughts and Arguments, Originally Treated* (1838), a collection of loosely versified commonplaces. It ran to over 50 editions in England, as well as being extremely popular in America. Tupper continued to write prolifically, publishing a continuation of COLERIDGE's CHRISTABEL (1838), three more series of *Proverbial Philosophy* (1842, 1867, 1869), three CONDITION OF ENGLAND NOVELS (*The Crock of Gold*, *The Twins* and *Heart*, all 1844), a historical novel (*Stephan Langton*, 1858), several plays, an autobiography and many occasional verses. Never well received by the critics, his work had lost popularity before his death.

Turn of the Screw, The A short novel by HENRY JAMES, first published in *Collier's Weekly*, and then with another story, 'Covering End', in a volume entitled *The Two Magics*, in 1898.

The story is about a governess who takes charge of two children at the lonely country house of Bly. Her employer, the children's uncle, has given her strict orders not to bother him with any of the details of their education or behaviour. The children, Flora and Miles, are attractive and intelligent, but also seem strained and secretive. Shortly after her arrival the governess sees two former members of the household, the steward Peter Quint and the previous governess Miss Jessel; later she learns that both of them are dead. She is convinced that the children see the ghosts too, but they display a remarkable talent for evading questions about them. She challenges Flora directly and provokes a hysterical reaction which

makes the girl ill. When she confronts Miles, Peter Quint appears at the window. She is determined to exorcize his influence, but despite her efforts to shield Miles from the apparition, the frantic and terrified boy dies in her arms. The fact that, after a brief introductory section, the story is told from the point of view of the governess raises doubts about whether the ghosts are 'real' or merely her hallucinations.

Turner, Ethel 1872–1958 Australian writer of CHILDREN'S LITERATURE. Born in Yorkshire, she emigrated to Australia with her family in 1880. Educated at the Sydney Girls' High School, She later contributed a children's column to *The Australian Town and Country Journal*. Her first novel, *Seven Little Australians* (1894), was an immediate success. It describes the unruly children of Captain Woolcott, an unsympathetic widower who has just remarried; far from mellowing, he becomes even more irritated by his family, finally sending his daughter Judy with her infant brother to a remote inland settlement. After learning about country ways, Judy dies saving her brother's life, and while this naturally sobers the other rebellious children they soon get back into trouble with authority in a sequel, *The Family at Misrule* (1895). The same theme reappears in many of the stories that followed, where good-hearted if mischievous children are constantly thwarted by parents who are either insensitive or negligent. Often very funny, Ethel Turner is comparable to E. NESBIT in her depictions of the ups and downs of family life and anticipates RICHMAL CROMPTON in her relish for children's ability to discomfort adults.

Turner, Frederick Jackson 1861–1932 American historian. He was born in Portage, Wisconsin, and educated at the University of Wisconsin and Johns Hopkins University. He taught at the University of Wisconsin and at Harvard. Turner read his famous essay, 'The Significance of the Frontier in American History', to the American Historical Association in Chicago in 1893. In it he advanced the notion that the continual challenge presented by the frontier was the primary factor in American development, more important than the European influences of ancestry and culture. American life and values, he argued, were shaped above all by the waves of western movement. 'The Significance of the Frontier' was published with some of his other essays as *The Frontier in American History* (1920). His earlier publications include *The Character and Influence of the Indian Trade in Wisconsin* (1891) and *Rise of the New West, 1819–1829* (1906). For *The Significance of Sections in American History* (1932), Turner was posthumously awarded the PULITZER PRIZE for history. He won a second posthumous Pulitzer for *The United States, 1830–1850, The Nation and Its Sections* (1935), a continuation of *Rise of the New West*.

Turner, Sharon 1768–1847 Historian. Born and educated in London, he abandoned it the law for the study of Old English manuscripts in the British Museum; he had long been interested in Norse antiquity and its connection with the history of England. Primarily an antiquarian, he nevertheless produced, after 16 years' work, *A History of England from the Earliest Period to the Norman Conquest* (1799–1805), which encouraged serious study of England's ancient past. Other books by Turner were *The History of England from the Norman Conquest to 1500* (1814–23), *The History of the Reign of Henry VIII* (1826) and *The Reigns of Edward VI, Mary and Elizabeth* (1829). He also published *A Vindication of the Genuineness of the Ancient British Poems of Aneurin, Taliesin, Llynwarch Hen and Merdhin, with Specimens* (1803).

Tusser, Thomas ?1524–80 Agricultural writer and poet. Tusser was educated at Eton and Cambridge, and farmed in Suffolk, where he introduced the cultivation of barley. *A Hundred Points of Good Husbandry* (1557) is a manual in verse about farming and gardening, adorned with aphorisms on behaviour which make it a rich source of proverbs and maxims. The work was enlarged by the addition of *A Hundred Good Points of Housewifery* in the 1570 edition; by 1573 the 100 good points had grown to 500.

Tutuola, Amos 1920– Nigerian writer. Born in Abeokuta, he became a farmer, blacksmith and office messenger. He inaugurated West African literature in English with *The Palm-Wine Drinkard* (1952), a sequence of 30 episodes of quest, endurance and the achievement of wisdom, mainly adapted from Yoruba folk-tales. Tutuola works in the tradition of the village storyteller but, instead of telling his stories in Yoruba, writes them in the best English his scanty schooling permits. His linguistic idiosyncrasy proves a strangely suitable means of conducting his readers into the rich expanses of the Yoruba imagination – to which indeed he adds his own inventions, like the television-handed goddess in *My Life in the Bush of Ghosts* (1954). His other books are: *Simbi and the Satyr of the Dark Jungle* (1955), *The Brave African Huntress* (1958), *Feather Woman of the Jungle* (1962), *Ajaiyi and His Inherited Poverty* (1967), *The Witch-Herbalist of the Remote Town* (1981) and *The Wild Hunter in the Bush of Ghosts* (1989).

Tuwhare, Hone 1922– New Zealand poet. Born in Kaikohe in Northland, he grew up in Auckland. He had no secondary schooling but was apprenticed as a boilermaker at the Railway Workshops; later he worked as a boilermaker on hydro-electric power projects in New Zealand, Western Samoa and Papua New Guinea. While a member of the Communist Party he came to know R. A. K. MASON, who encouraged his writing and contributed a preface to Tuwhare's first collection, *No Ordinary Sun* (1964). Reprinted 11 times, it was one of the best-selling poetry books ever published in New Zealand. *Mihi: Collected Poems* (1987) offers an overview of Tuwhare's work. His poetry is influenced by the rhythms and cadences of the oral Maori tradition and the Bible, by the English lyric, and by contemporary Maori and Pakeha (European) working-class vernacular. Out of this rich mixture of voices Tuwhare writes lyrics, ELEGIES, conversation poems and political poems. Like WITI IHIMAERA and PATRICIA GRACE, he is preoccupied with the Maori land issue. He has also written stories and plays.

Twain, Mark [Clemens, Samuel Langhorne] 1835–1910 American novelist, short-story writer and humorist. Born in Florida, Missouri, he moved with his family to the Mississippi River town of Hannibal when he was four. Later, he would make the scenes of his youth internationally famous in his most popular novels, THE ADVENTURES OF TOM SAWYER and ADVENTURES OF HUCKLEBERRY FINN. Although always associated with the Mississippi River region, he travelled widely. He left school at the age of 12, and later travelled throughout the East and Midwest as a journeyman printer. He served briefly in the Confederate Army during the Civil War, but his division deserted and he spent the remainder of the war out West, some of it prospecting for silver in Nevada with his brother Orion, and then working with BRET HARTE as a journalist in San Francisco. In 1863 he began using the name Mark Twain, and in 1865 made it famous with his story THE CELEBRATED JUMPING FROG OF CALAVERAS COUNTY.

Twain's rise to celebrity was impressive. His sparkling personality and his quotable phrases caught on fast and he soon began making lecture tours. His 1867 trip to Europe and the Holy Land produced his first major work, THE INNOCENTS ABROAD (1869). He returned to America to settle in the East, and in 1870 married Olivia Langdon, the wealthy daughter of a New York coal magnate. His popularity continued to grow, through a series of works: ROUGHING IT (1872), a humorous narrative of his early travels out West; THE GILDED AGE (1873), a satirical novel of the post-Civil War era which he co-wrote with CHARLES DUDLEY WARNER; the ever-popular *Adventures of Tom Sawyer* (1876); and *A Tramp Abroad* (1880), another travel narrative. On his frequent visits to England he was received even more enthusiastically than in the USA.

The last works of what might be called Twain's optimistic period were THE PRINCE AND THE PAUPER (1882) and LIFE ON THE MISSISSIPPI (1883). In 1884 his heavy investment in a badly managed publishing firm and an inefficient typesetting invention drove him into bankruptcy. Ironically, the products of this harsh awakening are among his best works, most no-

Mark Twain: a caricature
by Joseph Keppler

tably the renowned *Adventures of Huckleberry Finn* (1884), which has a moral dimension that is lacking in its predecessor *Tom Sawyer*. A CONNECTICUT YANKEE IN KING ARTHUR'S COURT (1889) and THE TRAGEDY OF PUDD'NHEAD WILSON (1894) are both characterized by a deep pessimism, though both were conceived simply as entertainments. In *The American Claimant* (1892), *Tom Sawyer Abroad* (1894), and *Tom Sawyer, Detective* (1896) he sought to recapture the innocent fun of his early works, but he was never quite able to write with his former casual ease.

He gradually overcame his debts, but after his daughter Susy died in 1896 Twain became increasingly alienated from the good-humoured wit on which his popularity was based. Books such as *The Man That Corrupted Hadleyburg* (1900) and *What is Man?* (1906), as well as much of his posthumously published work, reflect a severe pessimism and dissatisfaction. However, when his personal life was devastated (his wife died in 1904 and his second daughter in 1909), his professional life carried him through. He continued to lecture widely, in the USA and abroad, though his opinions were often controversial, and he was supremely proud of the honorary doctorate of letters awarded to him by Oxford University in 1907. When he died in 1910 he left a wealth of unpublished material, including *The Mysterious Stranger* (1916)

and *Letters from the Earth* (1962). His *Autobiography* was published in 1924.

***Twelfth Night:** or, What You Will* A comedy by WILLIAM SHAKESPEARE, first performed *c.* 1600 and published in the First Folio of 1623. The most direct source was probably BARNABE RICH's *Apolonius and Silla*, a story derived from the Italian of Matteo Bandello.

A shipwreck brings to the sea coast of Illyria a mournful but still resourceful Viola, saddened by the loss, in the same wreck, of her 'identical' twin brother, Sebastian. Disguised as a boy (Cesario), she seeks service in the court of Orsino, Duke of Illyria. Orsino is hopelessly in love with Olivia, a lady who rejects him ostensibly because she is mourning her dead brother. As Cesario, Viola is sent to Olivia's house with messages of love from Orsino. Olivia is attracted to Viola, who is secretly falling in love with Orsino. Unknown to Viola, Sebastian arrives in Illyria with his faithful friend Antonio. The two men are separated, and accidents of identical appearance and identical dress lead, through mistaken identity, to Antonio's belief that Sebastian has betrayed their friendship, to the astonished Sebastian's marriage to Olivia, and to a near-crisis when Orsino believes that Viola has stolen Olivia from him and threatens dire punishment. Only when, at the play's end, Sebastian and Viola are allowed on stage together do the confusions turn to clarity. Orsino is free to marry the loving Viola and Olivia to keep faith with her new husband, Sebastian.

In a busy sub-plot, Olivia's bibulous kinsman Sir Toby Belch takes advantage of the gullible Sir Andrew Aguecheek, plays an enthusiastic part in an inventive practical joke on Olivia's presumptuous steward Malvolio, and marries the plot's inventor, Olivia's lady-in-waiting Maria.

Twelfth Night is the most formally satisfying of Shakespeare's mature comedies. There is some evidence that the part of the worldly-wise clown, Feste, was rewritten to take account of the musical skills of ROBERT ARMIN, who had recently replaced WILL KEMP. That is speculative, but Feste certainly has three of Shakespeare's finest songs, and the play is uncommonly confident in its use of music.

Two Drovers, The See CHRONICLES OF THE CANONGATE.

Two Foscari, The A tragedy by BYRON, first published in 1821, the same year as his other Venetian tragedy, MARINO FALIERO. It was produced at COVENT GARDEN in 1837. Verdi's opera, based on Byron's tragedy, was first produced in Rome in 1844. It is set in the 15th century and Jacopo Foscari, son of the aged Doge Francesco Foscari, is being interrogated on the rack. He was twice exiled, first for accepting bribes and then for complicity in the murder of Donato, one of the Council of Ten who had sentenced him to his first exile. He has been brought back from his second exile in Crete to answer charges of treason, and faces execution. But the council sentence him to perpetual exile and the aged Francesco has to sign the decree. The sentence is too much for Jacopo, who dies when he hears the news. The council then demand the abdication of his father, who dies as he leaves the palace, while the bells of St Mark's toll for the election of a new Doge. The historical Jacopo Foscari died in Crete six months after his perpetual banishment, too soon for the reprieve which followed the confession of the real murderer of Donato.

Two Gentlemen of Verona, The A comedy by WILLIAM SHAKESPEARE, first performed *c.* 1593 and published in the First Folio of 1623. The source of the play is a story by Jorge de Montemayor, *Diana enamorada*, but Shakespeare may have come upon it by way of a lost play, *The History of Felix and Philiomena*, known to have been acted at court in 1585.

The two gentlemen are the friends Valentine and Proteus, who both fall in love with the Duke of Milan's daughter Silvia, though Proteus was originally contracted to Julia in Verona. Proteus betrays Valentine to the Duke, who wants his daughter to marry Thurio, and Valentine becomes the leader of an outlaw band.

Julia disguises herself as a boy and becomes page to Proteus. Silvia is captured by robbers and rescued by Proteus, still pressing his unwelcome suit. Eventually the confusions and identities are resolved; the Duke withdraws his objections to Valentine, allowing him to marry Silvia and Proteus to marry Julia.

The Two Gentlemen of Verona is a charming romantic comedy, without the emotional or imaginative range of Shakespeare's mature work in the genre. Proteus's servant Launce, much troubled by his dog, has some of the best theatrical opportunities. The part was probably written for WILL KEMP.

Two Noble Kinsmen, The A play first published in 1634, bearing on the title-page the inscription 'Written by the memorable Worthies of their Time; Mr JOHN FLETCHER, and Mr WILLIAM SHAKESPEARE. Gent.' Most critics agree that, whatever Shakespeare's contribution may have been, it was not sufficient to make a good play of it. It is based on CHAUCER's The *Knight's Tale* (see THE CANTERBURY TALES) with an additional character, the jailer's daughter, who helps in Palamon's escape and then goes mad with love for him.

Two on a Tower A novel by THOMAS HARDY, first published serially in *The Atlantic Monthly*, an American journal, between May and December 1882 and in book form the same year.

Swithin St Cleeve, a young astronomer and son of a curate who married beneath himself, is found by Lady Viviette Constantine (some ten years his senior) using as his observatory a column known as Rings-Hill Speer, on the estate of her husband, Sir Blount Constantine, an unpleasant man given to big-game hunting. Upon being informed of the latter's death in Africa Viviette and Swithin marry in secret. About the same time Swithin is left a generous inheritance, which he ignores because it is contingent on his remaining single until the age of 25. Then he and Viviette learn that Sir Blount, although now dead, was alive when they married, thus rendering the union void. Under pressure from Viviette, Swithin claims his inheritance and travels abroad. Viviette realizes she is pregnant and, to confer respectability on the child, accepts the hand of the Bishop of Melchester, who dies soon after their marriage. After an absence of a few years Swithin returns to England, meets Viviette once more and proposes anew. But the shock is too much and she dies.

Two Treatises of Government JOHN LOCKE began his refutation of the doctrine of absolute power, and his proposals for reconciling individual liberty with collective order, during the last two years of his employment in the house of the Earl of Shaftesbury. By the time his work appeared in 1690 the idea of Divine Right had already died a natural death: Shaftesbury had fallen, Charles II had died, his successor James II had abdicated and a revolution had placed William and Mary on the throne. Nevertheless, Locke's *Treatises* had enormous influence on liberal thought, in France and America as well as England. The second treatise proposed Locke's theory of social contract: the people consent to be governed, resigning total freedom so that life, property and liberty can be maintained, while for their part those who govern remain accountable and lose their authority when they exceed their powers.

Two Years before the Mast An account by RICHARD HENRY DANA of life at sea in the 1830s, published in 1840. After leaving Harvard University, he sailed on the brig *Pilgrim* from Boston around Cape Horn to California, and made the return trip on the *Alert*. His vivid portraits of his fellow seamen stress the cruelties and injustices they suffered. Another chapter, added 24 years later, tells of his return to California in 1859 and of the fortunes of some of the men described in the original narrative.

Tyler, Anne 1941– American novelist. Born in Minneapolis and educated at Duke University and Columbia, she now lives in Baltimore, the setting for most of her fiction. She has achieved greatest acclaim for *The Accidental Tourist* (1985), awarded a PULITZER PRIZE and filmed, about a lonely writer of guidebooks for business travellers. Its cast of oddball characters, its tone modulating from whimsical comedy to pathos and its emphasis on family life all typify her work and the continual danger of sentimentality it runs. Other novels include *If Morning Ever Comes* (1965), *A Slipping-Down Life* (1970), *Celestial Navigation* (1975), *Searching for Caleb* (1976), *Morgan's Passing* (1980), *Dinner at the Homesick Restaurant* (1982), *Breathing Lessons* (Pulitzer Prize, 1988) and *Saint Maybe* (1991).

Tyler, Royall 1757–1826 American playwright and novelist. He was born in Boston and educated at Harvard. A distinguished legal career culminated in his appointments as chief justice of the Supreme Court in Vermont (1807–13), and as professor of jurisprudence at the University of Vermont (1811–14).

His literary reputation is based largely on his first play, *THE CONTRAST* (1787), said to have been written in the three weeks following his attendance at a performance of *THE SCHOOL FOR SCANDAL* in New York. *The Contrast* was the first comedy by a native American writer to be professionally produced. Tyler's second and less successful play was *Mad Day in Town: or, New York in an Uproar* (1787), a comic opera of which the manuscript has not survived. Two other plays of which no copy exists are *The Farm House: or, The Female Duellists* (1796), possibly an adaptation of J. P. Kemble's *The Farm House* (1789), and *The Georgia*

Spec: or, Land in the Moon (1797), a satire of land speculation in Georgia. The texts of four other plays have survived, though none has been produced on stage: *The Island of Barrataria* is a three-act FARCE based on an episode from Cervantes's *Don Quixote*; *The Judgment of Solomon*, *The Origin of the Feast of Purim* and *Joseph and his Brethren* are all sacred verse dramas. *The Yankey in London* (1809) is a collection of essays and sketches. *THE ALGERINE CAPTIVE* (1797) was his only novel.

Tynan, Katharine 1861–1931 Irish poet, novelist and journalist. Born in County Dublin, she attended a convent school at Drogheda. A literary hostess and close friend of W. B. YEATS, she married Henry A. Hinkson in 1893 and moved to England, where she became a regular contributor to a number of English, Irish and American journals and magazines. Her journalism won her a large public but did not help her career as a poet. She and her family returned to Ireland in 1911 and maintained a strong pro-British stance throughout the insurrectionary period. After her husband's death in 1919 she travelled through Europe, writing journalistic pieces on the chaotic conditions she found. A prolific writer, she produced 105 novels, 18 volumes of poetry and 38 other miscellaneous volumes as well as journalistic pieces that were not collected. Her *Collected Poems* appeared in 1930. Much of her work is strongly Roman Catholic in its preoccupations. She is widely regarded as one of the most promising but blighted poets of the Irish revival.

Tynan, Kenneth (Peacock) 1927–80 Drama critic. A short career as an actor and director preceded his appointment as a reviewer of plays for *The Observer* in 1954. Tynan's lifelong delight in controversy was the mercurial aspect of his passionate belief in the neglected importance of theatre in society. During his first spell at *The Observer* (1954–8), English drama experienced a revival, and Tynan undoubtedly contributed to it, not only by his trenchantly witty reviews, but also by his engagement in theoretical debates in the short-lived but influential journal, *Encore*. He became Brecht's most articulate English advocate. After two years as dramatic critic for *THE NEW YORKER* (1958–60), Tynan returned to *The Observer* for a second spell (1960–3) and was then appointed literary manager of the ROYAL NATIONAL THEATRE (1963–9). It was he who spearheaded the assault on theatrical censorship in Britain and the erotic revue, *Oh! Calcutta!*, which he produced in 1968–9, was in part a celebration of the abolition of the Lord Chamberlain's powers. Tynan's theatrical criticism has been collected in several volumes, *He That Plays the King* (1950), *Curtains* (1961), *Tynan Right and Left* (1968) and *A View of the English Stage* (1975) among them. His enthusiasm for bullfighting is recorded in *Bull Fever* (1955). He spent his last years in the USA.

Tyndale, William ?1494–1536 Protestant martyr, humanist and translator of the Bible. He came from Gloucestershire, was educated at Oxford and later Cambridge. In 1522 he sought support for an English translation of the Bible, but finding such figures as Tunstall, Bishop of London, opposed to the project left England for the Continent in 1524, never to return. Printing of his English New Testament (translated from the Greek text of ERASMUS) was begun at Cologne and, after intervention by local magistrates, completed at Worms in 1525–6. Such copies as found their way to England were ordered by the bishops to be burned. Tyndale spent most of the rest of his life in Antwerp where he revised his New Testament and completed English translations of the Pentateuch (1530) and Jonah (1531). COVERDALE continued the work: see also THE BIBLE IN ENGLISH.

Doctrinally, he was close to Luther, whom he met at Wittenberg, on justification by faith, but was Zwinglian in his view of the Eucharist. His view of the king as sole authority in the state was expressed in his *The Obedience of a Christian Man* (1528), which won him the approval of Henry VIII. Nonetheless Tyndale later opposed the king's divorce. Tyndale entered into controversy with THOMAS MORE, notably in *An Answer unto Sir Thomas More's Dialogue* (1530). A translation of Erasmus' *Enchiridion militis christianae* as *The Manual of the Christian Knight* is also attributed to him.

Tyndale was arrested for heresy at Antwerp, imprisoned at Vilvorde near Brussels, and strangled and burned at the stake.

Tyndall, John 1820–93 Scientist. Born to small landowners at Leighlin Bridge, County Carlow, Ireland, Tyndall was educated at the local national school and then worked on the Ordnance Survey of Ireland. Later, he attended the Mechanics Institute at Preston, Lancashire, and became a railway engineer and teacher. His career as a scientist began when he studied for a D. Phil. at Marburg University in 1848–50. His work on magnetic force and radiant heat made him famous among scientists, and his graphic and graceful expository style made him perhaps the greatest popularizer of 19th-century physical science. His essays in this field are published as *Fragments of Science for Unscientific People* (1871; 8 vols. by 1889).

Tyndall is said to have had an extraordinarily developed mental awareness of relations in space, an intellectual talent trained, he suggested, by early study of the syntax of MILTON'S *PARADISE LOST*. The impact of his writing concerning wave-theory and the reasons for the blue colour of the sky can be traced in GEORGE ELIOT'S *MIDDLEMARCH* and *DANIEL DERONDA*. He is fleetingly, but significantly, referred to in VIRGINIA WOOLF'S *MRS DALLOWAY*. Her father, LESLIE STEPHEN, was, with THOMAS HENRY HUXLEY, among Tyndall's closest friends, and, with them, he was a leader of agnostic opinion.

Typee: *A Peep at Polynesian Life. During a Four Months' Residence in a Valley of the Marquesas* HERMAN MELVILLE's first novel, published in 1846. It is based on his own experiences in the South Seas.

Two seamen on a whaler, Tommo and Toby, jump ship in the Marquesas Islands and make their way to an inland valley. They have heard that the Typee tribe is particularly savage, and hope instead to fall in with the peace-loving Happars. They meet the Typees first, however, and find them fairly friendly. Then the two become separated, and Tommo is left alone among the Typees. The natives are kind and generous, and he enjoys his island paradise in the company of Fayaway, a beautiful native girl. A sympathetic though not always comprehending observer of island culture, he criticizes white missionary efforts and their destructive effects on the islanders, as well as the facile dichotomy between 'civilization' and 'savagery' by which the whites justify their actions. However, some native customs are strange to him – he has heard uncomfortable rumours about cannibalism – and he becomes increasingly homesick for the Western world. He sees evidence of ritual cannibalism among the Typees and begins to fear that he will be their next victim. He decides to flee the valley, and though the tribe pursues him into the sea he is rescued by the boat of an Australian whaler. *OMOO* is a sequel.

Tyrannic Love: *or, The Royal Martyr* A heroic tragedy in rhymed couplets by JOHN DRYDEN, produced in 1669 and published in 1670. The story concerns Princess Catharine of Alexandria, a Christian captive of the Roman Emperor Maximin. He falls in love with her but she does not respond. She succeeds in converting the Empress Berenice and the furious Maximin orders their death. Catharine is beheaded and becomes St Catharine, but Maximin is stabbed by Placidius, an officer who loves Berenice and is determined to save her.

Tyrwhitt, Thomas 1730–86 Scholar and editor. He was born at Westminster, educated at Eton College and The Queen's College, Oxford, and elected a fellow of Merton College in 1755. He was notable for the careful scholarship he brought to the study of CHAUCER's poetry. His edition of *THE CANTERBURY TALES* (1775–8) helped establish the Chaucer canon but was most important for explaining the principles of Chaucer's heroic line, which had gone undiscerned for four centuries. Tyrwhitt also edited the Rowley poems of THOMAS CHATTERTON in 1777, a time when they were still the object of great curiosity and dispute as to their authenticity. He himself became persuaded that they were forgeries and argued this view in an appendix added to his edition in the following year.

Udall [Uvedale], **Nicholas** 1505–56 Playwright. It is known that he was commissioned by Queen Mary to present masques and plays. Only *RALPH ROISTER DOISTER*, which vies with *GAMMER GURTON'S NEEDLE* for the title of the earliest English comedy, can be called his with any certainty, though several other works (e.g. *JACK JUGGLER* and *THERSITES*) have been attributed to him. Udall was born in Southampton and educated at Winchester and Corpus Christi College, Oxford, where he became a fellow in 1524. At Oxford he was suspected of Lutheranism and investigated in 1528 but seems to have emerged unscathed. With his friend JOHN LELAND he contributed songs and verses for the coronation procession of Anne Boleyn in 1533, and in 1534 Udall published a book of selections from Terence with English translations, *Flowers for Latin Speaking*. In the same year he became headmaster of Eton and was soon notorious for the readiness with which he ordered floggings. He was dismissed in 1541, charged with theft and homosexual practices. He was imprisoned in the Marshalsea but apparently not for long, since he was settled in London in 1542 and in that year published his translation of the *Apophthegmata* of ERASMUS. He was by now a declared supporter of the Reformation and in a lost play, *Ezechias*, celebrated the king's triumph over the Pope. Well on the way to rehabilitation with his translation of Erasmus's *Paraphrase upon Luke* (1545) under the patronage of Queen Catherine, he supervised the publication of the complete *Paraphrases* in 1549. He became canon of Windsor in 1551 and, in spite of his Reformist zeal, seems to have enjoyed the goodwill of Mary when she became queen. In 1555 he became headmaster of Westminster School.

Ulster Literary Theatre It was founded in 1902, with no encouragement from YEATS, by Bulmer Hobson and David Parkhill (Lewis Purcell), both of whom contributed plays. It proposed to enunciate a regional identity, a variant of the ABBEY THEATRE's work, often in good-humoured SATIRE. In 1915 its name changed to the Ulster Theatre. The company toured England and Ireland and gave the premières of some 50 Northern Irish plays. Apart from RUTHERFORD MAYNE, it cultivated no important dramatist and remained amateur to the end, though working to professional standards. Its demise in 1934 was due to the lack of either private or government financing.

Ulysses A DRAMATIC MONOLOGUE by ALFRED TENNYSON, published in 1842 but written in 1833. Its sources are Book IX of *The Odyssey* and Canto XXVI of Dante's *Inferno*. In old age Ulysses looks back on his past travels and forward to his last voyage, summoning the values of endurance, determination and hope to his aid. Tennyson said that there was more of himself in this poem than in *IN MEMORIAM*: it was 'written under the sense of loss and that all had gone by, but that still life must be fought out to the end'.

Ulysses A novel by JAMES JOYCE, written in Trieste, Zurich and Paris between 1914 and 1921. Its serialization by *THE LITTLE REVIEW*, begun in 1918, was suspended in 1920 after the 'Nausicaa' chapter provoked a prosecution for obscenity. The first edition was published in Paris by Harriet Shaw Weaver's Egoist Press on 2 February 1922, Joyce's 40th birthday. *Ulysses* was banned in the USA until 1933 and in Britain until 1937.

The action takes place in Dublin on a single day, 16 June 1904, now known as 'Bloomsday'. Its main protagonists are: Leopold Bloom, a Jewish advertisement canvasser; his unfaithful wife Molly, a concert singer; and Stephen Dedalus, from *A PORTRAIT OF THE ARTIST AS A YOUNG MAN*. Bloom and Stephen wander separately around Dublin until they meet at the end of the day, an event which may or may not alter the sense of futility, frustration and loneliness which possesses them.

The minutely detailed account of the mundane, and occasionally sordid, episodes of the day, and of the topography of Dublin, would seem to place *Ulysses* at the extreme edge of REALISM and to suggest that Joyce's ambition was to offer the largest 'slice of life' in the history of the English novel. A different purpose is implied by the systematic allusion to Homer's *Odyssey* which dominates the book's manifold references to literature, music, philosophy, history and myth. According to this scheme Bloom represents Odysseus (Ulysses), Molly is Penelope and Stephen is Telemachus. The titles Joyce originally gave to the novel's 18 chapters spell out the parallel: 1 'Telemachus' (Stephen and Buck Mulligan at the Martello Tower); 2 'Nestor' (Stephen at work as a schoolteacher); 3 'Proteus' (Stephen meditating on the beach); 4 'Calypso' (Bloom making breakfast for Molly); 5 'Lotos Eaters' (Bloom on Sir John Rogerson's Quay); 6 'Hades' (Bloom at Paddy Dignam's funeral); 7 'Aeolus' (Bloom in the newspaper office); 8 'Lestrygonians' (Bloom at lunch); 9 'Scylla and Charybdis' (Stephen in the National Library); 10 'Wandering Rocks' (the citizens of Dublin on the streets); 11 'Sirens' (Bloom in the Ormond hotel); 12 'Polyphemus' or 'Cyclops' (Bloom's encounter with an Irish nationalist); 13 'Nausicaa' (Bloom watching

Gertie McDowell on the beach); 14 'Oxen of the Sun' (Bloom and Stephen separately visiting the Holles Street Hospital); 15 'Circe' (Bloom and Stephen meeting in the Mabbot Street brothel district, 'Nighttown'); 16 'Eumaeus' (Stephen and Bloom at Bloom's home in Eccles Street); 17 'Ithaca' (Bloom falling asleep); 18 'Penelope' (Molly Bloom's soliloquy).

The Homeric parallel has a double and deliberately contradictory purpose: making SATIRE, or at least MOCK-HEROIC, of the contrast between ancient grandeur and pitiful modernity but also asserting that the present can provide valid material for EPIC. Joyce's relentlessly experimental method answers this complex challenge. He uses STREAM OF CONSCIOUSNESS (most notably in 'Penelope') without relying on it to sustain a book which also embraces PARODY (of journalese in 'Aeolus', women's magazine fiction in 'Nausicaa' and the whole history of English prose style in 'Oxen of the Sun') and EXPRESSIONISM in 'Circe'.

Uncle Remus: *His Songs and His Sayings* The first collection of JOEL CHANDLER HARRIS's verse and tales based on black folklore, published in 1881. Uncle Remus, once a slave, is a valued family servant; the son of the house is a fascinated audience to whom he recounts the traditional stories of his people. Harris attempts to reproduce the speech of plantation blacks, and endows the animals in his fables with human qualities. Among the characters are Br'er Rabbit, Br'er Fox and Br'er Wolf.

Uncle Silas: *A Tale of Bartram-Haugh* A novel of suspense by SHERIDAN LE FANU, published in 1864.

On her father's death Maud Ruthyn is made the ward of her uncle Silas, a sinister figure suspected of having murdered a gambling associate at his remote house, Bartram-Haugh, in Derbyshire. Silas, who will inherit if Maud should die, tries to force her into marriage to his own unpleasant son, Dudley. She escapes the marriage when it turns out that Dudley already has a wife, but Silas begins to plot her murder. The web of terror and intrigue tightens around the girl with the introduction of the grotesque and frightening French governess, Madame de la Rougierre. In the event, the plot against her fails, Dudley kills the governess by mistake and Maud makes her escape.

Uncle Tom's Cabin: *or, Life among the Lowly* An anti-slavery novel by HARRIET BEECHER STOWE, published serially in the *National Era* (1851–2) and in book form in 1852. It became the best-selling novel of the 19th century. Abraham Lincoln, in the midst of the Civil War, is reported to have remarked that Mrs Stowe was 'the little lady who wrote the book that made this great war'.

Uncle Tom is a saintly and faithful slave owned by the Shelby family. When the Shelbys find themselves in financial straits, Tom is separated from his wife and children and sold to a slave trader. Young George Shelby sympathizes with Tom and vows to redeem him some day. Tom is taken South, and on the voyage down the Mississippi he saves the life of Eva St Clare (known as little Eva) with the result that her father buys him out of gratitude. They go to the St Clare home in New Orleans, where Tom is happy and grows close to Eva and her black friend Topsy. After two years little Eva dies from a weakened constitution in a highly sentimental death scene. Her father is then killed in an accident and Tom is sold at auction to the villainous Simon Legree, a cruel and drunken Yankee. Two female slaves capitalize on Tom's ever-patient nature by pretending to escape and going into hiding. Tom will not reveal their whereabouts, and Legree has him brutally whipped to death. As he is dying, George Shelby arrives to rescue him but it is too late. In despair, Shelby pledges to fight for the Abolitionist cause. 'God wrote the book,' Mrs Stowe once said. 'I took His dictation.'

Unconditional Surrender See *SWORD OF HONOUR*.

Under Milk Wood A 'Play for voices' by DYLAN THOMAS, written in 1952, revised for its first public performance during his American tour in 1953, and first broadcast as a radio play in 1954. It describes, in liltingly poetic prose, a day in the life of some of the inhabitants of a small fishing town in South Wales. Called Llareggub (a jesting reversal of 'buggerall') in the play, the town is based on Laugharne, where Thomas lived.

Under the Greenwood Tree: *or, The Mellstock Quire* A novel by THOMAS HARDY, first published in 1872.

Termed 'a rural painting of the Dutch school', this pastoral tale set in and about Mellstock (Stinsford) concerns the love of Dick Dewey, a tranter, for the flighty but charming Fancy Day. The narrative also traces the decline of the old church music, to be supplanted at Mellstock by a 'cabinet-organ'. Fancy, the new teacher at the parish school and would-be organist, is sought not only by Dick (whom she really loves) but also by Farmer Shiner and Parson Maybold. In a weak moment she rashly agrees to marry the latter and then, recognizing her foolishness in time, breaks the engagement. The book ends with her cheery rustic marriage to Dick. *Under the Greenwood Tree* is a sunny, bucolic novel populated by simple, amusing countryfolk, but it is touched with regret at the changing of the old musical order and the duplicity of Fancy Day.

Under the Volcano A novel by MALCOLM LOWRY, published in 1947 and considered his masterpiece. It is the story of the final day in the life of Geoffrey

Firmin, the British Consul in Cuernavaca, Mexico, in 1938, on the date of the festival of the Day of the Dead. On this day (the events of which are recalled in flashback exactly a year later by Firmin's former neighbour, Jacques Laruelle), Firmin's estranged wife Yvonne (who has had an affair with Laruelle) returns to visit her husband, who has become incorrigibly alcoholic. During the day they and Firmin's brother Hugh visit the festival, amid alarming premonitions of incipient local violence and symbolic intimations of doom. Finally, as the Consul is separated from Yvonne and Hugh during a torrential storm, Yvonne is killed by a runaway horse which the Consul has unleashed, and the Consul is murdered by a band of fascist thugs.

Dense with SYMBOL and allusion to literature, religion and myth, the novel employs a complex, impacted time scheme and frequently achieves flights of remarkable prose reverie. It can be read as an unparalleled evocation of extreme alcoholism, as a virtuoso synthesis of arcane myth systems, or as an unforced ALLEGORY of a world in entropy as it stands on the brink of World War II.

Under Western Eyes A novel by JOSEPH CONRAD, published in 1911. The narrator, an elderly English teacher of languages in Geneva, tells the story of the Russian student Razumov, using Razumov's diary as well as his own observation.

Razumov's quiet life in St Petersburg is disrupted when Victor Haldin, a revolutionary idealist who has just assassinated a minister of state, seeks shelter with him. He betrays Haldin to the police, only to find that the autocracy now regards him as a suspect. His isolation intensifies when he is dispatched to Geneva as a secret agent. He arrives with the reputation of a hero among his fellow Russian exiles, since Haldin had written admiringly about him to his mother and young sister, Natalia. Natalia's innocent devotion to the man she thinks tried to help her brother makes Razumov's guilt the harder to bear. He is repelled, further, by the cynical idealism of the revolutionaries, epitomized in the grotesque figure of Peter Ivanovitch. When he attempts to break free from his life of deceit, confessing both to Natalia (whom he loves) and to the revolutionaries, he brings ghastly retribution on himself. They burst his eardrums, and he is struck down and crippled by a tram he cannot hear.

Underwoods A collection by BEN JONSON of what he called 'lesser poems', published in 1640. It includes the poem on SHAKESPEARE which had appeared in the First Folio of 1623; other notable pieces are 'An Ode: To Himself', 'A Celebration of Charis' and the 'Hymn on the Nativity'. ROBERT LOUIS STEVENSON also adopted the title for a volume of his own poetry, published in 1887.

Unfortunate Traveller, The A pamphlet by THOMAS NASHE, published in 1594. The dedicatory epistle (to the Earl of Southampton) promises 'some reasonable conveyance of history and variety of mirth' and the work has sometimes been claimed as the first PICARESQUE novel in English. The story follows the adventures of Jack Wilton, a young English page, in France and Italy. It opens with Jack's tricks at the English camp during the siege of Tournai in the reign of Henry VIII and follows his travels as page to the Earl of Surrey. There is an account of the slaughter of the Anabaptists at Munster. In Italy Jack's adventures are hair-raising: he is involved with rapes, murders, revenges and schemings, and the sensational descriptions culminate in the horrific torture and execution of the Jew Zadoch. Another execution, that of Cutwolfe, causes Jack to flee Italy and reform his way of life. Nashe is nowhere more brutal or sensational in his writing, perhaps self-consciously so, in an attempt to burlesque the stock situations and tone of popular Elizabethan journalism.

University Wits The name popularly given to a group of playwrights, among whom MARLOWE, GREENE, NASHE and PEELE are the most prominent, who received their education at Oxford or Cambridge, lived rashly in London and contributed significantly to the rapid development of a national repertoire of plays in the 1580s and 1590s. Most of the University Wits were hostile to the rising generation of playwrights, including JONSON and SHAKESPEARE, who lacked their educational advantages.

Unto this Last Essays on political economy by JOHN RUSKIN, first published in *THE CORNHILL MAGAZINE* in 1860 and in book form in 1862.

Unto this Last is Ruskin's most important and succinct social pronouncement, rejecting the *laissez-faire* doctrines of the 'Manchester School' of economic thought. So strongly were book and author reviled that publication in the *Cornhill*, then under THACKERAY's nervous editorship, was curtailed. The fundamental message of *Unto this Last* is that 'that country is the richest which nourishes the greatest number of noble and happy human beings'. Like his mentor, CARLYLE, Ruskin calls for a benevolent paternalism in which enlightened 'Captains of Industry' work with their employees towards a way of life that will yield true wealth in an atmosphere of harmonious relationships and humane understanding. Honesty, justice, kindness, 'social affection', purity of commercial engagement: these are the values of *Unto this Last*, whose idealistic message was respected by both Tolstoy and Gandhi. The book is notable for its clear, eloquent style, touched by mordant humour.

Updike, John (Hoyer) 1932– American novelist, short-story writer and poet. Born in Shillington,

John Updike

Pennsylvania, and educated at Harvard, he worked on the staff of THE NEW YORKER for two years. In 1958 he published a volume of verse, *The Carpentered Hen* (as *Hoping for a Hoopoe* in Britain); his first novel, *The Poorhouse Fair*, came in the following year.

Updike established a reputation as a keen observer of modern American life with the short stories in *The Same Door* (1959), and enjoyed major success with the novel *Rabbit Run* (1960), whose central character, Harry Angstrom, also appears in *Rabbit Redux* (1971), *Rabbit is Rich* (1981) and *Rabbit at Rest* (1990), the final and most admired volume of the tetralogy. Assured, urbane and ironic, his fiction is as versatile as it is prolific. *The Centaur* (1963), which won a National Book Award, mythologizes the life of a small-town teacher through the figure of Chiron, the wise centaur. *Bech: A Book* (1970) and its sequel *Bech is Back* (1982) follow the travels of a Jewish-American writer through Eastern Europe. *Couples* (1968) shows his abiding interest in marital and erotic themes. *The Coup* (1978), set in an imaginary African dictatorship, is an extreme example of his lush, sensuous prose. Later nov-

els, often tackling metaphysical subjects, include: *The Witches of Eastwick* (1982), in which the Devil materializes in a small New England town as a womanizing bachelor; *Roger's Version* (1986), about the interpenetration of physics and religion; *S* (1988), an EPISTOLARY NOVEL satirizing West Coast susceptibility to fake mysticism; and *Memories of the Ford Administration* (1993). His collections of short stories include *A Month of Sundays* (1975), *Marry Me* (1976) and *Trust Me* (1987). He has also published: poetry in, for example, *Tossing and Turning* (1977); CHILDREN'S LITERATURE; art criticism in *Just Looking* (1989); and autobiography in *Self-Consciousness* (1989). His large output of book reviews and essays, mostly for *The New Yorker* and *THE NEW YORK REVIEW OF BOOKS*, has been gathered in *Assorted Prose* (1965), *Picked-Up Pieces* (1978), *Hugging the Shore* (1983) and *Odd Jobs* (1991).

Upward, Edward (Falaise) 1903– Novelist. He was born at Romford in Essex and educated at Repton and Corpus Christi College, Cambridge. At school he met and became a lifelong friend of CHRISTOPHER

ISHERWOOD, who was also a contemporary at Cambridge. He won the Chancellor's Medal for poetry and worked closely with Isherwood when both began to write.

During the 1930s Upward became a member of the Communist Party, and his *Journey to the Border* (1938) is a Kafkaesque political allegory about a private tutor's progress towards radicalism and the Workers' Movement. Like many radicals of his generation, Upward was caught in the trap of Party dogmatism during the Stalin era. His political 'soul-searching' was largely responsible for a period of silence which lasted for over two decades. He became a schoolteacher and, in 1962, published *In the Thirties*, the first part of a trilogy which gave an account of his personal struggles during the intervening years. *Rotten Elements* followed in 1969, then *No Home But the Struggle* (1977). The completed trilogy, *The Spiral Ascent*, was published the same year and traced Upward's career (through the person of Alan Sebrill, schoolteacher and Marxist poet) over several decades. The final volume presented Upward's artistic and political credo about the need for harmony between personal and social commitment.

Urn Burial See HYDRIOTAPHIA.

Urquhart [Urchard], Sir **Thomas** *c.* 1611–*c.* 1660 Translator. A Scottish Royalist who fought against the Covenanters and was knighted in 1641, he took part in the Battle of Worcester and was imprisoned in the Tower for two years. On his return to Scotland he embarked on the spirited translation of Rabelais for which he is remembered; the first two books of *Gargantua and Pantagruel* appeared in 1653 and a third book was published posthumously (1693) by PETER ANTHONY MOTTEUX, who completed the remainder in 1694. Urquhart was also the author of curious treatises on mathematics and language to which he gave elaborate Greek titles.

USA A trilogy of novels by JOHN DOS PASSOS, consisting of *The 42nd Parallel* (1930), *1919* (1932) and *The Big Money* (1936). One of the most ambitious as well as saddest and most angry novels the USA has yet produced, it aims to chronicle the essential experience of the first 30 years of the 20th century. Only its immense length has prevented it finding a permanent readership. The most conventional, and least satisfactory, of its several approaches follows the lives of various 'typical' fictional characters, ending in disaster or disappointment. Their individual stories are supplemented by: 'Camera Eye' sections, written in STREAM OF CONSCIOUSNESS, which present the experiences of a young boy growing to manhood; 'Newsreels', or montages, of slogans, newspaper headlines, popular songs and political speeches; and, most fruitful of all, incisive miniature biographies of historical figures, who include Eugene V. Debs, RANDOLPH BOURNE, THORSTEIN VEBLEN, Thomas Edison, Frank Lloyd Wright, Theodore Roosevelt, Woodrow Wilson, Henry Ford, Isadora Duncan and Rudolph Valentino.

Usk, Thomas d. 1388 Author of a religious prose work, *The Testament of Love*. Little is known of his life, but he was confidential clerk to John of Northampton, whom he betrayed in 1384; he was executed in 1388. His sole surviving work, written *c.* 1387, is an ALLEGORY in three books describing how the imprisoned author was visited by Love (meaning divine love) after praying to Margaret, the Grace of God, for comfort. Love consoles him, condemns worldly fame and declares God's greatness and compassion. The second book contains complaints against the clergy, a discourse on women and a discussion on the route to salvation. The third book is concerned with predestination and free will; Love finally shows how Grace may be attained. The piece is obscure, poorly written and lacking in unity. It draws extensively on CHAUCER's BOECE and on THE HOUSE OF FAME and was included in early editions of Chaucer's works (see CHAUCERIAN APOCRYPHA).

Ussher, James 1581–1656 Irish churchman and scholar. Born in Dublin, he became one of the first students at Trinity College and its professor of divinity in 1607. A tireless preacher, controversialist and antagonist of Rome, he was appointed Bishop of Meath in 1620, and Archbishop of Armagh, Primate of the Anglican Church in Ireland, in 1625. In London during the 1630s he helped defend the episcopal system that was increasingly under attack, becoming a trusted associate of King Charles and moving with the court to Oxford in the 1640s. Ussher was admired by Cromwell, with whom he tried unsuccessfully to negotiate freedom of worship for Anglicans under the Protectorate. He had an incomparable knowledge of patristic literature and of the history of the primitive church; he was famed too for his skill in languages, including Anglo-Saxon, Hebrew, Arabic and Persian. Frequent visits to England brought him in touch with WILLIAM CAMDEN, SIR ROBERT COTTON and JOHN SELDEN, who described him as 'learned to a miracle'. Most of Ussher's many scholarly works are in Latin. They include *Britannicarum ecclesiarum antiquitates* (1639), a lengthy study of the early church in the British Isles, and *Annales veteris et Novi Testamenti* (1650), long accepted as providing a definitive chronology of the world up to the dispersion of the Jews. It determined that the Creation had taken place on 23 October 4004 BC and the Flood in 1656 BC, dates useful to contemporaries for working out the timetable of the Apocalypse.

Utilitarianism An ethical doctrine which judges an act to be right or wrong according to its tendency to promote the happiness of the majority affected by it. JEREMY BENTHAM is usually named as the founding father of Utilitarianism, although he acknowledged his debt to other 18th-century philosophers, including DAVID HUME and the Frenchman Helvetius. For Bentham, Utilitarianism formed the ideological basis for a programme of moral and legal reforms that he and his followers, JAMES MILL, DAVID RICARDO and John Austin, a professor of jurisprudence, wished to introduce. In the next generation JOHN STUART MILL was to widen the doctrine's scope, notably in the essay 'Utilitarianism' (1861), to include private as well as public moral sanctions and to refine the concept of 'pleasure'. Still working within the Utilitarian framework, later in the 19th century, HENRY SIDGWICK was to suggest that the method involved in determining the right course of action could frequently be more complex than early Utilitarian theory had allowed for, and in the early 20th century G. E. MOORE argued for the recognition of non-hedonistic values, independent of the pain-pleasure principle.

Initially conceived as a doctrine of public morality, Utilitarianism had its widest effects in the fields of 19th-century law, politics and economics. In the popular mid-19th-century mind political economy was seen as a branch of Utilitarian theory, partly because of the close connection of many leading economists with the 'philosophical radicals'. The premise of the early political economists that the market had a self-regulating tendency towards the ultimate welfare of the greatest number was discountenanced by experience, and later Utilitarians were prepared to admit a greater degree of state intervention.

Utopia THOMAS MORE's work was originally written in Latin and printed at Louvain in 1516 as *Libellus vere aureus, nec minus salutaris quam festivus, de optimo reipublicae statu deque nova insula Utopia* ('A truly golden little book, no less beneficial than entertaining, about the best state of a commonwealth and the new island of Utopia'). In the 16th century *Utopia* was translated into Dutch, French, Italian, Spanish and into English, Ralph Robinson's version being printed in 1551. GILBERT BURNET's translation was published in 1684.

It was begun in the Low Countries, completed in England, and opens with a historical event, a delegation to Bruges in 1515 in which More had taken part. More is then introduced to the traveller Raphael Hythlodaeus at Antwerp and enters into conversation with him. Raphael recalls conversations at the house of More's sometime patron Cardinal Morton which attempt criticism and analysis of contemporary European society, and offer solutions for its ills, in the course of which Raphael cites the example of the Utopians. Book I ends with More's request to hear further of Utopia and Book II (which was written first) contains Raphael's description of the happy island state where all things are held in common, gold is despised and the people live communally. The work ends with More's ambiguous reflections on the story: there are some things in Utopia he cannot agree with and others he would like to see implemented in Europe, although he doubts that they will be.

Interpretations of *Utopia* (the name plays on two Greek words *eutopos*, 'a good place', and *outopos*, 'no place') are many and diverse. It has been seen as a programme for an ideal state, a contemplative vision of the ideal, a satirical look at contemporary European society, and a humanist *jeu d'esprit*. Models for More's island state can be found in earlier literature. Plato's *Republic* is explicitly mentioned, while Plutarch had described an ideal Spartan commonwealth, and the most perfect island possible crops up in medieval theological debate. After the publication of *Utopia*, Italian humanists preoccupied themselves with works on ideal states, the most significant being Tommaso Campanella's *La città del sole* ('The City of the Sun', written *c.* 1602). BACON's *NEW ATLANTIS* (1627) was one of many such works in the 17th century, when 'Utopian' became current as an adjective. The ambiguities of More's island, whether it is ideal, possible or even desirable, continue in subsequent Utopian literature, as does More's use of imagined strange lands for satirical purposes (SWIFT's *GULLIVER'S TRAVELS*, SAMUEL BUTLER's *EREWHON*). 'Dystopian' was first used as an adjective in the late 19th century by J. S. MILL, to suggest an imagined state which was not desirable. But the desirability of Utopia is deliberately open to question even in More's own work. ALDOUS HUXLEY's *BRAVE NEW WORLD* and GEORGE ORWELL's *NINETEEN EIGHTY-FOUR* describe apparent Utopias that reveal themselves to be dystopian.

Uttley, Alison 1884–1976 Writer of CHILDREN'S LITERATURE. A farmer's daughter born in Derbyshire, she went from the village school to study physics at Cambridge. After teaching science in a London girls' school she married and began writing. Her first children's book, *The Little Grey Rabbit* (1929), was followed by over 30 titles in the same series, all illustrated by Margaret Tempest and appearing in the same small format. *Tales of Four Pigs and Brock the Badger* (1939) introduced Sam Pig, a popular character with small readers who went on to feature in 35 separate adventures. Sometimes reaching back into ancient legend and history, Alison Uttley's imaginary world is gentle, much taken up with the domestic details of humanized squirrels, hares and moles. A harsher side of rural life was brilliantly recorded in an autobiography, *The Country Child* (1931). In her finest story for older children, *A Traveller in Time* (1939), a modern child is transported back into dangerous 16th-century plots involving the imprisoned Mary, Queen of Scots.

Valentinian A tragedy by JOHN FLETCHER, performed about 1612 and published in 1647. The play has some basis in history – the last century of the Roman era – and includes some fine lyrics.

Valentinian III is guilty of dishonouring Lucina, wife of his general, Maximus. Lucina kills herself and Maximus plots his revenge. He poisons Valentinian's mind against his favourite general, Aecius, who commits suicide when he loses the emperor's favour. Two friends of Aecius kill Valentinian in revenge and Maximus is made emperor in his place. He takes Eudoxia, Valentinian's widow, as consort but makes the mistake of telling her how he reached the imperial throne. Eudoxia, revolted at hearing Maximus' false boast that he connived in the dishonour of Lucina, poisons him before he can be crowned.

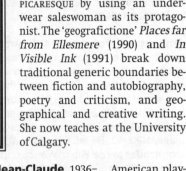

van der Post, Sir Laurens (Jan)

1906– South African man of letters. Of rural Afrikaner origin, he was born near Philippolis. His openness to other cultures, and to the intuitive and the mythopoeic, derives from childhood exposure to San (Bushman) and other African myths and survival skills, reinforced by his distinguished commando service in World War II and his friendship with Jung. His first and most convincing novel, *In a Province* (1934), is an early indictment of white South African racism. *The Face beside the Fire* (1953) is overburdened psychologically and symbolically, while *Flamingo Feather* (1955) is melodramatic. *The Hunter and the Whale* (1967), *A Story Like the Wind* (1972) and its sequel *A Far-off Place* (1974) are novels of vigorous action, emphasizing individualism and intuition as correctives to Marxism and modern rationalism. *The Seed and the Sower* (1963) consists of three connected stories of Japanese prisoner-of-war camps. He deploys his narrative skills most successfully, however, in non-fiction such as *Venture to the Interior* (1952), about exploration in Malawi, and his records of surviving San culture in *The Lost World of the Kalahari* (1958), *The Heart of the Hunter* (1961), *A Mantis Carol* (1975) and *Testament to the Bushman* (with Jane Taylor; 1984). His other books are: *The Dark Eye in Africa* (essays; 1955), *Journey into Russia* (as *A View of All the Russias* in the USA; 1964), *A Portrait of Japan* (1968), *The Night of the New Moon* (prisoner-of-war memoirs; 1970), *A Bar of Silence* (1972), *Jung and the Story of Our Time* (1976), *First Catch Your Eland: A Taste of Africa* (1977), *Yet Being Someone Other* (1982) and *A Walk with a White Bushman: Laurens van der Post in Conversation with Jean-Marc Pottiez* (1986).

Van Herk, Aritha

1954– Canadian novelist. She was born and grew up on a farm in Wetaskiwin, Alberta. She wrote her prize-winning first novel, *Judith* (1978), while a student of RUDY WIEBE's creative writing classes at the University of Alberta. About a woman who leaves the city to run a pig farm, it has affinities with the work of a fellow student, MARIAN ENGEL, particularly *Bear*. *The Tent Peg* (1981), in which a woman disguises herself to secure the job of cook for an all-male mining expedition in the Yukon, also displays strong feminist concerns. *No Fixed Address: An Amorous Journey* (1987) subverts the normal conventions of PICARESQUE by using an underwear saleswoman as its protagonist. The 'geografictione' *Places far from Ellesmere* (1990) and *In Visible Ink* (1991) break down traditional generic boundaries between fiction and autobiography, poetry and criticism, and geographical and creative writing. She now teaches at the University of Calgary.

Van Itallie, Jean-Claude

1936– American playwright, director and producer. Born in Brussels, he moved to the USA in 1940 and studied at Harvard. His experimental plays, which merge European traditions with a poetic vision of American experience, include *War* (1963), *America Hurrah* (1966), *King of the United States* (1972), *Mystery Play* (1973) and *Ancient Boys* (1991). He has also adapted several plays by Chekhov.

Van Vechten, Carl

1880–1966 American novelist. Born in Cedar Rapids, Iowa, he is best known for a series of novels which deal with the cultural life of New York in the 1920s. These include *Peter Whiffle* (1922), *The Blind Bow-Boy* (1923), *Firecrackers* (1925) and *Parties* (1930). His most highly acclaimed work is *Nigger Heaven* (1926), which takes place in the exotic world of Harlem's nightclubs and soirées, and which is often seen as epitomizing the renewed interest in black life shown by white writers during this period. His other novels include a SATIRE of Hollywood, *Spider Boy* (1928), and *The Tattooed Countess* (1924), set in his home state of Iowa. He was also active as a music and drama critic and wrote several memoirs, the most notable of which are *Sacred and Profane Memoirs* (1932) and an account of his friendship with GERTRUDE STEIN, published as an introduction to an edition of her *Three Lives* (1909).

van Vogt, A(lfred) E(lton)

1912– Canadian-born writer of SCIENCE FICTION. He became one of the most colourful pulp science fiction writers of the 1940s. His plots are convoluted, crowded with ideas, and often fail to make sense, but he compensates for these failings by the sheer verve of his inventiveness and the panache with which he delivers his imaginative flourishes. He has written many stories whose harassed heroes gradually achieve control of awesome superhuman powers, including *Slan* (1940; in book form, 1948), *The World of Null-A* (1945; in book form, 1946; revised, 1965) and the two stories in *Masters of Time* (1950). His writing career was interrupted for some years when he tried to make these fantasies real by becoming a follower of L. Ron Hubbard's Scientology. Although he is primarily an entertainer, his best work has intellectual substance, perhaps best displayed in his non-fantasy novel about brainwashing, *The Violent Man* (1962).

Vanbrugh, Sir **John** 1664–1726 Architect and playwright. Born in London, Vanbrugh was sent to school in Chester. He may have studied architecture in France, 1683–5. (His architectural training is otherwise something of a mystery.) Commissioned ensign in the 13th Foot Regiment, Vanbrugh saw service in France and was arrested and imprisoned for espionage, 1688–92. He left the army in 1702 to become Comptroller to the Public Works, remaining in that office for 12 years. He was appointed Carlisle Herald in 1703 and Clarenceux King-at-Arms from 1704 until his death. He was knighted in 1723.

Public honours came Vanbrugh's way more because of his work as an architect than as a dramatist. Among his most famous designs were those for Castle Howard (begun 1701), Blenheim Palace (begun 1705) and Seaton Delaval (begun 1720). He is said to have drafted a comedy during his French imprisonment, but his first performed play was provoked by his scepticism over the hero's reformation in COLLEY CIBBER'S *LOVE'S LAST SHIFT. THE RELAPSE* (1696) shows the rakish Loveless reverting to type. With his other major work, *THE PROVOKED WIFE* (1697), it was singled out for attack by JEREMY COLLIER in his *Short View of the Immorality and Profaneness of the English Stage* (1698). Vanbrugh was stung into replying with *A Short Vindication* (1698). His remaining plays are mostly adaptations, the two-part *Aesop* (1697) from Boursault, *The Country House* (1698) from Dancourt, *The Pilgrim* (1700) from JOHN FLETCHER, *The False Friend* (1702) from Le Sage, *THE CONFEDERACY* (1705) from Dancourt and *The Mistake* (1705) from Molière. He collaborated with CONGREVE and William Walsh in *Squire Trelooby* (1704), another version of Molière, wrote the unsuccessful *The Cuckold in Conceit* (1707) and left unfinished *A Journey to London*, which Cibber completed and staged as *The Provoked Husband* (1728).

Vancouver, George 1758–98 Explorer. He accompanied CAPTAIN COOK on his second voyage towards the South Pole (1772–5), and took part in Admiral Rodney's victory over the French at Les Saintes in the West Indies (1782). He was sent on a voyage of discovery (1791–5) during which he surveyed the south-west coast of Australia, the coast of New Zealand, and the Pacific coast of America. He returned by way of Vancouver Island (named after him) and Cape Horn. His *A Voyage of Discovery to the North Pacific* was published posthumously (1798).

Vanderhaeghe, Guy 1951– Canadian novelist and short-story writer. Born and raised in Esterhazy, Saskatchewan, he studied at the Universities of Saskatchewan and Regina. The 12 stories of his first collection, *Man Descending* (1982), which won the Governor-General's Award for Fiction, chronicle the disillusionment and pain of daily life in the seemingly hostile environment of the contemporary world. Seven earlier stories were gathered together in *The Trouble with Heroes and Other Stories* (1983). His novel, *My Present Age* (1984), further explores the loneliness of modern man through the eyes of its 31-year-old narrator. In 1987 Vanderhaeghe won the Geoffrey Faber Memorial Prize. Like many Canadian novels of recent years, *Homesick* (1989) deals with a female protagonist's need to return to and connect with her origins, in this case her father and her native Saskatchewan.

Vanity Fair: *A Novel without a Hero* A novel written and illustrated by W. M. THACKERAY, published in monthly parts from January 1847 to July 1848 and in volume form in 1848.

It traces the interwoven destinies of two contrasted heroines during the period of Waterloo and its aftermath. Becky Sharp, orphan daughter of a penniless artist, is resourceful and socially ambitious; her friend Amelia Sedley, at whose comfortable Bloomsbury home Becky goes to stay when the two leave school together, is affectionate, trusting and unworldly. Thwarted in her attempt to trap into marriage Amelia's brother, the fat Anglo-Indian Jos Sedley, Becky leaves to become governess at the Hampshire home of the Crawley family, where she soon makes herself indispensable to the dissolute old baronet, Sir Pitt, and charms his soldier son, Rawdon. On the death of his second wife, Sir Pitt proposes to Becky, only to find that she is already married to Rawdon. This news alienates the wealthy aunt on whose fortune Rawdon depends, and the couple are forced to live by their wits.

The clouds of war gather and Amelia's fortunes decline. Her stockbroker father is ruined; her love affair with George Osborne, the handsome but vain and selfish son of a wealthy merchant, is opposed by his purse-proud father. George is persuaded to marry her by his best friend and fellow officer, William Dobbin, who secretly loves Amelia, and is disinherited. The principal characters move with the army to Brussels, where George flirts with Becky and is then killed in the battle of Waterloo. The grieving Amelia dotes on her son, Georgy, and the memory of George. Becky also has a son, Rawdon, whom she neglects.

As Amelia in genteel poverty struggles to bring up her son, supported in secret by the faithful Dobbin, now in India, Becky and Rawdon attempt 'to live well on nothing a year'. Through gambling, deceit, and the patronage of the wealthy Lord Steyne, Becky pursues a life of fashion until she is discovered by Rawdon in a compromising situation with Steyne. Rejected by both and ostracized by society, Becky escapes from her creditors to the Continent, where she is discovered leading a Bohemian life by Amelia, whose fortunes have revived with the return of Dobbin and Jos from India and Georgy's adoption by his wealthy grandfather. Amelia's kindness to Becky is disapproved of by Dobbin, but leads to the revelation that George Osborne had proposed to elope with Becky on the eve of Waterloo, which destroys the sentimental memories of her husband Amelia has cherished. Older and disillusioned, Dobbin and Amelia can now marry. Becky meanwhile regains her hold over Jos, who gives her control of his finances and then dies in suspicious circumstances. Rawdon also dies abroad and his son inherits the Crawley estate. He pensions his mother but refuses to see her, and Becky ends the novel in the guise of a pious widow, busy with good works.

Vanity Fair is one of the greatest of English novels, a vast satirical panorama of a materialistic society and a landmark in the history of realistic fiction. Thackeray's sceptical, anti-heroic vision, and what BAGEHOT called his 'stern and humble realism', were important influences on the development of the Victorian domestic novel.

Vanity Fair An American magazine, published since 1859, though with interruptions and changes of character. Under its first editors, C. G. Leland and ARTEMUS WARD, it offered humorous commentary on contemporary affairs. Contributors included THOMAS ALDRICH, WILLIAM DEAN HOWELLS, FITZ-JAMES O'BRIEN and RICHARD HENRY STODDARD. It was revived in 1868. In 1913 it was purchased by Condé Nast and became a sophisticated review of literature, art and fashion. Frank Crowninshield was editor from 1914 to 1936, at which time it was absorbed by *Vogue*. It reappeared in 1983, chiefly as a magazine of high fashion and living, though it has also printed work by Márquez, Calvino, Joseph Brodsky and NORMAN MAILER.

Vanity of Human Wishes, The A poem by SAMUEL JOHNSON in IMITATION of Juvenal's Tenth Satire, published in 1749. With his customary generality of observation, the poet surveys the aspirations and delusions of mankind through the ages and across the busy geography of human ambition, selecting (as in the Latin original on which it is skilfully modelled) certain representative figures for examination.

Wolsey, Buckingham and CLARENDON are considered for their overreaching attitudes to power; the perils of intellectual eminence are adduced from the careers of Galileo and LAUD; and Charles XII of Sweden (about whom the poet was thinking of writing a play) is the military leader in a world of power politics, brought low by a stray bullet. The section on the fearsomeness of old age is especially effective (it includes a terrifying vignette of the senile SWIFT) as is the treatment of physical beauty, though the poem ends with an affirmation of faith. The atmosphere of weary inevitability and the tragic irony of the human examples are enhanced by the poem's intensely regular movement.

Vansittart, Peter 1920– Novelist. Born in Bedford, he was educated at Marlborough House School, Haileybury College and Worcester College, Oxford, where he read modern history. A distinctive though often neglected writer, preoccupied with language at the expense of narrative, he has frequently made imaginative use of historical settings. His many titles include *I am the World* (1942), *Broken Canes* (1950), *A Little Madness* (1953), *Carolina* (1961), *Quintet* (1976), *Aspects of Feeling* (1986) and *Parsifal* (1988). *Paths from the White Horse* (1985) is his autobiography.

Varieties of Religious Experience, The A book by WILLIAM JAMES, published in 1902, based on two courses of lectures delivered at Edinburgh University in 1901–2. He focuses on a personal instead of an organized religion, which he found to be a matter of 'ritual acts' rather than of private importance. His argument, based on scientific analysis of a number of examples of the conversion process, asserts that the particulars of religious faith are true insofar as they provide the believer with emotional fulfilment. The book was especially influential in stimulating the study of the psychology of religion.

Vassanji, Moyez G(ulamhussein) 1950– Kenyan novelist, short-story writer, publisher, editor and astrophysicist. Born in Nairobi, he was educated in Dar es Salaam before attending the Massachusetts Institute of Technology and the University of Pennsylvania. A research associate at the University of Toronto, he also publishes and edits *The Toronto South Asian Review*. His novel *The Gunny Sack* (1989) deals with Asian experience in East Africa over four generations. Beginning at Matamu on the Indian Ocean, it moves to East Africa during the period from German colonization to the final alienation of the Asian community through Amin's appropriations in Uganda and the spill-over effect in Tanzania. It ends as the family of Salim, the narrator, migrate to Canada. *No New Land* (1991), a much smaller novel, deals with Asian immigrants in Toronto. *Uhuru Street* (1992) is a collection of stories set in Dar es Salaam.

Vathek: *An Arabian Tale* A novel by WILLIAM BECKFORD, written in French and first published in English in 1786. The translation, probably by Samuel Henley, may have been undertaken at Beckford's request and with his help, but was presented as Henley's own version from the Arabic. Beckford issued the original in Paris and Lausanne (1786) and later revised the English text. *The Episodes of Vathek*, probably part of the original manuscript, were discovered and published with an English translation by F. T. Marzials in 1912.

The Caliph, Vathek, is the grandson of Haroun-al-Raschid; his mother, Catharis, is a Greek sorceress. Corrupted by power and a thirst for forbidden knowledge, Vathek becomes a servant of Eblis (the devil) in order to gain access to the treasures of the pre-Adamite sultans in the ruins of Istakar. He sacrifices 50 children and is given the power of death in the glance of one of his eyes, and sets off from his capital, Samarah. On his journey Vathek falls in love with Nouronihar, an emir's daughter, and she accompanies him. After exotic incidents in Istakar, Vathek gains admission to the halls of Eblis in the underworld, where he realizes the vanity of all the earthly treasures and wonders contained there. The story ends with Vathek and his companions awaiting their eternal torment: their bodies will remain intact but their hearts will burn for ever inside them.

Beckford's fantasy, finely sustained to its splendidly infernal conclusion, owes much to the contemporary fashion for the GOTHIC NOVEL. Its setting, however, allies it with the tradition of Orientalism already apparent in SAMUEL JOHNSON's *RASSELAS* and later to reach its full flowering in the work of BYRON and THOMAS MOORE.

Vaughan, Henry 1621/2-95 Poet. The twin brother of THOMAS VAUGHAN, he was born at Newton-upon-Usk in Wales. By 1638 he went up to Jesus College, Oxford, but did not take his degree, moving to London in 1640 to study law – 'which the sudden eruption of our late Civil Wars wholly frustrated'. He evidently fought on the Royalist side, then returned home to make his living as a physician.

In 1646 he published his *Poems, with the Tenth Satire of Juvenal Englished*, a slender offering of courtly Cavalier verse that he admitted was already out of fashion, although the translation of Juvenal remains a powerful and ominous work. *Olor iscanus* ('The Swan of Usk') was ready for the press in 1647, but publication was delayed until 1651. Here Vaughan tried to create a poetry of rural retreat in a Welsh pastoral setting, but the violence of the age could not be kept out. A complete change occurred in Vaughan's style and subject matter with *Silex scintillans* (1650), one of the outstanding volumes of meditative verse of the century. 'The Flashing Flint' of the title announces the theme of the hardened heart struck by affliction until it yields a holy fire. The experiences that lie behind the book are various: the sense of regeneration from sin, the death of a close friend, presumably the poet's younger brother William, moments of transcendence when the veil of mortality seems to lift, anticipations of the Day of Judgement. Stylistically the poems are deeply influenced by Vaughan's reading of GEORGE HERBERT. The character of Vaughan's religious poems is, however, notably different from Herbert's: at their finest they transmit a visionary sense of the divine presence pervading the natural world. Frequently they are coloured by a mood of wistfulness induced by Vaughan's desire to reach some spiritual home.

An enlarged edition of *Silex scintillans* appeared in 1655, and after a long silence came *Thalia rediviva* (1678), a dry miscellany of poems devoid of his earlier delicacy of spirit. His prose works include a meditative treatise, *The Mount of Olives: or, Solitary Devotions* (1652), and several translations of religious and medical writings. He liked to style himself Henry Vaughan, Silurist, a reference to his homeland in the border country of Wales once occupied by the ancient British tribe of the Silures.

Vaughan, Thomas 1621/2-66 Hermetic philosopher. Twin brother of the poet HENRY VAUGHAN, he was born at Newton-upon-Usk in Wales to a family belonging to the rural gentry. He went to Jesus College, Oxford, by 1638 and was ordained by 1645, although he did not exercise his calling. He probably fought on the Royalist side in the Civil War. He engaged in chemical research at Oxford and London, and died, according to ANTHONY À WOOD, as a result of an experiment with mercury, 'which getting up into his nose, marched him off'. Under the name Eugenius Philalethes ('The well-born lover of Truth') he published in the 1650s a number of treatises of hermetic philosophy, and was regarded as one of the most notable alchemists of his time. His works explore the occult influences that operate throughout the creation, and he writes to justify the pursuit of alchemy as the supreme philosophic quest. His prose is learned, allusive and cryptic; it may, however, be admired for its aggressive ebullience. Vaughan was lampooned by SAMUEL BUTLER in *HUDIBRAS*, and by SWIFT in *A TALE OF A TUB*. His writings are: *Anthroposophia theomagica: or, A Discourse of the Nature of Man and his State after Death* (1650), *Anima magica abscondita: or, A Discourse of the Universal Spirit of Nature* (1650), *Magica Adamica: or, The Antiquity of Magic, the Descent thereof from Adam Proved* (1650), *The Man-Mouse* (1650), a fulmination against HENRY MORE, the CAMBRIDGE PLATONIST, *Lumen de lumine: or, A New Magical Light Discovered* (1651), *The Second Wash: or, The Moore Scour'd* (1651), another attack on More for his scepticism about alchemy, *Aula lucis: or, The House of Light* (1651), *The Fame and Confession of* the *Fraternity of the Rosie Cross* (1653), a translation of the Rosicrucian manifestos, and *Euphrates* (1655), on the elements of generation. Some of his poems were printed in Henry Vaughan's collection *Thalia rediviva* (1678).

Vaux, Thomas, 2nd Baron Vaux of Harrowden 1510–56 Poet. Educated at Cambridge, he accompanied Wolsey on an embassy to France in 1527 and Henry VIII to Calais and Boulogne in 1532. He was made a Knight of the Bath in 1533. He contributed two poems to TOTTEL'S MISCELLANY, one of them his best-known poem, 'The aged Lover Renounceth Love'; three of its stanzas were later garbled by the gravedigger in HAMLET. THE PARADISE OF DAINTY DEVICES (1576) contains 13 poems by Vaux.

Veblen, Thorstein (Bunde) 1857–1929 American economist and social critic. The son of Norwegian immigrant farmers, he was born in Cato Township, Wisconsin, and educated at Carleton College, Johns Hopkins University and Yale. His first and most famous book, *The Theory of the Leisure Class: An Economic Study in the Evolution of Institutions* (1899), was popular among radicals for its attack on the caste system which grew out of the pursuit of wealth. *The Instinct of Workmanship* (1914) considers two opposing tendencies within men – the disposition to workmanship which survives in the modern capitalist system and the predatory impulse which thrives in it. *The Place of Science in Modern Civilization* (1919) is a study of the two main sources of science: disorderly knowledge of a utilitarian character and disinterested interpretation of this knowledge. Veblen's abiding interest in the economic determinants of modern society – in particular, his concern with the disjunction between those who produce goods and those who control the production process and the distribution of products – is evident in several of his other works: *The Theory of Business Enterprise* (1904), *The Vested Interests and the State of the Industrial Arts* (1919), *The Engineers and the Price System* (1921) and his last book, *Absentee Ownership* (1923).

Vein of Iron A novel by ELLEN GLASGOW, published in 1935. It tells the story of the Scottish-Irish Fincastle family, who have been ministers and leaders in Shut-In Valley in the Virginia mountains since colonial times. The story focuses on a daughter of the family, Ada, and follows her from her childhood through the years of the Depression. John, Ada's father, has lost his position in the church because of his unorthodox ideas, and has started teaching. Ada is in love with her father's student, Ralph McBride, and is jealous when he marries the beautiful Janet Rowan. When Janet divorces Ralph to marry a richer man, he and Ada become lovers. He goes to fight in World War I, un-

knowingly leaving Ada pregnant. Rejected by the community after the death of her grandmother, whose good reputation has helped sustain the family, Ada moves to Queenborough to give birth to her son, Rannie. Ralph returns and they are married. Their happy reunion is upset, however, when Ralph is temporarily paralysed in a car accident. Ada, with her 'vein of iron', her undaunted pride and courage, goes back to work to support her husband, son and ailing father. After John Fincastle's death, the family uses the insurance money to buy back the family home in Shut-In Valley.

Venice Preserved A tragedy in BLANK VERSE by THOMAS OTWAY, first performed in 1682, with Betterton as Jaffeir and Elizabeth Barry as Belvidera.

Priuli, a Venetian senator, has repudiated his daughter Belvidera because of her marriage to the nobly born Jaffeir. He also repudiates Jaffeir's desperate request for help against poverty. The rejected Jaffeir is persuaded by his brave friend, Pierre, to join a conspiracy against the Venetian republic, and entrusts Belvidera to Renault, leader of the conspiracy, as proof of his loyalty. But Renault forces his attentions on Belvidera, and the disillusioned Jaffeir breaks his oath and reveals the conspiracy to her. She persuades him to warn her father, and Jaffeir does so on condition that the lives of the conspirators will be spared. But the Venetian senators break their promise, and Jaffeir kills Pierre to save him the agony of being broken on the wheel. He then kills himself, and Belvidera, her mind unbalanced by the tragedies she has witnessed, dies.

A sub-plot of surprising comic potential matches a courtesan called Aquilina with a masochistic senator called Antonio. It was known to some of the contemporary audience that Antonio and Renault formed a composite caricature of the EARL OF SHAFTESBURY.

Venus and Adonis A narrative poem by SHAKESPEARE, printed in 1593. The seven editions by 1602 and the 14 by 1640 testify to its enthusiastic readership. Like the slightly later THE RAPE OF LUCRECE, it was dedicated, as 'the first heir of my invention', to the Earl of Southampton. In both poems Shakespeare was laying claim to the status of a recognized professional poet. The poem is a sensuous and witty erotic EPYLLION like MARLOWE's HERO AND LEANDER. It retells a favourite Renaissance myth which Shakespeare took mainly from Ovid's *Metamorphoses*. Ovid's version of the story is already a detached account of love and passion; Shakespeare's retelling increases the detachment and makes some changes. His coy, peevishly reluctant and epicene Adonis is unlike Ovid's willing lover, his Venus is aggressively sexual and the dominant partner. The poem tells of Venus' repeated, and simultaneously arousing and comic, attempts to woo Adonis. She warns him against hunting the boar but

Adonis goes off to the hunt and Venus, hearing its sounds, runs distracted through the woods in search of her boy. She finds him dead, laments over the corpse, and finds the anemone sprung from his blood.

Like *The Rape of Lucrece*, the poem is full of rhetorical display, ornamented language, verbal display, elaborate CONCEITS and witty play. In addition there are fine descriptions of the countryside and its animals. The poem is like many of Shakespeare's comedies in its alternately sympathetic and ironic scrutiny of the pains, humour and pathos of wooing.

Vercelli Book A 10th-century manuscript of Old English verse and prose preserved in the cathedral library at Vercelli in northern Italy. It contains two poems by CYNEWULF (*ELENE* and *The Fates of the Apostles*), *The Address of the Soul to the Body*, *ANDREAS* and *THE DREAM OF THE ROOD*, together with a prose life of ST GUTHLAC and 22 prose HOMILIES.

verse romance A poetic form originating in 12th-century France, where the greatest romances were the work of Chrétien de Troyes, and flourishing in England in the 13th and 14th centuries. Characteristically, the romance tells the story of a single knight, sometimes a character from ARTHURIAN LITERATURE. He is separated from the court and exposed to various adventures, which often involve the supernatural, before making his triumphant return to court and prosperity; his rewards frequently include marriage to his beloved. Occasionally two central figures are involved, either a couple (as in *FLORES AND BLANCHEFLOUR*) or close companions (as in *AMIS AND AMILOUN*). The romance is courtly, concerned with the chivalric codes governing behaviour and manners in all aspects of social life, love and battle.

Most English romances are translations from the French, though they rarely match the quality of their originals. Early romances without French counterparts – such as *ATHELSTON*, *KING HORN* and *THE TALE OF GAMELYN* – tell old English stories. The later romances which are not translations, like *THE SQUIRE OF LOW DEGREE*, draw from a stock of common motifs. This type appeared more frequently towards the end of the 15th century when the form was in decline, and these late romances often have little to recommend them.

Although romances are not concerned with individual characterization, the better ones explore the psychological development of the hero through his various adventures and hardships. Criticism or examination of the courtly life and society also appear in the more distinguished examples – like *SIR GAWAIN AND THE GREEN KNIGHT*, the best of the English romances. A love interest and some supernatural content are common but not necessarily central; some poems usually classified as verse romances (such as *THE SOWDON OF BABYLON*) are more concerned with military campaigns and the opposition of Christianity to pagan religions. The verse forms most frequently used are TAIL-RHYME, ALLITERATIVE VERSE and the octosyllabic couplet.

Verses on the Death of Dr Swift A poem by JONATHAN SWIFT himself, published in 1739. It imagines the circumstances of his own death, the reaction of those who had known him and his subsequent misrepresentation for posterity. The poet's IRONY and raillery about contemporary values, and his good-natured gibes at the expense of his friends, do not conceal the genuinely felt impression of the ingratitude and fickleness of human nature. Swift's auto-elegy is distinguished – like so much of his verse – by the superb modulation of its rhythms, which frequently imitate conversation or speech, and allow the satirist to duck in and out of his own arguments. It is one of the outstanding examples of an *apologia pro vita et satura sua*, a writer's defence of his life and satire.

Vertue, George 1684–1756 Engraver and antiquary. Born in London, Vertue learned the art of engraving from van der Gucht and was a member of Kneller's academy. Throughout his life he was constantly employed on major projects, such as Tindal's translation of Rapin's *History of England* (1736) and the Oxford Almanacks. He became a member of the Society of Antiquaries in 1717 and was appointed its official engraver. He spent a good deal of time collecting materials for a history of the arts in England and published *A Description of the Works of Wenceslaus Hollar* (1745) and a catalogue of Simon's numismatical collection in 1753. After his death HORACE WALPOLE bought all Vertue's working papers from his widow and incorporated much of the material in his *Andecdotes of Painting*. The notebooks have also been published separately (Walpole Society, 6 vols., 1929–52). Walpole also published Vertue's catalogue of the collection of Queen Caroline and his transcriptions of the catalogues of the collections of Charles I and James II.

Very, Jones 1813–80 American poet. He was born in Salem, Massachusetts, and educated at Harvard. His first book, *Essays and Poems* (1839), was edited and published by RALPH WALDO EMERSON. A mystic who believed in the absolute surrender of the will to God, he wrote devotional verse in the vein of the METAPHYSICAL POETS. His work was highly praised by WILLIAM CULLEN BRYANT and WILLIAM ELLERY CHANNING as well as by Emerson. Two volumes were published posthumously: *Poems* (1883) and *Poems and Essays* (1886).

Vicar of Bullhampton, The A novel by ANTHONY TROLLOPE, serialized in monthly numbers from July 1869 to May 1870, and published in volume form in 1870.

The vicar is Frank Fenwick, a clergyman 'who talked more of life with its sorrows, and vices, and chances of happiness, and possibilities of goodness, than he did of the requirements of his religion'. His vigorous, practical Christianity shows in his concern for two erring children of the local miller Jacob Brattle. When Sam Brattle is accused of complicity in the murder of a local farmer, the vicar saves him by helping to bring the real murderers to trial. He also rescues Sam's sister Carry, a fallen woman, from a life of destitution, restoring her to the home and eventual forgiveness of her stern old father. Frank's support of the Brattle family leads him into conflict with the local landowner, who causes a Dissenting chapel to be built at the vicarage gates only to have it pulled down when the land is discovered to belong to the vicarage after all. Love-interest is provided by the hopeless passion of the local squire, Harry Gilmore, for Mary Lowther and her eventual marriage to her cousin Walter Marrable.

The Vicar of Bullhampton is notable for its sympathetic, if conventional, handling of the fallen woman Carry Brattle, and for the portrayal of Gilmore's unhappiness and the flinty integrity of Jacob Brattle.

Vicar of Wakefield, The The only novel by OLIVER GOLDSMITH, written in 1761 or 1762 but not published until 1766.

The story is told by the Vicar himself, Dr Primrose. He has a wife, Deborah, and six children; despite Deborah's social aspirations the family is both comfortable and contented. Their hardships begin when Dr Primrose loses his personal fortune in the bankruptcy of a merchant company. He finds a new living through the patronage of Squire Thornhill but the Squire proves a villain, persuading the eldest daughter, Olivia, into a false marriage ceremony and then deserting her. She is found by her father and brought back to his modest vicarage but further misfortune follows when the house is destroyed by fire. Thornhill calls in Dr Primrose's debts but the Vicar cannot pay and is thrown into prison. His son George, a captain, challenges Thornhill to a duel but the Squire has him overpowered by thugs and put in prison as well. The younger daughter, Sophia, is abducted by an unknown villain and the deserted Olivia, so the Vicar is told, has died of grief. Dr Primrose endures all these blows with stoicism.

A kind-hearted but apparently seedy gentleman, Mr Burchell, whose advice to Mrs Primrose about her daughters' marriage prospects has been rejected by that socially ambitious lady, effects the rescue of Sophia and she begins to feel affection for him. Burchell proves to be Sir William Thornhill, uncle of the evil Squire. The Squire was Sophia's abductor, and Sir William proves also that Olivia's marriage was after all a true one and that she is not dead. George is able to marry his love, Arabella Wilmot, and Dr

Primrose's fortune is restored to him by the reformation of the swindler, Ephraim Jenkinson.

The story has the perennial charm of a fairy-tale: the rural setting is cosy, the characters are divided into stereotypes of good and evil, and their sufferings can be magically relieved by a happy ending. It incorporates three notable short poems: 'The Hermit: or, Edwin and Angelina', 'When Lovely Woman Stoops to Folly' and 'Elegy on the Death of a Mad Dog'. The novel was adapted for the stage by W. G. WILLS as *Olivia* (1878), the new title indicating the change of emphasis. Ellen Terry played the part with great success.

Vices and Virtues The earliest dialogue in Middle English to survive, written c. 1200 in or near Kent. The beginning is lost. A Soul confesses in detail its sins to Reason and the latter explains the nature and value of the Christian virtues. The Body complains that the Soul and Body are of different composition, and Reason answers that they should work in accord and continues to discuss various virtues. It is a dignified and carefully ordered series of expositions, held together by the loose dialogue form. It includes an interesting allegorical representation of the meeting between Mercy, Truth, Pity, Peace and Patience.

Victory A novel by JOSEPH CONRAD, published in 1915. The story is set in Indonesia.

On a rare impulse the solitary and cynical Axel Heyst helps Morrison, the captain of a trading brig, by paying his fines. He is offered a share in the Tropical Belt Coal Company and becomes its owner when Morrison dies. The Company fails but Heyst remains on the island of Samburan, alone except for his servant Wang. Schomberg, the hotel keeper in Sourabaya, circulates rumours that Heyst murdered Morrison and has secreted a fortune on the island. His malignancy increases when Heyst, on a rare visit, rescues an English girl, Lena, from his unwanted attentions and takes her home with him. Schomberg invites a trio of desperadoes to raid Heyst's island: the woman-hating 'plain Mr Jones', his 'secretary' Ricardo, and the Caliban-like Pedro. Found by Ricardo, Lena feigns sympathy for his plan to steal the illusory fortune. Jones finds her with Ricardo and fires at him; he dies and Lena is mortally wounded. Jones drowns while trying to escape from the island. Lena dies in Heyst's arms with the smile of private 'victory' on her lips. Heyst commits suicide in despair; the bungalow in which Lena dies becomes their joint pyre.

Vidal, Gore 1925– American novelist, playwright and essayist. Born in West Point, New York, he was educated at the University of New Hampshire. He served on army transports in the Aleutian Islands in World War II, making use of his experiences in two early novels, *Williwaw* (1946) and *In a Yellow Wood* (1947).

Gore Vidal

The City and the Pillar (1948, revised 1965), a bestseller dealing frankly with homosexuality, was followed by *The Season of Comfort* (1949), *A Search for the King* (1950), *The Judgement of Paris* (1952), *Messiah* (1954, revised 1965) and the collection of short stories *The Thirsty Evil* (1956). He became a playwright, first for television, with *Visit to a Small Planet* (published with others in 1957), and then for the theatre with *The Best Man* (1960), about an election campaign based on his own experience of running for Congress that year. *Rocking the Boat* (1962) was his first book of essays, *Washington DC* (1964) his first SATIRE on American politics. Since then a series of long, exhaustively researched novels has scrutinized famous lives and epochs from American history: *Burr* (1973), *1876* (1976), *Lincoln* (1984), *Empire* (1987) and *Hollywood* (1989). *Creation* (1982) tackles ancient history. Other novels are jaundiced, often apocalyptic comedies: *Myra Breckenridge* (1968) explores the weirder fringes of sexuality; *Kalki* (1978) and *Live from Golgotha* (1992) postulate false Messiahs and imminent Armageddon; *Duluth* (1983) ridicules TV soap opera. The evils of popular culture, American right-wing politics and fundamentalist religion are also favourite targets of Vidal's essays, which frequently plead for sexual liberation and tolerance. *Homage to Daniel Shays* (as *Collected Essays 1952–72* in Britain, 1972) has been followed by *Matters of Fact*

and Fiction (1977), *The Second American Revolution* (as *Pink Triangle and Yellow Star* in Britain, 1982) and *At Home* (as *Armageddon?* in Britain, 1988). *Screening History* (1992) is a series of essays on film. Vidal has also written DETECTIVE FICTION under the name of Edgar Box.

Village, The A poem in two books by GEORGE CRABBE, published in 1783. It opposes descriptions of pain, want and deprivation to the idyllic sentimentalism of conventional PASTORAL. Crabbe fails to sustain this kind of attack in the second book, and the poem ends with a rather lame homily on misery and distress as the general human condition, though both are earlier seen as the special preserve of the rural poor. Warmly approved by JOHNSON and BURKE, it established Crabbe's reputation.

Villette A novel by CHARLOTTE BRONTË, published in 1853. The story develops material that she had already used in her first novel, *THE PROFESSOR*, rejected by publishers and never issued during her lifetime.

Lucy Snowe, an English girl, gains a post as teacher in a girls' school at Villette, a town in Belgium based on the author's experience of Brussels. Though lacking in friends, beauty or money, she proves her worth to Madame Beck, the headmistress. She is condescendingly befriended by one of the pupils, the beautiful and vain Ginevra Fanshawe, who counts among her admirers Dr John Bretton, the son of Lucy's godmother. Observing his infatuation with Ginevra, Lucy represses her own feelings for him and Bretton, realizing Ginevra's vanity, falls in love with Paulina Home. Lucy buries herself in her work but gradually awakens to the fascination of the professor, Paul Emmanuel, a sharp-tongued, waspish, unattractive man who finds in her a response that mellows and softens him. When he is obliged to depart for the West Indies he leaves Lucy in charge of his school, promising to return in three years.

Vindication of the Rights of Woman, A See WOLLSTONECRAFT, MARY.

Virgin Martyr, The A tragedy by PHILIP MASSINGER and THOMAS DEKKER, first produced about 1620 and published in 1622. Dorothea, the martyr of the title, is usually called St Dorothy.

The Princess Artemia, daughter of Emperor Diocletian, is exhorted by her father to marry. She chooses Antoninus, the son of the governor of Caesarea; but Antoninus is devoted to Dorothea and declines the princess's hand. Theophilus, a tireless persecutor, and his secretary Harpax (who personifies evil) inform Artemia that Dorothea is a Christian. The furious princess finds Antoninus and Dorothea together and orders their execution; but she is persuaded by Theophilus to let him attempt to detach

Dorothea from the proscribed faith. He sends his daughters to convert Dorothea but, in fact, she converts them. The enraged Theophilus kills his own daughters, and Dorothea, attended by Angelo (who personifies good), suffers extremes of torture before being executed; Antoninus dies at her side. The last part of the play is concerned with the struggle between Harpax and Angelo for the soul of Theophilus. Angelo prevails and Theophilus himself suffers martyrdom as a Christian.

Virginian, The: *A Horseman of the Plains* A romantic novel of the old West by OWEN WISTER, published in 1902. Extremely popular in its day, it is the prototype for the whole genre of Western novels and the source of much Western lore. Set mostly in the Wyoming cattle country of the 1870s, it portrays a society which combines the unrefined manly life of the cowboys with signs of advancing civilization, like the pretty Vermont schoolteacher, Miss Molly Wood. The plot builds towards the wedding day of Miss Wood and the Virginian, when the hero is forced to kill his sworn enemy, Trampas, in a show-down duel (probably the first portrayed in literature). Molly has sworn to break the engagement if such an event were to occur, but she decides to accept the Virginian anyway. Thus the bond between the civilized and pioneer America is closed, but not without bitter-sweet nostalgia for a way of life that will be lost for ever.

Virginians, The A novel by W. M. THACKERAY, with illustrations by him, published in monthly numbers from November 1857 to September 1859, and in book form in 1858–9. A stately and rather static historical romance, it continues the story of the Esmond family from *THE HISTORY OF HENRY ESMOND* by following the fortunes of Esmond's twin grandsons, George and Harry Warrington.

George, heir to the Castlewood estate in Virginia, is a thoughtful and studious youth. He joins General Braddock's expedition against the French and is reported killed in action. Harry – the favourite of his mother, Rachel Warrington – is active, spirited and pleasure-loving. He comes to England after George's presumed death and visits his Castlewood relations, where he becomes a favourite of his aunt, the Baroness Bernstein (the Beatrix of *Esmond*) and falls in love with his middle-aged cousin, Lady Maria Esmond. Introduced to fashionable society, he gets into debt but is rescued by George, escaped from French imprisonment. Now that Harry is no longer the heir, Maria releases him from his engagement.

George settles in London, turns to writing plays, and marries Theo Lambert, daughter of the honest middle-class Lambert family. His mother disapproves and stops his allowance, and the couple are hard pressed until by the death of his English uncle, Sir Miles Warrington, George succeeds to the title and

the Warrington estates in England. Meanwhile Harry, taunted for his idleness by Theo's witty younger sister Hetty, who secretly loves him, joins the army, and serves with General Wolfe at the capture of Quebec. Later he sells his commission and buys an estate in Virginia, aided by a legacy from the Baroness Bernstein; he marries the daughter of his mother's companion. The brothers find themselves on opposing sides during the Revolution and George, who has fought for the King, resigns his Virginian estate to Harry and retires to England.

Vision, A An occult and historical study by W. B. YEATS, first published in Dublin in 1925, and revised, enlarged and published in London in 1937. It contains three sections: 'A Packet for Ezra Pound', 'Stories of Michael Robartes and His Friends' and 'The Phases of the Moon'. The text also includes four of Yeats's poems, 'The Phases of the Moon', 'Huddon, Duddon and Daniel O'Leary', 'Leda' and 'All Souls' Night', and there is a woodcarving of Yeats in the guise of Giraldus, fictional author of the fictional medieval source of the book, the *Speculum angelorum et hominum*. Based on the automatic writing of his wife, by whom the Instructors give him 'metaphors for poetry', and on the occult material of the Rosicrucian society, the Order of the Golden Dawn, it relates historical, occult and astrological material to three related symbols: the Phases of the Moon, the Great Wheel and the Gyres. These have in common that they are symbols of perpetual recurrence on many levels, and that Yeats never explicitly claims to believe in them other than as 'an impulse to create'. Their influence on his work can be seen in *The Tower*, *The Winding Stair*, *New Poems* and *Last Poems*, and in the play *The Resurrection*.

Vision of Judgement, A A poem by SOUTHEY, published in 1821. An apotheosis of George III, who had died the previous year, it describes the king's shade triumphing over his enemies and being admitted to Paradise. WILKES and JUNIUS retire discomfited, George Washington (of all people) speaks on the king's behalf, and the dead monarchs and great men of English history welcome George to his heavenly rest. An ill-judged performance from a POET LAUREATE despised by the younger generation of poets as an ex-radical turned apologist for the Establishment, it was made even more provocative by a savage attack on BYRON in the preface. Byron replied with *THE VISION OF JUDGEMENT*, taunting Southey again in the preface to *DON JUAN*.

Vision of Judgement, The A satirical poem by BYRON, prompted by SOUTHEY's eulogy of George III, *A VISION OF JUDGEMENT*. It was published in 1822 by LEIGH HUNT in *THE LIBERAL* after Byron's usual publisher, JOHN MURRAY, had refused it. Hunt incurred a

£100 fine and would probably have suffered a heavier penalty if he had included Byron's preface, which charged Southey with attempting 'to canonize a monarch, who, whatever were his household virtues, was neither a successful nor a patriotic king'.

Byron imitated Southey's poem closely, transforming its solemn heroics into comedy. His PARODY opens with St Peter sitting at Heaven's gate, bored for lack of work. When he is told of the king's death, he has no idea who he is. There is a striking encounter between the archangel Michael and Satan, and a series of comments by the king's critics. These are cut short, and Washington and BENJAMIN FRANKLIN prevented from speaking, by the entry of a devil carrying Southey. St Peter implores him to speak in prose but Southey insists on reading his *Vision of Judgement*. In the ensuing uproar St Peter fells Southey with his keys and George III slips unnoticed into Paradise, where Byron leaves him 'practising the hundredth psalm'.

Vittoria A novel by GEORGE MEREDITH, published in 1867. It continues the story begun in *SANDRA BELLONI*.

The setting is northern Italy in 1848, when the Italians, inspired by Mazzini, are moving towards revolt against their Austrian overlords. The singer, Sandra Belloni, places herself at the disposal of the independence movement and agrees to appear in the opera at Milan under the name 'Vittoria' to sing the song that will signal the revolt. Suspicion falls on her because her English friend, Wilfred Pole, is an officer in the Austrian army. She marries the gallant patriot Carlo Ammiani, but the climate of suspicion and the enmity of Violetta d'Isorella and Anna von Lenkenstein involve Vittoria, Carlo and Wilfred in a series of dangerous situations and Carlo is killed. Vittoria is comforted by the arrival of her friend Merthyr Powys.

Vivian Grey The first novel by BENJAMIN DISRAELI, written to pay off debts on a failed newspaper venture, and published in 1826. Although Disraeli had a good ear for society conversation, his characterization was unreliable and he failed, in this instance, to construct a plot. Vivian, a clever, manipulative young man, rejects Oxford to embark on political intrigue and overreaches himself. His beloved suddenly dies in his arms. He kills his man in a duel and is forced to go to Germany, where he is soon embroiled in German political intrigue. The book's most interesting character is Essper George, a conjuror of mysterious origins who gives up showmanship to become Vivian's servant and entertain his employer with tall stories. The book may owe something to the tradition of TOM JONES and PEREGRINE PICKLE, with their scapegrace heroes, accompanied by faithful servants.

Vizenor, Gerald 1934– Native American poet and novelist. A member of the Minnesota Chippewa tribe,

he was born in Minneapolis and educated at the University of Minnesota. His first collection of poetry, *Born in the Wind*, was privately printed in 1960. He has since published several volumes of English haiku poetry, including *Raising the Moon* (1964), *Seventeen Chirps* (1964), *Two Wings the Butterfly* (1967) and *Matsushima: Haiku* (1984). Recent works include *The Trickster of Liberty* (1988), *Griever: An American Monkey in China* (1990), *Bearheart* (1990), *Landfill Meditation: Wise Blood Stories* (1991) and *Dead Voices: Natural Agonies in the New World* (1992). A novel, *Darkness in Saint Louis Bearheart* (1978), is a self-reflexive exercise in POST-MODERNISM. He has also published several collections of Native American writing, including *Ojibwa Lyric Poems and Tribal Stories* (1981), *Earthdivers: Tribal Narratives on Mixed Descent* (1981) and *The People Named the Chippewa: Narrative Histories* (1984), as well as *Narrative Chance: Postmodern Discourses of Native American Indian Literature* (1989).

Volpone: or, The Fox A comedy by BEN JONSON, often regarded as his masterpiece. It was first performed by the KING'S MEN in 1605–6 (published 1607) and is the most frequently revived of Jonson's plays. Although formally set in Venice, *Volpone* directs its merciless moral scrutiny on the customs and values of the rising merchant classes of Jacobean London. Volpone, a wealthy Venetian without heirs, lets it be known that he is near death in the confident belief that avaricious legacy-hunters will flock to his bedside, there to be duped by himself and his quick-witted servant, Mosca (fly). On the promise of inheriting the dying man's fortune, three of Venice's leading citizens reveal their true corruption. The lawyer Voltore (vulture) is prepared to infringe the laws he claims to sustain. The decrepit Corbaccio (crow) will disinherit his own son. The sanctimonious Corvino (raven) will send his virtuous wife, Celia, to Volpone's bed. The exuberance of the two plotters, Volpone and Mosca, together with the vileness of their victims, comes close to excusing the criminality of their schemes, but Volpone overreaches himself when, having willed his property to Mosca, he pretends to be dead. The infuriated Voltore takes the matter to court, where Mosca recognizes and exploits the personal advantage of his master's 'death'. To thwart Mosca, Volpone has to come alive and reveal the whole plot, on the strength of which revelation he, along with everyone else, is appropriately punished. Only the virtuous – Corvino's wife and Corbaccio's son – are rewarded.

Vonnegut, Kurt, Jr 1922– American novelist, short-story writer, playwright and writer of SCIENCE FICTION. He was born in Indianapolis and educated at Cornell and the University of Chicago. His novels are ironic jeremiads, combining dark humour with

Kurt Vonnegut

unashamed sentimentality in lamenting our apparent inability to treat one another as well as we might and should. *Player Piano* (1952) is a dystopian novel about automation. *The Sirens of Titan* (1959) is satirical science fiction, introducing the Tralfamadorian aliens who reappear in his most substantial work, *Slaughterhouse-Five: or, The Children's Crusade* (1969), which draws upon his experiences as a prisoner of war during and after the firestorming of Dresden. *Cat's Cradle* (1963) and *Galapagos* (1985) are sarcastic apocalyptic fantasies. Vonnegut's non-fantastic novels, including *Mother Night* (1961), *God Bless You, Mr Rosewater* (1965), *Jailbird* (1979), *Deadeye Dick* (1985) and *Hocus Pocus* (1991), are char-

acter studies whose innocent and unlucky protagonists have difficulty coping with the paradoxical hostility of the world around them. His short fiction is collected in *Welcome to the Monkey House* (1968). Plays include *Happy Birthday, Wanda June* (1960) and *Timesteps* (1979). His non-fiction is collected in *Wampeters, Foma and Granfalloons* (1974) and two volumes of 'autobiographical collage', *Palm Sunday* (1981) and *Fates Worse Than Death* (1991).

vorticism A movement in British art, part of MODERNISM, which flourished in 1913–15 with the writer and painter WYNDHAM LEWIS as its leading figure. In October 1913 he quarrelled with the art critic Roger

Fry and broke away from the Omega Workshops, dominated by the BLOOMSBURY GROUP. His followers included the painters Frederick Etchells, Cuthbert Hamilton and Edward Wadsworth. In March 1914 they created the Rebel Art Centre, which attracted more artists – the sculptor Jacob Epstein and several poets of IMAGISM – who rejected the prevailing orthodoxy of post-impressionism. They preferred German aesthetics, EXPRESSIONISM, cubism and futurism to the decorative art of Matisse. The term 'vortex' had been first used by EZRA POUND to describe the *avant-garde* spirit of London's art world, and was adopted by Lewis to signify his version of the concentrated energy of the new arts of modernism. Vorticism, so its principal exponents claimed, was in favour of activity and significance in art, essential movement, and the energy of the individual human mind. Vorticist paintings and drawings tended towards sharp-lined and angular abstraction and non-representation, though they often celebrated modern machinery and industrial landscapes. The vorticist magazine *BLAST* – of which only two issues appeared, in July 1914 and July 1915 – was largely produced by Wyndham Lewis.

Voss A novel by PATRICK WHITE, published in 1957. The first part, which can be read as a fairly straightforward novel of manners, is set in Sydney in the 1840s and describes preparations for the expedition into the interior of Australia. The long central section, which employs a dense, metaphorical style, is the story of the journey itself and of how the megalomaniac explorer Voss, whose beliefs are based on Schopenhauer's theory of the Will, gradually comes to acknowledge humility. The final section returns to Sydney and deals ironically with the making of the myth of Voss, who has perished, along with all the members of the expedition except one. The novel incorporates aspects of Jungian theory, particularly the notions of the anima and the mandala. Voss's actual journey is complemented by the metaphorical journey of Laura Trevelyan, who remains in Sydney but functions as his anima and 'spiritual wife'. *Voss* was

inspired by White's reading of the journals of the Australian explorers Leichhardt and Eyre. These provided him with the starting-point for an epic novel about the creation of an Australian identity, which also explores psychological, spiritual and gender issues.

Voyage Out, The VIRGINIA WOOLF's first novel, written in 1912–13 but not published until 1915.

Unlike her later works, it is realistic in form, though it contains passages of lyrical intensity. The story concerns a young woman of 24, Rachel Vinrace, an innocent, 'unlicked' girl who voyages to South America on board her father's ship, the *Euphrosyne*. Accompanying her are her aunt, Helen Ambrose, and uncle Ridley, together with an assortment of English characters whose social interaction is delicately observed. During the voyage the ship puts in at Lisbon, and Rachel meets Richard and Clarissa Dalloway, who reappear more prominently in *MRS DALLOWAY*.

In South America Rachel meets a young Englishman, Terence Hewet, an aspiring writer working on his first novel: '"I want to write a novel about Silence," he said; "the things people don't say."' Rachel attempts to broaden her education by reading but finds herself out of sympathy with the male perspective of standard classics. Terence, in contrast to other men, is interested in women's experiences and concerned about their position in society. '"Doesn't it make your blood boil? If I were a woman I'd blow someone's brains out."' He and Rachel fall in love and become engaged, determined to establish their future marriage on a new basis of equality. However, during an expedition Rachel contracts an unspecified disease and is confined to her bed with a fever. After a fortnight's illness she dies. The novel concludes with an image of the English party at the hotel retiring: 'a procession of objects, black and indistinct, the figures of people picking up their books, their cards, their balls of wool, their work-baskets, and passing... one after another on their way to bed'.

Vulgar Errors See *PSEUDODOXIA EPIDEMICA*.

Wace See ARTHURIAN LITERATURE.

Waddell, Helen (Jane) 1889–1965 Scholar, translator and novelist. The daughter of an Ulster Presbyterian missionary, she was born in Tokyo and educated at Victoria College and Queen's University, Belfast. After an early career of miscellaneous writing, including *The Spoiled Buddha*, a play produced in 1915 by her brother RUTHERFORD MAYNE, and a volume of *Lyrics from the Chinese* (1915), she was able to go to Oxford in 1919 to study medieval literature. After further study in Paris and London she produced her masterpiece, *The Wandering Scholars* (1927), a pioneering study of European learning in the 12th century and the sometimes ribald goliardic verse associated with it. Her distinguished book of verse translations, *Medieval Latin Lyrics*, and her learned but lively and moving novel *Peter Abelard* were both published in 1933. Her other writings include wartime journalism, translations of medieval SAINTS' LIVES as *Beasts and Saints* (1934) and of the *Vitae patrum* as *The Desert Fathers* (1936), and a second play, *The Abbé Prévost* (1933). Her main achievement was to rekindle interest in the spirituality and the Latin literature of early medieval Europe.

Waddell, Samuel J. See MAYNE, RUTHERFORD.

Waddington [*née* Dworkin], **Miriam** 1917– Canadian poet. Born in Winnipeg, the daughter of Russian Jewish immigrants, she was educated at the universities of Toronto and Pennsylvania. She has been a social worker in Montreal and professor of English and Canadian literature at York University in Toronto (1964–83). Her first poems were published in 1943 in the Montreal little magazine *First Statement* and her first collection of poetry, *Green World*, in 1945. Her other volumes include *The Second Silence* (1955), *The Glass Trumpet* (1966), *Say Yes* (1969), *Driving Home* (1972), *The Price of Gold* (1976) and *The Visitants* (1981). Her short stories are collected in *Summer at Lonely Beach* (1982). With their meticulous craft and their lyric celebration of the baffling richness within common things, her poems have appeared in many Canadian anthologies, and some have been set to music by Canadian and American composers. She is also a distinguished critic and translator of prose and poetry from the Yiddish.

Wade, Thomas 1805–75 Poet and playwright. Born at Woodbridge in Suffolk, Wade published a volume of poetry, *Tasso and the Sisters* (1825), before turning to a play in verse and prose, *Woman's Love:*

or, The Trial of Patience (1829), which his friend Charles Kemble produced successfully at DRURY LANE. A FARCE, *The Phrenologists* (1830), was also successful but *The Jew of Arragon*, a tragedy produced in the same year, failed. Wade published some volumes of verse, wrote two other plays which were not produced, and was the editor of *Bell's Weekly Messenger* and *Wade's London Review*. His remarkable SONNETS were published in a volume entitled *Mundi et cordis: de rebus sempiternis et temporariis: carmina* (1835).

Wain, John 1925–94 Novelist, poet and critic. Born in Stoke-on-Trent, he was educated in Newcastle and at St John's College, Oxford, where he was subsequently a fellow in 1946–9. He lectured in English at Reading University in 1949–55 and was professor of poetry at Oxford in 1973–8. His own poetry, dry, cerebral and witty, is collected in *Poems 1949–79* (1981).

His most famous novel is still his first, *Hurry On Down* (1953), classed with AMIS's *LUCKY JIM* and JOHN BRAINE's *Room at the Top* as a leading example of the fiction produced by the ANGRY YOUNG MEN. It narrates the PICARESQUE career of the university graduate Charles Lumley, whose deliberate flight down the social scale leads him to work as a window-cleaner and thence into other increasingly unpropitious occupations. Later novels include: *The Contenders* (1958); *Strike the Father Dead* (1962); *The Smaller Sky* (1968); *A Winter in the Hills* (1971), a rampageous comedy about a linguist's researches in North Wales; *Young Shoulders* (1982), a sensitive study of juvenile bereavement; and two BILDUNGSROMANEN drawing on his knowledge of Oxford, *Where the River Meets* (1988) and *Comedies* (1990). *Nuncle* (1960) and *Death of the Hind Legs* (1966) are volumes of short stories. He also wrote a biography of SAMUEL JOHNSON (1974), several volumes of literary criticism and many radio plays.

Wainwright, Jeffrey 1944– Poet. He was born in Stoke-on-Trent and educated there and at the University of Leeds. He has taught at the University of Wales, Aberystwyth, Long Island University, Brooklyn, and Manchester Polytechnic. Early influences included GEOFFREY HILL, JON SILKIN and KEN SMITH. Wainwright's pamphlet *The Important Man* (1970) includes 'Three Poems on the Battle of Jutland 1916', '1815', 'Sentimental Education' and 'The Garden Master'. They are poems of political commitment although riven with irony and self-questioning, and his language is terse and humane. Poems from *The Important Man* were included in Wainwright's widely acclaimed first book, *Heart's Desire* (1978), which also added 'Thomas Muntzer', a major political poem about a 16th-century German radical and visionary executed during the Peasant War. Wainwright's adaptation of Péguy's *Le Mystère de la charité de Jeanne d'Arc* was performed by the ROYAL SHAKESPEARE COMPANY in 1984. *Selected Poems* appeared in 1985.

Waiting for Godot A play by BECKETT, originally written and performed in French (*En attendant Godot*, 1953), then translated by the author and performed in English in 1955. Its cryptic allusiveness was first greeted with derision and then admired to a degree that has made it one of the most influential works of the post-war European theatre.

In Act One, two tramps, Vladimir and Estragon, wait beside a leafless tree (the stage is otherwise bare) for the arrival of Godot, with whom they believe they have an appointment. In order to pass the time, or perhaps simply to accompany the passing of time, they play verbal games reminiscent of the cross-talk of music-hall comedians. When Pozzo arrives, holding his slave Lucky with a rope, the tramps wonder if he is Godot, but Pozzo denies all knowledge of Godot. To the discomfort and confusion of Vladimir, Estragon and the audience, he makes Lucky 'dance' and then 'think', in a long, incoherent tirade. Master and slave depart and a boy arrives to tell the tramps that Godot will not be coming that day 'but surely tomorrow'. In Act Two the tree has leaves, but there is little other evidence of change as Vladimir and Estragon continue waiting. Pozzo enters again, but blind and dependent on the guiding rope that binds Lucky to him. Lucky is now dumb, but Pozzo is unaware of any difference. When they have gone, a boy, who may or may not be the same boy but who claims to be his brother, arrives with the same message. Still determining to go, the tramps do not move.

Waiting for Lefty A play by CLIFFORD ODETS, first produced in New York in 1935. Its reference to the previous year's taxi strike gave it the urgency of political propaganda. It was published in England by the LEFT BOOK CLUB in 1937.

Within the framework of a corrupt union meeting – the theatre audience is addressed as if it were at the meeting – short naturalistic scenes involving characters and issues affected by the union's decision to strike are acted out. In the end the union bosses are exposed and a rallying call for action is flung out.

Wake, William 1657–1737 Divine. Born into a family of landowners at Blandford in Dorset, he completed his education at Christ Church, Oxford, and became chaplain to the English ambassador in Paris in 1682. His ambition to achieve a union between the Church of England and the Gallican Church came to

nothing, but he is remembered in religious literature for his translation, *The Genuine Epistles of the Apostolic Fathers* (1693), and for *The State of the Church and Clergy of England* (1703). Wake became Archbishop of Canterbury in 1716.

Wakefield cycle See MIRACLE PLAYS.

Wakoski, Diane 1937– American poet. She was born in Whittier, California, and educated at the University of California at Berkeley. *Coins and Coffins* (1962) was the first of more than 30 volumes. Much of her work resembles CONFESSIONAL POETRY, focusing in particular on her unhappy childhood and painful experiences with men. Other volumes include *Discrepancies and Apparitions* (1966), *The George Washington Poems* (1967), *Greed Parts One and Two* (1968), *Thanking My Mother for Piano Lessons* (1969), *The Lament of the Lady Bank Dick* (1970), *The Pumpkin Pie: or, Reassurances are Always False, Tho We Love Them, Only Physics Counts ...* (1972), *Dancing on the Grave of a Son of a Bitch* (1973), *Looking for the King of Spain* (1976), *Waiting for the King of Spain* (1976), *The Lady Who Drove Me to the Airport* (1982), *The Collected Greed, Parts 1–13* (1984), *The Rings of Saturn* (1986), *Roses* (1987) and *Medea the Sorceress* (1992). *Emerald Ice: Selected Poems 1962–1987* appeared in 1989. She has also published several volumes of prose, including *Form is an Extension of Content* (1972), *Creating a Personal Mythology* (1975) and *Toward a New Poetry* (1980).

Walcott, Derek (Alton) 1930– Caribbean poet, playwright and theatre director. He was born in Castries, St Lucia, and educated at the University of the West Indies, Jamaica. He lived in Trinidad for two decades, founding the Trinidad Theatre Workshop in 1959 and working as arts reviewer for *The Trinidad Guardian*. His first three volumes of verse were published in the Caribbean between 1948 and 1951 but his widespread recognition came with *In a Green Night* (1962), *The Castaway* (1965) and *The Gulf* (1970) – ironic, antithetical poetry of personal and artistic discovery, with delicate physical description as a means of taking psychological bearings and finding anchorage. Walcott has worked for a Caribbean culture subsuming African, Indian and European origins in the region he describes as 'Our hammock swung between Americas' ('Elegy', *The Gulf*). He tries to alchemize 'where nothing was/ the language of a race' ('Crusoe's Journal', *Castaway*) out of various Caribbean Creoles and metropolitan English, with which to confront Caribbean individual, historical and racial contradictions. With the impressive autobiographical poem, *Another Life* (1973), his poetry becomes both more supple in versification and even more linguistically disciplined. Poetry, detached and sceptical but simultaneously 'religious' in drift, has

Derek Walcott

followed in *Sea Grapes* (1976), *The Star-Apple Kingdom* (1980) and *The Fortunate Traveller* (1981). *Midsummer* (1983) disappointingly shows little further development. A volume of selected poetry appeared in 1981, *Collected Poems* in 1986 and *The Arkansas Testament* in 1987. Walcott's plays enact many of his interior explorations, combining much folk-activity, like singing, storytelling and dancing, with colloquial, richly metaphorical speech. They include *Henri Christophe* (1950), *Henri Dernier* (1951), *Ione* (1954), *Drums and Colours* (1961), *Dream on Monkey Mountain* with *Ti-Jean and His Brothers*, *Malcochon*, and *The Sea at Dauphin* (1971), *The Joker of Seville* with *O Babylon* (1978), *Remembrance* with *Pantomime* (1980), *Three Plays* (1982) – *The Last Carnival, Beef, No Chicken* and *A Branch of the Blue Nile* – and *Viva Detroit* (1992).

Throughout his career Walcott has been fascinated by parallels between Homer's Aegean and the Caribbean. This absorption has found its fullest expression in *Omeros* (1989), one of his finest poems to date, and *The Odyssey*, staged by the ROYAL SHAKESPEARE COMPANY in 1992. Though best known as a poet and playwright, he is also a fine prose stylist. 'What the Twilight Says', with which he introduces the *Monkey Mountain* volume, and 'The Muse of History'

are illuminating essays on the Caribbean creative imagination and New World history respectively. He was awarded the Nobel Prize for Literature in 1992.

Walden: *or, Life in the Woods* An autobiographical narrative by HENRY DAVID THOREAU, published in 1854. It describes a two-year period from March 1845 to September 1847 during which the author retired from the town of Concord to live alone at nearby Walden Pond. This was Thoreau's own experiment in TRANSCENDENTALISM, equivalent in many ways to that of BROOK FARM: he sought to put into action a programme of self-reliance, whereby the individual spirit might thrive in its detachment from the fractured world of mass society.

Much of the book was derived from the journals Thoreau kept during his stay. Comprising 18 essays, it effectively creates a sense of the multiple dimensions of the author's self. His prose can be complex and poetically evocative, but also lucid, even scientifically direct; at times he engages in ALLEGORY and parable. Other passages catalogue the various animals and plants in the area. The narrative often digresses into lengthy discussions of philosophy and poetry; famous sections describe visits to a Canadian woodcutter and an Irish family, a trip to Concord and his bean field.

Waldhere An Old English poem of which only two brief fragments survive. It was apparently quite long and told a well-known story recorded in a Latin poem by Ekkehard of St Gall (d. 973). Hildegund, Walter and Hagen are prisoners of Attila of the Huns. Hagen escapes to join Gunther, king of the Franks. Walter and Hildegund, who are lovers, also escape with much treasure and Gunther persuades the reluctant Hagen to accompany him and 11 warriors going to rob them. In a narrow pass Walter kills all but Hagen and Gunther, and these three are maimed. The surviving fragments are from speeches, the first by Hildegund and the second from the end of Gunther's speech with Walter's reply.

Waley, Arthur (David) 1889–1966 Poet and Sinologist. He was born Arthur David Schloss in Tunbridge Wells, Kent, and educated at Rugby and King's College, Cambridge. Waley (he adopted his mother's surname in 1914) taught himself Chinese and Japanese while working in the Print Room of the British Museum. He is best known for his translations: *A Hundred and Seventy Chinese Poems* (1918); *The Tale of Genji* (6 vols., 1925-33), an 11th-century Japanese novel; *The Pillow-Book of Sei Shonagon* (1928); *The Analects of Confucius* (1938); and *Monkey* (1942), a 16th-century Chinese novel. His other work included *The No Plays of Japan* (1921), *The Poetry and Career of Li Po, AD 701-762* (1951) and the miscellany *The Secret History of the Moguls* (1964). Waley's work, which contributed greatly to the interest in the East during the 1920s, was related to IMAGISM, especially to POUND's *Cathay* (1915) and AMY LOWELL's *Fir Flower Tablets* (1921).

Walker, Alice 1944– Black American novelist, short-story writer and poet. Born into a family of sharecroppers at Eatonton, Georgia, she was educated at Spelman College and Sarah Lawrence College. Her first publications were two collections of poetry: *Once: Poems* (1968), which reflects her experience of the civil rights movement and her travels in Africa, and *Revolutionary Petunias and Other Poems* (1973), a tribute to those who struggle against racism and oppression. Later volumes are *Good Night, Willie Lee, I'll See You in the Morning* (1979) and *Horses Make a Landscape Look More Beautiful: Poems* (1984). Her first novel, *The Third Life of Grange Copeland* (1970), is the story of three generations of black tenant farmers from 1900 to the 1960s. A book of short stories, *In Love and Trouble: Stories of Black Women* (1973), explores the experience and heritage of black women, a theme to which Walker returns in a second collection, *You Can't Keep a Good Woman Down* (1981). *The Color Purple* (1982), an EPISTOLARY NOVEL which won a PULITZER PRIZE, centres on the life of Celie, a black woman who has been raped by the man she believed to be her father. She bears his children, and then is forced to marry an older man whom she despises. The novel is made up of Celie's despairing letters to God and to her sister Nettie who has gone to Africa as a missionary, and of Nettie's letters to Celie. Walker's other novels are *Meridian* (1977), about civil rights workers in the South during the 1960s, *The Temple of My Familiar* (1989) and *Possessing the Secret of Joy* (1992), a harsh exploration of female circumcision. She has also published a biography of LANGSTON HUGHES for children (1974) and a volume of essays, *In Search of My Mother's Garden: Womanist Prose* (1983).

Walker, George (Frederick) 1947– Canadian playwright. He was born into a working-class family in Toronto's East End. Much of his work – including his first play, *The Prince of Naples* (1971), *Beyond Mozambique* (1974) and *Ramona and the White Slaves* (1976) – has resulted from his connection with the Factory Theatre Lab, where he has worked as playwright-in-residence and later as an associate director. *Gossip* (1977) and his Gothic comedy *Zastrozzi* (1977) have enjoyed productions in the USA, Britain and Australia. An urban playwright, Walker is influenced by the THEATRE OF THE ABSURD as well as television and films. In his own words, his plays 'try to walk that fine line between the serious and the comic', their characters finding their obsessions 'a way of coping with life and surviving'. Other plays include *Filthy Rich* (1979), *Theatre of the Film Noir* (1981), *The Art of War* (1982), *Criminals in Love* (1985) and

Nothing Sacred (1988), a reworking of Turgenev's *Fathers and Sons.*

Walker, Kath See OODGEROO.

Wallace A poem written *c.* 1477 by the Scottish poet BLIND HARRY, relating the life of Sir William Wallace and his struggle against the English. The work is divided into 12 books. The first two introduce the patriotic hero and Books III–VI give vivid descriptions of his battles and tell how he was made Guardian of Scotland. The poem continues to develop the figure of Wallace as a hero of mythic proportions. His final betrayal to the English and consequent execution by Edward I in 1305 (Book XII) are glossed over in favour of reinforcing the poem's image of Wallace as a saintly national hero. It enjoyed enduring popularity and influenced, amongst others, ROBERT BURNS and WILLIAM WORDSWORTH. Despite its exaggeration and the addition of some fictional incidents, the poem is a major source of information about the life of Wallace.

Wallace, (Richard Horatio) Edgar 1875–1932 Thriller writer. Born and brought up in the slums of south-east London, he worked in a printing firm, shoe shop and rubber factory and as a merchant seaman, plasterer, milk delivery boy and soldier before serving as correspondent for Reuters and *The Daily Mail* in the Boer War (1899–1902). For the rest of his life he combined newspaper work with a prodigious writing career which began with *The Four Just Men* (1906) and extended to nearly 100 more thrillers, over 50 volumes of short stories, nearly 30 plays and screenplays, four volumes of verse and many miscellaneous books, including three autobiographies and a ten-volume history of World War I. Critical success played no part in Wallace's ambition. He sought and gained the widest possible readership, becoming a wealthy and influential public figure. The 11 books featuring 'Sanders of the River' were among his most popular works. Of his DETECTIVE FICTION, the stories about J. G. Reeder were particularly successful: *Room 13* (1924), *The Mind of Mr J. G. Reeder* (1925), *Terror Keep* (1927), *Red Aces* (1929) and *The Guv'nor* (1932).

Wallace, Lew(is) 1827–1905 American novelist. Born in Indiana, he spent much of his life as a soldier, serving with distinction in the Mexican War and the Civil War and reaching the rank of major-general. He lived for a time in Mexico, then returned to Indiana to practise law and to write. *The Fair God* (1873) tells of the Spanish conquest of Mexico. His next book, *BEN-HUR* (1880), was an enormous success, selling over two million copies. His third book was a work of non-fiction, *The Boyhood of Christ* (1888). He served as governor of New Mexico and in 1881 became the US minister to Turkey. He also wrote other works of fiction, a tragic poem, *The Wooing of Malkatoon* (1897), and an autobiography.

Wallace-Crabbe, Chris(topher) (Keith) 1934– Australian poet and critic. Born in Melbourne, he was educated at Scotch College, Melbourne, and at Melbourne University. From 1965 to 1967 he was a Harkness Fellow at Yale University. He subsequently joined the department of English at Melbourne University, where he is now a professor. His poetry is frequently concerned with the shaping of beliefs. An early absorption in rationalism quickly crystallized itself into an attempt to write poetry which moved beyond a purely personal lyrical vision to a more objective consideration of social and political issues. Australian themes loom larger in his later work, though the voice which handles them is generally ironic. *Selected Poems* (1973) gathered work from earlier volumes together with new work such as a number of 'Meditations' inspired by Turner's paintings. Other collections are *Act in the Noon* (1974), *Foundations of Joy* (1976), *The Emotions Are Not Skilled Workers* (1980), *The Amorous Cannibal* (1985), *I'm Deadly Serious* (1988) and *For Crying Out Loud* (1990). *Splinters* (1981) is a novel about the underlying chaos of Melbourne life. He has edited several poetry anthologies and a collection of essays, *The Australian Nationalists* (1971). His own critical writing includes *Melbourne or the Bush* (1974), *Toil and Spin* (1980), *Three Absences in Australian Writing* (1983) and *Falling into Language* (1990).

Wallant, Edward (Lewis) 1926–62 American novelist. Born in New Haven, Connecticut, he served in the US Navy during World War II, graduated from Pratt Institute in 1950, and worked in New York advertising agencies until his death. His first story was published in 1955; *The Human Season*, his first novel, which appeared in 1960, is the story of a middle-aged immigrant Jew following the death of his wife. *The Pawnbroker* (1961), Wallant's most acclaimed work, is one of the first American novels to consider the atrocities that occurred during World War II. Sol Nazerman, a Polish Jew and the sole member of his family to have survived a Nazi concentration camp, owns a pawnshop in Harlem, where he relives the horrors he endured in nightmares and in flashbacks. Wallant's early death cut short a brief yet accomplished career. Two works were published posthumously: *The Tenants of Moonbloom* (1963) and *The Children at the Gate* (1965).

Waller, Edmund 1606–87 Poet. The eldest son of a wealthy landowner, Waller was born at Coleshill, now in Buckinghamshire, and educated at Eton and King's College, Cambridge. Elected to Parliament when he was only 16, he gained a reputation as a brilliant orator, possessing (said JOHN AUBREY) 'a great

mastership of the English Language'. A member of LUCIUS FALKLAND's circle at Great Tew, Waller sought, in the troubled 1640s, to steer a politically moderate course between the king and his opponents. In 1643, however, he plotted to oust the Parliamentary rebels and secure London for the royal cause. The plot was discovered and Waller confessed. Summoned before Parliament, he pleaded eloquently for clemency, was fined heavily and exiled. Settling in Paris, he also travelled in Italy and Switzerland with his friend, the diarist JOHN EVELYN. In 1652 he was allowed to come home to England, and was returned to Parliament and into royal favour at the Restoration. He died in his bed, aged 82.

For most of his long lifetime, Waller was a famous wit and poet, renowned for both lyric and panegyric. To DRYDEN, he embodied both sweetness and correctness. POPE acknowledged him as a master and, as late as 1766, the *Biographia Britannica* proclaimed him 'the most celebrated Lyric Poet that ever England produced'. Waller's subsequent reputation fast declined: SAMUEL JOHNSON found evidence of moral vacuity in his willingness to pen panegyrics on both the death of Cromwell and the return of Charles. (When Charles trenchantly observed that the former was much the better poem, Waller is said to have replied: 'Sir, we poets never succeed so well in writing truth as in fiction.') Waller's eulogy of the Dutch Wars, *Instructions to a Painter* (1666), is unread, survived by its parody, ANDREW MARVELL's *Last Instructions*. The lyrics addressed to Lady Dorothy Sidney, whom he courted in the 1630s, in the guise of Sacharissa, were renowned in his own century, but today only two of his short pieces are well known: 'On a Girdle' and the exquisite song, 'Go, Lovely Rose'. Waller deserves recognition for the refinement he brought to the HEROIC COUPLET and to standards of poetic eloquence and linguistic purity (he was a member of the Royal Society committee for 'improving the English tongue'). He proved a significant model for 18th-century ideals of literature.

Wallis, John 1616–1703 Mathematician. Educated at Felsted School, near his birthplace, and at Emmanuel College, Cambridge, at a time when 'Mathematicks... were scarce looked upon as Academical Studies', Wallis became Savilian Professor of Geometry at Oxford (1649–1703) and was one of the founders of the Royal Society. His *Arithmetica infinitorum* (1655) contains the first evaluation of π as a method of measurement, the first use of the symbol for infinity, and the germ of the differential calculus. A moderate Puritan, Wallis used his mathematical skill to decipher Royalist coded messages during the Civil War.

Walmsley, Leo 1892–1966 Novelist and playwright. Born in Shipley, West Yorkshire, Walmsley served with distinction in the Royal Flying Corps in Africa before settling first on the Yorkshire coast and later in Cornwall. He is best known for his regional novels, in which he portrayed the austere and often dangerous lives of the Yorkshire fishermen, with their loves, their hates, and their struggles with storm and tide. Of some dozen novels, charming for their simplicity and honesty rather than subtlety, *Three Fevers* (1932), *Foreigners* (1935) and *Sally Lunn* (1937; later dramatized) stand out. Walmsley also wrote an autobiography, *So Many Loves* (1944).

Walpole, Horace, 4th Earl of Orford 1717–97 Letter-writer and aesthetician. Born in London, the youngest son of Sir Robert Walpole, though malicious rumour of the time suggested that his true father was Lord Hervey, he was educated at Eton and King's College, Cambridge. In March 1739 he set off on a Grand Tour to Italy with GRAY (during the course of which they disagreed and separated), returning in 1741 to England where Walpole in his absence had been elected MP for Callington, Cornwall. His *Aedes Walpolianae* (1747), an annotated catalogue of the extensive family collection of paintings, was his first contribution to art studies.

In the same year he moved to Twickenham and started to Gothicize his house, Strawberry Hill, an activity which continued for nearly 25 years. The fame of this reconstruction, aided by the publication in 1774 of his *Description of the Villa of Horace Walpole*, was a major factor in the Gothic movement in both architecture and landscape gardening. The *Description* was printed on his own press installed at Strawberry Hill, the first important publication from which had been an edition of *Odes by Mr Gray* (1757). This was followed by Walpole's own *Catalogue of the Royal and Noble Authors of England* (1758), a combination of bibliography, antiquarianism and criticism which was a typical product of his interests and abilities. Other books were his reworking of GEORGE VERTUE's manuscripts as *Anecdotes of Painting in England* (1762–71), his own *Catalogue of Engravers Who Have Been Born or Resided in England* (1763), *Historic Doubts of the Life and Reign of Richard III* (1768), *Essay on Modern Gardening* (1785) and an edition of Lucan's *Pharsalia* with BENTLEY's notes (1760). These works were distinguished by both their scholarship and the quality of the printing.

In addition to contributing a number of minor pieces to journals, Walpole wrote THE CASTLE OF OTRANTO (1764). This tale, which he initially attempted to pass off as a translation from an Italian original, set out 'to blend the wonderful of old stories with the natural of modern novels'. Its main interest resides in the fact that it was the first of a long line of far more successful GOTHIC NOVELS by writers such as REEVE, RADCLIFFE and LEWIS. He followed *Otranto* with a blank-verse tragedy, *The Mysterious Mother*

(1768), which, having as its central theme the protagonist's remorse for an act of incest, was not regarded as a suitable piece for presentation on stage, though later it was admired by BYRON.

In 1769 CHATTERTON sent Walpole a number of his forgeries, to which Walpole replied showing some interest. He was speedily disabused by Gray and WILLIAM MASON, and wrote to Chatterton indicating that the pieces were not authentic. On hearing of the suicide of the forger Walpole appears to have been genuinely upset. Walpole's political connections and his own career as an MP for, successively, Callington, Castle Rising and Lynn, provided him with much inside information relating to government which he recorded and left sealed. His *Memoirs of the Last Ten Years of the Reign of George the Second* appeared in 1822; *Memoirs of the Reign of George the Third* in 1845; and *Journal of the Reign of King George the Third from the Year 1771 to 1783* in 1859. These editions are textually unreliable. All his other works are insignificant in comparison with his letters. Over 4000 survive, now gathered in the monumental 48-volume Yale edition (1937–83). Walpole discussed antiquarian topics with Cole; politics with Mann; literature with Gray, Mason and Madame du Deffand (whose correspondence with Walpole is preserved only in letters from her, he having requested that his own be destroyed, presumably because of a feeling of inadequacy in his French); and social gossip with George Montagu and the Countess of Upper Ossory. He wrote his letters with an eye to publication, successfully requesting the return of about 1000, which he then annotated for the benefit of future editors. The first group to be treated in this way, a batch originally sent to Mann, were returned to Walpole as early as 1749. His reputation was impugned by WORDSWORTH, COLERIDGE, KEATS and HAZLITT who wrongly thought him responsible for the death of Chatterton; his literary works were praised by Byron and SIR WALTER SCOTT; his political memoirs were considered poisonous by the Victorians.

Walpole, Sir **Hugh (Seymour)** 1884–1941 Novelist. Born in New Zealand, he was educated at King's School, Canterbury, and Emmanuel College, Cambridge. His first novels were *The Wooden Horse* (1910) and *Maradick at Forty* (1910), but it is for *Mr Perrin and Mr Traill* (1911) – which started the vogue for school stories and was based on his own brief experiences as a teacher – that he is chiefly remembered. *Fortitude* (1913) and *The Duchess of Wrexe* (1914) established his popular reputation.

During World War I he worked with the Russian Red Cross and was awarded the Order of St George. His experiences provided the background for *The Dark Forest* (1916) and *The Secret City* (1919), awarded the James Tait Black Memorial Prize. Other popular school stories followed with *Jeremy* (1919), *Jeremy and Hamlet* (1923) and *Jeremy at Crale* (1927). A family saga set in Cumberland, *The Herries Chronicle*, was enormously popular; it included *Rogue Herries* (1930), *Judith Paris* (1931), *The Fortress* (1932) and *Vanessa* (1933). *Farthing Hall* (1929) was written in collaboration with J. B. PRIESTLEY.

In total, Walpole produced over 40 popular novels, but he never achieved the literary status won by contemporaries like VIRGINIA WOOLF, whose MODERNISM he envied. His nonfiction includes studies of JOSEPH CONRAD (1916), JAMES BRANCH CABELL (1920) and TROLLOPE (1928). *The Crystal Box* (1924), *The Apple Trees* (1932) and *Roman Fountain* (1940) were autobiographical.

Walsh, Jill [Gillian] **Paton** 1937– Writer of CHILDREN'S LITERATURE. Born in London and educated at St Michael's Convent and St Anne's College, Oxford, she began writing after she left the teaching profession in 1962 to raise a family. *Farewell the Great King* (1972) and several subsequent novels use a historical setting. *The Emperor's Winding-Sheet*, winner of the Whitbread Award in 1974, is about an English boy caught up in the final siege of Constantinople, while *A Parcel of Patterns* (1983) takes place in the village of Eyam during the plague. *A Chance Child* (1978) mixes historical elements with fantasy, linking the brutality of life in a modern slum to the horrors of child labour in Victorian England. She has also produced several powerful novels dealing with the problems of adolescence: *Goldengrove* (1972) and its sequel *Unleaving* (1976), tracing the growth of the heroine Madge, are her most ambitious works. *The Dolphin Crossing* (1967) and *Fireweed* (1969) are set during World War II.

Walsh, William 1663–1708 Critic and poet. His PASTORALS and amorous verses were fashionable but Walsh's more enduring claim to attention rests on his encouragement of POPE in praising his *Pastorals* and suggesting improvements to them. He advised Pope to work towards an ideal of 'correctness' in his poetry. Pope published their letters in 1735. Walsh's *Works in Prose and Verse* appeared in 1736, and JOHNSON included a biography of him in LIVES OF THE POETS.

Walton, Izaak 1593–1683 Biographical and piscatorial writer. Born in Stafford, Walton went to London in 1618 and was apprenticed to a draper, and then an ironmonger, eventually making himself prosperous through his own drapery business. Until 1643 he lived in the parish of St Dunstan's, where JOHN DONNE was the vicar, and the two became friends. As a result of this, Walton made the acquaintance of GEORGE HERBERT, HENRY KING, and WOTTON, the distinguished Provost of Eton. From the latter, who died in 1639, Walton took over the writing of the 'Life' of Donne, which appeared in the 1640 edition of the poet's ser-

mons. This was followed by a further series of 'Lives', each of which the author scrupulously updated, in his characteristic fashion; these were of Wotton himself (1651), RICHARD HOOKER (1665), Herbert (1670) and Bishop Sanderson (1678), all Anglican churchmen. Walton was a robust Royalist – but no Laudian – and his several ecclesiastical connections included the families of his two wives. After the Restoration of the monarchy he moved to Worcester as Steward to Bishop Morley, and then to Winchester, where he died in his 90th year, and was buried in the Cathedral. His unique place in English letters, and his international reputation, are really the result of *THE COMPLEAT ANGLER*, a classic book on fishes and fishing which was published in 1653 and has since been reprinted on many hundreds of occasions.

Walwicz, Ania 1951– Australian experimental writer, playwright and painter. Born in Poland, she studied in Melbourne and has been writer-in-residence at several Australian universities. Her sense of herself as outsider, both as woman and migrant, and her late encounter with the language in which she now writes, left her free to break through structural formalities. The work in *Writing* (1982), *Boat* (1989) and *Red Roses* (1991) can be described as both poetry and prose: using no punctuation, it piles up apparently illogical connections which nevertheless accumulate profound rationality of meaning. The power of her experiment is widely acknowledged and her work is currently being represented in more collections than that of any other contemporary Australian writer. Her plays are *Girlboytalk* (1986), *Dissecting Mice* (1989) and *Elegant* (1990).

Wanderer, The An Old English poem preserved in the EXETER BOOK. The structure is somewhat ambiguous: the poem may represent a monologue containing two reported speeches or, alternatively, speeches by different characters. The first speech or quotation says that the solitary wanderer often experiences the grace of God despite the hardships he endures. There follows a long personal account of exile leading the speaker to wonder that his suffering and the general state of decay of the world do not make him miserable. Finally the voice of wisdom asserts that the world's wealth is transitory and faith in God is the only source of security. Although the dramatic form is obscure, the thought is clearly developed.

Wanley, Nathaniel 1634–80 Poet and cleric. He was born in Leicester, educated at Trinity College, Cambridge, and spent most of his adult life as vicar of Holy Trinity, Coventry. His religious verse, *Scintillulae sacrae*, declares its debt to HENRY VAUGHAN in its title; these meditations, and the narratives *The Witch of Endor* and *Lazarus* were first collected in 1928. His prose compilation, *The Wonders of* the *Little World* (1678), was one of the sources of ROBERT BROWNING'S *THE PIED PIPER OF HAMELIN*.

War of the Worlds, The A novel by H. G. WELLS, published as a serial in *Pearson's Magazine* in 1897 and reprinted in book form in 1898.

The first part of the novel describes how missiles fired from Mars land in England, arousing only mild interest until they disgorge fearful war machines to devastate the country. Panic spreads as resistance fails and London is destroyed. In the second part survivors of the catastrophe live in hiding; a curate and an artilleryman offer opposed philosophies in reaction to the invasion, the latter dreaming hopelessly of revolution against the world's new masters. In the end, though, the loathsome Martians are unprotected by their armoured weapons against the ravages of earthly bacteria, which succeed where men's best efforts failed in destroying them. Wells takes a certain delight in contemplating the destruction of English society, but with characteristic ambivalence also displays a sympathetic appreciation of the magnitude of the tragedy.

This archetypal story of alien invasion provided a model for countless cruder imitations; a famous radio adaptation by Orson Welles was realistic enough to cause panic in the USA in 1938.

Ward, Artemus [Browne, Charles Farrar] 1834–67 American humorist. He was born in Waterford, Maine, and was for the most part self-educated. From 1857 to 1859 he wrote for *The Cleveland Plain Dealer*, and during this period created Artemus Ward – the writer of mock letters to the editor, full of colloquial language and misspellings that result in puns or malapropisms. Browne left Ohio in 1859 to join the staff of New York's *VANITY FAIR*; later, as the journal's editor, he came to be known as the 'unofficial dean of American humour'.

He was a pioneer of the comic lecture – a form of entertainment MARK TWAIN would later capitalize on. His targets were Abolitionists, Mormons, Shakers, feminists, temperance advocates and anyone else he considered hypocritical or ineffectual. His publications include *Artemus Ward, His Book* (1862) and *Artemus Ward, His Travels* (1865). He died of tuberculosis while on a lecture tour in England, during which he had contributed to *PUNCH*. *Artemus Ward in London and Other Papers* was published posthumously in 1867.

Ward, Mrs Humphry (Mary Augusta) 1851–1920 Novelist. She was born in Hobart, Tasmania, where her father, Thomas Arnold, younger brother of MATTHEW ARNOLD, had become inspector of schools, a post he relinquished on his conversion to Roman Catholicism in 1856. In 1858, two years after the family's return to England, Mary was sent to the first of a series of private boarding schools whilst her father worked in Roman Catholic educational institutions in Dublin and Birmingham. She rejoined her family in 1867 when her father's return to Anglicanism enabled him to teach in Oxford. In 1876 her father's reconversion to Roman Catholicism necessitated another move, but by this time she had been married for four years to Thomas Humphry Ward, an Oxford don and later the art critic for *The Times*.

Acquaintance with leading Oxford figures such as J. R. GREEN, T. H. GREEN, BENJAMIN JOWETT, WALTER PATER and MARK PATTISON encouraged her academic interests. She contributed the lives of early Spanish ecclesiastics to the *Dictionary of Christian Biography* and became the first secretary of Somerville College in 1879. The Arnold family history, combined with her friendship with leading anti-dogmatic theologians, resulted in her defence, in pamphlet and novel form, of an unorthodox religious position close to that held by her uncle Matthew Arnold. She argued for a religious faith which, freed from the need to believe in the historical truth of the Gospel, could concentrate upon applying the spiritual truths of Christianity to practical humanitarian work. Her novel *ROBERT ELSMERE* (1888) records the intellectual and emotional implications of such a spiritual pilgrimage, whilst the next phase of her own life showed its practical results. In 1881 the Wards moved to London where, in addition to literary reviewing, editing, and the writing of further novels, she involved herself in the work of the Passmore Edwards Settlement opened in Bloomsbury in 1897. Here she instituted recreational activities for children and developed an educational programme for the physically handicapped.

Despite her support for higher education for women and her active political campaigning on behalf of her own son, she disapproved of female suffrage sufficiently to become president of the Women's Anti-Suffrage League (1908). During World War I President Theodore Roosevelt persuaded her to write for the American public a series of letters and articles describing the Allied war effort, later published in England as *England's Effort* (1916), *Towards the Goal* (1917) and *Fields of Victory* (1919). In the year of her death she was appointed one of the first seven women magistrates.

Apart from *Robert Elsmere*, the most notable of her 25 novels are *The History of David Grieve* (1892) and *Helbeck of Bannisdale* (1898) for their treatment of religious issues, and *Marcella* (1894) and *Delia Blanchflower* (1915) for their debate of social and political issues. *A Writer's Recollections* (1918) provides interesting accounts of the many major literary figures she had met, including GEORGE ELIOT and HENRY JAMES, and a record of the social and intellectual life of Oxford in her early years. Her translation of the *Journal Intime* of the Swiss mystic Henri Amiel (1885) long remained the standard English edition.

Ward, Nathaniel 1578–1652 American Puritan writer. Born in Essex, he emigrated to Massachusetts in 1634 and became influential in the colony's politics. His literary reputation rests on his THE SIMPLE COBBLER OF AGGAWAM, written in 1645 and published in London in 1647. He returned to England in 1646 and remained there for the rest of his life, but retained his ties with his American friends, and wrote a poem commending ANNE BRADSTREET's collection, *The Tenth Muse*, which was included in the first edition (1650).

Ward, Ned [Edward] 1667–1731 A London tavern keeper with a gift for doggerel verse, he was also a reporter of life in the capital. In *The London Spy*, begun in 1698, he uses the device of a countryman who meets a London friend while visiting the city and is taken everywhere to see almost everything. The 18 sketches were collected in 1703. Ward wrote quantities of verse in the manner of SAMUEL BUTLER and was notoriously indiscreet in his comments on the contemporary scene. He was sentenced to the pillory for passages in *Hudibras redivivus* (1705).

Warden, The The first of ANTHONY TROLLOPE's BARSETSHIRE NOVELS, published in 1855.

The Rev. Septimus Harding is an elderly clergyman who has been appointed by the Bishop of Barchester to be warden of Hiram's Hospital, an almshouse for 12 old men funded from a medieval charity. A gentle and unworldly man, Mr Harding never questions the discrepancy between his comfortable annual salary and the small weekly allowance given to the old men, until the issue is taken up by a local reformer, John Bold, and denounced as a flagrant church abuse by the *Jupiter* newspaper (*The Times*). Bold is the suitor of Mr Harding's youngest daughter, Eleanor, and abandons the campaign at her request. But battle has been joined between the metropolitan reformers and the conservative clerical party led by Archdeacon Grantly, Mr Harding's son-in-law, and the warden resigns, 'not so anxious to prove himself right, as to be so'. Bold marries Eleanor, and Mr Harding leaves his pleasant home and garden for lodgings in Barchester.

A subtle study of the clash between public rhetoric and individual conscience, *The Warden* is one of the finest and most characteristic of Trollope's works. It contains an implicit defence of his own art and moral vision in the portraits of CARLYLE as Dr Pessimist Anticant and DICKENS as Mr Popular Sentiment.

Ware, Sir James 1594–1666 Irish antiquarian and historian. Born in Dublin, he was educated at Trinity College. His father was Attorney-General of Ireland, an office to which Ware succeeded in 1632, three years after he had been knighted. His great work, *Antiquities of Ireland*, began to appear in 1626; the final instalment did not appear until 1654. During this time Ware's political position exposed him to the hazards of the contemporary crises in England. He was imprisoned by the Parliamentarians for 10 months in the Tower of London in 1644 and exiled to France for two years in 1649 on the orders of the Puritan Deputy in Dublin. Ware brought out a second edition of the *Antiquities* (1659), *Annals of Ireland* (1664), *Lives of the Irish Bishops* (1665) and *Works Ascribed to St Patrick* (1656). His most popular work for a time was *Writers of Ireland* (1639). His reputation as a reliable scholar and historian suffered grievously because of the later interpolations and forgeries introduced into his writings by his son Robert. The full extent of these corruptions was not exposed until 1917.

Warner, Charles Dudley 1829–1900 American novelist and essayist. Born in Massachusetts, he received his BA in 1851 from Hamilton College and, after working briefly as a railroad surveyor in Missouri, studied law at the University of Pennsylvania. He practised law in Chicago until 1860, when he turned to writing professionally. He is best remembered for THE GILDED AGE (1873), his first published novel, which was written in collaboration with MARK TWAIN. He also produced several collections of essays, including *Summer in a Garden* (1870), *Being a Boy* (1878) and *The Relation of Literature to Life* (1896). He devoted his later years to writing a trilogy of novels: *A Little Journey in the World* (1889), *The Golden House* (1894) and *That Fortune* (1899).

Warner, Marina (Sarah) 1946– Novelist and cultural historian. Educated at Oxford, she has been a Getty Scholar at the Getty Center for the History of Art and the Humanities in the USA and a professor at Erasmus University in Rotterdam. Although she has published novels, including *The Lost Father* (1988) and *Indigo* (1992), her reputation rests on works of female cultural history: *Alone of All Her Sex* (1976), a study of the Virgin Mary; *Joan of Arc* (1981); and *Monuments and Maidens* (1986), about 'The Allegory of the Female Form'.

Warner, Rex 1905–86 Poet, novelist and translator. Born in Gloucestershire, educated at St George's School, Harpenden, and Wadham College, Oxford, he became a schoolteacher in England and Egypt until the end of World War II. From 1945–7 he was director of the British Institute in Athens and became a respected translator. He was a professor at the University of Connecticut from 1964 to 1974.

Warner's first volume of poetry, *Poems* (1937), was inspired by an anti-totalitarian fervour which he shared with many of his contemporaries during the

1930s, notably W. H. AUDEN and CHRISTOPHER ISHERWOOD. *The Wild Goose Chase*, a novel published in the same year, and *The Professor* (1938) were more bleak, showing the influence of Kafka in their use of mysterious allegory and an atmosphere of threat and guilt. *The Aerodrome* (1941), his best-known novel, studies the conflict between an unnamed but quintessentially English village representing the fallen human condition, unregenerate but moderately happy, and the aerodrome, whose personnel believe in cleanliness, health and discipline.

Warner's many notable translations include: Euripides' *Medea* (1944), *Hippolytus* (1950) and *Helen* (1951); Aeschylus' *Prometheus Bound* (1947); Xenophon's *Anabasis* (1949); Thucydides (1954); and Plutarch (1958). In 1960 he produced a translation of the modern Greek poet George Seferis. His studies of classical subjects include *The Young Caesar* (1958) and *Pericles the Athenian* (1963).

Warner, Sylvia Townsend 1893–1978 Novelist, poet and short-story writer. The daughter of a master of Harrow School, she received no formal education but absorbed a wide range of knowledge from her parents and read voraciously. She joined the editorial board of the Church Music project in 1917 and spent the next 10 years working on the 10-volume *Tudor Church Music*. Her early poems were praised by HOUSMAN and YEATS, and Louis Untermeyer compared her to THOMAS HARDY. Other writers who influenced Warner were T. F. POWYS, whom she met in 1923, and DAVID GARNETT. She was a regular contributor to THE NEW YORKER for many years. Her first novel, *Lolly Willowes* (1926), is a supernatural story. *Mr Fortune's Maggot* (1927) relates the story of a missionary, Mr Fortune, who goes to the island of Fanua to convert the natives, with little success. A month spent in the mysterious world of the Essex marshes inspired *The True Heart* (1929), a story of love in its many forms, which shows Warner at her imaginative and lyrical best. Her volumes of poetry include *The Espalier* (1925), *Time Importuned* (1928), *Opus 7* (1931) and *Rainbow* (1932). Later novels include *Summer Will Show* (1936), *The Corner That Held Them* (1948) and *The Flint Anchor* (1954). *A Garland of Straw* (1943) and *Museum of Cheats* (1947) are volumes of short stories. Warner lived with the writer Valentine Ackland from the early 1930s until her death in 1969.

Warner, William ?1558–1609 Poet and translator. Warner was educated at Oxford and became an attorney in London. *Pan His Syrinx* (1584) is a collection of seven prose tales. Warner translated the *Menaechmi* of Plautus (1595), but it is unlikely that SHAKESPEARE had seen the unpublished manuscript when he wrote THE COMEDY OF ERRORS. Warner's major work is *Albion's England*, a verse history of Britain in 14-syl-lable lines, which enjoyed a high reputation in its own time. The first edition of 1586 tells the story from Noah to the Norman Conquest, with many mythical episodes. Later editions (1589, 1592) carry the history on to the accessions of Henry VII and Elizabeth, while the 1612 version reaches the reign of JAMES I.

Warren, Mercy Otis 1728–1814 American playwright. The sister of James Otis, a colonial political leader, and the wife of James Warren, the president of the Provincial Congress of Massachusetts, she was at the centre of Revolutionary politics and in frequent correspondence with Revolutionary leaders. She is best known for her anti-Loyalist political dramas, *The Adulateur* (1773) and *The Group* (1775). Other plays have been attributed to her, most notably *The Blockheads* (1776) and *The Motley Assembly* (1779). She also published a collection of dramatic verse, *Poems Dramatic and Miscellaneous* (1790), which contains two verse tragedies, 'The Sack of Rome' and 'The Ladies of Castille', and a three-volume *History of the Rise, Progress and Termination of the American Revolution* (1805), which serves as an important contemporary record of the Revolutionary years.

Warren, Robert Penn 1905–89 American poet, novelist and critic. He was born in Guthrie, Kentucky, and educated at Vanderbilt, the University of California at Berkeley, Yale and Oxford, where he was a Rhodes Scholar. A member of the FUGITIVES, he helped to found and edit the group's magazine, *The Fugitive* (1922–5). His first book was a biography, *John Brown, the Making of a Martyr* (1929; reissued 1992), and in 1930 he contributed to the Southern Agrarian manifesto, *I'll Take My Stand: The South and the Agrarian Tradition*. His first volume of poetry, *Thirty-Six Poems*, appeared in 1935, the year he took up the editorship of *The Southern Review* with CLEANTH BROOKS.

The next 20 years or so were the period of his greatest achievement, when he distinguished himself in poetry, fiction and criticism. Both his poetry and fiction are marked by a brooding, philosophical intelligence, and he wrote perceptively on writers with a similar cast of mind, notably CONRAD and FAULKNER. Among his many volumes of verse are *Selected Poems 1923–1943* (1944), *Brother to Dragons: A Tale in Verse and Voices* (1953, revised edition 1979), *Promises: Poems 1954-1956* (PULITZER PRIZE, 1957), *Selected Poems: New and Old 1923–1966* (1966), *Or Else: Poem/Poems 1968–1974* (1974), *Now and Then: Poems 1976-1978* (Pulitzer Prize, 1978), *Being Here: Poetry 1977–1980* (1980), *Chief Joseph of the Nez Perce* (1983), *New and Selected Poems 1923–1985* (1985) and *Portrait of a Father* (1988). *A Robert Penn Warren Reader* (1988) is a useful anthology of his poetry and prose. His fiction often deals with Southern history and generally has Southern settings. *Night Rider*

(1939) and *At Heaven's Gate* (1943) were followed by his best-known novel, *All the King's Men* (Pulitzer Prize, 1946). It tells the story of Willie Stark (apparently based on Governor Huey Long of Louisiana), a corrupt politician who becomes governor of a Southern state and dies a tragic death. Later novels include: *World Enough and Time* (1950), based on an 1826 murder trial in Kentucky; *Band of Angels* (1955), a tragedy of miscegenation; *The Cave* (1959); *Wilderness: A Tale of the Civil War* (1961); *Flood: A Romance of Our Times* (1964); *Meet Me in the Green Glen* (1971); and *A Place to Come To* (1977).

His many works of non-fiction include *Segregation: The Inner Conflict in the South* (1956), *Remember the Alamo!* (1958), *Who Speaks for the Negro?* (1965), *Homage to Theodore Dreiser* (1971), *Democracy and Poetry: A Lecture* (1975) and *Jefferson Davis Gets His Citizenship Back* (1980). *Selected Essays* (1958) was superseded by *New and Selected Essays* (1989). With Cleanth Brooks he edited several volumes of criticism and creative writing, including *Understanding Poetry: An Anthology for College Students* (1938; revised editions 1950, 1960 and 1976) and *Understanding Fiction* (1943; revised editions 1959 and 1979). In addition to his Pulitzer Prizes, he received the Shelley Memorial Award for Poetry, the Bollingen Prize and the Presidential Medal for Freedom. He became the first POET LAUREATE of the USA in 1986.

Warren, Samuel 1807–77 Novelist. Born in Lancashire of a devoutly religious family, he studied medicine at the University of Edinburgh, changed to the law and was called to the English Bar in 1837. He became a bencher of the Inner Temple in 1851, Recorder for Hull in 1852–74 and Conservative MP for Midhurst in 1856–9. His first work of fiction, the melodramatic *Passages from the Diary of a Late Physician*, appeared in BLACKWOOD'S EDINBURGH MAGAZINE in 1830–7. *Ten Thousand a Year*, serialized in *Blackwood's* from 1839 and published complete in 1841, scored a great success and led some reviewers to compare him favourably with the young DICKENS. Packed with sensational incident, as well as portraits of the legal profession and high society, the novel tells of the rise and fall of Mr Tittlebat Titmouse. *Now and Then* (1847) was less successful, and Warren turned to writing legal textbooks.

Warton, Joseph 1722–1800 Critic. The son of THOMAS WARTON THE ELDER and brother of THOMAS WARTON THE YOUNGER, he was born at Dunsfold in Surrey. He became headmaster of Winchester College, which he had attended before going to Oriel College, Oxford, and was prebendary of both Winchester and St Paul's cathedrals. He is remembered for his literary criticism, particularly his essays on POPE (1756, 1782), rather than for his own books of verse and his translations of the *Eclogues* and *Georgics* of Virgil. Warton also edited the works of Pope (1797) and SIDNEY's *APOLOGY FOR POETRY* (1787).

Warton, Thomas, the elder 1688–1745 Scholar, poet, and father of JOSEPH WARTON and THOMAS WARTON THE YOUNGER. He was educated at Hart Hall and Magdalen College, Oxford, where he was a fellow in 1717–24. He held the professorship of poetry from 1718 until 1728. In 1723 he also became vicar of Basingstoke and master of its grammar school, where GILBERT WHITE was one of his pupils. Joseph Warton prepared his father's *Poems on Several Occasions* for posthumous publication in 1748. The two 'Runic Odes' included in the volume influenced THOMAS GRAY.

Warton, Thomas, the younger 1728–90 Poet and literary historian. The younger son of THOMAS WARTON THE ELDER and younger brother of JOSEPH WARTON, he entered Trinity College, Oxford, in 1744 and became a fellow in 1751. He remained at Oxford all his life, following his father in serving as professor of poetry (1757–67). He was appointed POET LAUREATE in 1785.

As well as editing *The Oxford Sausage: or, Select Poetical Pieces Written by the Most Celebrated Wits of the University of Oxford* (1764), Warton produced occasional verse which includes 'The Pleasures of Melancholy' (1747), 'The Triumph of Isis' (1749) and 'Newmarket: A Satire' (1751). Much of his poetry imitated SPENSER and MILTON, and revived interest in the SONNET, a form important to the next generation of poets. A collected edition of his poems (1777) went through four editions before his death.

The most important of Warton's many scholarly works was his *History of English Poetry from the Close of the Eleventh to the Commencement of the Eighteenth Century* (3 vols. 1774–81; slightly expanded as 4 vols., 1824), which ranks with THOMAS PERCY's *Reliques of Ancient English Poetry* as a crucial document in the rediscovery of medieval and 16th-century poetry. In its shift away from exclusively classical tenets, it anticipates the spirit of ROMANTICISM. The same tendencies are apparent in his contribution to the CHATTERTON controversy, *An Enquiry into the Authenticity of the Poems Attributed to Rowley* (1782), and in the high regard for Gothic architecture which he shared with his contemporary FRANCIS GROSE, manifest in the posthumous *Essays on Gothic Architecture by the Rev. T. Warton, Rev. J. Bentham, Captain Grose, and the Rev. J. Milner* (1800). Warton was also instrumental in securing the degree of MA for his friend SAMUEL JOHNSON in 1755 and contributed three papers (Nos. 33, 93 and 96) to *The Idler*.

Washington, Booker T(aliaferro) 1856–1915 Black American leader, born in Hale's Ford, Virginia, the son of a slave mother and a white father. He urged a programme of gradual development for blacks, and emphasized training in the techniques of agricultural and industrial production. These policies soon brought him into conflict with W. E. B. DU BOIS and other black leaders. Du Bois attacked him for not taking a sufficiently forceful stand on disenfranchisement in the South, and criticized him for promoting vocational instruction at the expense of liberal education. Washington's publications include *The Future of the American Negro* (1899), *Sowing and Reaping* (1900), *Character Building* (1902), *Working with the Hands* (1904), *The Story of the Negro* (1909), *My Larger Education* (1911) and *The Man Farthest Down* (1912). His biography of FREDERICK DOUGLASS (1906) is widely considered to be a pioneering work in the field. His autobiography, *Up from Slavery*, was published in 1901.

Washington Square A short novel by HENRY JAMES, published serially in *THE CORNHILL MAGAZINE* in 1880 and in volume form in 1881. The motherless daughter of a wealthy New York physician, Catherine Sloper is unappreciated and ignored by her father, and leads a lonely and bleak existence until she is courted by Morris Townsend. She accepts his proposal of marriage, but her father refuses to give his consent when he discovers Townsend to be a penniless fortune-hunter. Exasperated by Catherine's obstinate attachment, Dr Sloper takes her away to Europe for a year. This does not change her mind, but Morris, faced with the prospect of Catherine having to forfeit her inheritance if she marries him, breaks off the engagement. Seventeen years later, after the death of her father has made Catherine a rich woman, Morris returns and proposes again. She rejects him absolutely and settles down to the life of a spinster in the family house in Washington Square.

Wasserstein, Wendy 1950– American playwright. Born in Brooklyn, she attended Mount Holyoke, the City College of New York and Yale Drama School. *Uncommon Women and Others* (1977) depicts the reunion of five women graduates of Mount Holyoke and their reflections on their college days. *Isn't It Romantic* (1983) follows two such women as they confront their parents, their lovers and their own unclear futures. *The Heidi Chronicles* (1989) traces the history of the women's movement through the life of one woman and her friends.

Waste Land, The A poem by T. S. ELIOT, published in 1922. At first attracting both praise and derision for its radically experimental technique, it became his most influential work and hence one of the most influential texts of MODERNISM.

The title – suggested by *From Ritual to Romance* (1920), Jessie L. Weston's study of the Grail legend (see ARTHURIAN LITERATURE) – refers to a dry and desolate country which can be revived by a fertility ritual. Using this as his central SYMBOL for European life after World War I, Eliot explores the various aspects of its sterility in five sections: 'The Burial of the Dead', 'A Game of Chess', 'The Fire Sermon', 'Death by Water' and 'What the Thunder Said'. The method throughout is deliberately fragmentary, abandoning traditional verse forms for FREE VERSE to juxtapose monologues or overheard snatches of conversation by the inhabitants of the waste land with allusions, not merely to the Grail legend, but to previous literature (SHAKESPEARE and Dante in particular), religious teaching (the Bible, St Augustine and the Upanishads) and myth. The resulting 'heap of broken images' both intensifies the portrait of spiritual decay and hints at the possibility of redemption. With its repeated chant of 'Shantih', which Eliot himself suggested can be translated as 'The Peace which passeth understanding', the ending is deliberately enigmatic. Much critical interpretation of *The Waste Land* has concentrated on gauging the extent of its pessimism.

The poem appeared in the first issue of *THE CRITERION*, which Eliot edited, in October 1922 and again a month later in THE DIAL (New York). When it appeared in book form, also in 1922, it included footnotes by Eliot, explaining his allusions but rarely resolving other complexities of the text. The original manuscript was published in facsimile, with an introduction by his widow, Valerie Eliot, in 1971. Considerably longer than the published version, it shows the cuts and revisions proposed by EZRA POUND, to whom the poem is dedicated.

Water-Babies, The: *A Fairy Tale for a Land Baby* A fantasy written by CHARLES KINGSLEY for his youngest son, as *THE HEROES* was written for his older children. It was serialized by *Macmillan's Magazine* in 1862–3 and published in volume form in 1863. Tom, a young chimney-sweep, runs away from his brutal employer, Grimes. In his flight he falls into a river and is transformed into a water baby. Thereafter, in the river and in the seas, he meets all sorts of creatures and learns a series of moral lessons.

Waterhouse, Keith (Spencer) 1929– Novelist, playwright and journalist. Born and educated in Leeds, he made his name as a novelist with *Billy Liar* (1959). Its superficial similarities with the provincial realism of contemporaries like JOHN BRAINE and STAN BARSTOW are tempered by a whimsical streak: Billy is a compulsive dreamer who inhabits his own fantasy world of Ambrosia. Subsequent novels have included a belated sequel taking up Billy's fortunes in London, *Billy Liar on the Moon* (1976), as well as *Maggie Muggins* (1981) and *Unsweet Charity* (1992). His collaborative work for stage, screen and television with Willis Hall includes an adaptation of *Billy Liar* (1960),

Celebration (1961), *All Things Bright and Beautiful* (1963) and a comedy of adulteries, *Say Who You Are* (1965). *Jeffrey Bernard is Unwell* (1989) is an ingenious stage adaptation of Jeffrey Bernard's columns in *The Spectator*. Waterhouse has also pursued a long career as a polemical, witty journalist

Waterman, Andrew (John) 1940– Poet. He grew up in the South London suburbia which is the carefully evoked setting for many of his poems. After leaving home at the age of 17 he did various clerical and manual jobs before reading English at the University of Leicester. He teaches at the New University of Ulster, Coleraine. His first collection, *Living Room* (1974), announced his preoccupation with the journey from London childhood to present-day Ulster and his interest in conversational or demotic language. *From the Other Country* (1977) was followed by *Over the Wall* (1980), which showed a new assurance. The remarkable title sequence of *Out for the Elements* (1981) – 187 stanzas in a form borrowed from Pushkin but in spirit Wordsworthian – traces the growth of a poet's mind and, true to WORDSWORTH's precepts, does so in determinedly ordinary language. *Selected Poems* appeared in 1986 and *In the Planetarium* in 1990.

Watership Down A novel by RICHARD ADAMS, published in 1972. A long and intricately plotted anthropomorphic fantasy about a community of rabbits who set out to found a new warren, it found a large adult readership only after initial success as CHILDREN'S LITERATURE. While its ALLEGORY of human society extends to the semi-mystical overtones of an enigmatic God-rabbit, El-a-H'rairah, Adams's novel is also notable for its authentic account of rabbit behaviour and its sensitive evocation of the natural world of the Berkshire Downs.

Watkins, Vernon (Phillips) 1906–67 Poet. Born in Maesteg, Glamorganshire, to Welsh-speaking parents, Watkins was educated at Swansea Grammar School, Repton School, and Magdalene College, Cambridge. He worked as a clerk at Lloyds Bank in Swansea until 1965, apart from wartime service in the RAF. His collections include *The Ballad of the Mari Lwyd and Other Poems* (1941), *The Lady with the Unicorn: Poems* (1948), *The Death Bell: Poems and Ballads* (1954), and the posthumous volumes *Fidelities* (1968) and *The Collected Poems* (1986). Throughout his poetic career, Watkins pursued one theme: the time-annulling revelation of the transcendent. His poetry aims to create a controlled music through which we may enter into an experience that is both simple and overwhelming. His admiration for YEATS helped to offset the influence of the NEW APOCALYPSE poets and DYLAN THOMAS, his long-standing friend.

Watson, Richard 1737–1816 Polymath. Born at Heversham in Westmorland, he studied mathematics at Trinity College, Cambridge. With no training in the subject, Watson succeeded in becoming professor of chemistry at Cambridge in 1764. With no training in divinity, he became Regius Professor in that subject (1771) and held several church livings; he was appointed to the see of Llandaff in 1782 and went to live on Lake Windermere. His *Apology for Christianity, in a Series of Letters to E. Gibbon* (1776), prompted by Chapters XV and XVI of the first volume of *THE DECLINE AND FALL OF THE ROMAN EMPIRE*, was courteously acknowledged by the historian. Watson was also the author of *Apology for the Bible, in Answer to Thomas Paine* (1796).

Watson, Sheila 1919– Canadian novelist and short-story writer. Born in New Westminster, British Columbia, she was educated at the University of British Columbia and later at the University of Toronto. She was a schoolteacher for many years and in the latter part of her career a professor at the University of Alberta. Her first story, 'Brother Oedipus', was published in the *Queen's Quarterly* in 1954. Her novel, *The Double Hook* (1959), received much critical and popular attention. An attack on the rural NATURALISM of much Canadian literature which draws on native myths, it is one of the few masterpieces of MODERNISM in Canada. *Four Stories* was published in 1980.

Watson, Thomas ?1557–92 Translator and poet. He was educated at Oxford and afterwards studied law in London. He probably first met Sir Thomas Walsingham, who was to become his patron, on a visit to Paris in 1581. Watson had a reputation as a considerable classicist even at Oxford. His translation of Sophocles' *Antigone* with appendices of Latin allegorical poems and metrical exercises was printed in 1581. His Latin hexameter paraphrase of Tasso's *Aminta* (1585) was translated into English by Abraham Fraunce without acknowledgement to Watson. *Raptus Helenae* (1586) is a Latin translation from the Greek of Coluthus. *The First Set of Italian Madrigals Englished* (1590) contains English versions of Italian madrigals, mainly those of Marenzio. Watson mourned his patron Walsingham's death in a Latin elegy (1590) which he translated into English and published in the same year. His Latin pastoral *Amintae Gaudia* was printed posthumously in 1592.

As a poet, Watson is notable largely for his SONNETS. *The Hekatompathia: or, Passionate Century of Love* (1582) is a collection of 18-line poems which he calls 'sonnets'. They are mainly imitations of classical, Italian and French models or contain paraphrases from classical and Continental authors. It may well be that SHAKESPEARE had one of these poems, an extended and highly wrought catalogue of a mistress's charms, in mind when he wrote sonnet 130, 'My mistress' eyes are nothing like the sun'. *The Tears of Fancy*, printed posthumously in 1593, contains 60 sonnets, largely inspired by Petrarch and Ronsard. The miscellanies also contain Watson's poems: *THE PHOENIX NEST* prints three previously unpublished poems, *ENGLAND'S HELICON* five (only one is new) and *A POETICAL RHAPSODY* prints ten poems from *Hekatompathia*.

Watson, Sir William 1858–1935 Poet. Born in Yorkshire, he published several volumes of poetry heavily indebted to TENNYSON, among them *Wordsworth's Grave* (1890), *Lachrymae Musarum* (1892) which included poems on the death of Tennyson, *The Year of Shame* (1896) and *The Heralds of Dawn* (1912). His *Collected Poems* appeared in 1899 and 1906.

Watts, Isaac 1674–1748 Hymn-writer. The son of a Nonconformist minister and teacher, Watts was born in Southampton. His abilities marked him out at the local grammar school and a patron offered him a university education. However, Watts preferred to attend the Dissenters' Academy at Stoke Newington, where educational standards were exacting and where DANIEL DEFOE had also been taught. In 1700 Watts became assistant pastor, and then pastor, at the Independent Congregation in Mark Lane, but his health deteriorated after 1703 and he resigned in 1712. Thereafter he lived at Abney Hall, in Stoke Newington.

Watts promoted the practice of hymn-singing in Nonconformist congregations where the Metrical Psalms had previously been the only music heard. His principal collections were *Hymns and Spiritual Songs* (1707) and *The Psalms of David* (1719); he also published *Divine Songs* (1715), the first hymn book composed for children, and a book of verse, *Horae Lyricae* (1706). His most popular hymns include 'Our God, Our Help in Ages Past' (JOHN WESLEY changed its opening to 'O God, our help in ages past'), 'Jesus Shall Reign Where'er the Sun' and 'When I Survey the Wondrous Cross'. LEWIS CARROLL parodied Watts in *ALICE'S ADVENTURES IN WONDERLAND* ('How Doth the Little Busy Bee').

Watts-Dunton, (Walter) Theodore 1832–1914 Novelist and critic. Born Theodore Watts (he changed his name by deed poll) at St Ives, now in Cambridgeshire, he went to school in Cambridge and practised as a solicitor in London. He published contributions to *THE ATHENAEUM*, some Shakespearean criticism, a volume of poetry and *Aylwin* (1898), a novel which includes a thinly disguised portrait of DANTE GABRIEL ROSSETTI. Also a student of gypsy-life, he edited GEORGE BORROW's *LAVENGRO* in 1893 and *THE ROMANY RYE* in 1900. His literary aspirations outpaced his abilities, and, if Watts-Dunton is remembered at all, it is for his care of the alcoholically ravaged SWINBURNE at The Pines, Putney, for the last 30 years of the poet's life.

Waugh, Alec [Alexander] **(Raban)** 1898–1981 Novelist. He was born in London, the elder brother of EVELYN WAUGH. Sherborne School in Dorset provided the background for his precocious first novel, *The Loom of Youth* (1917), which enjoyed some success (partly on account of its treatment of public-school homosexuality) and set him on a long career as a middlebrow novelist. His greatest commercial success was *Island in the Sun* (1956). He lived latterly in Morocco and the United States, and produced several volumes of autobiography.

Waugh, Evelyn (Arthur St John) 1902–66 Novelist. The son of the publisher Arthur Waugh and the younger brother of ALEC WAUGH, he was born in Hampstead and educated at Lancing and Hertford College, Oxford, where he became a close friend of HAROLD ACTON. After Oxford he became a teacher in various private schools, a frustrating experience, and then worked for *The Daily Express*.

A juvenile piece, *The World to Come: A Poem in Three Cantos* (1916), was followed by *PRB: An Essay on The Pre-Raphaelite Brotherhood 1847–1854* (1926), both of which were privately printed. *DECLINE AND FALL*, his first great success, based on his teaching experience, was published in 1928. In the same year he published *Rossetti: His Life and Works*, married Evelyn Gardner (whom he divorced in 1930), and was received into the Roman Catholic Church. Waugh's reputation as England's leading satirical novelist was established during the 1930s with *Vile Bodies* (1930), *Black Mischief* (1932), *A HANDFUL OF DUST* (1934) and *Scoop* (1938). These and *Put Out More Flags* (1942) caught the witty, cynical and irresponsible mood of upper-class life during the 1920s and 1930s. He travelled extensively throughout the 1930s and produced several travel books. *Labels: A Mediterranean Journal* (1930) was followed by *Remote People* (about Africa; 1931), *Ninety-Two Days* (about South America; 1934), *Waugh in Abyssinia* (about Mussolini's invasion; 1936) and *Robbery under Law: The Mexican Object Lesson*, published in 1939. His last travel book was *A Tourist in Africa* (1960).

In 1937 Waugh married Laura Herbert and settled in the West Country. Two chapters of an unfinished novel were published as *Work Suspended* (1942). He served in the Royal Marines during World War II, and was a member of the British Military Mission to Yugoslavia in 1944. *BRIDESHEAD REVISITED* (1945) marked a change from his earlier satirical mode. *Men at Arms* (1952), *Officers and Gentlemen* (1955) and *Unconditional Surrender* (1961) make up the trilogy *SWORD OF HONOUR*, published together in 1965.

The Loved One (1948), sub-titled 'An Anglo-American Tragedy', is a SATIRE based on Waugh's experiences in Hollywood. *Helena* (1950), a historical novel set in the Rome of the Emperor Constantine, was Waugh's favourite work, but not his readers'. *The Ordeal of Gilbert Pinfold* (1957), about a middle-aged writer who suffers a nervous breakdown but eventually finds salvation, is frankly autobiographical and held in high esteem by Waugh's admirers. *The Life of Ronald Knox* (1959) was a biography, and *A Little Learning* (1964) comprised a chapter of his autobiography, which he did not live to complete. His *Diaries* were edited by M. Davie (1976) and his equally frank and revealing *Letters* by M. Amory (1980).

Waverley SIR WALTER SCOTT's first novel, published anonymously in 1814. It is set during the period of the 1745 rebellion.

Edward Waverley, the hero, has been brought up partly by his uncle, Sir Edward Waverley, who has Jacobite sympathies. When Edward receives his commission in the army and joins his regiment in Scotland, he visits Digby's friend Bradwardine, another Jacobite, and is attracted to Rose, Bradwardine's gentle daughter. Waverley's romantic disposition leads him to visit the Highlands and seek out a free-booting character, Donald Bean Lean, and there he meets Fergus Mac-Ivor and his beautiful sister Flora, both ardent Jacobites and active in the Stuart cause. His connection with the Jacobites gets Waverley into trouble with his colonel. An incipient mutiny is laid at his door and he is cashiered; the intervention of Rose, who is devoted to him, saves him from prison. But injustice leads him to join the other side; he is encouraged by Flora and well received by the Young Pretender. At the Battle of Prestonpans which the Jacobite forces win, Waverley saves the life of Colonel Talbot, a family friend, who eventually secures a pardon for him. The other Jacobite rebels are severely dealt with and Fergus Mac-Ivor is convicted of high treason. Waverley, meanwhile, is rejected by the beautiful Flora, who enters a convent when Fergus is executed; he later marries Rose.

Waves, The A novel by VIRGINIA WOOLF, published in 1931.

The most experimental of Virginia Woolf's novels, it traces the lives of six characters – Bernard, Susan, Rhoda, Neville, Jinny and Louis – from childhood to old age in a rotating series of interior monologues. These are interspersed with italicized passages which record the ascent and descent of the sun, the rise and fall of the waves, and the passing of the seasons. Each character's life story is revealed incidentally and, although there is no differentiation in their speech, their individual personalities are revealed by recurring phrases and images.

At the very beginning, as children, all six share a house by the seashore and are taught by a governess, Miss Hudson. Their lives soon diverge, but they gather later, first at a dinner in a French restaurant in London (to mark the departure to India of a friend, Percival, who dies soon afterwards), and secondly at Hampton Court. In a final monologue, Bernard as an elderly man reviews his life, those of his friends, and their influence on each other. He feels himself flowing into their consciousnesses like a wave into other waves.

The novel explores the continuity of memory and celebrates the potential for communion and love between individuals in the face of change and death. It is widely considered to be Virginia Woolf's masterpiece.

Way of All Flesh, The A novel by SAMUEL BUTLER, posthumously published in 1903.

The hero, Ernest Pontifex, endures an unhappy upbringing in the Evangelical parsonage at Battersby. His father, Theo, re-enacts the tyrannical ways of his own father, George, a religious publisher, but justifies them with the sanctimonious dictates of a spiritually bankrupt religious piety. At Cambridge Ernest is converted and then ordained, in accordance with his parents' wishes. As a curate, Ernest falls prey to the conflicting influences of a duplicitous Tractarian and a free-thinking tinker, before breaking out in an incident where his naivety makes him mistake a respectable girl for a prostitute. The sudden shock of his subsequent imprisonment enables him to cast off his faith, his family and his class in an attempt to revert to the simple life of his artisan great-grandfather. Another false start leads him to marry a former maid-servant at the Rectory, sacked when she was found to be pregnant. This time his freedom is achieved when his drunken wife is discovered to be already married. Anxious to avoid a repetition of the Pontifex paternal tyranny, Ernest farms out the children of his union. Having inherited an income from his aunt Alethea, he embarks upon a solitary life, a literary vocation and eclectic interests much resembling Butler's own adult career.

The fortunes of the Pontifex family, as unfolded by the narrator, Overton, are designed to show that personal happiness stems from the liberating effect of acting upon inherited and largely unconscious stores of vitality. The play between the conscious and unconscious also fuels the thrust of the novel's attack upon the conventions and hypocrisies of Victorian family life.

Butler started writing the novel in 1873, began revision in 1880, but abandoned it when his friend Miss Savage, model for Alethea, died in 1885. Although the realistic details, including actual letters from the Butler family, are taken from his own mid-century upbringing, for many of its first readers, such as ARNOLD

BENNETT, E. M. FORSTER and G. B. SHAW, Butler's debunking novel articulated their reaction against a whole range of orthodox Victorian pieties.

Way of the World, The A comedy by WILLIAM CONGREVE, first performed in 1700, when its comparative failure contributed to Congreve's decision to turn away from the theatre. It is a complex play, whose elegant, witty dialogue polishes a plot that gradually reveals how far self-interest may go to make money and mar marriages.

In order to marry Millamant, Mirabell must win the consent of her aunt, Lady Wishfort. His best hope lies in Lady Wishfort's eagerness for a lover of her own. But Lady Wishfort is only one of the obstacles. More threatening is the spite of Mrs Marwood, whose love Mirabell had not returned. Her liaison with Lady Wishfort's avaricious son-in-law Fainall takes them into a conspiracy which carries the play to the point of near-tragic confrontation. Nor is Millamant easily won, as she makes clear in the famous 'proviso' scene in Act IV by laying down her conditions for marrying Mirabell. Lady Wishfort, gullible and constantly being gulled, is finally shaken into consenting to her niece's marriage when the villainies of Fainall and Mrs Marwood are exposed.

Way We Live Now, The A novel by ANTHONY TROLLOPE, serialized in monthly numbers from February 1874 to September 1875 and published in two volumes in 1875.

At the centre of this huge satirical panorama of contemporary manners – Trollope's longest novel – is the fitfully heroic figure of Augustus Melmotte, a financier of obscure origins and seemingly fabulous wealth. Through the corrupt American Hamilton Fisker, Melmotte becomes involved in promoting a grandiose but fictitious American railway company, and quickly rises to social prominence in London as a consequence. Courted by impecunious aristocrats eager to get on the boards of his companies, he is chosen to entertain the Emperor of China in his Grosvenor Square house and is elected to Parliament as a Conservative MP. But the bubble bursts with the discovery of fraud, his titled friends desert him, and after getting drunk in the House of Commons, Melmotte goes home and commits suicide. A related plot involves the efforts of Lady Carbury to arrange a marriage between her dissolute son Sir Felix and Melmotte's only child, Marie, which collapse when Felix drunkenly gambles away the money Marie, who loves him, has obtained for their elopement. The only character to speak out against the widespread corruption is Lady Carbury's cousin Roger Carbury, a middle-aged country squire in love with her daughter Hetta. Another plot concerns Roger and his friend Paul Montague, a business partner of Hamilton Fisker and the erstwhile lover of Winifred Hurtle, a passionate American woman. Mrs Hurtle comes to England to win him back, but fails, Paul having fallen in love with Hetta. Although the marriage of Paul and Hetta provides the conventional happy ending, the loneliness and disappointment of Mrs Hurtle and Roger Carbury ensure that the mood of this most sombre of Trollope's novels is sustained to the end.

A study of what Trollope called 'the commercial profligacy of the age', *The Way We Live Now* portrays a society in which gambling – on the Stock Exchange and in the gentlemen's club – has become a dominant activity. Undervalued in his own day, it is now seen as one of his finest works, a SATIRE comparable in scope to *VANITY FAIR* and *LITTLE DORRIT*.

Wealth of Nations, The A treatise on political economy by ADAM SMITH, fully titled *An Inquiry into the Nature and Causes of the Wealth of Nations* and first published in 1776. During Smith's lifetime it went through five editions, of which the third (1784) was definitive.

It analyses the effects of the pursuit of self-interest on different groups within an economic system and recommends that market forces be left to ensure the accumulation of wealth, albeit within a framework of law and with some government intervention. Book I analyses how the division of labour lies behind increased labour productivity and how the consequent benefits are distributed as wages, rents and profits to different groups in society. The pursuit of self-interest by one man will produce unintended benefits for others. Book II analyses the nature of capital (fixed and circulating), the means and effects of individual accumulation of it, and its different uses. He shows how the expenditure of savings results in increased income, thus making growth self-perpetuating. Book III attempts to explain, partly historically, different rates of growth in different countries, beginning with an analysis of the economic interdependence of country and town, and showing how the growth of the town has been beneficial to both. Book IV attacks mercantilism for regarding wealth as money and not the goods it can buy, and promotes the case for free trade among nations. Book V turns to domestic political economy and outlines the case for some government intervention: market systems cannot produce armies, courts, roads and canals, all of which increase welfare. The state has a duty to ensure the education of the young where private systems fail.

Eloquently argued, and showing Smith's mastery of ethics, history, sociology, jurisprudence and economics, *The Wealth of Nations* has exerted a profound influence over generations of economists; indeed, it virtually defined the content of the subject for over 150 years. Marx was influenced by its sociological underpinning, and Smith's economics provided a manifesto for British politicians seeking to reduce state intervention in economic life.

Webb [*née* Potter], **(Martha) Beatrice** 1858–1943 and **Webb, Sidney,** 1st Baron Passfield 1859–1947 Social historians. Beatrice and Sidney Webb constituted what has been called 'the most prolific partnership in 20th-century British history'. Committed Socialists before their marriage in 1892, they became leading figures in the Fabian Society (founded 1884) and collaborated on numerous social and political activities, which included founding the London School of Economics in 1895 and *The New Statesman* in 1913. As Lord Passfield, Sidney Webb served in the Labour governments of 1924 and 1929–31.

With *The History of Trade Unionism* (1894) and *Industrial Democracy* (1897) the Webbs established labour history as a separate study. Their minority report of the Poor Law Commission (1905–9) laid the foundations for the Welfare State. Other titles written in collaboration included the seven-volume *History of English Local Government* (1903–30), *The State and the Doctor* (1910), *The Prevention of Destitution* (1911), *The Decay of Capitalist Civilization* (1923), *Soviet Communism: A New Civilization?* (1935) and *The Truth about Soviet Russia* (1942). Beatrice Webb also wrote two autobiographical works, *My Apprenticeship* (1926) and *Our Partnership* (posthumously published, 1948), revealing an unsuspected gift for psychological perception which, combined with her acute social observation, has made them classics of their kind. Norman and Jeanne Mackenzie have edited her diary (1982–5).

Webb, Francis 1925–73 Australian poet. He was born in Adelaide and lived in Sydney. War service in the RAAF and spells in England took him out of Australia but schizophrenia prevented sustained work of any kind. It also raised the questions of identity and the role of the artist which he explored in his work, thus precipitating the first movement away from traditional Australian lyric verse. *A Drum for Ben Boyd* (1948), *Leichardt in Theatre* (1952), *The Birthday* (1953), *The Ghost of Cock Walk* (1964) and *Socrates and Other Poems* (1961) are represented in *Collected Poems* (1969), which finally secured his position. He has been seriously compared with both T. S. ELIOT and GERARD MANLEY HOPKINS.

Webb [*née* Meredith], **(Gladys) Mary** 1881–1927 Novelist. Born in Shropshire, she was educated at Southport. She and her husband worked as market gardeners before moving to London in 1921. Her early novels – *The Golden Arrow* (1916), *Gone to Earth* (1917), *The House in Dormer Forest* (1920) and *Seven for a Secret* (1922) – met with little success, but *Precious Bane* (1924), set in Shropshire, became a bestseller after it had been praised by the Prime Minister, Stanley Baldwin. He wrote an introduction to the 1928 edition of the novel, thereby assuring her a large posthumous readership. Her novels are infused with a romantic and often naive passion, unrelieved by any sense of humour – a style brilliantly parodied by Stella Gibbons in *COLD COMFORT FARM* (1932) – but many have found in her stark descriptions of the countryside and rural life an original lyrical intensity akin to that of D. H. LAWRENCE. *Armour Wherein He Trusted*, an unfinished novel, and *The Spring of Joy*, poems and essays, were both published posthumously in 1929.

Webb, Phyllis 1927– Canadian poet. Born in Victoria, she attended the University of British Columbia, where she was influenced by EARLE BIRNEY, and McGill. She has taught at the Universities of British Columbia and Victoria. Despite living in many cities in Canada and abroad, she sees herself as primarily a West Coast poet and settled on Saltspring Island, British Columbia, in 1969. She found her distinctive voice in the 1960s, when she moved away from a formal style to a spare, imagistic verse which has been compared with Japanese *haiku*. *Naked Poems* (1965) is reductive in the extreme, expressing enigmatic feelings in a minimalist style. *Wilson's Bowl* (1980) is more expansive but again unsentimentally chronicles stark emotions. Much of her poetry is about psychic fragmentation and the capacity of poetry to provide order in the face of primal chaos. Other volumes include *Even Your Right Eye* (1956), *The Sea is Also a Garden* (1962), *Selected Poems: 1954–1965* (1971), *The Vision Tree* (1982), *Water and Light: Ghazals and Anti-Ghazals* (1984) and *Hanging Fire* (1990). *Talking* (1982) is a collection of essays, reviews and talks.

Webbe, William d. 1591 Critic. After graduating from Cambridge, Webbe seems to have supported himself by tutoring. He is the author of *A Discourse of English Poetry* (1586).

Webster, John c. 1580–c. 1634 Playwright. Almost nothing is known of his life. HENSLOWE records payments made to him in 1602, but his first known work dates from 1604. Then he wrote an Induction for the revival of MARSTON's *THE MALCONTENT* by the KING's MEN, and collaborated with DEKKER on *WESTWARD HO*. Another collaboration with Dekker, *THE FAMOUS HISTORY OF SIR THOMAS WYATT*, may belong to the same year, and another, *NORTHWARD HO*, to 1605. *Appius and Virginia* (c. 1608), a retelling from Roman history of a father's loving murder of his daughter, was probably written with THOMAS HEYWOOD. There followed three plays which are normally supposed to be Webster's alone. *The Devil's Law Case* (c. 1610) is a sensational but uncharacteristically careless tragicomedy. *THE WHITE DEVIL* (c. 1612) and *THE DUCHESS OF MALFI* (? before 1614) are among the finest of all Jacobean tragedies. The new philosophy has put all in doubt, and Webster's characters strive unavailingly to fashion for themselves a meaningful life in a disintegrating world.

The last 20 years of Webster's life are as obscure as the first 20. A pageant survives (*Monuments of Honour*, 1624) and two collaborations, with MIDDLETON on *Any Thing for a Quiet Life* (*c.* 1621) and with WILLIAM ROWLEY on *A Cure for a Cuckold* (*c.* 1624). Other plays may have been lost. For so diligent a writer, the known output is improbably slight.

Webster's Dictionary The American Noah Webster (1758–1843) was the author of two dictionaries (1806 and 1828). Although trained as a lawyer, he took up teaching and, from 1783 onwards, published elementary schoolbooks and monographs on the English language. *The American Spelling Book* (1806), a reissue of the first of his publications, sold over 80,000,000 copies within a hundred years and was to a great extent responsible for those spellings now considered markedly American. The real ancestor of the dictionaries that today bear Webster's name is his *An American Dictionary of the English Language* (1828). The word 'American' remained in subsequent editions of Webster until replaced by 'International'. The current *Webster's Third New International Dictionary*, much the size of the *Shorter Oxford English Dictionary*, was, when first published in 1961, greatly criticized for its relative lack of editorial prescriptivism. See also ENGLISH DICTIONARIES.

Wedde, Ian 1946– New Zealand poet, novelist, short-story writer and editor. Born in Blenheim and educated at Auckland University, he has lived for long periods as a freelance writer, as well as working as art critic for a Wellington newspaper. He has travelled in Europe, North America, the Middle East and Asia.

Wedde was a leading proponent and exponent of the open forms, informal language and verbal collage characteristic of the work of the New Zealand poets who emerged in the late 1960s and early 1970s. Like BILL MANHIRE and MURRAY EDMOND, he was strongly influenced by modern American poetry, the work of WILLIAM CARLOS WILLIAMS and A. R. AMMONS being particularly important to him. His collections include *Homage to Matisse* (1971), *Earthly: Sonnets for Carlos* (1975), *Castalay* (1980), *Tales of Gotham City* (1984) and *Tendering* (1988). His poetry is notable for its energy, irreverence, informality of voice and control of tone. *Earthly*, a sequence of 60 SONNETS, and *Pathway to the Sea* (1975; later collected in *Castalay*), a long poem about digging a drain, also show his ability to make flexible and sustained use of more precise forms. His introduction to *The Penguin Book of New Zealand Verse* (1985), which he co-edited, is an important sequel to ALLEN CURNOW's introduction to the previous Penguin anthology (1960). Wedde argues that New Zealand poetry has now moved beyond nationalism and cultural alienation, developing a language which is fully acclimatized to its setting. He also co-edited *The Penguin Book of Contemporary New Zealand Poetry* (1989). His novels include: *Dick Seddon's Great Dive* (1976); *Symmes Hole* (1986), a rich, allusive work which counterpoints various 19th-century Pacific journeys (including MELVILLE's) with the narrator's quest for home in New Zealand in the 1980s; and *Survival Arts* (1988). *The Shirt Factory* (1981) is a volume of short stories. Wedde has won the New Zealand National Book Award for both fiction and poetry.

Wedding of Sir Gawen and Dame Ragnell, The A VERSE ROMANCE written *c.* 1450 in the east Midlands. While hunting, King Arthur meets Sir Gromer Somer Joure, who threatens to kill him. He lets Arthur go on condition that he return in a year to tell him what women most desire. Arthur and Gawen seek the answer and after 11 months a hideous hag tells them in return for a promise of marriage to Gawen. Gromer Somer Joure curses his sister for revealing the answer, but has to allow Arthur to go. Gawen marries Dame Ragnell and when he kisses her in bed she becomes young and beautiful. She asks him whether he would rather have her fair by day or night, and when he allows her the choice she promises to be beautiful always. The same story is told by GEOFFREY CHAUCER as *The Wife of Bath's Tale* in THE CANTERBURY TALES.

Wedgwood, Dame **C(icely) V(eronica)** 1910– Historian. Born in Northumberland, she was educated privately before going to Lady Margaret Hall, Oxford. *Strafford* (1935) and *The Thirty Years' War* (1938) established her as a successful popular historian of 17th-century Europe. *Oliver Cromwell* and her translation of Carl Brandi's *Charles V* (both 1939) were followed by *William the Silent* (1944), winner of the James Tait Black Memorial Prize. Other works during this period included a translation of Canetti's novel *Auto da Fé* (1946), *Richelieu and the French Monarchy* (1949) and *Seventeenth-Century English Literature* (1950).

The King's Peace (1955) began her major history of the English Civil War, completed by *The King's War* (1958) and *The Trial of Charles I* (1964; as *A Coffin for King Charles* in USA). *Thomas Wentworth: A Revaluation* (1961) was a reconsideration of her first subject, Strafford. Other works included *Velvet Studies* (1946), a collection of essays, *Truth and Opinion* and *Poetry and Politics* (both 1960), *The World of Rubens* (1967), *Milton and His World* (1970) and *The Political Career of Peter Paul Rubens* (1975).

The author was created a Dame of the British Empire in 1968. She was a member of the Institute of Advanced Studies at Princeton from 1953 to 1968.

Week on the Concord and Merrimack Rivers, A An account by HENRY DAVID THOREAU, published in

1849, of a boat trip to the White Mountains of New Hampshire, taken in 1839 with his brother John. Written during the period described in *WALDEN*, it resembles that better-known work in its thoughtful digressions on poetry, philosophy and religion. It was Thoreau's first major publication.

Weever, John 1576–1632 Poet and antiquary. Of Lancashire stock, Weever was educated at Queens' College, Cambridge. His early SATIRE, in *Epigrams* (1599) and *Faunus and Melliflora* (1600), is an important source of literary gossip. His later antiquarian studies culminated in the massive *Ancient Funeral Monuments within the United Monarchy of Great Britain* (1631).

Weir of Hermiston An unfinished novel by ROBERT LOUIS STEVENSON. The fragment published posthumously in 1896 does little more than set the scene and introduce the chief characters, but it is generally acknowledged as a potential masterpiece.

The Lord Justice-Clerk Adam Weir, Lord Hermiston, is a formidable hanging judge with a strength of character and will notably lacking in his son Archie. Archie's mother is dead, and he lives alone with his father, whom he loves and hates in equal proportions. Their relationship reaches a crisis when Archie, revolted by his father's brutal treatment of the defendant at a criminal trial, loses his temper and publicly insults him. He is banished to Hermiston, a remote and uncivilized village, where he lives as a recluse with his devoted housekeeper, Kirstie. Her four nephews, the 'Black Elliotts', are notorious for their ruthless hunting-down of the murderer of their father. Archie falls in love with their sister Christina. The couple's meetings become known to Kirstie and to Frank Innes, Archie's visitor and treacherous friend, and Archie tells Christina that their relationship must end.

The fragment ends here, but Stevenson's plans for the novel survive. Archie continues to avoid Christina and Frank Innes takes advantage of the situation by seducing her. The two men quarrel and Archie kills his rival. He is tried before his own father and condemned to death. Kirstie, meanwhile, has discovered the identity of Christina's seducer. She tells the 'Black Elliotts', who gather their followers and rescue Archie from prison. He escapes to America with Christina. Lord Hermiston is so much affected by the shock of having sentenced his own son that he collapses and dies.

Welch, Denton (Maurice) 1915–48 Novelist, short-story writer and artist. Born of British parents in Shanghai, he was educated at Repton School before going on to the Goldsmith School of Art in London. When he was 20 he suffered severe spinal injury in a cycling accident; he never recovered, and it greatly limited his life. This narrowing of capabilities caused him to concentrate almost exclusively on his writing and painting. Towards the end of his short life writing had become a painful and difficult exercise, performed only with great courage. Welch took pleasure in examining people and objects closely and in describing them in clear, vivid prose. He began by publishing an account of his meeting with the artist Walter Sickert (1942). It was followed by many poems, 60 short stories, three largely autobiographical novels – *Maiden Voyage* (1943), introduced by EDITH SITWELL, *In Youth is Pleasure* (1945) and *A Voice through a Cloud* (1950) – and his *Journals* (1952).

Welch, James 1940– American novelist and poet. A Blackfoot Indian on his father's side and Gros Ventre on his mother's, he was born in Browning, Montana, and educated at schools on the Blackfoot and Fort Belknap reservations before attending the universities of Minnesota and Montana. His first publication, *Riding the Earthboy 40: Poems*, appeared in 1971. His first novel, *Winter in the Blood* (1974), is about a young Indian trying to make sense of his heritage in the modern world. His second, *The Death of Jim Loney* (1979), though set in contemporary Midwestern society, is concerned with the traditional codes of behaviour found in the mythic stories of the Gros Ventres. *Fool's Crew* (1986) is set in the Two Medicines Indian region of Montana in the 1870s, while *The Indian Lawyer* (1990) is a fast-paced political thriller.

Weldon, Fay 1933– Novelist and television playwright. Born in Worcester, and later a student at the University of St Andrews, she worked as an advertising copywriter before turning to full-time authorship. Her prolific output has alternated between television plays and vigorous, resourceful novels articulating a contemporary feminist consciousness. These include: *Female Friends* (1975); *Praxis* (1978); *Puffball* (1980), unusual in essaying an extended evocation of the biological process of conception in the womb; *The President's Child* (1982) and *The Life and Loves of a She-Devil* (1983), caustic SATIRES of male-dominated society; *The Rules of Life* (1987), a novella; *The Hearts and Lives of Men* (1987); *Darcy's Utopia* (1990); *Growing Rich* (1992); and *Life Force* (1992). *Sacred Cows* (1989) is a trenchant pamphlet on the relationship of religion to society, prompted by her opposition to the *fatwa* pronounced against SALMAN RUSHDIE.

Well at the World's End, The A late prose romance by WILLIAM MORRIS, first published in 1896.

Ralph, youngest son of King Peter of Upmeads, sets out on a quest for the 'Well at the World's End', whose waters give the drinker long life and an ever-youthful 'lucky' appearance. He falls in love with the Lady of

Abundance who has drunk from the Well, but she is killed before she can lead him to it. After a period of despair Ralph's quest for the Well finds a parallel in his search for Ursula, his first love. Together they reach the Well, drink from it and eventually return to rule Upmeads and 'to live in peace and patience without fear or hatred, and to succour the oppressed and love the lovely'.

Though largely unpalatable to a modern readership, the epic scale, pseudo-medieval setting and archaic language of Morris's late romances are an integral part of his attempt to recapture the spirit of bardic narrative literature. In 1895 Morris stated that he 'had not the least intention of thrusting an allegory' into a prose romance, which was rather 'meant for a tale pure and simple'. Political didacticism is abandoned in favour of a broad philanthropy, of which social concerns are only a part. The Well, from which only the 'Strong of Heart' may drink, is a source of human love and moral value. In reviewing the book W. B. YEATS wrote: 'there is scarcely a chapter in which there is not some moment for which one might almost give one's soul'.

Well-Beloved, The: *A Sketch of a Temperament*
A novel by THOMAS HARDY, serialized as *The Pursuit of the Well-Beloved* in *The Illustrated London News* from October to December 1892 and substantially revised for book publication in 1897.

Jocelyn Pierston, sculptor and son of a prosperous stone merchant on the Isle of Slingers (Portland), seeks an ideal woman whose incarnation should take the form of the Well-Beloved. He pursues this myth by courting, successively, a mother, daughter and granddaughter all named Avice. As the years and generations pass it becomes apparent that the ideal eludes him and in old age he settles for marrying another old flame, Marcia Bencomb.

well-made play Used strictly, the term applies to English imitations of the *pièce bien faite*, whose formula was devised by the prolific French playwright Eugène Scribe (1791–1861). Its aim is less to create a finely shaped structure than to pace effects and revelations so as to keep the audience in suspense. Particularly suited to MELODRAMA, the formula has also been often used in FARCE. Successful English exponents include HENRY ARTHUR JONES and PINERO. See also DÉNOUEMENT and SCÈNE À FAIRE.

Weller, Archie (Kirk) [Irving Kirkwood] 1957– Australian part-Aboriginal novelist and short-story writer. Born in Western Australia, he has been a wharf operator, farm labourer, stablehand, printer, dishwasher, writer-in-residence at the Australian National University, landscape gardener and roustabout. His novel *The Day of the Dog* (1981) gives a vivid picture of the violence and want endured at the margins of urban society. *Going Home* (1986) explores the same settings, showing a mastery of the European short-story form as a frame for Aboriginal material. He has written two plays, *Sunset and Shadows* (1989) and *Nidjers* (1990), and co-edited *Us Fellas* (1988), essays and short stories by Aboriginal writers.

Weller, Michael 1942– American playwright. Born in New York, he was educated at Brandeis University and the University of Manchester. *Moonchildren* (1971) depicts the hangups and idealism of the 1960s, while *Loose Ends* (1979) shows the same generation dealing with the disillusion of the 1970s. Other plays include *23 Years Later* (1973), *Fishing* (1975), *Spoils of War* (1988) and *Lake No Bottom* (1990), a study of the relationship between artist and critic. He also wrote the screenplays for *Hair* (1979) and E. L. DOCTOROW's *Ragtime* (1980).

Wells, H(erbert) G(eorge) 1866–1946 Novelist, writer of SCIENCE FICTION and student of politics, history and society. He was born at Bromley, where his father was an unsuccessful tradesman. His early life reflected in the struggles of many of his novels' protagonists, and his father can be recognized in a number of fictional guises – most notably as Mr Polly. After two unhappy years as a draper's apprentice, Wells became a student assistant at Midhurst Grammar School. From here, in 1884, he won a scholarship to the Normal School of Science, now Imperial College, London. His year under T. H. HUXLEY, teacher of comparative anatomy, was seminal. Before taking a first-class honours degree in zoology in 1890, he had resumed the life of a schoolteacher. After an accident which damaged his kidneys, he determined that he would learn to write; his first full-length works were textbooks of biology and geography. In 1891 he made an unfortunate marriage to his cousin Isabel; his second marriage in 1895 to Amy Robbins (always 'Jane' to Wells) was to be lasting. From 1898 to 1909 they lived in Sandgate.

His literary career began with the publication of his first major novel, THE TIME MACHINE (1895). Other works of science fiction followed: *The Wonderful Visit* (1895), *The Island of Dr Moreau* (1896), a grim parable of the blind and bestial forces underlying civilization, *The Invisible Man* (1897), THE WAR OF THE WORLDS (1898), *When the Sleeper Wakes* (1899), *The First Men in the Moon* (1901) and *The War in the Air* (1908). By their SATIRE and their implicit note of warning, these fables about the impact of alien races or advanced science on established society prefigure Wells's later concern with social and political realities. His interest in the changing social order again unites with a lesser element of fantasy in *A Modern Utopia* (1905). This, with other works like the later 'discussion' novel, *The New Machiavelli* (1911), displays the didactic tendency in Wells. From 1903 he was a member of the Fabian Society, but his contact with its members was brief and mostly belligerent. His quarrel with G. B. SHAW was only one of his controversies with leading thinkers of the day.

Wells's major novels with a bias towards social realism drew heavily on his own experiences as a youth from the lower middle classes. *LOVE AND MR LEWISHAM* (1900) and *KIPPS* (1905) were followed by *TONO-BUNGAY* (1909), his most ambitious novel, and *THE HISTORY OF MR POLLY* (1910). *Ann Veronica* (1909) was considered scandalous for its portrayal of an emancipated woman.

Wells's public reputation survived the disgrace which attached to his views on sexual freedom. His liaison with REBECCA WEST between 1913 and 1923 attracted much attention. From 1912 until Jane's death in 1927, his home was in Essex. He wrote about his life there in *MR BRITLING SEES IT THROUGH* (1916), one of his popular successes. Wells was not despairing about the major international crises of the modern world – the Great War and the rise of fascism. He was an advocate of the League of Nations in 1919, and continued to see himself as an educator, writing *The Outline of History* (1920) for a large readership. His novel-writing continued, notably with *Mr Blettsworthy on Rampole Island* (1928) and *The Bulpington of Blup* (1932). At his last home in Regent's Park, which he refused to leave during the air raids of World War II, he wrote the lively and engaging self-portrait in *Experiment in Autobiography* (1934) as well as his pessimistic last work, *Mind at the End of Its Tether* (1945).

Wells, Robert 1947– Poet and translator. He was born in Oxford, where he received an intensively classical education before reading English and classics at King's College, Cambridge. He has taught in Italy and Iran, and translated Virgil's *Georgics* (1982) and Theocritus' *Idylls* (1988). Wells has worked for several years as a forester: it is the combination of classical precision with an intense physical awareness of the natural world which gives his work its unmistakable distinction. His poetry appeared in a Cambridge anthology, *Shade Mariners* (1970), which he shared with DICK DAVIS and CLIVE WILMER, and in Michael Schmidt's *Ten English Poets* (1976) before the publication of *The Winter's Task* in 1977. The finest poems here mix rapturous sensuousness and muscular clarity: the reader may be reminded of THOMAS TRAHERNE and THOM GUNN. Other poems are epigrammatic in a style perhaps learned from BEN JONSON via YVOR WINTERS and J. V. CUNNINGHAM. *Selected Poems* appeared in 1986, *Place by Pieces* in 1992.

Welty, Eudora 1909– American short-story writer and novelist. She was born in Jackson, Mississippi, and educated at Mississippi State College for Women, the University of Wisconsin, and Columbia. Her first collection, *A Curtain of Green, and Other Stories* (1941), introduced by KATHERINE ANNE PORTER, established her as a major Southern writer with a powerful sense of place. Her second collection, *The Wide Net, and Other Stories* (1943), was less well received. *The Golden Apples* (1949) contains seven related stories about three generations of the MacLain, Morrison, Stark, Rainey and Carmichael families in the fictitious small town of Morgana, Mississippi. *The Bride of the Innisfallen, and Other Stories* (1955) includes stories set in London, Italy and Greece, as well as in the South. Welty has also written a number of novels in the Southern Gothic tradition, among them *The Robber Bridegroom* (1942), *Delta Wedding* (1946), *The Ponder Heart* (1954), *Losing Battles* (1970) and *The Optimist's Daughter* (PULITZER PRIZE, 1972). Volumes of critical essays include *The Eye of the Story: Selected Essays and Reviews* (1979). Her literary autobiography, *One Writer's Beginnings*, appeared in 1984.

Wendt, Albert 1939– Western Samoan novelist, short-story writer, critic and poet. Of mixed German and Polynesian ancestry, he received most of his education in New Zealand, eventually gaining an MA in history from Victoria University, Wellington. He worked as a schoolteacher in New Zealand before returning to Western Samoa in 1965. Shortly afterwards he became principal of Samoa College and then, in 1974, moved to Fiji, where he became professor of South Pacific literature at the University of the South Pacific and founded *Mana*, the first literary journal in the South Pacific. In 1989 he returned to New Zealand as professor of literature at the University of Auckland.

The one writer from the South Pacific with an international reputation, he is best known for his novel, *Leaves of the Banyan Tree* (1979), a three-generation saga of Western Samoan life which, in addition to correcting sentimentalized Western versions of the 'South Seas', provides a complex and powerfully written account of the psychological effects of colonialism and the possibility of achieving liberation from them through an existentialist individualism. While drawing on traditional Polynesian culture, Wendt believes that its fragmentation under the impact of Western civilization has given the artist a new freedom to develop a personal style. His earlier novels were *Sons for the Return Home* (1973) and *Pouliuli* (1977). *Ola* (1991) moves for the first time outside the South Pacific. *Flying-Fox in a Freedom Tree* (1974) and *The Birth and Death of the Miracle Man* (1986) are collections of short stories. His poetry includes *Inside Us the Dead* (1976) and *Shaman of Visions* (1984). Wendt also edited the first anthology of Pacific writing, *Lali* (1980).

Wescott, Glenway 1901–87 American novelist. He was born and raised in Wisconsin. His first publication was *The Bitterns* (1920), a book of verse influenced by IMAGISM. His best-known works were published while he lived as an expatriate in France in the 1920s. They include *The Apple of the Eye* (1924) and his most successful novel, *The Grandmothers* (1926). Both are stories of frontier life in Wisconsin, and in both Wescott fashions a lyrical evocation of the past, a rich and deeply felt assessment of his heritage. *Good-Bye Wisconsin* (1928) is a collection of stories. He was friendly with GERTRUDE STEIN and her literary circle; ERNEST HEMINGWAY based his character Robert Prentiss, in THE SUN ALSO RISES, on him. After his return to the USA in 1933 his work grew more infrequent; his last publication of note, *The Pilgrim Hawk*, appeared in 1940. He published several collections of essays, among them *Fear and Trembling* (1932) and *Images of Truth: Remembrances and Criticism* (1962).

Wesker, Arnold 1932– Playwright. Born and educated in the East End of London, he tells much about his early life in his trilogy about Ronnie Kahn and his family and friends: *Chicken Soup with Barley* (1958), *Roots* (1959) and *I'm Talking about Jerusalem* (1960). *The Kitchen* (1959) draws on his experience as a kitchen porter and pastry cook, *Chips with Everything* (1962) on his experience of the RAF. In 1961–70 he was founder-director of Centre 42, an arts centre based at the Round House in London's Chalk Farm. His frustrations in raising money for this venture are reflected in *Their Very Own and Golden City* (1965) and *The Friends* (1970), both of which mourn the decline of utopian socialism in Britain. Later work, moving away from his earlier social optimism towards a more lyrical, disillusioned and introverted theatre, includes: *The Four Seasons* (1965), *The Wedding Feast* (1974), the frankly satirical *The Journalists* (1975), *Love Letters on Blue Paper* (1976), the provocative rewriting of SHAKESPEARE in *The Merchant* (1977), *Caritas* (1981) and a one-woman trilogy of short plays, *Annie Wobbler* (1984).

Wesley, John 1703–91 and **Wesley, Charles** 1707–88 Founders of Methodism. The two brothers were the 15th and 18th children of the rector of Epworth, Lincolnshire. A childhood rescue from their burning home in 1709 left John ever afterwards with a providential sense of mission, being 'a brand plucked out of the burning'. Both brothers were undergraduates at Christ Church, Oxford, though John had formerly attended Charterhouse and Charles had been at Westminster School. In 1726 John Wesley became a fellow of Lincoln College, Oxford, and spent two years acting as his father's curate. On his return to Oxford in 1729 he joined, and swiftly became leader of, a group variously nicknamed the 'Holy Club' or 'Methodists', of which Charles was already a member. Members, who were later to include JAMES HERVEY and George Whitefield, met for study and religious discussion, visited the poor, sick and imprisoned and practised strict self-discipline. Their self-examinations, frequently recorded in coded diaries, became the quarry for their *Journals*. John's was published periodically between 1739 and 1790 and Charles's posthumously in 1849. In 1735 the brothers embarked on an abortive mission to the settlers and Indians in Georgia. On the voyage out they had been impressed by the piety of the Moravian passengers and, on their return to England (Charles in 1736 and John in 1737), they came under the influence of the Moravian pastor Peter Bohler and experienced conversions to 'saving faith' (Charles on 21 May and John on 24 May 1738).

In 1739 both brothers, having first tried to work through Church of England pulpits, resorted to open-air preaching. Using Bristol, London and Newcastle as their chief centres, they embarked on the life of itinerant preachers, establishing societies wherever they went, to provide discipline and mutual support for their converts. In 1743 John Wesley drew up *Rules* for these classes and in 1744 held the first conference for lay preachers whose help he had increasingly used since 1738. The implicit incompatibility of Methodism's evolving structure with the parochial discipline and apostolic claims of the Anglican Church was never admitted by John Wesley, but caused his brother to retire from itinerant work in 1756. John continued, covering some 250,000 miles of the British Isles by foot, horse and post-chaise and preaching three or four times a day.

John Wesley's *Journal*, a textbook of experiential religion, served to maintain contact between far-flung societies. Something of his authoritarian personality emerges from this grandly impersonal document of well over a million words, but his voluminous letters provide a more intimate picture of the detailed concern he expended on his devoted followers. John also engaged in polemical debate with the Moravians and Calvinists, wrote religious tracts and treatises, produced practical handbooks on medicine and translated, edited or abridged the work of others for more popular consumption.

John and Charles both recognized the value of hymns in worship as a method of instruction and a channel for spiritual fervour. Of the thousands of hymns composed by Charles, and often edited by John, many are still in use well beyond the confines of Methodism. Such favourites include 'Love Divine, All Loves Excelling', 'Hark, the Herald-Angels Sing' and 'Jesu, Lover of My Soul'.

Wesley, Mary 1912– Novelist. Born in Windsor, she studied at the London School of Economics, worked at the War Office in 1939–41, and has also had experience in the antiques trade. Though she had earlier produced CHILDREN'S LITERATURE, she did not write her first adult novel, *The Camomile Lawn*

(1984), until she was in her 70s. Since then she has been prolific and successful with bizarre, vituperative comedies in which sex is a prime determinant of human behaviour. *Jumping the Queue* (1984), *The Vacillations of Polly Carew* (1986) and *Not That Sort of Girl* (1987) are typically spirited examples.

Wessex The name borrowed by THOMAS HARDY from Anglo-Saxon history for the West Country setting of most of his novels and many of his poems. It was first used in *FAR FROM THE MADDING CROWD*. It is centred on Dorset and particularly Dorchester, whose fictional name is Casterbridge. The slight transposition is typical of Hardy's use of real placenames to create a 'partly real, partly dream' landscape.

Wessex Poems and Other Verses The first collection of poetry published by THOMAS HARDY, appearing in 1898. These 51 poems (some dating from the 1860s) are characteristically Hardyan in their diversity of subject matter, verse forms and instinct for the dramatic moment. They range from the speculative 'Hap' to the embittered 'Neutral Tones', from the mildly Chaucerian 'The Bride-Night Fire' to the poignant 'Thoughts of Phena' and from the gravity of 'Nature's Questioning' to the hearty 'Sergeant's Song'. *Wessex Poems* is the prelude to 30 years of sustained poetic writing.

West, Nathanael [Weinstein, Nathan Wallenstein] 1903–40 American novelist. He was born in New York and educated at Brown University. His first novel, *The Dream Life of Balso Snell* (1931), is a garish and self-consciously *avant-garde* SATIRE on the inner life of the intellectual introvert of the title. West's preoccupation with the barrenness of contemporary life was given further expression in *Miss Lonelyhearts* (1933), the story of a newspaperman who writes an advice-to-the-lovelorn column and who becomes obsessed with the need to be more than a phoney saviour. His initial professional detachment from his suffering correspondents turns into a tragic involvement which ends in his murder. The mockery of his sadistic editor accompanies his downfall. *A Cool Million: The Dismantling of Lemuel Pitkin* (1934) is a satire of the American Dream itself: Lemuel is naive to the point of idiocy but this is no obstacle to his becoming a runner in the lethal race for riches and eminence. After he is murdered he is proclaimed a hero. West, who was earning his living as a journalist at the time, went to Hollywood in 1935 to write scripts for a minor studio. *The Day of the Locust* (1939) exposes the squalid hidden world of Hollywood – that apotheosis of the American Dream – of which the hypnotized public knows nothing.

West, Dame Rebecca [Andrews (née Fairfield), Cicily Isabel] 1892–1983 Novelist and journalist.

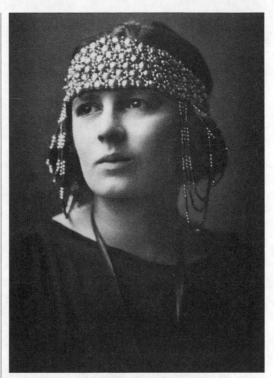

Rebecca West, photograph by E. O. Hoppé

Born in Kerry, Ireland, she was educated at George Watson's Ladies' College and briefly became an actress (her role in Ibsen's *Rosmersholm* suggesting the name she was to adopt). Turning to journalism, she reviewed books for *The Freewoman* and joined the staff of the *The Clarion* in 1912. She was deeply influenced by the Pankhursts and became an ardent and vocal supporter of women's suffrage. Her outspoken review of H. G. WELLS's *Marriage* (1912) began a liaison which lasted for ten years and resulted in the birth of a son, Anthony West, in 1914.

Rebecca West's first book was a critical study of HENRY JAMES (1916). Her first novel, *The Return of the Soldier* (1918), about a shell-shock victim, was adapted for the stage in 1928 by John van Druten. Other novels were published at intervals: *The Judge* (1922), *The Strange Necessity* (1928), *Harriet Hume* (1929), *The Thinking Reed* (1936), *The Fountain Overflows* (1957) and *The Birds Fall Down* (1966). *This Real Night*, a sequel to *The Fountain Overflows*, was published posthumously in 1984 and *Sunflower*, written during the 1920s, in 1986. Recent studies have applauded the strong characterization of her heroines and stressed the radical qualities in her writing.

Her other works included a study of D. H. LAWRENCE (1930), a two-volume study of Yugoslavia, *Black Lamb and Grey Falcon* (1941–2) and *The Meaning of Treason* (1949, revised 1952 and 1965), an account of the treason trials following World War II, updated to include later espionage trials. In *The Court and the Castle* (1958) she turned to the study of religion and politics in literature. This was followed by *McLuhan and the Future of Literature* (1969). *1900* (1982), her last work, was an evocation of the world of her childhood. Many earlier pieces were collected and reprinted as *The Young Rebecca* (edited by Jane Marcus; 1982).

Westall, Robert (Atkinson) 1929–93 Writer of CHILDREN'S LITERATURE. Educated at the University of Durham and the Slade School of Art in London, he taught in secondary schools after 1957. *The Machine-Gunners* (1975) made an immediate impact by its description of a gang of children brutalized by bombing and family disruption during World War II. *The Scarecrows* (1981) proved equally controversial in its account of the jealousy felt by a son about his mother's second marriage. Though still retaining their power to shock, subsequent stories concentrated more on the supernatural than the everyday.

Westminster Review, The A quarterly journal published between 1824 and 1914. It was conceived as the organ of 'philosophical radicalism' and intended to compete in its coverage of politics and literature with the Whig *EDINBURGH REVIEW* and the Tory *QUARTERLY REVIEW*. Initially funded and inspired by JEREMY BENTHAM, it drew heavily on free contributions from JAMES MILL, JOHN STUART MILL and their circles. Disenchanted with changes of proprietor and editor, the Mills began an alternative periodical, *The London Review*, in 1835. It was amalgamated with the *Westminster* under the effective but undeclared editorship of J. S. Mill in 1836–40. Under various changes of owner the review remained consistent in its radical campaign for social reform through legislation and education. When the publisher John Chapman bought it in 1851, he appointed GEORGE ELIOT as assistant editor (1851–3) and accepted contributions from such progressive intellectuals as J. A. FROUDE, T. H. HUXLEY, G. H. LEWES and JOHN TYNDALL. The review at this period also offered extensive coverage of imperial politics and systematic reviewing of contemporary literature. With a further change of ownership and its conversion to a monthly in 1887, the review lost its former high seriousness and eventually dropped its literary coverage.

Westward Ho A comedy by THOMAS DEKKER and JOHN WEBSTER, produced in 1604 and published in 1607. The main plot concerns three wives who enjoy an escapade with three admirers, but are discovered by their husbands at an inn in Brentford. However, the innocence of the escapade is established and all is forgiven. The sub-plot concerns Justiniano, an Italian merchant in London, who believes his wife to be unfaithful and leaves her. Adopting a disguise, he does his best to enjoy the comedy of London life.

Meanwhile, his wife nearly becomes involved with a dubious nobleman; but she loves her husband and they are reconciled at the end of the play.

Westward Ho! A historical novel by CHARLES KINGSLEY, published in 1855. Now remembered chiefly as CHILDREN'S LITERATURE, it was Kingsley's most ambitious novel, an epic of England's heroic victory over Spain and the fear of Catholic domination in the 16th century. Jesuits plot the ruin of England, the Inquisition tortures prisoners and roasts them alive; Englishmen fight fair, hang miscreants from the yardarm, and win against the powers of darkness. The singeing of the Spanish king's beard is justified as liberation of the South American Indians and revenge for the cruelties practised upon them. The story is packed with incident and clotted with pedantry and preaching: Drake, SIR WALTER RALEIGH, SPENSER and other real-life heroes crowd the pages, as do references to HAKLUYT and Plato. Its heady mixture of patriotism, sentiment and romance set the attitudes of English children for several generations.

Wetherell, Elizabeth [Warner, Susan Bogert] 1819–85 American writer of CHILDREN'S LITERATURE. Born in New York, she began writing at the age of 30 to help her family's finances. Two best-sellers, *The Wide Wide World* (1850) and *Queechy* (1852), launched her career producing moral and sentimental novels, some written in collaboration with her sister Anna: *Mrs Rutherford's Children* (1853–5), *The Old Helmet* (1863), *Melbourne House* (1864), *Daisy* (1868), *Wych Hazel* (1876), *My Desire* (1879), *Nobody* (1882) and *Stephan, MD* (1883).

Weyman, Stanley (John) 1855–1928 Novelist. Born in Shropshire, he was educated at Shrewsbury and Christ Church, Oxford. He was a history teacher, then read for the Bar in 1877 but abandoned the law in 1891. His first ventures into literature were short stories for *THE CORNHILL MAGAZINE* and *The English Illustrated Magazine*, but it was with *The House of the Wolf* (1890; previously serialized in the latter periodical in 1888–9) that he began his career as the author of highly successful historical romances. *A Gentleman of France* (1893), set in the period of Henry of Navarre, was praised by R. L. STEVENSON; it was followed by *Under the Red Robe* (1894; successfully dramatized in 1896), *The Red Cockade* (1895), *The Castle Inn* (1898), *Count Hannibal* (about the Massacre of St Bartholomew; 1901), *Chippinge* (set at the time of the Reform Bill; 1906) and many others. Weyman continued to write popular novels until the year of his death; they were described by HUGH WALPOLE as 'the finest English historical romances since SCOTT'.

Whale, The An Old English poem preserved in the EXETER BOOK. The first section tells a common story about the whale from a version of the *Physiologus*. The whale's practice of lying with its back exposed encourages sailors to land on it thinking it an island, but when they are moored and light their fires it dives and drowns them. This is interpreted as an ALLEGORY of the devil's use of deception to trap the unwary.

Whalen, Philip 1923– American poet and novelist. Born in Portland, Oregon, he served in the US Air Force during World War II before enrolling as a student at Reed College. He then moved to San Francisco, where he became involved in the vibrant local poetry scene and associated with members of the BEATS such as GREGORY CORSO and LAWRENCE FERLINGHETTI. His first volume was *Three Satires* (1951). *Self-Portrait from Another Direction* (1960) is more characteristic in its use of typographical layout to enhance and intensify linguistic meaning. Other volumes include *Like I Say* (1960), *Memoirs of an Interglacial Age* (1960), *Highgrade* (1966), *Enough Said* (1980) and *Heavy Breathing: Poems, 1967–1983* (1983). Like many of the Beats, he has an absorbing interest in Eastern religion, and was ordained as a Zen Buddhist priest in 1973.

Wharton, Edith (Newbold) 1862–1937 American novelist and short-story writer. She was born into the wealthy New York society whose standards of taste she criticized in her first book, *The Decoration of Houses* (with Ogden Codman Jr; 1897). In 1907 she moved to France with her husband, remaining there after her divorce in 1913. She was appointed a Chevalier of the Legion of Honour in 1916 for her relief work during World War I. Her close friend HENRY JAMES was a major influence on her work; she acknowledged the debt in *The Writing of Fiction* (1925).

A collection of short stories, *The Great Inclination* (1899), was followed by a short novel, *The Touchstone* (1900), and *The Valley of Decision* (1902), a novel set in 18th-century Italy. *THE HOUSE OF MIRTH* (1905) was her first popular success. *Madame de Treymes* (1907) tackled a characteristic theme, the difference between American and European social customs, though Edith Wharton's range extended to the study of rural New England which made *ETHAN FROME* (1911) enduringly popular. *The Reef* (1912) and *The Custom of the Country* (1913) continued her attack on the hypocrisies of New York society. Experience of the war provided the material for *The Marne* (1918) and *A Son at the Front* (1923). *THE AGE OF INNOCENCE* (1920) made her the first woman to receive a PULITZER PRIZE. *Old New York* (1924) consists of four novelettes. *The Mother's Recompense* (1925), *Twilight Sleep* (1927) and *The Children* (1928) deal with inter-generational differences in families. *Hudson River Bracketed* (1929) and *The Gods Arrive* (1932) examine the artistic temperament through the character of Vance Western, a struggling novelist. At the time of her death she was

working on *The Buccaneers* (1938), set in Saratoga in the 1860s. The best-known of her 11 collections of short stories is probably *Xingu and Other Stories* (1916). *A Backward Glance* (1934) is autobiographical.

Wharton, William [du Aime, Albert] 1925– American novelist. Born in Philadelphia and educated at the University of California, he drew on his experience of World War II in his most accomplished novel, *A Midnight Clear* (1982), about an encounter between American and German troops at the beginning of the Battle of the Bulge. The absurdity of human conflicts is a recurrent theme, from his first novel, *Birdy* (1979), onwards. He is also preoccupied with identity and self-definition: like *Birdy*, *Pride* (1986) uses an animal metaphor to underscore its story of a man's gradual reclamation of his honour. Other novels include *Dad* (1981), *Scumbler* (1984) and *Last Loves* (1991).

What Every Woman Knows A comedy by J. M. BARRIE, first performed at the Duke of York's Theatre, London, in 1908. The father and brother of Maggie Wylie determine to get her a husband, despite her plainness. When the police report that an intruder has been seen climbing into their house, they keep watch and trap him. He is John Shand, a railwayman forced by poverty to discontinue his studies at Glasgow University. He explains that he has been breaking in to read the Wylies' books. The Wylies agree to finance his studies if, after five years, he gives Maggie the right to marry him. The marriage takes place after he has been elected to Parliament, where he quickly establishes a reputation as a brilliantly witty speaker. When Shand falls for Lady Sybil Tenterden, Maggie arranges for them to meet at a country cottage, secretly hopeful that they will bore each other. She is proved right, and the humourless Shand realizes 'what every woman knows': that he owes his success to Maggie who, as his typist, has added the brilliance to his dull speeches.

What Maisie Knew A novel by HENRY JAMES, published in *The Chap Book* from January to August 1897. Later the same year a revised version was serialized in the *New Review* and published in volume form.

Though written in the third person, it is told from the point of view of the perceptive but somewhat naive Maisie. Her parents, Beale and Ida Farange, divorce when she is six and it is arranged that she spend half the year with her father and half with her mother. Beale marries Miss Overmore, who had been Maisie's governess; Ida marries Sir Claude but still has a succession of lovers. Maisie, now under the care of Mrs Wix, Miss Overmore's replacement, is shuttled back and forth between the two households. Her two new step-parents become attracted to one another and, when their marriages to her real parents dissolve, they marry. Abandoned to Mrs Wix's care by Ida and Beale, Maisie is invited by Sir Claude, who is fond of her, to make her home with him and the former Miss Overmore. Unfortunately, the former Miss Overmore cannot abide Mrs Wix, the one 'safe' adult whom Maisie absolutely refuses to give up. The final scene, which takes place in Boulogne, ends with Maisie's refusal to live with Sir Claude and his new wife: she departs for England with Mrs Wix, her means of subsistence guaranteed by Sir Claude. It is ambiguous what sort of 'knowledge' Maisie has achieved and debatable whether or not she has remained innocent in spite of the sordid worldliness that surrounds her.

Wheatley, Phillis 1753–84

Black American poet. She was born in Africa and sold as a slave in Boston at the age of eight to a tailor, John Wheatley, who educated her with his family. She studied English, Latin and Greek, and began to write poetry in her teens. She travelled to London when she was eighteen and there published *Poems on Various Subjects, Religious and Moral* in 1773. When she returned to the USA she married John Peters, a free black, and died in poverty at a young age. Her poetry contains frequent allusions to classical mythology, and mixes topical or contemporary matter with religious and moral concerns. Her subjects include tributes to friends and famous people; discourses on Imagination, Recollection and Friendship; and occasionally references to incidents in her own life. *Memoirs and Poems of Phillis Wheatley* was published in 1834 and a volume of her letters in 1864.

Phillis Wheatley: a portrait printed as the frontispiece to the first edition of her *Poems*, 1773

Wheelwright, John Brooks 1897–1940

American poet. He was born in Boston and educated at Harvard and the Massachusetts Institute of Technology. His poetry emphasizes his regional interests by focusing on Boston and its environs. It is frequently accompanied by prose 'arguments' which serve as interpretations rather than reiterations of the poems themselves. His first collection, *Rock and Shell*, was published in 1933. Like all the volumes published during his life, it was privately printed. A second, *Mirrors of Venus*, appeared in 1938, and a third,

Political Self-Portrait, in 1940. While working on *Dusk to Dusk* Wheelwright was killed in a car accident. This fourth volume was published posthumously in *The Collected Poems of John Wheelwright* in 1972.

Where Angels Fear to Tread

The first novel by E. M. FORSTER, published in 1905.

Lilia Herriton, a widow in her early thirties, is urged to spend a year in Italy by her brother-in-law, Philip, who believes that the experience will purify and ennoble her. Accompanying a younger but less impulsive neighbour, Caroline Abbott, Lilia departs. All goes well until news reaches the Herritons in Sawston that she intends to marry again. Mrs Herriton, her mother-in-law and a domineering social snob, dispatches Philip to prevent the catastrophe but he arrives too late. On reaching Monteriano he discovers that Lilia has already married Gino Carella, several years her junior and a dentist's son. Philip returns with Caroline to England.

The marriage fails and Lilia dies in childbirth. Mrs Herriton and her equally unsavoury daughter, Harriet, eventually decide to retrieve the baby from its father's dubious influence. Philip is again dispatched, this time with Harriet, and Caroline Abbott, guilt-ridden over her part in Lilia's downfall, determines to adopt the child herself. All three meet in Monteriano (where Forster supplies a delightfully comic description surrounding a performance of the opera *Lucia di Lammermoor*) and Philip and Caroline begin to succumb to the charm of Italy.

Gino proves to be a devoted father and the mission is more or less abandoned. Harriet refuses to admit defeat, however, and attempts to steal the baby. The carriage in which she, Philip and the baby are travelling is involved in a collision. It overturns and the baby is killed. Gino assaults Philip and the three English characters return home. On the journey Philip discovers that he has fallen in love with Caroline, but she has fallen in love with Gino; her future seems to hold spinsterhood and charitable works.

Whetstone, George ?1544–?1587

Writer of romances, playwright, poet. Whetstone seems to have attempted to support his unstable fortunes by a military life and literary production. He fought in the Low Countries and was present at Zutphen when SIR PHILIP SIDNEY received his fatal wound. *The Rock of Regard* (1576) is mainly a collection of tales (largely drawn from Italian sources) in prose and verse. His play *Promos and Cassandra* (1578) was never acted. Its story is from Cinthio's *Hecatommithi*. The story of Promos and Cassandra is also one of the prose romances in Whetstone's 1582 collection *An Heptameron of Civil Discourses* where again many of the stories are from Cinthio. Whetstone's version of this story, either as play or romance or both, is probably the immediate main source for SHAKESPEARE's *MEASURE FOR MEASURE*. Among Whetstone's other works are a verse eulogy in commemoration of GEORGE GASCOIGNE (1577), and a series of biographical elegies of distinguished contemporaries, including a verse biography of Sir Philip Sidney.

White [*née* Botting], **Antonia** 1899–1980 Novelist. Born in London, she was educated at the Convent of the Sacred Heart, Roehampton, and at St Paul's Girls' School. She married H. T. Hopkinson, subsequently editor of *Picture Post*, in 1930. Her first novel, *Frost in May* (1933), is a largely autobiographical account of Nanda Grey's convent education. Clara Batchelor, the heroine of *The Lost Traveller* (1950), *The Sugar House* (1952) and *Beyond the Glass* (1954), suffers in her relationships with men, is confined in an asylum, and eventually returns to the faith which she had rejected early in life. The conclusion echoes *The Hound and the Falcon* (1965), Antonia White's account of her own reconversion to Catholicism. She also wrote a play (*Three in a Room*, 1947) and CHILDREN'S LITERATURE (*Minka and Curdy*, 1957; *Living with Minka and Curdy*, 1970). She also translated many works from French, including novels by Christine Arnothy and Colette.

White, E(lwyn) B(rooks) 1899–1985 American essayist, journalist and critic. He was born in Mount Vernon, New York, and educated at Cornell. After a period in Seattle as a reporter, he moved to New York where he became a writer and contributing editor for *THE NEW YORKER* in 1926. His long-term friendship with JAMES THURBER included a collaboration, *Is Sex Necessary?*, in 1929. His other works include *Alice through the Cellophane* (1933), *Quo Vadimus? Or the Case for the Bicycle* (1938), *One Man's Meat* (1942), *The Second Tree from the Corner* (1954) and *The Points of My Compass* (1962). His contribution to CHILDREN'S LITERATURE includes two notable books, *Stuart Little* (1945) and *Charlotte's Web* (1952).

White, Edmund 1940– American novelist. A leading homosexual author, he has published: *Forgetting Elena* (1973); *Nocturnes for the King of Naples* (1978);

A Boy's Own Story (1982), his best-known work, about an adolescent becoming aware of his homosexuality and trying to find a place for himself in contemporary society; *Caracole* (1985); and *The Beautiful Room is Empty* (1988). His short stories appear with those of Adam Mars-Jones in a collection with a homosexual theme, *The Darker Proof* (1990). White has also published works of non-fiction dealing with issues of sociological and cultural interest. *States of Desire: Travels in Gay America* (1980) investigates the gay communities of several major American cities. With Dr Charles Silverstein he co-wrote *The Joy of Gay Sex* (1977).

White, Gilbert 1720–93 Naturalist. Born in Selborne, Hampshire, he was taught by THOMAS WARTON THE ELDER at the grammar school in Basingstoke and became a schoolfellow of JOSEPH WARTON and THOMAS WARTON THE YOUNGER at Winchester College. The poet WILLIAM COLLINS was his contemporary at Oriel College, Oxford. He returned to his native village in 1758 and remained there for the rest of his life, holding several local curacies.

White was a keen observer of wildlife and the changing seasons, with a gift for painstaking fieldwork and an eye for luminous detail. He recorded his observations of the local scene in letters to friends (chiefly the naturalists THOMAS PENNANT and Daines Barrington) and, at their urging, published them with an introductory description as *The Natural History and Antiquities of Selborne* (1789). *The Natural History of Selborne*, as it is usually called, is a scientific classic as well as a book of lasting charm. *A Naturalist's Calendar*, edited by JOHN AIKIN after White's death, appeared in 1795.

White, Henry Kirke 1785–1806 Poet. Born in Nottingham, where he received some elementary schooling, he educated himself further while serving as a solicitors' articled clerk. Increasingly evangelical in religion, he sought a university education to prepare for ordination, and published *Clifton Grove* (1803), a volume of verses in the style of GOLDSMITH's *DESERTED VILLAGE*, to raise funds. SOUTHEY encouraged his poetical bent, and others furthered his academic career. Already consumptive, he died at St John's College, Cambridge, where he was showing signs of promise as an undergraduate. Southey compiled *The Remains of Henry Kirke White* (1807) from his literary manuscripts; its evangelical tone ensured its brief popularity.

White, Kenneth 1936– Poet. Born in Glasgow and educated at the Universities of Glasgow, Munich and Paris, he travelled widely before becoming professor of 20th-century poetics at the Sorbonne in 1983. Better known and appreciated abroad than in Britain, he writes in French and English and is influenced by

Patrick White, photograph by Cecil Beaton

both WHITMAN and Nietzsche. Travel and drifting are recurrent themes in his work. His British titles include: *The Most Difficult Area* (1968), published in the now famous Cape Goliard editions, with which he was involved; *Ode to Charles Fourier* (1969), a translation of André Breton; *Walk along the Shore* (1977); *Two Stages on the Northern Route* (1985); *Late August on the Coast* (1986); *Travels in the Drifting Dawn* (1989), a record of real and internal travels between 1963 and 1975; *The Bird Path: Collected Longer Poems* (1989), which covers topics as disparate as a Glasgow boyhood, the sea, France, a journey to Asia and the Greenland sagas; *The Blue Road* (1990); *Handbook for the Diamond Country: Collected Shorter Poems 1960–90* (1990); and *Pilgrim of the Void* (1992).

White, Patrick 1912–90 Australian novelist, short-story writer and playwright. The son of a wealthy landowning family, he was born in London of Australian parents and educated at Cheltenham College and Cambridge. He wrote an early volume of poetry and his first novel, *The Happy Valley* (1939), in London. During World War II he served as an RAF Intelligence Officer in the Middle East and Greece, meeting Manoly Lascaris, a Greek officer who became his lifelong companion. After the war he settled with Lascaris at Castle Hill, near Sydney. The rediscovery of his Australianness ultimately led to three of his finest novels, about aspects of Australian identity: *The Tree of Man* (1955), covering a period from pioneer settlement to suburbanization, *Voss* (1957) and *Riders in* the *Chariot* (1961), which contains a powerful indictment of Australian suburban life. *The Solid Mandala* (1966), *The Vivisector* (1970) and *The Eye of the Storm* (1973) are all products of his own move to an inner suburb of Sydney. *A Fringe of Leaves* (1976), like *Voss*, takes its subject from 19th-century Australian history and uses it as a metaphor for self-exploration with national, psychological and gender implications. *The Twyborn Affair* (1979) is a wide-ranging work exploring dualities in human nature, including that of male and female sexuality. Though White declared it was to be his last novel, he broke his resolution in 1986 with *Memoirs of Many in One* 'by Alex Xenophon Demirjian Gray, edited by Patrick White'.

Other works include: *The Living and the Dead* (1941) and *The Aunt's Story* (1948), both novels; *The Burnt Ones* (1964) and *The Cockatoos* (1974), collections of short stories; and plays such as *The Season at Sarsaparilla* (1961), *Night on Bald Mountain* (1962) and *Signal Driver* (1983), which established him as one of Australia's finest non-naturalistic dramatists. His autobiography, *Flaws in the Glass* (1981), openly acknowledged his homosexuality. *Patrick White Speaks* (1990) is a collection of essays and speeches, often campaigning, from 1958 to 1988. He was awarded the Nobel Prize for Literature in 1973.

White, T(erence) H(anbury) 1906–64 Writer of CHILDREN'S LITERATURE. Born in Bombay, he was educated at Cheltenham College and Queens' College, Cambridge. For several years he was a schoolmaster at Stowe, then resigned his post to concentrate on his writing, living in a cottage at Stowe Ridings on the Stowe estate. His early works were hardly successful but *England Have My Bones* (1937), a paean of praise for the English countryside, its traditions and history, was admired by a number of contemporary readers. Profoundly affected by MALORY'S *LE MORTE DARTHUR*, which, as a pacifist, he considered to be about 'a quest for an antidote to war', White made a major contribution to ARTHURIAN LITERATURE with his quirky, humorous retelling of the legend in *The Sword in the Stone* (1939), *The Witch in the Wood* (1940), *The Ill-Made Knight* (1941) and *The Candle in the Wind* (1958). The series was revised as *The Once and Future King* (1958). A fifth volume, *The Book of Merlyn*, posthumously discovered among the author's papers, was published in 1977. Other works included *Mistress Masham's Repose* (1946), a fantasy about descendants of the Lilliputians from GULLIVER'S TRAVELS; *The Goshawk* (1951), about training a pet hawk; *The Book of Beasts* (1954), a translation from a medieval bestiary; and *The Master* (1957), part parable and part SCIENCE FICTION.

White, William Hale 1831–1913 Novelist and essayist under the pseudonym of Mark Rutherford. He was born in the Dissenting stronghold of Bedford,

where his father, a printer and bookseller, played a prominent part in local Dissenting politics. In a later capacity as doorman of the House of Commons his father, whom White continued to revere, wrote lively parliamentary sketches. White attended Bedford Modern School and, after the 'conversion' expected by his family's religious background, went to train as an Independent minister at the Countess of Huntingdon's college at Cheshunt and then to New College, St John's Wood, from which he and two other students were expelled in 1851 for raising issues of biblical criticism unacceptable to diehard orthodoxy. During the 1850s he preached in Unitarian chapels and thereafter occasionally attended preachers whose life and teaching he respected. White worked for John Chapman, publisher and editor of THE WESTMINSTER REVIEW, in whose offices he met GEORGE ELIOT, whom he greatly admired. In 1854 he entered the Civil Service, retiring in 1891 with the rank of assistant director of contracts at the Admiralty. Meanwhile, he had also turned to political and literary journalism, acting as London correspondent of *The Scotsman*.

In his fifties White began to publish in two distinct, but for him related, fields: fiction and philosophy. In 1881 he published *The Autobiography of Mark Rutherford, Dissenting Minister*, allegedly edited by Reuben Shapcott, which, in thinly veiled form, retold White's own spiritual history. Rutherford finishes his ministerial training, but becomes disillusioned with the spiritually moribund nature of the congregations he attempts to serve and embarks on a journey through Unitarianism to theism, agnosticism and finally a state of stoic resignation. What distinguishes White's account both here and in the sequel, *Mark Rutherford's Deliverance* (1885), is the narrator's air of absolute fidelity to the truth as he sees it, however drab, sombre or inconvenient to the demands of fictional structure. These two novels, together with *The Revolution in Tanner's Lane* (1887), provide a portrait of 19th-century dissent where nostalgia for the past glories of Puritanism informs the astringent analysis of its present decay. Under his own name White also published studies of BUNYAN, WORDSWORTH and Spinoza. His other writings, the novels *Catherine Furze* (1893), *Miriam's Schooling and Other Papers* (1893) and *Clara Hopgood* (1896), and the essays and stories published in *Pages from a Journal* (1900), *More Pages from a Journal* (1910) and *Last Pages from a Journal* (1915), all serve to confirm the picture of a deeply self-critical moral earnestness schooling an innately depressive temperament for survival in an often uncongenial world.

White Book of Rhydderch See MABINOGION, THE.

White Devil, The A tragedy by JOHN WEBSTER, first produced *c*. 1612 and published in 1612. The source of the play lies in historical events that took place in Italy in the 1580s.

The Duke of Brachiano is married to Isabella, sister of Francisco, the Duke of Florence. Brachiano is tired of Isabella and has fallen in love with Vittoria Corombona. Vittoria and Brachiano are encouraged and abetted in their adulterous relationship by Vittoria's brother, Flamineo, who helps Brachiano dispose of both Isabella and Vittoria's husband, Camillo. Flamineo also quarrels with his younger brother, Marcello, who is as honourable as Flamineo is evil; he kills him, and their mother, Cornelia, is an involuntary witness of the murder. Despite vigorous pleading in her own defence, Vittoria is convicted of murder and adultery. Brachiano rescues her from confinement and they flee to Padua.

Francisco is determined to avenge Isabella's death. Flamineo, meanwhile, feels entitled to rich rewards for his services to Vittoria and Brachiano; but Francisco's men Gasparo and Lodovico, disguised as Capuchin friars, succeed in murdering Brachiano with the greatest possible cruelty. Vittoria and Flamineo now confront each other. Flamineo presses his claim to reward and Vittoria knows that destruction is only a hair's breadth from either of them. She would willingly kill him, but Gasparo and Lodovico return to complete Francisco's vengeance on both of them.

White Goddess, The: *A Historical Grammar of Poetic Myth* A study by ROBERT GRAVES, published in 1948 and revised in 1952. It is an eclectic and highly original exploration of poetic thinking in terms of Celtic and Mediterranean archaeology, anthropology and mythology. The central theme is that the Muse, or Moon-goddess, inspires poetry of a magical quality, in contrast to rational, classical verse. This is elaborated in terms of seasonal rituals of sacrifice and rebirth, in which the poet is identified with the God of the Waxing Year and his muse with the triple goddess who represents the 'ancient power of fright and lust'. The anthropological arguments for an ancient matriarchy and for the figure of the Muse have been attacked as historically implausible. On the other hand, the book has been admired for the creation of an extended metaphor of poetic inspiration, and as a scholastic extravaganza, erudite, inventive and riddling.

White-Jacket: *or, The World in a Man-of-War* A novel by HERMAN MELVILLE, published in 1850. It is based on his experiences on the man-of-war *United States* in 1844.

The story describes the homeward voyage of the frigate *Neversink* from Peru eastward round the Horn to Virginia. The title refers to the nickname which the narrator earns by making himself a white jacket from scraps of cloth. The jacket causes him grief through-out the journey, alienating him from his fellows, providing him with no protection against the elements, appalling and frightening him with its ghastly colour, and indeed nearly causing his death when the wind wraps it around his head so that he falls from the yardarm into the sea.

Most of the book, though, is devoted to describing life on board the man-of-war, emphasizing the degrading conditions the men live in and the tyrannies practised by the captain and officers. The hierarchical organization of the navy, Melville argues, is dehumanizing to all involved and contradicts the spirit of American democracy. His criticism of flogging was timely, and copies of the book were sent to Congress during its debate of the issue.

White Peacock, The D. H. LAWRENCE's first novel, published in 1911. Narrated in the first person by Cyril Beardsall, it describes the relationships of his sister, Lettie, with George Saxton, a tenant farmer's son, and Leslie Tempest, heir of a wealthy mineowner. Lettie flirts with both men, but eventually decides to marry Tempest to gain material security. Saxton is tormented by the knowledge that he could have won her had he been more strong-willed. Instead he marries Meg, a commonplace girl – the beginning of a steady decline. Lettie makes the best of her prudent but unfulfilling marriage. Cyril himself shows a mild romantic interest in Saxton's sister, Emily, but nothing comes of it and she marries someone else. The most striking figure is the gamekeeper, Annable, the precursor of Oliver Mellors in LADY CHATTERLEY'S LOVER. The characters are based loosely on friends and family members, and the countryside is recognizably the country around Eastwood, Nottinghamshire.

Whitehead, Charles 1804–62 Novelist, poet and playwright. Whitehead was born in London, the son of a wine merchant. He was the author of several popular works: a poem, *The Solitary* (1831), two romantic novels, *Jack Ketch* (1834) and *Richard Savage* (1842), and a verse drama, *The Cavalier* (1836). His career was blighted by drunkenness and he ceased writing about 1850, dying in Australia.

Whitehead, William 1715–85 Poet and playwright. Born in Cambridge, he was educated at Winchester College and Clare College, Cambridge, where he was elected a fellow in 1742. Not wishing to be ordained, he resigned his fellowship in 1745 and became tutor to Viscount Villiers, son of the Earl of Jersey. The family remained his faithful patrons. Largely influenced by POPE, his early poems used the HEROIC COUPLET, but Whitehead explored BLANK VERSE too. GARRICK produced his tragedy *The Roman Father* with some success in 1750. HORACE WALPOLE and WILLIAM MASON praised *Creusa, Queen of Athens* (1754). *Elegies, with an Ode to the Tiber, Written*

Abroad (1757) was inspired by his experiences as tutor on the Grand Tour in 1754–6.

Whitehead became POET LAUREATE on the death of CIBBER in 1757, after GRAY had declined the post, and attracted the disapproval of various contemporaries by the ODES he wrote in performance of his duties. JOHNSON found his '*grand* nonsense... insupportable', but Whitehead's chief assailant was CHARLES CHURCHILL, who wrote in *The Ghost* (1762–3): 'DULL-NESS and METHOD still are one,/ and WHITEHEAD is their darling Son.' Whitehead made a dignified reply in *A Charge to the Poets* (1762) and in *A Pathetic Apology for All Laureates, Past, Present, and to Come*. The latter was circulated among his friends and published posthumously in Mason's memoir.

Whitehead produced a successful comedy, *The School for Lovers*, in 1762 and a FARCE, *The Trip to Scotland*, in 1770. His later poems include *Variety: A Tale for Married People* (1776) and *The Goat's Beard* (1777), his last separate publication. His collected works appeared in two volumes in 1774. Mason added a third volume with a memoir for the collected edition of 1788.

Whiteing, Richard 1840–1928 Novelist and journalist. Born in London, he trained as an engraver before turning to fiction at the age of 48 with *The Island* (1888) and its sequel, *Number 5 John Street* (1889). The novels depict social unrest in late Victorian Britain and criticize accepted values. A series of satirical articles which date from Whiteing's time in Paris were published in *The Evening Star* from 1866.

Whitfield, James M. 1823–78 Black American poet and Abolitionist. Born in Exeter, New Hampshire, he lived briefly in Boston and then settled in Buffalo, where he worked as a barber. His first volume, *Poems*, appeared in 1846, but it was not until the publication of *America, and Other Poems* (1853) that he gave up barbering. In 1858 he founded a journal, *African-American Repository*. His later poetry appeared primarily in magazines such as the *Liberator* and *Frederick Douglass' Paper* (see FREDERICK DOUGLASS). He died in California, en route to Central America to examine the possibility of establishing a colony of free blacks.

Whiting, John 1917–63 Playwright. He was born in Salisbury and educated at Taunton School and the Royal Academy of Dramatic Art. Whiting wrote against the stream of socially committed drama and acquired a following that was never quite large enough to constitute a paying audience. His best work includes a whimsical comedy, *A Penny for a Song* (1951), and several plays in which he dramatizes his own and his characters' spiritual struggles: *Saint's Day* (1951), *Marching Song* (1954), *The Gates of*

Summer (1956) and *The Devils* (1961), derived from ALDOUS HUXLEY's *The Devils of Loudun*. He also adapted French plays for the British stage and wrote screenplays for films and television. His perceptive criticism of the contemporary stage is collected in *Whiting on Theatre* (1966).

Whitman, Walt(er) 1819–92 American poet. He was born in West Hills on Long Island, though his family moved to Brooklyn in 1823. He left school in 1830 to become a printer's apprentice and then an itinerant teacher, returning in 1838 to Long Island, where he started *The Long Islander*, a newspaper which he delivered personally to subscribers. In 1842 he went back to Brooklyn and became editor of the New York *Aurora*. Four years later he assumed editorship of the Brooklyn *Eagle*, but, because of the radical tone of his editorials, he did not keep the post for long. While working for these various newspapers he also began to write poetry and short stories. His early works include a temperance tract, *Franklin Evans* (1842), written in the form of a novel. His early stories are recollected in *The Half-Breed and Other Stories* (1927).

In 1848 he travelled south to work on the New Orleans *Crescent*. The experience of the vastness of the American landscape and the variety of its people made a deep impression on him. He returned to New York later that year and turned his attention increasingly towards poetry. In 1855 he borrowed a press from some friends and set up the 12 poems, including an early version of 'Song of Myself', which made up the first edition of LEAVES OF GRASS. Although he himself published an anonymous laudatory review, the book received little attention. It did, however, elicit a letter of praise from RALPH WALDO EMERSON, which Whitman printed in the second edition (1856). This edition also included 20 new poems, among them 'Crossing Brooklyn Ferry'. In 1857 he became editor of the Brooklyn *Times*, his contributions to which were subsequently published in *I Sit and Look Out* (1932). In 1860 he found a publisher, Thayer and Eldridge, for a new edition of *Leaves of Grass* which contained 124 new poems, including the 'Calamus' and 'Children of Adam' sections.

Whitman's verse, with its frequent use of colloquial language and everyday events, represents a turning-point in the history of American poetry – a poetic form fashioned out of specifically American experience in a distinctively American idiom. Some of his finest poems grew out of his personal experience of the horrors of the Civil War (during which he served as a volunteer nurse in army hospitals and as a correspondent for *The New York Times*), and out of his attempt to reconcile the destruction of the war with his visionary idea of America. *Drum Taps* was published in 1865, and with its companion volume, *Sequel*, appeared in the 1867 edition of *Leaves of*

Walt Whitman: a portrait printed as the frontispiece to the first edition of *Leaves of Grass*, 1855

Grass. Sequel was written in the aftermath of Abraham Lincoln's assassination and includes Whitman's elegies for the dead president: 'When Lilacs Last in the Dooryard Bloom'd' and 'O Captain! My Captain!'.

After the war Whitman worked briefly as a clerk in the Department of the Interior, but was dismissed when the Secretary learned that he was the author of the sensual and shocking *Leaves of Grass*. He continued to hold minor posts in Washington, however, and his prose work *Democratic Vistas* (1871) is a passionate reaffirmation of democratic principles in the face of the widespread corruption of the Reconstruction era. In 1873 he suffered the first of a series of paralytic strokes. The 1871 edition of *Leaves of Grass* (which in-cluded the *Passage to India* group of poems) was reprinted in 1876 as the 'Author's' or 'Centennial' edition. In 1876 he also published a volume of prose pieces entitled *Two Rivulets*. In 1881 a newly augmented edition of *Leaves of Grass* appeared, then comprising 293 poems in all. The following year he published another volume of prose, *Specimen Days and Collect*. A collection of his newspaper pieces, *November Boughs*, appeared in 1888. His final volume was the 'Deathbed' edition of *Leaves of Grass*, which he prepared in 1891–2. It includes two annexes, the 'Sands at Seventy' and 'Good-bye My Fancy' groups of poems, and concludes with the prose piece 'A Backward Glance o'er Travel'd Roads', in which he attempts to explain his life and work.

Whittier, John Greenleaf *c*. 1807–92 American poet. He was born into a Quaker family in East Haverhill, Massachusetts. The Abolitionist WILLIAM LLOYD GARRISON published Whittier's first poems in *The Liberator* and helped him obtain an editorial job on a Boston newspaper in 1829. His first book was *Legends of New-England in Prose and Verse* (1831). Early New England life also provided the subject for two long poems, *Moll Pitcher* (1832) and *Mogg Megone* (1836).

A career in journalism and letters seemed set, but Whittier's Quaker conscience and the influence of Garrison brought him into politics. He became involved in the anti-slavery cause and was elected to the Massachusetts legislature in 1835. He edited the *Pennsylvania Freeman* from 1838 to 1840, and published *Poems Written during the Progress of the Abolition Question* in 1838. He then became increasingly uncomfortable with Garrison's politics and founded the Liberty Party, to which he contributed his skills as a journalist. *Lays of My Home and Other Poems* appeared in 1843, and further anti-slavery poems in *Voices of Freedom* in 1846. His first collected *Poems* (1849) testifies eloquently to his hatred of tyranny and his unshakeable concern for the suffering of others, as does *Songs of Labor* (1850).

He continued to write in support of Abolition throughout the Civil War, but also found time for creative efforts as a poet of the countryside with *The Chapel of the Hermits* (1853), *The Panorama and Other Poems* (1856) and *Home Ballads and Poems* (1860). The Civil War was the impulse for *In War Time and Other Poems* (1864). When the struggle was over, he turned back to New England and the countryside for his inspiration and produced what is probably his best work: *Snowbound* (1866), *The Tent on the Beach* (1867), *Among the Hills* (1869), *Miriam and Other Poems* (1871), *Hazel-Blossoms* (1875), *The Vision of Echard* (1878), *Saint Gregory's Guest* (1886) and *At Sundown* (1890).

Who's Afraid of Virginia Woolf? A play by EDWARD ALBEE, first performed in New York in 1962. The first of his three-act dramas, it is also the most admired of his plays.

George is a history professor at a small New England college. His wife Martha is the daughter of the college president. The play depicts the events of a single night, when George and Martha bring a young colleague and his nervous wife back from a party. The elder couple involve Nick and Honey in the verbal abuse that seems to be a nightly ritual with them. Honey drinks too much and becomes ill. Martha tries to seduce Nick. The sexuality of all four characters is impugned. Albee calls the second act a 'Walpurgisnacht', a night of conflict and purgation. The final purgative comes in Act Three, titled 'Exorcism', when George and Martha's imaginary son, created by them as some kind of sustenance, is declared dead by Martha, thereby acknowledging their illusions and allowing compassionate feelings to surface.

Whyte-Melville, G(eorge) J(ohn) 1821–78 Novelist. Born of aristocratic parents and educated at Eton, he entered the Army and served in the Crimea, thereafter devoting himself to writing and foxhunting. He published some 23 novels and a volume of verse. His subjects were historical, romantic and sporting and his work in the latter area is generally felt to have survived best, being perceptive, vivid and curiously undated. A good example is *Market Harborough* (1861). He was killed, characteristically, in a hunting accident.

Widow's Tears, The A sour comedy by GEORGE CHAPMAN, first performed by a BOYS' COMPANY in *c*. 1605 and published in 1612.

The play is oddly broken-backed. The first three acts are largely concerned with what emerges as the subplot, in which the widowed Eudora, despite her vows of faithfulness to her dead husband, is wooed and won by Tharsalio, who, though well-born, was formerly her servant. Cynthia, one of the people most shocked by Eudora's fall, becomes the focus of the last two acts, which are based on the story of the widow of Ephesus in the *Satyricon* of Petronius. Chapman has given the story a twist by having Lysander feign his own death in order to test Cynthia's constancy. Disguised as a soldier, he woos his 'widow' in the tomb and succeeds in cuckolding himself. *The Widow's Tears* relies on conventional cynicism about the fickleness of women.

Widowers' Houses GEORGE BERNARD SHAW's first play, produced in 1892. He insisted that it was both 'didactic' and 'realistic'. His aim, certainly, was to instruct the Victorian age in the economic realities of capitalism.

Dr Henry Trench, a member of an aristocratic family, has fallen in love with Blanche Sartorius. Her father will consent to the match only if it can be guaranteed that Trench's family will accept Blanche. When Trench learns that Sartorius has gained his wealth, and continues to gain it, by extorting rent from impoverished tenants, he is horrified. But Sartorius turns the tables on him by pointing out that Trench's income, however little he may concern himself with it, is derived from the same sources. Trench capitulates and agrees to marry Blanche, who is not much more admirable than her father and Trench.

Widsith An Old English poem preserved in the EXETER BOOK. Dating from the 7th century, it is one of the oldest surviving works in the vernacular. Purporting to be an account of the courts visited by the minstrel Widsith, the poem catalogues the heroes of the European tribes. The chronological span, from Eormanric (d. 375) to Aelfwine's invasion of Italy in 568, makes it impossible that the work was based on the reminiscences of a real minstrel.

Wiebe, Rudy (Henry) 1934– Canadian novelist and short-story writer. Born in Fairholme, Saskatchewan, of Russian parents, he grew up in a Mennonite community in Alberta and was educated at the University of Alberta where he now teaches. His first novel, *Peace Shall Destroy Many* (1962), has been followed by *First and Vital Candle* (1966), *The Blue Mountains of China* (1970), *The Temptations of Big Bear* (1973), *The Scorched-Wood People* (1977), *The Mad Trapper* (1980), *My Lovely Enemy* (1983), as well as *Where is the Voice Coming From?* (1974), a collection of stories, and *Playing Dead* (1989), 'a contemplation concerning the Arctic'. His work is notable for its revisionist accounts of the history of Canadian minorities: Mennonites in *The Blue Mountains of China*, Cree Indians in *The Temptations of Big Bear* and the Métis population of Manitoba in *The Scorched-Wood People*.

Wieland: or, The Transformation A GOTHIC NOVEL by CHARLES BROCKDEN BROWN, published in 1798, and generally recognized as one of America's first major novels. Cast in the form of a letter from Clara, the only surviving member of the Wieland family, to an unnamed friend, the story begins with a brief biography of Wieland senior, a mystic who emigrated from Germany to Pennsylvania and built a large estate there. While engaged one evening in an unidentified spiritual enterprise, he dies of spontaneous combustion. Following his wife's death, their children, Clara and Wieland Jr, are cared for by Catherine Pleyel, whom Wieland eventually marries. When Catherine's brother Henry arrives from Germany, Clara falls in love with him and the four enjoy each other's company insulated from the outside world.

The sense of spiritual and physical harmony is destroyed, however, following the intrusion of the mysterious Carwin. Shortly after his first appearance, disembodied voices issue various announcements and warnings. On one occasion they tell of the death of Henry Pleyel's fiancée, and this encourages him to fall in love with Clara. Later, when the voices suggest that Clara and Carwin are having an affair, Henry returns to Germany and, finding his fiancée alive, marries her. Back at the estate in Pennsylvania, the voices eventually drive Wieland insane; he murders his wife and children and is incarcerated in an asylum. He escapes, however, and returns on the very evening that Carwin confesses to Clara that he himself has created the voices by ventriloquism. Wieland's intention is to kill his sister, but when ordered not to by the concealed Carwin's voices, he commits suicide instead.

Carwin disappears, and in time Clara marries Henry, when he returns to the estate after the death of his wife.

Wieners, John 1934– American poet. Born in Boston, he was educated at Boston College and Black Mountain College, North Carolina, where he studied with ROBERT DUNCAN and CHARLES OLSON. His powerful evocations of city life, particularly in New York, were the hallmark of his first volume, *The Hotel Wentley Poems* (1958). His characteristically uneasy treatment of the city is developed in *Ace of Pentacles* (1964), *Pressed Wafer* (1967), *Asylum Poems* (1969) and *Nerves* (1970). *Behind the State Capitol: or, Cincinnati Pike* (1975) is a montage of poems, prose and photographs. Later volumes include *A Superficial Estimation* (1986) and *Conjugal Contraries and Quart* (1987), while *Selected Poems, 1958 to 1984* (1986) makes the ideal introduction to his work.

Wife of Bath's Tale, The See CANTERBURY TALES, THE.

Wife's Lament, The An Old English poem preserved in the EXETER BOOK, recording the lament of a wife whose husband is in exile. She is apparently an alien in his homeland and friendless; he has committed a crime and been banished. Consequently she lives in an earth-barrow in the forest. The chronology of events is not completely clear and the circumstances of the husband's exile are not fully explained. Despite this obscurity the woman's lament poignantly expresses her solitude, isolation and longing for her husband. The poem may be connected with THE HUSBAND'S MESSAGE, in the same collection.

Wiggin (*née* Smith), **Kate Douglas** 1856–1923 American writer of CHILDREN'S LITERATURE. Born and educated in Philadelphia, she trained as a teacher and for a time ran a free nursery school in San Francisco. Her first novels were written to raise money for this enterprise, but her great bestseller, *Rebecca of Sunnybrook Farm* (1903), came many years later. It is memorable for the conflict between the lively heroine and her spinster aunt, Matilda Sawyer, and the evocation of life in small-town Maine. Other works include the autobiographical *My Garden of Memory* (1923).

Wigglesworth, Michael 1631–1705 American Puritan minister and poet. Born in Yorkshire, he was taken by his family to New England in 1638 and settled in Quinnipiac (later named New Haven), Connecticut. He studied medicine at Harvard, and in 1656 he was ordained minister of the congregation at Malden, Massachusetts. Wigglesworth's writing not only states the most fundamental tenets of Puritan belief, but shows American Puritanism as it was lived by the individual and the community. His most widely read poems were written either to present the articles of faith in a form which allowed them to be easily memorized, or to prescribe behaviour fitting for a Christian. *THE DAY OF DOOM* (1662) deals with salvation and damnation, *Meat out of the Eater* (1670) with the uses the virtuous can find in the experience of ill health. A posthumously published verse jeremiad, 'God's Controversy with New England', interprets the drought of 1662 as a providential warning to reform. His *Diary* records the psychological struggle inherent in spiritual growth.

Wilbur, Richard (Purdy) 1921– American poet. Born in New York, he was educated at Amherst College and, with an interruption for service in World War II, at Harvard. He has taught at Harvard, Wellesley College, Wesleyan University, and currently teaches at Smith College. His first two volumes, *The Beautiful Changes* (1947) and *Ceremony and Other Poems* (1950), are in part responses to the personal and public dislocation he perceived in the war and its aftermath. *Things of This World* (1956) achieved the rare distinction of winning both a PULITZER PRIZE and the National Book Award for poetry. Subsequent volumes include *Poems, 1943-1956* (1957), *Advice to a Prophet and Other Poems* (1961), *The Poems* (1963), *The Pelican from a Bestiary of 1120* (1963), *Complaint* (1968), *Walking to Sleep: New Poems and Translations* (1969), *Seed Leaves: Homage to R. F.* (1974), *The Mind-Reader: New Poems* (1976), *Verses on the Times* (1981), *Seven Poems* (1981) and *New and Collected Poems* (Pulitzer Prize, 1988). His verse is oblique, witty and formally strict, qualities equipping him for his translations from Molière, which include *The Misanthrope* (1955), *Tartuffe* (1963), *The School for Wives* (1971) and *The Learned Ladies* (1978), and of Racine's *Andromaque* (1982). He has also published children's verse in *Loudmouse* (1963) and *Opposites* (1973). *Responses: Prose Pieces 1953-1976* (1976) is a collection of essays; *On My Own Work* (1983) an exercise in self-criticism.

Wild Wales A travel book by GEORGE BORROW, published in 1862.

Based upon Borrow's holiday visits and solitary walking tours, *Wild Wales* retains its place as a document celebrating the Victorian rediscovery of rural Britain, not so much for its factual accuracy, but for the immediacy of its narrative, the high colouring given to simple episodes and the raciness of the dialogue. The writing is so direct that the book will serve as a guide even in the late 20th century, though Borrow's affectionate interpretation of the Welsh and their history draws its strength from a lifelong academic interest in the Welsh language and its literature, some of which he had translated.

Wild-Goose Chase, The A comedy by JOHN FLETCHER, first performed *c.* 1621 and published in 1652. Its anticipation of RESTORATION COMEDY was recognized in FARQUHAR's revision of it as *The Inconstant* (1702). The wild goose of the title is Mirabell, whose aversion to marriage leads Oriana, his betrothed, to desperate measures. She eventually wins him after disguising herself as a rich Italian.

Wilde, Lady **Jane Francesca** 1820–96 Irish poet and journalist. The wife of SIR WILLIAM WILDE and mother of OSCAR WILDE, she became a regular contributor to *The Nation*, the newspaper of the Young Ireland movement, using the pen-name 'Speranza' for her fiercely nationalistic poems and prose pieces. One of her articles, 'Jacta Alea Est' ('The Die is Cast'), led to the suppression of the issue of 29 July 1848. After her marriage to Sir William Wilde, she made their home at Merrion Square one of the best-known and most-frequented social centres in Dublin. After his death in 1876, she moved to London and resumed her career as the hostess of a salon at Chelsea. She died in London while Oscar Wilde was in prison. More famous as a personality than as a writer, she made something of a reputation as the author of *Ancient Legends, Mystic Charms, and Superstitions of Ireland* (1887).

Wilde, Oscar (Fingal O'Flahertie Wills) 1854–1900 Playwright, novelist, essayist, poet and wit. He was born in Dublin, the son of SIR WILLIAM WILDE and LADY JANE FRANCESCA WILDE. He studied at Trinity College, Dublin, and later at Magdalen College, Oxford. A brilliant classicist, he won the Newdigate Prize in 1878 for his poem, 'Ravenna'. He made himself conspicuous by despising athleticism and espousing the AESTHETIC MOVEMENT: he collected blue china and peacock's feathers, declared himself a disciple of WALTER PATER and the cult of Art for Art's Sake (which GILBERT and Sullivan mocked in *Patience*, 1881). That year his first volume of poems was published. Wilde affected velvet knee-breeches and advocated rational dress (which meant flowing robes and no corsets) for women. He also proclaimed himself a socialist, though his concern was less with egalitarianism than freedom for the artist. He went on a lecture tour of the United States in 1882, where he is said to have made the famous reply to the customs official who asked him whether he had anything to declare: 'Only my genius'. In 1883 he attended the first night of his play *Vera* in New York, but it was unsuccessful.

The Happy Prince and Other Tales (1888) are fairy-stories written for the two sons by his marriage in 1884. A similar collection, *A House of Pomegranates*, followed in 1891, together with *Lord Arthur Savile's Crime and Other Stories* and *The Duchess of Padua*, an uninspired tragedy in verse. Altogether more important was the insolently epigrammatic WIT, and the fascination with the relations between serene art and decadent life, expressed in *THE PICTURE OF DORIAN GRAY* (1890). Wilde found his true theatrical voice with *LADY WINDERMERE'S FAN* (1892), *A WOMAN OF NO IMPORTANCE* (1893), *AN IDEAL HUSBAND* (1895) and his masterpiece, *THE IMPORTANCE OF BEING EARNEST* (1895). *SALOME*, written in French, was published in 1894 in an English translation by LORD ALFRED DOUGLAS. Wilde's homosexuality was an open secret. When the Marquess of Queensberry, Lord Alfred's father, publicly insulted him in a note accusing him of 'posing as a Somdomite' (*sic*), he sued for libel but lost his case. He was prosecuted and imprisoned for homosexual acts in 1895. His bitter letter of reproach to Lord Alfred was published (incomplete) as *DE PROFUNDIS* (1905), though his poem, *THE BALLAD OF READING GAOL* (1898), is a more characteristic, because more generous, reaction to the pain of imprisonment. On his release in 1897 he went to France, calling himself 'Sebastian Melmoth', a name which combines a martyred saint with the hero of *MELMOTH THE WANDERER*, by his distant ancestor MATURIN. He died in Paris after, it is said, becoming a Roman Catholic. ROBERT HICHENS's *The Green Carnation* (1894) remains the best attempt at PARODY of a literary style which invited imitation while remaining confident of its inimitability.

Wilde, Sir **William** 1815–76 Irish antiquarian, the husband of LADY JANE FRANCESCA WILDE and father of OSCAR WILDE. Born in County Roscommon, he trained at the Royal College of Surgeons in Dublin and became a specialist in diseases of the eye and ear. He was also a gifted writer. Most of his early work was biographical and topographical, but it was in the field of antiquarian and archaeological history that he won his most enduring reputation. His *Irish Popular Superstitions* (1852), legendary tales and superstitions collected by him in the West of Ireland, helped to preserve a vanishing culture.

Wilder, Laura Ingalls 1867–1957 American writer of CHILDREN'S LITERATURE. The daughter of a farmer, she was over 60 before she began to write stories remembered from her pioneering childhood. *Little House in the Big Woods* (1932) describes life in a log cabin with Laura herself, appearing in the third person, observing the simple life around her, never minimizing its hardships but always remembering it with love. *Little House on the Prairie* (1935) tells how Laura's father takes his family out West, where they survive more difficulties before returning nearer home, this time to try wheat farming. Further adventures see the family on the move again, finally settling in a small town where they experience seven months of snow and ice in *The Long Winter* (1940). Once again, poverty and near-starvation are described with realism tempered by compassion and under-

standing. Subsequent novels take Laura to marriage and a teaching career.

Wilder, Thornton (Niven) 1897–1975 American playwright and novelist. Born in Madison, Wisconsin, the son of Calvinist parents, he attended missionary schools from 1905 to 1909, while his father served as consul-general in Shanghai and Hong Kong. He completed high school in California, then attended Oberlin College, Yale, and Princeton.

His early writing included a series of 'three-minute' plays, 16 of which he later published in *The Angel That Troubled the Waters* (1928). His first publication, however, was the full-length play *The Trumpet Shall Sound*, which appeared serially in *The Yale Literary Magazine* in 1919. His first novel, *The Cabala*, was published in 1926. Two years later he won a PULITZER PRIZE for the novel *The Bridge of San Luis Rey* (1927), a complex study of the role of destiny, or providence, in the death of five travellers when the bridge near Lima, Peru, collapses in 1714. The story is supposedly taken from a manuscript written by a Franciscan monk, Brother Juniper. A third novel, *The Woman of Andros* (1930), set in ancient Greece, provoked an attack by critics who felt that Wilder was ignoring the bitter realities of contemporary American life. His other novels are *Heaven's My Destination* (1934), which concerns the fortunes of a good and simple man during the Depression; a historical novel of the last days of Julius Caesar, *The Ides of March* (1948), and two late works, *The Eighth Day* (1967) and *Theophilus North* (1973).

During the 1930s Wilder chose to concentrate most of his energies on the theatre. The six one-act sketches in *The Long Christmas Dinner and Other Plays* (1931) mingle REALISM and experimental modes, notably EXPRESSIONISM, designed to 'shake up' the American theatre. He received his second Pulitzer Prize for *OUR TOWN* (1938), a drama set in the small town of Grover's Corners, New Hampshire, and played without scenery. *The Skin of Our Teeth* (1942), also awarded the Pulitzer, is an expressionistic play about mankind's precarious survival. *The Matchmaker* (1955) was a revision of an earlier play called *The Merchant of Yonkers* (1939), and in turn became another success as the musical comedy *Hello Dolly!* (1963). Several of Wilder's essays on the theatre are included in *American Characteristics and Other Essays* (1979).

Wilding, Michael 1942– Australian short-story writer, novelist, critic and editor. Born at Worcester in England, he attended Oxford University and, after graduating in 1963, lectured in English at the Universities of Sydney, 1963–6, and Birmingham, 1967–8. In 1969 he returned to the University of Sydney, where he is now reader in English. He founded *Tabloid Story*, a magazine for experimental imaginative prose, with Frank Moorhouse in 1972 and has been an energetic champion of *avant-garde* fiction, publishing it under the imprint of Wild and Woolley and acting as Australian editor for the English magazine *Stand*. Influenced by North American post-modernism, his own work is characterized by a strong sense of literary awareness. He often incorporates parodic and self-reflexive elements into his short stories, as in 'Emma: Memoirs of a Woman of Pleasure', which playfully juxtaposes extracts from Jane Austen and John Cleland. His short-story collections are *Aspects of the Dying Process* (1972), *The West Midland Underground* (1975), *Scenic Drive* (1976), *The Phallic Forest* (1978), *Reading the Signs* (1985) and *A Man of Slow Feelings* (1985), selected from the previous volumes, and *Great Climate* (1991). *Under Saturn* (1988) is a collection of four novellas. His novels are *Living Together* (1974), *The Short Story Embassy* (1975), *Pacific Highway* (1982) and *The Paraguayan Experiment* (1985). His critical works include studies of Milton's *Paradise Lost* (1969) and Marcus Clarke (1977) and *Political Fictions* (1980).

Wilkes, John 1727–97 Politician and journalist. The son of a maltster, Wilkes was born in Clerkenwell, London, and received his early schooling from a Presbyterian minister. He completed his education at the University of Leiden, and before he was 21 was married to an heiress some years his senior. Wilkes was hungry for something more exciting than the company of his wife and mother-in-law, and after a few years a separation was agreed. He became a lively young rake and a member of the Hellfire Club.

Wilkes was elected Member of Parliament for Aylesbury in Buckinghamshire in 1755. He supported the elder Pitt, but turned to journalism when the Earl of Bute came to power, finding a ready-made subject in the incompetence of the new prime minister. He contributed to *The Monitor*, wrote successful pamphlets and in June 1762, with the help of Charles Churchill, launched *The North Briton* to oppose *The Briton*, which Bute had established with a fellow Scot, Smollett, as its editor. Bute's growing unpopularity made *The North Briton* a success, but Wilkes grew too bold. No. 45 of his journal libelled the Crown by impugning the truth of statements made in the speech from the throne about the Peace of Paris; he also published the 'obscene' *Essay on Woman*. The *North Briton* was suppressed in April 1763. Wilkes himself was expelled from the House of Commons and banished, though he escaped criminal prosecution by claiming parliamentary privilege.

He returned to England in 1768, when changes in the administration allowed his outlawry to be set aside. He became Member of Parliament for Middlesex but was expelled again in 1769 for a libel in *The St James's Chronicle*. Re-elected three times by his constituents, he was three times denied his seat in the Commons. His persistence in the face of authority made him a popular hero and in 1774, when he became first Sheriff and then Lord Mayor of London, he took his seat without further opposition.

Wilkinson, Anne 1910–61 Canadian poet. Born Anne Gibbons in Toronto and educated in Canada, England and the USA, she lived in Toronto for most of her life. She was a founding editor of *Tamarack Review* and published two volumes of poems, *Counterpoint to Sleep* (1951) and *The Hangman Ties the Holly* (1955). Her *Collected Poems*, edited by A. J. M. Smith, appeared in 1968. In their celebration of the elemental organic principles of life, her lyrics may be compared with the work of metaphysical poets like Marvell and Henry Vaughan, while her last poems, about death, stand with the best in Canadian literature.

Will to Believe, The, *and Other Essays in Popular Psychology* A treatise by William James, published in 1897. It sets out his philosophy of 'radical empiricism' in relation to scientific and religious issues. His work as a psychologist led him to emphasize the importance of instinct and to find a belief in absolute truth philosophically untenable.

William of Palerne A verse romance written *c*. 1350–61, probably in the south-west Midlands, and also known as *William and the Werewolf*. It is a translation in alliterative verse, from the French *Guillaume de Palerne* (*c*. 1194–7) by an unknown 'William' whose patron was Humphrey de Bohun (d. 1361). Though the beginning of this enchanting and well-told story is missing, the French poem opens with the infant prince William of Sicily being carried away by a werewolf to save him from the plots of his uncle. He is found and brought up by a cowherd and then by the emperor of Rome, who entrusts him to his daughter Melior. The couple fall in love and when the girl is promised to a Greek prince, they flee, dressed first in bearskins and later disguised as deer. With the help of the werewolf they reach Sicily and the plot is resolved. The werewolf, the bewitched heir of Spain, is released by his stepmother and marries William's sister. He identifies William who marries Melior. Although not a close translation of its French source, the poem is unusual among English romances of the period in preserving a detailed description of the symptoms of courtly love.

William of Shoreham 14th-century poet. Little is known of his life, but he lived in Kent, probably at Shoreham near Sevenoaks. He is reported to have been vicar of Chart. Of his seven poems to survive, four are didactic, explaining points of Christian doctrine, discussing sin, the sacraments and the commandments. The remaining three poems are in praise of the Virgin, one a translation of 'Patris sapientia, veritas divina' from the *Horae canonicae salvatoris*, and another a translation from the work of ROBERT GROSSETESTE. Although difficult theological points are sometimes considered they are lucidly and simply expressed. The verse itself is unremarkable, with frequent defects in metre and rhyme. The *Midland Prose Psalter* was at one time wrongly attributed to him.

Williams, Charles (Walter Stansby) 1886–1945 Poet, novelist, theologian and critic. Born in London, he was educated at St Albans and University College, London. He worked for Oxford University Press in London for most of his life. Imbued with his Christian faith, his writings are preoccupied with man's relation to God and with the problem of good and evil. Though he began publishing poetry with *The Silver Stair* (1912), it was some years before he found his distinctive poetic voice, intense, joyous and sometimes obscure. It emerged in the verse dramas, which include *Thomas Cranmer of Canterbury* and *The House of the Octopus*, written between 1936 and 1941 in the wake of ELIOT's *MURDER IN THE CATHEDRAL*. They are collected in JOHN HEATH-STUBBS's edition (1963). Equally characteristic is the contribution to ARTHURIAN LITERATURE in two volumes of poems, *Taliessin through Logres* (1938) and *The Region of the Summer Stars* (1944), admired by C. S. LEWIS.

His novels, which he called 'metaphysical thrillers', dramatize his theological concerns in sensational adventures and fantastic miracles. They include *War in Heaven* (1930), *Many Dimensions* (1931), *Descent into Hell* (1937) and *All Hallows' Eve* (1945). Of his theological writings *He Came down from Heaven* (1937) and *The Descent of the Dove* (1939) are probably the most important. His literary criticism includes a study of Dante, *The Figure of Beatrice* (1943).

Williams, Helen Maria ?1762–1827 Poet, novelist and essayist on politics. Born in London and brought up in Berwick-on-Tweed, she returned to the capital with the manuscript of her long poem, *Edwin and Eltruda* (1782), and mixed in literary and BLUESTOCKING circles. *Peru* (1784) attacked slavery and colonial exploitation. *Poems* (1786) contained the 'Sonnet to Twilight' which prompted WORDSWORTH to his first published poem, 'Sonnet, On Seeing Miss Helen Maria Williams Weep at a Tale of Distress', though he was later anxious to stress that he had not met her. In 1788 she went to France, where she spent most of her remaining life, her early liberalism quickly growing into ardent support of the Revolution. Despite her growing opposition to Jacobinism and the Girondist sympathies shown in her various *Letters from France* covering the years 1790–95, she became the embodiment of dangerous extremism to English conserva-

tives, who regularly attacked her in, for example, *THE ANTI-JACOBIN*. Her liaison with John Hurford Stone, whom she may or may not have married, further blackened her reputation. *Julia*, a SENTIMENTAL NOVEL, appeared in 1790; its successor, *Perourou, the Bellows-Mender* (1801), was later adapted for the stage by BULWER LYTTON as *The Lady of Lyons*. She also published *A Tour of Switzerland* (1798) as well as translations of Bernardin de Saint-Pierre's *Paul et Virginie* and Humboldt's voluminous travels.

Williams, Isaac 1802–65 Poet and follower of the OXFORD MOVEMENT. Born in Aberystwyth, he was educated at Harrow and Trinity College, Oxford, where he won the Chancellor's Prize for Latin verse in 1823, an achievement which brought him into close association with JOHN KEBLE. He was ordained in 1829, elected a Fellow of Trinity in 1831 and appointed Dean in 1833, when he also acted as curate to JOHN HENRY NEWMAN at St Mary's church. He contributed Tracts 80, 86 and 87 to *TRACTS FOR THE TIMES* and poems to *The British Magazine*, reprinted with verse by Newman and Keble in *Lyra Apostolica* (1836). After his support for the Oxford Movement stopped him succeeding Keble as professor of poetry in 1842, Williams left Oxford and eventually settled in Stinchcombe, Gloucestershire. His volumes of verse include *The Cathedral* (1838), *Thoughts in Past Years* (1838), *The Baptistery* (1842), *The Altar* (1847) and *The Christian Seasons* (1854).

Williams, John See *REDEEMED CAPTIVE, RETURNING TO ZION, THE*.

Williams, John (Alfred) 1925– Black American novelist. Born in Jackson, Mississippi, he served in the US Navy from 1943 to 1946 and graduated from Syracuse University in 1950. His first novel, *The Angry Ones* (1960), tells the story of Steve Hill, an artist who fights his own personal war against American racism. The protagonist of *Night Song* (1961) is a jazz musician who uses his art to combat discrimination. Williams's early work has often been compared to that of RICHARD WRIGHT, but in his biography of Wright, *The Most Native of Sons* (1970), he criticizes Wright's characterization of the black man as lacking racial and cultural consciousness. In *Sissie* (1963), *The Man Who Cried I Am* (1967), *Sons of Darkness, Sons of Light* (1969) and *Captain Blackman* (1972), his voice is increasingly militant. *Mothersill and the Foxes* (1975), *The Junior Bachelor Society* (1976), *Click Song* (1982), *The Berhama Account* (1985) and *Jacob's Ladder* (1987) are less radical, though still firm in their emphasis on black unity. His non-fiction includes *Africa: Her History, Lands and People* (1962), *This is My Country, Too* (1965), *The King God Didn't Save* (1970) and a biographical study of the comedian Richard Pryor (1991).

Williams, Raymond (Henry) 1921–88 Critic. The son of a railway signalman, Williams was born in the Welsh border village of Pandy, and attended the grammar school at Abergavenny. His studies at Trinity College, Cambridge, were interrupted by wartime service as an anti-tank captain. He edited *Politics and Letters* (1947–8), and worked as an adult education tutor until his appointment as lecturer in English at Cambridge and Fellow of Jesus College in 1961. He was professor of drama at Cambridge from 1974 to 1983, and wrote extensively on modern theatre in *Drama from Ibsen to Eliot* (1952; revised as *Drama from Ibsen to Brecht*, 1968), *Modern Tragedy* (1966) and elsewhere. His most influential work, especially in the celebrated *Culture and Society 1780–1950* (1958), and in *The Long Revolution* (1961) and *Keywords* (1976), was a sustained attempt to revise the concept of culture, away from the elitism of the Cambridge school and towards the socially responsible ideal of a 'common culture'. This has involved an extension of interests from literature to other media in *Communications* (1962) and *Television: Technology and Cultural Form* (1974). An active socialist, he showed a closer affiliation to Marxism in his later work, including *Orwell* (1971), *The Country and the City* (1973), *Marxism and Literature* (1977) and *Culture* (1981). His lectures on fiction were published in *The English Novel from Dickens to Lawrence* (1971), and his other lectures and essays were collected in *Problems in Materialism and Culture* (1980) and *Writings in Society* (1983).

Williams, Roger 1603–83 American Puritan minister. Born in London, he was educated at Charterhouse and Pembroke College, Cambridge. He emigrated to Massachusetts Bay in 1631, settling in Plymouth and then Salem but having difficulty finding a home for his views. He advocated a division between church and state and opposed the colony's attempt to establish synods at which representatives from each congregation would arrive at uniform answers to religious questions. He repeatedly angered the General Court and was finally banished from the colony in 1635. Williams then founded the first Rhode Island settlement, at Providence among the Narragansett Indians, whom he described in *A Key into the Language of America* (1643). The book was published during a visit to England to secure a charter for the Providence Plantations. The same stay also produced two works pursuing his quarrel with JOHN COTTON and others: *Mr Cotton's Letter Lately Printed, Examined, and Answered* (1644), his version of the events leading to his banishment, and THE BLOODY TENET OF PERSECUTION (1644). After his return to Providence he assumed an unofficial but highly influential role in determining its policies. He also wrote *Christenings Make Not Christians* (1645) and, though tolerant of both Jews and Quakers, a critique of

Quaker reliance on the 'inner light' in *George Fox Digged Out of his Burrows* (1672).

Williams, Tennessee (Thomas Lanier) 1911–83 American playwright. Born in Columbus, Mississippi, he graduated from the University of Iowa in 1938. His first plays were one-act pieces given in amateur and student performances between 1936 and 1940. They are partially collected in the volume *27 Wagons Full of Cotton and Other One-Act Plays* (1946; augmented 1953) and *Dragon Country: A Book of Plays* (1970).

His reputation was established by THE GLASS MENAGERIE (1944) and further enhanced by *A STREETCAR NAMED DESIRE* (1947). Both plays show Williams's sympathy for the lost and self-punishing individual, a characteristic of many of his subsequent dramas, such as *Summer and Smoke* (1947; revised as *The Eccentricities of a Nightingale*, 1964). His gift for comedy, often an undercurrent of his more serious dramas, is evident in *The Rose Tattoo* (1951). After the experimental *Camino Real* (1953), poorly received by the critics, he returned to the more familiar themes of the intricacies of Southern families and Southern culture with CAT ON A HOT TIN ROOF (1955), *Sweet Bird of Youth* (1956) and *The Night of the Iguana* (1959; revised 1961). Other plays include *Suddenly Last Summer* (1958), *The Milk Train Doesn't Stop Here Anymore* (1962), *In the Bar of a Tokyo Hotel* (1969), *Small Craft Warnings* (1974), *Vieux Carré* (1977) and *Clothes for a Summer Hotel* (1980).

Williams also published two volumes of poetry, *In the Winter of Cities* (1956) and *Androgyne, Mon Amour* (1977), several collections of prose and a novel, *The Roman Spring of Mrs Stone* (1950). His *Memoirs*, published in 1975, present an account of a life consumed with guilt, anger and a sense of failure, themes which are frequently associated with the major characters in his dramas. A volume of *Collected Stories* was issued in 1985.

Williams, William Carlos 1883–1963 American poet. Born in Rutherford, New Jersey, the son of an English father and a Puerto Rican mother, he attended Swiss and French schools before studying medicine at the University of Pennsylvania, where he met HILDA DOOLITTLE and EZRA POUND. After further medical study in New York and Leipzig, and a visit to London where he met YEATS, Williams settled down to practise medicine in Rutherford in 1909.

His poetry, recognized as one of the most original and influential achievements of the 20th century, is in fact deceptively simple. As critics have often noted, no object or occasion was 'unpoetic' to Williams. 'No ideas but in things,' he declared, finding his subjects in such homely items as refrigerated plums and wheelbarrows. His early work shows the influence of IMAGISM in its objective, precise manner of description; his later poems, however, went beyond the interests of that movement, and became more personal. They also display his metrical invention, the 'variable foot', which he felt approximated to colloquial American speech more closely than did traditional metres.

His first book, *Poems*, was privately printed in 1900. It was followed by *The Tempers* (1913), *Al Que Quiere!* (1917), *Kora in Hell: Improvisations* (1920), *Sour Grapes* (1921) and *Spring and All* (1923). Numerous other volumes followed. Among his last books were *The Desert Music and Other Poems* (1954), *Journey to Love* (1955) and *Pictures from Brueghel and Other Poems* (1962), for which he received the PULITZER PRIZE posthumously in 1963. Between 1946 and 1958 he published five books of the epic-length poem, *PATERSON*, the work for which he is best known. Set in Paterson, New Jersey, the poem deals with the history and people of the town from its origins to modern times. Fragments of a sixth book were published posthumously in 1963. A posthumously edited two-volume *Collected Poems* appeared in 1986–8.

Williams also published a number of prose works, both fiction and non-fiction, beginning with two collections of essays: *The Great American Novel* (1923) and *In the American Grain* (1925). *Selected Essays of William Carlos Williams* appeared in 1954. His short stories were collected in *The Farmer's Daughter: The Collected Stories* (1961); earlier volumes include *The Knife of the Times* (1932), *Life along the Passaic River* (1938) and *Make Light of It: Collected Stories* (1950). His novels are *A Voyage to Pagany* (1928), *White Mule* (1937), *In the Money* (1940) and *The Build-Up* (1952). *The Autobiography of William Carlos Williams* was published in 1951; a collection of plays, *Many Lives and Other Plays*, appeared in 1961.

Williamson, David (Keith) 1942– Australian playwright. Born in Melbourne, he was educated in Bairnsdale, Victoria, and at Monash University, where he studied mechanical engineering. He subsequently lectured at the Swinburne College of Technology in Melbourne, an experience which appears to have provided material for *The Department* (1974). His first full-length play, *The Coming of Stork* (1970) marked his emergence as one of the most important voices of the Australian 'New Wave'. *The Removalists* (1971) and *Don's Party* (1971) quickly established him as the nation's most popular contemporary playwright. Both deal with personal confrontations which occur when repressed tensions find expression. *The Department* and *The Club* (1977) are about institutional power struggles. Williamson is primarily a naturalistic dramatist who anatomizes the Australian vernacular experience in a witty and satirical style. Despite his early association with the *avant-garde*, his work is formally far from radical. His more recent plays continue the anatomy of contemporary Australian society, but the satirical dimension is less

David Williamson

prominent. His work is also notable for its portrayal of changing gender roles. Other plays include *Jugglers Three* (1972), *What If You Died Tomorrow* (1973), *A Handful of Friends* (1976), *Travelling North* (1979), *The Perfectionist* (1982), *Son of Cain* (1985) and *Emerald City* (1987). His work for the cinema includes versions of *Don's Party* (1976) and *The Club* (1980), and screenplays for *Gallipoli* (1981), *Phar Lap* (1983) and *The Year of Living Dangerously* (1985), the last written in collaboration with Peter Weir and CHRISTOPHER KOCH, author of the novel on which it is based.

Williamson, Henry 1895-1977 Novelist and naturalist. Born in Bedfordshire, he was educated at Colfe's Grammar School, Lewisham. He joined the army at 17 and saw action on the Western Front during World War I, an experience which left him psychologically scarred. He later recorded the horrors of trench warfare in *The Wet Flanders Plain* (1929) and *A Patriot's Progress* (1930), a powerful account rendered from the point of view of the common soldier. After the war Williamson spent a brief but unhappy period as a Fleet Street journalist, during which he began *The Flax of Dreams*, a sequence of novels comprising *The Beautiful Years* (1921), *Dandelion Days* (1922), *The Dream of Fair Women* (1924) and *The Pathway* (1928). Completed in Devon, to which he had retreated in 1921, it was much admired by T. E. LAWRENCE. The two became close friends and Williamson later wrote a biography, *T. E. Lawrence: Genius of Friendship* (1941).

It was as a nature writer that Williamson achieved wider recognition and success. *The Peregrine's Saga* (1923) and *The Old Stag* (1926) were followed by *Tarka the Otter* (1927), a minutely observed and moving tale of animal life. It won the Hawthornden Prize and has become a popular classic. There followed other tales in the same genre, *Salar the Salmon* (1935), *The Phasian Bird* (1948) and *Tales of Moorland and Estuary* (1953), which reflect Williamson's debt to the 19th-century naturalist RICHARD JEFFERIES. He published a selection of Jefferies's work in 1937.

A supporter of Oswald Mosley and an admirer of Hitler, he was briefly interned at the outbreak of World War II. His political sympathies did much to mar his reputation. His most ambitious work, begun in his mid-50s, was a 15-novel sequence called *A Chronicle of Ancient Sunlight: The Dark Lantern* (1951), *Donkey Boy* (1952), *Young Phillip Maddison* (1953), *How Dear is Life* (1954), *A Fox under My Cloak* (1955), *The Golden Virgin* (1957), *Love and Loveless* (1958), *A Test to Destruction* (1960), *The Innocent Moon* (1961), *It was the Nightingale* (1962), *The Power of the Dead* (1963), *The Phoenix Generation* (1965), *A Solitary War* (1966), *Lucifer before Sunrise* (1967) and *The Gale of the World* (1969). It recounts the career of Phillip Maddison, a writer whose life-story mirrors Williamson's own political and creative interests.

Willobie, Henry ?1574–?1596 Poet. Born in Wiltshire, he was educated at St John's College, Oxford. Willobie's reputation rests exclusively on a complex, riddling poem *Willobie His Avisa* (1594), the most comprehensive account of which explains it as a veiled history of the courtships of Queen Elizabeth. References within the poem to 'W. S.', characterized as 'the old player', have tantalized Shakespearean myth-makers.

Wills, William Gorman 1828–91 Anglo-Irish playwright and painter. He was born near Dublin. He provided the actor Henry Irving with many of his successes, including *Charles I* (1872), *Eugene Aram* (1873), *Vanderdecken* (1878) and *Faust* (1885). Wills believed poetry to be a higher form than drama, and his attempts to combine the two impressed contemporaries more than they have posterity. A noted clubman and an endearingly generous, if somewhat anachronistic, Bohemian, he made more money by painting fashionable portraits than by writing plays. His only enduring success was *Olivia* (1878), an adaptation of GOLDSMITH's *THE VICAR OF WAKEFIELD*, and even that endured only as long as Ellen Terry continued to perform in it.

Wilmer, Clive 1945– Poet and editor. Born in Harrogate, he was educated at King's College, Cambridge, and spent many years teaching abroad before returning to Britain in 1986. *The Dwelling Place* (1977), *Devotions* (1982) and *Of Earthly Paradise* (1992) have established him as an exact and disciplined poet, concerned to express a sense of continuity with the past and spiritual values, maintained outside any declared allegiance. His translations from the Hungarian with George Gomori include *Forced March: Selected Poems* (1979), from the work of Miklós Radnóti, and *Night Song of the Personal Shadow: Selected Poems* (1991), from the work of Gyorgy Petri. He has also edited a tribute to THOM GUNN (1982) and selections from JOHN RUSKIN (1985) and DANTE GABRIEL ROSSETTI (1991).

Wilmot, John, Earl of Rochester See ROCHESTER, JOHN WILMOT, EARL OF.

Wilson, A(ndrew) N(orman) 1950– Novelist, biographer and critic. He was born in Staffordshire and brought up in Wales. Without noticeable reluctance, he acquired a certain notoriety for his mordant book reviews while literary editor of *The Specator* and for his uncompromising High Church conservatism. His prolific output of fiction began with baleful comedies in the manner of EVELYN WAUGH, such as *The Sweets of Pimlico* (1977) and *Unguarded Hours* (1978), but his reputation rests mainly on *The Healing Art* (1980), *Who was Oswald Fish?* (1981) and *Wise Virgin* (1982), intricately plotted tragicomedies which confront perplexing moral dilemmas. Subsequent novels, such as *Scandal* (1983), *Gentlemen in England* (1985), *Incline Our Hearts* (1988) and *A Bottle in the Smoke* (1990), aspire to a more gentrified tone. He has also published acclaimed biographies of SIR WALTER SCOTT (1980), MILTON (1983), BELLOC (1984), Tolstoy (1988) and C. S. LEWIS (1990). His literary criticism is collected in *Penfriends from Porlock* (1988).

Wilson, Sir Angus (Frank Johnstone) 1913–91 Novelist, short-story writer and critic. Born of English and South African parents in Bexhill, Sussex, he was educated at Westminster School and Merton College, Oxford. He joined the staff of the British Museum Library in 1937 and, apart from service at the Foreign Office during World War II (1942–6), worked there until 1955. In 1966 he was appointed professor of English literature at the University of East Anglia, presiding with MALCOLM BRADBURY over Britain's only notable university course in creative writing. He was knighted in 1980.

Wilson's career as a writer began with two volumes of short stories, *The Wrong Set* (1949) and *Such Darling Dodos* (1950). *Hemlock and After* (1952), a novel about a middle-aged writer's attempt to establish a literary colony, was in part intended as 'a critique of the liberal humanism that is to be found in Forster's novels'. In fact, Wilson was often compared with FORSTER by critics who failed to observe his attempts to refute the tradition. *Anglo-Saxon Attitudes*

(1956), another study of middle age, was followed by a further volume of short stories, *A Bit off the Map* (1957). *The Middle Age of Mrs Eliot* (1958) recounts the traumatic effect of widowhood and financial hardship on a previously wealthy and contented wife. *The Old Men at the Zoo* (1961), an uncharacteristic novel, is a bizarre and often violent fable about the 'near future' when England is at war with an alliance of European powers, and *Late Call* (1964), narrated from the perspective of Sylvia Calvert, a retired hotel manager, explores the spiritual desolation of life in a new town in the English Midlands. In *No Laughing Matter* (1967), Wilson traces the fortunes of the Matthews family from 1912 to 1967. A long, ambitious work, its presentation of English social history and resourcefulness of language have been widely praised. Other works include *As If by Magic* (1973), about a world-ranging quest for meaning by Namo Langmuir and his god-daughter Alexandra, and *Setting the World on Fire* (1980), in which the lives and values of two brothers are contrasted.

Wilson's other work included studies of Zola (1950), DICKENS (1970) and KIPLING (1977), and *Diversity and Depth in Fiction: Selected Critical Writings* (1983). He was also the author of a play, *The Mulberry Bush* (1955).

Wilson, August 1945– Black American playwright. Drawing on his experience of growing up in a slum district of Pittsburgh, he has written a series of plays, each set in a different decade, which he terms his 'view of the black experience of the 20th century'. They include *Ma Rainey's Black Bottom* (1984), *Joe Turner's Come and Gone* (1986), *Fences* (1987), *The Piano Lesson* (1988) and *Two Trains Running* (1990).

Wilson, Colin (Henry) 1931– Critic, novelist and miscellaneous writer. Born in Leicester, he left school at the age of 16 to work in a variety of jobs – laboratory assistant, tax collector, labourer and hospital porter – before becoming a full-time writer in 1954. He shot to fame with his enthusiastic but disorganized study of alienation, *The Outsider* (1956). Its publication coincided with the first production of JOHN OSBORNE's *LOOK BACK IN ANGER* and Wilson was hailed by some as a key thinker of the ANGRY YOUNG MEN generation. The critical euphoria quickly evaporated, and Wilson himself has complained that he has not been dealt with seriously ever since. But he has survived his abrupt rejection and has, by his prolific output, to some extent succeeded in removing himself from the influence exercised by critics. The first of his 'psychological thrillers' was *Ritual in the Dark* (published in 1960 but in fact completed before *The Outsider*), based on the Jack the Ripper case. Other novels include *The Mind Parasites* (1967), *The Killer* (1970), *The Black Room* (1975) and *The Janus Murder Case* (1984). Numerous works of non-fiction deal with literature,

philosophy (particularly existentialism), psychology, the occult and the paranormal, and crime. They include *The Strength to Dream: Literature and the Imagination* (1962), *Beyond the Outsider: The Philosophy of the Future* (1965) and *Mysteries: An Investigation into the Occult, the Paranormal and the Supernatural* (1980).

Wilson, Edmund 1895–1972 American man of letters. He was born in Red Bank, New Jersey, and educated at Princeton. During World War I he served in the US Army, first as a hospital aide, then with the Intelligence Corps. He was managing editor of *VANITY FAIR* in 1920, associate editor of *THE NEW REPUBLIC* in 1926–31 and regular book reviewer for *THE NEW YORKER* in 1944–8. But Wilson was not simply a journalist. Widely recognized as a learned and incisive critic of politics as well as literature, he also wrote poetry, plays, novels and short stories. He was a close friend of several literary figures, among them JOHN DOS PASSOS, F. SCOTT FITZGERALD, and EDNA ST VINCENT MILLAY. The third of his four wives was MARY McCARTHY, to whom he was married from 1938 to 1946.

Among his works of non-fiction are: *Axel's Castle: A Study in the Imaginative Literature of 1870–1930* (1931), a standard work on SYMBOLISM; *Travels in Two Democracies* (1936), a Marxist critique of life in the USA and Russia; *To the Finland Station: A Study in the Writing and Acting of History* (1940), which describes the origins of the Russian Revolution; *The Boys in the Back Room: Notes on California Novelists* (1941); *The Wound and the Bow: Seven Studies in Literature* (1941), which contains an influential reassessment of DICKENS; and *Patriotic Gore: Studies in the Literature of the American Civil War* (1962). He also edited several volumes, including an anthology of American literary criticism, *The Shock of Recognition: The Development of Literature in the United States Recorded by the Men Who Made It* (1943; enlarged in 1955), and a volume of F. Scott Fitzgerald's uncollected pieces, *The Crack-Up: With Other Uncollected Pieces, Note-Books and Unpublished Letters* (1945). His own fiction consists of two novels, *I Thought of Daisy* (1929) and *Galahad* (1957), and a collection of short stories, *Memoirs of Hecate County* (1946; revised 1958). He published two autobiographies, *A Piece of My Mind: Reflections at Sixty* (1956) and *A Prelude: Landscapes, Characters and Conversations from the Earlier Years of My Life* (1967). Three volumes of memoirs appeared after his death: *The Twenties* (1975), *The Thirties* (1980) and *The Forties* (1983).

Wilson, Ethel 1890–1980 Canadian novelist and short-story writer. Born at Port Elizabeth in South Africa, Ethel Davis Bryant spent her early childhood in England, moving to Canada after the early deaths of her parents. She was educated in Vancouver and taught for some years. Her first novel, *Hetty Dorval* (1947), was followed by *The Innocent Traveller* (1949), *Swamp Angel* (1954) and *Love and Salt Water* (1956), developing her gift for poised studies of human relationships, their modest surface and apparently traditional structure belying a keen ironic intelligence. *The Equations of Love* (1952) brings together two novellas, and *Mrs Golightly and Other Stories* (1961) most of her important short stories.

Wilson, J(ohn) Dover 1881–1969 Literary scholar and critic. Born in Mortlake, Surrey, the son of an engraver, Wilson was educated at Lancing and at Gonville and Caius College, Cambridge, where he studied history. He spent three years teaching in Finland and another three years as lecturer at Goldsmiths' College, London (where he edited *Life in Shakespeare's England*, 1911), before becoming a school inspector in 1912 – thus following the example of MATTHEW ARNOLD, whose *CULTURE AND ANARCHY* he was to edit in 1932. His major contribution to literature began in 1919 when he was appointed co-editor of the New Cambridge Shakespeare series, which he saw through to completion in 1966 after publishing four books on SHAKESPEARE: *The Essential Shakespeare* (1932), *What Happens in Hamlet* (1935) – which became something of an academic best-seller – *The Fortunes of Falstaff* (1943) and *Shakespeare's Happy Comedies* (1962). As a school inspector and later as

J. Dover Wilson

professor of education at King's College, London (1924–35), Wilson was a keen advocate of literary education, contributing to the influential Newbolt Report on the teaching of English (1921) an impassioned appeal for literature to be taught to working-class children. From 1935 to 1945 he occupied the chair of English literature at Edinburgh. His autobiography, *Milestones on the Dover Road*, appeared in 1969.

Wilson, John 1626–*c.* 1695 Playwright. Wilson was born in Plymouth and educated at Exeter College, Oxford. After Oxford he entered Lincoln's Inn, became a barrister and eventually Recorder of Londonderry. He wrote two comedies in the manner of BEN JONSON, *The Cheats* (1664) and *The Projectors* (1665). *Belphegor: or, The Marriage of the Devil* (1690) is a tragicomedy based on Machiavelli's story and *Andronicus Comnenius* (1664) a tragedy about the career of the Byzantine emperor. Wilson also wrote occasional verse.

Wilson, John 1785–1854 Critic. He was born in Paisley, the son of a factory owner, and educated at Glasgow University and Magdalen College, Oxford, where he won the Newdigate Prize for poetry. Though he published several volumes of verse, including *The Isle of Palms* (1812) and *The City of the Plague* (1816), and novels, including *The Trials of Margaret Lyndsay* (1823), he is chiefly remembered for his connection with *BLACKWOOD'S EDINBURGH MAGAZINE*. With JAMES HOGG and JOHN GIBSON LOCKHART he wrote the satirical *Chaldee MS* (October 1817) which gave *Blackwood's* its first considerable success. Under the pseudonym of Christopher North he wrote the greatest number of the *Noctes Ambrosianae* papers (1822–35) and appeared as one of the characters in the dialogues. In 1820 he was elected to the chair of moral philosophy at Edinburgh University on the strength of his firm Tory principles.

Wilson, Lanford (Eugene) 1937– American playwright. Born in Lebanon, Missouri, he attended San Diego State College and the University of Missouri. He is best known for *The Hot l Baltimore* (1973), about social outcasts living in a condemned hotel, whose broken sign gives the play its title. Other works, which have prompted comparison with TENNESSEE WILLIAMS, include: *The Madness of Lady Bright* (1964), about a transvestite homosexual; *Balm in Gilead* (1965), about an all-night coffee shop in New York; *Rimers of Eldritch* (1966), about small-town spite and hypocrisy; *The Mound Builders* (1975); *5th of July* (1978); *Talley's Folly* (1979); *Angel's Fall* (1983); and *Burn This* (1988).

Wilson, Robert d. 1600 Actor and playwright. He was famous as an extemporizer but few details of his life have survived, except that he was a member of the Earl of Leicester's Men after 1572 and Queen Elizabeth's Men after 1583. Of several plays which he wrote or helped to write, the surviving three, *The Ladies of London* (c. 1581), *The Three Lords and Three Ladies of London* (c. 1589) and *The Cobbler's Prophecy* (c. 1594), show his ability to adapt the MORALITY PLAY to the changing taste of the early public theatres.

Wilson, Thomas ?1528–81 Humanist and diplomat. Educated at Eton and Cambridge, he was engaged to tutor the two sons of the Duke of Suffolk; their death of the plague occasioned his first publication, a Latin eulogy, in 1551. Wilson spent most of Mary's reign abroad, and after his return to England in 1560 was successful over a period of years on embassies to Portugal and the Netherlands. He became a Privy Councillor c. 1572 and Secretary of State in 1578. *The Rule of Reason* (1551) is an introduction to logic and the conduct of argument. *The Art of Rhetoric* (1553) urges the use of plain English and discourages the affectation of foreign phrases and 'inkhorn terms'. His translation of some of Demosthenes' orations was printed in 1570 and his treatise on usury in 1572.

Winchilsea, [Finch, Anne] **Countess of** 1661–1721 Poet. Born Anne Kingsmill, the daughter of a Hampshire family, she became a maid-of-honour to the Duchess of York in 1683. She married Heneage Finch, who became 6th Earl of Winchilsea, in 1684. Her first poems appeared in 1701 and a collection, in a variety of metres, was published as *Miscellany Poems* in 1713. Her nature poetry, particularly the 'Nocturnal Reverie', was praised by WORDSWORTH in *LYRICAL BALLADS* (1801) and her small output is believed to have influenced POPE's *ESSAY ON MAN* and SHELLEY's *Epipsychidion*.

Wind in the Willows, The A novel for children by KENNETH GRAHAME, published in 1908. Set on the banks of the Thames, it chronicles the adventures of three bachelor animals living the easy lives of Edwardian landed gentry. The timid but friendly Mole moves in with his new acquaintance the Water Rat, a forceful character forever worrying about Toad, the owner of the local great house, Toad Hall. Given to sudden enthusiasms, Toad takes up motoring to such dangerous effect that he is finally sent to prison, at which point Toad Hall is invaded by the distinctly proletarian stoats and weasels who normally live in the Wild Wood beyond. Escaping from prison dressed as a washerwoman, Toad recaptures his ancestral home with his two friends and the curmudgeonly Badger. The book ends with Toad back in residence and promising to reform – a vain hope, according to a letter Grahame sent to a child admirer.

The strength of the book lies in its animal characterizations, but their adventures are interspersed with charming descriptions of the countryside and a meeting with the god Pan, here depicted as a friend to all dumb animals. Helped in its popularity by the illustrations of E. H. SHEPARD and then ARTHUR RACKHAM, *The Wind in the Willows* has enjoyed a second and equally enduring life on the stage, usually in MILNE's adaptation as *Toad of Toad Hall* (1929).

Winesburg, Ohio A collection of 23 thematically related stories by SHERWOOD ANDERSON, published in 1919. They explore life in a fictional small town, in part based on the author's hometown in Ohio. They are further unified by the character of George Willard, a reporter for the local newspaper who has literary ambitions and to whom all the other characters gravitate in the course of the book. Their style and thematic focus reflect his naturalistic approach to American life as well as his interest in the unusual or unfamiliar aspects of human existence. The various characters in the collection, referred to as 'grotesques', are portrayed in a manner which stresses both their alienation and their desperate attempts to communicate with others in their daily lives.

Wings of the Dove, The A novel by HENRY JAMES, published in 1902. Kate Croy, the daughter of a discredited social adventurer, is secretly engaged to Merton Densher, a journalist. While Merton is in America, Kate becomes friends with the wealthy Milly Theale, who confides to her that she is suffering from a mysterious illness, and that her doctor has told her that only happiness can postpone her death. When Merton returns to London, Kate encourages him to take an interest in Milly, hoping that they will get married, thus soon making him a rich widower whom she herself can marry. The plot appears to be working until the fortune-hunting Lord Mark, rejected by Milly, reveals to her the true relationship between Kate and Merton. Milly's health deteriorates, and soon afterwards she dies in Venice. After her death Merton receives a letter from her: she has made him rich enough to marry Kate. In an agony of shame he confronts Kate and offers to marry her only if she agrees not to accept the wealth bestowed on him by Milly. Kate declines, and the novel closes as they separate for ever.

Winner and Waster A political ALLEGORY in ALLITERATIVE VERSE, written in the West of England c. 1352, perhaps by the author of *THE PARLIAMENT OF THE THREE AGES*. In a DREAM-VISION the narrator sees two armies arrayed for battle with all types of people under their two banners. The king forbids them to fight and calls upon their leaders to explain their respective causes. The first spokesman is Wynnere (Winner). He describes the practice and philosophy of those who produce and gain wealth through labour, and berates his opponent Wastoure (Waster), who spends freely and wastes resources. The ensuing debate sets Wynnere's selfish miserliness against Wastoure's laziness and profligacy, and reveals the disadvantages and scant benefits of each attitude. The king sends Wynnere to live with the Pope in Rome and Wastoure to Cheapside. The poem is satiric, with several contemporary political references, although its central issue is obviously relevant to all societies.

Winnie-the-Pooh See MILNE, A. A.

Winter Words in Various Moods and Metres A collection of verse by THOMAS HARDY, posthumously published in October 1928. Written mostly after 1925, the poems stem from incidents and feelings of many decades before, some reaching back to the 1860s. In its unique diversity the volume is an astonishing compendium of Hardy the poet. Its pages reveal him in a variety of moods: philosophic, humorous, dramatic, observant of nature, narrative, lyric. Varied, too, are the technical devices employed by the poet to convey his feelings. The final poem of the volume is appropriately and movingly entitled 'He Resolves to Say No More'.

Winter's Tale, The A play by WILLIAM SHAKESPEARE, first performed c. 1611 and published in the First Folio of 1623. The main source is ROBERT GREENE's romance, *Pandosto* (1588).

The first part of *The Winter's Tale* forms a rounded tragedy of jealousy. Leontes, King of Sicilia, has entertained his childhood friend, Polixenes, now King of Bohemia, for several months. Driven to a sudden and insane jealousy by the closeness of the friendship between his queen Hermione and Polixenes, he instructs his close adviser Camillo to poison Polixenes. Instead, Camillo warns Polixenes and escapes with him to Bohemia. Leontes claps his pregnant wife into prison and brings her to trial on a charge of adultery and a trumped-up accusation of conspiracy to poison him. When the Delphic oracle pronounces Hermione chaste and Leontes a 'jealous tyrant', he defies its message. His new-born daughter has already been carried off by Antigonus, unwillingly bound to expose the infant to the elements. Now comes news of the death of Leontes' son and a report from Antigonus' forceful and outraged wife Paulina that Hermione has also died. The shamed Leontes vows to spend the rest of his life in daily penance. Meanwhile Antigonus has brought the innocent daughter to the Bohemian shore, where he leaves her with a store of gold and a 'character', naming her Perdita. He is eaten by a bear while an old shepherd finds Perdita.

There follows a gap of 16 years, explained by Time as Chorus, and the second part, destined to be a comedy of rebirth and renewal, begins. Perdita,

though brought up in the shepherd's humble home, has attracted the love of Polixenes' son, Prince Florizel. But Polixenes comes in disguise to attend the sheep-shearing feast and shatters the joy of the event by disclosing himself and demanding the end of the match. With Camillo's help, Perdita and Florizel escape and sail to Sicilia, where they are welcomed by Leontes. The vengeful Polixenes, who has followed them, learns, as they all do, the secret of Perdita's birth and welcomes the forthcoming marriage as a guarantee of his reconciliation with Leontes. Paulina gathers all the leading characters to see the statue of Hermione, newly completed. As Leontes looks at it with wonder, Paulina calls for music and the statue comes to life. Hermione is 'reborn' into her marriage with Leontes.

The Winter's Tale belongs with Shakespeare's other last plays PERICLES, CYMBELINE and THE TEMPEST. It is a multi-faceted romance, written for indoor performance at the BLACKFRIARS, where the stylish work of JOHN FLETCHER was much favoured. The second half focuses on the reconciliation that can be achieved through grace, a word which is allowed its full range from spiritual to physical reference.

Winters, (Arthur) Yvor 1900–68 American poet and critic. He was born in Chicago and educated at the universities of Chicago, Colorado and Stanford. His verse, which is severely restrained and meticulously patterned, is among the first notable poetry of the American West. His first volume, *Poetry: The Immobile Wind*, was published in 1921. This was followed by *The Magpie's Shadow* (1922), *The Bare Hills* (1927) and *The Proof* (1930). During the 1930s and 1940s he published several more volumes, the last of which, *To the Holy Spirit*, appeared in 1947. His critical writings, which allied him with the NEW CRITICISM, include *In Defense of Reason* (1947), *The Function of Criticism* (1957) and *Forms of Discovery* (1967).

Winterson, Jeanette 1959– Novelist. She drew extensively on her Pentecostal Evangelist upbringing in *Oranges are Not the Only Fruit* (1985), a whimsical, often bizarre tale of a girl growing up in a militantly God-fearing Lancashire community. Its successors include: *Boating for Beginners* (1986), a hasty reworking of the story of Noah's Ark; *The Passion* (1987), admired for its blend of WIT and extravagant myth-making; *Sexing the Cherry* (1989), an ambitious, intermittently successful fantasy about a mythical Dog-Woman; and *Written on the Body* (1992).

Winthrop, John 1588–1649 American Puritan leader. He was born in Suffolk, and educated at Trinity College, Cambridge. In appreciation for his aid in negotiating the colony's charter, the Massachusetts Bay Company elected him governor in 1629. He sailed aboard the *Arbella* in 1630 and during the voyage wrote and delivered 'A Model of Christian Charity', a lay sermon which defined the social hierarchy he deemed necessary in order to preserve the commonwealth. He wrote a number of other pamphlets while serving, until his death, as governor or deputy governor. *A Defence of an Order of Court Made in the Year 1637* supports the legislation passed by the General Court after the trial of Anne Hutchinson, which denied citizenship to 'dissenters'. His account of the Hutchinson trial was incorporated into Thomas Welde's *A Short History of the Rise, Reign and Ruin of the Antinomians* (1644). His many comments on the political affairs of Puritan New England are collected in his journal, which was published in part in 1790 and complete in 1826, entitled *The History of New England 1630–1649*.

Winthrop, Theodore 1826–61 American novelist and travel-writer. He was born in Connecticut, and educated at Yale. None of his books was published before his death in the Civil War. His best-known work is *John Brent* (1862), a novel which exploits its Western setting to produce an exciting, melodramatic plot involving kidnappings and unscrupulous Mormons. Other works include two novels, *Cecil Dreeme* (1861) and *Edwin Brothertoft* (1862), and *Life in the Open Air* (1863) and *The Canoe and the Saddle* (1863), both travel books.

Winton, Tim(othy) (John) 1960– Australian novelist, short-story writer and writer of CHILDREN'S LITERATURE. Born in Perth, he wrote two novels while still at university: *An Open Swimmer* (1982) and *Shallows* (1984), winner of the Miles Franklin Award. His fiction lovingly records the land and seascape of Western Australia and the communities of its small towns, concentrating with particular compassion on the lives of the inarticulate: a 13-year-old boy in *That Eye, The Sky* (1986) and the frightened elderly in *In the Winter Dark* (1988). *Cloudstreet* (1991) is about the struggles of two families over 20 years. *Scission* (1985) and *Minimum of Two* (1987) are collections of short stories. *Jesse* (1989), *Lockie Leonard, Human Torpedo* (1990) and *The Bugalugs Bum Thief* (1991) are children's books.

Wisdom of the Ancients, The See DE SAPIENTIA VETERUM.

Wise, John *c.* 1652–1725 American Puritan minister. Born in Roxbury, Massachusetts, and educated at Harvard, he was ordained minister of the Second Church of Ipswich, Massachusetts, in 1682. In 1687 he incited a vehement protest against paying taxes that violated the colony's charter rights, an act for which he was imprisoned briefly by Royal Governor Andros. Signing a petition to vindicate those accused of witchcraft in 1703, he helped the colony recover from the social damage done by the trials of 1692. He opposed the attempt to centralize church government, and his advocacy of autonomous congregations produced his two most important and popular publications: *The Churches' Quarrel Espoused* (1710), a systematic refutation of the proposal for ecclesiastical centralization presented in *Questions and Proposals* by COTTON MATHER and INCREASE MATHER; and *A Vindication of the Government of New England Churches* (1717), a definition and defence of Congregationalism. That both works advance egalitarian principles explains their subsequent appeal to American Revolutionaries and Abolitionists in the 18th and 19th centuries, when they were reprinted in large quantities. *A Word of Comfort to a Melancholy Country* (1721) is a defence of paper money.

Wise, T(homas) J(ames) 1859–1937 Book collector, bibliographer and forger. A successful businessman, he gathered many honours by collecting and cataloguing a valuable library. In 1934 John Carter and Graham Pollard showed that he had also been forging first editions of major authors. Their work generated further investigation and at the present count it is known that Wise forged or pirated more than 50 works by, among others, MATTHEW ARNOLD, CHARLOTTE BRONTË, ELIZABETH BARRETT BROWNING, ROBERT BROWNING, DICKENS, GEORGE ELIOT, WILLIAM MORRIS, DANTE GABRIEL ROSSETTI, SHELLEY, SWINBURNE, TENNYSON, THACKERAY and WORDSWORTH. The forgeries took a variety of forms: type facsimiles of genuine pamphlets; genuine works to which bogus title-pages with false dates were added; and works to which bogus cancels were added. In 1959 David Foxon demonstrated that Wise had also taken advantage of his standing in bibliographical circles to gain unsupervised access to Jacobean plays in the British Museum, many of them in the priceless Garrick Collection, and had torn out leaves from perfect copies in order to make up his own imperfect copies, which he then sold.

Wise Blood A novel by FLANNERY O'CONNOR, published in 1952. A highly disturbing book, it attempts to analyse the effects of religious belief and the nature of such belief in the 'fallen' world of the post-bellum South.

It concerns the spiritual quest of Hazel Motes, a Southerner recently returned from World War II. He is obsessed by the idea that redemption is impossible and that the whole notion of Jesus as saviour is suspect. As he sets himself up as a preacher of non-belief he meets a variety of outcasts and social misfits. In particular, it is his encounter with the false preacher Asa Hawkes (who has supposedly blinded himself out of religious fervour) and his daughter Sabbath Lily that precipitates his downfall. Though apparently a non-believer, Hazel is devastated when he discovers that Asa is only pretending to be blind, having been too cowardly to carry out the act. Eventually, after Asa leaves town, Hazel murders another phoney preacher, who has been parodying Hazel's own 'Church of Christ Without Christ'. He then blinds himself and performs various acts of self-torture in atonement – although he cannot say for what. Finally, after being exposed to freezing wind and rain for two days, he is picked up by the police and clubbed into silence. He dies on the trip back to his landlady's house.

Wiseman, Adele 1928– Canadian novelist. Born in Winnipeg of Ukrainian Jewish parents, she attended the University of Manitoba and subsequently taught at McGill University and Sir George Williams University. She has also worked as a secretary and social worker. Her novels, *The Sacrifice* (1956) and *Crackpot* (1974), deal with the Jewish experience on the Canadian prairies. *The Sacrifice* is a modern version of the Abraham and Isaac story, which can be read both as a realistic saga of immigrant family life, spanning three generations, and as religious ALLE-GORY. *Crackpot*, also depicting the harshness of immigrants' ghetto lives and drawing on traditional Jewish symbolism and humour, is more experimental. She has also written two plays, a children's book and *Old Woman at Play* (1978), a fragmentary memoir of her mother.

Wister, Owen 1860–1938 American novelist and short-story writer. Born in Pennsylvania and educated at Harvard, he first travelled west (to Wyoming) in order to improve his health, and this experience became the basis for his early writings. *Red Man and White* (1896), *Lin McLean* (1896) and *The Jimmyjohn Boss* (1900) are collections of stories set in the Western cattle country. His best-known work, THE VIRGINIAN (1902), was an enormous popular success. Its heroic cowpuncher, unassumingly masterful, crude but innately gentle, set the mould for the Western hero in countless novels and movies. Having become famous for his Westerns, Wister decided to turn to the East for his subjects. *Philosophy Four* (1903) is a story about undergraduate life at Harvard. *Lady Baltimore* (1906) is a romantic novel set in Charleston. He also wrote a biography of Ulysses S. Grant (1900) and reminiscences of Theodore Roosevelt (1930), the boyhood friend to whom he had dedicated *The Virginian*.

wit Like humour – so often, and usefully, compared with it – a concept that has varied not only from period to period but also within each period. Yet of both concepts it may be said that practically all the variations share the common property of being in some way in touch with, or derivable from, their etymological origins. Wit (Old English 'witan', to know) in all its manifestations remains within hailing dis-

tance of the idea of intelligence, cleverness or judgement. Humour (Latin *humorem*, moisture) can always be seen to have some relationship – eventually a rather distant one – with its early medical meaning: a bodily fluid. Wit, that is to say, is associated with qualities of mind and manners, humour with qualities of body and mood. The epigrammatic statement, then, that wit is the perception of resemblances, humour the perception of incongruities, is nearly true – if we bear in mind that while the wit himself always sees the resemblances, the incongruities are usually seen only by the audience.

In Elizabethan medical theory man was governed by four humours: black bile, yellow bile (or choler), phlegm and blood. Properly mixed they rendered him a balanced, equable, 'good-humoured' person. An excess of any one, however, rendered him melancholic, choleric, phlegmatic or sanguine, respectively: unbalanced, obsessive and therefore absurd. BEN JONSON seizes on this medical theory and turns it into one for COMEDY (in the Prologue to EVERY MAN IN HIS HUMOUR, 1598) by generalizing it to include any kind of obsession, whether for silence, sex or money, or any other such unbalancing folly. Straight away, then, physical imbalance becomes associated with temperamental oddity. Taken along with the gradual disappearance of humours from medical theory, this makes understandable the transition to the modern idea of humour as geniality about others or good-natured deprecation of oneself; it is in fact a modulation of what 'good-humoured' originally implied. So humorous comedy now implies something less moralistic than it used to; it is now amusement without judgement, attack without malice. However, it still tends to be associated with situation and type-characters – with clever plotting that manoeuvres people into situations that expose their one-sided unadaptability. The difference is that a method has become a mood. For Jonson's audience the humour lay in the action, the method of demonstrating absurdity and pointing a moral; for the modern audience it lies in the tone. Jonson's comedies can usually also be styled SATIRE, whereas today a humorous satire is almost a contradiction in terms. Wit, on the other hand, has remained a method – which could in principle be used for any literary mode. Thus, a witty tragedy is not impossible, but a humorous tragedy is now inconceivable.

In Jonson and SHAKESPEARE wit is usually close to good sense, intelligence, inventiveness. In DONNE and the METAPHYSICAL POETS that shift towards ingenuity has begun which seems to be the source of the Restoration distinction between true wit and false wit – wit that illuminates and wit that merely dazzles. However, Shakespeare also sees wit as sharing some qualities of the imagination. Falstaff says of sherris-sack that: 'It ascends me into the brain; dries me there all the foolish and dull and crudy vapours which environ it; makes it apprehensive, forgetive, full of nimble fiery and delectable shapes; which, delivered over to the voice, the tongue, which is the birth, becomes excellent wit.'

This is not so far from HOBBES's definition of wit as a combination of Fancy (imagination) and Judgement, an association that never quite drops out of sight, though for the AUGUSTAN AGE wit was predominantly good sense, or propriety of idea and diction, or the natural civilized, or inventiveness, or perceptive cleverness. ROMANTICISM tended to deprecate wit as frivolity; and indeed the idea of wit as witticism or joke, its modern meaning, was in being before the modern period.

Freud's *Jokes and their Relation to the Unconscious* (translated by James Strachey, 1960) brilliantly analyses and codifies the nature of this kind of wit – a kind of which Shakespeare and Hobbes were clearly not unaware, though neither linked it so specifically to jokes as we do today. The essential perception is that such wit – as distinct from amusing cleverness of a fully conscious kind, like IRONY – has its roots in the subconscious, but only its roots. It combines cognitive cleverness with emotional release or aggression; taken in the round, it is preconscious rather than subconscious. That is why the joker, though he cannot deliberately make up a good joke, is not quite so surprised as the hearer when he does so. However, such wit shares with dream the characteristics of latent significance, unexpectedness, disguise and compression.

But this does not exhaust the meaning of wit in the post-Romantic period. OSCAR WILDE's remark that 'the tragedy of age is not that one feels old; it is that one feels young' is so unexpected and unpredictable that one feels it has to be counted as wit, so profound that it might almost be a product of the unconscious; yet, unlike jokes, it touches on no taboo, and shows all those signs of acute perception and high intelligence that were earlier hallmarks of wit. Though there is a difference of emphasis today, it would appear that earlier meanings of wit have not come to seem foreign – as, indeed, is the case with humour. So too, in literature, witty comedy still tends to be characterized by dialogue rather than situation, verbal cleverness rather than type-characters, surprising congruities rather than incongruities, in contrast to humour.

Witch of Edmonton, The A tragicomedy performed *c.* 1621 but not published until 1658, when the title-page named the leading collaborators as WILLIAM ROWLEY, THOMAS DEKKER and JOHN FORD.

The play suffers from two plots that do not really fit together. The witch of the title is a poor and lonely old woman, Elizabeth Sawyer, persecuted by her neighbours until, in desperation, she makes a pact with the Devil and becomes a witch who can exact retribution

for their thoughtless spite. The hand of Dekker is clearly discerned in these scenes, for they show his sympathy for the ill-used. The other part of the play, chiefly by Ford, is a domestic tragedy of crime and punishment. Frank Thorney secretly marries the servant Winifred against his father's wishes. Then his father orders him to marry a girl chosen for him, Susan Carter. Frank's inheritance depends on this, so he marries Susan and then murders her, having planned to throw the guilt on her two rejected suitors. But the truth is discovered and he is executed for the murder.

With the Procession A novel by HENRY BLAKE FULLER, published in 1895. Set in Fuller's native Chicago, it tells the story of a family of social climbers, focusing on the bourgeois convention that a man should amass as much money as possible and then put it at the disposal of his wife and children, who squander it. This is the situation in which David Marshall finds himself: his eldest daughter, Jane, has social ambitions for the family which change all their lives; his son Truesdale spends four years abroad at his father's expense; the youngest daughter, Rosey, a social butterfly, continually demands money from her father. Exhausted by the demands made upon him – to build a new house, to be a philanthropist, to cut a public figure – David Marshall dies, sacrificed to his family's ambition to march 'with the procession'.

Wither, George 1588–1667 Poet. He was born at Bentworth in Hampshire and educated at Magdalen College, Oxford. His main claim to be remembered is as a PASTORAL poet. He contributed seven eclogues to WILLIAM BROWNE's *The Shepherd's Pipe* (1614) and continued in the same vein the next year with *The Shepherd's Hunting*. *Fidelia* (1617) is a letter from a faithful nymph to her inconstant lover, *Fair Virtue* (1622) a hymn of love to his half-imagined mistress, Arete, and *Juvenilia* (1622) a collection of love and pastoral poetry. The merit of these verses has been obscured by the notoriety of Wither's SATIRE – *Abuses Stripped and Whipped: or, Satirical Essays* (1613) sent him to the Marshalsea prison, *Wither's Motto* (1621) to Newgate – and by the leaden didactic poetry of his later years: *The Hymns and Songs of the Church* (1624), *Britain's Remembrancer* (1628) and *Heleluiah: or, Britain's Second Remembrancer* (1641). A convinced Puritan, he attained the rank of major-general in the Civil War. JOHN AUBREY records how, after Wither's arrest at the Restoration, 'SIR JOHN DENHAM went to the king and desired his majesty not to hang him, for that while George Wither lived, he should not be the worst poet in England.' Wither also worked with Marchamont Needham on the *Mercurius Britannicus*.

Wives and Daughters The last novel by ELIZABETH GASKELL, almost complete at her untimely death in 1865. It was serialized in *THE CORNHILL MAGAZINE* from August 1864 until January 1866 and published in book form in 1866.

At the centre of its various skilfully interwoven plots is Molly Gibson's development from a confused, insecure girl to a poised young woman. She is the daughter of the local doctor of Hollingford who, after years as a widower, unwisely marries a flighty and vulgar widow, Clare Kirkpatrick. Molly is much beloved at Hamley Hall, home of Squire Hamley, an old-fashioned Tory landowner with two sons, Roger (who becomes a respected scientist) and Osborne (who dies soon after secretly marrying a French girl of lowly social status). Molly helps Cynthia Kirkpatrick, Clare's daughter by her first husband, extricate herself from an unwise commitment to Mr Preston – which has not prevented her being briefly engaged to the bemused Roger. Cynthia ultimately marries a London barrister, Henderson, and Molly secures Roger.

Socially, the novel ranges from Lord and Lady Cumnor, the Hamleys and the Gibsons down to mob-capped spinsters, tenant farmers and ordinary labourers to register a lively, informative picture of early 19th-century England. A host of lesser characters contribute a leavening humour, a dramatic moment or a small turn to the plot. *Wives and Daughters* is an enduring work as narrative, social history and psychological study.

Wodehouse, Sir **P(elham) G(renville)** 1881–1975 Novelist and short-story writer. Born in Guildford and educated at Dulwich College, he worked as a bank clerk before devoting himself to writing. Beginning in 1902, he published well over 100 books, as well as contributing lyrics to a number of successful musical comedies with Cole Porter, Irving Berlin and George Gershwin (*Oh, Kay!*, 1926; *Damsel in Distress*, 1928). His comic novels and short stories are sustained by romantic, gently farcical plots and a carefully wrought prose style which combines literary allusion, the slang of the day and the occasional audacious SIMILE. Their setting is leisured upper-class society between the two wars, presented as a world of almost PASTORAL innocence. Jeeves and Bertie Wooster, the omni-competent manservant and his amiably incompetent master, have proved his most enduring creations. Introduced in *The Man with Two Left Feet* (1917), they appear in a long series of novels and collections of short stories: *My Man Jeeves* (1917), *The Inimitable Jeeves* (1923), *Carry On, Jeeves!* (1925), *Very Good, Jeeves* (1930), *Right Ho, Jeeves* (1934), *The Code of the Woosters* (1938) and so on. Wodehouse adapted many of these stories for the stage in collaboration with IAN HAY and Guy Bolton. *Blandings Castle* (1935) began a similar series centred on the eccentric Lord Emsworth, forever preoccupied with his prize pig, the Empress of Blandings.

After 1909 Wodehouse lived largely abroad. Captured and interned by the Germans during World War II, he incautiously made several broadcasts from Berlin. The resulting controversy in Britain was partly responsible for his decision to settle in the USA after the war. He became a US citizen in 1955 and, in long-delayed recognition of his achievement, was knighted only weeks before his death. His later works include the autobiographical *Performing Flea* (1953) and *Over Seventy* (1957).

Wolcot, John See PINDAR, PETER.

Wolfe, Thomas (Clayton) 1900–38 American novelist and playwright, born in Asheville, North Carolina, and educated at the University of North Carolina and at Harvard. His first works were plays: *Welcome to Our City* (1923), set in his home town of Asheville, and *The Return of Buck Gavin* (1923). From 1924 to 1930 he taught English at New York University, where he wrote *Mannerhouse*, a play about the decay of a Southern family. He decided to become a full-time writer after the publication of *Look Homeward, Angel* (1929). This strongly autobiographical novel follows the life of Eugene Gant, the son of a stonecutter and a boarding-house matron, as he grows from a child in Altamont, Catawba, into the young adult who breaks with his family at the end. Wolfe's next book, a short novel entitled *A Portrait of Bascom Hawke* (1932), was later incorporated into *Of Time and the River* (1935), which continues the story of Eugene Gant, now at Harvard, and ends with his departure for Europe after a disappointing love affair. *From Death to Morning* (1935) is a collection of stories; *The Story of a Novel* (1936), Wolfe's last book to be published during his lifetime, is a critical examination of his own work. Wolfe died at the age of 38 after two operations for a brain infection following pneumonia. He left a considerable amount of material, from which Edward C. Aswell edited the semi-autobiographical novel *The Web and the Rock* (1939) and its sequel, *You Can't Go Home Again* (1940). A volume of short stories, *The Lost Boy*, was published in 1965.

Wolfe, Tom [Thomas] **(Kennerly)** 1930– American journalist and novelist. Born in Richmond, Virginia, and educated at Yale, he became a reporter for *The Washington Post* (1959–62) and *The New York Herald Tribune* (1962–6). He has been a major proponent of the New Journalism in the introduction to the anthology (1975) he co-edited with E. W. Johnson and in a succession of volumes: *The Kandy-Kolored Tangerine Flake Streamline Baby* (1966), *The Pump House Gang* (1968), *Radical Chic and Mau-Mauing the Flak-Catchers* (1971), *Mauve Gloves and Madmen, Clutter and Vine and Other Stories* (1976) and *In Our*

Time (1980). *The Electric Kool-Aid Acid Test* (1968), his account of the wild lifestyle of KEN KESEY and his friends, is regarded as an outstanding document of 1960s counter-culture. *The Right Stuff* (1979), about the first American astronauts' ascent into space, proved an ideal vehicle for his high-octane prose. Other works of non-fiction are *The Painted Word* (1975) and *From Bauhaus to Our House* (1982). Despite his earlier strictures against fiction, he scored a major success with *The Bonfire of the Vanities* (1988), a novel combining SATIRE with indignant reportage of Reagan's America.

Wollstonecraft, Mary 1759–97 Novelist, essayist and educational writer. She was born in Spitalfields, London. Her father dissipated his fortune in unsuccessful attempts to become a gentleman farmer, and she spent much of her childhood moving from farm to farm in England and Wales. Between the ages of 9 and 15 she received a certain amount of day-school instruction in Beverley, but like most of the educated women of her time she was largely self-taught. At 16 when living in Hoxton near London, she formed a close friendship with Fanny Blood, the accomplished daughter of a poor family, with whom she planned to live and work. At 19 she took a post as companion to a wealthy widow in Bath, a lonely and unhappy experience that quickened her distaste for the habits of the rich. In 1781 she returned to her family at Enfield to care for her sick mother, after whose death she assumed responsibility for the welfare of the younger children. With her sisters and Fanny Blood she opened a school at Newington Green, where she became acquainted with the famous polemicist RICHARD PRICE and other Dissenting ministers and intellectuals. Following the collapse of the school and the death of Fanny Blood, she began to write *Thoughts on the Education of Daughters*, published in 1787. In the same year she went to Ireland as governess to the daughters of Lord Kingsborough, another uncomfortable employment, during which she wrote *Mary: A Fiction* (1788), a self-pitying account of her childhood and friendship with Fanny Blood.

Upon her dismissal by Lady Kingsborough in 1787, Wollstonecraft resolved to try to make her living through writing and was soon working as translator and reader, and later as reviewer and editorial assistant, on Joseph Johnson's *Analytical Review*, a newly launched liberal journal. Through Johnson she met THOMAS PAINE, Henry Fuseli, WILLIAM BLAKE and WILLIAM GODWIN. Between 1787 and 1790 she wrote two books for children, *Original Stories from Real Life; with Conversations Calculated to Regulate the Affections, and Form the Mind to Truth and Goodness* and *The Female Reader*, a selection of texts for girls. She translated Jacques Necker's *Of the Importance of Religious Opinion* and Christian Gotthilf Salzmann's *Elements of Morality for the Use of Children*. Her

Vindication of the Rights of Men (1790) replied to BURKE's attack on Price, among other radicals, in *REFLECTIONS ON THE REVOLUTION IN FRANCE*. In it she defends the parliamentary reformers, identifies herself with the democratic programmes of the European Enlightenment and deplores both the complacency of British society and its trivialization of women. The latter theme is taken up at greater length in her most famous work, *A Vindication of the Rights of Woman* (1792), a sometimes chaotically written but rhetorically powerful plea for fundamental change in society's perception of the function, place and potential of women. It was dedicated to Talleyrand, in the vain hope of influencing the legislation on women's education before the French Assembly.

Following an obsessive, though unrewarding, relationship with Fuseli, she travelled alone to Revolutionary France in 1792. Her *History and Moral View of the Origin and Progress of the French Revolution* (1794) condemns many of the events of the Revolution, while continuing to hold to its basic principles. In Paris she met HELEN MARIA WILLIAMS, leading members of the Girondist faction and GILBERT IMLAY, with whom she fell in love. Their daughter, Fanny, was born in Le Havre in 1794, though Imlay rapidly lost interest in the relationship. Learning of his infidelities on her return to England in 1795, she tried to commit suicide, agreeing afterwards to an unlikely solo journey to Scandinavia as his business representative, which is fascinatingly described in *Letters Written during a Short Residence in Sweden, Norway and Denmark* (1796). Painful confirmation of Imlay's indifference awaited her in England, and she made another attempt on her own life. She slowly recovered from this affair and began to write and review again, meeting other writers such as Mary Hays, at whose home she again saw William Godwin. A mutual attachment developed, of which strong friendship was a welcome and stabilizing component after the near-fatality of passion. With Godwin's encouragement she began her last novel, *The Wrongs of Woman*, which expands many of her earlier ideas on the institutionalized oppression and enfeeblement of middle- and lower-class women, and the legal expropriation of their labour, property and sexuality. She married Godwin after becoming pregnant, though they continued to maintain separate houses for a time. She died in 1797, eleven days after the birth of her daughter, the future MARY SHELLEY.

In 1798 Godwin published his *Memoirs* of his wife and edited her *Posthumous Works*, which included letters to Imlay, an autobiographical fictional fragment, *The Cave of Fancy*, and the unfinished *Wrongs of Woman*. She is also portrayed in his novel *St Leon* (1799). By this time, conservative reaction had set in in England, and she was much attacked as an unsexed woman, 'a hyena in petticoats' and a 'philosophizing serpent'. *THE ANTI-JACOBIN* represented her work as tending to the propagation of whores.

Woman in White, The A novel by WILKIE COLLINS, published in *ALL THE YEAR ROUND* from November 1859 to August 1860 and in volume form in 1860.

The story is told through eyewitness accounts by the main characters. Walter Hartright goes to Limmeridge House in Cumberland as drawing master to Laura Fairlie and her half-sister Marian Halcombe. Laura is pretty and fair, while Marian is ugly and dark but also strong-minded and intelligent. Walter falls in love with Laura, even though she is to marry Sir Percival Glyde. Anne Catherick, a mysterious woman in white first encountered by Walter on his last night in London, reappears; she has escaped from the mental asylum to which she had been committed by Sir Percival because she and her mother know a discreditable secret about his past. Laura insists on going ahead with the marriage, and Walter leaves.

Determined to gain control of Laura's wealth, the baronet enlists the help of Count Fosco, a fat, suave and sinister Italian. Exploiting the resemblance between Laura and Anne Catherick, who has died, they bury Anne under Laura's name and commit Laura to an asylum as Anne. Marian helps her escape and is joined by Walter. They discover that Sir Percival's secret is his illegitimacy; he burns the parish registry containing the evidence and is killed in the resulting fire. Walter confronts Count Fosco, forcing him to admit his part in the conspiracy and so restore Laura to her true identity. The Count dies at the hand of the Italian secret societies he has betrayed, and Laura and Walter marry.

The novel shows Collins at the height of his powers. The careful plotting and manipulation of suspense are matched by his skill in creating atmosphere (notably in the scene where Walter first meets the woman in white) and his sharp eye for characterization. If he gives the reader a conventional heroine in Laura and a conventional villain in Sir Percival, he also offers, in Marian Halcombe and Count Fosco, the most interesting and evenly matched heroine and villain in the Victorian SENSATION NOVEL.

Woman Killed with Kindness, A A domestic tragedy by THOMAS HEYWOOD, first performed in 1603. It has claims to be considered, alongside *ARDEN OF FEVERSHAM*, as an early masterpiece of the form.

The main plot concerns the marriage of a country gentleman, John Frankford, to an exemplary wife, Anne Acton. Frankford's domestic peace is ruined for ever when he finds Anne in the arms of their guest Wendoll. He punishes her by sending her to live in comfort in a lonely house, barred from the sight of their children or himself. Living at ease but sick with remorse, Anne receives Frankford's forgiveness on her death-bed.

Woman of No Importance, A A play by OSCAR WILDE (1893). The illegitimate Gerald is torn between his father, Lord Illingworth, and his long-suffering mother, Mrs Arbuthnot. She refuses Lord Illingworth's proposal of marriage, which has come 20 years too late. Lord Illingworth betrays his baseness by attempting to kiss a young American heiress, in love with Gerald. Gerald is able to secure his future by marrying her.

Women Beware Women A tragedy by THOMAS MIDDLETON, perhaps dating from as late as 1625. Like most of Middleton's plays, it has a complex plot and finely drawn characters, but it moves, in its climax of demented vengeance, towards a kind of black farce.

Bianca, daughter of a noble house, marries Leantio, a merchant's clerk, but soon tires of living in reduced circumstances and becomes the mistress of the Duke of Florence. Livia, who plays bawd to the adulterers, is a monster of cynical depravity, also instrumental in furthering the incestuous lust of her brother Hippolito for their niece Isabella. When the cardinal, brother to the Duke of Florence, upbraids the duke for his adultery, Leantio becomes an obstacle to their passion. The duke decides to have him killed, and the scheme is made easier when he discovers that Livia has become Leantio's lover. The outraged Hippolito kills Leantio and Livia takes her revenge initially by denouncing Hippolito's incestuous lust. But the climax of the various revenges is reached during a masque in the final act. Lethal incense, poisoned arrows, fatal trapdoors and tainted gold are used to kill off the victims of their own depravity.

Women in Love A novel by D. H. LAWRENCE, first published in 1920.

Ursula and Gudrun Brangwen, from *THE RAINBOW*, are central characters in what is not strictly a sequel but rather a continuation of Lawrence's inquiry into the possibilities that human relationships hold amid the unpromising circumstances of modern industrial culture. At the beginning of the novel, the sisters have returned to teach at the grammar school in Beldover but are frustrated by the limitations of their environment. Ursula falls in love with Rupert Birkin, the school inspector, and Gudrun, an artist, is attracted to his friend, Gerald Crich, son of the local mineowner. Gerald replaces his father's benevolent management of the colliery with a more efficient but inhuman system. He has been haunted by feelings of guilt since the accidental death of his brother when they were children. These feelings are compounded when his sister, Diana, drowns during a water-party given by the Crich family. Birkin and Gerald experience both attraction and repulsion in their respective relationships with the Brangwen sisters, and are also drawn towards each other. Gerald, however, rejects Birkin's attempt to establish a closer intimacy between them.

He pursues his passionate and ultimately destructive relationship with Gudrun.

Ursula and Birkin marry. All four travel abroad, and at Innsbruck, after Birkin and Ursula have departed for Verona, Gudrun flirts with a decadent German sculptor, Loerke. Gerald attacks them before wandering off to die alone in the snow. Birkin grieves for Gerald and attempts to explain to a sceptical Ursula his vision of a male love to complement his love for her. The minor characters include a portrait of LADY OTTOLINE MORRELL as the neurotic Hermione Roddice.

Wonder-Working Providence of Sion's Saviour in New-England, The: *A History of New-England, from the English Planting of the Year 1628 until the Year 1652* A treatise by EDWARD JOHNSON, published anonymously in 1653. The work divides into three books and catalogues instances of divine intervention in New England's history which, Johnson argues, indicate God's approval of the New England Way. Book I (1628–37) considers the conditions in England which compelled removal to America, the journey across the Atlantic, and the settlement of towns and congregations. Book II (1637–45) and Book III (1645–51) portray the Puritans coping with those incidents – the Antinomian affair and the Pequot War, for example – which most seriously threatened the colony's existence.

Wongar, Banumbir [Bozic, Streten] 1936– Novelist. Streten Bozic was born in Yugoslavia, emigrated to Australia in 1960 and has lived with Aborigines in the Northern Territory, taking the Aboriginal name Banumbir Wongar ('messenger from the spirit world'). Described by his publisher as an Aborigine educated abroad, he is an elusive figure whose true identity was tracked down by ROBERT DREWE in 1981. His novels evoke Aboriginal culture and its bitter dilemma in the face of a still hostile society. They include: *The Trackers* (1978); *Walg* (1983), *Karan* (1985) and *Gabo Djara* (1987), making up *The Nuclear Trilogy*; *The Last Pack of Dingoes* (1992); and *Marngit* (1993). He has also published several volumes of stories, *The Sinners* (1972), *The Track to Bralgu* (1978) and *Babaru* (1982), and a collection, *Aboriginal Myths* (with Alan Marshall; 1972).

Wood, Anthony à 1632–95 Antiquary and diarist. Anthony Wood (he archaized his name in later life) was born in Oxford, attending New College School (1641–4) and Lord Williams's School at Thame (1644–6) before entering Merton College in 1647. He lived in Oxford all his life, though he never became a Fellow of his college, dying in the same house where he had been born.

The Antiquities of Warwickshire by SIR WILLIAM DUGDALE first aroused Wood's antiquarian interests, and he made collections for a similar book on Oxfordshire. Most of this work remained unpublished in his lifetime, but Dr John Fell saw that Wood's papers dealing with the University of Oxford went into print as *Historia et antiquitates universitatis oxoniensis* (1674). Wood made an English version, *The History and Antiquities of the University of Oxford*, which John Gutch prepared for publication in 1791–6. In the biographical sections of his *History* and in the later *Athenae oxonienses* (1691–2) – lives of illustrious Oxonians – Wood received the invaluable help of JOHN AUBREY, whom he later treated with ingratitude. In 1693 the *Athenae* was judged to contain a libel against CLARENDON. The relevant pages were publicly burned and the guilty Wood was expelled from the university, blaming Aubrey for misinformation.

Besides his antiquarian collections, Wood left an autobiography and a remarkable diary for the years 1657–95, fully edited by Andrew Clark and published in five volumes as *The Life and Times of Anthony Wood... As Described by Himself* (1891–1900).

Wood, Charles (Gerald) 1933– Playwright. Born into a theatrical family, he served as a trooper in the Lancers from 1950 to 1955. His three short plays about the army, produced as *Cockade* in 1963, revealed his gift for terse, vivid dialogue and bitter SATIRE. He has written attacks on militarism, British imperialism and the class system embodied in the army. *Dingo* (1967), set in North Africa during World War II, and *H: Being Monologues in Front of Burning Cities* (1969), about General Havelock and the Indian Mutiny, are epic tirades against the follies and hypocrisies of war. In lighter vein, he has written comedies: *Fill the Stage with Happy Hours* (1966), about a run-down repertory theatre; *Meals on Wheels* (1965), about the Welfare State; and *Veterans* (1972), *Has 'Washington' Legs?* (1978) and *Across from the Garden of Allah* (1986), about Hollywood. His work for television includes the controversial *Tumbledown* (1988), about the treatment of an officer wounded in the Falklands War

Wood, Mrs Henry (Ellen) 1814–87 Novelist. The daughter of a wealthy glove-manufacturer in Worcester, she spent 20 years living in France after her marriage at the age of 22. She started publishing magazine short stories in 1855 and won a prize offered for a temperance novel with *Danesbury House* (1860), written in a month. The mixture of sentiment, MELODRAMA and piety in her second novel, *EAST LYNNE* (1861), made it a worldwide success. Its many successors included *Mrs Halliburton's Troubles* (1862), *The Channings* (1862), *Verner's Pride* (1862–3) and *Roland Yorke* (1869). She considered *The Shadow of Ashlydat* (1863) her best novel. Much of her work was serialized in *The Argosy*, a journal she bought in 1867 and edited thereafter. A memoir by her son appeared in 1894.

Woodfall, Henry Sampson See JUNIUS and *PUBLIC ADVERTISER, THE*.

Woodforde, James 1740–1803 Diarist. His father was rector of Ansford and vicar of Castle Cary, Somerset. Educated at Winchester and New College, Oxford, Woodforde held several curacies in Somerset, including those of his father's parishes. In 1776 he moved to Weston Longville, Norfolk, and remained there as rector until his death.

His diary begins in 1758, when he was an undergraduate, and continues for 45 years. Public events are mentioned briefly but Woodforde concentrates on the daily minutiae of domestic and parish life: meals, cricket matches, charities ('To a poor old Man that plays on the Dulcimer gave 0.0.6'), a glimpse of the Royal Family at Lord Digby's park in Sherborne, Dorset, hare-coursing, gains and losses at games of whist and quadrille, bastard children, household remedies, the payment of five shillings for black 'ribband' to prevent sore throats. The diaries reflect no intellectual interests, merely the surface of everyday life: 'I wore my largest gouty Shoes to Church today.' The eccentricities of grammar and spelling add piquancy to this trivial fond record of life in the second half of the 18th century, a rural life when news of the great world often took ten days to arrive.

Woodlanders, The A novel by THOMAS HARDY, first published serially in *Macmillan's Magazine* from May 1886 to April 1887 and in book form in 1887.

Socially ambitious for his daughter Grace, whom he has educated above her class, the timber merchant George Melbury regrets committing her to the rustic Giles Winterbourne, and uses Winterbourne's financial and legal misfortunes as an excuse to end their relationship. Dr Edred Fitzpiers, scion of a once-prominent local family, expresses an interest in marrying Grace. She, knowing of Fitzpiers's dalliance with a local hoyden, Suke Damson, is not enthusiastic, but her father insists and the marriage takes place. Fitzpiers forms a liaison with Felice Charmond, who has returned from abroad to Hintock Manor House, and Melbury assaults him. Fitzpiers takes refuge with Mrs Charmond and they go to the Continent where, after a foolish quarrel, their association comes to an end. It is on the Continent, too, that the shadowy figure of the 'gentleman from South Carolina' appears and kills Mrs Charmond in a jealous rage. Fitzpiers returns to England. Grace, meanwhile, supported by her father's vain hope that she can obtain a divorce, encourages Giles and is forced to seek shelter at his cottage in bad weather. Out of propriety he takes to a hopelessly inadequate outdoor retreat of hay and hurdles; already weakened by a previous illness, he dies of exposure. Grace is reunited with Fitzpiers, and the faithful Marty South, an outdoor worker deeply in love with Giles, is left to mourn

him with the poignant elegy: 'But no, no, my love, I never can forget 'ee; for you was a good man, and did good things!'

Woodstock: or, The Cavalier. A Tale of the Year 1651 A novel by SIR WALTER SCOTT, published in 1826. It marks the beginning of Scott's unremitting labours to clear the huge debts which came as the result of improvident spending and his financial connection with James Ballantyne.

Sir Henry Lee, the old Cavalier, is ranger at Woodstock, the royal lodge. His daughter Alice loves her cousin Everard, but Lee disdains him because Everard serves Cromwell and has earned his favour. When Parliamentary commissioners come to seize Woodstock, however, Everard intervenes. They withdraw, but this is at Cromwell's orders. He knows Woodstock's royal connections and has it watched in the hope that Prince Charles, after his defeat at Worcester, will take refuge there.

Charles does arrive, as page to Albert, Alice's brother; he falls in love with Alice and this brings a clash with Everard, whereupon Charles reveals his identity. Everard gives his word not to betray Charles but Cromwell, informed of his presence, arrives with a force and surrounds the house. He orders the arrest of Everard. Albert Lee impersonates Charles, giving him a chance to escape. The furious Cromwell orders the execution of Everard and the Lees, but later relents and pardons them. Charles has left a parting message with his loyal friends at Woodstock, and this reconciles Sir Henry and Everard, who is now able to marry Alice.

Woodworth, Samuel 1785–1842 American poet and playwright. He was born in Massachusetts. Much of his poetry appeared in *Melodies, Duets, Songs, and Ballads* (1826). He published one novel, *The Champions of Freedom* (1816), a romance set during the war of 1812. His plays include a MELODRAMA, *Lafayette* (1824), a domestic tragedy of the Revolutionary period entitled *The Widow's Son* (1825) and a comedy, *The Forest Rose: or, American Farmers*, which presents the typical Yankee character, Jonathan Ploughboy.

Woolf, Leonard (Sidney) 1880–1969 Author and social reformer. Born in London, he was educated at St Paul's and Trinity College, Cambridge, where he became a member of the APOSTLES and was profoundly influenced by the teachings of the philosopher G. E. MOORE. He entered the Ceylon Civil Service in 1904 and served until 1911. On his return to England he wrote for various political journals and became an active member of the Fabian Society. He married Virginia Stephen (see VIRGINIA WOOLF) in 1912 and published his first novel, *The Village in the Jungle*, about life in Ceylon, in 1913. *The Wise Virgins*

(1914), his only other novel, and *Stones of the East* (1916) were also set in Ceylon.

Leonard and Virginia Woolf founded the Hogarth Press in 1917, and during the 1920s and 30s their Richmond house and later 52 Tavistock Square, London, remained a focus for the BLOOMSBURY GROUP. His own publications continued with works on politics and international affairs, among them *Economic Imperialism* (1920), *Imperialism and Civilization* (1928), *After the Deluge* (2 vols., 1931 and 1939), and *Principia politica* (1953). He was literary editor of *The Nation* from 1923 to 1930, and helped found *The Political Quarterly* (1931–59). His five volumes of autobiography are highly regarded for their literary qualities and for their portraits of notable figures: *Sowing* (1960), *Growing* (1961), *Beginning Again* (1964), *Downhill All the Way* (1967) and *The Journey Not the Arrival Matters* (1969).

Woolf, (Adeline) Virginia 1882–1941 Novelist. She was born Virginia Stephen, the daughter of SIR LESLIE STEPHEN by his second wife, Julia Duckworth. The family lived at Hyde Park Gate, London, and she was educated at home. After her father's death in 1904, she moved to 46 Gordon Square, Bloomsbury, with her sister Vanessa (later the wife of CLIVE BELL) and her brothers Thoby and Adrian. The house was to be the original meeting-place of the BLOOMSBURY GROUP. When Thoby died of typhoid fever in 1906, she suffered a prolonged mental breakdown; throughout her life she was subject to nervous illness.

In 1912 she married LEONARD WOOLF, and completed her first novel, *THE VOYAGE OUT*, the following year, though another breakdown delayed its publication until 1915. She and Leonard founded the Hogarth Press, working on a hand press installed in their home at Hogarth House, Richmond. They began by publishing *Two Stories* in 1917 ('The Mark on the Wall' by Virginia, and 'Three Jews' by Leonard); KATHERINE MANSFIELD's *Prelude* (1918) and T. S. ELIOT's *Poems* (1919) followed and they were established publishers by the time they printed Eliot's *THE WASTE LAND* in 1923.

Virginia Woolf's career continued with *Night and Day* (1919), a realistic novel set in London, which contrasted the lives of two friends: Katherine, the daughter of a famous literary family, and Mary, who becomes involved with the suffragette movement. *JACOB'S ROOM* (1922) was based upon the life and death of her brother, Thoby, and broke away from the realistic mode of her early writing. Like *MRS DALLOWAY* (1925) it fulfilled the purposes of fiction laid down in her essay 'Modern Fiction' (1919): 'Life is not a series of gig-lamps symmetrically arranged; life is a luminous halo, a semi-transparent envelope surrounding us from the beginning of consciousness to the end. Is it not the task of the novelist to convey this... with as little mixture of the alien and external

as possible?' With *TO THE LIGHTHOUSE* (1927) and *THE WAVES* (1931) she fully established herself as a leading exponent of MODERNISM.

ORLANDO (1928), a fantastic biography which traces the history of its androgynous protagonist through four centuries, is unlike any of her other novels and was her greatest commercial success. It was dedicated to VITA SACKVILLE-WEST, with whom the author had an intimate friendship. Another 'biography', *Flush* (1933), revolves around the life of ELIZABETH BARRETT BROWNING's pet spaniel and gives a dog's-eye view of the love affair between his mistress and ROBERT BROWNING.

THE YEARS (1937) was more conventional in form, but her last novel, *BETWEEN THE ACTS*, published posthumously in 1941, returned to the experimental and was completed just before the final attack of mental illness which drove her to suicide. In March 1941 she filled her pockets with stones and drowned herself in the River Ouse near her home at Rodmell in Sussex. Virginia Woolf is now generally acknowledged as one of the major innovative novelists of the 20th century, best known, perhaps, for her use of STREAM OF CONSCIOUSNESS. Her contribution to FEMINIST CRITICISM has been widely recognized: *A ROOM OF ONE'S OWN* (1929) and its still more radical sequel, *Three Guineas* (1938), are now established classics. Her critical works, which began when she became a reviewer for *THE TIMES LITERARY SUPPLEMENT* in 1905 (a connection lasting until just before her death), included several collections of essays, notably *The Common Reader* (1925) and *The Second Common Reader* (1932). They were reprinted in *Collected Essays of Virginia Woolf* (4 vols., 1966–7). Her letters, edited by Nigel Nicolson and J. Trautmann in six volumes (1975–80), include correspondence with nearly everyone associated with the Bloomsbury Group. Her diaries, edited in five volumes by Anne Olivier Bell and A. McNeillie (1977–84), give an invaluable picture of her creative method.

Woolson, Constance (Fenimore) 1840–94 American novelist. Born in Claremont, New Hampshire, she lived in various parts of the USA and used her wide knowledge of the country in her writings. *Castle Nowhere: Lake-Country Sketches* (1875) tells of the French settlers in the Great Lakes region. *Rodman the Keeper: Southern Sketches* (1880) contrasts the life of the Old South with the South during Reconstruction. *Anna* (1882) tells of a Mackinac Island (Michigan) girl in New York. *For the Major* (1883) is the story of a North Carolina woman helping to preserve her husband's illusions about the South. *East Angels* (1886) is set in Florida; *Jupiter Lights* (1889) portrays two sisters-in-law in conflict, one representing the North and the other the South. Her last novel, *Horace Chase* (1894), is a domestic drama about a woman who despises her self-made husband but discovers, almost

Virginia Woolf

too late, his sterling character. *Dorothy, and Other Italian Stories* (1896), her last book, is about Americans in Europe. HENRY JAMES portrayed her in *THE ASPERN PAPERS.*

Worde, Wynkyn de d. ?1534 Printer. He was born Jan van Wynkyn in Worth, Alsace, hence the name by which he is usually known (i. e. Wynkyn from Worth). He arrived in London *c.* 1476 and became apprentice and assistant to WILLIAM CAXTON, inheriting Caxton's press and materials on the latter's death in 1491. Unlike Caxton, he contented himself with printing and did not make forays into translation and editing. Many important books came from his press in

Westminster: editions of *The Golden Legend* of Jacobus de Voragine (1493), Caxton's translations of St Jerome's *Vitae patrum* (1495), MALORY'S *MORTE DARTHUR* (1498) and CHAUCER'S *CANTERBURY TALES* (1498). In about 1500 he moved to Fleet Street and after that time printed some 600 books, mainly those likely to have a popular appeal, such as small service books (e.g. the *Sarum Hours*), grammar books and some popular romances. He was the first English printer to use italic type, in 1524.

Wordsworth, Dorothy 1771–1855 Sister of WILLIAM WORDSWORTH and author of journals. Born a year and a half after William at Cockermouth,

Cumberland, Dorothy spent her later childhood, after her parents' early death, with various relatives in Halifax, Penrith and Norfolk. The bond between her and William was exceptionally strong, and when he was left a legacy by his friend Raisley Calvert in 1795, they were able to realize a long-cherished plan of setting up house together, settling first at Racedown in Dorset, and then in the Quantocks at Alfoxden, Somerset, in order to be close to COLERIDGE at Nether Stowey. They were to remain inseparable through William's marriage until his death in 1850.

Dorothy's *Alfoxden Journal*, of which only the entries for the months January–April 1798 have survived, is remarkable not only for the light it sheds on William and his friendship and collaboration with Coleridge in the *annus mirabilis* of the LYRICAL BALLADS, but also for its powerfully poetic quality as descriptive prose. Although she had no thought of professional authorship, and committed to paper her thoughts, impressions and responses to nature simply to 'give William pleasure by it', it is clear that the imaginative economy of her writing was an important source of stimulation to Wordsworth and Coleridge in the composition of individual poems. This is equally true of the *Grasmere Journals* for 1800–3, upon which William frequently drew for themes, motifs and images, most famously in the poem 'I Wandered Lonely As a Cloud', whose daffodils are first observed by Dorothy as they 'tossed and reeled and danced and seemed as if they verily laughed with the wind that blew upon them over the lake, they looked so gay ever glancing ever changing'.

In the winter of 1798–9 she accompanied the friends to Germany, and in December 1799 she and William moved to Dove Cottage, Grasmere, where she continued to stay after his marriage (1802), participating as a matter of course in subsequent family moves to Allan Bank and Rydal Mount. She was with William on countless walking tours, excursions and foreign travels, on which she kept journals which remained unpublished until after her death. The German sojourn is briefly captured in her *Visit to Hamburgh and a Journey to... Goslar 1798–99*, and in 1805 she finished *Recollections of a Tour made in Scotland 1803*. Her strikingly lively accounts of *An Excursion on the Banks of Ullswater 1805* and *An Excursion to Scawfell Pike 1818* were used by Wordsworth in his *Guide to the Lakes* (1825). *The Journal of a Tour on the Continent 1820* is remarkable for its deeply emotional passages on the Swiss landscape and its vivid portrait of Wordsworth in middle age. A *Journal of a Second Tour in Scotland* followed in 1822, and a *Journal of a Tour in the Isle of Man* in 1828. The unusual quality of Dorothy's personality left a deep impression on everyone who knew her. To Coleridge she was Wordsworth's 'exquisite sister... simple, ardent, innocent... her eye watchful in minutest observation of nature'; DE QUINCEY considered her

'the most... natural person I have ever known... quickest in sympathy with joy and sorrow', and Wordsworth himself pays tribute to her beneficent influence upon his life and work in numerous poems. In 1829 she became seriously ill and was henceforth an invalid. From 1835 she developed arteriosclerosis, and apart from brief periods of remission her mind was clouded for the remaining 20 years of her life.

Wordsworth, William 1770–1850 Poet. He was born at Cockermouth, Cumberland, the third of the five children of John Wordsworth, attorney to Sir James Lowther (later Earl of Lonsdale). He was educated at primary schools in Cockermouth and Penrith, and from 1779 to 1787 at the grammar school in Hawkshead, where he lived in lodgings. The children lost their mother when William was eight, and their father five years later, and were placed under the guardianship of uncles. Lowther's failure to pay large debts owing to his former employee left the orphans only modestly provided for, and new domestic arrangements caused William to be separated from his beloved sister, DOROTHY WORDSWORTH. His first published poem, a sonnet 'On Seeing Miss HELEN MARIA WILLIAMS Weep at a Tale of Distress', and signed 'Axiologus', appeared in *The European Magazine* for March 1787.

In October of that year he entered St John's College, Cambridge, where he was unsettled by the unfamiliar climate of worldliness and intellectual sophistication and read largely outside the curriculum, gradually shedding his awe of 'printed books and authorship'. The summer and autumn of 1790 were spent on a walking tour in France, Switzerland and Germany which is commemorated in *Descriptive Sketches* (composed 1792). At Cambridge he took an ordinary BA degree in January 1791, then spent some months in London and North Wales, before returning to France at the end of the year, where he stayed at Blois and Orléans, with occasional visits to Paris. This year in Revolutionary France was one of the most important periods of his life. His friendship with Michel de Beaupuy, an aristocratic supporter of the Revolution, and later general in the Republican army, inspired a deep and passionate faith in the Revolution, and he fell in love with Annette Vallon, the daughter of a surgeon at Blois, by whom he had a daughter (Caroline, born in December 1792). Their affair is the basis of the poem *Vaudracour and Julia*, first published in 1820. Wordsworth entertained ideas of offering his services to the Girondist faction of the Revolution in Paris, and of marrying Annette, but he ran out of money and his uncles refused to fund further residence abroad. Bowing to 'harsh necessity' he returned to England in December 1792. In January 1793 he made his debut as an author with 'An Evening Walk' and *Descriptive Sketches*, brought out by the radical publisher Joseph Johnson. He also wrote (but did not publish) a 'Letter

William Wordsworth: a drawing by Daniel Maclise for *Fraser's Magazine*

to the Bishop of Llandaff' criticizing his anti-Revolutionary sermon on 'The Wisdom and Goodness of God in having made both Rich and Poor', and identifying himself with the ideas laid down by PAINE in the recently published *RIGHTS OF MAN*.

The period 1793–5 was one of great personal unhappiness, uncertainty about his professional future, and moral and intellectual confusion, towards the end of which he seems to have been close to nervous breakdown. Despite dismay at the drift of the Revolution into the political terror of the Jacobin dictatorship, he held fast to his belief in the French experiment as the future model for all European countries, but England's declaration of war against France in February 1793 left him grievously divided in his national loyalties, and was effectively to separate him for good from Annette and his child. He fell briefly under the spell of GODWIN's *ENQUIRY CONCERNING POLITICAL JUSTICE*, but was soon repelled by its extreme rationalism. In the summer of 1793 he undertook a walking tour from Salisbury to North Wales, during which he first visited Tintern Abbey. Most of the first version of 'Salisbury Plain' (later 'Guilt and Sorrow'), published in part as 'The Female Vagrant' in the *LYRICAL BALLADS* of 1798, was written at this time. He probably visited Paris in late September and early October, where he witnessed the execution of Gorsas, the first Girondist to be guillotined. His Revolutionary sympathies continued undaunted, however, and his joy at hearing the news of the death of Robespierre in August 1794 was accompanied by the expectation that the 'golden time' would now really come. He was not finally to become disenchanted with France until her occupation of Switzerland in 1798.

Wordsworth's precarious financial circumstances changed for the better in 1795, when his Penrith friend Raisley Calvert died, leaving him a legacy of

£900. He was now in a position to follow his vocation as a poet, and to realize his long-cherished dream of setting up house with Dorothy, with whom he had been reunited in 1794. Taking charge of the small son of their widower friend, Basil Montagu, they settled first at Racedown in Dorset, where Wordsworth wrote the first version of 'The Ruined Cottage' and his only play, the BLANK-VERSE tragedy *The Borderers*, and then at the fine manor house at Alfoxden in Somerset, in order to be near to their exciting new friend, SAMUEL TAYLOR COLERIDGE, who was living at Nether Stowey. Wordsworth probably first met Coleridge, along with ROBERT SOUTHEY and the publisher Joseph Cottle, during a stay at Bristol in 1795. Encouraged and in many ways inspired by Dorothy, whose influence upon Coleridge was almost as strong as her influence upon her brother, both poets entered a period of intense creativity which produced the *Lyrical Ballads* (1798), a collection which inaugurated the Romantic epoch of English poetry. Largely in deference to Coleridge's desire to complete his philosophical education, the trio travelled to Germany in the autumn of 1798, splitting up to allow Coleridge to proceed to the University of Göttingen, while Dorothy and William entered winter quarters in the remote little town of Goslar. It was here that Wordsworth wrote the enigmatic 'Lucy' poems.

On their return to England in May 1799, the Wordsworths stayed at Sockburn-on-Tees, before moving into Dove Cottage, Grasmere, in December. In the next year Wordsworth completed Book I of 'The Recluse' (later *THE EXCURSION*) and wrote many of the poems included in the second edition of *Lyrical Ballads* (1800), as well as the controversial new Preface which became the aesthetic manifesto of conservative ROMANTICISM. On the death of Lord Lonsdale in 1802 his financial situation was substantially improved by the payment to the family of money owed to John Wordsworth. During the short-lived Peace of Amiens William travelled with Dorothy to France to visit Annette Vallon and his daughter, and in the same year married Mary Hutchinson, with whom he had been friendly since childhood. It was agreed that Dorothy should retain her membership of the household. This was also the year in which he composed 'Resolution and Independence' and parts of his ODE 'Intimations of Immortality from Recollections of Early Childhood', both of which appeared in *Poems in Two Volumes* (1807), along with other later work such as the 'Ode to Duty', 'Miscellaneous Sonnets' and 'Sonnets Dedicated to Liberty'. His son John, the first of five children by Mary, was born in 1803.

Wordsworth's life was now relatively uneventful, though the completion of the second, 13-book version of *THE PRELUDE*, his poetic autobiography, in 1805 showed him at the height of his creative powers. He had begun the poem in Germany in 1798 and completed a two-book version the following year. He would return again to it in later years, putting aside a 14-book version in 1839. It appeared posthumously in 1850. The head of an unswervingly devoted household, he maintained an unperturbed confidence in his fame despite sharp attacks in the literary press. New friends included SIR WALTER SCOTT, Sir George Beaumont, and the young DE QUINCEY, who wrote to him in tones bordering on hero-worship. His married life was contented, but the loss of his brother John at sea in February 1805 came as a cruel blow, and the Wordsworths' middle years were saddened by the deaths of two of their children in 1812. His estrangement from Coleridge in 1810 was a further disappointment for Wordsworth. A kind of reconciliation took place in 1812, but the old intimacy was never restored. In 1813 he was appointed to the sinecure of Distributor of Stamps for Westmorland, which carried the substantial salary of £400 a year, and moved from Allan Bank (where he had lived since 1808) to Rydal Mount, Ambleside, where he remained for the rest of his life. *The Excursion* was published in 1814, *The White Doe of Rylstone* in 1815, and *Poems, Including Lyrical Ballads* in 1815 – the first of many collected editions of old and new poetical work, frequently revised and reclassified, to appear over the next 35 years. *Peter Bell: A Tale in Verse* (composed 1798) and *The Waggoner* (composed 1805) were both published in 1819.

Arriving at Rydal Mount to pay his respects to the great poet in 1818, KEATS was dismayed to discover that Wordsworth was busy campaigning for the Tory Lord Lonsdale in the general election. He was indeed now a long way from the cosmopolitan radicalism of his youth, and the openly reactionary politics and priestly patriotism of his middle age increasingly became a bone of contention between him and the second generation of Romantic poets, who were nonetheless lastingly indebted to the great innovations of his poetry. Yet his poetic powers too began to decline as he neared 50, and the work of his later years is the inspiration of a less demanding muse. Much of the best of it commemorates his travels: *The River Duddon: A Series of Sonnets* was published in 1820, and a volume of poems entitled *Memorials of a Tour on the Continent* in 1822. In 1828 he toured the Rhineland with his daughter Dora, and Coleridge, and in 1831 stayed with Sir Walter Scott at Abbotsford, on the way to the Highlands. *Yarrow Revisited and Other Poems* was published in 1835. He was honoured by the Universities of Durham (1838) and Oxford (1839), and in 1842 received a Civil List pension of £300 a year. In 1843 he succeeded Southey as POET LAUREATE. His prose works include *The Convention of Cintra* (1809), an essay criticizing the agreement of Britain and Portugal to allow the beaten French army to return home during the Peninsular War; an 'Essay on Epitaphs', published in Coleridge's journal *The Friend* (1810); a guidebook to the Lake

District, originally designed as an introduction to Joseph Wilkinson's *Select Views of Cumberland* (1810) but later expanded and published separately, notably in an edition of 1835; and two famous public letters opposing the Kendal and Windermere railway (1845).

Workers in the Dawn The first novel by GEORGE GISSING, published in 1880. Naturalist in method, it is about rich and poor, degradation, drink, destitution and the effects of heredity. Two solutions are proposed: revolution, which the author rejects as leading to incendiary madness, and education, which he endorses. But to educate the masses is seen as a hard struggle: the noble Helen, who has embraced the doctrines of 'Schopenhauer, Comte and SHELLEY', wears herself out giving free lessons in adult literacy and dies of inherited consumption. Arthur, in love with Helen, carelessly marries Carrie, a woman of low morals who resists his efforts to get her to speak correctly and learn to spell. Though gifted, Arthur suffers from inherited instability, which leads to his defeat by misfortune, despite his ability and heroic struggles. Although the minor characters are predictable (Whiffle the wastrel, Maud the heartless socialite), Helen and Arthur hold our interest. The descriptions of squalor are memorable.

Wotton, Sir **Henry** 1568–1639 Poet and diplomat. A Kentish man, Wotton was educated at Winchester and then at New College and The Queen's College, Oxford, before entering the Middle Temple. In 1595 he was engaged by the Earl of Essex as agent and secretary, collecting foreign intelligence. He was later appointed ambassador to Venice and worked as a diplomat until 1624, when he became Provost of Eton.

The only work published during his lifetime was *The Elements of Architecture* (1624). His poems and miscellaneous writings were collected as *Reliquiae Wottonianae* in 1651, and later enlarged. Among them were three poems that became favourite anthology pieces: 'Elizabeth of Bohemia', 'The Character of a Happy Life' and 'Upon the Sudden Restraint of the Earl of Somerset'. Wotton planned to write a life of his friend JOHN DONNE but the task devolved on their mutual friend IZAAK WALTON, who contributed a memoir of Wotton to the *Reliquiae*. Wotton's definition of an ambassador is famous: 'An Ambassador is an honest man, sent to lie abroad for the good of his country.'

Wouk, Herman 1915– American novelist. He was born in New York and educated at Columbia University. His literary reputation chiefly depends on *The Caine Mutiny* (PULITZER PRIZE, 1951), a graphic tale of mutiny on a US destroyer in the Pacific during World War II. Later novels, usually long and tending towards melodrama, have included *Marjorie Morningstar* (1955), *Youngblood Hawke* (1962), *Don't Stop the Carnival* (1965), *The Winds of War* (1971) and *War and Remembrance* (1978), made into a TV mini-series, and *Inside, Outside* (1985).

Wren, P(ercival) (Christopher) 1885–1941 Novelist. He was born in Devon and educated at Oxford. He then travelled the world, working as a schoolmaster, journalist, explorer and farmhand, serving in a British cavalry regiment and the French Foreign Legion, and living in India. During World War I he was an officer with the Indian forces in East Africa. From these varied experiences he drew inspiration for his many popular novels of romance and adventure, which reflect his belief in the values of the British Empire. His most famous book, *Beau Geste* (1924), dealt with the Foreign Legion; it was followed by more stories about the three Geste brothers, *Beau Sabreur* (1926), *Beau Ideal* (1928) and *Good Gestes* (1929). Other titles include *Dew and Mildew* (1912), *The Wages of Virtue* (1916), *Valiant Dust* (1932), *Sinbad the Sailor* (1935), *Rough Shooting* (1938) and *The Uniform of Glory* (1941).

Wright, Charles 1935– American poet. He was born in Pickwick Dam, Tennessee, and educated at Davidson College, North Carolina, and the University of Iowa. He served with US Army Intelligence in Verona in 1957–63 and went on to the University of Rome before returning to take up an appointment at the University of California at Irvine. Since 1983 he has been a professor of English at the University of Virginia. His poetry, often compared with that of contemporaries such as MARK STRAND and W. S. MERWIN, is notable for its religious feeling and its use of the landscapes of the American South. Volumes include *Dream Animal* (1968), *Bloodlines* (1973), *Country Music: Selected Early Poems* (1974), *China Trace* (1977), *The Southern Cross* (1981), *Zone Journals* (1988) and *The World of Ten Thousand Things: Selected Poems, 1980–1990* (1990). He has also translated Eugenio Montale in *The Storm and Other Poems* (1978).

Wright, David (Murray) 1920– Poet and anthologist. Born in Johannesburg, he lost his hearing at the age of seven. In 1934 he came to England, where he attended the Northampton School for the Deaf and Keble College, Oxford. He was Gregory Poetry Fellow at the University of Leeds in 1965–7. With the painter Patrick Swift he edited the brilliant but short-lived quarterly *X* in 1959–62; it included contributions from GEORGE BARKER, SAMUEL BECKETT, HUGH MAC-DIARMID, PATRICK KAVANAGH and STEVIE SMITH. His anthologies include *The Faber Book of Twentieth-Century Verse* (with JOHN HEATH-STUBBS; 1953), *Mid-Century: English Poetry 1940-60* (1965), *The Penguin Book of English Romantic Verse* (1968) and *The*

Penguin Book of Everyday Verse (1976). In 1969 he published a remarkable autobiography, *Deafness*, and in 1985 a verse translation of THE CANTERBURY TALES. His volumes of poetry include *Moral Stories* (1954), *Monologue of a Deaf Man* (1958), *Adam at Evening* (1965), *Nerve Ends* (1969), *To the Gods the Shades: New and Selected Poems* (1976) and *Metrical Observations* (1980). His work is distinguished by its sense of the rhythm of ordinary speech, its vivid rendering of appearances and its power to celebrate, giving intimations of a deep-seated romanticism.

Wright, James 1927–80 American poet. Born in Martin's Ferry, Ohio, he was educated at Kenyon College and the University of Washington. He taught at Hunter College in New York from 1966 until his death. Whether writing about nature, politics, social outcasts or his home town, Wright emphasizes the common human element in the subjects of his poems. His language is colloquial and unadorned, and his tone compassionate. He himself said that he wanted his poems to 'say something humanly important instead of just showing off with language'. His first volume, *The Green Wall*, was published in 1957; it was followed by *Saint Judas* (1959), *The Lion's Tail and Eyes* (1962), *This Branch will Not Break* (1963), *Shall We Gather at the River?* (1968), *Collected Poems* (PULITZER PRIZE, 1971), *Two Citizens* (1973), *Moments of the Italian Summer* (1976) and *To a Blossoming Pear Tree* (1977).

Wright, Judith (Arundell) 1915– Australian poet, critic and essayist. She grew up in rural Arundale and was educated at New England Girls' School and Sydney University. Although love of the environment and concern for the Aboriginal community inform much of her work, she helped to ease the 'aggressive regionalism' of preceding Australian literature. *Preoccupations in Australian Poetry* (1965), a seminal critical text, throws light on her own interests and techniques. Her many volumes of verse, beginning with *The Moving Image* (1946), are best represented by *The Double Tree: Selected Poems 1942–1976* (1978) and *The Human Pattern: Selected Poems* (1990). *The Generations of Men* (1959) traces her family history, while *The Cry for the Dead* (1981) deals with the destruction of the Aborigines – also a prominent topic of the essays selected in *Born of the Conquerors* (1991). She has also written a volume of short stories, *The Nature of Love* (1968), several children's books and studies of CHARLES HARPUR (1963) and HENRY LAWSON (1967).

Wright, Richard 1908–60 Black American novelist and social critic. Born near Natchez, Mississippi, he lived in Memphis and Chicago before moving to New York in 1937. *Lawd Today*, a novel he was working on during this period, was published posthumously in 1963. His first published volume was a collection of short stories about Southern racism, ironically entitled *Uncle Tom's Children* (1938, enlarged edition 1940). The novel NATIVE SON (1940), with its memorable portrait of the rebellious Bigger Thomas, brought Wright widespread recognition.

In 1940 he left the USA to live in Mexico, and then in 1946 moved to Paris, where he remained for the rest of his life. His other novels are *The Outsider* (1953), chronicling a black intellectual's search for identity, *Savage Holiday* (1954) and *The Long Dream* (1958). *Eight Men*, published posthumously in 1961, is a collection of short stories, radio plays, a novella, and an autobiography. Wright's non-fictional work includes *Twelve Million Black Voices* (1941), an illustrated folk history of American blacks, and the acclaimed autobiography *Black Boy* (1945). *American Hunger*, a continuation of *Black Boy*, was published posthumously in 1977. He also published three books of social criticism inspired by his travels: *Black Power* (1954), about Africa, *The Color Curtain* (1956), about Asia, and *Pagan Spain* (1957). A collection of lectures on racial injustice, *White Man, Listen!*, appeared in 1957.

Wright, Thomas 1810–77 Antiquary. He was born at Tenbury, Shropshire, and educated at Ludlow and Trinity College, Cambridge. A founding member of the Camden Society (1838) and the Percy Society (1841), he edited many volumes of medieval texts for both societies. His most ambitious project was a biography of literary characters, *Biographia Britannica Literaria*, of which only the first two volumes were completed (1842 and 1846).

Wrightson, (Alice) Patricia 1921– Australian writer of CHILDREN'S LITERATURE. Born in New South Wales and educated largely through correspondence school, she worked in hospital administration before taking up writing. Her best-known novel, *I Own the Racecourse!* (1968), deals sympathetically with the tragicomic delusions of a backward Australian adolescent loyally supported by an understanding group of friends. Since then she has linked her talent for realistic description to an exploration of Aboriginal folk-tales, most notably in *The Nargun and the Stars* (1973).

Wulf and Eadwacer An Old English poem preserved in the EXETER BOOK. It is short and enigmatic, yet poignantly expresses the sorrow of a woman separated from her lover by the enmity of their clans. Apparently she has or will soon have Wulf's child and expects it to be persecuted, but the nature of the events related by the poem is unclear.

Wulfstan d. 1023 Author of Old English HOMILIES, tracts and law codes. He was Bishop of London (996–1002) and Worcester (1002–16) and Archbishop of York (1002–23), but nothing is known of his earlier life. His style is distinctive, enabling his homilies and legal texts to be identified, as well as his entries in a northern redaction of the ANGLO-SAXON CHRONICLE. His main concerns were with problems of political and social organization and church reform. His most famous work, written under the pseudonym Lupus, is *Sermo Lupi ad anglos* (1014); it calls for repentance and reformation after the defeat of Aethelred. He also wrote *The Canons of Edgar* and the *Institutes of Polity* as well as many lesser-known pieces, and contributed to a vernacular version of the Benedictine office.

Wuthering Heights The only novel by EMILY BRONTË, first published in 1847.

The story is told by Lockwood, a gentleman visiting the Yorkshire moors, and Mrs Dean, servant to the Earnshaw family. Heathcliff, a foundling from the streets of Liverpool, is brought to Wuthering Heights by Mr Earnshaw to be treated like his own children, Catherine and Hindley. But after Mr Earnshaw's death Heathcliff is bullied and degraded by Hindley, now married and head of the household. Heathcliff, who is of a passionate and ferocious nature, falls in love with Catherine, who returns his affection even though she feels it would be humiliating to marry him. Upon learning this Heathcliff slips quietly away. Meanwhile Hindley's wife has died, leaving him a son, Hareton. Catherine is attracted to the soft, luxurious life of the Lintons of Thrushcross Grange and marries Edgar Linton.

When Heathcliff returns to Wuthering Heights his vengeful nature begins to assert itself. His first victim is his beloved Catherine, whose death he hastens by incessant and vehement accusations of betrayal, of contempt for himself and of cruelty; she dies giving birth to a girl, another Catherine. A further victim is Edgar's sister Isabella, whom Heathcliff marries and mistreats until she runs away. He also destroys Hindley, a heavy drinker and gambler, and gains control of the Heights. To secure the Linton family property he forces a marriage between young Catherine and Linton, his sickly son by Isabella. When Linton dies the young widow develops an interest in Hareton, Hindley's son, whom Heathcliff has brought up in brutish ignorance. By now Heathcliff, all passion spent, longs for death and union with Catherine. Increasingly alienated from daily life, he experiences visions and supernatural portents of reconciliation with his beloved Catherine. He dies having failed to extirpate the Earnshaws and the Lintons, and leaves to the younger generation, Catherine and Hareton, hopes of a richer life.

The novel's stern power, which disturbed and shocked contemporaries but has impressed later generations of readers, owes much to the deliberately enigmatic portrait of Heathcliff. Hardly less remarkable is the way that the tortuous and violent plot, instead of seeming merely melodramatic, is given solidity by the precisely realized Yorkshire locations and subtlety by the shifting narrative viewpoints.

Wyatt, Sir **Thomas** ?1503–42 Poet. Wyatt was educated at St John's College, Cambridge, and became an important and popular member of the court of Henry VIII. In *c.* 1520 he married Elizabeth Brooke, from whom he separated *c.* 1525, charging her with adultery. He served Henry VIII on a number of missions (to the papal court and Venice in 1527), and in various offices (High Marshal of Calais in 1528–30), and was knighted in 1535. When Anne Boleyn lost the king's favour and was accused of adultery in 1536, Wyatt was arrested and imprisoned in the Tower, possibly on suspicion of being one of her lovers. He was released the same year and, in favour with the king again, was made ambassador to Charles V in 1537. In 1541 he was again arrested and confined to the Tower, this time on accusations of misconduct as ambassador first made against him in 1538 by Bonner, who was now Bishop of London. He wrote a spirited 'Defence' and was pardoned, perhaps at the request of Queen Catherine Howard. He died suddenly at Sherborne, Dorset, on his way abroad on another diplomatic mission. His son and namesake was executed for his rebellion against Mary I in 1554.

None of Wyatt's poems appeared in print in his lifetime and his first published work was *Certain Psalms... Drawn into English Metre* (1549), a version of the penitential psalms from a prose paraphrase by Aretino. More of his poetry, lyrics and satires appeared in TOTTEL'S MISCELLANY (1557); the rest remained in manuscript until the 19th and 20th centuries. With SURREY, he was the first to domesticate the SONNET into English, providing it with its characteristic final rhyming couplet. His versions of Petrarch show an extraordinary facility in the difficult task of imitation in another language: 'I Find No Peace' is a remarkably close rendering of Petrarch's '*Pace non trovo*'. Wyatt's most famous sonnet, 'Whoso List to Hunt', imitates and transforms Petrarch's '*Una candida cerva*' to produce a sonnet radically different in tone from its original. (It has sometimes been seen as containing covert allusions to Anne Boleyn, the hind with her diamond collar inscribed '*Noli me tangere* [do not touch me], for Caesar's I am'.) Wyatt was also successful in his handling of such new forms in English as the RONDEAU and the TERZA RIMA. With their song-like refrains, his poems also continued native traditions of the English lyric. Some, especially those referring to the poet's lute (e. g. 'My Lute Awake' and 'Blame Not My Lute'), may have been sung by Wyatt himself to a courtly audience. One of Wyatt's best and most famous poems, 'They Flee from Me', shows his ability to combine native traditions and classical influence.

Wycherley, William 1640–1716 Playwright. Born at Clive, near Shrewsbury, Wycherley was sent to France by his prosperous family in 1655–60. There he became a Catholic, absorbed French literary culture and developed the social ambitions and financial greed that tarnished much of his later life. He was briefly at Oxford in 1660 and then at the Inner Temple, but he pursued fashion rather than the law, associating with such Restoration wits as the EARL OF ROCHESTER, SIR GEORGE ETHEREGE and SIR CHARLES SEDLEY. *Hero and Leander* (1669), a verse BURLESQUE, was a bid for membership of the cleverly dismissive literary elite.

Wycherley may have had experience as an actor and a dabbler in theatrical management before he wrote his first play, *Love in a Wood: or, St James's Park* (1671). The mordant SATIRE of a sexually and financially rapacious society that characterizes his best plays is already present in his first. *The Gentleman Dancing-Master* (1672), derived from a play by Calderón, is more generous to its characters than either of Wycherley's greatest comedies, THE COUNTRY WIFE (1675) and THE PLAIN DEALER (1676). In these plays, Wycherley describes a world he knew. It is not a pleasant world, and although the comic contrivance is masterly, there is no affection in the portraiture.

After 1676, Wycherley turned his back on the theatre and proceeded to live almost like a character in one of his plays. He forfeited the patronage of Charles II when he married the Countess of Drogheda, a wealthy widow, in 1679. She died in 1681, and Wycherley was imprisoned for debt on her estate in 1682–6. *Epistles to the King and Duke* (1683) is an expression, in lame verse, of pathetic need. James II arranged his release from prison in 1686, gave him a pension of £200 and paid his debts. From the seclusion of the family estate in Clive, Wycherley tried to guard his literary reputation, wrote unimpressive and sometimes obscene poems (published as *Miscellany Poems*, 1704), and became increasingly cantankerous. When he married a second time, shortly before his death, he seems to have been motivated by a wish to disinherit his nephew.

The strange friendship between the ageing Wycherley and the youthful ALEXANDER POPE found expression in the edition by Pope and LEWIS THEOBALD of Wycherley's *Posthumous Works* (2 vols., 1729), in which original Wycherley cannot be easily distinguished from sub-standard Pope.

Wyclif [Wycliffe]**, John** *c.* 1320–84 Theologian and translator of the Bible. Born at Hipswell near Richmond into a wealthy family, he studied at Balliol College, Oxford, and later became Master of the college, resigning in 1361 to take up the living of Fillingham, Lincolnshire. In 1362 he accepted the prebend of Aust, Bristol, and in 1365 was appointed Warden of Canterbury Hall. This appointment was contested and he lost it. In 1368 he moved from Fillingham to the curacy of Ludgershall and became a canon in Lincoln in 1371. In 1374 he was rector of Lutterworth and retained the post until his death.

He became a renowned lecturer in theology and philosophy. His writings took on a militant aspect after his engagement in negotiations with papal envoys in Bruges in 1374. He began to attack Rome's control of the English church and his stance became increasingly anti-papal, resulting in condemnation of his teaching and threats of excommunication. He further antagonized the orthodox church by disputing the doctrine of transubstantiation. He amassed a great following, particularly in Oxford, which developed into the LOLLARD movement and spread throughout England.

The majority of his writings are in Latin but his crucial contribution to the history of English literature was his project for vernacular translation of the Bible. His part in its execution was probably restricted to an unfinished version of the New Testament. (See also THE BIBLE IN ENGLISH.) Of the many sermons, commentaries, glosses and tracts attributed to Wyclif, some are undoubtedly by Lollard followers drawing on his work in Latin.

Wyndham, John [Harris, John Wyndham Parkes Lucas Beynon] 1903–69 Novelist who used various combinations of his names in different phases of his career. Before World War II he was active as John Beynon and as John Beynon Harris, but became known as John Wyndham for his post-war SCIENCE FICTION novels, beginning with *The Day of the Triffids* (1951). His other novels include *The Kraken Wakes* (1953), *The Chrysalids* (1955), *The Midwich Cuckoos* (1957) and *The Trouble with Lichen* (1960). The best of his short fiction is in *Consider Her Ways and Others* (1961). His stories focus on the reactions of ordinary people to terrible circumstances which plunge them into a struggle for survival. These anxious fantasies, preoccupied with the difficulty of preserving the values of English decency in hostile conditions, found favour with the British public while more colourful American science fiction still seemed alien, allowing Wyndham to carve out his own literary niche. His work provides a bridge between traditional British scientific romance and the more varied science fiction which has replaced it.

Wynnere and Wastoure See WINNER AND WASTER.

Yates, Dornford [Mercer, Cecil William] 1885–1960 Novelist. Born in London and educated at Harrow and Oxford, Yates was called to the Bar before embarking on a career as a writer. His novels, almost invariably sustained by gently farcical plots and centred on an elegant leisured society, found a huge popular readership in the 1920s and 1930s. *Berry and Co.* (1921), *Jonah and Co.* (1922) and *Maiden Stakes* (1929) were among his many books about the activities of Berry Pleydell and his circle. *The Stolen March* (1926) was a fantasy of a hidden world; *Blind Corner* (1927) and *Perishable Goods* (1928) were among his 'Chandos' thrillers. *As Berry and I were Saying* (1952) and *Berry and I Look Back* (1958) were autobiographical.

Years, The A novel by VIRGINIA WOOLF, published in 1937.

Unlike her other late works, this novel is a conventional family saga with none of the experimental devices used elsewhere. It chronicles the lives of the Pargiters from 1880 to the 1930s. At the beginning, Colonel Pargiter's wife, Rose, is dying ('She was better today; would be worse tomorrow') and their seven children (ranging from early childhood to mid-20s) live under the oppressive weight of her illness. The first chapter ('1880') ends with her funeral. Subsequent chapters trace the lives of each of the children in a series of separate but connected episodes which form a recurring cycle. Each chapter comprises a year: from '1907', through the years of World War I, to the present in 1936 when there is a large family reunion. There are many vivid descriptions of London life, and the novel sold well despite the author's reservations about her return to the 'novel of fact'.

Yeast: A Problem A novel by CHARLES KINGSLEY, serialized in *FRASER'S MAGAZINE* in 1848 and published in book form in 1850. It is unashamedly a novel of ideas, in which Lancelot Smith, a gentleman and heedless atheist, learns about life from Paul Tregarva, one of the 'Dissenting poor'. Its interest lies in its analysis of problems which the author admitted he could not solve. The main anxieties are what Kingsley saw as the insidious lure of the Roman Catholic Church and the necessity for sanitary reform. The picture of rural degradation is vivid and the descriptions of the poor, sleeping 'like pilchards in a barrel', with no clean water and no sanitation, are memorable. Kingsley symbolically punishes the rich for their negligence by letting them catch fatal fevers, bred by filth. He deplores the waste of sewage, which fouls rivers when it should be fertilizing fields, attacks the game laws and defends the 'true idea of

Protestantism'. Though claiming to avoid taking sides, he preaches that art is a mere self-indulgence when political action (reformist, not revolutionary) is needed.

Yeats, William Butler 1865–1939 Irish poet and playwright. Born in Dublin, he spent two-thirds of his life out of Ireland. His father, John B. Yeats, was a lawyer turned painter, and in 1867 the family followed him to London, moving to the recently developed Bedford Park estate in Chiswick in 1879. Summer holidays, and two longer periods in 1869 and 1872, were spent with his mother's family, the Pollexfens, in Sligo. In 1881 the family returned to Dublin, and Yeats studied at the Metropolitan School of Art, where he met GEORGE WILLIAM RUSSELL (AE). Both were interested in mysticism, and in 1886 Yeats formed the Dublin Lodge of the Hermetic Society. At the Contemporary Club, a nationalist university debating group, he met WILLIAM MORRIS and, most importantly, the old Fenian leader John O'Leary, who encouraged in him a cultural nationalism. He also began to publish in *The Dublin University Review*: an Arcadian verse-drama, *The Island of Statues* (1885), and a short verse-drama, *Mosada* (1886).

In 1887 the family returned to Bedford Park, and he began to build a reputation as an anthologist of Irish literature and as a poet of the RHYMERS' CLUB, which he formed with Ernest Rhys in 1890. He visited Mme Blavatsky (recalled in his autobiography, *The Trembling of the Veil*) and joined the Esoteric Section of the Theosophical Society, but was later asked to resign because his experiments were becoming too enthusiastic. He also joined MacGregor Mathers's Rosicrucian society, the Hermetic Order of the Golden Dawn, and quickly became a leading member. He met Maud Gonne in 1889, and she became the subject of his early love poetry. In 1892 he formed the Irish Literary Society in London, and then the National Literary Society in Dublin, which aimed to promote the New Irish Library, as well as concerts and lectures on Irish themes. Through ARTHUR SYMONS he discovered French SYMBOLISM, and in Paris in 1896 met Verlaine and J. M. SYNGE. In the following year he formed another important friendship with LADY GREGORY; her estate, Coole Park, became the setting for several of his poems.

During the next decade he was preoccupied with 'theatre business'. With GEORGE MOORE and EDWARD MARTYN he formed the Irish Literary Theatre, inaugurated in 1899 with a production of *The Countess Kathleen*, and collaborated with the Fay brothers and their Irish actors to produce his most successful play, *Cathleen Ni Houlihan* (1902), a propaganda piece with Maud Gonne in the title-role. A few members of this team became the Irish National Theatre, subsidized by Annie Horniman, which opened the ABBEY THEATRE in December 1904. Yeats, Synge and Lady Gregory were joint directors. In 1912 he met POUND, who became his fencing master and secretary in the winters of 1913 and 1914, and who introduced him to Japanese Noh drama: this was a significant influence on his plays, starting with *At the Hawk's Well* (1916). Although he was out of Ireland at the time of the Easter Rising in 1916, he knew several of the executed rebels personally, as recorded in 'Easter, 1916'.

In early 1917 he bought Thoor Ballylee, a derelict Norman stone tower at Ballylee near Coole Park, and restored it as a summer home and a central symbol in his later poetry. In October 1917 he married Georgie Hyde-Lees, and on their honeymoon she began the automatic writing which led eventually to *A VISION* (1925, revised 1937). At the start of the guerrilla war in Ireland they settled in Oxford, but in 1922 returned to live in Dublin. The bridge at Thoor Ballylee was blown up, and shots were fired into their Dublin home. In the same year he became a Senator, and in 1923 was awarded the Nobel Prize for Literature. After a serious illness in 1929 he convalesced in Rapallo, Italy, where an emergency will had been witnessed by Pound and BASIL BUNTING. In 1932 he founded the Irish Academy of Letters, and in 1933 was briefly, but enthusiastically, involved with the fascist Blueshirts in Dublin. In 1936, while in Mallorca collaborating on a translation of the Upanishads, he again became seriously ill but survived to publish a controversial *Oxford Book of Modern Verse* (1936). He died at the Hôtel Idéal Séjour and was buried in Roquebrune, France. His coffin was disinterred and taken to Sligo in 1948; there is now some doubt as to the authenticity of the bones.

His work, which is now considered to be the most important in the revival of Irish literature, and which fruitfully engaged with Ireland's political independence, included poetry, drama, criticism, essays, journalism, novels and occult writings. A central theme is Ireland, its history, folklore and contemporary public life: 'Creative work must have a fatherland.' Beginning in the later years of the CELTIC REVIVAL, the poetry developed from long allegorical nationalist poems, and Arcadian lyrics and verse dramas influenced by SHELLEY and SPENSER, to a mature voice that was at once public and private in the work of the 1920s and a more deliberately passionate condemnation of Western civilization in the late poetry. A second important source was the occult, with which he was seriously involved throughout his life, because it provided a philosophy of poetry which emphasized the associative power of the imagination, and because it was a source of SYMBOLS, ideas and 'almost an infallible church of poetic tradition'. The obscure symbolism of *The Wind among the Reeds* (1899) was resolved in the later poetry into three symbols, themselves explained in *A Vision*: the Phases of the Moon, the Great Wheel and the Gyres.

His early work included *The Wanderings of Oisin and Other Poems* (1889), *The Countess Kathleen and Other Legends and Lyrics* (1892; the poetry from this volume was subsequently organized into two sections, 'Crossways' and 'The Rose'), *The Wind among the Reeds* (1899) and *In the Seven Woods* (1903). He wrote two short novels which deal with the opposition between the poet and the magician, *John Sherman and Dhoya* (1891) and *The Speckled Bird* (1897-1901), and published several anthologies of Irish writing and folklore, including *Fairy and Folk Tales of the Irish Peasantry* (1888), *Irish Fairy and Folk Tales* (1894), *The Celtic Twilight* (1893) and *The Secret Rose* (1897). *Ideas of Good and Evil* (1903) was a collection of essays, and 'Discoveries' (1906) was a long essay on art and drama. He also edited the poetry of WILLIAM BLAKE (1893), in collaboration with Edwin Ellis, and that of Spenser (1906).

The Green Helmet and Other Poems (1910) and *Responsibilities* (1914) showed him simplifying his poetry by turning to dramatic speech and public occasions, contrasting Greek mythology and Renaissance Italy with contemporary Dublin, the dispute over funding for the Municipal Gallery and the General Strike of 1913. *The Wild Swans at Coole* (1919) significantly extended his range, notably in the ELEGY 'In Memory of Major Robert Gregory', and introduced the symbols of *A Vision* and the magician-figure Michael Robartes, based on MacGregor Mathers, who appears in the occult stories *Rosa Alchemica* (1897) and the essays *Per Amica Silentia Lunae* (1917). *Michael Robartes and the Dancer* (1921) contained 'The Second Coming' and 'Easter, 1916', his elegy for those who had died in the Easter Rising, including THOMAS MACDONAGH and PATRICK PEARSE. He also published two collections of plays, *Plays for an Irish Theatre* (1911) and *Four Plays for Dancers* (1920); a collection of essays, *The Cutting of an Agate* (1918); and two volumes of autobiography, *Reveries over Childhood and Youth* (1914) and *The Trembling of the Veil* (1922).

The Tower (1928) included 'Sailing to Byzantium', 'Leda and the Swan', 'Among School Children' and two sequences on the Civil War. In these he achieved a rich lyricism that encompassed the apparent contradictions between art and politics. *The Winding Stair* (1933) was a powerfully pessimistic collection which included 'Byzantium', 'Coole Park, 1929' and 'Coole Park and Ballylee'. It also included the sequence 'Words for Music Perhaps', 25 songs written for the puppet-characters Crazy Jane, Jack the Journeyman, the Bishop, Old Tom and God, set in a world of dreams, rhymes, madness songs and riddling re-

William Butler Yeats

frains. *Parnell's Funeral and Other Poems* (1935) began the theme of 'lust and rage' which dominated *New Poems* (1938) and the posthumous *Last Poems and Two Plays* (1939); these included 'The Municipal Gallery Revisited' and 'The Circus Animals' Desertion', both retrospective judgements on the vision of Ireland in his work. 'Lapis Lazuli' drew on the ideas of Spengler, whose *The Decline of the West* had many similarities with his own *A Vision*. Other work included *Collected Poems* (1933), *Collected Plays* (1934), *Wheels and Butterflies* (1934), a further volume of autobiography in *Dramatis Personae* (1935), *Ten Principal Upanishads* (1937), *Essays 1931–36* (1937), *The Oxford Book of Modern Verse* (1936), and contributions to *Broadsides* and *On the Boiler*, intended as a bi-annual periodical, the only issue of which appeared in 1939.

Posthumous publications include *Collected Plays* (1953), *The Letters of W. B. Yeats* (1954), *Autobiographies* (1955), *Mythologies* (1959), *Essays and Introductions* (1961), *Explorations* (1962), *Uncollected Prose* (1970, 1975), *Memoirs* (1972) and *The Poems: A New Edition* (1984) edited by R. Finneran.

Variorum editions of the *Poems* (1957) and *Plays* (1966) were edited by R. Alspach and P. Allt. Several volumes of his correspondence have been published, including that with Dorothy Wellesley (1940, 1964), Florence Farr and G. B. Shaw (1946), T. STURGE MOORE (1953), KATHARINE TYNAN (1953) and Margot Ruddock (1970). The first volume of *The Collected Letters*, edited by J. Kelly, appeared in 1986. The *Senate Speeches* (1960) were edited by D. Pearce.

Yellow Book, The A literary and art periodical which ran from 1894 to 1897, published by John Lane and edited by HENRY HARLAND. Considered decadent and shocking by many readers, it had a distinctive yellow binding decorated by AUBREY BEARDSLEY, the art editor. The first issue included MAX BEERBOHM's controversial essay 'A Defence of Cosmetics'. Many of its contributors were to become major literary figures: HENRY JAMES, EDMUND GOSSE, ARNOLD BENNETT, H. G. WELLS and W. B. YEATS were all represented during its three years' existence, and Walter Sickert and Wilson Steer were among the many artists who also contributed.

Yellowplush Papers, The Comic sketches by W. M. THACKERAY, serialized as *The Yellowplush Correspondence* in FRASER'S MAGAZINE from November 1837 to August 1838 and in January 1840, reprinted under its present title in his *Comic Tales and Sketches* (1841).

These comic memoirs of a footman, Charles James Yellowplush, are told in his aspiring cockney idiom, and deal with his life under two masters. The first is a respectable gentleman who turns out to be a crossing-sweeper; the second a card-sharping aristocrat, the Hon. Algernon Deuceace, who is outwitted in his pursuit of a wealthy marriage by his even more rascally father, the Earl of Crabs.

Yemassee, The: *A Romance of Carolina* A novel by WILLIAM GILMORE SIMMS, published in 1835. Set in South Carolina, it is based on the 1715 uprising of the Yemassee Indians against the English colonists.

Sanutee, the Yemassee chief, perceives the threat the expanding colonies pose to his tribe. Urged on by the Spaniards, and aided by a renegade English officer named Chorley, he prepares to attack the white settlements. His son Occonestoga, who has been corrupted by white men's ways (and by alcohol in particular), sides with the whites against his tribe. Gabriel Harrison leads the defence of the settlement. Both he and Hugh Grayson, a young man who comes to emulate the naturally noble Harrison, are in love with Bess Matthews, who embodies the Southern ideal of womanhood. The Indians attack, led by Chorley, and kill many settlers. Harrison sends Occonestoga to spy on his tribe, but he is captured and formally expelled from the tribe. To be thus stripped of identity is a sentence more severe than death, and his mother kills him to save him from the disgrace. She also helps his friend Harrison to escape when he is captured by the Yemassee. Bess and her father are taken by Chorley, but Harrison saves them and kills Chorley. Matthews agrees to the union of Bess and Harrison, who then reveals his true identity: he is in fact Charles Craven, the governor of Carolina. He leaves Hugh Grayson in charge of the local forces and travels to Charleston to organize the force which finally destroys the Yemassee. The book ends with the death of Sanutee.

Yerby, Frank (Garvin) 1916– Black American novelist. He was born in Augusta, Georgia, and educated at Paine College in Augusta and Fisk University in Tennessee. Writing about racial injustice, he won early recognition for his stories 'Health Card' (1944) and 'The Homecoming' (1946). He received the O. Henry Award in 1944. Yerby then turned to historical novels, the first of which, *The Foxes of Harrow* (1947), won immediate success and sold over a million copies. He has since written many melodramatic costume novels, usually dealing with the 'eternal warfare of the sexes'. Several are set in the 19th century; he moves back to the 18th century in *The Devil's Laughter* (1953) and *Bride of Liberty* (1954), to the 17th century in *The Golden Hawk* (1948) and to biblical times in *Judas My Brother* (1968). Later novels include: *The Dahomean* (1971), dealing primarily with blacks; *Devilseed* (1984); and *McKenzie's Hundred* (1986).

Yezierska, Anzia *c*. 1885–1970 Russian-American novelist and short-story writer. She was born at Plinsk, in Russian Poland, and emigrated with her family to the USA in the 1890s. They settled in the ghetto of New York's Lower East Side. She attended night school to improve her English, won a scholarship which enabled her to become a domestic science teacher, and taught cooking from 1905 to 1913. Her stories and novels deal realistically with the lives of struggling immigrants living in the ghetto. Her protagonists are usually women. *Hungry Hearts*, a collection of ten short stories, appeared in 1920; *Salome of the Tenements*, her first novel, in 1922. Subsequent works include another collection of short stories, *Children of Loneliness* (1923), *Bread Givers: A Novel: A Struggle between a Father of the Old World and a Daughter of the New* (1925), *Arrogant Beggar* (1927), another novel, *All I Could Never Be* (1932), a semi-autobiographical novel, and her autobiography, *Red Ribbon on a White Horse* (1950). She died in poverty in Ontario, California.

Yonge, Charlotte M(ary) 1823–1901 Novelist and writer of CHILDREN'S LITERATURE. The daughter of a country gentleman who educated her himself, she lived all her life in the village of Otterbourne, Hampshire. JOHN KEBLE, vicar of the neighbouring parish of Hursley, deeply influenced her religious views. Tirelessly energetic, she edited a girls' magazine, *The Monthly Packet*, for nearly 50 years and produced 160 books, including biographies of Bishop Patterson (1874) and HANNAH MORE (1888), histories and textbooks as well as fiction aimed at young female readers. Her first novel was *Abbeychurch: or, Self-Control and Self-Conceit* (1844) but THE HEIR OF REDCLYFFE (1853) began her popular success. It was followed by THE DAISY CHAIN (1856) and several later volumes continuing the fortunes of the May family. The authentic home and family background makes these books an excellent source of information about Victorian middle-class life. An admirer of SIR WALTER SCOTT, she chose a historical setting for many of her novels, among them *The Little Duke* (1854), *The Lances of Lynwood* (1855), *The Prince and the Page* (1865) and *The Caged Lion* (1870).

York cycle See MIRACLE PLAYS.

Yorke, Henry Vincent See GREEN, HENRY.

Yorkshire Tragedy, A A domestic tragedy, probably first performed in 1606, when it was part of the repertoire of the KING'S MEN at the GLOBE THEATRE. The title-page of a 1608 edition claims it as SHAKESPEARE'S work (see SHAKESPEARE APOCRYPHA), but the most that could be supposed is that he had some hand in cutting the play down to the truncated form in which it has survived. THOMAS MIDDLETON has been suggested as a possible author.

The play is based on the story of Walter Calverley, executed for murder in 1605. It describes with grim haste his passage from gambling debts to the attempted murder of his family (wife and one son survive), arrest and final repentance.

Young, Andrew (John) 1885–1971 Poet. Born at Elgin and educated in Edinburgh, he was ordained first as a Free Church minister and then as an Anglican clergyman. He was appointed canon of Chichester Cathedral in 1948. His long poetic career began with *Songs of Night* (1910). After the short nature lyrics of *The Green Man* (1947), he wrote two long meditative poems, *Into Hades* (1952) and *A Traveller in Time*, published together as *Out of the World and Back* (1958). In the preface to *Into Hades* he wrote that 'while my interest in nature was intense, it was not so deep as the underlying interest that prompted me to change my style'. Both poems attempt to reconcile philosophical and religious generalization with visionary narrative. Young also published prose pieces, including *A Prospect of Flowers* (1945), *A Retrospect of Flowers* (1950), *A Prospect of Britain* (1950) and *The Poet and the Landscape* (1962).

Young, Arthur 1741–1820 Writer on agriculture and travel. The son of a Suffolk clergyman, he was born in London and published a pamphlet, *The War in North America*, at the age of 17, but did not find his true subject as a writer until he had tried, and failed, to be a farmer and worked as an Irish land agent.

He became known as an agricultural theorist with *A Farmer's Letters to the People of England* (1768), *A Six Weeks Tour through the Southern Counties of England and Wales* (1768), *A Six Months Tour through the North of England* (1771), *The Farmer's Tour through the East of England* (1771), *Political Arithmetic* (1774) and *A Tour in Ireland* (1780), works which also show him to be a shrewd observer of architecture, landscape and politics. The same qualities inform his most important work, *Travels during the Years 1787, 1788, 1789 and 1790, Undertaken with a View of Ascertaining the Cultivation, Wealth, Resources and National Prosperity of the Kingdom of France* (1792), usually known simply as *Travels in France*, a damning indictment of conditions immediately before the Revolution. *The Example of France a Warning to England* (1793) appeared in the year he

became Secretary to the Board of Agriculture. Young also founded and edited a periodical, *The Annals of Agriculture* (1784–1809). His family was connected to the Burneys, and FANNY BURNEY often mentions him in her diaries and letters.

Young, Edward 1683–1765 Poet and playwright. Born at Upham, near Winchester, he was educated at Winchester College and at New College and Corpus Christi College, Oxford, becoming a Fellow of All Souls in 1708. His early poems met with little success but his tragedy *Busiris, King of Egypt* (1719) was highly acclaimed. Another tragedy, *The Revenge* (1721), also became extremely popular after being coolly received at first. A series of seven SATIRES, *The Universal Passion* (1725–8; later called *The Love of Fame*), enjoyed a considerable vogue until eclipsed by POPE's great satires of the 1730s.

The slow development of his career made Young look to the church. In 1730 he became rector of Welwyn, where he spent the rest of his life. His only published poem in the next decade was a patriotic ODE, *The Foreign Address* (1735). The death of his stepdaughter in 1736 and his wife, Lady Elizabeth Lee, in 1740 prompted him to begin the work which made him famous. The first part of *The Complaint: or, Night-Thoughts on Life, Death and Immortality* appeared in 1742 and the last part (the ninth Night) in 1746. *NIGHT THOUGHTS*, as it is usually known, allied him with both an older tradition of moral writing and the contemporary GRAVEYARD POETS. Young's new fame brought him into contact with MARY DELANY, ELIZABETH MONTAGU and the BLUESTOCKING circle, as well as CIBBER, RICHARDSON and JOHNSON, who rashly judged him 'a man of genius and a poet'. Latterly, he published *The Brothers* (1753), a play he had written earlier, and *The Centaur Not Fabulous* (1755). *Conjectures on Original Composition* (1759) seems to have been prompted by conversations with Richardson about the *Essay on the Genius and Writings of Pope* (1756), which JOSEPH WARTON had dedicated to Young. His last published poem was the long *Resignation* (1762).

Young, Francis Brett 1884–1954 Novelist, short-story writer and poet. Born in Worcestershire, he was educated at Epsom School and at the University of Birmingham, where he studied medicine. He practised in Devon for several years, where he also began writing. His early novels, *Deep Sea* (1914), *The Dark Tower* (1914) and *The Iron Age* (1916), were all well received in critical circles.

During World War I he served in the Medical Corps in East Africa, and produced a valuable account of the campaign there, *Marching on Tanga* (1918). His post-war novels were situated in the west Midlands and included the titles for which he is best remembered, *Portrait of Clare* (1927) and *My Brother Jonathan*

(1928). Towards the end of his life he returned to Africa, where he lived until his death. Novels with a South African setting included *Jim Redlake* (1930), *They Seek a Country* (1937), about the Great Trek, and *The City of Gold* (1939). *The Island* (1944) is a verse history of England, using verse forms appropriate to each period.

Ywain and Gawain A VERSE ROMANCE probably written in the first half of the 14th century in the North of England. A condensed version of *Yvain*, a late 12th-century French romance by Chrétien de Troyes, it omits much of the descriptive and reflective material in its source. Colloquial language replaces much of Chrétien's sophisticated literary diction and the irony of the source has been replaced by a straightforward and fluent account. It is the only Middle English translation of any of Chrétien's works.

Ywain defeats a knight who appears when water is cast over a stone. With the help of a go-between, Lunet, he marries the knight's widow. Gawain persuades him to leave his wife for a year to live as a knight, and when Ywain forgets to return she rejects him. After Ywain has spent a period of madness in the woods and undergone several adventures, Lunet eventually effects a reconciliation between the couple. Ywain is known as the Knight of the Lion because he is accompanied and helped by a lion he saved and befriended during his period of solitude. (See also ARTHURIAN LITERATURE.)

Zangwill, Israel 1864–1926 Novelist, playwright and translator. Born in London of Russian-Jewish descent, he was educated at London University. For a number of years he edited the humorous periodical *Ariel* and worked as a teacher and journalist. After publishing several unsuccessful novels, he wrote *Children of the Ghetto* (1892), which brilliantly captured the stark reality of immigrant life in London. Other works in the same vein included *Ghetto Tragedies* (1893), *The Kings of Shnorrers* (1894) and *The Mantle of Elijah* (1900), which established him as a leading figure and powerful spokesman in the struggle for Jewish rights. *The Melting Pot* (1909), the best known of his plays, dealt with a similar theme, as did various non-fictional works, including *The War for the World* (1916) and *The Voice of Jerusalem* (1920). *The Big Bow Mystery* (1892) is Zangwill's one canny venture into DETECTIVE FICTION.

Zanoni A novel by EDWARD BULWER LYTTON, published in 1842, and set partly during the French Revolution. The hero is a mysterious sage and master of the occult arts possessed of the secret of eternal life, whose superhuman powers begin to fail him when he falls in love with a human being. Realizing that the affections of the heart, which he has hitherto shunned, can lead to a higher spiritual state than the abstractions of the intellect, he forsakes his immortality, marries the girl, and eventually dies in her place on the guillotine. His sacrifice prefigures the ending of DICKENS's *A TALE OF TWO CITIES*.

Zaturenska, Marya 1902–82 Russian-American poet. Born in Kiev, she emigrated to the USA in 1910 and attended Valparaiso University and the University of Wisconsin before marrying the poet HORACE GREGORY in 1925. With him she edited numerous anthologies and wrote *A History of American Poetry 1900–1940* (1946). *Threshold and Hearth* (1934) was her first volume of poetry. *Cold Morning Sky*, published in 1937, brought her critical acclaim and the PULITZER PRIZE in 1938. Other collections of her poetry include *The Listening Landscape* (1941), *Golden Mirror* (1943), *Terraces of Light* (1960) and *The Hidden Waterfalls* (1974).

Zen and the Art of Motorcycle Maintenance See PIRSIG, ROBERT.

zeugma See SYLLEPSIS.

Zimunya, Musaemura Bonas 1949– Zimbabwean poet. His country's leading literary figure, he was born in Mutare. In 1973 he was expelled from the University of Rhodesia for 'disturbing the peace'. While exiled in Britain he studied at the University of Kent, later publishing his MA dissertation as *Those Years of Hunger and Drought: The Birth of African Fiction in English in Zimbabwe* (1982). He is senior lecturer in English at the University of Zimbabwe and has been secretary-general of the Zimbabwean Writers' Union. His poetry is preoccupied with the beauty of Zimbabwe, but also with its poverty and legacy of suffering, and with the vulgarity and spiritual alienation of the city. Volumes are *A Patch of Blue Sky and Zimbabwean Ruins* (with D. E. Borrell; 1979), *Kingfisher, Jikinya and Other Poems* (1982), *Thought Tracks* (1983) and *Country Dawns and City Lights* (1986). With Kofi Anyidoho and PETER PORTER he has co-edited *The Fate of Vultures: New Poetry of Africa* (1989).

Zoo Story, The A long one-act play by EDWARD ALBEE. His first work to be performed professionally, it opened in Berlin in 1959 and in New York in 1960. It concerns a confrontation in Central Park between Jerry, an alienated and unhappy homosexual, and the middle-aged and distinctly ordinary Peter. Jerry frustrates all Peter's attempts to leave with harangues about his alienated condition and finally tricks Peter into helping him kill himself.

Zukofsky, Louis 1904–78 American poet. He was born in New York and educated at Columbia University. Associated with OBJECTIVISM, he published his first poetry in *An 'Objectivists' Anthology* (1932), which he edited. *First Half of 'A'* (1940) began a long poem expanded over the next 38 years and finally completed in 1978. It explores the interrelationship of poetry and music and treats questions of aesthetics, philosophy and history. Volumes of shorter poems include *55 Poems* (1941), *Anew* (1946), *Some Time* (1956), *Barely and Widely* (1958), *I's* (1963), *After I's* (1964) and *I Sent Thee Late* (1965). *All: The Collected Shorter Poems, 1923–1964* appeared in 1966. *A Test of Poetry* (1948) and *Prepositions* (1967) are collections of essays on modern poets and poetry. He also wrote a play, *Arise, Arise* (1965), and a novel, *Little: A Fragment for Careenagers* (1970).

Zuleika Dobson: or, An Oxford Love Story A novel by MAX BEERBOHM, published in 1911. Refusing to identify this witty performance as a SATIRE directed at particular targets, he preferred to label it a 'fantasy'.

When Zuleika visits her grandfather, the Warden of Judas College, during Eights Week, her beauty devastates the undergraduates, even the splendid and

Frontispiece by J. Godwin to Bulwer Lytton's *Zanoni* (1880). The virtuoso violinist, Gaetano Pisani, was based on the celebrated Niccolò Paganini.

haughty Duke of Dorset. She remains disappointed in her quest for a man 'who would not bow down to her'. The Duke fulfils his promise to lay down his life by drowning himself, and is followed by the entire undergraduate population, who plunge into the Isis 'like lemmings'. The only survivor is the pedestrian Noaks, less agile than the others. At the end of the novel Zuleika consults the train timetable to Cambridge.

Zwicky, (Julia) Fay 1933– Australian poet, short-story writer and critic. Born in Melbourne, she is also a concert pianist and university teacher. The relation between art and the artist, the paradoxes of life and themes of conflict dominate her collections of densely textured but elegant and direct verse, *Isaac Babel's Fiddle* (1975), *Kaddish and Other Poems* (1982) and *Ask Me* (1990). Her Jewishness and autobiographical experience provide much of the material, as they do for several of the stories in *Hostages and Other Stories* (1983). *The Lyre in the Pawnshop: Essays on Literature and Survival 1974–1984* (1986) demonstrates her commitment to both literature and social comment. She has edited three anthologies, *Quarry* (1981), *Journeys* (1982) and *Procession* (1987).

Illustration Acknowledgements

The Publishers gratefully acknowledge the following for supplying illustrations and granting permission for their use.

While every effort has been made to obtain copyright for illustrations that appear in this book, should anyone inadvertently have been overlooked we shall be pleased to make proper acknowledgement in future editions

Acknowledgements are listed according to page numbers.

3, Paul Freestone/print courtesy of Heinemann; 11, Mary Evans Picture Library/Fawcett Library; 22, Peter Jordan/Network Photographers; 32, 77, 553b, by permission of the British Library, London; 42, 893, Maggie Murray/ Format; 50, by permission of the Syndics of Cambridge University Library, from *Spedding et al: The Works of Francis Bacon*, vol. 1, 1857; 52, Bernard Charlon/Camera Press; 68, Francois-Marie Banier/Rex Features; 72, 667, Horst Tappe/Camera Press; 74, 754, 823, 1007, E.O. Hoppé/Mansell Collection; 91, 160, 226, 341, 363, 418, 427, 499, 517, 599, 632, 917, 934, 938, 1016, Hulton-Deutsch Collection; 96, by permission of the Syndics of Cambridge University Library, from *The Female Spectator*, vol. 1, ed. by Eliza Haywood, 1744-6; 125, 203, 293, 433, 446, 861, Mary Evans Picture Library; 141, 535, 814, 1039, National Portrait Gallery, London; 153, Herbie Knott/Rex Features; 156, 459, 544, 574, 791, 797, Fay Godwin/Network Photographers; 165, 614, Mary Evans Picture Library/Ida Kar; 181, by permission of the Syndics of Cambridge University Library, from *Richardson: Clarissa*, 1784 edition, plate XXI; 195, by permission of the Syndics of Cambridge University Library, from *Combe: The Tour of Doctor Syntax in Search of the Picturesque*, 1809; 246, 267, 409, 838, 896, Mansell Collection; 252, Anita Desai; 256, by permission of the Syndics of Cambridge University Library, from *The Illustrated London News*, 25 June 1870; 258, courtesy of the Robert Frost Library, Amherst College, Massachusetts; 279, 680, Val Wilmer/Format; 295, Douglas Glass/ Popperfoto; 325, Camera Press; 335, 567, 963, Hulton-Deutsch Collection/ Bettmann Archive; 354, Henry E. Huntington Library, San Marino, California; 358, by permission of the Syndics of Cambridge University Library, from *Thomas Middleton: A Game at Chess*, 1624; 372, courtesy of the Schlesinger Library, Radcliffe College, Cambridge, Massachusetts; 373, G. Freedman/ Camera Press; 384, by permission of the Syndics of Cambridge University Library, from *Walpole: The Description of Strawberry Hill*, 1784; 392, Karsh of Ottawa/Camera Press, London; 398, by permission of the Syndics of Cambridge University Library, engraving by Thomas Stothard in *The Novelists Magazine*, 1782; 421, George Hallett/print courtesy of Heinemann; 455, Tessa Colvin; 464, 879, 902, 1012, Cecil Beaton/Camera Press; 477, *The Return of Rip Van Winkle* by John Quidor (18[4?]9), National Gallery of Art, Washington, D.C., Andrew W. Mellon Collection, 1942; 482, reproduced by kind permission of the Smith College Archives, Northampton, Massachusetts, USA; 491, by permission of the Syndics of Cambridge University Library, an engraving by Thomas Rowlandson in *Johnson: The Picturesque Beauties of Boswell*, 1786; 508, Neil Libbert/Camera Press; 521, National Galleries of Scotland; 523, by permission of the Syndics of Cambridge University Library, from *Thomas Kyd: The Spanish Tragedy*, 1615; 553tr, Royal Commission on the Historical Monuments of England; 562, Nicholas Judd; 610, by permission of the Syndics of Cambridge University Library, from *Grose: The Antiquities of England and Wales*, 1773-6; 627, Shakespeare Centre Library, Stratford-upon-Avon; 629, by permission of the Syndics of Cambridge University Library, illustration by W.J. Allen in *George Eliot: The Mill on the Floss*, 1860; 652, Michaline Pelletier/Sygma; 660, 671, 708, courtesy of Noma Award for Publishing in Africa; 662, Tom Blau/ Camera Press; 669, courtesy of Heinemann; 690, 987, Popperfoto; 696, Douglas Brother/courtesy of Jonathan Cape; 701, 970, Rex Features; 707, ©Vernon Richards/George Orwell Archive, University College London; 730, Master and Fellows of Magdalene College, Cambridge; 741, by permission of the Syndics of Cambridge University Library, from *Black & White*, 10 June 1893; 763, from the collections of the Theatre Museum, by courtesy of the Trustees of the Victoria & Albert Museum; 795, courtesy of the Henry Handel Richardson Archive at the National Library, Canberra; 799, Mervyn Peake in *Rime of the Ancient Mariner*, Methuen; 811, Angus McBean; 829, Fitzwilliam Museum, Cambridge; 850, by permission of the Syndics of Cambridge University Library, from *The Gentlemen's Magazine*, July 1769; 853, A.F. Kersting; 859, Studio Lisa/Camera Press; 923, sketch by Satyajit Ray; 932, by permission of the Birmingham Museum & Art Gallery; 983, Frank Herrman/ Camera Press; 1010, New York Public Library; 1024, courtesy of The Currency Press Pty, Ltd, Paddington, Australia; 1041, by Daniel Maclise in *Fraser's Magazine*; 1049, BBC Photograph Library; 1054, by permission of the Syndics of Cambridge University Library, illustration by J. Godwin in *Bulwer Lytton: Zanoni*, 1880